PETERSON'S®
GRADUATE PROGRAMS IN THE PHYSICAL SCIENCES, MATHEMATICS, AGRICULTURAL SCIENCES, THE ENVIRONMENT & NATURAL RESOURCES

2020

 PETERSON'S®

About Peterson's®

Peterson's® has been your trusted educational publisher for over 50 years. It's a milestone we're quite proud of, as we continue to offer the most accurate, dependable, high-quality educational content in the field, providing you with everything you need to succeed. No matter where you are on your academic or professional path, you can rely on Peterson's for its books, online information, expert test-prep tools, the most up-to-date education exploration data, and the highest quality career success resources—everything you need to achieve your education goals. For our complete line of products, visit **www.petersons.com**.

For more information about Peterson's range of educational products, contact Peterson's, 8740 Lucent Blvd., Suite 400 Highlands Ranch, CO 80129, or find us online at **www.petersons.com**.

ISSN 1093-8443
ISBN: 978-0-7689-4316-0

Printed in the United States of America

10 9 8 7 6 5 4 3 2 1   21 20 19

Fifty-fourth Edition

CONTENTS

ACADEMIC AND PROFESSIONAL PROGRAMS IN THE AGRICULTURAL SCIENCES

ACADEMIC AND PROFESSIONAL PROGRAMS IN THE ENVIRONMENT AND NATURAL SCIENCES

APPENDIXES

INDEXES

iv   www.petersons.com

Peterson's Graduate Programs in the Physical Sciences, Mathematics, Agricultural Sciences, the Environment & Natural Resources 2020

A Note from the Peterson's Editors

The six volumes of Peterson's *Graduate and Professional Programs*, the only annually updated reference work of its kind, provide wide-ranging information on the graduate and professional programs offered by accredited colleges and universities in the United States, U.S. territories, and Canada and by those institutions outside the United States that are accredited by U.S. accrediting bodies. More than 44,000 individual academic and professional programs at nearly 2,300 institutions are listed. Peterson's *Graduate and Professional Programs* have been used for more than fifty years by prospective graduate and professional students, placement counselors, faculty advisers, and all others interested in postbaccalaureate education.

Graduate & Professional Programs: An Overview contains information on institutions as a whole, while the other books in the series are devoted to specific academic and professional fields:

- *Graduate Programs in the Biological/Biomedical Sciences & Health-Related Medical Professions*

- *Graduate Programs in Business, Education, Information Studies, Law & Social Work*

- *Graduate Programs in Engineering & Applied Sciences*

- *Graduate Programs in the Humanities, Arts & Social Sciences*

- *Graduate Programs in the Physical Sciences, Mathematics, Agricultural Sciences, the Environment & Natural Resources*

The books may be used individually or as a set. For example, if you have chosen a field of study but do not know what institution you want to attend or if you have a college or university in mind but have not chosen an academic field of study, it is best to begin with the Overview guide.

Graduate & Professional Programs: An Overview presents several directories to help you identify programs of study that might interest you; you can then research those programs further in the other books in the series by using the Directory of Graduate and Professional Programs by Field, which lists 500 fields and gives the names of those institutions that offer graduate degree programs in each.

For geographical or financial reasons, you may be interested in attending a particular institution and will want to know what it has to offer. You should turn to the Directory of Institutions and Their Offerings, which lists the degree programs available at each institution. As in the Directory of Graduate and Professional Programs by Field, the level of degrees offered is also indicated.

All books in the series include advice on graduate education, including topics such as admissions tests, financial aid, and accreditation. **The Graduate Adviser** includes two essays and information about accreditation. The first essay, "The Admissions Process," discusses general admission requirements, admission tests, factors to consider when selecting a graduate school or program, when and how to apply, and how admission decisions are made. Special information for international students and tips for minority students are also included. The second essay, "Financial Support," is an overview of the broad range of support available at the graduate level. Fellowships, scholarships, and grants; assistantships and internships; federal and private loan programs, as well as Federal Work-Study; and the GI bill are detailed. This essay concludes with advice on applying for need-based financial aid. "Accreditation and Accrediting Agencies" gives information on accreditation and its purpose and lists institutional accrediting agencies first and then specialized accrediting agencies relevant to each volume's specific fields of study.

With information on more than 40,000 graduate programs in more than 500 disciplines, Peterson's *Graduate and Professional Programs* give you all the information you need about the programs that are of interest to you in three formats: **Profiles** (capsule summaries of basic information), **Displays** (information that an institution or program wants to emphasize), and **Close-Ups** (written by administrators, with more expansive information than the **Profiles**, emphasizing different aspects of the programs). By using these various formats of program information, coupled with **Appendixes** and **Indexes** covering directories and subject areas for all six books, you will find that these guides provide the most comprehensive, accurate, and up-to-date graduate study information available.

Peterson's publishes a full line of resources with information you need to guide you through the graduate admissions process. Peterson's publications can be found at college libraries and career centers and your local bookstore or library—or visit us on the Web at www.petersons.com.

Colleges and universities will be pleased to know that Peterson's helped you in your selection. Admissions staff members are more than happy to answer questions, address specific problems, and help in any way they can. The editors at Peterson's wish you great success in your graduate program search!

THE GRADUATE ADVISER

The Admissions Process

Generalizations about graduate admissions practices are not always helpful because each institution has its own set of guidelines and procedures. Nevertheless, some broad statements can be made about the admissions process that may help you plan your strategy.

Factors Involved in Selecting a Graduate School or Program

Selecting a graduate school and a specific program of study is a complex matter. Quality of the faculty; program and course offerings; the nature, size, and location of the institution; admission requirements; cost; and the availability of financial assistance are among the many factors that affect one's choice of institution. Other considerations are job placement and achievements of the program's graduates and the institution's resources, such as libraries, laboratories, and computer facilities. If you are to make the best possible choice, you need to learn as much as you can about the schools and programs you are considering before you apply.

The following steps may help you narrow your choices.

- Talk to alumni of the programs or institutions you are considering to get their impressions of how well they were prepared for work in their fields of study.
- Remember that graduate school requirements change, so be sure to get the most up-to-date information possible.
- Talk to department faculty members and the graduate adviser at your undergraduate institution. They often have information about programs of study at other institutions.
- Visit the websites of the graduate schools in which you are interested to request a graduate catalog. Contact the department chair in your chosen field of study for additional information about the department and the field.
- Visit as many campuses as possible. Call ahead for an appointment with the graduate adviser in your field of interest and be sure to check out the facilities and talk to students.

General Requirements

Graduate schools and departments have requirements that applicants for admission must meet. Typically, these requirements include undergraduate transcripts (which provide information about undergraduate grade point average and course work applied toward a major), admission test scores, and letters of recommendation. Most graduate programs also ask for an essay or personal statement that describes your personal reasons for seeking graduate study. In some fields, such as art and music, portfolios or auditions may be required in addition to other evidence of talent. Some institutions require that the applicant have an undergraduate degree in the same subject as the intended graduate major.

Most institutions evaluate each applicant on the basis of the applicant's total record, and the weight accorded any given factor varies widely from institution to institution and from program to program.

The Application Process

You should begin the application process at least one year before you expect to begin your graduate study. Find out the application deadline for each institution (many are provided in the **Profile** section of this guide). Go to the institution's website and find out if you can apply online. If not, request a paper application form. Fill out this form thoroughly and neatly. Assume that the school needs all the information it is requesting and that the admissions officer will be sensitive to the neatness and overall quality of what you submit. Do not supply more information than the school requires.

The institution may ask at least one question that will require a three- or four-paragraph answer. Compose your response on the assumption that the admissions officer is interested in both what you think and how you express yourself. Keep your statement brief and to the point, but, at the same time, include all pertinent information about your past experiences and your educational goals. Individual statements vary greatly in style and content, which helps admissions officers differentiate among applicants. Many graduate departments give considerable weight to the statement in making their admissions decisions, so be sure to take the time to prepare a thoughtful and concise statement.

If recommendations are a part of the admissions requirements, carefully choose the individuals you ask to write them. It is generally best to ask current or former professors to write the recommendations, provided they are able to attest to your intellectual ability and motivation for doing the work required of a graduate student. It is advisable to provide stamped, preaddressed envelopes to people being asked to submit recommendations on your behalf.

Completed applications, including references, transcripts, and admission test scores, should be received at the institution by the specified date.

Be advised that institutions do not usually make admissions decisions until all materials have been received. Enclose a self-addressed postcard with your application, requesting confirmation of receipt. Allow at least ten days for the return of the postcard before making further inquiries.

If you plan to apply for financial support, it is imperative that you file your application early.

ADMISSION TESTS

The major testing program used in graduate admissions is the Graduate Record Examinations (GRE®) testing program, sponsored by the GRE Board and administered by Educational Testing Service, Princeton, New Jersey.

The Graduate Record Examinations testing program consists of a General Test and six Subject Tests. The General Test measures critical thinking, verbal reasoning, quantitative reasoning, and analytical writing skills. It is offered as an Internet-based test (iBT) in the United States, Canada, and many other countries.

The GRE® revised General Test's questions were designed to reflect the kind of thinking that students need to do in graduate or business school and demonstrate that students are indeed ready for graduate-level work.

- **Verbal Reasoning**—Measures ability to analyze and evaluate written material and synthesize information obtained from it, analyze relationships among component parts of sentences, and recognize relationships among words and concepts.
- **Quantitative Reasoning**—Measures problem-solving ability, focusing on basic concepts of arithmetic, algebra, geometry, and data analysis.
- **Analytical Writing**—Measures critical thinking and analytical writing skills, specifically the ability to articulate and support complex ideas clearly and effectively.

The computer-delivered GRE® revised General Test is offered year-round at Prometric™ test centers and on specific dates at testing locations outside of the Prometric test center network. Appointments are scheduled on a first-come, first-served basis. The GRE® revised General Test is also offered as a paper-based test three times a year in areas where computer-based testing is not available.

You can take the computer-delivered GRE® revised General Test once every twenty-one days, up to five times within any continuous rolling twelve-month period (365 days)—even if you canceled your scores on a previously taken test. You may take the paper-delivered GRE® revised General Test as often as it is offered.

Three scores are reported on the revised General Test:

1. A **Verbal Reasoning score** is reported on a 130–170 score scale, in 1-point increments.

2. A **Quantitative Reasoning score** is reported on a 130–170 score scale, in 1-point increments.

3. An **Analytical Writing score** is reported on a 0–6 score level, in half-point increments.

The GRE® Subject Tests measure achievement and assume undergraduate majors or extensive background in the following six disciplines:

- Biology
- Chemistry
- Literature in English
- Mathematics
- Physics
- Psychology

The Subject Tests are available three times per year as paper-based administrations around the world. Testing time is approximately 2 hours and 50 minutes. You can obtain more information about the GRE® by visiting the ETS website at **www.ets.org** or consulting the *GRE® Information Bulletin*. The *Bulletin* can be obtained at many undergraduate colleges. You can also download it from the ETS website or obtain it by contacting Graduate Record Examinations, Educational Testing Service, P.O. Box 6000, Princeton, NJ 08541-6000; phone: 609-771-7670 or 866-473-4373.

If you expect to apply for admission to a program that requires any of the GRE® tests, you should select a test date well in advance of the application deadline. Scores on the computer-based General Test are reported within ten to fifteen days; scores on the paper-based Subject Tests are reported within six weeks.

Another testing program, the Miller Analogies Test® (MAT®), is administered at more than 500 Controlled Testing Centers in the United States, Canada, and other countries. The MAT® computer-based test is now available. Testing time is 60 minutes. The test consists of 120 partial analogies. You can obtain the *Candidate Information Booklet,* which contains a list of test centers and instructions for taking the test, from **www.milleranalogies.com** or by calling 800-328-5999 (toll-free).

Check the specific requirements of the programs to which you are applying.

How Admission Decisions Are Made

The program you apply to is directly involved in the admissions process. Although the final decision is usually made by the graduate dean (or an associate) or the faculty admissions committee, recommendations from faculty members in your intended field are important. At some institutions, an interview is incorporated into the decision process.

A Special Note for International Students

In addition to the steps already described, there are some special considerations for international students who intend to apply for graduate study in the United States. All graduate schools require an indication of competence in English. The purpose of the Test of English as a Foreign Language (TOEFL®) is to evaluate the English proficiency of people who are nonnative speakers of English and want to study at colleges and universities where English is the language of instruction. The TOEFL® is administered by Educational Testing Service (ETS) under the general direction of a policy board established by the College Board and the Graduate Record Examinations Board.

The TOEFL iBT® assesses four basic language skills: listening, reading, writing, and speaking. The Internet-based test is administered at secure, official test centers. The testing time is approximately 4 hours.

The TOEFL® is also offered in a paper-based format in areas of the world where internet-based testing is not available. In 2017, ETS launched a revised TOEFL® Paper-delivered Test, that more closely aligned to the TOEFL iBT® test. This revised paper-based test consists of three sections—listening, reading, and writing. The testing time is approximately 3 hours.

You can obtain more information for both versions of the TOEFL® by visiting the ETS website at **www.ets.org/toefl**. Information can also be obtained by contacting TOEFL® Services, Educational Testing Service, P.O. Box 6151, Princeton, NJ 08541-6151. Phone: 609-771-7100 or 877-863-3546 (toll free).

International students should apply especially early because of the number of steps required to complete the admissions process. Furthermore, many United States graduate schools have a limited number of spaces for international students, and many more students apply than the schools can accommodate.

International students may find financial assistance from institutions very limited. The U.S. government requires international applicants to submit a certification of support, which is a statement attesting to the applicant's financial resources. In addition, international students *must* have health insurance coverage.

Tips for Minority Students

Indicators of a university's values in terms of diversity are found both in its recruitment programs and its resources directed to student success. Important questions: Does the institution vigorously recruit minorities for its graduate programs? Is there funding available to help with the costs associated with visiting the school? Are minorities represented in the institution's brochures or website or on their faculty rolls? What campus-based resources or services (including assistance in locating housing or career counseling and placement) are available? Is funding available to members of underrepresented groups?

At the program level, it is particularly important for minority students to investigate the "climate" of a program under consideration. How many minority students are enrolled and how many have graduated? What opportunities are there to work with diverse faculty and mentors whose research interests match yours? How are conflicts resolved or concerns addressed? How interested are faculty in building strong and supportive relations with students? "Climate" concerns should be addressed by posing questions to various individuals, including faculty members, current students, and alumni.

Information is also available through various organizations, such as the Hispanic Association of Colleges & Universities (HACU), and publications such as *Diverse Issues in Higher Education* and *Hispanic Outlook* magazine. There are also books devoted to this topic, such as *The Multicultural Student's Guide to Colleges* by Robert Mitchell.

4 www.petersons.com

Peterson's Graduate Programs in the Physical Sciences, Mathematics, Agricultural Sciences, the Environment & Natural Resources 2020

Financial Support

The range of financial support at the graduate level is very broad. The following descriptions will give you a general idea of what you might expect and what will be expected of you as a financial support recipient.

Fellowships, Scholarships, and Grants

These are usually outright awards of a few hundred to many thousands of dollars with no service to the institution required in return. Fellowships and scholarships are usually awarded on the basis of merit and are highly competitive. Grants are made on the basis of financial need or special talent in a field of study. Many fellowships, scholarships, and grants not only cover tuition, fees, and supplies but also include stipends for living expenses with allowances for dependents. However, the terms of each should be examined because some do not permit recipients to supplement their income with outside work. Fellowships, scholarships, and grants may vary in the number of years for which they are awarded.

In addition to the availability of these funds at the university or program level, many excellent fellowship programs are available at the national level and may be applied for before and during enrollment in a graduate program. A listing of many of these programs can be found at the Council of Graduate Schools' website, **https://cgsnet.org/**. There is a wealth of information in the "Programs" and "Awards" sections.

Assistantships and Internships

Many graduate students receive financial support through assistantships, particularly involving teaching or research duties. It is important to recognize that such appointments should not be viewed simply as employment relationships but rather should constitute an integral and important part of a student's graduate education. As such, the appointments should be accompanied by strong faculty mentoring and increasingly responsible apprenticeship experiences. The specific nature of these appointments in a given program should be considered in selecting that graduate program.

TEACHING ASSISTANTSHIPS

These usually provide a salary and full or partial tuition remission and may also provide health benefits. Unlike fellowships, scholarships, and grants, which require no service to the institution, teaching assistantships require recipients to provide the institution with a specific amount of undergraduate teaching, ideally related to the student's field of study. Some teaching assistants are limited to grading papers, compiling bibliographies, taking notes, or monitoring laboratories. At some graduate schools, teaching assistants must carry lighter course loads than regular full-time students.

RESEARCH ASSISTANTSHIPS

These are very similar to teaching assistantships in the manner in which financial assistance is provided. The difference is that recipients are given basic research assignments in their disciplines rather than teaching responsibilities. The work required is normally related to the student's field of study; in most instances, the assistantship supports the student's thesis or dissertation research.

ADMINISTRATIVE INTERNSHIPS

These are similar to assistantships in application of financial assistance funds, but the student is given an assignment on a part-time basis, usually as a special assistant with one of the university's administrative offices. The assignment may not necessarily be directly related to the recipient's discipline.

RESIDENCE HALL AND COUNSELING ASSISTANTSHIPS

These assistantships are frequently assigned to graduate students in psychology, counseling, and social work, but they may be offered to students in other disciplines, especially if the student has worked in this capacity during his or her undergraduate years. Duties can vary from being available in a dean's office for a specific number of hours for consultation with undergraduates to living in campus residences and being responsible for both counseling and administrative tasks or advising student activity groups. Residence hall assistantships often include a room and board allowance and, in some cases, tuition assistance and stipends. Contact the Housing and Student Life Office for more information.

Health Insurance

The availability and affordability of health insurance is an important issue and one that should be considered in an applicant's choice of institution and program. While often included with assistantships and fellowships, this is not always the case and, even if provided, the benefits may be limited. It is important to note that the U.S. government requires international students to have health insurance.

The GI Bill

This provides financial assistance for students who are veterans of the United States armed forces. If you are a veteran, contact your local Veterans Administration office to determine your eligibility and to get full details about benefits. There are a number of programs that offer educational benefits to current military enlistees. Some states have tuition assistance programs for members of the National Guard. Contact the VA office at the college for more information.

Federal Work-Study Program (FWS)

Employment is another way some students finance their graduate studies. The federally funded Federal Work-Study Program provides eligible students with employment opportunities, usually in public and private nonprofit organizations. Federal funds pay up to 75 percent of the wages, with the remainder paid by the employing agency. FWS is available to graduate students who demonstrate financial need. Not all schools have these funds, and some only award them to undergraduates. Each school sets its application deadline and workstudy earnings limits. Wages vary and are related to the type of work done. You must file the Free Application for Federal Student Aid (FAFSA) to be eligible for this program.

Loans

Many graduate students borrow to finance their graduate programs when other sources of assistance (which do not have to be repaid) prove insufficient. You should always read and understand the terms of any loan program before submitting your application.

FEDERAL DIRECT LOANS

Federal Direct Loans. The Federal Direct Loan Program offers a variable-fixed interest rate loan to graduate students with the Department of Education acting as the lender. Students receive a new rate with each new loan, but that rate is fixed for the life of the loan. Beginning with loans made on or after July 1, 2013, the interest rate for loans made each July 1st to June 30th period are determined based on the last 10-year Treasury note auction prior to June 1st of that year, plus an added percentage. The interest rate can be no higher than 9.5%.

Beginning July 1, 2012, the Federal Direct Loan for graduate students is an unsubsidized loan. Under the *unsubsidized* program, the grad borrower pays the interest on the loan from the day proceeds are issued and is responsible for paying interest during all periods. If the borrower chooses not to pay the interest while in school, or during the grace periods, deferment, or forbearance, the interest accrues and will be capitalized.

Graduate students may borrow up to $20,500 per year through the Direct Loan Program, up to a cumulative maximum of $138,500, including undergraduate borrowing. No more than $65,500 of the $138,500 can be from subsidized loans, including loans the grad borrower may have received for periods of enrollment that began before July 1, 2012, or for prior undergraduate borrowing. You may borrow up to the cost of attendance at the school in which you are enrolled or will attend, minus estimated financial assistance from other federal, state, and private sources, up to a maximum of $20,500. Grad borrowers who reach the aggregate loan limit over the course of their education cannot receive additional loans; however, if they repay some of their loans to bring the outstanding balance below the aggregate limit, they could be eligible to borrow again, up to that limit.

Under the *subsidized* Federal Direct Loan Program, repayment begins six months after your last date of enrollment on at least a half-time basis. Under the *unsubsidized* program, repayment of interest begins within thirty days from disbursement of the loan proceeds, and repayment of the principal begins six months after your last enrollment on at least a half-time basis. Some borrowers may choose to defer interest payments while they are in school. The accrued interest is added to the loan balance when the borrower begins repayment. There are several repayment options.

Federal Perkins Loans. The Federal Perkins Loan is available to students demonstrating financial need and is administered directly by the school. Not all schools have these funds, and some may award them to undergraduates only. Eligibility is determined from the information you provide on the FAFSA. The school will notify you of your eligibility.

Eligible graduate students may borrow up to $8,000 per year, up to a maximum of $60,000, including undergraduate borrowing (even if your previous Perkins Loans have been repaid). The interest rate for Federal Perkins Loans is 5 percent, and no interest accrues while you remain in school at least half-time. Students who are attending less than half-time need to check with their school to determine the length of their grace period. There are no guarantee, loan, or disbursement fees. Repayment begins nine months after your last date of enrollment on at least a half-time basis and may extend over a maximum of ten years with no prepayment penalty.

Federal Direct Graduate PLUS Loans. Effective July 1, 2006, graduate and professional students are eligible for Graduate PLUS loans. This program allows students to borrow up to the cost of attendance, less any other aid received. These loans have a fixed interest rate (7.08% for loans first disbursed on or after July 1, 2019, and before July 1, 2020) and interest begins to accrue at the time of disbursement. Beginning with loans made on or after July 1, 2013, the interest rate for loans made each July 1st to June 30th period are determined based on the last 10-year Treasury note auction prior to June 1st of that year. The interest rate can be no higher than 10.5%. The PLUS loans do involve a credit check; a PLUS borrower may obtain a loan with a cosigner if his or her credit is not good enough. Grad PLUS loans may be deferred while a student is in school and for the six months following a drop below half-time enrollment. For more information, you should contact a representative in your college's financial aid office.

Deferring Your Federal Loan Repayments. If you borrowed under the Federal Direct Loan Program, Federal Direct PLUS Loan Program, or the Federal Perkins Loan Program for previous undergraduate or graduate study, your payments may be deferred when you return to graduate school, depending on when you borrowed and under which program.

There are other deferment options available if you are temporarily unable to repay your loan. Information about these deferments is provided at your entrance and exit interviews. If you believe you are eligible for a deferment of your loan payments, you must contact your lender or loan servicer to request a deferment. The deferment must be filed prior to the time your payment is due, and it must be re-filed when it expires if you remain eligible for deferment at that time.

SUPPLEMENTAL (PRIVATE) LOANS

Many lending institutions offer supplemental loan programs and other financing plans, such as the ones described here, to students seeking additional assistance in meeting their education expenses. Some loan programs target all types of graduate students; others are designed specifically for business, law, or medical students. In addition, you can use private loans not specifically designed for education to help finance your graduate degree.

If you are considering borrowing through a supplemental or private loan program, you should carefully consider the terms and be sure to read the fine print. Check with the program sponsor for the most current terms that will be applicable to the amounts you intend to borrow for graduate study. Most supplemental loan programs for graduate study offer unsubsidized, credit-based loans. In general, a credit-ready borrower is one who has a satisfactory credit history or no credit history at all. A creditworthy borrower generally must pass a credit test to be eligible to borrow or act as a cosigner for the loan funds.

Many supplemental loan programs have minimum and maximum annual loan limits. Some offer amounts equal to the cost of attendance minus any other aid you will receive for graduate study. If you are planning to borrow for several years of graduate study, consider whether there is a cumulative or aggregate limit on the amount you may borrow. Often this cumulative or aggregate limit will include any amounts you borrowed and have not repaid for undergraduate or previous graduate study.

The combination of the annual interest rate, loan fees, and the repayment terms you choose will determine how much you will repay over time. Compare these features in combination before you decide which loan program to use. Some loans offer interest rates that are adjusted monthly, quarterly, or annually. Some offer interest rates that are lower during the in-school, grace, and deferment periods and then increase when you begin repayment. Some programs include a loan origination fee, which is usually deducted from the principal amount you receive when the loan is disbursed and must be repaid along with the interest and other principal when you graduate, withdraw from school, or drop below half-time study. Sometimes the loan fees are reduced if you borrow with a qualified cosigner. Some programs allow you to defer interest and/or principal payments while you are enrolled in graduate school. Many programs allow you to capitalize your interest payments; the interest due on your loan is added to the outstanding balance of your loan, so you don't have to repay immediately, but this increases the amount you owe. Other programs allow you to pay the interest as you go, which reduces the amount you later have to repay. The private loan market is very competitive, and your financial aid office can help you evaluate these programs.

Applying for Need-Based Financial Aid

Schools that award federal and institutional financial assistance based on need will require you to complete the FAFSA and, in some cases, an institutional financial aid application.

If you are applying for federal student assistance, you **must** complete the FAFSA. A service of the U.S. Department of Education, the FAFSA is free to all applicants. Most applicants apply online at **www.fafsa.ed.gov**. Paper applications are available at the financial aid office of your local college.

After your FAFSA information has been processed, you will receive a Student Aid Report (SAR). If you provided an e-mail address on the FAFSA, this will be sent to you electronically; otherwise, it will be mailed to your home address.

Follow the instructions on the SAR if you need to correct information reported on your original application. If your situation changes after you file your FAFSA, contact your financial aid officer to discuss amending

6 www.petersons.com

Peterson's Graduate Programs in the Physical Sciences, Mathematics, Agricultural Sciences, the Environment & Natural Resources 2020

your information. You can also appeal your financial aid award if you have extenuating circumstances.

If you would like more information on federal student financial aid, visit the FAFSA website or download the most recent version of *Do You Need Money for College* at www.studentaid.ed.gov/sa/sites/default/files/2018-19-do-you-need-money.pdf. This guide is also available in Spanish.

The U.S. Department of Education also has a toll-free number for questions concerning federal student aid programs. The number is 1-800-4-FED AID (1-800-433-3243). If you are hearing impaired, call toll-free, 1-800-730-8913.

Summary

Remember that these are generalized statements about financial assistance at the graduate level. Because each institution allots its aid differently, you should communicate directly with the school and the specific department of interest to you. It is not unusual, for example, to find that an endowment vested within a specific department supports one or more fellowships. You may fit its requirements and specifications precisely.

Peterson's Graduate Programs in the Physical Sciences, Mathematics, Agricultural Sciences, the Environment & Natural Resources 2020

www.petersons.com   **7**

Accreditation and Accrediting Agencies

Colleges and universities in the United States, and their individual academic and professional programs, are accredited by nongovernmental agencies concerned with monitoring the quality of education in this country. Agencies with both regional and national jurisdictions grant accreditation to institutions as a whole, while specialized bodies acting on a nationwide basis—often national professional associations—grant accreditation to departments and programs in specific fields.

Institutional and specialized accrediting agencies share the same basic concerns: the purpose an academic unit—whether university or program—has set for itself and how well it fulfills that purpose, the adequacy of its financial and other resources, the quality of its academic offerings, and the level of services it provides. Agencies that grant institutional accreditation take a broader view, of course, and examine university-wide or college-wide services with which a specialized agency may not concern itself.

Both types of agencies follow the same general procedures when considering an application for accreditation. The academic unit prepares a self-evaluation, focusing on the concerns mentioned above and usually including an assessment of both its strengths and weaknesses; a team of representatives of the accrediting body reviews this evaluation, visits the campus, and makes its own report; and finally, the accrediting body makes a decision on the application. Often, even when accreditation is granted, the agency makes a recommendation regarding how the institution or program can improve. All institutions and programs are also reviewed every few years to determine whether they continue to meet established standards; if they do not, they may lose their accreditation.

Accrediting agencies themselves are reviewed and evaluated periodically by the U.S. Department of Education and the Council for Higher Education Accreditation (CHEA). Recognized agencies adhere to certain standards and practices, and their authority in matters of accreditation is widely accepted in the educational community.

This does not mean, however, that accreditation is a simple matter, either for schools wishing to become accredited or for students deciding where to apply. Indeed, in certain fields the very meaning and methods of accreditation are the subject of a good deal of debate. For their part, those applying to graduate school should be aware of the safeguards provided by regional accreditation, especially in terms of degree acceptance and institutional longevity. Beyond this, applicants should understand the role that specialized accreditation plays in their field, as this varies considerably from one discipline to another. In certain professional fields, it is necessary to have graduated from a program that is accredited in order to be eligible for a license to practice, and in some fields the federal government also makes this a hiring requirement. In other disciplines, however, accreditation is not as essential, and there can be excellent programs that are not accredited. In fact, some programs choose not to seek accreditation, although most do.

Institutions and programs that present themselves for accreditation are sometimes granted the status of candidate for accreditation, or what is known as "preaccreditation." This may happen, for example, when an academic unit is too new to have met all the requirements for accreditation. Such status signifies initial recognition and indicates that the school or program in question is working to fulfill all requirements; it does not, however, guarantee that accreditation will be granted.

Institutional Accrediting Agencies—Regional

MIDDLE STATES COMMISSION ON HIGHER EDUCATION

Accredits institutions in Delaware, District of Columbia, Maryland, New Jersey, New York, Pennsylvania, Puerto Rico, and the Virgin Islands.

Dr. Elizabeth Sibolski, President
Middle States Commission on Higher Education
3624 Market Street, Second Floor West
Philadelphia, Pennsylvania 19104
Phone: 267-284-5000
Fax: 215-662-5501
E-mail: info@mscho.org
Website: www.msche.org

NEW ENGLAND ASSOCIATION OF SCHOOLS AND COLLEGES

Accredits institutions in Connecticut, Maine, Massachusetts, New Hampshire, Rhode Island, and Vermont.

Dr. Barbara E. Brittingham, President/Director
Commission on Institutions of Higher Education
3 Burlington Woods Drive, Suite 100
Burlington, Massachusetts 01803-4531
Phone: 855-886-3272 or 781-425-7714
Fax: 781-425-1001
E-mail: cihe@neasc.org
Website: https://cihe.neasc.org

THE HIGHER LEARNING COMMISSION

Accredits institutions in Arizona, Arkansas, Colorado, Illinois, Indiana, Iowa, Kansas, Michigan, Minnesota, Missouri, Nebraska, New Mexico, North Dakota, Ohio, Oklahoma, South Dakota, West Virginia, Wisconsin, and Wyoming.

Dr. Barbara Gellman-Danley, President
The Higher Learning Commission
230 South LaSalle Street, Suite 7-500
Chicago, Illinois 60604-1413
Phone: 800-621-7440 or 312-263-0456
Fax: 312-263-7462
E-mail: info@hlcommission.org
Website: www.hlcommission.org

NORTHWEST COMMISSION ON COLLEGES AND UNIVERSITIES

Accredits institutions in Alaska, Idaho, Montana, Nevada, Oregon, Utah, and Washington.

Dr. Sandra E. Elman, President
8060 165th Avenue, NE, Suite 100
Redmond, Washington 98052
Phone: 425-558-4224
Fax: 425-376-0596
E-mail: selman@nwccu.org
Website: www.nwccu.org

SOUTHERN ASSOCIATION OF COLLEGES AND SCHOOLS

Accredits institutions in Alabama, Florida, Georgia, Kentucky, Louisiana, Mississippi, North Carolina, South Carolina, Tennessee, Texas, and Virginia.

Dr. Belle S. Wheelan, President
Commission on Colleges
1866 Southern Lane
Decatur, Georgia 30033-4097
Phone: 404-679-4500 Ext. 4504
Fax: 404-679-4558
E-mail: questions@sacscoc.org
Website: www.sacscoc.org

WESTERN ASSOCIATION OF SCHOOLS AND COLLEGES

Accredits institutions in California, Guam, and Hawaii.

Jamienne S. Studley, President
WASC Senior College and University Commission
985 Atlantic Avenue, Suite 100
Alameda, California 94501
Phone: 510-748-9001
Fax: 510-748-9797
E-mail: wasc@wscuc.org
Website: https://www.wscuc.org/

Institutional Accrediting Agencies—Other

ACCREDITING COUNCIL FOR INDEPENDENT COLLEGES AND SCHOOLS
Michelle Edwards, President
750 FIrst Street NE, Suite 980
Washington, DC 20002-4223
Phone: 202-336-6780
Fax: 202-842-2593
E-mail: info@acics.org
Website: www.acics.org

DISTANCE EDUCATION ACCREDITING COMMISSION (DEAC)
Leah Matthews, Executive Director
1101 17th Street NW, Suite 808
Washington, DC 20036-4704
Phone: 202-234-5100
Fax: 202-332-1386
E-mail: info@deac.org
Website: www.deac.org

Specialized Accrediting Agencies

ACUPUNCTURE AND ORIENTAL MEDICINE
Mark S. McKenzie, LAc MsOM DiplOM, Executive Director
Accreditation Commission for Acupuncture and Oriental Medicine
8941 Aztec Drive, Suite 2
Eden Prairie, Minnesota 55347
Phone: 952-212-2434
Fax: 301-313-0912
E-mail: info@acaom.org
Website: www.acaom.org

ALLIED HEALTH
Kathleen Megivern, Executive Director
Commission on Accreditation of Allied Health Education Programs (CAAHEP)
25400 US Hwy 19 North, Suite 158
Clearwater, Florida 33763
Phone: 727-210-2350
Fax: 727-210-2354
E-mail: mail@caahep.org
Website: www.caahep.org

ART AND DESIGN
Karen P. Moynahan, Executive Director
National Association of Schools of Art and Design (NASAD)
Commission on Accreditation
11250 Roger Bacon Drive, Suite 21
Reston, Virginia 20190-5248
Phone: 703-437-0700
Fax: 703-437-6312
E-mail: info@arts-accredit.org
Website: http://nasad.arts-accredit.org

ATHLETIC TRAINING EDUCATION
Pamela Hansen, CAATE Director of Accreditation
Commission on Accreditation of Athletic Training Education (CAATE)
6850 Austin Center Blvd., Suite 100
Austin, Texas 78731-3184
Phone: 512-733-9700
E-mail: pamela@caate.net
Website: www.caate.net

AUDIOLOGY EDUCATION
Meggan Olek, Director
Accreditation Commission for Audiology Education (ACAE)
11480 Commerce Park Drive, Suite 220
Reston, Virginia 20191
Phone: 202-986-9500
Fax: 202-986-9550
E-mail: info@acaeaccred.org
Website: https://acaeaccred.org/

AVIATION
Dr. Gary J. Northam, President
Aviation Accreditation Board International (AABI)
3410 Skyway Drive
Auburn, Alabama 36830
Phone: 334-844-2431
Fax: 334-844-2432
E-mail: gary.northam@auburn.edu
Website: www.aabi.aero

BUSINESS
Stephanie Bryant, Executive Vice President and Chief Accreditation Officer
AACSB International—The Association to Advance Collegiate Schools of Business
777 South Harbour Island Boulevard, Suite 750
Tampa, Florida 33602
Phone: 813-769-6500
Fax: 813-769-6559
E-mail: stephanie.bryant@aacsb.edu
Website: www.aacsb.edu

BUSINESS EDUCATION
Dr. Phyllis Okrepkie, President
International Assembly for Collegiate Business Education (IACBE)
11374 Strang Line Road
Lenexa, Kansas 66215
Phone: 913-631-3009
Fax: 913-631-9154
E-mail: iacbe@iacbe.org
Website: www.iacbe.org

CHIROPRACTIC
Dr. Craig S. Little, President
Council on Chiropractic Education (CCE)
Commission on Accreditation
8049 North 85th Way
Scottsdale, Arizona 85258-4321
Phone: 480-443-8877 or 888-443-3506
Fax: 480-483-7333
E-mail: cce@cce-usa.org
Website: www.cce-usa.org

CLINICAL LABORATORY SCIENCES
Dianne M. Cearlock, Ph.D., Chief Executive Officer
National Accrediting Agency for Clinical Laboratory Sciences
5600 North River Road, Suite 720
Rosemont, Illinois 60018-5119
Phone: 773-714-8880 or 847-939-3597
Fax: 773-714-8886
E-mail: info@naacls.org
Website: www.naacls.org

CLINICAL PASTORAL EDUCATION
Trace Haythorn, Ph.D., Executive Director/CEO
Association for Clinical Pastoral Education, Inc.
One West Court Square, Suite 325
Decatur, Georgia 30030-2576
Phone: 678-363-6226
Fax: 404-320-0849
E-mail: acpe@acpe.edu
Website: www.acpe.edu

DANCE
Karen P. Moynahan, Executive Director
National Association of Schools of Dance (NASD)
Commission on Accreditation
11250 Roger Bacon Drive, Suite 21
Reston, Virginia 20190-5248
Phone: 703-437-0700
Fax: 703-437-6312
E-mail: info@arts-accredit.org
Website: http://nasd.arts-accredit.org

DENTISTRY
Dr. Kathleen T. O'Loughlin, Executive Director
Commission on Dental Accreditation
American Dental Association
211 East Chicago Avenue
Chicago, Illinois 60611
Phone: 312-440-2500
E-mail: accreditation@ada.org
Website: www.ada.org

DIETETICS AND NUTRITION
Mary B. Gregoire, Ph.D., Executive Director; RD, FADA, FAND
Academy of Nutrition and Dietetics
Accreditation Council for Education in Nutrition and Dietetics (ACEND)
120 South Riverside Plaza
Chicago, Illinois 60606-6995
Phone: 800-877-1600 or 312-899-0040
E-mail: acend@eatright.org
Website: www.eatright.org/cade

EDUCATION PREPARATION
Christopher Koch, President
Council for the Accreditation of Educator Preparation (CAEP)
1140 19th Street NW, Suite 400
Washington, DC 20036
Phone: 202-223-0077
Fax: 202-296-6620
E-mail: caep@caepnet.org
Website: www.caepnet.org

ENGINEERING
Michael Milligan, Ph.D., PE, Executive Director
Accreditation Board for Engineering and Technology, Inc. (ABET)
415 North Charles Street
Baltimore, Maryland 21201
Phone: 410-347-7700
E-mail: accreditation@abet.org
Website: www.abet.org

FORENSIC SCIENCES
Nancy J. Jackson, Director of Development and Accreditation
American Academy of Forensic Sciences (AAFS)
Forensic Science Education Program Accreditation Commission
(FEPAC)
410 North 21st Street
Colorado Springs, Colorado 80904
Phone: 719-636-1100
Fax: 719-636-1993
E-mail: njackson@aafs.org
Website: www.fepac-edu.org

FORESTRY
Carol L. Redelsheimer
Director of Science and Education
Society of American Foresters
10100 Laureate Way
Bethesda, Maryland 20814-2198
Phone: 301-897-8720 or 866-897-8720
Fax: 301-897-3690
E-mail: membership@safnet.org
Website: www.eforester.com

HEALTHCARE MANAGEMENT
Commission on Accreditation of Healthcare Management Education
(CAHME)
Anthony Stanowski, President and CEO
6110 Executive Boulevard, Suite 614
Rockville, Maryland 20852
Phone: 301-298-1820
E-mail: info@cahme.org
Website: www.cahme.org

HEALTH INFORMATICS AND HEALTH MANAGEMENT
Angela Kennedy, EdD, MBA, RHIA, Chief Executive Officer
Commission on Accreditation for Health Informatics and Information
Management Education (CAHIIM)
233 North Michigan Avenue, 21st Floor
Chicago, Illinois 60601-5800
Phone: 312-233-1134
Fax: 312-233-1948
E-mail: info@cahiim.org
Website: www.cahiim.org

HUMAN SERVICE EDUCATION
Dr. Elaine Green, President
Council for Standards in Human Service Education (CSHSE)
3337 Duke Street
Alexandria, Virginia 22314
Phone: 571-257-3959
E-mail: info@cshse.org
Website: www.cshse.org

INTERIOR DESIGN
Holly Mattson, Executive Director
Council for Interior Design Accreditation
206 Grandview Avenue, Suite 350
Grand Rapids, Michigan 49503-4014
Phone: 616-458-0400
Fax: 616-458-0460
E-mail: info@accredit-id.org
Website: www.accredit-id.org

JOURNALISM AND MASS COMMUNICATIONS
Patricia Thompson, Executive Director
Accrediting Council on Education in Journalism and Mass
Communications (ACEJMC)
201 Bishop Hall
P.O. Box 1848
University, MS 38677-1848
Phone: 662-915-5504
E-mail: pthomps1@olemiss.edu
Website: www.acejmc.org

LANDSCAPE ARCHITECTURE
Nancy Somerville, Executive Vice President, CEO
American Society of Landscape Architects (ASLA)
636 Eye Street, NW
Washington, DC 20001-3736
Phone: 202-898-2444
Fax: 202-898-1185
E-mail: info@asla.org
Website: www.asla.org

LAW
Barry Currier, Managing Director of Accreditation & Legal Education
American Bar Association
321 North Clark Street, 21st Floor
Chicago, Illinois 60654
Phone: 312-988-6738
Fax: 312-988-5681
E-mail: legaled@americanbar.org
Website: https://www.americanbar.org/groups/legal_education/
accreditation.html

LIBRARY
Karen O'Brien, Director
Office for Accreditation
American Library Association
50 East Huron Street
Chicago, Illinois 60611-2795
Phone: 800-545-2433, ext. 2432 or 312-280-2432
Fax: 312-280-2433
E-mail: accred@ala.org
Website: http://www.ala.org/aboutala/offices/accreditation/

Peterson's Graduate Programs in the Physical Sciences, Mathematics,
Agricultural Sciences, the Environment & Natural Resources 2020

www.petersons.com   11

MARRIAGE AND FAMILY THERAPY
Tanya A. Tamarkin, Director of Educational Affairs
Commission on Accreditation for Marriage and Family Therapy
   Education (COAMFTE)
American Association for Marriage and Family Therapy
112 South Alfred Street
Alexandria, Virginia 22314-3061
Phone: 703-838-9808
Fax: 703-838-9805
E-mail: coa@aamft.org
Website: www.aamft.org

MEDICAL ILLUSTRATION
Kathleen Megivern, Executive Director
Commission on Accreditation of Allied Health Education Programs
   (CAAHEP)
25400 US Highway 19 North, Suite 158
Clearwater, Florida 33756
Phone: 727-210-2350
Fax: 727-210-2354
E-mail: mail@caahep.org
Website: www.caahep.org

MEDICINE
Liaison Committee on Medical Education (LCME)
Robert B. Hash, M.D., LCME Secretary
American Medical Association
Council on Medical Education
330 North Wabash Avenue, Suite 39300
Chicago, Illinois 60611-5885
Phone: 312-464-4933
E-mail: lcme@aamc.org
Website: www.ama-assn.org

Liaison Committee on Medical Education (LCME)
Heather Lent, M.A., Director
Accreditation Services
Association of American Medical Colleges
655 K Street, NW
Washington, DC 20001-2399
Phone: 202-828-0596
E-mail: lcme@aamc.org
Website: www.lcme.org

MUSIC
Karen P. Moynahan, Executive Director
National Association of Schools of Music (NASM)
Commission on Accreditation
11250 Roger Bacon Drive, Suite 21
Reston, Virginia 20190-5248
Phone: 703-437-0700
Fax: 703-437-6312
E-mail: info@arts-accredit.org
Website: http://nasm.arts-accredit.org/

NATUROPATHIC MEDICINE
Daniel Seitz, J.D., Ed.D., Executive Director
Council on Naturopathic Medical Education
P.O. Box 178
Great Barrington, Massachusetts 01230
Phone: 413-528-8877
E-mail: https://cnme.org/contact-us/
Website: www.cnme.org

NURSE ANESTHESIA
Francis R.Gerbasi, Ph.D., CRNA, COA Executive Director
Council on Accreditation of Nurse Anesthesia Educational Programs
   (CoA-NAEP)
American Association of Nurse Anesthetists
222 South Prospect Avenue
Park Ridge, Illinois 60068-4001
Phone: 847-655-1160
Fax: 847-692-7137
E-mail: accreditation@coa.us.com
Website: http://www.coacrna.org

NURSE EDUCATION
Jennifer L. Butlin, Executive Director
Commission on Collegiate Nursing Education (CCNE)
One Dupont Circle, NW, Suite 530
Washington, DC 20036-1120
Phone: 202-887-6791
Fax: 202-887-8476
E-mail: jbutlin@aacn.nche.edu
Website: www.aacn.nche.edu/accreditation

Marsal P. Stoll, Chief Executive Officer
Accreditation Commission for Education in Nursing (ACEN)
3343 Peachtree Road, NE, Suite 850
Atlanta, Georgia 30326
Phone: 404-975-5000
Fax: 404-975-5020
E-mail: mstoll@acenursing.org
Website: www.acenursing.org

NURSE MIDWIFERY
Heather L. Maurer, M.A., Executive Director
Accreditation Commission for Midwifery Education (ACME)
American College of Nurse-Midwives
8403 Colesville Road, Suite 1550
Silver Spring, Maryland 20910
Phone: 240-485-1800
Fax: 240-485-1818
E-mail: info@acnm.org
Website: www.midwife.org/Program-Accreditation

NURSE PRACTITIONER
Gay Johnson, CEO
National Association of Nurse Practitioners in Women's Health
Council on Accreditation
505 C Street, NE
Washington, DC 20002
Phone: 202-543-9693 Ext. 1
Fax: 202-543-9858
E-mail: info@npwh.org
Website: www.npwh.org

NURSING
Marsal P. Stoll, Chief Executive Director
Accreditation Commission for Education in Nursing (ACEN)
3343 Peachtree Road, NE, Suite 850
Atlanta, Georgia 30326
Phone: 404-975-5000
Fax: 404-975-5020
E-mail: info@acenursing.org
Website: www.acenursing.org

OCCUPATIONAL THERAPY
Heather Stagliano, DHSc, OTR/L, Executive Director
The American Occupational Therapy Association, Inc.
4720 Montgomery Lane, Suite 200
Bethesda, Maryland 20814-3449
Phone: 301-652-6611 Ext. 2682
TDD: 800-377-8555
Fax: 240-762-5150
E-mail: accred@aota.org
Website: www.aoteonline.org

12 www.petersons.com

*Peterson's Graduate Programs in the Physical Sciences, Mathematics,
Agricultural Sciences, the Environment & Natural Resources 2020*

OPTOMETRY
Joyce L. Urbeck, Administrative Director
Accreditation Council on Optometric Education (ACOE)
American Optometric Association
243 North Lindbergh Boulevard
St. Louis, Missouri 63141-7881
Phone: 314-991-4100, Ext. 4246
Fax: 314-991-4101
E-mail: accredit@aoa.org
Website: www.theacoe.org

OSTEOPATHIC MEDICINE
Director, Department of Accreditation
Commission on Osteopathic College Accreditation (COCA)
American Osteopathic Association
142 East Ontario Street
Chicago, Illinois 60611
Phone: 312-202-8048
Fax: 312-202-8202
E-mail: predoc@osteopathic.org
Website: www.aoacoca.org

PHARMACY
Peter H. Vlasses, PharmD, Executive Director
Accreditation Council for Pharmacy Education
135 South LaSalle Street, Suite 4100
Chicago, Illinois 60603-4810
Phone: 312-664-3575
Fax: 312-664-4652
E-mail: csinfo@acpe-accredit.org
Website: www.acpe-accredit.org

PHYSICAL THERAPY
Sandra Wise, Senior Director
Commission on Accreditation in Physical Therapy Education (CAPTE)
American Physical Therapy Association (APTA)
1111 North Fairfax Street
Alexandria, Virginia 22314-1488
Phone: 703-706-3245
Fax: 703-706-3387
E-mail: accreditation@apta.org
Website: www.capteonline.org

PHYSICIAN ASSISTANT STUDIES
Sharon L. Luke, Executive Director
Accredittion Review Commission on Education for the Physician
    Assistant, Inc. (ARC-PA)
12000 Findley Road, Suite 275
Johns Creek, Georgia 30097
Phone: 770-476-1224
Fax: 770-476-1738
E-mail: arc-pa@arc-pa.org
Website: www.arc-pa.org

PLANNING
Jesmarie Soto Johnson, Executive Director
American Institute of Certified Planners/Association of Collegiate
    Schools of Planning/American Planning Association
Planning Accreditation Board (PAB)
2334 West Lawrence Avenue, Suite 209
Chicago, Illinois 60625
Phone: 773-334-7200
E-mail: smerits@planningaccreditationboard.org
Website: www.planningaccreditationboard.org

PODIATRIC MEDICINE
Heather Stagliano, OTR/L, DHSc, Executive Director
Council on Podiatric Medical Education (CPME)
American Podiatric Medical Association (APMA)
9312 Old Georgetown Road
Bethesda, Maryland 20814-1621
Phone: 301-581-9200
Fax: 301-571-4903
Website: www.cpme.org

PSYCHOLOGY AND COUNSELING
Jacqueline Remondet, Associate Executive Director, CEO of the
Accrediting Unit,
Office of Program Consultation and Accreditation
American Psychological Association
750 First Street, NE
Washington, DC 20002-4202
Phone: 202-336-5979 or 800-374-2721
TDD/TTY: 202-336-6123
Fax: 202-336-5978
E-mail: apaaccred@apa.org
Website: www.apa.org/ed/accreditation

Kelly Coker, Executive Director
Council for Accreditation of Counseling and Related Educational
    Programs (CACREP)
1001 North Fairfax Street, Suite 510
Alexandria, Virginia 22314
Phone: 703-535-5990
Fax: 703-739-6209
E-mail: cacrep@cacrep.org
Website: www.cacrep.org

Richard M. McFall, Executive Director
Psychological Clinical Science Accreditation System (PCSAS)
1101 East Tenth Street
IU Psychology Building
Bloomington, Indiana 47405-7007
Phone: 812-856-2570
Fax: 812-322-5545
E-mail: rmmcfall@pcsas.org
Website: www.pcsas.org

PUBLIC HEALTH
Laura Rasar King, M.P.H., MCHES, Executive Director
Council on Education for Public Health
1010 Wayne Avenue, Suite 220
Silver Spring, Maryland 20910
Phone: 202-789-1050
Fax: 202-789-1895
E-mail: Lking@ceph.org
Website: www.ceph.org

PUBLIC POLICY, AFFAIRS AND ADMINISTRATION
Crystal Calarusse, Chief Accreditation Officer
Commission on Peer Review and Accreditation
Network of Schools of Public Policy, Affairs, and Administration
(NASPAA-COPRA)
1029 Vermont Avenue, NW, Suite 1100
Washington, DC 20005
Phone: 202-628-8965
Fax: 202-626-4978
E-mail: copra@naspaa.org
Website: accreditation.naspaa.org

RADIOLOGIC TECHNOLOGY
Leslie Winter, Chief Executive Officer Joint Review Committee on
Education in Radiologic Technology (JRCERT)
20 North Wacker Drive, Suite 2850
Chicago, Illinois 60606-3182
Phone: 312-704-5300
Fax: 312-704-5304
E-mail: mail@jrcert.org
Website: www.jrcert.org

REHABILITATION EDUCATION
Frank Lane, Ph.D., Executive Director
Council for Accreditation of Counseling and Related Educational
    Programs (CACREP)
1001 North Fairfax Street, Suite 510
Alexandria, Virginia 22314
Phone: 703-535-5990
Fax: 703-739-6209
E-mail: cacrep@cacrep.org
Website: www.cacrep.org

Peterson's Graduate Programs in the Physical Sciences, Mathematics, Agricultural Sciences, the Environment & Natural Resources 2020

www.petersons.com 13

RESPIRATORY CARE
Thomas Smalling, Executive Director
Commission on Accreditation for Respiratory Care (CoARC)
1248 Harwood Road
Bedford, Texas 76021-4244
Phone: 817-283-2835
Fax: 817-354-8519
E-mail: tom@coarc.com
Website: www.coarc.com

SOCIAL WORK
Dr. Stacey Borasky, Director of Accreditation
Office of Social Work Accreditation
Council on Social Work Education
1701 Duke Street, Suite 200
Alexandria, Virginia 22314
Phone: 703-683-8080
Fax: 703-519-2078
E-mail: info@cswe.org
Website: www.cswe.org

SPEECH-LANGUAGE PATHOLOGY AND AUDIOLOGY
Kimberlee Moore, Accreditation Executive Director
American Speech-Language-Hearing Association
Council on Academic Accreditation in Audiology and Speech-Language
   Pathology
2200 Research Boulevard #310
Rockville, Maryland 20850-3289
Phone: 301-296-5700
Fax: 301-296-8750
E-mail: accreditation@asha.org
Website: http://caa.asha.org

TEACHER EDUCATION
Christopher A. Koch, President
National Council for Accreditation of Teacher Education (NCATE)
Teacher Education Accreditation Council (TEAC)
1140 19th Street, Suite 400
Washington, DC 20036
Phone: 202-223-0077
Fax: 202-296-6620
E-mail: caep@caepnet.org
Website: www.ncate.org

TECHNOLOGY
Michale S. McComis, Ed.D., Executive Director
Accrediting Commission of Career Schools and Colleges
2101 Wilson Boulevard, Suite 302
Arlington, Virginia 22201
Phone: 703-247-4212
Fax: 703-247-4533
E-mail: mccomis@accsc.org
Website: www.accsc.org

TECHNOLOGY, MANAGEMENT, AND APPLIED ENGINEERING
Kelly Schild, Director of Accreditation
The Association of Technology, Management, and Applied Engineering
(ATMAE)
275 N. York Street, Suite 401
Elmhurst, Illinois 60126
Phone: 630-433-4514
Fax: 630-563-9181
E-mail: Kelly@atmae.org
Website: www.atmae.org

THEATER
Karen P. Moynahan, Executive Director
National Association of Schools of Theatre Commission on
   Accreditation
11250 Roger Bacon Drive, Suite 21
Reston, Virginia 20190
Phone: 703-437-0700
Fax: 703-437-6312
E-mail: info@arts-accredit.org
Website: http://nast.arts-accredit.org/

THEOLOGY
Dr. Bernard Fryshman, Executive VP
Emeritus and Interim Executive Director
Association of Advanced Rabbinical and Talmudic Schools (AARTS)
Accreditation Commission
11 Broadway, Suite 405
New York, New York 10004
Phone: 212-363-1991
Fax: 212-533-5335
E-mail: k.sharfman.aarts@gmail.com

Frank Yamada, Executive Director
Association of Theological Schools in the United States and Canada
   (ATS)
Commission on Accrediting
10 Summit Park Drive
Pittsburgh, Pennsylvania 15275
Phone: 412-788-6505
Fax: 412-788-6510
E-mail: ats@ats.edu
Website: www.ats.edu

Dr. Timothy Eaton, President
Transnational Association of Christian Colleges and Schools (TRACS)
Accreditation Commission
15935 Forest Road
Forest, Virginia 24551
Phone: 434-525-9539
Fax: 434-525-9538
E-mail: info@tracs.org
Website: www.tracs.org

VETERINARY MEDICINE
Dr. Karen Brandt, Director of Education and Research
American Veterinary Medical Association (AVMA)
Council on Education
1931 North Meacham Road, Suite 100
Schaumburg, Illinois 60173-4360
Phone: 847-925-8070 Ext. 6674
Fax: 847-285-5732
E-mail: info@avma.org
Website: www.avma.org

14   www.petersons.com

Peterson's Graduate Programs in the Physical Sciences, Mathematics,
Agricultural Sciences, the Environment & Natural Resources 2020

How to Use These Guides

As you identify the particular programs and institutions that interest you, you can use both the *Graduate & Professional Programs: An Overview* volume and the specialized volumes in the series to obtain detailed information.

- *Graduate Programs in the Biological/Biomedical Sciences & Health-Related Professions*
- *Graduate Programs in Business, Education, Information Studies, Law & Social Work*
- *Graduate Programs in Engineering & Applied Sciences*
- *Graduate Programs the Humanities, Arts & Social Sciences*
- *Graduate Programs in the Physical Sciences, Mathematics, Agricultural Sciences, the Environment & Natural Resources*

Each of the specialized volumes in the series is divided into sections that contain one or more directories devoted to programs in a particular field. If you do not find a directory devoted to your field of interest in a specific volume, consult "Directories and Subject Areas" (located at the end of each volume). After you have identified the correct volume, consult the "Directories and Subject Areas in This Book" index, which shows (as does the more general directory) what directories cover subjects not specifically named in a directory or section title.

Each of the specialized volumes in the series has a number of general directories. These directories have entries for the largest unit at an institution granting graduate degrees in that field. For example, the general Engineering and Applied Sciences directory in the *Graduate Programs in Engineering & Applied Sciences* volume consists of **Profiles** for colleges, schools, and departments of engineering and applied sciences.

General directories are followed by other directories, or sections, that give more detailed information about programs in particular areas of the general field that has been covered. The general Engineering and Applied Sciences directory, in the previous example, is followed by nineteen sections with directories in specific areas of engineering, such as Chemical Engineering, Industrial/Management Engineering, and Mechanical Engineering.

Because of the broad nature of many fields, any system of organization is bound to involve a certain amount of overlap. Environmental studies, for example, is a field whose various aspects are studied in several types of departments and schools. Readers interested in such studies will find information on relevant programs in the *Graduate Programs in the Biological/Biomedical Sciences & Health-Related Professions* volume under Ecology and Environmental Biology and Environmental and Occupational Health; in the *Graduate Programs in the Physical Sciences, Mathematics, Agricultural Sciences, the Environment & Natural Resources* volume under Environmental Management and Policy and Natural Resources; and in the *Graduate Programs in Engineering & Applied Sciences* volume under Energy Management and Policy and Environmental Engineering. To help you find all of the programs of interest to you, the introduction to each section within the specialized volumes includes, if applicable, a paragraph suggesting other sections and directories with information on related areas of study.

Directory of Institutions with Programs in the Physical Sciences, Mathematics, Agricultural Sciences, the Environment & Natural Resources

This directory lists institutions in alphabetical order and includes beneath each name the academic fields in which each institution offers graduate programs. The degree level in each field is also indicated, provided that the institution has supplied that information in response to Peterson's Annual Survey of Graduate and Professional Institutions.

An M indicates that a master's degree program is offered; a D indicates that a doctoral degree program is offered; an O signifies that other advanced degrees (e.g., certificates or specialist degrees) are offered; and an * (asterisk) indicates that a **Close-Up** and/or **Display** is located in this volume. See the index, "Close-Ups and Displays," for the specific page number.

Profiles of Academic and Professional Programs in the Specialized Volumes

Each section of **Profiles** has a table of contents that lists the Program Directories, **Displays**, and **Close-Ups**. Program Directories consist of the **Profiles** of programs in the relevant fields, with **Displays** following if programs have chosen to include them. **Close-Ups,** which are more individualized statements, are also listed for those graduate schools or programs that have chosen to submit them.

The **Profiles** found in the 500 directories in the specialized volumes provide basic data about the graduate units in capsule form for quick reference. To make these directories as useful as possible, **Profiles** are generally listed for an institution's smallest academic unit within a subject area. In other words, if an institution has a College of Liberal Arts that administers many related programs, the **Profile** for the individual program (e.g., Program in History), not the entire College, appears in the directory.

There are some programs that do not fit into any current directory and are not given individual **Profiles**. The directory structure is reviewed annually in order to keep this number to a minimum and to accommodate major trends in graduate education.

The following outline describes the **Profile** information found in the guides and explains how best to use that information. Any item that does not apply to or was not provided by a graduate unit is omitted from its listing. The format of the **Profiles** is constant, making it easy to compare one institution with another and one program with another.

A ★ graphic next to the school's name indicates the institution has additional detailed information in a "Premium Profile" on Petersons.com. After reading their information here, you can learn more about the school by visiting www.petersons.com and searching for that particular college or university's graduate program.

Identifying Information. The institution's name, in boldface type, is followed by a complete listing of the administrative structure for that field of study. (For example, University of Akron, Buchtel College of Arts and Sciences, Department of Theoretical and Applied Mathematics, Program in Mathematics.) The last unit listed is the one to which all information in the **Profile** pertains. The institution's city, state, and ZIP code follow.

Offerings. Each field of study offered by the unit is listed with all postbaccalaureate degrees awarded. Degrees that are not preceded by a specific concentration are awarded in the general field listed in the unit name. Frequently, fields of study are broken down into subspecializations, and those appear following the degrees awarded; for example, "Offerings in secondary education (M.Ed.), including English education, mathematics education, science education." Students enrolled in the M.Ed. program would be able to specialize in any of the three fields mentioned.

Professional Accreditation. Some **Profiles** indicate whether a program is professionally accredited. Because it is possible for a program to receive or lose professional accreditation at any time, students entering fields in which accreditation is important to a career should verify the status of programs by contacting either the chairperson or the appropriate accrediting association.

Jointly Offered Degrees. Explanatory statements concerning programs that are offered in cooperation with other institutions are included in the list of degrees offered. This occurs most commonly on a regional basis (for example, two state universities offering a cooperative Ph.D. in special education) or where the specialized nature of the institutions encourages joint efforts (a J.D./M.B.A. offered by a law school at an institution with no formal business programs and an institution with a business school but lacking a law school). Only programs that are truly cooperative are listed; those involving only limited course work at another institution are not. Interested students should contact the heads of such units for further information.

Program Availability. This may include the following: part-time, evening/weekend, online only, blended/hybrid learning, and/or minimal on-campus study. When information regarding the availability of part-time or evening/weekend study appears in the **Profile**, it means that students are able to earn a degree exclusively through such study. Blended/hybrid learning describes those courses in which some traditional in-class time has been replaced by online learning activities. Hybrid courses take advantage of the best features of both face-to-face and online learning.

Faculty. Figures on the number of faculty members actively involved with graduate students through teaching or research are separated into full- and part-time as well as men and women whenever the information has been supplied.

Students. Figures for the number of students enrolled in graduate and professional programs pertain to the semester of highest enrollment from the 2018–19 academic year. These figures are broken down into full- and part-time and men and women whenever the data have been supplied. Information on the number of matriculated students enrolled in the unit who are members of a minority group or are international students appears here. The average age of the matriculated students is followed by the number of applicants, the percentage accepted, and the number enrolled for fall 2018.

Degrees Awarded. The number of degrees awarded in the calendar year is listed. Many doctoral programs offer a terminal master's degree if students leave the program after completing only part of the requirements for a doctoral degree; that is indicated here. All degrees are classified into one of four types: master's, doctoral, first professional, and other advanced degrees. A unit may award one or several degrees at a given level; however, the data are only collected by type and may therefore represent several different degree programs.

Degree Requirements. The information in this section is also broken down by type of degree, and all information for a degree level pertains to all degrees of that type unless otherwise specified. Degree requirements are collected in a simplified form to provide some very basic information on the nature of the program and on foreign language, thesis or dissertation, comprehensive exam, and registration requirements. Many units also provide a short list of additional requirements, such as fieldwork or an internship. For complete information on graduation requirements, contact the graduate school or program directly.

Entrance Requirements. Entrance requirements are broken down into the four degree levels of master's, doctoral, first professional, and other advanced degrees. Within each level, information may be provided in two basic categories: entrance exams and other requirements. The entrance exams are identified by the standard acronyms used by the testing agencies, unless they are not well known. Other entrance requirements are quite varied, but they often contain an undergraduate or graduate grade point average (GPA). Unless otherwise stated, the GPA is calculated on a 4.0 scale and is listed as a minimum required for admission. Additional exam requirements/recommendations for international students may be listed here. Application deadlines for domestic and international students, the application fee, and whether electronic applications are accepted may be listed here. Note that the deadline should be used for reference only; these dates are subject to change, and students interested in applying should always contact the graduate unit directly about application procedures and deadlines.

Expenses. The typical cost of study for the 2018–2019 academic year (2017–18 if 2018–19 figures were not available) is given in two basic categories: tuition and fees. Cost of study may be quite complex at a graduate institution. There are often sliding scales for part-time study, a different cost for first-year students, and other variables that make it impossible to completely cover the cost of study for each graduate program. To provide the most usable information, figures are given for full-time study for a full year where available and for part-time study in terms of a per-unit rate (per credit, per semester hour, etc.). Occa-

sionally, variances may be noted in tuition and fees for reasons such as the type of program, whether courses are taken during the day or evening, whether courses are at the master's or doctoral level, or other institution-specific reasons. Respondents were also given the opportunity to provide more specific and detailed tuition and fees information at the unit level. When provided, this information will appear in place of any typical costs entered elsewhere on the university-level survey. Expenses are usually subject to change; for exact costs at any given time, contact your chosen schools and programs directly. Keep in mind that the tuition of Canadian institutions is usually given in Canadian dollars.

Financial Support. This section contains data on the number of awards administered by the institution and given to graduate students during the 2018–19 academic year. The first figure given represents the total number of students receiving financial support enrolled in that unit. If the unit has provided information on graduate appointments, these are broken down into three major categories: fellowships give money to graduate students to cover the cost of study and living expenses and are not based on a work obligation or research commitment, research assistantships provide stipends to graduate students for assistance in a formal research project with a faculty member, and teaching assistantships provide stipends to graduate students for teaching or for assisting faculty members in teaching undergraduate classes. Within each category, figures are given for the total number of awards, the average yearly amount per award, and whether full or partial tuition reimbursements are awarded. In addition to graduate appointments, the availability of several other financial aid sources is covered in this section. Tuition waivers are routinely part of a graduate appointment, but units sometimes waive part or all of a student's tuition even if a graduate appointment is not available. Federal Work Study is made available to students who demonstrate need and meet the federal guidelines; this form of aid normally includes 10 or more hours of work per week in an office of the institution. Institutionally sponsored loans are low-interest loans available to graduate students to cover both educational and living expenses. Career-related internships or fieldwork offer money to students who are participating in a formal off-campus research project or practicum. Grants, scholarships, traineeships, unspecified assistantships, and other awards may also be noted. The availability of financial support to part-time students is also indicated here.

Some programs list the financial aid application deadline and the forms that need to be completed for students to be eligible for financial awards. There are two forms: FAFSA, the Free Application for Federal Student Aid, which is required for federal aid, and the CSS PROFILE®.

Faculty Research. Each unit has the opportunity to list several keyword phrases describing the current research involving faculty members and graduate students. Space limitations prevent the unit from listing complete information on all research programs. The total expenditure for funded research from the previous academic year may also be included.

Unit Head and Application Contact. The head of the graduate program for each unit may be listed with academic title, phone and fax numbers, and e-mail address. In addition to the unit head's contact information, many graduate programs also list a separate contact for application and admission information, followed by the graduate school, program, or department's website. If no unit head or application contact is given, you should contact the overall institution for information on graduate admissions.

Displays and Close-Ups

The **Displays** and **Close-Ups** are supplementary insertions submitted by deans, chairs, and other administrators who wish to offer an additional, more individualized statement to readers. A number of graduate school and program administrators have attached a **Display** ad near the **Profile** listing. Here you will find information that an institution or program wants to emphasize. The **Close-Ups** are by their very nature more expansive and flexible than the **Profiles**, and the administrators who have written them may emphasize different aspects of their programs. All of the **Close-Ups** are organized in the same way (with the exception of a few that describe research and training opportunities instead of degree programs), and in each one

16 www.petersons.com

Peterson's Graduate Programs in the Physical Sciences, Mathematics, Agricultural Sciences, the Environment & Natural Resources 2020

you will find information on the same basic topics, such as programs of study, research facilities, tuition and fees, financial aid, and application procedures. If an institution or program has submitted a **Close-Up**, a boldface cross-reference appears below its **Profile**. As with the **Displays**, all of the **Close-Ups** in the guides have been submitted by choice; the absence of a **Display** or **Close-Up** does not reflect any type of editorial judgment on the part of Peterson's, and their presence in the guides should not be taken as an indication of status, quality, or approval. Statements regarding a university's objectives and accomplishments are a reflection of its own beliefs and are not the opinions of the Peterson's editors.

Appendixes

This section contains two appendixes. The first, "Institutional Changes Since the 2018 Edition," lists institutions that have closed, merged, or changed their name or status since the last edition of the guides. The second, "Abbreviations Used in the Guides," gives abbreviations of degree names, along with what those abbreviations stand for. These appendixes are identical in all six volumes of *Peterson's Graduate and Professional Programs*.

Indexes

There are three indexes presented here. The first index, "Close-Ups and Displays," gives page references for all programs that have chosen to place **Close-Ups** and **Displays** in this volume. It is arranged alphabetically by institution; within institutions, the arrangement is alphabetical by subject area. It is not an index to all programs in the book's directories of **Profiles**; readers must refer to the directories themselves for **Profile** information on programs that have not submitted the additional, more individualized statements. The second index, "Directories and Subject Areas in Other Books in This Series", gives book references for the directories in the specialized volumes and also includes cross-references for subject area names not used in the directory structure, for example, "Computing Technology (see Computer Science)." The third index, "Directories and Subject Areas in This Book," gives page references for the directories in this volume and cross-references for subject area names not used in this volume's directory structure.

Data Collection Procedures

The information published in the directories and Profiles of all the books is collected through Peterson's Annual Survey of Graduate and Professional Institutions. The survey is sent each spring to nearly 2,300 institutions offering postbaccalaureate degree programs, including accredited institutions in the United States, U.S. territories, and Canada and those institutions outside the United States that are accredited by U.S. accrediting bodies. Deans and other administrators complete these surveys, providing information on programs in the 500 academic and professional fields covered in the guides as well as overall institutional information. While every effort has been made to ensure the accuracy and completeness of the data, information is sometimes unavailable or changes occur after publication deadlines. All usable information received in time for publication has been included. The omission of any particular item from a directory or Profile signifies either that the item is not applicable to the institution or program or that information was not available. Profiles of programs scheduled to begin during the 2018–19 academic year cannot, obviously, include statistics on enrollment or, in many cases, the number of faculty members. If no usable data were submitted by an institution, its name, address, and program name appear in order to indicate the availability of graduate work.

Criteria for Inclusion in This Guide

To be included in this guide, an institution must have full accreditation or be a candidate for accreditation (preaccreditation) status by an institutional or specialized accrediting body recognized by the U.S. Department of Education or the Council for Higher Education Accreditation (CHEA). Institutional accrediting bodies, which review each institution as a whole, include the six regional associations of schools and colleges (Middle States, New England, North Central, Northwest, Southern, and Western), each of which is responsible for a specified portion of the United States and its territories. Other institutional accrediting bodies are national in scope and accredit specific kinds of institutions (e.g., Bible colleges, independent colleges, and rabbinical and Talmudic schools). Program registration by the New York State Board of Regents is considered to be the equivalent of institutional accreditation, since the board requires that all programs offered by an institution meet its standards before recognition is granted. A Canadian institution must be chartered and authorized to grant degrees by the provincial government, affiliated with a chartered institution, or accredited by a recognized U.S. accrediting body. This guide also includes institutions outside the United States that are accredited by these U.S. accrediting bodies. There are recognized specialized or professional accrediting bodies in more than fifty different fields, each of which is authorized to accredit institutions or specific programs in its particular field. For specialized institutions that offer programs in one field only, we designate this to be the equivalent of institutional accreditation. A full explanation of the accrediting process and complete information on recognized institutional (regional and national) and specialized accrediting bodies can be found online at **www.chea.org** or at **www.ed.gov/admins/finaid/accred/index.html**.

Peterson's Graduate Programs in the Physical Sciences, Mathematics, Agricultural Sciences, the Environment & Natural Resources 2020

www.petersons.com   **17**

DIRECTORY OF INSTITUTIONS WITH PROGRAMS IN THE PHYSICAL SCIENCES, MATHEMATICS, AGRICULTURAL SCIENCES, THE ENVIRONMENT & NATURAL RESOURCES

ACADIA UNIVERSITY

Chemistry	M
Geology	M
Mathematics	M
Statistics	M

ADELPHI UNIVERSITY

Environmental Management and Policy	M
Environmental Sciences	M

AIR FORCE INSTITUTE OF TECHNOLOGY

Applied Mathematics	M,D
Applied Physics	M,D
Astrophysics	M,D
Environmental Management and Policy	M
Optical Sciences	M,D
Planetary and Space Sciences	M,D

ALABAMA AGRICULTURAL AND MECHANICAL UNIVERSITY

Agricultural Sciences— General	M,D
Agronomy and Soil Sciences	M,D
Food Science and Technology	M,D
Optical Sciences	M,D
Physics	M,D
Planetary and Space Sciences	M,D
Plant Sciences	M,D

ALABAMA STATE UNIVERSITY

Mathematics	M

ALASKA PACIFIC UNIVERSITY

Environmental Sciences	M

ALBANY STATE UNIVERSITY

Water Resources	M

ALCORN STATE UNIVERSITY

Agricultural Sciences— General	M
Agronomy and Soil Sciences	M
Animal Sciences	M

AMERICAN PUBLIC UNIVERSITY SYSTEM

Environmental Management and Policy	M,D

AMERICAN UNIVERSITY

Applied Statistics	M,O
Biostatistics	M,O
Chemistry	M
Environmental Management and Policy	M,D,O
Environmental Sciences	M,O
Mathematics	M,O
Natural Resources	M,D,O
Statistics	M,O

THE AMERICAN UNIVERSITY IN CAIRO

Chemistry	M,D,O
Physics	M,D,O

AMERICAN UNIVERSITY OF BEIRUT

Animal Sciences	M
Aquaculture	M
Biostatistics	M,D
Chemistry	M,D
Computational Sciences	M,D
Environmental Management and Policy	M,D
Environmental Sciences	M,D
Food Science and Technology	M
Geology	M,D
Mathematics	M,D
Physics	M,D
Plant Sciences	M
Theoretical Physics	M,D

THE AMERICAN UNIVERSITY OF ROME

Food Science and Technology	M

AMERICAN UNIVERSITY OF SHARJAH

Mathematics	M,D

ANGELO STATE UNIVERSITY

Agricultural Sciences— General	M

ANTIOCH UNIVERSITY NEW ENGLAND

Environmental Management and Policy	M,D
Environmental Sciences	M,D

APPALACHIAN STATE UNIVERSITY

Mathematics	M

ARIZONA STATE UNIVERSITY AT THE TEMPE CAMPUS

Applied Mathematics	M,D,O
Astrophysics	M,D
Chemistry	M,D
Environmental Management and Policy	M
Environmental Sciences	M,D,O
Geology	M,D
Geosciences	M,D
Mathematics	M,D,O
Physics	M,D
Planetary and Space Sciences	M,D
Statistics	M,D,O

ARKANSAS STATE UNIVERSITY

Agricultural Sciences— General	M,O
Chemistry	M,O
Environmental Sciences	M,D
Mathematics	M

ARKANSAS TECH UNIVERSITY

Fish, Game, and Wildlife Management	M

AUBURN UNIVERSITY

Agricultural Sciences— General	M,D
Agronomy and Soil Sciences	M,D
Analytical Chemistry	M,D
Animal Sciences	M,D
Applied Mathematics	M,D
Aquaculture	M,D
Chemistry	M,D
Fish, Game, and Wildlife Management	M,D
Food Science and Technology	M,D,O
Forestry	M,D
Geology	M
Horticulture	M,D
Inorganic Chemistry	M,D
Mathematics	M,D
Natural Resources	M,D
Organic Chemistry	M,D
Physical Chemistry	M,D
Physics	M,D
Statistics	M,D

AUGUSTANA UNIVERSITY

Mathematics	M

AURORA UNIVERSITY

Mathematics	M

AUSTIN PEAY STATE UNIVERSITY

Mathematical and Computational Finance	M

BALL STATE UNIVERSITY

Chemistry	M,D
Environmental Management and Policy	M,O
Environmental Sciences	D
Geology	M,D
Geosciences	M
Mathematics	M
Meteorology	M,O
Natural Resources	M,O
Physics	M
Statistics	M

BARD COLLEGE

Atmospheric Sciences	M,O
Environmental Management and Policy	M,O

BARUCH COLLEGE OF THE CITY UNIVERSITY OF NEW YORK

Statistics	M

BAYLOR UNIVERSITY

Chemistry	M,D
Environmental Management and Policy	M,D
Environmental Sciences	D
Geosciences	M,D
Mathematics	M,D
Physics	M,D
Statistics	M,D

BAY PATH UNIVERSITY

Applied Statistics	M

BEMIDJI STATE UNIVERSITY

Environmental Management and Policy	M
Mathematics	M

BERGIN UNIVERSITY OF CANINE STUDIES

Animal Sciences	M

BINGHAMTON UNIVERSITY, STATE UNIVERSITY OF NEW YORK

Analytical Chemistry	M,D
Applied Physics	M,D
Chemistry	M,D
Environmental Management and Policy	M,D
Geology	M,D
Inorganic Chemistry	M,D
Mathematics	M,D
Physical Chemistry	M,D
Physics	M,D
Statistics	M,D

BOISE STATE UNIVERSITY

Animal Sciences	M,D
Chemistry	M
Geophysics	M,D
Geosciences	M,D
Hydrology	M,D
Mathematics	M
Natural Resources	M,D,O

BOSTON COLLEGE

Chemistry	M,D
Geology	M
Geophysics	M
Inorganic Chemistry	M,D
Mathematics	D
Organic Chemistry	M,D
Physical Chemistry	M,D
Physics	M,D

BOSTON UNIVERSITY

Astronomy	M,D
Biostatistics	M,D
Chemistry	M,D
Environmental Sciences	M,D
Food Science and Technology	M
Geosciences	M,D
Mathematical and Computational Finance	M,D
Mathematics	M,D
Physics	D

BOWIE STATE UNIVERSITY

Applied Mathematics	M

BOWLING GREEN STATE UNIVERSITY

Applied Statistics	M
Chemistry	M,D
Geology	M
Geophysics	M
Mathematics	M,D
Physics	M,D
Statistics	M,D

BRADLEY UNIVERSITY

Chemistry	M

BRANDEIS UNIVERSITY

Chemistry	M,D
Inorganic Chemistry	M,D
Mathematics	M,D
Organic Chemistry	M,D
Physical Chemistry	M,D
Physics	M,D

BRIGHAM YOUNG UNIVERSITY

Agricultural Sciences— General	M,D
Analytical Chemistry	M,D
Animal Sciences	M,D
Applied Statistics	M
Astronomy	M,D
Chemistry	M,D
Environmental Sciences	M,D
Fish, Game, and Wildlife Management	M,D
Food Science and Technology	M
Geology	M
Mathematics	M,D
Physics	M,D
Plant Sciences	M,D
Statistics	M

BROCK UNIVERSITY

Chemistry	M,D
Geosciences	M
Mathematics	M
Physics	M
Statistics	M

BROOKLYN COLLEGE OF THE CITY UNIVERSITY OF NEW YORK

Chemistry	M,D
Geology	M,D
Geosciences	M
Mathematics	M
Physics	M

BROWN UNIVERSITY

Applied Mathematics	M,D
Biostatistics	M,D
Chemistry	D
Geosciences	D
Mathematics	D
Physics	M,D

BRYN MAWR COLLEGE

Chemistry	M,D
Mathematics	M,D
Physics	M,D

BUCKNELL UNIVERSITY

Chemistry	M
Mathematics	M

CABRINI UNIVERSITY

Chemistry	M,D
Mathematics	M,D

CALIFORNIA BAPTIST UNIVERSITY

Applied Mathematics	M

CALIFORNIA INSTITUTE OF TECHNOLOGY

Applied Mathematics	M,D
Applied Physics	M,D
Astronomy	D
Chemistry	M,D
Computational Sciences	M,D
Environmental Sciences	M,D
Geochemistry	M,D
Geology	M,D
Geophysics	M,D
Mathematics	D
Physics	D
Planetary and Space Sciences	M,D

CALIFORNIA POLYTECHNIC STATE UNIVERSITY, SAN LUIS OBISPO

Agricultural Sciences— General	M
Chemistry	M
Food Science and Technology	M
Forestry	M
Mathematics	M
Natural Resources	M

CALIFORNIA STATE POLYTECHNIC UNIVERSITY, POMONA

Agricultural Sciences— General	M
Applied Mathematics	M
Chemistry	M
Environmental Sciences	M
Geology	M
Mathematics	M

CALIFORNIA STATE UNIVERSITY, BAKERSFIELD

Geology	M
Hydrology	M

CALIFORNIA STATE UNIVERSITY CHANNEL ISLANDS

Mathematics	M

CALIFORNIA STATE UNIVERSITY, CHICO

Agricultural Sciences— General	M
Environmental Sciences	M
Geology	M
Geosciences	M

CALIFORNIA STATE UNIVERSITY, EAST BAY

Applied Statistics	M
Biostatistics	M
Chemistry	M
Environmental Sciences	M
Geology	M
Marine Sciences	M
Mathematics	M
Statistics	M

CALIFORNIA STATE UNIVERSITY, FRESNO

Animal Sciences	M
Chemistry	M
Geology	M
Marine Sciences	M
Mathematics	M
Physics	M
Plant Sciences	M
Viticulture and Enology	M

CALIFORNIA STATE UNIVERSITY, FULLERTON

Applied Mathematics	M
Chemistry	M
Environmental Management and Policy	M
Geology	M
Mathematics	M
Physics	M

CALIFORNIA STATE UNIVERSITY, LONG BEACH

Applied Mathematics	M,D
Applied Statistics	M
Chemistry	M
Geology	M
Mathematics	M
Physics	M

CALIFORNIA STATE UNIVERSITY, LOS ANGELES

Analytical Chemistry	M
Applied Mathematics	M
Chemistry	M
Geology	M
Mathematics	M
Physics	M

CALIFORNIA STATE UNIVERSITY, MONTEREY BAY

Marine Sciences	M
Water Resources	M

CALIFORNIA STATE UNIVERSITY, NORTHRIDGE

Applied Mathematics	M
Chemistry	M
Environmental Sciences	M
Geology	M
Mathematics	M
Physics	M

CALIFORNIA STATE UNIVERSITY, SACRAMENTO

Chemistry	M
Mathematics	M

CALIFORNIA STATE UNIVERSITY, SAN BERNARDINO

Environmental Sciences	M
Geosciences	M
Mathematics	M

CALIFORNIA STATE UNIVERSITY, SAN MARCOS

Mathematics	M

CARLETON UNIVERSITY

Chemistry	M,D
Geosciences	M,D
Mathematics	M,D
Physics	M,D

CARLOW UNIVERSITY

Mathematics	M

CARNEGIE MELLON UNIVERSITY

Applied Physics	M,D
Atmospheric Sciences	D
Chemistry	D
Environmental Sciences	D
Mathematical and Computational Finance	M,D
Mathematics	M,D
Physics	M,D
Statistics	M,D
Theoretical Chemistry	D

CASE WESTERN RESERVE UNIVERSITY

Applied Mathematics	M,D
Astronomy	M,D
Biostatistics	M,D
Chemistry	M,D
Geology	M,D
Geosciences	M,D
Mathematics	M,D
Physics	M,D

THE CATHOLIC UNIVERSITY OF AMERICA

Physics	M,D

CENTRAL CONNECTICUT STATE UNIVERSITY

Mathematics	M,O
Statistics	M,O

CENTRAL EUROPEAN UNIVERSITY

Applied Mathematics	M,D

20   www.petersons.com

Peterson's Graduate Programs in the Physical Sciences, Mathematics, Agricultural Sciences, the Environment & Natural Resources 2020

Environmental Management and Policy — M,D
Mathematics — M,D

CENTRAL MICHIGAN UNIVERSITY
Chemistry — M
Mathematics — M,D
Physics — M,D

CENTRAL WASHINGTON UNIVERSITY
Chemistry — M
Environmental Management and Policy — M
Fish, Game, and Wildlife Management — M
Geology — M
Natural Resources — M

CHAPMAN UNIVERSITY
Computational Sciences — M,D*
Food Science and Technology — M*

CHICAGO STATE UNIVERSITY
Mathematics — M

CHRISTOPHER NEWPORT UNIVERSITY
Applied Physics — M
Environmental Sciences — M
Physics — M

THE CITADEL, THE MILITARY COLLEGE OF SOUTH CAROLINA
Environmental Management and Policy — M,O

CITY COLLEGE OF THE CITY UNIVERSITY OF NEW YORK
Atmospheric Sciences — M
Chemistry — M,D
Geology — M
Geosciences — M
Mathematics — M
Physics — M,D

CLAREMONT GRADUATE UNIVERSITY
Applied Mathematics — M,D
Computational Sciences — M,D
Mathematics — M,D
Statistics — M,D

CLARK ATLANTA UNIVERSITY
Chemistry — M,D
Mathematics — M
Physics — M

CLARKSON UNIVERSITY
Chemistry — M,D
Environmental Management and Policy — M
Environmental Sciences — M,D
Mathematics — M,D
Physics — M,D

CLARK UNIVERSITY
Chemistry — D
Environmental Management and Policy — M
Environmental Sciences — M
Physics — D

CLEMSON UNIVERSITY
Agricultural Sciences—General — M,D
Animal Sciences — M,D
Applied Statistics — M,D
Chemistry — M,D
Environmental Management and Policy — M,D
Environmental Sciences — M,D
Fish, Game, and Wildlife Management — M,D
Food Science and Technology — M,D
Forestry — M,D
Hydrogeology — M,D
Mathematics — M,D
Physics — M,D
Statistics — M,D

CLEVELAND STATE UNIVERSITY
Applied Statistics — M
Chemistry — M,D
Environmental Management and Policy — M,O
Environmental Sciences — M,D
Mathematics — M
Organic Chemistry — M,D
Physical Chemistry — M,D
Physics — M

COASTAL CAROLINA UNIVERSITY
Marine Sciences — M,D,O

THE COLLEGE AT BROCKPORT, STATE UNIVERSITY OF NEW YORK
Chemistry — M,O
Environmental Sciences — M
Mathematics — M

COLLEGE OF CHARLESTON
Environmental Sciences — M
Marine Sciences — M
Mathematics — M

COLLEGE OF STATEN ISLAND OF THE CITY UNIVERSITY OF NEW YORK
Environmental Sciences — M

COLLEGE OF THE ATLANTIC
Environmental Management and Policy — M

THE COLLEGE OF WILLIAM AND MARY
Marine Sciences — M,D

COLORADO SCHOOL OF MINES
Applied Mathematics — M,D
Applied Physics — M,D
Applied Statistics — M,D
Chemistry — M,D
Environmental Sciences — M,D
Geochemistry — M,D
Geology — M,D
Geophysics — M,D
Hydrology — M,D
Physics — M,D

COLORADO STATE UNIVERSITY
Agricultural Sciences—General — M,D
Agronomy and Soil Sciences — M,D
Animal Sciences — M,D
Atmospheric Sciences — M,D
Chemistry — M,D
Environmental Management and Policy — M,D
Fish, Game, and Wildlife Management — M,D
Food Science and Technology — M,D
Geosciences — M,D
Horticulture — M,D
Mathematics — M,D
Natural Resources — M,D
Physics — M,D
Plant Sciences — M,D
Statistics — M,D
Water Resources — M,D

COLORADO STATE UNIVERSITY–PUEBLO
Chemistry — M

COLUMBIA UNIVERSITY
Applied Mathematics — M,D
Applied Physics — M,D
Astronomy — M,D
Atmospheric Sciences — M,D
Biostatistics — M,D
Chemical Physics — M,D
Chemistry — M,D
Environmental Management and Policy — M
Environmental Sciences — M,D
Geosciences — M,D
Mathematics — M,D
Physics — M,D
Statistics — M,D

COLUMBUS STATE UNIVERSITY
Chemistry — M,O
Environmental Management and Policy — M
Environmental Sciences — M,O
Mathematics — M,O

CONCORDIA UNIVERSITY (CANADA)
Chemistry — M,D
Environmental Management and Policy — M,D,O
Mathematics — M,D
Physics — M,D
Statistics — M,D

CORNELL UNIVERSITY
Agronomy and Soil Sciences — M,D
Analytical Chemistry — D
Animal Sciences — M,D
Applied Mathematics — M,D
Applied Physics — M,D
Applied Statistics — M,D
Astronomy — D
Astrophysics — D
Atmospheric Sciences — M,D
Biometry — M,D
Chemical Physics — D
Chemistry — M,D
Computational Sciences — M,D
Environmental Management and Policy — M,D
Environmental Sciences — M,D
Fish, Game, and Wildlife Management — M,D
Food Science and Technology — M,D
Forestry — M,D
Geochemistry — M,D
Geology — M,D
Geophysics — M,D
Geosciences — M,D
Horticulture — M,D
Hydrology — M,D
Inorganic Chemistry — D
Limnology — D
Marine Geology — M,D
Marine Sciences — M,D
Mathematics — D
Mineralogy — M,D
Natural Resources — M,D
Oceanography — D
Organic Chemistry — D
Paleontology — M,D
Physical Chemistry — D
Physics — D
Planetary and Space Sciences — D
Plant Sciences — M,D
Statistics — M,D
Theoretical Chemistry — D
Theoretical Physics — M,D
Viticulture and Enology — M,D
Water Resources — M,D

CREIGHTON UNIVERSITY
Physics — M

DALHOUSIE UNIVERSITY
Agricultural Sciences—General — M
Agronomy and Soil Sciences — M
Animal Sciences — M
Applied Mathematics — M,D
Aquaculture — M
Chemistry — M,D
Environmental Management and Policy — M
Environmental Sciences — M
Food Science and Technology — M,D
Geosciences — M,D
Horticulture — M
Marine Affairs — M
Mathematics — M,D
Natural Resources — M
Oceanography — M,D
Physics — M,D
Statistics — M,D
Water Resources — M

DARTMOUTH COLLEGE
Astronomy — D
Biostatistics — M,D
Chemistry — M,D
Geosciences — M,D
Mathematics — M,D
Physical Chemistry — M,D
Physics — D

DELAWARE STATE UNIVERSITY
Applied Mathematics — M,D
Chemistry — M,D
Mathematics — M
Natural Resources — M
Optical Sciences — M,D
Physics — M,D
Plant Sciences — M
Theoretical Physics — D

DEPAUL UNIVERSITY
Applied Mathematics — M,D
Applied Statistics — M,D
Chemistry — M,D
Environmental Sciences — M,D
Mathematical and Computational Finance — M,D
Mathematics — M,D
Physics — M,D

DREW UNIVERSITY
Chemistry — M,D,O
Mathematics — M,D,O

DREXEL UNIVERSITY
Biostatistics — M,D,O
Chemistry — M,D
Environmental Management and Policy — M
Environmental Sciences — M,D
Food Science and Technology — M
Hydrology — M,D
Mathematics — M,D
Physics — M,D

DUKE UNIVERSITY
Biostatistics — M
Chemistry — D
Computational Sciences — M,D
Environmental Management and Policy — D
Environmental Sciences — M,D
Geology — M,D
Geosciences — M,D
Marine Sciences — M,D
Mathematics — D
Natural Resources — M,D
Optical Sciences — M
Paleontology — D
Photonics — M
Physics — M
Statistics — M,D

DUQUESNE UNIVERSITY
Chemistry — D
Environmental Management and Policy — M,O
Environmental Sciences — M,O
Mathematics — M

EAST CAROLINA UNIVERSITY
Applied Physics — M,D
Chemistry — M
Geology — M,O
Hydrogeology — M,O
Mathematics — M
Physics — M
Statistics — M

EASTERN ILLINOIS UNIVERSITY
Chemistry — M
Mathematics — M

EASTERN KENTUCKY UNIVERSITY
Chemistry — M
Geology — M,D
Mathematics — M

EASTERN MICHIGAN UNIVERSITY
Chemistry — M
Geosciences — M
Mathematics — M
Physics — M

EASTERN NEW MEXICO UNIVERSITY
Analytical Chemistry — M
Chemistry — M
Organic Chemistry — M
Physical Chemistry — M

EAST TENNESSEE STATE UNIVERSITY
Biostatistics — M,D,O
Chemistry — M,O
Geosciences — M,O
Mathematics — M,O
Paleontology — M,O

ÉCOLE POLYTECHNIQUE DE MONTRÉAL
Applied Mathematics — M,D,O
Optical Sciences — M,D,O

ELIZABETH CITY STATE UNIVERSITY
Applied Mathematics — M
Mathematics — M

EMORY UNIVERSITY
Biostatistics — M,D
Chemistry — D
Mathematics — M,D
Physics — D

EMPORIA STATE UNIVERSITY
Geosciences — M,O
Mathematics — M

THE EVERGREEN STATE COLLEGE
Environmental Management and Policy — M

FAIRFIELD UNIVERSITY
Mathematics — M

FAIRLEIGH DICKINSON UNIVERSITY, FLORHAM CAMPUS
Chemistry — M

FAIRLEIGH DICKINSON UNIVERSITY, METROPOLITAN CAMPUS
Chemistry — M
Mathematics — M

FISK UNIVERSITY
Chemistry — M
Physics — M

FLORIDA AGRICULTURAL AND MECHANICAL UNIVERSITY
Chemistry — M
Environmental Sciences — M,D
Physics — M,D

FLORIDA ATLANTIC UNIVERSITY
Applied Mathematics — M,D
Chemistry — M,D
Geology — M,D
Geosciences — M,D
Mathematics — M,D
Physics — M,D
Statistics — M,D

FLORIDA GULF COAST UNIVERSITY
Environmental Management and Policy — M
Environmental Sciences — M
Mathematics — M

FLORIDA INSTITUTE OF TECHNOLOGY
Applied Mathematics — M,D
Chemistry — M,D
Environmental Management and Policy — M,D
Environmental Sciences — M,D
Geosciences — M
Marine Sciences — M,D
Meteorology — M
Oceanography — M,D
Physics — M,D
Planetary and Space Sciences — M,D

FLORIDA INTERNATIONAL UNIVERSITY
Biostatistics — M,D
Chemistry — M,D
Environmental Management and Policy — M,D
Geosciences — M,D
Mathematics — M
Natural Resources — M,D
Physics — M,D
Statistics — M

FLORIDA STATE UNIVERSITY
Analytical Chemistry — M,D
Applied Mathematics — M,D
Applied Statistics — M,D
Atmospheric Sciences — M,D
Biomathematics — M,D
Biostatistics — M,D
Computational Sciences — M,D
Environmental Sciences — M,D
Food Science and Technology — M,D
Geology — M,D
Geosciences — M,D
Inorganic Chemistry — M,D
Marine Sciences — M,D
Mathematical and Computational Finance — M,D
Meteorology — M,D
Oceanography — M,D
Organic Chemistry — M,D
Physical Chemistry — M,D
Physics — M,D

FORDHAM UNIVERSITY
Applied Statistics — M,D

FORT HAYS STATE UNIVERSITY
Geology — M
Geosciences — M

FORT VALLEY STATE UNIVERSITY
Animal Sciences — M

FROSTBURG STATE UNIVERSITY
Fish, Game, and Wildlife Management — M

FURMAN UNIVERSITY
Chemistry — M

GANNON UNIVERSITY
Environmental Sciences — M

---

*M—master's; D—doctorate; O—other advanced degree; *Close-Up and/or Display*

Peterson's Graduate Programs in the Physical Sciences, Mathematics, Agricultural Sciences, the Environment & Natural Resources 2020

www.petersons.com **21**

GEORGE MASON UNIVERSITY

Astronomy	M,D
Atmospheric Sciences	D
Biostatistics	M,D,O
Chemistry	M,D
Computational Sciences	M,D,O
Environmental Management and Policy	M,D
Environmental Sciences	M,D
Geosciences	M,D,O
Mathematics	M,D
Physics	M,D
Statistics	M,D,O

GEORGETOWN UNIVERSITY

Analytical Chemistry	D
Biostatistics	M,O
Chemistry	D
Inorganic Chemistry	D
Mathematics	M
Organic Chemistry	D
Statistics	M
Theoretical Chemistry	D

THE GEORGE WASHINGTON UNIVERSITY

Analytical Chemistry	M,D
Applied Mathematics	M,D,O
Biostatistics	M,D
Chemistry	M,D
Environmental Management and Policy	M
Inorganic Chemistry	M,D
Mathematical and Computational Finance	M,D,O
Mathematics	M,D,O
Organic Chemistry	M,D
Physical Chemistry	M,D
Physics	M,D
Statistics	M,D,O

GEORGIA INSTITUTE OF TECHNOLOGY

Atmospheric Sciences	M,D
Chemistry	M,D
Computational Sciences	M,D
Environmental Management and Policy	M,D
Geosciences	M,D
Mathematical and Computational Finance	M
Mathematics	M,D
Physics	M,D
Statistics	M

GEORGIA SOUTHERN UNIVERSITY

Applied Physics	M
Biostatistics	M,D
Mathematics	M

GEORGIA STATE UNIVERSITY

Analytical Chemistry	M,D
Astronomy	D
Biostatistics	M,D
Chemistry	M,D
Environmental Management and Policy	M,D,O
Geochemistry	M,D
Geology	M
Geosciences	M,D,O
Mathematics	M,D
Organic Chemistry	M,D
Physical Chemistry	M,D
Physics	M,D
Statistics	M,D

GOVERNORS STATE UNIVERSITY

Analytical Chemistry	M
Mathematics	M

THE GRADUATE CENTER, CITY UNIVERSITY OF NEW YORK

Chemistry	D
Environmental Sciences	D
Geosciences	D
Mathematics	D
Physics	D

GRAND VALLEY STATE UNIVERSITY

Biostatistics	M

HAMPTON UNIVERSITY

Applied Mathematics	M
Atmospheric Sciences	M,D
Chemistry	M
Computational Sciences	M
Physics	M,D
Planetary and Space Sciences	M,D
Statistics	M

HARVARD UNIVERSITY

Applied Mathematics	M,D
Applied Physics	M,D
Astronomy	D
Astrophysics	D
Biostatistics	M,D
Chemical Physics	D
Chemistry	D
Computational Sciences	M,D
Environmental Management and Policy	M,O
Environmental Sciences	M,O
Forestry	M
Geosciences	M,D
Inorganic Chemistry	D
Mathematics	D
Organic Chemistry	D
Physical Chemistry	D
Physics	D
Planetary and Space Sciences	M,D
Statistics	M,D
Theoretical Physics	D

HAWAI'I PACIFIC UNIVERSITY

Marine Sciences	M

HOFSTRA UNIVERSITY

Mathematics	M,D,O

HOUSTON BAPTIST UNIVERSITY

Mathematics	M,D

HOWARD UNIVERSITY

Analytical Chemistry	M,D
Applied Mathematics	M,D
Atmospheric Sciences	M,D
Chemistry	M,D
Environmental Sciences	M,D
Inorganic Chemistry	M,D
Mathematics	M,D
Organic Chemistry	M,D
Physical Chemistry	M,D
Physics	M,D

HUMBOLDT STATE UNIVERSITY

Environmental Management and Policy	M
Environmental Sciences	M
Fish, Game, and Wildlife Management	M
Forestry	M
Geology	M
Natural Resources	M
Water Resources	M

HUNTER COLLEGE OF THE CITY UNIVERSITY OF NEW YORK

Applied Mathematics	M
Astronomy	M,D
Chemistry	D
Geosciences	M
Mathematics	M
Physics	M,D
Statistics	M

IDAHO STATE UNIVERSITY

Applied Physics	M,D
Chemistry	M
Environmental Management and Policy	M
Environmental Sciences	M,O
Geology	M,O
Geophysics	M,O
Geosciences	M,O
Hydrology	M,O
Mathematics	M,D
Physics	M,D

ILLINOIS INSTITUTE OF TECHNOLOGY

Analytical Chemistry	M,D
Applied Mathematics	M,D
Applied Physics	M,D
Chemistry	M,D
Environmental Management and Policy	M
Food Science and Technology	M
Inorganic Chemistry	M,D
Mathematical and Computational Finance	M,D
Physics	M,D

ILLINOIS STATE UNIVERSITY

Agricultural Sciences—General	M
Mathematics	M
Plant Sciences	M,D

INDIANA STATE UNIVERSITY

Mathematics	M

INDIANA UNIVERSITY BLOOMINGTON

Analytical Chemistry	M,D
Applied Mathematics	M,D
Applied Statistics	M,D
Astronomy	M,D
Astrophysics	M,D
Atmospheric Sciences	M,D
Biostatistics	M,D
Chemistry	M,D
Environmental Management and Policy	M,D,O
Environmental Sciences	M,D,O
Geochemistry	M,D
Geophysics	M,D
Geosciences	M,D
Hydrogeology	M,D
Inorganic Chemistry	M,D
Mathematical Physics	M,D
Mathematics	M,D
Mineralogy	M,D
Organic Chemistry	M,D
Physical Chemistry	M,D
Physics	M,D
Statistics	M,D

INDIANA UNIVERSITY NORTHWEST

Environmental Management and Policy	M,O

INDIANA UNIVERSITY OF PENNSYLVANIA

Applied Mathematics	M
Chemistry	M
Environmental Management and Policy	M
Mathematics	M
Physics	M

INDIANA UNIVERSITY–PURDUE UNIVERSITY INDIANAPOLIS

Applied Mathematics	M,D
Applied Statistics	M,D
Biostatistics	M,D,O
Chemistry	M,D
Geology	M,D
Geosciences	M,D
Mathematics	M,D
Natural Resources	M,D,O
Physics	M,D
Statistics	M,D

INDIANA UNIVERSITY SOUTH BEND

Applied Mathematics	M,O

INSTITUTO TECNOLOGICO DE SANTO DOMINGO

Environmental Management and Policy	M,D,O
Environmental Sciences	M,D,O
Marine Sciences	M,D,O
Mathematics	M,D,O
Natural Resources	M,D,O

INSTITUTO TECNOLÓGICO Y DE ESTUDIOS SUPERIORES DE MONTERREY, CAMPUS CIUDAD DE MÉXICO

Environmental Sciences	M,D

INSTITUTO TECNOLÓGICO Y DE ESTUDIOS SUPERIORES DE MONTERREY, CAMPUS ESTADO DE MÉXICO

Environmental Management and Policy	M,D

INSTITUTO TECNOLÓGICO Y DE ESTUDIOS SUPERIORES DE MONTERREY, CAMPUS IRAPUATO

Environmental Management and Policy	M,D

INSTITUTO TECNOLÓGICO Y DE ESTUDIOS SUPERIORES DE MONTERREY, CAMPUS MONTERREY

Agricultural Sciences—General	M,D
Applied Statistics	M,D
Chemistry	M,D
Organic Chemistry	M,D

INTER AMERICAN UNIVERSITY OF PUERTO RICO, METROPOLITAN CAMPUS

Environmental Management and Policy	M

INTER AMERICAN UNIVERSITY OF PUERTO RICO, SAN GERMÁN CAMPUS

Applied Mathematics	M
Environmental Sciences	M

IOWA STATE UNIVERSITY OF SCIENCE AND TECHNOLOGY

Agricultural Sciences—General	M,D
Agronomy and Soil Sciences	M,D
Analytical Chemistry	M,D
Animal Sciences	M,D
Applied Mathematics	M,D
Applied Physics	M,D
Astrophysics	M,D
Biostatistics	M,D
Chemistry	M,D
Condensed Matter Physics	M,D
Environmental Sciences	M,D
Fish, Game, and Wildlife Management	M,D
Food Science and Technology	M,D
Forestry	M,D
Geology	M,D
Geosciences	M,D
Horticulture	M,D
Inorganic Chemistry	M,D
Mathematics	M,D
Meteorology	M,D
Natural Resources	M,D
Organic Chemistry	M,D
Physical Chemistry	M,D
Physics	M,D
Plant Sciences	M,D
Statistics	M,D

JACKSON STATE UNIVERSITY

Applied Mathematics	M
Atmospheric Sciences	M,D
Chemistry	M,D
Environmental Sciences	M
Geosciences	M,D
Mathematics	M
Physics	M,D
Statistics	M

JACKSONVILLE STATE UNIVERSITY

Mathematics	M

JACKSONVILLE UNIVERSITY

Marine Sciences	M
Mathematics	M

JAMES MADISON UNIVERSITY

Environmental Management and Policy	M

JOHN CARROLL UNIVERSITY

Mathematics	M

JOHNS HOPKINS UNIVERSITY

Applied Mathematics	M,D,O
Applied Physics	M,O
Astronomy	D
Biostatistics	M,D
Chemistry	M,D
Environmental Management and Policy	M,O
Environmental Sciences	M,O
Geosciences	M,D
Mathematical and Computational Finance	M,D,O
Mathematics	D
Photonics	M,O
Physics	D
Planetary and Space Sciences	M,D
Statistics	M,D

KANSAS STATE UNIVERSITY

Agricultural Sciences—General	M,D,O
Agronomy and Soil Sciences	M,D,O
Animal Sciences	M,D
Chemistry	M,D
Environmental Sciences	M,D,O
Food Science and Technology	M,D
Geology	M
Horticulture	M,D
Mathematics	M,D,O
Natural Resources	M,D
Physics	M,D
Plant Sciences	M,D,O
Range Science	M,D,O
Statistics	M,D,O

KENNESAW STATE UNIVERSITY

Applied Statistics	M
Chemistry	M

KENT STATE UNIVERSITY

Applied Mathematics	M,D
Biostatistics	M,D
Chemical Physics	M,D
Chemistry	M,D
Geology	M,D
Mathematics	M,D,O
Physics	M,D

KUTZTOWN UNIVERSITY OF PENNSYLVANIA

Mathematics	M,D

LAKE FOREST COLLEGE

Environmental Management and Policy	M

LAKEHEAD UNIVERSITY

Chemistry	M
Forestry	M,D
Geology	M
Mathematics	M
Physics	M

LAMAR UNIVERSITY

Chemistry	M
Mathematics	M

LAURENTIAN UNIVERSITY

Analytical Chemistry	M
Applied Physics	M
Chemistry	M
Environmental Sciences	M
Geology	M,D
Natural Resources	M,D
Organic Chemistry	M
Physical Chemistry	M
Theoretical Chemistry	M

LEE UNIVERSITY

Mathematics	M,O

LEHIGH UNIVERSITY

Applied Mathematics	M,D
Chemistry	M,D
Environmental Management and Policy	M,O
Environmental Sciences	M,D
Geology	M,D
Geosciences	M,D
Mathematics	M,D
Photonics	M,D
Physics	M,D
Statistics	M,D

LEHMAN COLLEGE OF THE CITY UNIVERSITY OF NEW YORK

Mathematics	M

LEWIS UNIVERSITY

Chemical Physics	M
Chemistry	M
Physics	M

LINCOLN UNIVERSITY (MO)

Environmental Sciences	M

LOMA LINDA UNIVERSITY

Biostatistics	M,D

LONDON METROPOLITAN UNIVERSITY

Food Science and Technology	M,D

LONG ISLAND UNIVERSITY–LIU BROOKLYN

Chemistry	M,D,O

LONG ISLAND UNIVERSITY–LIU POST

Applied Mathematics	M,O
Environmental Management and Policy	M,O
Geosciences	M,O

LOUISIANA STATE UNIVERSITY AND AGRICULTURAL & MECHANICAL COLLEGE

Agricultural Sciences—General	M,D
Agronomy and Soil Sciences	M,D
Animal Sciences	M,D
Applied Statistics	M
Astronomy	M,D
Astrophysics	M,D
Chemistry	M,D
Environmental Management and Policy	M,D
Environmental Sciences	M,D
Fish, Game, and Wildlife Management	M,D
Food Science and Technology	M,D
Forestry	M,D
Geology	M,D
Geophysics	M,D
Horticulture	M,D
Marine Affairs	M,D
Mathematics	M,D
Natural Resources	M,D
Oceanography	M,D
Physics	M,D
Statistics	M

LOUISIANA STATE UNIVERSITY HEALTH SCIENCES CENTER
Biostatistics — M,D

LOUISIANA TECH UNIVERSITY
Agricultural Sciences—
  General — M,D,O
Applied Physics — M,D
Chemistry — M,D,O
Mathematics — M,D,O

LOYOLA MARYMOUNT UNIVERSITY
Environmental Sciences — M

LOYOLA UNIVERSITY CHICAGO
Applied Statistics — M
Chemistry — M,D
Mathematics — M
Statistics — M

MANHATTAN COLLEGE
Applied Mathematics — M
Mathematics — M,O

MANHATTANVILLE COLLEGE
Chemistry — M,O
Geosciences — M,O
Mathematics — M,O
Physics — M,O

MARQUETTE UNIVERSITY
Analytical Chemistry — M,D
Chemical Physics — M,D
Chemistry — M,D
Computational Sciences — M,D
Inorganic Chemistry — M,D
Mathematics — M,D
Organic Chemistry — M,D
Physical Chemistry — M,D
Water Resources — M,D,O

MARSHALL UNIVERSITY
Chemistry — M
Environmental Sciences — M
Mathematics — M
Physics — M

MARYGROVE COLLEGE
Mathematics — M,O

MASSACHUSETTS INSTITUTE OF TECHNOLOGY
Atmospheric Sciences — M,D
Chemistry — D
Computational Sciences — M
Environmental Sciences — M,D,O
Geochemistry — M,D
Geology — M,D
Geophysics — M,D
Geosciences — M,D
Hydrology — M,D,O
Inorganic Chemistry — D
Marine Geology — M,D
Mathematics — D
Oceanography — M,D,O
Organic Chemistry — M,D,O
Physical Chemistry — D
Physics — M,D
Planetary and Space
  Sciences — M,D

MCGILL UNIVERSITY
Agricultural Sciences—
  General — M,D,O
Agronomy and Soil Sciences — M,D
Animal Sciences — M,D
Applied Mathematics — M,D
Atmospheric Sciences — M,D
Biostatistics — M,D
Chemistry — M,D
Computational Sciences — M,D
Environmental Management
  and Policy — M,D
Fish, Game, and Wildlife
  Management — M,D
Food Science and
  Technology — M,D
Forestry — M,D
Geosciences — M,D
Mathematics — M,D
Meteorology — M,D
Natural Resources — M,D
Oceanography — M,D
Physics — M,D
Planetary and Space
  Sciences — M,D
Plant Sciences — M,D,O
Statistics — M,D,O

MCMASTER UNIVERSITY
Analytical Chemistry — M,D
Applied Statistics — M
Astrophysics — D
Chemical Physics — M,D
Chemistry — M,D
Geochemistry — M,D
Geology — M,D
Geosciences — M,D
Inorganic Chemistry — M,D
Mathematics — M,D
Organic Chemistry — M,D
Physical Chemistry — M,D
Physics — D
Statistics — M,D

MCNEESE STATE UNIVERSITY
Agricultural Sciences—
  General — M
Chemistry — M
Environmental Sciences — M
Mathematics — M
Statistics — M

MCPHS UNIVERSITY
Chemistry — M,D

MEDICAL COLLEGE OF WISCONSIN
Biostatistics — D

MEDICAL UNIVERSITY OF SOUTH CAROLINA
Biostatistics — M,D
Marine Sciences — D

MEMORIAL UNIVERSITY OF NEWFOUNDLAND
Aquaculture — M
Chemistry — M,D
Computational Sciences — M
Condensed Matter Physics — M,D
Environmental Sciences — M,D
Fish, Game, and Wildlife
  Management — M,O
Food Science and
  Technology — M,D
Geology — M,D
Geophysics — M,D
Geosciences — M,D
Marine Affairs — M,D,O
Marine Sciences — M,O
Mathematics — M,D
Oceanography — M,D
Physics — M,D
Statistics — M,D

MERCER UNIVERSITY
Environmental Sciences — M
Mathematics — M,D,O

MIAMI UNIVERSITY
Chemistry — M,D
Environmental Sciences — M
Geology — M,D
Mathematics — M
Physics — M
Statistics — M

MICHIGAN STATE UNIVERSITY
Agricultural Sciences—
  General — M,D
Agronomy and Soil Sciences — M,D
Animal Sciences — M,D
Applied Mathematics — M,D
Applied Statistics — M,D
Astronomy — M,D
Astrophysics — M,D
Chemical Physics — M,D
Chemistry — M,D
Environmental Sciences — M,D
Fish, Game, and Wildlife
  Management — M,D
Food Science and
  Technology — M,D
Forestry — M,D
Geosciences — M,D
Horticulture — M,D
Mathematics — M,D
Natural Resources — M,D
Physics — M,D
Plant Sciences — M,D
Statistics — M,D

MICHIGAN TECHNOLOGICAL UNIVERSITY
Applied Physics — M,D
Chemistry — M,D
Computational Sciences — M,D,O
Forestry — M,D
Geophysics — M,D
Mathematics — M,D
Physics — M,D

MIDDLEBURY INSTITUTE OF INTERNATIONAL STUDIES AT MONTEREY
Environmental Management
  and Policy — M

MIDDLE TENNESSEE STATE UNIVERSITY
Biostatistics — M
Chemistry — M
Computational Sciences — D
Geosciences — O
Mathematics — M

MILLERSVILLE UNIVERSITY OF PENNSYLVANIA
Environmental Management
  and Policy — M
Meteorology — M

MINNESOTA STATE UNIVERSITY MANKATO
Applied Statistics — M
Astronomy — M
Environmental Sciences — M
Mathematics — M
Physics — M
Statistics — M

MISSISSIPPI COLLEGE
Chemistry — M
Mathematics — M

MISSISSIPPI STATE UNIVERSITY
Agricultural Sciences—
  General — M,D
Agronomy and Soil Sciences — M,D
Animal Sciences — M,D
Atmospheric Sciences — M,D
Chemistry — M,D
Fish, Game, and Wildlife
  Management — M,D
Food Science and
  Technology — M,D
Forestry — M,D
Geology — M,D
Geosciences — M,D
Horticulture — M,D

Mathematics — M,D
Meteorology — M,D
Physics — M,D
Plant Sciences — M,D
Statistics — M,D

MISSOURI STATE UNIVERSITY
Agricultural Sciences—
  General — M
Chemistry — M
Environmental Management
  and Policy — M,O
Geology — M,O
Geosciences — M,O
Mathematics — M
Physics — M
Plant Sciences — M

MISSOURI UNIVERSITY OF SCIENCE AND TECHNOLOGY
Applied Mathematics — M,D
Chemistry — M,D
Geochemistry — M,D
Geology — M,D
Geophysics — M,D
Mathematics — M,D
Physics — M,D
Statistics — M,D
Water Resources — M,D

MISSOURI WESTERN STATE UNIVERSITY
Animal Sciences — M
Chemistry — M

MONROE COLLEGE
Biostatistics — M

MONTANA STATE UNIVERSITY
Agricultural Sciences—
  General — M,D
Animal Sciences — M,D
Chemistry — M,D
Environmental Sciences — M,D
Fish, Game, and Wildlife
  Management — M,D
Geosciences — M,D
Mathematics — M,D
Natural Resources — M
Physics — M,D
Plant Sciences — M,D
Range Science — M,D
Statistics — M,D

MONTANA TECH OF THE UNIVERSITY OF MONTANA
Geochemistry — M
Geology — M
Geosciences — M
Hydrogeology — M

MONTCLAIR STATE UNIVERSITY
Applied Mathematics — M
Chemistry — M
Environmental Management
  and Policy — M,D
Environmental Sciences — M
Geosciences — M
Mathematics — M
Statistics — M
Water Resources — O

MOREHEAD STATE UNIVERSITY
Agricultural Sciences—
  General — M
Environmental Management
  and Policy — M

MORGAN STATE UNIVERSITY
Chemistry — M
Computational Sciences — M,D
Mathematics — M
Physics — M

MOUNT ALLISON UNIVERSITY
Chemistry — M

MURRAY STATE UNIVERSITY
Agricultural Sciences—
  General — M,O
Chemistry — M
Environmental Sciences — M,O
Geosciences — M,O
Mathematics — M
Statistics — M

NAVAL POSTGRADUATE SCHOOL
Acoustics — M,D
Applied Mathematics — M,D
Applied Physics — M,D,O
Meteorology — M,D
Oceanography — M,D
Physics — M,D

NEW JERSEY INSTITUTE OF TECHNOLOGY
Applied Mathematics — M,D,O
Applied Physics — M,D,O
Applied Statistics — M,D,O
Biostatistics — M,D,O
Chemistry — M,D,O
Environmental Management
  and Policy — M,D,O
Environmental Sciences — M,D,O
Mathematical and
  Computational Finance — M,D,O
Mathematics — M,D,O
Statistics — M,D,O

NEW MEXICO HIGHLANDS UNIVERSITY
Chemistry — M
Natural Resources — M

NEW MEXICO INSTITUTE OF MINING AND TECHNOLOGY
Applied Mathematics — M,D

Astrophysics — M,D
Atmospheric Sciences — M,D
Chemistry — M,D
Geochemistry — M,D
Geology — M,D
Geophysics — M,D
Geosciences — M,D
Hydrology — M,D
Mathematical Physics — M,D
Mathematics — M,D
Physics — M,D
Statistics — M,D

NEW MEXICO STATE UNIVERSITY
Agricultural Sciences—
  General — M,D
Applied Statistics — M,D,O
Astrophysics — M,D
Food Science and
  Technology — M
Hydrology — M,D
Water Resources — M,D

THE NEW SCHOOL
Environmental Management
  and Policy — M

NEW YORK INSTITUTE OF TECHNOLOGY
Environmental Management
  and Policy — O

NEW YORK MEDICAL COLLEGE
Biostatistics — M,D,O

NEW YORK UNIVERSITY
Applied Statistics — M
Chemistry — M,D
Environmental Management
  and Policy — M
Food Science and
  Technology — M,D
Mathematical and
  Computational Finance — M,D
Mathematics — M,D*
Physics — M,D
Statistics — M,D

NORFOLK STATE UNIVERSITY
Optical Sciences — M

NORTH CAROLINA AGRICULTURAL AND TECHNICAL STATE UNIVERSITY
Agricultural Sciences—
  General — M
Agronomy and Soil Sciences — M
Animal Sciences — M
Applied Mathematics — M
Chemistry — M
Computational Sciences — M
Environmental Sciences — M
Food Science and
  Technology — M
Mathematics — M
Natural Resources — M
Optical Sciences — M,D
Physics — M
Plant Sciences — M

NORTH CAROLINA CENTRAL UNIVERSITY
Chemistry — M
Environmental Sciences — M
Geosciences — M
Mathematics — M
Physics — M

NORTH CAROLINA STATE UNIVERSITY
Agricultural Sciences—
  General — M,D,O
Agronomy and Soil Sciences — M,D
Animal Sciences — M,D
Atmospheric Sciences — M,D
Chemistry — M,D
Food Science and
  Technology — M,D
Forestry — M,D
Geosciences — M,D
Horticulture — M,D,O
Marine Sciences — M,D
Mathematical and
  Computational Finance — M
Mathematics — M,D
Meteorology — M,D
Natural Resources — M,D
Oceanography — M,D
Physics — M,D
Statistics — M,D

NORTH DAKOTA STATE UNIVERSITY
Agricultural Sciences—
  General — M,D
Agronomy and Soil Sciences — M,D
Animal Sciences — M,D
Applied Mathematics — M,D
Chemistry — M,D
Environmental Sciences — M,D
Food Science and
  Technology — M,D
Horticulture — M,D
Mathematics — M,D
Natural Resources — M,D
Physics — M,D
Plant Sciences — M,D
Statistics — M,D

NORTHEASTERN ILLINOIS UNIVERSITY
Applied Mathematics — M
Chemistry — M
Environmental Management
  and Policy — M,O
Mathematics — M,O

NORTHEASTERN STATE UNIVERSITY
Natural Resources — M

---

*M—master's; D—doctorate; O—other advanced degree; *Close-Up and/or Display*

Peterson's Graduate Programs in the Physical Sciences, Mathematics, Agricultural Sciences, the Environment & Natural Resources 2020

www.petersons.com   **23**

NORTHEASTERN UNIVERSITY

Applied Mathematics	M,D
Chemistry	M,D
Environmental Management and Policy	M,D
Environmental Sciences	M,D
Mathematics	M,D
Physics	M,D

NORTHERN ARIZONA UNIVERSITY

Applied Physics	M,D
Applied Statistics	M,O
Atmospheric Sciences	M,D,O
Chemistry	M,D
Environmental Management and Policy	M,D,O
Environmental Sciences	M,D,O
Forestry	M,D
Geology	M,D,O
Mathematics	M,O
Meteorology	M,D,O
Physics	M,D
Statistics	M,O

NORTHERN ILLINOIS UNIVERSITY

Chemistry	M,D
Geology	M,D
Mathematics	M,D
Physics	M,D
Statistics	M

NORTHWESTERN UNIVERSITY

Applied Mathematics	M,D
Applied Physics	D
Astronomy	D
Biostatistics	D
Chemistry	D
Geology	D
Geosciences	D
Mathematics	D
Physics	D
Statistics	M,D

NORTHWEST MISSOURI STATE UNIVERSITY

Agricultural Sciences— General	M
Mathematics	M,O

NOVA SOUTHEASTERN UNIVERSITY

Oceanography	M,D

OAKLAND UNIVERSITY

Applied Mathematics	M,D
Applied Statistics	M
Chemistry	M,D
Environmental Sciences	M,D
Mathematics	M
Physics	M,D
Statistics	O

THE OHIO STATE UNIVERSITY

Agricultural Sciences— General	
Agronomy and Soil Sciences	M,D
Animal Sciences	M,D
Astronomy	M,D
Atmospheric Sciences	M,D
Biostatistics	M,D
Chemical Physics	M,D
Chemistry	M,D
Computational Sciences	M,D
Environmental Management and Policy	M,D
Environmental Sciences	M,D
Fish, Game, and Wildlife Management	M,D
Food Science and Technology	M,D
Forestry	M,D
Geodetic Sciences	M,D
Geology	M,D
Geosciences	M,D
Horticulture	M,D
Mathematics	M,D
Natural Resources	M,D
Optical Sciences	M,D
Physics	M,D
Plant Sciences	D
Statistics	M,D

OHIO UNIVERSITY

Astronomy	M,D
Environmental Management and Policy	M,O
Geochemistry	M
Geology	M
Mathematics	M,D
Physics	M,D

OKLAHOMA STATE UNIVERSITY

Agricultural Sciences— General	M,D
Agronomy and Soil Sciences	M,D
Animal Sciences	M,D
Applied Mathematics	M,D
Chemistry	M,D
Environmental Sciences	M,D,O
Food Science and Technology	M,D
Forestry	M,D
Geology	M,D
Horticulture	M,D
Mathematics	M,D
Natural Resources	M,D
Photonics	M,D
Physics	M,D
Plant Sciences	M,D
Statistics	M,D

OLD DOMINION UNIVERSITY

Analytical Chemistry	M,D
Applied Mathematics	M,D
Biostatistics	M,D
Chemistry	M,D
Environmental Sciences	M,D
Inorganic Chemistry	M,D

Mathematics	M,D
Oceanography	M,D
Organic Chemistry	M,D
Physical Chemistry	M,D
Physics	M,D
Statistics	M,D
Water Resources	M

OREGON HEALTH & SCIENCE UNIVERSITY

Environmental Sciences	M,D

OREGON STATE UNIVERSITY

Agronomy and Soil Sciences	M,D
Analytical Chemistry	M,D
Animal Sciences	M
Applied Mathematics	M,D
Aquaculture	M,D
Atmospheric Sciences	M,D
Biostatistics	M,D
Chemistry	M,D
Computational Sciences	M,D
Environmental Management and Policy	M,D
Environmental Sciences	M,D
Fish, Game, and Wildlife Management	M,D
Food Science and Technology	M,D
Forestry	M,D
Geochemistry	M,D
Geology	M,D
Geophysics	M,D
Horticulture	M,D
Hydrogeology	M,D
Hydrology	M,D
Limnology	M,D
Marine Affairs	M
Marine Sciences	M
Mathematical and Computational Finance	M,D
Mathematics	M,D
Natural Resources	M
Oceanography	M,D
Physics	M,D
Range Science	M,D
Statistics	M,D
Viticulture and Enology	M,D
Water Resources	M,D

PACE UNIVERSITY

Chemistry	M,O
Environmental Management and Policy	M
Environmental Sciences	M
Geosciences	M,O
Mathematics	M,O
Physics	M,O

PENN STATE HARRISBURG

Environmental Sciences	M,O

PENN STATE HERSHEY MEDICAL CENTER

Biostatistics	D

PENN STATE UNIVERSITY PARK

Acoustics	M,D
Agricultural Sciences— General	M,D,O
Agronomy and Soil Sciences	M,D
Animal Sciences	M,D
Applied Statistics	M,D
Astronomy	M,D
Astrophysics	M,D
Chemistry	M,D
Environmental Management and Policy	M
Environmental Sciences	M
Fish, Game, and Wildlife Management	M,D
Food Science and Technology	M,D
Forestry	M,D
Geosciences	M,D
Horticulture	M,D
Mathematics	M,D
Meteorology	M,D
Physics	M,D
Plant Sciences	M,D
Statistics	M,D

PITTSBURG STATE UNIVERSITY

Chemistry	M
Mathematics	M
Physics	M

POINT PARK UNIVERSITY

Environmental Management and Policy	M

POLYTECHNIC UNIVERSITY OF PUERTO RICO

Environmental Management and Policy	M

POLYTECHNIC UNIVERSITY OF PUERTO RICO, MIAMI CAMPUS

Environmental Management and Policy	M

POLYTECHNIC UNIVERSITY OF PUERTO RICO, ORLANDO CAMPUS

Environmental Management and Policy	M

PONTIFICAL CATHOLIC UNIVERSITY OF PUERTO RICO

Chemistry	M
Environmental Sciences	M

PORTLAND STATE UNIVERSITY

Applied Statistics	M,D,O
Chemistry	M,D
Environmental Management and Policy	M,D,O
Environmental Sciences	M,D,O

Food Science and Technology	M,D,O
Geology	M,D,O
Hydrology	M,D,O
Mathematics	M,D,O
Physics	M,D,O
Statistics	M,D,O

PRAIRIE VIEW A&M UNIVERSITY

Agricultural Sciences— General	M
Chemistry	M

PRESCOTT COLLEGE

Environmental Management and Policy	M

PRINCETON UNIVERSITY

Applied Mathematics	D
Astronomy	D
Astrophysics	D
Atmospheric Sciences	D
Chemistry	M,D
Computational Sciences	D
Geosciences	D
Mathematics	D
Oceanography	D
Photonics	D
Physics	D
Plasma Physics	D

PURDUE UNIVERSITY

Agricultural Sciences— General	M,D
Agronomy and Soil Sciences	M,D
Analytical Chemistry	M,D
Animal Sciences	M,D
Aquaculture	M,D
Atmospheric Sciences	M,D
Chemistry	M,D
Computational Sciences	D
Environmental Management and Policy	M,D
Fish, Game, and Wildlife Management	M,D
Food Science and Technology	M,D
Forestry	M,D
Geosciences	M,D
Horticulture	M,D
Inorganic Chemistry	M,D
Mathematics	M,D
Natural Resources	M,D
Organic Chemistry	M,D
Physical Chemistry	M,D
Physics	M,D
Plant Sciences	D
Statistics	M,D

PURDUE UNIVERSITY FORT WAYNE

Applied Mathematics	M,O
Applied Statistics	M,O
Mathematics	M,O

PURDUE UNIVERSITY NORTHWEST

Mathematics	M

QUEENS COLLEGE OF THE CITY UNIVERSITY OF NEW YORK

Applied Mathematics	M
Chemistry	M
Environmental Sciences	M
Geology	M
Geosciences	M
Mathematics	M
Photonics	M
Physics	M

QUEEN'S UNIVERSITY AT KINGSTON

Astronomy	M,D
Chemistry	M,D
Geology	M,D
Mathematics	M,D
Physics	M,D
Statistics	M,D

REGENT UNIVERSITY

Mathematics	M,D,O

RENSSELAER POLYTECHNIC INSTITUTE

Acoustics	D
Applied Mathematics	M
Astronomy	M
Chemistry	M,D
Geology	M,D
Mathematics	M,D
Physics	M,D

RHODE ISLAND COLLEGE

Mathematics	M,O

RICE UNIVERSITY

Applied Mathematics	M,D
Applied Physics	M,D
Astronomy	M,D
Biostatistics	M,D
Chemistry	M,D
Computational Sciences	M,D
Environmental Management and Policy	M
Environmental Sciences	M,D
Geophysics	M
Geosciences	M,D
Inorganic Chemistry	M,D
Mathematical and Computational Finance	
Mathematics	D
Organic Chemistry	M,D
Physical Chemistry	M,D
Physics	M,D
Statistics	M,D

RIVIER UNIVERSITY

Mathematics	M

ROCHESTER INSTITUTE OF TECHNOLOGY

Applied Mathematics	M

Applied Statistics	M,O
Astrophysics	M,D
Chemistry	M
Environmental Sciences	M
Mathematical and Computational Finance	M,D,O
Optical Sciences	M,D
Statistics	O

ROOSEVELT UNIVERSITY

Chemistry	M
Mathematics	M

ROSE-HULMAN INSTITUTE OF TECHNOLOGY

Optical Sciences	M

ROWAN UNIVERSITY

Mathematics	M

ROYAL MILITARY COLLEGE OF CANADA

Chemistry	M,D
Mathematics	M,D
Physics	M

ROYAL ROADS UNIVERSITY

Environmental Management and Policy	M,O

RUTGERS UNIVERSITY–CAMDEN

Applied Mathematics	M
Chemistry	M
Mathematics	M

RUTGERS UNIVERSITY–NEWARK

Analytical Chemistry	M,D
Applied Physics	M,D
Chemistry	M,D
Environmental Sciences	M,D
Geology	M
Inorganic Chemistry	M,D
Mathematics	D
Organic Chemistry	M,D
Physical Chemistry	M,D

RUTGERS UNIVERSITY–NEW BRUNSWICK

Animal Sciences	M,D
Applied Mathematics	M,D
Applied Statistics	M,D
Astronomy	M,D
Atmospheric Sciences	M,D
Biostatistics	M,D,O
Chemistry	M,D
Condensed Matter Physics	M,D
Environmental Sciences	M,D
Food Science and Technology	M,D
Geology	M,D
Horticulture	M,D
Inorganic Chemistry	M,D
Mathematics	M,D
Oceanography	M,D
Organic Chemistry	M,D
Physical Chemistry	M,D
Physics	M,D
Statistics	M,D
Theoretical Physics	M,D
Water Resources	M,D

SACRED HEART UNIVERSITY

Chemistry	M

ST. EDWARD'S UNIVERSITY

Environmental Management and Policy	M

ST. FRANCIS XAVIER UNIVERSITY

Chemistry	M
Geology	M
Geosciences	M

ST. JOHN FISHER COLLEGE

Chemistry	M
Physics	M

ST. JOHN'S UNIVERSITY (NY)

Applied Mathematics	M
Chemistry	M
Computational Sciences	M
Mathematics	M
Statistics	M

SAINT JOSEPH'S UNIVERSITY

Mathematics	M,O

SAINT LOUIS UNIVERSITY

Chemistry	M,D
Geophysics	M,D
Geosciences	M,D
Mathematics	M,D
Meteorology	M,D

SAINT MARY'S UNIVERSITY (CANADA)

Astronomy	M,D

ST. THOMAS UNIVERSITY

Geosciences	M,D,O
Planetary and Space Sciences	M,D,O

SALEM STATE UNIVERSITY

Mathematics	M

SAMFORD UNIVERSITY

Environmental Management and Policy	M

SAM HOUSTON STATE UNIVERSITY

Agricultural Sciences— General	M
Chemistry	M
Computational Sciences	M
Mathematics	M
Statistics	M

SAN DIEGO STATE UNIVERSITY

Applied Mathematics	M
Astronomy	M

Biometry	M
Biostatistics	M,D
Chemistry	M,D
Computational Sciences	M
Geology	M
Mathematics	M,D
Physics	M
Statistics	M

SAN FRANCISCO STATE UNIVERSITY
Astronomy	M
Chemistry	M
Environmental Management and Policy	M
Geosciences	M
Marine Sciences	M
Mathematics	M
Physics	M

SAN JOSE STATE UNIVERSITY
Chemistry	M
Environmental Management and Policy	M
Geology	M
Marine Sciences	M
Meteorology	M
Physics	M

SANTA CLARA UNIVERSITY
Applied Mathematics	M,D,O

SAVANNAH STATE UNIVERSITY
Marine Sciences	M

THE SCRIPPS RESEARCH INSTITUTE
Chemistry	D

SETON HALL UNIVERSITY
Analytical Chemistry	M,D
Chemistry	M,D
Inorganic Chemistry	M,D
Organic Chemistry	M,D
Physical Chemistry	M,D

SHIPPENSBURG UNIVERSITY OF PENNSYLVANIA
Environmental Management and Policy	M

SIMON FRASER UNIVERSITY
Applied Mathematics	M,D
Chemistry	M,D
Computational Sciences	M,D
Environmental Management and Policy	M,D,O
Fish, Game, and Wildlife Management	M,D,O
Geosciences	M,D
Mathematics	M,D
Physics	M,D
Statistics	M,D

SIT GRADUATE INSTITUTE
Environmental Management and Policy	M
Meteorology	M

SITTING BULL COLLEGE
Environmental Sciences	M

SLIPPERY ROCK UNIVERSITY OF PENNSYLVANIA
Environmental Management and Policy	M

SMITH COLLEGE
Chemistry	M
Mathematics	O

SOUTH CAROLINA STATE UNIVERSITY
Mathematics	M

SOUTH DAKOTA SCHOOL OF MINES AND TECHNOLOGY
Atmospheric Sciences	M,D
Environmental Sciences	D
Geology	M,D
Paleontology	M,D
Physics	M,D

SOUTH DAKOTA STATE UNIVERSITY
Agricultural Sciences— General	M,D
Animal Sciences	M,D
Chemistry	M,D
Computational Sciences	M,D
Fish, Game, and Wildlife Management	M,D
Food Science and Technology	M,D
Geosciences	D
Mathematics	M,D
Physics	M
Plant Sciences	M,D
Statistics	M,D

SOUTHEAST MISSOURI STATE UNIVERSITY
Chemistry	M
Environmental Management and Policy	M
Environmental Sciences	M
Mathematics	M

SOUTHERN ARKANSAS UNIVERSITY–MAGNOLIA
Agricultural Sciences— General	M

SOUTHERN CONNECTICUT STATE UNIVERSITY
Chemistry	M
Environmental Sciences	M,O
Marine Sciences	M,O
Mathematics	M

SOUTHERN ILLINOIS UNIVERSITY CARBONDALE
Agricultural Sciences— General	M
Agronomy and Soil Sciences	M
Animal Sciences	M
Applied Physics	M,D
Chemistry	M,D
Environmental Management and Policy	M,D
Environmental Sciences	D
Forestry	M
Geology	M,D
Geosciences	M,D
Mathematics	M,D
Physics	M,D
Plant Sciences	M

SOUTHERN ILLINOIS UNIVERSITY EDWARDSVILLE
Applied Mathematics	M
Chemistry	M
Computational Sciences	M
Environmental Management and Policy	M
Environmental Sciences	M
Mathematics	M
Statistics	M

SOUTHERN METHODIST UNIVERSITY
Applied Mathematics	M,D
Applied Statistics	M,D
Biostatistics	M,D
Chemistry	M,D
Computational Sciences	M,D
Geology	M,D
Geophysics	M,D
Mathematics	M,D
Physics	M,D
Statistics	M,D

SOUTHERN NEW HAMPSHIRE UNIVERSITY
Environmental Management and Policy	M,D,O

SOUTHERN UNIVERSITY AND AGRICULTURAL AND MECHANICAL COLLEGE
Agricultural Sciences— General	M
Analytical Chemistry	M
Chemistry	M
Environmental Sciences	M
Forestry	M
Inorganic Chemistry	M
Mathematics	M
Organic Chemistry	M
Physical Chemistry	M
Physics	M

STANFORD UNIVERSITY
Applied Physics	M,D
Biostatistics	M
Chemistry	D
Computational Sciences	M,D
Environmental Sciences	M,D,O
Geophysics	M
Geosciences	M,D,O
Hydrology	M,D,O
Mathematics	M,D
Physics	D
Statistics	M,D

STATE UNIVERSITY OF NEW YORK AT NEW PALTZ
Chemistry	M,O
Geosciences	M,O

STATE UNIVERSITY OF NEW YORK AT OSWEGO
Chemistry	M

STATE UNIVERSITY OF NEW YORK COLLEGE AT CORTLAND
Mathematics	M
Physics	M

STATE UNIVERSITY OF NEW YORK COLLEGE AT POTSDAM
Mathematics	M

STATE UNIVERSITY OF NEW YORK COLLEGE OF ENVIRONMENTAL SCIENCE AND FORESTRY
Chemistry	M,D
Environmental Management and Policy	M,D
Environmental Sciences	M,D
Fish, Game, and Wildlife Management	M,D
Forestry	M,D
Natural Resources	M,D
Organic Chemistry	M,D
Plant Sciences	M,D
Water Resources	M,D

STEPHEN F. AUSTIN STATE UNIVERSITY
Agricultural Sciences— General	M
Chemistry	M
Environmental Sciences	M
Forestry	M,D
Geology	M
Mathematics	M
Physics	M
Statistics	M

STEVENS INSTITUTE OF TECHNOLOGY
Applied Mathematics	M,D
Chemistry	M,D,O
Hydrology	M,D,O
Mathematics	M,D
Photonics	M,D,O

Statistics	M,O

STEVENSON UNIVERSITY
Chemistry	M

STOCKTON UNIVERSITY
Environmental Sciences	M

STONY BROOK UNIVERSITY, STATE UNIVERSITY OF NEW YORK
Applied Mathematics	M,D,O
Astronomy	D
Atmospheric Sciences	M,D
Chemistry	M,D
Environmental Management and Policy	M,O
Geosciences	M,D
Marine Affairs	M
Marine Sciences	M,D
Mathematics	M,D
Physics	M,D
Statistics	M,D,O

SUL ROSS STATE UNIVERSITY
Animal Sciences	M
Fish, Game, and Wildlife Management	M
Geology	M
Natural Resources	M
Range Science	M

SYRACUSE UNIVERSITY
Applied Statistics	M
Chemistry	M,D
Geology	M,D
Mathematics	M,D
Physics	M,D

TARLETON STATE UNIVERSITY
Agricultural Sciences— General	M
Environmental Sciences	M
Fish, Game, and Wildlife Management	M
Mathematics	M
Natural Resources	M

TEACHERS COLLEGE, COLUMBIA UNIVERSITY
Applied Statistics	M,D
Chemistry	M,D
Geosciences	M,D
Physics	M,D

TEMPLE UNIVERSITY
Applied Mathematics	M,D
Chemistry	M,D
Geology	M,D
Geosciences	M,D
Hydrology	M,O
Mathematics	M,D
Physics	M,D
Statistics	M,D

TENNESSEE STATE UNIVERSITY
Agricultural Sciences— General	M,D
Agronomy and Soil Sciences	M,D
Chemistry	M
Mathematics	M
Plant Sciences	M,D

TENNESSEE TECHNOLOGICAL UNIVERSITY
Agricultural Sciences— General	D
Chemistry	M,D
Environmental Management and Policy	M
Environmental Sciences	M,D
Fish, Game, and Wildlife Management	M
Geosciences	D
Mathematics	M

TEXAS A&M INTERNATIONAL UNIVERSITY
Mathematics	M

TEXAS A&M UNIVERSITY
Agricultural Sciences— General	M,D
Agronomy and Soil Sciences	M,D
Animal Sciences	M,D
Applied Physics	M,D
Astronomy	M,D
Biostatistics	M,D
Chemistry	M,D
Fish, Game, and Wildlife Management	M,D
Food Science and Technology	M,D
Forestry	M,D
Geology	M,D
Geophysics	M,D
Horticulture	M,D
Marine Sciences	M
Mathematics	M,D
Meteorology	M,D
Natural Resources	M,D
Oceanography	M,D
Physics	M,D
Statistics	M,D

TEXAS A&M UNIVERSITY–CENTRAL TEXAS
Mathematics	M,O

TEXAS A&M UNIVERSITY–COMMERCE
Agricultural Sciences— General	M,O
Chemistry	M,O
Computational Sciences	M,O
Environmental Sciences	M,O
Mathematics	M,O

Physics	M,O

TEXAS A&M UNIVERSITY–CORPUS CHRISTI
Aquaculture	M
Chemistry	M,D
Environmental Sciences	M,D
Marine Sciences	M,D
Mathematics	M

TEXAS A&M UNIVERSITY–KINGSVILLE
Agricultural Sciences— General	M,D
Agronomy and Soil Sciences	M,D
Animal Sciences	M
Chemistry	M
Fish, Game, and Wildlife Management	M,D
Horticulture	M,D
Mathematics	M
Plant Sciences	M
Range Science	M
Statistics	M

TEXAS CHRISTIAN UNIVERSITY
Applied Mathematics	M,D
Astrophysics	M,D
Chemistry	M,D
Environmental Sciences	M,D
Mathematics	M,D
Physics	M,D

TEXAS SOUTHERN UNIVERSITY
Chemistry	M
Environmental Management and Policy	M,D
Mathematics	M

TEXAS STATE UNIVERSITY
Chemistry	M
Fish, Game, and Wildlife Management	M
Mathematics	M
Physics	M

TEXAS TECH UNIVERSITY
Agricultural Sciences— General	M,D
Agronomy and Soil Sciences	M,D
Animal Sciences	M,D
Astronomy	M,D
Atmospheric Sciences	M,D
Chemistry	M,D
Environmental Management and Policy	M,D
Environmental Sciences	M,D
Fish, Game, and Wildlife Management	M,D
Food Science and Technology	M,D
Geosciences	M,D
Horticulture	M,D
Mathematics	M,D
Natural Resources	M,D
Physics	M,D
Plant Sciences	M,D
Statistics	M,D

TEXAS WOMAN'S UNIVERSITY
Chemistry	M
Food Science and Technology	M,D
Mathematics	M

THOMAS EDISON STATE UNIVERSITY
Environmental Management and Policy	M

THOMPSON RIVERS UNIVERSITY
Environmental Sciences	M

TOWSON UNIVERSITY
Applied Mathematics	M
Applied Physics	M
Environmental Management and Policy	M
Environmental Sciences	M,O

TRENT UNIVERSITY
Chemistry	M
Environmental Management and Policy	M,D
Physics	M

TROPICAL AGRICULTURE RESEARCH AND HIGHER EDUCATION CENTER
Agricultural Sciences— General	M,D
Environmental Management and Policy	M,D
Forestry	M,D
Water Resources	M,D

TROY UNIVERSITY
Environmental Management and Policy	M

TUFTS UNIVERSITY
Animal Sciences	M
Astrophysics	M,D
Biostatistics	M,D,O
Chemical Physics	M,D
Chemistry	M,D
Environmental Management and Policy	M,D,O
Mathematics	M,D
Physics	M,D
Water Resources	M,D

TULANE UNIVERSITY
Biostatistics	M,D
Chemistry	M,D
Mathematics	M,D
Physics	M,D

---

*M—master's; D—doctorate; O—other advanced degree; *Close-Up and/or Display*

Peterson's Graduate Programs in the Physical Sciences, Mathematics, Agricultural Sciences, the Environment & Natural Resources 2020

www.petersons.com **25**

TUSKEGEE UNIVERSITY
Agronomy and Soil Sciences	M
Animal Sciences	M
Chemistry	M
Environmental Sciences	M
Food Science and Technology	M
Plant Sciences	M

UNITY COLLEGE
Natural Resources	M

UNIVERSIDAD AUTONOMA DE GUADALAJARA
Environmental Management and Policy	M,D

UNIVERSIDAD DE LAS AMÉRICAS PUEBLA
Food Science and Technology	M

UNIVERSIDAD DEL TURABO
Chemistry	M,D
Environmental Management and Policy	M,D
Environmental Sciences	M,D

UNIVERSIDAD METROPOLITANA
Environmental Management and Policy	M
Natural Resources	M

UNIVERSIDAD NACIONAL PEDRO HENRIQUEZ URENA
Agricultural Sciences—General	M
Animal Sciences	M
Environmental Sciences	M
Horticulture	M
Natural Resources	M

UNIVERSITÉ DE MONCTON
Astronomy	M
Chemistry	M
Food Science and Technology	M
Mathematics	M
Physics	M

UNIVERSITÉ DE MONTRÉAL
Chemistry	M,D
Environmental Management and Policy	O
Mathematical and Computational Finance	M,D,O
Mathematics	M,D,O
Physics	M,D
Statistics	M,D,O

UNIVERSITÉ DE SHERBROOKE
Chemistry	M,D,O
Environmental Sciences	M,O
Mathematics	M,D
Physics	M,D

UNIVERSITÉ DU QUÉBEC À CHICOUTIMI
Environmental Management and Policy	M
Geosciences	M
Mineralogy	D

UNIVERSITÉ DU QUÉBEC À MONTRÉAL
Atmospheric Sciences	M,D,O
Chemistry	M,D
Environmental Sciences	M,D,O
Geology	M,D,O
Geosciences	M,D,O
Mathematics	M,D
Meteorology	M,D,O
Mineralogy	M,D,O
Natural Resources	M,D,O

UNIVERSITÉ DU QUÉBEC À RIMOUSKI
Fish, Game, and Wildlife Management	M,D,O
Marine Affairs	M,O
Oceanography	M,D

UNIVERSITÉ DU QUÉBEC À TROIS-RIVIÈRES
Chemistry	M
Environmental Sciences	M,D
Mathematics	M
Physics	M,D

UNIVERSITÉ DU QUÉBEC EN ABITIBI-TÉMISCAMINGUE
Environmental Sciences	M,D
Forestry	M,D
Natural Resources	M,D

UNIVERSITÉ DU QUÉBEC, INSTITUT NATIONAL DE LA RECHERCHE SCIENTIFIQUE
Environmental Management and Policy	M,D
Geosciences	M,D
Hydrology	M,D

UNIVERSITÉ LAVAL
Agricultural Sciences—General	M,D,O
Agronomy and Soil Sciences	M,D
Animal Sciences	M,D
Chemistry	M,D
Environmental Management and Policy	M,D,O
Environmental Sciences	M,D
Food Science and Technology	M,D
Forestry	M,D
Geodetic Sciences	M,D
Geology	M,D
Geosciences	M,D
Mathematics	M,D
Oceanography	D
Physics	M,D
Statistics	M

UNIVERSITY AT ALBANY, STATE UNIVERSITY OF NEW YORK
Atmospheric Sciences	M,D
Biostatistics	M,D
Chemistry	M,D
Mathematics	M,D
Physics	M,D

UNIVERSITY AT BUFFALO, THE STATE UNIVERSITY OF NEW YORK
Biostatistics	M,D
Chemistry	M,D
Computational Sciences	D,O
Environmental Sciences	M,D
Food Science and Technology	M,D,O
Geology	M,D
Geosciences	M,D
Mathematics	M,D
Physics	M,D

THE UNIVERSITY OF AKRON
Applied Mathematics	M
Chemistry	M,D
Geology	M
Geosciences	M
Mathematics	M
Statistics	M

THE UNIVERSITY OF ALABAMA
Applied Mathematics	M,D
Applied Statistics	M,D
Astronomy	M,D
Chemistry	M,D
Geology	M,D
Geosciences	M,D
Mathematics	M,D
Physics	M,D

THE UNIVERSITY OF ALABAMA AT BIRMINGHAM
Applied Mathematics	D
Biostatistics	M,D
Chemistry	M,D
Computational Sciences	D
Mathematics	M
Physics	M,D

THE UNIVERSITY OF ALABAMA IN HUNTSVILLE
Applied Mathematics	M,D
Astronomy	M,D
Atmospheric Sciences	M,D
Chemistry	M,D
Geosciences	M,D
Mathematics	M,D
Optical Sciences	M,D
Photonics	M,D
Physics	M,D

UNIVERSITY OF ALASKA FAIRBANKS
Astrophysics	M,D
Atmospheric Sciences	M,D
Chemistry	M,D
Computational Sciences	M,D
Environmental Management and Policy	M
Fish, Game, and Wildlife Management	M,D,O
Geophysics	M
Limnology	M,D
Marine Sciences	M,D
Mathematics	M,D,O
Natural Resources	M,D
Oceanography	M,D
Physics	M,D
Statistics	M,D,O

UNIVERSITY OF ALBERTA
Agricultural Sciences—General	M,D
Agronomy and Soil Sciences	M,D
Applied Mathematics	M,D,O
Astrophysics	M,D,O
Biostatistics	M,D,O
Chemistry	M,D
Condensed Matter Physics	M,D
Environmental Management and Policy	M,D
Environmental Sciences	M,D
Forestry	M,D
Geophysics	M,D
Geosciences	M,D
Mathematical and Computational Finance	M,D,O
Mathematical Physics	M,D,O
Mathematics	M,D,O
Natural Resources	M,D
Physics	M,D
Statistics	M,D,O

THE UNIVERSITY OF ARIZONA
Agricultural Sciences—General	M,D,O
Agronomy and Soil Sciences	M,D,O
Animal Sciences	M,D
Applied Mathematics	M,D
Astronomy	D
Atmospheric Sciences	M,D
Biostatistics	M,D
Chemistry	M,D
Environmental Management and Policy	M,D
Environmental Sciences	M,D,O
Forestry	M,D
Geosciences	M,D
Hydrology	D,O
Mathematics	M,D
Natural Resources	M,D
Optical Sciences	M,D,O
Physics	M,D
Planetary and Space Sciences	M,D
Plant Sciences	M,D
Range Science	M,D
Statistics	M,D

UNIVERSITY OF ARKANSAS
Agricultural Sciences—General	M,D
Agronomy and Soil Sciences	M,D
Animal Sciences	M,D
Applied Physics	M,D
Chemistry	M,D
Food Science and Technology	M,D
Geology	M
Horticulture	M
Mathematics	M,D
Photonics	M,D
Physics	M,D
Planetary and Space Sciences	M,D
Plant Sciences	D
Statistics	M,D

UNIVERSITY OF ARKANSAS AT LITTLE ROCK
Applied Mathematics	M,O
Applied Statistics	M,O
Chemistry	M
Geosciences	O
Mathematics	M,O

UNIVERSITY OF ARKANSAS AT MONTICELLO
Forestry	M,D
Natural Resources	M

UNIVERSITY OF ARKANSAS AT PINE BLUFF
Aquaculture	M,D
Fish, Game, and Wildlife Management	M,D

UNIVERSITY OF ARKANSAS FOR MEDICAL SCIENCES
Biostatistics	M,D,O

THE UNIVERSITY OF BRITISH COLUMBIA
Agricultural Sciences—General	M,D
Agronomy and Soil Sciences	M,D
Animal Sciences	M,D
Astronomy	M,D
Atmospheric Sciences	M,D
Chemistry	M,D
Environmental Management and Policy	M,D
Food Science and Technology	M,D
Forestry	M,D
Geology	M,D
Geophysics	M,D
Marine Sciences	M,D
Mathematics	M,D
Natural Resources	M,D
Oceanography	M,D
Physics	M,D
Plant Sciences	M,D
Statistics	M,D
Water Resources	M

UNIVERSITY OF CALGARY
Analytical Chemistry	M,D
Astronomy	M,D
Chemistry	M,D
Environmental Management and Policy	M,D,O
Geology	M,D
Geophysics	M,D
Geosciences	M,D
Hydrology	M,D
Inorganic Chemistry	M,D
Mathematics	M,D
Organic Chemistry	M,D
Physical Chemistry	M,D
Physics	M,D
Statistics	M,D
Theoretical Chemistry	M,D
Water Resources	M,D

UNIVERSITY OF CALIFORNIA, BERKELEY
Applied Mathematics	M,D
Astrophysics	D
Biostatistics	M,D
Chemistry	D
Environmental Management and Policy	M,D,O
Environmental Sciences	M,D
Forestry	M,D
Geology	M,D
Geophysics	M,D
Mathematics	M,D
Natural Resources	M,D
Physics	D
Range Science	M
Statistics	M,D

UNIVERSITY OF CALIFORNIA, DAVIS
Agricultural Sciences—General	M
Agronomy and Soil Sciences	M,D
Animal Sciences	M,D
Applied Mathematics	M,D
Atmospheric Sciences	M,D
Biostatistics	M,D
Chemistry	M,D
Environmental Sciences	M,D
Food Science and Technology	M,D
Geology	M,D
Horticulture	M
Hydrology	M,D
Mathematics	M,D
Physics	M,D
Statistics	M,D
Viticulture and Enology	M,D

UNIVERSITY OF CALIFORNIA, IRVINE
Applied Mathematics	M,D
Chemistry	M,D
Geosciences	M,D
Mathematics	M,D
Physics	M,D
Statistics	M,D

UNIVERSITY OF CALIFORNIA, LOS ANGELES
Astronomy	M,D
Astrophysics	M,D
Atmospheric Sciences	M,D
Biomathematics	M,D
Biostatistics	M,D
Chemistry	M,D
Environmental Sciences	M,D
Geochemistry	M,D
Geology	M,D
Geophysics	M,D
Geosciences	M,D
Mathematics	M,D
Oceanography	M,D
Physics	M,D
Planetary and Space Sciences	M,D
Statistics	M,D

UNIVERSITY OF CALIFORNIA, MERCED
Applied Mathematics	M,D
Chemistry	M,D
Physics	M,D

UNIVERSITY OF CALIFORNIA, RIVERSIDE
Agronomy and Soil Sciences	M,D
Chemistry	M,D
Environmental Sciences	M
Geology	M,D
Mathematics	M,D
Physics	M,D
Plant Sciences	M,D
Statistics	M,D
Water Resources	M,D

UNIVERSITY OF CALIFORNIA, SAN DIEGO
Applied Mathematics	M,D
Applied Physics	M,D
Biostatistics	D
Chemistry	M,D
Computational Sciences	M,D
Environmental Management and Policy	M
Geophysics	M,D
Geosciences	M,D
Marine Sciences	M
Mathematics	M,D
Meteorology	M
Oceanography	M,D
Photonics	M,D
Physics	M,D
Statistics	M,D

UNIVERSITY OF CALIFORNIA, SAN FRANCISCO
Chemistry	D

UNIVERSITY OF CALIFORNIA, SANTA BARBARA
Applied Mathematics	M,D
Applied Statistics	M,D
Chemistry	M,D
Computational Sciences	M,D
Environmental Management and Policy	M,D
Environmental Sciences	M,D
Geosciences	M,D
Marine Sciences	M,D
Mathematical and Computational Finance	M,D
Mathematics	M,D
Photonics	M,D
Physics	D
Statistics	M,D

UNIVERSITY OF CALIFORNIA, SANTA CRUZ
Applied Mathematics	M,D
Astronomy	D
Astrophysics	D
Chemistry	M,D
Environmental Management and Policy	D
Geosciences	M,D
Marine Sciences	M,D
Mathematics	M,D
Physics	M,D
Planetary and Space Sciences	M,D
Statistics	M,D

UNIVERSITY OF CENTRAL ARKANSAS
Applied Mathematics	M
Mathematics	M

UNIVERSITY OF CENTRAL FLORIDA
Chemistry	M,D,O
Mathematics	M,D,O
Optical Sciences	M,D
Photonics	M,D
Physics	M,D

UNIVERSITY OF CENTRAL MISSOURI
Applied Mathematics	M,D,O
Environmental Management and Policy	M,D,O
Mathematics	M,D,O

UNIVERSITY OF CENTRAL OKLAHOMA
Applied Mathematics	M
Computational Sciences	M
Mathematics	M
Physics	M
Statistics	M

UNIVERSITY OF CHICAGO
Applied Mathematics	D

26 www.petersons.com

Peterson's Graduate Programs in the Physical Sciences, Mathematics, Agricultural Sciences, the Environment & Natural Resources 2020

Applied Statistics	M
Astronomy	D
Astrophysics	D
Atmospheric Sciences	D
Chemistry	D
Computational Sciences	M
Environmental Management and Policy	M
Environmental Sciences	M
Geophysics	D
Geosciences	D
Mathematical and Computational Finance	M
Mathematics	D
Paleontology	D
Physics	M,D
Planetary and Space Sciences	D
Statistics	M,D,O

UNIVERSITY OF CINCINNATI

Analytical Chemistry	M,D
Applied Mathematics	M,D
Biostatistics	M,D
Chemistry	M,D
Environmental Sciences	M,D
Geology	M,D
Inorganic Chemistry	M,D
Mathematics	M,D
Organic Chemistry	M,D
Physical Chemistry	M,D
Physics	M,D
Statistics	M,D

UNIVERSITY OF COLORADO BOULDER

Applied Mathematics	M,D
Astrophysics	M,D
Atmospheric Sciences	M,D
Chemistry	M,D
Environmental Management and Policy	M,D
Geology	M,D
Geophysics	M,D
Mathematical Physics	M,D
Mathematics	M,D
Oceanography	M,D
Physics	M,D
Plasma Physics	M,D

UNIVERSITY OF COLORADO COLORADO SPRINGS

Applied Mathematics	M
Environmental Sciences	M
Mathematics	D
Physics	D

UNIVERSITY OF COLORADO DENVER

Applied Mathematics	M,D
Applied Statistics	M,D
Biostatistics	M,D
Chemistry	M
Computational Sciences	M,D
Environmental Management and Policy	M,D,O
Environmental Sciences	M
Hydrology	M,D
Mathematics	M,D
Statistics	M,D
Water Resources	M

UNIVERSITY OF CONNECTICUT

Agricultural Sciences— General	M,D
Agronomy and Soil Sciences	M,D
Animal Sciences	M,D
Applied Mathematics	M
Chemistry	M,D
Geology	M,D
Mathematical and Computational Finance	M
Natural Resources	M,D
Physics	M,D
Plant Sciences	M,D
Statistics	M,D

UNIVERSITY OF DAYTON

Applied Mathematics	M
Chemistry	M
Environmental Management and Policy	M,D
Mathematical and Computational Finance	M
Optical Sciences	M,D
Photonics	M,D

UNIVERSITY OF DELAWARE

Agricultural Sciences— General	M,D
Agronomy and Soil Sciences	M,D
Animal Sciences	M,D
Applied Mathematics	M,D
Astronomy	M,D
Chemistry	M,D
Environmental Management and Policy	M,D
Fish, Game, and Wildlife Management	M,D
Food Science and Technology	M,D
Geology	M,D
Horticulture	M
Marine Affairs	M,D
Marine Geology	M,D
Marine Sciences	M,D
Mathematics	M,D
Natural Resources	M
Oceanography	M,D
Physics	M,D
Plant Sciences	M,D
Statistics	M

UNIVERSITY OF DENVER

Chemistry	M,D

Environmental Management and Policy	M,O
Mathematics	M,D
Physics	M,D

UNIVERSITY OF DETROIT MERCY

Chemistry	M,D

THE UNIVERSITY OF FINDLAY

Environmental Management and Policy	M,D
Mathematics	M,D

UNIVERSITY OF FLORIDA

Agricultural Sciences— General	M,D,O
Agronomy and Soil Sciences	M,D
Animal Sciences	M,D
Aquaculture	M,D
Astronomy	M,D
Biostatistics	M,D,O
Chemistry	M,D
Fish, Game, and Wildlife Management	M,D,O
Food Science and Technology	M,D
Forestry	M,D
Geology	M,D
Geosciences	M,D
Horticulture	M,D
Hydrology	M,D
Limnology	M,D
Marine Sciences	M,D
Mathematics	M,D
Natural Resources	M,D
Physics	M,D
Plant Sciences	D
Statistics	M,D
Water Resources	M,D

UNIVERSITY OF GEORGIA

Agricultural Sciences— General	M,D
Agronomy and Soil Sciences	M,D
Analytical Chemistry	M,D
Animal Sciences	M,D
Applied Mathematics	M,D
Chemistry	M,D
Food Science and Technology	M,D
Forestry	M,D
Geology	M,D
Horticulture	M,D
Marine Sciences	M,D
Mathematics	M,D
Natural Resources	M,D
Physics	M,D
Plant Sciences	M,D
Statistics	M,D

UNIVERSITY OF GUAM

Environmental Sciences	M

UNIVERSITY OF GUELPH

Agricultural Sciences— General	M,D,O
Agronomy and Soil Sciences	M,D
Animal Sciences	M,D
Applied Mathematics	M,D
Applied Statistics	M,D
Aquaculture	M
Atmospheric Sciences	M,D
Chemistry	M,D
Environmental Management and Policy	M,D
Environmental Sciences	M,D
Food Science and Technology	M,D
Horticulture	M,D
Mathematics	M,D
Natural Resources	M,D
Physics	M,D
Statistics	M,D

UNIVERSITY OF HAWAII AT HILO

Environmental Sciences	M

UNIVERSITY OF HAWAII AT MANOA

Agricultural Sciences— General	M,D
Animal Sciences	M
Astronomy	M,D
Chemistry	M,D
Environmental Management and Policy	M,D,O
Food Science and Technology	M
Geochemistry	M,D
Geology	M,D
Geophysics	M,D
Horticulture	M,D
Hydrogeology	M,D
Marine Geology	M,D
Marine Sciences	O
Mathematics	M,D
Meteorology	M,D
Natural Resources	M,D
Oceanography	M,D
Physics	M,D
Planetary and Space Sciences	M,D
Plant Sciences	M,D

UNIVERSITY OF HOUSTON

Applied Mathematics	M,D
Atmospheric Sciences	M,D
Chemistry	M,D
Geology	M,D
Geophysics	M,D
Mathematics	M,D
Physics	M,D
Planetary and Space Sciences	M,D

UNIVERSITY OF HOUSTON–CLEAR LAKE

Chemistry	M
Environmental Management and Policy	M
Environmental Sciences	M
Mathematics	M
Physics	M
Statistics	M

UNIVERSITY OF IDAHO

Agronomy and Soil Sciences	M,D
Animal Sciences	M,D
Chemistry	M,D
Environmental Sciences	M,D
Food Science and Technology	M,D
Geology	M,D
Mathematics	M,D
Natural Resources	M,D
Physics	M,D
Plant Sciences	M,D
Statistics	M
Water Resources	M,D

UNIVERSITY OF ILLINOIS AT CHICAGO

Biostatistics	M,D
Chemistry	M,D
Geology	M,D
Geosciences	M,D
Mathematics	M,D
Physics	M,D
Statistics	M,D

UNIVERSITY OF ILLINOIS AT SPRINGFIELD

Environmental Management and Policy	M
Environmental Sciences	M

UNIVERSITY OF ILLINOIS AT URBANA–CHAMPAIGN

Agricultural Sciences— General	M
Agronomy and Soil Sciences	M,D
Animal Sciences	M,D
Applied Mathematics	M,D
Applied Statistics	M,D
Astronomy	M,D
Atmospheric Sciences	M,D
Chemical Physics	M,D
Chemistry	M,D
Environmental Sciences	M,D
Food Science and Technology	M,D
Geology	M,D
Geosciences	M,D
Mathematics	M,D
Natural Resources	M,D
Physics	M,D
Statistics	M,D

THE UNIVERSITY OF IOWA

Agricultural Sciences— General	M,D,O
Applied Mathematics	D
Astronomy	M
Biostatistics	M,D,O
Chemistry	D
Computational Sciences	M,D
Geosciences	M,D
Mathematics	M,D
Physics	M,D
Statistics	M,D,O
Water Resources	M,D

THE UNIVERSITY OF KANSAS

Acoustics	M,D,O
Applied Mathematics	M,D,O
Applied Statistics	M,D,O
Astronomy	M,D
Atmospheric Sciences	M,D,O
Biostatistics	M,D,O
Chemistry	M,D
Environmental Sciences	M,D
Geology	M,D
Mathematics	M,D,O
Physics	M,D
Statistics	M,D,O

UNIVERSITY OF KENTUCKY

Agricultural Sciences— General	M,D
Agronomy and Soil Sciences	M,D
Animal Sciences	M,D
Applied Mathematics	M,D
Astronomy	M,D
Biostatistics	D
Chemistry	M,D
Food Science and Technology	M,D
Forestry	M
Geology	M,D
Mathematics	M,D
Physics	M,D
Plant Sciences	M,D
Statistics	M,D

UNIVERSITY OF LETHBRIDGE

Agricultural Sciences— General	M,D
Chemistry	M,D
Computational Sciences	M,D
Environmental Sciences	M,D
Mathematics	M,D
Physics	M,D

UNIVERSITY OF LOUISIANA AT LAFAYETTE

Environmental Sciences	M
Geosciences	M
Mathematics	M,D
Natural Resources	M

Physics	M

UNIVERSITY OF LOUISVILLE

Analytical Chemistry	M,D
Applied Mathematics	M,D
Chemical Physics	M,D
Chemistry	M,D
Inorganic Chemistry	M,D
Mathematics	M,D
Organic Chemistry	M,D
Physical Chemistry	M,D
Physics	M,D

UNIVERSITY OF LYNCHBURG

Geosciences	M
Mathematics	M

UNIVERSITY OF MAINE

Agricultural Sciences— General	M,D,O
Chemistry	M,D
Environmental Management and Policy	D
Fish, Game, and Wildlife Management	M,D
Forestry	M,D
Geology	M,O
Geosciences	M,D
Horticulture	M,D,O
Marine Sciences	M,D
Mathematics	M
Physics	M,D
Water Resources	M,D

THE UNIVERSITY OF MANCHESTER

Analytical Chemistry	M,D
Applied Mathematics	M,D
Astronomy	M,D
Astrophysics	M,D
Atmospheric Sciences	M,D
Chemistry	M,D
Condensed Matter Physics	M,D
Environmental Management and Policy	M,D
Environmental Sciences	M,D
Geochemistry	M,D
Geosciences	M,D
Inorganic Chemistry	M,D
Mathematical and Computational Finance	M,D
Mathematics	M,D
Natural Resources	M,D
Organic Chemistry	M,D
Paleontology	M,D
Physical Chemistry	M,D
Physics	M,D
Plant Sciences	M,D
Statistics	M,D
Theoretical Chemistry	M,D
Theoretical Physics	M,D

UNIVERSITY OF MANITOBA

Agricultural Sciences— General	M,D
Agronomy and Soil Sciences	M,D
Animal Sciences	M,D
Chemistry	M,D
Computational Sciences	M
Environmental Sciences	M,D
Food Science and Technology	M,D
Geology	M,D
Geophysics	M,D
Horticulture	M,D
Mathematics	M,D
Natural Resources	M,D
Physics	M,D
Plant Sciences	M,D
Statistics	M,D

UNIVERSITY OF MARYLAND, BALTIMORE

Biostatistics	M,D
Environmental Sciences	M,D
Marine Sciences	M,D

UNIVERSITY OF MARYLAND, BALTIMORE COUNTY

Applied Mathematics	M,D
Atmospheric Sciences	M,D
Biostatistics	M,D
Chemistry	M,D,O
Environmental Management and Policy	M,D
Environmental Sciences	M,D
Marine Sciences	M,D
Physics	M,D
Statistics	M,D

UNIVERSITY OF MARYLAND, COLLEGE PARK

Agricultural Sciences— General	M,D
Analytical Chemistry	M,D
Animal Sciences	M,D
Applied Mathematics	M,D
Astronomy	M,D
Biostatistics	M,D
Chemical Physics	M,D
Chemistry	M,D
Environmental Sciences	M,D
Food Science and Technology	M,D
Geology	M,D
Horticulture	M,D
Inorganic Chemistry	M,D
Marine Sciences	M,D
Mathematics	M,D
Meteorology	M,D
Natural Resources	M,D
Oceanography	M,D
Organic Chemistry	M,D
Physical Chemistry	M,D

*M—master's; D—doctorate; O—other advanced degree; *Close-Up and/or Display*

Peterson's Graduate Programs in the Physical Sciences, Mathematics, Agricultural Sciences, the Environment & Natural Resources 2020

www.petersons.com **27**

Physics	M,D
Statistics	M,D

UNIVERSITY OF MARYLAND EASTERN SHORE
Agricultural Sciences— General	M
Chemistry	M,D
Environmental Management and Policy	M,D
Environmental Sciences	M,D
Fish, Game, and Wildlife Management	M,D
Food Science and Technology	M,D
Marine Sciences	M,D

UNIVERSITY OF MARYLAND UNIVERSITY COLLEGE
Environmental Management and Policy	M

UNIVERSITY OF MASSACHUSETTS AMHERST
Animal Sciences	M,D
Applied Mathematics	M,D
Astronomy	M,D
Biostatistics	M,D
Chemistry	M,D
Environmental Management and Policy	M,D
Fish, Game, and Wildlife Management	M,D
Food Science and Technology	M,D
Forestry	M,D
Geosciences	M,D
Marine Sciences	M,D
Mathematics	M,D
Physics	M,D
Plant Sciences	M,D
Statistics	M,D
Water Resources	M,D

UNIVERSITY OF MASSACHUSETTS BOSTON
Applied Physics	M
Chemistry	M,D
Computational Sciences	D
Environmental Sciences	M,D
Marine Sciences	M,D

UNIVERSITY OF MASSACHUSETTS DARTMOUTH
Chemistry	M,D
Environmental Management and Policy	M,O
Marine Affairs	M,D
Marine Sciences	M,D
Physics	M

UNIVERSITY OF MASSACHUSETTS LOWELL
Analytical Chemistry	M,D
Chemistry	M,D
Environmental Sciences	M,D
Inorganic Chemistry	M,D
Mathematics	D
Organic Chemistry	M,D
Physics	M,D

UNIVERSITY OF MEMPHIS
Analytical Chemistry	M,D
Applied Mathematics	M,D
Applied Statistics	M,D
Biostatistics	M,D
Chemistry	M,D
Computational Sciences	M
Geology	M,D,O
Geophysics	M,D,O
Inorganic Chemistry	M,D
Mathematics	M,D,O
Organic Chemistry	M,D
Physical Chemistry	M,D
Physics	M
Statistics	M,D

UNIVERSITY OF MIAMI
Biostatistics	M,D
Chemistry	M,D
Fish, Game, and Wildlife Management	M,D
Geophysics	M,D
Inorganic Chemistry	M,D
Marine Affairs	M
Marine Geology	M,D
Marine Sciences	M,D
Mathematical and Computational Finance	M,D
Mathematics	M,D
Meteorology	M,D
Oceanography	M,D
Organic Chemistry	M,D
Physical Chemistry	M,D
Physics	M,D

UNIVERSITY OF MICHIGAN
Analytical Chemistry	M,D
Applied Physics	D
Applied Statistics	M,D
Astronomy	D
Astrophysics	D
Atmospheric Sciences	M,D
Biostatistics	M,D
Chemistry	M,D
Environmental Management and Policy	M,D
Environmental Sciences	M,D
Geosciences	M,D
Inorganic Chemistry	M,D
Mathematics	M,D
Natural Resources	M,D
Organic Chemistry	M,D
Physical Chemistry	M,D
Physics	D
Planetary and Space Sciences	M,D

UNIVERSITY OF MICHIGAN–DEARBORN
Applied Mathematics	M
Computational Sciences	M
Environmental Sciences	M

UNIVERSITY OF MICHIGAN–FLINT
Mathematics	M

UNIVERSITY OF MINNESOTA, DULUTH
Applied Mathematics	M
Chemistry	M
Computational Sciences	M
Geology	M,D
Physics	M

UNIVERSITY OF MINNESOTA, TWIN CITIES CAMPUS
Agricultural Sciences— General	M,D
Agronomy and Soil Sciences	M,D
Animal Sciences	M,D
Astrophysics	M,D
Biostatistics	M,D
Chemical Physics	M,D
Chemistry	M,D
Computational Sciences	M,D
Environmental Management and Policy	M,D
Food Science and Technology	M,D
Forestry	M,D
Geology	M,D
Geophysics	M,D
Hydrology	M,D
Mathematics	M,D,O
Natural Resources	M,D
Physics	M,D
Plant Sciences	M,D
Statistics	M,D
Water Resources	M,D

UNIVERSITY OF MISSISSIPPI
Chemistry	M,D
Food Science and Technology	M,D
Geology	M,D
Hydrology	M,D
Mathematics	M,D
Physics	M,D

UNIVERSITY OF MISSOURI
Agricultural Sciences— General	M,D
Agronomy and Soil Sciences	M,D,O
Analytical Chemistry	D
Animal Sciences	M,D
Applied Mathematics	M,D
Astronomy	M,D
Chemistry	D
Environmental Sciences	M,D,O
Fish, Game, and Wildlife Management	M,D,O
Food Science and Technology	M,D
Forestry	M,D,O
Geology	M,D
Horticulture	M,D
Mathematics	M,D
Physics	M,D
Plant Sciences	M,D
Statistics	M,D
Water Resources	M,D,O

UNIVERSITY OF MISSOURI–KANSAS CITY
Analytical Chemistry	M,D
Chemistry	M,D
Geosciences	M,D
Inorganic Chemistry	M,D
Mathematics	M,D
Organic Chemistry	M,D
Physical Chemistry	M,D
Physics	M,D
Statistics	M,D

UNIVERSITY OF MISSOURI–ST. LOUIS
Applied Physics	M,D
Astrophysics	M,D
Chemistry	M,D
Mathematics	M,D
Physics	M,D

UNIVERSITY OF MONTANA
Analytical Chemistry	M,D
Chemistry	M,D
Environmental Management and Policy	M
Environmental Sciences	M
Fish, Game, and Wildlife Management	M,D
Forestry	M,D
Geology	M,D
Geosciences	M,D
Inorganic Chemistry	M,D
Mathematics	M,D
Natural Resources	M,D
Organic Chemistry	M,D
Physical Chemistry	M,D

UNIVERSITY OF NEBRASKA AT OMAHA
Mathematics	M

UNIVERSITY OF NEBRASKA–LINCOLN
Agricultural Sciences— General	M,D
Agronomy and Soil Sciences	M,D
Analytical Chemistry	M,D
Animal Sciences	M,D
Astronomy	M,D
Chemistry	M,D
Food Science and Technology	M,D
Geosciences	M,D
Horticulture	M,D
Inorganic Chemistry	M,D
Mathematics	M,D

UNIVERSITY OF NEBRASKA MEDICAL CENTER
Biostatistics	D

UNIVERSITY OF NEVADA, LAS VEGAS
Astronomy	M,D
Chemistry	M,D
Environmental Sciences	M,D,O
Geosciences	M,D
Mathematics	M,D
Physics	M,D
Water Resources	M

UNIVERSITY OF NEVADA, RENO
Agricultural Sciences— General	M,D
Animal Sciences	M
Atmospheric Sciences	M,D
Chemical Physics	D
Chemistry	M,D
Environmental Management and Policy	M
Environmental Sciences	M,D
Geochemistry	M,D
Geology	M,D
Geophysics	M,D
Hydrogeology	M,D
Hydrology	M,D
Mathematics	M
Physics	M,D
Range Science	M

UNIVERSITY OF NEW BRUNSWICK FREDERICTON
Chemistry	M,D
Environmental Management and Policy	M,D
Forestry	M,D
Geodetic Sciences	M,D
Geology	M,D
Hydrology	M,D
Mathematics	M,D
Physics	M,D
Statistics	M,D
Water Resources	M,D

UNIVERSITY OF NEW BRUNSWICK SAINT JOHN
Natural Resources	M

UNIVERSITY OF NEW ENGLAND
Marine Sciences	M

UNIVERSITY OF NEW HAMPSHIRE
Agricultural Sciences— General	M,D
Animal Sciences	M,D
Applied Mathematics	M,D,O
Chemistry	M,D
Environmental Management and Policy	M
Fish, Game, and Wildlife Management	M
Forestry	M
Geology	M
Geosciences	M
Hydrology	M
Mathematics	M,D,O
Natural Resources	M,D
Oceanography	M,D,O
Physics	M,D
Water Resources	M

UNIVERSITY OF NEW HAVEN
Environmental Management and Policy	M
Environmental Sciences	M
Geosciences	M

UNIVERSITY OF NEW MEXICO
Chemistry	M,D
Environmental Management and Policy	M
Geosciences	M,D
Mathematics	M,D
Natural Resources	M,D
Optical Sciences	M,D
Photonics	M,D
Physics	M,D
Planetary and Space Sciences	M,D
Statistics	M,D
Water Resources	M

UNIVERSITY OF NEW ORLEANS
Chemistry	M,D
Environmental Sciences	M,D
Geosciences	M,D
Mathematics	M,D
Physics	M,D

THE UNIVERSITY OF NORTH CAROLINA AT CHAPEL HILL
Astronomy	M,D
Astrophysics	M,D
Biostatistics	M,D
Chemistry	M,D
Environmental Sciences	M,D
Geology	M,D
Marine Sciences	M,D
Mathematics	M,D
Physics	M,D
Statistics	M,D

THE UNIVERSITY OF NORTH CAROLINA AT CHARLOTTE
Applied Mathematics	M,D
Applied Physics	M,D
Chemistry	M,D
Geosciences	M,D
Mathematical and Computational Finance	M,O

THE UNIVERSITY OF NORTH CAROLINA AT GREENSBORO
Chemistry	M
Mathematics	M,D

THE UNIVERSITY OF NORTH CAROLINA WILMINGTON
Applied Statistics	M,O
Chemistry	M
Environmental Management and Policy	M
Environmental Sciences	M
Geosciences	M,O
Marine Sciences	M,D,O
Mathematics	M,O
Statistics	M,O

UNIVERSITY OF NORTH DAKOTA
Astrophysics	M
Atmospheric Sciences	M,D
Chemistry	M,D
Fish, Game, and Wildlife Management	M,D
Geology	M,D
Geosciences	M,D
Mathematics	M
Physics	M,D
Planetary and Space Sciences	M

UNIVERSITY OF NORTHERN BRITISH COLUMBIA
Environmental Management and Policy	M,D,O
Mathematics	M,D,O
Natural Resources	M,D,O

UNIVERSITY OF NORTHERN COLORADO
Applied Statistics	M,D
Chemistry	M,D
Geosciences	M
Mathematics	M,D

UNIVERSITY OF NORTHERN IOWA
Applied Mathematics	M
Geosciences	M
Mathematics	M
Physics	M

UNIVERSITY OF NORTH FLORIDA
Mathematics	M
Statistics	M

UNIVERSITY OF NORTH TEXAS
Chemistry	M,D,O
Environmental Sciences	M,D,O
Mathematics	M,D,O

UNIVERSITY OF NORTH TEXAS HEALTH SCIENCE CENTER AT FORT WORTH
Biostatistics	M,D,O

UNIVERSITY OF NOTRE DAME
Applied Mathematics	M,D
Applied Statistics	M,D
Chemistry	M,D
Computational Sciences	M,D
Geosciences	M,D
Inorganic Chemistry	M,D
Mathematical and Computational Finance	M,D
Mathematics	M,D
Organic Chemistry	M,D
Physical Chemistry	M,D
Physics	M,D
Statistics	M,D

UNIVERSITY OF OKLAHOMA
Analytical Chemistry	M,D
Chemistry	M,D
Environmental Sciences	M,D
Geology	M,D
Geophysics	M,D
Inorganic Chemistry	M,D
Mathematics	M,D*
Meteorology	M,D
Organic Chemistry	M,D
Physical Chemistry	M,D
Physics	M,D

UNIVERSITY OF OKLAHOMA HEALTH SCIENCES CENTER
Biostatistics	M,D

UNIVERSITY OF OREGON
Chemistry	M,D
Environmental Management and Policy	M,D
Geology	M,D
Mathematics	M,D
Physics	M,D

UNIVERSITY OF OTTAWA
Chemistry	M,D
Geosciences	M,D
Mathematics	M,D
Physics	M,D
Statistics	M,D

UNIVERSITY OF PENNSYLVANIA
Applied Mathematics	D
Biostatistics	M,D
Chemistry	M,D
Computational Sciences	M,D
Environmental Management and Policy	M
Environmental Sciences	M,D
Geosciences	M,D
Mathematics	M,D
Physics	M,D
Statistics	M,D

UNIVERSITY OF PITTSBURGH
Applied Mathematics	M,D
Applied Statistics	M,D

28 www.petersons.com

Peterson's Graduate Programs in the Physical Sciences, Mathematics, Agricultural Sciences, the Environment & Natural Resources 2020

Biostatistics — M,D
Chemistry — M,D
Computational Sciences — M,D,O
Environmental Sciences — M,D
Geology — M,D
Mathematics — M,D
Physics — M,D*
Statistics — M,D

UNIVERSITY OF PRINCE EDWARD ISLAND
Chemistry — M,D
Environmental Sciences — M,D

UNIVERSITY OF PUERTO RICO–MAYAGÜEZ
Agricultural Sciences—
General — M
Agronomy and Soil Sciences — M
Animal Sciences — M
Applied Mathematics — M
Chemistry — M,D
Computational Sciences — M
Environmental Sciences — M,D
Food Science and
Technology — M
Geology — M
Horticulture — M
Marine Sciences — M,D
Mathematics — M
Physical Chemistry — M,D
Physics — M

UNIVERSITY OF PUERTO RICO–MEDICAL SCIENCES CAMPUS
Biostatistics — M

UNIVERSITY OF PUERTO RICO–RÍO PIEDRAS
Chemistry — M,D
Environmental Management
and Policy — M
Environmental Sciences — M,D
Mathematics — M,D
Physics — M,D

UNIVERSITY OF REGINA
Analytical Chemistry — M,D
Chemistry — M,D
Geology — M,D
Inorganic Chemistry — M,D
Mathematics — M,D
Organic Chemistry — M,D
Physics — M,D
Statistics — M,D
Theoretical Chemistry — M,D

UNIVERSITY OF RHODE ISLAND
Animal Sciences — M,D
Applied Mathematics — M,D
Aquaculture — M
Chemistry — M,D
Environmental Management
and Policy — M,D
Environmental Sciences — M,D
Fish, Game, and Wildlife
Management — M
Food Science and
Technology — M,D
Geophysics — M,D
Geosciences — M,D,O
Hydrology — M,D,O
Marine Affairs — M,D
Marine Geology — M,D
Marine Sciences — M,D
Mathematics — M,D
Natural Resources — M,D
Oceanography — M,D
Physics — M,D
Statistics — M,D,O

UNIVERSITY OF ROCHESTER
Astronomy — D
Biostatistics — M
Chemistry — D
Geology — M,D
Geosciences — M,D
Inorganic Chemistry — D
Mathematics — D
Optical Sciences — M,D
Organic Chemistry — D
Physical Chemistry — D
Physics — D
Statistics — M,D

UNIVERSITY OF SAINT JOSEPH
Chemistry — M

UNIVERSITY OF SAN DIEGO
Environmental Sciences — M
Mathematics — M
Oceanography — M

UNIVERSITY OF SAN FRANCISCO
Chemistry — M
Natural Resources — M

UNIVERSITY OF SASKATCHEWAN
Agricultural Sciences—
General — M,D,O
Agronomy and Soil Sciences — M,D
Animal Sciences — M,D
Chemistry — M,D
Environmental Sciences — M,D
Food Science and
Technology — M,D
Geology — M,D,O
Mathematics — M,D
Physics — M,D
Plant Sciences — M,D
Statistics — M,D

THE UNIVERSITY OF SCRANTON
Chemistry — M

UNIVERSITY OF SOUTH AFRICA
Agricultural Sciences—
General — M,D
Environmental Management
and Policy — M,D
Environmental Sciences — M,D
Horticulture — M,D
Natural Resources — M,D
Statistics — M,D

UNIVERSITY OF SOUTH ALABAMA
Chemistry — M,D
Environmental Management
and Policy — M,D
Marine Sciences — M,D
Mathematics — M

UNIVERSITY OF SOUTH CAROLINA
Applied Statistics — M,D,O
Astronomy — M,D
Biostatistics — M,D
Chemistry — M,D
Environmental Management
and Policy — M
Geology — M,D
Geosciences — M,D
Marine Sciences — M,D
Mathematics — M,D
Physics — M,D
Statistics — M,D,O

UNIVERSITY OF SOUTH DAKOTA
Chemistry — M,D
Mathematics — M
Physics — M,D

UNIVERSITY OF SOUTHERN CALIFORNIA
Applied Mathematics — M,D
Biostatistics — M,D
Chemistry — D
Food Science and
Technology — M,D,O
Geosciences — M,D
Marine Sciences — M,D
Mathematical and
Computational Finance — M,D
Mathematics — M,D
Oceanography — M,D
Physical Chemistry — D
Physics — M,D
Statistics — M,D
Water Resources — M,D,O

UNIVERSITY OF SOUTHERN MAINE
Statistics — M,O

UNIVERSITY OF SOUTHERN MISSISSIPPI
Biostatistics — M
Chemistry — M,D
Computational Sciences — M,D
Food Science and
Technology — M
Geology — M,D
Hydrology — M,D
Marine Sciences — M,D
Mathematics — M,D
Physics — M,D

UNIVERSITY OF SOUTH FLORIDA
Applied Mathematics — M,D
Applied Physics — M,D
Biostatistics — O
Chemistry — M,D
Environmental Management
and Policy — M,D,O
Environmental Sciences — M,D
Geology — M,D,O
Geosciences — M,D
Hydrogeology — O
Marine Sciences — M,D
Mathematics — M,D,O
Oceanography — M,D
Physics — M,D
Statistics — M,D

UNIVERSITY OF SOUTH FLORIDA, ST. PETERSBURG
Environmental Management
and Policy — M
Environmental Sciences — M

THE UNIVERSITY OF TENNESSEE
Agricultural Sciences—
General — M,D
Analytical Chemistry — M,D
Animal Sciences — M,D
Applied Mathematics — M,D
Chemical Physics — M,D
Chemistry — M,D
Environmental Management
and Policy — M,D
Fish, Game, and Wildlife
Management — M
Food Science and
Technology — M,D
Forestry — M
Geology — M,D
Inorganic Chemistry — M,D
Mathematics — M,D
Organic Chemistry — M,D
Physical Chemistry — M,D
Physics — M,D
Plant Sciences — M
Statistics — M,D
Theoretical Chemistry — M,D

THE UNIVERSITY OF TENNESSEE AT CHATTANOOGA
Applied Mathematics — M
Applied Statistics — M
Computational Sciences — D
Environmental Sciences — M

Mathematics — M

THE UNIVERSITY OF TENNESSEE AT MARTIN
Agricultural Sciences—
General — M
Food Science and
Technology — M

THE UNIVERSITY OF TEXAS AT ARLINGTON
Applied Mathematics — M,D
Chemistry — M,D
Environmental Sciences — M,D
Geology — M,D
Mathematics — M,D
Physics — M,D

THE UNIVERSITY OF TEXAS AT AUSTIN
Analytical Chemistry — D
Applied Mathematics — M,D
Applied Physics — M,D
Astronomy — M,D
Chemistry — D
Computational Sciences — M,D
Environmental Management
and Policy — M
Geology — M,D
Geosciences — M,D
Inorganic Chemistry — D
Marine Sciences — M,D
Mathematics — M,D
Natural Resources — M
Organic Chemistry — D
Physical Chemistry — D
Physics — M,D
Statistics — M,D

THE UNIVERSITY OF TEXAS AT DALLAS
Applied Mathematics — M,D
Chemistry — M,D
Geosciences — M,D
Mathematics — M,D
Mineralogy — M,D
Physics — M,D
Statistics — M,D

THE UNIVERSITY OF TEXAS AT EL PASO
Chemistry — M,D
Environmental Sciences — M,D
Geology — M,D
Geophysics — M,D
Mathematics — M
Physics — M
Statistics — M

THE UNIVERSITY OF TEXAS AT SAN ANTONIO
Applied Mathematics — M
Applied Statistics — M,D
Chemistry — M,D
Environmental Sciences — M,D
Geology — M
Mathematics — M
Physics — M,D
Statistics — M,D

THE UNIVERSITY OF TEXAS AT TYLER
Mathematics — M

THE UNIVERSITY OF TEXAS HEALTH SCIENCE CENTER AT HOUSTON
Biostatistics — M,D,O

THE UNIVERSITY OF TEXAS OF THE PERMIAN BASIN
Geology — M

THE UNIVERSITY OF TEXAS RIO GRANDE VALLEY
Agricultural Sciences—
General — M
Chemistry — M
Environmental Sciences — M
Geosciences — M
Mathematics — M
Oceanography — M
Physics — M

UNIVERSITY OF THE DISTRICT OF COLUMBIA
Water Resources — M

UNIVERSITY OF THE INCARNATE WORD
Applied Statistics — M
Mathematics — M

UNIVERSITY OF THE PACIFIC
Water Resources — M,D

UNIVERSITY OF THE SCIENCES
Chemistry — M,D

UNIVERSITY OF THE VIRGIN ISLANDS
Environmental Sciences — M
Marine Sciences — M
Mathematics — M

THE UNIVERSITY OF TOLEDO
Analytical Chemistry — M,D
Applied Mathematics — M,D
Astrophysics — M,D
Biostatistics — M,O
Chemistry — M,D
Environmental Sciences — M,D
Geology — M,D
Inorganic Chemistry — M,D
Mathematics — M,D
Organic Chemistry — M,D
Physical Chemistry — M,D
Physics — M,D
Statistics — M,D

UNIVERSITY OF TORONTO
Astronomy — M,D

Astrophysics — M,D
Biostatistics — M,D
Chemistry — M,D
Environmental Sciences — M,D
Forestry — M,D
Geology — M,D
Mathematical and
Computational Finance — M
Mathematics — M,D
Physics — M,D
Statistics — M,D

THE UNIVERSITY OF TULSA
Geophysics — M,D
Geosciences — M,D
Mathematics — M,D

UNIVERSITY OF UTAH
Atmospheric Sciences — M,D
Biostatistics — M,D
Chemical Physics — M,D
Chemistry — M,D
Computational Sciences — M
Environmental Sciences — M,D
Geology — M,D
Geophysics — M,D
Mathematics — M,D
Physics — M,D
Statistics — M,D,O

UNIVERSITY OF VERMONT
Agricultural Sciences—
General — M,D,O
Agronomy and Soil Sciences — M,D,O
Animal Sciences — M,D
Biostatistics — M
Chemistry — M,D
Environmental Sciences — M
Food Science and
Technology — M,D,O
Forestry — M,D,O
Geology — M
Horticulture — M,D,O
Mathematics — M,D
Natural Resources — M,D,O
Physics — M
Plant Sciences — M,D,O
Statistics — M

UNIVERSITY OF VICTORIA
Astronomy — M,D
Astrophysics — M,D
Chemistry — M,D
Condensed Matter Physics — M,D
Geosciences — M,D
Mathematics — M,D
Oceanography — M,D
Physics — M,D
Statistics — M,D
Theoretical Physics — M,D

UNIVERSITY OF VIRGINIA
Astronomy — M,D
Chemistry — M,D
Environmental Sciences — M,D
Mathematics — M,D
Physics — M,D
Statistics — M,D

UNIVERSITY OF WASHINGTON
Applied Mathematics — M,D
Applied Physics — M,D
Astronomy — M,D
Atmospheric Sciences — M,D
Biostatistics — M,D
Chemistry — M,D
Computational Sciences — M,D
Environmental Management
and Policy — M,D
Fish, Game, and Wildlife
Management — M,D
Forestry — M,D
Geology — M,D
Geophysics — M,D
Horticulture — M,D
Hydrology — M,D
Marine Affairs — M,O
Marine Geology — M,D
Mathematics — M,D
Natural Resources — M,D
Oceanography — M,D
Physics — M,D
Statistics — M,D

UNIVERSITY OF WATERLOO
Applied Mathematics — M,D
Biostatistics — M,D
Chemistry — M,D
Environmental Management
and Policy — M,D
Environmental Sciences — M,D
Geosciences — M,D
Mathematics — M,D
Physics — M,D
Statistics — M,D

THE UNIVERSITY OF WESTERN ONTARIO
Applied Mathematics — M,D
Astronomy — M,D
Biostatistics — M,D
Chemistry — M,D
Environmental Sciences — M,D
Geology — M,D
Geophysics — M,D
Geosciences — M,D
Mathematics — M,D
Physics — M,D
Statistics — M,D

UNIVERSITY OF WEST FLORIDA
Environmental Sciences — M
Mathematics — M

---

*M—master's; D—doctorate; O—other advanced degree; *Close-Up and/or Display*

Peterson's Graduate Programs in the Physical Sciences, Mathematics, Agricultural Sciences, the Environment & Natural Resources 2020

www.petersons.com **29**

UNIVERSITY OF WEST GEORGIA
Mathematics — M,O

UNIVERSITY OF WINDSOR
Chemistry — M,D
Environmental Sciences — M,D
Geosciences — M,D
Mathematics — M,D
Physics — M,D
Statistics — M,D

UNIVERSITY OF WISCONSIN–GREEN BAY
Environmental Management and Policy — M
Environmental Sciences — M

UNIVERSITY OF WISCONSIN–LA CROSSE
Marine Sciences — M

UNIVERSITY OF WISCONSIN–MADISON
Agricultural Sciences—General — M,D
Agronomy and Soil Sciences — M,D
Animal Sciences — M,D
Astronomy — D
Atmospheric Sciences — M,D
Biometry — M
Chemistry — M,D
Environmental Sciences — M
Fish, Game, and Wildlife Management — M,D
Food Science and Technology — M,D
Forestry — M,D
Geology — M,D
Geophysics — M,D
Horticulture — M,D
Marine Sciences — M,D
Mathematics — D
Natural Resources — M,D
Oceanography — M,D
Physics — M,D
Plant Sciences — M,D
Statistics — M,D
Water Resources — M

UNIVERSITY OF WISCONSIN–MILWAUKEE
Applied Mathematics — M,D
Atmospheric Sciences — M,D
Biostatistics — M,D,O
Chemistry — M,D
Environmental Sciences — M,D
Geology — M,D
Mathematics — M,D
Physics — M,D
Statistics — M,D
Water Resources — M,D

UNIVERSITY OF WISCONSIN–RIVER FALLS
Agricultural Sciences—General — M

UNIVERSITY OF WISCONSIN–STEVENS POINT
Natural Resources — M

UNIVERSITY OF WISCONSIN–STOUT
Applied Mathematics — M
Food Science and Technology — M

UNIVERSITY OF WYOMING
Agricultural Sciences—General — M,D
Agronomy and Soil Sciences — M,D
Animal Sciences — M,D
Applied Statistics — M,D
Atmospheric Sciences — M,D
Chemistry — M,D
Food Science and Technology — M
Geology — M,D
Geophysics — M,D
Mathematics — M,D
Natural Resources — M,D
Range Science — M,D
Water Resources — M,D

UTAH STATE UNIVERSITY
Agricultural Sciences—General — M,D
Agronomy and Soil Sciences — M,D
Animal Sciences — M,D
Applied Mathematics — M,D
Chemistry — M,D
Environmental Management and Policy — M,D
Fish, Game, and Wildlife Management — M,D
Food Science and Technology — M,D
Forestry — M,D
Geology — M

Horticulture — M,D
Mathematics — M,D
Meteorology — M,D
Natural Resources — M
Physics — M,D
Plant Sciences — M,D
Range Science — M,D
Statistics — M,D
Water Resources — M,D

VALPARAISO UNIVERSITY
Computational Sciences — M

VANDERBILT UNIVERSITY
Chemistry — M,D
Environmental Management and Policy — M,D
Environmental Sciences — M
Geology — M
Mathematics — M,D
Physics — M,D

VERMONT LAW SCHOOL
Environmental Management and Policy — M

VILLANOVA UNIVERSITY
Applied Statistics — M
Chemistry — M
Mathematics — M

VIRGINIA COMMONWEALTH UNIVERSITY
Analytical Chemistry — M,D
Applied Mathematics — M
Applied Physics — M
Biostatistics — M,D
Chemical Physics — M,D
Chemistry — M,D
Environmental Management and Policy — M
Inorganic Chemistry — M,D
Mathematics — M
Organic Chemistry — M,D
Physical Chemistry — M,D
Physics — M

VIRGINIA POLYTECHNIC INSTITUTE AND STATE UNIVERSITY
Agricultural Sciences—General — M,D,O
Agronomy and Soil Sciences — M,D
Animal Sciences — M,D
Applied Statistics — M,D
Chemistry — M,D
Environmental Management and Policy — M,D,O
Environmental Sciences — M,O
Fish, Game, and Wildlife Management — M,D
Forestry — M,D
Geosciences — M,D
Horticulture — M,D
Mathematics — M,D
Natural Resources — M,D,O
Physics — M,D
Statistics — M,D

VIRGINIA STATE UNIVERSITY
Mathematics — M

WAKE FOREST UNIVERSITY
Analytical Chemistry — M,D
Chemistry — M,D
Inorganic Chemistry — M,D
Mathematics — M
Organic Chemistry — M,D
Physical Chemistry — M,D
Physics — M,D

WASHINGTON STATE UNIVERSITY
Agronomy and Soil Sciences — M,D,O
Animal Sciences — M,D
Applied Mathematics — M,D
Chemistry — M,D
Environmental Sciences — M,D
Food Science and Technology — M,D
Geology — M,D
Horticulture — M,D
Mathematics — M,D
Natural Resources — M,D
Physics — M,D

WASHINGTON UNIVERSITY IN ST. LOUIS
Biostatistics — M,D,O
Chemistry — D
Geosciences — D
Mathematics — M,D
Physics — D
Planetary and Space Sciences — D
Statistics — M,D

WAYNE STATE UNIVERSITY
Analytical Chemistry — M,D
Applied Mathematics — M,D

Chemistry — M,D
Food Science and Technology — M,D,O
Geology — M
Mathematics — M,D,O
Physics — M,D
Statistics — M,D

WEBSTER UNIVERSITY
Environmental Management and Policy — M

WEILL CORNELL MEDICINE
Biostatistics — M

WESLEYAN UNIVERSITY
Astronomy — M
Chemical Physics — D
Chemistry — D
Environmental Sciences — M
Geosciences — M
Inorganic Chemistry — D
Mathematics — M,D
Organic Chemistry — D
Physics — D
Theoretical Chemistry — D

WESLEY COLLEGE
Environmental Management and Policy — M

WEST CHESTER UNIVERSITY OF PENNSYLVANIA
Applied Mathematics — M,O
Applied Statistics — M,O
Astronomy — M,O
Chemistry — O
Geosciences — M,O
Mathematics — M,O

WESTERN CAROLINA UNIVERSITY
Chemistry — M

WESTERN CONNECTICUT STATE UNIVERSITY
Geosciences — M
Mathematics — M
Planetary and Space Sciences — M

WESTERN ILLINOIS UNIVERSITY
Applied Statistics — M
Chemistry — M
Environmental Sciences — D
Mathematics — M
Physics — M

WESTERN KENTUCKY UNIVERSITY
Agricultural Sciences—General — M
Chemistry — M
Geology — M
Geosciences — M
Mathematics — M
Physics — M

WESTERN MICHIGAN UNIVERSITY
Applied Mathematics — M,D
Chemistry — M,D,O
Computational Sciences — M,D
Geosciences — M,D,O
Mathematics — M,D
Physics — M,D,O
Statistics — M,D,O

WESTERN STATE COLORADO UNIVERSITY
Environmental Management and Policy — M

WESTERN WASHINGTON UNIVERSITY
Chemistry — M
Environmental Sciences — M
Geology — M
Marine Sciences — M
Mathematics — M

WEST TEXAS A&M UNIVERSITY
Agricultural Sciences—General — M,D
Animal Sciences — M
Chemistry — M
Environmental Sciences — M
Mathematics — M
Plant Sciences — M

WEST VIRGINIA UNIVERSITY
Agricultural Sciences—General — M,D
Agronomy and Soil Sciences — M,D
Animal Sciences — M,D
Biostatistics — M,D
Chemistry — M,D
Fish, Game, and Wildlife Management — M,D
Food Science and Technology — M,D
Forestry — M,D
Geology — M,D

Horticulture — M,D
Mathematics — M,D
Natural Resources — M,D
Physics — M,D
Plant Sciences — M,D
Statistics — M,D

WICHITA STATE UNIVERSITY
Applied Mathematics — M,D
Chemistry — M,D
Environmental Sciences — M
Geology — M
Mathematics — M,D
Physics — M,D

WILFRID LAURIER UNIVERSITY
Chemistry — M
Environmental Management and Policy — M,D
Environmental Sciences — M,D
Mathematics — M

WILKES UNIVERSITY
Mathematics — M

WILMINGTON UNIVERSITY
Environmental Management and Policy — M,D

WOODS HOLE OCEANOGRAPHIC INSTITUTION
Marine Geology — D
Oceanography — D

WORCESTER POLYTECHNIC INSTITUTE
Applied Mathematics — M,D,O
Applied Statistics — M,D,O
Chemistry — M,D
Mathematics — M,D,O
Physics — M,D

WRIGHT STATE UNIVERSITY
Applied Mathematics — M
Applied Statistics — M
Chemistry — M
Environmental Sciences — D
Geology — O
Geophysics — M
Mathematics — M
Physics — M

YALE UNIVERSITY
Applied Mathematics — M,D
Applied Physics — M,D
Astronomy — M,D
Astrophysics — M,D
Atmospheric Sciences — D
Biostatistics — M,D
Chemistry — D
Environmental Management and Policy — M,D
Environmental Sciences — M,D
Forestry — M,D
Geochemistry — D
Geology — D
Geophysics — D
Geosciences — D
Inorganic Chemistry — D
Mathematics — M,D
Meteorology — D
Oceanography — D
Organic Chemistry — D
Paleontology — D
Physical Chemistry — D
Physics — D
Planetary and Space Sciences — M,D
Statistics — M,D
Theoretical Chemistry — D

YESHIVA UNIVERSITY
Mathematics — M

YORK UNIVERSITY
Applied Mathematics — M,D
Astronomy — M,D
Chemistry — M,D
Environmental Management and Policy — M,D
Geosciences — M,D
Mathematics — M,D
Physics — M,D
Planetary and Space Sciences — M,D
Statistics — M,D

YOUNGSTOWN STATE UNIVERSITY
Analytical Chemistry — M
Applied Mathematics — M
Chemistry — M
Environmental Management and Policy — M,O
Inorganic Chemistry — M
Mathematics — M
Organic Chemistry — M
Physical Chemistry — M
Statistics — M

30 www.petersons.com

Peterson's Graduate Programs in the Physical Sciences, Mathematics, Agricultural Sciences, the Environment & Natural Resources 2020

ACADEMIC AND PROFESSIONAL PROGRAMS IN THE PHYSICAL SCIENCES

Section 1
Astronomy and Astrophysics

This section contains a directory of institutions offering graduate work in astronomy and astrophysics. Additional information about programs listed in the directory but not augmented by an in-depth entry may be obtained by writing directly to the dean of a graduate school or chair of a department at the address given in the directory.

For programs offering related work, see also in this book *Geosciences*, *Meteorology and Atmospheric Sciences*, and *Physics*. In the other guides in this series:

Graduate Programs in the Biological/Biomedical Sciences & Health-Related Medical Professions

See *Biological and Biomedical Sciences* and *Biophysics*

Graduate Programs in Engineering & Applied Sciences

See *Aerospace/Aeronautical Engineering, Energy and Power Engineering (Nuclear Engineering), Engineering and Applied Sciences,* and *Mechanical Engineering and Mechanics*

CONTENTS

Program Directories

Astronomy

Boston University, Graduate School of Arts and Sciences, Department of Astronomy, Boston, MA 02215. Offers MA, PhD. *Students:* 34 full-time (11 women), 1 (woman) part-time; includes 4 minority (2 Asian, non-Hispanic/Latino; 2 Hispanic/Latino), 6 international. Average age 23. 109 applicants, 15% accepted, 8 enrolled. In 2018, 3 master's, 3 doctorates awarded. Terminal master's awarded for partial completion of doctoral program. *Degree requirements:* For master's, comprehensive exam, thesis or alternative; for doctorate, comprehensive exam, thesis/dissertation. *Entrance requirements:* For doctorate, GRE General Test, GRE Subject Test (physics), 3 letters of recommendation, transcripts, personal statement, resume/CV. Additional exam requirements/recommendations for international students: Required—TOEFL (minimum score 550 paper-based; 84 iBT). *Application deadline:* For fall admission, 12/15 for domestic and international students. Application fee: $95. Electronic applications accepted. *Financial support:* In 2018–19, 32 students received support, including 2 fellowships with full tuition reimbursements available (averaging $22,660 per year), 21 research assistantships with full tuition reimbursements available (averaging $22,660 per year), 9 teaching assistantships with full tuition reimbursements available (averaging $22,660 per year); Federal Work-Study, health care benefits, and unspecified assistantships also available. Support available to part-time students. Financial award application deadline: 12/15. *Unit head:* Dan Clemens, Chair, 617-353-6140, Fax: 617-353-5704, E-mail: clemens@bu.edu. *Application contact:* Anne Smartvlasak, Department Administrator, 617-363-2625, Fax: 617-353-5704, E-mail: asmart@bu.edu.
Website: http://www.bu.edu/astronomy

Brigham Young University, Graduate Studies, College of Physical and Mathematical Sciences, Department of Physics and Astronomy, Provo, UT 84602-1001. Offers physics (MS, PhD); physics and astronomy (PhD). *Program availability:* Part-time. *Faculty:* 25 full-time (3 women). *Students:* 38 full-time (4 women), 3 part-time (0 women); includes 3 minority (2 Hispanic/Latino; 1 Native Hawaiian or other Pacific Islander, non-Hispanic/Latino), 5 international. Average age 30. 33 applicants, 64% accepted, 13 enrolled. In 2018, 7 master's, 4 doctorates awarded. Terminal master's awarded for partial completion of doctoral program. *Degree requirements:* For master's, thesis; for doctorate, thesis/dissertation, qualifying exam, candidacy exam. *Entrance requirements:* For master's and doctorate, GRE Subject Test (physics), GRE General Test, minimum GPA of 3.0, ecclesiastical endorsement. Additional exam requirements/recommendations for international students: Required—TOEFL (minimum score 580 paper-based; 85 iBT), IELTS (minimum score 7), E3PT (overall 79; speaking, reading, listening 21 and writing 16), TOEFL iBT (listening, reading, writing 21 and speaking 22), CAE (185 or 'C' grade). *Application deadline:* For fall admission, 1/15 priority date for domestic and international students. Application fee: $50. Electronic applications accepted. *Financial support:* In 2018–19, 36 students received support, including 22 research assistantships with full tuition reimbursements available (averaging $22,430 per year), 7 teaching assistantships with full tuition reimbursements available (averaging $20,814 per year); fellowships, scholarships/grants, traineeships, and tuition waivers (full) also available. Support available to part-time students. Financial award application deadline: 1/15. *Faculty research:* Acoustics; atomic, molecular, and optical physics; theoretical and mathematical physics; condensed matter; astrophysics and plasma. *Total annual research expenditures:* $2 million. *Unit head:* Dr. Kent L. Gee, Chair, 801-422-1544, Fax: 801-422-0553, E-mail: kentgee@byu.edu. *Application contact:* Dr. Richard R. Vanfleet, Graduate Coordinator, 801-422-1702, Fax: 801-422-0553, E-mail: richard_vanfleet@byu.edu.
Website: http://physics.byu.edu/

California Institute of Technology, Division of Physics, Mathematics and Astronomy, Department of Astronomy, Pasadena, CA 91125-0001. Offers PhD. *Degree requirements:* For doctorate, one foreign language, thesis/dissertation, candidacy and final exams. *Entrance requirements:* For doctorate, GRE General Test, GRE Subject Test. Additional exam requirements/recommendations for international students: Required—TOEFL. *Faculty research:* Observational and theoretical astrophysics, cosmology, radio astronomy, solar physics.

Case Western Reserve University, School of Graduate Studies, Department of Astronomy, Cleveland, OH 44106. Offers MS, PhD. *Program availability:* Part-time. *Faculty:* 5 full-time (1 woman), 1 part-time/adjunct (0 women). *Students:* 4 full-time (1 woman), 1 international. Average age 27. 24 applicants, 29% accepted, 1 enrolled. *Degree requirements:* For doctorate, comprehensive exam, thesis/dissertation. *Entrance requirements:* For doctorate, GRE General Test, GRE Subject Test (physics). Additional exam requirements/recommendations for international students: Required—TOEFL (minimum score 577 paper-based; 90 iBT), IELTS (minimum score 7). *Application deadline:* For fall admission, 1/15 priority date for domestic students. Applications are processed on a rolling basis. Application fee: $50. Electronic applications accepted. *Expenses: Tuition:* Full-time $45,168; part-time $1939 per credit hour. *Required fees:* $36; $18 per semester. $18 per semester. *Financial support:* Fellowships, research assistantships, and health care benefits available. Financial award application deadline: 1/15; financial award applicants required to submit FAFSA. *Faculty research:* Optical observational astronomy, high- and low-dispersion spectroscopy, theoretical astrophysics, galactic structure, computational theory. *Unit head:* Prof. Stacy McGaugh, Professor and Chair, 216-368-1808, Fax: 216-368-5406, E-mail: stacy.mcgaugh@case.edu. *Application contact:* Agnes Torontali, Department Assistant, 216-368-3728, Fax: 216-368-5406, E-mail: agnes.torontali@case.edu.
Website: http://astronomy.case.edu/

Columbia University, Graduate School of Arts and Sciences, New York, NY 10027. Offers African-American studies (MA); American studies (MA); anthropology (MA, PhD); art history and archaeology (MA, PhD); astronomy (PhD); biological sciences (PhD); biotechnology (MA); chemical physics (PhD); chemistry (PhD); classical studies (MA, PhD); classics (MA, PhD); climate and society (MA); conservation biology (MA); earth and environmental sciences (PhD); East Asia: regional studies (MA); East Asian languages and cultures (MA, PhD); ecology, evolution and environmental biology (MA), including conservation biology; ecology, evolution, and environmental biology (PhD), including ecology and evolutionary biology, evolutionary primatology; economics (MA, PhD); English and comparative literature (MA, PhD); French and Romance philology (MA, PhD); Germanic languages (MA, PhD); global French studies (MA); global thought (MA); Hispanic cultural studies (MA); history (PhD); history and literature (MA); human rights studies (MA); Islamic studies (MA); Italian (MA, PhD); Japanese pedagogy (MA); Jewish studies (MA); Latin America and the Caribbean: regional studies (MA); Latin American and Iberian cultures (PhD); mathematics (MA, PhD), including finance (MA); medieval and Renaissance studies (MA); Middle Eastern, South Asian, and African studies (MA, PhD); modern art: critical and curatorial studies (MA); modern European studies (MA); museum anthropology (MA); music (DMA, PhD); oral history (MA); philosophical foundations of physics (MA); philosophy (MA, PhD); physics (PhD); political science (MA, PhD); psychology (PhD); quantitative methods in the social sciences (MA); religion (MA, PhD); Russia, Eurasia and East Europe: regional studies (MA); Russian translation (MA); Slavic cultures (MA); Slavic languages (MA, PhD); sociology (MA, PhD); South Asian studies (MA); statistics (MA, PhD); theatre (PhD). Dual-degree programs require admission to both Graduate School of Arts and Sciences and another Columbia school. *Program availability:* Part-time. Terminal master's awarded for partial completion of doctoral program. *Degree requirements:* For master's, variable foreign language requirement, comprehensive exam (for some programs), thesis (for some programs); for doctorate, variable foreign language requirement, comprehensive exam (for some programs), thesis/dissertation. *Entrance requirements:* For master's and doctorate, GRE General Test, GRE Subject Test (for some programs). Additional exam requirements/recommendations for international students: Required—TOEFL, IELTS. Electronic applications accepted.

Cornell University, Graduate School, Graduate Fields of Arts and Sciences, Field of Astronomy and Space Sciences, Ithaca, NY 14853. Offers astronomy (PhD); astrophysics (PhD); general space sciences (PhD); infrared astronomy (PhD); planetary studies (PhD); radio astronomy (PhD); radiophysics (PhD); theoretical astrophysics (PhD). *Degree requirements:* For doctorate, comprehensive exam, thesis/dissertation. *Entrance requirements:* For doctorate, GRE General Test, GRE Subject Test (physics), 3 letters of recommendation. Additional exam requirements/recommendations for international students: Required—TOEFL (minimum score 600 paper-based; 77 iBT). Electronic applications accepted. *Faculty research:* Observational astrophysics, planetary sciences, cosmology, instrumentation, gravitational astrophysics.

Dartmouth College, Guarini School of Graduate and Advanced Studies, Department of Physics and Astronomy, Hanover, NH 03755. Offers PhD. *Faculty:* 23 full-time (4 women), 4 part-time/adjunct (1 woman). *Students:* 40 full-time (17 women); includes 3 minority (2 Hispanic/Latino; 1 Two or more races, non-Hispanic/Latino), 17 international. Average age 26. 95 applicants, 25% accepted, 6 enrolled. In 2018, 7 doctorates awarded. *Entrance requirements:* For doctorate, GRE General Test, GRE Subject Test. Additional exam requirements/recommendations for international students: Required—TOEFL. *Application deadline:* For fall admission, 1/15 for domestic students. Application fee: $50. Electronic applications accepted. *Financial support:* Research assistantships, teaching assistantships, and scholarships/grants available. *Faculty research:* Matter physics, plasma and beam physics, space physics, astronomy, cosmology. *Unit head:* John R. Thorstensen, Chair, 603-646-2869. *Application contact:* Judy Lowell, Administrative Assistant, 603-646-2359.
Website: http://www.dartmouth.edu/~physics/

George Mason University, College of Science, Department of Physics and Astronomy, Fairfax, VA 22030. Offers MS, PhD. *Faculty:* 31 full-time (8 women), 8 part-time/adjunct (1 woman). *Students:* 31 full-time (2 women), 29 part-time (5 women); includes 11 minority (5 Black or African American, non-Hispanic/Latino; 1 Asian, non-Hispanic/Latino; 4 Hispanic/Latino; 1 Two or more races, non-Hispanic/Latino), 16 international. Average age 31. 49 applicants, 49% accepted, 10 enrolled. In 2018, 6 master's, 4 doctorates awarded. *Degree requirements:* For master's, thesis optional; for doctorate, comprehensive exam, thesis/dissertation. *Entrance requirements:* For master's, GRE General and Subject Tests (recommended), three letters of recommendation, preferably from former professors; personal statement; for doctorate, GRE General Test; GRE Subject Test (recommended), three letters of recommendation, preferably from former professors; personal statement with emphasis on research experience and goals. Additional exam requirements/recommendations for international students: Required—TOEFL (minimum score 575 paper-based; 88 iBT), IELTS (minimum score 6.5), PTE (minimum score 59). *Application deadline:* For fall admission, 2/15 priority date for domestic students, 2/1 priority date for international students. Application fee: $75 ($80 for international students). Electronic applications accepted. *Financial support:* In 2018–19, 28 students received support, including 2 fellowships, 13 research assistantships with tuition reimbursements available (averaging $16,421 per year), 14 teaching assistantships with tuition reimbursements available (averaging $19,643 per year); career-related internships or fieldwork, Federal Work-Study, scholarships/grants, unspecified assistantships, and health care benefits (for full-time research or teaching assistantship recipients) also available. Support available to part-time students. Financial award application deadline: 3/1; financial award applicants required to submit FAFSA. *Faculty research:* Astrophysics/space sciences; materials/condensed matter physics; biological physics/aerodynamics; applied mechanics; high energy physics. *Total annual research expenditures:* $2.9 million. *Unit head:* Dr. Paul So, Chair, 709-993-4377, E-mail: paso@gmu.edu. *Application contact:* Executive Assistant, 703-993-1280, E-mail: physics@gmu.edu.

Georgia State University, College of Arts and Sciences, Department of Physics and Astronomy, Program in Astronomy, Atlanta, GA 30302-3083. Offers PhD. Terminal master's awarded for partial completion of doctoral program. *Entrance requirements:* For doctorate, GRE General Test, GRE Subject Test (physics). Additional exam requirements/recommendations for international students: Required—TOEFL (minimum score 550 paper-based; 80 iBT). Application fee: $50. Electronic applications accepted. *Expenses: Tuition, area resident:* Full-time $9360; part-time $390 per credit hour. Tuition, state resident: full-time $9360; part-time $390 per credit hour. Tuition, nonresident: full-time $30,024; part-time $1251 per credit hour. *International tuition:* $30,024 full-time. *Required fees:* $2128. *Financial support:* Fellowships, research assistantships, teaching assistantships, institutionally sponsored loans, scholarships/grants, and unspecified assistantships available. Financial award application deadline: 1/15; financial award applicants required to submit FAFSA. *Faculty research:* Astrophysics, active galactic nuclei, exoplanet searches, missing mass and dark matter stellar. *Unit head:* Dr. Mike Crenshaw, Chair, 404-413-6020, E-mail: crenshaw@chara.gsu.edu. *Application contact:* Russel White, Graduate Director, 404-413-6018, Fax: 404-413-6025, E-mail: white@astro.gsu.edu.
Website: http://www.phy-astr.gsu.edu/

Harvard University, Graduate School of Arts and Sciences, Department of Astronomy, Cambridge, MA 02138. Offers astronomy (PhD); astrophysics (PhD). *Degree requirements:* For doctorate, thesis/dissertation, paper, research project, 2 semesters of teaching. *Entrance requirements:* For doctorate, GRE General Test, GRE Subject Test (physics). Additional exam requirements/recommendations for international students: Required—TOEFL. Electronic applications accepted. *Faculty research:* Atomic and molecular physics, electromagnetism, solar physics, nuclear physics, fluid dynamics.

Hunter College of the City University of New York, Graduate School, School of Arts and Sciences, Department of Physics and Astronomy, New York, NY 10065-5085. Offers MA, PhD. PhD offered jointly with The Graduate Center, City University of New

York. *Program availability:* Part-time. Terminal master's awarded for partial completion of doctoral program. *Degree requirements:* For master's, comprehensive exam or thesis. *Entrance requirements:* For master's, minimum 36 credits of course work in mathematics and physics. Additional exam requirements/recommendations for international students: Required—TOEFL. *Faculty research:* Experimental and theoretical quantum optics, experimental and theoretical condensed matter, mathematical physics.

Indiana University Bloomington, University Graduate School, College of Arts and Sciences, Department of Astronomy, Bloomington, IN 47405. Offers astronomy (MA, PhD); astrophysics (PhD). Terminal master's awarded for partial completion of doctoral program. *Degree requirements:* For master's, thesis or alternative, oral exam; for doctorate, comprehensive exam, thesis/dissertation, oral defense. *Entrance requirements:* For master's and doctorate, GRE General Test, BA or BS in science. Additional exam requirements/recommendations for international students: Required— TOEFL (minimum score 550 paper-based; 79 iBT), IELTS. Electronic applications accepted. *Expenses:* Contact institution. *Faculty research:* Stellar and galaxy dynamics, stellar chemical abundances, galaxy evolution, observational cosmology.

Johns Hopkins University, Zanvyl Krieger School of Arts and Sciences, Henry A. Rowland Department of Physics and Astronomy, Baltimore, MD 21218. Offers astronomy (PhD); physics (PhD). *Faculty:* 59 full-time (11 women). *Students:* 102 full-time (23 women). 351 applicants, 20% accepted, 21 enrolled. In 2018, 18 doctorates awarded. *Degree requirements:* For doctorate, comprehensive exam, thesis/dissertation, minimum B- on required coursework. *Entrance requirements:* For doctorate, GRE General Test, GRE Subject Test. Additional exam requirements/recommendations for international students: Required—TOEFL (minimum score 600 paper-based; 100 iBT), IELTS. *Application deadline:* For fall admission, 1/15 for domestic and international students. Application fee: $75. Electronic applications accepted. *Financial support:* In 2018–19, 100 students received support, including 3 fellowships with full tuition reimbursements available (averaging $33,333 per year), 45 research assistantships with full tuition reimbursements available (averaging $33,333 per year), 52 teaching assistantships with full tuition reimbursements available (averaging $33,333 per year); career-related internships or fieldwork, Federal Work-Study, institutionally sponsored loans, health care benefits, tuition waivers (full), and unspecified assistantships also available. Financial award application deadline: 4/15; financial award applicants required to submit FAFSA. *Faculty research:* High-energy physics, condensed-matter, astrophysics, particle and experimental physics, plasma physics. *Unit head:* Dr. Timothy Heckman, Chair, 410-516-7369, E-mail: theckma1@jhu.edu. *Application contact:* Richard Helman, Director of Graduate Admissions, 410-516-7125, E-mail: rhelman@jhu.edu. Website: http://physics-astronomy.jhu.edu/

Louisiana State University and Agricultural & Mechanical College, Graduate School, College of Science, Department of Physics and Astronomy, Baton Rouge, LA 70803. Offers astronomy (PhD); astrophysics (PhD); medical physics (MS); physics (MS, PhD).

Michigan State University, The Graduate School, College of Natural Science, Department of Physics and Astronomy, East Lansing, MI 48824. Offers astrophysics and astronomy (MS, PhD); physics (MS, PhD). *Entrance requirements:* Additional exam requirements/recommendations for international students: Required—TOEFL (minimum score 550 paper-based), Michigan State University ELT (minimum score 85), Michigan English Language Assessment Battery (minimum score 83). Electronic applications accepted. *Faculty research:* Nuclear and accelerator physics, high energy physics, condensed matter physics, biophysics, astrophysics and astronomy.

Minnesota State University Mankato, College of Graduate Studies and Research, College of Science, Engineering and Technology, Department of Physics and Astronomy, Mankato, MN 56001. Offers physics (MS); physics education (MS). *Degree requirements:* For master's, one foreign language, comprehensive exam, thesis or alternative. *Entrance requirements:* For master's, minimum GPA of 2.75, two recommendation letters, one-page personal statement. Additional exam requirements/ recommendations for international students: Required—TOEFL (minimum score 530 paper-based; 72 iBT). Electronic applications accepted.

Northwestern University, The Graduate School, Judd A. and Marjorie Weinberg College of Arts and Sciences, Department of Physics and Astronomy, Evanston, IL 60208. Offers PhD. Admissions and degrees offered through The Graduate School. *Degree requirements:* For doctorate, thesis/dissertation, qualifying exam. *Entrance requirements:* For doctorate, GRE General Test, GRE Subject Test. Additional exam requirements/recommendations for international students: Required—TOEFL. *Faculty research:* Nuclear and particle physics, condensed-matter physics, nonlinear physics, astrophysics.

The Ohio State University, Graduate School, College of Arts and Sciences, Division of Natural and Mathematical Sciences, Department of Astronomy, Columbus, OH 43210. Offers MS, PhD. *Faculty:* 17. *Students:* 27 full-time (12 women). Average age 25. In 2018, 2 master's, 5 doctorates awarded. Terminal master's awarded for partial completion of doctoral program. *Degree requirements:* For master's, comprehensive exam, thesis; for doctorate, comprehensive exam, thesis/dissertation. *Entrance requirements:* For master's and doctorate, GRE General Test, GRE Subject Test (physics). Additional exam requirements/recommendations for international students: Required—TOEFL (minimum score 550 paper-based; 79 iBT), Michigan English Language Assessment Battery (minimum score 82); Recommended—IELTS (minimum score 7). *Application deadline:* For fall admission, 12/15 priority date for domestic students, 11/30 priority date for international students. Applications are processed on a rolling basis. Application fee: $60 ($70 for international students). Electronic applications accepted. *Financial support:* Fellowships, research assistantships, teaching assistantships, Federal Work-Study, and institutionally sponsored loans available. Support available to part-time students. *Unit head:* Dr. David Weinberg, Chair, 614-292-6543, E-mail: weinberg.21@osu.edu. *Application contact:* Graduate and Professional Admissions, 614-292-9444, Fax: 614-292-3895, E-mail: gpadmissions@osu.edu. Website: http://astronomy.osu.edu/

Ohio University, Graduate College, College of Arts and Sciences, Department of Physics and Astronomy, Athens, OH 45701. Offers astronomy (MS, PhD); physics (MS, PhD). *Faculty:* 29 full-time (4 women), 1 part-time/adjunct (0 women). *Students:* 72 full-time (9 women), 46 international. 118 applicants, 36% accepted, 14 enrolled. In 2018, 11 master's, 11 doctorates awarded. Terminal master's awarded for partial completion of doctoral program. *Degree requirements:* For master's, thesis or alternative; for doctorate, comprehensive exam, thesis/dissertation. *Entrance requirements:* For master's and doctorate, minimum GPA of 3.0. Additional exam requirements/ recommendations for international students: Required—TOEFL (minimum score 590 paper-based; 95 iBT), IELTS (minimum score 7). *Application deadline:* For fall admission, 1/15 priority date for domestic and international students. Applications are processed on a rolling basis. Application fee: $50 ($55 for international students). Electronic applications accepted. *Financial support:* In 2018–19, 72 students received

support, including 5 fellowships with full tuition reimbursements available (averaging $28,710 per year), 35 research assistantships with full tuition reimbursements available (averaging $26,510 per year), 32 teaching assistantships with full tuition reimbursements available (averaging $24,504 per year); scholarships/grants also available. Financial award application deadline: 1/15. *Faculty research:* Nuclear physics, condensed-matter physics, nonlinear systems, astrophysics, biophysics. *Total annual research expenditures:* $1.9 million. *Unit head:* Dr. David Ingram, Chair, 740-593-0336, Fax: 740-593-0433, E-mail: ingram@ohio.edu. *Application contact:* Dr. Alexander Neiman, Graduate Admissions Chair, 740-593-1701, Fax: 740-593-0433, E-mail: physicsgradapps@ohio.edu. Website: http://www.ohio.edu/physastro/

Penn State University Park, Graduate School, Eberly College of Science, Department of Astronomy and Astrophysics, University Park, PA 16802. Offers astronomy and astrophysics (MS, PhD).

Princeton University, Graduate School, Department of Astrophysical Sciences, Princeton, NJ 08544-1019. Offers astronomy (PhD); plasma physics (PhD). *Degree requirements:* For doctorate, thesis/dissertation. *Entrance requirements:* For doctorate, GRE General Test, GRE Subject Test (physics). Additional exam requirements/ recommendations for international students: Required—TOEFL (minimum score 600 paper-based). Electronic applications accepted. *Faculty research:* Theoretical astrophysics, cosmology, galaxy formation, galactic dynamics, interstellar and intergalactic matter.

Queen's University at Kingston, School of Graduate Studies, Faculty of Arts and Science, Department of Physics, Engineering Physics and Astronomy, Kingston, ON K7L 3N6, Canada. Offers M Sc, M Sc Eng, PhD. *Program availability:* Part-time. *Degree requirements:* For master's, thesis; for doctorate, comprehensive exam, thesis/ dissertation. *Entrance requirements:* For doctorate, M Sc or M Sc Eng. Additional exam requirements/recommendations for international students: Required—TOEFL (minimum score 550 paper-based). *Faculty research:* Theoretical physics, astronomy and astrophysics, condensed matter.

Rensselaer Polytechnic Institute, Graduate School, School of Science, Program in Astronomy, Troy, NY 12180-3590. Offers MS. *Students:* 1 (woman) full-time. Average age 23. 7 applicants, 14% accepted, 1 enrolled. *Entrance requirements:* For master's, GRE. Additional exam requirements/recommendations for international students: Required—TOEFL (minimum score 600 paper-based; 100 iBT), IELTS (minimum score 7), PTE (minimum score 68). *Application deadline:* For fall admission, 1/1 for domestic and international students; for spring admission, 8/15 for domestic and international students. *Unit head:* Dr. Gyorgy Korniss, Graduate Program Director, 518-276-2555, E-mail: korniss@rpi.edu. *Application contact:* Jarron Decker, Director of Graduate Admissions, 518-276-6216, Fax: 518-276-4072, E-mail: gradadmissions@rpi.edu. Website: https://science.rpi.edu/physics/programs/graduate/ms-astronomy

Rice University, Graduate Programs, Wiess School of Natural Sciences, Department of Physics and Astronomy, Houston, TX 77251-1892. Offers nanoscale physics (MS); physics and astronomy (PhD); science teaching (MST). *Program availability:* Part-time. *Degree requirements:* For master's, thesis (for some programs); for doctorate, thesis/ dissertation, minimum B average. *Entrance requirements:* For master's, GRE General Test; for doctorate, GRE General Test, GRE Subject Test. Additional exam requirements/recommendations for international students: Required—TOEFL (minimum score 600 paper-based; 90 iBT). Electronic applications accepted. *Faculty research:* Optical physics; ultra cold atoms; membrane electr-statics, peptides, proteins and lipids; solar astrophysics; stellar activity; magnetic fields; young stars.

Rutgers University–New Brunswick, Graduate School-New Brunswick, Department of Physics and Astronomy, Piscataway, NJ 08854-8097. Offers astronomy (MS, PhD); biophysics (PhD); condensed matter physics (MS, PhD); elementary particle physics (MS, PhD); intermediate energy nuclear physics (MS); nuclear physics (MS, PhD); physics (MST); surface science (PhD); theoretical physics (MS, PhD). *Program availability:* Part-time. Terminal master's awarded for partial completion of doctoral program. *Degree requirements:* For master's, comprehensive exam, thesis or alternative; for doctorate, comprehensive exam, thesis/dissertation. *Entrance requirements:* For master's and doctorate, GRE General Test, GRE Subject Test. Additional exam requirements/recommendations for international students: Required— TOEFL (minimum score 560 paper-based). Electronic applications accepted. *Faculty research:* Astronomy, high energy, condensed matter, surface, nuclear physics.

Saint Mary's University, Faculty of Science, Department of Astronomy and Physics, Halifax, NS B3H 3C3, Canada. Offers astronomy (M Sc, PhD). *Program availability:* Part-time. *Degree requirements:* For master's, thesis optional; for doctorate, comprehensive exam, thesis/dissertation. *Entrance requirements:* For master's, honors degree with minimum GPA of 3.0. Additional exam requirements/recommendations for international students: Required—TOEFL. *Faculty research:* Young stellar objects, interstellar medium, star clusters, galactic structure, early-type galaxies.

San Diego State University, Graduate and Research Affairs, College of Sciences, Department of Astronomy, San Diego, CA 92182. Offers MS. *Degree requirements:* For master's, thesis. *Entrance requirements:* For master's, GRE General Test, letters of reference. Additional exam requirements/recommendations for international students: Required—TOEFL. Electronic applications accepted. *Faculty research:* Classical and dwarf novae, photometry, interactive binaries.

San Francisco State University, Division of Graduate Studies, College of Science and Engineering, Department of Physics and Astronomy, San Francisco, CA 94132-1722. Offers astronomy (MS); physics (MS). *Program availability:* Part-time. *Application deadline:* Applications are processed on a rolling basis. Electronic applications accepted. *Unit head:* Dr. Joseph Barranco, Chair, 415-338-2450, Fax: 415-338-2178, E-mail: barranco@sfsu.edu. *Application contact:* Dr. Kristan Jensen, Graduate Advisor, 415-338-1969, Fax: 415-338-2178, E-mail: kristanj@sfsu.edu. Website: http://www.physics.sfsu.edu/

Stony Brook University, State University of New York, Graduate School, College of Arts and Sciences, Department of Physics and Astronomy, Program in Astronomy, Stony Brook, NY 11794. Offers PhD. *Entrance requirements:* For doctorate, GRE General Test, minimum GPA of 3.0. Additional exam requirements/recommendations for international students: Required—TOEFL (minimum score 90 iBT). *Application deadline:* For fall admission, 1/15 for domestic students; for spring admission, 10/1 for domestic students. Application fee: $100. Electronic applications accepted. *Expenses:* Contact institution. *Financial support:* Fellowships, research assistantships, and teaching assistantships available. Financial award application deadline: 2/1. *Unit head:* Dr. Axel Drees, Chair, 631-632-8114, E-mail: axel.drees@stonybrook.edu. *Application contact:* Donald Sheehan, Coordinator, 631-632-1046, Fax: 631-632-8176, E-mail: donald.j.sheehan@stonybrook.edu.

Texas A&M University, College of Science, Department of Physics and Astronomy, College Station, TX 77843. Offers applied physics (PhD); astronomy (MS); physics

Peterson's Graduate Programs in the Physical Sciences, Mathematics, Agricultural Sciences, the Environment & Natural Resources 2020

www.petersons.com **35**

(PhD). *Faculty:* 61. *Students:* 150 full-time (24 women), 7 part-time (1 woman); includes 15 minority (1 Black or African American, non-Hispanic/Latino; 4 Asian, non-Hispanic/Latino; 7 Hispanic/Latino; 3 Two or more races, non-Hispanic/Latino), 82 international. Average age 27. 202 applicants, 34% accepted, 34 enrolled. In 2018, 11 master's, 29 doctorates awarded. Terminal master's awarded for partial completion of doctoral program. *Entrance requirements:* For master's and doctorate, GRE General Test, GRE Subject Test. Additional exam requirements/recommendations for international students: Required—TOEFL. *Application deadline:* For fall admission, 12/1 for domestic students, 12/15 for international students. Application fee: $50 ($90 for international students). Electronic applications accepted. *Expenses:* Contact institution. *Financial support:* In 2018–19, 151 students received support, including 39 fellowships with tuition reimbursements available (averaging $16,344 per year), 109 research assistantships with tuition reimbursements available (averaging $13,676 per year), 64 teaching assistantships with tuition reimbursements available (averaging $13,698 per year); career-related internships or fieldwork, institutionally sponsored loans, scholarships/grants, traineeships, health care benefits, tuition waivers (full and partial), and unspecified assistantships also available. Support available to part-time students. Financial award application deadline: 3/1; financial award applicants required to submit FAFSA. *Faculty research:* Condensed matter, atomic/molecular, high-energy and nuclear physics, quantum optics. *Unit head:* Dr. George R. Welch, Head, 979-845-1571, E-mail: welch@physics.tamu.edu. *Application contact:* Dr. Joe Ross, Graduate Advisor, 979-845-3842, Fax: 979-845-2590, E-mail: ross@physics.tamu.edu.
Website: http://physics.tamu.edu/

Texas Tech University, Graduate School, College of Arts and Sciences, Department of Physics and Astronomy, Lubbock, TX 79409-1051. Offers physics (MS, PhD). *Program availability:* Part-time. *Faculty:* 29 full-time (6 women), 1 part-time/adjunct (0 women). *Students:* 44 full-time (10 women), 3 part-time (2 women); includes 11 minority (1 Black or African American, non-Hispanic/Latino; 3 Asian, non-Hispanic/Latino; 4 Hispanic/Latino; 3 Two or more races, non-Hispanic/Latino), 31 international. Average age 29. 37 applicants, 35% accepted, 9 enrolled. In 2018, 20 master's, 5 doctorates awarded. *Degree requirements:* For master's, variable foreign language requirement, comprehensive exam (for some programs), thesis (for some programs); for doctorate, variable foreign language requirement, comprehensive exam, thesis/dissertation, proposal presentation. *Entrance requirements:* For master's and doctorate, GRE. Additional exam requirements/recommendations for international students: Required—TOEFL (minimum score 550 paper-based; 79 iBT), IELTS (minimum score 6.5). *Application deadline:* For fall admission, 6/1 priority date for domestic students, 1/15 priority date for international students; for spring admission, 9/1 priority date for domestic students, 6/15 priority date for international students. Applications are processed on a rolling basis. Application fee: $65. Electronic applications accepted. *Expenses:* Contact institution. *Financial support:* In 2018–19, 49 students received support, including 44 fellowships (averaging $1,797 per year), 15 research assistantships (averaging $22,828 per year), 33 teaching assistantships (averaging $16,857 per year); Federal Work-Study, scholarships/grants, health care benefits, and unspecified assistantships also available. Support available to part-time students. Financial award application deadline: 2/1; financial award applicants required to submit FAFSA. *Faculty research:* Astrophysics, biophysics, condensed matter physics, high energy physics, quantum optics and quantum materials physics. *Total annual research expenditures:* $3 million. *Unit head:* Dr. Sung-Won Lee, Professor and Chair, 806-834-8188, Fax: 806-742-1182, E-mail: Sungwon.Lee@ttu.edu. *Application contact:* Dr. Mahdi Sanati, Graduate Recruiter, 806-834-6169, Fax: 806-742-1182, E-mail: m.sanati@ttu.edu.
Website: www.depts.ttu.edu/phas/

Université de Moncton, Faculty of Sciences, Department of Physics and Astronomy, Moncton, NB E1A 3E9, Canada. Offers M Sc. *Program availability:* Part-time. *Degree requirements:* For master's, thesis. *Entrance requirements:* For master's, proficiency in French. Electronic applications accepted. *Faculty research:* Thin films, optical properties, solar selective surfaces, microgravity and photonic materials.

The University of Alabama, Graduate School, College of Arts and Sciences, Department of Physics and Astronomy, Tuscaloosa, AL 35487-0324. Offers MS, PhD. Terminal master's awarded for partial completion of doctoral program. *Degree requirements:* For master's, comprehensive exam, thesis optional, oral exam; for doctorate, comprehensive exam, thesis/dissertation, oral and written exams. *Entrance requirements:* For master's and doctorate, GRE General Test (minimum score of 300), minimum GPA of 3.0. Additional exam requirements/recommendations for international students: Required—TOEFL (minimum score 550 paper-based; 79 iBT). Electronic applications accepted. *Faculty research:* Condensed matter, particle physics, astrophysics, particle astrophysics, collider physics.

The University of Alabama in Huntsville, School of Graduate Studies, College of Science, Department of Space Science, Huntsville, AL 35899. Offers MS, PhD. *Program availability:* Part-time. *Faculty:* 8 full-time, 1 part-time/adjunct. *Students:* 22 full-time (7 women), 1 part-time; includes 1 minority (Black or African American, non-Hispanic/Latino), 11 international. Average age 28. 12 applicants, 58% accepted, 6 enrolled. In 2018, 6 master's, 2 doctorates awarded. *Degree requirements:* For master's, comprehensive exam, thesis or alternative, oral and written exams; for doctorate, comprehensive exam, thesis/dissertation, oral and written exams. *Entrance requirements:* For master's and doctorate, GRE General Test, minimum GPA of 3.0. Additional exam requirements/recommendations for international students: Required—TOEFL (minimum score 550 paper-based; 80 iBT), IELTS (minimum score 6.5). *Application deadline:* For fall admission, 7/15 priority date for domestic students, 4/1 priority date for international students; for spring admission, 11/30 priority date for domestic students, 9/1 priority date for international students. Applications are processed on a rolling basis. Application fee: $50. Electronic applications accepted. *Expenses: Tuition, area resident:* Full-time $10,632; part-time $412 per credit hour. Tuition, state resident: full-time $10,632. Tuition, nonresident: full-time $23,604; part-time $412 per credit hour. *Required fees:* $582; $582. Tuition and fees vary according to course load and program. *Financial support:* In 2018–19, 17 students received support, including 17 research assistantships with full tuition reimbursements available (averaging $9,500 per year); teaching assistantships with full tuition reimbursements available, career-related internships or fieldwork, Federal Work-Study, institutionally sponsored loans, scholarships/grants, health care benefits, and unspecified assistantships also available. Support available to part-time students. Financial award application deadline: 4/1; financial award applicants required to submit FAFSA. *Unit head:* Dr. Gary Zank, Distinguished Professor and Chair, 256-961-7536, Fax: 256-824-6819, E-mail: gary.zank@uah.edu. *Application contact:* Kim Gray, Graduate Studies Admissions Coordinator, 256-824-6002, Fax: 256-824-6405, E-mail: deangrad@uah.edu.
Website: http://www.uah.edu/science/departments/space-science

The University of Arizona, College of Science, Department of Astronomy, Tucson, AZ 85721. Offers PhD. *Degree requirements:* For doctorate, thesis/dissertation. *Entrance requirements:* For doctorate, GRE General Test, GRE Subject Test (physics), minimum GPA of 3.5, 3 letters of recommendation. Additional exam requirements/recommendations for international students: Required—TOEFL (minimum score 550 paper-based; 79 iBT). Electronic applications accepted. *Faculty research:* Astrophysics, submillimeter astronomy, infrared astronomy, Near Infrared Camera and Multi-Object Spectrometer (NICMOS), Spitzer Space Telescope.

The University of British Columbia, Faculty of Science, Department of Physics and Astronomy, Program in Astronomy, Vancouver, BC V6T 1Z1, Canada. Offers M Sc, PhD. *Expenses:* Contact institution.

University of Calgary, Faculty of Graduate Studies, Faculty of Science, Program in Physics and Astronomy, Calgary, AB T2N 1N4, Canada. Offers M Sc, PhD. *Program availability:* Part-time. *Degree requirements:* For master's, thesis; for doctorate, thesis/dissertation, oral candidacy exam, written qualifying exam. *Entrance requirements:* For master's and doctorate, GRE General Test, GRE Subject Test. Additional exam requirements/recommendations for international students: Required—TOEFL (minimum score 550 paper-based). Electronic applications accepted. *Faculty research:* Astronomy and astrophysics, mass spectrometry, atmospheric physics, space physics, medical physics.

University of California, Los Angeles, Graduate Division, College of Letters and Science, Department of Physics and Astronomy, Program in Astronomy, Los Angeles, CA 90095. Offers MAT, MS, PhD. Terminal master's awarded for partial completion of doctoral program. *Degree requirements:* For master's, comprehensive exam; for doctorate, thesis/dissertation, oral and written qualifying exams; 3 quarters of teaching experience. *Entrance requirements:* For master's and doctorate, GRE General Test, GRE Subject Test (physics), bachelor's degree; minimum undergraduate GPA of 3.0 (or its equivalent if letter grade system not used). Additional exam requirements/recommendations for international students: Required—TOEFL. Electronic applications accepted.

University of California, Santa Cruz, Division of Graduate Studies, Division of Physical and Biological Sciences, Department of Astronomy and Astrophysics, Santa Cruz, CA 95064. Offers PhD. *Degree requirements:* For doctorate, one foreign language, thesis/dissertation, qualifying exam. *Entrance requirements:* For doctorate, GRE General Test, GRE Subject Test. Additional exam requirements/recommendations for international students: Required—TOEFL (minimum score 550 paper-based; 83 iBT); Recommended—IELTS (minimum score 8). Electronic applications accepted. *Faculty research:* Solar system and the Milky Way to the most distant galaxies in the Universe, fundamental questions of cosmology.

University of Chicago, Division of the Physical Sciences, Department of Astronomy and Astrophysics, Chicago, IL 60637. Offers PhD. Terminal master's awarded for partial completion of doctoral program. *Degree requirements:* For doctorate, comprehensive exam, thesis/dissertation. *Entrance requirements:* For doctorate, GRE General Test, GRE Subject Test (physics), research statement, 3 letters of recommendation, transcripts for all previous degrees and institutions attended. Additional exam requirements/recommendations for international students: Required—TOEFL (minimum score 600 paper-based; 90 iBT), IELTS (minimum score 7). Electronic applications accepted. *Faculty research:* Cosmology, exoplanets, galaxy formation, interstellar and intergalactic matter, astroparticle physics, high-performance computation in astrophysics.

University of Delaware, College of Arts and Sciences, Department of Physics and Astronomy, Newark, DE 19716. Offers MS, PhD. *Program availability:* Part-time. Terminal master's awarded for partial completion of doctoral program. *Degree requirements:* For master's, thesis; for doctorate, thesis/dissertation. *Entrance requirements:* For master's and doctorate, GRE General Test, GRE Subject Test. Additional exam requirements/recommendations for international students: Required—TOEFL (minimum score 600 paper-based). Electronic applications accepted. *Faculty research:* Magnetoresistance and magnetic materials, ultrafast optical phenomena, superfluidity, elementary particle physics, stellar atmospheres and interiors.

University of Florida, Graduate School, College of Liberal Arts and Sciences, Department of Astronomy, Gainesville, FL 32611. Offers MS, MST, PhD. *Degree requirements:* For doctorate, one foreign language, comprehensive exam, thesis/dissertation. *Entrance requirements:* For master's and doctorate, GRE General Test, GRE Subject Test (physics), minimum GPA of 3.0. Additional exam requirements/recommendations for international students: Required—TOEFL (minimum score 550 paper-based; 80 iBT), IELTS (minimum score 6). Electronic applications accepted. *Faculty research:* Solar systems, stars and stellar populations, star formation and interstellar medium, structure and evolution of galaxies, extragalactic astronomy and cosmology, extrasolar planets and instrumentation.

University of Hawaii at Manoa, Office of Graduate Education, College of Natural Sciences, Department of Physics and Astronomy, Program in Astronomy, Honolulu, HI 96822. Offers MS, PhD. *Program availability:* Part-time. *Degree requirements:* For master's, thesis optional; for doctorate, comprehensive exam, thesis/dissertation. *Entrance requirements:* For master's and doctorate, GRE General Test. Additional exam requirements/recommendations for international students: Required—TOEFL (minimum score 560 paper-based; 83 iBT), IELTS (minimum score 5).

University of Illinois at Urbana–Champaign, Graduate College, College of Liberal Arts and Sciences, Department of Astronomy, Champaign, IL 61820. Offers MS, PhD.

The University of Iowa, Graduate College, College of Liberal Arts and Sciences, Department of Physics and Astronomy, Program in Astronomy, Iowa City, IA 52242-1316. Offers MS. *Degree requirements:* For master's, thesis optional, exam. *Entrance requirements:* For master's, GRE General Test, minimum GPA of 3.0. Additional exam requirements/recommendations for international students: Required—TOEFL (minimum score 550 paper-based; 81 iBT). Electronic applications accepted.

The University of Kansas, Graduate Studies, College of Liberal Arts and Sciences, Department of Physics and Astronomy, Lawrence, KS 66045. Offers physics and astronomy (MS, PhD); MS/PhD. *Students:* 54 full-time (11 women); includes 5 minority (1 American Indian or Alaska Native, non-Hispanic/Latino; 1 Asian, non-Hispanic/Latino; 3 Hispanic/Latino), 23 international. Average age 29. 72 applicants, 46% accepted, 13 enrolled. In 2018, 2 master's, 7 doctorates awarded. Terminal master's awarded for partial completion of doctoral program. *Entrance requirements:* For master's and doctorate, GRE Subject Test (physics), statement of personal goals, resume or curriculum vitae, official transcripts, three letters of recommendation. Additional exam requirements/recommendations for international students: Required—TOEFL, IELTS, TOEFL or IELTS. *Application deadline:* For fall admission, 12/31 priority date for domestic and international students; for spring admission, 10/1 priority date for domestic and international students. Application fee: $65 ($85 for international students). Electronic applications accepted. *Financial support:* Fellowships, research assistantships, teaching assistantships, scholarships/grants, health care benefits, and unspecified assistantships available. Financial award application deadline: 12/31; financial award applicants required to submit FAFSA. *Faculty research:* Astrophysics, biophysics, high energy physics, nanophysics, nuclear physics. *Unit head:* Hume A. Feldman, Chair, 785-864-4626, E-mail: feldman@ku.edu. *Application contact:* Joel Sauerwein, Graduate Secretary, 785-864-1225, E-mail: physics@ku.edu.
Website: http://www.physics.ku.edu

University of Kentucky, Graduate School, College of Arts and Sciences, Program in Physics and Astronomy, Lexington, KY 40506-0032. Offers MS, PhD. *Degree requirements:* For master's, comprehensive exam, thesis optional; for doctorate, comprehensive exam, thesis/dissertation. *Entrance requirements:* For master's, GRE General Test, minimum undergraduate GPA of 2.75; for doctorate, GRE General Test, minimum graduate GPA of 3.0. Additional exam requirements/recommendations for international students: Required—TOEFL (minimum score 550 paper-based). Electronic applications accepted. *Faculty research:* Astrophysics, active galactic nuclei, and radio astronomy; Rydbert atoms, and electron scattering; TOF spectroscopy, hyperon interactions and muons; particle theory, lattice gauge theory, quark, and skyrmion models.

The University of Manchester, School of Physics and Astronomy, Manchester, United Kingdom. Offers astronomy and astrophysics (M Sc, PhD); biological physics (M Sc, PhD); condensed matter physics (M Sc, PhD); nonlinear and liquid crystals physics (M Sc, PhD); nuclear physics (M Sc, PhD); particle physics (M Sc, PhD); photon physics (M Sc, PhD); physics (M Sc, PhD); theoretical physics (M Sc, PhD).

University of Maryland, College Park, Academic Affairs, College of Computer, Mathematical and Natural Sciences, Department of Astronomy, College Park, MD 20742. Offers MS, PhD. *Program availability:* Part-time, evening/weekend. Terminal master's awarded for partial completion of doctoral program. *Degree requirements:* For master's, thesis or alternative, written exam; for doctorate, thesis/dissertation, research project. *Entrance requirements:* For master's, GRE General Test, GRE Subject Test (physics), minimum GPA of 3.0, 3 letters of recommendation; for doctorate, GRE General Test, GRE Subject Test (physics), 3 letters of recommendation. Electronic applications accepted. *Faculty research:* Solar radio astronomy, plasma and high-energy astrophysics, galactic and extragalactic astronomy.

University of Massachusetts Amherst, Graduate School, College of Natural Sciences, Department of Astronomy, Amherst, MA 01003. Offers MS, PhD. *Program availability:* Part-time. Terminal master's awarded for partial completion of doctoral program. *Degree requirements:* For master's, thesis or alternative; for doctorate, comprehensive exam, thesis/dissertation. *Entrance requirements:* For master's and doctorate, GRE General Test, GRE Subject Test (physics). Additional exam requirements/recommendations for international students: Required—TOEFL (minimum score 550 paper-based; 80 iBT), IELTS (minimum score 6.5). Electronic applications accepted.

University of Michigan, Rackham Graduate School, College of Literature, Science, and the Arts, Department of Astronomy, Ann Arbor, MI 48109-1042. Offers astronomy and astrophysics (PhD). *Faculty:* 21 full-time (7 women). *Students:* 31 full-time (12 women); includes 6 minority (5 Hispanic/Latino; 1 Two or more races, non-Hispanic/Latino), 6 international. 254 applicants, 8% accepted, 6 enrolled. In 2018, 5 doctorates awarded. Terminal master's awarded for partial completion of doctoral program. *Degree requirements:* For doctorate, comprehensive exam, thesis/dissertation, preliminary exam to advance to candidacy, oral defense of dissertation. *Entrance requirements:* For doctorate, GRE General Test. Additional exam requirements/recommendations for international students: Required—TOEFL (minimum score 560 paper-based; 84 iBT), IELTS (minimum score 6.5). *Application deadline:* For fall admission, 12/15 for domestic and international students. Application fee: $75 ($90 for international students). Electronic applications accepted. *Financial support:* Fellowships, research assistantships, teaching assistantships, scholarships/grants, health care benefits, and unspecified assistantships available. *Faculty research:* Cosmology- extragalactic and galactic, stars and exoplanets, extreme astrophysics, instrumentation. *Unit head:* Dr. Edwin Bergin, Professor and Chair, 734-764-3440, Fax: 734-763-6317, E-mail: astrochair@umich.edu. *Application contact:* Andrea Nashar, PhD Program Coordinator, 734-763-3520, E-mail: astrophdprogram@umich.edu. Website: https://lsa.umich.edu/astro

University of Missouri, Office of Research and Graduate Studies, College of Arts and Science, Department of Physics and Astronomy, Columbia, MO 65211. Offers MS, PhD. Terminal master's awarded for partial completion of doctoral program. *Entrance requirements:* For master's and doctorate, GRE General Test, minimum GPA of 3.0. *Faculty research:* Experimental and theoretical condensed-matter physics, biological physics, astronomy/astrophysics.

University of Nebraska–Lincoln, Graduate College, College of Arts and Sciences, Department of Physics and Astronomy, Lincoln, NE 68588. Offers astronomy (MS, PhD); physics (MS, PhD). *Degree requirements:* For master's, thesis optional; for doctorate, comprehensive exam, thesis/dissertation. *Entrance requirements:* For master's and doctorate, GRE General Test. Additional exam requirements/recommendations for international students: Required—TOEFL (minimum score 550 paper-based). Electronic applications accepted. *Faculty research:* Electromagnetics of solids and thin films, photoionization, ion collisions with atoms, molecules and surfaces, nanostructures.

University of Nevada, Las Vegas, Graduate College, College of Sciences, Department of Physics and Astronomy, Las Vegas, NV 89154-4002. Offers astronomy (MS, PhD); physics (MS, PhD). *Program availability:* Part-time. *Faculty:* 15 full-time (1 woman). *Students:* 24 full-time (5 women), 6 part-time (0 women); includes 6 minority (1 American Indian or Alaska Native, non-Hispanic/Latino; 2 Asian, non-Hispanic/Latino; 2 Hispanic/Latino; 1 Two or more races, non-Hispanic/Latino), 5 international. Average age 30. 25 applicants, 24% accepted, 5 enrolled. In 2018, 2 master's, 5 doctorates awarded. *Degree requirements:* For master's, comprehensive exam (for some programs), thesis (for some programs); for doctorate, comprehensive exam, thesis/dissertation. *Entrance requirements:* For master's, GRE General Test, bachelor's degree; for doctorate, GRE General Test, bachelor's degree/master's degree. Additional exam requirements/recommendations for international students: Required—TOEFL (minimum score 550 paper-based; 80 iBT), IELTS (minimum score 7). *Application deadline:* For fall admission, 5/15 for domestic students, 5/1 for international students; for spring admission, 11/15 for domestic students, 10/1 for international students. Application fee: $60 ($95 for international students). Electronic applications accepted. *Expenses:* Contact institution. *Financial support:* In 2018–19, 25 students received support, including 5 research assistantships with full tuition reimbursements available (averaging $19,793 per year), 20 teaching assistantships with full tuition reimbursements available (averaging $17,520 per year); institutionally sponsored loans, scholarships/grants, health care benefits, and unspecified assistantships also available. Financial award application deadline: 3/15; financial award applicants required to submit FAFSA. *Faculty research:* High energy and gamma-ray bursters astrophysics, exoplanet astrophysics, experimental high pressure physics, theoretical condensed matter physics, atomic molecular and optical physics. *Total annual research expenditures:* $3.4 million. *Unit head:* Dr. Stephen Lepp, Chair/Professor, 702-895-4455, Fax: 702-895-0804, E-mail: physics.chair@unlv.edu. *Application contact:* Dr. Victor Kwong, Graduate Coordinator, 702-895-1700, Fax: 702-895-0804, E-mail: physics.gradcoord@unlv.edu. Website: http://www.physics.unlv.edu/academics.html

The University of North Carolina at Chapel Hill, Graduate School, College of Arts and Sciences, Department of Physics and Astronomy, Chapel Hill, NC 27599. Offers physics (MS, PhD). Terminal master's awarded for partial completion of doctoral program. *Degree requirements:* For master's, comprehensive exam; for doctorate, comprehensive exam, thesis/dissertation. *Entrance requirements:* For master's and doctorate, GRE General Test, minimum GPA of 3.0. Electronic applications accepted. *Faculty research:* Observational astronomy, fullerenes, polarized beams, nanotubes, nucleosynthesis in stars and supernovae, superstring theory, ballistic transport in semiconductors, gravitation.

University of Rochester, School of Arts and Sciences, Department of Physics and Astronomy, Rochester, NY 14627. Offers physics and astronomy (PhD). *Faculty:* 24 full-time (3 women). *Students:* 110 full-time (21 women); includes 17 minority (2 Black or African American, non-Hispanic/Latino; 4 Asian, non-Hispanic/Latino; 6 Hispanic/Latino; 5 Two or more races, non-Hispanic/Latino), 31 international. Average age 27. 327 applicants, 26% accepted, 17 enrolled. In 2018, 14 doctorates awarded. Terminal master's awarded for partial completion of doctoral program. *Degree requirements:* For doctorate, comprehensive exam, thesis/dissertation, qualifying exam. *Entrance requirements:* For doctorate, GRE General Test, GRE Subject Test (physics), statement of purpose, transcripts, three letters of recommendation. Additional exam requirements/recommendations for international students: Required—TOEFL, IELTS. *Application deadline:* For fall admission, 1/15 for domestic and international students. Application fee: $0. Electronic applications accepted. *Expenses: Tuition:* Full-time $52,974; part-time $1654 per credit hour. *Required fees:* $612. One-time fee: $30 part-time. Tuition and fees vary according to campus/location and program. *Financial support:* In 2018–19, 110 students received support, including 34 fellowships (averaging $32,000 per year), 59 research assistantships (averaging $27,744 per year), 17 teaching assistantships (averaging $27,744 per year). *Faculty research:* Theoretical optical physics, theoretical plasma physics, theoretical astrophysics, experimental atomic physics, plasma physics. *Total annual research expenditures:* $6.7 million. *Unit head:* Steven Manly, Chair and Professor, 585-275-8473, E-mail: steven.manly@rochester.edu. *Application contact:* Laura Blumkin, Graduate Program Coordinator, 585-275-4356, E-mail: laura.blumkin@rochester.edu. Website: https://www.pas.rochester.edu/graduate/index.html

University of South Carolina, The Graduate School, College of Arts and Sciences, Department of Physics and Astronomy, Columbia, SC 29208. Offers IMA, MAT, MS, PSM, PhD. IMA and MAT offered in cooperation with the College of Education. *Program availability:* Part-time. Terminal master's awarded for partial completion of doctoral program. *Degree requirements:* For master's, comprehensive exam, thesis; for doctorate, one foreign language, comprehensive exam, thesis/dissertation. *Entrance requirements:* For master's and doctorate, GRE General Test, GRE Subject Test. Additional exam requirements/recommendations for international students: Required—TOEFL (minimum score 570 paper-based; 75 iBT). Electronic applications accepted. *Faculty research:* Condensed matter, intermediate-energy nuclear physics, foundations of quantum mechanics, astronomy/astrophysics.

The University of Texas at Austin, Graduate School, College of Natural Sciences, Department of Astronomy, Austin, TX 78712-1111. Offers MA, PhD. *Entrance requirements:* For master's and doctorate, GRE General Test, GRE Subject Test (physics). Additional exam requirements/recommendations for international students: Required—TOEFL. Electronic applications accepted. *Faculty research:* Stars, interstellar medium, galaxies, planetary astronomy, cosmology.

University of Toronto, School of Graduate Studies, Faculty of Arts and Science, Department of Astronomy and Astrophysics, Toronto, ON M5S 1A1, Canada. Offers M Sc, PhD. *Program availability:* Part-time. *Degree requirements:* For doctorate, thesis/dissertation, qualifying exam, thesis defense. *Entrance requirements:* For master's, minimum B average, bachelor's degree in astronomy or equivalent, 3 letters of reference; for doctorate, GRE General Test, minimum B+ average, master's degree in astronomy or equivalent, demonstrated research competence, 3 letters of reference. Additional exam requirements/recommendations for international students: Required—TOEFL (minimum score 580 paper-based; 93 iBT), TWE (minimum score 4). Electronic applications accepted.

University of Victoria, Faculty of Graduate Studies, Faculty of Science, Department of Physics and Astronomy, Victoria, BC V8W 2Y2, Canada. Offers astronomy and astrophysics (M Sc, PhD); condensed matter physics (M Sc, PhD); experimental particle physics (M Sc, PhD); medical physics (M Sc, PhD); ocean physics (M Sc, PhD); theoretical physics (M Sc, PhD). *Degree requirements:* For master's, thesis; for doctorate, comprehensive exam, thesis/dissertation, candidacy exam. *Entrance requirements:* For master's and doctorate, GRE. Additional exam requirements/recommendations for international students: Required—TOEFL (minimum score 575 paper-based), IELTS (minimum score 7). Electronic applications accepted. *Faculty research:* Old stellar populations; observational cosmology and large scale structure; cp violation; atlas.

University of Virginia, College and Graduate School of Arts and Sciences, Department of Astronomy, Charlottesville, VA 22903. Offers MS, PhD. *Degree requirements:* For master's, comprehensive exam, thesis or alternative; for doctorate, comprehensive exam, thesis/dissertation. *Entrance requirements:* For master's and doctorate, GRE General Test, GRE Subject Test. Additional exam requirements/recommendations for international students: Required—TOEFL (minimum score 650 paper-based; 90 iBT), IELTS (minimum score 7). Electronic applications accepted.

University of Washington, Graduate School, College of Arts and Sciences, Department of Astronomy, Seattle, WA 98195. Offers MS, PhD. Terminal master's awarded for partial completion of doctoral program. *Degree requirements:* For doctorate, thesis/dissertation. *Entrance requirements:* For master's and doctorate, GRE General Test, GRE Subject Test, minimum GPA of 3.0. Additional exam requirements/recommendations for international students: Required—TOEFL. *Faculty research:* Solar system dust, space astronomy, high-energy astrophysics, galactic and extragalactic astronomy, stellar astrophysics.

The University of Western Ontario, School of Graduate and Postdoctoral Studies, Faculty of Science, Department of Physics and Astronomy, Program in Astronomy, London, ON N6A 3K7, Canada. Offers M Sc, PhD. Terminal master's awarded for partial completion of doctoral program. *Degree requirements:* For master's, thesis optional; for doctorate, comprehensive exam, thesis/dissertation. *Entrance requirements:* For master's, GRE Subject Test (physics), honors B Sc degree, minimum B average (Canadian), A - (international); for doctorate, M Sc degree, minimum B average (Canadian), A - (international). Additional exam requirements/recommendations for international students: Required—TOEFL (minimum score 580 paper-based). *Faculty research:* Observational and theoretical astrophysics spectroscopy, photometry, spectro-polarimetry, variable stars, cosmology.

University of Wisconsin–Madison, Graduate School, College of Letters and Science, Department of Astronomy, Madison, WI 53706-1380. Offers PhD. *Degree requirements:* For doctorate, comprehensive exam, thesis/dissertation. *Entrance requirements:* For doctorate, GRE General Test, GRE Subject Test (physics), bachelor's degree in related

Peterson's Graduate Programs in the Physical Sciences, Mathematics, Agricultural Sciences, the Environment & Natural Resources 2020

www.petersons.com   **37**

field. Additional exam requirements/recommendations for international students: Required—TOEFL. Electronic applications accepted. *Faculty research:* Kinematics, evolution of galaxies, cosmic distance, scale and large-scale structures, interstellar intergalactic medium, star formation and evolution, solar system chemistry and dynamics.

Wesleyan University, Graduate Studies, Department of Astronomy, Middletown, CT 06459. Offers MA. *Faculty:* 4 full-time (1 woman). *Students:* 6 full-time (2 women); includes 1 minority (Hispanic/Latino). Average age 25. 27 applicants, 15% accepted, 4 enrolled. In 2018, 4 master's awarded. *Degree requirements:* For master's, thesis. *Entrance requirements:* For master's, GRE General Test; GRE Subject Test in physics (recommended). Additional exam requirements/recommendations for international students: Required—TOEFL. *Application deadline:* For fall admission, 3/1 for domestic and international students. Application fee: $0. Electronic applications accepted. *Financial support:* In 2018–19, 4 students received support, including 1 research assistantship, 3 teaching assistantships with full tuition reimbursements available; tuition waivers (full) and full-year stipends also available. Financial award application deadline: 4/15. *Faculty research:* Observational-theoretical astronomy and astrophysics. *Unit head:* Dr. Seth Redfield, Chair, 860-685-3669, E-mail: sredfield@wesleyan.edu. *Application contact:* Linda Shettleworth, Administrative Assistant, 860-685-2130, Fax: 860-685-2131, E-mail: shettleworth@wesleyan.edu.
Website: http://www.wesleyan.edu/astro/

West Chester University of Pennsylvania, College of the Sciences and Mathematics, Department of Earth and Space Science, West Chester, PA 19383. Offers general science (Teaching Certificate); geoscience (MS). *Program availability:* Part-time, evening/weekend. *Degree requirements:* For master's, final project involving manuscript, presentation. *Entrance requirements:* For master's, minimum GPA of 2.8. Additional exam requirements/recommendations for international students: Required—TOEFL or IELTS. Electronic applications accepted. *Faculty research:* Environmental geology, coastal geomorphology (sea level change), geoscience education, water and soil remediation, hydrogeology, energy and sustainability, astronomy, short-term weather forecasting.

Yale University, Graduate School of Arts and Sciences, Department of Astronomy, New Haven, CT 06520. Offers astronomy (PhD); solar and terrestrial physics (PhD). *Degree requirements:* For doctorate, thesis/dissertation. *Entrance requirements:* For doctorate, GRE General Test, GRE Subject Test (physics).

York University, Faculty of Graduate Studies, Faculty of Science, Program in Physics and Astronomy, Toronto, ON M3J 1P3, Canada. Offers M Sc, PhD. *Program availability:* Part-time, evening/weekend. *Degree requirements:* For master's, thesis or alternative; for doctorate, comprehensive exam, thesis/dissertation. Electronic applications accepted.

Astrophysics

Air Force Institute of Technology, Graduate School of Engineering and Management, Department of Engineering Physics, Dayton, OH 45433-7765. Offers applied physics (MS, PhD); electro-optics (MS, PhD); materials science (PhD); nuclear engineering (MS, PhD); space physics (MS). *Program availability:* Part-time. *Degree requirements:* For master's, thesis; for doctorate, thesis/dissertation. *Entrance requirements:* For master's and doctorate, GRE General Test, minimum GPA of 3.0, U.S. citizenship. *Faculty research:* High-energy lasers, space physics, nuclear weapon effects, semiconductor physics.

Arizona State University at the Tempe campus, College of Liberal Arts and Sciences, School of Earth and Space Exploration, Tempe, AZ 85287-1404. Offers astrophysics (MS, PhD); exploration systems design (PhD); geological sciences (MS, PhD). PhD in exploration systems design is offered in collaboration with the Ira A. Fulton School of Engineering. Terminal master's awarded for partial completion of doctoral program. *Degree requirements:* For master's, thesis, interactive Program of Study (iPOS) submitted before completing 50 percent of required credit hours; for doctorate, thesis/dissertation, interactive Program of Study (iPOS) submitted before completing 50 percent of required credit hours. *Entrance requirements:* For master's and doctorate, GRE, minimum GPA of 3.0 or equivalent in last 2 years of work leading to bachelor's degree. Additional exam requirements/recommendations for international students: Required—TOEFL, IELTS, or PTE. Electronic applications accepted.

Cornell University, Graduate School, Graduate Fields of Arts and Sciences, Field of Astronomy and Space Sciences, Ithaca, NY 14853. Offers astronomy (PhD); astrophysics (PhD); general space sciences (PhD); infrared astronomy (PhD); planetary studies (PhD); radio astronomy (PhD); radiophysics (PhD); theoretical astrophysics (PhD). *Degree requirements:* For doctorate, comprehensive exam, thesis/dissertation. *Entrance requirements:* For doctorate, GRE General Test, GRE Subject Test (physics), 3 letters of recommendation. Additional exam requirements/recommendations for international students: Required—TOEFL (minimum score 600 paper-based; 77 iBT). Electronic applications accepted. *Faculty research:* Observational astrophysics, planetary sciences, cosmology, instrumentation, gravitational astrophysics.

Harvard University, Graduate School of Arts and Sciences, Department of Astronomy, Cambridge, MA 02138. Offers astronomy (PhD); astrophysics (PhD). *Degree requirements:* For doctorate, thesis/dissertation, paper, research project, 2 semesters of teaching. *Entrance requirements:* For doctorate, GRE General Test, GRE Subject Test (physics). Additional exam requirements/recommendations for international students: Required—TOEFL. Electronic applications accepted. *Faculty research:* Atomic and molecular physics, electromagnetism, solar physics, nuclear physics, fluid dynamics.

Indiana University Bloomington, University Graduate School, College of Arts and Sciences, Department of Astronomy, Bloomington, IN 47405. Offers astronomy (MA, PhD); astrophysics (PhD). Terminal master's awarded for partial completion of doctoral program. *Degree requirements:* For master's, thesis or alternative, oral exam; for doctorate, comprehensive exam, thesis/dissertation, oral defense. *Entrance requirements:* For master's and doctorate, GRE General Test, BA or BS in science. Additional exam requirements/recommendations for international students: Required—TOEFL (minimum score 550 paper-based; 79 iBT), IELTS. Electronic applications accepted. *Expenses:* Contact institution. *Faculty research:* Stellar and galaxy dynamics, stellar chemical abundances, galaxy evolution, observational cosmology.

Iowa State University of Science and Technology, Department of Physics and Astronomy, Ames, IA 50011. Offers applied physics (MS, PhD); astrophysics (MS, PhD); condensed matter physics (MS, PhD); high energy physics (MS, PhD); nuclear physics (MS, PhD); physics (MS, PhD). *Degree requirements:* For master's, thesis (for some programs); for doctorate, thesis/dissertation. *Entrance requirements:* For master's and doctorate, GRE General Test, GRE Subject Test (physics). Additional exam requirements/recommendations for international students: Required—TOEFL (minimum score 550 paper-based; 79 iBT), IELTS (minimum score 6.5). Electronic applications accepted. *Faculty research:* Condensed-matter physics, including superconductivity and new materials; high-energy and nuclear physics; astronomy and astrophysics; atmospheric and environmental physics.

Iowa State University of Science and Technology, Program in Astrophysics, Ames, IA 50011. Offers MS, PhD. *Entrance requirements:* For master's and doctorate, GRE. Additional exam requirements/recommendations for international students: Required—TOEFL (minimum score 550 paper-based; 79 iBT), IELTS (minimum score 6.5).

Louisiana State University and Agricultural & Mechanical College, Graduate School, College of Science, Department of Physics and Astronomy, Baton Rouge, LA 70803. Offers astronomy (PhD); astrophysics (PhD); medical physics (MS); physics (MS, PhD).

McMaster University, School of Graduate Studies, Faculty of Science, Department of Physics and Astronomy, Hamilton, ON L8S 4M2, Canada. Offers astrophysics (PhD); physics (PhD). *Program availability:* Part-time. *Degree requirements:* For doctorate, comprehensive exam, thesis/dissertation. *Entrance requirements:* For doctorate, minimum B+ average. Additional exam requirements/recommendations for international students: Required—TOEFL (minimum score 550 paper-based). *Faculty research:* Condensed matter, astrophysics, nuclear, medical, nonlinear dynamics.

Michigan State University, The Graduate School, College of Natural Science, Department of Physics and Astronomy, East Lansing, MI 48824. Offers astrophysics and astronomy (MS, PhD); physics (MS, PhD). *Entrance requirements:* Additional exam requirements/recommendations for international students: Required—TOEFL (minimum score 550 paper-based), Michigan State University ELT (minimum score 85), Michigan English Language Assessment Battery (minimum score 83). Electronic applications accepted. *Faculty research:* Nuclear and accelerator physics, high energy physics, condensed matter physics, biophysics, astrophysics and astronomy.

New Mexico Institute of Mining and Technology, Center for Graduate Studies, Department of Physics, Socorro, NM 87801. Offers astrophysics (PhD); atmospheric physics (PhD); instrumentation (MS); mathematical physics (PhD); physics (MS). *Degree requirements:* For master's, thesis optional; for doctorate, thesis/dissertation. *Entrance requirements:* For master's, GRE General Test; for doctorate, GRE General Test, GRE Subject Test. Additional exam requirements/recommendations for international students: Required—TOEFL (minimum score 540 paper-based). *Faculty research:* Cloud physics, stellar and extragalactic processes.

New Mexico State University, College of Arts and Sciences, Department of Physics, Las Cruces, NM 88003-8001. Offers space physics (MS). *Program availability:* Part-time. *Faculty:* 14 full-time (1 woman). *Students:* 34 full-time (8 women), 2 part-time (0 women); includes 2 minority (both Hispanic/Latino), 26 international. Average age 31. 45 applicants, 22% accepted, 5 enrolled. In 2018, 3 master's, 6 doctorates awarded. Terminal master's awarded for partial completion of doctoral program. *Degree requirements:* For master's, comprehensive exam, thesis optional, written qualifying exam; for doctorate, comprehensive exam, thesis/dissertation. *Entrance requirements:* For master's and doctorate, GRE General Test, GRE Subject Test. Additional exam requirements/recommendations for international students: Required—TOEFL (minimum score 550 paper-based; 79 iBT), IELTS (minimum score 6.5). *Application deadline:* For fall admission, 2/15 priority date for domestic and international students; for spring admission, 11/1 priority date for domestic students, 9/1 priority date for international students. Applications are processed on a rolling basis. Application fee: $40 ($50 for international students). Electronic applications accepted. *Expenses: Tuition, area resident:* Full-time $4216.70; part-time $252.70 per credit hour. Tuition, state resident: full-time $4216.70; part-time $252.70 per credit hour. Tuition, nonresident: full-time $12,769; part-time $881.10 per credit hour. *International tuition:* $12,769.30 full-time. *Required fees:* $878.40; $48.80 per credit hour. Full-time tuition and fees vary according to course load and reciprocity agreements. *Financial support:* In 2018–19, 32 students received support, including 1 fellowship (averaging $4,548 per year), 9 research assistantships (averaging $20,127 per year), 20 teaching assistantships (averaging $19,017 per year); career-related internships or fieldwork, Federal Work-Study, scholarships/grants, traineeships, health care benefits, and unspecified assistantships also available. Support available to part-time students. Financial award application deadline: 3/1. *Faculty research:* Nuclear and particle physics, condensed matter physics, materials science, geophysics, applied physics. *Total annual research expenditures:* $1.6 million. *Unit head:* Dr. Stefan Zollner, Department Head, 575-646-3831, Fax: 575-646-1934, E-mail: zollner@nmsu.edu. *Application contact:* Dr. Vassilios Papavassiliou, Graduate Program Head, 575-646-3831, Fax: 575-646-1934, E-mail: graduate-advisor@physics.nmsu.edu.
Website: http://physics.nmsu.edu

Penn State University Park, Graduate School, Eberly College of Science, Department of Astronomy and Astrophysics, University Park, PA 16802. Offers astronomy and astrophysics (MS, PhD).

Princeton University, Graduate School, Department of Astrophysical Sciences, Princeton, NJ 08544-1019. Offers astronomy (PhD); plasma physics (PhD). *Degree requirements:* For doctorate, thesis/dissertation. *Entrance requirements:* For doctorate, GRE General Test, GRE Subject Test (physics). Additional exam requirements/recommendations for international students: Required—TOEFL (minimum score 600 paper-based). Electronic applications accepted. *Faculty research:* Theoretical astrophysics, cosmology, galaxy formation, galactic dynamics, interstellar and intergalactic matter.

Rochester Institute of Technology, Graduate Enrollment Services, College of Science, School of Physics and Astronomy, MS Program in Astrophysical Science and Technology, Rochester, NY 14623-5603. Offers MS. *Program availability:* Part-time. *Students:* 5 full-time (3 women), 1 international. Average age 23. 15 applicants, 33% accepted, 2 enrolled. In 2018, 3 master's awarded. *Degree requirements:* For master's,

thesis. *Entrance requirements:* For master's, GRE, minimum GPA of 3.2 (recommended) in course work in mathematical, science, engineering, and computing subject areas; personal statement; resume; two letters of recommendation. Additional exam requirements/recommendations for international students: Required—TOEFL (minimum score 550 paper-based; 79 iBT), IELTS (minimum score 6.5), PTE (minimum score 58). *Application deadline:* For fall admission, 2/15 priority date for domestic and international students; for spring admission, 12/15 priority date for domestic and international students. Applications are processed on a rolling basis. Application fee: $65. Electronic applications accepted. *Financial support:* In 2018–19, 8 students received support. Research assistantships with partial tuition reimbursements available, teaching assistantships with partial tuition reimbursements available, career-related internships or fieldwork, scholarships/grants, and unspecified assistantships available. Financial award applicants required to submit FAFSA. *Faculty research:* Astronomical instrumentation and detectors; galaxy structure and evolution; observational cosmology; stellar evolution and planet formation; general relativity and gravitational wave astronomy. *Unit head:* Andrew Robinson, Graduate Program Director, 585-475-2726, E-mail: axrsps@rit.edu. *Application contact:* Diane Ellison, Senior Associate Vice President, Graduate Enrollment Services, 585-475-2229, Fax: 585-475-7164, E-mail: gradinfo@rit.edu.
Website: https://www.rit.edu/study/astrophysical-sciences-and-technology-ms

Rochester Institute of Technology, Graduate Enrollment Services, College of Science, School of Physics and Astronomy, PhD Program in Astrophysical Science and Technology, Rochester, NY 14623-5603. Offers PhD. *Students:* 24 full-time (13 women); includes 1 minority (Hispanic/Latino), 5 international. Average age 27. 64 applicants, 6% accepted, 2 enrolled. In 2018, 1 doctorate awarded. *Degree requirements:* For doctorate, comprehensive exam, thesis/dissertation. *Entrance requirements:* For doctorate, GRE, minimum GPA of 3.2 (recommended) in course work in mathematical, science, engineering, and computing subject areas. Personal statement. Resume. Two letters of recommendation. Additional exam requirements/recommendations for international students: Required—TOEFL (minimum score 550 paper-based; 79 iBT), IELTS (minimum score 6.5), PTE (minimum score 58). *Application deadline:* For fall admission, 1/15 priority date for domestic and international students. Applications are processed on a rolling basis. Application fee: $65. Electronic applications accepted. *Expenses:* Contact institution. *Financial support:* In 2018–19, 24 students received support. Research assistantships with full tuition reimbursements available, teaching assistantships with full tuition reimbursements available, career-related internships or fieldwork, scholarships/grants, health care benefits, and unspecified assistantships available. Financial award applicants required to submit FAFSA. *Faculty research:* Astronomical instrumentation and detectors; galaxy structure and evolution; observational cosmology; stellar evolution and planet formation; general relativity and gravitational wave astronomy. *Unit head:* Andrew Robinson, Graduate Program Director, 585-475-2726, E-mail: axrsps@rit.edu. *Application contact:* Diane Ellison, Senior Associate Vice President, Graduate Enrollment Services, 585-475-2229, Fax: 585-475-7164, E-mail: gradinfo@rit.edu.
Website: https://www.rit.edu/study/astrophysical-sciences-and-technology-phd

Texas Christian University, College of Science and Engineering, Department of Physics and Astronomy, Fort Worth, TX 76129-0002. Offers physics (MA, MS, PhD), including astrophysics (PhD), biophysics (PhD); PhD/MBA. *Program availability:* Part-time. *Faculty:* 8 full-time (3 women). *Students:* 17 full-time (6 women); includes 3 minority (1 Black or African American, non-Hispanic/Latino; 2 Hispanic/Latino), 6 international. Average age 25. 20 applicants, 20% accepted, 4 enrolled. In 2018, 3 master's, 4 doctorates awarded. Terminal master's awarded for partial completion of doctoral program. *Degree requirements:* For master's, one foreign language, comprehensive exam, thesis or alternative; for doctorate, comprehensive exam, thesis/dissertation. *Entrance requirements:* Additional exam requirements/recommendations for international students: Required—TOEFL (minimum score 550 paper-based; 80 iBT), IELTS (minimum score 6.5). *Application deadline:* For fall admission, 1/1 priority date for domestic and international students; for spring admission, 9/1 priority date for domestic and international students. Applications are processed on a rolling basis. Application fee: $0 ($60 for international students). Electronic applications accepted. *Expenses:* Contact institution. *Financial support:* In 2018–19, 16 students received support, including 3 research assistantships with full tuition reimbursements available (averaging $24,000 per year), 13 teaching assistantships with full tuition reimbursements available (averaging $21,000 per year); scholarships/grants and unspecified assistantships also available. Financial award application deadline: 1/1. *Faculty research:* Nanomaterials, computer simulations of biophysical processes, nonlinear dynamics, computational and observational studies of galaxy evolution using stars and gas, spectroscopy and fluorescence of biomolecules. *Total annual research expenditures:* $265,000. *Unit head:* Dr. Yuri M. Strzhemechny, Associate Professor/Chair, 817-257-5793, Fax: 817-257-7742, E-mail: y.strzhemechny@tcu.edu. *Application contact:* Dr. Peter M. Frinchaboy, III, Associate Professor, 817-257-6387, Fax: 817-257-7742, E-mail: p.frinchaboy@tcu.edu.
Website: http://physics.tcu.edu/

Tufts University, Graduate School of Arts and Sciences, Department of Physics and Astronomy, Medford, MA 02155. Offers astrophysics (MS, PhD); chemical physics (PhD); physics (MS, PhD); physics education (PhD). Terminal master's awarded for partial completion of doctoral program. *Degree requirements:* For master's, thesis optional; for doctorate, thesis/dissertation, oral qualifying exam. *Entrance requirements:* For master's and doctorate, GRE General Test. Additional exam requirements/recommendations for international students: Required—TOEFL (minimum score 550 paper-based; 80 iBT), IELTS (minimum score 6.5). Electronic applications accepted. *Expenses:* Contact institution.

University of Alaska Fairbanks, College of Natural Science and Mathematics, Department of Physics, Fairbanks, AK 99775-5920. Offers computational physics (MS); physics (MS, PhD); space physics (MS). *Program availability:* Part-time. *Faculty:* 8 full-time (2 women). *Students:* 22 full-time (3 women), 1 part-time (0 women); includes 3 minority (1 Asian, non-Hispanic/Latino; 2 Hispanic/Latino), 5 international. Average age 29. 35 applicants, 14% accepted, 5 enrolled. In 2018, 1 master's, 2 doctorates awarded. *Degree requirements:* For master's, comprehensive exam, oral defense of project or thesis; for doctorate, comprehensive exam, thesis/dissertation, oral defense of dissertation. *Entrance requirements:* For master's, GRE General Test, bachelor's degree from accredited institution with minimum cumulative undergraduate and major GPA of 3.0; for doctorate, GRE General Test, minimum cumulative GPA of 3.0. Additional exam requirements/recommendations for international students: Required—TOEFL (minimum score 550 paper-based; 80 iBT). *Application deadline:* For fall admission, 6/1 for domestic students, 3/1 for international students; for spring admission, 10/15 for domestic students, 9/1 for international students. Applications are processed on a rolling basis. Application fee: $60. Electronic applications accepted. *Expenses: Tuition, area resident:* Full-time $8802; part-time $5868 per credit hour. Tuition, state resident: full-time $8802; part-time $5868 per credit hour. Tuition, nonresident: full-time $18,504; part-time $12,336 per credit hour. *International tuition:* $18,504 full-time. *Required fees:* $1416; $944 per credit hour. $472 per semester. Tuition and fees vary according to course load and program. *Financial support:* In 2018–19, 11 research assistantships with full tuition reimbursements (averaging $9,421 per year), 12 teaching assistantships with full tuition reimbursements (averaging $12,712 per year) were awarded; fellowships with full tuition reimbursements, Federal Work-Study, scholarships/grants, health care benefits, and unspecified assistantships also available. Support available to part-time students. Financial award application deadline: 2/15; financial award applicants required to submit FAFSA. *Faculty research:* Atmospheric and ionospheric radar studies, space plasma theory, magnetospheric dynamics, space weather and auroral studies, turbulence and complex systems. *Total annual research expenditures:* $11.2 million. *Unit head:* Renate Wackerbauer, Department Chair, 907-474-7339, E-mail: uaf-physics@alaska.edu. *Application contact:* Samara Taber, Director of Admissions, 907-474-7500, E-mail: uaf-admissions@alaska.edu.
Website: http://www.uaf.edu/physics/

University of Alberta, Faculty of Graduate Studies and Research, Department of Physics, Edmonton, AB T6G 2E1, Canada. Offers astrophysics (M Sc, PhD); condensed matter (M Sc, PhD); geophysics (M Sc, PhD); medical physics (M Sc, PhD); subatomic physics (M Sc, PhD). *Degree requirements:* For master's, thesis; for doctorate, thesis/dissertation. *Entrance requirements:* For master's and doctorate, minimum GPA of 7.0 on a 9.0 scale. Additional exam requirements/recommendations for international students: Required—TOEFL. *Faculty research:* Cosmology, astroparticle physics, high-intermediate energy, magnetism, superconductivity.

University of California, Berkeley, Graduate Division, College of Letters and Science, Department of Astrophysics, Berkeley, CA 94720. Offers PhD. *Degree requirements:* For doctorate, thesis/dissertation, qualifying exam. *Entrance requirements:* For doctorate, GRE General Test, GRE Subject Test, minimum GPA of 3.0, 3 letters of recommendation. Additional exam requirements/recommendations for international students: Required—TOEFL (minimum score 570 paper-based; 90 iBT). Electronic applications accepted. *Faculty research:* Theory, cosmology, radio astronomy, extra solar planets, infrared instrumentation.

University of California, Los Angeles, Graduate Division, College of Letters and Science, Department of Earth and Space Sciences, Program in Geophysics and Space Physics, Los Angeles, CA 90095. Offers MS, PhD. Terminal master's awarded for partial completion of doctoral program. *Degree requirements:* For master's, comprehensive exam or thesis; for doctorate, thesis/dissertation, oral and written qualifying exams. *Entrance requirements:* For master's and doctorate, GRE General Test, bachelor's degree; minimum undergraduate GPA of 3.0 (or its equivalent if letter grade system not used). Additional exam requirements/recommendations for international students: Required—TOEFL. Electronic applications accepted.

University of California, Santa Cruz, Division of Graduate Studies, Division of Physical and Biological Sciences, Department of Astronomy and Astrophysics, Santa Cruz, CA 95064. Offers PhD. *Degree requirements:* For doctorate, one foreign language, thesis/dissertation, qualifying exam. *Entrance requirements:* For doctorate, GRE General Test, GRE Subject Test. Additional exam requirements/recommendations for international students: Required—TOEFL (minimum score 550 paper-based; 83 iBT); Recommended—IELTS (minimum score 8). Electronic applications accepted. *Faculty research:* Solar system and the Milky Way to the most distant galaxies in the Universe, fundamental questions of cosmology.

University of Chicago, Division of the Physical Sciences, Department of Astronomy and Astrophysics, Chicago, IL 60637. Offers PhD. Terminal master's awarded for partial completion of doctoral program. *Degree requirements:* For doctorate, comprehensive exam, thesis/dissertation. *Entrance requirements:* For doctorate, GRE General Test, GRE Subject Test (physics), research statement, 3 letters of recommendation, transcripts for all previous degrees and institutions attended. Additional exam requirements/recommendations for international students: Required—TOEFL (minimum score 600 paper-based; 90 iBT), IELTS (minimum score 7). Electronic applications accepted. *Faculty research:* Cosmology, exoplanets, galaxy formation, interstellar and intergalactic matter, astroparticle physics, high-performance computation in astrophysics.

University of Colorado Boulder, Graduate School, College of Arts and Sciences, Department of Astrophysical and Planetary Sciences, Boulder, CO 80309. Offers astrophysics (MS, PhD); planetary science (PhD). Terminal master's awarded for partial completion of doctoral program. *Degree requirements:* For master's, comprehensive exam, thesis or alternative; for doctorate, one foreign language, thesis/dissertation. *Entrance requirements:* For master's, GRE General Test, GRE Subject Test, minimum undergraduate GPA of 3.0; for doctorate, GRE General Test, GRE Subject Test. Electronic applications accepted. Application fee is waived when completed online. *Faculty research:* Astrophysics; astronomy; infrared/optical astronomy; spectroscopy; telescopes.

The University of Manchester, School of Physics and Astronomy, Manchester, United Kingdom. Offers astronomy and astrophysics (M Sc, PhD); biological physics (M Sc, PhD); condensed matter physics (M Sc, PhD); nonlinear and liquid crystals physics (M Sc, PhD); nuclear physics (M Sc, PhD); particle physics (M Sc, PhD); photon physics (M Sc, PhD); physics (M Sc, PhD); theoretical physics (M Sc, PhD).

University of Michigan, Rackham Graduate School, College of Literature, Science, and the Arts, Department of Astronomy, Ann Arbor, MI 48109-1042. Offers astronomy and astrophysics (PhD). *Faculty:* 21 full-time (7 women). *Students:* 31 full-time (12 women); includes 6 minority (5 Hispanic/Latino; 1 Two or more races, non-Hispanic/Latino), 6 international. 254 applicants, 8% accepted, 6 enrolled. In 2018, 5 doctorates awarded. Terminal master's awarded for partial completion of doctoral program. *Degree requirements:* For doctorate, comprehensive exam, thesis/dissertation, preliminary exam to advance to candidacy, oral defense of dissertation. *Entrance requirements:* For doctorate, GRE General Test. Additional exam requirements/recommendations for international students: Required—TOEFL (minimum score 560 paper-based; 84 iBT), IELTS (minimum score 6.5). *Application deadline:* For fall admission, 12/15 for domestic and international students. Application fee: $75 ($90 for international students). Electronic applications accepted. *Financial support:* Fellowships, research assistantships, teaching assistantships, scholarships/grants, health care benefits, and unspecified assistantships available. *Faculty research:* Cosmology- extragalactic and galactic, stars and exoplanets, extreme astrophysics, instrumentation. *Unit head:* Dr. Edwin Bergin, Professor and Chair, 734-764-3440, Fax: 734-763-6317, E-mail: astrochair@umich.edu. *Application contact:* Andrea Nashar, PhD Program Coordinator, 734-763-3520, E-mail: astrophdprogram@umich.edu.
Website: https://lsa.umich.edu/astro

University of Minnesota, Twin Cities Campus, College of Science and Engineering, School of Physics and Astronomy, Program in Astrophysics, Minneapolis, MN 55455-0213. Offers MS, PhD. Terminal master's awarded for partial completion of doctoral program. *Degree requirements:* For master's, thesis optional; for doctorate, thesis/dissertation. *Entrance requirements:* For master's and doctorate, GRE General Test,

Astrophysics

GRE Subject Test. Additional exam requirements/recommendations for international students: Required—TOEFL. *Faculty research:* Evolution of stars and galaxies; the interstellar medium; cosmology; observational, optical, infrared, and radio astronomy; computational astrophysics.

University of Missouri–St. Louis, College of Arts and Sciences, Department of Physics and Astronomy, St. Louis, MO 63121. Offers applied physics (MS); astrophysics (MS); physics (PhD). *Program availability:* Part-time, evening/weekend. Terminal master's awarded for partial completion of doctoral program. *Degree requirements:* For master's, thesis optional; for doctorate, thesis/dissertation. *Entrance requirements:* For master's, GRE General Test, minimum GPA of 2.75, 2 letters of recommendation; for doctorate, GRE General Test, 2 letters of recommendation, minimum GPA of 3.0. Additional exam requirements/recommendations for international students: Required—TOEFL (minimum score 550 paper-based; 79 iBT), IELTS (minimum score 6.5). Electronic applications accepted. *Faculty research:* Biophysics, astrophysics, materials science.

The University of North Carolina at Chapel Hill, Graduate School, College of Arts and Sciences, Department of Physics and Astronomy, Chapel Hill, NC 27599. Offers physics (MS, PhD). Terminal master's awarded for partial completion of doctoral program. *Degree requirements:* For master's, comprehensive exam; for doctorate, comprehensive exam, thesis/dissertation. *Entrance requirements:* For master's and doctorate, GRE General Test, minimum GPA of 3.0. Electronic applications accepted. *Faculty research:* Observational astronomy, fullerenes, polarized beams, nanotubes, nucleosynthesis in stars and supernovae, superstring theory, ballistic transport in semiconductors, gravitation.

University of North Dakota, Graduate School, College of Arts and Sciences, Department of Physics and Astrophysics, Grand Forks, ND 58202. Offers MA, MS, PhD. *Degree requirements:* For master's, thesis, final exam; for doctorate, comprehensive exam, thesis/dissertation, final exam. *Entrance requirements:* For master's, minimum GPA of 3.0; for doctorate, minimum GPA of 3.5. Additional exam requirements/recommendations for international students: Required—TOEFL (minimum score 550 paper-based; 79 iBT), IELTS (minimum score 6.5). Electronic applications accepted. *Faculty research:* Solid state physics, atomic and molecular physics, astrophysics, health physics.

The University of Toledo, College of Graduate Studies, College of Natural Sciences and Mathematics, Department of Physics and Astronomy, Toledo, OH 43606-3390.

Offers photovoltaics (PSM); physics (MS, PhD), including astrophysics (PhD), materials science, medical physics (PhD); MS/PhD. *Degree requirements:* For master's, thesis; for doctorate, thesis/dissertation, departmental qualifying exam. *Entrance requirements:* For master's and doctorate, GRE General Test, GRE Subject Test, minimum cumulative point-hour ratio of 2.7 for all previous academic work, three letters of recommendation, statement of purpose, transcripts from all prior institutions attended. Additional exam requirements/recommendations for international students: Required—TOEFL (minimum score 550 paper-based; 80 iBT). Electronic applications accepted. *Faculty research:* Atomic physics, solid-state physics, materials science, astrophysics.

University of Toronto, School of Graduate Studies, Faculty of Arts and Science, Department of Astronomy and Astrophysics, Toronto, ON M5S 1A1, Canada. Offers M Sc, PhD. *Program availability:* Part-time. *Degree requirements:* For doctorate, thesis/dissertation, qualifying exam, thesis defense. *Entrance requirements:* For master's, minimum B average, bachelor's degree in astronomy or equivalent, 3 letters of reference; for doctorate, GRE General Test, minimum B+ average, master's degree in astronomy or equivalent, demonstrated research competence, 3 letters of reference. Additional exam requirements/recommendations for international students: Required—TOEFL (minimum score 580 paper-based; 93 iBT), TWE (minimum score 4). Electronic applications accepted.

University of Victoria, Faculty of Graduate Studies, Faculty of Science, Department of Physics and Astronomy, Victoria, BC V8W 2Y2, Canada. Offers astronomy and astrophysics (M Sc, PhD); condensed matter physics (M Sc, PhD); experimental particle physics (M Sc, PhD); medical physics (M Sc, PhD); ocean physics (M Sc, PhD); theoretical physics (M Sc, PhD). *Degree requirements:* For master's, thesis; for doctorate, comprehensive exam, thesis/dissertation, candidacy exam. *Entrance requirements:* For master's and doctorate, GRE. Additional exam requirements/recommendations for international students: Required—TOEFL (minimum score 575 paper-based), IELTS (minimum score 7). Electronic applications accepted. *Faculty research:* Old stellar populations; observational cosmology and large scale structure; cp violation; atlas.

Yale University, Graduate School of Arts and Sciences, Department of Astronomy, New Haven, CT 06520. Offers astronomy (PhD); solar and terrestrial physics (PhD). *Degree requirements:* For doctorate, thesis/dissertation. *Entrance requirements:* For doctorate, GRE General Test, GRE Subject Test (physics).

40 www.petersons.com

Peterson's Graduate Programs in the Physical Sciences, Mathematics, Agricultural Sciences, the Environment & Natural Resources 2020

Section 2
Chemistry

This section contains a directory of institutions offering graduate work in chemistry, followed by in-depth entries submitted by institutions that chose to prepare detailed program descriptions. Additional information about programs listed in the directory but not augmented by an in-depth entry may be obtained by writing directly to the dean of a graduate school or chair of a department at the address given in the directory.

For programs offering related work, see also in this book *Geosciences* and *Physics.* In the other guides in this series:

Graduate Programs in the Biological/Biomedical Sciences & Health-Related Medical Professions

See *Biological and Biomedical Sciences, Biochemistry, Biophysics, Nutrition, Pharmacology and Toxicology,* and *Pharmacy and Pharmaceutical Sciences*

Graduate Programs in Engineering & Applied Sciences

See *Engineering and Applied Sciences; Agricultural Engineering; Chemical Engineering; Geological, Mineral/Mining, and Petroleum Engineering; Materials Sciences and Engineering;* and *Pharmaceutical Engineering*

CONTENTS

Program Directories

Analytical Chemistry

Auburn University, Graduate School, College of Sciences and Mathematics, Department of Chemistry and Biochemistry, Auburn University, AL 36849. Offers analytical chemistry (MS, PhD); biochemistry (MS, PhD); inorganic chemistry (MS); organic chemistry (PhD); physical chemistry (MS, PhD). *Program availability:* Part-time. *Degree requirements:* For master's, thesis (for some programs); for doctorate, thesis/dissertation, oral and written exams. *Entrance requirements:* For master's and doctorate, GRE General Test. Electronic applications accepted. *Expenses:* Tuition, state resident: full-time $11,282; part-time $535 per credit hour. Tuition, nonresident: full-time $30,542; part-time $1605 per credit hour. *Required fees:* $826 per semester. Tuition and fees vary according to degree level and program.

Binghamton University, State University of New York, Graduate School, Harpur College of Arts and Sciences, Department of Chemistry, Binghamton, NY 13902-6000. Offers analytical chemistry (PhD); chemistry (MA, MS); inorganic chemistry (PhD); physical chemistry (PhD). *Program availability:* Part-time. Terminal master's awarded for partial completion of doctoral program. *Degree requirements:* For master's, thesis; for doctorate, comprehensive exam, thesis/dissertation. *Entrance requirements:* For master's and doctorate, GRE General Test. Additional exam requirements/recommendations for international students: Required—TOEFL (minimum score 90 iBT). Electronic applications accepted.

Brigham Young University, Graduate Studies, College of Physical and Mathematical Sciences, Department of Chemistry and Biochemistry, Provo, UT 84602. Offers biochemistry (MS, PhD); chemistry (MS, PhD). *Faculty:* 37 full-time (5 women), 13 part-time/adjunct (5 women). *Students:* 95 full-time (34 women); includes 6 minority (1 Black or African American, non-Hispanic/Latino; 2 Hispanic/Latino; 3 Two or more races, non-Hispanic/Latino), 53 international. Average age 29. 63 applicants, 71% accepted, 30 enrolled. In 2018, 3 master's, 9 doctorates awarded. *Degree requirements:* For master's, thesis; for doctorate, thesis/dissertation, qualifying exam. *Entrance requirements:* For master's and doctorate, GRE General Test, minimum GPA of 3.0. Additional exam requirements/recommendations for international students: Required—TOEFL (minimum score 580 paper-based; 85 iBT), IELTS (minimum score 7). *Application deadline:* For fall admission, 2/1 priority date for domestic and international students. Applications are processed on a rolling basis. Application fee: $50. Electronic applications accepted. *Expenses:* $46,400 for Ph.D. in Chemistry and Biochemistry (covers student's tuition for the required 54 credit hours); $25,800 for MS in Chemistry and Biochemistry (covers student's tuition for the required 30 credit hours). *Financial support:* In 2018–19, 91 students received support, including 20 fellowships with full tuition reimbursements available (averaging $26,000 per year), 36 research assistantships with full tuition reimbursements available (averaging $26,000 per year), 34 teaching assistantships with full tuition reimbursements available (averaging $26,000 per year); scholarships/grants and supplementary awards also available. Financial award application deadline: 2/1. *Faculty research:* Separation science, molecular recognition, organic synthesis and biomedical application, biochemistry and molecular biology, molecular spectroscopy. *Total annual research expenditures:* $5.3 million. *Unit head:* Dr. David V. Dearden, Chair, 801-422-2355, Fax: 801-422-0153, E-mail: david_dearden@byu.edu. *Application contact:* Dr. Ken A. Christensen, Graduate Coordinator, 801-422-0249, Fax: 801-422-0153, E-mail: kenc@chem.byu.edu.
Website: http://www.chem.byu.edu/

California State University, Los Angeles, Graduate Studies, College of Natural and Social Sciences, Department of Chemistry and Biochemistry, Los Angeles, CA 90032-8530. Offers analytical chemistry (MS). *Program availability:* Part-time, evening/weekend. *Degree requirements:* For master's, one foreign language, comprehensive exam or thesis. *Entrance requirements:* Additional exam requirements/recommendations for international students: Required—TOEFL. *Faculty research:* Intercalation of heavy metal, carborane chemistry, conductive polymers and fabrics, titanium reagents, computer modeling and synthesis.

Cornell University, Graduate School, Graduate Fields of Arts and Sciences, Field of Chemistry and Chemical Biology, Ithaca, NY 14853. Offers analytical chemistry (PhD); bio-organic chemistry (PhD); biophysical chemistry (PhD); chemical biology (PhD); chemical physics (PhD); inorganic chemistry (PhD); materials chemistry (PhD); organic chemistry (PhD); organometallic chemistry (PhD); physical chemistry (PhD); polymer chemistry (PhD); theoretical chemistry (PhD). *Degree requirements:* For doctorate, comprehensive exam, thesis/dissertation. *Entrance requirements:* For doctorate, GRE General Test, GRE Subject Test (chemistry), 3 letters of recommendation. Additional exam requirements/recommendations for international students: Required—TOEFL (minimum score 600 paper-based; 77 iBT). Electronic applications accepted. *Faculty research:* Analytical, organic, inorganic, physical, materials, chemical biology.

Eastern New Mexico University, Graduate School, College of Liberal Arts and Sciences, Department of Physical Sciences, Portales, NM 88130. Offers chemistry (MS), including analytical chemistry, biochemistry, organic chemistry, physical chemistry. *Program availability:* Part-time. *Degree requirements:* For master's, thesis optional, seminar, oral and written comprehensive exams. *Entrance requirements:* For master's, ACS placement examination, minimum GPA of 3.0; 2 letters of recommendation; personal statement of career goals; bachelor's degree with minimum of one year each of general, organic, and analytical chemistry. Additional exam requirements/recommendations for international students: Required—TOEFL (minimum score 550 paper-based; 79 iBT), IELTS (minimum score 6). Electronic applications accepted. *Expenses: Tuition, area resident:* Full-time $6776. Tuition, state resident: full-time $6776; part-time $282 per credit hour. Tuition, nonresident: full-time $8986; part-time $374 per credit hour. *Required fees:* $60 per semester. One-time fee: $25. *Faculty research:* Synfuel, electrochemistry, protein chemistry.

Florida State University, The Graduate School, Department of Anthropology, Department of Chemistry and Biochemistry, Tallahassee, FL 32306-4390. Offers analytical chemistry (MS, PhD); biochemistry (MS, PhD); inorganic chemistry (MS, PhD); materials chemistry (PhD); organic chemistry (MS, PhD); physical chemistry (MS, PhD). *Faculty:* 29 full-time (4 women). *Students:* 159 full-time (57 women), 2 part-time (1 woman); includes 73 minority (9 Black or African American, non-Hispanic/Latino; 46 Asian, non-Hispanic/Latino; 9 Hispanic/Latino; 3 Native Hawaiian or other Pacific Islander, non-Hispanic/Latino; 6 Two or more races, non-Hispanic/Latino). Average age 26. 215 applicants, 49% accepted, 35 enrolled. In 2018, 33 master's, 30 doctorates awarded. Terminal master's awarded for partial completion of doctoral program. *Degree requirements:* For master's, thesis (for some programs); for doctorate, thesis/dissertation. *Entrance requirements:* For master's and doctorate, GRE General Test (minimum scores: 150 verbal, 151 quantitative), minimum upper-division GPA of 3.1 in undergraduate course work. Additional exam requirements/recommendations for international students: Required—TOEFL (minimum score 80 iBT). *Application deadline:* For fall admission, 12/15 priority date for domestic and international students. Applications are processed on a rolling basis. Application fee: $30. Electronic applications accepted. *Expenses: Tuition, area resident:* Part-time $479.32 per credit hour. Tuition and fees vary according to campus/location and program. *Financial support:* In 2018–19, 163 students received support, including 4 fellowships with full tuition reimbursements available (averaging $24,241 per year), 59 research assistantships with full tuition reimbursements available (averaging $24,241 per year), 102 teaching assistantships with full tuition reimbursements available (averaging $24,241 per year). Financial award application deadline: 12/15; financial award applicants required to submit FAFSA. *Faculty research:* Bioanalytical chemistry, separations, microfluidics, petroleomics; materials chemistry, solid state materials, magnets, polymers, catalysts, advanced spectroscopic methods, NMR and EPR, ultrafast, Raman, and mass spectrometry; organic synthesis, natural products, photochemistry, and supramolecular chemistry; biochemistry, structural biology, metabolomics, and anticancer drugs; nanochemistry, applications in energy, sustainability, biology, and technology development; radiochemistry. *Total annual research expenditures:* $7.1 million. *Unit head:* Dr. Geoffrey Strouse, Chairman, 850-644-1244, Fax: 850-644-8281, E-mail: gradinfo@chem.fsu.edu. *Application contact:* Dr. Wei Yang, Associate Chair for Graduate Studies, 850-645-6884, Fax: 850-644-8281, E-mail: gradinfo@chem.fsu.edu.
Website: http://www.chem.fsu.edu/

Georgetown University, Graduate School of Arts and Sciences, Department of Chemistry, Washington, DC 20057. Offers analytical chemistry (PhD); biochemistry (PhD); computational chemistry (PhD); inorganic chemistry (PhD); materials chemistry (PhD); organic chemistry (PhD); theoretical chemistry (PhD). Terminal master's awarded for partial completion of doctoral program. *Degree requirements:* For doctorate, comprehensive exam, thesis/dissertation. *Entrance requirements:* For doctorate, GRE General Test. Additional exam requirements/recommendations for international students: Required—TOEFL.

The George Washington University, Columbian College of Arts and Sciences, Department of Chemistry, Washington, DC 20052. Offers analytical chemistry (MS, PhD); inorganic chemistry (MS, PhD); materials science (MS, PhD); organic chemistry (MS, PhD); physical chemistry (MS, PhD). *Program availability:* Part-time, evening/weekend. *Students:* 29 full-time (15 women), 8 part-time (5 women); includes 3 minority (1 Black or African American, non-Hispanic/Latino; 2 Hispanic/Latino), 5 international. Average age 27. 96 applicants, 47% accepted, 9 enrolled. In 2018, 9 master's, 6 doctorates awarded. Terminal master's awarded for partial completion of doctoral program. *Degree requirements:* For master's, comprehensive exam, thesis or alternative; for doctorate, thesis/dissertation, general exam. *Entrance requirements:* For master's and doctorate, GRE General Test, interview, minimum GPA of 3.0. Additional exam requirements/recommendations for international students: Required—TOEFL (minimum score 550 paper-based; 80 iBT). *Application deadline:* For fall admission, 1/15 priority date for domestic and international students; for spring admission, 9/1 priority date for domestic and international students. Applications are processed on a rolling basis. Application fee: $75. Electronic applications accepted. *Financial support:* In 2018–19, 27 students received support. Fellowships, research assistantships, teaching assistantships, Federal Work-Study, and tuition waivers available. Financial award application deadline: 1/15. *Unit head:* Dr. Michael King, Chair, 202-994-6488. *Application contact:* Information Contact, 202-994-6121, E-mail: gwchem@gwu.edu.
Website: http://chemistry.columbian.gwu.edu/

Georgia State University, College of Arts and Sciences, Department of Chemistry, Atlanta, GA 30302-3083. Offers analytical chemistry (MS, PhD); biochemistry (MS, PhD); bioinformatics (MS, PhD); biophysical chemistry (PhD); computational chemistry (MS, PhD); geochemistry (PhD); organic/medicinal chemistry (MS, PhD); physical chemistry (MS). PhD in geochemistry offered jointly with Department of Geosciences. *Program availability:* Part-time. *Faculty:* 27 full-time (6 women), 1 part-time/adjunct (0 women). *Students:* 147 full-time (59 women), 15 part-time (10 women); includes 37 minority (21 Black or African American, non-Hispanic/Latino; 7 Asian, non-Hispanic/Latino; 4 Hispanic/Latino; 5 Two or more races, non-Hispanic/Latino), 84 international. Average age 29. 106 applicants, 40% accepted, 28 enrolled. In 2018, 37 master's, 13 doctorates awarded. Terminal master's awarded for partial completion of doctoral program. *Degree requirements:* For master's, one foreign language, comprehensive exam (for some programs), thesis (for some programs); for doctorate, one foreign language, comprehensive exam, thesis/dissertation. *Entrance requirements:* For master's and doctorate, GRE. *Application deadline:* For fall admission, 7/1 priority date for domestic and international students; for winter admission, 11/15 priority date for domestic and international students; for spring admission, 4/15 priority date for domestic and international students. Applications are processed on a rolling basis. Application fee: $50. Electronic applications accepted. *Expenses: Tuition, area resident:* Full-time $9360; part-time $390 per credit hour. Tuition, state resident: full-time $9360; part-time $390 per credit hour. Tuition, nonresident: full-time $30,024; part-time $1251 per credit hour. *International tuition:* $30,024 full-time. *Required fees:* $2128. *Financial support:* Fellowships with full tuition reimbursements, research assistantships with full tuition reimbursements, and teaching assistantships with full tuition reimbursements available. Financial award applicants required to submit FAFSA. *Faculty research:* Analytical chemistry, biological/biochemistry, biophysical/computational chemistry, chemical education, organic/medicinal chemistry. *Unit head:* Dr. Donald Hamelberg, Professor; Chair, 404-413-5564, Fax: 404-413-5505, E-mail: dhamelberg@gsu.edu. *Application contact:* Dr. Donald Hamelberg, Professor; Chair, 404-413-5564, Fax: 404-413-5505, E-mail: dhamelberg@gsu.edu.
Website: http://chemistry.gsu.edu/

Governors State University, College of Arts and Sciences, Program in Analytical Chemistry, University Park, IL 60484. Offers MS. *Program availability:* Part-time. *Faculty:* 39 full-time (14 women), 29 part-time/adjunct (12 women). *Students:* 3 full-time (0 women), 6 part-time (2 women); includes 3 minority (2 Black or African American, non-Hispanic/Latino; 1 Hispanic/Latino). Average age 31. 16 applicants, 69% accepted, 5 enrolled. In 2018, 6 master's awarded. *Application deadline:* For fall admission, 4/1 for domestic students. Applications are processed on a rolling basis. Application fee: $50. Electronic applications accepted. *Financial support:* Application deadline: 5/1; applicants required to submit FAFSA. *Unit head:* Mary Carrington, Interim Chair, Division of Science, Mathematics, and Technology, 708-534-5000 Ext. 4532, E-mail: mcarrington@govst.edu. *Application contact:* Mary Carrington, Interim Chair, Division of Science, Mathematics, and Technology, 708-534-5000 Ext. 4532, E-mail: mcarrington@govst.edu.

Howard University, Graduate School, Department of Chemistry, Washington, DC 20059-0002. Offers analytical chemistry (MS, PhD); atmospheric (MS, PhD); biochemistry (MS, PhD); environmental (MS, PhD); inorganic chemistry (MS, PhD); organic chemistry (MS, PhD); physical chemistry (MS, PhD). Terminal master's awarded for partial completion of doctoral program. *Degree requirements:* For master's, comprehensive exam, thesis, teaching experience; for doctorate, comprehensive exam, thesis/dissertation, teaching experience. *Entrance requirements:* For master's, GRE General Test, minimum GPA of 2.7; for doctorate, GRE General Test, minimum GPA of 3.0. Additional exam requirements/recommendations for international students: Required—TOEFL. Electronic applications accepted. *Faculty research:* Synthetic organics, materials, natural products, mass spectrometry.

Illinois Institute of Technology, Graduate College, College of Science, Department of Chemistry, Chicago, IL 60616. Offers analytical chemistry (MAS); chemistry (MAS, MS, PhD); materials chemistry (MAS), including inorganic, organic, or polymeric materials. *Program availability:* Part-time, evening/weekend, online learning. Terminal master's awarded for partial completion of doctoral program. *Degree requirements:* For master's, comprehensive exam, thesis (for some programs); for doctorate, comprehensive exam, thesis/dissertation. *Entrance requirements:* For master's, GRE General Test (minimum score 300 Quantitative and Verbal, 2.5 Analytical Writing), minimum undergraduate GPA of 3.0; for doctorate, GRE General Test (minimum score 310 Quantitative and Verbal, 3.0 Analytical Writing), GRE Subject Test, minimum undergraduate GPA of 3.0. Additional exam requirements/recommendations for international students: Required—TOEFL (minimum score 550 paper-based; 80 iBT); Recommended—IELTS. Electronic applications accepted. *Faculty research:* Materials science, biological chemistry, synthetic chemistry, computational chemistry, energy, sensor science and technology, scholarship of teaching and learning.

Indiana University Bloomington, University Graduate School, College of Arts and Sciences, Department of Chemistry, Bloomington, IN 47405. Offers analytical chemistry (PhD); chemical biology (PhD); chemistry (MAT); inorganic chemistry (PhD); materials chemistry (PhD); organic chemistry (PhD); physical chemistry (PhD); MSES/MS. Terminal master's awarded for partial completion of doctoral program. *Degree requirements:* For master's, thesis; for doctorate, thesis/dissertation. *Entrance requirements:* For master's and doctorate, GRE General Test, GRE Subject Test. Additional exam requirements/recommendations for international students: Required—TOEFL. Electronic applications accepted. *Faculty research:* Synthesis of complex natural products, organic reaction mechanisms, organic electrochemistry, transitive-metal chemistry, solid-state and surface chemistry.

Iowa State University of Science and Technology, Program in Analytical Chemistry, Ames, IA 50011. Offers MS, PhD. *Entrance requirements:* For doctorate, official academic transcripts, resume, three letters of recommendation. Additional exam requirements/recommendations for international students: Required—TOEFL (minimum score 570 paper-based; 89 iBT), IELTS (minimum score 6.5). Electronic applications accepted.

Laurentian University, School of Graduate Studies and Research, Programme in Chemistry and Biochemistry, Sudbury, ON P3E 2C6, Canada. Offers analytical chemistry (M Sc); biochemistry (M Sc); environmental chemistry (M Sc); organic chemistry (M Sc); physical/theoretical chemistry (M Sc). *Program availability:* Part-time. *Degree requirements:* For master's, thesis or alternative. *Entrance requirements:* For master's, honors degree with minimum second class. *Faculty research:* Cell cycle checkpoints, kinetic modeling, toxicology to metal stress, quantum chemistry, biogeochemistry metal speciation.

Marquette University, Graduate School, College of Arts and Sciences, Department of Chemistry, Milwaukee, WI 53201-1881. Offers analytical chemistry (MS, PhD); bioanalytical chemistry (MS, PhD); biophysical chemistry (MS, PhD); chemical physics (MS, PhD); inorganic chemistry (MS, PhD); organic chemistry (MS, PhD); physical chemistry (MS, PhD). *Program availability:* Part-time. Terminal master's awarded for partial completion of doctoral program. *Degree requirements:* For master's, comprehensive exam; for doctorate, thesis/dissertation, cumulative exams. *Entrance requirements:* For master's and doctorate, official transcripts from all current and previous colleges/universities except Marquette, three letters of recommendation from individuals familiar with the applicant's academic work. Additional exam requirements/recommendations for international students: Required—TOEFL. Electronic applications accepted. *Faculty research:* Inorganic complexes, laser Raman spectroscopy, organic synthesis, synthetic bioinorganic chemistry, electro-active organic molecules.

McMaster University, School of Graduate Studies, Faculty of Science, Department of Chemistry, Hamilton, ON L8S 4M2, Canada. Offers analytical chemistry (M Sc, PhD); chemical physics (M Sc, PhD); chemistry (M Sc, PhD); inorganic chemistry (M Sc, PhD); organic chemistry (M Sc, PhD); physical chemistry (M Sc, PhD); polymer chemistry (M Sc, PhD). *Program availability:* Part-time. Terminal master's awarded for partial completion of doctoral program. *Degree requirements:* For master's, thesis; for doctorate, comprehensive exam, thesis/dissertation. *Entrance requirements:* For master's, minimum B+ average. Additional exam requirements/recommendations for international students: Required—TOEFL (minimum score 550 paper-based).

Old Dominion University, College of Sciences, Program in Chemistry, Norfolk, VA 23529. Offers analytical chemistry (MS, PhD); biochemistry (MS, PhD); environmental chemistry (MS, PhD); inorganic chemistry (MS, PhD); organic chemistry (MS, PhD); physical chemistry (MS, PhD). *Program availability:* Part-time. Terminal master's awarded for partial completion of doctoral program. *Degree requirements:* For master's, comprehensive exam, thesis (for some programs); for doctorate, comprehensive exam, thesis/dissertation. *Entrance requirements:* For master's and doctorate, GRE General Test, minimum GPA of 3.0 in major, 2.5 overall, transcripts, essay, three letters of recommendation, resume. Additional exam requirements/recommendations for international students: Required—TOEFL (minimum score 84 iBT). Electronic applications accepted. *Expenses:* Contact institution. *Faculty research:* Biogeochemistry, materials chemistry, computational chemistry, organic chemistry, biofuels.

Oregon State University, College of Science, Program in Chemistry, Corvallis, OR 97331. Offers analytical chemistry (MA, MS, PhD). Terminal master's awarded for partial completion of doctoral program. *Degree requirements:* For master's, thesis (for some programs); for doctorate, thesis/dissertation. *Entrance requirements:* For master's and doctorate, GRE, minimum GPA of 3.0 in last 90 hours of course work. Additional exam requirements/recommendations for international students: Required—TOEFL (minimum score 80 iBT), IELTS (minimum score 6.5). *Faculty research:* Solid state chemistry, enzyme reaction mechanisms, structure and dynamics of gas molecules, chemiluminescence, nonlinear optical spectroscopy.

Purdue University, Graduate School, College of Science, Department of Chemistry, West Lafayette, IN 47907. Offers analytical chemistry (PhD); biochemistry (MS, PhD); chemical education (MS, PhD); inorganic chemistry (MS, PhD); organic chemistry (MS, PhD); physical chemistry (PhD). *Faculty:* 47 full-time (13 women), 2 part-time/adjunct (0 women). *Students:* 314 full-time (124 women), 18 part-time (13 women); includes 63 minority (16 Black or African American, non-Hispanic/Latino; 15 Asian, non-Hispanic/Latino; 25 Hispanic/Latino; 7 Two or more races, non-Hispanic/Latino), 146 international. Average age 26. 711 applicants, 27% accepted, 64 enrolled. In 2018, 9 master's, 50 doctorates awarded. Terminal master's awarded for partial completion of doctoral program. *Degree requirements:* For master's, thesis; for doctorate, comprehensive exam, thesis/dissertation. *Entrance requirements:* For master's and doctorate, minimum undergraduate GPA of 3.0. Additional exam requirements/recommendations for international students: Required—TOEFL (minimum score 550 paper-based; 77 iBT); Recommended—TWE. *Application deadline:* For fall admission, 2/15 priority date for domestic students, 1/1 for international students. Applications are processed on a rolling basis. Application fee: $60 ($75 for international students). Electronic applications accepted. *Financial support:* In 2018–19, 2 fellowships with partial tuition reimbursements (averaging $18,000 per year), 55 teaching assistantships with partial tuition reimbursements (averaging $18,000 per year) were awarded; research assistantships with partial tuition reimbursements and tuition waivers (partial) also available. Support available to part-time students. Financial award applicants required to submit FAFSA. *Unit head:* Christine A. Hrycyna, Head, 765-494-5203, E-mail: hrycyna@purdue.edu. *Application contact:* Betty L. Hatfield, Director of Graduate Admissions, 765-494-5208, E-mail: bettyh@purdue.edu.
Website: https://www.chem.purdue.edu/

Rutgers University–Newark, Graduate School, Program in Chemistry, Newark, NJ 07102. Offers analytical chemistry (MS, PhD); biochemistry (MS, PhD); inorganic chemistry (MS, PhD); organic chemistry (MS, PhD); physical chemistry (MS, PhD). *Program availability:* Part-time, evening/weekend. Terminal master's awarded for partial completion of doctoral program. *Degree requirements:* For master's, thesis optional, cumulative exams; for doctorate, thesis/dissertation, exams, research proposal. *Entrance requirements:* For master's and doctorate, GRE General Test, minimum undergraduate B average. Additional exam requirements/recommendations for international students: Required—TOEFL. Electronic applications accepted. *Faculty research:* Medicinal chemistry, natural products, isotope effects, biophysics and biorganic approaches to enzyme mechanisms, organic and organometallic synthesis.

Seton Hall University, College of Arts and Sciences, Department of Chemistry and Biochemistry, South Orange, NJ 07079-2697. Offers analytical chemistry (MS, PhD); biochemistry (MS, PhD); chemistry (MS); inorganic chemistry (MS, PhD); organic chemistry (MS, PhD); physical chemistry (MS, PhD). *Program availability:* Part-time, evening/weekend. Terminal master's awarded for partial completion of doctoral program. *Degree requirements:* For master's, thesis optional; for doctorate, comprehensive exam, thesis/dissertation. *Entrance requirements:* Additional exam requirements/recommendations for international students: Required—TOEFL. Electronic applications accepted. *Faculty research:* DNA metal reactions; chromatography; bioinorganic, biophysical, organometallic, polymer chemistry; heterogeneous catalyst; synthetic organic and carbohydrate chemistry.

Southern University and Agricultural and Mechanical College, Graduate School, College of Sciences and Engineering, Program in Chemistry, Baton Rouge, LA 70813. Offers analytical chemistry (MS); biochemistry (MS); environmental sciences (MS); inorganic chemistry (MS); organic chemistry (MS); physical chemistry (MS). *Degree requirements:* For master's, thesis. *Entrance requirements:* For master's, GMAT or GRE General Test. Additional exam requirements/recommendations for international students: Required—TOEFL (minimum score 525 paper-based). *Faculty research:* Synthesis of macrocyclic ligands, latex accelerators, anticancer drugs, biosensors, absorption isotheums, isolation of specific enzymes from plants.

University of Calgary, Faculty of Graduate Studies, Faculty of Science, Program in Chemistry, Calgary, AB T2N 1N4, Canada. Offers analytical chemistry (M Sc, PhD); applied chemistry (M Sc, PhD); inorganic chemistry (M Sc, PhD); organic chemistry (M Sc, PhD); physical chemistry (M Sc, PhD); polymer chemistry (M Sc, PhD); theoretical chemistry (M Sc, PhD). *Degree requirements:* For master's, thesis; for doctorate, thesis/dissertation, candidacy exam. *Entrance requirements:* For master's, minimum GPA of 3.0; for doctorate, honors B Sc degree with minimum GPA of 3.7 or M Sc with minimum GPA of 3.3. Additional exam requirements/recommendations for international students: Required—TOEFL (minimum score 580 paper-based). Electronic applications accepted. *Faculty research:* Chemical analysis, chemical dynamics, synthesis theory.

University of Cincinnati, Graduate School, McMicken College of Arts and Sciences, Department of Chemistry, Cincinnati, OH 45221. Offers analytical chemistry (MS, PhD); biochemistry (MS, PhD); inorganic chemistry (MS, PhD); organic chemistry (MS, PhD); physical chemistry (MS, PhD); polymer chemistry (MS, PhD); sensors (PhD). *Program availability:* Part-time, evening/weekend. Terminal master's awarded for partial completion of doctoral program. *Degree requirements:* For master's, thesis optional; for doctorate, comprehensive exam, thesis/dissertation. *Entrance requirements:* For master's and doctorate, GRE General Test. Additional exam requirements/recommendations for international students: Required—TOEFL (minimum score 580 paper-based). Electronic applications accepted. *Faculty research:* Biomedical chemistry, laser chemistry, surface science, chemical sensors, synthesis.

University of Georgia, Franklin College of Arts and Sciences, Department of Chemistry, Athens, GA 30602. Offers analytical chemistry (MS, PhD). Terminal master's awarded for partial completion of doctoral program. *Degree requirements:* For master's, thesis; for doctorate, one foreign language, thesis/dissertation. *Entrance requirements:* For master's and doctorate, GRE General Test. Additional exam requirements/recommendations for international students: Required—TOEFL. Electronic applications accepted.

University of Louisville, Graduate School, College of Arts and Sciences, Department of Chemistry, Louisville, KY 40292-0001. Offers analytical chemistry (MS, PhD); biochemistry (MS, PhD); chemical physics (PhD); inorganic chemistry (MS, PhD); organic chemistry (MS, PhD); physical chemistry (MS, PhD). *Faculty:* 26 full-time (9 women), 3 part-time/adjunct (1 woman). *Students:* 35 full-time (14 women), 17 part-time (4 women); includes 5 minority (2 Black or African American, non-Hispanic/Latino; 3 Asian, non-Hispanic/Latino), 39 international. Average age 31. 47 applicants, 36% accepted, 10 enrolled. In 2018, 18 master's, 3 doctorates awarded. Terminal master's awarded for partial completion of doctoral program. *Degree requirements:* For master's, thesis (for some programs), Literature Seminars; for doctorate, thesis/dissertation, Cumulative Exams, Literature Seminars; Research. *Entrance requirements:* For master's and doctorate, GRE General Test, official transcripts, recommendation letters (minimum of 2), personal statement. Additional exam requirements/recommendations for international students: Required—TOEFL (minimum score 550 paper-based; 79 iBT), IELTS can be taken in place of TOEFL; Recommended—IELTS (minimum score 6.5). *Application deadline:* For fall admission, 1/15 priority date for domestic and international students; for spring admission, 9/15 priority date for domestic and international students. Application fee: $65. Electronic applications accepted. *Expenses: Tuition, area resident:* Full-time $6500; part-time $723 per credit hour. Tuition, state resident: full-time $6500.

Tuition, nonresident: full-time $13,557; part-time $1507 per credit hour. Tuition and fees vary according to course load and program. *Financial support:* In 2018–19, 59 students received support, including 2 fellowships with full tuition reimbursements available (averaging $23,000 per year), 10 research assistantships with full tuition reimbursements available (averaging $23,000 per year), 41 teaching assistantships with full tuition reimbursements available (averaging $23,000 per year); scholarships/grants, health care benefits, and unspecified assistantships also available. Financial award application deadline: 1/15. *Faculty research:* Solid state chemistry, chemical synthesis, nanoparticle research, green chemistry, spectroscopic studies, computational chemistry, catalysis. *Total annual research expenditures:* $1 million. *Unit head:* Dr. Craig Grapperhaus, Professor, 502-852-8148, Fax: 502-852-8149, E-mail: craig.grapperhaus@louisville.edu. *Application contact:* Sherry Nalley, Graduate Program Assistant, 502-852-6798, Fax: 502-852-6536, E-mail: sherry.nalley@louisville.edu.
Website: http://louisville.edu/chemistry

The University of Manchester, School of Chemical Engineering and Analytical Science, Manchester, United Kingdom. Offers biocatalysis (M Phil, PhD); chemical engineering (M Phil, PhD); chemical engineering and analytical science (M Phil, D Eng, PhD); colloids, crystals, interfaces and materials (M Phil, PhD); environment and sustainable technology (M Phil, PhD); instrumentation (M Phil, PhD); multi-scale modeling (M Phil, PhD); process integration (M Phil, PhD); systems biology (M Phil, PhD).

University of Maryland, College Park, Academic Affairs, College of Computer, Mathematical and Natural Sciences, Department of Chemistry and Biochemistry, Chemistry Program, College Park, MD 20742. Offers analytical chemistry (MS, PhD); inorganic chemistry (MS, PhD); organic chemistry (MS, PhD); physical chemistry (MS, PhD). *Program availability:* Part-time, evening/weekend. Terminal master's awarded for partial completion of doctoral program. *Degree requirements:* For master's, thesis optional; for doctorate, thesis/dissertation, 2 seminar presentations, oral exam. *Entrance requirements:* For master's and doctorate, GRE General Test, GRE Subject Test (recommended), minimum GPA of 3.0, 3 letters of recommendation. Additional exam requirements/recommendations for international students: Required—TOEFL. Electronic applications accepted. *Faculty research:* Environmental chemistry, nuclear chemistry, lunar and environmental analysis, X-ray crystallography.

University of Massachusetts Lowell, College of Sciences, Department of Chemistry, Lowell, MA 01854. Offers analytical chemistry (PhD); biochemistry (PhD); chemistry (MS, PhD); environmental studies (PhD); green chemistry (PhD); inorganic chemistry (PhD); organic chemistry (PhD); polymer science (MS). Terminal master's awarded for partial completion of doctoral program. *Degree requirements:* For master's, thesis; for doctorate, 2 foreign languages, thesis/dissertation. *Entrance requirements:* For master's and doctorate, GRE General Test. Electronic applications accepted.

University of Memphis, Graduate School, College of Arts and Sciences, Department of Chemistry, Memphis, TN 38152. Offers analytical chemistry (MS, PhD); computational chemistry (MS, PhD); inorganic chemistry (MS, PhD); organic chemistry (MS, PhD); physical chemistry (MS, PhD). *Program availability:* Part-time. *Students:* 37 full-time (11 women), 14 part-time (5 women); includes 9 minority (2 Black or African American, non-Hispanic/Latino; 3 Asian, non-Hispanic/Latino; 4 Two or more races, non-Hispanic/Latino), 6 international. Average age 27. 24 applicants, 67% accepted, 14 enrolled. In 2018, 9 master's, 3 doctorates awarded. Terminal master's awarded for partial completion of doctoral program. *Degree requirements:* For master's, comprehensive exam, thesis or alternative; for doctorate, comprehensive exam, thesis/dissertation. *Entrance requirements:* For master's and doctorate, GRE General Test, admission to Graduate School plus 32 undergraduate hours in chemistry. Additional exam requirements/recommendations for international students: Required—TOEFL (minimum score 550 paper-based). *Application deadline:* For fall admission, 7/1 for domestic students, 5/1 for international students; for winter admission, 9/15 for international students; for spring admission, 12/1 for domestic students. Applications are processed on a rolling basis. Application fee: $35 ($60 for international students). Electronic applications accepted. *Expenses: Tuition, area resident:* Full-time $10,240; part-time $503 per credit hour. Tuition, state resident: full-time $10,464. Tuition, nonresident: full-time $20,224; part-time $991 per credit hour. *Required fees:* $850; $106 per credit hour. *Financial support:* Research assistantships with full tuition reimbursements, teaching assistantships with full tuition reimbursements, Federal Work-Study, scholarships/grants, and unspecified assistantships available. Financial award application deadline: 2/1; financial award applicants required to submit FAFSA. *Faculty research:* Computational chemistry, materials chemistry, organic/polymer synthesis, drug design/delivery, water chemistry. *Unit head:* Dr. Gary Emmert, Chair, 901-678-2638, Fax: 901-678-3447, E-mail: gemmert@memphis.edu. *Application contact:* Dr. Paul Simone, Coordinator of Graduate Studies, 901-678-3671, Fax: 901-678-3447, E-mail: gradchem@memphis.edu.
Website: http://www.memphis.edu/chem/

University of Michigan, Rackham Graduate School, College of Literature, Science, and the Arts, Department of Chemistry, Ann Arbor, MI 48109-1055. Offers analytical chemistry (PhD); chemical biology (PhD); chemical sciences (MS); inorganic chemistry (PhD); materials chemistry (PhD); organic chemistry (PhD); physical chemistry (PhD). *Program availability:* Part-time. *Faculty:* 40 full-time (14 women), 7 part-time/adjunct (3 women). *Students:* 262 full-time (112 women), 4 part-time (all women); includes 44 minority (11 Black or African American, non-Hispanic/Latino; 11 Asian, non-Hispanic/Latino; 19 Hispanic/Latino; 1 Native Hawaiian or other Pacific Islander, non-Hispanic/Latino; 2 Two or more races, non-Hispanic/Latino), 61 international. 692 applicants, 71 enrolled. In 2018, 47 master's, 46 doctorates awarded. *Degree requirements:* For doctorate, comprehensive exam, thesis/dissertation, oral defense of dissertation, organic cumulative proficiency exams. *Entrance requirements:* For master's, bachelor's degree, 3 letters of recommendation, personal statement; for doctorate, bachelor's degree, 3 letters of recommendation, personal statement, curriculum vitae/resume. Additional exam requirements/recommendations for international students: Required—TOEFL (minimum score 560 paper-based; 84 iBT) or IELTS. *Application deadline:* For fall admission, 12/1 for domestic and international students. Application fee: $0 ($90 for international students). Electronic applications accepted. *Financial support:* In 2018–19, 269 students received support, including 50 fellowships with full tuition reimbursements available (averaging $31,625 per year), 84 research assistantships with full tuition reimbursements available (averaging $31,625 per year), 133 teaching assistantships with full tuition reimbursements available (averaging $31,625 per year); career-related internships or fieldwork, Federal Work-Study, scholarships/grants, traineeships, health care benefits, tuition waivers (full), and unspecified assistantships also available. *Faculty research:* Biological catalysis, protein engineering, chemical sensors, de novo metalloprotein design, supramolecular architecture. *Total annual research expenditures:* $19.6 million. *Unit head:* Dr. Robert Kennedy, Professor of Chemistry/Chair, 734-763-9681, Fax: 734-647-4847. *Application contact:* Elizabeth Oxford, Graduate Program Coordinator, 734-764-7278, Fax: 734-647-4865, E-mail: chemadmissions@umich.edu.
Website: http://www.lsa.umich.edu/chem/

University of Missouri, Office of Research and Graduate Studies, College of Arts and Science, Department of Chemistry, Columbia, MO 65211. Offers analytical chemistry (PhD). *Degree requirements:* For doctorate, one foreign language, comprehensive exam, thesis/dissertation. *Entrance requirements:* For doctorate, GRE General Test (minimum score: Verbal 450, Quantitative 600, Analytical 3), minimum GPA of 3.0. Additional exam requirements/recommendations for international students: Required—TOEFL (minimum score 600 paper-based; 100 iBT). Electronic applications accepted.

University of Missouri–Kansas City, College of Arts and Sciences, Department of Chemistry, Kansas City, MO 64110-2499. Offers analytical chemistry (PhD); inorganic chemistry (PhD); organic chemistry (PhD); physical chemistry (PhD); polymer chemistry (MS, PhD). PhD (interdisciplinary) offered through the School of Graduate Studies. *Program availability:* Part-time, evening/weekend. *Degree requirements:* For master's, thesis (for some programs); for doctorate, thesis/dissertation. *Entrance requirements:* For master's, equivalent of American Chemical Society approved bachelor's degree in chemistry; for doctorate, GRE General Test, equivalent of American Chemical Society approved bachelor's degree in chemistry. Additional exam requirements/recommendations for international students: Required—TOEFL (minimum score 550 paper-based; 80 iBT), TWE. Electronic applications accepted. *Faculty research:* Molecular spectroscopy, characterization and synthesis of materials and compounds, computational chemistry, natural products, drug delivery systems and anti-tumor agents.

University of Montana, Graduate School, College of Humanities and Sciences, Department of Chemistry and Biochemistry, Missoula, MT 59812. Offers chemistry (MS, PhD), including environmental/analytical chemistry, inorganic chemistry, organic chemistry, physical chemistry. Terminal master's awarded for partial completion of doctoral program. *Degree requirements:* For master's, thesis (for some programs); for doctorate, thesis/dissertation. *Entrance requirements:* For master's and doctorate, GRE General Test. Additional exam requirements/recommendations for international students: Required—TOEFL (minimum score 575 paper-based). *Faculty research:* Reaction mechanisms and kinetics, inorganic and organic synthesis, analytical chemistry, natural products.

University of Nebraska–Lincoln, Graduate College, College of Arts and Sciences, Department of Chemistry, Lincoln, NE 68588. Offers analytical chemistry (PhD); biochemistry (PhD); chemistry (MS); inorganic chemistry (PhD); materials chemistry (PhD); organic chemistry (PhD); physical chemistry (PhD). *Degree requirements:* For master's, one foreign language, thesis optional, departmental qualifying exam; for doctorate, one foreign language, comprehensive exam, thesis/dissertation, departmental qualifying exams. *Entrance requirements:* For master's and doctorate, GRE. Additional exam requirements/recommendations for international students: Required—TOEFL (minimum score 550 paper-based). Electronic applications accepted. *Faculty research:* Bioorganic and bioinorganic chemistry, biophysical and bioanalytical chemistry, structure-function of DNA and proteins, organometallics, mass spectrometry.

University of Oklahoma, College of Arts and Sciences, Department of Chemistry and Biochemistry, Norman, OK 73019. Offers chemistry (MS, PhD), including analytical chemistry, biochemistry, chemical education, inorganic chemistry, inter-and/or multidisciplinary, organic chemistry, physical chemistry, structural biology. *Program availability:* Part-time. *Faculty:* 32 full-time (13 women). *Students:* 89 full-time (38 women), 33 part-time (15 women); includes 22 minority (2 Black or African American, non-Hispanic/Latino; 9 Asian, non-Hispanic/Latino; 6 Hispanic/Latino; 5 Two or more races, non-Hispanic/Latino), 46 international. Average age 26. 78 applicants, 71% accepted, 33 enrolled. In 2018, 15 master's, 21 doctorates awarded. Terminal master's awarded for partial completion of doctoral program. *Degree requirements:* For master's, comprehensive exam (for some programs), thesis (for some programs); for doctorate, comprehensive exam, thesis/dissertation, general exam. *Entrance requirements:* For master's and doctorate, GRE. Additional exam requirements/recommendations for international students: Required—TOEFL (minimum score 79 iBT) or IELTS (minimum score 6.5). *Application deadline:* For fall admission, 3/31 priority date for domestic and international students; for spring admission, 9/1 priority date for domestic and international students. Application fee: $50 ($100 for international students). Electronic applications accepted. *Expenses:* Tuition, state resident: full-time $5683.20; part-time $236.80 per credit hour. Tuition, nonresident: full-time $20,342; part-time $847.60 per credit hour. *International tuition:* $20,342.40 full-time. *Required fees:* $2894.20; $110.05 per credit hour. $126.50 per semester. Tuition and fees vary according to course load and program. *Financial support:* Research assistantships, teaching assistantships, institutionally sponsored loans, scholarships/grants, health care benefits, unspecified assistantships, and full tuition with qualifying graduate assistantship available. Support available to part-time students. Financial award application deadline: 6/1; financial award applicants required to submit FAFSA. *Faculty research:* Structural biology, solid state materials, natural products, membrane biochemistry, bioanalysis. *Unit head:* Dr. Ronald L. Halterman, Professor and Chair, 405-325-4812, Fax: 405-325-6111, E-mail: rhalterman@ou.edu. *Application contact:* Carol Jones, Operations Manager, 405-325-4811, Fax: 405-325-6111, E-mail: caroljones@ou.edu.
Website: http://www.ou.edu/cas/chemistry

University of Regina, Faculty of Graduate Studies and Research, Faculty of Science, Department of Chemistry and Biochemistry, Regina, SK S4S 0A2, Canada. Offers biophysics of biological interfaces (M Sc, PhD); computational chemistry (M Sc, PhD); environmental analytical chemistry (M Sc, PhD); enzymology/chemical biology (M Sc, PhD); inorganic/organometallic chemistry (M Sc, PhD); signal transduction and mechanisms of cancer cell regulation (M Sc, PhD); supramolecular organic photochemistry and photophysics (M Sc, PhD); synthetic organic chemistry (M Sc, PhD). *Program availability:* Part-time. *Faculty:* 12 full-time (2 women), 4 part-time/adjunct (0 women). *Students:* 12 full-time (6 women), 1 part-time (0 women). Average age 30. 23 applicants, 17% accepted. In 2018, 2 master's awarded. *Degree requirements:* For master's, thesis; for doctorate, comprehensive exam, thesis/dissertation. *Entrance requirements:* For master's, 4 years Bachelor degree in Chemistry or related program; for doctorate, completion of Master's in Chemistry. Additional exam requirements/recommendations for international students: Required—TOEFL (minimum score 580 paper-based; 80 iBT), IELTS (minimum score 6.5), PTE (minimum score 59), other options are CAEL, MELAB, Cantest and U of R ESL. *Application deadline:* Applications are processed on a rolling basis. Application fee: $100. Electronic applications accepted. Tuition and fees vary according to course level, course load, degree level and program. *Financial support:* Fellowships, research assistantships, teaching assistantships, career-related internships or fieldwork, Federal Work-Study, scholarships/grants, unspecified assistantships, and travel award & Graduate Scholarship Base Funds available. Support available to part-time students. Financial award application deadline: 9/30. *Faculty research:* Asymmetric synthesis and methodology, theoretical and computational chemistry, biophysical biochemistry, analytical and environmental chemistry, chemical biology. *Unit head:* Dr. Renata Raina-Fulton, Department Head, 306-585-4012, Fax: 306-337-2409, E-mail: renata.raina@uregina.ca. *Application contact:* Dr. Brian Sterenberg, Graduate Program Coordinator, 306-585-4106, Fax: 306-337-2409, E-mail: brian.sterenberg@uregina.ca.
Website: http://www.uregina.ca/science/chem-biochem/

The University of Tennessee, Graduate School, College of Arts and Sciences, Department of Chemistry, Knoxville, TN 37996. Offers analytical chemistry (MS, PhD); chemical physics (PhD); environmental chemistry (MS, PhD); inorganic chemistry (MS, PhD); organic chemistry (MS, PhD); physical chemistry (MS, PhD); polymer chemistry (MS, PhD); theoretical chemistry (PhD). *Program availability:* Part-time. Terminal master's awarded for partial completion of doctoral program. *Degree requirements:* For master's, thesis; for doctorate, thesis/dissertation. *Entrance requirements:* For master's and doctorate, GRE General Test, minimum GPA of 2.7. Additional exam requirements/recommendations for international students: Required—TOEFL. Electronic applications accepted.

The University of Texas at Austin, Graduate School, College of Natural Sciences, Department of Chemistry and Biochemistry, Austin, TX 78712-1111. Offers analytical chemistry (PhD); biochemistry (PhD); inorganic chemistry (PhD); organic chemistry (PhD); physical chemistry (PhD). *Entrance requirements:* For doctorate, GRE General Test.

The University of Toledo, College of Graduate Studies, College of Natural Sciences and Mathematics, Department of Chemistry, Toledo, OH 43606-3390. Offers analytical chemistry (MS, PhD); biological chemistry (MS, PhD); inorganic chemistry (MS, PhD); organic chemistry (MS, PhD); physical chemistry (MS, PhD). *Program availability:* Part-time. *Degree requirements:* For master's, thesis or alternative; for doctorate, thesis/dissertation. *Entrance requirements:* For master's and doctorate, GRE General Test, GRE Subject Test, minimum cumulative point-hour ratio of 2.7 for all previous academic work, three letters of recommendation, statement of purpose, transcripts from all prior institutions attended. Additional exam requirements/recommendations for international students: Required—TOEFL (minimum score 550 paper-based; 80 iBT). Electronic applications accepted. *Faculty research:* Enzymology, materials chemistry, crystallography, theoretical chemistry.

Virginia Commonwealth University, Graduate School, College of Humanities and Sciences, Department of Chemistry, Richmond, VA 23284-9005. Offers analytical chemistry (MS, PhD); chemical physics (PhD); inorganic chemistry (MS, PhD); organic chemistry (MS, PhD); physical chemistry (MS, PhD). *Program availability:* Part-time. Terminal master's awarded for partial completion of doctoral program. *Degree requirements:* For master's, thesis; for doctorate, thesis/dissertation, comprehensive cumulative exams, research proposal. *Entrance requirements:* For master's, GRE General Test, 30 undergraduate credits in chemistry; for doctorate, GRE General Test. Additional exam requirements/recommendations for international students: Required—TOEFL (minimum score 600 paper-based; 100 iBT) or IELTS (minimum score 6.5). Electronic applications accepted. *Faculty research:* Physical, organic, inorganic, analytical, and polymer chemistry; chemical physics.

Wake Forest University, Graduate School of Arts and Sciences, Department of Chemistry, Winston-Salem, NC 27109. Offers analytical chemistry (MS, PhD); inorganic chemistry (MS, PhD); organic chemistry (MS, PhD); physical chemistry (MS, PhD).

Program availability: Part-time. *Degree requirements:* For master's, one foreign language, comprehensive exam, thesis; for doctorate, 2 foreign languages, comprehensive exam, thesis/dissertation. *Entrance requirements:* For master's and doctorate, GRE General Test. Additional exam requirements/recommendations for international students: Required—TOEFL. Electronic applications accepted.

Wayne State University, College of Liberal Arts and Sciences, Department of Chemistry, Detroit, MI 48202. Offers analytical chemistry (PhD); chemistry (MA, MS). *Faculty:* 33. *Students:* 121 full-time (49 women), 3 part-time (all women); includes 12 minority (1 Black or African American, non-Hispanic/Latino; 2 Asian, non-Hispanic/Latino; 5 Hispanic/Latino; 1 Native Hawaiian or other Pacific Islander, non-Hispanic/Latino; 3 Two or more races, non-Hispanic/Latino), 74 international. Average age 28. 353 applicants, 20% accepted, 28 enrolled. In 2018, 4 master's, 22 doctorates awarded. *Entrance requirements:* For master's, GRE (strongly recommended), 1 year of physics, math through calculus, general chemistry (8 credits), organic chemistry (8 credits), physical chemistry (6 credits), quantitative analysis (4 credits), advanced chemistry (3 credits), minimum undergraduate GPA of 2.75 in chemistry and cognate sciences, statement of interest, three letters of recommendation; for doctorate, GRE (strongly recommended), minimum undergraduate GPA of 3.0 in chemistry and cognate science. Additional exam requirements/recommendations for international students: Required—TOEFL (minimum score 90 iBT), IELTS (minimum score 6.5), TWE. *Application deadline:* Applications are processed on a rolling basis. Electronic applications accepted. *Financial support:* In 2018–19, 116 students received support, including 21 fellowships with tuition reimbursements available (averaging $11,119 per year), 42 research assistantships with tuition reimbursements available (averaging $22,026 per year), 74 teaching assistantships with tuition reimbursements available (averaging $22,042 per year); scholarships/grants, health care benefits, and unspecified assistantships also available. Financial award applicants required to submit FAFSA. *Faculty research:* Natural products synthesis, molecular biology, molecular mechanics calculations, organometallic chemistry, experimental physical chemistry. *Unit head:* Dr. Matthew Allen, Chair, 313-577-2070, E-mail: mallen@chem.wayne.edu. *Application contact:* Melissa Rochon, Graduate Academic Services Officer, 313-577-2844, E-mail: melissa@chem.wayne.edu.
Website: http://chem.wayne.edu/

Youngstown State University, College of Graduate Studies, College of Science, Technology, Engineering and Mathematics, Department of Chemistry, Youngstown, OH 44555-0001. Offers analytical chemistry (MS); biochemistry (MS); chemistry education (MS); inorganic chemistry (MS); organic chemistry (MS); physical chemistry (MS). *Program availability:* Part-time. *Degree requirements:* For master's, thesis. *Entrance requirements:* For master's, bachelor's degree in chemistry, minimum GPA of 2.7. Additional exam requirements/recommendations for international students: Required—TOEFL. *Faculty research:* Analysis of antioxidants, chromatography, defects and disorder in crystalline oxides, hydrogen bonding, novel organic and organometallic materials.

Chemistry

Acadia University, Faculty of Pure and Applied Science, Department of Chemistry, Wolfville, NS B4P 2R6, Canada. Offers M Sc. *Entrance requirements:* Additional exam requirements/recommendations for international students: Required—TOEFL (minimum score 580 paper-based; 93 iBT), IELTS (minimum score 6.5). *Faculty research:* Atmospheric chemistry, chemical kinetics, bioelectrochemistry of proteins, self-assembling monolayers.

American University, College of Arts and Sciences, Department of Chemistry, Washington, DC 20016-8014. Offers MS. *Program availability:* Part-time, evening/weekend. *Faculty:* 14 full-time (7 women), 1 (woman) part-time/adjunct. *Students:* 5 full-time (4 women), 1 (woman) part-time; includes 2 minority (1 Black or African American, non-Hispanic/Latino; 1 Asian, non-Hispanic/Latino), 2 international. Average age 26. 7 applicants, 100% accepted, 3 enrolled. In 2018, 3 master's awarded. *Degree requirements:* For master's, comprehensive exam, thesis. *Entrance requirements:* For master's, GRE; Please see website: https://www.american.edu/cas/chemistry/, statement of purpose, transcripts, 2 letters of recommendation, resume. Additional exam requirements/recommendations for international students: Required—TOEFL. *Application deadline:* Applications are processed on a rolling basis. Application fee: $55. Electronic applications accepted. *Expenses:* Contact institution. *Financial support:* Research assistantships, teaching assistantships, and unspecified assistantships available. Financial award applicants required to submit FAFSA. *Unit head:* Dr. Shouzhong Zou, Chair, 202-885-1750, E-mail: afarran@american.edu. *Application contact:* Jonathan Harper, Assistant Director, Graduate Recruitment, 202-855-3622, E-mail: jharper@american.edu.
Website: http://www.american.edu/cas/chemistry/

The American University in Cairo, School of Sciences and Engineering, Cairo, Egypt. Offers biotechnology (MS); chemistry (MS); computer science (MS); computing (M Comp); construction engineering (M Eng, MS); electronics and communications engineering (M Eng); environmental engineering (MS); environmental system design (M Eng); mechanical engineering (M Eng, MS); nanotechnology (MS); physics (MS); robotics, control and smart systems (MS); sciences and engineering (PhD); sustainable development (MS, Graduate Diploma). *Program availability:* Part-time, evening/weekend. *Degree requirements:* For master's, comprehensive exam (for some programs), thesis (for some programs); for doctorate, comprehensive exam (for some programs), thesis/dissertation. *Entrance requirements:* Additional exam requirements/recommendations for international students: Required—TOEFL (minimum score 450 paper-based; 45 iBT), IELTS (minimum score 5). Electronic applications accepted. *Faculty research:* Construction, mechanical, and electronics engineering; physics; computer science; biotechnology; nanotechnology; chemistry; robotics.

American University of Beirut, Graduate Programs, Faculty of Arts and Sciences, Beirut 1107 2020, Lebanon. Offers anthropology (MA); Arab and Middle Eastern history (PhD); Arabic language and literature (MA, PhD); archaeology (MA); art history and curating (MA); biology (MS); cell and molecular biology (PhD); chemistry (MS); clinical psychology (MA); computational sciences (MS); computer science (MS); economics (MA); education (MA), including administration and policy studies, elementary education, mathematics education, psychology school guidance, psychology test and measurements, science education, teaching English as a foreign language; English language (MA); English literature (MA); environmental policy planning (MS); financial economics (MAFE); general psychology (MA); geology (MS); history (MA); Islamic

studies (MA); mathematics (MS); media studies (MA); Middle East studies (MA); philosophy (MA); physics (MS); political studies (MA); public administration (MA); public policy and international affairs (MA); sociology (MA); theoretical physics (PhD). *Program availability:* Part-time. *Faculty:* 187 full-time (64 women), 27 part-time/adjunct (15 women). *Students:* 292 full-time (215 women), 216 part-time (148 women). Average age 27. 422 applicants, 64% accepted, 124 enrolled. In 2018, 90 master's, 3 doctorates awarded. *Degree requirements:* For master's, comprehensive exam, thesis (for some programs), project; for doctorate, comprehensive exam, thesis/dissertation (for some programs). *Entrance requirements:* For master's, GRE General Test (for archaeology, clinical psychology, general psychology, economics, financial economics and biology); for doctorate, GRE General Test for all PhD programs, GRE Subject Test for theoretical physics. Additional exam requirements/recommendations for international students: Required—TOEFL (minimum score 583 paper-based; 97 iBT), IELTS (minimum score 7). *Application deadline:* For fall admission, 3/18 for domestic students; for spring admission, 11/5 for domestic students. Application fee: $50. Electronic applications accepted. *Expenses:* MA/MS: Humanities and social sciences=$912/credit. Sciences=$943/credit. Financial economics=$986/credit. Thesis: Humanities/social sciences=$6565 and sciences=$6865. *Financial support:* In 2018–19, 227 fellowships with full tuition reimbursements, 17 research assistantships with full tuition reimbursements, 83 teaching assistantships with full tuition reimbursements were awarded; scholarships/grants, tuition waivers (full and partial), and unspecified assistantships also available. Financial award application deadline: 3/18. *Faculty research:* Sciences: Physics: High energy, Particle, Polymer and Soft Matter, Thermal, Plasma; String Theory, Mathematical physics, Astrophysics (stellar evolution, planet and galaxy formation and evolution, astrophysical dynamics), Solid State physics/thin films, Spintronics, Magnetic properties of materials, Mineralogy, Petrology, and Geochemistry of Hard Rocks, Geophysics and Petrophysics, Hydrogeology, Micropaleontology, Sedimentology, and Stratigraphy, Structural Geology and Geotectonics, Renewable en. *Total annual research expenditures:* $4.3 million. *Unit head:* Dr. Nadia Maria El Cheikh, Dean, Faculty of Arts and Sciences, 961-1-350000 Ext. 3800, Fax: 961-1-744461, E-mail: nmcheikh@aub.edu.lb. *Application contact:* Adriana Michelle Zanaty, Curriculum and Graduate Studies Officer, 961-1-350000 Ext. 3833, Fax: 961-1-744461, E-mail: az48@aub.edu.lb.
Website: https://www.aub.edu.lb/fas/Pages/default.aspx

Arizona State University at the Tempe campus, College of Liberal Arts and Sciences, Department of Chemistry and Biochemistry, Tempe, AZ 85287-1604. Offers biochemistry (MS, PhD); chemistry (MS, PhD); nanoscience (PSM). Terminal master's awarded for partial completion of doctoral program. *Degree requirements:* For master's, thesis, interactive Program of Study (iPOS) submitted before completing 50 percent of required credit hours; for doctorate, comprehensive exam, thesis/dissertation, interactive Program of Study (iPOS) submitted before completing 50 percent of required credit hours. *Entrance requirements:* For master's and doctorate, GRE, minimum GPA of 3.0 or equivalent in last 2 years of work leading to bachelor's degree. Additional exam requirements/recommendations for international students: Required—TOEFL, IELTS, or PTE. Electronic applications accepted.

Arkansas State University, Graduate School, College of Sciences and Mathematics, Department of Chemistry and Physics, State University, AR 72467. Offers chemistry (MS); chemistry education (MSE, SCCT). *Program availability:* Part-time. *Degree requirements:* For master's, comprehensive exam, thesis or alternative; for SCCT,

Peterson's Graduate Programs in the Physical Sciences, Mathematics, Agricultural Sciences, the Environment & Natural Resources 2020

www.petersons.com **45**

comprehensive exam. *Entrance requirements:* For master's, GRE General Test or MAT, appropriate bachelor's degree, official transcript, immunization records, valid teaching certificate (for MSE); for SCCT, GRE General Test or MAT, interview, master's degree, official transcript, immunization records. Additional exam requirements/recommendations for international students: Required—TOEFL (minimum score 550 paper-based; 79 iBT), IELTS (minimum score 6), PTE (minimum score 56). Electronic applications accepted.

Auburn University, Graduate School, College of Sciences and Mathematics, Department of Chemistry and Biochemistry, Auburn University, AL 36849. Offers analytical chemistry (MS, PhD); biochemistry (MS, PhD); inorganic chemistry (MS); organic chemistry (PhD); physical chemistry (MS, PhD). *Program availability:* Part-time. *Degree requirements:* For master's, thesis (for some programs); for doctorate, thesis/dissertation, oral and written exams. *Entrance requirements:* For master's and doctorate, GRE General Test. Electronic applications accepted. *Expenses:* Tuition, state resident: full-time $11,282; part-time $535 per credit hour. Tuition, nonresident: full-time $30,542; part-time $1605 per credit hour. *Required fees:* $826 per semester. Tuition and fees vary according to degree level and program.

Ball State University, Graduate School, College of Sciences and Humanities, Department of Chemistry, Muncie, IN 47306. Offers chemistry (MA, MS). *Program availability:* Part-time. *Entrance requirements:* For master's, minimum baccalaureate GPA of 2.75 or 3.0 in latter half of baccalaureate, two letters of reference, academic transcripts. Additional exam requirements/recommendations for international students: Required—TOEFL (minimum score 550 paper-based; 79 iBT), IELTS (minimum score 6.5). Electronic applications accepted. *Faculty research:* Synthetic and analytical chemistry, biochemistry, theoretical chemistry.

Ball State University, Graduate School, College of Sciences and Humanities, Interdepartmental Program in Environmental Sciences, Muncie, IN 47306. Offers environmental science (PhD), including biology, chemistry, geological sciences. *Program availability:* Part-time. *Degree requirements:* For doctorate, thesis/dissertation. *Entrance requirements:* For doctorate, GRE General Test, minimum cumulative GPA of 3.0 (chemistry), 3.2 (biology and geological sciences); acknowledged arrangement for doctoral environmental sciences research with faculty mentor; three letters of recommendation. Additional exam requirements/recommendations for international students: Required—TOEFL (minimum score 550 paper-based; 79 iBT), IELTS (minimum score 6.5). Electronic applications accepted.

Baylor University, Graduate School, College of Arts and Sciences, Department of Chemistry and Biochemistry, Waco, TX 76798. Offers biochemistry (MS, PhD); chemistry (MS, PhD). *Faculty:* 18 full-time (3 women). *Students:* 74 full-time (23 women); includes 12 minority (1 Black or African American, non-Hispanic/Latino; 2 Asian, non-Hispanic/Latino; 6 Hispanic/Latino; 3 Two or more races, non-Hispanic/Latino), 15 international. Average age 25. 95 applicants, 48% accepted, 23 enrolled. In 2018, 7 master's, 9 doctorates awarded. Terminal master's awarded for partial completion of doctoral program. *Degree requirements:* For master's, thesis or alternative; for doctorate, comprehensive exam, thesis/dissertation. *Entrance requirements:* For doctorate, GRE General Test, transcripts, 3 letters of recommendation, personal statement. Additional exam requirements/recommendations for international students: Required—TOEFL (minimum score 90 iBT). *Application deadline:* For fall admission, 1/7 for domestic and international students. Applications are processed on a rolling basis. Application fee: $50. Electronic applications accepted. *Expenses:* Contact institution. *Financial support:* In 2018–19, 42 students received support, including 6 research assistantships with full tuition reimbursements available (averaging $23,000 per year), 36 teaching assistantships with full tuition reimbursements available (averaging $23,000 per year); tuition waivers (full) also available. Financial award application deadline: 1/7. *Faculty research:* Total synthesis, proteomics, computational materials, enzymology. *Total annual research expenditures:* $2.7 million. *Unit head:* Dr. Michael Trakselis, Director of Graduate Affairs, 254-710-2581, E-mail: michael_trakselis@baylor.edu. *Application contact:* Dr. Kevin Shuford, Director of Graduate Recruiting, 254-710-2576, E-mail: kevin_shuford@baylor.edu.
Website: http://www.baylor.edu/chemistry/

Binghamton University, State University of New York, Graduate School, Harpur College of Arts and Sciences, Department of Chemistry, Binghamton, NY 13902-6000. Offers analytical chemistry (PhD); chemistry (MA, MS); inorganic chemistry (PhD); physical chemistry (PhD). *Program availability:* Part-time. Terminal master's awarded for partial completion of doctoral program. *Degree requirements:* For master's, thesis; for doctorate, comprehensive exam, thesis/dissertation. *Entrance requirements:* For master's and doctorate, GRE General Test. Additional exam requirements/recommendations for international students: Required—TOEFL (minimum score 90 iBT). Electronic applications accepted.

Boise State University, College of Arts and Sciences, Department of Chemistry and Biochemistry, Boise, ID 83725. Offers chemistry (MS). *Program availability:* Part-time. *Degree requirements:* For master's, thesis. *Entrance requirements:* For master's, GRE General Test, minimum GPA of 3.0 for all upper-division credits. Additional exam requirements/recommendations for international students: Required—TOEFL (minimum score 550 paper-based; 80 iBT), IELTS (minimum score 6). Electronic applications accepted.

Boston College, Morrissey Graduate School of Arts and Sciences, Department of Chemistry, Chestnut Hill, MA 02467-3800. Offers biochemistry (PhD); inorganic chemistry (PhD); organic chemistry (PhD); physical chemistry (PhD); science education (MST). *Degree requirements:* For doctorate, thesis/dissertation, qualifying exam. *Entrance requirements:* For doctorate, GRE General Test, GRE Subject Test. Additional exam requirements/recommendations for international students: Required—TOEFL (minimum score 600 paper-based; 100 iBT), IELTS (minimum score 8). Electronic applications accepted. *Faculty research:* Organic and organometallic chemistry, chemical biology and biochemistry, physical and theoretical chemistry, inorganic chemistry.

Boston University, Graduate School of Arts and Sciences, Department of Chemistry, Boston, MA 02215. Offers MA, PhD. *Students:* 118 full-time (57 women); includes 19 minority (1 Black or African American, non-Hispanic/Latino; 6 Asian, non-Hispanic/Latino; 9 Hispanic/Latino; 1 Native Hawaiian or other Pacific Islander, non-Hispanic/Latino; 2 Two or more races, non-Hispanic/Latino), 35 international. Average age 24. 320 applicants, 20% accepted, 20 enrolled. In 2018, 14 master's, 13 doctorates awarded. Terminal master's awarded for partial completion of doctoral program. *Degree requirements:* For doctorate, comprehensive exam, thesis/dissertation. *Entrance requirements:* For master's and doctorate, GRE General Test, GRE Subject Test in chemistry (recommended), 3 letters of recommendation, transcripts, personal statement. Additional exam requirements/recommendations for international students: Required—TOEFL (minimum score 550 paper-based; 84 iBT). *Application deadline:* For fall admission, 12/15 for domestic and international students. Application fee: $95. Electronic applications accepted. *Financial support:* In 2018–19, 116 students received support, including 3 fellowships with full tuition reimbursements available (averaging $22,660 per year), 53 research assistantships with full tuition reimbursements available (averaging $22,660 per year), 58 teaching assistantships with full tuition reimbursements available (averaging $22,660 per year); Federal Work-Study, scholarships/grants, health care benefits, and tuition waivers (full) also available. Support available to part-time students. Financial award application deadline: 12/15. *Unit head:* Karen Allen, Chair, 617-353-5544, Fax: 617-353-6466, E-mail: drkallen@bu.edu. *Application contact:* Marley O'Neil, Graduate Academic Administrator, 617-353-2503, Fax: 617-353-6466, E-mail: chemgaa@bu.edu.
Website: http://www.bu.edu/chemistry/

Bowling Green State University, Graduate College, College of Arts and Sciences, Center for Photochemical Sciences, Bowling Green, OH 43403. Offers PhD. *Degree requirements:* For doctorate, comprehensive exam, thesis/dissertation. *Entrance requirements:* For doctorate, GRE General Test. Additional exam requirements/recommendations for international students: Required—TOEFL. Electronic applications accepted. *Faculty research:* Laser-initiated photo polymerization, spectroscopic and kinetic studies, optoelectronics of semiconductor multiple quantum wells, electron transfer processes, carotenoid pigments.

Bowling Green State University, Graduate College, College of Arts and Sciences, Department of Chemistry, Bowling Green, OH 43403. Offers MS, PhD. *Program availability:* Part-time. *Degree requirements:* For master's, thesis or alternative. *Entrance requirements:* For master's, GRE General Test. Additional exam requirements/recommendations for international students: Required—TOEFL. Electronic applications accepted. *Faculty research:* Organic, inorganic, physical, and analytical chemistry; biochemistry; surface science.

Bradley University, The Graduate School, College of Liberal Arts and Sciences, Mund-Lagowski Department of Chemistry and Biochemistry, Peoria, IL 61625-0002. Offers biochemistry (MS); chemistry (MS). *Program availability:* Part-time, evening/weekend. *Faculty:* 10 full-time (2 women). *Students:* 10 full-time (1 woman), 4 part-time (2 women); includes 4 minority (1 Asian, non-Hispanic/Latino; 3 Hispanic/Latino), 1 international. Average age 26. 26 applicants, 96% accepted, 6 enrolled. In 2018, 4 master's awarded. *Degree requirements:* For master's, comprehensive exam, thesis. *Entrance requirements:* Additional exam requirements/recommendations for international students: Required—TOEFL (minimum score 550 paper-based; 79 iBT), IELTS (minimum score 6.5). *Application deadline:* For fall admission, 5/15 priority date for domestic students; for spring admission, 10/15 priority date for domestic students. Applications are processed on a rolling basis. Application fee: $40 ($50 for international students). Electronic applications accepted. *Expenses: Tuition:* Part-time $890 per credit. *Required fees:* $50 per unit. *Financial support:* In 2018–19, 7 students received support, including 4 research assistantships with partial tuition reimbursements available (averaging $5,785 per year); scholarships/grants, tuition waivers (partial), and unspecified assistantships also available. Support available to part-time students. Financial award application deadline: 4/1. *Faculty research:* Materials chemistry, computational chemistry, biological chemistry, green chemistry, pharmaceutical chemistry. *Unit head:* Brad Andersh, Chairperson, 309-677-3493. *Application contact:* Rachel Webb, Director of On-Campus Graduate Admissions & International Student and Scholar Services, 309-677-2375, E-mail: rkwebb@bradley.edu.
Website: http://www.bradley.edu/academic/departments/chemistry/

Brandeis University, Graduate School of Arts and Sciences, Department of Chemistry, Waltham, MA 02454-9110. Offers inorganic chemistry (MA, MS, PhD); organic chemistry (MA, MS, PhD); physical chemistry (MS, PhD). *Program availability:* Part-time. *Faculty:* 13 full-time (5 women), 3 part-time/adjunct (0 women). *Students:* 33 full-time (12 women); includes 5 minority (3 Black or African American, non-Hispanic/Latino; 2 Hispanic/Latino), 19 international. Average age 26. 91 applicants, 41% accepted, 9 enrolled. In 2018, 3 master's, 8 doctorates awarded. Terminal master's awarded for partial completion of doctoral program. *Degree requirements:* For master's, comprehensive exam, thesis (for some programs); for doctorate, comprehensive exam, thesis/dissertation. *Entrance requirements:* For master's and doctorate, GRE General Test; GRE Subject Test (recommended), resume, statement of purpose, letters of recommendation, transcripts. Additional exam requirements/recommendations for international students: Required—TOEFL, IELTS, PTE. *Application deadline:* For fall admission, 12/15 priority date for domestic students. Applications are processed on a rolling basis. Application fee: $75. Electronic applications accepted. *Financial support:* In 2018–19, 21 fellowships with full tuition reimbursements (averaging $30,000 per year), 13 research assistantships with full tuition reimbursements (averaging $30,000 per year), 23 teaching assistantships with full tuition reimbursements (averaging $6,400 per year) were awarded; scholarships/grants, health care benefits, and tuition waivers (full and partial) also available. Support available to part-time students. *Faculty research:* Inorganic and organic chemistry, physical chemistry, chemical biology, biophysical chemistry, materials chemistry. *Unit head:* Dr. Klaus Schmidt-Rohr, Director of Graduate Study, 781-736-2520, E-mail: srohr@brandeis.edu. *Application contact:* Maryanna Aldrich, Administrator, 781-736-2352, E-mail: scigradoffice@brandeis.edu.
Website: http://www.brandeis.edu/gsas/programs/chemistry.html

Brigham Young University, Graduate Studies, College of Physical and Mathematical Sciences, Department of Chemistry and Biochemistry, Provo, UT 84602. Offers biochemistry (MS, PhD); chemistry (MS, PhD). *Faculty:* 37 full-time (5 women), 13 part-time/adjunct (5 women). *Students:* 95 full-time (34 women); includes 6 minority (1 Black or African American, non-Hispanic/Latino; 2 Hispanic/Latino; 3 Two or more races, non-Hispanic/Latino), 53 international. Average age 29. 63 applicants, 71% accepted, 30 enrolled. In 2018, 3 master's, 9 doctorates awarded. *Degree requirements:* For master's, thesis; for doctorate, thesis/dissertation, qualifying exam. *Entrance requirements:* For master's and doctorate, GRE General Test, minimum GPA of 3.0. Additional exam requirements/recommendations for international students: Required—TOEFL (minimum score 580 paper-based; 85 iBT), IELTS (minimum score 7). *Application deadline:* For fall admission, 2/1 priority date for domestic and international students. Applications are processed on a rolling basis. Application fee: $50. Electronic applications accepted. *Expenses:* $46,400 for Ph.D. in Chemistry and Biochemistry (covers student's tuition for the required 54 credit hours); $25,800 for MS in Chemistry and Biochemistry (covers student's tuition for the required 30 credit hours). *Financial support:* In 2018–19, 91 students received support, including 20 fellowships with full tuition reimbursements available (averaging $26,000 per year), 36 research assistantships with full tuition reimbursements available (averaging $26,000 per year), 34 teaching assistantships with full tuition reimbursements available (averaging $26,000 per year); scholarships/grants and supplementary awards also available. Financial award application deadline: 2/1. *Faculty research:* Separation science, molecular recognition, organic synthesis and biomedical application, biochemistry and molecular biology, molecular spectroscopy. *Total annual research expenditures:* $5.3 million. *Unit head:* Dr. David V. Dearden, Chair, 801-422-2355, Fax: 801-422-0153, E-mail: david_dearden@byu.edu. *Application contact:* Dr. Ken A. Christensen, Graduate Coordinator, 801-422-0249, Fax: 801-422-0153, E-mail: kenc@chem.byu.edu.
Website: http://www.chem.byu.edu/

Brock University, Faculty of Graduate Studies, Faculty of Mathematics and Science, Program in Chemistry, St. Catharines, ON L2S 3A1, Canada. Offers M Sc, PhD. *Program availability:* Part-time. *Degree requirements:* For master's, thesis; for doctorate, thesis/dissertation. *Entrance requirements:* For master's, honors B Sc in chemistry; for doctorate, M Sc. Additional exam requirements/recommendations for international students: Required—TOEFL (minimum score 550 paper-based; 80 iBT), IELTS (minimum score 6.5), TWE (minimum score 4). Electronic applications accepted. *Faculty research:* Bioorganic chemistry, trace element analysis, organic synthesis, electrochemistry, structural inorganic chemistry.

Brooklyn College of the City University of New York, School of Education, Program in Middle Childhood Science Education, Brooklyn, NY 11210-2889. Offers biology (MA); chemistry (MA); earth science (MA); general science (MA); physics (MA). *Program availability:* Part-time, evening/weekend. *Entrance requirements:* For master's, LAST, interview, previous course work in education and mathematics, resume, 2 letters of recommendation, essay. Additional exam requirements/recommendations for international students: Required—TOEFL (minimum score 500 paper-based; 61 iBT). Electronic applications accepted. *Faculty research:* Geometric thinking, mastery of basic facts, problem-solving strategies, history of mathematics.

Brooklyn College of the City University of New York, School of Natural and Behavioral Sciences, Department of Chemistry, Brooklyn, NY 11210-2889. Offers MA, MS, PhD. *Program availability:* Part-time. *Degree requirements:* For master's, one foreign language, thesis or alternative, 30 credits. *Entrance requirements:* For master's, 2 letters of recommendation. Additional exam requirements/recommendations for international students: Required—TOEFL (minimum score 500 paper-based; 61 iBT). Electronic applications accepted.

Brown University, Graduate School, Department of Chemistry, Providence, RI 02912. Offers PhD. *Degree requirements:* For doctorate, one foreign language, thesis/dissertation. Electronic applications accepted.

Bryn Mawr College, Graduate School of Arts and Sciences, Department of Chemistry, Bryn Mawr, PA 19010-2899. Offers MA, PhD. *Program availability:* Part-time. *Degree requirements:* For master's, thesis; for doctorate, comprehensive exam, thesis/ dissertation. *Entrance requirements:* For master's and doctorate, GRE General Test, transcripts, three letters of recommendation, statement of interest, resume or curriculum vitae. Additional exam requirements/recommendations for international students: Required—TOEFL (minimum score 600 paper-based; 100 iBT), IELTS (minimum score 7). Electronic applications accepted.

Bucknell University, Graduate Studies, College of Arts and Sciences, Department of Chemistry, Lewisburg, PA 17837. Offers MA, MS. *Degree requirements:* For master's, thesis. *Entrance requirements:* For master's, GRE General Test, GRE Subject Test, minimum GPA of 3.0. Additional exam requirements/recommendations for international students: Required—TOEFL (minimum score 600 paper-based).

Cabrini University, Academic Affairs, Radnor, PA 19087. Offers accounting (M Acc); autism spectrum disorder (M Ed); biological sciences (MS), including civic leadership; criminology and criminal justice (MA); curriculum, instruction, and assessment (M Ed); educational leadership (M Ed, Ed D), including curriculum and instructional leadership (Ed D), preK-12 leadership (Ed D); English as a second language (M Ed); organizational leadership (DBA, PhD); preK to 4 (M Ed); reading specialist (M Ed); secondary education (M Ed), including biology, chemistry, English, English/communication, mathematics, social studies; special education grades 7-12 (M Ed); special education preK-8 (M Ed); teaching and learning (M Ed). *Program availability:* Part-time, evening/ weekend. *Degree requirements:* For master's, comprehensive exam (for some programs), thesis (for some programs); for doctorate, comprehensive exam (for some programs), thesis/dissertation. *Entrance requirements:* For master's, professional resume, personal statement, two recommendations, official transcripts; for doctorate, official transcripts, minimum master's GPA of 3.0, two recommendations, interview with admissions committee. Additional exam requirements/recommendations for international students: Required—TOEFL (minimum score 80 iBT). Electronic applications accepted. Application fee is waived when completed online. *Expenses:* Contact institution.

California Institute of Technology, Division of Chemistry and Chemical Engineering, Program in Chemistry, Pasadena, CA 91125-0001. Offers MS, PhD. Terminal master's awarded for partial completion of doctoral program. *Degree requirements:* For master's, thesis; for doctorate, thesis/dissertation. *Entrance requirements:* Additional exam requirements/recommendations for international students: Required—TOEFL; Recommended—IELTS, TWE. Electronic applications accepted. *Faculty research:* Biochemistry and molecular biophysics, inorganic and electrochemistry, organic chemistry, physical chemistry (both experimental and theoretical).

California Polytechnic State University, San Luis Obispo, College of Science and Mathematics, Department of Chemistry and Biochemistry, San Luis Obispo, CA 93407. Offers polymers and coating science (MS). *Program availability:* Part-time. *Faculty:* 3 full-time (1 woman). *Students:* 5 full-time (1 woman), 2 part-time (0 women); includes 4 minority (1 Asian, non-Hispanic/Latino; 3 Hispanic/Latino), 1 international. Average age 24. 7 applicants, 71% accepted, 3 enrolled. In 2018, 5 master's awarded. *Degree requirements:* For master's, thesis. *Entrance requirements:* For master's, GRE. Additional exam requirements/recommendations for international students: Required— TOEFL (minimum score 80 iBT). *Application deadline:* For fall admission, 4/1 for domestic and international students; for spring admission, 2/1 for domestic students. Applications are processed on a rolling basis. Application fee: $55. Electronic applications accepted. *Expenses:* Tuition, area resident: Full-time $7176; part-time $4164 per year. Tuition, state resident: full-time $10,965. Tuition, nonresident: full-time $10,965. *Required fees:* $6336; $3711. *Financial support:* Fellowships, research assistantships, career-related internships or fieldwork, Federal Work-Study, and scholarships/grants available. Support available to part-time students. Financial award application deadline: 3/2; financial award applicants required to submit FAFSA. *Faculty research:* Polymer physical chemistry and analysis, polymer synthesis, coatings formulation. *Unit head:* Dr. Raymond Fernando, Graduate Coordinator, 805-756-2395, E-mail: rhfernan@calpoly.edu. *Application contact:* Dr. Raymond Fernando, Graduate Coordinator, 805-756-2395, E-mail: rhfernan@calpoly.edu. Website: http://www.chemistry.calpoly.edu/

California State Polytechnic University, Pomona, Program in Chemistry, Pomona, CA 91768-2557. Offers chemistry (MS). *Program availability:* Part-time, evening/ weekend. *Students:* 9 full-time (3 women), 11 part-time (3 women); includes 9 minority (1 Black or African American, non-Hispanic/Latino; 7 Asian, non-Hispanic/Latino; 1 Hispanic/Latino), 3 international. Average age 28. 16 applicants, 44% accepted, 5 enrolled. In 2018, 6 master's awarded. *Entrance requirements:* Additional exam requirements/recommendations for international students: Required—TOEFL (minimum score 550 paper-based). *Application deadline:* Applications are processed on a rolling basis. Application fee: $55. Electronic applications accepted. *Expenses:* Contact institution. *Financial support:* Application deadline: 3/2; applicants required to submit

FAFSA. *Unit head:* Dr. Gregory Barding, Graduate Coordinator, 909-869-3681, Fax: 909-869-4344, E-mail: gabarding@cpp.edu. *Application contact:* Dr. Gregory Barding, Graduate Coordinator, 909-869-3681, Fax: 909-869-4344, E-mail: gabarding@cpp.edu. Website: http://www.cpp.edu/~sci/chemistry-biochemistry/graduate-students/

California State University, East Bay, Office of Graduate Studies, College of Science, Department of Chemistry and Biochemistry, Hayward, CA 94542-3000. Offers biochemistry (MS). *Degree requirements:* For master's, comprehensive exam or thesis. *Entrance requirements:* For master's, minimum GPA of 2.6 in field during previous 2 years of course work. Additional exam requirements/recommendations for international students: Required—TOEFL (minimum score 550 paper-based). Electronic applications accepted.

California State University, Fresno, Division of Research and Graduate Studies, College of Science and Mathematics, Department of Chemistry, Fresno, CA 93740-8027. Offers MS. *Program availability:* Part-time. *Degree requirements:* For master's, thesis or alternative. *Entrance requirements:* For master's, GRE General Test, minimum GPA of 2.5. Additional exam requirements/recommendations for international students: Required—TOEFL. Electronic applications accepted. *Faculty research:* Genetics, viticulture, DNA, soils, molecular modeling, analysis of Quinone.

California State University, Fullerton, Graduate Studies, College of Natural Science and Mathematics, Department of Chemistry and Biochemistry, Fullerton, CA 92831-3599. Offers biology (MS); chemistry (MA, MS). *Program availability:* Part-time. *Degree requirements:* For master's, thesis, departmental qualifying exam. *Entrance requirements:* For master's, minimum GPA of 2.5 in last 60 units of course work, major in chemistry or related field.

California State University, Long Beach, Graduate Studies, College of Natural Sciences and Mathematics, Department of Chemistry and Biochemistry, Long Beach, CA 90840. Offers biochemistry (MS); chemistry (MS). *Program availability:* Part-time. *Degree requirements:* For master's, thesis, departmental qualifying exam. *Application deadline:* For fall admission, 6/1 for domestic students; for spring admission, 11/1 for domestic students. Applications are processed on a rolling basis. Application fee: $55. Electronic applications accepted. *Expenses:* Required fees: $2628 per term. Tuition and fees vary according to class time, course level, course load, degree level, campus/ location and program. *Financial support:* Research assistantships, teaching assistantships, Federal Work-Study, institutionally sponsored loans, scholarships/ grants, and unspecified assistantships available. Financial award application deadline: 3/2; financial award applicants required to submit FAFSA. *Faculty research:* Enzymology, organic synthesis, molecular modeling, environmental chemistry, reaction kinetics. *Unit head:* Christopher R. Brazier, Chair, 562-985-4941, Fax: 562-985-8557. *Application contact:* Christopher R. Brazier, Chair, 562-985-4941, Fax: 562-985-8557. Website: http://www.csulb.edu/chemistry-biochemistry/students/graduate-degree-programs

California State University, Los Angeles, Graduate Studies, College of Natural and Social Sciences, Department of Chemistry and Biochemistry, Los Angeles, CA 90032-8530. Offers analytical chemistry (MS). *Program availability:* Part-time, evening/ weekend. *Degree requirements:* For master's, one foreign language, comprehensive exam or thesis. *Entrance requirements:* Additional exam requirements/ recommendations for international students: Required—TOEFL. *Faculty research:* Intercalation of heavy metal, carborane chemistry, conductive polymers and fabrics, titanium reagents, computer modeling and synthesis.

California State University, Northridge, Graduate Studies, College of Science and Mathematics, Department of Chemistry and Biochemistry, Northridge, CA 91330. Offers biochemistry (MS); chemistry (MS), including chemistry, environmental chemistry. *Degree requirements:* For master's, thesis. *Entrance requirements:* For master's, GRE General Test or minimum GPA of 3.0. Additional exam requirements/recommendations for international students: Required—TOEFL. Electronic applications accepted.

California State University, Sacramento, College of Natural Sciences and Mathematics, Department of Chemistry, Sacramento, CA 95819. Offers biochemistry (MS); chemistry (MS). *Program availability:* Part-time. *Degree requirements:* For master's, thesis or project; qualifying exam; writing proficiency exam. *Entrance requirements:* For master's, minimum GPA of 2.5 during previous 2 years of course work, BA in chemistry or equivalent. Additional exam requirements/recommendations for international students: Required—TOEFL (minimum score 550 paper-based; 80 iBT); Recommended—IELTS, TSE. Electronic applications accepted. *Expenses:* Contact institution.

Carleton University, Faculty of Graduate Studies, Faculty of Science, Department of Chemistry, Ottawa, ON K1S 5B6, Canada. Offers M Sc, PhD. Programs offered jointly with University of Ottawa. *Degree requirements:* For master's, thesis; for doctorate, comprehensive exam, thesis/dissertation. *Entrance requirements:* For master's, honors degree; for doctorate, M Sc. Additional exam requirements/recommendations for international students: Required—TOEFL. *Faculty research:* Bioorganic chemistry, analytical toxicology, theoretical and physical chemistry, inorganic chemistry.

Carnegie Mellon University, Mellon College of Science, Department of Chemistry, Pittsburgh, PA 15213-3891. Offers atmospheric chemistry (PhD); bioinorganic chemistry (PhD); bioorganic chemistry and chemical biology (PhD); biophysical chemistry (PhD); catalysis (PhD); green and environmental chemistry (PhD); materials and nanoscience (PhD); renewable energy (PhD); sensors, probes, and imaging (PhD); spectroscopy and single molecule analysis (PhD); theoretical and computational chemistry (PhD). *Program availability:* Part-time. Terminal master's awarded for partial completion of doctoral program. *Degree requirements:* For doctorate, thesis/dissertation, departmental qualifying and oral exams, teaching experience. *Entrance requirements:* For doctorate, GRE General Test, GRE Subject Test. Additional exam requirements/recommendations for international students: Required—TOEFL. Electronic applications accepted. *Faculty research:* Physical and theoretical chemistry, chemical synthesis, biophysical/ bioinorganic chemistry.

Case Western Reserve University, School of Graduate Studies, Department of Chemistry, Cleveland, OH 44106. Offers MS, PhD. *Program availability:* Part-time. *Faculty:* 19 full-time (6 women). *Students:* 72 full-time (26 women), 3 part-time (2 women); includes 13 minority (1 Black or African American, non-Hispanic/Latino; 2 Asian, non-Hispanic/Latino; 8 Hispanic/Latino; 2 Two or more races, non-Hispanic/ Latino), 37 international. Average age 27. 142 applicants, 32% accepted, 19 enrolled. In 2018, 5 master's, 7 doctorates awarded. Terminal master's awarded for partial completion of doctoral program. *Degree requirements:* For master's, thesis optional; for doctorate, thesis/dissertation. *Entrance requirements:* For master's, GRE General Test, GRE Subject Test, three letters of recommendation; resume; for doctorate, GRE General Test, GRE Subject Test. Additional exam requirements/recommendations for international students: Required—TOEFL (minimum score 577 paper-based; 90 iBT); Recommended—IELTS (minimum score 7). *Application deadline:* For fall admission, 1/ 15 priority date for domestic students. Applications are processed on a rolling basis. Application fee: $50. Electronic applications accepted. *Expenses:* Tuition: Full-time

Peterson's Graduate Programs in the Physical Sciences, Mathematics, Agricultural Sciences, the Environment & Natural Resources 2020

www.petersons.com **47**

Chemistry

$45,168; part-time $1939 per credit hour. *Required fees:* $36; $18 per semester. $18 per semester. *Financial support:* Fellowships, research assistantships, teaching assistantships, health care benefits, and unspecified assistantships available. Financial award application deadline: 1/15; financial award applicants required to submit FAFSA. *Faculty research:* Electrochemistry, synthetic chemistry, chemistry of life process, spectroscopy, kinetics. *Unit head:* Prof. John D. Protasiewicz, Chair, 216-368-5060, Fax: 216-368-3006, E-mail: protasiewicz@case.edu. *Application contact:* Sarah Elashram, Department Assistant, Academic Affairs, 216-368.5030, Fax: 216-368-3006, E-mail: sxe171@case.edu.
Website: http://chemistry.case.edu/

Central Michigan University, College of Graduate Studies, College of Science and Engineering, Department of Chemistry, Mount Pleasant, MI 48859. Offers chemistry (MS); teaching chemistry (MA), including teaching college chemistry, teaching high school chemistry. *Program availability:* Part-time. *Degree requirements:* For master's, comprehensive exam, thesis or alternative. *Entrance requirements:* For master's, GRE. Electronic applications accepted. *Faculty research:* Analytical and organic-inorganic chemistry, biochemistry, catalysis, dendrimer and polymer studies, nanotechnology.

Central Washington University, School of Graduate Studies and Research, College of the Sciences, Department of Chemistry, Ellensburg, WA 98926. Offers MS. *Program availability:* Part-time. *Entrance requirements:* For master's, GRE General Test, minimum GPA of 3.0. Additional exam requirements/recommendations for international students: Required—TOEFL (minimum score 550 paper-based; 79 iBT), IELTS (minimum score 6.5). Electronic applications accepted.

City College of the City University of New York, Graduate School, Division of Science, Department of Chemistry, Program in Chemistry, New York, NY 10031-9198. Offers MS, PhD. PhD program offered jointly with Graduate School and University Center of the City University of New York. Terminal master's awarded for partial completion of doctoral program. *Degree requirements:* For doctorate, one foreign language, thesis/dissertation. *Entrance requirements:* For master's and doctorate, GRE. Additional exam requirements/recommendations for international students: Required—TOEFL (minimum score 500 paper-based). *Faculty research:* Laser spectroscopy, bioorganic chemistry, polymer chemistry and crystallography, electroanalytical chemistry, ESR of metal clusters.

Clark Atlanta University, School of Arts and Sciences, Department of Chemistry, Atlanta, GA 30314. Offers MS, PhD. *Program availability:* Part-time. *Degree requirements:* For master's, one foreign language, thesis; for doctorate, 2 foreign languages, thesis/dissertation. *Entrance requirements:* For master's, GRE General Test, minimum GPA of 2.5; for doctorate, GRE General Test, GRE Subject Test, minimum graduate GPA of 3.0. Additional exam requirements/recommendations for international students: Required—TOEFL (minimum score 500 paper-based; 61 iBT).

Clarkson University, School of Arts and Sciences, Department of Chemistry and Biomolecular Science, Potsdam, NY 13699. Offers MS, PhD. *Faculty:* 11 full-time (2 women), 2 part-time/adjunct (0 women). *Students:* 25 full-time (11 women); includes 1 minority (Asian, non-Hispanic/Latino), 14 international. 28 applicants, 61% accepted, 8 enrolled. In 2018, 3 master's, 4 doctorates awarded. *Degree requirements:* For master's, thesis; for doctorate, comprehensive exam, thesis/dissertation. *Entrance requirements:* For master's and doctorate, GRE. Additional exam requirements/recommendations for international students: Required—TOEFL (minimum score 550 paper-based, 80 iBT) or IELTS (6.5). *Application deadline:* Applications are processed on a rolling basis. Application fee: $50. Electronic applications accepted. *Expenses: Tuition:* Full-time $24,984; part-time $1388 per credit hour. *Required fees:* $225. Tuition and fees vary according to campus/location and program. *Financial support:* Scholarships/grants and unspecified assistantships available. *Unit head:* Dr. Devon Shipp, Chair of Chemistry and Biomolecular Science, 315-268-2389, E-mail: dshipp@clarkson.edu. *Application contact:* Dan Capogna, Director of Graduate Admissions & Recruitment, 518-631-9910, E-mail: graduate@clarkson.edu.
Website: https://www.clarkson.edu/academics/graduate

Clark University, Graduate School, Gustav H. Carlson School of Chemistry, Worcester, MA 01610-1477. Offers biochemistry (PhD); chemistry (PhD). Terminal master's awarded for partial completion of doctoral program. *Degree requirements:* For doctorate, one foreign language, thesis/dissertation. *Entrance requirements:* For doctorate, GRE General Test. Additional exam requirements/recommendations for international students: Required—TOEFL (minimum score 575 paper-based; 90 iBT), IELTS (minimum score 6.5). Electronic applications accepted. *Expenses: Tuition:* Full-time $34,110. *Required fees:* $40. Tuition and fees vary according to course load and program. *Faculty research:* Nuclear chemistry, molecular biology simulation, NMR studies, biochemistry, protein folding mechanisms.

Clemson University, Graduate School, College of Science, Department of Chemistry, Clemson, SC 29634. Offers MS, PhD. *Faculty:* 37 full-time (7 women). *Students:* 91 full-time (45 women), 5 part-time (1 woman); includes 9 minority (2 Black or African American, non-Hispanic/Latino; 4 Asian, non-Hispanic/Latino; 3 Hispanic/Latino), 42 international. Average age 26. 136 applicants, 44% accepted, 19 enrolled. In 2018, 1 master's, 13 doctorates awarded. *Degree requirements:* For master's, thesis; for doctorate, comprehensive exam, thesis/dissertation. *Entrance requirements:* For master's and doctorate, GRE General Test, unofficial transcripts, letters of recommendation. Additional exam requirements/recommendations for international students: Required—TOEFL (minimum score 80 iBT); Recommended—IELTS (minimum score 6.5), TSE (minimum score 54). *Application deadline:* For fall admission, 1/15 priority date for domestic and international students. Applications are processed on a rolling basis. Application fee: $80 ($90 for international students). Electronic applications accepted. *Expenses: Tuition, area resident:* Full-time $11,270; part-time $8688 per credit hour. Tuition, state resident: full-time $11,796. Tuition, nonresident: full-time $23,802; part-time $17,412 per credit hour. *International tuition:* $23,246 full-time. *Required fees:* $1196; $497 per semester. Tuition and fees vary according to course load, degree level, campus/location and program. *Financial support:* In 2018–19, 42 students received support, including 24 research assistantships with full and partial tuition reimbursements available (averaging $22,333 per year), 78 teaching assistantships with full and partial tuition reimbursements available (averaging $22,030 per year); career-related internships or fieldwork also available. *Faculty research:* Fluorine chemistry, organic synthetic methods and natural products, metal and non-metal clusters, analytical spectroscopies, polymers. *Total annual research expenditures:* $2.8 million. *Unit head:* Dr. Bill Pennington, Department Chair, 864-656-4200, E-mail: billp@clemson.edu. *Application contact:* Dr. George Chumanov, Graduate Program Coordinator, 864-656-2339, E-mail: gchumak@clemson.edu.
Website: https://www.clemson.edu/science/departments/chemistry/

Cleveland State University, College of Graduate Studies, College of Sciences and Health Professions, Department of Chemistry, Cleveland, OH 44115. Offers clinical chemistry (PhD), including cellular and molecular medicine, clinical/bioanalytical chemistry; organic chemistry (MS); physical chemistry (MS). *Program availability:* Part-time, evening/weekend. *Faculty:* 17 full-time (3 women). *Students:* 55 full-time (30 women), 16 part-time (10 women); includes 4 minority (3 Black or African American, non-Hispanic/Latino; 1 Asian, non-Hispanic/Latino), 38 international. Average age 30. 63 applicants, 63% accepted, 11 enrolled. In 2018, 3 master's, 15 doctorates awarded. *Entrance requirements:* For master's and doctorate, GRE General Test. Additional exam requirements/recommendations for international students: Required—TOEFL (minimum score 550 paper-based; 78 iBT). *Application deadline:* Applications are processed on a rolling basis. Application fee: $40. Electronic applications accepted. *Expenses:* Tuition, state resident: full-time $7232.55; part-time $6676 per credit hour. Tuition, nonresident: full-time $12,375. *International tuition:* $18,914 full-time. *Required fees:* $80; $80 $40. Tuition and fees vary according to program. *Financial support:* In 2018–19, 44 students received support. Fellowships, research assistantships, teaching assistantships, scholarships/grants, and unspecified assistantships available. Financial award application deadline: 1/15. *Faculty research:* Bioanalytical techniques and molecular diagnostics, glycoproteomics and antithrombotic agents, drug discovery and innovation, analytical pharmacology, inflammatory disease research. *Total annual research expenditures:* $3 million. *Unit head:* Dr. David W. Ball, Chair, 216-687-2467, Fax: 216-687-9298, E-mail: d.ball@csuohio.edu. *Application contact:* Richelle P. Emery, Administrative Coordinator, 216-687-2457, Fax: 216-687-9298, E-mail: r.emery@csuohio.edu.
Website: http://www.csuohio.edu/sciences/chemistry

The College at Brockport, State University of New York, School of Education, Health, and Human Services, Department of Education and Human Development, Brockport, NY 14420-2997. Offers adolescence education (MS Ed), including adolescence biology education, adolescence chemistry education, adolescence English, adolescence mathematics, adolescence physics, adolescence physics education, adolescence social studies education; bilingual education (MS Ed, AGC); childhood curriculum specialist (MS Ed); inclusive generalist education (MS Ed, AGC, Advanced Certificate), including biology (MS Ed, AGC), chemistry (MS Ed), English (MS Ed, Advanced Certificate), mathematics (MS Ed, Advanced Certificate), science (MS Ed, Advanced Certificate), social studies (MS Ed, Advanced Certificate); literacy education B-12 (MS Ed). *Accreditation:* NCATE. *Faculty:* 12 full-time (7 women), 10 part-time/adjunct (6 women). *Students:* 60 full-time (39 women), 227 part-time (157 women); includes 9 minority (1 Asian, non-Hispanic/Latino; 8 Hispanic/Latino). 135 applicants, 71% accepted, 59 enrolled. In 2018, 107 master's, 13 AGCs awarded. *Degree requirements:* For master's, thesis or alternative. *Entrance requirements:* For master's, minimum GPA of 3.0, letters of recommendation, interview (for some programs); statement of objectives, current resume. Additional exam requirements/recommendations for international students: Required—TOEFL (minimum score 550 paper-based; 79 iBT), IELTS (minimum score 6.5). *Application deadline:* For fall admission, 3/15 priority date for domestic and international students; for spring admission, 10/15 priority date for domestic and international students; for summer admission, 3/15 priority date for domestic and international students. Application fee: $80. Electronic applications accepted. *Expenses:* Tuition, state resident: part-time $471 per credit. Tuition, nonresident: part-time $963 per credit. *Financial support:* In 2018–19, 1 fellowship with full tuition reimbursement (averaging $7,500 per year), 1 teaching assistantship with full tuition reimbursement (averaging $6,000 per year) were awarded; Federal Work-Study, scholarships/grants, and unspecified assistantships also available. Support available to part-time students. Financial award application deadline: 3/15; financial award applicants required to submit FAFSA. *Faculty research:* Educational assessment, literacy education, inclusive education, teacher preparation, qualitative methodology. *Unit head:* Dr. Janka Szilagyi, Chairperson, 585-395-5945, Fax: 585-395-2172, E-mail: jszilagy@brockport.edu. *Application contact:* Buffie Edick, Graduate Program Director, 585-395-2326, Fax: 585-395-2172, E-mail: bedick@brockport.edu.
Website: https://www.brockport.edu/academics/education_human_development/department.html

Colorado School of Mines, Office of Graduate Studies, Department of Chemistry and Geochemistry, Golden, CO 80401. Offers chemistry (MS, PhD), including applied chemistry; geochemistry (MS, PhD); materials science (MS, PhD); nuclear engineering (MS, PhD). *Program availability:* Part-time. *Faculty:* 38 full-time (14 women), 2 part-time/adjunct (1 woman). *Students:* 58 full-time (23 women), 3 part-time (2 women); includes 11 minority (4 Asian, non-Hispanic/Latino; 6 Hispanic/Latino; 1 Two or more races, non-Hispanic/Latino), 6 international. Average age 26. 90 applicants, 38% accepted, 14 enrolled. In 2018, 11 master's, 14 doctorates awarded. *Degree requirements:* For master's, thesis (for some programs); for doctorate, comprehensive exam, thesis/dissertation. *Entrance requirements:* For master's and doctorate, GRE General Test. Additional exam requirements/recommendations for international students: Required—TOEFL (minimum score 550 paper-based; 79 iBT). *Application deadline:* For fall admission, 12/15 priority date for domestic and international students; for spring admission, 9/1 priority date for domestic and international students. Application fee: $60 ($80 for international students). Electronic applications accepted. *Expenses:* Tuition, state resident: full-time $16,650; part-time $925 per contact hour. Tuition, nonresident: full-time $36,270; part-time $2015 per contact hour. *International tuition:* $36,270 full-time. *Required fees:* $2314; $2314 per semester. *Financial support:* In 2018–19, 27 research assistantships with full tuition reimbursements, 19 teaching assistantships with full tuition reimbursements were awarded; fellowships, scholarships/grants, health care benefits, and unspecified assistantships also available. Financial award application deadline: 12/15; financial award applicants required to submit FAFSA. *Faculty research:* Environmental chemistry, exploration geochemistry, biogeochemistry, organic geochemistry, catalysis and surface chemistry. *Unit head:* Dr. Tom Gennett, Head, 303-273-3622, Fax: 303-273-3629, E-mail: tgennett@mines.edu. *Application contact:* Megan Rose, Program Manager, 303-273-3637, E-mail: meganrose@mines.edu.
Website: http://chemistry.mines.edu

Colorado State University, College of Natural Sciences, Department of Chemistry, Fort Collins, CO 80523-1872. Offers MS, PhD. Terminal master's awarded for partial completion of doctoral program. *Degree requirements:* For master's, comprehensive exam, thesis (for some programs), seminar; for doctorate, comprehensive exam, thesis/dissertation, seminar, independent research proposal. *Entrance requirements:* For master's and doctorate, GRE, minimum GPA of 3.0; resume; research experience; recommendation letters; transcript; statement of purpose. Additional exam requirements/recommendations for international students: Required—TOEFL (minimum score 600 paper-based; 90 iBT), IELTS (minimum score 7). Electronic applications accepted. *Expenses:* Tuition, state resident: full-time $10,520; part-time $4675 per credit hour. Tuition, nonresident: full-time $25,791; part-time $11,462 per credit hour. *International tuition:* $25,791 full-time. *Required fees:* $2392; $576 $288. Tuition and fees vary according to course level, course load, degree level, program and student level. *Faculty research:* Atmospheric biogeochemistry and mass spectrometry; physical and synthetic approaches to magnetic resonance and reactivity; microscale bioanalytical and environmental chemistry; synthetic methods for nanostructured materials with applications in renewable energy; functional inorganic materials for energy and biomineralization.

Colorado State University–Pueblo, College of Science and Mathematics, Pueblo, CO 81001-4901. Offers applied natural science (MS), including biochemistry, biology, chemistry. *Program availability:* Part-time, evening/weekend. *Degree requirements:* For master's, comprehensive exam (for some programs), thesis (for some programs), internship report (if non-thesis). *Entrance requirements:* For master's, GRE General Test (minimum score 1000), 2 letters of reference, minimum GPA of 3.0. Additional exam requirements/recommendations for international students: Required—TOEFL (minimum score 500 paper-based), IELTS (minimum score 5). *Faculty research:* Fungal cell walls, molecular biology, bioactive materials synthesis, atomic force microscopy-surface chemistry, nanoscience.

Columbia University, Graduate School of Arts and Sciences, New York, NY 10027. Offers African-American studies (MA); American studies (MA); anthropology (MA, PhD); art history and archaeology (MA, PhD); astronomy (PhD); biological sciences (PhD); biotechnology (MA); chemical physics (PhD); chemistry (PhD); classical studies (MA, PhD); classics (MA, PhD); climate and society (MA); conservation biology (MA); earth and environmental sciences (PhD); East Asia: regional studies (MA); East Asian languages and cultures (MA, PhD); ecology, evolution and environmental biology (MA), including conservation biology; ecology, evolution, and environmental biology (PhD), including ecology and evolutionary biology, evolutionary primatology; economics (MA, PhD); English and comparative literature (MA, PhD); French and Romance philology (MA, PhD); Germanic languages (MA, PhD); global French studies (MA); global thought (MA); Hispanic cultural studies (MA); history (PhD); history and literature (MA); human rights studies (MA); Islamic studies (MA); Italian (MA, PhD); Japanese pedagogy (MA); Jewish studies (MA); Latin America and the Caribbean: regional studies (MA); Latin American and Iberian cultures (PhD); mathematics (MA, PhD), including finance (MA); medieval and Renaissance studies (MA); Middle Eastern, South Asian, and African studies (MA, PhD); modern art: critical and curatorial studies (MA); modern European studies (MA); museum anthropology (MA); music (DMA, PhD); oral history (MA); philosophical foundations of physics (MA); philosophy (MA, PhD); physics (PhD); political science (MA, PhD); psychology (PhD); quantitative methods in the social sciences (MA); religion (MA, PhD); Russia, Eurasia and East Europe: regional studies (MA); Russian translation (MA); Slavic cultures (MA); Slavic languages (MA, PhD); sociology (MA, PhD); South Asian studies (MA); statistics (MA, PhD); theatre (PhD). Dual-degree programs require admission to both Graduate School of Arts and Sciences and another Columbia school. *Program availability:* Part-time. Terminal master's awarded for partial completion of doctoral program. *Degree requirements:* For master's, variable foreign language requirement, comprehensive exam (for some programs), thesis (for some programs); for doctorate, variable foreign language requirement, comprehensive exam (for some programs), thesis/dissertation. *Entrance requirements:* For master's and doctorate, GRE General Test, GRE Subject Test (for some programs). Additional exam requirements/recommendations for international students: Required—TOEFL, IELTS. Electronic applications accepted.

Columbus State University, Graduate Studies, College of Education and Health Professions, Department of Teacher Education, Columbus, GA 31907-5645. Offers curriculum and instruction in accomplished teaching (M Ed); early childhood education (M Ed, MAT, Ed S); middle grades education (M Ed, MAT, Ed S); secondary education (M Ed, MAT, Ed S), including biology (MAT), chemistry (MAT), earth and space science (MAT), English/language arts, general science (M Ed), history (MAT), mathematics, science (Ed S), social science (M Ed, Ed S); special education (M Ed, MAT, Ed S), including general curriculum (M Ed, MAT); teacher leadership (M Ed). *Accreditation:* NCATE. *Program availability:* Part-time, evening/weekend, 100% online, blended/hybrid learning. *Faculty:* 20 full-time (12 women), 20 part-time/adjunct (15 women). *Students:* 110 full-time (84 women), 143 part-time (115 women); includes 105 minority (96 Black or African American, non-Hispanic/Latino; 4 Hispanic/Latino; 5 Two or more races, non-Hispanic/Latino). Average age 33. 147 applicants, 56% accepted, 62 enrolled. In 2018, 112 master's, 11 other advanced degrees awarded. *Degree requirements:* For Ed S, thesis or alternative. *Entrance requirements:* For master's, GRE General Test, minimum undergraduate GPA of 2.75; for Ed S, GRE General Test, minimum undergraduate GPA of 2.75, graduate 3.0. Additional exam requirements/recommendations for international students: Required—TOEFL (minimum score 550 paper-based; 79 iBT). *Application deadline:* For fall admission, 6/30 for domestic students, 5/1 for international students; for spring admission, 11/1 for domestic and international students; for summer admission, 3/1 for domestic and international students. Applications are processed on a rolling basis. Application fee: $50. Electronic applications accepted. *Expenses: Tuition, area resident:* Full-time $4924; part-time $618 per credit hour. Tuition, state resident: full-time $4924; part-time $618 per credit hour. Tuition, nonresident: full-time $19,218; part-time $2403 per credit hour. *International tuition:* $19,218 full-time. *Required fees:* $1870; $802. Tuition and fees vary according to course load, degree level and program. *Financial support:* In 2018–19, 29 students received support, including 7 research assistantships with partial tuition reimbursements available (averaging $3,000 per year); career-related internships or fieldwork, Federal Work-Study, institutionally sponsored loans, scholarships/grants, tuition waivers (partial), and unspecified assistantships also available. Support available to part-time students. Financial award application deadline: 5/1; financial award applicants required to submit FAFSA. *Unit head:* Dr. Jan Burcham, Department Chair, 706-507-8519, Fax: 706-568-3134, E-mail: burcham_jan@columbusstate.edu. *Application contact:* Catrina Smith-Edmond, Assistant Director for Graduate and Global Admission, 706-507-8824, Fax: 706-568-5091, E-mail: smithedmond_catrina@columbusstate.edu. Website: http://te.columbusstate.edu/

Columbus State University, Graduate Studies, College of Letters and Sciences, Department of Earth and Space Sciences, Columbus, GA 31907-5645. Offers natural sciences (MS), including biology, chemistry, environmental science, geosciences. *Program availability:* Part-time, evening/weekend. *Faculty:* 5 full-time (2 women), 8 part-time/adjunct (0 women). *Students:* 19 full-time (7 women), 10 part-time (5 women); includes 7 minority (4 Black or African American, non-Hispanic/Latino; 2 Hispanic/Latino; 1 Two or more races, non-Hispanic/Latino), 4 international. Average age 27. 21 applicants, 48% accepted, 7 enrolled. In 2018, 6 master's awarded. *Degree requirements:* For master's, thesis. *Entrance requirements:* For master's, GRE General Test, minimum GPA of 3.0. Additional exam requirements/recommendations for international students: Required—TOEFL (minimum score 550 paper-based; 79 iBT). *Application deadline:* For fall admission, 6/30 priority date for domestic students, 5/1 for international students; for spring admission, 11/1 for domestic and international students; for summer admission, 3/1 for domestic and international students. Applications are processed on a rolling basis. Application fee: $50. Electronic applications accepted. *Expenses: Tuition, area resident:* Full-time $4924; part-time $618 per credit hour. Tuition, state resident: full-time $4924; part-time $618 per credit hour. Tuition, nonresident: full-time $19,218; part-time $2403 per credit hour. *International tuition:* $19,218 full-time. *Required fees:* $1870; $802. Tuition and fees vary according to course load, degree level and program. *Financial support:* In 2018–19, 1 student received support, including 15 research assistantships with partial tuition reimbursements available (averaging $3,000 per year); career-related internships or fieldwork, Federal Work-Study, institutionally sponsored loans, scholarships/grants, and unspecified assistantships also available. Support available to part-time students. Financial award application deadline: 5/1; financial award applicants required to submit FAFSA. *Unit head:* Dr. Clint Barineau, Department Chair, 706-569-3026, E-mail: barineau_clinton@columbusstate.edu. *Application contact:* Catrina Smith-Edmond, Assistant Director for Graduate and Global Admission, 706-507-8824, Fax: 706-568-5091, E-mail: smithedmond_catrina@columbusstate.edu. Website: http://ess.columbusstate.edu/

Concordia University, School of Graduate Studies, Faculty of Arts and Science, Department of Chemistry and Biochemistry, Montréal, QC H3G 1M8, Canada. Offers chemistry (M Sc, PhD). *Degree requirements:* For master's, thesis; for doctorate, thesis/dissertation. *Entrance requirements:* For master's, honors degree in chemistry; for doctorate, M Sc in biochemistry, biology, or chemistry. *Faculty research:* Bioanalytical, bio-organic, and inorganic chemistry; materials and solid-state chemistry.

Cornell University, Graduate School, Graduate Fields of Arts and Sciences, Field of Chemistry and Chemical Biology, Ithaca, NY 14853. Offers analytical chemistry (PhD); bio-organic chemistry (PhD); biophysical chemistry (PhD); chemical biology (PhD); chemical physics (PhD); inorganic chemistry (PhD); materials chemistry (PhD); organic chemistry (PhD); organometallic chemistry (PhD); physical chemistry (PhD); polymer chemistry (PhD); theoretical chemistry (PhD). *Degree requirements:* For doctorate, comprehensive exam, thesis/dissertation. *Entrance requirements:* For doctorate, GRE General Test, GRE Subject Test (chemistry), 3 letters of recommendation. Additional exam requirements/recommendations for international students: Required—TOEFL (minimum score 600 paper-based; 77 iBT). Electronic applications accepted. *Faculty research:* Analytical, organic, inorganic, physical, materials, chemical biology.

Dalhousie University, Faculty of Science, Department of Chemistry, Halifax, NS B3H 4R2, Canada. Offers M Sc, PhD. *Program availability:* Part-time. Terminal master's awarded for partial completion of doctoral program. *Degree requirements:* For master's, thesis; for doctorate, thesis/dissertation. *Entrance requirements:* Additional exam requirements/recommendations for international students: Required—TOEFL (minimum score 600 paper-based; 92 iBT), IELTS (minimum score 7). Electronic applications accepted. *Faculty research:* Analytical, inorganic, organic, physical, and theoretical chemistry.

Dartmouth College, Guarini School of Graduate and Advanced Studies, Department of Chemistry, Hanover, NH 03755. Offers biophysical chemistry (MS); chemistry (PhD). *Faculty:* 17 full-time (4 women), 1 (woman) part-time/adjunct. *Students:* 41 full-time (14 women); includes 8 minority (4 Asian, non-Hispanic/Latino; 1 Hispanic/Latino; 3 Two or more races, non-Hispanic/Latino), 11 international. Average age 26. 149 applicants, 12% accepted, 10 enrolled. In 2018, 3 master's, 5 doctorates awarded. *Entrance requirements:* For doctorate, GRE General Test, GRE Subject Test. Additional exam requirements/recommendations for international students: Required—TOEFL. *Application deadline:* For fall admission, 1/2 for domestic students. Application fee: $0. Electronic applications accepted. *Financial support:* Fellowships, research assistantships, teaching assistantships, institutionally sponsored loans, scholarships/grants, traineeships, tuition waivers (full), and unspecified assistantships available. Financial award application deadline: 4/1; financial award applicants required to submit CSS PROFILE or FAFSA. *Faculty research:* Organic and polymer synthesis, bioinorganic chemistry, magnetic resonance parameters. *Unit head:* Dr. Dean E. Wilcox, Chair, 603-646-2501. *Application contact:* Phyllis Ford, Administrative Assistant, 603-646-2501, E-mail: phyllis.p.ford@dartmouth.edu. Website: http://www.dartmouth.edu/~chem/

Delaware State University, Graduate Programs, Department of Chemistry, Dover, DE 19901-2277. Offers applied chemistry (MS, PhD); chemistry (MS). *Program availability:* Part-time, evening/weekend. *Entrance requirements:* For master's, GRE, minimum GPA of 3.0 in major, 2.75 overall; for doctorate, GRE. Additional exam requirements/recommendations for international students: Required—TOEFL (minimum score 550 paper-based). Electronic applications accepted. *Faculty research:* Chemiluminescence, environmental chemistry, forensic chemistry, heteropoly anions anti-cancer and antiviral agents, low temperature infrared studies of lithium salts.

DePaul University, College of Science and Health, Chicago, IL 60604-2287. Offers applied mathematics (MS); applied statistics (MS); biological sciences (MA, MS); chemistry (MS); environmental science (MS); mathematics education (MA); mathematics for teaching (MS); nursing (MS); nursing practice (DNP); physics (MS); polymer and coatings science (MS); psychology (MS); pure mathematics (MS); science education (MS); MA/PhD. *Accreditation:* AACN. Electronic applications accepted.

Drew University, Caspersen School of Graduate Studies, Madison, NJ 07940-1403. Offers conflict resolution and leadership (Certificate), including community leadership, moderation, peace building; education (M Ed); finance (MA); history and culture (MA, PhD), including American history, book history, British history, European history, intellectual history, Irish history, print culture, public history; K-12 education (MAT), including art, biology, chemistry, elementary education, English, French, Italian, math, secondary education, special education, teacher of students with disabilities; liberal studies (M Litt, D Litt), including history, Irish/Irish-American studies, literature (M Litt, MMH, D Litt, DMH, CMH), religion, spirituality, teaching in the two-year college, writing; medical humanities (MMH, DMH, CMH), including arts, health, healthcare, literature (M Litt, MMH, D Litt, DMH, CMH); scientific research; poetry (MFA). *Program availability:* Part-time, evening/weekend. *Faculty:* 3 full-time (2 women), 27 part-time/adjunct (13 women). *Students:* 66 full-time (38 women), 179 part-time (117 women); includes 37 minority (15 Black or African American, non-Hispanic/Latino; 2 Asian, non-Hispanic/Latino; 15 Hispanic/Latino; 5 Two or more races, non-Hispanic/Latino), 14 international. Average age 42. 157 applicants, 82% accepted, 57 enrolled. In 2018, 34 master's, 24 doctorates, 17 other advanced degrees awarded. Terminal master's awarded for partial completion of doctoral program. *Degree requirements:* For master's and other advanced degree, thesis (for some programs); for doctorate, one foreign language, comprehensive exam (for some programs), thesis/dissertation. *Entrance requirements:* For master's, PRAXIS Core and Subject Area tests (for MAT), GRE/GMAT (for MFin MS in Data Analytics), resume, transcripts, writing sample, personal statement, letters of recommendation; for doctorate, GRE (PhD in history and culture), resume, transcripts, writing sample, personal statement, letters of recommendation; for other advanced degree, resume, transcripts, personal statement. Additional exam requirements/recommendations for international students: Required—TOEFL (minimum score 587 paper-based; 80 iBT), IELTS (minimum score 6), TWE (minimum score 4). *Application deadline:* For fall admission, 8/1 for domestic students; 6/1 for international students; for spring admission, 12/1 for domestic students, 10/1 for international students. Applications are processed on a rolling basis. Application fee: $35. Electronic applications accepted. *Financial support:* Fellowships, research assistantships, teaching assistantships, career-related internships or fieldwork, Federal Work-Study, scholarships/grants, and unspecified assistantships available. Support available to part-time students. Financial award applicants required to submit FAFSA. *Unit head:* Dr. Debra Liebowitz, Provost and Dean of the College of Liberal Arts & Caspersen School of Graduate Studies, 973-4083139, E-mail: dliebowi@drew.edu. *Application contact:* Amo-Augustus Kubeyinje, Associate Vice President for Graduate Enrollment, 973-408-3111, E-mail: akubeyinje@drew.edu. Website: http://www.drew.edu/caspersen

Peterson's Graduate Programs in the Physical Sciences, Mathematics, Agricultural Sciences, the Environment & Natural Resources 2020

www.petersons.com **49**

Chemistry

Drexel University, College of Arts and Sciences, Department of Chemistry, Philadelphia, PA 19104-2875. Offers MS, PhD. *Program availability:* Part-time. Terminal master's awarded for partial completion of doctoral program. *Degree requirements:* For master's, thesis optional; for doctorate, one foreign language, thesis/dissertation. *Entrance requirements:* For master's and doctorate, GRE. Additional exam requirements/recommendations for international students: Required—TOEFL. Electronic applications accepted. *Faculty research:* Inorganic, analytical, organic, physical, and atmospheric polymer chemistry.

Duke University, Graduate School, Department of Chemistry, Durham, NC 27708. Offers PhD. *Degree requirements:* For doctorate, one foreign language, thesis/dissertation. *Entrance requirements:* For doctorate, GRE General Test, GRE Subject Test (recommended). Additional exam requirements/recommendations for international students: Required—TOEFL (minimum score 577 paper-based; 90 iBT) or IELTS (minimum score 7). Electronic applications accepted.

Duquesne University, Bayer School of Natural and Environmental Sciences, Department of Chemistry and Biochemistry, Pittsburgh, PA 15282-0001. Offers chemistry (PhD). *Program availability:* Part-time. *Faculty:* 17 full-time (5 women), 1 (woman) part-time/adjunct. *Students:* 36 full-time (17 women), 1 (woman) part-time; includes 4 minority (1 Black or African American, non-Hispanic/Latino; 1 Asian, non-Hispanic/Latino; 2 Hispanic/Latino), 1 international. Average age 28. 22 applicants, 86% accepted, 4 enrolled. In 2018, 4 doctorates awarded. Terminal master's awarded for partial completion of doctoral program. *Entrance requirements:* For doctorate, GRE General Test, BS in chemistry or related field, statement of purpose, official transcripts, 3 letters of recommendation with recommendation forms. Additional exam requirements/recommendations for international students: Required—TOEFL (minimum score 100 iBT) or IELTS. *Application deadline:* For fall admission, 1/4 priority date for domestic students, 2/15 for international students; for spring admission, 10/1 for international students. Applications are processed on a rolling basis. Application fee: $0. Electronic applications accepted. *Expenses:* $1376/credit hour. *Financial support:* In 2018–19, 39 students received support, including 1 fellowship with tuition reimbursement available (averaging $25,200 per year), 8 research assistantships with full tuition reimbursements available (averaging $24,230 per year), 30 teaching assistantships with full tuition reimbursements available (averaging $24,230 per year); scholarships/grants and unspecified assistantships also available. Financial award application deadline: 5/31. *Faculty research:* Computational physical chemistry, bioinorganic chemistry, analytical chemistry, biophysics, synthetic organic chemistry. *Total annual research expenditures:* $1.4 million. *Unit head:* Dr. Ellen Gawalt, Chair, 412-396-4709, Fax: 412-396-5683, E-mail: gawalte@duq.edu. *Application contact:* Heather Costello, Senior Graduate Academic Advisor, 412-396-6339, E-mail: costelloh@duq.edu.
Website: http://www.duq.edu/academics/schools/natural-and-environmental-sciences/academic-programs/chemistry-and-biochemistry

East Carolina University, Graduate School, Thomas Harriot College of Arts and Sciences, Department of Chemistry, Greenville, NC 27858-4353. Offers MS. *Program availability:* Part-time. *Application deadline:* For fall admission, 6/1 for domestic students, 3/1 for international students; for spring admission, 11/1 for domestic students, 10/1 for international students; for summer admission, 3/1 for domestic and international students. *Expenses: Tuition, area resident:* Full-time $4749. Tuition, state resident: full-time $4749. Tuition, nonresident: full-time $17,898. *International tuition:* $17,898 full-time. *Required fees:* $2787. Part-time tuition and fees vary according to course load and program. *Financial support:* Application deadline: 3/1. *Unit head:* Dr. Andrew Morehead, Chair, 252-328-9702, E-mail: moreheada@ecu.edu. *Application contact:* Graduate School Admissions, 252-328-6012, Fax: 252-328-6071, E-mail: gradschool@ecu.edu.
Website: http://www.ecu.edu/cs-cas/chem/

Eastern Illinois University, Graduate School, College of Liberal Arts and Sciences, Department of Chemistry and Biochemistry, Charleston, IL 61920. Offers chemistry (MS). *Program availability:* Part-time, evening/weekend. *Degree requirements:* For master's, thesis. *Entrance requirements:* For master's, GMAT or GRE. Additional exam requirements/recommendations for international students: Required—TOEFL (minimum score 500 paper-based; 61 iBT), IELTS (minimum score 6). Electronic applications accepted. *Expenses:* Tuition, state resident: part-time $299 per credit hour. Tuition, nonresident: part-time $718 per credit hour. *Required fees:* $214.50 per credit hour.

Eastern Kentucky University, The Graduate School, College of Arts and Sciences, Department of Chemistry, Richmond, KY 40475-3102. Offers MS. *Program availability:* Part-time, evening/weekend. *Entrance requirements:* For master's, GRE General Test, minimum GPA of 2.5. *Faculty research:* Organic synthesis, surface chemistry, inorganic chemistry, analytical chemistry.

Eastern Michigan University, Graduate School, College of Arts and Sciences, Department of Chemistry, Ypsilanti, MI 48197. Offers MS. *Program availability:* Part-time, evening/weekend. *Faculty:* 21 full-time (8 women). *Students:* 3 full-time (2 women), 31 part-time (20 women); includes 5 minority (1 Black or African American, non-Hispanic/Latino; 1 Asian, non-Hispanic/Latino; 3 Hispanic/Latino), 2 international. Average age 27. 20 applicants, 70% accepted, 11 enrolled. In 2018, 9 master's awarded. *Entrance requirements:* For master's, GRE General Test. Additional exam requirements/recommendations for international students: Required—TOEFL. *Application deadline:* For fall admission, 8/1 for domestic students, 5/1 for international students; for winter admission, 12/1 for domestic students, 8/1 for international students; for spring admission, 4/1 for domestic students, 3/1 for international students. Applications are processed on a rolling basis. Application fee: $45. *Financial support:* Fellowships, research assistantships with full tuition reimbursements, teaching assistantships with full tuition reimbursements, career-related internships or fieldwork, Federal Work-Study, institutionally sponsored loans, scholarships/grants, tuition waivers (partial), and unspecified assistantships available. Support available to part-time students. Financial award applicants required to submit FAFSA. *Unit head:* Dr. Deborah Heyl-Clegg, Department Head, 734-487-0106, Fax: 734-487-1496, E-mail: dheylcle@emich.edu. *Application contact:* Dr. Timothy Brewer, Graduate Coordinator, 734-487-9613, Fax: 734-487-1496, E-mail: tbrewer@emich.edu.
Website: http://www.emich.edu/chemistry/

Eastern New Mexico University, Graduate School, College of Liberal Arts and Sciences, Department of Physical Sciences, Portales, NM 88130. Offers chemistry (MS), including analytical chemistry, biochemistry, organic chemistry, physical chemistry. *Program availability:* Part-time. *Degree requirements:* For master's, thesis optional, seminar, oral and written comprehensive exams. *Entrance requirements:* For master's, ACS placement examination, minimum GPA of 3.0; 2 letters of recommendation; personal statement of career goals; bachelor's degree with minimum of one year each of general, organic, and analytical chemistry. Additional exam requirements/recommendations for international students: Required—TOEFL (minimum score 550 paper-based; 79 iBT), IELTS (minimum score 6). Electronic applications accepted. *Expenses: Tuition, area resident:* Full-time $6776. Tuition, state resident: full-time $6776; part-time $282 per credit hour. Tuition, nonresident: full-time $8086; part-time $374 per credit hour. *Required fees:* $60 per semester. One-time fee: $25. *Faculty research:* Synfuel, electrochemistry, protein chemistry.

East Tennessee State University, School of Graduate Studies, College of Arts and Sciences, Department of Chemistry, Johnson City, TN 37614. Offers MS. *Program availability:* Part-time, evening/weekend. *Degree requirements:* For master's, comprehensive exam, thesis. *Entrance requirements:* For master's, prerequisites in physical chemistry with lab requiring calculus, 2 letters of recommendation, bachelor's degree with adequate undergraduate background for the advanced work in chemistry. Additional exam requirements/recommendations for international students: Required—TOEFL (minimum score 550 paper-based; 79 iBT). Electronic applications accepted. *Faculty research:* Analytical chemistry, inorganic chemistry, organic chemistry, physical chemistry.

Emory University, Laney Graduate School, Department of Chemistry, Atlanta, GA 30322-1100. Offers PhD. *Degree requirements:* For doctorate, comprehensive exam, thesis/dissertation. *Entrance requirements:* For doctorate, GRE General Test, 3 letters of recommendation, curriculum vitae. Additional exam requirements/recommendations for international students: Required—TOEFL. Electronic applications accepted. *Faculty research:* Organometallic synthesis and catalysis, synthesis of natural products, x-ray crystallography, mass spectrometry, analytical neurochemistry.

Fairleigh Dickinson University, Florham Campus, Maxwell Becton College of Arts and Sciences, Department of Chemistry and Geological Sciences, Program in Chemistry, Madison, NJ 07940-1099. Offers MS.

Fairleigh Dickinson University, Metropolitan Campus, University College: Arts, Sciences, and Professional Studies, School of Natural Sciences, Program in Chemistry, Teaneck, NJ 07666-1914. Offers MS.

Fairleigh Dickinson University, Metropolitan Campus, University College: Arts, Sciences, and Professional Studies, School of Natural Sciences, Program in Cosmetic Science, Teaneck, NJ 07666-1914. Offers MS.

Fisk University, Division of Graduate Studies, Department of Chemistry, Nashville, TN 37208-3051. Offers MA. *Program availability:* Part-time. *Degree requirements:* For master's, comprehensive exam, thesis. *Entrance requirements:* For master's, GRE General Test, minimum GPA of 3.0. Electronic applications accepted. *Faculty research:* Environmental studies, lithium compound synthesis, HIU compound synthesis.

Florida Agricultural and Mechanical University, Division of Graduate Studies, Research, and Continuing Education, College of Science and Technology, Department of Chemistry, Tallahassee, FL 32307-3200. Offers MS. *Degree requirements:* For master's, comprehensive exam, thesis optional. *Entrance requirements:* For master's, GRE General Test, minimum GPA of 3.0.

Florida Atlantic University, Charles E. Schmidt College of Science, Department of Chemistry and Biochemistry, Boca Raton, FL 33431-0991. Offers chemistry (MS, MST, PhD). *Program availability:* Part-time. *Faculty:* 15 full-time (4 women), 1 part-time/adjunct (0 women). *Students:* 13 full-time (4 women), 21 part-time (10 women); includes 9 minority (2 Asian, non-Hispanic/Latino; 6 Hispanic/Latino; 1 Two or more races, non-Hispanic/Latino), 11 international. Average age 28. 20 applicants, 25% accepted, 5 enrolled. In 2018, 3 master's, 5 doctorates awarded. Terminal master's awarded for partial completion of doctoral program. *Degree requirements:* For master's, thesis; for doctorate, comprehensive exam, thesis/dissertation. *Entrance requirements:* For master's, GRE General Test, minimum GPA of 3.0; for doctorate, GRE, minimum GPA of 3.0. Additional exam requirements/recommendations for international students: Required—TOEFL (minimum score 500 paper-based; 61 iBT), IELTS (minimum score 6). *Application deadline:* For fall admission, 7/1 priority date for domestic students, 2/15 priority date for international students; for spring admission, 11/1 priority date for domestic students, 7/15 priority date for international students. Applications are processed on a rolling basis. Application fee: $30. *Expenses: Tuition, area resident:* Full-time $7400; part-time $369.82 per credit. Tuition, state resident: full-time $7400; part-time $369.82 per credit. Tuition, nonresident: full-time $20,496; part-time $1024.81 per credit. *Financial support:* Fellowships, research assistantships, teaching assistantships, and Federal Work-Study available. *Faculty research:* Polymer synthesis and characterization, spectroscopy, geochemistry, environmental chemistry, biomedical chemistry. *Unit head:* Dr. Predrag Cudic, Chair, 561-799-8375, E-mail: pcudic@fau.edu. *Application contact:* Dr. Salvatore D. Lepore, Professor, 561-297-0330, Fax: 561-297-2759, E-mail: slepore@fau.edu.
Website: http://www.science.fau.edu/chemistry/

Florida Institute of Technology, College of Engineering and Science, Program in Chemistry, Melbourne, FL 32901-6975. Offers MS, PhD. *Program availability:* Part-time. *Students:* 36 full-time (17 women), 3 part-time (0 women); includes 1 minority (Black or African American, non-Hispanic/Latino), 30 international. Average age 30. 38 applicants, 66% accepted, 8 enrolled. In 2018, 4 master's, 5 doctorates awarded. Terminal master's awarded for partial completion of doctoral program. *Degree requirements:* For master's, comprehensive exam (for some programs), thesis optional, research proposal, oral examination in defense of the thesis, or final program examination and research project, 30 credit hours; for doctorate, comprehensive exam, thesis/dissertation, six cumulative examinations, research proposal, completion of original research study, preparation and defense of dissertation, presentation of seminar on dissertation. *Entrance requirements:* For master's, GRE General Test (recommended), undergraduate degree in chemistry or related area; for doctorate, GRE General Test (recommended), 3 letters of recommendation, resume, statement of objectives, minimum GPA of 3.2. Additional exam requirements/recommendations for international students: Required—TOEFL (minimum score 550 paper-based; 79 iBT). *Application deadline:* For fall admission, 4/1 for international students; for spring admission, 9/30 for international students. Applications are processed on a rolling basis. Application fee: $50. Electronic applications accepted. *Expenses: Tuition:* Full-time $22,338; part-time $1241 per credit hour. Tuition and fees vary according to degree level, campus/location and program. *Financial support:* Career-related internships or fieldwork, institutionally sponsored loans, tuition waivers (partial), unspecified assistantships, and tuition remissions available. Support available to part-time students. Financial award application deadline: 3/1; financial award applicants required to submit FAFSA. *Faculty research:* Energy storage applications, marine and organic chemistry, stereochemistry, medicinal chemistry, environmental chemistry. *Unit head:* Dr. Ted Conway, Department Head, 321-674-8491, E-mail: tconway@fit.edu. *Application contact:* Mike Perry, Executive Director of Admissions, 321-674-7127, E-mail: perrymj@fit.edu.
Website: https://www.fit.edu/programs/chemistry-ms/

Florida International University, College of Arts, Sciences, and Education, Department of Chemistry and Biochemistry, Miami, FL 33199. Offers chemistry (MS, PhD); forensic science (MS, PSM, PhD). *Program availability:* Part-time, evening/weekend. *Faculty:* 38 full-time (12 women), 4 part-time/adjunct (1 woman). *Students:* 148 full-time (82 women), 11 part-time (9 women); includes 64 minority (13 Black or African American, non-Hispanic/Latino; 6 Asian, non-Hispanic/Latino; 43 Hispanic/Latino; 2 Two or more races, non-Hispanic/Latino), 56 international. Average age 28. 181 applicants, 40% accepted, 60 enrolled. In 2018, 21 master's, 27 doctorates awarded. *Degree requirements:* For master's, thesis (for some programs); for doctorate, comprehensive exam, thesis/dissertation. *Entrance requirements:* For master's and doctorate, GRE General Test, minimum GPA of 3.0, 3 letters of recommendation, resume, letter of intent. Additional exam requirements/recommendations for international students: Required—TOEFL (minimum score 550 paper-based; 80 iBT). *Application deadline:* For fall admission, 6/1 for domestic students, 4/1 for international students; for spring admission, 10/1 for domestic students, 9/1 for international students. Applications are processed on a rolling basis. Application fee: $30. Electronic applications accepted. *Financial support:* Institutionally sponsored loans and scholarships/grants available. Financial award application deadline: 3/1; financial award applicants required to submit FAFSA. *Faculty research:* Organic synthesis and reaction catalysis, environmental chemistry, molecular beam studies, organic geochemistry, bioinorganic and organometallic chemistry. *Unit head:* Dr. Yong Cai, Chair, 305-348-6210, Fax: 305-348-3772, E-mail: yong.cai@fiu.edu. *Application contact:* Nanett Rojas, Manager, Admissions Operations, 305-348-7464, Fax: 305-348-7441, E-mail: gradadm@fiu.edu.

Furman University, Graduate Division, Department of Chemistry, Greenville, SC 29613. Offers MS. *Degree requirements:* For master's, comprehensive exam, thesis. *Entrance requirements:* For master's, GRE General Test, GRE Subject Test. *Expenses: Tuition:* Full-time $27,500; part-time $7290 per credit. Tuition and fees vary according to program. *Faculty research:* Computer-assisted chemical analysis, DNA-metal interactions, laser-initiated reactions, nucleic acid chemistry and biochemistry.

George Mason University, College of Science, Department of Chemistry and Biochemistry, Fairfax, VA 22030. Offers MS, PhD. *Faculty:* 18 full-time (6 women), 10 part-time/adjunct (5 women). *Students:* 28 full-time (16 women), 18 part-time (13 women); includes 18 minority (6 Black or African American, non-Hispanic/Latino; 1 American Indian or Alaska Native, non-Hispanic/Latino; 8 Asian, non-Hispanic/Latino; 1 Hispanic/Latino; 2 Two or more races, non-Hispanic/Latino), 6 international. Average age 32. 27 applicants, 78% accepted, 10 enrolled. In 2018, 5 master's, 4 doctorates awarded. *Degree requirements:* For master's, comprehensive exam (for some programs), thesis (for some programs); for doctorate, comprehensive exam, thesis/dissertation, exit seminar. *Entrance requirements:* For doctorate, GRE, BS or MS in chemistry or related discipline. Additional exam requirements/recommendations for international students: Required—TOEFL (minimum score 575 paper-based; 88 iBT), IELTS (minimum score 6.5), PTE (minimum score 59). Application fee: $75 ($80 for international students). Electronic applications accepted. *Financial support:* In 2018–19, 25 students received support, including 1 fellowship, 6 research assistantships with tuition reimbursements available (averaging $18,667 per year), 18 teaching assistantships with tuition reimbursements available (averaging $18,597 per year); career-related internships or fieldwork, Federal Work-Study, scholarships/grants, unspecified assistantships, and health care benefits (for full-time research or teaching assistantship recipients) also available. Support available to part-time students. Financial award application deadline: 3/1; financial award applicants required to submit FAFSA. *Faculty research:* Nanomaterials; metabolomics; aquatic and environmental chemistry, biodegradation; antimicrobial, peptides; synthetic and medicinal chemistry, drug discovery. *Total annual research expenditures:* $827,939. *Unit head:* Gerald Weatherspoon, Chair, 703-993-1456, Fax: 703-993-1055, E-mail: grobert1@gmu.edu. *Application contact:* Robert Honeychuck, Graduate Coordinator and Associate Professor, 703-993-1076, Fax: 703-993-1055, E-mail: rhoneych@gmu.edu.
Website: http://chemistry.gmu.edu/

Georgetown University, Graduate School of Arts and Sciences, Department of Chemistry, Washington, DC 20057. Offers analytical chemistry (PhD); biochemistry (PhD); computational chemistry (PhD); inorganic chemistry (PhD); materials chemistry (PhD); organic chemistry (PhD); theoretical chemistry (PhD). Terminal master's awarded for partial completion of doctoral program. *Degree requirements:* For doctorate, comprehensive exam, thesis/dissertation. *Entrance requirements:* For doctorate, GRE General Test. Additional exam requirements/recommendations for international students: Required—TOEFL.

The George Washington University, Columbian College of Arts and Sciences, Department of Chemistry, Washington, DC 20052. Offers analytical chemistry (MS, PhD); inorganic chemistry (MS, PhD); materials science (MS, PhD); organic chemistry (MS, PhD); physical chemistry (MS, PhD). *Program availability:* Part-time, evening/weekend. *Students:* 29 full-time (15 women), 8 part-time (5 women); includes 3 minority (1 Black or African American, non-Hispanic/Latino; 2 Hispanic/Latino), 5 international. Average age 27. 96 applicants, 47% accepted, 9 enrolled. In 2018, 9 master's, 6 doctorates awarded. Terminal master's awarded for partial completion of doctoral program. *Degree requirements:* For master's, comprehensive exam, thesis or alternative; for doctorate, thesis/dissertation, general exam. *Entrance requirements:* For master's and doctorate, GRE General Test, interview, minimum GPA of 3.0. Additional exam requirements/recommendations for international students: Required—TOEFL (minimum score 550 paper-based; 80 iBT). *Application deadline:* For fall admission, 1/15 priority date for domestic and international students; for spring admission, 9/1 priority date for domestic and international students. Applications are processed on a rolling basis. Application fee: $75. Electronic applications accepted. *Financial support:* In 2018–19, 27 students received support. Fellowships, research assistantships, teaching assistantships, Federal Work-Study, and tuition waivers available. Financial award application deadline: 1/15. *Unit head:* Dr. Michael King, Chair, 202-994-6488. *Application contact:* Information Contact, 202-994-6121, E-mail: gwchem@gwu.edu.
Website: http://chemistry.columbian.gwu.edu/

Georgia Institute of Technology, Graduate Studies, College of Sciences, School of Chemistry and Biochemistry, Atlanta, GA 30332-0001. Offers MS, PhD. *Program availability:* Part-time. Terminal master's awarded for partial completion of doctoral program. *Degree requirements:* For master's, thesis optional; for doctorate, comprehensive exam, thesis/dissertation. *Entrance requirements:* For master's and doctorate, GRE General Test, GRE Subject Test. Additional exam requirements/recommendations for international students: Required—TOEFL (minimum score 600 paper-based; 100 iBT). Electronic applications accepted. *Faculty research:* Inorganic, organic, physical, and analytical chemistry.

Georgia State University, College of Arts and Sciences, Department of Chemistry, Atlanta, GA 30302-3083. Offers analytical chemistry (MS, PhD); biochemistry (MS, PhD); bioinformatics (MS, PhD); biophysical chemistry (PhD); computational chemistry (MS, PhD); geochemistry (PhD); organic/medicinal chemistry (MS, PhD); physical chemistry (MS). PhD in geochemistry offered jointly with Department of Geosciences. *Program availability:* Part-time. *Faculty:* 27 full-time (6 women), 1 part-time/adjunct (0 women). *Students:* 147 full-time (59 women), 15 part-time (10 women); includes 37 minority (21 Black or African American, non-Hispanic/Latino; 7 Asian, non-Hispanic/Latino; 4 Hispanic/Latino; 5 Two or more races, non-Hispanic/Latino), 84 international. Average age 29. 106 applicants, 40% accepted, 28 enrolled. In 2018, 37 master's, 13 doctorates awarded. Terminal master's awarded for partial completion of doctoral program. *Degree requirements:* For master's, one foreign language, comprehensive exam (for some programs), thesis (for some programs); for doctorate, one foreign language, comprehensive exam, thesis/dissertation. *Entrance requirements:* For master's and doctorate, GRE. *Application deadline:* For fall admission, 7/1 priority date for domestic and international students; for winter admission, 11/15 priority date for domestic and international students; for spring admission, 4/15 priority date for domestic and international students. Applications are processed on a rolling basis. Application fee: $50. Electronic applications accepted. *Expenses: Tuition, area resident:* Full-time $9360; part-time $390 per credit hour. Tuition, state resident: full-time $9360; part-time $390 per credit hour. Tuition, nonresident: full-time $30,024; part-time $1251 per credit hour. *International tuition:* $30,024 full-time. *Required fees:* $2128. *Financial support:* Fellowships with full tuition reimbursements, research assistantships with full tuition reimbursements, and teaching assistantships with full tuition reimbursements available. Financial award applicants required to submit FAFSA. *Faculty research:* Analytical chemistry, biological/biochemistry, biophysical/computational chemistry, chemical education, organic/medicinal chemistry. *Unit head:* Dr. Donald Hamelberg, Professor; Chair, 404-413-5564, Fax: 404-413-5505, E-mail: dhamelberg@gsu.edu. *Application contact:* Dr. Donald Hamelberg, Professor; Chair, 404-413-5564, Fax: 404-413-5505, E-mail: dhamelberg@gsu.edu.
Website: http://chemistry.gsu.edu/

Georgia State University, College of Education and Human Development, Department of Middle and Secondary Education, Atlanta, GA 30302-3083. Offers curriculum and instruction (Ed D); English education (MAT); mathematics education (M Ed, MAT); middle level education (MAT); reading, language and literacy education (M Ed, MAT), including reading instruction (M Ed); science education (M Ed, MAT), including biology (MAT), broad field science (MAT), chemistry (MAT), earth science (MAT), physics (MAT); social studies education (M Ed, MAT), including economics (MAT), geography (MAT), history (MAT), political science (MAT); teaching and learning (PhD), including language and literacy, mathematics education, music education, science education, social studies education, teaching and teacher education. *Accreditation:* NCATE. *Program availability:* Part-time, evening/weekend, online learning. *Faculty:* 19 full-time (15 women), 9 part-time/adjunct (7 women). *Students:* 217 full-time (136 women), 203 part-time (140 women); includes 229 minority (156 Black or African American, non-Hispanic/Latino; 23 Asian, non-Hispanic/Latino; 31 Hispanic/Latino; 19 Two or more races, non-Hispanic/Latino), 3 international. Average age 34. 149 applicants, 60% accepted, 70 enrolled. In 2018, 112 master's, 23 doctorates awarded. *Entrance requirements:* For master's, GRE; GACE I (for initial teacher preparation programs), baccalaureate degree or equivalent, resume, goals statement, two letters of recommendation, minimum undergraduate GPA of 2.5; proof of initial teacher certification in the content area (for M Ed); for doctorate, GRE, resume, goals statement, writing sample, two letters of recommendation, minimum graduate GPA of 3.3, interview. *Application deadline:* For fall admission, 1/15 priority date for domestic and international students; for spring admission, 10/1 for domestic and international students. Application fee: $50. Electronic applications accepted. *Expenses: Tuition, area resident:* Full-time $9360; part-time $390 per credit hour. Tuition, state resident: full-time $9360; part-time $390 per credit hour. Tuition, nonresident: full-time $30,024; part-time $1251 per credit hour. *International tuition:* $30,024 full-time. *Required fees:* $2128. *Financial support:* In 2018–19, fellowships with full tuition reimbursements (averaging $19,667 per year), research assistantships with full tuition reimbursements (averaging $5,436 per year), teaching assistantships with full tuition reimbursements (averaging $2,779 per year) were awarded; career-related internships or fieldwork, Federal Work-Study, scholarships/grants, health care benefits, tuition waivers (full and partial), and unspecified assistantships also available. Financial award application deadline: 3/15. *Faculty research:* Teacher education in language and literacy, mathematics, science, and social studies in urban middle and secondary school settings; learning technologies in school, community, and corporate settings; multicultural education and education for social justice; urban education; international education. *Unit head:* Dr. Gertrude Marilyn Tinker Sachs, Chair, 404-413-8384, Fax: 404-413-8063, E-mail: gtinkersachs@gsu.edu. *Application contact:* Shaleen Tibbs, Administrative Specialist, 404-413-8385, Fax: 404-413-8063, E-mail: stibbs@gsu.edu.
Website: http://mse.education.gsu.edu/

The Graduate Center, City University of New York, Graduate Studies, Program in Chemistry, New York, NY 10016-4039. Offers PhD. *Degree requirements:* For doctorate, one foreign language, thesis/dissertation. *Entrance requirements:* For doctorate, GRE General Test. Additional exam requirements/recommendations for international students: Required—TOEFL. Electronic applications accepted.

Hampton University, School of Science, Department of Chemistry and Biochemistry, Hampton, VA 23668. Offers chemistry (MS). *Students:* 4 full-time (1 woman); includes 2 minority (1 Black or African American, non-Hispanic/Latino; 1 Asian, non-Hispanic/Latino), 2 international. Average age 28. 7 applicants, 43% accepted, 1 enrolled. *Degree requirements:* For master's, one foreign language, comprehensive exam, thesis. *Entrance requirements:* For master's, GRE General Test. *Application deadline:* For fall admission, 6/1 priority date for domestic students, 4/1 priority date for international students; for winter admission, 11/1 priority date for domestic students, 9/1 priority date for international students; for spring admission, 11/1 for domestic students; for summer admission, 4/1 priority date for domestic students, 2/1 priority date for international students. Applications are processed on a rolling basis. Application fee: $35. Electronic applications accepted. *Financial support:* Fellowships, research assistantships, teaching assistantships, career-related internships or fieldwork, Federal Work-Study, institutionally sponsored loans, and scholarships/grants available. Support available to part-time students. Financial award application deadline: 5/1; financial award applicants required to submit FAFSA. *Faculty research:* Nanoscience, organic synthesis, analytical chemistry, environmental chemistry, bioinorganic chemistry, biochemistry, inorganic chemistry, material science, electrochemistry. *Unit head:* Dr. Willie Darby, Interim Chairman, 757-727-5249. *Application contact:* Dr. Willie Darby, Interim Chairman, 757-727-5249.
Website: http://science.hamptonu.edu/chem/

Harvard University, Graduate School of Arts and Sciences, Department of Chemistry and Chemical Biology, Cambridge, MA 02138. Offers biochemical chemistry (PhD); inorganic chemistry (PhD); organic chemistry (PhD); physical chemistry (PhD). *Degree requirements:* For doctorate, thesis/dissertation, cumulative exams. *Entrance requirements:* For doctorate, GRE General Test, GRE Subject Test. Additional exam requirements/recommendations for international students: Required—TOEFL.

Howard University, Graduate School, Department of Chemistry, Washington, DC 20059-0002. Offers analytical chemistry (MS, PhD); atmospheric (MS, PhD); biochemistry (MS, PhD); environmental (MS, PhD); inorganic chemistry (MS, PhD); organic chemistry (MS, PhD); physical chemistry (MS, PhD). Terminal master's awarded for partial completion of doctoral program. *Degree requirements:* For master's, comprehensive exam, thesis, teaching experience; for doctorate, comprehensive exam, thesis/dissertation, teaching experience. *Entrance requirements:* For master's, GRE General Test, minimum GPA of 2.7; for doctorate, GRE General Test, minimum GPA of 3.0. Additional exam requirements/recommendations for international students: Required—TOEFL. Electronic applications accepted. *Faculty research:* Synthetic organics, materials, natural products, mass spectrometry.

Chemistry

Hunter College of the City University of New York, Graduate School, School of Arts and Sciences, Department of Chemistry, Program in Chemistry, New York, NY 10065-5085. Offers PhD.

Idaho State University, Graduate School, College of Science and Engineering, Department of Chemistry, Pocatello, ID 83209-8023. Offers MNS, MS. MS students must enter as undergraduates. *Program availability:* Part-time. *Degree requirements:* For master's, comprehensive exam, thesis (for some programs). *Entrance requirements:* For master's, GRE General Test, minimum GPA of 3.0 in all upper-division classes; 1 semester of calculus, inorganic chemistry, and analytical chemistry; 1 year of physics, organic chemistry and physical chemistry. Additional exam requirements/recommendations for international students: Required—TOEFL (minimum score 550 paper-based; 80 iBT). Electronic applications accepted. *Faculty research:* Low temperature plasma, organic chemistry, physical chemistry, inorganic chemistry, analytical chemistry.

Illinois Institute of Technology, Graduate College, College of Science, Department of Chemistry, Chicago, IL 60616. Offers analytical chemistry (MAS); chemistry (MAS, MS, PhD); materials chemistry (MAS), including inorganic, organic, or polymeric materials. *Program availability:* Part-time, evening/weekend, online learning. Terminal master's awarded for partial completion of doctoral program. *Degree requirements:* For master's, comprehensive exam, thesis (for some programs); for doctorate, comprehensive exam, thesis/dissertation. *Entrance requirements:* For master's, GRE General Test (minimum score 300 Quantitative and Verbal, 2.5 Analytical Writing), minimum undergraduate GPA of 3.0; for doctorate, GRE General Test (minimum score 310 Quantitative and Verbal, 3.0 Analytical Writing), GRE Subject Test, minimum undergraduate GPA of 3.0. Additional exam requirements/recommendations for international students: Required—TOEFL (minimum score 550 paper-based; 80 iBT); Recommended—IELTS. Electronic applications accepted. *Faculty research:* Materials science, biological chemistry, synthetic chemistry, computational chemistry, energy, sensor science and technology, scholarship of teaching and learning.

Indiana University Bloomington, University Graduate School, College of Arts and Sciences, Department of Chemistry, Bloomington, IN 47405. Offers analytical chemistry (PhD); chemical biology (PhD); chemistry (MAT); inorganic chemistry (PhD); materials chemistry (PhD); organic chemistry (PhD); physical chemistry (PhD); MSES/MS. Terminal master's awarded for partial completion of doctoral program. *Degree requirements:* For master's, thesis; for doctorate, thesis/dissertation. *Entrance requirements:* For master's and doctorate, GRE General Test, GRE Subject Test. Additional exam requirements/recommendations for international students: Required—TOEFL. Electronic applications accepted. *Faculty research:* Synthesis of complex natural products, organic reaction mechanisms, organic electrochemistry, transitive-metal chemistry, solid-state and surface chemistry.

Indiana University of Pennsylvania, School of Graduate Studies and Research, College of Natural Sciences and Mathematics, Department of Chemistry, Program in Applied and Industrial Chemistry, Indiana, PA 15705. Offers PSM. *Program availability:* Part-time. *Faculty:* 5 full-time (3 women). *Students:* 5 full-time (1 woman), 1 (woman) part-time; includes 1 minority (Two or more races, non-Hispanic/Latino), 1 international. Average age 22. 15 applicants, 73% accepted, 5 enrolled. In 2018, 1 master's awarded. *Degree requirements:* For master's, thesis. *Entrance requirements:* For master's, 2 letters of recommendation. Additional exam requirements/recommendations for international students: Required—TOEFL (minimum score 540 paper-based). *Application deadline:* Applications are processed on a rolling basis. Application fee: $50. Electronic applications accepted. *Expenses:* Tuition, state resident: full-time $12,384; part-time $516 per credit hour. Tuition, nonresident: full-time $18,576; part-time $774 per credit hour. *Required fees:* $4454; $186 per credit hour. $65 per semester. Tuition and fees vary according to program and reciprocity agreements. *Financial support:* In 2018–19, 3 research assistantships with tuition reimbursements (averaging $2,467 per year) were awarded; career-related internships or fieldwork, Federal Work-Study, scholarships/grants, and unspecified assistantships also available. *Unit head:* Dr. Andrada Maicaneanu, Coordinator, 724-357-2277, E-mail: Sanda.Maicaneanu@iup.edu. *Application contact:* Dr. Andrada Maicaneanu, Coordinator, 724-357-2277, E-mail: Sanda.Maicaneanu@iup.edu.

Indiana University–Purdue University Indianapolis, School of Science, Department of Chemistry and Chemical Biology, Indianapolis, IN 46202. Offers MS, PhD, MD/PhD. MD/PhD offered jointly with Indiana University School of Medicine and Purdue University. *Program availability:* Part-time, evening/weekend. Terminal master's awarded for partial completion of doctoral program. *Degree requirements:* For master's, thesis (for some programs); for doctorate, comprehensive exam, thesis/dissertation. *Entrance requirements:* For master's and doctorate, minimum GPA of 3.0. Additional exam requirements/recommendations for international students: Required—TOEFL (minimum score 106 iBT). Electronic applications accepted. *Faculty research:* Analytical, biological, inorganic, organic, and physical chemistry.

Instituto Tecnológico y de Estudios Superiores de Monterrey, Campus Monterrey, Graduate and Research Division, Program in Natural and Social Sciences, Monterrey, Mexico. Offers biotechnology (MS); chemistry (MS, PhD); communications (MS); education (MA). *Program availability:* Part-time. *Degree requirements:* For master's, one foreign language, thesis; for doctorate, one foreign language, thesis/dissertation. *Entrance requirements:* For master's, EXADEP; for doctorate, EXADEP, master's degree in related field. Additional exam requirements/recommendations for international students: Required—TOEFL. *Faculty research:* Cultural industries, mineral substances, bioremediation, food processing, CQ in industrial chemical processing.

Iowa State University of Science and Technology, Department of Chemistry, Ames, IA 50011. Offers MS, PhD. *Degree requirements:* For master's, thesis; for doctorate, thesis/dissertation. *Entrance requirements:* Additional exam requirements/recommendations for international students: Required—TOEFL (minimum score 570 paper-based; 89 iBT), IELTS (minimum score 6.5). Electronic applications accepted.

Jackson State University, Graduate School, College of Science, Engineering and Technology, Department of Chemistry and Biochemistry, Jackson, MS 39217. Offers MS, PhD. *Program availability:* Part-time, evening/weekend. *Degree requirements:* For master's, comprehensive exam, thesis; for doctorate, comprehensive exam, thesis/dissertation. *Entrance requirements:* For master's, GRE General Test; for doctorate, MAT. Additional exam requirements/recommendations for international students: Required—TOEFL (minimum score 520 paper-based; 67 iBT). *Faculty research:* Electrochemical and spectroscopic studies on charge transfer and energy transfer processes, spectroscopy of trapped molecular ions, respirable mine dust.

Johns Hopkins University, Zanvyl Krieger School of Arts and Sciences, Chemistry-Biology Interface Program, Baltimore, MD 21218. Offers chemical biology (MS, PhD). *Students:* 30 full-time (10 women). 85 applicants, 16% accepted, 4 enrolled. Terminal master's awarded for partial completion of doctoral program. *Degree requirements:* For master's, comprehensive exam, 8 one-semester courses, oral exam; for doctorate, comprehensive exam, thesis/dissertation, 8 one-semester courses, research proposal,

oral exam. *Entrance requirements:* For doctorate, GRE General Test; GRE Subject Test in biochemistry, cell and molecular biology, biology or chemistry (strongly recommended), 3 letters of recommendation, transcripts, statement of purpose, resume/curriculum vitae, interview. Additional exam requirements/recommendations for international students: Required—TOEFL (minimum score 600 paper-based). *Application deadline:* For fall admission, 1/15 for domestic and international students. Applications are processed on a rolling basis. Application fee: $75. Electronic applications accepted. *Expenses:* Contact institution. *Financial support:* Fellowships, teaching assistantships, Federal Work-Study, scholarships/grants, health care benefits, unspecified assistantships, and stipends (averaging $32,470) available. Financial award application deadline: 4/15; financial award applicants required to submit FAFSA. *Faculty research:* Enzyme mechanisms, inhibitors, and metabolic pathways; DNA replication, damaged, and repair; using small molecules to probe signal transduction, gene regulation, angiogenesis, and other biological processes; synthetic methods and medicinal chemistry; synthetic modeling of metalloenzymes. *Unit head:* Dr. David Yarkony, Chair, 410-516-4663, Fax: 410-516-8420, E-mail: yarkony@jhu.edu. *Application contact:* Richard Helman, Director of Graduate Admissions, 410-516-7125, E-mail: rhelman@jhu.edu.
Website: http://www.cbi.jhu.edu

Johns Hopkins University, Zanvyl Krieger School of Arts and Sciences, Department of Chemistry, Baltimore, MD 21218. Offers MA, PhD. *Faculty:* 31 full-time (4 women). *Students:* 120 full-time (41 women). 196 applicants, 19% accepted, 14 enrolled. In 2018, 24 master's, 21 doctorates awarded. Terminal master's awarded for partial completion of doctoral program. *Degree requirements:* For master's, comprehensive exam, 6 one-semester courses, department oral exam; for doctorate, comprehensive exam, thesis/dissertation, 6 one-semester courses, literature seminar, department oral exam, graduate board oral exam. *Entrance requirements:* For doctorate, GRE General Test, GRE Subject Test (recommended), 3 letters of recommendation, transcripts, statement of purpose, resume/curriculum vitae. Additional exam requirements/recommendations for international students: Required—TOEFL (minimum score 600 paper-based), IELTS. *Application deadline:* For fall admission, 1/15 for domestic and international students. Applications are processed on a rolling basis. Application fee: $75. Electronic applications accepted. *Expenses:* Contact institution. *Financial support:* In 2018–19, 8 students received support, including 7 fellowships with partial tuition reimbursements available; teaching assistantships, Federal Work-Study, scholarships/grants, health care benefits, unspecified assistantships, and stipends (averaging $32,470) also available. Financial award application deadline: 4/15; financial award applicants required to submit FAFSA. *Faculty research:* Experimental physical chemistry, biophysical chemistry, inorganic/materials chemistry, organic/bioorganic chemistry, theoretical chemistry. *Unit head:* Dr. David Yarkony, Chair, 410-516-4663, E-mail: yarkony@jhu.edu. *Application contact:* Richard Helman, Director of Graduate Admissions, 410-516-7125, E-mail: rhelman@jhu.edu.
Website: http://chemistry.jhu.edu/

Kansas State University, Graduate School, College of Arts and Sciences, Department of Chemistry, Manhattan, KS 66506. Offers MS, PhD. Terminal master's awarded for partial completion of doctoral program. *Degree requirements:* For master's, thesis; for doctorate, thesis/dissertation, cumulative exams, oral proposal. *Entrance requirements:* For master's and doctorate, GRE, minimum GPA of 3.0. Additional exam requirements/recommendations for international students: Required—TOEFL (minimum score 550 paper-based; 79 iBT). Electronic applications accepted. *Faculty research:* Inorganic chemistry, organic and biological chemistry, analytical chemistry, physical chemistry, materials chemistry and nanotechnology.

Kennesaw State University, College of Science and Mathematics, Program in Chemical Sciences, Kennesaw, GA 30144. Offers biochemistry (MS); chemistry (MS). *Students:* 16 full-time (8 women); includes 7 minority (2 Black or African American, non-Hispanic/Latino; 1 Asian, non-Hispanic/Latino; 2 Hispanic/Latino; 1 Native Hawaiian or other Pacific Islander, non-Hispanic/Latino; 1 Two or more races, non-Hispanic/Latino), 2 international. Average age 28. 18 applicants, 67% accepted, 8 enrolled. In 2018, 3 master's awarded. *Degree requirements:* For master's, thesis. *Entrance requirements:* For master's, GRE. Additional exam requirements/recommendations for international students: Required—TOEFL (minimum score 550 paper-based; 80 iBT), IELTS (minimum score 6.5). *Application deadline:* For fall admission, 4/1 for domestic and international students. Application fee: $60. Electronic applications accepted. *Expenses: Tuition, area resident:* Full-time $6960; part-time $290 per credit hour. Tuition, state resident: full-time $6960; part-time $290 per credit hour. Tuition, nonresident: full-time $25,080; part-time $1045 per credit hour. *International tuition:* $25,080 full-time. *Required fees:* $2006; $1706 per semester. $853 per semester. *Financial support:* Teaching assistantships with full tuition reimbursements and unspecified assistantships available. Financial award applicants required to submit FAFSA. *Unit head:* Dr. Chris Dockery, Assistant Department Chair, 470-578-2047, E-mail: mscb@kennesaw.edu. *Application contact:* Admissions Counselor, 470-578-4377, Fax: 470-578-9172, E-mail: ksugrad@kennesaw.edu.
Website: http://csm.kennesaw.edu/chemistry-biochemistry/programs/mscb.php

Kent State University, College of Arts and Sciences, Department of Chemistry and Biochemistry, Kent, OH 44242-0001. Offers chemistry (MA, MS, PhD). *Program availability:* Part-time. *Faculty:* 13 full-time (0 women). *Students:* 50 full-time (19 women), 2 part-time (1 woman), 39 international. Average age 30. 76 applicants, 14% accepted, 7 enrolled. In 2018, 2 master's, 6 doctorates awarded. Terminal master's awarded for partial completion of doctoral program. *Degree requirements:* For master's, thesis; for doctorate, comprehensive exam, thesis/dissertation. *Entrance requirements:* For master's, GRE General Test (minimum score 600/143 quantitative); GRE Subject Test (encouraged), transcripts; goal statement; completion of undergraduate courses consisting of one year each in analytical chemistry or biochemistry, organic chemistry, physical chemistry, calculus and physics; for doctorate, GRE General Test (minimum score 600/143 quantitative); GRE Subject Test (encouraged), 3 letters of recommendation; transcripts; goal statement; minimum undergraduate GPA of 3.0, 3.25 graduate; completion of undergraduate courses consisting of one year each in analytical chemistry or biochemistry, organic chemistry, physical chemistry, calculus and physics. Additional exam requirements/recommendations for international students: Required—TOEFL (minimum score 525 paper-based, 71 iBT), Michigan English Language Assessment Battery (minimum score 74), IELTS (minimum score 6.0) or PTE (minimum score 50). *Application deadline:* For fall admission, 1/15 for domestic and international students. Applications are processed on a rolling basis. Application fee: $45 ($70 for international students). Electronic applications accepted. *Expenses:* Tuition, state resident: full-time $11,766; part-time $536 per credit. Tuition, nonresident: full-time $21,952; part-time $999 per credit. *International tuition:* $21,952 full-time. Tuition and fees vary according to course load. *Financial support:* Research assistantships with full tuition reimbursements, teaching assistantships with full tuition reimbursements, Federal Work-Study, scholarships/grants, and unspecified assistantships available. Financial award application deadline: 1/15. *Unit head:* Dr. Soumitra Basu, Professor/Chair, 330-672-3906, E-mail: sbasu@kent.edu. *Application contact:* Erin Michael-McLaughlin, Academic Program Coordinator, 330-672-0030, E-mail: enmichae@kent.edu.
Website: http://www.kent.edu/chemistry/

Lakehead University, Graduate Studies, Department of Chemistry, Thunder Bay, ON P7B 5E1, Canada. Offers M Sc. *Program availability:* Part-time, evening/weekend. *Degree requirements:* For master's, thesis, oral examination. *Entrance requirements:* For master's, minimum B+ average. Additional exam requirements/recommendations for international students: Required—TOEFL. *Faculty research:* Physical inorganic chemistry, photochemistry, physical chemistry.

Lamar University, College of Graduate Studies, College of Arts and Sciences, Department of Chemistry and Biochemistry, Beaumont, TX 77710. Offers MS. *Program availability:* Part-time. *Faculty:* 13 full-time (4 women), 2 part-time/adjunct (both women). *Students:* 10 full-time (6 women), 10 part-time (8 women); includes 3 minority (1 Black or African American, non-Hispanic/Latino; 2 Two or more races, non-Hispanic/Latino), 14 international. Average age 26. 16 applicants, 94% accepted, 5 enrolled. In 2018, 25 master's awarded. *Degree requirements:* For master's, thesis, practicum. *Entrance requirements:* For master's, GRE General Test, minimum GPA of 2.5 in last 60 hours of course work. Additional exam requirements/recommendations for international students: Required—TOEFL (minimum score 527 paper-based; 71 iBT), IELTS (minimum score 6). *Application deadline:* Applications are processed on a rolling basis. Application fee: $25 ($50 for international students). Electronic applications accepted. *Expenses:* Tuition, state resident: full-time $6234; part-time $346 per credit hour. Tuition, nonresident: full-time $6852; part-time $761 per credit hour. *International tuition:* $6852 full-time. *Required fees:* $1940; $327 per credit hour. Tuition and fees vary according to course load, campus/location, program and reciprocity agreements. *Financial support:* In 2018–19, 1 student received support, including 5 teaching assistantships with partial tuition reimbursements available (averaging $9,000 per year); tuition waivers (partial) and unspecified assistantships also available. *Faculty research:* Environmental chemistry, surface chemistry, polymer chemistry, organic synthesis, computational chemistry. *Unit head:* Dr. Xiangyang Lei, Interim Department Chair, 409-880-8267, Fax: 409-880-8270. *Application contact:* Celeste Contreas, Director, Admissions and Academic Services, 409-880-8888, Fax: 409-880-7419, E-mail: gradmissions@lamar.edu. *Website:* http://artssciences.lamar.edu/chemistry-and-biochemistry/

Laurentian University, School of Graduate Studies and Research, Programme in Chemistry and Biochemistry, Sudbury, ON P3E 2C6, Canada. Offers analytical chemistry (M Sc); biochemistry (M Sc); environmental chemistry (M Sc); organic chemistry (M Sc); physical/theoretical chemistry (M Sc). *Program availability:* Part-time. *Degree requirements:* For master's, thesis or alternative. *Entrance requirements:* For master's, honors degree with minimum second class. *Faculty research:* Cell cycle checkpoints, kinetic modeling, toxicology to metal stress, quantum chemistry, biogeochemistry metal speciation.

Lehigh University, College of Arts and Sciences, Department of Chemistry, Bethlehem, PA 18015. Offers MS, PhD. *Faculty:* 16 full-time (2 women), 3 part-time/adjunct (2 women). *Students:* 31 full-time (15 women), 3 part-time (0 women); includes 1 minority (Hispanic/Latino), 9 international. Average age 26. 48 applicants, 38% accepted, 6 enrolled. In 2018, 5 master's, 7 doctorates awarded. Terminal master's awarded for partial completion of doctoral program. *Degree requirements:* For doctorate, comprehensive exam, thesis/dissertation. *Entrance requirements:* For master's, pass 2 proficiency exams; total of five areas: organic, inorganic, physical, biochemistry, analytical; for doctorate, pass 3 proficiency exams; total of five areas: organic, inorganic, physical, biochemistry, analytical. Additional exam requirements/recommendations for international students: Required—TOEFL (minimum score 85 iBT), IELTS (minimum score 6.5). *Application deadline:* For fall admission, 1/1 priority date for domestic and international students. Applications are processed on a rolling basis. Application fee: $75. Electronic applications accepted. *Expenses:* $1500 per credit. *Financial support:* In 2018–19, 5 fellowships with full tuition reimbursements (averaging $30,500 per year), 4 research assistantships, 24 teaching assistantships with full tuition reimbursements (averaging $28,500 per year) were awarded. Financial award application deadline: 1/1. *Faculty research:* Analytical chemistry, biochemistry, computational chemistry, inorganic chemistry, materials and polymer chemistry. *Total annual research expenditures:* $2.5 million. *Unit head:* Prof. Gregory S. Ferguson, Professor/Chair, 610-758-3462, Fax: 610-758-6536, E-mail: gf03@lehigh.edu. *Application contact:* Dr. Kai Landskron, Graduate Admissions Director, 610-758-5788, Fax: 610-758-6536, E-mail: kal205@lehigh.edu. *Website:* http://www.lehigh.edu/chemistry

Lewis University, College of Arts and Sciences, Program in Chemistry, Romeoville, IL 60446. Offers MS. *Program availability:* Part-time. *Students:* 2 full-time (both women), 15 part-time (11 women); includes 4 minority (1 Asian, non-Hispanic/Latino; 2 Hispanic/Latino; 1 Two or more races, non-Hispanic/Latino). Average age 24. *Entrance requirements:* For master's, bachelor's degree in chemistry, or in another area of study with work experience in chemical industry; minimum GPA of 3.0; 3 letters of recommendation; personal statement. Additional exam requirements/recommendations for international students: Required—TOEFL (minimum score 550 paper-based; 79 iBT), IELTS (minimum score 6). *Application deadline:* For fall admission, 5/1 for international students; for winter admission, 11/1 for international students. Applications are processed on a rolling basis. Application fee: $40. Electronic applications accepted. *Financial support:* Federal Work-Study and unspecified assistantships available. Financial award application deadline: 5/1; financial award applicants required to submit FAFSA. *Unit head:* Jason Keleher, Program Director. *Application contact:* Linda Campbell, Graduate Admissions Counselor, 815-836-5610, E-mail: grad@lewisu.edu. *Website:* http://www.lewisu.edu/academics/mschemistry/index.htm

Long Island University–LIU Brooklyn, Richard L. Conolly College of Liberal Arts and Sciences, Brooklyn, NY 11201-8423. Offers biology (MS); chemistry (MS); clinical psychology (PhD); creative writing (MFA); English (MA); media arts (MA, MFA); political science (MA); psychology (MA); social science (MS); United Nations (Advanced Certificate); urban studies (MA); writing and production for television (MFA). *Program availability:* Part-time. Terminal master's awarded for partial completion of doctoral program. *Degree requirements:* For master's, comprehensive exam (for some programs), thesis (for some programs); for doctorate, thesis/dissertation. *Entrance requirements:* For doctorate, GRE. Additional exam requirements/recommendations for international students: Required—TOEFL (minimum score 550 paper-based, 79 iBT) or IELTS. Electronic applications accepted. *Faculty research:* Quantum gravity and astrophysics; string theory; pharmaceutical biotechnology with a focus on molecular details of drug susceptibility/resistance mechanisms; entomology, population and community ecology, agroecology, and biodiversity; psychotherapy process-outcome, particularly therapeutic alliance development, the role of common factors, and the study of treatment failures; personality pathology, borderline personality disorder and pathological narcissism.

Louisiana State University and Agricultural & Mechanical College, Graduate School, College of Science, Department of Chemistry, Baton Rouge, LA 70803. Offers MS, PhD.

Louisiana Tech University, Graduate School, College of Education, Ruston, LA 71272. Offers counseling and guidance (MA), including clinical mental health counseling, human services, orientation and mobility; counseling psychology (PhD); curriculum and instruction (M Ed); cyber education (Graduate Certificate); dynamics of domestic and family violence (Graduate Certificate); early childhood education - PreK-3 (MAT); educational leadership (M Ed, Ed D); elementary education and special education mild/moderate grades 1-5 (MAT); higher education administration (Graduate Certificate); industrial/organizational psychology (MA, PhD); kinesiology (MS); middle school education (MAT), including mathematics; orientation and mobility (Graduate Certificate); rehabilitation teaching for the blind (Graduate Certificate); secondary education (MAT), including agriculture, biology, business, chemistry, English; special education: visually impaired (MAT); teacher leader education (Graduate Certificate); visual impairments - blind education (Graduate Certificate). *Accreditation:* NCATE. *Program availability:* Part-time. *Degree requirements:* For master's, thesis; for doctorate, thesis/dissertation. *Entrance requirements:* For master's and doctorate, GRE General Test. Additional exam requirements/recommendations for international students: Required—TOEFL (minimum score 550 paper-based; 80 iBT), IELTS (minimum score 6.5). Electronic applications accepted. *Faculty research:* Blindness and the best methods for increasing independence for individuals who are blind or visually impaired; educating and investigating factors contributing to improvements in human performance across the lifespan and a reduction in injury rates during training.

Loyola University Chicago, Graduate School, Department of Chemistry and Biochemistry, Chicago, IL 60660. Offers chemistry (PhD); chemistry/biochemistry (MS). *Program availability:* Part-time, evening/weekend. *Faculty:* 16 full-time (2 women). *Students:* 34 full-time (22 women), 5 part-time (0 women); includes 12 minority (4 Asian, non-Hispanic/Latino; 6 Hispanic/Latino; 2 Two or more races, non-Hispanic/Latino), 8 international. Average age 27. 46 applicants, 50% accepted, 12 enrolled. In 2018, 5 master's, 7 doctorates awarded. Terminal master's awarded for partial completion of doctoral program. *Degree requirements:* For master's, thesis (for some programs); for doctorate, comprehensive exam, thesis/dissertation. *Entrance requirements:* For master's and doctorate, GRE General Test, GRE Subject Test. Additional exam requirements/recommendations for international students: Required—TOEFL (minimum score 550 paper-based). *Application deadline:* For fall admission, 8/1 priority date for domestic students; for spring admission, 12/1 for domestic students. Applications are processed on a rolling basis. Application fee: $0. Electronic applications accepted. Application fee is waived when completed online. *Expenses:* Tuition: Full-time $1033; part-time $788 per credit hour. *Required fees:* $700; $400 per credit hour. $400. One-time fee: $100. Tuition and fees vary according to course level, course load, degree level, program and student level. *Financial support:* In 2018–19, 19 students received support, including 3 fellowships with full tuition reimbursements available (averaging $23,000 per year), 6 research assistantships with tuition reimbursements available (averaging $23,000 per year), 16 teaching assistantships with full tuition reimbursements available (averaging $23,000 per year); Federal Work-Study, scholarships/grants, traineeships, and unspecified assistantships also available. Financial award application deadline: 2/1; financial award applicants required to submit FAFSA. *Faculty research:* Magnetic resonance of membrane/protein systems, organometallic catalysis, novel synthesis of natural products. *Total annual research expenditures:* $682,510. *Unit head:* Dr. Martina Schmeling, Graduate Program Director, 773-508-3124, Fax: 773-508-3086, E-mail: mschmel@luc.edu. *Application contact:* Sandy Orozco, Graduate Program Coordinator, 773-508-3104, E-mail: sorozco1@luc.edu. *Website:* http://www.luc.edu/chemistry/

Manhattanville College, School of Education, Program in Middle Childhood/Adolescence Education (Grades 5-12), Purchase, NY 10577-2132. Offers biology and special education (MPS); chemistry and special education (MPS); education for sustainability (Advanced Certificate); English and special education (MPS); literacy and special education (MPS); literacy specialist (MPS); math and special education (MPS); mathematics (Advanced Certificate); middle childhood/adolescence ed science (biology or chemistry grades 5-12) or (physics grades 7-12) (MAT); middle childhood/adolescence education (grades 5-12) English (MAT, Advanced Certificate); middle childhood/adolescence education (grades 5-12) mathematics (MAT, Advanced Certificate); middle childhood/adolescence education (grades 5-12) science (biology chemistry, physics, earth science) (Advanced Certificate); middle childhood/adolescence education (grades 5-12) social studies (MAT, Advanced Certificate); physics (MAT, Advanced Certificate); social studies (MAT); social studies and special education (MPS); special education generalist (MPS). *Program availability:* Part-time, evening/weekend. *Faculty:* 3 full-time (2 women), 9 part-time/adjunct (4 women). *Students:* 11 full-time (6 women), 17 part-time (12 women); includes 3 minority (1 Black or African American, non-Hispanic/Latino; 2 Hispanic/Latino). Average age 31. 17 applicants, 71% accepted, 7 enrolled. In 2018, 8 master's, 3 other advanced degrees awarded. *Degree requirements:* For master's, comprehensive exam (for some programs), thesis (for some programs), student teaching, research seminars, portfolios, internships, writing assessment; for Advanced Certificate, comprehensive exam (for some programs). *Entrance requirements:* For master's, for programs leading to certification, candidates must submit scores from GRE or MAT(Miller Analogies Test), minimum undergraduate GPA of 3.0, all transcripts from all colleges and universities attended, 2 letters of recommendation, interview, essay (2-3 page personal statement that describes reasons for choosing education as profession and personal philosophy of education), proof of immunization (for those born after 1957). Additional exam requirements/recommendations for international students: Required—TOEFL (minimum score 600 paper-based; 110 iBT); Recommended—IELTS (minimum score 8). *Application deadline:* Applications are processed on a rolling basis. Application fee: $75. Electronic applications accepted. *Expenses:* 935 per credit. *Financial support:* Teaching assistantships, career-related internships or fieldwork, Federal Work-Study, institutionally sponsored loans, scholarships/grants, and unspecified assistantships available. Financial award application deadline: 3/15; financial award applicants required to submit FAFSA. *Faculty research:* Education for sustainability. *Unit head:* Dr. Shelley Wepner, Dean, 914-323-3153, Fax: 914-323-5493, E-mail: Shelley.Wepner@mville.edu. *Application contact:* Alissa Wilson, Director, Graduate Admissions, 914-323-3150, Fax: 914-694-1732, E-mail: edschool@mville.edu. *Website:* http://www.mville.edu/programs#/search/19

Marquette University, Graduate School, College of Arts and Sciences, Department of Chemistry, Milwaukee, WI 53201-1881. Offers analytical chemistry (MS, PhD); bioanalytical chemistry (MS, PhD); biophysical chemistry (MS, PhD); chemical physics (MS, PhD); inorganic chemistry (MS, PhD); organic chemistry (MS, PhD); physical chemistry (MS, PhD). *Program availability:* Part-time. Terminal master's awarded for partial completion of doctoral program. *Degree requirements:* For master's, comprehensive exam; for doctorate, thesis/dissertation, cumulative exams. *Entrance requirements:* For master's and doctorate, official transcripts from all current and previous colleges/universities except Marquette, three letters of recommendation from individuals familiar with the applicant's academic work. Additional exam requirements/recommendations for international students: Required—TOEFL. Electronic applications accepted. *Faculty research:* Inorganic complexes, laser Raman spectroscopy, organic synthesis, synthetic bioinorganic chemistry, electro-active organic molecules.

Peterson's Graduate Programs in the Physical Sciences, Mathematics, Agricultural Sciences, the Environment & Natural Resources 2020

www.petersons.com **53**

Chemistry

Marshall University, Academic Affairs Division, College of Science, Department of Chemistry, Huntington, WV 25755. Offers MS. *Degree requirements:* For master's, thesis.

Massachusetts Institute of Technology, School of Science, Department of Chemistry, Cambridge, MA 02139. Offers biological chemistry (PhD); inorganic chemistry (PhD); organic chemistry (PhD); physical chemistry (PhD). *Degree requirements:* For doctorate, comprehensive exam, thesis/dissertation, teaching assistantship during two semesters. *Entrance requirements:* For doctorate, GRE General Test. Additional exam requirements/recommendations for international students: Required—TOEFL, IELTS. Electronic applications accepted. *Expenses: Tuition:* Full-time $51,520; part-time $800 per credit hour. *Required fees:* $312. *Faculty research:* Synthetic organic and organometallic chemistry including catalysis; biological chemistry including bioorganic chemistry; physical chemistry including chemical dynamics, theoretical chemistry and biophysical chemistry; inorganic chemistry including synthesis, catalysis, bioinorganic and physical inorganic chemistry; materials chemistry including surface science, nanoscience and polymers.

McGill University, Faculty of Graduate and Postdoctoral Studies, Faculty of Science, Department of Chemistry, Montréal, QC H3A 2T5, Canada. Offers chemical biology (M Sc, PhD); chemistry (M Sc, PhD).

McMaster University, School of Graduate Studies, Faculty of Science, Department of Chemistry, Hamilton, ON L8S 4M2, Canada. Offers analytical chemistry (M Sc, PhD); chemical physics (M Sc, PhD); chemistry (M Sc, PhD); inorganic chemistry (M Sc, PhD); organic chemistry (M Sc, PhD); physical chemistry (M Sc, PhD); polymer chemistry (M Sc, PhD). *Program availability:* Part-time. Terminal master's awarded for partial completion of doctoral program. *Degree requirements:* For master's, thesis; for doctorate, comprehensive exam, thesis/dissertation. *Entrance requirements:* For master's, minimum B+ average. Additional exam requirements/recommendations for international students: Required—TOEFL (minimum score 550 paper-based).

McNeese State University, Doré School of Graduate Studies, College of Science and Agriculture, Department of Chemistry and Physics, Program in Environmental and Chemical Sciences, Lake Charles, LA 70609. Offers environmental and chemical sciences (MS), including chemistry. *Program availability:* Evening/weekend. *Degree requirements:* For master's, comprehensive exam, thesis or alternative. *Entrance requirements:* For master's, GRE.

MCPHS University, Graduate Studies, Program in Medicinal Chemistry, Boston, MA 02115-5896. Offers MS, PhD. Terminal master's awarded for partial completion of doctoral program. *Degree requirements:* For master's, thesis, oral defense of thesis; for doctorate, one foreign language, comprehensive exam, thesis/dissertation, oral defense of dissertation, qualifying exam. *Entrance requirements:* For master's and doctorate, GRE General Test, minimum GPA of 3.0. Additional exam requirements/recommendations for international students: Required—TOEFL (minimum score 550 paper-based; 79 iBT). Electronic applications accepted. *Faculty research:* Analytical chemistry, medicinal chemistry, organic chemistry, neurochemistry.

Memorial University of Newfoundland, School of Graduate Studies, Department of Chemistry, St. John's, NL A1C 5S7, Canada. Offers chemistry (M Sc, PhD); instrumental analysis (M Sc). *Program availability:* Part-time. *Degree requirements:* For master's, thesis, research seminar, American Chemical Society Exam; for doctorate, comprehensive exam, thesis/dissertation, seminars, oral thesis defense, American Chemical Society Exam. *Entrance requirements:* For master's, B Sc or honors degree in chemistry (preferred); for doctorate, master's degree in chemistry or honors bachelor's degree. Electronic applications accepted. *Faculty research:* Analytical/environmental chemistry; medicinal electrochemistry; inorganic, marine, organic, physical, and theoretical/computational chemistry, environmental science and instrumental analysis.

Miami University, College of Arts and Science, Department of Chemistry and Biochemistry, Oxford, OH 45056. Offers MS, PhD. *Faculty:* 23 full-time (7 women). *Students:* 64 full-time (31 women), 1 part-time (0 women); includes 2 minority (1 Black or African American, non-Hispanic/Latino; 1 Hispanic/Latino), 37 international. Average age 27. In 2018, 2 master's, 7 doctorates awarded. *Unit head:* Dr. Michael Crowder, Professor and Chair, 513-529-7274, E-mail: crowdemw@miamioh.edu. *Application contact:* Dr. Scott Hartley, Professor, 513-529-1731, E-mail: hartlecs@miamioh.edu.
Website: http://www.miamioh.edu/cas/academics/departments/chemistry-biochemistry/

Michigan State University, The Graduate School, College of Natural Science, Department of Chemistry, East Lansing, MI 48824. Offers chemical physics (PhD); chemistry (MS, PhD); chemistry-environmental toxicology (PhD); computational chemistry (MS). *Entrance requirements:* Additional exam requirements/recommendations for international students: Required—TOEFL. Electronic applications accepted. *Faculty research:* Analytical chemistry, inorganic and organic chemistry, nuclear chemistry, physical chemistry, theoretical and computational chemistry.

Michigan State University, National Superconducting Cyclotron Laboratory, East Lansing, MI 48824. Offers chemistry (PhD); physics (PhD).

Michigan Technological University, Graduate School, College of Sciences and Arts, Department of Chemistry, Houghton, MI 49931. Offers MS, PhD. *Faculty:* 20 full-time (9 women), 3 part-time/adjunct. *Students:* 34 full-time (15 women); includes 2 minority (1 Black or African American, non-Hispanic/Latino; 1 Two or more races, non-Hispanic/Latino), 26 international. Average age 28. 116 applicants, 43% accepted, 12 enrolled. In 2018, 1 master's, 4 doctorates awarded. Terminal master's awarded for partial completion of doctoral program. *Degree requirements:* For master's, thesis; for doctorate, comprehensive exam, thesis/dissertation. *Entrance requirements:* For master's and doctorate, statement of purpose, personal statement, official transcripts, 3 letters of recommendation, resume/curriculum vitae. Additional exam requirements/recommendations for international students: Required—TOEFL (recommended minimum score 88 iBT) or IELTS (recommended minimum score of 6.5). *Application deadline:* For fall admission, 1/1 priority date for domestic and international students. Applications are processed on a rolling basis. Electronic applications accepted. *Expenses: Tuition, area resident:* Full-time $18,126; part-time $1007 per credit. Tuition, state resident: full-time $18,126; part-time $1007 per credit. Tuition, nonresident: full-time $18,126; part-time $1007 per credit. *International tuition:* $18,126 full-time. *Required fees:* $248; $124 per semester. Tuition and fees vary according to course load and program. *Financial support:* In 2018–19, 34 students received support, including 6 fellowships with tuition reimbursements available (averaging $16,590 per year), 4 research assistantships with tuition reimbursements available (averaging $16,590 per year), 21 teaching assistantships with tuition reimbursements available (averaging $16,590 per year); career-related internships or fieldwork, Federal Work-Study, scholarships/grants, traineeships, health care benefits, unspecified assistantships, and cooperative program also available. Financial award applicants required to submit FAFSA. *Faculty research:* Inorganic chemistry, physical/theoretical chemistry, bio/organic chemistry, polymer/materials chemistry, analytical/environmental chemistry. *Total annual research expenditures:* $509,827. *Unit head:* Dr. John Jaszczak, Interim Chair, 906-487-2048, Fax: 906-487-2061, E-mail: cfchabal@mtu.edu. *Application contact:* Kimberly McMullan, Office Assistant, 906-487-2048, Fax: 906-487-2061, E-mail: klmcmull@mtu.edu.
Website: http://www.mtu.edu/chemistry/

Middle Tennessee State University, College of Graduate Studies, College of Basic and Applied Sciences, Department of Chemistry, Murfreesboro, TN 37132. Offers MS. *Program availability:* Part-time, evening/weekend, online learning. *Degree requirements:* For master's, comprehensive exam, thesis. *Entrance requirements:* For master's, GRE. Additional exam requirements/recommendations for international students: Required—TOEFL (minimum score 525 paper-based; 71 iBT) or IELTS (minimum score 6). Electronic applications accepted.

Mississippi College, Graduate School, College of Arts and Sciences, School of Science and Mathematics, Department of Chemistry and Biochemistry, Clinton, MS 39058. Offers MCS, MS. *Program availability:* Part-time. *Degree requirements:* For master's, comprehensive exam, thesis (for some programs). *Entrance requirements:* For master's, GRE. Additional exam requirements/recommendations for international students: Recommended—TOEFL, IELTS. Electronic applications accepted.

Mississippi State University, College of Arts and Sciences, Department of Chemistry, Mississippi State, MS 39762. Offers MA, MS, PhD. MA offered online only. *Program availability:* Blended/hybrid learning. *Faculty:* 16 full-time (4 women). *Students:* 68 full-time (31 women), 5 part-time (2 women); includes 9 minority (7 Black or African American, non-Hispanic/Latino; 2 Hispanic/Latino), 50 international. Average age 30. 94 applicants, 74% accepted, 18 enrolled. In 2018, 5 master's, 6 doctorates awarded. Terminal master's awarded for partial completion of doctoral program. *Degree requirements:* For master's, thesis, comprehensive oral or written exam; for doctorate, thesis/dissertation, comprehensive oral or written exam. *Entrance requirements:* For master's, minimum GPA of 2.75 on last two years of undergraduate courses; for doctorate, minimum GPA of 2.75. Additional exam requirements/recommendations for international students: Required—TOEFL (minimum score 477 paper-based; 53 iBT); Recommended—IELTS (minimum score 4.5). *Application deadline:* For fall admission, 7/1 for domestic students, 5/1 for international students; for spring admission, 11/1 for domestic students, 9/1 for international students. Applications are processed on a rolling basis. Application fee: $60 ($80 for international students). Electronic applications accepted. *Expenses:* Tuition, state resident: full-time $8450; part-time $360.59 per credit hour. Tuition, nonresident: full-time $23,140; part-time $969.09 per credit hour. *Required fees:* $110. One-time fee: $55 full-time. Part-time tuition and fees vary according to course load, degree level, campus/location and reciprocity agreements. *Financial support:* In 2018–19, 10 research assistantships with full tuition reimbursements (averaging $18,896 per year), 54 teaching assistantships with full tuition reimbursements (averaging $18,110 per year) were awarded; Federal Work-Study, institutionally sponsored loans, scholarships/grants, and unspecified assistantships also available. Financial award application deadline: 4/1; financial award applicants required to submit FAFSA. *Faculty research:* Spectroscopy, fluorometry, organic and inorganic synthesis, electrochemistry. *Total annual research expenditures:* $5.2 million. *Unit head:* Dr. Dennis W. Smith, Professor/Head/Director, 662-325-3584, Fax: 662-325-1618, E-mail: ds2754@msstate.edu. *Application contact:* Nathan Drake, Admissions and Enrollment Assistant, 662-325-3804, E-mail: ndrake@grad.msstate.edu.
Website: http://www.chemistry.msstate.edu/graduate/

Missouri State University, Graduate College, College of Natural and Applied Sciences, Department of Chemistry, Springfield, MO 65897. Offers chemistry (MS); natural and applied science (MNAS), including chemistry (MNAS, MS Ed); secondary education (MS Ed), including chemistry (MNAS, MS Ed). *Program availability:* Part-time. *Faculty:* 15 full-time (2 women). *Students:* 12 full-time (5 women), 9 part-time (4 women); includes 2 minority (1 Hispanic/Latino; 1 Two or more races, non-Hispanic/Latino), 5 international. Average age 23. 11 applicants, 45% accepted. In 2018, 8 master's awarded. *Degree requirements:* For master's, comprehensive exam, thesis. *Entrance requirements:* For master's, GRE General Test (MS, MNAS), minimum undergraduate GPA of 3.0 (MS and MNAS), 9-12 teacher certification (MS Ed). Additional exam requirements/recommendations for international students: Required—TOEFL (minimum score 550 paper-based; 79 iBT), IELTS (minimum score 6). *Application deadline:* For fall admission, 7/20 priority date for domestic students, 5/1 for international students; for spring admission, 12/20 priority date for domestic students, 9/1 for international students; for summer admission, 5/20 priority date for domestic students. Applications are processed on a rolling basis. Application fee: $55 ($60 for international students). Electronic applications accepted. Tuition and fees vary according to class time, course level, course load, degree level, campus/location, program and student level. *Financial support:* In 2018–19, 17 teaching assistantships with full tuition reimbursements (averaging $8,772 per year) were awarded; Federal Work-Study, institutionally sponsored loans, scholarships/grants, and unspecified assistantships also available. Financial award application deadline: 1/31; financial award applicants required to submit FAFSA. *Faculty research:* Polyethylene glycol derivatives, electrochemiluminescence of environmental systems, enzymology, environmental organic pollutants, DNA repair via nuclear magnetic resonance (NMR). *Unit head:* Dr. Bryan Breyfogle, Department Head, 417-836-5601, Fax: 417-836-5507, E-mail: chemistry@missouristate.edu. *Application contact:* Lakan Drinker, Director, Graduate Enrollment Management, 417-836-5330, Fax: 417-836-6200, E-mail: lakandrinker@missouristate.edu.
Website: http://chemistry.missouristate.edu/

Missouri University of Science and Technology, Department of Chemistry, Rolla, MO 65401. Offers MS, MST, PhD. Terminal master's awarded for partial completion of doctoral program. *Degree requirements:* For doctorate, one foreign language, thesis/dissertation. *Entrance requirements:* For master's, GRE (minimum score 600 quantitative, 3 writing), minimum GPA of 3.0; for doctorate, GRE (minimum score: quantitative 600, writing 3.5), minimum GPA of 3.0. Additional exam requirements/recommendations for international students: Required—TOEFL (minimum score 550 paper-based). Electronic applications accepted. *Expenses:* Tuition, state resident: full-time $7545.60; part-time $419.20 per credit hour. Tuition, nonresident: full-time $22,169; part-time $1231.60 per credit hour. *International tuition:* $23,518.80 full-time. *Required fees:* $4523.05. Full-time tuition and fees vary according to course load, campus/location, program and reciprocity agreements. *Faculty research:* Structure and properties of materials; bioanalytical, environmental, and polymer chemistry.

Missouri Western State University, Program in Applied Science, St. Joseph, MO 64507-2294. Offers chemistry (MAS); engineering technology management (MAS); industrial life science (MAS); sport and fitness management (MAS). *Accreditation:* AACSB. *Program availability:* Part-time. *Students:* 35 full-time (11 women), 14 part-time (5 women); includes 4 minority (1 Black or African American, non-Hispanic/Latino; 1 Asian, non-Hispanic/Latino; 1 Hispanic/Latino; 1 Two or more races, non-Hispanic/Latino), 10 international. Average age 25. 31 applicants, 94% accepted, 20 enrolled. In 2018, 18 master's awarded. *Entrance requirements:* Additional exam requirements/recommendations for international students: Recommended—TOEFL (minimum score 79 iBT), IELTS (minimum score 6). *Application deadline:* For fall admission, 7/15 for domestic and international students; for spring admission, 11/1 for domestic and international students; for summer admission, 4/29 for domestic and international students. Applications are processed on a rolling basis. Application fee: $45 ($50 for international students). Electronic applications accepted. *Expenses: Tuition, area resident:* Part-time $359.39 per credit hour. Tuition, state resident: part-time $359.39 per credit hour. Tuition, nonresident: part-time $643.39 per credit hour. Tuition and fees vary according to program. *Financial support:* Scholarships/grants and unspecified assistantships available. Support available to part-time students. *Unit head:* Dr. Susan Bashinski, Dean of the Graduate School, 816-271-4394, Fax: 816-271-4525, E-mail: graduate@missouriwestern.edu. *Application contact:* Dr. Susan Bashinski, Dean of the Graduate School, 816-271-4394, Fax: 816-271-4525, E-mail: graduate@missouriwestern.edu.

Montana State University, The Graduate School, College of Letters and Science, Department of Chemistry and Biochemistry, Bozeman, MT 59717. Offers biochemistry (MS, PhD); chemistry (MS, PhD). *Program availability:* Part-time. *Degree requirements:* For master's, comprehensive exam, thesis (for some programs); for doctorate, comprehensive exam, thesis/dissertation. *Entrance requirements:* For master's and doctorate, GRE General Test, transcripts, letter of recommendation. Additional exam requirements/recommendations for international students: Required—TOEFL (minimum score 550 paper-based). Electronic applications accepted. *Faculty research:* Proteomics, nano-materials chemistry, computational chemistry, optical spectroscopy, photochemistry.

Montclair State University, The Graduate School, College of Science and Mathematics, Program in Chemistry, Montclair, NJ 07043-1624. Offers MS. *Degree requirements:* For master's, thesis. *Entrance requirements:* For master's, GRE General Test, 24 undergraduate credits in chemistry, 2 letters of recommendation, essay. Additional exam requirements/recommendations for international students: Required—TOEFL (minimum score 83 iBT), IELTS (minimum score 6.5). Electronic applications accepted. *Faculty research:* Computational chemistry, nanochemistry, pharmaceutical biochemistry, medicinal chemistry, biophysical chemistry.

Morgan State University, School of Graduate Studies, School of Computer, Mathematical, and Natural Sciences, Department of Chemistry, Baltimore, MD 21251. Offers MS. *Degree requirements:* For master's, comprehensive exam, thesis, oral defense of thesis. *Entrance requirements:* For master's, GRE General Test, minimum GPA of 2.5.

Mount Allison University, Department of Chemistry and Biochemistry, Sackville, NB E4L 1E4, Canada. Offers chemistry (M Sc). *Degree requirements:* For master's, thesis. *Entrance requirements:* For master's, honors degree in chemistry. *Faculty research:* Organometallic and main group chemistry; medicinal, bio-organic, and bio-inorganic chemistry; materials chemistry; surface chemistry; environmental chemistry; nuclear resonance spectroscopy; green chemistry.

Murray State University, Jesse D. Jones College of Science, Engineering and Technology, Department of Chemistry, Murray, KY 42071. Offers MS. *Program availability:* Part-time. *Entrance requirements:* For master's, GRE or GMAT, minimum university GPA of 2.75. Additional exam requirements/recommendations for international students: Required—TOEFL (minimum score 527 paper-based; 71 iBT). Electronic applications accepted.

New Jersey Institute of Technology, College of Science and Liberal Arts, Newark, NJ 07102. Offers applied mathematics (MS); applied physics (MS, PhD); applied statistics (MS, Certificate); biology (MS, PhD); biostatistics (MS); chemistry (MS, PhD); environmental and sustainability policy (MS); environmental science (MS, PhD); history (MA, MAT); materials science and engineering (MS, PhD); mathematical and computational finance (MS); mathematical sciences (PhD); pharmaceutical chemistry (MS); professional and technical communications (MS); technical communication essentials (Certificate). *Program availability:* Part-time, evening/weekend. *Faculty:* 150 full-time (43 women), 115 part-time/adjunct (47 women). *Students:* 200 full-time (79 women), 63 part-time (29 women); includes 61 minority (17 Black or African American, non-Hispanic/Latino; 29 Asian, non-Hispanic/Latino; 11 Hispanic/Latino; 4 Two or more races, non-Hispanic/Latino), 136 international. Average age 28. 429 applicants, 49% accepted, 89 enrolled. In 2018, 43 master's, 16 doctorates, 2 other advanced degrees awarded. Terminal master's awarded for partial completion of doctoral program. *Degree requirements:* For master's, thesis (for some programs); for doctorate, thesis/dissertation. *Entrance requirements:* For master's and doctorate, GRE General Test, Minimum GPA of 3.0, personal statement, three (3) letters of recommendation, and transcripts. Additional exam requirements/recommendations for international students: Required—TOEFL (minimum score 550 paper-based; 79 iBT), IELTS (minimum score 6.5). *Application deadline:* For fall admission, 6/1 priority date for domestic students, 5/1 priority date for international students; for spring admission, 11/15 priority date for domestic and international students. Applications are processed on a rolling basis. Application fee: $75. Electronic applications accepted. *Expenses:* $22,690 per year (in-state), $32,136 per year (out-of-state). *Financial support:* In 2018–19, 134 students received support, including 17 fellowships with full tuition reimbursements available (averaging $22,000 per year), 74 research assistantships with full tuition reimbursements available (averaging $22,000 per year), 71 teaching assistantships with full tuition reimbursements available (averaging $22,000 per year); scholarships/grants, traineeships, health care benefits, and unspecified assistantships also available. Financial award application deadline: 1/15. *Faculty research:* Biophotonics and bioimaging, morphogenetic patterning, embryogenesis, biological fluid dynamics, applied research in the mathematical sciences. *Total annual research expenditures:* $29.2 million. *Unit head:* Dr. Kevin Belfield, Dean, 973-596-3676, Fax: 973-565-0586, E-mail: kevin.d.belfield@njit.edu. *Application contact:* Stephen Eck, Director of Admissions, 973-596-3300, Fax: 973-596-3461, E-mail: admissions@njit.edu.
Website: http://csla.njit.edu/

New Mexico Highlands University, Graduate Studies, College of Arts and Sciences, Department of Biology and Chemistry, Las Vegas, NM 87701. Offers chemistry (MS). *Program availability:* Part-time. *Degree requirements:* For master's, comprehensive exam, thesis. *Entrance requirements:* For master's, minimum undergraduate GPA of 3.0. Additional exam requirements/recommendations for international students: Required—TOEFL (minimum score 540 paper-based). *Faculty research:* Invasive organisms in managed and wildland ecosystems, juniper and pinyon ecology and management, vegetation and community structure, big game management, quantitative forestry.

New Mexico Highlands University, Graduate Studies, College of Arts and Sciences, Department of Natural Resources Management, Las Vegas, NM 87701. Offers natural science (MS), including chemistry.

New Mexico Institute of Mining and Technology, Center for Graduate Studies, Department of Chemistry, Socorro, NM 87801. Offers MS, PhD. *Program availability:* Part-time. *Degree requirements:* For master's, thesis; for doctorate, thesis/dissertation. *Entrance requirements:* For master's, GRE General Test; for doctorate, GRE General Test, GRE Subject Test. Additional exam requirements/recommendations for international students: Required—TOEFL (minimum score 540 paper-based). Electronic applications accepted. *Faculty research:* Organic, analytical, environmental, and explosives chemistry.

New York University, Graduate School of Arts and Science, Department of Chemistry, New York, NY 10012-1019. Offers MS, PhD. *Students:* 136 full-time (55 women), 4 part-time (2 women); includes 26 minority (2 Black or African American, non-Hispanic/Latino; 10 Asian, non-Hispanic/Latino; 9 Hispanic/Latino; 5 Two or more races, non-Hispanic/Latino), 72 international. Average age 25. 278 applicants, 33% accepted, 36 enrolled. In 2018, 2 master's, 23 doctorates awarded. *Degree requirements:* For master's, thesis or alternative; for doctorate, one foreign language, thesis/dissertation. *Entrance requirements:* For master's and doctorate, GRE General Test; GRE Subject Test (strongly recommended). Additional exam requirements/recommendations for international students: Required—TOEFL, IELTS. *Application deadline:* For fall admission, 12/12 for domestic and international students. Application fee: $110. *Financial support:* Fellowships, research assistantships, teaching assistantships, career-related internships or fieldwork, Federal Work-Study, institutionally sponsored loans, scholarships/grants, health care benefits, and unspecified assistantships available. Financial award application deadline: 12/12; financial award applicants required to submit FAFSA. *Faculty research:* Biomolecular chemistry, theoretical and computational chemistry, physical chemistry, nanotechnology, bio-organic chemistry. *Unit head:* James Canary, Chair, 212-998-8400, Fax: 212-260-7905, E-mail: chemistry.grad@nyu.edu. *Application contact:* Kent Kirshenbaum, Director of Graduate Studies, 212-998-8400, Fax: 212-260-7905, E-mail: chemistry.grad@nyu.edu.
Website: http://www.nyu.edu/pages/chemistry/

North Carolina Agricultural and Technical State University, The Graduate College, College of Science and Technology, Department of Chemistry, Greensboro, NC 27411. Offers MAT, MS. *Program availability:* Part-time, evening/weekend. *Degree requirements:* For master's, comprehensive exam, thesis or alternative, qualifying exam. *Entrance requirements:* For master's, GRE General Test, minimum GPA of 3.0. *Faculty research:* Tobacco pesticides.

North Carolina Central University, College of Arts and Sciences, Department of Chemistry and Biochemistry, Durham, NC 27707-3129. Offers chemistry (MS). *Degree requirements:* For master's, one foreign language, comprehensive exam, thesis. *Entrance requirements:* For master's, GRE, minimum GPA of 3.0 in major, 2.5 overall. Additional exam requirements/recommendations for international students: Required—TOEFL.

North Carolina State University, Graduate School, College of Sciences, Department of Chemistry, Raleigh, NC 27695. Offers MS, PhD. *Program availability:* Part-time. Terminal master's awarded for partial completion of doctoral program. *Degree requirements:* For master's, thesis (for some programs); for doctorate, thesis/dissertation. *Entrance requirements:* For master's and doctorate, GRE General Test (recommended). Electronic applications accepted. *Faculty research:* Biological chemistry, electrochemistry, organic/inorganic materials, natural products, organometallics.

North Dakota State University, College of Graduate and Interdisciplinary Studies, College of Science and Mathematics, Department of Chemistry and Biochemistry, Program in Chemistry, Fargo, ND 58102. Offers MS, PhD.

Northeastern Illinois University, College of Graduate Studies and Research, College of Arts and Sciences, Program in Chemistry, Chicago, IL 60625. Offers chemistry (MS), including chemical education, general chemistry, separation science. *Program availability:* Part-time, evening/weekend. *Degree requirements:* For master's, comprehensive exam, final exam or thesis. *Entrance requirements:* For master's, 2 semesters each of chemistry, calculus, organic chemistry, physical chemistry, and physics; 1 semester of analytic chemistry; minimum GPA of 2.75. Additional exam requirements/recommendations for international students: Required—TOEFL (minimum score 550 paper-based; 79 iBT). Electronic applications accepted. *Faculty research:* Liquid chromatographic separation of pharmaceuticals, Diels-Alder reaction products, organogermanium chemistry, mass spectroscopy.

Northeastern University, College of Science, Boston, MA 02115-5096. Offers applied mathematics (MS); bioinformatics (MS); biology (PhD); biotechnology (MS); chemistry and chemical biology (MS, PhD); environmental science and policy (MS); marine and environmental sciences (PhD); marine biology (MS); mathematics (MS, PhD); operations research (MSOR); physics (MS, PhD); psychology (PhD). *Program availability:* Part-time. Terminal master's awarded for partial completion of doctoral program. *Degree requirements:* For master's, comprehensive exam (for some programs), thesis; for doctorate, comprehensive exam (for some programs), thesis/dissertation. *Entrance requirements:* For master's, GRE General Test. Electronic applications accepted. *Expenses:* Contact institution.

Northern Arizona University, College of Environment, Forestry, and Natural Sciences, Department of Chemistry and Biochemistry, Flagstaff, AZ 86011. Offers chemistry (MS). *Program availability:* Part-time. *Degree requirements:* For master's, variable foreign language requirement, comprehensive exam (for some programs), thesis, oral defense, individualized research. *Entrance requirements:* Additional exam requirements/recommendations for international students: Required—TOEFL (minimum score 80 iBT), IELTS (minimum score 6.5). Electronic applications accepted.

Northern Illinois University, Graduate School, College of Liberal Arts and Sciences, Department of Chemistry and Biochemistry, De Kalb, IL 60115-2854. Offers MS, PhD. *Faculty:* 16 full-time (1 woman), 3 part-time/adjunct (1 woman). *Students:* 34 full-time (15 women), 9 part-time (3 women); includes 7 minority (2 Black or African American, non-Hispanic/Latino; 2 Asian, non-Hispanic/Latino; 3 Hispanic/Latino), 19 international. Average age 30. 52 applicants, 73% accepted, 12 enrolled. In 2018, 4 master's, 5 doctorates awarded. Terminal master's awarded for partial completion of doctoral program. *Degree requirements:* For master's, comprehensive exam, thesis optional, research seminar; for doctorate, one foreign language, thesis/dissertation, candidacy exam, dissertation defense, research seminar. *Entrance requirements:* For master's, GRE General Test, bachelor's degree in mathematics or science, minimum GPA of 2.75; for doctorate, GRE General Test, bachelor's degree in mathematics or science; minimum undergraduate GPA of 2.75, 3.2 graduate. Additional exam requirements/recommendations for international students: Required—TOEFL (minimum score 550 paper-based). *Application deadline:* For fall admission, 6/1 for domestic students, 5/1 for international students; for spring admission, 11/1 for domestic students, 10/1 for international students. Applications are processed on a rolling basis. Application fee: $40. Electronic applications accepted. *Financial support:* In 2018–19, 10 research assistantships with full tuition reimbursements, 33 teaching assistantships with full tuition reimbursements were awarded; fellowships with full tuition reimbursements, career-related internships or fieldwork, Federal Work-Study, scholarships/grants, tuition waivers (full), and unspecified assistantships also available. Support available to part-time students. Financial award applicants required to submit FAFSA. *Faculty research:* Viscoelastic properties of polymers, lig and buding tocytochrome coxidases, computational inorganic chemistry, chemistry of organosilanes. *Unit head:* Dr. Ralph Wheeler, Chair, 815-753-1181, Fax: 815-753-4802, E-mail: rwheeler@niu.edu. *Application contact:* Graduate School Office, 815-753-0395, E-mail: gradsch@niu.edu. Website: http://www.chembio.niu.edu/

Northwestern University, The Graduate School, Judd A. and Marjorie Weinberg College of Arts and Sciences, Department of Chemistry, Evanston, IL 60208. Offers PhD. Admissions and degrees offered through The Graduate School. *Degree requirements:* For doctorate, thesis/dissertation. *Entrance requirements:* For doctorate, GRE General Test, GRE Subject Test (chemistry). Additional exam requirements/recommendations for international students: Required—TOEFL. Electronic applications accepted. *Faculty research:* Inorganic, organic, physical, environmental, materials, and chemistry of life processes.

Oakland University, Graduate Study and Lifelong Learning, College of Arts and Sciences, Department of Chemistry, Rochester, MI 48309-4479. Offers biomedical sciences (PhD), including health and environmental chemistry; chemistry (MS). *Degree requirements:* For master's, thesis; for doctorate, thesis/dissertation. *Entrance requirements:* For master's, minimum GPA of 3.0; for doctorate, GRE Subject Test, minimum GPA of 3.0. Additional exam requirements/recommendations for international students: Required—TOEFL (minimum score 550 paper-based). Electronic applications accepted.

The Ohio State University, Graduate School, College of Arts and Sciences, Division of Natural and Mathematical Sciences, Department of Chemistry and Biochemistry, Columbus, OH 43210. Offers biochemistry (MS); chemistry (MS, PhD). *Faculty:* 50. *Students:* 250 (103 women); includes 28 minority (5 Black or African American, non-Hispanic/Latino; 5 Asian, non-Hispanic/Latino; 14 Hispanic/Latino; 4 Two or more races, non-Hispanic/Latino), 108 international. Average age 26. In 2018, 12 master's, 39 doctorates awarded. *Entrance requirements:* For master's and doctorate, GRE General Test. Additional exam requirements/recommendations for international students: Required—TOEFL (minimum score 550 paper-based; 79 iBT), Michigan English Language Assessment Battery (minimum score 82); Recommended—IELTS (minimum score 7). *Application deadline:* For fall admission, 12/15 for domestic and international students. Applications are processed on a rolling basis. Application fee: $60 ($70 for international students). Electronic applications accepted. *Financial support:* Fellowships, research assistantships, teaching assistantships, Federal Work-Study, and institutionally sponsored loans available. Support available to part-time students. *Unit head:* Dr. Claudia Turro, Chair, 614-292-6708, E-mail: chair@chemistry.ohio-state.edu. *Application contact:* Graduate and Professional Admissions, 614-292-9444, Fax: 614-292-3895, E-mail: gpadmissions@osu.edu.
Website: https://chemistry.osu.edu/

Oklahoma State University, College of Arts and Sciences, Department of Chemistry, Stillwater, OK 74078. Offers MS, PhD. *Faculty:* 24 full-time (4 women), 1 part-time/adjunct (0 women). *Students:* 16 full-time (7 women), 50 part-time (15 women); includes 3 minority (1 Black or African American, non-Hispanic/Latino; 2 Hispanic/Latino), 43 international. Average age 30. 98 applicants, 19% accepted, 15 enrolled. In 2018, 3 master's, 13 doctorates awarded. *Entrance requirements:* For master's and doctorate, GRE or GMAT. Additional exam requirements/recommendations for international students: Required—TOEFL (minimum score 550 paper-based; 79 iBT). *Application deadline:* For fall admission, 3/1 priority date for international students; for spring admission, 8/1 priority date for international students. Applications are processed on a rolling basis. Application fee: $40 ($75 for international students). Electronic applications accepted. *Expenses: Tuition, area resident:* Full-time $4148. Tuition, state resident: full-time $4148. Tuition, nonresident: full-time $10,517. *International tuition:* $10,517 full-time. *Required fees:* $4394; $2929 per credit hour. Tuition and fees vary according to course load and program. *Financial support:* Research assistantships, teaching assistantships, career-related internships or fieldwork, Federal Work-Study, scholarships/grants, health care benefits, tuition waivers (partial), and unspecified assistantships available. Support available to part-time students. Financial award application deadline: 3/1; financial award applicants required to submit FAFSA. *Faculty research:* Materials science, surface chemistry, and nanoparticles; theoretical physical chemistry; synthetic and medicinal chemistry; bioanalytical chemistry; electromagnetic, mass, and X-ray spectroscopes. *Unit head:* Dr. Nicholas Materer, Department Head, 405-744-5920, Fax: 405-744-6007, E-mail: nicholas.materer@okstate.edu. *Application contact:* Dr. Jimmie Weaver, Graduate Recruiter, 405-744-3966, E-mail: jimmie.weaver@okstate.edu.
Website: http://chemistry.okstate.edu

Old Dominion University, College of Sciences, Program in Chemistry, Norfolk, VA 23529. Offers analytical chemistry (MS, PhD); biochemistry (MS, PhD); environmental chemistry (MS, PhD); inorganic chemistry (MS, PhD); organic chemistry (MS, PhD); physical chemistry (MS, PhD). *Program availability:* Part-time. Terminal master's awarded for partial completion of doctoral program. *Degree requirements:* For master's, comprehensive exam, thesis (for some programs); for doctorate, comprehensive exam, thesis/dissertation. *Entrance requirements:* For master's and doctorate, GRE General Test, minimum GPA of 3.0 in major, 2.5 overall, transcripts, essay, three letters of recommendation, resume. Additional exam requirements/recommendations for international students: Required—TOEFL (minimum score 84 iBT). Electronic applications accepted. *Expenses:* Contact institution. *Faculty research:* Biogeochemistry, materials chemistry, computational chemistry, organic chemistry, biofuels.

Old Dominion University, Darden College of Education, Programs in Secondary Education, Norfolk, VA 23529. Offers chemistry (MS Ed); English (MS Ed); secondary education (MS Ed). *Accreditation:* NCATE. *Program availability:* Part-time, evening/weekend, online learning. *Degree requirements:* For master's, comprehensive exam, thesis. *Entrance requirements:* For master's, GRE General Test or MAT, PRAXIS I (for licensure), minimum GPA of 2.8, teaching certificate. Additional exam requirements/recommendations for international students: Required—TOEFL. Electronic applications accepted. *Faculty research:* Use of technology, writing project for teachers, geography teaching, reading.

Oregon State University, College of Science, Program in Chemistry, Corvallis, OR 97331. Offers analytical chemistry (MA, MS, PhD). Terminal master's awarded for partial completion of doctoral program. *Degree requirements:* For master's, thesis (for some programs); for doctorate, thesis/dissertation. *Entrance requirements:* For master's and doctorate, GRE, minimum GPA of 3.0 in last 90 hours of course work. Additional exam requirements/recommendations for international students: Required—TOEFL (minimum score 80 iBT), IELTS (minimum score 6.5). *Faculty research:* Solid state chemistry, enzyme reaction mechanisms, structure and dynamics of gas molecules, chemiluminescence, nonlinear optical spectroscopy.

Pace University, School of Education, New York, NY 10038. Offers adolescent education (MST), including biology, chemistry, earth science, English, foreign languages, mathematics, physics, social studies; childhood education (MST); early childhood development, learning and intervention (MST); educational technology studies (MS); inclusive adolescent education (MST), including biology, chemistry, earth science, English, foreign languages, mathematics, physics, social studies; integrated instruction for educational technology (Certificate); integrated instruction for literacy and technology (Certificate); literacy (MS Ed); special education (MS Ed). *Accreditation:* NCATE. *Program availability:* Part-time, evening/weekend, 100% online, blended/hybrid learning. *Faculty:* 19 full-time (13 women), 86 part-time/adjunct (49 women). *Students:* 98 full-time (82 women), 542 part-time (391 women); includes 256 minority (116 Black or African American, non-Hispanic/Latino; 2 American Indian or Alaska Native, non-Hispanic/Latino; 45 Asian, non-Hispanic/Latino; 83 Hispanic/Latino; 10 Two or more races, non-Hispanic/Latino), 4 international. Average age 30. 223 applicants, 89% accepted, 130 enrolled. In 2018, 269 master's, 12 other advanced degrees awarded. *Degree requirements:* For master's and Certificate, certification exams. *Entrance requirements:* For master's, GRE (for initial certification programs only), teaching certificate (for MS Ed in literacy and special education programs only). Additional exam requirements/recommendations for international students: Required—TOEFL (minimum score 88 iBT), IELTS or PTE. *Application deadline:* For fall admission, 8/1 priority date for domestic students, 6/1 for international students; for spring admission, 12/1 priority date for domestic students, 10/1 for international students. Applications are processed on a rolling basis. Application fee: $70. Electronic applications accepted. *Expenses:* Contact institution. *Financial support:* In 2018–19, 17 students received support, including 17 research assistantships with partial tuition reimbursements available (averaging $6,020 per year); career-related internships or fieldwork, Federal Work-Study, scholarships/grants, and unspecified assistantships also available. Financial award application deadline: 9/1; financial award applicants required to submit FAFSA. *Faculty research:* STEM education, TESOL, teacher education, special education, language and literary development. *Total annual research expenditures:* $1.4 million. *Unit head:* Dr. Harriet Feldman, Dean, School of Education, 914-773-3829, E-mail: hfeldman@pace.edu. *Application contact:* Susan Ford-Goldschein, Director of Graduate Admissions, 212-346-1531, Fax: 212-346-1585, E-mail: graduateadmission@pace.edu.
Website: http://www.pace.edu/school-of-education

Penn State University Park, Graduate School, Eberly College of Science, Department of Chemistry, University Park, PA 16802. Offers MS, PhD.

Pittsburg State University, Graduate School, College of Arts and Sciences, Department of Chemistry, Pittsburg, KS 66762. Offers chemistry (MS); polymer chemistry (MS). *Degree requirements:* For master's, comprehensive exam (for some programs), thesis or alternative. *Entrance requirements:* Additional exam requirements/recommendations for international students: Required—TOEFL (minimum score 520 paper-based; 68 iBT), IELTS (minimum score 6), PTE (minimum score 47). Electronic applications accepted. *Expenses:* Contact institution.

Pontifical Catholic University of Puerto Rico, College of Sciences, Department of Chemistry, Ponce, PR 00717-0777. Offers MS. *Program availability:* Part-time, evening/weekend. *Degree requirements:* For master's, thesis. *Entrance requirements:* For master's, GRE General Test, 2 letters of recommendation, minimum GPA of 3.0, minimum 37 credits in chemistry. Electronic applications accepted.

Portland State University, Graduate Studies, College of Liberal Arts and Sciences, Department of Chemistry, Portland, OR 97207-0751. Offers MA, MS, PhD. *Program availability:* Part-time. *Degree requirements:* For master's, one foreign language, thesis; for doctorate, one foreign language, thesis/dissertation, cumulative exams, seminar presentations. *Entrance requirements:* For master's, GRE General Test, GRE Subject Test, minimum GPA of 3.0 in upper-division course work or 2.75 overall, 2 letters of recommendation. Additional exam requirements/recommendations for international students: Required—TOEFL (minimum score 550 paper-based; 80 iBT). *Faculty research:* Synthetic inorganic chemistry, atmospheric chemistry, organic photochemistry, enzymology, analytical chemistry.

Prairie View A&M University, College of Arts and Sciences, Department of Chemistry, Prairie View, TX 77446. Offers MS. *Program availability:* Part-time, evening/weekend. *Faculty:* 5 full-time (0 women). *Students:* 14 full-time (8 women), 3 part-time (all women); includes 12 minority (all Black or African American, non-Hispanic/Latino), 4 international. Average age 29. 14 applicants, 93% accepted, 11 enrolled. In 2018, 3 master's awarded. *Degree requirements:* For master's, thesis. *Entrance requirements:* For master's, GRE General Test. Additional exam requirements/recommendations for international students: Required—TOEFL (minimum score 550 paper-based; 79 iBT). *Application deadline:* For fall admission, 5/1 priority date for domestic and international students; for spring admission, 10/1 priority date for domestic students, 9/1 priority date for international students; for summer admission, 3/1 priority date for domestic students, 2/1 priority date for international students. Applications are processed on a rolling basis. Application fee: $50. Electronic applications accepted. *Expenses: Tuition, area resident:* Full-time $3172; part-time $317 per credit. Tuition, state resident: full-time $3172; part-time $317 per credit. Tuition, nonresident: full-time $7965; part-time $796 per credit. *Required fees:* $4847; $485 per credit. *Financial support:* In 2018–19, 9 students received support, including 13 fellowships (averaging $11,908 per year), 4 research assistantships (averaging $4,800 per year); tuition waivers (full) and unspecified assistantships also available. Financial award application deadline: 4/1; financial award applicants required to submit FAFSA. *Faculty research:* Material science, environmental characterization (surface phenomena), theoretical modelling, polymer modifications, organic synthesis. *Unit head:* Dr. Remi R. Oki, Head, 936-261-3106, Fax: 936-261-3117, E-mail: aroki@pvamu.edu. *Application contact:* Pauline Walker, Office of Graduate Admissions, 936-261-3521, Fax: 936-261-3529, E-mail: gradadmissions@pvamu.edu.

Princeton University, Graduate School, Department of Chemistry, Princeton, NJ 08544-1019. Offers chemistry (PhD); industrial chemistry (MS). *Degree requirements:* For doctorate, thesis/dissertation, general exams. *Entrance requirements:* For master's, GRE General Test; for doctorate, GRE General Test, GRE Subject Test (recommended). Additional exam requirements/recommendations for international students: Required—TOEFL. Electronic applications accepted. *Faculty research:* Chemistry of interfaces, organic synthesis, organometallic chemistry, inorganic reactions, biostructural chemistry.

Purdue University, Graduate School, College of Science, Department of Chemistry, West Lafayette, IN 47907. Offers analytical chemistry (PhD); biochemistry (MS, PhD); chemical education (MS, PhD); inorganic chemistry (MS, PhD); organic chemistry (MS, PhD); physical chemistry (PhD). *Faculty:* 47 full-time (13 women), 2 part-time/adjunct (0 women). *Students:* 314 full-time (124 women), 18 part-time (13 women); includes 63 minority (16 Black or African American, non-Hispanic/Latino; 15 Asian, non-Hispanic/Latino; 25 Hispanic/Latino; 7 Two or more races, non-Hispanic/Latino), 146 international. Average age 26. 711 applicants, 27% accepted, 64 enrolled. In 2018, 9 master's, 50 doctorates awarded. Terminal master's awarded for partial completion of doctoral program. *Degree requirements:* For master's, thesis; for doctorate, comprehensive exam, thesis/dissertation. *Entrance requirements:* For master's and doctorate, minimum undergraduate GPA of 3.0. Additional exam requirements/recommendations for international students: Required—TOEFL (minimum score 550 paper-based; 77 iBT); Recommended—TWE. *Application deadline:* For fall admission,

2/15 priority date for domestic students, 1/1 for international students. Applications are processed on a rolling basis. Application fee: $60 ($75 for international students). Electronic applications accepted. *Financial support:* In 2018–19, 2 fellowships with partial tuition reimbursements (averaging $18,000 per year), 55 teaching assistantships with partial tuition reimbursements (averaging $18,000 per year) were awarded; research assistantships with partial tuition reimbursements and tuition waivers (partial) also available. Support available to part-time students. Financial award applicants required to submit FAFSA. *Unit head:* Christine A. Hrycyna, Head, 765-494-5203, E-mail: hrycyna@purdue.edu. *Application contact:* Betty L. Hatfield, Director of Graduate Admissions, 765-494-5208, E-mail: bettyh@purdue.edu. Website: https://www.chem.purdue.edu/

Queens College of the City University of New York, Mathematics and Natural Sciences Division, Department of Chemistry and Biochemistry, Queens, NY 11367-1597. Offers chemistry (MA). *Program availability:* Part-time. *Faculty:* 14 full-time (3 women). *Students:* 1 (woman) full-time, 11 part-time (9 women); includes 5 minority (4 Asian, non-Hispanic/Latino; 1 Two or more races, non-Hispanic/Latino), 4 international. Average age 26. 19 applicants, 79% accepted, 6 enrolled. In 2018, 7 master's awarded. *Degree requirements:* For master's, thesis optional. *Entrance requirements:* Additional exam requirements/recommendations for international students: Required—TOEFL (minimum score 61 iBT), IELTS (minimum score 5). *Application deadline:* For fall admission, 4/1 for domestic students; for spring admission, 11/1 for domestic students. Applications are processed on a rolling basis. Application fee: $125. Electronic applications accepted. *Financial support:* In 2018–19, 3 teaching assistantships (averaging $6,000 per year) were awarded; career-related internships or fieldwork and unspecified assistantships also available. Financial award application deadline: 4/1; financial award applicants required to submit FAFSA. *Faculty research:* Medicinal chemistry, computational and theoretical chemistry, nanoelectrochemistry, transition metal catalysis, materials science. *Total annual research expenditures:* $800,000. *Unit head:* Dr. Seogjoo Julian Jang, Chair, 718-997-4100, Fax: 718-997-5531, E-mail: sjang@qc.cuny.edu. *Application contact:* Elizabeth D'Amico-Ramirez, Assistant Director of Graduate Admissions, 718-997-5203, E-mail: elizabeth.damicoramirez@qc.cuny.edu.

Queen's University at Kingston, School of Graduate Studies, Faculty of Arts and Science, Department of Chemistry, Kingston, ON K7L 3N6, Canada. Offers M Sc, PhD. *Program availability:* Part-time. *Degree requirements:* For master's, thesis (for some programs); for doctorate, comprehensive exam, thesis/dissertation. *Entrance requirements:* Additional exam requirements/recommendations for international students: Required—TOEFL (minimum score 580 paper-based). *Faculty research:* Medicinal/biological chemistry, materials chemistry, environmental/analytical chemistry, theoretical/computational chemistry.

Rensselaer Polytechnic Institute, Graduate School, School of Science, Program in Chemistry, Troy, NY 12180-3590. Offers MS, PhD. *Faculty:* 17 full-time (3 women). *Students:* 37 full-time (17 women), 3 part-time (1 woman); includes 8 minority (2 Black or African American, non-Hispanic/Latino; 1 Asian, non-Hispanic/Latino; 3 Hispanic/Latino; 2 Two or more races, non-Hispanic/Latino), 9 international. Average age 25. 115 applicants, 21% accepted, 7 enrolled. In 2018, 3 master's, 8 doctorates awarded. Terminal master's awarded for partial completion of doctoral program. *Degree requirements:* For master's, thesis (for some programs); for doctorate, comprehensive exam, thesis/dissertation. *Entrance requirements:* For master's and doctorate, GRE. Additional exam requirements/recommendations for international students: Required—TOEFL (minimum score 600 paper-based; 100 iBT), IELTS (minimum score 7), PTE (minimum score 68). *Application deadline:* For fall admission, 1/1 priority date for domestic and international students; for spring admission, 8/15 priority date for domestic and international students. Applications are processed on a rolling basis. Application fee: $75. Electronic applications accepted. *Financial support:* In 2018–19, research assistantships (averaging $23,000 per year), teaching assistantships (averaging $23,000 per year) were awarded; fellowships also available. Financial award application deadline: 1/1. *Faculty research:* Analytical and bioanalytical chemistry; biotechnology; chemical biology and biochemistry; chemistry; inorganic and organometallic chemistry; nanotechnology, organic and medicinal chemistry; physical and computational chemistry; polymer and materials chemistry. *Total annual research expenditures:* $8.3 million. *Unit head:* Dr. Peter Dinolfo, Graduate Program Director, 518-276-2326, E-mail: dinolp@rpi.edu. *Application contact:* Jarron Decker, Director of Graduate Admissions, 518-276-6216, Fax: 518-276-4072, E-mail: gradadmissions@rpi.edu. Website: https://science.rpi.edu/chemistry

Rice University, Graduate Programs, Wiess School of Natural Sciences, Department of Chemistry, Houston, TX 77251-1892. Offers chemistry (MA); inorganic chemistry (PhD); organic chemistry (PhD); physical chemistry (PhD). Terminal master's awarded for partial completion of doctoral program. *Degree requirements:* For master's, thesis; for doctorate, thesis/dissertation. *Entrance requirements:* For master's and doctorate, GRE General Test, minimum GPA of 3.0. Additional exam requirements/recommendations for international students: Required—TOEFL (minimum score 600 paper-based; 90 iBT). Electronic applications accepted. *Faculty research:* Nanoscience, biomaterials, nanobioinformatics, fullerene pharmaceuticals.

Rochester Institute of Technology, Graduate Enrollment Services, College of Science, School of Chemistry and Materials Science, MS Program in Chemistry, Rochester, NY 14623-5603. Offers MS. *Program availability:* Part-time. *Students:* 17 full-time (12 women), 2 part-time (1 woman); includes 1 minority (Hispanic/Latino), 4 international. Average age 25. 19 applicants, 63% accepted, 4 enrolled. In 2018, 2 master's awarded. *Degree requirements:* For master's, thesis or alternative, thesis or project report. *Entrance requirements:* For master's, GRE (taking the chemistry GRE is encouraged), minimum GPA of 3.0 (recommended), two letters of recommendation. Additional exam requirements/recommendations for international students: Required—TOEFL (minimum score 550 paper-based; 79 iBT), IELTS (minimum score 6.5), PTE (minimum score 58). *Application deadline:* For fall admission, 2/15 priority date for domestic and international students; for spring admission, 12/15 priority date for domestic and international students. Applications are processed on a rolling basis. Application fee: $65. Electronic applications accepted. *Financial support:* In 2018–19, 18 students received support. Research assistantships with partial tuition reimbursements available, teaching assistantships with partial tuition reimbursements available, career-related internships or fieldwork, scholarships/grants, and unspecified assistantships available. Support available to part-time students. Financial award applicants required to submit FAFSA. *Faculty research:* Atmospheric chemistry; imaging contrast agents; low frequency electron paramagnetic resonance spectroscopy; membrane proteins; natural product synthesis. *Unit head:* Dr. Michael G. Coleman, Director, 585-475-5108, Fax: 585-475-7800, E-mail: mgcsch@rit.edu. *Application contact:* Diane Ellison, Senior Associate Vice President, Graduate Enrollment Services, 585-475-2229, Fax: 585-475-7164, E-mail: gradinfo@rit.edu. Website: https://www.rit.edu/study/chemistry-ms

Roosevelt University, Graduate Division, College of Arts and Sciences, Department of Biological, Chemical, and Physical Sciences, Chicago, IL 60605. Offers biology (MS); biomedical sciences (MA); biotechnology and chemical science (MS), including biotechnology, biotechnology management, chemical science. *Program availability:* Part-time, evening/weekend. *Degree requirements:* For master's, thesis optional. Electronic applications accepted. *Expenses:* Contact institution.

Royal Military College of Canada, Division of Graduate Studies, Faculty of Science, Department of Chemistry and Chemical Engineering, Kingston, ON K7K 7B4, Canada. Offers chemical engineering (M Eng, MA Sc, PhD); chemistry (M Sc, PhD). *Degree requirements:* For master's, thesis; for doctorate, comprehensive exam, thesis/dissertation. *Entrance requirements:* For master's, honour's degree with second-class standing; for doctorate, master's degree. Electronic applications accepted.

Rutgers University–Camden, Graduate School of Arts and Sciences, Program in Chemistry, Camden, NJ 08102. Offers MS. *Program availability:* Part-time, evening/weekend. *Degree requirements:* For master's, comprehensive exam, thesis (for some programs), 30 credits. *Entrance requirements:* For master's, GRE (for assistantships), 3 letters of recommendation; statement of personal, professional and academic goals; chemistry or related undergraduate degree (preferred). Additional exam requirements/recommendations for international students: Required—TOEFL, IELTS; Recommended—TWE. Electronic applications accepted. *Faculty research:* Organic and inorganic synthesis, enzyme biochemistry, trace metal analysis, theoretical and molecular modeling.

Rutgers University–Newark, Graduate School, Program in Chemistry, Newark, NJ 07102. Offers analytical chemistry (MS, PhD); biochemistry (MS, PhD); inorganic chemistry (MS, PhD); organic chemistry (MS, PhD); physical chemistry (MS, PhD). *Program availability:* Part-time, evening/weekend. Terminal master's awarded for partial completion of doctoral program. *Degree requirements:* For master's, thesis optional, cumulative exams; for doctorate, thesis/dissertation, exams, research proposal. *Entrance requirements:* For master's and doctorate, GRE General Test, minimum undergraduate B average. Additional exam requirements/recommendations for international students: Required—TOEFL. Electronic applications accepted. *Faculty research:* Medicinal chemistry, natural products, isotope effects, biophysics and biorganic approaches to enzyme mechanisms, organic and organometallic synthesis.

Rutgers University–New Brunswick, Graduate School-New Brunswick, Department of Chemistry and Chemical Biology, Piscataway, NJ 08854-8097. Offers biological chemistry (MS, PhD); inorganic chemistry (MS, PhD); organic chemistry (MS, PhD); physical chemistry (MS, PhD). *Program availability:* Part-time, evening/weekend. Terminal master's awarded for partial completion of doctoral program. *Degree requirements:* For master's, thesis or alternative, exam; for doctorate, thesis/dissertation, 1 year residency. *Entrance requirements:* For master's and doctorate, GRE General Test, GRE Subject Test. Additional exam requirements/recommendations for international students: Required—TOEFL. Electronic applications accepted. *Faculty research:* Biophysical organic/bioorganic, inorganic/bioinorganic, theoretical, and solid-state/surface chemistry.

Rutgers University–New Brunswick, Graduate School-New Brunswick, Department of Environmental Sciences, Piscataway, NJ 08854-8097. Offers air pollution and resources (MS, PhD); aquatic biology (MS, PhD); aquatic chemistry (MS, PhD); atmospheric science (MS, PhD); chemistry and physics of aerosol and hydrosol systems (MS, PhD); environmental chemistry (MS, PhD); environmental microbiology (MS, PhD); environmental toxicology (PhD); exposure assessment (PhD); fate and effects of pollutants (MS, PhD); pollution prevention and control (MS, PhD); water and wastewater treatment (MS, PhD); water resources (MS, PhD). Terminal master's awarded for partial completion of doctoral program. *Degree requirements:* For master's, comprehensive exam, thesis or alternative, oral final exam; for doctorate, comprehensive exam, thesis/dissertation, thesis defense, qualifying exam. *Entrance requirements:* For master's and doctorate, GRE General Test. Additional exam requirements/recommendations for international students: Required—TOEFL. Electronic applications accepted. *Faculty research:* Biological waste treatment; contaminant fate and transport; air, soil and water quality.

Sacred Heart University, Graduate Programs, College of Arts and Sciences, Department of Chemistry, Fairfield, CT 06825. Offers bioinformatics (MS); chemistry (MS); molecular biology (MS). *Program availability:* Part-time, evening/weekend. *Degree requirements:* For master's, thesis optional. *Entrance requirements:* For master's, bachelor's degree in related area (natural science with a heavy concentration in chemistry), minimum GPA of 2.75. Additional exam requirements/recommendations for international students: Required—TOEFL (minimum score 570 paper-based, 80 iBT), TWE, or IELTS (6.5); Recommended—TSE. Electronic applications accepted. *Expenses:* Contact institution.

St. Francis Xavier University, Graduate Studies, Department of Chemistry, Antigonish, NS B2G 2W5, Canada. Offers M Sc. *Degree requirements:* For master's, thesis. *Entrance requirements:* Additional exam requirements/recommendations for international students: Required—TOEFL (minimum score 580 paper-based). *Expenses: Tuition, area resident:* Full-time $7547 Canadian dollars. Tuition, state resident: full-time $7547 Canadian dollars; part-time $804.19 Canadian dollars per course. Tuition, nonresident: full-time $8839 Canadian dollars; part-time $932.49 Canadian dollars per course. International tuition: $932.49 Canadian dollars full-time. Required fees: $90.20 Canadian dollars; $90.20 Canadian dollars per course. One-time fee: $6 Canadian dollars. Tuition and fees vary according to course load, degree level and program. *Faculty research:* Photoelectron spectroscopy, synthesis and properties of surfactants, nucleic acid synthesis, transition metal chemistry, colloids.

St. John Fisher College, Ralph C. Wilson Jr. School of Education, Program in Adolescence Education and Special Education, Rochester, NY 14618-3597. Offers adolescence education: biology with special education (MS Ed); adolescence education: chemistry with special education (MS Ed); adolescence education: English with special education (MS Ed); adolescence education: French with special education (MS Ed); adolescence education: math with special education (MS Ed); adolescence education: physics with special education (MS Ed); adolescence education: social studies with special education (MS Ed); adolescence education: Spanish with special education (MS Ed). *Program availability:* Part-time, evening/weekend. *Faculty:* 8 full-time (6 women), 2 part-time/adjunct (both women). *Students:* 13 full-time (4 women), 2 part-time (1 woman); includes 2 minority (1 Black or African American, non-Hispanic/Latino; 1 Two or more races, non-Hispanic/Latino). Average age 27. 24 applicants, 58% accepted, 4 enrolled. In 2018, 9 master's awarded. *Degree requirements:* For master's, field experiences, student teaching. *Entrance requirements:* For master's, LAST, 2 letters of recommendation, personal statement, current resume. Additional exam requirements/recommendations for international students: Required—TOEFL (minimum score 575 paper-based; 80 iBT). *Application deadline:* Applications are processed on a rolling basis. Application fee: $30. Electronic applications accepted. *Expenses:* Contact institution. *Financial support:* Scholarships/grants available. Financial award applicants required to submit FAFSA. *Faculty research:* Arts and humanities, urban schools, constructivist learning, at-risk students, mentoring. *Unit head:* Dr. Susan Hildenbrand, Program Director, 585-385-7297, E-mail: shildenbrand@sjfc.edu. *Application contact:* Michelle Gosier, Director of Transfer and Graduate Admissions, 585-385-8064, E-mail: mgosier@sjfc.edu.

Peterson's Graduate Programs in the Physical Sciences, Mathematics, Agricultural Sciences, the Environment & Natural Resources 2020

www.petersons.com **57**

Chemistry

St. John's University, St. John's College of Liberal Arts and Sciences, Department of Chemistry, Queens, NY 11439. Offers MS. *Program availability:* Part-time, evening/ weekend. *Degree requirements:* For master's, comprehensive exam (for some programs), thesis (for some programs). *Entrance requirements:* For master's, GRE, letters of recommendation, transcripts, resume, personal statement. Additional exam requirements/recommendations for international students: Required—TOEFL (minimum score 80 iBT), IELTS (minimum score 6.5). Electronic applications accepted. *Faculty research:* Synthesis and reactions of alpha-lactams, co-solvent effects of proteins, analytical chemistry of sensors, DNA-based mesoscale molecular engineering, and photochemistry of transition metal complexes.

Saint Louis University, Graduate Programs, College of Arts and Sciences, Department of Chemistry, St. Louis, MO 63103. Offers MS, MS-R, PhD. *Program availability:* Part-time, evening/weekend. *Degree requirements:* For master's, thesis; for doctorate, comprehensive exam, thesis/dissertation. *Entrance requirements:* For master's, letters of recommendation, resume, interview; for doctorate, letters of recommendation, resumé, interview, transcripts, goal statement. Additional exam requirements/ recommendations for international students: Required—TOEFL (minimum score 550 paper-based; 80 iBT). Electronic applications accepted. *Faculty research:* Photochemistry, energy, materials, biomaterials, nanomaterials.

Sam Houston State University, College of Sciences, Department of Chemistry, Huntsville, TX 77341. Offers MS. *Program availability:* Part-time. *Degree requirements:* For master's, comprehensive exam, thesis optional. *Entrance requirements:* For master's, GRE General Test, letters of recommendation. Additional exam requirements/ recommendations for international students: Required—TOEFL (minimum score 550 paper-based; 79 iBT), IELTS (minimum score 6.5). Electronic applications accepted.

San Diego State University, Graduate and Research Affairs, College of Sciences, Department of Chemistry and Biochemistry, San Diego, CA 92182. Offers MA, MS, PhD. PhD offered jointly with University of California, San Diego. Terminal master's awarded for partial completion of doctoral program. *Degree requirements:* For doctorate, thesis/dissertation. *Entrance requirements:* For master's, GRE General Test, bachelor's degree in related field, 3 letters of reference; for doctorate, GRE General Test, GRE Subject Test. Additional exam requirements/recommendations for international students: Required—TOEFL. Electronic applications accepted. *Faculty research:* Nonlinear, laser, and electrochemistry; surface reaction dynamics; catalysis, synthesis, and organometallics; proteins, enzymology, and gene expression regulation.

San Francisco State University, Division of Graduate Studies, College of Science and Engineering, Department of Chemistry and Biochemistry, San Francisco, CA 94132-1722. Offers biochemistry (MS); chemistry (MS). *Program availability:* Part-time. *Application deadline:* Applications are processed on a rolling basis. Electronic applications accepted. *Unit head:* Dr. Teaster Baird, Jr., Chair, 415-338-1288, Fax: 415-338-2384, E-mail: tbaird@sfsu.edu. *Application contact:* Dr. Andrew Ichimura, Graduate Coordinator, 415-405-0721, Fax: 415-338-2384, E-mail: ichimura@sfsu.edu.
Website: http://www.chembiochem.sfsu.edu/0home/0layout.php

San Jose State University, Program in Chemistry, San Jose, CA 95192-0001. Offers MA, MS. *Program availability:* Part-time, evening/weekend. *Degree requirements:* For master's, thesis or alternative. *Entrance requirements:* For master's, GRE. Electronic applications accepted. *Faculty research:* Intercalated compounds, organic/biochemical reaction mechanisms, complexing agents in biochemistry, DNA repair, metabolic inhibitors.

The Scripps Research Institute, Kellogg School of Science and Technology, La Jolla, CA 92037. Offers chemical and biological sciences (PhD). *Degree requirements:* For doctorate, thesis/dissertation. *Entrance requirements:* For doctorate, GRE General Test, GRE Subject Test, 3 letters of recommendation, official transcripts. Additional exam requirements/recommendations for international students: Required—TOEFL. Electronic applications accepted. *Faculty research:* Molecular structure and function, plant biology, immunology, bioorganic chemistry and molecular design, synthetic organic chemistry and natural product synthesis.

Seton Hall University, College of Arts and Sciences, Department of Chemistry and Biochemistry, South Orange, NJ 07079-2697. Offers analytical chemistry (MS, PhD); biochemistry (MS, PhD); chemistry (MS); inorganic chemistry (MS, PhD); organic chemistry (MS, PhD); physical chemistry (MS, PhD). *Program availability:* Part-time, evening/weekend. Terminal master's awarded for partial completion of doctoral program. *Degree requirements:* For master's, thesis optional; for doctorate, comprehensive exam, thesis/dissertation. *Entrance requirements:* Additional exam requirements/recommendations for international students: Required—TOEFL. Electronic applications accepted. *Faculty research:* DNA metal reactions; chromatography; bioinorganic, biophysical, organometallic, polymer chemistry; heterogeneous catalyst; synthetic organic and carbohydrate chemistry.

Simon Fraser University, Office of Graduate Studies and Postdoctoral Fellows, Faculty of Science, Department of Chemistry, Burnaby, BC V5A 1S6, Canada. Offers M Sc, PhD. *Degree requirements:* For master's, thesis; for doctorate, thesis/dissertation. *Entrance requirements:* For master's, minimum GPA of 3.0 (on scale of 4.33) or 3.33 based on last 60 credits of undergraduate courses; for doctorate, minimum GPA of 3.5 (on scale of 4.33). Additional exam requirements/recommendations for international students: Recommended—TOEFL (minimum score 580 paper-based; 93 iBT), IELTS (minimum score 7), TWE (minimum score 5). Electronic applications accepted. *Faculty research:* Analytical chemistry, inorganic and bioinorganic chemistry, organic and biological chemistry, physical and nuclear chemistry, chemical biology.

Smith College, Graduate and Special Programs, Department of Chemistry, Northampton, MA 01063. Offers secondary education (MAT), including chemistry. *Program availability:* Part-time. *Students:* 2 full-time (both women); includes 1 minority (Asian, non-Hispanic/Latino). Average age 22. 2 applicants, 100% accepted, 2 enrolled. In 2018, 2 master's awarded. *Entrance requirements:* Additional exam requirements/ recommendations for international students: Required—TOEFL (minimum score 595 paper-based; 97 iBT), IELTS (minimum score 7.5). *Application deadline:* For fall admission, 4/15 for domestic students, 1/15 for international students; for spring admission, 12/1 for domestic students. Applications are processed on a rolling basis. Application fee: $60. *Expenses:* The total tuition cost to each M.A.T. student (the full program fee, after 'built-in' scholarship award) is $18,500. *Financial support:* In 2018–19, 2 students received support, including 2 fellowships with full tuition reimbursements available; scholarships/grants also available. Support available to part-time students. Financial award application deadline: 4/15; financial award applicants required to submit CSS PROFILE or FAFSA. *Unit head:* Kate Queeney, Department Chair, 413-585-3835, E-mail: kqueeney@smith.edu. *Application contact:* Ruth Morgan, Program Coordinator, 413-585-3050, Fax: 413-585-3054, E-mail: gradstdy@smith.edu.
Website: http://www.science.smith.edu/departments/chem/

South Dakota State University, Graduate School, College of Natural Sciences, Department of Chemistry and Biochemistry, Brookings, SD 57007. Offers biochemistry (PhD); chemistry (MS, PhD). *Degree requirements:* For master's, thesis, oral exam; for doctorate, thesis/dissertation, preliminary oral and written exams, research tool. *Entrance requirements:* For master's and doctorate, bachelor's degree in chemistry or closely related discipline. Additional exam requirements/recommendations for international students: Required—TOEFL (minimum score 580 paper-based; 92 iBT). *Faculty research:* Environmental chemistry, computational chemistry, organic synthesis and photochemistry, novel material development and characterization.

Southeast Missouri State University, School of Graduate Studies, Department of Chemistry, Cape Girardeau, MO 63701-4799. Offers MNS. *Program availability:* Part-time. *Faculty:* 8 full-time (3 women), 3 part-time/adjunct (all women). *Students:* 6 full-time (5 women), 4 part-time (1 woman); includes 2 minority (1 Black or African American, non-Hispanic/Latino; 1 Hispanic/Latino), 5 international. Average age 27. 7 applicants, 86% accepted, 5 enrolled. In 2018, 4 master's awarded. *Degree requirements:* For master's, comprehensive exam (for some programs), thesis and oral defense, or research paper and comprehensive exam. *Entrance requirements:* Additional exam requirements/recommendations for international students: Required—TOEFL (minimum score 550 paper-based; 79 iBT), IELTS (minimum score 6), PTE (minimum score 53). *Application deadline:* For fall admission, 4/1 for domestic and international students; for spring admission, 11/21 for domestic students, 10/1 for international students. Applications are processed on a rolling basis. Application fee: $30 ($40 for international students). Electronic applications accepted. *Expenses:* Contact institution. *Financial support:* In 2018–19, 4 students received support, including 7 teaching assistantships with full tuition reimbursements available; career-related internships or fieldwork, Federal Work-Study, scholarships/grants, traineeships, tuition waivers (full), and unspecified assistantships also available. Financial award application deadline: 6/30; financial award applicants required to submit FAFSA. *Faculty research:* Electrochemistry of molecules of biological interest, environmental trace metal analysis, fingerprint age determination by chemometric analysis, green chemistry methodology and synthesis, X-ray diffraction of crystals. *Unit head:* Dr. Philip W. Crawford, Chairperson and Professor, 573-651-2166, Fax: 573-651-2508, E-mail: pcrawford@semo.edu. *Application contact:* Dr. Mohammed H. Ali, Professor, 573-651-2983, Fax: 573-651-2508, E-mail: mhali@semo.edu.
Website: http://www.semo.edu/chemistry/

Southern Connecticut State University, School of Graduate Studies, School of Arts and Sciences, Department of Chemistry, New Haven, CT 06515-1355. Offers MS. *Program availability:* Part-time, evening/weekend. *Degree requirements:* For master's, thesis or alternative. *Entrance requirements:* For master's, interview, undergraduate work in chemistry. Electronic applications accepted.

Southern Illinois University Carbondale, Graduate School, College of Science, Department of Chemistry and Biochemistry, Carbondale, IL 62901-4701. Offers MS, PhD. *Program availability:* Part-time. Terminal master's awarded for partial completion of doctoral program. *Degree requirements:* For master's, one foreign language, thesis; for doctorate, variable foreign language requirement, thesis/dissertation. *Entrance requirements:* For master's, GRE, minimum GPA of 2.7; for doctorate, GRE General Test, minimum GPA of 3.25. Additional exam requirements/recommendations for international students: Required—TOEFL. *Faculty research:* Materials, separations, computational chemistry, synthetics.

Southern Illinois University Edwardsville, Graduate School, College of Arts and Sciences, Department of Chemistry, Edwardsville, IL 62026. Offers MS. *Program availability:* Part-time, evening/weekend. *Degree requirements:* For master's, thesis optional, research paper. *Entrance requirements:* Additional exam requirements/ recommendations for international students: Required—TOEFL (minimum score 550 paper-based; 79 iBT), IELTS (minimum score 6.5). Electronic applications accepted.

Southern Methodist University, Dedman College of Humanities and Sciences, Department of Chemistry, Dallas, TX 75275-0314. Offers chemistry (MS); experimental chemistry (PhD); theoretical and computational chemistry (PhD). Terminal master's awarded for partial completion of doctoral program. *Degree requirements:* For master's, thesis; for doctorate, comprehensive exam, thesis/dissertation. *Entrance requirements:* For master's, GRE General Test, bachelor's degree in chemistry, minimum GPA of 3.0; for doctorate, GRE General Test, bachelor's degree in chemistry or closely-related field, minimum GPA of 3.0. Additional exam requirements/recommendations for international students: Required—TOEFL (minimum score 550 paper-based; 80 iBT). Electronic applications accepted. *Faculty research:* Materials/polymer, medicinal/bioorganic, theoretical and computational, organic/ inorganic/organometallic synthesis, inorganic polymer chemistry.

Southern University and Agricultural and Mechanical College, Graduate School, College of Sciences and Engineering, Program in Chemistry, Baton Rouge, LA 70813. Offers analytical chemistry (MS); biochemistry (MS); environmental sciences (MS); inorganic chemistry (MS); organic chemistry (MS); physical chemistry (MS). *Degree requirements:* For master's, thesis. *Entrance requirements:* For master's, GMAT or GRE General Test. Additional exam requirements/recommendations for international students: Required—TOEFL (minimum score 525 paper-based). *Faculty research:* Synthesis of macrocyclic ligands, latex accelerators, anticancer drugs, biosensors, absorption isotheums, isolation of specific enzymes from plants.

Stanford University, School of Humanities and Sciences, Department of Chemistry, Stanford, CA 94305-2004. Offers PhD. *Expenses: Tuition:* Full-time $50,703; part-time $32,970 per year. *Required fees:* $651.
Website: http://www.stanford.edu/dept/chemistry/

State University of New York at New Paltz, Graduate and Extended Learning School, School of Education, Department of Teaching and Learning, New Paltz, NY 12561. Offers adolescence education: biology (MAT, MS Ed); adolescence education: chemistry (MAT, MS Ed); adolescence education: earth science (MAT, MS Ed); adolescence education: English (MAT, MS Ed); adolescence education: French (MAT, MS Ed); adolescence education: social studies (MAT, MS Ed); adolescence education: Spanish (MAT, MS Ed); second language education (MS Ed, AC), including second language education (MS Ed), teaching English language learners (AC). *Accreditation:* NCATE. *Program availability:* Part-time, evening/weekend. *Faculty:* 21 full-time (16 women), 15 part-time/adjunct (12 women). *Students:* 127 full-time (91 women), 171 part-time (149 women); includes 48 minority (5 Black or African American, non-Hispanic/ Latino; 2 Asian, non-Hispanic/Latino; 37 Hispanic/Latino; 4 Two or more races, non-Hispanic/Latino). 152 applicants, 84% accepted, 104 enrolled. In 2018, 135 master's, 19 other advanced degrees awarded. *Degree requirements:* For master's, comprehensive exam (for some programs), portfolio. *Entrance requirements:* For master's, minimum GPA of 3.0, New York state teaching certificate (MS Ed). Additional exam requirements/ recommendations for international students: Required—TOEFL (minimum score 550 paper-based; 80 iBT), IELTS (minimum score 6.5). *Application deadline:* For fall admission, 3/1 priority date for domestic students, 3/1 for international students; for spring admission, 10/1 priority date for domestic students, 10/1 for international students. Application fee: $50. Electronic applications accepted. *Financial support:* Application deadline: 8/1. *Unit head:* Dr. Aaron Isabelle, Associate Dean, 845-257-2837, E-mail: isabella@newpaltz.edu. *Application contact:* Vika Shock, Director of Graduate Admissions, 845-257-3285, Fax: 845-257-3284, E-mail: gradstudies@newpaltz.edu.
Website: http://www.newpaltz.edu/secondaryed/

State University of New York at Oswego, Graduate Studies, College of Liberal Arts and Sciences, Department of Chemistry, Oswego, NY 13126. Offers MS. *Program availability:* Part-time. *Degree requirements:* For master's, comprehensive exam, thesis. *Entrance requirements:* For master's, GRE General Test, GRE Subject Test, BA or BS in chemistry. Additional exam requirements/recommendations for international students: Required—TOEFL (minimum score 560 paper-based).

State University of New York College of Environmental Science and Forestry, Department of Chemistry, Syracuse, NY 13210-2779. Offers biochemistry (MPS, MS, PhD); environmental chemistry (MPS, MS, PhD); organic chemistry of natural products (MPS, MS, PhD); polymer chemistry (MPS, MS, PhD). *Program availability:* Part-time. *Faculty:* 14 full-time (1 woman), 1 part-time/adjunct (0 women). *Students:* 37 full-time (14 women), 3 part-time (2 women); includes 1 minority (Asian, non-Hispanic/Latino), 13 international. Average age 28. 51 applicants, 53% accepted, 13 enrolled. In 2018, 4 master's, 5 doctorates awarded. Terminal master's awarded for partial completion of doctoral program. *Degree requirements:* For master's, thesis; for doctorate, comprehensive exam, thesis/dissertation. *Entrance requirements:* For master's and doctorate, GRE General Test, GRE Subject Test, minimum GPA of 3.0. Additional exam requirements/recommendations for international students: Required—TOEFL (minimum score 550 paper-based; 80 iBT), IELTS (minimum score 6). *Application deadline:* For fall admission, 2/1 priority date for domestic and international students; for spring admission, 11/1 priority date for domestic and international students. Applications are processed on a rolling basis. Application fee: $60. Electronic applications accepted. *Expenses:* Tuition, area resident: Full-time $11,090; part-time $462 per credit hour. Tuition, state resident: full-time $11,090; part-time $462 per credit hour. Tuition, nonresident: full-time $22,650; part-time $944 per credit hour. *International tuition:* $22,650 full-time. *Required fees:* $1733; $178.58 per credit hour. *Financial support:* In 2018–19, 13 students received support. Unspecified assistantships available. Financial award application deadline: 6/30; financial award applicants required to submit FAFSA. *Faculty research:* Polymer chemistry, biochemistry, environmental chemistry, natural products chemistry. *Total annual research expenditures:* $1.3 million. *Unit head:* Dr. Avik Chatterjee, Chair, 315-470-4747, Fax: 315-470-6855, E-mail: achatter@esf.edu. *Application contact:* Scott Shannon, Associate Provost for Instruction/Dean of the Graduate School, 315-470-6599, Fax: 315-470-6978, E-mail: sshannon@esf.edu. Website: http://www.esf.edu/chemistry

Stephen F. Austin State University, Graduate School, College of Sciences and Mathematics, Department of Chemistry and Biochemistry, Nacogdoches, TX 75962. Offers chemistry (MS). *Program availability:* Part-time. *Degree requirements:* For master's, comprehensive exam. *Entrance requirements:* For master's, GRE General Test, minimum GPA of 2.8 in last 60 hours, 2.5 overall. Additional exam requirements/recommendations for international students: Required—TOEFL. *Faculty research:* Synthesis and chemistry of ferrate ion, properties of fluoroberyllates, polymer chemistry.

Stevens Institute of Technology, Graduate School, Charles V. Schaefer Jr. School of Engineering and Science, Department of Chemistry, Chemical Biology and Biomedical Engineering, Chemistry, Hoboken, NJ 07030. Offers MS, PhD, Certificate. *Program availability:* Part-time, evening/weekend. *Faculty:* 15 full-time (6 women). *Students:* 23 full-time (11 women), 4 part-time (2 women); includes 3 minority (all Asian, non-Hispanic/Latino), 17 international. Average age 27. In 2018, 7 master's, 3 doctorates awarded. Terminal master's awarded for partial completion of doctoral program. *Degree requirements:* For master's, thesis optional, minimum B average in major field and overall; for doctorate, comprehensive exam (for some programs), thesis/dissertation; for Certificate, minimum B average. *Entrance requirements:* For master's, GRE/GMAT scores: GRE scores are required for all applicants applying to a full-time graduate program in the Schaefer School of Engineering and Science (SES). International applicants must submit TOEFL/IELTS scores and fulfill the English Language Proficiency Requirements in order to be considered. Additional exam requirements/recommendations for international students: Required—TOEFL (minimum score 74 iBT), IELTS (minimum score 6). *Application deadline:* For fall admission, 4/15 for domestic and international students; for spring admission, 11/1 for domestic and international students; for summer admission, 5/1 for domestic students. Applications are processed on a rolling basis. Application fee: $60. Electronic applications accepted. *Expenses: Tuition:* Full-time $35,960; part-time $1620 per credit. *Required fees:* $1290; $600 per semester. Tuition and fees vary according to course load. *Financial support:* Fellowships, research assistantships, teaching assistantships, career-related internships or fieldwork, Federal Work-Study, and unspecified assistantships available. Financial award application deadline: 2/15; financial award applicants required to submit FAFSA. *Unit head:* Dr. Jean Zu, Dean of SES, 201-216.8233, Fax: 201-216.8372, E-mail: Jean.Zu@stevens.edu. *Application contact:* Graduate Admissions, 888-783-8367, Fax: 888-511-1306, E-mail: graduate@stevens.edu.

Stevenson University, Master of Forensic Science, Owings Mills, MD 21153. Offers biology (MS); chemistry (MS); crime scene investigation (MS). Program offered in partnership with Maryland State Police Forensic Sciences Division. *Program availability:* Part-time. *Faculty:* 1 full-time (0 women), 7 part-time/adjunct (3 women). *Students:* 29 full-time (26 women), 37 part-time (34 women); includes 39 minority (33 Black or African American, non-Hispanic/Latino; 1 American Indian or Alaska Native, non-Hispanic/Latino; 3 Asian, non-Hispanic/Latino; 2 Hispanic/Latino). Average age 27. 45 applicants, 67% accepted, 19 enrolled. In 2018, 15 master's awarded. *Degree requirements:* For master's, capstone course. *Entrance requirements:* For master's, bachelor's degree in a natural science from regionally-accredited institution; official college transcripts from all previous academic work; minimum cumulative GPA of 3.0 in past academic work. *Application deadline:* Applications are processed on a rolling basis. Application fee: $0. Electronic applications accepted. *Expenses:* Contact institution. *Financial support:* Unspecified assistantships available. Financial award applicants required to submit FAFSA. *Unit head:* Carolyn Johnson, Program Coordinator, E-mail: CHJOHNSON@stevenson.edu. *Application contact:* Amanda Millar, Director, Admissions, 443-333-3334, Fax: 443-394-0538, E-mail: amillar@stevenson.edu. Website: http://www.stevenson.edu

Stony Brook University, State University of New York, Graduate School, College of Arts and Sciences, Department of Chemistry, Stony Brook, NY 11794. Offers MS, PhD. *Faculty:* 39 full-time (10 women), 3 part-time/adjunct (0 women). *Students:* 183 full-time (75 women), 1 part-time (0 women); includes 37 minority (5 Black or African American, non-Hispanic/Latino; 15 Asian, non-Hispanic/Latino; 15 Hispanic/Latino; 2 Two or more races, non-Hispanic/Latino), 99 international. Average age 26. 275 applicants, 52% accepted, 33 enrolled. In 2018, 20 master's, 19 doctorates awarded. Terminal master's awarded for partial completion of doctoral program. *Degree requirements:* For master's, thesis; for doctorate, one foreign language, thesis/dissertation. *Entrance requirements:* For master's and doctorate, GRE General Test. Additional exam requirements/recommendations for international students: Required—TOEFL (minimum score 90 iBT). *Application deadline:* For fall admission, 1/15 for domestic students; for spring admission, 10/1 for domestic students. Application fee: $100. Electronic applications accepted. *Expenses:* Contact institution. *Financial support:* In 2018–19, 8 fellowships, 68 research assistantships, 79 teaching assistantships were awarded. *Faculty research:* Bioimaging, chemical sciences, chemistry, spectroscopy, enzymology. *Total annual research expenditures:* $7.4 million. *Unit head:* Dr. Peter Tong, Chair, 631-632-7885, E-mail: peter.tonge@stonybrook.edu. *Application contact:* Katherine Hughes, Coordinator, 631-632-7886, E-mail: katherine.hughes@stonybrook.edu. Website: http://ws.cc.stonybrook.edu/chemistry

Syracuse University, College of Arts and Sciences, Department of Chemistry, Syracuse, NY 13244. Offers MS, PhD. *Degree requirements:* For master's, comprehensive exam, thesis or alternative; for doctorate, comprehensive exam, thesis/dissertation. *Entrance requirements:* For master's and doctorate, GRE General Test, official transcripts, three letters of recommendation, curriculum vitae, personal statement. Additional exam requirements/recommendations for international students: Required—TOEFL (minimum score 100 iBT). *Application deadline:* For fall admission, 2/1 priority date for domestic and international students. Application fee: $75. Electronic applications accepted. *Financial support:* Fellowships with full tuition reimbursements, research assistantships, teaching assistantships, and scholarships/grants available. Financial award application deadline: 1/1. *Faculty research:* Synthetic organic chemistry, biophysical spectroscopy, solid state in organic chemistry, biochemistry, organometallic chemistry. *Unit head:* Dr. Timothy M. Korter, Chair, 315-443-0269, E-mail: tmkorter@syr.edu. *Application contact:* Jodi Randall, Graduate Admissions Coordinator, 315-443-3992, E-mail: chemgrad@syr.edu. Website: http://chemistry.syr.edu/graduate-program/overview.html

Syracuse University, School of Education, Programs in Science Education, Syracuse, NY 13244. Offers biology (MS); chemistry (MS, PhD). *Program availability:* Part-time. *Students:* Average age 38. In 2018, 4 doctorates awarded. *Degree requirements:* For doctorate, comprehensive exam, thesis/dissertation. *Entrance requirements:* For master's, GRE General Test or MAT, official transcripts from previous academic institutions, 3 letters of recommendation (preferably from faculty), personal statement that makes a clear and compelling argument for why applicant wants to teach secondary science; for doctorate, GRE General Test or MAT, master's degree, interview. Additional exam requirements/recommendations for international students: Required—TOEFL (minimum score 100 iBT). *Application deadline:* For fall admission, 1/15 priority date for domestic and international students; for spring admission, 10/15 priority date for domestic and international students. Applications are processed on a rolling basis. Application fee: $75. Electronic applications accepted. *Financial support:* Fellowships with full tuition reimbursements, research assistantships, teaching assistantships, and scholarships/grants available. Financial award application deadline: 1/15. *Faculty research:* Diverse field experiences and theoretical and practical knowledge in research-based science teaching, biology, chemistry, earth science, and physics. *Unit head:* Dr. Sharon Dotger, Program Coordinator, 315-443-9138, E-mail: sdotger@syr.edu. *Application contact:* Speranza Migliore, Graduate Admissions Recruiter, 315-443-2505, E-mail: gradrcrt@syr.edu. Website: http://soe.syr.edu/academic/teaching_and_leadership/graduate/masters/science_education/

Teachers College, Columbia University, Department of Mathematics, Science and Technology, New York, NY 10027-6696. Offers biology 7-12 (MA); chemistry 7-12 (MA); communication and education (MA, Ed D); computing in education (MA); earth science 7-12 (MA); instructional technology and media (Ed M, MA, Ed D); mathematics education (Ed M, MA, Ed D, Ed DCT, PhD); physics 7-12 (MA); science and dental education (MA); science education (Ed M, MS, Ed DCT, PhD); supervisor/teacher of science education (MA); technology specialist (MA). *Program availability:* Part-time, evening/weekend, online learning. *Students:* 155 full-time (114 women), 254 part-time (162 women); includes 136 minority (44 Black or African American, non-Hispanic/Latino; 1 American Indian or Alaska Native, non-Hispanic/Latino; 59 Asian, non-Hispanic/Latino; 23 Hispanic/Latino; 9 Two or more races, non-Hispanic/Latino), 140 international. Average age 31. 484 applicants, 60% accepted, 138 enrolled. Terminal master's awarded for partial completion of doctoral program. *Unit head:* Prof. Erica Walker, Chair, 212-678-8246, E-mail: ewalker@tc.columbia.edu. *Application contact:* Kelly Sutton Skinner, Director of Admission & New Student Enrollment, E-mail: kms2237@tc.columbia.edu. Website: http://www.tc.columbia.edu/mathematics-science-and-technology/

Temple University, College of Science and Technology, Department of Chemistry, Philadelphia, PA 19122. Offers MA, PhD. *Program availability:* Part-time. *Faculty:* 30 full-time (9 women), 3 part-time/adjunct (0 women). *Students:* 123 full-time (40 women), 11 part-time (7 women); includes 18 minority (10 Black or African American, non-Hispanic/Latino; 5 Asian, non-Hispanic/Latino; 1 Hispanic/Latino; 2 Two or more races, non-Hispanic/Latino), 60 international. 139 applicants, 50% accepted, 29 enrolled. In 2018, 13 master's, 5 doctorates awarded. *Degree requirements:* For master's, comprehensive exam, thesis; for doctorate, thesis/dissertation, original research proposal, cumulative examinations, literature seminar. *Entrance requirements:* For master's and doctorate, GRE, 3 letters of recommendation, statement of goals, resume. Additional exam requirements/recommendations for international students: Required—TOEFL (minimum score 88 iBT), IELTS (minimum score 6.5), PTE (minimum score 60), one of three is required. *Application deadline:* For fall admission, 12/15 for domestic students, 1/1 for international students; for spring admission, 9/15 for domestic students, 8/1 for international students. Application fee: $60. Electronic applications accepted. *Expenses:* Contact institution. *Financial support:* Research assistantships, teaching assistantships, Federal Work-Study, and health care benefits available. Financial award applicants required to submit FAFSA. *Faculty research:* Synthetic chemistry, biochemistry, ultra-fast laser chemistry, spectroscopy and smart detectors. *Unit head:* Daniel R Strongin, Chairperson, 215-204-7119, E-mail: dstrongin@temple.edu. *Application contact:* Rodrigo Andrade, Graduate Chair, 215-204-7155, E-mail: chemgrad@temple.edu. Website: https://chem.cst.temple.edu/

Tennessee State University, The School of Graduate Studies and Research, College of Agriculture, Human and Natural Sciences, Department of Chemistry, Nashville, TN 37209-1561. Offers MS. *Program availability:* Part-time. *Degree requirements:* For master's, thesis optional. *Entrance requirements:* For master's, GRE General Test. Electronic applications accepted.

Tennessee Technological University, College of Graduate Studies, College of Arts and Sciences, Department of Chemistry, Cookeville, TN 38505. Offers MS. *Program availability:* Part-time. *Faculty:* 16 full-time (1 woman). *Students:* 8 full-time (5 women), 8 part-time (4 women); includes 1 minority (Two or more races, non-Hispanic/Latino), 4 international. 17 applicants, 53% accepted, 6 enrolled. In 2018, 5 master's awarded. *Degree requirements:* For master's, thesis. *Entrance requirements:* For master's, GRE. Additional exam requirements/recommendations for international students: Required—TOEFL (minimum score 527 paper-based; 71 iBT), IELTS (minimum score 5.5), PTE (minimum score 48), or TOEIC (Test of English as an International Communication). *Application deadline:* For fall admission, 8/1 for domestic students, 5/1 for international students; for spring admission, 12/1 for domestic students, 10/1 for international students; for summer admission, 5/1 for domestic students, 2/1 for international students. Applications are processed on a rolling basis. Application fee: $35 ($40 for international students). Electronic applications accepted. *Financial support:* In 2018–19,

Peterson's Graduate Programs in the Physical Sciences, Mathematics, Agricultural Sciences, the Environment & Natural Resources 2020

www.petersons.com **59**

14 teaching assistantships (averaging $7,500 per year) were awarded; research assistantships and career-related internships or fieldwork also available. Financial award application deadline: 4/1. *Unit head:* Dr. Jeffrey Boles, Chairperson, 931-372-3421, Fax: 931-372-3434, E-mail: jboles@tntech.edu. *Application contact:* Shelia K. Kendrick, Coordinator of Graduate Studies, 931-372-3808, Fax: 931-372-3497, E-mail: skendrick@tntech.edu.

Tennessee Technological University, College of Graduate Studies, College of Interdisciplinary Studies, School of Environmental Studies, Department of Environmental Sciences, Cookeville, TN 38505. Offers agriculture (PhD); biology (PhD); chemistry (PhD); geosciences (PhD); integrated research (PhD). *Program availability:* Part-time. *Students:* 3 full-time (all women), 17 part-time (6 women); includes 2 minority (1 Asian, non-Hispanic/Latino; 1 Two or more races, non-Hispanic/Latino), 5 international. 14 applicants, 29% accepted, 2 enrolled. In 2018, 3 doctorates awarded. *Degree requirements:* For doctorate, comprehensive exam, thesis/dissertation. *Entrance requirements:* For doctorate, GRE. Additional exam requirements/recommendations for international students: Required—TOEFL (minimum score 527 paper-based; 71 iBT), IELTS (minimum score 5.5), PTE (minimum score 48), or TOEIC (Test of English as an International Communication). *Application deadline:* For fall admission, 7/1 for domestic students, 5/1 for international students; for spring admission, 12/1 for domestic students, 10/2 for international students; for summer admission, 5/1 for domestic students, 2/1 for international students. Applications are processed on a rolling basis. Application fee: $35 ($40 for international students). Electronic applications accepted. *Financial support:* Fellowships, research assistantships, and teaching assistantships available. Financial award application deadline: 4/1. *Unit head:* Dr. Hayden Mattingly, Interim Director, 931-372-6246, E-mail: hmattingly@tntech.edu. *Application contact:* Shelia K. Kendrick, Coordinator of Graduate Studies, 931-372-3808, Fax: 931-372-3497, E-mail: skendrick@tntech.edu.

Texas A&M University, College of Science, Department of Chemistry, College Station, TX 77843. Offers chemistry (MS). *Faculty:* 43. *Students:* 281 full-time (92 women), 4 part-time (2 women); includes 42 minority (4 Black or African American, non-Hispanic/Latino; 1 American Indian or Alaska Native, non-Hispanic/Latino; 15 Asian, non-Hispanic/Latino; 16 Hispanic/Latino; 6 Two or more races, non-Hispanic/Latino), 144 international. Average age 26. 314 applicants, 61% accepted, 64 enrolled. In 2018, 45 doctorates awarded. Terminal master's awarded for partial completion of doctoral program. *Degree requirements:* For master's, thesis; for doctorate, thesis/dissertation. *Entrance requirements:* For master's and doctorate, GRE General Test. Additional exam requirements/recommendations for international students: Required—TOEFL. *Application deadline:* For fall admission, 12/15 priority date for domestic students. Applications are processed on a rolling basis. Application fee: $50 ($90 for international students). Electronic applications accepted. *Expenses:* Contact institution. *Financial support:* In 2018–19, 283 students received support, including 48 fellowships with tuition reimbursements available (averaging $9,921 per year), 90 research assistantships with tuition reimbursements available (averaging $18,000 per year), 186 teaching assistantships with tuition reimbursements available (averaging $19,736 per year); career-related internships or fieldwork, institutionally sponsored loans, scholarships/grants, traineeships, health care benefits, tuition waivers (full and partial), and unspecified assistantships also available. Support available to part-time students. Financial award application deadline: 3/1; financial award applicants required to submit FAFSA. *Faculty research:* Biological chemistry, spectroscopy, structure and bonding, reactions and mechanisms, theoretical chemistry. *Unit head:* Simon North, Department Head, 979-845-4947. *Application contact:* Simon North, Department Head, 979-845-4947.
Website: http://www.chem.tamu.edu/

Texas A&M University–Commerce, College of Science and Engineering, Commerce, TX 75429. Offers biological sciences (MS); broadfield science biology (MS); broadfield science chemistry (MS); broadfield science physics (MS); chemistry (MS); computational linguistics (Graduate Certificate); computational science (MS); computer science (MS); environmental science (Graduate Certificate); mathematics (MS); physics (MS); technology management (MS). *Program availability:* Part-time. *Faculty:* 44 full-time (7 women), 7 part-time/adjunct (0 women). *Students:* 178 full-time (67 women), 234 part-time (104 women); includes 82 minority (19 Black or African American, non-Hispanic/Latino; 1 American Indian or Alaska Native, non-Hispanic/Latino; 14 Asian, non-Hispanic/Latino; 37 Hispanic/Latino; 11 Two or more races, non-Hispanic/Latino), 158 international. Average age 30. 481 applicants, 52% accepted, 105 enrolled. In 2018, 218 master's awarded. *Degree requirements:* For master's, comprehensive exam, thesis optional. *Entrance requirements:* For master's, GRE, official transcripts, letters of recommendation, resume, statement of goals. Additional exam requirements/recommendations for international students: Required—TOEFL (minimum score 550 paper-based; 79 iBT), IELTS (minimum score 6), PTE (minimum score 53). *Application deadline:* For fall admission, 6/1 priority date for international students; for spring admission, 10/15 priority date for international students; for summer admission, 3/15 priority date for international students. Applications are processed on a rolling basis. Application fee: $50 ($75 for international students). Electronic applications accepted. *Expenses:* Contact institution. *Financial support:* In 2018–19, 46 students received support, including 43 research assistantships with partial tuition reimbursements available (averaging $2,418 per year), 135 teaching assistantships with partial tuition reimbursements available (averaging $3,376 per year); scholarships/grants, health care benefits, and unspecified assistantships also available. Financial award application deadline: 5/1; financial award applicants required to submit FAFSA. *Faculty research:* Biomedical, Catalytic Material & Processes, Nuclear Theory/Astrophysics, Cybersecurity, STEM Education. *Total annual research expenditures:* $1.8 million. *Unit head:* Dr. Brent L. Donham, Dean, 903-886-5321, Fax: 903-886-5199, E-mail: brent.donham@tamuc.edu. *Application contact:* Dayla Burgin, Graduate Student Services Coordinator, 903-886-5134, E-mail: dayla.burgin@tamuc.edu.
Website: https://new.tamuc.edu/science-engineering/

Texas A&M University–Corpus Christi, College of Graduate Studies, College of Science and Engineering, Corpus Christi, TX 78412. Offers biology (MS, PhD); chemistry (MS); coastal and marine system science (MS, PhD); computer science (MS); environmental science (MS); fisheries and mariculture (MS); geospatial computing sciences (PhD); geospatial surveying engineering (MS); marine biology (MS, PhD); mathematics (MS). *Program availability:* Part-time, evening/weekend. *Degree requirements:* For master's, comprehensive exam, thesis. *Entrance requirements:* For master's, GRE General Test. Additional exam requirements/recommendations for international students: Required—TOEFL (minimum score 550 paper-based; 69 iBT), IELTS (minimum score 6.5). Electronic applications accepted.

Texas A&M University–Kingsville, College of Graduate Studies, College of Arts and Sciences, Department of Chemistry, Kingsville, TX 78363. Offers MS. *Entrance requirements:* Additional exam requirements/recommendations for international students: Required—TOEFL (minimum score 525 paper-based; 79 iBT); Recommended—IELTS. Electronic applications accepted.

Texas Christian University, College of Science and Engineering, Department of Chemistry and Biochemistry, Fort Worth, TX 76129-0002. Offers MA, MS, PhD. *Program availability:* Part-time. *Faculty:* 11 full-time (1 woman). *Students:* 17 full-time (8 women), 1 part-time (0 women); includes 6 minority (2 Asian, non-Hispanic/Latino; 4 Hispanic/Latino). Average age 27. 11 applicants, 45% accepted, 2 enrolled. In 2018, 12 doctorates awarded. Terminal master's awarded for partial completion of doctoral program. *Degree requirements:* For master's, thesis; for doctorate, thesis/dissertation, literature seminar, cumulative exams, research progress report, independent research proposal, teaching of undergraduate labs. *Entrance requirements:* Additional exam requirements/recommendations for international students: Required—TOEFL (minimum score 80 iBT). *Application deadline:* For fall admission, 3/1 for domestic and international students; for spring admission, 10/1 for domestic and international students. Applications are processed on a rolling basis. Application fee: $60. Electronic applications accepted. *Financial support:* In 2018–19, 18 students received support, including 18 fellowships with full tuition reimbursements available (averaging $21,000 per year); scholarships/grants, traineeships, health care benefits, tuition waivers, and unspecified assistantships also available. Support available to part-time students. Financial award application deadline: 4/1. *Faculty research:* Bioinorganic chemistry, materials chemistry, protein folding, aggregation and transport phenomena, synthetic methodology and total synthesis, synthetic switches for sensing applications, electronic structure approximations, polymer chemistry, science education, protein modification, ribozymes. *Total annual research expenditures:* $460,000. *Unit head:* Dr. Eric Simanek, Chair/Professor, 817-257-5355, Fax: 817-257-5851, E-mail: e.simanek@tcu.edu. *Application contact:* Dr. Benjamin G. Janesko, Director of Graduate Studies/Associate Professor, 817-257-6202, Fax: 817-257-5851, E-mail: b.janesko@tcu.edu.
Website: http://www.chm.tcu.edu/

Texas Southern University, School of Science and Technology, Department of Chemistry, Houston, TX 77004-4584. Offers MS. *Degree requirements:* For master's, one foreign language, comprehensive exam, thesis. *Entrance requirements:* For master's, GRE General Test, minimum GPA of 2.5. Additional exam requirements/recommendations for international students: Required—TOEFL. Electronic applications accepted. *Faculty research:* Analytical and physical chemistry, geochemistry, inorganic chemistry, biochemistry, organic chemistry.

Texas State University, The Graduate College, College of Science and Engineering, Program in Chemistry, San Marcos, TX 78666. Offers MA, MS. *Program availability:* Part-time. *Faculty:* 10 full-time (1 woman), 2 part-time/adjunct (1 woman). *Students:* 11 full-time (6 women), 4 part-time (3 women); includes 6 minority (2 Black or African American, non-Hispanic/Latino; 1 Asian, non-Hispanic/Latino; 3 Hispanic/Latino). Average age 26. 23 applicants, 52% accepted, 9 enrolled. In 2018, 3 master's awarded. *Degree requirements:* For master's, comprehensive exam, thesis (for some programs). *Entrance requirements:* For master's, official GRE (general test only) required with competitive scores in the verbal reasoning and quantitative reasoning sections, baccalaureate degree from regionally-accredited university; undergraduate major in chemistry; minimum GPA of 3.0 on last 60 undergraduate semester hours; 2 letters of reference; statement of purpose. Additional exam requirements/recommendations for international students: Required—TOEFL (minimum score 550 paper-based; 78 iBT), IELTS (minimum score 6.5). *Application deadline:* For fall admission, 2/1 priority date for domestic and international students; for spring admission, 10/1 for domestic and international students. Applications are processed on a rolling basis. Application fee: $55 ($90 for international students). Electronic applications accepted. *Expenses:* Tuition, state resident: full-time $8102; part-time $4051 per semester. Tuition, nonresident: full-time $18,229; part-time $9115 per semester. *International tuition:* $18,229 full-time. *Required fees:* $2116; $120 per credit hour. Tuition and fees vary according to course load. *Financial support:* In 2018–19, 8 students received support, including 1 research assistantship (averaging $14,850 per year), 7 teaching assistantships (averaging $13,500 per year); career-related internships or fieldwork, Federal Work-Study, institutionally sponsored loans, scholarships/grants, health care benefits, and unspecified assistantships also available. Support available to part-time students. Financial award application deadline: 1/15; financial award applicants required to submit FAFSA. *Faculty research:* Main Group Organometallic Chemistry; Polymer Science/Polymer Materials; Photochromism - Mechanism and Bioapplications; Chemistry Education. *Total annual research expenditures:* $164,781. *Unit head:* Dr. Chang Ji, Graduate Advisor, 512-245-4949, Fax: 512-245-2374, E-mail: cj22@txstate.edu. *Application contact:* Dr. Andrea Golato, Dean of Graduate School, 512-245-2581, Fax: 512-245-8365, E-mail: gradcollege@txstate.edu.
Website: http://www.gradcollege.txstate.edu/programs/chemistry.html

Texas Tech University, Graduate School, College of Arts and Sciences, Department of Chemistry and Biochemistry, Lubbock, TX 79409-1061. Offers chemical biology (MS); chemistry (MS, PhD). *Program availability:* Part-time. *Faculty:* 42 full-time (7 women). *Students:* 97 full-time (46 women), 2 part-time (1 woman); includes 13 minority (1 American Indian or Alaska Native, non-Hispanic/Latino; 2 Asian, non-Hispanic/Latino; 9 Hispanic/Latino; 1 Native Hawaiian or other Pacific Islander, non-Hispanic/Latino), 72 international. Average age 28. 88 applicants, 33% accepted, 21 enrolled. In 2018, 4 master's, 7 doctorates awarded. *Degree requirements:* For master's, thesis; for doctorate, thesis/dissertation. *Entrance requirements:* For master's and doctorate, GRE General Test, diagnostic examination in area of specialization. Additional exam requirements/recommendations for international students: Required—TOEFL (minimum score 550 paper-based; 79 iBT); Recommended—IELTS (minimum score 6.5). *Application deadline:* For fall admission, 6/1 priority date for domestic students, 1/15 priority date for international students; for spring admission, 9/1 priority date for domestic students, 6/15 priority date for international students. Applications are processed on a rolling basis. Application fee: $65. Electronic applications accepted. *Expenses:* Contact institution. *Financial support:* In 2018–19, 105 students received support, including 103 fellowships (averaging $1,811 per year), 40 research assistantships (averaging $20,649 per year), 65 teaching assistantships (averaging $19,205 per year); career-related internships or fieldwork, Federal Work-Study, scholarships/grants, and tuition waivers (partial) also available. Financial award application deadline: 4/1; financial award applicants required to submit FAFSA. *Faculty research:* Chemical biology and plant biochemistry an, theoretical and computational chemistry, mass spectrometry and spectroscopic analysis, materials and supramolecular chemistry, medicinal and natural product synthesis. *Total annual research expenditures:* $3.6 million. *Unit head:* Dr. Yehia Mechref, Paul Whitfield Horn Professor, Department Chair, and Director of the TTU Center for Biotechnology & Genomics, 806-834-8246, Fax: 806-742-1289, E-mail: yehia.mechref@ttu.edu. *Application contact:* Ellyn Anthony, Senior Graduate Advisor, 806-742-3057, Fax: 806-742-1289, E-mail: chemgrad@ttu.edu.
Website: www.depts.ttu.edu/chemistry/

Texas Woman's University, Graduate School, College of Arts and Sciences, Department of Chemistry and Biochemistry, Denton, TX 76204. Offers chemistry (MS). *Program availability:* Part-time. *Faculty:* 5 full-time (3 women). *Students:* 2 full-time (both women), 8 part-time (5 women); includes 4 minority (1 Black or African American, non-Hispanic/Latino; 2 Hispanic/Latino; 1 Two or more races, non-Hispanic/Latino), 2 international. Average age 29. 7 applicants, 43% accepted, 1 enrolled. In 2018, 3

master's awarded. *Degree requirements:* For master's, comprehensive exam, thesis (for some programs), professional paper or thesis; oral exam given by the research committee. *Entrance requirements:* For master's, GRE General Test (preferred minimum score 146 [400 old version] verbal, 146 [550 old version] quantitative), 2 reference contacts, bachelor's degree or equivalent, minimum GPA of 3.0 in last 60 undergraduate hours or all prior graduate courses. Additional exam requirements/recommendations for international students: Required—TOEFL (minimum score 79 iBT); Recommended—IELTS (minimum score 6.5), TSE (minimum score 53). *Application deadline:* For fall admission, 3/1 for domestic students, 3/1 priority date for international students; for spring admission, 11/1 priority date for domestic students, 7/1 priority date for international students; for summer admission, 5/1 priority date for domestic students, 2/1 priority date for international students. Applications are processed on a rolling basis. Application fee: $50 ($75 for international students). Electronic applications accepted. *Expenses: Tuition, area resident:* Full-time $4852; part-time $270 per semester hour. Tuition, state resident: full-time $4852; part-time $270 per semester hour. Tuition, nonresident: full-time $12,322; part-time $685 per semester hour. *International tuition:* $12,322 full-time. *Required fees:* $2714; $113 per semester hour. $296 per semester. Tuition and fees vary according to course level, course load, degree level, campus/location and program. *Financial support:* In 2018–19, 3 students received support, including 3 teaching assistantships; research assistantships, career-related internships or fieldwork, Federal Work-Study, institutionally sponsored loans, scholarships/grants, traineeships, health care benefits, and unspecified assistantships also available. Support available to part-time students. Financial award application deadline: 3/1; financial award applicants required to submit FAFSA. *Faculty research:* Enzyme catalytic events using the shifting specificity model, chemical education, organic nitrogen compounds, properties of nucleic acids, dna sequence transitions and binding. *Unit head:* Dr. Richard Sheardy, Chair, 940-898-2550, Fax: 940-898-2548, E-mail: chawkins@twu.edu. *Application contact:* Korie Hawkins, Associate Director of Admissions, Graduate Recruitment, 940-898-3188, Fax: 940-898-3081, E-mail: admissions@twu.edu.
Website: http://www.twu.edu/chemistry-biochemistry/

Trent University, Graduate Studies, Program in Applications of Modeling in the Natural and Social Sciences, Department of Chemistry, Peterborough, ON K9J 7B8, Canada. Offers M Sc. *Program availability:* Part-time. *Degree requirements:* For master's, thesis. *Entrance requirements:* For master's, honours degree. *Faculty research:* Synthetic-organic chemistry, mass spectrometry and ion storage.

Tufts University, Graduate School of Arts and Sciences, Department of Chemistry, Medford, MA 02155. Offers chemical physics (PhD); chemistry (MS, PhD); chemistry/biotechnology (PhD). Terminal master's awarded for partial completion of doctoral program. *Degree requirements:* For master's, thesis optional; for doctorate, comprehensive exam, thesis/dissertation. *Entrance requirements:* For master's and doctorate, GRE General Test; GRE Subject Test (recommended). Additional exam requirements/recommendations for international students: Required—TOEFL (minimum score 550 paper-based; 80 iBT), IELTS (minimum score 6.5). Electronic applications accepted. *Expenses:* Contact institution.

Tulane University, School of Science and Engineering, Department of Chemistry, New Orleans, LA 70118-5669. Offers MS, PhD. Terminal master's awarded for partial completion of doctoral program. *Degree requirements:* For master's, thesis; for doctorate, thesis/dissertation. *Entrance requirements:* For master's, GRE General Test, minimum B average in undergraduate course work; for doctorate, GRE General Test. Additional exam requirements/recommendations for international students: Required—TOEFL. Electronic applications accepted. *Expenses: Tuition:* Full-time $52,856; part-time $2937 per credit hour. *Required fees:* $2040; $44.50 per credit hour. $580 per term. Tuition and fees vary according to course load, degree level and program. *Faculty research:* Enzyme mechanisms, organic synthesis, photochemistry, theory of polymer dynamics.

Tuskegee University, Graduate Programs, College of Arts and Sciences, Department of Chemistry, Tuskegee, AL 36088. Offers MS. *Degree requirements:* For master's, thesis. *Entrance requirements:* For master's, GRE General Test. Additional exam requirements/recommendations for international students: Required—TOEFL (minimum score 500 paper-based).

Universidad del Turabo, Graduate Programs, Programs in Science and Technology, Gurabo, PR 00778-3030. Offers environmental analysis (MSE), including environmental chemistry, environmental management (MSE), including pollution management; environmental science (D Sc), including environmental biology. *Entrance requirements:* For master's, GRE, EXADEP, GMAT, interview, official transcript, essay, recommendation letters; for doctorate, GRE, EXADEP, GMAT, official transcript, recommendation letters, essay, curriculum vitae, interview. Electronic applications accepted.

Université de Moncton, Faculty of Sciences, Department of Chemistry and Biochemistry, Moncton, NB E1A 3E9, Canada. Offers biochemistry (M Sc); chemistry (M Sc). *Program availability:* Part-time. *Degree requirements:* For master's, one foreign language, thesis. *Entrance requirements:* For master's, minimum GPA of 3.0. Electronic applications accepted. *Faculty research:* Environmental contaminants, natural products synthesis, nutraceutical, organic catalysis, molecular biology of cancer.

Université de Montréal, Faculty of Arts and Sciences, Department of Chemistry, Montréal, QC H3C 3J7, Canada. Offers M Sc, PhD. *Degree requirements:* For master's, thesis; for doctorate, thesis/dissertation, general exam. *Entrance requirements:* For master's, B Sc in chemistry or the equivalent; for doctorate, M Sc in chemistry or equivalent. Electronic applications accepted. *Faculty research:* Analytical, inorganic, physical, and organic chemistry.

Université de Sherbrooke, Faculty of Sciences, Department of Chemistry, Sherbrooke, QC J1K 2R1, Canada. Offers M Sc, PhD, Diploma. *Degree requirements:* For master's, thesis; for doctorate, thesis/dissertation. *Entrance requirements:* For doctorate, master's degree. Electronic applications accepted. *Faculty research:* Organic, electro-, theoretical, and physical chemistry.

Université du Québec à Montréal, Graduate Programs, Program in Chemistry, Montréal, QC H3C 3P8, Canada. Offers M Sc, PhD. M Sc offered jointly with Université du Québec à Trois-Rivières. *Program availability:* Part-time. *Degree requirements:* For master's, thesis. *Entrance requirements:* For master's, appropriate bachelor's degree or equivalent and proficiency in French.

Université du Québec à Trois-Rivières, Graduate Programs, Program in Chemistry, Trois-Rivières, QC G9A 5H7, Canada. Offers M Sc. *Program availability:* Part-time. *Degree requirements:* For master's, thesis. *Entrance requirements:* For master's, appropriate bachelor's degree, proficiency in French.

Université Laval, Faculty of Sciences and Engineering, Department of Chemistry, Programs in Chemistry, Québec, QC G1K 7P4, Canada. Offers M Sc, PhD. *Program availability:* Part-time. Terminal master's awarded for partial completion of doctoral

program. *Degree requirements:* For master's, thesis; for doctorate, comprehensive exam, thesis/dissertation. *Entrance requirements:* For master's and doctorate, knowledge of French, comprehension of written English. Electronic applications accepted.

University at Albany, State University of New York, College of Arts and Sciences, Department of Chemistry, Albany, NY 12222-0001. Offers MS, PhD. *Faculty:* 22 full-time (3 women). *Students:* 56 full-time (34 women), 45 part-time (27 women); includes 14 minority (9 Asian, non-Hispanic/Latino; 4 Hispanic/Latino; 1 Two or more races, non-Hispanic/Latino), 43 international. 84 applicants, 71% accepted, 25 enrolled. In 2018, 10 master's, 10 doctorates awarded. *Degree requirements:* For master's, one foreign language, thesis, major field exam; for doctorate, 2 foreign languages, thesis/dissertation, cumulative exams, oral proposition. *Entrance requirements:* For doctorate, GRE. Additional exam requirements/recommendations for international students: Required—TOEFL (minimum score 550 paper-based). *Application deadline:* For fall admission, 6/1 for domestic and international students; for spring admission, 6/1 for international students. Applications are processed on a rolling basis. Application fee: $75. Electronic applications accepted. *Financial support:* Research assistantships, teaching assistantships, and minority assistantships available. Financial award application deadline: 6/1. *Faculty research:* Synthetic, organic, and inorganic chemistry; polymer chemistry; ESR and NMR spectroscopy; theoretical chemistry; physical biochemistry. *Unit head:* Li Niu, Chair, 518-442-4400, Fax: 518-442-3462, E-mail: lniu@albany.edu. *Application contact:* Michael DeRensis, Director, Graduate Admissions, 518-442-3980, Fax: 518-442-3922, E-mail: graduate@albany.edu.
Website: http://www.albany.edu/chemistry/

University at Albany, State University of New York, School of Public Health, Department of Environmental Health Sciences, Albany, NY 12222-0001. Offers environmental and occupational health (MS, PhD); environmental chemistry (MS, PhD); toxicology (MS, PhD). *Faculty:* 9 full-time (7 women), 11 part-time/adjunct (5 women). *Students:* 10 full-time (7 women), 9 part-time (8 women); includes 6 minority (4 Black or African American, non-Hispanic/Latino; 2 Asian, non-Hispanic/Latino), 5 international. 16 applicants, 75% accepted, 3 enrolled. In 2018, 2 doctorates awarded. *Degree requirements:* For master's, thesis; for doctorate, comprehensive exam, thesis/dissertation. *Entrance requirements:* For master's and doctorate, GRE General Test, GRE Subject Test, 3 letters of reference. Additional exam requirements/recommendations for international students: Required—TOEFL (minimum score 600 paper-based). *Application deadline:* For fall admission, 1/15 for domestic and international students; for winter admission, 4/1 for domestic and international students; for spring admission, 10/1 for domestic students, 11/1 for international students. Applications are processed on a rolling basis. Application fee: $75. Electronic applications accepted. *Financial support:* Fellowships, research assistantships with full tuition reimbursements, teaching assistantships with full tuition reimbursements, scholarships/grants, health care benefits, tuition waivers (partial), and unspecified assistantships available. Financial award application deadline: 1/15. *Faculty research:* Xenobiotic metabolism, neurotoxicity of halogenated hydrocarbons, pharmacy/toxic genomics, environmental analytical chemistry. *Unit head:* Dr. David Lawrence, Chair, 518-474-7161, E-mail: dalawrence@albany.edu. *Application contact:* Dr. David Lawrence, Chair, 518-474-7161, E-mail: dalawrence@albany.edu.
Website: http://www.albany.edu/sph/eht/index.html

University at Buffalo, the State University of New York, Graduate School, College of Arts and Sciences, Department of Chemistry, Buffalo, NY 14260. Offers chemistry (MA, PhD); medicinal chemistry (MS, PhD). *Program availability:* Part-time. *Faculty:* 33 full-time (7 women), 2 part-time/adjunct (both women). *Students:* 175 full-time (81 women); includes 28 minority (5 Black or African American, non-Hispanic/Latino; 10 Asian, non-Hispanic/Latino; 11 Hispanic/Latino; 2 Two or more races, non-Hispanic/Latino), 58 International. Average age 26. 221 applicants, 45% accepted, 43 enrolled. In 2018, 7 master's, 19 doctorates awarded. Terminal master's awarded for partial completion of doctoral program. *Degree requirements:* For master's, thesis or alternative, project; for doctorate, thesis/dissertation, synopsis and proposal and 8th semester presentation. *Entrance requirements:* For master's and doctorate, GRE General Test, 3.0 GPA, letters of recommendation, baccalaureate degree or its equivalent. Additional exam requirements/recommendations for international students: Required—TOEFL (minimum score 550 paper-based; 79 iBT). *Application deadline:* For fall admission, 3/1 for domestic and international students; for spring admission, 11/1 for domestic and international students. Applications are processed on a rolling basis. Application fee: $75. Electronic applications accepted. *Expenses:* State resident full time $7,005.00 per semester; state resident per credit $671.01 per semester. *Financial support:* In 2018–19, 21 students received support, including 3 fellowships with full tuition reimbursements available (averaging $27,000 per year), 53 research assistantships with full tuition reimbursements available (averaging $23,000 per year), 75 teaching assistantships with full tuition reimbursements available (averaging $23,000 per year); Federal Work-Study, institutionally sponsored loans, scholarships/grants, and unspecified assistantships also available. Financial award application deadline: 3/1; financial award applicants required to submit FAFSA. *Faculty research:* Synthesis, measurements, structure theory, translation. *Total annual research expenditures:* $5.3 million. *Unit head:* Dr. David F. Watson, Chairman, 716-645-6824, Fax: 716-645-6963, E-mail: chechair@buffalo.edu. *Application contact:* Dr. Jason B. Benedict, Director of Graduate Studies, 716-645-4276, Fax: 716-645-6963, E-mail: jbb6@buffalo.edu.
Website: https://arts-sciences.buffalo.edu/chemistry.html

The University of Akron, Graduate School, Buchtel College of Arts and Sciences, Department of Chemistry, Akron, OH 44325. Offers MS, PhD. *Program availability:* Part-time, evening/weekend. Terminal master's awarded for partial completion of doctoral program. *Entrance requirements:* For master's and doctorate, GRE General Test (strongly recommended), baccalaureate degree in chemistry, biochemistry, or related field; three letters of recommendation; statement of purpose. Additional exam requirements/recommendations for international students: Required—TOEFL (minimum score 90 iBT), IELTS (minimum score 7.5). Electronic applications accepted. *Faculty research:* NMR and mass spectrometric characterization of biological and synthetic polymers, synthesis and characterization of new organic and inorganic material, metals in medicine, enzymology of gene regulation, high-resolution spectroscopy and ultrafast characterization of organic materials.

The University of Alabama, Graduate School, College of Arts and Sciences, Department of Chemistry, Tuscaloosa, AL 35487-0336. Offers MS, PhD. Terminal master's awarded for partial completion of doctoral program. *Degree requirements:* For master's, comprehensive exam, thesis (for some programs); for doctorate, comprehensive exam, thesis/dissertation, research proposal, oral defense, research seminar. *Entrance requirements:* For master's and doctorate, GRE General Test, minimum GPA of 3.0. Additional exam requirements/recommendations for international students: Recommended—TOEFL (minimum score 550 paper-based; 79 iBT), IELTS (minimum score 6.5), TSE (minimum score 59). Electronic applications accepted. *Faculty research:* Molecular synthesis and assembly, materials and measurements for alternative energy, electronic and magnetic nanomaterials, biochemical processes and biomaterials, environmental and green chemistry.

Peterson's Graduate Programs in the Physical Sciences, Mathematics, Agricultural Sciences, the Environment & Natural Resources 2020

www.petersons.com **61**

Chemistry

The University of Alabama at Birmingham, College of Arts and Sciences, Program in Chemistry, Birmingham, AL 35294. Offers MS, PhD. Terminal master's awarded for partial completion of doctoral program. *Degree requirements:* For master's, thesis (for some programs); for doctorate, thesis/dissertation. *Entrance requirements:* For master's and doctorate, GRE General Test, letters of recommendation. Additional exam requirements/recommendations for international students: Required—TOEFL. *Expenses: Tuition, area resident:* Full-time $8100; part-time $8100 per year. Tuition, state resident: full-time $8100. Tuition, nonresident: full-time $19,188; part-time $19,188 per year. Tuition and fees vary according to program. *Faculty research:* Drug discovery and synthesis, structural biochemistry and physical biochemistry, synthesis and characterization of advanced materials and polymers.

The University of Alabama in Huntsville, School of Graduate Studies, College of Science, Department of Chemistry, Huntsville, AL 35899. Offers biotechnology science and engineering (PhD); chemistry (MS); education (MS); materials science (MS, PhD). *Program availability:* Part-time. *Faculty:* 5 full-time (3 women). *Students:* 14 full-time (5 women), 8 part-time (5 women); includes 5 minority (all Black or African American, non-Hispanic/Latino), 4 international. Average age 29. 26 applicants, 77% accepted, 9 enrolled. In 2018, 3 master's awarded. *Degree requirements:* For master's, comprehensive exam, thesis or alternative, oral and written exams. *Entrance requirements:* For master's, GRE General Test, minimum GPA of 3.0. Additional exam requirements/recommendations for international students: Required—TOEFL (minimum score 550 paper-based; 80 iBT), IELTS (minimum score 6.5). *Application deadline:* For fall admission, 7/15 priority date for domestic students, 4/1 priority date for international students; for spring admission, 11/30 priority date for domestic students, 9/1 priority date for international students. Applications are processed on a rolling basis. Application fee: $50. Electronic applications accepted. *Expenses: Tuition, area resident:* Full-time $10,632; part-time $412 per credit hour. Tuition, state resident: full-time $10,632. Tuition, nonresident: full-time $23,604; part-time $412 per credit hour. *Required fees:* $582; $582. Tuition and fees vary according to course load and program. *Financial support:* In 2018–19, 8 students received support, including 1 research assistantship with full tuition reimbursement available (averaging $6,000 per year), 7 teaching assistantships with full tuition reimbursements available (averaging $6,000 per year); career-related internships or fieldwork, Federal Work-Study, institutionally sponsored loans, scholarships/grants, health care benefits, tuition waivers (full and partial), and unspecified assistantships also available. Support available to part-time students. Financial award application deadline: 4/1; financial award applicants required to submit FAFSA. *Faculty research:* Natural products drug discovery, protein biochemistry, macromolecular biophysics, polymer synthesis, surface modification and analysis of materials. *Unit head:* Dr. John Foster, Professor and Chair, 256-824-6253, Fax: 256-824-6349, E-mail: john.foster@uah.edu. *Application contact:* Kim Gray, Graduate Studies Admissions Coordinator, 256-824-6002, Fax: 256-824-6405, E-mail: deangrad@uah.edu.
Website: http://chemistry.uah.edu

University of Alaska Fairbanks, College of Natural Science and Mathematics, Department of Chemistry and Biochemistry, Fairbanks, AK 99775-6160. Offers biochemistry and neuroscience (PhD); chemistry (MA, MS), including chemistry (MS); environmental chemistry (PhD). *Program availability:* Part-time. *Faculty:* 9 full-time (2 women). *Students:* 27 full-time (17 women), 7 part-time (4 women); includes 7 minority (1 American Indian or Alaska Native, non-Hispanic/Latino; 2 Asian, non-Hispanic/Latino; 1 Hispanic/Latino; 3 Two or more races, non-Hispanic/Latino), 11 international. Average age 29. 37 applicants, 19% accepted, 6 enrolled. In 2018, 2 master's, 5 doctorates awarded. *Degree requirements:* For master's, comprehensive exam, thesis (for some programs), oral defense of project or thesis; for doctorate, comprehensive exam, thesis/dissertation, oral defense of dissertation. *Entrance requirements:* For master's, GRE General Test (for MS), bachelor's degree from accredited institution with minimum cumulative undergraduate and major GPA of 3.0; for doctorate, GRE General Test, minimum cumulative GPA of 3.0. Additional exam requirements/recommendations for international students: Required—TOEFL (minimum score 550 paper-based; 79 iBT), TWE. *Application deadline:* For fall admission, 6/1 for domestic students, 3/1 for international students; for spring admission, 10/15 for domestic students, 9/1 for international students. Applications are processed on a rolling basis. Application fee: $60. Electronic applications accepted. *Expenses: Tuition, area resident:* Full-time $8802; part-time $5868 per credit hour. Tuition, state resident: full-time $8802; part-time $5868 per credit hour. Tuition, nonresident: full-time $18,504; part-time $12,336 per credit hour. *International tuition:* $18,504 full-time. *Required fees:* $1416; $944 per credit hour. $472 per semester. Tuition and fees vary according to course load and program. *Financial support:* In 2018–19, 9 research assistantships with full tuition reimbursements (averaging $18,914 per year), 17 teaching assistantships with full tuition reimbursements (averaging $9,279 per year) were awarded; fellowships with full tuition reimbursements, Federal Work-Study, scholarships/grants, health care benefits, and unspecified assistantships also available. Support available to part-time students. Financial award application deadline: 7/1; financial award applicants required to submit FAFSA. *Faculty research:* Atmospheric aerosols, cold adaptation, hibernation and neuroprotection, liganogated ion channels, arctic contaminants. *Unit head:* Tom Green, Department Chair, 907-474-5510, E-mail: uaf-chem-biochem@alaska.edu. *Application contact:* Samara Taber, Director of Admissions, 907-474-7500, E-mail: uaf-admissions@alaska.edu.
Website: http://www.uaf.edu/chem

University of Alberta, Faculty of Graduate Studies and Research, Department of Chemistry, Edmonton, AB T6G 2E1, Canada. Offers M Sc, PhD. *Program availability:* Part-time. Terminal master's awarded for partial completion of doctoral program. *Degree requirements:* For master's, thesis; for doctorate, thesis/dissertation. *Entrance requirements:* For master's and doctorate, minimum GPA of 6.5 on 9.0 scale. *Expenses:* Contact institution. *Faculty research:* Synthetic inorganic and organic chemistry, chemical biology and biochemical analysis, materials and surface chemistry, spectroscopy and instrumentation, computational chemistry.

The University of Arizona, College of Science, Department of Chemistry and Biochemistry, Tucson, AZ 85721. Offers biochemistry (PhD); chemistry (MA, MS, PhD). *Program availability:* Part-time. *Degree requirements:* For doctorate, comprehensive exam, thesis/dissertation. *Entrance requirements:* For doctorate, GRE General Test, 3 letters of recommendation, statement of purpose. Additional exam requirements/recommendations for international students: Required—TOEFL (minimum score 550 paper-based; 79 iBT). Electronic applications accepted. *Faculty research:* Analytical, inorganic, organic, physical chemistry, biological chemistry.

University of Arkansas, Graduate School, J. William Fulbright College of Arts and Sciences, Department of Chemistry and Biochemistry, Fayetteville, AR 72701. Offers chemistry (MS, PhD). In 2018, 5 doctorates awarded. *Degree requirements:* For master's, one foreign language, thesis; for doctorate, one foreign language, thesis/dissertation. *Application deadline:* For fall admission, 8/1 for domestic students, 4/1 for international students; for spring admission, 12/1 for domestic students, 10/1 for international students; for summer admission, 4/15 for domestic students, 3/1 for international students. Applications are processed on a rolling basis. Application fee: $60. Electronic applications accepted. *Financial support:* In 2018–19, 17 research assistantships, 32 teaching assistantships were awarded; fellowships with tuition reimbursements, career-related internships or fieldwork, and Federal Work-Study also available. Support available to part-time students. Financial award application deadline: 4/1; financial award applicants required to submit FAFSA. *Unit head:* Dr. Wesley Stites, Department Chair, 479-575-4362, E-mail: wstites@uark.edu. *Application contact:* Julie Stenken, Director of Graduate Studies, 479-575-7945, E-mail: jstenken@uark.edu.
Website: https://fulbright.uark.edu/departments/chemistry/

University of Arkansas at Little Rock, Graduate School, College of Arts, Letters, and Sciences, Department of Chemistry, Little Rock, AR 72204-1099. Offers MA, MS. *Program availability:* Part-time, evening/weekend. *Degree requirements:* For master's, thesis (MS). *Entrance requirements:* For master's, minimum GPA of 2.7.

The University of British Columbia, Faculty of Science, Department of Chemistry, Vancouver, BC V6T 1Z1, Canada. Offers M Sc, PhD. Terminal master's awarded for partial completion of doctoral program. *Degree requirements:* For master's, thesis; for doctorate, comprehensive exam, thesis/dissertation. *Entrance requirements:* For master's and doctorate, GRE General Test, GRE Subject Test. Additional exam requirements/recommendations for international students: Required—TOEFL, IELTS. Electronic applications accepted. Application fee is waived when completed online. *Expenses:* Contact institution. *Faculty research:* Analytical chemistry, biological chemistry, environmental chemistry, inorganic chemistry, materials chemistry, organic chemistry, physical chemistry, theoretical chemistry.

University of Calgary, Faculty of Graduate Studies, Faculty of Science, Program in Chemistry, Calgary, AB T2N 1N4, Canada. Offers analytical chemistry (M Sc, PhD); applied chemistry (M Sc, PhD); inorganic chemistry (M Sc, PhD); organic chemistry (M Sc, PhD); physical chemistry (M Sc, PhD); polymer chemistry (M Sc, PhD); theoretical chemistry (M Sc, PhD). *Degree requirements:* For master's, thesis; for doctorate, thesis/dissertation, candidacy exam. *Entrance requirements:* For master's, minimum GPA of 3.0; for doctorate, honors B Sc degree with minimum GPA of 3.7 or M Sc with minimum GPA of 3.3. Additional exam requirements/recommendations for international students: Required—TOEFL (minimum score 580 paper-based). Electronic applications accepted. *Faculty research:* Chemical analysis, chemical dynamics, synthesis theory.

University of California, Berkeley, Graduate Division, College of Chemistry, Department of Chemistry, Berkeley, CA 94720. Offers PhD. *Degree requirements:* For doctorate, thesis/dissertation, qualifying exam. *Entrance requirements:* For doctorate, GRE General Test, GRE Subject Test, minimum GPA of 3.0, 3 letters of recommendation. Additional exam requirements/recommendations for international students: Required—TOEFL (minimum score 570 paper-based; 90 iBT). Electronic applications accepted. *Faculty research:* Analytical bioinorganic, bio-organic, biophysical environmental, inorganic and organometallic.

University of California, Davis, Graduate Studies, Graduate Group in Agricultural and Environmental Chemistry, Davis, CA 95616. Offers MS, PhD. *Degree requirements:* For master's, thesis; for doctorate, thesis/dissertation. *Entrance requirements:* For master's and doctorate, GRE General Test, minimum GPA of 3.0. Additional exam requirements/recommendations for international students: Required—TOEFL (minimum score 550 paper-based). Electronic applications accepted.

University of California, Davis, Graduate Studies, Program in Chemistry, Davis, CA 95616. Offers MS, PhD. Terminal master's awarded for partial completion of doctoral program. *Degree requirements:* For master's, thesis; for doctorate, thesis/dissertation. *Entrance requirements:* For master's, minimum GPA of 3.0; for doctorate, GRE, minimum GPA of 3.0. Additional exam requirements/recommendations for international students: Required—TOEFL (minimum score 550 paper-based). Electronic applications accepted. *Faculty research:* Analytical, biological, organic, inorganic, and theoretical chemistry.

University of California, Irvine, School of Physical Sciences, Department of Chemistry, Irvine, CA 92697. Offers MS, PhD. *Students:* 222 full-time (99 women), 2 part-time (0 women); includes 65 minority (3 Black or African American, non-Hispanic/Latino; 34 Asian, non-Hispanic/Latino; 16 Hispanic/Latino; 12 Two or more races, non-Hispanic/Latino), 35 international. Average age 26. 431 applicants, 41% accepted, 51 enrolled. In 2018, 17 master's, 35 doctorates awarded. *Entrance requirements:* For master's and doctorate, GRE General Test, GRE Subject Test, minimum GPA of 3.0. Additional exam requirements/recommendations for international students: Required—TOEFL (minimum score 550 paper-based). *Application deadline:* For fall admission, 1/15 priority date for domestic students, 1/15 for international students. Applications are processed on a rolling basis. Application fee: $105 ($125 for international students). Electronic applications accepted. *Financial support:* Fellowships, research assistantships with full tuition reimbursements, teaching assistantships, institutionally sponsored loans, traineeships, health care benefits, and unspecified assistantships available. Financial award application deadline: 3/1; financial award applicants required to submit FAFSA. *Faculty research:* Analytical, organic, inorganic, physical, and atmospheric chemistry; biogeochemistry and climate; synthetic chemistry. *Unit head:* Dr. Reginald M. Penner, Chair, 949-824-8572, Fax: 949-824-8571, E-mail: rmpenner@uci.edu. *Application contact:* Jaime M. Albano, Graduate Affairs Manager, 949-824-4261, Fax: 949-824-8571, E-mail: jmalbano@uci.edu.
Website: http://www.chem.uci.edu/

University of California, Los Angeles, Graduate Division, College of Letters and Science, Department of Chemistry and Biochemistry, Program in Chemistry, Los Angeles, CA 90095. Offers MS, PhD. *Degree requirements:* For master's, comprehensive exam or thesis; for doctorate, thesis/dissertation, oral and written exams, 1 year of teaching experience. *Entrance requirements:* For doctorate, GRE General Test, GRE Subject Test (recommended), bachelor's degree; minimum undergraduate GPA of 3.0 (or its equivalent if letter grade system not used). Additional exam requirements/recommendations for international students: Required—TOEFL. Electronic applications accepted.

University of California, Merced, Graduate Division, School of Natural Sciences, Merced, CA 95343. Offers applied mathematics (MS, PhD); chemistry and chemical biology (MS, PhD); physics (MS, PhD); quantitative and systems biology (MS, PhD), including molecular and cellular biology (PhD). *Faculty:* 77 full-time (30 women). *Students:* 232 full-time (98 women), 2 part-time (0 women); includes 79 minority (8 Black or African American, non-Hispanic/Latino; 22 Asian, non-Hispanic/Latino; 41 Hispanic/Latino; 8 Two or more races, non-Hispanic/Latino), 65 international. Average age 28. 302 applicants, 42% accepted, 58 enrolled. In 2018, 13 master's, 23 doctorates awarded. Terminal master's awarded for partial completion of doctoral program. *Degree requirements:* For master's, variable foreign language requirement, comprehensive exam, thesis or alternative, oral defense; for doctorate, variable foreign language requirement, comprehensive exam, thesis/dissertation, oral defense. *Entrance requirements:* For master's and doctorate, GRE. Additional exam requirements/recommendations for international students: Required—TOEFL (minimum score 550 paper-based; 80 iBT); Recommended—IELTS (minimum score 6.5). *Application deadline:* For fall admission, 1/15 for domestic and international students. Application fee: $105 ($125 for international students). Electronic applications accepted. *Expenses: Tuition, area resident:* Full-time $11,442; part-time $5721 per year. Tuition, state resident: full-time $11,442; part-time $5721 per year. Tuition, nonresident: full-time $26,544; part-time $13,272 per year. *International tuition:* $26,544 full-time. *Required fees:* $1765; $1765 per unit. $883 per semester. *Financial support:* In 2018–19, 229 students received support, including 12 fellowships with full tuition reimbursements available (averaging $21,865 per year), 47 research assistantships with full tuition reimbursements available (averaging $19,123 per year), 170 teaching assistantships with full tuition reimbursements available (averaging $20,710 per year); scholarships/grants, traineeships, and health care benefits also available. *Faculty research:* Biomedical sciences; soft matter physics; applied math and computational science; environmental and biological systems; biological and materials chemistry. *Total annual research expenditures:* $4.1 million. *Unit head:* Dr. Elizabeth Dumont, Dean, 209-228-4487, Fax: 209-228-4060, E-mail: edumont@ucmerced.edu. *Application contact:* Tsu Ya, Director of Graduate Admissions and Academic Services, 209-228-4521, Fax: 209-228-6906, E-mail: tya@ucmerced.edu.

University of California, Riverside, Graduate Division, Department of Chemistry, Riverside, CA 92521-0403. Offers MS, PhD. Terminal master's awarded for partial completion of doctoral program. *Degree requirements:* For master's, qualifying exams or thesis; for doctorate, thesis/dissertation, qualifying exams, 3 quarters of teaching experience, research proposition. *Entrance requirements:* For master's and doctorate, GRE General Test, minimum GPA of 3.0. Additional exam requirements/recommendations for international students: Required—TOEFL (minimum score 550 paper-based; 80 iBT). Electronic applications accepted. *Faculty research:* Analytical, inorganic, organic, and physical chemistry; chemical physics.

University of California, San Diego, Graduate Division, Department of Chemistry and Biochemistry, La Jolla, CA 92093. Offers chemistry (MS, PhD). PhD offered jointly with San Diego State University. *Students:* 293 full-time (111 women), 8 part-time (3 women). 676 applicants, 32% accepted, 79 enrolled. In 2018, 56 master's, 30 doctorates awarded. *Degree requirements:* For master's, comprehensive exam (for some programs), thesis (for some programs); for doctorate, comprehensive exam, thesis/dissertation. *Entrance requirements:* For master's, GRE General Test, MS Thesis Agreement Form, letters of recommendation, statement of purpose; for doctorate, GRE General Test, GRE Subject Test, letters of recommendation, statement of purpose. Additional exam requirements/recommendations for international students: Required—TOEFL (minimum score 550 paper-based; 80 iBT), IELTS (minimum score 7), PTE (minimum score 65). *Application deadline:* For fall admission, 3/18 for domestic students. Application fee: $105 ($125 for international students). Electronic applications accepted. *Financial support:* Fellowships, research assistantships, teaching assistantships, scholarships/grants, and traineeships available. Financial award applicants required to submit FAFSA. *Faculty research:* Analytical and atmospheric chemistry, biochemistry and biophysics, cellular and systems biochemistry, chemical biology, inorganic chemistry, organic chemistry, physical chemistry, quantitative biology, structural biology, theoretical and computational chemistry. *Unit head:* Edward Dennis, Chair, 858-534-3055, E-mail: edennis@ucsd.edu. *Application contact:* Jeff Rances, Admissions Coordinator, 858-534-9728, E-mail: chemgradinfo@ucsd.edu.
Website: http://chemistry.ucsd.edu

University of California, San Francisco, School of Pharmacy and Graduate Division, Chemistry and Chemical Biology Graduate Program, San Francisco, CA 94143. Offers PhD. *Degree requirements:* For doctorate, thesis/dissertation. *Entrance requirements:* For doctorate, GRE General Test, minimum GPA of 3.0, bachelor's degree. Additional exam requirements/recommendations for international students: Required—TOEFL (minimum score 550 paper-based; 80 iBT). Electronic applications accepted. *Faculty research:* Macromolecular structure function and dynamics, computational chemistry and biology, biological chemistry and synthetic biology, chemical biology and molecular design, nanomolecular design.

University of California, Santa Barbara, Graduate Division, College of Letters and Sciences, Division of Mathematics, Life, and Physical Sciences, Department of Chemistry and Biochemistry, Santa Barbara, CA 93106-9510. Offers chemistry (MA, MS, PhD). Terminal master's awarded for partial completion of doctoral program. *Degree requirements:* For master's, comprehensive exam (for some programs), thesis (for some programs); for doctorate, comprehensive exam, thesis/dissertation, annual faculty committee meetings; minimum 1 year of teaching experience; proposal exam. *Entrance requirements:* For master's and doctorate, GRE General Test, GRE Subject Test in chemistry (recommended), 3 letters of recommendation, statement of purpose, personal achievements essay, resume/curriculum vitae, transcripts. Additional exam requirements/recommendations for international students: Required—TOEFL (minimum score 550 paper-based; 80 iBT), IELTS (minimum score 7). Electronic applications accepted. *Faculty research:* Organic, inorganic, physical, biochemistry, and materials chemistry.

University of California, Santa Cruz, Division of Graduate Studies, Division of Physical and Biological Sciences, Department of Chemistry and Biochemistry, Santa Cruz, CA 95064. Offers MS, PhD. *Degree requirements:* For master's, thesis optional; for doctorate, one foreign language, thesis/dissertation, qualifying exam. *Entrance requirements:* For master's and doctorate, GRE General Test, GRE Subject Test. Additional exam requirements/recommendations for international students: Required—TOEFL (minimum score 570 paper-based; 89 iBT); Recommended—IELTS (minimum score 8). Electronic applications accepted. *Faculty research:* Marine chemistry; biochemistry; inorganic, organic, and physical chemistry.

University of Central Florida, College of Sciences, Department of Chemistry, Orlando, FL 32816. Offers MS, PhD, Certificate. *Program availability:* Part-time, evening/weekend. *Students:* 90 full-time (37 women), 7 part-time (2 women); includes 20 minority (3 Black or African American, non-Hispanic/Latino; 4 Asian, non-Hispanic/Latino; 10 Hispanic/Latino; 3 Two or more races, non-Hispanic/Latino), 25 international. Average age 29. 131 applicants, 42% accepted, 14 enrolled. In 2018, 9 master's, 14 doctorates awarded. *Degree requirements:* For master's, thesis or alternative, qualifying examinations; for doctorate, thesis/dissertation, candidacy examination, qualifying examinations. *Entrance requirements:* For master's, GRE General Test, minimum GPA of 3.0 in last 60 hours, letters of recommendation; for doctorate, GRE General Test, letters of recommendation, resume, statement of purpose. Additional exam requirements/recommendations for international students: Required—TOEFL. *Application deadline:* For fall admission, 7/15 for domestic students; for spring admission, 12/1 for domestic students. Application fee: $30. Electronic applications accepted. *Financial support:* In 2018–19, 82 students received support, including 11 fellowships with partial tuition reimbursements available (averaging $8,727 per year), 40 research assistantships with partial tuition reimbursements available (averaging $10,829 per year), 64 teaching assistantships with partial tuition reimbursements available (averaging $14,612 per year); career-related internships or fieldwork, Federal Work-Study, institutionally sponsored loans, health care benefits, tuition waivers (partial), and unspecified assistantships also available. Financial award application deadline: 3/1; financial award applicants required to submit FAFSA. *Unit head:* Dr. Cherie Yestrebsky, Chair, 407-823-2135, Fax: 407-823-2252, E-mail: cherie.yestrebsky@ucf.edu. *Application contact:* Associate Director, Graduate Admissions, 407-823-2766, Fax: 407-823-6442, E-mail: gradadmissions@ucf.edu.
Website: http://chemistry.cos.ucf.edu/

University of Chicago, Division of the Physical Sciences, Department of Chemistry, Chicago, IL 60637. Offers PhD. *Degree requirements:* For doctorate, comprehensive exam, thesis/dissertation. *Entrance requirements:* For doctorate, GRE General Test; GRE Subject Test in chemistry (recommended), research statement, 3 letters of recommendation, transcripts for all previous degrees and institutions attended. Additional exam requirements/recommendations for international students: Required—TOEFL (minimum score 600 paper-based; 90 iBT), IELTS (minimum score 7). Electronic applications accepted. *Expenses:* Contact institution. *Faculty research:* Organic, inorganic, physical, theoretical, materials, and biological chemistry.

University of Cincinnati, Graduate School, McMicken College of Arts and Sciences, Department of Chemistry, Cincinnati, OH 45221. Offers analytical chemistry (MS, PhD); biochemistry (MS, PhD); inorganic chemistry (MS, PhD); organic chemistry (MS, PhD); physical chemistry (MS, PhD); polymer chemistry (MS, PhD); sensors (PhD). *Program availability:* Part-time, evening/weekend. Terminal master's awarded for partial completion of doctoral program. *Degree requirements:* For master's, thesis optional; for doctorate, comprehensive exam, thesis/dissertation. *Entrance requirements:* For master's and doctorate, GRE General Test. Additional exam requirements/recommendations for international students: Required—TOEFL (minimum score 580 paper-based). Electronic applications accepted. *Faculty research:* Biomedical chemistry, laser chemistry, surface science, chemical sensors, synthesis.

University of Colorado Boulder, Graduate School, College of Arts and Sciences, Department of Chemistry and Biochemistry, Boulder, CO 80309. Offers MS, PhD. Terminal master's awarded for partial completion of doctoral program. *Degree requirements:* For master's, comprehensive exam or thesis; for doctorate, comprehensive exam, thesis/dissertation, cumulative exam. *Entrance requirements:* For master's, GRE General Test, GRE Subject Test, minimum undergraduate GPA of 2.75; for doctorate, GRE General Test, GRE Subject Test, minimum GPA of 3.0. Electronic applications accepted. Application fee is waived when completed online. *Faculty research:* Physical chemistry; biochemistry; biochemistry: proteins; catalysis/kinetics; analytical chemistry.

University of Colorado Denver, College of Liberal Arts and Sciences, Department of Chemistry, Denver, CO 80217-3364. Offers MS. *Program availability:* Part-time. *Degree requirements:* For master's, comprehensive exam, thesis optional, 30-33 credit hours. *Entrance requirements:* For master's, GRE General Test and GRE Subject Test in chemistry (recommended), undergraduate degree in chemistry; minimum undergraduate GPA of 3.0. Additional exam requirements/recommendations for international students: Required—TOEFL (minimum score 550 paper-based; 79 iBT); Recommended—IELTS (minimum score 6). *Expenses:* Tuition, state resident: full-time $6786; part-time $337 per credit hour. Tuition, nonresident: full-time $22,590; part-time $1255 per credit hour. *Required fees:* $1231; $137 per credit hour. Tuition and fees vary according to program and reciprocity agreements.

University of Connecticut, Graduate School, College of Liberal Arts and Sciences, Department of Chemistry, Storrs, CT 06269. Offers MS, PhD. Terminal master's awarded for partial completion of doctoral program. *Degree requirements:* For master's, comprehensive exam; for doctorate, thesis/dissertation. *Entrance requirements:* For master's and doctorate, GRE General Test, GRE Subject Test. Additional exam requirements/recommendations for international students: Required—TOEFL (minimum score 550 paper-based). Electronic applications accepted.

University of Dayton, Department of Chemistry and Biochemistry, Dayton, OH 45469. Offers MS. *Program availability:* Part-time. *Degree requirements:* For master's, thesis, 30 credit hours. *Entrance requirements:* For master's, BS in chemistry or closely-related discipline. Additional exam requirements/recommendations for international students: Required—TOEFL (minimum score 550 paper-based; 80 iBT), GRE; Recommended—IELTS. Electronic applications accepted. *Faculty research:* DNA reactive metals, antibiotic efflux inhibitors, flame retardants, medicinal chiral phosphates, supramolecular chemistry.

University of Delaware, College of Arts and Sciences, Department of Chemistry and Biochemistry, Newark, DE 19716. Offers biochemistry (MA, MS, PhD); chemistry (MA, MS, PhD). *Program availability:* Part-time. Terminal master's awarded for partial completion of doctoral program. *Degree requirements:* For master's, one foreign language, thesis (for some programs); for doctorate, one foreign language, thesis/dissertation, cumulative exam. *Entrance requirements:* For master's and doctorate, GRE General Test. Additional exam requirements/recommendations for international students: Required—TOEFL (minimum score 600 paper-based). Electronic applications accepted. *Faculty research:* Micro-organisms, bone, cancer metastosis, developmental biology, cell biology, molecular biology.

University of Denver, Division of Natural Sciences and Mathematics, Department of Chemistry and Biochemistry, Denver, CO 80208. Offers chemistry (MA, MS, PhD). *Program availability:* Part-time. *Faculty:* 18 full-time (4 women). *Students:* 14 full-time (4 women), 11 part-time (6 women); includes 11 minority (3 Black or African American, non-Hispanic/Latino; 1 Asian, non-Hispanic/Latino; 5 Hispanic/Latino; 2 Two or more races, non-Hispanic/Latino), 4 international. Average age 28. 55 applicants, 58% accepted, 9 enrolled. In 2018, 3 master's, 4 doctorates awarded. Terminal master's awarded for partial completion of doctoral program. *Degree requirements:* For master's, thesis (for some programs); for doctorate, comprehensive exam, thesis/dissertation. *Entrance requirements:* For master's, GRE General Test, bachelor's degree in chemistry, biochemistry, or a related field; transcripts; personal statement; three letters of recommendation; for doctorate, GRE General Test, bachelor's degree in chemistry, biochemistry, or a related field; transcripts; personal statement, resume or curriculum vitae; three letters of recommendation. Additional exam requirements/recommendations for international students: Required—TOEFL (minimum score 550 paper-based; 80 iBT). *Application deadline:* For fall admission, 1/15 priority date for domestic and international students. Applications are processed on a rolling basis. Application fee: $65. Electronic applications accepted. *Expenses:* $33,183 per year full-time. *Financial support:* In 2018–19, 25 students received support, including 15 research assistantships with tuition reimbursements available (averaging $13,306 per year), 19 teaching assistantships with tuition reimbursements available (averaging $13,794 per year); career-related internships or fieldwork, Federal Work-Study, institutionally sponsored loans, and scholarships/grants also available. Support available to part-time students. Financial award application deadline: 2/15; financial award applicants required to submit FAFSA. *Faculty research:* Protein folding, atmospheric environmental chemistry, electron paramagnetic resonance, applied organic chemistry, biophysical chemistry. *Total annual research expenditures:* $2.2 million. *Unit head:* Dr. Sandra S. Eaton, Professor and Chair, 303-871-3100, E-mail: seaton@du.edu. *Application contact:* Mary Shonk, Assistant to the Chair, 303-871-2436, E-mail: cheminfo@du.edu.
Website: http://www.du.edu/nsm/departments/chemistryandbiochemistry

Chemistry

University of Detroit Mercy, College of Engineering and Science, Detroit, MI 48221. Offers chemistry (MS); civil and environmental engineering (DE); electrical and computer engineering (ME); electrical engineering (DE); engineering management (M Eng Mgt); environmental engineering (MEE); mechanical engineering (MME, DE); product development (MS); software engineering (MSSE); teaching of mathematics (MATM). *Program availability:* Part-time, evening/weekend. *Degree requirements:* For doctorate, thesis/dissertation. Electronic applications accepted. Application fee is waived when completed online. *Expenses:* Contact institution.

University of Florida, Graduate School, College of Liberal Arts and Sciences, Department of Chemistry, Gainesville, FL 32611. Offers chemistry (MS, MST, PhD); clinical and translational science (PhD); imaging science and technology (PhD). Terminal master's awarded for partial completion of doctoral program. *Degree requirements:* For master's, thesis; for doctorate, comprehensive exam, thesis/dissertation. *Entrance requirements:* For master's and doctorate, GRE General Test, minimum GPA of 3.0. Additional exam requirements/recommendations for international students: Required—TOEFL (minimum score 550 paper-based; 80 iBT), IELTS (minimum score 6). Electronic applications accepted. *Faculty research:* Organic, analytical, physical, inorganic, and biological chemistry.

University of Georgia, Franklin College of Arts and Sciences, Department of Chemistry, Athens, GA 30602. Offers analytical chemistry (MS, PhD). Terminal master's awarded for partial completion of doctoral program. *Degree requirements:* For master's, thesis; for doctorate, one foreign language, thesis/dissertation. *Entrance requirements:* For master's and doctorate, GRE General Test. Additional exam requirements/recommendations for international students: Required—TOEFL. Electronic applications accepted.

University of Guelph, Office of Graduate and Postdoctoral Studies, College of Physical and Engineering Science, Guelph-Waterloo Centre for Graduate Work in Chemistry and Biochemistry, Guelph, ON N1G 2W1, Canada. Offers M Sc, PhD. M Sc, PhD offered jointly with University of Waterloo. *Program availability:* Part-time. *Degree requirements:* For master's, thesis; for doctorate, thesis/dissertation. *Faculty research:* Inorganic, analytical, biological, physical/theoretical, polymer, and organic chemistry.

University of Hawaii at Manoa, Office of Graduate Education, College of Natural Sciences, Department of Chemistry, Honolulu, HI 96822. Offers MS, PhD. *Program availability:* Part-time. *Degree requirements:* For master's, comprehensive exam, thesis; for doctorate, comprehensive exam, thesis/dissertation. *Entrance requirements:* For master's and doctorate, GRE General Test, GRE Subject Test. Additional exam requirements/recommendations for international students: Required—TOEFL (minimum score 500 paper-based; 61 iBT), IELTS (minimum score 5). *Faculty research:* Marine natural products, biophysical spectroscopy, zeolites, organometallic hydrides, new visual pigments, theory of surfaces.

University of Houston, College of Natural Sciences and Mathematics, Department of Chemistry, Houston, TX 77204. Offers MA, PhD. *Program availability:* Part-time. Terminal master's awarded for partial completion of doctoral program. *Degree requirements:* For master's, thesis; for doctorate, thesis/dissertation, oral presentation. *Entrance requirements:* For master's and doctorate, GRE General Test. Additional exam requirements/recommendations for international students: Required—TOEFL (minimum score 79 iBT), IELTS (minimum score 6.5). Electronic applications accepted. *Faculty research:* Materials, molecular design, surface science, structural chemistry, synthesis.

University of Houston–Clear Lake, School of Science and Computer Engineering, Program in Chemistry, Houston, TX 77058-1002. Offers MS. *Program availability:* Part-time, evening/weekend. *Entrance requirements:* For master's, GRE General Test. Additional exam requirements/recommendations for international students: Required—TOEFL (minimum score 550 paper-based).

University of Idaho, College of Graduate Studies, College of Science, Department of Chemistry, Moscow, ID 83844-2343. Offers MS, PhD. *Faculty:* 10. *Students:* 21. Average age 29. In 2018, 1 master's, 3 doctorates awarded. *Degree requirements:* For master's, thesis or alternative; for doctorate, thesis/dissertation. *Entrance requirements:* For master's, GRE, minimum GPA of 3.0; for doctorate, minimum GPA of 3.0. Additional exam requirements/recommendations for international students: Required—TOEFL (minimum score 79 iBT). *Application deadline:* For fall admission, 5/1 for domestic students; for spring admission, 11/1 for domestic students. Applications are processed on a rolling basis. Application fee: $60. Electronic applications accepted. *Expenses:* Tuition, state resident: full-time $7266.44; part-time $474.50 per credit hour. Tuition, nonresident: full-time $24,902; part-time $1453.50 per credit hour. *Required fees:* $2085.56; $45.50 per credit hour. *Financial support:* Fellowships, research assistantships, and teaching assistantships available. Financial award applicants required to submit FAFSA. *Faculty research:* Analytical chemistry, energetic materials, green techniques for nuclear waste management, organic chemistry, physical chemistry. *Unit head:* Dr. Ray von Wandruszka, Chair, 208-885-6552, E-mail: chemoff@uidaho.edu. *Application contact:* Dr. Ray von Wandruszka, Chair, 208-885-6552, E-mail: chemoff@uidaho.edu.
Website: https://www.uidaho.edu/sci/chem

University of Illinois at Chicago, College of Liberal Arts and Sciences, Department of Chemistry, Chicago, IL 60607-7128. Offers MS, PhD. *Program availability:* Part-time. Terminal master's awarded for partial completion of doctoral program. *Degree requirements:* For master's, thesis or cumulative exam; for doctorate, one foreign language, thesis/dissertation, cumulative exams. *Entrance requirements:* For master's and doctorate, GRE Subject Test, minimum GPA of 3.0. Additional exam requirements/recommendations for international students: Required—TOEFL. Electronic applications accepted. *Expenses:* Contact institution. *Faculty research:* Analytical, biological, inorganic, organic and physical chemistry; chemical biology, nanotechnology and neurochemistry.

University of Illinois at Urbana–Champaign, Graduate College, College of Liberal Arts and Sciences, School of Chemical Sciences, Department of Chemistry, Champaign, IL 61820. Offers astrochemistry (PhD); chemical physics (PhD); chemistry (MA, MS, PhD); teaching of chemistry (MS); MS/JD; MS/MBA.

The University of Iowa, Graduate College, College of Liberal Arts and Sciences, Department of Chemistry, Iowa City, IA 52242-1316. Offers PhD. *Degree requirements:* For doctorate, comprehensive exam, thesis/dissertation. *Entrance requirements:* For doctorate, GRE General Test, minimum GPA of 3.0. Additional exam requirements/recommendations for international students: Required—TOEFL (minimum score 550 paper-based; 81 iBT). Electronic applications accepted.

The University of Kansas, Graduate Studies, College of Liberal Arts and Sciences, Department of Chemistry, Lawrence, KS 66045. Offers MS, PhD. *Program availability:* Part-time. *Students:* 108 full-time (50 women), 6 part-time (4 women); includes 10 minority (1 American Indian or Alaska Native, non-Hispanic/Latino; 4 Asian, non-Hispanic/Latino; 3 Hispanic/Latino; 2 Two or more races, non-Hispanic/Latino), 55 international. Average age 27. 123 applicants, 41% accepted, 25 enrolled. In 2018, 3 master's, 16 doctorates awarded. *Entrance requirements:* For master's and doctorate, GRE General Test (recommended), original transcript, three letters of recommendation; personal statement and resume (recommended). Additional exam requirements/recommendations for international students: Required—TOEFL, IELTS. *Application deadline:* For fall admission, 12/15 priority date for domestic and international students; for spring admission, 10/15 priority date for domestic and international students. Application fee: $65 ($85 for international students). Electronic applications accepted. *Financial support:* Fellowships, research assistantships, teaching assistantships, scholarships/grants, traineeships, tuition waivers (full), and unspecified assistantships available. Financial award application deadline: 4/15. *Faculty research:* Organometallic and inorganic synthetic methodology, bioanalytical chemistry, computational materials science, proteomics, physical chemistry. *Unit head:* Prof. Brian B. Laird, Chair, 785-864-4632, E-mail: blaird@ku.edu. *Application contact:* Megan Belaire, Graduate Affairs Administrator, 785-864-8287, E-mail: mbelaire@ku.edu.
Website: http://www.chem.ku.edu/

University of Kentucky, Graduate School, College of Arts and Sciences, Program in Chemistry, Lexington, KY 40506-0032. Offers MS, PhD. *Program availability:* Part-time. Terminal master's awarded for partial completion of doctoral program. *Degree requirements:* For master's, comprehensive exam, thesis optional; for doctorate, comprehensive exam, thesis/dissertation. *Entrance requirements:* For master's, GRE General Test, minimum undergraduate GPA of 2.75; for doctorate, GRE General Test, minimum graduate GPA of 3.0. Additional exam requirements/recommendations for international students: Required—TOEFL (minimum score 550 paper-based). Electronic applications accepted. *Faculty research:* Analytical, inorganic, organic, and physical chemistry; biological chemistry; nuclear chemistry; radiochemistry; materials chemistry.

University of Lethbridge, School of Graduate Studies, Lethbridge, AB T1K 3M4, Canada. Offers addictions counseling (M Sc); agricultural biotechnology (M Sc); agricultural studies (M Sc, MA); anthropology (MA); archaeology (M Sc, MA); art (MA, MFA); biochemistry (M Sc); biological sciences (M Sc); biomolecular science (PhD); biosystems and biodiversity (PhD); Canadian studies (MA); chemistry (M Sc); computer science (M Sc); computer science and geographical information science (M Sc); counseling (MC); counseling psychology (M Ed); dramatic arts (MA); earth, space, and physical science (PhD); economics (MA); education (MA, PhD); educational leadership (M Ed); English (MA); environmental science (M Sc); evolution and behavior (PhD); exercise science (M Sc); French (MA); French/German (MA); French/Spanish (MA); general education (M Ed); geography (M Sc, MA); German (MA); health sciences (M Sc); individualized multidisciplinary (M Sc, MA); kinesiology (M Sc, MA); management (M Sc), including accounting, finance, human resource management and labor relations, information systems, international management, marketing, policy and strategy; mathematics (M Sc); music (M Mus, MA); Native American studies (MA); neuroscience (M Sc, PhD); new media (MA, MFA); nursing (M Sc, MN); philosophy (MA); physics (M Sc); political science (MA); psychology (M Sc, MA); religious studies (MA); sociology (MA); theatre and dramatic arts (MFA); theoretical and computational science (PhD); urban and regional studies (MA); women and gender studies (MA). *Program availability:* Part-time, evening/weekend. *Degree requirements:* For master's, thesis (for some programs); for doctorate, comprehensive exam, thesis/dissertation. *Entrance requirements:* For master's, GMAT (for M Sc in management), bachelor's degree in related field, minimum GPA of 3.0 during previous 20 graded semester courses, 2 years' teaching or related experience (M Ed); for doctorate, master's degree, minimum graduate GPA of 3.5. Additional exam requirements/recommendations for international students: Required—TOEFL (minimum score 580 paper-based; 93 iBT). Electronic applications accepted. *Faculty research:* Movement and brain plasticity, gibberellin physiology, photosynthesis, carbon cycling, molecular properties of main-group ring components.

University of Louisville, Graduate School, College of Arts and Sciences, Department of Chemistry, Louisville, KY 40292-0001. Offers analytical chemistry (MS, PhD); biochemistry (MS, PhD); chemical physics (PhD); inorganic chemistry (MS, PhD); organic chemistry (MS, PhD); physical chemistry (MS, PhD). *Faculty:* 26 full-time (9 women), 3 part-time/adjunct (1 woman). *Students:* 35 full-time (14 women), 17 part-time (4 women); includes 5 minority (2 Black or African American, non-Hispanic/Latino; 3 Asian, non-Hispanic/Latino), 39 international. Average age 31. 47 applicants, 36% accepted, 10 enrolled. In 2018, 18 master's, 3 doctorates awarded. Terminal master's awarded for partial completion of doctoral program. *Degree requirements:* For master's, thesis (for some programs), Literature Seminars; for doctorate, thesis/dissertation, Cumulative Exams, Literature Seminars; Research. *Entrance requirements:* For master's and doctorate, GRE General Test, official transcripts, recommendation letters (minimum of 2), personal statement. Additional exam requirements/recommendations for international students: Required—TOEFL (minimum score 550 paper-based; 79 iBT), IELTS can be taken in place of TOEFL; Recommended—IELTS (minimum score 6.5). *Application deadline:* For fall admission, 1/15 priority date for domestic and international students; for spring admission, 9/15 priority date for domestic and international students. Application fee: $65. Electronic applications accepted. *Expenses: Tuition, area resident:* Full-time $6500; part-time $723 per credit hour. Tuition, state resident: full-time $6500. Tuition, nonresident: full-time $13,557; part-time $1507 per credit hour. Tuition and fees vary according to course load and program. *Financial support:* In 2018–19, 59 students received support, including 2 fellowships with full tuition reimbursements available (averaging $23,000 per year), 10 research assistantships with full tuition reimbursements available (averaging $23,000 per year), 41 teaching assistantships with full tuition reimbursements available (averaging $23,000 per year); scholarships/grants, health care benefits, and unspecified assistantships also available. Financial award application deadline: 1/15. *Faculty research:* Solid state chemistry, chemical synthesis, nanoparticle research, green chemistry, spectroscopic studies, computational chemistry, catalysis. *Total annual research expenditures:* $1 million. *Unit head:* Dr. Craig Grapperhaus, Professor, 502-852-8148, Fax: 502-852-8149, E-mail: craig.grapperhaus@louisville.edu. *Application contact:* Sherry Nalley, Graduate Program Assistant, 502-852-6798, Fax: 502-852-6536, E-mail: sherry.nalley@louisville.edu.
Website: http://louisville.edu/chemistry

University of Maine, Graduate School, College of Liberal Arts and Sciences, Department of Chemistry, Orono, ME 04469. Offers MS, PhD. *Faculty:* 12 full-time (2 women). *Students:* 38 full-time (12 women); includes 4 minority (2 American Indian or Alaska Native, non-Hispanic/Latino; 2 Asian, non-Hispanic/Latino), 25 international. Average age 29. 26 applicants, 42% accepted, 5 enrolled. In 2018, 1 master's, 1 doctorate awarded. Terminal master's awarded for partial completion of doctoral program. *Degree requirements:* For master's, thesis; for doctorate, comprehensive exam, thesis/dissertation. *Entrance requirements:* For master's and doctorate, GRE General Test. Additional exam requirements/recommendations for international students: Required—TOEFL (minimum score 80 iBT), IELTS (minimum score 6.5), PTE (minimum score 60). *Application deadline:* Applications are processed on a rolling basis. Application fee: $65. Electronic applications accepted. *Financial support:* In 2018–19, 34 students received support, including 11 research assistantships with full tuition reimbursements available (averaging $21,000 per year), 23 teaching assistantships with

full tuition reimbursements available (averaging $18,700 per year); tuition waivers (full and partial) also available. Financial award application deadline: 3/1. *Faculty research:* Nanomaterials, surface chemistry and catalysis; synthesis of biologically active organic and inorganic compounds; sustainable polymers and chemicals; electrochemistry; computational chemistry. *Total annual research expenditures:* $1.1 million. *Unit head:* Dr. Barbara Cole, Chair, 207-581-1196, E-mail: cole@maine.edu. *Application contact:* Scott G. Delcourt, Assistant Vice President for Graduate Studies and Senior Associate Dean, 207-581-3291, Fax: 207-581-3232, E-mail: graduate@maine.edu.
Website: http://umaine.edu/chemistry

The University of Manchester, School of Chemical Engineering and Analytical Science, Manchester, United Kingdom. Offers biocatalysis (M Phil, PhD); chemical engineering (M Phil, PhD); chemical engineering and analytical science (M Phil, D Eng, PhD); colloids, crystals, interfaces and materials (M Phil, PhD); environment and sustainable technology (M Phil, PhD); instrumentation (M Phil, PhD); multi-scale modeling (M Phil, PhD); process integration (M Phil, PhD); systems biology (M Phil, PhD).

The University of Manchester, School of Chemistry, Manchester, United Kingdom. Offers biological chemistry (PhD); chemistry (M Ent, M Phil, M Sc, D Ent, PhD); inorganic chemistry (PhD); materials chemistry (PhD); nanoscience (PhD); nuclear fission (PhD); organic chemistry (PhD); physical chemistry (PhD); theoretical chemistry (PhD).

The University of Manchester, School of Earth and Environmental Sciences, Manchester, United Kingdom. Offers atmospheric sciences (M Phil, M Sc, PhD); basin studies and petroleum geosciences (M Phil, M Sc, PhD); earth, atmospheric and environmental sciences (M Phil, M Sc, PhD); environmental geochemistry and cosmochemistry (M Phil, M Sc, PhD); isotope geochemistry and cosmochemistry (M Phil, M Sc, PhD); paleontology (M Phil, M Sc, PhD); physics and chemistry of minerals and fluids (M Phil, M Sc, PhD); structural and petrological geosciences (M Phil, M Sc, PhD).

University of Manitoba, Faculty of Graduate Studies, Faculty of Science, Department of Chemistry, Winnipeg, MB R3T 2N2, Canada. Offers M Sc, PhD. *Degree requirements:* For master's, thesis; for doctorate, one foreign language, thesis/dissertation.

University of Maryland, Baltimore County, The Graduate School, College of Natural and Mathematical Sciences, Department of Chemistry and Biochemistry, Baltimore, MD 21250. Offers chemistry (MS, PhD); chemistry and biochemistry (Postbaccalaureate Certificate). *Program availability:* Part-time. Terminal master's awarded for partial completion of doctoral program. *Degree requirements:* For master's, comprehensive exam (for some programs), thesis (for some programs); for doctorate, comprehensive exam, thesis/dissertation. *Entrance requirements:* For master's, GRE General Test, minimum GPA of 3.0; for doctorate, GRE General Test, GRE Subject Test (recommended), minimum GPA of 3.0. Additional exam requirements/recommendations for international students: Required—TOEFL (minimum score 550 paper-based; 80 iBT), IELTS (minimum score 6.5). Electronic applications accepted. Application fee is waived when completed online. *Faculty research:* Protein structures, bio-organic chemistry, enzyme catalysis, molecular biology, metabolism, nanotechnology.

University of Maryland, College Park, Academic Affairs, College of Computer, Mathematical and Natural Sciences, Department of Chemistry and Biochemistry, Chemistry Program, College Park, MD 20742. Offers analytical chemistry (MS, PhD); inorganic chemistry (MS, PhD); organic chemistry (MS, PhD); physical chemistry (MS, PhD). *Program availability:* Part-time, evening/weekend. Terminal master's awarded for partial completion of doctoral program. *Degree requirements:* For master's, thesis optional; for doctorate, thesis/dissertation, 2 seminar presentations, oral exam. *Entrance requirements:* For master's and doctorate, GRE General Test, GRE Subject Test (recommended), minimum GPA of 3.0, 3 letters of recommendation. Additional exam requirements/recommendations for international students: Required—TOEFL. Electronic applications accepted. *Faculty research:* Environmental chemistry, nuclear chemistry, lunar and environmental analysis, X-ray crystallography.

University of Maryland Eastern Shore, Graduate Programs, Department of Natural Sciences, Princess Anne, MD 21853. Offers chemistry (MS); quantitative fisheries and resource economics (PMS); toxicology (MS, PhD). *Degree requirements:* For master's, thesis; for doctorate, comprehensive exam, thesis/dissertation. *Entrance requirements:* For master's and doctorate, GRE General Test, minimum GPA of 3.0. Additional exam requirements/recommendations for international students: Required—TOEFL (minimum score 80 iBT). Electronic applications accepted. *Faculty research:* Environmental chemistry (air/water pollution), fin fish ecology.

University of Massachusetts Amherst, Graduate School, College of Natural Sciences, Department of Chemistry, Amherst, MA 01003. Offers MS, PhD. *Program availability:* Part-time. Terminal master's awarded for partial completion of doctoral program. *Degree requirements:* For master's, thesis (for some programs); for doctorate, comprehensive exam, thesis/dissertation. *Entrance requirements:* For master's and doctorate, GRE General Test. Additional exam requirements/recommendations for international students: Required—TOEFL (minimum score 550 paper-based; 80 iBT), IELTS (minimum score 6.5). Electronic applications accepted.

University of Massachusetts Boston, College of Science and Mathematics, Program in Chemistry, Boston, MA 02125-3393. Offers MS, PhD. *Program availability:* Part-time, evening/weekend. *Faculty:* 16 full-time (5 women), 3 part-time/adjunct (2 women). *Students:* 37 full-time (22 women), 7 part-time (2 women); includes 13 minority (2 Black or African American, non-Hispanic/Latino; 7 Asian, non-Hispanic/Latino; 4 Hispanic/Latino), 9 international. Average age 28. 45 applicants, 69% accepted, 15 enrolled. In 2018, 1 master's, 6 doctorates awarded. *Entrance requirements:* For master's, GRE General Test, GRE Subject Test, minimum GPA of 2.75. *Application deadline:* For fall admission, 6/1 for domestic students; for spring admission, 11/1 for domestic students. *Expenses: Tuition, area resident:* Full-time $17,896. Tuition, state resident: full-time $17,896. Tuition, nonresident: full-time $34,932. *International tuition:* $34,932 full-time. *Required fees:* $355. *Financial support:* Research assistantships, teaching assistantships, career-related internships or fieldwork, Federal Work-Study, and unspecified assistantships available. Support available to part-time students. Financial award application deadline: 3/1; financial award applicants required to submit FAFSA. *Faculty research:* Synthesis and mechanisms of organic nitrogen compounds, application of spin resonance in the study of structure and dynamics, chemical education and teacher training, new synthetic reagents, structural study of inorganic solids by infrared and Raman spectroscopy. *Unit head:* Dr. Hannah Sevian, Professor of Chemistry, 617-287-7724, E-mail: Hannah.Sevian@umb.edu. *Application contact:* Graduate Admissions Coordinator, 617-287-6400, Fax: 617-287-6236, E-mail: graduate.admissions@umb.edu.

University of Massachusetts Dartmouth, Graduate School, College of Arts and Sciences, Department of Chemistry and Biochemistry, North Dartmouth, MA 02747-2300. Offers chemistry (MS, PhD). *Program availability:* Part-time. *Faculty:* 20 full-time (7 women), 4 part-time/adjunct (2 women). *Students:* 20 full-time (8 women), 20 part-time (9 women); includes 4 minority (1 Black or African American, non-Hispanic/Latino; 3 Asian, non-Hispanic/Latino), 18 international. Average age 29. 25 applicants, 72% accepted, 10 enrolled. In 2018, 11 master's awarded. *Degree requirements:* For master's, thesis, thesis or project; for doctorate, comprehensive exam, thesis/dissertation, Dissertation. *Entrance requirements:* For master's, GRE (recommended), statement of purpose (minimum of 300 words), resume, official transcripts, 2 letters of recommendation (3 recommended); for doctorate, GRE, statement of purpose (minimum of 300 words), resume, official transcripts, 2 letters of recommendation (3 recommended). Additional exam requirements/recommendations for international students: Required—TOEFL (minimum score 550 paper-based; 79 iBT), IELTS (minimum score 6.5). *Application deadline:* For fall admission, 3/15 priority date for domestic students, 2/15 priority date for international students; for spring admission, 11/1 priority date for domestic students, 10/1 priority date for international students. Application fee: $60. Electronic applications accepted. *Financial support:* In 2018–19, 1 fellowship (averaging $6,000 per year), 6 research assistantships (averaging $9,548 per year), 23 teaching assistantships (averaging $12,217 per year) were awarded; career-related internships or fieldwork, tuition waivers (full), unspecified assistantships, and dissertation writing support also available. Support available to part-time students. Financial award application deadline: 3/1; financial award applicants required to submit FAFSA. *Faculty research:* Molecular imaging probes for iron and reactive oxygen species detection in living systems, self-assembly of peptide nanotubes, host-guest complexes, mechanical and optical properties of carbon nanotubes, cellular antioxidant chemistry. *Total annual research expenditures:* $996,000. *Unit head:* Yuegang Zuo, Graduate Program Director, Chemistry, 508-999-8959, E-mail: yzuo@umassd.edu. *Application contact:* Scott Webster, Director of Graduate Studies & Admissions, 508-999-8604, Fax: 508-999-8183, E-mail: graduate@umassd.edu.
Website: http://www.umassd.edu/cas/chemistry

University of Massachusetts Lowell, College of Sciences, Department of Chemistry, Lowell, MA 01854. Offers analytical chemistry (PhD); biochemistry (PhD); chemistry (MS, PhD); environmental studies (PhD); green chemistry (PhD); inorganic chemistry (PhD); organic chemistry (PhD); polymer science (MS). Terminal master's awarded for partial completion of doctoral program. *Degree requirements:* For master's, thesis; for doctorate, 2 foreign languages, thesis/dissertation. *Entrance requirements:* For master's and doctorate, GRE General Test. Electronic applications accepted.

University of Memphis, Graduate School, College of Arts and Sciences, Department of Chemistry, Memphis, TN 38152. Offers analytical chemistry (MS, PhD); computational chemistry (MS, PhD); inorganic chemistry (MS, PhD); organic chemistry (MS, PhD); physical chemistry (MS, PhD). *Program availability:* Part-time. *Students:* 37 full-time (11 women), 14 part-time (5 women); includes 9 minority (2 Black or African American, non-Hispanic/Latino; 3 Asian, non-Hispanic/Latino; 4 Two or more races, non-Hispanic/Latino), 6 international. Average age 27. 24 applicants, 67% accepted, 14 enrolled. In 2018, 9 master's, 3 doctorates awarded. Terminal master's awarded for partial completion of doctoral program. *Degree requirements:* For master's, comprehensive exam, thesis or alternative; for doctorate, comprehensive exam, thesis/dissertation. *Entrance requirements:* For master's and doctorate, GRE General Test, admission to Graduate School plus 32 undergraduate hours in chemistry. Additional exam requirements/recommendations for international students: Required—TOEFL (minimum score 550 paper-based). *Application deadline:* For fall admission, 7/1 for domestic students, 5/1 for international students; for winter admission, 9/15 for international students; for spring admission, 12/1 for domestic students. Applications are processed on a rolling basis. Application fee: $35 ($60 for international students). Electronic applications accepted. *Expenses: Tuition, area resident:* Full-time $10,240; part-time $503 per credit hour. Tuition, state resident: full-time $10,464. Tuition, nonresident: full-time $20,224; part-time $991 per credit hour. *Required fees:* $850; $106 per credit hour. *Financial support:* Research assistantships with full tuition reimbursements, teaching assistantships with full tuition reimbursements, Federal Work-Study, scholarships/grants, and unspecified assistantships available. Financial award application deadline: 2/1; financial award applicants required to submit FAFSA. *Faculty research:* Computational chemistry, materials chemistry, organic/polymer synthesis, drug design/delivery, water chemistry. *Unit head:* Dr. Gary Emmert, Chair, 901-678-2638, Fax: 901-678-3447, E-mail: gemmert@memphis.edu. *Application contact:* Dr. Paul Simone, Coordinator of Graduate Studies, 901-678-3671, Fax: 901-678-3447, E-mail: gradchem@memphis.edu.
Website: http://www.memphis.edu/chem/

University of Miami, Graduate School, College of Arts and Sciences, Department of Chemistry, Coral Gables, FL 33124. Offers chemistry (MS); inorganic chemistry (PhD); organic chemistry (PhD); physical chemistry (PhD). Terminal master's awarded for partial completion of doctoral program. *Degree requirements:* For master's, comprehensive exam; for doctorate, comprehensive exam, thesis/dissertation. *Entrance requirements:* For master's and doctorate, GRE General Test. Additional exam requirements/recommendations for international students: Required—TOEFL (minimum score 550 paper-based). Electronic applications accepted. *Faculty research:* Supramolecular chemistry, electrochemistry, surface chemistry, catalysis, organometalic.

University of Michigan, Rackham Graduate School, College of Literature, Science, and the Arts, Department of Chemistry, Ann Arbor, MI 48109-1055. Offers analytical chemistry (PhD); chemical biology (PhD); chemical sciences (MS); inorganic chemistry (PhD); materials chemistry (PhD); organic chemistry (PhD); physical chemistry (PhD). *Program availability:* Part-time. *Faculty:* 40 full-time (14 women), 7 part-time/adjunct (3 women). *Students:* 262 full-time (112 women), 4 part-time (all women); includes 44 minority (11 Black or African American, non-Hispanic/Latino; 11 Asian, non-Hispanic/Latino; 19 Hispanic/Latino; 1 Native Hawaiian or other Pacific Islander, non-Hispanic/Latino; 2 Two or more races, non-Hispanic/Latino), 61 international. 692 applicants, 71 enrolled. In 2018, 47 master's, 46 doctorates awarded. *Degree requirements:* For doctorate, comprehensive exam, thesis/dissertation, oral defense of dissertation, organic cumulative proficiency exams. *Entrance requirements:* For master's, bachelor's degree, 3 letters of recommendation, personal statement; for doctorate, bachelor's degree, 3 letters of recommendation, personal statement, curriculum vitae/resume. Additional exam requirements/recommendations for international students: Required—TOEFL (minimum score 560 paper-based; 84 iBT) or IELTS. *Application deadline:* For fall admission, 12/1 for domestic and international students. Application fee: $0 ($90 for international students). Electronic applications accepted. *Financial support:* In 2018–19, 269 students received support, including 50 fellowships with full tuition reimbursements available (averaging $31,625 per year), 84 research assistantships with full tuition reimbursements available (averaging $31,625 per year), 133 teaching assistantships with full tuition reimbursements available (averaging $31,625 per year); career-related internships or fieldwork, Federal Work-Study, scholarships/grants, traineeships, health care benefits, tuition waivers (full), and unspecified assistantships also available. *Faculty research:* Biological catalysis, protein engineering, chemical sensors, de novo metalloprotein design, supramolecular architecture. *Total annual research expenditures:* $19.6 million. *Unit head:* Dr. Robert Kennedy, Professor of Chemistry/Chair, 734-763-

9681, Fax: 734-647-4847. *Application contact:* Elizabeth Oxford, Graduate Program Coordinator, 734-764-7278, Fax: 734-647-4865, E-mail: chemadmissions@umich.edu.
Website: http://www.lsa.umich.edu/chem/

University of Minnesota, Duluth, Graduate School, Swenson College of Science and Engineering, Department of Chemistry and Biochemistry, Duluth, MN 55812-2496. Offers MS. *Program availability:* Part-time. *Degree requirements:* For master's, thesis. *Entrance requirements:* For master's, bachelor's degree in chemistry, minimum GPA of 3.0. Additional exam requirements/recommendations for international students: Required—TOEFL (minimum score 550 paper-based; 79 iBT), IELTS (minimum score 6.5). *Faculty research:* Physical, inorganic, organic, and analytical chemistry; biochemistry and molecular biology.

University of Minnesota, Twin Cities Campus, College of Science and Engineering, Department of Chemistry, Minneapolis, MN 55455-0213. Offers chemical physics (MS, PhD); chemistry (MS, PhD). *Program availability:* Part-time. Terminal master's awarded for partial completion of doctoral program. *Degree requirements:* For master's, thesis or alternative; for doctorate, thesis/dissertation, preliminary candidacy exams. *Entrance requirements:* For master's and doctorate, GRE General Test. Additional exam requirements/recommendations for international students: Required—TOEFL. Electronic applications accepted. *Faculty research:* Analytical chemistry, environmental chemistry, organic chemistry, inorganic chemistry, materials chemistry, polymer chemistry, computational chemistry, experimental physical chemistry, chemical biology.

University of Minnesota, Twin Cities Campus, School of Public Health, Division of Environmental Health Sciences, Area in Environmental Chemistry, Minneapolis, MN 55455-0213. Offers MS, PhD. *Degree requirements:* For doctorate, thesis/dissertation. *Entrance requirements:* For master's and doctorate, GRE General Test. Electronic applications accepted.

University of Mississippi, Graduate School, College of Liberal Arts, University, MS 38677-1848. Offers anthropology (MA); biology (MS, PhD); chemistry (MS, DA, PhD); creative writing (MFA); documentary expression (MFA); economics (MA, PhD); English (MA, PhD); experimental psychology (PhD); history (MA, PhD); mathematics (MS, PhD); modern languages (MA); music (MM); philosophy (MA); physics (MA, MS, PhD); political science (MA, PhD); Southern studies (MA); studio art (MFA). *Program availability:* Part-time. *Faculty:* 474 full-time (209 women), 71 part-time/adjunct (38 women). *Students:* 471 full-time (241 women), 80 part-time (39 women); includes 90 minority (43 Black or African American, non-Hispanic/Latino; 14 Asian, non-Hispanic/Latino; 23 Hispanic/Latino; 10 Two or more races, non-Hispanic/Latino), 136 international. *Degree requirements:* For doctorate, thesis/dissertation. *Entrance requirements:* For master's, GRE General Test, minimum GPA of 3.0; for doctorate, GRE General Test. Additional exam requirements/recommendations for international students: Required—TOEFL. *Application deadline:* Applications are processed on a rolling basis. Application fee: $50. Electronic applications accepted. *Financial support:* Fellowships, research assistantships, teaching assistantships, career-related internships or fieldwork, Federal Work-Study, institutionally sponsored loans, scholarships/grants, and unspecified assistantships available. Financial award application deadline: 3/1; financial award applicants required to submit FAFSA. *Unit head:* Dr. Lee Michael Cohen, Dean, 662-915-7177, Fax: 662-915-5792, E-mail: libarts@olemiss.edu. *Application contact:* Tameka Smith, Graduate Activities Specialist for Admissions, 662-915-7474, Fax: 662-915-7577, E-mail: gschool@olemiss.edu.
Website: ventress@olemiss.edu

University of Missouri, Office of Research and Graduate Studies, College of Arts and Science, Department of Chemistry, Columbia, MO 65211. Offers analytical chemistry (PhD). *Degree requirements:* For doctorate, one foreign language, comprehensive exam, thesis/dissertation. *Entrance requirements:* For doctorate, GRE General Test (minimum score: Verbal 450, Quantitative 600, Analytical 3), minimum GPA of 3.0. Additional exam requirements/recommendations for international students: Required—TOEFL (minimum score 600 paper-based; 100 iBT). Electronic applications accepted.

University of Missouri–Kansas City, College of Arts and Sciences, Department of Chemistry, Kansas City, MO 64110-2499. Offers analytical chemistry (PhD); inorganic chemistry (PhD); organic chemistry (PhD); physical chemistry (PhD); polymer chemistry (MS, PhD). PhD (interdisciplinary) offered through the School of Graduate Studies. *Program availability:* Part-time, evening/weekend. *Degree requirements:* For master's, thesis (for some programs); for doctorate, thesis/dissertation. *Entrance requirements:* For master's, equivalent of American Chemical Society approved bachelor's degree in chemistry; for doctorate, GRE General Test, equivalent of American Chemical Society approved bachelor's degree in chemistry. Additional exam requirements/recommendations for international students: Required—TOEFL (minimum score 550 paper-based; 80 iBT), TWE. Electronic applications accepted. *Faculty research:* Molecular spectroscopy, characterization and synthesis of materials and compounds, computational chemistry, natural products, drug delivery systems and anti-tumor agents.

University of Missouri–St. Louis, College of Arts and Sciences, Department of Chemistry and Biochemistry, St. Louis, MO 63121. Offers biochemistry and biotechnology (MS); chemistry (MS, PhD). *Program availability:* Part-time, evening/weekend. Terminal master's awarded for partial completion of doctoral program. *Degree requirements:* For master's, thesis optional; for doctorate, thesis/dissertation. *Entrance requirements:* For master's, 2 letters of recommendation; for doctorate, GRE General Test, 3 letters of recommendation. Additional exam requirements/recommendations for international students: Required—TOEFL (minimum score 550 paper-based; 79 iBT), IELTS (minimum score 6.5). Electronic applications accepted. *Faculty research:* Metallaborane chemistry, serum transferrin chemistry, natural products chemistry, organic synthesis.

University of Montana, Graduate School, College of Humanities and Sciences, Department of Chemistry and Biochemistry, Missoula, MT 59812. Offers chemistry (MS, PhD), including environmental/analytical chemistry, inorganic chemistry, organic chemistry, physical chemistry. Terminal master's awarded for partial completion of doctoral program. *Degree requirements:* For master's, thesis (for some programs); for doctorate, thesis/dissertation. *Entrance requirements:* For master's and doctorate, GRE General Test. Additional exam requirements/recommendations for international students: Required—TOEFL (minimum score 575 paper-based). *Faculty research:* Reaction mechanisms and kinetics, inorganic and organic synthesis, analytical chemistry, natural products.

University of Nebraska–Lincoln, Graduate College, College of Arts and Sciences, Department of Chemistry, Lincoln, NE 68588. Offers analytical chemistry (PhD); biochemistry (PhD); chemistry (MS); inorganic chemistry (PhD); materials chemistry (PhD); organic chemistry (PhD); physical chemistry (PhD). *Degree requirements:* For master's, one foreign language, thesis optional, departmental qualifying exam; for doctorate, one foreign language, comprehensive exam, thesis/dissertation, departmental qualifying exams. *Entrance requirements:* For master's and doctorate, GRE. Additional exam requirements/recommendations for international students: Required—TOEFL (minimum score 550 paper-based). Electronic applications accepted. *Faculty research:* Bioorganic and bioinorganic chemistry, biophysical and bioanalytical chemistry, structure-function of DNA and proteins, organometallics, mass spectrometry.

University of Nevada, Las Vegas, Graduate College, College of Sciences, Department of Chemistry and Biochemistry, Las Vegas, NV 89154-4003. Offers biochemistry (MS); chemistry (MS, PhD); radio chemistry (PhD). *Program availability:* Part-time. *Faculty:* 15 full-time (2 women), 1 (woman) part-time/adjunct. *Students:* 37 full-time (16 women), 2 part-time (both women); includes 13 minority (1 Black or African American, non-Hispanic/Latino; 4 Asian, non-Hispanic/Latino; 6 Hispanic/Latino; 2 Two or more races, non-Hispanic/Latino), 2 international. Average age 30. 34 applicants, 38% accepted, 10 enrolled. In 2018, 4 master's, 11 doctorates awarded. Terminal master's awarded for partial completion of doctoral program. *Degree requirements:* For master's, thesis, departmental seminar; for doctorate, comprehensive exam (for some programs), thesis/dissertation, oral exam. *Entrance requirements:* For master's, GRE General Test, bachelor's degree; 2 letters of recommendation; for doctorate, GRE General Test, bachelor's degree/master's degree with minimum GPA of 3.0; statement of interest; 3 letters of recommendation. Additional exam requirements/recommendations for international students: Required—TOEFL (minimum score 550 paper-based; 80 iBT), IELTS (minimum score 7). *Application deadline:* For fall admission, 2/1 for domestic and international students; for spring admission, 10/1 for domestic and international students. Application fee: $60 ($95 for international students). Electronic applications accepted. *Expenses:* Contact institution. *Financial support:* In 2018–19, 37 students received support, including 15 research assistantships with full tuition reimbursements available (averaging $20,191 per year), 22 teaching assistantships with full tuition reimbursements available (averaging $20,786 per year); institutionally sponsored loans, scholarships/grants, health care benefits, and unspecified assistantships also available. Financial award application deadline: 3/15; financial award applicants required to submit FAFSA. *Faculty research:* Material science, biochemistry, chemical education, physical chemistry and theoretical computation, analytical and organic chemistry. *Total annual research expenditures:* $3.4 million. *Unit head:* Dr. Spencer Steinberg, Chair, 702-895-3599, Fax: 702-895-4072, E-mail: chemistry.chair@unlv.edu. *Application contact:* Dr. Kathleen Robins, Graduate Coordinator, 702-895-4304, Fax: 702-895-4072, E-mail: chemistry.gradcoord@unlv.edu.
Website: http://www.unlv.edu/chemistry

University of Nevada, Reno, Graduate School, College of Science, Department of Chemistry, Reno, NV 89557. Offers MS, PhD. Terminal master's awarded for partial completion of doctoral program. *Degree requirements:* For master's, thesis; for doctorate, one foreign language, thesis/dissertation. *Entrance requirements:* For master's, GRE, minimum GPA of 2.75; for doctorate, GRE, minimum GPA of 3.0. Additional exam requirements/recommendations for international students: Required—TOEFL (minimum score 500 paper-based; 61 iBT), IELTS (minimum score 6). Electronic applications accepted. *Faculty research:* Organic/inorganic chemistry, physical chemistry, chemical chemistry, physics, organometallic chemistry.

University of New Brunswick Fredericton, School of Graduate Studies, Faculty of Science, Department of Chemistry, Fredericton, NB E3B 5A3, Canada. Offers M Sc, PhD. Terminal master's awarded for partial completion of doctoral program. *Degree requirements:* For master's, thesis; for doctorate, comprehensive exam, thesis/dissertation. *Entrance requirements:* For master's, bachelor's degree in chemistry or biochemistry; minimum GPA of 3.0; for doctorate, minimum GPA of 3.0. Additional exam requirements/recommendations for international students: Required—TOEFL (minimum score 580 paper-based), IELTS (minimum score 7.5), TWE (minimum score 4). Electronic applications accepted. *Faculty research:* Analytical, inorganic, organic, bio-organic, physical chemistry, pulp and paper, theoretical and computational chemistry.

University of New Hampshire, Graduate School, College of Engineering and Physical Sciences, Department of Chemistry, Durham, NH 03824. Offers chemistry (MS, PhD); chemistry education (PhD). Terminal master's awarded for partial completion of doctoral program. *Entrance requirements:* For master's and doctorate, GRE. Additional exam requirements/recommendations for international students: Required—TOEFL (minimum score 550 paper-based; 80 iBT). Electronic applications accepted.

University of New Mexico, Graduate Studies, College of Arts and Sciences, Program in Chemistry, Albuquerque, NM 87131-2039. Offers MS, PhD. *Students:* Average age 30. 52 applicants, 21% accepted, 11 enrolled. In 2018, 9 master's, 4 doctorates awarded. Terminal master's awarded for partial completion of doctoral program. *Degree requirements:* For master's, comprehensive exam, thesis (for some programs); for doctorate, comprehensive exam, thesis/dissertation. *Entrance requirements:* For master's and doctorate, department exams. Additional exam requirements/recommendations for international students: Required—TOEFL (minimum score 550 paper-based; 79 iBT). *Application deadline:* For fall admission, 2/1 for domestic and international students. Applications are processed on a rolling basis. Application fee: $50 ($100 for international students). *Financial support:* Fellowships, research assistantships, teaching assistantships, scholarships/grants, health care benefits, and unspecified assistantships available. Financial award application deadline: 2/1; financial award applicants required to submit FAFSA. *Faculty research:* Materials, inorganic, organic, physical, and biological chemistry. *Total annual research expenditures:* $2.7 million. *Unit head:* Dr. Stephen Cabaniss, Chair, 505-277-6655, Fax: 505-277-2609, E-mail: cabaniss@unm.edu. *Application contact:* Coordinator, Program Advisement, 505-277-6655, Fax: 505-277-2609, E-mail: kamc@unm.edu.
Website: http://chemistry.unm.edu/

University of New Orleans, Graduate School, College of Sciences, Department of Chemistry, New Orleans, LA 70148. Offers MS, PhD. *Degree requirements:* For master's, variable foreign language requirement, thesis, departmental qualifying exam; for doctorate, variable foreign language requirement, thesis/dissertation, departmental qualifying exam. *Entrance requirements:* For master's and doctorate, GRE General Test. Additional exam requirements/recommendations for international students: Required—TOEFL (minimum score 550 paper-based; 79 iBT), IELTS (minimum score 6.5). Electronic applications accepted. *Faculty research:* Synthesis and reactions of novel compounds, high-temperature kinetics, calculations of molecular electrostatic potentials, structures and reactions of metal complexes.

The University of North Carolina at Chapel Hill, Graduate School, College of Arts and Sciences, Department of Chemistry, Chapel Hill, NC 27599. Offers MA, MS, PhD. *Degree requirements:* For master's, comprehensive exam, thesis (for some programs); for doctorate, comprehensive exam, thesis/dissertation. *Entrance requirements:* For master's and doctorate, GRE General Test, GRE Subject Test, minimum GPA of 3.0.

The University of North Carolina at Charlotte, College of Liberal Arts and Sciences, Department of Chemistry, Charlotte, NC 28223-0001. Offers chemistry (MS); nanoscale science (PhD). *Program availability:* Part-time. *Students:* 26 full-time (15 women), 16 part-time (5 women); includes 9 minority (3 Black or African American, non-Hispanic/Latino; 2 Asian, non-Hispanic/Latino; 2 Hispanic/Latino; 2 Two or more races, non-Hispanic/Latino), 10 international. Average age 27. 31 applicants, 39% accepted, 9 enrolled. In 2018, 5 master's, 1 doctorate awarded. Terminal master's awarded for partial completion of doctoral program. *Entrance requirements:* For master's, GRE,

minimum GPA of 3.0 in undergraduate major, 2.75 overall; for doctorate, GRE, bachelor's or master's degree in a science or engineering field relevant to nanoscale science, minimum GPA of 3.0, recommendation letters. Additional exam requirements/recommendations for international students: Required—TOEFL (minimum score 523 paper-based; 70 iBT), IELTS (minimum score 6), TOEFL (minimum score 523 paper-based, 70 iBT) or IELTS (6). *Application deadline:* Applications are processed on a rolling basis. Application fee: $75. Electronic applications accepted. Tuition and fees vary according to course load and program. *Financial support:* Fellowships, research assistantships, teaching assistantships, career-related internships or fieldwork, Federal Work-Study, institutionally sponsored loans, scholarships/grants, and unspecified assistantships available. Support available to part-time students. Financial award application deadline: 3/1; financial award applicants required to submit FAFSA. *Faculty research:* Nanoscale science, computational chemistry, organic synthesis, polymer chemistry, organometallic chemistry, electrochemistry, structural and mechanistic organic chemistry, materials and interfacial chemistry, catalysis, biochemistry, bioanalytical chemistry, and biophysical chemistry. *Total annual research expenditures:* $867,670. *Unit head:* Dr. Bernadette T. Donovan-Merkert, Chair, 704-687-1300, E-mail: bdonovan@uncc.edu. *Application contact:* Kathy B. Giddings, Director of Graduate Admissions, 704-687-5503, Fax: 704-687-1668, E-mail: gradadm@uncc.edu.
Website: http://chemistry.uncc.edu/

The University of North Carolina at Greensboro, Graduate School, College of Arts and Sciences, Department of Chemistry and Biochemistry, Greensboro, NC 27412-5001. Offers biochemistry (MS); chemistry (MS). *Degree requirements:* For master's, one foreign language, thesis. *Entrance requirements:* For master's, GRE General Test. Additional exam requirements/recommendations for international students: Required—TOEFL. Electronic applications accepted. *Faculty research:* Synthesis of novel cyclopentadienes, molybdenum hydroxylase-cata ladder polymers, vinyl silicones.

The University of North Carolina Wilmington, College of Arts and Sciences, Department of Chemistry and Biochemistry, Wilmington, NC 28403-3297. Offers chemistry (MS). *Program availability:* Part-time, 100% online. *Degree requirements:* For master's, comprehensive exam, thesis. *Entrance requirements:* For master's, GRE General Test, 3 letters of recommendation, baccalaureate degree in chemistry. Additional exam requirements/recommendations for international students: Required—TOEFL (minimum score 550 paper-based; 79 iBT), IELTS (minimum score 6.5). Electronic applications accepted.

University of North Dakota, Graduate School, College of Arts and Sciences, Department of Chemistry, Grand Forks, ND 58202. Offers MS, PhD. Terminal master's awarded for partial completion of doctoral program. *Degree requirements:* For master's, thesis, final exam; for doctorate, comprehensive exam, thesis/dissertation, final exam. *Entrance requirements:* For master's and doctorate, GRE General Test, GRE Subject Test, minimum GPA of 3.0. Additional exam requirements/recommendations for international students: Required—TOEFL (minimum score 550 paper-based; 79 iBT), IELTS (minimum score 6.5). Electronic applications accepted. *Faculty research:* Synthetic and structural organometallic chemistry, photochemistry, theoretical chemistry, chromatographic chemistry, x-ray crystallography.

University of Northern Colorado, Graduate School, College of Natural and Health Sciences, Department of Chemistry and Biochemistry, Greeley, CO 80639. Offers chemical education (MS, PhD); chemistry (MS). *Program availability:* Part-time. *Degree requirements:* For master's, comprehensive exam, thesis or alternative; for doctorate, comprehensive exam, thesis/dissertation. *Entrance requirements:* For master's, 3 letters of reference; for doctorate, GRE General Test, 3 letters of reference. Electronic applications accepted.

University of North Texas, Toulouse Graduate School, Denton, TX 76203-5459. Offers accounting (MS); applied anthropology (MA, MS); applied behavior analysis (Certificate); applied geography (MA); applied technology and performance improvement (M Ed, MS); art education (MA); art history (MA); arts leadership (Certificate); audiology (Au D); behavior analysis (MS); behavioral science (PhD); biochemistry and molecular biology (MS); biology (MA, MS); biomedical engineering (MS); business analysis (MS); chemistry (MS); clinical health psychology (PhD); communication studies (MA, MS); computer engineering (MS); computer science (MS); counseling (M Ed, MS), including clinical mental health counseling (MS), college and university counseling, elementary school counseling, secondary school counseling; creative writing (MA); criminal justice (MS); curriculum and instruction (M Ed); decision sciences (MBA); design (MA, MFA), including fashion design (MFA), innovation studies, interior design (MFA); early childhood studies (MS); economics (MS); educational leadership (M Ed, Ed D); educational psychology (MS, PhD), including family studies (MS), gifted and talented (MS), human development (MS), learning and cognition (MS), research, measurement and evaluation (MS); electrical engineering (MS); emergency management (MPA); engineering technology (MS); English (MA); English as a second language (MA); environmental science (MS); finance (MBA, MS); financial management (MPA); French (MA); health services management (MBA); higher education (M Ed, Ed D); history (MA, MS); hospitality management (MS); human resources management (MPA); information science (MS); information systems (PhD); information technologies (MBA); interdisciplinary studies (MA, MS); international studies (MA); international sustainable tourism (MS); jazz studies (MM); journalism (MA, MJ, Graduate Certificate), including interactive and virtual digital communication (Graduate Certificate), narrative journalism (Graduate Certificate), public relations (Graduate Certificate); kinesiology (MS); linguistics (MA); local government management (MPA); logistics (PhD); logistics and supply chain management (MBA); long-term care, senior housing, and aging services (MA); management (PhD); marketing (MBA); mathematics (MA, MS); mechanical and energy engineering (MS, PhD); music (MA), including ethnomusicology, music theory, musicology, performance; music composition (PhD); music education (MM Ed, PhD); nonprofit management (MPA); operations and supply chain management (MBA); performance (MM, DMA); philosophy (MA); political science (MA); professional and technical communication (MA); radio, television and film (MA, MFA); rehabilitation counseling (Certificate); sociology (MA); Spanish (MA); special education (M Ed); speech-language pathology (MA); strategic management (MBA); studio art (MFA); teaching (M Ed); MBA/MS. *Program availability:* Part-time, evening/weekend, online learning. Terminal master's awarded for partial completion of doctoral program. *Degree requirements:* For master's, variable foreign language requirement, comprehensive exam (for some programs), thesis (for some programs); for doctorate, variable foreign language requirement, comprehensive exam (for some programs), thesis/dissertation; for other advanced degree, variable foreign language requirement, comprehensive exam (for some programs). *Entrance requirements:* For master's and doctorate, GRE, GMAT. Additional exam requirements/recommendations for international students: Required—TOEFL (minimum score 550 paper-based; 79 iBT). Electronic applications accepted.

University of Notre Dame, The Graduate School, College of Science, Department of Chemistry and Biochemistry, Notre Dame, IN 46556. Offers biochemistry (MS, PhD); inorganic chemistry (MS, PhD); organic chemistry (MS, PhD); physical chemistry (MS, PhD). Terminal master's awarded for partial completion of doctoral program. *Degree requirements:* For master's, comprehensive exam, thesis; for doctorate, thesis/dissertation, qualifying exam. *Entrance requirements:* For master's and doctorate, GRE General Test, GRE Subject Test (strongly recommended). Additional exam requirements/recommendations for international students: Required—TOEFL (minimum score 600 paper-based; 80 iBT). Electronic applications accepted. *Faculty research:* Reaction design and mechanistic studies; reactive intermediates; synthesis, structure and reactivity of organometallic cluster complexes and biologically active natural products; bioorganic chemistry; enzymology.

University of Oklahoma, College of Arts and Sciences, Department of Chemistry and Biochemistry, Norman, OK 73019. Offers chemistry (MS, PhD), including analytical chemistry, biochemistry, chemical education, inorganic chemistry, inter-and/or multidisciplinary, organic chemistry, physical chemistry, structural biology. *Program availability:* Part-time. *Faculty:* 32 full-time (13 women). *Students:* 89 full-time (38 women), 33 part-time (15 women); includes 22 minority (2 Black or African American, non-Hispanic/Latino; 9 Asian, non-Hispanic/Latino; 6 Hispanic/Latino; 5 Two or more races, non-Hispanic/Latino), 46 international. Average age 26. 78 applicants, 71% accepted, 33 enrolled. In 2018, 15 master's, 21 doctorates awarded. Terminal master's awarded for partial completion of doctoral program. *Degree requirements:* For master's, comprehensive exam (for some programs), thesis (for some programs); for doctorate, comprehensive exam, thesis/dissertation, general exam. *Entrance requirements:* For master's and doctorate, GRE. Additional exam requirements/recommendations for international students: Required—TOEFL (minimum score 79 iBT) or IELTS (minimum score 6.5). *Application deadline:* For fall admission, 3/31 priority date for domestic and international students; for spring admission, 9/1 priority date for domestic and international students. Application fee: $50 ($100 for international students). Electronic applications accepted. *Expenses:* Tuition, state resident: full-time $5683.20; part-time $236.80 per credit hour. Tuition, nonresident: full-time $20,342; part-time $847.60 per credit hour. *International tuition:* $20,342.40 full-time. *Required fees:* $2894.20; $110.05 per credit hour. $126.50 per semester. Tuition and fees vary according to course load and program. *Financial support:* Research assistantships, teaching assistantships, institutionally sponsored loans, scholarships/grants, health care benefits, unspecified assistantships, and full tuition with qualifying graduate assistantship available. Support available to part-time students. Financial award application deadline: 6/1; financial award applicants required to submit FAFSA. *Faculty research:* Structural biology, solid state materials, natural products, membrane biochemistry, bioanalysis. *Unit head:* Dr. Ronald L. Halterman, Professor and Chair, 405-325-4812, Fax: 405-325-6111, E-mail: rhalterman@ou.edu. *Application contact:* Carol Jones, Operations Manager, 405-325-4811, Fax: 405-325-6111, E-mail: caroljones@ou.edu.
Website: http://www.ou.edu/cas/chemistry

University of Oregon, Graduate School, College of Arts and Sciences, Department of Chemistry, Eugene, OR 97403. Offers biochemistry (MA, MS, PhD); chemistry (MA, MS, PhD). Terminal master's awarded for partial completion of doctoral program. *Degree requirements:* For doctorate, thesis/dissertation. *Entrance requirements:* For master's and doctorate, GRE General Test, minimum GPA of 3.0. Additional exam requirements/recommendations for international students: Required—TOEFL. *Faculty research:* Organic chemistry, organometallic chemistry, inorganic chemistry, physical chemistry, materials science, biochemistry, chemical physics, molecular or cell biology.

University of Ottawa, Faculty of Graduate and Postdoctoral Studies, Faculty of Science, Ottawa-Carleton Chemistry Institute, Ottawa, ON K1N 6N5, Canada. Offers M Sc, PhD. M Sc, PhD offered jointly with Carleton University. *Degree requirements:* For master's, thesis, seminar; for doctorate, comprehensive exam, thesis/dissertation, 2 seminars. *Entrance requirements:* For master's, honors B Sc degree or equivalent, minimum B average; for doctorate, honors B Sc with minimum B average or M Sc in chemistry with minimum B+ average. Electronic applications accepted. *Faculty research:* Organic chemistry, physical chemistry, inorganic chemistry.

University of Pennsylvania, School of Arts and Sciences, College of Liberal and Professional Studies, Philadelphia, PA 19104. Offers applied geosciences (MSAG); applied positive psychology (MAP); chemical sciences (MCS); environmental studies (MES); individualized study (MLA); liberal arts (M Phil); medical physics (MMP); organization dynamics (M Phil). *Students:* 219 full-time (144 women), 295 part-time (178 women); includes 101 minority (31 Black or African American, non-Hispanic/Latino; 1 American Indian or Alaska Native, non-Hispanic/Latino; 35 Asian, non-Hispanic/Latino; 16 Hispanic/Latino; 1 Native Hawaiian or other Pacific Islander, non-Hispanic/Latino; 17 Two or more races, non-Hispanic/Latino), 103 international. Average age 34. 633 applicants, 52% accepted, 249 enrolled. In 2018, 180 master's awarded. *Unit head:* Nora Lewis, Vice Dean, Professional and Liberal Education, 215-898-7326, E-mail: nlewis@sas.upenn.edu. *Application contact:* Nora Lewis, Vice Dean, Professional and Liberal Education, 215-898-7326, E-mail: nlewis@sas.upenn.edu.
Website: http://www.sas.upenn.edu/lps/graduate

University of Pennsylvania, School of Arts and Sciences, Graduate Group in Chemistry, Philadelphia, PA 19104. Offers MS, PhD. *Faculty:* 37 full-time (9 women), 2 part-time/adjunct (1 woman). *Students:* 181 full-time (70 women); includes 14 minority (1 Black or African American, non-Hispanic/Latino; 9 Asian, non-Hispanic/Latino; 2 Hispanic/Latino; 2 Two or more races, non-Hispanic/Latino), 80 international. Average age 26. 437 applicants, 26% accepted, 56 enrolled. In 2018, 29 master's, 29 doctorates awarded. Application fee: $80. *Financial support:* Application deadline: 12/1.
Website: http://www.sas.upenn.edu/graduate-division

University of Pittsburgh, Kenneth P. Dietrich School of Arts and Sciences, Department of Chemistry, Pittsburgh, PA 15216. Offers MS, PhD. *Program availability:* Part-time, evening/weekend. Terminal master's awarded for partial completion of doctoral program. *Degree requirements:* For master's, comprehensive exam, thesis; for doctorate, comprehensive exam, thesis/dissertation, original research proposal. *Entrance requirements:* For master's and doctorate, GRE General Test, GRE Subject Test. Additional exam requirements/recommendations for international students: Required—TOEFL (minimum score 600 paper-based; 100 iBT), IELTS (minimum score 7). Electronic applications accepted. *Expenses:* Contact institution. *Faculty research:* Analytical, biological, inorganic and materials chemistry including nanostructured materials, organic, physical and theoretical chemistry.

University of Prince Edward Island, Faculty of Science, Charlottetown, PE C1A 4P3, Canada. Offers environmental sciences (M Sc, PhD); human biology (M Sc); molecular and macromolecular sciences (M Sc, PhD); sustainable design engineering (M Sc). *Degree requirements:* For master's, thesis. *Entrance requirements:* Additional exam requirements/recommendations for international students: Required—TOEFL (minimum score 550 paper-based; 80 iBT), Canadian Academic English Language Assessment, Michigan English Language Assessment Battery, Canadian Test of English for Scholars and Trainees. *Faculty research:* Ecology and wildlife biology, molecular, genetics and biotechnology, organometallic, bio-organic, supramolecular and synthetic organic chemistry, neurobiology and stoke materials science.

University of Puerto Rico–Mayagüez, Graduate Studies, College of Arts and Sciences, Department of Chemistry, Mayagüez, PR 00681-9000. Offers applied chemistry (MS, PhD), including biophysical chemistry (PhD), chemistry of materials (PhD), environmental chemistry (PhD). *Program availability:* Part-time. Terminal master's awarded for partial completion of doctoral program. *Degree requirements:* For master's, one foreign language, comprehensive exam, thesis; for doctorate, one foreign language, comprehensive exam, thesis/dissertation. *Entrance requirements:* For master's, GRE General Test or minimum GPA of 2.0, BS in chemistry or the equivalent; minimum GPA of 2.8; for doctorate, GRE General Test or minimum GPA of 2.0. Electronic applications accepted. *Faculty research:* Synthesis of heterocyclic moieties, protein structure and function, chemistry of explosives, bio-nanocomposites, process analytical technology.

University of Puerto Rico–Río Piedras, College of Natural Sciences, Department of Chemistry, San Juan, PR 00931-3300. Offers MS, PhD. *Program availability:* Part-time. *Degree requirements:* For master's, one foreign language, comprehensive exam, thesis; for doctorate, one foreign language, comprehensive exam, thesis/dissertation. *Entrance requirements:* For master's, GRE General Test, GRE Subject Test, interview, minimum GPA of 3.0, letter of recommendation; for doctorate, GRE General Test, GRE Subject Test, minimum GPA of 3.0, letter of recommendation. Additional exam requirements/recommendations for international students: Required—TOEFL.

University of Regina, Faculty of Graduate Studies and Research, Faculty of Science, Department of Chemistry and Biochemistry, Regina, SK S4S 0A2, Canada. Offers biophysics of biological interfaces (M Sc, PhD); computational chemistry (M Sc, PhD); environmental analytical chemistry (M Sc, PhD); enzymology/chemical biology (M Sc, PhD); inorganic/organometallic chemistry (M Sc, PhD); signal transduction and mechanisms of cancer cell regulation (M Sc, PhD); supramolecular organic photochemistry and photophysics (M Sc, PhD); synthetic organic chemistry (M Sc, PhD). *Program availability:* Part-time. *Faculty:* 12 full-time (2 women), 4 part-time/adjunct (0 women). *Students:* 12 full-time (6 women), 1 part-time (0 women). Average age 30. 23 applicants, 17% accepted. In 2018, 2 master's awarded. *Degree requirements:* For master's, thesis; for doctorate, comprehensive exam, thesis/dissertation. *Entrance requirements:* For master's, 4 years Bachelor degree in Chemistry or related program; for doctorate, completion of Master's in Chemistry. Additional exam requirements/recommendations for international students: Required—TOEFL (minimum score 580 paper-based; 80 iBT), IELTS (minimum score 6.5), PTE (minimum score 59), other options are CAEL, MELAB, Cantest and U of R ESL. *Application deadline:* Applications are processed on a rolling basis. Application fee: $100. Electronic applications accepted. Tuition and fees vary according to course level, course load, degree level and program. *Financial support:* Fellowships, research assistantships, teaching assistantships, career-related internships or fieldwork, Federal Work-Study, scholarships/grants, unspecified assistantships, and travel award & Graduate Scholarship Base Funds available. Support available to part-time students. Financial award application deadline: 9/30. *Faculty research:* Asymmetric synthesis and methodology, theoretical and computational chemistry, biophysical biochemistry, analytical and environmental chemistry, chemical biology. *Unit head:* Dr. Renata Raina-Fulton, Department Head, 306-585-4012, Fax: 306-337-2409, E-mail: renata.raina@uregina.ca. *Application contact:* Dr. Brian Sterenberg, Graduate Program Coordinator, 306-585-4106, Fax: 306-337-2409, E-mail: brian.sterenberg@uregina.ca.
Website: http://www.uregina.ca/science/chem-biochem/

University of Rhode Island, Graduate School, College of Arts and Sciences, Department of Chemistry, Kingston, RI 02881. Offers MS, PhD. *Program availability:* Part-time, evening/weekend. *Faculty:* 21 full-time (8 women). *Students:* 48 full-time (26 women), 2 part-time (1 woman); includes 5 minority (3 Asian, non-Hispanic/Latino; 1 Hispanic/Latino; 1 Native Hawaiian or other Pacific Islander, non-Hispanic/Latino), 19 international. 42 applicants, 57% accepted, 15 enrolled. In 2018, 3 master's, 14 doctorates awarded. *Entrance requirements:* For master's and doctorate, GRE General Test (for graduates of non-U.S. universities), GRE Subject Test in chemistry (recommended), 2 letters of recommendation (3 for non-U.S. graduates). Additional exam requirements/recommendations for international students: Required—TOEFL. *Application deadline:* Applications are processed on a rolling basis. Application fee: $65. Electronic applications accepted. *Expenses: Tuition, area resident:* Full-time $13,226; part-time $735 per credit. Tuition, state resident: full-time $13,226; part-time $735 per credit. Tuition, nonresident: full-time $25,854; part-time $1436 per credit. *International tuition:* $25,854 full-time. *Required fees:* $1698; $50 per credit. $35 per semester. One-time fee: $165. *Financial support:* In 2018–19, 8 research assistantships with tuition reimbursements (averaging $8,525 per year), 41 teaching assistantships with tuition reimbursements (averaging $14,061 per year) were awarded; unspecified assistantships also available. Financial award applicants required to submit FAFSA. *Unit head:* Dr. James Smith, Chairperson, 401-874-2438, E-mail: chair@chm.uri.edu. *Application contact:* Brenton DeBoef, Graduate Program Director, 401-874-9480, E-mail: bdeboef@uri.edu.
Website: http://www.chm.uri.edu/index.php

University of Rochester, School of Arts and Sciences, Department of Chemistry, Rochester, NY 14627. Offers inorganic chemistry (PhD); organic chemistry (PhD); physical chemistry (PhD). *Faculty:* 17 full-time (5 women). *Students:* 91 full-time (42 women); includes 10 minority (1 Black or African American, non-Hispanic/Latino; 2 Asian, non-Hispanic/Latino; 7 Hispanic/Latino), 24 international. Average age 27. 247 applicants, 25% accepted, 16 enrolled. In 2018, 9 doctorates awarded. Terminal master's awarded for partial completion of doctoral program. *Degree requirements:* For doctorate, thesis/dissertation, qualifying exam. *Entrance requirements:* For doctorate, GRE General Test, GRE Subject Test (recommended), transcripts, three letters of recommendation. Additional exam requirements/recommendations for international students: Required—TOEFL (minimum score 100 iBT), IELTS (minimum score 6.5). *Application deadline:* For fall admission, 12/15 for domestic and international students. Electronic applications accepted. *Expenses: Tuition:* Full-time $52,974; part-time $1654 per credit hour. *Required fees:* $612. One-time fee: $30 part-time. Tuition and fees vary according to campus/location and program. *Financial support:* In 2018–19, 34 students received support, including 13 research assistantships (averaging $26,000 per year), 4 teaching assistantships (averaging $26,000 per year); Federal Work-Study, scholarships/grants, and tuition waivers (full) also available. Financial award application deadline: 12/15. *Faculty research:* Organic chemistry, physical chemistry, theoretical chemistry, biological chemistry, materials chemistry. *Total annual research expenditures:* $4.2 million. *Unit head:* Todd D. Krauss, Chair, 585-275-5093, E-mail: todd.krauss@rochester.edu. *Application contact:* Robin Clark, Administrative Assistant, 585-275-0635, E-mail: robin.clark@rochester.edu.
Website: http://www.sas.rochester.edu/chm/graduate/index.html

University of Saint Joseph, Department of Chemistry, West Hartford, CT 06117-2700. Offers biochemistry (MS); chemistry (MS). *Program availability:* Part-time, evening/weekend, online learning. *Degree requirements:* For master's, comprehensive exam, thesis optional. *Entrance requirements:* For master's, 2 letters of recommendation, official undergraduate transcript. Electronic applications accepted. Application fee is waived when completed online.

University of San Francisco, College of Arts and Sciences, Chemistry Program, San Francisco, CA 94117. Offers MS. *Program availability:* Part-time, evening/weekend. *Students:* 8 full-time (3 women); includes 4 minority (1 Asian, non-Hispanic/Latino; 3 Hispanic/Latino), 2 international. Average age 24. 26 applicants, 23% accepted, 4 enrolled. In 2018, 4 master's awarded. *Degree requirements:* For master's, thesis. *Entrance requirements:* For master's, GRE General Test, GRE Subject Test (recommended), BS in chemistry or related field. Additional exam requirements/recommendations for international students: Required—TOEFL (minimum score 90 iBT), IELTS (minimum score 6.5), PTE (minimum score 61). *Application deadline:* For fall admission, 2/1 for domestic and international students; for spring admission, 10/15 for domestic and international students. Applications are processed on a rolling basis. Application fee: $55. Electronic applications accepted. Application fee is waived when completed online. *Financial support:* In 2018–19, 13 students received support. Fellowships with full tuition reimbursements available, research assistantships, teaching assistantships, career-related internships or fieldwork, and institutionally sponsored loans available. Financial award applicants required to submit FAFSA. *Faculty research:* Organic photochemistry, genetics of chromatic adaptation, electron transfer processes in solution, metabolism of protein hormones. *Unit head:* Dr. Ryan West, Graduate Director, 415-422-4914, E-mail: rmwest2@usfca.edu. *Application contact:* Information Contact, 415-422-5101, E-mail: asgraduate@usfca.edu.
Website: https://www.usfca.edu/arts-sciences/graduate-programs/chemistry

University of Saskatchewan, College of Graduate and Postdoctoral Studies, College of Arts and Science, Department of Chemistry, Saskatoon, SK S7N 5A2, Canada. Offers M Sc, PhD. *Degree requirements:* For master's, thesis; for doctorate, comprehensive exam (for some programs), thesis/dissertation. *Entrance requirements:* Additional exam requirements/recommendations for international students: Required—TOEFL (minimum score 80 iBT); Recommended—IELTS (minimum score 6.5). Electronic applications accepted.

The University of Scranton, College of Arts and Sciences, Department of Chemistry, Program in Chemistry, Scranton, PA 18510. Offers MS. *Program availability:* Part-time, evening/weekend. *Degree requirements:* For master's, comprehensive exam (for some programs), thesis (for some programs), capstone experience. *Entrance requirements:* For master's, minimum GPA of 3.0, three letters of reference. Additional exam requirements/recommendations for international students: Required—TOEFL (minimum score 500 paper-based; 80 iBT), IELTS (minimum score 6.5). Electronic applications accepted.

The University of Scranton, College of Arts and Sciences, Department of Chemistry, Program in Clinical Chemistry, Scranton, PA 18510. Offers MS. *Program availability:* Part-time, evening/weekend. *Degree requirements:* For master's, comprehensive exam (for some programs), thesis (for some programs), capstone experience. *Entrance requirements:* For master's, minimum GPA of 3.0, three letters of reference. Additional exam requirements/recommendations for international students: Required—TOEFL (minimum score 500 paper-based; 80 iBT), IELTS (minimum score 6.5). Electronic applications accepted.

University of South Alabama, Graduate School, Program in Environmental Toxicology, Mobile, AL 36688. Offers basic medical sciences (MS); biology (MS); chemistry (MS); environmental toxicology (MS); exposure route and chemical transport (MS). *Degree requirements:* For master's, comprehensive exam, research project or thesis. *Entrance requirements:* For master's, GRE, BA/BS in related discipline, minimum undergraduate GPA of 3.0. Additional exam requirements/recommendations for international students: Required—TOEFL (minimum score 525 paper-based; 71 iBT). Electronic applications accepted.

University of South Carolina, The Graduate School, College of Arts and Sciences, Department of Chemistry and Biochemistry, Columbia, SC 29208. Offers IMA, MAT, MS, PhD. IMA and MAT offered in cooperation with the College of Education. *Program availability:* Part-time. Terminal master's awarded for partial completion of doctoral program. *Degree requirements:* For master's, comprehensive exam, thesis; for doctorate, comprehensive exam, thesis/dissertation. *Entrance requirements:* For master's and doctorate, GRE General Test. Additional exam requirements/recommendations for international students: Required—TOEFL. Electronic applications accepted. *Faculty research:* Spectroscopy, crystallography, organic and organometallic synthesis, analytical chemistry, materials.

University of South Dakota, Graduate School, College of Arts and Sciences, Department of Chemistry, Vermillion, SD 57069. Offers MS, PhD. *Degree requirements:* For master's, comprehensive exam, thesis. *Entrance requirements:* For master's, minimum GPA of 2.7; for doctorate, GRE, minimum GPA of 2.7. Additional exam requirements/recommendations for international students: Required—TOEFL (minimum score 550 paper-based; 79 iBT), GRE. Electronic applications accepted. *Faculty research:* Electrochemistry, photochemistry, inorganic synthesis, environmental and solid-state chemistry.

University of Southern California, Graduate School, Dana and David Dornsife College of Letters, Arts and Sciences, Department of Chemistry, Los Angeles, CA 90089. Offers chemistry (PhD); physical chemistry (PhD). Terminal master's awarded for partial completion of doctoral program. *Degree requirements:* For doctorate, thesis/dissertation. *Entrance requirements:* For doctorate, GRE General Test. Additional exam requirements/recommendations for international students: Required—TOEFL. Electronic applications accepted. *Faculty research:* Biological chemistry, inorganic chemistry, organic chemistry, physical chemistry, theoretical chemistry.

University of Southern Mississippi, College of Arts and Sciences, Department of Chemistry and Biochemistry, Hattiesburg, MS 39406-0001. Offers MS, PhD. *Degree requirements:* For master's, comprehensive exam, thesis; for doctorate, comprehensive exam, thesis/dissertation. *Entrance requirements:* For master's, GRE General Test, minimum GPA of 2.75 in last 60 hours; for doctorate, GRE General Test, minimum GPA of 3.5. Additional exam requirements/recommendations for international students: Required—TOEFL, IELTS. *Faculty research:* Plant biochemistry, photo chemistry, polymer chemistry, x-ray analysis, enzyme chemistry.

University of Southern Mississippi, College of Arts and Sciences, Division of Marine Science, Stennis Space Center, MS 39529. Offers hydrographic science (MS); marine science (MS, PhD). *Program availability:* Part-time. *Degree requirements:* For master's, comprehensive exam, thesis, oral qualifying exam (marine science); for doctorate, 2 foreign languages, comprehensive exam, thesis/dissertation, oral qualifying exam. *Entrance requirements:* For master's, GRE General Test, minimum GPA of 3.0; for doctorate, GRE General Test, minimum GPA of 3.0 (undergraduate), 3.5 (graduate). Additional exam requirements/recommendations for international students: Required—TOEFL (minimum score 567 paper-based; 86 iBT), IELTS (minimum score 6.5). Electronic applications accepted. *Expenses:* Contact institution. *Faculty research:* Bioacoustics, biological oceanography, bio-optics, coastal geology, coastal hazards, computational biology, geological oceanography, hydrography, marine chemistry, marine phytoplankton ecology, marine science, numerical modeling, paleontology, physical oceanography, remote sensing, signal processing, zooplankton.

University of South Florida, College of Arts and Sciences, Department of Chemistry, Tampa, FL 33620-9951. Offers MA, MS, PhD. *Program availability:* Part-time. *Faculty:* 26 full-time (4 women). *Students:* 139 full-time (56 women), 5 part-time (4 women); includes 24 minority (2 Black or African American, non-Hispanic/Latino; 1 American Indian or Alaska Native, non-Hispanic/Latino; 6 Asian, non-Hispanic/Latino; 14 Hispanic/Latino; 1 Two or more races, non-Hispanic/Latino), 71 international. Average age 27. 135 applicants, 39% accepted, 28 enrolled. In 2018, 7 master's, 9 doctorates awarded. Terminal master's awarded for partial completion of doctoral program. *Degree requirements:* For master's, comprehensive exam, thesis (for some programs); for doctorate, comprehensive exam, thesis/dissertation. *Entrance requirements:* For master's, GRE - A preferred minimum score of 149 V (430/800, 47th percentile) and 147 Q (570/800, 28th percentile) on the GRE (the Chemistry subject exam is not required), minimum GPA of 3.0 in last two years of undergraduate chemistry coursework, three letters of recommendation; for doctorate, GRE - A preferred minimum score of 149 V (430/800, 47th percentile) and 147 Q (470/800, 28th percentile) on the GRE (the Chemistry subject exam is not required), minimum GPA of 3.0 in last two years of chemistry coursework, three letters of recommendation. Additional exam requirements/recommendations for international students: Required—TOEFL, TOEFL (minimum score 550 paper-based; 79 iBT) or IELTS (minimum score 6.5). *Application deadline:* For fall admission, 2/15 priority date for domestic students, 1/15 priority date for international students; for spring admission, 10/1 priority date for domestic students, 9/15 priority date for international students. Applications are processed on a rolling basis. Application fee: $30. Electronic applications accepted. *Expenses:* Tuition, state resident: full-time $6350. Tuition, nonresident: full-time $19,048. *International tuition:* $19,048 full-time. *Required fees:* $2079. *Financial support:* In 2018–19, 39 students received support, including 28 research assistantships with tuition reimbursements available (averaging $15,020 per year), 108 teaching assistantships with tuition reimbursements available (averaging $15,164 per year); unspecified assistantships also available. *Faculty research:* Synthesis, bio-organic chemistry, bioinorganic chemistry, environmental chemistry, nuclear magnetic resonance (NMR). *Total annual research expenditures:* $3.6 million. *Unit head:* Dr. Wayne Guida, Chairperson and Professor, Chemistry Department, 813-974-0169, E-mail: wguida@usf.edu. *Application contact:* Dr. James Leahy, Professor/Graduate Program Director, 813-974-0274, E-mail: jwleahy@usf.edu.
Website: http://chemistry.usf.edu/

The University of Tennessee, Graduate School, College of Arts and Sciences, Department of Chemistry, Knoxville, TN 37996. Offers analytical chemistry (MS, PhD); chemical physics (PhD); environmental chemistry (MS, PhD); inorganic chemistry (MS, PhD); organic chemistry (MS, PhD); physical chemistry (MS, PhD); polymer chemistry (MS, PhD); theoretical chemistry (PhD). *Program availability:* Part-time. Terminal master's awarded for partial completion of doctoral program. *Degree requirements:* For master's, thesis; for doctorate, thesis/dissertation. *Entrance requirements:* For master's and doctorate, GRE General Test, minimum GPA of 2.7. Additional exam requirements/recommendations for international students: Required—TOEFL. Electronic applications accepted.

The University of Texas at Arlington, Graduate School, College of Science, Department of Chemistry and Biochemistry, Arlington, TX 76019. Offers chemistry (MS, PhD). *Program availability:* Part-time. Terminal master's awarded for partial completion of doctoral program. *Degree requirements:* For master's, comprehensive exam (for some programs), thesis optional; for doctorate, comprehensive exam, thesis/dissertation, internship, oral defense of dissertation. *Entrance requirements:* For master's and doctorate, GRE General Test, minimum GPA of 3.0 in last 60 hours of course work; BS in STEM field (preferably chemistry or biochemistry) or equivalent 4-year minimum program. Additional exam requirements/recommendations for international students: Required—TOEFL (minimum score 550 paper-based; 80 iBT), TOEFL Speaking Score: 23; IELTS Speaking Score: 7. Electronic applications accepted.

The University of Texas at Austin, Graduate School, College of Natural Sciences, Department of Chemistry and Biochemistry, Austin, TX 78712-1111. Offers analytical chemistry (PhD); biochemistry (PhD); inorganic chemistry (PhD); organic chemistry (PhD); physical chemistry (PhD). *Entrance requirements:* For doctorate, GRE General Test.

The University of Texas at Dallas, School of Natural Sciences and Mathematics, Department of Chemistry and Biochemistry, Richardson, TX 75080. Offers MS, PhD. *Program availability:* Part-time, evening/weekend. *Faculty:* 22 full-time (4 women), 1 part-time/adjunct (0 women). *Students:* 91 full-time (45 women), 6 part-time (5 women); includes 24 minority (4 Black or African American, non-Hispanic/Latino; 10 Asian, non-Hispanic/Latino; 10 Hispanic/Latino), 49 international. Average age 28. 118 applicants, 27% accepted, 24 enrolled. In 2018, 2 master's, 19 doctorates awarded. *Degree requirements:* For master's, thesis or internship; for doctorate, comprehensive exam, thesis/dissertation, research practica. *Entrance requirements:* For master's and doctorate, GRE General Test, minimum GPA of 3.0 in upper-level course work in field. Additional exam requirements/recommendations for international students: Required—TOEFL (minimum score 600 paper-based). *Application deadline:* For fall admission, 7/15 for domestic students, 5/1 priority date for international students; for spring admission, 11/15 for domestic students, 9/1 priority date for international students. Applications are processed on a rolling basis. Application fee: $50 ($100 for international students). Electronic applications accepted. *Expenses: Tuition, area resident:* Full-time $13,458. Tuition, state resident: full-time $13,458. Tuition, nonresident: full-time $26,852. *International tuition:* $26,852 full-time. Tuition and fees vary according to course load. *Financial support:* In 2018–19, 80 students received support, including 44 research assistantships with partial tuition reimbursements available (averaging $23,925 per year), 40 teaching assistantships with partial tuition reimbursements available (averaging $17,528 per year); fellowships, career-related internships or fieldwork, Federal Work-Study, institutionally sponsored loans, scholarships/grants, and unspecified assistantships also available. Support available to part-time students. Financial award application deadline: 4/30; financial award applicants required to submit FAFSA. *Faculty research:* Advanced nano-materials; novel MRI agents; peptidomimetics to treat diabetes; semiconducting polymers for organic electronics; macrocyclic receptors for catalysis, medicine, materials science; electroactive polymers. *Unit head:* Dr. Ken Balkus, Department Head, 972-883-2659, Fax: 972-883-2925, E-mail: chemistry@utdallas.edu. *Application contact:* Dr. Ken Balkus, Department Head, 972-883-2659, Fax: 972-883-2925, E-mail: chemistry@utdallas.edu.
Website: http://www.utdallas.edu/chemistry/

The University of Texas at El Paso, Graduate School, College of Science, Department of Chemistry and Biochemistry, El Paso, TX 79968-0001. Offers MS, PhD. *Program availability:* Part-time, evening/weekend. *Degree requirements:* For master's, thesis; for doctorate, thesis/dissertation. *Entrance requirements:* For master's, GRE, minimum GPA of 3.0; for doctorate, GRE, letters of recommendation. Additional exam requirements/recommendations for international students: Required—TOEFL; Recommended—IELTS. Electronic applications accepted.

The University of Texas at San Antonio, College of Sciences, Department of Chemistry, San Antonio, TX 78249-0617. Offers MS, PhD. *Degree requirements:* For master's, comprehensive exam, thesis optional; for doctorate, comprehensive exam, thesis/dissertation. *Entrance requirements:* For master's, GRE General Test, minimum GPA of 3.0 in all undergraduate chemistry courses, 2 letters of recommendation; for doctorate, GRE, official transcripts from all colleges and universities attended, resume or curriculum vitae, at least 2 letters of recommendation, statement of purpose. Additional exam requirements/recommendations for international students: Required—TOEFL (minimum score 550 paper-based; 79 iBT), IELTS (minimum score 6.5). Electronic applications accepted. *Faculty research:* Medicinal chemistry, biosensors, mass spectrometry, organic synthesis, enzymatic mechanisms.

The University of Texas Rio Grande Valley, College of Sciences, Department of Chemistry, Edinburg, TX 78539. Offers MS. *Program availability:* Part-time, evening/weekend. *Degree requirements:* For master's, thesis optional. *Entrance requirements:* For master's, GRE General Test, minimum GPA of 3.0 in the last 32 hours of the completed undergraduate degree; 32 credit hours of undergraduate coursework in chemistry. Additional exam requirements/recommendations for international students: Required—TOEFL or IELTS. Electronic applications accepted. *Expenses: Tuition, area resident:* Full-time $6888. Tuition, state resident: full-time $6888. Tuition, nonresident: full-time $14,484. *International tuition:* $14,484 full-time. *Required fees:* $1468.

University of the Sciences, Program in Chemistry, Biochemistry and Pharmacognosy, Philadelphia, PA 19104-4495. Offers biochemistry (MS, PhD); chemistry (MS, PhD); pharmacognosy (MS, PhD). *Program availability:* Part-time. *Degree requirements:* For master's, thesis, qualifying exams; for doctorate, comprehensive exam, thesis/dissertation, qualifying exams. *Entrance requirements:* For master's and doctorate, GRE General Test, GRE Subject Test. Additional exam requirements/recommendations for international students: Required—TOEFL, TWE. *Expenses:* Contact institution.

The University of Toledo, College of Graduate Studies, College of Natural Sciences and Mathematics, Department of Chemistry, Toledo, OH 43606-3390. Offers analytical chemistry (MS, PhD); biological chemistry (MS, PhD); inorganic chemistry (MS, PhD); organic chemistry (MS, PhD); physical chemistry (MS, PhD). *Program availability:* Part-time. *Degree requirements:* For master's, thesis or alternative; for doctorate, thesis/dissertation. *Entrance requirements:* For master's and doctorate, GRE General Test, GRE Subject Test, minimum cumulative point-hour ratio of 2.7 for all previous academic work, three letters of recommendation, statement of purpose, transcripts from all prior institutions attended. Additional exam requirements/recommendations for international students: Required—TOEFL (minimum score 550 paper-based; 80 iBT). Electronic applications accepted. *Faculty research:* Enzymology, materials chemistry, crystallography, theoretical chemistry.

University of Toronto, School of Graduate Studies, Faculty of Arts and Science, Department of Chemistry, Toronto, ON M5S 1A1, Canada. Offers M Sc, PhD. *Degree requirements:* For master's, thesis; for doctorate, thesis/dissertation, oral exam, thesis defense. *Entrance requirements:* For master's, bachelor's degree in chemistry or a related field; for doctorate, master's degree in chemistry or a related field. Additional exam requirements/recommendations for international students: Required—TOEFL (minimum score 580 paper-based; 93 iBT), TWE (minimum score 4). Electronic applications accepted.

University of Utah, Graduate School, College of Science, Department of Chemistry, Salt Lake City, UT 84112-0850. Offers chemistry (MS, PhD); science teacher education (MS). *Program availability:* Part-time, online learning. *Faculty:* 29 full-time (9 women), 15 part-time/adjunct (3 women). *Students:* 137 full-time (64 women), 22 part-time (2 women); includes 20 minority (1 American Indian or Alaska Native, non-Hispanic/Latino; 10 Asian, non-Hispanic/Latino; 7 Hispanic/Latino; 2 Two or more races, non-Hispanic/Latino), 38 international. Average age 27. 298 applicants, 34% accepted, 37 enrolled. In 2018, 11 master's, 24 doctorates awarded. Terminal master's awarded for partial completion of doctoral program. *Degree requirements:* For master's, thesis optional, 20 hours of course work, 10 hours of research; for doctorate, thesis/dissertation, 18 hours of course work, 14 hours of research. *Entrance requirements:* For master's and doctorate, GRE General Test, minimum GPA of 3.0. Additional exam requirements/recommendations for international students: Required—TOEFL (minimum score 620 paper-based; 105 iBT). *Application deadline:* For fall admission, 4/1 for domestic students, 2/1 for international students; for spring admission, 11/1 for domestic and international students. Application fee: $55 ($65 for international students). Electronic applications accepted. Application fee is waived when completed online. *Expenses:* Contact institution. *Financial support:* In 2018–19, 175 students received support, including 1 fellowship with full tuition reimbursement available (averaging $25,000 per year), 119 research assistantships with tuition reimbursements available (averaging $25,500 per year), 55 teaching assistantships with tuition reimbursements available (averaging $25,000 per year); scholarships/grants and tuition waivers (full) also available. Financial award application deadline: 4/1; financial award applicants required to submit FAFSA. *Faculty research:* Analytical, biological, inorganic, materials, organic, physical and theoretical chemistry. *Unit head:* Dr. Cynthia J. Burrows, Chair, 801-585-7290, Fax: 801-581-8433, E-mail: chair@chemistry.utah.edu. *Application contact:* Jo Vallejo, Graduate Coordinator, 801-581-4393, E-mail: jvallejo@chem.utah.edu.
Website: http://www.chem.utah.edu/

University of Vermont, Graduate College, College of Arts and Sciences, Department of Chemistry, Burlington, VT 05405. Offers MS, PhD. *Degree requirements:* For master's, thesis; for doctorate, thesis/dissertation. *Entrance requirements:* For master's and doctorate, GRE General Test. Additional exam requirements/recommendations for international students: Required—TOEFL (minimum score 550 paper-based, 90 iBT) or IELTS (6.5). Electronic applications accepted.

University of Victoria, Faculty of Graduate Studies, Faculty of Science, Department of Chemistry, Victoria, BC V8W 2Y2, Canada. Offers M Sc, PhD. *Degree requirements:* For master's, thesis; for doctorate, thesis/dissertation, candidacy exam. *Entrance requirements:* For master's and doctorate, GRE Subject Test. Additional exam requirements/recommendations for international students: Required—TOEFL (minimum score 575 paper-based), IELTS (minimum score 7). Electronic applications accepted. *Faculty research:* Laser spectroscopy and dynamics; inorganic, organic, and organometallic synthesis; electro and surface chemistry.

University of Virginia, College and Graduate School of Arts and Sciences, Department of Chemistry, Charlottesville, VA 22903. Offers MA, MS, PhD. *Degree requirements:* For master's, comprehensive exam, thesis; for doctorate, comprehensive exam, thesis/dissertation. *Entrance requirements:* For master's and doctorate, GRE General Test; GRE Subject Test (recommended). Additional exam requirements/recommendations for international students: Required—TOEFL (minimum score 600 paper-based; 90 iBT), IELTS (minimum score 7). Electronic applications accepted.

University of Washington, Graduate School, College of Arts and Sciences, Department of Chemistry, Seattle, WA 98195. Offers MS, PhD. Terminal master's awarded for partial completion of doctoral program. *Degree requirements:* For master's, thesis (for some programs); for doctorate, thesis/dissertation. *Entrance requirements:* For master's and doctorate, GRE Subject Test, minimum GPA of 3.0. Additional exam requirements/recommendations for international students: Required—TOEFL. *Faculty research:* Biopolymers, material science and nanotechnology, organometallic chemistry, analytical chemistry, bioorganic chemistry.

University of Waterloo, Graduate Studies and Postdoctoral Affairs, Faculty of Science, Department of Chemistry, Waterloo, ON N2L 3G1, Canada. Offers M Sc, PhD. *Program availability:* Part-time. *Degree requirements:* For master's and doctorate, project or thesis. *Entrance requirements:* For master's, GRE, honors degree, minimum B average; for doctorate, GRE, master's degree, minimum B average. Additional exam requirements/recommendations for international students: Required—TOEFL, IELTS, PTE. *Application deadline:* Applications are processed on a rolling basis. Application fee: $125 Canadian dollars. Electronic applications accepted. *Financial support:* Research assistantships, teaching assistantships, and scholarships/grants available. *Faculty research:* Polymer, physical, inorganic, organic, and theoretical chemistry.
Website: https://uwaterloo.ca/chemistry/

The University of Western Ontario, School of Graduate and Postdoctoral Studies, Faculty of Science, Department of Chemistry, London, ON N6A 3K7, Canada. Offers M Sc, PhD. *Degree requirements:* For master's, thesis; for doctorate, thesis/dissertation. *Entrance requirements:* For master's, minimum B+ average, honors B Sc in chemistry; for doctorate, M Sc or equivalent in chemistry. Additional exam requirements/recommendations for international students: Required—TOEFL (paper-based 570) or IELTS (6). *Faculty research:* Materials, inorganic, organic, physical and theoretical chemistry.

University of Windsor, Faculty of Graduate Studies, Faculty of Science, Department of Chemistry and Biochemistry, Windsor, ON N9B 3P4, Canada. Offers M Sc, PhD. *Program availability:* Part-time. *Degree requirements:* For master's, thesis; for doctorate, comprehensive exam, thesis/dissertation. *Entrance requirements:* For master's and doctorate, minimum B average. Additional exam requirements/recommendations for international students: Required—TOEFL (minimum score 560 paper-based). Electronic applications accepted. *Faculty research:* Molecular biology/recombinant DNA techniques (PCR, cloning mutagenesis), No/02 detectors, western immunoblotting and detection, CD/NMR protein/peptide structure determination, confocal/electron microscopes.

University of Wisconsin–Madison, Graduate School, College of Engineering, Program in Environmental Chemistry and Technology, Madison, WI 53706. Offers MS, PhD. *Program availability:* Part-time. *Faculty:* 15 full-time (4 women). *Students:* 18 full-time (14 women); includes 3 minority (1 American Indian or Alaska Native, non-Hispanic/Latino; 1 Hispanic/Latino; 1 Two or more races, non-Hispanic/Latino), 2 international. Average age 26. 51 applicants, 18% accepted, 2 enrolled. In 2018, 5 doctorates awarded. Terminal master's awarded for partial completion of doctoral program. *Degree requirements:* For master's, thesis or alternative, minimum of 30 credits; minimum GPA of 3.0; for doctorate, comprehensive exam, thesis/dissertation, minimum of 51 credits; minimum GPA of 3.0. *Entrance requirements:* For master's and doctorate, GRE General Test, BS; minimum GPA of 3.0. Additional exam requirements/recommendations for international students: Required—TOEFL (minimum score 580 paper-based; 92 iBT), IELTS (minimum score 7). *Application deadline:* For fall admission, 12/15 for domestic and international students. Application fee: $75 ($81 for international students). Electronic applications accepted. *Financial support:* Fellowships with full tuition reimbursements, research assistantships with full tuition reimbursements, Federal Work-Study, and institutionally sponsored loans available. Financial award application deadline: 12/1; financial award applicants required to submit FAFSA. *Faculty research:* Chemical limnology, chemical remediation, geochemistry, photo catalysis, water quality. *Unit head:* Dr. William Likos, Chair and Professor, 608-263-9490. *Application contact:* Cheryl Loschko, Student Services Coordinator, 608-890-2420, E-mail: loschko@wisc.edu.
Website: http://www.engr.wisc.edu//academics/graduate-academics/environmental-chemistry-technology/

University of Wisconsin–Madison, Graduate School, College of Letters and Science, Department of Chemistry, Madison, WI 53706-1380. Offers MS, PhD. *Program availability:* Part-time. Terminal master's awarded for partial completion of doctoral program. *Degree requirements:* For master's, thesis (for some programs); for doctorate, thesis/dissertation, cumulative exams, research proposal, seminar. *Entrance requirements:* For master's and doctorate, GRE, minimum GPA of 3.0. Additional exam requirements/recommendations for international students: Required—TOEFL. Electronic applications accepted. *Faculty research:* Analytical, inorganic, organic, physical, and macromolecular chemistry.

University of Wisconsin–Milwaukee, Graduate School, College of Letters and Science, Department of Chemistry and Biochemistry, Milwaukee, WI 53201-0413. Offers MS, PhD. *Students:* 67 full-time (20 women), 9 part-time (4 women); includes 5 minority (1 Black or African American, non-Hispanic/Latino; 2 Asian, non-Hispanic/Latino; 2 Two or more races, non-Hispanic/Latino), 36 international. Average age 31. 53 applicants, 28% accepted, 9 enrolled. In 2018, 2 master's, 9 doctorates awarded. *Entrance requirements:* For doctorate, GRE General Test. Additional exam requirements/recommendations for international students: Required—TOEFL (minimum score 600 paper-based; 79 iBT), IELTS (minimum score 6.5). *Application deadline:* For fall admission, 1/1 priority date for domestic students; for spring admission, 9/1 for domestic students. Application fee: $56 ($96 for international students). Electronic applications accepted. *Financial support:* In 2018–19, 3 fellowships, 30 research assistantships, 46 teaching assistantships were awarded; career-related internships or fieldwork, unspecified assistantships, and project assistantships also available. Support available to part-time students. Financial award application deadline: 4/15; financial award applicants required to submit FAFSA. *Faculty research:* Analytical chemistry, biochemistry, inorganic chemistry, organic chemistry, physical chemistry. *Unit head:* Peter Geissinger, Department Chair, 414-229-4098, E-mail: geissing@uwm.edu. *Application contact:* General Information Contact, 414-229-4982, Fax: 414-229-6967, E-mail: gradschool@uwm.edu.
Website: https://uwm.edu/chemistry/

University of Wyoming, College of Arts and Sciences, Department of Chemistry, Laramie, WY 82071. Offers MS, PhD. *Degree requirements:* For master's, thesis; for doctorate, thesis/dissertation. *Entrance requirements:* For master's and doctorate, GRE General Test, minimum GPA of 3.0. Additional exam requirements/recommendations for international students: Required—TOEFL (minimum score 600 paper-based). Electronic applications accepted. *Expenses: Tuition, area resident:* Full-time $6504; part-time $271 per credit hour. Tuition, state resident: full-time $6504; part-time $271 per credit hour. Tuition, nonresident: full-time $19,464; part-time $811 per credit hour. *International tuition:* $19,464 full-time. *Required fees:* $1410.94; $343.82 per semester. $343.82 per semester. Tuition and fees vary according to course load, program and reciprocity agreements. *Faculty research:* Organic chemistry, inorganic chemistry, analytical chemistry, physical chemistry.

Utah State University, School of Graduate Studies, College of Science, Department of Chemistry and Biochemistry, Logan, UT 84322. Offers biochemistry (MS, PhD); chemistry (MS, PhD). *Program availability:* Part-time. Terminal master's awarded for partial completion of doctoral program. *Degree requirements:* For master's, thesis, oral and written exams; for doctorate, thesis/dissertation, oral and written exams. *Entrance requirements:* For master's and doctorate, GRE General Test, minimum GPA of 3.0. Additional exam requirements/recommendations for international students: Required—TOEFL. *Faculty research:* Analytical, inorganic, organic, and physical chemistry; iron in asbestos chemistry and carcinogenicity; dicopper complexes; photothermal spectrometry; metal molecule clusters.

Vanderbilt University, Department of Chemistry, Nashville, TN 37240-1001. Offers MAT, MS, PhD. *Faculty:* 21 full-time (4 women). *Students:* 111 full-time (54 women); includes 29 minority (8 Black or African American, non-Hispanic/Latino; 6 Asian, non-Hispanic/Latino; 10 Hispanic/Latino; 5 Two or more races, non-Hispanic/Latino), 3 international. Average age 26. 227 applicants, 24% accepted, 13 enrolled. In 2018, 3 master's, 20 doctorates awarded. Terminal master's awarded for partial completion of doctoral program. *Degree requirements:* For master's, thesis; for doctorate, thesis/dissertation, area, qualifying, and final exams. *Entrance requirements:* For master's and doctorate, GRE General Test, GRE Subject Test (recommended). Additional exam requirements/recommendations for international students: Required—TOEFL (minimum score 570 paper-based; 88 iBT). *Application deadline:* For fall admission, 1/15 for domestic and international students. Application fee: $0. Electronic applications accepted. *Expenses: Tuition:* Full-time $47,208; part-time $2026 per credit hour. *Required fees:* $478. *Financial support:* Fellowships with tuition reimbursements, research assistantships with full tuition reimbursements, teaching assistantships with full tuition reimbursements, Federal Work-Study, institutionally sponsored loans, scholarships/grants, traineeships, and health care benefits available. Financial award application deadline: 1/15; financial award applicants required to submit CSS PROFILE or FAFSA. *Faculty research:* Chemical synthesis; mechanistic, theoretical, bioorganic, analytical, and spectroscopic chemistry. *Unit head:* Dr. David Cliffel, Chair, 615-343-3937, Fax: 615-322-4936, E-mail: d.cliffel@vanderbilt.edu. *Application contact:* Carmello Rizzo, Director of Graduate Studies, 615-322-2861, Fax: 615-322-4936, E-mail: c.rizzo@vanderbilt.edu.
Website: http://www.vanderbilt.edu/chemistry/

Villanova University, Graduate School of Liberal Arts and Sciences, Department of Chemistry, Villanova, PA 19085-1699. Offers MS. *Program availability:* Part-time, evening/weekend. *Degree requirements:* For master's, comprehensive exam (for some programs), thesis (for some programs). *Entrance requirements:* For master's, GRE General Test, minimum GPA of 3.0, 3 recommendation letters, statement of goals. Additional exam requirements/recommendations for international students: Required—TOEFL. Electronic applications accepted.

Virginia Commonwealth University, Graduate School, College of Humanities and Sciences, Department of Chemistry, Richmond, VA 23284-9005. Offers analytical chemistry (MS, PhD); chemical physics (PhD); inorganic chemistry (MS, PhD); organic chemistry (MS, PhD); physical chemistry (MS, PhD). *Program availability:* Part-time. Terminal master's awarded for partial completion of doctoral program. *Degree requirements:* For master's, thesis; for doctorate, thesis/dissertation, comprehensive cumulative exams, research proposal. *Entrance requirements:* For master's, GRE General Test, 30 undergraduate credits in chemistry; for doctorate, GRE General Test. Additional exam requirements/recommendations for international students: Required—TOEFL (minimum score 600 paper-based; 100 iBT) or IELTS (minimum score 6.5). Electronic applications accepted. *Faculty research:* Physical, organic, inorganic, analytical, and polymer chemistry; chemical physics.

Virginia Polytechnic Institute and State University, Graduate School, College of Science, Blacksburg, VA 24061. Offers biological sciences (MS, PhD); biomedical technology development and management (MS); chemistry (MS, PhD); data analysis and applied statistics (MA); economics (PhD); geosciences (MS, PhD); mathematics (MS, PhD); physics (MS, PhD); psychology (MS, PhD); statistics (MS, PhD). *Faculty:* 349 full-time (109 women), 3 part-time/adjunct (2 women). *Students:* 542 full-time (202 women), 39 part-time (19 women); includes 71 minority (11 Black or African American, non-Hispanic/Latino; 1 American Indian or Alaska Native, non-Hispanic/Latino; 18 Asian, non-Hispanic/Latino; 32 Hispanic/Latino; 9 Two or more races, non-Hispanic/Latino), 220 international. Average age 27. 977 applicants, 25% accepted, 110 enrolled. In 2018, 75 master's, 69 doctorates awarded. *Degree requirements:* For master's, comprehensive exam (for some programs), thesis (for some programs); for doctorate, comprehensive exam (for some programs), thesis/dissertation (for some programs). *Entrance requirements:* For master's and doctorate, GRE/GMAT. Additional exam requirements/recommendations for international students: Required—TOEFL (minimum score 90 iBT). *Application deadline:* For fall admission, 8/1 for domestic students, 4/1 for international students; for spring admission, 1/1 for domestic students, 9/1 for international students. Applications are processed on a rolling basis. Application fee: $75. Electronic applications accepted. *Expenses:* Tuition, state resident: full-time $15,510; part-time $739.50 per credit hour. Tuition, nonresident: full-time $29,629; part-time $1490.25 per credit hour. *Required fees:* $2804; $550 per semester. Tuition and fees vary according to course load, campus/location and program. *Financial support:* In 2018–19, 7 fellowships with full tuition reimbursements (averaging $29,657 per year), 260 research assistantships with full tuition reimbursements (averaging $15,888 per year), 383 teaching assistantships with full tuition reimbursements (averaging $18,063 per year) were awarded; unspecified assistantships also available. Financial award application deadline: 3/1; financial award applicants required to submit FAFSA. *Total annual research expenditures:* $27.3 million. *Unit head:* Dr. Sally C. Morton, Dean, 540-231-5422, Fax: 540-231-3380, E-mail: scmorton@vt.edu. *Application contact:* Allison Craft, Executive Assistant, 540-231-6394, Fax: 540-231-3380, E-mail: crafta@vt.edu.
Website: http://www.science.vt.edu/

Wake Forest University, Graduate School of Arts and Sciences, Department of Chemistry, Winston-Salem, NC 27109. Offers analytical chemistry (MS, PhD); inorganic chemistry (MS, PhD); organic chemistry (MS, PhD); physical chemistry (MS, PhD). *Program availability:* Part-time. *Degree requirements:* For master's, one foreign language, comprehensive exam, thesis; for doctorate, 2 foreign languages, comprehensive exam, thesis/dissertation. *Entrance requirements:* For master's and doctorate, GRE General Test. Additional exam requirements/recommendations for international students: Required—TOEFL. Electronic applications accepted.

Washington State University, College of Arts and Sciences, Department of Chemistry, Pullman, WA 99164. Offers MS, PhD. Program applications must be made through the Pullman campus. *Program availability:* Part-time, evening/weekend. Terminal master's awarded for partial completion of doctoral program. *Degree requirements:* For master's, comprehensive exam (for some programs), thesis (for some programs), oral exam, teaching experience; for doctorate, comprehensive exam, thesis/dissertation, oral exam, written exam, teaching experience. *Entrance requirements:* For master's and doctorate, GRE General Test, GRE Subject Test (recommended), transcripts from each post-secondary school attended (photocopies acceptable); three letters of recommendation.

Additional exam requirements/recommendations for international students: Required—TOEFL. Electronic applications accepted. *Faculty research:* Chemistry of biological systems, chemistry of materials, chemistry of energy and the environment, radiochemistry.

Washington University in St. Louis, The Graduate School, Department of Chemistry, St. Louis, MO 63130-4899. Offers PhD. Terminal master's awarded for partial completion of doctoral program. *Degree requirements:* For doctorate, thesis/dissertation. *Entrance requirements:* For doctorate, GRE General Test, GRE Subject Test. Additional exam requirements/recommendations for international students: Required—TOEFL. Electronic applications accepted. *Faculty research:* Bioinorganic chemistry; biological chemistry; biorganic chemistry; biophysical chemistry; inorganic chemistry; materials chemistry; nuclear chemistry; organic chemistry; organometallic chemistry; physical chemistry; polymer chemistry; radiochemistry; spectroscopy; theoretical chemistry.

Wayne State University, College of Liberal Arts and Sciences, Department of Chemistry, Detroit, MI 48202. Offers analytical chemistry (PhD); chemistry (MA, MS). *Faculty:* 33. *Students:* 121 full-time (49 women), 3 part-time (all women); includes 12 minority (1 Black or African American, non-Hispanic/Latino; 2 Asian, non-Hispanic/Latino; 5 Hispanic/Latino; 1 Native Hawaiian or other Pacific Islander, non-Hispanic/Latino; 3 Two or more races, non-Hispanic/Latino), 74 international. Average age 28. 353 applicants, 20% accepted, 28 enrolled. In 2018, 4 master's, 22 doctorates awarded. *Entrance requirements:* For master's, GRE (strongly recommended), 1 year of physics, math through calculus, general chemistry (8 credits), organic chemistry (8 credits), physical chemistry (6 credits), quantitative analysis (4 credits), advanced chemistry (3 credits), minimum undergraduate GPA of 2.75 in chemistry and cognate sciences, statement of interest, three letters of recommendation; for doctorate, GRE (strongly recommended), minimum undergraduate GPA of 3.0 in chemistry and cognate science. Additional exam requirements/recommendations for international students: Required—TOEFL (minimum score 90 iBT), IELTS (minimum score 6.5), TWE. *Application deadline:* Applications are processed on a rolling basis. Electronic applications accepted. *Financial support:* In 2018–19, 116 students received support, including 21 fellowships with tuition reimbursements available (averaging $11,119 per year), 42 research assistantships with tuition reimbursements available (averaging $22,026 per year), 74 teaching assistantships with tuition reimbursements available (averaging $22,042 per year); scholarships/grants, health care benefits, and unspecified assistantships also available. Financial award applicants required to submit FAFSA. *Faculty research:* Natural products synthesis, molecular biology, molecular mechanics calculations, organometallic chemistry, experimental physical chemistry. *Unit head:* Dr. Matthew Allen, Chair, 313-577-2070, E-mail: mallen@chem.wayne.edu. *Application contact:* Melissa Rochon, Graduate Academic Services Officer, 313-577-2844, E-mail: melissa@chem.wayne.edu.
Website: http://chem.wayne.edu/

Wesleyan University, Graduate Studies, Department of Chemistry, Middletown, CT 06459. Offers biochemistry (PhD); chemical physics (PhD); inorganic chemistry (PhD); organic chemistry (PhD); physical chemistry (PhD); theoretical chemistry (PhD). *Faculty:* 11 full-time (3 women), 1 part-time/adjunct (0 women). *Students:* 16 full-time (9 women). Average age 25. In 2018, 4 doctorates awarded. Terminal master's awarded for partial completion of doctoral program. *Degree requirements:* For doctorate, thesis/dissertation. *Entrance requirements:* For doctorate, GRE General Test, 3 recommendations. Additional exam requirements/recommendations for international students: Required—TOEFL, IELTS. *Application deadline:* 1/1 for domestic and international students; for summer admission, 1/1 for domestic and international students. Application fee: $0. Electronic applications accepted. *Financial support:* In 2018–19, 15 students received support, including 4 research assistantships with full tuition reimbursements available, 13 teaching assistantships with full tuition reimbursements available; institutionally sponsored loans and health care benefits also available. Financial award application deadline: 4/30. *Faculty research:* The synthesis of noble metal and noble metal alloy nanoparticles with well-defined shapes and catalytically-active high-energy surfaces; inorganic chemistry; materials science; scanning electron microscopy (SEM);transition organometallic complexes. *Unit head:* Michael A. Calter, Chair, 860-685-2633 Ext. 2633, Fax: 860-685-2211, E-mail: mcalter@wesleyan.edu. *Application contact:* Aracely Suto, Administrative Assistant, 860-685-2572, Fax: 860-685-2211, E-mail: chemistry@wesleyan.edu.
Website: http://www.wesleyan.edu/chem/

West Chester University of Pennsylvania, College of the Sciences and Mathematics, Department of Chemistry, West Chester, PA 19383. Offers Teaching Certificate. *Degree requirements:* For Teaching Certificate, minimum overall GPA of 3.0, chemistry PRAXIS. *Entrance requirements:* For degree, minimum GPA of 2.8 in most recent 48 credits. Additional exam requirements/recommendations for international students: Required—TOEFL or IELTS. Electronic applications accepted. *Faculty research:* Nanomaterials synthesis and characterization, medicinal chemistry synthesis, biosensor development and testing, atmospheric chemistry, forensic analysis of drug microcrystals.

Western Carolina University, Graduate School, College of Arts and Sciences, Department of Chemistry and Physics, Cullowhee, NC 28723. Offers chemistry (MS). *Degree requirements:* For master's, thesis. *Entrance requirements:* For master's, GRE General Test, undergraduate science degree with minimum GPA of 3.0, 3 letters of recommendation, 1-2 page statement outlining goals and research interests. Additional exam requirements/recommendations for international students: Required—TOEFL (minimum score 550 paper-based, 79 iBT) or IELTS (6.5). Electronic applications accepted. *Expenses: Tuition, area resident:* Full-time $4435. Tuition, state resident: full-time $4435. Tuition, nonresident: full-time $14,842. *International tuition:* $14,842 full-time. *Required fees:* $2979. Part-time tuition and fees vary according to course load, degree level and program. *Faculty research:* Trace metal analysis, metal waste reduction, supramolecular chemistry, free radical biophysical chemistry.

Western Illinois University, School of Graduate Studies, College of Arts and Sciences, Department of Chemistry, Macomb, IL 61455-1390. Offers MS. *Program availability:* Part-time. *Students:* 30 full-time (17 women), 7 part-time (3 women); includes 5 minority (2 Asian, non-Hispanic/Latino; 2 Hispanic/Latino; 1 Two or more races, non-Hispanic/Latino), 20 international. Average age 25. 28 applicants, 86% accepted, 14 enrolled. In 2018, 16 master's awarded. *Entrance requirements:* Additional exam requirements/recommendations for international students: Required—TOEFL (minimum score 530 paper-based; 71 iBT). *Application deadline:* Applications are processed on a rolling basis. Application fee: $30. Electronic applications accepted. *Financial support:* In 2018–19, 22 students received support, including 12 teaching assistantships with full tuition reimbursements available (averaging $8,688 per year); unspecified assistantships also available. Financial award applicants required to submit FAFSA. *Unit head:* Dr. Rose McConnell, Chairperson, 309-298-1538. *Application contact:* Dr. Mark Mossman, Associate Provost and Director of Graduate Studies, 309-298-1806, Fax: 309-298-2345, E-mail: grad-office@wiu.edu.
Website: http://wiu.edu/chemistry

Western Kentucky University, Graduate School, Ogden College of Science and Engineering, Department of Chemistry, Bowling Green, KY 42101. Offers MA Ed, MS. *Degree requirements:* For master's, comprehensive exam, thesis. *Entrance requirements:* For master's, GRE General Test, minimum GPA of 2.75. Additional exam requirements/recommendations for international students: Required—TOEFL (minimum score 555 paper-based). *Faculty research:* Catatonic surfactants, directed orthometalation reactions, thermal stability and degradation mechanisms, co-firing refused derived fuels, laser fluorescence.

Western Michigan University, Graduate College, College of Arts and Sciences, Department of Chemistry, Kalamazoo, MI 49008. Offers MS, PhD. *Degree requirements:* For master's, thesis; for doctorate, thesis/dissertation.

Western Michigan University, Graduate College, College of Arts and Sciences, Department of Interdisciplinary Arts and Sciences, Kalamazoo, MI 49008. Offers science education (MA, PhD), including biological sciences (PhD), chemistry (PhD), geosciences (PhD), physical geography (PhD), physics (PhD), science education (PhD). *Degree requirements:* For doctorate, thesis/dissertation.

Western Washington University, Graduate School, College of Sciences and Technology, Department of Chemistry, Bellingham, WA 98225-5996. Offers MS. *Program availability:* Part-time. *Degree requirements:* For master's, thesis (for some programs). *Entrance requirements:* For master's, GRE General Test, minimum GPA of 3.0 in last 60 semester hours or last 90 quarter hours. Additional exam requirements/recommendations for international students: Required—TOEFL (minimum score 567 paper-based). Electronic applications accepted. *Faculty research:* Bio-, organic, inorganic, physical, analytical chemistry.

West Texas A&M University, College of Agriculture and Natural Sciences, Department of Chemistry and Physics, Canyon, TX 79015. Offers chemistry (MS). *Program availability:* Part-time. *Degree requirements:* For master's, comprehensive exam, thesis optional. *Entrance requirements:* For master's, GRE General Test. Additional exam requirements/recommendations for international students: Required—TOEFL (minimum score 550 paper-based). Electronic applications accepted. *Faculty research:* Biochemistry; inorganic, organic, and physical chemistry; vibrational spectroscopy; magnetic susceptibilities; carbine chemistry.

West Virginia University, Eberly College of Arts and Sciences, Morgantown, WV 26506. Offers biology (MS, PhD); chemistry (MS, PhD); communication studies (MA, PhD); computational statistics (PhD); creative writing (MFA); English (MA, PhD); forensic and investigative science (MS); forensic science (PhD); geography (MA); geology (MA, PhD); history (MA, PhD); legal studies (MLS); mathematics (MS); physics (MS, PhD); political science (MA, PhD); professional writing and editing (MA); psychology (MA); public administration (MPA); social work (MSW); sociology (MA, PhD); statistics (MS). *Program availability:* Part-time, evening/weekend, online learning. *Students:* 803 full-time (434 women), 237 part-time (138 women); includes 99 minority (31 Black or African American, non-Hispanic/Latino; 1 American Indian or Alaska Native, non-Hispanic/Latino; 16 Asian, non-Hispanic/Latino; 25 Hispanic/Latino; 26 Two or more races, non-Hispanic/Latino), 208 international. In 2018, 285 master's, 63 doctorates awarded. Terminal master's awarded for partial completion of doctoral program. *Degree requirements:* For master's, thesis (for some programs); for doctorate, comprehensive exam, thesis/dissertation. *Entrance requirements:* For master's and doctorate, GRE. Additional exam requirements/recommendations for international students: Required—TOEFL (minimum score 600 paper-based); Recommended—TWE. *Application deadline:* For spring admission, 2/15 priority date for domestic and international students. Applications are processed on a rolling basis. Application fee: $45. Electronic applications accepted. *Financial support:* Fellowships with full tuition reimbursements, research assistantships with full tuition reimbursements, teaching assistantships with full tuition reimbursements, career-related internships or fieldwork, Federal Work-Study, institutionally sponsored loans, scholarships/grants, health care benefits, tuition waivers (full and partial), unspecified assistantships, and administrative assistantships available. Financial award application deadline: 2/1; financial award applicants required to submit FAFSA. *Faculty research:* Humanities, social sciences, life science, physical sciences, mathematics. *Unit head:* Dr. Gregory Dunaway, Dean, 304-293-4611, Fax: 304-293-6858, E-mail: gregory.dunaway@mail.wvu.edu. *Application contact:* Dr. Jessica Queener, Director of Graduate Studies, 304-293-7476 Ext. 5205, Fax: 304-293-6858, E-mail: Jessica.queener@mail.wvu.edu.
Website: http://www.as.wvu.edu/

Wichita State University, Graduate School, Fairmount College of Liberal Arts and Sciences, Department of Chemistry, Wichita, KS 67260. Offers MS, PhD. *Unit head:* Dr. Doug English, Chair, 316-978-3120, Fax: 316-978-3431, E-mail: doug.english@wichita.edu. *Application contact:* Jordan Oleson, Admission Coordinator, 316-978-3095, E-mail: jordan.oleson@wichita.edu.
Website: http://www.wichita.edu/chemistry

Wilfrid Laurier University, Faculty of Graduate and Postdoctoral Studies, Faculty of Science, Department of Chemistry, Waterloo, ON N2L 3C5, Canada. Offers M Sc. *Degree requirements:* For master's, thesis. *Entrance requirements:* For master's, honors degree or equivalent in chemistry, biochemistry or a related discipline; minimum B average in last two full-time undergraduate years. Additional exam requirements/recommendations for international students: Required—TOEFL (minimum score 89 iBT). Electronic applications accepted. *Faculty research:* Cold regions water science, biophysical methods, biochemistry, nanochemistry.

Worcester Polytechnic Institute, Graduate Admissions, Department of Chemistry and Biochemistry, Worcester, MA 01609-2280. Offers biochemistry (MS, PhD); chemistry (MS, PhD). *Program availability:* Part-time, evening/weekend. *Students:* 22 full-time (12 women), 6 part-time (0 women); includes 2 minority (1 Black or African American, non-Hispanic/Latino; 1 Hispanic/Latino), 6 international. Average age 27. 33 applicants, 39% accepted, 7 enrolled. In 2018, 1 master's, 3 doctorates awarded. *Degree requirements:* For doctorate, comprehensive exam, thesis/dissertation. *Entrance requirements:* For master's and doctorate, GRE General Test, 3 letters of recommendation, statement of purpose. Additional exam requirements/recommendations for international students: Required—TOEFL (minimum score 563 paper-based; 84 iBT), IELTS (minimum score 7). *Application deadline:* For fall admission, 1/1 priority date for domestic and international students; for spring admission, 10/1 priority date for domestic and international students. Applications are processed on a rolling basis. Application fee: $70. Electronic applications accepted. *Financial support:* Fellowships, research assistantships, teaching assistantships, career-related internships or fieldwork, institutionally sponsored loans, scholarships/grants, and unspecified assistantships available. Financial award application deadline: 1/1. *Unit head:* Dr. Arne Gericke, Department Head, 508-831-5371, Fax: 508-831-5933, E-mail: agericke@wpi.edu. *Application contact:* Dr. Anita Mattson, Graduate Coordinator, 508-831-5371, Fax: 508-831-5933, E-mail: aemattson@wpi.edu.
Website: https://www.wpi.edu/academics/departments/chemistry-biochemistry

Wright State University, Graduate School, College of Science and Mathematics, Department of Chemistry, Dayton, OH 45435. Offers chemistry (MS). *Program availability:* Part-time, evening/weekend. *Degree requirements:* For master's, oral defense of thesis, seminar. *Entrance requirements:* Additional exam requirements/recommendations for international students: Required—TOEFL. *Faculty research:* Polymer synthesis and characterization, laser kinetics, organic and inorganic synthesis, analytical and environmental chemistry.

Yale University, Graduate School of Arts and Sciences, Department of Chemistry, New Haven, CT 06520. Offers biophysical chemistry (PhD); inorganic chemistry (PhD); organic chemistry (PhD); physical and theoretical chemistry (PhD). *Degree requirements:* For doctorate, thesis/dissertation. *Entrance requirements:* For doctorate, GRE General Test, GRE Subject Test. Additional exam requirements/recommendations for international students: Required—TOEFL.

York University, Faculty of Graduate Studies, Faculty of Science, Program in Chemistry, Toronto, ON M3J 1P3, Canada. Offers M Sc, PhD. *Program availability:* Part-time, evening/weekend. *Degree requirements:* For master's, thesis or alternative; for doctorate, thesis/dissertation. Electronic applications accepted.

Youngstown State University, College of Graduate Studies, College of Science, Technology, Engineering and Mathematics, Department of Chemistry, Youngstown, OH 44555-0001. Offers analytical chemistry (MS); biochemistry (MS); chemistry education (MS); inorganic chemistry (MS); organic chemistry (MS); physical chemistry (MS). *Program availability:* Part-time. *Degree requirements:* For master's, thesis. *Entrance requirements:* For master's, bachelor's degree in chemistry, minimum GPA of 2.7. Additional exam requirements/recommendations for international students: Required—TOEFL. *Faculty research:* Analysis of antioxidants, chromatography, defects and disorder in crystalline oxides, hydrogen bonding, novel organic and organometallic materials.

Inorganic Chemistry

Auburn University, Graduate School, College of Sciences and Mathematics, Department of Chemistry and Biochemistry, Auburn University, AL 36849. Offers analytical chemistry (MS, PhD); biochemistry (MS, PhD); inorganic chemistry (MS, PhD); organic chemistry (PhD); physical chemistry (MS, PhD). *Program availability:* Part-time. *Degree requirements:* For master's, thesis (for some programs); for doctorate, thesis/dissertation, oral and written exams. *Entrance requirements:* For master's and doctorate, GRE General Test. Electronic applications accepted. *Expenses:* Tuition, state resident: full-time $11,282; part-time $535 per credit hour. Tuition, nonresident: full-time $30,542; part-time $1605 per credit hour. *Required fees:* $826 per semester. Tuition and fees vary according to degree level and program.

Binghamton University, State University of New York, Graduate School, Harpur College of Arts and Sciences, Department of Chemistry, Binghamton, NY 13902-6000. Offers analytical chemistry (PhD); chemistry (MA, MS); inorganic chemistry (PhD); physical chemistry (PhD). *Program availability:* Part-time. Terminal master's awarded for partial completion of doctoral program. *Degree requirements:* For master's, thesis; for doctorate, comprehensive exam, thesis/dissertation. *Entrance requirements:* For master's and doctorate, GRE General Test. Additional exam requirements/recommendations for international students: Required—TOEFL (minimum score 90 iBT). Electronic applications accepted.

Boston College, Morrissey Graduate School of Arts and Sciences, Department of Chemistry, Chestnut Hill, MA 02467-3800. Offers biochemistry (PhD); inorganic chemistry (PhD); organic chemistry (PhD); physical chemistry (PhD); science education (MST). *Degree requirements:* For doctorate, thesis/dissertation, qualifying exam. *Entrance requirements:* For doctorate, GRE General Test, GRE Subject Test. Additional exam requirements/recommendations for international students: Required—TOEFL (minimum score 600 paper-based; 100 iBT), IELTS (minimum score 8). Electronic applications accepted. *Faculty research:* Organic and organometallic chemistry, chemical biology and biochemistry, physical and theoretical chemistry, inorganic chemistry.

Brandeis University, Graduate School of Arts and Sciences, Department of Chemistry, Waltham, MA 02454-9110. Offers inorganic chemistry (MA, MS, PhD); organic chemistry (MA, MS, PhD); physical chemistry (MS, PhD). *Program availability:* Part-time. *Faculty:* 13 full-time (5 women), 3 part-time/adjunct (0 women). *Students:* 33 full-time (12 women); includes 5 minority (3 Black or African American, non-Hispanic/Latino; 2 Hispanic/Latino), 19 international. Average age 26. 91 applicants, 41% accepted, 9 enrolled. In 2018, 3 master's, 8 doctorates awarded. Terminal master's awarded for partial completion of doctoral program. *Degree requirements:* For master's, comprehensive exam, thesis (for some programs); for doctorate, comprehensive exam, thesis/dissertation. *Entrance requirements:* For master's and doctorate, GRE General Test; GRE Subject Test (recommended), resume, statement of purpose, letters of recommendation, transcripts. Additional exam requirements/recommendations for international students: Required—TOEFL, IELTS, PTE. *Application deadline:* For fall admission, 12/15 priority date for domestic students. Applications are processed on a rolling basis. Application fee: $75. Electronic applications accepted. *Financial support:* In 2018–19, 21 fellowships with full tuition reimbursements (averaging $30,000 per year), 13 research assistantships with full tuition reimbursements (averaging $30,000 per year), 23 teaching assistantships with full tuition reimbursements (averaging $6,400 per year) were awarded; scholarships/grants, health care benefits, and tuition waivers (full and partial) also available. Support available to part-time students. *Faculty research:* Inorganic and organic chemistry, physical chemistry, chemical biology, biophysical chemistry, materials chemistry. *Unit head:* Dr. Klaus Schmidt-Rohr, Director of Graduate Study, 781-736-2520, E-mail: srohr@brandeis.edu. *Application contact:* Maryanna Aldrich, Administrator, 781-736-2352, E-mail: scigradoffice@brandeis.edu.
Website: http://www.brandeis.edu/gsas/programs/chemistry.html

Cornell University, Graduate School, Graduate Fields of Arts and Sciences, Field of Chemistry and Chemical Biology, Ithaca, NY 14853. Offers analytical chemistry (PhD); bio-organic chemistry (PhD); biophysical chemistry (PhD); chemical biology (PhD); chemical physics (PhD); inorganic chemistry (PhD); materials chemistry (PhD); organic chemistry (PhD); organometallic chemistry (PhD); physical chemistry (PhD); polymer chemistry (PhD); theoretical chemistry (PhD). *Degree requirements:* For doctorate, comprehensive exam, thesis/dissertation. *Entrance requirements:* For doctorate, GRE General Test, GRE Subject Test (chemistry), 3 letters of recommendation. Additional exam requirements/recommendations for international students: Required—TOEFL (minimum score 600 paper-based; 77 iBT). Electronic applications accepted. *Faculty research:* Analytical, organic, inorganic, physical, materials, chemical biology.

Florida State University, The Graduate School, Department of Anthropology, Department of Chemistry and Biochemistry, Tallahassee, FL 32306-4390. Offers analytical chemistry (MS, PhD); biochemistry (MS, PhD); inorganic chemistry (MS, PhD); materials chemistry (PhD); organic chemistry (MS, PhD); physical chemistry (MS, PhD). *Faculty:* 29 full-time (4 women). *Students:* 159 full-time (57 women), 2 part-time (1 woman); includes 73 minority (9 Black or African American, non-Hispanic/Latino; 46 Asian, non-Hispanic/Latino; 9 Hispanic/Latino; 3 Native Hawaiian or other Pacific Islander, non-Hispanic/Latino; 6 Two or more races, non-Hispanic/Latino). Average age 26. 215 applicants, 49% accepted, 35 enrolled. In 2018, 33 master's, 30 doctorates awarded. Terminal master's awarded for partial completion of doctoral program. *Degree requirements:* For master's, thesis (for some programs); for doctorate, thesis/dissertation. *Entrance requirements:* For master's and doctorate, GRE General Test (minimum scores: 150 verbal, 151 quantitative), minimum upper-division GPA of 3.1 in undergraduate course work. Additional exam requirements/recommendations for international students: Required—TOEFL (minimum score 80 iBT). *Application deadline:* For fall admission, 12/15 priority date for domestic and international students. Applications are processed on a rolling basis. Application fee: $30. Electronic applications accepted. *Expenses: Tuition, area resident:* Part-time $479.32 per credit hour. Tuition and fees vary according to campus/location and program. *Financial support:* In 2018–19, 163 students received support, including 4 fellowships with full tuition reimbursements available (averaging $24,241 per year), 59 research assistantships with full tuition reimbursements available (averaging $24,241 per year), 102 teaching assistantships with full tuition reimbursements available (averaging $24,241 per year). Financial award application deadline: 12/15; financial award applicants required to submit FAFSA. *Faculty research:* Bioanalytical chemistry, separations, microfluidics, petroleomics; materials chemistry, solid state materials, magnets, polymers, catalysts, advanced spectroscopic methods, NMR and EPR, ultrafast, Raman, and mass spectrometry; organic synthesis, natural products, photochemistry, and supramolecular chemistry; biochemistry, structural biology, metabolomics, and anticancer drugs; nanochemistry, applications in energy, sustainability, biology, and technology development; radiochemistry. *Total annual research expenditures:* $7.1 million. *Unit head:* Dr. Geoffrey Strouse, Chairman, 850-644-1244, Fax: 850-644-8281, E-mail: gradinfo@chem.fsu.edu. *Application contact:* Dr. Wei Yang, Associate Chair for Graduate Studies, 850-645-6884, Fax: 850-644-8281, E-mail: gradinfo@chem.fsu.edu.
Website: http://www.chem.fsu.edu/

Georgetown University, Graduate School of Arts and Sciences, Department of Chemistry, Washington, DC 20057. Offers analytical chemistry (PhD); biochemistry (PhD); computational chemistry (PhD); inorganic chemistry (PhD); materials chemistry (PhD); organic chemistry (PhD); theoretical chemistry (PhD). Terminal master's awarded for partial completion of doctoral program. *Degree requirements:* For doctorate, comprehensive exam, thesis/dissertation. *Entrance requirements:* For doctorate, GRE General Test. Additional exam requirements/recommendations for international students: Required—TOEFL.

The George Washington University, Columbian College of Arts and Sciences, Department of Chemistry, Washington, DC 20052. Offers analytical chemistry (MS, PhD); inorganic chemistry (MS, PhD); materials science (MS, PhD); organic chemistry (MS, PhD); physical chemistry (MS, PhD). *Program availability:* Part-time, evening/weekend. *Students:* 29 full-time (15 women), 8 part-time (5 women); includes 3 minority (1 Black or African American, non-Hispanic/Latino; 2 Hispanic/Latino), 5 international. Average age 27. 96 applicants, 47% accepted, 9 enrolled. In 2018, 9 master's, 6 doctorates awarded. Terminal master's awarded for partial completion of doctoral program. *Degree requirements:* For master's, comprehensive exam, thesis or alternative; for doctorate, thesis/dissertation, general exam. *Entrance requirements:* For master's and doctorate, GRE General Test, interview, minimum GPA of 3.0. Additional exam requirements/recommendations for international students: Required—TOEFL (minimum score 550 paper-based; 80 iBT). *Application deadline:* For fall admission, 1/15 priority date for domestic and international students; for spring admission, 9/1 priority date for domestic and international students. Applications are processed on a rolling basis. Application fee: $75. Electronic applications accepted. *Financial support:* In 2018–19, 27 students received support. Fellowships, research assistantships, teaching assistantships, Federal Work-Study, and tuition waivers available. Financial award application deadline: 1/15. *Unit head:* Dr. Michael King, Chair, 202-994-6488. *Application contact:* Information Contact, 202-994-6121, E-mail: gwchem@gwu.edu.
Website: http://chemistry.columbian.gwu.edu/

Harvard University, Graduate School of Arts and Sciences, Department of Chemistry and Chemical Biology, Cambridge, MA 02138. Offers biochemical chemistry (PhD); inorganic chemistry (PhD); organic chemistry (PhD); physical chemistry (PhD). *Degree requirements:* For doctorate, thesis/dissertation, cumulative exams. *Entrance requirements:* For doctorate, GRE General Test, GRE Subject Test. Additional exam requirements/recommendations for international students: Required—TOEFL.

Howard University, Graduate School, Department of Chemistry, Washington, DC 20059-0002. Offers analytical chemistry (MS, PhD); atmospheric (MS, PhD); biochemistry (MS, PhD); environmental (MS, PhD); inorganic chemistry (MS, PhD); organic chemistry (MS, PhD); physical chemistry (MS, PhD). Terminal master's awarded for partial completion of doctoral program. *Degree requirements:* For master's, comprehensive exam, thesis, teaching experience; for doctorate, comprehensive exam, thesis/dissertation, teaching experience. *Entrance requirements:* For master's, GRE General Test, minimum GPA of 2.7; for doctorate, GRE General Test, minimum GPA of 3.0. Additional exam requirements/recommendations for international students: Required—TOEFL. Electronic applications accepted. *Faculty research:* Synthetic organics, materials, natural products, mass spectrometry.

Illinois Institute of Technology, Graduate College, College of Science, Department of Chemistry, Chicago, IL 60616. Offers analytical chemistry (MAS); chemistry (MAS, MS, PhD); materials chemistry (MAS), including inorganic, organic, or polymeric materials. *Program availability:* Part-time, evening/weekend, online learning. Terminal master's awarded for partial completion of doctoral program. *Degree requirements:* For master's, comprehensive exam, thesis (for some programs); for doctorate, comprehensive exam, thesis/dissertation. *Entrance requirements:* For master's, GRE General Test (minimum score 300 Quantitative and Verbal, 2.5 Analytical Writing), minimum undergraduate GPA of 3.0; for doctorate, GRE General Test (minimum score 310 Quantitative and Verbal, 3.0 Analytical Writing), GRE Subject Test, minimum undergraduate GPA of 3.0. Additional exam requirements/recommendations for international students: Required—TOEFL (minimum score 550 paper-based; 80 iBT); Recommended—IELTS. Electronic applications accepted. *Faculty research:* Materials science, biological chemistry, synthetic chemistry, computational chemistry, energy, sensor science and technology, scholarship of teaching and learning.

Indiana University Bloomington, University Graduate School, College of Arts and Sciences, Department of Chemistry, Bloomington, IN 47405. Offers analytical chemistry (PhD); chemical biology (PhD); chemistry (MAT); inorganic chemistry (PhD); materials chemistry (PhD); organic chemistry (PhD); physical chemistry (PhD); MSES/MS. Terminal master's awarded for partial completion of doctoral program. *Degree requirements:* For master's, thesis; for doctorate, thesis/dissertation. *Entrance requirements:* For master's and doctorate, GRE General Test, GRE Subject Test. Additional exam requirements/recommendations for international students: Required—TOEFL. Electronic applications accepted. *Faculty research:* Synthesis of complex natural products, organic reaction mechanisms, organic electrochemistry, transitive-metal chemistry, solid-state and surface chemistry.

Iowa State University of Science and Technology, Program in Inorganic Chemistry, Ames, IA 50011. Offers MS, PhD. *Entrance requirements:* Additional exam requirements/recommendations for international students: Required—TOEFL (minimum score 570 paper-based; 89 iBT), IELTS (minimum score 6.5). Electronic applications accepted.

Marquette University, Graduate School, College of Arts and Sciences, Department of Chemistry, Milwaukee, WI 53201-1881. Offers analytical chemistry (MS, PhD); bioanalytical chemistry (MS, PhD); biophysical chemistry (MS, PhD); chemical physics (MS, PhD); inorganic chemistry (MS, PhD); organic chemistry (MS, PhD); physical chemistry (MS, PhD). *Program availability:* Part-time. Terminal master's awarded for partial completion of doctoral program. *Degree requirements:* For master's, comprehensive exam; for doctorate, thesis/dissertation, cumulative exams. *Entrance requirements:* For master's and doctorate, official transcripts from all current and previous colleges/universities except Marquette, three letters of recommendation from individuals familiar with the applicant's academic work. Additional exam requirements/recommendations for international students: Required—TOEFL. Electronic applications accepted. *Faculty research:* Inorganic complexes, laser Raman spectroscopy, organic synthesis, synthetic bioinorganic chemistry, electro-active organic molecules.

Massachusetts Institute of Technology, School of Science, Department of Chemistry, Cambridge, MA 02139. Offers biological chemistry (PhD); inorganic chemistry (PhD); organic chemistry (PhD); physical chemistry (PhD). *Degree requirements:* For doctorate, comprehensive exam, thesis/dissertation, teaching assistantship during two semesters. *Entrance requirements:* For doctorate, GRE General Test. Additional exam requirements/recommendations for international students: Required—TOEFL, IELTS. Electronic applications accepted. *Expenses: Tuition:* Full-time $51,520; part-time $800 per credit hour. *Required fees:* $312. *Faculty research:* Synthetic organic and organometallic chemistry including catalysis; biological chemistry including bioorganic chemistry; physical chemistry including chemical dynamics, theoretical chemistry and biophysical chemistry; inorganic chemistry including synthesis, catalysis, bioinorganic and physical inorganic chemistry; materials chemistry including surface science, nanoscience and polymers.

McMaster University, School of Graduate Studies, Faculty of Science, Department of Chemistry, Hamilton, ON L8S 4M2, Canada. Offers analytical chemistry (M Sc, PhD); chemical physics (M Sc, PhD); chemistry (M Sc, PhD); inorganic chemistry (M Sc, PhD); organic chemistry (M Sc, PhD); physical chemistry (M Sc, PhD); polymer chemistry (M Sc, PhD). *Program availability:* Part-time. Terminal master's awarded for partial completion of doctoral program. *Degree requirements:* For master's, thesis; for doctorate, comprehensive exam, thesis/dissertation. *Entrance requirements:* For master's, minimum B+ average. Additional exam requirements/recommendations for international students: Required—TOEFL (minimum score 550 paper-based).

Old Dominion University, College of Sciences, Program in Chemistry, Norfolk, VA 23529. Offers analytical chemistry (MS, PhD); biochemistry (MS, PhD); environmental chemistry (MS, PhD); inorganic chemistry (MS, PhD); organic chemistry (MS, PhD); physical chemistry (MS, PhD). *Program availability:* Part-time. Terminal master's awarded for partial completion of doctoral program. *Degree requirements:* For master's, comprehensive exam, thesis (for some programs); for doctorate, comprehensive exam, thesis/dissertation. *Entrance requirements:* For master's and doctorate, GRE General Test, minimum GPA of 3.0 in major, 2.5 overall, transcripts, essay, three letters of recommendation, resume. Additional exam requirements/recommendations for international students: Required—TOEFL (minimum score 84 iBT). Electronic applications accepted. *Expenses:* Contact institution. *Faculty research:* Biogeochemistry, materials chemistry, computational chemistry, organic chemistry, biofuels.

Purdue University, Graduate School, College of Science, Department of Chemistry, West Lafayette, IN 47907. Offers analytical chemistry (PhD); biochemistry (MS, PhD); chemical education (MS, PhD); inorganic chemistry (MS, PhD); organic chemistry (MS, PhD); physical chemistry (PhD). *Faculty:* 47 full-time (13 women), 2 part-time/adjunct (0 women). *Students:* 314 full-time (124 women), 18 part-time (13 women); includes 63 minority (16 Black or African American, non-Hispanic/Latino; 15 Asian, non-Hispanic/Latino; 25 Hispanic/Latino; 7 Two or more races, non-Hispanic/Latino), 146 international. Average age 26. 711 applicants, 27% accepted, 64 enrolled. In 2018, 9 master's, 50 doctorates awarded. Terminal master's awarded for partial completion of doctoral program. *Degree requirements:* For master's, thesis; for doctorate, comprehensive exam, thesis/dissertation. *Entrance requirements:* For master's and doctorate, minimum undergraduate GPA of 3.0. Additional exam requirements/recommendations for international students: Required—TOEFL (minimum score 550 paper-based; 77 iBT); Recommended—TWE. *Application deadline:* For fall admission, 2/15 priority date for domestic students, 1/1 for international students. Applications are processed on a rolling basis. Application fee: $60 ($75 for international students). Electronic applications accepted. *Financial support:* In 2018–19, 2 fellowships with partial tuition reimbursements (averaging $18,000 per year), 55 teaching assistantships with partial tuition reimbursements (averaging $18,000 per year) were awarded; research assistantships with partial tuition reimbursements and tuition waivers (partial) also available. Support available to part-time students. Financial award applicants required to submit FAFSA. *Unit head:* Christine A. Hrycyna, Head, 765-494-5203, E-mail: hrycyna@purdue.edu. *Application contact:* Betty L. Hatfield, Director of Graduate Admissions, 765-494-5208, E-mail: bettyh@purdue.edu.
Website: https://www.chem.purdue.edu/

Rice University, Graduate Programs, Wiess School of Natural Sciences, Department of Chemistry, Houston, TX 77251-1892. Offers chemistry (MA); inorganic chemistry (PhD); organic chemistry (PhD); physical chemistry (PhD). Terminal master's awarded for partial completion of doctoral program. *Degree requirements:* For master's, thesis; for doctorate, thesis/dissertation. *Entrance requirements:* For master's and doctorate, GRE General Test, minimum GPA of 3.0. Additional exam requirements/recommendations for international students: Required—TOEFL (minimum score 600 paper-based; 90 iBT). Electronic applications accepted. *Faculty research:* Nanoscience, biomaterials, nanobioinformatics, fullerene pharmaceuticals.

Rutgers University–Newark, Graduate School, Program in Chemistry, Newark, NJ 07102. Offers analytical chemistry (MS, PhD); biochemistry (MS, PhD); inorganic chemistry (MS, PhD); organic chemistry (MS, PhD); physical chemistry (MS, PhD). *Program availability:* Part-time, evening/weekend. Terminal master's awarded for partial completion of doctoral program. *Degree requirements:* For master's, thesis optional, cumulative exams; for doctorate, thesis/dissertation, exams, research proposal. *Entrance requirements:* For master's and doctorate, GRE General Test, minimum undergraduate B average. Additional exam requirements/recommendations for international students: Required—TOEFL. Electronic applications accepted. *Faculty research:* Medicinal chemistry, natural products, isotope effects, biophysics and biorganic approaches to enzyme mechanisms, organic and organometallic synthesis.

Rutgers University–New Brunswick, Graduate School-New Brunswick, Department of Chemistry and Chemical Biology, Piscataway, NJ 08854-8097. Offers biological chemistry (MS, PhD); inorganic chemistry (MS, PhD); organic chemistry (MS, PhD); physical chemistry (MS, PhD). *Program availability:* Part-time, evening/weekend. Terminal master's awarded for partial completion of doctoral program. *Degree requirements:* For master's, thesis or alternative, exam; for doctorate, thesis/dissertation, 1 year residency. *Entrance requirements:* For master's and doctorate, GRE General Test, GRE Subject Test. Additional exam requirements/recommendations for international students: Required—TOEFL. Electronic applications accepted. *Faculty research:* Biophysical organic/bioorganic, inorganic/bioinorganic, theoretical, and solid-state/surface chemistry.

Seton Hall University, College of Arts and Sciences, Department of Chemistry and Biochemistry, South Orange, NJ 07079-2697. Offers analytical chemistry (MS, PhD); biochemistry (MS, PhD); chemistry (MS); inorganic chemistry (MS, PhD); organic chemistry (MS, PhD); physical chemistry (MS, PhD). *Program availability:* Part-time, evening/weekend. Terminal master's awarded for partial completion of doctoral program. *Degree requirements:* For master's, thesis optional; for doctorate, comprehensive exam, thesis/dissertation. *Entrance requirements:* Additional exam requirements/recommendations for international students: Required—TOEFL. Electronic applications accepted. *Faculty research:* DNA metal reactions; chromatography; bioinorganic, biophysical, organometallic, polymer chemistry; heterogeneous catalyst; synthetic organic and carbohydrate chemistry.

Southern University and Agricultural and Mechanical College, Graduate School, College of Sciences and Engineering, Program in Chemistry, Baton Rouge, LA 70813. Offers analytical chemistry (MS); biochemistry (MS); environmental sciences (MS); inorganic chemistry (MS); organic chemistry (MS); physical chemistry (MS). *Degree requirements:* For master's, thesis. *Entrance requirements:* For master's, GMAT or GRE General Test. Additional exam requirements/recommendations for international students: Required—TOEFL (minimum score 525 paper-based). *Faculty research:* Synthesis of macrocyclic ligands, latex accelerators, anticancer drugs, biosensors, absorption isotheums, isolation of specific enzymes from plants.

University of Calgary, Faculty of Graduate Studies, Faculty of Science, Program in Chemistry, Calgary, AB T2N 1N4, Canada. Offers analytical chemistry (M Sc, PhD); applied chemistry (M Sc, PhD); inorganic chemistry (M Sc, PhD); organic chemistry (M Sc, PhD); physical chemistry (M Sc, PhD); polymer chemistry (M Sc, PhD); theoretical chemistry (M Sc, PhD). *Degree requirements:* For master's, thesis; for doctorate, thesis/dissertation, candidacy exam. *Entrance requirements:* For master's, minimum GPA of 3.0; for doctorate, honors B Sc degree with minimum GPA of 3.7 or M Sc with minimum GPA of 3.3. Additional exam requirements/recommendations for international students: Required—TOEFL (minimum score 580 paper-based). Electronic applications accepted. *Faculty research:* Chemical analysis, chemical dynamics, synthesis theory.

University of Cincinnati, Graduate School, McMicken College of Arts and Sciences, Department of Chemistry, Cincinnati, OH 45221. Offers analytical chemistry (MS, PhD); biochemistry (MS, PhD); inorganic chemistry (MS, PhD); organic chemistry (MS, PhD); physical chemistry (MS, PhD); polymer chemistry (MS, PhD), sensors (PhD). *Program availability:* Part-time, evening/weekend. Terminal master's awarded for partial completion of doctoral program. *Degree requirements:* For master's, thesis optional; for doctorate, comprehensive exam, thesis/dissertation. *Entrance requirements:* For master's and doctorate, GRE General Test. Additional exam requirements/recommendations for international students: Required—TOEFL (minimum score 580 paper-based). Electronic applications accepted. *Faculty research:* Biomedical chemistry, laser chemistry, surface science, chemical sensors, synthesis.

University of Louisville, Graduate School, College of Arts and Sciences, Department of Chemistry, Louisville, KY 40292-0001. Offers analytical chemistry (MS, PhD); biochemistry (MS, PhD); chemical physics (PhD); inorganic chemistry (MS, PhD); organic chemistry (MS, PhD); physical chemistry (MS, PhD). *Faculty:* 26 full-time (9 women), 3 part-time/adjunct (1 woman). *Students:* 35 full-time (14 women), 17 part-time (4 women); includes 5 minority (2 Black or African American, non-Hispanic/Latino; 3 Asian, non-Hispanic/Latino), 39 international. Average age 31. 47 applicants, 36% accepted, 10 enrolled. In 2018, 18 master's, 3 doctorates awarded. Terminal master's awarded for partial completion of doctoral program. *Degree requirements:* For master's, thesis (for some programs), Literature Seminars; for doctorate, thesis/dissertation, Cumulative Exams, Literature Seminars; Research. *Entrance requirements:* For master's and doctorate, GRE General Test, official transcripts, recommendation letters (minimum of 2), personal statement. Additional exam requirements/recommendations for international students: Required—TOEFL (minimum score 550 paper-based; 79 iBT), IELTS can be taken in place of TOEFL; Recommended—IELTS (minimum score 6.5). *Application deadline:* For fall admission, 1/15 priority date for domestic and international students; for spring admission, 9/15 priority date for domestic and international students. Application fee: $65. Electronic applications accepted. *Expenses: Tuition, area resident:* Full-time $6500; part-time $723 per credit hour. Tuition, state resident: full-time $6500. Tuition, nonresident: full-time $13,557; part-time $1507 per credit hour. Tuition and fees vary according to course load and program. *Financial support:* In 2018–19, 59 students received support, including 2 fellowships with full tuition reimbursements available (averaging $23,000 per year), 10 research assistantships with full tuition reimbursements available (averaging $23,000 per year), 41 teaching assistantships with full tuition reimbursements available (averaging $23,000 per year); scholarships/grants, health care benefits, and unspecified assistantships also available. Financial award application deadline: 1/15. *Faculty research:* Solid state chemistry, chemical synthesis, nanoparticle research, green chemistry, spectroscopic studies, computational chemistry, catalysis. *Total annual research expenditures:* $1 million. *Unit head:* Dr. Craig Grapperhaus, Professor, 502-852-8148, Fax: 502-852-8149, E-mail: craig.grapperhaus@louisville.edu.

Inorganic Chemistry

Application contact: Sherry Nalley, Graduate Program Assistant, 502-852-6798, Fax: 502-852-6536, E-mail: sherry.nalley@louisville.edu.
Website: http://louisville.edu/chemistry

The University of Manchester, School of Chemistry, Manchester, United Kingdom. Offers biological chemistry (PhD); chemistry (M Ent, M Phil, M Sc, D Ent, PhD); inorganic chemistry (PhD); materials chemistry (PhD); nanoscience (PhD); nuclear fission (PhD); organic chemistry (PhD); physical chemistry (PhD); theoretical chemistry (PhD).

University of Maryland, College Park, Academic Affairs, College of Computer, Mathematical and Natural Sciences, Department of Chemistry and Biochemistry, Chemistry Program, College Park, MD 20742. Offers analytical chemistry (MS, PhD); inorganic chemistry (MS, PhD); organic chemistry (MS, PhD); physical chemistry (MS, PhD). *Program availability:* Part-time, evening/weekend. Terminal master's awarded for partial completion of doctoral program. *Degree requirements:* For master's, thesis optional; for doctorate, thesis/dissertation, 2 seminar presentations, oral exam. *Entrance requirements:* For master's and doctorate, GRE General Test, GRE Subject Test (recommended), minimum GPA of 3.0, 3 letters of recommendation. Additional exam requirements/recommendations for international students: Required—TOEFL. Electronic applications accepted. *Faculty research:* Environmental chemistry, nuclear chemistry, lunar and environmental analysis, X-ray crystallography.

University of Massachusetts Lowell, College of Sciences, Department of Chemistry, Lowell, MA 01854. Offers analytical chemistry (PhD); biochemistry (PhD); chemistry (MS, PhD); environmental studies (PhD); green chemistry (PhD); inorganic chemistry (PhD); organic chemistry (PhD); polymer science (MS). Terminal master's awarded for partial completion of doctoral program. *Degree requirements:* For master's, thesis; for doctorate, 2 foreign languages, thesis/dissertation. *Entrance requirements:* For master's and doctorate, GRE General Test. Electronic applications accepted.

University of Memphis, Graduate School, College of Arts and Sciences, Department of Chemistry, Memphis, TN 38152. Offers analytical chemistry (MS, PhD); computational chemistry (MS, PhD); inorganic chemistry (MS, PhD); organic chemistry (MS, PhD); physical chemistry (MS, PhD). *Program availability:* Part-time. *Students:* 37 full-time (11 women), 14 part-time (5 women); includes 9 minority (2 Black or African American, non-Hispanic/Latino; 3 Asian, non-Hispanic/Latino; 4 Two or more races, non-Hispanic/Latino), 6 international. Average age 27. 24 applicants, 67% accepted, 14 enrolled. In 2018, 9 master's, 3 doctorates awarded. Terminal master's awarded for partial completion of doctoral program. *Degree requirements:* For master's, comprehensive exam, thesis or alternative; for doctorate, comprehensive exam, thesis/dissertation. *Entrance requirements:* For master's and doctorate, GRE General Test, admission to Graduate School plus 32 undergraduate hours in chemistry. Additional exam requirements/recommendations for international students: Required—TOEFL (minimum score 550 paper-based). *Application deadline:* For fall admission, 7/1 for domestic students, 5/1 for international students; for winter admission, 9/15 for international students; for spring admission, 12/1 for domestic students. Applications are processed on a rolling basis. Application fee: $35 ($60 for international students). Electronic applications accepted. *Expenses: Tuition, area resident:* Full-time $10,240; part-time $503 per credit hour. Tuition, state resident: full-time $10,464. Tuition, nonresident: full-time $20,224; part-time $991 per credit hour. *Required fees:* $850; $106 per credit hour. *Financial support:* Research assistantships with full tuition reimbursements, teaching assistantships with full tuition reimbursements, Federal Work-Study, scholarships/grants, and unspecified assistantships available. Financial award application deadline: 2/1; financial award applicants required to submit FAFSA. *Faculty research:* Computational chemistry, materials chemistry, organic/polymer synthesis, drug design/delivery, water chemistry. *Unit head:* Dr. Gary Emmert, Chair, 901-678-2638, Fax: 901-678-3447, E-mail: gemmert@memphis.edu. *Application contact:* Dr. Paul Simone, Coordinator of Graduate Studies, 901-678-3671, Fax: 901-678-3447, E-mail: gradchem@memphis.edu.
Website: http://www.memphis.edu/chem/

University of Miami, Graduate School, College of Arts and Sciences, Department of Chemistry, Coral Gables, FL 33124. Offers chemistry (MS); inorganic chemistry (PhD); organic chemistry (PhD); physical chemistry (PhD). Terminal master's awarded for partial completion of doctoral program. *Degree requirements:* For master's, comprehensive exam; for doctorate, comprehensive exam, thesis/dissertation. *Entrance requirements:* For master's and doctorate, GRE General Test. Additional exam requirements/recommendations for international students: Required—TOEFL (minimum score 550 paper-based). Electronic applications accepted. *Faculty research:* Supramolecular chemistry, electrochemistry, surface chemistry, catalysis, organometalic.

University of Michigan, Rackham Graduate School, College of Literature, Science, and the Arts, Department of Chemistry, Ann Arbor, MI 48109-1055. Offers analytical chemistry (PhD); chemical biology (PhD); chemical sciences (MS); inorganic chemistry (PhD); materials chemistry (PhD); organic chemistry (PhD); physical chemistry (PhD). *Program availability:* Part-time. *Faculty:* 40 full-time (14 women), 7 part-time/adjunct (3 women). *Students:* 262 full-time (112 women), 4 part-time (all women); includes 44 minority (11 Black or African American, non-Hispanic/Latino; 11 Asian, non-Hispanic/Latino; 19 Hispanic/Latino; 1 Native Hawaiian or other Pacific Islander, non-Hispanic/Latino; 2 Two or more races, non-Hispanic/Latino), 61 international. 692 applicants, 71 enrolled. In 2018, 47 master's, 46 doctorates awarded. *Degree requirements:* For doctorate, comprehensive exam, thesis/dissertation, oral defense of dissertation, organic cumulative proficiency exams. *Entrance requirements:* For master's, bachelor's degree, 3 letters of recommendation, personal statement; for doctorate, bachelor's degree, 3 letters of recommendation, personal statement, curriculum vitae/resume. Additional exam requirements/recommendations for international students: Required—TOEFL (minimum score 560 paper-based; 84 iBT) or IELTS. *Application deadline:* For fall admission, 12/1 for domestic and international students. Application fee: $0 ($90 for international students). Electronic applications accepted. *Financial support:* In 2018–19, 269 students received support, including 50 fellowships with full tuition reimbursements available (averaging $31,625 per year), 84 research assistantships with full tuition reimbursements available (averaging $31,625 per year), 133 teaching assistantships with full tuition reimbursements available (averaging $31,625 per year); career-related internships or fieldwork, Federal Work-Study, scholarships/grants, traineeships, health care benefits, tuition waivers (full), and unspecified assistantships also available. *Faculty research:* Biological catalysis, protein engineering, chemical sensors, de novo metalloprotein design, supramolecular architecture. *Total annual research expenditures:* $19.6 million. *Unit head:* Dr. Robert Kennedy, Professor of Chemistry/Chair, 734-763-9681, Fax: 734-647-4847. *Application contact:* Elizabeth Oxford, Graduate Program Coordinator, 734-764-7278, Fax: 734-647-4865, E-mail: chemadmissions@umich.edu.
Website: http://www.lsa.umich.edu/chem/

University of Missouri–Kansas City, College of Arts and Sciences, Department of Chemistry, Kansas City, MO 64110-2499. Offers analytical chemistry (PhD); inorganic chemistry (PhD); organic chemistry (PhD); physical chemistry (PhD); polymer chemistry (MS, PhD). PhD (interdisciplinary) offered through the School of Graduate Studies. *Program availability:* Part-time, evening/weekend. *Degree requirements:* For master's, thesis (for some programs); for doctorate, thesis/dissertation. *Entrance requirements:* For master's, equivalent of American Chemical Society approved bachelor's degree in chemistry; for doctorate, GRE General Test, equivalent of American Chemical Society approved bachelor's degree in chemistry. Additional exam requirements/recommendations for international students: Required—TOEFL (minimum score 550 paper-based; 80 iBT), TWE. Electronic applications accepted. *Faculty research:* Molecular spectroscopy, characterization and synthesis of materials and compounds, computational chemistry, natural products, drug delivery systems and anti-tumor agents.

University of Montana, Graduate School, College of Humanities and Sciences, Department of Chemistry and Biochemistry, Missoula, MT 59812. Offers chemistry (MS, PhD), including environmental/analytical chemistry, inorganic chemistry, organic chemistry, physical chemistry. Terminal master's awarded for partial completion of doctoral program. *Degree requirements:* For master's, thesis (for some programs); for doctorate, thesis/dissertation. *Entrance requirements:* For master's and doctorate, GRE General Test. Additional exam requirements/recommendations for international students: Required—TOEFL (minimum score 575 paper-based). *Faculty research:* Reaction mechanisms and kinetics, inorganic and organic synthesis, analytical chemistry, natural products.

University of Nebraska–Lincoln, Graduate College, College of Arts and Sciences, Department of Chemistry, Lincoln, NE 68588. Offers analytical chemistry (PhD); biochemistry (PhD); chemistry (MS); inorganic chemistry (PhD); materials chemistry (PhD); organic chemistry (PhD); physical chemistry (PhD). *Degree requirements:* For master's, one foreign language, thesis optional, departmental qualifying exam; for doctorate, one foreign language, comprehensive exam, thesis/dissertation, departmental qualifying exams. *Entrance requirements:* For master's and doctorate, GRE. Additional exam requirements/recommendations for international students: Required—TOEFL (minimum score 550 paper-based). Electronic applications accepted. *Faculty research:* Bioorganic and bioinorganic chemistry, biophysical and bioanalytical chemistry, structure-function of DNA and proteins, organometallics, mass spectrometry.

University of Notre Dame, The Graduate School, College of Science, Department of Chemistry and Biochemistry, Notre Dame, IN 46556. Offers biochemistry (MS, PhD); inorganic chemistry (MS, PhD); organic chemistry (MS, PhD); physical chemistry (MS, PhD). Terminal master's awarded for partial completion of doctoral program. *Degree requirements:* For master's, comprehensive exam, thesis; for doctorate, thesis/dissertation, qualifying exam. *Entrance requirements:* For master's and doctorate, GRE General Test, GRE Subject Test (strongly recommended). Additional exam requirements/recommendations for international students: Required—TOEFL (minimum score 600 paper-based; 80 iBT). Electronic applications accepted. *Faculty research:* Reaction design and mechanistic studies; reactive intermediates; synthesis, structure and reactivity of organometallic cluster complexes and biologically active natural products; bioorganic chemistry; enzymology.

University of Oklahoma, College of Arts and Sciences, Department of Chemistry and Biochemistry, Norman, OK 73019. Offers chemistry (MS, PhD), including analytical chemistry, biochemistry, chemical education, inorganic chemistry, inter-and/or multidisciplinary, organic chemistry, physical chemistry, structural biology. *Program availability:* Part-time. *Faculty:* 32 full-time (13 women). *Students:* 89 full-time (38 women), 33 part-time (15 women); includes 22 minority (2 Black or African American, non-Hispanic/Latino; 9 Asian, non-Hispanic/Latino; 6 Hispanic/Latino; 5 Two or more races, non-Hispanic/Latino), 46 international. Average age 26. 78 applicants, 71% accepted, 33 enrolled. In 2018, 15 master's, 21 doctorates awarded. Terminal master's awarded for partial completion of doctoral program. *Degree requirements:* For master's, comprehensive exam (for some programs), thesis (for some programs); for doctorate, comprehensive exam, thesis/dissertation, general exam. *Entrance requirements:* For master's and doctorate, GRE. Additional exam requirements/recommendations for international students: Required—TOEFL (minimum score 79 iBT) or IELTS (minimum score 6.5). *Application deadline:* For fall admission, 3/31 priority date for domestic and international students; for spring admission, 9/1 priority date for domestic and international students. Application fee: $50 ($100 for international students). Electronic applications accepted. *Expenses:* Tuition, state resident: full-time $5683.20; part-time $236.80 per credit hour. Tuition, nonresident: full-time $20,342; part-time $847.60 per credit hour. *International tuition:* $20,342.40 full-time. *Required fees:* $2894.20; $110.05 per credit hour. $126.50 per semester. Tuition and fees vary according to course load and program. *Financial support:* Research assistantships, teaching assistantships, institutionally sponsored loans, scholarships/grants, health care benefits, unspecified assistantships, and full tuition with qualifying graduate assistantship available. Support available to part-time students. Financial award application deadline: 6/1; financial award applicants required to submit FAFSA. *Faculty research:* Structural biology, solid state materials, natural products, membrane biochemistry, bioanalysis. *Unit head:* Dr. Ronald L. Halterman, Professor and Chair, 405-325-4812, Fax: 405-325-6111, E-mail: rhalterman@ou.edu. *Application contact:* Carol Jones, Operations Manager, 405-325-4811, Fax: 405-325-6111, E-mail: caroljones@ou.edu.
Website: http://www.ou.edu/cas/chemistry

University of Regina, Faculty of Graduate Studies and Research, Faculty of Science, Department of Chemistry and Biochemistry, Regina, SK S4S 0A2, Canada. Offers biophysics of biological interfaces (M Sc, PhD); computational chemistry (M Sc, PhD); environmental analytical chemistry (M Sc, PhD); enzymology/chemical biology (M Sc, PhD); inorganic/organometallic chemistry (M Sc, PhD); signal transduction and mechanisms of cancer cell regulation (M Sc, PhD); supramolecular organic photochemistry and photophysics (M Sc, PhD); synthetic organic chemistry (M Sc, PhD). *Program availability:* Part-time. *Faculty:* 12 full-time (2 women), 4 part-time/adjunct (0 women). *Students:* 12 full-time (6 women), 1 part-time (0 women). Average age 30. 23 applicants, 17% accepted. In 2018, 2 master's awarded. *Degree requirements:* For master's, thesis; for doctorate, comprehensive exam, thesis/dissertation. *Entrance requirements:* For master's, 4 years Bachelor degree in Chemistry or related program; for doctorate, completion of Master's in Chemistry. Additional exam requirements/recommendations for international students: Required—TOEFL (minimum score 580 paper-based; 80 iBT), IELTS (minimum score 6.5), PTE (minimum score 59), other options are CAEL, MELAB, Cantest and U of R ESL. *Application deadline:* Applications are processed on a rolling basis. Application fee: $100. Electronic applications accepted. Tuition and fees vary according to course level, course load, degree level and program. *Financial support:* Fellowships, research assistantships, teaching assistantships, career-related internships or fieldwork, Federal Work-Study, scholarships/grants, unspecified assistantships, and travel award & Graduate Scholarship Base Funds available. Support available to part-time students. Financial award application deadline: 9/30. *Faculty research:* Asymmetric synthesis and methodology, theoretical and computational chemistry, biophysical biochemistry, analytical and environmental chemistry, chemical biology. *Unit head:* Dr. Renata Raina-Fulton, Department Head, 306-585-4012, Fax: 306-337-2409, E-mail: renata.raina@uregina.ca. *Application contact:* Dr. Brian Sterenberg, Graduate Program Coordinator, 306-585-4106, Fax: 306-337-2409, E-mail: brian.sterenberg@uregina.ca.
Website: http://www.uregina.ca/science/chem-biochem/

University of Rochester, School of Arts and Sciences, Department of Chemistry, Rochester, NY 14627. Offers inorganic chemistry (PhD); organic chemistry (PhD); physical chemistry (PhD). *Faculty:* 17 full-time (5 women). *Students:* 91 full-time (42 women); includes 10 minority (1 Black or African American, non-Hispanic/Latino; 2 Asian, non-Hispanic/Latino; 7 Hispanic/Latino), 24 international. Average age 27. 247 applicants, 25% accepted, 16 enrolled. In 2018, 9 doctorates awarded. Terminal master's awarded for partial completion of doctoral program. *Degree requirements:* For doctorate, thesis/dissertation, qualifying exam. *Entrance requirements:* For doctorate, GRE General Test, GRE Subject Test (recommended), transcripts, three letters of recommendation. Additional exam requirements/recommendations for international students: Required—TOEFL (minimum score 100 iBT), IELTS (minimum score 6.5). *Application deadline:* For fall admission, 12/15 for domestic and international students. Electronic applications accepted. *Expenses: Tuition:* Full-time $52,974; part-time $1654 per credit hour. *Required fees:* $612. One-time fee: $30 part-time. Tuition and fees vary according to campus/location and program. *Financial support:* In 2018–19, 34 students received support, including 13 research assistantships (averaging $26,000 per year), 4 teaching assistantships (averaging $26,000 per year); Federal Work-Study, scholarships/grants, and tuition waivers (full) also available. Financial award application deadline: 12/15. *Faculty research:* Organic chemistry, physical chemistry, theoretical chemistry, biological chemistry, materials chemistry. *Total annual research expenditures:* $4.2 million. *Unit head:* Todd D. Krauss, Chair, 585-275-5093, E-mail: todd.krauss@rochester.edu. *Application contact:* Robin Clark, Administrative Assistant, 585-275-0635, E-mail: robin.clark@rochester.edu.
Website: http://www.sas.rochester.edu/chm/graduate/index.html

The University of Tennessee, Graduate School, College of Arts and Sciences, Department of Chemistry, Knoxville, TN 37996. Offers analytical chemistry (MS, PhD); chemical physics (PhD); environmental chemistry (MS, PhD); inorganic chemistry (MS, PhD); organic chemistry (MS, PhD); physical chemistry (MS, PhD); polymer chemistry (MS, PhD); theoretical chemistry (PhD). *Program availability:* Part-time. Terminal master's awarded for partial completion of doctoral program. *Degree requirements:* For master's, thesis; for doctorate, thesis/dissertation. *Entrance requirements:* For master's and doctorate, GRE General Test, minimum GPA of 2.7. Additional exam requirements/recommendations for international students: Required—TOEFL. Electronic applications accepted.

The University of Texas at Austin, Graduate School, College of Natural Sciences, Department of Chemistry and Biochemistry, Austin, TX 78712-1111. Offers analytical chemistry (PhD); biochemistry (PhD); inorganic chemistry (PhD); organic chemistry (PhD); physical chemistry (PhD). *Entrance requirements:* For doctorate, GRE General Test.

The University of Toledo, College of Graduate Studies, College of Natural Sciences and Mathematics, Department of Chemistry, Toledo, OH 43606-3390. Offers analytical chemistry (MS, PhD); biological chemistry (MS, PhD); inorganic chemistry (MS, PhD); organic chemistry (MS, PhD); physical chemistry (MS, PhD). *Program availability:* Part-time. *Degree requirements:* For master's, thesis or alternative; for doctorate, thesis/dissertation. *Entrance requirements:* For master's and doctorate, GRE General Test, GRE Subject Test, minimum cumulative point-hour ratio of 2.7 for all previous academic work, three letters of recommendation, statement of purpose, transcripts from all prior institutions attended. Additional exam requirements/recommendations for international students: Required—TOEFL (minimum score 550 paper-based; 80 iBT). Electronic applications accepted. *Faculty research:* Enzymology, materials chemistry, crystallography, theoretical chemistry.

Virginia Commonwealth University, Graduate School, College of Humanities and Sciences, Department of Chemistry, Richmond, VA 23284-9005. Offers analytical chemistry (MS, PhD); chemical physics (PhD); inorganic chemistry (MS, PhD); organic chemistry (MS, PhD); physical chemistry (MS, PhD). *Program availability:* Part-time. Terminal master's awarded for partial completion of doctoral program. *Degree requirements:* For master's, thesis; for doctorate, thesis/dissertation, comprehensive cumulative exams, research proposal. *Entrance requirements:* For master's, GRE General Test, 30 undergraduate credits in chemistry; for doctorate, GRE General Test. Additional exam requirements/recommendations for international students: Required—TOEFL (minimum score 600 paper-based; 100 iBT) or IELTS (minimum score 6.5). Electronic applications accepted. *Faculty research:* Physical, organic, inorganic, analytical, and polymer chemistry; chemical physics.

Wake Forest University, Graduate School of Arts and Sciences, Department of Chemistry, Winston-Salem, NC 27109. Offers analytical chemistry (MS, PhD); inorganic chemistry (MS, PhD); organic chemistry (MS, PhD); physical chemistry (MS, PhD). *Program availability:* Part-time. *Degree requirements:* For master's, one foreign language, comprehensive exam, thesis; for doctorate, 2 foreign languages, comprehensive exam, thesis/dissertation. *Entrance requirements:* For master's and doctorate, GRE General Test. Additional exam requirements/recommendations for international students: Required—TOEFL. Electronic applications accepted.

Wesleyan University, Graduate Studies, Department of Chemistry, Middletown, CT 06459. Offers biochemistry (PhD); chemical physics (PhD); inorganic chemistry (PhD); organic chemistry (PhD); physical chemistry (PhD); theoretical chemistry (PhD). *Faculty:* 11 full-time (3 women), 1 part-time/adjunct (0 women). *Students:* 16 full-time (9 women). Average age 25. In 2018, 4 doctorates awarded. Terminal master's awarded for partial completion of doctoral program. *Degree requirements:* For doctorate, thesis/dissertation. *Entrance requirements:* For doctorate, GRE General Test, 3 recommendations. Additional exam requirements/recommendations for international students: Required—TOEFL, IELTS. *Application deadline:* 1/1 for domestic and international students; for summer admission, 1/1 for domestic and international students. Application fee: $0. Electronic applications accepted. *Financial support:* In 2018–19, 15 students received support, including 4 research assistantships with full tuition reimbursements available, 13 teaching assistantships with full tuition reimbursements available; institutionally sponsored loans and health care benefits also available. Financial award application deadline: 4/30. *Faculty research:* The synthesis of noble metal and noble metal alloy nanoparticles with well-defined shapes and catalytically-active high-energy surfaces; inorganic chemistry; materials science; scanning electron microscopy (SEM);transition organometallic complexes. *Unit head:* Michael A. Calter, Chair, 860-685-2633 Ext. 2633, Fax: 860-685-2211, E-mail: mcalter@wesleyan.edu. *Application contact:* Aracely Suto, Administrative Assistant, 860-685-2572, Fax: 860-685-2211, E-mail: chemistry@wesleyan.edu.
Website: http://www.wesleyan.edu/chem/

Yale University, Graduate School of Arts and Sciences, Department of Chemistry, New Haven, CT 06520. Offers biophysical chemistry (PhD); inorganic chemistry (PhD); organic chemistry (PhD); physical and theoretical chemistry (PhD). *Degree requirements:* For doctorate, thesis/dissertation. *Entrance requirements:* For doctorate, GRE General Test, GRE Subject Test. Additional exam requirements/recommendations for international students: Required—TOEFL.

Youngstown State University, College of Graduate Studies, College of Science, Technology, Engineering and Mathematics, Department of Chemistry, Youngstown, OH 44555-0001. Offers analytical chemistry (MS); biochemistry (MS); chemistry education (MS); inorganic chemistry (MS); organic chemistry (MS); physical chemistry (MS). *Program availability:* Part-time. *Degree requirements:* For master's, thesis. *Entrance requirements:* For master's, bachelor's degree in chemistry, minimum GPA of 2.7. Additional exam requirements/recommendations for international students: Required—TOEFL. *Faculty research:* Analysis of antioxidants, chromatography, defects and disorder in crystalline oxides, hydrogen bonding, novel organic and organometallic materials.

Organic Chemistry

Auburn University, Graduate School, College of Sciences and Mathematics, Department of Chemistry and Biochemistry, Auburn University, AL 36849. Offers analytical chemistry (MS, PhD); biochemistry (MS, PhD); inorganic chemistry (MS, PhD); organic chemistry (PhD); physical chemistry (MS, PhD). *Program availability:* Part-time. *Degree requirements:* For master's, thesis (for some programs); for doctorate, thesis/dissertation, oral and written exams. *Entrance requirements:* For master's and doctorate, GRE General Test. Electronic applications accepted. *Expenses:* Tuition, state resident: full-time $11,282; part-time $535 per credit hour. Tuition, nonresident: full-time $30,542; part-time $1605 per credit hour. *Required fees:* $826 per semester. Tuition and fees vary according to degree level and program.

Boston College, Morrissey Graduate School of Arts and Sciences, Department of Chemistry, Chestnut Hill, MA 02467-3800. Offers biochemistry (PhD); inorganic chemistry (PhD); organic chemistry (PhD); physical chemistry (PhD); science education (MST). *Degree requirements:* For doctorate, thesis/dissertation, qualifying exam. *Entrance requirements:* For doctorate, GRE General Test, GRE Subject Test. Additional exam requirements/recommendations for international students: Required—TOEFL (minimum score 600 paper-based; 100 iBT), IELTS (minimum score 8). Electronic applications accepted. *Faculty research:* Organic and organometallic chemistry, chemical biology and biochemistry, physical and theoretical chemistry, inorganic chemistry.

Brandeis University, Graduate School of Arts and Sciences, Department of Chemistry, Waltham, MA 02454-9110. Offers inorganic chemistry (MA, MS, PhD); organic chemistry (MA, MS, PhD); physical chemistry (MS, PhD). *Program availability:* Part-time. *Faculty:* 13 full-time (5 women), 3 part-time/adjunct (0 women). *Students:* 33 full-time (12 women); includes 5 minority (3 Black or African American, non-Hispanic/Latino; 2 Hispanic/Latino), 19 international. Average age 26. 91 applicants, 41% accepted, 9 enrolled. In 2018, 3 master's, 8 doctorates awarded. Terminal master's awarded for partial completion of doctoral program. *Degree requirements:* For master's, comprehensive exam, thesis (for some programs); for doctorate, comprehensive exam, thesis/dissertation. *Entrance requirements:* For master's and doctorate, GRE General Test; GRE Subject Test (recommended), resume, statement of purpose, letters of recommendation, transcripts. Additional exam requirements/recommendations for international students: Required—TOEFL, IELTS, PTE. *Application deadline:* For fall admission, 12/15 priority date for domestic students. Applications are processed on a rolling basis. Application fee: $75. Electronic applications accepted. *Financial support:* In 2018–19, 21 fellowships with full tuition reimbursements (averaging $30,000 per year), 13 research assistantships with full tuition reimbursements (averaging $30,000 per year), 23 teaching assistantships with full tuition reimbursements (averaging $6,400 per year) were awarded; scholarships/grants, health care benefits, and tuition waivers (full and partial) also available. Support available to part-time students. *Faculty research:* Inorganic and organic chemistry, physical chemistry, chemical biology, biophysical chemistry, materials chemistry. *Unit head:* Dr. Klaus Schmidt-Rohr, Director of Graduate Study, 781-736-2520, E-mail: srohr@brandeis.edu. *Application contact:* Maryanna Aldrich, Administrator, 781-736-2352, E-mail: scigradoffice@brandeis.edu.
Website: http://www.brandeis.edu/gsas/programs/chemistry.html

Cleveland State University, College of Graduate Studies, College of Sciences and Health Professions, Department of Chemistry, Cleveland, OH 44115. Offers clinical chemistry (PhD), including cellular and molecular medicine, clinical/bioanalytical chemistry; organic chemistry (MS); physical chemistry (MS). *Program availability:* Part-time, evening/weekend. *Faculty:* 17 full-time (3 women). *Students:* 55 full-time (30 women), 16 part-time (10 women); includes 4 minority (3 Black or African American, non-Hispanic/Latino; 1 Asian, non-Hispanic/Latino), 38 international. Average age 30. 63 applicants, 63% accepted, 11 enrolled. In 2018, 3 master's, 15 doctorates awarded. *Entrance requirements:* For master's and doctorate, GRE General Test. Additional exam requirements/recommendations for international students: Required—TOEFL (minimum score 550 paper-based; 78 iBT). *Application deadline:* Applications are processed on a rolling basis. Application fee: $40. Electronic applications accepted. *Expenses:* Tuition, state resident: full-time $7232.55; part-time $6676 per credit hour. Tuition, nonresident: full-time $12,375. *International tuition:* $18,914 full-time. *Required fees:* $80; $80 $40. Tuition and fees vary according to program. *Financial support:* In 2018–19, 44 students received support. Fellowships, research assistantships, teaching assistantships, scholarships/grants, and unspecified assistantships available. Financial award application deadline: 1/15. *Faculty research:* Bioanalytical techniques and molecular diagnostics, glycoproteomics and antithrombotic agents, drug discovery and innovation, analytical pharmacology, inflammatory disease research. *Total annual research expenditures:* $3 million. *Unit head:* Dr. David W. Ball, Chair, 216-687-2467, Fax: 216-687-9298, E-mail: d.ball@csuohio.edu. *Application contact:* Richelle P. Emery, Administrative Coordinator, 216-687-2457, Fax: 216-687-9298, E-mail: r.emery@csuohio.edu.
Website: http://www.csuohio.edu/sciences/chemistry

Cornell University, Graduate School, Graduate Fields of Arts and Sciences, Field of Chemistry and Chemical Biology, Ithaca, NY 14853. Offers analytical chemistry (PhD);

bio-organic chemistry (PhD); biophysical chemistry (PhD); chemical biology (PhD); chemical physics (PhD); inorganic chemistry (PhD); materials chemistry (PhD); organic chemistry (PhD); organometallic chemistry (PhD); physical chemistry (PhD); polymer chemistry (PhD); theoretical chemistry (PhD). *Degree requirements:* For doctorate, comprehensive exam, thesis/dissertation. *Entrance requirements:* For doctorate, GRE General Test, GRE Subject Test (chemistry), 3 letters of recommendation. Additional exam requirements/recommendations for international students: Required—TOEFL (minimum score 600 paper-based; 77 iBT). Electronic applications accepted. *Faculty research:* Analytical, organic, inorganic, physical, materials, chemical biology.

Eastern New Mexico University, Graduate School, College of Liberal Arts and Sciences, Department of Physical Sciences, Portales, NM 88130. Offers chemistry (MS), including analytical chemistry, biochemistry, organic chemistry, physical chemistry. *Program availability:* Part-time. *Degree requirements:* For master's, thesis optional, seminar, oral and written comprehensive exams. *Entrance requirements:* For master's, ACS placement examination, minimum GPA of 3.0; 2 letters of recommendation; personal statement of career goals; bachelor's degree with minimum of one year each of general, organic, and analytical chemistry. Additional exam requirements/recommendations for international students: Required—TOEFL (minimum score 550 paper-based; 79 iBT), IELTS (minimum score 6). Electronic applications accepted. *Expenses: Tuition, area resident:* Full-time $6776. Tuition, state resident: full-time $6776; part-time $282 per credit hour. Tuition, nonresident: full-time $8986; part-time $374 per credit hour. *Required fees:* $60 per semester. One-time fee: $25. *Faculty research:* Synfuel, electrochemistry, protein chemistry.

Florida State University, The Graduate School, Department of Anthropology, Department of Chemistry and Biochemistry, Tallahassee, FL 32306-4390. Offers analytical chemistry (MS, PhD); biochemistry (MS, PhD); inorganic chemistry (MS, PhD); materials chemistry (PhD); organic chemistry (MS, PhD); physical chemistry (MS, PhD). *Faculty:* 29 full-time (4 women). *Students:* 159 full-time (57 women), 2 part-time (1 woman); includes 73 minority (9 Black or African American, non-Hispanic/Latino; 46 Asian, non-Hispanic/Latino; 9 Hispanic/Latino; 3 Native Hawaiian or other Pacific Islander, non-Hispanic/Latino; 6 Two or more races, non-Hispanic/Latino). Average age 26. 215 applicants, 49% accepted, 35 enrolled. In 2018, 33 master's, 30 doctorates awarded. Terminal master's awarded for partial completion of doctoral program. *Degree requirements:* For master's, thesis (for some programs); for doctorate, thesis/dissertation. *Entrance requirements:* For master's and doctorate, GRE General Test (minimum scores: 150 verbal, 151 quantitative), minimum upper-division GPA of 3.1 in undergraduate course work. Additional exam requirements/recommendations for international students: Required—TOEFL (minimum score 80 iBT). *Application deadline:* For fall admission, 12/15 priority date for domestic and international students. Applications are processed on a rolling basis. Application fee: $30. Electronic applications accepted. *Expenses: Tuition, area resident:* Part-time $479.32 per credit hour. Tuition and fees vary according to campus/location and program. *Financial support:* In 2018–19, 163 students received support, including 4 fellowships with full tuition reimbursements available (averaging $24,241 per year), 59 research assistantships with full tuition reimbursements available (averaging $24,241 per year), 102 teaching assistantships with full tuition reimbursements available (averaging $24,241 per year). Financial award application deadline: 12/15; financial award applicants required to submit FAFSA. *Faculty research:* Bioanalytical chemistry, separations, microfluidics, petroleomics; materials chemistry, solid state materials, magnets, polymers, catalysts, advanced spectroscopic methods, NMR and EPR, ultrafast, Raman, and mass spectrometry; organic synthesis, natural products, photochemistry, and supramolecular chemistry; biochemistry, structural biology, metabolomics, and anticancer drugs; nanochemistry, applications in energy, sustainability, biology, and technology development; radiochemistry. *Total annual research expenditures:* $7.1 million. *Unit head:* Dr. Geoffrey Strouse, Chairman, 850-644-1244, Fax: 850-644-8281, E-mail: gradinfo@chem.fsu.edu. *Application contact:* Dr. Wei Yang, Associate Chair for Graduate Studies, 850-645-6884, Fax: 850-644-8281, E-mail: gradinfo@chem.fsu.edu.
Website: http://www.chem.fsu.edu/

Georgetown University, Graduate School of Arts and Sciences, Department of Chemistry, Washington, DC 20057. Offers analytical chemistry (PhD); biochemistry (PhD); computational chemistry (PhD); inorganic chemistry (PhD); materials chemistry (PhD); organic chemistry (PhD); theoretical chemistry (PhD). Terminal master's awarded for partial completion of doctoral program. *Degree requirements:* For doctorate, comprehensive exam, thesis/dissertation. *Entrance requirements:* For doctorate, GRE General Test. Additional exam requirements/recommendations for international students: Required—TOEFL.

The George Washington University, Columbian College of Arts and Sciences, Department of Chemistry, Washington, DC 20052. Offers analytical chemistry (MS, PhD); inorganic chemistry (MS, PhD); materials science (MS, PhD); organic chemistry (MS, PhD); physical chemistry (MS, PhD). *Program availability:* Part-time, evening/weekend. *Students:* 29 full-time (15 women), 8 part-time (5 women); includes 3 minority (1 Black or African American, non-Hispanic/Latino; 2 Hispanic/Latino), 5 international. Average age 27. 96 applicants, 47% accepted, 9 enrolled. In 2018, 9 master's, 6 doctorates awarded. Terminal master's awarded for partial completion of doctoral program. *Degree requirements:* For master's, comprehensive exam, thesis or alternative; for doctorate, thesis/dissertation, general exam. *Entrance requirements:* For master's and doctorate, GRE General Test, interview, minimum GPA of 3.0. Additional exam requirements/recommendations for international students: Required—TOEFL (minimum score 550 paper-based; 80 iBT). *Application deadline:* For fall admission, 1/15 priority date for domestic and international students; for spring admission, 9/1 priority date for domestic and international students. Applications are processed on a rolling basis. Application fee: $75. Electronic applications accepted. *Financial support:* In 2018–19, 27 students received support. Fellowships, research assistantships, teaching assistantships, Federal Work-Study, and tuition waivers available. Financial award application deadline: 1/15. *Unit head:* Dr. Michael King, Chair, 202-994-6488. *Application contact:* Information Contact, 202-994-6121, E-mail: gwchem@gwu.edu.
Website: http://chemistry.columbian.gwu.edu/

Georgia State University, College of Arts and Sciences, Department of Chemistry, Atlanta, GA 30302-3083. Offers analytical chemistry (MS, PhD); biochemistry (MS, PhD); bioinformatics (MS, PhD); biophysical chemistry (PhD); computational chemistry (MS, PhD); geochemistry (PhD); organic/medicinal chemistry (MS, PhD); physical chemistry (MS). PhD in geochemistry offered jointly with Department of Geosciences. *Program availability:* Part-time. *Faculty:* 27 full-time (6 women), 1 part-time/adjunct (0 women). *Students:* 147 full-time (59 women), 15 part-time (10 women); includes 37 minority (21 Black or African American, non-Hispanic/Latino; 7 Asian, non-Hispanic/Latino; 4 Hispanic/Latino; 5 Two or more races, non-Hispanic/Latino), 84 international. Average age 29. 106 applicants, 40% accepted, 28 enrolled. In 2018, 37 master's, 13 doctorates awarded. Terminal master's awarded for partial completion of doctoral program. *Degree requirements:* For master's, one foreign language, comprehensive exam (for some programs), thesis (for some programs); for doctorate, one foreign language, comprehensive exam, thesis/dissertation. *Entrance requirements:* For master's and doctorate, GRE. *Application deadline:* For fall admission, 7/1 priority date for domestic and international students; for winter admission, 11/15 priority date for domestic and international students; for spring admission, 4/15 priority date for domestic and international students. Applications are processed on a rolling basis. Application fee: $50. Electronic applications accepted. *Expenses: Tuition, area resident:* Full-time $9360; part-time $390 per credit hour. Tuition, state resident: full-time $9360; part-time $390 per credit hour. Tuition, nonresident: full-time $30,024; part-time $1251 per credit hour. *International tuition:* $30,024 full-time. *Required fees:* $2128. *Financial support:* Fellowships with full tuition reimbursements, research assistantships with full tuition reimbursements, and teaching assistantships with full tuition reimbursements available. Financial award applicants required to submit FAFSA. *Faculty research:* Analytical chemistry, biological/biochemistry, biophysical/computational chemistry, chemical education, organic/medicinal chemistry. *Unit head:* Dr. Donald Hamelberg, Professor; Chair, 404-413-5564, Fax: 404-413-5505, E-mail: dhamelberg@gsu.edu. *Application contact:* Dr. Donald Hamelberg, Professor; Chair, 404-413-5564, Fax: 404-413-5505, E-mail: dhamelberg@gsu.edu.
Website: http://chemistry.gsu.edu/

Harvard University, Graduate School of Arts and Sciences, Department of Chemistry and Chemical Biology, Cambridge, MA 02138. Offers biochemical chemistry (PhD); inorganic chemistry (PhD); organic chemistry (PhD); physical chemistry (PhD). *Degree requirements:* For doctorate, thesis/dissertation, cumulative exams. *Entrance requirements:* For doctorate, GRE General Test, GRE Subject Test. Additional exam requirements/recommendations for international students: Required—TOEFL.

Howard University, Graduate School, Department of Chemistry, Washington, DC 20059-0002. Offers analytical chemistry (MS, PhD); atmospheric (MS, PhD); biochemistry (MS, PhD); environmental (MS, PhD); inorganic chemistry (MS, PhD); organic chemistry (MS, PhD); physical chemistry (MS, PhD). Terminal master's awarded for partial completion of doctoral program. *Degree requirements:* For master's, comprehensive exam, thesis, teaching experience; for doctorate, comprehensive exam, thesis/dissertation, teaching experience. *Entrance requirements:* For master's, GRE General Test, minimum GPA of 2.7; for doctorate, GRE General Test, minimum GPA of 3.0. Additional exam requirements/recommendations for international students: Required—TOEFL. Electronic applications accepted. *Faculty research:* Synthetic organics, materials, natural products, mass spectrometry.

Indiana University Bloomington, University Graduate School, College of Arts and Sciences, Department of Chemistry, Bloomington, IN 47405. Offers analytical chemistry (PhD); chemical biology (PhD); chemistry (MAT); inorganic chemistry (PhD); materials chemistry (PhD); organic chemistry (PhD); physical chemistry (PhD); MSES/MS. Terminal master's awarded for partial completion of doctoral program. *Degree requirements:* For master's, thesis; for doctorate, thesis/dissertation. *Entrance requirements:* For master's and doctorate, GRE General Test, GRE Subject Test. Additional exam requirements/recommendations for international students: Required—TOEFL. Electronic applications accepted. *Faculty research:* Synthesis of complex natural products, organic reaction mechanisms, organic electrochemistry, transitive-metal chemistry, solid-state and surface chemistry.

Instituto Tecnológico y de Estudios Superiores de Monterrey, Campus Monterrey, Graduate and Research Division, Program in Natural and Social Sciences, Monterrey, Mexico. Offers biotechnology (MS); chemistry (MS, PhD); communications (MS); education (MA). *Program availability:* Part-time. *Degree requirements:* For master's, one foreign language, thesis; for doctorate, one foreign language, thesis/dissertation. *Entrance requirements:* For master's, EXADEP; for doctorate, EXADEP, master's degree in related field. Additional exam requirements/recommendations for international students: Required—TOEFL. *Faculty research:* Cultural industries, mineral substances, bioremediation, food processing, CQ in industrial chemical processing.

Iowa State University of Science and Technology, Program in Organic Chemistry, Ames, IA 50011. Offers MS, PhD. *Entrance requirements:* Additional exam requirements/recommendations for international students: Required—TOEFL (minimum score 570 paper-based; 89 iBT), IELTS (minimum score 6.5). Electronic applications accepted.

Laurentian University, School of Graduate Studies and Research, Programme in Chemistry and Biochemistry, Sudbury, ON P3E 2C6, Canada. Offers analytical chemistry (M Sc); biochemistry (M Sc); environmental chemistry (M Sc); organic chemistry (M Sc); physical/theoretical chemistry (M Sc). *Program availability:* Part-time. *Degree requirements:* For master's, thesis or alternative. *Entrance requirements:* For master's, honors degree with minimum second class. *Faculty research:* Cell cycle checkpoints, kinetic modeling, toxicology to metal stress, quantum chemistry, biogeochemistry metal speciation.

Marquette University, Graduate School, College of Arts and Sciences, Department of Chemistry, Milwaukee, WI 53201-1881. Offers analytical chemistry (MS, PhD); bioanalytical chemistry (MS, PhD); biophysical chemistry (MS, PhD); chemical physics (MS, PhD); inorganic chemistry (MS, PhD); organic chemistry (MS, PhD); physical chemistry (MS, PhD). *Program availability:* Part-time. Terminal master's awarded for partial completion of doctoral program. *Degree requirements:* For master's, comprehensive exam; for doctorate, thesis/dissertation, cumulative exams. *Entrance requirements:* For master's and doctorate, official transcripts from all current and previous colleges/universities except Marquette, three letters of recommendation from individuals familiar with the applicant's academic work. Additional exam requirements/recommendations for international students: Required—TOEFL. Electronic applications accepted. *Faculty research:* Inorganic complexes, laser Raman spectroscopy, organic synthesis, synthetic bioinorganic chemistry, electro-active organic molecules.

Massachusetts Institute of Technology, School of Engineering, Department of Civil and Environmental Engineering, Cambridge, MA 02139. Offers biological oceanography (PhD, Sc D); chemical oceanography (PhD, Sc D); civil and environmental engineering (M Eng, SM, PhD, Sc D); civil and environmental systems (PhD, Sc D); civil engineering (PhD, Sc D, CE); civil engineering and computation (PhD); coastal engineering (PhD, Sc D); construction engineering and management (PhD, Sc D); environmental biology (PhD, Sc D); environmental chemistry (PhD, Sc D); environmental engineering (PhD, Sc D); environmental engineering and computation (PhD); environmental fluid mechanics (PhD, Sc D); geotechnical and geoenvironmental engineering (PhD, Sc D); hydrology (PhD, Sc D); information technology (PhD, Sc D); oceanographic engineering (PhD, Sc D); structures and materials (PhD, Sc D); transportation (PhD, Sc D); SM/MBA. *Degree requirements:* For master's, thesis; for doctorate, comprehensive exam, thesis/dissertation; for CE, comprehensive exam, thesis. *Entrance requirements:* For master's, doctorate, and CE, GRE General Test. Additional exam requirements/recommendations for international students: Required—TOEFL, IELTS. Electronic applications accepted. *Expenses: Tuition:* Full-time $51,520; part-time $800 per credit hour. *Required fees:* $312. *Faculty research:* Environmental chemistry, environmental fluid mechanics and coastal engineering, environmental microbiology, geotechnical engineering and geomechanics, hydrology and hydro climatology, infrastructure systems, mechanics of materials and structures, transportation systems.

Massachusetts Institute of Technology, School of Science, Department of Chemistry, Cambridge, MA 02139. Offers biological chemistry (PhD); inorganic chemistry (PhD); organic chemistry (PhD); physical chemistry (PhD). *Degree requirements:* For doctorate, comprehensive exam, thesis/dissertation, teaching assistantship during two semesters. *Entrance requirements:* For doctorate, GRE General Test. Additional exam requirements/recommendations for international students: Required—TOEFL, IELTS. Electronic applications accepted. *Expenses: Tuition:* Full-time $51,520; part-time $800 per credit hour. *Required fees:* $312. *Faculty research:* Synthetic organic and organometallic chemistry including catalysis; biological chemistry including bioorganic chemistry; physical chemistry including chemical dynamics, theoretical chemistry and biophysical chemistry; inorganic chemistry including synthesis, catalysis, bioinorganic and physical inorganic chemistry; materials chemistry including surface science, nanoscience and polymers.

McMaster University, School of Graduate Studies, Faculty of Science, Department of Chemistry, Hamilton, ON L8S 4M2, Canada. Offers analytical chemistry (M Sc, PhD); chemical physics (M Sc, PhD); chemistry (M Sc, PhD); inorganic chemistry (M Sc, PhD); organic chemistry (M Sc, PhD); physical chemistry (M Sc, PhD); polymer chemistry (M Sc, PhD). *Program availability:* Part-time. Terminal master's awarded for partial completion of doctoral program. *Degree requirements:* For master's, thesis; for doctorate, comprehensive exam, thesis/dissertation. *Entrance requirements:* For master's, minimum B+ average. Additional exam requirements/recommendations for international students: Required—TOEFL (minimum score 550 paper-based).

Old Dominion University, College of Sciences, Program in Chemistry, Norfolk, VA 23529. Offers analytical chemistry (MS, PhD); biochemistry (MS, PhD); environmental chemistry (MS, PhD); inorganic chemistry (MS, PhD); organic chemistry (MS, PhD); physical chemistry (MS, PhD). *Program availability:* Part-time. Terminal master's awarded for partial completion of doctoral program. *Degree requirements:* For master's, comprehensive exam, thesis (for some programs); for doctorate, comprehensive exam, thesis/dissertation. *Entrance requirements:* For master's and doctorate, GRE General Test, minimum GPA of 3.0 in major, 2.5 overall, transcripts, essay, three letters of recommendation, resume. Additional exam requirements/recommendations for international students: Required—TOEFL (minimum score 84 iBT). Electronic applications accepted. *Expenses:* Contact institution. *Faculty research:* Biogeochemistry, materials chemistry, computational chemistry, organic chemistry, biofuels.

Purdue University, Graduate School, College of Science, Department of Chemistry, West Lafayette, IN 47907. Offers analytical chemistry (PhD); biochemistry (MS, PhD); chemical education (MS, PhD); inorganic chemistry (MS, PhD); organic chemistry (MS, PhD); physical chemistry (PhD). *Faculty:* 47 full-time (13 women), 2 part-time/adjunct (0 women). *Students:* 314 full-time (124 women), 18 part-time (13 women); includes 63 minority (16 Black or African American, non-Hispanic/Latino; 15 Asian, non-Hispanic/Latino; 25 Hispanic/Latino; 7 Two or more races, non-Hispanic/Latino), 146 international. Average age 26. 711 applicants, 27% accepted, 64 enrolled. In 2018, 9 master's, 50 doctorates awarded. Terminal master's awarded for partial completion of doctoral program. *Degree requirements:* For master's, thesis; for doctorate, comprehensive exam, thesis/dissertation. *Entrance requirements:* For master's and doctorate, minimum undergraduate GPA of 3.0. Additional exam requirements/recommendations for international students: Required—TOEFL (minimum score 550 paper-based; 77 iBT); Recommended—TWE. *Application deadline:* For fall admission, 2/15 priority date for domestic students, 1/1 for international students. Applications are processed on a rolling basis. Application fee: $60 ($75 for international students). Electronic applications accepted. *Financial support:* In 2018–19, 2 fellowships with partial tuition reimbursements (averaging $18,000 per year), 55 teaching assistantships with partial tuition reimbursements (averaging $18,000 per year) were awarded; research assistantships with partial tuition reimbursements and tuition waivers (partial) also available. Support available to part-time students. Financial award applicants required to submit FAFSA. *Unit head:* Christine A. Hrycyna, Head, 765-494-5203, E-mail: hrycyna@purdue.edu. *Application contact:* Betty L. Hatfield, Director of Graduate Admissions, 765-494-5208, E-mail: bettyh@purdue.edu. Website: https://www.chem.purdue.edu/

Rice University, Graduate Programs, Wiess School of Natural Sciences, Department of Chemistry, Houston, TX 77251-1892. Offers chemistry (MA); inorganic chemistry (PhD); organic chemistry (PhD); physical chemistry (PhD). Terminal master's awarded for partial completion of doctoral program. *Degree requirements:* For master's, thesis; for doctorate, thesis/dissertation. *Entrance requirements:* For master's and doctorate, GRE General Test, minimum GPA of 3.0. Additional exam requirements/recommendations for international students: Required—TOEFL (minimum score 600 paper-based; 90 iBT). Electronic applications accepted. *Faculty research:* Nanoscience, biomaterials, nanobioinformatics, fullerene pharmaceuticals.

Rutgers University–Newark, Graduate School, Program in Chemistry, Newark, NJ 07102. Offers analytical chemistry (MS, PhD); biochemistry (MS, PhD); inorganic chemistry (MS, PhD); organic chemistry (MS, PhD); physical chemistry (MS, PhD). *Program availability:* Part-time, evening/weekend. Terminal master's awarded for partial completion of doctoral program. *Degree requirements:* For master's, thesis optional, cumulative exams; for doctorate, thesis/dissertation, exams, research proposal. *Entrance requirements:* For master's and doctorate, GRE General Test, minimum undergraduate B average. Additional exam requirements/recommendations for international students: Required—TOEFL. Electronic applications accepted. *Faculty research:* Medicinal chemistry, natural products, isotope effects, biophysics and biorganic approaches to enzyme mechanisms, organic and organometallic synthesis.

Rutgers University–New Brunswick, Graduate School-New Brunswick, Department of Chemistry and Chemical Biology, Piscataway, NJ 08854-8097. Offers biological chemistry (MS, PhD); inorganic chemistry (MS, PhD); organic chemistry (MS, PhD); physical chemistry (MS, PhD). *Program availability:* Part-time, evening/weekend. Terminal master's awarded for partial completion of doctoral program. *Degree requirements:* For master's, thesis or alternative, exam; for doctorate, thesis/dissertation, 1 year residency. *Entrance requirements:* For master's and doctorate, GRE General Test, GRE Subject Test. Additional exam requirements/recommendations for international students: Required—TOEFL. Electronic applications accepted. *Faculty research:* Biophysical organic/bioorganic, inorganic/bioinorganic, theoretical, and solid-state/surface chemistry.

Seton Hall University, College of Arts and Sciences, Department of Chemistry and Biochemistry, South Orange, NJ 07079-2697. Offers analytical chemistry (MS, PhD); biochemistry (MS, PhD); chemistry (MS); inorganic chemistry (MS, PhD); organic chemistry (MS, PhD); physical chemistry (MS, PhD). *Program availability:* Part-time, evening/weekend. Terminal master's awarded for partial completion of doctoral program. *Degree requirements:* For master's, thesis optional; for doctorate, comprehensive exam, thesis/dissertation. *Entrance requirements:* Additional exam requirements/recommendations for international students: Required—TOEFL. Electronic applications accepted. *Faculty research:* DNA metal reactions; chromatography; bioinorganic, biophysical, organometallic, polymer chemistry; heterogeneous catalyst; synthetic organic and carbohydrate chemistry.

Southern University and Agricultural and Mechanical College, Graduate School, College of Sciences and Engineering, Program in Chemistry, Baton Rouge, LA 70813. Offers analytical chemistry (MS); biochemistry (MS); environmental sciences (MS); inorganic chemistry (MS); organic chemistry (MS); physical chemistry (MS). *Degree requirements:* For master's, thesis. *Entrance requirements:* For master's, GMAT or GRE General Test. Additional exam requirements/recommendations for international students: Required—TOEFL (minimum score 525 paper-based). *Faculty research:* Synthesis of macrocyclic ligands, latex accelerators, anticancer drugs, biosensors, absorption isotheums, isolation of specific enzymes from plants.

State University of New York College of Environmental Science and Forestry, Department of Chemistry, Syracuse, NY 13210-2779. Offers biochemistry (MPS, MS, PhD); environmental chemistry (MPS, MS, PhD); organic chemistry of natural products (MPS, MS, PhD); polymer chemistry (MPS, MS, PhD). *Program availability:* Part-time. *Faculty:* 14 full-time (1 woman), 1 part-time/adjunct (0 women). *Students:* 37 full-time (14 women), 3 part-time (2 women); includes 1 minority (Asian, non-Hispanic/Latino), 13 international. Average age 28. 51 applicants, 53% accepted, 13 enrolled. In 2018, 4 master's, 5 doctorates awarded. Terminal master's awarded for partial completion of doctoral program. *Degree requirements:* For master's, thesis; for doctorate, comprehensive exam, thesis/dissertation. *Entrance requirements:* For master's and doctorate, GRE General Test, GRE Subject Test, minimum GPA of 3.0. Additional exam requirements/recommendations for international students: Required—TOEFL (minimum score 550 paper-based; 80 iBT), IELTS (minimum score 6). *Application deadline:* For fall admission, 2/1 priority date for domestic and international students; for spring admission, 11/1 priority date for domestic and international students. Applications are processed on a rolling basis. Application fee: $60. Electronic applications accepted. *Expenses: Tuition, area resident:* Full-time $11,090; part-time $462 per credit hour. Tuition, state resident: full-time $11,090; part-time $462 per credit hour. Tuition, nonresident: full-time $22,650; part-time $944 per credit hour. *International tuition:* $22,650 full-time. *Required fees:* $1733; $178.58 per credit hour. *Financial support:* In 2018–19, 13 students received support. Unspecified assistantships available. Financial award application deadline: 6/30; financial award applicants required to submit FAFSA. *Faculty research:* Polymer chemistry, biochemistry, environmental chemistry, natural products chemistry. *Total annual research expenditures:* $1.3 million. *Unit head:* Dr. Avik Chatterrjee, Chair, 315-470-4747, Fax: 315-470-6855, E-mail: achatter@esf.edu. *Application contact:* Scott Shannon, Associate Provost for Instruction/Dean of the Graduate School, 315-470-6599, Fax: 315-470-6978, E-mail: sshannon@esf.edu. Website: http://www.esf.edu/chemistry

University of Calgary, Faculty of Graduate Studies, Faculty of Science, Program in Chemistry, Calgary, AB T2N 1N4, Canada. Offers analytical chemistry (M Sc, PhD); applied chemistry (M Sc, PhD); inorganic chemistry (M Sc, PhD); organic chemistry (M Sc, PhD); physical chemistry (M Sc, PhD); polymer chemistry (M Sc, PhD); theoretical chemistry (M Sc, PhD). *Degree requirements:* For master's, thesis; for doctorate, thesis/dissertation, candidacy exam. *Entrance requirements:* For master's, minimum GPA of 3.0; for doctorate, honors B Sc degree with minimum GPA of 3.7 or M Sc with minimum GPA of 3.3. Additional exam requirements/recommendations for international students: Required—TOEFL (minimum score 580 paper-based). Electronic applications accepted. *Faculty research:* Chemical analysis, chemical dynamics, synthesis theory.

University of Cincinnati, Graduate School, McMicken College of Arts and Sciences, Department of Chemistry, Cincinnati, OH 45221. Offers analytical chemistry (MS, PhD); biochemistry (MS, PhD); inorganic chemistry (MS, PhD); organic chemistry (MS, PhD); physical chemistry (MS, PhD); polymer chemistry (MS, PhD); sensors (PhD). *Program availability:* Part-time, evening/weekend. Terminal master's awarded for partial completion of doctoral program. *Degree requirements:* For master's, thesis optional; for doctorate, comprehensive exam, thesis/dissertation. *Entrance requirements:* For master's and doctorate, GRE General Test. Additional exam requirements/recommendations for international students: Required—TOEFL (minimum score 580 paper-based). Electronic applications accepted. *Faculty research:* Biomedical chemistry, laser chemistry, surface science, chemical sensors, synthesis.

University of Louisville, Graduate School, College of Arts and Sciences, Department of Chemistry, Louisville, KY 40292-0001. Offers analytical chemistry (MS, PhD); biochemistry (MS, PhD); chemical physics (PhD); inorganic chemistry (MS, PhD); organic chemistry (MS, PhD); physical chemistry (MS, PhD). *Faculty:* 26 full-time (9 women), 3 part-time/adjunct (1 woman). *Students:* 35 full-time (14 women), 17 part-time (4 women); includes 5 minority (2 Black or African American, non-Hispanic/Latino; 3 Asian, non-Hispanic/Latino), 39 international. Average age 31. 47 applicants, 36% accepted, 10 enrolled. In 2018, 18 master's, 3 doctorates awarded. Terminal master's awarded for partial completion of doctoral program. *Degree requirements:* For master's, thesis (for some programs), Literature Seminars; for doctorate, thesis/dissertation, Cumulative Exams, Literature Seminars; Research. *Entrance requirements:* For master's and doctorate, GRE General Test, official transcripts, recommendation letters (minimum of 2), personal statement. Additional exam requirements/recommendations for international students: Required—TOEFL (minimum score 550 paper-based; 79 iBT), IELTS can be taken in place of TOEFL; Recommended—IELTS (minimum score 6.5). *Application deadline:* For fall admission, 1/15 priority date for domestic and international students; for spring admission, 9/15 priority date for domestic and international students. Application fee: $65. Electronic applications accepted. *Expenses: Tuition, area resident:* Full-time $6500; part-time $723 per credit hour. Tuition, state resident: full-time $6500. Tuition, nonresident: full-time $13,557; part-time $1507 per credit hour. Tuition and fees vary according to course load and program. *Financial support:* In 2018–19, 59 students received support, including 2 fellowships with full tuition reimbursements available (averaging $23,000 per year), 10 research assistantships with full tuition reimbursements available (averaging $23,000 per year), 41 teaching assistantships with full tuition reimbursements available (averaging $23,000 per year); scholarships/grants, health care benefits, and unspecified assistantships also available. Financial award application deadline: 1/15. *Faculty research:* Solid state chemistry, chemical synthesis, nanoparticle research, green chemistry, spectroscopic studies, computational chemistry, catalysis. *Total annual research expenditures:* $1 million. *Unit head:* Dr. Craig Grapperhaus, Professor, 502-852-8148, Fax: 502-852-8149, E-mail: craig.grapperhaus@louisville.edu. *Application contact:* Sherry Nalley, Graduate Program Assistant, 502-852-6798, Fax: 502-852-6536, E-mail: sherry.nalley@louisville.edu. Website: http://louisville.edu/chemistry

The University of Manchester, School of Chemistry, Manchester, United Kingdom. Offers biological chemistry (PhD); chemistry (M Ent, M Phil, M Sc, D Ent, PhD); inorganic chemistry (PhD); materials chemistry (PhD); nanoscience (PhD); nuclear fission (PhD); organic chemistry (PhD); physical chemistry (PhD); theoretical chemistry (PhD).

Peterson's Graduate Programs in the Physical Sciences, Mathematics, Agricultural Sciences, the Environment & Natural Resources 2020

www.petersons.com **77**

Organic Chemistry

University of Maryland, College Park, Academic Affairs, College of Computer, Mathematical and Natural Sciences, Department of Chemistry and Biochemistry, Chemistry Program, College Park, MD 20742. Offers analytical chemistry (MS, PhD); inorganic chemistry (MS, PhD); organic chemistry (MS, PhD); physical chemistry (MS, PhD). *Program availability:* Part-time, evening/weekend. Terminal master's awarded for partial completion of doctoral program. *Degree requirements:* For master's, thesis optional; for doctorate, thesis/dissertation, 2 seminar presentations, oral exam. *Entrance requirements:* For master's and doctorate, GRE General Test, GRE Subject Test (recommended), minimum GPA of 3.0, 3 letters of recommendation. Additional exam requirements/recommendations for international students: Required—TOEFL. Electronic applications accepted. *Faculty research:* Environmental chemistry, nuclear chemistry, lunar and environmental analysis, X-ray crystallography.

University of Massachusetts Lowell, College of Sciences, Department of Chemistry, Lowell, MA 01854. Offers analytical chemistry (PhD); biochemistry (PhD); chemistry (MS, PhD); environmental studies (PhD); green chemistry (PhD); inorganic chemistry (PhD); organic chemistry (PhD); polymer science (MS). Terminal master's awarded for partial completion of doctoral program. *Degree requirements:* For master's, thesis; for doctorate, 2 foreign languages, thesis/dissertation. *Entrance requirements:* For master's and doctorate, GRE General Test. Electronic applications accepted.

University of Memphis, Graduate School, College of Arts and Sciences, Department of Chemistry, Memphis, TN 38152. Offers analytical chemistry (MS, PhD); computational chemistry (MS, PhD); inorganic chemistry (MS, PhD); organic chemistry (MS, PhD); physical chemistry (MS, PhD). *Program availability:* Part-time. *Students:* 37 full-time (11 women), 14 part-time (5 women); includes 9 minority (2 Black or African American, non-Hispanic/Latino; 3 Asian, non-Hispanic/Latino; 4 Two or more races, non-Hispanic/Latino), 6 international. Average age 27. 24 applicants, 67% accepted, 14 enrolled. In 2018, 9 master's, 3 doctorates awarded. Terminal master's awarded for partial completion of doctoral program. *Degree requirements:* For master's, comprehensive exam, thesis or alternative; for doctorate, comprehensive exam, thesis/dissertation. *Entrance requirements:* For master's and doctorate, GRE General Test, admission to Graduate School plus 32 undergraduate hours in chemistry. Additional exam requirements/recommendations for international students: Required—TOEFL (minimum score 550 paper-based). *Application deadline:* For fall admission, 7/1 for domestic students, 5/1 for international students; for winter admission, 9/15 for international students; for spring admission, 12/1 for domestic students. Applications are processed on a rolling basis. Application fee: $35 ($60 for international students). Electronic applications accepted. *Expenses: Tuition,* area resident: Full-time $10,240; part-time $503 per credit hour. Tuition, state resident: full-time $10,464. Tuition, nonresident: full-time $20,224; part-time $991 per credit hour. *Required fees:* $850; $106 per credit hour. *Financial support:* Research assistantships with full tuition reimbursements, teaching assistantships with full tuition reimbursements, Federal Work-Study, scholarships/grants, and unspecified assistantships available. Financial award application deadline: 2/1; financial award applicants required to submit FAFSA. *Faculty research:* Computational chemistry, materials chemistry, organic/polymer synthesis, drug design/delivery, water chemistry. *Unit head:* Dr. Gary Emmert, Chair, 901-678-2638, Fax: 901-678-3447, E-mail: gemmert@memphis.edu. *Application contact:* Dr. Paul Simone, Coordinator of Graduate Studies, 901-678-3671, Fax: 901-678-3447, E-mail: gradchem@memphis.edu.
Website: http://www.memphis.edu/chem/

University of Miami, Graduate School, College of Arts and Sciences, Department of Chemistry, Coral Gables, FL 33124. Offers chemistry (MS); inorganic chemistry (PhD); organic chemistry (PhD); physical chemistry (PhD). Terminal master's awarded for partial completion of doctoral program. *Degree requirements:* For master's, comprehensive exam; for doctorate, comprehensive exam, thesis/dissertation. *Entrance requirements:* For master's and doctorate, GRE General Test. Additional exam requirements/recommendations for international students: Required—TOEFL (minimum score 550 paper-based). Electronic applications accepted. *Faculty research:* Supramolecular chemistry, electrochemistry, surface chemistry, catalysis, organometalic.

University of Michigan, Rackham Graduate School, College of Literature, Science, and the Arts, Department of Chemistry, Ann Arbor, MI 48109-1055. Offers analytical chemistry (PhD); chemical biology (PhD); chemical sciences (MS); inorganic chemistry (PhD); materials chemistry (PhD); organic chemistry (PhD); physical chemistry (PhD). *Program availability:* Part-time. *Faculty:* 40 full-time (14 women), 7 part-time/adjunct (3 women). *Students:* 262 full-time (112 women), 4 part-time (all women); includes 44 minority (11 Black or African American, non-Hispanic/Latino; 11 Asian, non-Hispanic/Latino; 19 Hispanic/Latino; 1 Native Hawaiian or other Pacific Islander, non-Hispanic/Latino; 2 Two or more races, non-Hispanic/Latino), 61 international. 692 applicants, 71 enrolled. In 2018, 47 master's, 46 doctorates awarded. *Degree requirements:* For doctorate, comprehensive exam, thesis/dissertation, oral defense of dissertation, organic cumulative proficiency exams. *Entrance requirements:* For master's, bachelor's degree, 3 letters of recommendation, personal statement; for doctorate, bachelor's degree, 3 letters of recommendation, personal statement, curriculum vitae/resume. Additional exam requirements/recommendations for international students: Required—TOEFL (minimum score 560 paper-based; 84 iBT) or IELTS. *Application deadline:* For fall admission, 12/1 for domestic and international students. Application fee: $0 ($90 for international students). Electronic applications accepted. *Financial support:* In 2018–19, 269 students received support, including 50 fellowships with full tuition reimbursements available (averaging $31,625 per year), 84 research assistantships with full tuition reimbursements available (averaging $31,625 per year), 133 teaching assistantships with full tuition reimbursements available (averaging $31,625 per year); career-related internships or fieldwork, Federal Work-Study, scholarships/grants, traineeships, health care benefits, tuition waivers (full), and unspecified assistantships also available. *Faculty research:* Biological catalysis, protein engineering, chemical sensors, de novo metalloprotein design, supramolecular architecture. *Total annual research expenditures:* $19.6 million. *Unit head:* Dr. Robert Kennedy, Professor of Chemistry/Chair, 734-763-9681, Fax: 734-647-4847. *Application contact:* Elizabeth Oxford, Graduate Program Coordinator, 734-764-7278, Fax: 734-647-4865, E-mail: chemadmissions@umich.edu.
Website: http://www.lsa.umich.edu/chem/

University of Missouri–Kansas City, College of Arts and Sciences, Department of Chemistry, Kansas City, MO 64110-2499. Offers analytical chemistry (PhD); inorganic chemistry (PhD); organic chemistry (PhD); physical chemistry (PhD); polymer chemistry (MS, PhD). PhD (interdisciplinary) offered through the School of Graduate Studies. *Program availability:* Part-time, evening/weekend. *Degree requirements:* For master's, thesis (for some programs); for doctorate, thesis/dissertation. *Entrance requirements:* For master's, equivalent of American Chemical Society approved bachelor's degree in chemistry; for doctorate, GRE General Test, equivalent of American Chemical Society approved bachelor's degree in chemistry. Additional exam requirements/recommendations for international students: Required—TOEFL (minimum score 550 paper-based; 80 iBT), TWE. Electronic applications accepted. *Faculty research:* Molecular spectroscopy, characterization and synthesis of materials and compounds, computational chemistry, natural products, drug delivery systems and anti-tumor agents.

University of Montana, Graduate School, College of Humanities and Sciences, Department of Chemistry and Biochemistry, Missoula, MT 59812. Offers chemistry (MS, PhD), including environmental/analytical chemistry, inorganic chemistry, organic chemistry, physical chemistry. Terminal master's awarded for partial completion of doctoral program. *Degree requirements:* For master's, thesis (for some programs); for doctorate, thesis/dissertation. *Entrance requirements:* For master's and doctorate, GRE General Test. Additional exam requirements/recommendations for international students: Required—TOEFL (minimum score 575 paper-based). *Faculty research:* Reaction mechanisms and kinetics, inorganic and organic synthesis, analytical chemistry, natural products.

University of Nebraska–Lincoln, Graduate College, College of Arts and Sciences, Department of Chemistry, Lincoln, NE 68588. Offers analytical chemistry (PhD); biochemistry (PhD); chemistry (MS); inorganic chemistry (PhD); materials chemistry (PhD); organic chemistry (PhD); physical chemistry (PhD). *Degree requirements:* For master's, one foreign language, thesis optional, departmental qualifying exam; for doctorate, one foreign language, comprehensive exam, thesis/dissertation, departmental qualifying exams. *Entrance requirements:* For master's and doctorate, GRE. Additional exam requirements/recommendations for international students: Required—TOEFL (minimum score 550 paper-based). Electronic applications accepted. *Faculty research:* Bioorganic and bioinorganic chemistry, biophysical and bioanalytical chemistry, structure-function of DNA and proteins, organometallics, mass spectrometry.

University of Notre Dame, The Graduate School, College of Science, Department of Chemistry and Biochemistry, Notre Dame, IN 46556. Offers biochemistry (MS, PhD); inorganic chemistry (MS, PhD); organic chemistry (MS, PhD); physical chemistry (MS, PhD). Terminal master's awarded for partial completion of doctoral program. *Degree requirements:* For master's, comprehensive exam, thesis; for doctorate, thesis/dissertation, qualifying exam. *Entrance requirements:* For master's and doctorate, GRE General Test, GRE Subject Test (strongly recommended). Additional exam requirements/recommendations for international students: Required—TOEFL (minimum score 600 paper-based; 80 iBT). Electronic applications accepted. *Faculty research:* Reaction design and mechanistic studies; reactive intermediates; synthesis, structure and reactivity of organometallic cluster complexes and biologically active natural products; bioorganic chemistry; enzymology.

University of Oklahoma, College of Arts and Sciences, Department of Chemistry and Biochemistry, Norman, OK 73019. Offers chemistry (MS, PhD), including analytical chemistry, biochemistry, chemical education, inorganic chemistry, inter-and/or multidisciplinary, organic chemistry, physical chemistry, structural biology. *Program availability:* Part-time. *Faculty:* 32 full-time (13 women). *Students:* 89 full-time (38 women), 33 part-time (15 women); includes 22 minority (2 Black or African American, non-Hispanic/Latino; 9 Asian, non-Hispanic/Latino; 6 Hispanic/Latino; 5 Two or more races, non-Hispanic/Latino), 46 international. Average age 26. 78 applicants, 71% accepted, 33 enrolled. In 2018, 15 master's, 21 doctorates awarded. Terminal master's awarded for partial completion of doctoral program. *Degree requirements:* For master's, comprehensive exam (for some programs), thesis (for some programs); for doctorate, comprehensive exam, thesis/dissertation, general exam. *Entrance requirements:* For master's and doctorate, GRE. Additional exam requirements/recommendations for international students: Required—TOEFL (minimum score 79 iBT) or IELTS (minimum score 6.5). *Application deadline:* For fall admission, 3/31 priority date for domestic and international students; for spring admission, 9/1 priority date for domestic and international students. Application fee: $50 ($100 for international students). Electronic applications accepted. *Expenses:* Tuition, state resident: full-time $5683.20; part-time $236.80 per credit hour. Tuition, nonresident: full-time $20,342; part-time $847.60 per credit hour. *International tuition:* $20,342.40 full-time. *Required fees:* $2894.20; $110.05 per credit hour. $126.50 per semester. Tuition and fees vary according to course load and program. *Financial support:* Research assistantships, teaching assistantships, institutionally sponsored loans, scholarships/grants, health care benefits, unspecified assistantships, and full tuition with qualifying graduate assistantship available. Support available to part-time students. Financial award application deadline: 6/1; financial award applicants required to submit FAFSA. *Faculty research:* Structural biology, solid state materials, natural products, membrane biochemistry, bioanalysis. *Unit head:* Dr. Ronald L. Halterman, Professor and Chair, 405-325-4812, Fax: 405-325-6111, E-mail: rhalterman@ou.edu. *Application contact:* Carol Jones, Operations Manager, 405-325-4811, Fax: 405-325-6111, E-mail: caroljones@ou.edu.
Website: http://www.ou.edu/cas/chemistry

University of Regina, Faculty of Graduate Studies and Research, Faculty of Science, Department of Chemistry and Biochemistry, Regina, SK S4S 0A2, Canada. Offers biophysics of biological interfaces (M Sc, PhD); computational chemistry (M Sc, PhD); environmental analytical chemistry (M Sc, PhD); enzymology/chemical biology (M Sc, PhD); inorganic/organometallic chemistry (M Sc, PhD); signal transduction and mechanisms of cancer cell regulation (M Sc, PhD); supramolecular organic photochemistry and photophysics (M Sc, PhD); synthetic organic chemistry (M Sc, PhD). *Program availability:* Part-time. *Faculty:* 12 full-time (2 women), 4 part-time/adjunct (0 women). *Students:* 12 full-time (6 women), 1 part-time (0 women). Average age 30. 23 applicants, 17% accepted. In 2018, 2 master's awarded. *Degree requirements:* For master's, thesis; for doctorate, comprehensive exam, thesis/dissertation. *Entrance requirements:* For master's, 4 years Bachelor degree in Chemistry or related program; for doctorate, completion of Master's in Chemistry. Additional exam requirements/recommendations for international students: Required—TOEFL (minimum score 580 paper-based; 80 iBT), IELTS (minimum score 6.5), PTE (minimum score 59), other options are CAEL, MELAB, Cantest and U of R ESL. *Application deadline:* Applications are processed on a rolling basis. Application fee: $100. Electronic applications accepted. Tuition and fees vary according to course level, course load, degree level and program. *Financial support:* Fellowships, research assistantships, teaching assistantships, career-related internships or fieldwork, Federal Work-Study, scholarships/grants, unspecified assistantships, and travel award & Graduate Scholarship Base Funds available. Support available to part-time students. Financial award application deadline: 9/30. *Faculty research:* Asymmetric synthesis and methodology, theoretical and computational chemistry, biophysical biochemistry, analytical and environmental chemistry, chemical biology. *Unit head:* Dr. Renata Raina-Fulton, Department Head, 306-585-4012, Fax: 306-337-2409, E-mail: renata.raina@uregina.ca. *Application contact:* Dr. Brian Sterenberg, Graduate Program Coordinator, 306-585-4106, Fax: 306-337-2409, E-mail: brian.sterenberg@uregina.ca.
Website: http://www.uregina.ca/science/chem-biochem/

University of Rochester, School of Arts and Sciences, Department of Chemistry, Rochester, NY 14627. Offers inorganic chemistry (PhD); organic chemistry (PhD); physical chemistry (PhD). *Faculty:* 17 full-time (5 women). *Students:* 91 full-time (42 women); includes 10 minority (1 Black or African American, non-Hispanic/Latino; 2 Asian, non-Hispanic/Latino; 7 Hispanic/Latino), 24 international. Average age 27. 247 applicants, 25% accepted, 16 enrolled. In 2018, 9 doctorates awarded. Terminal master's awarded for partial completion of doctoral program. *Degree requirements:* For doctorate, thesis/dissertation, qualifying exam. *Entrance requirements:* For doctorate, GRE General Test, GRE Subject Test (recommended), transcripts, three letters of

recommendation. Additional exam requirements/recommendations for international students: Required—TOEFL (minimum score 100 iBT), IELTS (minimum score 6.5). *Application deadline:* For fall admission, 12/15 for domestic and international students. Electronic applications accepted. *Expenses: Tuition:* Full-time $52,974; part-time $1654 per credit hour. *Required fees:* $612. One-time fee: $30 part-time. Tuition and fees vary according to campus/location and program. *Financial support:* In 2018–19, 34 students received support, including 13 research assistantships (averaging $26,000 per year), 4 teaching assistantships (averaging $26,000 per year); Federal Work-Study, scholarships/grants, and tuition waivers (full) also available. Financial award application deadline: 12/15. *Faculty research:* Organic chemistry, physical chemistry, theoretical chemistry, biological chemistry, materials chemistry. *Total annual research expenditures:* $4.2 million. *Unit head:* Todd D. Krauss, Chair, 585-275-5093, E-mail: todd.krauss@rochester.edu. *Application contact:* Robin Clark, Administrative Assistant, 585-275-0635, E-mail: robin.clark@rochester.edu.
Website: http://www.sas.rochester.edu/chm/graduate/index.html

The University of Tennessee, Graduate School, College of Arts and Sciences, Department of Chemistry, Knoxville, TN 37996. Offers analytical chemistry (MS, PhD); chemical physics (PhD); environmental chemistry (MS, PhD); inorganic chemistry (MS, PhD); organic chemistry (MS, PhD); physical chemistry (MS, PhD); polymer chemistry (MS, PhD); theoretical chemistry (PhD). *Program availability:* Part-time. Terminal master's awarded for partial completion of doctoral program. *Degree requirements:* For master's, thesis; for doctorate, thesis/dissertation. *Entrance requirements:* For master's and doctorate, GRE General Test, minimum GPA of 2.7. Additional exam requirements/recommendations for international students: Required—TOEFL. Electronic applications accepted.

The University of Texas at Austin, Graduate School, College of Natural Sciences, Department of Chemistry and Biochemistry, Austin, TX 78712-1111. Offers analytical chemistry (PhD); biochemistry (PhD); inorganic chemistry (PhD); organic chemistry (PhD); physical chemistry (PhD). *Entrance requirements:* For doctorate, GRE General Test.

The University of Toledo, College of Graduate Studies, College of Natural Sciences and Mathematics, Department of Chemistry, Toledo, OH 43606-3390. Offers analytical chemistry (MS, PhD); biological chemistry (MS, PhD); inorganic chemistry (MS, PhD); organic chemistry (MS, PhD); physical chemistry (MS, PhD). *Program availability:* Part-time. *Degree requirements:* For master's, thesis or alternative; for doctorate, thesis/dissertation. *Entrance requirements:* For master's and doctorate, GRE General Test, GRE Subject Test, minimum cumulative point-hour ratio of 2.7 for all previous academic work, three letters of recommendation, statement of purpose, transcripts from all prior institutions attended. Additional exam requirements/recommendations for international students: Required—TOEFL (minimum score 550 paper-based; 80 iBT). Electronic applications accepted. *Faculty research:* Enzymology, materials chemistry, crystallography, theoretical chemistry.

Virginia Commonwealth University, Graduate School, College of Humanities and Sciences, Department of Chemistry, Richmond, VA 23284-9005. Offers analytical chemistry (MS, PhD); chemical physics (PhD); inorganic chemistry (MS, PhD); organic chemistry (MS, PhD); physical chemistry (MS, PhD). *Program availability:* Part-time. Terminal master's awarded for partial completion of doctoral program. *Degree requirements:* For master's, thesis; for doctorate, thesis/dissertation, comprehensive cumulative exams, research proposal. *Entrance requirements:* For master's, GRE General Test, 30 undergraduate credits in chemistry; for doctorate, GRE General Test. Additional exam requirements/recommendations for international students: Required—TOEFL (minimum score 600 paper-based; 100 iBT) or IELTS (minimum score 6.5). Electronic applications accepted. *Faculty research:* Physical, organic, inorganic, analytical, and polymer chemistry; chemical physics.

Wake Forest University, Graduate School of Arts and Sciences, Department of Chemistry, Winston-Salem, NC 27109. Offers analytical chemistry (MS, PhD); inorganic chemistry (MS, PhD); organic chemistry (MS, PhD); physical chemistry (MS, PhD). *Program availability:* Part-time. *Degree requirements:* For master's, one foreign language, comprehensive exam, thesis; for doctorate, 2 foreign languages, comprehensive exam, thesis/dissertation. *Entrance requirements:* For master's and doctorate, GRE General Test. Additional exam requirements/recommendations for international students: Required—TOEFL. Electronic applications accepted.

Wesleyan University, Graduate Studies, Department of Chemistry, Middletown, CT 06459. Offers biochemistry (PhD); chemical physics (PhD); inorganic chemistry (PhD); organic chemistry (PhD); physical chemistry (PhD); theoretical chemistry (PhD). *Faculty:* 11 full-time (3 women), 1 part-time/adjunct (0 women). *Students:* 16 full-time (9 women). Average age 25. In 2018, 4 doctorates awarded. Terminal master's awarded for partial completion of doctoral program. *Degree requirements:* For doctorate, thesis/dissertation. *Entrance requirements:* For doctorate, GRE General Test, 3 recommendations. Additional exam requirements/recommendations for international students: Required—TOEFL, IELTS. *Application deadline:* 1/1 for domestic and international students; for summer admission, 1/1 for domestic and international students. Application fee: $0. Electronic applications accepted. *Financial support:* In 2018–19, 15 students received support, including 4 research assistantships with full tuition reimbursements available, 13 teaching assistantships with full tuition reimbursements available; institutionally sponsored loans and health care benefits also available. Financial award application deadline: 4/30. *Faculty research:* The synthesis of noble metal and noble metal alloy nanoparticles with well-defined shapes and catalytically-active high-energy surfaces; inorganic chemistry; materials science; scanning electron microscopy (SEM);transition organometallic complexes. *Unit head:* Michael A. Calter, Chair, 860-685-2633 Ext. 2633, Fax: 860-685-2211, E-mail: mcalter@wesleyan.edu. *Application contact:* Aracely Suto, Administrative Assistant, 860-685-2572, Fax: 860-685-2211, E-mail: chemistry@wesleyan.edu.
Website: http://www.wesleyan.edu/chem/

Yale University, Graduate School of Arts and Sciences, Department of Chemistry, New Haven, CT 06520. Offers biophysical chemistry (PhD); inorganic chemistry (PhD); organic chemistry (PhD); physical and theoretical chemistry (PhD). *Degree requirements:* For doctorate, thesis/dissertation. *Entrance requirements:* For doctorate, GRE General Test, GRE Subject Test. Additional exam requirements/recommendations for international students: Required—TOEFL.

Youngstown State University, College of Graduate Studies, College of Science, Technology, Engineering and Mathematics, Department of Chemistry, Youngstown, OH 44555-0001. Offers analytical chemistry (MS); biochemistry (MS); chemistry education (MS); inorganic chemistry (MS); organic chemistry (MS); physical chemistry (MS). *Program availability:* Part-time. *Degree requirements:* For master's, thesis. *Entrance requirements:* For master's, bachelor's degree in chemistry, minimum GPA of 2.7. Additional exam requirements/recommendations for international students: Required—TOEFL. *Faculty research:* Analysis of antioxidants, chromatography, defects and disorder in crystalline oxides, hydrogen bonding, novel organic and organometallic materials.

Physical Chemistry

Auburn University, Graduate School, College of Sciences and Mathematics, Department of Chemistry and Biochemistry, Auburn University, AL 36849. Offers analytical chemistry (MS, PhD); biochemistry (MS, PhD); inorganic chemistry (MS); organic chemistry (PhD); physical chemistry (MS, PhD). *Program availability:* Part-time. *Degree requirements:* For master's, thesis (for some programs); for doctorate, thesis/dissertation, oral and written exams. *Entrance requirements:* For master's and doctorate, GRE General Test. Electronic applications accepted. *Expenses:* Tuition, state resident: full-time $11,282; part-time $535 per credit hour. Tuition, nonresident: full-time $30,542; part-time $1605 per credit hour. *Required fees:* $826 per semester. Tuition and fees vary according to degree level and program.

Binghamton University, State University of New York, Graduate School, Harpur College of Arts and Sciences, Department of Chemistry, Binghamton, NY 13902-6000. Offers analytical chemistry (PhD); chemistry (MA, MS); inorganic chemistry (PhD); physical chemistry (PhD). *Program availability:* Part-time. Terminal master's awarded for partial completion of doctoral program. *Degree requirements:* For master's, thesis; for doctorate, comprehensive exam, thesis/dissertation. *Entrance requirements:* For master's and doctorate, GRE General Test. Additional exam requirements/recommendations for international students: Required—TOEFL (minimum score 90 iBT). Electronic applications accepted.

Boston College, Morrissey Graduate School of Arts and Sciences, Department of Chemistry, Chestnut Hill, MA 02467-3800. Offers biochemistry (PhD); inorganic chemistry (PhD); organic chemistry (PhD); physical chemistry (PhD); science education (MST). *Degree requirements:* For doctorate, thesis/dissertation, qualifying exam. *Entrance requirements:* For doctorate, GRE General Test, GRE Subject Test. Additional exam requirements/recommendations for international students: Required—TOEFL (minimum score 600 paper-based; 100 iBT), IELTS (minimum score 8). Electronic applications accepted. *Faculty research:* Organic and organometallic chemistry, chemical biology and biochemistry, physical and theoretical chemistry, inorganic chemistry.

Brandeis University, Graduate School of Arts and Sciences, Department of Chemistry, Waltham, MA 02454-9110. Offers inorganic chemistry (MA, MS, PhD); organic chemistry (MA, MS, PhD); physical chemistry (MS, PhD). *Program availability:* Part-time. *Faculty:* 13 full-time (5 women), 3 part-time/adjunct (0 women). *Students:* 33 full-time (12 women); includes 5 minority (3 Black or African American, non-Hispanic/Latino; 2 Hispanic/Latino), 19 international. Average age 26. 91 applicants, 41% accepted, 0 enrolled. In 2018, 3 master's, 8 doctorates awarded. Terminal master's awarded for partial completion of doctoral program. *Degree requirements:* For master's, comprehensive exam, thesis (for some programs); for doctorate, comprehensive exam, thesis/dissertation. *Entrance requirements:* For master's and doctorate, GRE General Test; GRE Subject Test (recommended), resume, statement of purpose, letters of recommendation, transcripts. Additional exam requirements/recommendations for international students: Required—TOEFL, IELTS, PTE. *Application deadline:* For fall admission, 12/15 priority date for domestic students. Applications are processed on a rolling basis. Application fee: $75. Electronic applications accepted. *Financial support:* In 2018–19, 21 fellowships with full tuition reimbursements (averaging $30,000 per year), 13 research assistantships with full tuition reimbursements (averaging $30,000 per year), 23 teaching assistantships with full tuition reimbursements (averaging $6,400 per year) were awarded; scholarships/grants, health care benefits, and tuition waivers (full and partial) also available. Support available to part-time students. *Faculty research:* Inorganic and organic chemistry, physical chemistry, chemical biology, biophysical chemistry, materials chemistry. *Unit head:* Dr. Klaus Schmidt-Rohr, Director of Graduate Study, 781-736-2520, E-mail: srohr@brandeis.edu. *Application contact:* Maryanna Aldrich, Administrator, 781-736-2352, E-mail: scigradoffice@brandeis.edu.
Website: http://www.brandeis.edu/gsas/programs/chemistry.html

Cleveland State University, College of Graduate Studies, College of Sciences and Health Professions, Department of Chemistry, Cleveland, OH 44115. Offers clinical chemistry (PhD), including cellular and molecular medicine, clinical/bioanalytical chemistry; organic chemistry (MS); physical chemistry (MS). *Program availability:* Part-time, evening/weekend. *Faculty:* 17 full-time (3 women). *Students:* 55 full-time (30 women), 16 part-time (10 women); includes 4 minority (3 Black or African American, non-Hispanic/Latino; 1 Asian, non-Hispanic/Latino), 38 international. Average age 30. 63 applicants, 63% accepted, 11 enrolled. In 2018, 3 master's, 15 doctorates awarded. *Entrance requirements:* For master's and doctorate, GRE General Test. Additional exam requirements/recommendations for international students: Required—TOEFL (minimum score 550 paper-based; 78 IBT). *Application deadline:* Applications are processed on a rolling basis. Application fee: $40. Electronic applications accepted. *Expenses:* Tuition, state resident: full-time $7232.55; part-time $6676 per credit hour. Tuition, nonresident: full-time $12,375. *International tuition:* $18,914 full-time. *Required fees:* $80; $80 $40. Tuition and fees vary according to program. *Financial support:* In 2018–19, 44 students received support. Fellowships, research assistantships, teaching assistantships, scholarships/grants, and unspecified assistantships available. Financial award application deadline: 1/15. *Faculty research:* Bioanalytical techniques and molecular diagnostics, glycoproteomics and antithrombotic agents, drug discovery and innovation, analytical pharmacology, inflammatory disease research. *Total annual research expenditures:* $3 million. *Unit head:* Dr. David W. Ball, Chair, 216-687-2467, Fax: 216-687-9298, E-mail: d.ball@csuohio.edu. *Application contact:* Richelle P. Emory, Administrative Coordinator, 216-687-2457, Fax: 216-687-9298, E-mail: r.emery@csuohio.edu.
Website: http://www.csuohio.edu/sciences/chemistry

Cornell University, Graduate School, Graduate Fields of Arts and Sciences, Field of Chemistry and Chemical Biology, Ithaca, NY 14853. Offers analytical chemistry (PhD);

bio-organic chemistry (PhD); biophysical chemistry (PhD); chemical biology (PhD); chemical physics (PhD); inorganic chemistry (PhD); materials chemistry (PhD); organic chemistry (PhD); organometallic chemistry (PhD); physical chemistry (PhD); polymer chemistry (PhD); theoretical chemistry (PhD). *Degree requirements:* For doctorate, comprehensive exam, thesis/dissertation. *Entrance requirements:* For doctorate, GRE General Test, GRE Subject Test (chemistry), 3 letters of recommendation. Additional exam requirements/recommendations for international students: Required—TOEFL (minimum score 600 paper-based; 77 iBT). Electronic applications accepted. *Faculty research:* Analytical, organic, inorganic, physical, materials, chemical biology.

Dartmouth College, Guarini School of Graduate and Advanced Studies, Department of Chemistry, Hanover, NH 03755. Offers biophysical chemistry (MS); chemistry (PhD). *Faculty:* 17 full-time (4 women), 1 (woman) part-time/adjunct. *Students:* 41 full-time (14 women); includes 8 minority (4 Asian, non-Hispanic/Latino; 1 Hispanic/Latino; 3 Two or more races, non-Hispanic/Latino), 11 international. Average age 26. 149 applicants, 12% accepted, 10 enrolled. In 2018, 3 master's, 5 doctorates awarded. *Entrance requirements:* For doctorate, GRE General Test, GRE Subject Test. Additional exam requirements/recommendations for international students: Required—TOEFL. *Application deadline:* For fall admission, 1/2 for domestic students. Application fee: $0. Electronic applications accepted. *Financial support:* Fellowships, research assistantships, teaching assistantships, institutionally sponsored loans, scholarships/grants, traineeships, tuition waivers (full), and unspecified assistantships available. Financial award application deadline: 4/1; financial award applicants required to submit CSS PROFILE or FAFSA. *Faculty research:* Organic and polymer synthesis, bioinorganic chemistry, magnetic resonance parameters. *Unit head:* Dr. Dean E. Wilcox, Chair, 603-646-2501. *Application contact:* Phyllis Ford, Administrative Assistant, 603-646-2501, E-mail: phyllis.p.ford@dartmouth.edu.
Website: http://www.dartmouth.edu/~chem/

Eastern New Mexico University, Graduate School, College of Liberal Arts and Sciences, Department of Physical Sciences, Portales, NM 88130. Offers chemistry (MS), including analytical chemistry, biochemistry, organic chemistry, physical chemistry. *Program availability:* Part-time. *Degree requirements:* For master's, thesis optional, seminar, oral and written comprehensive exams. *Entrance requirements:* For master's, ACS placement examination, minimum GPA of 3.0; 2 letters of recommendation; personal statement of career goals; bachelor's degree with minimum of one year each of general, organic, and analytical chemistry. Additional exam requirements/recommendations for international students: Required—TOEFL (minimum score 550 paper-based; 79 iBT), IELTS (minimum score 6). Electronic applications accepted. *Expenses: Tuition, area resident:* Full-time $6776. Tuition, state resident: full-time $6776; part-time $282 per credit hour. Tuition, nonresident: full-time $8986; part-time $374 per credit hour. *Required fees:* $60 per semester. One-time fee: $25. *Faculty research:* Synfuel, electrochemistry, protein chemistry.

Florida State University, The Graduate School, Department of Anthropology, Department of Chemistry and Biochemistry, Tallahassee, FL 32306-4390. Offers analytical chemistry (MS, PhD); biochemistry (MS, PhD); inorganic chemistry (MS, PhD); materials chemistry (PhD); organic chemistry (MS, PhD); physical chemistry (MS, PhD). *Faculty:* 29 full-time (4 women). *Students:* 159 full-time (57 women), 2 part-time (1 woman); includes 73 minority (9 Black or African American, non-Hispanic/Latino; 46 Asian, non-Hispanic/Latino; 9 Hispanic/Latino; 3 Native Hawaiian or other Pacific Islander, non-Hispanic/Latino; 6 Two or more races, non-Hispanic/Latino). Average age 26. 215 applicants, 49% accepted, 35 enrolled. In 2018, 33 master's, 30 doctorates awarded. Terminal master's awarded for partial completion of doctoral program. *Degree requirements:* For master's, thesis (for some programs); for doctorate, thesis/dissertation. *Entrance requirements:* For master's and doctorate, GRE General Test (minimum scores: 150 verbal, 151 quantitative), minimum upper-division GPA of 3.1 in undergraduate course work. Additional exam requirements/recommendations for international students: Required—TOEFL (minimum score 80 iBT). *Application deadline:* For fall admission, 12/15 priority date for domestic and international students. Applications are processed on a rolling basis. Application fee: $30. Electronic applications accepted. *Expenses: Tuition, area resident:* Part-time $479.32 per credit hour. Tuition and fees vary according to campus/location and program. *Financial support:* In 2018–19, 163 students received support, including 4 fellowships with full tuition reimbursements available (averaging $24,241 per year), 59 research assistantships with full tuition reimbursements available (averaging $24,241 per year), 102 teaching assistantships with full tuition reimbursements available (averaging $24,241 per year). Financial award application deadline: 12/15; financial award applicants required to submit FAFSA. *Faculty research:* Bioanalytical chemistry, separations, microfluidics, petroleomics; materials chemistry, solid state materials, magnets, polymers, catalysts, advanced spectroscopic methods, NMR and EPR, ultrafast, Raman, and mass spectrometry; organic synthesis, natural products, photochemistry, and supramolecular chemistry; biochemistry, structural biology, metabolomics, and anticancer drugs; nanochemistry, applications in energy, sustainability, biology, and technology development; radiochemistry. *Total annual research expenditures:* $7.1 million. *Unit head:* Dr. Geoffrey Strouse, Chairman, 850-644-1244, Fax: 850-644-8281, E-mail: gradinfo@chem.fsu.edu. *Application contact:* Dr. Wei Yang, Associate Chair for Graduate Studies, 850-645-6884, Fax: 850-644-8281, E-mail: gradinfo@chem.fsu.edu.
Website: http://www.chem.fsu.edu/

The George Washington University, Columbian College of Arts and Sciences, Department of Chemistry, Washington, DC 20052. Offers analytical chemistry (MS, PhD); inorganic chemistry (MS, PhD); materials science (MS, PhD); organic chemistry (MS, PhD); physical chemistry (MS, PhD). *Program availability:* Part-time, evening/weekend. *Students:* 29 full-time (15 women), 8 part-time (5 women); includes 3 minority (1 Black or African American, non-Hispanic/Latino; 2 Hispanic/Latino), 5 international. Average age 27. 96 applicants, 47% accepted, 9 enrolled. In 2018, 9 master's, 6 doctorates awarded. Terminal master's awarded for partial completion of doctoral program. *Degree requirements:* For master's, comprehensive exam, thesis or alternative; for doctorate, thesis/dissertation, general exam. *Entrance requirements:* For master's and doctorate, GRE General Test, interview, minimum GPA of 3.0. Additional exam requirements/recommendations for international students: Required—TOEFL (minimum score 550 paper-based; 80 iBT). *Application deadline:* For fall admission, 1/15 priority date for domestic and international students; for spring admission, 9/1 priority date for domestic and international students. Applications are processed on a rolling basis. Application fee: $75. Electronic applications accepted. *Financial support:* In 2018–19, 27 students received support. Fellowships, research assistantships, teaching assistantships, Federal Work-Study, and tuition waivers available. Financial award application deadline: 1/15. *Unit head:* Dr. Michael King, Chair, 202-994-6488. *Application contact:* Information Contact, 202-994-6121, E-mail: gwchem@gwu.edu.
Website: http://chemistry.columbian.gwu.edu/

Georgia State University, College of Arts and Sciences, Department of Chemistry, Atlanta, GA 30302-3083. Offers analytical chemistry (MS, PhD); biochemistry (MS, PhD); bioinformatics (MS, PhD); biophysical chemistry (PhD); computational chemistry (MS, PhD); geochemistry (PhD); organic/medicinal chemistry (MS, PhD); physical chemistry (MS). PhD in geochemistry offered jointly with Department of Geosciences. *Program availability:* Part-time. *Faculty:* 27 full-time (6 women), 1 part-time/adjunct (0 women). *Students:* 147 full-time (59 women), 15 part-time (10 women); includes 37 minority (21 Black or African American, non-Hispanic/Latino; 7 Asian, non-Hispanic/Latino; 4 Hispanic/Latino; 5 Two or more races, non-Hispanic/Latino), 84 international. Average age 29. 106 applicants, 40% accepted, 28 enrolled. In 2018, 37 master's, 13 doctorates awarded. Terminal master's awarded for partial completion of doctoral program. *Degree requirements:* For master's, one foreign language, comprehensive exam (for some programs), thesis (for some programs); for doctorate, one foreign language, comprehensive exam, thesis/dissertation. *Entrance requirements:* For master's and doctorate, GRE. *Application deadline:* For fall admission, 7/1 priority date for domestic and international students; for winter admission, 11/15 priority date for domestic and international students; for spring admission, 4/15 priority date for domestic and international students. Applications are processed on a rolling basis. Application fee: $50. Electronic applications accepted. *Expenses: Tuition, area resident:* Full-time $9360; part-time $390 per credit hour. Tuition, state resident: full-time $9360; part-time $390 per credit hour. Tuition, nonresident: full-time $30,024; part-time $1251 per credit hour. *International tuition:* $30,024 full-time. *Required fees:* $2128. *Financial support:* Fellowships with full tuition reimbursements, research assistantships with full tuition reimbursements, and teaching assistantships with full tuition reimbursements available. Financial award applicants required to submit FAFSA. *Faculty research:* Analytical chemistry, biological/biochemistry, biophysical/computational chemistry, chemical education, organic/medicinal chemistry. *Unit head:* Dr. Donald Hamelberg, Professor; Chair, 404-413-5564, Fax: 404-413-5505, E-mail: dhamelberg@gsu.edu. *Application contact:* Dr. Donald Hamelberg, Professor; Chair, 404-413-5564, Fax: 404-413-5505, E-mail: dhamelberg@gsu.edu.
Website: http://chemistry.gsu.edu/

Harvard University, Graduate School of Arts and Sciences, Department of Chemistry and Chemical Biology, Cambridge, MA 02138. Offers biochemical chemistry (PhD); inorganic chemistry (PhD); organic chemistry (PhD); physical chemistry (PhD). *Degree requirements:* For doctorate, thesis/dissertation, cumulative exams. *Entrance requirements:* For doctorate, GRE General Test, GRE Subject Test. Additional exam requirements/recommendations for international students: Required—TOEFL.

Howard University, Graduate School, Department of Chemistry, Washington, DC 20059-0002. Offers analytical chemistry (MS, PhD); atmospheric (MS, PhD); biochemistry (MS, PhD); environmental (MS, PhD); inorganic chemistry (MS, PhD); organic chemistry (MS, PhD); physical chemistry (MS, PhD). Terminal master's awarded for partial completion of doctoral program. *Degree requirements:* For master's, comprehensive exam, thesis, teaching experience; for doctorate, comprehensive exam, thesis/dissertation, teaching experience. *Entrance requirements:* For master's, GRE General Test, minimum GPA of 2.7; for doctorate, GRE General Test, minimum GPA of 3.0. Additional exam requirements/recommendations for international students: Required—TOEFL. Electronic applications accepted. *Faculty research:* Synthetic organics, materials, natural products, mass spectrometry.

Indiana University Bloomington, University Graduate School, College of Arts and Sciences, Department of Chemistry, Bloomington, IN 47405. Offers analytical chemistry (PhD); chemical biology (PhD); chemistry (MAT); inorganic chemistry (PhD); materials chemistry (PhD); organic chemistry (PhD); physical chemistry (PhD); MSES/MS. Terminal master's awarded for partial completion of doctoral program. *Degree requirements:* For master's, thesis; for doctorate, thesis/dissertation. *Entrance requirements:* For master's and doctorate, GRE General Test, GRE Subject Test. Additional exam requirements/recommendations for international students: Required—TOEFL. Electronic applications accepted. *Faculty research:* Synthesis of complex natural products, organic reaction mechanisms, organic electrochemistry, transitive-metal chemistry, solid-state and surface chemistry.

Iowa State University of Science and Technology, Program in Physical Chemistry, Ames, IA 50011. Offers MS, PhD. *Entrance requirements:* Additional exam requirements/recommendations for international students: Required—TOEFL (minimum score 570 paper-based; 89 iBT), IELTS (minimum score 6.5). Electronic applications accepted.

Laurentian University, School of Graduate Studies and Research, Programme in Chemistry and Biochemistry, Sudbury, ON P3E 2C6, Canada. Offers analytical chemistry (M Sc); biochemistry (M Sc); environmental chemistry (M Sc); organic chemistry (M Sc); physical/theoretical chemistry (M Sc). *Program availability:* Part-time. *Degree requirements:* For master's, thesis or alternative. *Entrance requirements:* For master's, honors degree with minimum second class. *Faculty research:* Cell cycle checkpoints, kinetic modeling, toxicology to metal stress, quantum chemistry, biogeochemistry metal speciation.

Marquette University, Graduate School, College of Arts and Sciences, Department of Chemistry, Milwaukee, WI 53201-1881. Offers analytical chemistry (MS, PhD); bioanalytical chemistry (MS, PhD); biophysical chemistry (MS, PhD); chemical physics (MS, PhD); inorganic chemistry (MS, PhD); organic chemistry (MS, PhD); physical chemistry (MS, PhD). *Program availability:* Part-time. Terminal master's awarded for partial completion of doctoral program. *Degree requirements:* For master's, comprehensive exam; for doctorate, thesis/dissertation, cumulative exams. *Entrance requirements:* For master's and doctorate, official transcripts from all current and previous colleges/universities except Marquette, three letters of recommendation from individuals familiar with the applicant's academic work. Additional exam requirements/recommendations for international students: Required—TOEFL. Electronic applications accepted. *Faculty research:* Inorganic complexes, laser Raman spectroscopy, organic synthesis, synthetic bioinorganic chemistry, electro-active organic molecules.

Massachusetts Institute of Technology, School of Science, Department of Chemistry, Cambridge, MA 02139. Offers biological chemistry (PhD); inorganic chemistry (PhD); organic chemistry (PhD); physical chemistry (PhD). *Degree requirements:* For doctorate, comprehensive exam, thesis/dissertation, teaching assistantship during two semesters. *Entrance requirements:* For doctorate, GRE General Test. Additional exam requirements/recommendations for international students: Required—TOEFL, IELTS. Electronic applications accepted. *Expenses: Tuition:* Full-time $51,520; part-time $800 per credit hour. *Required fees:* $312. *Faculty research:* Synthetic organic and organometallic chemistry including catalysis; biological chemistry including bioorganic chemistry; physical chemistry including chemical dynamics, theoretical chemistry and biophysical chemistry; inorganic chemistry including synthesis, catalysis, bioinorganic and physical inorganic chemistry; materials chemistry including surface science, nanoscience and polymers.

McMaster University, School of Graduate Studies, Faculty of Science, Department of Chemistry, Hamilton, ON L8S 4M2, Canada. Offers analytical chemistry (M Sc, PhD); chemical physics (M Sc, PhD); chemistry (M Sc, PhD); inorganic chemistry (M Sc, PhD); organic chemistry (M Sc, PhD); physical chemistry (M Sc, PhD); polymer chemistry (M Sc, PhD). *Program availability:* Part-time. Terminal master's awarded for partial completion of doctoral program. *Degree requirements:* For master's, thesis; for doctorate, comprehensive exam, thesis/dissertation. *Entrance requirements:* For master's, minimum B+ average. Additional exam requirements/recommendations for international students: Required—TOEFL (minimum score 550 paper-based).

Old Dominion University, College of Sciences, Program in Chemistry, Norfolk, VA 23529. Offers analytical chemistry (MS, PhD); biochemistry (MS, PhD); environmental chemistry (MS, PhD); inorganic chemistry (MS, PhD); organic chemistry (MS, PhD); physical chemistry (MS, PhD). *Program availability:* Part-time. Terminal master's awarded for partial completion of doctoral program. *Degree requirements:* For master's, comprehensive exam, thesis (for some programs); for doctorate, comprehensive exam, thesis/dissertation. *Entrance requirements:* For master's and doctorate, GRE General Test, minimum GPA of 3.0 in major, 2.5 overall, transcripts, essay, three letters of recommendation, resume. Additional exam requirements/recommendations for international students: Required—TOEFL (minimum score 84 iBT). Electronic applications accepted. *Expenses:* Contact institution. *Faculty research:* Biogeochemistry, materials chemistry, computational chemistry, organic chemistry, biofuels.

Purdue University, Graduate School, College of Science, Department of Chemistry, West Lafayette, IN 47907. Offers analytical chemistry (PhD); biochemistry (MS, PhD); chemical education (MS, PhD); inorganic chemistry (MS, PhD); organic chemistry (MS, PhD); physical chemistry (PhD). *Faculty:* 47 full-time (13 women), 2 part-time/adjunct (0 women). *Students:* 314 full-time (124 women), 18 part-time (13 women); includes 63 minority (16 Black or African American, non-Hispanic/Latino; 15 Asian, non-Hispanic/Latino; 25 Hispanic/Latino; 7 Two or more races, non-Hispanic/Latino), 146 international. Average age 26. 711 applicants, 27% accepted, 64 enrolled. In 2018, 9 master's, 50 doctorates awarded. Terminal master's awarded for partial completion of doctoral program. *Degree requirements:* For master's, thesis; for doctorate, comprehensive exam, thesis/dissertation. *Entrance requirements:* For master's and doctorate, minimum undergraduate GPA of 3.0. Additional exam requirements/recommendations for international students: Required—TOEFL (minimum score 550 paper-based; 77 iBT); Recommended—TWE. *Application deadline:* For fall admission, 2/15 priority date for domestic students, 1/1 for international students. Applications are processed on a rolling basis. Application fee: $60 ($75 for international students). Electronic applications accepted. *Financial support:* In 2018–19, 2 fellowships with partial tuition reimbursements (averaging $18,000 per year), 55 teaching assistantships with partial tuition reimbursements (averaging $18,000 per year) were awarded; research assistantships with partial tuition reimbursements and tuition waivers (partial) also available. Support available to part-time students. Financial award applicants required to submit FAFSA. *Unit head:* Christine A. Hrycyna, Head, 765-494-5203, E-mail: hrycyna@purdue.edu. *Application contact:* Betty L. Hatfield, Director of Graduate Admissions, 765-494-5208, E-mail: bettyh@purdue.edu. Website: https://www.chem.purdue.edu/

Rice University, Graduate Programs, Wiess School of Natural Sciences, Department of Chemistry, Houston, TX 77251-1892. Offers chemistry (MA); inorganic chemistry (PhD); organic chemistry (PhD); physical chemistry (PhD). Terminal master's awarded for partial completion of doctoral program. *Degree requirements:* For master's, thesis; for doctorate, thesis/dissertation. *Entrance requirements:* For master's and doctorate, GRE General Test, minimum GPA of 3.0. Additional exam requirements/recommendations for international students: Required—TOEFL (minimum score 600 paper-based; 90 iBT). Electronic applications accepted. *Faculty research:* Nanoscience, biomaterials, nanobioinformatics, fullerene pharmaceuticals.

Rutgers University–Newark, Graduate School, Program in Chemistry, Newark, NJ 07102. Offers analytical chemistry (MS, PhD); biochemistry (MS, PhD); inorganic chemistry (MS, PhD); organic chemistry (MS, PhD); physical chemistry (MS, PhD). *Program availability:* Part-time, evening/weekend. Terminal master's awarded for partial completion of doctoral program. *Degree requirements:* For master's, thesis optional, cumulative exams; for doctorate, thesis/dissertation, exams, research proposal. *Entrance requirements:* For master's and doctorate, GRE General Test, minimum undergraduate B average. Additional exam requirements/recommendations for international students: Required—TOEFL. Electronic applications accepted. *Faculty research:* Medicinal chemistry, natural products, isotope effects, biophysics and bioorganic approaches to enzyme mechanisms, organic and organometallic synthesis.

Rutgers University–New Brunswick, Graduate School-New Brunswick, Department of Chemistry and Chemical Biology, Piscataway, NJ 08854-8097. Offers biological chemistry (MS, PhD); inorganic chemistry (MS, PhD); organic chemistry (MS, PhD); physical chemistry (MS, PhD). *Program availability:* Part-time, evening/weekend. Terminal master's awarded for partial completion of doctoral program. *Degree requirements:* For master's, thesis or alternative, exam; for doctorate, thesis/dissertation, 1 year residency. *Entrance requirements:* For master's and doctorate, GRE General Test, GRE Subject Test. Additional exam requirements/recommendations for international students: Required—TOEFL. Electronic applications accepted. *Faculty research:* Biophysical organic/bioorganic, inorganic/bioinorganic, theoretical, and solid-state/surface chemistry.

Seton Hall University, College of Arts and Sciences, Department of Chemistry and Biochemistry, South Orange, NJ 07079-2697. Offers analytical chemistry (MS, PhD); biochemistry (MS, PhD); chemistry (MS); inorganic chemistry (MS, PhD); organic chemistry (MS, PhD); physical chemistry (MS, PhD). *Program availability:* Part-time, evening/weekend. Terminal master's awarded for partial completion of doctoral program. *Degree requirements:* For master's, thesis optional; for doctorate, comprehensive exam, thesis/dissertation. *Entrance requirements:* Additional exam requirements/recommendations for international students: Required—TOEFL. Electronic applications accepted. *Faculty research:* DNA metal reactions; chromatography; bioinorganic, biophysical, organometallic, polymer chemistry; heterogeneous catalyst; synthetic organic and carbohydrate chemistry.

Southern University and Agricultural and Mechanical College, Graduate School, College of Sciences and Engineering, Program in Chemistry, Baton Rouge, LA 70813. Offers analytical chemistry (MS); biochemistry (MS); environmental sciences (MS); inorganic chemistry (MS); organic chemistry (MS); physical chemistry (MS). *Degree requirements:* For master's, thesis. *Entrance requirements:* For master's, GMAT or GRE General Test. Additional exam requirements/recommendations for international students: Required—TOEFL (minimum score 525 paper-based). *Faculty research:* Synthesis of macrocyclic ligands, latex accelerators, anticancer drugs, biosensors, absorption isotheums, isolation of specific enzymes from plants.

University of Calgary, Faculty of Graduate Studies, Faculty of Science, Program in Chemistry, Calgary, AB T2N 1N4, Canada. Offers analytical chemistry (M Sc, PhD); applied chemistry (M Sc, PhD); inorganic chemistry (M Sc, PhD); organic chemistry (M Sc, PhD); physical chemistry (M Sc, PhD); polymer chemistry (M Sc, PhD); theoretical chemistry (M Sc, PhD). *Degree requirements:* For master's, thesis; for doctorate, thesis/dissertation, candidacy exam. *Entrance requirements:* For master's, minimum GPA of 3.0; for doctorate, honors B Sc degree with minimum GPA of 3.7 or M Sc with minimum GPA of 3.3. Additional exam requirements/recommendations for

international students: Required—TOEFL (minimum score 580 paper-based). Electronic applications accepted. *Faculty research:* Chemical analysis, chemical dynamics, synthesis theory.

University of Cincinnati, Graduate School, McMicken College of Arts and Sciences, Department of Chemistry, Cincinnati, OH 45221. Offers analytical chemistry (MS, PhD); biochemistry (MS, PhD); inorganic chemistry (MS, PhD); organic chemistry (MS, PhD); physical chemistry (MS, PhD); polymer chemistry (MS, PhD); sensors (PhD). *Program availability:* Part-time, evening/weekend. Terminal master's awarded for partial completion of doctoral program. *Degree requirements:* For master's, thesis optional; for doctorate, comprehensive exam, thesis/dissertation. *Entrance requirements:* For master's and doctorate, GRE General Test. Additional exam requirements/recommendations for international students: Required—TOEFL (minimum score 580 paper-based). Electronic applications accepted. *Faculty research:* Biomedical chemistry, laser chemistry, surface science, chemical sensors, synthesis.

University of Louisville, Graduate School, College of Arts and Sciences, Department of Chemistry, Louisville, KY 40292-0001. Offers analytical chemistry (MS, PhD); biochemistry (MS, PhD); chemical physics (PhD); inorganic chemistry (MS, PhD); organic chemistry (MS, PhD); physical chemistry (MS, PhD). *Faculty:* 26 full-time (9 women), 3 part-time/adjunct (1 woman). *Students:* 35 full-time (14 women), 17 part-time (4 women); includes 5 minority (2 Black or African American, non-Hispanic/Latino; 3 Asian, non-Hispanic/Latino), 39 international. Average age 31. 47 applicants, 36% accepted, 10 enrolled. In 2018, 18 master's, 3 doctorates awarded. Terminal master's awarded for partial completion of doctoral program. *Degree requirements:* For master's, thesis (for some programs), Literature Seminars; for doctorate, thesis/dissertation, Cumulative Exams, Literature Seminars; Research. *Entrance requirements:* For master's and doctorate, GRE General Test, official transcripts, recommendation letters (minimum of 2), personal statement. Additional exam requirements/recommendations for international students: Required—TOEFL (minimum score 550 paper-based; 79 iBT), IELTS can be taken in place of TOEFL; Recommended—IELTS (minimum score 6.5). *Application deadline:* For fall admission, 1/15 priority date for domestic and international students; for spring admission, 9/15 priority date for domestic and international students. Application fee: $65. Electronic applications accepted. *Expenses: Tuition, area resident:* Full-time $6500; part-time $723 per credit hour. Tuition, state resident: full-time $6500. Tuition, nonresident: full-time $13,557; part-time $1507 per credit hour. Tuition and fees vary according to course load and program. *Financial support:* In 2018–19, 59 students received support, including 2 fellowships with full tuition reimbursements available (averaging $23,000 per year), 10 research assistantships with full tuition reimbursements available (averaging $23,000 per year), 41 teaching assistantships with full tuition reimbursements available (averaging $23,000 per year); scholarships/grants, health care benefits, and unspecified assistantships also available. Financial award application deadline: 1/15. *Faculty research:* Solid state chemistry, chemical synthesis, nanoparticle research, green chemistry, spectroscopic studies, computational chemistry, catalysis. *Total annual research expenditures:* $1 million. *Unit head:* Dr. Craig Grapperhaus, Professor, 502-852-8148, Fax: 502-852-8149, E-mail: craig.grapperhaus@louisville.edu. *Application contact:* Sherry Nalley, Graduate Program Assistant, 502-852-6798, Fax: 502-852-6536, E-mail: sherry.nalley@louisville.edu.
Website: http://louisville.edu/chemistry

The University of Manchester, School of Chemistry, Manchester, United Kingdom. Offers biological chemistry (PhD); chemistry (M Ent, M Phil, M Sc, D Ent, PhD); inorganic chemistry (PhD); materials chemistry (PhD); nanoscience (PhD); nuclear fission (PhD); organic chemistry (PhD); physical chemistry (PhD); theoretical chemistry (PhD).

University of Maryland, College Park, Academic Affairs, College of Computer, Mathematical and Natural Sciences, Department of Chemistry and Biochemistry, Chemistry Program, College Park, MD 20742. Offers analytical chemistry (MS, PhD); inorganic chemistry (MS, PhD); organic chemistry (MS, PhD); physical chemistry (MS, PhD). *Program availability:* Part-time, evening/weekend. Terminal master's awarded for partial completion of doctoral program. *Degree requirements:* For master's, thesis optional; for doctorate, thesis/dissertation, 2 seminar presentations, oral exam. *Entrance requirements:* For master's and doctorate, GRE General Test, GRE Subject Test (recommended), minimum GPA of 3.0, 3 letters of recommendation. Additional exam requirements/recommendations for international students: Required—TOEFL. Electronic applications accepted. *Faculty research:* Environmental chemistry, nuclear chemistry, lunar and environmental analysis, X-ray crystallography.

University of Memphis, Graduate School, College of Arts and Sciences, Department of Chemistry, Memphis, TN 38152. Offers analytical chemistry (MS, PhD); computational chemistry (MS, PhD); inorganic chemistry (MS, PhD); organic chemistry (MS, PhD); physical chemistry (MS, PhD). *Program availability:* Part-time. *Students:* 37 full-time (11 women), 14 part-time (5 women); includes 9 minority (2 Black or African American, non-Hispanic/Latino; 3 Asian, non-Hispanic/Latino; 4 Two or more races, non-Hispanic/Latino), 6 international. Average age 27. 24 applicants, 67% accepted, 14 enrolled. In 2018, 9 master's, 3 doctorates awarded. Terminal master's awarded for partial completion of doctoral program. *Degree requirements:* For master's, comprehensive exam, thesis or alternative; for doctorate, comprehensive exam, thesis/dissertation. *Entrance requirements:* For master's and doctorate, GRE General Test, admission to Graduate School plus 32 undergraduate hours in chemistry. Additional exam requirements/recommendations for international students: Required—TOEFL (minimum score 550 paper-based). *Application deadline:* For fall admission, 7/1 for domestic students, 5/1 for international students; for winter admission, 9/15 for international students; for spring admission, 12/1 for domestic students. Applications are processed on a rolling basis. Application fee: $35 ($60 for international students). Electronic applications accepted. *Expenses: Tuition, area resident:* Full-time $10,240; part-time $503 per credit hour. Tuition, state resident: full-time $10,464. Tuition, nonresident: full-time $20,224; part-time $991 per credit hour. *Required fees:* $850; $106 per credit hour. *Financial support:* Research assistantships with full tuition reimbursements, teaching assistantships with full tuition reimbursements, Federal Work-Study, scholarships/grants, and unspecified assistantships available. Financial award application deadline: 2/1; financial award applicants required to submit FAFSA. *Faculty research:* Computational chemistry, materials chemistry, organic/polymer synthesis, drug design/delivery, water chemistry. *Unit head:* Dr. Gary Emmert, Chair, 901-678-2638, Fax: 901-678-3447, E-mail: gemmert@memphis.edu. *Application contact:* Dr. Paul Simone, Coordinator of Graduate Studies, 901-678-3671, Fax: 901-678-3447, E-mail: gradchem@memphis.edu.
Website: http://www.memphis.edu/chem/

University of Miami, Graduate School, College of Arts and Sciences, Department of Chemistry, Coral Gables, FL 33124. Offers chemistry (MS); inorganic chemistry (PhD); organic chemistry (PhD); physical chemistry (PhD). Terminal master's awarded for partial completion of doctoral program. *Degree requirements:* For master's, comprehensive exam; for doctorate, comprehensive exam, thesis/dissertation. *Entrance requirements:* For master's and doctorate, GRE General Test. Additional exam requirements/

Peterson's Graduate Programs in the Physical Sciences, Mathematics, Agricultural Sciences, the Environment & Natural Resources 2020

www.petersons.com **81**

recommendations for international students: Required—TOEFL (minimum score 550 paper-based). Electronic applications accepted. *Faculty research:* Supramolecular chemistry, electrochemistry, surface chemistry, catalysis, organometalic.

University of Michigan, Rackham Graduate School, College of Literature, Science, and the Arts, Department of Chemistry, Ann Arbor, MI 48109-1055. Offers analytical chemistry (PhD); chemical biology (PhD); chemical sciences (MS); inorganic chemistry (PhD); materials chemistry (PhD); organic chemistry (PhD); physical chemistry (PhD). *Program availability:* Part-time. *Faculty:* 40 full-time (14 women), 7 part-time/adjunct (3 women). *Students:* 262 full-time (112 women), 4 part-time (all women); includes 44 minority (11 Black or African American, non-Hispanic/Latino; 11 Asian, non-Hispanic/Latino; 19 Hispanic/Latino; 1 Native Hawaiian or other Pacific Islander, non-Hispanic/Latino; 2 Two or more races, non-Hispanic/Latino), 61 international. 692 applicants, 71 enrolled. In 2018, 47 master's, 46 doctorates awarded. *Degree requirements:* For doctorate, comprehensive exam, thesis/dissertation, oral defense of dissertation, organic cumulative proficiency exams. *Entrance requirements:* For master's, bachelor's degree, 3 letters of recommendation, personal statement; for doctorate, bachelor's degree, 3 letters of recommendation, personal statement, curriculum vitae/resume. Additional exam requirements/recommendations for international students: Required—TOEFL (minimum score 560 paper-based; 84 iBT) or IELTS. *Application deadline:* For fall admission, 12/1 for domestic and international students. Application fee: $0 ($90 for international students). Electronic applications accepted. *Financial support:* In 2018–19, 269 students received support, including 50 fellowships with full tuition reimbursements available (averaging $31,625 per year), 84 research assistantships with full tuition reimbursements available (averaging $31,625 per year), 133 teaching assistantships with full tuition reimbursements available (averaging $31,625 per year); career-related internships or fieldwork, Federal Work-Study, scholarships/grants, traineeships, health care benefits, tuition waivers (full), and unspecified assistantships also available. *Faculty research:* Biological catalysis, protein engineering, chemical sensors, de novo metalloprotein design, supramolecular architecture. *Total annual research expenditures:* $19.6 million. *Unit head:* Dr. Robert Kennedy, Professor of Chemistry/Chair, 734-763-9681, Fax: 734-647-4847. *Application contact:* Elizabeth Oxford, Graduate Program Coordinator, 734-764-7278, Fax: 734-647-4865, E-mail: chemadmissions@umich.edu.
Website: http://www.lsa.umich.edu/chem/

University of Missouri–Kansas City, College of Arts and Sciences, Department of Chemistry, Kansas City, MO 64110-2499. Offers analytical chemistry (PhD); inorganic chemistry (PhD); organic chemistry (PhD); physical chemistry (PhD); polymer chemistry (MS, PhD). PhD (interdisciplinary) offered through the School of Graduate Studies. *Program availability:* Part-time, evening/weekend. *Degree requirements:* For master's, thesis (for some programs); for doctorate, thesis/dissertation. *Entrance requirements:* For master's, equivalent of American Chemical Society approved bachelor's degree in chemistry; for doctorate, GRE General Test, equivalent of American Chemical Society approved bachelor's degree in chemistry. Additional exam requirements/recommendations for international students: Required—TOEFL (minimum score 550 paper-based; 80 iBT), TWE. Electronic applications accepted. *Faculty research:* Molecular spectroscopy, characterization and synthesis of materials and compounds, computational chemistry, natural products, drug delivery systems and anti-tumor agents.

University of Montana, Graduate School, College of Humanities and Sciences, Department of Chemistry and Biochemistry, Missoula, MT 59812. Offers chemistry (MS, PhD), including environmental/analytical chemistry, inorganic chemistry, organic chemistry, physical chemistry. Terminal master's awarded for partial completion of doctoral program. *Degree requirements:* For master's, thesis (for some programs); for doctorate, thesis/dissertation. *Entrance requirements:* For master's and doctorate, GRE General Test. Additional exam requirements/recommendations for international students: Required—TOEFL (minimum score 575 paper-based). *Faculty research:* Reaction mechanisms and kinetics, inorganic and organic synthesis, analytical chemistry, natural products.

University of Nebraska–Lincoln, Graduate College, College of Arts and Sciences, Department of Chemistry, Lincoln, NE 68588. Offers analytical chemistry (PhD); biochemistry (PhD); chemistry (MS); inorganic chemistry (PhD); materials chemistry (PhD); organic chemistry (PhD); physical chemistry (PhD). *Degree requirements:* For master's, one foreign language, thesis optional, departmental qualifying exam; for doctorate, one foreign language, comprehensive exam, thesis/dissertation, departmental qualifying exams. *Entrance requirements:* For master's and doctorate, GRE. Additional exam requirements/recommendations for international students: Required—TOEFL (minimum score 550 paper-based). Electronic applications accepted. *Faculty research:* Bioorganic and bioinorganic chemistry, biophysical and bioanalytical chemistry, structure-function of DNA and proteins, organometallics, mass spectrometry.

University of Notre Dame, The Graduate School, College of Science, Department of Chemistry and Biochemistry, Notre Dame, IN 46556. Offers biochemistry (MS, PhD); inorganic chemistry (MS, PhD); organic chemistry (MS, PhD); physical chemistry (MS, PhD). Terminal master's awarded for partial completion of doctoral program. *Degree requirements:* For master's, comprehensive exam, thesis; for doctorate, thesis/dissertation, qualifying exam. *Entrance requirements:* For master's and doctorate, GRE General Test, GRE Subject Test (strongly recommended). Additional exam requirements/recommendations for international students: Required—TOEFL (minimum score 600 paper-based; 80 iBT). Electronic applications accepted. *Faculty research:* Reaction design and mechanistic studies; reactive intermediates; synthesis, structure and reactivity of organometallic cluster complexes and biologically active natural products; bioorganic chemistry; enzymology.

University of Oklahoma, College of Arts and Sciences, Department of Chemistry and Biochemistry, Norman, OK 73019. Offers chemistry (MS, PhD), including analytical chemistry, biochemistry, chemical education, inorganic chemistry, inter-and/or multidisciplinary, organic chemistry, physical chemistry, structural biology. *Program availability:* Part-time. *Faculty:* 32 full-time (13 women). *Students:* 89 full-time (38 women), 33 part-time (15 women); includes 22 minority (2 Black or African American, non-Hispanic/Latino; 9 Asian, non-Hispanic/Latino; 6 Hispanic/Latino; 5 Two or more races, non-Hispanic/Latino), 46 international. Average age 26. 78 applicants, 71% accepted, 33 enrolled. In 2018, 15 master's, 21 doctorates awarded. Terminal master's awarded for partial completion of doctoral program. *Degree requirements:* For master's, comprehensive exam (for some programs), thesis (for some programs); for doctorate, comprehensive exam, thesis/dissertation, general exam. *Entrance requirements:* For master's and doctorate, GRE. Additional exam requirements/recommendations for international students: Required—TOEFL (minimum score 79 iBT) or IELTS (minimum score 6.5). *Application deadline:* For fall admission, 3/31 priority date for domestic and international students; for spring admission, 9/1 priority date for domestic and international students. Application fee: $50 ($100 for international students). Electronic applications accepted. *Expenses:* Tuition, state resident: full-time $5683.20; part-time $236.80 per credit hour. Tuition, nonresident: full-time $20,342; part-time $847.60 per credit hour. *International tuition:* $20,342.40 full-time. *Required fees:* $2894.20; $110.05 per credit hour. $126.50 per semester. Tuition and fees vary according to course load and program. *Financial support:* Research assistantships, teaching assistantships, institutionally sponsored loans, scholarships/grants, health care benefits, unspecified assistantships, and full tuition with qualifying graduate assistantship available. Support available to part-time students. Financial award application deadline: 6/1; financial award applicants required to submit FAFSA. *Faculty research:* Structural biology, solid state materials, natural products, membrane biochemistry, bioanalysis. *Unit head:* Dr. Ronald L. Halterman, Professor and Chair, 405-325-4812, Fax: 405-325-6111, E-mail: rhalterman@ou.edu. *Application contact:* Carol Jones, Operations Manager, 405-325-4811, Fax: 405-325-6111, E-mail: caroljones@ou.edu.
Website: http://www.ou.edu/cas/chemistry

University of Puerto Rico–Mayagüez, Graduate Studies, College of Arts and Sciences, Department of Chemistry, Mayagüez, PR 00681-9000. Offers applied chemistry (MS, PhD), including biophysical chemistry (PhD), chemistry of materials (PhD), environmental chemistry (PhD). *Program availability:* Part-time. Terminal master's awarded for partial completion of doctoral program. *Degree requirements:* For master's, one foreign language, comprehensive exam, thesis; for doctorate, one foreign language, comprehensive exam, thesis/dissertation. *Entrance requirements:* For master's, GRE General Test or minimum GPA of 2.0, BS in chemistry or the equivalent; minimum GPA of 2.8; for doctorate, GRE General Test or minimum GPA of 2.0. Electronic applications accepted. *Faculty research:* Synthesis of heterocyclic moieties, protein structure and function, chemistry of explosives, bio-nanocomposites, process analytical technology.

University of Rochester, School of Arts and Sciences, Department of Chemistry, Rochester, NY 14627. Offers inorganic chemistry (PhD); organic chemistry (PhD); physical chemistry (PhD). *Faculty:* 17 full-time (5 women). *Students:* 91 full-time (42 women); includes 10 minority (1 Black or African American, non-Hispanic/Latino; 2 Asian, non-Hispanic/Latino; 7 Hispanic/Latino), 24 international. Average age 27. 247 applicants, 25% accepted, 16 enrolled. In 2018, 9 doctorates awarded. Terminal master's awarded for partial completion of doctoral program. *Degree requirements:* For doctorate, thesis/dissertation, qualifying exam. *Entrance requirements:* For doctorate, GRE General Test, GRE Subject Test (recommended), transcripts, three letters of recommendation. Additional exam requirements/recommendations for international students: Required—TOEFL (minimum score 100 iBT), IELTS (minimum score 6.5). *Application deadline:* For fall admission, 12/15 for domestic and international students. Electronic applications accepted. *Expenses: Tuition:* Full-time $52,974; part-time $1654 per credit hour. *Required fees:* $612. One-time fee: $30 part-time. Tuition and fees vary according to campus/location and program. *Financial support:* In 2018–19, 34 students received support, including 13 research assistantships (averaging $26,000 per year), 4 teaching assistantships (averaging $26,000 per year); Federal Work-Study, scholarships/grants, and tuition waivers (full) also available. Financial award application deadline: 12/15. *Faculty research:* Organic chemistry, physical chemistry, theoretical chemistry, biological chemistry, materials chemistry. *Total annual research expenditures:* $4.2 million. *Unit head:* Todd D. Krauss, Chair, 585-275-5093, E-mail: todd.krauss@rochester.edu. *Application contact:* Robin Clark, Administrative Assistant, 585-275-0635, E-mail: robin.clark@rochester.edu.
Website: http://www.sas.rochester.edu/chm/graduate/index.html

University of Southern California, Graduate School, Dana and David Dornsife College of Letters, Arts and Sciences, Department of Chemistry, Los Angeles, CA 90089. Offers chemistry (PhD); physical chemistry (PhD). Terminal master's awarded for partial completion of doctoral program. *Degree requirements:* For doctorate, thesis/dissertation. *Entrance requirements:* For doctorate, GRE General Test. Additional exam requirements/recommendations for international students: Required—TOEFL. Electronic applications accepted. *Faculty research:* Biological chemistry, inorganic chemistry, organic chemistry, physical chemistry, theoretical chemistry.

The University of Tennessee, Graduate School, College of Arts and Sciences, Department of Chemistry, Knoxville, TN 37996. Offers analytical chemistry (MS, PhD); chemical physics (PhD); environmental chemistry (MS, PhD); inorganic chemistry (MS, PhD); organic chemistry (MS, PhD); physical chemistry (MS, PhD); polymer chemistry (MS, PhD); theoretical chemistry (PhD). *Program availability:* Part-time. Terminal master's awarded for partial completion of doctoral program. *Degree requirements:* For master's, thesis; for doctorate, thesis/dissertation. *Entrance requirements:* For master's and doctorate, GRE General Test, minimum GPA of 2.7. Additional exam requirements/recommendations for international students: Required—TOEFL. Electronic applications accepted.

The University of Texas at Austin, Graduate School, College of Natural Sciences, Department of Chemistry and Biochemistry, Austin, TX 78712-1111. Offers analytical chemistry (PhD); biochemistry (PhD); inorganic chemistry (PhD); organic chemistry (PhD); physical chemistry (PhD). *Entrance requirements:* For doctorate, GRE General Test.

The University of Toledo, College of Graduate Studies, College of Natural Sciences and Mathematics, Department of Chemistry, Toledo, OH 43606-3390. Offers analytical chemistry (MS, PhD); biological chemistry (MS, PhD); inorganic chemistry (MS, PhD); organic chemistry (MS, PhD); physical chemistry (MS, PhD). *Program availability:* Part-time. *Degree requirements:* For master's, thesis or alternative; for doctorate, thesis/dissertation. *Entrance requirements:* For master's and doctorate, GRE General Test, GRE Subject Test, minimum cumulative point-hour ratio of 2.7 for all previous academic work, three letters of recommendation, statement of purpose, transcripts from all prior institutions attended. Additional exam requirements/recommendations for international students: Required—TOEFL (minimum score 550 paper-based; 80 iBT). Electronic applications accepted. *Faculty research:* Enzymology, materials chemistry, crystallography, theoretical chemistry.

Virginia Commonwealth University, Graduate School, College of Humanities and Sciences, Department of Chemistry, Richmond, VA 23284-9005. Offers analytical chemistry (MS, PhD); chemical physics (PhD); inorganic chemistry (MS, PhD); organic chemistry (MS, PhD); physical chemistry (MS, PhD). *Program availability:* Part-time. Terminal master's awarded for partial completion of doctoral program. *Degree requirements:* For master's, thesis; for doctorate, thesis/dissertation, comprehensive cumulative exams, research proposal. *Entrance requirements:* For master's, GRE General Test, 30 undergraduate credits in chemistry; for doctorate, GRE General Test. Additional exam requirements/recommendations for international students: Required—TOEFL (minimum score 600 paper-based; 100 iBT) or IELTS (minimum score 6.5). Electronic applications accepted. *Faculty research:* Physical, organic, inorganic, analytical, and polymer chemistry; chemical physics.

Wake Forest University, Graduate School of Arts and Sciences, Department of Chemistry, Winston-Salem, NC 27109. Offers analytical chemistry (MS, PhD); inorganic chemistry (MS, PhD); organic chemistry (MS, PhD); physical chemistry (MS, PhD). *Program availability:* Part-time. *Degree requirements:* For master's, one foreign language, comprehensive exam, thesis; for doctorate, 2 foreign languages, comprehensive exam, thesis/dissertation. *Entrance requirements:* For master's and doctorate, GRE General Test. Additional exam requirements/recommendations for international students: Required—TOEFL. Electronic applications accepted.

Yale University, Graduate School of Arts and Sciences, Department of Chemistry, New Haven, CT 06520. Offers biophysical chemistry (PhD); inorganic chemistry (PhD); organic chemistry (PhD); physical and theoretical chemistry (PhD). *Degree requirements:* For doctorate, thesis/dissertation. *Entrance requirements:* For doctorate, GRE General Test, GRE Subject Test. Additional exam requirements/recommendations for international students: Required—TOEFL.

Youngstown State University, College of Graduate Studies, College of Science, Technology, Engineering and Mathematics, Department of Chemistry, Youngstown, OH

44555-0001. Offers analytical chemistry (MS); biochemistry (MS); chemistry education (MS); inorganic chemistry (MS); organic chemistry (MS); physical chemistry (MS). *Program availability:* Part-time. *Degree requirements:* For master's, thesis. *Entrance requirements:* For master's, bachelor's degree in chemistry, minimum GPA of 2.7. Additional exam requirements/recommendations for international students: Required—TOEFL. *Faculty research:* Analysis of antioxidants, chromatography, defects and disorder in crystalline oxides, hydrogen bonding, novel organic and organometallic materials.

Theoretical Chemistry

Carnegie Mellon University, Mellon College of Science, Department of Chemistry, Pittsburgh, PA 15213-3891. Offers atmospheric chemistry (PhD); bioinorganic chemistry (PhD); bioorganic chemistry and chemical biology (PhD); biophysical chemistry (PhD); catalysis (PhD); green and environmental chemistry (PhD); materials and nanoscience (PhD); renewable energy (PhD); sensors, probes, and imaging (PhD); spectroscopy and single molecule analysis (PhD); theoretical and computational chemistry (PhD). *Program availability:* Part-time. Terminal master's awarded for partial completion of doctoral program. *Degree requirements:* For doctorate, thesis/dissertation, departmental qualifying and oral exams, teaching experience. *Entrance requirements:* For doctorate, GRE General Test, GRE Subject Test. Additional exam requirements/recommendations for international students: Required—TOEFL. Electronic applications accepted. *Faculty research:* Physical and theoretical chemistry, chemical synthesis, biophysical/bioinorganic chemistry.

Cornell University, Graduate School, Graduate Fields of Arts and Sciences, Field of Chemistry and Chemical Biology, Ithaca, NY 14853. Offers analytical chemistry (PhD); bio-organic chemistry (PhD); biophysical chemistry (PhD); chemical biology (PhD); chemical physics (PhD); inorganic chemistry (PhD); materials chemistry (PhD); organic chemistry (PhD); organometallic chemistry (PhD); physical chemistry (PhD); polymer chemistry (PhD); theoretical chemistry (PhD). *Degree requirements:* For doctorate, comprehensive exam, thesis/dissertation. *Entrance requirements:* For doctorate, GRE General Test, GRE Subject Test (chemistry), 3 letters of recommendation. Additional exam requirements/recommendations for international students: Required—TOEFL (minimum score 600 paper-based; 77 iBT). Electronic applications accepted. *Faculty research:* Analytical, organic, inorganic, physical, materials, chemical biology.

Georgetown University, Graduate School of Arts and Sciences, Department of Chemistry, Washington, DC 20057. Offers analytical chemistry (PhD); biochemistry (PhD); computational chemistry (PhD); inorganic chemistry (PhD); materials chemistry (PhD); organic chemistry (PhD); theoretical chemistry (PhD). Terminal master's awarded for partial completion of doctoral program. *Degree requirements:* For doctorate, comprehensive exam, thesis/dissertation. *Entrance requirements:* For doctorate, GRE General Test. Additional exam requirements/recommendations for international students: Required—TOEFL.

Laurentian University, School of Graduate Studies and Research, Programme in Chemistry and Biochemistry, Sudbury, ON P3E 2C6, Canada. Offers analytical chemistry (M Sc); biochemistry (M Sc); environmental chemistry (M Sc); organic chemistry (M Sc); physical/theoretical chemistry (M Sc). *Program availability:* Part-time. *Degree requirements:* For master's, thesis or alternative. *Entrance requirements:* For master's, honors degree with minimum second class. *Faculty research:* Cell cycle checkpoints, kinetic modeling, toxicology to metal stress, quantum chemistry, biogeochemistry metal speciation.

University of Calgary, Faculty of Graduate Studies, Faculty of Science, Program in Chemistry, Calgary, AB T2N 1N4, Canada. Offers analytical chemistry (M Sc, PhD); applied chemistry (M Sc, PhD); inorganic chemistry (M Sc, PhD); organic chemistry (M Sc, PhD); physical chemistry (M Sc, PhD); polymer chemistry (M Sc, PhD); theoretical chemistry (M Sc, PhD). *Degree requirements:* For master's, thesis; for doctorate, thesis/dissertation, candidacy exam. *Entrance requirements:* For master's, minimum GPA of 3.0; for doctorate, honors B Sc degree with minimum GPA of 3.7 or M Sc with minimum GPA of 3.3. Additional exam requirements/recommendations for international students: Required—TOEFL (minimum score 580 paper-based). Electronic applications accepted. *Faculty research:* Chemical analysis, chemical dynamics, synthesis theory.

The University of Manchester, School of Chemistry, Manchester, United Kingdom. Offers biological chemistry (PhD); chemistry (M Ent, M Phil, M Sc, D Ent, PhD); inorganic chemistry (PhD); materials chemistry (PhD); nanoscience (PhD); nuclear fission (PhD); organic chemistry (PhD); physical chemistry (PhD); theoretical chemistry (PhD).

University of Regina, Faculty of Graduate Studies and Research, Faculty of Science, Department of Chemistry and Biochemistry, Regina, SK S4S 0A2, Canada. Offers biophysics of biological interfaces (M Sc, PhD); computational chemistry (M Sc, PhD); environmental analytical chemistry (M Sc, PhD); enzymology/chemical biology (M Sc, PhD); inorganic/organometallic chemistry (M Sc, PhD); signal transduction and

mechanisms of cancer cell regulation (M Sc, PhD); supramolecular organic photochemistry and photophysics (M Sc, PhD); synthetic organic chemistry (M Sc, PhD). *Program availability:* Part-time. *Faculty:* 12 full-time (2 women), 4 part-time/adjunct (0 women). *Students:* 12 full-time (6 women), 1 part-time (0 women). Average age 30. 23 applicants, 17% accepted. In 2018, 2 master's awarded. *Degree requirements:* For master's, thesis; for doctorate, comprehensive exam, thesis/dissertation. *Entrance requirements:* For master's, 4 years Bachelor degree in Chemistry or related program; for doctorate, completion of Master's in Chemistry. Additional exam requirements/recommendations for international students: Required—TOEFL (minimum score 580 paper-based; 80 iBT), IELTS (minimum score 6.5), PTE (minimum score 59), other options are CAEL, MELAB, Cantest and U of R ESL. *Application deadline:* Applications are processed on a rolling basis. Application fee: $100. Electronic applications accepted. Tuition and fees vary according to course level, course load, degree level and program. *Financial support:* Fellowships, research assistantships, teaching assistantships, career-related internships or fieldwork, Federal Work-Study, scholarships/grants, unspecified assistantships, and travel award & Graduate Scholarship Base Funds available. Support available to part-time students. Financial award application deadline: 9/30. *Faculty research:* Asymmetric synthesis and methodology, theoretical and computational chemistry, biophysical biochemistry, analytical and environmental chemistry, chemical biology. *Unit head:* Dr. Renata Raina-Fulton, Department Head, 306-585-4012, Fax: 306-337-2409, E-mail: renata.raina@uregina.ca. *Application contact:* Dr. Brian Sterenberg, Graduate Program Coordinator, 306-585-4106, Fax: 306-337-2409, E-mail: brian.sterenberg@uregina.ca. Website: http://www.uregina.ca/science/chem-biochem/

The University of Tennessee, Graduate School, College of Arts and Sciences, Department of Chemistry, Knoxville, TN 37996. Offers analytical chemistry (MS, PhD); chemical physics (PhD); environmental chemistry (MS, PhD); inorganic chemistry (MS, PhD); organic chemistry (MS, PhD); physical chemistry (MS, PhD); polymer chemistry (MS, PhD); theoretical chemistry (PhD). *Program availability:* Part-time. Terminal master's awarded for partial completion of doctoral program. *Degree requirements:* For master's, thesis; for doctorate, thesis/dissertation. *Entrance requirements:* For master's and doctorate, GRE General Test, minimum GPA of 2.7. Additional exam requirements/recommendations for international students: Required—TOEFL. Electronic applications accepted.

Wesleyan University, Graduate Studies, Department of Chemistry, Middletown, CT 06459. Offers biochemistry (PhD); chemical physics (PhD); inorganic chemistry (PhD); organic chemistry (PhD); physical chemistry (PhD); theoretical chemistry (PhD). *Faculty:* 11 full-time (3 women), 1 part-time/adjunct (0 women). *Students:* 16 full-time (9 women). Average age 25. In 2018, 4 doctorates awarded. Terminal master's awarded for partial completion of doctoral program. *Degree requirements:* For doctorate, thesis/dissertation. *Entrance requirements:* For doctorate, GRE General Test, 3 recommendations. Additional exam requirements/recommendations for international students: Required—TOEFL, IELTS. *Application deadline:* 1/1 for domestic and international students; for summer admission, 1/1 for domestic and international students. Application fee: $0. Electronic applications accepted. *Financial support:* In 2018–19, 15 students received support, including 4 research assistantships with full tuition reimbursements available, 13 teaching assistantships with full tuition reimbursements available; institutionally sponsored loans and health care benefits also available. Financial award application deadline: 4/30. *Faculty research:* The synthesis of noble metal and noble metal alloy nanoparticles with well-defined shapes and catalytically-active high-energy surfaces; inorganic chemistry; materials science; scanning electron microscopy (SEM);transition organometallic complexes. *Unit head:* Michael A. Calter, Chair, 860-685-2633 Ext. 2633, Fax: 860-685-2211, E-mail: mcalter@wesleyan.edu. *Application contact:* Aracely Suto, Administrative Assistant, 860-685-2572, Fax: 860-685-2211, E-mail: chemistry@wesleyan.edu. Website: http://www.wesleyan.edu/chem/

Yale University, Graduate School of Arts and Sciences, Department of Chemistry, New Haven, CT 06520. Offers biophysical chemistry (PhD); inorganic chemistry (PhD); organic chemistry (PhD); physical and theoretical chemistry (PhD). *Degree requirements:* For doctorate, thesis/dissertation. *Entrance requirements:* For doctorate, GRE General Test, GRE Subject Test. Additional exam requirements/recommendations for international students: Required—TOEFL.

Peterson's Graduate Programs in the Physical Sciences, Mathematics, Agricultural Sciences, the Environment & Natural Resources 2020

www.petersons.com **83**

Section 3
Geosciences

This section contains a directory of institutions offering graduate work in geosciences. Additional information about programs listed in the directory may be obtained by writing directly to the dean of a graduate school or chair of a department at the address given in the directory.

For programs offering related work, see all other areas in this book. In the other guides in this series:

Graduate Programs in the Humanities, Arts & Social Sciences
See *Geography*

Graduate Programs in the Biological/Biomedical Sciences & Health-Related Medical Professions
See *Biological and Biomedical Sciences, Biophysics,* and *Botany and Plant Biology*

Graduate Programs in Engineering & Applied Sciences
See *Aerospace/Aeronautical Engineering; Agricultural Engineering and Bioengineering; Civil and Environmental Engineering; Energy and Power Engineering (Nuclear Engineering); Engineering and Applied Sciences; Geological, Mineral/Mining, and Petroleum Engineering;* and *Mechanical Engineering and Mechanics*

CONTENTS

Geochemistry

California Institute of Technology, Division of Geological and Planetary Sciences, Pasadena, CA 91125-0001. Offers environmental science and engineering (MS, PhD); geobiology (MS, PhD); geochemistry (MS, PhD); geology (MS, PhD); geophysics (MS, PhD); planetary science (MS, PhD). *Degree requirements:* For doctorate, thesis/dissertation. *Entrance requirements:* For doctorate, GRE General Test. Additional exam requirements/recommendations for international students: Required—TOEFL; Recommended—IELTS, TWE. Electronic applications accepted. *Faculty research:* Planetary surfaces, evolution of anaerobic respiratory processes, structural geology and tectonics, theoretical and numerical seismology, global biogeochemical cycles.

Colorado School of Mines, Office of Graduate Studies, Department of Chemistry and Geochemistry, Golden, CO 80401. Offers chemistry (MS, PhD), including applied chemistry; geochemistry (MS, PhD); materials science (MS, PhD); nuclear engineering (MS, PhD). *Program availability:* Part-time. *Faculty:* 38 full-time (14 women), 2 part-time/adjunct (1 woman). *Students:* 58 full-time (23 women), 3 part-time (2 women); includes 11 minority (4 Asian, non-Hispanic/Latino; 6 Hispanic/Latino; 1 Two or more races, non-Hispanic/Latino), 6 international. Average age 26. 90 applicants, 38% accepted, 14 enrolled. In 2018, 11 master's, 14 doctorates awarded. *Degree requirements:* For master's, thesis (for some programs); for doctorate, comprehensive exam, thesis/dissertation. *Entrance requirements:* For master's and doctorate, GRE General Test. Additional exam requirements/recommendations for international students: Required—TOEFL (minimum score 550 paper-based; 79 iBT). *Application deadline:* For fall admission, 12/15 priority date for domestic and international students; for spring admission, 9/1 priority date for domestic and international students. Application fee: $60 ($80 for international students). Electronic applications accepted. *Expenses:* Tuition, state resident: full-time $16,650; part-time $925 per contact hour. Tuition, nonresident: full-time $36,270; part-time $2015 per contact hour. *International tuition:* $36,270 full-time. *Required fees:* $2314; $2314 per semester. *Financial support:* In 2018–19, 27 research assistantships with full tuition reimbursements, 19 teaching assistantships with full tuition reimbursements were awarded; fellowships, scholarships/grants, health care benefits, and unspecified assistantships also available. Financial award application deadline: 12/15; financial award applicants required to submit FAFSA. *Faculty research:* Environmental chemistry, exploration geochemistry, biogeochemistry, organic geochemistry, catalysis and surface chemistry. *Unit head:* Dr. Tom Gennett, Head, 303-273-3622, Fax: 303-273-3629, E-mail: tgennett@mines.edu. *Application contact:* Megan Rose, Program Manager, 303-273-3637, E-mail: meganrose@mines.edu.
Website: http://chemistry.mines.edu

Colorado School of Mines, Office of Graduate Studies, Department of Geology and Geological Engineering, Golden, CO 80401. Offers environmental geochemistry (PMS); geochemistry (MS, PhD); geological engineering (ME, MS, PhD); geology (MS, PhD); hydrology (MS, PhD); mineral exploration (PMS); petroleum reservoir systems (PMS); underground construction and tunneling (MS). *Program availability:* Part-time. *Faculty:* 30 full-time (12 women), 6 part-time/adjunct (5 women). *Students:* 129 full-time (44 women), 32 part-time (12 women); includes 20 minority (1 Black or African American, non-Hispanic/Latino; 2 American Indian or Alaska Native, non-Hispanic/Latino; 3 Asian, non-Hispanic/Latino; 10 Hispanic/Latino; 4 Two or more races, non-Hispanic/Latino), 30 international. Average age 29. 244 applicants, 41% accepted, 54 enrolled. In 2018, 39 master's, 11 doctorates awarded. *Degree requirements:* For master's, thesis (for some programs); for doctorate, comprehensive exam, thesis/dissertation. *Entrance requirements:* For master's and doctorate, GRE General Test. Additional exam requirements/recommendations for international students: Required—TOEFL (minimum score 550 paper-based; 79 iBT). *Application deadline:* For fall admission, 12/15 priority date for domestic and international students; for spring admission, 9/1 priority date for domestic and international students. Application fee: $60 ($80 for international students). Electronic applications accepted. *Expenses:* Tuition, state resident: full-time $16,650; part-time $925 per contact hour. Tuition, nonresident: full-time $36,270; part-time $2015 per contact hour. *International tuition:* $36,270 full-time. *Required fees:* $2314; $2314 per semester. *Financial support:* In 2018–19, 48 research assistantships with full tuition reimbursements, 20 teaching assistantships with full tuition reimbursements were awarded; fellowships, scholarships/grants, health care benefits, and unspecified assistantships also available. Financial award application deadline: 12/15; financial award applicants required to submit FAFSA. *Faculty research:* Predictive sediment modeling, petrophysics, aquifer-contaminant flow modeling, water-rock interactions, geotechnical engineering. *Unit head:* Dr. Wendy Bohrson, Head, 303-273-3066, E-mail: bohrson@mines.edu. *Application contact:* Dr. Christian Shorey, Lecturer/Program Manager, 303-273-3556, E-mail: cshorey@mines.edu.
Website: http://geology.mines.edu

Cornell University, Graduate School, Graduate Fields of Agriculture and Life Sciences, Field of Natural Resources, Ithaca, NY 14853. Offers community-based natural resources management (MS, PhD); conservation biology (MS, PhD); ecosystem biology and biogeochemistry (MPS, MS, PhD); environmental management (MPS); fishery and aquatic science (MPS, MS, PhD); forest science (MPS, MS, PhD); human dimensions of natural resources management (MPS, MS, PhD); policy and institutional analysis (MS, PhD); program development and evaluation (MPS, MS, PhD); quantitative ecology (MS, PhD); wildlife science (MPS, MS, PhD). *Degree requirements:* For master's, thesis (MS), project paper (MPS); for doctorate, comprehensive exam, thesis/dissertation. *Entrance requirements:* For master's and doctorate, GRE General Test, 2 letters of recommendation. Additional exam requirements/recommendations for international students: Required—TOEFL (minimum score 550 paper-based; 77 iBT). Electronic applications accepted. *Faculty research:* Ecosystem-level dynamics, systems modeling, conservation biology/management, resource management's human dimensions, biogeochemistry.

Cornell University, Graduate School, Graduate Fields of Engineering, Field of Geological Sciences, Ithaca, NY 14853. Offers economic geology (M Eng, MS, PhD); engineering geology (M Eng, MS, PhD); environmental geophysics (M Eng, MS, PhD); general geology (M Eng, MS, PhD); geobiology (M Eng, MS, PhD); geochemistry and isotope geology (M Eng, MS, PhD); geohydrology (M Eng, MS, PhD); geomorphology (M Eng, MS, PhD); geophysics (M Eng, MS, PhD); geotectonics (M Eng, MS, PhD); marine geology (MS, PhD); mineralogy (M Eng, MS, PhD); paleontology (M Eng, MS, PhD); petroleum geology (M Eng, MS, PhD); petrology (M Eng, MS, PhD); planetary geology (M Eng, MS, PhD); Precambrian geology (M Eng, MS, PhD); Quaternary geology (M Eng, MS, PhD); rock mechanics (M Eng, MS, PhD); sedimentology (M Eng, MS, PhD); seismology (M Eng, MS, PhD); stratigraphy (M Eng, MS, PhD); structural geology (M Eng, MS, PhD). *Degree requirements:* For master's, thesis (MS); for doctorate, comprehensive exam, thesis/dissertation. *Entrance requirements:* For master's and doctorate, GRE General Test, 3 letters of recommendation. Additional exam requirements/recommendations for international students: Required—TOEFL (minimum score 550 paper-based; 77 iBT). Electronic applications accepted. *Faculty research:* Geophysics, structural geology, petrology, geochemistry, geodynamics.

Georgia State University, College of Arts and Sciences, Department of Chemistry, Atlanta, GA 30302-3083. Offers analytical chemistry (MS, PhD); biochemistry (MS, PhD); bioinformatics (MS, PhD); biophysical chemistry (PhD); computational chemistry (MS, PhD); geochemistry (PhD); organic/medicinal chemistry (MS, PhD); physical chemistry (MS). PhD in geochemistry offered jointly with Department of Geosciences. *Program availability:* Part-time. *Faculty:* 27 full-time (6 women), 1 part-time/adjunct (0 women). *Students:* 147 full-time (59 women), 15 part-time (10 women); includes 37 minority (21 Black or African American, non-Hispanic/Latino; 7 Asian, non-Hispanic/Latino; 4 Hispanic/Latino; 5 Two or more races, non-Hispanic/Latino), 84 international. Average age 29. 106 applicants, 40% accepted, 28 enrolled. In 2018, 37 master's, 13 doctorates awarded. Terminal master's awarded for partial completion of doctoral program. *Degree requirements:* For master's, one foreign language, comprehensive exam (for some programs), thesis (for some programs); for doctorate, one foreign language, comprehensive exam, thesis/dissertation. *Entrance requirements:* For master's and doctorate, GRE. *Application deadline:* For fall admission, 7/1 priority date for domestic and international students; for winter admission, 11/15 priority date for domestic and international students; for spring admission, 4/15 priority date for domestic and international students. Applications are processed on a rolling basis. Application fee: $50. Electronic applications accepted. *Expenses: Tuition, area resident:* Full-time $9360; part-time $390 per credit hour. Tuition, state resident: full-time $9360; part-time $390 per credit hour. Tuition, nonresident: full-time $30,024; part-time $1251 per credit hour. *International tuition:* $30,024 full-time. *Required fees:* $2128. *Financial support:* Fellowships with full tuition reimbursements, research assistantships with full tuition reimbursements, and teaching assistantships with full tuition reimbursements available. Financial award applicants required to submit FAFSA. *Faculty research:* Analytical chemistry, biological/biochemistry, biophysical/computational chemistry, chemical education, organic/medicinal chemistry. *Unit head:* Dr. Donald Hamelberg, Professor; Chair, 404-413-5564, Fax: 404-413-5505, E-mail: dhamelberg@gsu.edu. *Application contact:* Dr. Donald Hamelberg, Professor; Chair, 404-413-5564, Fax: 404-413-5505, E-mail: dhamelberg@gsu.edu.
Website: http://chemistry.gsu.edu/

Indiana University Bloomington, University Graduate School, College of Arts and Sciences, Department of Earth and Atmospheric Sciences, Bloomington, IN 47405-7000. Offers biogeochemistry (MS, PhD); economic geology (MS, PhD); geobiology (MS, PhD); geophysics, structural geology and tectonics (MS, PhD); hydrogeology (MS, PhD); mineralogy (MS, PhD); stratigraphy and sedimentology (MS, PhD). Terminal master's awarded for partial completion of doctoral program. *Degree requirements:* For master's, thesis or alternative; for doctorate, comprehensive exam, thesis/dissertation. *Entrance requirements:* For master's and doctorate, GRE General Test. Additional exam requirements/recommendations for international students: Required—TOEFL. *Faculty research:* Geophysics, geochemistry, hydrogeology, geobiology, planetary science.

Massachusetts Institute of Technology, School of Science, Department of Earth, Atmospheric, and Planetary Sciences, Cambridge, MA 02139. Offers atmospheric chemistry (PhD, Sc D); atmospheric science (SM, PhD, Sc D); chemical oceanography (SM, PhD, Sc D); climate physics and chemistry (SM, PhD, Sc D); earth and planetary sciences (SM); geochemistry (PhD, Sc D); geology (PhD, Sc D); geophysics (PhD, Sc D); marine geology and geophysics (SM, PhD, Sc D); physical oceanography (SM, PhD, Sc D); planetary sciences (PhD, Sc D). Terminal master's awarded for partial completion of doctoral program. *Degree requirements:* For master's, thesis; for doctorate, comprehensive exam, thesis/dissertation. *Entrance requirements:* For master's and doctorate, GRE General Test. Additional exam requirements/recommendations for international students: Required—TOEFL, IELTS. Electronic applications accepted. *Expenses: Tuition:* Full-time $51,520; part-time $800 per credit hour. *Required fees:* $312. *Faculty research:* Earth: origin, composition, structure, and dynamics of (and interactions between) the atmosphere, oceans, surface, and interior of the earth; planets: formation, dynamics, and evolution of planetary systems and the characterization of exoplanets; climate: characterization of past, present, and potential future climates; studies of the causes and consequences of climate change; life: co-evolution of life and environmental systems.

McMaster University, School of Graduate Studies, Faculty of Science, School of Geography and Earth Sciences, Hamilton, ON L8S 4M2, Canada. Offers geochemistry (PhD); geology (M Sc, PhD); human geography (MA, PhD); physical geography (M Sc, PhD). *Program availability:* Part-time. Terminal master's awarded for partial completion of doctoral program. *Degree requirements:* For master's, thesis; for doctorate, comprehensive exam, thesis/dissertation. *Entrance requirements:* For master's, minimum B+ average. Additional exam requirements/recommendations for international students: Required—TOEFL (minimum score 550 paper-based).

Missouri University of Science and Technology, Department of Geosciences and Geological and Petroleum Engineering, Rolla, MO 65401. Offers geological engineering (MS, DE, PhD); geology and geophysics (MS, PhD), including geochemistry, geology, geophysics, groundwater and environmental geology; petroleum engineering (MS, DE, PhD). *Program availability:* Part-time. *Degree requirements:* For master's, thesis optional; for doctorate, comprehensive exam, thesis/dissertation. *Entrance requirements:* For master's, GRE General Test (minimum score 600 quantitative, writing 3.5), minimum GPA of 3.0 in last 4 semesters; for doctorate, GRE General Test (minimum scores: Quantitative 600, Writing 3.5). Additional exam requirements/recommendations for international students: Required—TOEFL (minimum score 550 paper-based). Electronic applications accepted. *Expenses:* Tuition, state resident: full-time $7545.60; part-time $419.20 per credit hour. Tuition, nonresident: full-time $22,169; part-time $1231.60 per credit hour. *International tuition:* $23,518.80 full-time. *Required fees:* $4523.05. Full-time tuition and fees vary according to course load, campus/location, program and reciprocity agreements. *Faculty research:* Digital image processing and geographic information systems, mineralogy, igneous and sedimentary petrology-geochemistry, sedimentology groundwater hydrology and contaminant transport.

Montana Tech of The University of Montana, Geosciences Programs, Butte, MT 59701-8997. Offers geochemistry (MS); geological engineering (MS); geology (MS); geophysical engineering (MS); hydrogeological engineering (MS); hydrogeology (MS). *Program availability:* Part-time. *Degree requirements:* For master's, comprehensive exam (for some programs), thesis (for some programs). *Entrance requirements:* For master's, GRE General Test, minimum GPA of 3.0. Additional exam requirements/recommendations for international students: Required—TOEFL (minimum score 545 paper-based; 78 iBT), IELTS (minimum score 6.5). Electronic applications accepted. *Faculty research:* Water resource development, seismic processing, petroleum reservoir characterization, environmental geochemistry, geologic mapping.

New Mexico Institute of Mining and Technology, Center for Graduate Studies, Department of Earth and Environmental Science, Program in Geochemistry, Socorro, NM 87801. Offers MS, PhD. *Degree requirements:* For doctorate, thesis/dissertation.

Ohio University, Graduate College, College of Arts and Sciences, Department of Geological Sciences, Athens, OH 45701-2979. Offers environmental geochemistry (MS). *Program availability:* Part-time. *Degree requirements:* For master's, thesis. *Entrance requirements:* Additional exam requirements/recommendations for international students: Required—TOEFL (minimum score 550 paper-based; 80 iBT) or IELTS (minimum score 6.5). Electronic applications accepted. *Faculty research:* Geoscience education, tectonics, fluvial geomorphology, invertebrate paleontology, mine/hydrology.

Oregon State University, College of Earth, Ocean, and Atmospheric Sciences, Program in Geology, Corvallis, OR 97331. Offers geochemistry (MA, MS, PhD); geomorphology (MA, MS, PhD); geophysics (MA, MS, PhD); glacial geology (MA, MS, PhD); hydrology and hydrogeology (MA, MS, PhD); igneous petrology (MA, MS, PhD); neotonics (MA, MS, PhD); paleoclimatology (MA); structural geology (MA, MS, PhD). Terminal master's awarded for partial completion of doctoral program. *Entrance requirements:* For master's and doctorate, GRE, minimum GPA of 3.0 in last 90 hours. Additional exam requirements/recommendations for international students: Required—TOEFL (minimum score 80 iBT), IELTS (minimum score 6.5). *Faculty research:* Hydrogeology, geomorphology, ocean geology, geochemistry, earthquake geology.

Oregon State University, Interdisciplinary/Institutional Programs, Program in Environmental Sciences, Corvallis, OR 97331. Offers biogeochemistry (MA, MS, PSM, PhD); ecology (MA, MS, PSM, PhD); environmental education (MA, MS, PhD); quantitative analysis (PSM); social science (MA, MS, PSM, PhD); water resources (MA, MS, PhD). *Program availability:* Part-time. *Degree requirements:* For master's, variable foreign language requirement, thesis; for doctorate, thesis/dissertation. *Entrance requirements:* For master's and doctorate, GRE. Additional exam requirements/ recommendations for international students: Required—TOEFL (minimum score 80 iBT), IELTS (minimum score 6.5).

University of California, Los Angeles, Graduate Division, College of Letters and Science, Department of Earth and Space Sciences, Program in Geochemistry, Los Angeles, CA 90095. Offers MS, PhD. *Degree requirements:* For master's, comprehensive exam, thesis; for doctorate, thesis/dissertation, oral and written qualifying exams. *Entrance requirements:* For master's, GRE General and Subject Tests, bachelor's degree; minimum undergraduate GPA of 3.0 (or its equivalent if letter grade system not used); for doctorate, bachelor's degree; minimum undergraduate GPA

of 3.0 (or its equivalent if letter grade system not used). Additional exam requirements/ recommendations for international students: Required—TOEFL. Electronic applications accepted.

University of Hawaii at Manoa, Office of Graduate Education, School of Ocean and Earth Science and Technology, Department of Geology and Geophysics, Honolulu, HI 96822. Offers high-pressure geophysics and geochemistry (MS, PhD); hydrogeology and engineering geology (MS, PhD); marine geology and geophysics (MS, PhD); planetary geosciences and remote sensing (MS, PhD); seismology and solid-earth geophysics (MS, PhD); volcanology, petrology, and geochemistry (MS, PhD). *Program availability:* Part-time. Terminal master's awarded for partial completion of doctoral program. *Degree requirements:* For master's, thesis optional; for doctorate, comprehensive exam, thesis/dissertation. *Entrance requirements:* For master's and doctorate, GRE General Test, minimum GPA of 3.0. Additional exam requirements/ recommendations for international students: Required—TOEFL (minimum score 580 paper-based; 92 iBT), IELTS (minimum score 5).

The University of Manchester, School of Earth and Environmental Sciences, Manchester, United Kingdom. Offers atmospheric sciences (M Phil, M Sc, PhD); basin studies and petroleum geosciences (M Phil, M Sc, PhD); earth, atmospheric and environmental sciences (M Phil, M Sc, PhD); environmental geochemistry and cosmochemistry (M Phil, M Sc, PhD); isotope geochemistry and cosmochemistry (M Phil, M Sc, PhD); paleontology (M Phil, M Sc, PhD); physics and chemistry of minerals and fluids (M Phil, M Sc, PhD); structural and petrological geosciences (M Phil, M Sc, PhD).

University of Nevada, Reno, Graduate School, College of Science, Mackay School of Earth Sciences and Engineering, Department of Geological Sciences and Engineering, Program in Geochemistry, Reno, NV 89557. Offers MS, PhD. Terminal master's awarded for partial completion of doctoral program. *Degree requirements:* For master's, thesis optional; for doctorate, thesis/dissertation. *Entrance requirements:* For master's, GRE General Test, minimum GPA of 2.75; for doctorate, GRE General Test, minimum GPA of 3.0. Additional exam requirements/recommendations for international students: Required—TOEFL (minimum score 500 paper-based; 61 iBT), IELTS (minimum score 6). Electronic applications accepted.

Yale University, Graduate School of Arts and Sciences, Department of Geology and Geophysics, New Haven, CT 06520. Offers biogeochemistry (PhD); climate dynamics (PhD); geochemistry (PhD); geophysics (PhD); meteorology (PhD); oceanography (PhD); paleontology (PhD); paleooceanography (PhD); petrology (PhD); tectonics (PhD). *Degree requirements:* For doctorate, thesis/dissertation. *Entrance requirements:* For doctorate, GRE General Test. Additional exam requirements/recommendations for international students: Required—TOEFL.

Geodetic Sciences

The Ohio State University, Graduate School, College of Arts and Sciences, Division of Natural and Mathematical Sciences, School of Earth Sciences, Columbus, OH 43210. Offers earth sciences (MS, PhD); geodetic science (MS, PhD); geological sciences (MS, PhD). *Faculty:* 27. *Students:* 67 (27 women). Average age 28. In 2018, 18 master's, 12 doctorates awarded. *Entrance requirements:* For master's, GRE, undergraduate degree in biological science, geological sciences, physical science or engineering (recommended); minimum GPA of 3.2; for doctorate, GRE, undergraduate degree in biological science, geological sciences, physical science or engineering (recommended); minimum GPA of 3.4. Additional exam requirements/recommendations for international students: Required—TOEFL (minimum score 550 paper-based; 79 iBT), Michigan English Language Assessment Battery (minimum score 82); Recommended— IELTS (minimum score 8). *Application deadline:* For fall admission, 12/13 priority date for domestic students, 11/30 priority date for international students; for spring admission, 11/30 for domestic and international students; for summer admission, 7/24 for domestic students, 3/13 for international students. Applications are processed on a rolling basis. Application fee: $60 ($70 for international students). Electronic applications accepted. *Financial support:* Fellowships, research assistantships, and teaching assistantships available. *Unit head:* Dr. Matthew Saltzman, Director, 614-292-0481, Fax: 614-292-7688, E-mail: saltzman.11@osu.edu. *Application contact:* Graduate and Professional Admissions, 614-292-9444, Fax: 614-292-3895, E-mail: gpadmissions@osu.edu. Website: http://earthsciences.osu.edu/

Université Laval, Faculty of Forestry, Geography and Geomatics, Department of Geomatics Sciences, Programs in Geomatics Sciences, Québec, QC G1K 7P4, Canada. Offers M Sc, PhD. Terminal master's awarded for partial completion of doctoral program. *Degree requirements:* For master's, thesis (for some programs); for doctorate, comprehensive exam, thesis/dissertation. *Entrance requirements:* For master's and doctorate, knowledge of French and English. Electronic applications accepted.

University of New Brunswick Fredericton, School of Graduate Studies, Faculty of Engineering, Department of Geodesy and Geomatics Engineering, Fredericton, NB E3B 5A3, Canada. Offers M Eng, M Sc E, PhD. *Degree requirements:* For master's, thesis; for doctorate, comprehensive exam, thesis/dissertation, qualifying exam. *Entrance requirements:* For master's and doctorate, minimum GPA of 3.0. Additional exam requirements/recommendations for international students: Required—TOEFL (minimum score 550 paper-based; 80 iBT), IELTS (minimum score 7), TWE (minimum score 4), Michigan English Language Assessment Battery (minimum score 85) or CanTest (minimum score 4.5). Electronic applications accepted. *Faculty research:* GIS, GPS, remote sensing, ocean mapping, land administration, hydrography, engineering surveys.

Geology

Acadia University, Faculty of Pure and Applied Science, Program in Geology, Wolfville, NS B4P 2R6, Canada. Offers M Sc. *Entrance requirements:* For master's, BSC (honours) in geology or equivalent. Additional exam requirements/recommendations for international students: Required—TOEFL (minimum score 580 paper-based; 93 iBT), IELTS (minimum score 6.5). *Faculty research:* Igneous, metamorphic, and Quaternary geology; stratigraphy; remote sensing; tectonics; carbonate sedimentology.

American University of Beirut, Graduate Programs, Faculty of Arts and Sciences, Beirut 1107 2020, Lebanon. Offers anthropology (MA); Arab and Middle Eastern history (PhD); Arabic language and literature (MA, PhD); archaeology (MA); art history and curating (MA); biology (MS); cell and molecular biology (PhD); chemistry (MS); clinical psychology (MA); computational sciences (MS); computer science (MS); economics (MA); education (MA), including administration and policy studies, elementary education, mathematics education, psychology school guidance, psychology test and measurements, science education, teaching English as a foreign language; English language (MA); English literature (MA); environmental policy planning (MS); financial economics (MAFE); general psychology (MA); geology (MS); history (MA); Islamic studies (MA); mathematics (MS); media studies (MA); Middle East studies (MA); philosophy (MA); physics (MS); political studies (MA); public administration (MA); public policy and international affairs (MA); sociology (MA); theoretical physics (PhD). *Program availability:* Part-time. *Faculty:* 187 full-time (64 women), 27 part-time/adjunct (15

women). *Students:* 292 full-time (215 women), 216 part-time (148 women). Average age 27. 422 applicants, 64% accepted, 124 enrolled. In 2018, 90 master's, 3 doctorates awarded. *Degree requirements:* For master's, comprehensive exam, thesis (for some programs), project; for doctorate, comprehensive exam, thesis/dissertation (for some programs). *Entrance requirements:* For master's, GRE General Test (for archaeology, clinical psychology, general psychology, economics, financial economics and biology); for doctorate, GRE General Test for all PhD programs, GRE Subject Test for theoretical physics. Additional exam requirements/recommendations for international students: Required—TOEFL (minimum score 583 paper-based; 97 iBT), IELTS (minimum score 7). *Application deadline:* For fall admission, 3/18 for domestic students; for spring admission, 11/5 for domestic students. Application fee: $50. Electronic applications accepted. *Expenses:* MA/MS: Humanities and social sciences=$912/credit. Sciences=$943/credit. Financial economics=$986/credit. Thesis: Humanities/social sciences=$6565 and sciences=$6865. *Financial support:* In 2018–19, 227 fellowships with full tuition reimbursements, 17 research assistantships with full tuition reimbursements, 83 teaching assistantships with full tuition reimbursements were awarded; scholarships/grants, tuition waivers (full and partial), and unspecified assistantships also available. Financial award application deadline: 3/18. *Faculty research:* Sciences: Physics: High energy, Particle, Polymer and Soft Matter, Thermal, Plasma; String Theory, Mathematical physics, Astrophysics (stellar evolution, planet and galaxy formation and evolution, astrophysical dynamics), Solid State physics/thin films,

Peterson's Graduate Programs in the Physical Sciences, Mathematics, Agricultural Sciences, the Environment & Natural Resources 2020

www.petersons.com **87**

Spintronics, Magnetic properties of materials, Mineralogy, Petrology, and Geochemistry of Hard Rocks, Geophysics and Petrophysics, Hydrogeology, Micropaleontology, Sedimentology, and Stratigraphy, Structural Geology and Geotectonics, Renewable en. *Total annual research expenditures:* $4.3 million. *Unit head:* Dr. Nadia Maria El Cheikh, Dean, Faculty of Arts and Sciences, 961-1-350000 Ext. 3800, Fax: 961-1-744461, E-mail: nmcheikh@aub.edu.lb. *Application contact:* Adriana Michelle Zanaty, Curriculum and Graduate Studies Officer, 961-1-350000 Ext. 3833, Fax: 961-1-744461, E-mail: az48@aub.edu.lb.
Website: https://www.aub.edu.lb/fas/Pages/default.aspx

Arizona State University at the Tempe campus, College of Liberal Arts and Sciences, School of Earth and Space Exploration, Tempe, AZ 85287-1404. Offers astrophysics (MS, PhD); exploration systems design (PhD); geological sciences (MS, PhD). PhD in exploration systems design is offered in collaboration with the Ira A. Fulton School of Engineering. Terminal master's awarded for partial completion of doctoral program. *Degree requirements:* For master's, thesis, interactive Program of Study (iPOS) submitted before completing 50 percent of required credit hours; for doctorate, thesis/dissertation, interactive Program of Study (iPOS) submitted before completing 50 percent of required credit hours. *Entrance requirements:* For master's and doctorate, GRE, minimum GPA of 3.0 or equivalent in last 2 years of work leading to bachelor's degree. Additional exam requirements/recommendations for international students: Required—TOEFL, IELTS, or PTE. Electronic applications accepted.

Auburn University, Graduate School, College of Sciences and Mathematics, Department of Geology and Geography, Auburn University, AL 36849. Offers MS. *Program availability:* Part-time. *Degree requirements:* For master's, computer language or geographic information systems, field camp. *Entrance requirements:* For master's, GRE General Test. Electronic applications accepted. *Expenses:* Tuition, state resident: full-time $11,282; part-time $535 per credit hour. Tuition, nonresident: full-time $30,542; part-time $1605 per credit hour. *Required fees:* $826 per semester. Tuition and fees vary according to degree level and program. *Faculty research:* Empirical magma dynamics and melt migration, ore mineralogy, role of terrestrial plant biomass in deposition, metamorphic petrology and isotope geochemistry, reef development, crinoid topology.

Ball State University, Graduate School, College of Sciences and Humanities, Department of Geological Sciences, Muncie, IN 47306. Offers geology (MA, MS). *Program availability:* Part-time. *Entrance requirements:* For master's, GRE General Test, minimum baccalaureate GPA of 2.75 or 3.0 in latter half of baccalaureate. Additional exam requirements/recommendations for international students: Required—TOEFL (minimum score 550 paper-based; 79 iBT), IELTS (minimum score 6.5). Electronic applications accepted. *Faculty research:* Environmental geology, geophysics, stratigraphy.

Ball State University, Graduate School, College of Sciences and Humanities, Interdepartmental Program in Environmental Sciences, Muncie, IN 47306. Offers environmental science (PhD), including biology, chemistry, geological sciences. *Program availability:* Part-time. *Degree requirements:* For doctorate, thesis/dissertation. *Entrance requirements:* For doctorate, GRE General Test, minimum cumulative GPA of 3.0 (chemistry), 3.2 (biology and geological sciences); acknowledged arrangement for doctoral environmental sciences research with faculty mentor; three letters of recommendation. Additional exam requirements/recommendations for international students: Required—TOEFL (minimum score 550 paper-based; 79 iBT), IELTS (minimum score 6.5). Electronic applications accepted.

Binghamton University, State University of New York, Graduate School, Harpur College of Arts and Sciences, Department of Geological Sciences and Environmental Studies, Binghamton, NY 13902-6000. Offers environmental studies (MS); geological sciences (MS, PhD). *Program availability:* Part-time. Terminal master's awarded for partial completion of doctoral program. *Degree requirements:* For master's, thesis; for doctorate, one foreign language, comprehensive exam, thesis/dissertation. *Entrance requirements:* For master's and doctorate, GRE General Test. Additional exam requirements/recommendations for international students: Required—TOEFL (minimum score 550 paper-based; 80 iBT). Electronic applications accepted.

Boston College, Morrissey Graduate School of Arts and Sciences, Department of Earth and Environmental Sciences, Chestnut Hill, MA 02467-3800. Offers MS, MBA/MS. *Degree requirements:* For master's, thesis. *Entrance requirements:* For master's, GRE General Test. Additional exam requirements/recommendations for international students: Required—TOEFL (minimum score 600 paper-based; 100 iBT), IELTS (minimum score 8). Electronic applications accepted. *Faculty research:* Coastal and estuarine processes, earthquake and exploration seismology, environmental geology and geophysics, earth surface processes, paleoclimate, groundwater hydrology, igneous and metamorphic petrology, geochemistry, dynamics and processes of sedimentary systems, plate tectonics, structural geology.

Bowling Green State University, Graduate College, College of Arts and Sciences, Department of Geology, Bowling Green, OH 43403. Offers MS. *Program availability:* Part-time. *Degree requirements:* For master's, thesis. *Entrance requirements:* For master's, GRE General Test. Additional exam requirements/recommendations for international students: Required—TOEFL. Electronic applications accepted. *Faculty research:* Remote sensing, environmental geology, geological information systems, structural geology, geochemistry.

Brigham Young University, Graduate Studies, College of Physical and Mathematical Sciences, Department of Geological Sciences, Provo, UT 84602-1001. Offers MS. *Faculty:* 15 full-time (1 woman), 1 part-time/adjunct (0 women). *Students:* 19 full-time (5 women), 13 part-time (4 women); includes 2 minority (1 Asian, non-Hispanic/Latino; 1 Hispanic/Latino). Average age 27. 19 applicants, 58% accepted, 11 enrolled. In 2018, 5 master's awarded. *Degree requirements:* For master's, thesis. *Entrance requirements:* For master's, GRE General Test, minimum GPA of 3.0 in last 60 hours of course work. Additional exam requirements/recommendations for international students: Required—TOEFL. *Application deadline:* For fall admission, 2/1 priority date for domestic students, 2/1 for international students. Applications are processed on a rolling basis. Application fee: $50. Electronic applications accepted. *Financial support:* In 2018–19, 1 student received support, including 5 research assistantships (averaging $18,309 per year), 15 teaching assistantships with full tuition reimbursements available (averaging $19,620 per year); career-related internships or fieldwork, institutionally sponsored loans, scholarships/grants, and tuition waivers (partial) also available. Financial award application deadline: 2/15. *Faculty research:* Economic geology, geochemistry, geomorphology, planetary geology, geophysics, hydrogeology, environmental geology, mineralogy, petrology, paleontology, petroleum geology, sedimentology, stratigraphy, structural geology, tectonics, volcanology. *Total annual research expenditures:* $550,312. *Unit head:* Dr. Michael J. Dorais, Chairman, 801-422-1347, Fax: 801-422-0267, E-mail: dorais@byu.edu. *Application contact:* Dr. John McBride, Graduate Coordinator, 801-422-1347, Fax: 801-422-0267, E-mail: john_mcbride@byu.edu.
Website: http://www.geology.byu.edu/

Brooklyn College of the City University of New York, School of Natural and Behavioral Sciences, Department of Earth and Environmental Sciences, Brooklyn, NY 11210-2889. Offers MA, PhD. *Program availability:* Evening/weekend. Terminal master's awarded for partial completion of doctoral program. *Degree requirements:* For master's, comprehensive exam, thesis or alternative, qualifying exams, 30 credits. *Entrance requirements:* For master's, bachelor's degree in geology or equivalent, 2 letters of recommendation; for doctorate, GRE. Additional exam requirements/recommendations for international students: Required—TOEFL (minimum score 550 paper-based; 79 iBT). Electronic applications accepted. *Faculty research:* Geochemistry, petrology, tectonophysics, hydrogeology, sedimentary geology, environmental geology.

California Institute of Technology, Division of Geological and Planetary Sciences, Pasadena, CA 91125-0001. Offers environmental science and engineering (MS, PhD); geobiology (MS, PhD); geochemistry (MS, PhD); geology (MS, PhD); geophysics (MS, PhD); planetary science (MS, PhD). *Degree requirements:* For doctorate, thesis/dissertation. *Entrance requirements:* For doctorate, GRE General Test. Additional exam requirements/recommendations for international students: Required—TOEFL; Recommended—IELTS, TWE. Electronic applications accepted. *Faculty research:* Planetary surfaces, evolution of anaerobic respiratory processes, structural geology and tectonics, theoretical and numerical seismology, global biogeochemical cycles.

California State Polytechnic University, Pomona, Program in Geology, Pomona, CA 91768-2557. Offers geology (MS). *Program availability:* Part-time, evening/weekend. *Students:* 7 full-time (3 women), 22 part-time (10 women); includes 13 minority (2 Black or African American, non-Hispanic/Latino; 2 Asian, non-Hispanic/Latino; 8 Hispanic/Latino; 1 Two or more races, non-Hispanic/Latino). Average age 29. 10 applicants, 100% accepted, 8 enrolled. In 2018, 6 master's awarded. *Entrance requirements:* Additional exam requirements/recommendations for international students: Required—TOEFL (minimum score 550 paper-based). *Application deadline:* Applications are processed on a rolling basis. Electronic applications accepted. *Expenses:* Contact institution. *Financial support:* Application deadline: 3/2; applicants required to submit FAFSA. *Unit head:* Dr. Jonathan A. Nourse, Department Chair/Coordinator, 909-869-3460, Fax: 909-869-2920, E-mail: janourse@cpp.edu. *Application contact:* Dr. Jonathan A. Nourse, Department Chair/Coordinator, 909-869-3460, Fax: 909-869-2920, E-mail: janourse@cpp.edu.
Website: http://www.cpp.edu/~sci/geological-sciences/masters-program/

California State University, Bakersfield, Division of Graduate Studies, School of Natural Sciences, Mathematics, and Engineering, Program in Geological Sciences, Bakersfield, CA 93311. Offers geological sciences (MS); hydrogeology (MS); petroleum geology (MS); science education (MS). *Program availability:* Part-time, evening/weekend. *Faculty:* 4 full-time (0 women). *Students:* 6 full-time (2 women), 17 part-time (7 women); includes 13 minority (1 Black or African American, non-Hispanic/Latino; 1 American Indian or Alaska Native, non-Hispanic/Latino; 10 Hispanic/Latino; 1 Two or more races, non-Hispanic/Latino). Average age 30. 18 applicants, 94% accepted, 15 enrolled. In 2018, 12 master's awarded. *Degree requirements:* For master's, thesis. *Entrance requirements:* For master's, GRE General Test, BS in geology. *Application deadline:* Applications are processed on a rolling basis. Application fee: $55. *Financial support:* In 2018–19, fellowships (averaging $1,850 per year) were awarded; Federal Work-Study, scholarships/grants, and tuition waivers (full and partial) also available. Financial award application deadline: 3/2; financial award applicants required to submit FAFSA. *Unit head:* Dr. William Krugh, Director, 661-654-3126, Fax: 661-654-2040, E-mail: wkrugh@csub.edu. *Application contact:* Martha Manriquez, Graduate Student Center Coordinator, 661-654-2786, Fax: 661-654-2791, E-mail: gsc@csub.edu.
Website: https://www.csub.edu/geology/index.html

California State University, Chico, Office of Graduate Studies, College of Natural Sciences, Department of Geological and Environmental Sciences, Chico, CA 95929-0722. Offers environmental science (MS, PSM), including environmental science; geosciences (MS). *Program availability:* Part-time. *Faculty:* 5 full-time (all women), 5 part-time/adjunct (2 women). *Students:* 5 full-time (4 women), 9 part-time (4 women); includes 7 minority (2 Asian, non-Hispanic/Latino; 2 Hispanic/Latino; 3 Two or more races, non-Hispanic/Latino). 17 applicants, 41% accepted, 7 enrolled. In 2018, 6 master's awarded. *Degree requirements:* For master's, thesis or project. *Entrance requirements:* For master's, GRE General Test, identification of faculty mentor, 2 letters of recommendation, statement of purpose, curriculum vitae, department letter of recommendation access waiver form. Additional exam requirements/recommendations for international students: Required—TOEFL (minimum score 550 paper-based; 80 iBT), IELTS (minimum score 6.5), PTE (minimum score 59). *Application deadline:* For fall admission, 3/2 priority date for domestic and international students; for spring admission, 11/1 priority date for domestic and international students. Application fee: $55. Electronic applications accepted. *Expenses: Tuition, area resident:* Full-time $4622; part-time $3116 per unit. Tuition, state resident: full-time $4622; part-time $3116 per unit. Tuition, nonresident: full-time $10,634. *Required fees:* $2160; $1620 per year. Tuition and fees vary according to class time and program. *Financial support:* Fellowships, research assistantships, teaching assistantships, career-related internships or fieldwork, Federal Work-Study, scholarships/grants, traineeships, health care benefits, unspecified assistantships, and stipends available. Support available to part-time students. Financial award application deadline: 3/2; financial award applicants required to submit FAFSA. *Unit head:* Dr. Todd J. Greene, Chair, 530-898-5262, E-mail: geos@csuchico.edu. *Application contact:* Micah Lehner, Graduate Admissions Coordinator, 530-898-5416, Fax: 530-898-3342, E-mail: mlehner@csuchico.edu.
Website: http://www.csuchico.edu/geos/

California State University, East Bay, Office of Graduate Studies, College of Science, Department of Earth and Environmental Sciences, Hayward, CA 94542-3000. Offers geology (MS), including environmental geology, geology. *Program availability:* Part-time, evening/weekend. *Degree requirements:* For master's, thesis or project. *Entrance requirements:* For master's, GRE, minimum GPA of 2.75 in field, 2.5 overall; 2 letters of recommendation. Additional exam requirements/recommendations for international students: Required—TOEFL (minimum score 550 paper-based). Electronic applications accepted. *Faculty research:* Hydrology, seismic activity; origins of life.

California State University, Fresno, Division of Research and Graduate Studies, College of Science and Mathematics, Department of Earth and Environmental Sciences, Fresno, CA 93740-8027. Offers geology (MS). *Program availability:* Part-time. *Degree requirements:* For master's, thesis. *Entrance requirements:* For master's, GRE General Test, undergraduate geology degree, minimum GPA of 2.7. Additional exam requirements/recommendations for international students: Required—TOEFL. Electronic applications accepted. *Faculty research:* Water drainage, pollution, cartography, creek restoration, nitrate contamination.

California State University, Fullerton, Graduate Studies, College of Natural Science and Mathematics, Department of Geological Sciences, Fullerton, CA 92831-3599. Offers MS. *Program availability:* Part-time. *Entrance requirements:* For master's, bachelor's degree in geology, minimum GPA of 3.0 in geology courses.

California State University, Long Beach, Graduate Studies, College of Natural Sciences and Mathematics, Department of Geological Sciences, Long Beach, CA 90840. Offers geology (MS). *Program availability:* Part-time. *Degree requirements:* For master's, thesis. *Entrance requirements:* For master's, GRE General Test. *Application deadline:* For fall admission, 2/15 for domestic students; for spring admission, 10/1 for domestic students. Applications are processed on a rolling basis. Application fee: $55. Electronic applications accepted. *Expenses: Required fees:* $2628 per term. Tuition and fees vary according to class time, course level, course load, degree level, campus/location and program. *Financial support:* Research assistantships, teaching assistantships, Federal Work-Study, institutionally sponsored loans, and scholarships/grants available. Financial award application deadline: 3/2; financial award applicants required to submit FAFSA. *Faculty research:* Paleontology, geophysics, structural geology, organic geochemistry, sedimentary geology. *Unit head:* Rick Behl, Chair, 562-985-5850, Fax: 562-985-8638, E-mail: richard.behl@csulb.edu. *Application contact:* Dr. Lora Stevens-London, Graduate Advisor, 562-985-4817, Fax: 562-985-8638, E-mail: lora.stevens@csulb.edu.
Website: http://web.csulb.edu/depts/geology/

California State University, Los Angeles, Graduate Studies, College of Natural and Social Sciences, Department of Geological Sciences, Los Angeles, CA 90032-8530. Offers MS. Program offered jointly with California State University, Northridge. *Program availability:* Part-time, evening/weekend. *Degree requirements:* For master's, comprehensive exam or thesis. *Entrance requirements:* Additional exam requirements/recommendations for international students: Required—TOEFL (minimum score 500 paper-based). Electronic applications accepted.

California State University, Northridge, Graduate Studies, College of Science and Mathematics, Department of Geological Sciences, Northridge, CA 91330. Offers geology (MS). *Program availability:* Part-time, evening/weekend. *Degree requirements:* For master's, thesis. *Entrance requirements:* For master's, GRE General Test, minimum GPA of 2.75. Additional exam requirements/recommendations for international students: Required—TOEFL. *Faculty research:* Petrology of California Miocene volcanics, sedimentology of California Miocene formations, Eocene gastropods, structure of White/Inyo Mountains, seismology of Californian and Mexican earthquakes.

Case Western Reserve University, School of Graduate Studies, Department of Earth, Environmental, and Planetary Sciences, Cleveland, OH 44106. Offers MS, PhD. *Program availability:* Part-time. *Faculty:* 8 full-time (2 women), 2 part-time/adjunct (1 woman). *Students:* 8 full-time (3 women); includes 3 minority (1 Black or African American, non-Hispanic/Latino; 1 Hispanic/Latino; 1 Two or more races, non-Hispanic/Latino), 2 international. Average age 29. 10 applicants, 30% accepted, 1 enrolled. In 2018, 1 master's, 1 doctorate awarded. Terminal master's awarded for partial completion of doctoral program. *Degree requirements:* For master's, thesis or alternative; for doctorate, thesis/dissertation. *Entrance requirements:* For master's and doctorate, GRE General Test, GRE Subject Test, three letters of recommendation. Additional exam requirements/recommendations for international students: Required—TOEFL (minimum score 577 paper-based; 90 iBT); Recommended—IELTS (minimum score 7). *Application deadline:* For fall admission, 1/15 priority date for domestic students; for spring admission, 11/1 for domestic students. Applications are processed on a rolling basis. Application fee: $50. Electronic applications accepted. *Expenses: Tuition:* Full-time $45,168; part-time $1939 per credit hour. *Required fees:* $36; $18 per semester. $18 per semester. *Financial support:* Research assistantships, teaching assistantships, Federal Work-Study, health care benefits, and tuition waivers (partial) available. Support available to part-time students. Financial award application deadline: 1/15; financial award applicants required to submit FAFSA. *Faculty research:* Geochemistry, hydrology, ecology, geomorphology, planetary science, stratigraphy and basin analysis, igneous petrology. *Unit head:* Steven A. Hauck, II, Professor and Chair, 216-368.3675, Fax: 216-368-3691, E-mail: steven.hauck@case.edu. *Application contact:* Steven A. Hauck, II, Professor and Chair, 216-368.3675, Fax: 216-368-3691, E-mail: steven.hauck@case.edu.
Website: http://geology.case.edu/

Central Washington University, School of Graduate Studies and Research, College of the Sciences, Department of Geological Sciences, Ellensburg, WA 98926. Offers active and regional tectonics (MS); continental dynamics and seismology (MS); environmental geochemistry (MS); geomorphology (MS); geomorphology and climate change (MS); paleohydrology and volcanology (MS). *Program availability:* Part-time. *Entrance requirements:* For master's, GRE General Test, minimum GPA of 3.0. Additional exam requirements/recommendations for international students: Required—TOEFL (minimum score 550 paper-based; 79 iBT) or IELTS. Electronic applications accepted.

City College of the City University of New York, Graduate School, Division of Science, Department of Earth and Atmospheric Sciences, New York, NY 10031-9198. Offers geology (MS). *Degree requirements:* For master's, comprehensive exam, thesis. *Entrance requirements:* Additional exam requirements/recommendations for international students: Required—TOEFL (minimum score 500 paper-based; 61 iBT). Electronic applications accepted. *Faculty research:* Water resources, high-temperature geochemistry, sedimentary basin analysis, tectonics.

Colorado School of Mines, Office of Graduate Studies, Department of Geology and Geological Engineering, Golden, CO 80401. Offers environmental geochemistry (PMS); geochemistry (MS, PhD); geological engineering (ME, MS, PhD); geology (MS, PhD); hydrology (MS, PhD); mineral exploration (PMS); petroleum reservoir systems (PMS); underground construction and tunneling (MS). *Program availability:* Part-time. *Faculty:* 30 full-time (12 women), 6 part-time/adjunct (5 women). *Students:* 129 full-time (44 women), 32 part-time (12 women); includes 20 minority (1 Black or African American, non-Hispanic/Latino; 2 American Indian or Alaska Native, non-Hispanic/Latino; 3 Asian, non-Hispanic/Latino; 10 Hispanic/Latino; 4 Two or more races, non-Hispanic/Latino), 30 international. Average age 29. 244 applicants, 41% accepted, 54 enrolled. In 2018, 39 master's, 11 doctorates awarded. *Degree requirements:* For master's, thesis (for some programs); for doctorate, comprehensive exam, thesis/dissertation. *Entrance requirements:* For master's and doctorate, GRE General Test. Additional exam requirements/recommendations for international students: Required—TOEFL (minimum score 550 paper-based; 79 iBT). *Application deadline:* For fall admission, 12/15 priority date for domestic and international students; for spring admission, 9/1 priority date for domestic and international students. Application fee: $60 ($80 for international students). Electronic applications accepted. *Expenses:* Tuition, state resident: full-time $16,650; part-time $925 per contact hour. Tuition, nonresident: full-time $36,270; part-time $2015 per contact hour. *International tuition:* $36,270 full-time. *Required fees:* $2314; $2314 per semester. *Financial support:* In 2018–19, 48 research assistantships with full tuition reimbursements, 20 teaching assistantships with full tuition reimbursements were awarded; fellowships, scholarships/grants, health care benefits, and unspecified assistantships also available. Financial award application deadline: 12/15; financial award applicants required to submit FAFSA. *Faculty research:* Predictive sediment modeling, petrophysics, aquifer-contaminant flow modeling, water-rock interactions, geotechnical engineering. *Unit head:* Dr. Wendy Bohrson, Head, 303-273-3066, E-mail: bohrson@mines.edu. *Application contact:* Dr. Christian Shorey, Lecturer/Program Manager, 303-273-3556, E-mail: cshorey@mines.edu.
Website: http://geology.mines.edu

Cornell University, Graduate School, Graduate Fields of Engineering, Field of Geological Sciences, Ithaca, NY 14853. Offers economic geology (M Eng, MS, PhD); engineering geology (M Eng, MS, PhD); environmental geophysics (M Eng, MS, PhD); general geology (M Eng, MS, PhD); geobiology (M Eng, MS, PhD); geochemistry and isotope geology (M Eng, MS, PhD); geohydrology (M Eng, MS, PhD); geomorphology (M Eng, MS, PhD); geophysics (M Eng, MS, PhD); geotectonics (M Eng, MS, PhD); marine geology (MS, PhD); mineralogy (M Eng, MS, PhD); paleontology (M Eng, MS, PhD); petroleum geology (M Eng, MS, PhD); petrology (M Eng, MS, PhD); planetary geology (M Eng, MS, PhD); Precambrian geology (M Eng, MS, PhD); Quaternary geology (M Eng, MS, PhD); rock mechanics (M Eng, MS, PhD); sedimentology (M Eng, MS, PhD); seismology (M Eng, MS, PhD); stratigraphy (M Eng, MS, PhD); structural geology (M Eng, MS, PhD). *Degree requirements:* For master's, thesis (MS); for doctorate, comprehensive exam, thesis/dissertation. *Entrance requirements:* For master's and doctorate, GRE General Test, 3 letters of recommendation. Additional exam requirements/recommendations for international students: Required—TOEFL (minimum score 550 paper-based; 77 iBT). Electronic applications accepted. *Faculty research:* Geophysics, structural geology, petrology, geochemistry, geodynamics.

Duke University, Graduate School, Division of Earth and Ocean Sciences, Durham, NC 27708. Offers MS, PhD. *Program availability:* Part-time. Terminal master's awarded for partial completion of doctoral program. *Degree requirements:* For master's, thesis; for doctorate, thesis/dissertation. *Entrance requirements:* For master's and doctorate, GRE General Test. Additional exam requirements/recommendations for international students: Required—TOEFL (minimum score 577 paper-based; 90 iBT) or IELTS (minimum score 7). Electronic applications accepted.

East Carolina University, Graduate School, Thomas Harriot College of Arts and Sciences, Department of Geological Sciences, Greenville, NC 27858-4353. Offers geology (MS); hydrogeology and environmental geology (Certificate). *Program availability:* Part-time. *Application deadline:* For fall admission, 6/1 priority date for domestic students, 12/15 priority date for international students; for spring admission, 11/1 priority date for domestic students, 8/15 priority date for international students. *Expenses: Tuition, area resident:* Full-time $4749. Tuition, state resident: full-time $4749. Tuition, nonresident: full-time $17,898. *International tuition:* $17,898 full-time. *Required fees:* $2787. Part-time tuition and fees vary according to course load and program. *Financial support:* Application deadline: 2/1. *Unit head:* Dr. Stephen Culver, Chair, 252-328-6360, Fax: 252-328-4391, E-mail: culvers@ecu.edu. *Application contact:* Graduate School Admissions, 252-328-6012, Fax: 252-328-6071, E-mail: gradschool@ecu.edu.
Website: http://www.ecu.edu/geology/

Eastern Kentucky University, The Graduate School, College of Arts and Sciences, Department of Earth Sciences, Richmond, KY 40475-3102. Offers geology (MS, PhD). PhD program offered jointly with University of Kentucky. *Program availability:* Part-time. *Degree requirements:* For master's, thesis. *Entrance requirements:* For master's, GRE General Test, minimum GPA of 2.5. *Faculty research:* Hydrogeology, sedimentary geology, geochemistry, environmental geology, tectonics.

Florida Atlantic University, Charles E. Schmidt College of Science, Department of Geosciences, Boca Raton, FL 33431-0991. Offers geology (MS); geosciences (PhD). *Program availability:* Part-time. *Faculty:* 18 full-time (5 women), 2 part-time/adjunct (1 woman). *Students:* 28 full-time (12 women), 34 part-time (16 women); includes 10 minority (1 Asian, non-Hispanic/Latino; 7 Hispanic/Latino; 2 Two or more races, non-Hispanic/Latino), 7 international. Average age 31. 40 applicants, 48% accepted, 11 enrolled. In 2018, 9 master's, 2 doctorates awarded. *Entrance requirements:* For master's, GRE General Test, minimum GPA of 3.0. Additional exam requirements/recommendations for international students: Required—TOEFL (minimum score 500 paper-based; 61 iBT), IELTS (minimum score 6). *Application deadline:* For fall admission, 3/15 for domestic and international students; for spring admission, 10/15 for domestic and international students. Applications are processed on a rolling basis. Application fee: $30. Electronic applications accepted. *Expenses: Tuition, area resident:* Full-time $7400; part-time $369.82 per credit. Tuition, state resident: full-time $7400; part-time $369.82 per credit. Tuition, nonresident: full-time $20,496; part-time $1024.81 per credit. *Financial support:* Research assistantships with partial tuition reimbursements, teaching assistantships with partial tuition reimbursements, career-related internships or fieldwork, Federal Work-Study, institutionally sponsored loans, and unspecified assistantships available. *Faculty research:* GIS applications, paleontology, hydrogeology, economic development. *Unit head:* Zhixiao Xie, Chair and Professor, 561-297-2852, E-mail: xie@fau.edu. *Application contact:* Tobin Hindle, Graduate Program Director, 561-297-2846, E-mail: thindle@fau.edu.
Website: http://www.geosciences.fau.edu/

Florida State University, The Graduate School, Department of Anthropology, Department of Earth, Ocean and Atmospheric Science, Program in Geological Sciences, Tallahassee, FL 32306. Offers MS, PhD. *Faculty:* 12 full-time (1 woman). *Students:* 32 full-time (13 women), 2 part-time (1 woman); includes 2 minority (both Two or more races, non-Hispanic/Latino), 10 international. Average age 26. 35 applicants, 29% accepted, 5 enrolled. In 2018, 6 master's awarded. *Degree requirements:* For master's, comprehensive exam, thesis; for doctorate, comprehensive exam, thesis/dissertation. *Entrance requirements:* For master's and doctorate, GRE General Test, minimum GPA of 3.0. Additional exam requirements/recommendations for international students: Required—TOEFL (minimum score 550 paper-based; 80 iBT). *Application deadline:* For fall admission, 1/15 priority date for domestic and international students; for spring admission, 9/15 priority date for domestic and international students. Application fee: $35. Electronic applications accepted. *Expenses: Tuition, area resident:* Part-time $479.32 per credit hour. Tuition and fees vary according to campus/location and program. *Financial support:* In 2018–19, 28 students received support, including 7 research assistantships with full tuition reimbursements available, 20 teaching assistantships with full tuition reimbursements available; fellowships, career-related internships or fieldwork, and Federal Work-Study also available. Financial award application deadline: 1/15; financial award applicants required to submit FAFSA. *Faculty research:* Appalachian and collisional tectonics, surface and groundwater hydrogeology, micropaleontology, isotope and trace element geochemistry, coastal and estuarine studies. *Unit head:* Dr. Mainak Mookherjee, Graduate Program Chair, 850-644-6205, Fax: 850-644-4214, E-mail: mmookherjee@fsu.edu. *Application contact:* Michaela Lupiani, Academic Coordinator, 850-644-6205, Fax: 850-644-4214, E-mail: mlupiani@fsu.edu.
Website: http://www.eoas.fsu.edu

Fort Hays State University, Graduate School, Peter Werth College of Science, Technology and Mathematics, Department of Geosciences, Program in Geosciences, Hays, KS 67601-4099. Offers geography (MS); geology (MS). *Degree requirements:* For master's, comprehensive exam, thesis. *Entrance requirements:* For master's, GRE General Test. Additional exam requirements/recommendations for international students: Required—TOEFL (minimum score 550 paper-based). Electronic applications accepted. *Faculty research:* Cretaceous and late Cenozoic stratigraphy, sedimentation, paleontology.

Georgia State University, College of Arts and Sciences, Department of Geosciences, Program in Geology, Atlanta, GA 30302-3083. Offers MS. *Entrance requirements:* For master's, GRE General Test, minimum GPA of 2.75. Additional exam requirements/recommendations for international students: Required—TOEFL. Application fee: $50. *Expenses: Tuition, area resident:* Full-time $9360; part-time $390 per credit hour. Tuition, state resident: full-time $9360; part-time $390 per credit hour. Tuition, nonresident: full-time $30,024; part-time $1251 per credit hour. *International tuition:* $30,024 full-time. *Required fees:* $2128. *Financial support:* Research assistantships, teaching assistantships, and tuition waivers (partial) available. *Unit head:* Dr. Katherin Hankings, Chair, 404-413-5775, E-mail: khankins@gsu.edu. *Application contact:* Dr. Katherin Hankings, Chair, 404-413-5775, E-mail: khankins@gsu.edu.
Website: http://geosciences.gsu.edu/grad-programs/m-s-degree-in-geosciences/

Humboldt State University, Academic Programs, College of Natural Resources and Sciences, Programs in Environmental Systems, Arcata, CA 95521-8299. Offers environmental systems (MS), including energy, environment and society, environmental resources engineering, geology, math modeling. *Faculty:* 34 full-time (14 women), 37 part-time/adjunct (17 women). *Students:* 18 full-time (8 women), 6 part-time (2 women); includes 7 minority (3 Asian, non-Hispanic/Latino; 3 Hispanic/Latino; 1 Two or more races, non-Hispanic/Latino), 4 international. Average age 28. 48 applicants, 52% accepted, 11 enrolled. In 2018, 12 master's awarded. *Degree requirements:* For master's, thesis. *Entrance requirements:* For master's, GRE, appropriate bachelor's degree, minimum GPA of 2.5, 3 letters of recommendation. Additional exam requirements/recommendations for international students: Required—TOEFL. *Application deadline:* For fall admission, 2/15 for domestic students; for spring admission, 10/15 for domestic students. Applications are processed on a rolling basis. Application fee: $55. *Expenses: Tuition:* Part-time $4649 per semester. *Required fees:* $2121; $1673. Tuition and fees vary according to program. *Financial support:* Application deadline: 3/1; applicants required to submit FAFSA. *Faculty research:* Mathematical modeling, international development technology, geology, environmental resources engineering. *Unit head:* Dr. Margaret Lang, Graduate Program Coordinator, 707-826-3256, E-mail: CNRSmast@humboldt.edu. *Application contact:* Dr. Margaret Lang, Graduate Program Coordinator, 707-826-3256, E-mail: CNRSmast@humboldt.edu.

Idaho State University, Graduate School, College of Science and Engineering, Department of Geosciences, Pocatello, ID 83209-8072. Offers geographic information science (MS); geology (MNS, MS); geology with emphasis in environmental geoscience (MS); geophysics/hydrology/geology (MS); geotechnology (Postbaccalaureate Certificate). *Program availability:* Part-time. *Degree requirements:* For master's, comprehensive exam, thesis, oral colloquium; for Postbaccalaureate Certificate, thesis optional, minimum 19 credits. *Entrance requirements:* For master's, GRE General Test (minimum 50th percentile in 2 sections), 3 letters of recommendation; for Postbaccalaureate Certificate, GRE General Test, 3 letters of recommendation, bachelor's degree, statement of goals. Additional exam requirements/recommendations for international students: Required—TOEFL (minimum score 550 paper-based; 80 iBT). Electronic applications accepted. *Faculty research:* Quantitative field mapping and sampling: microscopic, geochemical, and isotopic analysis of rocks, minerals and water; remote sensing, geographic information systems, and global positioning systems: environmental and watershed management; surficial and fluvial processes: landscape change; regional tectonics, structural geology; planetary geology.

Indiana University–Purdue University Indianapolis, School of Science, Department of Earth Sciences, Indianapolis, IN 46202-3272. Offers applied earth sciences (PhD); geology (MS). *Program availability:* Part-time, evening/weekend. *Degree requirements:* For master's, thesis (for some programs). *Entrance requirements:* For master's, GRE General Test, minimum GPA of 3.0. *Faculty research:* Wetland hydrology, groundwater contamination, soils, sedimentology, sediment chemistry.

Iowa State University of Science and Technology, Department of Geological and Atmospheric Sciences, Ames, IA 50011. Offers earth science (MS, PhD); environmental science (MS, PhD); geology (MS, PhD); meteorology (MS, PhD). *Degree requirements:* For master's, thesis (for some programs); for doctorate, thesis/dissertation. *Entrance requirements:* For master's and doctorate, GRE General Test. Additional exam requirements/recommendations for international students: Required—TOEFL (minimum score 550 paper-based; 79 iBT), IELTS (minimum score 6.5). Electronic applications accepted.

Kansas State University, Graduate School, College of Arts and Sciences, Department of Geology, Manhattan, KS 66506. Offers MS. *Degree requirements:* For master's, thesis. *Entrance requirements:* For master's, GRE General Test, minimum GPA of 3.0 in all geology undergraduate coursework, two semesters of calculus. Additional exam requirements/recommendations for international students: Required—TOEFL. Electronic applications accepted. *Faculty research:* Chemical hydrogeology, petroleum geology, geophysics, Quaternary geology, igneous petrology, isotope geology, volcanology, paleoclimatology, sedimentology, luminescence dating, geomicrobiology, environmental geology, structural geology, economic geology, tectonics.

Kent State University, College of Arts and Sciences, Department of Geology, Kent, OH 44242-0001. Offers applied geology (PhD); geology (MS). *Program availability:* Part-time. *Faculty:* 6 full-time (2 women), 1 part-time/adjunct. *Students:* 27 full-time (13 women), 20 part-time (17 women); includes 1 minority (Hispanic/Latino), 7 international. Average age 27. 37 applicants, 65% accepted, 11 enrolled. In 2018, 3 master's awarded. *Degree requirements:* For master's, thesis. *Entrance requirements:* For master's, GRE, goal statement, 3 letters of recommendation, resume, transcripts, minimum GPA of 3.0; for doctorate, GRE, minimum GPA of 3.0, goal statement, 3 letters of recommendation, transcripts. Additional exam requirements/recommendations for international students: Required—TOEFL (minimum score 550 paper-based, 79 iBT), Michigan English Language Assessment Battery (minimum score 77), IELTS (minimum score 6.5) or PTE (minimum score 58). *Application deadline:* For fall admission, 1/15 for domestic students, 12/15 for international students. Applications are processed on a rolling basis. Application fee: $45 ($70 for international students). Electronic applications accepted. *Expenses:* Tuition, state resident: full-time $11,766; part-time $536 per credit. Tuition, nonresident: full-time $21,952; part-time $999 per credit. *International tuition:* $21,952 full-time. Tuition and fees vary according to course load. *Financial support:* Teaching assistantships with full tuition reimbursements, scholarships/grants, and unspecified assistantships available. Financial award application deadline: 1/15. *Unit head:* Dr. Daniel K. Holm, Professor and Chair, 330-672-4094, E-mail: dholm@kent.edu. *Application contact:* Dr. Anne Jefferson, Associate Professor and Graduate Coordinator, 330-672-2746, E-mail: ajeffer9@kent.edu.
Website: http://www.kent.edu/geology/

Lakehead University, Graduate Studies, Department of Geology, Thunder Bay, ON P7B 5E1, Canada. Offers M Sc. *Program availability:* Part-time, evening/weekend. *Degree requirements:* For master's, thesis, department seminar, oral exam. *Entrance requirements:* For master's, minimum B average, honours bachelors degree in geology. Additional exam requirements/recommendations for international students: Required—TOEFL. *Faculty research:* Rock physics, sedimentology, mineralogy and economic geology, geochemistry, petrology of alkaline rocks.

Laurentian University, School of Graduate Studies and Research, Programme in Geology (Earth Sciences), Sudbury, ON P3E 2C6, Canada. Offers geology (M Sc); mineral deposits and precambrian geology (PhD); mineral exploration (M Sc). *Program availability:* Part-time. *Degree requirements:* For master's, thesis. *Entrance requirements:* For master's, honors degree with second class or better. *Faculty research:* Localization and metallogenesis of Ni-Cu-(PGE) sulfide mineralization in the Thompson Nickel Belt, mapping lithology and ore-grade and monitoring dissolved organic carbon in lakes using remote sensing, global reefs, volcanic effects on VMS deposits.

Lehigh University, College of Arts and Sciences, Department of Earth and Environmental Sciences, Bethlehem, PA 18015. Offers MS, PhD. *Faculty:* 15 full-time (3 women). *Students:* 21 full-time (9 women); includes 1 minority (Hispanic/Latino), 5 international. Average age 31. 24 applicants, 33% accepted, 4 enrolled. In 2018, 2 master's, 1 doctorate awarded. Terminal master's awarded for partial completion of doctoral program. *Degree requirements:* For master's, thesis; for doctorate, thesis/dissertation. *Entrance requirements:* For master's and doctorate, GRE General Test, transcripts, recommendation letters, research statement, faculty advocates. Additional exam requirements/recommendations for international students: Required—TOEFL (minimum score 85 iBT). *Application deadline:* For fall admission, 1/1 for domestic and international students. Application fee: $75. Tuition and fees vary according to program. *Financial support:* In 2018–19, 14 students received support, including 6 fellowships with full tuition reimbursements available (averaging $21,310 per year), 10 research assistantships with partial tuition reimbursements available (averaging $21,310 per year), 18 teaching assistantships with full tuition reimbursements available (averaging $21,310 per year); scholarships/grants also available. Financial award application deadline: 1/1. *Faculty research:* Geochemistry, petrology, climate modeling, seismology, geomorphology, tectonics, surficial processes, ecology, environmental change, remote sensing. *Total annual research expenditures:* $851,337. *Unit head:* Dr. Gray E. Bebout, Chairman, 610-758-5831, Fax: 610-758-3677, E-mail: geb0@lehigh.edu. *Application contact:* Dr. Robert K. Booth, Graduate Coordinator, 610-758-6580, Fax: 610-758-3677, E-mail: rkb205@lehigh.edu.
Website: http://www.ees.lehigh.edu/

Louisiana State University and Agricultural & Mechanical College, Graduate School, College of Science, Department of Geology and Geophysics, Baton Rouge, LA 70803. Offers MS, PhD.

Massachusetts Institute of Technology, School of Science, Department of Earth, Atmospheric, and Planetary Sciences, Cambridge, MA 02139. Offers atmospheric chemistry (PhD, Sc D); atmospheric science (SM, PhD, Sc D); chemical oceanography (SM, PhD, Sc D); climate physics and chemistry (SM, PhD, Sc D); earth and planetary sciences (SM); geochemistry (PhD, Sc D); geology (PhD, Sc D); geophysics (PhD, Sc D); marine geology and geophysics (SM, PhD, Sc D); physical oceanography (SM, PhD, Sc D); planetary sciences (PhD, Sc D). Terminal master's awarded for partial completion of doctoral program. *Degree requirements:* For master's, thesis; for doctorate, comprehensive exam, thesis/dissertation. *Entrance requirements:* For master's and doctorate, GRE General Test. Additional exam requirements/recommendations for international students: Required—TOEFL, IELTS. Electronic applications accepted. *Expenses: Tuition:* Full-time $51,520; part-time $800 per credit hour. *Required fees:* $312. *Faculty research:* Earth: origin, composition, structure, and dynamics of (and interactions between) the atmosphere, oceans, surface, and interior of the earth; planets: formation, dynamics, and evolution of planetary systems and the characterization of exoplanets; climate: characterization of past, present, and potential future climates; studies of the causes and consequences of climate change; life: co-evolution of life and environmental systems.

McMaster University, School of Graduate Studies, Faculty of Science, School of Geography and Earth Sciences, Hamilton, ON L8S 4M2, Canada. Offers geochemistry (PhD); geology (M Sc, PhD); human geography (MA, PhD); physical geography (M Sc, PhD). *Program availability:* Part-time. Terminal master's awarded for partial completion of doctoral program. *Degree requirements:* For master's, thesis; for doctorate, comprehensive exam, thesis/dissertation. *Entrance requirements:* For master's, minimum B+ average. Additional exam requirements/recommendations for international students: Required—TOEFL (minimum score 550 paper-based).

Memorial University of Newfoundland, School of Graduate Studies, Department of Earth Sciences, St. John's, NL A1C 5S7, Canada. Offers geology (M Sc, PhD); geophysics (M Sc, PhD). *Program availability:* Part-time. *Degree requirements:* For master's, thesis; for doctorate, comprehensive exam, thesis/dissertation, oral thesis defense, entry evaluation. *Entrance requirements:* For master's, honors B Sc; for doctorate, M Sc. Electronic applications accepted. *Faculty research:* Geochemistry, sedimentology, paleoceanography and global change, mineral deposits, petroleum geology, hydrology.

Miami University, College of Arts and Science, Department of Geology, Oxford, OH 45056. Offers MA, MS, PhD. *Faculty:* 11 full-time (3 women). *Students:* 24 full-time (15 women), 2 part-time (1 woman); includes 3 minority (1 Black or African American, non-Hispanic/Latino; 1 American Indian or Alaska Native, non-Hispanic/Latino; 1 Hispanic/Latino), 6 international. Average age 27. In 2018, 8 master's, 1 doctorate awarded. *Unit head:* Dr. Elisabeth Widom, Department Chair and Professor, 513-529-5048, E-mail: widome@miamioh.edu. *Application contact:* Cathy Edwards, Administrative Assistant, 513-529-3216, E-mail: edwardca@miamioh.edu.
Website: http://www.MiamiOH.edu/geology/

Mississippi State University, College of Arts and Sciences, Department of Geosciences, Mississippi State, MS 39762. Offers applied meteorology (MS); broadcast meteorology (MS); earth and atmospheric science (PhD); environmental geosciences (MS); geography (MS); geology (MS); geospatial sciences (MS); professional meteorology/climatology (MS); teachers in geosciences (MS). *Program availability:* Blended/hybrid learning. *Faculty:* 20 full-time (6 women), 1 part-time/adjunct (0 women). *Students:* 62 full-time (21 women), 204 part-time (87 women); includes 44 minority (12 Black or African American, non-Hispanic/Latino; 1 American Indian or Alaska Native, non-Hispanic/Latino; 1 Asian, non-Hispanic/Latino; 25 Hispanic/Latino; 1 Native Hawaiian or other Pacific Islander, non-Hispanic/Latino; 4 Two or more races, non-Hispanic/Latino), 16 international. Average age 33. 130 applicants, 84% accepted, 89 enrolled. In 2018, 76 master's, 4 doctorates awarded. *Degree requirements:* For master's, thesis (for some programs), comprehensive oral or written exam; for doctorate, thesis/dissertation, comprehensive oral or written exam. *Entrance requirements:* For master's, GRE (for on-campus applicants), minimum undergraduate GPA of 2.75; for doctorate, thesis-based MS with background in one department emphasis area. Additional exam requirements/recommendations for international students: Required—

TOEFL (minimum score 477 paper-based; 53 iBT); Recommended—IELTS (minimum score 4.5). *Application deadline:* For fall admission, 7/1 for domestic students, 5/1 for international students; for spring admission, 11/1 for domestic students, 9/1 for international students. Applications are processed on a rolling basis. Application fee: $60 ($80 for international students). Electronic applications accepted. *Expenses:* Tuition, state resident: full-time $8450; part-time $360.59 per credit hour. Tuition, nonresident: full-time $23,140; part-time $969.09 per credit hour. *Required fees:* $110. One-time fee: $55 full-time. Part-time tuition and fees vary according to course load, degree level, campus/location and reciprocity agreements. *Financial support:* In 2018–19, 7 research assistantships with full tuition reimbursements (averaging $16,483 per year), 28 teaching assistantships with full tuition reimbursements (averaging $19,000 per year) were awarded; Federal Work-Study, institutionally sponsored loans, scholarships/grants, tuition waivers (partial), and unspecified assistantships also available. Financial award application deadline: 4/1; financial award applicants required to submit FAFSA. *Faculty research:* Climatology, hydrogeology, sedimentology, meteorology. *Total annual research expenditures:* $8.9 million. *Unit head:* Dr. John C. Rodgers, III, Professor and Interim Head, 662-325-1032, Fax: 662-325-9423, E-mail: jcr100@msstate.edu. *Application contact:* Nathan Drake, Admissions and Enrollment Assistant, 662-325-3804, E-mail: ndrake@grad.msstate.edu. Website: http://www.geosciences.msstate.edu

Missouri State University, Graduate College, College of Natural and Applied Sciences, Department of Geography, Geology, and Planning, Springfield, MO 65897. Offers geography, geology, and planning (Certificate); natural and applied science (MNAS), including geography, geology and planning; secondary education (MS Ed), including earth science, physical geography. *Program availability:* Part-time, evening/weekend. *Faculty:* 18 full-time (4 women), 1 part-time/adjunct (0 women). *Students:* 24 full-time (10 women), 10 part-time (5 women); includes 2 minority (1 Hispanic/Latino; 1 Two or more races, non-Hispanic/Latino), 5 international. Average age 25. 26 applicants, 50% accepted. In 2018, 8 master's awarded. *Degree requirements:* For master's, comprehensive exam, thesis (for some programs). *Entrance requirements:* For master's, GRE General Test (MS, MNAS), minimum undergraduate GPA of 3.0 (MS, MNAS), 9-12 teacher certification (MS Ed). Additional exam requirements/recommendations for international students: Required—TOEFL (minimum score 550 paper-based; 79 iBT), IELTS (minimum score 6). *Application deadline:* For fall admission, 7/20 priority date for domestic students, 5/1 for international students; for spring admission, 12/20 priority date for domestic students, 9/1 for international students. Applications are processed on a rolling basis. Application fee: $55 ($60 for international students). Electronic applications accepted. Tuition and fees vary according to class time, course level, course load, degree level, campus/location, program and student level. *Financial support:* In 2018–19, 3 research assistantships with full tuition reimbursements (averaging $11,574 per year), 15 teaching assistantships with full tuition reimbursements (averaging $9,365 per year) were awarded; career-related internships or fieldwork, Federal Work-Study, institutionally sponsored loans, scholarships/grants, and unspecified assistantships also available. Financial award application deadline: 1/31; financial award applicants required to submit FAFSA. *Faculty research:* Stratigraphy and ancient meteorite impacts, environmental geochemistry of karst, hyperspectral image processing, water quality, small town planning. *Unit head:* Dr. Toby Dogwiler, Department Head, 417-836-5800, Fax: 417-836-6934, E-mail: tobydogwiler@missouristate.edu. *Application contact:* Lakan Drinker, Director, Graduate Enrollment Management, 417-836-5330, Fax: 417-836-6200, E-mail: lakandrinker@missouristate.edu.
Website: http://geosciences.missouristate.edu/

Missouri University of Science and Technology, Department of Geosciences and Geological and Petroleum Engineering, Rolla, MO 65401. Offers geological engineering (MS, DE, PhD); geology and geophysics (MS, PhD), including geochemistry, geology, geophysics, groundwater and environmental geology; petroleum engineering (MS, DE, PhD). *Program availability:* Part-time. *Degree requirements:* For master's, thesis optional; for doctorate, comprehensive exam, thesis/dissertation. *Entrance requirements:* For master's, GRE General Test (minimum score 600 quantitative, writing 3.5), minimum GPA of 3.0 In last 4 semesters; for doctorate, GRE General Test (minimum scores: Quantitative 600, Writing 3.5). Additional exam requirements/recommendations for international students: Required—TOEFL (minimum score 550 paper-based). Electronic applications accepted. *Expenses:* Tuition, state resident: full-time $7545.60; part-time $419.20 per credit hour. Tuition, nonresident: full-time $22,169; part-time $1231.60 per credit hour. *International tuition:* $23,518.80 full-time. *Required fees:* $4523.05. Full-time tuition and fees vary according to course load, campus/location, program and reciprocity agreements. *Faculty research:* Digital image processing and geographic information systems, mineralogy, igneous and sedimentary petrology-geochemistry, sedimentology groundwater hydrology and contaminant transport.

Montana Tech of The University of Montana, Geosciences Programs, Butte, MT 59701-8997. Offers geochemistry (MS); geological engineering (MS); geology (MS); geophysical engineering (MS); hydrogeological engineering (MS); hydrogeology (MS). *Program availability:* Part-time. *Degree requirements:* For master's, comprehensive exam (for some programs), thesis (for some programs). *Entrance requirements:* For master's, GRE General Test, minimum GPA of 3.0. Additional exam requirements/recommendations for international students: Required—TOEFL (minimum score 545 paper-based; 78 iBT), IELTS (minimum score 6.5). Electronic applications accepted. *Faculty research:* Water resource development, seismic processing, petroleum reservoir characterization, environmental geochemistry, geologic mapping.

New Mexico Institute of Mining and Technology, Center for Graduate Studies, Department of Earth and Environmental Science, Program in Geology, Socorro, NM 87801. Offers MS, PhD. *Degree requirements:* For master's, thesis optional; for doctorate, thesis/dissertation. *Entrance requirements:* For master's, GRE General Test; for doctorate, GRE General Test, GRE Subject Test. Additional exam requirements/recommendations for international students: Required—TOEFL (minimum score 540 paper-based). Electronic applications accepted. *Faculty research:* Care and karst topography, soil/water chemistry and properties, geochemistry of ore deposits.

Northern Arizona University, College of Environment, Forestry, and Natural Sciences, School of Earth Sciences and Environmental Sustainability, Flagstaff, AZ 86011. Offers climate science and solutions (MS); conservation ecology (Graduate Certificate); earth sciences and environmental sustainability (PhD); environmental sciences and policy (MS); geology (MS). *Program availability:* Part-time. *Degree requirements:* For master's, variable foreign language requirement, comprehensive exam (for some programs), thesis (for some programs); for doctorate, variable foreign language requirement, comprehensive exam (for some programs), thesis/dissertation (for some programs); for Graduate Certificate, comprehensive exam (for some programs). *Entrance requirements:* For master's and doctorate, GRE General Test. Additional exam requirements/recommendations for international students: Required—TOEFL (minimum score 80 iBT), IELTS (minimum score 6.5). Electronic applications accepted.

Northern Illinois University, Graduate School, College of Liberal Arts and Sciences, Department of Geology and Environmental Geosciences, De Kalb, IL 60115-2854. Offers MS, PhD. *Program availability:* Part-time. *Faculty:* 11 full-time (1 woman), 1 (woman) part-time/adjunct. *Students:* 15 full-time (5 women), 11 part-time (6 women); includes 6 minority (1 Asian, non-Hispanic/Latino; 2 Hispanic/Latino; 3 Two or more races, non-Hispanic/Latino), 1 international. Average age 28. 20 applicants, 70% accepted. In 2018, 7 master's, 1 doctorate awarded. Terminal master's awarded for partial completion of doctoral program. *Degree requirements:* For master's, comprehensive exam, thesis optional, research seminar; for doctorate, thesis/dissertation, candidacy exam, dissertation defense, internship, research seminar. *Entrance requirements:* For master's, GRE General Test, bachelor's degree in engineering or science, minimum GPA of 2.75; for doctorate, GRE General Test, bachelor's or master's degree in engineering or science, minimum graduate GPA of 3.2. Additional exam requirements/recommendations for international students: Required—TOEFL (minimum score 550 paper-based). *Application deadline:* For fall admission, 6/1 for domestic students, 5/1 for international students; for spring admission, 11/1 for domestic students, 10/1 for international students. Applications are processed on a rolling basis. Application fee: $40. Electronic applications accepted. *Financial support:* In 2018–19, 3 research assistantships with full tuition reimbursements, 20 teaching assistantships with full tuition reimbursements were awarded; fellowships with full tuition reimbursements, career-related internships or fieldwork, Federal Work-Study, scholarships/grants, tuition waivers (full), and unspecified assistantships also available. Support available to part-time students. Financial award applicants required to submit FAFSA. *Faculty research:* Micropaleontology, environmental geochemistry, glacial geology, igneous petrology, statistical analyses of fracture networks. *Unit head:* Dr. Mark Fischer, Chair, 815-753-0523, Fax: 815-753-1945, E-mail: mfischer@niu.edu. *Application contact:* Graduate School Office, 815-753-0395, E-mail: gradsch@niu.edu. Website: http://www.niu.edu/geology/

Northwestern University, The Graduate School, Judd A. and Marjorie Weinberg College of Arts and Sciences, Department of Earth and Planetary Sciences, Evanston, IL 60208. Offers PhD. Admissions and degrees offered through The Graduate School. *Program availability:* Part-time. *Degree requirements:* For doctorate, thesis/dissertation. *Entrance requirements:* For doctorate, GRE General Test. Additional exam requirements/recommendations for international students: Required—TOEFL. Electronic applications accepted.

The Ohio State University, Graduate School, College of Arts and Sciences, Division of Natural and Mathematical Sciences, School of Earth Sciences, Columbus, OH 43210. Offers earth sciences (MS, PhD); geodetic science (MS, PhD); geological sciences (MS, PhD). *Faculty:* 27. *Students:* 67 (27 women). Average age 28. In 2018, 18 master's, 12 doctorates awarded. *Entrance requirements:* For master's, GRE, undergraduate degree in biological science, geological sciences, physical science or engineering (recommended); minimum GPA of 3.2; for doctorate, GRE, undergraduate degree in biological science, geological sciences, physical science or engineering (recommended); minimum GPA of 3.4. Additional exam requirements/recommendations for international students: Required—TOEFL (minimum score 550 paper-based; 79 iBT), Michigan English Language Assessment Battery (minimum score 82); Recommended—IELTS (minimum score 8). *Application deadline:* For fall admission, 12/13 priority date for domestic students, 11/30 priority date for international students; for spring admission, 11/30 for domestic and international students; for summer admission, 7/24 for domestic students, 3/13 for international students. Applications are processed on a rolling basis. Application fee: $60 ($70 for international students). Electronic applications accepted. *Financial support:* Fellowships, research assistantships, and teaching assistantships available. *Unit head:* Dr. Matthew Saltzman, Director, 614-292-0481, Fax: 614-292-7688, E-mail: saltzman.11@osu.edu. *Application contact:* Graduate and Professional Admissions, 614-292-9444, Fax: 614-292-3895, E-mail: gpadmissions@osu.edu. Website: http://earthsciences.osu.edu/

Ohio University, Graduate College, College of Arts and Sciences, Department of Geological Sciences, Athens, OH 45701-2979. Offers environmental geochemistry (MS). *Program availability:* Part-time. *Degree requirements:* For master's, thesis. *Entrance requirements:* Additional exam requirements/recommendations for international students: Required—TOEFL (minimum score 550 paper-based; 80 iBT) or IELTS (minimum score 6.5). Electronic applications accepted. *Faculty research:* Geoscience education, tectonics, fluvial geomorphology, invertebrate paleontology, mine/hydrology.

Oklahoma State University, College of Arts and Sciences, Boone Pickens School of Geology, Stillwater, OK 74078. Offers MS, PhD. *Faculty:* 15 full-time (3 women), 1 (woman) part-time/adjunct. *Students:* 28 full-time (8 women), 51 part-time (14 women); includes 8 minority (2 Black or African American, non-Hispanic/Latino; 1 American Indian or Alaska Native, non-Hispanic/Latino; 3 Hispanic/Latino; 2 Two or more races, non-Hispanic/Latino), 20 international. Average age 30. 85 applicants, 20% accepted, 14 enrolled. In 2018, 23 master's, 2 doctorates awarded. *Entrance requirements:* For master's and doctorate, GRE. Additional exam requirements/recommendations for international students: Required—TOEFL (minimum score 550 paper-based; 79 iBT). *Application deadline:* For fall admission, 3/1 priority date for international students; for spring admission, 8/1 priority date for international students. Applications are processed on a rolling basis. Application fee: $40 ($75 for international students). Electronic applications accepted. *Expenses:* Tuition, area resident: Full-time $4148. Tuition, state resident: full-time $4148. Tuition, nonresident: full-time $10,517. *International tuition:* $10,517 full-time. *Required fees:* $4394; $2929 per credit hour. Tuition and fees vary according to course load and program. *Financial support:* Research assistantships, teaching assistantships, career-related internships or fieldwork, Federal Work-Study, scholarships/grants, health care benefits, tuition waivers (partial), and unspecified assistantships available. Support available to part-time students. Financial award application deadline: 3/1; financial award applicants required to submit FAFSA. *Faculty research:* Groundwater hydrology, petroleum geology. *Unit head:* Dr. Camelia Knapp, Department Head, 405-744-6358, Fax: 405-744-7841, E-mail: camelia.knapp@okstate.edu. *Application contact:* Dr. Sheryl Tucker, Dean, 405-744-6368, Fax: 405-744-0355, E-mail: gradi@okstate.edu. Website: http://geology.okstate.edu

Oregon State University, College of Earth, Ocean, and Atmospheric Sciences, Program in Geology, Corvallis, OR 97331. Offers geochemistry (MA, MS, PhD); geomorphology (MA, MS, PhD); geophysics (MA, MS, PhD); glacial geology (MA, MS, PhD); hydrology and hydrogeology (MA, MS, PhD); igneous petrology (MA, MS, PhD); neotonics (MA, MS, PhD); paleoclimatology (MA); structural geology (MA, MS, PhD). Terminal master's awarded for partial completion of doctoral program. *Entrance requirements:* For master's and doctorate, GRE, minimum GPA of 3.0 in last 90 hours. Additional exam requirements/recommendations for international students: Required—TOEFL (minimum score 80 iBT), IELTS (minimum score 6.5). *Faculty research:* Hydrogeology, geomorphology, ocean geology, geochemistry, earthquake geology.

Portland State University, Graduate Studies, College of Liberal Arts and Sciences, Department of Geology, Portland, OR 97207-0751. Offers environmental sciences and

Peterson's Graduate Programs in the Physical Sciences, Mathematics, Agricultural Sciences, the Environment & Natural Resources 2020

www.petersons.com **91**

resources (PhD); geology (MA, MS, Certificate); science/geology (MAT, MST). *Program availability:* Part-time. *Degree requirements:* For master's, comprehensive exam, thesis or alternative, field comprehensive; for doctorate, thesis/dissertation. *Entrance requirements:* For master's, GRE General Test, GRE Subject Test, BA/BS in geology, minimum GPA of 3.0 in geology-related and allied sciences, resume, statement of intent, 2 letters of recommendation. Additional exam requirements/recommendations for international students: Required—TOEFL (minimum score 550 paper-based; 80 iBT). Electronic applications accepted. *Faculty research:* Sediment transport, volcanic environmental geology, coastal and fluvial processes.

Queens College of the City University of New York, Mathematics and Natural Sciences Division, School of Earth and Environmental Sciences, Queens, NY 11367-1597. Offers applied environmental geosciences (MS); geological and environmental sciences (MA). *Program availability:* Part-time, evening/weekend. *Faculty:* 17 full-time (5 women), 16 part-time/adjunct (8 women). *Students:* 1 (woman) full-time, 14 part-time (5 women); includes 3 minority (2 Black or African American, non-Hispanic/Latino; 1 Asian, non-Hispanic/Latino), 1 international. Average age 28. 11 applicants, 73% accepted, 6 enrolled. In 2018, 11 master's awarded. *Degree requirements:* For master's, thesis (for some programs), internship (MS) or thesis (MA) required. *Entrance requirements:* For master's, previous course work in calculus, physics, geology, and chemistry; minimum GPA of 3.0. Additional exam requirements/recommendations for international students: Required—TOEFL, IELTS. *Application deadline:* For fall admission, 4/1 for domestic students; for spring admission, 11/1 for domestic students. Applications are processed on a rolling basis. Application fee: $125. Electronic applications accepted. *Financial support:* In 2018–19, 10 teaching assistantships (averaging $11,968 per year) were awarded; career-related internships or fieldwork and unspecified assistantships also available. Financial award application deadline: 4/1; financial award applicants required to submit FAFSA. *Unit head:* Jeffrey Bird, Chair, 718-997-3300, E-mail: jeffrey.bird@qc.cuny.edu. *Application contact:* Gregory O'Mullan, Graduate Advisor, 718-997-3452, E-mail: gomullan@qc.cuny.edu.
Website: http://www.qc.cuny.edu/Academics/Degrees/DMNS/sees/Pages/default.aspx

Queen's University at Kingston, School of Graduate Studies, Faculty of Arts and Science, Department of Geological Sciences and Geological Engineering, Kingston, ON K7L 3N6, Canada. Offers M Sc, PhD. *Program availability:* Part-time. *Degree requirements:* For master's, thesis (for some programs); for doctorate, comprehensive exam, thesis/dissertation. *Entrance requirements:* Additional exam requirements/recommendations for international students: Required—TOEFL. *Faculty research:* Geochemistry, sedimentology, geophysics, economic geology, structural geology.

Rensselaer Polytechnic Institute, Graduate School, School of Science, Program in Geology, Troy, NY 12180-3590. Offers MS, PhD. *Faculty:* 9 full-time (3 women). *Students:* 11 full-time (4 women); includes 2 minority (both Hispanic/Latino), 3 international. Average age 26. 33 applicants, 30% accepted, 3 enrolled. In 2018, 4 master's, 3 doctorates awarded. Terminal master's awarded for partial completion of doctoral program. *Degree requirements:* For master's, comprehensive exam, thesis (for some programs); for doctorate, comprehensive exam, thesis/dissertation. *Entrance requirements:* For master's and doctorate, GRE. Additional exam requirements/recommendations for international students: Required—TOEFL (minimum score 570 paper-based; 88 iBT), IELTS (minimum score 6.5), PTE (minimum score 60). *Application deadline:* For fall admission, 1/1 priority date for domestic and international students; for spring admission, 8/15 priority date for domestic and international students. Applications are processed on a rolling basis. Application fee: $75. Electronic applications accepted. *Financial support:* In 2018–19, research assistantships (averaging $23,000 per year), teaching assistantships (averaging $23,000 per year) were awarded; fellowships also available. Financial award application deadline: 1/1; financial award applicants required to submit FAFSA. *Faculty research:* Astrobiology, carbon in deep earth, climate assessment, ecosystem studies, environmental and freshwater geochemistry, geoinformatics, geomicrobiology, geophysical simulation, inorganic and igneous experimental geochemistry, isotopic and organic geochemistry, lithosphere dynamics and tectonophysics, metamorphic petrology and geochemistry, microbial geochemistry, paleoceanography and micropaleontology, seismology and solid earth geophysics. *Total annual research expenditures:* $403,292. *Unit head:* Dr. Mimi Katz, Graduate Program Director, 518-276-8521, E-mail: katzm@rpi.edu. *Application contact:* Jarron Decker, Director of Graduate Admissions, 518-276-6216, Fax: 518-276-4072, E-mail: gradadmissions@rpi.edu.
Website: https://science.rpi.edu/earth

Rutgers University–Newark, Graduate School, Program in Environmental Geology, Newark, NJ 07102. Offers MS. *Program availability:* Part-time, evening/weekend. *Degree requirements:* For master's, comprehensive exam, thesis optional. *Entrance requirements:* For master's, GRE General Test, minimum B average. Electronic applications accepted. *Faculty research:* Environmental geology, plate tectonics, geoarchaeology, geophysics, mineralogy-petrology.

Rutgers University–New Brunswick, Graduate School-New Brunswick, Department of Earth and Planetary Sciences, Piscataway, NJ 08854-8097. Offers geological sciences (MS, PhD). *Program availability:* Part-time. *Degree requirements:* For master's, thesis; for doctorate, comprehensive exam, thesis/dissertation. *Entrance requirements:* For master's and doctorate, GRE General Test, GRE Subject Test (recommended). Electronic applications accepted. *Faculty research:* Basin analysis, volcanology, quaternary studies, engineering geophysics, marine geology, biogeochemistry and paleoceanography.

St. Francis Xavier University, Graduate Studies, Department of Earth Sciences, Antigonish, NS B2G 2W5, Canada. Offers M Sc. *Degree requirements:* For master's, thesis. *Entrance requirements:* Additional exam requirements/recommendations for international students: Required—TOEFL (minimum score 580 paper-based). *Expenses: Tuition, area resident:* Full-time $7547 Canadian dollars. Tuition, state resident: full-time $7547 Canadian dollars; part-time $804.19 Canadian dollars per course. Tuition, nonresident: full-time $8839 Canadian dollars; part-time $932.49 Canadian dollars per course. *International tuition:* $932.49 Canadian dollars full-time. *Required fees:* $90.20 Canadian dollars; $90.20 Canadian dollars per course. One-time fee: $6 Canadian dollars. Tuition and fees vary according to course load, degree level and program. *Faculty research:* Environmental earth sciences, global change tectonics, paleoclimatology, crustal fluids.

San Diego State University, Graduate and Research Affairs, College of Sciences, Department of Geological Sciences, San Diego, CA 92182. Offers MS. *Program availability:* Part-time. *Degree requirements:* For master's, thesis. *Entrance requirements:* For master's, GRE General Test, bachelor's degree in related field, 2 letters of reference. Additional exam requirements/recommendations for international students: Required—TOEFL. Electronic applications accepted. *Faculty research:* Earthquakes, hydrology, meteorological analysis and tomography studies.

San Jose State University, Program in Geology, San Jose, CA 95192-0001. Offers MS. *Degree requirements:* For master's, thesis. *Entrance requirements:* For master's, GRE. Electronic applications accepted.

South Dakota School of Mines and Technology, Graduate Division, Department of Geology and Geological Engineering, Rapid City, SD 57701-3995. Offers geology and geological engineering (MS, PhD); paleontology (MS). *Program availability:* Part-time. *Degree requirements:* For master's, thesis; for doctorate, thesis/dissertation. *Entrance requirements:* For master's and doctorate, GRE General Test, GRE Subject Test. Additional exam requirements/recommendations for international students: Required—TOEFL (minimum score 520 paper-based; 68 iBT), TWE. Electronic applications accepted. *Faculty research:* Contaminants in soil, nitrate leaching, environmental changes, fracture formations, greenhouse effect.

Southern Illinois University Carbondale, Graduate School, College of Science, Department of Geology, Carbondale, IL 62901-4701. Offers environmental resources and policy (PhD); geology (MS); geosciences (PhD). *Degree requirements:* For master's, thesis; for doctorate, one foreign language, thesis/dissertation. *Entrance requirements:* For master's, GRE, minimum GPA of 2.7; for doctorate, GRE General Test, minimum GPA of 3.25. Additional exam requirements/recommendations for international students: Required—TOEFL.

Southern Methodist University, Dedman College of Humanities and Sciences, Roy M. Huffington Department of Earth Sciences, Dallas, TX 75275. Offers applied geophysics (MS); earth sciences (MS, PhD). *Program availability:* Part-time. *Degree requirements:* For master's, thesis (for some programs), qualifying exam; for doctorate, thesis/dissertation, qualifying exam. *Entrance requirements:* For master's and doctorate, GRE General Test, minimum GPA of 3.0, letters of recommendation. Additional exam requirements/recommendations for international students: Required—TOEFL. Electronic applications accepted. *Faculty research:* Sedimentology, geochemistry, igneous and metamorphic petrology, vertebrate paleontology, seismology.

Stephen F. Austin State University, Graduate School, College of Sciences and Mathematics, Department of Geology, Nacogdoches, TX 75962. Offers MS, MSNS. *Degree requirements:* For master's, comprehensive exam. *Entrance requirements:* For master's, GRE General Test, minimum GPA of 2.8 in last 60 hours, 2.5 overall. Additional exam requirements/recommendations for international students: Required—TOEFL. *Faculty research:* Stratigraphy of Kaibab limestone, Utah; structure of Ouachita Mountains, Arkansas; groundwater chemistry of Carrizo Sand, Texas.

Sul Ross State University, College of Arts and Sciences, Department of Earth and Physical Sciences, Alpine, TX 79832. Offers geology (MS). *Program availability:* Part-time. *Degree requirements:* For master's, thesis optional. *Entrance requirements:* For master's, GRE General Test, minimum GPA of 2.5 in last 60 hours of undergraduate work.

Syracuse University, College of Arts and Sciences, Department of Earth Sciences, Syracuse, NY 13244. Offers MS, PhD. *Degree requirements:* For master's, thesis, research tool; for doctorate, thesis/dissertation, 2 research tools. *Entrance requirements:* For master's, GRE General Test, personal statement, including research and/or teaching experience, research interests, and career goals; three letters of recommendation; official transcripts; for doctorate, GRE General Test. Additional exam requirements/recommendations for international students: Required—TOEFL (minimum score 85 iBT). *Application deadline:* For fall admission, 1/15 priority date for domestic and international students. Application fee: $75. Electronic applications accepted. *Financial support:* Fellowships with full tuition reimbursements, research assistantships, teaching assistantships, and scholarships/grants available. Financial award application deadline: 1/1. *Faculty research:* Environmental geology, thermochronology, tectonics, isotope geochemistry, paleobiology. *Application contact:* Dr. Zunli Lu, Associate Professor/Director of Graduate Studies, 315-443-0281, E-mail: zunlilu@syr.edu.
Website: http://earthsciences.syr.edu/academics/g-program.html

Temple University, College of Science and Technology, Department of Earth and Environmental Science, Philadelphia, PA 19122. Offers geology (MS); geoscience (PhD). *Faculty:* 12 full-time (5 women). *Students:* 17 full-time (5 women), 2 international. 26 applicants, 35% accepted, 5 enrolled. In 2018, 3 master's awarded. *Degree requirements:* For master's, comprehensive exam, thesis; for doctorate, thesis/dissertation. *Entrance requirements:* For master's, GRE, bachelor's degree in related discipline, statement of goals, 2 letters of recommendation; for doctorate, GRE, bachelor's degree in related discipline, statement of goals, 3 letters of recommendation, writing sample. Additional exam requirements/recommendations for international students: Required—TOEFL (minimum score 105 iBT), IELTS (minimum score 7), PTE (minimum score 72), one of three is required. *Application deadline:* For fall admission, 2/1 for domestic students. Application fee: $60. Electronic applications accepted. *Expenses:* Contact institution. *Financial support:* Fellowships, research assistantships, teaching assistantships, Federal Work-Study, health care benefits, and unspecified assistantships available. Financial award applicants required to submit FAFSA. *Faculty research:* Coastal dynamics, environmental geophysics, hydrogeology and groundwater contamination, nanomaterials, paleontology-fossil provenance. *Unit head:* Nicholas Davatzes, Department Chair, 215-204-2319, E-mail: nicholas.davatzes@temple.edu. *Application contact:* Dennis Terry, Graduate Chair, 215-204-8226, E-mail: eesgrad@temple.edu.
Website: https://ees.cst.temple.edu/

Texas A&M University, College of Geosciences, Department of Geology and Geophysics, College Station, TX 77843. Offers geology (MS, PhD); geophysics (PhD). *Faculty:* 37. *Students:* 85 full-time (30 women), 29 part-time (13 women); includes 10 minority (1 Black or African American, non-Hispanic/Latino; 4 Asian, non-Hispanic/Latino; 4 Hispanic/Latino; 1 Two or more races, non-Hispanic/Latino), 51 international. Average age 30. 145 applicants, 12% accepted, 13 enrolled. In 2018, 22 master's, 5 doctorates awarded. *Degree requirements:* For master's, thesis; for doctorate, thesis/dissertation. *Entrance requirements:* For master's and doctorate, GRE General Test. Additional exam requirements/recommendations for international students: Required—TOEFL (minimum score 550 paper-based; 80 iBT), IELTS (minimum score 6), PTE (minimum score 53). *Application deadline:* For fall admission, 1/1 priority date for domestic students; for spring admission, 8/15 priority date for domestic students. Applications are processed on a rolling basis. Application fee: $50 ($90 for international students). Electronic applications accepted. *Expenses:* Contact institution. *Financial support:* In 2018–19, 81 students received support, including 38 fellowships with tuition reimbursements available (averaging $6,947 per year), 34 research assistantships with tuition reimbursements available (averaging $12,517 per year), 31 teaching assistantships with tuition reimbursements available (averaging $12,385 per year); career-related internships or fieldwork, institutionally sponsored loans, scholarships/grants, traineeships, health care benefits, tuition waivers (full and partial), and unspecified assistantships also available. Support available to part-time students. Financial award application deadline: 3/15; financial award applicants required to submit FAFSA. *Faculty research:* Environmental and engineering geology and geophysics, petroleum geology, tectonophysics, geochemistry. *Unit head:* Dr. Mike Pope, Professor and Department Head, 979-845-4376, E-mail: mcpope@tamu.edu. *Application contact:* Dr. Mark E. Everett, Professor and Associate Department Head for Graduate Affairs, 979-862-2129, E-mail: everett@geo.tamu.edu.
Website: http://geoweb.tamu.edu

Université du Québec à Montréal, Graduate Programs, Program in Earth Sciences, Montreal, QC H3C 3P8, Canada. Offers earth sciences (M Sc); mineral resources (PhD); non-renewable resources (DESS). *Program availability:* Part-time. Terminal master's awarded for partial completion of doctoral program. *Degree requirements:* For master's, thesis (for some programs); for doctorate, thesis/dissertation. *Entrance requirements:* For master's, appropriate bachelor's degree or equivalent, proficiency in French. *Faculty research:* Economic geology, structural geology, geochemistry, Quaternary geology, isotopic geochemistry.

Université Laval, Faculty of Sciences and Engineering, Department of Geology and Geological Engineering, Québec, QC G1K 7P4, Canada. Offers earth sciences (M Sc, PhD), including earth sciences, environmental technologies (M Sc); geology (M Sc, PhD). Terminal master's awarded for partial completion of doctoral program. *Degree requirements:* For master's, thesis (for some programs); for doctorate, comprehensive exam, thesis/dissertation. *Entrance requirements:* For master's and doctorate, knowledge of French. Electronic applications accepted. *Faculty research:* Engineering, economics, regional geology.

University at Buffalo, the State University of New York, Graduate School, College of Arts and Sciences, Department of Geology, Buffalo, NY 14260. Offers MA, MS, PhD. *Program availability:* Part-time. *Faculty:* 17 full-time (8 women), 3 part-time/adjunct (2 women). *Students:* 44 full-time (17 women); includes 3 minority (2 Black or African American, non-Hispanic/Latino; 1 Asian, non-Hispanic/Latino), 2 international. Average age 26. 89 applicants, 55% accepted, 21 enrolled. In 2018, 19 master's, 5 doctorates awarded. Terminal master's awarded for partial completion of doctoral program. *Degree requirements:* For master's, project or thesis; for doctorate, thesis/dissertation, dissertation defense. *Entrance requirements:* For master's and doctorate, GRE General Test. Additional exam requirements/recommendations for international students: Required—TOEFL (minimum score 550 paper-based; 79 iBT). *Application deadline:* For fall admission, 1/1 priority date for domestic and international students; for spring admission, 10/1 priority date for domestic and international students. Applications are processed on a rolling basis. Application fee: $75. Electronic applications accepted. *Financial support:* In 2018–19, 3 fellowships with full tuition reimbursements, 9 research assistantships with full and partial tuition reimbursements, 16 teaching assistantships with full and partial tuition reimbursements were awarded; Federal Work-Study, scholarships/grants, health care benefits, and unspecified assistantships also available. Financial award application deadline: 2/1; financial award applicants required to submit FAFSA. *Faculty research:* Climate, water and the environment, ecosystems and adaptation, geohazards, volcanoes and geodynamics. *Unit head:* Dr. Beata Csatho, Professor and Chair, 716-645-3489, Fax: 716-645-3999, E-mail: geology@buffalo.edu. *Application contact:* Dr. Chris Lowry, Director of Graduate Studies, 716-645-4266, Fax: 716-645-3999, E-mail: cslowry@buffalo.edu. Website: http://www.geology.buffalo.edu/

The University of Akron, Graduate School, Buchtel College of Arts and Sciences, Department of Geosciences, Akron, OH 44325. Offers earth science (MS); engineering geology (MS); environmental geology (MS); geology (MS). *Program availability:* Part-time. *Entrance requirements:* For master's, minimum GPA of 2.75, three letters of recommendation, statement of purpose. Additional exam requirements/recommendations for international students: Required—TOEFL (minimum score 79 iBT), IELTS (minimum score 6.5). Electronic applications accepted. *Faculty research:* Terrestrial environmental change, karst hydrogeology, lacustrine paleo environments, environmental magnetism and geophysics.

The University of Alabama, Graduate School, College of Arts and Sciences, Department of Geological Sciences, Tuscaloosa, AL 35487. Offers MS, PhD. Terminal master's awarded for partial completion of doctoral program. *Degree requirements:* For master's, comprehensive exam, thesis; for doctorate, comprehensive exam, thesis/dissertation. *Entrance requirements:* For master's and doctorate, GRE. Additional exam requirements/recommendations for international students: Recommended—TOEFL (minimum score 550 paper-based; 79 iBT). Electronic applications accepted. *Faculty research:* Energy, hydrology, geochemistry, structure, petrology.

University of Arkansas, Graduate School, J. William Fulbright College of Arts and Sciences, Department of Geosciences, Program in Geology, Fayetteville, AR 72701. Offers MS. *Program availability:* Part-time. In 2018, 7 master's awarded. *Application deadline:* For fall admission, 8/1 for domestic students, 4/1 for international students; for spring admission, 12/1 for domestic students, 10/1 for international students; for summer admission, 4/15 for domestic students, 3/1 for international students. Applications are processed on a rolling basis. Application fee: $60. Electronic applications accepted. *Financial support:* In 2018–19, 1 research assistantship, 10 teaching assistantships were awarded; fellowships, career-related internships or fieldwork, and Federal Work-Study also available. Support available to part-time students. Financial award application deadline: 4/1; financial award applicants required to submit FAFSA. *Unit head:* Dr. Christopher Liner, Department Chair, 479-575-3355, Fax: 479-575-3469, E-mail: liner@uark.edu. *Application contact:* Dr. Celina Suarez, Graduate Coordinator of Geology, 479-575-4866, Fax: 479-575-3469, E-mail: casuarez@uark.edu. Website: https://fulbright.uark.edu/departments/geosciences/

The University of British Columbia, Faculty of Science, Department of Earth, Ocean and Atmospheric Sciences, Vancouver, BC V6T 1Z4, Canada. Offers atmospheric science (M Sc, PhD); geological engineering (M Eng, MA Sc, PhD); geological sciences (M Sc, PhD); geophysics (M Sc, MA Sc, PhD); oceanography (M Sc, PhD). *Degree requirements:* For master's, one foreign language, thesis (for some programs); for doctorate, one foreign language, comprehensive exam, thesis/dissertation. *Entrance requirements:* Additional exam requirements/recommendations for international students: Required—TOEFL. *Expenses:* Contact institution. *Faculty research:* Oceans and atmosphere, environmental earth science, hydro geology, mineral deposits, geophysics.

University of Calgary, Faculty of Graduate Studies, Faculty of Science, Program in Geoscience, Calgary, AB T2N 1N4, Canada. Offers geology (M Sc, PhD); geophysics (M Sc, PhD); hydrology (M Sc, PhD). *Program availability:* Part-time. Terminal master's awarded for partial completion of doctoral program. *Degree requirements:* For master's, thesis; for doctorate, thesis/dissertation, candidacy exam. *Entrance requirements:* For master's, B Sc; for doctorate, honors B Sc or M Sc. Additional exam requirements/recommendations for international students: Required—TOEFL. Electronic applications accepted. *Faculty research:* Geochemistry, petrology, paleontology, stratigraphy, exploration and solid-earth geophysics.

University of California, Berkeley, Graduate Division, College of Letters and Science, Department of Earth and Planetary Science, Berkeley, CA 94720. Offers geology (MA, MS, PhD); geophysics (MA, MS, PhD). Terminal master's awarded for partial completion of doctoral program. *Degree requirements:* For master's, oral exam (MA), thesis (MS); for doctorate, comprehensive exam, thesis/dissertation, candidacy exams. *Entrance requirements:* For master's and doctorate, GRE General Test, minimum GPA of 3.0, 3 letters of recommendation. Additional exam requirements/recommendations for international students: Required—TOEFL (minimum score 570 paper-based; 90 iBT).

Electronic applications accepted. *Faculty research:* Tectonics, environmental geology, high-pressure geophysics and seismology, economic geology, geochemistry.

University of California, Davis, Graduate Studies, Program in Geology, Davis, CA 95616. Offers MS, PhD. Terminal master's awarded for partial completion of doctoral program. *Degree requirements:* For master's, thesis; for doctorate, thesis/dissertation. *Entrance requirements:* For master's and doctorate, GRE General Test, GRE Subject Test, minimum GPA of 3.0. Additional exam requirements/recommendations for international students: Required—TOEFL (minimum score 550 paper-based). Electronic applications accepted. *Faculty research:* Petrology, paleontology, geophysics, sedimentology, structure/tectonics.

University of California, Los Angeles, Graduate Division, College of Letters and Science, Department of Earth and Space Sciences, Program in Geology, Los Angeles, CA 90095. Offers MS, PhD. Terminal master's awarded for partial completion of doctoral program. *Degree requirements:* For master's, comprehensive exam or thesis; for doctorate, thesis/dissertation, oral and written qualifying exams. *Entrance requirements:* For master's and doctorate, GRE General Test, bachelor's degree; minimum undergraduate GPA of 3.0 (or its equivalent if letter grade system not used). Additional exam requirements/recommendations for international students: Required—TOEFL. Electronic applications accepted.

University of California, Riverside, Graduate Division, Department of Earth Sciences, Riverside, CA 92521-0102. Offers geological sciences (MS, PhD). Terminal master's awarded for partial completion of doctoral program. *Degree requirements:* For master's, thesis, final oral exam; for doctorate, thesis/dissertation, qualifying exams, final oral exam. *Entrance requirements:* For master's and doctorate, GRE General Test, minimum GPA of 3.2. Additional exam requirements/recommendations for international students: Required—TOEFL (minimum score 550 paper-based; 80 iBT). Electronic applications accepted. *Faculty research:* Applied and solid earth geophysics, tectonic geomorphology, fluid-rock interaction, paleobiology-ecology, sedimentary-geochemistry.

University of Cincinnati, Graduate School, McMicken College of Arts and Sciences, Department of Geology, Cincinnati, OH 45221. Offers MS, PhD. *Program availability:* Part-time. *Degree requirements:* For master's, thesis; for doctorate, comprehensive exam, thesis/dissertation. *Entrance requirements:* For master's and doctorate, GRE General Test, 1 year of course work in physics, chemistry, and calculus. Additional exam requirements/recommendations for international students: Required—TOEFL. Electronic applications accepted. *Faculty research:* Paleobiology, sequence stratigraphy, earth systems history, quaternary, groundwater.

University of Colorado Boulder, Graduate School, College of Arts and Sciences, Department of Geological Sciences, Boulder, CO 80309. Offers geology (MS, PhD); geophysics (PhD). Terminal master's awarded for partial completion of doctoral program. *Degree requirements:* For master's, comprehensive exam, thesis; for doctorate, comprehensive exam, thesis/dissertation. *Entrance requirements:* For master's, GRE General Test, minimum undergraduate GPA of 3.0; for doctorate, GRE General Test, minimum GPA of 2.75. Electronic applications accepted. Application fee is waived when completed online. *Faculty research:* Geology; earth sciences; tectonics; geophysics; geosciences.

University of Connecticut, Graduate School, College of Liberal Arts and Sciences, Center for Integrative Geosciences, Storrs, CT 06269. Offers geological sciences (MS, PhD). *Degree requirements:* For doctorate, thesis/dissertation. *Entrance requirements:* For master's and doctorate, GRE General Test. Additional exam requirements/recommendations for international students: Required—TOEFL (minimum score 550 paper-based). Electronic applications accepted.

University of Delaware, College of Earth, Ocean, and Environment, Department of Geological Sciences, Newark, DE 19716. Offers MA, PhD.

University of Florida, Graduate School, College of Liberal Arts and Sciences, Department of Geological Sciences, Gainesville, FL 32611. Offers geology (MS, MST, PhD); hydrologic sciences (MS, PhD); tropical conservation and development (MS, MST, PhD); wetland sciences (MS, MST, PhD). Terminal master's awarded for partial completion of doctoral program. *Degree requirements:* For master's, thesis (for some programs); for doctorate, one foreign language, thesis/dissertation. *Entrance requirements:* For master's and doctorate, GRE General Test, minimum GPA of 3.0. Additional exam requirements/recommendations for international students: Required—TOEFL (minimum score 550 paper-based; 80 iBT), IELTS (minimum score 6). Electronic applications accepted. *Faculty research:* Paleoclimatology, tectonophysics, petrochemistry, marine geology, geochemistry, hydrology.

University of Georgia, Franklin College of Arts and Sciences, Department of Geology, Athens, GA 30602. Offers MS, PhD. *Degree requirements:* For master's, thesis; for doctorate, one foreign language, thesis/dissertation. *Entrance requirements:* For master's and doctorate, GRE General Test. Electronic applications accepted.

University of Hawaii at Manoa, Office of Graduate Education, School of Ocean and Earth Science and Technology, Department of Geology and Geophysics, Honolulu, HI 96822. Offers high-pressure geophysics and geochemistry (MS, PhD); hydrogeology and engineering geology (MS, PhD); marine geology and geophysics (MS, PhD); planetary geosciences and remote sensing (MS, PhD); seismology and solid-earth geophysics (MS, PhD); volcanology, petrology, and geochemistry (MS, PhD). *Program availability:* Part-time. Terminal master's awarded for partial completion of doctoral program. *Degree requirements:* For master's, thesis optional; for doctorate, comprehensive exam, thesis/dissertation. *Entrance requirements:* For master's and doctorate, GRE General Test, minimum GPA of 3.0. Additional exam requirements/recommendations for international students: Required—TOEFL (minimum score 580 paper-based; 92 iBT), IELTS (minimum score 5).

University of Houston, College of Natural Sciences and Mathematics, Department of Earth and Atmospheric Sciences, Houston, TX 77204. Offers atmospheric science (PhD); geology (MA, PhD); geophysics (PhD). *Program availability:* Part-time. *Degree requirements:* For master's, thesis; for doctorate, comprehensive exam, thesis/dissertation. *Entrance requirements:* For master's and doctorate, GRE General Test. Additional exam requirements/recommendations for international students: Required—TOEFL (minimum score 550 paper-based; 79 iBT), IELTS (minimum score 6.5). Electronic applications accepted. *Faculty research:* Atmospherics sciences, seismic and solid earth geophysics, tectonics, environmental hydrochemistry, carbonates, micropaleontology, structure and tectonics, petroleum geology.

University of Idaho, College of Graduate Studies, College of Science, Department of Geological Sciences, Moscow, ID 83844-3022. Offers geology (MS, PhD). *Faculty:* 8. *Students:* 18. Average age 30. In 2018, 5 master's, 1 doctorate awarded. *Degree requirements:* For master's, thesis or alternative; for doctorate, thesis/dissertation. *Entrance requirements:* For master's, GRE, minimum GPA of 3.0; for doctorate, minimum GPA of 3.0. Additional exam requirements/recommendations for international students: Required—TOEFL (minimum score 79 iBT). *Application deadline:* For fall

Peterson's Graduate Programs in the Physical Sciences, Mathematics, Agricultural Sciences, the Environment & Natural Resources 2020

www.petersons.com 93

admission, 1/15 for domestic students; for spring admission, 12/15 for domestic students. Applications are processed on a rolling basis. Application fee: $60. Electronic applications accepted. *Expenses:* Tuition, state resident: full-time $7266.44; part-time $474.50 per credit hour. Tuition, nonresident: full-time $24,902; part-time $1453.50 per credit hour. *Required fees:* $2085.56; $45.50 per credit hour. *Financial support:* Fellowships, research assistantships, and teaching assistantships available. Financial award applicants required to submit FAFSA. *Faculty research:* Health effects of mineral dust, geomicrobiology, glacial and arctic sciences, optical mineralogy, planetary and terrestrial geomechanics. *Unit head:* Dr. Leslie Baker, Chair, 208-885-6192, E-mail: geology@uidaho.edu. *Application contact:* Dr. Leslie Baker, Chair, 208-885-6192, E-mail: geology@uidaho.edu.
Website: http://www.uidaho.edu/sci/geology

University of Illinois at Chicago, College of Liberal Arts and Sciences, Department of Earth and Environmental Sciences, Chicago, IL 60607-7128. Offers MS, PhD. *Degree requirements:* For master's, thesis; for doctorate, thesis/dissertation. *Entrance requirements:* For master's and doctorate, GRE General Test, minimum GPA of 2.75. Additional exam requirements/recommendations for international students: Required—TOEFL. Electronic applications accepted. *Expenses:* Contact institution. *Faculty research:* Geochemistry, mineralogy and petrology, geophysics, tectonics, global change, hydrology, geobiology.

University of Illinois at Urbana–Champaign, Graduate College, College of Liberal Arts and Sciences, School of Earth, Society and Environment, Department of Geology, Champaign, IL 61820. Offers geology (MS, PhD); teaching of earth sciences (MS). Terminal master's awarded for partial completion of doctoral program.

The University of Kansas, Graduate Studies, College of Liberal Arts and Sciences, Department of Geology, Lawrence, KS 66045. Offers MS, PhD. *Program availability:* Part-time. *Students:* 53 full-time (15 women), 14 part-time (6 women); includes 8 minority (1 Asian, non-Hispanic/Latino; 3 Hispanic/Latino; 4 Two or more races, non-Hispanic/Latino), 9 international. Average age 29. 73 applicants, 30% accepted, 13 enrolled. In 2018, 14 master's, 4 doctorates awarded. *Entrance requirements:* For master's and doctorate, GRE General Test, official transcripts, 3 letters of recommendation, statement of purpose, resume. Additional exam requirements/ recommendations for international students: Required—TOEFL, IELTS, TOEFL or IELTS. *Application deadline:* For fall admission, 1/15 for domestic and international students; for spring admission, 10/31 for domestic and international students. Application fee: $65 ($85 for international students). Electronic applications accepted. *Financial support:* Fellowships, research assistantships, teaching assistantships, scholarships/grants, and unspecified assistantships available. *Faculty research:* Sedimentology, paleontology, tectonics, geophysics, hydrogeology. *Unit head:* Jennifer A. Roberts, Chair, 785-864-1960, E-mail: jaroberts@ku.edu. *Application contact:* Cicily Riggs, Graduate Admissions Contact, 785-864-0937, Fax: 785-864-5276, E-mail: csriggs@ku.edu.
Website: http://www.geo.ku.edu

University of Kentucky, Graduate School, College of Arts and Sciences, Program in Geology, Lexington, KY 40506-0032. Offers MS, PhD. *Degree requirements:* For master's, comprehensive exam, thesis; for doctorate, comprehensive exam, thesis/ dissertation. *Entrance requirements:* For master's, GRE General Test, minimum undergraduate GPA of 2.75; for doctorate, GRE General Test, minimum graduate GPA of 3.0. Additional exam requirements/recommendations for international students: Required—TOEFL (minimum score 550 paper-based). Electronic applications accepted. *Faculty research:* Structure tectonics, geophysics, stratigraphy, hydrogeology, coal geology.

University of Maine, Graduate School, Climate Change Institute, Orono, ME 04469. Offers MS, CGS. *Program availability:* Part-time. *Faculty:* 39 full-time (11 women). *Students:* 8 full-time (6 women), 3 part-time (2 women); includes 1 minority (American Indian or Alaska Native, non-Hispanic/Latino), 1 international. Average age 28. 17 applicants, 47% accepted, 1 enrolled. In 2018, 2 master's awarded. *Degree requirements:* For master's, thesis. *Entrance requirements:* For master's, GRE General Test. Additional exam requirements/recommendations for international students: Required—TOEFL (minimum score 80 iBT), IELTS (minimum score 6.5). *Application deadline:* For fall admission, 11/1 priority date for domestic and international students; for spring admission, 2/1 priority date for domestic and international students. Applications are processed on a rolling basis. Application fee: $65. Electronic applications accepted. *Financial support:* In 2018–19, 28 students received support, including 24 research assistantships with full tuition reimbursements available (averaging $15,200 per year), 1 teaching assistantship with full tuition reimbursement available (averaging $15,200 per year); institutionally sponsored loans, tuition waivers (full and partial), and unspecified assistantships also available. Financial award application deadline: 3/1. *Faculty research:* Climatology, paleoclimate, glaciology, ecosystems, anthropology. *Total annual research expenditures:* $145,825. *Unit head:* Dr. Paul Mayewski, Director, 207-581-3019, Fax: 207-581-1203, E-mail: paul.mayewski@maine.edu. *Application contact:* Dr. Karl Kreutz, Graduate Coordinator, 207-581-3011, E-mail: karl.kreutz@maine.edu.
Website: http://climatechange.umaine.edu/

University of Manitoba, Faculty of Graduate Studies, Clayton H. Riddell Faculty of Environment, Earth, and Resources, Department of Geological Sciences, Winnipeg, MB R3T 2N2, Canada. Offers geology (M Sc, PhD); geophysics (M Sc, PhD). *Degree requirements:* For master's, thesis; for doctorate, thesis/dissertation. *Entrance requirements:* For master's and doctorate, GRE General Test, GRE Subject Test (geology), minimum GPA of 3.0. Additional exam requirements/recommendations for international students: Required—TOEFL.

University of Maryland, College Park, Academic Affairs, College of Computer, Mathematical and Natural Sciences, Department of Geology, College Park, MD 20742. Offers MS, PhD. *Degree requirements:* For master's, thesis, oral defense; for doctorate, thesis/dissertation. *Entrance requirements:* For master's, GRE General Test, minimum GPA of 3.0, 3 letters of recommendation; for doctorate, GRE General Test, 3 letters of recommendation. Additional exam requirements/recommendations for international students: Required—TOEFL. Electronic applications accepted.

University of Memphis, Graduate School, College of Arts and Sciences, Department of Earth Sciences, Memphis, TN 38152. Offers earth sciences (MA, MS, PhD), including archaeology (MS), geography (MS), geology (MS), geophysics (MS), interdisciplinary studies (MS); geographic information systems (Graduate Certificate), including geographic information systems, GIS educator, GIS planning, GIS professional. *Program availability:* Part-time, evening/weekend. *Students:* 44 full-time (19 women), 30 part-time (10 women); includes 9 minority (7 Asian, non-Hispanic/Latino; 2 Hispanic/ Latino), 25 international. Average age 31. 19 applicants, 89% accepted, 16 enrolled. In 2018, 13 master's, 5 doctorates, 8 other advanced degrees awarded. Terminal master's awarded for partial completion of doctoral program. *Degree requirements:* For master's, comprehensive exam, thesis, seminar presentation; for doctorate, comprehensive exam, thesis/dissertation, qualifying exam, submission of two manuscripts for publication in peer-reviewed journal or books. *Entrance requirements:* For master's, GRE General Test, 3 letters of recommendation, statement of research interests; for doctorate, GRE General Test, 2 letters of recommendation, resume, personal statement. Additional exam requirements/recommendations for international students: Required—TOEFL (minimum score 550 paper-based; 79 iBT). *Application deadline:* For fall admission, 1/15 for domestic students; for spring admission, 11/1 for domestic students. Applications are processed on a rolling basis. Application fee: $35 ($60 for international students). Electronic applications accepted. *Expenses: Tuition, area resident:* Full-time $10,240; part-time $503 per credit hour. Tuition, state resident: full-time $10,464. Tuition, nonresident: full-time $20,224; part-time $991 per credit hour. *Required fees:* $850; $106 per credit hour. *Financial support:* Fellowships with full tuition reimbursements, research assistantships with full tuition reimbursements, teaching assistantships with full tuition reimbursements, Federal Work-Study, scholarships/grants, and unspecified assistantships available. Financial award application deadline: 2/1; financial award applicants required to submit FAFSA. *Faculty research:* Hazards, active tectonics, geophysics, hydrology and water resources, spatial analysis. *Unit head:* Dr. Daniel Larsen, Chair, 901-678-4358, Fax: 901-678-2178, E-mail: dlarsen@memphis.edu. *Application contact:* Dr. Andrew Mickelson, Graduate Coordinator, 901-678-4505, Fax: 901-678-2178, E-mail: amicklsn@memphis.edu.
Website: http://www.memphis.edu/earthsciences/

University of Minnesota, Duluth, Graduate School, Swenson College of Science and Engineering, Department of Geological Sciences, Duluth, MN 55812-2496. Offers MS, PhD. PhD offered jointly with University of Minnesota, Twin Cities Campus. *Program availability:* Part-time. *Degree requirements:* For master's, thesis, final oral exam, written and oral research proposal. *Entrance requirements:* For master's, GRE General Test, minimum GPA of 3.0. Additional exam requirements/recommendations for international students: Required—TOEFL (minimum score 550 paper-based). Electronic applications accepted. *Faculty research:* Surface processes, tectonics, planetary geology, paleoclimate, petrology.

University of Minnesota, Twin Cities Campus, College of Science and Engineering, Department of Earth Sciences, Minneapolis, MN 55455-0213. Offers MS, PhD. Terminal master's awarded for partial completion of doctoral program. *Degree requirements:* For master's, thesis; for doctorate, thesis/dissertation. *Entrance requirements:* For master's and doctorate, GRE General Test, 3 letters of recommendation. Additional exam requirements/recommendations for international students: Required—TOEFL (minimum score 550 paper-based). Electronic applications accepted. *Faculty research:* Geology, geophysics, geochemistry, geobiology, climate and environmental geosciences.

University of Mississippi, Graduate School, School of Engineering, University, MS 38677. Offers aeroacoustics (MS, PhD); chemical engineering (MS, PhD); civil engineering (MS, PhD); computational hydroscience (MS, PhD); computer science (MS, PhD); electrical engineering (MS, PhD); electromagnetics (MS, PhD); environmental engineering (MS, PhD); geology and geological engineering (MS, PhD); hydrology (MS); material science (MS); mechanical engineering (MS, PhD); telecommunications (MS). *Faculty:* 76 full-time (16 women), 3 part-time/adjunct (1 woman). *Students:* 129 full-time (33 women), 21 part-time (5 women); includes 15 minority (7 Black or African American, non-Hispanic/Latino; 6 Asian, non-Hispanic/Latino; 1 Hispanic/Latino; 1 Two or more races, non-Hispanic/Latino), 73 international. Average age 29. In 2018, 36 master's, 17 doctorates awarded. *Entrance requirements:* For master's, GRE General Test, minimum GPA of 3.0; for doctorate, GRE General Test. Additional exam requirements/ recommendations for international students: Required—TOEFL. *Application deadline:* Applications are processed on a rolling basis. Application fee: $50. Electronic applications accepted. *Financial support:* Scholarships/grants available. Financial award application deadline: 3/1; financial award applicants required to submit FAFSA. *Unit head:* Dr. David Puleo, Dean, 662-915-5780, Fax: 662-915-5387, E-mail: engineer@olemiss.edu. *Application contact:* Temeka Smith, Graduate Activities Specialist for Admissions, 662-915-7474, Fax: 662-915-7577, E-mail: gschool@olemiss.edu.

University of Missouri, Office of Research and Graduate Studies, College of Arts and Science, Department of Geological Sciences, Columbia, MO 65211. Offers MS, PhD. *Degree requirements:* For doctorate, variable foreign language requirement, thesis/ dissertation. *Entrance requirements:* For master's and doctorate, GRE General Test, minimum GPA of 3.0. *Faculty research:* Geochemistry, tectonics, economic geology, biogeochemistry, geophysics.

University of Montana, Graduate School, College of Humanities and Sciences, Department of Geosciences, Missoula, MT 59812. Offers MS, PhD. *Degree requirements:* For doctorate, thesis/dissertation. *Entrance requirements:* For master's and doctorate, GRE General Test. Additional exam requirements/recommendations for international students: Required—TOEFL (minimum score 525 paper-based). *Faculty research:* Environmental geoscience, regional structure and tectonics, groundwater geology, petrology, mineral deposits.

University of Nevada, Reno, Graduate School, College of Science, Mackay School of Earth Sciences and Engineering, Department of Geological Sciences and Engineering, Program in Geology, Reno, NV 89557. Offers MS, PhD. Terminal master's awarded for partial completion of doctoral program. *Degree requirements:* For master's, thesis optional; for doctorate, thesis/dissertation. *Entrance requirements:* For master's, GRE General Test, minimum GPA of 2.75; for doctorate, GRE General Test, minimum GPA of 3.0. Additional exam requirements/recommendations for international students: Required—TOEFL (minimum score 500 paper-based; 61 iBT), IELTS (minimum score 6). Electronic applications accepted. *Faculty research:* Mineral exploration, geochemistry, hydrology.

University of New Brunswick Fredericton, School of Graduate Studies, Faculty of Science, Department of Earth Sciences, Fredericton, NB E3B 5A3, Canada. Offers M Sc, PhD. *Program availability:* Part-time. *Degree requirements:* For master's, thesis; for doctorate, thesis/dissertation. *Entrance requirements:* For master's, minimum GPA of 3.0, B Sc in earth sciences or related subject; for doctorate, minimum GPA of 3.0; M Sc in earth science or related subject. Additional exam requirements/recommendations for international students: Required—TOEFL, IELTS, TWE. Electronic applications accepted. *Faculty research:* Applied geophysics and rock physics; applied glacial and quaternary geology; aqueous and environmental geochemistry and hydrogeology; lithogeochemistry and mineral deposits; igneous, metamorphic and experimental petrology; isotope geochemistry and U-Pb geochronology; paleontology and ichnology; sedimentology, stratigraphy and petroleum geology; shock metamorphism, impact and planetary geology; structural geology and rock mechanics.

University of New Hampshire, Graduate School, College of Engineering and Physical Sciences, Department of Earth Sciences, Durham, NH 03824. Offers geochemical systems (MS); geology (MS); hydrology (MS); ocean mapping (MS); oceanography (MS). *Degree requirements:* For master's, thesis. *Entrance requirements:* For master's, GRE General Test. Additional exam requirements/recommendations for international students: Required—TOEFL (minimum score 550 paper-based; 80 iBT). Electronic applications accepted.

The University of North Carolina at Chapel Hill, Graduate School, College of Arts and Sciences, Department of Geological Sciences, Chapel Hill, NC 27599. Offers MS, PhD. *Degree requirements:* For master's, comprehensive exam, thesis; for doctorate, one foreign language, comprehensive exam, thesis/dissertation. *Entrance requirements:* For master's and doctorate, GRE General Test, minimum GPA of 3.0. Electronic applications accepted. *Faculty research:* Paleoceanography, igneous petrology, paleontology, geophysics, structural geology.

University of North Dakota, Graduate School, School of Engineering and Mines, Department of Geology, Grand Forks, ND 58202. Offers MA, MS, PhD. *Degree requirements:* For master's, thesis, final exam; for doctorate, one foreign language, comprehensive exam, thesis/dissertation, final exam. *Entrance requirements:* For master's and doctorate, GRE General Test, minimum GPA of 3.0. Additional exam requirements/recommendations for international students: Required—TOEFL (minimum score 550 paper-based; 79 iBT), IELTS (minimum score 6.5). Electronic applications accepted. *Faculty research:* Hydrogeology, environmental geology, geological engineering, sedimentology, geomorphology.

University of Oklahoma, Mewbourne College of Earth and Energy, ConocoPhillips School of Geology and Geophysics, Norman, OK 73019. Offers geology (MS, PhD); geophysics (MS, PhD). *Program availability:* Part-time. *Degree requirements:* For master's, thesis; for doctorate, thesis/dissertation. *Entrance requirements:* For master's and doctorate, GRE. Additional exam requirements/recommendations for international students: Required—TOEFL (minimum score 79 iBT) or IELTS (minimum score 6.5). Electronic applications accepted. *Expenses:* Tuition, state resident: full-time $5683.20; part-time $236.80 per credit hour. Tuition, nonresident: full-time $20,342; part-time $847.60 per credit hour. *International tuition:* $20,342.40 full-time. *Required fees:* $2894.20; $110.05 per credit hour. $126.50 per semester. Tuition and fees vary according to course load and program. *Faculty research:* Energy; geochemistry; geophysics; earth systems; lithospheric dynamics.

University of Oregon, Graduate School, College of Arts and Sciences, Department of Geological Sciences, Eugene, OR 97403. Offers MA, MS, PhD. *Degree requirements:* For master's, foreign language (MA). *Entrance requirements:* For master's and doctorate, GRE General Test, GRE Subject Test.

University of Pittsburgh, Kenneth P. Dietrich School of Arts and Sciences, Department of Geology and Environmental Science, Pittsburgh, PA 15260. Offers geographical information systems and remote sensing (Pro-MS); geology and environmental science (MS, PhD). *Program availability:* Part-time. *Degree requirements:* For master's, comprehensive exam, thesis; for doctorate, comprehensive exam, thesis/dissertation. *Entrance requirements:* For master's and doctorate, GRE. Additional exam requirements/recommendations for international students: Required—TOEFL (minimum score 100 iBT); Recommended—IELTS (minimum score 7). Electronic applications accepted. *Expenses:* Contact institution. *Faculty research:* Volcanology; sedimentary geology; geochemistry; hydrology; geophysics; geomorphology; remote sensing.

University of Puerto Rico–Mayagüez, Graduate Studies, College of Arts and Sciences, Department of Geology, Mayagüez, PR 00681-9000. Offers MS. *Program availability:* Part-time. *Degree requirements:* For master's, comprehensive exam, thesis. *Entrance requirements:* For master's, GRE General Test, BS in geology or its equivalent; minimum GPA of 2.8. Electronic applications accepted. *Faculty research:* Seismology, applied geophysics, geographic information systems, environmental remote sensing, petrology.

University of Regina, Faculty of Graduate Studies and Research, Faculty of Science, Department of Geology, Regina, SK S4S 0A2, Canada. Offers M Sc, PhD. *Program availability:* Part-time. *Faculty:* 9 full-time (3 women), 10 part-time/adjunct (1 woman). *Students:* 13 full-time (5 women), 6 part-time (2 women). Average age 30. 15 applicants, 13% accepted, 2 enrolled. In 2018, 4 master's awarded. *Degree requirements:* For master's, thesis; for doctorate, thesis/dissertation. *Entrance requirements:* For master's, 4 years Bachelor degree in Geology or related program; for doctorate, applicants must have obtained a thesis-based Master's degree in the discipline to qualify as a doctoral student. Applicants must have academic credentials consistent with being fully-qualified to undertake graduate work at the doctoral level. Additional exam requirements/recommendations for international students: Required—TOEFL (minimum score 580 paper-based; 80 iBT), IELTS (minimum score 6.5), PTE (minimum score 59), other options are CAEL, MELAB, Cantest and U of R ESL. *Application deadline:* Applications are processed on a rolling basis. Application fee: $100. Electronic applications accepted. Tuition and fees vary according to course level, course load, degree level and program. *Financial support:* Fellowships, research assistantships, teaching assistantships, career-related internships or fieldwork, Federal Work-Study, scholarships/grants, unspecified assistantships, and travel award and Graduate Scholarship Base Funds available. Support available to part-time students. Financial award application deadline: 9/30. *Faculty research:* Quaternary and economic geology; volcanology; organic, igneous, and metamorphic petrology; carbonate sedimentology and basin analysis; mineralogy. *Unit head:* Dr. Hairuo Qing, Department Head/coordinator, Geology, 306-585-4677, Fax: 306-585-5433, E-mail: guoxiang.chi@uregina.ca. *Application contact:* Dr. Hairuo Qing, Department Head/coordinator, Geology, 306-585-4677, Fax: 306-585-5433, E-mail: guoxiang.chi@uregina.ca.
Website: http://www.uregina.ca/geology/

University of Rochester, School of Arts and Sciences, Department of Earth and Environmental Sciences, Rochester, NY 14627. Offers geological sciences (MS); geosciences (PhD). *Faculty:* 11 full-time (2 women). *Students:* 23 full-time (12 women); includes 2 minority (1 American Indian or Alaska Native, non-Hispanic/Latino; 1 Hispanic/Latino), 10 international. Average age 29. 38 applicants, 29% accepted, 5 enrolled. In 2018, 1 master's, 1 doctorate awarded. Terminal master's awarded for partial completion of doctoral program. *Degree requirements:* For master's, thesis; for doctorate, comprehensive exam, thesis/dissertation. *Entrance requirements:* For master's and doctorate, GRE General Test, transcripts, letters of recommendation. Additional exam requirements/recommendations for international students: Required—TOEFL, IELTS. *Application deadline:* For fall admission, 1/15 for domestic and international students. Application fee: $60. Electronic applications accepted. *Expenses:* Tuition: Full-time $52,974; part-time $1654 per credit hour. *Required fees:* $612. One-time fee: $30 part-time. Tuition and fees vary according to campus/location and program. *Financial support:* In 2018–19, 48 students received support, including 24 research assistantships (averaging $26,900 per year), 24 teaching assistantships (averaging $26,900 per year); career-related internships or fieldwork, scholarships/grants, traineeships, tuition waivers (full), and unspecified assistantships also available. Support available to part-time students. Financial award application deadline: 1/15. *Faculty research:* Isotope geochemistry, ice core, paleomagnetism, atmospheric chemistry and climate modeling, early earth and experimental geochemistry. *Total annual research expenditures:* $2.4 million. *Unit head:* John A. Tarduno, Chair, 585-275-5713, E-mail: john.tarduno@rochester.edu. *Application contact:* Marissa Sette, Program Coordinator, 585-275-5713, E-mail: msette@ur.rochester.edu.
Website: http://www.sas.rochester.edu/ees/graduate/index.html

University of Saskatchewan, College of Graduate and Postdoctoral Studies, College of Arts and Science and College of Engineering, Department of Geological Sciences, Saskatoon, SK S7N 5A2, Canada. Offers M Sc, PhD, Diploma. *Degree requirements:* For master's, thesis; for doctorate, comprehensive exam (for some programs), thesis/dissertation. *Entrance requirements:* Additional exam requirements/recommendations for international students: Required—TOEFL (minimum score 80 iBT); Recommended—IELTS (minimum score 6.5). Electronic applications accepted.

University of South Carolina, The Graduate School, College of Arts and Sciences, Department of Geological Sciences, Columbia, SC 29208. Offers MS, PhD. Terminal master's awarded for partial completion of doctoral program. *Degree requirements:* For master's, thesis; for doctorate, comprehensive exam, thesis/dissertation, published paper. *Entrance requirements:* For master's and doctorate, GRE General Test. Additional exam requirements/recommendations for international students: Required—TOEFL (minimum score 570 paper-based; 75 iBT). Electronic applications accepted. *Faculty research:* Environmental geology, tectonics, petrology, coastal processes, paleoclimatology.

University of Southern Mississippi, College of Arts and Sciences, Department of Geography and Geology, Hattiesburg, MS 39406-0001. Offers geography (PhD); geography and geology (MS). *Program availability:* Part-time. *Degree requirements:* For master's, comprehensive exam, thesis (for some programs), internships; for doctorate, comprehensive exam, thesis/dissertation. *Entrance requirements:* For master's, GMAT, GRE General Test, minimum GPA of 3.0 for last 60 hours; for doctorate, GRE, minimum GPA of 3.5. Additional exam requirements/recommendations for international students: Required—TOEFL, IELTS. Electronic applications accepted. *Faculty research:* City and regional planning, geographic techniques, physical geography, human geography.

University of South Florida, College of Arts and Sciences, School of Geosciences, Tampa, FL 33620-9951. Offers environmental science and policy (MS); geography (MA), including environmental geography, geographic information science and spatial analysis, human geography; geography and environmental science and policy (PhD); geology (MS, PhD). *Program availability:* Part-time, evening/weekend. *Faculty:* 33 full-time (6 women). *Students:* 93 full-time (43 women), 48 part-time (23 women); includes 24 minority (8 Black or African American, non-Hispanic/Latino; 6 Asian, non-Hispanic/Latino; 5 Hispanic/Latino; 5 Two or more races, non-Hispanic/Latino), 42 international. Average age 31. 107 applicants, 50% accepted, 23 enrolled. In 2018, 14 master's, 11 doctorates awarded. *Degree requirements:* For master's, comprehensive exam, thesis (for some programs); for doctorate, comprehensive exam, thesis/dissertation. *Entrance requirements:* For master's, GRE General Test, minimum GPA of 3.0, letter of intent, 3 letters of recommendation; for doctorate, GRE General Test, master's in geography, environmental science and policy or related field; GPA of at least 3.2 in graduate credits; letter of intent; 3 letters of recommendation. Additional exam requirements/recommendations for international students: Required—TOEFL, TOEFL minimum score 550 paper-based; 79 iBT or IELTS minimum score 6.5 (for MA and MURP); TOEFL minimum score 600 paper-based (for MS and PhD). *Application deadline:* For fall admission, 2/15 priority date for domestic students, 2/15 for international students; for spring admission, 10/15 priority date for domestic students, 9/15 for international students; for summer admission, 2/15 priority date for domestic students, 1/15 for international students. Application fee: $30. Electronic applications accepted. *Expenses:* Tuition, state resident: full-time $6350. Tuition, nonresident: full-time $19,048. *International tuition:* $19,048 full-time. *Required fees:* $2079. *Financial support:* In 2018–19, 45 students received support, including 3 research assistantships (averaging $12,345 per year), 25 teaching assistantships with tuition reimbursements available (averaging $12,807 per year); unspecified assistantships also available. Financial award application deadline: 3/1. *Faculty research:* Geography: human geography, environmental geography, geographic information science and spatial analysis, urban geography, social theory; environmental science, policy, and planning: water resources, wildlife ecology, Karst and wetland environments, natural hazards, soil contamination, meteorology and climatology, environmental sustainability and policy, urban and regional planning. *Total annual research expenditures:* $3 million. *Unit head:* Dr. Mark Rains, Professor and Chair, 813-974-3310, Fax: 813-974-5911, E-mail: mrains@usf.edu. *Application contact:* Dr. Ruiliang Pu, Associate Professor and Graduate Program Coordinator, 813-974-1508, Fax: 813-974-5911, E-mail: rpu@usf.edu.
Website: http://hennarot.forest.usf.edu/main/depts/geosci/

University of South Florida, Innovative Education, Tampa, FL 33620-9951. Offers adult, career and higher education (Graduate Certificate), including college teaching, leadership in developing human resources, leadership in higher education; Africana studies (Graduate Certificate), including diasporas and health disparities, genocide and human rights; aging studies (Graduate Certificate), including gerontology; art research (Graduate Certificate), including museum studies; business foundations (Graduate Certificate); chemical and biomedical engineering (Graduate Certificate), including materials science and engineering, water, health and sustainability; child and family studies (Graduate Certificate), including positive behavior support; civil and industrial engineering (Graduate Certificate), including transportation systems analysis; community and family health (Graduate Certificate), including maternal and child health, social marketing and public health, violence and injury: prevention and intervention, women's health; criminology (Graduate Certificate), including criminal justice administration; data science for public administration (Graduate Certificate); digital humanities (Graduate Certificate); educational measurement and research (Graduate Certificate), including evaluation; English (Graduate Certificate), including comparative literary studies, creative writing, professional and technical communication; entrepreneurship (Graduate Certificate); environmental health (Graduate Certificate), including safety management; epidemiology and biostatistics (Graduate Certificate), including applied biostatistics, biostatistics, concepts and tools of epidemiology, epidemiology, epidemiology of infectious diseases; geography, environment and planning (Graduate Certificate), including community development, environmental policy and management, geographical information systems; geology (Graduate Certificate), including hydrogeology; global health (Graduate Certificate), including disaster management, global health and Latin American and Caribbean studies, global health practice, humanitarian assistance, infection control; government and international affairs (Graduate Certificate), including Cuban studies, globalization studies; health policy and management (Graduate Certificate), including health management and leadership, public health policy and programs; hearing specialist: early intervention (Graduate Certificate); industrial and management systems engineering (Graduate Certificate), including systems engineering, technology management; information studies (Graduate Certificate), including school library media specialist; information systems/decision sciences (Graduate Certificate), including analytics and business intelligence; instructional technology (Graduate Certificate), including distance education, Florida digital/virtual educator, instructional design, multimedia design, Web design; internal medicine, bioethics and medical humanities (Graduate Certificate), including biomedical ethics; Latin American and Caribbean studies (Graduate Certificate); leadership for coastal resiliency planning (Graduate Certificate); mass communications (Graduate Certificate), including multimedia journalism; mathematics and statistics (Graduate

Peterson's Graduate Programs in the Physical Sciences, Mathematics, Agricultural Sciences, the Environment & Natural Resources 2020

www.petersons.com **95**

Certificate), including mathematics; medicine (Graduate Certificate), including aging and neuroscience, bioinformatics, biotechnology, brain fitness and memory management, clinical investigation, hand and upper limb rehabilitation, health informatics, health sciences, integrative weight management, intellectual property, medicine and gender, metabolic and nutritional medicine, metabolic cardiology, pharmacy sciences; national and competitive intelligence (Graduate Certificate); nursing (Graduate Certificate), including simulation based academic fellowship in advanced pain management; psychological and social foundations (Graduate Certificate), including career counseling, college teaching, diversity in education, mental health counseling, school counseling; public affairs (Graduate Certificate), including nonprofit management, public management, research administration; public health (Graduate Certificate), including assessing chemical toxicity and public health risks, health equity, pharmacoepidemiology, public health generalist, toxicology, translational research in adolescent behavioral health; public health practices (Graduate Certificate), including planning for healthy communities; rehabilitation and mental health counseling (Graduate Certificate), including integrative mental health care, marriage and family therapy, rehabilitation technology; secondary education (Graduate Certificate), including ESOL, foreign language education: culture and content, foreign language education: professional; social work (Graduate Certificate), including geriatric social work/clinical gerontology; special education (Graduate Certificate), including autism spectrum disorder, disabilities education: severe/profound; world languages (Graduate Certificate), including teaching English as a second language (TESL) or foreign language. *Expenses:* Tuition, state resident: full-time $6350. Tuition, nonresident: full-time $19,048. *International tuition:* $19,048 full-time. *Required fees:* $2079. *Unit head:* Dr. Cynthia DeLuca, Associate Vice President and Assistant Vice Provost, 813-974-3077, Fax: 813-974-7061, E-mail: deluca@usf.edu. *Application contact:* Owen Hooper, Director, Summer and Alternative Calendar Programs, 813-974-6917, E-mail: hooper@usf.edu.
Website: http://www.usf.edu/innovative-education/

The University of Tennessee, Graduate School, College of Arts and Sciences, Department of Geological Sciences, Knoxville, TN 37996. Offers geology (MS, PhD). *Program availability:* Part-time. *Degree requirements:* For master's, thesis; for doctorate, one foreign language, thesis/dissertation. *Entrance requirements:* For master's and doctorate, GRE General Test, minimum GPA of 2.7. Additional exam requirements/recommendations for international students: Required—TOEFL. Electronic applications accepted.

The University of Texas at Arlington, Graduate School, College of Science, Department of Earth and Environmental Sciences, Arlington, TX 76019. Offers MS, PhD. *Program availability:* Part-time, evening/weekend. Terminal master's awarded for partial completion of doctoral program. *Degree requirements:* For master's, thesis optional; for doctorate, comprehensive exam, thesis/dissertation. *Entrance requirements:* For master's, GRE General Test. Additional exam requirements/recommendations for international students: Required—TOEFL (minimum score 550 paper-based). Electronic applications accepted. *Faculty research:* Hydrology, aqueous geochemistry, biostratigraphy, structural geology, petroleum geology.

The University of Texas at Austin, Graduate School, Jackson School of Geosciences, Austin, TX 78712-1111. Offers MA, MS, PhD. *Program availability:* Part-time. *Degree requirements:* For master's, report (MA), thesis (MS); for doctorate, thesis/dissertation. *Entrance requirements:* For master's and doctorate, GRE General Test. Electronic applications accepted. *Faculty research:* Sedimentary geology, geophysics, hydrogeology, structure/tectonics, vertebrate paleontology.

The University of Texas at El Paso, Graduate School, College of Science, Department of Geological Sciences, El Paso, TX 79968-0001. Offers geological sciences (MS, PhD); geophysics (MS). *Program availability:* Part-time, evening/weekend. *Degree requirements:* For master's, thesis; for doctorate, one foreign language, comprehensive exam, thesis/dissertation. *Entrance requirements:* For master's, GRE, minimum GPA of 3.0, BS in geology or equivalent; for doctorate, GRE, minimum GPA of 3.0, MS in geology or equivalent. Additional exam requirements/recommendations for international students: Required—TOEFL. Electronic applications accepted.

The University of Texas at San Antonio, College of Sciences, Department of Geological Sciences, San Antonio, TX 78249-0617. Offers MS. *Program availability:* Part-time. *Degree requirements:* For master's, comprehensive exam, thesis (for some programs). *Entrance requirements:* For master's, GRE General Test, three letters of recommendation, statement of research interest, undergraduate transcripts. Additional exam requirements/recommendations for international students: Required—TOEFL (minimum score 550 paper-based; 79 iBT), IELTS (minimum score 6.5). Electronic applications accepted. *Faculty research:* Hydrogeology, sedimentary and stratigraphy, structure, paleontology, geographic information science.

The University of Texas of the Permian Basin, Office of Graduate Studies, College of Arts and Sciences, Department of Physical Sciences, Program in Geology, Odessa, TX 79762-0001. Offers MS. *Degree requirements:* For master's, comprehensive exam, thesis or alternative. *Entrance requirements:* For master's, GRE General Test. Additional exam requirements/recommendations for international students: Required—TOEFL (minimum score 550 paper-based)

The University of Toledo, College of Graduate Studies, College of Natural Sciences and Mathematics, Department of Environmental Sciences, Toledo, OH 43606-3390. Offers biology (MS, PhD), including ecology; geology (MS), including earth surface processes. *Program availability:* Part-time. *Degree requirements:* For master's, thesis or alternative. *Entrance requirements:* For master's, GRE General Test, minimum cumulative point-hour ratio of 2.7 for all previous academic work, three letters of recommendation, statement of purpose, transcripts from all prior institutions attended. Additional exam requirements/recommendations for international students: Required—TOEFL (minimum score 550 paper-based; 80 iBT). Electronic applications accepted. *Faculty research:* Environmental geochemistry, geophysics, petrology and mineralogy, paleontology, geohydrology.

University of Toronto, School of Graduate Studies, Faculty of Arts and Science, Department of Earth Sciences, Toronto, ON M5S 1A1, Canada. Offers M Sc, MA Sc, PhD. *Program availability:* Part-time. *Degree requirements:* For master's, thesis (for some programs); for doctorate, thesis/dissertation. *Entrance requirements:* For master's, B Sc, BA Sc, or equivalent; letters of reference; for doctorate, M Sc or equivalent, minimum B+ average, letters of reference. Additional exam requirements/recommendations for international students: Required—TOEFL (minimum score 580 paper-based; 93 iBT), TWE (minimum score 4). Electronic applications accepted.

University of Utah, Graduate School, College of Mines and Earth Sciences, Department of Geology and Geophysics, Salt Lake City, UT 84112. Offers geological engineering (ME, MS, PhD); geology (MS, PhD); geophysics (MS, PhD). *Faculty:* 23 full-time (6 women), 15 part-time/adjunct (6 women). *Students:* 53 full-time (22 women), 12 part-time (2 women); includes 11 minority (1 American Indian or Alaska Native, non-Hispanic/Latino; 1 Asian, non-Hispanic/Latino; 8 Hispanic/Latino; 1 Two or more races, non-Hispanic/Latino), 11 international. Average age 25. 228 applicants, 14% accepted, 22 enrolled. In 2018, 12 master's, 2 doctorates awarded. Terminal master's awarded for partial completion of doctoral program. *Entrance requirements:* For master's and doctorate, GRE General Test, minimum GPA of 3.25. Additional exam requirements/recommendations for international students: Required—TOEFL (minimum score 500 paper-based; 61 iBT). Application fee: $55 ($65 for international students). Electronic applications accepted. *Expenses: Tuition, area resident:* Full-time $7190.66; part-time $2112.48 per year. Tuition, state resident: full-time $7190.66. Tuition, nonresident: full-time $25,195. *Required fees:* $558; $555.04 per unit. Tuition and fees vary according to course level, course load, degree level, program and student level. *Financial support:* In 2018–19, 62 students received support, including 14 fellowships with full tuition reimbursements available (averaging $18,500 per year), 32 research assistantships with full tuition reimbursements available (averaging $24,000 per year), 16 teaching assistantships with full tuition reimbursements available (averaging $18,500 per year); career-related internships or fieldwork, institutionally sponsored loans, scholarships/grants, health care benefits, unspecified assistantships, and stipends also available. Financial award application deadline: 1/15; financial award applicants required to submit FAFSA. *Faculty research:* Igneous, metamorphic, and sedimentary petrology; stratigraphy; paleoclimatology; hydrology; seismology. *Total annual research expenditures:* $4.1 million. *Unit head:* Dr. John Bartley, Chair, 801-585-1670, Fax: 801-581-7065, E-mail: john.bartley@utah.edu. *Application contact:* Dr. Gabriel J. Bowen, Director of Graduate Studies, 801-585-7925, Fax: 801-581-7065, E-mail: gabe.bowen@utah.edu.
Website: http://www.earth.utah.edu/

University of Vermont, Graduate College, College of Arts and Sciences, Department of Geology, Burlington, VT 05405-1758. Offers MS. *Degree requirements:* For master's, thesis. *Entrance requirements:* For master's, GRE General Test. Additional exam requirements/recommendations for international students: Required—TOEFL (minimum score 550 paper-based, 90 iBT) or IELTS (6.5). Electronic applications accepted. *Faculty research:* Mineralogy, lake sediments, structural geology.

University of Washington, Graduate School, College of the Environment, Department of Earth and Space Sciences, Seattle, WA 98195. Offers geology (MS, PhD); geophysics (MS, PhD). *Degree requirements:* For master's, thesis or alternative, departmental qualifying exam, final exam; for doctorate, thesis/dissertation, departmental qualifying exam, general and final exams. *Entrance requirements:* For master's and doctorate, GRE General Test, minimum GPA of 3.0. Additional exam requirements/recommendations for international students: Required—TOEFL (minimum score 580 paper-based). Electronic applications accepted.

The University of Western Ontario, School of Graduate and Postdoctoral Studies, Faculty of Science, Department of Earth Sciences, London, ON N6A 3K7, Canada. Offers environment and sustainability (MES); geology (M Sc, PhD); geology and environmental science (M Sc, PhD); geophysics (M Sc, PhD); geophysics and environmental science (M Sc, PhD). *Degree requirements:* For master's, thesis; for doctorate, thesis/dissertation, qualifying exam. *Entrance requirements:* For master's, honors in B Sc; for doctorate, M Sc. Additional exam requirements/recommendations for international students: Required—TOEFL. *Faculty research:* Geophysics, geochemistry, paleontology, sedimentology/stratigraphy, glaciology/quaternary.

University of Wisconsin–Madison, Graduate School, College of Letters and Science, Department of Geology and Geophysics, Program in Geology, Madison, WI 53706-1380. Offers MS, PhD. *Degree requirements:* For master's, thesis; for doctorate, one foreign language, thesis/dissertation. *Entrance requirements:* For master's and doctorate, GRE General Test.

University of Wisconsin–Milwaukee, Graduate School, College of Letters and Science, Department of Geosciences, Milwaukee, WI 53201-0413. Offers geological sciences (MS, PhD). *Students:* 19 full-time (9 women), 7 part-time (2 women); includes 1 minority (Black or African American, non-Hispanic/Latino), 2 international. Average age 31. 32 applicants, 38% accepted, 11 enrolled. In 2018, 2 master's, 2 doctorates awarded. *Degree requirements:* For master's, thesis; for doctorate, one foreign language, thesis/dissertation. *Entrance requirements:* For master's, GRE General Test, minimum GPA of 3.0; for doctorate, GRE General Test, master's degree. Additional exam requirements/recommendations for international students: Required—TOEFL (minimum score 550 paper-based; 79 iBT), IELTS (minimum score 6.5). *Application deadline:* For fall admission, 1/1 priority date for domestic students; for spring admission, 9/1 for domestic students. Application fee: $56 ($96 for international students). Electronic applications accepted. *Financial support:* In 2018–19, 4 research assistantships, 11 teaching assistantships were awarded; career-related internships or fieldwork and unspecified assistantships also available. Support available to part-time students. Financial award application deadline: 4/15; financial award applicants required to submit FAFSA. *Faculty research:* Geology, geosciences, geophysics, hydrogeology, paleontology. *Unit head:* Dr. Barry Cameron, Department Chair, 414-229-3136, E-mail: bcameron@uwm.edu. *Application contact:* General Information Contact, 414-229-4982, Fax: 414-229-6967, E-mail: gradschool@uwm.edu.
Website: http://www.uwm.edu/dept/geosciences/

University of Wyoming, College of Arts and Sciences, Department of Geology and Geophysics, Laramie, WY 82071. Offers geology (MS, PhD); geophysics (MS, PhD). *Program availability:* Part-time. *Degree requirements:* For master's, comprehensive exam, thesis; for doctorate, comprehensive exam, thesis/dissertation. *Entrance requirements:* For master's and doctorate, GRE General Test, minimum GPA of 3.0. *Expenses: Tuition, area resident:* Full-time $6504; part-time $271 per credit hour. Tuition, state resident: full-time $6504; part-time $271 per credit hour. Tuition, nonresident: full-time $19,464; part-time $811 per credit hour. *International tuition:* $19,464 full-time. *Required fees:* $1410.94; $343.82 per semester. $343.82 per semester. Tuition and fees vary according to course load, program and reciprocity agreements. *Faculty research:* Low-temp geochemistry, geohydrology, paleontology, structure/tectonics, sedimentation and petroleum geology, petrology, geophysics/seismology.

Utah State University, School of Graduate Studies, College of Science, Department of Geology, Logan, UT 84322. Offers MS. *Degree requirements:* For master's, thesis. *Entrance requirements:* For master's, GRE General Test, minimum GPA of 3.0. Additional exam requirements/recommendations for international students: Required—TOEFL. *Faculty research:* Sedimentary geology, structural geology, regional tectonics, hydrogeology petrology.

Vanderbilt University, Department of Earth and Environmental Sciences, Nashville, TN 37240-1001. Offers MAT, MS. *Faculty:* 9 full-time (2 women), 1 part-time/adjunct. *Students:* 13 full-time (8 women), 4 part-time (1 woman); includes 2 minority (both Hispanic/Latino). Average age 26. 39 applicants, 13% accepted, 4 enrolled. In 2018, 5 master's awarded. *Degree requirements:* For master's, thesis. *Entrance requirements:* For master's, GRE General Test, GRE Subject Test (recommended). Additional exam requirements/recommendations for international students: Required—TOEFL (minimum score 570 paper-based; 88 iBT). *Application deadline:* For fall admission, 1/15 for domestic and international students. Application fee: $0. Electronic applications accepted. *Expenses: Tuition:* Full-time $47,208; part-time $2026 per credit hour. *Required fees:* $478. *Financial support:* Fellowships with tuition reimbursements, research assistantships with tuition reimbursements, teaching assistantships with full tuition reimbursements, career-related internships or fieldwork, Federal Work-Study, institutionally sponsored loans, and health care benefits available. Financial award application deadline: 1/15; financial award applicants required to submit CSS PROFILE or FAFSA. *Faculty research:* Geochemical processes, magmatic processes and crustal evolution, paleoecology and paleo environments, sedimentary systems, transport phenomena, environmental policy. *Unit head:* Dr. Steven Goodbred, Chair, 615-322-2976, E-mail: g.gualda@vanderbilt.edu. *Application contact:* David Furbish, Director of Graduate Studies, 615-322-2137, E-mail: david.j.furbish@vanderbilt.edu. Website: http://www.vanderbilt.edu/ees/

Washington State University, College of Arts and Sciences, School of the Environment, Pullman, WA 99164. Offers environmental and natural resource sciences (PhD); environmental science (MS); geology (MS, PhD); natural resource science (MS). *Degree requirements:* For master's, comprehensive exam (for some programs), thesis (for some programs), oral exam; for doctorate, comprehensive exam, thesis/dissertation, oral exam, written exam. *Entrance requirements:* For master's, 3 undergraduate semester hours each in sociology or cultural anthropology, environmental science, biological sciences, and calculus or statistics; 4 in general ecology; and 6 in general chemistry or general physics; for doctorate, minimum GPA of 3.0. Additional exam requirements/recommendations for international students: Required—TOEFL, IELTS.

Wayne State University, College of Liberal Arts and Sciences, Department of Geology, Detroit, MI 48202. Offers MS. *Faculty:* 4. *Students:* 1 full-time (0 women), 2 part-time (1 woman), 1 international. Average age 30. 14 applicants, 29% accepted, 2 enrolled. In 2018, 2 master's awarded. *Entrance requirements:* For master's, GRE, personal statement; resume; three letters of recommendation; undergraduate major in geology or strong background in geology; minimum GPA of 3.0 in major; prerequisite study in mineralogy, petrology, sedimentation, geomorphology, environmental geochemistry, and structural geology. Additional exam requirements/recommendations for international students: Required—TOEFL (minimum score 550 paper-based; 79 iBT), TWE (minimum score 5.5), Michigan English Language Assessment Battery (minimum score 85); Recommended—IELTS (minimum score 6.5). *Application deadline:* For fall admission, 6/1 priority date for domestic students, 5/1 priority date for international students; for winter admission, 11/1 for domestic students, 9/1 priority date for international students; for spring admission, 3/15 for domestic students, 1/1 priority date for international students. Applications are processed on a rolling basis. Application fee: $50. Electronic applications accepted. *Financial support:* In 2018–19, 1 student received support, including 1 fellowship with tuition reimbursement available (averaging $12,429 per year), 2 research assistantships with tuition reimbursements available (averaging $17,606 per year); scholarships/grants, health care benefits, and unspecified assistantships also available. Financial award applicants required to submit FAFSA. *Faculty research:* Isotope geochemistry, hydrogeology, geochronology, sedimentology/stratigraphy, quaternary geology, soils and soil pollution, contaminate fate and transport, geophysics and crustal processes. *Unit head:* Dr. David Njus, Chair, 313-577-3105, Fax: 313-577-6891, E-mail: dnjus@wayne.edu. *Application contact:* Dr. Sarah Brownlee, Geology Graduate Program Director, 313-577-6223, E-mail: sarah.brownlee@wayne.edu. Website: http://clas.wayne.edu/geology/

Western Kentucky University, Graduate School, Ogden College of Science and Engineering, Department of Geography and Geology, Bowling Green, KY 42101. Offers geoscience (MS). *Degree requirements:* For master's, comprehensive exam, thesis or alternative. *Entrance requirements:* For master's, GRE General Test, minimum GPA of 2.75. Additional exam requirements/recommendations for international students: Required—TOEFL (minimum score 555 paper-based; 79 iBT). *Faculty research:* Hydroclimatology, electronic data sets, groundwater, sinkhole liquification potential, meteorological analysis.

Western Washington University, Graduate School, College of Sciences and Technology, Department of Geology, Bellingham, WA 98225-5996. Offers MS. *Program availability:* Part-time. *Degree requirements:* For master's, thesis. *Entrance requirements:* For master's, GRE General Test, minimum GPA of 3.0 in last 60 semester hours or last 90 quarter hours. Additional exam requirements/recommendations for international students: Required—TOEFL (minimum score 567 paper-based). Electronic applications accepted. *Faculty research:* Structure/tectonics; sedimentary, glacial and quaternary geomorphology; igneous and metamorphic petrology; hydrology, geophysics.

West Virginia University, Eberly College of Arts and Sciences, Morgantown, WV 26506. Offers biology (MS, PhD); chemistry (MS, PhD); communication studies (MA, PhD); computational statistics (PhD); creative writing (MFA); English (MA, PhD); forensic and investigative science (MS); forensic science (PhD); geography (MA); geology (MA, PhD); history (MA, PhD); legal studies (MLS); mathematics (MS); physics (MS, PhD); political science (MA, PhD); professional writing and editing (MA); psychology (MA); public administration (MPA); social work (MSW); sociology (MA, PhD); statistics (MS). *Program availability:* Part-time, evening/weekend, online learning. *Students:* 803 full-time (434 women), 237 part-time (138 women); includes 99 minority (31 Black or African American, non-Hispanic/Latino; 1 American Indian or Alaska Native, non-Hispanic/Latino; 16 Asian, non-Hispanic/Latino; 25 Hispanic/Latino; 26 Two or more races, non-Hispanic/Latino), 208 international. In 2018, 285 master's, 63 doctorates awarded. Terminal master's awarded for partial completion of doctoral program. *Degree requirements:* For master's, thesis (for some programs); for doctorate, comprehensive exam, thesis/dissertation. *Entrance requirements:* For master's and doctorate, GRE. Additional exam requirements/recommendations for international students: Required—TOEFL (minimum score 600 paper-based); Recommended—TWE. *Application deadline:* For spring admission, 2/15 priority date for domestic and international students. Applications are processed on a rolling basis. Application fee: $45. Electronic applications accepted. *Financial support:* Fellowships with full tuition reimbursements, research assistantships with full tuition reimbursements, teaching assistantships with full tuition reimbursements, career-related internships or fieldwork, Federal Work-Study, institutionally sponsored loans, scholarships/grants, health care benefits, tuition waivers (full and partial), unspecified assistantships, and administrative assistantships available. Financial award application deadline: 2/1; financial award applicants required to submit FAFSA. *Faculty research:* Humanities, social sciences, life science, physical sciences, mathematics. *Unit head:* Dr. Gregory Dunaway, Dean, 304-293-4611, Fax: 304-293-6858, E-mail: gregory.dunaway@mail.wvu.edu. *Application contact:* Dr. Jessica Queener, Director of Graduate Studies, 304-293-7476 Ext. 5205, Fax: 304-293-6858, E-mail: Jessica.queener@mail.wvu.edu. Website: http://www.as.wvu.edu/

Wichita State University, Graduate School, Fairmount College of Liberal Arts and Sciences, Department of Geology, Wichita, KS 67260. Offers earth, environmental, and physical sciences (MS). *Program availability:* Part-time. *Unit head:* Dr. William Parcell, Chair, 316-978-3140, E-mail: william.parcell@wichita.edu. *Application contact:* Jordan Oleson, Admissions Coordinator, 316-978-3095, Fax: 316-978-3253, E-mail: jordan.oleson@wichita.edu. Website: http://www.wichita.edu/geology

Wright State University, Graduate School, College of Science and Mathematics, Department of Earth and Environmental Sciences, Program in Geological Sciences, Dayton, OH 45435. Offers Graduate Certificate. *Program availability:* Part-time. *Entrance requirements:* Additional exam requirements/recommendations for international students: Required—TOEFL.

Yale University, Graduate School of Arts and Sciences, Department of Geology and Geophysics, New Haven, CT 06520. Offers biogeochemistry (PhD); climate dynamics (PhD); geochemistry (PhD); geophysics (PhD); meteorology (PhD); oceanography (PhD); paleontology (PhD); paleooceanography (PhD); petrology (PhD); tectonics (PhD). *Degree requirements:* For doctorate, thesis/dissertation. *Entrance requirements:* For doctorate, GRE General Test. Additional exam requirements/recommendations for international students: Required—TOEFL.

Geophysics

Boise State University, College of Arts and Sciences, Department of Geosciences, Boise, ID 83725-0399. Offers earth science (M E Sci); geophysics (MS, PhD); geoscience (MS); geosciences (PhD); hydrologic sciences (MS). *Program availability:* Part-time. Terminal master's awarded for partial completion of doctoral program. *Degree requirements:* For master's, thesis (for some programs); for doctorate, thesis/dissertation. *Entrance requirements:* For master's, GRE General Test, BS in related field, minimum GPA of 3.0; for doctorate, GRE General Test. Additional exam requirements/recommendations for international students: Required—TOEFL (minimum score 550 paper-based; 80 iBT), IELTS (minimum score 6). Electronic applications accepted. *Faculty research:* Seismology, geothermal aquifers, sedimentation, tectonics, seismo-acoustic propagation.

Boston College, Morrissey Graduate School of Arts and Sciences, Department of Earth and Environmental Sciences, Chestnut Hill, MA 02467-3800. Offers MS, MBA/MS. *Degree requirements:* For master's, thesis. *Entrance requirements:* For master's, GRE General Test. Additional exam requirements/recommendations for international students: Required—TOEFL (minimum score 600 paper-based; 100 iBT), IELTS (minimum score 8). Electronic applications accepted. *Faculty research:* Coastal and estuarine processes, earthquake and exploration seismology, environmental geology and geophysics, earth surface processes, paleoclimate, groundwater hydrology, igneous and metamorphic petrology, geochemistry, dynamics and processes of sedimentary systems, plate tectonics, structural geology.

Bowling Green State University, Graduate College, College of Arts and Sciences, Department of Physics and Astronomy, Bowling Green, OH 43403. Offers geophysics (MS); physics (MAT, MS). *Degree requirements:* For master's, thesis or alternative. *Entrance requirements:* For master's, GRE General Test. Additional exam requirements/recommendations for international students: Required—TOEFL. Electronic applications accepted. *Faculty research:* Computational physics, solid state physics, materials science, theoretical physics.

California Institute of Technology, Division of Geological and Planetary Sciences, Pasadena, CA 91125-0001. Offers environmental science and engineering (MS, PhD); geobiology (MS, PhD); geochemistry (MS, PhD); geology (MS, PhD); geophysics (MS, PhD); planetary science (MS, PhD). *Degree requirements:* For doctorate, thesis/

dissertation. *Entrance requirements:* For doctorate, GRE General Test. Additional exam requirements/recommendations for international students: Required—TOEFL; Recommended—IELTS, TWE. Electronic applications accepted. *Faculty research:* Planetary surfaces, evolution of anaerobic respiratory processes, structural geology and tectonics, theoretical and numerical seismology, global biogeochemical cycles.

Colorado School of Mines, Office of Graduate Studies, Department of Geophysics, Golden, CO 80401. Offers geophysical engineering (ME, MS, PhD); geophysics (MS, PhD); hydrology (MS, PhD); mineral exploration and mining geosciences (PMS); petroleum reservoir systems (PMS). *Program availability:* Part-time. *Faculty:* 14 full-time (5 women), 4 part-time/adjunct (0 women). *Students:* 62 full-time (17 women), 2 part-time (0 women); includes 5 minority (2 Asian, non-Hispanic/Latino; 1 Hispanic/Latino; 2 Two or more races, non-Hispanic/Latino), 33 international. Average age 28. 142 applicants, 26% accepted, 23 enrolled. In 2018, 12 master's, 12 doctorates awarded. *Degree requirements:* For master's, thesis (for some programs); for doctorate, comprehensive exam, thesis/dissertation. *Entrance requirements:* For master's and doctorate, GRE General Test. Additional exam requirements/recommendations for international students: Required—TOEFL (minimum score 550 paper-based; 79 iBT). *Application deadline:* For fall admission, 12/15 priority date for domestic and international students; for spring admission, 9/1 priority date for domestic students, 9/1 for international students. Application fee: $60 ($80 for international students). Electronic applications accepted. *Expenses:* Tuition, state resident: full-time $16,650; part-time $925 per contact hour. Tuition, nonresident: full-time $36,270; part-time $2015 per contact hour. *International tuition:* $36,270 full-time. *Required fees:* $2314; $2314 per semester. *Financial support:* In 2018–19, 40 research assistantships with full tuition reimbursements, 9 teaching assistantships with full tuition reimbursements were awarded; fellowships, career-related internships or fieldwork, scholarships/grants, health care benefits, and unspecified assistantships also available. Financial award application deadline: 12/15; financial award applicants required to submit FAFSA. *Faculty research:* Seismic exploration, gravity and geomagnetic fields, electrical mapping and sounding, bore hole measurements, environmental physics. *Unit head:* Dr. Paul Sava, Head, 303-384-2362, E-mail: psava@mines.edu. *Application contact:* Michelle Szobody, Program Assistant, 303-273-3935, E-mail: mszobody@mines.edu. Website: http://geophysics.mines.edu

Peterson's Graduate Programs in the Physical Sciences, Mathematics, Agricultural Sciences, the Environment & Natural Resources 2020

www.petersons.com **97**

Geophysics

Cornell University, Graduate School, Graduate Fields of Engineering, Field of Geological Sciences, Ithaca, NY 14853. Offers economic geology (M Eng, MS, PhD); engineering geology (M Eng, MS, PhD); environmental geophysics (M Eng, MS, PhD); general geology (M Eng, MS, PhD); geobiology (M Eng, MS, PhD); geochemistry and isotope geology (M Eng, MS, PhD); geohydrology (M Eng, MS, PhD); geomorphology (M Eng, MS, PhD); geophysics (M Eng, MS, PhD); geotectonics (M Eng, MS, PhD); marine geology (MS, PhD); mineralogy (M Eng, MS, PhD); paleontology (M Eng, MS, PhD); petroleum geology (M Eng, MS, PhD); petrology (M Eng, MS, PhD); planetary geology (M Eng, MS, PhD); Precambrian geology (M Eng, MS, PhD); Quaternary geology (M Eng, MS, PhD); rock mechanics (M Eng, MS, PhD); sedimentology (M Eng, MS, PhD); seismology (M Eng, MS, PhD); stratigraphy (M Eng, MS, PhD); structural geology (M Eng, MS, PhD). *Degree requirements:* For master's, thesis (MS); for doctorate, comprehensive exam, thesis/dissertation. *Entrance requirements:* For master's and doctorate, GRE General Test, 3 letters of recommendation. Additional exam requirements/recommendations for international students: Required—TOEFL (minimum score 550 paper-based; 77 iBT). Electronic applications accepted. *Faculty research:* Geophysics, structural geology, petrology, geochemistry, geodynamics.

Idaho State University, Graduate School, College of Science and Engineering, Department of Geosciences, Pocatello, ID 83209-8072. Offers geographic information science (MS); geology (MNS, MS); geology with emphasis in environmental geoscience (MS); geophysics/hydrology/geology (MS); geotechnology (Postbaccalaureate Certificate). *Program availability:* Part-time. *Degree requirements:* For master's, comprehensive exam, thesis, oral colloquium; for Postbaccalaureate Certificate, thesis optional, minimum 19 credits. *Entrance requirements:* For master's, GRE General Test (minimum 50th percentile in 2 sections), 3 letters of recommendation; for Postbaccalaureate Certificate, GRE General Test, 3 letters of recommendation, bachelor's degree, statement of goals. Additional exam requirements/recommendations for international students: Required—TOEFL (minimum score 550 paper-based; 80 iBT). Electronic applications accepted. *Faculty research:* Quantitative field mapping and sampling: microscopic, geochemical, and isotopic analysis of rocks, minerals and water; remote sensing, geographic information systems, and global positioning systems: environmental and watershed management; surficial and fluvial processes: landscape change; regional tectonics, structural geology; planetary geology.

Indiana University Bloomington, University Graduate School, College of Arts and Sciences, Department of Earth and Atmospheric Sciences, Bloomington, IN 47405-7000. Offers biogeochemistry (MS, PhD); economic geology (MS, PhD); geobiology (MS, PhD); geophysics, structural geology and tectonics (MS, PhD); hydrogeology (MS, PhD); mineralogy (MS, PhD); stratigraphy and sedimentology (MS, PhD). Terminal master's awarded for partial completion of doctoral program. *Degree requirements:* For master's, thesis or alternative; for doctorate, comprehensive exam, thesis/dissertation. *Entrance requirements:* For master's and doctorate, GRE General Test. Additional exam requirements/recommendations for international students: Required—TOEFL. *Faculty research:* Geophysics, geochemistry, hydrogeology, geobiology, planetary science.

Louisiana State University and Agricultural & Mechanical College, Graduate School, College of Science, Department of Geology and Geophysics, Baton Rouge, LA 70803. Offers MS, PhD.

Massachusetts Institute of Technology, School of Science, Department of Earth, Atmospheric, and Planetary Sciences, Cambridge, MA 02139. Offers atmospheric chemistry (PhD, Sc D); atmospheric science (SM, PhD, Sc D); chemical oceanography (SM, PhD, Sc D); climate physics and chemistry (SM, PhD, Sc D); earth and planetary sciences (SM); geochemistry (PhD, Sc D); geology (PhD, Sc D); geophysics (PhD, Sc D); marine geology and geophysics (SM, PhD, Sc D); physical oceanography (SM, PhD, Sc D); planetary sciences (PhD, Sc D). Terminal master's awarded for partial completion of doctoral program. *Degree requirements:* For master's, thesis; for doctorate, comprehensive exam, thesis/dissertation. *Entrance requirements:* For master's and doctorate, GRE General Test. Additional exam requirements/recommendations for international students: Required—TOEFL, IELTS. Electronic applications accepted. *Expenses: Tuition:* Full-time $51,520; part-time $800 per credit hour. *Required fees:* $312. *Faculty research:* Earth: origin, composition, structure, and dynamics of (and interactions between) the atmosphere, oceans, surface, and interior of the earth; planets: formation, dynamics, and evolution of planetary systems and the characterization of exoplanets; climate: characterization of past, present, and potential future climates; studies of the causes and consequences of climate change; life: co-evolution of life and environmental systems.

Memorial University of Newfoundland, School of Graduate Studies, Department of Earth Sciences, St. John's, NL A1C 5S7, Canada. Offers geology (M Sc, PhD); geophysics (M Sc, PhD). *Program availability:* Part-time. *Degree requirements:* For master's, thesis; for doctorate, comprehensive exam, thesis/dissertation, oral thesis defense, entry evaluation. *Entrance requirements:* For master's, honors B Sc; for doctorate, M Sc. Electronic applications accepted. *Faculty research:* Geochemistry, sedimentology, paleoceanography and global change, mineral deposits, petroleum geology, hydrology.

Michigan Technological University, Graduate School, College of Engineering, Department of Geological and Mining Engineering and Sciences, Houghton, MI 49931. Offers geology (MS); geophysics (PhD); mining engineering (PhD). *Program availability:* Part-time. *Faculty:* 28 full-time, 23 part-time/adjunct. *Students:* 34 full-time (15 women), 16 part-time (6 women); includes 5 minority (1 Black or African American, non-Hispanic/Latino; 1 Asian, non-Hispanic/Latino; 2 Hispanic/Latino; 1 Two or more races, non-Hispanic/Latino), 17 international. Average age 28. 156 applicants, 29% accepted, 14 enrolled. In 2018, 7 master's awarded. *Degree requirements:* For master's, comprehensive exam (for some programs), thesis optional, Thesis, Report or Coursework-only; for doctorate, comprehensive exam, thesis/dissertation. *Entrance requirements:* For master's and doctorate, GRE, statement of purpose, personal statement, official transcripts, 3 letters of recommendation. Additional exam requirements/recommendations for international students: Required—TOEFL, TOEFL (recommended minimum score 79 iBT) or IELTS (recommended minimum score of 6.5). *Application deadline:* For fall admission, 2/1 priority date for domestic and international students. Applications are processed on a rolling basis. Electronic applications accepted. *Expenses:* $1,143 per credit. *Financial support:* In 2018–19, 27 students received support, including 5 fellowships with tuition reimbursements available (averaging $16,590 per year), 6 research assistantships with tuition reimbursements available (averaging $16,590 per year), 6 teaching assistantships with tuition reimbursements available (averaging $16,590 per year); career-related internships or fieldwork, Federal Work-Study, scholarships/grants, health care benefits, unspecified assistantships, and cooperative program also available. Financial award application deadline: 2/1; financial award applicants required to submit FAFSA. *Faculty research:* Natural hazards, geophysics, remote sensing, geostatistics, atmospheric modeling. *Total annual research expenditures:* $816,942. *Unit head:* Dr. John S. Gierke, Chair, 906-487-2535, Fax: 906-487-3371, E-mail: jsgierke@mtu.edu. *Application contact:* Brittany Buschell, Graduate Program Coordinator, 906-487-2531, Fax: 906-487-3371, E-mail: babusche@mtu.edu.
Website: http://www.mtu.edu/geo/

Missouri University of Science and Technology, Department of Geosciences and Geological and Petroleum Engineering, Rolla, MO 65401. Offers geological engineering (MS, DE, PhD); geology and geophysics (MS, PhD), including geochemistry, geology, geophysics, groundwater and environmental geology; petroleum engineering (MS, DE, PhD). *Program availability:* Part-time. *Degree requirements:* For master's, thesis optional; for doctorate, comprehensive exam, thesis/dissertation. *Entrance requirements:* For master's, GRE General Test (minimum score 600 quantitative, writing 3.5), minimum GPA of 3.0 in last 4 semesters; for doctorate, GRE General Test (minimum scores: Quantitative 600, Writing 3.5). Additional exam requirements/recommendations for international students: Required—TOEFL (minimum score 550 paper-based). Electronic applications accepted. *Expenses:* Tuition, state resident: full-time $7545.60; part-time $419.20 per credit hour. Tuition, nonresident: full-time $22,169; part-time $1231.60 per credit hour. *International tuition:* $23,518.80 full-time. *Required fees:* $4523.05. Full-time tuition and fees vary according to course load, campus/location, program and reciprocity agreements. *Faculty research:* Digital image processing and geographic information systems, mineralogy, igneous and sedimentary petrology-geochemistry, sedimentology groundwater hydrology and contaminant transport.

New Mexico Institute of Mining and Technology, Center for Graduate Studies, Department of Earth and Environmental Science, Program in Geophysics, Socorro, NM 87801. Offers MS, PhD. *Degree requirements:* For master's, thesis optional; for doctorate, thesis/dissertation. *Entrance requirements:* For master's, GRE General Test; for doctorate, GRE General Test, GRE Subject Test. Additional exam requirements/recommendations for international students: Required—TOEFL (minimum score 540 paper-based). *Faculty research:* Earthquake and volcanic seismology, subduction zone tectonics, network seismology, physical properties of sediments in fault zones.

Oregon State University, College of Earth, Ocean, and Atmospheric Sciences, Program in Ocean, Earth, and Atmospheric Sciences, Corvallis, OR 97331. Offers atmospheric sciences (MA, MS, PhD); oceanography (MA, MS, PhD). *Program availability:* Part-time. *Entrance requirements:* For master's, GRE. Additional exam requirements/recommendations for international students: Required—TOEFL (minimum score 80 iBT), IELTS (minimum score 6.5).

Rice University, Graduate Programs, Wiess School–Professional Science Master's Programs, Professional Master's Program in Subsurface Geosciences, Houston, TX 77251-1892. Offers geophysics (MS). *Program availability:* Part-time. *Degree requirements:* For master's, internship. *Entrance requirements:* For master's, GRE, letters of recommendation (4). Additional exam requirements/recommendations for international students: Required—TOEFL (minimum score 600 paper-based; 90 iBT). Electronic applications accepted. *Faculty research:* Seismology, geodynamics, wave propagation, bio-geochemistry, remote sensing.

Saint Louis University, Graduate Programs, College of Arts and Sciences, Department of Earth and Atmospheric Sciences, St. Louis, MO 63103. Offers geophysics (PhD); geoscience (MS); meteorology (M Pr Met, MS-R, PhD). *Program availability:* Part-time. *Degree requirements:* For master's, thesis (for some programs), comprehensive oral exam; for doctorate, thesis/dissertation, preliminary exams. *Entrance requirements:* For master's, GRE General Test, letters of recommendation, resume; for doctorate, GRE General Test, letters of recommendation, resumé, goal statement, transcripts. Additional exam requirements/recommendations for international students: Required—TOEFL (minimum score 525 paper-based). Electronic applications accepted. *Faculty research:* Structural geology, mesoscale meteorology and severe storms, weather and climate change prediction.

Southern Methodist University, Dedman College of Humanities and Sciences, Roy M. Huffington Department of Earth Sciences, Dallas, TX 75275. Offers applied geophysics (MS); earth sciences (MS, PhD). *Program availability:* Part-time. *Degree requirements:* For master's, thesis (for some programs), qualifying exam; for doctorate, thesis/dissertation, qualifying exam. *Entrance requirements:* For master's and doctorate, GRE General Test, minimum GPA of 3.0, letters of recommendation. Additional exam requirements/recommendations for international students: Required—TOEFL. Electronic applications accepted. *Faculty research:* Sedimentology, geochemistry, igneous and metamorphic petrology, vertebrate paleontology, seismology.

Stanford University, School of Earth, Energy and Environmental Sciences, Department of Geophysics, Stanford, CA 94305-2004. Offers MS, PhD. *Expenses: Tuition:* Full-time $50,703; part-time $32,970 per year. *Required fees:* $651.
Website: http://pangea.stanford.edu/departments/geophysics/

Texas A&M University, College of Geosciences, Department of Geology and Geophysics, College Station, TX 77843. Offers geology (MS, PhD); geophysics (PhD). *Faculty:* 37. *Students:* 85 full-time (30 women), 29 part-time (13 women); includes 10 minority (1 Black or African American, non-Hispanic/Latino; 4 Asian, non-Hispanic/Latino; 4 Hispanic/Latino; 1 Two or more races, non-Hispanic/Latino), 51 international. Average age 30. 145 applicants, 12% accepted, 13 enrolled. In 2018, 22 master's, 5 doctorates awarded. *Degree requirements:* For master's, thesis; for doctorate, thesis/dissertation. *Entrance requirements:* For master's and doctorate, GRE General Test. Additional exam requirements/recommendations for international students: Required—TOEFL (minimum score 550 paper-based; 80 iBT), IELTS (minimum score 6), PTE (minimum score 53). *Application deadline:* For fall admission, 1/1 priority date for domestic students; for spring admission, 8/15 priority date for domestic students. Applications are processed on a rolling basis. Application fee: $50 ($90 for international students). Electronic applications accepted. *Expenses:* Contact institution. *Financial support:* In 2018–19, 81 students received support, including 38 fellowships with tuition reimbursements available (averaging $6,947 per year), 34 research assistantships with tuition reimbursements available (averaging $12,517 per year), 31 teaching assistantships with tuition reimbursements available (averaging $12,385 per year); career-related internships or fieldwork, institutionally sponsored loans, scholarships/grants, traineeships, health care benefits, tuition waivers (full and partial), and unspecified assistantships also available. Support available to part-time students. Financial award application deadline: 3/15; financial award applicants required to submit FAFSA. *Faculty research:* Environmental and engineering geology and geophysics, petroleum geology, tectonophysics, geochemistry. *Unit head:* Dr. Mike Pope, Professor and Department Head, 979-845-4376, E-mail: mcpope@tamu.edu. *Application contact:* Dr. Mark E. Everett, Professor and Associate Department Head for Graduate Affairs, 979-862-2129, E-mail: everett@geo.tamu.edu.
Website: http://geoweb.tamu.edu

University of Alaska Fairbanks, College of Natural Science and Mathematics, Department of Geosciences, Fairbanks, AK 99775-5780. Offers geophysics (MS), including remote sensing geophysics, snow, ice, and permafrost geophysics, solid-earth geophysics. *Program availability:* Part-time. *Faculty:* 11 full-time (4 women), 1 part-time/adjunct (0 women). *Students:* 43 full-time (17 women), 21 part-time (6 women); includes

3 minority (1 Asian, non-Hispanic/Latino; 2 Two or more races, non-Hispanic/Latino), 9 international. Average age 31. 51 applicants, 24% accepted, 12 enrolled. In 2018, 3 master's awarded. *Degree requirements:* For master's, comprehensive exam, thesis, oral defense of thesis. *Entrance requirements:* For master's, GRE General Test, bachelor's degree in geology, geophysics, or an appropriate physical science or engineering with minimum cumulative undergraduate and major GPA of 3.0. Additional exam requirements/recommendations for international students: Required—TOEFL (minimum score 550 paper-based; 79 iBT), IELTS (minimum score 6.5). *Application deadline:* For fall admission, 6/1 for domestic students, 3/1 for international students; for spring admission, 10/15 for domestic students, 9/1 for international students. Applications are processed on a rolling basis. Application fee: $60. Electronic applications accepted. *Expenses: Tuition, area resident:* Full-time $8802; part-time $5868 per credit hour. Tuition, state resident: full-time $8802; part-time $5868 per credit hour. Tuition, nonresident: full-time $18,504; part-time $12,336 per credit hour. *International tuition:* $18,504 full-time. *Required fees:* $1416; $944 per credit hour. $472 per semester. Tuition and fees vary according to course load and program. *Financial support:* In 2018–19, 23 research assistantships with full tuition reimbursements (averaging $8,372 per year), 12 teaching assistantships with full tuition reimbursements (averaging $13,265 per year) were awarded; fellowships with full tuition reimbursements, Federal Work-Study, scholarships/grants, health care benefits, and unspecified assistantships also available. Support available to part-time students. Financial award application deadline: 2/15; financial award applicants required to submit FAFSA. *Faculty research:* Glacial surging, volcanology, geochronology, impact cratering, permafrost geophysics. *Total annual research expenditures:* $6.4 million. *Unit head:* Dr. Paul McCarthy, Department Chair, 907-474-7565, E-mail: uaf-geosciences@alaska.edu. *Application contact:* Samara Taber, Director of Admissions, 907-474-7500, E-mail: uaf-admissions@alaska.edu.
Website: http://www.uaf.edu/geology/

University of Alberta, Faculty of Graduate Studies and Research, Department of Physics, Edmonton, AB T6G 2E1, Canada. Offers astrophysics (M Sc, PhD); condensed matter (M Sc, PhD); geophysics (M Sc, PhD); medical physics (M Sc, PhD); subatomic physics (M Sc, PhD). *Degree requirements:* For master's, thesis; for doctorate, thesis/dissertation. *Entrance requirements:* For master's and doctorate, minimum GPA of 7.0 on a 9.0 scale. Additional exam requirements/recommendations for international students: Required—TOEFL. *Faculty research:* Cosmology, astroparticle physics, high-intermediate energy, magnetism, superconductivity.

The University of British Columbia, Faculty of Science, Department of Earth, Ocean and Atmospheric Sciences, Vancouver, BC V6T 1Z4, Canada. Offers atmospheric science (M Sc, PhD); geological engineering (M Eng, MA Sc, PhD); geological sciences (M Sc, PhD); geophysics (M Sc, MA Sc, PhD); oceanography (M Sc, PhD). *Degree requirements:* For master's, one foreign language, thesis (for some programs); for doctorate, one foreign language, comprehensive exam, thesis/dissertation. *Entrance requirements:* Additional exam requirements/recommendations for international students: Required—TOEFL. *Expenses:* Contact institution. *Faculty research:* Oceans and atmosphere, environmental earth science, hydro geology, mineral deposits, geophysics.

University of Calgary, Faculty of Graduate Studies, Faculty of Science, Program in Geoscience, Calgary, AB T2N 1N4, Canada. Offers geology (M Sc, PhD); geophysics (M Sc, PhD); hydrology (M Sc, PhD). *Program availability:* Part-time. Terminal master's awarded for partial completion of doctoral program. *Degree requirements:* For master's, thesis; for doctorate, thesis/dissertation, candidacy exam. *Entrance requirements:* For master's, B Sc; for doctorate, honors B Sc or M Sc. Additional exam requirements/recommendations for international students: Required—TOEFL. Electronic applications accepted. *Faculty research:* Geochemistry, petrology, paleontology, stratigraphy, exploration and solid-earth geophysics.

University of California, Berkeley, Graduate Division, College of Letters and Science, Department of Earth and Planetary Science, Berkeley, CA 94720. Offers geology (MA, MS, PhD); geophysics (MA, MS, PhD). Terminal master's awarded for partial completion of doctoral program. *Degree requirements:* For master's, oral exam (MA), thesis (MS); for doctorate, comprehensive exam, thesis/dissertation, candidacy exams. *Entrance requirements:* For master's and doctorate, GRE General Test, minimum GPA of 3.0, 3 letters of recommendation. Additional exam requirements/recommendations for international students: Required—TOEFL (minimum score 570 paper-based; 90 iBT). Electronic applications accepted. *Faculty research:* Tectonics, environmental geology, high-pressure geophysics and seismology, economic geology, geochemistry.

University of California, Los Angeles, Graduate Division, College of Letters and Science, Department of Earth and Space Sciences, Program in Geophysics and Space Physics, Los Angeles, CA 90095. Offers MS, PhD. Terminal master's awarded for partial completion of doctoral program. *Degree requirements:* For master's, comprehensive exam or thesis; for doctorate, thesis/dissertation, oral and written qualifying exams. *Entrance requirements:* For master's and doctorate, GRE General Test, bachelor's degree; minimum undergraduate GPA of 3.0 (or its equivalent if letter grade system not used). Additional exam requirements/recommendations for international students: Required—TOEFL. Electronic applications accepted.

University of California, San Diego, Graduate Division, Scripps Institution of Oceanography, La Jolla, CA 92093. Offers climate science and policy (MAS); earth sciences (PhD); geophysics (PhD); marine biodiversity and conservation (MAS); oceanography (MS, PhD). PhD in geophysics offered jointly with San Diego State University. *Students:* 265 full-time (143 women), 1 (woman) part-time. 407 applicants, 21% accepted, 55 enrolled. In 2018, 34 master's, 44 doctorates awarded. Terminal master's awarded for partial completion of doctoral program. *Degree requirements:* For master's, comprehensive exam (for some programs), thesis (for some programs); for doctorate, comprehensive exam, thesis/dissertation. *Entrance requirements:* For master's and doctorate, GRE General Test, GRE Subject Test (encouraged for ocean biosciences applicants), minimum GPA of 3.0. Additional exam requirements/recommendations for international students: Required—TOEFL (minimum score 550 paper-based; 80 iBT), IELTS (minimum score 7). *Application deadline:* For fall admission, 1/15 for domestic students. Application fee: $105 ($125 for international students). Electronic applications accepted. *Financial support:* Fellowships, research assistantships, teaching assistantships, scholarships/grants, traineeships, and unspecified assistantships available. Financial award applicants required to submit FAFSA. *Faculty research:* Biodiversity and conservation, earth and planetary chemistry, alternative energy, global environmental monitoring, air-sea boundary, tectonic margins and the interactions between systems and environments. *Unit head:* Peter Franks, Chair, 858-534-7528, E-mail: pfranks@ucsd.edu. *Application contact:* Gilbert Bretado, Graduate Coordinator, 858-534-1694, E-mail: siodept@sio.ucsd.edu.
Website: https://scripps.ucsd.edu/education

University of Chicago, Division of the Physical Sciences, Department of the Geophysical Sciences, Chicago, IL 60637. Offers atmospheric sciences (PhD); earth sciences (PhD); paleobiology (PhD); planetary and space sciences (PhD). Terminal master's awarded for partial completion of doctoral program. *Degree requirements:* For doctorate, comprehensive exam, thesis/dissertation. *Entrance requirements:* For doctorate, GRE General Test, research statement, 3 letters of recommendation, transcripts for all previous degrees and institutions attended. Additional exam requirements/recommendations for international students: Required—TOEFL (minimum score 600 paper-based; 95 iBT), IELTS (minimum score 7). Electronic applications accepted. *Faculty research:* Climatology, evolutionary paleontology, cosmochemistry, geochemistry, oceanic sciences.

University of Colorado Boulder, Graduate School, College of Arts and Sciences, Department of Geological Sciences, Boulder, CO 80309. Offers geology (MS, PhD); geophysics (PhD). Terminal master's awarded for partial completion of doctoral program. *Degree requirements:* For master's, comprehensive exam, thesis; for doctorate, comprehensive exam, thesis/dissertation. *Entrance requirements:* For master's, GRE General Test, minimum undergraduate GPA of 3.0; for doctorate, GRE General Test, minimum GPA of 2.75. Electronic applications accepted. Application fee is waived when completed online. *Faculty research:* Geology; earth sciences; tectonics; geophysics; geosciences.

University of Hawaii at Manoa, Office of Graduate Education, School of Ocean and Earth Science and Technology, Department of Geology and Geophysics, Honolulu, HI 96822. Offers high-pressure geophysics and geochemistry (MS, PhD); hydrogeology and engineering geology (MS, PhD); marine geology and geophysics (MS, PhD); planetary geosciences and remote sensing (MS, PhD); seismology and solid-earth geophysics (MS, PhD); volcanology, petrology, and geochemistry (MS, PhD). *Program availability:* Part-time. Terminal master's awarded for partial completion of doctoral program. *Degree requirements:* For master's, thesis optional; for doctorate, comprehensive exam, thesis/dissertation. *Entrance requirements:* For master's and doctorate, GRE General Test, minimum GPA of 3.0. Additional exam requirements/recommendations for international students: Required—TOEFL (minimum score 580 paper-based; 92 iBT), IELTS (minimum score 5).

University of Houston, College of Natural Sciences and Mathematics, Department of Earth and Atmospheric Sciences, Houston, TX 77204. Offers atmospheric science (PhD); geology (MA, PhD); geophysics (PhD). *Program availability:* Part-time. *Degree requirements:* For master's, thesis; for doctorate, comprehensive exam, thesis/dissertation. *Entrance requirements:* For master's and doctorate, GRE General Test. Additional exam requirements/recommendations for international students: Required—TOEFL (minimum score 550 paper-based; 79 iBT), IELTS (minimum score 6.5). Electronic applications accepted. *Faculty research:* Atmospherics sciences, seismic and solid earth geophysics, tectonics, environmental hydrochemistry, carbonates, micropaleontology, structure and tectonics, petroleum geology.

University of Manitoba, Faculty of Graduate Studies, Clayton H. Riddell Faculty of Environment, Earth, and Resources, Department of Geological Sciences, Winnipeg, MB R3T 2N2, Canada. Offers geology (M Sc, PhD); geophysics (M Sc, PhD). *Degree requirements:* For master's, thesis; for doctorate, thesis/dissertation. *Entrance requirements:* For master's and doctorate, GRE General Test, GRE Subject Test (geology), minimum GPA of 3.0. Additional exam requirements/recommendations for international students: Required—TOEFL.

University of Memphis, Graduate School, College of Arts and Sciences, Department of Earth Sciences, Memphis, TN 38152. Offers earth sciences (MA, MS, PhD), including archaeology (MS), geography (MS), geology (MS), geophysics (MS), interdisciplinary studies (MS); geographic information systems (Graduate Certificate), including geographic information systems, GIS educator, GIS planning, GIS professional. *Program availability:* Part-time, evening/weekend. *Students:* 44 full-time (19 women), 30 part-time (10 women); includes 9 minority (7 Asian, non-Hispanic/Latino; 2 Hispanic/Latino), 25 international. Average age 31. 19 applicants, 89% accepted, 16 enrolled. In 2018, 13 master's, 5 doctorates, 8 other advanced degrees awarded. Terminal master's awarded for partial completion of doctoral program. *Degree requirements:* For master's, comprehensive exam, thesis, seminar presentation; for doctorate, comprehensive exam, thesis/dissertation, qualifying exam, submission of two manuscripts for publication in peer-reviewed journal or books. *Entrance requirements:* For master's, GRE General Test, 3 letters of recommendation, statement of research interests; for doctorate, GRE General Test, 2 letters of recommendation, resume, personal statement. Additional exam requirements/recommendations for international students: Required—TOEFL (minimum score 550 paper-based; 79 iBT). *Application deadline:* For fall admission, 1/15 for domestic students; for spring admission, 11/1 for domestic students. Applications are processed on a rolling basis. Application fee: $35 ($60 for international students). Electronic applications accepted. *Expenses: Tuition, area resident:* Full-time $10,240; part-time $503 per credit hour. Tuition, state resident: full-time $10,464. Tuition, nonresident: full-time $20,224; part-time $991 per credit hour. *Required fees:* $850; $106 per credit hour. *Financial support:* Fellowships with full tuition reimbursements, research assistantships with full tuition reimbursements, teaching assistantships with full tuition reimbursements, Federal Work-Study, scholarships/grants, and unspecified assistantships available. Financial award application deadline: 2/1; financial award applicants required to submit FAFSA. *Faculty research:* Hazards, active tectonics, geophysics, hydrology and water resources, spatial analysis. *Unit head:* Dr. Daniel Larsen, Chair, 901-678-4358, Fax: 901-678-2178, E-mail: dlarsen@memphis.edu. *Application contact:* Dr. Andrew Mickelson, Graduate Coordinator, 901-678-4505, Fax: 901-678-2178, E-mail: amicklsn@memphis.edu.
Website: http://www.memphis.edu/earthsciences/

University of Miami, Graduate School, Rosenstiel School of Marine and Atmospheric Science, Division of Marine Geology and Geophysics, Coral Gables, FL 33124. Offers MS, PhD. Terminal master's awarded for partial completion of doctoral program. *Degree requirements:* For master's, comprehensive exam, thesis; for doctorate, comprehensive exam, thesis/dissertation. *Entrance requirements:* For master's and doctorate, GRE General Test. Additional exam requirements/recommendations for international students: Required—TOEFL (minimum score 550 paper-based). Electronic applications accepted. *Faculty research:* Carbonate sedimentology, low-temperature geochemistry, paleoceanography, geodesy and tectonics.

University of Minnesota, Twin Cities Campus, College of Science and Engineering, Department of Earth Sciences, Minneapolis, MN 55455-0213. Offers MS, PhD. Terminal master's awarded for partial completion of doctoral program. *Degree requirements:* For master's, thesis; for doctorate, thesis/dissertation. *Entrance requirements:* For master's and doctorate, GRE General Test, 3 letters of recommendation. Additional exam requirements/recommendations for international students: Required—TOEFL (minimum score 550 paper-based). Electronic applications accepted. *Faculty research:* Geology, geophysics, geochemistry, geobiology, climate and environmental geosciences.

University of Nevada, Reno, Graduate School, College of Science, Mackay School of Earth Sciences and Engineering, Department of Geological Sciences and Engineering, Program in Geophysics, Reno, NV 89557. Offers MS, PhD. Terminal master's awarded for partial completion of doctoral program. *Degree requirements:* For master's, thesis optional; for doctorate, thesis/dissertation. *Entrance requirements:* For master's, GRE

General Test, minimum GPA of 2.75; for doctorate, GRE General Test, minimum GPA of 3.0. Additional exam requirements/recommendations for international students: Required—TOEFL (minimum score 500 paper-based; 61 iBT), IELTS (minimum score 6). Electronic applications accepted. *Faculty research:* Geophysics exploration, seismology, remote sensing.

University of Oklahoma, Mewbourne College of Earth and Energy, ConocoPhillips School of Geology and Geophysics, Norman, OK 73019. Offers geology (MS, PhD); geophysics (MS, PhD). *Program availability:* Part-time. *Degree requirements:* For master's, thesis; for doctorate, thesis/dissertation. *Entrance requirements:* For master's and doctorate, GRE. Additional exam requirements/recommendations for international students: Required—TOEFL (minimum score 79 iBT) or IELTS (minimum score 6.5). Electronic applications accepted. *Expenses:* Tuition, state resident: full-time $5683.20; part-time $236.80 per credit hour. Tuition, nonresident: full-time $20,342; part-time $847.60 per credit hour. *International tuition:* $20,342.40 full-time. *Required fees:* $2894.20; $110.05 per credit hour. $126.50 per semester. Tuition and fees vary according to course load and program. *Faculty research:* Energy; geochemistry; geophysics; earth systems; lithospheric dynamics.

University of Rhode Island, Graduate School, Graduate School of Oceanography, Narragansett, RI 02882. Offers biological oceanography (MS, PhD); coastal ocean management (MO); coastal systems (MO); fisheries (MO); general oceanography (MO); marine and atmospheric chemistry (MS, PhD); marine fisheries management (MO); marine geology and geophysics (MS, PhD); ocean technology and data (MO); physical oceanography (MS, PhD); MBA/MO; PhD/MA; PhD/MMA. *Program availability:* Part-time. *Faculty:* 29 full-time (10 women). *Students:* 56 full-time (33 women), 10 part-time (5 women); includes 1 minority (Asian, non-Hispanic/Latino), 10 international. 76 applicants, 72% accepted, 17 enrolled. In 2018, 15 master's, 5 doctorates awarded. *Entrance requirements:* For master's, GRE, 2 letters of recommendation; for doctorate, GRE, 3 letters of recommendation. Additional exam requirements/recommendations for international students: Required—TOEFL. *Application deadline:* For fall admission, 1/15 for domestic and international students. Application fee: $65. Electronic applications accepted. *Expenses: Tuition, area resident:* Full-time $13,226; part-time $735 per credit. Tuition, state resident: full-time $13,226; part-time $735 per credit. Tuition, nonresident: full-time $25,854; part-time $1436 per credit. *International tuition:* $25,854 full-time. *Required fees:* $1698; $50 per credit. $35 per semester. One-time fee: $165. *Financial support:* In 2018–19, 31 research assistantships with tuition reimbursements (averaging $9,647 per year), 14 teaching assistantships with tuition reimbursements (averaging $10,563 per year) were awarded. Financial award application deadline: 1/15; financial award applicants required to submit FAFSA. *Faculty research:* Subduction, life in extreme environments, the marine nitrogen cycle, hurricane prediction, Antarctic ocean circulation. *Unit head:* Dr. Bruce Corliss, Dean, 401-874-6222, Fax: 401-874-6931, E-mail: bruce.corliss@gso.uri.edu. *Application contact:* Dr. David Smith, Professor of Oceanography/Associate Dean for Academic Affairs, 401-874-6172, E-mail: dcsmith@uri.edu.
Website: http://www.gso.uri.edu/

The University of Texas at El Paso, Graduate School, College of Science, Department of Geological Sciences, El Paso, TX 79968-0001. Offers geological sciences (MS, PhD); geophysics (MS). *Program availability:* Part-time, evening/weekend. *Degree requirements:* For master's, thesis; for doctorate, one foreign language, comprehensive exam, thesis/dissertation. *Entrance requirements:* For master's, GRE, minimum GPA of 3.0, BS in geology or equivalent; for doctorate, GRE, minimum GPA of 3.0, MS in geology or equivalent. Additional exam requirements/recommendations for international students: Required—TOEFL. Electronic applications accepted.

The University of Tulsa, Graduate School, College of Engineering and Natural Sciences, Department of Geosciences, Tulsa, OK 74104-3189. Offers geophysics (MS); geosciences (MS, PhD); JD/MS. *Program availability:* Part-time. *Faculty:* 11 full-time (2 women), 4 part-time/adjunct (0 women). *Students:* 20 full-time (4 women), 1 part-time (0 women); includes 1 minority (Hispanic/Latino), 8 international. Average age 27. 28 applicants, 71% accepted, 12 enrolled. In 2018, 9 master's awarded. Terminal master's awarded for partial completion of doctoral program. *Degree requirements:* For master's, thesis (for some programs); for doctorate, comprehensive exam, thesis/dissertation. *Entrance requirements:* For master's and doctorate, GRE General Test. Additional exam requirements/recommendations for international students: Required—TOEFL (minimum score 550 paper-based; 80 iBT), IELTS (minimum score 6). *Application deadline:* For fall admission, 2/1 for domestic and international students; for spring admission, 8/1 for domestic and international students. Applications are processed on a rolling basis. Application fee: $55. Electronic applications accepted. *Expenses: Tuition:* Full-time $22,230; part-time $1235 per credit hour. *Required fees:* $2100; $6 per credit hour. One-time fee: $400 full-time. Tuition and fees vary according to course level, course load and program. *Financial support:* In 2018–19, 10 students received support, including 3 fellowships with full tuition reimbursements available (averaging $5,023 per year), 2 research assistantships with full tuition reimbursements available (averaging $7,822 per year), 7 teaching assistantships with full tuition reimbursements available (averaging $12,758 per year); career-related internships or fieldwork, scholarships/grants, health care benefits, and unspecified assistantships also available. Support available to part-time students. Financial award application deadline: 2/1; financial award applicants required to submit FAFSA. *Faculty research:* Petroleum exploration/production and environmental science, including clastic sedimentology, petroleum seismology, seismic stratigraphy, structural geology, geochemistry, and biogeoscience. *Unit head:* Dr. Dennis Kerr, Chairperson, 918-631-3020, Fax: 918-631-2091, E-mail: dennis-kerr@utulsa.edu. *Application contact:* Dr. Peter Michael, Adviser, 918-631-3017, Fax: 918-631-2156, E-mail: pjm@utulsa.edu.
Website: http://engineering.utulsa.edu/academics/geosciences/

University of Utah, Graduate School, College of Mines and Earth Sciences, Department of Geology and Geophysics, Salt Lake City, UT 84112. Offers geological engineering (ME, MS, PhD); geology (MS, PhD); geophysics (MS, PhD). *Faculty:* 23 full-time (6 women), 15 part-time/adjunct (6 women). *Students:* 53 full-time (22 women), 12 part-time (2 women); includes 11 minority (1 American Indian or Alaska Native, non-Hispanic/Latino; 1 Asian, non-Hispanic/Latino; 8 Hispanic/Latino; 1 Two or more races, non-Hispanic/Latino), 11 international. Average age 25. 228 applicants, 14% accepted, 22 enrolled. In 2018, 12 master's, 2 doctorates awarded. Terminal master's awarded for partial completion of doctoral program. *Entrance requirements:* For master's and doctorate, GRE General Test, minimum GPA of 3.25. Additional exam requirements/recommendations for international students: Required—TOEFL (minimum score 500 paper-based; 61 iBT). Application fee: $55 ($65 for international students). Electronic applications accepted. *Expenses: Tuition, area resident:* Full-time $7190.66; part-time $2112.48 per year. Tuition, state resident: full-time $7190.66. Tuition, nonresident: full-time $25,195. *Required fees:* $558; $555.04 per unit. Tuition and fees vary according to course level, course load, degree level, program and student level. *Financial support:* In 2018–19, 62 students received support, including 14 fellowships with full tuition reimbursements available (averaging $18,500 per year), 32 research assistantships with full tuition reimbursements available (averaging $24,000 per year), 16 teaching assistantships with full tuition reimbursements available (averaging $18,500 per year); career-related internships or fieldwork, institutionally sponsored loans, scholarships/grants, health care benefits, unspecified assistantships, and stipends also available. Financial award application deadline: 1/15; financial award applicants required to submit FAFSA. *Faculty research:* Igneous, metamorphic, and sedimentary petrology; stratigraphy; paleoclimatology; hydrology; seismology. *Total annual research expenditures:* $4.1 million. *Unit head:* Dr. John Bartley, Chair, 801-585-1670, Fax: 801-581-7065, E-mail: john.bartley@utah.edu. *Application contact:* Dr. Gabriel J. Bowen, Director of Graduate Studies, 801-585-7925, Fax: 801-581-7065, E-mail: gabe.bowen@utah.edu.
Website: http://www.earth.utah.edu/

University of Washington, Graduate School, College of the Environment, Department of Earth and Space Sciences, Seattle, WA 98195. Offers geology (MS, PhD); geophysics (MS, PhD). *Degree requirements:* For master's, thesis or alternative, departmental qualifying exam, final exam; for doctorate, thesis/dissertation, departmental qualifying exam, general and final exams. *Entrance requirements:* For master's and doctorate, GRE General Test, minimum GPA of 3.0. Additional exam requirements/recommendations for international students: Required—TOEFL (minimum score 580 paper-based). Electronic applications accepted.

The University of Western Ontario, School of Graduate and Postdoctoral Studies, Faculty of Science, Department of Earth Sciences, London, ON N6A 3K7, Canada. Offers environment and sustainability (MES); geology (M Sc, PhD); geology and environmental science (M Sc, PhD); geophysics (M Sc, PhD); geophysics and environmental science (M Sc, PhD). *Degree requirements:* For master's, thesis; for doctorate, thesis/dissertation, qualifying exam. *Entrance requirements:* For master's, honors in B Sc; for doctorate, M Sc. Additional exam requirements/recommendations for international students: Required—TOEFL. *Faculty research:* Geophysics, geochemistry, paleontology, sedimentology/stratigraphy, glaciology/quaternary.

University of Wisconsin–Madison, Graduate School, College of Letters and Science, Department of Geology and Geophysics, Program in Geophysics, Madison, WI 53706-1380. Offers MS, PhD. *Degree requirements:* For master's, thesis; for doctorate, one foreign language, thesis/dissertation. *Entrance requirements:* For master's and doctorate, GRE General Test.

University of Wyoming, College of Arts and Sciences, Department of Geology and Geophysics, Laramie, WY 82071. Offers geology (MS, PhD); geophysics (MS, PhD). *Program availability:* Part-time. *Degree requirements:* For master's, comprehensive exam, thesis; for doctorate, comprehensive exam, thesis/dissertation. *Entrance requirements:* For master's and doctorate, GRE General Test, minimum GPA of 3.0. *Expenses: Tuition, area resident:* Full-time $6504; part-time $271 per credit hour. Tuition, state resident: full-time $6504; part-time $271 per credit hour. Tuition, nonresident: full-time $19,464; part-time $811 per credit hour. *International tuition:* $19,464 full-time. *Required fees:* $1410.94; $343.82 per semester. $343.82 per semester. Tuition and fees vary according to course load, program and reciprocity agreements. *Faculty research:* Low-temp geochemistry, geohydrology, paleontology, structure/tectonics, sedimentation and petroleum geology, petrology, geophysics/seismology.

Wright State University, Graduate School, College of Science and Mathematics, Department of Physics, Program in Physics, Dayton, OH 45435. Offers geophysics (MS). *Program availability:* Part-time, evening/weekend. *Degree requirements:* For master's, thesis. *Entrance requirements:* Additional exam requirements/recommendations for international students: Required—TOEFL. *Faculty research:* Solid-state physics, optics, geophysics.

Yale University, Graduate School of Arts and Sciences, Department of Geology and Geophysics, New Haven, CT 06520. Offers biogeochemistry (PhD); climate dynamics (PhD); geochemistry (PhD); geophysics (PhD); meteorology (PhD); oceanography (PhD); paleontology (PhD); paleooceanography (PhD); petrology (PhD); tectonics (PhD). *Degree requirements:* For doctorate, thesis/dissertation. *Entrance requirements:* For doctorate, GRE General Test. Additional exam requirements/recommendations for international students: Required—TOEFL.

Geosciences

Arizona State University at the Tempe campus, College of Liberal Arts and Sciences, School of Earth and Space Exploration, Tempe, AZ 85287-1404. Offers astrophysics (MS, PhD); exploration systems design (PhD); geological sciences (MS, PhD). PhD in exploration systems design is offered in collaboration with the Ira A. Fulton School of Engineering. Terminal master's awarded for partial completion of doctoral program. *Degree requirements:* For master's, thesis, interactive Program of Study (iPOS) submitted before completing 50 percent of required credit hours; for doctorate, thesis/dissertation, interactive Program of Study (iPOS) submitted before completing 50 percent of required credit hours. *Entrance requirements:* For master's and doctorate, GRE, minimum GPA of 3.0 or equivalent in last 2 years of work leading to bachelor's degree. Additional exam requirements/recommendations for international students: Required—TOEFL, IELTS, or PTE. Electronic applications accepted.

Ball State University, Graduate School, College of Sciences and Humanities, Department of Geological Sciences, Muncie, IN 47306. Offers geology (MA, MS). *Program availability:* Part-time. *Entrance requirements:* For master's, GRE General Test, minimum baccalaureate GPA of 2.75 or 3.0 in latter half of baccalaureate. Additional exam requirements/recommendations for international students: Required—TOEFL (minimum score 550 paper-based; 79 iBT), IELTS (minimum score 6.5). Electronic applications accepted. *Faculty research:* Environmental geology, geophysics, stratigraphy.

Baylor University, Graduate School, College of Arts and Sciences, Department of Geosciences, Waco, TX 76798. Offers MS, PhD. *Faculty:* 18 full-time (1 woman). *Students:* 40 full-time (18 women), 2 part-time (1 woman); includes 4 minority (1 Black or African American, non-Hispanic/Latino; 1 Asian, non-Hispanic/Latino; 2 Hispanic/Latino), 12 international. Average age 23. 56 applicants, 30% accepted, 12 enrolled. In 2018, 5 master's, 1 doctorate awarded. *Degree requirements:* For master's, comprehensive exam, thesis, preliminary exam, thesis proposal, thesis defense; for doctorate, comprehensive exam, thesis/dissertation, preliminary exam, dissertation proposal, dissertation defense. *Entrance requirements:* For master's and doctorate, GRE General Test. Additional exam requirements/recommendations for international students: Required—TOEFL (minimum score 550 paper-based; 80 iBT), IELTS (minimum score 6.5), PTE (minimum score 58). *Application deadline:* For fall admission, 1/15 priority date for domestic and international students. Applications are processed on a rolling basis. Application fee: $56. Electronic applications accepted. *Financial support:* In 2018–19, 33 students received support, including 6 research assistantships with full tuition reimbursements available (averaging $24,000 per year), 18 teaching assistantships with full tuition reimbursements available (averaging $24,000 per year); career-related internships or fieldwork, Federal Work-Study, institutionally sponsored loans, scholarships/grants, health care benefits, tuition waivers (full and partial), and unspecified assistantships also available. Support available to part-time students. Financial award application deadline: 2/28; financial award applicants required to submit FAFSA. *Faculty research:* Terrestrial paleoclimatology, applied petroleum studies, applied and solid earth geophysics, hydro geoscience, high temperature geochemistry and volcanology. *Total annual research expenditures:* $800,000. *Unit head:* Dr. Daniel Peppe, Graduate Program Director, 254-710-2629, Fax: 254-710-2673, E-mail: daniel_peppe@baylor.edu. *Application contact:* Jamie Ruth, Graduate Program Coordinator, 254-710-2361, Fax: 254-710-2673, E-mail: jamie_ruth@baylor.edu. Website: http://www.baylor.edu/geology/

Baylor University, Graduate School, College of Arts and Sciences, The Institute of Ecological, Earth and Environmental Sciences, Waco, TX 76798. Offers PhD. *Faculty:* 24 full-time (4 women). *Students:* 5 full-time (1 woman); includes 2 minority (1 Asian, non-Hispanic/Latino; 1 Hispanic/Latino), 2 international. Average age 25. 8 applicants, 25% accepted, 1 enrolled. In 2018, 1 doctorate awarded. *Degree requirements:* For doctorate, comprehensive exam, thesis/dissertation. *Entrance requirements:* For doctorate, GRE. Additional exam requirements/recommendations for international students: Required—TOEFL (minimum score 550 paper-based; 80 iBT); Recommended—IELTS (minimum score 6.5). *Application deadline:* For fall admission, 2/15 priority date for domestic and international students. Application fee: $40. Electronic applications accepted. *Expenses:* Contact institution. *Financial support:* In 2018–19, 5 students received support, including 5 research assistantships with full and partial tuition reimbursements available (averaging $22,000 per year), 5 teaching assistantships with full and partial tuition reimbursements available (averaging $22,000 per year); scholarships/grants, health care benefits, tuition waivers (partial), and unspecified assistantships also available. Financial award application deadline: 2/15. *Faculty research:* Ecosystem processes, environmental toxicology and risk assessment, biogeochemical cycling, chemical fate and transport, conservation management. *Unit head:* Dr. Joe C. Yelderman, Jr., Director, 254-710-2185, E-mail: joe_yelderman@baylor.edu. *Application contact:* Shannon Koehler, Office Manager, 254-710-2224, Fax: 254-710-2298, E-mail: shannon_koehler@baylor.edu. Website: http://www.baylor.edu/TIEEES/

Boise State University, College of Arts and Sciences, Department of Geosciences, Boise, ID 83725-0399. Offers earth science (M E Sci); geophysics (MS, PhD); geoscience (MS); geosciences (PhD); hydrologic sciences (MS). *Program availability:* Part-time. Terminal master's awarded for partial completion of doctoral program. *Degree requirements:* For master's, thesis (for some programs); for doctorate, thesis/dissertation. *Entrance requirements:* For master's, GRE General Test, BS in related field, minimum GPA of 3.0; for doctorate, GRE General Test. Additional exam requirements/recommendations for international students: Required—TOEFL (minimum score 550 paper-based; 80 iBT), IELTS (minimum score 6). Electronic applications accepted. *Faculty research:* Seismology, geothermal aquifers, sedimentation, tectonics, seismo-acoustic propagation.

Boston University, Graduate School of Arts and Sciences, Department of Earth and Environment, Boston, MA 02215. Offers earth and environment (MA, PhD); energy and environment (MA); remote sensing and geospatial sciences (MA). *Students:* 73 full-time (41 women), 5 part-time (3 women); includes 7 minority (3 Asian, non-Hispanic/Latino; 4 Hispanic/Latino), 38 international. Average age 25. 195 applicants, 53% accepted, 31 enrolled. In 2018, 30 master's, 4 doctorates awarded. Terminal master's awarded for partial completion of doctoral program. *Degree requirements:* For master's, comprehensive exam (for some programs), thesis (for some programs); for doctorate, comprehensive exam, thesis/dissertation. *Entrance requirements:* For master's and doctorate, GRE General Test, 3 letters of recommendation, official transcripts, personal statement. Additional exam requirements/recommendations for international students: Required—TOEFL (minimum score 550 paper-based; 84 iBT). *Application deadline:* For fall admission, 12/19 for domestic and international students; for winter admission, 11/1 for domestic and international students. Application fee: $95. Electronic applications accepted. *Financial support:* In 2018–19, 50 students received support, including 4 fellowships with full tuition reimbursements available (averaging $22,660 per year), 24 research assistantships with full tuition reimbursements available (averaging $22,660 per year), 12 teaching assistantships with full tuition reimbursements available (averaging $22,660 per year); Federal Work-Study, scholarships/grants, traineeships, and health care benefits also available. Financial award application deadline: 12/19. *Faculty research:* Biogeosciences, climate and surface processes; energy, environment and society; geographical sciences; geology, geochemistry and geophysics. *Unit head:* Guido Salvucci, Interim Chair, 617-353-8344, E-mail: gdsalvuc@bu.edu. *Application contact:* Matt DiCintio, Graduate Program Coordinator, 617-353-2529, Fax: 617-353-8399, E-mail: dicintio@bu.edu. Website: http://www.bu.edu/earth/

Brock University, Faculty of Graduate Studies, Faculty of Mathematics and Science, Program in Earth Sciences, St. Catharines, ON L2S 3A1, Canada. Offers M Sc. *Program availability:* Part-time. *Degree requirements:* For master's, thesis. *Entrance requirements:* For master's, honors B Sc in earth sciences. Additional exam requirements/recommendations for international students: Required—TOEFL (minimum score 550 paper-based; 80 iBT), IELTS (minimum score 6.5), TWE (minimum score 4). Electronic applications accepted. *Faculty research:* Clastic sedimentology, environmental geology, geochemistry, micropaleontology, structural geology.

Brooklyn College of the City University of New York, School of Education, Program in Adolescence Science Education and Special Subjects, Brooklyn, NY 11210-2889. Offers adolescence science education (MAT); biology teacher (7-12) (MA); chemistry teacher (7-12) (MA); earth science teacher (7-12) (MAT); English teacher (7-12) (MA); French teacher (7-12) (MA); mathematics teacher (7-12) (MA); music teacher (7-12) (MA); physics teacher (7-12) (MA); social studies teacher (7-12) (MA); Spanish teacher (7-12) (MA). *Program availability:* Part-time, evening/weekend. *Degree requirements:* For

master's, comprehensive exam (for some programs), thesis (for some programs). *Entrance requirements:* For master's, LAST, previous course work in education, resume, 2 letters of recommendation, essay. Additional exam requirements/recommendations for international students: Required—TOEFL (minimum score 500 paper-based; 61 iBT). Electronic applications accepted. *Faculty research:* Interdisciplinary education, semiotics, discourse analysis, autobiography, teacher identity.

Brooklyn College of the City University of New York, School of Education, Program in Middle Childhood Science Education, Brooklyn, NY 11210-2889. Offers biology (MA); chemistry (MA); earth science (MA); general science (MA); physics (MA). *Program availability:* Part-time, evening/weekend. *Entrance requirements:* For master's, LAST, interview, previous course work in education and mathematics, resume, 2 letters of recommendation, essay. Additional exam requirements/recommendations for international students: Required—TOEFL (minimum score 500 paper-based; 61 iBT). Electronic applications accepted. *Faculty research:* Geometric thinking, mastery of basic facts, problem-solving strategies, history of mathematics.

Brown University, Graduate School, Department of Earth, Environmental and Planetary Sciences, Providence, RI 02912. Offers PhD. *Degree requirements:* For doctorate, thesis/dissertation, 1 semester of teaching experience, preliminary exam. *Faculty research:* Geochemistry, mineral kinetics, igneous and metamorphic petrology, tectonophysics including geophysics and structural geology, paleoclimatology, paleoceanography, sedimentation, planetary geology.

California State University, Chico, Office of Graduate Studies, College of Natural Sciences, Department of Geological and Environmental Sciences, Program in Geosciences, Chico, CA 95929-0722. Offers MS. *Program availability:* Part-time. *Students:* 2 full-time (1 woman), 7 part-time (1 woman); includes 3 minority (1 American Indian or Alaska Native, non-Hispanic/Latino; 1 Hispanic/Latino; 1 Two or more races, non-Hispanic/Latino). 10 applicants, 90% accepted, 6 enrolled. *Degree requirements:* For master's, thesis or comprehensive exam. *Entrance requirements:* For master's, GRE, identification of faculty mentor, 2 letters of recommendation, statement of purpose, curriculum vitae, department letter of recommendation access waiver form. Additional exam requirements/recommendations for international students: Required—TOEFL (minimum score 550 paper-based; 80 iBT), IELTS (minimum score 6.5), PTE (minimum score 59). *Application deadline:* For fall admission, 3/1 priority date for domestic students, 3/1 for international students; for spring admission, 9/15 priority date for domestic students, 9/15 for international students. Application fee: $55. Electronic applications accepted. *Expenses: Tuition, area resident:* Full-time $4622; part-time $3116 per unit. *Tuition, state resident:* full-time $4622; part-time $3116 per unit. *Tuition, nonresident:* full-time $10,634. *Required fees:* $2160; $1620 per year. Tuition and fees vary according to class time and program. *Financial support:* Fellowships, research assistantships, teaching assistantships, career-related internships or fieldwork, Federal Work-Study, scholarships/grants, traineeships, health care benefits, unspecified assistantships, and stipends available. Support available to part-time students. Financial award application deadline: 3/2; financial award applicants required to submit FAFSA. *Unit head:* Dr. Todd J. Greene, Chair, 530-898-5262, E-mail: geos@csuchico.edu. *Application contact:* Micah Lehner, Graduate Admissions Coordinator, 530-898-5416, Fax: 530-898-3342, E-mail: mlehner@csuchico.edu. Website: http://catalog.csuchico.edu/viewer/15/GEOS/GEOSNONEPN.html

California State University, San Bernardino, Graduate Studies, College of Natural Sciences, Program in Earth and Environmental Sciences, San Bernardino, CA 92407. Offers MS. *Faculty:* 1 (woman) full-time. *Students:* 8 full-time (3 women), 1 (woman) part-time; includes 6 minority (all Hispanic/Latino). Average age 27. 9 applicants, 44% accepted, 2 enrolled. *Entrance requirements:* Additional exam requirements/recommendations for international students: Required—TOEFL. *Application deadline:* For fall admission, 7/16 for domestic students; for winter admission, 10/16 for domestic students; for spring admission, 1/22 for domestic students. Application fee: $55. *Unit head:* Dr. Joan E. Fryxell, Graduate Coordinator, 909-537-5311, E-mail: jfryxell@csusb.edu. *Application contact:* Dr. Dorota Huizinga, Dean of Graduate Studies, 909-537-3064, E-mail: dorota.huizinga@csusb.edu.

Carleton University, Faculty of Graduate Studies, Faculty of Science, Department of Earth Sciences, Ottawa, ON K1S 5B6, Canada. Offers M Sc, PhD. Programs offered jointly with University of Ottawa. *Degree requirements:* For master's, thesis, seminar; for doctorate, comprehensive exam, thesis/dissertation, seminar. *Entrance requirements:* For master's, honors degree in science; for doctorate, M Sc. Additional exam requirements/recommendations for international students: Required—TOEFL. *Faculty research:* Resource geology, geophysics, basin analysis, lithosphere dynamics.

Case Western Reserve University, School of Graduate Studies, Department of Earth, Environmental, and Planetary Sciences, Cleveland, OH 44106. Offers MS, PhD. *Program availability:* Part-time. *Faculty:* 8 full-time (2 women), 2 part-time/adjunct (1 woman). *Students:* 8 full-time (3 women); includes 3 minority (1 Black or African American, non-Hispanic/Latino; 1 Hispanic/Latino; 1 Two or more races, non-Hispanic/Latino), 2 international. Average age 29. 10 applicants, 30% accepted, 1 enrolled. In 2018, 1 master's, 1 doctorate awarded. Terminal master's awarded for partial completion of doctoral program. *Degree requirements:* For master's, thesis or alternative; for doctorate, thesis/dissertation. *Entrance requirements:* For master's and doctorate, GRE General Test, GRE Subject Test, three letters of recommendation. Additional exam requirements/recommendations for international students: Required—TOEFL (minimum score 577 paper-based; 90 iBT); Recommended—IELTS (minimum score 7). *Application deadline:* For fall admission, 1/15 priority date for domestic students; for spring admission, 11/1 for domestic students. Applications are processed on a rolling basis. Application fee: $50. Electronic applications accepted. *Expenses: Tuition:* Full-time $45,168; part-time $1939 per credit hour. *Required fees:* $36; $18 per semester. $18 per semester. *Financial support:* Research assistantships, teaching assistantships, Federal Work-Study, health care benefits, and tuition waivers (partial) available. Support available to part-time students. Financial award application deadline: 1/15; financial award applicants required to submit FAFSA. *Faculty research:* Geochemistry, hydrology, ecology, geomorphology, planetary science, stratigraphy and basin analysis, igneous petrology. *Unit head:* Steven A. Hauck, II, Professor and Chair, 216-368.3675, Fax: 216-368-3691, E-mail: steven.hauck@case.edu. *Application contact:* Steven A. Hauck, II, Professor and Chair, 216-368.3675, Fax: 216-368-3691, E-mail: steven.hauck@case.edu. Website: http://geology.case.edu/

City College of the City University of New York, Graduate School, Division of Science, Department of Earth and Atmospheric Sciences, New York, NY 10031-9198. Offers geology (MS). *Degree requirements:* For master's, comprehensive exam, thesis. *Entrance requirements:* Additional exam requirements/recommendations for international students: Required—TOEFL (minimum score 500 paper-based; 61 iBT). Electronic applications accepted. *Faculty research:* Water resources, high-temperature geochemistry, sedimentary basin analysis, tectonics.

Peterson's Graduate Programs in the Physical Sciences, Mathematics, Agricultural Sciences, the Environment & Natural Resources 2020

www.petersons.com **101**

Geosciences

Colorado State University, Warner College of Natural Resources, Department of Geosciences, Fort Collins, CO 80523-1482. Offers earth sciences (PhD), including geosciences, watershed science. Terminal master's awarded for partial completion of doctoral program. *Degree requirements:* For master's, thesis; for doctorate, comprehensive exam, thesis/dissertation. *Entrance requirements:* For master's, GRE General Test, minimum GPA of 3.3, letters of recommendation; for doctorate, GRE General Test, minimum GPA of 3.3, letters of recommendation; MS (preferred). Additional exam requirements/recommendations for international students: Required—TOEFL (minimum score 550 paper-based; 80 iBT), IELTS (minimum score 6.5). Electronic applications accepted. *Expenses:* Tuition, state resident: full-time $10,520; part-time $4675 per credit hour. Tuition, nonresident: full-time $25,791; part-time $11,462 per credit hour. *International tuition:* $25,791 full-time. *Required fees:* $2392; $576 $288. Tuition and fees vary according to course level, course load, degree level, program and student level. *Faculty research:* Geophysics, cryosphere, hydrogeology, geomorphology, geology.

Columbia University, Graduate School of Arts and Sciences, New York, NY 10027. Offers African-American studies (MA); American studies (MA); anthropology (MA, PhD); art history and archaeology (MA, PhD); astronomy (PhD); biological sciences (PhD); biotechnology (MA); chemical physics (PhD); chemistry (PhD); classical studies (MA, PhD); classics (MA, PhD); climate and society (MA); conservation biology (MA); earth and environmental sciences (PhD); East Asia: regional studies (MA); East Asian languages and cultures (MA, PhD); ecology, evolution and environmental biology (MA), including conservation biology; ecology, evolution, and environmental biology (PhD), including ecology and evolutionary biology, evolutionary primatology; economics (MA, PhD); English and comparative literature (MA, PhD); French and Romance philology (MA, PhD); Germanic languages (MA, PhD); global French studies (MA); global thought (MA); Hispanic cultural studies (MA); history (PhD); history and literature (MA); human rights studies (MA); Islamic studies (MA); Italian (MA, PhD); Japanese pedagogy (MA); Jewish studies (MA); Latin America and the Caribbean: regional studies (MA); Latin American and Iberian cultures (PhD); mathematics (MA, PhD), including finance (MA); medieval and Renaissance studies (MA); Middle Eastern, South Asian, and African studies (MA, PhD); modern art: critical and curatorial studies (MA); modern European studies (MA); museum anthropology (MA); music (DMA, PhD); oral history (MA); philosophical foundations of physics (MA); philosophy (MA, PhD); physics (PhD); political science (MA, PhD); psychology (PhD); quantitative methods in the social sciences (MA); religion (MA, PhD); Russia, Eurasia and East Europe: regional studies (MA); Russian translation (MA); Slavic cultures (MA); Slavic languages (MA, PhD); sociology (MA, PhD); South Asian studies (MA); statistics (MA, PhD); theatre (PhD). Dual-degree programs require admission to both Graduate School of Arts and Sciences and another Columbia school. *Program availability:* Part-time. Terminal master's awarded for partial completion of doctoral program. *Degree requirements:* For master's, variable foreign language requirement, comprehensive exam (for some programs), thesis (for some programs); for doctorate, variable foreign language requirement, comprehensive exam (for some programs), thesis/dissertation. *Entrance requirements:* For master's and doctorate, GRE General Test, GRE Subject Test (for some programs). Additional exam requirements/recommendations for international students: Required—TOEFL, IELTS. Electronic applications accepted.

Cornell University, Graduate School, Graduate Fields of Engineering, Field of Geological Sciences, Ithaca, NY 14853. Offers economic geology (M Eng, MS, PhD); engineering geology (M Eng, MS, PhD); environmental geophysics (M Eng, MS, PhD); general geology (M Eng, MS, PhD); geobiology (M Eng, MS, PhD); geochemistry and isotope geology (M Eng, MS, PhD); geohydrology (M Eng, MS, PhD); geomorphology (M Eng, MS, PhD); geophysics (M Eng, MS, PhD); geotectonics (M Eng, MS, PhD); marine geology (MS, PhD); mineralogy (M Eng, MS, PhD); paleontology (M Eng, MS, PhD); petroleum geology (M Eng, MS, PhD); petrology (M Eng, MS, PhD); planetary geology (M Eng, MS, PhD); Precambrian geology (M Eng, MS, PhD); Quaternary geology (M Eng, MS, PhD); rock mechanics (M Eng, MS, PhD); sedimentology (M Eng, MS, PhD); seismology (M Eng, MS, PhD); stratigraphy (M Eng, MS, PhD); structural geology (M Eng, MS, PhD). *Degree requirements:* For master's, thesis (MS); for doctorate, comprehensive exam, thesis/dissertation. *Entrance requirements:* For master's and doctorate, GRE General Test, 3 letters of recommendation. Additional exam requirements/recommendations for international students: Required—TOEFL (minimum score 550 paper-based; 77 iBT). Electronic applications accepted. *Faculty research:* Geophysics, structural geology, petrology, geochemistry, geodynamics.

Dalhousie University, Faculty of Science, Department of Earth Sciences, Halifax, NS B3H 4R2, Canada. Offers M Sc, PhD. *Degree requirements:* For master's, one foreign language, thesis; for doctorate, one foreign language, thesis/dissertation. *Entrance requirements:* Additional exam requirements/recommendations for international students: Required—TOEFL, IELTS, CANTEST, CAEL, or Michigan English Language Assessment Battery. *Faculty research:* Marine geology and geophysics, Appalachian and Grenville geology, micropaleontology, geodynamics and structural geology, geochronology.

Dartmouth College, Guarini School of Graduate and Advanced Studies, Department of Earth Sciences, Hanover, NH 03755. Offers MS, PhD. *Faculty:* 12 full-time (4 women). *Students:* 22 full-time (11 women); includes 3 minority (all Asian, non-Hispanic/Latino), 5 international. Average age 26. 58 applicants, 24% accepted, 7 enrolled. In 2018, 5 master's, 3 doctorates awarded. Terminal master's awarded for partial completion of doctoral program. *Entrance requirements:* For master's and doctorate, GRE General Test, GRE Subject Test. Additional exam requirements/recommendations for international students: Required—TOEFL. *Application deadline:* For fall admission, 1/15 for domestic students. Application fee: $50. Electronic applications accepted. *Financial support:* Fellowships, research assistantships, teaching assistantships, career-related internships or fieldwork, institutionally sponsored loans, scholarships/grants, tuition waivers (full), and unspecified assistantships available. Financial award application deadline: 4/1; financial award applicants required to submit FAFSA. *Faculty research:* Geochemistry, remote sensing, geophysics, hydrology, economic geology. *Unit head:* Dr. William B. Dade, Chair, 603-646-0286. *Application contact:* Patty Alves, Department Administrator, 603-646-2373, Fax: 603-646-3922.
Website: http://www.dartmouth.edu/~earthsci/

Duke University, Nicholas School of the Environment, Durham, NC 27708. Offers earth and ocean sciences (PhD); environment (MEM, MF, PhD); marine science and conservation (PhD). *Faculty:* 50. *Students:* 365 full-time (243 women); includes 67 minority (7 Black or African American, non-Hispanic/Latino; 4 American Indian or Alaska Native, non-Hispanic/Latino; 36 Asian, non-Hispanic/Latino; 20 Hispanic/Latino), 93 international. Average age 27. 428 applicants, 83% accepted, 151 enrolled. In 2018, 181 master's awarded. *Degree requirements:* For master's, project; for doctorate, variable foreign language requirement, thesis/dissertation. *Entrance requirements:* For master's, GRE General Test, previous course work in natural or social sciences relevant to environmental interests; college calculus, college statistics, and concentration-specific prerequisites. Additional exam requirements/recommendations for international students: Required—TOEFL, IELTS. *Application deadline:* For fall admission, 12/15 priority date for domestic and international students. Application fee: $400. Electronic applications accepted. *Financial support:* Research assistantships, career-related internships or fieldwork, Federal Work-Study, institutionally sponsored loans, scholarships/grants, and unspecified assistantships available. Financial award application deadline: 12/15; financial award applicants required to submit CSS PROFILE or FAFSA. *Faculty research:* Global environmental change, energy and the environment, water resource management, ecosystem science and conservation, ecotoxicology and environmental health, business and environment, environmental economics and policy, coastal environmental management, forest resource management. *Unit head:* Sherri Nevius, Associate Dean, Student Services, 919-613-8063, E-mail: sherri.nevius@duke.edu. *Application contact:* Benjamin Spain, Associate Director of Enrollment Services, 919-684-1155, E-mail: admissions@nicholas.duke.edu.
Website: http://nicholas.duke.edu/

Eastern Michigan University, Graduate School, College of Arts and Sciences, Department of Geography and Geology, Program in Earth Science Education, Ypsilanti, MI 48197. Offers MS. *Students:* 1 (woman) part-time; minority (Hispanic/Latino). Average age 26. Application fee: $45. *Application contact:* Dr. Katherine Ryker, Program Advisor, 734-487-6712, E-mail: kryker@emich.edu.

East Tennessee State University, School of Graduate Studies, College of Arts and Sciences, Department of Geosciences, Johnson City, TN 37614-1709. Offers geographic information systems (Postbaccalaureate Certificate); geospatial analysis (MS); paleontology (MS). *Program availability:* Part-time. *Degree requirements:* For master's, thesis. *Entrance requirements:* For master's, bachelor's degree in geosciences or related discipline, minimum GPA of 3.0, three letters of recommendation, resume, two-page letter that discusses career goals and specific academic and research interests; for Postbaccalaureate Certificate, minimum undergraduate GPA of 2.5, personal essay. Additional exam requirements/recommendations for international students: Required—TOEFL (minimum score 550 paper-based; 79 iBT). Electronic applications accepted. *Faculty research:* Vertebrate paleontology; volcanology; soils and geological engineering; geological hazards stemming from volcanoes and tsunamis and the sociological responses; applications of geospatial analysis to meteorology, weather and climate, and geomorphology/watershed management; shallow surface geophysics, sedimentology, and stratigraphy.

Emporia State University, Department of Physical Sciences, Emporia, KS 66801-5415. Offers forensic science (MS); geospatial analysis (Postbaccalaureate Certificate); physical science (MS). *Program availability:* Part-time, online learning. *Degree requirements:* For master's, comprehensive exam or thesis; qualifying exam. *Entrance requirements:* For master's, appropriate undergraduate degree. Additional exam requirements/recommendations for international students: Required—TOEFL (minimum score 520 paper-based; 68 iBT). Electronic applications accepted. *Faculty research:* Bredigite, larnite, and dicalcium silicates from Marble Canyon.

Florida Atlantic University, Charles E. Schmidt College of Science, Department of Geosciences, Boca Raton, FL 33431-0991. Offers geology (MS); geosciences (PhD). *Program availability:* Part-time. *Faculty:* 18 full-time (5 women), 2 part-time/adjunct (1 woman). *Students:* 28 full-time (12 women), 34 part-time (16 women); includes 10 minority (1 Asian, non-Hispanic/Latino; 7 Hispanic/Latino; 2 Two or more races, non-Hispanic/Latino), 7 international. Average age 31. 40 applicants, 48% accepted, 11 enrolled. In 2018, 9 master's, 2 doctorates awarded. *Entrance requirements:* For master's, GRE General Test, minimum GPA of 3.0. Additional exam requirements/recommendations for international students: Required—TOEFL (minimum score 500 paper-based; 61 iBT), IELTS (minimum score 6). *Application deadline:* For fall admission, 3/15 for domestic and international students; for spring admission, 10/15 for domestic and international students. Applications are processed on a rolling basis. Application fee: $30. Electronic applications accepted. *Expenses: Tuition, area resident:* Full-time $7400; part-time $369.82 per credit. Tuition, state resident: full-time $7400; part-time $369.82 per credit. Tuition, nonresident: full-time $20,496; part-time $1024.81 per credit. *Financial support:* Research assistantships with partial tuition reimbursements, teaching assistantships with partial tuition reimbursements, career-related internships or fieldwork, Federal Work-Study, institutionally sponsored loans, and unspecified assistantships available. *Faculty research:* GIS applications, paleontology, hydrogeology, economic development. *Unit head:* Zhixiao Xie, Chair and Professor, 561-297-2852, E-mail: xie@fau.edu. *Application contact:* Tobin Hindle, Graduate Program Director, 561-297-2846, E-mail: thindle@fau.edu.
Website: http://www.geosciences.fau.edu/

Florida Institute of Technology, College of Engineering and Science, Program in Earth Remote Sensing, Melbourne, FL 32901-6975. Offers MS. *Program availability:* Part-time. In 2018, 1 master's awarded. *Degree requirements:* For master's, comprehensive exam (for some programs), thesis (with 30 credit hours) or final exam (with 33 credit hours). *Entrance requirements:* For master's, GRE, 3 letters of recommendation, resume, statement of objectives. Additional exam requirements/recommendations for international students: Required—TOEFL (minimum score 550 paper-based; 79 iBT). *Application deadline:* Applications are processed on a rolling basis. Electronic applications accepted. *Expenses: Tuition:* Full-time $22,338; part-time $1241 per credit hour. Tuition and fees vary according to degree level, campus/location and program. *Financial support:* Applicants required to submit FAFSA. *Unit head:* Dr. Thomas Waite, Department Head, 321-674-7344, E-mail: twaite@fit.edu. *Application contact:* Mike Perry, Executive Director of Admissions, 321-674-7127, E-mail: perrymj@fit.edu.
Website: https://www.fit.edu/programs/earth-remote-sensing-ms/

Florida International University, College of Arts, Sciences, and Education, Department of Earth and Environment, Miami, FL 33199. Offers earth science (PhD); environmental studies (MS); geosciences (MS, PhD); natural resources management and policy (PSM). *Program availability:* Part-time, evening/weekend. *Faculty:* 33 full-time (11 women), 15 part-time/adjunct (5 women). *Students:* 92 full-time (45 women), 6 part-time (4 women); includes 42 minority (5 Black or African American, non-Hispanic/Latino; 1 Asian, non-Hispanic/Latino; 32 Hispanic/Latino; 4 Two or more races, non-Hispanic/Latino), 22 international. Average age 30. 80 applicants, 55% accepted, 27 enrolled. In 2018, 22 master's, 4 doctorates awarded. *Degree requirements:* For master's, thesis; for doctorate, comprehensive exam, thesis/dissertation. *Entrance requirements:* For master's and doctorate, GRE General Test, 3 letters of recommendation, minimum GPA of 3.0, resume. Additional exam requirements/recommendations for international students: Required—TOEFL (minimum score 550 paper-based; 80 iBT). *Application deadline:* For fall admission, 2/15 for domestic and international students; for spring admission, 9/1 for domestic and international students. Applications are processed on a rolling basis. Application fee: $30. Electronic applications accepted. *Financial support:* Institutionally sponsored loans and scholarships/grants available. Financial award application deadline: 3/1; financial award applicants required to submit FAFSA. *Faculty research:* Determination of dispersivity and hydraulic conductivity in the Biscayne Aquifer. *Unit head:* Dr. Rene Price, Chair, 305-348-3119, E-mail: rene.price@fiu.edu. *Application contact:* Nanett Rojas, Manager, Admissions Operations, 305-348-7464, Fax: 305-348-7441, E-mail: gradadm@fiu.edu.

Florida State University, The Graduate School, Department of Anthropology, Department of Scientific Computing, Tallahassee, FL 32306-4120. Offers computational science (MS, PhD), including atmospheric science (PhD), biochemistry (PhD), biological science (PhD), computational science (PhD), geological science (PhD), materials science (PhD), physics (PhD). *Program availability:* Part-time. *Faculty:* 9 full-time (1 woman), 2 part-time/adjunct (1 woman). *Students:* 34 full-time (6 women); includes 17 minority (10 Asian, non-Hispanic/Latino; 3 Hispanic/Latino; 4 Two or more races, non-Hispanic/Latino), 13 international. Average age 26. 64 applicants, 23% accepted, 6 enrolled. In 2018, 10 master's, 8 doctorates awarded. Terminal master's awarded for partial completion of doctoral program. *Degree requirements:* For master's, comprehensive exam, thesis (for some programs); for doctorate, comprehensive exam, thesis/dissertation. *Entrance requirements:* For master's and doctorate, GRE General Test, knowledge of at least one object-oriented computing language, 3 letters of recommendation, resume, statement of purpose. Additional exam requirements/recommendations for international students: Required—TOEFL (minimum score 550 paper-based; 80 iBT). *Application deadline:* For fall admission, 1/15 for domestic and international students. Applications are processed on a rolling basis. Application fee: $30. Electronic applications accepted. *Expenses: Tuition, area resident:* Part-time $479.32 per credit hour. Tuition and fees vary according to campus/location and program. *Financial support:* In 2018–19, 32 students received support, including 10 research assistantships with full tuition reimbursements available (averaging $26,670 per year), 23 teaching assistantships with full tuition reimbursements available (averaging $23,000 per year); scholarships/grants, health care benefits, tuition waivers (full), and unspecified assistantships also available. Financial award application deadline: 1/15. *Faculty research:* Morphometrics, mathematical and systems biology, mining proteomic and metabolic data, computational materials research, computational fluid dynamics, astrophysics, deep learning, computational neuroscience. *Total annual research expenditures:* $500,000. *Unit head:* Dr. Gordon Erlebacher, Chair, 850-644-7024, E-mail: gerlebacher@fsu.edu. *Application contact:* Karey Fowler, Academic Program Specialist, 850-644-0143, Fax: 850-644-0098, E-mail: kgfowler@fsu.edu. Website: http://www.sc.fsu.edu

Fort Hays State University, Graduate School, Peter Werth College of Science, Technology and Mathematics, Department of Geosciences, Program in Geosciences, Hays, KS 67601-4099. Offers geography (MS); geology (MS). *Degree requirements:* For master's, comprehensive exam, thesis. *Entrance requirements:* For master's, GRE General Test. Additional exam requirements/recommendations for international students: Required—TOEFL (minimum score 550 paper-based). Electronic applications accepted. *Faculty research:* Cretaceous and late Cenozoic stratigraphy, sedimentation, paleontology.

George Mason University, College of Science, Department of Geography and Geoinformation Science, Fairfax, VA 22030. Offers earth system science (MS); earth systems and geoinformation sciences (PhD); environmental geoinformation science and biodiversity conservation (Certificate); geography and geoinformation science (Certificate). *Faculty:* 18 full-time (3 women), 3 part-time/adjunct (0 women). *Students:* 54 full-time (25 women), 102 part-time (31 women); includes 26 minority (5 Black or African American, non-Hispanic/Latino; 11 Asian, non-Hispanic/Latino; 8 Hispanic/Latino; 2 Two or more races, non-Hispanic/Latino), 38 international. Average age 34. 70 applicants, 91% accepted, 31 enrolled. In 2018, 28 master's, 13 doctorates, 7 other advanced degrees awarded. *Degree requirements:* For master's, comprehensive exam (for some programs), thesis (for some programs); for doctorate, comprehensive exam, thesis/dissertation. *Entrance requirements:* For master's, GRE, bachelor's degree with minimum GPA of 3.0; 2 copies of official transcripts; current resume; expanded goals statement; 3 letters of recommendation; for doctorate, GRE, bachelor's degree with minimum GPA of 3.0; 2 copies of official transcripts; 3 letters of recommendation; resume; expanded goals statement; for Certificate, GRE, baccalaureate degree with minimum GPA of 3.0; 2 official copies of transcripts; expanded goals statement; 3 letters of recommendation; resume. Additional exam requirements/recommendations for international students: Required—TOEFL (minimum score 575 paper-based; 88 iBT), IELTS (minimum score 6.5), PTE (minimum score 59). *Application deadline:* For fall admission, 2/1 priority date for domestic and international students. Application fee: $75 ($80 for international students). Electronic applications accepted. *Expenses:* $689 per credit in-state tuition, $1,546.75 per credit out-of-state tuition. *Financial support:* In 2018–19, 33 students received support, including 21 research assistantships with tuition reimbursements available (averaging $17,476 per year), 12 teaching assistantships with tuition reimbursements available (averaging $13,918 per year); career-related internships or fieldwork, Federal Work-Study, scholarships/grants, unspecified assistantships, and health care benefits (for full-time research or teaching assistantship recipients) also available. Support available to part-time students. Financial award application deadline: 3/1; financial award applicants required to submit FAFSA. *Faculty research:* Urban geography; remote sensing; spatial databases; crowdsourcing geospatial data; spatial data mining. *Total annual research expenditures:* $1.2 million. *Unit head:* Anthony Stefanidis, Acting Chair, 703-993-9237, Fax: 703-993-9230, E-mail: astefani@gmu.edu. *Application contact:* Samantha Cooke, Department Manager, 703-993-1212, E-mail: scooke4@gmu.edu. Website: http://ggs.gmu.edu/

Georgia Institute of Technology, Graduate Studies, College of Sciences, School of Earth and Atmospheric Sciences, Atlanta, GA 30332-0340. Offers MS, PhD. *Program availability:* Part-time. Terminal master's awarded for partial completion of doctoral program. *Degree requirements:* For master's, thesis optional; for doctorate, comprehensive exam, thesis/dissertation. *Entrance requirements:* For master's and doctorate, GRE. Additional exam requirements/recommendations for international students: Required—TOEFL (minimum score 550 paper-based; 79 iBT). Electronic applications accepted. *Faculty research:* Geophysics; atmospheric chemistry, aerosols and clouds; dynamics of weather and climate; geochemistry; oceanography; paleoclimate; planetary science; remote sensing.

Georgia State University, College of Arts and Sciences, Department of Geosciences, Atlanta, GA 30302-3083. Offers geographic information systems (Certificate); geography (MS); geology (MS). *Program availability:* Part-time. *Faculty:* 15 full-time (4 women), 1 (woman) part-time/adjunct. *Students:* 40 full-time (18 women), 8 part-time (5 women); includes 13 minority (6 Black or African American, non-Hispanic/Latino; 7 Two or more races, non-Hispanic/Latino), 16 international. Average age 30. 36 applicants, 72% accepted, 16 enrolled. In 2018, 16 master's, 4 other advanced degrees awarded. *Entrance requirements:* For master's and Certificate, GRE. Additional exam requirements/recommendations for international students: Required—TOEFL (minimum score 550 paper-based; 80 iBT). *Application deadline:* For fall admission, 4/15 for domestic and international students; for spring admission, 11/15 for domestic and international students. Applications are processed on a rolling basis. Application fee: $50. Electronic applications accepted. *Expenses: Tuition, area resident:* Full-time $9360; part-time $390 per credit hour. Tuition, state resident: full-time $9360; part-time $390 per credit hour. Tuition, nonresident: full-time $30,024; part-time $1251 per credit hour. International tuition: $30,024 full-time. *Required fees:* $2128. *Financial support:* In 2018–19, research assistantships with full tuition reimbursements (averaging $12,000

per year), teaching assistantships with full tuition reimbursements (averaging $6,000 per year) were awarded; fellowships, career-related internships or fieldwork, Federal Work-Study, and unspecified assistantships also available. Support available to part-time students. Financial award application deadline: 4/15; financial award applicants required to submit FAFSA. *Faculty research:* Sedimentology, mineralogy, climatology, geographic information science, hydrology. *Unit head:* Dr. Katherine Hankins, Chair, 404-413-5775, Fax: 404-413-5768, E-mail: khankins@gsu.edu. *Application contact:* Dr. Katherine Hankins, Chair, 404-413-5775, Fax: 404-413-5768, E-mail: khankins@gsu.edu. Website: http://geosciences.gsu.edu/

Georgia State University, College of Education and Human Development, Department of Middle and Secondary Education, Atlanta, GA 30302-3083. Offers curriculum and instruction (Ed D); English education (MAT); mathematics education (M Ed, MAT); middle level education (MAT); reading, language and literacy education (M Ed, MAT), including reading instruction (M Ed); science education (M Ed, MAT), including biology (MAT), broad field science (MAT), chemistry (MAT), earth science (MAT), physics (MAT); social studies education (M Ed, MAT), including economics (MAT), geography (MAT), history (MAT), political science (MAT); teaching and learning (PhD), including language and literacy, mathematics education, music education, science education, social studies education, teaching and teacher education. *Accreditation:* NCATE. *Program availability:* Part-time, evening/weekend, online learning. *Faculty:* 19 full-time (15 women), 9 part-time/adjunct (7 women). *Students:* 217 full-time (136 women), 203 part-time (140 women); includes 229 minority (156 Black or African American, non-Hispanic/Latino; 23 Asian, non-Hispanic/Latino; 31 Hispanic/Latino; 19 Two or more races, non-Hispanic/Latino), 3 international. Average age 34. 149 applicants, 60% accepted, 70 enrolled. In 2018, 112 master's, 23 doctorates awarded. *Entrance requirements:* For master's, GRE; GACE I (for initial teacher preparation programs), baccalaureate degree or equivalent, resume, goals statement, two letters of recommendation, minimum undergraduate GPA of 2.5; proof of initial teacher certification in the content area (for M Ed); for doctorate, GRE, resume, goals statement, writing sample, two letters of recommendation, minimum graduate GPA of 3.3, interview. *Application deadline:* For fall admission, 1/15 priority date for domestic and international students; for spring admission, 10/1 for domestic and international students. Application fee: $50. Electronic applications accepted. *Expenses: Tuition, area resident:* Full-time $9360; part-time $390 per credit hour. Tuition, state resident: full-time $9360; part-time $390 per credit hour. Tuition, nonresident: full-time $30,024; part-time $1251 per credit hour. International tuition: $30,024 full-time. *Required fees:* $2128. *Financial support:* In 2018–19, fellowships with full tuition reimbursements (averaging $19,667 per year), research assistantships with full tuition reimbursements (averaging $5,436 per year), teaching assistantships with full tuition reimbursements (averaging $2,779 per year) were awarded; career-related internships or fieldwork, Federal Work-Study, scholarships/grants, health care benefits, tuition waivers (full and partial), and unspecified assistantships also available. Financial award application deadline: 3/15. *Faculty research:* Teacher education in language and literacy, mathematics, science, and social studies in urban middle and secondary school settings; learning technologies in school, community, and corporate settings; multicultural education and education for social justice; urban education; international education. *Unit head:* Dr. Gertrude Marilyn Tinker Sachs, Chair, 404-413-8384, Fax: 404-413-8063, E-mail: gtinkersachs@gsu.edu. *Application contact:* Shaleen Tibbs, Administrative Specialist, 404-413-8385, Fax: 404-413-8063, E-mail: stibbs@gsu.edu. Website: http://mse.education.gsu.edu/

The Graduate Center, City University of New York, Graduate Studies, Program in Earth and Environmental Sciences, New York, NY 10016-4039. Offers PhD. *Degree requirements:* For doctorate, one foreign language, comprehensive exam, thesis/dissertation. *Entrance requirements:* For doctorate, GRE General Test. Additional exam requirements/recommendations for international students: Required—TOEFL. Electronic applications accepted.

Harvard University, Graduate School of Arts and Sciences, Department of Earth and Planetary Sciences, Cambridge, MA 02138. Offers AM, PhD. Terminal master's awarded for partial completion of doctoral program. *Degree requirements:* For doctorate, comprehensive exam, thesis/dissertation. *Entrance requirements:* For doctorate, GRE General Test. Additional exam requirements/recommendations for international students: Required—TOEFL. Electronic applications accepted. *Faculty research:* Economic geography, geochemistry, geophysics, mineralogy, crystallography.

Hunter College of the City University of New York, Graduate School, School of Education, Programs in Secondary Education, New York, NY 10065-5085. Offers biology education (MA); chemistry education (MA); earth science (MA); English education (MA); French education (MA); Italian education (MA); mathematics education (MA); physics education (MA); social studies education (MA); Spanish education (MA). *Accreditation:* NCATE. *Degree requirements:* For master's, thesis. *Entrance requirements:* Additional exam requirements/recommendations for international students: Required—TOEFL.

Idaho State University, Graduate School, College of Science and Engineering, Department of Geosciences, Pocatello, ID 83209-8072. Offers geographic information science (MS); geology (MNS, MS); geology with emphasis in environmental geoscience (MS); geophysics/hydrology/geology (MS); geotechnology (Postbaccalaureate Certificate). *Program availability:* Part-time. *Degree requirements:* For master's, comprehensive exam, thesis, oral colloquium; for Postbaccalaureate Certificate, thesis optional, minimum 19 credits. *Entrance requirements:* For master's, GRE General Test (minimum 50th percentile in 2 sections), 3 letters of recommendation; for Postbaccalaureate Certificate, GRE General Test, 3 letters of recommendation, bachelor's degree, statement of goals. Additional exam requirements/recommendations for international students: Required—TOEFL (minimum score 550 paper-based; 80 iBT). Electronic applications accepted. *Faculty research:* Quantitative field mapping and sampling: microscopic, geochemical, and isotopic analysis of rocks, minerals and water; remote sensing, geographic information systems, and global positioning systems: environmental and watershed management; surficial and fluvial processes: landscape change; regional tectonics, structural geology; planetary geology.

Indiana University Bloomington, University Graduate School, College of Arts and Sciences, Department of Earth and Atmospheric Sciences, Bloomington, IN 47405-7000. Offers biogeochemistry (MS, PhD); economic geology (MS, PhD); geobiology (MS, PhD); geophysics, structural geology and tectonics (MS, PhD); hydrogeology (MS, PhD); mineralogy (MS, PhD); stratigraphy and sedimentology (MS, PhD). Terminal master's awarded for partial completion of doctoral program. *Degree requirements:* For master's, thesis or alternative; for doctorate, comprehensive exam, thesis/dissertation. *Entrance requirements:* For master's and doctorate, GRE General Test. Additional exam requirements/recommendations for international students: Required—TOEFL. *Faculty research:* Geophysics, geochemistry, hydrogeology, geobiology, planetary science.

Indiana University–Purdue University Indianapolis, School of Science, Department of Earth Sciences, Indianapolis, IN 46202-3272. Offers applied earth sciences (PhD);

Peterson's Graduate Programs in the Physical Sciences, Mathematics, Agricultural Sciences, the Environment & Natural Resources 2020

www.petersons.com **103**

geology (MS). *Program availability:* Part-time, evening/weekend. *Degree requirements:* For master's, thesis (for some programs). *Entrance requirements:* For master's, GRE General Test, minimum GPA of 3.0. *Faculty research:* Wetland hydrology, groundwater contamination, soils, sedimentology, sediment chemistry.

Iowa State University of Science and Technology, Department of Geological and Atmospheric Sciences, Ames, IA 50011. Offers earth science (MS, PhD); environmental science (MS, PhD); geology (MS, PhD); meteorology (MS, PhD). *Degree requirements:* For master's, thesis (for some programs); for doctorate, thesis/dissertation. *Entrance requirements:* For master's and doctorate, GRE General Test. Additional exam requirements/recommendations for international students: Required—TOEFL (minimum score 550 paper-based; 79 iBT), IELTS (minimum score 6.5). Electronic applications accepted.

Iowa State University of Science and Technology, Program in Earth Science, Ames, IA 50011. Offers MS, PhD. *Entrance requirements:* For master's and doctorate, GRE. Additional exam requirements/recommendations for international students: Required—TOEFL (minimum score 550 paper-based; 79 iBT), IELTS (minimum score 6.5). Electronic applications accepted.

Jackson State University, Graduate School, College of Science, Engineering and Technology, Department of Physics, Atmospheric Sciences, and Geoscience, Jackson, MS 39217. Offers physical science (MS, PhD); science education (MST). *Program availability:* Part-time, evening/weekend. *Degree requirements:* For master's, comprehensive exam. *Entrance requirements:* For master's, GRE General Test. Additional exam requirements/recommendations for international students: Required—TOEFL (minimum score 520 paper-based; 67 iBT).

Johns Hopkins University, Zanvyl Krieger School of Arts and Sciences, The Morton K. Blaustein Department of Earth and Planetary Sciences, Baltimore, MD 21218. Offers MA, PhD. *Faculty:* 21 full-time (10 women). *Students:* 40 full-time (22 women). 56 applicants, 21% accepted, 4 enrolled. In 2018, 8 master's, 7 doctorates awarded. *Degree requirements:* For doctorate, comprehensive exam, thesis/dissertation. *Entrance requirements:* For master's and doctorate, GRE General Test. Additional exam requirements/recommendations for international students: Required—TOEFL (minimum score 600 paper-based; 100 iBT), IELTS. *Application deadline:* For fall admission, 1/15 for domestic and international students. Application fee: $75. Electronic applications accepted. *Financial support:* Fellowships with full tuition reimbursements, research assistantships with full tuition reimbursements, teaching assistantships with full tuition reimbursements, institutionally sponsored loans, scholarships/grants, traineeships, health care benefits, tuition waivers (full), and unspecified assistantships available. Financial award application deadline: 4/15; financial award applicants required to submit FAFSA. *Faculty research:* Oceanography, atmospheric sciences, geophysics, geology, geochemistry. *Unit head:* Dr. Anand Gnanadesikan, Chair, 410-516-0722, E-mail: gnanades@jhu.edu. *Application contact:* Richard Helman, Director of Graduate Admissions, 410-516-7125, E-mail: rhelman@jhu.edu.
Website: http://eps.jhu.edu/

Lehigh University, College of Arts and Sciences, Department of Earth and Environmental Sciences, Bethlehem, PA 18015. Offers MS, PhD. *Faculty:* 15 full-time (3 women). *Students:* 21 full-time (9 women); includes 1 minority (Hispanic/Latino), 5 international. Average age 31. 24 applicants, 33% accepted, 4 enrolled. In 2018, 2 master's, 1 doctorate awarded. Terminal master's awarded for partial completion of doctoral program. *Degree requirements:* For master's, thesis; for doctorate, thesis/dissertation. *Entrance requirements:* For master's and doctorate, GRE General Test, transcripts, recommendation letters, research statement, faculty advocates. Additional exam requirements/recommendations for international students: Required—TOEFL (minimum score 85 iBT). *Application deadline:* For fall admission, 1/1 for domestic and international students. Application fee: $75. Tuition and fees vary according to program. *Financial support:* In 2018–19, 14 students received support, including 6 fellowships with full tuition reimbursements available (averaging $21,310 per year), 10 research assistantships with partial tuition reimbursements available (averaging $21,310 per year), 18 teaching assistantships with full tuition reimbursements available (averaging $21,310 per year); scholarships/grants also available. Financial award application deadline: 1/1. *Faculty research:* Geochemistry, petrology, climate modeling, seismology, geomorphology, tectonics, surficial processes, ecology, environmental change, remote sensing. *Total annual research expenditures:* $851,337. *Unit head:* Dr. Gray E. Bebout, Chairman, 610-758-5831, Fax: 610-758-3677, E-mail: geb0@lehigh.edu. *Application contact:* Dr. Robert K. Booth, Graduate Coordinator, 610-758-6580, Fax: 610-758-3677, E-mail: rkb205@lehigh.edu.
Website: http://www.ees.lehigh.edu/

Long Island University–LIU Post, College of Liberal Arts and Sciences, Brookville, NY 11548-1300. Offers applied mathematics (MS); behavior analysis (MA); biology (MS); criminal justice (MS); earth science (MS); English (MA); environmental sustainability (MS); genetic counseling (MS); history (MA); interdisciplinary studies (MA, MS); political science (MA); psychology (MA). *Program availability:* Part-time, evening/weekend, blended/hybrid learning. Terminal master's awarded for partial completion of doctoral program. *Degree requirements:* For master's, comprehensive exam (for some programs), thesis (for some programs). *Entrance requirements:* Additional exam requirements/recommendations for international students: Required—TOEFL, IELTS, or PTE. Electronic applications accepted. *Faculty research:* Biology, environmental sustainability, mathematics, psychology, genetic counseling.

Manhattanville College, School of Education, Program in Middle Childhood/Adolescence Education (Grades 5-12), Purchase, NY 10577-2132. Offers biology and special education (MPS); chemistry and special education (MPS); education for sustainability (Advanced Certificate); English and special education (MPS); literacy and special education (MPS); literacy specialist (MPS); math and special education (MPS); mathematics (Advanced Certificate); middle childhood/adolescence ed science (biology or chemistry grades 5-12) or (physics grades 7-12) (MAT); middle childhood/adolescence education (grades 5-12) English (MAT, Advanced Certificate); middle childhood/adolescence education (grades 5-12) mathematics (MAT, Advanced Certificate); middle childhood/adolescence education (grades 5-12) science (biology chemistry, physics, earth science) (Advanced Certificate); middle childhood/adolescence education (grades 5-12) social studies (MAT, Advanced Certificate); physics (MAT, Advanced Certificate); social studies (MAT); social studies and special education (MPS); special education generalist (MPS). *Program availability:* Part-time, evening/weekend. *Faculty:* 3 full-time (2 women), 9 part-time/adjunct (4 women). *Students:* 11 full-time (6 women), 17 part-time (12 women); includes 3 minority (1 Black or African American, non-Hispanic/Latino; 2 Hispanic/Latino). Average age 31. 17 applicants, 71% accepted, 7 enrolled. In 2018, 8 master's, 3 other advanced degrees awarded. *Degree requirements:* For master's, comprehensive exam (for some programs), thesis (for some programs), student teaching, research seminars, portfolios, internships, writing assessment; for Advanced Certificate, comprehensive exam (for some programs). *Entrance requirements:* For master's, for programs leading to certification, candidates must submit scores from GRE or MAT(Miller Analogies Test), minimum undergraduate GPA of 3.0, all transcripts from all colleges and universities attended, 2 letters of recommendation, interview, essay (2-3 page personal statement that describes reasons for choosing education as profession and personal philosophy of education), proof of immunization (for those born after 1957). Additional exam requirements/recommendations for international students: Required—TOEFL (minimum score 600 paper-based; 110 iBT); Recommended—IELTS (minimum score 8). *Application deadline:* Applications are processed on a rolling basis. Application fee: $75. Electronic applications accepted. *Expenses:* 935 per credit. *Financial support:* Teaching assistantships, career-related internships or fieldwork, Federal Work-Study, institutionally sponsored loans, scholarships/grants, and unspecified assistantships available. Financial award application deadline: 3/15; financial award applicants required to submit FAFSA. *Faculty research:* Education for sustainability. *Unit head:* Dr. Shelley Wepner, Dean, 914-323-3153, Fax: 914-323-5493, E-mail: Shelley.Wepner@mville.edu. *Application contact:* Alissa Wilson, Director, Graduate Admissions, 914-323-3150, Fax: 914-694-1732, E-mail: edschool@mville.edu.
Website: http://www.mville.edu/programs#/search/19

Massachusetts Institute of Technology, School of Science, Department of Earth, Atmospheric, and Planetary Sciences, Cambridge, MA 02139. Offers atmospheric chemistry (PhD, Sc D); atmospheric science (SM, PhD, Sc D); chemical oceanography (SM, PhD, Sc D); climate physics and chemistry (SM, PhD, Sc D); earth and planetary sciences (SM); geochemistry (PhD, Sc D); geology (PhD, Sc D); geophysics (PhD, Sc D); marine geology and geophysics (SM, PhD, Sc D); physical oceanography (SM, PhD, Sc D); planetary sciences (PhD, Sc D). Terminal master's awarded for partial completion of doctoral program. *Degree requirements:* For master's, thesis; for doctorate, comprehensive exam, thesis/dissertation. *Entrance requirements:* For master's and doctorate, GRE General Test. Additional exam requirements/recommendations for international students: Required—TOEFL, IELTS. Electronic applications accepted. *Expenses: Tuition:* Full-time $51,520; part-time $800 per credit hour. *Required fees:* $312. *Faculty research:* Earth: origin, composition, structure, and dynamics of (and interactions between) the atmosphere, oceans, surface, and interior of the earth; planets: formation, dynamics, and evolution of planetary systems and the characterization of exoplanets; climate: characterization of past, present, and potential future climates; studies of the causes and consequences of climate change; life: co-evolution of life and environmental systems.

McGill University, Faculty of Graduate and Postdoctoral Studies, Faculty of Science, Department of Earth and Planetary Sciences, Montréal, QC H3A 2T5, Canada. Offers M Sc, PhD.

McMaster University, School of Graduate Studies, Faculty of Science, School of Geography and Earth Sciences, Hamilton, ON L8S 4M2, Canada. Offers geochemistry (PhD); geology (M Sc, PhD); human geography (MA, PhD); physical geography (M Sc, PhD). *Program availability:* Part-time. Terminal master's awarded for partial completion of doctoral program. *Degree requirements:* For master's, thesis; for doctorate, comprehensive exam, thesis/dissertation. *Entrance requirements:* For master's, minimum B+ average. Additional exam requirements/recommendations for international students: Required—TOEFL (minimum score 550 paper-based).

Memorial University of Newfoundland, School of Graduate Studies, Department of Earth Sciences, St. John's, NL A1C 5S7, Canada. Offers geology (M Sc, PhD); geophysics (M Sc, PhD). *Program availability:* Part-time. *Degree requirements:* For master's, thesis; for doctorate, comprehensive exam, thesis/dissertation, oral thesis defense, entry evaluation. *Entrance requirements:* For master's, honors B Sc; for doctorate, M Sc. Electronic applications accepted. *Faculty research:* Geochemistry, sedimentology, paleoceanography and global change, mineral deposits, petroleum geology, hydrology.

Michigan State University, The Graduate School, College of Natural Science, Department of Earth and Environmental Sciences, East Lansing, MI 48824. Offers environmental geosciences (MS, PhD); environmental geosciences-environmental toxicology (PhD); geological sciences (MS, PhD). *Degree requirements:* For master's, thesis (for those without prior thesis work); for doctorate, thesis/dissertation. *Entrance requirements:* For master's, GRE General Test, minimum GPA of 3.0, course work in geoscience, 3 letters of recommendation; for doctorate, GRE General Test, 3 letters of recommendation. Additional exam requirements/recommendations for international students: Required—TOEFL (minimum score 550 paper-based), Michigan State University ELT (minimum score 85), Michigan English Language Assessment Battery (minimum score 83). Electronic applications accepted. *Faculty research:* Water in the environment, global and biological change, crystal dynamics.

Middle Tennessee State University, College of Graduate Studies, College of Liberal Arts, Department of Geosciences, Murfreesboro, TN 37132. Offers Graduate Certificate. *Program availability:* Part-time, evening/weekend, online learning. *Entrance requirements:* Additional exam requirements/recommendations for international students: Required—TOEFL (minimum score 525 paper-based; 71 iBT) or IELTS (minimum score 6). Electronic applications accepted.

Mississippi State University, College of Arts and Sciences, Department of Geosciences, Mississippi State, MS 39762. Offers applied meteorology (MS); broadcast meteorology (MS); earth and atmospheric science (PhD); environmental geosciences (MS); geography (MS); geology (MS); geospatial sciences (MS); professional meteorology/climatology (MS); teachers in geosciences (MS). *Program availability:* Blended/hybrid learning. *Faculty:* 20 full-time (6 women), 1 part-time/adjunct (0 women). *Students:* 62 full-time (21 women), 204 part-time (87 women); includes 44 minority (12 Black or African American, non-Hispanic/Latino; 1 American Indian or Alaska Native, non-Hispanic/Latino; 1 Asian, non-Hispanic/Latino; 25 Hispanic/Latino; 1 Native Hawaiian or other Pacific Islander, non-Hispanic/Latino; 4 Two or more races, non-Hispanic/Latino), 16 international. Average age 33. 130 applicants, 84% accepted, 89 enrolled. In 2018, 76 master's, 4 doctorates awarded. *Degree requirements:* For master's, thesis (for some programs), comprehensive oral or written exam; for doctorate, thesis/dissertation, comprehensive oral or written exam. *Entrance requirements:* For master's, GRE (for on-campus applicants), minimum undergraduate GPA of 2.75; for doctorate, thesis-based MS with background in one department emphasis area. Additional exam requirements/recommendations for international students: Required—TOEFL (minimum score 477 paper-based; 53 iBT); Recommended—IELTS (minimum score 4.5). *Application deadline:* For fall admission, 7/1 for domestic students, 5/1 for international students; for spring admission, 11/1 for domestic students, 9/1 for international students. Applications are processed on a rolling basis. Application fee: $60 ($80 for international students). Electronic applications accepted. *Expenses:* Tuition, state resident: full-time $8450; part-time $360.59 per credit hour. Tuition, nonresident: full-time $23,140; part-time $969.09 per credit hour. *Required fees:* $110. One-time fee: $55 full-time. Part-time tuition and fees vary according to course load, degree level, campus/location and reciprocity agreements. *Financial support:* In 2018–19, 7 research assistantships with full tuition reimbursements (averaging $16,483 per year), 28 teaching assistantships with full tuition reimbursements (averaging $19,000 per year) were awarded; Federal Work-Study, institutionally sponsored loans,

scholarships/grants, tuition waivers (partial), and unspecified assistantships also available. Financial award application deadline: 4/1; financial award applicants required to submit FAFSA. *Faculty research:* Climatology, hydrogeology, sedimentology, meteorology. *Total annual research expenditures:* $8.9 million. *Unit head:* Dr. John C. Rodgers, III, Professor and Interim Head, 662-325-1032, Fax: 662-325-9423, E-mail: jcr100@msstate.edu. *Application contact:* Nathan Drake, Admissions and Enrollment Assistant, 662-325-3804, E-mail: ndrake@grad.msstate.edu.
Website: http://www.geosciences.msstate.edu

Missouri State University, Graduate College, College of Natural and Applied Sciences, Department of Geography, Geology, and Planning, Springfield, MO 65897. Offers geography, geology, and planning (Certificate); natural and applied science (MNAS), including geography, geology and planning; secondary education (MS Ed), including earth science, physical geography. *Program availability:* Part-time, evening/weekend. *Faculty:* 18 full-time (4 women), 1 part-time/adjunct (0 women). *Students:* 24 full-time (10 women), 10 part-time (5 women); includes 2 minority (1 Hispanic/Latino; 1 Two or more races, non-Hispanic/Latino), 5 international. Average age 25. 26 applicants, 50% accepted. In 2018, 8 master's awarded. *Degree requirements:* For master's, comprehensive exam, thesis (for some programs). *Entrance requirements:* For master's, GRE General Test (MS, MNAS), minimum undergraduate GPA of 3.0 (MS, MNAS), 9-12 teacher certification (MS Ed). Additional exam requirements/recommendations for international students: Required—TOEFL (minimum score 550 paper-based; 79 iBT), IELTS (minimum score 6). *Application deadline:* For fall admission, 7/20 priority date for domestic students, 5/1 for international students; for spring admission, 12/20 priority date for domestic students, 9/1 for international students. Applications are processed on a rolling basis. Application fee: $55 ($60 for international students). Electronic applications accepted. Tuition and fees vary according to class time, course level, course load, degree level, campus/location, program and student level. *Financial support:* In 2018–19, 3 research assistantships with full tuition reimbursements (averaging $11,574 per year), 15 teaching assistantships with full tuition reimbursements (averaging $9,365 per year) were awarded; career-related internships or fieldwork, Federal Work-Study, institutionally sponsored loans, scholarships/grants, and unspecified assistantships also available. Financial award application deadline: 1/31; financial award applicants required to submit FAFSA. *Faculty research:* Stratigraphy and ancient meteorite impacts, environmental geochemistry of karst, hyperspectral image processing, water quality, small town planning. *Unit head:* Dr. Toby Dogwiler, Department Head, 417-836-5800, Fax: 417-836-6934, E-mail: tobydogwiler@missouristate.edu. *Application contact:* Lakan Drinker, Director, Graduate Enrollment Management, 417-836-5330, Fax: 417-836-6200, E-mail: lakandrinker@missouristate.edu.
Website: http://geosciences.missouristate.edu/

Montana State University, The Graduate School, College of Letters and Science, Department of Earth Sciences, Bozeman, MT 59717. Offers MS, PhD. *Program availability:* Part-time. *Degree requirements:* For master's, comprehensive exam, thesis (for some programs); for doctorate, comprehensive exam, thesis/dissertation. *Entrance requirements:* For master's and doctorate, GRE General Test, minimum GPA of 3.0. Additional exam requirements/recommendations for international students: Required—TOEFL (minimum score 550 paper-based). Electronic applications accepted. *Faculty research:* Dinosaur paleontology, climate history/geomicrobiology, stratigraphy/sedimentology/structure/carbon sequestration, igneous petrology South America, historical/urban economic geography western U.S. and China.

Montana Tech of The University of Montana, Geosciences Programs, Butte, MT 59701-8997. Offers geochemistry (MS); geological engineering (MS); geology (MS); geophysical engineering (MS); hydrogeological engineering (MS); hydrogeology (MS). *Program availability:* Part-time. *Degree requirements:* For master's, comprehensive exam (for some programs), thesis (for some programs). *Entrance requirements:* For master's, GRE General Test, minimum GPA of 3.0. Additional exam requirements/recommendations for international students: Required—TOEFL (minimum score 545 paper-based; 78 iBT), IELTS (minimum score 6.5). Electronic applications accepted. *Faculty research:* Water resource development, seismic processing, petroleum reservoir characterization, environmental geochemistry, geologic mapping.

Montclair State University, The Graduate School, College of Science and Mathematics, Program in Earth and Environmental Science, Montclair, NJ 07043-1624. Offers MS. *Program availability:* Part-time, evening/weekend. *Degree requirements:* For master's, comprehensive exam, thesis or alternative. *Entrance requirements:* For master's, GRE General Test, 2 letters of recommendation, essay. Additional exam requirements/recommendations for international students: Required—TOEFL (minimum score 83 iBT) or IELTS (minimum score 6.5). Electronic applications accepted. *Faculty research:* Environmental geochemistry/remediation/forensics, environmental law and policy, regional climate modeling, remote sensing, Cenozoic marine sediment records from polar regions, sustainability science.

Montclair State University, The Graduate School, College of Science and Mathematics, Program in Geoscience, Montclair, NJ 07043-1624. Offers MS. *Program availability:* Part-time, evening/weekend. *Degree requirements:* For master's, thesis. *Entrance requirements:* Additional exam requirements/recommendations for international students: Required—TOEFL (minimum score 83 iBT), IELTS (minimum score 6.5). Electronic applications accepted. *Faculty research:* Environmental geochemistry, flood hydrology, geomorphology and weathering processes, regional climate modeling, remote sensing, Cenozoic marine sediment records from polar regions, igneous and metamorphic petrology.

Murray State University, Jesse D. Jones College of Science, Engineering and Technology, Department of Earth and Environmental Sciences, Murray, KY 42071. Offers geosciences (MS); geospatial data science (Certificate). *Program availability:* Part-time. *Entrance requirements:* For master's and Certificate, GRE or GMAT, minimum university GPA of 2.75. Additional exam requirements/recommendations for international students: Required—TOEFL (minimum score 527 paper-based; 71 iBT). Electronic applications accepted.

New Mexico Institute of Mining and Technology, Center for Graduate Studies, Department of Earth and Environmental Science, Socorro, NM 87801. Offers geochemistry (MS, PhD); geology (MS, PhD); geophysics (MS, PhD); hydrology (MS, PhD). *Degree requirements:* For master's, thesis optional; for doctorate, thesis/dissertation. *Entrance requirements:* For master's, GRE General Test; for doctorate, GRE General Test, GRE Subject Test. Additional exam requirements/recommendations for international students: Required—TOEFL. *Faculty research:* Seismology, geochemistry, caves and karst topography, hydrology, volcanology.

North Carolina Central University, College of Arts and Sciences, Department of Environmental, Earth and Geospatial Sciences, Durham, NC 27707-3129. Offers earth sciences (MS); environmental and geographic sciences (MS). *Degree requirements:* For master's, one foreign language, comprehensive exam. *Entrance requirements:* For master's, GRE, minimum GPA of 3.0 in major, 2.5 overall. Additional exam requirements/recommendations for international students: Required—TOEFL.

North Carolina State University, Graduate School, College of Sciences, Department of Marine, Earth, and Atmospheric Sciences, Raleigh, NC 27695. Offers marine, earth, and atmospheric sciences (MS, PhD); meteorology (MS, PhD); oceanography (MS, PhD). PhD offered jointly with The University of North Carolina Wilmington. Terminal master's awarded for partial completion of doctoral program. *Degree requirements:* For master's, thesis (for some programs), final oral exam; for doctorate, comprehensive exam, thesis/dissertation, final oral exam, preliminary oral and written exams. *Entrance requirements:* For master's, GRE General Test, minimum GPA of 3.0; for doctorate, GRE General Test, GRE Subject Test (for disciplines in biological oceanography and geology), minimum GPA of 3.0. Additional exam requirements/recommendations for international students: Required—TOEFL (minimum score 550 paper-based). Electronic applications accepted. *Faculty research:* Boundary layer and air quality meteorology; climate and mesoscale dynamics; biological, chemical, geological, and physical oceanography; hard rock, soft rock, environmental, and paleo-geology.

Northwestern University, The Graduate School, Judd A. and Marjorie Weinberg College of Arts and Sciences, Department of Earth and Planetary Sciences, Evanston, IL 60208. Offers PhD. Admissions and degrees offered through The Graduate School. *Program availability:* Part-time. *Degree requirements:* For doctorate, thesis/dissertation. *Entrance requirements:* For doctorate, GRE General Test. Additional exam requirements/recommendations for international students: Required—TOEFL. Electronic applications accepted.

The Ohio State University, Graduate School, College of Arts and Sciences, Division of Natural and Mathematical Sciences, School of Earth Sciences, Columbus, OH 43210. Offers earth sciences (MS, PhD); geodetic science (MS, PhD); geological sciences (MS, PhD). *Faculty:* 27. *Students:* 67 (27 women). Average age 28. In 2018, 18 master's, 12 doctorates awarded. *Entrance requirements:* For master's, GRE, undergraduate degree in biological science, geological sciences, physical science or engineering (recommended); minimum GPA of 3.2; for doctorate, GRE, undergraduate degree in biological science, geological sciences, physical science or engineering (recommended); minimum GPA of 3.4. Additional exam requirements/recommendations for international students: Required—TOEFL (minimum score 550 paper-based; 79 iBT), Michigan English Language Assessment Battery (minimum score 82); Recommended—IELTS (minimum score 8). *Application deadline:* For fall admission, 12/13 priority date for domestic students, 11/30 priority date for international students; for spring admission, 11/30 for domestic and international students; for summer admission, 7/24 for domestic students, 3/13 for international students. Applications are processed on a rolling basis. Application fee: $60 ($70 for international students). Electronic applications accepted. *Financial support:* Fellowships, research assistantships, and teaching assistantships available. *Unit head:* Dr. Matthew Saltzman, Director, 614-292-0481, Fax: 614-292-7688, E-mail: saltzman.11@osu.edu. *Application contact:* Graduate and Professional Admissions, 614-292-9444, Fax: 614-292-3895, E-mail: gpadmissions@osu.edu.
Website: http://earthsciences.osu.edu/

Pace University, School of Education, New York, NY 10038. Offers adolescent education (MST), including biology, chemistry, earth science, English, foreign languages, mathematics, physics, social studies; childhood education (MST); early childhood development, learning and intervention (MST); educational technology studies (MS); inclusive adolescent education (MST), including biology, chemistry, earth science, English, foreign languages, mathematics, physics, social studies; integrated instruction for educational technology (Certificate); integrated instruction for literacy and technology (Certificate); literacy (MS Ed); special education (MS Ed). *Accreditation:* NCATE. *Program availability:* Part-time, evening/weekend, 100% online, blended/hybrid learning. *Faculty:* 19 full-time (13 women), 86 part-time/adjunct (49 women). *Students:* 98 full-time (82 women), 542 part-time (391 women); includes 256 minority (116 Black or African American, non-Hispanic/Latino; 2 American Indian or Alaska Native, non-Hispanic/Latino; 45 Asian, non-Hispanic/Latino; 83 Hispanic/Latino; 10 Two or more races, non-Hispanic/Latino), 4 international. Average age 30. 223 applicants, 89% accepted, 130 enrolled. In 2018, 269 master's, 12 other advanced degrees awarded. *Degree requirements:* For master's and Certificate, certification exams. *Entrance requirements:* For master's, GRE (for initial certification programs only), teaching certificate (for MS Ed in literacy and special education programs only). Additional exam requirements/recommendations for international students: Required—TOEFL (minimum score 88 iBT), IELTS or PTE. *Application deadline:* For fall admission, 8/1 priority date for domestic students, 6/1 for international students; for spring admission, 12/1 priority date for domestic students, 10/1 for international students. Applications are processed on a rolling basis. Application fee: $70. Electronic applications accepted. *Expenses:* Contact institution. *Financial support:* In 2018–19, 17 students received support, including 17 research assistantships with partial tuition reimbursements available (averaging $6,020 per year); career-related internships or fieldwork, Federal Work-Study, scholarships/grants, and unspecified assistantships also available. Financial award application deadline: 9/1; financial award applicants required to submit FAFSA. *Faculty research:* STEM education, TESOL, teacher education, special education, language and literary development. *Total annual research expenditures:* $1.4 million. *Unit head:* Dr. Harriet Feldman, Dean, School of Education, 914-773-3829, E-mail: hfeldman@pace.edu. *Application contact:* Susan Ford-Goldschein, Director of Graduate Admissions, 212-346-1531, Fax: 212-346-1585, E-mail: graduateadmission@pace.edu.
Website: http://www.pace.edu/school-of-education

Penn State University Park, Graduate School, College of Earth and Mineral Sciences, Department of Geosciences, University Park, PA 16802. Offers geosciences (MS, PhD).

Princeton University, Graduate School, Department of Geosciences, Princeton, NJ 08544-1019. Offers atmospheric and oceanic sciences (PhD); geosciences (PhD); ocean sciences and marine biology (PhD). *Degree requirements:* For doctorate, one foreign language, thesis/dissertation. *Entrance requirements:* For doctorate, GRE General Test. Additional exam requirements/recommendations for international students: Required—TOEFL (minimum score 600 paper-based). Electronic applications accepted. *Faculty research:* Biogeochemistry, climate science, earth history, regional geology and tectonics, solid–earth geophysics.

Purdue University, Graduate School, College of Science, Department of Earth and Atmospheric Sciences, West Lafayette, IN 47907. Offers MS, PhD. *Faculty:* 33 full-time (9 women). *Students:* 67 full-time (31 women), 2 part-time (0 women); includes 7 minority (3 American Indian or Alaska Native, non-Hispanic/Latino; 2 Asian, non-Hispanic/Latino; 1 Hispanic/Latino; 1 Two or more races, non-Hispanic/Latino), 28 international. Average age 27. 130 applicants, 25% accepted, 21 enrolled. In 2018, 14 master's, 12 doctorates awarded. *Degree requirements:* For master's, comprehensive exam, thesis; for doctorate, one foreign language, comprehensive exam, thesis/dissertation. *Entrance requirements:* For master's, GRE General Test, minimum undergraduate GPA of 3.0 or equivalent; for doctorate, GRE General Test, minimum undergraduate or master's GPA of 3.0 or equivalent. Additional exam requirements/recommendations for international students: Required—TOEFL (minimum score 550 paper-based; 77 iBT); Recommended—TWE. *Application deadline:* For fall admission, 1/2 priority date for domestic and international students; for spring admission, 9/1 for domestic and international students. Applications are processed on a rolling basis.

Application fee: $60 ($75 for international students). Electronic applications accepted. *Financial support:* Fellowships with partial tuition reimbursements, research assistantships with partial tuition reimbursements, and teaching assistantships with partial tuition reimbursements available. Support available to part-time students. Financial award application deadline: 3/1; financial award applicants required to submit FAFSA. *Faculty research:* Geology, geophysics, hydrogeology, paleoclimatology, environmental science. *Unit head:* Daniel J. Cziczo, Head of the Graduate Program, 765-494-3258, E-mail: djcziczo@purdue.edu. *Application contact:* Kathy S. Kincade, Graduate Secretary, 765-494-5984, E-mail: kkincade@purdue.edu.
Website: http://www.eas.purdue.edu

Queens College of the City University of New York, Mathematics and Natural Sciences Division, School of Earth and Environmental Sciences, Queens, NY 11367-1597. Offers applied environmental geosciences (MS); geological and environmental sciences (MA). *Program availability:* Part-time, evening/weekend. *Faculty:* 17 full-time (5 women), 16 part-time/adjunct (8 women). *Students:* 1 (woman) full-time, 14 part-time (5 women); includes 3 minority (2 Black or African American, non-Hispanic/Latino; 1 Asian, non-Hispanic/Latino), 1 international. Average age 28. 11 applicants, 73% accepted, 6 enrolled. In 2018, 11 master's awarded. *Degree requirements:* For master's, thesis (for some programs), internship (MS) or thesis (MA) required. *Entrance requirements:* For master's, previous course work in calculus, physics, geology, and chemistry; minimum GPA of 3.0. Additional exam requirements/recommendations for international students: Required—TOEFL, IELTS. *Application deadline:* For fall admission, 4/1 for domestic students; for spring admission, 11/1 for domestic students. Applications are processed on a rolling basis. Application fee: $125. Electronic applications accepted. *Financial support:* In 2018–19, 10 teaching assistantships (averaging $11,968 per year) were awarded; career-related internships or fieldwork and unspecified assistantships also available. Financial award application deadline: 4/1; financial award applicants required to submit FAFSA. *Unit head:* Jeffrey Bird, Chair, 718-997-3300, E-mail: jeffrey.bird@qc.cuny.edu. *Application contact:* Gregory O'Mullan, Graduate Advisor, 718-997-997-3452, E-mail: gomullan@qc.cuny.edu.
Website: http://www.qc.cuny.edu/Academics/Degrees/DMNS/sees/Pages/default.aspx

Rice University, Graduate Programs, Wiess School of Natural Sciences, Department of Earth Science, Houston, TX 77251-1892. Offers MS, PhD. Terminal master's awarded for partial completion of doctoral program. *Degree requirements:* For master's, comprehensive exam, thesis, annual department report and presentation, qualifying exam, orals, 2 publications; for doctorate, comprehensive exam, thesis/dissertation, annual department report and presentation, qualifying exam, orals, 3 publications. *Entrance requirements:* For master's and doctorate, GRE. Additional exam requirements/recommendations for international students: Required—TOEFL (minimum score 600 paper-based; 90 iBT), IELTS. Electronic applications accepted. *Faculty research:* Seismology, structural geology, tectonics and paleomagnetism, geodynamics, high temperature geochemistry, volcanic processes.

Rice University, Graduate Programs, Wiess School–Professional Science Master's Programs, Professional Master's Program in Subsurface Geosciences, Houston, TX 77251-1892. Offers geophysics (MS). *Program availability:* Part-time. *Degree requirements:* For master's, internship. *Entrance requirements:* For master's, GRE, letters of recommendation (4). Additional exam requirements/recommendations for international students: Required—TOEFL (minimum score 600 paper-based; 90 iBT). Electronic applications accepted. *Faculty research:* Seismology, geodynamics, wave propagation, bio-geochemistry, remote sensing.

St. Francis Xavier University, Graduate Studies, Department of Earth Sciences, Antigonish, NS B2G 2W5, Canada. Offers M Sc. *Degree requirements:* For master's, thesis. *Entrance requirements:* Additional exam requirements/recommendations for international students: Required—TOEFL (minimum score 580 paper-based). *Expenses: Tuition, area resident:* Full-time $7547 Canadian dollars. Tuition, state resident: full-time $7547 Canadian dollars; part-time $804.19 Canadian dollars per course. Tuition, nonresident: full-time $8839 Canadian dollars; part-time $932.49 Canadian dollars per course. *International tuition:* $932.49 Canadian dollars full-time. *Required fees:* $90.20 Canadian dollars; $90.20 Canadian dollars per course. One-time fee: $6 Canadian dollars. Tuition and fees vary according to course load, degree level and program. *Faculty research:* Environmental earth sciences, global change tectonics, paleoclimatology, crustal fluids.

Saint Louis University, Graduate Programs, College of Arts and Sciences, Department of Earth and Atmospheric Sciences, St. Louis, MO 63103. Offers geophysics (PhD); geoscience (MS); meteorology (M Pr Met, MS-R, PhD). *Program availability:* Part-time. *Degree requirements:* For master's, thesis (for some programs), comprehensive oral exam; for doctorate, thesis/dissertation, preliminary exams. *Entrance requirements:* For master's, GRE General Test, letters of recommendation, resume; for doctorate, GRE General Test, letters of recommendation, resumé, goal statement, transcripts. Additional exam requirements/recommendations for international students: Required—TOEFL (minimum score 525 paper-based). Electronic applications accepted. *Faculty research:* Structural geology, mesoscale meteorology and severe storms, weather and climate change prediction.

St. Thomas University, School of Leadership Studies, Institute for Education, Miami Gardens, FL 33054-6459. Offers earth/space science (Certificate); educational administration (MS, Certificate); educational leadership (Ed D); elementary education (MS); ESOL (Certificate); gifted education (Certificate); instructional technology (MS, Certificate); professional/studies (Certificate); reading (MS, Certificate); special education (MS). *Program availability:* Part-time, evening/weekend. *Degree requirements:* For master's, comprehensive exam; for doctorate, comprehensive exam, thesis/dissertation. *Entrance requirements:* For master's, interview, minimum GPA of 3.0 or GRE; for doctorate, GRE or MAT. Additional exam requirements/recommendations for international students: Required—TOEFL (minimum score 550 paper-based; 79 iBT). Electronic applications accepted.

San Francisco State University, Division of Graduate Studies, College of Science and Engineering, Department of Earth and Climate Sciences, San Francisco, CA 94132-1722. Offers geosciences (MS). *Application deadline:* Applications are processed on a rolling basis. *Unit head:* Dr. Petra Dekens, Chair, 415-338-6015, Fax: 415-338-7705, E-mail: dekens@sfsu.edu. *Application contact:* Roger Dang, Office Manager, 415-338-2993, Fax: 415-338-7705, E-mail: rogerd@sfsu.edu.
Website: http://tornado.sfsu.edu

Simon Fraser University, Office of Graduate Studies and Postdoctoral Fellows, Faculty of Science, Department of Earth Sciences, Burnaby, BC V5A 1S6, Canada. Offers M Sc, PhD. *Degree requirements:* For master's, thesis; for doctorate, comprehensive exam, thesis/dissertation. *Entrance requirements:* For master's, minimum GPA of 3.0 (on scale of 4.33) or 3.33 based on last 60 credits of undergraduate courses; for doctorate, minimum GPA of 3.5 (on scale of 4.33). Additional exam requirements/recommendations for international students: Recommended—TOEFL (minimum score 580 paper-based; 93 iBT), IELTS (minimum score 7), TWE (minimum score 5). Electronic applications accepted. *Faculty research:* Glaciology, structural geology, quaternary and environmental earth sciences, geochronology, and tectonics; exploration or earthquake seismology.

South Dakota State University, Graduate School, Geospatial Science and Engineering Program, Brookings, SD 57007. Offers PhD. *Program availability:* Part-time. *Degree requirements:* For doctorate, comprehensive exam, thesis/dissertation. *Entrance requirements:* For doctorate, GRE. Additional exam requirements/recommendations for international students: Required—TOEFL (minimum score 525 paper-based; 71 iBT). *Faculty research:* Deforestation, land use/cover change, GIS spatial modeling.

Southern Illinois University Carbondale, Graduate School, College of Science, Department of Geology, Carbondale, IL 62901-4701. Offers environmental resources and policy (PhD); geology (MS); geosciences (PhD). *Degree requirements:* For master's, thesis; for doctorate, one foreign language, thesis/dissertation. *Entrance requirements:* For master's, GRE, minimum GPA of 2.7; for doctorate, GRE General Test, minimum GPA of 3.25. Additional exam requirements/recommendations for international students: Required—TOEFL.

Stanford University, School of Earth, Energy and Environmental Sciences, Department of Earth System Science, Stanford, CA 94305-2004. Offers MS, PhD. *Expenses: Tuition:* Full-time $50,703; part-time $32,970 per year. *Required fees:* $651.

Stanford University, School of Earth, Energy and Environmental Sciences, Department of Geological Sciences, Stanford, CA 94305-2004. Offers MS, PhD, Eng. *Expenses: Tuition:* Full-time $50,703; part-time $32,970 per year. *Required fees:* $651.
Website: http://pangea.stanford.edu/departments/ges/

State University of New York at New Paltz, Graduate and Extended Learning School, School of Education, Department of Teaching and Learning, New Paltz, NY 12561. Offers adolescence education: biology (MAT, MS Ed); adolescence education: chemistry (MAT, MS Ed); adolescence education: earth science (MAT, MS Ed); adolescence education: English (MAT, MS Ed); adolescence education: French (MAT, MS Ed); adolescence education: social studies (MAT, MS Ed); adolescence education: Spanish (MAT, MS Ed); second language education (MS Ed, AC), including second language education (MS Ed), teaching English language learners (AC). *Accreditation:* NCATE. *Program availability:* Part-time, evening/weekend. *Faculty:* 21 full-time (16 women), 15 part-time/adjunct (12 women). *Students:* 127 full-time (91 women), 171 part-time (149 women); includes 48 minority (5 Black or African American, non-Hispanic/Latino; 2 Asian, non-Hispanic/Latino; 37 Hispanic/Latino; 4 Two or more races, non-Hispanic/Latino). 152 applicants, 84% accepted, 104 enrolled. In 2018, 135 master's, 19 other advanced degrees awarded. *Degree requirements:* For master's, comprehensive exam (for some programs), portfolio. *Entrance requirements:* For master's, minimum GPA of 3.0, New York state teaching certificate (MS Ed). Additional exam requirements/recommendations for international students: Required—TOEFL (minimum score 550 paper-based; 80 iBT), IELTS (minimum score 6.5). *Application deadline:* For fall admission, 3/1 priority date for domestic students, 3/1 for international students; for spring admission, 10/1 priority date for domestic students, 10/1 for international students. Application fee: $50. Electronic applications accepted. *Financial support:* Application deadline: 8/1. *Unit head:* Dr. Aaron Isabelle, Associate Dean, 845-257-2837, E-mail: isabella@newpaltz.edu. *Application contact:* Vika Shock, Director of Graduate Admissions, 845-257-3285, Fax: 845-257-3284, E-mail: gradstudies@newpaltz.edu.
Website: http://www.newpaltz.edu/secondaryed/

Stony Brook University, State University of New York, Graduate School, College of Arts and Sciences, Department of Geosciences, Stony Brook, NY 11794. Offers MAT, MS, PhD. MAT offered through the School of Professional Development. *Faculty:* 13 full-time (3 women), 2 part-time/adjunct (0 women). *Students:* 33 full-time (18 women), 9 part-time (3 women); includes 5 minority (1 Black or African American, non-Hispanic/Latino; 1 Asian, non-Hispanic/Latino; 3 Hispanic/Latino), 10 international. Average age 27. 54 applicants, 37% accepted, 8 enrolled. In 2018, 3 master's, 7 doctorates awarded. Terminal master's awarded for partial completion of doctoral program. *Entrance requirements:* For master's and doctorate, GRE General Test, minimum GPA of 3.0. Additional exam requirements/recommendations for international students: Required—TOEFL. *Application deadline:* For fall admission, 1/15 for domestic students; for spring admission, 10/1 for domestic students. Application fee: $100. Electronic applications accepted. *Expenses:* Contact institution. *Financial support:* In 2018–19, 1 fellowship, 18 research assistantships, 5 teaching assistantships were awarded. *Faculty research:* Geology, petrology, planetary studies, planetary geology, mineralogy. *Total annual research expenditures:* $2.3 million. *Unit head:* Dr. Brian Phillips, Chair, 631-632-8217, Fax: 631-632-8240, E-mail: brian.phillips@stonybrook.edu. *Application contact:* Jamie Brazier, Graduate Program Coordinator, 631-632-8554, Fax: 631-632-8240, E-mail: jamie.brazier@stonybrook.edu.
Website: http://www.geosciences.stonybrook.edu/

Teachers College, Columbia University, Department of Mathematics, Science and Technology, New York, NY 10027-6696. Offers biology 7-12 (MA); chemistry 7-12 (MA); communication and education (MA, Ed D); computing in education (MA); earth science 7-12 (MA); instructional technology and media (Ed M, MA, Ed D); mathematics education (Ed M, MA, Ed D, Ed DCT, PhD); physics 7-12 (MA); science and dental education (MA); science education (Ed M, MS, Ed DCT, PhD); supervisor/teacher of science education (MA); technology specialist (MA). *Program availability:* Part-time, evening/weekend, online learning. *Students:* 155 full-time (114 women), 254 part-time (162 women); includes 136 minority (44 Black or African American, non-Hispanic/Latino; 1 American Indian or Alaska Native, non-Hispanic/Latino; 59 Asian, non-Hispanic/Latino; 23 Hispanic/Latino; 9 Two or more races, non-Hispanic/Latino), 140 international. Average age 31. 484 applicants, 60% accepted, 138 enrolled. Terminal master's awarded for partial completion of doctoral program. *Unit head:* Prof. Erica Walker, Chair, 212-678-8246, E-mail: ewalker@tc.columbia.edu. *Application contact:* Kelly Sutton Skinner, Director of Admission & New Student Enrollment, E-mail: kms2237@tc.columbia.edu.
Website: http://www.tc.columbia.edu/mathematics-science-and-technology/

Temple University, College of Science and Technology, Department of Earth and Environmental Science, Philadelphia, PA 19122. Offers geology (MS); geoscience (PhD). *Faculty:* 12 full-time (5 women). *Students:* 17 full-time (5 women), 2 international. 26 applicants, 35% accepted, 5 enrolled. In 2018, 3 master's awarded. *Degree requirements:* For master's, comprehensive exam, thesis; for doctorate, thesis/dissertation. *Entrance requirements:* For master's, GRE, bachelor's degree in related discipline, statement of goals, 2 letters of recommendation; for doctorate, GRE, bachelor's degree in related discipline, statement of goals, 3 letters of recommendation, writing sample. Additional exam requirements/recommendations for international students: Required—TOEFL (minimum score 105 iBT), IELTS (minimum score 7), PTE (minimum score 72), one of three is required. *Application deadline:* For fall admission, 2/1 for domestic students. Application fee: $60. Electronic applications accepted. *Expenses:* Contact institution. *Financial support:* Fellowships, research assistantships, teaching assistantships, Federal Work-Study, health care benefits, and unspecified assistantships available. Financial award applicants required to submit FAFSA. *Faculty research:* Coastal dynamics, environmental geophysics, hydrogeology and groundwater contamination, nanomaterials,

paleontology-fossil provenance. *Unit head:* Nicholas Davatzes, Department Chair, 215-204-2319, E-mail: nicholas.davatzes@temple.edu. *Application contact:* Dennis Terry, Graduate Chair, 215-204-8226, E-mail: eesgrad@temple.edu.
Website: https://ees.cst.temple.edu/

Tennessee Technological University, College of Graduate Studies, College of Interdisciplinary Studies, School of Environmental Studies, Department of Environmental Sciences, Cookeville, TN 38505. Offers agriculture (PhD); biology (PhD); chemistry (PhD); geosciences (PhD); integrated research (PhD). *Program availability:* Part-time. *Students:* 3 full-time (all women), 17 part-time (6 women); includes 2 minority (1 Asian, non-Hispanic/Latino; 1 Two or more races, non-Hispanic/Latino), 5 international. 14 applicants, 29% accepted, 2 enrolled. In 2018, 3 doctorates awarded. *Degree requirements:* For doctorate, comprehensive exam, thesis/dissertation. *Entrance requirements:* For doctorate, GRE. Additional exam requirements/recommendations for international students: Required—TOEFL (minimum score 527 paper-based; 71 iBT), IELTS (minimum score 5.5), PTE (minimum score 48), or TOEIC (Test of English as an International Communication). *Application deadline:* For fall admission, 7/1 for domestic students, 5/1 for international students; for spring admission, 12/1 for domestic students, 10/2 for international students; for summer admission, 5/1 for domestic students, 2/1 for international students. Applications are processed on a rolling basis. Application fee: $35 ($40 for international students). Electronic applications accepted. *Financial support:* Fellowships, research assistantships, and teaching assistantships available. Financial award application deadline: 4/1. *Unit head:* Dr. Hayden Mattingly, Interim Director, 931-372-6246, E-mail: hmattingly@tntech.edu. *Application contact:* Shelia K. Kendrick, Coordinator of Graduate Studies, 931-372-3808, Fax: 931-372-3497, E-mail: skendrick@tntech.edu.

Texas Tech University, Graduate School, College of Arts and Sciences, Department of Geosciences, Lubbock, TX 79409-1053. Offers atmospheric science (MS); geography (MS); geosciences (MS, PhD). *Program availability:* Part-time. *Faculty:* 30 full-time (4 women), 4 part-time/adjunct (2 women). *Students:* 72 full-time (26 women), 10 part-time (3 women); includes 7 minority (1 Asian, non-Hispanic/Latino; 5 Hispanic/Latino; 1 Two or more races, non-Hispanic/Latino), 17 international. Average age 27. 95 applicants, 36% accepted, 27 enrolled. In 2018, 11 master's, 5 doctorates awarded. Terminal master's awarded for partial completion of doctoral program. *Degree requirements:* For master's, thesis; for doctorate, comprehensive exam, thesis/dissertation. *Entrance requirements:* For master's and doctorate, GRE General Test. Additional exam requirements/recommendations for international students: Required—TOEFL (minimum score 550 paper-based; 79 iBT). *Application deadline:* For fall admission, 6/1 priority date for domestic students, 1/15 priority date for international students; for spring admission, 9/1 priority date for domestic students, 6/15 priority date for international students. Applications are processed on a rolling basis. Application fee: $65. Electronic applications accepted. *Expenses:* Contact institution. *Financial support:* In 2018–19, 80 students received support, including 60 fellowships (averaging $3,178 per year), 35 research assistantships (averaging $18,032 per year), 43 teaching assistantships (averaging $15,850 per year); Federal Work-Study, scholarships/grants, health care benefits, tuition waivers (partial), and unspecified assistantships also available. Financial award application deadline: 2/15; financial award applicants required to submit FAFSA. *Faculty research:* Geology, geophysics, geochemistry, geospatial technology, atmospheric sciences. *Total annual research expenditures:* $2.8 million. *Unit head:* Dr. Kevin R. Mulligan, Associate Professor and Chair, 806-834-0391, E-mail: kevin.mulligan@ttu.edu. *Application contact:* Dr. Juske Horita, Professor, 806-834-7027, E-mail: juske.horita@ttu.edu.
Website: www.depts.ttu.edu/geosciences/

Université du Québec à Chicoutimi, Graduate Programs, Program in Earth Sciences, Chicoutimi, QC G7H 2B1, Canada. Offers M Sc A. *Program availability:* Part-time. *Degree requirements:* For master's, thesis. *Entrance requirements:* For master's, appropriate bachelor's degree, proficiency in French.

Université du Québec à Montréal, Graduate Programs, Program in Earth and Atmospheric Sciences, Montréal, QC H3C 3P8, Canada. Offers atmospheric sciences (M Sc); Earth and atmospheric sciences (PhD); Earth science (M Sc); meteorology (PhD, Diploma). PhD programs offered jointly with McGill University. *Program availability:* Part-time. *Degree requirements:* For master's, thesis. *Entrance requirements:* For master's and Diploma, appropriate bachelor's degree or equivalent, proficiency in French; for doctorate, appropriate master's degree or equivalent, proficiency in French.

Université du Québec à Montréal, Graduate Programs, Program in Earth Sciences, Montreal, QC H3C 3P8, Canada. Offers earth sciences (M Sc); mineral resources (PhD); non-renewable resources (DESS). *Program availability:* Part-time. Terminal master's awarded for partial completion of doctoral program. *Degree requirements:* For master's, thesis (for some programs); for doctorate, thesis/dissertation. *Entrance requirements:* For master's, appropriate bachelor's degree or equivalent, proficiency in French. *Faculty research:* Economic geology, structural geology, geochemistry, Quaternary geology, isotopic geochemistry.

Université du Québec, Institut National de la Recherche Scientifique, Graduate Programs, Research Center–Water Earth Environment, Québec, QC G1K 9A9, Canada. Offers earth sciences (M Sc, PhD); earth sciences - environmental technologies (M Sc); water sciences (M Sc, PhD). *Program availability:* Part-time. *Faculty:* 34 full-time. *Students:* 169 full-time (87 women), 19 part-time (11 women), 132 international. Average age 33. 58 applicants, 66% accepted, 32 enrolled. In 2018, 34 master's, 24 doctorates awarded. *Degree requirements:* For master's, thesis (for some programs); for doctorate, thesis/dissertation. *Entrance requirements:* For master's, appropriate bachelor's degree, proficiency in French; for doctorate, appropriate master's degree, proficiency in French. *Application deadline:* For fall admission, 3/30 for domestic and international students; for winter admission, 11/1 for domestic and international students; for spring admission, 3/1 for domestic and international students. Application fee: $45. Electronic applications accepted. *Financial support:* In 2018–19, fellowships (averaging $16,500 per year) were awarded; research assistantships also available. *Faculty research:* Land use, impacts of climate change, adaptation to climate change, integrated management of resources (mineral and water). *Unit head:* Jean-François Blais, Director, 418-654-2575, Fax: 418-654-2600, E-mail: jean-francois.blais@ete.inrs.ca. *Application contact:* Sean Otto, Registrar, 418-654-2518, Fax: 418-654-3858, E-mail: sean.otto@inrs.ca.
Website: http://www.ete.inrs.ca/

Université Laval, Faculty of Sciences and Engineering, Department of Geology and Geological Engineering, Programs in Earth Sciences, Québec, QC G1K 7P4, Canada. Offers earth sciences (M Sc, PhD); environmental technologies (M Sc). Offered jointly with INRS-Géressources. Terminal master's awarded for partial completion of doctoral program. *Degree requirements:* For master's, thesis (for some programs); for doctorate, comprehensive exam, thesis/dissertation. *Entrance requirements:* For master's and doctorate, knowledge of French. Electronic applications accepted.

University at Buffalo, the State University of New York, Graduate School, College of Arts and Sciences, Department of Geography, Buffalo, NY 14260. Offers earth systems science (MA, MS); economic geography and business geographics (MS); environmental modeling and analysis (MA); geographic information science (MA, MS); geography (MA, PhD); health geography (MS); international trade (MA); urban and regional analysis (MA). *Program availability:* Part-time. Terminal master's awarded for partial completion of doctoral program. *Degree requirements:* For master's, thesis (for some programs), project or portfolio; for doctorate, thesis/dissertation. *Entrance requirements:* For master's, GRE General Test, minimum GPA of 2.9; for doctorate, GRE General Test, minimum GPA of 3.0. Additional exam requirements/recommendations for international students: Required—TOEFL (minimum score 550 paper-based; 79 iBT). Electronic applications accepted. *Expenses:* Contact institution. *Faculty research:* International business and world trade, geographic information systems and cartography, transportation, urban and regional analysis, physical and environmental geography.

The University of Akron, Graduate School, Buchtel College of Arts and Sciences, Department of Geosciences, Akron, OH 44325. Offers earth science (MS); engineering geology (MS); environmental geology (MS); geology (MS). *Program availability:* Part-time. *Entrance requirements:* For master's, minimum GPA of 2.75, three letters of recommendation, statement of purpose. Additional exam requirements/recommendations for international students: Required—TOEFL (minimum score 79 iBT), IELTS (minimum score 6.5). Electronic applications accepted. *Faculty research:* Terrestrial environmental change, karst hydrogeology, lacustrine paleo environments, environmental magnetism and geophysics.

The University of Alabama, Graduate School, College of Arts and Sciences, Department of Geography, Tuscaloosa, AL 35487. Offers earth system science (MS, PhD); environment and natural resources (MS, PhD); environment and society (MS, PhD); geographic information science (MS, PhD). *Program availability:* Part-time. *Degree requirements:* For master's, comprehensive exam, thesis; for doctorate, comprehensive exam, thesis/dissertation. *Entrance requirements:* For master's, GRE, minimum GPA of 3.0. Additional exam requirements/recommendations for international students: Required—TOEFL (minimum score 550 paper-based; 79 iBT). Electronic applications accepted. *Faculty research:* Earth system science; geographic information science; environment and natural resources; environment and society.

The University of Alabama in Huntsville, School of Graduate Studies, College of Science, Department of Atmospheric Science, Huntsville, AL 35899. Offers atmospheric science (MS, PhD); earth system science (MS). *Program availability:* Part-time. *Faculty:* 14 full-time (2 women), 2 part-time/adjunct (1 woman). *Students:* 42 full-time (21 women), 17 part-time (8 women); includes 3 minority (2 Hispanic/Latino; 1 Two or more races, non-Hispanic/Latino), 7 international. Average age 30. 43 applicants, 67% accepted, 18 enrolled. In 2018, 14 master's, 4 doctorates awarded. *Degree requirements:* For master's, comprehensive exam, thesis or alternative, oral and written exams; for doctorate, comprehensive exam, thesis/dissertation, oral and written exams. *Entrance requirements:* For master's, GRE General Test, minimum GPA of 3.0; sequence of courses in calculus (including the calculus of vector-valued functions); courses in linear algebra and ordinary differential equations; two semesters each of chemistry and calculus-based physics; proficiency in at least one high-level computer programming language; for doctorate, GRE General Test, minimum GPA of 3.0. Additional exam requirements/recommendations for international students: Required—TOEFL (minimum score 550 paper-based; 80 iBT), IELTS (minimum score 6.5). *Application deadline:* For fall admission, 7/15 priority date for domestic students, 4/1 priority date for international students; for spring admission, 11/30 priority date for domestic students, 9/1 priority date for international students. Applications are processed on a rolling basis. Application fee: $50. Electronic applications accepted. *Expenses: Tuition, area resident:* Full-time $10,632; part-time $412 per credit hour. Tuition, state resident: full-time $10,632. Tuition, nonresident: full-time $23,604; part-time $412 per credit hour. *Required fees:* $582; $582. Tuition and fees vary according to course load and program. *Financial support:* In 2018–19, 34 students received support, including 32 research assistantships with full tuition reimbursements available (averaging $9,359 per year), 2 teaching assistantships with full tuition reimbursements available (averaging $9,000 per year); career-related internships or fieldwork, Federal Work-Study, institutionally sponsored loans, scholarships/grants, health care benefits, and unspecified assistantships also available. Support available to part-time students. Financial award application deadline: 4/1; financial award applicants required to submit FAFSA. *Faculty research:* Severe weather, climate, satellite remote sensing, numerical modeling, air pollution. *Unit head:* Dr. John Mecikalski, Interim Chair, 256-961-7877, Fax: 256-922-7755, E-mail: johnm@nsstc.uah.edu. *Application contact:* Kim Gray, Graduate Studies Admissions Coordinator, 256-824-6002, Fax: 256-824-6405, E-mail: deangrad@uah.edu.
Website: http://www.uah.edu/science/departments/atmospheric-science

University of Alberta, Faculty of Graduate Studies and Research, Department of Earth and Atmospheric Sciences, Edmonton, AB T6G 2E1, Canada. Offers M Sc, MA, PhD. *Degree requirements:* For master's, thesis, residency; for doctorate, thesis/dissertation, residency. *Entrance requirements:* For master's, B Sc, minimum GPA of 6.5 on a 9.0 scale; for doctorate, M Sc. Additional exam requirements/recommendations for international students: Required—TOEFL or Michigan English Language Assessment Battery. Electronic applications accepted. *Faculty research:* Geology, human geography, physical geography, meteorology.

The University of Arizona, College of Science, Department of Geosciences, Tucson, AZ 85721. Offers MS, PSM, PhD. *Program availability:* Part-time. Terminal master's awarded for partial completion of doctoral program. *Degree requirements:* For master's, thesis or prepublication; for doctorate, comprehensive exam, thesis/dissertation. *Entrance requirements:* For master's, GRE General Test, 3 letters of recommendation, curriculum vitae; for doctorate, GRE General Test, statement of purpose, 3 letters of recommendation, curriculum vitae. Additional exam requirements/recommendations for international students: Required—TOEFL (minimum score 550 paper-based; 79 iBT). Electronic applications accepted. *Faculty research:* Tectonics, geophysics, geochemistry/petrology, economic geology, Quaternary studies, stratigraphy/paleontology.

University of Arkansas at Little Rock, Graduate School, George W. Donaghey College of Engineering and Information Technology, Program in Geospatial Technology, Little Rock, AR 72204-1099. Offers Graduate Certificate. *Entrance requirements:* For degree, baccalaureate degree, minimum cumulative GPA of 2.75.

University of Calgary, Faculty of Graduate Studies, Faculty of Science, Program in Geoscience, Calgary, AB T2N 1N4, Canada. Offers geology (M Sc, PhD); geophysics (M Sc, PhD); hydrology (M Sc, PhD). *Program availability:* Part-time. Terminal master's awarded for partial completion of doctoral program. *Degree requirements:* For master's, thesis; for doctorate, thesis/dissertation, candidacy exam. *Entrance requirements:* For master's, B Sc; for doctorate, honors B Sc or M Sc. Additional exam requirements/recommendations for international students: Required—TOEFL. Electronic applications accepted. *Faculty research:* Geochemistry, petrology, paleontology, stratigraphy, exploration and solid-earth geophysics.

Geosciences

University of California, Irvine, School of Physical Sciences, Department of Earth System Science, Irvine, CA 92697. Offers MS, PhD. *Students:* 55 full-time (24 women); includes 13 minority (1 Asian, non-Hispanic/Latino; 5 Hispanic/Latino; 7 Two or more races, non-Hispanic/Latino), 14 international. Average age 28. 81 applicants, 38% accepted, 16 enrolled. In 2018, 14 master's, 6 doctorates awarded. *Entrance requirements:* For master's and doctorate, GRE General Test, GRE Subject Test, minimum GPA of 3.0. Additional exam requirements/recommendations for international students: Required—TOEFL (minimum score 550 paper-based). *Application deadline:* For fall admission, 1/15 priority date for domestic students, 1/15 for international students. Applications are processed on a rolling basis. Application fee: $105 ($125 for international students). Electronic applications accepted. *Financial support:* Fellowships, research assistantships with full tuition reimbursements, teaching assistantships, career-related internships or fieldwork, institutionally sponsored loans, traineeships, health care benefits, and unspecified assistantships available. Financial award application deadline: 3/1; financial award applicants required to submit FAFSA. *Faculty research:* Atmospheric chemistry, climate change, isotope biogeochemistry, global environmental chemistry. *Unit head:* Gudrun Magnusdottir, Chair, 949-824-3250, Fax: 949-824-3874, E-mail: gudrun@uci.edu. *Application contact:* Morgan Sibley, Student Affairs Manager, 949-824-1604, Fax: 949-824-3874, E-mail: msibley@uci.edu.
Website: http://www.ess.uci.edu/

University of California, Los Angeles, Graduate Division, College of Letters and Science, Department of Earth and Space Sciences, Los Angeles, CA 90095. Offers geochemistry (MS, PhD); geology (MS, PhD); geophysics and space physics (MS, PhD). Terminal master's awarded for partial completion of doctoral program. *Degree requirements:* For master's, comprehensive exams or thesis; for doctorate, thesis/dissertation, oral and written qualifying exams. *Entrance requirements:* For master's, GRE General Test; GRE Subject Test, bachelor's degree; minimum undergraduate GPA of 3.0 (or its equivalent if letter grade system not used); for doctorate, GRE General Test, bachelor's degree; minimum undergraduate GPA of 3.0 (or its equivalent if letter grade system not used). Additional exam requirements/recommendations for international students: Required—TOEFL. Electronic applications accepted.

University of California, San Diego, Graduate Division, Scripps Institution of Oceanography, La Jolla, CA 92093. Offers climate science and policy (MAS); earth sciences (PhD); geophysics (PhD); marine biodiversity and conservation (MAS); oceanography (MS, PhD). PhD in geophysics offered jointly with San Diego State University. *Students:* 265 full-time (143 women), 1 (woman) part-time. 407 applicants, 21% accepted, 55 enrolled. In 2018, 34 master's, 44 doctorates awarded. Terminal master's awarded for partial completion of doctoral program. *Degree requirements:* For master's, comprehensive exam (for some programs), thesis (for some programs); for doctorate, comprehensive exam, thesis/dissertation. *Entrance requirements:* For master's and doctorate, GRE General Test, GRE Subject Test (encouraged for ocean biosciences applicants), minimum GPA of 3.0. Additional exam requirements/recommendations for international students: Required—TOEFL (minimum score 550 paper-based; 80 iBT), IELTS (minimum score 7). *Application deadline:* For fall admission, 1/15 for domestic students. Application fee: $105 ($125 for international students). Electronic applications accepted. *Financial support:* Fellowships, research assistantships, teaching assistantships, scholarships/grants, traineeships, and unspecified assistantships available. Financial award applicants required to submit FAFSA. *Faculty research:* Biodiversity and conservation, earth and planetary chemistry, alternative energy, global environmental monitoring, air-sea boundary, tectonic margins and the interactions between systems and environments. *Unit head:* Peter Franks, Chair, 858-534-7528, E-mail: pfranks@ucsd.edu. *Application contact:* Gilbert Bretado, Graduate Coordinator, 858-534-1694, E-mail: siodept@sio.ucsd.edu.
Website: https://scripps.ucsd.edu/education

University of California, Santa Barbara, Graduate Division, College of Letters and Sciences, Division of Mathematics, Life, and Physical Sciences, Department of Earth Science, Santa Barbara, CA 93106-9620. Offers MS, PhD. Terminal master's awarded for partial completion of doctoral program. *Degree requirements:* For master's, comprehensive exam, thesis, 30 units; for doctorate, comprehensive exam, thesis/dissertation, 30 units, qualifying exam, defense. *Entrance requirements:* For master's and doctorate, GRE General Test. Additional exam requirements/recommendations for international students: Required—TOEFL (minimum score 550 paper-based; 80 iBT), IELTS (minimum score 7). Electronic applications accepted. *Faculty research:* Geology, geomaterials and earth's structure; geomorphology, tectonics; geophysics, seismology; paleoclimatology, paleoceanography and geochemistry; paleobiology, evolution and paleontology.

University of California, Santa Cruz, Division of Graduate Studies, Division of Physical and Biological Sciences, Department of Earth and Planetary Sciences, Santa Cruz, CA 95064. Offers MS, PhD. Terminal master's awarded for partial completion of doctoral program. *Degree requirements:* For master's, thesis; for doctorate, one foreign language, thesis/dissertation, qualifying exam. *Entrance requirements:* For master's and doctorate, GRE General Test. Additional exam requirements/recommendations for international students: Required—TOEFL (minimum score 550 paper-based; 83 iBT); Recommended—IELTS (minimum score 8). Electronic applications accepted. *Faculty research:* Evolution of continental margins and orogenic belts, geologic processes occurring at plate boundaries, deep-sea sediment diagenesis, paleoecology, hydrogeology.

University of Chicago, Division of the Physical Sciences, Department of the Geophysical Sciences, Chicago, IL 60637. Offers atmospheric sciences (PhD); earth sciences (PhD); paleobiology (PhD); planetary and space sciences (PhD). Terminal master's awarded for partial completion of doctoral program. *Degree requirements:* For doctorate, comprehensive exam, thesis/dissertation. *Entrance requirements:* For doctorate, GRE General Test, research statement, 3 letters of recommendation, transcripts for all previous degrees and institutions attended. Additional exam requirements/recommendations for international students: Required—TOEFL (minimum score 600 paper-based; 95 iBT), IELTS (minimum score 7). Electronic applications accepted. *Faculty research:* Climatology, evolutionary paleontology, cosmochemistry, geochemistry, oceanic sciences.

University of Florida, Graduate School, College of Liberal Arts and Sciences, Department of Geological Sciences, Gainesville, FL 32611. Offers geology (MS, MST, PhD); hydrologic sciences (MS, PhD); tropical conservation and development (MS, MST, PhD); wetland sciences (MS, MST, PhD). Terminal master's awarded for partial completion of doctoral program. *Degree requirements:* For master's, thesis (for some programs); for doctorate, one foreign language, thesis/dissertation. *Entrance requirements:* For master's and doctorate, GRE General Test, minimum GPA of 3.0. Additional exam requirements/recommendations for international students: Required—TOEFL (minimum score 550 paper-based; 80 iBT), IELTS (minimum score 6). Electronic applications accepted. *Faculty research:* Paleoclimatology, tectonophysics, petrochemistry, marine geology, geochemistry, hydrology.

University of Illinois at Chicago, College of Liberal Arts and Sciences, Department of Earth and Environmental Sciences, Chicago, IL 60607-7128. Offers MS, PhD. *Degree requirements:* For master's, thesis; for doctorate, thesis/dissertation. *Entrance requirements:* For master's and doctorate, GRE General Test, minimum GPA of 2.75. Additional exam requirements/recommendations for international students: Required—TOEFL. Electronic applications accepted. *Expenses:* Contact institution. *Faculty research:* Geochemistry, mineralogy and petrology, geophysics, tectonics, global change, hydrology, geobiology.

University of Illinois at Urbana–Champaign, Graduate College, College of Liberal Arts and Sciences, School of Earth, Society and Environment, Department of Geology, Champaign, IL 61820. Offers geology (MS, PhD); teaching of earth sciences (MS). Terminal master's awarded for partial completion of doctoral program.

The University of Iowa, Graduate College, College of Liberal Arts and Sciences, Department of Earth and Environmental Science, Iowa City, IA 52242-1316. Offers MS, PhD. *Degree requirements:* For master's, thesis optional, exam; for doctorate, comprehensive exam, thesis/dissertation. *Entrance requirements:* For master's and doctorate, GRE General Test, minimum GPA of 3.0. Additional exam requirements/recommendations for international students: Required—TOEFL (minimum score 550 paper-based; 81 iBT). Electronic applications accepted.

University of Louisiana at Lafayette, College of Sciences, School of Geosciences, Lafayette, LA 70504. Offers environmental resource science (MS); geosciences (MS). *Program availability:* Part-time. *Degree requirements:* For master's, comprehensive exam, thesis. *Entrance requirements:* For master's, GRE General Test, minimum GPA of 2.75. Additional exam requirements/recommendations for international students: Required—TOEFL (minimum score 550 paper-based). Electronic applications accepted. *Faculty research:* Aquifer contamination, coastal erosion, geochemistry of peat, petroleum geology and geophysics, remote sensing and geographic information systems applications.

University of Lynchburg, Graduate Studies, M Ed Program in Science Education, Lynchburg, VA 24501-3199. Offers science education (M Ed), including earth science, math. *Program availability:* Part-time, evening/weekend. *Degree requirements:* For master's, comprehensive exam. *Entrance requirements:* For master's, GRE, minimum GPA of 3.0 (preferred), official transcripts (bachelor's, others as relevant), three letters of recommendation, career goals statement. Additional exam requirements/recommendations for international students: Required—TOEFL (minimum score 550 paper-based; 80 iBT), IELTS (minimum score 6). Electronic applications accepted. Application fee is waived when completed online. *Expenses:* Contact institution.

University of Maine, Graduate School, College of Natural Sciences, Forestry, and Agriculture, School of Earth and Climate Sciences, Orono, ME 04469. Offers MS, PhD. *Program availability:* Part-time. *Faculty:* 23 full-time (6 women), 28 part-time/adjunct (8 women). *Students:* 37 full-time (18 women), 5 part-time (2 women); includes 3 minority (1 Asian, non-Hispanic/Latino; 2 Hispanic/Latino), 5 international. Average age 31. 55 applicants, 33% accepted, 13 enrolled. In 2018, 6 master's, 2 doctorates awarded. *Degree requirements:* For master's, thesis; for doctorate, one foreign language, comprehensive exam, thesis/dissertation. *Entrance requirements:* For master's and doctorate, GRE General Test. Additional exam requirements/recommendations for international students: Required—TOEFL (minimum score 80 iBT). *Application deadline:* For fall admission, 1/15 for domestic and international students. Applications are processed on a rolling basis. Application fee: $65. Electronic applications accepted. *Financial support:* In 2018–19, 54 students received support, including 1 fellowship with full tuition reimbursement available (averaging $16,000 per year), 37 research assistantships with full tuition reimbursements available (averaging $18,500 per year), 10 teaching assistantships with full tuition reimbursements available (averaging $15,600 per year); Federal Work-Study, institutionally sponsored loans, tuition waivers (full and partial), and unspecified assistantships also available. Financial award application deadline: 3/1. *Faculty research:* Geodynamics, climate change, environmental geology, marine geology. *Total annual research expenditures:* $2.2 million. *Unit head:* Dr. Scott Johnson, Chair, 207-581-2142, Fax: 207-581-2202. *Application contact:* Scott G. Delcourt, Assistant Vice President for Graduate Studies and Senior Associate Dean, 207-581-3291, Fax: 207-581-3232, E-mail: graduate@maine.edu.
Website: http://umaine.edu/earthclimate/

The University of Manchester, School of Earth and Environmental Sciences, Manchester, United Kingdom. Offers atmospheric sciences (M Phil, M Sc, PhD); basin studies and petroleum geosciences (M Phil, M Sc, PhD); earth, atmospheric and environmental sciences (M Phil, M Sc, PhD); environmental geochemistry and cosmochemistry (M Phil, M Sc, PhD); isotope geochemistry and cosmochemistry (M Phil, M Sc, PhD); paleontology (M Phil, M Sc, PhD); physics and chemistry of minerals and fluids (M Phil, M Sc, PhD); structural and petrological geosciences (M Phil, M Sc, PhD).

University of Massachusetts Amherst, Graduate School, College of Natural Sciences, Department of Geosciences, Program in Geosciences, Amherst, MA 01003. Offers MS, PhD. *Program availability:* Part-time. Terminal master's awarded for partial completion of doctoral program. *Degree requirements:* For master's, thesis or alternative; for doctorate, comprehensive exam, thesis/dissertation. *Entrance requirements:* For master's and doctorate, GRE General Test. Additional exam requirements/recommendations for international students: Required—TOEFL (minimum score 550 paper-based; 80 iBT), IELTS (minimum score 6.5). Electronic applications accepted.

University of Michigan, Rackham Graduate School, College of Literature, Science, and the Arts, Department of Earth and Environmental Sciences, Ann Arbor, MI 48109-1005. Offers MS, PhD. Terminal master's awarded for partial completion of doctoral program. *Degree requirements:* For master's, thesis; for doctorate, comprehensive exam, thesis/dissertation, oral defense of dissertation. *Entrance requirements:* For master's and doctorate, GRE General Test. Additional exam requirements/recommendations for international students: Required—TOEFL (minimum score 100 iBT). Electronic applications accepted. *Faculty research:* Isotope geochemistry, paleoclimatology, mineral physics, tectonics, paleontology.

University of Missouri–Kansas City, College of Arts and Sciences, Department of Geosciences, Kansas City, MO 64110-2499. Offers MS, PhD. PhD (interdisciplinary) offered through the School of Graduate Studies. *Program availability:* Part-time. *Degree requirements:* For master's, thesis; for doctorate, thesis/dissertation, qualifying exam. *Entrance requirements:* For master's, GRE General Test, minimum GPA of 3.0. Additional exam requirements/recommendations for international students: Required—TOEFL (minimum score 550 paper-based; 80 iBT). Electronic applications accepted. *Faculty research:* Geotectonics and applied geophysics, environmental geosciences, urban geoscience, geoinformatics-remote sensing, atmospheric research.

University of Montana, Graduate School, College of Humanities and Sciences, Department of Geosciences, Missoula, MT 59812. Offers MS, PhD. *Degree requirements:* For doctorate, thesis/dissertation. *Entrance requirements:* For master's and doctorate, GRE General Test. Additional exam requirements/recommendations for international students: Required—TOEFL (minimum score 525 paper-based). *Faculty research:* Environmental geoscience, regional structure and tectonics, groundwater geology, petrology, mineral deposits.

University of Nebraska–Lincoln, Graduate College, College of Arts and Sciences, Department of Geosciences, Lincoln, NE 68588. Offers MS, PhD. *Degree requirements:* For master's, thesis optional, departmental qualifying exam; for doctorate, comprehensive exam, thesis/dissertation, departmental qualifying exams. *Entrance requirements:* For master's and doctorate, GRE General Test. Additional exam requirements/recommendations for international students: Required—TOEFL (minimum score 550 paper-based). Electronic applications accepted. *Faculty research:* Hydrogeology, sedimentology, environmental geology, vertebrate paleontology.

University of Nevada, Las Vegas, Graduate College, College of Sciences, Department of Geoscience, Las Vegas, NV 89154-4010. Offers MS, PhD. *Program availability:* Part-time. *Faculty:* 8 full-time (3 women), 1 part-time/adjunct (0 women). *Students:* 29 full-time (15 women), 11 part-time (5 women); includes 6 minority (4 Asian, non-Hispanic/Latino; 2 Hispanic/Latino), 4 international. Average age 30. 52 applicants, 21% accepted, 7 enrolled. In 2018, 6 master's, 1 doctorate awarded. *Degree requirements:* For master's, thesis; for doctorate, comprehensive exam, thesis/dissertation. *Entrance requirements:* For master's, GRE General Test, bachelor's degree; letter of recommendation; statement of interest; for doctorate, GRE General Test, bachelor's degree/master's degree; letter of recommendation; statement of interest. Additional exam requirements/recommendations for international students: Required—TOEFL (minimum score 550 paper-based; 80 iBT), IELTS (minimum score 7). *Application deadline:* For fall admission, 2/1 for domestic and international students; for spring admission, 10/1 for domestic and international students. Application fee: $60 ($95 for international students). Electronic applications accepted. *Expenses:* Contact institution. *Financial support:* In 2018–19, 29 students received support, including 3 research assistantships with full tuition reimbursements available (averaging $17,750 per year), 26 teaching assistantships with full tuition reimbursements available (averaging $16,921 per year); institutionally sponsored loans, scholarships/grants, health care benefits, and unspecified assistantships also available. Financial award application deadline: 3/15; financial award applicants required to submit FAFSA. *Faculty research:* Petrology, geochemistry, planetary science, tectonics, hydrology. *Total annual research expenditures:* $2.9 million. *Unit head:* Dr. Rod Metcalf, Chair/Professor, 702-895-4442, Fax: 702-895-4064, E-mail: geoscience.chair@unlv.edu. *Application contact:* Dr. Ganqing Jiang, Graduate Coordinator, 702-895-2708, Fax: 702-895-4064, E-mail: geoscience.gradcoord@unlv.edu.
Website: http://geoscience.unlv.edu/

University of New Hampshire, Graduate School, College of Engineering and Physical Sciences, Department of Earth Sciences, Durham, NH 03824. Offers geochemical systems (MS); geology (MS); hydrology (MS); ocean mapping (MS); oceanography (MS). *Degree requirements:* For master's, thesis. *Entrance requirements:* For master's, GRE General Test. Additional exam requirements/recommendations for international students: Required—TOEFL (minimum score 550 paper-based; 80 iBT). Electronic applications accepted.

University of New Hampshire, Graduate School, College of Life Sciences and Agriculture, Department of Natural Resources and the Environment, Durham, NH 03824. Offers environmental conservation (MS); environmental economics (MS); forestry (MS); natural resources (MS); resource administration and management (MS); soil and water resource management (MS); wildlife and conservation biology (MS). *Program availability:* Part-time. *Entrance requirements:* For master's, GRE General Test. Additional exam requirements/recommendations for international students: Required—TOEFL (minimum score 550 paper-based; 80 iBT). Electronic applications accepted.

University of New Haven, Graduate School, College of Arts and Sciences, Program in Environmental Science, West Haven, CT 06516. Offers environmental ecology (MS); environmental geoscience (MS); environmental health and management (MS); environmental science (MS); geographical information systems (MS). *Program availability:* Part-time, evening/weekend. *Students:* 14 full-time (8 women), 13 part-time (6 women); includes 7 minority (3 Black or African American, non-Hispanic/Latino; 3 Hispanic/Latino; 1 Native Hawaiian or other Pacific Islander, non-Hispanic/Latino), 4 international. Average age 29. 59 applicants, 86% accepted, 10 enrolled. In 2018, 17 master's awarded. *Entrance requirements:* Additional exam requirements/recommendations for international students: Required—TOEFL (minimum score 80 iBT), IELTS, PTE. *Application deadline:* Applications are processed on a rolling basis. Application fee: $50. Electronic applications accepted. Application fee is waived when completed online. *Expenses:* Tuition: Full-time $16,470; part-time $915 per credit hour. *Required fees:* $230; $95 per term. *Financial support:* Research assistantships with partial tuition reimbursements, teaching assistantships with partial tuition reimbursements, Federal Work-Study, scholarships/grants, and unspecified assistantships available. Support available to part-time students. Financial award applicants required to submit FAFSA. *Unit head:* Dr. Roman Zajac, Professor, 203-932-7114, E-mail: rzajac@newhaven.edu. *Application contact:* Selina O'Toole, Senior Associate Director of Graduate Admissions, 203-932-7337, E-mail: SOToole@newhaven.edu.
Website: https://www.newhaven.edu/arts-sciences/graduate-programs/environmental-science/

University of New Mexico, Graduate Studies, College of Arts and Sciences, Program in Earth and Planetary Sciences, Albuquerque, NM 87131-2039. Offers MS, PhD. *Program availability:* Part-time. *Students:* Average age 30. 56 applicants, 27% accepted, 15 enrolled. In 2018, 1 master's, 3 doctorates awarded. Terminal master's awarded for partial completion of doctoral program. *Degree requirements:* For master's, comprehensive exam, thesis; for doctorate, comprehensive exam, thesis/dissertation. *Entrance requirements:* For master's and doctorate, GRE General Test. Additional exam requirements/recommendations for international students: Required—TOEFL. *Application deadline:* For fall admission, 1/15 priority date for domestic and international students; for spring admission, 11/1 priority date for domestic and international students. Application fee: $50. Electronic applications accepted. *Financial support:* Fellowships with full tuition reimbursements, research assistantships with full tuition reimbursements, teaching assistantships with full tuition reimbursements, scholarships/grants, and health care benefits available. Financial award application deadline: 1/15. *Faculty research:* Climatology, experimental petrology, geochemistry, geographic information technologies, geomorphology, geophysics, hydrogeology, igneous petrology, metamorphic petrology, meteoritic, meteorology, micrometeorites, mineralogy, paleoclimatology, paleontology, pedology, petrology, physical volcanology, planetary sciences, Precambrian geology, quaternary geology, sedimentary geochemistry, sedimentology, stable isotope geochemistry, stratigraphy, structural geology, tectonics, volcanology. *Total annual research expenditures:* $2.5 million. *Unit head:* Dr. Adrian J. Brearley, Chair, 505-277-4204, Fax: 505-277-8843, E-mail: brearley@unm.edu. *Application contact:* Cindy Jaramillo, Administrative Assistant III, 505-277-1635, Fax: 505-277-8843, E-mail: epsdept@unm.edu.
Website: http://epswww.unm.edu/

University of New Orleans, Graduate School, College of Sciences, Department of Earth and Environmental Sciences, New Orleans, LA 70148. Offers MS, PhD. *Program availability:* Evening/weekend. *Degree requirements:* For master's, thesis. *Entrance requirements:* For master's, GRE General Test. Additional exam requirements/recommendations for international students: Required—TOEFL (minimum score 550 paper-based; 79 iBT), IELTS. Electronic applications accepted. *Faculty research:* Continental margin structure and seismology, tectonics at convergent plate margins, continental shelf sediment stability, early diagenesis of carbonates.

The University of North Carolina at Charlotte, College of Liberal Arts and Sciences, Department of Geography and Earth Sciences, Charlotte, NC 28223-0001. Offers earth sciences (MS); geography (MA), including community planning, geographic information science and technologies, location analysis, urban-regional analysis; geography and urban regional analysis (PhD). *Program availability:* Part-time, evening/weekend. *Students:* 45 full-time (19 women), 24 part-time (5 women); includes 9 minority (2 Black or African American, non-Hispanic/Latino; 3 Asian, non-Hispanic/Latino; 3 Hispanic/Latino; 1 Two or more races, non-Hispanic/Latino), 18 international. Average age 30. 47 applicants, 83% accepted, 21 enrolled. In 2018, 23 master's, 4 doctorates awarded. Terminal master's awarded for partial completion of doctoral program. *Entrance requirements:* For master's, GRE General Test or MAT, minimum GPA of 2.75, 3.0 for junior and senior years, transcripts, letters of recommendation, and personal essays (for MS); minimum GPA of 3.1 overall or for the last 2 years, 3.2 in major, three letters of reference, and personal essay (for MA); for doctorate, GRE, MA or MS in geography or a field related to the primary emphases of the program; minimum master's-level GPA of 3.5; GIS proficiency. Additional exam requirements/recommendations for international students: Required—TOEFL (minimum score 523 paper-based; 70 iBT), IELTS (minimum score 6), TOEFL (minimum score 523 paper-based, 70 iBT) or IELTS (6). *Application deadline:* Applications are processed on a rolling basis. Application fee: $75. Electronic applications accepted. Tuition and fees vary according to course load and program. *Financial support:* Research assistantships, teaching assistantships, career-related internships or fieldwork, institutionally sponsored loans, scholarships/grants, and unspecified assistantships available. Support available to part-time students. Financial award application deadline: 3/1; financial award applicants required to submit FAFSA. *Total annual research expenditures:* $494,867. *Unit head:* Dr. Craig Allan, Chair, 704-687-5999, E-mail: ges@uncc.edu. *Application contact:* Kathy B. Giddings, Director of Graduate Admissions, 704-687-5503, Fax: 704-687-1668, E-mail: gradadm@uncc.edu.
Website: https://geoearth.uncc.edu/

The University of North Carolina Wilmington, College of Arts and Sciences, Department of Earth and Ocean Sciences, Wilmington, NC 28403-3297. Offers geographic information science (Graduate Certificate); geoscience (MS). *Program availability:* Part-time. *Degree requirements:* For master's, comprehensive exam, thesis (for some programs). *Entrance requirements:* For master's, GRE General Test, 3 recommendations, research essay. Additional exam requirements/recommendations for international students: Required—TOEFL (minimum score 550 paper-based; 79 iBT), IELTS (minimum score 6.5). Electronic applications accepted.

University of North Dakota, Graduate School, John D. Odegard School of Aerospace Sciences, Program in Earth System Science and Policy, Grand Forks, ND 58202. Offers MEM, MS, PhD. *Program availability:* Part-time. *Degree requirements:* For master's, thesis (for some programs); for doctorate, thesis/dissertation (for some programs). *Entrance requirements:* For master's and doctorate, GRE General Test, minimum GPA of 3.0. Additional exam requirements/recommendations for international students: Required—TOEFL (minimum score 550 paper-based; 79 iBT), IELTS (minimum score 6.5). Electronic applications accepted.

University of Northern Colorado, Graduate School, College of Natural and Health Sciences, Program in Earth Sciences, Greeley, CO 80639. Offers MA. *Program availability:* Part-time. *Degree requirements:* For master's, comprehensive exam. *Entrance requirements:* For master's, GRE General Test, 3 letters of recommendation. Electronic applications accepted.

University of Northern Iowa, Graduate College, College of Humanities, Arts and Sciences, MA Program in Science Education, Cedar Falls, IA 50614. Offers earth science education (MA); physics education (MA); science education (MA). *Degree requirements:* For master's, comprehensive exam (for some programs), thesis or alternative. *Entrance requirements:* For master's, minimum GPA of 3.0. Additional exam requirements/recommendations for international students: Required—TOEFL (minimum score 500 paper-based; 61 iBT). Electronic applications accepted.

University of Notre Dame, The Graduate School, College of Engineering, Department of Civil and Environmental Engineering and Earth Sciences, Notre Dame, IN 46556. Offers bioengineering (MS Bio E); civil engineering (MSCE); civil engineering and geological sciences (PhD); earth sciences (MS); environmental engineering (MS Env E). Terminal master's awarded for partial completion of doctoral program. *Degree requirements:* For master's, comprehensive exam; for doctorate, thesis/dissertation, candidacy exam. *Entrance requirements:* For master's and doctorate, GRE General Test. Additional exam requirements/recommendations for international students: Required—TOEFL (minimum score 600 paper-based; 80 iBT). Electronic applications accepted. *Faculty research:* Environmental modeling, biological-waste treatment, petrology, environmental geology, geochemistry.

University of Ottawa, Faculty of Graduate and Postdoctoral Studies, Faculty of Science, Ottawa-Carleton Geoscience Centre, Ottawa, ON K1N 6N5, Canada. Offers earth sciences (M Sc, PhD). M Sc, PhD offered jointly with Carleton University. *Degree requirements:* For master's, thesis, seminar; for doctorate, comprehensive exam, thesis/dissertation, seminar. *Entrance requirements:* For master's, honors B Sc degree or equivalent, minimum B average; for doctorate, honors B Sc with minimum B average or M Sc with minimum B+ average. Electronic applications accepted. *Faculty research:* Environmental geoscience, geochemistry/petrology, geomatics/geomathematics, mineral resource studies.

University of Pennsylvania, School of Arts and Sciences, College of Liberal and Professional Studies, Philadelphia, PA 19104. Offers applied geosciences (MSAG); applied positive psychology (MAP); chemical sciences (MCS); environmental studies (MES); individualized study (MLA); liberal arts (M Phil); medical physics (MMP); organization dynamics (M Phil). *Students:* 219 full-time (144 women), 295 part-time (178 women); includes 101 minority (31 Black or African American, non-Hispanic/Latino; 1 American Indian or Alaska Native, non-Hispanic/Latino; 35 Asian, non-Hispanic/Latino; 16 Hispanic/Latino, 1 Native Hawaiian or other Pacific Islander, non-Hispanic/Latino; 17 Two or more races, non-Hispanic/Latino), 103 international. Average age 34. 633 applicants, 52% accepted, 249 enrolled. In 2018, 180 master's awarded. *Unit head:* Nora Lewis, Vice Dean, Professional and Liberal Education, 215-898-7326, E-mail: nlewis@sas.upenn.edu. *Application contact:* Nora Lewis, Vice Dean, Professional and Liberal Education, 215-898-7326, E-mail: nlewis@sas.upenn.edu.
Website: http://www.sas.upenn.edu/lps/graduate

Peterson's Graduate Programs in the Physical Sciences, Mathematics, Agricultural Sciences, the Environment & Natural Resources 2020

www.petersons.com **109**

Geosciences

University of Pennsylvania, School of Arts and Sciences, Graduate Group in Earth and Environmental Science, Philadelphia, PA 19104. Offers MS, PhD. *Program availability:* Part-time. *Faculty:* 10 full-time (3 women), 2 part-time/adjunct (0 women). *Students:* 13 full-time (4 women); includes 6 minority (2 Black or African American, non-Hispanic/Latino; 4 Two or more races, non-Hispanic/Latino), 2 international. Average age 27. 57 applicants, 18% accepted, 2 enrolled. In 2018, 1 doctorate awarded. Application fee: $80.
Website: http://www.sas.upenn.edu/graduate-division

University of Rhode Island, Graduate School, College of the Environment and Life Sciences, Department of Biological Sciences, Kingston, RI 02881. Offers cell and molecular biology (MS, PhD); earth and environmental sciences (MS, PhD); ecology and ecosystem sciences (MS, PhD); evolutionary and marine biology (MS, PhD); sustainable agriculture and food systems (MS, PhD). *Program availability:* Part-time. *Faculty:* 20 full-time (10 women). *Students:* 105 full-time (65 women), 7 part-time (3 women); includes 10 minority (4 Black or African American, non-Hispanic/Latino; 3 Asian, non-Hispanic/Latino; 2 Hispanic/Latino; 1 Two or more races, non-Hispanic/Latino), 23 international. 121 applicants, 31% accepted, 28 enrolled. In 2018, 17 master's, 11 doctorates awarded. *Entrance requirements:* Additional exam requirements/recommendations for international students: Required—TOEFL. *Application deadline:* For fall admission, 1/15 for domestic and international students. Application fee: $65. Electronic applications accepted. *Expenses: Tuition, area resident:* Full-time $13,226; part-time $735 per credit. Tuition, state resident: full-time $13,226; part-time $735 per credit. Tuition, nonresident: full-time $25,854; part-time $1436 per credit. *International tuition:* $25,854 full-time. *Required fees:* $1698; $50 per credit. $35 per semester. One-time fee: $165. *Financial support:* In 2018–19, 11 research assistantships with tuition reimbursements (averaging $10,985 per year) were awarded. Financial award application deadline: 1/15; financial award applicants required to submit FAFSA. *Faculty research:* Physiological constraints on predators in the Antarctic, effects of CO2 absorption in salt water particularly as it impacts pteropods. *Unit head:* Dr. Evan Preisser, Chair, 401-874-2120, E-mail: preisser@uri.edu. *Application contact:* Dr. Evan Preisser, Chair, 401-874-2120, E-mail: preisser@uri.edu.
Website: http://web.uri.edu/bio/

University of Rhode Island, Graduate School, College of the Environment and Life Sciences, Department of Geosciences, Kingston, RI 02881. Offers environmental and earth sciences (MS, PhD); environmental science and management (MESM); hydrology (Graduate Certificate). *Program availability:* Part-time. *Faculty:* 8 full-time (4 women). *Students:* 1 part-time (0 women). In 2018, 1 master's, 9 other advanced degrees awarded. *Entrance requirements:* For master's and doctorate, GRE, 2 letters of recommendation. Additional exam requirements/recommendations for international students: Required—TOEFL. *Application deadline:* For fall admission, 7/15 for domestic students, 2/1 for international students; for spring admission, 11/15 for domestic students, 7/15 for international students. Application fee: $65. Electronic applications accepted. *Expenses: Tuition, area resident:* Full-time $13,226; part-time $735 per credit. Tuition, state resident: full-time $13,226; part-time $735 per credit. Tuition, nonresident: full-time $25,854; part-time $1436 per credit. *International tuition:* $25,854 full-time. *Required fees:* $1698; $50 per credit. $35 per semester. One-time fee: $165. *Financial support:* In 2018–19, 16 research assistantships with tuition reimbursements (averaging $11,641 per year) were awarded. Financial award application deadline: 2/1; financial award applicants required to submit FAFSA. *Unit head:* Dr. Brian Savage, Professor and Chair, 401-874-5392, E-mail: savage@uri.edu. *Application contact:* Dr. Thomas Boving, Professor, 401-874-7053, E-mail: tboving@uri.edu.
Website: http://web.uri.edu/geo/

University of Rochester, School of Arts and Sciences, Department of Earth and Environmental Sciences, Rochester, NY 14627. Offers geological sciences (MS); geosciences (PhD). *Faculty:* 11 full-time (2 women). *Students:* 23 full-time (12 women); includes 2 minority (1 American Indian or Alaska Native, non-Hispanic/Latino; 1 Hispanic/Latino), 10 international. Average age 29. 38 applicants, 29% accepted, 5 enrolled. In 2018, 1 master's, 1 doctorate awarded. Terminal master's awarded for partial completion of doctoral program. *Degree requirements:* For master's, thesis; for doctorate, comprehensive exam, thesis/dissertation. *Entrance requirements:* For master's and doctorate, GRE General Test, transcripts, letters of recommendation. Additional exam requirements/recommendations for international students: Required—TOEFL, IELTS. *Application deadline:* For fall admission, 1/15 for domestic and international students. Application fee: $60. Electronic applications accepted. *Expenses: Tuition:* Full-time $52,974; part-time $1654 per credit hour. *Required fees:* $612. One-time fee: $30 part-time. Tuition and fees vary according to campus/location and program. *Financial support:* In 2018–19, 48 students received support, including 24 research assistantships (averaging $26,900 per year), 24 teaching assistantships (averaging $26,900 per year); career-related internships or fieldwork, scholarships/grants, traineeships, tuition waivers (full), and unspecified assistantships also available. Support available to part-time students. Financial award application deadline: 1/15. *Faculty research:* Isotope geochemistry, ice core, paleomagnetism, atmospheric chemistry and climate modeling, early earth and experimental geochemistry. *Total annual research expenditures:* $2.4 million. *Unit head:* John A. Tarduno, Chair, 585-275-5713, E-mail: john.tarduno@rochester.edu. *Application contact:* Marissa Sette, Program Coordinator, 585-275-5713, E-mail: msette@ur.rochester.edu.
Website: http://www.sas.rochester.edu/ees/graduate/index.html

University of South Carolina, The Graduate School, College of Arts and Sciences, Department of Geological Sciences, Columbia, SC 29208. Offers MS, PhD. Terminal master's awarded for partial completion of doctoral program. *Degree requirements:* For master's, thesis; for doctorate, comprehensive exam, thesis/dissertation, published paper. *Entrance requirements:* For master's and doctorate, GRE General Test. Additional exam requirements/recommendations for international students: Required—TOEFL (minimum score 570 paper-based; 75 iBT). Electronic applications accepted. *Faculty research:* Environmental geology, tectonics, petrology, coastal processes, paleoclimatology.

University of Southern California, Graduate School, Dana and David Dornsife College of Letters, Arts and Sciences, Department of Earth Sciences, Los Angeles, CA 90089. Offers MS, PhD. *Program availability:* Part-time. Terminal master's awarded for partial completion of doctoral program. *Degree requirements:* For master's, thesis; for doctorate, comprehensive exam, thesis/dissertation. *Entrance requirements:* For master's and doctorate, GRE. Additional exam requirements/recommendations for international students: Required—TOEFL. Electronic applications accepted. *Faculty research:* Geophysics, paleoceanography, geochemistry, geobiology, structure, tectonics.

University of South Florida, College of Arts and Sciences, School of Geosciences, Tampa, FL 33620-9951. Offers environmental science and policy (MS); geography (MA), including environmental geography, geographic information science and spatial analysis, human geography; geography and environmental science and policy (PhD); geology (MS, PhD). *Program availability:* Part-time, evening/weekend. *Faculty:* 33 full-time (6 women). *Students:* 93 full-time (43 women), 48 part-time (23 women); includes 24 minority (8 Black or African American, non-Hispanic/Latino; 6 Asian, non-Hispanic/Latino; 5 Hispanic/Latino; 5 Two or more races, non-Hispanic/Latino), 42 international. Average age 31. 107 applicants, 50% accepted, 23 enrolled. In 2018, 14 master's, 11 doctorates awarded. *Degree requirements:* For master's, comprehensive exam, thesis (for some programs); for doctorate, comprehensive exam, thesis/dissertation. *Entrance requirements:* For master's, GRE General Test, minimum GPA of 3.0, letter of intent, 3 letters of recommendation; for doctorate, GRE General Test, master's in geography, environmental science and policy or related field; GPA of at least 3.2 in graduate credits; letter of intent; 3 letters of recommendation. Additional exam requirements/recommendations for international students: Required—TOEFL, TOEFL minimum score 550 paper-based; 79 iBT or IELTS minimum score 6.5 (for MA and MURP); TOEFL minimum score 600 paper-based (for MS and PhD). *Application deadline:* For fall admission, 2/15 priority date for domestic students, 2/15 for international students; for spring admission, 10/15 priority date for domestic students, 9/15 for international students; for summer admission, 2/15 priority date for domestic students, 1/15 for international students. Application fee: $30. Electronic applications accepted. *Expenses:* Tuition, state resident: full-time $6350. Tuition, nonresident: full-time $19,048. *International tuition:* $19,048 full-time. *Required fees:* $2079. *Financial support:* In 2018–19, 45 students received support, including 3 research assistantships (averaging $12,345 per year), 25 teaching assistantships with tuition reimbursements available (averaging $12,807 per year); unspecified assistantships also available. Financial award application deadline: 3/1. *Faculty research:* Geography: human geography, environmental geography, geographic information science and spatial analysis, urban geography, social theory; environmental science, policy, and planning: water resources, wildlife ecology, Karst and wetland environments, natural hazards, soil contamination, meteorology and climatology, environmental sustainability and policy, urban and regional planning. *Total annual research expenditures:* $3 million. *Unit head:* Dr. Mark Rains, Professor and Chair, 813-974-3310, Fax: 813-974-5911, E-mail: mrains@usf.edu. *Application contact:* Dr. Ruiliang Pu, Associate Professor and Graduate Program Coordinator, 813-974-1508, Fax: 813-974-5911, E-mail: rpu@usf.edu.
Website: http://hennarot.forest.usf.edu/main/depts/geosci/

The University of Texas at Austin, Graduate School, Jackson School of Geosciences, Austin, TX 78712-1111. Offers MA, MS, PhD. *Program availability:* Part-time. *Degree requirements:* For master's, report (MA), thesis (MS); for doctorate, thesis/dissertation. *Entrance requirements:* For master's and doctorate, GRE General Test. Electronic applications accepted. *Faculty research:* Sedimentary geology, geophysics, hydrogeology, structure/tectonics, vertebrate paleontology.

The University of Texas at Dallas, School of Natural Sciences and Mathematics, Department of Geosciences, Richardson, TX 75080. Offers geosciences (MS, PhD); geosciences - petrology and mineralogy (MS, PhD); geosciences - sedimentology (MS, PhD); geosciences - stratigraphy (MS, PhD). *Program availability:* Part-time, evening/weekend. *Faculty:* 9 full-time (0 women), 2 part-time/adjunct (0 women). *Students:* 42 full-time (11 women), 25 part-time (11 women); includes 11 minority (3 Black or African American, non-Hispanic/Latino; 1 American Indian or Alaska Native, non-Hispanic/Latino; 4 Asian, non-Hispanic/Latino; 2 Hispanic/Latino; 1 Two or more races, non-Hispanic/Latino), 27 international. Average age 30. 40 applicants, 35% accepted, 10 enrolled. In 2018, 14 master's, 4 doctorates awarded. *Degree requirements:* For master's, thesis optional; for doctorate, thesis/dissertation. *Entrance requirements:* For master's and doctorate, GRE General Test, minimum GPA of 3.0 in upper-level course work in field. Additional exam requirements/recommendations for international students: Required—TOEFL (minimum score 550 paper-based). *Application deadline:* For fall admission, 7/15 for domestic students, 5/1 priority date for international students; for spring admission, 11/15 for domestic students, 9/1 priority date for international students. Applications are processed on a rolling basis. Application fee: $50 ($100 for international students). Electronic applications accepted. *Expenses: Tuition, area resident:* Full-time $13,458. Tuition, state resident: full-time $13,458. Tuition, nonresident: full-time $26,852. *International tuition:* $26,852 full-time. Tuition and fees vary according to course load. *Financial support:* In 2018–19, 19 students received support, including 6 research assistantships with partial tuition reimbursements available (averaging $22,800 per year), 14 teaching assistantships with partial tuition reimbursements available (averaging $17,100 per year); career-related internships or fieldwork, Federal Work-Study, institutionally sponsored loans, scholarships/grants, and unspecified assistantships also available. Support available to part-time students. Financial award application deadline: 4/30; financial award applicants required to submit FAFSA. *Faculty research:* Cyber mapping, GPS applications for geophysics and geology, seismology and ground-penetrating radar, numerical modeling, signal processing and inverse modeling techniques in seismology. *Unit head:* Dr. John Geissman, Department Head, 972-883-2401, Fax: 972-883-2537, E-mail: geosciences@utdallas.edu. *Application contact:* Gloria Eby, Graduate Support Assistant, 972-883-2401, Fax: 972-883-2537, E-mail: geosciences@utdallas.edu.
Website: http://www.utdallas.edu/geosciences

The University of Texas Rio Grande Valley, College of Sciences, School of Earth, Environmental, and Marine Sciences, Edinburg, TX 78539. Offers agricultural, environmental, and sustainability sciences (MS); ocean, coastal, and earth sciences (MS). *Expenses: Tuition, area resident:* Full-time $6888. Tuition, state resident: full-time $6888. Tuition, nonresident: full-time $14,484. *International tuition:* $14,484 full-time. *Required fees:* $1468.

The University of Tulsa, Graduate School, College of Engineering and Natural Sciences, Department of Geosciences, Tulsa, OK 74104-3189. Offers geophysics (MS); geosciences (MS, PhD); JD/MS. *Program availability:* Part-time. *Faculty:* 11 full-time (2 women), 4 part-time/adjunct (0 women). *Students:* 20 full-time (4 women), 1 part-time (0 women); includes 1 minority (Hispanic/Latino), 8 international. Average age 27. 28 applicants, 71% accepted, 12 enrolled. In 2018, 9 master's awarded. Terminal master's awarded for partial completion of doctoral program. *Degree requirements:* For master's, thesis (for some programs); for doctorate, comprehensive exam, thesis/dissertation. *Entrance requirements:* For master's and doctorate, GRE General Test. Additional exam requirements/recommendations for international students: Required—TOEFL (minimum score 550 paper-based; 80 iBT), IELTS (minimum score 6). *Application deadline:* For fall admission, 2/1 for domestic and international students; for spring admission, 8/1 for domestic and international students. Applications are processed on a rolling basis. Application fee: $55. Electronic applications accepted. *Expenses: Tuition:* Full-time $22,230; part-time $1235 per credit hour. *Required fees:* $2100; $6 per credit hour. One-time fee: $400 full-time. Tuition and fees vary according to course level, course load and program. *Financial support:* In 2018–19, 10 students received support, including 3 fellowships with full tuition reimbursements available (averaging $5,023 per year), 2 research assistantships with full tuition reimbursements available (averaging $7,822 per year), 7 teaching assistantships with full tuition reimbursements available (averaging $12,758 per year); career-related internships or fieldwork, scholarships/grants, health care benefits, and unspecified assistantships also available. Support available to part-time students. Financial award application deadline: 2/1; financial award applicants required to submit FAFSA. *Faculty research:* Petroleum exploration/production and

environmental science, including clastic sedimentology, petroleum seismology, seismic stratigraphy, structural geology, geochemistry, and biogeoscience. *Unit head:* Dr. Dennis Kerr, Chairperson, 918-631-3020, Fax: 918-631-2091, E-mail: dennis-kerr@utulsa.edu. *Application contact:* Dr. Peter Michael, Adviser, 918-631-3017, Fax: 918-631-2156, E-mail: pjm@utulsa.edu.
Website: http://engineering.utulsa.edu/academics/geosciences/

University of Victoria, Faculty of Graduate Studies, Faculty of Science, School of Earth and Ocean Sciences, Victoria, BC V8W 2Y2, Canada. Offers M Sc, PhD. *Program availability:* Part-time. *Degree requirements:* For master's, thesis; for doctorate, thesis/dissertation, candidacy exam. *Entrance requirements:* For master's and doctorate, GRE. Additional exam requirements/recommendations for international students: Required—TOEFL (minimum score 575 paper-based), IELTS (minimum score 7). Electronic applications accepted. *Faculty research:* Climate modeling, geology.

University of Waterloo, Graduate Studies and Postdoctoral Affairs, Faculty of Science, Department of Earth and Environmental Sciences, Waterloo, ON N2L 3G1, Canada. Offers M Sc, PhD. *Program availability:* Part-time. *Degree requirements:* For master's, research paper or thesis; for doctorate, comprehensive exam, thesis/dissertation. *Entrance requirements:* For master's, GRE, honors degree, minimum B average; for doctorate, GRE, master's degree, minimum B average. Additional exam requirements/recommendations for international students: Required—TOEFL, IELTS, PTE. *Application deadline:* Applications are processed on a rolling basis. Application fee: $125 Canadian dollars. Electronic applications accepted. *Financial support:* Research assistantships, teaching assistantships, career-related internships or fieldwork, and institutionally sponsored loans available. *Faculty research:* Environmental geology, soil physics.
Website: https://uwaterloo.ca/earth-environmental-sciences/

The University of Western Ontario, School of Graduate and Postdoctoral Studies, Faculty of Science, Department of Earth Sciences, London, ON N6A 3K7, Canada. Offers environment and sustainability (MES); geology (M Sc, PhD); geology and environmental science (M Sc, PhD); geophysics (M Sc, PhD); geophysics and environmental science (M Sc, PhD). *Degree requirements:* For master's, thesis; for doctorate, thesis/dissertation, qualifying exam. *Entrance requirements:* For master's, honors in B Sc; for doctorate, M Sc. Additional exam requirements/recommendations for international students: Required—TOEFL. *Faculty research:* Geophysics, geochemistry, paleontology, sedimentology/stratigraphy, glaciology/quaternary.

University of Windsor, Faculty of Graduate Studies, Faculty of Science, Department of Earth and Environmental Sciences, Windsor, ON N9B 3P4, Canada. Offers earth sciences (M Sc, PhD). *Program availability:* Part-time. *Degree requirements:* For master's, thesis; for doctorate, comprehensive exam, thesis/dissertation. *Entrance requirements:* For master's, minimum B average; for doctorate, minimum B average, copies of publication abstract. Additional exam requirements/recommendations for international students: Required—TOEFL (minimum score 560 paper-based). *Faculty research:* Aqueous geochemistry and hydrothermal processes, igneous petrochemistry, radiogenic isotopes, radiometric age-dating, diagenetic and sedimentary geochemistry.

Virginia Polytechnic Institute and State University, Graduate School, College of Science, Blacksburg, VA 24061. Offers biological sciences (MS, PhD); biomedical technology development and management (MS); chemistry (MS, PhD); data analysis and applied statistics (MA); economics (PhD); geosciences (MS, PhD); mathematics (MS, PhD); physics (MS, PhD); psychology (MS, PhD); statistics (MS, PhD). *Faculty:* 349 full-time (109 women), 3 part-time/adjunct (2 women). *Students:* 542 full-time (202 women), 39 part-time (19 women); includes 71 minority (11 Black or African American, non-Hispanic/Latino; 1 American Indian or Alaska Native, non-Hispanic/Latino; 18 Asian, non-Hispanic/Latino; 32 Hispanic/Latino; 9 Two or more races, non-Hispanic/Latino), 220 international. Average age 27. 977 applicants, 25% accepted, 110 enrolled. In 2018, 75 master's, 69 doctorates awarded. *Degree requirements:* For master's, comprehensive exam (for some programs), thesis (for some programs); for doctorate, comprehensive exam (for some programs), thesis/dissertation (for some programs). *Entrance requirements:* For master's and doctorate, GRE/GMAT. Additional exam requirements/recommendations for international students: Required—TOEFL (minimum score 90 iBT). *Application deadline:* For fall admission, 8/1 for domestic students, 4/1 for international students; for spring admission, 1/1 for domestic students, 9/1 for international students. Applications are processed on a rolling basis. Application fee: $75. Electronic applications accepted. *Expenses:* Tuition, state resident: full-time $15,510; part-time $739.50 per credit hour. Tuition, nonresident: full-time $29,629; part-time $1490.25 per credit hour. *Required fees:* $2804; $550 per semester. Tuition and fees vary according to course load, campus/location and program. *Financial support:* In 2018–19, 7 fellowships with full tuition reimbursements (averaging $29,657 per year), 260 research assistantships with full tuition reimbursements (averaging $15,888 per year), 383 teaching assistantships with full tuition reimbursements (averaging $18,063 per year) were awarded; unspecified assistantships also available. Financial award application deadline: 3/1; financial award applicants required to submit FAFSA. *Total annual research expenditures:* $27.3 million. *Unit head:* Dr. Sally C. Morton, Dean, 540-231-5422, Fax: 540-231-3380, E-mail: scmorton@vt.edu. *Application contact:* Allison Craft, Executive Assistant, 540-231-6394, Fax: 540-231-3380, E-mail: crafta@vt.edu. Website: http://www.science.vt.edu/

Washington University in St. Louis, The Graduate School, Department of Earth and Planetary Sciences, St. Louis, MO 63130-4899. Offers PhD. Terminal master's awarded for partial completion of doctoral program. *Degree requirements:* For doctorate, thesis/dissertation. *Entrance requirements:* For doctorate, GRE General Test. Additional exam requirements/recommendations for international students: Required—TOEFL. Electronic applications accepted. *Faculty research:* Planetary sciences; geology; geobiology; geochemistry; geodynamics.

Wesleyan University, Graduate Studies, Department of Earth and Environmental Sciences, Middletown, CT 06459. Offers MA. *Degree requirements:* For master's, thesis. *Entrance requirements:* For master's, GRE General Test, official transcripts, three recommendation letters, essay. Additional exam requirements/recommendations for international students: Required—TOEFL. Electronic applications accepted. *Faculty research:* Tectonics, volcanology, stratigraphy, coastal processes, geochemistry.

West Chester University of Pennsylvania, College of the Sciences and Mathematics, Department of Earth and Space Science, West Chester, PA 19383. Offers general science (Teaching Certificate); geoscience (MS). *Program availability:* Part-time, evening/weekend. *Degree requirements:* For master's, final project involving manuscript, presentation. *Entrance requirements:* For master's, minimum GPA of 2.8. Additional exam requirements/recommendations for international students: Required—TOEFL or IELTS. Electronic applications accepted. *Faculty research:* Environmental geology, coastal geomorphology (sea level change), geoscience education, water and soil remediation, hydrogeology, energy and sustainability, astronomy, short-term weather forecasting.

Western Connecticut State University, Division of Graduate Studies, Maricostas School of Arts and Sciences, Department of Physics, Astronomy and Meteorology, Danbury, CT 06810-6885. Offers earth and planetary sciences (MA). *Program availability:* Part-time. *Students:* 4 part-time (2 women). Average age 34. *Degree requirements:* For master's, thesis, completion of program in 6 years. *Entrance requirements:* For master's, minimum GPA of 2.5 or GRE; one year each of calculus-based physics and calculus; semester course in differential equations. Additional exam requirements/recommendations for international students: Recommended—TOEFL (minimum score 550 paper-based; 79 iBT), IELTS (minimum score 6). *Application deadline:* For fall admission, 8/5 priority date for domestic students; for spring admission, 1/5 priority date for domestic students. Applications are processed on a rolling basis. Application fee: $50. *Expenses:* Contact institution. *Financial support:* Application deadline: 5/1; applicants required to submit FAFSA. *Faculty research:* Data collection and analysis of Gulf Stream surface temperature and circulation; science for visually impaired students including investigations of a satellite orbit, the Moon's surface, spectra of chemical elements and stars, the rotation of the Sun, and the spiral structure of our galaxy. *Unit head:* Dr. Dennis Dawson, Graduate Coordinator, 203-837-8671, E-mail: dawsond@wcsu.edu. *Application contact:* Dr. Chris Shankle, Associate Director of Graduate Admissions, 203-837-9005, Fax: 203-837-8326, E-mail: shanklec@wcsu.edu.
Website: http://www.wcsu.edu/physics/

Western Kentucky University, Graduate School, Ogden College of Science and Engineering, Department of Geography and Geology, Bowling Green, KY 42101. Offers geoscience (MS). *Degree requirements:* For master's, comprehensive exam, thesis or alternative. *Entrance requirements:* For master's, GRE General Test, minimum GPA of 2.75. Additional exam requirements/recommendations for international students: Required—TOEFL (minimum score 555 paper-based; 79 iBT). *Faculty research:* Hydroclimatology, electronic data sets, groundwater, sinkhole liquification potential, meteorological analysis.

Western Michigan University, Graduate College, College of Arts and Sciences, Department of Geosciences, Kalamazoo, MI 49008. Offers earth science (MA); geosciences (MS, PhD). *Degree requirements:* For master's, thesis; for doctorate, one foreign language, thesis/dissertation.

Western Michigan University, Graduate College, College of Arts and Sciences, Department of Interdisciplinary Arts and Sciences, Kalamazoo, MI 49008. Offers science education (MA, PhD), including biological sciences (PhD), chemistry (PhD), geosciences (PhD), physical geography (PhD), physics (PhD), science education (PhD). *Degree requirements:* For doctorate, thesis/dissertation.

Yale University, Graduate School of Arts and Sciences, Department of Geology and Geophysics, New Haven, CT 06520. Offers biogeochemistry (PhD); climate dynamics (PhD); geochemistry (PhD); geophysics (PhD); meteorology (PhD); oceanography (PhD); paleontology (PhD); paleooceanography (PhD); petrology (PhD); tectonics (PhD). *Degree requirements:* For doctorate, thesis/dissertation. *Entrance requirements:* For doctorate, GRE General Test. Additional exam requirements/recommendations for international students: Required—TOEFL.

York University, Faculty of Graduate Studies, Lassonde School of Engineering, Program in Earth and Space Science, Toronto, ON M3J 1P3, Canada. Offers M Sc, PhD. *Program availability:* Part-time, evening/weekend. *Degree requirements:* For master's, thesis or alternative; for doctorate, thesis/dissertation. Electronic applications accepted.

Hydrogeology

Clemson University, Graduate School, College of Engineering, Computing and Applied Sciences, Department of Environmental Engineering and Earth Sciences, Anderson, SC 29625. Offers biosystems engineering (MS, PhD); environmental engineering and science (MS, PhD); environmental health physics (MS); hydrogeology (MS). *Program availability:* Part-time. *Faculty:* 20 full-time (4 women). *Students:* 75 full-time (30 women), 16 part-time (5 women); includes 5 minority (1 Black or African American, non-Hispanic/Latino; 1 Native Hawaiian or other Pacific Islander, non-Hispanic/Latino; 3 Two or more races, non-Hispanic/Latino), 30 international. Average age 26. 118 applicants, 72% accepted, 24 enrolled. In 2018, 31 master's, 4 doctorates awarded. *Degree requirements:* For master's, thesis or alternative; for doctorate, comprehensive exam, thesis/dissertation. *Entrance requirements:* For master's and doctorate, GRE General Test, unofficial transcripts, letters of recommendation. Additional exam requirements/recommendations for international students: Required—TOEFL (minimum score 80 paper-based; 80 iBT); Recommended—IELTS (minimum score 6.5), TSE (minimum score 54). *Application deadline:* For fall admission, 2/15 for domestic and international students. Applications are processed on a rolling basis. Application fee: $80 ($90 for

international students). Electronic applications accepted. *Expenses:* $6823 per semester full-time resident, $14023 per semester full-time non-resident, $833 per credit hour part-time resident, $1731 per credit hour part-time non-resident, online $1264 per credit hour, $4938 doctoral programs resident, $10405 doctoral programs non-resident, $1144 full-time graduate assistant, other fees may apply per session. *Financial support:* In 2018–19, 60 students received support, including 5 fellowships with full and partial tuition reimbursements available (averaging $3,573 per year), 34 research assistantships with full and partial tuition reimbursements available (averaging $18,464 per year), 19 teaching assistantships with full and partial tuition reimbursements available (averaging $18,021 per year); career-related internships or fieldwork and unspecified assistantships also available. Financial award application deadline: 2/15. *Faculty research:* Environmental engineering, bioprocess and ecological engineering, nuclear environmental engineering and science, hydrogeology, environmental chemistry and microbiology. *Total annual research expenditures:* $5.4 million. *Unit head:* Dr. David Freedman, Department Chair, 864-656-5566, E-mail: dfreedm@clemson.edu. *Application contact:* Dr. Mark Schlautman, Graduate Program Coordinator, 864-656-

Peterson's Graduate Programs in the Physical Sciences, Mathematics, Agricultural Sciences, the Environment & Natural Resources 2020

www.petersons.com **111**

4059, E-mail: mschlau@clemson.edu.
Website: https://www.clemson.edu/cecas/departments/eees/

East Carolina University, Graduate School, Thomas Harriot College of Arts and Sciences, Department of Geological Sciences, Greenville, NC 27858-4353. Offers geology (MS); hydrogeology and environmental geology (Certificate). *Program availability:* Part-time. *Application deadline:* For fall admission, 6/1 priority date for domestic students, 12/15 priority date for international students; for spring admission, 11/1 priority date for domestic students, 8/15 priority date for international students. *Expenses: Tuition, area resident:* Full-time $4749. Tuition, state resident: full-time $4749. Tuition, nonresident: full-time $17,898. *International tuition:* $17,898 full-time. *Required fees:* $2787. Part-time tuition and fees vary according to course load and program. *Financial support:* Application deadline: 2/1. *Unit head:* Dr. Stephen Culver, Chair, 252-328-6360, Fax: 252-328-4391, E-mail: culvers@ecu.edu. *Application contact:* Graduate School Admissions, 252-328-6012, Fax: 252-328-6071, E-mail: gradschool@ecu.edu.
Website: http://www.ecu.edu/geology/

Indiana University Bloomington, University Graduate School, College of Arts and Sciences, Department of Earth and Atmospheric Sciences, Bloomington, IN 47405-7000. Offers biogeochemistry (MS, PhD); economic geology (MS, PhD); geobiology (MS, PhD); geophysics, structural geology and tectonics (MS, PhD); hydrogeology (MS, PhD); mineralogy (MS, PhD); stratigraphy and sedimentology (MS, PhD). Terminal master's awarded for partial completion of doctoral program. *Degree requirements:* For master's, thesis or alternative; for doctorate, comprehensive exam, thesis/dissertation. *Entrance requirements:* For master's and doctorate, GRE General Test. Additional exam requirements/recommendations for international students: Required—TOEFL. *Faculty research:* Geophysics, geochemistry, hydrogeology, geobiology, planetary science.

Montana Tech of The University of Montana, Geosciences Programs, Butte, MT 59701-8997. Offers geochemistry (MS); geological engineering (MS); geology (MS); geophysical engineering (MS); hydrogeological engineering (MS); hydrogeology (MS). *Program availability:* Part-time. *Degree requirements:* For master's, comprehensive exam (for some programs), thesis (for some programs). *Entrance requirements:* For master's, GRE General Test, minimum GPA of 3.0. Additional exam requirements/recommendations for international students: Required—TOEFL (minimum score 545 paper-based; 78 iBT), IELTS (minimum score 6.5). Electronic applications accepted. *Faculty research:* Water resource development, seismic processing, petroleum reservoir characterization, environmental geochemistry, geologic mapping.

Oregon State University, College of Earth, Ocean, and Atmospheric Sciences, Program in Geology, Corvallis, OR 97331. Offers geochemistry (MA, MS, PhD); geomorphology (MA, MS, PhD); geophysics (MA, MS, PhD); glacial geology (MA, MS, PhD); hydrology and hydrogeology (MA, MS, PhD); igneous petrology (MA, MS, PhD); neotonics (MA, MS, PhD); paleoclimatology (MA); structural geology (MA, MS, PhD). Terminal master's awarded for partial completion of doctoral program. *Entrance requirements:* For master's and doctorate, GRE, minimum GPA of 3.0 in last 90 hours. Additional exam requirements/recommendations for international students: Required—TOEFL (minimum score 80 iBT), IELTS (minimum score 6.5). *Faculty research:* Hydrogeology, geomorphology, ocean geology, geochemistry, earthquake geology.

University of Hawaii at Manoa, Office of Graduate Education, School of Ocean and Earth Science and Technology, Department of Geology and Geophysics, Honolulu, HI 96822. Offers high-pressure geophysics and geochemistry (MS, PhD); hydrogeology and engineering geology (MS, PhD); marine geology and geophysics (MS, PhD); planetary geosciences and remote sensing (MS, PhD); seismology and solid-earth geophysics (MS, PhD); volcanology, petrology, and geochemistry (MS, PhD). *Program availability:* Part-time. Terminal master's awarded for partial completion of doctoral program. *Degree requirements:* For master's, thesis optional; for doctorate, comprehensive exam, thesis/dissertation. *Entrance requirements:* For master's and doctorate, GRE General Test, minimum GPA of 3.0. Additional exam requirements/recommendations for international students: Required—TOEFL (minimum score 580 paper-based; 92 iBT), IELTS (minimum score 5).

University of Nevada, Reno, Graduate School, Interdisciplinary Program in Hydrologic Sciences, Reno, NV 89557. Offers hydrogeology (MS, PhD); hydrology (MS, PhD). Offered through the M. C. Fleischmann College of Agriculture, the College of Engineering, the Mackay School of Mines, and the Desert Research Institute. Terminal master's awarded for partial completion of doctoral program. *Degree requirements:* For master's, thesis optional; for doctorate, thesis/dissertation. *Entrance requirements:* For master's and doctorate, GRE General Test, minimum GPA of 3.0. Additional exam requirements/recommendations for international students: Required—TOEFL (minimum score 500 paper-based; 61 iBT), IELTS (minimum score 6). Electronic applications accepted. *Faculty research:* Groundwater, water resources, surface water, soil science.

University of South Florida, Innovative Education, Tampa, FL 33620-9951. Offers adult, career and higher education (Graduate Certificate), including college teaching, leadership in developing human resources, leadership in higher education; Africana studies (Graduate Certificate), including diasporas and health disparities, genocide and human rights; aging studies (Graduate Certificate), including gerontology; art research (Graduate Certificate), including museum studies; business foundations (Graduate Certificate); chemical and biomedical engineering (Graduate Certificate), including materials science and engineering, water, health and sustainability; child and family studies (Graduate Certificate), including positive behavior support; civil and industrial engineering (Graduate Certificate), including transportation systems analysis; community and family health (Graduate Certificate), including maternal and child health, social marketing and public health, violence and injury: prevention and intervention, women's health; criminology (Graduate Certificate), including criminal justice administration; data science for public administration (Graduate Certificate); digital humanities (Graduate Certificate); educational measurement and research (Graduate Certificate), including evaluation; English (Graduate Certificate), including comparative literary studies, creative writing, professional and technical communication; entrepreneurship (Graduate Certificate); environmental health (Graduate Certificate), including safety management; epidemiology and biostatistics (Graduate Certificate), including applied biostatistics, biostatistics, concepts and tools of epidemiology, epidemiology, epidemiology of infectious diseases; geography, environment and planning (Graduate Certificate), including community development, environmental policy and management, geographical information systems; geology (Graduate Certificate), including hydrogeology; global health (Graduate Certificate), including disaster management, global health and Latin American and Caribbean studies, global health practice, humanitarian assistance, infection control; government and international affairs (Graduate Certificate), including Cuban studies, globalization studies; health policy and management (Graduate Certificate), including health management and leadership, public health policy and programs; hearing specialist: early intervention (Graduate Certificate); industrial and management systems engineering (Graduate Certificate), including systems engineering, technology management; information studies (Graduate Certificate), including school library media specialist; information systems/decision sciences (Graduate Certificate), including analytics and business intelligence; instructional technology (Graduate Certificate), including distance education, Florida digital/virtual educator, instructional design, multimedia design, Web design; internal medicine, bioethics and medical humanities (Graduate Certificate), including biomedical ethics; Latin American and Caribbean studies (Graduate Certificate); leadership for coastal resiliency planning (Graduate Certificate); mass communications (Graduate Certificate), including multimedia journalism; mathematics and statistics (Graduate Certificate), including mathematics; medicine (Graduate Certificate), including aging and neuroscience, bioinformatics, biotechnology, brain fitness and memory management, clinical investigation, hand and upper limb rehabilitation, health informatics, health sciences, integrative weight management, intellectual property, medicine and gender, metabolic and nutritional medicine, metabolic cardiology, pharmacy sciences; national and competitive intelligence (Graduate Certificate); nursing (Graduate Certificate), including simulation based academic fellowship in advanced pain management; psychological and social foundations (Graduate Certificate), including career counseling, college teaching, diversity in education, mental health counseling, school counseling; public affairs (Graduate Certificate), including nonprofit management, public management, research administration; public health (Graduate Certificate), including assessing chemical toxicity and public health risks, health equity, pharmacoepidemiology, public health generalist, toxicology, translational research in adolescent behavioral health; public health practices (Graduate Certificate), including planning for healthy communities; rehabilitation and mental health counseling (Graduate Certificate), including integrative mental health care, marriage and family therapy, rehabilitation technology; secondary education (Graduate Certificate), including ESOL, foreign language education: culture and content, foreign language education: professional; social work (Graduate Certificate), including geriatric social work/clinical gerontology; special education (Graduate Certificate), including autism spectrum disorder, disabilities education: severe/profound; world languages (Graduate Certificate), including teaching English as a second language (TESL) or foreign language. *Expenses:* Tuition, state resident: full-time $6350. Tuition, nonresident: full-time $19,048. *International tuition:* $19,048 full-time. *Required fees:* $2079. *Unit head:* Dr. Cynthia DeLuca, Associate Vice President and Assistant Vice Provost, 813-974-3077, Fax: 813-974-7061, E-mail: deluca@usf.edu. *Application contact:* Owen Hooper, Director, Summer and Alternative Calendar Programs, 813-974-6917, E-mail: hooper@usf.edu.
Website: http://www.usf.edu/innovative-education/

Hydrology

Boise State University, College of Arts and Sciences, Department of Geosciences, Boise, ID 83725-0399. Offers earth science (M E Sci); geophysics (MS, PhD); geoscience (MS); geosciences (PhD); hydrologic sciences (MS). *Program availability:* Part-time. Terminal master's awarded for partial completion of doctoral program. *Degree requirements:* For master's, thesis (for some programs); for doctorate, thesis/dissertation. *Entrance requirements:* For master's, GRE General Test, BS in related field, minimum GPA of 3.0; for doctorate, GRE General Test. Additional exam requirements/recommendations for international students: Required—TOEFL (minimum score 550 paper-based; 80 iBT), IELTS (minimum score 6). Electronic applications accepted. *Faculty research:* Seismology, geothermal aquifers, sedimentation, tectonics, seismo-acoustic propagation.

California State University, Bakersfield, Division of Graduate Studies, School of Natural Sciences, Mathematics, and Engineering, Program in Geological Sciences, Bakersfield, CA 93311. Offers geological sciences (MS); hydrogeology (MS); petroleum geology (MS); science education (MS). *Program availability:* Part-time, evening/weekend. *Faculty:* 4 full-time (0 women). *Students:* 6 full-time (2 women), 17 part-time (7 women); includes 13 minority (1 Black or African American, non-Hispanic/Latino; 1 American Indian or Alaska Native, non-Hispanic/Latino; 10 Hispanic/Latino; 1 Two or more races, non-Hispanic/Latino). Average age 30. 18 applicants, 94% accepted, 15 enrolled. In 2018, 12 master's awarded. *Degree requirements:* For master's, thesis. *Entrance requirements:* For master's, GRE General Test, BS in geology. *Application deadline:* Applications are processed on a rolling basis. Application fee: $55. *Financial support:* In 2018–19, fellowships (averaging $1,850 per year) were awarded; Federal Work-Study, scholarships/grants, and tuition waivers (full and partial) also available. Financial award application deadline: 3/2; financial award applicants required to submit FAFSA. *Unit head:* Dr. William Krugh, Director, 661-654-3126, Fax: 661-654-2040, E-mail: wkrugh@csub.edu. *Application contact:* Martha Manriquez, Graduate Student Center Coordinator, 661-654-2786, Fax: 661-654-2791, E-mail: gsc@csub.edu.
Website: https://www.csub.edu/geology/index.html

Colorado School of Mines, Office of Graduate Studies, Department of Geology and Geological Engineering, Golden, CO 80401. Offers environmental geochemistry (PMS); geochemistry (MS, PhD); geological engineering (ME, MS, PhD); geology (MS, PhD); hydrology (MS, PhD); mineral exploration (PMS); petroleum reservoir systems (PMS); underground construction and tunneling (MS). *Program availability:* Part-time. *Faculty:* 30 full-time (12 women), 6 part-time/adjunct (5 women). *Students:* 129 full-time (44 women), 32 part-time (12 women); includes 20 minority (1 Black or African American, non-Hispanic/Latino; 2 American Indian or Alaska Native, non-Hispanic/Latino; 3 Asian, non-Hispanic/Latino; 10 Hispanic/Latino; 4 Two or more races, non-Hispanic/Latino), 30 international. Average age 29. 244 applicants, 41% accepted, 54 enrolled. In 2018, 39 master's, 11 doctorates awarded. *Degree requirements:* For master's, thesis (for some programs); for doctorate, comprehensive exam, thesis/dissertation. *Entrance requirements:* For master's and doctorate, GRE General Test. Additional exam requirements/recommendations for international students: Required—TOEFL (minimum score 550 paper-based; 79 iBT). *Application deadline:* For fall admission, 12/15 priority date for domestic and international students; for spring admission, 9/1 priority date for domestic and international students. Application fee: $60 ($80 for international

students). Electronic applications accepted. *Expenses:* Tuition, state resident: full-time $16,650; part-time $925 per contact hour. Tuition, nonresident: full-time $36,270; part-time $2015 per contact hour. *International tuition:* $36,270 full-time. *Required fees:* $2314; $2314 per semester. *Financial support:* In 2018–19, 48 research assistantships with full tuition reimbursements, 20 teaching assistantships with full tuition reimbursements were awarded; fellowships, scholarships/grants, health care benefits, and unspecified assistantships also available. Financial award application deadline: 12/15; financial award applicants required to submit FAFSA. *Faculty research:* Predictive sediment modeling, petrophysics, aquifer-contaminant flow modeling, water-rock interactions, geotechnical engineering. *Unit head:* Dr. Wendy Bohrson, Head, 303-273-3066, E-mail: bohrson@mines.edu. *Application contact:* Dr. Christian Shorey, Lecturer/Program Manager, 303-273-3556, E-mail: cshorey@mines.edu.
Website: http://geology.mines.edu

Colorado School of Mines, Office of Graduate Studies, Department of Geophysics, Golden, CO 80401. Offers geophysical engineering (ME, MS, PhD); geophysics (MS, PhD); hydrology (MS, PhD); mineral exploration and mining geosciences (PMS); petroleum reservoir systems (PMS). *Program availability:* Part-time. *Faculty:* 14 full-time (5 women), 4 part-time/adjunct (0 women). *Students:* 62 full-time (17 women), 2 part-time (0 women); includes 5 minority (2 Asian, non-Hispanic/Latino; 1 Hispanic/Latino; 2 Two or more races, non-Hispanic/Latino), 33 international. Average age 28. 142 applicants, 26% accepted, 23 enrolled. In 2018, 12 master's, 12 doctorates awarded. *Degree requirements:* For master's, thesis (for some programs); for doctorate, comprehensive exam, thesis/dissertation. *Entrance requirements:* For master's and doctorate, GRE General Test. Additional exam requirements/recommendations for international students: Required—TOEFL (minimum score 550 paper-based; 79 iBT). *Application deadline:* For fall admission, 12/15 priority date for domestic and international students; for spring admission, 9/1 priority date for domestic students, 9/1 for international students. Application fee: $60 ($80 for international students). Electronic applications accepted. *Expenses:* Tuition, state resident: full-time $16,650; part-time $925 per contact hour. Tuition, nonresident: full-time $36,270; part-time $2015 per contact hour. *International tuition:* $36,270 full-time. *Required fees:* $2314; $2314 per semester. *Financial support:* In 2018–19, 40 research assistantships with full tuition reimbursements, 9 teaching assistantships with full tuition reimbursements were awarded; fellowships, career-related internships or fieldwork, scholarships/grants, health care benefits, and unspecified assistantships also available. Financial award application deadline: 12/15; financial award applicants required to submit FAFSA. *Faculty research:* Seismic exploration, gravity and geomagnetic fields, electrical mapping and sounding, bore hole measurements, environmental physics. *Unit head:* Dr. Paul Sava, Head, 303-384-2362, E-mail: psava@mines.edu. *Application contact:* Michelle Szobody, Program Assistant, 303-273-3935, E-mail: mszobody@mines.edu.
Website: http://geophysics.mines.edu

Cornell University, Graduate School, Graduate Fields of Engineering, Field of Civil and Environmental Engineering, Ithaca, NY 14853. Offers engineering management (M Eng, MS, PhD); environmental engineering (M Eng, MS, PhD); environmental fluid mechanics and hydrology (M Eng, MS, PhD); environmental systems engineering (M Eng, MS, PhD); geotechnical engineering (M Eng, MS, PhD); remote sensing (M Eng, MS, PhD); structural engineering (M Eng, MS, PhD); structural mechanics (M Eng, MS); transportation engineering (MS, PhD); transportation systems engineering (M Eng); water resource systems (M Eng, MS, PhD). Terminal master's awarded for partial completion of doctoral program. *Degree requirements:* For master's, thesis (MS); for doctorate, comprehensive exam, thesis/dissertation. *Entrance requirements:* For master's and doctorate, GRE General Test (recommended), 2 letters of recommendation. Additional exam requirements/recommendations for international students: Required—TOEFL (minimum score 600 paper-based; 77 iBT). Electronic applications accepted. *Faculty research:* Environmental engineering, geotechnical engineering, remote sensing, environmental fluid mechanics and hydrology, structural engineering.

Cornell University, Graduate School, Graduate Fields of Engineering, Field of Geological Sciences, Ithaca, NY 14853. Offers economic geology (M Eng, MS, PhD); engineering geology (M Eng, MS, PhD); environmental geophysics (M Eng, MS, PhD); general geology (M Eng, MS, PhD); geobiology (M Eng, MS, PhD); geochemistry and isotope geology (M Eng, MS, PhD); geohydrology (M Eng, MS, PhD); geomorphology (M Eng, MS, PhD); geophysics (M Eng, MS, PhD); geotectonics (M Eng, MS, PhD); marine geology (MS, PhD); mineralogy (M Eng, MS, PhD); paleontology (M Eng, MS, PhD); petroleum geology (M Eng, MS, PhD); petrology (M Eng, MS, PhD); planetary geology (M Eng, MS, PhD); Precambrian geology (M Eng, MS, PhD); Quaternary geology (M Eng, MS, PhD); rock mechanics (M Eng, MS, PhD); sedimentology (M Eng, MS, PhD); seismology (M Eng, MS, PhD); stratigraphy (M Eng, MS, PhD); structural geology (M Eng, MS, PhD). *Degree requirements:* For master's, thesis (MS); for doctorate, comprehensive exam, thesis/dissertation. *Entrance requirements:* For master's and doctorate, GRE General Test, 3 letters of recommendation. Additional exam requirements/recommendations for international students: Required—TOEFL (minimum score 550 paper-based; 77 iBT). Electronic applications accepted. *Faculty research:* Geophysics, structural geology, petrology, geochemistry, geodynamics.

Drexel University, College of Engineering, Department of Civil, Architectural, and Environmental Engineering, Philadelphia, PA 19104-2875. Offers architectural/building systems engineering (MS, PhD); civil engineering (MS, PhD); environmental engineering (MS, PhD); geotechnical, geoenvironmental and geosynthetics engineering (MS, PhD); hydraulics, hydrology and water resources engineering (MS, PhD); structures (MS). *Program availability:* Part-time, evening/weekend. *Degree requirements:* For master's, thesis optional; for doctorate, thesis/dissertation. *Entrance requirements:* For master's, minimum GPA of 3.0; for doctorate, minimum GPA of 3.5, MS in civil engineering. Additional exam requirements/recommendations for international students: Required—TOEFL. Electronic applications accepted. *Faculty research:* Structural dynamics, hazardous wastes, water resources, pavement materials, groundwater.

Idaho State University, Graduate School, College of Science and Engineering, Department of Geosciences, Pocatello, ID 83209-8072. Offers geographic information science (MS); geology (MNS, MS); geology with emphasis in environmental geoscience (MS); geophysics/hydrology/geology (MS); geotechnology (Postbaccalaureate Certificate). *Program availability:* Part-time. *Degree requirements:* For master's, comprehensive exam, thesis, oral colloquium; for Postbaccalaureate Certificate, thesis optional, minimum 19 credits. *Entrance requirements:* For master's, GRE General Test (minimum 50th percentile in 2 sections), 3 letters of recommendation; for Postbaccalaureate Certificate, GRE General Test, 3 letters of recommendation, bachelor's degree, statement of goals. Additional exam requirements/recommendations for international students: Required—TOEFL (minimum score 550 paper-based; 80 iBT). Electronic applications accepted. *Faculty research:* Quantitative field mapping and sampling: microscopic, geochemical, and isotopic analysis of rocks, minerals and water; remote sensing, geographic information systems, and global positioning systems: environmental and watershed management; surficial and fluvial processes: landscape change; regional tectonics, structural geology; planetary geology.

Massachusetts Institute of Technology, School of Engineering, Department of Civil and Environmental Engineering, Cambridge, MA 02139. Offers biological oceanography (PhD, Sc D); chemical oceanography (PhD, Sc D); civil and environmental engineering (M Eng, SM, PhD, Sc D); civil and environmental systems (PhD, Sc D); civil engineering (PhD, Sc D, CE); civil engineering and computation (PhD); coastal engineering (PhD, Sc D); construction engineering and management (PhD, Sc D); environmental biology (PhD, Sc D); environmental chemistry (PhD, Sc D); environmental engineering (PhD, Sc D); environmental engineering and computation (PhD); environmental fluid mechanics (PhD, Sc D); geotechnical and geoenvironmental engineering (PhD, Sc D); hydrology (PhD, Sc D); information technology (PhD, Sc D); oceanographic engineering (PhD, Sc D); structures and materials (PhD, Sc D); transportation (PhD, Sc D); SM/MBA. *Degree requirements:* For master's, thesis; for doctorate, comprehensive exam, thesis/dissertation; for CE, comprehensive exam, thesis. *Entrance requirements:* For master's, doctorate, and CE, GRE General Test. Additional exam requirements/recommendations for international students: Required—TOEFL, IELTS. Electronic applications accepted. *Expenses: Tuition:* Full-time $51,520; part-time $800 per credit hour. *Required fees:* $312. *Faculty research:* Environmental chemistry, environmental fluid mechanics and coastal engineering, environmental microbiology, geotechnical engineering and geomechanics, hydrology and hydro climatology, infrastructure systems, mechanics of materials and structures, transportation systems.

New Mexico Institute of Mining and Technology, Center for Graduate Studies, Department of Earth and Environmental Science, Program in Hydrology, Socorro, NM 87801. Offers MS, PhD. *Degree requirements:* For master's, thesis; for doctorate, thesis/dissertation. *Entrance requirements:* For master's, GRE General Test; for doctorate, GRE General Test, GRE Subject Test. Additional exam requirements/recommendations for international students: Required—TOEFL (minimum score 540 paper-based). *Faculty research:* Surface and subsurface hydrology, numerical simulation, stochastic hydrology, water quality, modeling.

New Mexico State University, College of Agricultural, Consumer and Environmental Sciences, Department of Agricultural Economics and Agricultural Business, Las Cruces, NM 88003-8001. Offers agribusiness (MBA); agriculture (M Ag); economic development (DED); water science management (MS). *Program availability:* Part-time. *Faculty:* 4 full-time (1 woman), 2 part-time/adjunct (0 women). *Students:* 7 full-time (4 women), 3 part-time (1 woman); includes 4 minority (all Hispanic/Latino), 1 international. Average age 24. 11 applicants, 45% accepted, 4 enrolled. In 2018, 4 master's awarded. *Degree requirements:* For master's, thesis (for some programs); for doctorate, comprehensive exam, thesis/dissertation. *Entrance requirements:* For master's, GRE; GMAT (for MBA), previous course work in intermediate microeconomics, intermediate macroeconomics, college-level calculus, statistics; for doctorate, previous course work in intermediate microeconomics, intermediate macroeconomics, college-level calculus, statistics, related MS or equivalent, minimum GPA of 3.0. Additional exam requirements/recommendations for international students: Required—TOEFL (minimum score 550 paper-based; 79 iBT), IELTS (minimum score 6.5). *Application deadline:* For fall admission, 7/1 priority date for domestic and international students; for spring admission, 11/1 priority date for domestic and international students. Applications are processed on a rolling basis. Application fee: $40 ($50 for international students). Electronic applications accepted. *Expenses: Tuition, area resident:* Full-time $4216.70; part-time $252.70 per credit hour. Tuition, state resident: full-time $4216.70; part-time $252.70 per credit hour. Tuition, nonresident: full-time $12,769; part-time $881.10 per credit hour. *International tuition:* $12,769.30 full-time. *Required fees:* $878.40; $48.80 per credit hour. Full-time tuition and fees vary according to course load and reciprocity agreements. *Financial support:* In 2018–19, 8 students received support, including 5 research assistantships (averaging $16,380 per year), 4 teaching assistantships (averaging $16,964 per year); career-related internships or fieldwork, Federal Work-Study, scholarships/grants, traineeships, health care benefits, and unspecified assistantships also available. Support available to part-time students. Financial award application deadline: 3/1. *Faculty research:* Natural resource policy, production economics and farm/ranch management, agribusiness and marketing, international marketing and trade, agricultural risk management. *Total annual research expenditures:* $917,292. *Unit head:* Dr. Jay Lillywhite, Department Head, 575-646-3215, Fax: 575-646-3808, E-mail: lillywhi@nmsu.edu. *Application contact:* Dr. Ram Acharya, Graduate Committee Chair, 575-646-2524, Fax: 575-646-3808, E-mail: acharyar@nmsu.edu.
Website: http://aces.nmsu.edu/academics/aeab/

Oregon State University, College of Earth, Ocean, and Atmospheric Sciences, Program in Geology, Corvallis, OR 97331. Offers geochemistry (MA, MS, PhD); geomorphology (MA, MS, PhD); geophysics (MA, MS, PhD); glacial geology (MA, MS, PhD); hydrology and hydrogeology (MA, MS, PhD); igneous petrology (MA, MS, PhD); neotonics (MA, MS, PhD); paleoclimatology (MA); structural geology (MA, MS, PhD). Terminal master's awarded for partial completion of doctoral program. *Entrance requirements:* For master's and doctorate, GRE, minimum GPA of 3.0 in last 90 hours. Additional exam requirements/recommendations for international students: Required—TOEFL (minimum score 80 iBT), IELTS (minimum score 6.5). *Faculty research:* Hydrogeology, geomorphology, ocean geology, geochemistry, earthquake geology.

Portland State University, Graduate Studies, College of Liberal Arts and Sciences, Department of Environmental Sciences and Management, Portland, OR 97207-0751. Offers environmental management (MEM); environmental science and management (PSM); environmental sciences/biology (PhD); environmental sciences/chemistry (PhD); environmental sciences/civil engineering (PhD); environmental sciences/geography (PhD); environmental sciences/geology (PhD); environmental sciences/physics (PhD); environmental studies (MS); hydrology (Certificate). *Program availability:* Part-time. *Degree requirements:* For master's, thesis or alternative; for doctorate, variable foreign language requirement, comprehensive exam, thesis/dissertation, oral and qualifying exams. *Entrance requirements:* For master's, GRE General Test, science-based BA/BS or equivalent training, 3 letters of recommendation, identification of potential advisor; for doctorate, minimum GPA of 3.0 in upper-division course work or 2.75 overall. Additional exam requirements/recommendations for international students: Required—TOEFL (minimum score 550 paper-based; 80 iBT), IELTS (minimum score 6.5). *Faculty research:* Environmental aspects of biology, chemistry, civil engineering, geology, physics.

Stanford University, School of Engineering, Department of Civil and Environmental Engineering, Stanford, CA 94305-2004. Offers atmosphere and energy (MS, PhD); construction (MS), including construction engineering and management, design-construction integration, sustainable design and construction; environmental engineering and science (MS, PhD, Eng); environmental fluid mechanics and hydrology (PhD); geomechanics (MS); structural engineering (MS). *Expenses: Tuition:* Full-time $50,703; part-time $32,970 per year. *Required fees:* $651.
Website: http://www-ce.stanford.edu/

Stevens Institute of Technology, Graduate School, Charles V. Schaefer Jr. School of Engineering and Science, Department of Civil, Environmental, and Ocean Engineering, Program in Civil Engineering, Hoboken, NJ 07030. Offers civil engineering (PhD, Certificate), including geotechnical engineering (Certificate); geotechnical/

geoenvironmental engineering (M Eng, Engr); hydrologic modeling (M Eng); stormwater management (M Eng); structural engineering (M Eng, Engr); transportation engineering (M Eng); water resources engineering (M Eng). *Program availability:* Part-time, evening/weekend. *Faculty:* 28 full-time (7 women), 2 part-time/adjunct (1 woman). *Students:* 37 full-time (8 women), 27 part-time (8 women); includes 8 minority (1 Black or African American, non-Hispanic/Latino; 1 American Indian or Alaska Native, non-Hispanic/Latino; 6 Asian, non-Hispanic/Latino), 30 international. Average age 25. In 2018, 44 master's awarded. Terminal master's awarded for partial completion of doctoral program. *Degree requirements:* For master's, thesis optional, minimum B average in major field and overall; for doctorate, comprehensive exam (for some programs), thesis/dissertation; for other advanced degree, minimum B average. *Entrance requirements:* For master's, GRE/GMAT scores: GRE scores are required for all applicants applying to a full-time graduate program in the Schaefer School of Engineering and Science (SES). International applicants must submit TOEFL/IELTS scores and fulfill the English Language Proficiency Requirements in order to be considered. Additional exam requirements/recommendations for international students: Required—TOEFL (minimum score 74 iBT), IELTS (minimum score 6). *Application deadline:* For fall admission, 4/15 for domestic and international students; for spring admission, 11/1 for domestic and international students; for summer admission, 5/1 for domestic students. Applications are processed on a rolling basis. Application fee: $60. Electronic applications accepted. *Expenses: Tuition:* Full-time $35,960; part-time $1620 per credit. *Required fees:* $1290; $600 per semester. Tuition and fees vary according to course load. *Financial support:* Fellowships, research assistantships, teaching assistantships, career-related internships or fieldwork, Federal Work-Study, scholarships/grants, and unspecified assistantships available. Financial award application deadline: 2/15; financial award applicants required to submit FAFSA. *Unit head:* Dr. Jean Zu, Dean of SES, 201-216.8233, Fax: 201-216.8372, E-mail: Jean.Zu@stevens.edu. *Application contact:* Graduate Admission, 888-783-8367, Fax: 888-511-1306, E-mail: graduate@stevens.edu.

Temple University, College of Engineering, Department of Civil and Environmental Engineering, Philadelphia, PA 19122-6096. Offers civil engineering (MSCE); environmental engineering (MS Env E); storm water management (Graduate Certificate). *Program availability:* Part-time, evening/weekend. Terminal master's awarded for partial completion of doctoral program. *Degree requirements:* For master's, thesis optional. *Entrance requirements:* For master's, GRE General Test, minimum GPA of 3.0; BS in engineering from ABET-accredited or equivalent institution; resume; goals statement; three letters of reference; official transcripts. Additional exam requirements/recommendations for international students: Required—TOEFL (minimum score 550 paper-based; 79 iBT), IELTS (minimum score 6.5), PTE (minimum score 53). Electronic applications accepted. *Expenses:* Contact institution. *Faculty research:* Analysis of the effect of scour on bridge stability, design of sustainable buildings, development of new highway pavement material using plastic waste, characterization of by-products and waste materials for pavement and geotechnical engineering applications, development of effective traffic signals in urban and rural settings, development of techniques for effective construction management.

Université du Québec, Institut National de la Recherche Scientifique, Graduate Programs, Research Center–Water Earth Environment, Québec, QC G1K 9A9, Canada. Offers earth sciences (M Sc, PhD); earth sciences - environmental technologies (M Sc); water sciences (M Sc, PhD). *Program availability:* Part-time. *Faculty:* 34 full-time. *Students:* 169 full-time (87 women), 19 part-time (11 women), 132 international. Average age 33. 58 applicants, 66% accepted, 32 enrolled. In 2018, 34 master's, 24 doctorates awarded. *Degree requirements:* For master's, thesis (for some programs); for doctorate, thesis/dissertation. *Entrance requirements:* For master's, appropriate bachelor's degree, proficiency in French; for doctorate, appropriate master's degree, proficiency in French. *Application deadline:* For fall admission, 3/30 for domestic and international students; for winter admission, 11/1 for domestic and international students; for spring admission, 3/1 for domestic and international students. Application fee: $45. Electronic applications accepted. *Financial support:* In 2018–19, fellowships (averaging $16,500 per year) were awarded; research assistantships also available. *Faculty research:* Land use, impacts of climate change, adaptation to climate change, integrated management of resources (mineral and water). *Unit head:* Jean-François Blais, Director, 418-654-2575, Fax: 418-654-2600, E-mail: jean-francois.blais@ete.inrs.ca. *Application contact:* Sean Otto, Registrar, 418-654-2518, Fax: 418-654-3858, E-mail: sean.otto@inrs.ca.
Website: http://www.ete.inrs.ca/

The University of Arizona, College of Science, Department of Hydrology and Water Resources, Tucson, AZ 85721. Offers hydrology (PhD). *Program availability:* Part-time. *Degree requirements:* For doctorate, thesis/dissertation. *Entrance requirements:* For doctorate, GRE General Test, minimum undergraduate GPA of 3.2, graduate 3.4; 3 letters of recommendation; master's degree in related field; master's thesis abstract. Additional exam requirements/recommendations for international students: Required—TOEFL (minimum score 550 paper-based; 79 iBT). Electronic applications accepted. *Faculty research:* Subsurface and surface hydrology, hydrometeorology/climatology, applied remote sensing, water resource systems, environmental hydrology and water quality.

University of Calgary, Faculty of Graduate Studies, Faculty of Science, Program in Geoscience, Calgary, AB T2N 1N4, Canada. Offers geology (M Sc, PhD); geophysics (M Sc, PhD); hydrology (M Sc, PhD). *Program availability:* Part-time. Terminal master's awarded for partial completion of doctoral program. *Degree requirements:* For master's, thesis; for doctorate, thesis/dissertation, candidacy exam. *Entrance requirements:* For master's, B Sc; for doctorate, honors B Sc or M Sc. Additional exam requirements/recommendations for international students: Required—TOEFL. Electronic applications accepted. *Faculty research:* Geochemistry, petrology, paleontology, stratigraphy, exploration and solid-earth geophysics.

University of California, Davis, Graduate Studies, Graduate Group in Hydrologic Sciences, Davis, CA 95616. Offers MS, PhD. Terminal master's awarded for partial completion of doctoral program. *Degree requirements:* For master's, comprehensive exam (for some programs), thesis (for some programs); for doctorate, thesis/dissertation. *Entrance requirements:* For master's, GRE General Test, minimum GPA of 3.0; for doctorate, GRE. Additional exam requirements/recommendations for international students: Required—TOEFL (minimum score 550 paper-based). Electronic applications accepted. *Faculty research:* Pollutant transport in surface and subsurface waters, subsurface heterogeneity, micrometeorology evaporation, biodegradation.

University of Colorado Denver, College of Engineering, Design and Computing, Department of Civil Engineering, Denver, CO 80217. Offers civil engineering (EASPh D); civil engineering systems (PhD); environmental and sustainability engineering (MS, PhD); geographic information systems (MS); geotechnical engineering (MS, PhD); hydrology and hydraulics (MS, PhD); structural engineering (MS, PhD); transportation engineering (MS, PhD). *Program availability:* Part-time, evening/weekend. *Degree requirements:* For master's, comprehensive exam, 30 credit hours, project or thesis; for doctorate, comprehensive exam, thesis/dissertation, 60 credit hours (30 of which are dissertation research). *Entrance requirements:* For master's, GRE, statement of purpose, transcripts, three references; for doctorate, GRE, statement of purpose, transcripts, references, letter of support from faculty stating willingness to serve as dissertation advisor and outlining plan for financial support. Additional exam requirements/recommendations for international students: Required—TOEFL (minimum score 537 paper-based; 75 iBT); Recommended—IELTS (minimum score 6.5). Electronic applications accepted. *Expenses:* Tuition, state resident: full-time $6786; part-time $337 per credit hour. Tuition, nonresident: full-time $22,590; part-time $1255 per credit hour. *Required fees:* $1231; $137 per credit hour. Tuition and fees vary according to program and reciprocity agreements.

University of Florida, Graduate School, College of Liberal Arts and Sciences, Department of Geological Sciences, Gainesville, FL 32611. Offers geology (MS, MST, PhD); hydrologic sciences (MS, PhD); tropical conservation and development (MS, MST, PhD); wetland sciences (MS, MST, PhD). Terminal master's awarded for partial completion of doctoral program. *Degree requirements:* For master's, thesis (for some programs); for doctorate, one foreign language, thesis/dissertation. *Entrance requirements:* For master's and doctorate, GRE General Test, minimum GPA of 3.0. Additional exam requirements/recommendations for international students: Required—TOEFL (minimum score 550 paper-based; 80 iBT), IELTS (minimum score 6). Electronic applications accepted. *Faculty research:* Paleoclimatology, tectonophysics, petrochemistry, marine geology, geochemistry, hydrology.

University of Minnesota, Twin Cities Campus, Graduate School, College of Food, Agricultural and Natural Resource Sciences, Program in Natural Resources Science and Management, St. Paul, MN 55108. Offers assessment, monitoring, and geospatial analysis (MS, PhD); economics, policy, management, and society (MS, PhD); forest hydrology and watershed management (MS, PhD); forest products (MS, PhD); forests: biology, ecology, conservation, and management (MS, PhD); natural resources science and management (MS, PhD); paper science and engineering (MS, PhD); recreation resources, tourism, and environmental education (MS, PhD). *Program availability:* Part-time. Terminal master's awarded for partial completion of doctoral program. *Degree requirements:* For master's, comprehensive exam, thesis (for some programs); for doctorate, comprehensive exam, thesis/dissertation. *Entrance requirements:* For master's and doctorate, GRE General Test. Additional exam requirements/recommendations for international students: Required—TOEFL (minimum score 550 paper-based; 79 iBT); Recommended—IELTS (minimum score 6.5). Electronic applications accepted. *Faculty research:* Forest hydrology, biology, ecology, conservation, and management; recreation resources and environmental education; wildlife ecology; economics, policy, and society; geographic information systems (GIS); forest products and paper science.

University of Mississippi, Graduate School, School of Engineering, University, MS 38677. Offers aeroacoustics (MS, PhD); chemical engineering (MS, PhD); civil engineering (MS, PhD); computational hydroscience (MS, PhD); computer science (MS, PhD); electrical engineering (MS, PhD); electromagnetics (MS, PhD); environmental engineering (MS, PhD); geology and geological engineering (MS, PhD); hydrology (MS); material science (MS); mechanical engineering (MS, PhD); telecommunications (MS). *Faculty:* 76 full-time (16 women), 3 part-time/adjunct (1 woman). *Students:* 129 full-time (33 women), 21 part-time (5 women); includes 15 minority (7 Black or African American, non-Hispanic/Latino; 6 Asian, non-Hispanic/Latino; 1 Hispanic/Latino; 1 Two or more races, non-Hispanic/Latino), 73 international. Average age 29. In 2018, 36 master's, 17 doctorates awarded. *Entrance requirements:* For master's, GRE General Test, minimum GPA of 3.0; for doctorate, GRE General Test. Additional exam requirements/recommendations for international students: Required—TOEFL. *Application deadline:* Applications are processed on a rolling basis. Application fee: $50. Electronic applications accepted. *Financial support:* Scholarships/grants available. Financial award application deadline: 3/1; financial award applicants required to submit FAFSA. *Unit head:* Dr. David Puleo, Dean, 662-915-5780, Fax: 662-915-5387, E-mail: engineer@olemiss.edu. *Application contact:* Temeka Smith, Graduate Activities Specialist for Admissions, 662-915-7474, Fax: 662-915-7577, E-mail: gschool@olemiss.edu.

University of Nevada, Reno, Graduate School, Interdisciplinary Program in Hydrologic Sciences, Reno, NV 89557. Offers hydrogeology (MS, PhD); hydrology (MS, PhD). Offered through the M. C. Fleischmann College of Agriculture, the College of Engineering, the Mackay School of Mines, and the Desert Research Institute. Terminal master's awarded for partial completion of doctoral program. *Degree requirements:* For master's, thesis optional; for doctorate, thesis/dissertation. *Entrance requirements:* For master's and doctorate, GRE General Test, minimum GPA of 3.0. Additional exam requirements/recommendations for international students: Required—TOEFL (minimum score 500 paper-based; 61 iBT), IELTS (minimum score 6). Electronic applications accepted. *Faculty research:* Groundwater, water resources, surface water, soil science.

University of New Brunswick Fredericton, School of Graduate Studies, Faculty of Engineering, Department of Civil Engineering, Fredericton, NB E3B 5A3, Canada. Offers construction engineering and management (M Eng, M Sc E, PhD); environmental engineering (M Eng, M Sc E, PhD); environmental studies (M Eng); geotechnical engineering (M Eng, M Sc E, PhD); groundwater/hydrology (M Eng, M Sc E, PhD); materials (M Eng, M Sc E, PhD); pavements (M Eng, M Sc E, PhD); structures (M Eng, M Sc E, PhD); transportation (M Eng, M Sc E, PhD). *Program availability:* Part-time. *Degree requirements:* For master's, thesis; for doctorate, comprehensive exam, thesis/dissertation, qualifying exam; 27 credit hours of courses. *Entrance requirements:* For master's, minimum GPA of 3.0; B Sc E in civil engineering or related engineering degree; for doctorate, minimum GPA of 3.0; graduate degree in engineering or applied science. Additional exam requirements/recommendations for international students: Required—IELTS (minimum score 7.5), TWE (minimum score 4), Michigan English Language Assessment Battery (minimum score 85) or CanTest (minimum score 4.5); Recommended—TOEFL (minimum score 580 paper-based). Electronic applications accepted. *Faculty research:* Construction engineering and management; engineering materials and infrastructure renewal; highway and pavement research; structures and solid mechanics; geotechnical and geoenvironmental engineering; structure interaction; transportation and planning; environment, solid waste management; structural engineering; water and environmental engineering.

University of New Hampshire, Graduate School, College of Engineering and Physical Sciences, Department of Earth Sciences, Durham, NH 03824. Offers geochemical systems (MS); geology (MS); hydrology (MS); ocean mapping (MS); oceanography (MS). *Degree requirements:* For master's, thesis. *Entrance requirements:* For master's, GRE General Test. Additional exam requirements/recommendations for international students: Required—TOEFL (minimum score 550 paper-based; 80 iBT). Electronic applications accepted.

University of Rhode Island, Graduate School, College of Engineering, Department of Ocean Engineering, Narragansett, RI 02882. Offers ocean engineering (MS, PhD), including acoustics, geomechanics (MS), hydrodynamics (MS), ocean instrumentation (MS), offshore energy (MS), offshore structures (MS), water wave mechanics (MS).

Program availability: Part-time. *Faculty:* 9 full-time (1 woman). *Students:* 24 full-time (6 women), 19 part-time (4 women); includes 2 minority (both Asian, non-Hispanic/Latino), 6 international. 27 applicants, 70% accepted, 9 enrolled. In 2018, 10 master's, 1 doctorate awarded. *Entrance requirements:* Additional exam requirements/ recommendations for international students: Required—TOEFL. *Application deadline:* For fall admission, 7/15 for domestic students, 2/1 for international students; for spring admission, 11/15 for domestic students, 7/15 for international students; for summer admission, 4/15 for domestic students. Application fee: $65. Electronic applications accepted. *Expenses: Tuition, area resident:* Full-time $13,226; part-time $735 per credit. Tuition, state resident: full-time $13,226; part-time $735 per credit. Tuition, nonresident: full-time $25,854; part-time $1436 per credit. *International tuition:* $25,854 full-time. *Required fees:* $1698; $50 per credit. $35 per semester. One-time fee: $165. *Financial support:* In 2018–19, 8 research assistantships with tuition reimbursements (averaging $9,512 per year), 3 teaching assistantships with tuition reimbursements (averaging $13,338 per year) were awarded. Financial award application deadline: 2/1; financial award applicants required to submit FAFSA. *Unit head:* Dr. Stephen Grilli, Chairman, 401-874-6636, E-mail: grilli@uri.edu. *Application contact:* Christopher Baxter, Graduate Program Director, 401-874-6575, E-mail: cbaxter@uri.edu.
Website: http://www.oce.uri.edu/

University of Rhode Island, Graduate School, College of the Environment and Life Sciences, Department of Geosciences, Kingston, RI 02881. Offers environmental and earth sciences (MS, PhD); environmental science and management (MESM); hydrology (Graduate Certificate). *Program availability:* Part-time. *Faculty:* 8 full-time (4 women). *Students:* 1 part-time (0 women). In 2018, 1 master's, 9 other advanced degrees awarded. *Entrance requirements:* For master's and doctorate, GRE, 2 letters of recommendation. Additional exam requirements/recommendations for international students: Required—TOEFL. *Application deadline:* For fall admission, 7/15 for domestic students, 2/1 for international students; for spring admission, 11/15 for domestic students, 7/15 for international students. Application fee: $65. Electronic applications accepted. *Expenses: Tuition, area resident:* Full-time $13,226; part-time $735 per credit. Tuition, state resident: full-time $13,226; part-time $735 per credit. Tuition, nonresident: full-time $25,854; part-time $1436 per credit. *International tuition:* $25,854 full-time. *Required fees:* $1698; $50 per credit. $35 per semester. One-time fee: $165. *Financial support:* In 2018–19, 16 research assistantships with tuition reimbursements (averaging $11,641 per year) were awarded. Financial award application deadline: 2/1; financial award applicants required to submit FAFSA. *Unit head:* Dr. Brian Savage, Professor and Chair, 401-874-5392, E-mail: savage@uri.edu. *Application contact:* Dr. Thomas Boving, Professor, 401-874-7053, E-mail: tboving@uri.edu.
Website: http://web.uri.edu/geo/

University of Southern Mississippi, College of Arts and Sciences, Division of Marine Science, Stennis Space Center, MS 39529. Offers hydrographic science (MS); marine science (MS, PhD). *Program availability:* Part-time. *Degree requirements:* For master's, comprehensive exam, thesis, oral qualifying exam (marine science); for doctorate, 2 foreign languages, comprehensive exam, thesis/dissertation, oral qualifying exam. *Entrance requirements:* For master's, GRE General Test, minimum GPA of 3.0; for doctorate, GRE General Test, minimum GPA of 3.0 (undergraduate), 3.5 (graduate). Additional exam requirements/recommendations for international students: Required—TOEFL (minimum score 567 paper-based; 86 iBT), IELTS (minimum score 6.5). Electronic applications accepted. *Expenses:* Contact institution. *Faculty research:* Bioacoustics, biological oceanography, bio-optics, coastal geology, coastal hazards, computational biology, geological oceanography, hydrography, marine chemistry, marine phytoplankton ecology, marine science, numerical modeling, paleontology, physical oceanography, remote sensing, signal processing, zooplankton.

University of Washington, Graduate School, College of Engineering, Department of Civil and Environmental Engineering, Seattle, WA 98195-2700. Offers construction engineering (MSCE, PhD); environmental engineering (MSCE, PhD); geotechnical engineering (MSCE, PhD); hydrology and hydrodynamics (MSCE, PhD); structural engineering and mechanics (MSCE, PhD); transportation engineering (MSCE, PhD). *Program availability:* Part-time, 100% online. *Faculty:* 38 full-time (10 women). *Students:* 239 full-time (104 women), 172 part-time (51 women); includes 91 minority (3 Black or African American, non-Hispanic/Latino; 2 American Indian or Alaska Native, non-Hispanic/Latino; 42 Asian, non-Hispanic/Latino; 26 Hispanic/Latino; 18 Two or more races, non-Hispanic/Latino), 120 international. Average age 28. 787 applicants, 57% accepted, 163 enrolled. In 2018, 161 master's, 11 doctorates awarded. Terminal master's awarded for partial completion of doctoral program. *Degree requirements:* For master's, thesis optional; for doctorate, comprehensive exam, thesis/dissertation, qualifying, general and final exams; completion of degree within 10 years. *Entrance requirements:* For master's, GRE General Test, minimum GPA of 3.0, statement of purpose, letters of recommendation, transcripts; for doctorate, GRE General Test, minimum GPA of 3.5, statement of purpose, letters of recommendation, transcripts, resume. Additional exam requirements/recommendations for international students: Required—TOEFL (minimum score 580 paper-based; 92 iBT); Recommended—IELTS (minimum score 7), TSE. *Application deadline:* For fall admission, 12/15 for domestic and international students. Applications are processed on a rolling basis. Application fee: $85. Electronic applications accepted. *Expenses:* Research-focused Master's and PhD: $18,852 resident; $32,760 nonresident. *Financial support:* In 2018–19, 120 students received support, including 23 fellowships with tuition reimbursements available (averaging $30,240 per year), 78 research assistantships with full tuition reimbursements available (averaging $30,240 per year), 28 teaching assistantships with full tuition reimbursements available (averaging $30,240 per year); scholarships/grants also available. Financial award application deadline: 12/15; financial award applicants required to submit FAFSA. *Faculty research:* Structural and geotechnical engineering, transportation and construction engineering, water and environmental engineering. *Total annual research expenditures:* $16.4 million. *Unit head:* Dr. Timothy V. Larson, Professor/Chair, 206-543-6815, Fax: 206-543-1543, E-mail: tlarson@uw.edu. *Application contact:* Melissa Pritchard, Graduate Adviser, 206-543-2574, Fax: 206-543-1543, E-mail: ceginfo@u.washington.edu.
Website: http://www.ce.washington.edu/

Limnology

Cornell University, Graduate School, Graduate Fields of Agriculture and Life Sciences, Field of Ecology and Evolutionary Biology, Ithaca, NY 14853. Offers ecology (PhD), including animal ecology, applied ecology, biogeochemistry, community and ecosystem ecology, limnology, oceanography, physiological ecology, plant ecology, population ecology, theoretical ecology, vertebrate zoology; evolutionary biology (PhD), including ecological genetics, paleobiology, population biology, systematics. *Degree requirements:* For doctorate, comprehensive exam, thesis/dissertation, 2 semesters of teaching experience. *Entrance requirements:* For doctorate, GRE General Test, GRE Subject Test (biology), 2 letters of recommendation. Additional exam requirements/ recommendations for international students: Required—TOEFL (minimum score 550 paper-based; 77 iBT). Electronic applications accepted. *Faculty research:* Population and organismal biology, population and evolutionary genetics, systematics and macroevolution, biochemistry, conservation biology.

Oregon State University, College of Agricultural Sciences, Program in Fisheries Science, Corvallis, OR 97331. Offers aquaculture (MS); conservation biology (MS, PhD); fish genetics (MS, PhD); ichthyology (MS, PhD); limnology (MS, PhD); parasites and diseases (MS, PhD); physiology and ecology of marine and freshwater fishes (MS, PhD); stream ecology (MS, PhD); toxicology (MS, PhD); water pollution biology (MS, PhD). *Program availability:* Part-time. *Entrance requirements:* For master's and doctorate, GRE, minimum GPA of 3.0 in last 90 hours. Additional exam requirements/ recommendations for international students: Required—TOEFL (minimum score 80 iBT), IELTS (minimum score 6.5). *Faculty research:* Fisheries ecology, fish toxicology, stream ecology, quantitative analyses of marine and freshwater fish populations.

University of Alaska Fairbanks, College of Fisheries and Ocean Sciences, Department of Marine Biology, Fairbanks, AK 99775-7220. Offers marine biology (MS, PhD); oceanography (MS, PhD). *Program availability:* Part-time. *Faculty:* 9 full-time (5 women). *Students:* 23 full-time (17 women), 13 part-time (7 women); includes 3 minority (2 Asian, non-Hispanic/Latino; 1 Two or more races, non-Hispanic/Latino), 6 international. Average age 31. 26 applicants, 27% accepted, 5 enrolled. In 2018, 3 master's, 3 doctorates awarded. *Degree requirements:* For master's, comprehensive exam, thesis, oral defense of thesis; for doctorate, comprehensive exam, thesis/ dissertation, oral defense of dissertation. *Entrance requirements:* For master's, GRE General Test, bachelor's degree from accredited institution with minimum cumulative undergraduate and major GPA of 3.0; for doctorate, GRE General Test, minimum cumulative GPA of 3.0. Additional exam requirements/recommendations for international students: Required—TOEFL (minimum score 550 paper-based; 79 iBT), IELTS (minimum score 6.5). *Application deadline:* For fall admission, 5/1 for domestic students, 3/1 for international students; for spring admission, 9/15 for domestic students, 8/15 for international students. Applications are processed on a rolling basis. Application fee: $60. Electronic applications accepted. *Expenses: Tuition, area resident:* Full-time $8802; part-time $5868 per credit hour. Tuition, state resident: full-time $8802; part-time $5868 per credit hour. Tuition, nonresident: full-time $18,504; part-time $12,336 per credit hour. *International tuition:* $18,504 full-time. *Required fees:* $1416; $944 per credit hour. $472 per semester. Tuition and fees vary according to course load and program. *Financial support:* In 2018–19, 13 research assistantships with full tuition reimbursements (averaging $8,919 per year), 5 teaching assistantships with full tuition reimbursements (averaging $14,433 per year) were awarded; fellowships with full tuition reimbursements, career-related internships or fieldwork, Federal Work-Study, scholarships/grants, health care benefits, and unspecified assistantships also available. Support available to part-time students. Financial award application deadline: 7/1; financial award applicants required to submit FAFSA. *Total annual research expenditures:* $9.4 million. *Unit head:* Dr. Lara Horstman, Chair, 907-474-7724, E-mail: info@sfos.uaf.edu. *Application contact:* Samara Taber, Director of Admissions, 907-474-7500, Fax: 907-474-7097, E-mail: uaf-admissions@alaska.edu.
Website: http://www.uaf.edu/cfos/academics/graduate/

University of Florida, Graduate School, College of Agricultural and Life Sciences, School of Forest Resources and Conservation, Department of Fisheries and Aquatic Sciences, Gainesville, FL 32611. Offers MFAS, MS, PhD. *Program availability:* Part-time, online learning. *Degree requirements:* For master's, thesis (for MS); technical paper (for MFAS); for doctorate, comprehensive exam, thesis/dissertation. *Entrance requirements:* For master's and doctorate, GRE General Test, minimum GPA of 3.0. Additional exam requirements/recommendations for international students: Required—TOEFL (minimum score 550 paper-based; 80 iBT), IELTS (minimum score 6). Electronic applications accepted.

Marine Geology

Cornell University, Graduate School, Graduate Fields of Engineering, Field of Geological Sciences, Ithaca, NY 14853. Offers economic geology (M Eng, MS, PhD); engineering geology (M Eng, MS, PhD); environmental geophysics (M Eng, MS, PhD); general geology (M Eng, MS, PhD); geobiology (M Eng, MS, PhD); geochemistry and isotope geology (M Eng, MS, PhD); geohydrology (M Eng, MS, PhD); geomorphology (M Eng, MS, PhD); geophysics (M Eng, MS, PhD); geotectonics (M Eng, MS, PhD); marine geology (MS, PhD); mineralogy (M Eng, MS, PhD); paleontology (M Eng, MS, PhD); petroleum geology (M Eng, MS, PhD); petrology (M Eng, MS, PhD); planetary geology (M Eng, MS, PhD); Precambrian geology (M Eng, MS, PhD); Quaternary geology (M Eng, MS, PhD); rock mechanics (M Eng, MS, PhD); sedimentology (M Eng, MS, PhD); seismology (M Eng, MS, PhD); stratigraphy (M Eng, MS, PhD); structural geology (M Eng, MS, PhD). *Degree requirements:* For master's, thesis (MS); for doctorate, comprehensive exam, thesis/dissertation. *Entrance requirements:* For master's and doctorate, GRE General Test, 3 letters of recommendation. Additional exam requirements/recommendations for international students: Required—TOEFL (minimum score 550 paper-based; 77 iBT). Electronic applications accepted. *Faculty research:* Geophysics, structural geology, petrology, geochemistry, geodynamics.

Massachusetts Institute of Technology, School of Science, Department of Earth, Atmospheric, and Planetary Sciences, Cambridge, MA 02139. Offers atmospheric chemistry (PhD, Sc D); atmospheric science (SM, PhD, Sc D); chemical oceanography (SM, PhD, Sc D); climate physics and chemistry (SM, PhD, Sc D); earth and planetary sciences (SM); geochemistry (PhD, Sc D); geology (PhD, Sc D); geophysics (PhD, Sc D); marine geology and geophysics (SM, PhD, Sc D); physical oceanography (SM, PhD, Sc D); planetary sciences (PhD, Sc D). Terminal master's awarded for partial completion of doctoral program. *Degree requirements:* For master's, thesis; for doctorate, comprehensive exam, thesis/dissertation. *Entrance requirements:* For master's and doctorate, GRE General Test. Additional exam requirements/recommendations for international students: Required—TOEFL, IELTS. Electronic applications accepted. *Expenses: Tuition:* Full-time $51,520; part-time $800 per credit hour. *Required fees:* $312. *Faculty research:* Earth: origin, composition, structure, and dynamics of (and interactions between) the atmosphere, oceans, surface, and interior of the earth; planets: formation, dynamics, and evolution of planetary systems and the characterization of exoplanets; climate: characterization of past, present, and potential future climates; studies of the causes and consequences of climate change; life: co-evolution of life and environmental systems.

University of Delaware, College of Earth, Ocean, and Environment, Newark, DE 19716. Offers geography (MA, MS, PhD); geology (MS, PhD); marine science and policy (MMP, MS, PhD), including marine policy (MMP), marine studies (MS, PhD), oceanography (PhD); ocean engineering (MS, PhD). *Degree requirements:* For master's, thesis; for doctorate, thesis/dissertation. *Entrance requirements:* For master's and doctorate, GRE General Test. Additional exam requirements/recommendations for international students: Required—TOEFL. Electronic applications accepted. *Faculty research:* Marine biology and biochemistry, oceanography, marine policy, physical ocean science and engineering, ocean engineering.

University of Hawaii at Manoa, Office of Graduate Education, School of Ocean and Earth Science and Technology, Department of Geology and Geophysics, Honolulu, HI 96822. Offers high-pressure geophysics and geochemistry (MS, PhD); hydrogeology and engineering geology (MS, PhD); marine geology and geophysics (MS, PhD); planetary geosciences and remote sensing (MS, PhD); seismology and solid-earth geophysics (MS, PhD); volcanology, petrology, and geochemistry (MS, PhD). *Program availability:* Part-time. Terminal master's awarded for partial completion of doctoral program. *Degree requirements:* For master's, thesis optional; for doctorate, comprehensive exam, thesis/dissertation. *Entrance requirements:* For master's and doctorate, GRE General Test, minimum GPA of 3.0. Additional exam requirements/recommendations for international students: Required—TOEFL (minimum score 580 paper-based; 92 iBT), IELTS (minimum score 5).

University of Miami, Graduate School, Rosenstiel School of Marine and Atmospheric Science, Division of Marine Geology and Geophysics, Coral Gables, FL 33124. Offers MS, PhD. Terminal master's awarded for partial completion of doctoral program. *Degree requirements:* For master's, comprehensive exam, thesis; for doctorate, comprehensive exam, thesis/dissertation. *Entrance requirements:* For master's and doctorate, GRE General Test. Additional exam requirements/recommendations for international students: Required—TOEFL (minimum score 550 paper-based). Electronic applications accepted. *Faculty research:* Carbonate sedimentology, low-temperature geochemistry, paleoceanography, geodesy and tectonics.

University of Rhode Island, Graduate School, Graduate School of Oceanography, Narragansett, RI 02882. Offers biological oceanography (MS, PhD); coastal ocean management (MO); coastal systems (MO); fisheries (MO); general oceanography (MO); marine and atmospheric chemistry (MS, PhD); marine fisheries management (MO); marine geology and geophysics (MS, PhD); ocean technology and data (MO); physical oceanography (MS, PhD); MBA/MO; PhD/MA; PhD/MMA. *Program availability:* Part-time. *Faculty:* 29 full-time (10 women). *Students:* 56 full-time (33 women), 10 part-time (5 women); includes 1 minority (Asian, non-Hispanic/Latino), 10 international. 76 applicants, 72% accepted, 17 enrolled. In 2018, 15 master's, 5 doctorates awarded. *Entrance requirements:* For master's, GRE, 2 letters of recommendation; for doctorate, GRE, 3 letters of recommendation. Additional exam requirements/recommendations for international students: Required—TOEFL. *Application deadline:* For fall admission, 1/15 for domestic and international students. Application fee: $65. Electronic applications accepted. *Expenses: Tuition, area resident:* Full-time $13,226; part-time $735 per credit. Tuition, state resident: full-time $13,226; part-time $735 per credit. Tuition, nonresident: full-time $25,854; part-time $1436 per credit. *International tuition:* $25,854 full-time. *Required fees:* $1698; $50 per credit. $35 per semester. One-time fee: $165. *Financial support:* In 2018–19, 31 research assistantships with tuition reimbursements (averaging $9,647 per year), 14 teaching assistantships with tuition reimbursements (averaging $10,563 per year) were awarded. Financial award application deadline: 1/15; financial award applicants required to submit FAFSA. *Faculty research:* Subduction, life in extreme environments, the marine nitrogen cycle, hurricane prediction, Antarctic ocean circulation. *Unit head:* Dr. Bruce Corliss, Dean, 401-874-6222, Fax: 401-874-6931, E-mail: bruce.corliss@gso.uri.edu. *Application contact:* Dr. David Smith, Professor of Oceanography/Associate Dean for Academic Affairs, 401-874-6172, E-mail: dcsmith@uri.edu.
Website: http://www.gso.uri.edu/

University of Washington, Graduate School, College of the Environment, School of Oceanography, Seattle, WA 98195. Offers biological oceanography (MS, PhD); chemical oceanography (MS, PhD); marine geology and geophysics (MS, PhD); physical oceanography (MS, PhD). Terminal master's awarded for partial completion of doctoral program. *Degree requirements:* For master's, research project; for doctorate, thesis/dissertation. *Entrance requirements:* For master's and doctorate, GRE General Test, minimum GPA of 3.0. Additional exam requirements/recommendations for international students: Required—TOEFL. Electronic applications accepted. *Faculty research:* Global climate change, hydrothermal vent systems, marine microbiology, marine and freshwater biogeochemistry, biological-physical interactions.

Woods Hole Oceanographic Institution, MIT/WHOI Joint Program in Oceanography/Applied Ocean Science and Engineering, Woods Hole, MA 02543-1541. Offers applied ocean science and engineering (PhD); biological oceanography (PhD); chemical oceanography (PhD); marine geology and geophysics (PhD); physical oceanography (PhD). Program offered jointly with Massachusetts Institute of Technology. *Degree requirements:* For doctorate, thesis/dissertation. *Entrance requirements:* For doctorate, GRE General Test. Additional exam requirements/recommendations for international students: Required—TOEFL or IELTS. Electronic applications accepted.

Mineralogy

Cornell University, Graduate School, Graduate Fields of Engineering, Field of Geological Sciences, Ithaca, NY 14853. Offers economic geology (M Eng, MS, PhD); engineering geology (M Eng, MS, PhD); environmental geophysics (M Eng, MS, PhD); general geology (M Eng, MS, PhD); geobiology (M Eng, MS, PhD); geochemistry and isotope geology (M Eng, MS, PhD); geohydrology (M Eng, MS, PhD); geomorphology (M Eng, MS, PhD); geophysics (M Eng, MS, PhD); geotectonics (M Eng, MS, PhD); marine geology (MS, PhD); mineralogy (M Eng, MS, PhD); paleontology (M Eng, MS, PhD); petroleum geology (M Eng, MS, PhD); petrology (M Eng, MS, PhD); planetary geology (M Eng, MS, PhD); Precambrian geology (M Eng, MS, PhD); Quaternary geology (M Eng, MS, PhD); rock mechanics (M Eng, MS, PhD); sedimentology (M Eng, MS, PhD); seismology (M Eng, MS, PhD); stratigraphy (M Eng, MS, PhD); structural geology (M Eng, MS, PhD). *Degree requirements:* For master's, thesis (MS); for doctorate, comprehensive exam, thesis/dissertation. *Entrance requirements:* For master's and doctorate, GRE General Test, 3 letters of recommendation. Additional exam requirements/recommendations for international students: Required—TOEFL (minimum score 550 paper-based; 77 iBT). Electronic applications accepted. *Faculty research:* Geophysics, structural geology, petrology, geochemistry, geodynamics.

Indiana University Bloomington, University Graduate School, College of Arts and Sciences, Department of Earth and Atmospheric Sciences, Bloomington, IN 47405-7000. Offers biogeochemistry (MS, PhD); economic geology (MS, PhD); geobiology (MS, PhD); geophysics, structural geology and tectonics (MS, PhD); hydrogeology (MS, PhD); mineralogy (MS, PhD); stratigraphy and sedimentology (MS, PhD). Terminal master's awarded for partial completion of doctoral program. *Degree requirements:* For master's, thesis or alternative; for doctorate, comprehensive exam, thesis/dissertation. *Entrance requirements:* For master's and doctorate, GRE General Test. Additional exam requirements/recommendations for international students: Required—TOEFL. *Faculty research:* Geophysics, geochemistry, hydrogeology, geobiology, planetary science.

Université du Québec à Chicoutimi, Graduate Programs, Program in Mineral Resources, Chicoutimi, QC G7H 2B1, Canada. Offers PhD. Program offered jointly with Université du Québec à Montréal. *Program availability:* Part-time. *Degree requirements:* For doctorate, thesis/dissertation. *Entrance requirements:* For doctorate, appropriate master's degree, proficiency in French.

Université du Québec à Montréal, Graduate Programs, Program in Earth Sciences, Montreal, QC H3C 3P8, Canada. Offers earth sciences (M Sc); mineral resources (PhD); non-renewable resources (DESS). *Program availability:* Part-time. Terminal master's awarded for partial completion of doctoral program. *Degree requirements:* For master's, thesis (for some programs); for doctorate, thesis/dissertation. *Entrance requirements:* For master's, appropriate bachelor's degree or equivalent, proficiency in French. *Faculty research:* Economic geology, structural geology, geochemistry, Quaternary geology, isotopic geochemistry.

Université du Québec à Montréal, Graduate Programs, Program in Mineral Resources, Montréal, QC H3C 3P8, Canada. Offers PhD. Program offered jointly with Université du Québec à Chicoutimi. *Program availability:* Part-time. *Degree requirements:* For doctorate, thesis/dissertation. *Entrance requirements:* For doctorate, appropriate master's degree or equivalent, proficiency in French.

The University of Texas at Dallas, School of Natural Sciences and Mathematics, Department of Geosciences, Richardson, TX 75080. Offers geosciences (MS, PhD); geosciences - petrology and mineralogy (MS, PhD); geosciences - sedimentology (MS, PhD); geosciences - stratigraphy (MS, PhD). *Program availability:* Part-time, evening/weekend. *Faculty:* 9 full-time (0 women), 2 part-time/adjunct (0 women). *Students:* 42 full-time (11 women), 25 part-time (11 women); includes 11 minority (3 Black or African American, non-Hispanic/Latino; 1 American Indian or Alaska Native, non-Hispanic/Latino; 4 Asian, non-Hispanic/Latino; 2 Hispanic/Latino; 1 Two or more races, non-Hispanic/Latino), 27 international. Average age 30. 40 applicants, 35% accepted, 10 enrolled. In 2018, 14 master's, 4 doctorates awarded. *Degree requirements:* For master's, thesis optional; for doctorate, thesis/dissertation. *Entrance requirements:* For master's and doctorate, GRE General Test, minimum GPA of 3.0 in upper-level course work in field. Additional exam requirements/recommendations for international students: Required—TOEFL (minimum score 550 paper-based). *Application deadline:* For fall admission, 7/15 for domestic students, 5/1 priority date for international students; for spring admission, 11/15 for domestic students, 9/1 priority date for international students. Applications are processed on a rolling basis. Application fee: $50 ($100 for international students). Electronic applications accepted. *Expenses: Tuition, area resident:* Full-time $13,458. Tuition, state resident: full-time $13,458. Tuition, nonresident: full-time $26,852. *International tuition:* $26,852 full-time. Tuition and fees vary according to course load. *Financial support:* In 2018–19, 19 students received support, including 6 research assistantships with partial tuition reimbursements available (averaging $22,800 per year), 14 teaching assistantships with partial tuition reimbursements available (averaging $17,100 per year); career-related internships or fieldwork, Federal Work-Study, institutionally sponsored loans, scholarships/grants, and unspecified assistantships also available. Support available to part-time students. Financial award application deadline: 4/30; financial award applicants required to submit FAFSA. *Faculty research:* Cyber mapping, GPS applications for geophysics and geology, seismology and ground-penetrating radar, numerical modeling, signal processing and inverse modeling techniques in seismology. *Unit head:* Dr. John Geissman, Department Head, 972-883-2401, Fax: 972-883-2537, E-mail: geosciences@utdallas.edu. *Application contact:* Gloria Eby, Graduate Support Assistant, 972-883-2401, Fax: 972-883-2537, E-mail: geosciences@utdallas.edu.
Website: http://www.utdallas.edu/geosciences

Paleontology

Cornell University, Graduate School, Graduate Fields of Engineering, Field of Geological Sciences, Ithaca, NY 14853. Offers economic geology (M Eng, MS, PhD); engineering geology (M Eng, MS, PhD); environmental geophysics (M Eng, MS, PhD); general geology (M Eng, MS, PhD); geobiology (M Eng, MS, PhD); geochemistry and isotope geology (M Eng, MS, PhD); geohydrology (M Eng, MS, PhD); geomorphology (M Eng, MS, PhD); geophysics (M Eng, MS, PhD); geotectonics (M Eng, MS, PhD); marine geology (MS, PhD); mineralogy (M Eng, MS, PhD); paleontology (M Eng, MS, PhD); petroleum geology (M Eng, MS, PhD); petrology (M Eng, MS, PhD); planetary geology (M Eng, MS, PhD); Precambrian geology (M Eng, MS, PhD); Quaternary geology (M Eng, MS, PhD); rock mechanics (M Eng, MS, PhD); sedimentology (M Eng, MS, PhD); seismology (M Eng, MS, PhD); stratigraphy (M Eng, MS, PhD); structural geology (M Eng, MS, PhD). *Degree requirements:* For master's, thesis (MS); for doctorate, comprehensive exam, thesis/dissertation. *Entrance requirements:* For master's and doctorate, GRE General Test, 3 letters of recommendation. Additional exam requirements/recommendations for international students: Required—TOEFL (minimum score 550 paper-based; 77 iBT). Electronic applications accepted. *Faculty research:* Geophysics, structural geology, petrology, geochemistry, geodynamics.

Duke University, Graduate School, Department of Evolutionary Anthropology, Durham, NC 27708. Offers cellular and molecular biology (PhD); gross anatomy and physical anthropology (PhD), including comparative morphology of human and non-human primates, primate social behavior, vertebrate paleontology; neuroanatomy (PhD). *Degree requirements:* For doctorate, one foreign language, thesis/dissertation. *Entrance requirements:* For doctorate, GRE General Test. Additional exam requirements/recommendations for international students: Required—TOEFL (minimum score 577 paper-based; 90 iBT) or IELTS (minimum score 7). Electronic applications accepted.

East Tennessee State University, School of Graduate Studies, College of Arts and Sciences, Department of Geosciences, Johnson City, TN 37614-1709. Offers geographic information systems (Postbaccalaureate Certificate); geospatial analysis (MS); paleontology (MS). *Program availability:* Part-time. *Degree requirements:* For master's, thesis. *Entrance requirements:* For master's, bachelor's degree in geosciences or related discipline, minimum GPA of 3.0, three letters of recommendation, resume, two-page letter that discusses career goals and specific academic and research interests; for Postbaccalaureate Certificate, minimum undergraduate GPA of 2.5, personal essay. Additional exam requirements/recommendations for international students: Required—TOEFL (minimum score 550 paper-based; 79 iBT). Electronic applications accepted. *Faculty research:* Vertebrate paleontology; volcanology; soils and geological engineering; geological hazards stemming from volcanoes and tsunamis and the sociological responses; applications of geospatial analysis to meteorology, weather and climate, and geomorphology/watershed management; shallow surface geophysics, sedimentology, and stratigraphy.

South Dakota School of Mines and Technology, Graduate Division, Department of Geology and Geological Engineering, Rapid City, SD 57701-3995. Offers geology and geological engineering (MS, PhD); paleontology (MS). *Program availability:* Part-time. *Degree requirements:* For master's, thesis; for doctorate, thesis/dissertation. *Entrance requirements:* For master's and doctorate, GRE General Test, GRE Subject Test. Additional exam requirements/recommendations for international students: Required—TOEFL (minimum score 520 paper-based; 68 iBT), TWE. Electronic applications accepted. *Faculty research:* Contaminants in soil, nitrate leaching, environmental changes, fracture formations, greenhouse effect.

South Dakota School of Mines and Technology, Graduate Division, Program in Paleontology, Rapid City, SD 57701-3995. Offers MS. *Program availability:* Part-time. *Degree requirements:* For master's, thesis. *Entrance requirements:* For master's, GRE General Test, GRE Subject Test. Additional exam requirements/recommendations for international students: Required—TOEFL (minimum score 520 paper-based; 68 iBT), TWE. Electronic applications accepted.

University of Chicago, Division of the Physical Sciences, Department of the Geophysical Sciences, Chicago, IL 60637. Offers atmospheric sciences (PhD); earth sciences (PhD); paleobiology (PhD); planetary and space sciences (PhD). Terminal master's awarded for partial completion of doctoral program. *Degree requirements:* For doctorate, comprehensive exam, thesis/dissertation. *Entrance requirements:* For doctorate, GRE General Test, research statement, 3 letters of recommendation, transcripts for all previous degrees and institutions attended. Additional exam requirements/recommendations for international students: Required—TOEFL (minimum score 600 paper-based; 95 iBT), IELTS (minimum score 7). Electronic applications accepted. *Faculty research:* Climatology, evolutionary paleontology, cosmochemistry, geochemistry, oceanic sciences.

The University of Manchester, School of Earth and Environmental Sciences, Manchester, United Kingdom. Offers atmospheric sciences (M Phil, M Sc, PhD); basin studies and petroleum geosciences (M Phil, M Sc, PhD); earth, atmospheric and environmental sciences (M Phil, M Sc, PhD); environmental geochemistry and cosmochemistry (M Phil, M Sc, PhD); isotope geochemistry and cosmochemistry (M Phil, M Sc, PhD); paleontology (M Phil, M Sc, PhD); physics and chemistry of minerals and fluids (M Phil, M Sc, PhD); structural and petrological geosciences (M Phil, M Sc, PhD).

Yale University, Graduate School of Arts and Sciences, Department of Geology and Geophysics, New Haven, CT 06520. Offers biogeochemistry (PhD); climate dynamics (PhD); geochemistry (PhD); geophysics (PhD); meteorology (PhD); oceanography (PhD); paleontology (PhD); paleooceanography (PhD); petrology (PhD); tectonics (PhD). *Degree requirements:* For doctorate, thesis/dissertation. *Entrance requirements:* For doctorate, GRE General Test. Additional exam requirements/recommendations for international students: Required—TOEFL.

Planetary and Space Sciences

Air Force Institute of Technology, Graduate School of Engineering and Management, Department of Operational Sciences, Dayton, OH 45433-7765. Offers logistics management (MS); operations research (MS, PhD); space operations (MS). *Program availability:* Part-time. *Degree requirements:* For master's, thesis; for doctorate, thesis/dissertation. *Entrance requirements:* For doctorate, GRE General Test, minimum GPA of 3.0, U.S. citizenship. *Faculty research:* Optimization, simulation, combat modeling and analysis, reliability and maintainability, resource scheduling.

Alabama Agricultural and Mechanical University, School of Graduate Studies, College of Engineering, Technology, and Physical Sciences, Department of Physics, Chemistry and Mathematics, Huntsville, AL 35811. Offers physics (MS, PhD), including materials science (PhD), optics/lasers (PhD), space science (PhD). *Program availability:* Part-time, evening/weekend. *Degree requirements:* For doctorate, thesis/dissertation. *Entrance requirements:* For master's and doctorate, GRE General Test. Additional exam requirements/recommendations for international students: Required—TOEFL (minimum score 500 paper-based; 61 iBT). Electronic applications accepted.

Arizona State University at the Tempe campus, College of Liberal Arts and Sciences, School of Earth and Space Exploration, Tempe, AZ 85287-1404. Offers astrophysics (MS, PhD); exploration systems design (PhD); geological sciences (MS, PhD). PhD in exploration systems design is offered in collaboration with the Ira A. Fulton School of Engineering. Terminal master's awarded for partial completion of doctoral program. *Degree requirements:* For master's, thesis, interactive Program of Study (iPOS) submitted before completing 50 percent of required credit hours; for doctorate, thesis/dissertation, interactive Program of Study (iPOS) submitted before completing 50 percent of required credit hours. *Entrance requirements:* For master's and doctorate, GRE, minimum GPA of 3.0 or equivalent in last 2 years of work leading to bachelor's degree. Additional exam requirements/recommendations for international students: Required—TOEFL, IELTS, or PTE. Electronic applications accepted.

California Institute of Technology, Division of Geological and Planetary Sciences, Pasadena, CA 91125-0001. Offers environmental science and engineering (MS, PhD); geobiology (MS, PhD); geochemistry (MS, PhD); geology (MS, PhD); geophysics (MS, PhD); planetary science (MS, PhD). *Degree requirements:* For doctorate, thesis/dissertation. *Entrance requirements:* For doctorate, GRE General Test. Additional exam requirements/recommendations for international students: Required—TOEFL; Recommended—IELTS, TWE. Electronic applications accepted. *Faculty research:* Planetary surfaces, evolution of anaerobic respiratory processes, structural geology and tectonics, theoretical and numerical seismology, global biogeochemical cycles.

Cornell University, Graduate School, Graduate Fields of Arts and Sciences, Field of Astronomy and Space Sciences, Ithaca, NY 14853. Offers astronomy (PhD); astrophysics (PhD); general space sciences (PhD); infrared astronomy (PhD); planetary studies (PhD); radio astronomy (PhD); radiophysics (PhD); theoretical astrophysics (PhD). *Degree requirements:* For doctorate, comprehensive exam, thesis/dissertation. *Entrance requirements:* For doctorate, GRE General Test, GRE Subject Test (physics), 3 letters of recommendation. Additional exam requirements/recommendations for international students: Required—TOEFL (minimum score 600 paper-based; 77 iBT). Electronic applications accepted. *Faculty research:* Observational astrophysics, planetary sciences, cosmology, instrumentation, gravitational astrophysics.

Florida Institute of Technology, College of Engineering and Science, Program in Space Sciences, Melbourne, FL 32901-6975. Offers MS, PhD. *Program availability:* Part-time. *Students:* 16 full-time (6 women), 7 part-time (2 women); includes 2 minority (1 Black or African American, non-Hispanic/Latino; 1 Hispanic/Latino), 4 international. Average age 29. 16 applicants, 56% accepted, 2 enrolled. In 2018, 1 master's, 2 doctorates awarded. Terminal master's awarded for partial completion of doctoral program. *Degree requirements:* For master's, comprehensive exam, thesis optional, minimum of 30 credit hours, all course grades of C or higher; for doctorate, comprehensive exam, thesis/dissertation, minimum of 45 credit hours. *Entrance requirements:* For master's, GRE General Test, GRE Subject Test, undergraduate degree is any subfield of space sciences, physics, or a related engineering field, minimum GPA of 3.0, 3 letters of recommendation, resume, statement of objectives; for doctorate, GRE General Test, GRE Subject Test, minimum GPA of 3.2, resume. Additional exam requirements/recommendations for international students: Required—TOEFL (minimum score 550 paper-based; 79 iBT). *Application deadline:* Applications are processed on a rolling basis. Application fee: $50. Electronic applications accepted. *Expenses: Tuition:* Full-time $22,338; part-time $1241 per credit hour. Tuition and fees vary according to degree level, campus/location and program. *Financial support:* Research assistantships, teaching assistantships, and tuition remissions available. Financial award application deadline: 3/1; financial award applicants required to submit FAFSA. *Faculty research:* Observational astronomy, theoretical astrophysics, space plasma physics. *Unit head:* Dr. Daniel Batcheldor, Department Head, 321-674-7717, Fax: 321-674-7482, E-mail: dbatcheldor@fit.edu. *Application contact:* Mike Perry, Executive Director of Admissions, 321-674-7127, E-mail: perrymj@fit.edu.
Website: https://www.fit.edu/programs/space-sciences-ms/

Hampton University, School of Science, Department of Atmospheric and Planetary Sciences, Hampton, VA 23668. Offers atmospheric science (MS, PhD); planetary science (MS, PhD). *Program availability:* Part-time. *Students:* 13 full-time (4 women), 3 part-time (0 women); includes 6 minority (3 Black or African American, non-Hispanic/Latino; 3 Asian, non-Hispanic/Latino), 1 international. Average age 30. 5 applicants, 20% accepted, 1 enrolled. In 2018, 2 doctorates awarded. Terminal master's awarded for partial completion of doctoral program. *Degree requirements:* For master's, thesis; for doctorate, comprehensive exam, thesis/dissertation. *Entrance requirements:* For master's, GRE. Additional exam requirements/recommendations for international students: Required—TOEFL (minimum score 525 paper-based) or IELTS (6.5). *Application deadline:* For fall admission, 6/1 priority date for domestic students, 4/1 priority date for international students; for spring admission, 11/1 priority date for domestic students, 9/1 priority date for international students; for summer admission, 4/1 priority date for domestic students, 2/1 priority date for international students.

Applications are processed on a rolling basis. Application fee: $35. Electronic applications accepted. *Financial support:* In 2018–19, 11 research assistantships with full tuition reimbursements (averaging $21,000 per year) were awarded; career-related internships or fieldwork, scholarships/grants, health care benefits, and unspecified assistantships also available. Financial award application deadline: 6/30; financial award applicants required to submit FAFSA. *Faculty research:* Remote sensing, polar stratospheric and mesospheric clouds, lidar and related technologies, astrobiology, atmospheric dynamics, weather prediction and tracking. *Unit head:* Dr. Robert P. Loughman, Chairperson, 757-727-5108, Fax: 757-727-5090, E-mail: robert.loughman@hamptonu.edu. *Application contact:* Dr. Robert P. Loughman, Chairperson, 757-727-5108, Fax: 757-727-5090, E-mail: robert.loughman@hamptonu.edu.
Website: http://science.hamptonu.edu/aps/

Harvard University, Graduate School of Arts and Sciences, Department of Earth and Planetary Sciences, Cambridge, MA 02138. Offers AM, PhD. Terminal master's awarded for partial completion of doctoral program. *Degree requirements:* For doctorate, comprehensive exam, thesis/dissertation. *Entrance requirements:* For doctorate, GRE General Test. Additional exam requirements/recommendations for international students: Required—TOEFL. Electronic applications accepted. *Faculty research:* Economic geography, geochemistry, geophysics, mineralogy, crystallography.

Johns Hopkins University, Zanvyl Krieger School of Arts and Sciences, The Morton K. Blaustein Department of Earth and Planetary Sciences, Baltimore, MD 21218. Offers MA, PhD. *Faculty:* 21 full-time (10 women). *Students:* 40 full-time (22 women). 56 applicants, 21% accepted, 4 enrolled. In 2018, 8 master's, 7 doctorates awarded. *Degree requirements:* For doctorate, comprehensive exam, thesis/dissertation. *Entrance requirements:* For master's and doctorate, GRE General Test. Additional exam requirements/recommendations for international students: Required—TOEFL (minimum score 600 paper-based; 100 iBT), IELTS. *Application deadline:* For fall admission, 1/15 for domestic and international students. Application fee: $75. Electronic applications accepted. *Financial support:* Fellowships with full tuition reimbursements, research assistantships with full tuition reimbursements, teaching assistantships with full tuition reimbursements, institutionally sponsored loans, scholarships/grants, traineeships, health care benefits, tuition waivers (full), and unspecified assistantships available. Financial award application deadline: 4/15; financial award applicants required to submit FAFSA. *Faculty research:* Oceanography, atmospheric sciences, geophysics, geology, geochemistry. *Unit head:* Dr. Anand Gnanadesikan, Chair, 410-516-0722, E-mail: gnanades@jhu.edu. *Application contact:* Richard Helman, Director of Graduate Admissions, 410-516-7125, E-mail: rhelman@jhu.edu.
Website: http://eps.jhu.edu/

Massachusetts Institute of Technology, School of Science, Department of Earth, Atmospheric, and Planetary Sciences, Cambridge, MA 02139. Offers atmospheric chemistry (PhD, Sc D); atmospheric science (SM, PhD, Sc D); chemical oceanography (SM, PhD, Sc D); climate physics and chemistry (SM, PhD, Sc D); earth and planetary sciences (SM); geochemistry (PhD, Sc D); geology (PhD, Sc D); geophysics (PhD, Sc D); marine geology and geophysics (SM, PhD, Sc D); physical oceanography (SM, PhD, Sc D); planetary sciences (PhD, Sc D). Terminal master's awarded for partial completion of doctoral program. *Degree requirements:* For master's, thesis; for doctorate, comprehensive exam, thesis/dissertation. *Entrance requirements:* For master's and doctorate, GRE General Test. Additional exam requirements/recommendations for international students: Required—TOEFL, IELTS. Electronic applications accepted. *Expenses: Tuition:* Full-time $51,520; part-time $800 per credit hour. *Required fees:* $312. *Faculty research:* Earth: origin, composition, structure, and dynamics of (and interactions between) the atmosphere, oceans, surface, and interior of the earth; planets: formation, dynamics, and evolution of planetary systems and the characterization of exoplanets; climate: characterization of past, present, and potential future climates; studies of the causes and consequences of climate change; life: co-evolution of life and environmental systems.

McGill University, Faculty of Graduate and Postdoctoral Studies, Faculty of Science, Department of Earth and Planetary Sciences, Montréal, QC H3A 2T5, Canada. Offers M Sc, PhD.

St. Thomas University, School of Leadership Studies, Institute for Education, Miami Gardens, FL 33054-6459. Offers earth/space science (Certificate); educational administration (MS, Certificate); educational leadership (Ed D); elementary education (MS); ESOL (Certificate); gifted education (Certificate); instructional technology (MS, Certificate); professional/studies (Certificate); reading (MS, Certificate); special education (MS). *Program availability:* Part-time, evening/weekend. *Degree requirements:* For master's, comprehensive exam; for doctorate, comprehensive exam, thesis/dissertation. *Entrance requirements:* For master's, interview, minimum GPA of 3.0 or GRE; for doctorate, GRE or MAT. Additional exam requirements/recommendations for international students: Required—TOEFL (minimum score 550 paper-based; 79 iBT). Electronic applications accepted.

The University of Arizona, College of Science, Department of Planetary Sciences, Tucson, AZ 85721. Offers MS, PhD. *Degree requirements:* For master's, thesis (for some programs); for doctorate, one foreign language, thesis/dissertation. *Entrance requirements:* For master's and doctorate, 3 letters of recommendation. Additional exam requirements/recommendations for international students: Required—TOEFL (minimum score 550 paper-based; 79 iBT). Electronic applications accepted. *Faculty research:* Cosmochemistry, planetary geology, astronomy, space physics, planetary physics.

University of Arkansas, Graduate School, Interdisciplinary Program in Space and Planetary Sciences, Fayetteville, AR 72701. Offers MS, PhD. In 2018, 1 master's, 2 doctorates awarded. *Application deadline:* For fall admission, 8/1 for domestic students, 4/1 for international students; for spring admission, 12/1 for domestic students, 10/1 for international students; for summer admission, 4/15 for domestic students, 3/1 for international students. Applications are processed on a rolling basis. Application fee: $60. Electronic applications accepted. *Financial support:* In 2018–19, 7 research assistantships, 12 teaching assistantships were awarded; fellowships also available. *Unit head:* Dr. Larry Roe, Department Chair, 479-575-3750, E-mail: lar@uark.edu. *Application contact:* Larry Roe, Program Coordinator, 479-575-3750, E-mail: lar@uark.edu.
Website: https://spacecenter.uark.edu

University of California, Los Angeles, Graduate Division, College of Letters and Science, Department of Earth and Space Sciences, Los Angeles, CA 90095. Offers geochemistry (MS, PhD); geology (MS, PhD); geophysics and space physics (MS, PhD). Terminal master's awarded for partial completion of doctoral program. *Degree requirements:* For master's, comprehensive exams or thesis; for doctorate, thesis/dissertation, oral and written qualifying exams. *Entrance requirements:* For master's, GRE General Test; GRE Subject Test, bachelor's degree; minimum undergraduate GPA of 3.0 (or its equivalent if letter grade system not used); for doctorate, GRE General Test, bachelor's degree; minimum undergraduate GPA of 3.0 (or its equivalent if letter grade system not used). Additional exam requirements/recommendations for international students: Required—TOEFL. Electronic applications accepted.

University of California, Santa Cruz, Division of Graduate Studies, Division of Physical and Biological Sciences, Department of Earth and Planetary Sciences, Santa Cruz, CA 95064. Offers MS, PhD. Terminal master's awarded for partial completion of doctoral program. *Degree requirements:* For master's, thesis; for doctorate, one foreign language, thesis/dissertation, qualifying exam. *Entrance requirements:* For master's and doctorate, GRE General Test. Additional exam requirements/recommendations for international students: Required—TOEFL (minimum score 550 paper-based; 83 iBT); Recommended—IELTS (minimum score 8). Electronic applications accepted. *Faculty research:* Evolution of continental margins and orogenic belts, geologic processes occurring at plate boundaries, deep-sea sediment diagenesis, paleoecology, hydrogeology.

University of Chicago, Division of the Physical Sciences, Department of the Geophysical Sciences, Chicago, IL 60637. Offers atmospheric sciences (PhD); earth sciences (PhD); paleobiology (PhD); planetary and space sciences (PhD). Terminal master's awarded for partial completion of doctoral program. *Degree requirements:* For doctorate, comprehensive exam, thesis/dissertation. *Entrance requirements:* For doctorate, GRE General Test, research statement, 3 letters of recommendation, transcripts for all previous degrees and institutions attended. Additional exam requirements/recommendations for international students: Required—TOEFL (minimum score 600 paper-based; 95 iBT), IELTS (minimum score 7). Electronic applications accepted. *Faculty research:* Climatology, evolutionary paleontology, cosmochemistry, geochemistry, oceanic sciences.

University of Hawaii at Manoa, Office of Graduate Education, School of Ocean and Earth Science and Technology, Department of Geology and Geophysics, Honolulu, HI 96822. Offers high-pressure geophysics and geochemistry (MS, PhD); hydrogeology and engineering geology (MS, PhD); marine geology and geophysics (MS, PhD); planetary geosciences and remote sensing (MS, PhD); seismology and solid-earth geophysics (MS, PhD); volcanology, petrology, and geochemistry (MS, PhD). *Program availability:* Part-time. Terminal master's awarded for partial completion of doctoral program. *Degree requirements:* For master's, thesis optional; for doctorate, comprehensive exam, thesis/dissertation. *Entrance requirements:* For master's and doctorate, GRE General Test, minimum GPA of 3.0. Additional exam requirements/recommendations for international students: Required—TOEFL (minimum score 580 paper-based; 92 iBT), IELTS (minimum score 5).

University of Houston, College of Liberal Arts and Social Sciences, Department of Health and Human Performance, Houston, TX 77204. Offers exercise science (MS); human nutrition (MS); human space exploration sciences (MS); kinesiology (PhD); physical education (M Ed). *Accreditation:* NCATE (one or more programs are accredited). *Program availability:* Part-time, evening/weekend. *Degree requirements:* For master's, comprehensive exam (for some programs), thesis (for some programs); for doctorate, comprehensive exam, thesis/dissertation, qualifying exam, candidacy paper. *Entrance requirements:* For master's, GRE (minimum 35th percentile on each section), minimum cumulative GPA of 3.0; for doctorate, GRE (minimum 35th percentile on each section), minimum cumulative GPA of 3.3. Additional exam requirements/recommendations for international students: Required—TOEFL (minimum score 550 paper-based; 79 iBT). Electronic applications accepted. *Faculty research:* Biomechanics, exercise physiology, obesity, nutrition, space exploration science.

University of Michigan, College of Engineering, Department of Climate and Space Sciences and Engineering, Ann Arbor, MI 48109. Offers applied climate (M Eng); atmospheric, oceanic and space sciences (MS, PhD); geoscience and remote sensing (PhD); space and planetary sciences (PhD); space engineering (M Eng). *Program availability:* Part-time. *Students:* 83 full-time (29 women). 103 applicants, 19% accepted, 9 enrolled. In 2018, 42 master's, 10 doctorates awarded. Terminal master's awarded for partial completion of doctoral program. *Degree requirements:* For master's, thesis (for some programs); for doctorate, thesis/dissertation, oral defense of dissertation, preliminary exams. *Entrance requirements:* For master's and doctorate, GRE General Test. Additional exam requirements/recommendations for international students: Required—TOEFL. *Application deadline:* Applications are processed on a rolling basis. Electronic applications accepted. *Financial support:* Fellowships, research assistantships, teaching assistantships, career-related internships or fieldwork, Federal Work-Study, institutionally sponsored loans, and health care benefits available. Support available to part-time students. Financial award applicants required to submit FAFSA. *Faculty research:* Planetary environments, space instrumentation, air pollution meteorology, global climate change, sun-earth connection, space weather. *Total annual research expenditures:* $29.9 million. *Unit head:* Tuija Pulkkinen, Department Chair, 734-780-4079, Fax: 734-763-0437, E-mail: tuija@umich.edu. *Application contact:* Sandra Pytlinski, Graduate Student Services Coordinator, 734-936-0482, Fax: 734-763-0437, E-mail: sanpyt@umich.edu.
Website: https://clasp.engin.umich.edu/

University of New Mexico, Graduate Studies, College of Arts and Sciences, Program in Earth and Planetary Sciences, Albuquerque, NM 87131-2039. Offers MS, PhD. *Program availability:* Part-time. *Students:* Average age 30. 56 applicants, 27% accepted, 15 enrolled. In 2018, 1 master's, 3 doctorates awarded. Terminal master's awarded for partial completion of doctoral program. *Degree requirements:* For master's, comprehensive exam, thesis; for doctorate, comprehensive exam, thesis/dissertation. *Entrance requirements:* For master's and doctorate, GRE General Test. Additional exam requirements/recommendations for international students: Required—TOEFL. *Application deadline:* For fall admission, 1/15 priority date for domestic and international students; for spring admission, 11/1 priority date for domestic and international students. Application fee: $50. Electronic applications accepted. *Financial support:* Fellowships with full tuition reimbursements, research assistantships with full tuition reimbursements, teaching assistantships with full tuition reimbursements, scholarships/grants, and health care benefits available. Financial award application deadline: 1/15. *Faculty research:* Climatology, experimental petrology, geochemistry, geographic information technologies, geomorphology, geophysics, hydrogeology, igneous petrology, metamorphic petrology, meteoritic, meteorology, micrometeorites, mineralogy, paleoclimatology, paleontology, pedology, petrology, physical volcanology, planetary sciences, Precambrian geology, quaternary geology, sedimentary geochemistry, sedimentology, stable isotope geochemistry, stratigraphy, structural geology, tectonics, volcanology. *Total annual research expenditures:* $2.5 million. *Unit head:* Dr. Adrian J. Brearley, Chair, 505-277-4204, Fax: 505-277-8843, E-mail: brearley@unm.edu. *Application contact:* Cindy Jaramillo, Administrative Assistant III, 505-277-1635, Fax: 505-277-8843, E-mail: epsdept@unm.edu.
Website: http://epswww.unm.edu/

University of North Dakota, Graduate School, John D. Odegard School of Aerospace Sciences, Space Studies Program, Grand Forks, ND 58202. Offers MS. *Program availability:* Part-time, online learning. *Degree requirements:* For master's, comprehensive exam, thesis or alternative. *Entrance requirements:* For master's, minimum GPA of 3.0. Additional exam requirements/recommendations for international students: Required—TOEFL (minimum score 550 paper-based; 79 iBT), IELTS (minimum score 6.5). Electronic applications accepted. *Faculty research:* Earth-approaching asteroids, international remote sensing statutes, Mercury fly-by design, origin of meteorites, craters on Venus.

Washington University in St. Louis, The Graduate School, Department of Earth and Planetary Sciences, St. Louis, MO 63130-4899. Offers PhD. Terminal master's awarded for partial completion of doctoral program. *Degree requirements:* For doctorate, thesis/dissertation. *Entrance requirements:* For doctorate, GRE General Test. Additional exam requirements/recommendations for international students: Required—TOEFL. Electronic applications accepted. *Faculty research:* Planetary sciences; geology; geobiology; geochemistry; geodynamics.

Western Connecticut State University, Division of Graduate Studies, Maricostas School of Arts and Sciences, Department of Physics, Astronomy and Meteorology, Danbury, CT 06810-6885. Offers earth and planetary sciences (MA). *Program availability:* Part-time. *Students:* 4 part-time (2 women). Average age 34. *Degree requirements:* For master's, thesis, completion of program in 6 years. *Entrance requirements:* For master's, minimum GPA of 2.5 or GRE; one year each of calculus-based physics and calculus; semester course in differential equations. Additional exam requirements/recommendations for international students: Recommended—TOEFL (minimum score 550 paper-based; 79 iBT), IELTS (minimum score 6). *Application deadline:* For fall admission, 8/5 priority date for domestic students; for spring admission, 1/5 priority date for domestic students. Applications are processed on a rolling basis. Application fee: $50. *Expenses:* Contact institution. *Financial support:* Application deadline: 5/1; applicants required to submit FAFSA. *Faculty research:* Data collection and analysis of Gulf Stream surface temperature and circulation; science for visually impaired students including investigations of a satellite orbit, the Moon's surface, spectra of chemical elements and stars, the rotation of the Sun, and the spiral structure of our galaxy. *Unit head:* Dr. Dennis Dawson, Graduate Coordinator, 203-837-8671, E-mail: dawsond@wcsu.edu. *Application contact:* Dr. Chris Shankle, Associate Director of Graduate Admissions, 203-837-9005, Fax: 203-837-8326, E-mail: shanklec@wcsu.edu.
Website: http://www.wcsu.edu/physics/

Yale University, Graduate School of Arts and Sciences, Department of Astronomy, New Haven, CT 06520. Offers astronomy (PhD); solar and terrestrial physics (PhD). *Degree requirements:* For doctorate, thesis/dissertation. *Entrance requirements:* For doctorate, GRE General Test, GRE Subject Test (physics).

York University, Faculty of Graduate Studies, Lassonde School of Engineering, Program in Earth and Space Science, Toronto, ON M3J 1P3, Canada. Offers M Sc, PhD. *Program availability:* Part-time, evening/weekend. *Degree requirements:* For master's, thesis or alternative; for doctorate, thesis/dissertation. Electronic applications accepted.

Peterson's Graduate Programs in the Physical Sciences, Mathematics, Agricultural Sciences, the Environment & Natural Resources 2020

www.petersons.com   **119**

Section 4
Marine Sciences and Oceanography

This section contains a directory of institutions offering graduate work in marine sciences and oceanography. Additional information about programs listed in the directory may be obtained by writing directly to the dean of a graduate school or chair of a department at the address given in the directory.

For programs offering related work, see also in this book *Chemistry, Geosciences, Meteorology and Atmospheric Sciences,* and *Physics.* In the other guides in this series:

Graduate Programs in the Biological/Biomedical Sciences & Health-Related Medical Professions

See *Biological and Biomedical Sciences; Environmental Biology, and Evolutionary Biology;* and *Marine Biology*

Graduate Programs in Engineering & Applied Sciences

See *Civil and Environmental Engineering, Engineering and Applied Sciences,* and *Ocean Engineering*

CONTENTS

Program Directories

Marine Sciences

California State University, East Bay, Office of Graduate Studies, College of Science, Department of Biological Sciences, Marine Science Program, Moss Landing, CA 95039. Offers MS. *Degree requirements:* For master's, thesis. *Entrance requirements:* For master's, GRE Subject Test, minimum GPA of 3.0 in field, 2.75 overall; 3 letters of reference; statement of purpose. Additional exam requirements/recommendations for international students: Required—TOEFL.

California State University, Fresno, Division of Research and Graduate Studies, College of Science and Mathematics, Program in Marine Science, Fresno, CA 93740-8027. Offers MS. *Program availability:* Part-time, online learning. *Degree requirements:* For master's, thesis. *Entrance requirements:* For master's, GRE General Test, minimum GPA of 3.0. Additional exam requirements/recommendations for international students: Required—TOEFL. Electronic applications accepted. *Faculty research:* Wetlands ecology, land/water conservation, water irrigation.

California State University, Monterey Bay, College of Science, Moss Landing Marine Laboratories, Seaside, CA 93955-8001. Offers MS. *Program availability:* Part-time. *Degree requirements:* For master's, thesis, thesis defense. *Entrance requirements:* For master's, selected MLML faculty member to serve as potential thesis advisor and selected consortium institution to serve as home campus. Additional exam requirements/recommendations for international students: Required—TOEFL (minimum score 525 paper-based; 71 iBT). Electronic applications accepted. *Faculty research:* Remote sensing microbiology trace elements, chemistry ecology of birds, mammals, turtles and fish, invasive species, marine phycology.

Coastal Carolina University, College of Science, Conway, SC 29528-6054. Offers applied computing and information systems (Certificate); coastal marine and wetland studies (MS); information systems technology (MS); marine science (PhD); sports management (MS). *Program availability:* Part-time, evening/weekend, 100% online. *Degree requirements:* For master's, thesis or internship; for doctorate, comprehensive exam, thesis/dissertation. *Entrance requirements:* For master's, GRE, 3 letters of recommendation, resume, official transcripts, written statement of educational and career goals, baccalaureate degree; for doctorate, GRE, official transcripts; baccalaureate or master's degree; minimum GPA of 3.0 for all collegiate coursework; successful completion of at least two semesters of college-level calculus, physics, and chemistry; 3 letters of recommendation; written statement of educational and career goals; resume; for Certificate, 2 letters of reference, official transcripts, minimum GPA of 3.0 in all computing and information systems courses, documentation of graduation from accredited four-year college or university. Additional exam requirements/recommendations for international students: Required—TOEFL (minimum score 550 paper-based; 79 iBT), IELTS (minimum score 6.5). Electronic applications accepted.

College of Charleston, Graduate School, School of Sciences and Mathematics, Program in Marine Biology, Charleston, SC 29412. Offers MS. *Degree requirements:* For master's, comprehensive exam, thesis. *Entrance requirements:* For master's, GRE General Test, 3 letters of recommendation. Additional exam requirements/recommendations for international students: Required—TOEFL (minimum score 81 iBT). Electronic applications accepted. *Faculty research:* Ecology, environmental physiology, marine genomics, bioinformatics, toxicology, cell biology, population biology, fisheries science, animal physiology, biodiversity, estuarine ecology, evolution and systematics, microbial processes, plant physiology, immunology.

The College of William and Mary, Virginia Institute of Marine Science, Gloucester Point, VA 23062. Offers MS, PhD. *Faculty:* 49 full-time (14 women), 1 part-time/adjunct (0 women). *Students:* 73 full-time (48 women), 1 part-time (0 women); includes 8 minority (1 Asian, non-Hispanic/Latino; 3 Hispanic/Latino; 4 Two or more races, non-Hispanic/Latino), 14 international. Average age 27. 84 applicants, 31% accepted, 14 enrolled. In 2018, 8 master's, 12 doctorates awarded. *Degree requirements:* For master's, thesis, qualifying exam; for doctorate, comprehensive exam, thesis/dissertation, qualifying exam. *Entrance requirements:* For master's, GRE, appropriate bachelor's degree; for doctorate, GRE, appropriate bachelor's and master's degrees. Additional exam requirements/recommendations for international students: Required—TOEFL (minimum score 94 iBT). *Application deadline:* For fall admission, 1/5 for domestic students, 1/6 for international students. Application fee: $50. Electronic applications accepted. *Financial support:* In 2018–19, 64 students received support, including research assistantships with full tuition reimbursements available (averaging $20,452 per year), teaching assistantships with full tuition reimbursements available (averaging $20,452 per year). Financial award application deadline: 1/5. *Faculty research:* Marine science, oceanography, marine ecology, fisheries, environmental science and ecotoxicology. *Total annual research expenditures:* $19.5 million. *Unit head:* Dr. John T. Wells, Dean/Director, 804-684-7103, Fax: 804-684-7009, E-mail: wells@vims.edu. *Application contact:* Dr. Linda C. Schaffner, Associate Dean of Academic Studies, 804-684-7105, Fax: 804-684-7881, E-mail: admissions@vims.edu.
Website: http://www.vims.edu/

Cornell University, Graduate School, Graduate Fields of Agriculture and Life Sciences, Field of Natural Resources, Ithaca, NY 14853. Offers community-based natural resources management (MS, PhD); conservation biology (MS, PhD); ecosystem biology and biogeochemistry (MPS, MS, PhD); environmental management (MPS); fishery and aquatic science (MPS, MS, PhD); forest science (MPS, MS, PhD); human dimensions of natural resources management (MPS, MS, PhD); policy and institutional analysis (MS, PhD); program development and evaluation (MPS, MS, PhD); quantitative ecology (MS, PhD); wildlife science (MPS, MS, PhD). *Degree requirements:* For master's, thesis (MS), project paper (MPS); for doctorate, comprehensive exam, thesis/dissertation. *Entrance requirements:* For master's and doctorate, GRE General Test, 2 letters of recommendation. Additional exam requirements/recommendations for international students: Required—TOEFL (minimum score 550 paper-based; 77 iBT). Electronic applications accepted. *Faculty research:* Ecosystem-level dynamics, systems modeling, conservation biology/management, resource management's human dimensions, biogeochemistry.

Duke University, Graduate School, Program in Marine Science and Conservation, Beaufort, NC 28516. Offers PhD. *Entrance requirements:* For doctorate, GRE General Test. Additional exam requirements/recommendations for international students: Required—TOEFL (minimum score 577 paper-based; 90 iBT) or IELTS.

Duke University, Nicholas School of the Environment, Durham, NC 27708. Offers earth and ocean sciences (PhD); environment (MEM, MF, PhD); marine science and conservation (PhD). *Faculty:* 50. *Students:* 365 full-time (243 women); includes 67 minority (7 Black or African American, non-Hispanic/Latino; 4 American Indian or Alaska Native, non-Hispanic/Latino; 36 Asian, non-Hispanic/Latino; 20 Hispanic/Latino), 93 international. Average age 27. 428 applicants, 83% accepted, 151 enrolled. In 2018, 181 master's awarded. *Degree requirements:* For master's, project; for doctorate, variable foreign language requirement, thesis/dissertation. *Entrance requirements:* For master's, GRE General Test, previous course work in natural or social sciences relevant to environmental interests; college calculus, college statistics, and concentration-specific prerequisites. Additional exam requirements/recommendations for international students: Required—TOEFL, IELTS. *Application deadline:* For fall admission, 12/15 priority date for domestic and international students. Application fee: $400. Electronic applications accepted. *Financial support:* Research assistantships, career-related internships or fieldwork, Federal Work-Study, institutionally sponsored loans, scholarships/grants, and unspecified assistantships available. Financial award application deadline: 12/15; financial award applicants required to submit CSS PROFILE or FAFSA. *Faculty research:* Global environmental change, energy and the environment, water resource management, ecosystem science and conservation, ecotoxicology and environmental health, business and environment, environmental economics and policy, coastal environmental management, forest resource management. *Unit head:* Sherri Nevius, Associate Dean, Student Services, 919-613-8063, E-mail: sherri.nevius@duke.edu. *Application contact:* Benjamin Spain, Associate Director of Enrollment Services, 919-684-1155, E-mail: admissions@nicholas.duke.edu.
Website: http://nicholas.duke.edu/

Florida Institute of Technology, College of Engineering and Science, Program in Oceanography, Melbourne, FL 32901-6975. Offers biological oceanography (MS); coastal management (MS). *Program availability:* Part-time. *Students:* 16 full-time (10 women), 2 part-time (both women); includes 1 minority (Two or more races, non-Hispanic/Latino), 2 international. Average age 28. 13 applicants, 69% accepted, 4 enrolled. In 2018, 4 master's, 1 doctorate awarded. *Degree requirements:* For master's, comprehensive exam, thesis optional; for doctorate, comprehensive exam, thesis/dissertation, seminar, internships, publications, original research. *Entrance requirements:* For master's, GRE General Test, minimum GPA of 3.0, 3 letters of recommendation, resume, transcripts, statement of objectives, appropriate bachelor's degree; for doctorate, GRE General Test, minimum GPA of 3.3, resume, 3 letters of recommendation, statement of objectives, on-campus interview (highly recommended). Additional exam requirements/recommendations for international students: Required—TOEFL (minimum score 550 paper-based; 79 iBT). *Application deadline:* Applications are processed on a rolling basis. Electronic applications accepted. *Expenses: Tuition:* Full-time $22,338; part-time $1241 per credit hour. Tuition and fees vary according to degree level, campus/location and program. *Financial support:* Career-related internships or fieldwork, institutionally sponsored loans, tuition waivers (partial), unspecified assistantships, and tuition remissions available. Support available to part-time students. Financial award application deadline: 3/1; financial award applicants required to submit FAFSA. *Faculty research:* Deep-sea, coastal and estuarine environmental factors affected by pollution, climate change and natural processes. *Unit head:* Dr. Richard Aronson, Department Head, 321-674-8034, E-mail: raronson@fit.edu. *Application contact:* Mike Perry, Executive Director of Admissions, 321-674-7127, E-mail: perrymj@fit.edu.
Website: https://www.fit.edu/programs/oceanography-ms/

Florida State University, The Graduate School, Department of Anthropology, Department of Earth, Ocean and Atmospheric Science, Program in Oceanography, Tallahassee, FL 32306-4320. Offers aquatic environmental science (MS, PSM); oceanography (MS, PhD). *Faculty:* 15 full-time (4 women). *Students:* 49 full-time (29 women), 4 part-time (2 women); includes 5 minority (1 Black or African American, non-Hispanic/Latino; 2 Asian, non-Hispanic/Latino; 2 Hispanic/Latino), 9 international. Average age 26. 77 applicants, 34% accepted, 22 enrolled. In 2018, 13 master's, 2 doctorates awarded. *Degree requirements:* For master's, thesis; for doctorate, comprehensive exam, thesis/dissertation. *Entrance requirements:* For master's and doctorate, GRE General Test, minimum upper-division GPA of 3.0. Additional exam requirements/recommendations for international students: Required—TOEFL (minimum score 550 paper-based; 80 iBT). *Application deadline:* For fall admission, 2/15 priority date for domestic and international students; for spring admission, 9/15 priority date for domestic and international students. Applications are processed on a rolling basis. Application fee: $35. Electronic applications accepted. *Expenses: Tuition, area resident:* Part-time $479.32 per credit hour. Tuition and fees vary according to campus/location and program. *Financial support:* In 2018–19, 38 students received support, including 2 fellowships with full tuition reimbursements available, 24 research assistantships with full tuition reimbursements available, 12 teaching assistantships with full tuition reimbursements available. Financial award application deadline: 2/15; financial award applicants required to submit FAFSA. *Faculty research:* Trace metals in seawater, currents and waves, modeling, benthic ecology, marine biogeochemistry. *Unit head:* Dr. Jeffrey Chanton, Area Coordinator, 850-644-6205, Fax: 850-644-2581, E-mail: jchanton@fsu.edu. *Application contact:* Michaela Lupiani, Academic Coordinator, 850-644-6205, Fax: 850-644-2581, E-mail: mlupiani@fsu.edu.
Website: http://www.eoas.fsu.edu

Hawai`i Pacific University, College of Natural and Computational Sciences, Program in Marine Science, Honolulu, HI 96813. Offers MS. *Program availability:* Part-time. *Entrance requirements:* For master's, GRE, baccalaureate degree in a natural science discipline, minimum undergraduate GPA of 3.0. Additional exam requirements/recommendations for international students: Recommended—TOEFL (minimum score 550 paper-based; 80 iBT), IELTS (minimum score 6), TWE (minimum score 5). Electronic applications accepted. *Expenses:* Contact institution.

Instituto Tecnologico de Santo Domingo, Graduate School, Area of Basic And Environmental Sciences, Santo Domingo, Dominican Republic. Offers environmental science (M En S), including environmental education, environmental management, marine resources, natural resources management; mathematics (MS, PhD); renewable energy technology (MS, Certificate).

Jacksonville University, College of Arts and Sciences, Marine Science Research Institute, Jacksonville, FL 32211. Offers MA, MS, MPP/MS. MPP/MS offered jointly with JU's Public Policy Institute. *Program availability:* Part-time. *Degree requirements:* For master's, comprehensive exam, thesis optional, thesis in preparation research, thesis defense, and 1 semester of practical experience as teaching assistant in undergraduate marine science or biology lab (for MS); 30 credit hours with minimum 6 of lab courses and comprehensive exam (for MA). *Entrance requirements:* For master's, GRE, official transcripts of academic work, 2-page statement of research and professional goals, resume, three letters of recommendation, interview with program advisor. Additional exam requirements/recommendations for international students: Required—TOEFL (minimum score 540 paper-based; 76 iBT), IELTS (minimum score 6). Electronic applications accepted. *Expenses:* Contact institution. *Faculty research:* Tagging; satellites to predict weather, ocean drifters and more.

Medical University of South Carolina, College of Graduate Studies, Program in Molecular and Cellular Biology and Pathobiology, Charleston, SC 29425. Offers cancer biology (PhD); cardiovascular biology (PhD); cardiovascular imaging (PhD); cell regulation (PhD); craniofacial biology (PhD); genetics and development (PhD); marine biomedicine (PhD); DMD/PhD; MD/PhD. *Degree requirements:* For doctorate, thesis/dissertation, oral and written exams. *Entrance requirements:* For doctorate, GRE General Test, interview, minimum GPA of 3.0. Additional exam requirements/recommendations for international students: Required—TOEFL (minimum score 600 paper-based; 100 iBT). Electronic applications accepted.

Memorial University of Newfoundland, School of Graduate Studies, Interdisciplinary Program in Marine Studies, St. John's, NL A1C 5S7, Canada. Offers fisheries resource management (MMS, Graduate Diploma); marine spatial planning and management (MMS). *Program availability:* Part-time. *Degree requirements:* For master's, report. *Entrance requirements:* For master's, high 2nd class degree from a recognized university; demonstrated commitment to the fishery through employment or experience in a sector of the fishery, in a regulatory agency or government department connected to the fisheries, in a non-governmental agency, or through self-employment or relevant professional consulting activities; for Graduate Diploma, high 2nd class degree from a recognized university. Electronic applications accepted. *Faculty research:* Biological, ecological and oceanographic aspects of world fisheries; economics; political science; sociology.

North Carolina State University, Graduate School, College of Sciences, Department of Marine, Earth, and Atmospheric Sciences, Raleigh, NC 27695. Offers marine, earth, and atmospheric sciences (MS, PhD); meteorology (MS, PhD); oceanography (MS, PhD). PhD offered jointly with The University of North Carolina Wilmington. Terminal master's awarded for partial completion of doctoral program. *Degree requirements:* For master's, thesis (for some programs), final oral exam; for doctorate, comprehensive exam, thesis/dissertation, final oral exam, preliminary oral and written exams. *Entrance requirements:* For master's, GRE General Test, minimum GPA of 3.0; for doctorate, GRE General Test, GRE Subject Test (for disciplines in biological oceanography and geology), minimum GPA of 3.0. Additional exam requirements/recommendations for international students: Required—TOEFL (minimum score 550 paper-based). Electronic applications accepted. *Faculty research:* Boundary layer and air quality meteorology; climate and mesoscale dynamics; biological, chemical, geological, and physical oceanography; hard rock, soft rock, environmental, and paleo-geology.

Oregon State University, College of Earth, Ocean, and Atmospheric Sciences, Program in Marine Resource Management, Corvallis, OR 97331. Offers MS. *Program availability:* Part-time. *Entrance requirements:* For master's, GRE, minimum GPA of 3.0 in last 90 hours of course work. Additional exam requirements/recommendations for international students: Required—TOEFL (minimum score 575 paper-based). *Faculty research:* Ocean and coastal resources, fisheries resources, marine pollution, marine recreation and tourism.

San Francisco State University, Division of Graduate Studies, College of Science and Engineering, Department of Biology, Program in Interdisciplinary Marine and Estuarine Science, San Francisco, CA 94132-1722. Offers MS. Program offered through the Moss Landing Marine Laboratories. *Application deadline:* Applications are processed on a rolling basis. *Unit head:* Dr. Ellen Hines, Program Coordinator, 415-338-3512, Fax: 415-338-2295, E-mail: ehines@sfsu.edu. *Application contact:* Dr. Ellen Hines, Program Coordinator, 415-338-3512, Fax: 415-338-2295, E-mail: ehines@sfsu.edu.
Website: http://biology.sfsu.edu/graduate/marine_sciencesRTC

San Jose State University, Moss Landing Marine Laboratories, San Jose, CA 95192-0001. Offers MS. *Degree requirements:* For master's, thesis, qualifying exam. *Entrance requirements:* For master's, GRE. Electronic applications accepted. *Faculty research:* Physical oceanography, marine geology, ecology, ichthyology, invertebrate zoology.

Savannah State University, Master of Science in Marine Sciences Program, Savannah, GA 31404. Offers applied marine science (MSMS); marine science research (MSMS); professional advancement (MSMS). *Program availability:* Part-time. *Degree requirements:* For master's, comprehensive exam, field paper or thesis. *Entrance requirements:* For master's, GRE General Test, minimum GPA of 3.0, 3 letters of recommendation, essay, official transcripts, resume, immunization certificate, interview (recommended). Additional exam requirements/recommendations for international students: Required—TOEFL. Electronic applications accepted. *Expenses:* Contact institution.

Southern Connecticut State University, School of Graduate Studies, School of Arts and Sciences, Department of Environment, Geography and Marine Sciences, New Haven, CT 06515-1355. Offers environmental education (MS); science education (MS, Diploma). *Accreditation:* NCATE. *Program availability:* Part-time, evening/weekend. *Degree requirements:* For master's, thesis or alternative. *Entrance requirements:* For master's, interview; for Diploma, master's degree. Electronic applications accepted.

Stony Brook University, State University of New York, Graduate School, School of Marine and Atmospheric Sciences, Program in Marine Sciences, Stony Brook, NY 11794. Offers MS, PhD. *Program availability:* Evening/weekend. *Degree requirements:* For doctorate, one foreign language, comprehensive exam, thesis/dissertation. *Entrance requirements:* For master's, GRE General Test, official transcripts, minimum GPA of 3.0, 3 letters of recommendation; for doctorate, GRE General Test, minimum GPA of 3.0, 3 letters of recommendation. Additional exam requirements/recommendations for international students: Required—TOEFL (minimum score 600 paper-based; 90 iBT). *Application deadline:* For fall admission, 1/15 priority date for domestic students; for spring admission, 10/1 priority date for domestic students. Application fee: $100. Electronic applications accepted. *Expenses:* Contact institution. *Financial support:* In 2018–19, 13 fellowships, 42 research assistantships, 25 teaching assistantships were awarded; career-related internships or fieldwork also available. *Unit head:* Dr. Larry Swanson, Interim Dean, 631-632-8700, E-mail: larry.swanson@stonybrook.edu. *Application contact:* Ginny Clancy, Coordinator, 631-632-8681, Fax: 631-632-8200, E-mail: ginny.clancy@stonybrook.edu.
Website: http://you.stonybrook.edu/somas/education/graduate/marine-sciences-track/

Texas A&M University, Galveston Campus, Department of Marine Sciences, College Station, TX 77843. Offers marine resources management (MMRM). *Program availability:* Part-time. *Faculty:* 15. *Students:* 18 full-time (9 women), 4 part-time (2 women); includes 5 minority (4 Hispanic/Latino; 1 Two or more races, non-Hispanic/Latino). Average age 27. 7 applicants, 100% accepted, 4 enrolled. In 2018, 14 master's awarded. Terminal master's awarded for partial completion of doctoral program. *Entrance requirements:* For master's, GRE, course work in economics. Additional exam requirements/recommendations for international students: Required—TOEFL (minimum score 550 paper-based; 80 iBT), IELTS (minimum score 6). *Application deadline:* For fall admission, 5/1 for domestic and international students; for spring admission, 10/15 for domestic students, 10/1 for international students. Application fee: $50 ($90 for international students). Electronic applications accepted. *Expenses:* Contact institution. *Financial support:* In 2018–19, 17 students received support, including 7 research assistantships (averaging $9,686 per year), 12 teaching assistantships (averaging $14,785 per year); scholarships/grants, health care benefits, and unspecified assistantships also available. Financial award application deadline: 3/31; financial award applicants required to submit FAFSA. *Faculty research:* Biogeochemistry, physical oceanography, theoretical chemistry, marine policy. *Unit head:* Dr. Kyeong Park, Department Head, 409-740-4710. *Application contact:* Dr. Wesley Highfield, Assistant Professor/Graduate Advisor, 409-740-4518, Fax: 409-740-4429, E-mail: schlemme@tamug.edu.
Website: http://www.tamug.edu/mars/

Texas A&M University–Corpus Christi, College of Graduate Studies, College of Science and Engineering, Program in Coastal and Marine System Science, Corpus Christi, TX 78412. Offers MS, PhD. *Program availability:* Part-time. *Degree requirements:* For master's, comprehensive exam, thesis; for doctorate, comprehensive exam, thesis/dissertation. *Entrance requirements:* For master's and doctorate, GRE (taken within 5 years), essay (up to 1,000 words), curriculum vitae, 3 letters of recommendation. Additional exam requirements/recommendations for international students: Required—TOEFL (minimum score 550 paper-based; 79 iBT), IELTS (minimum score 6.5). Electronic applications accepted.

University of Alaska Fairbanks, College of Fisheries and Ocean Sciences, Department of Marine Biology, Fairbanks, AK 99775-7220. Offers marine biology (MS, PhD); oceanography (MS, PhD). *Program availability:* Part-time. *Faculty:* 9 full-time (5 women). *Students:* 23 full-time (17 women), 13 part-time (7 women); includes 3 minority (2 Asian, non-Hispanic/Latino; 1 Two or more races, non-Hispanic/Latino), 6 international. Average age 31. 26 applicants, 27% accepted, 5 enrolled. In 2018, 3 master's, 3 doctorates awarded. *Degree requirements:* For master's, comprehensive exam, thesis, oral defense of thesis; for doctorate, comprehensive exam, thesis/dissertation, oral defense of dissertation. *Entrance requirements:* For master's, GRE General Test, bachelor's degree from accredited institution with minimum cumulative undergraduate and major GPA of 3.0; for doctorate, GRE General Test, minimum cumulative GPA of 3.0. Additional exam requirements/recommendations for international students: Required—TOEFL (minimum score 550 paper-based; 79 iBT), IELTS (minimum score 6.5). *Application deadline:* For fall admission, 5/1 for domestic students, 3/1 for international students; for spring admission, 9/15 for domestic students, 8/15 for international students. Applications are processed on a rolling basis. Application fee: $60. Electronic applications accepted. *Expenses: Tuition, area resident:* Full-time $8802; part-time $5868 per credit hour. Tuition, state resident: full-time $8802; part-time $5868 per credit hour. Tuition, nonresident: full-time $18,504; part-time $12,336 per credit hour. *International tuition:* $18,504 full-time. *Required fees:* $1416; $944 per credit hour. $472 per semester. Tuition and fees vary according to course load and program. *Financial support:* In 2018–19, 13 research assistantships with full tuition reimbursements (averaging $8,919 per year), 5 teaching assistantships with full tuition reimbursements (averaging $14,433 per year) were awarded; fellowships with full tuition reimbursements, career-related internships or fieldwork, Federal Work-Study, scholarships/grants, health care benefits, and unspecified assistantships also available. Support available to part-time students. Financial award application deadline: 7/1; financial award applicants required to submit FAFSA. *Total annual research expenditures:* $9.4 million. *Unit head:* Dr. Lara Horstman, Chair, 907-474-7724, E-mail: info@sfos.uaf.edu. *Application contact:* Samara Taber, Director of Admissions, 907-474-7500, Fax: 907-474-7097, E-mail: uaf-admissions@alaska.edu.
Website: http://www.uaf.edu/cfos/academics/graduate/

The University of British Columbia, Faculty of Science, Department of Earth, Ocean and Atmospheric Sciences, Vancouver, BC V6T 1Z4, Canada. Offers atmospheric science (M Sc, PhD); geological engineering (M Eng, MA Sc, PhD); geological sciences (M Sc, PhD); geophysics (M Sc, MA Sc, PhD); oceanography (M Sc, PhD). *Degree requirements:* For master's, one foreign language, thesis (for some programs); for doctorate, one foreign language, comprehensive exam, thesis/dissertation. *Entrance requirements:* Additional exam requirements/recommendations for international students: Required—TOEFL. *Expenses:* Contact institution. *Faculty research:* Oceans and atmosphere, environmental earth science, hydro geology, mineral deposits, geophysics.

University of California, San Diego, Graduate Division, Scripps Institution of Oceanography, Program in Marine Biodiversity and Conservation, La Jolla, CA 92093. Offers MAS. *Students:* 23 full-time (14 women), 2 part-time (both women). 63 applicants, 52% accepted, 23 enrolled. In 2018, 18 master's awarded. *Degree requirements:* For master's, capstone/independent study project. *Entrance requirements:* For master's, minimum GPA of 3.0, statement of purpose, 3 letters of recommendation, current resume or curriculum vitae. Additional exam requirements/recommendations for international students: Required—TOEFL (minimum score 550 paper-based; 80 iBT), IELTS (minimum score 7). *Application deadline:* For summer admission, 1/18 for domestic students. Application fee: $105 ($125 for international students). Electronic applications accepted. *Expenses:* Contact institution. *Financial support:* Fellowships and scholarships/grants available. Financial award applicants required to submit FAFSA. *Faculty research:* Marine ecosystems, policy analysis, economics. *Unit head:* Dr. Mark Jacobsen, Program Co-Chair, 858-534-7040, E-mail: m3jacobsen@ucsd.edu. *Application contact:* Risa Farrell, Program Coordinator, 858-822-2886, E-mail: mbc@ucsd.edu.
Website: https://scripps.ucsd.edu/masters/mas/mbc

University of California, Santa Barbara, Graduate Division, College of Letters and Sciences, Division of Mathematics, Life, and Physical Sciences, Interdepartmental Graduate Program in Marine Science, Santa Barbara, CA 93106-9620. Offers MS, PhD. *Degree requirements:* For master's, thesis, 39 units; for doctorate, comprehensive exam, thesis/dissertation, 31 units. *Entrance requirements:* For master's and doctorate, GRE. Additional exam requirements/recommendations for international students: Required—TOEFL (minimum score 550 paper-based; 80 iBT), IELTS (minimum score 7). Electronic applications accepted. *Faculty research:* Ocean carbon cycling, paleoceanography, physiology of marine organisms, bio-optical oceanography, biological oceanography.

University of California, Santa Cruz, Division of Graduate Studies, Division of Physical and Biological Sciences, Department of Ocean Sciences, Santa Cruz, CA 95064. Offers MS, PhD. Terminal master's awarded for partial completion of doctoral program. *Degree requirements:* For master's, thesis; for doctorate, comprehensive exam, thesis/dissertation, seminar, qualifying exam. *Entrance requirements:* For master's and doctorate, GRE General Test, GRE Subject Test, 3 letters of recommendation. Additional exam requirements/recommendations for international students: Required—TOEFL (minimum score 550 paper-based; 83 iBT); Recommended—IELTS (minimum score 8). Electronic applications accepted. *Faculty research:* Sediment, marine organic and trace metal biogeochemistry; paleoceanography; remote sensing (satellite oceanography); coastal circulation processes; the development of software applications for real-time data acquisition and data visualization; climatology.

Marine Sciences

University of Delaware, College of Earth, Ocean, and Environment, School of Marine Science and Policy, Newark, DE 19716. Offers marine policy (MMP); marine studies (MS, PhD), including marine biosciences, oceanography, physical ocean science and engineering; oceanography (PhD).

University of Florida, Graduate School, College of Agricultural and Life Sciences, School of Forest Resources and Conservation, Department of Fisheries and Aquatic Sciences, Gainesville, FL 32611. Offers MFAS, MS, PhD. *Program availability:* Part-time, online learning. *Degree requirements:* For master's, thesis (for MS); technical paper (for MFAS); for doctorate, comprehensive exam, thesis/dissertation. *Entrance requirements:* For master's and doctorate, GRE General Test, minimum GPA of 3.0. Additional exam requirements/recommendations for international students: Required—TOEFL (minimum score 550 paper-based; 80 iBT), IELTS (minimum score 6). Electronic applications accepted.

University of Georgia, Franklin College of Arts and Sciences, Department of Marine Sciences, Athens, GA 30602. Offers MS, PhD. *Degree requirements:* For master's, thesis; for doctorate, comprehensive exam, thesis/dissertation, teaching experience, field research experience. *Entrance requirements:* For master's and doctorate, GRE General Test. Additional exam requirements/recommendations for international students: Required—TOEFL. Electronic applications accepted. *Faculty research:* Microbial ecology, biogeochemistry, polar biology, coastal ecology, coastal circulation.

University of Hawaii at Manoa, Office of Graduate Education, College of Social Sciences, Department of Geography, Graduate Ocean Policy Certificate Program, Honolulu, HI 96822. Offers Graduate Certificate. *Program availability:* Part-time. *Entrance requirements:* Additional exam requirements/recommendations for international students: Required—TOEFL (minimum score 500 paper-based; 61 iBT), IELTS (minimum score 5).

University of Maine, Graduate School, College of Natural Sciences, Forestry, and Agriculture, School of Marine Sciences, Orono, ME 04469. Offers MS, PSM, PhD. *Program availability:* Part-time. *Faculty:* 26 full-time (9 women), 11 part-time/adjunct (0 women). *Students:* 49 full-time (28 women), 4 part-time (2 women); includes 5 minority (1 American Indian or Alaska Native, non-Hispanic/Latino; 1 Asian, non-Hispanic/Latino; 1 Hispanic/Latino; 2 Two or more races, non-Hispanic/Latino), 8 international. Average age 27. 64 applicants, 22% accepted, 14 enrolled. In 2018, 19 master's, 4 doctorates awarded. *Degree requirements:* For master's, thesis; for doctorate, comprehensive exam, thesis/dissertation. *Entrance requirements:* For master's and doctorate, GRE General Test. Additional exam requirements/recommendations for international students: Required—TOEFL (minimum score 550 paper-based; 79 iBT). *Application deadline:* For fall admission, 8/1 priority date for domestic students. Applications are processed on a rolling basis. Application fee: $65. Electronic applications accepted. *Financial support:* In 2018–19, 100 students received support, including 1 fellowship with full tuition reimbursement available (averaging $21,400 per year), 63 research assistantships with full tuition reimbursements available (averaging $16,000 per year), 10 teaching assistantships with full tuition reimbursements available (averaging $15,600 per year); career-related internships or fieldwork, Federal Work-Study, tuition waivers (full and partial), and unspecified assistantships also available. Support available to part-time students. Financial award application deadline: 3/1. *Faculty research:* Oceanography, marine biology, marine policy, aquaculture and fisheries. *Total annual research expenditures:* $11 million. *Unit head:* Dr. Fei Chai, Director, 207-581-3321, Fax: 207-581-4388. *Application contact:* Scott G. Delcourt, Assistant Vice President for Graduate Studies and Senior Associate Dean, 207-581-3291, Fax: 207-581-3232, E-mail: graduate@maine.edu.
Website: http://www.umaine.edu/marine/

University of Maryland, Baltimore, Graduate School, Program in Marine-Estuarine-Environmental Sciences, College Park, MD 20740. Offers MS, PhD. *Program availability:* Part-time. Terminal master's awarded for partial completion of doctoral program. *Degree requirements:* For doctorate, comprehensive exam, thesis/dissertation, proposal defense, oral defense. *Entrance requirements:* For doctorate, GRE General Test, minimum GPA of 3.0, curriculum vitae, essay, 3 letters of recommendation. Additional exam requirements/recommendations for international students: Required—TOEFL (minimum score 80 iBT); Recommended—IELTS (minimum score 7). Electronic applications accepted.

University of Maryland, Baltimore County, The Graduate School, Marine-Estuarine-Environmental Sciences Graduate Program, College Park, MD 20742. Offers MS, PhD. *Program availability:* Part-time. *Degree requirements:* For master's, thesis, oral defense; for doctorate, comprehensive exam, thesis/dissertation, proposal defense, oral defense. *Entrance requirements:* For master's and doctorate, GRE General Test, minimum GPA of 3.0. Additional exam requirements/recommendations for international students: Required—TOEFL. Electronic applications accepted.

University of Maryland, College Park, Academic Affairs, College of Computer, Mathematical and Natural Sciences, Program in Marine-Estuarine-Environmental Sciences, College Park, MD 20742. Offers MS, PhD. *Program availability:* Part-time. Terminal master's awarded for partial completion of doctoral program. *Degree requirements:* For master's, thesis, oral defense; for doctorate, comprehensive exam, thesis/dissertation, proposal defense, oral defense. *Entrance requirements:* For master's and doctorate, GRE General Test, minimum GPA of 3.0. Additional exam requirements/recommendations for international students: Required—TOEFL. Electronic applications accepted. *Faculty research:* Ecology, environmental chemistry, environmental molecular biology/biotechnology, environmental sciences, fisheries science, oceanography.

University of Maryland Eastern Shore, Graduate Programs, Program in Marine-Estuarine-Environmental Sciences, College Park, MD 20740. Offers MS, PhD. *Program availability:* Part-time. *Degree requirements:* For master's, thesis; for doctorate, comprehensive exam, thesis/dissertation, proposal defense. *Entrance requirements:* For master's and doctorate, GRE General Test, minimum GPA of 3.0. Additional exam requirements/recommendations for international students: Required—TOEFL. Electronic applications accepted.

University of Massachusetts Amherst, Graduate School, Interdisciplinary Programs, Program in Marine Science and Technology, Amherst, MA 01003. Offers MS, PhD. *Program availability:* Part-time. Terminal master's awarded for partial completion of doctoral program. *Degree requirements:* For master's, thesis or alternative; for doctorate, comprehensive exam, thesis/dissertation. *Entrance requirements:* For master's and doctorate, GRE General Test, 3 letters of recommendation. Additional exam requirements/recommendations for international students: Required—TOEFL (minimum score 550 paper-based; 80 iBT), IELTS (minimum score 6.5). Electronic applications accepted.

University of Massachusetts Boston, School for the Environment, Program in Marine Science and Technology, Boston, MA 02125-3393. Offers MS, PhD. *Students:* 8 full-time (4 women), 8 part-time (4 women); includes 2 minority (1 Hispanic/Latino; 1 Two or more races, non-Hispanic/Latino). Average age 31. 5 applicants. In 2018, 2 master's, 1 doctorate awarded. *Application deadline:* For fall admission, 1/15 for domestic students; for spring admission, 10/15 for domestic students. *Expenses: Tuition, area resident:* Full-time $17,896. Tuition, state resident: full-time $17,896. Tuition, nonresident: full-time $34,932. *International tuition:* $34,932 full-time. *Required fees:* $355. *Unit head:* Dr. Juanita Urban-Rich, Associate Professor, 617-287.7485, E-mail: Juanita.Urban-Rich@umb.edu. *Application contact:* Graduate Admissions Coordinator, 617-287-6400, Fax: 617-287-6236, E-mail: graduate.admissions@umb.edu.

University of Massachusetts Dartmouth, Graduate School, School for Marine Science and Technology, New Bedford, MA 02747-2300. Offers coastal and ocean administration science and technology (MS); marine science and technology (MS, PhD). *Program availability:* Part-time. *Faculty:* 14 full-time (1 woman). *Students:* 21 full-time (13 women), 31 part-time (15 women); includes 3 minority (1 Asian, non-Hispanic/Latino; 2 Two or more races, non-Hispanic/Latino), 8 international. Average age 31. 30 applicants, 73% accepted, 10 enrolled. In 2018, 7 master's, 4 doctorates awarded. Terminal master's awarded for partial completion of doctoral program. *Degree requirements:* For master's, thesis; for doctorate, comprehensive exam, thesis/dissertation. *Entrance requirements:* For master's, GRE, statement of interest (minimum of 300 words), resume, 3 letters of recommendation, official transcripts; for doctorate, GRE, statement of intent (minimum of 300 words), statement of interest (minimum of 300 words), resume, 3 letters of recommendation, official transcripts. Additional exam requirements/recommendations for international students: Required—TOEFL (minimum score 577 paper-based; 90 iBT). *Application deadline:* For fall admission, 2/15 priority date for domestic students, 1/15 priority date for international students; for spring admission, 11/15 priority date for domestic students, 10/15 priority date for international students. Application fee: $60. Electronic applications accepted. *Financial support:* In 2018–19, 3 fellowships (averaging $14,000 per year), 30 research assistantships (averaging $17,994 per year), 1 teaching assistantship (averaging $9,250 per year) were awarded; tuition waivers (full and partial) and doctoral support, dissertation writing support also available. Financial award application deadline: 3/1; financial award applicants required to submit FAFSA. *Faculty research:* Major marine biogeochemical cycles, atmospheric co2 concentration, resource assessment and bycatch avoidance, air sea interaction, dynamics/kinematics of coastal fonts, estuarian circulation, storm-force and internal wave dynamics stock assessment, oceanic frontal processes, arctic ocean and climate change. *Total annual research expenditures:* $11.1 million. *Unit head:* Steven Lohrenz, Dean, School for Marine Science and Technology, 508-910-6550, E-mail: slohrenz@umassd.edu. *Application contact:* Scott Webster, Director of Graduate Studies and Admissions, 508-999-8604, Fax: 508-999-8183, E-mail: graduate@umassd.edu.
Website: http://www.umassd.edu/smast

University of Miami, Graduate School, Rosenstiel School of Marine and Atmospheric Science, Division of Applied Marine Physics, Coral Gables, FL 33124. Offers applied marine physics (MS, PhD), including coastal ocean dynamics, underwater acoustics and geoacoustics (PhD), wave surface dynamics and air-sea interaction (PhD). *Program availability:* Part-time. Terminal master's awarded for partial completion of doctoral program. *Degree requirements:* For master's, comprehensive exam, thesis; for doctorate, comprehensive exam, thesis/dissertation. *Entrance requirements:* For master's and doctorate, GRE General Test. Additional exam requirements/recommendations for international students: Required—TOEFL (minimum score 550 paper-based). Electronic applications accepted.

University of Miami, Graduate School, Rosenstiel School of Marine and Atmospheric Science, Division of Marine and Atmospheric Chemistry, Coral Gables, FL 33124. Offers MS, PhD. Terminal master's awarded for partial completion of doctoral program. *Degree requirements:* For master's, comprehensive exam, thesis; for doctorate, comprehensive exam, thesis/dissertation. *Entrance requirements:* For master's and doctorate, GRE General Test. Additional exam requirements/recommendations for international students: Required—TOEFL (minimum score 550 paper-based). Electronic applications accepted. *Faculty research:* Global change issues, chemistry of marine waters and marine atmosphere.

University of New England, College of Arts and Sciences, Biddeford, ME 04005-9526. Offers biological sciences (MS); marine sciences (MS). *Program availability:* Part-time. *Faculty:* 13 full-time (5 women). *Students:* 13 full-time (9 women), 3 part-time (all women). Average age 26. 46 applicants, 37% accepted, 12 enrolled. In 2018, 8 master's awarded. *Application deadline:* Applications are processed on a rolling basis. Electronic applications accepted. *Financial support:* Fellowships, research assistantships, teaching assistantships, career-related internships or fieldwork, scholarships/grants, traineeships, and unspecified assistantships available. Financial award application deadline: 5/1; financial award applicants required to submit FAFSA. *Unit head:* Dr. Jonathan H. Millen, Dean, College of Arts and Sciences, 207-602-2371, E-mail: jmillen@une.edu. *Application contact:* Scott Steinberg, Vice President of University Admissions, 207-221-4225, Fax: 207-523-1925, E-mail: ssteinberg@une.edu.
Website: http://www.une.edu/cas/programs/graduate

The University of North Carolina at Chapel Hill, Graduate School, College of Arts and Sciences, Department of Marine Sciences, Chapel Hill, NC 27599. Offers MS, PhD. *Degree requirements:* For master's, comprehensive exam, thesis; for doctorate, comprehensive exam, thesis/dissertation. *Entrance requirements:* For master's and doctorate, GRE General Test, minimum GPA of 3.0. Additional exam requirements/recommendations for international students: Required—TOEFL. Electronic applications accepted. *Faculty research:* Physical oceanography, marine biology and ecology, marine geochemistry, marine geology and coastal meteorology.

The University of North Carolina Wilmington, Center for Marine Science, Wilmington, NC 28403-3297. Offers MS. *Program availability:* Part-time. *Degree requirements:* For master's, comprehensive exam, thesis. *Entrance requirements:* For master's, GRE, 3 recommendations, statement of research interest, baccalaureate degree in a natural science or mathematics. Additional exam requirements/recommendations for international students: Required—TOEFL (minimum score 550 paper-based; 79 iBT), IELTS (minimum score 6.5). Electronic applications accepted.

The University of North Carolina Wilmington, College of Arts and Sciences, Department of Biology and Marine Biology, Wilmington, NC 28403-3297. Offers biology (MS); marine biology (MS, PhD). *Program availability:* Part-time. *Degree requirements:* For master's, comprehensive exam, thesis; for doctorate, comprehensive exam, thesis/dissertation. *Entrance requirements:* For master's, GRE General Test, 3 recommendations, research interests form and statement, resume or curriculum vitae, baccalaureate degree from biology-related field; for doctorate, GRE General Test, 3 recommendations, resume or curriculum vitae, summary of MS thesis research, statement of PhD research interests, copies of publications, master's degree or BS and 1 year of completed work in the MS in biology program. Additional exam requirements/recommendations for international students: Required—TOEFL (minimum score 550 paper-based; 79 iBT), IELTS (minimum score 6.5). Electronic applications accepted. *Faculty research:* Ecology, physiology, cell and molecular biology, systematics, biomechanics.

The University of North Carolina Wilmington, College of Arts and Sciences, Department of Earth and Ocean Sciences, Wilmington, NC 28403-3297. Offers geographic information science (Graduate Certificate); geoscience (MS). *Program availability:* Part-time. *Degree requirements:* For master's, comprehensive exam, thesis (for some programs). *Entrance requirements:* For master's, GRE General Test, 3 recommendations, research essay. Additional exam requirements/recommendations for international students: Required—TOEFL (minimum score 550 paper-based; 79 iBT), IELTS (minimum score 6.5). Electronic applications accepted.

The University of North Carolina Wilmington, College of Arts and Sciences, Department of Public and International Affairs, Wilmington, NC 28403-3297. Offers coastal and ocean policy (MS); conflict management and resolution (MA); public administration (MPA), including coastal management. *Accreditation:* NASPAA. *Program availability:* Blended/hybrid learning. *Degree requirements:* For master's, thesis (for some programs), internship, practicum, capstone project. *Entrance requirements:* For master's, GRE, GMAT, 3 letters of recommendation, statement of interest, resume, essay. Additional exam requirements/recommendations for international students: Required—TOEFL (minimum score 550 paper-based; 79 iBT), IELTS (minimum score 6.5). Electronic applications accepted.

University of Puerto Rico–Mayagüez, Graduate Studies, College of Arts and Sciences, Department of Marine Sciences, Mayagüez, PR 00681-9000. Offers MS, PhD. *Program availability:* Part-time. *Degree requirements:* For master's, one foreign language, comprehensive exam, thesis, departmental final exams; for doctorate, one foreign language, comprehensive exam, thesis/dissertation, qualifying and departmental final exams. *Entrance requirements:* For master's, GRE, minimum GPA of 3.0; for doctorate, GRE, minimum GPA of 3.5. Electronic applications accepted. *Faculty research:* Marine botany, ecology, chemistry, and parasitology; fisheries; ichthyology; aquaculture.

University of Rhode Island, Graduate School, College of the Environment and Life Sciences, Department of Fisheries, Animal and Veterinary Sciences, Kingston, RI 02881. Offers animal health and disease (MS); animal science (MS); aquaculture (MS); aquatic pathology (MS); environmental sciences (PhD), including animal science, aquaculture science, aquatic pathology, fisheries science; fisheries (MS). *Faculty:* 12 full-time (7 women). *Entrance requirements:* Additional exam requirements/recommendations for international students: Required—TOEFL. *Application deadline:* For fall admission, 7/15 for domestic students, 2/1 for international students; for spring admission, 11/15 for domestic students, 7/15 for international students. Application fee: $65. Electronic applications accepted. *Expenses: Tuition, area resident:* Full-time $13,226; part-time $735 per credit. Tuition, state resident: full-time $13,226; part-time $735 per credit. Tuition, nonresident: full-time $25,854; part-time $1436 per credit. *International tuition:* $25,854 full-time. *Required fees:* $1698; $50 per credit. $35 per semester. One-time fee: $165. *Financial support:* Application deadline: 2/1; applicants required to submit FAFSA. *Unit head:* Dr. Marta Gomez-Chiarri, Chair, 401-874-2917, Fax: 401-874-7575, E-mail: gomezchi@uri.edu. *Application contact:* Dr. Marta Gomez-Chiarri, Chair, 401-874-2917, Fax: 401-874-7575, E-mail: gomezchi@uri.edu. Website: http://web.uri.edu/favs/

University of South Alabama, College of Arts and Sciences, Department of Marine Sciences, Mobile, AL 36688. Offers marine conservation and resource management (MS); marine sciences (MS, PhD). *Degree requirements:* For master's, comprehensive exam, thesis optional; for doctorate, comprehensive exam, thesis/dissertation, research project. *Entrance requirements:* For master's, GRE, minimum GPA of 3.0, BS in marine sciences or related discipline; for doctorate, GRE, BS or MS in marine sciences or related discipline; minimum undergraduate GPA of 3.0, graduate 3.25. Additional exam requirements/recommendations for international students: Required—TOEFL (minimum score 525 paper-based; 71 iBT). Electronic applications accepted. *Faculty research:* Marine ecosystem response, coastal ecosystems, marine fisheries ecology, overfishing, climate change.

University of South Carolina, The Graduate School, College of Arts and Sciences, Marine Science Program, Columbia, SC 29208. Offers MS, PhD. *Degree requirements:* For master's, thesis; for doctorate, comprehensive exam, thesis/dissertation. *Entrance requirements:* For master's and doctorate, GRE General Test. Additional exam requirements/recommendations for international students: Required—TOEFL (minimum score 570 paper-based). Electronic applications accepted. *Faculty research:* Biological, chemical, geological, and physical oceanography; policy.

University of Southern California, Graduate School, Dana and David Dornsife College of Letters, Arts and Sciences, Graduate Program in Ocean Sciences, Los Angeles, CA 90089. Offers MS, PhD. Only Ph.D. and M.S./Ph.D. students are funded. *Program availability:* Part-time. Terminal master's awarded for partial completion of doctoral program. *Degree requirements:* For master's, thesis; for doctorate, comprehensive exam, thesis/dissertation. *Entrance requirements:* For master's and doctorate, GRE. Additional exam requirements/recommendations for international students: Required—TOEFL. Electronic applications accepted. *Faculty research:* Microbial ecology, biogeochemical cycles, marine chemistry, marine biology, global change.

University of Southern Mississippi, College of Arts and Sciences, Division of Coastal Sciences, Ocean Springs, MS 39566-7000. Offers MS, PhD. *Program availability:* Part-time. Terminal master's awarded for partial completion of doctoral program. *Degree requirements:* For master's, comprehensive exam, thesis; for doctorate, comprehensive exam, thesis/dissertation. *Entrance requirements:* For master's, GRE General Test, minimum GPA of 3.0 for last 60 hours; for doctorate, GRE General Test, minimum undergraduate GPA of 3.0, graduate 3.5. Additional exam requirements/recommendations for international students: Required—TOEFL, IELTS. Electronic applications accepted.

University of Southern Mississippi, College of Arts and Sciences, Division of Marine Science, Stennis Space Center, MS 39529. Offers hydrographic science (MS); marine science (MS, PhD). *Program availability:* Part-time. *Degree requirements:* For master's, comprehensive exam, thesis, oral qualifying exam (marine science); for doctorate, 2 foreign languages, comprehensive exam, thesis/dissertation, oral qualifying exam. *Entrance requirements:* For master's, GRE General Test, minimum GPA of 3.0; for doctorate, GRE General Test, minimum GPA of 3.0 (undergraduate), 3.5 (graduate). Additional exam requirements/recommendations for international students: Required—TOEFL (minimum score 567 paper-based; 86 iBT), IELTS (minimum score 6.5).

Electronic applications accepted. *Expenses:* Contact institution. *Faculty research:* Bioacoustics, biological oceanography, bio-optics, coastal geology, coastal hazards, computational biology, geological oceanography, hydrography, marine chemistry, marine phytoplankton ecology, marine science, numerical modeling, paleontology, physical oceanography, remote sensing, signal processing, zooplankton.

University of South Florida, College of Marine Science, St. Petersburg, FL 33701. Offers marine science (MS, PhD), including biological oceanography, chemical oceanography, geological oceanography, interdisciplinary, marine resource assessment, physical oceanography. *Program availability:* Part-time. *Faculty:* 27 full-time (8 women). *Students:* 67 full-time (39 women), 21 part-time (12 women); includes 10 minority (1 Black or African American, non-Hispanic/Latino; 6 Hispanic/Latino; 3 Two or more races, non-Hispanic/Latino), 16 international. Average age 30. 79 applicants, 25% accepted, 17 enrolled. In 2018, 14 master's, 14 doctorates awarded. Terminal master's awarded for partial completion of doctoral program. *Degree requirements:* For master's, comprehensive exam, thesis; for doctorate, comprehensive exam, thesis/dissertation. *Entrance requirements:* For master's and doctorate, GRE General Test, bachelor's degree from regionally-accredited university, preferably in biology, chemistry, geology, physics or math; minimum GPA of 3.0 in upper-division coursework; research interest statement; resume; three letters of recommendation; commitment of faculty to serve as advisor. Additional exam requirements/recommendations for international students: Required—TOEFL, TOEFL (minimum score 550 paper-based; 79 iBT) or IELTS (minimum score 6.5). *Application deadline:* For fall admission, 1/10 for domestic and international students; for spring admission, 10/1 for domestic and international students. Applications are processed on a rolling basis. Application fee: $30. Electronic applications accepted. *Expenses:* Tuition, state resident: full-time $6350. Tuition, nonresident: full-time $19,048. *International tuition:* $19,048 full-time. *Required fees:* $2079. *Financial support:* In 2018–19, 41 students received support, including 45 research assistantships with partial tuition reimbursements available (averaging $14,199 per year), 10 teaching assistantships with partial tuition reimbursements available (averaging $14,196 per year); health care benefits and unspecified assistantships also available. Financial award application deadline: 1/15. *Faculty research:* Problems in shelf, coastal and estuarine waters, in the deep ocean, and in the watershed that drains to the coastal zone such as long-term sea-level rise, coral reef demise, recent paleo-climate change, ocean acidification, harmful algal blooms, fisheries management, water quality, shoreline change, and oil-drilling. *Total annual research expenditures:* $14.8 million. *Unit head:* Dr. Jacqueline E. Dixon, Dean, 727-553-3369, Fax: 727-553-1189, E-mail: jdixon@usf.edu. *Application contact:* Dr. David F. Naar, Associate Professor and Director of Academic Affairs, 727-553-1637, Fax: 727-553-1189, E-mail: naar@usf.edu. Website: http://www.marine.usf.edu/

The University of Texas at Austin, Graduate School, College of Natural Sciences, Department of Marine Science, Austin, TX 78712-1111. Offers MS, PhD. *Degree requirements:* For master's, thesis; for doctorate, thesis/dissertation. *Entrance requirements:* For master's and doctorate, GRE General Test. Additional exam requirements/recommendations for international students: Required—TOEFL.

University of the Virgin Islands, College of Science and Mathematics, St. Thomas, VI 00802. Offers marine and environmental science (MS); mathematics for secondary teachers (MA). *Faculty:* 5 full-time (4 women), 7 part-time/adjunct (2 women). *Students:* 16 full-time (13 women), 19 part-time (13 women); includes 10 minority (4 Black or African American, non-Hispanic/Latino; 1 American Indian or Alaska Native, non-Hispanic/Latino; 2 Hispanic/Latino; 1 Native Hawaiian or other Pacific Islander, non-Hispanic/Latino; 2 Two or more races, non-Hispanic/Latino), 1 international. Average age 27. In 2018, 8 master's awarded. *Degree requirements:* For master's, comprehensive exam, thesis. *Entrance requirements:* For master's, GRE, minimum GPA of 2.5. Additional exam requirements/recommendations for international students: Required—TOEFL (minimum score 550 paper-based). *Application deadline:* For fall admission, 4/30 for domestic and international students; for spring admission, 10/30 for domestic and international students. Application fee: $30. Electronic applications accepted. *Expenses:* Tuition, state resident: full-time $6948; part-time $386 per credit. Tuition, nonresident: full-time $13,230; part-time $735 per credit. *International tuition:* $13,230 full-time. *Required fees:* $508. *Financial support:* Fellowships, research assistantships, teaching assistantships, career-related internships or fieldwork, and scholarships/grants available. Financial award application deadline: 4/15; financial award applicants required to submit FAFSA. *Unit head:* Dr. Sandra Romano, Dean, 340-693-1230, Fax: 340-693-1245, E-mail: sromano@uvi.edu. *Application contact:* Charmaine Smith, Director of Admissions, 340-690-4070, E-mail: csmith@uvi.edu.

University of Wisconsin–La Crosse, College of Science and Health, Department of Biology, La Crosse, WI 54601-3742. Offers aquatic sciences (MS); biology (MS); cellular and molecular biology (MS); clinical microbiology (MS); microbiology (MS); nurse anesthesia (MS); physiology (MS). *Accreditation:* AANA/CANAEP. *Program availability:* Part-time. *Degree requirements:* For master's, comprehensive exam, thesis. *Entrance requirements:* For master's, GRE General Test, minimum GPA of 2.85. Additional exam requirements/recommendations for international students: Required—TOEFL (minimum score 550 paper-based; 79 iBT). Electronic applications accepted.

University of Wisconsin–Madison, Graduate School, College of Letters and Science, Department of Atmospheric and Oceanic Sciences, Madison, WI 53706-1380. Offers MS, PhD. *Program availability:* Part-time. *Degree requirements:* For master's, thesis (for some programs); for doctorate, thesis/dissertation. *Entrance requirements:* For master's and doctorate, GRE General Test, minimum GPA of 3.0; previous course work in chemistry, mathematics, and physics. Electronic applications accepted. *Faculty research:* Satellite meteorology, weather systems, global climate change, numerical modeling, atmosphere-ocean interaction.

Western Washington University, Graduate School, Huxley College of the Environment, Department of Environmental Sciences, Bellingham, WA 98225-5996. Offers environmental science (MS); marine and estuarine science (MS). *Program availability:* Part-time. *Degree requirements:* For master's, thesis. *Entrance requirements:* For master's, GRE General Test, minimum GPA of 3.0 in last 60 semester hours or last 90 quarter hours. Additional exam requirements/recommendations for international students: Required—TOEFL (minimum score 567 paper-based). Electronic applications accepted. *Faculty research:* Landscape ecology, climate change, watershed studies, environmental toxicology and risk assessment, aquatic toxicology, toxic algae, invasive species.

Peterson's Graduate Programs in the Physical Sciences, Mathematics, Agricultural Sciences, the Environment & Natural Resources 2020

www.petersons.com   **125**

Oceanography

Cornell University, Graduate School, Graduate Fields of Agriculture and Life Sciences, Field of Ecology and Evolutionary Biology, Ithaca, NY 14853. Offers ecology (PhD), including animal ecology, applied ecology, biogeochemistry, community and ecosystem ecology, limnology, oceanography, physiological ecology, plant ecology, population ecology, theoretical ecology, vertebrate zoology; evolutionary biology (PhD), including ecological genetics, paleobiology, population biology, systematics. *Degree requirements:* For doctorate, comprehensive exam, thesis/dissertation, 2 semesters of teaching experience. *Entrance requirements:* For doctorate, GRE General Test, GRE Subject Test (biology), 2 letters of recommendation. Additional exam requirements/recommendations for international students: Required—TOEFL (minimum score 550 paper-based; 77 iBT). Electronic applications accepted. *Faculty research:* Population and organismal biology, population and evolutionary genetics, systematics and macroevolution, biochemistry, conservation biology.

Dalhousie University, Faculty of Science, Department of Oceanography, Halifax, NS B3H 4R2, Canada. Offers M Sc, PhD. *Degree requirements:* For master's, thesis; for doctorate, thesis/dissertation. *Entrance requirements:* Additional exam requirements/recommendations for international students: Required—TOEFL, IELTS, CANTEST, CAEL, or Michigan English Language Assessment Battery. Electronic applications accepted. *Faculty research:* Biological and physical oceanography, chemical and geological oceanography, atmospheric sciences.

Florida Institute of Technology, College of Engineering and Science, Program in Oceanography, Melbourne, FL 32901-6975. Offers biological oceanography (MS); coastal management (MS). *Program availability:* Part-time. *Students:* 16 full-time (10 women), 2 part-time (both women); includes 1 minority (Two or more races, non-Hispanic/Latino), 2 international. Average age 28. 13 applicants, 69% accepted, 4 enrolled. In 2018, 4 master's, 1 doctorate awarded. *Degree requirements:* For master's, comprehensive exam, thesis optional; for doctorate, comprehensive exam, thesis/dissertation, seminar, internships, publications, original research. *Entrance requirements:* For master's, GRE General Test, minimum GPA of 3.0, 3 letters of recommendation, resume, transcripts, statement of objectives, appropriate bachelor's degree; for doctorate, GRE General Test, minimum GPA of 3.3, resume, 3 letters of recommendation, statement of objectives, on-campus interview (highly recommended). Additional exam requirements/recommendations for international students: Required—TOEFL (minimum score 550 paper-based; 79 iBT). *Application deadline:* Applications are processed on a rolling basis. Electronic applications accepted. *Expenses: Tuition:* Full-time $22,338; part-time $1241 per credit hour. Tuition and fees vary according to degree level, campus/location and program. *Financial support:* Career-related internships or fieldwork, institutionally sponsored loans, tuition waivers (partial), unspecified assistantships, and tuition remissions available. Support available to part-time students. Financial award application deadline: 3/1; financial award applicants required to submit FAFSA. *Faculty research:* Deep-sea, coastal and estuarine environmental factors affected by pollution, climate change and natural processes. *Unit head:* Dr. Richard Aronson, Department Head, 321-674-8034, E-mail: raronson@fit.edu. *Application contact:* Mike Perry, Executive Director of Admissions, 321-674-7127, E-mail: perrymj@fit.edu.
Website: https://www.fit.edu/programs/oceanography-ms/

Florida State University, The Graduate School, Department of Anthropology, Department of Earth, Ocean and Atmospheric Science, Program in Oceanography, Tallahassee, FL 32306-4320. Offers aquatic environmental science (MS, PSM); oceanography (MS, PhD). *Faculty:* 15 full-time (4 women). *Students:* 49 full-time (29 women), 4 part-time (2 women); includes 5 minority (1 Black or African American, non-Hispanic/Latino; 2 Asian, non-Hispanic/Latino; 2 Hispanic/Latino), 9 international. Average age 26. 77 applicants, 34% accepted, 22 enrolled. In 2018, 13 master's, 2 doctorates awarded. *Degree requirements:* For master's, thesis; for doctorate, comprehensive exam, thesis/dissertation. *Entrance requirements:* For master's and doctorate, GRE General Test, minimum upper-division GPA of 3.0. Additional exam requirements/recommendations for international students: Required—TOEFL (minimum score 550 paper-based; 80 iBT). *Application deadline:* For fall admission, 2/15 priority date for domestic and international students; for spring admission, 9/15 priority date for domestic and international students. Applications are processed on a rolling basis. Application fee: $35. Electronic applications accepted. *Expenses: Tuition, area resident:* Part-time $479.32 per credit hour. Tuition and fees vary according to campus/location and program. *Financial support:* In 2018–19, 38 students received support, including 2 fellowships with full tuition reimbursements available, 24 research assistantships with full tuition reimbursements available, 12 teaching assistantships with full tuition reimbursements available. Financial award application deadline: 2/15; financial award applicants required to submit FAFSA. *Faculty research:* Trace metals in seawater, currents and waves, modeling, benthic ecology, marine biogeochemistry. *Unit head:* Dr. Jeffrey Chanton, Area Coordinator, 850-644-6205, Fax: 850-644-2581, E-mail: jchanton@fsu.edu. *Application contact:* Michaela Lupiani, Academic Coordinator, 850-644-6205, Fax: 850-644-2581, E-mail: mlupiani@fsu.edu.
Website: http://www.eoas.fsu.edu

Louisiana State University and Agricultural & Mechanical College, Graduate School, School of the Coast and Environment, Department of Oceanography and Coastal Sciences, Baton Rouge, LA 70803. Offers MS, PhD.

Massachusetts Institute of Technology, School of Engineering, Department of Civil and Environmental Engineering, Cambridge, MA 02139. Offers biological oceanography (PhD, Sc D); chemical oceanography (PhD, Sc D); civil and environmental engineering (M Eng, SM, PhD, Sc D); civil and environmental systems (PhD, Sc D); civil engineering (PhD, Sc D, CE); civil engineering and computation (PhD); coastal engineering (PhD, Sc D); construction engineering and management (PhD, Sc D); environmental biology (PhD, Sc D); environmental chemistry (PhD, Sc D); environmental engineering (PhD, Sc D); environmental engineering and computation (PhD); environmental fluid mechanics (PhD, Sc D); geotechnical and geoenvironmental engineering (PhD, Sc D); hydrology (PhD, Sc D); information technology (PhD, Sc D); oceanographic engineering (PhD, Sc D); structures and materials (PhD, Sc D); transportation (PhD, Sc D); SM/MBA. *Degree requirements:* For master's, thesis; for doctorate, comprehensive exam, thesis/dissertation; for CE, comprehensive exam, thesis. *Entrance requirements:* For master's, doctorate, and CE, GRE General Test. Additional exam requirements/recommendations for international students: Required—TOEFL, IELTS. Electronic applications accepted. *Expenses: Tuition:* Full-time $51,520; part-time $800 per credit hour. *Required fees:* $312. *Faculty research:* Environmental chemistry, environmental fluid mechanics and coastal engineering, environmental microbiology, geotechnical engineering and geomechanics, hydrology and hydro climatology, infrastructure systems, mechanics of materials and structures, transportation systems.

Massachusetts Institute of Technology, School of Science, Department of Biology, Cambridge, MA 02139. Offers biochemistry (PhD); biological oceanography (PhD); biology (PhD); biophysical chemistry and molecular structure (PhD); cell biology (PhD); computational and systems biology (PhD); developmental biology (PhD); genetics (PhD); immunology (PhD); microbiology (PhD); molecular biology (PhD); neurobiology (PhD). *Degree requirements:* For doctorate, comprehensive exam, thesis/dissertation, teaching assistantship during two semesters. *Entrance requirements:* For doctorate, GRE General Test. Additional exam requirements/recommendations for international students: Required—TOEFL, IELTS. Electronic applications accepted. *Expenses: Tuition:* Full-time $51,520; part-time $800 per credit hour. *Required fees:* $312. *Faculty research:* Cellular, developmental and molecular (plant and animal) biology; biochemistry, bioengineering, biophysics and structural biology; classical and molecular genetics, stem cell and epigenetics; immunology and microbiology; cancer biology, molecular medicine, neurobiology and human disease; computational and systems biology.

Massachusetts Institute of Technology, School of Science, Department of Earth, Atmospheric, and Planetary Sciences, Cambridge, MA 02139. Offers atmospheric chemistry (PhD, Sc D); atmospheric science (SM, PhD, Sc D); chemical oceanography (SM, PhD, Sc D); climate physics and chemistry (SM, PhD, Sc D); earth and planetary sciences (SM); geochemistry (PhD, Sc D); geology (PhD, Sc D); geophysics (PhD, Sc D); marine geology and geophysics (SM, PhD, Sc D); physical oceanography (SM, PhD, Sc D); planetary sciences (PhD, Sc D). Terminal master's awarded for partial completion of doctoral program. *Degree requirements:* For master's, thesis; for doctorate, comprehensive exam, thesis/dissertation. *Entrance requirements:* For master's and doctorate, GRE General Test. Additional exam requirements/recommendations for international students: Required—TOEFL, IELTS. Electronic applications accepted. *Expenses: Tuition:* Full-time $51,520; part-time $800 per credit hour. *Required fees:* $312. *Faculty research:* Earth: origin, composition, structure, and dynamics of (and interactions between) the atmosphere, oceans, surface, and interior of the earth; planets: formation, dynamics, and evolution of planetary systems and the characterization of exoplanets; climate: characterization of past, present, and potential future climates; studies of the causes and consequences of climate change; life: co-evolution of life and environmental systems.

McGill University, Faculty of Graduate and Postdoctoral Studies, Faculty of Science, Department of Atmospheric and Oceanic Sciences, Montréal, QC H3A 2T5, Canada. Offers atmospheric science (M Sc, PhD); physical oceanography (M Sc, PhD). PhD program in physical oceanography offered jointly with Université Laval.

Memorial University of Newfoundland, School of Graduate Studies, Department of Physics and Physical Oceanography, St. John's, NL A1C 5S7, Canada. Offers atomic and molecular physics (PhD); condensed matter physics (PhD); physical oceanography (M Sc, PhD); physics (M Sc). *Program availability:* Part-time. *Degree requirements:* For master's, thesis, seminar presentation on thesis topic; for doctorate, comprehensive exam, thesis/dissertation, oral defense of thesis. *Entrance requirements:* For master's, honors B Sc or equivalent; for doctorate, M Sc or equivalent. Electronic applications accepted. *Faculty research:* Experiment and theory in atomic and molecular physics, condensed matter physics, physical oceanography, theoretical geophysics and applied nuclear physics.

Naval Postgraduate School, Departments and Academic Groups, Department of Meteorology, Monterey, CA 93943. Offers meteorology (MS, PhD); meteorology and physical oceanography (MS). Program only open to commissioned officers of the United States and friendly nations and selected United States federal civilian employees. *Program availability:* Part-time. *Degree requirements:* For master's, thesis; for doctorate, one foreign language, thesis/dissertation. *Faculty research:* Air-sea interactions, boundary layer meteorology, climate dynamics, numerical weather prediction, tropical cyclones.

Naval Postgraduate School, Departments and Academic Groups, Department of Oceanography, Monterey, CA 93943. Offers physical oceanography (MS, PhD). Program only open to commissioned officers of the United States and friendly nations and selected United States federal civilian employees. *Program availability:* Part-time. *Degree requirements:* For master's, thesis; for doctorate, thesis/dissertation. *Faculty research:* Lagrangian acoustic subsurface technology, naval ocean analysis prediction, nearshore processes, unmanned vehicles, ocean acoustics, turbulence, waves.

Naval Postgraduate School, Departments and Academic Groups, Undersea Warfare Academic Group, Monterey, CA 93943. Offers applied mathematics (MS); applied physics (MS); applied science (MS), including acoustics, operations research, physical oceanography, signal processing; electrical engineering (MS); engineering acoustics (MS, PhD); engineering science (MS), including electrical engineering, mechanical engineering; mechanical engineer (ME); mechanical engineering (MS, MSME); meteorology (MS); operations research (MS); physical oceanography (MS). Program only open to commissioned officers of the United States and friendly nations and selected United States federal civilian employees. *Program availability:* Part-time. *Degree requirements:* For master's, thesis. *Faculty research:* Unmanned/autonomous vehicles, sea mines and countermeasures, submarine warfare in the twentieth and twenty-first centuries.

North Carolina State University, Graduate School, College of Sciences, Department of Marine, Earth, and Atmospheric Sciences, Raleigh, NC 27695. Offers marine, earth, and atmospheric sciences (MS, PhD); meteorology (MS, PhD); oceanography (MS, PhD). PhD offered jointly with The University of North Carolina Wilmington. Terminal master's awarded for partial completion of doctoral program. *Degree requirements:* For master's, thesis (for some programs), final oral exam; for doctorate, comprehensive exam, thesis/dissertation, final oral exam, preliminary oral and written exams. *Entrance requirements:* For master's, GRE General Test, minimum GPA of 3.0; for doctorate, GRE General Test, GRE Subject Test (for disciplines in biological oceanography and geology), minimum GPA of 3.0. Additional exam requirements/recommendations for international students: Required—TOEFL (minimum score 550 paper-based). Electronic applications accepted. *Faculty research:* Boundary layer and air quality meteorology; climate and mesoscale dynamics; biological, chemical, geological, and physical oceanography; hard rock, soft rock, environmental, and paleo-geology.

Nova Southeastern University, Halmos College of Natural Sciences and Oceanography, Fort Lauderdale, FL 33314-7796. Offers biological sciences (MS), including health studies; marine biology and oceanography (PhD), including marine biology, oceanography. *Program availability:* Part-time, evening/weekend, blended/hybrid learning. *Degree requirements:* For master's, thesis; for doctorate, comprehensive exam, thesis/dissertation, departmental qualifying exam. *Entrance requirements:* For master's, GRE General Test, 3 letters of recommendation; BS/BA in natural science (for marine biology program); BS/BA in biology (for biological sciences program); minor in the natural sciences or equivalent (for coastal zone management and marine environmental sciences); for doctorate, GRE General Test, master's degree. Additional exam requirements/recommendations for international students: Required—TOEFL (minimum score 550 paper-based); Recommended—IELTS. Electronic applications accepted. *Expenses:* Contact institution. *Faculty research:* Physical and biological oceanography, molecular and microbiology, ecology and evolution, coral reefs, marine ecosystems.

Old Dominion University, College of Sciences, Department of Ocean, Earth and Atmospheric Sciences, Norfolk, VA 23529. Offers ocean and earth sciences (MS); oceanography (PhD). *Program availability:* Part-time. Terminal master's awarded for partial completion of doctoral program. *Degree requirements:* For master's, comprehensive exam (for some programs), thesis (for some programs), 10 days of ship time or fieldwork; for doctorate, comprehensive exam, thesis/dissertation, 10 days of ship time or fieldwork. *Entrance requirements:* For master's and doctorate, GRE General Test, minimum GPA of 3.0 in major, 2.8 overall. Additional exam requirements/recommendations for international students: Required—TOEFL (minimum score 550 paper-based). Electronic applications accepted. *Faculty research:* Biological, chemical, geological, and physical oceanography.

Oregon State University, College of Earth, Ocean, and Atmospheric Sciences, Program in Ocean, Earth, and Atmospheric Sciences, Corvallis, OR 97331. Offers atmospheric sciences (MA, MS, PhD); oceanography (MA, MS, PhD). *Program availability:* Part-time. *Entrance requirements:* For master's, GRE. Additional exam requirements/recommendations for international students: Required—TOEFL (minimum score 80 iBT), IELTS (minimum score 6.5).

Princeton University, Graduate School, Department of Geosciences, Program in Atmospheric and Oceanic Sciences, Princeton, NJ 08544-1019. Offers PhD. *Degree requirements:* For doctorate, one foreign language, thesis/dissertation. *Entrance requirements:* For doctorate, GRE General Test, GRE Subject Test. Additional exam requirements/recommendations for international students: Required—TOEFL (minimum score 600 paper-based). Electronic applications accepted. *Faculty research:* Climate dynamics, middle atmosphere dynamics and chemistry, oceanic circulation, marine geochemistry, numerical modeling.

Rutgers University–New Brunswick, Graduate School-New Brunswick, Program in Oceanography, Piscataway, NJ 08854-8097. Offers MS, PhD. Terminal master's awarded for partial completion of doctoral program. *Degree requirements:* For master's, thesis; for doctorate, comprehensive exam, thesis/dissertation. *Entrance requirements:* For master's and doctorate, GRE General Test, 1 year course work in calculus, physics, chemistry. Additional exam requirements/recommendations for international students: Required—TOEFL. Electronic applications accepted. *Faculty research:* Coastal observations and modeling, estuarine ecology/fish/benthos, geochemistry, deep sea ecology/hydrothermal vents, molecular biology applications.

Texas A&M University, College of Geosciences, Department of Oceanography, College Station, TX 77843. Offers oceanography (PhD). *Faculty:* 24. *Students:* 63 full-time (31 women), 10 part-time (6 women); includes 12 minority (1 Black or African American, non-Hispanic/Latino; 7 Hispanic/Latino; 4 Two or more races, non-Hispanic/Latino), 28 international. Average age 28. 48 applicants, 50% accepted, 20 enrolled. In 2018, 12 master's, 8 doctorates awarded. *Degree requirements:* For master's, thesis; for doctorate, thesis/dissertation. *Entrance requirements:* For master's and doctorate, GRE General Test. Additional exam requirements/recommendations for international students: Required—TOEFL (minimum score 550 paper-based; 80 iBT), IELTS (minimum score 6), PTE (minimum score 53). *Application deadline:* For fall admission, 1/1 priority date for domestic students; for spring admission, 9/1 for domestic students. Applications are processed on a rolling basis. Application fee: $50 ($90 for international students). Electronic applications accepted. *Expenses:* Contact institution. *Financial support:* In 2018–19, 63 students received support, including 11 fellowships with tuition reimbursements available (averaging $14,276 per year), 28 research assistantships with tuition reimbursements available (averaging $14,032 per year), 15 teaching assistantships with tuition reimbursements available (averaging $13,807 per year); career-related internships or fieldwork, institutionally sponsored loans, scholarships/grants, traineeships, health care benefits, tuition waivers (full and partial), and unspecified assistantships also available. Support available to part-time students. Financial award application deadline: 3/15; financial award applicants required to submit FAFSA. *Faculty research:* Ocean circulation, climate studies, coastal and shelf dynamics, marine phytoplankton, stable isotope geochemistry. *Unit head:* Dr. Debbie Thomas, Professor and Department Head, 979-862-7248, Fax: 979-845-6331. *Application contact:* Brady Dennis, Academic Advisor II, 979-845-5346, Fax: 979-845-6331, E-mail: brady-dennis@tamu.edu.
Website: http://ocean.tamu.edu

Université du Québec à Rimouski, Graduate Programs, Program in Oceanography, Rimouski, QC G5L 3A1, Canada. Offers M Sc, PhD. *Program availability:* Part-time. *Degree requirements:* For master's, thesis; for doctorate, thesis/dissertation. *Entrance requirements:* For master's, appropriate bachelor's degree, proficiency in French; for doctorate, appropriate master's degree, proficiency in French.

Université Laval, Faculty of Sciences and Engineering, Program in Oceanography, Québec, QC G1K 7P4, Canada. Offers PhD. Program offered jointly with McGill University and Université du Québec à Rimouski. *Degree requirements:* For doctorate, comprehensive exam, thesis/dissertation. *Entrance requirements:* For doctorate, knowledge of French, knowledge of English. Additional exam requirements/recommendations for international students: Required—TOEFL. Electronic applications accepted.

University of Alaska Fairbanks, College of Fisheries and Ocean Sciences, Department of Marine Biology, Fairbanks, AK 99775-7220. Offers marine biology (MS, PhD); oceanography (MS, PhD). *Program availability:* Part-time. *Faculty:* 9 full-time (5 women). *Students:* 23 full-time (17 women), 13 part-time (7 women); includes 3 minority (2 Asian, non-Hispanic/Latino; 1 Two or more races, non-Hispanic/Latino), 6 international. Average age 31. 26 applicants, 27% accepted, 5 enrolled. In 2018, 3 master's, 3 doctorates awarded. *Degree requirements:* For master's, comprehensive exam, thesis, oral defense of thesis; for doctorate, comprehensive exam, thesis/dissertation, oral defense of dissertation. *Entrance requirements:* For master's, GRE General Test, bachelor's degree from accredited institution with minimum cumulative undergraduate and major GPA of 3.0; for doctorate, GRE General Test, minimum cumulative GPA of 3.0. Additional exam requirements/recommendations for international students: Required—TOEFL (minimum score 550 paper-based; 79 iBT), IELTS (minimum score 6.5). *Application deadline:* For fall admission, 5/1 for domestic students, 3/1 for international students; for spring admission, 9/15 for domestic students, 8/15 for international students. Applications are processed on a rolling basis. Application fee: $60. Electronic applications accepted. *Expenses: Tuition, area resident:* Full-time $8802; part-time $5868 per credit hour. Tuition, state resident: full-time $8802; part-time $5868 per credit hour. Tuition, nonresident: full-time $18,504; part-time $12,336 per credit hour. *International tuition:* $18,504 full-time. *Required fees:* $1416; $944 per credit hour. $472 per semester. Tuition and fees vary according to course load and program. *Financial support:* In 2018–19, 13 research assistantships with full tuition reimbursements (averaging $8,919 per year), 5 teaching assistantships with full tuition reimbursements (averaging $14,433 per year) were awarded; fellowships with full tuition reimbursements, career-related internships or fieldwork, Federal Work-Study, scholarships/grants, health care benefits, and unspecified assistantships also available. Support available to part-time students. Financial award application deadline: 7/1; financial award applicants required to submit FAFSA. *Total annual research expenditures:* $9.4 million. *Unit head:* Dr. Lara Horstman, Chair, 907-474-7724, E-mail: info@sfos.uaf.edu. *Application contact:* Samara Taber, Director of Admissions, 907-474-7500, Fax: 907-474-7097, E-mail: uaf-admissions@alaska.edu.
Website: http://www.uaf.edu/cfos/academics/graduate/

The University of British Columbia, Faculty of Science, Department of Earth, Ocean and Atmospheric Sciences, Vancouver, BC V6T 1Z4, Canada. Offers atmospheric science (M Sc, PhD); geological engineering (M Eng, MA Sc, PhD); geological sciences (M Sc, PhD); geophysics (M Sc, MA Sc, PhD); oceanography (M Sc, PhD). *Degree requirements:* For master's, one foreign language, thesis (for some programs); for doctorate, one foreign language, comprehensive exam, thesis/dissertation. *Entrance requirements:* Additional exam requirements/recommendations for international students: Required—TOEFL. *Expenses:* Contact institution. *Faculty research:* Oceans and atmosphere, environmental earth science, hydro geology, mineral deposits, geophysics.

University of California, Los Angeles, Graduate Division, College of Letters and Science, Department of Atmospheric and Oceanic Sciences, Los Angeles, CA 90095. Offers MS, PhD. Terminal master's awarded for partial completion of doctoral program. *Degree requirements:* For master's, comprehensive exam or thesis; for doctorate, thesis/dissertation, oral and written qualifying exams; 2 quarters of teaching experience. *Entrance requirements:* For master's and doctorate, GRE General Test, bachelor's degree; minimum undergraduate GPA of 3.0 (or its equivalent if letter grade system not used). Additional exam requirements/recommendations for international students: Required—TOEFL. Electronic applications accepted.

University of California, San Diego, Graduate Division, Scripps Institution of Oceanography, La Jolla, CA 92093. Offers climate science and policy (MAS); earth sciences (PhD); geophysics (PhD); marine biodiversity and conservation (MAS); oceanography (MS, PhD). PhD in geophysics offered jointly with San Diego State University. *Students:* 265 full-time (143 women), 1 (woman) part-time. 407 applicants, 21% accepted, 55 enrolled. In 2018, 34 master's, 44 doctorates awarded. Terminal master's awarded for partial completion of doctoral program. *Degree requirements:* For master's, comprehensive exam (for some programs), thesis (for some programs); for doctorate, comprehensive exam, thesis/dissertation. *Entrance requirements:* For master's and doctorate, GRE General Test, GRE Subject Test (encouraged for ocean biosciences applicants), minimum GPA of 3.0. Additional exam requirements/recommendations for international students: Required—TOEFL (minimum score 550 paper-based; 80 iBT), IELTS (minimum score 7). *Application deadline:* For fall admission, 1/15 for domestic students. Application fee: $105 ($125 for international students). Electronic applications accepted. *Financial support:* Fellowships, research assistantships, teaching assistantships, scholarships/grants, traineeships, and unspecified assistantships available. Financial award applicants required to submit FAFSA. *Faculty research:* Biodiversity and conservation, earth and planetary chemistry, alternative energy, global environmental monitoring, air-sea boundary, tectonic margins and the interactions between systems and environments. *Unit head:* Peter Franks, Chair, 858-534-7528, E-mail: pfranks@ucsd.edu. *Application contact:* Gilbert Bretado, Graduate Coordinator, 858-534-1694, E-mail: siodept@sio.ucsd.edu.
Website: https://scripps.ucsd.edu/education

University of Colorado Boulder, Graduate School, College of Arts and Sciences, Department of Atmospheric and Oceanic Sciences, Boulder, CO 80309. Offers MS, PhD. *Entrance requirements:* For master's, minimum undergraduate GPA of 3.0. Electronic applications accepted. Application fee is waived when completed online. *Faculty research:* Atmospheric sciences; atmospheric physics; atmospheric structure and dynamics; climate change; climatology.

University of Delaware, College of Earth, Ocean, and Environment, School of Marine Science and Policy, Newark, DE 19716. Offers marine policy (MMP); marine studies (MS, PhD), including marine biosciences, oceanography, physical ocean science and engineering; oceanography (PhD).

University of Hawaii at Manoa, Office of Graduate Education, School of Ocean and Earth Science and Technology, Department of Oceanography, Honolulu, HI 96822. Offers MS, PhD. *Program availability:* Part-time. Terminal master's awarded for partial completion of doctoral program. *Degree requirements:* For master's, one foreign language, comprehensive exam, thesis, field experience; for doctorate, one foreign language, comprehensive exam, thesis/dissertation, field experience. *Entrance requirements:* For master's and doctorate, GRE General Test. Additional exam requirements/recommendations for international students: Required—TOEFL (minimum score 560 paper-based; 83 iBT), IELTS (minimum score 5). *Faculty research:* Physical oceanography, marine chemistry, biological oceanography, atmospheric chemistry, marine geology.

University of Maryland, College Park, Academic Affairs, College of Computer, Mathematical and Natural Sciences, Department of Atmospheric and Oceanic Science, College Park, MD 20742. Offers MS, PMS, PhD. *Program availability:* Part-time, evening/weekend, online learning. Terminal master's awarded for partial completion of doctoral program. *Degree requirements:* For master's, comprehensive exam, scholarly paper, written and oral exams; for doctorate, thesis/dissertation, exam. *Entrance requirements:* For master's, GRE General Test, background in mathematics, experience in scientific computer languages, 3 letters of recommendation; for doctorate, GRE General Test. Electronic applications accepted. *Faculty research:* Weather, atmospheric chemistry, air pollution, global change, radiation.

University of Miami, Graduate School, Rosenstiel School of Marine and Atmospheric Science, Division of Meteorology and Physical Oceanography, Coral Gables, FL 33124. Offers meteorology (MS, PhD); physical oceanography (MS, PhD). Terminal master's awarded for partial completion of doctoral program. *Degree requirements:* For master's, comprehensive exam, thesis; for doctorate, comprehensive exam, thesis/dissertation. *Entrance requirements:* For master's and doctorate, GRE General Test. Additional exam requirements/recommendations for international students: Required—TOEFL (minimum score 550 paper-based). Electronic applications accepted.

University of New Hampshire, Graduate School, College of Engineering and Physical Sciences, Department of Earth Sciences, Durham, NH 03824. Offers geochemical systems (MS); geology (MS); hydrology (MS); ocean mapping (MS); oceanography

(MS). *Degree requirements:* For master's, thesis. *Entrance requirements:* For master's, GRE General Test. Additional exam requirements/recommendations for international students: Required—TOEFL (minimum score 550 paper-based; 80 iBT). Electronic applications accepted.

University of New Hampshire, Graduate School, School of Marine Science and Ocean Engineering, Durham, NH 03824. Offers ocean engineering (MS, PhD); ocean mapping (MS, Postbaccalaureate Certificate). *Degree requirements:* For master's, thesis. *Entrance requirements:* Additional exam requirements/recommendations for international students: Required—TOEFL (minimum score 550 paper-based; 80 iBT). Electronic applications accepted.

University of Rhode Island, Graduate School, Graduate School of Oceanography, Narragansett, RI 02882. Offers biological oceanography (MS, PhD); coastal ocean management (MO); coastal systems (MO); fisheries (MO); general oceanography (MO); marine and atmospheric chemistry (MS, PhD); marine fisheries management (MO); marine geology and geophysics (MS, PhD); ocean technology and data (MO); physical oceanography (MS, PhD); MBA/MO; PhD/MA; PhD/MMA. *Program availability:* Part-time. *Faculty:* 29 full-time (10 women). *Students:* 56 full-time (33 women), 10 part-time (5 women); includes 1 minority (Asian, non-Hispanic/Latino), 10 international. 76 applicants, 72% accepted, 17 enrolled. In 2018, 15 master's, 5 doctorates awarded. *Entrance requirements:* For master's, GRE, 2 letters of recommendation; for doctorate, GRE, 3 letters of recommendation. Additional exam requirements/recommendations for international students: Required—TOEFL. *Application deadline:* For fall admission, 1/15 for domestic and international students. Application fee: $65. Electronic applications accepted. *Expenses: Tuition, area resident:* Full-time $13,226; part-time $735 per credit. Tuition, state resident: full-time $13,226; part-time $735 per credit. Tuition, nonresident: full-time $25,854; part-time $1436 per credit. *International tuition:* $25,854 full-time. *Required fees:* $1698; $50 per credit. $35 per semester. One-time fee: $165. *Financial support:* In 2018–19, 31 research assistantships with tuition reimbursements (averaging $9,647 per year), 14 teaching assistantships with tuition reimbursements (averaging $10,563 per year) were awarded. Financial award application deadline: 1/15; financial award applicants required to submit FAFSA. *Faculty research:* Subduction, life in extreme environments, the marine nitrogen cycle, hurricane prediction, Antarctic ocean circulation. *Unit head:* Dr. Bruce Corliss, Dean, 401-874-6222, Fax: 401-874-6931, E-mail: bruce.corliss@gso.uri.edu. *Application contact:* Dr. David Smith, Professor of Oceanography/Associate Dean for Academic Affairs, 401-874-6172, E-mail: dcsmith@uri.edu.
Website: http://www.gso.uri.edu/

University of San Diego, College of Arts and Sciences, Environmental and Ocean Sciences Program, San Diego, CA 92110-2492. Offers MS. *Program availability:* Part-time. *Faculty:* 6 full-time (3 women), 1 part-time/adjunct (0 women). *Students:* 5 full-time (all women), 13 part-time (10 women); includes 4 minority (2 Asian, non-Hispanic/Latino; 2 Two or more races, non-Hispanic/Latino), 1 international. Average age 27. 17 applicants, 41% accepted, 4 enrolled. In 2018, 6 master's awarded. *Degree requirements:* For master's, thesis. *Entrance requirements:* For master's, GRE General Test, minimum GPA of 3.0; 1 semester each of biology with lab, physics with lab, and calculus; 1 year of chemistry with lab. Additional exam requirements/recommendations for international students: Required—TOEFL (minimum score 580 paper-based; 83 iBT), TWE. *Application deadline:* For fall admission, 4/1 for domestic and international students. Applications are processed on a rolling basis. Application fee: $45. Electronic applications accepted. *Financial support:* In 2018–19, 12 students received support. Teaching assistantships, career-related internships or fieldwork, Federal Work-Study, institutionally sponsored loans, scholarships/grants, and unspecified assistantships available. Support available to part-time students. Financial award application deadline: 4/1; financial award applicants required to submit FAFSA. *Faculty research:* Marine biology and ecology, environmental geology and geochemistry, climatology and geomorphology, physiological ecology, fisheries and aquaculture. *Unit head:* Dr. Ronald S. Kaufmann, Director, 619-260-4795, Fax: 619-260-6874, E-mail: soroya@sandiego.edu. *Application contact:* Erika Garwood, Associate Director of Graduate Admissions, 619-260-4524, Fax: 619-260-4158, E-mail: grads@sandiego.edu.
Website: http://www.sandiego.edu/cas/ms-environmental-ocean-sciences/

University of Southern California, Graduate School, Dana and David Dornsife College of Letters, Arts and Sciences, Department of Biological Sciences, Program in Marine Biology and Biological Oceanography, Los Angeles, CA 90089. Offers marine and environmental biology (MS); marine biology and biological oceanography (PhD). Terminal master's awarded for partial completion of doctoral program. *Degree requirements:* For master's, research paper; for doctorate, comprehensive exam, thesis/dissertation, qualifying examination, dissertation defense. *Entrance requirements:* For master's and doctorate, GRE, 3 letters of recommendation, personal statement, resume, minimum GPA of 3.0. Additional exam requirements/recommendations for international students: Required—TOEFL (minimum score 600 paper-based; 100 iBT). Electronic applications accepted. *Faculty research:* Microbial ecology, biogeochemistry, and geobiology; biodiversity and molecular ecology; integrative organismal biology; conservation biology; marine genomics.

University of South Florida, College of Marine Science, St. Petersburg, FL 33701. Offers marine science (MS, PhD), including biological oceanography, chemical oceanography, geological oceanography, interdisciplinary, marine resource assessment, physical oceanography. *Program availability:* Part-time. *Faculty:* 27 full-time (8 women). *Students:* 67 full-time (39 women), 21 part-time (12 women); includes 10 minority (1 Black or African American, non-Hispanic/Latino; 6 Hispanic/Latino; 3 Two or more races, non-Hispanic/Latino), 16 international. Average age 30. 79 applicants, 25% accepted, 17 enrolled. In 2018, 14 master's, 14 doctorates awarded. Terminal master's awarded for partial completion of doctoral program. *Degree requirements:* For master's, comprehensive exam, thesis; for doctorate, comprehensive exam, thesis/dissertation. *Entrance requirements:* For master's and doctorate, GRE General Test, bachelor's degree from regionally-accredited university, preferably in biology, chemistry, geology, physics or math; minimum GPA of 3.0 in upper-division coursework; research interest statement; resume; three letters of recommendation; commitment of faculty to serve as advisor. Additional exam requirements/recommendations for international students: Required—TOEFL, TOEFL (minimum score 550 paper-based; 79 iBT) or IELTS (minimum score 6.5). *Application deadline:* For fall admission, 1/10 for domestic and international students; for spring admission, 10/1 for domestic and international students. Applications are processed on a rolling basis. Application fee: $30. Electronic applications accepted. *Expenses:* Tuition, state resident: full-time $6350. Tuition, nonresident: full-time $19,048. *International tuition:* $19,048 full-time. *Required fees:* $2079. *Financial support:* In 2018–19, 41 students received support, including 45 research assistantships with partial tuition reimbursements available (averaging $14,199 per year), 10 teaching assistantships with partial tuition reimbursements available (averaging $14,196 per year); health care benefits and unspecified assistantships also available. Financial award application deadline: 1/15. *Faculty research:* Problems in shelf, coastal and estuarine waters, in the deep ocean, and in the watershed that drains to the coastal zone such as long-term sea-level rise, coral reef demise, recent paleo-climate change, ocean acidification, harmful algal blooms, fisheries management, water quality, shoreline change, and oil-drilling. *Total annual research expenditures:* $14.8 million. *Unit head:* Dr. Jacqueline E. Dixon, Dean, 727-553-3369, Fax: 727-553-1189, E-mail: jdixon@usf.edu. *Application contact:* Dr. David F. Naar, Associate Professor and Director of Academic Affairs, 727-553-1637, Fax: 727-553-1189, E-mail: naar@usf.edu.
Website: http://www.marine.usf.edu/

The University of Texas Rio Grande Valley, College of Sciences, School of Earth, Environmental, and Marine Sciences, Edinburg, TX 78539. Offers agricultural, environmental, and sustainability sciences (MS); ocean, coastal, and earth sciences (MS). *Expenses: Tuition, area resident:* Full-time $6888. Tuition, state resident: full-time $6888. Tuition, nonresident: full-time $14,484. *International tuition:* $14,484 full-time. *Required fees:* $1468.

University of Victoria, Faculty of Graduate Studies, Faculty of Science, School of Earth and Ocean Sciences, Victoria, BC V8W 2Y2, Canada. Offers M Sc, PhD. *Program availability:* Part-time. *Degree requirements:* For master's, thesis; for doctorate, thesis/dissertation, candidacy exam. *Entrance requirements:* For master's and doctorate, GRE. Additional exam requirements/recommendations for international students: Required—TOEFL (minimum score 575 paper-based), IELTS (minimum score 7). Electronic applications accepted. *Faculty research:* Climate modeling, geology.

University of Washington, Graduate School, College of the Environment, School of Oceanography, Seattle, WA 98195. Offers biological oceanography (MS, PhD); chemical oceanography (MS, PhD); marine geology and geophysics (MS, PhD); physical oceanography (MS, PhD). Terminal master's awarded for partial completion of doctoral program. *Degree requirements:* For master's, research project; for doctorate, thesis/dissertation. *Entrance requirements:* For master's and doctorate, GRE General Test, minimum GPA of 3.0. Additional exam requirements/recommendations for international students: Required—TOEFL. Electronic applications accepted. *Faculty research:* Global climate change, hydrothermal vent systems, marine microbiology, marine and freshwater biogeochemistry, biological-physical interactions.

University of Wisconsin–Madison, Graduate School, College of Letters and Science, Department of Atmospheric and Oceanic Sciences, Madison, WI 53706-1380. Offers MS, PhD. *Program availability:* Part-time. *Degree requirements:* For master's, thesis (for some programs); for doctorate, thesis/dissertation. *Entrance requirements:* For master's and doctorate, GRE General Test, minimum GPA of 3.0; previous course work in chemistry, mathematics, and physics. Electronic applications accepted. *Faculty research:* Satellite meteorology, weather systems, global climate change, numerical modeling, atmosphere-ocean interaction.

Woods Hole Oceanographic Institution, MIT/WHOI Joint Program in Oceanography/Applied Ocean Science and Engineering, Woods Hole, MA 02543-1541. Offers applied ocean science and engineering (PhD); biological oceanography (PhD); chemical oceanography (PhD); marine geology and geophysics (PhD); physical oceanography (PhD). Program offered jointly with Massachusetts Institute of Technology. *Degree requirements:* For doctorate, thesis/dissertation. *Entrance requirements:* For doctorate, GRE General Test. Additional exam requirements/recommendations for international students: Required—TOEFL or IELTS. Electronic applications accepted.

Yale University, Graduate School of Arts and Sciences, Department of Geology and Geophysics, New Haven, CT 06520. Offers biogeochemistry (PhD); climate dynamics (PhD); geochemistry (PhD); geophysics (PhD); meteorology (PhD); oceanography (PhD); paleontology (PhD); paleooceanography (PhD); petrology (PhD); tectonics (PhD). *Degree requirements:* For doctorate, thesis/dissertation. *Entrance requirements:* For doctorate, GRE General Test. Additional exam requirements/recommendations for international students: Required—TOEFL.

Section 5
Meteorology and Atmospheric Sciences

This section contains a directory of institutions offering graduate work in meteorology and atmospheric sciences. Additional information about programs listed in the directory may be obtained by writing directly to the dean of a graduate school or chair of a department at the address given in the directory.

For programs offering related work, see also in this book *Astronomy and Astrophysics, Geosciences, Marine Sciences and Oceanography,* and *Physics.* In the other guides in this series:

Graduate Programs in the Biological/Biomedical Sciences & Health-Related Medical Professions
See *Biological and Biomedical Sciences* and *Biophysics*

Graduate Programs in Engineering & Applied Sciences
See *Aerospace/Aeronautical Engineering, Civil and Environmental Engineering, Engineering and Applied Sciences,* and *Mechanical Engineering and Mechanics*

CONTENTS

Program Directories

Atmospheric Sciences

Bard College, Bard Center for Environmental Policy, Annandale-on-Hudson, NY 12504. Offers climate science and policy (MS, Professional Certificate), including agriculture (MS), ecosystems (MS); environmental policy (MS, Professional Certificate); sustainability (MBA); MS/JD; MS/MAT. *Program availability:* Part-time. *Degree requirements:* For master's, thesis, 4-month, full-time internship. *Entrance requirements:* For master's, GRE, coursework in statistics, chemistry and one other semester of college science; personal statement; curriculum vitae; 3 letters of recommendation; sample of written work. Additional exam requirements/recommendations for international students: Required—TOEFL (minimum score 600 paper-based; 100 iBT). Electronic applications accepted. *Expenses:* Contact institution. *Faculty research:* Climate and agriculture, alternative energy, environmental economics, environmental toxicology, EPA law, sustainable development, international relations, literature and composition, human rights, agronomy, advocacy, leadership.

Carnegie Mellon University, Mellon College of Science, Department of Chemistry, Pittsburgh, PA 15213-3891. Offers atmospheric chemistry (PhD); bioinorganic chemistry (PhD); bioorganic chemistry and chemical biology (PhD); biophysical chemistry (PhD); catalysis (PhD); green and environmental chemistry (PhD); materials and nanoscience (PhD); renewable energy (PhD); sensors, probes, and imaging (PhD); spectroscopy and single molecule analysis (PhD); theoretical and computational chemistry (PhD). *Program availability:* Part-time. Terminal master's awarded for partial completion of doctoral program. *Degree requirements:* For doctorate, thesis/dissertation, departmental qualifying and oral exams, teaching experience. *Entrance requirements:* For doctorate, GRE General Test, GRE Subject Test. Additional exam requirements/recommendations for international students: Required—TOEFL. Electronic applications accepted. *Faculty research:* Physical and theoretical chemistry, chemical synthesis, biophysical/bioinorganic chemistry.

City College of the City University of New York, Graduate School, Division of Science, Department of Earth and Atmospheric Sciences, New York, NY 10031-9198. Offers geology (MS). *Degree requirements:* For master's, comprehensive exam, thesis. *Entrance requirements:* Additional exam requirements/recommendations for international students: Required—TOEFL (minimum score 500 paper-based; 61 iBT). Electronic applications accepted. *Faculty research:* Water resources, high-temperature geochemistry, sedimentary basin analysis, tectonics.

Colorado State University, Walter Scott, Jr. College of Engineering, Department of Atmospheric Science, Fort Collins, CO 80523-1371. Offers MS, PhD. *Program availability:* Part-time. *Degree requirements:* For master's, thesis; for doctorate, thesis/dissertation, preliminary exam. *Entrance requirements:* For master's, GRE General Test, BS in physics, math, engineering, chemistry, or related field with minimum cumulative GPA of 3.0; calculus-based math course sequence including differential equations and vector analysis; calculus-based physics course sequence including kinetics, electricity and magnetism, and some modern topics; for doctorate, GRE General Test, MS with thesis in field of atmospheric science or related field and minimum cumulative GPA of 3.0; demonstration of basic principles of atmospheric science and aptitude for research. Additional exam requirements/recommendations for international students: Required—TOEFL (minimum score 550 paper-based; 80 iBT), IELTS (minimum score 6.5), PTE (minimum score 58). Electronic applications accepted. *Expenses:* Contact institution. *Faculty research:* Cloud microphysics, severe storms and mesoscale meteorology, atmospheric chemistry and air quality, radiation and remote sensing, climate and atmosphere-ocean dynamics, global biogeochemical cycles and ecosystems.

Columbia University, Graduate School of Arts and Sciences, New York, NY 10027. Offers African-American studies (MA); American studies (MA); anthropology (MA, PhD); art history and archaeology (MA, PhD); astronomy (PhD); biological sciences (PhD); biotechnology (MA); chemical physics (PhD); chemistry (PhD); classical studies (MA, PhD); classics (MA, PhD); climate and society (MA); conservation biology (MA); earth and environmental sciences (PhD); East Asia: regional studies (MA); East Asian languages and cultures (MA, PhD); ecology, evolution and environmental biology (MA), including conservation biology; ecology, evolution, and environmental biology (PhD), including ecology and evolutionary biology, evolutionary primatology; economics (MA, PhD); English and comparative literature (MA, PhD); French and Romance philology (MA, PhD); Germanic languages (MA, PhD); global French studies (MA); global thought (MA); Hispanic cultural studies (MA); history (PhD); history and literature (MA); human rights studies (MA); Islamic studies (MA); Italian (MA, PhD); Japanese pedagogy (MA); Jewish studies (MA); Latin America and the Caribbean: regional studies (MA); Latin American and Iberian cultures (PhD); mathematics (MA, PhD), including finance (MA); medieval and Renaissance studies (MA); Middle Eastern, South Asian, and African studies (MA, PhD); modern art: critical and curatorial studies (MA); modern European studies (MA); museum anthropology (MA); music (DMA, PhD); oral history (MA); philosophical foundations of physics (MA); philosophy (MA, PhD); physics (PhD); political science (MA, PhD); psychology (PhD); quantitative methods in the social sciences (MA); religion (MA, PhD); Russia, Eurasia and East Europe: regional studies (MA); Russian translation (MA); Slavic cultures (MA); Slavic languages (MA, PhD); sociology (MA, PhD); South Asian studies (MA); statistics (MA, PhD); theatre (PhD). Dual-degree programs require admission to both Graduate School of Arts and Sciences and another Columbia school. *Program availability:* Part-time. Terminal master's awarded for partial completion of doctoral program. *Degree requirements:* For master's, variable foreign language requirement, comprehensive exam (for some programs), thesis (for some programs); for doctorate, variable foreign language requirement, comprehensive exam (for some programs), thesis/dissertation. *Entrance requirements:* For master's and doctorate, GRE General Test, GRE Subject Test (for some programs). Additional exam requirements/recommendations for international students: Required—TOEFL, IELTS. Electronic applications accepted.

Cornell University, Graduate School, Graduate Fields of Agriculture and Life Sciences, Field of Atmospheric Science, Ithaca, NY 14853. Offers MS, PhD. *Degree requirements:* For master's, thesis; for doctorate, comprehensive exam, thesis/dissertation. *Entrance requirements:* For master's and doctorate, GRE General Test, 2 letters of recommendation. Additional exam requirements/recommendations for international students: Required—TOEFL (minimum score 550 paper-based; 77 iBT). Electronic applications accepted. *Faculty research:* Applied climatology, climate dynamics, statistical meteorology/climatology, synoptic meteorology, upper atmospheric science.

Florida State University, The Graduate School, Department of Anthropology, Department of Scientific Computing, Tallahassee, FL 32306-4120. Offers computational science (MS, PhD), including atmospheric science (PhD), biochemistry (PhD), biological science (PhD), computational science (PhD), geological science (PhD), materials science (PhD), physics (PhD). *Program availability:* Part-time. *Faculty:* 9 full-time (1 woman), 2 part-time/adjunct (1 woman). *Students:* 34 full-time (6 women); includes 17 minority (10 Asian, non-Hispanic/Latino; 3 Hispanic/Latino; 4 Two or more races, non-Hispanic/Latino), 13 international. Average age 26. 64 applicants, 23% accepted, 6 enrolled. In 2018, 10 master's, 8 doctorates awarded. Terminal master's awarded for partial completion of doctoral program. *Degree requirements:* For master's, comprehensive exam, thesis (for some programs); for doctorate, comprehensive exam, thesis/dissertation. *Entrance requirements:* For master's and doctorate, GRE General Test, knowledge of at least one object-oriented computing language, 3 letters of recommendation, resume, statement of purpose. Additional exam requirements/recommendations for international students: Required—TOEFL (minimum score 550 paper-based; 80 iBT). *Application deadline:* For fall admission, 1/15 for domestic and international students. Applications are processed on a rolling basis. Application fee: $30. Electronic applications accepted. *Expenses: Tuition, area resident:* Part-time $479.32 per credit hour. Tuition and fees vary according to campus/location and program. *Financial support:* In 2018–19, 32 students received support, including 10 research assistantships with full tuition reimbursements available (averaging $26,670 per year), 23 teaching assistantships with full tuition reimbursements available (averaging $23,000 per year); scholarships/grants, health care benefits, tuition waivers (full), and unspecified assistantships also available. Financial award application deadline: 1/15. *Faculty research:* Morphometrics, mathematical and systems biology, mining proteomic and metabolic data, computational materials research, computational fluid dynamics, astrophysics, deep learning, computational neuroscience. *Total annual research expenditures:* $500,000. *Unit head:* Dr. Gordon Erlebacher, Chair, 850-644-7024, E-mail: gerlebacher@fsu.edu. *Application contact:* Karey Fowler, Academic Program Specialist, 850-644-0143, Fax: 850-644-0098, E-mail: kgfowler@fsu.edu.
Website: http://www.sc.fsu.edu

George Mason University, College of Science, Program in Climate Dynamics, Fairfax, VA 22030. Offers PhD. *Faculty:* 20 full-time (6 women), 3 part-time/adjunct (0 women). *Students:* 19 full-time (7 women), 2 part-time (1 woman); includes 3 minority (1 Black or African American, non-Hispanic/Latino; 1 Asian, non-Hispanic/Latino; 1 Hispanic/Latino), 7 international. Average age 29. 29 applicants, 72% accepted, 7 enrolled. In 2018, 5 doctorates awarded. *Degree requirements:* For doctorate, comprehensive exam, thesis/dissertation. *Entrance requirements:* For doctorate, GRE (verbal and quantitative), undergraduate degree with minimum GPA of 3.0; 2 copies of official transcripts; current resume; expanded goals statement; 3 letters of recommendation. Additional exam requirements/recommendations for international students: Required—TOEFL (minimum score 575 paper-based; 88 iBT), IELTS (minimum score 6.5), PTE (minimum score 59). *Application deadline:* For fall admission, 12/31 priority date for domestic and international students. Application fee: $75 ($80 for international students). Electronic applications accepted. *Financial support:* In 2018–19, 16 students received support, including 15 research assistantships with tuition reimbursements available (averaging $19,867 per year), 1 teaching assistantship; career-related internships or fieldwork, Federal Work-Study, scholarships/grants, unspecified assistantships, and health care benefits (for full-time research or teaching assistantship recipients) also available. Support available to part-time students. Financial award application deadline: 3/1; financial award applicants required to submit FAFSA. *Faculty research:* Climate dynamics; climate predictability; atmospheric and ocean variability; atmospheric-land interactions; atmospheric-ocean interactions. *Unit head:* Jagadish Shukla, Director, 703-993-1983, Fax: 703-993-9300, E-mail: jshukla@gmu.edu. *Application contact:* Dr. Barry Klinger, Graduate Coordinator, 703-993-9227, Fax: 703-993-9300, E-mail: bklinger@gmu.edu.
Website: https://cos.gmu.edu/aoes/academics/climate-dynamics-graduate-program/

Georgia Institute of Technology, Graduate Studies, College of Sciences, School of Earth and Atmospheric Sciences, Atlanta, GA 30332-0340. Offers MS, PhD. *Program availability:* Part-time. Terminal master's awarded for partial completion of doctoral program. *Degree requirements:* For master's, thesis optional; for doctorate, comprehensive exam, thesis/dissertation. *Entrance requirements:* For master's and doctorate, GRE. Additional exam requirements/recommendations for international students: Required—TOEFL (minimum score 550 paper-based; 79 iBT). Electronic applications accepted. *Faculty research:* Geophysics; atmospheric chemistry, aerosols and clouds; dynamics of weather and climate; geochemistry; oceanography; paleoclimate; planetary science; remote sensing.

Hampton University, School of Science, Department of Atmospheric and Planetary Sciences, Hampton, VA 23668. Offers atmospheric science (MS, PhD); planetary science (MS, PhD). *Program availability:* Part-time. *Students:* 13 full-time (4 women), 3 part-time (0 women); includes 6 minority (3 Black or African American, non-Hispanic/Latino; 3 Asian, non-Hispanic/Latino), 1 international. Average age 30. 5 applicants, 20% accepted, 1 enrolled. In 2018, 2 doctorates awarded. Terminal master's awarded for partial completion of doctoral program. *Degree requirements:* For master's, thesis; for doctorate, comprehensive exam, thesis/dissertation. *Entrance requirements:* For master's, GRE. Additional exam requirements/recommendations for international students: Required—TOEFL (minimum score 525 paper-based) or IELTS (6.5). *Application deadline:* For fall admission, 6/1 priority date for domestic students, 4/1 priority date for international students; for spring admission, 11/1 priority date for domestic students, 9/1 priority date for international students; for summer admission, 4/1 priority date for domestic students, 2/1 priority date for international students. Applications are processed on a rolling basis. Application fee: $35. Electronic applications accepted. *Financial support:* In 2018–19, 11 research assistantships with full tuition reimbursements (averaging $21,000 per year) were awarded; career-related internships or fieldwork, scholarships/grants, health care benefits, and unspecified assistantships also available. Financial award application deadline: 6/30; financial award applicants required to submit FAFSA. *Faculty research:* Remote sensing, polar stratospheric and mesospheric clouds, lidar and related technologies, astrobiology, atmospheric dynamics, weather prediction and tracking. *Unit head:* Dr. Robert P. Loughman, Chairperson, 757-727-5108, Fax: 757-727-5090, E-mail: robert.loughman@hamptonu.edu. *Application contact:* Dr. Robert P. Loughman, Chairperson, 757-727-5108, Fax: 757-727-5090, E-mail: robert.loughman@hamptonu.edu.
Website: http://science.hamptonu.edu/aps/

Howard University, Graduate School and School of Engineering and Computer Science, Department of Atmospheric Sciences, Washington, DC 20059-0002. Offers MS, PhD. *Program availability:* Part-time. Terminal master's awarded for partial completion of doctoral program. *Degree requirements:* For master's, thesis; for doctorate, one foreign language, comprehensive exam, thesis/dissertation. *Entrance requirements:* For master's, GRE General Test, minimum GPA of 3.0; for doctorate,

GRE General Test, minimum GPA of 3.2. Additional exam requirements/recommendations for international students: Required—TOEFL (minimum score 550 paper-based). *Faculty research:* Atmospheric chemistry, climate, atmospheric radiation, gravity waves, aerosols, extraterrestrial atmospheres, turbulence.

Howard University, Graduate School, Department of Chemistry, Washington, DC 20059-0002. Offers analytical chemistry (MS, PhD); atmospheric (MS, PhD); biochemistry (MS, PhD); environmental (MS, PhD); inorganic chemistry (MS, PhD); organic chemistry (MS, PhD); physical chemistry (MS, PhD). Terminal master's awarded for partial completion of doctoral program. *Degree requirements:* For master's, comprehensive exam, thesis, teaching experience; for doctorate, comprehensive exam, thesis/dissertation, teaching experience. *Entrance requirements:* For master's, GRE General Test, minimum GPA of 2.7; for doctorate, GRE General Test, minimum GPA of 3.0. Additional exam requirements/recommendations for international students: Required—TOEFL. Electronic applications accepted. *Faculty research:* Synthetic organics, materials, natural products, mass spectrometry.

Indiana University Bloomington, University Graduate School, College of Arts and Sciences, Department of Earth and Atmospheric Sciences, Bloomington, IN 47405-7000. Offers biogeochemistry (MS, PhD); economic geology (MS, PhD); geobiology (MS, PhD); geophysics, structural geology and tectonics (MS, PhD); hydrogeology (MS, PhD); mineralogy (MS, PhD); stratigraphy and sedimentology (MS, PhD). Terminal master's awarded for partial completion of doctoral program. *Degree requirements:* For master's, thesis or alternative; for doctorate, comprehensive exam, thesis/dissertation. *Entrance requirements:* For master's and doctorate, GRE General Test. Additional exam requirements/recommendations for international students: Required—TOEFL. *Faculty research:* Geophysics, geochemistry, hydrogeology, geobiology, planetary science.

Jackson State University, Graduate School, College of Science, Engineering and Technology, Department of Physics, Atmospheric Sciences, and Geoscience, Jackson, MS 39217. Offers physical science (MS, PhD); science education (MST). *Program availability:* Part-time, evening/weekend. *Degree requirements:* For master's, comprehensive exam. *Entrance requirements:* For master's, GRE General Test. Additional exam requirements/recommendations for international students: Required—TOEFL (minimum score 520 paper-based; 67 iBT).

Massachusetts Institute of Technology, School of Science, Department of Earth, Atmospheric, and Planetary Sciences, Cambridge, MA 02139. Offers atmospheric chemistry (PhD, Sc D); atmospheric science (SM, PhD, Sc D); chemical oceanography (SM, PhD, Sc D); climate physics and chemistry (SM, PhD, Sc D); earth and planetary sciences (SM); geochemistry (PhD, Sc D); geology (PhD, Sc D); geophysics (PhD, Sc D); marine geology and geophysics (SM, PhD, Sc D); physical oceanography (SM, PhD, Sc D); planetary sciences (PhD, Sc D). Terminal master's awarded for partial completion of doctoral program. *Degree requirements:* For master's, thesis; for doctorate, comprehensive exam, thesis/dissertation. *Entrance requirements:* For master's and doctorate, GRE General Test. Additional exam requirements/recommendations for international students: Required—TOEFL, IELTS. Electronic applications accepted. *Expenses: Tuition:* Full-time $51,520; part-time $800 per credit hour. *Required fees:* $312. *Faculty research:* Earth: origin, composition, structure, and dynamics of (and interactions between) the atmosphere, oceans, surface, and interior of the earth; planets: formation, dynamics, and evolution of planetary systems and the characterization of exoplanets; climate: characterization of past, present, and potential future climates; studies of the causes and consequences of climate change; life: co-evolution of life and environmental systems.

McGill University, Faculty of Graduate and Postdoctoral Studies, Faculty of Science, Department of Atmospheric and Oceanic Sciences, Montréal, QC H3A 2T5, Canada. Offers atmospheric science (M Sc, PhD); physical oceanography (M Sc, PhD). PhD program in physical oceanography offered jointly with Université Laval.

Mississippi State University, College of Arts and Sciences, Department of Geosciences, Mississippi State, MS 39762. Offers applied meteorology (MS); broadcast meteorology (MS); earth and atmospheric science (PhD); environmental geosciences (MS); geography (MS); geology (MS); geospatial sciences (MS); professional meteorology/climatology (MS); teachers in geosciences (MS). *Program availability:* Blended/hybrid learning. *Faculty:* 20 full-time (6 women), 1 part-time/adjunct (0 women). *Students:* 62 full-time (21 women), 204 part-time (87 women); includes 44 minority (12 Black or African American, non-Hispanic/Latino; 1 American Indian or Alaska Native, non-Hispanic/Latino; 1 Asian, non-Hispanic/Latino; 25 Hispanic/Latino; 1 Native Hawaiian or other Pacific Islander, non-Hispanic/Latino; 4 Two or more races, non-Hispanic/Latino), 16 international. Average age 33. 130 applicants, 84% accepted, 89 enrolled. In 2018, 76 master's, 4 doctorates awarded. *Degree requirements:* For master's, thesis (for some programs), comprehensive oral or written exam; for doctorate, thesis/dissertation, comprehensive oral or written exam. *Entrance requirements:* For master's, GRE (for on-campus applicants), minimum undergraduate GPA of 2.75; for doctorate, thesis-based MS with background in one department emphasis area. Additional exam requirements/recommendations for international students: Required—TOEFL (minimum score 477 paper-based; 53 iBT); Recommended—IELTS (minimum score 4.5). *Application deadline:* For fall admission, 7/1 for domestic students, 5/1 for international students; for spring admission, 11/1 for domestic students, 9/1 for international students. Applications are processed on a rolling basis. Application fee: $60 ($80 for international students). Electronic applications accepted. *Expenses:* Tuition, state resident: full-time $8450; part-time $360.59 per credit hour. Tuition, nonresident: full-time $23,140; part-time $969.09 per credit hour. *Required fees:* $110. One-time fee: $55 full-time. Part-time tuition and fees vary according to course load, degree level, campus/location and reciprocity agreements. *Financial support:* In 2018–19, 7 research assistantships with full tuition reimbursements (averaging $16,483 per year), 28 teaching assistantships with full tuition reimbursements (averaging $19,000 per year) were awarded; Federal Work-Study, institutionally sponsored loans, scholarships/grants, tuition waivers (partial), and unspecified assistantships also available. Financial award application deadline: 4/1; financial award applicants required to submit FAFSA. *Faculty research:* Climatology, hydrogeology, sedimentology, meteorology. *Total annual research expenditures:* $8.9 million. *Unit head:* Dr. John C. Rodgers, III, Professor and Interim Head, 662-325-1032, Fax: 662-325-9423, E-mail: jcr100@msstate.edu. *Application contact:* Nathan Drake, Admissions and Enrollment Assistant, 662-325-3804, E-mail: ndrake@grad.msstate.edu. Website: http://www.geosciences.msstate.edu

New Mexico Institute of Mining and Technology, Center for Graduate Studies, Department of Physics, Socorro, NM 87801. Offers astrophysics (PhD); atmospheric physics (PhD); instrumentation (PhD); mathematical physics (PhD); physics (MS). *Degree requirements:* For master's, thesis optional; for doctorate, thesis/dissertation. *Entrance requirements:* For master's, GRE General Test; for doctorate, GRE General Test, GRE Subject Test. Additional exam requirements/recommendations for international students: Required—TOEFL (minimum score 540 paper-based). *Faculty research:* Cloud physics, stellar and extragalactic processes.

North Carolina State University, Graduate School, College of Sciences, Department of Marine, Earth, and Atmospheric Sciences, Raleigh, NC 27695. Offers marine, earth, and atmospheric sciences (MS, PhD); meteorology (MS, PhD); oceanography (MS, PhD). PhD offered jointly with The University of North Carolina Wilmington. Terminal master's awarded for partial completion of doctoral program. *Degree requirements:* For master's, thesis (for some programs), final oral exam; for doctorate, comprehensive exam, thesis/dissertation, final oral exam, preliminary oral and written exams. *Entrance requirements:* For master's, GRE General Test, minimum GPA of 3.0; for doctorate, GRE General Test, GRE Subject Test (for disciplines in biological oceanography and geology), minimum GPA of 3.0. Additional exam requirements/recommendations for international students: Required—TOEFL (minimum score 550 paper-based). Electronic applications accepted. *Faculty research:* Boundary layer and air quality meteorology; climate and mesoscale dynamics; biological, chemical, geological, and physical oceanography; hard rock, soft rock, environmental, and paleo-geology.

Northern Arizona University, College of Environment, Forestry, and Natural Sciences, School of Earth Sciences and Environmental Sustainability, Flagstaff, AZ 86011. Offers climate science and solutions (MS); conservation ecology (Graduate Certificate); earth sciences and environmental sustainability (PhD); environmental sciences and policy (MS); geology (MS). *Program availability:* Part-time. *Degree requirements:* For master's, variable foreign language requirement, comprehensive exam (for some programs), thesis (for some programs); for doctorate, variable foreign language requirement, comprehensive exam (for some programs), thesis/dissertation (for some programs); for Graduate Certificate, comprehensive exam (for some programs). *Entrance requirements:* For master's and doctorate, GRE General Test. Additional exam requirements/recommendations for international students: Required—TOEFL (minimum score 80 iBT), IELTS (minimum score 6.5). Electronic applications accepted.

The Ohio State University, Graduate School, College of Arts and Sciences, Division of Social and Behavioral Sciences, Department of Geography, Columbus, OH 43210. Offers atmospheric sciences (MS, PhD); geography (MA, PhD). *Faculty:* 20. *Students:* 47 full-time (24 women). Average age 27. In 2018, 5 master's, 5 doctorates awarded. *Degree requirements:* For doctorate, variable foreign language requirement, thesis/dissertation. *Entrance requirements:* For master's and doctorate, GRE. Additional exam requirements/recommendations for international students: Required—Michigan English Language Assessment Battery (minimum score 86); Recommended—TOEFL (minimum score 600 paper-based; 100 iBT), IELTS (minimum score 8). *Application deadline:* For fall admission, 12/13 priority date for domestic students, 11/30 priority date for international students. Applications are processed on a rolling basis. Application fee: $60 ($70 for international students). Electronic applications accepted. *Financial support:* Fellowships, research assistantships, teaching assistantships, Federal Work-Study, and institutionally sponsored loans available. Support available to part-time students. *Unit head:* Dr. Darla Monroe, Professor and Chair, 614-247-8382, E-mail: munroe.9@osu.edu. *Application contact:* Graduate and Professional Admissions, 614-292-9444, Fax: 614-292-3895, E-mail: gpadmissions@osu.edu. Website: http://geography.osu.edu/

Oregon State University, College of Earth, Ocean, and Atmospheric Sciences, Program in Ocean, Earth, and Atmospheric Sciences, Corvallis, OR 97331. Offers atmospheric sciences (MA, MS, PhD); oceanography (MA, MS, PhD). *Program availability:* Part-time. *Entrance requirements:* For master's, GRE. Additional exam requirements/recommendations for international students: Required—TOEFL (minimum score 80 iBT), IELTS (minimum score 6.5).

Princeton University, Graduate School, Department of Geosciences, Program in Atmospheric and Oceanic Sciences, Princeton, NJ 08544-1019. Offers PhD. *Degree requirements:* For doctorate, one foreign language, thesis/dissertation. *Entrance requirements:* For doctorate, GRE General Test, GRE Subject Test. Additional exam requirements/recommendations for international students: Required—TOEFL (minimum score 600 paper-based). Electronic applications accepted. *Faculty research:* Climate dynamics, middle atmosphere dynamics and chemistry, oceanic circulation, marine geochemistry, numerical modeling.

Purdue University, Graduate School, College of Science, Department of Earth and Atmospheric Sciences, West Lafayette, IN 47907. Offers MS, PhD. *Faculty:* 33 full-time (9 women). *Students:* 67 full-time (31 women), 2 part-time (0 women); includes 7 minority (3 American Indian or Alaska Native, non-Hispanic/Latino; 2 Asian, non-Hispanic/Latino; 1 Hispanic/Latino; 1 Two or more races, non-Hispanic/Latino), 28 international. Average age 27. 130 applicants, 25% accepted, 21 enrolled. In 2018, 14 master's, 12 doctorates awarded. *Degree requirements:* For master's, comprehensive exam, thesis; for doctorate, one foreign language, comprehensive exam, thesis/dissertation. *Entrance requirements:* For master's, GRE General Test, minimum undergraduate GPA of 3.0 or equivalent; for doctorate, GRE General Test, minimum undergraduate or master's GPA of 3.0 or equivalent. Additional exam requirements/recommendations for international students: Required—TOEFL (minimum score 550 paper-based; 77 iBT); Recommended—TWE. *Application deadline:* For fall admission, 1/2 priority date for domestic and international students; for spring admission, 9/1 for domestic and international students. Applications are processed on a rolling basis. Application fee: $60 ($75 for international students). Electronic applications accepted. *Financial support:* Fellowships with partial tuition reimbursements, research assistantships with partial tuition reimbursements, and teaching assistantships with partial tuition reimbursements available. Support available to part-time students. Financial award application deadline: 3/1; financial award applicants required to submit FAFSA. *Faculty research:* Geology, geophysics, hydrogeology, paleoclimatology, environmental science. *Unit head:* Daniel J. Cziczo, Head of the Graduate Program, 765-494-3258, E-mail: djcziczo@purdue.edu. *Application contact:* Kathy S. Kincade, Graduate Secretary, 765-494-5984, E-mail: kkincade@purdue.edu. Website: http://www.eas.purdue.edu

Rutgers University–New Brunswick, Graduate School-New Brunswick, Department of Environmental Sciences, Piscataway, NJ 08854-8097. Offers air pollution and resources (MS, PhD); aquatic biology (MS, PhD); aquatic chemistry (MS, PhD); atmospheric science (MS, PhD); chemistry and physics of aerosol and hydrosol systems (MS, PhD); environmental chemistry (MS, PhD); environmental microbiology (MS, PhD); environmental toxicology (PhD); exposure assessment (PhD); fate and effects of pollutants (MS, PhD); pollution prevention and control (MS, PhD); water and wastewater treatment (MS, PhD); water resources (MS, PhD). Terminal master's awarded for partial completion of doctoral program. *Degree requirements:* For master's, comprehensive exam, thesis or alternative, oral final exam; for doctorate, comprehensive exam, thesis/dissertation, thesis defense, qualifying exam. *Entrance requirements:* For master's and doctorate, GRE General Test. Additional exam requirements/recommendations for international students: Required—TOEFL. Electronic applications accepted. *Faculty research:* Biological waste treatment; contaminant fate and transport; air, soil and water quality.

South Dakota School of Mines and Technology, Graduate Division, MS Program in Atmospheric and Environmental Sciences, Rapid City, SD 57701-3995. Offers MS.

Peterson's Graduate Programs in the Physical Sciences, Mathematics, Agricultural Sciences, the Environment & Natural Resources 2020

www.petersons.com **131**

Program availability: Part-time. *Degree requirements:* For master's, thesis. *Entrance requirements:* For master's, GRE General Test. Additional exam requirements/ recommendations for international students: Required—TOEFL (minimum score 520 paper-based; 68 iBT), TWE. Electronic applications accepted. *Faculty research:* Hailstorm observations and numerical modeling, microbursts and lightning, radioactive transfer, remote sensing.

South Dakota School of Mines and Technology, Graduate Division, PhD Program in Atmospheric and Environmental Sciences, Rapid City, SD 57701-3995. Offers PhD. Program offered jointly with South Dakota State University. *Program availability:* Part-time. *Degree requirements:* For doctorate, comprehensive exam, thesis/dissertation. *Entrance requirements:* For doctorate, GRE General Test, GRE Subject Test. Additional exam requirements/recommendations for international students: Required—TOEFL (minimum score 520 paper-based; 68 iBT), TWE. Electronic applications accepted.

Stony Brook University, State University of New York, Graduate School, School of Marine and Atmospheric Sciences, Program in Atmospheric Sciences, Stony Brook, NY 11794. Offers MS, PhD. *Program availability:* Evening/weekend. *Degree requirements:* For doctorate, one foreign language, comprehensive exam, thesis/dissertation. *Entrance requirements:* For master's, GRE, minimum GPA of 3.0, 3 letters of recommendation; for doctorate, GRE, official transcripts, minimum GPA of 3.0, 3 letters of recommendation. Additional exam requirements/recommendations for international students: Required—TOEFL (minimum score 600 paper-based). *Application deadline:* For fall admission, 1/15 priority date for domestic students; for spring admission, 10/1 priority date for domestic students. Application fee: $100. Electronic applications accepted. *Expenses:* Contact institution. *Financial support:* Fellowships, research assistantships, teaching assistantships, and career-related internships or fieldwork available. *Unit head:* Dr. Larry Swanson, Interim Dean, 631-632-8700, E-mail: larry.swanson@stonybrook.edu. *Application contact:* Ginny Clancy, Educational Programs Coordinator, 631-632-8681, Fax: 631-632-8200, E-mail: somas@stonybrook.edu.
Website: http://you.stonybrook.edu/somas/education/graduate/atmospheric-sciences-track/

Texas Tech University, Graduate School, College of Arts and Sciences, Department of Geosciences, Lubbock, TX 79409-1053. Offers atmospheric science (MS); geography (MS); geosciences (MS, PhD). *Program availability:* Part-time. *Faculty:* 30 full-time (4 women), 4 part-time/adjunct (2 women). *Students:* 72 full-time (26 women), 10 part-time (3 women); includes 7 minority (1 Asian, non-Hispanic/Latino; 5 Hispanic/Latino; 1 Two or more races, non-Hispanic/Latino), 17 international. Average age 27. 95 applicants, 36% accepted, 27 enrolled. In 2018, 11 master's, 5 doctorates awarded. Terminal master's awarded for partial completion of doctoral program. *Degree requirements:* For master's, thesis; for doctorate, comprehensive exam, thesis/dissertation. *Entrance requirements:* For master's and doctorate, GRE General Test. Additional exam requirements/recommendations for international students: Required—TOEFL (minimum score 550 paper-based; 79 iBT). *Application deadline:* For fall admission, 6/1 priority date for domestic students, 1/15 priority date for international students; for spring admission, 9/1 priority date for domestic students, 6/15 priority date for international students. Applications are processed on a rolling basis. Application fee: $65. Electronic applications accepted. *Expenses:* Contact institution. *Financial support:* In 2018–19, 80 students received support, including 60 fellowships (averaging $3,178 per year), 35 research assistantships (averaging $18,032 per year), 43 teaching assistantships (averaging $15,850 per year); Federal Work-Study, scholarships/grants, health care benefits, tuition waivers (partial), and unspecified assistantships also available. Financial award application deadline: 2/15; financial award applicants required to submit FAFSA. *Faculty research:* Geology, geophysics, geochemistry, geospatial technology, atmospheric sciences. *Total annual research expenditures:* $2.8 million. *Unit head:* Dr. Kevin R. Mulligan, Associate Professor and Chair, 806-834-0391, E-mail: kevin.mulligan@ttu.edu. *Application contact:* Dr. Juske Horita, Professor, 806-834-7027, E-mail: juske.horita@ttu.edu.
Website: www.depts.ttu.edu/geosciences/

Université du Québec à Montréal, Graduate Programs, Program in Earth and Atmospheric Sciences, Montréal, QC H3C 3P8, Canada. Offers atmospheric sciences (M Sc); Earth and atmospheric sciences (PhD); Earth science (M Sc); meteorology (PhD, Diploma). PhD programs offered jointly with McGill University. *Program availability:* Part-time. *Degree requirements:* For master's, thesis. *Entrance requirements:* For master's and Diploma, appropriate bachelor's degree or equivalent, proficiency in French; for doctorate, appropriate master's degree or equivalent, proficiency in French.

University at Albany, State University of New York, College of Arts and Sciences, Department of Atmospheric and Environmental Sciences, Albany, NY 12222-0001. Offers atmospheric science (MS, PhD). *Faculty:* 25 full-time (5 women), 1 part-time/adjunct (0 women). *Students:* 60 full-time (21 women), 18 part-time (3 women); includes 5 minority (2 Asian, non-Hispanic/Latino; 3 Hispanic/Latino), 26 international. In 2018, 7 master's, 11 doctorates awarded. *Degree requirements:* For master's, one foreign language, comprehensive exam, thesis; for doctorate, 2 foreign languages, comprehensive exam, thesis/dissertation, oral exams. *Entrance requirements:* For master's and doctorate, GRE General Test. Additional exam requirements/ recommendations for international students: Required—TOEFL (minimum score 550 paper-based). *Application deadline:* For fall admission, 6/1 for domestic students, 5/1 for international students; for spring admission, 11/1 for domestic students, 11/11 for international students. Applications are processed on a rolling basis. Application fee: $75. Electronic applications accepted. *Financial support:* Fellowships, research assistantships, teaching assistantships, and minority assistantships available. Financial award application deadline: 3/1. *Faculty research:* Environmental geochemistry, tectonics, mesoscale meteorology, atmospheric chemistry. *Unit head:* Chrisopher Thorncroft, Chair, 518-442-4556, Fax: 518-442-5825, E-mail: cthorncroft@albany.edu. *Application contact:* Michael DeRensis, Director, Graduate Admissions, 518-442-3980, Fax: 518-442-3980, E-mail: graduate@albany.edu.
Website: http://www.atmos.albany.edu/

The University of Alabama in Huntsville, School of Graduate Studies, College of Science, Department of Atmospheric Science, Huntsville, AL 35899. Offers atmospheric science (MS, PhD); earth system science (MS). *Program availability:* Part-time. *Faculty:* 14 full-time (2 women), 2 part-time/adjunct (1 woman). *Students:* 42 full-time (21 women), 17 part-time (8 women); includes 3 minority (2 Hispanic/Latino; 1 Two or more races, non-Hispanic/Latino), 7 international. Average age 30. 43 applicants, 67% accepted, 18 enrolled. In 2018, 14 master's, 4 doctorates awarded. *Degree requirements:* For master's, comprehensive exam, thesis or alternative, oral and written exams; for doctorate, comprehensive exam, thesis/dissertation, oral and written exams. *Entrance requirements:* For master's, GRE General Test, minimum GPA of 3.0; sequence of courses in calculus (including the calculus of vector-valued functions); courses in linear algebra and ordinary differential equations; two semesters each of chemistry and calculus-based physics; proficiency in at least one high-level computer programming language; for doctorate, GRE General Test, minimum GPA of 3.0. Additional exam requirements/recommendations for international students: Required—TOEFL (minimum score 550 paper-based; 80 iBT), IELTS (minimum score 6.5). *Application deadline:* For fall admission, 7/15 priority date for domestic students, 4/1 priority date for international students; for spring admission, 11/30 priority date for domestic students, 9/1 priority date for international students. Applications are processed on a rolling basis. Application fee: $50. Electronic applications accepted. *Expenses: Tuition, area resident:* Full-time $10,632; part-time $412 per credit hour. Tuition, state resident: full-time $10,632. Tuition, nonresident: full-time $23,604; part-time $412 per credit hour. *Required fees:* $582; $582. Tuition and fees vary according to course load and program. *Financial support:* In 2018–19, 34 students received support, including 32 research assistantships with full tuition reimbursements available (averaging $9,359 per year), 2 teaching assistantships with full tuition reimbursements available (averaging $9,000 per year); career-related internships or fieldwork, Federal Work-Study, institutionally sponsored loans, scholarships/grants, health care benefits, and unspecified assistantships also available. Support available to part-time students. Financial award application deadline: 4/1; financial award applicants required to submit FAFSA. *Faculty research:* Severe weather, climate, satellite remote sensing, numerical modeling, air pollution. *Unit head:* Dr. John Mecikalski, Interim Chair, 256-961-7877, Fax: 256-922-7755, E-mail: johnm@nsstc.uah.edu. *Application contact:* Kim Gray, Graduate Studies Admissions Coordinator, 256-824-6002, Fax: 256-824-6405, E-mail: deangrad@uah.edu.
Website: http://www.uah.edu/science/departments/atmospheric-science

University of Alaska Fairbanks, College of Natural Science and Mathematics, Department of Atmospheric Sciences, Fairbanks, AK 99775-7320. Offers MS, PhD. *Program availability:* Part-time. *Faculty:* 1 full-time (0 women). *Students:* 7 full-time (4 women), 2 part-time (1 woman); includes 2 minority (1 American Indian or Alaska Native, non-Hispanic/Latino; 1 Hispanic/Latino), 6 international. Average age 33. 6 applicants. In 2018, 3 doctorates awarded. *Degree requirements:* For master's, comprehensive exam, thesis, oral defense of thesis; for doctorate, comprehensive exam, thesis/dissertation, oral defense of dissertation. *Entrance requirements:* For master's, GRE General Test, bachelor's degree in a scientific discipline with minimum cumulative undergraduate and major GPA of 3.0; one year of calculus-based physics, math through differential equations, and one semester of chemistry; for doctorate, GRE General Test, degree in a scientific discipline with minimum GPA of 3.0; one year of calculus-based physics, math through differential equations, and one semester of chemistry. Additional exam requirements/recommendations for international students: Required—TOEFL (minimum score 550 paper-based; 80 iBT), IELTS (minimum score 6.5). *Application deadline:* For fall admission, 6/1 for domestic students, 3/1 for international students; for spring admission, 10/15 for domestic students, 9/1 for international students. Applications are processed on a rolling basis. Application fee: $60. Electronic applications accepted. *Expenses: Tuition, area resident:* Full-time $8802; part-time $5868 per credit hour. Tuition, state resident: full-time $8802; part-time $5868 per credit hour. Tuition, nonresident: full-time $18,504; part-time $12,336 per credit hour. *International tuition:* $18,504 full-time. *Required fees:* $1416; $944 per credit hour. $472 per semester. Tuition and fees vary according to course load and program. *Financial support:* In 2018–19, 4 research assistantships with full tuition reimbursements (averaging $8,183 per year), 1 teaching assistantship with full tuition reimbursement (averaging $4,587 per year) were awarded; fellowships with full tuition reimbursements, Federal Work-Study, scholarships/grants, health care benefits, and unspecified assistantships also available. Support available to part-time students. Financial award application deadline: 2/15; financial award applicants required to submit FAFSA. *Faculty research:* Sea ice, climate modeling, atmospheric chemistry, global change, cloud and aerosol physics. *Total annual research expenditures:* $906,000. *Unit head:* Dr. Javier Fochesatto, Department Chair, 907-474-7290, E-mail: atmos@gi.alaska.edu. *Application contact:* Samara Taber, Director of Admissions, 907-474-7500, E-mail: uaf-admissions@alaska.edu.
Website: http://www.uaf.edu/asp

The University of Arizona, College of Science, Department of Atmospheric Sciences, Tucson, AZ 85721. Offers MS, PhD. *Degree requirements:* For master's, thesis or alternative; for doctorate, comprehensive exam, thesis/dissertation. *Entrance requirements:* For master's, GRE General Test, 3 letters of recommendation; for doctorate, GRE General Test, 3 letters of recommendation, statement of purpose. Additional exam requirements/recommendations for international students: Required—TOEFL (minimum score 550 paper-based; 79 iBT). Electronic applications accepted. *Faculty research:* Climate dynamics, radiative transfer and remote sensing, atmospheric chemistry, atmosphere dynamics, atmospheric electricity.

The University of British Columbia, Faculty of Science, Department of Earth, Ocean and Atmospheric Sciences, Vancouver, BC V6T 1Z4, Canada. Offers atmospheric science (M Sc, PhD); geological engineering (M Eng, MA Sc, PhD); geological sciences (M Sc, PhD); geophysics (M Sc, MA Sc, PhD); oceanography (M Sc, PhD). *Degree requirements:* For master's, one foreign language, thesis (for some programs); for doctorate, one foreign language, comprehensive exam, thesis/dissertation. *Entrance requirements:* Additional exam requirements/recommendations for international students: Required—TOEFL. *Expenses:* Contact institution. *Faculty research:* Oceans and atmosphere, environmental earth science, hydro geology, mineral deposits, geophysics.

University of California, Davis, Graduate Studies, Graduate Group in Atmospheric Sciences, Davis, CA 95616. Offers MS, PhD. *Degree requirements:* For master's, comprehensive exam or thesis; for doctorate, thesis/dissertation, 3 part qualifying exam. *Entrance requirements:* For master's and doctorate, GRE General Test, minimum GPA of 3.0. Additional exam requirements/recommendations for international students: Required—TOEFL (minimum score 550 paper-based). Electronic applications accepted. *Faculty research:* Air quality, biometeorology, climate dynamics, boundary layer large-scale dynamics.

University of California, Los Angeles, Graduate Division, College of Letters and Science, Department of Atmospheric and Oceanic Sciences, Los Angeles, CA 90095. Offers MS, PhD. Terminal master's awarded for partial completion of doctoral program. *Degree requirements:* For master's, comprehensive exam or thesis; for doctorate, thesis/dissertation, oral and written qualifying exams; 2 quarters of teaching experience. *Entrance requirements:* For master's and doctorate, GRE General Test, bachelor's degree; minimum undergraduate GPA of 3.0 (or its equivalent if letter grade system not used). Additional exam requirements/recommendations for international students: Required—TOEFL. Electronic applications accepted.

University of Chicago, Division of the Physical Sciences, Department of the Geophysical Sciences, Chicago, IL 60637. Offers atmospheric sciences (PhD); earth sciences (PhD); paleobiology (PhD); planetary and space sciences (PhD). Terminal master's awarded for partial completion of doctoral program. *Degree requirements:* For doctorate, comprehensive exam, thesis/dissertation. *Entrance requirements:* For doctorate, GRE General Test, research statement, 3 letters of recommendation, transcripts for all previous degrees and institutions attended. Additional exam requirements/recommendations for international students: Required—TOEFL (minimum score 600 paper-based; 95 iBT), IELTS (minimum score 7). Electronic applications accepted. *Faculty research:* Climatology, evolutionary paleontology, cosmochemistry, geochemistry, oceanic sciences.

University of Colorado Boulder, Graduate School, College of Arts and Sciences, Department of Atmospheric and Oceanic Sciences, Boulder, CO 80309. Offers MS, PhD. *Entrance requirements:* For master's, minimum undergraduate GPA of 3.0. Electronic applications accepted. Application fee is waived when completed online. *Faculty research:* Atmospheric sciences; atmospheric physics; atmospheric structure and dynamics; climate change; climatology.

University of Guelph, Office of Graduate and Postdoctoral Studies, Ontario Agricultural College, Department of Land Resource Science, Guelph, ON N1G 2W1, Canada. Offers atmospheric science (M Sc, PhD); environmental and agricultural earth sciences (M Sc, PhD); land resources management (M Sc, PhD); soil science (M Sc, PhD). *Program availability:* Part-time. *Degree requirements:* For master's, thesis (for some programs), research project (non-thesis track); for doctorate, comprehensive exam, thesis/dissertation. *Entrance requirements:* For master's, minimum B- average during previous 2 years of course work; for doctorate, minimum B average during previous 2 years of course work. Additional exam requirements/recommendations for international students: Required—TOEFL (minimum score 550 paper-based). Electronic applications accepted. *Faculty research:* Soil science, environmental earth science, land resource management.

University of Houston, College of Natural Sciences and Mathematics, Department of Earth and Atmospheric Sciences, Houston, TX 77204. Offers atmospheric science (PhD); geology (MA, PhD); geophysics (PhD). *Program availability:* Part-time. *Degree requirements:* For master's, thesis; for doctorate, comprehensive exam, thesis/dissertation. *Entrance requirements:* For master's and doctorate, GRE General Test. Additional exam requirements/recommendations for international students: Required—TOEFL (minimum score 550 paper-based; 79 iBT), IELTS (minimum score 6.5). Electronic applications accepted. *Faculty research:* Atmospherics sciences, seismic and solid earth geophysics, tectonics, environmental hydrochemistry, carbonates, micropaleontology, structure and tectonics, petroleum geology.

University of Illinois at Urbana–Champaign, Graduate College, College of Liberal Arts and Sciences, School of Earth, Society and Environment, Department of Atmospheric Sciences, Champaign, IL 61820. Offers MS, PhD.

The University of Kansas, Graduate Studies, College of Liberal Arts and Sciences, Department of Geography and Atmospheric Science, Lawrence, KS 66045-7613. Offers atmospheric science (MS); geographic information science (Graduate Certificate); geography (MA, PhD); MUP/MA. *Program availability:* Part-time. *Students:* 54 full-time (28 women), 3 part-time (1 woman); includes 9 minority (8 American Indian or Alaska Native, non-Hispanic/Latino; 1 Hispanic/Latino), 6 international. Average age 32. 26 applicants, 50% accepted, 9 enrolled. In 2018, 12 master's, 5 doctorates, 2 other advanced degrees awarded. *Entrance requirements:* For master's and doctorate, GRE General Test, 3 letters of reference, transcripts, statement of interests, resume. Additional exam requirements/recommendations for international students: Required—TOEFL, IELTS. *Application deadline:* For fall admission, 1/15 priority date for domestic and international students; for spring admission, 11/1 for domestic and international students; for summer admission, 4/1 for domestic and international students. Application fee: $65 ($85 for international students). Electronic applications accepted. *Financial support:* Fellowships, research assistantships, teaching assistantships, and unspecified assistantships available. Financial award application deadline: 1/15. *Faculty research:* Physical geography, human/cultural/regional geography, geographic information science, atmospheric science. *Unit head:* Nathaniel Brunsell, Chair, 785-864-2021, E-mail: brunsell@ku.edu. *Application contact:* Cicily Riggs, Graduate Admission Contact, 785-864-0937, E-mail: csriggs@ku.edu.
Website: http://www.geog.ku.edu/

The University of Manchester, School of Earth and Environmental Sciences, Manchester, United Kingdom. Offers atmospheric sciences (M Phil, M Sc, PhD); basin studies and petroleum geosciences (M Phil, M Sc, PhD); earth, atmospheric and environmental sciences (M Phil, M Sc, PhD); environmental geochemistry and cosmochemistry (M Phil, M Sc, PhD); isotope geochemistry and cosmochemistry (M Phil, M Sc, PhD); paleontology (M Phil, M Sc, PhD); physics and chemistry of minerals and fluids (M Phil, M Sc, PhD); structural and petrological geosciences (M Phil, M Sc, PhD).

University of Maryland, Baltimore County, The Graduate School, College of Natural and Mathematical Sciences, Department of Physics, Program in Atmospheric Physics, Baltimore, MD 21250. Offers MS, PhD. *Program availability:* Part-time. Terminal master's awarded for partial completion of doctoral program. *Degree requirements:* For master's, comprehensive exam (for some programs), thesis optional; for doctorate, comprehensive exam, thesis/dissertation. *Entrance requirements:* For master's and doctorate, GRE General Test, minimum GPA of 3.0. Additional exam requirements/recommendations for international students: Required—TOEFL (minimum score 587 paper-based; 95 iBT). Electronic applications accepted. *Faculty research:* Atmospheric dynamics, aerosols and clouds, satellite and aircraft remote sensing, optics and instrumentation development, LIDAR and in situ aerosol measurements.

University of Michigan, College of Engineering, Department of Climate and Space Sciences and Engineering, Ann Arbor, MI 48109. Offers applied climate (M Eng); atmospheric, oceanic and space sciences (MS, PhD); geoscience and remote sensing (PhD); space and planetary sciences (PhD); space engineering (M Eng). *Program availability:* Part-time. *Students:* 83 full-time (29 women). 103 applicants, 19% accepted, 9 enrolled. In 2018, 42 master's, 10 doctorates awarded. Terminal master's awarded for partial completion of doctoral program. *Degree requirements:* For master's, thesis (for some programs); for doctorate, thesis/dissertation, oral defense of dissertation, preliminary exams. *Entrance requirements:* For master's and doctorate, GRE General Test. Additional exam requirements/recommendations for international students: Required—TOEFL. *Application deadline:* Applications are processed on a rolling basis. Electronic applications accepted. *Financial support:* Fellowships, research assistantships, teaching assistantships, career-related internships or fieldwork, Federal Work-Study, institutionally sponsored loans, and health care benefits available. Support available to part-time students. Financial award applicants required to submit FAFSA. *Faculty research:* Planetary environments, space instrumentation, air pollution meteorology, global climate change, sun-earth connection, space weather. *Total annual research expenditures:* $29.9 million. *Unit head:* Tuija Pulkkinen, Department Chair, 734-780-4079, Fax: 734-763-0437, E-mail: tuija@umich.edu. *Application contact:* Sandra Pytlinski, Graduate Student Services Coordinator, 734-936-0482, Fax: 734-763-0437, E-mail: sanpyt@umich.edu.
Website: https://clasp.engin.umich.edu/

University of Nevada, Reno, Graduate School, Interdisciplinary Program in Atmospheric Sciences, Reno, NV 89557. Offers MS, PhD. Terminal master's awarded for partial completion of doctoral program. *Degree requirements:* For master's, thesis optional; for doctorate, thesis/dissertation. *Entrance requirements:* For master's, GRE (recommended), minimum GPA of 2.75; for doctorate, GRE (recommended), minimum GPA of 3.0. Additional exam requirements/recommendations for international students: Required—TOEFL (minimum score 500 paper-based; 61 iBT), IELTS (minimum score 6). Electronic applications accepted. *Faculty research:* Atmospheric chemistry, cloud and aerosol physics, atmospheric optics, mesoscale meterology.

University of North Dakota, Graduate School, John D. Odegard School of Aerospace Sciences, Department of Atmospheric Sciences, Grand Forks, ND 58202. Offers MS, PhD. *Program availability:* Part-time. *Degree requirements:* For master's, comprehensive exam, thesis or alternative. *Entrance requirements:* For master's and doctorate, GRE General Test, minimum GPA of 3.0. Additional exam requirements/recommendations for international students: Required—TOEFL (minimum score 550 paper-based; 79 iBT), IELTS (minimum score 6.5). Electronic applications accepted.

University of Utah, Graduate School, College of Mines and Earth Sciences, Department of Atmospheric Sciences, Salt Lake City, UT 84112. Offers MS, PhD. *Program availability:* Part-time. *Faculty:* 11 full-time (2 women), 11 part-time/adjunct (1 woman). *Students:* 25 full-time (7 women), 9 part-time (3 women); includes 2 minority (both Black or African American, non-Hispanic/Latino), 11 international. Average age 28. 34 applicants, 32% accepted, 9 enrolled. In 2018, 10 master's, 5 doctorates awarded. Terminal master's awarded for partial completion of doctoral program. *Degree requirements:* For master's, comprehensive exam, thesis; for doctorate, comprehensive exam, thesis/dissertation. *Entrance requirements:* For master's and doctorate, GRE General Test, minimum GPA of 3.0, 3 letters of reference, personal statement, resume/curriculum vitae, official transcript. Additional exam requirements/recommendations for international students: Required—TOEFL (minimum score 550 paper-based; 80 iBT); Recommended—IELTS (minimum score 6.5). *Application deadline:* For fall admission, 1/7 priority date for domestic and international students. Applications are processed on a rolling basis. Application fee: $55 ($65 for international students). Electronic applications accepted. *Expenses:* Contact institution. *Financial support:* In 2018–19, 31 students received support, including 2 fellowships (averaging $25,000 per year), 31 research assistantships (averaging $25,500 per year), 3 teaching assistantships (averaging $5,000 per year); traineeships also available. Financial award application deadline: 1/7. *Faculty research:* Air quality and land-atmosphere interactions; cloud-aerosol-climate interactions; mountain weather and wildfires; climate modeling, physics, and dynamics; tropical meteorology. *Total annual research expenditures:* $5.4 million. *Unit head:* Dr. John D. Horel, Chair, Fax: 801-581-7091, E-mail: john.horel@utah.edu. *Application contact:* Holly Moreno, Administrative Program Coordinator, 801-581-6136, Fax: 801-585-3681, E-mail: atmos-advising@lists.utah.edu.
Website: http://www.atmos.utah.edu/

University of Washington, Graduate School, College of the Environment, Department of Atmospheric Sciences, Seattle, WA 98195. Offers MS, PhD. *Degree requirements:* For master's, thesis; for doctorate, thesis/dissertation, qualifying exam. *Entrance requirements:* For master's and doctorate, GRE General Test, minimum GPA of 3.0. Additional exam requirements/recommendations for international students: Required—TOEFL. *Faculty research:* Climate change, synoptic and mesoscale meteorology, atmospheric chemistry, cloud physics, dynamics of the atmosphere.

University of Wisconsin–Madison, Graduate School, College of Letters and Science, Department of Atmospheric and Oceanic Sciences, Madison, WI 53706-1380. Offers MS, PhD. *Program availability:* Part-time. *Degree requirements:* For master's, thesis (for some programs); for doctorate, thesis/dissertation. *Entrance requirements:* For master's and doctorate, GRE General Test, minimum GPA of 3.0; previous course work in chemistry, mathematics, and physics. Electronic applications accepted. *Faculty research:* Satellite meteorology, weather systems, global climate change, numerical modeling, atmosphere-ocean interaction.

University of Wisconsin–Milwaukee, Graduate School, College of Letters and Science, Department of Mathematical Sciences, Milwaukee, WI 53201-0413. Offers mathematics (MS, PhD), including actuarial science, algebra (PhD), applied and computational mathematics (PhD), atmospheric science, foundations of advanced studies (MS), industrial mathematics, probability and statistics (PhD), standard mathematics (MS), statistics (MS), topology (PhD). *Students:* 56 full-time (11 women), 10 part-time (2 women); includes 4 minority (2 Black or African American, non-Hispanic/Latino; 1 Asian, non-Hispanic/Latino; 1 Two or more races, non-Hispanic/Latino), 28 international. Average age 30. 136 applicants, 22% accepted, 20 enrolled. In 2018, 16 master's, 8 doctorates awarded. *Degree requirements:* For master's, comprehensive exam, thesis optional; for doctorate, 2 foreign languages, thesis/dissertation. *Entrance requirements:* Additional exam requirements/recommendations for international students: Required—TOEFL (minimum score 550 paper-based; 79 iBT), IELTS (minimum score 6.5). *Application deadline:* For fall admission, 1/1 priority date for domestic students; for spring admission, 9/1 for domestic students. Application fee: $56 ($96 for international students). Electronic applications accepted. *Financial support:* Fellowships, research assistantships, teaching assistantships, career-related internships or fieldwork, health care benefits, and unspecified assistantships available. Support available to part-time students. Financial award application deadline: 4/15; financial award applicants required to submit FAFSA. *Faculty research:* Algebra, applied mathematics, atmospheric science, probability and statistics, topology. *Unit head:* Richard Stockbridge, Department Chair, 414-229-4568, E-mail: stockbri@uwm.edu. *Application contact:* General Information Contact, 414-229-4982, Fax: 414-229-6967, E-mail: gradschool@uwm.edu.
Website: http://www.uwm.edu/dept/math/

University of Wyoming, College of Engineering and Applied Science, Department of Atmospheric Science, Laramie, WY 82071. Offers MS, PhD. *Program availability:* Online learning. Terminal master's awarded for partial completion of doctoral program. *Degree requirements:* For master's, thesis; for doctorate, comprehensive exam, thesis/dissertation. *Entrance requirements:* For master's and doctorate, GRE General Test, minimum GPA of 3.0. Additional exam requirements/recommendations for international students: Required—TOEFL (minimum score 525 paper-based). Electronic applications accepted. *Expenses:* Contact institution. *Faculty research:* Cloud physics; aerosols, boundary layer processes; airborne observations; stratospheric aerosols and gases.

Yale University, Graduate School of Arts and Sciences, Department of Geology and Geophysics, New Haven, CT 06520. Offers biogeochemistry (PhD); climate dynamics (PhD); geochemistry (PhD); geophysics (PhD); meteorology (PhD); oceanography (PhD); paleontology (PhD); paleooceanography (PhD); petrology (PhD); tectonics (PhD). *Degree requirements:* For doctorate, thesis/dissertation. *Entrance requirements:* For doctorate, GRE General Test. Additional exam requirements/recommendations for international students: Required—TOEFL.

Meteorology

Ball State University, Graduate School, College of Sciences and Humanities, Department of Geography, Muncie, IN 47306. Offers geographic information systems (Certificate); geography (MS); professional meteorology and climatology (Certificate). *Program availability:* Part-time. *Entrance requirements:* For master's, minimum baccalaureate GPA of 2.75 or 3.0 in latter half of baccalaureate, letter of interest, three letters of recommendation, resume or curriculum vitae, official transcripts. Additional exam requirements/recommendations for international students: Required—TOEFL (minimum score 550 paper-based; 79 iBT), IELTS (minimum score 6.5). Electronic applications accepted. *Faculty research:* Remote sensing, tourism and recreation, Latin American urbanization.

Florida Institute of Technology, College of Engineering and Science, Program in Meteorology, Melbourne, FL 32901-6975. Offers MS. *Program availability:* Part-time. *Students:* 4 full-time (3 women), 1 (woman) part-time; includes 1 minority (Two or more races, non-Hispanic/Latino), 1 international. Average age 26. 4 applicants, 50% accepted, 2 enrolled. In 2018, 1 master's awarded. *Degree requirements:* For master's, comprehensive exam (for some programs), thesis optional, 30 credit hours, seminar, oral presentation. *Entrance requirements:* For master's, GRE General Test, 3 letters of recommendation, resume, statement of objectives, undergraduate degree in physical sciences or engineering. Additional exam requirements/recommendations for international students: Required—TOEFL (minimum score 550 paper-based; 79 iBT). *Application deadline:* Applications are processed on a rolling basis. Application fee: $50. Electronic applications accepted. *Expenses: Tuition:* Full-time $22,338; part-time $1241 per credit hour. Tuition and fees vary according to degree level, campus/location and program. *Financial support:* Research assistantships and teaching assistantships available. Financial award applicants required to submit FAFSA. *Faculty research:* wind and wave nowcasting, gamma rays, and hurricane and lightning research (involving access to largest X-ray array in the world for measuring lightning). *Unit head:* Dr. Richard Aronson, Department Head, 321-674-8034, E-mail: oems@fit.edu. *Application contact:* Mike Perry, Executive Director of Admissions, 321-674-7127, E-mail: perrymj@fit.edu.
Website: https://www.fit.edu/programs/meteorology-ms/

Florida State University, The Graduate School, Department of Anthropology, Department of Earth, Ocean and Atmospheric Science, Program in Meteorology, Tallahassee, FL 32306-4520. Offers MS, PhD. *Faculty:* 16 full-time (2 women). *Students:* 46 full-time (17 women); includes 7 minority (1 Black or African American, non-Hispanic/Latino; 4 Asian, non-Hispanic/Latino; 1 Hispanic/Latino; 1 Two or more races, non-Hispanic/Latino), 5 international. Average age 28. 54 applicants, 46% accepted, 9 enrolled. In 2018, 12 master's, 2 doctorates awarded. Terminal master's awarded for partial completion of doctoral program. *Degree requirements:* For master's, thesis optional; for doctorate, comprehensive exam, thesis/dissertation. *Entrance requirements:* For master's, GRE General Test (minimum score 300 combined verbal and quantitative), minimum GPA of 3.0 in upper-division work; for doctorate, GRE General Test (minimum combined Verbal and Quantitative score: 300), minimum GPA of 3.0, faculty sponsor. Additional exam requirements/recommendations for international students: Required—TOEFL (minimum score 550 paper-based; 80 iBT). *Application deadline:* For fall admission, 1/15 for domestic students, 1/1 for international students; for spring admission, 11/1 for domestic and international students. Applications are processed on a rolling basis. Application fee: $30. Electronic applications accepted. *Expenses: Tuition, area resident:* Part-time $479.32 per credit hour. Tuition and fees vary according to campus/location and program. *Financial support:* In 2018–19, 42 students received support, including 2 fellowships with full tuition reimbursements available (averaging $25,000 per year), 15 research assistantships with full tuition reimbursements available (averaging $25,000 per year), 24 teaching assistantships with full tuition reimbursements available (averaging $25,000 per year); career-related internships or fieldwork, scholarships/grants, and unspecified assistantships also available. Financial award application deadline: 1/15; financial award applicants required to submit FAFSA. *Faculty research:* Physical, dynamic, and synoptic meteorology; climate. *Total annual research expenditures:* $600,000. *Unit head:* Dr. Vincent Salters, Chairman, 850-644-1934, Fax: 850-644-9642, E-mail: salters@magnet.fsu.edu. *Application contact:* Shel McGuire, Academic Program Specialist, 850-644-8582, Fax: 850-644-9642, E-mail: smcguire@fsu.edu.
Website: http://www.eoas.fsu.edu

Iowa State University of Science and Technology, Department of Geological and Atmospheric Sciences, Ames, IA 50011. Offers earth science (MS, PhD); environmental science (MS, PhD); geology (MS, PhD); meteorology (MS, PhD). *Degree requirements:* For master's, thesis (for some programs); for doctorate, thesis/dissertation. *Entrance requirements:* For master's and doctorate, GRE General Test. Additional exam requirements/recommendations for international students: Required—TOEFL (minimum score 550 paper-based; 79 iBT), IELTS (minimum score 6.5). Electronic applications accepted.

Iowa State University of Science and Technology, Program in Agricultural Meteorology, Ames, IA 50011. Offers MS, PhD. *Entrance requirements:* Additional exam requirements/recommendations for international students: Required—TOEFL (minimum score 550 paper-based; 79 iBT), IELTS (minimum score 6.5). Electronic applications accepted.

Iowa State University of Science and Technology, Program in Meteorology, Ames, IA 50011. Offers MS, PhD. *Entrance requirements:* For master's and doctorate, GRE. Additional exam requirements/recommendations for international students: Required—TOEFL (minimum score 550 paper-based; 79 iBT), IELTS (minimum score 6.5). Electronic applications accepted.

McGill University, Faculty of Graduate and Postdoctoral Studies, Faculty of Agricultural and Environmental Sciences, Department of Natural Resource Sciences, Montréal, QC H3A 2T5, Canada. Offers entomology (M Sc, PhD); environmental assessment (M Sc); forest science (M Sc, PhD); microbiology (M Sc, PhD); micrometeorology (M Sc, PhD); neotropical environment (M Sc, PhD); soil science (M Sc, PhD); wildlife biology (M Sc, PhD).

Millersville University of Pennsylvania, College of Graduate Studies and Adult Learning, College of Science and Technology, Department of Earth Sciences, Millersville, PA 17551-0302. Offers integrated scientific applications (MS). *Program availability:* Part-time. *Faculty:* 3 full-time (0 women), 5 part-time/adjunct (1 woman). *Students:* 7 full-time (3 women), 7 part-time (3 women); includes 3 minority (1 Black or African American, non-Hispanic/Latino; 1 Asian, non-Hispanic/Latino; 1 Hispanic/Latino). Average age 26. 10 applicants, 100% accepted, 8 enrolled. In 2018, 3 master's awarded. *Degree requirements:* For master's, thesis optional, capstone experience such as internship or applied research. *Entrance requirements:* For master's, GRE or MAT or GMAT, required only if cumulative GPA is lower than 3.0, Resume. Additional exam requirements/recommendations for international students: Required—TOEFL, IELTS (minimum score 6), PTE (minimum score 60). *Application deadline:* Applications are processed on a rolling basis. Application fee: $40. Electronic applications accepted. *Expenses: Tuition, area resident:* Full-time $9288; part-time $516 per credit. Tuition, state resident: full-time $9288; part-time $516 per credit. Tuition, nonresident: full-time $13,932; part-time $774 per credit. *International tuition:* $13,932 full-time. *Required fees:* $2623.50; $145.75 per credit. Tuition and fees vary according to course load, degree level and program. *Financial support:* In 2018–19, 4 students received support. Unspecified assistantships available. Financial award application deadline: 3/15; financial award applicants required to submit FAFSA. *Faculty research:* Meteorology, ocean sciences and coastal studies, physical oceanography, geology, earth sciences, environmental geology, earth sciences education, heliophysics and space weather. *Total annual research expenditures:* $50,000. *Unit head:* Dr. Richard D. Clark, Chairperson and Graduate Program Coordinator, 717-871-7434, Fax: 717-871-7918, E-mail: richard.clark@millersville.edu. *Application contact:* Dr. James A. Delle, Acting Dean of College of Graduate Studies and Adult Learning/Associate Provost, Academic Administration, 717-871-7462, E-mail: James.Delle@millersville.edu.
Website: https://www.millersville.edu/esci/index.php

Mississippi State University, College of Arts and Sciences, Department of Geosciences, Mississippi State, MS 39762. Offers applied meteorology (MS); broadcast meteorology (MS); earth and atmospheric science (PhD); environmental geosciences (MS); geography (MS); geology (MS); geospatial sciences (MS); professional meteorology/climatology (MS); teachers in geosciences (MS). *Program availability:* Blended/hybrid learning. *Faculty:* 20 full-time (6 women), 1 part-time/adjunct (0 women). *Students:* 62 full-time (21 women), 204 part-time (87 women); includes 44 minority (12 Black or African American, non-Hispanic/Latino; 1 American Indian or Alaska Native, non-Hispanic/Latino; 1 Asian, non-Hispanic/Latino; 25 Hispanic/Latino; 1 Native Hawaiian or other Pacific Islander, non-Hispanic/Latino; 4 Two or more races, non-Hispanic/Latino), 16 international. Average age 33. 130 applicants, 84% accepted, 89 enrolled. In 2018, 76 master's, 4 doctorates awarded. *Degree requirements:* For master's, thesis (for some programs), comprehensive oral or written exam; for doctorate, thesis/dissertation, comprehensive oral or written exam. *Entrance requirements:* For master's, GRE (for on-campus applicants), minimum undergraduate GPA of 2.75; for doctorate, thesis-based MS with background in one department emphasis area. Additional exam requirements/recommendations for international students: Required—TOEFL (minimum score 477 paper-based; 53 iBT); Recommended—IELTS (minimum score 4.5). *Application deadline:* For fall admission, 7/1 for domestic students, 5/1 for international students; for spring admission, 11/1 for domestic students, 9/1 for international students. Applications are processed on a rolling basis. Application fee: $60 ($80 for international students). Electronic applications accepted. *Expenses:* Tuition, state resident: full-time $8450; part-time $360.59 per credit hour. Tuition, nonresident: full-time $23,140; part-time $969.09 per credit hour. *Required fees:* $110. One-time fee: $55 full-time. Part-time tuition and fees vary according to course load, degree level, campus/location and reciprocity agreements. *Financial support:* In 2018–19, 7 research assistantships with full tuition reimbursements (averaging $16,483 per year), 28 teaching assistantships with full tuition reimbursements (averaging $19,000 per year) were awarded; Federal Work-Study, institutionally sponsored loans, scholarships/grants, tuition waivers (partial), and unspecified assistantships also available. Financial award application deadline: 4/1; financial award applicants required to submit FAFSA. *Faculty research:* Climatology, hydrogeology, sedimentology, meteorology. *Total annual research expenditures:* $8.9 million. *Unit head:* Dr. John C. Rodgers, III, Professor and Interim Head, 662-325-1032, Fax: 662-325-9423, E-mail: jcr100@msstate.edu. *Application contact:* Nathan Drake, Admissions and Enrollment Assistant, 662-325-3804, E-mail: ndrake@grad.msstate.edu.
Website: http://www.geosciences.msstate.edu

Naval Postgraduate School, Departments and Academic Groups, Department of Meteorology, Monterey, CA 93943. Offers meteorology (MS, PhD); meteorology and physical oceanography (MS). Program only open to commissioned officers of the United States and friendly nations and selected United States federal civilian employees. *Program availability:* Part-time. *Degree requirements:* For master's, thesis; for doctorate, one foreign language, thesis/dissertation. *Faculty research:* Air-sea interactions, boundary layer meteorology, climate dynamics, numerical weather prediction, tropical cyclones.

Naval Postgraduate School, Departments and Academic Groups, Undersea Warfare Academic Group, Monterey, CA 93943. Offers applied mathematics (MS); applied physics (MS); applied science (MS), including acoustics, operations research, physical oceanography, signal processing; electrical engineering (MS); engineering acoustics (MS, PhD); engineering science (MS), including electrical engineering, mechanical engineering; mechanical engineer (ME); mechanical engineering (MS, MSME); meteorology (MS); operations research (MS); physical oceanography (MS). Program only open to commissioned officers of the United States and friendly nations and selected United States federal civilian employees. *Program availability:* Part-time. *Degree requirements:* For master's, thesis. *Faculty research:* Unmanned/autonomous vehicles, sea mines and countermeasures, submarine warfare in the twentieth and twenty-first centuries.

North Carolina State University, Graduate School, College of Sciences, Department of Marine, Earth, and Atmospheric Sciences, Raleigh, NC 27695. Offers marine, earth, and atmospheric sciences (MS, PhD); meteorology (MS, PhD); oceanography (MS, PhD). PhD offered jointly with The University of North Carolina Wilmington. Terminal master's awarded for partial completion of doctoral program. *Degree requirements:* For master's, thesis (for some programs), final oral exam; for doctorate, comprehensive exam, thesis/dissertation, final oral exam, preliminary oral and written exams. *Entrance requirements:* For master's, GRE General Test, minimum GPA of 3.0; for doctorate, GRE General Test, GRE Subject Test (for disciplines in biological oceanography and geology), minimum GPA of 3.0. Additional exam requirements/recommendations for international students: Required—TOEFL (minimum score 550 paper-based). Electronic applications accepted. *Faculty research:* Boundary layer and air quality meteorology; climate and mesoscale dynamics; biological, chemical, geological, and physical oceanography; hard rock, soft rock, environmental, and paleo-geology.

Northern Arizona University, College of Environment, Forestry, and Natural Sciences, School of Earth Sciences and Environmental Sustainability, Flagstaff, AZ 86011. Offers climate science and solutions (MS); conservation ecology (Graduate Certificate); earth sciences and environmental sustainability (PhD); environmental sciences and policy

(MS); geology (MS). *Program availability:* Part-time. *Degree requirements:* For master's, variable foreign language requirement, comprehensive exam (for some programs), thesis (for some programs); for doctorate, variable foreign language requirement, comprehensive exam (for some programs), thesis/dissertation (for some programs); for Graduate Certificate, comprehensive exam (for some programs). *Entrance requirements:* For master's and doctorate, GRE General Test. Additional exam requirements/recommendations for international students: Required—TOEFL (minimum score 80 iBT), IELTS (minimum score 6.5). Electronic applications accepted.

Penn State University Park, Graduate School, College of Earth and Mineral Sciences, Department of Meteorology, University Park, PA 16802. Offers MS, PhD.

Saint Louis University, Graduate Programs, College of Arts and Sciences, Department of Earth and Atmospheric Sciences, St. Louis, MO 63103. Offers geophysics (PhD); geoscience (MS); meteorology (M Pr Met, MS-R, PhD). *Program availability:* Part-time. *Degree requirements:* For master's, thesis (for some programs), comprehensive oral exam; for doctorate, thesis/dissertation, preliminary exams. *Entrance requirements:* For master's, GRE General Test, letters of recommendation, resume; for doctorate, GRE General Test, letters of recommendation, resumé, goal statement, transcripts. Additional exam requirements/recommendations for international students: Required—TOEFL (minimum score 525 paper-based). Electronic applications accepted. *Faculty research:* Structural geology, mesoscale meteorology and severe storms, weather and climate change prediction.

San Jose State University, Program in Meteorology and Climate Science, San Jose, CA 95192-0001. Offers meteorology (MS). *Degree requirements:* For master's, thesis or alternative. *Entrance requirements:* For master's, GRE. Electronic applications accepted.

SIT Graduate Institute, Graduate Programs, Master's Program in Climate Change and Global Sustainability, Brattleboro, VT 05302-0676. Offers MA.

Texas A&M University, College of Geosciences, Department of Atmospheric Sciences, College Station, TX 77843. Offers atmospheric science (MS). *Faculty:* 16. *Students:* 39 full-time (13 women), 3 part-time (1 woman); includes 4 minority (1 Black or African American, non-Hispanic/Latino; 1 Asian, non-Hispanic/Latino; 2 Hispanic/Latino), 21 international. Average age 28. 79 applicants, 28% accepted, 10 enrolled. In 2018, 9 master's, 8 doctorates awarded. *Degree requirements:* For master's, thesis; for doctorate, thesis/dissertation. *Entrance requirements:* For master's and doctorate, GRE General Test. Additional exam requirements/recommendations for international students: Required—TOEFL (minimum score 550 paper-based; 80 iBT), IELTS (minimum score 6), PTE (minimum score 53). *Application deadline:* For fall admission, 1/15 for domestic students; for spring admission, 10/1 for domestic students. Applications are processed on a rolling basis. Application fee: $50 ($90 for international students). Electronic applications accepted. *Expenses:* Contact institution. *Financial support:* In 2018–19, 40 students received support, including 1 fellowship with tuition reimbursement available (averaging $150 per year), 38 research assistantships with tuition reimbursements available (averaging $16,920 per year), 8 teaching assistantships with tuition reimbursements available (averaging $13,121 per year); career-related internships or fieldwork, institutionally sponsored loans, scholarships/grants, traineeships, health care benefits, tuition waivers (full and partial), and unspecified assistantships also available. Support available to part-time students. Financial award application deadline: 3/15; financial award applicants required to submit FAFSA *Faculty research:* Radar and satellite rainfall relationships, mesoscale dynamics and numerical modeling, climatology. *Unit head:* Dr. Ping Yang, Department Head, 979-845-7679, E-mail: pyang@tamu.edu. *Application contact:* Roxanne R. Russell, Senior Academic Advisor II, 979-862-3240, Fax: 979-862-4466, E-mail: rrussell@tamu.edu. Website: http://atmo.tamu.edu/

Université du Québec à Montréal, Graduate Programs, Program in Earth and Atmospheric Sciences, Montréal, QC H3C 3P8, Canada. Offers atmospheric sciences (M Sc); Earth and atmospheric sciences (PhD); Earth science (M Sc); meteorology (PhD, Diploma). PhD programs offered jointly with McGill University. *Program availability:* Part-time. *Degree requirements:* For master's, thesis. *Entrance requirements:* For master's and Diploma, appropriate bachelor's degree or equivalent, proficiency in French; for doctorate, appropriate master's degree or equivalent, proficiency in French.

University of California, San Diego, Graduate Division, Scripps Institution of Oceanography, Program in Climate Science and Policy, La Jolla, CA 92093. Offers MAS. *Program availability:* Part-time. *Students:* 9 full-time (5 women), 2 part-time (1 woman). 23 applicants, 87% accepted, 9 enrolled. In 2018, 7 master's awarded. *Degree requirements:* For master's, capstone project. *Entrance requirements:* For master's, minimum GPA of 3.0, resume or curriculum vitae, 3 letters of recommendation. Additional exam requirements/recommendations for international students: Required—TOEFL (minimum score 550 paper-based; 80 iBT), IELTS (minimum score 7). *Application deadline:* For summer admission, 4/16 for domestic students. Application fee: $105 ($125 for international students). Electronic applications accepted. *Expenses:* Contact institution. *Financial support:* Scholarships/grants available. Financial award applicants required to submit FAFSA. *Faculty research:* Climate, atmospheric science, policy analysis. *Unit head:* Corey J. Gabriel, Chair, 858-534-0748, E-mail: mas-csp@sio.ucsd.edu. *Application contact:* Risa Farrell, Program Coordinator, 858-822-2886, E-mail: mas-csp@sio.ucsd.edu. Website: https://scripps.ucsd.edu/masters/mas/climate-science-and-policy

University of Hawaii at Manoa, Office of Graduate Education, School of Ocean and Earth Science and Technology, Department of Meteorology, Honolulu, HI 96822. Offers MS, PhD. *Program availability:* Part-time. *Degree requirements:* For master's, comprehensive exam, thesis; for doctorate, comprehensive exam, thesis/dissertation. *Entrance requirements:* For master's and doctorate, GRE General Test. Additional exam requirements/recommendations for international students: Required—TOEFL (minimum score 560 paper-based; 83 iBT), IELTS (minimum score 5). *Faculty research:* Tropical cyclones, air-sea interactions, mesoscale meteorology, intraseasonal oscillations, tropical climate.

University of Maryland, College Park, Academic Affairs, College of Computer, Mathematical and Natural Sciences, Department of Atmospheric and Oceanic Science, College Park, MD 20742. Offers MS, PMS, PhD. *Program availability:* Part-time, evening/weekend, online learning. Terminal master's awarded for partial completion of doctoral program. *Degree requirements:* For master's, comprehensive exam, scholarly paper, written and oral exams; for doctorate, thesis/dissertation, exam. *Entrance requirements:* For master's, GRE General Test, background in mathematics, experience in scientific computer languages, 3 letters of recommendation; for doctorate, GRE General Test. Electronic applications accepted. *Faculty research:* Weather, atmospheric chemistry, air pollution, global change, radiation.

University of Miami, Graduate School, Rosenstiel School of Marine and Atmospheric Science, Division of Meteorology and Physical Oceanography, Coral Gables, FL 33124. Offers meteorology (MS, PhD); physical oceanography (MS, PhD). Terminal master's awarded for partial completion of doctoral program. *Degree requirements:* For master's, comprehensive exam, thesis; for doctorate, comprehensive exam, thesis/dissertation. *Entrance requirements:* For master's and doctorate, GRE General Test. Additional exam requirements/recommendations for international students: Required—TOEFL (minimum score 550 paper-based). Electronic applications accepted.

University of Oklahoma, College of Atmospheric and Geographic Sciences, School of Meteorology, Norman, OK 73072. Offers MS, PhD. *Faculty:* 43 full-time (8 women). *Students:* 50 full-time (12 women), 29 part-time (10 women); includes 7 minority (1 Black or African American, non-Hispanic/Latino; 2 Asian, non-Hispanic/Latino; 4 Hispanic/Latino), 13 international. Average age 25. 86 applicants, 27% accepted, 22 enrolled. In 2018, 12 master's, 7 doctorates awarded. Terminal master's awarded for partial completion of doctoral program. *Degree requirements:* For master's, thesis; for doctorate, thesis/dissertation, general exam. *Entrance requirements:* For master's and doctorate, GRE, transcripts with all academic work. Additional exam requirements/recommendations for international students: Required—TOEFL (minimum score 79 iBT) or IELTS (minimum score 6.5). *Application deadline:* For fall admission, 1/15 for domestic students, 2/1 for international students; for spring admission, 10/1 for domestic and international students. Applications are processed on a rolling basis. Application fee: $50 ($100 for international students). Electronic applications accepted. *Expenses:* Tuition, state resident: full-time $5683.20; part-time $236.80 per credit hour. Tuition, nonresident: full-time $20,342; part-time $847.60 per credit hour. *International tuition:* $20,342.40 full-time. *Required fees:* $2894.20; $110.05 per credit hour. $126.50 per semester. Tuition and fees vary according to course load and program. *Financial support:* In 2018–19, 70 students received support, including 2 fellowships with tuition reimbursements available (averaging $4,500 per year), 41 research assistantships with full tuition reimbursements available (averaging $20,415 per year), 19 teaching assistantships with full tuition reimbursements available (averaging $20,837 per year); health care benefits, tuition waivers (full and partial), and unspecified assistantships also available. Support available to part-time students. Financial award application deadline: 6/1; financial award applicants required to submit FAFSA. *Faculty research:* High impact weather; radar; climate and global circulation; atmospheric chemistry; numerical modeling and data assimilation. *Total annual research expenditures:* $3.5 million. *Unit head:* Dr. David Parsons, Director, 405-325-6561, Fax: 405-325-7689, E-mail: dparsons@ou.edu. *Application contact:* Christie Upchurch, Academic Coordinator, Graduate Program, 405-325-6571, Fax: 405-325-7689, E-mail: cupchurch@ou.edu. Website: http://meteorology.ou.edu

Utah State University, School of Graduate Studies, College of Agriculture and Applied Sciences, Department of Plants, Soils and Climate, Logan, UT 84322. Offers climate sciences (MS, PhD); ecology (MS, PhD); horticulture (MPS); plant science (MS, PhD); soil science (MS, PhD). *Program availability:* Part-time. Terminal master's awarded for partial completion of doctoral program. *Degree requirements:* For master's, thesis; for doctorate, thesis/dissertation. *Entrance requirements:* For master's, GRE General Test, BS in plant, soil, atmospheric science, or related field; minimum GPA of 3.0; for doctorate, GRE General Test, minimum GPA of 3.0. Additional exam requirements/recommendations for international students: Required—TOEFL. Electronic applications accepted. *Faculty research:* Biotechnology and genomics, plant physiology and biology, nutrient and water efficient landscapes, physical-chemical-biological processes in soil, environmental biophysics and climate.

Yale University, Graduate School of Arts and Sciences, Department of Geology and Geophysics, New Haven, CT 06520. Offers biogeochemistry (PhD); climate dynamics (PhD); geochemistry (PhD); geophysics (PhD); meteorology (PhD); oceanography (PhD); paleontology (PhD); paleooceanography (PhD); petrology (PhD); tectonics (PhD). *Degree requirements:* For doctorate, thesis/dissertation. *Entrance requirements:* For doctorate, GRE General Test. Additional exam requirements/recommendations for international students: Required—TOEFL.

Peterson's Graduate Programs in the Physical Sciences, Mathematics, Agricultural Sciences, the Environment & Natural Resources 2020

www.petersons.com **135**

Section 6
Physics

This section contains a directory of institutions offering graduate work in physics, followed by in-depth entries submitted by institutions that chose to prepare detailed program descriptions. Additional information about programs listed in the directory but not augmented by an in-depth entry may be obtained by writing directly to the dean of a graduate school or chair of a department at the address given in the directory.

For programs offering related work, see all other areas in this book. In the other guides in this series:

Graduate Programs in the Biological/Biomedical Sciences & Health-Related Medical Professions

See *Allied Health, Biological and Biomedical Sciences, Biophysics,* and *Vision Sciences*

Graduate Programs in Engineering & Applied Sciences

See *Aerospace/Aeronautical Engineering, Electrical and Computer Engineering, Energy and Power Engineering (Nuclear Engineering), Engineering and Applied Sciences, Engineering Physics, Materials Sciences and Engineering,* and *Mechanical Engineering and Mechanics*

CONTENTS

Acoustics

Naval Postgraduate School, Departments and Academic Groups, Undersea Warfare Academic Group, Monterey, CA 93943. Offers applied mathematics (MS); applied physics (MS); applied science (MS), including acoustics, operations research, physical oceanography, signal processing; electrical engineering (MS); engineering acoustics (MS, PhD); engineering science (MS), including electrical engineering, mechanical engineering; mechanical engineer (ME); mechanical engineering (MS, MSME); meteorology (MS); operations research (MS); physical oceanography (MS). Program only open to commissioned officers of the United States and friendly nations and selected United States federal civilian employees. *Program availability:* Part-time. *Degree requirements:* For master's, thesis. *Faculty research:* Unmanned/autonomous vehicles, sea mines and countermeasures, submarine warfare in the twentieth and twenty-first centuries.

Penn State University Park, Graduate School, Intercollege Graduate Programs and College of Engineering, Intercollege Graduate Program in Acoustics, University Park, PA 16802. Offers acoustics (PhD).

Rensselaer Polytechnic Institute, Graduate School, School of Architecture, Program in Architectural Sciences, Troy, NY 12180-3590. Offers architectural acoustics (PhD); built ecologies (PhD); lighting (PhD). *Faculty:* 33 full-time (8 women), 13 part-time/adjunct (1 woman). *Students:* 24 full-time (8 women), 3 part-time (1 woman); includes 5 minority (1 Black or African American, non-Hispanic/Latino; 2 Asian, non-Hispanic/Latino; 1 Hispanic/Latino; 1 Two or more races, non-Hispanic/Latino), 8 international. Average age 29. 40 applicants, 68% accepted, 13 enrolled. In 2018, 4 doctorates awarded. *Degree requirements:* For doctorate, comprehensive exam (for some programs), thesis/dissertation. *Entrance requirements:* For doctorate, GRE, portfolio/personal statement. Additional exam requirements/recommendations for international students: Required—TOEFL (minimum score 570 paper-based; 88 iBT), IELTS (minimum score 6.5), PTE (minimum score 60). *Application deadline:* For fall admission, 1/1 priority date for domestic and international students. Applications are processed on a rolling basis. Application fee: $75. Electronic applications accepted. *Financial support:* In 2018–19, research assistantships (averaging $23,000 per year), teaching assistantships with full tuition reimbursements (averaging $23,000 per year) were awarded; fellowships also available. Financial award application deadline: 1/1. *Unit head:* Evan Douglis, Dean, School of Architecture, 518-276-3034, E-mail: douglis@rpi.edu. *Application contact:* Jarron Decker, Director of Graduate Admissions, 518-276-6216, Fax: 518-276-4072, E-mail: gradadmissions@rpi.edu.
Website: http://www.arch.rpi.edu/academic/graduate/phd-program/

The University of Kansas, Graduate Studies, School of Architecture and Design, Department of Architecture, Lawrence, KS 66045. Offers architectural acoustics (Certificate); architecture (M Arch, PhD); health and wellness (Certificate); historic preservation (Certificate); urban design (Certificate). *Students:* 87 full-time (43 women), 19 part-time (9 women); includes 21 minority (5 Black or African American, non-Hispanic/Latino; 3 Asian, non-Hispanic/Latino; 9 Hispanic/Latino; 4 Two or more races, non-Hispanic/Latino), 20 international. Average age 25. 87 applicants, 74% accepted, 26 enrolled. In 2018, 70 master's, 3 doctorates, 11 other advanced degrees awarded. Terminal master's awarded for partial completion of doctoral program. *Entrance requirements:* For master's, GRE, transcript; resume; minimum GPA of 3.0; statement of purpose; letters of recommendation; portfolio of design work, or samples of written work or other creative artifacts produced if previous degree was not in a design-related discipline; for doctorate, GRE, transcript, resume, minimum GPA of 3.0, statement of purpose, letters of recommendation, research-informed writing sample, exhibit of work illustrating applicant's interests and abilities in areas related to the design disciplines. Additional exam requirements/recommendations for international students: Required—TOEFL, IELTS. *Application deadline:* For fall admission, 1/15 priority date for domestic and international students; for summer admission, 1/15 priority date for domestic and international students. Application fee: $65 ($85 for international students). Electronic applications accepted. *Financial support:* Fellowships, research assistantships, teaching assistantships, scholarships/grants, health care benefits, and unspecified assistantships available. Financial award application deadline: 1/15; financial award applicants required to submit FAFSA. *Faculty research:* Design build, sustainability, emergent technology, healthy places, urban design. *Unit head:* Frank Zilm, Dean, 816-561-7186, E-mail: frankzilm@ku.edu. *Application contact:* Joan Weaver, Graduate Admissions Contact, 785-864-3709, Fax: 785-864-5185, E-mail: jweaver@ku.edu.
Website: http://architecture.ku.edu/

Applied Physics

Air Force Institute of Technology, Graduate School of Engineering and Management, Department of Engineering Physics, Dayton, OH 45433-7765. Offers applied physics (MS, PhD); electro-optics (MS, PhD); materials science (PhD); nuclear engineering (MS, PhD); space physics (MS). *Program availability:* Part-time. *Degree requirements:* For master's, thesis; for doctorate, thesis/dissertation. *Entrance requirements:* For master's and doctorate, GRE General Test, minimum GPA of 3.0, U.S. citizenship. *Faculty research:* High-energy lasers, space physics, nuclear weapon effects, semiconductor physics.

Binghamton University, State University of New York, Graduate School, Harpur College of Arts and Sciences, Department of Physics, Applied Physics, and Astronomy, Binghamton, NY 13902-6000. Offers MS, PhD. *Program availability:* Part-time. Terminal master's awarded for partial completion of doctoral program. *Degree requirements:* For master's, comprehensive exam (for some programs), thesis or alternative; for doctorate, comprehensive exam, thesis/dissertation. *Entrance requirements:* For master's and doctorate, GRE General Test. Additional exam requirements/recommendations for international students: Required—TOEFL (minimum score 550 paper-based; 80 iBT). Electronic applications accepted.

California Institute of Technology, Division of Engineering and Applied Science, Option in Applied Physics, Pasadena, CA 91125-0001. Offers MS, PhD. *Degree requirements:* For doctorate, thesis/dissertation. Electronic applications accepted. *Faculty research:* Solid-state electronics, quantum electronics, plasmas, linear and nonlinear laser optics, electromagnetic theory.

Carnegie Mellon University, Mellon College of Science, Department of Physics, Pittsburgh, PA 15213-3891. Offers applied physics (PhD); physics (MS, PhD). *Degree requirements:* For doctorate, thesis/dissertation, qualifying exam. *Entrance requirements:* For doctorate, GRE General Test, GRE Subject Test. Additional exam requirements/recommendations for international students: Required—TOEFL. Electronic applications accepted. *Faculty research:* Astrophysics, condensed matter physics, biological physics, medium energy and nuclear physics, high-energy physics.

Christopher Newport University, Graduate Studies, Department of Physics, Computer Science, and Engineering, Newport News, VA 23606-3072. Offers applied physics and computer science (MS). *Program availability:* Part-time. *Degree requirements:* For master's, comprehensive exam (for some programs), thesis (for some programs). *Entrance requirements:* For master's, GRE General Test, minimum GPA of 3.0. Additional exam requirements/recommendations for international students: Required—TOEFL (minimum score 580 paper-based; 92 iBT), IELTS (minimum score 7). Electronic applications accepted. *Faculty research:* Advanced programming methodologies, experimental nuclear physics, computer architecture, semiconductor nanophysics, laser and optical fiber sensors.

Colorado School of Mines, Office of Graduate Studies, Department of Physics, Golden, CO 80401. Offers applied physics (MS, PhD); materials science (MS, PhD); nuclear engineering (ME, MS, PhD). *Program availability:* Part-time. *Faculty:* 34 full-time (4 women), 9 part-time/adjunct (3 women). *Students:* 61 full-time (14 women), 5 part-time (1 woman); includes 7 minority (4 Hispanic/Latino; 3 Two or more races, non-Hispanic/Latino), 8 international. Average age 27. 70 applicants, 33% accepted, 15 enrolled. In 2018, 5 master's, 10 doctorates awarded. *Degree requirements:* For master's, thesis (for some programs); for doctorate, comprehensive exam, thesis/dissertation. *Entrance requirements:* For master's and doctorate, GRE General Test, GRE Subject Test. Additional exam requirements/recommendations for international students: Required—TOEFL (minimum score 550 paper-based; 79 iBT). *Application deadline:* For fall admission, 12/15 priority date for domestic and international students; for spring admission, 9/1 priority date for domestic and international students. Application fee: $60 ($80 for international students). Electronic applications accepted. *Expenses:* Tuition, state resident: full-time $16,650; part-time $925 per contact hour. Tuition, nonresident: full-time $36,270; part-time $2015 per contact hour. *International tuition:* $36,270 full-time. *Required fees:* $2314; $2314 per semester. *Financial support:* In 2018–19, 32 research assistantships with full tuition reimbursements, 13 teaching assistantships with full tuition reimbursements were awarded; fellowships, scholarships/grants, health care benefits, and unspecified assistantships also available. Financial award application deadline: 12/15; financial award applicants required to submit FAFSA. *Faculty research:* Light scattering, low-energy nuclear physics, high fusion plasma diagnostics, laser operations, mathematical physics. *Unit head:* Dr. Uwe Greife, Head, 303-273-3618, E-mail: ugreife@mines.edu. *Application contact:* Dr. Kyle Leach, Professor, 303-273-3044, E-mail: kleach@mines.edu.
Website: http://physics.mines.edu

Columbia University, Fu Foundation School of Engineering and Applied Science, Department of Applied Physics and Applied Mathematics, New York, NY 10027. Offers applied mathematics (MS, Eng Sc D, PhD); applied physics (MS, Eng Sc D, PhD); materials science and engineering (MS, Eng Sc D, PhD); medical physics (MS). *Program availability:* Part-time, online learning. Terminal master's awarded for partial completion of doctoral program. *Degree requirements:* For master's, comprehensive exam; for doctorate, thesis/dissertation, qualifying exam. *Entrance requirements:* For master's, GRE General Test, GRE Subject Test (strongly recommended); for doctorate, GRE General Test, GRE Subject Test (applied physics). Additional exam requirements/recommendations for international students: Required—TOEFL, IELTS, PTE. Electronic applications accepted. *Faculty research:* Plasma physics and fusion energy; optical and laser physics; atmospheric, oceanic and earth physics; applied mathematics; solid state science and processing of materials, their properties, and their structure; medical physics.

Cornell University, Graduate School, Graduate Fields of Engineering, Field of Applied Physics, Ithaca, NY 14853. Offers applied physics (PhD); engineering physics (M Eng). *Degree requirements:* For doctorate, comprehensive exam, thesis/dissertation, written exams. *Entrance requirements:* For master's, GRE General Test, 3 letters of recommendation; for doctorate, GRE General Test, GRE Subject Test (physics), GRE Writing Assessment, 3 letters of recommendation. Additional exam requirements/recommendations for international students: Required—TOEFL (minimum score 600 paper-based; 77 iBT). Electronic applications accepted. *Faculty research:* Quantum and nonlinear optics, plasma physics, solid state physics, condensed matter physics and nanotechnology, electron and X-ray spectroscopy.

East Carolina University, Graduate School, Thomas Harriot College of Arts and Sciences, Department of Physics, Greenville, NC 27858-4353. Offers applied physics (MS); biomedical physics (PhD); health physics (MS); medical physics (MS). *Program availability:* Part-time. *Application deadline:* For fall admission, 3/1 priority date for domestic and international students. *Expenses: Tuition, area resident:* Full-time $4749. Tuition, state resident: full-time $4749. Tuition, nonresident: full-time $17,898. *International tuition:* $17,898 full-time. *Required fees:* $2787. Part-time tuition and fees vary according to course load and program. *Financial support:* Application deadline: 3/1. *Unit head:* Dr. Jefferson Shinpaugh, Chair, 252-328-6739, E-mail: shinpaughj@ecu.edu. *Application contact:* Graduate School Admissions, 252-328-6012, Fax: 252-328-6071, E-mail: gradschool@ecu.edu.
Website: http://www.ecu.edu/cs-cas/physics/

Georgia Southern University, Jack N. Averitt College of Graduate Studies, College of Science and Mathematics, Program in Applied Physical Science, Statesboro, GA 30458. Offers applied physical science (MS). *Faculty:* 12 full-time (4 women). *Students:* 22 full-time (7 women), 3 part-time (1 woman); includes 6 minority (5 Black or African American, non-Hispanic/Latino; 1 Hispanic/Latino), 10 international. Average age 27. 9 applicants, 78% accepted, 7 enrolled. In 2018, 11 master's awarded. *Degree requirements:* For master's, comprehensive exam (for some programs), thesis (for some programs). *Entrance requirements:* For master's, GRE, minimum GPA of 2.75, 2 letters of recommendation, statement of purpose. Additional exam requirements/recommendations for international students: Required—TOEFL (minimum score 550 paper-based; 80 iBT), IELTS (minimum score 6). *Application deadline:* For fall admission, 3/15 priority date for domestic and international students; for spring admission, 10/15 priority date for domestic and international students. Application fee: $4 ($3 for international students). Electronic applications accepted. *Expenses: Tuition, area resident:* Part-time $3324 per semester. Tuition, state resident: full-time $5814; part-time $3324 per semester. Tuition, nonresident: full-time $23,204; part-time $13,260 per semester. *Required fees:* $2092; $2092. Tuition and fees vary according to course load, degree level, campus/location and program. *Financial support:* In 2018–19, 25 students received support, including 1 research assistantship with full tuition reimbursement available (averaging $10,000 per year), 9 teaching assistantships with full tuition reimbursements available (averaging $10,000 per year); scholarships/grants, tuition waivers (full), and unspecified assistantships also available. Financial award application deadline: 4/20; financial award applicants required to submit FAFSA. *Faculty research:* Cancer Research, Materials and Coatings Science, Protein Structure and Function, Nano materials. *Unit head:* Dr. Michele Davis McGibony, Program Director, 912-478-5919, E-mail: mdavis@georgiasouthern.edu. *Application contact:* Dr. Michele Davis McGibony, Program Director, 912-478-5919, E-mail: mdavis@georgiasouthern.edu.

Harvard University, Graduate School of Arts and Sciences, Department of Physics, Cambridge, MA 02138. Offers experimental physics (PhD); medical engineering/medical physics (PhD), including applied physics, engineering sciences, physics; theoretical physics (PhD). *Degree requirements:* For doctorate, thesis/dissertation, final exams, laboratory experience. *Entrance requirements:* For doctorate, GRE General Test, GRE Subject Test. Additional exam requirements/recommendations for international students: Required—TOEFL. *Faculty research:* Particle physics, condensed matter physics, atomic physics.

Harvard University, Graduate School of Arts and Sciences, Harvard John A. Paulson School of Engineering and Applied Sciences, Cambridge, MA 02138. Offers applied mathematics (PhD); applied physics (PhD); computational science and engineering (ME, SM); computer science (PhD); data science (SM); design engineering (MDE); engineering science (ME), including electrical engineering (ME, SM, PhD); engineering sciences (SM, PhD), including bioengineering (PhD), electrical engineering (ME, SM, PhD), environmental science and engineering (PhD), materials science and mechanical engineering (PhD). MDE offered in collaboration with Graduate School of Design. *Program availability:* Part-time. Terminal master's awarded for partial completion of doctoral program. *Degree requirements:* For master's, thesis (for ME); for doctorate, comprehensive exam, thesis/dissertation. *Entrance requirements:* For master's and doctorate, GRE General Test, GRE Subject Test (recommended), 3 letters of recommendation. Additional exam requirements/recommendations for international students: Required—TOEFL (minimum score 80 iBT). Electronic applications accepted. *Expenses:* Contact institution. *Faculty research:* Applied mathematics, applied physics, computer science and electrical engineering, environmental engineering, mechanical and biomedical engineering.

Idaho State University, Graduate School, College of Science and Engineering, Department of Physics, Pocatello, ID 83209-8106. Offers applied physics (PhD); health physics (MS); physics (MNS). *Program availability:* Part-time. *Degree requirements:* For master's, comprehensive exam, thesis (for some programs), oral exam (for some programs); for doctorate, comprehensive exam, thesis/dissertation (for some programs), oral exam, written qualifying exam in physics or health physics after 1st year. *Entrance requirements:* For master's, GRE General Test, 3 letters of recommendation, BS or BA in physics, teaching certificate (MNS); for doctorate, GRE General Test (minimum 50th percentile), 3 letters of recommendation, statement of career goals. Additional exam requirements/recommendations for international students: Required—TOEFL (minimum score 550 paper-based; 80 iBT). Electronic applications accepted. *Faculty research:* Ion beam applications, low-energy nuclear physics, relativity and cosmology, observational astronomy.

Illinois Institute of Technology, Graduate College, College of Science, Department of Physics, Chicago, IL 60616. Offers applied physics (MS); health physics (MAS); physics (MS, PhD). *Program availability:* Part-time, evening/weekend, online learning. Terminal master's awarded for partial completion of doctoral program. *Degree requirements:* For master's, comprehensive exam (for some programs), thesis (for some programs); for doctorate, comprehensive exam, thesis/dissertation. *Entrance requirements:* For master's, GRE General Test (minimum score 295 Quantitative and Verbal, 2.5 Analytical Writing), minimum undergraduate GPA of 3.0; for doctorate, GRE General Test (minimum score 310 Quantitative and Verbal, 3.0 Analytical Writing); GRE Subject Test in physics (strongly recommended), minimum undergraduate GPA of 3.0. Additional exam requirements/recommendations for international students: Required—TOEFL (minimum score 550 paper-based; 80 iBT). Electronic applications accepted. *Faculty research:* Elementary particle physics, condensed matter, superconductivity, experimental and computational biophysics.

Iowa State University of Science and Technology, Department of Physics and Astronomy, Ames, IA 50011. Offers applied physics (MS, PhD); astrophysics (MS, PhD); condensed matter physics (MS, PhD); high energy physics (MS, PhD); nuclear physics (MS, PhD); physics (MS, PhD). *Degree requirements:* For master's, thesis (for some programs); for doctorate, thesis/dissertation. *Entrance requirements:* For master's and doctorate, GRE General Test, GRE Subject Test (physics). Additional exam requirements/recommendations for international students: Required—TOEFL (minimum score 550 paper-based; 79 iBT), IELTS (minimum score 6.5). Electronic applications accepted. *Faculty research:* Condensed-matter physics, including superconductivity and new materials; high-energy and nuclear physics; astronomy and astrophysics; atmospheric and environmental physics.

Iowa State University of Science and Technology, Program in Applied Physics, Ames, IA 50011. Offers MS, PhD. *Entrance requirements:* For master's and doctorate, GRE. Additional exam requirements/recommendations for international students: Required—TOEFL (minimum score 550 paper-based; 79 iBT), IELTS (minimum score 6.5). Electronic applications accepted.

Johns Hopkins University, Engineering Program for Professionals, Part-time Program in Applied Physics, Baltimore, MD 21218. Offers MS, Post-Master's Certificate. *Program availability:* Part-time, evening/weekend, blended/hybrid learning. *Faculty:* 17 part-time/adjunct. *Students:* 53 part-time (11 women). 18 applicants, 72% accepted, 8 enrolled. In 2018, 13 master's awarded. *Entrance requirements:* Additional exam requirements/recommendations for international students: Required—TOEFL (minimum score 600 paper-based; 100 iBT). *Application deadline:* Applications are processed on a rolling basis. Application fee: $0. Electronic applications accepted. *Unit head:* Dr. Harry K. Charles, Jr., Chair, 443-778-8050, E-mail: harry.charles@jhuapl.edu. *Application contact:* Doug Schiller, Admissions Director, 410-516-2300, Fax: 410-579-8049, E-mail: schiller@jhu.edu.
Website: http://www.ep.jhu.edu

Laurentian University, School of Graduate Studies and Research, Programme in Physics, Sudbury, ON P3E 2C6, Canada. Offers M Sc. *Program availability:* Part-time. *Degree requirements:* For master's, thesis or alternative. *Entrance requirements:* For master's, honors degree with second class or better. *Faculty research:* Solar neutrino physics and astrophysics, applied acoustics and ultrasonics, powder science and technology, solid state physics, theoretical physics.

Louisiana Tech University, Graduate School, College of Engineering and Science, Ruston, LA 71272. Offers applied physics (MS); biomedical engineering (PhD); computer science (MS); engineering (MS, PhD), including cyberspace engineering (PhD), engineering education (PhD), engineering physics (PhD), materials and infrastructure systems (PhD), micro/nanoscale systems (PhD); engineering and technology management (MS); mathematics (MS); molecular science and nanotechnology (MS, PhD). *Program availability:* Part-time-only. Terminal master's awarded for partial completion of doctoral program. *Degree requirements:* For master's, thesis (for some programs); for doctorate, thesis/dissertation. *Entrance requirements:* For master's and Graduate Certificate, GRE General Test, minimum GPA of 3.0 in last 60 hours. Additional exam requirements/recommendations for international students: Required—TOEFL (minimum score 550 paper-based; 80 iBT), IELTS (minimum score 6.5). Electronic applications accepted. *Faculty research:* Trenchless technology, micromanufacturing, radionuclide transport, microbial liquefaction, hazardous waste treatment.

Michigan Technological University, Graduate School, College of Sciences and Arts, Department of Physics, Houghton, MI 49931. Offers applied physics (MS, PhD); physics (MS, PhD). *Program availability:* Part-time. *Faculty:* 32 full-time, 11 part-time/adjunct. *Students:* 38 full-time (12 women), 1 part-time, 24 international. Average age 28. 133 applicants, 51% accepted, 11 enrolled. In 2018, 6 master's, 2 doctorates awarded. Terminal master's awarded for partial completion of doctoral program. *Degree requirements:* For master's, comprehensive exam (for some programs), thesis (for some programs); for doctorate, comprehensive exam, thesis/dissertation, qualifying exam, research proposal exam. *Entrance requirements:* For master's and doctorate, GRE (recommended minimum quantitative score of 156 and analytical score of 3.0), statement of purpose, personal statement, official transcripts, 3 letters of recommendation. Additional exam requirements/recommendations for international students: Required—TOEFL, IELTS, TOEFL (recommended minimum score 88 iBT) or IELTS (recommended minimum score of 6.5). *Application deadline:* For fall and spring admission, 2/1 priority date for domestic and international students. Applications are processed on a rolling basis. Electronic applications accepted. *Expenses: Tuition, area resident:* Full-time $18,126; part-time $1007 per credit. Tuition, state resident: full-time $18,126; part-time $1007 per credit. Tuition, nonresident: full-time $18,126; part-time $1007 per credit. *International tuition:* $18,126 full-time. *Required fees:* $248; $124 per semester. Tuition and fees vary according to course load and program. *Financial support:* In 2018–19, 38 students received support, including 9 fellowships with tuition reimbursements available (averaging $16,590 per year), 8 research assistantships with tuition reimbursements available (averaging $16,590 per year), 14 teaching assistantships with tuition reimbursements available (averaging $16,590 per year); career-related internships or fieldwork, Federal Work-Study, scholarships/grants, health care benefits, unspecified assistantships, and cooperative program also available. Financial award applicants required to submit FAFSA. *Faculty research:* Atmospheric physics, astrophysics, biophysics, materials physics, atomic/molecular physics. *Total annual research expenditures:* $1.3 million. *Unit head:* Dr. Ravindra Pandey, Chair, 906-487-2086, Fax: 906-487-2933, E-mail: physics@mtu.edu. *Application contact:* Dr. Ravindra Pandey, Chair, 906-487-2086, Fax: 906-487-2933, E-mail: physics@mtu.edu.
Website: http://www.mtu.edu/physics/

Naval Postgraduate School, Departments and Academic Groups, Department of Physics, Monterey, CA 93943. Offers applied physics (MS, PhD); combat systems technology (MS); engineering acoustics (MS, PhD); physics (MS, PhD). Program only open to commissioned officers of the United States and friendly nations and selected United States federal civilian employees. *Program availability:* Part-time. *Degree requirements:* For master's, thesis; for doctorate, thesis/dissertation. *Faculty research:* Acoustics, free electron laser, sensors, weapons and effects.

Naval Postgraduate School, Departments and Academic Groups, Space Systems Academic Group, Monterey, CA 93943. Offers applied physics (MS); astronautical engineering (MS); computer science (MS); electrical engineering (MS); mechanical engineering (MS); space systems (Engr); space systems operations (MS). Program only open to commissioned officers of the United States and friendly nations and selected United States federal civilian employees. *Program availability:* Part-time. *Degree requirements:* For master's and Engr, thesis; for doctorate, thesis/dissertation. *Faculty research:* Military applications for space; space reconnaissance and remote sensing; radiation-hardened electronics for space; design, construction and operations of small satellites; satellite communications systems.

Naval Postgraduate School, Departments and Academic Groups, Undersea Warfare Academic Group, Monterey, CA 93943. Offers applied mathematics (MS); applied physics (MS); applied science (MS), including acoustics, operations research, physical oceanography, signal processing; electrical engineering (MS); engineering acoustics (MS, PhD); engineering science (MS), including electrical engineering, mechanical engineering; mechanical engineer (ME); mechanical engineering (MS, MSME); meteorology (MS); operations research (MS); physical oceanography (MS). Program only open to commissioned officers of the United States and friendly nations and selected United States federal civilian employees. *Program availability:* Part-time. *Degree requirements:* For master's, thesis. *Faculty research:* Unmanned/autonomous vehicles, sea mines and countermeasures, submarine warfare in the twentieth and twenty-first centuries.

New Jersey Institute of Technology, College of Science and Liberal Arts, Newark, NJ 07102. Offers applied mathematics (MS); applied physics (MS, PhD); applied statistics (MS, Certificate); biology (MS, PhD); biostatistics (MS); chemistry (MS, PhD); environmental and sustainability policy (MS); environmental science (MS, PhD); history (MA, MAT); materials science and engineering (MS, PhD); mathematical and computational finance (MS); mathematical sciences (PhD); pharmaceutical chemistry (MS); professional and technical communications (MS); technical communication essentials (Certificate). *Program availability:* Part-time, evening/weekend. *Faculty:* 150 full-time (43 women), 115 part-time/adjunct (47 women). *Students:* 200 full-time (70 women), 63 part-time (29 women); includes 61 minority (17 Black or African American, non-Hispanic/Latino; 29 Asian, non-Hispanic/Latino; 11 Hispanic/Latino; 4 Two or more races, non-Hispanic/Latino), 136 international. Average age 28. 429 applicants, 49% accepted, 89 enrolled. In 2018, 43 master's, 16 doctorates, 2 other advanced degrees awarded. Terminal master's awarded for partial completion of doctoral program. *Degree requirements:* For master's, thesis (for some programs); for doctorate, thesis/

dissertation. *Entrance requirements:* For master's and doctorate, GRE General Test, Minimum GPA of 3.0, personal statement, three (3) letters of recommendation, and transcripts. Additional exam requirements/recommendations for international students: Required—TOEFL (minimum score 550 paper-based; 79 iBT), IELTS (minimum score 6.5). *Application deadline:* For fall admission, 6/1 priority date for domestic students, 5/1 priority date for international students; for spring admission, 11/15 priority date for domestic and international students. Applications are processed on a rolling basis. Application fee: $75. Electronic applications accepted. *Expenses:* $22,690 per year (in-state), $32,136 per year (out-of-state). *Financial support:* In 2018–19, 134 students received support, including 17 fellowships with full tuition reimbursements available (averaging $22,000 per year), 74 research assistantships with full tuition reimbursements available (averaging $22,000 per year), 71 teaching assistantships with full tuition reimbursements available (averaging $22,000 per year); scholarships/grants, traineeships, health care benefits, and unspecified assistantships also available. Financial award application deadline: 1/15. *Faculty research:* Biophotonics and bioimaging, morphogenetic patterning, embryogenesis, biological fluid dynamics, applied research in the mathematical sciences. *Total annual research expenditures:* $29.2 million. *Unit head:* Dr. Kevin Belfield, Dean, 973-596-3676, Fax: 973-565-0586, E-mail: kevin.d.belfield@njit.edu. *Application contact:* Stephen Eck, Director of Admissions, 973-596-3300, Fax: 973-596-3461, E-mail: admissions@njit.edu.
Website: http://csla.njit.edu/

Northern Arizona University, College of Environment, Forestry, and Natural Sciences, Department of Physics and Astronomy, Flagstaff, AZ 86011. Offers applied physics (MS); astronomy and planetary science (PhD). *Program availability:* Part-time. *Degree requirements:* For master's, variable foreign language requirement, comprehensive exam (for some programs), thesis (for some programs); for doctorate, variable foreign language requirement, comprehensive exam (for some programs), thesis/dissertation (for some programs). *Entrance requirements:* For master's and doctorate, GRE General Test. Additional exam requirements/recommendations for international students: Required—TOEFL (minimum score 80 iBT), IELTS (minimum score 6.5). Electronic applications accepted.

Northwestern University, The Graduate School, Judd A. and Marjorie Weinberg College of Arts and Sciences and McCormick School of Engineering and Applied Science, Program in Applied Physics, Evanston, IL 60208. Offers PhD.

Rice University, Rice Quantum Institute, Houston, TX 77251-1892. Offers MS, PhD. *Degree requirements:* For master's, thesis; for doctorate, thesis/dissertation. *Entrance requirements:* For master's and doctorate, GRE General Test, GRE Subject Test (physics), minimum GPA of 3.0. Additional exam requirements/recommendations for international students: Required—TOEFL (minimum score 600 paper-based; 90 iBT). Electronic applications accepted. *Faculty research:* Nanotechnology, solid state materials, atomic physics, thin films.

Rutgers University–Newark, Graduate School, Program in Applied Physics, Newark, NJ 07102. Offers MS, PhD. MS, PhD offered jointly with New Jersey Institute of Technology. *Entrance requirements:* For master's and doctorate, GRE. Additional exam requirements/recommendations for international students: Required—TOEFL.

Southern Illinois University Carbondale, Graduate School, College of Science, Department of Physics, Carbondale, IL 62901-4701. Offers MS, PhD. *Degree requirements:* For master's, one foreign language, thesis; for doctorate, thesis/dissertation. *Entrance requirements:* For master's, minimum GPA of 2.7; for doctorate, GRE, minimum GPA of 3.25. Additional exam requirements/recommendations for international students: Required—TOEFL. *Faculty research:* Atomic, molecular, nuclear, and mathematical physics; statistical mechanics; solid-state and low-temperature physics; rheology; material science.

Stanford University, School of Humanities and Sciences, Department of Applied Physics, Stanford, CA 94305-2004. Offers applied and engineering physics (MS); applied physics (PhD). *Expenses: Tuition:* Full-time $50,703; part-time $32,970 per year. *Required fees:* $651.
Website: http://www.stanford.edu/dept/app-physics/

Texas A&M University, College of Science, Department of Physics and Astronomy, College Station, TX 77843. Offers applied physics (PhD); astronomy (MS); physics (PhD). *Faculty:* 61. *Students:* 150 full-time (24 women), 7 part-time (1 woman); includes 15 minority (1 Black or African American, non-Hispanic/Latino; 4 Asian, non-Hispanic/Latino; 7 Hispanic/Latino; 3 Two or more races, non-Hispanic/Latino), 82 international. Average age 27. 202 applicants, 34% accepted, 34 enrolled. In 2018, 11 master's, 29 doctorates awarded. Terminal master's awarded for partial completion of doctoral program. *Entrance requirements:* For master's and doctorate, GRE General Test, GRE Subject Test. Additional exam requirements/recommendations for international students: Required—TOEFL. *Application deadline:* For fall admission, 12/1 for domestic students, 12/15 for international students. Application fee: $50 ($90 for international students). Electronic applications accepted. *Expenses:* Contact institution. *Financial support:* In 2018–19, 151 students received support, including 39 fellowships with tuition reimbursements available (averaging $16,344 per year), 109 research assistantships with tuition reimbursements available (averaging $13,676 per year), 64 teaching assistantships with tuition reimbursements available (averaging $13,698 per year); career-related internships or fieldwork, institutionally sponsored loans, scholarships/grants, traineeships, health care benefits, tuition waivers (full and partial), and unspecified assistantships also available. Support available to part-time students. Financial award application deadline: 3/1; financial award applicants required to submit FAFSA. *Faculty research:* Condensed matter, atomic/molecular, high-energy and nuclear physics, quantum optics. *Unit head:* Dr. George R. Welch, Head, 979-845-1571, E-mail: welch@physics.tamu.edu. *Application contact:* Dr. Joe Ross, Graduate Advisor, 979-845-3842, Fax: 979-845-2590, E-mail: ross@physics.tamu.edu.
Website: http://physics.tamu.edu/

Towson University, Jess and Mildred Fisher College of Science and Mathematics, Program in Applied Physics, Towson, MD 21252-0001. Offers MS. *Entrance requirements:* For master's, bachelor's degree, minimum GPA of 3.0, resume, letter of recommendation, statement of purpose. Electronic applications accepted. *Expenses: Tuition, area resident:* Full-time $9196; part-time $418 per unit. Tuition, state resident: full-time $9196; part-time $418 per unit. Tuition, nonresident: full-time $19,030; part-time $865 per unit. *International tuition:* $19,030 full-time. *Required fees:* $3102; $141 per year. $423 per term. Tuition and fees vary according to campus/location and program.

University of Arkansas, Graduate School, J. William Fulbright College of Arts and Sciences, Department of Physics, Fayetteville, AR 72701. Offers applied physics (MS); physics (MS, PhD); physics education (MA). In 2018, 3 master's, 7 doctorates awarded. *Application deadline:* For fall admission, 8/1 for domestic students, 4/1 for international students; for spring admission, 12/1 for domestic students, 10/1 for international students; for summer admission, 4/15 for domestic students, 3/1 for international students. Applications are processed on a rolling basis. Application fee: $60. Electronic applications accepted. *Financial support:* In 2018–19, 21 research assistantships, 22 teaching assistantships were awarded; fellowships with tuition reimbursements, career-related internships or fieldwork, and Federal Work-Study also available. Support available to part-time students. Financial award application deadline: 4/1; financial award applicants required to submit FAFSA. *Unit head:* William Oliver, Department Chair, 479-575-6571, Fax: 479-575-6595, E-mail: woliver@uark.edu. *Application contact:* Dr. Surendra Singh, Graduate Coordinator, 479-575-6058, Fax: 479-575-6595, E-mail: ssingh@uark.edu.
Website: https://fulbright.uark.edu/departments/physics/

University of California, San Diego, Graduate Division, Department of Electrical and Computer Engineering, La Jolla, CA 92093. Offers applied ocean science (MS, PhD); applied physics (MS, PhD); communication theory and systems (MS, PhD); computer engineering (MS, PhD); electronic circuits and systems (MS, PhD); intelligent systems, robotics and control (MS, PhD); medical devices and systems (MS, PhD); nanoscale devices and systems (MS, PhD); photonics (MS, PhD); signal and image processing (MS, PhD). Program offered jointly with San Diego State University. *Students:* 830 full-time (174 women), 69 part-time (8 women). 2,810 applicants, 40% accepted, 399 enrolled. In 2018, 226 master's, 42 doctorates awarded. Terminal master's awarded for partial completion of doctoral program. *Degree requirements:* For master's, comprehensive exam (for some programs), thesis (for some programs); for doctorate, comprehensive exam, thesis/dissertation. *Entrance requirements:* For master's and doctorate, GRE General Test, minimum GPA of 3.0, resume or curriculum vitae (recommended). Additional exam requirements/recommendations for international students: Required—TOEFL (minimum score 550 paper-based; 80 iBT), IELTS (minimum score 7), PTE (minimum score 65). *Application deadline:* For fall admission, 12/13 for domestic students. Application fee: $105 ($125 for international students). Electronic applications accepted. *Financial support:* Fellowships, research assistantships, teaching assistantships, scholarships/grants, traineeships, and unspecified assistantships available. Financial award applicants required to submit FAFSA. *Faculty research:* Applied ocean science; applied physics; communication theory and systems; computer engineering; electronic circuits and systems; intelligent systems, robotics and control; medical devices and systems; nanoscale devices and systems; photonics; signal and image processing. *Unit head:* Bill Lin, Chair, 858-822-1383, E-mail: billin@ucsd.edu. *Application contact:* Sean Jones, Graduate Admissions Coordinator, 858-534-3213, E-mail: ecegradapps@ece.ucsd.edu.
Website: http://ece.ucsd.edu/

University of Massachusetts Boston, College of Science and Mathematics, Program in Applied Physics, Boston, MA 02125-3393. Offers MS. *Program availability:* Part-time, evening/weekend. *Faculty:* 12 full-time (0 women). *Students:* 4 full-time (1 woman), 22 part-time (3 women); includes 3 minority (1 Black or African American, non-Hispanic/Latino; 1 Asian, non-Hispanic/Latino; 1 Hispanic/Latino), 5 international. Average age 35. 19 applicants, 79% accepted, 11 enrolled. In 2018, 10 master's awarded. *Entrance requirements:* For master's, minimum GPA of 2.75. *Application deadline:* For fall admission, 3/15 for domestic students; for spring admission, 10/15 for domestic students. *Expenses: Tuition, area resident:* Full-time $17,896. Tuition, state resident: full-time $17,896. Tuition, nonresident: full-time $34,932. *International tuition:* $34,932 full-time. *Required fees:* $355. *Financial support:* Research assistantships, teaching assistantships, career-related internships or fieldwork, Federal Work-Study, and unspecified assistantships available. Support available to part-time students. Financial award application deadline: 3/1; financial award applicants required to submit FAFSA. *Faculty research:* Experimental laser research, nonlinear optics, experimental and theoretical solid state physics, semiconductor devices, opto-electronics. *Unit head:* Dr. Jon Celli, Assistant Professor of Physics, 617-287.5715, E-mail: Jonathan.Celli@umb.edu. *Application contact:* Graduate Admissions Coordinator, 617-287-6400, Fax: 617-287-6236, E-mail: graduate.admissions@umb.edu.

University of Michigan, Rackham Graduate School, College of Literature, Science, and the Arts, Applied Physics Program, Ann Arbor, MI 48198. Offers PhD. *Degree requirements:* For doctorate, oral defense of dissertation, preliminary and qualifying exams. *Entrance requirements:* For doctorate, GRE General Test. Additional exam requirements/recommendations for international students: Required—TOEFL. *Application deadline:* For fall admission, 1/15 for domestic and international students. Applications are processed on a rolling basis. Application fee: $60 ($75 for international students). Electronic applications accepted. *Financial support:* Fellowships with full tuition reimbursements, research assistantships with full tuition reimbursements, teaching assistantships with full tuition reimbursements, traineeships, health care benefits, and unspecified assistantships available. Financial award application deadline: 1/15; financial award applicants required to submit FAFSA. *Faculty research:* Optical sciences, materials research, quantum structures, medical imaging, environment and science policy. *Unit head:* Dr. Cagliyan Kurdak, Director, 734-647-4650, Fax: 734-764-2193, E-mail: kurdak@umich.edu. *Application contact:* Cynthia L. McNabb, Program Manager, 734-936-0653, Fax: 734-764-2193, E-mail: cyndia@umich.edu.
Website: https://lsa.umich.edu/appliedphysics

University of Missouri–St. Louis, College of Arts and Sciences, Department of Physics and Astronomy, St. Louis, MO 63121. Offers applied physics (MS); astrophysics (MS); physics (PhD). *Program availability:* Part-time, evening/weekend. Terminal master's awarded for partial completion of doctoral program. *Degree requirements:* For master's, thesis optional; for doctorate, thesis/dissertation. *Entrance requirements:* For master's, GRE General Test, minimum GPA of 2.75, 2 letters of recommendation; for doctorate, GRE General Test, 2 letters of recommendation, minimum GPA of 3.0. Additional exam requirements/recommendations for international students: Required—TOEFL (minimum score 550 paper-based; 79 iBT), IELTS (minimum score 6.5). Electronic applications accepted. *Faculty research:* Biophysics, astrophysics, materials science.

The University of North Carolina at Charlotte, College of Liberal Arts and Sciences, Department of Physics and Optical Science, Charlotte, NC 28223-0001. Offers applied physics (MS); optical science and engineering (MS, PhD). *Students:* 46 full-time (14 women), 11 part-time (2 women); includes 3 minority (1 Black or African American, non-Hispanic/Latino; 1 Hispanic/Latino; 1 Two or more races, non-Hispanic/Latino), 27 international. Average age 28. 35 applicants, 49% accepted, 7 enrolled. In 2018, 10 master's, 14 doctorates awarded. *Entrance requirements:* For master's, GRE, bachelor's degree in physics or closely-allied field; minimum overall GPA of 2.75, major 3.0; demonstrated evidence of sufficient interest, ability, and preparation in physics to adequately profit from graduate study; for doctorate, GRE, baccalaureate or master's degree in physics, chemistry, mathematics, engineering, optics, or related field with minimum undergraduate GPA of 3.0 overall, 3.2 in major and graduate; letters of recommendation. Additional exam requirements/recommendations for international students: Required—TOEFL (minimum score 523 paper-based; 70 iBT), IELTS (minimum score 6), TOEFL (minimum score 523 paper-based, 70 iBT) or IELTS (6). *Application deadline:* Applications are processed on a rolling basis. Application fee: $75. Electronic applications accepted. Tuition and fees vary according to course load and program. *Financial support:* Fellowships, research assistantships, teaching assistantships, career-related internships or fieldwork, institutionally sponsored loans, scholarships/grants, and unspecified assistantships available. Support available to part-time students. Financial award application deadline: 3/1; financial award applicants required to submit FAFSA. *Total annual research expenditures:* $2.1 million. *Unit head:* Dr. Glen Boreman, Chair, 704-687-8132. *Application contact:* Kathy B. Giddings, Director of Graduate Admissions, 704-687-5503, Fax: 704-687-1668, E-mail: gradadm@uncc.edu. Website: http://physics.uncc.edu/

University of South Florida, College of Arts and Sciences, Department of Physics, Tampa, FL 33620-9951. Offers applied physics (PhD), including medical physics; physics (MS), including applied physics, atomic and molecular physics, laser physics, materials physics, optical physics, semiconductor physics, solid state physics. *Program availability:* Part-time. *Faculty:* 24 full-time (2 women), 1 (woman) part-time/adjunct. *Students:* 53 full-time (17 women), 4 part-time (0 women); includes 10 minority (1 Asian, non-Hispanic/Latino; 9 Hispanic/Latino), 27 international. Average age 29. 89 applicants, 27% accepted, 7 enrolled. In 2018, 7 master's, 5 doctorates awarded. *Degree requirements:* For master's, comprehensive exam, thesis optional; for doctorate, comprehensive exam, thesis/dissertation. *Entrance requirements:* For master's and doctorate, GRE General Test; GRE Subject Test in physics (recommended), minimum GPA of 3.0, three letters of recommendation, statement of purpose. Additional exam requirements/recommendations for international students: Required—TOEFL, TOEFL (minimum score 550 paper-based; 79 iBT) or IELTS (minimum score 6.5). *Application deadline:* For fall admission, 2/1 priority date for domestic students, 2/1 for international students; for spring admission, 9/1 for domestic and international students. Applications are processed on a rolling basis. Application fee: $30. Electronic applications accepted. *Expenses:* Tuition, state resident: full-time $6350. Tuition, nonresident: full-time $19,048. *International tuition:* $19,048 full-time. *Required fees:* $2079. *Financial support:* In 2018–19, 15 students received support, including 27 research assistantships with tuition reimbursements available (averaging $15,272 per year), 43 teaching assistantships with tuition reimbursements available (averaging $16,267 per year); unspecified assistantships also available. *Faculty research:* Molecular organization of collagen, lipid rafts in biological membranes, formation of Alzheimer plaques, the role of cellular ion pumps in wound healing, carbon nanotubes as biological detectors, optical imaging of neuronal activity, three-dimensional imaging of intact tissues, motility of cancer cells, optical detection of pathogens in water. *Total annual research expenditures:* $2.9 million. *Unit head:* Dr. David Rabson, Professor and Chairperson, 813-974-1207, E-mail: davidra@ewald.cas.usf.edu. *Application contact:* Dr. Xiaomei Jiang, Associate Professor and Director of Graduate Admissions, 813-974-7765, E-mail: xjiang@usf.edu. Website: http://physics.usf.edu/

The University of Texas at Austin, Graduate School, College of Natural Sciences, Department of Physics, Austin, TX 78712-1111. Offers MA, MS, PhD. *Degree requirements:* For master's, thesis; for doctorate, thesis/dissertation. *Entrance requirements:* For master's and doctorate, GRE General Test, GRE Subject Test (physics). Electronic applications accepted.

University of Washington, Graduate School, College of Arts and Sciences, Department of Physics, Seattle, WA 98195. Offers MS, PhD. *Program availability:* Part-time, evening/weekend. Terminal master's awarded for partial completion of doctoral program. *Degree requirements:* For doctorate, thesis/dissertation. *Entrance requirements:* For master's, GRE; for doctorate, GRE General Test, GRE Subject Test. Additional exam requirements/recommendations for international students: Required—TOEFL. Electronic applications accepted. *Faculty research:* Astro-, atomic, condensed-matter, nuclear, and particle physics; physics education.

Virginia Commonwealth University, Graduate School, College of Humanities and Sciences, Department of Physics, Program in Physics and Applied Physics, Richmond, VA 23284-9005. Offers MS. *Entrance requirements:* For master's, GRE. Additional exam requirements/recommendations for international students: Required—TOEFL (minimum score 600 paper-based; 100 iBT); Recommended—IELTS (minimum score 6.5). Electronic applications accepted. *Faculty research:* Theoretical and experimental condensed matter physics, general relativity and cosmology, physics education.

Yale University, Graduate School of Arts and Sciences, School of Engineering and Applied Science, Department of Applied Physics, New Haven, CT 06520. Offers MS, PhD. Terminal master's awarded for partial completion of doctoral program. *Degree requirements:* For doctorate, thesis/dissertation, area exam. *Entrance requirements:* For master's and doctorate, GRE General Test. Additional exam requirements/recommendations for international students: Required—TOEFL. *Faculty research:* Condensed-matter physics, optical physics, materials science.

Chemical Physics

Columbia University, Graduate School of Arts and Sciences, New York, NY 10027. Offers African-American studies (MA); American studies (MA); anthropology (MA, PhD); art history and archaeology (MA, PhD); astronomy (PhD); biological sciences (PhD); biotechnology (MA); chemical physics (PhD); chemistry (PhD); classical studies (MA, PhD); classics (MA, PhD); climate and society (MA); conservation biology (MA); earth and environmental sciences (PhD); East Asia: regional studies (MA); East Asian languages and cultures (MA, PhD); ecology, evolution and environmental biology (MA), including conservation biology; ecology, evolution, and environmental biology (PhD), including ecology and evolutionary biology, evolutionary primatology; economics (MA, PhD); English and comparative literature (MA, PhD); French and Romance philology (MA, PhD); Germanic languages (MA, PhD); global French studies (MA); global thought (MA); Hispanic cultural studies (MA); history (PhD); history and literature (MA); human rights studies (MA); Islamic studies (MA); Italian (MA, PhD); Japanese pedagogy (MA); Jewish studies (MA); Latin America and the Caribbean: regional studies (MA); Latin American and Iberian cultures (PhD); mathematics (MA, PhD), including finance (MA); medieval and Renaissance studies (MA); Middle Eastern, South Asian, and African studies (MA, PhD); modern art: critical and curatorial studies (MA); modern European studies (MA); museum anthropology (MA); music (DMA, PhD); oral history (MA); philosophical foundations of physics (MA); philosophy (MA, PhD); physics (PhD); political science (MA, PhD); psychology (PhD); quantitative methods in the social sciences (MA); religion (MA, PhD); Russia, Eurasia and East Europe: regional studies (MA); Russian translation (MA); Slavic cultures (MA); Slavic languages (MA, PhD); sociology (MA, PhD); South Asian studies (MA); statistics (MA, PhD); theatre (PhD). Dual-degree programs require admission to both Graduate School of Arts and Sciences and another Columbia school. *Program availability:* Part-time. Terminal master's awarded for partial completion of doctoral program. *Degree requirements:* For master's, variable foreign language requirement, comprehensive exam (for some programs), thesis (for some programs); for doctorate, variable foreign language requirement, comprehensive exam (for some programs), thesis/dissertation. *Entrance requirements:* For master's and doctorate, GRE General Test, GRE Subject Test (for some programs). Additional exam requirements/recommendations for international students: Required—TOEFL, IELTS. Electronic applications accepted.

Cornell University, Graduate School, Graduate Fields of Arts and Sciences, Field of Chemistry and Chemical Biology, Ithaca, NY 14853. Offers analytical chemistry (PhD); bio-organic chemistry (PhD); biophysical chemistry (PhD); chemical biology (PhD); chemical physics (PhD); inorganic chemistry (PhD); materials chemistry (PhD); organic chemistry (PhD); organometallic chemistry (PhD); physical chemistry (PhD); polymer chemistry (PhD); theoretical chemistry (PhD). *Degree requirements:* For doctorate, comprehensive exam, thesis/dissertation. *Entrance requirements:* For doctorate, GRE General Test, GRE Subject Test (chemistry), 3 letters of recommendation. Additional exam requirements/recommendations for international students: Required—TOEFL (minimum score 600 paper-based; 77 iBT). Electronic applications accepted. *Faculty research:* Analytical, organic, inorganic, physical, materials, chemical biology.

Harvard University, Graduate School of Arts and Sciences, Committee on Chemical Physics, Cambridge, MA 02138. Offers PhD. *Degree requirements:* For doctorate, one foreign language, thesis/dissertation, cumulative exams. *Entrance requirements:* For doctorate, GRE General Test, GRE Subject Test. Additional exam requirements/recommendations for international students: Required—TOEFL.

Kent State University, College of Arts and Sciences, Chemical Physics Interdisciplinary Program, Kent, OH 44242-0001. Offers chemical physics (MS, PhD), including liquid crystal engineering. *Program availability:* Part-time. *Faculty:* 12 full-time (2 women), 1 part-time/adjunct (0 women). *Students:* 36 full-time (13 women); includes 3 minority (1 Asian, non-Hispanic/Latino; 2 Two or more races, non Hispanic/Latino), 26 international. Average age 29. 24 applicants, 42% accepted, 6 enrolled. In 2018, 5 master's, 6 doctorates awarded. Terminal master's awarded for partial completion of doctoral program. *Degree requirements:* For master's, thesis optional, project; for doctorate, comprehensive exam, thesis/dissertation. *Entrance requirements:* For master's and doctorate, GRE General Test and GRE Subject Test in physics or chemistry (strongly recommended), official transcript(s), goal statement, two letters of recommendation. Additional exam requirements/recommendations for international students: Required—TOEFL (minimum score 525 paper-based; 71 iBT), IELTS (minimum score 6), PTE (minimum score 50), Michigan English Language Assessment Battery (minimum score 74). *Application deadline:* Applications are processed on a rolling basis. Application fee: $45 ($70 for international students). Electronic applications accepted. *Expenses:* Tuition, state resident: full-time $11,766; part-time $536 per credit. Tuition, nonresident: full-time $21,952; part-time $999 per credit. *International tuition:* $21,952 full-time. Tuition and fees vary according to course load. *Financial support:* Research assistantships with full tuition reimbursements, Federal Work-Study, and health care benefits available. Financial award application deadline: 2/1; financial award applicants required to submit FAFSA. *Unit head:* Dr. Torsten Hegmann, Director, 330-672-7770, E-mail: thegmann@kent.edu. *Application contact:* Dr. Antal Jakli, Professor of Chemical Physics and Graduate Coordinator, 672-4886, E-mail: ajakli@kent.edu. Website: http://www.kent.edu/cpip

Lewis University, College of Arts and Sciences, Program in Chemical Physics, Romeoville, IL 60446. Offers MS. *Program availability:* Part-time. *Students:* 5 part-time (2 women); includes 1 minority (Hispanic/Latino). Average age 23. *Entrance requirements:* For master's, bachelor's degree in chemistry, physics, or chemical physics with minimum GPA of 3.0; 3 letters of recommendation; personal statement. Additional exam requirements/recommendations for international students: Required—TOEFL (minimum score 550 paper-based; 79 iBT), IELTS (minimum score 6). *Application deadline:* For fall admission, 5/1 priority date for international students; for spring admission, 11/15 priority date for international students. Applications are processed on a rolling basis. Application fee: $40. Electronic applications accepted. *Financial support:* Federal Work-Study and unspecified assistantships available. Financial award application deadline: 5/1; financial award applicants required to submit FAFSA. *Unit head:* Dr. Jason Keleher, Program Director. *Application contact:* Linda Campbell, Graduate Admission Counselor, 815-836-5610, E-mail: grad@lewisu.edu. Website: http://www.lewisu.edu/academics/mschemicalphysics/index.htm

Marquette University, Graduate School, College of Arts and Sciences, Department of Chemistry, Milwaukee, WI 53201-1881. Offers analytical chemistry (MS, PhD); bioanalytical chemistry (MS, PhD); biophysical chemistry (MS, PhD); chemical physics (MS, PhD); inorganic chemistry (MS, PhD); organic chemistry (MS, PhD); physical chemistry (MS, PhD). *Program availability:* Part-time. Terminal master's awarded for partial completion of doctoral program. *Degree requirements:* For master's, comprehensive exam; for doctorate, thesis/dissertation, cumulative exams. *Entrance requirements:* For master's and doctorate, official transcripts from all current and previous colleges/universities except Marquette, three letters of recommendation from individuals familiar with the applicant's academic work. Additional exam requirements/recommendations for international students: Required—TOEFL. Electronic applications accepted. *Faculty research:* Inorganic complexes, laser Raman spectroscopy, organic synthesis, synthetic bioinorganic chemistry, electro-active organic molecules.

McMaster University, School of Graduate Studies, Faculty of Science, Department of Chemistry, Hamilton, ON L8S 4M2, Canada. Offers analytical chemistry (M Sc, PhD); chemical physics (M Sc, PhD); chemistry (M Sc, PhD); inorganic chemistry (M Sc, PhD); organic chemistry (M Sc, PhD); physical chemistry (M Sc, PhD); polymer chemistry (M Sc, PhD). *Program availability:* Part-time. Terminal master's awarded for partial completion of doctoral program. *Degree requirements:* For master's, thesis; for doctorate, comprehensive exam, thesis/dissertation. *Entrance requirements:* For master's, minimum B+ average. Additional exam requirements/recommendations for international students: Required—TOEFL (minimum score 550 paper-based).

Michigan State University, The Graduate School, College of Natural Science, Department of Chemistry, East Lansing, MI 48824. Offers chemical physics (PhD); chemistry (MS, PhD); chemistry-environmental toxicology (PhD); computational chemistry (MS). *Entrance requirements:* Additional exam requirements/recommendations for international students: Required—TOEFL. Electronic applications accepted. *Faculty research:* Analytical chemistry, inorganic and organic chemistry, nuclear chemistry, physical chemistry, theoretical and computational chemistry.

Peterson's Graduate Programs in the Physical Sciences, Mathematics, Agricultural Sciences, the Environment & Natural Resources 2020

www.petersons.com   **141**

The Ohio State University, Graduate School, College of Arts and Sciences, Division of Natural and Mathematical Sciences, Program in Chemical Physics, Columbus, OH 43210. Offers MS, PhD. *Students:* 6 full-time (4 women). Average age 25. In 2018, 1 doctorate awarded. *Entrance requirements:* For doctorate, GRE General Test, GRE Subject Test in chemistry or physics (recommended). Additional exam requirements/ recommendations for international students: Required—Michigan English Language Assessment Battery (minimum score 86); Recommended—TOEFL (minimum score 600 paper-based; 100 iBT), IELTS (minimum score 8). *Application deadline:* For fall admission, 12/13 priority date for domestic students, 11/30 priority date for international students; for spring admission, 3/1 for domestic students, 2/1 for international students. Applications are processed on a rolling basis. Application fee: $60 ($70 for international students). Electronic applications accepted. *Financial support:* Fellowships, research assistantships, teaching assistantships, Federal Work-Study, and institutionally sponsored loans available. Support available to part-time students. *Unit head:* Dr. Sherwin Singer, Graduate Studies Chair, 614-292-5185, E-mail: singer.2@osu.edu. *Application contact:* E-mail: chemphys@osu.edu.
Website: https://chemphys.osu.edu/

Tufts University, Graduate School of Arts and Sciences, Department of Chemistry, Medford, MA 02155. Offers chemical physics (PhD); chemistry (MS, PhD); chemistry/ biotechnology (PhD). Terminal master's awarded for partial completion of doctoral program. *Degree requirements:* For master's, thesis optional; for doctorate, comprehensive exam, thesis/dissertation. *Entrance requirements:* For master's and doctorate, GRE General Test; GRE Subject Test (recommended). Additional exam requirements/recommendations for international students: Required—TOEFL (minimum score 550 paper-based; 80 iBT), IELTS (minimum score 6.5). Electronic applications accepted. *Expenses:* Contact institution.

Tufts University, Graduate School of Arts and Sciences, Department of Physics and Astronomy, Medford, MA 02155. Offers astrophysics (MS, PhD); chemical physics (PhD); physics (MS, PhD); physics education (PhD). Terminal master's awarded for partial completion of doctoral program. *Degree requirements:* For master's, thesis optional; for doctorate, thesis/dissertation, oral qualifying exam. *Entrance requirements:* For master's and doctorate, GRE General Test. Additional exam requirements/ recommendations for international students: Required—TOEFL (minimum score 550 paper-based; 80 iBT), IELTS (minimum score 6.5). Electronic applications accepted. *Expenses:* Contact institution.

University of Illinois at Urbana–Champaign, Graduate College, College of Liberal Arts and Sciences, School of Chemical Sciences, Department of Chemistry, Champaign, IL 61820. Offers astrochemistry (PhD); chemical physics (PhD); chemistry (MA, MS, PhD); teaching of chemistry (MS); MS/JD; MS/MBA.

University of Louisville, Graduate School, College of Arts and Sciences, Department of Chemistry, Louisville, KY 40292-0001. Offers analytical chemistry (MS, PhD); biochemistry (MS, PhD); chemical physics (PhD); inorganic chemistry (MS, PhD); organic chemistry (MS, PhD); physical chemistry (MS, PhD). *Faculty:* 26 full-time (9 women), 3 part-time/adjunct (1 woman). *Students:* 35 full-time (14 women), 17 part-time (4 women); includes 5 minority (2 Black or African American, non-Hispanic/Latino; 3 Asian, non-Hispanic/Latino), 39 international. Average age 31. 47 applicants, 36% accepted, 10 enrolled. In 2018, 18 master's, 3 doctorates awarded. Terminal master's awarded for partial completion of doctoral program. *Degree requirements:* For master's, thesis (for some programs), Literature Seminars; for doctorate, thesis/dissertation, Cumulative Exams, Literature Seminars; Research. *Entrance requirements:* For master's and doctorate, GRE General Test, official transcripts, recommendation letters (minimum of 2), personal statement. Additional exam requirements/recommendations for international students: Required—TOEFL (minimum score 550 paper-based; 79 iBT), IELTS can be taken in place of TOEFL; Recommended—IELTS (minimum score 6.5). *Application deadline:* For fall admission, 1/15 priority date for domestic and international students; for spring admission, 9/15 priority date for domestic and international students. Application fee: $65. Electronic applications accepted. *Expenses: Tuition, area resident:* Full-time $6500; part-time $723 per credit hour. Tuition, state resident: full-time $6500. Tuition, nonresident: full-time $13,557; part-time $1507 per credit hour. Tuition and fees vary according to course load and program. *Financial support:* In 2018–19, 59 students received support, including 2 fellowships with full tuition reimbursements available (averaging $23,000 per year), 10 research assistantships with full tuition reimbursements available (averaging $23,000 per year), 41 teaching assistantships with full tuition reimbursements available (averaging $23,000 per year); scholarships/grants, health care benefits, and unspecified assistantships also available. Financial award application deadline: 1/15. *Faculty research:* Solid state chemistry, chemical synthesis, nanoparticle research, green chemistry, spectroscopic studies, computational chemistry, catalysis. *Total annual research expenditures:* $1 million. *Unit head:* Dr. Craig Grapperhaus, Professor, 502-852-8148, Fax: 502-852-8149, E-mail: craig.grapperhaus@louisville.edu. *Application contact:* Sherry Nalley, Graduate Program Assistant, 502-852-6798, Fax: 502-852-6536, E-mail: sherry.nalley@louisville.edu.
Website: http://louisville.edu/chemistry

University of Maryland, College Park, Academic Affairs, College of Computer, Mathematical and Natural Sciences, Institute for Physical Science and Technology, Program in Chemical Physics, College Park, MD 20742. Offers MS, PhD. *Program availability:* Part-time, evening/weekend. Terminal master's awarded for partial completion of doctoral program. *Degree requirements:* For master's, thesis optional, paper, qualifying exam; for doctorate, thesis/dissertation, seminars. *Entrance requirements:* For master's, GRE General Test, GRE Subject Test (chemistry, math or physics), minimum GPA of 3.3, 3 letters of recommendation; for doctorate, GRE Subject Test (chemistry, math, or physics), GRE General Test, minimum GPA of 3.3, 3 letters of recommendation. Electronic applications accepted. *Faculty research:* Discrete molecules and gases; dynamic phenomena; thermodynamics, statistical mechanical theory and quantum mechanical theory; atmospheric physics; biophysics.

University of Minnesota, Twin Cities Campus, College of Science and Engineering, Department of Chemistry, Minneapolis, MN 55455-0213. Offers chemical physics (MS, PhD); chemistry (MS, PhD). *Program availability:* Part-time. Terminal master's awarded for partial completion of doctoral program. *Degree requirements:* For master's, thesis or alternative; for doctorate, thesis/dissertation, preliminary candidacy exams. *Entrance requirements:* For master's and doctorate, GRE General Test. Additional exam requirements/recommendations for international students: Required—TOEFL. Electronic applications accepted. *Faculty research:* Analytical chemistry, environmental chemistry, organic chemistry, inorganic chemistry, materials chemistry, polymer chemistry, computational chemistry, experimental physical chemistry, chemical biology.

University of Nevada, Reno, Graduate School, Interdisciplinary Program in Chemical Physics, Reno, NV 89557. Offers PhD. *Degree requirements:* For doctorate, thesis/ dissertation. *Entrance requirements:* For doctorate, GRE, minimum GPA of 3.0. Additional exam requirements/recommendations for international students: Required—TOEFL (minimum score 500 paper-based; 61 iBT). Electronic applications accepted. *Faculty research:* Atomic and molecular physics, physical chemistry.

The University of Tennessee, Graduate School, College of Arts and Sciences, Department of Chemistry, Knoxville, TN 37996. Offers analytical chemistry (MS, PhD); chemical physics (PhD); environmental chemistry (MS, PhD); inorganic chemistry (MS, PhD); organic chemistry (MS, PhD); physical chemistry (MS, PhD); polymer chemistry (MS, PhD); theoretical chemistry (PhD). *Program availability:* Part-time. Terminal master's awarded for partial completion of doctoral program. *Degree requirements:* For master's, thesis; for doctorate, thesis/dissertation. *Entrance requirements:* For master's and doctorate, GRE General Test, minimum GPA of 2.7. Additional exam requirements/ recommendations for international students: Required—TOEFL. Electronic applications accepted.

University of Utah, Graduate School, College of Science, Department of Physics and Astronomy, Salt Lake City, UT 84112. Offers chemical physics (PhD); medical physics (MS, PhD); physics (MA, MS, PhD); physics teaching (PhD). *Program availability:* Part-time. *Faculty:* 37 full-time (4 women), 15 part-time/adjunct (2 women). *Students:* 69 full-time (21 women); includes 3 minority (all Hispanic/Latino), 30 international. Average age 27. In 2018, 3 master's, 17 doctorates awarded. Terminal master's awarded for partial completion of doctoral program. *Degree requirements:* For master's, comprehensive exam, https://gradschool.utah.edu/graduate-catalog/degree-requirements/; for doctorate, comprehensive exam, thesis/dissertation, https://gradschool.utah.edu/ graduate-catalog/degree-requirements/. *Entrance requirements:* For master's and doctorate, GRE General Test (Subject Test not required), minimum GPA of 3.0. Additional exam requirements/recommendations for international students: Required—TOEFL (minimum score 550 paper-based; 85 iBT). *Application deadline:* For fall admission, 1/15 for domestic and international students. Application fee: $55 ($65 for international students). Electronic applications accepted. *Expenses:* Https:// fbs.admin.utah.edu/income/tuition/. *Financial support:* In 2018–19, 67 students received support, including 66 research assistantships with full tuition reimbursements available (averaging $25,000 per year), 66 teaching assistantships with full tuition reimbursements available (averaging $25,000 per year); scholarships/grants, health care benefits, and unspecified assistantships also available. Financial award application deadline: 2/15; financial award applicants required to submit FAFSA. *Faculty research:* High-energy, cosmic-ray, medical physics, condensed matter, relativity applied physics, biophysics, astronomy and astrophysics. *Total annual research expenditures:* $6 million. *Unit head:* Dr. Christoph Bhoehme, Chair, 801-581-6806, Fax: 801-581-4801, E-mail: bhoeme@physics.utah.edu. *Application contact:* Bryce Nelson, Graduate Coordinator, 801-581-6861, Fax: 801-581-4801, E-mail: bryce@physics.utah.edu.
Website: http://www.physics.utah.edu/

Virginia Commonwealth University, Graduate School, College of Humanities and Sciences, Department of Chemistry, Richmond, VA 23284-9005. Offers analytical chemistry (MS, PhD); chemical physics (PhD); inorganic chemistry (MS, PhD); organic chemistry (MS, PhD); physical chemistry (MS, PhD). *Program availability:* Part-time. Terminal master's awarded for partial completion of doctoral program. *Degree requirements:* For master's, thesis; for doctorate, thesis/dissertation, comprehensive cumulative exams, research proposal. *Entrance requirements:* For master's, GRE General Test, 30 undergraduate credits in chemistry; for doctorate, GRE General Test. Additional exam requirements/recommendations for international students: Required—TOEFL (minimum score 600 paper-based; 100 iBT) or IELTS (minimum score 6.5). Electronic applications accepted. *Faculty research:* Physical, organic, inorganic, analytical, and polymer chemistry; chemical physics.

Wesleyan University, Graduate Studies, Department of Chemistry, Middletown, CT 06459. Offers biochemistry (PhD); chemical physics (PhD); inorganic chemistry (PhD); organic chemistry (PhD); physical chemistry (PhD); theoretical chemistry (PhD). *Faculty:* 11 full-time (3 women), 1 part-time/adjunct (0 women). *Students:* 16 full-time (9 women). Average age 25. In 2018, 4 doctorates awarded. Terminal master's awarded for partial completion of doctoral program. *Degree requirements:* For doctorate, thesis/ dissertation. *Entrance requirements:* For doctorate, GRE General Test, 3 recommendations. Additional exam requirements/recommendations for international students: Required—TOEFL, IELTS. *Application deadline:* 1/1 for domestic and international students; for summer admission, 1/1 for domestic and international students. Application fee: $0. Electronic applications accepted. *Financial support:* In 2018–19, 15 students received support, including 4 research assistantships with full tuition reimbursements available, 13 teaching assistantships with full tuition reimbursements available; institutionally sponsored loans and health care benefits also available. Financial award application deadline: 4/30. *Faculty research:* The synthesis of noble metal and noble metal alloy nanoparticles with well-defined shapes and catalytically-active high-energy surfaces; inorganic chemistry; materials science; scanning electron microscopy (SEM);transition organometallic complexes. *Unit head:* Michael A. Calter, Chair, 860-685-2633 Ext. 2633, Fax: 860-685-2211, E-mail: mcalter@wesleyan.edu. *Application contact:* Aracely Suto, Administrative Assistant, 860-685-2572, Fax: 860-685-2211, E-mail: chemistry@wesleyan.edu.
Website: http://www.wesleyan.edu/chem/

Condensed Matter Physics

Iowa State University of Science and Technology, Department of Physics and Astronomy, Ames, IA 50011. Offers applied physics (MS, PhD); astrophysics (MS, PhD); condensed matter physics (MS, PhD); high energy physics (MS, PhD); nuclear physics (MS, PhD); physics (MS, PhD). *Degree requirements:* For master's, thesis (for some programs); for doctorate, thesis/dissertation. *Entrance requirements:* For master's and doctorate, GRE General Test, GRE Subject Test (physics). Additional exam requirements/recommendations for international students: Required—TOEFL (minimum score 550 paper-based; 79 iBT), IELTS (minimum score 6.5). Electronic applications accepted. *Faculty research:* Condensed-matter physics, including superconductivity and new materials; high-energy and nuclear physics; astronomy and astrophysics; atmospheric and environmental physics.

Iowa State University of Science and Technology, Program in Condensed Matter Physics, Ames, IA 50011. Offers MS, PhD. *Entrance requirements:* For master's and doctorate, GRE. Additional exam requirements/recommendations for international students: Required—TOEFL (minimum score 550 paper-based; 79 iBT), IELTS (minimum score 6.5). Electronic applications accepted.

Memorial University of Newfoundland, School of Graduate Studies, Department of Physics and Physical Oceanography, St. John's, NL A1C 5S7, Canada. Offers atomic and molecular physics (PhD); condensed matter physics (PhD); physical oceanography (M Sc, PhD); physics (M Sc). *Program availability:* Part-time. *Degree requirements:* For master's, thesis, seminar presentation on thesis topic; for doctorate, comprehensive exam, thesis/dissertation, oral defense of thesis. *Entrance requirements:* For master's, honors B Sc or equivalent; for doctorate, M Sc or equivalent. Electronic applications accepted. *Faculty research:* Experiment and theory in atomic and molecular physics, condensed matter physics, physical oceanography, theoretical geophysics and applied nuclear physics.

Rutgers University–New Brunswick, Graduate School-New Brunswick, Department of Physics and Astronomy, Piscataway, NJ 08854-8097. Offers astronomy (MS, PhD); biophysics (PhD); condensed matter physics (MS, PhD); elementary particle physics (MS, PhD); intermediate energy nuclear physics (MS); nuclear physics (MS, PhD); physics (MST); surface science (PhD); theoretical physics (MS, PhD). *Program availability:* Part-time. Terminal master's awarded for partial completion of doctoral program. *Degree requirements:* For master's, comprehensive exam, thesis or alternative; for doctorate, comprehensive exam, thesis/dissertation. *Entrance requirements:* For master's and doctorate, GRE General Test, GRE Subject Test.

Additional exam requirements/recommendations for international students: Required—TOEFL (minimum score 560 paper-based). Electronic applications accepted. *Faculty research:* Astronomy, high energy, condensed matter, surface, nuclear physics.

University of Alberta, Faculty of Graduate Studies and Research, Department of Physics, Edmonton, AB T6G 2E1, Canada. Offers astrophysics (M Sc, PhD); condensed matter (M Sc, PhD); geophysics (M Sc, PhD); medical physics (M Sc, PhD); subatomic physics (M Sc, PhD). *Degree requirements:* For master's, thesis; for doctorate, thesis/dissertation. *Entrance requirements:* For master's and doctorate, minimum GPA of 7.0 on a 9.0 scale. Additional exam requirements/recommendations for international students: Required—TOEFL. *Faculty research:* Cosmology, astroparticle physics, high-intermediate energy, magnetism, superconductivity.

The University of Manchester, School of Physics and Astronomy, Manchester, United Kingdom. Offers astronomy and astrophysics (M Sc, PhD); biological physics (M Sc, PhD); condensed matter physics (M Sc, PhD); nonlinear and liquid crystals physics (M Sc, PhD); nuclear physics (M Sc, PhD); particle physics (M Sc, PhD); photon physics (M Sc, PhD); physics (M Sc, PhD); theoretical physics (M Sc, PhD).

University of Victoria, Faculty of Graduate Studies, Faculty of Science, Department of Physics and Astronomy, Victoria, BC V8W 2Y2, Canada. Offers astronomy and astrophysics (M Sc, PhD); condensed matter physics (M Sc, PhD); experimental particle physics (M Sc, PhD); medical physics (M Sc, PhD); ocean physics (M Sc, PhD); theoretical physics (M Sc, PhD). *Degree requirements:* For master's, thesis; for doctorate, comprehensive exam, thesis/dissertation, candidacy exam. *Entrance requirements:* For master's and doctorate, GRE. Additional exam requirements/recommendations for international students: Required—TOEFL (minimum score 575 paper-based), IELTS (minimum score 7). Electronic applications accepted. *Faculty research:* Old stellar populations; observational cosmology and large scale structure; cp violation; atlas.

Mathematical Physics

Indiana University Bloomington, University Graduate School, College of Arts and Sciences, Department of Mathematics, Bloomington, IN 47405. Offers applied mathematics (MA); mathematical physics (PhD); mathematics education (MAT); pure mathematics (MA, PhD). Terminal master's awarded for partial completion of doctoral program. *Degree requirements:* For doctorate, one foreign language, thesis/dissertation. *Entrance requirements:* For master's and doctorate, GRE General Test, GRE Subject Test. Additional exam requirements/recommendations for international students: Required—TOEFL. Electronic applications accepted. *Expenses:* Contact institution. *Faculty research:* Topology, geometry, algebra, applied mathematics, analysis.

New Mexico Institute of Mining and Technology, Center for Graduate Studies, Department of Physics, Socorro, NM 87801. Offers astrophysics (PhD); atmospheric physics (PhD); instrumentation (MS); mathematical physics (PhD); physics (MS). *Degree requirements:* For master's, thesis optional; for doctorate, thesis/dissertation. *Entrance requirements:* For master's, GRE General Test; for doctorate, GRE General Test, GRE Subject Test. Additional exam requirements/recommendations for international students: Required—TOEFL (minimum score 540 paper-based). *Faculty research:* Cloud physics, stellar and extragalactic processes.

University of Alberta, Faculty of Graduate Studies and Research, Department of Mathematical and Statistical Sciences, Edmonton, AB T6G 2E1, Canada. Offers applied

mathematics (M Sc, PhD); biostatistics (M Sc); mathematical finance (M Sc, PhD); mathematical physics (M Sc, PhD); mathematics (M Sc, PhD); statistics (M Sc, PhD, Postgraduate Diploma). *Program availability:* Part-time. Terminal master's awarded for partial completion of doctoral program. *Degree requirements:* For master's, thesis (for some programs); for doctorate, comprehensive exam, thesis/dissertation. *Entrance requirements:* Additional exam requirements/recommendations for international students: Required—TOEFL (minimum score 580 paper-based). Electronic applications accepted. *Faculty research:* Classical and functional analysis, algebra, differential equations, geometry.

University of Colorado Boulder, Graduate School, College of Arts and Sciences, Department of Physics, Boulder, CO 80309. Offers mathematical physics (PhD). Terminal master's awarded for partial completion of doctoral program. *Degree requirements:* For master's, comprehensive exam, thesis or alternative; for doctorate, comprehensive exam, thesis/dissertation. *Entrance requirements:* For master's and doctorate, GRE General Test, GRE Subject Test, minimum undergraduate GPA of 3.0. Additional exam requirements/recommendations for international students: Required—TOEFL. Electronic applications accepted. Application fee is waived when completed online. *Faculty research:* Physics; experimental physics; theoretical physics; high energy physics; optics.

Optical Sciences

Air Force Institute of Technology, Graduate School of Engineering and Management, Department of Electrical and Computer Engineering, Dayton, OH 45433-7765. Offers computer engineering (MS, PhD); computer systems/science (MS); electrical engineering (MS, PhD); electro-optics (MS, PhD). *Accreditation:* ABET (one or more programs are accredited). *Program availability:* Part-time. *Degree requirements:* For master's, thesis; for doctorate, thesis/dissertation. *Entrance requirements:* For master's and doctorate, GRE General Test, minimum GPA of 3.0, U.S. citizenship. *Faculty research:* Remote sensing, information survivability, microelectronics, computer networks, artificial intelligence.

Air Force Institute of Technology, Graduate School of Engineering and Management, Department of Engineering Physics, Dayton, OH 45433-7765. Offers applied physics (MS, PhD); electro-optics (MS, PhD); materials science (PhD); nuclear engineering (MS, PhD); space physics (MS). *Program availability:* Part-time. *Degree requirements:* For master's, thesis; for doctorate, thesis/dissertation. *Entrance requirements:* For master's and doctorate, GRE General Test, minimum GPA of 3.0, U.S. citizenship. *Faculty research:* High-energy lasers, space physics, nuclear weapon effects, semiconductor physics.

Alabama Agricultural and Mechanical University, School of Graduate Studies, College of Engineering, Technology, and Physical Sciences, Department of Physics, Chemistry and Mathematics, Huntsville, AL 35811. Offers physics (MS, PhD), including materials science (PhD), optics/lasers (PhD), space science (PhD). *Program availability:* Part-time, evening/weekend. *Degree requirements:* For doctorate, thesis/dissertation. *Entrance requirements:* For master's and doctorate, GRE General Test. Additional exam requirements/recommendations for international students: Required—TOEFL (minimum score 500 paper-based; 61 iBT). Electronic applications accepted.

Delaware State University, Graduate Programs, Department of Physics, Dover, DE 19901-2277. Offers applied optics (MS); optics (PhD); physics (MS); physics teaching (MS). *Program availability:* Part-time, evening/weekend. *Entrance requirements:* For master's, minimum GPA of 3.0 in major, 2.75 overall. Additional exam requirements/recommendations for international students: Required—TOEFL. Electronic applications accepted. *Faculty research:* Thermal properties of solids, nuclear physics, radiation damage in solids.

Duke University, Graduate School, Pratt School of Engineering, Master of Engineering Program, Durham, NC 27708-0271. Offers biomedical engineering (M Eng); civil engineering (M Eng); computational mechanics and scientific computing (M Eng); electrical and computer engineering (M Eng); environmental engineering (M Eng); materials science and engineering (M Eng); mechanical engineering (M Eng); photonics and optical sciences (M Eng); risk engineering (M Eng). *Program availability:* Part-time. *Entrance requirements:* For master's, GRE General Test, resume, 3 letters of recommendation, statement of purpose, transcripts. Additional exam requirements/recommendations for international students: Required—TOEFL. Electronic applications accepted.

École Polytechnique de Montréal, Graduate Programs, Department of Engineering Physics, Montréal, QC H3C 3A7, Canada. Offers optical engineering (M Eng, M Sc A, PhD); solid-state physics and engineering (M Eng, M Sc A, PhD). *Program availability:* Part-time. *Degree requirements:* For master's, one foreign language, thesis; for doctorate, one foreign language, thesis/dissertation. *Entrance requirements:* For master's, minimum GPA of 2.75; for doctorate, minimum GPA of 3.0. *Faculty research:* Optics, thin-film physics, laser spectroscopy, plasmas, photonic devices.

Norfolk State University, School of Graduate Studies, School of Science and Technology, Program in Optical Engineering, Norfolk, VA 23504. Offers MS.

North Carolina Agricultural and Technical State University, The Graduate College, College of Engineering, Department of Electrical and Computer Engineering, Greensboro, NC 27411. Offers electrical engineering (MSEE, PhD), including communications and signal processing, computer engineering, electronic and optical materials and devices, power systems and control. *Program availability:* Part-time. *Degree requirements:* For master's, project, thesis defense; for doctorate, thesis/dissertation. *Entrance requirements:* For master's, GRE General Test, GRE Subject Test, minimum GPA of 2.8; for doctorate, GRE General Test, minimum GPA of 3.0. *Faculty research:* Semiconductor compounds, VLSI design, image processing, optical systems and devices, fault-tolerant computing.

The Ohio State University, College of Optometry, Columbus, OH 43210. Offers optometry (OD); vision science (MS, PhD); OD/MS. *Accreditation:* AOA (one or more programs are accredited). *Faculty:* 34. *Students:* 275 (185 women); includes 52 minority (14 Black or African American, non-Hispanic/Latino; 21 Asian, non-Hispanic/Latino; 7

Peterson's Graduate Programs in the Physical Sciences, Mathematics, Agricultural Sciences, the Environment & Natural Resources 2020

www.petersons.com **143**

Hispanic/Latino; 10 Two or more races, non-Hispanic/Latino). Average age 24. In 2018, 14 master's, 67 doctorates awarded. *Degree requirements:* For master's, thesis; for doctorate, thesis/dissertation. *Entrance requirements:* For master's, GRE; for doctorate, GRE (for PhD); OAT (for OD). Additional exam requirements/recommendations for international students: Required—TOEFL minimum score 550 paper-based, 79 iBT, Michigan English Language Assessment Battery minimum score 82, IELTS minimum score 7 (for MS and PhD); TOEFL minimum score 577 paper-based; 90 iBT, Michigan English Language Assessment Battery minimum score 84, IELTS minimum score 7.5 (for OD). *Application deadline:* For fall admission, 3/31 for domestic and international students; for spring admission, 12/1 for domestic students, 11/1 for international students. Applications are processed on a rolling basis. Application fee: $60 ($70 for international students). Electronic applications accepted. *Expenses:* Contact institution. *Financial support:* Research assistantships with full tuition reimbursements, teaching assistantships with full tuition reimbursements, institutionally sponsored loans, and scholarships/grants available. Financial award application deadline: 2/15; financial award applicants required to submit FAFSA. *Unit head:* Dr. Karla Zadnik, Dean, 614-292-6603, E-mail: zadnik.4@osu.edu. *Application contact:* Office of Student Affairs, College of Optometry, 614-292-2647, Fax: 614-292-7493, E-mail: admissions@optometry.osu.edu.
Website: http://www.optometry.osu.edu/

Rochester Institute of Technology, Graduate Enrollment Services, College of Science, Center for Imaging Science, MS Program in Color Science, Rochester, NY 14623-5603. Offers MS. *Program availability:* Part-time. *Students:* 1 full-time (0 women), 1 part-time, 1 international. Average age 29. 2 applicants, 50% accepted. In 2018, 2 master's awarded. *Degree requirements:* For master's, thesis. *Entrance requirements:* For master's, GRE, minimum GPA of 3.0 (recommended), one-page personal statement, resume, two letters of recommendation, on-campus interview (when possible). Additional exam requirements/recommendations for international students: Required—TOEFL (minimum score 600 paper-based; 100 iBT), IELTS (minimum score 7), PTE (minimum score 68). *Application deadline:* For fall admission, 2/15 priority date for domestic and international students; for spring admission, 12/15 priority date for domestic and international students. Applications are processed on a rolling basis. Application fee: $65. Electronic applications accepted. *Financial support:* Research assistantships with partial tuition reimbursements, teaching assistantships with partial tuition reimbursements, career-related internships or fieldwork, scholarships/grants, and unspecified assistantships available. Support available to part-time students. Financial award applicants required to submit FAFSA. *Faculty research:* Individual differences in color vision, color and appearance reproduction of cultural heritage, color perception in augmented reality; color measurement and specification of materials, perceptual psychophysics of color and images. *Unit head:* Dr. Mark Fairchild, Head of the Integrated Sciences Academy, 585-475-2784, Fax: 585-475-5988, E-mail: fairchild@cis.rit.edu. *Application contact:* Diane Ellison, Senior Associate Vice President, Graduate Enrollment Services, 585-475-2229, Fax: 585-475-7164, E-mail: gradinfo@rit.edu.
Website: https://www.rit.edu/study/color-science-ms

Rochester Institute of Technology, Graduate Enrollment Services, College of Science, Center for Imaging Science, MS Program in Imaging Science, Rochester, NY 14623-5603. Offers MS. *Program availability:* Part-time, evening/weekend, 100% online, blended/hybrid learning. *Students:* 11 full-time (2 women), 10 part-time; includes 1 minority (Two or more races, non-Hispanic/Latino), 9 international. Average age 28. 16 applicants, 75% accepted, 9 enrolled. In 2018, 5 master's awarded. *Degree requirements:* For master's, thesis or alternative, Thesis or paper/project. *Entrance requirements:* For master's, GRE, minimum GPA of 3.0 (recommended), personal statement, resume, two letters of recommendation. Additional exam requirements/recommendations for international students: Required—TOEFL (minimum score 600 paper-based; 100 iBT), IELTS (minimum score 7), PTE (minimum score 68). *Application deadline:* For fall admission, 2/15 priority date for domestic and international students; for spring admission, 12/15 priority date for domestic students, 12/14 priority date for international students. Applications are processed on a rolling basis. Application fee: $65. Electronic applications accepted. *Financial support:* In 2018–19, 9 students received support. Research assistantships with partial tuition reimbursements available, teaching assistantships with partial tuition reimbursements available, career-related internships or fieldwork, scholarships/grants, and unspecified assistantships available. Support available to part-time students. Financial award applicants required to submit FAFSA. *Faculty research:* Astronomy and space science, biomedical imaging, cultural artifact document imaging, detector research, disaster response, nano-imaging and materials, optics, printing, remote sensing, vision, document library. *Unit head:* Charles Bachmann, Graduate Program Director, 585-475-7238, Fax: 585-475-5988, E-mail: cmbpci@rit.edu. *Application contact:* Diane Ellison, Senior Associate Vice President, Graduate Enrollment Services, 585-475-2229, Fax: 585-475-7164, E-mail: gradinfo@rit.edu.
Website: https://www.rit.edu/study/imaging-science-ms

Rochester Institute of Technology, Graduate Enrollment Services, College of Science, Center for Imaging Science, PhD Program in Color Science, Rochester, NY 14623-5603. Offers PhD. *Program availability:* Part-time. *Students:* 11 full-time (5 women), 4 part-time (3 women); includes 1 minority (Two or more races, non-Hispanic/Latino), 9 international. Average age 28. 9 applicants, 56% accepted, 4 enrolled. Terminal master's awarded for partial completion of doctoral program. *Degree requirements:* For doctorate, comprehensive exam, thesis/dissertation. *Entrance requirements:* For doctorate, GRE, minimum GPA of 3.0 (recommended), one-page personal statement, resume, two letters of recommendation. Additional exam requirements/recommendations for international students: Required—TOEFL (minimum score 600 paper-based; 100 iBT), IELTS (minimum score 7), PTE (minimum score 68). *Application deadline:* For fall admission, 1/15 priority date for domestic and international students. Applications are processed on a rolling basis. Application fee: $65. Electronic applications accepted. *Expenses:* Contact institution. *Financial support:* In 2018–19, 14 students received support. Research assistantships with full tuition reimbursements available, teaching assistantships with partial tuition reimbursements available, career-related internships or fieldwork, scholarships/grants, health care benefits, and unspecified assistantships available. Financial award applicants required to submit FAFSA. *Faculty research:* Individual differences in color vision, color and appearance reproduction of cultural heritage, color perception in augmented reality; color measurement and specification of materials, perceptual psychophysics of color and images. *Unit head:* Dr. Mark Fairchild, Graduate Program Director, 585-475-2784, E-mail: fairchild@cis.rit.edu. *Application contact:* Diane Ellison, Senior Associate Vice President, Graduate Enrollment Services, 585-475-2229, Fax: 585-475-7164, E-mail: gradinfo@rit.edu.
Website: https://www.rit.edu/study/color-science-phd

Rochester Institute of Technology, Graduate Enrollment Services, College of Science, Center for Imaging Science, PhD Program in Imaging Science, Rochester, NY 14623-5603. Offers PhD. *Program availability:* Part-time. *Students:* 76 full-time (16 women), 19 part-time (3 women); includes 2 minority (1 Asian, non-Hispanic/Latino; 1 Two or more races, non-Hispanic/Latino), 63 international. Average age 28. 41 applicants, 71% accepted, 15 enrolled. In 2018, 2 doctorates awarded. Terminal master's awarded for partial completion of doctoral program. *Degree requirements:* For doctorate, comprehensive exam, thesis/dissertation. *Entrance requirements:* For doctorate, GRE, Hold a bachalaureate degree in engineering, computer science, applied mathematics, or a natural science. Completed courses in calculus, university physics, modern physics, and a computer language. Personal statement. Resume. Two letters of recommendation. Additional exam requirements/recommendations for international students: Required—TOEFL (minimum score 600 paper-based; 100 iBT), IELTS (minimum score 7), PTE (minimum score 68). *Application deadline:* For fall admission, 1/15 priority date for domestic and international students. Applications are processed on a rolling basis. Application fee: $65. Electronic applications accepted. *Expenses:* Contact institution. *Financial support:* In 2018–19, 76 students received support. Research assistantships with full tuition reimbursements available, teaching assistantships with partial tuition reimbursements available, career-related internships or fieldwork, scholarships/grants, health care benefits, and unspecified assistantships available. Support available to part-time students. Financial award applicants required to submit FAFSA. *Faculty research:* Astronomy and space science, biomedical imaging, cultural artifact document imaging, detector research, disaster response, nano-imaging and materials, optics, printing, remote sensing, vision, document library. *Unit head:* Charles Bachmann, Graduate Program Director, 585-475-7238, Fax: 585-475-5988, E-mail: cmbpci@rit.edu. *Application contact:* Diane Ellison, Senior Associate Vice President, Graduate Enrollment Services, 585-475-2229, Fax: 585-475-7164, E-mail: gradinfo@rit.edu.
Website: https://www.rit.edu/study/imaging-science-phd

Rose-Hulman Institute of Technology, Graduate Studies, Department of Physics and Optical Engineering, Terre Haute, IN 47803-3999. Offers optical engineering (MS). *Program availability:* Part-time. *Faculty:* 18 full-time (2 women), 1 part-time/adjunct (0 women). *Students:* 4 full-time (0 women), 6 part-time (0 women); includes 2 minority (both Asian, non-Hispanic/Latino), 5 international. Average age 25. 10 applicants, 50% accepted, 3 enrolled. In 2018, 5 master's awarded. *Degree requirements:* For master's, thesis. *Entrance requirements:* For master's, GRE, minimum GPA of 3.0. Additional exam requirements/recommendations for international students: Required—TOEFL (minimum score 580 paper-based; 94 iBT), IELTS (minimum score 7). *Application deadline:* For fall admission, 2/1 priority date for domestic and international students; for winter admission, 10/1 for domestic students, 4/1 for international students; for spring admission, 1/15 for domestic students, 11/1 for international students. Applications are processed on a rolling basis. Application fee: $0. Electronic applications accepted. *Expenses: Tuition:* Full-time $46,641. *Financial support:* In 2018–19, 10 students received support. Fellowships with tuition reimbursements available, research assistantships with tuition reimbursements available, institutionally sponsored loans, scholarships/grants, and tuition waivers (full and partial) available. *Faculty research:* Non-linear optics/laser physics and photo refractive materials; integrated optics and optical MEMS; fiber optics, fiber optic communications, and optical system design; semiconductor materials, acoustics, and asteroid photometry; holography and speckles; micro- and nano-technology and nanomedicine. *Total annual research expenditures:* $373,779. *Unit head:* Dr. Galen Duree, Department Head, 812-872-6025, Fax: 812-877-8023, E-mail: duree@rose-hulman.edu. *Application contact:* Dr. Craig Downing, Associate Dean of Lifelong Learning, 812-877-8822, E-mail: downing@rose-hulman.edu.
Website: https://www.rose-hulman.edu/academics/academic-departments/physics-and-optical-engineering/index.html

The University of Alabama in Huntsville, School of Graduate Studies, College of Engineering, Department of Electrical and Computer Engineering, Huntsville, AL 35899. Offers computer engineering (MSE, PhD); electrical engineering (MSE, PhD), including optics and photonics technology (MSE); optical science and engineering (PhD); software engineering (MSSE). *Program availability:* Part-time. *Faculty:* 22 full-time (4 women), 4 part-time/adjunct. *Students:* 65 full-time (12 women), 125 part-time (12 women); includes 12 minority (5 Black or African American, non-Hispanic/Latino; 5 Asian, non-Hispanic/Latino; 2 Hispanic/Latino), 61 international. Average age 31. 199 applicants, 78% accepted, 46 enrolled. In 2018, 42 master's, 11 doctorates awarded. *Degree requirements:* For master's, comprehensive exam, thesis or alternative, oral and written exams; for doctorate, comprehensive exam, thesis/dissertation, oral and written exams. *Entrance requirements:* For master's, GRE General Test, appropriate bachelor's degree, minimum GPA of 3.0; for doctorate, GRE General Test, minimum GPA of 3.0. Additional exam requirements/recommendations for international students: Required—TOEFL (minimum score 500 paper-based; 80 iBT), IELTS (minimum score 6.5). *Application deadline:* For fall admission, 7/15 priority date for domestic students, 4/1 priority date for international students; for spring admission, 11/30 priority date for domestic students, 9/1 priority date for international students. Applications are processed on a rolling basis. Application fee: $50. Electronic applications accepted. *Expenses: Tuition, area resident:* Full-time $10,632; part-time $412 per credit hour. Tuition, state resident: full-time $10,632. Tuition, nonresident: full-time $23,604; part-time $412 per credit hour. *Required fees:* $582; $582. Tuition and fees vary according to course load and program. *Financial support:* In 2018–19, 37 students received support, including 18 research assistantships with full tuition reimbursements available (averaging $5,783 per year), 19 teaching assistantships with full tuition reimbursements available (averaging $5,813 per year); career-related internships or fieldwork, Federal Work-Study, institutionally sponsored loans, scholarships/grants, health care benefits, tuition waivers (full and partial), and unspecified assistantships also available. Support available to part-time students. Financial award application deadline: 4/1; financial award applicants required to submit FAFSA. *Faculty research:* Advanced computer architecture and systems, fault tolerant computing and verification, computational electro-magnetics, nano-photonics and plasmonics, micro electro-mechanical (MEMS) systems. *Unit head:* Dr. Ravi Gorur, Chair, 256-824-6316, Fax: 256-824-6803, E-mail: ravi.gorur@uah.edu. *Application contact:* Kim Gray, Graduate Studies Admissions Coordinator, 256-824-6002, Fax: 256-824-6405, E-mail: deangrad@uah.edu.
Website: http://www.ece.uah.edu/

The University of Arizona, College of Optical Sciences, Tucson, AZ 85721. Offers MS, PhD, Graduate Certificate. *Program availability:* Part-time. *Degree requirements:* For master's, thesis (for some programs), exam; for doctorate, thesis/dissertation, oral and written exams. *Entrance requirements:* For master's, GRE General Test, GRE Subject Test (recommended), minimum GPA of 3.0, 2 letters of recommendation, resume; for doctorate, GRE General Test, GRE Subject Test (recommended), minimum GPA of 3.0, 2 letters of recommendation, statement of purpose, resume. Additional exam requirements/recommendations for international students: Required—TOEFL. Electronic applications accepted. *Faculty research:* Medical optics, medical imaging, optical data storage, optical bistability, nonlinear optical effects.

University of Central Florida, College of Optics and Photonics, Orlando, FL 32816. Offers MS, PhD. *Program availability:* Part-time, evening/weekend. *Faculty:* 41 full-time (3 women), 9 part-time/adjunct (1 woman). *Students:* 121 full-time (28 women), 21 part-time (2 women); includes 14 minority (1 Black or African American, non-Hispanic/Latino;

4 Asian, non-Hispanic/Latino; 8 Hispanic/Latino; 1 Two or more races, non-Hispanic/Latino), 90 international. Average age 28. 167 applicants, 43% accepted, 27 enrolled. In 2018, 21 master's, 12 doctorates awarded. *Degree requirements:* For master's, thesis or alternative; for doctorate, thesis/dissertation, departmental qualifying exam, candidacy exam. *Entrance requirements:* For master's and doctorate, GRE General Test, minimum GPA of 3.0 in last 60 hours, goal statement, letters of recommendation, resume. Additional exam requirements/recommendations for international students: Required—TOEFL. *Application deadline:* For fall admission, 7/15 for domestic students; for spring admission, 12/1 for domestic students. Application fee: $30. Electronic applications accepted. *Financial support:* In 2018–19, 116 students received support, including 25 fellowships with partial tuition reimbursements available (averaging $22,304 per year), 106 research assistantships with partial tuition reimbursements available (averaging $15,182 per year), 9 teaching assistantships with partial tuition reimbursements available (averaging $14,404 per year); career-related internships or fieldwork, Federal Work-Study, institutionally sponsored loans, health care benefits, tuition waivers (partial), and unspecified assistantships also available. Financial award application deadline: 3/1; financial award applicants required to submit FAFSA. *Faculty research:* Lasers, fiber optics, optoelectronics and integrated photonics, nonlinear and quantum optics, imaging, sensing and display. *Unit head:* Dr. Bahaa E. Saleh, Dean and Director, 407-823-6817, E-mail: besaleh@creol.ucf.edu. *Application contact:* Associate Director, Graduate Admissions, 407-823-2766, Fax: 407-823-6442, E-mail: gradadmissions@ucf.edu.
Website: http://www.creol.ucf.edu/

University of Dayton, Department of Electro-Optics and Photonics, Dayton, OH 45469. Offers electro-optics (MSEO, PhD). *Degree requirements:* For master's, thesis, 30 credits, minimum GPA of 3.0; for doctorate, comprehensive exam, thesis/dissertation, 60 credits beyond master's degree, candidacy exam, minimum GPA of 3.0, 6 credits of math. *Entrance requirements:* For master's, minimum GPA of 3.0 in electrical engineering, physics or other related disciplines; for doctorate, master's degree with minimum GPA of 3.5. Additional exam requirements/recommendations for international students: Required—TOEFL (minimum score 550 paper-based; 80 iBT); Recommended—IELTS. Electronic applications accepted. *Faculty research:* Non-linear optics, polarization, nano-optics, adaptive optics.

University of New Mexico, Graduate Studies, College of Arts and Sciences, Program in Optical Science and Engineering, Albuquerque, NM 87131-2039. Offers imaging science (MS, PhD); optical science and engineering (MS, PhD); photonics (MS, PhD). Program held jointly with the Department of Physics and Astronomy and the Department of Electrical and Computer Engineering. *Program availability:* Part-time. *Students:* Average age 30. 50 applicants, 24% accepted, 8 enrolled. In 2018, 4 master's, 8 doctorates awarded. Terminal master's awarded for partial completion of doctoral program. *Degree requirements:* For master's, comprehensive exam (for some programs), thesis (for some programs); for doctorate, comprehensive exam, thesis/dissertation. *Entrance requirements:* For master's, GRE General Test, GRE Subject Test in physics (preferred), relevant undergraduate coursework, curriculum vitae, letters of recommendation, letter of intent/personal statement; for doctorate, GRE General Test, GRE Subject Test in physics (preferred), relevant undergraduate coursework, curriculum vitae, letters of recommendation. Additional exam requirements/recommendations for international students: Required—TOEFL (minimum score 575 paper-based; 79 iBT), IELTS (minimum score 7). *Application deadline:* For fall admission, 1/15 priority date for domestic and international students; for spring admission, 8/1 priority date for domestic and international students. Application fee: $50. Electronic applications accepted. *Financial support:* Fellowships with full tuition reimbursements, research assistantships with full tuition reimbursements, teaching assistantships with full tuition reimbursements, career-related internships or fieldwork, scholarships/grants, health care benefits, and unspecified assistantships available. Support available to part-time students. Financial award application deadline: 2/1; financial award applicants required to submit FAFSA. *Faculty research:* Advanced materials, atom optics, biomedical optics, fiber optics, laser cooling, high intensity interactions, lithography, nano-photonics, nonlinear optics, optical imaging, optical sensors, optoelectronics, quantum optics, spectroscopy, ultrafast phenomena. *Unit head:* Dr. Majeed Hayat, Chair, 505-272-7095, Fax: 505-277-7801, E-mail: hayat@ece.unm.edu. *Application contact:* Doris Williams, Advisor, 505-277-7764, Fax: 505-277-7801, E-mail: dorisw@chtm.unm.edu.
Website: http://www.optics.unm.edu/

The University of North Carolina at Charlotte, College of Liberal Arts and Sciences, Department of Physics and Optical Science, Charlotte, NC 28223-0001. Offers applied physics (MS); optical science and engineering (MS, PhD). *Students:* 46 full-time (14 women), 11 part-time (2 women); includes 3 minority (1 Black or African American, non-Hispanic/Latino; 1 Hispanic/Latino; 1 Two or more races, non-Hispanic/Latino), 27 international. Average age 28. 35 applicants, 49% accepted, 7 enrolled. In 2018, 10 master's, 14 doctorates awarded. *Entrance requirements:* For master's, GRE, bachelor's degree in physics or closely-allied field; minimum overall GPA of 2.75, major 3.0; demonstrated evidence of sufficient interest, ability, and preparation in physics to adequately profit from graduate study; for doctorate, GRE, baccalaureate or master's degree in physics, chemistry, mathematics, engineering, optics, or related field with minimum undergraduate GPA of 3.0 overall, 3.2 in major and graduate; letters of recommendation. Additional exam requirements/recommendations for international students: Required—TOEFL (minimum score 523 paper-based; 70 iBT), IELTS (minimum score 6), TOEFL (minimum score 523 paper-based, 70 iBT) or IELTS (6). *Application deadline:* Applications are processed on a rolling basis. Application fee: $75. Electronic applications accepted. Tuition and fees vary according to course load and program. *Financial support:* Fellowships, research assistantships, teaching assistantships, career-related internships or fieldwork, institutionally sponsored loans, scholarships/grants, and unspecified assistantships available. Support available to part-time students. Financial award application deadline: 3/1; financial award applicants required to submit FAFSA. *Total annual research expenditures:* $2.1 million. *Unit head:* Dr. Glen Boreman, Chair, 704-687-8132. *Application contact:* Kathy B. Giddings, Director of Graduate Admissions, 704-687-5503, Fax: 704-687-1668, E-mail: gradadm@uncc.edu.
Website: http://physics.uncc.edu/

University of Rochester, Hajim School of Engineering and Applied Sciences, Institute of Optics, Rochester, NY 14627. Offers MS, PhD. *Program availability:* Part-time. *Faculty:* 19 full-time (1 woman). *Students:* 127 full-time (27 women), 6 part-time (1 woman); includes 21 minority (2 Black or African American, non-Hispanic/Latino; 10 Asian, non-Hispanic/Latino; 6 Hispanic/Latino; 3 Two or more races, non-Hispanic/Latino), 67 international. Average age 26. 275 applicants, 55% accepted, 45 enrolled. In 2018, 31 master's, 15 doctorates awarded. *Degree requirements:* For master's, thesis (for some programs); for doctorate, thesis/dissertation. *Entrance requirements:* For master's and doctorate, GRE, transcripts, three letters of recommendation, statement of purpose, resume/curriculum vitae. Additional exam requirements/recommendations for international students: Required—TOEFL (minimum score 620 paper-based; 105 iBT), IELTS (minimum score 7.2). Application fee: $60. Electronic applications accepted. *Expenses: Tuition:* Full-time $52,974; part-time $1654 per credit hour. *Required fees:* $612. One-time fee: $30 part-time. Tuition and fees vary according to campus/location and program. *Financial support:* In 2018–19, 154 students received support, including 26 fellowships with full and partial tuition reimbursements available (averaging $30,000 per year), 86 research assistantships with full and partial tuition reimbursements available (averaging $30,000 per year), 42 teaching assistantships with full and partial tuition reimbursements available (averaging $9,996 per year); health care benefits and tuition waivers (full and partial) also available. *Faculty research:* Biomedical optics, fibers and optical communication, image science and systems, nanooptics and nanophotonics, optical engineering and design. *Total annual research expenditures:* $14.6 million. *Unit head:* Scott Carney, Director/Professor of Optics, 585-274-0113, E-mail: scott.carney@rochester.edu. *Application contact:* Kai Davies, Graduate Program Coordinator, 585-275-7629, E-mail: kai.davies@rochester.edu.
Website: http://www.hajim.rochester.edu/optics/graduate/index.html

Photonics

Duke University, Graduate School, Pratt School of Engineering, Master of Engineering Program, Durham, NC 27708-0271. Offers biomedical engineering (M Eng); civil engineering (M Eng); computational mechanics and scientific computing (M Eng); electrical and computer engineering (M Eng); environmental engineering (M Eng); materials science and engineering (M Eng); mechanical engineering (M Eng); photonics and optical sciences (M Eng); risk engineering (M Eng). *Program availability:* Part-time. *Entrance requirements:* For master's, GRE General Test, resume, 3 letters of recommendation, statement of purpose, transcripts. Additional exam requirements/recommendations for international students: Required—TOEFL. Electronic applications accepted.

Johns Hopkins University, Engineering Program for Professionals, Part-time Program in Electrical and Computer Engineering, Baltimore, MD 21218. Offers communications and networking (MS); electrical and computer engineering (Graduate Certificate, Post-Master's Certificate); photonics (MS). *Program availability:* Part-time, evening/weekend, 100% online, blended/hybrid learning. *Faculty:* 1 full-time, 47 part-time/adjunct (2 women). *Students:* 364 part-time (60 women). 119 applicants, 68% accepted, 53 enrolled. In 2018, 101 master's awarded. *Entrance requirements:* Additional exam requirements/recommendations for international students: Required—TOEFL (minimum score 600 paper-based; 100 iBT). *Application deadline:* Applications are processed on a rolling basis. Application fee: $0. Electronic applications accepted. *Unit head:* Dr. Brian Jennison, Program Chair, 443-778-6421, E-mail: brian.jennison@jhuapl.edu. *Application contact:* Doug Schiller, Admissions Director, 410-516-2300, Fax: 410-579-8049, E-mail: schiller@jhu.edu.
Website: http://www.ep.jhu.edu/

Lehigh University, College of Arts and Sciences, Department of Physics, Bethlehem, PA 18015. Offers photonics (MS); physics (MS, PhD). *Faculty:* 15 full-time (4 women), 3 part-time/adjunct (0 women). *Students:* 43 full-time (16 women), 1 part-time (0 women); includes 3 minority (all Asian, non-Hispanic/Latino), 15 international. Average age 27. 106 applicants, 26% accepted, 11 enrolled. In 2018, 6 master's, 6 doctorates awarded. *Degree requirements:* For doctorate, comprehensive exam, thesis/dissertation. *Entrance requirements:* For master's and doctorate, GRE General Test. Additional exam requirements/recommendations for international students: Required—TOEFL (minimum score 85 iBT), TOEFL required unless attended another school in US for two or more years. *Application deadline:* For fall admission, 1/15 for domestic and international students. Application fee: $75. Electronic applications accepted. Tuition and fees vary according to program. *Financial support:* In 2018–19, 39 students received support, including 1 fellowship with full tuition reimbursement available (averaging $34,000 per year), 10 research assistantships with full tuition reimbursements available (averaging $29,340 per year), 28 teaching assistantships with full tuition reimbursements available (averaging $29,340 per year); scholarships/grants and health care benefits also available. Financial award application deadline: 1/15. *Faculty research:* Condensed matter physics; atomic, molecular and optical physics; biophysics; nonlinear optics and photonics; astronomy and astrophysics; high energy nuclear physics. *Total annual research expenditures:* $1.2 million. *Unit head:* Dr. Volkmar Dierolf, Chair, 610-758-3909, Fax: 610-758-5730, E-mail: vod2@lehigh.edu. *Application contact:* Dr. Joshua Pepper, Graduate Admissions Officer, 610-758-3649, Fax: 610-758-5730, E-mail: jap612@lehigh.edu.
Website: http://www.physics.cas2.lehigh.edu

Lehigh University, P.C. Rossin College of Engineering and Applied Science, Department of Electrical and Computer Engineering, Bethlehem, PA 18015. Offers electrical engineering (M Eng, MS, PhD); photonics (MS). *Program availability:* Part-time. *Faculty:* 16 full-time (4 women). *Students:* 79 full-time (8 women), 73 international. Average age 25. 269 applicants, 27% accepted, 19 enrolled. In 2018, 35 master's, 7 doctorates awarded. Terminal master's awarded for partial completion of doctoral program. *Degree requirements:* For master's, thesis optional; for doctorate, thesis/dissertation, qualifying or comprehensive exam for all 1st year PhD's; general exam 7 months or more prior to completion/dissertation defense. *Entrance requirements:* For master's and doctorate, GRE General Test, BS in field or related field. Additional exam requirements/recommendations for international students: Required—TOEFL (minimum score 79 iBT), IELTS (minimum score 6.5), TOEFL or IELTS; Recommended—TSE. *Application deadline:* For fall admission, 4/1 for domestic and international students; for spring admission, 11/1 for domestic and international students. Application fee: $75. Electronic applications accepted. Tuition and fees vary according to program. *Financial support:* In 2018–19, 52 students received support, including 5 fellowships with full tuition reimbursements available (averaging $29,400 per year), 40 research assistantships with full tuition reimbursements available (averaging $29,400 per year), 7 teaching assistantships with full tuition reimbursements available (averaging $29,400 per year). Financial award application deadline: 1/15. *Faculty research:* Bio-electrical engineering, communications and signal processing, computer engineering, electric

energy, electronics and photonics. *Total annual research expenditures:* $4 million. *Unit head:* Dr. Chengshan Xiao, Chair, 610-758-4069, Fax: 610-758-6279, E-mail: chx417@lehigh.edu. *Application contact:* Diane Hubinsky, Graduate Coordinator, 610-758-4072, Fax: 610-758-6279, E-mail: dih2@lehigh.edu.
Website: http://www.ece.lehigh.edu/

Lehigh University, P.C. Rossin College of Engineering and Applied Science, Department of Materials Science and Engineering, Bethlehem, PA 18015. Offers materials science and engineering (M Eng, MS, PhD); photonics (MS); polymer science/engineering (M Eng, MS, PhD); MBA/E. *Program availability:* Part-time. *Faculty:* 16 full-time (4 women). *Students:* 24 full-time (6 women), 2 part-time (1 woman); includes 4 minority (1 Black or African American, non-Hispanic/Latino; 1 Hispanic/Latino; 2 Two or more races, non-Hispanic/Latino), 5 international. Average age 25. 107 applicants, 19% accepted, 8 enrolled. In 2018, 4 master's, 7 doctorates awarded. *Degree requirements:* For master's, thesis; for doctorate, comprehensive exam, thesis/dissertation. *Entrance requirements:* For master's and doctorate, GRE General Test, minimum GPA of 3.60. Additional exam requirements/recommendations for international students: Required—TOEFL (minimum score 487 paper-based; 85 iBT), IELTS (minimum score 6.5), TOEFL or IELTS required. *Application deadline:* For fall admission, 1/15 priority date for domestic students, 1/15 for international students; for spring admission, 12/1 priority date for domestic students, 12/1 for international students. Application fee: $75. Tuition and fees vary according to program. *Financial support:* In 2018–19, 26 students received support, including 9 fellowships with tuition reimbursements available (averaging $12,848 per year), 14 research assistantships with tuition reimbursements available (averaging $29,640 per year), 12 teaching assistantships with tuition reimbursements available (averaging $7,350 per year); scholarships/grants and health care benefits also available. Financial award application deadline: 1/15. *Faculty research:* Metals, ceramics, crystals, polymers, fatigue crack propagation, biomaterials. *Total annual research expenditures:* $2.7 million. *Unit head:* Dr. Wojciech Misiolek, Chairperson, 610-758-4252, Fax: 610-758-4244, E-mail: wzm2@lehigh.edu. *Application contact:* Lisa Carreras Arechiga, Graduate Administrative Coordinator, 610-758-4222, Fax: 610-758-4244, E-mail: lia4@lehigh.edu.
Website: https://engineering.lehigh.edu/matsci

Oklahoma State University, College of Arts and Sciences, Department of Physics, Stillwater, OK 74078. Offers photonics (MS, PhD). *Faculty:* 27 full-time (6 women). *Students:* 2 full-time (0 women), 37 part-time (5 women); includes 2 minority (1 Hispanic/Latino; 1 Two or more races, non-Hispanic/Latino), 23 international. Average age 28. 70 applicants, 24% accepted, 11 enrolled. In 2018, 4 master's, 6 doctorates awarded. *Entrance requirements:* For master's and doctorate, GRE. Additional exam requirements/recommendations for international students: Required—TOEFL (minimum score 550 paper-based; 79 iBT). *Application deadline:* For fall admission, 3/1 priority date for international students; for spring admission, 8/1 priority date for international students. Applications are processed on a rolling basis. Application fee: $40 ($75 for international students). Electronic applications accepted. *Expenses: Tuition, area resident:* Full-time $4148. Tuition, state resident: full-time $4148. Tuition, nonresident: full-time $10,517. *International tuition:* $10,517 full-time. *Required fees:* $4394; $2929 per credit hour. Tuition and fees vary according to course load and program. *Financial support:* Research assistantships, teaching assistantships, career-related internships or fieldwork, Federal Work-Study, scholarships/grants, health care benefits, tuition waivers (partial), and unspecified assistantships available. Support available to part-time students. Financial award application deadline: 3/1; financial award applicants required to submit FAFSA. *Faculty research:* Lasers and photonics, non-linear optical materials, turbulence, structure and function of biological membranes, particle theory. *Unit head:* Dr. David N McIlroy, Department Head, 405-744-5796, Fax: 405-744-6811, E-mail: dave.mcilroy@okstate.edu. *Application contact:* Dr. Albert T. Rosenberger, Graduate Coordinator, 405-744-6742, Fax: 405-744-6811, E-mail: physics.grad.coordinator@okstate.edu.
Website: http://physics.okstate.edu/

Princeton University, Princeton Institute for the Science and Technology of Materials (PRISM), Princeton, NJ 08544-1019. Offers materials (PhD).

Queens College of the City University of New York, Mathematics and Natural Sciences Division, Department of Physics, Queens, NY 11367-1597. Offers photonics (MS); physics (MA). *Program availability:* Part-time. *Faculty:* 12 full-time, 1 part-time/adjunct. *Students:* 5 full-time (3 women), 12 part-time (5 women); includes 5 minority (1 Black or African American, non-Hispanic/Latino; 1 Hispanic/Latino; 3 Two or more races, non-Hispanic/Latino), 7 international. Average age 30. In 2018, 3 master's awarded. *Degree requirements:* For master's, thesis optional. *Entrance requirements:* For master's, previous course work in calculus, minimum GPA of 3.0. Additional exam requirements/recommendations for international students: Required—TOEFL (minimum score 61 iBT), IELTS (minimum score 5). *Application deadline:* For fall admission, 6/1 for domestic students; for spring admission, 11/1 for domestic students. Applications are processed on a rolling basis. Application fee: $125. Electronic applications accepted. *Financial support:* Teaching assistantships, career-related internships or fieldwork, Federal Work-Study, and institutionally sponsored loans available. Financial award application deadline: 4/1; financial award applicants required to submit FAFSA. *Faculty research:* Photonics, devices, spectroscopy and transport in condensed matter, bio-mimetics. *Unit head:* Dr. Steven Schwarz, Chair, 718-997-3385, E-mail: steven.schwarz@qc.cuny.edu. *Application contact:* Elizabeth D'Amico-Ramirez, Assistant Director of Graduate Admissions, 718-997-5203, E-mail: elizabeth.damicoramirez@qc.cuny.edu.
Website: http://physics.qc.cuny.edu/

Stevens Institute of Technology, Graduate School, Charles V. Schaefer Jr. School of Engineering and Science, Department of Electrical and Computer Engineering, Program in Electrical Engineering, Hoboken, NJ 07030. Offers autonomous robotics (Certificate); electrical engineering (M Eng, PhD, Certificate), including computer architecture and digital systems (M Eng), microelectronics and photonics science and technology (M Eng), signal processing for communications (M Eng), telecommunications systems engineering (M Eng), wireless communications (M Eng, Certificate). *Program availability:* Part-time, evening/weekend. *Faculty:* 19 full-time (5 women), 5 part-time/adjunct (1 woman). *Students:* 149 full-time (25 women), 23 part-time (4 women); includes 8 minority (1 Black or African American, non-Hispanic/Latino; 6 Asian, non-Hispanic/Latino; 1 Hispanic/Latino), 143 international. Average age 25. In 2018, 68 master's, 1 doctorate, 29 other advanced degrees awarded. Terminal master's awarded for partial completion of doctoral program. *Degree requirements:* For master's, thesis optional, minimum B average in major field and overall; for doctorate, comprehensive exam (for some programs), thesis/dissertation; for Certificate, minimum B average. *Entrance requirements:* For master's, GRE/GMAT scores: GRE scores are required for all applicants applying to a full-time graduate program in the Schaefer School of Engineering and Science (SES). International applicants must submit TOEFL/IELTS scores and fulfill the English Language Proficiency Requirements in order to be considered. Additional exam requirements/recommendations for international students: Required—TOEFL (minimum score 74 iBT), IELTS (minimum score 6). *Application deadline:* For fall admission, 4/15 for domestic and international students; for spring admission, 11/1 for domestic and international students; for summer admission, 5/1 for domestic students. Applications are processed on a rolling basis. Application fee: $60. Electronic applications accepted. *Expenses: Tuition:* Full-time $35,960; part-time $1620 per credit. *Required fees:* $1290; $600 per semester. Tuition and fees vary according to course load. *Financial support:* Fellowships, research assistantships, teaching assistantships, career-related internships or fieldwork, Federal Work-Study, scholarships/grants, and unspecified assistantships available. Financial award application deadline: 2/15; financial award applicants required to submit FAFSA. *Unit head:* Dr. Jean Zu, Dean of SES, 201-216.8233, Fax: 201-216.8372, E-mail: Jean.Zu@stevens.edu. *Application contact:* Graduate Admissions, 888-783-8367, Fax: 888-511-1306, E-mail: graduate@stevens.edu.

The University of Alabama in Huntsville, School of Graduate Studies, College of Engineering, Department of Electrical and Computer Engineering, Huntsville, AL 35899. Offers computer engineering (MSE, PhD); electrical engineering (MSE, PhD), including optics and photonics technology (MSE); optical science and engineering (PhD); software engineering (MSSE). *Program availability:* Part-time. *Faculty:* 22 full-time (4 women), 4 part-time/adjunct. *Students:* 65 full-time (12 women), 125 part-time (12 women); includes 12 minority (5 Black or African American, non-Hispanic/Latino; 5 Asian, non-Hispanic/Latino; 2 Hispanic/Latino), 61 international. Average age 31. 199 applicants, 78% accepted, 46 enrolled. In 2018, 42 master's, 11 doctorates awarded. *Degree requirements:* For master's, comprehensive exam, thesis or alternative, oral and written exams; for doctorate, comprehensive exam, thesis/dissertation, oral and written exams. *Entrance requirements:* For master's, GRE General Test, appropriate bachelor's degree, minimum GPA of 3.0; for doctorate, GRE General Test, minimum GPA of 3.0. Additional exam requirements/recommendations for international students: Required—TOEFL (minimum score 500 paper-based; 80 iBT), IELTS (minimum score 6.5). *Application deadline:* For fall admission, 7/15 priority date for domestic students, 4/1 priority date for international students; for spring admission, 11/30 priority date for domestic students, 9/1 priority date for international students. Applications are processed on a rolling basis. Application fee: $50. Electronic applications accepted. *Expenses: Tuition, area resident:* Full-time $10,632; part-time $412 per credit hour. Tuition, state resident: full-time $10,632. Tuition, nonresident: full-time $23,604; part-time $412 per credit hour. *Required fees:* $582; $582. Tuition and fees vary according to course load and program. *Financial support:* In 2018–19, 37 students received support, including 18 research assistantships with full tuition reimbursements available (averaging $5,783 per year), 19 teaching assistantships with full tuition reimbursements available (averaging $5,813 per year); career-related internships or fieldwork, Federal Work-Study, institutionally sponsored loans, scholarships/grants, health care benefits, tuition waivers (full and partial), and unspecified assistantships also available. Support available to part-time students. Financial award application deadline: 4/1; financial award applicants required to submit FAFSA. *Faculty research:* Advanced computer architecture and systems, fault tolerant computing and verification, computational electro-magnetics, nano-photonics and plasmonics, micro electro-mechanical (MEMS) systems. *Unit head:* Dr. Ravi Gorur, Chair, 256-824-6316, Fax: 256-824-6803, E-mail: ravi.gorur@uah.edu. *Application contact:* Kim Gray, Graduate Studies Admissions Coordinator, 256-824-6002, Fax: 256-824-6405, E-mail: deangrad@uah.edu.
Website: http://www.ece.uah.edu/

The University of Alabama in Huntsville, School of Graduate Studies, College of Science, Department of Physics, Huntsville, AL 35899. Offers education (MS); optics and photonics technology (MS); physics (MS, PhD). *Program availability:* Part-time. *Faculty:* 5 full-time, 2 part-time/adjunct. *Students:* 20 full-time (7 women), 12 part-time (1 woman); includes 2 minority (1 Black or African American, non-Hispanic/Latino; 1 Two or more races, non-Hispanic/Latino), 8 international. Average age 31. 22 applicants, 73% accepted, 6 enrolled. In 2018, 4 master's, 2 doctorates awarded. *Degree requirements:* For master's, comprehensive exam, thesis or alternative, oral and written exams; for doctorate, comprehensive exam, thesis/dissertation, oral and written exams. *Entrance requirements:* For master's and doctorate, GRE General Test, minimum GPA of 3.0. Additional exam requirements/recommendations for international students: Required—TOEFL (minimum score 550 paper-based; 80 iBT), IELTS (minimum score 6.5). *Application deadline:* For fall admission, 7/15 priority date for domestic students, 4/1 priority date for international students; for spring admission, 11/30 priority date for domestic students, 9/1 priority date for international students. Applications are processed on a rolling basis. Application fee: $50. Electronic applications accepted. *Expenses: Tuition, area resident:* Full-time $10,632; part-time $412 per credit hour. Tuition, state resident: full-time $10,632. Tuition, nonresident: full-time $23,604; part-time $412 per credit hour. *Required fees:* $582; $582. Tuition and fees vary according to course load and program. *Financial support:* In 2018–19, 18 students received support, including 7 research assistantships with full tuition reimbursements available (averaging $9,130 per year), 10 teaching assistantships with full tuition reimbursements available (averaging $7,444 per year); career-related internships or fieldwork, Federal Work-Study, institutionally sponsored loans, scholarships/grants, health care benefits, and unspecified assistantships also available. Support available to part-time students. Financial award application deadline: 4/1; financial award applicants required to submit FAFSA. *Faculty research:* Space and solar physics, computational physics, optics, high energy astrophysics. *Unit head:* Dr. James A. Miller, Chair, 256-824-2483, Fax: 256-824-6873, E-mail: millerja@uah.edu. *Application contact:* Kim Gray, Graduate Studies Admissions Coordinator, 256-824-6002, Fax: 256-824-6405, E-mail: deangrad@uah.edu.
Website: http://physics.uah.edu/

University of Arkansas, Graduate School, Interdisciplinary Program in Microelectronics and Photonics, Fayetteville, AR 72701. Offers MS, PhD. In 2018, 5 master's, 6 doctorates awarded. *Application deadline:* For fall admission, 8/1 for domestic students, 4/1 for international students; for spring admission, 12/1 for domestic students, 10/1 for international students; for summer admission, 4/15 for domestic students, 3/1 for international students. Applications are processed on a rolling basis. Application fee: $60. Electronic applications accepted. *Financial support:* In 2018–19, 25 research assistantships, 4 teaching assistantships were awarded; fellowships with tuition reimbursements also available. Financial award application deadline: 4/1; financial award applicants required to submit FAFSA. *Unit head:* Dr. Rick Wise, Director, 479-575-2875, E-mail: rickwise@uark.edu. *Application contact:* Dr. Rick Wise, Director, 479-575-2875, E-mail: rickwise@uark.edu.
Website: https://microelectronics-photonics.uark.edu/

University of California, San Diego, Graduate Division, Department of Electrical and Computer Engineering, La Jolla, CA 92093. Offers applied ocean science (MS, PhD); applied physics (MS, PhD); communication theory and systems (MS, PhD); computer engineering (MS, PhD); electronic circuits and systems (MS, PhD); intelligent systems, robotics and control (MS, PhD); medical devices and systems (MS, PhD); nanoscale devices and systems (MS, PhD); photonics (MS, PhD); signal and image processing (MS, PhD). Program offered jointly with San Diego State University. *Students:* 830 full-time (174 women), 69 part-time (8 women). 2,810 applicants, 40% accepted, 399 enrolled. In 2018, 226 master's, 42 doctorates awarded. Terminal master's awarded for partial completion of doctoral program. *Degree requirements:* For master's,

comprehensive exam (for some programs), thesis (for some programs); for doctorate, comprehensive exam, thesis/dissertation. *Entrance requirements:* For master's and doctorate, GRE General Test, minimum GPA of 3.0, resume or curriculum vitae (recommended). Additional exam requirements/recommendations for international students: Required—TOEFL (minimum score 550 paper-based; 80 iBT), IELTS (minimum score 7), PTE (minimum score 65). *Application deadline:* For fall admission, 12/13 for domestic students. Application fee: $105 ($125 for international students). Electronic applications accepted. *Financial support:* Fellowships, research assistantships, teaching assistantships, scholarships/grants, traineeships, and unspecified assistantships available. Financial award applicants required to submit FAFSA. *Faculty research:* Applied ocean science; applied physics; communication theory and systems; computer engineering; electronic circuits and systems; intelligent systems, robotics and control; medical devices and systems; nanoscale devices and systems; photonics; signal and image processing. *Unit head:* Bill Lin, Chair, 858-822-1383, E-mail: billin@ucsd.edu. *Application contact:* Sean Jones, Graduate Admissions Coordinator, 858-534-3213, E-mail: ecegradapps@ece.ucsd.edu.
Website: http://ece.ucsd.edu/

University of California, Santa Barbara, Graduate Division, College of Engineering, Department of Electrical and Computer Engineering, Santa Barbara, CA 93106-2014. Offers communications, control and signal processing (MS, PhD); computer engineering (MS, PhD); electronics and photonics (MS, PhD); MS/PhD. *Degree requirements:* For master's, comprehensive exam, thesis; for doctorate, thesis/dissertation. *Entrance requirements:* For master's and doctorate, GRE General Test. Additional exam requirements/recommendations for international students: Required—TOEFL (minimum score 550 paper-based; 80 iBT), IELTS (minimum score 7). Electronic applications accepted. *Faculty research:* Communications, signal processing, computer engineering, control, electronics and photonics.

University of Central Florida, College of Optics and Photonics, Orlando, FL 32816. Offers MS, PhD. *Program availability:* Part-time, evening/weekend. *Faculty:* 41 full-time (3 women), 9 part-time/adjunct (1 woman). *Students:* 121 full-time (28 women), 21 part-time (2 women); includes 14 minority (1 Black or African American, non-Hispanic/Latino; 4 Asian, non-Hispanic/Latino; 8 Hispanic/Latino; 1 Two or more races, non-Hispanic/Latino), 90 international. Average age 28. 167 applicants, 43% accepted, 27 enrolled. In 2018, 21 master's, 12 doctorates awarded. *Degree requirements:* For master's, thesis or alternative; for doctorate, thesis/dissertation, departmental qualifying exam, candidacy exam. *Entrance requirements:* For master's and doctorate, GRE General Test, minimum GPA of 3.0 in last 60 hours, goal statement, letters of recommendation, resume. Additional exam requirements/recommendations for international students: Required—TOEFL. *Application deadline:* For fall admission, 7/15 for domestic students; for spring admission, 12/1 for domestic students. Application fee: $30. Electronic applications accepted. *Financial support:* In 2018–19, 116 students received support, including 25 fellowships with partial tuition reimbursements available (averaging $22,304 per year), 106 research assistantships with partial tuition reimbursements available (averaging $15,182 per year), 9 teaching assistantships with partial tuition reimbursements available (averaging $14,404 per year); career-related internships or fieldwork, Federal Work-Study, institutionally sponsored loans, health care benefits, tuition waivers (partial), and unspecified assistantships also available. Financial award application deadline: 3/1; financial award applicants required to submit FAFSA. *Faculty research:*

Lasers, fiber optics, optoelectronics and integrated photonics, nonlinear and quantum optics, imaging, sensing and display. *Unit head:* Dr. Bahaa E. Saleh, Dean and Director, 407-823-6817, E-mail: besaleh@creol.ucf.edu. *Application contact:* Associate Director, Graduate Admissions, 407-823-2766, Fax: 407-823-6442, E-mail: gradadmissions@ucf.edu.
Website: http://www.creol.ucf.edu/

University of Dayton, Department of Electro-Optics and Photonics, Dayton, OH 45469. Offers electro-optics (MSEO, PhD). *Degree requirements:* For master's, thesis, 30 credits, minimum GPA of 3.0; for doctorate, comprehensive exam, thesis/dissertation, 60 credits beyond master's degree, candidacy exam, minimum GPA of 3.0, 6 credits of math. *Entrance requirements:* For master's, minimum GPA of 3.0 in electrical engineering, physics or other related disciplines; for doctorate, master's degree with minimum GPA of 3.5. Additional exam requirements/recommendations for international students: Required—TOEFL (minimum score 550 paper-based; 80 iBT); Recommended—IELTS. Electronic applications accepted. *Faculty research:* Non-linear optics, polarization, nano-optics, adaptive optics.

University of New Mexico, Graduate Studies, College of Arts and Sciences, Program in Optical Science and Engineering, Albuquerque, NM 87131-2039. Offers imaging science (MS, PhD); optical science and engineering (MS, PhD); photonics (MS, PhD). Program held jointly with the Department of Physics and Astronomy and the Department of Electrical and Computer Engineering. *Program availability:* Part-time. *Students:* Average age 30. 50 applicants, 24% accepted, 8 enrolled. In 2018, 4 master's, 8 doctorates awarded. Terminal master's awarded for partial completion of doctoral program. *Degree requirements:* For master's, comprehensive exam (for some programs), thesis (for some programs); for doctorate, comprehensive exam, thesis/dissertation. *Entrance requirements:* For master's, GRE General Test, GRE Subject Test in physics (preferred), relevant undergraduate coursework, curriculum vitae, letters of recommendation, letter of intent/personal statement; for doctorate, GRE General Test, GRE Subject Test in physics (preferred), relevant undergraduate coursework, curriculum vitae, letters of recommendation. Additional exam requirements/recommendations for international students: Required—TOEFL (minimum score 575 paper-based; 79 iBT), IELTS (minimum score 7). *Application deadline:* For fall admission, 1/15 priority date for domestic and international students; for spring admission, 8/1 priority date for domestic and international students. Application fee: $50. Electronic applications accepted. *Financial support:* Fellowships with full tuition reimbursements, research assistantships with full tuition reimbursements, teaching assistantships with full tuition reimbursements, career-related internships or fieldwork, scholarships/grants, health care benefits, and unspecified assistantships available. Support available to part-time students. Financial award application deadline: 2/1; financial award applicants required to submit FAFSA. *Faculty research:* Advanced materials, atom optics, biomedical optics, fiber optics, laser cooling, high intensity interactions, lithography, nano-photonics, nonlinear optics, optical imaging, optical sensors, optoelectronics, quantum optics, spectroscopy, ultrafast phenomena. *Unit head:* Dr. Majeed Hayat, Chair, 505-272-7095, Fax: 505-277-7801, E-mail: hayat@ece.unm.edu. *Application contact:* Doris Williams, Advisor, 505-277-7764, Fax: 505-277-7801, E-mail: dorisw@chtm.unm.edu.
Website: http://www.optics.unm.edu/

Physics

Alabama Agricultural and Mechanical University, School of Graduate Studies, College of Engineering, Technology, and Physical Sciences, Department of Physics, Chemistry and Mathematics, Huntsville, AL 35811. Offers physics (MS, PhD), including materials science (PhD), optics/lasers (PhD), space science (PhD). *Program availability:* Part-time, evening/weekend. *Degree requirements:* For doctorate, thesis/dissertation. *Entrance requirements:* For master's and doctorate, GRE General Test. Additional exam requirements/recommendations for international students: Required—TOEFL (minimum score 500 paper-based; 61 iBT). Electronic applications accepted.

The American University in Cairo, School of Sciences and Engineering, Cairo, Egypt. Offers biotechnology (MS); chemistry (MS); computer science (MS); computing (M Comp); construction engineering (M Eng, MS); electronics and communications engineering (M Eng); environmental engineering (MS); environmental system design (M Eng); mechanical engineering (M Eng, MS); nanotechnology (MS); physics (MS); robotics, control and smart systems (MS); sciences and engineering (PhD); sustainable development (MS, Graduate Diploma). *Program availability:* Part-time, evening/weekend. *Degree requirements:* For master's, comprehensive exam (for some programs), thesis (for some programs); for doctorate, comprehensive exam (for some programs), thesis/dissertation. *Entrance requirements:* Additional exam requirements/recommendations for international students: Required—TOEFL (minimum score 450 paper-based; 45 iBT), IELTS (minimum score 5). Electronic applications accepted. *Faculty research:* Construction, mechanical, and electronics engineering; physics; computer science; biotechnology; nanotechnology; chemistry; robotics.

American University of Beirut, Graduate Programs, Faculty of Arts and Sciences, Beirut 1107 2020, Lebanon. Offers anthropology (MA); Arab and Middle Eastern history (PhD); Arabic language and literature (MA, PhD); archaeology (MA); art history and curating (MA); biology (MS); cell and molecular biology (PhD); chemistry (MS); clinical psychology (MA); computational sciences (MS); computer science (MS); economics (MA); education (MA), including administration and policy studies, elementary education, mathematics education, psychology school guidance, psychology test and measurements, science education, teaching English as a foreign language; English language (MA); English literature (MA); environmental policy planning (MS); financial economics (MAFE); general psychology (MA); geology (MS); history (MA); Islamic studies (MA); mathematics (MS); media studies (MA); Middle East studies (MA); philosophy (MA); physics (MS); political studies (MA); public administration (MA); public policy and international affairs (MA); sociology (MA); theoretical physics (PhD). *Program availability:* Part-time. *Faculty:* 187 full-time (64 women), 27 part-time/adjunct (15 women). *Students:* 292 full-time (215 women), 216 part-time (148 women). Average age 27. 422 applicants, 61% accepted, 124 enrolled. In 2018, 90 master's, 3 doctorates awarded. *Degree requirements:* For master's, comprehensive exam, thesis (for some programs), project; for doctorate, comprehensive exam, thesis/dissertation (for some programs). *Entrance requirements:* For master's, GRE General Test (for archaeology, clinical psychology, general psychology, economics, financial economics and biology); for doctorate, GRE General Test for all PhD programs, GRE Subject Test for theoretical physics. Additional exam requirements/recommendations for international students:

Required—TOEFL (minimum score 583 paper-based; 97 iBT), IELTS (minimum score 7). *Application deadline:* For fall admission, 3/18 for domestic students; for spring admission, 11/5 for domestic students. Application fee: $50. Electronic applications accepted. *Expenses:* MA/MS: Humanities and social sciences=$912/credit. Sciences=$943/credit. Financial economics=$986/credit. Thesis: Humanities/social sciences=$6565 and sciences=$6865. *Financial support:* In 2018–19, 227 fellowships with full tuition reimbursements, 17 research assistantships with full tuition reimbursements, 83 teaching assistantships with full tuition reimbursements were awarded; scholarships/grants, tuition waivers (full and partial), and unspecified assistantships also available. Financial award application deadline: 3/18. *Faculty research:* Sciences: Physics: High energy, Particle, Polymer and Soft Matter, Thermal, Plasma; String Theory, Mathematical physics, Astrophysics (stellar evolution, planet and galaxy formation and evolution, astrophysical dynamics), Solid State physics/thin films, Spintronics, Magnetic properties of materials, Mineralogy, Petrology, and Geochemistry of Hard Rocks, Geophysics and Petrophysics, Hydrogeology, Micropaleontology, Sedimentology, and Stratigraphy, Structural Geology and Geotectonics, Renewable en. *Total annual research expenditures:* $4.3 million. *Unit head:* Dr. Nadia Maria El Cheikh, Dean, Faculty of Arts and Sciences, 961-1-350000 Ext. 3800, Fax: 961-1-744461, E-mail: nmcheikh@aub.edu.lb. *Application contact:* Adriana Michelle Zanaty, Curriculum and Graduate Studies Officer, 961-1-350000 Ext. 3833, Fax: 961-1-744461, E-mail: az48@aub.edu.lb.
Website: https://www.aub.edu.lb/fas/Pages/default.aspx

Arizona State University at the Tempe campus, College of Liberal Arts and Sciences, Department of Physics, Tempe, AZ 85287-1504. Offers nanoscience (PSM); physics (MNS, PhD). *Program availability:* Part-time. Terminal master's awarded for partial completion of doctoral program. *Degree requirements:* For master's, comprehensive exam, thesis or alternative, interactive Program of Study (iPOS) submitted before completing 50 percent of required credit hours; for doctorate, comprehensive exam, thesis/dissertation, interactive Program of Study (iPOS) submitted before completing 50 percent of required credit hours. *Entrance requirements:* For master's and doctorate, GRE, minimum GPA of 3.0 or equivalent in last 2 years of work leading to bachelor's degree. Additional exam requirements/recommendations for international students: Required—TOEFL, IELTS, or PTE. Electronic applications accepted. *Expenses:* Contact institution.

Auburn University, Graduate School, College of Sciences and Mathematics, Department of Physics, Auburn University, AL 36849. Offers MS, PhD. *Program availability:* Part-time. *Degree requirements:* For doctorate, thesis/dissertation, oral and written exams. *Entrance requirements:* For master's and doctorate, GRE General Test. Electronic applications accepted. *Expenses:* Tuition, state resident: full-time $11,282; part-time $535 per credit hour. Tuition, nonresident: full-time $30,542; part-time $1605 per credit hour. *Required fees:* $826 per semester. Tuition and fees vary according to degree level and program. *Faculty research:* Atomic/radioactive physics, plasma physics, condensed matter physics, space physics, nonlinear dynamics.

Peterson's Graduate Programs in the Physical Sciences, Mathematics, Agricultural Sciences, the Environment & Natural Resources 2020

www.petersons.com **147**

Physics

Ball State University, Graduate School, College of Sciences and Humanities, Department of Physics and Astronomy, Muncie, IN 47306. Offers physics (MA, MAE, MS). *Program availability:* Part-time. *Entrance requirements:* For master's, GRE General Test, minimum baccalaureate GPA of 2.75 or 3.0 in latter half of baccalaureate. Additional exam requirements/recommendations for international students: Required—TOEFL (minimum score 550 paper-based; 79 iBT), IELTS (minimum score 6.5). Electronic applications accepted.

Baylor University, Graduate School, College of Arts and Sciences, Department of Physics, Waco, TX 76798. Offers MA, MS, PhD. *Faculty:* 17 full-time (3 women). *Students:* 38 full-time (6 women), 3 part-time (0 women); includes 3 minority (1 Asian, non-Hispanic/Latino; 2 Hispanic/Latino), 22 international. 59 applicants, 29% accepted, 10 enrolled. In 2018, 1 master's, 6 doctorates awarded. Terminal master's awarded for partial completion of doctoral program. *Degree requirements:* For master's, comprehensive exam (for some programs), thesis or alternative; for doctorate, comprehensive exam, thesis/dissertation. *Entrance requirements:* For master's and doctorate, GRE General Test, GRE Subject Test (physics). Additional exam requirements/recommendations for international students: Required—TOEFL (minimum score 80 iBT), IELTS (minimum score 6.5). *Application deadline:* For fall admission, 1/15 for domestic students, 2/1 for international students; for spring admission, 12/1 for international students. Application fee: $50. Electronic applications accepted. *Financial support:* In 2018–19, 42 students received support, including 42 fellowships with full tuition reimbursements available (averaging $5,500 per year), 11 research assistantships with full tuition reimbursements available (averaging $23,402 per year), 27 teaching assistantships with full tuition reimbursements available (averaging $22,100 per year); scholarships/grants and health care benefits also available. Financial award application deadline: 1/15. *Faculty research:* Elementary particle physics and cosmology, gravity, condensed matter physics, space science physics, nonlinear dynamics, atomic and molecular physics. *Total annual research expenditures:* $545,988. *Unit head:* Prof. Gerald B. Cleaver, Graduate Program Director, 254-710-2283, Fax: 254-710-3878, E-mail: gerald_cleaver@baylor.edu. *Application contact:* Marian Nunn-Graves, Administrative Assistant, 254-710-2511, Fax: 254-710-3878, E-mail: marian_nunn-graves@baylor.edu.
Website: http://www.baylor.edu/physics/

Binghamton University, State University of New York, Graduate School, Harpur College of Arts and Sciences, Department of Physics, Applied Physics, and Astronomy, Binghamton, NY 13902-6000. Offers MS, PhD. *Program availability:* Part-time. Terminal master's awarded for partial completion of doctoral program. *Degree requirements:* For master's, comprehensive exam (for some programs), thesis or alternative; for doctorate, comprehensive exam, thesis/dissertation. *Entrance requirements:* For master's and doctorate, GRE General Test. Additional exam requirements/recommendations for international students: Required—TOEFL (minimum score 550 paper-based; 80 iBT). Electronic applications accepted.

Boston College, Morrissey Graduate School of Arts and Sciences, Department of Physics, Chestnut Hill, MA 02467-3800. Offers MS, PhD. Terminal master's awarded for partial completion of doctoral program. *Degree requirements:* For master's, thesis (for some programs); for doctorate, thesis/dissertation. *Entrance requirements:* For master's and doctorate, GRE General Test, GRE Subject Test. Additional exam requirements/recommendations for international students: Required—TOEFL (minimum score 600 paper-based; 100 iBT), IELTS (minimum score 8). Electronic applications accepted. *Faculty research:* Superconductivity, photovoltaics, metamaterials, thermoelectrics, nanostructures and nanomaterials for biosensing, plasmonics, plasmas, topological insulators, novel electronic materials.

Boston University, Graduate School of Arts and Sciences, Department of Physics, Boston, MA 02215. Offers PhD. *Students:* 81 full-time (7 women); includes 4 minority (2 Asian, non-Hispanic/Latino; 1 Hispanic/Latino; 1 Two or more races, non-Hispanic/Latino), 49 international. Average age 23. 373 applicants, 25% accepted, 28 enrolled. In 2018, 14 doctorates awarded. Terminal master's awarded for partial completion of doctoral program. *Degree requirements:* For doctorate, comprehensive exam, thesis/dissertation, interim progress report, departmental seminar. *Entrance requirements:* For doctorate, GRE General Test, GRE Subject Test (physics), 3 letters of recommendation, transcripts, personal statement, curriculum vitae. Additional exam requirements/recommendations for international students: Required—TOEFL (minimum score 600 paper-based; 84 iBT). *Application deadline:* For fall admission, 1/5 for domestic and international students. Application fee: $95. Electronic applications accepted. *Financial support:* In 2018–19, 81 students received support, including 3 fellowships with full tuition reimbursements available (averaging $22,660 per year), 40 research assistantships with full tuition reimbursements available (averaging $22,660 per year), 35 teaching assistantships with full tuition reimbursements available (averaging $22,660 per year); Federal Work-Study, scholarships/grants, and health care benefits also available. Support available to part-time students. Financial award application deadline: 1/5. *Unit head:* Andrei Ruckenstein, Chair, 617-358-4791, Fax: 617-353-9393, E-mail: andreir@bu.edu. *Application contact:* Mirtha M. Cabello, Administrative Coordinator, 617-353-2623, Fax: 617-353-9393, E-mail: cabello@bu.edu.
Website: http://buphy.bu.edu/

Bowling Green State University, Graduate College, College of Arts and Sciences, Department of Physics and Astronomy, Bowling Green, OH 43403. Offers geophysics (MS); physics (MAT, MS). *Degree requirements:* For master's, thesis or alternative. *Entrance requirements:* For master's, GRE General Test. Additional exam requirements/recommendations for international students: Required—TOEFL. Electronic applications accepted. *Faculty research:* Computational physics, solid-state physics, materials science, theoretical physics.

Brandeis University, Graduate School of Arts and Sciences, Department of Physics, Waltham, MA 02454-9110. Offers physics (MS, PhD); quantitative biology (PhD). *Program availability:* Part-time. *Faculty:* 15 full-time (4 women), 1 part-time/adjunct (0 women). *Students:* 50 full-time (18 women); includes 3 minority (1 Asian, non-Hispanic/Latino; 2 Hispanic/Latino), 27 international. Average age 26. 152 applicants, 16% accepted, 8 enrolled. In 2018, 1 master's, 3 doctorates awarded. Terminal master's awarded for partial completion of doctoral program. *Degree requirements:* For master's, thesis optional, qualifying exam, 1-year residency; for doctorate, comprehensive exam, thesis/dissertation, qualifying and advanced exams. *Entrance requirements:* For master's and doctorate, GRE; GRE Subject Test (recommended), resume, letters of recommendation, statement of purpose, transcripts. Additional exam requirements/recommendations for international students: Required—TOEFL, IELTS, PTE. *Application deadline:* For fall admission, 1/15 priority date for domestic students. Application fee: $75. Electronic applications accepted. *Financial support:* In 2018–19, 16 fellowships with full tuition reimbursements (averaging $30,000 per year), 38 research assistantships with full tuition reimbursements (averaging $30,000 per year), 19 teaching assistantships with full tuition reimbursements (averaging $6,400 per year) were awarded; scholarships/grants, health care benefits, and tuition waivers (full and partial) also available. *Faculty research:* Astrophysics, condensed-matter and biophysics, high energy and gravitational theory, particle physics, microfluidics, radio astronomy, string theory. *Unit head:* Dr. Craig Blocker, Director of Graduate Study, 781-736-2879, E-mail: blocker@brandeis.edu. *Application contact:* Maryanna Aldrich, Administrator, 781-736-2352, E-mail: scigradoffice@brandeis.edu.
Website: http://www.brandeis.edu/gsas/programs/physics.html

Brigham Young University, Graduate Studies, College of Physical and Mathematical Sciences, Department of Physics and Astronomy, Provo, UT 84602-1001. Offers physics (MS, PhD); physics and astronomy (PhD). *Program availability:* Part-time. *Faculty:* 25 full-time (3 women). *Students:* 38 full-time (4 women), 3 part-time (0 women); includes 3 minority (2 Hispanic/Latino; 1 Native Hawaiian or other Pacific Islander, non-Hispanic/Latino), 5 international. Average age 30. 33 applicants, 64% accepted, 13 enrolled. In 2018, 7 master's, 4 doctorates awarded. Terminal master's awarded for partial completion of doctoral program. *Degree requirements:* For master's, thesis; for doctorate, thesis/dissertation, qualifying exam, candidacy exam. *Entrance requirements:* For master's and doctorate, GRE Subject Test (physics), GRE General Test, minimum GPA of 3.0, ecclesiastical endorsement. Additional exam requirements/recommendations for international students: Required—TOEFL (minimum score 580 paper-based; 85 iBT), IELTS (minimum score 7), E3PT (overall 79; speaking, reading, listening 21 and writing 16), TOEFL iBT (listening, reading, writing 21 and speaking 22), CAE (185 or 'C' grade). *Application deadline:* For fall admission, 1/15 priority date for domestic and international students. Application fee: $50. Electronic applications accepted. *Financial support:* In 2018–19, 36 students received support, including 22 research assistantships with full tuition reimbursements available (averaging $22,430 per year), 7 teaching assistantships with full tuition reimbursements available (averaging $20,814 per year); fellowships, scholarships/grants, traineeships, and tuition waivers (full) also available. Support available to part-time students. Financial award application deadline: 1/15. *Faculty research:* Acoustics; atomic, molecular, and optical physics; theoretical and mathematical physics; condensed matter; astrophysics and plasma. *Total annual research expenditures:* $2 million. *Unit head:* Dr. Kent L. Gee, Chair, 801-422-1544, Fax: 801-422-0553, E-mail: kentgee@byu.edu. *Application contact:* Dr. Richard R. Vanfleet, Graduate Coordinator, 801-422-1702, Fax: 801-422-0553, E-mail: richard_vanfleet@byu.edu.
Website: http://physics.byu.edu/

Brock University, Faculty of Graduate Studies, Faculty of Mathematics and Science, Program in Physics, St. Catharines, ON L2S 3A1, Canada. Offers M Sc. *Program availability:* Part-time. *Degree requirements:* For master's, thesis. *Entrance requirements:* For master's, honors B Sc in physics. Additional exam requirements/recommendations for international students: Required—TOEFL (minimum score 550 paper-based; 80 iBT), IELTS (minimum score 6.5), TWE (minimum score 4). Electronic applications accepted. *Faculty research:* Quantum physics, optical properties, non-crystalline materials, condensed matter physics, biophysics.

Brooklyn College of the City University of New York, School of Education, Program in Middle Childhood Science Education, Brooklyn, NY 11210-2889. Offers biology (MA); chemistry (MA); earth science (MA); general science (MA); physics (MA). *Program availability:* Part-time, evening/weekend. *Entrance requirements:* For master's, LAST, interview, previous course work in education and mathematics, resume, 2 letters of recommendation, essay. Additional exam requirements/recommendations for international students: Required—TOEFL (minimum score 500 paper-based; 61 iBT). Electronic applications accepted. *Faculty research:* Geometric thinking, mastery of basic facts, problem-solving strategies, history of mathematics.

Brooklyn College of the City University of New York, School of Natural and Behavioral Sciences, Department of Physics, Brooklyn, NY 11210-2889. Offers MA. *Program availability:* Part-time. Terminal master's awarded for partial completion of doctoral program. *Degree requirements:* For master's, comprehensive exam, thesis or alternative, 30 credits. *Entrance requirements:* For master's, 2 letters of recommendation, 12 credits in advanced physics. Additional exam requirements/recommendations for international students: Required—TOEFL (minimum score 500 paper-based; 61 iBT). Electronic applications accepted.

Brown University, Graduate School, Department of Physics, Providence, RI 02912. Offers Sc M, PhD. *Program availability:* Part-time. *Faculty:* 29 full-time (5 women). *Students:* 135 full-time (26 women), 1 part-time (0 women); includes 10 minority (1 Black or African American, non-Hispanic/Latino; 5 Asian, non-Hispanic/Latino; 3 Hispanic/Latino; 1 Two or more races, non-Hispanic/Latino), 91 international. 459 applicants, 28% accepted, 39 enrolled. In 2018, 32 master's, 10 doctorates awarded. Terminal master's awarded for partial completion of doctoral program. *Degree requirements:* For master's, thesis optional, Master's thesis is optional, no dissertation requirement; for doctorate, comprehensive exam, thesis/dissertation, qualifying and oral exams. *Entrance requirements:* For doctorate, GRE General Test; GRE Subject Test (recommended). Additional exam requirements/recommendations for international students: Required—TOEFL (minimum score 577 paper-based; 90 iBT), IELTS (minimum score 7), TOEFL (minimum score 577 paper-based, 90 iBT) or IELTS (7). *Application deadline:* For fall admission, 1/2 for domestic and international students; for spring admission, 4/15 for domestic and international students. Application fee: $75. Electronic applications accepted. *Expenses:* Master's Degree tuition is $59,758 for all eight courses for the degree, students are billed for each course taken, typically two courses each semester (full time). *Financial support:* In 2018–19, 12 students received support, including fellowships with full tuition reimbursements available (averaging $28,483 per year), research assistantships with full tuition reimbursements available (averaging $28,483 per year), teaching assistantships with full tuition reimbursements available (averaging $28,483 per year). Financial award application deadline: 1/2. *Faculty research:* Astrophysics/cosmology, condensed matter, elementary particles. *Unit head:* Gang Xiao, Chair of the Physics Department, 401-863-2644. *Application contact:* Student Affairs, 401-863-2641, E-mail: physics@brown.edu.
Website: https://www.brown.edu/academics/physics/

Bryn Mawr College, Graduate School of Arts and Sciences, Department of Physics, Bryn Mawr, PA 19010-2899. Offers MA, PhD. Terminal master's awarded for partial completion of doctoral program. *Degree requirements:* For master's, thesis; for doctorate, comprehensive exam, thesis/dissertation. *Entrance requirements:* For master's and doctorate, GRE General Test, GRE Subject Test, transcripts, three letters of recommendation, statement of interest, resume or curriculum vitae. Additional exam requirements/recommendations for international students: Required—TOEFL (minimum score 600 paper-based; 100 iBT), IELTS (minimum score 7). Electronic applications accepted.

California Institute of Technology, Division of Physics, Mathematics and Astronomy, Department of Physics, Pasadena, CA 91125-0001. Offers PhD. *Degree requirements:* For doctorate, thesis/dissertation, candidacy and final exams. *Entrance requirements:* For doctorate, GRE General Test, GRE Subject Test. Additional exam requirements/recommendations for international students: Required—TOEFL. *Faculty research:* High-energy physics, nuclear physics, condensed-matter physics, theoretical physics and astrophysics, gravity physics.

California State University, Fresno, Division of Research and Graduate Studies, College of Science and Mathematics, Department of Physics, Fresno, CA 93740-8027. Offers MS. *Program availability:* Part-time. *Degree requirements:* For master's, thesis or alternative. *Entrance requirements:* For master's, GRE General Test, minimum GPA of 2.5. Additional exam requirements/recommendations for international students: Required—TOEFL. Electronic applications accepted. *Faculty research:* Energy, astronomy, silicon vertex detector, neuroimaging, particle physics.

California State University, Fullerton, Graduate Studies, College of Natural Science and Mathematics, Department of Physics, Fullerton, CA 92831-3599. Offers MS. *Program availability:* Part-time.

California State University, Long Beach, Graduate Studies, College of Natural Sciences and Mathematics, Department of Physics and Astronomy, Long Beach, CA 90840. Offers physics (MS). *Program availability:* Part-time. *Degree requirements:* For master's, comprehensive exam or thesis. *Application deadline:* For fall admission, 6/1 for domestic students. Applications are processed on a rolling basis. Application fee: $55. Electronic applications accepted. *Expenses: Required fees:* $2628 per term. Tuition and fees vary according to class time, course level, course load, degree level, campus/location and program. *Financial support:* Federal Work-Study, institutionally sponsored loans, and scholarships/grants available. Financial award application deadline: 3/2; financial award applicants required to submit FAFSA. *Faculty research:* Musical acoustics, modern optics, neutrino physics, quantum gravity, atomic physics. *Unit head:* Dr. Andreas Bill, Chair, 562-985-7925, Fax: 562-985-7924, E-mail: andreas.bill@csulb.edu. *Application contact:* Prashanth Jaikumar, Graduate Advisor, 562-985-5592, E-mail: prashanth.jaikumar@csulb.edu.

California State University, Los Angeles, Graduate Studies, College of Natural and Social Sciences, Department of Physics and Astronomy, Los Angeles, CA 90032-8530. Offers physics (MS). *Program availability:* Part-time, evening/weekend. *Degree requirements:* For master's, comprehensive exam or thesis. *Entrance requirements:* Additional exam requirements/recommendations for international students: Required—TOEFL (minimum score 500 paper-based). Electronic applications accepted. *Faculty research:* Intermediate energy, nuclear physics, condensed-matter physics, biophysics.

California State University, Northridge, Graduate Studies, College of Science and Mathematics, Department of Physics and Astronomy, Northridge, CA 91330. Offers physics (MS). *Program availability:* Part-time, evening/weekend. *Degree requirements:* For master's, thesis or comprehensive exam. *Entrance requirements:* For master's, GRE General Test or minimum GPA of 3.0. Additional exam requirements/recommendations for international students: Required—TOEFL.

Carleton University, Faculty of Graduate Studies, Faculty of Science, Department of Physics, Ottawa, ON K1S 5B6, Canada. Offers M Sc, PhD. Programs offered jointly with University of Ottawa. *Degree requirements:* For master's, thesis optional, seminar; for doctorate, comprehensive exam, thesis/dissertation, seminar. *Entrance requirements:* For master's, honors degree in science; for doctorate, M Sc. Additional exam requirements/recommendations for international students: Required—TOEFL. *Faculty research:* Experimental and theoretical elementary particle physics, medical physics.

Carnegie Mellon University, Mellon College of Science, Department of Physics, Pittsburgh, PA 15213-3891. Offers applied physics (PhD); physics (MS, PhD). *Degree requirements:* For doctorate, thesis/dissertation, qualifying exam. *Entrance requirements:* For doctorate, GRE General Test, GRE Subject Test. Additional exam requirements/recommendations for international students: Required—TOEFL. Electronic applications accepted. *Faculty research:* Astrophysics, condensed matter physics, biological physics, medium energy and nuclear physics, high-energy physics.

Case Western Reserve University, School of Graduate Studies, Department of Physics, Cleveland, OH 44106. Offers MS, PhD. *Program availability:* Part-time. *Faculty:* 26 full-time (4 women). *Students:* 73 full-time (15 women); includes 4 minority (1 Black or African American, non-Hispanic/Latino; 3 Asian, non-Hispanic/Latino), 40 international. Average age 28. 137 applicants, 18% accepted, 10 enrolled. In 2018, 4 master's, 11 doctorates awarded. Terminal master's awarded for partial completion of doctoral program. *Degree requirements:* For master's, comprehensive exam; for doctorate, comprehensive exam, thesis/dissertation. *Entrance requirements:* For master's and doctorate, GRE General Test, GRE Subject Test (physics), statement of objective; three letters of recommendation. Additional exam requirements/recommendations for international students: Required—TOEFL (minimum score 577 paper-based; 90 iBT); Recommended—IELTS (minimum score 7). *Application deadline:* For fall admission, 1/15 priority date for domestic students. Application fee: $50. Electronic applications accepted. *Expenses: Tuition:* Full-time $45,168; part-time $1939 per credit hour. *Required fees:* $36; $18 per semester. $18 per semester. *Financial support:* Research assistantships, teaching assistantships, health care benefits, tuition waivers, and unspecified assistantships available. Financial award application deadline: 1/15; financial award applicants required to submit FAFSA. *Faculty research:* Condensed-matter, optics and optical materials, cosmology and astrophysics, and biophysics, medical and imaging physics. *Unit head:* Prof. Glenn Starkman, Distinguished University Professor and Co-chair Department of Physics, 216-368.3660, E-mail: glenn.starkman@case.edu. *Application contact:* Prof. Corbin Covault, Professor and Co-chair Department of Physics, 216-368-4006, Fax: 216-368-4671, E-mail: corbin.covault@case.edu.
Website: http://www.phys.cwru.edu/

The Catholic University of America, School of Arts and Sciences, Department of Physics, Washington, DC 20064. Offers nuclear environmental protection (MS); physics (MS, PhD). *Program availability:* Part-time. *Faculty:* 13 full-time (3 women). *Students:* 10 full-time (7 women), 24 part-time (15 women); includes 5 minority (1 Black or African American, non-Hispanic/Latino; 1 Asian, non-Hispanic/Latino; 1 Hispanic/Latino; 2 Two or more races, non-Hispanic/Latino), 16 international. Average age 30. 25 applicants, 60% accepted, 5 enrolled. In 2018, 12 master's, 3 doctorates awarded. *Degree requirements:* For master's, comprehensive exam, thesis or alternative; for doctorate, comprehensive exam, thesis/dissertation, oral exam. *Entrance requirements:* For master's and doctorate, GRE General Test, statement of purpose, official copies of academic transcripts, three letters of recommendation. Additional exam requirements/recommendations for international students: Required—TOEFL (minimum score 550 paper-based; 80 iBT). *Application deadline:* For fall admission, 7/15 priority date for domestic students, 7/1 for international students; for spring admission, 11/15 priority date for domestic students, 11/1 for international students. Applications are processed on a rolling basis. Application fee: $55. Electronic applications accepted. *Expenses:* Contact institution. *Financial support:* Fellowships, research assistantships, teaching assistantships, Federal Work-Study, scholarships/grants, tuition waivers (full and partial), and unspecified assistantships available. Financial award application deadline: 2/1; financial award applicants required to submit FAFSA. *Faculty research:* Glass and ceramics technologies, astrophysics and computational sciences, the role of evolution in galaxy properties, nuclear physics, biophysics. *Unit head:* Dr. John Philip, Chair, 202-319-5856, Fax: 202-319-4448, E-mail: kraemer@cua.edu. *Application contact:* Dr. Steven Brown, Director of Graduate Admissions, 202-319-5057, Fax: 202-319-6533, E-mail: cua-admissions@cua.edu.
Website: http://physics.cua.edu/

Central Michigan University, College of Graduate Studies, College of Science and Engineering, Department of Physics, Mount Pleasant, MI 48859. Offers physics (MS); science of advanced materials (PhD). PhD is an interdisciplinary program. *Program availability:* Part-time. *Degree requirements:* For master's, thesis or alternative; for doctorate, comprehensive exam, thesis/dissertation. *Entrance requirements:* For doctorate, GRE, bachelor's degree in physics, chemistry, biochemistry, biology, geology, engineering, mathematics, or other relevant area. Electronic applications accepted. *Faculty research:* Science of advanced materials, polymer physics, laser spectroscopy, observational astronomy, nuclear physics.

Christopher Newport University, Graduate Studies, Department of Physics, Computer Science, and Engineering, Newport News, VA 23606-3072. Offers applied physics and computer science (MS). *Program availability:* Part-time. *Degree requirements:* For master's, comprehensive exam (for some programs), thesis (for some programs). *Entrance requirements:* For master's, GRE General Test, minimum GPA of 3.0. Additional exam requirements/recommendations for international students: Required—TOEFL (minimum score 580 paper-based; 92 iBT), IELTS (minimum score 7). Electronic applications accepted. *Faculty research:* Advanced programming methodologies, experimental nuclear physics, computer architecture, semiconductor nanophysics, laser and optical fiber sensors.

City College of the City University of New York, Graduate School, Division of Science, Department of Physics, New York, NY 10031-9198. Offers MS, PhD. PhD program offered jointly with Graduate School and University Center of the City University of New York. Terminal master's awarded for partial completion of doctoral program. *Degree requirements:* For master's, comprehensive exam; for doctorate, thesis/dissertation. *Entrance requirements:* For doctorate, GRE. Additional exam requirements/recommendations for international students: Required—TOEFL (minimum score 500 paper-based; 61 iBT). Electronic applications accepted.

Clark Atlanta University, School of Arts and Sciences, Department of Physics, Atlanta, GA 30314. Offers MS. *Program availability:* Part-time. *Degree requirements:* For master's, one foreign language, comprehensive exam, thesis optional. *Entrance requirements:* For master's, GRE General Test, minimum GPA of 2.5. Additional exam requirements/recommendations for international students: Required—TOEFL (minimum score 500 paper-based; 61 iBT). *Faculty research:* Fusion energy, investigations of nonlinear differential equations, difference schemes, collisions in dense plasma.

Clarkson University, School of Arts and Sciences, Department of Physics, Potsdam, NY 13699. Offers MS, PhD. *Faculty:* 8 full-time (2 women), 1 part-time/adjunct (0 women). *Students:* 15 full-time (1 woman), 1 part-time (0 women), 4 international. 35 applicants, 14% accepted, 2 enrolled. In 2018, 6 master's, 1 doctorate awarded. *Degree requirements:* For master's, thesis; for doctorate, comprehensive exam, thesis/dissertation. *Entrance requirements:* For master's and doctorate, GRE. Additional exam requirements/recommendations for international students: Required—TOEFL (minimum score 550 paper-based, 80 iBT) or IELTS (6.5). *Application deadline:* Applications are processed on a rolling basis. Application fee: $50. Electronic applications accepted. *Expenses: Tuition:* Full-time $24,984; part-time $1388 per credit hour. *Required fees:* $225. Tuition and fees vary according to campus/location and program. *Financial support:* Scholarships/grants and unspecified assistantships available. *Unit head:* Dr. Dipankar Roy, Chair of Physics, 315-268-6676, E-mail: droy@clarkson.edu. *Application contact:* Dan Capogna, Director of Graduate Admissions & Recruitment, 518-631-9910, E-mail: graduate@clarkson.edu.
Website: https://www.clarkson.edu/academics/graduate

Clark University, Graduate School, Department of Physics, Worcester, MA 01610-1477. Offers PhD. *Program availability:* Part-time. Terminal master's awarded for partial completion of doctoral program. *Degree requirements:* For doctorate, one foreign language, thesis/dissertation. *Entrance requirements:* For doctorate, GRE. Additional exam requirements/recommendations for international students: Required—TOEFL (minimum score 575 paper-based; 90 iBT), IELTS (minimum score 6.5). Electronic applications accepted. *Expenses: Tuition:* Full-time $34,110. *Required fees:* $40. Tuition and fees vary according to course load and program. *Faculty research:* Statistical and thermal physics, magnetic properties of materials, computer simulation, particle diffusion.

Clemson University, Graduate School, College of Science, Department of Physics and Astronomy, Clemson, SC 29634. Offers physics (MS, PhD). *Faculty:* 28 full-time (5 women). *Students:* 72 full-time (19 women); includes 2 minority (1 Asian, non-Hispanic/Latino; 1 Hispanic/Latino), 41 international. Average age 26. 86 applicants, 44% accepted, 18 enrolled. In 2018, 2 master's, 8 doctorates awarded. *Degree requirements:* For master's, comprehensive exam, thesis optional; for doctorate, comprehensive exam, thesis/dissertation, qualifying exam. *Entrance requirements:* For master's and doctorate, GRE General Test, unofficial transcripts, letters of recommendation. Additional exam requirements/recommendations for international students: Required—TOEFL (minimum score 80 paper-based; 80 iBT), PTE (minimum score 54); Recommended—IELTS (minimum score 6.5). *Application deadline:* For fall admission, 1/1 for domestic and international students. Applications are processed on a rolling basis. Application fee: $80 ($90 for international students). Electronic applications accepted. *Expenses: Tuition, area resident:* Full-time $11,270; part-time $8688 per credit hour. Tuition, state resident: full-time $11,796. Tuition, nonresident: full-time $23,802; part-time $17,412 per credit hour. *International tuition:* $23,246 full-time. *Required fees:* $1196; $497 per semester. Tuition and fees vary according to course load, degree level, campus/location and program. *Financial support:* In 2018–19, 73 students received support, including 3 fellowships with full and partial tuition reimbursements available (averaging $2,417 per year), 20 research assistantships with full and partial tuition reimbursements available (averaging $18,583 per year), 50 teaching assistantships with full and partial tuition reimbursements available (averaging $18,970 per year); career-related internships or fieldwork also available. Financial award application deadline: 1/1. *Faculty research:* Astrophysics, atmospheric physics, atomic physics, biophysics, condensed matter physics. *Total annual research expenditures:* $3.5 million. *Unit head:* Dr. Sean Brittain, Department Chair, 864-656-3416, E-mail: sbritt@clemson.edu. *Application contact:* Dr. Murray Daw, Graduate Program Coordinator, 864-656-6702, E-mail: daw@clemson.edu.
Website: https://clemson.edu/science/departments/physics-astro/

Cleveland State University, College of Graduate Studies, College of Sciences and Health Professions, Department of Physics, Cleveland, OH 44115. Offers MS. *Program availability:* Part-time, evening/weekend. *Faculty:* 4 full-time (0 women), 1 part-time/adjunct (0 women). *Students:* 11 full-time (5 women), 3 part-time (0 women); includes 1 minority (Black or African American, non-Hispanic/Latino), 1 international. Average age 29. 40 applicants, 50% accepted, 5 enrolled. In 2018, 9 master's awarded. *Entrance requirements:* For master's, undergraduate degree in engineering, physics, chemistry or mathematics. Additional exam requirements/recommendations for international students: Required—TOEFL (minimum score 550 paper-based; 78 iBT). *Application deadline:* Applications are processed on a rolling basis. Application fee: $40. Electronic applications accepted. *Expenses:* Tuition, state resident: full-time $7232.55; part-time $6676 per credit

Peterson's Graduate Programs in the Physical Sciences, Mathematics, Agricultural Sciences, the Environment & Natural Resources 2020

www.petersons.com **149**

hour. Tuition, nonresident: full-time $12,375. *International tuition:* $18,914 full-time. *Required fees:* $80; $80 $40. Tuition and fees vary according to program. *Financial support:* In 2018–19, 1 research assistantship with tuition reimbursement (averaging $6,960 per year), 7 teaching assistantships (averaging $6,960 per year) were awarded; fellowships and tuition waivers (full) also available. Financial award applicants required to submit FAFSA. *Faculty research:* Statistical physics, experimental solid-state physics, theoretical optics, experimental biological physics (macromolecular crystallography), experimental optics. *Total annual research expenditures:* $350,000. *Unit head:* Dr. Petru Fodor, Chairperson/Associate Professor, 216-523-7520, Fax: 216-523-7268, E-mail: p.fodor@csuohio.edu. *Application contact:* Karen Colston, Administrative Coordinator, 216-687-2425, Fax: 216-523-7268, E-mail: k.colston@csuohio.edu.
Website: http://www.csuohio.edu/sciences/physics/physics

Colorado School of Mines, Office of Graduate Studies, Department of Physics, Golden, CO 80401. Offers applied physics (MS, PhD); materials science (MS, PhD); nuclear engineering (ME, MS, PhD). *Program availability:* Part-time. *Faculty:* 34 full-time (4 women), 9 part-time/adjunct (3 women). *Students:* 61 full-time (14 women), 5 part-time (1 woman); includes 7 minority (4 Hispanic/Latino; 3 Two or more races, non-Hispanic/Latino), 8 international. Average age 27. 70 applicants, 33% accepted, 15 enrolled. In 2018, 5 master's, 10 doctorates awarded. *Degree requirements:* For master's, thesis (for some programs); for doctorate, comprehensive exam, thesis/dissertation. *Entrance requirements:* For master's and doctorate, GRE General Test, GRE Subject Test. Additional exam requirements/recommendations for international students: Required—TOEFL (minimum score 550 paper-based; 79 iBT). *Application deadline:* For fall admission, 12/15 priority date for domestic and international students; for spring admission, 9/1 priority date for domestic and international students. Application fee: $60 ($80 for international students). Electronic applications accepted. *Expenses:* Tuition, state resident: full-time $16,650; part-time $925 per contact hour. Tuition, nonresident: full-time $36,270; part-time $2015 per contact hour. *International tuition:* $36,270 full-time. *Required fees:* $2314; $2314 per semester. *Financial support:* In 2018–19, 32 research assistantships with full tuition reimbursements, 13 teaching assistantships with full tuition reimbursements were awarded; fellowships, scholarships/grants, health care benefits, and unspecified assistantships also available. Financial award application deadline: 12/15; financial award applicants required to submit FAFSA. *Faculty research:* Light scattering, low-energy nuclear physics, high fusion plasma diagnostics, laser operations, mathematical physics. *Unit head:* Dr. Uwe Greife, Head, 303-273-3618, E-mail: ugreife@mines.edu. *Application contact:* Dr. Kyle Leach, Professor, 303-273-3044, E-mail: kleach@mines.edu.
Website: http://physics.mines.edu

Colorado State University, College of Natural Sciences, Department of Physics, Fort Collins, CO 80523-1875. Offers MS, PhD. Terminal master's awarded for partial completion of doctoral program. *Degree requirements:* For master's, thesis (for some programs); for doctorate, thesis/dissertation. *Entrance requirements:* For master's and doctorate, GRE General Test, GRE Subject Test (physics), minimum GPA of 3.0; transcripts; resume/curriculum vitae; personal statement; 3 recommendation letters. Additional exam requirements/recommendations for international students: Required—TOEFL (minimum score 550 paper-based; 80 iBT), IELTS (minimum score 6.5). Electronic applications accepted. *Expenses:* Tuition, state resident: full-time $10,520; part-time $4675 per credit hour. Tuition, nonresident: full-time $25,791; part-time $11,462 per credit hour. *International tuition:* $25,791 full-time. *Required fees:* $2392; $576 $288. Tuition and fees vary according to course level, course load, degree level, program and student level. *Faculty research:* Atomic, molecular and optical physics; condensed matter experiment and theory; high energy particle and astroparticle physics.

Columbia University, Graduate School of Arts and Sciences, New York, NY 10027. Offers African-American studies (MA); American studies (MA); anthropology (MA, PhD); art history and archaeology (MA, PhD); astronomy (PhD); biological sciences (PhD); biotechnology (MA); chemical physics (PhD); chemistry (PhD); classical studies (MA, PhD); classics (MA, PhD); climate and society (MA); conservation biology (MA); earth and environmental sciences (PhD); East Asia: regional studies (MA); East Asian languages and cultures (MA, PhD); ecology, evolution and environmental biology (MA), including conservation biology; ecology, evolution, and environmental biology (PhD), including ecology and evolutionary biology, evolutionary primatology; economics (MA, PhD); English and comparative literature (MA, PhD); French and Romance philology (MA, PhD); Germanic languages (MA, PhD); global French studies (MA); global thought (MA); Hispanic cultural studies (MA); history (PhD); history and literature (MA); human rights studies (MA); Islamic studies (MA); Italian (MA, PhD); Japanese pedagogy (MA); Jewish studies (MA); Latin America and the Caribbean: regional studies (MA); Latin American and Iberian cultures (PhD); mathematics (MA, PhD), including finance (MA); medieval and Renaissance studies (MA); Middle Eastern, South Asian, and African studies (MA, PhD); modern art: critical and curatorial studies (MA); modern European studies (MA); museum anthropology (MA); music (DMA, PhD); oral history (MA); philosophical foundations of physics (MA); philosophy (MA, PhD); physics (PhD); political science (MA, PhD); psychology (PhD); quantitative methods in the social sciences (MA); religion (MA, PhD); Russia, Eurasia and East Europe: regional studies (MA); Russian translation (MA); Slavic cultures (MA); Slavic languages (MA, PhD); sociology (MA, PhD); South Asian studies (MA); statistics (MA, PhD); theatre (PhD). Dual-degree programs require admission to both Graduate School of Arts and Sciences and another Columbia school. *Program availability:* Part-time. Terminal master's awarded for partial completion of doctoral program. *Degree requirements:* For master's, variable foreign language requirement, comprehensive exam (for some programs), thesis (for some programs); for doctorate, variable foreign language requirement, comprehensive exam (for some programs), thesis/dissertation. *Entrance requirements:* For master's and doctorate, GRE General Test, GRE Subject Test (for some programs). Additional exam requirements/recommendations for international students: Required—TOEFL, IELTS. Electronic applications accepted.

Concordia University, School of Graduate Studies, Faculty of Arts and Science, Department of Physics, Montréal, QC H3G 1M8, Canada. Offers M Sc, PhD.

Cornell University, Graduate School, Graduate Fields of Arts and Sciences, Field of Physics, Ithaca, NY 14853. Offers experimental physics (MS, PhD); physics (MS, PhD); theoretical physics (MS, PhD). *Degree requirements:* For doctorate, comprehensive exam, thesis/dissertation. *Entrance requirements:* For doctorate, GRE General Test, GRE Subject Test (physics), 3 letters of recommendation. Additional exam requirements/recommendations for international students: Required—TOEFL (minimum score 620 paper-based; 105 iBT). Electronic applications accepted. *Faculty research:* Experimental condensed matter physics, theoretical condensed matter physics, experimental high energy particle physics, theoretical particle physics and field theory, theoretical astrophysics.

Creighton University, Graduate School, College of Arts and Sciences, Program in Physics, Omaha, NE 68178-0001. Offers MS. *Program availability:* Part-time. *Faculty:* 11 full-time (2 women), 2 part-time/adjunct (0 women). *Students:* 10 full-time (2 women), 1 part-time (0 women), 4 international. Average age 25. 17 applicants, 76% accepted, 5 enrolled. In 2018, 2 master's awarded. *Degree requirements:* For master's, comprehensive exam, thesis (for some programs). *Entrance requirements:* For master's, GRE General Test, 3 letters of recommendation. Additional exam requirements/recommendations for international students: Required—TOEFL (minimum score 90 iBT). *Application deadline:* For fall admission, 3/1 for domestic and international students. Applications are processed on a rolling basis. Application fee: $50. Electronic applications accepted. *Financial support:* In 2018–19, 9 students received support, including 9 teaching assistantships with full tuition reimbursements available (averaging $11,576 per year). Financial award applicants required to submit FAFSA. *Unit head:* Dr. Michael Nichols, Chair, 402-280-2159, E-mail: mnichols@creighton.edu. *Application contact:* Lindsay Johnson, Director of Graduate and Adult Recruitment, 402-280-2703, Fax: 402-280-2423, E-mail: gradschool@creighton.edu.

Dalhousie University, Faculty of Science, Department of Physics and Atmospheric Science, Halifax, NS B3H 4R2, Canada. Offers M Sc, PhD. *Degree requirements:* For master's, thesis; for doctorate, thesis/dissertation. *Entrance requirements:* Additional exam requirements/recommendations for international students: Required—TOEFL, IELTS, CANTEST, CAEL, or Michigan English Language Assessment Battery. Electronic applications accepted. *Faculty research:* Applied, experimental, and solid-state physics.

Dartmouth College, Guarini School of Graduate and Advanced Studies, Department of Physics and Astronomy, Hanover, NH 03755. Offers PhD. *Faculty:* 23 full-time (4 women), 4 part-time/adjunct (1 woman). *Students:* 40 full-time (17 women); includes 3 minority (2 Hispanic/Latino; 1 Two or more races, non-Hispanic/Latino), 17 international. Average age 26. 95 applicants, 25% accepted, 6 enrolled. In 2018, 7 doctorates awarded. *Entrance requirements:* For doctorate, GRE General Test, GRE Subject Test. Additional exam requirements/recommendations for international students: Required—TOEFL. *Application deadline:* For fall admission, 1/15 for domestic students. Application fee: $50. Electronic applications accepted. *Financial support:* Research assistantships, teaching assistantships, and scholarships/grants available. *Faculty research:* Matter physics, plasma and beam physics, space physics, astronomy, cosmology. *Unit head:* John R. Thorstensen, Chair, 603-646-2869. *Application contact:* Judy Lowell, Administrative Assistant, 603-646-2359.
Website: http://www.dartmouth.edu/~physics/

Delaware State University, Graduate Programs, Department of Physics, Dover, DE 19901-2277. Offers applied optics (MS); optics (PhD); physics (MS); physics teaching (MS). *Program availability:* Part-time, evening/weekend. *Entrance requirements:* For master's, minimum GPA of 3.0 in major, 2.75 overall. Additional exam requirements/recommendations for international students: Required—TOEFL. Electronic applications accepted. *Faculty research:* Thermal properties of solids, nuclear physics, radiation damage in solids.

DePaul University, College of Science and Health, Chicago, IL 60604-2287. Offers applied mathematics (MS); applied statistics (MS); biological sciences (MA, MS); chemistry (MS); environmental science (MS); mathematics education (MA); mathematics for teaching (MS); nursing (MS); nursing practice (DNP); physics (MS); polymer and coatings science (MS); psychology (MS); pure mathematics (MS); science education (MS); MA/PhD. *Accreditation:* AACN. Electronic applications accepted.

Drexel University, College of Arts and Sciences, Department of Physics, Philadelphia, PA 19104-2875. Offers MS, PhD. Terminal master's awarded for partial completion of doctoral program. *Degree requirements:* For doctorate, thesis/dissertation. *Entrance requirements:* For master's and doctorate, GRE. Additional exam requirements/recommendations for international students: Required—TOEFL. Electronic applications accepted. *Faculty research:* Nuclear structure, mesoscale meteorology, numerical astrophysics, numerical weather prediction, earth energy radiation budget.

Duke University, Graduate School, Department of Physics, Durham, NC 27708. Offers PhD. *Degree requirements:* For doctorate, thesis/dissertation. *Entrance requirements:* For doctorate, GRE General Test, GRE Subject Test. Additional exam requirements/recommendations for international students: Required—TOEFL (minimum score 577 paper-based; 90 iBT) or IELTS (minimum score 7).

East Carolina University, Graduate School, Thomas Harriot College of Arts and Sciences, Department of Physics, Greenville, NC 27858-4353. Offers applied physics (MS); biomedical physics (PhD); health physics (MS); medical physics (MS). *Program availability:* Part-time. *Application deadline:* For fall admission, 3/1 priority date for domestic and international students. *Expenses: Tuition, area resident:* Full-time $4749. Tuition, state resident: full-time $4749. Tuition, nonresident: full-time $17,898. *International tuition:* $17,898 full-time. *Required fees:* $2787. Part-time tuition and fees vary according to course load and program. *Financial support:* Application deadline: 3/1. *Unit head:* Dr. Jefferson Shinpaugh, Chair, 252-328-6739, E-mail: shinpaughj@ecu.edu. *Application contact:* Graduate School Admissions, 252-328-6012, Fax: 252-328-6071, E-mail: gradschool@ecu.edu.
Website: http://www.ecu.edu/cs-cas/physics/

Eastern Michigan University, Graduate School, College of Arts and Sciences, Department of Physics and Astronomy, Ypsilanti, MI 48197. Offers physics (MS). *Program availability:* Part-time, evening/weekend, online learning. *Faculty:* 10 full-time (2 women). *Students:* 8 part-time (2 women), 1 international. Average age 27. 29 applicants, 48% accepted, 5 enrolled. In 2018, 4 master's awarded. *Entrance requirements:* Additional exam requirements/recommendations for international students: Required—TOEFL. *Application deadline:* Applications are processed on a rolling basis. Application fee: $45. *Financial support:* Fellowships, research assistantships with full tuition reimbursements, teaching assistantships with full tuition reimbursements, career-related internships or fieldwork, Federal Work-Study, institutionally sponsored loans, scholarships/grants, tuition waivers, and unspecified assistantships available. Support available to part-time students. Financial award applicants required to submit FAFSA. *Unit head:* Dr. Alexandria Oakes, Department Head, 734-487-4144, Fax: 734-487-0989, E-mail: aoakes@emich.edu. *Application contact:* Dr. Alexandria Oakes, Department Head, 734-487-4144, Fax: 734-487-0989, E-mail: aoakes@emich.edu.
Website: http://www.emich.edu/physics/

Emory University, Laney Graduate School, Department of Physics, Atlanta, GA 30322-1100. Offers PhD, MS/PhD. *Degree requirements:* For doctorate, thesis/dissertation, qualifier proposal. *Entrance requirements:* For doctorate, GRE General Test, minimum GPA of 3.0. Additional exam requirements/recommendations for international students: Required—TOEFL (minimum score 600 paper-based). Electronic applications accepted. *Faculty research:* Experimental studies of the structure and function of metalloproteins, soft condensed matter, granular materials, biophotonics and fluorescence correlation spectroscopy, single molecule studies of DNA-protein systems.

Fisk University, Division of Graduate Studies, Department of Physics, Nashville, TN 37208-3051. Offers MA. *Degree requirements:* For master's, thesis. *Entrance requirements:* For master's, GRE General Test, GRE Subject Test, minimum GPA of 3.0. Electronic applications accepted. *Faculty research:* Molecular physics, astrophysics, surface physics, nanobase materials, optical processing.

Florida Agricultural and Mechanical University, Division of Graduate Studies, Research, and Continuing Education, College of Science and Technology, Department of Physics, Tallahassee, FL 32307-3200. Offers MS, PhD. *Degree requirements:* For master's, comprehensive exam, thesis optional; for doctorate, comprehensive exam, thesis/dissertation. *Entrance requirements:* For master's, GRE General Test, minimum GPA of 3.0; for doctorate, GRE General Test, minimum GPA of 3.0, letters of recommendation (2). Additional exam requirements/recommendations for international students: Required—TOEFL (minimum score 550 paper-based). *Faculty research:* Plasma physics, quantum mechanics, condensed matter physics, astrophysics, laser ablation.

Florida Atlantic University, Charles E. Schmidt College of Science, Department of Physics, Boca Raton, FL 33431-0991. Offers physics (MS, MST, PhD). *Program availability:* Part-time. *Faculty:* 12 full-time (2 women), 4 part-time/adjunct (1 woman). *Students:* 23 full-time (10 women), 26 part-time (6 women); includes 6 minority (1 Asian, non-Hispanic/Latino; 4 Hispanic/Latino; 1 Two or more races, non-Hispanic/Latino), 28 international. Average age 31. 28 applicants, 46% accepted, 13 enrolled. In 2018, 4 master's, 2 doctorates awarded. *Entrance requirements:* For master's, GRE General Test, minimum GPA of 3.0; for doctorate, GRE General Test. Additional exam requirements/recommendations for international students: Required—TOEFL (minimum score 500 paper-based; 61 iBT), IELTS (minimum score 6). *Application deadline:* For fall admission, 7/1 for domestic students, 2/15 for international students; for spring admission, 11/1 for domestic students, 7/15 for international students. Applications are processed on a rolling basis. Application fee: $30. *Expenses: Tuition, area resident:* Full-time $7400; part-time $369.82 per credit. Tuition, state resident: full-time $7400; part-time $369.82 per credit. Tuition, nonresident: full-time $20,496; part-time $1024.81 per credit. *Financial support:* Fellowships, research assistantships, teaching assistantships, Federal Work-Study, and unspecified assistantships available. *Faculty research:* Astrophysics, spectroscopy, mathematical physics, theory of metals, superconductivity. *Unit head:* Luc Wille, Professor/Chair, 561-297-3380, E-mail: willel@fau.edu. *Application contact:* Luc Wille, Professor/Chair, 561-297-3380, E-mail: willel@fau.edu. Website: http://physics.fau.edu/

Florida Institute of Technology, College of Engineering and Science, Program in Physics, Melbourne, FL 32901-6975. Offers MS, PhD. *Program availability:* Part-time. *Students:* 13 full-time (3 women), 2 part-time (0 women); includes 2 minority (both Black or African American, non-Hispanic/Latino), 7 international. Average age 29. 22 applicants, 55% accepted, 4 enrolled. In 2018, 3 master's, 1 doctorate awarded. Terminal master's awarded for partial completion of doctoral program. *Degree requirements:* For master's, comprehensive exam, thesis optional, minimum of 30 credit hours; for doctorate, comprehensive exam, thesis/dissertation, oral defense of dissertation, 45 credit hours. *Entrance requirements:* For master's, GRE General Test and GRE Subject Test in physics (recommended), 3 letters of recommendation, resume, statement of objectives, undergraduate degree in physics or related field; for doctorate, GRE General Test (recommended). Additional exam requirements/recommendations for international students: Required—TOEFL (minimum score 550 paper-based; 79 iBT). *Application deadline:* For fall admission, 4/1 for international students; for spring admission, 9/30 for international students. Applications are processed on a rolling basis. Application fee: $50. Electronic applications accepted. *Expenses: Tuition:* Full-time $22,338; part-time $1241 per credit hour. Tuition and fees vary according to degree level, campus/location and program. *Financial support:* Research assistantships, teaching assistantships, career-related internships or fieldwork, and tuition remissions available. Financial award application deadline: 3/1; financial award applicants required to submit FAFSA. *Faculty research:* Lasers, semiconductors, magnetism, quantum devices, solid state physics, optics. *Unit head:* Dr. Daniel Batcheldor, Department Head, 321-674-8098, E-mail: dbatcheldor@fit.edu. *Application contact:* Mike Perry, Executive Director of Admissions, 321-674-7127, E-mail: perrymj@flt.edu. Website: https://www.fit.edu/programs/physics-ms/

Florida International University, College of Arts, Sciences, and Education, Department of Physics, Miami, FL 33199. Offers MS, PhD. *Program availability:* Part-time, evening/weekend. *Faculty:* 24 full-time (3 women), 12 part-time/adjunct (1 woman). *Students:* 40 full-time (8 women); includes 11 minority (1 Black or African American, non-Hispanic/Latino; 10 Hispanic/Latino), 24 international. Average age 30. 84 applicants, 10% accepted, 6 enrolled. In 2018, 2 master's, 5 doctorates awarded. *Degree requirements:* For master's, one foreign language, thesis; for doctorate, one foreign language, comprehensive exam, thesis/dissertation. *Entrance requirements:* For master's and doctorate, GRE General Test, 2 letters of recommendation. Additional exam requirements/recommendations for international students: Required—TOEFL (minimum score 550 paper-based; 80 iBT). *Application deadline:* For fall admission, 6/1 for domestic students, 4/1 for international students; for spring admission, 10/1 for domestic students, 9/1 for international students. Applications are processed on a rolling basis. Application fee: $30. Electronic applications accepted. *Financial support:* Institutionally sponsored loans and scholarships/grants available. Financial award application deadline: 3/1; financial award applicants required to submit FAFSA. *Faculty research:* Molecular collision processes (molecular beams), biophysical optics. *Unit head:* Dr. Werner Boeglin, Chair, 305-348-1711, Fax: 305-348-6700, E-mail: werner.boeglin@fiu.edu. *Application contact:* Nanett Rojas, Manager, Admissions Operations, 305-348-7464, Fax: 305-348-7441, E-mail: gradadm@fiu.edu.

Florida State University, The Graduate School, Department of Anthropology, Department of Scientific Computing, Tallahassee, FL 32306-4120. Offers computational science (MS, PhD), including atmospheric science (PhD), biochemistry (PhD), biological science (PhD), computational science (PhD), geological science (PhD), materials science (PhD), physics (PhD). *Program availability:* Part-time. *Faculty:* 9 full-time (1 woman), 2 part-time/adjunct (1 woman). *Students:* 34 full-time (6 women); includes 17 minority (10 Asian, non-Hispanic/Latino; 3 Hispanic/Latino; 4 Two or more races, non-Hispanic/Latino), 13 international. Average age 26. 64 applicants, 23% accepted, 6 enrolled. In 2018, 10 master's, 8 doctorates awarded. Terminal master's awarded for partial completion of doctoral program. *Degree requirements:* For master's, comprehensive exam, thesis (for some programs); for doctorate, comprehensive exam, thesis/dissertation. *Entrance requirements:* For master's and doctorate, GRE General Test, knowledge of at least one object-oriented computing language, 3 letters of recommendation, resume, statement of purpose. Additional exam requirements/recommendations for international students: Required—TOEFL (minimum score 550 paper-based; 80 iBT). *Application deadline:* For fall admission, 1/15 for domestic and international students. Applications are processed on a rolling basis. Application fee: $30. Electronic applications accepted. *Expenses: Tuition, area resident:* Part-time $479.32 per credit hour. Tuition and fees vary according to campus/location and program. *Financial support:* In 2018–19, 32 students received support, including 10 research assistantships with full tuition reimbursements available (averaging $26,670 per year), 23 teaching assistantships with full tuition reimbursements available (averaging $23,000 per year); scholarships/grants, health care benefits, tuition waivers (full), and unspecified assistantships also available. Financial award application deadline: 1/15. *Faculty research:* Morphometrics, mathematical and systems biology, mining proteomic and metabolic data, computational materials research, computational

fluid dynamics, astrophysics, deep learning, computational neuroscience. *Total annual research expenditures:* $500,000. *Unit head:* Dr. Gordon Erlebacher, Chair, 850-644-7024, E-mail: gerlebacher@fsu.edu. *Application contact:* Karey Fowler, Academic Program Specialist, 850-644-0143, Fax: 850-644-0098, E-mail: kgfowler@fsu.edu. Website: http://www.sc.fsu.edu

George Mason University, College of Science, Department of Physics and Astronomy, Fairfax, VA 22030. Offers MS, PhD. *Faculty:* 31 full-time (8 women), 8 part-time/adjunct (1 woman). *Students:* 31 full-time (2 women), 29 part-time (5 women); includes 11 minority (5 Black or African American, non-Hispanic/Latino; 1 Asian, non-Hispanic/Latino; 4 Hispanic/Latino; 1 Two or more races, non-Hispanic/Latino), 16 international. Average age 31. 49 applicants, 49% accepted, 10 enrolled. In 2018, 6 master's, 4 doctorates awarded. *Degree requirements:* For master's, thesis optional; for doctorate, comprehensive exam, thesis/dissertation. *Entrance requirements:* For master's, GRE General and Subject Tests (recommended), three letters of recommendation, preferably from former professors; personal statement; for doctorate, GRE General Test; GRE Subject Test (recommended), three letters of recommendation, preferably from former professors; personal statement with emphasis on research experience and goals. Additional exam requirements/recommendations for international students: Required—TOEFL (minimum score 575 paper-based; 88 iBT), IELTS (minimum score 6.5), PTE (minimum score 59). *Application deadline:* For fall admission, 2/15 priority date for domestic students, 2/1 priority date for international students. Application fee: $75 ($80 for international students). Electronic applications accepted. *Financial support:* In 2018–19, 28 students received support, including 2 fellowships, 13 research assistantships with tuition reimbursements available (averaging $16,421 per year), 14 teaching assistantships with tuition reimbursements available (averaging $19,643 per year); career-related internships or fieldwork, Federal Work-Study, scholarships/grants, unspecified assistantships, and health care benefits (for full-time research or teaching assistantship recipients) also available. Support available to part-time students. Financial award application deadline: 3/1; financial award applicants required to submit FAFSA. *Faculty research:* Astrophysics/space sciences; materials/condensed matter physics; biological physics/aerodynamics; applied mechanics; high energy physics. *Total annual research expenditures:* $2.9 million. *Unit head:* Dr. Paul So, Chair, 709-993-4377, E-mail: paso@gmu.edu. *Application contact:* Executive Assistant, 703-993-1280, E-mail: physics@gmu.edu.

The George Washington University, Columbian College of Arts and Sciences, Department of Physics, Washington, DC 20052. Offers MA, PhD. *Program availability:* Part-time, evening/weekend. *Students:* 24 full-time (9 women), 16 part-time (3 women); includes 2 minority (1 Asian, non-Hispanic/Latino; 1 Two or more races, non-Hispanic/Latino), 21 international. Average age 27. 71 applicants, 27% accepted, 6 enrolled. In 2018, 16 master's, 9 doctorates awarded. *Degree requirements:* For doctorate, thesis/dissertation, general exam. *Entrance requirements:* For master's and doctorate, GRE General Test, minimum GPA of 3.0. Additional exam requirements/recommendations for international students: Required—TOEFL (minimum score 550 paper-based; 80 iBT). *Application deadline:* For fall admission, 1/15 priority date for domestic and international students; for spring admission, 10/1 priority date for domestic students, 9/1 priority date for international students. Applications are processed on a rolling basis. Application fee: $75. Electronic applications accepted. *Financial support:* In 2018–19, 24 students received support. Fellowships with full tuition reimbursements available, research assistantships, teaching assistantships, Federal Work-Study, and tuition waivers available. Financial award application deadline: 1/15. *Unit head:* Dr. Briscoe J. William, Chair, 202-994-6788, E-mail: briscoe@gwu.edu. *Application contact:* Dr. Mark Reeves, Director, 202-994-6279, Fax: 202-994-3001, E-mail: reevesme@gwu.edu. Website: http://www.gwu.edu/~physics/

Georgia Institute of Technology, Graduate Studies, College of Sciences, School of Physics, Atlanta, GA 30332-0001. Offers MS, PhD. *Program availability:* Part-time. Terminal master's awarded for partial completion of doctoral program. *Degree requirements:* For doctorate, comprehensive exam, thesis/dissertation. *Entrance requirements:* For master's and doctorate, GRE General Test, GRE Subject Test. Additional exam requirements/recommendations for international students: Required—TOEFL (minimum score 625 paper-based; 106 iBT). Electronic applications accepted. *Faculty research:* Atomic and molecular physics, chemical physics, condensed matter, optics, nonlinear physics and chaos.

Georgia State University, College of Arts and Sciences, Department of Physics and Astronomy, Program in Physics, Atlanta, GA 30302-3083. Offers MS, PhD. *Program availability:* Part-time, evening/weekend. Terminal master's awarded for partial completion of doctoral program. *Entrance requirements:* For master's and doctorate, GRE General Test, GRE Subject Test. Additional exam requirements/recommendations for international students: Required—TOEFL (minimum score 550 paper-based; 80 iBT). *Application deadline:* Applications are processed on a rolling basis. Application fee: $50. Electronic applications accepted. *Expenses: Tuition, area resident:* Full-time $9360; part-time $390 per credit hour. Tuition, state resident: full-time $9360; part-time $390 per credit hour. Tuition, nonresident: full-time $30,024; part-time $1251 per credit hour. *International tuition:* $30,024 full-time. *Required fees:* $2128. *Financial support:* Fellowships, research assistantships, teaching assistantships, scholarships/grants, and unspecified assistantships available. Financial award application deadline: 2/15; financial award applicants required to submit FAFSA. *Faculty research:* Experimental and theoretical condensed matter physics, nuclear physics (relativistic heavy ion collisions, proton and neutron spin, cosmic ray radiation), biophysics and brain sciences, theoretical atomic and molecular structure and collisions, physics education research. *Unit head:* Dr. Murad Sarsour, Physics Graduate Director, 404-413-6077, Fax: 404-413-6025, E-mail: msar@phy-astr.gsu.edu. *Application contact:* Amber Amari, Director, Graduate and Scheduling Services, 404-413-5037, E-mail: aamari@gsu.edu. Website: http://www.phy-astr.gsu.edu/

Georgia State University, College of Education and Human Development, Department of Middle and Secondary Education, Atlanta, GA 30302-3083. Offers curriculum and instruction (Ed D); English education (MAT); mathematics education (M Ed, MAT); middle level education (MAT); reading, language and literacy education (M Ed, MAT), including reading instruction (M Ed); science education (M Ed, MAT), including biology (MAT), broad field science (MAT), chemistry (MAT), earth science (MAT), physics (MAT); social studies education (M Ed, MAT), including economics (MAT), geography (MAT), history (MAT), political science (MAT); teaching and learning (PhD), including language and literacy, mathematics education, music education, science education, social studies education, teaching and teacher education. *Accreditation:* NCATE. *Program availability:* Part-time, evening/weekend, online learning. *Faculty:* 19 full-time (15 women), 9 part-time/adjunct (7 women). *Students:* 217 full-time (136 women), 203 part-time (140 women); includes 229 minority (156 Black or African American, non-Hispanic/Latino; 23 Asian, non-Hispanic/Latino; 31 Hispanic/Latino; 19 Two or more races, non-Hispanic/Latino), 3 international. Average age 34. 149 applicants, 60% accepted, 70 enrolled. In 2018, 112 master's, 23 doctorates awarded. *Entrance requirements:* For master's, GRE; GACE I (for initial teacher preparation programs), baccalaureate degree or equivalent, resume, goals statement, two letters of recommendation, minimum undergraduate GPA of 2.5; proof of initial teacher

Peterson's Graduate Programs in the Physical Sciences, Mathematics, Agricultural Sciences, the Environment & Natural Resources 2020

www.petersons.com 151

certification in the content area (for M Ed); for doctorate, GRE, resume, goals statement, writing sample, two letters of recommendation, minimum graduate GPA of 3.3, interview. *Application deadline:* For fall admission, 1/15 priority date for domestic and international students; for spring admission, 10/1 for domestic and international students. Application fee: $50. Electronic applications accepted. *Expenses: Tuition, area resident:* Full-time $9360; part-time $390 per credit hour. Tuition, state resident: full-time $9360; part-time $390 per credit hour. Tuition, nonresident: full-time $30,024; part-time $1251 per credit hour. *International tuition:* $30,024 full-time. *Required fees:* $2128. *Financial support:* In 2018–19, fellowships with full tuition reimbursements (averaging $19,667 per year), research assistantships with full tuition reimbursements (averaging $5,436 per year), teaching assistantships with full tuition reimbursements (averaging $2,779 per year) were awarded; career-related internships or fieldwork, Federal Work-Study, scholarships/grants, health care benefits, tuition waivers (full and partial), and unspecified assistantships also available. Financial award application deadline: 3/15. *Faculty research:* Teacher education in language and literacy, mathematics, science, and social studies in urban middle and secondary school settings; learning technologies in school, community, and corporate settings; multicultural education and education for social justice; urban education; international education. *Unit head:* Dr. Gertrude Marilyn Tinker Sachs, Chair, 404-413-8384, Fax: 404-413-8063, E-mail: gtinkersachs@gsu.edu. *Application contact:* Shaleen Tibbs, Administrative Specialist, 404-413-8385, Fax: 404-413-8063, E-mail: stibbs@gsu.edu.
Website: http://mse.education.gsu.edu/

The Graduate Center, City University of New York, Graduate Studies, Program in Physics, New York, NY 10016-4039. Offers PhD. *Degree requirements:* For doctorate, thesis/dissertation. *Entrance requirements:* For doctorate, GRE General Test. Additional exam requirements/recommendations for international students: Required—TOEFL or IELTS. Electronic applications accepted. *Faculty research:* Condensed-matter; particle, nuclear, and high energy physics; astrophysics and cosmology; biophysics and neuroscience; materials science; photonics and nanotechnology; quantum information and quantum optics; computational and statistical physics.

Hampton University, School of Science, Department of Physics, Hampton, VA 23668. Offers medical physics (PhD); nuclear physics (MS, PhD); optical physics (MS, PhD). *Students:* 14 full-time (4 women), 1 part-time (0 women); includes 5 minority (3 Black or African American, non-Hispanic/Latino; 2 Asian, non-Hispanic/Latino), 7 international. Average age 33. 7 applicants, 29% accepted. In 2018, 2 master's, 1 doctorate awarded. *Degree requirements:* For master's, thesis optional; for doctorate, thesis/dissertation, oral defense, qualifying exam. *Entrance requirements:* For master's, GRE General Test; for doctorate, GRE General Test, minimum GPA of 3.0 or master's degree in physics or related field. Additional exam requirements/recommendations for international students: Required—TOEFL (minimum score 525 paper-based) or IELTS (6.5). *Application deadline:* For fall admission, 6/1 priority date for domestic students, 4/1 priority date for international students; for spring admission, 11/1 priority date for domestic students, 9/1 priority date for international students; for summer admission, 4/1 priority date for domestic students, 2/1 priority date for international students. Applications are processed on a rolling basis. Application fee: $35. Electronic applications accepted. *Financial support:* In 2018–19, 17 research assistantships were awarded; fellowships, teaching assistantships, career-related internships or fieldwork, Federal Work-Study, institutionally sponsored loans, and scholarships/grants also available. Support available to part-time students. Financial award application deadline: 6/30; financial award applicants required to submit FAFSA. *Faculty research:* Laser optics, remote sensing, particle and nuclear physics, proton therapy, the effect of two-photon exchange by comparison of positron-proton and electron-proton elastic scattering, TREK (Time Reversal Experiment with Kaons) aims to discover violation of time reversal invariance beyond the Standard Model in the decay of positive kaons. *Unit head:* Dr. Paul Gueye, Chairperson, 757-727-5277. *Application contact:* Dr. Paul Gueye, Chairperson, 757-727-5277.
Website: http://science.hamptonu.edu/physics/

Harvard University, Graduate School of Arts and Sciences, Department of Physics, Cambridge, MA 02138. Offers experimental physics (PhD); medical engineering/medical physics (PhD), including applied physics, engineering sciences, physics; theoretical physics (PhD). *Degree requirements:* For doctorate, thesis/dissertation, final exams, laboratory experience. *Entrance requirements:* For doctorate, GRE General Test, GRE Subject Test. Additional exam requirements/recommendations for international students: Required—TOEFL. *Faculty research:* Particle physics, condensed matter physics, atomic physics.

Howard University, Graduate School, Department of Physics and Astronomy, Washington, DC 20059-0002. Offers physics (MS, PhD). *Degree requirements:* For master's, comprehensive exam (for some programs), thesis (for some programs); for doctorate, comprehensive exam, thesis/dissertation, departmental qualifying exam. *Entrance requirements:* For master's, GRE General Test, bachelor's degree in physics or related field, minimum GPA of 3.0; for doctorate, GRE General Test, bachelor's or master's degree in physics or related field, minimum GPA of 3.0. Additional exam requirements/recommendations for international students: Required—TOEFL (minimum score 550 paper-based). Electronic applications accepted. *Faculty research:* Atmospheric physics, spectroscopy and optical physics, high energy physics, condensed matter.

Hunter College of the City University of New York, Graduate School, School of Arts and Sciences, Department of Physics and Astronomy, New York, NY 10065-5085. Offers MA, PhD. PhD offered jointly with The Graduate Center, City University of New York. *Program availability:* Part-time. Terminal master's awarded for partial completion of doctoral program. *Degree requirements:* For master's, comprehensive exam or thesis. *Entrance requirements:* For master's, minimum 36 credits of course work in mathematics and physics. Additional exam requirements/recommendations for international students: Required—TOEFL. *Faculty research:* Experimental and theoretical quantum optics, experimental and theoretical condensed matter, mathematical physics.

Idaho State University, Graduate School, College of Science and Engineering, Department of Physics, Pocatello, ID 83209-8106. Offers applied physics (PhD); health physics (MS); physics (MNS). *Program availability:* Part-time. *Degree requirements:* For master's, comprehensive exam, thesis (for some programs), oral exam (for some programs); for doctorate, comprehensive exam, thesis/dissertation (for some programs), oral exam, written qualifying exam in physics or health physics after 1st year. *Entrance requirements:* For master's, GRE General Test, 3 letters of recommendation, BS or BA in physics, teaching certificate (MNS); for doctorate, GRE General Test (minimum 50th percentile), 3 letters of recommendation, statement of career goals. Additional exam requirements/recommendations for international students: Required—TOEFL (minimum score 550 paper-based; 80 iBT). Electronic applications accepted. *Faculty research:* Ion beam applications, low-energy nuclear physics, relativity and cosmology, observational astronomy.

Illinois Institute of Technology, Graduate College, College of Science, Department of Physics, Chicago, IL 60616. Offers applied physics (MS); health physics (MAS); physics (MS, PhD). *Program availability:* Part-time, evening/weekend, online learning. Terminal master's awarded for partial completion of doctoral program. *Degree requirements:* For master's, comprehensive exam (for some programs), thesis (for some programs); for doctorate, comprehensive exam, thesis/dissertation. *Entrance requirements:* For master's, GRE General Test (minimum score 295 Quantitative and Verbal, 2.5 Analytical Writing), minimum undergraduate GPA of 3.0; for doctorate, GRE General Test (minimum score 310 Quantitative and Verbal, 3.0 Analytical Writing); GRE Subject Test in physics (strongly recommended), minimum undergraduate GPA of 3.0. Additional exam requirements/recommendations for international students: Required—TOEFL (minimum score 550 paper-based; 80 iBT). Electronic applications accepted. *Faculty research:* Elementary particle physics, condensed matter, superconductivity, experimental and computational biophysics.

Indiana University Bloomington, University Graduate School, College of Arts and Sciences, Department of Physics, Bloomington, IN 47405. Offers medical physics (MS); physics (MAT, MS, PhD). *Program availability:* Part-time, online learning. Terminal master's awarded for partial completion of doctoral program. *Degree requirements:* For master's, comprehensive exam (for some programs), thesis (for some programs), qualifying exam; for doctorate, comprehensive exam, thesis/dissertation, qualifying exam. *Entrance requirements:* For master's and doctorate, GRE General Test, GRE Subject Test (physics), minimum GPA of 3.0. Additional exam requirements/recommendations for international students: Required—TOEFL (minimum score 550 paper-based; 80 iBT) or IELTS (minimum score 6.5). Electronic applications accepted. *Expenses:* Contact institution. *Faculty research:* Accelerator physics, astrophysics and cosmology, biophysics (biocomplexity, neural networks, visual systems, chemical signaling), condensed matter physics (neutron scattering, complex fluids, quantum computing), particle physics (collider physics, hybrid mesons, lattice gauge, symmetries, collider phenomenology), neutrino physics, nuclear physics (proton and neutron physics, neutrinos, symmetries, nuclear astrophysics, hadron structure).

Indiana University of Pennsylvania, School of Graduate Studies and Research, College of Natural Sciences and Mathematics, Department of Physics, Indiana, PA 15705. Offers nanoscience/industrial materials (PSM); physics (MA, PSM). *Program availability:* Part-time. *Faculty:* 4 full-time (0 women). *Students:* 2 full-time (1 woman), 1 international. Average age 25. 6 applicants, 50% accepted. In 2018, 1 master's awarded. *Entrance requirements:* For master's, 2 letters of recommendation. Additional exam requirements/recommendations for international students: Required—TOEFL (minimum score 540 paper-based). *Application deadline:* Applications are processed on a rolling basis. Application fee: $50. Electronic applications accepted. *Expenses:* Tuition, state resident: full-time $12,384; part-time $516 per credit hour. Tuition, nonresident: full-time $18,576; part-time $774 per credit hour. *Required fees:* $4454; $186 per credit hour. $65 per semester. Tuition and fees vary according to program and reciprocity agreements. *Financial support:* In 2018–19, 2 research assistantships (averaging $3,173 per year) were awarded; fellowships, career-related internships or fieldwork, Federal Work-Study, scholarships/grants, and unspecified assistantships also available. Support available to part-time students. Financial award application deadline: 4/15; financial award applicants required to submit FAFSA. *Unit head:* Dr. Muhammad Numan, Chairperson, 724-357-2371, E-mail: mznuman@iup.edu. *Application contact:* Dr. John Bradshaw, Graduate Coordinator, 724-357-7731, E-mail: bradshaw@iup.edu.
Website: http://www.iup.edu/physics

Indiana University–Purdue University Indianapolis, School of Science, Department of Physics, Indianapolis, IN 46202. Offers MS, PhD. *Program availability:* Part-time. Terminal master's awarded for partial completion of doctoral program. *Degree requirements:* For master's, thesis optional; for doctorate, thesis/dissertation. *Entrance requirements:* For master's and doctorate, GRE. Additional exam requirements/recommendations for international students: Required—TOEFL (minimum score 79 iBT). *Faculty research:* Magnetic resonance, photosynthesis, optical physics, biophysics, physics of materials.

Iowa State University of Science and Technology, Department of Physics and Astronomy, Ames, IA 50011. Offers applied physics (MS, PhD); astrophysics (MS, PhD); condensed matter physics (MS, PhD); high energy physics (MS, PhD); nuclear physics (MS, PhD); physics (MS, PhD). *Degree requirements:* For master's, thesis (for some programs); for doctorate, thesis/dissertation. *Entrance requirements:* For master's and doctorate, GRE General Test, GRE Subject Test (physics). Additional exam requirements/recommendations for international students: Required—TOEFL (minimum score 550 paper-based; 79 iBT), IELTS (minimum score 6.5). Electronic applications accepted. *Faculty research:* Condensed-matter physics, including superconductivity and new materials; high-energy and nuclear physics; astronomy and astrophysics; atmospheric and environmental physics.

Iowa State University of Science and Technology, Program in High Energy Physics, Ames, IA 50011. Offers MS, PhD. *Entrance requirements:* For master's and doctorate, GRE. Additional exam requirements/recommendations for international students: Required—TOEFL (minimum score 550 paper-based; 79 iBT), IELTS (minimum score 6.5). Electronic applications accepted.

Iowa State University of Science and Technology, Program in Nuclear Physics, Ames, IA 50011. Offers MS, PhD. *Entrance requirements:* For master's and doctorate, GRE. Additional exam requirements/recommendations for international students: Required—TOEFL (minimum score 550 paper-based; 79 iBT), IELTS (minimum score 6.5). Electronic applications accepted.

Jackson State University, Graduate School, College of Science, Engineering and Technology, Department of Physics, Atmospheric Sciences, and Geoscience, Jackson, MS 39217. Offers physical science (MS, PhD); science education (MST). *Program availability:* Part-time, evening/weekend. *Degree requirements:* For master's, comprehensive exam. *Entrance requirements:* For master's, GRE General Test. Additional exam requirements/recommendations for international students: Required—TOEFL (minimum score 520 paper-based; 67 iBT).

Johns Hopkins University, Zanvyl Krieger School of Arts and Sciences, Henry A. Rowland Department of Physics and Astronomy, Baltimore, MD 21218. Offers astronomy (PhD); physics (PhD). *Faculty:* 59 full-time (11 women). *Students:* 102 full-time (23 women). 351 applicants, 20% accepted, 21 enrolled. In 2018, 18 doctorates awarded. *Degree requirements:* For doctorate, comprehensive exam, thesis/dissertation, minimum B- on required coursework. *Entrance requirements:* For doctorate, GRE General Test, GRE Subject Test. Additional exam requirements/recommendations for international students: Required—TOEFL (minimum score 600 paper-based; 100 iBT), IELTS. *Application deadline:* For fall admission, 1/15 for domestic and international students. Application fee: $75. Electronic applications accepted. *Financial support:* In 2018–19, 100 students received support, including 3 fellowships with full tuition reimbursements available (averaging $33,333 per year), 45 research assistantships with full tuition reimbursements available (averaging $33,333 per year), 52 teaching assistantships with full tuition reimbursements available

(averaging $33,333 per year); career-related internships or fieldwork, Federal Work-Study, institutionally sponsored loans, health care benefits, tuition waivers (full), and unspecified assistantships also available. Financial award application deadline: 4/15; financial award applicants required to submit FAFSA. *Faculty research:* High-energy physics, condensed-matter, astrophysics, particle and experimental physics, plasma physics. *Unit head:* Dr. Timothy Heckman, Chair, 410-516-7369, E-mail: theckma1@jhu.edu. *Application contact:* Richard Helman, Director of Graduate Admissions, 410-516-7125, E-mail: rhelman@jhu.edu.
Website: http://physics-astronomy.jhu.edu/

Kansas State University, Graduate School, College of Arts and Sciences, Department of Physics, Manhattan, KS 66506. Offers MS, PhD. Terminal master's awarded for partial completion of doctoral program. *Degree requirements:* For master's, thesis; for doctorate, comprehensive exam, thesis/dissertation, preliminary exams, thesis defense. *Entrance requirements:* For master's and doctorate, BS in physics, minimum GPA of 3.0. Additional exam requirements/recommendations for international students: Required—TOEFL (minimum scores 550 paper-based, 79 iBT), IELTS or PTE. Electronic applications accepted. *Faculty research:* Atomic, molecular, optical physics; soft matter and biological physics; high energy physics; physics education; cosmology.

Kent State University, College of Arts and Sciences, Department of Physics, Kent, OH 44242-0001. Offers MA, MS, PhD. *Program availability:* Part-time. *Faculty:* 24 full-time (6 women). *Students:* 65 full-time (16 women), 1 (woman) part-time; includes 2 minority (both Asian, non-Hispanic/Latino), 50 international. Average age 30. 88 applicants, 22% accepted, 8 enrolled. In 2018, 6 master's, 9 doctorates awarded. Terminal master's awarded for partial completion of doctoral program. *Degree requirements:* For master's, thesis (for some programs); for doctorate, comprehensive exam, thesis/dissertation, colloquium presentation. *Entrance requirements:* For master's, GRE General Test; GRE Subject Test (physics), goal statement, 3 letters of recommendation, transcripts, resume or vita, minimum GPA of 3.0; for doctorate, GRE General Test; GRE Subject Test (physics), goal statement, 3 letters of recommendation, transcripts, minimum GPA of 3.0, resume. Additional exam requirements/recommendations for international students: Required—TOEFL (minimum score of 525 paper-based, 71 iBT), IELTS (minimum score of 6), Michigan English Language Assessment Battery (minimum score of 75), or PTE (minimum score of 48). *Application deadline:* For fall admission, 1/31 for domestic and international students; for spring admission, 8/31 for domestic and international students. Applications are processed on a rolling basis. Application fee: $45 ($70 for international students). Electronic applications accepted. *Expenses:* Tuition, state resident: full-time $11,766; part-time $536 per credit. Tuition, nonresident: full-time $21,952; part-time $999 per credit. *International tuition:* $21,952 full-time. Tuition and fees vary according to course load. *Financial support:* Fellowships with full tuition reimbursements, research assistantships with full tuition reimbursements, teaching assistantships with full tuition reimbursements, scholarships/grants, and unspecified assistantships available. Financial award application deadline: 1/31. *Unit head:* Dr. James T. Gleeson, Professor and Chair, 330-672-9592, E-mail: jgleeson@kent.edu. *Application contact:* Dr. John Portman, Professor and Graduate Coordinator, 330-672-9518, E-mail: jportman@kent.edu.
Website: http://www.kent.edu/cas/physics/

Lakehead University, Graduate Studies, Department of Physics, Thunder Bay, ON P7B 5E1, Canada. Offers M Sc. *Degree requirements:* For master's, thesis or alternative. *Entrance requirements:* For master's, minimum B average. Additional exam requirements/recommendations for international students: Required—TOEFL. *Faculty research:* Absorbed water, radiation reaction, superlattices and quantum well structures, polaron interactions.

Lehigh University, College of Arts and Sciences, Department of Physics, Bethlehem, PA 18015. Offers photonics (MS); physics (MS, PhD). *Faculty:* 15 full-time (4 women), 3 part-time/adjunct (0 women). *Students:* 43 full-time (16 women), 1 part-time (0 women); includes 3 minority (all Asian, non-Hispanic/Latino), 15 international. Average age 27. 106 applicants, 26% accepted, 11 enrolled. In 2018, 6 master's, 6 doctorates awarded. *Degree requirements:* For doctorate, comprehensive exam, thesis/dissertation. *Entrance requirements:* For master's and doctorate, GRE General Test. Additional exam requirements/recommendations for international students: Required—TOEFL (minimum score 85 iBT), TOEFL required unless attended another school in US for two or more years. *Application deadline:* For fall admission, 1/15 for domestic and international students. Application fee: $75. Electronic applications accepted. Tuition and fees vary according to program. *Financial support:* In 2018–19, 39 students received support, including 1 fellowship with full tuition reimbursement available (averaging $34,000 per year), 10 research assistantships with full tuition reimbursements available (averaging $29,340 per year), 28 teaching assistantships with full tuition reimbursements available (averaging $29,340 per year); scholarships/grants and health care benefits also available. Financial award application deadline: 1/15. *Faculty research:* Condensed matter physics; atomic, molecular and optical physics; biophysics; nonlinear optics and photonics; astronomy and astrophysics; high energy nuclear physics. *Total annual research expenditures:* $1.2 million. *Unit head:* Dr. Volkmar Dierolf, Chair, 610-758-3909, Fax: 610-758-5730, E-mail: vod2@lehigh.edu. *Application contact:* Dr. Joshua Pepper, Graduate Admissions Officer, 610-758-3649, Fax: 610-758-5730, E-mail: jap612@lehigh.edu.
Website: http://www.physics.cas2.lehigh.edu

Lewis University, College of Arts and Sciences, Program in Physics, Romeoville, IL 60446. Offers MS. *Program availability:* Part-time, evening/weekend. *Students:* 1 (woman) full-time, 2 part-time (0 women); includes 1 minority (Hispanic/Latino). Average age 24. *Entrance requirements:* For master's, bachelor's degree in physics, or bachelor's degree and work experience in industries related to physics; minimum undergraduate GPA of 3.0; personal statement; 3 letters of recommendation. Additional exam requirements/recommendations for international students: Required—TOEFL (minimum score 550 paper-based; 79 iBT), IELTS (minimum score 6). *Application deadline:* For fall admission, 5/1 priority date for international students. Applications are processed on a rolling basis. Application fee: $40. Electronic applications accepted. *Financial support:* Federal Work-Study, scholarships/grants, and unspecified assistantships available. Financial award application deadline: 5/1; financial award applicants required to submit FAFSA. *Unit head:* Dr. Joseph Kozminski, Program Director. *Application contact:* Linda Campbell, Graduate Admissions Counselor, 815-836-5610, E-mail: grad@lewisu.edu.
Website: http://www.lewisu.edu/academics/msphysics/index.htm

Louisiana State University and Agricultural & Mechanical College, Graduate School, College of Science, Department of Physics and Astronomy, Baton Rouge, LA 70803. Offers astronomy (PhD); astrophysics (PhD); medical physics (MS); physics (MS, PhD).

Manhattanville College, School of Education, Program in Middle Childhood/Adolescence Education (Grades 5-12), Purchase, NY 10577-2132. Offers biology and special education (MPS); chemistry and special education (MPS); education for sustainability (Advanced Certificate); English and special education (MPS); literacy and

special education (MPS); literacy specialist (MPS); math and special education (MPS); mathematics (Advanced Certificate); middle childhood/adolescence ed science (biology or chemistry grades 5-12) or (physics grades 7-12) (MAT); middle childhood/adolescence education (grades 5-12) English (MAT, Advanced Certificate); middle childhood/adolescence education (grades 5-12) mathematics (MAT, Advanced Certificate); middle childhood/adolescence education (grades 5-12) science (biology chemistry, physics, earth science) (Advanced Certificate); middle childhood/adolescence education (grades 5-12) social studies (MAT, Advanced Certificate); physics (MAT, Advanced Certificate); social studies (MAT); social studies and special education (MPS); special education generalist (MPS). *Program availability:* Part-time, evening/weekend. *Faculty:* 3 full-time (2 women), 9 part-time/adjunct (4 women). *Students:* 11 full-time (6 women), 17 part-time (12 women); includes 3 minority (1 Black or African American, non-Hispanic/Latino; 2 Hispanic/Latino). Average age 31. 17 applicants, 71% accepted, 7 enrolled. In 2018, 8 master's, 3 other advanced degrees awarded. *Degree requirements:* For master's, comprehensive exam (for some programs), thesis (for some programs), student teaching, research seminars, portfolios, internships, writing assessment; for Advanced Certificate, comprehensive exam (for some programs). *Entrance requirements:* For master's, for programs leading to certification, candidates must submit scores from GRE or MAT(Miller Analogies Test), minimum undergraduate GPA of 3.0, all transcripts from all colleges and universities attended, 2 letters of recommendation, interview, essay (2-3 page personal statement that describes reasons for choosing education as profession and personal philosophy of education), proof of immunization (for those born after 1957). Additional exam requirements/recommendations for international students: Required—TOEFL (minimum score 600 paper-based; 110 iBT); Recommended—IELTS (minimum score 8). *Application deadline:* Applications are processed on a rolling basis. Application fee: $75. Electronic applications accepted. *Expenses:* 935 per credit. *Financial support:* Teaching assistantships, career-related internships or fieldwork, Federal Work-Study, institutionally sponsored loans, scholarships/grants, and unspecified assistantships available. Financial award application deadline: 3/15; financial award applicants required to submit FAFSA. *Faculty research:* Education for sustainability. *Unit head:* Dr. Shelley Wepner, Dean, 914-323-3153, Fax: 914-323-5493, E-mail: Shelley.Wepner@mville.edu. *Application contact:* Alissa Wilson, Director, Graduate Admissions, 914-323-3150, Fax: 914-694-1732, E-mail: edschool@mville.edu.
Website: http://www.mville.edu/programs#/search/19

Marshall University, Academic Affairs Division, College of Science, Department of Physical and Applied Science, Huntington, WV 25755. Offers MS. *Degree requirements:* For master's, thesis optional.

Massachusetts Institute of Technology, School of Science, Department of Physics, Cambridge, MA 02139. Offers SM, PhD. Terminal master's awarded for partial completion of doctoral program. *Degree requirements:* For master's, thesis; for doctorate, comprehensive exam, thesis/dissertation. *Entrance requirements:* For master's and doctorate, GRE General Test, GRE Subject Test. Additional exam requirements/recommendations for international students: Required—TOEFL, IELTS. Electronic applications accepted. *Expenses:* Tuition: Full-time $51,520; part-time $800 per credit hour. *Required fees:* $312. *Faculty research:* High-energy and nuclear physics, condensed matter physics, astrophysics, atomic physics, biophysics, plasma physics.

McGill University, Faculty of Graduate and Postdoctoral Studies, Faculty of Science, Department of Physics, Montréal, QC H3A 2T5, Canada. Offers M Sc, PhD.

McMaster University, School of Graduate Studies, Faculty of Science, Department of Physics and Astronomy, Hamilton, ON L8S 4M2, Canada. Offers astrophysics (PhD); physics (PhD). *Program availability:* Part-time. *Degree requirements:* For doctorate, comprehensive exam, thesis/dissertation. *Entrance requirements:* For doctorate, minimum B+ average. Additional exam requirements/recommendations for international students: Required—TOEFL (minimum score 550 paper-based). *Faculty research:* Condensed matter, astrophysics, nuclear, medical, nonlinear dynamics.

Memorial University of Newfoundland, School of Graduate Studies, Department of Physics and Physical Oceanography, St. John's, NL A1C 5S7, Canada. Offers atomic and molecular physics (PhD); condensed matter physics (PhD); physical oceanography (M Sc, PhD); physics (M Sc). *Program availability:* Part-time. *Degree requirements:* For master's, thesis, seminar presentation on thesis topic; for doctorate, comprehensive exam, thesis/dissertation, oral defense of thesis. *Entrance requirements:* For master's, honors B Sc or equivalent; for doctorate, M Sc or equivalent. Electronic applications accepted. *Faculty research:* Experiment and theory in atomic and molecular physics, condensed matter physics, physical oceanography, theoretical geophysics and applied nuclear physics.

Miami University, College of Arts and Science, Department of Physics, Oxford, OH 45056. Offers MS. *Faculty:* 12 full-time (2 women). *Students:* 21 full-time (2 women); includes 1 minority (Native Hawaiian or other Pacific Islander, non-Hispanic/Latino), 12 international. Average age 26. In 2018, 10 master's awarded. *Unit head:* Dr. Herbert Jaeger, Chair, 513-529-5515, E-mail: jaegerh@miamioh.edu. *Application contact:* Dr. Mahmud Khan, Graduate Program Director, 513-529-2557, E-mail: khanm2@miamioh.edu.
Website: http://www.MiamiOH.edu/physics

Michigan State University, The Graduate School, College of Natural Science, Department of Physics and Astronomy, East Lansing, MI 48824. Offers astrophysics and astronomy (MS, PhD); physics (MS, PhD). *Entrance requirements:* Additional exam requirements/recommendations for international students: Required—TOEFL (minimum score 550 paper-based), Michigan State University ELT (minimum score 85), Michigan English Language Assessment Battery (minimum score 83). Electronic applications accepted. *Faculty research:* Nuclear and accelerator physics, high energy physics, condensed matter physics, biophysics, astrophysics and astronomy.

Michigan State University, National Superconducting Cyclotron Laboratory, East Lansing, MI 48824. Offers chemistry (PhD); physics (PhD).

Michigan Technological University, Graduate School, College of Sciences and Arts, Department of Physics, Houghton, MI 49931. Offers applied physics (MS, PhD); physics (MS, PhD). *Program availability:* Part-time. *Faculty:* 32 full-time, 11 part-time/adjunct. *Students:* 38 full-time (12 women), 1 part-time, 24 international. Average age 28. 133 applicants, 51% accepted, 11 enrolled. In 2018, 6 master's, 2 doctorates awarded. Terminal master's awarded for partial completion of doctoral program. *Degree requirements:* For master's, comprehensive exam (for some programs), thesis (for some programs), for doctorate, comprehensive exam, thesis/dissertation, qualifying exam, research proposal exam. *Entrance requirements:* For master's and doctorate, GRE (recommended minimum quantitative score of 156 and analytical score of 3.0), statement of purpose, personal statement, official transcripts, 3 letters of recommendation. Additional exam requirements/recommendations for international students: Required—TOEFL, IELTS, TOEFL (recommended minimum score 88 iBT) or IELTS (recommended minimum score of 6.5). *Application deadline:* For fall and spring

Peterson's Graduate Programs in the Physical Sciences, Mathematics, Agricultural Sciences, the Environment & Natural Resources 2020

www.petersons.com **153**

admission, 2/1 priority date for domestic and international students. Applications are processed on a rolling basis. Electronic applications accepted. *Expenses: Tuition, area resident:* Full-time $18,126; part-time $1007 per credit. Tuition, state resident: full-time $18,126; part-time $1007 per credit. Tuition, nonresident: full-time $18,126; part-time $1007 per credit. *International tuition:* $18,126 full-time. *Required fees:* $248; $124 per semester. Tuition and fees vary according to course load and program. *Financial support:* In 2018–19, 38 students received support, including 9 fellowships with tuition reimbursements available (averaging $16,590 per year), 8 research assistantships with tuition reimbursements available (averaging $16,590 per year), 14 teaching assistantships with tuition reimbursements available (averaging $16,590 per year); career-related internships or fieldwork, Federal Work-Study, scholarships/grants, health care benefits, unspecified assistantships, and cooperative program also available. Financial award applicants required to submit FAFSA. *Faculty research:* Atmospheric physics, astrophysics, biophysics, materials physics, atomic/molecular physics. *Total annual research expenditures:* $1.3 million. *Unit head:* Dr. Ravindra Pandey, Chair, 906-487-2086, Fax: 906-487-2933, E-mail: physics@mtu.edu. *Application contact:* Dr. Ravindra Pandey, Chair, 906-487-2086, Fax: 906-487-2933, E-mail: physics@mtu.edu.
Website: http://www.mtu.edu/physics/

Minnesota State University Mankato, College of Graduate Studies and Research, College of Science, Engineering and Technology, Department of Physics and Astronomy, Mankato, MN 56001. Offers physics (MS); physics education (MS). *Degree requirements:* For master's, one foreign language, comprehensive exam, thesis or alternative. *Entrance requirements:* For master's, minimum GPA of 2.75, two recommendation letters, one-page personal statement. Additional exam requirements/recommendations for international students: Required—TOEFL (minimum score 530 paper-based; 72 iBT). Electronic applications accepted.

Mississippi State University, College of Arts and Sciences, Department of Physics and Astronomy, Mississippi State, MS 39762. Offers physics (MS, PhD). PhD in applied physics offered jointly with College of Engineering. *Program availability:* Part-time. *Faculty:* 15 full-time (3 women). *Students:* 47 full-time (16 women), 1 part-time (0 women); includes 2 minority (both Asian, non-Hispanic/Latino), 39 international. Average age 30. 48 applicants, 42% accepted, 16 enrolled. In 2018, 8 master's, 7 doctorates awarded. *Degree requirements:* For master's, thesis optional, comprehensive oral or written exam; for doctorate, thesis/dissertation, comprehensive oral or written exam. *Entrance requirements:* For master's, GRE, minimum GPA of 2.75 on last two years of undergraduate courses; for doctorate, GRE. Additional exam requirements/recommendations for international students: Required—TOEFL (minimum score 477 paper-based; 53 iBT); Recommended—IELTS (minimum score 4.5). *Application deadline:* For fall admission, 7/1 priority date for domestic students, 5/1 for international students; for spring admission, 11/1 priority date for domestic students, 9/1 for international students. Applications are processed on a rolling basis. Application fee: $60 ($80 for international students). Electronic applications accepted. *Expenses:* Tuition, state resident: full-time $8450; part-time $360.59 per credit hour. Tuition, nonresident: full-time $23,140; part-time $969.09 per credit hour. *Required fees:* $110. One-time fee: $55 full-time. Part-time tuition and fees vary according to course load, degree level, campus/location and reciprocity agreements. *Financial support:* In 2018–19, 10 research assistantships with full tuition reimbursements (averaging $15,820 per year), 28 teaching assistantships with full tuition reimbursements (averaging $14,807 per year) were awarded; Federal Work-Study, institutionally sponsored loans, and unspecified assistantships also available. Financial award application deadline: 3/15; financial award applicants required to submit FAFSA. *Faculty research:* Atomic/molecular spectroscopy, theoretical optics, gamma-ray astronomy, experimental nuclear physics, computational physics. *Total annual research expenditures:* $4.9 million. *Unit head:* Dr. Mark Novotny, Professor and Head, 662-325-2688, Fax: 662-325-8898, E-mail: man40@msstate.edu. *Application contact:* Nathan Drake, Admissions and Enrollment Assistant, 662-325-3804, E-mail: ndrake@grad.msstate.edu.
Website: http://www.physics.msstate.edu

Missouri State University, Graduate College, College of Natural and Applied Sciences, Department of Physics, Astronomy, and Materials Science, Springfield, MO 65897. Offers materials science (MS); natural and applied science (MNAS), including physics (MNAS, MS Ed); secondary education (MS Ed), including physics (MNAS, MS Ed). *Program availability:* Part-time. *Faculty:* 9 full-time (0 women). *Students:* 11 full-time (1 woman), 4 part-time (1 woman); includes 1 minority (Hispanic/Latino), 13 international. Average age 26. 12 applicants, 92% accepted. In 2018, 9 master's awarded. *Degree requirements:* For master's, comprehensive exam, thesis. *Entrance requirements:* For master's, GRE (MS, MNAS), minimum undergraduate GPA of 3.0 (MS and MNAS), 9-12 teaching certification (MS Ed). Additional exam requirements/recommendations for international students: Required—TOEFL (minimum score 550 paper-based; 79 iBT), IELTS (minimum score 6). *Application deadline:* For fall admission, 7/20 priority date for domestic students, 5/1 for international students; for spring admission, 12/20 priority date for domestic students, 9/1 for international students. Applications are processed on a rolling basis. Application fee: $55 ($60 for international students). Electronic applications accepted. Tuition and fees vary according to class time, course level, course load, degree level, campus/location, program and student level. *Financial support:* In 2018–19, 6 research assistantships with full tuition reimbursements (averaging $10,672 per year), 11 teaching assistantships with full tuition reimbursements (averaging $10,672 per year) were awarded; Federal Work-Study, institutionally sponsored loans, scholarships/grants, and unspecified assistantships also available. Financial award application deadline: 1/31; financial award applicants required to submit FAFSA. *Faculty research:* Nanocomposites, ferroelectricity, infrared focal plane array sensors, biosensors, pulsating stars. *Unit head:* Dr. Robert Mayanovic, Department Head, 417-836-5131, Fax: 417-836-6226, E-mail: physics@missouristate.edu. *Application contact:* Lakan Drinker, Director, Graduate Enrollment Management, 417-836-5330, Fax: 417-836-6200, E-mail: lakandrinker@missouristate.edu.
Website: http://physics.missouristate.edu/

Missouri University of Science and Technology, Department of Physics, Rolla, MO 65401. Offers MS, MST, PhD. *Entrance requirements:* For master's, GRE (minimum score 600 quantitative, 3 writing); for doctorate, GRE (minimum score: 600 quantitative, 3.5 writing). Additional exam requirements/recommendations for international students: Required—TOEFL (minimum score 550 paper-based). Electronic applications accepted. *Expenses:* Tuition, state resident: full-time $7545.60; part-time $419.20 per credit hour. Tuition, nonresident: full-time $22,169; part-time $1231.60 per credit hour. *International tuition:* $23,518.80 full-time. *Required fees:* $4523.05. Full-time tuition and fees vary according to course load, campus/location, program and reciprocity agreements.

Montana State University, The Graduate School, College of Letters and Science, Department of Physics, Bozeman, MT 59717. Offers MS, PhD. *Program availability:* Part-time. *Degree requirements:* For master's, comprehensive exam, thesis (for some programs); for doctorate, comprehensive exam, thesis/dissertation. *Entrance requirements:* For master's and doctorate, GRE General Test, GRE Subject Test (physics). Additional exam requirements/recommendations for international students: Required—TOEFL (minimum score 550 paper-based). Electronic applications accepted. *Faculty research:* Nanotechnology, gravitational wave, astronomy, photodynamic theory, diode laser development, solar radiation transfer.

Morgan State University, School of Graduate Studies, School of Computer, Mathematical, and Natural Sciences, Department of Physics, Baltimore, MD 21251. Offers MS.

Naval Postgraduate School, Departments and Academic Groups, Department of Physics, Monterey, CA 93943. Offers applied physics (MS, PhD); combat systems technology (MS); engineering acoustics (MS, PhD); physics (MS, PhD). Program only open to commissioned officers of the United States and friendly nations and selected United States federal civilian employees. *Program availability:* Part-time. *Degree requirements:* For master's, thesis; for doctorate, thesis/dissertation. *Faculty research:* Acoustics, free electron laser, sensors, weapons and effects.

New Mexico Institute of Mining and Technology, Center for Graduate Studies, Department of Physics, Socorro, NM 87801. Offers astrophysics (PhD); atmospheric physics (PhD); instrumentation (MS); mathematical physics (PhD); physics (MS). *Degree requirements:* For master's, thesis optional; for doctorate, thesis/dissertation. *Entrance requirements:* For master's, GRE General Test; for doctorate, GRE General Test, GRE Subject Test. Additional exam requirements/recommendations for international students: Required—TOEFL (minimum score 540 paper-based). *Faculty research:* Cloud physics, stellar and extragalactic processes.

New York University, Graduate School of Arts and Science, Department of Physics, New York, NY 10012-1019. Offers MS, PhD. *Program availability:* Part-time. *Faculty:* 25 full-time (1 woman), 5 part-time/adjunct (0 women). *Students:* 99 full-time (20 women), 4 part-time (1 woman); includes 6 minority (3 Asian, non-Hispanic/Latino; 1 Hispanic/Latino; 2 Two or more races, non-Hispanic/Latino), 70 international. Average age 26. 337 applicants, 20% accepted, 18 enrolled. In 2018, 8 master's, 11 doctorates awarded. Terminal master's awarded for partial completion of doctoral program. *Degree requirements:* For master's, thesis (for some programs); for doctorate, one foreign language, thesis/dissertation, research seminar, teaching experience. *Entrance requirements:* For master's, GRE General Test, GRE Subject Test, bachelor's degree in physics; for doctorate, GRE General Test, GRE Subject Test. Additional exam requirements/recommendations for international students: Required—TOEFL, IELTS. *Application deadline:* For fall admission, 12/18 for domestic and international students. Application fee: $110. *Financial support:* Fellowships with tuition reimbursements, research assistantships with tuition reimbursements, teaching assistantships with tuition reimbursements, Federal Work-Study, institutionally sponsored loans, scholarships/grants, health care benefits, and unspecified assistantships available. Financial award application deadline: 12/18; financial award applicants required to submit FAFSA. *Faculty research:* Atomic physics, elementary particles and fields, astrophysics, condensed-matter physics, neuromagnetism. *Unit head:* Gregory Gabadadze, Chairman, 212-998-7700, Fax: 212-995-4016, E-mail: dgphys@nyu.edu. *Application contact:* Aditi Mitra, Acting Director of Graduate Studies, 212-998-7700, Fax: 212-995-4016, E-mail: dgsphys@nyu.edu.
Website: http://www.physics.nyu.edu/

North Carolina Agricultural and Technical State University, The Graduate College, College of Science and Technology, Department of Physics, Greensboro, NC 27411. Offers computational sciences (MS); physics (MS).

North Carolina Central University, College of Arts and Sciences, Department of Mathematics and Physics, Durham, NC 27707-3129. Offers mathematics (MS); physics (MS). *Program availability:* Part-time, evening/weekend. *Degree requirements:* For master's, one foreign language, comprehensive exam, thesis. *Entrance requirements:* For master's, minimum GPA of 3.0 in major, 2.5 overall. Additional exam requirements/recommendations for international students: Required—TOEFL.

North Carolina Central University, College of Arts and Sciences, Department of Physics, Durham, NC 27707-3129. Offers MS.

North Carolina State University, Graduate School, College of Sciences, Department of Physics, Raleigh, NC 27695. Offers MS, PhD. *Program availability:* Part-time. Terminal master's awarded for partial completion of doctoral program. *Degree requirements:* For master's, thesis (for some programs); for doctorate, thesis/dissertation. *Entrance requirements:* For master's and doctorate, GRE General Test, GRE Subject Test. Electronic applications accepted. *Faculty research:* Astrophysics, optics, physics education, biophysics, geophysics.

North Dakota State University, College of Graduate and Interdisciplinary Studies, College of Science and Mathematics, Department of Physics, Fargo, ND 58102. Offers MS, PhD. *Program availability:* Part-time. Terminal master's awarded for partial completion of doctoral program. *Entrance requirements:* Additional exam requirements/recommendations for international students: Required—TOEFL (minimum score 550 paper-based; 79 iBT). Electronic applications accepted.

Northeastern University, College of Science, Boston, MA 02115-5096. Offers applied mathematics (MS); bioinformatics (MS); biology (PhD); biotechnology (MS); chemistry and chemical biology (MS, PhD); environmental science and policy (MS); marine and environmental sciences (PhD); marine biology (MS); mathematics (MS, PhD); operations research (MSOR); physics (MS, PhD); psychology (PhD). *Program availability:* Part-time. Terminal master's awarded for partial completion of doctoral program. *Degree requirements:* For master's, comprehensive exam (for some programs), thesis; for doctorate, comprehensive exam (for some programs), thesis/dissertation. *Entrance requirements:* For master's, GRE General Test. Electronic applications accepted. *Expenses:* Contact institution.

Northern Arizona University, College of Environment, Forestry, and Natural Sciences, Department of Physics and Astronomy, Flagstaff, AZ 86011. Offers applied physics (MS); astronomy and planetary science (PhD). *Program availability:* Part-time. *Degree requirements:* For master's, variable foreign language requirement, comprehensive exam (for some programs), thesis (for some programs); for doctorate, variable foreign language requirement, comprehensive exam (for some programs), thesis/dissertation (for some programs). *Entrance requirements:* For master's and doctorate, GRE General Test. Additional exam requirements/recommendations for international students: Required—TOEFL (minimum score 80 iBT), IELTS (minimum score 6.5). Electronic applications accepted.

Northern Illinois University, Graduate School, College of Liberal Arts and Sciences, Department of Physics, De Kalb, IL 60115-2854. Offers MS, PhD. *Program availability:* Part-time. *Faculty:* 18 full-time (3 women), 3 part-time/adjunct (0 women). *Students:* 33 full-time (7 women), 20 part-time (2 women); includes 4 minority (1 Black or African American, non-Hispanic/Latino; 3 Asian, non-Hispanic/Latino), 21 international. Average age 28. 61 applicants, 72% accepted, 7 enrolled. In 2018, 6 master's, 3 doctorates awarded. Terminal master's awarded for partial completion of doctoral program. *Degree requirements:* For master's, comprehensive exam, thesis or alternative, research seminar; for doctorate, thesis/dissertation, candidacy exam, dissertation defense, research seminar. *Entrance requirements:* For master's, GRE General Test, minimum GPA of 2.75; for doctorate, GRE General Test, GRE Subject Test (physics), bachelor's degree in physics or related field; minimum undergraduate GPA of 2.75, graduate 3.2.

Additional exam requirements/recommendations for international students: Required—TOEFL (minimum score 550 paper-based). *Application deadline:* For fall admission, 6/1 for domestic students, 5/1 for international students; for spring admission, 11/1 for domestic students, 10/1 for international students. Applications are processed on a rolling basis. Application fee: $40. Electronic applications accepted. *Financial support:* In 2018–19, 28 research assistantships with full tuition reimbursements, 18 teaching assistantships with full tuition reimbursements were awarded; fellowships with full tuition reimbursements, career-related internships or fieldwork, Federal Work-Study, scholarships/grants, and unspecified assistantships also available. Support available to part-time students. Financial award applicants required to submit FAFSA. *Faculty research:* Band-structure interpolation schemes, nonlinear procession beams, Mossbauer spectroscopy, beam physics. *Unit head:* Dr. Laurence Lurio, Chair, 815-753-6470, Fax: 815-753-8565, E-mail: lluio@niu.edu. *Application contact:* Graduate School Office, 815-753-0395, E-mail: gradsch@niu.edu.
Website: http://www.physics.niu.edu/

Northwestern University, The Graduate School, Judd A. and Marjorie Weinberg College of Arts and Sciences, Department of Physics and Astronomy, Evanston, IL 60208. Offers PhD. Admissions and degrees offered through The Graduate School. *Degree requirements:* For doctorate, thesis/dissertation, qualifying exam. *Entrance requirements:* For doctorate, GRE General Test, GRE Subject Test. Additional exam requirements/recommendations for international students: Required—TOEFL. *Faculty research:* Nuclear and particle physics, condensed-matter physics, nonlinear physics, astrophysics.

Oakland University, Graduate Study and Lifelong Learning, College of Arts and Sciences, Department of Physics, Rochester, MI 48309-4401. Offers medical physics (PhD); physics (MS). *Degree requirements:* For doctorate, thesis/dissertation. *Entrance requirements:* For master's, minimum GPA of 3.0; for doctorate, GRE Subject Test, GRE General Test, minimum GPA of 3.0. Additional exam requirements/recommendations for international students: Required—TOEFL (minimum score 550 paper-based). Electronic applications accepted. *Expenses:* Contact institution.

The Ohio State University, Graduate School, College of Arts and Sciences, Division of Natural and Mathematical Sciences, Department of Physics, Columbus, OH 43210. Offers MS, PhD. *Faculty:* 54. *Students:* 201 (37 women). Average age 26. In 2018, 34 master's, 34 doctorates awarded. *Entrance requirements:* For doctorate, GRE General Test, GRE Subject Test (physics). Additional exam requirements/recommendations for international students: Required—TOEFL (minimum score 550 paper-based; 79 iBT), Michigan English Language Assessment Battery (minimum score 82); Recommended—IELTS (minimum score 7). *Application deadline:* For fall admission, 12/13 priority date for domestic students, 11/30 priority date for international students; for spring admission, 3/1 for domestic students, 2/1 for international students. Applications are processed on a rolling basis. Application fee: $60 ($70 for international students). Electronic applications accepted. *Financial support:* Fellowships, research assistantships, teaching assistantships, Federal Work-Study, and institutionally sponsored loans available. Support available to part-time students. *Unit head:* Dr. Brian Winer, Chair and Professor, 614-292-8996, E-mail: winer.12@osu.edu. *Application contact:* Graduate and Professional Admissions, 614-292-9444, Fax: 614-292-3895, E-mail: gpadmissions@osu.edu.
Website: http://www.physics.osu.edu/

Ohio University, Graduate College, College of Arts and Sciences, Department of Physics and Astronomy, Athens, OH 45701. Offers astronomy (MS, PhD); physics (MS, PhD). *Faculty:* 29 full-time (4 women), 1 part-time/adjunct (0 women). *Students:* 72 full-time (9 women), 46 international. 118 applicants, 36% accepted, 14 enrolled. In 2018, 11 master's, 11 doctorates awarded. Terminal master's awarded for partial completion of doctoral program. *Degree requirements:* For master's, thesis or alternative; for doctorate, comprehensive exam, thesis/dissertation. *Entrance requirements:* For master's and doctorate, minimum GPA of 3.0. Additional exam requirements/recommendations for international students: Required—TOEFL (minimum score 590 paper-based; 95 iBT), IELTS (minimum score 7). *Application deadline:* For fall admission, 1/15 priority date for domestic and international students. Applications are processed on a rolling basis. Application fee: $50 ($55 for international students). Electronic applications accepted. *Financial support:* In 2018–19, 72 students received support, including 5 fellowships with full tuition reimbursements available (averaging $28,710 per year), 35 research assistantships with full tuition reimbursements available (averaging $20,510 per year), 32 teaching assistantships with full tuition reimbursements available (averaging $24,504 per year); scholarships/grants also available. Financial award application deadline: 1/15. *Faculty research:* Nuclear physics, condensed-matter physics, nonlinear systems, astrophysics, biophysics. *Total annual research expenditures:* $1.9 million. *Unit head:* Dr. David Ingram, Chair, 740-593-0336, Fax: 740-593-0433, E-mail: ingram@ohio.edu. *Application contact:* Dr. Alexander Neiman, Graduate Admissions Chair, 740-593-1701, Fax: 740-593-0433, E-mail: physicsgradapps@ohio.edu.
Website: http://www.ohio.edu/physastro/

Oklahoma State University, College of Arts and Sciences, Department of Physics, Stillwater, OK 74078. Offers photonics (MS, PhD). *Faculty:* 27 full-time (6 women). *Students:* 2 full-time (0 women), 37 part-time (5 women); includes 2 minority (1 Hispanic/Latino; 1 Two or more races, non-Hispanic/Latino), 23 international. Average age 28. 70 applicants, 24% accepted, 11 enrolled. In 2018, 4 master's, 6 doctorates awarded. *Entrance requirements:* For master's and doctorate, GRE. Additional exam requirements/recommendations for international students: Required—TOEFL (minimum score 550 paper-based; 79 iBT). *Application deadline:* For fall admission, 3/1 priority date for international students; for spring admission, 8/1 priority date for international students. Applications are processed on a rolling basis. Application fee: $40 ($75 for international students). Electronic applications accepted. *Expenses: Tuition, area resident:* Full-time $4148. Tuition, state resident: full-time $4148. Tuition, nonresident: full-time $10,517. *International tuition:* $10,517 full-time. *Required fees:* $4394; $2929 per credit hour. Tuition and fees vary according to course load and program. *Financial support:* Research assistantships, teaching assistantships, career-related internships or fieldwork, Federal Work-Study, scholarships/grants, health care benefits, tuition waivers (partial), and unspecified assistantships available. Support available to part-time students. Financial award application deadline: 3/1; financial award applicants required to submit FAFSA. *Faculty research:* Lasers and photonics, non-linear optical materials, turbulence, structure and function of biological membranes, particle theory. *Unit head:* Dr. David N McIlroy, Department Head, 405-744-5796, Fax: 405-744-6811, E-mail: dave.mcilroy@okstate.edu. *Application contact:* Dr. Albert T. Rosenberger, Graduate Coordinator, 405-744-6742, Fax: 405-744-6811, E-mail: physics.grad.coordinator@okstate.edu.
Website: http://physics.okstate.edu/

Old Dominion University, College of Sciences, Program in Physics, Norfolk, VA 23529. Offers MS, PhD. Terminal master's awarded for partial completion of doctoral program. *Degree requirements:* For master's, comprehensive exam, thesis optional; for doctorate, comprehensive exam, thesis/dissertation. *Entrance requirements:* For master's, GRE General Test, BS in physics or closely related field, minimum GPA of 3.0 in major, 2 reference letters; for doctorate, GRE General Test; GRE Subject Test (strongly recommended), minimum GPA of 3.0; three reference letters. Additional exam requirements/recommendations for international students: Required—TOEFL (minimum score 550 paper-based; 79 iBT), IELTS (minimum score 6.5). Electronic applications accepted. *Expenses:* Contact institution. *Faculty research:* Nuclear and particle physics, atomic physics, condensed-matter physics, plasma physics, accelerator physics.

Oregon State University, College of Science, Program in Physics, Corvallis, OR 97331. Offers atomic physics (MA, MS, PhD); computational physics (MA, MS, PhD); experimental physics (MA, MS, PhD); nuclear and particle physics (MA, MS, PhD); optical physics (MA, MS, PhD); solid state physics (MA, MS, PhD). *Entrance requirements:* Additional exam requirements/recommendations for international students: Required—TOEFL (minimum score 600 paper-based; 100 iBT). Electronic applications accepted.

Pace University, School of Education, New York, NY 10038. Offers adolescent education (MST), including biology, chemistry, earth science, English, foreign languages, mathematics, physics, social studies; childhood education (MST); early childhood development, learning and intervention (MST); educational technology studies (MS); inclusive adolescent education (MST), including biology, chemistry, earth science, English, foreign languages, mathematics, physics, social studies; integrated instruction for educational technology (Certificate); integrated instruction for literacy and technology (Certificate); literacy (MS Ed); special education (MS Ed). *Accreditation:* NCATE. *Program availability:* Part-time, evening/weekend, 100% online, blended/hybrid learning. *Faculty:* 19 full-time (13 women), 86 part-time/adjunct (49 women). *Students:* 98 full-time (82 women), 542 part-time (391 women); includes 256 minority (116 Black or African American, non-Hispanic/Latino; 2 American Indian or Alaska Native, non-Hispanic/Latino; 45 Asian, non-Hispanic/Latino; 83 Hispanic/Latino; 10 Two or more races, non-Hispanic/Latino), 4 international. Average age 30. 223 applicants, 89% accepted, 130 enrolled. In 2018, 269 master's, 12 other advanced degrees awarded. *Degree requirements:* For master's and Certificate, certification exams. *Entrance requirements:* For master's, GRE (for initial certification programs only), teaching certificate (for MS Ed in literacy and special education programs only). Additional exam requirements/recommendations for international students: Required—TOEFL (minimum score 88 iBT), IELTS or PTE. *Application deadline:* For fall admission, 8/1 priority date for domestic students, 6/1 for international students; for spring admission, 12/1 priority date for domestic students, 10/1 for international students. Applications are processed on a rolling basis. Application fee: $70. Electronic applications accepted. *Expenses:* Contact institution. *Financial support:* In 2018–19, 17 students received support, including 17 research assistantships with partial tuition reimbursements available (averaging $6,020 per year); career-related internships or fieldwork, Federal Work-Study, scholarships/grants, and unspecified assistantships also available. Financial award application deadline: 9/1; financial award applicants required to submit FAFSA. *Faculty research:* STEM education, TESOL, teacher education, special education, language and literary development. *Total annual research expenditures:* $1.4 million. *Unit head:* Dr. Harriet Feldman, Dean, School of Education, 914-773-3829, E-mail: hfeldman@pace.edu. *Application contact:* Susan Ford-Goldschein, Director of Graduate Admissions, 212-346-1531, Fax: 212-346-1585, E-mail: graduateadmission@pace.edu.
Website: http://www.pace.edu/school-of-education

Penn State University Park, Graduate School, Eberly College of Science, Department of Physics, University Park, PA 16802. Offers M Ed, MS, PhD.

Pittsburg State University, Graduate School, College of Arts and Sciences, Department of Physics, Pittsburg, KS 66762. Offers MS. *Degree requirements:* For master's, thesis or alternative. *Entrance requirements:* Additional exam requirements/recommendations for international students: Required—TOEFL (minimum score 520 paper-based; 68 iBT), IELTS (minimum score 6), PTE (minimum score 47). Electronic applications accepted. *Expenses:* Contact institution.

Portland State University, Graduate Studies, College of Liberal Arts and Sciences, Department of Physics, Portland, OR 97207-0751. Offers applied physics (PhD); physics (MA, MS). *Program availability:* Part-time. *Degree requirements:* For master's, variable foreign language requirement, thesis, oral exam, written report; for doctorate, thesis/dissertation. *Entrance requirements:* For master's, GRE General Test, statement of purpose, minimum GPA of 3.0 in upper-division course work or 2.75 overall, 2 letters of recommendation. Additional exam requirements/recommendations for international students: Required—TOEFL (minimum score 550 paper-based; 90 iBT). *Faculty research:* Statistical physics, membrane biophysics, low-temperature physics, electron microscopy, atmospheric physics.

Princeton University, Graduate School, Department of Physics, Princeton, NJ 08544-1019. Offers PhD. *Degree requirements:* For doctorate, thesis/dissertation, qualifying exam. *Entrance requirements:* For doctorate, GRE General Test, GRE Subject Test. Additional exam requirements/recommendations for international students: Required—TOEFL (minimum score 600 paper-based). Electronic applications accepted.

Purdue University, Graduate School, College of Science, Department of Physics, West Lafayette, IN 47907. Offers MS, PhD. *Program availability:* Part-time. *Faculty:* 51 full-time (6 women). *Students:* 124 full-time (21 women), 23 part-time (1 woman); includes 5 minority (2 Black or African American, non-Hispanic/Latino; 1 Asian, non-Hispanic/Latino; 1 Hispanic/Latino; 1 Two or more races, non-Hispanic/Latino), 106 international. Average age 26. 273 applicants, 32% accepted, 33 enrolled. In 2018, 12 master's, 26 doctorates awarded. Terminal master's awarded for partial completion of doctoral program. *Degree requirements:* For master's, thesis optional, qualifying exam; for doctorate, thesis/dissertation, qualifying exam. *Entrance requirements:* For master's and doctorate, GRE General Test, GRE Subject Test (physics), minimum undergraduate GPA of 3.0 or equivalent. Additional exam requirements/recommendations for international students: Required—TOEFL (minimum score 550 paper-based; 77 iBT); Recommended—TWE. *Application deadline:* For fall admission, 1/1 for domestic and international students; for spring admission, 9/1 for domestic and international students. Applications are processed on a rolling basis. Application fee: $60 ($75 for international students). Electronic applications accepted. *Financial support:* Fellowships with partial tuition reimbursements, research assistantships with partial tuition reimbursements, and teaching assistantships with partial tuition reimbursements available. Support available to part-time students. Financial award application deadline: 2/1; financial award applicants required to submit FAFSA. *Faculty research:* Solid-state, elementary particle, and nuclear physics; biological physics; acoustics; astrophysics. *Unit head:* John P. Finley, Head, 765-494-3000, E-mail: finley@purdue.edu. *Application contact:* Janice V. Thomaz, Graduate Contact, 765-494-3099, E-mail: thomazj@purdue.edu.
Website: http://www.physics.purdue.edu/

Queens College of the City University of New York, Mathematics and Natural Sciences Division, Department of Physics, Queens, NY 11367-1597. Offers photonics (MS); physics (MA). *Program availability:* Part-time. *Faculty:* 12 full-time, 1 part-time/adjunct. *Students:* 5 full-time (3 women), 12 part-time (5 women); includes 5 minority (1 Black or African American, non-Hispanic/Latino; 1 Hispanic/Latino; 3 Two or more races,

Physics

non-Hispanic/Latino), 7 international. Average age 30. In 2018, 3 master's awarded. *Degree requirements:* For master's, thesis optional. *Entrance requirements:* For master's, previous course work in calculus, minimum GPA of 3.0. Additional exam requirements/recommendations for international students: Required—TOEFL (minimum score 61 iBT), IELTS (minimum score 5). *Application deadline:* For fall admission, 6/1 for domestic students; for spring admission, 11/1 for domestic students. Applications are processed on a rolling basis. Application fee: $125. Electronic applications accepted. *Financial support:* Teaching assistantships, career-related internships or fieldwork, Federal Work-Study, and institutionally sponsored loans available. Financial award application deadline: 4/1; financial award applicants required to submit FAFSA. *Faculty research:* Photonics, devices, spectroscopy and transport in condensed matter, biomimetics. *Unit head:* Dr. Steven Schwarz, Chair, 718-997-3385, E-mail: steven.schwarz@qc.cuny.edu. *Application contact:* Elizabeth D'Amico-Ramirez, Assistant Director of Graduate Admissions, 718-997-5203, E-mail: elizabeth.damicoramirez@qc.cuny.edu.
Website: http://physics.qc.cuny.edu/

Queen's University at Kingston, School of Graduate Studies, Faculty of Arts and Science, Department of Physics, Engineering Physics and Astronomy, Kingston, ON K7L 3N6, Canada. Offers M Sc, M Sc Eng, PhD. *Program availability:* Part-time. *Degree requirements:* For master's, thesis; for doctorate, comprehensive exam, thesis/dissertation. *Entrance requirements:* For doctorate, M Sc or M Sc Eng. Additional exam requirements/recommendations for international students: Required—TOEFL (minimum score 550 paper-based). *Faculty research:* Theoretical physics, astronomy and astrophysics, condensed matter.

Rensselaer Polytechnic Institute, Graduate School, School of Science, Program in Physics, Troy, NY 12180-3590. Offers MS, PhD. *Faculty:* 24 full-time (6 women), 1 part-time/adjunct (0 women). *Students:* 40 full-time (4 women); includes 4 minority (2 Asian, non-Hispanic/Latino; 1 Hispanic/Latino; 1 Two or more races, non-Hispanic/Latino), 5 international. Average age 25. 130 applicants, 36% accepted, 9 enrolled. In 2018, 6 master's, 6 doctorates awarded. *Degree requirements:* For doctorate, thesis/dissertation. *Entrance requirements:* For master's and doctorate, GRE General Test, GRE Subject Test (physics). Additional exam requirements/recommendations for international students: Required—TOEFL (minimum score 600 paper-based; 100 iBT), IELTS (minimum score 7), PTE (minimum score 68). *Application deadline:* For fall admission, 1/1 priority date for domestic and international students; for spring admission, 8/15 priority date for domestic and international students. Applications are processed on a rolling basis. Application fee: $75. Electronic applications accepted. *Financial support:* In 2018–19, research assistantships (averaging $23,000 per year), teaching assistantships (averaging $23,000 per year) were awarded; fellowships also available. Financial award application deadline: 1/1. *Faculty research:* Astronomy and astrophysics, biological physics, condensed matter physics, optical physics, particle physics, stochastic dynamic on complex networks. *Total annual research expenditures:* $5.3 million. *Unit head:* Dr. Gyorgy Korniss, Graduate Program Director, 518-276-2555, E-mail: korniss@rpi.edu. *Application contact:* Jarron Decker, Director of Graduate Admissions, 518-276-6216, Fax: 518-276-4072, E-mail: gradadmissions@rpi.edu.
Website: https://science.rpi.edu/physics

Rice University, Graduate Programs, Wiess School of Natural Sciences, Department of Physics and Astronomy, Houston, TX 77251-1892. Offers nanoscale physics (MS); physics and astronomy (PhD); science teaching (MST). *Program availability:* Part-time. *Degree requirements:* For master's, thesis (for some programs); for doctorate, thesis/dissertation, minimum B average. *Entrance requirements:* For master's, GRE General Test; for doctorate, GRE General Test, GRE Subject Test. Additional exam requirements/recommendations for international students: Required—TOEFL (minimum score 600 paper-based; 90 iBT). Electronic applications accepted. *Faculty research:* Optical physics; ultra cold atoms; membrane electr-statics, peptides, proteins and lipids; solar astrophysics; stellar activity; magnetic fields; young stars.

Rice University, Graduate Programs, Wiess School—Professional Science Master's Programs, Professional Master's Program in Nanoscale Physics, Houston, TX 77251-1892. Offers MS. *Degree requirements:* For master's, internship. *Entrance requirements:* For master's, GRE General Test, bachelor's degree in physics and related field, 4 letters of recommendation. Additional exam requirements/recommendations for international students: Required—TOEFL (minimum score 600 paper-based; 90 iBT). Electronic applications accepted. *Faculty research:* Atomic, molecular, and applied physics, surface and condensed matter physics.

Royal Military College of Canada, Division of Graduate Studies, Faculty of Science, Department of Physics and Space Science, Kingston, ON K7K 7B4, Canada. Offers physics (M Sc). *Degree requirements:* For master's, thesis. *Entrance requirements:* For master's, honour's degree with second-class standing. Electronic applications accepted.

Rutgers University–New Brunswick, Graduate School-New Brunswick, Department of Physics and Astronomy, Piscataway, NJ 08854-8097. Offers astronomy (MS, PhD); biophysics (PhD); condensed matter physics (MS, PhD); elementary particle physics (MS, PhD); intermediate energy nuclear physics (MS); nuclear physics (MS, PhD); physics (MST); surface science (PhD); theoretical physics (MS, PhD). *Program availability:* Part-time. Terminal master's awarded for partial completion of doctoral program. *Degree requirements:* For master's, comprehensive exam, thesis or alternative; for doctorate, comprehensive exam, thesis/dissertation. *Entrance requirements:* For master's and doctorate, GRE General Test, GRE Subject Test. Additional exam requirements/recommendations for international students: Required—TOEFL (minimum score 560 paper-based). Electronic applications accepted. *Faculty research:* Astronomy, high energy, condensed matter, surface, nuclear physics.

St. John Fisher College, Ralph C. Wilson Jr. School of Education, Program in Adolescence Education and Special Education, Rochester, NY 14618-3597. Offers adolescence education: biology with special education (MS Ed); adolescence education: chemistry with special education (MS Ed); adolescence education: English with special education (MS Ed); adolescence education: French with special education (MS Ed); adolescence education: math with special education (MS Ed); adolescence education: physics with special education (MS Ed); adolescence education: social studies with special education (MS Ed); adolescence education: Spanish with special education (MS Ed). *Program availability:* Part-time, evening/weekend. *Faculty:* 8 full-time (6 women), 2 part-time/adjunct (both women). *Students:* 13 full-time (4 women), 2 part-time (1 woman); includes 2 minority (1 Black or African American, non-Hispanic/Latino; 1 Two or more races, non-Hispanic/Latino). Average age 27. 24 applicants, 58% accepted, 4 enrolled. In 2018, 9 master's awarded. *Degree requirements:* For master's, field experiences, student teaching. *Entrance requirements:* For master's, LAST, 2 letters of recommendation, personal statement, current resume. Additional exam requirements/recommendations for international students: Required—TOEFL (minimum score 575 paper-based; 80 iBT). *Application deadline:* Applications are processed on a rolling basis. Application fee: $30. Electronic applications accepted. *Expenses:* Contact institution. *Financial support:* Scholarships/grants available. Financial award applicants required to submit FAFSA. *Faculty research:* Arts and humanities, urban schools,

constructivist learning, at-risk students, mentoring. *Unit head:* Dr. Susan Hildenbrand, Program Director, 585-385-7297, E-mail: shildenbrand@sjfc.edu. *Application contact:* Michelle Gosier, Director of Transfer and Graduate Admissions, 585-385-8064, E-mail: mgosier@sjfc.edu.

San Diego State University, Graduate and Research Affairs, College of Sciences, Department of Physics, Program in Physics, San Diego, CA 92182. Offers MA, MS. *Program availability:* Part-time. *Degree requirements:* For master's, thesis, oral exam. *Entrance requirements:* For master's, GRE General Test, GRE Subject Test (physics), 2 letters of recommendation. Additional exam requirements/recommendations for international students: Required—TOEFL. Electronic applications accepted.

San Francisco State University, Division of Graduate Studies, College of Science and Engineering, Department of Physics and Astronomy, San Francisco, CA 94132-1722. Offers astronomy (MS); physics (MS). *Program availability:* Part-time. *Application deadline:* Applications are processed on a rolling basis. Electronic applications accepted. *Unit head:* Dr. Joseph Barranco, Chair, 415-338-2450, Fax: 415-338-2178, E-mail: barranco@sfsu.edu. *Application contact:* Dr. Kristan Jensen, Graduate Advisor, 415-338-1969, Fax: 415-338-2178, E-mail: kristanj@sfsu.edu.
Website: http://www.physics.sfsu.edu/

San Jose State University, Program in Physics and Astronomy, San Jose, CA 95192-0001. Offers computational physics (MS); physics (MS). *Program availability:* Part-time, evening/weekend. *Degree requirements:* For master's, thesis optional. *Entrance requirements:* For master's, GRE. Electronic applications accepted. *Faculty research:* Astrophysics, atmospheric physics, elementary particles, dislocation theory, general relativity.

Simon Fraser University, Office of Graduate Studies and Postdoctoral Fellows, Faculty of Science, Department of Physics, Burnaby, BC V5A 1S6, Canada. Offers M Sc, PhD. *Degree requirements:* For master's, thesis; for doctorate, thesis/dissertation. *Entrance requirements:* For master's, minimum GPA of 3.0 (on scale of 4.33) or 3.33 based on last 60 credits of undergraduate courses; for doctorate, minimum GPA of 3.5 (on scale of 4.33). Additional exam requirements/recommendations for international students: Recommended—TOEFL (minimum score 580 paper-based; 93 iBT), IELTS (minimum score 7), TWE (minimum score 5). Electronic applications accepted. *Faculty research:* Biophysics and soft condensed matter, particle physics, quantum matter, superconductivity, theoretical physics.

South Dakota School of Mines and Technology, Graduate Division, Program in Physics, Rapid City, SD 57701-3995. Offers MS, PhD. *Program availability:* Part-time. *Degree requirements:* For master's, thesis (for some programs). *Entrance requirements:* Additional exam requirements/recommendations for international students: Required—TOEFL (minimum score 520 paper-based; 68 iBT). Electronic applications accepted.

South Dakota State University, Graduate School, College of Natural Sciences, Department of Physics, Brookings, SD 57007. Offers engineering (MS). *Program availability:* Part-time. *Degree requirements:* For master's, comprehensive exam (for some programs), thesis (for some programs), oral exam. *Entrance requirements:* Additional exam requirements/recommendations for international students: Required—TOEFL (minimum score 580 paper-based). *Faculty research:* Materials science, astrophysics, remote sensing and atmospheric corrections, theoretical and computational physics, applied physics.

Southern Illinois University Carbondale, Graduate School, College of Science, Department of Physics, Carbondale, IL 62901-4701. Offers MS, PhD. *Degree requirements:* For master's, one foreign language, thesis; for doctorate, thesis/dissertation. *Entrance requirements:* For master's, minimum GPA of 2.7; for doctorate, GRE, minimum GPA of 3.25. Additional exam requirements/recommendations for international students: Required—TOEFL. *Faculty research:* Atomic, molecular, nuclear, and mathematical physics; statistical mechanics; solid-state and low-temperature physics; rheology; material science.

Southern Methodist University, Dedman College of Humanities and Sciences, Department of Physics, Dallas, TX 75275. Offers MS, PhD. *Program availability:* Part-time. Terminal master's awarded for partial completion of doctoral program. *Degree requirements:* For master's, thesis optional, oral exam; for doctorate, thesis/dissertation, written exam. *Entrance requirements:* For master's and doctorate, GRE General Test, GRE Subject Test (physics), minimum GPA of 3.0. Additional exam requirements/recommendations for international students: Required—TOEFL. Electronic applications accepted. *Faculty research:* Particle physics, cosmology, astrophysics, mathematics physics, computational physics.

Southern University and Agricultural and Mechanical College, Graduate School, College of Sciences and Engineering, Program in Physics, Baton Rouge, LA 70813. Offers MS. *Degree requirements:* For master's, thesis. *Entrance requirements:* For master's, GMAT or GRE General Test. Additional exam requirements/recommendations for international students: Required—TOEFL (minimum score 525 paper-based). *Faculty research:* Piezoelectric materials and devices, predictive ab-instio calculations, high energy physics, surface growth studies, semiconductor and intermetallics.

Stanford University, School of Humanities and Sciences, Department of Physics, Stanford, CA 94305-2004. Offers PhD. *Expenses:* Tuition: Full-time $50,703; part-time $32,970 per year. *Required fees:* $651.
Website: http://www.stanford.edu/dept/physics/

State University of New York College at Cortland, Graduate Studies, School of Arts and Sciences, Programs in Adolescence Education, Cortland, NY 13045. Offers biology (MAT); chemistry (MAT); English (MAT, MS Ed); mathematics (MAT); mathematics and physics (MS Ed); physics (MAT, MS Ed). *Accreditation:* NCATE. *Program availability:* Part-time, evening/weekend. *Degree requirements:* For master's, one foreign language, comprehensive exam (for some programs), thesis (for some programs). *Entrance requirements:* For master's, GRE General Test.

Stephen F. Austin State University, Graduate School, College of Sciences and Mathematics, Department of Physics, Engineering and Astronomy, Nacogdoches, TX 75962. Offers physics (MS, PhD). *Program availability:* Part-time. *Degree requirements:* For master's, comprehensive exam. *Entrance requirements:* For master's, GRE General Test, minimum GPA of 2.8 in last 60 hours, 2.5 overall. Additional exam requirements/recommendations for international students: Required—TOEFL. *Faculty research:* Low-temperature physics, x-ray spectroscopy and metallic glasses, infrared spectroscopy.

Stony Brook University, State University of New York, Graduate School, College of Arts and Sciences, Department of Physics and Astronomy, Program in Physics, Stony Brook, NY 11794. Offers MA, MAT, MS, PhD. *Faculty:* 55 full-time (7 women), 3 part-time/adjunct (1 woman). *Students:* 214 full-time (35 women), 5 part-time (0 women); includes 23 minority (2 Black or African American, non-Hispanic/Latino; 14 Asian, non-Hispanic/Latino; 7 Hispanic/Latino), 152 international. 560 applicants, 26% accepted, 66 enrolled. In 2018, 17 master's, 15 doctorates awarded. *Degree requirements:* For doctorate, one foreign language, thesis/dissertation. *Entrance requirements:* For master's and doctorate, GRE General Test. Additional exam requirements/ recommendations for international students: Required—TOEFL (minimum score 90 iBT). *Application deadline:* For fall admission, 1/15 for domestic students; for spring admission, 10/1 for domestic students. Application fee: $100. Electronic applications accepted. *Expenses:* Contact institution. *Financial support:* In 2018–19, 5 fellowships, 69 research assistantships, 55 teaching assistantships were awarded. Financial award application deadline: 2/1. *Total annual research expenditures:* $19.4 million. *Unit head:* Dr. Axel Drees, Chair, 631-632-8114, E-mail: axel.drees@stonybrook.edu. *Application contact:* Donald Sheehan, Coordinator, 631-632-1046, Fax: 631-632-8176, E-mail: donald.j.sheehan@stonybrook.edu.

Syracuse University, College of Arts and Sciences, Department of Physics, Syracuse, NY 13244. Offers MS, PhD. Terminal master's awarded for partial completion of doctoral program. *Degree requirements:* For master's, comprehensive exam, thesis or alternative; for doctorate, comprehensive exam, thesis/dissertation. *Entrance requirements:* For master's and doctorate, GRE General Test, GRE Subject Test, three letters of recommendation, statement of purpose, transcripts. Additional exam requirements/recommendations for international students: Required—TOEFL (minimum score 100 iBT). *Application deadline:* For fall admission, 1/15 priority date for domestic and international students. Application fee: $75. Electronic applications accepted. *Financial support:* Fellowships with full tuition reimbursements, research assistantships, teaching assistantships, and scholarships/grants available. Financial award application deadline: 1/1. *Faculty research:* Methods of theoretical physics, classical mechanics, quantum mechanics, thermodynamics and statistical mechanics, electromagnetic theory. *Unit head:* Dr. Eric A. Schiff, Director, Graduate Studies, 315-443-3901, E-mail: easchiff@syr.edu. *Application contact:* Tomasz Skwarnicki, Graduate Admissions Coordinator, 315-443-5973, E-mail: graduate@physics.syr.edu.
Website: http://physics.syr.edu/graduate/grad-home.html

Teachers College, Columbia University, Department of Mathematics, Science and Technology, New York, NY 10027-6696. Offers biology 7-12 (MA); chemistry 7-12 (MA); communication and education (MA, Ed D); computing in education (MA); earth science 7-12 (MA); instructional technology and media (Ed M, MA, Ed D); mathematics education (Ed M, MA, Ed D, Ed DCT, PhD); physics 7-12 (MA); science and dental education (MA); science education (Ed M, MS, Ed DCT, PhD); supervisor/teacher of science education (MA); technology specialist (MA). *Program availability:* Part-time, evening/weekend, online learning. *Students:* 155 full-time (114 women), 254 part-time (162 women); includes 136 minority (44 Black or African American, non-Hispanic/Latino; 1 American Indian or Alaska Native, non-Hispanic/Latino; 59 Asian, non-Hispanic/ Latino; 23 Hispanic/Latino; 9 Two or more races, non-Hispanic/Latino), 140 international. Average age 31. 484 applicants, 60% accepted, 138 enrolled. Terminal master's awarded for partial completion of doctoral program. *Unit head:* Prof. Erica Walker, Chair, 212-678-8246, E-mail: ewalker@tc.columbia.edu. *Application contact:* Kelly Sutton Skinner, Director of Admission & New Student Enrollment, E-mail: kms2237@tc.columbia.edu.
Website: http://www.tc.columbia.edu/mathematics-science-and-technology/

Temple University, College of Science and Technology, Department of Physics, Philadelphia, PA 19122-1801. Offers MS, PhD. *Program availability:* Part-time. *Faculty:* 24 full-time (5 women). *Students:* 59 full-time (11 women), 1 part-time (0 women); includes 3 minority (1 Black or African American, non-Hispanic/Latino; 2 Asian, non-Hispanic/Latino), 42 international. 58 applicants, 36% accepted, 6 enrolled. In 2018, 2 master's, 7 doctorates awarded. *Degree requirements:* For master's, comprehensive exam (for some programs), thesis; for doctorate, thesis/dissertation. *Entrance requirements:* For master's and doctorate, GRE General Test required, subject test in physics strongly recommended but not required, statement of goals, 2 letters of recommendation. Additional exam requirements/recommendations for international students: Required—TOEFL (minimum score 79 iBT), IELTS (minimum score 6.5), PTE (minimum score 53), one of three is required. *Application deadline:* For fall admission, 3/1 for domestic students, 12/15 for international students; for spring admission, 11/1 for domestic students, 8/1 for international students. Applications are processed on a rolling basis. Application fee: $60. Electronic applications accepted. *Expenses:* Contact institution. *Financial support:* Fellowships, research assistantships, teaching assistantships, Federal Work-Study, health care benefits, and unspecified assistantships available. Financial award applicants required to submit FAFSA. *Faculty research:* Theoretical and experimental elementary particle physics, condensed matter physics, atomic, molecular and optical physics, statistical mechanics. *Unit head:* James Napolitano, Chair, 215-204-7027, E-mail: napolj@temple.edu. *Application contact:* John Perdew, Graduate Chair, 215-204-1407, E-mail: physgrad@temple.edu.
Website: https://phys.cst.temple.edu/

Texas A&M University, College of Science, Department of Physics and Astronomy, College Station, TX 77843. Offers applied physics (PhD); astronomy (MS); physics (PhD). *Faculty:* 61. *Students:* 150 full-time (24 women), 7 part-time (1 woman); includes 15 minority (1 Black or African American, non-Hispanic/Latino; 4 Asian, non-Hispanic/ Latino; 7 Hispanic/Latino; 3 Two or more races, non-Hispanic/Latino), 82 international. Average age 27. 202 applicants, 34% accepted, 34 enrolled. In 2018, 11 master's, 29 doctorates awarded. Terminal master's awarded for partial completion of doctoral program. *Entrance requirements:* For master's and doctorate, GRE General Test, GRE Subject Test. Additional exam requirements/recommendations for international students: Required—TOEFL. *Application deadline:* For fall admission, 12/1 for domestic students, 12/15 for international students. Application fee: $50 ($90 for international students). Electronic applications accepted. *Expenses:* Contact institution. *Financial support:* In 2018–19, 151 students received support, including 39 fellowships with tuition reimbursements available (averaging $16,344 per year), 109 research assistantships with tuition reimbursements available (averaging $13,676 per year), 64 teaching assistantships with tuition reimbursements available (averaging $13,698 per year); career-related internships or fieldwork, institutionally sponsored loans, scholarships/grants, traineeships, health care benefits, tuition waivers (full and partial), and unspecified assistantships also available. Support available to part-time students. Financial award application deadline: 3/1; financial award applicants required to submit FAFSA. *Faculty research:* Condensed matter, atomic/molecular, high-energy and nuclear physics, quantum optics. *Unit head:* Dr. George R. Welch, Head, 979-845-1571, E-mail: welch@physics.tamu.edu. *Application contact:* Dr. Joe Ross, Graduate Advisor, 979-845-3842, Fax: 979-845-2590, E-mail: ross@physics.tamu.edu.
Website: http://physics.tamu.edu/

Texas A&M University–Commerce, College of Science and Engineering, Commerce, TX 75429. Offers biological sciences (MS); broadfield science biology (MS); broadfield science chemistry (MS); broadfield science physics (MS); chemistry (MS); computational linguistics (Graduate Certificate), computational science (MS); computer science (MS); environmental science (Graduate Certificate); mathematics (MS); physics (MS); technology management (MS). *Program availability:* Part-time. *Faculty:* 44 full-time (7 women), 7 part-time/adjunct (0 women). *Students:* 178 full-time (67 women), 234 part-time (104 women); includes 82 minority (19 Black or African American, non-Hispanic/Latino; 1 American Indian or Alaska Native, non-Hispanic/Latino; 14 Asian, non-Hispanic/Latino; 37 Hispanic/Latino; 11 Two or more races, non-Hispanic/Latino), 158 international. Average age 30. 481 applicants, 52% accepted, 105 enrolled. In 2018, 218 master's awarded. *Degree requirements:* For master's, comprehensive exam, thesis optional. *Entrance requirements:* For master's, GRE, official transcripts, letters of recommendation, resume, statement of goals. Additional exam requirements/ recommendations for international students: Required—TOEFL (minimum score 550 paper-based; 79 iBT), IELTS (minimum score 6), PTE (minimum score 53). *Application deadline:* For fall admission, 6/1 priority date for international students; for spring admission, 10/15 priority date for international students; for summer admission, 3/15 priority date for international students. Applications are processed on a rolling basis. Application fee: $50 ($75 for international students). Electronic applications accepted. *Expenses:* Contact institution. *Financial support:* In 2018–19, 46 students received support, including 43 research assistantships with partial tuition reimbursements available (averaging $2,418 per year), 135 teaching assistantships with partial tuition reimbursements available (averaging $3,376 per year); scholarships/grants, health care benefits, and unspecified assistantships also available. Financial award application deadline: 5/1; financial award applicants required to submit FAFSA. *Faculty research:* Biomedical, Catalytic Material & Processes, Nuclear Theory/Astrophysics, Cybersecurity, STEM Education. *Total annual research expenditures:* $1.8 million. *Unit head:* Dr. Brent L. Donham, Dean, 903-886-5321, Fax: 903-886-5199, E-mail: brent.donham@tamuc.edu. *Application contact:* Dayla Burgin, Graduate Student Services Coordinator, 903-886-5134, E-mail: dayla.burgin@tamuc.edu.
Website: https://new.tamuc.edu/science-engineering/

Texas Christian University, College of Science and Engineering, Department of Physics and Astronomy, Fort Worth, TX 76129-0002. Offers physics (MA, MS, PhD), including astrophysics (PhD), biophysics (PhD); PhD/MBA. *Program availability:* Part-time. *Faculty:* 8 full-time (3 women). *Students:* 17 full-time (6 women); includes 3 minority (1 Black or African American, non-Hispanic/Latino; 2 Hispanic/Latino), 6 international. Average age 25. 20 applicants, 20% accepted, 4 enrolled. In 2018, 3 master's, 4 doctorates awarded. Terminal master's awarded for partial completion of doctoral program. *Degree requirements:* For master's, one foreign language, comprehensive exam, thesis or alternative; for doctorate, comprehensive exam, thesis/ dissertation. *Entrance requirements:* Additional exam requirements/recommendations for international students: Required—TOEFL (minimum score 550 paper-based; 80 iBT), IELTS (minimum score 6.5). *Application deadline:* For fall admission, 1/1 priority date for domestic and international students; for spring admission, 9/1 priority date for domestic and international students. Applications are processed on a rolling basis. Application fee: $0 ($60 for international students). Electronic applications accepted. *Expenses:* Contact institution. *Financial support:* In 2018–19, 16 students received support, including 3 research assistantships with full tuition reimbursements available (averaging $24,000 per year), 13 teaching assistantships with full tuition reimbursements available (averaging $21,000 per year); scholarships/grants and unspecified assistantships also available. Financial award application deadline: 1/1. *Faculty research:* Nanomaterials, computer simulations of biophysical processes, nonlinear dynamics, computational and observational studies of galaxy evolution using stars and gas, spectroscopy and fluorescence of biomolecules. *Total annual research expenditures:* $265,000. *Unit head:* Dr. Yuri M. Strzhemechny, Associate Professor/Chair, 817-257-5793, Fax: 817-257-7742, E-mail: y.strzhemechny@tcu.edu. *Application contact:* Dr. Peter M. Frinchaboy, III, Associate Professor, 817-257-6387, Fax: 817-257-7742, E-mail: p.frinchaboy@tcu.edu.
Website: http://physics.tcu.edu/

Texas State University, The Graduate College, College of Science and Engineering, Program in Physics, San Marcos, TX 78666. Offers MS. *Program availability:* Part-time, evening/weekend. *Faculty:* 12 full-time (3 women), 1 part-time/adjunct (0 women). *Students:* 20 full-time (5 women), 7 part-time; includes 4 minority (3 Hispanic/Latino; 1 Two or more races, non-Hispanic/Latino), 9 international. Average age 29. 32 applicants, 34% accepted, 5 enrolled. In 2018, 8 master's awarded. *Degree requirements:* For master's, comprehensive exam, thesis optional. *Entrance requirements:* For master's, baccalaureate degree from regionally-accredited university with minimum GPA of 2.75 on last 60 undergraduate semester hours, 3.0 in upper-level physics courses; statement of purpose; resume/curriculum vitae; 3 letters of recommendation. Additional exam requirements/recommendations for international students: Required—TOEFL (minimum score 550 paper-based; 78 iBT), IELTS (minimum score 6.5). *Application deadline:* For fall admission, 2/1 priority date for domestic and international students; for spring admission, 9/15 priority date for domestic and international students. Applications are processed on a rolling basis. Application fee: $55 ($90 for international students). Electronic applications accepted. *Expenses:* Tuition, state resident: full-time $8102; part-time $4051 per semester. Tuition, nonresident: full-time $18,229; part-time $9115 per semester. *International tuition:* $18,229 full-time. *Required fees:* $2116; $120 per credit hour. Tuition and fees vary according to course load. *Financial support:* In 2018–19, 21 students received support, including 6 research assistantships (averaging $18,600 per year), 14 teaching assistantships (averaging $13,204 per year); career-related internships or fieldwork, Federal Work-Study, institutionally sponsored loans, scholarships/grants, health care benefits, and unspecified assistantships also available. Support available to part-time students. Financial award application deadline: 1/15; financial award applicants required to submit FAFSA. *Faculty research:* Negotiating energy dynamics through embodied action in a materially structured environment; developing body engagement activities that will assist the student in accessing mathematical ideas used in physics; working in nanoscale materials, particularly on questions relating to group III-nitride and II-VI semiconductors, diamond, device self-heating, and thermal properties; semiconductor fabrication, and performance optimization of wide bandgap materials for solid-state device applications. *Total annual research expenditures:* $1.4 million. *Unit head:* Dr. Edwin Piner, Graduate Advisor, 512-245-7049, E-mail: ep26@txstate.edu. *Application contact:* Dr. Andrea Golato, Dean of Graduate School, 512-245-2581, Fax: 512-245-8365, E-mail: gradcollege@txstate.edu.
Website: https://www.txstate.edu/physics/Degrees-Programs/Graduate.html

Texas Tech University, Graduate School, College of Arts and Sciences, Department of Physics and Astronomy, Lubbock, TX 79409-1051. Offers physics (MS, PhD). *Program availability:* Part-time. *Faculty:* 29 full-time (6 women), 1 part-time/adjunct (0 women). *Students:* 44 full-time (10 women), 3 part-time (2 women); includes 11 minority (1 Black or African American, non-Hispanic/Latino; 3 Asian, non-Hispanic/Latino; 4 Hispanic/ Latino; 3 Two or more races, non-Hispanic/Latino), 31 international. Average age 29. 37 applicants, 35% accepted, 9 enrolled. In 2018, 20 master's, 5 doctorates awarded. *Degree requirements:* For master's, variable foreign language requirement, comprehensive exam (for some programs), thesis (for some programs); for doctorate, variable foreign language requirement, comprehensive exam, thesis/dissertation, proposal presentation. *Entrance requirements:* For master's and doctorate, GRE. Additional exam requirements/recommendations for international students: Required—TOEFL (minimum score 550 paper-based; 79 iBT), IELTS (minimum score 6.5). *Application deadline:* For fall admission, 6/1 priority date for domestic students, 1/15 priority date for international students; for spring admission, 9/1 priority date for domestic students, 6/15 priority date for international students. Applications are processed on a rolling basis. Application fee: $65. Electronic applications accepted. *Expenses:* Contact

institution. *Financial support:* In 2018–19, 49 students received support, including 44 fellowships (averaging $1,797 per year), 15 research assistantships (averaging $22,828 per year), 33 teaching assistantships (averaging $16,857 per year); Federal Work-Study, scholarships/grants, health care benefits, and unspecified assistantships also available. Support available to part-time students. Financial award application deadline: 2/1; financial award applicants required to submit FAFSA. *Faculty research:* Astrophysics, biophysics, condensed matter physics, high energy physics, quantum optics and quantum materials physics. *Total annual research expenditures:* $3 million. *Unit head:* Dr. Sung-Won Lee, Professor and Chair, 806-834-8188, Fax: 806-742-1182, E-mail: Sungwon.Lee@ttu.edu. *Application contact:* Dr. Mahdi Sanati, Graduate Recruiter, 806-834-6169, Fax: 806-742-1182, E-mail: m.sanati@ttu.edu.
Website: www.depts.ttu.edu/phas/

Trent University, Graduate Studies, Program in Applications of Modeling in the Natural and Social Sciences, Department of Physics, Peterborough, ON K9J 7B8, Canada. Offers M Sc. *Program availability:* Part-time. *Degree requirements:* For master's, thesis. *Entrance requirements:* For master's, honours degree. *Faculty research:* Radiation physics, chemical physics.

Tufts University, Graduate School of Arts and Sciences, Department of Physics and Astronomy, Medford, MA 02155. Offers astrophysics (MS, PhD); chemical physics (PhD); physics (MS, PhD); physics education (PhD). Terminal master's awarded for partial completion of doctoral program. *Degree requirements:* For master's, thesis optional; for doctorate, thesis/dissertation, oral qualifying exam. *Entrance requirements:* For master's and doctorate, GRE General Test. Additional exam requirements/recommendations for international students: Required—TOEFL (minimum score 550 paper-based; 80 iBT), IELTS (minimum score 6.5). Electronic applications accepted. *Expenses:* Contact institution.

Tulane University, School of Science and Engineering, Department of Physics and Engineering Physics, New Orleans, LA 70118-5669. Offers physics (PhD). *Degree requirements:* For master's, thesis or alternative; for doctorate, thesis/dissertation. *Entrance requirements:* For master's, GRE General Test, minimum B average in undergraduate course work; for doctorate, GRE General Test. Additional exam requirements/recommendations for international students: Required—TOEFL. Electronic applications accepted. *Expenses: Tuition:* Full-time $52,856; part-time $2937 per credit hour. *Required fees:* $2040; $44.50 per credit hour. $580 per term. Tuition and fees vary according to course load, degree level and program. *Faculty research:* Surface physics, condensed-matter experiment, condensed-matter theory, nuclear theory, polymers.

Université de Moncton, Faculty of Sciences, Department of Physics and Astronomy, Moncton, NB E1A 3E9, Canada. Offers M Sc. *Program availability:* Part-time. *Degree requirements:* For master's, thesis. *Entrance requirements:* For master's, proficiency in French. Electronic applications accepted. *Faculty research:* Thin films, optical properties, solar selective surfaces, microgravity and photonic materials.

Université de Montréal, Faculty of Arts and Sciences, Department of Physics, Montréal, QC H3C 3J7, Canada. Offers M Sc, PhD. *Degree requirements:* For doctorate, thesis/dissertation, general exam. Electronic applications accepted. *Faculty research:* Astronomy; biophysics; solid-state, plasma, and nuclear physics.

Université de Sherbrooke, Faculty of Sciences, Department of Physics, Sherbrooke, QC J1K 2R1, Canada. Offers M Sc, PhD. *Degree requirements:* For master's, thesis; for doctorate, comprehensive exam, thesis/dissertation. *Entrance requirements:* For doctorate, master's degree. Electronic applications accepted. *Faculty research:* Solid-state physics, quantum computing.

Université du Québec à Trois-Rivières, Graduate Programs, Program in Physics, Trois-Rivières, QC G9A 5H7, Canada. Offers matter and energy (MS, PhD).

Université Laval, Faculty of Sciences and Engineering, Department of Physics, Physical Engineering, and Optics, Programs in Physics, Québec, QC G1K 7P4, Canada. Offers M Sc, PhD. Terminal master's awarded for partial completion of doctoral program. *Degree requirements:* For master's, thesis; for doctorate, comprehensive exam, thesis/dissertation. *Entrance requirements:* For master's and doctorate, knowledge of French, comprehension of written English. Electronic applications accepted.

University at Albany, State University of New York, College of Arts and Sciences, Department of Physics, Albany, NY 12222-0001. Offers MS, PhD. *Faculty:* 17 full-time (2 women). *Students:* 13 full-time (1 woman); includes 5 minority (1 Black or African American, non-Hispanic/Latino; 1 Asian, non-Hispanic/Latino; 1 Hispanic/Latino; 2 Two or more races, non-Hispanic/Latino), 16 international. 62 applicants, 32% accepted, 8 enrolled. In 2018, 4 master's, 6 doctorates awarded. *Degree requirements:* For master's, one foreign language; for doctorate, one foreign language, thesis/dissertation. *Entrance requirements:* Additional exam requirements/recommendations for international students: Required—TOEFL (minimum score 550 paper-based). *Application deadline:* For fall admission, 6/15 for domestic students, 5/1 for international students. Applications are processed on a rolling basis. Application fee: $75. Electronic applications accepted. *Financial support:* Fellowships, research assistantships, teaching assistantships, and minority assistantships available. Financial award application deadline: 6/15. *Faculty research:* Condensed-matter physics, high-energy physics, applied physics, electronic materials, theoretical particle physics. *Unit head:* Keith Earle, Chair, 518-442-4502, Fax: 518-442-4259, E-mail: acaticha@albany.edu. *Application contact:* Michael DeRensis, Director, Graduate Admissions, 518-442-3980, Fax: 518-442-3922, E-mail: graduate@albany.edu.
Website: http://www.albany.edu/physics/

University at Buffalo, the State University of New York, Graduate School, College of Arts and Sciences, Department of Physics, Buffalo, NY 14260. Offers MS, PhD. *Faculty:* 23 full-time (3 women). *Students:* 93 full-time (17 women); includes 48 minority (2 Black or African American, non-Hispanic/Latino; 1 American Indian or Alaska Native, non-Hispanic/Latino; 45 Asian, non-Hispanic/Latino). Average age 29. 146 applicants, 26% accepted, 20 enrolled. In 2018, 1 master's, 12 doctorates awarded. Terminal master's awarded for partial completion of doctoral program. *Degree requirements:* For master's, thesis optional; for doctorate, comprehensive exam, thesis/dissertation. *Entrance requirements:* For master's and doctorate, GRE General Test, GRE Subject Test (physics), undergraduate degree, letters of recommendation, statement of purpose. Additional exam requirements/recommendations for international students: Required—TOEFL (minimum score 550 paper-based; 79 iBT). *Application deadline:* For fall admission, 2/1 priority date for domestic and international students. Application fee: $75. Electronic applications accepted. *Financial support:* In 2018–19, 64 students received support, including 4 fellowships with full tuition reimbursements available (averaging $6,000 per year), 13 research assistantships with full tuition reimbursements available (averaging $17,000 per year), 48 teaching assistantships with full tuition reimbursements available (averaging $16,500 per year); institutionally sponsored loans, scholarships/grants, health care benefits, and unspecified assistantships also available. Financial award application deadline: 2/1; financial award applicants required to submit FAFSA. *Faculty research:* Condensed-matter physics (experimental and theoretical), cosmology (theoretical), high energy and particle physics (experimental and theoretical), computational physics, biophysics (experimental and theoretical), materials physics. *Total annual research expenditures:* $3.8 million. *Unit head:* Dr. Sambandamurthy Ganapathy, Chairman, 716-645-2906, Fax: 716-645-2507, E-mail: sg82@buffalo.edu. *Application contact:* Dr. Xuedong Hu, Director of Graduate Studies, 716-645-5444, Fax: 716-645-2507, E-mail: xhu@buffalo.edu.
Website: http://www.physics.buffalo.edu/

The University of Alabama, Graduate School, College of Arts and Sciences, Department of Physics and Astronomy, Tuscaloosa, AL 35487-0324. Offers MS, PhD. Terminal master's awarded for partial completion of doctoral program. *Degree requirements:* For master's, comprehensive exam, thesis optional, oral exam; for doctorate, comprehensive exam, thesis/dissertation, oral and written exams. *Entrance requirements:* For master's and doctorate, GRE General Test (minimum score of 300), minimum GPA of 3.0. Additional exam requirements/recommendations for international students: Required—TOEFL (minimum score 550 paper-based; 79 iBT). Electronic applications accepted. *Faculty research:* Condensed matter, particle physics, astrophysics, particle astrophysics, collider physics.

The University of Alabama at Birmingham, College of Arts and Sciences, Program in Physics, Birmingham, AL 35294. Offers MS, PhD. Terminal master's awarded for partial completion of doctoral program. *Degree requirements:* For master's, thesis optional; for doctorate, thesis/dissertation. *Entrance requirements:* For master's and doctorate, GRE General Test; GRE Subject Test (recommended), minimum GPA of 3.0. Additional exam requirements/recommendations for international students: Required—TOEFL, TWE. Electronic applications accepted. *Expenses: Tuition, area resident:* Full-time $8100; part-time $8100 per year. Tuition, state resident: full-time $8100. Tuition, nonresident: full-time $19,188; part-time $19,188 per year. Tuition and fees vary according to program. *Faculty research:* Condensed matter physics, material physics, laser physics, optics, biophysics, computational physics.

The University of Alabama in Huntsville, School of Graduate Studies, College of Science, Department of Physics, Huntsville, AL 35899. Offers education (MS); optics and photonics technology (MS); physics (MS, PhD). *Program availability:* Part-time. *Faculty:* 5 full-time, 2 part-time/adjunct. *Students:* 20 full-time (7 women), 12 part-time (1 woman); includes 2 minority (1 Black or African American, non-Hispanic/Latino; 1 Two or more races, non-Hispanic/Latino), 8 international. Average age 31. 22 applicants, 73% accepted, 6 enrolled. In 2018, 4 master's, 2 doctorates awarded. *Degree requirements:* For master's, comprehensive exam, thesis or alternative, oral and written exams; for doctorate, comprehensive exam, thesis/dissertation, oral and written exams. *Entrance requirements:* For master's and doctorate, GRE General Test, minimum GPA of 3.0. Additional exam requirements/recommendations for international students: Required—TOEFL (minimum score 550 paper-based; 80 iBT), IELTS (minimum score 6.5). *Application deadline:* For fall admission, 7/15 priority date for domestic students, 4/1 priority date for international students; for spring admission, 11/30 priority date for domestic students, 9/1 priority date for international students. Applications are processed on a rolling basis. Application fee: $50. Electronic applications accepted. *Expenses: Tuition, area resident:* Full-time $10,632; part-time $412 per credit hour. Tuition, state resident: full-time $10,632. Tuition, nonresident: full-time $23,604; part-time $412 per credit hour. *Required fees:* $582; $582. Tuition and fees vary according to course load and program. *Financial support:* In 2018–19, 18 students received support, including 7 research assistantships with full tuition reimbursements available (averaging $9,130 per year), 10 teaching assistantships with full tuition reimbursements available (averaging $7,444 per year); career-related internships or fieldwork, Federal Work-Study, institutionally sponsored loans, scholarships/grants, health care benefits, and unspecified assistantships also available. Support available to part-time students. Financial award application deadline: 4/1; financial award applicants required to submit FAFSA. *Faculty research:* Space and solar physics, computational physics, optics, high energy astrophysics. *Unit head:* Dr. James A. Miller, Chair, 256-824-2483, Fax: 256-824-6873, E-mail: millerja@uah.edu. *Application contact:* Kim Gray, Graduate Studies Admissions Coordinator, 256-824-6002, Fax: 256-824-6405, E-mail: deangrad@uah.edu.
Website: http://physics.uah.edu/

University of Alaska Fairbanks, College of Natural Science and Mathematics, Department of Physics, Fairbanks, AK 99775-5920. Offers computational physics (MS); physics (MS, PhD); space physics (MS). *Program availability:* Part-time. *Faculty:* 8 full-time (2 women). *Students:* 22 full-time (3 women), 1 part-time (0 women); includes 3 minority (1 Asian, non-Hispanic/Latino; 2 Hispanic/Latino), 5 international. Average age 29. 35 applicants, 14% accepted, 5 enrolled. In 2018, 1 master's, 2 doctorates awarded. *Degree requirements:* For master's, comprehensive exam, oral defense of project or thesis; for doctorate, comprehensive exam, thesis/dissertation, oral defense of dissertation. *Entrance requirements:* For master's, GRE General Test, bachelor's degree from accredited institution with minimum cumulative undergraduate and major GPA of 3.0; for doctorate, GRE General Test, minimum cumulative GPA of 3.0. Additional exam requirements/recommendations for international students: Required—TOEFL (minimum score 550 paper-based; 80 iBT). *Application deadline:* For fall admission, 6/1 for domestic students, 3/1 for international students; for spring admission, 10/15 for domestic students, 9/1 for international students. Applications are processed on a rolling basis. Application fee: $60. Electronic applications accepted. *Expenses: Tuition, area resident:* Full-time $8802; part-time $5868 per credit hour. Tuition, state resident: full-time $8802; part-time $5868 per credit hour. Tuition, nonresident: full-time $18,504; part-time $12,336 per credit hour. *International tuition:* $18,504 full-time. *Required fees:* $1416; $944 per credit hour. $472 per semester. Tuition and fees vary according to course load and program. *Financial support:* In 2018–19, 11 research assistantships with full tuition reimbursements (averaging $9,421 per year), 12 teaching assistantships with full tuition reimbursements (averaging $12,712 per year) were awarded; fellowships with full tuition reimbursements, Federal Work-Study, scholarships/grants, health care benefits, and unspecified assistantships also available. Support available to part-time students. Financial award application deadline: 2/15; financial award applicants required to submit FAFSA. *Faculty research:* Atmospheric and ionospheric radar studies, space plasma theory, magnetospheric dynamics, space weather and auroral studies, turbulence and complex systems. *Total annual research expenditures:* $11.2 million. *Unit head:* Renate Wackerbauer, Department Chair, 907-474-7339, E-mail: uaf-physics@alaska.edu. *Application contact:* Samara Taber, Director of Admissions, 907-474-7500, E-mail: uaf-admissions@alaska.edu.
Website: http://www.uaf.edu/physics/

University of Alberta, Faculty of Graduate Studies and Research, Department of Physics, Edmonton, AB T6G 2E1, Canada. Offers astrophysics (M Sc, PhD); condensed matter (M Sc, PhD); geophysics (M Sc, PhD); medical physics (M Sc, PhD); subatomic physics (M Sc, PhD). *Degree requirements:* For master's, thesis; for doctorate, thesis/dissertation. *Entrance requirements:* For master's and doctorate, minimum GPA of 7.0 on a 9.0 scale. Additional exam requirements/recommendations for international students: Required—TOEFL. *Faculty research:* Cosmology, astroparticle physics, high-intermediate energy, magnetism, superconductivity.

The University of Arizona, College of Science, Department of Physics, Tucson, AZ 85721. Offers medical physics (PSM); physics (PhD). *Program availability:* Part-time. Terminal master's awarded for partial completion of doctoral program. *Degree requirements:* For master's, comprehensive exam (for some programs), thesis optional; for doctorate, comprehensive exam, thesis/dissertation. *Entrance requirements:* For master's and doctorate, GRE General Test, GRE Subject Test, minimum GPA of 3.2, 3 letters of recommendation. Additional exam requirements/recommendations for international students: Required—TOEFL (minimum score 550 paper-based; 79 iBT). Electronic applications accepted. *Faculty research:* Astrophysics; high-energy, condensed-matter, atomic and molecular physics; optics.

University of Arkansas, Graduate School, J. William Fulbright College of Arts and Sciences, Department of Physics, Fayetteville, AR 72701. Offers applied physics (MS); physics (MS, PhD); physics education (MA). In 2018, 3 master's, 7 doctorates awarded. *Application deadline:* For fall admission, 8/1 for domestic students, 4/1 for international students; for spring admission, 12/1 for domestic students, 10/1 for international students; for summer admission, 4/15 for domestic students, 3/1 for international students. Applications are processed on a rolling basis. Application fee: $60. Electronic applications accepted. *Financial support:* In 2018–19, 21 research assistantships, 22 teaching assistantships were awarded; fellowships with tuition reimbursements, career-related internships or fieldwork, and Federal Work-Study also available. Support available to part-time students. Financial award application deadline: 4/1; financial award applicants required to submit FAFSA. *Unit head:* William Oliver, Department Chair, 479-575-6571, Fax: 479-575-6595, E-mail: woliver@uark.edu. *Application contact:* Dr. Surendra Singh, Graduate Coordinator, 479-575-6058, Fax: 479-575-6595, E-mail: ssingh@uark.edu.
Website: https://fulbright.uark.edu/departments/physics/

The University of British Columbia, Faculty of Science, Department of Physics and Astronomy, Program in Physics, Vancouver, BC V6T 1Z1, Canada. Offers M Sc, PhD. *Degree requirements:* For master's, thesis; for doctorate, comprehensive exam, thesis/dissertation. *Entrance requirements:* For master's, GRE General Test, honors degree; for doctorate, GRE General Test, master's degree. Additional exam requirements/recommendations for international students: Required—TOEFL. *Expenses:* Contact institution. *Faculty research:* Applied physics, astrophysics, condensed matter, plasma physics, subatomic physics, astronomy.

University of Calgary, Faculty of Graduate Studies, Faculty of Science, Program in Physics and Astronomy, Calgary, AB T2N 1N4, Canada. Offers M Sc, PhD. *Program availability:* Part-time. *Degree requirements:* For master's, thesis; for doctorate, thesis/dissertation, oral candidacy exam, written qualifying exam. *Entrance requirements:* For master's and doctorate, GRE General Test, GRE Subject Test. Additional exam requirements/recommendations for international students: Required—TOEFL (minimum score 550 paper-based). Electronic applications accepted. *Faculty research:* Astronomy and astrophysics, mass spectrometry, atmospheric physics, space physics, medical physics.

University of California, Berkeley, Graduate Division, College of Letters and Science, Department of Physics, Berkeley, CA 94720. Offers PhD. *Degree requirements:* For doctorate, thesis/dissertation, qualifying exam. *Entrance requirements:* For doctorate, GRE General Test, GRE Subject Test, minimum GPA of 3.0, 3 letters of recommendation. Additional exam requirements/recommendations for international students: Required—TOEFL (minimum score 570 paper-based; 90 iBT). Electronic applications accepted. *Faculty research:* Astrophysics (experimental and theoretical), condensed matter physics (experimental and theoretical), particle physics (experimental and theoretical), atomic/molecular physics, biophysics and complex systems.

University of California, Davis, Graduate Studies, Program in Physics, Davis, CA 95616. Offers MS, PhD. Terminal master's awarded for partial completion of doctoral program. *Degree requirements:* For master's, comprehensive exam (for some programs), thesis (for some programs); for doctorate, thesis/dissertation. *Entrance requirements:* For master's and doctorate, GRE General Test, GRE Subject Test, minimum GPA of 3.0. Additional exam requirements/recommendations for international students: Required—TOEFL (minimum score 550 paper-based). Electronic applications accepted. *Faculty research:* Astrophysics, condensed-matter physics, nuclear physics, particle physics, quantum optics.

University of California, Irvine, School of Physical Sciences, Department of Physics and Astronomy, Irvine, CA 92697. Offers physics (MS, PhD), MD/PhD. *Students:* 95 full-time (23 women), 1 part-time (0 women); includes 28 minority (1 Black or African American, non-Hispanic/Latino; 4 Asian, non-Hispanic/Latino; 15 Hispanic/Latino; 8 Two or more races, non-Hispanic/Latino), 15 international. Average age 26. 354 applicants, 19% accepted, 18 enrolled. In 2018, 16 master's, 16 doctorates awarded. Terminal master's awarded for partial completion of doctoral program. *Entrance requirements:* For master's and doctorate, GRE General Test, GRE Subject Test, minimum GPA of 3.0. Additional exam requirements/recommendations for international students: Required—TOEFL (minimum score 550 paper-based). *Application deadline:* For fall admission, 1/15 priority date for domestic and international students. Application fee: $105 ($125 for international students). Electronic applications accepted. *Financial support:* Fellowships with full tuition reimbursements, research assistantships with full tuition reimbursements, teaching assistantships with partial tuition reimbursements, institutionally sponsored loans, traineeships, health care benefits, and unspecified assistantships available. Financial award application deadline: 3/1; financial award applicants required to submit FAFSA. *Faculty research:* Condensed-matter physics, plasma physics, astrophysics, particle physics, chemical and materials physics, biophysics. *Unit head:* Peter Taborek, Chair, 949-824-2254, Fax: 949-824-2174, E-mail: ptaborek@uci.edu. *Application contact:* My Banh, Graduate Student Affairs Officer, 949-824-3496, Fax: 949-824-7988, E-mail: mbanh@uci.edu.
Website: http://www.physics.uci.edu/

University of California, Los Angeles, Graduate Division, College of Letters and Science, Department of Physics and Astronomy, Program in Physics, Los Angeles, CA 90095. Offers MS, PhD. Terminal master's awarded for partial completion of doctoral program. *Degree requirements:* For master's, comprehensive exam, thesis; for doctorate, thesis/dissertation, oral and written qualifying exams. *Entrance requirements:* For master's and doctorate, GRE General Test, GRE Subject Test (physics), bachelor's degree; minimum undergraduate GPA of 3.0 (or its equivalent if letter grade system not used). Additional exam requirements/recommendations for international students: Required—TOEFL. Electronic applications accepted.

University of California, Merced, Graduate Division, School of Natural Sciences, Merced, CA 95343. Offers applied mathematics (MS, PhD), chemistry and chemical biology (MS, PhD); physics (MS, PhD); quantitative and systems biology (MS, PhD), including molecular and cellular biology (PhD). *Faculty:* 77 full-time (30 women). *Students:* 232 full-time (98 women), 2 part-time (0 women); includes 79 minority (8 Black or African American, non-Hispanic/Latino; 22 Asian, non-Hispanic/Latino; 41 Hispanic/Latino; 8 Two or more races, non-Hispanic/Latino), 65 international. Average age 28. 302 applicants, 42% accepted, 58 enrolled. In 2018, 13 master's, 23 doctorates awarded. Terminal master's awarded for partial completion of doctoral program. *Degree requirements:* For master's, variable foreign language requirement, comprehensive exam, thesis or alternative, oral defense; for doctorate, variable foreign language requirement, comprehensive exam, thesis/dissertation, oral defense. *Entrance requirements:* For master's and doctorate, GRE. Additional exam requirements/recommendations for international students: Required—TOEFL (minimum score 550 paper-based; 80 iBT); Recommended—IELTS (minimum score 6.5). *Application deadline:* For fall admission, 1/15 for domestic and international students. Application fee: $105 ($125 for international students). Electronic applications accepted. *Expenses: Tuition, area resident:* Full-time $11,442; part-time $5721 per year. *Tuition, state resident:* full-time $11,442; part-time $5721 per year. *Tuition, nonresident:* full-time $26,544; part-time $13,272 per year. *International tuition:* $26,544 full-time. *Required fees:* $1765; $1765 per unit. $883 per semester. *Financial support:* In 2018–19, 229 students received support, including 12 fellowships with full tuition reimbursements available (averaging $21,865 per year), 47 research assistantships with full tuition reimbursements available (averaging $19,123 per year), 170 teaching assistantships with full tuition reimbursements available (averaging $20,710 per year); scholarships/grants, traineeships, and health care benefits also available. *Faculty research:* Biomedical sciences; soft matter physics; applied math and computational science; environmental and biological systems; biological and materials chemistry. *Total annual research expenditures:* $4.1 million. *Unit head:* Dr. Elizabeth Dumont, Dean, 209-228-4487, Fax: 209-228-4060, E-mail: edumont@ucmerced.edu. *Application contact:* Tsu Ya, Director of Graduate Admissions and Academic Services, 209-228-4521, Fax: 209-228-6906, E-mail: tya@ucmerced.edu.

University of California, Riverside, Graduate Division, Department of Physics and Astronomy, Riverside, CA 92521-0102. Offers physics (MS, PhD). *Degree requirements:* For master's, comprehensive exams or thesis; for doctorate, thesis/dissertation, qualifying exams. *Entrance requirements:* For master's and doctorate, GRE General Test, GRE Subject Test, minimum GPA of 3.0. Additional exam requirements/recommendations for international students: Required—TOEFL (minimum score 550 paper-based; 80 iBT). Electronic applications accepted. *Faculty research:* Laser physics and surface science, elementary particle and heavy ion physics, plasma physics, optical physics, astrophysics.

University of California, San Diego, Graduate Division, Department of Physics, La Jolla, CA 92093. Offers biophysics (PhD); computational neuroscience (PhD); computational science (PhD); multi-scale biology (PhD); physics (MS, PhD); quantitative biology (PhD). *Students:* 172 full-time (29 women), 1 part-time (0 women). 570 applicants, 27% accepted, 48 enrolled. In 2018, 11 master's, 26 doctorates awarded. *Degree requirements:* For doctorate, comprehensive exam, thesis/dissertation, 1-quarter teaching assistantship. *Entrance requirements:* For doctorate, GRE General Test, GRE Subject Test, statement of purpose, three letters of reference. Additional exam requirements/recommendations for international students: Required—TOEFL (minimum score 550 paper-based; 80 iBT), IELTS (minimum score 7). *Application deadline:* For fall admission, 12/19 for domestic students. Application fee: $105 ($125 for international students). Electronic applications accepted. *Financial support:* Fellowships, research assistantships, teaching assistantships, scholarships/grants, and unspecified assistantships available. Financial award applicants required to submit FAFSA. *Faculty research:* Astrophysics/Astronomy; Atomic/Molecular; Biophysics; Computational Science; Condensed Matter/Material Science; High Energy Physics; Mathematical Physics; Nonlinear Dynamics; Physics; Plasma/Fusion; Quantitative Biology; Statistical/Thermal Physics. *Unit head:* Benjamin Grinstein, Chair, 858-534-6857, E-mail: chair@physics.ucsd.edu. *Application contact:* Saixious Dominguez-Kilday, Graduate Admissions Coordinator, 858-534-3293, E-mail: skilday@physics.ucsd.edu. Website: http://physics.ucsd.edu/

University of California, Santa Barbara, Graduate Division, College of Letters and Sciences, Division of Mathematics, Life, and Physical Sciences, Department of Physics, Santa Barbara, CA 93106-9530. Offers astrophysics (PhD); physics (PhD). Terminal master's awarded for partial completion of doctoral program. *Degree requirements:* For doctorate, comprehensive exam, thesis/dissertation. *Entrance requirements:* For doctorate, GRE General Test, GRE Subject Test (physics). Additional exam requirements/recommendations for international students: Required—TOEFL (minimum score 550 paper-based; 80 iBT), IELTS (minimum score 7). Electronic applications accepted. *Faculty research:* High energy theoretical/experimental physics, condensed matter theoretical/experimental physics, astrophysics and cosmology, biophysics, gravity and relativity.

University of California, Santa Cruz, Division of Graduate Studies, Division of Physical and Biological Sciences, Department of Physics, Santa Cruz, CA 95064. Offers MS, PhD. Terminal master's awarded for partial completion of doctoral program. *Degree requirements:* For master's, written qualifying exam or thesis; for doctorate, one foreign language, thesis/dissertation, written and oral qualifying exam. *Entrance requirements:* For master's and doctorate, GRE Subject Test in physics (recommended). Additional exam requirements/recommendations for international students: Required—TOEFL (minimum score 550 paper-based; 83 iBT); Recommended—IELTS (minimum score 8). Electronic applications accepted. *Expenses:* Contact institution. *Faculty research:* Theoretical and experimental particle physics, astrophysics and cosmology, condensed matter physics, biophysics.

University of Central Florida, College of Sciences, Department of Physics, Orlando, FL 32816. Offers MS, PhD. *Program availability:* Part-time. *Students:* 97 full-time (32 women); includes 24 minority (10 Black or African American, non-Hispanic/Latino; 13 Hispanic/Latino; 1 Two or more races, non-Hispanic/Latino), 39 international. Average age 28. 118 applicants, 33% accepted, 18 enrolled. In 2018, 14 master's, 13 doctorates awarded. *Degree requirements:* For master's, thesis or alternative; for doctorate, thesis/dissertation, candidacy and qualifying exams. *Entrance requirements:* For master's, resume, goal statement, letters of recommendation; for doctorate, GRE General Test, GRE Subject Test (recommended), resume, goal statement, letters of recommendation. Additional exam requirements/recommendations for international students: Required—TOEFL. *Application deadline:* For fall admission, 6/15 for domestic students; for spring admission, 11/1 for domestic students. Application fee: $30. Electronic applications accepted. *Financial support:* In 2018–19, 90 students received support, including 18 fellowships with partial tuition reimbursements available (averaging $6,748 per year), 87 research assistantships with partial tuition reimbursements available (averaging $9,478 per year), 58 teaching assistantships with partial tuition reimbursements available (averaging $11,789 per year); career-related internships or fieldwork, Federal Work-Study, institutionally sponsored loans, tuition waivers (partial), and unspecified assistantships also available. Financial award application deadline: 3/1; financial award applicants required to submit FAFSA. *Faculty research:* Atomic-molecular physics, condensed-matter physics, quantum information science, planetary sciences. *Unit head:* Dr. Eduardo Mucciolo, Chair, 407-823-1882, E-mail: eduardo.mucciolo@ucf.edu. *Application contact:* Associate Director, Graduate Admissions, 407-823-2766, Fax: 407-823-6442, E-mail: gradadmissions@ucf.edu.
Website: http://www.physics.ucf.edu/

Peterson's Graduate Programs in the Physical Sciences, Mathematics, Agricultural Sciences, the Environment & Natural Resources 2020

www.petersons.com **159**

SECTION 6: PHYSICS

Physics

University of Central Oklahoma, The Jackson College of Graduate Studies, College of Mathematics and Science, Department of Engineering and Physics, Edmond, OK 73034-5209. Offers engineering physics (MS), including biomedical engineering, electrical engineering, mechanical systems, physics. *Program availability:* Part-time. *Degree requirements:* For master's, thesis optional. *Entrance requirements:* For master's, GRE, 24 hours of course work in physics or equivalent, mathematics through differential equations, minimum GPA of 2.75 overall and 3.0 in last 60 hours attempted, two letters of recommendation. Additional exam requirements/recommendations for international students: Required—TOEFL (minimum score 550 paper-based; 79 iBT), IELTS (minimum score 6.5). Electronic applications accepted.

University of Chicago, Division of the Physical Sciences, Department of Physics, Chicago, IL 60637. Offers PhD. *Degree requirements:* For doctorate, comprehensive exam, thesis/dissertation. *Entrance requirements:* For doctorate, GRE General Test, GRE Subject Test, research statement, 3 letters of recommendation, transcripts for all previous degrees and institutions attended. Additional exam requirements/ recommendations for international students: Required—TOEFL (minimum score 90 iBT), IELTS (minimum score 7). Electronic applications accepted. *Faculty research:* High energy physics experiment and theory; condensed matter experiment and theory; astrophysics; atomic, molecular, and optical physics; general relativity.

University of Chicago, Division of the Physical Sciences, Master of Science in Physical Sciences Programs, Chicago, IL 60637. Offers MS. *Program availability:* Part-time. *Degree requirements:* For master's, thesis. *Entrance requirements:* For master's, GRE General Test, research statement, 3 letters of recommendation, transcripts for all previous degrees and institutions attended. Additional exam requirements/ recommendations for international students: Required—TOEFL (minimum score 90 iBT), IELTS (minimum score 7). Electronic applications accepted.

University of Cincinnati, Graduate School, McMicken College of Arts and Sciences, Department of Physics, Cincinnati, OH 45221-0011. Offers MS, PhD. Terminal master's awarded for partial completion of doctoral program. *Degree requirements:* For master's, thesis optional; for doctorate, thesis/dissertation. *Entrance requirements:* For master's and doctorate, GRE General Test, GRE Subject Test. Additional exam requirements/ recommendations for international students: Required—TOEFL (minimum score 540 paper-based). Electronic applications accepted. *Faculty research:* Condensed matter physics, experimental particle physics, theoretical high energy physics, astronomy and astrophysics, computational physics.

University of Colorado Boulder, Graduate School, College of Arts and Sciences, Department of Physics, Boulder, CO 80309. Offers mathematical physics (PhD). Terminal master's awarded for partial completion of doctoral program. *Degree requirements:* For master's, comprehensive exam, thesis or alternative; for doctorate, comprehensive exam, thesis/dissertation. *Entrance requirements:* For master's and doctorate, GRE General Test, GRE Subject Test, minimum undergraduate GPA of 3.0. Additional exam requirements/recommendations for international students: Required—TOEFL. Electronic applications accepted. Application fee is waived when completed online. *Faculty research:* Physics; experimental physics; theoretical physics; high energy physics; optics.

University of Colorado Colorado Springs, College of Letters, Arts and Sciences, Program in Interdisciplinary Applied Sciences, Colorado Springs, CO 80918. Offers applied sciences (PhD), including math, physics. *Program availability:* Part-time, evening/weekend. *Faculty:* 10 full-time (2 women), 10 part-time/adjunct (0 women). *Students:* 2 full-time (1 woman), 43 part-time (14 women); includes 6 minority (1 American Indian or Alaska Native, non-Hispanic/Latino; 2 Asian, non-Hispanic/Latino; 1 Hispanic/Latino; 2 Two or more races, non-Hispanic/Latino), 6 international. Average age 31. 13 applicants, 92% accepted, 12 enrolled. In 2018, 3 doctorates awarded. *Degree requirements:* For doctorate, comprehensive exam, thesis/dissertation. *Entrance requirements:* For doctorate, GRE or minimum GPA of 3.0 with baccalaureate degree in biological sciences, mathematics, physics or equivalent from accredited college or university and appropriate background of undergraduate physics courses. Additional exam requirements/recommendations for international students: Required—TOEFL (minimum score 80 iBT), IELTS (minimum score 6.5). *Application deadline:* Applications are processed on a rolling basis. Application fee: $60 ($100 for international students). Electronic applications accepted. *Expenses:* Tuition and fees vary by program, course load, and residency type. Please visit the University of Colorado Colorado Springs Student Financial Services website to estimate current program costs: https://www.uccs.edu/bursar/index.php/estimate-your-bill. *Financial support:* In 2018–19, 15 students received support, including 11 teaching assistantships (averaging $3,500 per year); Federal Work-Study, scholarships/grants, and unspecified assistantships also available. Support available to part-time students. Financial award application deadline: 3/1; financial award applicants required to submit FAFSA. *Faculty research:* Solid-state/condensed-matter physics, surface science, electron spectroscopies, nonlinear physics. *Total annual research expenditures:* $695,442. *Unit head:* Dr. Robert Camley, Professor, 719-255-3512, E-mail: rcamley@uccs.edu. *Application contact:* Dr. Karen Livesey, Assistant Professor, 719-255-5116, E-mail: klivesey@uccs.edu.

University of Connecticut, Graduate School, College of Liberal Arts and Sciences, Department of Physics, Storrs, CT 06269. Offers MS, PhD. *Degree requirements:* For master's, comprehensive exam; for doctorate, thesis/dissertation. *Entrance requirements:* For master's and doctorate, GRE General Test, GRE Subject Test. Additional exam requirements/recommendations for international students: Required—TOEFL (minimum score 550 paper-based). Electronic applications accepted.

University of Delaware, College of Arts and Sciences, Department of Physics and Astronomy, Newark, DE 19716. Offers MS, PhD. *Program availability:* Part-time. Terminal master's awarded for partial completion of doctoral program. *Degree requirements:* For master's, thesis; for doctorate, thesis/dissertation. *Entrance requirements:* For master's and doctorate, GRE General Test, GRE Subject Test. Additional exam requirements/recommendations for international students: Required—TOEFL (minimum score 600 paper-based). Electronic applications accepted. *Faculty research:* Magnetoresistance and magnetic materials, ultrafast optical phenomena, superfluidity, elementary particle physics, stellar atmospheres and interiors.

University of Denver, Division of Natural Sciences and Mathematics, Department of Physics and Astronomy, Denver, CO 80208. Offers physics (MS, PhD). *Program availability:* Part-time. *Faculty:* 12 full-time (4 women), 2 part-time/adjunct (0 women). *Students:* 12 part-time (3 women); includes 3 minority (1 Hispanic/Latino; 2 Two or more races, non-Hispanic/Latino). Average age 27. 64 applicants, 19% accepted, 6 enrolled. In 2018, 1 master's, 1 doctorate awarded. Terminal master's awarded for partial completion of doctoral program. *Degree requirements:* For master's, comprehensive exam (for some programs), thesis (for some programs), Regular attendance at Physics and Astronomy colloquia; for doctorate, comprehensive exam, thesis/dissertation, Regular attendance and annual presentation at Physics and Astronomy colloquia. *Entrance requirements:* For master's and doctorate, GRE General Test, GRE Subject Test in physics (strongly preferred), bachelor's degree, transcripts, personal statement, three letters of recommendation, required essay questions, resume. Additional exam requirements/recommendations for international students: Required—TOEFL (minimum score 550 paper-based; 80 iBT). *Application deadline:* For fall admission, 2/1 priority date for domestic and international students. Applications are processed on a rolling basis. Application fee: $65. Electronic applications accepted. *Expenses:* $33,183 per year full-time. *Financial support:* In 2018–19, 12 students received support, including 4 research assistantships with tuition reimbursements available (averaging $16,667 per year), 9 teaching assistantships with tuition reimbursements available (averaging $20,000 per year); career-related internships or fieldwork, Federal Work-Study, institutionally sponsored loans, scholarships/grants, and unspecified assistantships also available. Support available to part-time students. Financial award application deadline: 2/15; financial award applicants required to submit FAFSA. *Faculty research:* Astronomy and astrophysics, biophysics, condensed matter and materials physics. *Unit head:* Dr. Davor Balzar, Associate Professor and Chair, 303-871-2137, E-mail: davor.balzar@du.edu. *Application contact:* Faun Lee, Assistant to the Chair, 303-871-2238, E-mail: faun.lee@du.edu.
Website: https://www.physics.du.edu/

University of Florida, Graduate School, College of Liberal Arts and Sciences, Department of Physics, Gainesville, FL 32611. Offers imaging science and technology (PhD); physics (MS, MST, PhD). Terminal master's awarded for partial completion of doctoral program. *Degree requirements:* For doctorate, comprehensive exam, thesis/ dissertation. *Entrance requirements:* For master's and doctorate, GRE General Test, minimum GPA of 3.0. Additional exam requirements/recommendations for international students: Required—TOEFL (minimum score 550 paper-based; 80 iBT), IELTS (minimum score 6). Electronic applications accepted. *Faculty research:* Astrophysics, biological physics (molecular, magnetic resonance imaging, spectroscopy, biomagnetism), chemical physics (molecular, nano-scale physics, solid state, surface physics, quantum chemistry, quantum electron dynamics, molecular biology), experimental and theory condensed matter physics, low temperature physics (theory and experimental, mathematical physics.

University of Georgia, Franklin College of Arts and Sciences, Department of Physics and Astronomy, Athens, GA 30602. Offers physics (MS, PhD). *Degree requirements:* For master's, thesis; for doctorate, one foreign language, thesis/dissertation. *Entrance requirements:* For master's and doctorate, GRE General Test. Electronic applications accepted.

University of Guelph, Office of Graduate and Postdoctoral Studies, College of Physical and Engineering Science, Guelph-Waterloo Physics Institute, Guelph, ON N1G 2W1, Canada. Offers M Sc, PhD. M Sc, PhD offered jointly with University of Waterloo. *Program availability:* Part-time. *Degree requirements:* For master's, project or thesis; for doctorate, comprehensive exam, thesis/dissertation. *Entrance requirements:* For master's, GRE Subject Test, minimum B average for honors degree; for doctorate, GRE Subject Test, minimum B average. Additional exam requirements/recommendations for international students: Required—TOEFL (minimum score 550 paper-based), TWE (minimum score 4). *Faculty research:* Condensed matter and material physics, quantum computing, astrophysics and gravitation, industrial and applied physics, subatomic physics.

University of Hawaii at Manoa, Office of Graduate Education, College of Natural Sciences, Department of Physics and Astronomy, Program in Physics, Honolulu, HI 96822. Offers MS, PhD. *Program availability:* Part-time. *Degree requirements:* For master's, thesis optional; for doctorate, comprehensive exam, thesis/dissertation. *Entrance requirements:* For master's and doctorate, GRE General Test. Additional exam requirements/recommendations for international students: Required—TOEFL (minimum score 560 paper-based; 83 iBT), IELTS (minimum score 5).

University of Houston, College of Natural Sciences and Mathematics, Department of Physics, Houston, TX 77204. Offers MA, PhD. *Program availability:* Part-time. Terminal master's awarded for partial completion of doctoral program. *Entrance requirements:* For master's and doctorate, GRE General Test. Electronic applications accepted. *Faculty research:* Condensed-matter, particle physics; high-temperature superconductivity; material/space physics; chaos.

University of Houston–Clear Lake, School of Science and Computer Engineering, Program in Physics, Houston, TX 77058-1002. Offers MS. *Program availability:* Part-time, evening/weekend. *Entrance requirements:* For master's, GRE General Test. Additional exam requirements/recommendations for international students: Required—TOEFL (minimum score 550 paper-based).

University of Idaho, College of Graduate Studies, College of Science, Department of Physics, Moscow, ID 83844-0903. Offers MS, PhD. *Faculty:* 9. *Students:* 25. Average age 30. In 2018, 1 master's, 2 doctorates awarded. *Degree requirements:* For master's, thesis or alternative; for doctorate, thesis/dissertation. *Entrance requirements:* For master's and doctorate, minimum GPA of 3.0. Additional exam requirements/ recommendations for international students: Required—TOEFL (minimum score 79 iBT). *Application deadline:* For fall admission, 8/1 for domestic students; for spring admission, 12/15 for domestic students. Applications are processed on a rolling basis. Application fee: $60. Electronic applications accepted. *Expenses:* Tuition, state resident: full-time $7266.44; part-time $474.50 per credit hour. Tuition, nonresident: full-time $24,902; part-time $1453.50 per credit hour. *Required fees:* $2085.56; $45.50 per credit hour. *Financial support:* Research assistantships and teaching assistantships available. Financial award applicants required to submit FAFSA. *Faculty research:* Growth and synthesis of luminescent materials, extrasolar planets, theoretical nuclear physics. *Unit head:* Dr. Ray von Wandruszka, Interim Chair, 208-885-6380, E-mail: physics@uidaho.edu. *Application contact:* Dr. Ray von Wandruszka, Interim Chair, 208-885-6380, E-mail: physics@uidaho.edu.
Website: http://www.uidaho.edu/sci/physics

University of Illinois at Chicago, College of Liberal Arts and Sciences, Department of Physics, Chicago, IL 60607-7128. Offers MS, PhD. Terminal master's awarded for partial completion of doctoral program. *Degree requirements:* For doctorate, thesis/ dissertation. *Entrance requirements:* For master's and doctorate, GRE General Test, minimum GPA of 3.0. Additional exam requirements/recommendations for international students: Required—TOEFL. Electronic applications accepted. *Expenses:* Contact institution. *Faculty research:* High-energy, laser, and solid-state physics.

University of Illinois at Urbana–Champaign, Graduate College, College of Engineering, Department of Physics, Champaign, IL 61820. Offers physics (MS, PhD); teaching of physics (MS).

The University of Iowa, Graduate College, College of Liberal Arts and Sciences, Department of Physics and Astronomy, Program in Physics, Iowa City, IA 52242-1316. Offers MS, PhD. *Degree requirements:* For master's, thesis optional, exam; for doctorate, comprehensive exam, thesis/dissertation. *Entrance requirements:* For master's and doctorate, GRE General Test, minimum GPA of 3.0. Additional exam requirements/recommendations for international students: Required—TOEFL (minimum score 550 paper-based; 81 iBT). Electronic applications accepted.

The University of Kansas, Graduate Studies, College of Liberal Arts and Sciences, Department of Physics and Astronomy, Lawrence, KS 66045. Offers physics and astronomy (MS, PhD); MS/PhD. *Students:* 54 full-time (11 women); includes 5 minority (1 American Indian or Alaska Native, non-Hispanic/Latino; 1 Asian, non-Hispanic/Latino; 3 Hispanic/Latino), 23 international. Average age 29. 72 applicants, 46% accepted, 13 enrolled. In 2018, 2 master's, 7 doctorates awarded. Terminal master's awarded for partial completion of doctoral program. *Entrance requirements:* For master's and doctorate, GRE Subject Test (physics), statement of personal goals, resume or curriculum vitae, official transcripts, three letters of recommendation. Additional exam requirements/recommendations for international students: Required—TOEFL, IELTS, TOEFL or IELTS. *Application deadline:* For fall admission, 12/31 priority date for domestic and international students; for spring admission, 10/1 priority date for domestic and international students. Application fee: $65 ($85 for international students). Electronic applications accepted. *Financial support:* Fellowships, research assistantships, teaching assistantships, scholarships/grants, health care benefits, and unspecified assistantships available. Financial award application deadline: 12/31; financial award applicants required to submit FAFSA. *Faculty research:* Astrophysics, biophysics, high energy physics, nanophysics, nuclear physics. *Unit head:* Hume A. Feldman, Chair, 785-864-4626, E-mail: feldman@ku.edu. *Application contact:* Joel Sauerwein, Graduate Secretary, 785-864-1225, E-mail: physics@ku.edu. Website: http://www.physics.ku.edu

University of Kentucky, Graduate School, College of Arts and Sciences, Program in Physics and Astronomy, Lexington, KY 40500-0032. Offers MS, PhD. *Degree requirements:* For master's, comprehensive exam, thesis optional; for doctorate, comprehensive exam, thesis/dissertation. *Entrance requirements:* For master's, GRE General Test, minimum undergraduate GPA of 2.75; for doctorate, GRE General Test, minimum graduate GPA of 3.0. Additional exam requirements/recommendations for international students: Required—TOEFL (minimum score 550 paper-based). Electronic applications accepted. *Faculty research:* Astrophysics, active galactic nuclei, and radio astronomy; Rydbert atoms, and electron scattering; TOF spectroscopy, hyperon interactions and muons; particle theory, lattice gauge theory, quark, and skyrmion models.

University of Lethbridge, School of Graduate Studies, Lethbridge, AB T1K 3M4, Canada. Offers addictions counseling (M Sc); agricultural biotechnology (M Sc); agricultural studies (M Sc, MA); anthropology (MA); archaeology (M Sc, MA); art (MA, MFA); biochemistry (M Sc); biological sciences (M Sc); biomolecular science (PhD); biosystems and biodiversity (PhD); Canadian studies (MA); chemistry (M Sc); computer science (M Sc); computer science and geographical information science (M Sc); counseling (MC); counseling psychology (M Ed); dramatic arts (MA); earth, space, and physical science (PhD); economics (MA); education (MA, PhD); educational leadership (M Ed); English (MA); environmental science (M Sc); evolution and behavior (PhD); exercise science (M Sc); French (MA); French/German (MA); French/Spanish (MA); general education (M Ed); geography (M Sc, MA); German (MA); health sciences (M Sc); individualized multidisciplinary (M Sc, MA); kinesiology (M Sc, MA); management (M Sc), including accounting, finance, human resource management and labor relations, information systems, international management, marketing, policy and strategy; mathematics (M Sc); music (M Mus, MA); Native American studies (MA); neuroscience (M Sc, PhD); new media (MA, MFA); nursing (M Sc, MN); philosophy (MA); physics (M Sc); political science (MA); psychology (M Sc, MA); religious studies (MA); sociology (MA); theatre and dramatic arts (MFA); theoretical and computational science (PhD); urban and regional studies (MA); women and gender studies (MA). *Program availability:* Part-time, evening/weekend. *Degree requirements:* For master's, thesis (for some programs); for doctorate, comprehensive exam, thesis/dissertation. *Entrance requirements:* For master's, GMAT (for M Sc in management), bachelor's degree in related field, minimum GPA of 3.0 during previous 20 graded semester courses, 2 years' teaching or related experience (M Ed); for doctorate, master's degree, minimum graduate GPA of 3.5. Additional exam requirements/recommendations for international students: Required—TOEFL (minimum score 580 paper-based; 93 iBT). Electronic applications accepted. *Faculty research:* Movement and brain plasticity, gibberellin physiology, photosynthesis, carbon cycling, molecular properties of main-group ring components.

University of Louisiana at Lafayette, College of Sciences, Department of Physics, Lafayette, LA 70504. Offers MS. *Program availability:* Part-time. *Entrance requirements:* For master's, GRE General Test, minimum GPA of 2.75. Additional exam requirements/recommendations for international students: Required—TOEFL (minimum score 550 paper-based). Electronic applications accepted. *Faculty research:* Environmental physics, geophysics, astrophysics, acoustics, atomic physics.

University of Louisville, Graduate School, College of Arts and Sciences, Department of Physics and Astronomy, Louisville, KY 40292. Offers physics (MS, PhD). *Program availability:* Part-time. *Faculty:* 17 full-time (3 women), 1 part-time/adjunct (0 women). *Students:* 33 full-time (10 women), 5 part-time (1 woman); includes 2 minority (both Asian, non-Hispanic/Latino), 22 international. Average age 32. 36 applicants, 39% accepted, 8 enrolled. In 2018, 2 master's, 1 doctorate awarded. Terminal master's awarded for partial completion of doctoral program. *Degree requirements:* For master's, thesis optional; for doctorate, comprehensive exam, thesis/dissertation. *Entrance requirements:* Additional exam requirements/recommendations for international students: Required—TOEFL (minimum score 550 paper-based; 79 iBT), IELTS can be used in place of TOEFL; Recommended—IELTS (minimum score 6.5). *Application deadline:* For fall admission, 2/1 priority date for domestic students, 12/31 priority date for international students; for spring admission, 10/15 priority date for domestic students, 10/31 priority date for international students. Applications are processed on a rolling basis. Application fee: $65. Electronic applications accepted. *Expenses:* Contact institution. *Financial support:* In 2018–19, 31 students received support, including 2 research assistantships with full tuition reimbursements available (averaging $22,000 per year), 16 teaching assistantships with full tuition reimbursements available (averaging $22,000 per year); fellowships, scholarships/grants, health care benefits, and unspecified assistantships also available. Financial award application deadline: 2/1. *Faculty research:* Applied Optics, Astronomy, Atmospheric Physics, Condensed Matter Physics, and Experimental High Energy Physics. *Total annual research expenditures:* $606,489. *Unit head:* Dr. Chakram S. Jayanthi, Professor/Chair, 502-852-6790, Fax: 502-852-0742, E-mail: csjaya01@louisville.edu. *Application contact:* Gamini Sumanasekera, Professor of Physics, 502-852-1558, Fax: 502-852-0742, E-mail: gamini.sumanasekera@louisville.edu. Website: http://www.physics.louisville.edu/

University of Maine, Graduate School, College of Liberal Arts and Sciences, Department of Physics and Astronomy, Orono, ME 04469. Offers ME, MS, PhD. *Faculty:* 12 full-time (1 woman), 2 part-time/adjunct (0 women). *Students:* 39 full-time (15 women), 7 part-time (2 women); includes 2 minority (1 Asian, non-Hispanic/Latino; 1 Two or more races, non-Hispanic/Latino), 4 international. Average age 28. 50 applicants, 30% accepted, 11 enrolled. In 2018, 11 master's, 2 doctorates awarded. Terminal master's awarded for partial completion of doctoral program. *Degree requirements:* For master's, thesis; for doctorate, comprehensive exam, thesis/

dissertation. *Entrance requirements:* For master's, GRE General Test, GRE Subject Test; for doctorate, GRE General Test. Additional exam requirements/recommendations for international students: Required—TOEFL (minimum score 92 iBT), IELTS (minimum score 7). *Application deadline:* For fall admission, 1/15 priority date for domestic students. Applications are processed on a rolling basis. Application fee: $65. Electronic applications accepted. *Financial support:* In 2018–19, 47 students received support, including 1 fellowship with full tuition reimbursement available (averaging $18,000 per year), 15 research assistantships with full tuition reimbursements available (averaging $15,600 per year), 25 teaching assistantships with full tuition reimbursements available (averaging $16,500 per year); tuition waivers (full and partial) and unspecified assistantships also available. Financial award application deadline: 3/1. *Faculty research:* Super-resolution fluorescence microscopy and spectroscopy; sensor technology and surface physics; electronic structure of nanoscale materials; development of physics student reasoning skills and metacognitive skills; astronomy and astrophysics. *Total annual research expenditures:* $1.2 million. *Unit head:* Dr. David Batuski, Chair, 207-581-1015, Fax: 207-581-3410. *Application contact:* Scott G. Delcourt, Associate Dean of the Graduate School, 207-581-3291, Fax: 207-581-3232, E-mail: graduate@maine.edu. Website: http://www.physics.umaine.edu/

The University of Manchester, School of Earth and Environmental Sciences, Manchester, United Kingdom. Offers atmospheric sciences (M Phil, M Sc, PhD); basin studies and petroleum geosciences (M Phil, M Sc, PhD); earth, atmospheric and environmental sciences (M Phil, M Sc, PhD); environmental geochemistry and cosmochemistry (M Phil, M Sc, PhD); isotope geochemistry and cosmochemistry (M Phil, M Sc, PhD); paleontology (M Phil, M Sc, PhD); physics and chemistry of minerals and fluids (M Phil, M Sc, PhD); structural and petrological geosciences (M Phil, M Sc, PhD).

The University of Manchester, School of Physics and Astronomy, Manchester, United Kingdom. Offers astronomy and astrophysics (M Sc, PhD); biological physics (M Sc, PhD); condensed matter physics (M Sc, PhD); nonlinear and liquid crystals physics (M Sc, PhD); nuclear physics (M Sc, PhD); particle physics (M Sc, PhD); photon physics (M Sc, PhD); physics (M Sc, PhD); theoretical physics (M Sc, PhD).

University of Manitoba, Faculty of Graduate Studies, Faculty of Science, Department of Physics and Astronomy, Winnipeg, MB R3T 2N2, Canada. Offers M Sc, PhD. *Degree requirements:* For master's, thesis; for doctorate, one foreign language, thesis/dissertation.

University of Maryland, Baltimore County, The Graduate School, College of Natural and Mathematical Sciences, Department of Physics, Program in Physics, Baltimore, MD 21250. Offers MS, PhD. *Program availability:* Part-time. Terminal master's awarded for partial completion of doctoral program. *Degree requirements:* For master's, thesis optional; for doctorate, comprehensive exam, thesis/dissertation. *Entrance requirements:* For master's, GRE General Test, GRE Subject Test (recommended), minimum GPA of 3.0; for doctorate, GRE General Test, GRE Subject Test (strongly recommended), minimum GPA of 3.0. Additional exam requirements/recommendations for international students: Required—TOEFL. Electronic applications accepted. *Faculty research:* Astrophysics, atmospheric physics, condensed matter physics, quantum optics and quantum information.

University of Maryland, College Park, Academic Affairs, College of Computer, Mathematical and Natural Sciences, Department of Physics, College Park, MD 20742. Offers MS, PhD. *Program availability:* Part-time, evening/weekend. Terminal master's awarded for partial completion of doctoral program. *Degree requirements:* For master's, thesis optional; for doctorate, thesis/dissertation. *Entrance requirements:* For master's, GRE General Test, GRE Subject Test (physics), minimum GPA of 3.0, 3 letters of recommendation; for doctorate, GRE General Test, GRE Subject Test (physics), 3 letters of recommendation. Electronic applications accepted. *Faculty research:* Astrometeorology, superconductivity, particle astrophysics, plasma physics, elementary particle theory.

University of Massachusetts Amherst, Graduate School, College of Natural Sciences, Department of Physics, Amherst, MA 01003. Offers MS, PhD. *Program availability:* Part-time. Terminal master's awarded for partial completion of doctoral program. *Degree requirements:* For master's, thesis or alternative; for doctorate, comprehensive exam, thesis/dissertation. *Entrance requirements:* For master's and doctorate, GRE General Test, GRE Subject Test (physics). Additional exam requirements/recommendations for international students: Required—TOEFL (minimum score 550 paper-based; 80 iBT), IELTS (minimum score 6.5). Electronic applications accepted.

University of Massachusetts Dartmouth, Graduate School, College of Engineering, Department of Physics, North Dartmouth, MA 02747-2300. Offers MS. *Program availability:* Part-time. *Faculty:* 10 full-time (2 women). *Students:* 8 full-time (2 women), 5 part-time (2 women); includes 1 minority (Hispanic/Latino), 6 international. Average age 25. 19 applicants, 100% accepted, 6 enrolled. In 2018, 7 master's awarded. *Degree requirements:* For master's, comprehensive exam, thesis, thesis, project or comprehensive exam. *Entrance requirements:* For master's, GRE, statement of purpose (minimum of 300 words), resume, 3 letters of recommendation, official transcripts. Additional exam requirements/recommendations for international students: Required—TOEFL (minimum score 533 paper-based; 72 iBT), IELTS (minimum score 6). *Application deadline:* For fall admission, 3/31 priority date for domestic students, 2/28 priority date for international students; for spring admission, 11/15 priority date for domestic students, 10/15 priority date for international students. Application fee: $60. Electronic applications accepted. *Financial support:* In 2018–19, 1 fellowship (averaging $16,000 per year), 2 research assistantships (averaging $11,422 per year), 8 teaching assistantships (averaging $14,384 per year) were awarded; scholarships/grants and tuition waivers (full and partial) also available. Support available to part-time students. Financial award application deadline: 3/1; financial award applicants required to submit FAFSA. *Faculty research:* Astrophysics, computational and theoretical physics, black holes, gravitation, high performance computing. *Total annual research expenditures:* $212,000. *Unit head:* Robert Fisher, Graduate Program Director, Physics, 508-999-8353, E-mail: robert.fisher@umassd.edu. *Application contact:* Scott Webster, Director of Graduate Studies and Admissions, 508-999-8604, Fax: 508-999-8183, E-mail: graduate@umassd.edu. Website: http://www.umassd.edu/engineering/phy/graduate

University of Massachusetts Lowell, College of Sciences, Department of Physics, Program in Physics, Lowell, MA 01854. Offers MS, PhD. *Degree requirements:* For master's, thesis; for doctorate, 2 foreign languages, thesis/dissertation. *Entrance requirements:* For master's, GRE General Test, 3 letters of reference; for doctorate, GRE General Test, transcripts, 3 letters of reference. Additional exam requirements/recommendations for international students: Required—TOEFL.

University of Memphis, Graduate School, College of Arts and Sciences, Department of Physics, Memphis, TN 38152. Offers computational physics (MS); general physics (MS); material science (MS). *Program availability:* Part-time. *Students:* 14 full-time (4 women),

Peterson's Graduate Programs in the Physical Sciences, Mathematics, Agricultural Sciences, the Environment & Natural Resources 2020

www.petersons.com **161**

Physics

7 part-time (3 women); includes 3 minority (1 Black or African American, non-Hispanic/Latino; 1 Asian, non-Hispanic/Latino; 1 Hispanic/Latino), 13 international. Average age 26. 18 applicants, 83% accepted, 10 enrolled. In 2018, 7 master's awarded. *Degree requirements:* For master's, comprehensive exam, thesis or alternative. *Entrance requirements:* For master's, GRE General Test, 21 undergraduate hours of course work in physics. *Application deadline:* For fall admission, 8/1 for domestic students; for spring admission, 12/1 for domestic students. Applications are processed on a rolling basis. Application fee: $35 ($60 for international students). Electronic applications accepted. *Expenses: Tuition, area resident:* Full-time $10,240; part-time $503 per credit hour. Tuition, state resident: full-time $10,464. Tuition, nonresident: full-time $20,224; part-time $991 per credit hour. *Required fees:* $850; $106 per credit hour. *Financial support:* Research assistantships with full tuition reimbursements, teaching assistantships with full tuition reimbursements, Federal Work-Study, institutionally sponsored loans, scholarships/grants, and unspecified assistantships available. Financial award application deadline: 2/1; financial award applicants required to submit FAFSA. *Faculty research:* Solid-state physics, materials science, biophysics, astrophysics, physics education. *Unit head:* Dr. Jingbiao Cui, Chair, 901-678-3657, Fax: 901-678-4733, E-mail: jcui@memphis.edu. *Application contact:* Dr. X Shen, Coordinator of Graduate Studies, 901-678-1668, Fax: 901-678-4733, E-mail: xshen1@memphis.edu.
Website: http://www.memphis.edu/physics

University of Miami, Graduate School, College of Arts and Sciences, Department of Physics, Coral Gables, FL 33124. Offers MS, PhD. Terminal master's awarded for partial completion of doctoral program. *Degree requirements:* For master's, comprehensive exam; for doctorate, comprehensive exam, thesis/dissertation. *Entrance requirements:* For master's and doctorate, GRE General Test, GRE Subject Test. Additional exam requirements/recommendations for international students: Required—TOEFL (minimum score 550 paper-based; 80 iBT). Electronic applications accepted. *Faculty research:* High-energy theory, marine and atmospheric optics, plasma physics, solid-state physics.

University of Michigan, Rackham Graduate School, College of Literature, Science, and the Arts, Department of Physics, Ann Arbor, MI 48109. Offers PhD. Terminal master's awarded for partial completion of doctoral program. *Degree requirements:* For doctorate, thesis/dissertation, oral defense of dissertation, preliminary exam. *Entrance requirements:* For doctorate, GRE General Test; GRE Subject Test in physics (recommended). Additional exam requirements/recommendations for international students: Required—TOEFL (minimum score 600 paper-based; 100 iBT). Electronic applications accepted. *Faculty research:* Elementary particle, solid-state, atomic, and molecular physics (theoretical and experimental).

University of Minnesota, Duluth, Graduate School, Swenson College of Science and Engineering, Department of Physics, Duluth, MN 55812-2496. Offers MS. *Program availability:* Part-time. *Degree requirements:* For master's, thesis optional, final oral exam. *Entrance requirements:* For master's, minimum GPA of 3.0 (preferred). Additional exam requirements/recommendations for international students: Required—TOEFL (minimum score 550 paper-based; 79 iBT), IELTS (minimum score 6.5), or Michigan English Language Assessment Battery (minimum score 80). Electronic applications accepted. *Faculty research:* Computational physics, neutrino physics, oceanography, computational particle physics, optics, condensed matter.

University of Minnesota, Twin Cities Campus, College of Science and Engineering, School of Physics and Astronomy, Program in Physics, Minneapolis, MN 55455-0213. Offers MS, PhD. *Program availability:* Part-time. *Degree requirements:* For master's, thesis; for doctorate, thesis/dissertation. *Entrance requirements:* For master's and doctorate, GRE General Test, GRE Subject Test. Additional exam requirements/recommendations for international students: Required—TOEFL. Electronic applications accepted. *Faculty research:* Elementary particles, condensed matter, cosmology, nuclear physics, space physics, biological physics, physics education.

University of Mississippi, Graduate School, College of Liberal Arts, University, MS 38677-1848. Offers anthropology (MA); biology (MS, PhD); chemistry (MS, DA, PhD); creative writing (MFA); documentary expression (MFA); economics (MA, PhD); English (MA, PhD); experimental psychology (PhD); history (MA, PhD); mathematics (MS, PhD); modern languages (MA); music (MM); philosophy (MA); physics (MA, MS, PhD); political science (MA, PhD); Southern studies (MA); studio art (MFA). *Program availability:* Part-time. *Faculty:* 474 full-time (209 women), 71 part-time/adjunct (38 women). *Students:* 471 full-time (241 women), 80 part-time (39 women); includes 90 minority (43 Black or African American, non-Hispanic/Latino; 14 Asian, non-Hispanic/Latino; 23 Hispanic/Latino; 10 Two or more races, non-Hispanic/Latino), 136 international. *Degree requirements:* For doctorate, thesis/dissertation. *Entrance requirements:* For master's, GRE General Test, minimum GPA of 3.0; for doctorate, GRE General Test. Additional exam requirements/recommendations for international students: Required—TOEFL. *Application deadline:* Applications are processed on a rolling basis. Application fee: $50. Electronic applications accepted. *Financial support:* Fellowships, research assistantships, teaching assistantships, career-related internships or fieldwork, Federal Work-Study, institutionally sponsored loans, scholarships/grants, and unspecified assistantships available. Financial award application deadline: 3/1; financial award applicants required to submit FAFSA. *Unit head:* Dr. Lee Michael Cohen, Dean, 662-915-7177, Fax: 662-915-5792, E-mail: libarts@olemiss.edu. *Application contact:* Tameka Smith, Graduate Activities Specialist for Admissions, 662-915-7474, Fax: 662-915-7577, E-mail: gschool@olemiss.edu.
Website: ventress@olemiss.edu

University of Missouri, Office of Research and Graduate Studies, College of Arts and Science, Department of Physics and Astronomy, Columbia, MO 65211. Offers MS, PhD. Terminal master's awarded for partial completion of doctoral program. *Entrance requirements:* For master's and doctorate, GRE General Test, minimum GPA of 3.0. *Faculty research:* Experimental and theoretical condensed-matter physics, biological physics, astronomy/astrophysics.

University of Missouri–Kansas City, College of Arts and Sciences, Department of Physics and Astronomy, Kansas City, MO 64110-2499. Offers physics (MS, PhD). PhD (interdisciplinary) offered through the School of Graduate Studies. *Program availability:* Part-time, evening/weekend. Terminal master's awarded for partial completion of doctoral program. *Degree requirements:* For master's, comprehensive exam, thesis optional; for doctorate, comprehensive exam, thesis/dissertation. *Entrance requirements:* For master's and doctorate, GRE General Test. Additional exam requirements/recommendations for international students: Required—TOEFL (minimum score 550 paper-based; 80 iBT). Electronic applications accepted. *Faculty research:* Surface physics, material science, statistical mechanics, computational physics, relativity and quantum theory.

University of Missouri–St. Louis, College of Arts and Sciences, Department of Physics and Astronomy, St. Louis, MO 63121. Offers applied physics (MS); astrophysics (MS); physics (PhD). *Program availability:* Part-time, evening/weekend. Terminal master's awarded for partial completion of doctoral program. *Degree requirements:* For master's, thesis optional; for doctorate, thesis/dissertation. *Entrance requirements:* For master's, GRE General Test, minimum GPA of 2.75, 2 letters of recommendation; for doctorate, GRE General Test, 2 letters of recommendation, minimum GPA of 3.0. Additional exam requirements/recommendations for international students: Required—TOEFL (minimum score 550 paper-based; 79 iBT), IELTS (minimum score 6.5). Electronic applications accepted. *Faculty research:* Biophysics, astrophysics, materials science.

University of Nebraska–Lincoln, Graduate College, College of Arts and Sciences, Department of Physics and Astronomy, Lincoln, NE 68588. Offers astronomy (MS, PhD); physics (MS, PhD). *Degree requirements:* For master's, thesis optional; for doctorate, comprehensive exam, thesis/dissertation. *Entrance requirements:* For master's and doctorate, GRE General Test. Additional exam requirements/recommendations for international students: Required—TOEFL (minimum score 550 paper-based). Electronic applications accepted. *Faculty research:* Electromagnetics of solids and thin films, photoionization, ion collisions with atoms, molecules and surfaces, nanostructures.

University of Nevada, Las Vegas, Graduate College, College of Sciences, Department of Physics and Astronomy, Las Vegas, NV 89154-4002. Offers astronomy (MS, PhD); physics (MS, PhD). *Program availability:* Part-time. *Faculty:* 15 full-time (1 woman). *Students:* 24 full-time (5 women), 6 part-time (0 women); includes 6 minority (1 American Indian or Alaska Native, non-Hispanic/Latino; 2 Asian, non-Hispanic/Latino; 2 Hispanic/Latino; 1 Two or more races, non-Hispanic/Latino), 5 international. Average age 30. 25 applicants, 24% accepted, 5 enrolled. In 2018, 2 master's, 5 doctorates awarded. *Degree requirements:* For master's, comprehensive exam (for some programs), thesis (for some programs); for doctorate, comprehensive exam, thesis/dissertation. *Entrance requirements:* For master's, GRE General Test, bachelor's degree; for doctorate, GRE General Test, bachelor's degree/master's degree. Additional exam requirements/recommendations for international students: Required—TOEFL (minimum score 550 paper-based; 80 iBT), IELTS (minimum score 7). *Application deadline:* For fall admission, 5/15 for domestic students, 5/1 for international students; for spring admission, 11/15 for domestic students, 10/1 for international students. Application fee: $60 ($95 for international students). Electronic applications accepted. *Expenses:* Contact institution. *Financial support:* In 2018–19, 25 students received support, including 5 research assistantships with full tuition reimbursements available (averaging $19,793 per year), 20 teaching assistantships with full tuition reimbursements available (averaging $17,520 per year); institutionally sponsored loans, scholarships/grants, health care benefits, and unspecified assistantships also available. Financial award application deadline: 3/15; financial award applicants required to submit FAFSA. *Faculty research:* High energy and gamma-ray bursters astrophysics, exoplanet astrophysics, experimental high pressure physics, theoretical condensed matter physics, atomic molecular and optical physics. *Total annual research expenditures:* $3.4 million. *Unit head:* Dr. Stephen Lepp, Chair/Professor, 702-895-4455, Fax: 702-895-0804, E-mail: physics.chair@unlv.edu. *Application contact:* Dr. Victor Kwong, Graduate Coordinator, 702-895-1700, Fax: 702-895-0804, E-mail: physics.gradcoord@unlv.edu.
Website: http://www.physics.unlv.edu/academics.html

University of Nevada, Reno, Graduate School, College of Science, Department of Physics, Reno, NV 89557. Offers MS, PhD. Terminal master's awarded for partial completion of doctoral program. *Degree requirements:* For master's, thesis optional; for doctorate, thesis/dissertation. *Entrance requirements:* For master's, GRE General Test, GRE Subject Test, minimum GPA of 2.75; for doctorate, GRE General Test, GRE Subject Test, minimum GPA of 3.0. Additional exam requirements/recommendations for international students: Required—TOEFL (minimum score 500 paper-based; 61 iBT), IELTS (minimum score 6). Electronic applications accepted. *Faculty research:* Atomic and molecular physics.

University of New Brunswick Fredericton, School of Graduate Studies, Faculty of Science, Department of Physics, Fredericton, NB E3B 5A3, Canada. Offers M Sc, PhD. *Program availability:* Part-time. *Degree requirements:* For master's, thesis; for doctorate, comprehensive exam, thesis/dissertation. *Entrance requirements:* For master's, B Sc with minimum B average; for doctorate, M Sc, minimum GPA of 3.0. Additional exam requirements/recommendations for international students: Required—TOEFL, TWE. Electronic applications accepted. *Faculty research:* Optical and laser spectroscopy, infrared and microwave spectroscopy, magnetic resonance and magnetic resonance imaging, space and atmospheric physics, theoretical atomic and molecular physics, space plasma theory, theoretical molecular spectroscopy.

University of New Hampshire, Graduate School, College of Engineering and Physical Sciences, Department of Physics, Durham, NH 03824. Offers MS, PhD. Terminal master's awarded for partial completion of doctoral program. *Entrance requirements:* For master's and doctorate, GRE General Test. Additional exam requirements/recommendations for international students: Required—TOEFL (minimum score 550 paper-based; 80 iBT). Electronic applications accepted.

University of New Mexico, Graduate Studies, College of Arts and Sciences, Program in Physics, Albuquerque, NM 87131-2039. Offers MS, PhD. *Program availability:* Part-time. *Students:* Average age 28. 105 applicants, 10% accepted, 10 enrolled. In 2018, 12 master's, 9 doctorates awarded. Terminal master's awarded for partial completion of doctoral program. *Degree requirements:* For master's, comprehensive exam (for some programs), preliminary exams or thesis; for doctorate, comprehensive exam, thesis/dissertation. *Entrance requirements:* For master's and doctorate, GRE General Test; GRE Subject Test (physics). Additional exam requirements/recommendations for international students: Required—TOEFL (minimum score 550 paper-based; 80 iBT), IELTS (minimum score 7). *Application deadline:* For fall admission, 1/15 for domestic students, 1/15 priority date for international students; for spring admission, 8/1 for domestic students, 8/1 priority date for international students. Application fee: $50. Electronic applications accepted. *Financial support:* Fellowships, research assistantships with full tuition reimbursements, teaching assistantships with full tuition reimbursements, career-related internships or fieldwork, scholarships/grants, traineeships, health care benefits, and unspecified assistantships available. Support available to part-time students. Financial award application deadline: 2/1; financial award applicants required to submit FAFSA. *Faculty research:* Astronomy and astrophysics, biological physics, condensed-matter physics, nonlinear science and complexity, optics and photonics, quantum information, subatomic physics. *Unit head:* Dr. Wolfgang Rudolph, Chair, 505-277-1517, Fax: 505-277-1520, E-mail: wrudolph@unm.edu. *Application contact:* Alisa Gibson, Coordinator, Academic Programs, 505-277-1514, Fax: 505-277-1520, E-mail: agibson@unm.edu.
Website: http://panda.unm.edu

University of New Orleans, Graduate School, College of Sciences, Department of Physics, New Orleans, LA 70148. Offers MS, PhD. *Program availability:* Part-time, evening/weekend. *Degree requirements:* For master's, thesis (for some programs). *Entrance requirements:* For master's, GRE General Test. Additional exam requirements/recommendations for international students: Required—TOEFL (minimum score 550 paper-based; 79 iBT), IELTS. Electronic applications accepted. *Faculty research:* Underwater acoustics, applied electromagnetics, experimental atomic beams, digital signal processing, astrophysics.

The University of North Carolina at Chapel Hill, Graduate School, College of Arts and Sciences, Department of Physics and Astronomy, Chapel Hill, NC 27599. Offers physics (MS, PhD). Terminal master's awarded for partial completion of doctoral program. *Degree requirements:* For master's, comprehensive exam; for doctorate, comprehensive exam, thesis/dissertation. *Entrance requirements:* For master's and doctorate, GRE General Test, minimum GPA of 3.0. Electronic applications accepted. *Faculty research:* Observational astronomy, fullerenes, polarized beams, nanotubes, nucleosynthesis in stars and supernovae, superstring theory, ballistic transport in semiconductors, gravitation.

University of North Dakota, Graduate School, College of Arts and Sciences, Department of Physics and Astrophysics, Grand Forks, ND 58202. Offers MA, MS, PhD. *Degree requirements:* For master's, thesis, final exam; for doctorate, comprehensive exam, thesis/dissertation, final exam. *Entrance requirements:* For master's, minimum GPA of 3.0; for doctorate, minimum GPA of 3.5. Additional exam requirements/recommendations for international students: Required—TOEFL (minimum score 550 paper-based; 79 iBT), IELTS (minimum score 6.5). Electronic applications accepted. *Faculty research:* Solid state physics, atomic and molecular physics, astrophysics, health physics.

University of Northern Iowa, Graduate College, College of Humanities, Arts and Sciences, MA Program in Science Education, Cedar Falls, IA 50614. Offers earth science education (MA); physics education (MA); science education (MA). *Degree requirements:* For master's, comprehensive exam (for some programs), thesis or alternative. *Entrance requirements:* For master's, minimum GPA of 3.0. Additional exam requirements/recommendations for international students: Required—TOEFL (minimum score 500 paper-based; 61 iBT). Electronic applications accepted.

University of Notre Dame, The Graduate School, College of Science, Department of Physics, Notre Dame, IN 46556. Offers MS, PhD. *Degree requirements:* For doctorate, thesis/dissertation, candidacy exam. *Entrance requirements:* For doctorate, GRE General Test, GRE Subject Test. Additional exam requirements/recommendations for international students: Required—TOEFL (minimum score 600 paper-based; 80 iBT). Electronic applications accepted. *Faculty research:* High energy, nuclear, atomic, condensed-matter physics; astrophysics; biophysics.

University of Oklahoma, College of Arts and Sciences, Homer L. Dodge Department of Physics and Astronomy, Norman, OK 73019. Offers engineering physics (MS); physics (MS, PhD). *Faculty:* 27 full-time (3 women). *Students:* 46 full-time (12 women), 10 part-time (1 woman); includes 3 minority (2 Hispanic/Latino; 1 Two or more races, non-Hispanic/Latino), 38 international. Average age 27. 98 applicants, 20% accepted, 18 enrolled. In 2018, 6 master's, 9 doctorates awarded. Terminal master's awarded for partial completion of doctoral program. *Degree requirements:* For master's, comprehensive exam, thesis (for some programs), thesis or qualifying exams; for doctorate, comprehensive exam, thesis/dissertation, qualifying exams. *Entrance requirements:* For master's and doctorate, GRE General Test and GRE Subject Test in physics (recommended), transcripts, statement of purpose, three letters of recommendation. Additional exam requirements/recommendations for international students: Required—TOEFL (minimum score 79 iBT) or IELTS (minimum score 6.5). *Application deadline:* For fall admission, 2/1 for domestic and international students; for spring admission, 9/1 for domestic and international students. Applications are processed on a rolling basis. Application fee: $50 ($100 for international students). Electronic applications accepted. *Expenses:* Tuition, state resident: full-time $5683.20; part-time $236.80 per credit hour. Tuition, nonresident: full-time $20,342; part-time $847.60 per credit hour. *International tuition:* $20,342.40 full-time. *Required fees:* $2894.20; $110.05 per credit hour. $126.50 per semester. Tuition and fees vary according to course load and program. *Financial support:* Fellowships, research assistantships, teaching assistantships, scholarships/grants, health care benefits, and unspecified assistantships available. Financial award application deadline: 6/1; financial award applicants required to submit FAFSA. *Faculty research:* Astrophysics; atomic, molecular, and optical physics; high energy physics; condensed matter physics. *Unit head:* Dr. Phillip Gutierrez, Chair, 405-325-3961, Fax: 405-325-7557, E-mail: chair@nhn.ou.edu. *Application contact:* Dr. Lloyd Bumm, Professor, 405-325-6053, Fax: 405-325-7557, E-mail: grad@nhn.ou.edu.
Website: http://www.nhn.ou.edu

University of Oregon, Graduate School, College of Arts and Sciences, Department of Physics, Eugene, OR 97403. Offers MA, MS, PhD. Terminal master's awarded for partial completion of doctoral program. *Degree requirements:* For doctorate, thesis/dissertation. *Entrance requirements:* For master's and doctorate, GRE General Test, GRE Subject Test, minimum GPA of 3.0. Additional exam requirements/recommendations for international students: Required—TOEFL. *Faculty research:* Solid-state and chemical physics, optical physics, elementary particle physics, astrophysics, atomic and molecular physics.

University of Ottawa, Faculty of Graduate and Postdoctoral Studies, Faculty of Science, Ottawa-Carleton Institute for Physics, Ottawa, ON K1N 6N5, Canada. Offers M Sc, PhD. M Sc, PhD offered jointly with Carleton University. *Degree requirements:* For master's, thesis or alternative; for doctorate, comprehensive exam, thesis/dissertation, seminar. *Entrance requirements:* For master's, honors B Sc degree or equivalent, minimum B average; for doctorate, M Sc, minimum B+ average. Electronic applications accepted. *Faculty research:* Condensed matter physics and statistical physics (CMS); subatomic physics (SAP); medical physics (Med).

University of Pennsylvania, School of Arts and Sciences, Graduate Group in Physics and Astronomy, Philadelphia, PA 19104. Offers medical physics (MS); physics (PhD). *Program availability:* Faculty: 45 full-time (8 women), 12 part-time/adjunct (0 women). *Students:* 104 full-time (27 women), 1 part-time (0 women); includes 21 minority (1 Black or African American, non-Hispanic/Latino; 8 Asian, non-Hispanic/Latino; 8 Hispanic/Latino; 4 Two or more races, non-Hispanic/Latino), 28 international. Average age 26. 466 applicants, 12% accepted, 27 enrolled. In 2018, 18 master's, 11 doctorates awarded. Application fee: $80. *Financial support:* Application deadline: 12/1. Website: http://www.physics.upenn.edu/graduate/

University of Pittsburgh, Kenneth P. Dietrich School of Arts and Sciences, Department of Physics and Astronomy, Pittsburgh, PA 15260. Offers MS, PhD. *Program availability:* Part-time. Terminal master's awarded for partial completion of doctoral program. *Degree requirements:* For master's, comprehensive exam, thesis or alternative, minimum of 30 credits; for doctorate, comprehensive exam, thesis/dissertation, preliminary evaluation, 2 terms of student teaching, admission to candidacy, minimum of 72 credits. *Entrance requirements:* For master's and doctorate, minimum GPA of 3.0. Additional exam requirements/recommendations for international students: Required—TOEFL (minimum score 90 iBT, 22 in each component) or IELTS (minimum score 7.0, 6.5 in each section). Electronic applications accepted. *Expenses:* Contact institution. *Faculty research:* Astrophysics/cosmology; particle physics; condensed matter/solid state/nanoscience; biological physics; physics education research.

See Display below and Close-Up on page 169.

University of Puerto Rico–Mayagüez, Graduate Studies, College of Arts and Sciences, Department of Physics, Mayagüez, PR 00681-9000. Offers MS. *Program availability:* Part-time. *Degree requirements:* For master's, one foreign language, comprehensive exam, thesis. *Entrance requirements:* For master's, bachelor's degree in

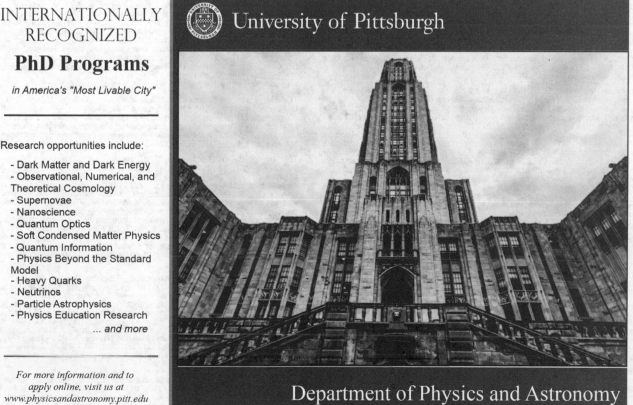

Peterson's Graduate Programs in the Physical Sciences, Mathematics, Agricultural Sciences, the Environment & Natural Resources 2020

www.petersons.com 163

physics or its equivalent. Electronic applications accepted. *Faculty research:* Atomic and molecular physics, nuclear physics, nonlinear thermostatics, fluid dynamics, molecular spectroscopy.

University of Puerto Rico–Río Piedras, College of Natural Sciences, Department of Physics, San Juan, PR 00931-3300. Offers chemical physics (PhD); physics (MS). *Program availability:* Part-time. *Degree requirements:* For master's, comprehensive exam, thesis; for doctorate, comprehensive exam, thesis/dissertation. *Entrance requirements:* For master's, GRE General Test, GRE Subject Test, interview, minimum GPA of 3.0, letter of recommendation (3); for doctorate, GRE, master's degree, minimum GPA of 3.0, letter of recommendation (3). Additional exam requirements/recommendations for international students: Required—TOEFL. *Faculty research:* Energy transfer process through Van der Vacqs interactions, study of the photodissociation of ketene.

University of Regina, Faculty of Graduate Studies and Research, Faculty of Science, Department of Physics, Regina, SK S4S 0A2, Canada. Offers M Sc, PhD. *Program availability:* Part-time. *Faculty:* 9 full-time (0 women), 4 part-time/adjunct (0 women). *Students:* 11 full-time (5 women), 3 part-time (0 women). Average age 30. 8 applicants, 50% accepted, 4 enrolled. In 2018, 2 master's, 2 doctorates awarded. *Degree requirements:* For master's, thesis; for doctorate, thesis/dissertation, seminar. *Entrance requirements:* For master's, GRE is highly recommended, bachelor honors degree in physics or engineering physics; minimum average of 75% in all physics and mathematics courses, and an overall average of 70%, is required; for doctorate, applicants must have obtained a thesis-based Master's degree in the discipline to qualify as a doctoral student. Applicants must have academic credentials consistent with being fully-qualified to undertake graduate work at the doctoral level. Additional exam requirements/recommendations for international students: Required—TOEFL (minimum score 580 paper-based; 80 iBT), IELTS (minimum score 6.5), PTE (minimum score 59), other options are CAEL, MELAB, Cantest and U of R ESL. *Application deadline:* For fall admission, 5/15 for domestic and international students; for winter admission, 8/15 for domestic and international students. Applications are processed on a rolling basis. Application fee: $100. Electronic applications accepted. Tuition and fees vary according to course level, course load, degree level and program. *Financial support:* Fellowships, research assistantships, teaching assistantships, career-related internships or fieldwork, Federal Work-Study, scholarships/grants, unspecified assistantships, and travel award and Graduate Scholarship Base funds available. Support available to part-time students. Financial award application deadline: 9/30. *Faculty research:* High energy physics, weak interactions and neutrino physics, hadronic QCD physics. *Unit head:* Dr. Zisis Papandreou, Department Head, 306-585-5379, Fax: 306-585-5659, E-mail: Zisis.Papandreou@uregina.ca. *Application contact:* Dr. Mauricio Barbi, Graduate Program Coordinator, 306-585-4260, Fax: 306-585-5659, E-mail: physgrad@uregina.ca.
Website: http://www.uregina.ca/science/physics/

University of Rhode Island, Graduate School, College of Arts and Sciences, Department of Physics, Kingston, RI 02881. Offers medical physics (MS); physics (MS, PhD). *Program availability:* Part-time, evening/weekend. *Faculty:* 15 full-time (1 woman). *Students:* 18 full-time (4 women), 2 part-time (0 women); includes 2 minority (1 Black or African American, non-Hispanic/Latino; 1 Asian, non-Hispanic/Latino), 6 international. 60 applicants, 17% accepted, 8 enrolled. In 2018, 3 master's, 2 doctorates awarded. *Entrance requirements:* For master's and doctorate, GRE General Test; GRE Subject Test in physics (recommended), 2 letters of recommendation. Additional exam requirements/recommendations for international students: Required—TOEFL. *Application deadline:* For fall admission, 3/1 for domestic students, 2/1 for international students; for spring admission, 7/15 for international students. Application fee: $65. Electronic applications accepted. *Expenses: Tuition, area resident:* Full-time $13,226; part-time $735 per credit. Tuition, state resident: full-time $13,226; part-time $735 per credit. Tuition, nonresident: full-time $25,854; part-time $1436 per credit. *International tuition:* $25,854 full-time. *Required fees:* $1698; $50 per credit. $35 per semester. One-time fee: $165. *Financial support:* In 2018–19, 16 teaching assistantships with tuition reimbursements (averaging $16,316 per year) were awarded. Financial award application deadline: 3/1; financial award applicants required to submit FAFSA. *Unit head:* Dr. Oleg Andreev, Chair, 401-874-2060, Fax: 401-874-2380, E-mail: andreev@mail.uri.edu. *Application contact:* Dr. Leonard M. Kahn, Director of Graduate Studies, 401-874-2503, Fax: 401-874-2380, E-mail: lkahn@uri.edu.
Website: https://web.uri.edu/physics/

University of Rochester, School of Arts and Sciences, Department of Physics and Astronomy, Rochester, NY 14627. Offers physics and astronomy (PhD). *Faculty:* 24 full-time (3 women). *Students:* 110 full-time (21 women); includes 17 minority (2 Black or African American, non-Hispanic/Latino; 4 Asian, non-Hispanic/Latino; 6 Hispanic/Latino; 5 Two or more races, non-Hispanic/Latino), 31 international. Average age 27. 327 applicants, 26% accepted, 17 enrolled. In 2018, 14 doctorates awarded. Terminal master's awarded for partial completion of doctoral program. *Degree requirements:* For doctorate, comprehensive exam, thesis/dissertation, qualifying exam. *Entrance requirements:* For doctorate, GRE General Test, GRE Subject Test (physics), statement of purpose, transcripts, three letters of recommendation. Additional exam requirements/recommendations for international students: Required—TOEFL, IELTS. *Application deadline:* For fall admission, 1/15 for domestic and international students. Application fee: $0. Electronic applications accepted. *Expenses: Tuition:* Full-time $52,974; part-time $1654 per credit hour. *Required fees:* $612. One-time fee: $30 part-time. Tuition and fees vary according to campus/location and program. *Financial support:* In 2018–19, 110 students received support, including 34 fellowships (averaging $32,000 per year), 59 research assistantships (averaging $27,744 per year), 17 teaching assistantships (averaging $27,744 per year). *Faculty research:* Theoretical optical physics, theoretical plasma physics, theoretical astrophysics, experimental atomic physics, plasma physics. *Total annual research expenditures:* $6.7 million. *Unit head:* Steven Manly, Chair and Professor, 585-275-8473, E-mail: steven.manly@rochester.edu. *Application contact:* Laura Blumkin, Graduate Program Coordinator, 585-275-4356, E-mail: laura.blumkin@rochester.edu.
Website: https://www.pas.rochester.edu/graduate/index.html

University of Saskatchewan, College of Graduate and Postdoctoral Studies, College of Arts and Science, Department of Physics and Engineering Physics, Saskatoon, SK S7N 5A2, Canada. Offers M Sc, PhD. *Degree requirements:* For master's, thesis; for doctorate, comprehensive exam (for some programs), thesis/dissertation. *Entrance requirements:* Additional exam requirements/recommendations for international students: Required—TOEFL (minimum score 80 iBT); Recommended—IELTS (minimum score 6.5). Electronic applications accepted.

University of South Carolina, The Graduate School, College of Arts and Sciences, Department of Physics and Astronomy, Columbia, SC 29208. Offers IMA, MAT, MS, PSM, PhD. IMA and MAT offered in cooperation with the College of Education. *Program availability:* Part-time. Terminal master's awarded for partial completion of doctoral program. *Degree requirements:* For master's, comprehensive exam, thesis; for doctorate, one foreign language, comprehensive exam, thesis/dissertation. *Entrance requirements:* For master's and doctorate, GRE General Test, GRE Subject Test. Additional exam requirements/recommendations for international students: Required—TOEFL (minimum score 570 paper-based; 75 iBT). Electronic applications accepted. *Faculty research:* Condensed matter, intermediate-energy nuclear physics, foundations of quantum mechanics, astronomy/astrophysics.

University of South Dakota, Graduate School, College of Arts and Sciences, Department of Physics, Vermillion, SD 57069. Offers MS, PhD. PhD program offered jointly with South Dakota School of Mines and Technology and South Dakota State University. *Entrance requirements:* For master's and doctorate, GRE. Additional exam requirements/recommendations for international students: Required—TOEFL (minimum score 550 paper-based; 79 iBT), IELTS (minimum score 6). Electronic applications accepted.

University of Southern California, Graduate School, Dana and David Dornsife College of Letters, Arts and Sciences, Department of Physics and Astronomy, Los Angeles, CA 90089. Offers physics (MA, MS, PhD). *Program availability:* Part-time. Terminal master's awarded for partial completion of doctoral program. *Degree requirements:* For master's, comprehensive exam, thesis (for some programs); for doctorate, comprehensive exam, thesis/dissertation. *Entrance requirements:* For doctorate, GRE General Test, GRE Subject Test (physics), 3 letters of recommendation, statement of purpose. Additional exam requirements/recommendations for international students: Required—TOEFL (minimum score 550 paper-based; 80 iBT). Electronic applications accepted. *Faculty research:* High-energy particle theory, condensed matter physics, astrophysics, solar and cosmology, biophysics, computational physics.

University of Southern Mississippi, College of Arts and Sciences, Department of Physics and Astronomy, Hattiesburg, MS 39406-0001. Offers computational science (PhD), including physics; physics (MS). *Degree requirements:* For master's, comprehensive exam, thesis; for doctorate, comprehensive exam, thesis/dissertation. *Entrance requirements:* For master's, GRE General Test, minimum GPA of 2.75 in last 60 hours; for doctorate, GRE General Test, minimum GPA of 3.5. Additional exam requirements/recommendations for international students: Required—TOEFL, IELTS. *Faculty research:* Polymers, atomic physics, fluid mechanics, liquid crystals, refractory materials.

University of South Florida, College of Arts and Sciences, Department of Physics, Tampa, FL 33620-9951. Offers applied physics (PhD), including medical physics; physics (MS), including applied physics, atomic and molecular physics, laser physics, materials physics, optical physics, semiconductor physics, solid state physics. *Program availability:* Part-time. *Faculty:* 24 full-time (2 women), 1 (woman) part-time/adjunct. *Students:* 53 full-time (17 women), 4 part-time (0 women); includes 10 minority (1 Asian, non-Hispanic/Latino; 9 Hispanic/Latino), 27 international. Average age 29. 89 applicants, 27% accepted, 7 enrolled. In 2018, 7 master's, 5 doctorates awarded. *Degree requirements:* For master's, comprehensive exam, thesis optional; for doctorate, comprehensive exam, thesis/dissertation. *Entrance requirements:* For master's and doctorate, GRE General Test; GRE Subject Test in physics (recommended), minimum GPA of 3.0, three letters of recommendation, statement of purpose. Additional exam requirements/recommendations for international students: Required—TOEFL, TOEFL (minimum score 550 paper-based; 79 iBT) or IELTS (minimum score 6.5). *Application deadline:* For fall admission, 2/1 priority date for domestic students, 2/1 for international students; for spring admission, 9/1 for domestic and international students. Applications are processed on a rolling basis. Application fee: $30. Electronic applications accepted. *Expenses:* Tuition, state resident: full-time $6350. Tuition, nonresident: full-time $19,048. *International tuition:* $19,048 full-time. *Required fees:* $2079. *Financial support:* In 2018–19, 15 students received support, including 27 research assistantships with tuition reimbursements available (averaging $15,272 per year), 43 teaching assistantships with tuition reimbursements available (averaging $16,267 per year); unspecified assistantships also available. *Faculty research:* Molecular organization of collagen, lipid rafts in biological membranes, formation of Alzheimer plaques, the role of cellular ion pumps in wound healing, carbon nanotubes as biological detectors, optical imaging of neuronal activity, three-dimensional imaging of intact tissues, motility of cancer cells, optical detection of pathogens in water. *Total annual research expenditures:* $2.9 million. *Unit head:* Dr. David Rabson, Professor and Chairperson, 813-974-1207, E-mail: davidra@ewald.cas.usf.edu. *Application contact:* Dr. Xiaomei Jiang, Associate Professor and Director of Graduate Admissions, 813-974-7765, E-mail: xjiang@usf.edu.
Website: http://physics.usf.edu/

The University of Tennessee, Graduate School, College of Arts and Sciences, Department of Physics and Astronomy, Knoxville, TN 37996. Offers physics (MS, PhD). *Program availability:* Part-time. *Degree requirements:* For master's, thesis or alternative; for doctorate, thesis/dissertation. *Entrance requirements:* For master's and doctorate, minimum GPA of 2.7. Additional exam requirements/recommendations for international students: Required—TOEFL. Electronic applications accepted.

The University of Tennessee, The University of Tennessee Space Institute, Tullahoma, TN 37388. Offers aerospace engineering (MS, PhD); biomedical engineering (MS, PhD); engineering science (MS, PhD); industrial and systems engineering/engineering management (MS, PhD); mechanical engineering (MS, PhD); physics (MS, PhD). *Program availability:* Part-time, blended/hybrid learning. Terminal master's awarded for partial completion of doctoral program. *Degree requirements:* For doctorate, one foreign language, thesis/dissertation. *Entrance requirements:* Additional exam requirements/recommendations for international students: Required—TOEFL (minimum score 550 paper-based; 80 iBT), IELTS (minimum score 6.5). Electronic applications accepted. *Expenses:* Contact institution. *Faculty research:* Fluid mechanics/aerodynamics, chemical and electric propulsion and laser diagnostics, computational mechanics and simulations, carbon fiber production and composite materials.

The University of Texas at Arlington, Graduate School, College of Science, Department of Physics, Arlington, TX 76019. Offers physics (MS); physics and applied physics (PhD). *Program availability:* Part-time. Terminal master's awarded for partial completion of doctoral program. *Degree requirements:* For master's, thesis optional; for doctorate, comprehensive exam, thesis/dissertation, internship or substitute. *Entrance requirements:* For master's, GRE General Test, minimum GPA of 3.0 in last 60 hours of course work; for doctorate, GRE General Test, minimum GPA of 3.0 in last 60 hours of course work, 30 hours graduate course work in physics. Additional exam requirements/recommendations for international students: Required—TOEFL (minimum score 550 paper-based; 79 iBT). *Faculty research:* Particle physics, astrophysics, condensed matter theory and experiment.

The University of Texas at Austin, Graduate School, College of Natural Sciences, Department of Physics, Austin, TX 78712-1111. Offers MA, MS, PhD. *Degree requirements:* For master's, thesis; for doctorate, thesis/dissertation. *Entrance requirements:* For master's and doctorate, GRE General Test, GRE Subject Test (physics). Electronic applications accepted.

The University of Texas at Dallas, School of Natural Sciences and Mathematics, Department of Physics, Richardson, TX 75080. Offers MS, PhD. *Program availability:* Part-time, evening/weekend. *Faculty:* 25 full-time (1 woman), 1 part-time/adjunct (0 women). *Students:* 77 full-time (12 women), 3 part-time (0 women); includes 6 minority (3 Asian, non-Hispanic/Latino; 2 Hispanic/Latino; 1 Two or more races, non-Hispanic/Latino), 51 international. Average age 28. 116 applicants, 26% accepted, 20 enrolled. In 2018, 12 master's, 16 doctorates awarded. *Degree requirements:* For master's, thesis optional, industrial internship; for doctorate, thesis/dissertation, publishable paper. *Entrance requirements:* For master's and doctorate, GRE General Test, minimum GPA of 3.0 in upper-level coursework in field. Additional exam requirements/recommendations for international students: Required—TOEFL (minimum score 550 paper-based). *Application deadline:* For fall admission, 7/15 for domestic students, 5/1 priority date for international students; for spring admission, 11/15 for domestic students, 9/1 priority date for international students. Applications are processed on a rolling basis. Application fee: $50 ($100 for international students). Electronic applications accepted. *Expenses: Tuition, area resident:* Full-time $13,458. Tuition, state resident: full-time $13,458. Tuition, nonresident: full-time $26,852. *International tuition:* $26,852 full-time. Tuition and fees vary according to course load. *Financial support:* In 2018–19, 70 students received support, including 25 research assistantships with partial tuition reimbursements available (averaging $23,668 per year), 46 teaching assistantships with partial tuition reimbursements available (averaging $17,100 per year); fellowships with partial tuition reimbursements available, career-related internships or fieldwork, Federal Work-Study, institutionally sponsored loans, scholarships/grants, and unspecified assistantships also available. Support available to part-time students. Financial award application deadline: 4/30; financial award applicants required to submit FAFSA. *Faculty research:* Ionospheric and magnetospheric electrodynamics; high-energy proton collisions and muon detector design and construction; condensed matter physics with emphasis on nanoscience; optical properties of solids including semiconductors, thermoelectric materials and nanomaterials; gravitational lensing and applications to cosmology. *Unit head:* Dr. Mark Lee, Department Head, 972-883-2835, Fax: 972-883-2848, E-mail: marklee@utdallas.edu. *Application contact:* Dr. Matthew Goeckner, Associate Dean, 972-883-2835, Fax: 972-883-2848, E-mail: physdept@exchange.utdallas.edu. Website: http://www.utdallas.edu/physics/

The University of Texas at El Paso, Graduate School, College of Science, Department of Physics, El Paso, TX 79968-0001. Offers MS. *Program availability:* Part-time, evening/weekend. *Degree requirements:* For master's, thesis optional. *Entrance requirements:* For master's, GRE, minimum GPA of 3.0. Additional exam requirements/recommendations for international students: Required—TOEFL; Recommended—IELTS. Electronic applications accepted.

The University of Texas at San Antonio, College of Sciences, Department of Physics and Astronomy, San Antonio, TX 78249-0617. Offers physics (MS, PhD). *Program availability:* Part-time. Terminal master's awarded for partial completion of doctoral program. *Degree requirements:* For master's, comprehensive exam, thesis; for doctorate, comprehensive exam, thesis/dissertation, at least 1 publication. *Entrance requirements:* For master's, GRE, resume, two letters of recommendation, statement of purpose; for doctorate, GRE, minimum GPA of 3.0 on last 60 hours of undergraduate or graduate coursework, resume, two letters of recommendation, statement of purpose. Additional exam requirements/recommendations for international students: Required—TOEFL (minimum score 550 paper-based; 79 iBT), IELTS (minimum score 6.5). Electronic applications accepted. *Expenses:* Contact institution. *Faculty research:* Ultramicroscopy, computational physics, terahertz spectroscopy, space physics, biophysics, nanotechnology materials, physics, astrophysics and cosmology, theoretical condensed matter and experimental condensed matter.

The University of Texas Rio Grande Valley, College of Sciences, Department of Physics, Edinburg, TX 78539. Offers MS. *Program availability:* Part-time. Terminal master's awarded for partial completion of doctoral program. *Degree requirements:* For master's, thesis optional. *Entrance requirements:* For master's, GRE, three letters of recommendation. Additional exam requirements/recommendations for international students: Required—TOEFL or IELTS. *Expenses: Tuition, area resident:* Full-time $6888. Tuition, state resident: full-time $6888. Tuition, nonresident: full-time $14,484. *International tuition:* $14,484 full-time. *Required fees:* $1468. *Faculty research:* Gravitational wave astronomy, nano-photonics, modern optics and lasers, radio astronomy, nano-technology, experimental and nano-scale biophysics, astrophysics, computational physics, applied and experimental physics, condensed matter physics, medical physics.

The University of Toledo, College of Graduate Studies, College of Natural Sciences and Mathematics, Department of Physics and Astronomy, Toledo, OH 43606-3390. Offers photovoltaics (PSM); physics (MS, PhD), including astrophysics (PhD), materials science, medical physics (PhD); MS/PhD. *Degree requirements:* For master's, thesis; for doctorate, thesis/dissertation, departmental qualifying exam. *Entrance requirements:* For master's and doctorate, GRE General Test, GRE Subject Test, minimum cumulative point-hour ratio of 2.7 for all previous academic work, three letters of recommendation, statement of purpose, transcripts from all prior institutions attended. Additional exam requirements/recommendations for international students: Required—TOEFL (minimum score 550 paper-based; 80 iBT). Electronic applications accepted. *Faculty research:* Atomic physics, solid-state physics, materials science, astrophysics.

University of Toronto, School of Graduate Studies, Faculty of Arts and Science, Department of Physics, Toronto, ON M5S 1A1, Canada. Offers M Sc, PhD. *Degree requirements:* For master's, thesis optional; for doctorate, thesis/dissertation. *Entrance requirements:* For master's, minimum B+ average in an honors physics program or equivalent, 2 letters of reference; for doctorate, M Sc in physics or related field, 2 letters of reference. Additional exam requirements/recommendations for international students: Required—TOEFL (minimum score 580 paper-based; 93 iBT), TWE (minimum score 4). Electronic applications accepted.

University of Utah, Graduate School, College of Science, Department of Physics and Astronomy, Salt Lake City, UT 84112. Offers chemical physics (PhD); medical physics (MS, PhD); physics (MA, MS, PhD); physics teaching (PhD). *Program availability:* Part-time. *Faculty:* 37 full-time (4 women), 15 part-time/adjunct (2 women). *Students:* 69 full-time (21 women); includes 3 minority (all Hispanic/Latino), 30 international. Average age 27. In 2018, 3 master's, 17 doctorates awarded. Terminal master's awarded for partial completion of doctoral program. *Degree requirements:* For master's, comprehensive exam, https://gradschool.utah.edu/graduate-catalog/degree-requirements/; for doctorate, comprehensive exam, thesis/dissertation, https://gradschool.utah.edu/graduate-catalog/degree-requirements/. *Entrance requirements:* For master's and doctorate, GRE General Test (Subject Test not required), minimum GPA of 3.0. Additional exam requirements/recommendations for international students: Required—TOEFL (minimum score 550 paper-based; 85 iBT). *Application deadline:* For fall admission, 1/15 for domestic and international students. Application fee: $55 ($65 for international students). Electronic applications accepted. *Expenses:* Https://fbs.admin.utah.edu/income/tuition/. *Financial support:* In 2018–19, 67 students received support, including 66 research assistantships with full tuition reimbursements available (averaging $25,000 per year), 66 teaching assistantships with full tuition reimbursements available (averaging $25,000 per year); scholarships/grants, health care benefits, and unspecified assistantships also available. Financial award application deadline: 2/15; financial award applicants required to submit FAFSA. *Faculty research:* High-energy, cosmic-ray, medical physics, condensed matter, relativity applied physics, biophysics, astronomy and astrophysics. *Total annual research expenditures:* $6 million. *Unit head:* Dr. Christoph Bhoehme, Chair, 801-581-6806, Fax: 801-581-4801, E-mail: bhoeme@physics.utah.edu. *Application contact:* Bryce Nelson, Graduate Coordinator, 801-581-6861, Fax: 801-581-4801, E-mail: bryce@physics.utah.edu. Website: http://www.physics.utah.edu/

University of Vermont, Graduate College, College of Arts and Sciences, Program in Physics, Burlington, VT 05405-0125. Offers MS. *Entrance requirements:* For master's, GRE General Test. Additional exam requirements/recommendations for international students: Required—TOEFL (minimum score 550 paper-based, 90 iBT) or IELTS (6.5). Electronic applications accepted.

University of Victoria, Faculty of Graduate Studies, Faculty of Science, Department of Physics and Astronomy, Victoria, BC V8W 2Y2, Canada. Offers astronomy and astrophysics (M Sc, PhD); condensed matter physics (M Sc, PhD); experimental particle physics (M Sc, PhD); medical physics (M Sc, PhD); ocean physics (M Sc, PhD); theoretical physics (M Sc, PhD). *Degree requirements:* For master's, thesis; for doctorate, comprehensive exam, thesis/dissertation, candidacy exam. *Entrance requirements:* For master's and doctorate, GRE. Additional exam requirements/recommendations for international students: Required—TOEFL (minimum score 575 paper-based), IELTS (minimum score 7). Electronic applications accepted. *Faculty research:* Old stellar populations; observational cosmology and large scale structure; cp violation; atlas.

University of Virginia, College and Graduate School of Arts and Sciences, Department of Physics, Charlottesville, VA 22903. Offers physics (MA, MS, PhD); physics education (MAPE). *Degree requirements:* For master's, thesis (for some programs); for doctorate, comprehensive exam, thesis/dissertation. *Entrance requirements:* For master's and doctorate, GRE General Test, GRE Subject Test, 2 or more letters of recommendation. Additional exam requirements/recommendations for international students: Required—TOEFL (minimum score 600 paper-based; 90 iBT), IELTS. Electronic applications accepted.

University of Washington, Graduate School, College of Arts and Sciences, Department of Physics, Seattle, WA 98195. Offers MS, PhD. *Program availability:* Part-time, evening/weekend. Terminal master's awarded for partial completion of doctoral program. *Degree requirements:* For doctorate, thesis/dissertation. *Entrance requirements:* For master's, GRE; for doctorate, GRE General Test, GRE Subject Test. Additional exam requirements/recommendations for international students: Required—TOEFL. Electronic applications accepted. *Faculty research:* Astro-, atomic, condensed-matter, nuclear, and particle physics; physics education.

University of Waterloo, Graduate Studies and Postdoctoral Affairs, Faculty of Science, Department of Physics and Astronomy, Waterloo, ON N2L 3G1, Canada. Offers M Sc, PhD. *Program availability:* Part-time. *Degree requirements:* For master's, project or thesis; for doctorate, thesis/dissertation. *Entrance requirements:* For master's, GRE Subject Test, honors degree, minimum B average; for doctorate, GRE Subject Test, master's degree, minimum B average. Additional exam requirements/recommendations for international students: Required—TOEFL, IELTS, PTE. *Application deadline:* Applications are processed on a rolling basis. Application fee: $125 Canadian dollars. Electronic applications accepted. *Financial support:* Research assistantships, teaching assistantships, career-related internships or fieldwork, scholarships/grants, and unspecified assistantships available. *Faculty research:* Condensed-matter and materials physics; industrial and applied physics; subatomic physics; astrophysics and gravitation; atomic, molecular, and optical physics. Website: https://uwaterloo.ca/physics-astronomy/

The University of Western Ontario, School of Graduate and Postdoctoral Studies, Faculty of Science, Department of Applied Mathematics, London, ON N6A 3K7, Canada. Offers applied mathematics (M Sc, PhD); theoretical physics (PhD). *Degree requirements:* For master's, thesis or alternative; for doctorate, comprehensive exam, thesis/dissertation. *Entrance requirements:* For master's and doctorate, minimum B average. Additional exam requirements/recommendations for international students: Required—TOEFL. *Faculty research:* Fluid dynamics, mathematical and computational methods, theoretical physics.

The University of Western Ontario, School of Graduate and Postdoctoral Studies, Faculty of Science, Department of Physics and Astronomy, Program in Physics, London, ON N6A 3K7, Canada. Offers M Sc, PhD. Terminal master's awarded for partial completion of doctoral program. *Degree requirements:* For master's, thesis; for doctorate, comprehensive exam, thesis/dissertation. *Entrance requirements:* For master's, GRE Subject Test (physics), honors B Sc degree, minimum B average (Canadian), A- (international); for doctorate, minimum B average (Canadian), A- (international). Additional exam requirements/recommendations for international students: Required—TOEFL (minimum score 580 paper-based). *Faculty research:* Condensed-matter and surface science, space and atmospheric physics, atomic and molecular physics, medical physics, theoretical physics.

University of Windsor, Faculty of Graduate Studies, Faculty of Science, Department of Physics, Windsor, ON N9B 3P4, Canada. Offers M Sc, PhD. *Program availability:* Part-time. *Degree requirements:* For master's, thesis or alternative; for doctorate, thesis/dissertation. *Entrance requirements:* For master's, GRE General Test, minimum B average; for doctorate, GRE General Test, master's degree. Additional exam requirements/recommendations for international students: Required—TOEFL (minimum score 560 paper-based). Electronic applications accepted. *Faculty research:* Electrodynamics, plasma physics, atomic structure/particles, spectroscopy, quantum mechanics.

University of Wisconsin–Madison, Graduate School, College of Letters and Science, Department of Physics, Madison, WI 53706-1380. Offers MA, MS, PhD. Terminal master's awarded for partial completion of doctoral program. *Degree requirements:* For master's, qualifying exam, thesis (MS); for doctorate, thesis/dissertation, preliminary and qualifying exams. *Entrance requirements:* For master's and doctorate, GRE, minimum GPA of 3.0. Additional exam requirements/recommendations for international students: Required—TOEFL. Electronic applications accepted. *Faculty research:* Atomic, physics, condensed matter, astrophysics, particles and fields.

University of Wisconsin–Milwaukee, Graduate School, College of Letters and Science, Department of Physics, Milwaukee, WI 53201-0413. Offers MS, PhD. *Students:* 20 full-time (6 women), 18 part-time (1 woman); includes 2 minority (both Two or more races, non-Hispanic/Latino), 20 international. Average age 29. 112 applicants, 5% accepted, 6 enrolled. In 2018, 2 doctorates awarded. *Degree requirements:* For master's, thesis or alternative; for doctorate, one foreign language, thesis/dissertation. *Entrance requirements:* For master's, GRE General Test, curriculum vitae; for doctorate, GRE General Test. Additional exam requirements/recommendations for international students: Required—TOEFL (minimum score 550 paper-based; 79 iBT), IELTS (minimum score 6.5). *Application deadline:* For fall admission, 1/1 priority date for

Peterson's Graduate Programs in the Physical Sciences, Mathematics, Agricultural Sciences, the Environment & Natural Resources 2020

www.petersons.com **165**

domestic students; for spring admission, 9/1 for domestic students. Application fee: $56 ($96 for international students). Electronic applications accepted. *Financial support:* Fellowships, research assistantships, teaching assistantships, career-related internships or fieldwork, and unspecified assistantships available. Support available to part-time students. Financial award application deadline: 4/15; financial award applicants required to submit FAFSA. *Faculty research:* Gravitation, biophysics, condensed matter, optics. *Unit head:* Valerica Raicu, Department Chair, 414-229-4969, E-mail: vraicu@uwm.edu. *Application contact:* General Information Contact, 414-229-4982, Fax: 414-229-6967, E-mail: gradschool@uwm.edu.
Website: http://www.uwm.edu/dept/physics

Utah State University, School of Graduate Studies, College of Science, Department of Physics, Logan, UT 84322. Offers MS, PhD. *Program availability:* Part-time. Terminal master's awarded for partial completion of doctoral program. *Degree requirements:* For master's, thesis; for doctorate, comprehensive exam, thesis/dissertation. *Entrance requirements:* For master's and doctorate, GRE General Test, minimum GPA of 3.0. Additional exam requirements/recommendations for international students: Required—TOEFL (minimum score 550 paper-based). Electronic applications accepted. *Faculty research:* Upper-atmosphere physics, relativity, gravitational magnetism, particle physics, nanotechnology.

Vanderbilt University, Department of Physics and Astronomy, Nashville, TN 37240-1001. Offers MA, MAT, MS, PhD. *Faculty:* 25 full-time (5 women). *Students:* 40 full-time (7 women); includes 8 minority (2 Black or African American, non-Hispanic/Latino; 1 Asian, non-Hispanic/Latino; 4 Hispanic/Latino; 1 Two or more races, non-Hispanic/Latino), 8 international. Average age 27. 61 applicants, 28% accepted, 8 enrolled. In 2018, 6 master's, 8 doctorates awarded. *Degree requirements:* For master's, thesis; for doctorate, comprehensive exam, thesis/dissertation, final and qualifying exams. *Entrance requirements:* For master's, GRE General Test; for doctorate, GRE General Test, GRE Subject Test. Additional exam requirements/recommendations for international students: Required—TOEFL (minimum score 570 paper-based; 88 iBT). *Application deadline:* For fall admission, 1/1 for domestic and international students. Electronic applications accepted. *Expenses:* Tuition: Full-time $47,208; part-time $2026 per credit hour. *Required fees:* $478. *Financial support:* Fellowships, research assistantships with full tuition reimbursements, teaching assistantships with full tuition reimbursements, career-related internships or fieldwork, Federal Work-Study, and institutionally sponsored loans available. Financial award application deadline: 1/15; financial award applicants required to submit CSS PROFILE or FAFSA. *Faculty research:* Experimental and theoretical physics, free electron laser, living-state physics, heavy-ion physics, nuclear structure. *Unit head:* Dr. Shane Hutson, Chair, 615-343-9980, E-mail: shane.hutson@Vanderbilt.Edu. *Application contact:* Julia Velkovska, Director of Graduate Studies, 615-322-2828, E-mail: julia.velkovska@vanderbilt.edu.
Website: http://www.vanderbilt.edu/physics/

Virginia Commonwealth University, Graduate School, College of Humanities and Sciences, Department of Physics, Program in Physics and Applied Physics, Richmond, VA 23284-9005. Offers MS. *Entrance requirements:* For master's, GRE. Additional exam requirements/recommendations for international students: Required—TOEFL (minimum score 600 paper-based; 100 iBT); Recommended—IELTS (minimum score 6.5). Electronic applications accepted. *Faculty research:* Theoretical and experimental condensed matter physics, general relativity and cosmology, physics education.

Virginia Polytechnic Institute and State University, Graduate School, College of Science, Blacksburg, VA 24061. Offers biological sciences (MS, PhD); biomedical technology development and management (MS); chemistry (MS, PhD); data analysis and applied statistics (MA); economics (PhD); geosciences (MS, PhD); mathematics (MS, PhD); physics (MS, PhD); psychology (MS, PhD); statistics (MS, PhD). *Faculty:* 349 full-time (109 women), 3 part-time/adjunct (2 women). *Students:* 542 full-time (202 women), 39 part-time (19 women); includes 71 minority (11 Black or African American, non-Hispanic/Latino; 1 American Indian or Alaska Native, non-Hispanic/Latino; 18 Asian, non-Hispanic/Latino; 32 Hispanic/Latino; 9 Two or more races, non-Hispanic/Latino), 220 international. Average age 27. 977 applicants, 25% accepted, 110 enrolled. In 2018, 75 master's, 69 doctorates awarded. *Degree requirements:* For master's, comprehensive exam (for some programs), thesis (for some programs); for doctorate, comprehensive exam (for some programs), thesis/dissertation (for some programs). *Entrance requirements:* For master's and doctorate, GRE/GMAT. Additional exam requirements/recommendations for international students: Required—TOEFL (minimum score 90 iBT). *Application deadline:* For fall admission, 8/1 for domestic students, 4/1 for international students; for spring admission, 1/1 for domestic students, 9/1 for international students. Applications are processed on a rolling basis. Application fee: $75. Electronic applications accepted. *Expenses:* Tuition, state resident: full-time $15,510; part-time $739.50 per credit hour. Tuition, nonresident: full-time $29,629; part-time $1490.25 per credit hour. *Required fees:* $2804; $550 per semester. Tuition and fees vary according to course load, campus/location and program. *Financial support:* In 2018–19, 7 fellowships with full tuition reimbursements (averaging $29,657 per year), 260 research assistantships with full tuition reimbursements (averaging $15,888 per year), 383 teaching assistantships with full tuition reimbursements (averaging $18,063 per year) were awarded; unspecified assistantships also available. Financial award application deadline: 3/1; financial award applicants required to submit FAFSA. *Total annual research expenditures:* $27.3 million. *Unit head:* Dr. Sally C. Morton, Dean, 540-231-5422, Fax: 540-231-3380, E-mail: scmorton@vt.edu. *Application contact:* Allison Craft, Executive Assistant, 540-231-6394, Fax: 540-231-3380, E-mail: crafta@vt.edu.
Website: http://www.science.vt.edu/

Wake Forest University, Graduate School of Arts and Sciences, Department of Physics, Winston-Salem, NC 27109. Offers MS, PhD. *Program availability:* Part-time. *Degree requirements:* For master's, thesis; for doctorate, comprehensive exam, thesis/dissertation. *Entrance requirements:* For master's and doctorate, GRE General Test. Additional exam requirements/recommendations for international students: Required—TOEFL (minimum score 79 iBT). Electronic applications accepted.

Washington State University, College of Arts and Sciences, Department of Physics and Astronomy, Pullman, WA 99164-2814. Offers MS, PhD. Programs offered at the Pullman campus. Terminal master's awarded for partial completion of doctoral program. *Degree requirements:* For master's, comprehensive exam (for some programs), thesis (for some programs), oral exam; for doctorate, comprehensive exam, thesis/dissertation, oral exam, written exam. *Entrance requirements:* For master's and doctorate, GRE General Test, GRE Subject Test (recommended), minimum GPA of 3.0. Additional exam requirements/recommendations for international students: Required—TOEFL (minimum score 550 paper-based; 80 iBT), IELTS. Electronic applications accepted. *Faculty research:* Astrophysics, matters under extreme conditions, materials and optical physics, novel states of matter.

Washington University in St. Louis, The Graduate School, Department of Physics, St. Louis, MO 63130-4899. Offers PhD. Terminal master's awarded for partial completion of doctoral program. *Degree requirements:* For doctorate, thesis/dissertation. *Entrance requirements:* For doctorate, GRE General Test. Additional exam requirements/

recommendations for international students: Required—TOEFL. Electronic applications accepted.

Wayne State University, College of Liberal Arts and Sciences, Department of Physics and Astronomy, Detroit, MI 48202. Offers physics (MA, MS, PhD). *Faculty:* 24. *Students:* 45 full-time (10 women), 5 part-time (1 woman); includes 5 minority (2 Black or African American, non-Hispanic/Latino; 2 Asian, non-Hispanic/Latino; 1 Hispanic/Latino), 24 international. Average age 30. 108 applicants, 6% accepted, 6 enrolled. In 2018, 3 master's, 10 doctorates awarded. Terminal master's awarded for partial completion of doctoral program. *Degree requirements:* For master's, comprehensive exam, thesis (for some programs); for doctorate, thesis/dissertation. *Entrance requirements:* For master's and doctorate, GRE General Test; GRE Subject Test in physics (recommended), bachelor's degree from recognized college or university, completion of general college physics with laboratory, fifteen credits in intermediate physics courses, general chemistry and lab, calculus 3 and differential equations and matrix algebra. Additional exam requirements/recommendations for international students: Required—TOEFL (minimum score 550 paper-based; 79 iBT), TWE (minimum score 5.5), Michigan English Language Assessment Battery (minimum score 85); Recommended—IELTS (minimum score 6.5). *Application deadline:* For fall admission, 1/15 priority date for domestic and international students. Applications are processed on a rolling basis. Application fee: $50. Electronic applications accepted. *Financial support:* In 2018–19, 46 students received support, including 5 fellowships with tuition reimbursements available (averaging $19,824 per year), 14 research assistantships with tuition reimbursements available (averaging $19,663 per year), 27 teaching assistantships with tuition reimbursements available (averaging $20,166 per year); scholarships/grants, health care benefits, and unspecified assistantships also available. Financial award applicants required to submit FAFSA. *Faculty research:* Applied physics and optics, astrophysics, atomic physics, biomedical physics, condensed matter and materials physics, nuclear physics, high energy particle physics, energy materials research. *Unit head:* Dr. David Cinabro, Professor and Chair, 313-577-2918, E-mail: cinabro@physics.wayne.edu. *Application contact:* Dr. Jogindra Wadehra, Associate Department Chair and Graduate Programs Advisor, 313-577-2740, E-mail: gradadm@physics.wayne.edu.
Website: http://physics.clas.wayne.edu/

Wesleyan University, Graduate Studies, Department of Physics, Middletown, CT 06459. Offers PhD. *Faculty:* 11 full-time (3 women). *Students:* 16 full-time (5 women), 13 international. Average age 29. Terminal master's awarded for partial completion of doctoral program. *Degree requirements:* For doctorate, thesis/dissertation. *Entrance requirements:* For doctorate, GRE General and Subject Tests (highly recommended). Additional exam requirements/recommendations for international students: Required—TOEFL (minimum score 550 paper-based; 80 iBT). *Application deadline:* For fall admission, 1/31 priority date for domestic and international students. Application fee: $0. Electronic applications accepted. *Financial support:* In 2018–19, 13 students received support. Research assistantships, teaching assistantships, institutionally sponsored loans, scholarships/grants, and health care benefits available. Financial award application deadline: 4/15; financial award applicants required to submit FAFSA. *Faculty research:* Rydberg states in strong fields, molecular collisions, photo-ionization, laser-produced plasmas, quantum fluids, granular and turbulent fluid flows, lipid membranes and hydration dynamics, single-molecule biophysics, optoelectronics of renewable energy materials, nonlinear dynamics, quantum chaos, properties of nanostructures, soft condensed matter, wave transport in complex media. *Unit head:* Fred Ellis, Chair, 860-685-2046, E-mail: fellis@wesleyan.edu. *Application contact:* Administrative Assistant, 860-685-2030, Fax: 860-685-2031, E-mail: dgordongannu@wesleyan.edu.
Website: http://www.wesleyan.edu/physics/

Western Illinois University, School of Graduate Studies, College of Arts and Sciences, Department of Physics, Macomb, IL 61455-1390. Offers MS. *Program availability:* Part-time. *Students:* 16 full-time (4 women), 3 part-time (1 woman); includes 1 minority (Hispanic/Latino), 15 international. Average age 31. 31 applicants, 45% accepted, 8 enrolled. In 2018, 11 master's awarded. *Entrance requirements:* Additional exam requirements/recommendations for international students: Required—TOEFL (minimum score 550 paper-based; 80 iBT). *Application deadline:* Applications are processed on a rolling basis. Application fee: $30. Electronic applications accepted. *Financial support:* In 2018–19, 12 students received support. Unspecified assistantships available. Financial award applicants required to submit FAFSA. *Unit head:* Dr. Kishor Kapale, Interim Chairperson, 309-298-1538. *Application contact:* Dr. Mark Mossman, Associate Provost and Director of Graduate Studies, 309-298-1806, Fax: 309-298-2345, E-mail: grad-office@wiu.edu.
Website: http://wiu.edu/physics

Western Kentucky University, Graduate School, Ogden College of Science and Engineering, Department of Physics and Astronomy, Bowling Green, KY 42101. Offers homeland security sciences (MS); physics (MA Ed).

Western Michigan University, Graduate College, College of Arts and Sciences, Department of Interdisciplinary Arts and Sciences, Kalamazoo, MI 49008. Offers science education (MA, PhD), including biological sciences (PhD), chemistry (PhD), geosciences (PhD), physical geography (PhD), physics (PhD), science education (PhD). *Degree requirements:* For doctorate, thesis/dissertation.

Western Michigan University, Graduate College, College of Arts and Sciences, Department of Physics, Kalamazoo, MI 49008. Offers MA, PhD. *Degree requirements:* For master's, thesis; for doctorate, thesis/dissertation.

West Virginia University, Eberly College of Arts and Sciences, Morgantown, WV 26506. Offers biology (MS, PhD); chemistry (MS, PhD); communication studies (MA, PhD); computational statistics (PhD); creative writing (MFA); English (MA, PhD); forensic and investigative science (MS); forensic science (PhD); geography (MA); geology (MA, PhD); history (MA, PhD); legal studies (MLS); mathematics (MS); physics (MS, PhD); political science (MA, PhD); professional writing and editing (MA); psychology (MA); public administration (MPA); social work (MSW); sociology (MA, PhD); statistics (MS). *Program availability:* Part-time, evening/weekend, online learning. *Students:* 803 full-time (434 women), 237 part-time (138 women); includes 99 minority (31 Black or African American, non-Hispanic/Latino; 1 American Indian or Alaska Native, non-Hispanic/Latino; 16 Asian, non-Hispanic/Latino; 25 Hispanic/Latino; 26 Two or more races, non-Hispanic/Latino), 208 international. In 2018, 285 master's, 63 doctorates awarded. Terminal master's awarded for partial completion of doctoral program. *Degree requirements:* For master's, thesis (for some programs); for doctorate, comprehensive exam, thesis/dissertation. *Entrance requirements:* For master's and doctorate, GRE. Additional exam requirements/recommendations for international students: Required—TOEFL (minimum score 600 paper-based); Recommended—TWE. *Application deadline:* For spring admission, 2/15 priority date for domestic and international students. Applications are processed on a rolling basis. Application fee: $45. Electronic applications accepted. *Financial support:* Fellowships with full tuition reimbursements, research assistantships with full tuition reimbursements, teaching assistantships with full tuition reimbursements, career-related internships or fieldwork, Federal Work-Study, institutionally sponsored loans, scholarships/grants, health care benefits, tuition waivers

166 www.petersons.com

Peterson's Graduate Programs in the Physical Sciences, Mathematics, Agricultural Sciences, the Environment & Natural Resources 2020

(full and partial), unspecified assistantships, and administrative assistantships available. Financial award application deadline: 2/1; financial award applicants required to submit FAFSA. *Faculty research:* Humanities, social sciences, life science, physical sciences, mathematics. *Unit head:* Dr. Gregory Dunaway, Dean, 304-293-4611, Fax: 304-293-6858, E-mail: gregory.dunaway@mail.wvu.edu. *Application contact:* Dr. Jessica Queener, Director of Graduate Studies, 304-293-7476 Ext. 5205, Fax: 304-293-6858, E-mail: Jessica.queener@mail.wvu.edu.
Website: http://www.as.wvu.edu/

Wichita State University, Graduate School, Fairmount College of Liberal Arts and Sciences, Department of Mathematics, Statistics and Physics, Wichita, KS 67260. Offers applied mathematics (PhD); mathematics (MS); physics (MS). *Program availability:* Part-time. *Unit head:* Dr. Ziqi Sun, Interim Chair, 316-978-3160, Fax: 316-978-3748, E-mail: ziqi.sun@wichita.edu. *Application contact:* Jordan Oleson, Admissions Coordinator, 316-978-3095, Fax: 316-978-3253, E-mail: jordan.oleson@wichita.edu.
Website: http://www.wichita.edu/math

Worcester Polytechnic Institute, Graduate Admissions, Department of Physics, Worcester, MA 01609-2280. Offers physics (MS). *Students:* 16 full-time (2 women), 11 part-time (1 woman); includes 2 minority (both Hispanic/Latino), 12 international. Average age 27. 21 applicants, 62% accepted, 4 enrolled. In 2018, 1 master's awarded. Terminal master's awarded for partial completion of doctoral program. *Degree requirements:* For master's, thesis; for doctorate, comprehensive exam, thesis/dissertation. *Entrance requirements:* For master's, GRE Subject Test (recommended), 3 letters of recommendation, statement of purpose; for doctorate, GRE Subject Test (physics), 3 letters of recommendation, statement of purpose. Additional exam requirements/recommendations for international students: Required—TOEFL (minimum score 563 paper-based; 84 iBT), IELTS (minimum score 7). *Application deadline:* For fall admission, 1/1 priority date for domestic students, 1/1 for international students; for spring admission, 10/1 priority date for domestic students, 10/1 for international students. Applications are processed on a rolling basis. Application fee: $70. Electronic applications accepted. *Financial support:* Fellowships, research assistantships, teaching assistantships, career-related internships or fieldwork, institutionally sponsored loans, scholarships/grants, and unspecified assistantships available. Financial award application deadline: 1/1. *Unit head:* Dr. Douglas Petkie, Head, 508-831-5258, Fax: 508-831-5886, E-mail: dtpetkie@wpi.edu. *Application contact:* Dr. Lyubov Titova, Graduate Coordinator, 508-831-5258, Fax: 508-831-5886, E-mail: ltitova@wpi.edu.
Website: https://www.wpi.edu/academics/departments/physics

Wright State University, Graduate School, College of Science and Mathematics, Department of Physics, Program in Physics, Dayton, OH 45435. Offers geophysics (MS). *Program availability:* Part-time, evening/weekend. *Degree requirements:* For master's, thesis. *Entrance requirements:* Additional exam requirements/recommendations for international students: Required—TOEFL. *Faculty research:* Solid-state physics, optics, geophysics.

Yale University, Graduate School of Arts and Sciences, Department of Physics, New Haven, CT 06520. Offers PhD. *Degree requirements:* For doctorate, thesis/dissertation. *Entrance requirements:* For doctorate, GRE General Test, GRE Subject Test.

York University, Faculty of Graduate Studies, Faculty of Science, Program in Physics and Astronomy, Toronto, ON M3J 1P3, Canada. Offers M Sc, PhD. *Program availability:* Part-time, evening/weekend. *Degree requirements:* For master's, thesis or alternative; for doctorate, comprehensive exam, thesis/dissertation. Electronic applications accepted.

Plasma Physics

Princeton University, Graduate School, Department of Astrophysical Sciences, Program in Plasma Physics, Princeton, NJ 08544-1019. Offers PhD. *Degree requirements:* For doctorate, thesis/dissertation. *Entrance requirements:* For doctorate, GRE General Test, GRE Subject Test. Additional exam requirements/recommendations for international students: Required—TOEFL (minimum score 600 paper-based). *Faculty research:* Magnetic fusion energy research, plasma physics, x-ray laser studies.

University of Colorado Boulder, Graduate School, College of Arts and Sciences, Department of Astrophysical and Planetary Sciences, Boulder, CO 80309. Offers astrophysics (MS, PhD); planetary science (PhD). Terminal master's awarded for partial completion of doctoral program. *Degree requirements:* For master's, comprehensive exam, thesis or alternative; for doctorate, one foreign language, thesis/dissertation. *Entrance requirements:* For master's, GRE General Test, GRE Subject Test, minimum undergraduate GPA of 3.0; for doctorate, GRE General Test, GRE Subject Test. Electronic applications accepted. Application fee is waived when completed online. *Faculty research:* Astrophysics; astronomy; infrared/optical astronomy; spectroscopy; telescopes.

Theoretical Physics

American University of Beirut, Graduate Programs, Faculty of Arts and Sciences, Beirut 1107 2020, Lebanon. Offers anthropology (MA); Arab and Middle Eastern history (PhD); Arabic language and literature (MA, PhD); archaeology (MA); art history and curating (MA); biology (MS); cell and molecular biology (PhD); chemistry (MS); clinical psychology (MA); computational sciences (MS); computer science (MS); economics (MA); education (MA), including administration and policy studies, elementary education, mathematics education, psychology school guidance, psychology test and measurements, science education, teaching English as a foreign language; English language (MA); English literature (MA); environmental policy planning (MS); financial economics (MAFE); general psychology (MA); geology (MS); history (MA); Islamic studies (MA); mathematics (MS); media studies (MA); Middle East studies (MA); philosophy (MA); physics (MS); political studies (MA); public administration (MA); public policy and international affairs (MA); sociology (MA); theoretical physics (PhD). *Program availability:* Part-time. *Faculty:* 187 full-time (64 women), 27 part-time/adjunct (15 women). *Students:* 292 full-time (215 women), 216 part-time (148 women). Average age 27. 422 applicants, 64% accepted, 124 enrolled. In 2018, 90 master's, 3 doctorates awarded. *Degree requirements:* For master's, comprehensive exam, thesis (for some programs), project; for doctorate, comprehensive exam, thesis/dissertation (for some programs). *Entrance requirements:* For master's, GRE General Test (for archaeology, clinical psychology, general psychology, economics, financial economics and biology); for doctorate, GRE General Test for all PhD programs, GRE Subject Test for theoretical physics. Additional exam requirements/recommendations for international students: Required—TOEFL (minimum score 583 paper-based; 97 iBT), IELTS (minimum score 7). *Application deadline:* For fall admission, 3/18 for domestic students; for spring admission, 11/5 for domestic students. Application fee: $50. Electronic applications accepted. *Expenses:* MA/MS: Humanities and social sciences=$912/credit. Sciences=$943/credit. Financial economics=$986/credit. Thesis: Humanities/social sciences=$6565 and sciences=$6865. *Financial support:* In 2018–19, 227 fellowships with full tuition reimbursements, 17 research assistantships with full tuition reimbursements, 83 teaching assistantships with full tuition reimbursements were awarded; scholarships/grants, tuition waivers (full and partial), and unspecified assistantships also available. Financial award application deadline: 3/18. *Faculty research:* Sciences: Physics: High energy, Particle, Polymer and Soft Matter, Thermal, Plasma; String Theory, Mathematical physics, Astrophysics (stellar evolution, planet and galaxy formation and evolution, astrophysical dynamics), Solid State physics/thin films, Spintronics, Magnetic properties of materials, Mineralogy, Petrology, and Geochemistry of Hard Rocks, Geophysics and Petrophysics, Hydrogeology, Micropaleontology, Sedimentology, and Stratigraphy, Structural Geology and Geotectonics, Renewable en. *Total annual research expenditures:* $4.3 million. *Unit head:* Dr. Nadia Maria El Cheikh, Dean, Faculty of Arts and Sciences, 961-1-350000 Ext. 3800, Fax: 961-1-744461, E-mail: nmcheikh@aub.edu.lb. *Application contact:* Adriana Michelle Zanaty, Curriculum and Graduate Studies Officer, 961-1-350000 Ext. 3833, Fax: 961-1-744461, E-mail: az48@aub.edu.lb.
Website: https://www.aub.edu.lb/fas/Pages/default.aspx

Cornell University, Graduate School, Graduate Fields of Arts and Sciences, Field of Physics, Ithaca, NY 14853. Offers experimental physics (MS, PhD); physics (MS, PhD); theoretical physics (MS, PhD). *Degree requirements:* For doctorate, comprehensive exam, thesis/dissertation. *Entrance requirements:* For doctorate, GRE General Test, GRE Subject Test (physics), 3 letters of recommendation. Additional exam requirements/recommendations for international students: Required—TOEFL (minimum score 620 paper-based; 105 iBT). Electronic applications accepted. *Faculty research:* Experimental condensed matter physics, theoretical condensed matter physics, experimental high energy particle physics, theoretical particle physics and field theory, theoretical astrophysics.

Delaware State University, Graduate Programs, Department of Mathematics, Interdisciplinary Program in Applied Mathematics and Theoretical Physics, Dover, DE 19901-2277. Offers PhD. *Degree requirements:* For doctorate, one foreign language, thesis defense. *Entrance requirements:* For doctorate, GRE General Test, MS degree in physics or mathematics. Additional exam requirements/recommendations for international students: Required—TOEFL (minimum score 550 paper-based).

Harvard University, Graduate School of Arts and Sciences, Department of Physics, Cambridge, MA 02138. Offers experimental physics (PhD); medical engineering/medical physics (PhD), including applied physics, engineering sciences, physics; theoretical physics (PhD). *Degree requirements:* For doctorate, thesis/dissertation, final exams, laboratory experience. *Entrance requirements:* For doctorate, GRE General Test, GRE Subject Test. Additional exam requirements/recommendations for international students: Required—TOEFL. *Faculty research:* Particle physics, condensed matter physics, atomic physics.

Rutgers University–New Brunswick, Graduate School-New Brunswick, Department of Physics and Astronomy, Piscataway, NJ 08854-8097. Offers astronomy (MS, PhD); biophysics (PhD); condensed matter physics (MS, PhD); elementary particle physics (MS, PhD); intermediate energy nuclear physics (MS); nuclear physics (MS, PhD); physics (MST); surface science (PhD); theoretical physics (MS, PhD). *Program availability:* Part-time. Terminal master's awarded for partial completion of doctoral program. *Degree requirements:* For master's, comprehensive exam, thesis or alternative; for doctorate, comprehensive exam, thesis/dissertation. *Entrance requirements:* For master's and doctorate, GRE General Test, GRE Subject Test. Additional exam requirements/recommendations for international students: Required—TOEFL (minimum score 560 paper-based). Electronic applications accepted. *Faculty research:* Astronomy, high energy, condensed matter, surface, nuclear physics.

The University of Manchester, School of Physics and Astronomy, Manchester, United Kingdom. Offers astronomy and astrophysics (M Sc, PhD); biological physics (M Sc, PhD); condensed matter physics (M Sc, PhD); nonlinear and liquid crystals physics (M Sc, PhD); nuclear physics (M Sc, PhD); particle physics (M Sc, PhD); photon physics (M Sc, PhD); physics (M Sc, PhD); theoretical physics (M Sc, PhD).

University of Victoria, Faculty of Graduate Studies, Faculty of Science, Department of Physics and Astronomy, Victoria, BC V8W 2Y2, Canada. Offers astronomy and astrophysics (M Sc, PhD); condensed matter physics (M Sc, PhD); experimental particle physics (M Sc, PhD); medical physics (M Sc, PhD); ocean physics (M Sc, PhD); theoretical physics (M Sc, PhD). *Degree requirements:* For master's, thesis; for doctorate, comprehensive exam, thesis/dissertation, candidacy exam. *Entrance requirements:* For master's and doctorate, GRE. Additional exam requirements/recommendations for international students: Required—TOEFL (minimum score 575 paper-based), IELTS (minimum score 7). Electronic applications accepted. *Faculty research:* Old stellar populations; observational cosmology and large scale structure; cp violation; atlas.

Peterson's Graduate Programs in the Physical Sciences, Mathematics, Agricultural Sciences, the Environment & Natural Resources 2020

www.petersons.com **167**

UNIVERSITY OF PITTSBURGH

Department of Physics and Astronomy

Programs of Study

The graduate programs in the Department of Physics and Astronomy are designed primarily for students who wish to obtain the Ph.D. degree, although the M.S. degree is also offered. The Ph.D. program provides high-quality training for students without excessive emphasis on formal requirements. Prior to arrival, each graduate student is appointed a faculty academic adviser to provide personalized guidance through the core curriculum. A set of basic courses is to be taken by all graduate students unless the equivalent material has been demonstrably mastered in other ways. These basic courses include mathematical methods, dynamical systems, quantum mechanics, electromagnetic theory, and statistical physics and thermodynamics. More advanced courses are offered in a range of areas, including, but not limited to, condensed matter, statistical, solid state, and biological physics; high-energy and particle physics; nanoscience; astrophysics; cosmology; particle astrophysics; relativity; and astronomical techniques.

Students have a wide variety of research programs from which to choose a thesis topic. Faculty members maintain active research programs in astrophysics, condensed matter physics, cosmology, particle physics, and physics education research. Topics in astrophysics and cosmology include: observational, numerical, and theoretical cosmology; dark matter and dark energy; galaxy formation and evolution; active galactic nuclei and quasars; galactic and intergalactic medium; stellar atmospheres and massive stars; supernovae; and physics of the early universe. Topics in condensed matter physics include: biological physics; nanoscience; quantum information; quantum kinetics; quantum optics; quantum states of matter; semiconductor physics; soft condensed matter physics; statistical physics; superconductivity and superfluidity; and ultrafast optics. Topics in particle physics include: the origin of mass and flavor; the search for new symmetries of nature; neutrino physics; CP violation; heavy quarks; leptoquarks; supersymmetry; extra dimensions; baryogenesis; effective field theory; and strongly interacting field theory. Topics in physics education research include: cognitive issues in learning physics; and development and evaluation of research-based curricula for introductory and advanced physics courses. Multidisciplinary thesis research may also be carried out in, for example, particle astrophysics, biophysics, chemical physics, laser physics, materials science, nanoscience, and surface science. This research may be done in collaboration with faculty from other departments within the University.

Interdisciplinary research programs may be arranged on a case-by-case basis. Previous students have performed their thesis research in collaboration with faculty members in the Department of Biological Sciences, the Department of Chemistry, the Department of Mathematics, the Department of Mechanical Engineering and Materials Science, the Departments of Electrical and Chemical Engineering, the Department of Computational Biology, the Department of Radiological Sciences, and the Department of Radiology in the School of Medicine, among others.

Research Facilities

The Department of Physics and Astronomy is located on the University of Pittsburgh's main campus and housed in a complex of five interconnected buildings, containing numerous cutting-edge research laboratories and educational facilities. The department houses a number of cross-disciplinary centers including the PITTsburgh Particle physics, Astrophysics, and Cosmology Center (PITT PACC); the Discipline-Based Science Education Research Center (dB-SERC); and Pittsburgh Quantum Institute (PQI, www.pqi.org). The department also has access to a number of facilities including machine, electric, and glass shops; the Gertrude E. and John M. Peterson Institute of NanoScience and Engineering (PINSE); the Nano Fabrication and Characterization Facility (NFCF); the Center for Simulation and Modeling (SAM); and the Pittsburgh Super-computing Center (PSC). Other local facilities include University of Pittsburgh's Allegheny Observatory (AO, www.pitt.edu/~aobsvtry).

Experiments in particle physics are carried out at national and international facilities such as Fermilab near Chicago (www.fnal.gov/), CERN in Switzerland (home.web.cern.ch/), and J–PARC in Japan (j-park.jp/index-e.html). This includes, for example, the Large Hadron Collider ATLAS experiment at CERN and various neutrino experiments (MINOS www-numi.fnal.gov/, MINERvA minerva.fnal.gov/, and T2K t2k-experiment.org/). Observational programs in astrophysics and cosmology are conducted at national and international ground-based observatories such as Kitt Peak and Mount Hopkins in Arizona, Cerro Tololo in Chile, Mauna Kea in Hawaii, and Apache Point in New Mexico for collection of Sloan Digital Sky Survey data. Faculty also make use of space-based telescopes, including the Hubble Space Telescope, the Chandra X-Ray Telescope, and the GALEX UV Telescope. University of Pittsburgh faculty are members of several current and/or future large-telescope consortia: the Sloan Digital Sky Survey (SDSS, www.sdss.org), the Atacama Cosmology Telescope (ACT, www.physics.princeton.edu/act/), the Panoramic Survey Telescope & Rapid Response System (Pan-STARRS, www.ps1sc.org), the Dark Energy Spectroscopic Instrument (DESI, desi.lbl.gov), and the Large Synoptic Survey Telescope (LSST, www.lsst.org). Many members of the department have significant leadership roles in these projects. More information is available at http://www.gradschoolshopper.com/gradschool/sclisting.jsp?rec=353#equipment.

Financial Aid

Financial aid is normally provided through teaching assistantships and fellowships during the first year and through research assistantships, teaching assistantships, or fellowships thereafter. These awards carry benefits as well as tuition and fee merit scholarships. The University provides individual health insurance under the Graduate Student Medical Plan, with options for spouse or family upgrades, with additional cost to the student, as well as dental and vision options. In addition to several University competitive predoctoral fellowships, the Department's predoctoral fellowships such as the Elizabeth Baranger, Whittington and Andrew Mellon, include the Dietrich School of Arts and Sciences Graduate Fellowships, the Dietrich School of Arts and Sciences Summer Research Fellowship, the K. Leroy Irvis Predoctoral Fellowship, and the Warga Predoctoral Fellowship for entering graduate students. They are awarded on a competitive basis with all qualified applicants automatically considered. These also carry tuition and fee scholarships. Currently, the University provides health insurance for fellows to purchase. The Department's financial support package generally covers five consecutive years of graduate study, provided students maintain good academic standing, make progress toward their degree, and are in residence in the Department or at an appropriate research facility. Teaching and research assistantship appointments carried a stipend of $9,225 per term in 2017, bringing the annual stipend to $27,675 for students supported throughout the year. This includes a full-tuition scholarship and benefits. Research assistantship appointments may be held in connection with most of the Department's research programs.

Cost of Study

For full-time students who are not Pennsylvania residents, tuition per term in 2018–19 was $19,368, including fees. Part-time students paid $1,583 per credit. Full-time students who are Pennsylvania residents paid $11,423 per term, including fees, and part-time students who were Pennsylvania residents paid $920 per credit. Fees for all part-time students were $270 per term.

Living and Housing Costs

Housing is particularly reasonable in both quality and price. Most University of Pittsburgh students live in apartments in the Oakland and surrounding areas. The typical cost of apartments ranges from $400 to $800 per month for housing. Pittsburgh's low cost of living affords extremely reasonable and numerous food and beverage prices. Further information may be found online at http://www.ocl.pitt.edu. A valid PITT student ID serves many purposes, including free transportation around campus and in and around the city.

Student Group

The Department's graduate student body for the fall of 2018 will consist of approximately 115 PhD students, all of whom receive financial support.

Student Outcomes

Many Ph.D. graduates accept postdoctoral positions at major research universities, often leading to teaching and research positions at outstanding universities in the United States and around the world. Other recent graduates have entered research careers in the private sector and national labs. One former graduate, Patrick D. Gallagher, became the eighteenth Chancellor and Chief Executive Officer of the University of Pittsburgh.

Location

Pittsburgh is internationally recognized as a hub of education, culture, and technology, offering affordable urban living, racial and ethnic diversity, and a thriving sports and arts community. Pittsburgh is an extraordinary American city in many respects. There's the striking geography of bridges and rivers. The nationally recognized cultural and art scene that includes a world-class symphony orchestra, opera, and many theaters. The pride that comes with cheering for three major league sports teams: the Penguins, Pirates, and Steelers. And the rich tapestry of 89 distinctive neighborhoods—including the University of Pittsburgh's own, Oakland—give Pittsburgh its genuineness and warmth. With a booming economy fueled by intellectual capital, Pittsburgh is a globally renowned success story. It is home to major corporate and nonprofit organizations, including eight Fortune 500 companies, such as U.S. Steel, PNC Bank, and Mylan Pharmaceuticals; research centers and offices from powerhouses such as Google, Apple, Disney, and Microsoft and a variety of strong small businesses and nonprofits. Combine this wealth of opportunity with an affordable cost of living and it is no surprise that *Forbes* magazine ranked Pittsburgh one of the most livable and affordable cities in the United States. More information about Pittsburgh can be found at coolpgh.edu.

The Department

The Department has a long history of high-impact research and is internationally recognized for its excellence in research and education. With accessibility to more than 40 core faculty members and lecturers, students have an unparalleled opportunity for individualized training, interaction, and mentorship. The Department has guided Ph.D. candidates to success for more than 80 years. In that time, many alumni have gone on to build distinguished careers as researchers at major academic and industrial laboratories, educators at universities and colleges, and independent scientific entrepreneurs. Close cooperation exists between this Department and the physics department of Carnegie Mellon University; all seminars, colloquiums, and advanced courses are shared. The graduate students of both institutions benefit from belonging to one of the largest communities of active physicists in the country. Furthermore, basic research, conducted at the University of Pittsburgh Medical Center and the School of Medicine, provides additional opportunities for research with multidisciplinary perspectives.

Applying

Students who wish to apply for admission or financial aid should apply online and take the GRE (the Subject Test in physics is strongly recommended), and have a cumulative grade point average of at least 3.0 on a 4.0 scale. Applicants are asked to view the department's "How To Apply" graduate webpage to select and rank their areas of interest when completing the online application. Applicants should upload CLEAR copies of their undergraduate transcripts and when applicable, graduate transcripts, with their online application. Once fall grades become available, if not on the originally downloaded application, and updated copy must be sent to the department to add to the student's materials. Include translations, if applicable. Certified transcripts (with final grades and degrees posted) of all undergraduate and graduate study are required no later than time of enrollment. Three letters of recommendation are required for admission with aid. Unless English is the applicant's native language, the TOEFL (IBT) or IELTS exam is required, except in cases in which an international applicant has received an advanced degree from a U.S. institution. Acceptable minimum scores are listed in the application instructions. The application deadline is January 15. The application fee is waived for U.S. citizens and permanent residents (refer to instructions). Through early March, late applications are accepted on the basis of space availability.

Correspondence and Information

Professor Robert P. Devaty
Admissions Committee
Department of Physics and Astronomy
University of Pittsburgh
Pittsburgh, Pennsylvania 15260
United States
Phone: 412-624-9009
Website: http://www.physicsandastronomy.pitt.edu/

THE FACULTY AND THEIR RESEARCH

Carles Badeness, Associate Professor; Ph.D., Politecnia de Catalunya (Spain). Type 1a supernovae, supernova remnants, large astronomical data bases, extragalactic astronomy, observational cosmology.

Brian Batell, Assistant Professor; Ph.D., Minnesota. Theoretical particle physics.

Rachel Bezanson, Assistant Professor (starting 2017); Ph.D., Yale. Observational astronomy, galaxy evolution in the early universe, the evolution of black holes in galaxies.

Joseph Boudreau, Professor; Ph.D., Wisconsin. Experimental particle physics.

Daniel Boyanovsky, Professor; Ph.D., California, Santa Barbara. Theoretical condensed matter physics, particle astrophysics, astrophysics and cosmology.

Matteo Broccio, Lecturer; Ph.D., Messina (Italy). Biophysics, physics, physics education research.

Guanglei Cheng, Adjunct Professor; Ph.D., Pittsburgh. Experimental condensed matter physics.

Russell Clark, Senior Lecturer/Lab Supervisor; Ph.D., LSU. Physics education research, neutrino physics.

Xuefeng Cui, Adjunct Assistant Professor; Ph.D., University of Science and Technology of China. Experimental Condensed Matter Physics.

Rob Coalson, Professor; Ph.D., Harvard. Chemical physics.

Istvan Danko, Lab Instructor; Ph.D., Vanderbilt. Experimental particle physics.

Robert P. Devaty, Associate Professor and Chair of the Graduate Admissions Committee; Ph.D., Cornell. Experimental solid-state physics, semiconductor physics.

Gurudev Dutt, Associate Professor; Ph.D., Michigan. Quantum optics, quantum information.

Steven A. Dytman, Professor; Ph.D., Carnegie Mellon. Experimental particle physics, neutrino physics.

Min Feng, Adjunct Professor; Ph.D., Chinese Academy of Sciences (Beijing). Experimental condensed matter.

Ayres Freitas, Associate Professor; Ph.D., Hamburg. Theoretical particle physics.

Sergey Frolov, Assistant Professor and member of the Peterson Institute of Nanoscience and Engineering Executive Committee (PINSE); Ph.D., Illinois. Experimental condensed matter physics, quantum nanowires, Majorana fermions in nanowires, nanowire quantum bits.

Melanie Good, Lecturer; Ph.D., University of Pittsburgh, Physics Education Research.

Tao Han, Distinguished Professor and Director of the PITTsburgh Particle physics, Astrophysics, and Cosmology Center (PITT PACC); Ph.D., Wisconsin. Theoretical particle physics.

Michael Hatridge, Assistant Professor; Ph.D., Berkeley. Experimental condensed matter, superconducting qubits and amplifier, quantum-limited measurement, quantum information.

D. John Hillier, Professor; Ph.D., Australian National. Theoretical and observational astrophysics, computational physics.

Tae Min Hong, Assistant Professor; Ph.D., California, Santa Barbara. Experimental high energy physics, dark matter, supersymmetry.

Kunie Ishioka, Adjunct Professor; Ph.D., Kyoto (Japan). Experimental condensed matter.

Patrick Irvin, Research Assistant Professor; Ph.D., Pittsburgh. Experimental condensed matter physics.

Arthur Kosowsky, Professor and Department Chair, Ph.D., University of Chicago, Astrophysics, cosmology, theoretical physics.

Sangyeop Lee, Assistant Professor; Ph.D., MIT. Mechanical engineering, material science.

Adam Leibovich, Professor and Associate Dean; Ph.D., Caltech. Theoretical particle physics.

Jeremy Levy, Distinguished Professor and Director of the Pittsburgh Quantum Institute (PQI); Ph.D., California, Santa Barbara. Experimental condensed matter, nanoscience, quantum information.

W. Vincent Liu, Professor; Ph.D., Texas at Austin. Theoretical condensed matter physics, cold atoms.

Emily Marshman, Lecturer; Ph.D., University of Pittsburgh, Physics Education Research.

Roger Mong, Assistant Professor; Ph.D., Berkeley. Theoretical condensed matter physics, topological insulators and superconductors, fractional quantum Hall, quantum information, disorder and transport in topological systems.

James Mueller, Professor; Ph.D., Cornell. Experimental particle physics.

Donna Naples, Professor; Ph.D., Maryland. Experimental neutrino physics.

David Nero, Lecturer; Ph.D., Toledo. Astronomy, physics, physics education research.

Jeffrey Newman, Professor; Ph.D., Berkeley. Astrophysics, extragalactic astronomy, observational cosmology.

Max Niedermaier, Research Associate Professor; Ph.D., Hamburg (Germany). Theoretical particle physics.

Vittorio Paolone, Professor; Ph.D., California, Davis. Experimental particle physics, neutrino physics.

David Pekker, Assistant Professor; Ph.D., Illinois at Urbana-Champaign. Atomic, molecular, and optical physics; computational physics; condensed matter physics.

Hrvoje Petek, Mellon Professor; Ph.D., Berkeley. Experimental condensed matter/AMO physics, nanoscience, solid-state physics.

Thomas Purdy, Assistant Professor; Ph.D.

Sandhya Rao, Research Professor; Ph.D., Pittsburgh. Astrophysics, extragalactic astronomy, observational cosmology.

Ralph Z. Roskies, Professor and Scientific Director of the Pittsburgh Supercomputing Center; Ph.D., Princeton. Theoretical particle physics, use of computers in theoretical physics.

Hanna Salman, Associate Professor; Ph.D., Weizmann Institute (Israel). Experimental biological physics.

Vladimir Savinov, Professor; Ph.D., Minnesota. Experimental particle physics.

Chandralekha Singh, Professor and Director of the Discipline Based Science Education Research Center (dB SERC); Ph.D., California, Santa Barbara. Physics education research, polymer physics.

David Snoke, Professor; Ph.D., Illinois at Urbana-Champaign. Experimental condensed matter physics, nanoscience, solid-state physics.

Eric Swanson, Professor; Ph.D., Toronto. Theoretical particle physics.

Shijing Tan, Adjunct Professor; Ph.D.; University of Science and Technology of China. Experimental condensed matter physics.

David A. Turnshek, Professor and Director of Allegheny Observatory; Ph.D., Arizona. Astrophysics, extragalactic astronomy, observational cosmology.

Michael Wood-Vasey, Associate Professor and Undergraduate Program Director; Ph.D., Berkeley. Astrophysics, extragalactic astronomy, observational cosmology.

Xiao-Lun Wu, Professor; Ph.D., Cornell. Experimental condensed matter physics, biological physics.

Yan Xu, Professor; Ph.D., Stony Brook, SUNY. Biophysics.

Judith Yang, Professor; Ph.D., Cornell. Materials science and engineering.

Andrew Zentner, Professor and Director of the Graduate Program; Ph.D., Ohio State. Theoretical cosmology.

Jin Zhao, Adjunct Research Professor; Ph.D., University of Sciences and Technology of China. Theoretical condensed matter.

EMERITUS FACULTY

Wolfgang J. Choyke, Research Professor; Ph.D., Ohio State. Experimental solid-state physics, defect states in semiconductors, large-bandgap spectroscopy.

Wilfred W. Cleland, Professor; Ph.D., Yale. Experimental particle physics.

H. E. Anthony Duncan, Professor; Ph.D., MIT. Theoretical particle physics.

Eugene Engels Jr., Professor; Ph.D., Princeton. Experimental particle physics.

Allen I. Janis, Professor; Ph.D., Syracuse. General relativity, philosophy of science.

David M. Jasnow, Professor; Ph.D., Illinois at Urbana–Champaign. Theory of phase transitions, statistical physics, biological physics.

Rainer Johnsen, Professor; Ph.D., Kiel (Germany). Experimental atomic and plasma physics.

Peter F. M. Koehler, Professor and Academic Assistant to Dean of University Honors College; Ph.D., Rochester. Experimental high-energy physics, physics education research.

James V. Maher, Professor Emeritus; Ph.D., Yale. Experimental statistical physics, critical phenomena, physics of fluids.

Ezra T. Newman, Professor; Ph.D., Syracuse. General relativity, gravitational lensing.

Richard H. Pratt, Professor; Ph.D., Chicago. Theoretical atomic physics.

Regina E. Schulte-Ladbeck, Professor Emeritus; Ph.D., Heidelberg. Extragalactic astronomy, observational cosmology.

Paul Shepard, Professor; Ph.D., Princeton. Experimental particle physics.

C. Martin Vincent, Professor; Ph.D., Witwatersrand (South Africa). Theoretical intermediate-energy physics.

Jeffrey Winicour, Professor; Ph.D., Syracuse. General relativity, numerical relativity.

Allen Hall, home to the Department.

Graduate student is connecting coaxial cables for superconducting qubit measurement on a dilution refrigerator in Dr. Michael Hatridge's lab.

170 www.petersons.com

Peterson's Graduate Programs in the Physical Sciences, Mathematics, Agricultural Sciences, the Environment & Natural Resources 2020

ACADEMIC AND PROFESSIONAL PROGRAMS IN MATHEMATICS

Section 7
Mathematical Sciences

This section contains a directory of institutions offering graduate work in mathematical sciences, followed by in-depth entries submitted by institutions that chose to prepare detailed program descriptions. Additional information about programs listed in the directory but not augmented by an in-depth entry may be obtained by writing directly to the dean of a graduate school or chair of a department at the address given in the directory.

For programs offering work in related fields, see all other areas in this book. In the other guides in this series:

Graduate Programs in the Humanities, Arts & Social Sciences

See *Economics* and *Psychology and Counseling*

Graduate Programs in the Biological/Biomedical Sciences & Health-Related Medical Professions

See *Biological and Biomedical Sciences; Biophysics; Genetics, Developmental Biology, and Reproductive Biology; Pharmacology and Toxicology* and *Public Health*

Graduate Programs in Engineering & Applied Sciences

See *Biomedical Engineering and Biotechnology; Chemical Engineering (Biochemical Engineering); Computer Science and Information Technology; Electrical and Computer Engineering; Engineering and Applied Sciences;* and *Industrial Engineering*

Graduate Programs in Business, Education, Information Studies, Law & Social Work

See *Business Administration and Management* and *Library and Information Studies*

CONTENTS

Program Directories

Featured Schools: Displays and Close-Ups

Applied Mathematics

Air Force Institute of Technology, Graduate School of Engineering and Management, Department of Mathematics and Statistics, Dayton, OH 45433-7765. Offers applied mathematics (MS, PhD). *Program availability:* Part-time. *Degree requirements:* For master's, thesis; for doctorate, thesis/dissertation. *Entrance requirements:* For master's, GRE General Test, minimum GPA of 3.0, U.S. citizenship or permanent U.S. residency; for doctorate, GRE General Test, minimum GPA of 3.5, U.S. citizenship or permanent U.S. residency. *Faculty research:* Electromagnetics, groundwater modeling, nonlinear diffusion, goodness of fit, finite element analysis.

Arizona State University at the Tempe campus, College of Liberal Arts and Sciences, School of Human Evolution and Social Change, Tempe, AZ 85287-2402. Offers anthropology (MA, PhD), including anthropology (PhD), archaeology (PhD), bioarchaeology (PhD), evolutionary (PhD), museum studies (MA), sociocultural (PhD); applied mathematics for the life and social sciences (PhD); environmental social science (PhD), including environmental social science, urbanism; global health (MA, PhD), including complex adaptive systems science (PhD), evolutionary global health sciences (PhD), health and culture (PhD), urbanism (PhD); immigration studies (Graduate Certificate). Terminal master's awarded for partial completion of doctoral program. *Degree requirements:* For master's, thesis or alternative, interactive Program of Study (iPOS) submitted before completing 50 percent of required credit hours; for doctorate, comprehensive exam, thesis/dissertation, interactive Program of Study (iPOS) submitted before completing 50 percent of required credit hours. *Entrance requirements:* For master's and doctorate, GRE, minimum GPA of 3.0 or equivalent in last 2 years of work leading to bachelor's degree. Additional exam requirements/recommendations for international students: Required—TOEFL, IELTS, or PTE. Electronic applications accepted.

Arizona State University at the Tempe campus, College of Liberal Arts and Sciences, School of Mathematical and Statistical Sciences, Tempe, AZ 85287-1804. Offers applied mathematics (PhD); mathematics (MA, PhD); mathematics education (PhD); statistics (MS, PhD, Graduate Certificate). *Program availability:* Part-time. Terminal master's awarded for partial completion of doctoral program. *Degree requirements:* For master's, thesis or alternative, interactive Program of Study (iPOS) submitted before completing 50 percent of required credit hours; for doctorate, comprehensive exam, thesis/dissertation, interactive Program of Study (iPOS) submitted before completing 50 percent of required credit hours. *Entrance requirements:* For master's and doctorate, GRE General Test, minimum GPA of 3.0 or equivalent in last 2 years of work leading to bachelor's degree. Additional exam requirements/recommendations for international students: Required—TOEFL, IELTS, or PTE. Electronic applications accepted. *Expenses:* Contact institution.

Auburn University, Graduate School, College of Sciences and Mathematics, Department of Mathematics and Statistics, Auburn University, AL 36849. Offers applied mathematics (MAM, MS); mathematics (MS, PhD); probability and statistics (M Prob S); statistics (MS). *Degree requirements:* For doctorate, thesis/dissertation. *Entrance requirements:* For master's, GRE General Test, undergraduate mathematics background; for doctorate, GRE General Test, GRE Subject Test. Electronic applications accepted. *Expenses:* Tuition, state resident: full-time $11,282; part-time $535 per credit hour. Tuition, nonresident: full-time $30,542; part-time $1605 per credit hour. *Required fees:* $826 per semester. Tuition and fees vary according to degree level and program. *Faculty research:* Pure and applied mathematics.

Bowie State University, Graduate Programs, Program in Applied and Computational Mathematics, Bowie, MD 20715-9465. Offers MS. *Program availability:* Part-time, evening/weekend. *Degree requirements:* For master's, comprehensive exam. *Entrance requirements:* For master's, calculus sequence, differential equations, linear algebra, mathematical probability and statistics. Electronic applications accepted.

Brown University, Graduate School, Division of Applied Mathematics, Providence, RI 02912. Offers Sc M, PhD. *Degree requirements:* For master's, thesis or alternative; for doctorate, one foreign language, thesis/dissertation, oral exam. *Entrance requirements:* For master's and doctorate, GRE General Test.

California Baptist University, Program in Applied Mathematics, Riverside, CA 92504-3206. Offers MS. *Program availability:* Part-time. *Faculty:* 6 full-time (2 women). *Students:* 3 full-time (2 women), 7 part-time (5 women); includes 5 minority (all Hispanic/Latino). Average age 28. 2 applicants, 100% accepted, 2 enrolled. In 2018, 9 master's awarded. *Entrance requirements:* For master's, minimum undergraduate GPA of 3.0, two letters of recommendation, essay, interview. Additional exam requirements/recommendations for international students: Required—TOEFL (minimum score 80 iBT). *Application deadline:* For fall admission, 8/1 priority date for domestic students, 7/1 priority date for international students; for spring admission, 12/1 priority date for domestic students, 11/1 priority date for international students. Applications are processed on a rolling basis. Application fee: $45. Electronic applications accepted. *Expenses:* $605 per unit. *Financial support:* In 2018–19, 3 students received support. Federal Work-Study, scholarships/grants, and unspecified assistantships available. Financial award applicants required to submit CSS PROFILE or FAFSA. *Faculty research:* Time-dependent Schrodinger equations, mathematical modeling, computational statistics, probability statistics, knot theory, several complex variables. *Unit head:* Dr. Lisa Hernandez, Dean, College of Arts and Science, 951-343-4767, E-mail: lihernandez@calbaptist.edu. *Application contact:* Dr. Linn Carothers, Department Chair, Mathematical Sciences, 951-343-4961, E-mail: lcarothers@calbaptist.edu.

California Institute of Technology, Division of Engineering and Applied Science, Option in Applied and Computational Mathematics, Pasadena, CA 91125-0001. Offers MS, PhD. *Degree requirements:* For doctorate, thesis/dissertation. *Entrance requirements:* For doctorate, GRE Subject Test. Electronic applications accepted. *Faculty research:* Theoretical and computational fluid mechanics, numerical analysis, ordinary and partial differential equations, linear and nonlinear wave propagation, perturbation and asymptotic methods.

California State Polytechnic University, Pomona, Program in Mathematics, Pomona, CA 91768-2557. Offers mathematics (MS). *Program availability:* Part-time, evening/weekend. *Students:* 14 full-time (5 women), 42 part-time (14 women); includes 33 minority (2 Black or African American, non-Hispanic/Latino; 9 Asian, non-Hispanic/Latino; 19 Hispanic/Latino; 3 Two or more races, non-Hispanic/Latino), 7 international. Average age 27. 67 applicants, 58% accepted, 25 enrolled. In 2018, 14 master's awarded. *Entrance requirements:* Additional exam requirements/recommendations for international students: Required—TOEFL (minimum score 550 paper-based). *Application deadline:* Applications are processed on a rolling basis. Application fee: $55. Electronic applications accepted. *Expenses:* Contact institution. *Financial support:* Application deadline: 3/2; applicants required to submit FAFSA. *Unit head:* Dr. Adam King, Assistant Professor/Graduate Coordinator, 909-979-5595, Fax: 909-869-4904, E-mail: king@cpp.edu. *Application contact:* Dr. Adam King, Assistant Professor/Graduate Coordinator, 909-979-5595, Fax: 909-869-4904, E-mail: king@cpp.edu.
Website: http://www.cpp.edu/~sci/mathematics-statistics/graduate-students/

California State University, Fullerton, Graduate Studies, College of Natural Science and Mathematics, Department of Mathematics, Fullerton, CA 92831-3599. Offers applied mathematics (MA); mathematics education (MA). *Program availability:* Part-time. *Entrance requirements:* For master's, minimum GPA of 2.5 in last 60 units of course work, major in mathematics or related field.

California State University, Long Beach, Graduate Studies, College of Engineering, Department of Mechanical and Aerospace Engineering, Long Beach, CA 90840. Offers aerospace engineering (MSAE); engineering and industrial applied mathematics (PhD); interdisciplinary engineering (MSE); management engineering (MSE); mechanical engineering (MSME). *Program availability:* Part-time. *Entrance requirements:* Additional exam requirements/recommendations for international students: Required—TOEFL. *Application deadline:* For fall admission, 4/15 for domestic students; for spring admission, 10/1 for domestic students. Application fee: $55. Electronic applications accepted. *Expenses: Required fees:* $2628 per term. Tuition and fees vary according to class time, course level, course load, degree level, campus/location and program. *Financial support:* Career-related internships or fieldwork, Federal Work-Study, institutionally sponsored loans, scholarships/grants, and unspecified assistantships available. Financial award application deadline: 3/2; financial award applicants required to submit FAFSA. *Faculty research:* Unsteady turbulent flows, solar energy, energy conversion, CAD/CAM, computer-assisted instruction. *Unit head:* Jalal Torabzadeh, Chair, 562-985-4398, E-mail: leanne.hayes@csulb.edu. *Application contact:* Dr. Jalal Torabzadeh, Graduate Advisor, 562-985-1512, Fax: 562-985-7561, E-mail: leanne.hayes@csulb.edu.
Website: http://www.csulb.edu/college-of-engineering/mechanical-aerospace-engineering

California State University, Long Beach, Graduate Studies, College of Natural Sciences and Mathematics, Department of Mathematics and Statistics, Long Beach, CA 90840. Offers mathematics (MS), including applied mathematics, applied statistics, mathematics education for secondary school teachers. *Program availability:* Part-time. *Degree requirements:* For master's, comprehensive exam or thesis. *Application deadline:* For fall admission, 6/1 for domestic students; for spring admission, 11/1 for domestic students. Applications are processed on a rolling basis. Application fee: $55. Electronic applications accepted. *Expenses: Required fees:* $2628 per term. Tuition and fees vary according to class time, course level, course load, degree level, campus/location and program. *Financial support:* Teaching assistantships, Federal Work-Study, institutionally sponsored loans, scholarships/grants, and traineeships available. Financial award application deadline: 3/2; financial award applicants required to submit FAFSA. *Faculty research:* Algebra, functional analysis, partial differential equations, operator theory, numerical analysis. *Unit head:* Dr. Tangan Gao, Chair, 562-985-4721, Fax: 562-985-8227, E-mail: tangan.gao@csulb.edu. *Application contact:* Dr. Tangan Gao, Chair, 562-985-4721, Fax: 562-985-8227, E-mail: tangan.gao@csulb.edu.

California State University, Los Angeles, Graduate Studies, College of Natural and Social Sciences, Department of Mathematics, Los Angeles, CA 90032-8530. Offers mathematics (MS), including applied mathematics. *Program availability:* Part-time, evening/weekend. *Degree requirements:* For master's, comprehensive exam or thesis. *Entrance requirements:* For master's, previous course work in mathematics. Additional exam requirements/recommendations for international students: Required—TOEFL (minimum score 500 paper-based). Electronic applications accepted. *Faculty research:* Group theory, functional analysis, convexity theory, ordered geometry.

California State University, Northridge, Graduate Studies, College of Science and Mathematics, Department of Mathematics, Northridge, CA 91330. Offers applied mathematics (MS); mathematics (MS). *Program availability:* Part-time, evening/weekend. *Degree requirements:* For master's, thesis (for some programs). *Entrance requirements:* For master's, GRE (if cumulative undergraduate GPA less than 3.0). Additional exam requirements/recommendations for international students: Required—TOEFL.

Case Western Reserve University, School of Graduate Studies, Department of Mathematics, Applied Mathematics and Statistics, Cleveland, OH 44106. Offers applied mathematics (MS, PhD); mathematics (MS, PhD). *Program availability:* Part-time. *Faculty:* 33 full-time (15 women), 2 part-time/adjunct (both women). *Students:* 35 full-time (15 women); includes 6 minority (1 Black or African American, non-Hispanic/Latino; 4 Asian, non-Hispanic/Latino; 1 Hispanic/Latino), 16 international. Average age 26. 185 applicants, 17% accepted, 15 enrolled. In 2018, 13 master's, 3 doctorates awarded. Terminal master's awarded for partial completion of doctoral program. *Degree requirements:* For master's, thesis or alternative; for doctorate, comprehensive exam, thesis/dissertation. *Entrance requirements:* For master's and doctorate, GRE General Test, 3 letters of recommendation. Additional exam requirements/recommendations for international students: Required—TOEFL (minimum score 577 paper-based; 90 iBT); Recommended—IELTS (minimum score 7). *Application deadline:* For fall admission, 4/1 priority date for domestic students; for spring admission, 11/1 priority date for domestic students. Applications are processed on a rolling basis. Application fee: $50. Electronic applications accepted. *Expenses: Tuition:* Full-time $45,168; part-time $1939 per credit hour. *Required fees:* $36; $18 per semester. $18 per semester. *Financial support:* Research assistantships, teaching assistantships, institutionally sponsored loans, health care benefits, and unspecified assistantships available. Financial award application deadline: 12/1; financial award applicants required to submit CSS PROFILE or FAFSA. *Faculty research:* Probability theory, convexity and high-dimensional phenomena, imaging, geometric evaluation of curves, dynamical systems, large scale scientific computing, life sciences. *Unit head:* Mary Ann Horn, Professor and Chair, 216-216.368.0470, Fax: 216-368-5163, E-mail: maryann.horn@case.edu. *Application contact:* Sakeenah Bari-Harold, Department Administrator, 216-368-0463, Fax: 216-368-5163, E-mail: sakeenah.bari-harold@case.edu.
Website: http://math.case.edu/

Central European University, Department of Mathematics and its Applications, 1051, Hungary. Offers mathematics and its applications (MS, PhD). *Degree requirements:* For master's, one foreign language, thesis (for some programs); for doctorate, comprehensive exam, thesis/dissertation. *Entrance requirements:* For master's and doctorate, entrance exam or GRE, statement of purpose. Additional exam requirements/

recommendations for international students: Required—TOEFL (minimum score 570 paper-based); Recommended—IELTS (minimum score 6.5). Electronic applications accepted. *Faculty research:* Algebra, algebraic geometry, bioinformatics, calculus of variations, computational biology, cryptography, discrete mathematics, evolutions equations, fluid mechanics, geometry, number theory, numerical analysis, optimization, ordinary and partial differential equations, probability theory, quantum mechanics, statistics, stochastic processes.

Claremont Graduate University, Graduate Programs, Institute of Mathematical Sciences, Claremont, CA 91711-6160. Offers computational and systems biology (PhD); computational mathematics and numerical analysis (MA, MS); computational science (PhD); engineering and industrial applied mathematics (PhD); mathematics (PhD); operations research and statistics (MA, MS); physical applied mathematics (MA, MS); pure mathematics (MA, MS); scientific computing (MA, MS); systems and control theory (MA, MS). PhD programs offered jointly with San Diego State University and California State University, Long Beach. *Program availability:* Part-time. Terminal master's awarded for partial completion of doctoral program. *Entrance requirements:* For master's and doctorate, GRE General Test. Additional exam requirements/ recommendations for international students: Required—TOEFL (minimum score 75 iBT). Electronic applications accepted.

Colorado School of Mines, Office of Graduate Studies, Department of Applied Mathematics and Statistics, Golden, CO 80401. Offers computational and applied mathematics (MS, PhD); statistics (MS, PhD). *Program availability:* Part-time. *Faculty:* 25 full-time (9 women), 7 part-time/adjunct (3 women). *Students:* 24 full-time (9 women), 7 part-time (3 women); includes 6 minority (1 Black or African American, non-Hispanic/ Latino; 1 American Indian or Alaska Native, non-Hispanic/Latino; 2 Hispanic/Latino; 1 Native Hawaiian or other Pacific Islander, non-Hispanic/Latino; 1 Two or more races, non-Hispanic/Latino), 1 international. Average age 27. 52 applicants, 60% accepted, 8 enrolled. In 2018, 7 master's, 1 doctorate awarded. *Degree requirements:* For master's, thesis (for some programs); for doctorate, comprehensive exam, thesis/dissertation. *Entrance requirements:* For master's and doctorate, GRE General Test. Additional exam requirements/recommendations for international students: Required—TOEFL (minimum score 550 paper-based; 79 iBT). *Application deadline:* For fall admission, 12/15 priority date for domestic and international students; for spring admission, 9/1 priority date for domestic and international students. Application fee: $60 ($80 for international students). Electronic applications accepted. *Expenses:* Tuition, state resident: full-time $16,650; part-time $925 per contact hour. Tuition, nonresident: full-time $36,270; part-time $2015 per contact hour. *International tuition:* $36,270 full-time. *Required fees:* $2314; $2314 per semester. *Financial support:* In 2018–19, 4 research assistantships with full tuition reimbursements, 10 teaching assistantships with full tuition reimbursements were awarded; fellowships, scholarships/grants, health care benefits, and unspecified assistantships also available. Financial award application deadline: 12/ 15; financial award applicants required to submit FAFSA. *Faculty research:* Applied statistics, numerical computation, artificial intelligence, linear optimization. *Unit head:* Dr. Debra Carney, Head, 303-273-3977, E-mail: dcarney@mines.edu. *Application contact:* Jaime Bachmeier, Program Manager, 303-273-3860, E-mail: jbachmeier@mines.edu.
Website: http://ams.mines.edu/

Columbia University, Fu Foundation School of Engineering and Applied Science, Department of Applied Physics and Applied Mathematics, New York, NY 10027. Offers applied mathematics (MS, Eng Sc D, PhD); applied physics (MS, Eng Sc D, PhD); materials science and engineering (MS, Eng Sc D, PhD); medical physics (MS). *Program availability:* Part-time, online learning. Terminal master's awarded for partial completion of doctoral program. *Degree requirements:* For master's, comprehensive exam; for doctorate, thesis/dissertation, qualifying exam. *Entrance requirements:* For master's, GRE General Test, GRE Subject Test (strongly recommended); for doctorate, GRE General Test, GRE Subject Test (applied physics). Additional exam requirements/ recommendations for international students: Required—TOEFL, IELTS, PTE. Electronic applications accepted. *Faculty research:* Plasma physics and fusion energy; optical and laser physics; atmospheric, oceanic and earth physics; applied mathematics; solid state science and processing of materials, their properties, and their structure; medical physics.

Cornell University, Graduate School, Graduate Fields of Arts and Sciences, Center for Applied Mathematics, Ithaca, NY 14853. Offers PhD. *Degree requirements:* For doctorate, one foreign language, comprehensive exam, thesis/dissertation. *Entrance requirements:* For doctorate, GRE General Test, GRE Subject Test in mathematics (recommended), 3 letters of recommendation. Additional exam requirements/ recommendations for international students: Required—TOEFL (minimum score 550 paper-based; 77 iBT). Electronic applications accepted. *Faculty research:* Nonlinear systems and PDEs, numerical methods, signal and image processing, mathematical biology, discrete mathematics and optimization.

Cornell University, Graduate School, Graduate Fields of Engineering, Field of Chemical Engineering, Ithaca, NY 14853. Offers advanced materials processing (M Eng, MS, PhD); applied mathematics and computational methods (M Eng, MS, PhD); biochemical engineering (M Eng, MS, PhD); chemical reaction engineering (M Eng, MS, PhD); classical and statistical thermodynamics (M Eng, MS, PhD); fluid dynamics, rheology and biorheology (M Eng, MS, PhD); heat and mass transfer (M Eng, MS, PhD); kinetics and catalysis (M Eng, MS, PhD); polymers (M Eng, MS, PhD); surface science (M Eng, MS, PhD). *Degree requirements:* For master's, thesis (MS); for doctorate, comprehensive exam, thesis/dissertation. *Entrance requirements:* For master's and doctorate, GRE General Test, 2 letters of recommendation. Additional exam requirements/recommendations for international students: Required—TOEFL (minimum score 600 paper-based; 77 iBT). Electronic applications accepted. *Faculty research:* Biochemical, biomedical and metabolic engineering; fluid and polymer dynamics; surface science and chemical kinetics; electronics materials; microchemical systems and nanotechnology.

Cornell University, Graduate School, Graduate Fields of Engineering, Field of Operations Research and Information Engineering, Ithaca, NY 14853. Offers applied probability and statistics (PhD); manufacturing systems engineering (PhD); mathematical programming (PhD); operations research and industrial engineering (M Eng). *Degree requirements:* For doctorate, comprehensive exam, thesis/dissertation. *Entrance requirements:* For master's and doctorate, GRE General Test, 3 letters of recommendation. Additional exam requirements/recommendations for international students: Required—TOEFL (minimum score 600 paper-based; 100 iBT). Electronic applications accepted. *Faculty research:* Mathematical programming and combinatorial optimization, statistics, stochastic processes, mathematical finance, simulation, manufacturing, e-commerce.

Dalhousie University, Faculty of Engineering, Department of Engineering Mathematics and Internetworking, Halifax, NS B3J 2X4, Canada. Offers engineering mathematics (M Sc, PhD); internetworking (M Eng). *Degree requirements:* For master's, thesis; for doctorate, thesis/dissertation. *Entrance requirements:* Additional exam requirements/ recommendations for international students: Required—TOEFL, IELTS, CANTEST, CAEL, or Michigan English Language Assessment Battery. Electronic applications accepted. *Faculty research:* Piecewise regression and robust statistics, random field theory, dynamical systems, wave loads on offshore structures, digital signal processing.

Delaware State University, Graduate Programs, Department of Mathematics, Interdisciplinary Program in Applied Mathematics and Theoretical Physics, Dover, DE 19901-2277. Offers PhD. *Degree requirements:* For doctorate, one foreign language, thesis defense. *Entrance requirements:* For doctorate, GRE General Test, MS degree in physics or mathematics. Additional exam requirements/recommendations for international students: Required—TOEFL (minimum score 550 paper-based).

Delaware State University, Graduate Programs, Department of Mathematics, Program in Applied Mathematics, Dover, DE 19901-2277. Offers MS. *Entrance requirements:* Additional exam requirements/recommendations for international students: Required—TOEFL (minimum score 550 paper-based). Electronic applications accepted.

DePaul University, College of Science and Health, Chicago, IL 60604-2287. Offers applied mathematics (MS); applied statistics (MS); biological sciences (MA, MS); chemistry (MS); environmental science (MS); mathematics education (MA); mathematics for teaching (MS); nursing (MS); nursing practice (DNP); physics (MS); polymer and coatings science (MS); psychology (MS); pure mathematics (MS); science education (MS); MA/PhD. *Accreditation:* AACN. Electronic applications accepted.

École Polytechnique de Montréal, Graduate Programs, Department of Mathematics and Industrial Engineering, Montréal, QC H3C 3A7, Canada. Offers ergonomy (M Eng, M Sc A, DESS); mathematical method in CA engineering (M Eng, M Sc A, PhD); operational research (M Eng, M Sc A, PhD); production (M Eng, M Sc A); technology management (M Eng, M Sc A). DESS program offered jointly with HEC Montreal and Université de Montréal. *Program availability:* Part-time. *Degree requirements:* For master's, one foreign language, thesis. *Entrance requirements:* For master's, minimum GPA of 2.75. *Faculty research:* Use of computers in organizations.

Elizabeth City State University, Department of Mathematics and Computer Science, Master of Science in Mathematics Program, Elizabeth City, NC 27909-7806. Offers applied mathematics (MS); community college teaching (MS); mathematics education (MS); remote sensing (MS). *Program availability:* Part-time, evening/weekend. *Degree requirements:* For master's, thesis. *Entrance requirements:* For master's, MAT and/or GRE, minimum GPA of 3.0, 3 letters of recommendation, two official transcripts from all undergraduate/graduate schools attended, typewritten one-page request for entry into program that includes description of student's educational preparation. Additional exam requirements/recommendations for international students: Required—TOEFL (minimum score 550 paper-based, 80 iBT) or IELTS (minimum score 6.5). Electronic applications accepted. *Faculty research:* Oceanic temperature effects, mathematics strategies in elementary schools, multimedia, Antarctic temperature mapping, computer networks, water quality, remote sensing, polar ice, satellite imagery.

Florida Atlantic University, Charles E. Schmidt College of Science, Department of Mathematical Sciences, Boca Raton, FL 33431-0991. Offers applied mathematics and statistics (MS); mathematics (MST, PhD). *Program availability:* Part-time. *Faculty:* 36 full-time (7 women), 1 part-time/adjunct (0 women). *Students:* 20 full-time (7 women), 38 part-time (10 women); includes 23 minority (7 Black or African American, non-Hispanic/ Latino; 3 Asian, non-Hispanic/Latino; 9 Hispanic/Latino; 4 Two or more races, non-Hispanic/Latino), 16 international. Average age 31. 47 applicants, 21% accepted, 10 enrolled. In 2018, 15 master's, 6 doctorates awarded. Terminal master's awarded for partial completion of doctoral program. *Entrance requirements:* For master's and doctorate, GRE General Test, minimum GPA of 3.0. Additional exam requirements/ recommendations for international students: Required—TOEFL (minimum score 500 paper-based; 61 iBT), IELTS (minimum score 6). *Application deadline:* For fall admission, 7/1 priority date for domestic students, 2/15 priority date for international students; for spring admission, 11/1 priority date for domestic students, 7/15 priority date for international students. Applications are processed on a rolling basis. Application fee: $30. Electronic applications accepted. *Expenses: Tuition, area resident:* Full-time $7400; part-time $369.82 per credit. Tuition, state resident: full-time $7400; part-time $369.82 per credit. Tuition, nonresident: full-time $20,496; part-time $1024.81 per credit. *Financial support:* Fellowships, teaching assistantships, and Federal Work-Study available. Financial award application deadline: 4/1. *Faculty research:* Cryptography, statistics, algebra, analysis, combinatorics. *Application contact:* Sonia Clayton, 561-297-4629, E-mail: mathgraduate@fau.edu.
Website: http://www.math.fau.edu/

Florida Institute of Technology, College of Engineering and Science, Program in Applied Mathematics, Melbourne, FL 32901-6975. Offers MS, PhD. *Program availability:* Part-time. *Students:* 27 full-time (12 women), 5 part-time (2 women); includes 2 minority (both Hispanic/Latino), 21 international. Average age 31. 14 applicants, 93% accepted, 7 enrolled. In 2018, 3 master's, 6 doctorates awarded. Terminal master's awarded for partial completion of doctoral program. *Degree requirements:* For master's, comprehensive exam (for some programs), thesis optional, minimum of 30 credit hours; for doctorate, comprehensive exam, thesis/dissertation, minimum of 75 credit hours. *Entrance requirements:* For master's, undergraduate degree in mathematics; for doctorate, GRE General Test, minimum GPA of 3.2, resume, 3 letters of recommendation, statement of objectives, good English-speaking skills. Additional exam requirements/recommendations for international students: Required—TOEFL (minimum score 550 paper-based; 79 iBT). *Application deadline:* For fall admission, 4/1 for international students; for spring admission, 9/30 for international students. Applications are processed on a rolling basis. Application fee: $50. Electronic applications accepted. *Expenses: Tuition:* Full-time $22,338; part-time $1241 per credit hour. Tuition and fees vary according to degree level, campus/location and program. *Financial support:* In 2018–19, 17 students received support. Research assistantships, teaching assistantships, career-related internships or fieldwork, and tuition remissions available. Financial award application deadline: 3/1; financial award applicants required to submit FAFSA. *Faculty research:* Methods of nonlinear analysis, spectral theory of operators, reaction diffusion equations, mathematical modeling. *Unit head:* Dr. Munevver Subasi, Interim Department Head, 717-674-7486, E-mail: msubasi@fit.edu. *Application contact:* Mike Perry, Executive Director of Admissions, 321-674-7127, E-mail: perrymj@fit.edu.
Website: https://www.fit.edu/programs/applied-mathematics-ms/

Florida State University, The Graduate School, Department of Anthropology, Department of Mathematics, Tallahassee, FL 32306-4510. Offers applied and computational mathematics (MS, PhD); biomathematics (MS, PhD); financial mathematics (MS, PhD), including actuarial science (MS); pure mathematics (MS, PhD). *Program availability:* Part-time. *Students:* 114 full-time (31 women); includes 8 minority (1 Black or African American, non-Hispanic/Latino; 1 Asian, non-Hispanic/Latino; 2 Hispanic/Latino; 4 Two or more races, non-Hispanic/Latino), 74 international. 225 applicants, 45% accepted, 47 enrolled. In 2018, 13 master's, 11 doctorates awarded. Terminal master's awarded for partial completion of doctoral program. *Degree requirements:* For master's, comprehensive exam (for some programs), thesis optional; for doctorate, comprehensive exam, thesis/dissertation, candidacy exam (including written qualifying examinations which differ by degree concentration). *Entrance*

requirements: For master's and doctorate, GRE General Test, minimum upper-division GPA of 3.0, 4-year bachelor's degree. Additional exam requirements/recommendations for international students: Required—TOEFL (minimum score 550 paper-based; 80 iBT), IELTS (minimum score 6.5). *Application deadline:* For fall admission, 12/15 priority date for domestic and international students; for spring admission, 4/30 for domestic and international students. Application fee: $30. Electronic applications accepted. *Expenses: Tuition, area resident:* Part-time $479.32 per credit hour. Tuition and fees vary according to campus/location and program. *Financial support:* In 2018–19, 109 students received support, including 2 fellowships with full tuition reimbursements available (averaging $24,053 per year), 10 research assistantships with full tuition reimbursements available (averaging $20,053 per year), 83 teaching assistantships with full tuition reimbursements available (averaging $20,053 per year); career-related internships or fieldwork, scholarships/grants, health care benefits, tuition waivers (full and partial), and unspecified assistantships also available. Financial award application deadline: 12/15; financial award applicants required to submit FAFSA. *Faculty research:* Low-dimensional and geometric topology, mathematical modeling in neuroscience, computational stochastics and Monte Carlo methods, mathematical physics, applied analysis. *Total annual research expenditures:* $1.3 million. *Unit head:* Dr. Philip L. Bowers, Chairperson, 850-644-2202, Fax: 850-644-4053, E-mail: bowers@math.fsu.edu. *Application contact:* Elizabeth Scott, Graduate Advisor and Admissions Coordinator, 850-644-2278, Fax: 850-644-4053, E-mail: emscott2@fsu.edu.
Website: http://www.math.fsu.edu/

The George Washington University, Columbian College of Arts and Sciences, Department of Mathematics, Washington, DC 20052. Offers applied mathematics (MS); financial mathematics (Graduate Certificate); mathematics (MA, PhD, Graduate Certificate). *Program availability:* Part-time, evening/weekend. *Students:* 29 full-time (10 women), 15 part-time (5 women); includes 9 minority (1 Black or African American, non-Hispanic/Latino; 4 Asian, non-Hispanic/Latino; 4 Hispanic/Latino), 21 international. Average age 27. 86 applicants, 73% accepted, 20 enrolled. In 2018, 7 master's, 6 doctorates awarded. Terminal master's awarded for partial completion of doctoral program. *Degree requirements:* For master's, comprehensive exam; for doctorate, one foreign language, thesis/dissertation, general exam. *Entrance requirements:* For master's and doctorate, GRE General Test, minimum GPA of 3.0, interview. Additional exam requirements/recommendations for international students: Required—TOEFL (minimum score 550 paper-based; 80 iBT). *Application deadline:* For fall admission, 1/15 priority date for domestic and international students; for spring admission, 10/1 priority date for domestic students, 9/1 priority date for international students. Applications are processed on a rolling basis. Application fee: $75. Electronic applications accepted. *Financial support:* In 2018–19, 17 students received support. Fellowships with full tuition reimbursements available, teaching assistantships, Federal Work-Study, and tuition waivers available. Financial award application deadline: 1/15. *Unit head:* Frank Baginski, Chair, 202-994-6269, E-mail: baginski@gwu.edu. *Application contact:* Frank Baginski, Chair, 202-994-6269, E-mail: baginski@gwu.edu.
Website: http://math.columbian.gwu.edu/

Hampton University, School of Science, Program in Applied Mathematics, Hampton, VA 23668. Offers computational mathematics (MS); nonlinear science (MS); statistics and probability (MS). *Program availability:* Part-time. *Faculty:* 1. *Students:* 2 full-time (1 woman), 1 (woman) part-time; all minorities (all Black or African American, non-Hispanic/Latino). Average age 37. 4 applicants, 50% accepted, 2 enrolled. In 2018, 1 master's awarded. *Degree requirements:* For master's, thesis optional. *Entrance requirements:* For master's, GRE General Test. Additional exam requirements/recommendations for international students: Required—TOEFL (minimum score 525 paper-based) or IELTS (6.5). *Application deadline:* For fall admission, 6/1 priority date for domestic students, 4/1 priority date for international students; for spring admission, 11/1 priority date for domestic students, 9/1 priority date for international students; for summer admission, 4/1 priority date for domestic students, 2/1 priority date for international students. Applications are processed on a rolling basis. Application fee: $35. Electronic applications accepted. *Financial support:* Application deadline: 6/30; applicants required to submit FAFSA. *Faculty research:* Stochastic processes, nonlinear dynamics, approximation theory, hydrodynamical stability, Clifford Analysis, Functional Analysis, Operator Theory, Hilbert Space, Polyconvex Integrand, Ordinary Differential Equations, and Calculus of Variations, Longitudinal Data Analysis and Logistic Regression Modeling. *Unit head:* Dr. Arun K. Verma, Professor/Chair, 757-727-5352, Fax: 757-637-2378, E-mail: arun.verma@hamptonu.edu. *Application contact:* Dr. Arun K. Verma, Professor/Chair, 757-727-5352, Fax: 757-637-2378, E-mail: arun.verma@hamptonu.edu.

Harvard University, Graduate School of Arts and Sciences, Harvard John A. Paulson School of Engineering and Applied Sciences, Cambridge, MA 02138. Offers applied mathematics (PhD); applied physics (PhD); computational science and engineering (ME, SM); computer science (PhD); data science (SM); design engineering (MDE); engineering science (ME), including electrical engineering (ME, SM, PhD); engineering sciences (SM, PhD), including bioengineering (PhD), electrical engineering (ME, SM, PhD), environmental science and engineering (PhD), materials science and mechanical engineering (PhD). MDE offered in collaboration with Graduate School of Design. *Program availability:* Part-time. Terminal master's awarded for partial completion of doctoral program. *Degree requirements:* For master's, thesis (for ME); for doctorate, comprehensive exam, thesis/dissertation. *Entrance requirements:* For master's and doctorate, GRE General Test, GRE Subject Test (recommended), 3 letters of recommendation. Additional exam requirements/recommendations for international students: Required—TOEFL (minimum score 80 iBT). Electronic applications accepted. *Expenses:* Contact institution. *Faculty research:* Applied mathematics, applied physics, computer science and electrical engineering, environmental engineering, mechanical and biomedical engineering.

Howard University, Graduate School, Department of Mathematics, Washington, DC 20059-0002. Offers applied mathematics (MS, PhD); mathematics (MS, PhD). *Program availability:* Part-time. Terminal master's awarded for partial completion of doctoral program. *Degree requirements:* For master's, comprehensive exam, thesis or alternative, qualifying exam; for doctorate, 2 foreign languages, comprehensive exam, thesis/dissertation, qualifying exams. *Entrance requirements:* For master's, GRE General Test, minimum GPA of 3.0; for doctorate, GRE General Test. Additional exam requirements/recommendations for international students: Required—TOEFL. Electronic applications accepted.

Hunter College of the City University of New York, Graduate School, School of Arts and Sciences, Department of Mathematics and Statistics, New York, NY 10065-5085. Offers adolescent mathematics education (MA); applied mathematics (MA); bioinformatics (MA); pure mathematics (MA); statistics (MA). *Program availability:* Part-time, evening/weekend. *Degree requirements:* For master's, one foreign language, comprehensive exam, thesis (for some programs). *Entrance requirements:* For master's, GRE General Test, 24 credits in mathematics. Additional exam requirements/recommendations for international students: Required—TOEFL. *Faculty research:* Data analysis, dynamical systems, computer graphics, topology, statistical decision theory.

Illinois Institute of Technology, Graduate College, College of Science, Department of Applied Mathematics, Chicago, IL 60616. Offers applied mathematics (MS, PhD); data science (MAS); mathematical finance (MAS). MAS in mathematical finance program held jointly with Stuart School of Business. Terminal master's awarded for partial completion of doctoral program. *Degree requirements:* For master's, comprehensive exam, thesis; for doctorate, comprehensive exam, thesis/dissertation. *Entrance requirements:* For master's, GRE General Test (minimum scores: 304 Quantitative and Verbal, 2.5 Analytical Writing), minimum undergraduate GPA of 3.0; three letters of recommendation; for doctorate, GRE General Test (minimum scores: 304 Quantitative and Verbal, 3.0 Analytical Writing), minimum undergraduate GPA of 3.5; three letters of recommendation. Additional exam requirements/recommendations for international students: Required—TOEFL (minimum score 550 paper-based; 80 iBT). Electronic applications accepted. *Faculty research:* Applied analysis, computational mathematics, discrete applied mathematics, stochastics (including financial mathematics).

Indiana University Bloomington, University Graduate School, College of Arts and Sciences, Department of Mathematics, Bloomington, IN 47405. Offers applied mathematics (MA); mathematical physics (PhD); mathematics education (MAT); pure mathematics (MA, PhD). Terminal master's awarded for partial completion of doctoral program. *Degree requirements:* For doctorate, one foreign language, thesis/dissertation. *Entrance requirements:* For master's and doctorate, GRE General Test, GRE Subject Test. Additional exam requirements/recommendations for international students: Required—TOEFL. Electronic applications accepted. *Expenses:* Contact institution. *Faculty research:* Topology, geometry, algebra, applied mathematics, analysis.

Indiana University of Pennsylvania, School of Graduate Studies and Research, College of Natural Sciences and Mathematics, Department of Mathematics, Program in Applied Mathematics, Indiana, PA 15705. Offers MS. *Program availability:* Part-time. *Faculty:* 11 full-time (4 women). *Students:* 9 full-time (2 women), 1 international. Average age 25. 11 applicants, 82% accepted, 4 enrolled. In 2018, 4 master's awarded. *Degree requirements:* For master's, thesis optional. *Entrance requirements:* For master's, 2 letters of recommendation. Additional exam requirements/recommendations for international students: Required—TOEFL (minimum score 540 paper-based). *Application deadline:* Applications are processed on a rolling basis. Application fee: $50. Electronic applications accepted. *Expenses:* Tuition, state resident: full-time $12,384; part-time $516 per credit hour. Tuition, nonresident: full-time $18,576; part-time $774 per credit hour. *Required fees:* $4454; $186 per credit hour. $65 per semester. Tuition and fees vary according to program and reciprocity agreements. *Financial support:* In 2018–19, 5 research assistantships with tuition reimbursements (averaging $4,500 per year) were awarded; fellowships with full tuition reimbursements, Federal Work-Study, scholarships/grants, and unspecified assistantships also available. Support available to part-time students. Financial award application deadline: 4/15; financial award applicants required to submit FAFSA. *Unit head:* Dr. Yu-Ju Kuo, Graduate Co-Coordinator, 724-357-3797, E-mail: Yu-Ju.Kuo@iup.edu. *Application contact:* Dr. Frederick Adkins, Graduate Co-Coordinator, 724-357-3790, E-mail: Frederick.Adkins@iup.edu.
Website: http://www.iup.edu/grad/appliedmath/default.aspx

Indiana University–Purdue University Indianapolis, School of Science, Department of Mathematical Sciences, Indianapolis, IN 46202-3216. Offers mathematics (MS, PhD), including applied mathematics, applied statistics (MS), mathematical statistics (PhD), mathematics, mathematics education (MS). *Program availability:* Part-time, evening/weekend. *Degree requirements:* For master's, thesis optional; for doctorate, one foreign language, comprehensive exam, thesis/dissertation. *Entrance requirements:* For doctorate, GRE General Test (recommended). Additional exam requirements/recommendations for international students: Required—TOEFL (minimum score 79 iBT), IELTS (minimum score 6.5), GRE General Test. Electronic applications accepted. *Faculty research:* Mathematical physics, integral systems, partial differential equations, noncommutative geometry, biomathematics, computational neurosciences.

Indiana University South Bend, College of Liberal Arts and Sciences, South Bend, IN 46615. Offers advanced computer programming (Graduate Certificate); applied informatics (Graduate Certificate); applied mathematics and computer science (MS); behavior modification (Graduate Certificate); computer applications (Graduate Certificate); computer programming (Graduate Certificate); correctional management and supervision (Graduate Certificate); English (MA); health systems management (Graduate Certificate); international studies (Graduate Certificate); liberal studies (MLS); nonprofit management (Graduate Certificate); paralegal studies (Graduate Certificate); professional writing (Graduate Certificate); public affairs (MPA); public management (Graduate Certificate); social and cultural diversity (Graduate Certificate); strategic sustainability leadership (Graduate Certificate); technology for administration (Graduate Certificate). *Program availability:* Part-time, evening/weekend. *Degree requirements:* For master's, variable foreign language requirement, thesis (for some programs). *Entrance requirements:* For master's, minimum GPA of 3.0. Additional exam requirements/recommendations for international students: Required—TOEFL (minimum score 550 paper-based; 80 iBT). *Expenses:* Contact institution. *Faculty research:* Artificial intelligence, bioinformatics, English language and literature, creative writing, computer networks.

Inter American University of Puerto Rico, San Germán Campus, Graduate Studies Center, Program in Mathematics Education, San Germán, PR 00683-5008. Offers applied mathematics (MA). *Program availability:* Part-time, evening/weekend. *Degree requirements:* For master's, comprehensive exam. *Entrance requirements:* For master's, EXADEP or GRE General Test, minimum GPA of 3.0. *Expenses: Tuition:* Full-time $212; part-time $212 per credit. *Required fees:* $366 per semester. One-time fee: $31. Tuition and fees vary according to degree level and program.

Iowa State University of Science and Technology, Department of Mathematics, Ames, IA 50011. Offers applied mathematics (MS, PhD); mathematics (MS, PhD); school mathematics (MSM). *Degree requirements:* For master's, thesis or alternative; for doctorate, thesis/dissertation. *Entrance requirements:* For master's and doctorate, GRE General Test. Additional exam requirements/recommendations for international students: Required—TOEFL (minimum score 550 paper-based; 79 iBT), IELTS (minimum score 6.5). Electronic applications accepted.

Iowa State University of Science and Technology, Program in Applied Mathematics, Ames, IA 50011. Offers MS, PhD. *Entrance requirements:* For master's and doctorate, GRE. Additional exam requirements/recommendations for international students: Required—TOEFL (minimum score 550 paper-based; 79 iBT), IELTS (minimum score 6.5). Electronic applications accepted.

Jackson State University, Graduate School, College of Science, Engineering and Technology, Department of Mathematics and Statistical Sciences, Jackson, MS 39217. Offers applied mathematics (MS); mathematics education (MST); pure mathematics (MS). *Program availability:* Part-time, evening/weekend. *Degree requirements:* For master's, comprehensive exam, thesis (for some programs). *Entrance requirements:* For master's, GRE General Test. Additional exam requirements/recommendations for international students: Required—TOEFL (minimum score 520 paper-based; 67 iBT).

Johns Hopkins University, Engineering Program for Professionals, Part-time Program in Applied and Computational Mathematics, Baltimore, MD 21218. Offers MS, Post-Master's Certificate. *Program availability:* Part-time, evening/weekend, blended/hybrid learning. *Faculty:* 2 full-time (1 woman), 19 part-time/adjunct (6 women). *Students:* 136 part-time (45 women). 71 applicants, 66% accepted, 18 enrolled. In 2018, 24 master's awarded. *Degree requirements:* For master's and Post-Master's Certificate, thesis optional. *Entrance requirements:* Additional exam requirements/recommendations for international students: Required—TOEFL (minimum score 600 paper-based; 100 iBT). *Application deadline:* Applications are processed on a rolling basis. Application fee: $0. Electronic applications accepted. *Financial support:* Applicants required to submit FAFSA. *Unit head:* Dr. Jim Spall, Program Chair, 443-778-4960, E-mail: james.spall@jhuapl.edu. *Application contact:* Doug Schiller, Admissions Director, 410-516-2300, Fax: 410-579-8049, E-mail: schiller@jhu.edu. Website: http://www.ep.jhu.edu.

Johns Hopkins University, G. W. C. Whiting School of Engineering, Department of Applied Mathematics and Statistics, Baltimore, MD 21218. Offers computational medicine (PhD); discrete mathematics (MA, MSE, PhD); financial mathematics (MSE); operations research/optimization (MA, MSE, PhD); statistics/probability (MA, MSE, PhD). *Faculty:* 25 full-time (4 women). *Students:* 173 full-time (67 women), 13 part-time (10 women). 1,406 applicants, 25% accepted, 89 enrolled. In 2018, 60 master's, 5 doctorates awarded. Terminal master's awarded for partial completion of doctoral program. *Degree requirements:* For master's, thesis (for some programs); for doctorate, thesis/dissertation, oral exam, introductory exam. *Entrance requirements:* For master's and doctorate, GRE General Test, 3 letters of recommendation, statement of purpose, transcripts. Additional exam requirements/recommendations for international students: Required—TOEFL (minimum score 600 paper-based; 100 iBT), IELTS (minimum score 7). *Application deadline:* For fall admission, 1/15 for domestic and international students; for spring admission, 9/15 for domestic and international students. Application fee: $75. Electronic applications accepted. *Financial support:* In 2018–19, 57 students received support, including 14 fellowships with full tuition reimbursements available (averaging $24,750 per year), 13 research assistantships with full tuition reimbursements available (averaging $23,000 per year), 30 teaching assistantships with full tuition reimbursements available (averaging $2,300 per year); Federal Work-Study, health care benefits, and tuition waivers (full and partial) also available. Financial award application deadline: 1/15; financial award applicants required to submit FAFSA. *Faculty research:* Matrix and numerical analysis, differential equation modeling, optimization and operations research, probability and statistics, discrete mathematics, financial mathematics. *Unit head:* Dr. Laurent Younes, Chair, 410-516-5103, Fax: 410-516-7459, E-mail: laurent.younes@jhu.edu. *Application contact:* Kristin Bechtel, Academic Program Coordinator, 410-516-7198, Fax: 410-516-7459, E-mail: kbechtel@jhu.edu. Website: http://engineering.jhu.edu/ams

Kent State University, College of Arts and Sciences, Department of Mathematical Sciences, Kent, OH 44242-0001. Offers applied mathematics (MA, MS, PhD); mathematics for secondary teachers (MA); pure mathematics (MA, MS, PhD). *Program availability:* Part-time. *Faculty:* 23 full-time (7 women). *Students:* 84 full-time (33 women), 39 part-time (17 women); includes 7 minority (2 Black or African American, non-Hispanic/Latino; 4 Asian, non-Hispanic/Latino; 1 Hispanic/Latino), 43 international. Average age 31. 66 applicants, 79% accepted, 12 enrolled. In 2018, 16 master's, 10 doctorates awarded. *Degree requirements:* For master's, comprehensive exam (for some programs), thesis (for some programs); for doctorate, comprehensive exam, thesis/dissertation. *Entrance requirements:* For master's, bachelor's degree with proficiency in numerical analysis and statistics, goal statement, resume or vita, 3 letters of recommendation; for doctorate, official transcript(s), goal statement, three letters of recommendation, resume or vita, passage of the departmental qualifying examination at the master's level. Additional exam requirements/recommendations for international students: Required—TOEFL (minimum score 525 paper-based, 71 iBT), Michigan English Language Assessment Battery (minimum score 74), IELTS (minimum score 6.0) or PTE (minimum score 50). *Application deadline:* For fall admission, 5/1 for domestic and international students; for spring admission, 10/1 for domestic and international students; for summer admission, 2/1 for domestic and international students. Applications are processed on a rolling basis. Application fee: $45 ($70 for international students). Electronic applications accepted. *Expenses:* Tuition, state resident: full-time $11,766; part-time $536 per credit. Tuition, nonresident: full-time $21,952; part-time $999 per credit. International tuition: $21,952 full-time. Tuition and fees vary according to course load. *Financial support:* Fellowships with full tuition reimbursements, research assistantships with full tuition reimbursements, teaching assistantships with full tuition reimbursements, scholarships/grants, and unspecified assistantships available. Financial award application deadline: 1/31. *Unit head:* Dr. Andrew Tonge, Professor and Chair, 330-672-9046, E-mail: atonge@kent.edu. *Application contact:* Artem Zvavitch, Professor and Graduate Coordinator, 330-672-3316, E-mail: zvavitch@math.kent.edu. Website: http://www.kent.edu/math/

Lehigh University, College of Arts and Sciences, Department of Mathematics, Bethlehem, PA 18015. Offers applied mathematics (MS, PhD); mathematics (MS, PhD); statistics (MS). *Program availability:* Part-time. *Faculty:* 23 full-time (5 women). *Students:* 37 full-time (10 women), 4 part-time (1 woman); includes 4 minority (1 Black or African American, non-Hispanic/Latino; 1 Asian, non-Hispanic/Latino; 1 Hispanic/Latino; 1 Two or more races, non-Hispanic/Latino), 22 international. Average age 24. 127 applicants, 53% accepted, 13 enrolled. In 2018, 14 master's, 3 doctorates awarded. Terminal master's awarded for partial completion of doctoral program. *Degree requirements:* For master's, comprehensive exam, thesis optional; for doctorate, comprehensive exam, thesis/dissertation, qualifying examination, general examination, advanced topic examination. *Entrance requirements:* For master's and doctorate, GRE General Test (strongly recommended), minimum undergraduate GPA of 2.75, 3.0 for last two semesters; adequate background in math. Additional exam requirements/recommendations for international students: Required—TOEFL. *Application deadline:* For fall admission, 1/1 for domestic and international students; for spring admission, 12/1 for domestic and international students. Application fee: $75. Electronic applications accepted. *Expenses:* $1500 per credit. *Financial support:* In 2018–19, 35 students received support, including fellowships with full tuition reimbursements available (averaging $25,000 per year), 2 research assistantships with full tuition reimbursements available (averaging $21,800 per year), 26 teaching assistantships with full tuition reimbursements available (averaging $21,500 per year); scholarships/grants and tuition waivers (full and partial) also available. Support available to part-time students. Financial award application deadline: 1/1. *Faculty research:* Probability and statistics, geometry and topology, algebra, discrete mathematics, differential equations. *Total annual research expenditures:* $173,233. *Unit head:* Dr. Garth Isaak, Chairman, 610-758-3732, Fax: 610-758-3767, E-mail: gisaak@lehigh.edu. *Application contact:* Dr. Robert Neel, Graduate Director, 610-758-5631, E-mail: robert.neel@lehigh.edu. Website: http://www.math.cas2.lehigh.edu/graduate-programs-mathematics

Long Island University–LIU Post, College of Liberal Arts and Sciences, Brookville, NY 11548-1300. Offers applied mathematics (MS); behavior analysis (MA); biology (MS); criminal justice (MS); earth science (MS); English (MA); environmental sustainability

(MS); genetic counseling (MS); history (MA); interdisciplinary studies (MA, MS); political science (MA); psychology (MA). *Program availability:* Part-time, evening/weekend, blended/hybrid learning. Terminal master's awarded for partial completion of doctoral program. *Degree requirements:* For master's, comprehensive exam (for some programs), thesis (for some programs). *Entrance requirements:* Additional exam requirements/recommendations for international students: Required—TOEFL, IELTS, or PTE. Electronic applications accepted. *Faculty research:* Biology, environmental sustainability, mathematics, psychology, genetic counseling.

Manhattan College, Graduate Programs, School of Science, Program in Applied Mathematics - Data Analytics, Riverdale, NY 10471. Offers MS. *Program availability:* Part-time. *Faculty:* 10 full-time (4 women). *Students:* 7 full-time (2 women), 3 part-time; includes 4 minority (1 Black or African American, non-Hispanic/Latino; 3 Hispanic/Latino), 2 international. Average age 24. 7 applicants, 86% accepted, 4 enrolled. In 2018, 4 master's awarded. *Degree requirements:* For master's, comprehensive exam. *Entrance requirements:* Additional exam requirements/recommendations for international students: Required—TOEFL (minimum score 550 paper-based; 80 iBT), IELTS (minimum score 6.5), TOEFL or IELTS is required. *Application deadline:* Applications are processed on a rolling basis. Application fee: $75. Electronic applications accepted. *Financial support:* In 2018–19, 4 students received support. Unspecified assistantships available. *Faculty research:* Machine learning, probabilistic modeling, statistical learning, operations research, network theory. *Unit head:* Dr. Constantine Theodosiou, Dean of Science, 718-862-7368, E-mail: constantine.theodosiou@manhattan.edu. *Application contact:* Doina Lawler, Assistant Director of Graduate Admissions, 718-862-8649, E-mail: dlawler01@manhattan.edu. Website: https://manhattan.edu/academics/5-year-programs/applied-mathematics-data-analytics.php

McGill University, Faculty of Graduate and Postdoctoral Studies, Faculty of Science, Department of Mathematics and Statistics, Montréal, QC H3A 2T5, Canada. Offers computational science and engineering (M Sc); mathematics and statistics (M Sc, MA, PhD), including applied mathematics (M Sc, MA), pure mathematics (M Sc, MA), statistics (M Sc, MA).

Michigan State University, The Graduate School, College of Natural Science, Department of Mathematics, East Lansing, MI 48824. Offers applied mathematics (MS, PhD); industrial mathematics (MS); mathematics (MAT, MS, PhD). *Entrance requirements:* Additional exam requirements/recommendations for international students: Required—TOEFL. Electronic applications accepted.

Missouri University of Science and Technology, Department of Mathematics and Statistics, Rolla, MO 65401. Offers applied mathematics (MS); mathematics (MST, PhD), including mathematics (PhD), mathematics education (MST), statistics (PhD). Terminal master's awarded for partial completion of doctoral program. *Degree requirements:* For master's, thesis or alternative; for doctorate, one foreign language, thesis/dissertation. *Entrance requirements:* For master's and doctorate, GRE General Test, GRE Subject Test. Additional exam requirements/recommendations for international students: Required—TOEFL (minimum score 550 paper-based). Electronic applications accepted. *Expenses:* Tuition, state resident: full-time $7545.60; part-time $419.20 per credit hour. Tuition, nonresident: full-time $22,169; part-time $1231.60 per credit hour. International tuition: $23,518.80 full-time. *Required fees:* $4523.05. Full-time tuition and fees vary according to course load, campus/location, program and reciprocity agreements. *Faculty research:* Analysis, differential equations, topology, statistics.

Montclair State University, The Graduate School, College of Science and Mathematics, Program in Mathematics, Montclair, NJ 07043-1624. Offers mathematics education (MS); pure and applied mathematics (MS). *Program availability:* Part-time, evening/weekend. *Degree requirements:* For master's, comprehensive exam. *Entrance requirements:* For master's, GRE General Test, 2 letters of recommendation, essay. Additional exam requirements/recommendations for international students: Required—TOEFL (minimum score 83 iBT), IELTS (minimum score 6.5). Electronic applications accepted. *Faculty research:* Computation, applied analysis.

Naval Postgraduate School, Departments and Academic Groups, Department of Applied Mathematics, Monterey, CA 93943. Offers MS, PhD. Program only open to commissioned officers of the United States and friendly nations and selected United States federal civilian employees. *Program availability:* Part-time. *Degree requirements:* For master's, thesis; for doctorate, one foreign language, thesis/dissertation. *Faculty research:* Compact S-box for Advanced Encryption Standard (AES), rotation symmetric Boolean functions - count and crytogprahic properties, pseudospectral method for the optimal control of constrained feedback linearizable systems, nodal triangle-based spectral element method for the shallow water equations on the sphere, axisymmetric equilibria of three-dimensional Smoluchowski equation.

Naval Postgraduate School, Departments and Academic Groups, Undersea Warfare Academic Group, Monterey, CA 93943. Offers applied mathematics (MS); applied physics (MS); applied science (MS), including acoustics, operations research, physical oceanography, signal processing; electrical engineering (MS); engineering acoustics (MS, PhD); engineering science (MS), including electrical engineering, mechanical engineering; mechanical engineer (ME); mechanical engineering (MS, MSME); meteorology (MS); operations research (MS); physical oceanography (MS). Program only open to commissioned officers of the United States and friendly nations and selected United States federal civilian employees. *Program availability:* Part-time. *Degree requirements:* For master's, thesis. *Faculty research:* Unmanned/autonomous vehicles, sea mines and countermeasures, submarine warfare in the twentieth and twenty-first centuries.

New Jersey Institute of Technology, College of Science and Liberal Arts, Newark, NJ 07102. Offers applied mathematics (MS); applied physics (MS, PhD); applied statistics (MS, Certificate); biology (MS, PhD); biostatistics (MS); chemistry (MS, PhD); environmental and sustainability policy (MS); environmental science (MS, PhD); history (MA, MAT); materials science and engineering (MS, PhD); mathematical and computational finance (MS); mathematical sciences (PhD); pharmaceutical chemistry (MS); professional and technical communications (MS); technical communication essentials (Certificate). *Program availability:* Part-time, evening/weekend. *Faculty:* 150 full-time (43 women), 115 part-time/adjunct (47 women). *Students:* 200 full-time (79 women), 63 part-time (29 women); includes 61 minority (17 Black or African American, non-Hispanic/Latino; 29 Asian, non-Hispanic/Latino; 11 Hispanic/Latino; 4 Two or more races, non-Hispanic/Latino), 136 international. Average age 28. 429 applicants, 49% accepted, 89 enrolled. In 2018, 43 master's, 16 doctorates, 2 other advanced degrees awarded. Terminal master's awarded for partial completion of doctoral program. *Degree requirements:* For master's, thesis (for some programs); for doctorate, thesis/dissertation. *Entrance requirements:* For master's and doctorate, GRE General Test, Minimum GPA of 3.0, personal statement, three (3) letters of recommendation, and transcripts. Additional exam requirements/recommendations for international students: Required—TOEFL (minimum score 550 paper-based; 79 iBT), IELTS (minimum score 6.5). *Application deadline:* For fall admission, 6/1 priority date for domestic students, 5/1 priority date for international students; for spring admission, 11/15 priority date for

Peterson's Graduate Programs in the Physical Sciences, Mathematics, Agricultural Sciences, the Environment & Natural Resources 2020

www.petersons.com   **177**

domestic and international students. Applications are processed on a rolling basis. Application fee: $75. Electronic applications accepted. *Expenses:* $22,690 per year (in-state), $32,136 per year (out-of-state). *Financial support:* In 2018–19, 134 students received support, including 17 fellowships with full tuition reimbursements available (averaging $22,000 per year), 74 research assistantships with full tuition reimbursements available (averaging $22,000 per year), 71 teaching assistantships with full tuition reimbursements available (averaging $22,000 per year); scholarships/grants, traineeships, health care benefits, and unspecified assistantships also available. Financial award application deadline: 1/15. *Faculty research:* Biophotonics and bioimaging, morphogenetic patterning, embryogenesis, biological fluid dynamics, applied research in the mathematical sciences. *Total annual research expenditures:* $29.2 million. *Unit head:* Dr. Kevin Belfield, Dean, 973-596-3676, Fax: 973-565-0586, E-mail: kevin.d.belfield@njit.edu. *Application contact:* Stephen Eck, Director of Admissions, 973-596-3300, Fax: 973-596-3461, E-mail: admissions@njit.edu.
Website: http://csla.njit.edu/

New Mexico Institute of Mining and Technology, Center for Graduate Studies, Department of Mathematics, Socorro, NM 87801. Offers applied and industrial mathematics (PhD); industrial mathematics (MS); mathematics (MS); operations research and statistics (MS). *Degree requirements:* For master's, thesis optional; for doctorate, thesis/dissertation. *Entrance requirements:* For master's, GRE General Test. Additional exam requirements/recommendations for international students: Required—TOEFL (minimum score 540 paper-based). *Faculty research:* Applied mathematics, differential equations, industrial mathematics, numerical analysis, stochastic processes.

North Carolina Agricultural and Technical State University, The Graduate College, College of Science and Technology, Department of Mathematics, Greensboro, NC 27411. Offers applied mathematics (MS), including secondary education; mathematics (MAT). *Accreditation:* NCATE (one or more programs are accredited). *Program availability:* Part-time, evening/weekend. *Degree requirements:* For master's, comprehensive exam, thesis or alternative, qualifying exam. *Entrance requirements:* For master's, GRE General Test, minimum GPA of 3.0.

North Dakota State University, College of Graduate and Interdisciplinary Studies, College of Science and Mathematics, Department of Mathematics, Fargo, ND 58102. Offers applied mathematics (MS, PhD); mathematics (MS, PhD). *Entrance requirements:* For master's and doctorate, GRE General Test. Additional exam requirements/recommendations for international students: Required—TOEFL (minimum score 525 paper-based; 71 iBT), IELTS. Electronic applications accepted.

Northeastern Illinois University, College of Graduate Studies and Research, College of Arts and Sciences, Program in Mathematics, Chicago, IL 60625. Offers mathematics (MS), including applied mathematics. *Program availability:* Part-time, evening/weekend. *Degree requirements:* For master's, comprehensive exam, thesis optional, project. *Entrance requirements:* For master's, minimum GPA of 2.75, 6 undergraduate courses in mathematics. Additional exam requirements/recommendations for international students: Required—TOEFL (minimum score 550 paper-based; 79 iBT). Electronic applications accepted. *Faculty research:* Numerical analysis, mathematical biology, operations research, statistics, geometry and mathematics of finance.

Northeastern University, College of Science, Boston, MA 02115-5096. Offers applied mathematics (MS); bioinformatics (MS); biology (PhD); biotechnology (MS); chemistry and chemical biology (MS, PhD); environmental science and policy (MS); marine and environmental sciences (PhD); marine biology (MS); mathematics (MS, PhD); operations research (MSOR); physics (MS, PhD); psychology (PhD). *Program availability:* Part-time. Terminal master's awarded for partial completion of doctoral program. *Degree requirements:* For master's, comprehensive exam (for some programs), thesis; for doctorate, comprehensive exam (for some programs), thesis/dissertation. *Entrance requirements:* For master's, GRE General Test. Electronic applications accepted. *Expenses:* Contact institution.

Northwestern University, McCormick School of Engineering and Applied Science, Department of Engineering Sciences and Applied Mathematics, Evanston, IL 60208. Offers MS, PhD. Admissions and degrees offered through The Graduate School. *Program availability:* Part-time. Terminal master's awarded for partial completion of doctoral program. *Degree requirements:* For master's, comprehensive exam; for doctorate, comprehensive exam, thesis/dissertation. *Entrance requirements:* For master's and doctorate, GRE General Test. Additional exam requirements/recommendations for international students: Required—TOEFL (minimum score 577 paper-based; 90 iBT), IELTS (minimum score 7). Electronic applications accepted. *Faculty research:* Acoustics, asymptotic analysis, bifurcation theory, combustion theory, fluid dynamics, information technology, math biology, microfluidics, moving boundary problems, nonlinear dynamics, pattern formation, waves.

Oakland University, Graduate Study and Lifelong Learning, College of Arts and Sciences, Department of Mathematics and Statistics, Program in Applied Mathematical Sciences, Rochester, MI 48309-4401. Offers PhD.

Oakland University, Graduate Study and Lifelong Learning, College of Arts and Sciences, Department of Mathematics and Statistics, Program in Industrial Applied Mathematics, Rochester, MI 48309-4401. Offers MS. *Program availability:* Part-time, evening/weekend. *Entrance requirements:* For master's, minimum GPA of 3.0. Additional exam requirements/recommendations for international students: Required—TOEFL (minimum score 550 paper-based). Electronic applications accepted. *Expenses:* Contact institution.

Oklahoma State University, College of Arts and Sciences, Department of Mathematics, Stillwater, OK 74078. Offers applied mathematics (MS, PhD). *Faculty:* 44 full-time (10 women), 9 part-time/adjunct (6 women). *Students:* 15 full-time (3 women), 32 part-time (13 women); includes 10 minority (4 Black or African American, non-Hispanic/Latino; 2 American Indian or Alaska Native, non-Hispanic/Latino; 2 Hispanic/Latino; 2 Two or more races, non-Hispanic/Latino), 17 international. Average age 29. 50 applicants, 32% accepted, 14 enrolled. In 2018, 5 master's awarded. *Entrance requirements:* For master's and doctorate, GRE (recommended). Additional exam requirements/recommendations for international students: Required—TOEFL (minimum score 550 paper-based; 79 iBT). *Application deadline:* For fall admission, 3/1 for domestic and international students; for spring admission, 10/15 for domestic students, 10/15 priority date for international students. Applications are processed on a rolling basis. Application fee: $40 ($75 for international students). Electronic applications accepted. *Expenses: Tuition, area resident:* Full-time $4148. Tuition, state resident: full-time $4148. Tuition, nonresident: full-time $10,517. *International tuition:* $10,517 full-time. *Required fees:* $4394; $2929 per credit hour. Tuition and fees vary according to course load and program. *Financial support:* Research assistantships, teaching assistantships, health care benefits, and tuition waivers (partial) available. Financial award application deadline: 3/1; financial award applicants required to submit FAFSA. *Unit head:* Dr. Willam Jaco, Department Head, 405-744-5688, Fax: 405-744-8225, E-mail: william.jaco@okstate.edu. *Application contact:* Dr. Sheryl Tucker, Dean, 405-744-6368, Fax: 405-744-0355, E-mail: gradi@okstate.edu.
Website: http://math.okstate.edu/

Old Dominion University, College of Sciences, Programs in Computational and Applied Mathematics, Norfolk, VA 23529. Offers applied mathematics (MS, PhD); biostatistics (MS); statistics (MS); statistics/biostatistics (PhD). *Program availability:* Part-time. Terminal master's awarded for partial completion of doctoral program. *Degree requirements:* For master's, project; for doctorate, comprehensive exam, thesis/dissertation, candidacy exam. *Entrance requirements:* For master's, minimum GPA of 3.0 in major, 2.8 overall; for doctorate, GRE General Test, 3 recommendation letters, transcripts, essay. Additional exam requirements/recommendations for international students: Required—TOEFL (minimum score 550 paper-based; 79 iBT); Recommended—IELTS (minimum score 6.5). Electronic applications accepted. *Faculty research:* Numerical analysis, integral equations, continuum mechanics, statistics, direct and inverse scattering.

Oregon State University, College of Science, Program in Mathematics, Corvallis, OR 97331. Offers differential geometry (MA, MS, PhD); financial and actuarial mathematics (MA, MS, PhD); mathematical biology (MA, MS, PhD); mathematics education (MS, PhD); number theory (MA, MS, PhD); numerical analysis (MA, MS, PhD); probability (MA). Terminal master's awarded for partial completion of doctoral program. *Degree requirements:* For master's, thesis or alternative; for doctorate, thesis/dissertation, qualifying exams. *Entrance requirements:* For master's and doctorate, GRE. Additional exam requirements/recommendations for international students: Required—TOEFL (minimum score 100 iBT). Electronic applications accepted.

Princeton University, Graduate School, Program in Applied and Computational Mathematics, Princeton, NJ 08544-1019. Offers PhD. *Degree requirements:* For doctorate, thesis/dissertation. *Entrance requirements:* For doctorate, GRE General Test, GRE Subject Test. Additional exam requirements/recommendations for international students: Required—TOEFL (minimum score 600 paper-based). Electronic applications accepted.

Purdue University Fort Wayne, College of Arts and Sciences, Department of Mathematical Sciences, Fort Wayne, IN 46805-1499. Offers applied mathematics (MS); applied statistics (Certificate); mathematics (MS); operations research (MS); teaching (MAT). *Program availability:* Part-time, evening/weekend. *Entrance requirements:* For master's, minimum GPA of 3.0, major or minor in mathematics, three letters of recommendation. Additional exam requirements/recommendations for international students: Required—TOEFL (minimum score 550 paper-based; 79 iBT); Recommended—TWE. Electronic applications accepted. *Faculty research:* Eves' Theorem, paired-placements for student teaching, holomorphic maps.

Queens College of the City University of New York, Mathematics and Natural Sciences Division, Department of Mathematics, Queens, NY 11367-1597. Offers applied mathematics (MA); pure mathematics (MA). *Program availability:* Part-time, evening/weekend. *Faculty:* 34 full-time (8 women), 65 part-time/adjunct (26 women). *Students:* 3 full-time (0 women), 34 part-time (12 women); includes 19 minority (5 Black or African American, non-Hispanic/Latino; 11 Asian, non-Hispanic/Latino; 3 Hispanic/Latino), 2 international. Average age 33. 39 applicants, 62% accepted, 13 enrolled. In 2018, 11 master's awarded. *Degree requirements:* For master's, comprehensive exam, oral exam (for pure mathematics); written exam (for applied mathematics). *Entrance requirements:* For master's, minimum GPA of 3.0. Additional exam requirements/recommendations for international students: Required—TOEFL (minimum score 61 iBT), IELTS (minimum score 5). *Application deadline:* For fall admission, 4/1 for domestic and international students; for spring admission, 11/1 for domestic and international students. Applications are processed on a rolling basis. Application fee: $125. Electronic applications accepted. *Financial support:* Career-related internships or fieldwork and Federal Work-Study available. Financial award application deadline: 4/1; financial award applicants required to submit FAFSA. *Faculty research:* Number theory, probability, complex analysis, algebra, topology. *Unit head:* Dr. Alan Sultan, Chair, 718-997-5811, Fax: 718-997-5882, E-mail: alan.sultan@qc.cuny.edu. *Application contact:* Elizabeth D'Amico-Ramirez, Assistant Director of Graduate Admissions, 718-997-5203, E-mail: elizabeth.damicoramirez@qc.cuny.edu.

Rensselaer Polytechnic Institute, Graduate School, School of Science, Program in Applied Mathematics, Troy, NY 12180-3590. Offers MS. *Program availability:* Part-time. *Faculty:* 24 full-time (5 women). *Students:* 4 full-time (2 women), 1 part-time (0 women); includes 1 minority (Hispanic/Latino), 2 international. Average age 24. 22 applicants, 18% accepted. In 2018, 4 master's awarded. *Entrance requirements:* For master's, GRE. Additional exam requirements/recommendations for international students: Required—TOEFL (minimum score 600 paper-based; 100 iBT), IELTS (minimum score 7), PTE (minimum score 68). *Application deadline:* For fall admission, 1/1 priority date for domestic and international students; for spring admission, 8/15 priority date for domestic and international students. Applications are processed on a rolling basis. Application fee: $75. Electronic applications accepted. *Financial support:* In 2018–19, 8 students received support, including teaching assistantships with full tuition reimbursements available (averaging $23,000 per year). Financial award application deadline: 1/1. *Total annual research expenditures:* $1.7 million. *Unit head:* Dr. John Mitchell, Graduate Program Director, 518-276-6519, E-mail: mitchj@rpi.edu. *Application contact:* Jarron Decker, Director of Graduate Admissions, 518-276-6216, Fax: 518-276-4072, E-mail: gradadmissions@rpi.edu.
Website: https://science.rpi.edu/mathematical-sciences/programs/graduate/ms-applied-mathematics

Rice University, Graduate Programs, George R. Brown School of Engineering, Department of Computational and Applied Mathematics, Houston, TX 77251-1892. Offers computational and applied mathematics (MA, MCAM, PhD); computational science and engineering (PhD). *Degree requirements:* For master's, comprehensive exam (for some programs), thesis (for some programs); for doctorate, comprehensive exam, thesis/dissertation. *Entrance requirements:* For master's and doctorate, GRE General Test, minimum GPA of 3.0. Additional exam requirements/recommendations for international students: Required—TOEFL (minimum score 600 paper-based; 90 iBT). Electronic applications accepted. *Faculty research:* Inverse problems, partial differential equations, computer algorithms, computational modeling, optimization theory.

Rochester Institute of Technology, Graduate Enrollment Services, College of Science, School of Mathematical Sciences, MS Program in Applied and Computational Mathematics, Rochester, NY 14623-5603. Offers MS. *Program availability:* Part-time. *Students:* 8 full-time (4 women), 11 part-time (3 women); includes 2 minority (both Asian, non-Hispanic/Latino), 2 international. Average age 26. 19 applicants, 53% accepted. In 2018, 3 master's awarded. *Degree requirements:* For master's, thesis or alternative, Thesis or Project. *Entrance requirements:* For master's, minimum GPA of 3.0 (recommended), personal statement, two letters of recommendation. Additional exam requirements/recommendations for international students: Required—TOEFL (minimum score 550 paper-based; 79 iBT), IELTS (minimum score 6.5), PTE (minimum score 58). *Application deadline:* For fall admission, 2/15 priority date for domestic and international students; for spring admission, 12/15 priority date for domestic and international

students. Applications are processed on a rolling basis. Application fee: $65. Electronic applications accepted. *Financial support:* In 2018–19, 9 students received support. Teaching assistantships with partial tuition reimbursements available, career-related internships or fieldwork, scholarships/grants, and unspecified assistantships available. Support available to part-time students. Financial award applicants required to submit FAFSA. *Faculty research:* Mathematical biology, graph theory, fluid dynamics, earth systems modeling, inverse problems. *Unit head:* Matthew Hoffman, Graduate Program Director, 585-420-6288, E-mail: mjhsma@rit.edu. *Application contact:* Diane Ellison, Senior Associate Vice President, Graduate Enrollment Services, 585-475-2229, Fax: 585-475-7164, E-mail: gradinfo@rit.edu.
Website: https://www.rit.edu/study/applied-and-computational-mathematics-ms

Rutgers University–Camden, Graduate School of Arts and Sciences, Program in Mathematical Sciences, Camden, NJ 08102. Offers industrial mathematics (MBS); industrial/applied mathematics (MS); mathematical computer science (MS); pure mathematics (MS); teaching in mathematical sciences (MS). *Program availability:* Part-time, evening/weekend. *Degree requirements:* For master's, comprehensive exam, thesis optional, survey paper, 30 credits. *Entrance requirements:* For master's, GRE, BS/BA in math or related subject, 2 letters of recommendation. Additional exam requirements/recommendations for international students: Required—TOEFL (minimum score 550 paper-based), IELTS. Electronic applications accepted. *Faculty research:* Differential geometry, dynamical systems, vertex operator algebra, automorphic forms, CR-structures.

Rutgers University–New Brunswick, Graduate School-New Brunswick, Department of Mathematics, Piscataway, NJ 08854-8097. Offers applied mathematics (MS, PhD); mathematics (MS, PhD). *Program availability:* Part-time. *Degree requirements:* For doctorate, one foreign language, comprehensive exam, thesis/dissertation. *Entrance requirements:* For master's and doctorate, GRE General Test, GRE Subject Test. Additional exam requirements/recommendations for international students: Required—TOEFL. *Faculty research:* Logic and set theory, number theory, mathematical physics, control theory, partial differential equations.

St. John's University, St. John's College of Liberal Arts and Sciences, Department of Mathematics and Computer Science, Queens, NY 11439. Offers applied and computational mathematics (MA). *Program availability:* Part-time, evening/weekend. *Degree requirements:* For master's, comprehensive exam. *Entrance requirements:* For master's, letters of recommendation, transcripts, resume, personal statement. Additional exam requirements/recommendations for international students: Required—TOEFL (minimum score 80 iBT), IELTS (minimum score 6.5). Electronic applications accepted.

San Diego State University, Graduate and Research Affairs, College of Sciences, Department of Mathematics and Statistics, Program in Applied Mathematics, San Diego, CA 92182. Offers MS. *Program availability:* Part-time. *Degree requirements:* For master's, comprehensive exam. *Entrance requirements:* For master's, GRE General Test. Additional exam requirements/recommendations for international students: Required—TOEFL. Electronic applications accepted. *Faculty research:* Modeling, computational fluid dynamics, biomathematics, thermodynamics.

Santa Clara University, School of Engineering, Santa Clara, CA 95053. Offers applied mathematics (MS); bioengineering (MS); civil, environmental, and sustainable engineering (MS); computer science and engineering (MS, PhD, Engineer); electrical engineering (MS, PhD, Engineer); engineering management and leadership (MS); mechanical engineering (MS, PhD, Engineer); power systems and sustainable energy (MS); software engineering (MS). *Program availability:* Part-time. *Faculty:* 72 full-time (24 women), 52 part-time/adjunct (9 women). *Students:* 555 full-time (211 women), 269 part-time (91 women); includes 208 minority (8 Black or African American, non-Hispanic/Latino; 1 American Indian or Alaska Native, non-Hispanic/Latino; 145 Asian, non-Hispanic/Latino; 28 Hispanic/Latino; 26 Two or more races, non-Hispanic/Latino), 472 international. Average age 27. 1,309 applicants, 36% accepted, 269 enrolled. In 2018, 320 master's, 7 doctorates awarded. *Entrance requirements:* For master's, GRE, official transcript; for doctorate, GRE, Official transcript, 500 word statement of purpose, three letters of recommendation. Additional exam requirements/recommendations for international students: Required—TOEFL (minimum score 79 iBT), IELTS (minimum score 6.5). *Application deadline:* For fall admission, 6/1 for domestic students; for winter admission, 9/6 for domestic students; for spring admission, 1/10 for domestic students; for summer admission, 3/6 for domestic students. Application fee: $60. Electronic applications accepted. *Financial support:* Fellowships, Federal Work-Study, and scholarships/grants available. Support available to part-time students. Financial award applicants required to submit FAFSA. *Unit head:* Dr. Elaine Scott, Dean, 408-554-3512, E-mail: epscott@scu.edu. *Application contact:* Stacey Tinker, Director of Admissions and Marketing, 408-554-4748, Fax: 408-554-4323, E-mail: stinker@scu.edu.
Website: http://www.scu.edu/engineering/graduate/

Simon Fraser University, Office of Graduate Studies and Postdoctoral Fellows, Faculty of Science, Department of Mathematics, Burnaby, BC V5A 1S6, Canada. Offers applied and computational mathematics (M Sc, PhD); mathematics (M Sc, PhD); operations research (M Sc, PhD). *Degree requirements:* For master's, thesis or alternative; for doctorate, comprehensive exam, thesis/dissertation. *Entrance requirements:* For master's, GRE General Test, GRE Subject Test (mathematics), minimum GPA of 3.0 (on scale of 4.33) or 3.33 based on last 60 credits of undergraduate courses; for doctorate, GRE General Test, GRE Subject Test (mathematics), minimum GPA of 3.5 (on scale of 4.33). Additional exam requirements/recommendations for international students: Recommended—TOEFL (minimum score 580 paper-based; 93 iBT), IELTS (minimum score 7), TWE (minimum score 5). Electronic applications accepted. *Faculty research:* Computer algebra, discrete mathematics, fluid dynamics, nonlinear partial differential equations and variation methods, numerical analysis and scientific computing.

Southern Illinois University Edwardsville, Graduate School, College of Arts and Sciences, Department of Mathematics and Statistics, Program in Computational and Applied Mathematics, Edwardsville, IL 62026. Offers MS. *Program availability:* Part-time. *Degree requirements:* For master's, thesis (for some programs), research paper. *Entrance requirements:* Additional exam requirements/recommendations for international students: Required—TOEFL (minimum score 550 paper-based, 79 iBT), IELTS (minimum score 6.5), Michigan Test of English Language Proficiency or PTE. Electronic applications accepted.

Southern Methodist University, Dedman College of Humanities and Sciences, Department of Mathematics, Dallas, TX 75275. Offers computational and applied mathematics (MS, PhD). *Degree requirements:* For master's, oral exams; for doctorate, thesis/dissertation, oral and written exams. *Entrance requirements:* For master's and doctorate, GRE General Test, minimum GPA of 3.0, 18 undergraduate hours in mathematics beyond first- and second-year calculus. Additional exam requirements/recommendations for international students: Required—TOEFL. Electronic applications accepted. *Faculty research:* Numerical analysis and scientific computation, fluid dynamics, optics, wave propagation, mathematical biology.

Stevens Institute of Technology, Graduate School, Charles V. Schaefer Jr. School of Engineering and Science, Department of Mathematical Sciences, Program in Applied Mathematics, Hoboken, NJ 07030. Offers MS. *Program availability:* Part-time, evening/weekend. *Faculty:* 21 full-time (2 women), 1 part-time/adjunct (0 women). *Students:* 13 full-time (3 women), 11 international. Average age 24. In 2018, 6 master's awarded. Terminal master's awarded for partial completion of doctoral program. *Degree requirements:* For master's, thesis optional, minimum B average in major field and overall. *Entrance requirements:* For master's, GRE/GMAT scores: GRE scores are required for all applicants applying to a full-time graduate program in the Schaefer School of Engineering and Science (SES). International applicants must submit TOEFL/IELTS scores and fulfill the English Language Proficiency Requirements in order to be considered. Additional exam requirements/recommendations for international students: Required—TOEFL (minimum score 74 iBT), IELTS (minimum score 6). *Application deadline:* For fall admission, 4/15 for domestic and international students; for spring admission, 11/1 for domestic and international students; for summer admission, 5/1 for domestic students. Applications are processed on a rolling basis. Application fee: $60. Electronic applications accepted. *Expenses: Tuition:* Full-time $35,960; part-time $1620 per credit. *Required fees:* $1290; $600 per semester. Tuition and fees vary according to course load. *Financial support:* Fellowships, research assistantships, teaching assistantships, career-related internships or fieldwork, Federal Work-Study, scholarships/grants, and unspecified assistantships available. Financial award application deadline: 2/15; financial award applicants required to submit FAFSA. *Unit head:* Dr. Jean Zu, Dean of SES, 201-216.8233, Fax: 201-216.8372, E-mail: Jean.Zu@stevens.edu. *Application contact:* Graduate Admission, 888-783-8367, Fax: 888-511-1306, E-mail: graduate@stevens.edu.

Stony Brook University, State University of New York, Graduate School, College of Engineering and Applied Sciences, Department of Applied Mathematics and Statistics, Stony Brook, NY 11794. Offers MS, PhD, Advanced Certificate. *Faculty:* 28 full-time (6 women), 5 part-time/adjunct (0 women). *Students:* 242 full-time (79 women), 30 part-time (15 women); includes 29 minority (23 Asian, non-Hispanic/Latino; 5 Hispanic/Latino; 1 Two or more races, non-Hispanic/Latino), 195 international. Average age 26. 388 applicants, 70% accepted, 58 enrolled. In 2018, 47 master's, 28 doctorates awarded. *Degree requirements:* For master's, thesis or alternative; for doctorate, one foreign language, comprehensive exam, thesis/dissertation. *Entrance requirements:* For master's and doctorate, GRE General Test. Additional exam requirements/recommendations for international students: Required—TOEFL (minimum score 90 iBT). *Application deadline:* For fall admission, 1/15 for domestic students; for spring admission, 10/1 for domestic students. Application fee: $100. *Expenses:* Contact institution. *Financial support:* In 2018–19, 3 fellowships, 36 research assistantships, 47 teaching assistantships were awarded. *Faculty research:* Computational mathematics, computational modeling, applied mathematics, computational physics, computational chemistry. *Total annual research expenditures:* $2.8 million. *Unit head:* Dr. Joseph Mitchell, Chair, 631-632-8366, Fax: 631-632-8490, E-mail: joseph.mitchell@stonybrook.edu. *Application contact:* Christine Rota, Coordinator, 631-632-8360, Fax: 631-632-8490, E-mail: christine.rota@stonybrook.edu.
Website: https://www.stonybrook.edu/commcms/ams/

Temple University, College of Science and Technology, Department of Mathematics, Philadelphia, PA 19122. Offers applied and computational mathematics (MS); mathematics (MS, PhD). *Program availability:* Part-time. *Faculty:* 30 full-time (3 women). *Students:* 32 full-time (12 women), 2 part-time (1 woman); includes 6 minority (5 Asian, non-Hispanic/Latino; 1 Hispanic/Latino), 17 international. 74 applicants, 35% accepted, 10 enrolled. In 2018, 6 master's, 6 doctorates awarded. *Degree requirements:* For master's, thesis optional; for doctorate, comprehensive exam, thesis/dissertation. *Entrance requirements:* For master's, GRE General Test, 3 letters of recommendation, statement of goals, resume; for doctorate, GRE General Test, GRE Subject Test, 3 letters of recommendation, statement of goals, resume. Additional exam requirements/recommendations for international students: Required—TOEFL (minimum score 79 iBT), IELTS (minimum score 6.5), PTE (minimum score 53), one of three is required. *Application deadline:* Applications are processed on a rolling basis. Application fee: $60. Electronic applications accepted. *Expenses:* Contact institution. *Financial support:* Research assistantships, teaching assistantships, Federal Work-Study, health care benefits, and unspecified assistantships available. Financial award applicants required to submit FAFSA. *Faculty research:* Complex analysis, partial differential equations, low dimensional topology, geometric group theory, applied mathematics. *Unit head:* Brian Rider, Department Chair, 215-204-7589, E-mail: brian.rider@temple.edu. *Application contact:* David Futer, Graduate Chairperson, 215-204-7854, E-mail: grad.math@temple.edu.
Website: http://math.temple.edu/

Texas Christian University, College of Science and Engineering, Department of Mathematics, Fort Worth, TX 76129-0002. Offers applied mathematics (MS); mathematics (MAT, PhD); pure mathematics (MS). *Program availability:* Part-time, evening/weekend. *Faculty:* 13 full-time (2 women). *Students:* 12 full-time (5 women), 1 part-time (0 women); includes 4 minority (1 Asian, non-Hispanic/Latino; 2 Hispanic/Latino; 1 Two or more races, non-Hispanic/Latino), 2 international. Average age 28. 11 applicants, 45% accepted, 4 enrolled. In 2018, 2 master's awarded. Terminal master's awarded for partial completion of doctoral program. *Degree requirements:* For master's, thesis optional; for doctorate, comprehensive exam, thesis/dissertation. *Entrance requirements:* For master's and doctorate, GRE General Test, 24 hours of math, including courses in elementary calculus of one and several variables, linear algebra, abstract algebra and real analysis. Additional exam requirements/recommendations for international students: Recommended—TOEFL (minimum score 550 paper-based; 80 iBT), IELTS (minimum score 6.5). *Application deadline:* For fall admission, 1/1 priority date for domestic and international students; for spring admission, 9/1 priority date for domestic and international students. Application fee: $60. Electronic applications accepted. *Financial support:* In 2018–19, 9 students received support, including 9 teaching assistantships with full tuition reimbursements available (averaging $15,000 per year); tuition waivers (full) also available. Support available to part-time students. Financial award application deadline: 1/1. *Faculty research:* Algebraic geometry, differential geometry and global analysis, algebraic topology, K-theory and operator algebras, number theory. *Total annual research expenditures:* $60,000. *Unit head:* Dr. Greg Friedman, Professor/Chair, 817-257-6343, Fax: 817-257-7766, E-mail: g.friedman@tcu.edu. *Application contact:* Dr. Ken Richardson, Professor/Director, Graduate Program, 817-257-6128, E-mail: k.richardson@tcu.edu.
Website: http://mathematics.tcu.edu/

Towson University, Jess and Mildred Fisher College of Science and Mathematics, Program in Applied and Industrial Mathematics, Towson, MD 21252-0001. Offers MS. *Program availability:* Part-time, evening/weekend. *Entrance requirements:* For master's, bachelor's degree in mathematics or related field; minimum GPA of 3.0 over last 60 credits, including 3 terms of calculus, course in differential equations, and course in linear algebra. Electronic applications accepted. *Expenses: Tuition, area resident:* Full-time $9196; part-time $418 per unit. Tuition, state resident: full-time $9196; part-time $418 per unit. Tuition, nonresident: full-time $19,030; part-time $865 per unit. *International tuition:* $19,030 full-time. *Required fees:* $3102; $141 per year. $423 per term. Tuition and fees vary according to campus/location and program.

Applied Mathematics

The University of Akron, Graduate School, Buchtel College of Arts and Sciences, Department of Mathematics, Program in Applied Mathematics, Akron, OH 44325. Offers MS. *Degree requirements:* For master's, thesis optional. *Entrance requirements:* For master's, minimum GPA of 2.75, three letters of recommendation, statement of purpose. Additional exam requirements/recommendations for international students: Required— TOEFL (minimum score 550 paper-based; 79 iBT), IELTS (minimum score 6.5). Electronic applications accepted. *Faculty research:* Analysis of nonlinear partial differential equations, finite groups and character theory, mathematics education, modeling and simulation of continuum and nanoscale systems, numerical analysis and scientific computation.

The University of Alabama, Graduate School, College of Arts and Sciences, Department of Mathematics, Tuscaloosa, AL 35487. Offers applied mathematics (PhD); mathematics (MA, PhD); pure mathematics (PhD). Terminal master's awarded for partial completion of doctoral program. *Degree requirements:* For master's, thesis or alternative, 24 semester hours of course work, plus thesis in mathematics, or 27 semester hours of courses plus 3 hours of work on project supervised by member of graduate faculty in mathematics; for doctorate, comprehensive exam, thesis/ dissertation, 48 hours of coursework with minimum of 39 hours in mathematics; qualifying exams in two areas of mathematics; candidacy; completion of at least 24 semester hours of dissertation research; written dissertation and oral defense. *Entrance requirements:* For master's and doctorate, GRE (minimum of 300 total combined Verbal/ Quantitative subscores), statement of purpose; three letters of recommendation; official transcripts; BA, BS or B Sc in mathematics or closely-related subject with minimum GPA of 3.0. Additional exam requirements/recommendations for international students: Recommended—TOEFL (minimum score 550 paper-based; 79 iBT), IELTS (minimum score 6.5). Electronic applications accepted. *Faculty research:* Algebra, analysis, topology, mathematics education, applied and computational mathematics, statistics.

The University of Alabama at Birmingham, College of Arts and Sciences, Program in Applied Mathematics, Birmingham, AL 35294. Offers PhD. Program offered jointly with The University of Alabama (Tuscaloosa) and The University of Alabama in Huntsville. *Degree requirements:* For doctorate, comprehensive exam, thesis/dissertation. *Entrance requirements:* For doctorate, GRE General Test (minimum score of 150 on Quantitative Reasoning portion), minimum B average in previous coursework, letters of recommendation. Additional exam requirements/recommendations for international students: Required—TOEFL. Electronic applications accepted. *Expenses: Tuition, area resident:* Full-time $8100; part-time $8100 per year. Tuition, state resident: full-time $8100. Tuition, nonresident: full-time $19,188; part-time $19,188 per year. Tuition and fees vary according to program. *Faculty research:* Inverse problems, mathematical modeling, mathematical biology.

The University of Alabama in Huntsville, School of Graduate Studies, College of Science, Department of Mathematical Sciences, Huntsville, AL 35899. Offers applied mathematics (PhD); education (MA); mathematics (MA, MS). PhD offered jointly with The University of Alabama (Tuscaloosa) and The University of Alabama at Birmingham. *Program availability:* Part-time. *Faculty:* 7 full-time. *Students:* 18 full-time (4 women), 12 part-time (4 women); includes 5 minority (3 Black or African American, non-Hispanic/ Latino; 2 Asian, non-Hispanic/Latino), 2 international. Average age 31. 25 applicants, 80% accepted, 10 enrolled. In 2018, 6 master's, 3 doctorates awarded. *Degree requirements:* For master's, comprehensive exam, thesis or alternative, oral and written exams; for doctorate, comprehensive exam, thesis/dissertation, oral and written exams. *Entrance requirements:* For master's and doctorate, GRE General Test, minimum GPA of 3.0. Additional exam requirements/recommendations for international students: Required—TOEFL (minimum score 550 paper-based; 80 iBT), IELTS (minimum score 6.5). *Application deadline:* For fall admission, 7/15 priority date for domestic students, 4/ 1 priority date for international students; for spring admission, 11/30 priority date for domestic students, 9/1 priority date for international students. Applications are processed on a rolling basis. Application fee: $50. Electronic applications accepted. *Expenses: Tuition, area resident:* Full-time $10,632; part-time $412 per credit hour. Tuition, state resident: full-time $10,632. Tuition, nonresident: full-time $23,604; part-time $412 per credit hour. *Required fees:* $582; $582. Tuition and fees vary according to course load and program. *Financial support:* In 2018–19, 7 students received support, including 6 teaching assistantships with full tuition reimbursements available (averaging $6,000 per year); career-related internships or fieldwork, Federal Work-Study, institutionally sponsored loans, scholarships/grants, health care benefits, and unspecified assistantships also available. Support available to part-time students. Financial award application deadline: 4/1; financial award applicants required to submit FAFSA. *Faculty research:* Combinatorics and graph theory, computational mathematics, differential equations and applications, mathematical biology, probability and stochastic processes. *Unit head:* Dr. Toka Diagana, Professor and Chair, 256-824-6470, Fax: 256-824-6173, E-mail: mathchair@uah.edu. *Application contact:* Kim Gray, Graduate Studies Admissions Coordinator, 256-824-6002, Fax: 256-824-6405, E-mail: deangrad@uah.edu.
Website: http://www.math.uah.edu/

University of Alberta, Faculty of Graduate Studies and Research, Department of Mathematical and Statistical Sciences, Edmonton, AB T6G 2E1, Canada. Offers applied mathematics (M Sc, PhD); biostatistics (M Sc); mathematical finance (M Sc, PhD); mathematical physics (M Sc, PhD); mathematics (M Sc, PhD); statistics (M Sc, PhD, Postgraduate Diploma). *Program availability:* Part-time. Terminal master's awarded for partial completion of doctoral program. *Degree requirements:* For master's, thesis (for some programs); for doctorate, comprehensive exam, thesis/dissertation. *Entrance requirements:* Additional exam requirements/recommendations for international students: Required—TOEFL (minimum score 580 paper-based). Electronic applications accepted. *Faculty research:* Classical and functional analysis, algebra, differential equations, geometry.

The University of Arizona, Graduate Interdisciplinary Programs, Graduate Interdisciplinary Program in Applied Mathematics, Tucson, AZ 85721. Offers applied mathematics (MS, PhD); mathematical sciences (PMS). Terminal master's awarded for partial completion of doctoral program. *Degree requirements:* For master's, thesis (for some programs); for doctorate, comprehensive exam, thesis/dissertation. *Entrance requirements:* For master's, GRE, 3 letters of recommendation; for doctorate, GRE, 3 letters of recommendation, statement of purpose. Additional exam requirements/ recommendations for international students: Required—TOEFL (minimum score 575 paper-based; 80 iBT). Electronic applications accepted. *Faculty research:* Dynamical systems and chaos, partial differential equations, pattern formation, fluid dynamics and turbulence, scientific computation, mathematical physics, mathematical biology, medical imaging, applied probability and stochastic processes.

University of Arkansas at Little Rock, Graduate School, College of Arts, Letters, and Sciences, Department of Mathematics and Statistics, Little Rock, AR 72204-1099. Offers applied statistics (Graduate Certificate); mathematical sciences (MS). *Program availability:* Part-time, evening/weekend. *Degree requirements:* For master's, comprehensive exam. *Entrance requirements:* For master's, GRE General Test, GRE Subject Test, minimum GPA of 2.7, previous course work in advanced mathematics.

University of California, Berkeley, Graduate Division, College of Letters and Science, Department of Mathematics, Berkeley, CA 94720. Offers applied mathematics (PhD); mathematics (MA, PhD). Terminal master's awarded for partial completion of doctoral program. *Degree requirements:* For master's, exam or thesis; for doctorate, 2 foreign languages, thesis/dissertation, qualifying exam. *Entrance requirements:* For master's and doctorate, GRE General Test, GRE Subject Test, minimum GPA of 3.0, 3 letters of recommendation. Electronic applications accepted. *Faculty research:* Algebra, analysis, logic, geometry/topology.

University of California, Davis, Graduate Studies, Graduate Group in Applied Mathematics, Davis, CA 95616. Offers MS, PhD. Terminal master's awarded for partial completion of doctoral program. *Degree requirements:* For master's, thesis; for doctorate, one foreign language, thesis/dissertation. *Entrance requirements:* For master's, GRE General Test, GRE Subject Test, minimum GPA of 3.0; for doctorate, GRE General Test, GRE Subject Test, master's degree, minimum GPA of 3.0. Additional exam requirements/recommendations for international students: Required— TOEFL (minimum score 550 paper-based). Electronic applications accepted. *Faculty research:* Mathematical biology, control and optimization, atmospheric sciences, theoretical chemistry, mathematical physics.

University of California, Irvine, School of Social Sciences, Institute for Mathematical Behavioral Sciences, Irvine, CA 92697. Offers games, decisions, and dynamical systems (PhD); mathematical behavioral sciences (MA). *Students:* 8 full-time (4 women), 2 part-time (0 women); includes 3 minority (1 Asian, non-Hispanic/Latino; 2 Two or more races, non-Hispanic/Latino), 2 international. Average age 36. 8 applicants, 13% accepted. In 2018, 2 master's, 1 doctorate awarded. *Entrance requirements:* For master's and doctorate, GRE General Test, minimum GPA of 3.0. *Application deadline:* For fall admission, 1/15 priority date for domestic students, 1/15 for international students. Applications are processed on a rolling basis. Application fee: $105 ($125 for international students). Electronic applications accepted. *Financial support:* Fellowships, research assistantships with full tuition reimbursements, teaching assistantships, institutionally sponsored loans, traineeships, health care benefits, and unspecified assistantships available. Financial award application deadline: 3/1; financial award applicants required to submit FAFSA. *Faculty research:* Representational measurement theory, mathematical models of learning and memory, mathematical psychology, utility theory, artificial intelligence. *Unit head:* Jean-Paul Carvalho, Interim Director, 949-824-3417, Fax: 949-824-3733, E-mail: jpcarv@uci.edu. *Application contact:* Joanna Kerner, Administrative Manager, 949-824-8651, Fax: 949-824-3733, E-mail: kernerj@uci.edu.
Website: http://www.imbs.uci.edu/

University of California, Merced, Graduate Division, School of Natural Sciences, Merced, CA 95343. Offers applied mathematics (MS, PhD); chemistry and chemical biology (MS, PhD); physics (MS, PhD); quantitative and systems biology (MS, PhD), including molecular and cellular biology (PhD). *Faculty:* 77 full-time (30 women). *Students:* 232 full-time (98 women), 2 part-time (0 women); includes 79 minority (8 Black or African American, non-Hispanic/Latino; 22 Asian, non-Hispanic/Latino; 41 Hispanic/ Latino; 8 Two or more races, non-Hispanic/Latino), 65 international. Average age 28. 302 applicants, 42% accepted, 58 enrolled. In 2018, 13 master's, 23 doctorates awarded. Terminal master's awarded for partial completion of doctoral program. *Degree requirements:* For master's, variable foreign language requirement, comprehensive exam, thesis or alternative, oral defense; for doctorate, variable foreign language requirement, comprehensive exam, thesis/dissertation, oral defense. *Entrance requirements:* For master's and doctorate, GRE. Additional exam requirements/ recommendations for international students: Required—TOEFL (minimum score 550 paper-based; 80 iBT); Recommended—IELTS (minimum score 6.5). *Application deadline:* For fall admission, 1/15 for domestic and international students. Application fee: $105 ($125 for international students). Electronic applications accepted. *Expenses: Tuition, area resident:* Full-time $11,442; part-time $5721 per year. Tuition, state resident: Full-time $11,442; part-time $5721 per year. Tuition, nonresident: full-time $26,544; part-time $13,272 per year. *International tuition:* $26,544 full-time. *Required fees:* $1765; $1765 per unit. $883 per semester. *Financial support:* In 2018–19, 229 students received support, including 12 fellowships with full tuition reimbursements available (averaging $21,865 per year), 47 research assistantships with full tuition reimbursements available (averaging $19,123 per year), 170 teaching assistantships with full tuition reimbursements available (averaging $20,710 per year); scholarships/ grants, traineeships, and health care benefits also available. *Faculty research:* Biomedical sciences; soft matter physics; applied math and computational science; environmental and biological systems; biological and materials chemistry. *Total annual research expenditures:* $4.1 million. *Unit head:* Dr. Elizabeth Dumont, Dean, 209-228-4487, Fax: 209-228-4060, E-mail: edumont@ucmerced.edu. *Application contact:* Tsu Ya, Director of Graduate Admissions and Academic Services, 209-228-4521, Fax: 209-228-6906, E-mail: tya@ucmerced.edu.

University of California, San Diego, Graduate Division, Department of Mathematics, La Jolla, CA 92093. Offers applied mathematics (MA); computational science (PhD); mathematics (MA, PhD); statistics (MS, PhD). *Students:* 171 full-time (36 women), 3 part-time (1 woman). 713 applicants, 25% accepted, 55 enrolled. In 2018, 12 master's, 13 doctorates awarded. Terminal master's awarded for partial completion of doctoral program. *Degree requirements:* For master's, comprehensive exam; for doctorate, comprehensive exam, thesis/dissertation. *Entrance requirements:* For master's, GRE General Test; GRE Subject Test (for MA), minimum GPA of 3.0; for doctorate, GRE General Test, GRE Subject Test, minimum GPA of 3.0. Additional exam requirements/ recommendations for international students: Required—TOEFL (minimum score 550 paper-based; 80 iBT), IELTS (minimum score 7); Recommended—TSE. *Application deadline:* For fall admission, 1/16 for domestic students. Application fee: $105 ($125 for international students). Electronic applications accepted. *Financial support:* Fellowships, research assistantships, teaching assistantships, and scholarships/grants available. Financial award applicants required to submit FAFSA. *Faculty research:* Combinatorics, bioinformatics, differential equations, logic and computational complexity, probability theory and statistics, Algebra, Algebraic Geometry, Analysis, Applied Math, Combinatorics, Computational Science, Geometry, Math Physics, Number Theory, Other, Partial Differential Equations, Probability, Representation Theory, Statistics, Topology. *Unit head:* Lei Ni, Chair, 858-534-2734, E-mail: lni@math.ucsd.edu. *Application contact:* Mark Whelan, Admissions Specialist, 858-534-2642, E-mail: mathgradadmissions@math.ucsd.edu.
Website: http://math.ucsd.edu.

University of California, Santa Barbara, Graduate Division, College of Letters and Sciences, Division of Mathematics, Life, and Physical Sciences, Department of Mathematics, Santa Barbara, CA 93106-3080. Offers applied mathematics (MA), including computational science and engineering; mathematics (MA, PhD), including computational science and engineering (PhD), mathematics (MA); MA/PhD. Terminal master's awarded for partial completion of doctoral program. *Degree requirements:* For master's, comprehensive exam (for some programs), thesis (for some programs); for doctorate, comprehensive exam, thesis/dissertation. *Entrance requirements:* For master's and doctorate, GRE General Test, GRE Subject Test (math). Additional exam requirements/recommendations for international students: Required—TOEFL (minimum score 575 paper-based; 80 iBT), IELTS (minimum score 7). Electronic applications accepted. *Faculty research:* Topology, differential geometry, algebra, applied mathematics, partial differential equations.

University of California, Santa Cruz, Jack Baskin School of Engineering, Department of Applied Mathematics, Santa Cruz, CA 95064. Offers scientific computing and applied mathematics (MS); statistics and applied mathematics (MS, PhD), including applied mathematics, statistics. *Program availability:* Part-time. Terminal master's awarded for partial completion of doctoral program. *Degree requirements:* For master's, thesis, seminar, capstone project; for doctorate, thesis/dissertation, seminar, first-year exam, qualifying exam. *Entrance requirements:* For master's and doctorate, GRE General Test; GRE Subject Test in math (recommended). Additional exam requirements/recommendations for international students: Required—TOEFL (minimum score 570 paper-based; 89 iBT); Recommended—IELTS (minimum score 8). Electronic applications accepted. *Expenses:* Contact institution. *Faculty research:* Bayesian nonparametric methods; computationally intensive Bayesian inference, prediction, and decision-making; envirometrics; fluid mechanics; mathematical biology.

University of Central Arkansas, Graduate School, College of Natural Sciences and Math, Department of Mathematics, Conway, AR 72035-0001. Offers applied mathematics (MS); math education (MA). *Program availability:* Part-time. *Degree requirements:* For master's, comprehensive exam, thesis optional. *Entrance requirements:* For master's, GRE General Test, minimum GPA of 2.7. Additional exam requirements/recommendations for international students: Required—TOEFL (minimum score 550 paper-based; 80 iBT). Electronic applications accepted.

University of Central Missouri, The Graduate School, Warrensburg, MO 64093. Offers accountancy (MA); accounting (MBA); applied mathematics (MS); aviation safety (MA); biology (MS); business administration (MBA); career and technical education leadership (MS); college student personnel administration (MS); communication (MA); computer science (MS); counseling (MS); criminal justice (MS); educational leadership (Ed D); educational technology (MS); elementary and early childhood education (MSE); English (MA); environmental studies (MA); finance (MBA); history (MA); human services/educational technology (Ed S); human services/learning resources (Ed S); human services/professional counseling (Ed S); industrial hygiene (MS); industrial management (MS); information systems (MBA); information technology (MS); kinesiology (MS); library science and information services (MS); literacy education (MSE); marketing (MBA); mathematics (MS); music (MA); occupational safety management (MS); psychology (MS); rural family nursing (MS); school administration (MSE); social gerontology (MS); sociology (MA); special education (MSE); speech language pathology (MS); superintendency (Ed S); teaching (MAT); teaching English as a second language (MA); technology (MS); technology management (PhD); theatre (MA). *Accreditation:* ASHA. *Program availability:* Part-time, 100% online, blended/hybrid learning. *Degree requirements:* For master's and Ed S, comprehensive exam (for some programs), thesis (for some programs). *Entrance requirements:* Additional exam requirements/recommendations for international students: Required—TOEFL (minimum score 550 paper-based; 79 iBT). Electronic applications accepted.

University of Central Oklahoma, The Jackson College of Graduate Studies, College of Mathematics and Science, Department of Mathematics and Statistics, Edmond, OK 73034-5209. Offers applied mathematical science (MS), including mathematics, statistics, teaching; applied mathematics and computer science (MS). *Program availability:* Part-time. *Degree requirements:* For master's, comprehensive exam (for some programs), thesis (for some programs). *Entrance requirements:* Additional exam requirements/recommendations for international students: Required—TOEFL (minimum score 550 paper-based; 79 iBT), IELTS (minimum score 6.5). Electronic applications accepted.

University of Chicago, Division of the Physical Sciences, Committee on Computational and Applied Mathematics, Chicago, IL 60637-1513. Offers PhD. *Degree requirements:* For doctorate, one foreign language, thesis/dissertation, 2 qualifying exams. *Entrance requirements:* For doctorate, GRE General Test, GRE Subject Test, 3 letters of recommendation, Statement of purpose, Transcripts, Resume or CV. Additional exam requirements/recommendations for international students: Required—TOEFL (minimum score 104 iBT). Electronic applications accepted. *Faculty research:* Applied analysis, dynamical systems, theoretical biology, math-physics.

University of Cincinnati, Graduate School, McMicken College of Arts and Sciences, Department of Mathematical Sciences, Cincinnati, OH 45221. Offers applied mathematics (MS, PhD); mathematics education (MAT); pure mathematics (MS, PhD); statistics (MS, PhD). *Program availability:* Part-time. *Faculty:* 39 full-time (4 women), 12 part-time/adjunct (4 women). *Students:* 44 full-time (24 women), 19 part-time (9 women); includes 28 minority (2 Black or African American, non-Hispanic/Latino; 25 Asian, non-Hispanic/Latino; 1 Hispanic/Latino), 42 international. 91 applicants, 35% accepted, 27 enrolled. In 2018, 5 master's, 4 doctorates awarded. Terminal master's awarded for partial completion of doctoral program. *Degree requirements:* For master's, comprehensive exam, thesis or alternative; for doctorate, comprehensive exam, thesis/dissertation. *Entrance requirements:* For master's and doctorate, GRE. Additional exam requirements/recommendations for international students: Required—TOEFL, IELTS. *Application deadline:* For fall admission, 2/1 priority date for domestic and international students. Applications are processed on a rolling basis. Application fee: $65. Electronic applications accepted. *Financial support:* In 2018–19, 51 students received support, including 2 fellowships with full tuition reimbursements available (averaging $13,500 per year), 2 research assistantships with full tuition reimbursements available (averaging $13,000 per year), 26 teaching assistantships with full tuition reimbursements available (averaging $18,500 per year); career-related internships or fieldwork, scholarships/grants, and unspecified assistantships also available. Support available to part-time students. Financial award application deadline: 2/1. *Faculty research:* Algebra, analysis, differential equations, numerical analysis, statistics. *Unit head:* Dr. Shuang Zhang, Professor and Department Head, 513-556-4052, Fax: 513-556-3417, E-mail: zhangs@ucmail.uc.edu. *Application contact:* Kamellia Smith, Program Coordinator, 513-5564053, Fax: 513-556-3417, E-mail: kamellia.smith@uc.edu.
Website: https://www.artsci.uc.edu/departments/math.html

University of Colorado Boulder, Graduate School, College of Arts and Sciences, Department of Applied Mathematics, Boulder, CO 80309. Offers MS, PhD. Terminal master's awarded for partial completion of doctoral program. *Degree requirements:* For master's, comprehensive exam, thesis or alternative; for doctorate, one foreign language, comprehensive exam, thesis/dissertation. *Entrance requirements:* For master's, GRE General Test, minimum undergraduate GPA of 2.75; for doctorate, GRE General Test. Additional exam requirements/recommendations for international students: Required—TOEFL. Electronic applications accepted. Application fee is waived when completed online. *Faculty research:* Applied mathematics; wave equations; nonlinear dynamics; numerical analysis; stochastic processes.

University of Colorado Colorado Springs, College of Letters, Arts and Sciences, Department of Mathematics, Colorado Springs, CO 80918. Offers applied mathematics (MS). *Program availability:* Part-time, evening/weekend. *Faculty:* 21 full-time (5 women), 14 part-time/adjunct (10 women). *Students:* 1 full-time (0 women), 7 part-time (3 women); includes 1 minority (Two or more races, non-Hispanic/Latino). Average age 27. 10 applicants, 80% accepted, 2 enrolled. In 2018, 3 master's awarded. *Degree requirements:* For master's, thesis, qualifying exam. *Entrance requirements:* For master's, bachelor degree in mathematics (or a bachelor degree in some other field, with extensive course work in mathematics), including a course in analysis comparable to the UCCS course Math 4310; minimum grade point average of 3.0; under special circumstances students may be admitted with a lower grade point average or without a course in analysis. Additional exam requirements/recommendations for international students: Required—TOEFL (minimum score 80 iBT); Recommended—IELTS (minimum score 6.5). *Application deadline:* Applications are processed on a rolling basis. Application fee: $60 ($100 for international students). Electronic applications accepted. *Expenses:* Program tuition and fees vary by course load and residency classification. Please visit the University of Colorado Colorado Springs Student Financial Services website to see current program costs: https://www.uccs.edu/bursar/index.php/estimate-your-bill. *Financial support:* In 2018–19, 5 students received support, including 15 teaching assistantships (averaging $9,000 per year); Federal Work-Study and scholarships/grants also available. Financial award application deadline: 3/1; financial award applicants required to submit FAFSA. *Faculty research:* Associative rings and modules, spectral theory for quantum graphs, spectral theory of integrable systems, percolation theory, interacting particle systems, Abelian groups. *Total annual research expenditures:* $111,770. *Unit head:* Dr. Zachary Mesyan, Professor, 719-255-3428, Fax: 719-255-3605, E-mail: zmesyan@uccs.edu. *Application contact:* Emanuelita Martinez, Department Assistant, 719-255-3311, Fax: 719-255-3605, E-mail: emartine@uccs.edu.
Website: https://www.uccs.edu/math/future-students/graduate-programs

University of Colorado Denver, College of Liberal Arts and Sciences, Department of Mathematical and Statistical Sciences, Denver, CO 80217. Offers applied mathematics (MS, PhD), including applied mathematics, applied probability (MS), applied statistics (MS), computational biology (PhD), computational mathematics (PhD), discrete mathematics, finite geometry (PhD), mathematics education (PhD), mathematics of engineering and science (MS), numerical analysis, operations research (MS), optimization and operations research (PhD), probability (PhD), statistics (PhD). *Program availability:* Part-time. *Degree requirements:* For master's, comprehensive exam, thesis optional, 30 hours of course work with minimum GPA of 3.0; for doctorate, comprehensive exam, thesis/dissertation, 42 hours of course work with minimum GPA of 3.25. *Entrance requirements:* For master's, GRE General Test; GRE Subject Test in math (recommended), 30 hours of course work in mathematics (24 of which must be upper-division mathematics), bachelor's degree with minimum GPA of 3.0; for doctorate, GRE General Test; GRE Subject Test in math (recommended), 30 hours of course work in mathematics (24 of which must be upper-division mathematics), master's degree with minimum GPA of 3.25. Additional exam requirements/recommendations for international students: Required—TOEFL (minimum score 537 paper-based; 75 iBT); Recommended—IELTS (minimum score 6.5). Electronic applications accepted. *Expenses:* Tuition, state resident: full-time $6786; part-time $337 per credit hour. Tuition, nonresident: full-time $22,590; part-time $1255 per credit hour. *Required fees:* $1231; $137 per credit hour. Tuition and fees vary according to program and reciprocity agreements. *Faculty research:* Computational mathematics, computational biology, discrete mathematics and geometry, probability and statistics, optimization.

University of Connecticut, Graduate School, College of Liberal Arts and Sciences, Department of Mathematics, Field of Applied Financial Mathematics, Storrs, CT 06269. Offers MS. *Degree requirements:* For master's, comprehensive exam. *Entrance requirements:* Additional exam requirements/recommendations for international students: Required—TOEFL (minimum score 550 paper-based). Electronic applications accepted.

University of Dayton, Department of Mathematics, Dayton, OH 45469. Offers applied mathematics (MAS); financial mathematics (MFM). *Program availability:* Part-time. *Degree requirements:* For master's, research in mathematics clinic. *Entrance requirements:* For master's, minimum undergraduate GPA of 2.8 (MAS), 3.0 (MFM, MME). Additional exam requirements/recommendations for international students: Required—TOEFL (minimum score 550 paper-based; 80 iBT). Electronic applications accepted. *Faculty research:* Differential equations, applied statistics, financial models, numerical analysis, coding/graph theory.

University of Delaware, College of Arts and Sciences, Department of Mathematical Sciences, Newark, DE 19716. Offers applied mathematics (MS, PhD); mathematics (MS, PhD). *Program availability:* Part-time. Terminal master's awarded for partial completion of doctoral program. *Degree requirements:* For master's, thesis (for some programs); for doctorate, one foreign language, thesis/dissertation, qualifying exam. *Entrance requirements:* For master's and doctorate, GRE General Test. Additional exam requirements/recommendations for international students: Required—TOEFL. Electronic applications accepted. *Faculty research:* Scattering theory, inverse problems, fluid dynamics, numerical analysis, combinatorics.

University of Georgia, Franklin College of Arts and Sciences, Department of Mathematics, Athens, GA 30602. Offers applied mathematical science (MAMS); mathematics (MA, PhD). *Degree requirements:* For master's, one foreign language, thesis (for some programs); for doctorate, 2 foreign languages, thesis/dissertation. *Entrance requirements:* For master's and doctorate, GRE General Test. Electronic applications accepted.

University of Guelph, Office of Graduate and Postdoctoral Studies, College of Physical and Engineering Science, Department of Mathematics and Statistics, Guelph, ON N1G 2W1, Canada. Offers applied mathematics (PhD); applied statistics (PhD); mathematics and statistics (M Sc). *Program availability:* Part-time. *Degree requirements:* For master's, thesis (for some programs); for doctorate, thesis/dissertation. *Entrance requirements:* For master's, minimum B- average during previous 2 years of course work; for doctorate, minimum B average. Additional exam requirements/recommendations for international students: Required—TOEFL (minimum score 550 paper-based; 89 iBT), IELTS (minimum score 6.5). *Faculty research:* Dynamical systems, mathematical biology, numerical analysis, linear and nonlinear models, reliability and bioassay.

University of Houston, College of Natural Sciences and Mathematics, Department of Mathematics, Houston, TX 77204. Offers applied mathematics (MS); mathematics (MA, PhD). *Program availability:* Part-time. *Degree requirements:* For master's, thesis optional. *Entrance requirements:* For master's and doctorate, GRE (Verbal and Quantitative). Additional exam requirements/recommendations for international students: Required—TOEFL (minimum score 550 paper-based; 79 iBT), IELTS (minimum score 6.5). Electronic applications accepted. *Faculty research:* Applied mathematics, modern analysis, computational science, geometry, dynamical systems.

University of Illinois at Urbana–Champaign, Graduate College, College of Liberal Arts and Sciences, Department of Mathematics, Champaign, IL 61820. Offers applied mathematics (MS); applied mathematics: actuarial science (MS); mathematics (MS, PhD); teaching of mathematics (MS).

Applied Mathematics

The University of Iowa, Graduate College, Program in Applied Mathematical and Computational Sciences, Iowa City, IA 52242-1316. Offers PhD. *Degree requirements:* For doctorate, comprehensive exam, thesis/dissertation. *Entrance requirements:* For doctorate, GRE General Test, minimum GPA of 3.0. Additional exam requirements/recommendations for international students: Required—TOEFL (minimum score 620 paper-based; 105 iBT). Electronic applications accepted.

The University of Kansas, Graduate Studies, College of Liberal Arts and Sciences, Department of Mathematics, Lawrence, KS 66045. Offers applied mathematics (Graduate Certificate); mathematics (MA, PhD); PhD/MA. *Program availability:* Part-time. *Students:* 73 full-time (17 women); includes 5 minority (4 Asian, non-Hispanic/Latino; 1 Two or more races, non-Hispanic/Latino), 32 international. Average age 28. 83 applicants, 49% accepted, 15 enrolled. In 2018, 9 master's, 7 doctorates, 1 other advanced degree awarded. Terminal master's awarded for partial completion of doctoral program. *Entrance requirements:* For master's and doctorate, GRE, official transcripts, three letters of recommendation, resume/curriculum vitae, statement of purpose. Additional exam requirements/recommendations for international students: Required—TOEFL, IELTS. *Application deadline:* For fall admission, 12/31 priority date for domestic and international students; for spring admission, 10/15 for domestic and international students. Application fee: $65 ($85 for international students). Electronic applications accepted. *Financial support:* Fellowships, research assistantships, teaching assistantships, institutionally sponsored loans, scholarships/grants, health care benefits, and unspecified assistantships available. Support available to part-time students. Financial award application deadline: 12/31. *Faculty research:* Algebra and algebraic geometry; analysis, partial differential equations and dynamical systems; probability, stochastic analysis and stochastic control; numerical analysis; geometry. *Unit head:* Weizhang Huang, Chair, 785-864-3651, E-mail: whuang@ku.edu. *Application contact:* Lori Springs, Graduate Admissions Contact, 785-864-7300, E-mail: lsprings@ku.edu.
Website: http://www.math.ku.edu/

University of Kentucky, Graduate School, College of Arts and Sciences, Program in Mathematics, Lexington, KY 40506-0032. Offers applied mathematics (MS); mathematics (MA, MS, PhD). *Degree requirements:* For master's, comprehensive exam, thesis optional; for doctorate, one foreign language, comprehensive exam, thesis/dissertation. *Entrance requirements:* For master's, GRE General Test, minimum undergraduate GPA of 2.75; for doctorate, GRE General Test, minimum graduate GPA of 3.0. Additional exam requirements/recommendations for international students: Required—TOEFL (minimum score 550 paper-based). Electronic applications accepted. *Faculty research:* Numerical analysis, combinatorics, partial differential equations, algebra and number theory, real and complex analysis.

University of Louisville, Graduate School, College of Arts and Sciences, Department of Mathematics, Louisville, KY 40292. Offers applied and industrial mathematics (PhD); mathematics (MA). *Program availability:* Part-time. *Faculty:* 32 full-time (6 women). *Students:* 28 full-time (9 women), 7 part-time (1 woman); includes 4 minority (2 Asian, non-Hispanic/Latino; 1 Hispanic/Latino; 1 Two or more races, non-Hispanic/Latino), 6 international. Average age 30. 21 applicants, 86% accepted, 13 enrolled. In 2018, 5 master's awarded. Terminal master's awarded for partial completion of doctoral program. *Degree requirements:* For master's, variable foreign language requirement, thesis or alternative; for doctorate, comprehensive exam, thesis/dissertation. *Entrance requirements:* For master's and doctorate, GRE. Additional exam requirements/recommendations for international students: Required—TOEFL (minimum score 550 paper-based; 79 iBT), IELTS (minimum score 6.5). *Application deadline:* For fall admission, 3/1 priority date for domestic and international students; for winter admission, 11/1 priority date for domestic and international students; for spring admission, 11/1 priority date for domestic and international students; for summer admission, 3/1 priority date for domestic and international students. Applications are processed on a rolling basis. Application fee: $65. Electronic applications accepted. *Expenses: Tuition, area resident:* Full-time $6500; part-time $723 per credit hour. Tuition, state resident: full-time $6500. Tuition, nonresident: full-time $13,557; part-time $1507 per credit hour. Tuition and fees vary according to course load and program. *Financial support:* In 2018–19, 32 students received support, including 3 fellowships with full tuition reimbursements available (averaging $22,000 per year), 1 research assistantship with partial tuition reimbursement available (averaging $20,000 per year), 24 teaching assistantships with full tuition reimbursements available (averaging $20,000 per year); health care benefits and unspecified assistantships also available. Financial award application deadline: 2/3. *Faculty research:* Mathematical biology, partial differential equations, statistics, combinatorics, analysis. *Total annual research expenditures:* $135,462. *Unit head:* Dr. David Swanson, Chair, 502-852-6234, E-mail: david.swanson@louisville.edu. *Application contact:* Dr. Hamid Kulosman, Graduate Director/Professor, 502-852-3403, E-mail: hamid.kulosman@louisville.edu.
Website: http://www.math.louisville.edu

The University of Manchester, School of Mathematics, Manchester, United Kingdom. Offers actuarial science (PhD); applied mathematics (M Phil, PhD); applied numerical computing (M Phil, PhD); financial mathematics (M Phil, PhD); mathematical logic (M Phil); probability (M Phil, PhD); pure mathematics (M Phil, PhD); statistics (M Phil, PhD).

University of Maryland, Baltimore County, The Graduate School, College of Natural and Mathematical Sciences, Department of Mathematics and Statistics, Program in Applied Mathematics, Baltimore, MD 21250. Offers MS, PhD. *Program availability:* Part-time, evening/weekend. Terminal master's awarded for partial completion of doctoral program. *Degree requirements:* For master's, comprehensive exam (for some programs), thesis (for some programs); for doctorate, comprehensive exam, thesis/dissertation. *Entrance requirements:* For master's and doctorate, GRE General Test, minimum GPA of 3.0. Additional exam requirements/recommendations for international students: Required—TOEFL (minimum score 600 paper-based; 100 iBT). Electronic applications accepted. *Faculty research:* Numerical analysis and scientific computation, optimization theory and algorithms, differential equations and mathematical modeling, mathematical biology and bioinformatics.

University of Maryland, College Park, Academic Affairs, College of Computer, Mathematical and Natural Sciences, Department of Mathematics, Applied Mathematics Program, College Park, MD 20742. Offers MS, PhD. *Program availability:* Part-time, evening/weekend. Terminal master's awarded for partial completion of doctoral program. *Degree requirements:* For master's, thesis optional, seminar, scholarly paper; for doctorate, comprehensive exam, thesis/dissertation, exams, seminars. *Entrance requirements:* For master's and doctorate, GRE General Test, GRE Subject Test, minimum GPA of 3.0, 3 letters of recommendation. Electronic applications accepted.

University of Massachusetts Amherst, Graduate School, College of Natural Sciences, Department of Mathematics and Statistics, Amherst, MA 01003. Offers applied mathematics (MS); mathematics (MS, PhD); statistics (MS, PhD). Terminal master's awarded for partial completion of doctoral program. *Degree requirements:* For master's, thesis or alternative; for doctorate, comprehensive exam, thesis/dissertation. *Entrance requirements:* For master's and doctorate, GRE General Test, GRE Subject Test (mathematics). Additional exam requirements/recommendations for international students: Required—TOEFL (minimum score 550 paper-based; 80 iBT), IELTS (minimum score 6.5). Electronic applications accepted.

University of Memphis, Graduate School, College of Arts and Sciences, Department of Mathematical Sciences, Memphis, TN 38152. Offers applied mathematics (MS); applied statistics (PhD); mathematics (MS, PhD); statistics (MS); teaching of mathematics (MS). *Program availability:* Part-time. *Students:* 35 full-time (11 women), 41 part-time (13 women); includes 33 minority (14 Black or African American, non-Hispanic/Latino; 12 Asian, non-Hispanic/Latino; 5 Hispanic/Latino; 2 Two or more races, non-Hispanic/Latino), 22 international. Average age 34. 35 applicants, 83% accepted, 17 enrolled. In 2018, 10 master's, 5 doctorates awarded. Terminal master's awarded for partial completion of doctoral program. *Degree requirements:* For master's, comprehensive exam, thesis or alternative; for doctorate, one foreign language, comprehensive exam, thesis/dissertation, qualifying exam, final exam. *Entrance requirements:* For master's, GRE General Test, minimum GPA of 2.5, undergraduate degree in math or statistics, two letters of recommendation; for doctorate, GRE General Test, minimum GPA of 2.5, three letters of recommendation. Additional exam requirements/recommendations for international students: Required—TOEFL (minimum score 550 paper-based; 79 iBT). *Application deadline:* For fall admission, 8/1 for domestic students, 5/1 priority date for international students; for spring admission, 12/1 for domestic students, 9/1 priority date for international students. Applications are processed on a rolling basis. Application fee: $35 ($60 for international students). Electronic applications accepted. *Expenses: Tuition, area resident:* Full-time $10,240; part-time $503 per credit hour. Tuition, state resident: full-time $10,464. Tuition, nonresident: full-time $20,224; part-time $991 per credit hour. *Required fees:* $850; $106 per credit hour. *Financial support:* Fellowships with full tuition reimbursements, research assistantships with full tuition reimbursements, teaching assistantships with full tuition reimbursements, career-related internships or fieldwork, Federal Work-Study, scholarships/grants, and unspecified assistantships available. Financial award application deadline: 2/1; financial award applicants required to submit FAFSA. *Faculty research:* Combinatorics, ergodic theory, graph theory, Ramsey theory, applied statistics. *Unit head:* Dr. Irena Lasiecka, Chair, 901-678-2482, Fax: 901-678-2480, E-mail: lasiecka@memphis.edu. *Application contact:* Dr. Fernanda Botelho, Graduate Advising Coordinator, 901-678-3131, Fax: 901-678-2480, E-mail: mbotelho@memphis.edu.
Website: https://www.memphis.edu/msci

University of Michigan–Dearborn, College of Arts, Sciences, and Letters, Master of Science in Applied and Computational Mathematics Program, Dearborn, MI 48128. Offers MS. *Program availability:* Part-time, evening/weekend. *Faculty:* 9 full-time (4 women). *Students:* 3 full-time (2 women), 9 part-time (2 women); includes 4 minority (1 Black or African American, non-Hispanic/Latino; 2 Asian, non-Hispanic/Latino; 1 Hispanic/Latino). Average age 29. 9 applicants, 78% accepted, 5 enrolled. In 2018, 5 master's awarded. *Degree requirements:* For master's, thesis or alternative. *Entrance requirements:* For master's, 3 letters of recommendation, minimum GPA of 3.0, 2 years of course work in math. Additional exam requirements/recommendations for international students: Required—TOEFL (minimum score 560 paper-based; 84 iBT), IELTS (minimum score 6.5). *Application deadline:* For fall admission, 8/1 priority date for domestic students, 5/1 priority date for international students; for winter admission, 12/1 priority date for domestic students, 9/1 priority date for international students; for spring admission, 4/1 priority date for domestic students, 1/1 priority date for international students. Applications are processed on a rolling basis. Application fee: $60. Electronic applications accepted. *Expenses:* FT in-state: $12,140; FT out-state: $20,708. *Financial support:* In 2018–19, 2 students received support. Scholarships/grants and non-resident tuition scholarships available. Financial award application deadline: 3/1; financial award applicants required to submit FAFSA. *Faculty research:* Stochastic differential equations, inverse problems, applied harmonic analysis, applied statistics, numerical analysis. *Unit head:* Dr. Yulia Hristova, Director, 313-593-5175, E-mail: yuliagh@umich.edu. *Application contact:* Office of Graduate Studies, 313-583-6321, E-mail: umd-graduatestudies@umich.edu.
Website: https://umdearborn.edu/casl/graduate-programs/programs/master-science-applied-and-computational-mathematics

University of Minnesota, Duluth, Graduate School, Swenson College of Science and Engineering, Department of Mathematics and Statistics, Duluth, MN 55812-2496. Offers applied and computational mathematics (MS). *Program availability:* Part-time. *Degree requirements:* For master's, thesis or alternative. *Entrance requirements:* For master's, GRE General Test, minimum GPA of 3.0. Additional exam requirements/recommendations for international students: Required—TOEFL (minimum score 550 paper-based; 79 iBT); Recommended—TWE. Electronic applications accepted. *Faculty research:* Discrete mathematics, diagnostic markers, combinatorics, biostatistics, mathematical modeling and scientific computation.

University of Missouri, Office of Research and Graduate Studies, College of Arts and Science, Department of Mathematics, Columbia, MO 65211. Offers applied mathematics (MS); mathematics (MA, PhD). *Entrance requirements:* For master's and doctorate, GRE General Test, minimum GPA of 3.0; bachelor's degree from accredited institution. *Faculty research:* Algebraic geometry, analysis (real, complex, functional and harmonic), analytic functions, applied mathematics, financial mathematics and mathematics of insurance, commutative rings, scattering theory, differential equations (ordinary and partial), differential geometry, dynamical systems, general relativity, mathematical physics, number theory, probabilistic analysis and topology.

University of New Hampshire, Graduate School, College of Engineering and Physical Sciences, Department of Mathematics and Statistics, Durham, NH 03824. Offers applied mathematics (PhD); industrial statistics (Certificate); mathematics (MS, MST, PhD); mathematics education (PhD); mathematics: applied mathematics (MS); mathematics: statistics (MS, PhD). Terminal master's awarded for partial completion of doctoral program. *Entrance requirements:* Additional exam requirements/recommendations for international students: Required—TOEFL (minimum score 550 paper-based; 80 iBT). Electronic applications accepted.

The University of North Carolina at Charlotte, College of Liberal Arts and Sciences, Department of Mathematics and Statistics, Charlotte, NC 28223-0001. Offers applied mathematics (PhD); mathematics (MS). *Program availability:* Part-time, evening/weekend. *Students:* 48 full-time (20 women), 20 part-time (13 women); includes 8 minority (2 Black or African American, non-Hispanic/Latino; 5 Asian, non-Hispanic/Latino; 1 Hispanic/Latino), 38 international. Average age 29. 48 applicants, 92% accepted, 20 enrolled. In 2018, 14 master's, 6 doctorates awarded. Terminal master's awarded for partial completion of doctoral program. *Entrance requirements:* For master's, GRE General Test, bachelor's degree, or its U.S. equivalent, from regionally-accredited college or university; minimum overall GPA of 3.0 on all previous work beyond high school; for doctorate, GRE General Test, at least 27 hours of courses in the mathematical sciences, as approved by the department Graduate Committee, with minimum C grades and minimum overall GPA in mathematics or statistics courses of 3.0. Additional exam requirements/recommendations for international students: Required—TOEFL (minimum score 523 paper-based; 70 iBT), IELTS (minimum score

6), TOEFL (minimum score 523 paper-based, 70 iBT) or IELTS (6). *Application deadline:* Applications are processed on a rolling basis. Application fee: $75. Electronic applications accepted. Tuition and fees vary according to course load and program. *Financial support:* Fellowships, research assistantships, teaching assistantships, career-related internships or fieldwork, Federal Work-Study, institutionally sponsored loans, scholarships/grants, and unspecified assistantships available. Support available to part-time students. Financial award application deadline: 3/1; financial award applicants required to submit FAFSA. *Total annual research expenditures:* $844,249. *Unit head:* Dr. Yuanan Diao, Chair, 704-687-0620, E-mail: ydiao@uncc.edu. *Application contact:* Kathy B. Giddings, Director of Graduate Admissions, 704-687-5503, Fax: 704-687-1668, E-mail: gradadm@uncc.edu.
Website: http://math.uncc.edu/

University of Northern Iowa, Graduate College, College of Humanities, Arts and Sciences, Department of Mathematics, PSM Program in Industrial Mathematics, Cedar Falls, IA 50614. Offers PSM.

University of Notre Dame, The Graduate School, College of Science, Department of Mathematics, Notre Dame, IN 46556. Offers algebra (PhD); algebraic geometry (PhD); applied mathematics (MSAM); complex analysis (PhD); differential geometry (PhD); logic (PhD); partial differential equations (PhD); topology (PhD). Terminal master's awarded for partial completion of doctoral program. *Degree requirements:* For doctorate, one foreign language, thesis/dissertation, qualifying exam. *Entrance requirements:* For master's and doctorate, GRE General Test, GRE Subject Test. Additional exam requirements/recommendations for international students: Required—TOEFL (minimum score 600 paper-based; 80 iBT). Electronic applications accepted. *Faculty research:* Algebra, analysis, geometry/topology, logic, applied math.

University of Pennsylvania, School of Arts and Sciences, Graduate Group in Applied Mathematics and Computational Science, Philadelphia, PA 19104. Offers PhD. *Faculty:* 32 full-time (4 women), 3 part-time/adjunct (0 women). *Students:* 40 full-time (9 women), 36 international. Average age 25. 203 applicants, 23% accepted, 15 enrolled. In 2018, 2 doctorates awarded. Application fee: $80.
Website: http://www.amcs.upenn.edu

University of Pittsburgh, Kenneth P. Dietrich School of Arts and Sciences, Department of Mathematics, Pittsburgh, PA 15260. Offers applied mathematics (MA, MS); mathematics (MA, MS, PhD). *Program availability:* Part-time. Terminal master's awarded for partial completion of doctoral program. *Degree requirements:* For master's, thesis; for doctorate, comprehensive exam, thesis/dissertation. *Entrance requirements:* For master's and doctorate, GRE General Test; GRE Subject Test (recommended), minimum GPA of 3.0. Additional exam requirements/recommendations for international students: Required—TOEFL (minimum score 90 iBT) or IELTS (minimum score 7.0). Electronic applications accepted. *Faculty research:* Algebra, combinatorics, and geometry; analysis and partial differential equations; applied analysis; complex biological systems; mathematical finance.

University of Puerto Rico–Mayagüez, Graduate Studies, College of Arts and Sciences, Department of Mathematical Sciences, Mayagüez, PR 00681-9000. Offers applied mathematics (MS); pre-college math education (MS); pure mathematics (MS); scientific computing (MS); statistics (MS). *Program availability:* Part-time. *Degree requirements:* For master's, one foreign language, comprehensive exam, thesis. *Entrance requirements:* For master's, undergraduate degree in mathematics or its equivalent. Electronic applications accepted. *Faculty research:* Automata theory, linear algebra, logic.

University of Rhode Island, Graduate School, College of Arts and Sciences, Department of Mathematics, Kingston, RI 02881. Offers applied analysis (MS); applied mathematical sciences (PhD); combinatorics and graph theory (MS); complex dynamical systems (MS); difference equations (MS); numerical analysis (MS); pure mathematics (PhD). *Program availability:* Part-time. *Faculty:* 24 full-time (8 women). *Students:* 17 full-time (7 women), 6 part-time (1 woman); includes 3 minority (2 Black or African American, non-Hispanic/Latino; 1 Hispanic/Latino), 1 international. 27 applicants, 81% accepted, 8 enrolled. In 2018, 3 master's, 3 doctorates awarded. *Entrance requirements:* For master's and doctorate, 2 letters of reference, one of which must address the candidate's abilities to teach in English (3 for international candidates). Additional exam requirements/recommendations for international students: Required—TOEFL. *Application deadline:* For fall admission, 7/15 for domestic students, 2/1 for international students; for spring admission, 11/15 for domestic students, 7/15 for international students. Application fee: $65. Electronic applications accepted. *Expenses:* Tuition, area resident: Full-time $13,226; part-time $735 per credit. Tuition, state resident: full-time $13,226; part-time $735 per credit. Tuition, nonresident: full-time $25,854; part-time $1436 per credit. *International tuition:* $25,854 full-time. *Required fees:* $1698; $50 per credit. $35 per semester. One-time fee: $165. *Financial support:* In 2018–19, 14 teaching assistantships with tuition reimbursements (averaging $17,996 per year) were awarded. Financial award application deadline: 2/1; financial award applicants required to submit FAFSA. *Unit head:* Dr. James Baglama, Chair, 401-874-2709, Fax: 401-874-4454, E-mail: jbaglama@math.uri.edu. *Application contact:* Dr. Tom Sharland, Director of Graduate Studies, 401-874-2314, E-mail: tsharland@uri.edu.
Website: http://www.math.uri.edu/

University of Southern California, Graduate School, Dana and David Dornsife College of Letters, Arts and Sciences, Department of Mathematics, Los Angeles, CA 90089. Offers applied mathematics (MA, MS, PhD); mathematical finance (MS); mathematics (MA, PhD); statistics (MS). *Program availability:* Part-time. Terminal master's awarded for partial completion of doctoral program. *Degree requirements:* For master's, comprehensive exam (for some programs), thesis (for some programs); for doctorate, one foreign language, comprehensive exam, thesis/dissertation. *Entrance requirements:* For master's, GRE General Test, GMAT; for doctorate, GRE General Test, GRE Subject Test (mathematics). Additional exam requirements/recommendations for international students: Required—TOEFL (minimum score 100 iBT). Electronic applications accepted. *Faculty research:* Algebra, algebraic geometry and number theory, analysis/partial differential equations, applied mathematics, financial mathematics, probability, combinatorics and statistics.

University of South Florida, College of Arts and Sciences, Department of Mathematics and Statistics, Tampa, FL 33620-9951. Offers mathematics (MA, PhD), including pure and applied mathematics, statistics (PhD); statistics (MA). *Program availability:* Part-time, evening/weekend. *Faculty:* 24 full-time (2 women). *Students:* 65 full-time (24 women), 16 part-time (3 women); includes 8 minority (2 Black or African American, non-Hispanic/Latino; 2 Asian, non-Hispanic/Latino; 1 Hispanic/Latino; 3 Two or more races, non-Hispanic/Latino), 43 international. Average age 29. 77 applicants, 57% accepted, 22 enrolled. In 2018, 14 master's, 11 doctorates awarded. Terminal master's awarded for partial completion of doctoral program. *Degree requirements:* For master's, comprehensive exam, thesis (for some programs); for doctorate, comprehensive exam, thesis/dissertation. *Entrance requirements:* For master's, GRE (minimum 55th percentile Quantitative score; Verbal and Analytical Writing scores also considered), BA in mathematical sciences, statistics, or related area. 3.00 GPA in undergraduate math

courses, and in Elementary Abstract Algebra, Bridge to Abstract Mathematics, and Intermediate Analysis (for Math) 3.50 GPA (for Statistics). 3 letters of recommendation; Dept Application with goals statement; TA application; for doctorate, GRE (minimum 55th percentile Quantitative; Verbal and Analytical Writing scores also considered), minimum GPA of 3.5 in graduate mathematics courses, three letters of recommendation, statement of goals, master's or bachelor's degree in mathematical sciences or related field. Department Application, TA Application. Additional exam requirements/recommendations for international students: Required—TOEFL, TOEFL (minimum score 550 paper-based; 79 iBT) or IELTS (minimum score 6.5). *Application deadline:* For fall admission, 2/1 priority date for domestic and international students; for spring admission, 10/1 priority date for domestic students, 9/15 for international students. Application fee: $30. Electronic applications accepted. *Expenses:* Tuition, state resident: full-time $6350. Tuition, nonresident: full-time $19,048. *International tuition:* $19,048 full-time. *Required fees:* $2079. *Financial support:* In 2018–19, 9 students received support, including 6 research assistantships (averaging $16,990 per year), 55 teaching assistantships with partial tuition reimbursements available (averaging $13,742 per year); unspecified assistantships also available. Financial award application deadline: 2/1. *Faculty research:* Mathematics: algebra and number theory, harmonic and complex analysis, approximation theory, theory of orthogonal polynomials, Banach space theory and operator theory, differential equations and nonlinear analysis, discrete mathematics, geometry and topology; statistics: linear and nonlinear statistical models for health sciences, operations research problems, economic systems; stochastic control problems; dynamic reliability analysis and control. *Total annual research expenditures:* $654,045. *Unit head:* Dr. Leslaw Skrzypek, Associate Professor and Chairperson, 813-974-1268, Fax: 813-974-2700, E-mail: skrzypek@usf.edu. *Application contact:* Dr. Brian Curtin, Professor/Director of Graduate Mathematics Program, 813-974-4929, E-mail: bcurtin@usf.edu.
Website: http://math.usf.edu/

The University of Tennessee, Graduate School, College of Arts and Sciences, Department of Mathematics, Knoxville, TN 37996. Offers applied mathematics (MS); mathematical ecology (PhD); mathematics (M Math, MS, PhD). *Program availability:* Part-time. *Degree requirements:* For master's, thesis or alternative; for doctorate, one foreign language, thesis/dissertation. *Entrance requirements:* For master's and doctorate, minimum GPA of 2.7. Additional exam requirements/recommendations for international students: Required—TOEFL. Electronic applications accepted.

The University of Tennessee at Chattanooga, Program in Mathematics, Chattanooga, TN 37403. Offers applied mathematics (MS); applied statistics (MS); mathematics education (MS); pre-professional mathematics (MS). *Program availability:* Part-time. *Degree requirements:* For master's, internship or thesis. *Entrance requirements:* For master's, GRE (if applying for an assistantship), two letters of recommendation. Additional exam requirements/recommendations for international students: Required—TOEFL (minimum score 550 paper-based; 61 iBT), IELTS (minimum score 6). Electronic applications accepted. *Expenses:* Contact institution.

The University of Texas at Arlington, Graduate School, College of Science, Department of Mathematics, Arlington, TX 76019. Offers applied math (MS); mathematics (PhD); mathematics education (MA). *Program availability:* Part-time, evening/weekend. *Degree requirements:* For master's, comprehensive exam, thesis or alternative; for doctorate, comprehensive exam, thesis/dissertation, preliminary examinations. *Entrance requirements:* For master's, GRE General Test (minimum score 350 verbal, 650 quantitative); for doctorate, GRE General Test (minimum score 350 verbal, 700 quantitative), 30 hours of graduate course work in mathematics, minimum GPA of 3.0 in last 60 hours of course work. Additional exam requirements/recommendations for international students: Required—TOEFL (minimum score 550 paper-based; 79 iBT). Electronic applications accepted. *Faculty research:* Algebra, combinatorics and geometry, applied mathematics and mathematical biology, computational mathematics, mathematics education, probability and statistics.

The University of Texas at Austin, Graduate School, Program in Computational Science, Engineering, and Mathematics, Austin, TX 78712-1111. Offers MS, PhD. Terminal master's awarded for partial completion of doctoral program. *Degree requirements:* For master's, thesis optional; for doctorate, thesis/dissertation, 3 area qualifying exams. Electronic applications accepted.

The University of Texas at Dallas, School of Natural Sciences and Mathematics, Department of Mathematical Sciences, Richardson, TX 75080. Offers actuarial science (MS); mathematics (MS, PhD), including applied mathematics, data science (MS), engineering mathematics (MS), mathematics (MS); statistics (MS, PhD). *Program availability:* Part-time, evening/weekend. *Faculty:* 29 full-time (6 women), 3 part-time/adjunct (0 women). *Students:* 155 full-time (58 women), 35 part-time (9 women); includes 34 minority (4 Black or African American, non-Hispanic/Latino; 19 Asian, non-Hispanic/Latino; 7 Hispanic/Latino; 4 Two or more races, non-Hispanic/Latino), 116 international. Average age 32. 264 applicants, 37% accepted, 48 enrolled. In 2018, 48 master's, 11 doctorates awarded. *Degree requirements:* For master's, thesis optional; for doctorate, thesis/dissertation. *Entrance requirements:* For master's, GRE General Test, minimum GPA of 3.0 in upper-level course work in field; for doctorate, GRE General Test, minimum GPA of 3.5 in upper-level course work in field. Additional exam requirements/recommendations for international students: Required—TOEFL (minimum score 550 paper-based). *Application deadline:* For fall admission, 7/15 for domestic students, 5/1 priority date for international students; for spring admission, 11/15 for domestic students, 9/1 priority date for international students. Applications are processed on a rolling basis. Application fee: $50 ($100 for international students). Electronic applications accepted. *Expenses: Tuition, area resident:* Full-time $13,458. Tuition, state resident: full-time $13,458. Tuition, nonresident: full-time $26,852. *International tuition:* $26,852 full-time. Tuition and fees vary according to course load. *Financial support:* In 2018–19, 92 students received support, including 10 research assistantships (averaging $24,110 per year), 89 teaching assistantships with partial tuition reimbursements available (averaging $17,110 per year); fellowships, career-related internships or fieldwork, Federal Work-Study, institutionally sponsored loans, scholarships/grants, and unspecified assistantships also available. Support available to part-time students. Financial award application deadline: 4/30; financial award applicants required to submit FAFSA. *Faculty research:* Sequential analysis, applications in semiconductor manufacturing, medical image analysis, computational anatomy, information theory, probability theory. *Unit head:* Dr. Vladimir Dragovic, Department Head, 972-883-2161, Fax: 972-883-6622, E-mail: utdmath@utdallas.edu. *Application contact:* Evangelina Bustamante, Graduate Student Coordinator, 972-883-2163, Fax: 972-883-6622, E-mail: utdmath@utdallas.edu.
Website: http://www.utdallas.edu/math

The University of Texas at San Antonio, College of Sciences, Department of Mathematics, San Antonio, TX 78249-0617. Offers applied mathematics (MS), including industrial mathematics; mathematics (MS); mathematics education (MS). *Program availability:* Part-time, evening/weekend. *Degree requirements:* For master's, comprehensive exam (for some programs), thesis or alternative. *Entrance requirements:* For master's, GRE General Test, minimum GPA of 3.0 in last 60 hours. Additional exam

Peterson's Graduate Programs in the Physical Sciences, Mathematics, Agricultural Sciences, the Environment & Natural Resources 2020

www.petersons.com   **183**

requirements/recommendations for international students: Required—TOEFL (minimum score 550 paper-based; 79 iBT), IELTS (minimum score 6.5). Electronic applications accepted. *Faculty research:* Differential equations, functional analysis, numerical analysis, number theory, logic.

The University of Toledo, College of Graduate Studies, College of Natural Sciences and Mathematics, Department of Mathematics, Toledo, OH 43606-3390. Offers applied mathematics (MS, PhD); statistics (MS, PhD). *Program availability:* Part-time. *Degree requirements:* For master's, comprehensive exam (for some programs), thesis (for some programs); for doctorate, 2 foreign languages, thesis/dissertation. *Entrance requirements:* For master's and doctorate, GRE General Test, GRE Subject Test, minimum cumulative point-hour ratio of 2.7 for all previous academic work, three letters of recommendation, statement of purpose, transcripts from all prior institutions attended. Additional exam requirements/recommendations for international students: Required—TOEFL (minimum score 550 paper-based; 80 iBT). Electronic applications accepted.

University of Washington, Graduate School, College of Arts and Sciences, Department of Applied Mathematics, Seattle, WA 98195. Offers MS, PhD. Terminal master's awarded for partial completion of doctoral program. *Degree requirements:* For master's, thesis optional; for doctorate, thesis/dissertation. *Entrance requirements:* For master's and doctorate, GRE, minimum GPA of 3.0. Additional exam requirements/recommendations for international students: Required—TOEFL. Electronic applications accepted. *Faculty research:* Mathematical modeling for physical, biological, social, and engineering sciences; development of mathematical methods for analysis, including perturbation, asymptotic, transform, vocational, and numerical methods.

University of Washington, Graduate School, College of Arts and Sciences, Department of Mathematics, Seattle, WA 98195. Offers mathematics (MA, MS, PhD); numerical analysis (MS); optimization (MS). *Program availability:* Part-time. Terminal master's awarded for partial completion of doctoral program. *Degree requirements:* For master's, thesis optional; for doctorate, 2 foreign languages, thesis/dissertation. *Entrance requirements:* For master's, GRE, minimum GPA of 3.0; for doctorate, GRE General Test, GRE Subject Test (mathematics), minimum GPA of 3.0. Additional exam requirements/recommendations for international students: Required—TOEFL. Electronic applications accepted. *Faculty research:* Algebra, analysis, probability, combinatorics and geometry.

University of Waterloo, Graduate Studies and Postdoctoral Affairs, Faculty of Mathematics, Department of Applied Mathematics, Waterloo, ON N2L 3G1, Canada. Offers M Math, PhD. *Program availability:* Part-time. *Degree requirements:* For master's, research paper or thesis; for doctorate, thesis/dissertation. *Entrance requirements:* For master's, honors degree in field, minimum B+ average; for doctorate, master's degree, minimum B+ average. Additional exam requirements/recommendations for international students: Required—TOEFL, IELTS, PTE. *Application deadline:* For fall admission, 2/1 for domestic and international students. Applications are processed on a rolling basis. Application fee: $125 Canadian dollars. Electronic applications accepted. *Financial support:* Research assistantships and teaching assistantships available. *Faculty research:* Differential equations, quantum theory, statistical mechanics, fluid mechanics, relativity, control theory.
Website: https://uwaterloo.ca/applied-mathematics/

The University of Western Ontario, School of Graduate and Postdoctoral Studies, Faculty of Science, Department of Applied Mathematics, London, ON N6A 3K7, Canada. Offers applied mathematics (M Sc, PhD); theoretical physics (PhD). *Degree requirements:* For master's, thesis or alternative; for doctorate, comprehensive exam, thesis/dissertation. *Entrance requirements:* For master's and doctorate, minimum B average. Additional exam requirements/recommendations for international students: Required—TOEFL. *Faculty research:* Fluid dynamics, mathematical and computational methods, theoretical physics.

University of Wisconsin–Milwaukee, Graduate School, College of Letters and Science, Department of Mathematical Sciences, Milwaukee, WI 53201-0413. Offers mathematics (MS, PhD), including actuarial science, algebra (PhD), applied and computational mathematics (PhD), atmospheric science, foundations of advanced studies (MS), industrial mathematics, probability and statistics (PhD), standard mathematics (MS), statistics (MS), topology (PhD). *Students:* 56 full-time (11 women), 10 part-time (2 women); includes 4 minority (2 Black or African American, non-Hispanic/Latino; 1 Asian, non-Hispanic/Latino; 1 Two or more races, non-Hispanic/Latino), 28 international. Average age 30. 136 applicants, 22% accepted, 20 enrolled. In 2018, 16 master's, 8 doctorates awarded. *Degree requirements:* For master's, comprehensive exam, thesis optional; for doctorate, 2 foreign languages, thesis/dissertation. *Entrance requirements:* Additional exam requirements/recommendations for international students: Required—TOEFL (minimum score 550 paper-based; 79 iBT), IELTS (minimum score 6.5). *Application deadline:* For fall admission, 1/1 priority date for domestic students; for spring admission, 9/1 for domestic students. Application fee: $56 ($96 for international students). Electronic applications accepted. *Financial support:* Fellowships, research assistantships, teaching assistantships, career-related internships or fieldwork, health care benefits, and unspecified assistantships available. Support available to part-time students. Financial award application deadline: 4/15; financial award applicants required to submit FAFSA. *Faculty research:* Algebra, applied mathematics, atmospheric science, probability and statistics, topology. *Unit head:* Richard Stockbridge, Department Chair, 414-229-4568, E-mail: stockbri@uwm.edu. *Application contact:* General Information Contact, 414-229-4982, Fax: 414-229-6967, E-mail: gradschool@uwm.edu.
Website: http://www.uwm.edu/dept/math/

University of Wisconsin–Stout, Graduate School, College of Science, Technology, Engineering and Mathematics, Program in Industrial and Applied Mathematics, Menomonie, WI 54751. Offers PSM. *Program availability:* Online learning.

Utah State University, School of Graduate Studies, College of Science, Department of Mathematics and Statistics, Logan, UT 84322. Offers industrial mathematics (MS); mathematical sciences (PhD); mathematics (M Math, MS); statistics (MS). *Program availability:* Part-time. Terminal master's awarded for partial completion of doctoral program. *Degree requirements:* For master's, thesis optional, qualifying exam; for doctorate, one foreign language, comprehensive exam, thesis/dissertation. *Entrance requirements:* For master's and doctorate, GRE General Test, minimum GPA of 3.0. Additional exam requirements/recommendations for international students: Required—TOEFL. *Faculty research:* Differential equations, computational mathematics, dynamical systems, probability and statistics, pure mathematics.

Virginia Commonwealth University, Graduate School, College of Humanities and Sciences, Department of Mathematics and Applied Mathematics, Richmond, VA 23284-9005. Offers applied mathematics (MS). *Degree requirements:* For master's, thesis optional. *Entrance requirements:* For master's, GRE General Test, GRE Subject Test, 30 undergraduate semester credits in the mathematical sciences or closely-related fields. Additional exam requirements/recommendations for international students: Required—TOEFL (minimum score 600 paper-based; 100 iBT); Recommended—IELTS (minimum score 6.5). Electronic applications accepted. *Faculty research:* Mathematics, applied mathematics.

Washington State University, College of Arts and Sciences, Department of Mathematics, Pullman, WA 99164. Offers applied mathematics (MS, PhD); mathematics (MS, PhD); mathematics teaching (MS, PhD). Programs offered at the Pullman campus. *Program availability:* Part-time. Terminal master's awarded for partial completion of doctoral program. *Degree requirements:* For master's, comprehensive exam (for some programs), thesis or alternative, oral exam, project; for doctorate, 2 foreign languages, comprehensive exam, thesis/dissertation, oral exam, written exam. *Entrance requirements:* For master's and doctorate, minimum GPA of 3.0, 3 letters of recommendation. Additional exam requirements/recommendations for international students: Required—TOEFL (minimum score 600 paper-based; 100 iBT) or IELTS (minimum score 7). Electronic applications accepted. *Faculty research:* Computational mathematics, operations research, modeling in the natural sciences, applied statistics.

Wayne State University, College of Liberal Arts and Sciences, Department of Mathematics, Detroit, MI 48202. Offers applied mathematics (MA); mathematical statistics (MA); mathematics (MA, MS, PhD). *Faculty:* 18. *Students:* 33 full-time (12 women), 17 part-time (5 women); includes 7 minority (1 Black or African American, non-Hispanic/Latino; 2 Asian, non-Hispanic/Latino; 1 Hispanic/Latino; 3 Two or more races, non-Hispanic/Latino), 28 international. Average age 30. 70 applicants, 40% accepted, 8 enrolled. In 2018, 16 master's, 4 doctorates awarded. *Degree requirements:* For master's, comprehensive exam, thesis (for some programs), essays, oral exams; for doctorate, comprehensive exam, thesis/dissertation. *Entrance requirements:* For master's, twelve semester credits in mathematics beyond sophomore calculus, including advanced calculus and linear or modern algebra; for doctorate, master's degree in mathematics or equivalent level of advancement. Additional exam requirements/recommendations for international students: Required—TOEFL (minimum score 550 paper-based; 79 iBT), TWE (minimum score 5.5), Michigan English Language Assessment Battery (minimum score 85); Recommended—IELTS (minimum score 6.5). Application fee: $50. Electronic applications accepted. *Financial support:* In 2018–19, 33 students received support, including 2 fellowships with tuition reimbursements available (averaging $20,000 per year), 3 research assistantships with tuition reimbursements available (averaging $21,107 per year), 25 teaching assistantships with tuition reimbursements available (averaging $20,216 per year); scholarships/grants, health care benefits, and unspecified assistantships also available. Financial award applicants required to submit FAFSA. *Faculty research:* Algebra, analysis, applied mathematics, geometry and topology, probability and statistics. *Unit head:* Dr. Hengguang Li, Associate Professor and Chair, 313-577-2479, E-mail: li@wayne.edu. *Application contact:* Dr. Hengguang Li, Associate Professor and Chair, 313-577-2479, E-mail: li@wayne.edu.
Website: http://clas.wayne.edu/math/

West Chester University of Pennsylvania, College of the Sciences and Mathematics, Department of Mathematics, West Chester, PA 19383. Offers applied and computational mathematics (MS); applied statistics (MS, Certificate); mathematics (MA, Teaching Certificate); mathematics education (MA). *Program availability:* Part-time, evening/weekend. *Degree requirements:* For master's, comprehensive exam or thesis (for MA). *Entrance requirements:* For master's, GMAT or GRE General Test (for MA in mathematics, may be waived under certain circumstances), interview (for MA in mathematics); for other advanced degree, GMAT or GRE General Test (for Certificate in applied statistics). Additional exam requirements/recommendations for international students: Required—TOEFL or IELTS. Electronic applications accepted. *Faculty research:* Teachers teaching with technology in service training program, biostatistics, hierarchical linear models, clustered binary outcome data, mathematics biology, stochastic analysis.

Western Michigan University, Graduate College, College of Arts and Sciences, Department of Mathematics, Kalamazoo, MI 49008. Offers applied and computational mathematics (MS); mathematics education (MA, PhD), including collegiate mathematics education (PhD). *Degree requirements:* For doctorate, one foreign language, thesis/dissertation.

Wichita State University, Graduate School, Fairmount College of Liberal Arts and Sciences, Department of Mathematics, Statistics and Physics, Wichita, KS 67260. Offers applied mathematics (PhD); mathematics (MS); physics (MS). *Program availability:* Part-time. *Unit head:* Dr. Ziqi Sun, Interim Chair, 316-978-3160, Fax: 316-978-3748, E-mail: ziqi.sun@wichita.edu. *Application contact:* Jordan Oleson, Admissions Coordinator, 316-978-3095, Fax: 316-978-3253, E-mail: jordan.oleson@wichita.edu.
Website: http://www.wichita.edu/math

Worcester Polytechnic Institute, Graduate Admissions, Department of Mathematical Sciences, Worcester, MA 01609-2280. Offers applied mathematics (MS); applied statistics (MS); financial mathematics (MS); industrial mathematics (MS); mathematical sciences (PhD, Graduate Certificate); mathematics for educators (MME). *Program availability:* Part-time, evening/weekend. *Students:* 56 full-time (26 women), 34 part-time (13 women); includes 3 minority (1 Black or African American, non-Hispanic/Latino; 1 Asian, non-Hispanic/Latino; 1 Hispanic/Latino), 51 international. Average age 27. 284 applicants, 63% accepted, 33 enrolled. In 2018, 35 master's, 6 doctorates awarded. Terminal master's awarded for partial completion of doctoral program. *Degree requirements:* For master's, thesis (for some programs); for doctorate, comprehensive exam, thesis/dissertation. *Entrance requirements:* For master's, GRE Subject Test in math (for teaching assistantship; strongly recommended for all others), 3 letters of recommendation; for doctorate, GRE General Test, GRE Subject Test (math), 3 letters of recommendation. Additional exam requirements/recommendations for international students: Required—TOEFL (minimum score 563 paper-based; 84 iBT), IELTS (minimum score 7). *Application deadline:* For fall admission, 1/1 priority date for domestic students, 1/1 for international students; for spring admission, 10/1 priority date for domestic students, 10/1 for international students. Applications are processed on a rolling basis. Application fee: $70. Electronic applications accepted. *Financial support:* Fellowships, research assistantships, teaching assistantships, career-related internships or fieldwork, institutionally sponsored loans, scholarships/grants, and unspecified assistantships available. Financial award application deadline: 1/1. *Unit head:* Dr. Luca Capogna, Department Head, 508-831-5241, Fax: 508-831-5824, E-mail: lcapogna@wpi.edu. *Application contact:* Dr. Sarah Olsen, Graduate Coordinator, 508-831-5241, Fax: 508-831-5824, E-mail: sdolsen@wpi.edu.
Website: https://www.wpi.edu/academics/departments/mathematical-sciences

Wright State University, Graduate School, College of Science and Mathematics, Department of Mathematics and Statistics, Program in Applied Mathematics, Dayton, OH 45435. Offers MS. *Degree requirements:* For master's, comprehensive exam. *Entrance requirements:* For master's, bachelor's degree in mathematics or related field. Additional exam requirements/recommendations for international students: Required—TOEFL. *Faculty research:* Control theory, ordinary differential equations, partial differential equations, numerical analysis, mathematical modeling.

Yale University, Graduate School of Arts and Sciences, Program in Applied Mathematics, New Haven, CT 06520. Offers M Phil, MS, PhD. *Entrance requirements:* For doctorate, GRE General Test.

York University, Faculty of Graduate Studies, Faculty of Science, Program in Mathematics and Statistics, Toronto, ON M3J 1P3, Canada. Offers industrial and applied mathematics (M Sc); mathematics and statistics (MA, PhD). *Program availability:* Part-time. *Degree requirements:* For master's, thesis optional; for doctorate, one foreign language, comprehensive exam, thesis/dissertation. Electronic applications accepted.

Youngstown State University, College of Graduate Studies, College of Science, Technology, Engineering and Mathematics, Department of Mathematics and Statistics, Youngstown, OH 44555-0001. Offers actuarial science (MS); applied mathematics (MS); computer science (MS); mathematics (MS); secondary/community college mathematics (MS); statistics (MS). *Program availability:* Part-time. *Degree requirements:* For master's, comprehensive exam, thesis optional. *Entrance requirements:* For master's, minimum GPA of 2.7 in computer science and mathematics. Additional exam requirements/recommendations for international students: Required—TOEFL. *Faculty research:* Regression analysis, numerical analysis, statistics, Markov chain, topology and fuzzy sets.

Applied Statistics

American University, College of Arts and Sciences, Department of Mathematics and Statistics, Washington, DC 22016-8050. Offers applied statistics (Certificate); biostatistics (MS); data science (Certificate); mathematics (MA); professional science: quantitative analysis (MS); statistics (MS). *Program availability:* Part-time, evening/weekend. *Faculty:* 36 full-time (13 women), 8 part-time/adjunct (1 woman). *Students:* 19 full-time (4 women), 21 part-time (9 women); includes 14 minority (7 Black or African American, non-Hispanic/Latino; 2 Asian, non-Hispanic/Latino; 4 Hispanic/Latino; 1 Two or more races, non-Hispanic/Latino), 10 international. Average age 29. 64 applicants, 92% accepted, 19 enrolled. In 2018, 10 master's, 9 other advanced degrees awarded. *Degree requirements:* For master's, comprehensive exam, thesis or alternative. *Entrance requirements:* For master's, GRE; please see website: https://www.american.edu/cas/mathstat/, statement of purpose, transcripts, 2 letters of recommendation, resume; for Certificate, bachelor's degree, statement of purpose, transcripts, resume. Additional exam requirements/recommendations for international students: Required—TOEFL (minimum score 600 paper-based; 100 iBT). Application fee: $55. *Expenses:* Contact institution. *Financial support:* Scholarships/grants and unspecified assistantships available. Financial award applicants required to submit FAFSA. *Unit head:* Dr. Stephen Casey, Department Chair, 202-885-3120, E-mail: mathstat@american.edu. *Application contact:* Jonathan Harper, Assistant Director, Graduate Recruitment, 202-855-3620, E-mail: casgrad@american.edu.
Website: http://www.american.edu/cas/mathstat/

Bay Path University, Program in Applied Data Science, Longmeadow, MA 01106-2292. Offers MS. *Program availability:* Part-time, 100% online. *Students:* 5 full-time (2 women), 12 part-time (6 women); includes 8 minority (4 Black or African American, non-Hispanic/Latino; 2 Asian, non-Hispanic/Latino; 2 Hispanic/Latino). Average age 37. *Application deadline:* Applications are processed on a rolling basis. Electronic applications accepted. Application fee is waived when completed online. *Expenses:* Contact institution. *Financial support:* Applicants required to submit FAFSA. *Unit head:* Ning Jia, DIRECTOR, MS APPLIED DATA SCIENCE, E-mail: njia@baypath.edu. *Application contact:* Elise Carrier, Assistant Director of Graduate Admissions, 413-565-1621, Fax: 413-565-1250, E-mail: ecarrier@baypath.edu.
Website: https://www.baypath.edu/academics/graduate-programs/applied-data-science-ms/

Bowling Green State University, Graduate College, College of Business, Program in Applied Statistics, Bowling Green, OH 43403. Offers MS. Program offered jointly with Department of Mathematics and Statistics. *Program availability:* Part-time. *Degree requirements:* For master's, thesis or alternative. *Entrance requirements:* For master's, GRE General Test. Additional exam requirements/recommendations for international students: Required—TOEFL. Electronic applications accepted. *Faculty research:* Reliability, linear models, time series, statistical quality control.

Brigham Young University, Graduate Studies, College of Physical and Mathematical Sciences, Department of Statistics, Provo, UT 84602-1001. Offers applied statistics (MS). *Faculty:* 17 full-time (3 women). *Students:* 24 full-time (9 women); includes 2 minority (both Asian, non-Hispanic/Latino). Average age 25. 17 applicants, 18% accepted, 3 enrolled. In 2018, 17 master's awarded. *Degree requirements:* For master's, comprehensive exam, thesis (for some programs). *Entrance requirements:* For master's, GRE General Test, bachelor's degree from an accredited US university or equivalent, minimum 3.3 undergraduate GPA, 2 methods courses beyond introductory statistics, 2 courses in calculus-based statistical theory, differential calculus, integral calculus, multivariate calculus, a course in linear algebra. Additional exam requirements/recommendations for international students: Required—TOEFL (minimum score 580 paper-based; 85 iBT). *Application deadline:* For fall admission, 2/1 for domestic and international students. Application fee: $50. Electronic applications accepted. *Expenses:* Contact institution. *Financial support:* In 2018–19, 15 students received support, including 11 research assistantships (averaging $11,500 per year), 10 teaching assistantships (averaging $11,500 per year); scholarships/grants and tuition waivers also available. Financial award application deadline: 3/1. *Faculty research:* Statistical genetics, reliability and pollution monitoring, Bayesian methods. *Total annual research expenditures:* $750,637. *Unit head:* Dr. Scott D Grimshaw, Chair, 801-422-6251, Fax: 801-422-0635, E-mail: sdg@stat.byu.edu. *Application contact:* Dr. David B Dahl, Graduate Coordinator, 801-422-9222, Fax: 801-422-0635, E-mail: dahl@stat.byu.edu.
Website: http://statistics.byu.edu/

California State University, East Bay, Office of Graduate Studies, College of Science, Department of Statistics and Biostatistics, Statistics Program, Hayward, CA 94542-3000. Offers actuarial science (MS); applied statistics (MS); computational statistics (MS); mathematical statistics (MS). *Program availability:* Part-time, evening/weekend. *Degree requirements:* For master's, comprehensive exam. *Entrance requirements:* For master's, letters of recommendation, minimum GPA of 3.0, math through lower-division calculus. Additional exam requirements/recommendations for international students: Required—TOEFL (minimum score 550 paper-based). Electronic applications accepted.

California State University, Long Beach, Graduate Studies, College of Natural Sciences and Mathematics, Department of Mathematics and Statistics, Long Beach, CA 90840. Offers mathematics (MS), including applied mathematics, applied statistics, mathematics education for secondary school teachers. *Program availability:* Part-time. *Degree requirements:* For master's, comprehensive exam or thesis. *Application deadline:* For fall admission, 6/1 for domestic students; for spring admission, 11/1 for domestic students. Applications are processed on a rolling basis. Application fee: $55. Electronic applications accepted. *Expenses: Required fees:* $2628 per term. Tuition and fees vary according to class time, course level, course load, degree level, campus/location and program. *Financial support:* Teaching assistantships, Federal Work-Study, institutionally sponsored loans, scholarships/grants, and traineeships available. Financial award application deadline: 3/2; financial award applicants required to submit FAFSA. *Faculty research:* Algebra, functional analysis, partial differential equations, operator theory, numerical analysis. *Unit head:* Dr. Tangan Gao, Chair, 562-985-4721, Fax: 562-985-8227, E-mail: tangan.gao@csulb.edu. *Application contact:* Dr. Tangan Gao, Chair, 562-985-4721, Fax: 562-985-8227, E-mail: tangan.gao@csulb.edu.

Clemson University, Graduate School, College of Business, John E. Walker Department of Economics, Clemson, SC 29634. Offers applied economics (PhD); applied economics and statistics (MS); economics (MA, PhD). *Faculty:* 30 full-time (4 women), 4 part-time/adjunct (1 woman). *Students:* 71 full-time (25 women), 2 part-time (1 woman); includes 4 minority (2 Black or African American, non-Hispanic/Latino; 1 Hispanic/Latino; 1 Two or more races, non-Hispanic/Latino), 39 international. Average age 27. 106 applicants, 57% accepted, 14 enrolled. In 2018, 6 master's, 12 doctorates awarded. Terminal master's awarded for partial completion of doctoral program. *Degree requirements:* For master's, thesis, 24 course hours, 6 thesis hours; for doctorate, comprehensive exam, thesis/dissertation, 42 course hours, 18 dissertation hours. *Entrance requirements:* For master's and doctorate, GRE General Test or GMAT, unofficial transcripts, letters of recommendation, courses in intermediate microeconomic theory and multivariable calculus. Additional exam requirements/recommendations for international students: Required—TOEFL (minimum score 80 paper-based; 80 iBT); Recommended—IELTS (minimum score 6.5), TSE (minimum score 54). *Application deadline:* For fall admission, 4/15 for international students; for spring admission, 10/15 for international students. Applications are processed on a rolling basis. Application fee: $80 ($90 for international students). Electronic applications accepted. *Expenses:* $6823 per semester full-time resident, $14023 per semester full-time non-resident, $833 per credit hour part-time resident, $1731 per credit hour part-time non-resident, online $1264 per credit hour, $4938 doctoral programs resident, $10405 doctoral programs non-resident, $1144 full-time graduate assistant, other fees may apply per session. *Financial support:* In 2018–19, 68 students received support, including 12 fellowships with full and partial tuition reimbursements available (averaging $4,291 per year), 14 teaching assistantships with full and partial tuition reimbursements available (averaging $13,874 per year); unspecified assistantships also available. *Faculty research:* Public economics, public choice and political economy; econometrics (focus on data envelope analysis), industrial organization (focus on pricing), labor and development economics, international economics (focus on free trade agreements). *Total annual research expenditures:* $42,200. *Unit head:* Dr. Scott Baier, Department Chair, 864-656-4534, E-mail: sbaier@clemson.edu. *Application contact:* Dr. Curtis Simon, PhD Program Coordinator, 864-656-3966, E-mail: cjsmn@clemson.edu.
Website: http://economics.clemson.edu/

Cleveland State University, College of Graduate Studies, College of Sciences and Health Professions, Department of Mathematics, Cleveland, OH 44115. Offers applied statistics (MS); mathematics (MS). *Program availability:* Part-time, evening/weekend. *Faculty:* 17 full-time (7 women), 1 part-time/adjunct (0 women). *Students:* 22 full-time (9 women), 18 part-time (9 women); includes 3 minority (2 Black or African American, non-Hispanic/Latino; 1 Asian, non-Hispanic/Latino), 13 international. Average age 29. 66 applicants, 86% accepted, 18 enrolled. In 2018, 23 master's awarded. *Entrance requirements:* Additional exam requirements/recommendations for international students: Required—TOEFL (minimum score 550 paper-based; 78 iBT). *Application deadline:* Applications are processed on a rolling basis. Application fee: $40. Electronic applications accepted. *Expenses:* Tuition, state resident: full-time $7232.55; part-time $6676 per credit hour. Tuition, nonresident: full-time $12,375. *International tuition:* $18,914 full-time. *Required fees:* $80; $80 $40. Tuition and fees vary according to program. *Financial support:* In 2018–19, 14 students received support, including 12 teaching assistantships with full tuition reimbursements available (averaging $6,960 per year); unspecified assistantships also available. Financial award application deadline: 3/15. *Faculty research:* Algebraic topology, algebraic geometry, statistics, mathematical biology, applied mathematics. *Total annual research expenditures:* $132,202. *Unit head:* Dr. Ivan Soprunov, Chairperson/Professor, 216-687-4681, Fax: 216-523-7340, E-mail: i.soprunov@csuohio.edu. *Application contact:* Elaine Chuha, Administrative Coordinator, 216-523-7162, Fax: 216-523-7340, E-mail: e.hoff@csuohio.edu.
Website: http://www.csuohio.edu/sciences/dept/mathematics/

Colorado School of Mines, Office of Graduate Studies, Department of Applied Mathematics and Statistics, Golden, CO 80401. Offers computational and applied mathematics (MS, PhD); statistics (MS, PhD). *Program availability:* Part-time. *Faculty:* 25 full-time (9 women), 7 part-time/adjunct (3 women). *Students:* 24 full-time (9 women), 7 part-time (3 women); includes 6 minority (1 Black or African American, non-Hispanic/Latino; 1 American Indian or Alaska Native, non-Hispanic/Latino; 2 Hispanic/Latino; 1 Native Hawaiian or other Pacific Islander, non-Hispanic/Latino; 1 Two or more races, non-Hispanic/Latino), 1 international. Average age 27. 52 applicants, 60% accepted, 8 enrolled. In 2018, 7 master's, 1 doctorate awarded. *Degree requirements:* For master's, thesis (for some programs); for doctorate, comprehensive exam, thesis/dissertation. *Entrance requirements:* For master's and doctorate, GRE General Test. Additional exam requirements/recommendations for international students: Required—TOEFL (minimum score 550 paper-based; 79 iBT). *Application deadline:* For fall admission, 12/15 priority date for domestic and international students; for spring admission, 9/1 priority date for domestic and international students. Application fee: $60 ($80 for international students). Electronic applications accepted. *Expenses:* Tuition, state resident: full-time $16,650; part-time $925 per contact hour. Tuition, nonresident: full-time $36,270; part-time $2015 per contact hour. *International tuition:* $36,270 full-time. *Required fees:* $2314; $2314 per semester. *Financial support:* In 2018–19, 4 research assistantships with full tuition reimbursements, 10 teaching assistantships with full tuition reimbursements were awarded; fellowships, scholarships/grants, health care benefits, and unspecified assistantships also available. Financial award application deadline: 12/15; financial award applicants required to submit FAFSA. *Faculty research:* Applied

statistics, numerical computation, artificial intelligence, linear optimization. *Unit head:* Dr. Debra Carney, Head, 303-273-3977, E-mail: dcarney@mines.edu. *Application contact:* Jaime Bachmeier, Program Manager, 303-273-3860, E-mail: jbachmeier@mines.edu.
Website: http://ams.mines.edu/

Cornell University, Graduate School, Graduate Fields of Engineering, Field of Statistics, Ithaca, NY 14853. Offers applied statistics (MPS); biometry (MS, PhD); decision theory (MS, PhD); economic and social statistics (MS, PhD); engineering statistics (MS, PhD); experimental design (MS, PhD); mathematical statistics (MS, PhD); probability (MS, PhD); sampling (MS, PhD); statistical computing (MS, PhD); stochastic processes (MS, PhD). Terminal master's awarded for partial completion of doctoral program. *Degree requirements:* For master's, project (MPS), thesis (MS); for doctorate, one foreign language, thesis/dissertation. *Entrance requirements:* For master's, GRE General Test (for MS), 2 letters of recommendation (MS, MPS); for doctorate, GRE General Test, 2 letters of recommendation. Additional exam requirements/ recommendations for international students: Required—TOEFL (minimum score 550 paper-based; 77 iBT). Electronic applications accepted. *Faculty research:* Bayesian analysis, survival analysis, nonparametric statistics, stochastic processes, mathematical statistics.

DePaul University, College of Science and Health, Chicago, IL 60604-2287. Offers applied mathematics (MS); applied statistics (MS); biological sciences (MA, MS); chemistry (MS); environmental science (MS); mathematics education (MA); mathematics for teaching (MS); nursing (MS); nursing practice (DNP); physics (MS); polymer and coatings science (MS); psychology (MS); pure mathematics (MS); science education (MS); MA/PhD. *Accreditation:* AACN. Electronic applications accepted.

Florida State University, The Graduate School, Department of Anthropology, Department of Statistics, Tallahassee, FL 32306-4330. Offers applied statistics (MS); biostatistics (MS, PhD); mathematical statistics (MS, PhD); statistical data science (MS). *Program availability:* Part-time. *Faculty:* 23 full-time (5 women). *Students:* 166 full-time (73 women), 27 part-time (6 women); includes 18 minority (2 Black or African American, non-Hispanic/Latino; 8 Asian, non-Hispanic/Latino; 2 Hispanic/Latino; 6 Two or more races, non-Hispanic/Latino), 151 international. Average age 26. 386 applicants, 62% accepted, 50 enrolled. In 2018, 59 master's, 23 doctorates awarded. Terminal master's awarded for partial completion of doctoral program. *Degree requirements:* For master's, thesis optional; for doctorate, comprehensive exam, thesis/dissertation, departmental qualifying exam. *Entrance requirements:* For master's, GRE General Test, calculus, linear algebra, one course each in applied statistics and probability, minimum GPA of 3.0; for doctorate, GRE General Test, minimum GPA of 3.0, two semesters of advanced calculus (intermediate analysis, real analysis with proofs). Additional exam requirements/recommendations for international students: Required—TOEFL (minimum score 80 iBT), IELTS (minimum score 6.5). *Application deadline:* For fall admission, 7/1 for domestic and international students. Application fee: $30. Electronic applications accepted. *Expenses: Tuition, area resident:* Part-time $479.32 per credit hour. Tuition and fees vary according to campus/location and program. *Financial support:* In 2018–19, 89 students received support, including 10 research assistantships with full tuition reimbursements available (averaging $23,000 per year), 66 teaching assistantships with full tuition reimbursements available (averaging $20,500 per year); institutionally sponsored loans, scholarships/grants, health care benefits, tuition waivers (full and partial), and unspecified assistantships also available. Support available to part-time students. Financial award application deadline: 2/1; financial award applicants required to submit FAFSA. *Faculty research:* Statistical inference, high dimensional data analysis, biostatistics, nonparametric estimation, automatic target recognition. *Total annual research expenditures:* $813,343. *Unit head:* Dr. Xufeng Niu, Chairman, 850-644-4008, Fax: 850-644-5271, E-mail: niu@stat.fsu.edu. *Application contact:* Natalie Webster, Academic Program Specialist, 850-644-3514, Fax: 850-644-5271, E-mail: nwebster@fsu.edu.
Website: http://www.stat.fsu.edu/

Fordham University, Gabelli School of Business, New York, NY 10023. Offers accounting (MBA, MS); applied statistics and decision-making (MS); business economics (DPS); capital markets (DPS); communications and media management (MBA); electronic business (MBA); entrepreneurship (MBA); finance (MBA, PhD); global finance (MS); global sustainability (MBA); health administration (MS); healthcare management (MBA); information systems (MBA, MS); investor relations (MS); management (EMBA, MBA, MS, PhD); marketing (MBA); marketing intelligence (MS); media management (MS); nonprofit leadership (MS); quantitative finance (MS); strategy and decision-making (DPS); taxation (MS); JD/MBA; MS/MBA. *Accreditation:* AACSB. *Program availability:* Part-time, evening/weekend. Terminal master's awarded for partial completion of doctoral program. *Degree requirements:* For master's, internships (for some degrees); for doctorate, comprehensive exam (for some programs), thesis/ dissertation. *Entrance requirements:* For master's, GMAT/GRE, 2 letters of recommendation, resume, 2 essays, transcripts, interview. Additional exam requirements/recommendations for international students: Required—TOEFL (minimum score 100 iBT), IELTS (minimum score 7). Electronic applications accepted. *Expenses:* Contact institution.

Indiana University Bloomington, University Graduate School, College of Arts and Sciences, Department of Statistics, Bloomington, IN 47405. Offers applied statistics (MS); statistical science (MS, PhD). *Program availability:* Part-time. Terminal master's awarded for partial completion of doctoral program. *Degree requirements:* For master's, thesis or alternative; for doctorate, comprehensive exam, thesis/dissertation. *Entrance requirements:* For master's and doctorate, GRE. Additional exam requirements/ recommendations for international students: Required—TOEFL (minimum score 100 iBT). *Faculty research:* Spatial statistics, Bayesian statistics, statistical learning, network science, applied statistics.

Indiana University–Purdue University Indianapolis, School of Science, Department of Mathematical Sciences, Indianapolis, IN 46202-3216. Offers mathematics (MS, PhD), including applied mathematics, applied statistics (MS), mathematical statistics (PhD), mathematics, mathematics education (MS). *Program availability:* Part-time, evening/ weekend. *Degree requirements:* For master's, thesis optional; for doctorate, one foreign language, comprehensive exam, thesis/dissertation. *Entrance requirements:* For doctorate, GRE General Test (recommended). Additional exam requirements/ recommendations for international students: Required—TOEFL (minimum score 79 iBT), IELTS (minimum score 6.5), GRE General Test. Electronic applications accepted. *Faculty research:* Mathematical physics, integral systems, partial differential equations, noncommutative geometry, biomathematics, computational neurosciences.

Instituto Tecnológico y de Estudios Superiores de Monterrey, Campus Monterrey, Graduate and Research Division, Programs in Engineering, Monterrey, Mexico. Offers applied statistics (M Eng); artificial intelligence (PhD); automation engineering (M Eng); chemical engineering (M Eng); civil engineering (M Eng); electrical engineering (M Eng); electronic engineering (M Eng); environmental engineering (M Eng); industrial engineering (M Eng, PhD); manufacturing engineering (M Eng); mechanical engineering (M Eng); systems and quality engineering (M Eng). M Eng program offered jointly with University of Waterloo; PhD in industrial engineering with Texas A&M University. *Program availability:* Part-time, evening/weekend. Terminal master's awarded for partial completion of doctoral program. *Degree requirements:* For master's, one foreign language, thesis; for doctorate, one foreign language, thesis/dissertation. *Entrance requirements:* For master's, EXADEP; for doctorate, GRE, master's degree in related field. Additional exam requirements/recommendations for international students: Required—TOEFL. *Faculty research:* Flexible manufacturing cells, materials, statistical methods, environmental prevention, control and evaluation.

Kennesaw State University, College of Science and Mathematics, Program in Applied Statistics, Kennesaw, GA 30144. Offers MSAS. *Program availability:* Part-time, evening/ weekend. *Students:* 25 full-time (8 women), 29 part-time (14 women); includes 14 minority (6 Black or African American, non-Hispanic/Latino; 4 Asian, non-Hispanic/ Latino; 3 Hispanic/Latino; 1 Two or more races, non-Hispanic/Latino), 2 international. Average age 34. 60 applicants, 63% accepted, 25 enrolled. In 2018, 25 master's awarded. *Entrance requirements:* For master's, GRE, minimum GPA of 2.75, resume. Additional exam requirements/recommendations for international students: Required—TOEFL (minimum score 550 paper-based; 80 iBT), IELTS (minimum score 6.5). *Application deadline:* For fall admission, 6/1 for domestic and international students; for spring admission, 11/1 for domestic and international students. Applications are processed on a rolling basis. Application fee: $60. Electronic applications accepted. *Expenses: Tuition, area resident:* Full-time $6960; part-time $290 per credit hour. Tuition, state resident: full-time $6960; part-time $290 per credit hour. Tuition, nonresident: full-time $25,080; part-time $1045 per credit hour. *International tuition:* $25,080 full-time. *Required fees:* $2006; $1706 per semester. $853 per semester. *Financial support:* Research assistantships and unspecified assistantships available. Financial award applicants required to submit FAFSA. *Unit head:* Dr. Joseph DeMaio, Coordinator, 470-578-6568, E-mail: jdemaio@kennesaw.edu. *Application contact:* Admissions Counselor, 470-578-4377, Fax: 470-578-9172, E-mail: ksugrad@kennesaw.edu.
Website: http://csm.kennesaw.edu/statistics/msas/

Louisiana State University and Agricultural & Mechanical College, Graduate School, College of Agriculture, Department of Experimental Statistics, Baton Rouge, LA 70803. Offers applied statistics (M App St).

Loyola University Chicago, Graduate School, Department of Mathematics and Statistics, Chicago, IL 60660. Offers applied statistics (MS); mathematics (MS). *Program availability:* Part-time. *Faculty:* 19 full-time (3 women). *Students:* 41 full-time (21 women), 7 part-time (1 woman); includes 10 minority (1 Black or African American, non-Hispanic/Latino; 7 Asian, non-Hispanic/Latino; 1 Hispanic/Latino; 1 Two or more races, non-Hispanic/Latino), 9 international. Average age 26. 69 applicants, 62% accepted, 22 enrolled. In 2018, 28 master's awarded. *Entrance requirements:* For master's, GRE General Test. Additional exam requirements/recommendations for international students: Required—TOEFL (minimum score 550 paper-based; 79 iBT), IELTS (minimum score 6.5). *Application deadline:* For fall admission, 8/1 for domestic students; for spring admission, 12/1 for domestic students. Applications are processed on a rolling basis. Application fee: $0. Electronic applications accepted. *Expenses:* Contact institution. *Financial support:* In 2018–19, 12 students received support, including 4 fellowships with full and partial tuition reimbursements available (averaging $12,000 per year), 6 teaching assistantships with tuition reimbursements available (averaging $10,000 per year); career-related internships or fieldwork, Federal Work-Study, institutionally sponsored loans, and tuition waivers (partial) also available. Financial award application deadline: 3/15; financial award applicants required to submit FAFSA. *Faculty research:* Nonlinear analysis and partial differential equations, algebra and combinatorics, knot theory, control theory and engineering, probability and applied statistics. *Total annual research expenditures:* $70,000. *Unit head:* Dr. Timothy O'Brien, Graduate Program Director for Applied Statistics, 773-508-2129, Fax: 773-508-2123, E-mail: tobrie1@luc.edu. *Application contact:* Dr. Rafal Goebel, Graduate Program Director for Mathematics, 773-508-3558, E-mail: rgoebel1@luc.edu.
Website: http://www.luc.edu/math/

McMaster University, School of Graduate Studies, Faculty of Science, Department of Mathematics and Statistics, Program in Statistics, Hamilton, ON L8S 4M2, Canada. Offers applied statistics (M Sc); medical statistics (M Sc); statistical theory (M Sc). *Degree requirements:* For master's, thesis or alternative. *Entrance requirements:* For master's, honors degree background in mathematics and statistics. Additional exam requirements/recommendations for international students: Required—TOEFL (minimum score 550 paper-based). *Faculty research:* Development of polymer production technology, quality of life in patients who use pharmaceutical agents, mathematical modeling, order statistics from progressively censored samples, nonlinear stochastic model in genetics.

Michigan State University, The Graduate School, College of Natural Science, Department of Statistics and Probability, East Lansing, MI 48824. Offers applied statistics (MS); statistics (MS, PhD). *Entrance requirements:* Additional exam requirements/recommendations for international students: Required—TOEFL. Electronic applications accepted.

Minnesota State University Mankato, College of Graduate Studies and Research, College of Science, Engineering and Technology, Department of Mathematics and Statistics, Program in Statistics, Mankato, MN 56001. Offers applied statistics (MS). *Degree requirements:* For master's, one foreign language, comprehensive exam, thesis or alternative. *Entrance requirements:* For master's, GRE General Test, minimum GPA of 3.0 during previous 2 years. Additional exam requirements/recommendations for international students: Required—TOEFL. Electronic applications accepted.

New Jersey Institute of Technology, College of Science and Liberal Arts, Newark, NJ 07102. Offers applied mathematics (MS); applied physics (MS, PhD); applied statistics (MS, Certificate); biology (MS, PhD); biostatistics (MS); chemistry (MS, PhD); environmental and sustainability policy (MS); environmental science (MS, PhD); history (MA, MAT); materials science and engineering (MS, PhD); mathematical and computational finance (MS); mathematical sciences (PhD); pharmaceutical chemistry (MS); professional and technical communications (MS); technical communication essentials (Certificate). *Program availability:* Part-time, evening/weekend. *Faculty:* 150 full-time (43 women), 115 part-time/adjunct (47 women). *Students:* 200 full-time (79 women), 63 part-time (29 women); includes 61 minority (17 Black or African American, non-Hispanic/Latino; 29 Asian, non-Hispanic/Latino; 11 Hispanic/Latino; 4 Two or more races, non-Hispanic/Latino), 136 international. Average age 28. 429 applicants, 49% accepted, 89 enrolled. In 2018, 43 master's, 16 doctorates, 2 other advanced degrees awarded. Terminal master's awarded for partial completion of doctoral program. *Degree requirements:* For master's, thesis (for some programs); for doctorate, thesis/ dissertation. *Entrance requirements:* For master's and doctorate, GRE General Test, Minimum GPA of 3.0, personal statement, three (3) letters of recommendation, and transcripts. Additional exam requirements/recommendations for international students: Required—TOEFL (minimum score 550 paper-based; 79 iBT), IELTS (minimum score 6.5). *Application deadline:* For fall admission, 6/1 priority date for domestic students, 5/1 priority date for international students; for spring admission, 11/15 priority date for domestic and international students. Applications are processed on a rolling basis. Application fee: $75. Electronic applications accepted. *Expenses:* $22,690 per year (in-state), $32,136 per year (out-of-state). *Financial support:* In 2018–19, 134 students received support, including 17 fellowships with full tuition reimbursements available (averaging $22,000 per year), 74 research assistantships with full tuition reimbursements available (averaging $22,000 per year), 71 teaching assistantships with full tuition reimbursements available (averaging $22,000 per year); scholarships/grants, traineeships, health care benefits, and unspecified assistantships also available. Financial award application deadline: 1/15. *Faculty research:* Biophotonics and bioimaging, morphogenetic patterning, embryogenesis, biological fluid dynamics, applied research in the mathematical sciences. *Total annual research expenditures:* $29.2 million. *Unit head:* Dr. Kevin Belfield, Dean, 973-596-3676, Fax: 973-565-0586, E-mail: kevin.d.belfield@njit.edu. *Application contact:* Stephen Eck, Director of Admissions, 973-596-3300, Fax: 973-596-3461, E-mail: admissions@njit.edu. Website: http://csla.njit.edu/

New Mexico State University, College of Business, Department of Economics, Applied Statistics and International Business, Las Cruces, NM 88003. Offers applied statistics (MS); economic development (DED); economics (MA); public utility regulation and economics (Graduate Certificate). *Program availability:* Part-time, online learning. *Faculty:* 14 full-time (3 women). *Students:* 43 full-time (21 women), 25 part-time (6 women); includes 25 minority (4 Black or African American, non-Hispanic/Latino; 1 American Indian or Alaska Native, non-Hispanic/Latino; 1 Asian, non-Hispanic/Latino; 18 Hispanic/Latino; 1 Two or more races, non-Hispanic/Latino), 28 international. Average age 34. 59 applicants, 59% accepted, 12 enrolled. In 2018, 16 master's, 9 doctorates, 14 other advanced degrees awarded. Terminal master's awarded for partial completion of doctoral program. *Degree requirements:* For master's, comprehensive exam, thesis or alternative; for doctorate, comprehensive exam, thesis/dissertation, internship. *Entrance requirements:* For master's, minimum GPA of 3.0; for doctorate, appropriate master's degree, minimum GPA of 3.0 with particular classes required. Additional exam requirements/recommendations for international students: Required—TOEFL (minimum score 550 paper-based; 79 iBT), IELTS (minimum score 6.5). *Application deadline:* For fall admission, 3/1 priority date for domestic and international students. Applications are processed on a rolling basis. Application fee: $40 ($50 for international students). Electronic applications accepted. *Expenses: Tuition, area resident:* Full-time $4216.70; part-time $252.70 per credit hour. *Tuition, state resident:* full-time $4216.70; part-time $252.70 per credit hour. *Tuition, nonresident:* full-time $12,769; part-time $881.10 per credit hour. *International tuition:* $12,769.30 full-time. *Required fees:* $878.40; $48.80 per credit hour. Full-time tuition and fees vary according to course load and reciprocity agreements. *Financial support:* In 2018–19, 39 students received support, including 1 fellowship (averaging $4,548 per year), 12 research assistantships (averaging $11,672 per year), 15 teaching assistantships (averaging $12,071 per year); career-related internships or fieldwork, Federal Work-Study, scholarships/grants, traineeships, health care benefits, and unspecified assistantships also available. Support available to part-time students. Financial award application deadline: 3/1. *Faculty research:* Public utilities, environment, linear models, biological sampling, public policy, economic development, energy, regional economics. *Total annual research expenditures:* $17,362. Website: http://business.nmsu.edu/departments/economics

New York University, Steinhardt School of Culture, Education, and Human Development, Applied Statistics, Social Science, and Humanities, Program in Applied Statistics for Social Science Research, New York, NY 10012-1019. Offers MS. *Entrance requirements:* For master's, GRE, statement of purpose, resume/curriculum vitae, two letters of recommendation, transcripts. Additional exam requirements/recommendations for international students: Required—TOEFL. Electronic applications accepted. *Faculty research:* Causal inference, multi-level models, multivariate analysis, psychometrics, survey research and design.

Northern Arizona University, College of Environment, Forestry, and Natural Sciences, Department of Mathematics and Statistics, Flagstaff, AZ 86011. Offers applied statistics (Graduate Certificate); mathematics (MS); mathematics education (MS); statistics (MS); teaching introductory community college mathematics (Graduate Certificate). *Program availability:* Part-time. *Degree requirements:* For master's, variable foreign language requirement, comprehensive exam (for some programs), thesis (for some programs); for Graduate Certificate, comprehensive exam (for some programs). *Entrance requirements:* Additional exam requirements/recommendations for international students: Required—TOEFL (minimum score 80 iBT), IELTS (minimum score 6.5), TOEFL minimum iBT score of 89 (for MS and Graduate Certificate). Electronic applications accepted.

Oakland University, Graduate Study and Lifelong Learning, College of Arts and Sciences, Department of Mathematics and Statistics, Program in Applied Statistics, Rochester, MI 48309-4401. Offers MS. *Program availability:* Part-time, evening/weekend. *Entrance requirements:* For master's, minimum GPA of 3.0. Additional exam requirements/recommendations for international students: Required—TOEFL (minimum score 550 paper-based). Electronic applications accepted. *Expenses:* Contact institution.

Penn State University Park, Graduate School, Eberly College of Science, Department of Statistics, University Park, PA 16802. Offers applied statistics (MAS); statistics (MA, MS, PhD).

Portland State University, Graduate Studies, College of Liberal Arts and Sciences, Fariborz Maseeh Department of Mathematics and Statistics, Portland, OR 97207-0751. Offers applied statistics (Certificate); mathematical sciences (PhD); mathematics education (PhD); mathematics for middle school (Certificate); mathematics for teachers (MS); statistics (MS); MA/MS. *Degree requirements:* For master's, comprehensive exam, thesis or alternative, 2 written examinations; for doctorate, thesis/dissertation, preliminary and comprehensive examinations. *Entrance requirements:* For master's, GRE General Test, GRE Subject Test, minimum GPA of 3.0 in upper-division course work or 2.75 cumulative undergraduate; for doctorate, GRE General Test. Additional exam requirements/recommendations for international students: Required—TOEFL (minimum score 550 paper-based; 80 iBT). *Faculty research:* Algebra, topology, statistical distribution theory, control theory, statistical robustness.

Purdue University Fort Wayne, College of Arts and Sciences, Department of Mathematical Sciences, Fort Wayne, IN 46805-1499. Offers applied mathematics (MS); applied statistics (Certificate); mathematics (MS); operations research (MS); teaching (MAT). *Program availability:* Part-time, evening/weekend. *Entrance requirements:* For master's, minimum GPA of 3.0, major or minor in mathematics, three letters of recommendation. Additional exam requirements/recommendations for international students: Required—TOEFL (minimum score 550 paper-based; 79 iBT); Recommended—TWE. Electronic applications accepted. *Faculty research:* Eves' Theorem, paired-placements for student teaching, holomorphic maps.

Rochester Institute of Technology, Graduate Enrollment Services, College of Science, School of Mathematical Sciences, Advanced Certificate Program in Applied Statistics, Rochester, NY 14623-5603. Offers Advanced Certificate. *Program availability:* Part-time, evening/weekend, 100% online. *Students:* 2 part-time; both minorities (both Hispanic/Latino). Average age 39. 1 applicant, 100% accepted, 1 enrolled. In 2018, 3 Advanced Certificates awarded. *Entrance requirements:* For degree, GRE, minimum GPA of 3.0 (recommended). Additional exam requirements/recommendations for international students: Required—TOEFL (minimum score 550 paper-based; 79 iBT), IELTS (minimum score 6), PTE (minimum score 58). *Application deadline:* Applications are processed on a rolling basis. Application fee: $65. Electronic applications accepted. *Expenses:* Contact institution. *Financial support:* Scholarships/grants available. Support available to part-time students. Financial award applicants required to submit FAFSA. *Faculty research:* Applied statistics; application of statistics in imaging science; application of statistics in cryptography. *Unit head:* Robert Parody, Associate Professor, 585-475-5288, E-mail: rjpeqa@rit.edu. *Application contact:* Diane Ellison, Senior Associate Vice President, Graduate Enrollment Services, 585-475-2229, Fax: 585-475-7164, E-mail: gradinfo@rit.edu. Website: https://www.rit.edu/study/applied-statistics-adv-cert

Rochester Institute of Technology, Graduate Enrollment Services, College of Science, School of Mathematical Sciences, MS Program in Applied Statistics, Rochester, NY 14623-5603. Offers MS. *Program availability:* Part-time, evening/weekend, 100% online, blended/hybrid learning. *Students:* 27 full-time (14 women), 43 part-time (20 women); includes 12 minority (1 Black or African American, non-Hispanic/Latino; 6 Asian, non-Hispanic/Latino; 2 Hispanic/Latino; 3 Two or more races, non-Hispanic/Latino), 26 international. Average age 28. 59 applicants, 73% accepted, 20 enrolled. In 2018, 20 master's awarded. *Degree requirements:* For master's, thesis or alternative, capstone. *Entrance requirements:* For master's, GRE is not required, but some applicants may be asked to submit scores to strengthen their application., minimum GPA of 3.0 (recommended), one year of differential equations and integral calculus, two courses in probability and statistics, knowledge of a programming language, resume, two letters of recommendation. Additional exam requirements/recommendations for international students: Required—TOEFL (minimum score 550 paper-based; 79 iBT), IELTS (minimum score 6.5), PTE (minimum score 58). *Application deadline:* Applications are processed on a rolling basis. Application fee: $65. Electronic applications accepted. *Financial support:* In 2018–19, 33 students received support. Research assistantships with partial tuition reimbursements available, teaching assistantships with partial tuition reimbursements available, career-related internships or fieldwork, scholarships/grants, and unspecified assistantships available. Support available to part-time students. Financial award applicants required to submit FAFSA. *Faculty research:* Applied statistics; application of statistics in imaging science; application of statistics in cryptography. *Unit head:* Robert Parody, Associate Professor, 585-475-5288, E-mail: rjpeqa@rit.edu. *Application contact:* Diane Ellison, Senior Associate Vice President, Graduate Enrollment Services, 585-475-2229, Fax: 585-475-7164, E-mail: gradinfo@rit.edu. Website: https://www.rit.edu/study/applied-statistics-ms

Rutgers University–New Brunswick, Graduate School-New Brunswick, Program in Statistics, Piscataway, NJ 08854-8097. Offers applied statistics (MS); biostatistics (MS); data mining (MS); quality and productivity management (MS); statistics (MS, PhD). *Program availability:* Part-time. Terminal master's awarded for partial completion of doctoral program. *Degree requirements:* For master's, comprehensive exam, essay, exam, non-thesis essay paper; for doctorate, one foreign language, thesis/dissertation, qualifying oral and written exams. *Entrance requirements:* For master's, GRE General Test; for doctorate, GRE General Test, GRE Subject Test (recommended). Additional exam requirements/recommendations for international students: Required—TOEFL (minimum score 550 paper-based). Electronic applications accepted. *Faculty research:* Probability, decision theory, linear models, multivariate statistics, statistical computing.

Southern Methodist University, Dedman College of Humanities and Sciences, Department of Statistical Science, Dallas, TX 75275-0332. Offers applied statistics and data analytics (MS); biostatistics (PhD); statistical science (PhD). *Program availability:* Part-time. *Degree requirements:* For master's, thesis, oral and written exams; for doctorate, thesis/dissertation, oral and written exams. *Entrance requirements:* For master's, GRE General Test, 12 hours of advanced math courses; for doctorate, GRE General Test, minimum GPA of 3.0. Additional exam requirements/recommendations for international students: Required—TOEFL. Electronic applications accepted. *Faculty research:* Regression, time series, linear models sampling, nonparametrics, biostatistics.

Syracuse University, College of Arts and Sciences, MS Program in Applied Statistics, Syracuse, NY 13244. Offers MS. *Program availability:* Part-time. *Students:* Average age 23. *Entrance requirements:* For master's, GRE General Test, letters of recommendation, personal statement, resume. Additional exam requirements/recommendations for international students: Required—TOEFL (minimum score 100 iBT). *Application deadline:* For fall admission, 3/15 for domestic and international students. Applications are processed on a rolling basis. Application fee: $75. Electronic applications accepted. *Financial support:* Fellowships with full tuition reimbursements, teaching assistantships, and tuition waivers available. Financial award application deadline: 1/1; financial award applicants required to submit FAFSA. *Faculty research:* Cutting-edge statistical methodologies, statistical theory, applied statistics, mathematical statistics, statistical consulting. *Unit head:* Dr. Pinyuen Chen, Graduate Contact, 315-443-1577, E-mail: pinchen@syr.edu. *Application contact:* Dr. Pinyuen Chen, Graduate Contact, 315-443-1577, E-mail: pinchen@syr.edu. Website: http://thecollege.syr.edu/academics/interdisciplinary/AppliedStats.html

Teachers College, Columbia University, Department of Human Development, New York, NY 10027-6696. Offers applied statistics (MS); cognitive studies in education (MA, Ed D, PhD); developmental psychology (MA, Ed D, PhD); educational psychology-human cognition and learning (Ed M, MA, Ed D, PhD); learning analytics (MS); measurement and evaluation (ME, Ed D, PhD); measurement, evaluation, and statistics (MA, MS, Ed D, PhD). *Program availability:* Part-time. *Students:* 114 full-time (89 women), 168 part-time (119 women); includes 75 minority (19 Black or African American, non-Hispanic/Latino; 36 Asian, non-Hispanic/Latino; 18 Hispanic/Latino; 2 Two or more races, non-Hispanic/Latino), 132 international. Average age 29. 401 applicants, 56% accepted, 109 enrolled. *Unit head:* Jim Corter, Chair, 212-678-3843, E-mail: jec34@tc.columbia.edu. *Application contact:* Kelly Sutton-Skinner, Director of Admission & New Student Enrollment, E-mail: kms2237@tc.columbia.edu. Website: http://www.tc.columbia.edu/human-development/

The University of Alabama, Graduate School, Manderson Graduate School of Business, Department of Information Systems, Statistics, and Management Science, Program in Applied Statistics, Tuscaloosa, AL 35487. Offers MS, PhD. *Program availability:* Part-time. Terminal master's awarded for partial completion of doctoral program. *Degree requirements:* For master's, comprehensive exam; for doctorate, comprehensive exam, thesis/dissertation. *Entrance requirements:* For master's and doctorate, GMAT or GRE, 3 semesters of calculus and linear algebra. Additional exam

Peterson's Graduate Programs in the Physical Sciences, Mathematics, Agricultural Sciences, the Environment & Natural Resources 2020

www.petersons.com **187**

requirements/recommendations for international students: Required—TOEFL (minimum score 550 paper-based; 100 iBT), IELTS (minimum score 6.5). Electronic applications accepted. *Faculty research:* Data mining, regression analysis, statistical quality control, nonparametric statistics, design of experiments.

University of Arkansas at Little Rock, Graduate School, College of Arts, Letters, and Sciences, Department of Mathematics and Statistics, Little Rock, AR 72204-1099. Offers applied statistics (Graduate Certificate); mathematical sciences (MS). *Program availability:* Part-time, evening/weekend. *Degree requirements:* For master's, comprehensive exam. *Entrance requirements:* For master's, GRE General Test, GRE Subject Test, minimum GPA of 2.7, previous course work in advanced mathematics.

University of California, Santa Barbara, Graduate Division, College of Letters and Sciences, Division of Mathematics, Life, and Physical Sciences, Department of Statistics and Applied Probability, Santa Barbara, CA 93106-3110. Offers bioengineering (PhD); financial mathematics and statistics (PhD); quantitative methods in the social sciences (PhD); statistics (MA), including applied statistics, mathematical statistics; statistics and applied probability (PhD); MA/PhD. Terminal master's awarded for partial completion of doctoral program. *Degree requirements:* For master's, comprehensive exam, thesis optional; for doctorate, comprehensive exam, thesis/dissertation. *Entrance requirements:* For master's and doctorate, GRE General Test. Additional exam requirements/recommendations for international students: Required—TOEFL (minimum score 550 paper-based; 80 iBT), IELTS (minimum score 7). Electronic applications accepted. *Faculty research:* Bayesian inference, financial mathematics, stochastic processes, environmental statistics, biostatistical modeling.

University of Chicago, Graham School of Continuing Liberal and Professional Studies, Master of Science Program in Analytics, Chicago, IL 60637. Offers M Sc. *Program availability:* Part-time, evening/weekend. *Degree requirements:* For master's, capstone project. *Entrance requirements:* For master's, 3 letters of recommendation, statement of purpose, transcripts, resume or curriculum vitae. Additional exam requirements/recommendations for international students: Required—TOEFL (minimum score 104 iBT), IELTS (minimum score 7). Electronic applications accepted.

University of Colorado Denver, College of Liberal Arts and Sciences, Department of Mathematical and Statistical Sciences, Denver, CO 80217. Offers applied mathematics (MS, PhD), including applied mathematics, applied probability (MS), applied statistics (MS), computational biology (PhD), computational mathematics (PhD), discrete mathematics, finite geometry (PhD), mathematics education (PhD), mathematics of engineering and science (MS), numerical analysis, operations research (MS), optimization and operations research (PhD), probability (PhD), statistics (PhD). *Program availability:* Part-time. *Degree requirements:* For master's, comprehensive exam, thesis optional, 30 hours of course work with minimum GPA of 3.0; for doctorate, comprehensive exam, thesis/dissertation, 42 hours of course work with minimum GPA of 3.25. *Entrance requirements:* For master's, GRE General Test; GRE Subject Test in math (recommended), 30 hours of course work in mathematics (24 of which must be upper-division mathematics), bachelor's degree with minimum GPA of 3.0; for doctorate, GRE General Test; GRE Subject Test in math (recommended), 30 hours of course work in mathematics (24 of which must be upper-division mathematics), master's degree with minimum GPA of 3.25. Additional exam requirements/recommendations for international students: Required—TOEFL (minimum score 537 paper-based; 75 iBT); Recommended—IELTS (minimum score 6.5). Electronic applications accepted. *Expenses:* Tuition, state resident: full-time $6786; part-time $337 per credit hour. Tuition, nonresident: full-time $22,590; part-time $1255 per credit hour. *Required fees:* $1231; $137 per credit hour. Tuition and fees vary according to program and reciprocity agreements. *Faculty research:* Computational mathematics, computational biology, discrete mathematics and geometry, probability and statistics, optimization.

University of Guelph, Office of Graduate and Postdoctoral Studies, College of Physical and Engineering Science, Department of Mathematics and Statistics, Guelph, ON N1G 2W1, Canada. Offers applied mathematics (PhD); applied statistics (PhD); mathematics and statistics (M Sc). *Program availability:* Part-time. *Degree requirements:* For master's, thesis (for some programs); for doctorate, thesis/dissertation. *Entrance requirements:* For master's, minimum B- average during previous 2 years of course work; for doctorate, minimum B average. Additional exam requirements/recommendations for international students: Required—TOEFL (minimum score 550 paper-based; 89 iBT), IELTS (minimum score 6.5). *Faculty research:* Dynamical systems, mathematical biology, numerical analysis, linear and nonlinear models, reliability and bioassay.

University of Illinois at Urbana–Champaign, Graduate College, College of Liberal Arts and Sciences, Department of Statistics, Champaign, IL 61820. Offers analytics (MS); applied statistics (MS); statistics (MS, PhD).

The University of Kansas, University of Kansas Medical Center, School of Medicine, Department of Biostatistics & Data Science, Kansas City, KS 66160. Offers applied statistics and analytics (MS); biostatistics (MS, PhD, Graduate Certificate); statistical applications (Graduate Certificate). *Faculty:* 21. *Students:* 36 full-time (16 women), 86 part-time (32 women); includes 32 minority (10 Black or African American, non-Hispanic/Latino; 12 Asian, non-Hispanic/Latino; 6 Hispanic/Latino; 4 Two or more races, non-Hispanic/Latino), 23 international. Average age 31. 52 applicants, 88% accepted, 42 enrolled. In 2018, 10 master's, 2 doctorates, 1 other advanced degree awarded. *Degree requirements:* For master's, comprehensive exam; for doctorate, comprehensive exam, thesis/dissertation. *Entrance requirements:* For master's, GRE, coursework in calculus, computer programming, linear algebra, differential equations, and numerical analysis; for doctorate, master's degree. Additional exam requirements/recommendations for international students: Required—TOEFL. Application fee: $60. Electronic applications accepted. *Financial support:* In 2018–19, 1 fellowship with full tuition reimbursement (averaging $25,000 per year), 25 research assistantships with full and partial tuition reimbursements (averaging $19,200 per year) were awarded; scholarships/grants, traineeships, and unspecified assistantships also available. Financial award application deadline: 3/1; financial award applicants required to submit FAFSA. *Faculty research:* Biostatistics, clinical trials. *Total annual research expenditures:* $451,667. *Unit head:* Dr. Matthew Mayo, Professor and Chair, 913-588-4735 Ext. 913, Fax: 913-588-0252, E-mail: mmayo@kumc.edu. *Application contact:* Dr. Jo A. Wick, Assistant Director of Graduate Education, 913-588-4790, Fax: 913-588-0252, E-mail: jwick@kumc.edu.
Website: http://www.kumc.edu/school-of-medicine/department-of-biostatistics.html

University of Memphis, Graduate School, College of Arts and Sciences, Department of Mathematical Sciences, Memphis, TN 38152. Offers applied mathematics (MS); applied statistics (PhD); mathematics (MS, PhD); statistics (MS); teaching of mathematics (MS). *Program availability:* Part-time. *Students:* 35 full-time (11 women), 41 part-time (13 women); includes 33 minority (14 Black or African American, non-Hispanic/Latino; 12 Asian, non-Hispanic/Latino; 5 Hispanic/Latino; 2 Two or more races, non-Hispanic/Latino), 22 international. Average age 34. 35 applicants, 83% accepted, 17 enrolled. In 2018, 10 master's, 5 doctorates awarded. Terminal master's awarded for partial completion of doctoral program. *Degree requirements:* For master's, comprehensive exam, thesis or alternative; for doctorate, one foreign language, comprehensive exam, thesis/dissertation, qualifying exam, final exam. *Entrance requirements:* For master's, GRE General Test, minimum GPA of 2.5, undergraduate degree in math or statistics, two letters of recommendation; for doctorate, GRE General Test, minimum GPA of 2.5, three letters of recommendation. Additional exam requirements/recommendations for international students: Required—TOEFL (minimum score 550 paper-based; 79 iBT). *Application deadline:* For fall admission, 8/1 for domestic students, 5/1 priority date for international students; for spring admission, 12/1 for domestic students, 9/1 priority date for international students. Applications are processed on a rolling basis. Application fee: $35 ($60 for international students). Electronic applications accepted. *Expenses: Tuition, area resident:* Full-time $10,240; part-time $503 per credit hour. Tuition, state resident: full-time $10,464. Tuition, nonresident: full-time $20,224; part-time $991 per credit hour. *Required fees:* $850; $106 per credit hour. *Financial support:* Fellowships with full tuition reimbursements, research assistantships with full tuition reimbursements, teaching assistantships with full tuition reimbursements, career-related internships or fieldwork, Federal Work-Study, scholarships/grants, and unspecified assistantships available. Financial award application deadline: 2/1; financial award applicants required to submit FAFSA. *Faculty research:* Combinatorics, ergodic theory, graph theory, Ramsey theory, applied statistics. *Unit head:* Dr. Irena Lasiecka, Chair, 901-678-2482, Fax: 901-678-2480, E-mail: lasiecka@memphis.edu. *Application contact:* Dr. Fernanda Botelho, Graduate Advising Coordinator, 901-678-3131, Fax: 901-678-2480, E-mail: mbotelho@memphis.edu.
Website: https://www.memphis.edu/msci

University of Michigan, Rackham Graduate School, College of Literature, Science, and the Arts, Department of Statistics, Ann Arbor, MI 48109. Offers applied statistics (MS); data science (MS); statistics (AM, PhD). *Faculty:* 23 full-time (5 women). *Students:* 216 full-time (88 women), 1 part-time (0 women); includes 25 minority (1 Black or African American, non-Hispanic/Latino; 20 Asian, non-Hispanic/Latino; 2 Hispanic/Latino; 2 Two or more races, non-Hispanic/Latino), 157 international. 1,267 applicants, 27% accepted, 102 enrolled. In 2018, 70 master's, 14 doctorates awarded. Terminal master's awarded for partial completion of doctoral program. *Degree requirements:* For doctorate, comprehensive exam, thesis/dissertation, oral defense of dissertation, preliminary exams. *Entrance requirements:* For master's and doctorate, GRE General Test. Additional exam requirements/recommendations for international students: Required—TOEFL (minimum score 560 paper-based; 84 iBT), IELTS (minimum score 6.5). *Application deadline:* For fall admission, 12/31 for domestic and international students. Application fee: $75 ($90 for international students). Electronic applications accepted. *Financial support:* Fellowships, research assistantships, teaching assistantships, career-related internships or fieldwork, Federal Work-Study, institutionally sponsored loans, scholarships/grants, health care benefits, and unspecified assistantships available. *Faculty research:* Reliability and degradation modeling, biological and legal applications, bioinformatics, statistical computing, covariance estimation. *Unit head:* Prof. Xuming He, Chair, 734-7645981, E-mail: statchair@umich.edu. *Application contact:* Andrea Nashar, PhD Program Coordinator, 734-763-3520, E-mail: statsphdprogram@umich.edu.
Website: http://www.lsa.umich.edu/stats/

The University of North Carolina Wilmington, College of Arts and Sciences, Department of Mathematics and Statistics, Wilmington, NC 28403-3297. Offers applied statistics (Professional Certificate); mathematics (MS). *Program availability:* Part-time. *Degree requirements:* For master's, comprehensive exam, thesis (for some programs). *Entrance requirements:* For master's, GRE General Test, 3 letters of recommendation. Additional exam requirements/recommendations for international students: Required—TOEFL (minimum score 550 paper-based; 79 iBT), IELTS (minimum score 6.5). Electronic applications accepted.

University of Northern Colorado, Graduate School, College of Education and Behavioral Sciences, Department of Applied Statistics and Research Methods, Greeley, CO 80639. Offers MS, PhD. *Program availability:* Part-time. *Degree requirements:* For master's, comprehensive exam; for doctorate, comprehensive exam, thesis/dissertation. *Entrance requirements:* For master's, 3 letters of reference; for doctorate, GRE General Test, 3 letters of reference. Electronic applications accepted.

University of Notre Dame, The Graduate School, College of Science, Department of Applied and Computational Mathematics and Statistics, Notre Dame, IN 46556. Offers applied and computational mathematics and statistics (PhD); applied statistics (MS); computational finance (MS).

University of Pittsburgh, Kenneth P. Dietrich School of Arts and Sciences, Department of Statistics, Pittsburgh, PA 15260. Offers applied statistics (MA, MS); statistics (MA, MS, PhD). *Program availability:* Part-time. Terminal master's awarded for partial completion of doctoral program. *Degree requirements:* For master's, thesis (for some programs); for doctorate, comprehensive exam, thesis/dissertation. *Entrance requirements:* For master's and doctorate, 3 semesters of calculus, 1 semester of linear algebra, 1 year of mathematical statistics. Additional exam requirements/recommendations for international students: Required—TOEFL (minimum score 90 iBT). Electronic applications accepted. *Faculty research:* Multivariate analysis, time series, quantile research analysis, stochastic models, high dimensional statistical inference.

University of South Carolina, The Graduate School, College of Arts and Sciences, Department of Statistics, Columbia, SC 29208. Offers applied statistics (CAS); industrial statistics (MIS); statistics (MS, PhD). *Program availability:* Part-time, evening/weekend, online learning. Terminal master's awarded for partial completion of doctoral program. *Degree requirements:* For master's, thesis; for doctorate, comprehensive exam, thesis/dissertation. *Entrance requirements:* For master's, GRE General Test or GMAT, 2 years of work experience (MIS); for doctorate, GRE General Test; for CAS, GRE General Test or GMAT. Additional exam requirements/recommendations for international students: Required—TOEFL (minimum score 600 paper-based; 100 iBT). Electronic applications accepted. *Expenses:* Contact institution. *Faculty research:* Reliability, environmentrics, statistics computing, psychometrics, bioinformatics.

The University of Tennessee at Chattanooga, Program in Mathematics, Chattanooga, TN 37403. Offers applied mathematics (MS); applied statistics (MS); mathematics education (MS); pre-professional mathematics (MS). *Program availability:* Part-time. *Degree requirements:* For master's, internship or thesis. *Entrance requirements:* For master's, GRE (if applying for an assistantship), two letters of recommendation. Additional exam requirements/recommendations for international students: Required—TOEFL (minimum score 550 paper-based; 61 iBT), IELTS (minimum score 6). Electronic applications accepted. *Expenses:* Contact institution.

The University of Texas at San Antonio, College of Business, Department of Management Science and Statistics, San Antonio, TX 78249-0617. Offers applied statistics (MS, PhD); management science (MBA). *Accreditation:* AACSB. *Program availability:* Part-time, evening/weekend. *Degree requirements:* For master's, comprehensive exam (for some programs), thesis or alternative; for doctorate, comprehensive exam, thesis/dissertation. *Entrance requirements:* For master's, GMAT, minimum of 36 semester credit hours of coursework beyond any hours acquired in the

MBA-leveling courses; statement of purpose; for doctorate, GRE, minimum cumulative GPA of 3.3 in the last 60 hours of coursework; transcripts from all colleges and universities attended; curriculum vitae; statement of academic work experiences, interests, and goals; three letters of recommendation; BA, BS, or MS in mathematics, statistics, or closely-related field. Additional exam requirements/recommendations for international students: Required—TOEFL (minimum score 550 paper-based; 79 iBT), IELTS (minimum score 6.5). Electronic applications accepted. *Faculty research:* Statistical signal processing, reliability and life-testing experiments, modeling decompression sickness using survival analysis.

University of the Incarnate Word, School of Mathematics, Science, and Engineering, San Antonio, TX 78209-6397. Offers applied statistics (MS); biology (MA, MS); mathematics (MA), including teaching; multidisciplinary sciences (MA); nutrition (MS). *Program availability:* Part-time, evening/weekend. *Faculty:* 6 full-time (4 women), 1 (woman) part-time/adjunct. *Students:* 30 full-time (24 women), 9 part-time (7 women); includes 20 minority (1 Black or African American, non-Hispanic/Latino; 1 American Indian or Alaska Native, non-Hispanic/Latino; 1 Asian, non-Hispanic/Latino; 17 Hispanic/Latino), 5 international. 34 applicants, 88% accepted, 13 enrolled. In 2018, 10 master's awarded. *Degree requirements:* For master's, comprehensive exam (for some programs), thesis optional, capstone. *Entrance requirements:* For master's, GRE, recommendation letter. Additional exam requirements/recommendations for international students: Required—TOEFL (minimum score 560 paper-based; 83 iBT). *Application deadline:* Applications are processed on a rolling basis. Application fee: $20. Electronic applications accepted. *Expenses: Tuition:* Full-time $22,560; part-time $940 per credit hour. *Required fees:* $2484; $94 per credit hour. Tuition and fees vary according to degree level, program and student level. *Financial support:* Research assistantships, Federal Work-Study, scholarships/grants, tuition waivers (partial), and unspecified assistantships available. Financial award applicants required to submit FAFSA. *Faculty research:* Neural morphallaxis in lumbriculus variegatus, igneous and metamorphic petrology, applied cloud and precipitation physics, DNA-protein interactions, evolution of adenoviruses and picornaviruses. *Unit head:* Dr. Carlos A. Garcia, Dean, 210-829-2717, Fax: 210-829-3153, E-mail: cagarci9@uiwtx.edu. *Application contact:* Jessica Delarosa, Associate Director of Admissions, 210-829-6005, Fax: 210-829-3921, E-mail: admis@uiwtx.edu. Website: https://www.uiw.edu/smse/index.html

University of Wyoming, College of Arts and Sciences, Department of Mathematics and Statistics, Laramie, WY 82071. Offers applied statistics (MS); mathematics (MA, MAT, MS, MST, PhD). *Program availability:* Part-time. Terminal master's awarded for partial completion of doctoral program. *Degree requirements:* For master's, comprehensive exam, thesis, qualifying exam; for doctorate, comprehensive exam, thesis/dissertation, preliminary exam. *Entrance requirements:* For master's and doctorate, GRE General Test, minimum GPA of 3.0. Additional exam requirements/recommendations for international students: Required—TOEFL (minimum score 540 paper-based; 76 iBT). *Expenses: Tuition,* area resident: Full-time $6504; part-time $271 per credit hour. Tuition, state resident: full-time $6504; part-time $271 per credit hour. Tuition, nonresident: full-time $19,464; part-time $811 per credit hour. International tuition: $19,464 full-time. *Required fees:* $1410.94; $343.82 per semester. $343.82 per semester. Tuition and fees vary according to course load, program and reciprocity agreements. *Faculty research:* Numerical analysis, classical analysis, mathematical modeling, algebraic combinations.

Villanova University, Graduate School of Liberal Arts and Sciences, Department of Mathematics and Statistics, Villanova, PA 19085-1699. Offers applied statistics (MS); mathematics (MA). *Program availability:* Part-time, evening/weekend. *Degree requirements:* For master's, comprehensive exam. *Entrance requirements:* For master's, GRE, minimum GPA of 3.0. Additional exam requirements/recommendations for international students: Required—TOEFL. Electronic applications accepted.

Virginia Polytechnic Institute and State University, Graduate School, College of Science, Blacksburg, VA 24061. Offers biological sciences (MS, PhD); biomedical technology development and management (MS); chemistry (MS, PhD); data analysis and applied statistics (MA); economics (PhD); geosciences (MS, PhD); mathematics (MS, PhD); physics (MS, PhD); psychology (MS, PhD); statistics (MS, PhD). *Faculty:* 349 full-time (109 women), 3 part-time/adjunct (2 women). *Students:* 542 full-time (202 women), 39 part-time (19 women); includes 71 minority (11 Black or African American, non-Hispanic/Latino; 1 American Indian or Alaska Native, non-Hispanic/Latino; 18 Asian, non-Hispanic/Latino; 32 Hispanic/Latino; 9 Two or more races, non-Hispanic/Latino), 220 international. Average age 27. 977 applicants, 25% accepted, 110 enrolled. In 2018, 75 master's, 69 doctorates awarded. *Degree requirements:* For master's, comprehensive exam (for some programs), thesis (for some programs); for doctorate, comprehensive exam (for some programs), thesis/dissertation (for some programs). *Entrance requirements:* For master's and doctorate, GRE/GMAT. Additional exam requirements/recommendations for international students: Required—TOEFL (minimum score 90 iBT). *Application deadline:* For fall admission, 8/1 for domestic students, 4/1 for international students; for spring admission, 1/1 for domestic students, 9/1 for international students. Applications are processed on a rolling basis. Application fee:

$75. Electronic applications accepted. *Expenses:* Tuition, state resident: full-time $15,510; part-time $739.50 per credit hour. Tuition, nonresident: full-time $29,629; part-time $1490.25 per credit hour. *Required fees:* $2804; $550 per semester. Tuition and fees vary according to course load, campus/location and program. *Financial support:* In 2018–19, 7 fellowships with full tuition reimbursements (averaging $29,657 per year), 260 research assistantships with full tuition reimbursements (averaging $15,888 per year), 383 teaching assistantships with full tuition reimbursements (averaging $18,063 per year) were awarded; unspecified assistantships also available. Financial award application deadline: 3/1; financial award applicants required to submit FAFSA. *Total annual research expenditures:* $27.3 million. *Unit head:* Dr. Sally C. Morton, Dean, 540-231-5422, Fax: 540-231-3380, E-mail: scmorton@vt.edu. *Application contact:* Allison Craft, Executive Assistant, 540-231-6394, Fax: 540-231-3380, E-mail: crafta@vt.edu. Website: http://www.science.vt.edu/

West Chester University of Pennsylvania, College of the Sciences and Mathematics, Department of Mathematics, West Chester, PA 19383. Offers applied and computational mathematics (MS); applied statistics (MS, Certificate); mathematics (MA, Teaching Certificate); mathematics education (MA). *Program availability:* Part-time, evening/weekend. *Degree requirements:* For master's, comprehensive exam or thesis (for MA). *Entrance requirements:* For master's, GMAT or GRE General Test (for MA in mathematics, may be waived under certain circumstances), interview (for MA in mathematics); for other advanced degree, GMAT or GRE General Test (for Certificate in applied statistics). Additional exam requirements/recommendations for international students: Required—TOEFL or IELTS. Electronic applications accepted. *Faculty research:* Teachers teaching with technology in service training program, biostatistics, hierarchical linear models, clustered binary outcome data, mathematics biology, stochastic analysis.

Western Illinois University, School of Graduate Studies, College of Business and Technology, Department of Economics and Decision Sciences, Program in Applied Statistics and Decision Analytics, Macomb, IL 61455-1390. Offers MS. *Program availability:* Part-time. *Students:* 9 full-time (3 women), 8 part-time (2 women); includes 6 minority (2 Black or African American, non-Hispanic/Latino; 2 Asian, non-Hispanic/Latino; 2 Two or more races, non-Hispanic/Latino), 8 international. Average age 32. 16 applicants, 44% accepted, 4 enrolled. In 2018, 5 master's awarded. *Application deadline:* Applications are processed on a rolling basis. Application fee: $30. Electronic applications accepted. *Financial support:* Unspecified assistantships available. *Unit head:* Dr. Tara Feld, Chairperson, 309-298-2442. *Application contact:* Dr. Mark Mossman, Assistant Director of Graduate Studies, 309-298-1806, Fax: 309-298-2345, E-mail: grad-office@wiu.edu. Website: http://www.wiu.edu/cbt/eds/graduate-appliedstats.php

Worcester Polytechnic Institute, Graduate Admissions, Department of Mathematical Sciences, Worcester, MA 01609-2280. Offers applied mathematics (MS); applied statistics (MS); financial mathematics (MS); industrial mathematics (MS); mathematical sciences (PhD, Graduate Certificate); mathematics for educators (MMF). *Program availability:* Part-time, evening/weekend. *Students:* 56 full-time (26 women), 34 part-time (13 women); includes 3 minority (1 Black or African American, non-Hispanic/Latino; 1 Asian, non-Hispanic/Latino; 1 Hispanic/Latino), 51 international. Average age 27. 284 applicants, 63% accepted, 33 enrolled. In 2018, 35 master's, 6 doctorates awarded. Terminal master's awarded for partial completion of doctoral program. *Degree requirements:* For master's, thesis (for some programs); for doctorate, comprehensive exam, thesis/dissertation. *Entrance requirements:* For master's, GRE Subject Test in math (for teaching assistantship; strongly recommended for all others), 3 letters of recommendation; for doctorate, GRE General Test, GRE Subject Test (math), 3 letters of recommendation. Additional exam requirements/recommendations for international students: Required—TOEFL (minimum score 563 paper-based; 84 iBT), IELTS (minimum score 7). *Application deadline:* For fall admission, 1/1 priority date for domestic students, 1/1 for international students; for spring admission, 10/1 priority date for domestic students, 10/1 for international students. Applications are processed on a rolling basis. Application fee: $70. Electronic applications accepted. *Financial support:* Fellowships, research assistantships, teaching assistantships, career-related internships or fieldwork, institutionally sponsored loans, scholarships/grants, and unspecified assistantships available. Financial award application deadline: 1/1. *Unit head:* Dr. Luca Capogna, Department Head, 508-831-5241, Fax: 508-831-5824, E-mail: lcapogna@wpi.edu. *Application contact:* Dr. Sarah Olsen, Graduate Coordinator, 508-831-5241, Fax: 508-831-5824, E-mail: sdolsen@wpi.edu. Website: https://www.wpi.edu/academics/departments/mathematical-sciences

Wright State University, Graduate School, College of Science and Mathematics, Department of Mathematics and Statistics, Program in Applied Statistics, Dayton, OH 45435. Offers MS. *Degree requirements:* For master's, comprehensive exam. *Entrance requirements:* For master's, 1 year of course work in calculus and matrix algebra, previous course work in computer programming and statistics. Additional exam requirements/recommendations for international students: Required—TOEFL. *Faculty research:* Reliability theory, stochastic process, nonparametric statistics, design of experiments, multivariate statistics.

Biomathematics

Florida State University, The Graduate School, Department of Anthropology, Department of Mathematics, Tallahassee, FL 32306-4510. Offers applied and computational mathematics (MS, PhD); biomathematics (MS, PhD); financial mathematics (MS, PhD), including actuarial science (MS); pure mathematics (MS, PhD). *Program availability:* Part-time. *Students:* 114 full-time (31 women); includes 8 minority (1 Black or African American, non-Hispanic/Latino; 1 Asian, non-Hispanic/Latino; 2 Hispanic/Latino; 4 Two or more races, non-Hispanic/Latino), 74 international. 225 applicants, 45% accepted, 47 enrolled. In 2018, 13 master's, 11 doctorates awarded. Terminal master's awarded for partial completion of doctoral program. *Degree requirements:* For master's, comprehensive exam (for some programs), thesis optional; for doctorate, comprehensive exam, thesis/dissertation, candidacy exam (including written qualifying examinations which differ by degree concentration). *Entrance requirements:* For master's and doctorate, GRE General Test, minimum upper-division GPA of 3.0, 4-year bachelor's degree. Additional exam requirements/recommendations for international students: Required—TOEFL (minimum score 550 paper-based; 80 iBT), IELTS (minimum score 6.5). *Application deadline:* For fall admission, 12/15 priority date for domestic and international students; for spring admission, 4/30 for domestic and international students. Application fee: $30. Electronic applications accepted. *Expenses: Tuition,* area resident: Part-time $479.32 per credit hour. Tuition and fees vary according

to campus/location and program. *Financial support:* In 2018–19, 109 students received support, including 2 fellowships with full tuition reimbursements available (averaging $24,053 per year), 10 research assistantships with full tuition reimbursements available (averaging $20,053 per year), 83 teaching assistantships with full tuition reimbursements available (averaging $20,053 per year); career-related internships or fieldwork, scholarships/grants, health care benefits, tuition waivers (full and partial), and unspecified assistantships also available. Financial award application deadline: 12/15; financial award applicants required to submit FAFSA. *Faculty research:* Low-dimensional and geometric topology, mathematical modeling in neuroscience, computational stochastics and Monte Carlo methods, mathematical physics, applied analysis. *Total annual research expenditures:* $1.3 million. *Unit head:* Dr. Philip L. Bowers, Chairperson, 850-644-2202, Fax: 850-644-4053, E-mail: bowers@math.fsu.edu. *Application contact:* Elizabeth Scott, Graduate Advisor and Admissions Coordinator, 850-644-2278, Fax: 850-644-4053, E-mail: emscott2@fsu.edu. Website: http://www.math.fsu.edu/

University of California, Los Angeles, David Geffen School of Medicine and Graduate Division, Graduate Programs in Medicine, Department of Biomathematics, Program in Biomathematics, Los Angeles, CA 90095. Offers MS, PhD. *Degree requirements:* For

Peterson's Graduate Programs in the Physical Sciences, Mathematics, Agricultural Sciences, the Environment & Natural Resources 2020

www.petersons.com **189**

master's, comprehensive exam, thesis; for doctorate, thesis/dissertation, written and oral qualifying exams; 2 quarters of teaching experience. *Entrance requirements:* For master's and doctorate, GRE General and Subject Tests, bachelor's degree; minimum undergraduate GPA of 3.0 (or its equivalent if letter grade system not used). Additional exam requirements/recommendations for international students: Required—TOEFL. Electronic applications accepted.

Biometry

Cornell University, Graduate School, Graduate Fields of Agriculture and Life Sciences, Field of Biometry, Ithaca, NY 14853. Offers MS, PhD. Terminal master's awarded for partial completion of doctoral program. *Degree requirements:* For master's, thesis; for doctorate, comprehensive exam, thesis/dissertation. *Entrance requirements:* For master's and doctorate, GRE General Test, 2 letters of recommendation. Additional exam requirements/recommendations for international students: Required—TOEFL (minimum score 550 paper-based; 77 iBT). Electronic applications accepted. *Faculty research:* Environmental, agricultural, and biological statistics; biomathematics; modern nonparametric statistics; statistical genetics; computational statistics.

Cornell University, Graduate School, Graduate Fields of Engineering, Field of Statistics, Ithaca, NY 14853. Offers applied statistics (MPS); biometry (MS, PhD); decision theory (MS, PhD); economic and social statistics (MS, PhD); engineering statistics (MS, PhD); experimental design (MS, PhD); mathematical statistics (MS, PhD); probability (MS, PhD); sampling (MS, PhD); statistical computing (MS, PhD); stochastic processes (MS, PhD). Terminal master's awarded for partial completion of doctoral program. *Degree requirements:* For master's, project (MPS), thesis (MS); for doctorate, one foreign language, thesis/dissertation. *Entrance requirements:* For master's, GRE General Test (for MS), 2 letters of recommendation (MS, MPS); for doctorate, GRE General Test, 2 letters of recommendation. Additional exam requirements/recommendations for international students: Required—TOEFL (minimum score 550 paper-based; 77 iBT). Electronic applications accepted. *Faculty research:* Bayesian analysis, survival analysis, nonparametric statistics, stochastic processes, mathematical statistics.

San Diego State University, Graduate and Research Affairs, College of Health and Human Services, Program in Biostatistics and Biometry, San Diego, CA 92182. Offers biometry (MPH). Electronic applications accepted.

University of Wisconsin–Madison, Graduate School, College of Letters and Science, Department of Statistics, Biometry Program, Madison, WI 53706-1380. Offers MS.

Biostatistics

American University, College of Arts and Sciences, Department of Mathematics and Statistics, Washington, DC 22016-8050. Offers applied statistics (Certificate); biostatistics (MS); data science (Certificate); mathematics (MA); professional science: quantitative analysis (MS); statistics (MS). *Program availability:* Part-time, evening/weekend. *Faculty:* 36 full-time (13 women), 8 part-time/adjunct (1 woman). *Students:* 19 full-time (4 women), 21 part-time (9 women); includes 14 minority (7 Black or African American, non-Hispanic/Latino; 2 Asian, non-Hispanic/Latino; 4 Hispanic/Latino; 1 Two or more races, non-Hispanic/Latino), 10 international. Average age 29. 64 applicants, 92% accepted, 19 enrolled. In 2018, 10 master's, 9 other advanced degrees awarded. *Degree requirements:* For master's, comprehensive exam, thesis or alternative. *Entrance requirements:* For master's, GRE; please see website: https://www.american.edu/cas/mathstat/, statement of purpose, transcripts, 2 letters of recommendation, resume; for Certificate, bachelor's degree, statement of purpose, transcripts, resume. Additional exam requirements/recommendations for international students: Required—TOEFL (minimum score 600 paper-based; 100 iBT). Application fee: $55. *Expenses:* Contact institution. *Financial support:* Scholarships/grants and unspecified assistantships available. Financial award applicants required to submit FAFSA. *Unit head:* Dr. Stephen Casey, Department Chair, 202-885-3120, E-mail: mathstat@american.edu. *Application contact:* Jonathan Harper, Assistant Director, Graduate Recruitment, 202-855-3620, E-mail: casgrad@american.edu.
Website: http://www.american.edu/cas/mathstat/

American University of Beirut, Graduate Programs, Faculty of Health Sciences, Beirut 1107 2020, Lebanon. Offers environmental sciences (MS), including environmental health; epidemiology (MS, PhD); epidemiology and biostatistics (MPH); health care leadership (EMHCL); health management and policy (MPH), including health service administration; health promotion and community health (MPH); health research (MS); public health nutrition (MS). *Program availability:* Part-time, evening/weekend. *Faculty:* 33 full-time (20 women), 10 part-time/adjunct (5 women). *Students:* 65 full-time (56 women), 84 part-time (77 women). Average age 26. 391 applicants, 42% accepted, 64 enrolled. In 2018, 136 master's awarded. *Degree requirements:* For master's, one foreign language, comprehensive exam, thesis, no thesis is required for the MPH program; for doctorate, one foreign language, comprehensive exam, thesis/dissertation. *Entrance requirements:* For master's, 2 letters of recommendations, personal statement for each program, transcript of grades, letter explaining the grading system and passing grade; for doctorate, GRE, Official transcripts(all levels) and certified copies of degrees, 3 letters of recommendations, personal statement, CV, interview. Additional exam requirements/recommendations for international students: Required—TOEFL (minimum score 97 iBT), IELTS (minimum score 7). *Application deadline:* For fall admission, 4/4 for domestic and international students; for spring admission, 11/5 for domestic and international students. Application fee: $50. Electronic applications accepted. *Expenses: Tuition:* Full-time $17,748; part-time $986 per credit. *Required fees:* $762. Tuition and fees vary according to course load and program. *Financial support:* In 2018–19, 50 students received support, including 3 fellowships with full and partial tuition reimbursements available (averaging $14,400 per year), 9 research assistantships with full and partial tuition reimbursements available (averaging $6,816 per year), 6 teaching assistantships with full and partial tuition reimbursements available (averaging $3,808 per year); scholarships/grants and unspecified assistantships also available. Financial award application deadline: 4/4. *Faculty research:* Conflict and health; refugees health; sexual and reproductive health; tobacco control; health care quality and access and environmental management. *Total annual research expenditures:* $2.3 million. *Unit head:* Prof. Iman Adel Nuwayhid, Dean/Professor, 961-1-759683 Ext. 4600, Fax: 961-1-744470, E-mail: nuwayhid@aub.edu.lb. *Application contact:* Lama El Kadi, Administrative Coordinator, 961-1-350000 Ext. 4687, E-mail: le19@aub.edu.lb.
Website: http://www.aub.edu.lb/fhs/Pages/default.aspx

Boston University, Graduate School of Arts and Sciences, Intercollegiate Program in Biostatistics, Boston, MA 02215. Offers MA, PhD. *Students:* 50 full-time (33 women), 7 part-time (5 women); includes 9 minority (6 Asian, non-Hispanic/Latino; 1 Hispanic/Latino; 2 Two or more races, non-Hispanic/Latino), 21 international. Average age 26. 244 applicants, 36% accepted, 15 enrolled. In 2018, 6 master's, 7 doctorates awarded. Terminal master's awarded for partial completion of doctoral program. *Degree requirements:* For master's, comprehensive exam; for doctorate, comprehensive exam, thesis/dissertation, teaching requirement. *Entrance requirements:* For master's and doctorate, GRE General Test, 3 letters of recommendation, transcripts, personal statement, curriculum vitae/resume, previous coursework document. Additional exam requirements/recommendations for international students: Required—TOEFL (minimum score 550 paper-based; 84 iBT). *Application deadline:* For fall admission, 12/1 for domestic and international students. Application fee: $95. Electronic applications accepted. *Financial support:* In 2018–19, 43 students received support, including 6 fellowships with full tuition reimbursements available (averaging $22,660 per year), 36 research assistantships with full tuition reimbursements available (averaging $22,660 per year); traineeships and health care benefits also available. Support available to part-time students. Financial award application deadline: 12/1. *Unit head:* Dr. Josee Dupuis, Chair, 617-638-5880, E-mail: dupuis@bu.edu. *Application contact:* Kaitlyn Grevera, Program Coordinator, 617-638-5163, Fax: 617-638-6484, E-mail: kgrevera@bu.edu.
Website: https://www.bu.edu/sph/education/degrees-and-programs/doctor-of-philosophy-phd/biostatistics-phd-program/

Boston University, School of Public Health, Biostatistics Department, Boston, MA 02215. Offers MA, MPH, PhD. *Program availability:* Part-time, evening/weekend. *Faculty:* 26 full-time, 18 part-time/adjunct. *Students:* 14 full-time (9 women), 4 part-time (3 women); includes 6 minority (5 Asian, non-Hispanic/Latino; 1 Two or more races, non-Hispanic/Latino), 4 international. Average age 25. *Entrance requirements:* For master's, GRE, GMAT, MCAT; for doctorate, GRE. Additional exam requirements/recommendations for international students: Required—TOEFL (minimum score 600 paper-based; 100 iBT), IELTS (minimum score 7). *Application deadline:* For fall admission, 12/1 priority date for domestic and international students; for spring admission, 10/1 priority date for domestic students. Applications are processed on a rolling basis. Application fee: $120. Electronic applications accepted. *Financial support:* Fellowships, research assistantships, teaching assistantships, career-related internships or fieldwork, Federal Work-Study, institutionally sponsored loans, scholarships/grants, traineeships, health care benefits, and unspecified assistantships available. Support available to part-time students. Financial award application deadline: 3/1; financial award applicants required to submit FAFSA. *Faculty research:* Statistical genetics, clinical trials, research methods. *Unit head:* Dr. Josee Dupuis, Interim Chair, 617-638-5880, Fax: 617-638-4458, E-mail: dupuis@bu.edu. *Application contact:* Marisa Crowley, Educational Program Manager, 617-638-4640, Fax: 617-638-5207, E-mail: marisac@bu.edu.
Website: http://www.bu.edu/sph/bio

Brown University, Graduate School, Division of Biology and Medicine, School of Public Health, Department of Biostatistics, Providence, RI 02912. Offers AM, Sc M, PhD. *Degree requirements:* For doctorate, thesis/dissertation, preliminary exam. *Entrance requirements:* For master's and doctorate, GRE General Test.

California State University, East Bay, Office of Graduate Studies, College of Science, Department of Statistics and Biostatistics, Biostatistics Program, Hayward, CA 94542-3000. Offers MS. *Program availability:* Part-time, evening/weekend. *Degree requirements:* For master's, comprehensive exam. *Entrance requirements:* For master's, minimum GPA of 3.0; math through lower-division calculus; statement of purpose; 2-3 letters of recommendation or GRE. Additional exam requirements/recommendations for international students: Required—TOEFL (minimum score 550 paper-based). Electronic applications accepted.

Case Western Reserve University, School of Medicine and School of Graduate Studies, Graduate Programs in Medicine, Department of Population and Quantitative Health Sciences, Program in Biostatistics, Cleveland, OH 44106. Offers MS. *Program availability:* Part-time. Terminal master's awarded for partial completion of doctoral program. *Degree requirements:* For master's, comprehensive exam, thesis, exam/practicum. *Entrance requirements:* For master's, GRE General Test or MCAT, 3 recommendations. Additional exam requirements/recommendations for international students: Required—TOEFL (minimum score 550 paper-based). Electronic applications accepted. *Expenses: Tuition:* Full-time $45,168; part-time $1939 per credit hour. *Required fees:* $36; $18 per semester. $18 per semester. *Faculty research:* Survey sampling and statistical computing, generalized linear models, statistical modeling, models in breast cancer survival.

Case Western Reserve University, School of Medicine and School of Graduate Studies, Graduate Programs in Medicine, Department of Population and Quantitative Health Sciences, Program in Epidemiology and Biostatistics, Cleveland, OH 44106. Offers PhD. *Program availability:* Part-time. Terminal master's awarded for partial completion of doctoral program. *Degree requirements:* For doctorate, comprehensive exam, thesis/dissertation. *Entrance requirements:* For doctorate, GRE General Test, 3 recommendations. Additional exam requirements/recommendations for international students: Required—TOEFL (minimum score 550 paper-based). Electronic applications accepted. *Expenses: Tuition:* Full-time $45,168; part-time $1939 per credit hour. *Required fees:* $36; $18 per semester. $18 per semester. *Faculty research:* Cardiovascular epidemiology, cancer risk factors, HIV in underserved populations, effectiveness studies in Medicare patients.

Columbia University, Columbia University Mailman School of Public Health, Department of Biostatistics, New York, NY 10032. Offers MPH, MS, Dr PH, PhD. PhD offered in cooperation with the Graduate School of Arts and Sciences. *Program availability:* Part-time. *Degree requirements:* For doctorate, thesis/dissertation. *Entrance requirements:* For master's, GRE General Test; for doctorate, GRE General Test, MPH or equivalent (for Dr PH). Additional exam requirements/recommendations for international students: Required—TOEFL (minimum score 600 paper-based; 100 iBT). Electronic applications accepted. *Faculty research:* Statistical methods and public health implications of biomedical experiments, clinical trials, functional data analysis, statistical genetics, observational studies.

Dartmouth College, Guarini School of Graduate and Advanced Studies, Institute for Quantitative Biomedical Sciences, Hanover, NH 03755. Offers epidemiology (MS); health data science (MS); quantitative biomedical sciences (PhD). PhD offered in collaboration with the Department of Genetics and the Department of Community and Family Medicine. *Students:* 57 full-time (30 women); includes 10 minority (2 Black or African American, non-Hispanic/Latino; 5 Asian, non-Hispanic/Latino; 2 Hispanic/Latino; 1 Two or more races, non-Hispanic/Latino), 27 international. Average age 26. 155 applicants, 35% accepted, 29 enrolled. In 2018, 1 doctorate awarded. *Entrance requirements:* For doctorate, GRE (minimum scores: 1200 old scoring, 308 new scoring verbal and quantitative; analytical writing 4.5; verbal 500 old scoring, 153 new scoring). *Application deadline:* For fall admission, 3/1 for domestic students. Applications are processed on a rolling basis. Application fee: $75. Electronic applications accepted. *Financial support:* Fellowships available. *Unit head:* Dr. Micheal Whitfield, Director, 603-650-1109. *Application contact:* Gary Hutchins, Assistant Dean, School of Arts and Sciences, 603-646-2107, Fax: 603-646-3488, E-mail: g.hutchins@dartmouth.edu.
Website: https://www.dartmouth.edu/~qbs/index.html

Drexel University, Dornsife School of Public Health, Department of Epidemiology and Biostatistics, Philadelphia, PA 19104-2875. Offers biostatistics (MS); epidemiology (PhD); epidemiology and biostatistics (Certificate).

Drexel University, School of Biomedical Engineering, Science and Health Systems, Philadelphia, PA 19104-2875. Offers biomedical engineering (MS, PhD); biomedical science (MS, PhD); biostatistics (MS); clinical/rehabilitation engineering (MS); MD/PhD. *Degree requirements:* For doctorate, thesis/dissertation, 1 year of residency, qualifying exam. *Entrance requirements:* For master's, minimum GPA of 3.0; for doctorate, minimum GPA of 3.0, MS. Additional exam requirements/recommendations for international students: Required—TOEFL. Electronic applications accepted. *Faculty research:* Cardiovascular dynamics, diagnostic and therapeutic ultrasound.

Duke University, School of Medicine, Program in Biostatistics, Durham, NC 27708. Offers MS. *Program availability:* Part-time. *Faculty:* 56 full-time (23 women), 17 part-time/adjunct (8 women). *Students:* 52 full-time (32 women); includes 3 minority (2 Black or African American, non-Hispanic/Latino; 1 American Indian or Alaska Native, non-Hispanic/Latino), 30 international. 251 applicants, 64% accepted, 28 enrolled. In 2018, 28 master's awarded. *Degree requirements:* For master's, project. *Entrance requirements:* For master's, GRE, 2 semesters of calculus plus linear algebra, Bachelor's Degree. Additional exam requirements/recommendations for international students: Required—TOEFL, IELTS, GRE. *Application deadline:* For fall admission, 1/15 for domestic students. Application fee: $75. *Financial support:* In 2018–19, 23 students received support. Scholarships/grants available. Financial award application deadline: 4/16; financial award applicants required to submit FAFSA. *Unit head:* Dr. Greg Samsa, Professor of Biostatistics, 919-613-5212, E-mail: megan.neely@duke.edu. *Application contact:* Michelle Evans, Assistant Director of Education, 919-613-6137, Fax: 919-681-4569, E-mail: michelle.evans@duke.edu.
Website: http://biostat.duke.edu/master-biostatistics-program/program-overview

East Tennessee State University, School of Graduate Studies, College of Public Health, Program in Public Health, Johnson City, TN 37614. Offers biostatistics (MPH, Postbaccalaureate Certificate); community health (MPH, DPH); environmental health (MPH); epidemiology (MPH, DPH, Postbaccalaureate Certificate); gerontology (Postbaccalaureate Certificate); global health (Postbaccalaureate Certificate); health care management (Postbaccalaureate Certificate); health management and policy (DPH); public health (Postbaccalaureate Certificate); public health services administration (MPH); rural health (Postbaccalaureate Certificate). *Accreditation:* CEPH. *Program availability:* Part-time, online learning. *Degree requirements:* For master's, comprehensive exam, field experience; for doctorate, thesis/dissertation, practicum. *Entrance requirements:* For master's, GRE General Test, minimum GPA of 2.75, SOPHAS application, three letters of recommendation; for doctorate, GRE General Test, SOPHAS application, three letters of recommendation; for Postbaccalaureate Certificate, minimum GPA of 2.5, three letters of recommendation, resume. Additional exam requirements/recommendations for international students: Required—TOEFL (minimum score 550 paper-based; 79 iBT), IELTS (minimum score 6.5). Electronic applications accepted.

Emory University, Rollins School of Public Health, Department of Biostatistics and Bioinformatics, Atlanta, GA 30322-1100. Offers bioinformatics (PhD); biostatistics (MPH, MSPH); public health informatics (MSPH). PhD offered through the Graduate School of Arts and Sciences. *Program availability:* Part-time. *Degree requirements:* For master's, thesis, practicum. *Entrance requirements:* For master's, GRE General Test. Additional exam requirements/recommendations for international students: Required—TOEFL (minimum score 550 paper-based; 80 iBT). Electronic applications accepted.

Florida International University, Robert Stempel College of Public Health and Social Work, Programs in Public Health, Miami, FL 33199. Offers biostatistics (MPH); environmental and occupational health (MPH, PhD); epidemiology (MPH, PhD); health policy and management (MPH); health promotion and disease prevention (MPH, PhD). PhD program has fall admissions only; MPH offered jointly with University of Miami. *Accreditation:* CEPH. *Program availability:* Part-time, evening/weekend, online learning. *Faculty:* 34 full-time (15 women), 3 part-time/adjunct (all women). *Students:* 175 full-time (118 women), 49 part-time (38 women); includes 156 minority (58 Black or African American, non-Hispanic/Latino; 1 American Indian or Alaska Native, non-Hispanic/Latino; 15 Asian, non-Hispanic/Latino; 78 Hispanic/Latino; 4 Two or more races, non-Hispanic/Latino), 34 international. Average age 29. 300 applicants, 71% accepted, 90 enrolled. In 2018, 57 master's, 10 doctorates awarded. *Degree requirements:* For master's, thesis optional; for doctorate, comprehensive exam, thesis/dissertation. *Entrance requirements:* For master's, minimum GPA of 3.0, letters of recommendation; for doctorate, GRE, resume, minimum GPA of 3.0, letters of recommendation, letter of intent. Additional exam requirements/recommendations for international students: Required—TOEFL (minimum score 550 paper-based; 80 iBT). *Application deadline:* For fall admission, 6/1 for domestic students, 4/1 for international students; for spring admission, 10/1 for domestic students, 9/1 for international students. Applications are processed on a rolling basis. Application fee: $30. Electronic applications accepted. *Expenses:* Contact institution. *Financial support:* Institutionally sponsored loans, scholarships/grants, and tuition waivers (full) available. Financial award application deadline: 3/1; financial award applicants required to submit FAFSA. *Faculty research:* Drugs/AIDS intervention among migrant workers, provision of services for active/recovering drug users with HIV. *Unit head:* Dr. Benjamin C. Amick, III, Chair, 305-348-7527, Fax: 305-348-7803, E-mail: benjamin.amickiii@fiu.edu. *Application contact:* Nanett Rojas, Manager, Admissions Operations, 305-348-7464, Fax: 305-348-7441, E-mail: gradadm@fiu.edu.

Florida State University, The Graduate School, Department of Anthropology, Department of Statistics, Tallahassee, FL 32306-4330. Offers applied statistics (MS); biostatistics (MS, PhD); mathematical statistics (MS, PhD); statistical data science (MS). *Program availability:* Part-time. *Faculty:* 23 full-time (5 women). *Students:* 166 full-time (73 women), 27 part-time (6 women); includes 18 minority (2 Black or African American, non-Hispanic/Latino; 8 Asian, non-Hispanic/Latino; 2 Hispanic/Latino; 6 Two or more races, non-Hispanic/Latino), 151 international. Average age 26. 386 applicants, 62% accepted, 50 enrolled. In 2018, 59 master's, 23 doctorates awarded. Terminal master's awarded for partial completion of doctoral program. *Degree requirements:* For master's, thesis optional; for doctorate, comprehensive exam, thesis/dissertation, departmental qualifying exam. *Entrance requirements:* For master's, GRE General Test, calculus, linear algebra, one course each in applied statistics and probability, minimum GPA of 3.0; for doctorate, GRE General Test, minimum GPA of 3.0, two semesters of advanced calculus (intermediate analysis, real analysis with proofs). Additional exam requirements/recommendations for international students: Required—TOEFL (minimum score 80 iBT), IELTS (minimum score 6.5). *Application deadline:* For fall admission, 7/1 for domestic and international students. Application fee: $30. Electronic applications accepted. *Expenses: Tuition, area resident:* Part-time $479.32 per credit hour. Tuition and fees vary according to campus/location and program. *Financial support:* In 2018–19, 89 students received support, including 10 research assistantships with full tuition reimbursements available (averaging $23,000 per year), 66 teaching assistantships with full tuition reimbursements available (averaging $20,500 per year); institutionally sponsored loans, scholarships/grants, health care benefits, tuition waivers (full and partial), and unspecified assistantships also available. Support available to part-time students. Financial award application deadline: 2/1; financial award applicants required to submit FAFSA. *Faculty research:* Statistical inference, high dimensional data analysis, biostatistics, nonparametric estimation, automatic target recognition. *Total annual research expenditures:* $813,343. *Unit head:* Dr. Xufeng Niu, Chairman, 850-644-4008, Fax: 850-644-5271, E-mail: niu@stat.fsu.edu. *Application contact:* Natalie Webster, Academic Program Specialist, 850-644-3514, Fax: 850-644-5271, E-mail: nwebster@fsu.edu.
Website: http://www.stat.fsu.edu/

George Mason University, Volgenau School of Engineering, Department of Statistics, Fairfax, VA 22030. Offers biostatistics (MS); statistical science (MS, PhD); statistics (Certificate). *Faculty:* 17 full-time (4 women), 5 part-time/adjunct (0 women). *Students:* 35 full-time (16 women), 30 part-time (14 women); includes 13 minority (3 Black or African American, non-Hispanic/Latino; 8 Asian, non-Hispanic/Latino; 1 Hispanic/Latino; 1 Two or more races, non-Hispanic/Latino), 28 international. Average age 29. 71 applicants, 77% accepted, 23 enrolled. In 2018, 24 master's, 3 doctorates, 5 other advanced degrees awarded. *Degree requirements:* For master's, thesis optional; for doctorate, comprehensive exam, thesis/dissertation, qualifying exams. *Entrance requirements:* For master's, GRE/GMAT, bachelor's degree from accredited institution with minimum GPA of 3.0 in major that includes calculus, matrix algebra, calculus-based probability and statistics; personal goal statement; 2 official copies of transcripts; 3 letters of recommendation; resume; official bank statement; proof of financial support; photocopy of passport; for doctorate, GRE, MS in math-intensive discipline with minimum GPA of 3.5, personal goals statement, 2 official copies of transcripts, 3 letters of recommendation, resume, official bank statement, proof of financial support, photocopy of passport; for Certificate, bachelor's degree with 2 courses in calculus and probability or statistics, personal goals statement, 2 official copies of transcripts, 1-3 letters of recommendation (depending on program), resume, official bank statement, proof of financial support, photocopy of passport. Additional exam requirements/recommendations for international students: Required—TOEFL (minimum score 575 paper-based; 80 iBT), IELTS (minimum score 6.5), PTE. *Application deadline:* For fall admission, 12/15 priority date for domestic and international students; for spring admission, 8/15 priority date for domestic and international students. Application fee: $65 ($80 for international students). Electronic applications accepted. *Expenses:* $589 per credit in-state, $1,346.75 per credit out-of-state. *Financial support:* In 2018–19, 25 students received support, including 9 research assistantships with tuition reimbursements available (averaging $17,522 per year), 16 teaching assistantships with tuition reimbursements available (averaging $17,851 per year); career-related internships or fieldwork, Federal Work-Study, scholarships/grants, unspecified assistantships, and health care benefits (for full-time research or teaching assistantship recipients) also available. Support available to part-time students. Financial award application deadline: 3/1; financial award applicants required to submit FAFSA. *Faculty research:* Data analytics; visualization; biostatistics; time series; statistical modeling. *Total annual research expenditures:* $368,545. *Unit head:* William F. Rosenberger, Chair, 703-993-3645, Fax: 703-993-1700, E-mail: wrosenbe@gmu.edu. *Application contact:* Elizabeth Quigley, Administrative Assistant, 703-993-9107, Fax: 703-993-1700, E-mail: equigley@gmu.edu.
Website: http://statistics.gmu.edu/

Georgetown University, Graduate School of Arts and Sciences, Department of Biostatistics, Bioinformatics and Biomathematics, Washington, DC 20057-1484. Offers biostatistics (MS, Certificate), including bioinformatics (MS); epidemiology (MS); epidemiology (Certificate). *Entrance requirements:* For master's, GRE General Test. Additional exam requirements/recommendations for international students: Required—TOEFL. *Faculty research:* Occupation epidemiology, cancer.

The George Washington University, Columbian College of Arts and Sciences, Program in Biostatistics, Washington, DC 20052. Offers MS, PhD. *Students:* 13 full-time (11 women), 13 part-time (4 women); includes 5 minority (1 Black or African American, non-Hispanic/Latino; 4 Asian, non-Hispanic/Latino), 19 international. Average age 30. 110 applicants, 39% accepted, 8 enrolled. In 2018, 7 master's awarded. *Degree requirements:* For master's, comprehensive exam; for doctorate, thesis/dissertation, general exam. *Entrance requirements:* For master's and doctorate, GRE General Test, minimum GPA of 3.0. Additional exam requirements/recommendations for international students: Required—TOEFL (minimum score 550 paper-based; 80 iBT). *Application deadline:* For fall admission, 1/15 priority date for domestic and international students; for spring admission, 10/1 priority date for domestic students, 9/1 priority date for international students. Applications are processed on a rolling basis. Application fee: $75. Electronic applications accepted. *Financial support:* In 2018–19, 1 student received support. Fellowships with full tuition reimbursements available, teaching

Peterson's Graduate Programs in the Physical Sciences, Mathematics, Agricultural Sciences, the Environment & Natural Resources 2020

www.petersons.com **191**

assistantships, and tuition waivers available. *Unit head:* Dr. Zhaohai Li, Director, 202-994-7844, Fax: 202-994-6917, E-mail: zli@gwu.edu. *Application contact:* Dr. Zhaohai Li, Director, 202-994-7844, Fax: 202-994-6917, E-mail: zli@gwu.edu.

The George Washington University, Milken Institute School of Public Health, Department of Epidemiology and Biostatistics, Washington, DC 20052. Offers biostatistics (MPH); epidemiology (MPH); microbiology and emerging infectious diseases (MSPH). *Students:* 76 full-time (62 women), 78 part-time (59 women); includes 63 minority (15 Black or African American, non-Hispanic/Latino; 25 Asian, non-Hispanic/Latino; 19 Hispanic/Latino; 4 Two or more races, non-Hispanic/Latino), 9 international. Average age 28. 602 applicants, 58% accepted, 58 enrolled. In 2018, 89 master's awarded. *Entrance requirements:* For master's, GMAT, GRE General Test, or MCAT. Additional exam requirements/recommendations for international students: Required—TOEFL. *Application deadline:* For fall admission, 4/15 priority date for domestic students, 4/15 for international students; for spring admission, 11/1 for domestic and international students. Applications are processed on a rolling basis. Application fee: $75. *Financial support:* In 2018–19, 6 students received support. Tuition waivers available. Financial award application deadline: 2/15. *Unit head:* Dr. Alan E. Greenberg, Chair, 202-994-0612, E-mail: aeg1@gwu.edu. *Application contact:* Jane Smith, Director of Admissions, 202-994-0248, Fax: 202-994-1860, E-mail: sphhsinfo@gwumc.edu.

Georgia Southern University, Jack N. Averitt College of Graduate Studies, Jiann-Ping Hsu College of Public Health, Program in Public Health, Statesboro, GA 30460. Offers biostatistics (MPH, Dr PH); community health behavior and education (Dr PH); community health education (MPH); environmental health sciences (MPH); epidemiology (MPH); health policy and management (MPH, Dr PH). *Program availability:* Part-time. *Degree requirements:* For master's, thesis optional, practicum; for doctorate, comprehensive exam, thesis/dissertation, preceptorship. *Entrance requirements:* For master's, GRE General Test, minimum GPA of 2.75, 3 letters of recommendation, statement of purpose, resume or curriculum vitae; for doctorate, GRE, GMAT, MCAT, LSAT, minimum GPA of 3.0, 3 letters of recommendation, statement of purpose, resume or curriculum vitae. Additional exam requirements/recommendations for international students: Required—TOEFL (minimum score 537 paper-based; 75 iBT), IELTS (minimum score 6). Electronic applications accepted. *Expenses:* Contact institution. *Faculty research:* Rural public health best practices, health disparity elimination, community initiatives to enhance public health, cost effectiveness analysis, epidemiology of rural public health, environmental health issues, health care system assessment, rural health care, health policy and healthcare financing, survival analysis, nonparametric statistics and resampling methods, micro-arrays and genomics, data imputation techniques and clinical trial methodology.

Georgia State University, College of Arts and Sciences, Department of Mathematics and Statistics, Atlanta, GA 30302-3083. Offers bioinformatics (MS, PhD); biostatistics (MS, PhD); discrete mathematics (MS); mathematics (MS, PhD); scientific computing (MS); statistics (MS). *Program availability:* Part-time. *Faculty:* 28 full-time (8 women), 1 part-time/adjunct (0 women). *Students:* 88 full-time (46 women), 15 part-time (8 women); includes 27 minority (7 Black or African American, non-Hispanic/Latino; 14 Asian, non-Hispanic/Latino; 4 Hispanic/Latino; 2 Two or more races, non-Hispanic/Latino), 57 international. Average age 32. 109 applicants, 65% accepted, 37 enrolled. In 2018, 29 master's, 11 doctorates awarded. Terminal master's awarded for partial completion of doctoral program. *Entrance requirements:* For master's and doctorate, GRE. Additional exam requirements/recommendations for international students: Required—TOEFL (minimum score 550 paper-based; 80 iBT). *Application deadline:* For fall admission, 7/1 priority date for domestic and international students; for spring admission, 11/15 priority date for domestic and international students. Application fee: $50. Electronic applications accepted. *Expenses: Tuition, area resident:* Full-time $9360; part-time $390 per credit hour. Tuition, state resident: full-time $9360; part-time $390 per credit hour. Tuition, nonresident: full-time $30,024; part-time $1251 per credit hour. *International tuition:* $30,024 full-time. *Required fees:* $2128. *Financial support:* In 2018–19, fellowships with full tuition reimbursements (averaging $22,000 per year), research assistantships with full tuition reimbursements (averaging $9,000 per year), teaching assistantships with full tuition reimbursements (averaging $9,000 per year) were awarded; institutionally sponsored loans, scholarships/grants, health care benefits, and unspecified assistantships also available. Financial award application deadline: 2/1. *Faculty research:* Algebra, matrix theory, graph theory and combinatorics; applied mathematics and analysis; collegiate mathematics education; statistics, biostatistics and applications; bioinformatics, dynamical systems. *Unit head:* Dr. Guantao Chen, Chair, 404-413-6436, Fax: 404-413-6403, E-mail: gchen@gsu.edu. *Application contact:* Dr. Guantao Chen, Chair, 404-413-6436, Fax: 404-413-6403, E-mail: gchen@gsu.edu.
Website: https://www.mathstat.gsu.edu/

Grand Valley State University, College of Liberal Arts and Sciences, Program in Biostatistics, Allendale, MI 49401-9403. Offers MS. *Program availability:* Part-time, evening/weekend. *Faculty:* 8 full-time (3 women). *Students:* 28 full-time (14 women), 6 part-time (2 women); includes 7 minority (3 Black or African American, non-Hispanic/Latino; 1 Hispanic/Latino; 3 Two or more races, non-Hispanic/Latino), 2 international. Average age 26. 23 applicants, 96% accepted, 12 enrolled. In 2018, 14 master's awarded. *Entrance requirements:* For master's, minimum GPA of 3.0 or GRE, SAS-based intermediate statistics undergraduate course, resume, personal statement, minimum of 2 letters of recommendation. Additional exam requirements/recommendations for international students: Required—TOEFL (minimum iBT score of 80), IELTS (6.5), or Michigan English Language Assessment Battery (77). *Application deadline:* Applications are processed on a rolling basis. Application fee: $30. Electronic applications accepted. *Expenses:* $682 per credit hour, 37 credit hours. *Financial support:* In 2018–19, 19 students received support, including 1 fellowship, 18 research assistantships with full and partial tuition reimbursements available (averaging $4,000 per year); unspecified assistantships also available. *Faculty research:* Biometrical models, spatial methods, medical statistics, design of experiments. *Unit head:* Dr. Paul Stephenson, Department Chair, 616-331-2081, Fax: 616-331-2910, E-mail: stephenp@gvsu.edu. *Application contact:* Dr. Robert Downer, Graduate Program Director, 616-331-2247, Fax: 616-331-2910, E-mail: downerr@gvsu.edu.

Harvard University, Cyprus International Institute for the Environment and Public Health in Association with Harvard School of Public Health, Cambridge, MA 02138. Offers environmental health (MS); environmental/public health (PhD); epidemiology and biostatistics (MS). *Entrance requirements:* For master's and doctorate, GRE, resume/curriculum vitae, 3 letters of recommendation, BA or BS (including diploma and official transcripts). Additional exam requirements/recommendations for international students: Required—TOEFL, IELTS (minimum score 7). Electronic applications accepted. *Faculty research:* Air pollution, climate change, biostatistics, sustainable development, environmental management.

Harvard University, Graduate School of Arts and Sciences, Department of Biostatistics, Cambridge, MA 02138. Offers PhD.

Harvard University, Harvard T.H. Chan School of Public Health, Department of Biostatistics, Boston, MA 02115-6096. Offers biostatistics (SM, PhD); health data science (SM). *Program availability:* Part-time. *Faculty:* 54 full-time (20 women), 11 part-time/adjunct (4 women). *Students:* 142 full-time (74 women), 5 part-time (3 women); includes 37 minority (4 Black or African American, non-Hispanic/Latino; 25 Asian, non-Hispanic/Latino; 4 Hispanic/Latino; 4 Two or more races, non-Hispanic/Latino), 62 international. Average age 29. 210 applicants, 27% accepted, 38 enrolled. In 2018, 20 master's, 16 doctorates awarded. *Degree requirements:* For doctorate, thesis/dissertation, oral and written qualifying exams. *Entrance requirements:* For master's, GRE, MCAT, prior training in mathematics and/or statistics; for doctorate, GRE, prior training in mathematics and/or statistics. Additional exam requirements/recommendations for international students: Recommended—TOEFL (minimum score 600 paper-based; 100 iBT), IELTS (minimum score 7). *Application deadline:* For fall admission, 12/1 for domestic and international students. Application fee: $135. Electronic applications accepted. *Financial support:* Fellowships, research assistantships, teaching assistantships, Federal Work-Study, scholarships/grants, traineeships, and unspecified assistantships available. Support available to part-time students. Financial award application deadline: 2/15; financial award applicants required to submit FAFSA. *Faculty research:* Statistical genetics, clinical trials, cancer and AIDS research, environmental and mental health, dose response modeling. *Unit head:* Dr. John Quackenbush, Chair/Professor of Biostatistics, 617-432-1056, E-mail: johnq@hsph.harvard.edu. *Application contact:* Vincent W. James, Director of Admissions, 617-432-1031, Fax: 617-432-7080, E-mail: admissions@hsph.harvard.edu.
Website: http://www.hsph.harvard.edu/biostatistics/

Indiana University Bloomington, School of Public Health, Department of Epidemiology and Biostatistics, Bloomington, IN 47405. Offers biostatistics (MPH); epidemiology (MPH, PhD). *Degree requirements:* For master's, thesis or alternative; for doctorate, comprehensive exam, thesis/dissertation. *Entrance requirements:* For master's, GRE (for applicants with cumulative undergraduate GPA less than 2.8); for doctorate, GRE. Additional exam requirements/recommendations for international students: Required—TOEFL (minimum score 550 paper-based; 80 iBT). Electronic applications accepted. *Faculty research:* Nutritional epidemiology, cancer epidemiology, global health, biostatistics.

Indiana University–Purdue University Indianapolis, Richard M. Fairbanks School of Public Health, Indianapolis, IN 46202. Offers biostatistics (MS, PhD); environmental health (MPH); epidemiology (MPH, PhD); global health leadership (Dr PH); health administration (MHA); health policy (Graduate Certificate); health policy and management (MPH, PhD); health systems management (Graduate Certificate); product stewardship (MS); public health (Graduate Certificate); social and behavioral sciences (MPH). *Accreditation:* CAHME; CEPH. *Expenses:* Contact institution.

Iowa State University of Science and Technology, Bioinformatics and Computational Biology Program, Ames, IA 50011. Offers MS, PhD. *Degree requirements:* For doctorate, thesis/dissertation. *Entrance requirements:* For master's and doctorate, GRE General Test. Additional exam requirements/recommendations for international students: Recommended—TOEFL, IELTS. Electronic applications accepted. *Faculty research:* Functional and structural genomics, genome evolution, macromolecular structure and function, mathematical biology and biological statistics, metabolic and developmental networks.

Johns Hopkins University, Bloomberg School of Public Health, Department of Biostatistics, Baltimore, MD 21205-2179. Offers biostatistics (MHS, Sc M, PhD). *Program availability:* Part-time. *Faculty:* 44 full-time. *Students:* 68 (31 women). 424 applicants, 8% accepted, 13 enrolled. In 2018, 11 master's, 6 doctorates awarded. *Degree requirements:* For master's, comprehensive exam (for some programs), thesis (for some programs), written exam, final project; for doctorate, comprehensive exam, thesis/dissertation, 1-year full-time residency, oral and written exams. *Entrance requirements:* For master's and doctorate, GRE General Test, course work in calculus and matrix algebra, 3 letters of recommendation, curriculum vitae. Additional exam requirements/recommendations for international students: Required—TOEFL (minimum score 100 iBT), IELTS (minimum score 7). Application fee: $135. Electronic applications accepted. *Financial support:* Fellowships, research assistantships, Federal Work-Study, institutionally sponsored loans, scholarships/grants, traineeships, health care benefits, and unspecified assistantships available. *Faculty research:* Statistical genetics, bioinformatics, statistical computing, statistical methods, environmental statistics. *Unit head:* Dr. Karen Bandeen-Roche, Chair, 410-955-3067, Fax: 410-955-0958, E-mail: kbandee1@jhu.edu. *Application contact:* Mary Joy Argo, Academic Administrator, 410-614-4454, Fax: 410-955-0958, E-mail: margo@jhu.edu.
Website: http://www.biostat.jhsph.edu/

Kent State University, College of Public Health, Kent, OH 44242-0001. Offers public health (MPH, PhD), including biostatistics (MPH), environmental health sciences (MPH), epidemiology, health policy and management, prevention science (PhD), social and behavioral sciences (MPH). *Accreditation:* CEPH. *Program availability:* Part-time, 100% online. *Faculty:* 20 full-time (10 women), 1 part-time/adjunct (0 women). *Students:* 136 full-time (95 women), 178 part-time (140 women); includes 71 minority (47 Black or African American, non-Hispanic/Latino; 10 Asian, non-Hispanic/Latino; 6 Hispanic/Latino; 8 Two or more races, non-Hispanic/Latino), 45 international. Average age 32. 197 applicants, 85% accepted, 112 enrolled. In 2018, 77 master's, 6 doctorates awarded. *Degree requirements:* For master's, comprehensive exam, 300 hours' placement at public health agency, final portfolio and presentation; for doctorate, comprehensive exam, thesis/dissertation. *Entrance requirements:* For master's, GRE, minimum GPA of 3.0, transcripts, goal statement, 3 letters of recommendation; for doctorate, GRE, minimum GPA of 3.0, personal statement, resume, interview, 3 letters of recommendation. Additional exam requirements/recommendations for international students: Required—TOEFL (minimum score 550 paper-based; 79 iBT), IELTS (minimum score 6.5), PTE (minimum score 58), Michigan English Language Assessment Battery. *Application deadline:* For fall admission, 6/15 for domestic and international students; for spring admission, 10/15 for domestic and international students; for summer admission, 3/15 for domestic and international students. Applications are processed on a rolling basis. Application fee: $45 ($70 for international students). Electronic applications accepted. *Expenses:* Tuition, state resident: full-time $11,766; part-time $536 per credit. Tuition, nonresident: full-time $21,952; part-time $999 per credit. *International tuition:* $21,952 full-time. Tuition and fees vary according to course load. *Financial support:* Career-related internships or fieldwork, Federal Work-Study, scholarships/grants, and unspecified assistantships available. *Unit head:* Dr. Sonia Alemagno, Dean and Professor of Health Policy and Management, 330-672-6500, E-mail: salemagn@kent.edu. *Application contact:* Dr. Jeffrey S. Hallam, Professor/Associate Dean for Research and Graduate Studies, 330-672-0679, E-mail: jhallam1@kent.edu.
Website: http://www.kent.edu/publichealth/

Loma Linda University, School of Public Health, Programs in Epidemiology and Biostatistics, Loma Linda, CA 92350. Offers biostatistics (MPH); epidemiology (MPH, Dr PH, PhD). *Entrance requirements:* Additional exam requirements/recommendations for international students: Required—Michigan English Language Assessment Battery or TOEFL.

Louisiana State University Health Sciences Center, School of Public Health, New Orleans, LA 70112. Offers behavioral and community health sciences (MPH); biostatistics (MPH, MS, PhD); community health sciences (PhD); environmental and occupational health sciences (MPH); epidemiology (MPH, PhD); health policy and systems management (MPH). *Accreditation:* CEPH. *Program availability:* Part-time. *Degree requirements:* For doctorate, thesis/dissertation. *Entrance requirements:* For master's, GRE General Test. Additional exam requirements/recommendations for international students: Recommended—TOEFL (minimum score 550 paper-based; 79 iBT), IELTS. Electronic applications accepted.

McGill University, Faculty of Graduate and Postdoctoral Studies, Faculty of Medicine, Department of Epidemiology, Biostatistics and Occupational Health, Montréal, QC H3A 2T5, Canada. Offers biostatistics (M Sc, PhD); epidemiology (M Sc, PhD); occupational health (M Sc A); public health (MSPH). M Sc A also offered as distance education program. *Program availability:* Part-time, online learning. *Degree requirements:* For doctorate, thesis/dissertation. *Entrance requirements:* For master's, B Sc in chemistry, engineering physics, environmental sciences, medicine, nursing, or other health science (for occupational health); MD or B Sc in nursing (for distance education); minimum GPA of 3.0; for doctorate, TOEFL, M Sc in environmental health, chemistry, engineering, community health, physics, epidemiology, medicine, nursing, or occupational health. *Faculty research:* Epidemiology of occupational diseases and cancer, effect of the environment on respiratory health, industrial safety.

Medical College of Wisconsin, Graduate School, Program in Biostatistics, Milwaukee, WI 53226-0509. Offers PhD. *Program availability:* Part-time. *Degree requirements:* For doctorate, comprehensive exam, thesis/dissertation. *Entrance requirements:* For doctorate, GRE, official transcripts, three letters of recommendation. Additional exam requirements/recommendations for international students: Required—TOEFL. Electronic applications accepted. *Faculty research:* Survival analysis, spatial statistics, time series, genetic statistics, Bayesian statistics.

Medical University of South Carolina, College of Graduate Studies, Division of Biostatistics and Epidemiology, Charleston, SC 29425. Offers biostatistics (MS, PhD); epidemiology (MS, PhD); DMD/PhD; MD/PhD. Terminal master's awarded for partial completion of doctoral program. *Degree requirements:* For master's, comprehensive exam, thesis (for some programs); for doctorate, comprehensive exam, oral and written exams. *Entrance requirements:* For master's, GRE General Test, two semesters of college-level calculus; for doctorate, GRE General Test, interview, minimum GPA of 3.0, two semesters of college-level calculus. Additional exam requirements/recommendations for international students: Required—TOEFL (minimum score 600 paper-based; 100 iBT). Electronic applications accepted. *Faculty research:* Health disparities, central nervous system injuries, radiation exposure, analysis of clinical trial data, biomedical information.

Middle Tennessee State University, College of Graduate Studies, College of Basic and Applied Sciences, Program in Professional Science, Murfreesboro, TN 37132. Offers actuarial sciences (MS); biostatistics (MS); biotechnology (MS); engineering management (MS); health care informatics (MS). *Program availability:* Part-time, evening/weekend, online learning. *Degree requirements:* For master's, comprehensive exam. *Entrance requirements:* For master's, GRE. Additional exam requirements/recommendations for international students: Required—TOEFL (minimum score 525 paper-based; 71 iBT) or IELTS (minimum score 6).

Monroe College, King Graduate School, Bronx, NY 10468. Offers accounting (MS); business administration (MBA), including entrepreneurship, finance, general business administration, healthcare management, human resources, information technology, marketing; computer science (MS); criminal justice (MS); hospitality management (MS); public health (MPH), including biostatistics and epidemiology, community health, health administration and leadership. *Program availability:* Online learning.

New Jersey Institute of Technology, College of Science and Liberal Arts, Newark, NJ 07102. Offers applied mathematics (MS); applied physics (MS, PhD); applied statistics (MS, Certificate); biology (MS, PhD); biostatistics (MS); chemistry (MS, PhD); environmental and sustainability policy (MS); environmental science (MS, PhD); history (MA, MAT); materials science and engineering (MS, PhD); mathematical and computational finance (MS); mathematical sciences (PhD); pharmaceutical chemistry (MS); professional and technical communications (MS); technical communication essentials (Certificate). *Program availability:* Part-time, evening/weekend. *Faculty:* 150 full-time (43 women), 115 part-time/adjunct (47 women). *Students:* 200 full-time (79 women), 63 part-time (29 women); includes 61 minority (17 Black or African American, non-Hispanic/Latino; 29 Asian, non-Hispanic/Latino; 11 Hispanic/Latino; 4 Two or more races, non-Hispanic/Latino), 136 international. Average age 28. 429 applicants, 49% accepted, 89 enrolled. In 2018, 43 master's, 16 doctorates, 2 other advanced degrees awarded. Terminal master's awarded for partial completion of doctoral program. *Degree requirements:* For master's, thesis (for some programs); for doctorate, thesis/dissertation. *Entrance requirements:* For master's and doctorate, GRE General Test, Minimum GPA of 3.0, personal statement, three (3) letters of recommendation, and transcripts. Additional exam requirements/recommendations for international students: Required—TOEFL (minimum score 550 paper-based; 79 iBT), IELTS (minimum score 6.5). *Application deadline:* For fall admission, 6/1 priority date for domestic students, 5/1 priority date for international students; for spring admission, 11/15 priority date for domestic and international students. Applications are processed on a rolling basis. Application fee: $75. Electronic applications accepted. *Expenses:* $22,690 per year (in-state), $32,136 per year (out-of-state). *Financial support:* In 2018–19, 134 students received support, including 17 fellowships with full tuition reimbursements available (averaging $22,000 per year), 74 research assistantships with full tuition reimbursements available (averaging $22,000 per year), 71 teaching assistantships with full tuition reimbursements available (averaging $22,000 per year); scholarships/grants, traineeships, health care benefits, and unspecified assistantships also available. Financial award application deadline: 1/15. *Faculty research:* Biophotonics and bioimaging, morphogenetic patterning, embryogenesis, biological fluid dynamics, applied research in the mathematical sciences. *Total annual research expenditures:* $29.2 million. *Unit head:* Dr. Kevin Belfield, Dean, 973-596-3676, Fax: 973-565-0586, E-mail: kevin.d.belfield@njit.edu. *Application contact:* Stephen Eck, Director of Admissions, 973-596-3300, Fax: 973-596-3461, E-mail: admissions@njit.edu.
Website: http://csla.njit.edu/

New York Medical College, School of Health Sciences and Practice, Valhalla, NY 10595. Offers behavioral sciences and health promotion (MPH); biostatistics (MS); children with special health care (Graduate Certificate); emergency preparedness (Graduate Certificate); environmental health science (MPH); epidemiology (MPH, MS); global health (Graduate Certificate); health education (Graduate Certificate); health policy and management (MPH, DrPH); industrial hygiene (Graduate Certificate); pediatric dysphagia (Post-Graduate Certificate); physical therapy (DPT); public health (Graduate Certificate); speech-language pathology (MS). *Accreditation:* ASHA; CEPH. *Program availability:* Part-time, evening/weekend, 100% online, blended/hybrid learning. *Faculty:* 47 full-time (34 women), 239 part-time/adjunct (141 women). *Students:* 245 full-time (181 women), 233 part-time (167 women); includes 208 minority (79 Black or African American, non-Hispanic/Latino; 2 American Indian or Alaska Native, non-Hispanic/Latino; 59 Asian, non-Hispanic/Latino; 57 Hispanic/Latino; 1 Native Hawaiian or other Pacific Islander, non-Hispanic/Latino; 10 Two or more races, non-Hispanic/Latino), 13 international. Average age 27. 484 applicants, 68% accepted, 88 enrolled. In 2018, 113 master's, 47 doctorates awarded. *Degree requirements:* For master's, comprehensive exam (for some programs), thesis (for some programs); for doctorate, thesis/dissertation. *Entrance requirements:* For master's, GRE (for MS in speech-language pathology); for doctorate, GRE (for Doctor of Physical Therapy and Doctor of Public Health). Additional exam requirements/recommendations for international students: Required—TOEFL (minimum score 96 paper-based; 24 iBT), IELTS (minimum score 7). *Application deadline:* For fall admission, 8/1 for domestic students, 4/15 for international students; for spring admission, 12/1 for domestic students; for summer admission, 5/1 for domestic students, 4/15 for international students. Applications are processed on a rolling basis. Application fee: $128 ($120 for international students). Electronic applications accepted. *Expenses:* $1165 per credit, $645 fees. *Financial support:* In 2018–19, 4 students received support. Federal Work-Study, scholarships/grants, unspecified assistantships, and Federal student loans available. Financial award application deadline: 4/30; financial award applicants required to submit FAFSA. *Faculty research:* Disaster medicine, environmental health, health policy, speech-language pathology including dysphagia, biomechanics of human motion in activities of daily living and occupations. *Total annual research expenditures:* $325,000. *Unit head:* Ben Johnson, PhD, Vice Dean, 914-594-4531, E-mail: bjohnson23@nymc.edu. *Application contact:* Irene Bundziak, Assistant to Director of Admissions, 914-594-4905, E-mail: irene_bundziak@nymc.edu.
Website: http://www.nymc.edu/school-of-health-sciences-and-practice-shsp/

Northwestern University, Feinberg School of Medicine, Driskill Graduate Program in Life Sciences, Chicago, IL 60611. Offers biostatistics (PhD); epidemiology (PhD); health and biomedical informatics (PhD); health services and outcomes research (PhD); healthcare quality and patient safety (PhD); translational outcomes in science (PhD). *Degree requirements:* For doctorate, comprehensive exam, thesis/dissertation, written and oral qualifying exams. *Entrance requirements:* For doctorate, GRE General Test. Additional exam requirements/recommendations for international students: Required—TOEFL (minimum score 600 paper-based). Electronic applications accepted.

The Ohio State University, Graduate School, College of Arts and Sciences, Division of Natural and Mathematical Sciences, Department of Statistics, Columbus, OH 43210. Offers biostatistics (PhD); statistics (M Appl Stat, MS, PhD). *Program availability:* Part-time. *Faculty:* 25. *Students:* 72 (30 women). Average age 26. In 2018, 19 master's, 12 doctorates awarded. Terminal master's awarded for partial completion of doctoral program. *Entrance requirements:* For master's and doctorate, GRE General Test. Additional exam requirements/recommendations for international students: Required—TOEFL (minimum score 600 paper-based; 100 iBT); Recommended—IELTS (minimum score 8). *Application deadline:* For fall admission, 1/1 priority date for domestic students, 12/1 priority date for international students; for spring admission, 12/1 for domestic students, 11/1 for international students. Applications are processed on a rolling basis. Application fee: $60 ($70 for international students). Electronic applications accepted. *Financial support:* Fellowships, research assistantships, teaching assistantships, Federal Work-Study, and institutionally sponsored loans available. Support available to part-time students. *Unit head:* Dr. Steve MacEachern, Chair, 614-292-5843, Fax: 614-292-2096, E-mail: maceachern.1@osu.edu. *Application contact:* Graduate and Professional Admissions, 614-292-9444, Fax: 614-292-3895, E-mail: gpadmissions@osu.edu.
Website: http://www.stat.osu.edu/

The Ohio State University, Graduate School, Program in Biostatistics, Columbus, OH 43210. Offers PhD. *Students:* 28 full-time (15 women). Average age 26. In 2018, 2 doctorates awarded. *Degree requirements:* For doctorate, thesis/dissertation. *Entrance requirements:* For doctorate, GRE General Test. Additional exam requirements/recommendations for international students: Required—TOEFL (minimum score 600 paper-based; 100 iBT), IELTS (minimum score 8), Michigan English Language Assessment Battery (minimum score 86). *Application deadline:* For fall admission, 1/1 priority date for domestic students, 12/1 priority date for international students; for spring admission, 12/12 for domestic students, 11/10 for international students; for summer admission, 4/10 for domestic students, 3/13 for international students. Applications are processed on a rolling basis. Application fee: $60 ($70 for international students). Electronic applications accepted. *Financial support:* Fellowships, research assistantships, teaching assistantships, Federal Work-Study, and institutionally sponsored loans available. Support available to part-time students. *Unit head:* Dr. Michael Pennell, Graduate Studies Committee Chair, 614-247-7936, E-mail: pennell.28@osu.edu. *Application contact:* Graduate and Professional Admissions, 614-292-9444, Fax: 614-292-3895, E-mail: gpadmissions@osu.edu.
Website: http://biostatprograms.osu.edu

Old Dominion University, College of Sciences, Programs in Computational and Applied Mathematics, Norfolk, VA 23529. Offers applied mathematics (MS, PhD); biostatistics (MS); statistics (MS); statistics/biostatistics (PhD). *Program availability:* Part-time. Terminal master's awarded for partial completion of doctoral program. *Degree requirements:* For master's, project; for doctorate, comprehensive exam, thesis/dissertation, candidacy exam. *Entrance requirements:* For master's, minimum GPA of 3.0 in major, 2.8 overall; for doctorate, GRE General Test, 3 recommendation letters, transcripts, essay. Additional exam requirements/recommendations for international students: Required—TOEFL (minimum score 550 paper-based; 79 iBT); Recommended—IELTS (minimum score 6.5). Electronic applications accepted. *Faculty research:* Numerical analysis, integral equations, continuum mechanics, statistics, direct and inverse scattering.

Oregon State University, College of Public Health and Human Sciences, Program in Public Health, Corvallis, OR 97331. Offers biostatistics (MPH); environmental and occupational health (MPH, PhD); epidemiology (MPH, PhD); global health (MPH, PhD). *Accreditation:* CEPH. Terminal master's awarded for partial completion of doctoral program. *Entrance requirements:* For master's and doctorate, GRE, minimum GPA of 3.0 in last 90 hours. Additional exam requirements/recommendations for international students: Required—TOEFL (minimum score 80 iBT), IELTS (minimum score 6.5). Electronic applications accepted. *Expenses:* Contact institution.

Penn State Hershey Medical Center, College of Medicine, Graduate School Programs in the Biomedical Sciences, Program in Biostatistics, Hershey, PA 17033. Offers PhD. *Entrance requirements:* For doctorate, GRE General Test, previous coursework or master's degree in biostatistics or statistics. Additional exam requirements/recommendations for international students: Required—TOEFL (minimum score 81 iBT). Electronic applications accepted.

Rice University, Graduate Programs, George R. Brown School of Engineering, Department of Statistics, Houston, TX 77251-1892. Offers bioinformatics (PhD); biostatistics (PhD); computational finance (PhD); general statistics (PhD); statistics

(M Stat, MA); MBA/M Stat. *Program availability:* Part-time. *Degree requirements:* For master's, comprehensive exam; for doctorate, comprehensive exam, thesis/dissertation. *Entrance requirements:* For master's and doctorate, GRE General Test, minimum GPA of 3.0. Additional exam requirements/recommendations for international students: Required—TOEFL (minimum score 630 paper-based; 90 iBT). Electronic applications accepted. *Faculty research:* Statistical genetics, non parametric function estimation, computational statistics and visualization, stochastic processes.

Rutgers University–New Brunswick, Graduate School-New Brunswick, BioMaPS Institute for Quantitative Biology, Piscataway, NJ 08854-8097. Offers computational biology and molecular biophysics (PhD). *Degree requirements:* For doctorate, comprehensive exam, thesis/dissertation. *Entrance requirements:* For doctorate, GRE. Additional exam requirements/recommendations for international students: Required—TOEFL. Electronic applications accepted. *Faculty research:* Structural biology, systems biology, bioinformatics, translational medicine, genomics.

Rutgers University–New Brunswick, Graduate School-New Brunswick, Program in Statistics, Piscataway, NJ 08854-8097. Offers applied statistics (MS); biostatistics (MS); data mining (MS); quality and productivity management (MS); statistics (MS, PhD). *Program availability:* Part-time. Terminal master's awarded for partial completion of doctoral program. *Degree requirements:* For master's, comprehensive exam, essay, exam, non-thesis essay paper; for doctorate, one foreign language, thesis/dissertation, qualifying oral and written exams. *Entrance requirements:* For master's, GRE General Test; for doctorate, GRE General Test, GRE Subject Test (recommended). Additional exam requirements/recommendations for international students: Required—TOEFL (minimum score 550 paper-based). Electronic applications accepted. *Faculty research:* Probability, decision theory, linear models, multivariate statistics, statistical computing.

Rutgers University–New Brunswick, School of Public Health, Piscataway, NJ 08854. Offers biostatistics (MPH, MS, Dr PH, PhD); clinical epidemiology (Certificate); environmental and occupational health (MPH, Dr PH, PhD, Certificate); epidemiology (MPH, Dr PH, PhD); general public health (Certificate); health education and behavioral science (MPH, Dr PH, PhD); health systems and policy (MPH, PhD); public health (MPH, Dr PH, PhD); public health preparedness (Certificate); DO/MPH; JD/MPH; MBA/MPH; MD/MPH; MPH/MBA; MPH/MSPA; MS/MPH; Psy D/MPH. *Accreditation:* CEPH. *Program availability:* Part-time, evening/weekend. *Degree requirements:* For master's, thesis, internship; for doctorate, comprehensive exam, thesis/dissertation. *Entrance requirements:* For master's, GRE General Test; for doctorate, GRE General Test, MPH (Dr PH); MA, MPH, or MS (PhD). Additional exam requirements/recommendations for international students: Required—TOEFL. Electronic applications accepted.

San Diego State University, Graduate and Research Affairs, College of Health and Human Services, School of Public Health, San Diego, CA 92182. Offers environmental health (MPH); epidemiology (MPH, PhD), including biostatistics (MPH); global emergency preparedness and response (MS); global health (PhD); health behavior (PhD); health promotion (MPH); health services administration (MPH); toxicology (MS); MPH/MA; MSW/MPH. *Accreditation:* CAHME (one or more programs are accredited); CEPH. *Program availability:* Part-time. *Degree requirements:* For master's, comprehensive exam (for some programs), thesis (for some programs); for doctorate, thesis/dissertation. *Entrance requirements:* For master's, GMAT (MPH in health services administration), GRE General Test; for doctorate, GRE General Test. Additional exam requirements/recommendations for international students: Required—TOEFL. *Faculty research:* Evaluation of tobacco, AIDS prevalence and prevention, mammography, infant death project, Alzheimer's in elderly Chinese.

Southern Methodist University, Dedman College of Humanities and Sciences, Department of Statistical Science, Dallas, TX 75275-0332. Offers applied statistics and data analytics (MS); biostatistics (PhD); statistical science (PhD). *Program availability:* Part-time. *Degree requirements:* For master's, thesis, oral and written exams; for doctorate, thesis/dissertation, oral and written exams. *Entrance requirements:* For master's, GRE General Test, 12 hours of advanced math courses; for doctorate, GRE General Test, minimum GPA of 3.0. Additional exam requirements/recommendations for international students: Required—TOEFL. Electronic applications accepted. *Faculty research:* Regression, time series, linear models sampling, nonparametrics, biostatistics.

Stanford University, School of Medicine, Graduate Programs in Medicine, Department of Health Research and Policy, Stanford, CA 94305-2004. Offers biostatistics (PhD); epidemiology and clinical research (MS, PhD); health policy (MS, PhD). *Expenses: Tuition:* Full-time $50,703; part-time $32,970 per year. *Required fees:* $651.
Website: http://med.stanford.edu/hsr/

Texas A&M University, School of Public Health, College Station, TX 77843. Offers biostatistics (MPH, MSPH); environmental health (MPH, MSPH); epidemiology (MPH, MSPH); health administration (MHA); health policy and management (MPH); health services research (PhD); occupational safety and health (MPH). *Accreditation:* CAHME; CEPH. *Program availability:* Part-time, blended/hybrid learning. *Faculty:* 59. *Students:* 278 full-time (184 women), 80 part-time (53 women); includes 147 minority (44 Black or African American, non-Hispanic/Latino; 31 Asian, non-Hispanic/Latino; 66 Hispanic/Latino; 6 Two or more races, non-Hispanic/Latino), 80 international. Average age 29. 169 applicants, 100% accepted, 135 enrolled. In 2018, 142 master's, 9 doctorates awarded. *Entrance requirements:* For master's, GRE General Test, 3 letters of recommendation; statement of purpose; current curriculum vitae or resume; official transcripts; for doctorate, GRE General Test, 3 letters of recommendation; statement of purpose; current curriculum vitae or resume; official transcripts; interview (in some cases). Additional exam requirements/recommendations for international students: Required—TOEFL (minimum score 597 paper-based, 95 iBT) or GRE (minimum verbal score 153). Application fee: $120. Electronic applications accepted. *Expenses:* Contact institution. *Financial support:* In 2018–19, 199 students received support, including 6 fellowships with tuition reimbursements available (averaging $18,326 per year), 53 research assistantships with tuition reimbursements available (averaging $13,190 per year), 28 teaching assistantships with tuition reimbursements available (averaging $17,245 per year); career-related internships or fieldwork, institutionally sponsored loans, scholarships/grants, traineeships, health care benefits, tuition waivers (full and partial), and unspecified assistantships also available. Support available to part-time students. Financial award applicants required to submit FAFSA. *Unit head:* Dr. Jay Maddock, Dean, 979-436-9322, Fax: 979-458-1878, E-mail: maddock@tamhsc.edu. *Application contact:* Erin E. Schneider, Associate Director of Admissions and Recruitment, 979-436-9380, E-mail: eschneider@sph.tamhsc.edu.
Website: http://sph.tamhsc.edu/

Tufts University, School of Medicine, Public Health and Professional Degree Programs, Boston, MA 02111. Offers biomedical sciences (MS); health communication (MS, Certificate); pain research, education and policy (MS, Certificate); physician assistant (MS); public health (MPH, Dr PH), including behavioral science (MPH), biostatistics (MPH), epidemiology (MPH), health communication (MPH), health services (MPH), management and policy (MPH), nutrition (MPH); DMD/MPH; DVM/MPH; JD/MPH; MD/MPH; MMS/MPH; MS/MBA; MS/MPH. *Accreditation:* CEPH (one or more programs are accredited). *Program availability:* Part-time, evening/weekend. Terminal master's awarded for partial completion of doctoral program. *Degree requirements:* For master's, thesis (for some programs); for doctorate, thesis/dissertation. *Entrance requirements:* For master's, GRE General Test, MCAT, or GMAT; for doctorate, GRE General Test or MCAT. Additional exam requirements/recommendations for international students: Required—TOEFL (minimum score 100 iBT); Recommended—IELTS (minimum score 7). Electronic applications accepted. *Expenses:* Contact institution. *Faculty research:* Environmental and occupational health, nutrition, epidemiology, health communication, biostatics, obesity/chronic disease, health policy and health care delivery, global health, health inequality and social determinants of health.

Tulane University, School of Public Health and Tropical Medicine, Department of Global Biostatistics and Data Science, New Orleans, LA 70118-5669. Offers MS, MSPH, PhD, MD/MSPH. MS and PhD offered through the Graduate School. *Program availability:* Part-time. *Degree requirements:* For doctorate, comprehensive exam, thesis/dissertation. *Entrance requirements:* For master's and doctorate, GRE General Test. Additional exam requirements/recommendations for international students: Required—TOEFL. Electronic applications accepted. *Expenses: Tuition:* Full-time $52,856; part-time $2937 per credit hour. *Required fees:* $2040; $44.50 per credit hour. $580 per term. Tuition and fees vary according to course load, degree level and program. *Faculty research:* Clinical trials, measurement, longitudinal analyses.

University at Albany, State University of New York, School of Public Health, Department of Epidemiology and Biostatistics, Albany, NY 12222-0001. Offers epidemiology and biostatistics (MS, PhD). *Faculty:* 14 full-time (5 women), 5 part-time/adjunct (4 women). *Students:* 25 full-time (13 women), 33 part-time (15 women); includes 9 minority (7 Asian, non-Hispanic/Latino; 2 Hispanic/Latino), 23 international. 75 applicants, 31% accepted, 12 enrolled. In 2018, 10 master's, 2 doctorates awarded. *Degree requirements:* For master's, thesis; for doctorate, thesis/dissertation. *Entrance requirements:* For master's and doctorate, GRE General Test. Additional exam requirements/recommendations for international students: Required—TOEFL (minimum score 550 paper-based). *Application deadline:* For fall admission, 6/30 for domestic students, 5/1 for international students; for spring admission, 11/30 for domestic students, 11/1 for international students. Applications are processed on a rolling basis. Application fee: $75. Electronic applications accepted. *Financial support:* Application deadline: 4/1. *Faculty research:* Developmental origins of disease, psychosocial adversity, epigenetics, cardiovascular epidemiology, non-parametric and semi-parametric statistical methods, Bayesian computational algorithms, adverse health effects of environmental and occupational exposures to toxic agents, diabetes and chronic disease epidemiology and others. *Unit head:* Dr. Recai Ycel, Chair, 518-402-0372. *Application contact:* Dr. Recai Ycel, Chair, 518-402-0372.
Website: http://www.albany.edu/sph/epi/index.html

University at Buffalo, the State University of New York, Graduate School, School of Public Health and Health Professions, Department of Biostatistics, Buffalo, NY 14260. Offers MA, MPH, MS, PhD. Terminal master's awarded for partial completion of doctoral program. *Entrance requirements:* For master's, GRE, 3 semesters of course work in calculus (for mathematics), course work in real analysis (preferred), course work in linear algebra; for doctorate, GRE, master's degree in statistics, biostatistics or equivalent. Additional exam requirements/recommendations for international students: Required—TOEFL (minimum score 640 paper-based; 79 iBT). Electronic applications accepted. *Faculty research:* Biostatistics, longitudinal data analysis, nonparametrics, statistical genetics, epidemiology.

The University of Alabama at Birmingham, School of Public Health, Program in Health Care Organization and Policy, Birmingham, AL 35294. Offers applied epidemiology and pharmacoepidemiology (MSPH); biostatistics (MPH); clinical and translational science (MSPH); environmental health (MPH); environmental health and toxicology (MSPH); epidemiology (MPH); general theory and practice (MPH); health behavior (MPH); health care organization (MPH, Dr PH); health policy (MPH); industrial hygiene (MPH, MSPH); maternal and child health policy (Dr PH); maternal and child health policy and leadership (MPH); occupational health and safety (MPH); outcomes research (MSPH, Dr PH); public health (PhD); public health preparedness management (MPH). *Accreditation:* CEPH. *Program availability:* Part-time, 100% online, blended/hybrid learning. *Faculty:* 14 full-time (6 women). *Students:* 53 full-time (37 women), 61 part-time (45 women); includes 37 minority (12 Black or African American, non-Hispanic/Latino; 20 Asian, non-Hispanic/Latino; 1 Hispanic/Latino; 4 Two or more races, non-Hispanic/Latino), 17 international. Average age 31. 136 applicants, 59% accepted, 44 enrolled. In 2018, 36 master's, 4 doctorates awarded. *Degree requirements:* For master's, comprehensive exam (for some programs), thesis (for some programs); for doctorate, comprehensive exam, thesis/dissertation. *Entrance requirements:* For doctorate, GRE. Additional exam requirements/recommendations for international students: Required—TOEFL (minimum score 80 iBT), IELTS (minimum score 6.5). *Application deadline:* For fall admission, 4/1 priority date for domestic students, 4/1 for international students; for spring admission, 11/1 for domestic students; for summer admission, 4/1 for domestic students. Application fee: $50 ($60 for international students). Electronic applications accepted. *Expenses: Tuition, area resident:* Full-time $8100; part-time $8100 per year. Tuition, state resident: full-time $8100. Tuition, nonresident: full-time $19,188; part-time $19,188 per year. Tuition and fees vary according to program. *Financial support:* Fellowships, research assistantships, teaching assistantships, scholarships/grants, traineeships, and unspecified assistantships available. Financial award application deadline: 3/1; financial award applicants required to submit FAFSA. *Unit head:* Dr. Martha Wingate, Program Director, 205-934-6783, Fax: 205-975-5484, E-mail: mslay@uab.edu. *Application contact:* Dustin Shaw, Coordinator, Student Admissions and Record, 205-934-3939, E-mail: bcampbel@uab.edu.
Website: http://www.soph.uab.edu

University of Alberta, Faculty of Graduate Studies and Research, Department of Mathematical and Statistical Sciences, Edmonton, AB T6G 2E1, Canada. Offers applied mathematics (M Sc, PhD); biostatistics (M Sc); mathematical finance (M Sc, PhD); mathematical physics (M Sc, PhD); mathematics (M Sc, PhD); statistics (M Sc, PhD, Postgraduate Diploma). *Program availability:* Part-time. Terminal master's awarded for partial completion of doctoral program. *Degree requirements:* For master's, thesis (for some programs); for doctorate, comprehensive exam, thesis/dissertation. *Entrance requirements:* Additional exam requirements/recommendations for international students: Required—TOEFL (minimum score 580 paper-based). Electronic applications accepted. *Faculty research:* Classical and functional analysis, algebra, differential equations, geometry.

The University of Arizona, Mel and Enid Zuckerman College of Public Health, Program in Biostatistics, Tucson, AZ 85721. Offers MS, PhD. *Entrance requirements:* Additional exam requirements/recommendations for international students: Required—TOEFL (minimum score 550 paper-based; 79 iBT). Electronic applications accepted.

University of Arkansas for Medical Sciences, Fay W. Boozman College of Public Health, Little Rock, AR 72205-7199. Offers biostatistics (MPH); environmental and occupational health (MPH, Certificate); epidemiology (MPH, PhD); health behavior and health education (MPH); health policy and management (MPH); health promotion and prevention research (PhD); health services administration (MHSA); health systems research (PhD); public health (Certificate); public health leadership (Dr PH). *Accreditation:* CAHME; CEPH. *Program availability:* Part-time. *Degree requirements:* For master's, preceptorship, culminating experience, internship; for doctorate, comprehensive exam, capstone. *Entrance requirements:* For master's, GRE, GMAT, LSAT, PCAT, MCAT, DAT; for doctorate, GRE. Additional exam requirements/recommendations for international students: Required—TOEFL (minimum score 80 iBT), IELTS. Electronic applications accepted. *Expenses:* Contact institution. *Faculty research:* Health systems, tobacco prevention control, obesity prevention, environmental and occupational exposure, cancer prevention.

University of California, Berkeley, Graduate Division, School of Public Health, Group in Biostatistics, Berkeley, CA 94720. Offers MA, PhD. *Accreditation:* CEPH (one or more programs are accredited). *Degree requirements:* For master's, oral exam; for doctorate, thesis/dissertation, oral exam. *Entrance requirements:* For master's and doctorate, GRE General Test, minimum GPA of 3.0, 3 letters of recommendation. Additional exam requirements/recommendations for international students: Required—TOEFL (minimum score 570 paper-based; 90 iBT). Electronic applications accepted.

University of California, Davis, Graduate Studies, Graduate Group in Biostatistics, Davis, CA 95616. Offers MS, PhD. *Degree requirements:* For master's, comprehensive exam; for doctorate, thesis/dissertation. *Entrance requirements:* Additional exam requirements/recommendations for international students: Required—TOEFL (minimum score 550 paper-based). Electronic applications accepted.

University of California, Los Angeles, Graduate Division, Fielding School of Public Health, Department of Biostatistics, Los Angeles, CA 90095. Offers MPH, MS, Dr PH, PhD. *Degree requirements:* For master's, comprehensive exam; for doctorate, thesis/dissertation, oral and written qualifying exams. *Entrance requirements:* For master's, GRE General Test, minimum GPA of 3.0; for doctorate, GRE General Test, minimum undergraduate GPA of 3.0. Electronic applications accepted.

University of California, San Diego, School of Medicine, Program in Biostatistics, La Jolla, CA 92093. Offers PhD. *Students:* 12 full-time (5 women), 1 (woman) part-time. 107 applicants, 5% accepted, 4 enrolled. *Degree requirements:* For doctorate, comprehensive exam, thesis/dissertation. *Entrance requirements:* For doctorate, GRE, 3 letters of recommendation, statement of purpose, resume/curriculum vitae, official transcripts with minimum GPA of 3.0. Additional exam requirements/recommendations for international students: Required—TOEFL (minimum score 550 paper-based; 80 iBT), IELTS (minimum score 7). *Application deadline:* For fall admission, 1/10 for domestic students. Application fee: $105 ($125 for international students). Electronic applications accepted. *Financial support:* Fellowships, research assistantships, and teaching assistantships available. Financial award applicants required to submit FAFSA. *Faculty research:* Biostatistics, mathematical statistics, computer sciences, survival analysis, prognostic modeling, longitudinal data analysis, statistical genetics. *Unit head:* Dr. Loki Natarajan, Director, 858-822-4763. *Application contact:* Sarah Dauchez, Coordinator, 858-246-2595, E-mail: sdauchez@ucsd.edu.
Website: http://biostat.ucsd.edu/phd-program/index.html

University of Cincinnati, Graduate School, College of Medicine, Graduate Programs in Biomedical Sciences, Department of Environmental Health, Cincinnati, OH 45221. Offers environmental and industrial hygiene (MS, PhD); environmental and occupational medicine (MS); environmental genetics and molecular toxicology (MS, PhD); epidemiology and biostatistics (MS, PhD); occupational safety and ergonomics (MS, PhD). *Accreditation:* ABET (one or more programs are accredited); CEPH. Terminal master's awarded for partial completion of doctoral program. *Degree requirements:* For master's, thesis; for doctorate, thesis/dissertation, qualifying exam. *Entrance requirements:* For master's, GRE General Test, bachelor's degree in science; for doctorate, GRE General Test. Additional exam requirements/recommendations for international students: Required—TOEFL (minimum score 600 paper-based; 100 iBT). Electronic applications accepted. *Faculty research:* Carcinogens and mutagenesis, pulmonary studies, reproduction and development.

University of Colorado Denver, Colorado School of Public Health, Department of Biostatistics and Informatics, Aurora, CO 80045. Offers MS, PhD. *Program availability:* Part-time. Terminal master's awarded for partial completion of doctoral program. *Degree requirements:* For master's, 34 credit hours, project or thesis; for doctorate, comprehensive exam, thesis/dissertation, 70 credit hours (25 of which can be completed while completing a master's degree). *Entrance requirements:* For master's, GRE General Test, baccalaureate degree in scientific field, minimum GPA of 3.0, math course work through integral calculus, two official copies of all academic transcripts, four letters of recommendation/reference, essays describing the applicant's career goals and reasons for applying to the program, resume; for doctorate, GRE General Test, baccalaureate degree in scientific field; master's degree in biostatistics, statistics or equivalent; minimum GPA of 3.0; math course work through integral calculus; two official copies of all academic transcripts; four letters of recommendation/reference; essays; resume. Additional exam requirements/recommendations for international students: Required—TOEFL (minimum score 550 paper-based; 80 iBT). Electronic applications accepted. *Expenses:* Tuition, state resident: full-time $6786; part-time $337 per credit hour. Tuition, nonresident: full-time $22,590; part-time $1255 per credit hour. *Required fees:* $1231; $137 per credit hour. Tuition and fees vary according to program and reciprocity agreements. *Faculty research:* Health policy research, nonlinear mixed effects models for longitudinal data, statistical methods in nutrition, clinical trials.

University of Florida, Graduate School, College of Public Health and Health Professions, Department of Biostatistics, Gainesville, FL 32611. Offers MS, PhD. *Degree requirements:* For doctorate, comprehensive exam, thesis/dissertation. *Entrance requirements:* For master's, GRE General Test, minimum GPA of 3.0. Additional exam requirements/recommendations for international students: Required—TOEFL (minimum score 550 paper-based; 80 iBT), IELTS (minimum score 6). *Faculty research:* Stochastic modeling of infectious diseases, medical image processing and jump regression analysis, causal modeling and inference for clinical trials and observational studies, modeling of dose-response curves, simultaneous statistical inference.

University of Florida, Graduate School, College of Public Health and Health Professions, Programs in Public Health, Gainesville, FL 32611. Offers biostatistics (MPH); clinical and translational science (PhD); environmental health (MPH); epidemiology (MPH); health management and policy (MPH); public health (MPH, PhD, Certificate); public health practice (MPH); rehabilitation science (PhD); social and behavioral sciences (MPH); DPT/MPH, DVM/MPH, JD/MPH, MD/MPH, Pharm D/MPH. *Accreditation:* CEPH. *Program availability:* Online learning. *Degree requirements:* For master's, internship. *Entrance requirements:* For master's, GRE General Test, minimum GPA of 3.0. Additional exam requirements/recommendations for international students: Required—TOEFL (minimum score 550 paper-based; 80 iBT), IELTS (minimum score 6).

University of Illinois at Chicago, School of Public Health, Epidemiology and Biostatistics Division, Chicago, IL 60607-7128. Offers biostatistics (MPH, MS, PhD); epidemiology (MPH, MS, PhD). *Program availability:* Part-time. Terminal master's awarded for partial completion of doctoral program. *Degree requirements:* For master's, thesis, field practicum; for doctorate, thesis/dissertation, independent research, internship. *Entrance requirements:* For master's and doctorate, GRE General Test, minimum GPA of 2.75. Additional exam requirements/recommendations for international students: Required—TOEFL. Electronic applications accepted. *Expenses:* Contact institution. *Faculty research:* Quantitative methods.

The University of Iowa, Graduate College, College of Public Health, Department of Biostatistics, Iowa City, IA 52242-1316. Offers biostatistics (MS, PhD, Certificate); quantitative methods (MPH). *Degree requirements:* For master's, thesis optional, exam; for doctorate, comprehensive exam, thesis/dissertation. *Entrance requirements:* For master's and doctorate, GRE General Test, minimum GPA of 3.0. Additional exam requirements/recommendations for international students: Required—TOEFL (minimum score 600 paper-based; 100 iBT). Electronic applications accepted.

The University of Kansas, University of Kansas Medical Center, School of Medicine, Department of Biostatistics & Data Science, Kansas City, KS 66160. Offers applied statistics and analytics (MS); biostatistics (MS, PhD, Graduate Certificate); statistical applications (Graduate Certificate). *Faculty:* 21. *Students:* 36 full-time (16 women), 86 part-time (32 women); includes 32 minority (10 Black or African American, non-Hispanic/Latino; 12 Asian, non-Hispanic/Latino; 6 Hispanic/Latino; 4 Two or more races, non-Hispanic/Latino), 23 international. Average age 31. 52 applicants, 88% accepted, 42 enrolled. In 2018, 10 master's, 2 doctorates, 1 other advanced degree awarded. *Degree requirements:* For master's, comprehensive exam; for doctorate, comprehensive exam, thesis/dissertation. *Entrance requirements:* For master's, GRE, coursework in calculus, computer programming, linear algebra, differential equations, and numerical analysis; for doctorate, master's degree. Additional exam requirements/recommendations for international students: Required—TOEFL. Application fee: $60. Electronic applications accepted. *Financial support:* In 2018–19, 1 fellowship with full tuition reimbursement (averaging $25,000 per year), 25 research assistantships with full and partial tuition reimbursements (averaging $19,200 per year) were awarded; scholarships/grants, traineeships, and unspecified assistantships also available. Financial award application deadline: 3/1; financial award applicants required to submit FAFSA. *Faculty research:* Biostatistics, clinical trials. *Total annual research expenditures:* $451,667. *Unit head:* Dr. Matthew Mayo, Professor and Chair, 913-588-4735 Ext. 913, Fax: 913-588-0252, E-mail: mmayo@kumc.edu. *Application contact:* Dr. Jo A. Wick, Assistant Director of Graduate Education, 913-588-4790, Fax: 913-588-0252, E-mail: jwick@kumc.edu. Website: http://www.kumc.edu/school-of-medicine/department-of-biostatistics.html

University of Kentucky, Graduate School, College of Public Health, Program in Epidemiology and Biostatistics, Lexington, KY 40506-0032. Offers PhD.

University of Maryland, Baltimore, School of Medicine, Department of Epidemiology and Public Health, Baltimore, MD 21201. Offers biostatistics (MS); clinical research (MS); epidemiology and preventive medicine (MPH, MS, PhD); gerontology (PhD); human genetics and genomic medicine (MS, PhD); molecular epidemiology (MS, PhD); toxicology (MS, PhD); JD/MS; MD/PhD; MS/PhD. *Accreditation:* CEPH. *Program availability:* Part-time. *Degree requirements:* For doctorate, comprehensive exam, thesis/dissertation. *Entrance requirements:* For master's and doctorate, GRE General Test. Additional exam requirements/recommendations for international students: Required—TOEFL (minimum score 550 paper-based; 80 iBT); Recommended—IELTS (minimum score 7). Electronic applications accepted. *Expenses:* Contact institution.

University of Maryland, Baltimore County, The Graduate School, College of Natural and Mathematical Sciences, Department of Mathematics and Statistics, Program in Statistics, Baltimore, MD 21250. Offers biostatistics (PhD); environmental statistics (MS); statistics (MS, PhD). *Program availability:* Part-time, evening/weekend. Terminal master's awarded for partial completion of doctoral program. *Degree requirements:* For master's, comprehensive exam (for some programs), thesis (for some programs); for doctorate, comprehensive exam, thesis/dissertation. *Entrance requirements:* For master's and doctorate, GRE General Test, minimum GPA of 3.0. Additional exam requirements/recommendations for international students: Required—TOEFL (minimum score 600 paper-based; 100 iBT). Electronic applications accepted. *Faculty research:* Design of experiments, statistical decision theory and inference, time series analysis, biostatistics and environmental statistics, bioinformatics.

University of Maryland, College Park, Academic Affairs, School of Public Health, Department of Epidemiology and Biostatistics, College Park, MD 20742. Offers biostatistics (MPH); epidemiology (MPH, PhD).

University of Massachusetts Amherst, Graduate School, School of Public Health and Health Sciences, Department of Public Health, Amherst, MA 01003. Offers biostatistics (MPH, MS, PhD); community health education (MPH, MS, PhD); environmental health sciences (MPH, MS, PhD); epidemiology (MPH, MS, PhD); health policy and management (MPH, MS, PhD); nutrition (MPH, PhD); public health practice (MPH); MPH/MPPA. *Accreditation:* CEPH. *Program availability:* Part-time, evening/weekend, online learning. Terminal master's awarded for partial completion of doctoral program. *Degree requirements:* For master's, thesis (for some programs); for doctorate, comprehensive exam, thesis/dissertation. *Entrance requirements:* For master's and doctorate, GRE General Test. Additional exam requirements/recommendations for international students: Required—TOEFL (minimum score 550 paper-based; 80 iBT), IELTS (minimum score 6.5). Electronic applications accepted.

University of Memphis, Graduate School, School of Public Health, Memphis, TN 38152. Offers biostatistics (MPH); environmental health (MPH); epidemiology (MPH, PhD); health systems and policy (PhD); health systems management (MPH); public health (MHA); social and behavioral sciences (MPH, PhD). *Accreditation:* CAHME; CEPH. *Program availability:* Part-time, evening/weekend. *Faculty:* 19 full-time (5 women), 7 part-time/adjunct (2 women). *Students:* 123 full-time (84 women), 75 part-time (54 women); includes 77 minority (46 Black or African American, non-Hispanic/Latino; 20 Asian, non-Hispanic/Latino; 7 Hispanic/Latino; 4 Two or more races, non-Hispanic/Latino), 31 international. Average age 31. 109 applicants, 93% accepted, 76 enrolled. In 2018, 47 master's, 9 doctorates awarded. *Degree requirements:* For master's, comprehensive exam, thesis (for some programs), practicum/field experience; for doctorate, comprehensive exam, thesis/dissertation, residency. *Entrance requirements:* For master's, GRE or GMAT, letters of recommendation; letter of intent; for doctorate, GRE, letters of recommendation; personal statement. Additional exam requirements/recommendations for international students: Required—TOEFL (minimum score 550 paper-based; 79 iBT). *Application deadline:* For fall admission, 4/1 for domestic students; for spring admission, 11/1 for domestic students. Application fee: $35 ($60 for international students). Electronic applications accepted. *Expenses:* Tuition, area resident: Full-time $10,240; part-time $503 per credit hour. Tuition, state resident: full-time $10,464. Tuition, nonresident: full-time $20,224; part-time $991 per credit hour. *Required fees:* $850; $106 per credit hour. *Financial support:* Research assistantships with full tuition reimbursements, Federal Work-Study, scholarships/

Peterson's Graduate Programs in the Physical Sciences, Mathematics, Agricultural Sciences, the Environment & Natural Resources 2020

www.petersons.com   **195**

grants, and unspecified assistantships available. Financial award application deadline: 2/1; financial award applicants required to submit FAFSA. *Faculty research:* Health and medical savings accounts, adoption rates, health informatics, Telehealth technologies, biostatistics, environmental health, epidemiology, health systems management, social and behavioral sciences. *Unit head:* Dr. James Gurney, Dean, 901-678-1673, E-mail: jggurney@memphis.edu. *Application contact:* Dr. Marian Levy, Associate Dean, 901-678-4514, E-mail: mlevy@memphis.edu.
Website: http://www.memphis.edu/sph/

University of Miami, Graduate School, Miller School of Medicine, Graduate Programs in Medicine, Department of Public Health Sciences, Miami, FL 33186. Offers biostatistics (MS, PhD); climate and health (MS); epidemiology (PhD); epidemiology, biostatistics, prevention science and community health (MD/PhD); generalist (MPH, MSPH); prevention science and community health (MS, PhD); JD/MPH; MD/MPH; MD/PhD; MPA/MPH; MPH/MAIA. *Accreditation:* CEPH (one or more programs are accredited). *Faculty:* 32 full-time (13 women), 25 part-time/adjunct (12 women). *Students:* 331 full-time (220 women), 19 part-time (14 women); includes 146 minority (30 Black or African American, non-Hispanic/Latino; 1 American Indian or Alaska Native, non-Hispanic/Latino; 42 Asian, non-Hispanic/Latino; 47 Hispanic/Latino; 7 Native Hawaiian or other Pacific Islander, non-Hispanic/Latino; 19 Two or more races, non-Hispanic/Latino), 40 international. In 2018, 88 master's, 8 doctorates awarded. *Degree requirements:* For master's, thesis (for some programs), project, practicum; for doctorate, comprehensive exam, thesis/dissertation. *Entrance requirements:* For master's, GRE General Test, MCAT, LSAT (for joint MPH/JD applicants), minimum GPA of 3.0, official transcripts, statement of purpose, 3 letters of recommendation, resume/CV; for doctorate, GRE General Test, minimum GPA of 3.0, pre-requisite coursework, 3 letters of recommendation, official transcripts, resume/CV. Additional exam requirements/recommendations for international students: Required—TOEFL (minimum score 550 paper-based; 80 iBT). Application fee: $135. Electronic applications accepted. *Faculty research:* Behavioral epidemiology, substance abuse, infectious disease, cardiovascular diseases, women's health, occupational health. *Total annual research expenditures:* $10.5 million. *Unit head:* Dr. J.Sunil Rao, Chair, E-mail: jrao@miami.edu. *Application contact:* Andria Williams, Director of Admissions, 305-243-0291, E-mail: alw157@med.miami.edu.
Website: https://www.publichealth.med.miami.edu/

University of Michigan, School of Public Health, Department of Biostatistics, Ann Arbor, MI 48109. Offers MPH, MS, PhD. MS and PhD offered through the Rackham Graduate School. Terminal master's awarded for partial completion of doctoral program. *Degree requirements:* For doctorate, oral defense of dissertation, qualifying exam. *Entrance requirements:* For master's, GRE General Test; for doctorate, GRE General Test, master's degree. Additional exam requirements/recommendations for international students: Required—TOEFL (minimum score 100 iBT). Electronic applications accepted. *Faculty research:* Statistical genetics, categorical data analysis, incomplete data, survival analysis, modeling.

University of Michigan, School of Public Health, Program in Clinical Research Design and Statistical Analysis, Ann Arbor, MI 48109. Offers MS. Offered through the Rackham Graduate School; program admits applicants in odd-numbered calendar years only. *Program availability:* Evening/weekend. *Degree requirements:* For master's, comprehensive exam. *Entrance requirements:* For master's, GRE General Test or MCAT. Additional exam requirements/recommendations for international students: Recommended—TOEFL (minimum score 560 paper-based; 100 iBT). Electronic applications accepted. *Expenses:* Contact institution. *Faculty research:* Survival analysis, missing data, Bayesian inference, health economics, quality of life.

University of Minnesota, Twin Cities Campus, School of Public Health, Major in Biostatistics, Minneapolis, MN 55455-0213. Offers MPH, MS, PhD. *Program availability:* Part-time. Terminal master's awarded for partial completion of doctoral program. *Degree requirements:* For master's, comprehensive exam; for doctorate, comprehensive exam, thesis/dissertation. *Entrance requirements:* For master's, GRE General Test, course work in applied statistics, computer programming, multivariable calculus, linear algebra; for doctorate, GRE General Test, bachelor's or master's degree in statistics, biostatistics or mathematics. Additional exam requirements/recommendations for international students: Required—TOEFL (minimum score 600 paper-based; 90 iBT). Electronic applications accepted. *Faculty research:* Analysis of spatial and longitudinal data, Bayes/Empirical Bayes methods, survival analysis, longitudinal models, generalized linear models.

University of Nebraska Medical Center, Department of Biostatistics, Omaha, NE 68198-4375. Offers biostatistics (PhD). *Program availability:* Part-time. *Faculty:* 7 full-time (4 women). *Students:* 5 full-time (0 women), 5 part-time (2 women); includes 3 minority (2 Black or African American, non-Hispanic/Latino; 1 Asian, non-Hispanic/Latino), 3 international. Average age 37. 5 applicants, 60% accepted, 2 enrolled. *Degree requirements:* For doctorate, comprehensive exam, thesis/dissertation, qualifying exam. *Entrance requirements:* For doctorate, GRE. Additional exam requirements/recommendations for international students: Required—TOEFL (minimum score 550 paper-based). *Application deadline:* For fall admission, 6/1 for domestic students, 4/1 for international students. Applications are processed on a rolling basis. Application fee: $60. Electronic applications accepted. *Expenses: Tuition, area resident:* Full-time $8721; part-time $2907 per credit hour. Tuition, state resident: full-time $8721; part-time $2907 per credit hour. Tuition, nonresident: full-time $24,975; part-time $8325 per credit hour. *International tuition:* $24,975 full-time. *Required fees:* $582. *Financial support:* In 2018–19, 1 research assistantship with full tuition reimbursement, 4 teaching assistantships with full tuition reimbursements were awarded; health care benefits and unspecified assistantships also available. Financial award application deadline: 4/1. *Faculty research:* Clinical trials, small area estimation, statistical genetics/genomics, statistical models in survival analysis, high dimensional data. *Unit head:* Dr. Kendra Schmid, Campus Director of Assessment, Assistant Dean Graduate Studies, Professor and Interim Chair, 402-559-8117, E-mail: kkschmid@unmc.edu. *Application contact:* Dr. Gleb Haynatzki, Graduate Program Director/Professor, 402-559-3294, E-mail: ghaynatzki@unmc.edu.
Website: http://www.unmc.edu/publichealth/departments/biostatistics/

The University of North Carolina at Chapel Hill, Graduate School, Gillings School of Global Public Health, Department of Biostatistics, Chapel Hill, NC 27599-7420. Offers MPH, MS, Dr PH, PhD, PhD/MD. *Faculty:* 33 full-time (8 women), 19 part-time/adjunct (5 women). *Students:* 112 full-time (64 women), 69 part-time (31 women); includes 45 minority (5 Black or African American, non-Hispanic/Latino; 31 Asian, non-Hispanic/Latino; 4 Hispanic/Latino; 1 Native Hawaiian or other Pacific Islander, non-Hispanic/Latino; 4 Two or more races, non-Hispanic/Latino), 62 international. Average age 28. 427 applicants, 40% accepted, 64 enrolled. In 2018, 21 master's, 15 doctorates awarded. *Degree requirements:* For master's, comprehensive exam, thesis or alternative, paper or formal thesis; for doctorate, comprehensive exam, thesis/dissertation. *Entrance requirements:* For master's, GRE General Test, coursework in multivariable calculus and linear algebra, 3 letters of recommendation; for doctorate, GRE General Test, prior mathematics training including advanced calculus and linear algebra, 3 letters of recommendation. Additional exam requirements/recommendations for international students: Required—TOEFL (minimum score 90 iBT), IELTS (minimum score 7). *Application deadline:* For fall admission, 1/8 for domestic and international students. Application fee: $90. Electronic applications accepted. *Expenses:* Contact institution. *Financial support:* Fellowships with tuition reimbursements, research assistantships with tuition reimbursements, teaching assistantships with tuition reimbursements, Federal Work-Study, institutionally sponsored loans, scholarships/grants, traineeships, health care benefits, and unspecified assistantships available. Financial award application deadline: 12/10; financial award applicants required to submit FAFSA. *Faculty research:* Cancer, cardiovascular, environmental biostatistics; AIDS and other infectious diseases; statistical genetics and computational biology; missing data methods. *Unit head:* Dr. Michael Kosorok, Chair, 919-966-8107, E-mail: kosorok@unc.edu. *Application contact:* Veronica Stallings, Student Services Manager, 919-966-7262, Fax: 919-966-3804, E-mail: stalling@bios.unc.edu.
Website: https://sph.unc.edu/bios/biostatistics/

University of North Texas Health Science Center at Fort Worth, School of Public Health, Fort Worth, TX 76107-2699. Offers biostatistics (MS); epidemiology (MPH, MS, PhD); food security and public health (Graduate Certificate); GIS in public health (Graduate Certificate); global health (Graduate Certificate); global health for medical professionals (Graduate Certificate); health administration (MHA); health behavior research (MS, PhD); maternal and child health (MPH); public health (Graduate Certificate); public health practice (MPH); DO/MPH; MS/MPH. *Accreditation:* CAHME; CEPH. *Program availability:* Part-time, evening/weekend, 100% online. *Degree requirements:* For master's, thesis or alternative, supervised internship; for doctorate, thesis/dissertation, supervised internship. *Entrance requirements:* For master's, GRE General Test. Additional exam requirements/recommendations for international students: Required—TOEFL. Electronic applications accepted. *Expenses:* Contact institution.

University of Oklahoma Health Sciences Center, Graduate College, Hudson College of Public Health, Department of Biostatistics and Epidemiology, Oklahoma City, OK 73190. Offers biostatistics (MPH, MS, Dr PH, PhD); epidemiology (MPH, MS, Dr PH, PhD). *Accreditation:* CEPH (one or more programs are accredited). *Program availability:* Part-time. *Degree requirements:* For master's, comprehensive exam, thesis (for some programs); for doctorate, comprehensive exam, thesis/dissertation. *Entrance requirements:* For master's, 3 letters of recommendation, resume; for doctorate, GRE General Test, letters of recommendation. Additional exam requirements/recommendations for international students: Required—TOEFL (minimum score 570 paper-based), TWE. *Faculty research:* Statistical methodology, applied statistics, acute and chronic disease epidemiology.

University of Pennsylvania, Perelman School of Medicine, Biomedical Graduate Studies, Graduate Group in Epidemiology and Biostatistics, Philadelphia, PA 19104. Offers biostatistics (MS, PhD); epidemiology (PhD). Terminal master's awarded for partial completion of doctoral program. *Degree requirements:* For master's, thesis; for doctorate, thesis/dissertation. *Entrance requirements:* For master's, GRE, 1 year of course work in calculus, 1 semester of course work in linear algebra, working knowledge of programming language; for doctorate, GRE, 1 year of course work in calculus, 1 semester of course work in linear algebra, and working knowledge of programming language (for biostatistics); training and experience in epidemiology, clinical sciences or a public health-related field (for epidemiology). Additional exam requirements/recommendations for international students: Required—TOEFL. *Faculty research:* Design of clinical trials; statistical methods for genetics, genomes and genetic epidemiology; causal inference and observation data; statistical methods for survival and longitudinal data; statistical methods for big data.

University of Pennsylvania, Perelman School of Medicine, Center for Clinical Epidemiology and Biostatistics, Philadelphia, PA 19104. Offers clinical epidemiology (MSCE), including bioethics, clinical trials, human genetics, patient centered outcome research, pharmacoepidemiology. *Program availability:* Part-time. *Degree requirements:* For master's, comprehensive exam, thesis. *Entrance requirements:* For master's, GRE General Test or MCAT, advanced degree, clinical experience. Additional exam requirements/recommendations for international students: Required—TOEFL. Electronic applications accepted. *Expenses:* Contact institution. *Faculty research:* Patient-centered outcomes, pharmacoepidemiology, women's health, cancer epidemiology, genetic epidemiology.

University of Pittsburgh, Graduate School of Public Health, Department of Biostatistics, Pittsburgh, PA 15261. Offers MS, PhD. *Program availability:* Part-time. Terminal master's awarded for partial completion of doctoral program. *Degree requirements:* For master's, thesis, comprehensive exam (for MS); for doctorate, comprehensive exam, thesis/dissertation, preliminary exam, dissertation defense. *Entrance requirements:* For master's and doctorate, GRE General Test, previous course work in biology and calculus. Additional exam requirements/recommendations for international students: Required—TOEFL (minimum score 550 paper-based, 80 iBT) or IELTS (minimum score 6.5). Electronic applications accepted. *Expenses:* Contact institution. *Faculty research:* Preconception of stress exposure, impact of mycoplasma on reproductive, mitochondrial determinants of cognitive outcomes, enhanced detection system for infection.

University of Puerto Rico–Medical Sciences Campus, Graduate School of Public Health, Department of Social Sciences, Program in Biostatistics, San Juan, PR 00936-5067. Offers MPH. *Program availability:* Part-time. *Entrance requirements:* For master's, GRE, previous course work in algebra. *Expenses:* Contact institution.

University of Rochester, School of Medicine and Dentistry, Graduate Programs in Medicine and Dentistry, Department of Biostatistics and Computational Biology, Program in Medical Statistics, Rochester, NY 14642. Offers MS. *Degree requirements:* For master's, internship/applied project. *Expenses: Tuition:* Full-time $52,974; part-time $1654 per credit hour. *Required fees:* $612. One-time fee: $30 part-time. Tuition and fees vary according to campus/location and program.

University of South Carolina, The Graduate School, Arnold School of Public Health, Department of Epidemiology and Biostatistics, Program in Biostatistics, Columbia, SC 29208. Offers MPH, MSPH, Dr PH, PhD. *Program availability:* Part-time. *Degree requirements:* For master's, comprehensive exam, thesis (for some programs), practicum (MPH); for doctorate, comprehensive exam, thesis/dissertation (for some programs), practicum (Dr PH). *Entrance requirements:* For master's, GRE General Test; for doctorate, GRE General Test, master's degree. Additional exam requirements/recommendations for international students: Required—TOEFL (minimum score 570 paper-based; 88 iBT). Electronic applications accepted. *Faculty research:* Bayesian methods, biometric modeling, nonlinear regression, health survey methodology, measurement of health status.

University of Southern California, Keck School of Medicine and Graduate School, Graduate Programs in Medicine, Department of Preventive Medicine, Division of Biostatistics, Los Angeles, CA 90089. Offers applied biostatistics and epidemiology

(MS); biostatistics (MS, PhD); epidemiology (PhD); molecular epidemiology (MS). *Program availability:* Part-time. *Faculty:* 47 full-time (8 women), 7 part-time/adjunct (3 women). *Students:* 93 full-time (59 women); includes 23 minority (3 Black or African American, non-Hispanic/Latino; 1 American Indian or Alaska Native, non-Hispanic/Latino; 17 Asian, non-Hispanic/Latino; 2 Native Hawaiian or other Pacific Islander, non-Hispanic/Latino), 55 international. Average age 30. 108 applicants, 55% accepted, 22 enrolled. In 2018, 15 master's, 12 doctorates awarded. Terminal master's awarded for partial completion of doctoral program. *Degree requirements:* For master's, thesis; for doctorate, thesis/dissertation. *Entrance requirements:* For master's, GRE General Test (minimum scores of 150 each on Verbal and Quantitative sections), minimum GPA of 3.0; for doctorate, GRE General Test (minimum scores of 160 each on Verbal and Quantitative sections), minimum GPA of 3.5. Additional exam requirements/recommendations for international students: Required—TOEFL (minimum score 600 paper-based; 100 iBT), IELTS (minimum score 7). *Application deadline:* For fall admission, 12/1 priority date for domestic and international students; for winter admission, 5/15 priority date for domestic and international students; for spring admission, 11/1 priority date for domestic and international students; for summer admission, 3/1 priority date for domestic and international students. Applications are processed on a rolling basis. Application fee: $85. Electronic applications accepted. *Expenses:* Contact institution. *Financial support:* In 2018–19, 38 students received support, including 10 fellowships with full tuition reimbursements available (averaging $32,000 per year), 36 research assistantships with tuition reimbursements available (averaging $32,000 per year), 15 teaching assistantships with tuition reimbursements available (averaging $32,000 per year); career-related internships or fieldwork, Federal Work-Study, institutionally sponsored loans, scholarships/grants, traineeships, health care benefits, and unspecified assistantships also available. Financial award application deadline: 12/1; financial award applicants required to submit CSS PROFILE or FAFSA. *Faculty research:* Clinical trials in ophthalmology and cancer research, methods of analysis for epidemiological studies, genetic epidemiology. *Total annual research expenditures:* $1.3 million. *Unit head:* Dr. Kiros Berhane, Director, Graduate Programs in Biostatistics and Epidemiology, 323-442-1994, Fax: 323-442-2993, E-mail: kiros@usc.edu. *Application contact:* Mary L. Trujillo, Student Advisor/Program Manager, 323-442-2633, Fax: 323-442-2993, E-mail: mtrujill@usc.edu.

University of Southern California, Keck School of Medicine and Graduate School, Graduate Programs in Medicine, Department of Preventive Medicine, Master of Public Health Program, Los Angeles, CA 90032. Offers biostatistics and epidemiology (MPH); child and family health (MPH); community health promotion (MPH); environmental health (MPH); geohealth (MPH); global health leadership (MPH); health communication (MPH); health services and policy (MPH). *Accreditation:* CEPH. *Program availability:* Part-time, evening/weekend, 100% online. *Faculty:* 38 full-time (30 women), 10 part-time/adjunct (6 women). *Students:* 213 full-time (164 women), 108 part-time (81 women); includes 195 minority (55 Black or African American, non-Hispanic/Latino; 2 American Indian or Alaska Native, non-Hispanic/Latino; 82 Asian, non-Hispanic/Latino; 56 Hispanic/Latino), 39 international. Average age 28. 460 applicants, 69% accepted, 77 enrolled. In 2018, 130 master's awarded. *Degree requirements:* For master's, practicum, final report, oral presentation. *Entrance requirements:* For master's, GRE General Test, MCAT, GMAT, minimum GPA of 3.0. Additional exam requirements/recommendations for international students: Required—TOEFL (minimum score 600 paper-based; 90 iBT). *Application deadline:* For fall admission, 12/1 priority date for domestic students, 5/1 priority date for international students; for spring admission, 9/1 priority date for domestic and international students; for summer admission, 3/1 for domestic and international students. Applications are processed on a rolling basis. Application fee: $135. Electronic applications accepted. *Financial support:* Career-related internships or fieldwork, Federal Work-Study, institutionally sponsored loans, and scholarships/grants available. Support available to part-time students. Financial award application deadline: 5/4; financial award applicants required to submit CSS PROFILE or FAFSA. *Faculty research:* Cancer and heart disease epidemiology and prevention, mass media and health communication, effects of air pollution on health, tobacco control, global health. *Total annual research expenditures:* $9.6 million. *Unit head:* Dr. Louise A. Rohrbach, Director, 323-442-8237, Fax: 323-442-8297, E-mail: rohrbac@usc.edu. *Application contact:* Valerie Burris, Admissions Counselor, 323-442-7257, Fax: 323-442-8297, E-mail: valeriem@usc.edu.
Website: https://preventivemedicine.usc.edu/education/graduate-programs/mph/

University of Southern Mississippi, College of Nursing and Health Professions, School of Health Professions, Hattiesburg, MS 39406-0001. Offers epidemiology and biostatistics (MPH); health policy and administration (MPH). *Accreditation:* CEPH. *Program availability:* Part-time, evening/weekend. *Degree requirements:* For master's, comprehensive exam, thesis (for some programs). *Entrance requirements:* For master's, GRE General Test, minimum GPA of 2.75 in last 60 hours. Additional exam requirements/recommendations for international students: Required—TOEFL, IELTS. Electronic applications accepted. *Faculty research:* Rural health care delivery, school health, nutrition of pregnant teens, risk factor reduction, sexually transmitted diseases.

University of South Florida, Innovative Education, Tampa, FL 33620-9951. Offers adult, career and higher education (Graduate Certificate), including college teaching, leadership in developing human resources, leadership in higher education; Africana studies (Graduate Certificate), including diasporas and health disparities, genocide and human rights; aging studies (Graduate Certificate), including gerontology; art research (Graduate Certificate), including museum studies; business foundations (Graduate Certificate); chemical and biomedical engineering (Graduate Certificate), including materials science and engineering, water, health and sustainability; child and family studies (Graduate Certificate), including positive behavior support; civil and industrial engineering (Graduate Certificate), including transportation systems analysis; community and family health (Graduate Certificate), including maternal and child health, social marketing and public health, violence and injury: prevention and intervention, women's health; criminology (Graduate Certificate), including criminal justice administration; data science for public administration (Graduate Certificate); digital humanities (Graduate Certificate); educational measurement and research (Graduate Certificate), including evaluation; English (Graduate Certificate), including comparative literary studies, creative writing, professional and technical communication; entrepreneurship (Graduate Certificate); environmental health (Graduate Certificate), including safety management; epidemiology and biostatistics (Graduate Certificate), including applied biostatistics, biostatistics, concepts and tools of epidemiology, epidemiology, epidemiology of infectious diseases; geography, environment and planning (Graduate Certificate), including community development, environmental policy and management, geographical information systems; geology (Graduate Certificate), including hydrogeology; global health (Graduate Certificate), including disaster management, global health and Latin American and Caribbean studies, global health practice, humanitarian assistance, infection control; government and international affairs (Graduate Certificate), including Cuban studies, globalization studies; health policy and management (Graduate Certificate), including health management and leadership, public health policy and programs; hearing specialist: early intervention (Graduate Certificate); industrial and management systems engineering (Graduate Certificate), including systems engineering, technology management; information studies (Graduate Certificate), including school library media specialist; information systems/decision sciences (Graduate Certificate), including analytics and business intelligence; instructional technology (Graduate Certificate), including distance education, Florida digital/virtual educator, instructional design, multimedia design, Web design; internal medicine, bioethics and medical humanities (Graduate Certificate), including biomedical ethics; Latin American and Caribbean studies (Graduate Certificate); leadership for coastal resiliency planning (Graduate Certificate); mass communications (Graduate Certificate), including multimedia journalism; mathematics and statistics (Graduate Certificate), including mathematics; medicine (Graduate Certificate), including aging and neuroscience, bioinformatics, biotechnology, brain fitness and memory management, clinical investigation, hand and upper limb rehabilitation, health informatics, health sciences, integrative weight management, intellectual property, medicine and gender, metabolic and nutritional medicine, metabolic cardiology, pharmacy sciences; national and competitive intelligence (Graduate Certificate); nursing (Graduate Certificate), including simulation based academic fellowship in advanced pain management; psychological and social foundations (Graduate Certificate), including career counseling, college teaching, diversity in education, mental health counseling, school counseling; public affairs (Graduate Certificate), including nonprofit management, public management, research administration; public health (Graduate Certificate), including assessing chemical toxicity and public health risks, health equity, pharmacoepidemiology, public health generalist, toxicology, translational research in adolescent behavioral health; public health practices (Graduate Certificate), including planning for healthy communities; rehabilitation and mental health counseling (Graduate Certificate), including integrative mental health care, marriage and family therapy, rehabilitation technology; secondary education (Graduate Certificate), including ESOL, foreign language education: culture and content, foreign language education: professional; social work (Graduate Certificate), including geriatric social work/clinical gerontology; special education (Graduate Certificate), including autism spectrum disorder, disabilities education: severe/profound; world languages (Graduate Certificate), including teaching English as a second language (TESL) or foreign language. *Expenses:* Tuition, state resident: full-time $6350. Tuition, nonresident: full-time $19,048. *International tuition:* $19,048 full-time. *Required fees:* $2079. *Unit head:* Dr. Cynthia DeLuca, Associate Vice President and Assistant Vice Provost, 813-974-3077, Fax: 813-974-7061, E-mail: deluca@usf.edu. *Application contact:* Owen Hooper, Director, Summer and Alternative Calendar Programs, 813-974-6917, E-mail: hooper@usf.edu.
Website: http://www.usf.edu/innovative-education/

The University of Texas Health Science Center at Houston, School of Public Health, Houston, TX 77030. Offers behavioral science (PhD); biostatistics (MPH, MS, PhD); environmental health (MPH); epidemiology (MPH, MS, PhD); general public health (Certificate); genomics and bioinformatics (Certificate); health disparities (Certificate); health promotion/health education (MPH, Dr PH); healthcare management (Certificate); management, policy and community health (MPH, Dr PH, PhD); maternal and child health (Certificate); public health informatics (Certificate); DDS/MPH; JD/MPH; MBA/MPH; MD/MPH; MGPS/MPH; MP Aff/MPH; MS/MPH; MSN/MPH; MSW/MPH; PhD/MPH. Specific programs are offered at each of our six campuses in Texas (Austin, Brownsville, Dallas, El Paso, Houston, and San Antonio). *Accreditation:* CAHME; CEPH. *Program availability:* Part-time. *Degree requirements:* For master's, thesis (for some programs); for doctorate, comprehensive exam, thesis/dissertation. *Entrance requirements:* For master's and doctorate, GRE General Test. Additional exam requirements/recommendations for international students: Required—TOEFL (minimum score 600 paper-based, 100 iBT) or IELTS (7.5). Electronic applications accepted. *Expenses:* Contact institution. *Faculty research:* Chronic and infectious disease epidemiology; health promotion and health education; applied and theoretical biostatistics; healthcare management, policy and economics; environmental and occupational health.

The University of Toledo, College of Graduate Studies, College of Medicine and Life Sciences, Department of Public Health and Preventative Medicine, Toledo, OH 43606-3390. Offers biostatistics and epidemiology (Certificate); contemporary gerontological practice (Certificate); environmental and occupational health and safety (MPH); epidemiology (Certificate); global public health (Certificate); health promotion and education (MPH); industrial hygiene (MSOH); medical and health science teaching and learning (Certificate); occupational health (Certificate); public health administration (MPH); public health and emergency response (Certificate); public health epidemiology (MPH); public health nutrition (MPH); MD/MPH. *Program availability:* Part-time, evening/weekend. *Degree requirements:* For master's, thesis or alternative. *Entrance requirements:* For master's, GRE, minimum undergraduate GPA of 3.0, three letters of recommendation, statement of purpose, transcripts from all prior institutions attended, resume; for Certificate, minimum undergraduate GPA of 3.0, three letters of recommendation, statement of purpose, transcripts from all prior institutions attended, resume. Additional exam requirements/recommendations for international students: Required—TOEFL (minimum score 550 paper-based; 80 iBT), IELTS (minimum score 6.5). Electronic applications accepted.

University of Toronto, School of Graduate Studies, Department of Public Health Sciences, Toronto, ON M5S 1A1, Canada. Offers biostatistics (M Sc, PhD); community health (M Sc); community nutrition (MPH), including nutrition and dietetics; epidemiology (MPH, PhD); family and community medicine (MPH); occupational and environmental health (MPH); social and behavioral health science (PhD); social and behavioral health sciences (MPH), including health promotion. *Accreditation:* CAHME (one or more programs are accredited). *Program availability:* Part-time. *Degree requirements:* For master's, thesis (for some programs), practicum; for doctorate, comprehensive exam, thesis/dissertation, oral thesis defense. *Entrance requirements:* For master's, 2 letters of reference, relevant professional/research experience, minimum B average in final year; for doctorate, 2 letters of reference, relevant professional/research experience, minimum B+ average. Additional exam requirements/recommendations for international students: Required—TOEFL (minimum score 580 paper-based; 93 iBT), TWE (minimum score 5). Electronic applications accepted. *Expenses:* Contact institution.

University of Utah, School of Medicine and Graduate School, Graduate Programs in Medicine, Department of Family and Preventive Medicine, Programs in Public Health, Salt Lake City, UT 84112-1107. Offers biostatistics (M Stat); public health (MPH, MSPH, PhD). *Accreditation:* CEPH (one or more programs are accredited). *Program availability:* Part-time. *Degree requirements:* For master's, comprehensive exam, thesis or project (MSPH); for doctorate, comprehensive exam, thesis/dissertation. *Entrance requirements:* For master's and doctorate, GRE General Test, 3 letters of reference, in-person interviews, minimum GPA of 3.0. Additional exam requirements/recommendations for international students: Required—TOEFL (minimum score 550 paper-based). Electronic applications accepted. *Expenses: Tuition, area resident:* Full-time $7190.66; part-time $2112.48 per year. Tuition, state resident: full-time $7190.66. Tuition, nonresident: full-time $25,195. *Required fees:* $558; $555.04 per unit. Tuition and fees vary according to course level, course load, degree level, program and student level. *Faculty research:* Health services, health policy, epidemiology of chronic disease, infectious disease epidemiology, cancer epidemiology.

University of Vermont, Graduate College, College of Engineering and Mathematical Sciences, Department of Mathematics and Statistics, Program in Biostatistics, Burlington, VT 05401. Offers MS. *Degree requirements:* For master's, thesis or alternative. *Entrance requirements:* For master's, GRE General Test. Additional exam requirements/recommendations for international students: Required—TOEFL (minimum score 90 iBT), IELTS (minimum score 6.5). Electronic applications accepted. *Faculty research:* Statistical genetics, bioengineering experiment design, community intervention studies, population-based health surveys.

University of Washington, Graduate School, Interdisciplinary Graduate Program in Quantitative Ecology and Resource Management, Seattle, WA 98195. Offers MS, PhD. *Degree requirements:* For master's, thesis; for doctorate, thesis/dissertation. *Entrance requirements:* For master's and doctorate, GRE General Test, minimum GPA of 3.0. Additional exam requirements/recommendations for international students: Required—TOEFL. Electronic applications accepted. *Faculty research:* Population dynamics, statistical analysis, ecological modeling and systems analysis of aquatic and terrestrial ecosystems.

University of Washington, Graduate School, School of Public Health, Department of Biostatistics, Seattle, WA 98195. Offers biostatistics (MPH, MS, PhD); statistical genetics (PhD). *Faculty:* 40 full-time (18 women), 6 part-time/adjunct (4 women). *Students:* 80 full-time (44 women), 4 part-time (2 women); includes 13 minority (2 Black or African American, non-Hispanic/Latino; 10 Asian, non-Hispanic/Latino; 1 Hispanic/Latino), 48 international. Average age 27. 357 applicants, 15% accepted, 18 enrolled. In 2018, 7 master's, 8 doctorates awarded. Terminal master's awarded for partial completion of doctoral program. *Degree requirements:* For master's, thesis (for some programs); for doctorate, thesis/dissertation. *Entrance requirements:* Additional exam requirements/recommendations for international students: Required—TOEFL (minimum score 500 paper-based; 80 iBT). *Application deadline:* For fall admission, 12/1 for domestic and international students. Application fee: $85. Electronic applications accepted. *Financial support:* In 2018–19, 14 research assistantships with full tuition reimbursements (averaging $26,592 per year), 28 teaching assistantships with full tuition reimbursements (averaging $62,048 per year) were awarded; traineeships, health care benefits, and tuition for employed students also available. Financial award application deadline: 12/1. *Faculty research:* Cystic Fibrosis, survival analysis, decision theory, biomarkers, longitudinal and multilevel data. *Unit head:* Dr. Patrick Heagerty, Chair/Professor, 206-543-1044, E-mail: bchair@uw.edu. *Application contact:* Biostatistics Admissions, E-mail: bioadmit@uw.edu.
Website: http://www.biostat.washington.edu/

University of Waterloo, Graduate Studies and Postdoctoral Affairs, Faculty of Mathematics, Department of Statistics and Actuarial Science, Waterloo, ON N2L 3G1, Canada. Offers actuarial science (M Math, MAS, PhD); biostatistics (PhD); statistics (M Math, PhD); statistics-biostatistics (M Math); statistics-computing (M Math); statistics-finance (M Math). *Degree requirements:* For master's, research paper or thesis; for doctorate, comprehensive exam, thesis/dissertation. *Entrance requirements:* For master's, honors degree in field, minimum B+ average; for doctorate, master's degree, minimum B+ average. Additional exam requirements/recommendations for international students: Required—TOEFL, IELTS, PTE. *Application deadline:* Applications are processed on a rolling basis. Application fee: $125 Canadian dollars. Electronic applications accepted. *Financial support:* Fellowships, research assistantships, teaching assistantships, career-related internships or fieldwork, and scholarships/grants available. *Faculty research:* Data analysis, risk theory, inference, stochastic processes, quantitative finance.
Website: https://uwaterloo.ca/statistics-and-actuarial-science/

The University of Western Ontario, Schulich School of Medicine and Dentistry, Department of Epidemiology and Biostatistics, London, ON N6A 3K7, Canada. Offers M Sc, PhD. *Program availability:* Part-time. *Degree requirements:* For master's, thesis; for doctorate, comprehensive exam, thesis proposal defense. *Entrance requirements:* For master's, BA or B Sc honors degree, minimum B+ average in last 10 courses; for doctorate, M Sc or equivalent, minimum B+ average in last 10 courses. *Faculty research:* Chronic disease epidemiology, clinical epidemiology.

University of Wisconsin–Milwaukee, Graduate School, Joseph J. Zilber School of Public Health, Program in Public Health, Milwaukee, WI 53201-0413. Offers biostatistics (MPH); community and behavioral health promotion (MPH); environmental health sciences (MPH); epidemiology (MPH, PhD); public and population health (Graduate Certificate); public health policy and administration (MPH); public health: biostatistics (PhD); public health: community and behavioral health promotion (PhD). *Students:* 77 full-time (62 women), 21 part-time (14 women); includes 27 minority (5 Black or African American, non-Hispanic/Latino; 11 Asian, non-Hispanic/Latino; 11 Two or more races, non-Hispanic/Latino), 9 international. Average age 31. 85 applicants, 76% accepted, 57 enrolled. In 2018, 18 master's awarded. Electronic applications accepted. *Application contact:* Darcie K. G. Warren, Graduate Program Manager, 414-229-5633, E-mail: darcie@uwm.edu.

Virginia Commonwealth University, Medical College of Virginia-Professional Programs, School of Medicine, Graduate Programs in Medicine, Department of Biostatistics, Richmond, VA 23298-0032. Offers MS, PhD, MD/PhD. *Program availability:* Part-time. Terminal master's awarded for partial completion of doctoral program. *Degree requirements:* For doctorate, thesis/dissertation, theoretical and applied qualifying exams; dissertation proposal. *Entrance requirements:* For master's, GRE, MCAT or DAT; for doctorate, GRE. Additional exam requirements/recommendations for international students: Required—TOEFL (minimum score 600 paper-based; 100 iBT). Electronic applications accepted. *Faculty research:* Health services, linear and nonlinear models, response surfaces, adaptive designs in clinical trials, genomic biostatistics, data mining/machine learning.

Washington University in St. Louis, Brown School, St. Louis, MO 63110. Offers American Indian/Alaska native (MSW); children, youth and families (MSW); epidemiology/biostatistics (MPH); generalist (MPH); global health (MPH); health (MSW); health policy analysis (MPH); individualized (MSW), including health; mental health (MSW); older adults and aging societies (MSW); public health sciences (PhD); social and economic development (MSW), including domestic, international; social work (PhD); urban design (MPH); violence and injury prevention (MSW); JD/MSW; M Arch/MSW; MPH/MBA; MSW/M Div; MSW/M Ed; MSW/MAPS; MSW/MBA; MSW/MPH; MUD/MSW. MSW/M Div and MSW/MAPS offered in partnership with Eden Theological Seminary. *Accreditation:* CEPH; CSWE (one or more programs are accredited). *Degree requirements:* For master's, 60 credit hours (for MSW); 52 credit hours (for MPH); practicum; for doctorate, comprehensive exam, thesis/dissertation. *Entrance requirements:* For master's, GRE (preferred), GMAT, LSAT, MCAT, PCAT, or United States Medical Licensing Exam (for MPH); for doctorate, GRE. Additional exam requirements/recommendations for international students: Required—TOEFL (minimum score 100 iBT), IELTS (minimum score 7). Electronic applications accepted. *Expenses:* Contact institution. *Faculty research:* Mental health, social policy, health policy, epidemiology, social and economic development.

Washington University in St. Louis, School of Medicine, Division of Biostatistics, St. Louis, MO 63110. Offers biostatistics (MS); genetic epidemiology (Certificate). *Program availability:* Part-time. *Entrance requirements:* For master's, GRE, proficiency in computer programming, statistics and biology/genetics. Additional exam requirements/recommendations for international students: Required—TOEFL (minimum score 600 paper-based; 100 iBT), TWE. Electronic applications accepted. *Expenses:* Contact institution. *Faculty research:* Biostatistics, clinical trials, cardiovascular diseases, genetics, genetic epidemiology.

Weill Cornell Medicine, Weill Cornell Graduate School of Medical Sciences, Program in Healthcare Policy and Research, New York, NY 10065. Offers biostatistics and data science (MS); health informatics (MS); health policy and economics (MS). *Program availability:* Part-time. *Students:* 62 full-time, 27 part-time; includes 3 minority (2 Asian, non-Hispanic/Latino; 1 Hispanic/Latino). In 2018, 4 master's awarded. *Degree requirements:* For master's, thesis. *Entrance requirements:* For master's, GRE, MCAT, or GMAT (recommended), official transcripts, resume, personal statement, 3 letters of reference.. Additional exam requirements/recommendations for international students: Required—TOEFL. *Application deadline:* For fall admission, 3/1 priority date for domestic and international students. Application fee: $75. *Expenses:* Contact institution. *Unit head:* William Tseng, Admissions Manager, 646-962-8083, E-mail: wit2006@med.cornell.edu. *Application contact:* William Tseng, Admissions Manager, 646-962-8083, E-mail: wit2006@med.cornell.edu.
Website: http://hpr.weill.cornell.edu/education/

West Virginia University, School of Public Health, Morgantown, WV 26506. Offers biostatistics (MPH, MS, PhD); epidemiology (MPH, PhD); health policy (MPH); occupational and environmental health sciences (MPH, PhD); public health (MPH); school health education (MS); social and behavioral science (MPH, PhD). *Accreditation:* CEPH. *Program availability:* Part-time, online learning. *Students:* 52 full-time (34 women), 26 part-time (15 women); includes 13 minority (4 Black or African American, non-Hispanic/Latino; 5 Asian, non-Hispanic/Latino; 2 Hispanic/Latino; 2 Two or more races, non-Hispanic/Latino), 10 international. In 2018, 38 master's, 9 doctorates awarded. *Degree requirements:* For master's, practicum, project. *Entrance requirements:* For master's, GRE General Test, MCAT, medical degree, medical internship. Additional exam requirements/recommendations for international students: Required—TOEFL (minimum score 550 paper-based; 80 iBT). *Application deadline:* For fall admission, 4/15 priority date for domestic students; for spring admission, 12/1 for domestic students. Applications are processed on a rolling basis. Application fee: $60. *Expenses:* Contact institution. *Financial support:* Research assistantships, teaching assistantships, scholarships/grants, and health care benefits available. Financial award application deadline: 2/1; financial award applicants required to submit FAFSA. *Faculty research:* Occupational health, environmental health, clinical epidemiology, health care management, prevention. *Unit head:* Dr. Jeffrey Coben, Dean, 304-293-5775, E-mail: jcoben@hsc.wvu.edu. *Application contact:* Leah Adkins, Senior Program Coordinator, 304-293-1097, E-mail: leadkins@hsc.wvu.edu.
Website: http://publichealth.hsc.wvu.edu/

Yale University, Yale School of Medicine, Yale School of Public Health, New Haven, CT 06520. Offers applied biostatistics and epidemiology (APMPH); biostatistics (MPH, MS, PhD), including global health (MPH); chronic disease epidemiology (MPH, PhD), including global health (MPH); environmental health sciences (MPH, PhD), including global health (MPH); epidemiology of microbial diseases (MPH, PhD), including global health (MPH); global health (APMPH); health management (MPH), including global health; health policy (MPH), including global health; health policy and administration (APMPH, PhD); occupational and environmental medicine (APMPH); preventive medicine (APMPH); social and behavioral sciences (APMPH, MPH), including global health (MPH); JD/MPH; M Div/MPH; MBA/MPH; MD/MPH; MEM/MPH; MFS/MPH; MM Sc/MPH; MPH/MA; MSN/MPH. MS and PhD offered through the Graduate School. *Accreditation:* CEPH. *Program availability:* Part-time. Terminal master's awarded for partial completion of doctoral program. *Degree requirements:* For master's, thesis, summer internship; for doctorate, comprehensive exam, thesis/dissertation, residency. *Entrance requirements:* For master's, GMAT, GRE, or MCAT, two years of undergraduate coursework in math and science; for doctorate, GRE General Test. Additional exam requirements/recommendations for international students: Required—TOEFL (minimum score 100 iBT). Electronic applications accepted. *Expenses:* Contact institution. *Faculty research:* Genetic and emerging infections epidemiology, virology, cost/quality, vector biology, quantitative methods, aging, asthma, cancer.

Computational Sciences

American University of Beirut, Graduate Programs, Faculty of Arts and Sciences, Beirut 1107 2020, Lebanon. Offers anthropology (MA); Arab and Middle Eastern history (PhD); Arabic language and literature (MA, PhD); archaeology (MA); art history and curating (MA); biology (MS); cell and molecular biology (PhD); chemistry (MS); clinical psychology (MA); computational sciences (MS); computer science (MS); economics (MA); education (MA), including administration and policy studies, elementary education, mathematics education, psychology school guidance, psychology test and measurements, science education, teaching English as a foreign language; English language (MA); English literature (MA); environmental policy planning (MS); financial economics (MAFE); general psychology (MA); geology (MS); history (MA); Islamic studies (MA); mathematics (MS); media studies (MA); Middle East studies (MA); philosophy (MA); physics (MS); political studies (MA); public administration (MA); public policy and international affairs (MA); sociology (MA); theoretical physics (PhD). *Program availability:* Part-time. *Faculty:* 187 full-time (64 women), 27 part-time/adjunct (15 women). *Students:* 292 full-time (215 women), 216 part-time (148 women). Average age 27. 422 applicants, 64% accepted, 124 enrolled. In 2018, 90 master's, 3 doctorates awarded. *Degree requirements:* For master's, comprehensive exam, thesis (for some programs), project; for doctorate, comprehensive exam, thesis/dissertation (for some

programs). *Entrance requirements:* For master's, GRE General Test (for archaeology, clinical psychology, general psychology, economics, financial economics and biology); for doctorate, GRE General Test for all PhD programs, GRE Subject Test for theoretical physics. Additional exam requirements/recommendations for international students: Required—TOEFL (minimum score 583 paper-based; 97 iBT), IELTS (minimum score 7). *Application deadline:* For fall admission, 3/18 for domestic students; for spring admission, 11/5 for domestic students. Application fee: $50. Electronic applications accepted. *Expenses:* MA/MS: Humanities and social sciences=$912/credit. Sciences=$943/credit. Financial economics=$986/credit. Thesis: Humanities/social sciences=$6565 and sciences=$6865. *Financial support:* In 2018–19, 227 fellowships with full tuition reimbursements, 17 research assistantships with full tuition reimbursements, 83 teaching assistantships with full tuition reimbursements were awarded; scholarships/grants, tuition waivers (full and partial), and unspecified assistantships also available. Financial award application deadline: 3/18. *Faculty research:* Sciences: Physics: High energy, Particle, Polymer and Soft Matter, Thermal, Plasma; String Theory, Mathematical physics, Astrophysics (stellar evolution, planet and galaxy formation and evolution, astrophysical dynamics), Solid State physics/thin films, Spintronics, Magnetic properties of materials, Mineralogy, Petrology, and Geochemistry of Hard Rocks, Geophysics and Petrophysics, Hydrogeology, Micropaleontology, Sedimentology, and Stratigraphy, Structural Geology and Geotectonics, Renewable en. *Total annual research expenditures:* $4.3 million. *Unit head:* Dr. Nadia Maria El Cheikh, Dean, Faculty of Arts and Sciences, 961-1-350000 Ext. 3800, Fax: 961-1-744461, E-mail: nmcheikh@aub.edu.lb. *Application contact:* Adriana Michelle Zanaty, Curriculum and Graduate Studies Officer, 961-1-350000 Ext. 3833, Fax: 961-1-744461, E-mail: az48@aub.edu.lb.
Website: https://www.aub.edu.lb/fas/Pages/default.aspx

California Institute of Technology, Division of Engineering and Applied Science, Option in Computation and Neural Systems, Pasadena, CA 91125-0001. Offers MS, PhD. Terminal master's awarded for partial completion of doctoral program. *Degree requirements:* For doctorate, thesis/dissertation, qualifying exam. *Entrance requirements:* For doctorate, GRE General Test. *Faculty research:* Biological and artificial computational devices, modeling of sensory processes and learning, theory of collective computation.

Chapman University, Schmid College of Science and Technology, Computational and Data Sciences Program, Orange, CA 92866. Offers MS, PhD. *Program availability:* Part-time. *Degree requirements:* For master's, thesis or alternative; for doctorate, thesis/dissertation. *Entrance requirements:* For master's and doctorate, GRE. Additional exam requirements/recommendations for international students: Required—TOEFL (minimum score 550 paper-based; 80 iBT), IELTS (minimum score 6.5), PTE (minimum score 53), CAE. Electronic applications accepted. *Expenses:* Contact institution.
See Display on this page and Close-Up on page 251.

Claremont Graduate University, Graduate Programs, Institute of Mathematical Sciences, Claremont, CA 91711-6160. Offers computational and systems biology (PhD); computational mathematics and numerical analysis (MA, MS); computational science (PhD); engineering and industrial applied mathematics (PhD); mathematics (PhD); operations research and statistics (MA, MS); physical applied mathematics (MA, MS); pure mathematics (MA, MS); scientific computing (MA, MS); systems and control theory (MA, MS). PhD programs offered jointly with San Diego State University and California State University, Long Beach. *Program availability:* Part-time. Terminal master's awarded for partial completion of doctoral program. *Entrance requirements:* For master's and doctorate, GRE General Test. Additional exam requirements/recommendations for international students: Required—TOEFL (minimum score 75 iBT). Electronic applications accepted.

Cornell University, Graduate School, Graduate Fields of Engineering, Field of Chemical Engineering, Ithaca, NY 14853. Offers advanced materials processing (M Eng, MS, PhD); applied mathematics and computational methods (M Eng, MS, PhD); biochemical engineering (M Eng, MS, PhD); chemical reaction engineering (M Eng, MS, PhD); classical and statistical thermodynamics (M Eng, MS, PhD); fluid dynamics, rheology and biorheology (M Eng, MS, PhD); heat and mass transfer (M Eng, MS, PhD); kinetics and catalysis (M Eng, MS, PhD); polymers (M Eng, MS, PhD); surface science (M Eng, MS, PhD). *Degree requirements:* For master's, thesis (MS); for doctorate, comprehensive exam, thesis/dissertation. *Entrance requirements:* For master's and doctorate, GRE General Test, 2 letters of recommendation. Additional exam requirements/recommendations for international students: Required—TOEFL (minimum score 600 paper-based; 77 iBT). Electronic applications accepted. *Faculty research:* Biochemical, biomedical and metabolic engineering; fluid and polymer dynamics; surface science and chemical kinetics; electronics materials; microchemical systems and nanotechnology.

Duke University, Graduate School, Pratt School of Engineering, Department of Civil and Environmental Engineering, Durham, NC 27708. Offers civil and environmental engineering (MS, PhD); civil engineering (M Eng); computational mechanics and scientific computing (M Eng); environmental engineering (M Eng, MS, PhD); risk engineering (M Eng). Terminal master's awarded for partial completion of doctoral program. *Degree requirements:* For doctorate, thesis/dissertation. *Entrance requirements:* For master's and doctorate, GRE General Test. Additional exam requirements/recommendations for international students: Required—TOEFL (minimum score 550 paper-based; 90 iBT), IELTS (minimum score 7). Electronic applications accepted. *Faculty research:* Environmental process engineering, hydrology and fluid dynamics, materials, structures and geo-systems.

Duke University, Graduate School, Pratt School of Engineering, Master of Engineering Program, Durham, NC 27708-0271. Offers biomedical engineering (M Eng); civil engineering (M Eng); computational mechanics and scientific computing (M Eng); electrical and computer engineering (M Eng); environmental engineering (M Eng); materials science and engineering (M Eng); mechanical engineering (M Eng); photonics and optical sciences (M Eng); risk engineering (M Eng). *Program availability:* Part-time. *Entrance requirements:* For master's, GRE General Test, resume, 3 letters of recommendation, statement of purpose, transcripts. Additional exam requirements/recommendations for international students: Required—TOEFL. Electronic applications accepted.

Florida State University, The Graduate School, Department of Anthropology, Department of Scientific Computing, Tallahassee, FL 32306-4120. Offers computational science (MS), including atmospheric science (PhD), biochemistry (PhD), biological science (PhD), computational science (PhD), geological science (PhD), materials science (PhD), physics (PhD). *Program availability:* Part-time. *Faculty:* 9 full-time (1 woman), 2 part-time/adjunct (1 woman). *Students:* 34 full-time (6 women); includes 17 minority (10 Asian, non-Hispanic/Latino; 3 Hispanic/Latino; 4 Two or more races, non-Hispanic/Latino), 13 international. Average age 26. 64 applicants, 23% accepted, 6 enrolled. In 2018, 10 master's, 8 doctorates awarded. Terminal master's awarded for partial completion of doctoral program. *Degree requirements:* For master's, comprehensive exam, thesis (for some programs); for doctorate, comprehensive exam,

Peterson's Graduate Programs in the Physical Sciences, Mathematics, Agricultural Sciences, the Environment & Natural Resources 2020

www.petersons.com **199**

thesis/dissertation. *Entrance requirements:* For master's and doctorate, GRE General Test, knowledge of at least one object-oriented computing language, 3 letters of recommendation, resume, statement of purpose. Additional exam requirements/ recommendations for international students: Required—TOEFL (minimum score 550 paper-based; 80 iBT). *Application deadline:* For fall admission, 1/15 for domestic and international students. Applications are processed on a rolling basis. Application fee: $30. Electronic applications accepted. *Expenses: Tuition, area resident:* Part-time $479.32 per credit hour. Tuition and fees vary according to campus/location and program. *Financial support:* In 2018–19, 32 students received support, including 10 research assistantships with full tuition reimbursements available (averaging $26,670 per year), 23 teaching assistantships with full tuition reimbursements available (averaging $23,000 per year); scholarships/grants, health care benefits, tuition waivers (full), and unspecified assistantships also available. Financial award application deadline: 1/15. *Faculty research:* Morphometrics, mathematical and systems biology, mining proteomic and metabolic data, computational materials research, computational fluid dynamics, astrophysics, deep learning, computational neuroscience. *Total annual research expenditures:* $500,000. *Unit head:* Dr. Gordon Erlebacher, Chair, 850-644-7024, E-mail: gerlebacher@fsu.edu. *Application contact:* Karey Fowler, Academic Program Specialist, 850-644-0143, Fax: 850-644-0098, E-mail: kgfowler@fsu.edu.
Website: http://www.sc.fsu.edu

Florida State University, The Graduate School, Department of Anthropology, Interdisciplinary Program in Geophysical Fluid Dynamics, Tallahassee, FL 32306. Offers computational sciences (PhD), including fire dynamics, geophysical fluid dynamics. *Faculty:* 24 full-time (1 woman). *Students:* 5 full-time (2 women), 2 international. Average age 30. 5 applicants, 60% accepted, 2 enrolled. In 2018, 2 doctorates awarded. *Degree requirements:* For doctorate, thesis/dissertation, departmental qualifying exam. *Entrance requirements:* For doctorate, GRE General Test, GRE Subject Test, minimum GPA of 3.0. Additional exam requirements/recommendations for international students: Required—TOEFL (minimum score 550 paper-based; 80 iBT). *Application deadline:* For fall admission, 3/30 for domestic and international students; for spring admission, 9/30 for domestic and international students; for summer admission, 12/15 for domestic students, 12/17 for international students. Application fee: $30. Electronic applications accepted. *Expenses: Tuition, area resident:* Part-time $479.32 per credit hour. Tuition and fees vary according to campus/location and program. *Financial support:* In 2018–19, 2 research assistantships with partial tuition reimbursements (averaging $21,500 per year) were awarded; fellowships and unspecified assistantships also available. Financial award application deadline: 2/15; financial award applicants required to submit FAFSA. *Faculty research:* Hurricane dynamics, convection, air-sea interaction, wave-mean flow interaction, numerical models, ground water flows, Karst environmental dynamics, fire dynamics. *Total annual research expenditures:* $934,702. *Unit head:* Dr. Kevin Speer, Director, 850-645-5625, Fax: 850-644-8972, E-mail: kspeer@fsu.edu. *Application contact:* Vijaya Challa, Academic Coordinator, 850-644-5594, Fax: 850-644-8972, E-mail: vijaya@fsu.edu.
Website: http://www.gfdi.fsu.edu/

George Mason University, College of Science, Department of Computational and Data Sciences, Fairfax, VA 22030. Offers computational science (MS); computational sciences and informatics (PhD); computational social science (PhD, Certificate); data science (Certificate). *Faculty:* 9 full-time (2 women), 10 part-time/adjunct (1 woman). *Students:* 30 full-time (6 women), 78 part-time (24 women); includes 34 minority (11 Black or African American, non-Hispanic/Latino; 20 Asian, non-Hispanic/Latino; 3 Hispanic/Latino), 19 international. Average age 39. 70 applicants, 63% accepted, 19 enrolled. In 2018, 5 master's, 12 doctorates, 1 other advanced degree awarded. *Degree requirements:* For master's, comprehensive exam (for some programs), thesis optional; for doctorate, comprehensive exam, thesis/dissertation. *Entrance requirements:* For master's, GRE general required for students with degrees outside US. TOEFL required for students with degrees outside US., GPA of at least 3.00 in their last 60 credits of undergraduate study. Applicants should have taken at least one course in differential equations. Applicant should have proficiency in using a high-level computer programming language.; for doctorate, GRE required for students with degrees outside US. TOEFL required for students with degrees outside US., GPA of at least 3.00 in their last 60 credits of undergraduate study. Applicants should have taken at least one course in differential equations. Applicants should have knowledge of a computer programming language such as C, C++, Fortran, Python, etc.; for Certificate, TOEFL required for students with degrees outside US., GPA of at least 3.00 in their last 60 credits of undergraduate study. Applicants should have taken at least one course in differential equation. Applicants should have knowledge of a computer programming language such as C, C++, Fortran, Python, etc. Additional exam requirements/recommendations for international students: Required—TOEFL. *Financial support:* In 2018–19, 12 students received support, including 10 research assistantships (averaging $16,004 per year), 3 teaching assistantships (averaging $14,397 per year); scholarships/grants and unspecified assistantships also available. *Faculty research:* Computational social science; material science; computational science; image analysis; data science. *Total annual research expenditures:* $262,807. *Unit head:* Jason Kinser, Acting Chair, 703-993-3785, E-mail: jkinser@gmu.edu. *Application contact:* Melissa C. Hayes, Graduate Programs Director, 703-993-3430, Fax: 703-993-9033, E-mail: mhayes5@gmu.edu.
Website: http://cos.gmu.edu/cds/

Georgia Institute of Technology, Graduate Studies, Multidisciplinary Program in Computational Science and Engineering, Atlanta, GA 30332-0001. Offers MS, PhD. *Program availability:* Part-time, online learning. Terminal master's awarded for partial completion of doctoral program. *Degree requirements:* For master's, thesis optional; for doctorate, comprehensive exam, thesis/dissertation. *Entrance requirements:* For master's and doctorate, GRE General Test. Additional exam requirements/ recommendations for international students: Required—TOEFL (minimum score 600 paper-based; 100 iBT). Electronic applications accepted.

Hampton University, School of Science, Program in Applied Mathematics, Hampton, VA 23668. Offers computational mathematics (MS); nonlinear science (MS); statistics and probability (MS). *Program availability:* Part-time. *Faculty:* 1. *Students:* 2 full-time (1 woman), 1 (woman) part-time; all minorities (all Black or African American, non-Hispanic/Latino). Average age 37. 4 applicants, 50% accepted, 2 enrolled. In 2018, 1 master's awarded. *Degree requirements:* For master's, thesis optional. *Entrance requirements:* For master's, GRE General Test. Additional exam requirements/ recommendations for international students: Required—TOEFL (minimum score 525 paper-based) or IELTS (6.5). *Application deadline:* For fall admission, 6/1 priority date for domestic students, 4/1 priority date for international students; for spring admission, 11/1 priority date for domestic students, 9/1 priority date for international students; for summer admission, 4/1 priority date for domestic students, 2/1 priority date for international students. Applications are processed on a rolling basis. Application fee: $35. Electronic applications accepted. *Financial support:* Application deadline: 6/30; applicants required to submit FAFSA. *Faculty research:* Stochastic processes, nonlinear dynamics, approximation theory, hydrodynamical stability, Clifford Analysis, Functional Analysis, Operator Theory, Hilbert Space, Polyconvex Integrand, Ordinary Differential Equations, and Calculus of Variations, Longitudinal Data Analysis and Logistic Regression Modeling. *Unit head:* Dr. Arun K. Verma, Professor/Chair, 757-727-5352, Fax: 757-637-2378, E-mail: arun.verma@hamptonu.edu. *Application contact:* Dr. Arun K. Verma, Professor/Chair, 757-727-5352, Fax: 757-637-2378, E-mail: arun.verma@hamptonu.edu.

Harvard University, Graduate School of Arts and Sciences, Harvard John A. Paulson School of Engineering and Applied Sciences, Cambridge, MA 02138. Offers applied mathematics (PhD); applied physics (PhD); computational science and engineering (ME, SM); computer science (PhD); data science (SM); design engineering (MDE); engineering science (ME), including electrical engineering (ME, SM, PhD); engineering sciences (SM, PhD), including bioengineering (PhD), electrical engineering (ME, SM, PhD), environmental science and engineering (PhD), materials science and mechanical engineering (PhD). MDE offered in collaboration with Graduate School of Design. *Program availability:* Part-time. Terminal master's awarded for partial completion of doctoral program. *Degree requirements:* For master's, thesis (for ME); for doctorate, comprehensive exam, thesis/dissertation. *Entrance requirements:* For master's and doctorate, GRE General Test, GRE Subject Test (recommended), 3 letters of recommendation. Additional exam requirements/recommendations for international students: Required—TOEFL (minimum score 80 iBT). Electronic applications accepted. *Expenses:* Contact institution. *Faculty research:* Applied mathematics, applied physics, computer science and electrical engineering, environmental engineering, mechanical and biomedical engineering.

Marquette University, Graduate School, College of Arts and Sciences, Department of Mathematics, Statistics, and Computer Science, Milwaukee, WI 53201-1881. Offers bioinformatics (MS); computational sciences (MS, PhD); computing (MS); mathematics education (MS). *Program availability:* Part-time, evening/weekend, online learning. Terminal master's awarded for partial completion of doctoral program. *Degree requirements:* For master's, thesis (for some programs), essay with oral presentation; for doctorate, comprehensive exam, thesis/dissertation, qualifying examination. *Entrance requirements:* For master's, official transcripts from all current and previous colleges/ universities except Marquette, three letters of recommendation; for doctorate, GRE General Test, official transcripts from all current and previous colleges/universities except Marquette, three letters of recommendation. Additional exam requirements/ recommendations for international students: Required—TOEFL (minimum score 530 paper-based). Electronic applications accepted. *Faculty research:* Models of physiological systems, mathematical immunology, computational group theory, mathematical logic, computational science.

Massachusetts Institute of Technology, School of Engineering and School of Science, Program in Computation for Design and Optimization, Cambridge, MA 02139. Offers SM. *Degree requirements:* For master's, thesis. *Entrance requirements:* For master's, GRE General Test. Additional exam requirements/recommendations for international students: Required—IELTS. Electronic applications accepted. *Expenses: Tuition:* Full-time $51,520; part-time $800 per credit hour. *Required fees:* $312. *Faculty research:* Numerical methods; partial differential equations; optimization; computational mechanics.

McGill University, Faculty of Graduate and Postdoctoral Studies, Faculty of Science, Department of Mathematics and Statistics, Montréal, QC H3A 2T5, Canada. Offers computational science and engineering (M Sc); mathematics and statistics (M Sc, MA, PhD), including applied mathematics (M Sc, MA), pure mathematics (M Sc, MA), statistics (M Sc, MA).

Memorial University of Newfoundland, School of Graduate Studies, Interdisciplinary Program in Scientific Computing, St. John's, NL A1C 5S7, Canada. Offers M Sc. *Degree requirements:* For master's, thesis. *Entrance requirements:* For master's, honors B Sc or significant background in the field. Electronic applications accepted. *Faculty research:* Scientific computing, modeling and simulation, computational fluid dynamics, polymer physics, computational chemistry.

Michigan Technological University, Graduate School, Interdisciplinary Programs, Houghton, MI 49931. Offers automotive systems and controls (Graduate Certificate); biochemistry and molecular biology (PhD); computational science and engineering (PhD); data science (Graduate Certificate); sustainability (Graduate Certificate). *Program availability:* Part-time. *Faculty:* 120 full-time (25 women), 8 part-time/adjunct. *Students:* 67 full-time (28 women), 24 part-time; includes 5 minority (2 Black or African American, non-Hispanic/Latino; 1 American Indian or Alaska Native, non-Hispanic/ Latino; 2 Two or more races, non-Hispanic/Latino), 59 international. Average age 29. 479 applicants, 24% accepted, 17 enrolled. In 2018, 19 master's, 8 doctorates, 10 other advanced degrees awarded. Terminal master's awarded for partial completion of doctoral program. *Degree requirements:* For master's, comprehensive exam (for some programs), thesis (for some programs); for doctorate, comprehensive exam, thesis/ dissertation. *Entrance requirements:* For master's, doctorate, and Graduate Certificate, GRE, statement of purpose, personal statement, official transcripts, 2-3 letters of recommendation. Additional exam requirements/recommendations for international students: Required—TOEFL or IELTS. *Application deadline:* Applications are processed on a rolling basis. Electronic applications accepted. *Expenses: Tuition, area resident:* Full-time $18,126; part-time $1007 per credit. Tuition, state resident: full-time $18,126; part-time $1007 per credit. Tuition, nonresident: full-time $18,126; part-time $1007 per credit. *International tuition:* $18,126 full-time. *Required fees:* $248; $124 per semester. Tuition and fees vary according to course load and program. *Financial support:* In 2018–19, 64 students received support, including 14 fellowships with tuition reimbursements available (averaging $16,590 per year), 14 research assistantships with tuition reimbursements available (averaging $16,590 per year), 12 teaching assistantships with tuition reimbursements available (averaging $16,590 per year); career-related internships or fieldwork, Federal Work-Study, scholarships/grants, health care benefits, unspecified assistantships, and cooperative program also available. Financial award applicants required to submit FAFSA. *Faculty research:* Big data, atmospheric sciences, bioinformatics and systems biology, molecular dynamics, environmental studies. *Unit head:* Dr. Pushpalatha Murthy, Dean of the Graduate School/Associate Provost for Graduate Education, 906-487-3007, Fax: 906-487-2284, E-mail: ppmurthy@mtu.edu. *Application contact:* Carol T. Wingerson, Administrative Aide, 906-487-2328, Fax: 906-487-2284, E-mail: gradadms@mtu.edu.

Middle Tennessee State University, College of Graduate Studies, College of Basic and Applied Sciences, Interdisciplinary Program in Computational Science, Murfreesboro, TN 37132. Offers PhD. *Entrance requirements:* For doctorate, GRE. Additional exam requirements/recommendations for international students: Required—TOEFL (minimum score 525 paper-based; 71 iBT) or IELTS (minimum score 6).

Morgan State University, School of Graduate Studies, School of Computer, Mathematical, and Natural Sciences, Department of Mathematics, Baltimore, MD 21251. Offers industrial and computational mathematics (PhD); mathematics (MA). *Program availability:* Part-time, evening/weekend. *Degree requirements:* For master's, comprehensive exam, thesis. *Entrance requirements:* For master's, GRE. Additional exam requirements/recommendations for international students: Required—TOEFL (minimum score 550 paper-based). *Faculty research:* Number theory, semigroups, analysis, operations research.

North Carolina Agricultural and Technical State University, The Graduate College, College of Science and Technology, Department of Physics, Greensboro, NC 27411. Offers computational sciences (MS); physics (MS).

The Ohio State University, Graduate School, College of Arts and Sciences, Division of Natural and Mathematical Sciences, Department of Mathematics, Columbus, OH 43210. Offers actuarial and quantitative risk management (MAQRM); computational sciences (MMS); mathematical biosciences (MMS); mathematics (PhD); mathematics for educators (MMS). *Faculty:* 61. *Students:* 150 full-time (32 women); includes 16 minority (9 Asian, non-Hispanic/Latino; 5 Hispanic/Latino; 2 Two or more races, non-Hispanic/Latino), 84 international. Average age 26. In 2018, 24 master's, 21 doctorates awarded. *Degree requirements:* For master's, thesis optional; for doctorate, one foreign language, thesis/dissertation. *Entrance requirements:* For master's, GRE General Test; for doctorate, GRE General Test (recommended), GRE Subject Test (mathematics). Additional exam requirements/recommendations for international students: Required—TOEFL (minimum score 550 paper-based; 79 iBT), Michigan English Language Assessment Battery (minimum score 82); Recommended—IELTS (minimum score 7). *Application deadline:* For fall admission, 12/15 priority date for domestic and international students. Applications are processed on a rolling basis. Application fee: $60 ($70 for international students). Electronic applications accepted. *Financial support:* Fellowships, research assistantships, teaching assistantships, Federal Work-Study, institutionally sponsored loans, and unspecified assistantships available. Support available to part-time students. *Unit head:* Dr. Jean-Francois Lafont, Chair, 614-292-7173, E-mail: lafont.1@osu.edu. *Application contact:* Erin Anthony, Graduate Studies Coordinator, 614-292-6274, Fax: 614-292-1479, E-mail: grad-info@math.osu.edu.
Website: http://www.math.osu.edu/

Oregon State University, College of Science, Program in Physics, Corvallis, OR 97331. Offers atomic physics (MA, MS, PhD); computational physics (MA, MS, PhD); experimental physics (MA, MS, PhD); nuclear and particle physics (MA, MS, PhD); optical physics (MA, MS, PhD); solid state physics (MA, MS, PhD). *Entrance requirements:* Additional exam requirements/recommendations for international students: Required—TOEFL (minimum score 600 paper-based; 100 iBT). Electronic applications accepted.

Princeton University, Graduate School, Program in Applied and Computational Mathematics, Princeton, NJ 08544-1019. Offers PhD. *Degree requirements:* For doctorate, thesis/dissertation. *Entrance requirements:* For doctorate, GRE General Test, GRE Subject Test. Additional exam requirements/recommendations for international students: Required—TOEFL (minimum score 600 paper-based). Electronic applications accepted.

Purdue University, Graduate School, College of Health and Human Sciences, Department of Psychological Sciences, West Lafayette, IN 47907. Offers behavioral neuroscience (PhD); clinical psychology (PhD); cognitive psychology (PhD); industrial/organizational psychology (PhD); mathematical and computational cognitive science (PhD). *Accreditation:* APA. *Faculty:* 45 full-time (20 women), 1 part-time/adjunct (0 women). *Students:* 62 full-time (47 women), 3 part-time (1 woman); includes 21 minority (3 Black or African American, non-Hispanic/Latino; 6 Asian, non-Hispanic/Latino; 9 Hispanic/Latino; 3 Two or more races, non-Hispanic/Latino), 12 international. Average age 27. 281 applicants, 10% accepted, 14 enrolled. In 2018, 9 doctorates awarded. Terminal master's awarded for partial completion of doctoral program. *Degree requirements:* For doctorate, thesis/dissertation. *Entrance requirements:* For doctorate, GRE General Test, minimum undergraduate GPA of 3.0 or equivalent. Additional exam requirements/recommendations for international students: Required—TOEFL (minimum score 550 paper-based; 77 iBT); Recommended—TWE. *Application deadline:* For fall admission, 12/3 for domestic and international students. Applications are processed on a rolling basis. Application fee: $60 ($75 for international students). Electronic applications accepted. *Financial support:* Fellowships with partial tuition reimbursements, research assistantships with partial tuition reimbursements, teaching assistantships with partial tuition reimbursements, and career-related internships or fieldwork available. Support available to part-time students. Financial award applicants required to submit FAFSA. *Faculty research:* Career development of women in science, development of friendships during childhood and adolescence, social competence, human information processing. *Unit head:* Dr. David Rollock, Head, 765-494-6061, E-mail: rollock@purdue.edu. *Application contact:* Nancy A. O'Brien, Graduate Contact, 765-494-6067, E-mail: nobrien@psych.purdue.edu.
Website: http://www.psych.purdue.edu/

Rice University, Graduate Programs, George R. Brown School of Engineering, Department of Computational and Applied Mathematics, Houston, TX 77251-1892. Offers computational and applied mathematics (MA, MCAM, PhD); computational science and engineering (PhD). *Degree requirements:* For master's, comprehensive exam (for some programs), thesis (for some programs); for doctorate, comprehensive exam, thesis/dissertation. *Entrance requirements:* For master's and doctorate, GRE General Test, minimum GPA of 3.0. Additional exam requirements/recommendations for international students: Required—TOEFL (minimum score 600 paper-based; 90 iBT). Electronic applications accepted. *Faculty research:* Inverse problems, partial differential equations, computer algorithms, computational modeling, optimization theory.

Rice University, Graduate Programs, George R. Brown School of Engineering, Program in Computational Science and Engineering, Houston, TX 77251-1892. Offers MCSE.

St. John's University, St. John's College of Liberal Arts and Sciences, Department of Mathematics and Computer Science, Queens, NY 11439. Offers applied and computational mathematics (MA). *Program availability:* Part-time, evening/weekend. *Degree requirements:* For master's, comprehensive exam. *Entrance requirements:* For master's, letters of recommendation, transcripts, resume, personal statement. Additional exam requirements/recommendations for international students: Required—TOEFL (minimum score 80 iBT), IELTS (minimum score 6.5). Electronic applications accepted.

Sam Houston State University, College of Sciences, Department of Computer Science, Huntsville, TX 77341. Offers computing and information science (MS); digital forensics (MS); information assurance and security (MS). *Program availability:* Part-time. *Degree requirements:* For master's, comprehensive exam, thesis optional, internship; for doctorate, comprehensive exam, thesis/dissertation. *Entrance requirements:* For master's, GRE General Test, letters of recommendation. Additional exam requirements/recommendations for international students: Required—TOEFL (minimum score 550 paper-based; 79 iBT), IELTS (minimum score 6.5). Electronic applications accepted.

San Diego State University, Graduate and Research Affairs, College of Sciences, Program in Computational Science, San Diego, CA 92182. Offers MS, PhD. *Degree requirements:* For master's, thesis; for doctorate, thesis/dissertation. *Entrance requirements:* For master's, GRE General Test, 3 letters of recommendation; for doctorate, GRE, 3 letters of recommendation. Additional exam requirements/recommendations for international students: Required—TOEFL. Electronic applications accepted.

Simon Fraser University, Office of Graduate Studies and Postdoctoral Fellows, Faculty of Science, Department of Mathematics, Burnaby, BC V5A 1S6, Canada. Offers applied and computational mathematics (M Sc, PhD); mathematics (M Sc, PhD); operations research (M Sc, PhD). *Degree requirements:* For master's, thesis or alternative; for doctorate, comprehensive exam, thesis/dissertation. *Entrance requirements:* For master's, GRE General Test, GRE Subject Test (mathematics), minimum GPA of 3.0 (on scale of 4.33) or 3.33 based on last 60 credits of undergraduate courses; for doctorate, GRE General Test, GRE Subject Test (mathematics), minimum GPA of 3.5 (on scale of 4.33). Additional exam requirements/recommendations for international students: Recommended—TOEFL (minimum score 580 paper-based; 93 iBT), IELTS (minimum score 7), TWE (minimum score 5). Electronic applications accepted. *Faculty research:* Computer algebra, discrete mathematics, fluid dynamics, nonlinear partial differential equations and variation methods, numerical analysis and scientific computing.

South Dakota State University, Graduate School, Jerome J. Lohr College of Engineering, Department of Mathematics and Statistics, Brookings, SD 57007. Offers computational science and statistics (PhD); mathematics (MS); statistics (MS). *Program availability:* Part-time. Terminal master's awarded for partial completion of doctoral program. *Degree requirements:* For master's, thesis (for some programs), oral exam; for doctorate, comprehensive exam, thesis/dissertation, oral and written exams. *Entrance requirements:* Additional exam requirements/recommendations for international students: Required—TOEFL (minimum score 550 paper-based; 80 iBT); Recommended—IELTS. *Faculty research:* Financial mathematics, predictive analytics, operations research, bioinformatics, biostatistics, computational science, statistics, number theory, abstract algebra.

Southern Illinois University Edwardsville, Graduate School, College of Arts and Sciences, Department of Mathematics and Statistics, Program in Computational and Applied Mathematics, Edwardsville, IL 62026. Offers MS. *Program availability:* Part-time. *Degree requirements:* For master's, thesis (for some programs), research paper. *Entrance requirements:* Additional exam requirements/recommendations for international students: Required—TOEFL (minimum score 550 paper-based, 79 iBT), IELTS (minimum score 6.5), Michigan Test of English Language Proficiency or PTE. Electronic applications accepted.

Southern Methodist University, Dedman College of Humanities and Sciences, Department of Mathematics, Dallas, TX 75275. Offers computational and applied mathematics (MS, PhD). *Degree requirements:* For master's, oral exams; for doctorate, thesis/dissertation, oral and written exams. *Entrance requirements:* For master's and doctorate, GRE General Test, minimum GPA of 3.0, 18 undergraduate hours in mathematics beyond first- and second-year calculus. Additional exam requirements/recommendations for international students: Required—TOEFL. Electronic applications accepted. *Faculty research:* Numerical analysis and scientific computation, fluid dynamics, optics, wave propagation, mathematical biology.

Stanford University, School of Engineering, Institute for Computational and Mathematical Engineering, Stanford, CA 94305-2004. Offers MS, PhD. *Expenses: Tuition:* Full-time $50,703; part-time $32,970 per year. *Required fees:* $651.
Website: http://icme.stanford.edu/

Texas A&M University–Commerce, College of Science and Engineering, Commerce, TX 75429. Offers biological sciences (MS); broadfield science biology (MS); broadfield science chemistry (MS); broadfield science physics (MS); chemistry (MS); computational linguistics (Graduate Certificate); computational science (MS); computer science (MS); environmental science (Graduate Certificate); mathematics (MS); physics (MS); technology management (MS). *Program availability:* Part-time. *Faculty:* 44 full-time (7 women), 7 part-time/adjunct (0 women). *Students:* 178 full-time (67 women), 234 part-time (104 women); includes 82 minority (19 Black or African American, non-Hispanic/Latino; 1 American Indian or Alaska Native, non-Hispanic/Latino; 14 Asian, non-Hispanic/Latino; 37 Hispanic/Latino; 11 Two or more races, non-Hispanic/Latino), 158 international. Average age 30. 481 applicants, 52% accepted, 105 enrolled. In 2018, 218 master's awarded. *Degree requirements:* For master's, comprehensive exam, thesis optional. *Entrance requirements:* For master's, GRE, official transcripts, letters of recommendation, resume, statement of goals. Additional exam requirements/recommendations for international students: Required—TOEFL (minimum score 550 paper-based; 79 iBT), IELTS (minimum score 6), PTE (minimum score 53). *Application deadline:* For fall admission, 6/1 priority date for international students; for spring admission, 10/15 priority date for international students; for summer admission, 3/15 priority date for international students. Applications are processed on a rolling basis. Application fee: $50 ($75 for international students). Electronic applications accepted. *Expenses:* Contact institution. *Financial support:* In 2018–19, 46 students received support, including 43 research assistantships with partial tuition reimbursements available (averaging $2,418 per year), 135 teaching assistantships with partial tuition reimbursements available (averaging $3,376 per year); scholarships/grants, health care benefits, and unspecified assistantships also available. Financial award application deadline: 5/1; financial award applicants required to submit FAFSA. *Faculty research:* Biomedical, Catalytic Material & Processes, Nuclear Theory/Astrophysics, Cybersecurity, STEM Education. *Total annual research expenditures:* $1.8 million. *Unit head:* Dr. Brent L. Donham, Dean, 903-886-5321, Fax: 903-886-5199, E-mail: brent.donham@tamuc.edu. *Application contact:* Dayla Burgin, Graduate Student Services Coordinator, 903-886-5134, E-mail: dayla.burgin@tamuc.edu.
Website: https://new.tamuc.edu/science-engineering/

University at Buffalo, the State University of New York, Graduate School, College of Arts and Sciences, Center for Computational Research, Buffalo, NY 14260. Offers computational science (Advanced Certificate).

University at Buffalo, the State University of New York, Graduate School, School of Engineering and Applied Sciences, Program in Computational and Data Enabled Sciences, Buffalo, NY 14260. Offers PhD.

The University of Alabama at Birmingham, School of Engineering, Program in Interdisciplinary Engineering, Birmingham, AL 35294. Offers computational engineering (PhD). *Program availability:* Part-time. *Faculty:* 1 full-time (0 women), 1 (woman) part-time/adjunct. *Students:* 11 full-time (0 women), 18 part-time (3 women); includes 7 minority (5 Black or African American, non-Hispanic/Latino; 1 Asian, non-Hispanic/Latino; 1 Two or more races, non-Hispanic/Latino), 7 international. Average age 40. 4 applicants, 50% accepted. In 2018, 1 doctorate awarded. *Degree requirements:* For doctorate, comprehensive exam, thesis/dissertation, publication of three first-author original research articles in peer-reviewed journal. *Entrance requirements:* For doctorate, The GRE general test is required for all applicants. Applicants must score a 156 or higher on the quantitative section of the GRE to be considered for admission., Undergraduate or graduate degree in Engineering. Minimum 3.0 on a 4.0 scale on most recent degree. Personal statement identifying research interest. CV/résumé. 3

recommendations from academic or professional contact. Additional exam requirements/recommendations for international students: Required—TOEFL (minimum score 80 iBT); Recommended—IELTS (minimum score 6.5). *Application deadline:* For fall admission, 8/1 for domestic and international students; for spring admission, 12/1 for domestic and international students; for summer admission, 5/1 for domestic and international students. Applications are processed on a rolling basis. Application fee: $50 ($60 for international students). Electronic applications accepted. *Expenses:* Contact institution. *Faculty research:* Aerospace systems, environmental engineering, mathematical foundations of quantum electronics, digital circuits and systems design, CO2 enhanced oil production. *Unit head:* Dr. Gregg Janowski, Program Director, 205-934-8524, E-mail: janowski@uab.edu. *Application contact:* Jesse Keppley, Director of Student and Academic Services, 205-996-5696, E-mail: gradschool@uab.edu.
Website: http://www.uab.edu/engineering/home/degrees-cert/phd?id-189:phd-in-interdisciplinary-engineering&catid-3

University of Alaska Fairbanks, College of Natural Science and Mathematics, Department of Physics, Fairbanks, AK 99775-5920. Offers computational physics (MS); physics (MS, PhD); space physics (MS). *Program availability:* Part-time. *Faculty:* 8 full-time (2 women). *Students:* 22 full-time (3 women), 1 part-time (0 women); includes 3 minority (1 Asian, non-Hispanic/Latino; 2 Hispanic/Latino), 5 international. Average age 29. 35 applicants, 14% accepted, 5 enrolled. In 2018, 1 master's, 2 doctorates awarded. *Degree requirements:* For master's, comprehensive exam, oral defense of project or thesis; for doctorate, comprehensive exam, thesis/dissertation, oral defense of dissertation. *Entrance requirements:* For master's, GRE General Test, bachelor's degree from accredited institution with minimum cumulative undergraduate and major GPA of 3.0; for doctorate, GRE General Test, minimum cumulative GPA of 3.0. Additional exam requirements/recommendations for international students: Required—TOEFL (minimum score 550 paper-based; 80 iBT). *Application deadline:* For fall admission, 6/1 for domestic students, 3/1 for international students; for spring admission, 10/15 for domestic students, 9/1 for international students. Applications are processed on a rolling basis. Application fee: $60. Electronic applications accepted. *Expenses: Tuition, area resident:* Full-time $8802; part-time $5868 per credit hour. Tuition, state resident: full-time $8802; part-time $5868 per credit hour. Tuition, nonresident: full-time $18,504; part-time $12,336 per credit hour. *International tuition:* $18,504 full-time. *Required fees:* $1416; $944 per credit hour. $472 per semester. Tuition and fees vary according to course load and program. *Financial support:* In 2018–19, 11 research assistantships with full tuition reimbursements (averaging $9,421 per year), 12 teaching assistantships with full tuition reimbursements (averaging $12,712 per year) were awarded; fellowships with full tuition reimbursements, Federal Work-Study, scholarships/grants, health care benefits, and unspecified assistantships also available. Support available to part-time students. Financial award application deadline: 2/15; financial award applicants required to submit FAFSA. *Faculty research:* Atmospheric and ionospheric radar studies, space plasma theory, magnetospheric dynamics, space weather and auroral studies, turbulence and complex systems. *Total annual research expenditures:* $11.2 million. *Unit head:* Renate Wackerbauer, Department Chair, 907-474-7339, E-mail: uaf-physics@alaska.edu. *Application contact:* Samara Taber, Director of Admissions, 907-474-7500, E-mail: uaf-admissions@alaska.edu.
Website: http://www.uaf.edu/physics/

University of California, San Diego, Graduate Division, Department of Mathematics, La Jolla, CA 92093. Offers applied mathematics (MA); computational science (PhD); mathematics (MA, PhD); statistics (MS, PhD). *Students:* 171 full-time (36 women), 3 part-time (1 woman). 713 applicants, 25% accepted, 55 enrolled. In 2018, 12 master's, 13 doctorates awarded. Terminal master's awarded for partial completion of doctoral program. *Degree requirements:* For master's, comprehensive exam; for doctorate, comprehensive exam, thesis/dissertation. *Entrance requirements:* For master's, GRE General Test; GRE Subject Test (for MA), minimum GPA of 3.0; for doctorate, GRE General Test, GRE Subject Test, minimum GPA of 3.0. Additional exam requirements/recommendations for international students: Required—TOEFL (minimum score 550 paper-based; 80 iBT), IELTS (minimum score 7); Recommended—TSE. *Application deadline:* For fall admission, 1/16 for domestic students. Application fee: $105 ($125 for international students). Electronic applications accepted. *Financial support:* Fellowships, research assistantships, teaching assistantships, and scholarships/grants available. Financial award applicants required to submit FAFSA. *Faculty research:* Combinatorics, bioinformatics, differential equations, logic and computational complexity, probability theory and statistics, Algebra, Algebraic Geometry, Analysis, Applied Math, Combinatorics, Computational Science, Geometry, Math Physics, Number Theory, Other, Partial Differential Equations, Probability, Representation Theory, Statistics, Topology. *Unit head:* Lei Ni, Chair, 858-534-2734, E-mail: lni@math.ucsd.edu. *Application contact:* Mark Whelan, Admissions Specialist, 858-534-2642, E-mail: mathgradadmissions@math.ucsd.edu.
Website: http://math.ucsd.edu/

University of California, San Diego, Graduate Division, Department of Mechanical and Aerospace Engineering, La Jolla, CA 92023-0515. Offers aerospace engineering (MS, PhD); applied mechanics (MS, PhD); applied ocean science (MS, PhD); engineering physics (MS, PhD); engineering sciences (PhD), including computational science, multi-scale biology; mechanical engineering (MS, PhD). PhD in engineering sciences offered jointly with San Diego State University. *Students:* 283 full-time (58 women), 48 part-time (12 women). 867 applicants, 46% accepted, 131 enrolled. In 2018, 78 master's, 21 doctorates awarded. Terminal master's awarded for partial completion of doctoral program. *Degree requirements:* For master's, comprehensive exam (for some programs), thesis (for some programs), comprehensive exam or thesis; for doctorate, comprehensive exam, thesis/dissertation. *Entrance requirements:* For master's and doctorate, GRE General Test, minimum GPA of 3.0. Additional exam requirements/recommendations for international students: Required—TOEFL (minimum score 550 paper-based; 80 iBT), IELTS (minimum score 7). *Application deadline:* For fall admission, 1/17 for domestic students. Application fee: $105 ($125 for international students). Electronic applications accepted. *Financial support:* Fellowships, research assistantships, teaching assistantships, scholarships/grants, and traineeships available. Financial award applicants required to submit FAFSA. *Faculty research:* Solid mechanics; materials; fluid mechanics and heat transfer; dynamics, systems and controls; energy, including combustion and renewables, plasmas. *Unit head:* Carlos Coimbra, Chair, 858-534-4285, E-mail: mae-chair-l@ucsd.edu. *Application contact:* Joana Halnez, Graduate Coordinator, 858-534-4387, E-mail: mae-gradadm-l@ucsd.edu.
Website: http://maeweb.ucsd.edu/

University of California, San Diego, Graduate Division, Department of Physics, La Jolla, CA 92093. Offers biophysics (PhD); computational neuroscience (PhD); computational science (PhD); multi-scale biology (PhD); physics (MS, PhD); quantitative biology (PhD). *Students:* 172 full-time (29 women), 1 part-time (0 women). 570 applicants, 27% accepted, 48 enrolled. In 2018, 11 master's, 26 doctorates awarded. *Degree requirements:* For doctorate, comprehensive exam, thesis/dissertation, 1-quarter teaching assistantship. *Entrance requirements:* For doctorate, GRE General Test, GRE Subject Test, statement of purpose, three letters of reference. Additional exam requirements/recommendations for international students: Required—TOEFL (minimum score 550 paper-based; 80 iBT), IELTS (minimum score 7). *Application deadline:* For fall admission, 12/19 for domestic students. Application fee: $105 ($125 for international students). Electronic applications accepted. *Financial support:* Fellowships, research assistantships, teaching assistantships, scholarships/grants, and unspecified assistantships available. Financial award applicants required to submit FAFSA. *Faculty research:* Astrophysics/Astronomy; Atomic/Molecular; Biophysics; Computational Science; Condensed Matter/Material Science; High Energy Physics; Mathematical Physics; Nonlinear Dynamics; Physics; Plasma/Fusion; Quantitative Biology; Statistical/Thermal Physics. *Unit head:* Benjamin Grinstein, Chair, 858-534-6857, E-mail: chair@physics.ucsd.edu. *Application contact:* Saixious Dominguez-Kilday, Graduate Admissions Coordinator, 858-534-3293, E-mail: skilday@physics.ucsd.edu.
Website: http://physics.ucsd.edu/

University of California, San Diego, Graduate Division, Program in Computational Science, Mathematics and Engineering, La Jolla, CA 92093. Offers MS. *Students:* 30 full-time (7 women), 9 part-time (3 women). 106 applicants, 39% accepted, 19 enrolled. In 2018, 22 master's awarded. *Degree requirements:* For master's, comprehensive exam. *Entrance requirements:* For master's, GRE General Test, 3 letters of recommendation, statement of purpose, minimum GPA of 3.0, 2 years of calculus. Additional exam requirements/recommendations for international students: Required—TOEFL (minimum score 550 paper-based; 80 iBT), IELTS (minimum score 7). *Application deadline:* For fall admission, 2/5 for domestic students. Application fee: $105 ($125 for international students). Electronic applications accepted. *Financial support:* Teaching assistantships available. Financial award applicants required to submit FAFSA. *Faculty research:* Computational fluid dynamics, atmospheric science, climate modeling, particle physics, multi-scale and multi-physics modeling. *Unit head:* Michael Holst, Co-Director, 858-534-4899, E-mail: mholst@ucsd.edu. *Application contact:* Juan Rodriguez, 858-534-9056, E-mail: csmeadmissions@math.ucsd.edu.
Website: http://csme.ucsd.edu

University of California, Santa Barbara, Graduate Division, College of Engineering, Department of Computer Science, Santa Barbara, CA 93106-5110. Offers computer science (MS, PhD), including cognitive science (PhD), computational science and engineering (PhD), technology and society (PhD). Terminal master's awarded for partial completion of doctoral program. *Degree requirements:* For master's, comprehensive exam (for some programs), thesis (for some programs), project (for some programs); for doctorate, thesis/dissertation. *Entrance requirements:* For master's and doctorate, GRE. Additional exam requirements/recommendations for international students: Required—TOEFL (minimum score 600 paper-based; 100 iBT), IELTS (minimum score 7). Electronic applications accepted. *Faculty research:* Algorithms and theory, computational science and engineering, computer architecture, database and information systems, machine learning and data mining, networking, operating systems and distributed systems, programming languages and software engineering, security and cryptography, social computing, visual computing and interaction.

University of California, Santa Barbara, Graduate Division, College of Letters and Sciences, Division of Mathematics, Life, and Physical Sciences, Department of Mathematics, Santa Barbara, CA 93106-3080. Offers applied mathematics (MA), including computational science and engineering; mathematics (MA, PhD), including computational science and engineering (PhD), mathematics (MA); MA/PhD. Terminal master's awarded for partial completion of doctoral program. *Degree requirements:* For master's, comprehensive exam (for some programs), thesis (for some programs); for doctorate, comprehensive exam, thesis/dissertation. *Entrance requirements:* For master's and doctorate, GRE General Test, GRE Subject Test (math). Additional exam requirements/recommendations for international students: Required—TOEFL (minimum score 575 paper-based; 80 iBT), IELTS (minimum score 7). Electronic applications accepted. *Faculty research:* Topology, differential geometry, algebra, applied mathematics, partial differential equations.

University of Central Oklahoma, The Jackson College of Graduate Studies, College of Mathematics and Science, Center for Research and Education in Interdisciplinary Computation, Edmond, OK 73034-5209. Offers computational science (PSM), including computational engineering, computational mathematics, computer science. *Degree requirements:* For master's, comprehensive exam (for some programs), thesis (for some programs), capstone project. *Entrance requirements:* For master's, official transcripts, two letters of recommendation. Additional exam requirements/recommendations for international students: Required—TOEFL (minimum score 550 paper-based; 79 iBT), IELTS (minimum score 6.5). Electronic applications accepted.

University of Chicago, Division of the Social Sciences, Master of Arts Program in Computational Social Science, Chicago, IL 60637. Offers MA. *Degree requirements:* For master's, thesis. *Entrance requirements:* For master's, GRE General Test, 3 letters of recommendation, statement of purpose, transcripts, resume or curriculum vitae, writing sample (dependent on department). Additional exam requirements/recommendations for international students: Required—TOEFL (minimum score 104 iBT), IELTS (minimum score 7). Electronic applications accepted. *Expenses:* Contact institution. *Faculty research:* Social science data analytics, modeling social systems, cognitive neuroimaging, quantitative social science.

University of Chicago, Harris School of Public Policy, Master of Science Program in Computational Analysis and Public Policy, Chicago, IL 60637. Offers MS. Offered jointly with Department of Computer Science. *Entrance requirements:* For master's, GRE General Test, transcripts, resume, 3 letters of recommendation. Additional exam requirements/recommendations for international students: Required—TOEFL (minimum score 104 iBT), IELTS (minimum score 7). Electronic applications accepted.

University of Colorado Denver, College of Liberal Arts and Sciences, Department of Mathematical and Statistical Sciences, Denver, CO 80217. Offers applied mathematics (MS, PhD), including applied mathematics, applied probability (MS), applied statistics (MS), computational biology (PhD), computational mathematics (PhD), discrete mathematics, finite geometry (PhD), mathematics education (PhD), mathematics of engineering and science (MS), numerical analysis, operations research (MS), optimization and operations research (PhD), probability (PhD), statistics (PhD). *Program availability:* Part-time. *Degree requirements:* For master's, comprehensive exam, thesis optional, 30 hours of course work with minimum GPA of 3.0; for doctorate, comprehensive exam, thesis/dissertation, 42 hours of course work with minimum GPA of 3.25. *Entrance requirements:* For master's, GRE General Test; GRE Subject Test in math (recommended), 30 hours of course work in mathematics (24 of which must be upper-division mathematics), bachelor's degree with minimum GPA of 3.0; for doctorate, GRE General Test; GRE Subject Test in math (recommended), 30 hours of course work in mathematics (24 of which must be upper-division mathematics), master's degree with minimum GPA of 3.25. Additional exam requirements/recommendations for international students: Required—TOEFL (minimum score 537 paper-based; 75 iBT); Recommended—IELTS (minimum score 6.5). Electronic applications accepted. *Expenses:* Tuition, state resident: full-time $6786; part-time $337 per credit hour.

Tuition, nonresident: full-time $22,590; part-time $1255 per credit hour. *Required fees:* $1231; $137 per credit hour. Tuition and fees vary according to program and reciprocity agreements. *Faculty research:* Computational mathematics, computational biology, discrete mathematics and geometry, probability and statistics, optimization.

The University of Iowa, Graduate College, Program in Applied Mathematical and Computational Sciences, Iowa City, IA 52242-1316. Offers PhD. *Degree requirements:* For doctorate, comprehensive exam, thesis/dissertation. *Entrance requirements:* For doctorate, GRE General Test, minimum GPA of 3.0. Additional exam requirements/ recommendations for international students: Required—TOEFL (minimum score 620 paper-based; 105 iBT). Electronic applications accepted.

University of Lethbridge, School of Graduate Studies, Lethbridge, AB T1K 3M4, Canada. Offers addictions counseling (M Sc); agricultural biotechnology (M Sc); agricultural studies (M Sc, MA); anthropology (MA); archaeology (M Sc, MA); art (MA, MFA); biochemistry (M Sc); biological sciences (M Sc); biomolecular science (PhD); biosystems and biodiversity (PhD); Canadian studies (MA); chemistry (M Sc); computer science (M Sc); computer science and geographical information science (M Sc); counseling (MC); counseling psychology (M Ed); dramatic arts (MA); earth, space, and physical science (PhD); economics (MA); education (MA, PhD); educational leadership (M Ed); English (MA); environmental science (M Sc); evolution and behavior (PhD); exercise science (M Sc); French (MA); French/German (MA); French/Spanish (MA); general education (M Ed); geography (M Sc, MA); German (MA); health sciences (M Sc); individualized multidisciplinary (M Sc, MA); kinesiology (M Sc, MA); management (M Sc), including accounting, finance, human resource management and labor relations, information systems, international management, marketing, policy and strategy; mathematics (M Sc); music (M Mus, MA); Native American studies (MA); neuroscience (M Sc, PhD); new media (MA, MFA); nursing (M Sc, MN); philosophy (MA); physics (M Sc); political science (MA); psychology (M Sc, MA); religious studies (MA); sociology (MA); theatre and dramatic arts (MFA); theoretical and computational science (PhD); urban and regional studies (MA); women and gender studies (MA). *Program availability:* Part-time, evening/weekend. *Degree requirements:* For master's, thesis (for some programs); for doctorate, comprehensive exam, thesis/dissertation. *Entrance requirements:* For master's, GMAT (for M Sc in management), bachelor's degree in related field, minimum GPA of 3.0 during previous 20 graded semester courses, 2 years' teaching or related experience (M Ed); for doctorate, master's degree, minimum graduate GPA of 3.5. Additional exam requirements/recommendations for international students: Required—TOEFL (minimum score 580 paper-based; 93 iBT). Electronic applications accepted. *Faculty research:* Movement and brain plasticity, gibberellin physiology, photosynthesis, carbon cycling, molecular properties of main-group ring components.

University of Manitoba, Faculty of Graduate Studies, Faculty of Science, Program in Mathematical, Computational and Statistical Sciences, Winnipeg, MB R3T 2N2, Canada. Offers MMCSS.

University of Massachusetts Boston, College of Science and Mathematics, Program in Computational Sciences, Boston, MA 02125-3393. Offers PhD. *Faculty:* 20 full-time (4 women), 3 part-time/adjunct (0 women). *Students:* 7 full-time (2 women), 5 international. Average age 31. 9 applicants, 22% accepted, 2 enrolled. *Application deadline:* For fall admission, 6/1 for domestic students; for spring admission, 11/15 for domestic students. *Expenses: Tuition, area resident:* Full-time $17,896. Tuition, state resident: full-time $17,896. Tuition, nonresident: full-time $34,932. *International tuition:* $34,932 full-time. *Required fees:* $355. *Unit head:* Dr. Ricardo Castano-Bernard, Associate Professor, 617-287.6494, E-mail: rcastanobernard@umb.edu. *Application contact:* Graduate Admissions Coordinator, 617-287-6400, Fax: 617-287-6236, E-mail: graduate.admissions@umb.edu.
Website: https://www.umb.edu/academics/csm/interdisciplinary_programs/computational_sciences_phd

University of Memphis, Graduate School, College of Arts and Sciences, Department of Physics, Memphis, TN 38152. Offers computational physics (MS); general physics (MS); material science (MS). *Program availability:* Part-time. *Students:* 14 full-time (4 women), 7 part-time (3 women); includes 3 minority (1 Black or African American, non-Hispanic/Latino; 1 Asian, non-Hispanic/Latino; 1 Hispanic/Latino), 13 international. Average age 26. 18 applicants, 83% accepted, 10 enrolled. In 2018, 7 master's awarded. *Degree requirements:* For master's, comprehensive exam, thesis or alternative. *Entrance requirements:* For master's, GRE General Test, 21 undergraduate hours of course work in physics. *Application deadline:* For fall admission, 8/1 for domestic students; for spring admission, 12/1 for domestic students. Applications are processed on a rolling basis. Application fee: $35 ($60 for international students). Electronic applications accepted. *Expenses: Tuition, area resident:* Full-time $10,240; part-time $503 per credit hour. Tuition, state resident: full-time $10,464. Tuition, nonresident: full-time $20,224; part-time $991 per credit hour. *Required fees:* $850; $106 per credit hour. *Financial support:* Research assistantships with full tuition reimbursements, teaching assistantships with full tuition reimbursements, Federal Work-Study, institutionally sponsored loans, scholarships/grants, and unspecified assistantships available. Financial award application deadline: 2/1; financial award applicants required to submit FAFSA. *Faculty research:* Solid-state physics, materials science, biophysics, astrophysics, physics education. *Unit head:* Dr. Jingbiao Cui, Chair, 901-678-3657, Fax: 901-678-4733, E-mail: jcui@memphis.edu. *Application contact:* Dr. X Shen, Coordinator of Graduate Studies, 901-678-1668, Fax: 901-678-4733, E-mail: xshen1@memphis.edu.
Website: http://www.memphis.edu/physics

University of Michigan–Dearborn, College of Arts, Sciences, and Letters, Master of Science in Applied and Computational Mathematics Program, Dearborn, MI 48128. Offers MS. *Program availability:* Part-time, evening/weekend. *Faculty:* 9 full-time (4 women). *Students:* 3 full-time (2 women), 9 part-time (2 women); includes 4 minority (1 Black or African American, non-Hispanic/Latino; 2 Asian, non-Hispanic/Latino; 1 Hispanic/Latino). Average age 29. 9 applicants, 78% accepted, 5 enrolled. In 2018, 5 master's awarded. *Degree requirements:* For master's, thesis or alternative. *Entrance requirements:* For master's, 3 letters of recommendation, minimum GPA of 3.0, 2 years of course work in math. Additional exam requirements/recommendations for international students: Required—TOEFL (minimum score 560 paper-based; 84 iBT), IELTS (minimum score 6.5). *Application deadline:* For fall admission, 8/1 priority date for domestic students, 5/1 priority date for international students; for winter admission, 12/1 priority date for domestic students, 9/1 priority date for international students; for spring admission, 4/1 priority date for domestic students, 1/1 priority date for international students. Applications are processed on a rolling basis. Application fee: $60. Electronic applications accepted. *Expenses:* FT in-state: $12,140; FT out-state: $20,708. *Financial support:* In 2018–19, 2 students received support. Scholarships/grants and non resident tuition scholarships available. Financial award application deadline: 3/1; financial award applicants required to submit FAFSA. *Faculty research:* Stochastic differential equations, inverse problems, applied harmonic analysis, applied statistics, numerical analysis. *Unit head:* Dr. Yulia Hristova, Director, 313-593-5175, E-mail: yuliagh@umich.edu. *Application contact:* Office of Graduate Studies, 313-583-6321, E-mail: umd-graduatestudies@umich.edu.

Website: https://umdearborn.edu/casl/graduate-programs/programs/master-science-applied-and-computational-mathematics

University of Minnesota, Duluth, Graduate School, Swenson College of Science and Engineering, Department of Mathematics and Statistics, Duluth, MN 55812-2496. Offers applied and computational mathematics (MS). *Program availability:* Part-time. *Degree requirements:* For master's, thesis or alternative. *Entrance requirements:* For master's, GRE General Test, minimum GPA of 3.0. Additional exam requirements/ recommendations for international students: Required—TOEFL (minimum score 550 paper-based; 79 iBT); Recommended—TWE. Electronic applications accepted. *Faculty research:* Discrete mathematics, diagnostic markers, combinatorics, biostatistics, mathematical modeling and scientific computation.

University of Minnesota, Twin Cities Campus, College of Science and Engineering, Scientific Computation Program, Minneapolis, MN 55455-0213. Offers MS, PhD. *Program availability:* Part-time. *Degree requirements:* For master's, thesis; for doctorate, thesis/dissertation. *Entrance requirements:* For master's and doctorate, GRE General Test. Additional exam requirements/recommendations for international students: Required—TOEFL (minimum score 550 paper-based; 79 iBT), IELTS (minimum score 6.5). Electronic applications accepted. *Faculty research:* Parallel computations, quantum mechanical dynamics, computational materials science, computational fluid dynamics, computational neuroscience.

University of Notre Dame, The Graduate School, College of Science, Department of Applied and Computational Mathematics and Statistics, Notre Dame, IN 46556. Offers applied and computational mathematics and statistics (PhD); applied statistics (MS); computational finance (MS).

University of Pennsylvania, School of Arts and Sciences, Graduate Group in Applied Mathematics and Computational Science, Philadelphia, PA 19104. Offers PhD. *Faculty:* 32 full-time (4 women), 3 part-time/adjunct (0 women). *Students:* 40 full-time (9 women), 36 international. Average age 25. 203 applicants, 23% accepted, 15 enrolled. In 2018, 2 doctorates awarded. Application fee: $80.
Website: http://www.amcs.upenn.edu

University of Pennsylvania, School of Engineering and Applied Science, Program in Scientific Computing, Philadelphia, PA 19104. Offers MSE. *Program availability:* Part-time. *Students:* 10 full-time (2 women), 2 part-time (1 woman); includes 1 minority (Asian, non-Hispanic/Latino), 11 international. Average age 25. 73 applicants, 34% accepted, 17 enrolled. In 2018, 10 master's awarded. *Degree requirements:* For master's, comprehensive exam, thesis optional. *Entrance requirements:* For master's, GRE, bachelor's degree, letters of recommendation, resume, personal statement. Additional exam requirements/recommendations for international students: Required—TOEFL (minimum score 100 iBT), IELTS (minimum score 7). *Application deadline:* For fall admission, 2/1 priority date for domestic and international students. Application fee: $80. Electronic applications accepted. *Expenses:* Contact institution. *Faculty research:* Numerical methods, algorithm development, high performance computational platforms. *Application contact:* William Fenton, Assistant Director of Graduate Admissions, 215-898-4542, Fax: 215-573-5577, E-mail: gradstudies@seas.upenn.edu.
Website: http://pics.upenn.edu/masters-of-engineering-in-scientific-computing

University of Pittsburgh, School of Computing and Information, Pittsburgh, PA 15260. Offers MLIS, MS, MSIS, MST, PhD, Certificate. *Program availability:* Part-time, evening/ weekend, 100% online. *Degree requirements:* For master's, thesis optional; for doctorate, comprehensive exam, thesis/dissertation. *Entrance requirements:* For master's, GRE General Test, GMAT, baccalaureate degree from accredited university or college with minimum GPA of 3.0; for doctorate, GRE General Test, GMAT, MAT, master's degree from accredited university or college; for Certificate, master's degree from accredited university or college. Additional exam requirements/recommendations for international students: Required—TOEFL (minimum score 550 paper-based; 80 iBT), IELTS (minimum score 6.5). Electronic applications accepted. *Expenses:* Contact institution. *Faculty research:* Databases, informatics theory and machine learning, big data, data streams and sensor networks, artificial intelligence, data analytics, algorithms and modeling techniques, human factors, visualization, adaptive hypermedia, embedded systems for improved energy, performance and reliability.

University of Puerto Rico–Mayagüez, Graduate Studies, College of Arts and Sciences, Department of Mathematical Sciences, Mayagüez, PR 00681-9000. Offers applied mathematics (MS); pre-college math education (MS); pure mathematics (MS); scientific computing (MS); statistics (MS). *Program availability:* Part-time. *Degree requirements:* For master's, one foreign language, comprehensive exam, thesis. *Entrance requirements:* For master's, undergraduate degree in mathematics or its equivalent. Electronic applications accepted. *Faculty research:* Automata theory, linear algebra, logic.

University of Southern Mississippi, College of Arts and Sciences, Department of Mathematics, Hattiesburg, MS 39406-0001. Offers computational science (PhD), including mathematics; mathematics (MS). *Program availability:* Part-time. *Degree requirements:* For master's, comprehensive exam, thesis or alternative; for doctorate, comprehensive exam, thesis/dissertation. *Entrance requirements:* For master's, GRE General Test, minimum GPA of 2.75 in last 60 hours; for doctorate, GRE General Test, minimum GPA of 3.5. Additional exam requirements/recommendations for international students: Required—TOEFL, IELTS. Electronic applications accepted. *Faculty research:* Dynamical systems, numerical analysis and multigrid methods, random number generation, matrix theory, group theory.

University of Southern Mississippi, College of Arts and Sciences, Department of Physics and Astronomy, Hattiesburg, MS 39406-0001. Offers computational science (PhD), including physics; physics (MS). *Degree requirements:* For master's, comprehensive exam, thesis; for doctorate, comprehensive exam, thesis/dissertation. *Entrance requirements:* For master's, GRE General Test, minimum GPA of 2.75 in last 60 hours; for doctorate, GRE General Test, minimum GPA of 3.5. Additional exam requirements/recommendations for international students: Required—TOEFL, IELTS. *Faculty research:* Polymers, atomic physics, fluid mechanics, liquid crystals, refractory materials.

University of Southern Mississippi, College of Arts and Sciences, School of Computing Sciences and Computer Engineering, Hattiesburg, MS 39406-0001. Offers computational science (MS, PhD); computer science (MS). *Degree requirements:* For master's, comprehensive exam, thesis; for doctorate, comprehensive exam, thesis/ dissertation. *Entrance requirements:* For master's, GRE General Test, minimum GPA of 2.75 in last 60 hours; for doctorate, GRE General Test, minimum GPA of 3.5. Additional exam requirements/recommendations for international students: Required—TOEFL, IELTS. Electronic applications accepted. *Faculty research:* Satellite telecommunications, advanced life-support systems, artificial intelligence.

The University of Tennessee at Chattanooga, Program in Computational Science, Chattanooga, TN 37403. Offers PhD. *Degree requirements:* For doctorate, comprehensive exam, thesis/dissertation. *Entrance requirements:* For doctorate, GRE

Peterson's Graduate Programs in the Physical Sciences, Mathematics, Agricultural Sciences, the Environment & Natural Resources 2020

www.petersons.com **203**

General Test, 3 letters of recommendation. Additional exam requirements/ recommendations for international students: Required—TOEFL (minimum score 550 paper-based; 79 iBT), IELTS (minimum score 6). Electronic applications accepted. *Expenses:* Contact institution. *Faculty research:* Computational fluid dynamics, design optimization, solution algorithms, hydronamics and propulsion.

The University of Texas at Austin, Graduate School, Program in Computational Science, Engineering, and Mathematics, Austin, TX 78712-1111. Offers MS, PhD. Terminal master's awarded for partial completion of doctoral program. *Degree requirements:* For master's, thesis optional; for doctorate, thesis/dissertation, 3 area qualifying exams. Electronic applications accepted.

University of Utah, Graduate School, Professional Master of Science and Technology Program, Salt Lake City, UT 84112-9016. Offers biotechnology (PSM); computational science (PSM); environmental science (PSM); science instrumentation (PSM). *Program availability:* Part-time. *Degree requirements:* For master's, professional experience project (internship). *Entrance requirements:* For master's, GRE (recommended), minimum undergraduate GPA of 3.0, bachelor's degree from accredited university or college. Additional exam requirements/recommendations for international students: Required—TOEFL (minimum score 550 paper-based; 80 iBT), IELTS (minimum score 6.5). Electronic applications accepted. *Expenses:* Contact institution.

University of Washington, Graduate School, College of Arts and Sciences, Department of Mathematics, Seattle, WA 98195. Offers mathematics (MA, MS, PhD); numerical analysis (MS); optimization (MS). *Program availability:* Part-time. Terminal master's awarded for partial completion of doctoral program. *Degree requirements:* For master's, thesis optional; for doctorate, 2 foreign languages, thesis/dissertation. *Entrance requirements:* For master's, GRE, minimum GPA of 3.0; for doctorate, GRE General Test, GRE Subject Test (mathematics), minimum GPA of 3.0. Additional exam requirements/recommendations for international students: Required—TOEFL. Electronic applications accepted. *Faculty research:* Algebra, analysis, probability, combinatorics and geometry.

Valparaiso University, Graduate School and Continuing Education, Program in Analytics and Modeling, Valparaiso, IN 46383. Offers MS. *Program availability:* Part-time, evening/weekend. *Degree requirements:* For master's, internship or research project. *Entrance requirements:* For master's, minimum GPA of 3.0; letters of recommendation; transcripts; personal essay; equivalent of minor in a science or engineering field; coursework in mathematics, statistics, and computer science. Additional exam requirements/recommendations for international students: Required—TOEFL (minimum score 550 paper-based; 80 iBT), IELTS (minimum score 6). Electronic applications accepted.

Western Michigan University, Graduate College, College of Arts and Sciences, Department of Mathematics, Kalamazoo, MI 49008. Offers applied and computational mathematics (MS); mathematics education (MA, PhD), including collegiate mathematics education (PhD). *Degree requirements:* For doctorate, one foreign language, thesis/ dissertation.

Mathematical and Computational Finance

Austin Peay State University, College of Graduate Studies, College of Science, Technology, Engineering and Mathematics, Professional Science Master's Program, Clarksville, TN 37044. Offers data management and analysis (MS, PSM); information assurance and security (MS, PSM); mathematical finance (MS, PSM); mathematics instruction (MS); predictive analytics (MS, PSM). *Program availability:* Part-time, online learning. *Faculty:* 7 full-time (0 women), 1 part-time/adjunct (0 women). *Students:* 48 full-time (11 women), 72 part-time (29 women); includes 22 minority (9 Black or African American, non-Hispanic/Latino; 5 Asian, non-Hispanic/Latino; 4 Hispanic/Latino; 4 Two or more races, non-Hispanic/Latino), 41 international. Average age 32. 76 applicants, 88% accepted, 41 enrolled. In 2018, 16 master's awarded. *Entrance requirements:* For master's, GRE, minimum undergraduate GPA of 2.5. Additional exam requirements/ recommendations for international students: Required—TOEFL (minimum score 500 paper-based). *Application deadline:* For fall admission, 8/21 priority date for domestic students. Applications are processed on a rolling basis. Application fee: $45 ($55 for international students). Electronic applications accepted. *Expenses: Tuition, area resident:* Part-time $450 per credit hour. Tuition, state resident: full-time $5987; part-time $450 per credit hour. Tuition, nonresident: full-time $8757; part-time $806 per credit hour. *Required fees:* $1583; $79.15 per credit hour. *Financial support:* Research assistantships with full tuition reimbursements, career-related internships or fieldwork, Federal Work-Study, institutionally sponsored loans, scholarships/grants, and unspecified assistantships available. Support available to part-time students. Financial award application deadline: 7/1; financial award applicants required to submit FAFSA. *Unit head:* Dr. Matt Jones, Graduate Coordinator, 931-221-7814, E-mail: gradpsm@apsu.edu. *Application contact:* Megan Mitchell, Coordinator of Graduate Admissions, 800-859-4723, Fax: 931-221-7641, E-mail: gradadmissions@apsu.edu.
Website: http://www.apsu.edu/csci/masters_degrees/index.php

Boston University, Questrom School of Business, Boston, MA 02215. Offers business (EMBA, MBA); business analytics (MS); management (PhD); management studies (MSMS); mathematical finance (MS, PhD); JD/MBA; MBA/MA; MBA/MPH; MBA/MS; MD/MBA. *Accreditation:* AACSB. *Program availability:* Part-time, evening/weekend. *Faculty:* 85 full-time (23 women), 28 part-time/adjunct (10 women). *Students:* 724 full-time (322 women), 636 part-time (286 women); includes 225 minority (43 Black or African American, non-Hispanic/Latino; 1 American Indian or Alaska Native, non-Hispanic/Latino; 104 Asian, non-Hispanic/Latino; 57 Hispanic/Latino; 20 Two or more races, non-Hispanic/Latino), 451 international. Average age 28. 1,069 applicants, 40% accepted, 164 enrolled. In 2018, 585 master's, 11 doctorates awarded. *Degree requirements:* For doctorate, comprehensive exam, thesis/dissertation. *Entrance requirements:* For master's, GMAT or GRE (for MBA and MS in mathematical finance programs), essay, resume, 2 letters of recommendation, official transcripts; for doctorate, GMAT or GRE, personal statement, resume, 3 letters of recommendation, official transcripts. Additional exam requirements/recommendations for international students: Required—TOEFL (minimum score 600 paper-based, 90 iBT), IELTS (6.5), or PTE. *Application deadline:* For fall admission, 3/18 for domestic and international students; for spring admission, 11/7 for domestic and international students. Application fee: $125. Electronic applications accepted. *Expenses:* Contact institution. *Financial support:* Career-related internships or fieldwork, Federal Work-Study, institutionally sponsored loans, scholarships/grants, and tuition waivers (partial) available. Support available to part-time students. Financial award applicants required to submit FAFSA. *Faculty research:* Digital innovation, sustainable energy, corporate social responsibility, finance, marketing. *Unit head:* Kenneth W. Freeman, Professor/Dean, 617-353-9720, Fax: 617-353-5581, E-mail: kfreeman@bu.edu. *Application contact:* Meredith C. Siegel, Assistant Dean, Graduate Admissions Office, 617-353-2670, Fax: 617-353-7368, E-mail: mba@bu.edu.
Website: http://www.bu.edu/questrom/

Carnegie Mellon University, Mellon College of Science, Department of Mathematical Sciences, Pittsburgh, PA 15213-3891. Offers algorithms, combinatorics, and optimization (PhD); computational finance (MS); mathematical finance (PhD); mathematical sciences (DA, PhD); pure and applied logic (PhD). *Program availability:* Part-time. Terminal master's awarded for partial completion of doctoral program. *Degree requirements:* For doctorate, thesis/dissertation. *Entrance requirements:* For master's and doctorate, GRE General Test, GRE Subject Test. Additional exam requirements/ recommendations for international students: Required—TOEFL. Electronic applications accepted. *Faculty research:* Continuum mechanics, discrete mathematics, applied and computational mathematics.

Carnegie Mellon University, Tepper School of Business, Pittsburgh, PA 15213-3891. Offers accounting (PhD); business management and software engineering (MBMSE); business technologies (PhD); civil engineering and industrial management (MS); computational finance (MSCF); economics (PhD); environmental engineering and management (MEEM); financial economics (PhD); industrial administration (MBA), including administration and public management; marketing (PhD); mathematical finance (PhD); operations management (PhD); operations research (PhD); organizational behavior and theory (PhD); production and operations management (PhD); public policy and management (MS, MSED); software engineering and business management (MS); JD/MS; JD/MSIA; M Div/MS; MOM/MSIA; MSCF/MSIA. JD/MSIA offered jointly with University of Pittsburgh. *Program availability:* Part-time. Terminal master's awarded for partial completion of doctoral program. *Degree requirements:* For doctorate, thesis/dissertation. *Entrance requirements:* For master's, GMAT. Additional exam requirements/recommendations for international students: Required—TOEFL. *Expenses:* Contact institution.

DePaul University, College of Computing and Digital Media, Chicago, IL 60604. Offers animation (MA, MFA); applied technology (MS); business information technology (MS); computational finance (MS); computer and information sciences (PhD); computer science (MS); creative producing (MFA); cybersecurity (MS); data science (MS); digital communication and media arts (MA); documentary (MFA); e-commerce technology (MS); experience design (MA); film and television (MS); film and television directing (MFA); game design (MFA); game programming (MS); health informatics (MS); human centered design (PhD); human-computer interaction (MS); information systems (MS); network engineering and security (MS); product innovation and computing (MS); screenwriting (MFA); software engineering (MS); JD/MS. *Program availability:* Part-time, evening/weekend, online learning. *Degree requirements:* For master's, thesis (for some programs); for doctorate, comprehensive exam, thesis/dissertation. *Entrance requirements:* For master's, GRE or GMAT (for MS in computational finance only), bachelor's degree, resume (MS in predictive analytics only), IT experience (MS in information technology project management only), portfolio review (all MFA programs and MA in animation); for doctorate, GRE, master's degree in computer science. Additional exam requirements/recommendations for international students: Required—TOEFL (minimum score 590 paper-based; 80 iBT), IELTS (minimum score 6.5), PTE (minimum score 53). Electronic applications accepted. *Expenses:* Contact institution. *Faculty research:* Data mining, computer science, human-computer interaction, security, animation and film.

DePaul University, Kellstadt Graduate School of Business, Chicago, IL 60604. Offers accountancy (MBA, MSA); applied economics (MBA); audit and advisory services (MS); business administration (DBA); business analytics (MS); business strategy and decision-making (MBA); computational finance (MS); economics and policy analysis (MS); enterprise risk management (MS); entrepreneurship (MBA, MS); finance (MBA, MS); general business (MBA); hospitality leadership (MBA); hospitality leadership and operational performance (MS); human resources (MS); international business (MBA); management (MBA, MS); management information systems (MBA); marketing (MBA, MS); marketing analysis (MS); marketing strategy and planning (MBA); real estate (MS); real estate finance and investment (MBA); strategy, execution and valuation (MBA); supply chain management (MS); sustainable management (MS); taxation (MS); JD/ MBA. *Accreditation:* AACSB. *Program availability:* Part-time, evening/weekend, online learning. *Entrance requirements:* For master's, GMAT/GRE, 2 letters of recommendation, resume, essay, official transcripts. Additional exam requirements/ recommendations for international students: Required—TOEFL (minimum score 550 paper-based; 80 iBT). Electronic applications accepted. *Expenses:* Contact institution.

Florida State University, The Graduate School, Department of Anthropology, Department of Mathematics, Tallahassee, FL 32306-4510. Offers applied and computational mathematics (MS, PhD); biomathematics (MS, PhD); financial mathematics (MS, PhD), including actuarial science (MS); pure mathematics (MS, PhD). *Program availability:* Part-time. *Students:* 114 full-time (31 women); includes 8 minority (1 Black or African American, non-Hispanic/Latino; 1 Asian, non-Hispanic/Latino; 2 Hispanic/Latino; 4 Two or more races, non-Hispanic/Latino), 74 international. 225 applicants, 45% accepted, 47 enrolled. In 2018, 13 master's, 11 doctorates awarded. Terminal master's awarded for partial completion of doctoral program. *Degree requirements:* For master's, comprehensive exam (for some programs), thesis optional; for doctorate, comprehensive exam, thesis/dissertation, candidacy exam (including written qualifying examinations which differ by degree concentration). *Entrance requirements:* For master's and doctorate, GRE General Test, minimum upper-division GPA of 3.0, 4-year bachelor's degree. Additional exam requirements/recommendations for international students: Required—TOEFL (minimum score 550 paper-based; 80 iBT), IELTS (minimum score 6.5). *Application deadline:* For fall admission, 12/15 priority date for domestic and international students; for spring admission, 4/30 for domestic and international students. Application fee: $30. Electronic applications accepted. *Expenses: Tuition, area resident:* Part-time $479.32 per credit hour. Tuition and fees vary according to campus/location and program. *Financial support:* In 2018–19, 109 students received support, including 2 fellowships with full tuition reimbursements available (averaging $24,053 per year), 10 research assistantships with full tuition reimbursements available (averaging $20,053 per year), 83 teaching assistantships with full tuition reimbursements available (averaging $20,053 per year); career-related internships or fieldwork, scholarships/grants, health care benefits, tuition waivers (full and partial), and unspecified assistantships also available. Financial award application deadline: 12/15; financial award applicants required to submit FAFSA. *Faculty research:* Low-dimensional and geometric topology, mathematical modeling in neuroscience, computational stochastics and Monte Carlo methods, mathematical physics, applied analysis. *Total annual research expenditures:* $1.3 million. *Unit head:* Dr. Philip L. Bowers, Chairperson, 850-644-2202, Fax: 850-644-4053, E-mail: bowers@math.fsu.edu. *Application contact:* Elizabeth Scott, Graduate Advisor and Admissions Coordinator, 850-644-2278, Fax: 850-644-4053, E-mail: emscott2@fsu.edu. Website: http://www.math.fsu.edu/

The George Washington University, Columbian College of Arts and Sciences, Department of Mathematics, Washington, DC 20052. Offers applied mathematics (MS); financial mathematics (Graduate Certificate); mathematics (MA, PhD, Graduate Certificate). *Program availability:* Part-time, evening/weekend. *Students:* 29 full-time (10 women), 15 part-time (5 women); includes 9 minority (1 Black or African American, non-Hispanic/Latino; 4 Asian, non-Hispanic/Latino; 4 Hispanic/Latino), 21 international. Average age 27. 86 applicants, 73% accepted, 20 enrolled. In 2018, 7 master's, 6 doctorates awarded. Terminal master's awarded for partial completion of doctoral program. *Degree requirements:* For master's, comprehensive exam; for doctorate, one foreign language, thesis/dissertation, general exam. *Entrance requirements:* For master's and doctorate, GRE General Test, minimum GPA of 3.0, interview. Additional exam requirements/recommendations for international students: Required—TOEFL (minimum score 550 paper-based; 80 iBT). *Application deadline:* For fall admission, 1/15 priority date for domestic and international students; for spring admission, 10/1 priority date for domestic students, 9/1 priority date for international students. Applications are processed on a rolling basis. Application fee: $75. Electronic applications accepted. *Financial support:* In 2018–19, 17 students received support. Fellowships with full tuition reimbursements available, teaching assistantships, Federal Work-Study, and tuition waivers available. Financial award application deadline: 1/15. *Unit head:* Frank Baginski, Chair, 202-994-6269, E-mail: baginski@gwu.edu. *Application contact:* Frank Baginski, Chair, 202-994-6269, E-mail: baginski@gwu.edu. Website: http://math.columbian.gwu.edu/

Georgia Institute of Technology, Graduate Studies, Multidisciplinary Program in Quantitative and Computational Finance, Atlanta, GA 30332-0001. Offers MS. Program offered jointly with Scheller College of Business, School of Industrial and Systems Engineering, and School of Mathematics. *Program availability:* Part-time. *Entrance requirements:* For master's, GRE General Test or GMAT. Additional exam requirements/recommendations for international students: Required—TOEFL (minimum score 570 paper-based; 95 iBT). Electronic applications accepted. *Expenses:* Contact institution.

Illinois Institute of Technology, Graduate College, College of Science, Department of Applied Mathematics, Chicago, IL 60616. Offers applied mathematics (MS, PhD); data science (MAS); mathematical finance (MAS). MAS in mathematical finance program held jointly with Stuart School of Business. Terminal master's awarded for partial completion of doctoral program. *Degree requirements:* For master's, comprehensive exam, thesis; for doctorate, comprehensive exam, thesis/dissertation. *Entrance requirements:* For master's, GRE General Test (minimum scores: 304 Quantitative and Verbal, 2.5 Analytical Writing), minimum undergraduate GPA of 3.0; three letters of recommendation; for doctorate, GRE General Test (minimum scores: 304 Quantitative and Verbal, 3.0 Analytical Writing), minimum undergraduate GPA of 3.5; three letters of recommendation. Additional exam requirements/recommendations for international students: Required—TOEFL (minimum score 550 paper-based; 80 iBT). Electronic applications accepted. *Faculty research:* Applied analysis, computational mathematics, discrete applied mathematics, stochastics (including financial mathematics).

Illinois Institute of Technology, Stuart School of Business, Program in Mathematical Finance, Chicago, IL 60661. Offers MMF. *Program availability:* Part-time, evening/weekend. *Entrance requirements:* For master's, GRE (minimum score 1200 old scoring, 310 new scoring), essay. Additional exam requirements/recommendations for international students: Required—TOEFL (minimum score 600 paper-based; 100 iBT); Recommended—IELTS (minimum score 7). Electronic applications accepted. *Expenses:* Contact institution. *Faculty research:* Factor models for investment management, credit rating and credit risk management, hedge fund performance analysis, option trading and risk management, global asset allocation strategies.

Johns Hopkins University, Engineering Program for Professionals, Part-time Program in Financial Mathematics, Baltimore, MD 21218. Offers financial mathematics (MS); financial risk management (Graduate Certificate); quantitative portfolio management (Graduate Certificate); securitization (Graduate Certificate). *Program availability:* Part-time, evening/weekend, online only, 100% online. *Faculty:* 1 full-time, 1 part-time/adjunct. *Students:* 31 part-time (10 women). 23 applicants, 43% accepted, 9 enrolled. In 2018, 5 master's awarded. *Entrance requirements:* For master's, undergraduate or graduate degree in a quantitative discipline; minimum of two years of relevant full-time work experience in finance or a related field. Additional exam requirements/recommendations for international students: Required—TOEFL (minimum score 600 paper-based; 100 iBT). *Unit head:* Dr. David Audley, Program Chair, 410-516-7136, E-mail: daudley1@jhu.edu. *Application contact:* Doug Schiller, Admissions Director, 410-516-2300, Fax: 410-579-8049, E-mail: schiller@jhu.edu. Website: https://ep.jhu.edu/programs-and-courses/programs/financial-mathematics

Johns Hopkins University, G. W. C. Whiting School of Engineering, Department of Applied Mathematics and Statistics, Baltimore, MD 21218. Offers computational medicine (PhD); discrete mathematics (MA, MSE, PhD); financial mathematics (MSE); operations research/optimization (MA, MSE, PhD); statistics/probability (MA, MSE, PhD). *Faculty:* 25 full-time (4 women). *Students:* 173 full-time (67 women), 13 part-time (10 women). 1,406 applicants, 25% accepted, 89 enrolled. In 2018, 60 master's, 5 doctorates awarded. Terminal master's awarded for partial completion of doctoral program. *Degree requirements:* For master's, thesis (for some programs); for doctorate, thesis/dissertation, oral exam, introductory exam. *Entrance requirements:* For master's and doctorate, GRE General Test, 3 letters of recommendation, statement of purpose, transcripts. Additional exam requirements/recommendations for international students: Required—TOEFL (minimum score 600 paper-based; 100 iBT), IELTS (minimum score 7). *Application deadline:* For fall admission, 1/15 for domestic and international students; for spring admission, 9/15 for domestic and international students. Application fee: $75. Electronic applications accepted. *Financial support:* In 2018–19, 57 students received support, including 14 fellowships with full tuition reimbursements available (averaging $24,750 per year), 13 research assistantships with full tuition reimbursements available (averaging $23,000 per year), 30 teaching assistantships with full tuition reimbursements available (averaging $2,300 per year); Federal Work-Study, health care benefits, and tuition waivers (full and partial) also available. Financial award application deadline: 1/15; financial award applicants required to submit FAFSA. *Faculty research:* Matrix and numerical analysis, differential equation modeling, optimization and

operations research, probability and statistics, discrete mathematics, financial mathematics. *Unit head:* Dr. Laurent Younes, Chair, 410-516-5103, Fax: 410-516-7459, E-mail: laurent.younes@jhu.edu. *Application contact:* Kristin Bechtel, Academic Program Coordinator, 410-516-7198, Fax: 410-516-7459, E-mail: kbechtel@jhu.edu. Website: http://engineering.jhu.edu/ams

New Jersey Institute of Technology, College of Science and Liberal Arts, Newark, NJ 07102. Offers applied mathematics (MS); applied physics (MS, PhD); applied statistics (MS, Certificate); biology (MS, PhD); biostatistics (MS); chemistry (MS, PhD); environmental and sustainability policy (MS); environmental science (MS, PhD); history (MA, MAT); materials science and engineering (MS, PhD); mathematical and computational finance (MS); mathematical sciences (PhD); pharmaceutical chemistry (MS); professional and technical communications (MS); technical communication essentials (Certificate). *Program availability:* Part-time, evening/weekend. *Faculty:* 150 full-time (43 women), 115 part-time/adjunct (47 women). *Students:* 200 full-time (79 women), 63 part-time (29 women); includes 61 minority (17 Black or African American, non-Hispanic/Latino; 29 Asian, non-Hispanic/Latino; 11 Hispanic/Latino; 4 Two or more races, non-Hispanic/Latino), 136 international. Average age 28. 429 applicants, 49% accepted, 89 enrolled. In 2018, 43 master's, 16 doctorates, 2 other advanced degrees awarded. Terminal master's awarded for partial completion of doctoral program. *Degree requirements:* For master's, thesis (for some programs); for doctorate, thesis/dissertation. *Entrance requirements:* For master's and doctorate, GRE General Test, Minimum GPA of 3.0, personal statement, three (3) letters of recommendation, and transcripts. Additional exam requirements/recommendations for international students: Required—TOEFL (minimum score 550 paper-based; 79 iBT), IELTS (minimum score 6.5). *Application deadline:* For fall admission, 6/1 priority date for domestic students, 5/1 priority date for international students; for spring admission, 11/15 priority date for domestic and international students. Applications are processed on a rolling basis. Application fee: $75. Electronic applications accepted. *Expenses:* $22,690 per year (in-state), $32,136 per year (out-of-state). *Financial support:* In 2018–19, 134 students received support, including 17 fellowships with full tuition reimbursements available (averaging $22,000 per year), 74 research assistantships with full tuition reimbursements available (averaging $22,000 per year), 71 teaching assistantships with full tuition reimbursements available (averaging $22,000 per year); scholarships/grants, traineeships, health care benefits, and unspecified assistantships also available. Financial award application deadline: 1/15. *Faculty research:* Biophotonics and bioimaging, morphogenetic patterning, embryogenesis, biological fluid dynamics, applied research in the mathematical sciences. *Total annual research expenditures:* $29.2 million. *Unit head:* Dr. Kevin Belfield, Dean, 973-596-3676, Fax: 973-565-0586, E-mail: kevin.d.belfield@njit.edu. *Application contact:* Stephen Eck, Director of Admissions, 973-596-3300, Fax: 973-596-3461, E-mail: admissions@njit.edu. Website: http://csla.njit.edu/

New York University, Graduate School of Arts and Science, Courant Institute of Mathematical Sciences, Department of Mathematics, New York, NY 10012-1019. Offers mathematics (MS); mathematics and statistics/operations research (MS); mathematics in finance (MS); scientific computing (MS). *Program availability:* Part-time, evening/weekend. *Students:* 195 full-time (78 women), 55 part-time (9 women); includes 32 minority (1 Black or African American, non-Hispanic/Latino; 21 Asian, non-Hispanic/Latino; 7 Hispanic/Latino; 3 Two or more races, non-Hispanic/Latino), 208 international. Average age 25. 1,477 applicants, 27% accepted, 122 enrolled. In 2018, 86 master's, 12 doctorates awarded. *Degree requirements:* For master's, thesis optional; for doctorate, one foreign language, thesis/dissertation, oral and written exams. *Entrance requirements:* For master's, GRE General Test, GRE Subject Test; for doctorate, GRE General Test, GRE Subject Test (recommended). Additional exam requirements/recommendations for international students: Required—TOEFL, IELTS. *Application deadline:* For fall admission, 1/4 for domestic and international students; for spring admission, 12/1 for domestic and international students. Application fee: $110. *Financial support:* Fellowships, research assistantships, teaching assistantships, Federal Work-Study, institutionally sponsored loans, scholarships/grants, health care benefits, and unspecified assistantships available. Financial award application deadline: 1/4; financial award applicants required to submit FAFSA. *Faculty research:* Partial differential equations, computational science, applied mathematics, geometry and topology, probability and stochastic processes. *Unit head:* Fedor Bogomolov, Director of Graduate Studies, 212-998-3238, Fax: 212-995-4121, E-mail: admissions@math.nyu.edu. *Application contact:* Tamar Arnon, Graduate Program Administrator, 212-998-3238, Fax: 212-995-4121, E-mail: admissions@math.nyu.edu. Website: http://www.math.nyu.edu/

See Close-Up on page 253.

New York University, Tandon School of Engineering, Department of Finance and Risk Engineering, New York, NY 10012-1019. Offers financial engineering (MS), including capital markets, computational finance, financial technology. *Program availability:* Part-time, evening/weekend. *Faculty:* 8 full-time (2 women), 42 part-time/adjunct (5 women). *Students:* 271 full-time (124 women), 5 part-time (1 woman); includes 132 minority (9 Asian, non-Hispanic/Latino; 123 Two or more races, non-Hispanic/Latino), 259 international. Average age 25. 1,905 applicants, 20% accepted, 110 enrolled. In 2018, 146 master's awarded. *Degree requirements:* For master's, comprehensive exam (for some programs), thesis (for some programs). *Entrance requirements:* For master's, GMAT, minimum B average in undergraduate course work. Additional exam requirements/recommendations for international students: Required—TOEFL (minimum score 550 paper-based; 90 iBT); Recommended—IELTS (minimum score 7). *Application deadline:* For fall admission, 2/15 priority date for domestic and international students; for spring admission, 11/1 priority date for domestic and international students. Applications are processed on a rolling basis. Application fee: $75. Electronic applications accepted. *Expenses:* Contact institution. *Financial support:* In 2018–19, 253 students received support. Fellowships, research assistantships, teaching assistantships, career-related internships or fieldwork, scholarships/grants, tuition waivers, and unspecified assistantships available. Support available to part-time students. Financial award application deadline: 2/15. *Faculty research:* Optimal control theory, general modeling and analysis, risk parity optimality, a new algorithmic approach to entangled political economy. *Total annual research expenditures:* $775,200. *Unit head:* Dr. Peter Paul Carr, Department Chair, 646-997-3539, E-mail: petercarr@nyu.edu. *Application contact:* Elizabeth Ensweiler, Senior Director of Graduate Enrollment and Graduate Admissions, 646-997-3182, E-mail: elizabeth.ensweiler@nyu.edu.

North Carolina State University, Graduate School, College of Agriculture and Life Sciences and College of Engineering and College of Sciences, Program in Financial Mathematics, Raleigh, NC 27695. Offers MFM. *Program availability:* Part-time. *Degree requirements:* For master's, thesis optional, project/internship. *Entrance requirements:* For master's, GRE General Test. Additional exam requirements/recommendations for international students: Required—TOEFL (minimum score 550 paper-based). Electronic applications accepted. *Faculty research:* Financial mathematics modeling and computation, futures, options and commodities markets, real options, credit risk, portfolio optimization.

Peterson's Graduate Programs in the Physical Sciences, Mathematics, Agricultural Sciences, the Environment & Natural Resources 2020

www.petersons.com **205**

Mathematical and Computational Finance

Oregon State University, College of Science, Program in Mathematics, Corvallis, OR 97331. Offers differential geometry (MA, MS, PhD); financial and actuarial mathematics (MA, MS, PhD); mathematical biology (MA, MS, PhD); mathematics education (MS, PhD); number theory (MA, MS, PhD); numerical analysis (MA, MS, PhD); probability (MA). Terminal master's awarded for partial completion of doctoral program. *Degree requirements:* For master's, thesis or alternative; for doctorate, thesis/dissertation, qualifying exams. *Entrance requirements:* For master's and doctorate, GRE. Additional exam requirements/recommendations for international students: Required—TOEFL (minimum score 100 iBT). Electronic applications accepted.

Rice University, Graduate Programs, George R. Brown School of Engineering, Department of Statistics, Houston, TX 77251-1892. Offers bioinformatics (PhD); biostatistics (PhD); computational finance (PhD); general statistics (PhD); statistics (M Stat, MA); MBA/M Stat. *Program availability:* Part-time. *Degree requirements:* For master's, comprehensive exam; for doctorate, comprehensive exam, thesis/dissertation. *Entrance requirements:* For master's and doctorate, GRE General Test, minimum GPA of 3.0. Additional exam requirements/recommendations for international students: Required—TOEFL (minimum score 630 paper-based; 90 iBT). Electronic applications accepted. *Faculty research:* Statistical genetics, non parametric function estimation, computational statistics and visualization, stochastic processes.

Rochester Institute of Technology, Graduate Enrollment Services, Saunders College of Business, Accounting and Finance Department, MS Program in Computational Finance, Rochester, NY 14623-5603. Offers MS. Program offered jointly with Saunders College of Business. *Program availability:* Part-time. *Students:* 9 full-time (4 women), 5 part-time (4 women); includes 3 minority (1 Asian, non-Hispanic/Latino; 1 Hispanic/Latino; 1 Two or more races, non-Hispanic/Latino), 11 international. Average age 24. 39 applicants, 72% accepted, 7 enrolled. In 2018, 6 master's awarded. *Degree requirements:* For master's, comprehensive exam. *Entrance requirements:* For master's, GRE or GMAT, minimum GPA of 3.0 (recommended), personal statement, resume. Additional exam requirements/recommendations for international students: Required—TOEFL (minimum score 580 paper-based; 92 iBT), IELTS (minimum score 7), PTE (minimum score 63). *Application deadline:* For fall admission, 2/15 priority date for domestic and international students; for spring admission, 12/15 priority date for domestic and international students. Applications are processed on a rolling basis. Application fee: $65. Electronic applications accepted. *Financial support:* In 2018–19, 17 students received support. Teaching assistantships with partial tuition reimbursements available, career-related internships or fieldwork, scholarships/grants, and unspecified assistantships available. Support available to part-time students. Financial award applicants required to submit FAFSA. *Faculty research:* Trading algorithms, short selling effects, corporate governance effects, optimal incentive compensation contracts, debt contract parameters, tax policy. *Unit head:* Matt Cornwell, Assistant Director of Student Services and Outreach, 585-475-6916, E-mail: mcornwell@saunders.rit.edu. *Application contact:* Diane Ellison, Senior Associate Vice President, Graduate Enrollment Services, 585-475-2229, Fax: 585-475-7164, E-mail: gradinfo@rit.edu.
Website: https://www.rit.edu/study/computational-finance-ms

Université de Montréal, Faculty of Arts and Sciences, Department of Economic Sciences, Montréal, QC H3C 3J7, Canada. Offers economics (M Sc, PhD); mathematical and computational finance (M Sc). *Degree requirements:* For master's, one foreign language, thesis; for doctorate, one foreign language, thesis/dissertation, general exam. Electronic applications accepted. *Faculty research:* Applied and economic theory, public choice, international trade, labor economics, industrial organization.

Université de Montréal, Faculty of Arts and Sciences, Department of Mathematics and Statistics, Montréal, QC H3C 3J7, Canada. Offers mathematical and computational finance (M Sc, DESS); mathematics (M Sc, PhD); statistics (M Sc, PhD). *Degree requirements:* For master's, thesis; for doctorate, thesis/dissertation, general exam. *Entrance requirements:* For master's and doctorate, proficiency in French. Electronic applications accepted. *Faculty research:* Pure and applied mathematics, actuarial mathematics.

University of Alberta, Faculty of Graduate Studies and Research, Department of Mathematical and Statistical Sciences, Edmonton, AB T6G 2E1, Canada. Offers applied mathematics (M Sc, PhD); biostatistics (M Sc); mathematical finance (M Sc, PhD); mathematical physics (M Sc, PhD); mathematics (M Sc, PhD); statistics (M Sc, PhD, Postgraduate Diploma). *Program availability:* Part-time. Terminal master's awarded for partial completion of doctoral program. *Degree requirements:* For master's, thesis (for some programs); for doctorate, comprehensive exam, thesis/dissertation. *Entrance requirements:* Additional exam requirements/recommendations for international students: Required—TOEFL (minimum score 580 paper-based). Electronic applications accepted. *Faculty research:* Classical and functional analysis, algebra, differential equations, geometry.

University of California, Santa Barbara, Graduate Division, College of Letters and Sciences, Division of Mathematics, Life, and Physical Sciences, Department of Statistics and Applied Probability, Santa Barbara, CA 93106-3110. Offers bioengineering (PhD); financial mathematics and statistics (PhD); quantitative methods in the social sciences (PhD); statistics (MA), including applied statistics, mathematical statistics; statistics and applied probability (PhD); MA/PhD. Terminal master's awarded for partial completion of doctoral program. *Degree requirements:* For master's, comprehensive exam, thesis optional; for doctorate, comprehensive exam, thesis/dissertation. *Entrance requirements:* For master's and doctorate, GRE General Test. Additional exam requirements/recommendations for international students: Required—TOEFL (minimum score 550 paper-based; 80 iBT), IELTS (minimum score 7). Electronic applications accepted. *Faculty research:* Bayesian inference, financial mathematics, stochastic processes, environmental statistics, biostatistical modeling.

University of Chicago, Division of the Physical Sciences, Master of Science in Financial Mathematics Program, Chicago, IL 60637. Offers MS. *Program availability:* Part-time, evening/weekend. *Entrance requirements:* For master's, GRE General Test, 3 letters of recommendation, transcripts for all previous degrees and institutions attended. Additional exam requirements/recommendations for international students: Required—TOEFL (minimum score 90 iBT), IELTS (minimum score 7). Electronic applications accepted. *Expenses:* Contact institution.

University of Connecticut, Graduate School, College of Liberal Arts and Sciences, Department of Mathematics, Field of Applied Financial Mathematics, Storrs, CT 06269. Offers MS. *Degree requirements:* For master's, comprehensive exam. *Entrance requirements:* Additional exam requirements/recommendations for international students: Required—TOEFL (minimum score 550 paper-based). Electronic applications accepted.

University of Dayton, Department of Mathematics, Dayton, OH 45469. Offers applied mathematics (MAS); financial mathematics (MFM). *Program availability:* Part-time. *Degree requirements:* For master's, research in mathematics clinic. *Entrance requirements:* For master's, minimum undergraduate GPA of 2.8 (MAS), 3.0 (MFM, MME). Additional exam requirements/recommendations for international students: Required—TOEFL (minimum score 550 paper-based; 80 iBT). Electronic applications accepted. *Faculty research:* Differential equations, applied statistics, financial models, numerical analysis, coding/graph theory.

The University of Manchester, School of Mathematics, Manchester, United Kingdom. Offers actuarial science (PhD); applied mathematics (M Phil, PhD); applied numerical computing (M Phil, PhD); financial mathematics (M Phil, PhD); mathematical logic (M Phil); probability (M Phil, PhD); pure mathematics (M Phil, PhD); statistics (M Phil, PhD).

University of Miami, Graduate School, College of Arts and Sciences, Department of Mathematics, Coral Gables, FL 33124. Offers mathematical finance (MS); mathematics (MA, MS, PhD). *Program availability:* Part-time, evening/weekend. Terminal master's awarded for partial completion of doctoral program. *Degree requirements:* For master's, comprehensive exam, qualifying exams; for doctorate, one foreign language, thesis/dissertation, qualifying exams. *Entrance requirements:* For master's and doctorate, GRE General Test, minimum GPA of 3.0. Additional exam requirements/recommendations for international students: Required—TOEFL (minimum score 550 paper-based; 59 iBT). Electronic applications accepted. *Faculty research:* Applied mathematics, probability, geometric analysis, differential equations, algebraic combinatorics.

The University of North Carolina at Charlotte, Belk College of Business, Interdisciplinary Business Programs, Charlotte, NC 28223-0001. Offers mathematical finance (MS); real estate (MS, Graduate Certificate). *Program availability:* Part-time, evening/weekend. *Students:* 59 full-time (17 women), 49 part-time (11 women); includes 18 minority (7 Black or African American, non-Hispanic/Latino; 5 Asian, non-Hispanic/Latino; 3 Hispanic/Latino; 3 Two or more races, non-Hispanic/Latino), 48 international. Average age 33. 130 applicants, 81% accepted, 47 enrolled. In 2018, 69 master's awarded. *Entrance requirements:* For master's, GRE or GMAT, baccalaureate degree in related field with minimum GPA of 3.0 overall and in junior and senior years; transcript of all previous academic work; resume; recommendations; for Graduate Certificate, basic proficiency in using spreadsheet computer software, to be demonstrated by past project or certificate from completion of training course in Excel; previous coursework in financial management. Additional exam requirements/recommendations for international students: Required—TOEFL (minimum score 523 paper-based; 70 iBT), IELTS (minimum score 6), TOEFL (minimum score 523 paper-based, 70 iBT) or IELTS (6). *Application deadline:* Applications are processed on a rolling basis. Application fee: $75. Electronic applications accepted. *Expenses:* Contact institution. *Financial support:* Research assistantships, teaching assistantships, career-related internships or fieldwork, scholarships/grants, and unspecified assistantships available. Support available to part-time students. Financial award application deadline: 3/1; financial award applicants required to submit FAFSA. *Unit head:* Dr. Steven Ott, Dean, 704-687-7577, Fax: 704-687-1393, E-mail: cob-dean@uncc.edu. *Application contact:* Kathy B. Giddings, Director of Graduate Admissions, 704-687-5503, Fax: 704-687-1668, E-mail: gradadm@uncc.edu.
Website: http://belkcollege.uncc.edu/

University of Notre Dame, The Graduate School, College of Science, Department of Applied and Computational Mathematics and Statistics, Notre Dame, IN 46556. Offers applied and computational mathematics and statistics (PhD); applied statistics (MS); computational finance (MS).

University of Southern California, Graduate School, Dana and David Dornsife College of Letters, Arts and Sciences, Department of Economics, Los Angeles, CA 90089. Offers economic development programming (MA, PhD); mathematical finance (MS); M Pl/MA; MA/JD. Terminal master's awarded for partial completion of doctoral program. *Degree requirements:* For master's, comprehensive exam; for doctorate, comprehensive exam, thesis/dissertation. *Entrance requirements:* For master's and doctorate, GRE. Additional exam requirements/recommendations for international students: Required—TOEFL (minimum score 93 iBT). Electronic applications accepted. *Faculty research:* Macro theory, development economics, econometrics.

University of Southern California, Graduate School, Dana and David Dornsife College of Letters, Arts and Sciences, Department of Mathematics, Los Angeles, CA 90089. Offers applied mathematics (MA, MS, PhD); mathematical finance (MS); mathematics (MA, PhD); statistics (MS). *Program availability:* Part-time. Terminal master's awarded for partial completion of doctoral program. *Degree requirements:* For master's, comprehensive exam (for some programs), thesis (for some programs); for doctorate, one foreign language, comprehensive exam, thesis/dissertation. *Entrance requirements:* For master's, GRE General Test, GMAT; for doctorate, GRE General Test, GRE Subject Test (mathematics). Additional exam requirements/recommendations for international students: Required—TOEFL (minimum score 100 iBT). Electronic applications accepted. *Faculty research:* Algebra, algebraic geometry and number theory, analysis/partial differential equations, applied mathematics, financial mathematics, probability, combinatorics and statistics.

University of Toronto, School of Graduate Studies, Faculty of Arts and Science, Department of Mathematics, Program in Mathematical Finance, Toronto, ON M5S 1A1, Canada. Offers MMF. *Entrance requirements:* For master's, four-year bachelor's degree in a quantitative, technical discipline from recognized university with minimum of the equivalent of the University of Toronto mid-B (75%) standing in final two years of program or equivalent number of most senior courses. Additional exam requirements/recommendations for international students: Required—TOEFL (minimum score 580 paper-based; 93 iBT), TWE (minimum score 5). Electronic applications accepted.

Mathematics

Acadia University, Faculty of Pure and Applied Science, Department of Mathematics and Statistics, Wolfville, NS B4P 2R6, Canada. Offers applied mathematics and statistics (M Sc). *Entrance requirements:* For master's, honors degree in mathematics, statistics or equivalent. Additional exam requirements/recommendations for international students: Required—TOEFL (minimum score 580 paper-based; 93 iBT), IELTS (minimum score 6.5). *Faculty research:* Geophysical fluid dynamics, machine scheduling problems, control theory, stochastic optimization, survival analysis.

Alabama State University, College of Science, Mathematics and Technology, Department of Mathematics and Computer Science, Montgomery, AL 36101-0271. Offers mathematics (MS). *Faculty:* 4 full-time (1 woman). *Students:* 3 part-time (0 women); all minorities (2 Black or African American, non-Hispanic/Latino; 1 Hispanic/Latino). Average age 28. 6 applicants, 33% accepted. *Degree requirements:* For master's, comprehensive exam, thesis. *Entrance requirements:* For master's, GRE General Test, GRE Subject Test, writing competency test. Additional exam requirements/recommendations for international students: Required—TOEFL (minimum score 500 paper-based). *Application deadline:* For fall admission, 4/15 for domestic and international students; for spring admission, 11/15 for domestic and international students; for summer admission, 3/15 for domestic and international students. Applications are processed on a rolling basis. Application fee: $25. Electronic applications accepted. *Financial support:* Research assistantships, teaching assistantships, scholarships/grants, tuition waivers (partial), and unspecified assistantships available. Financial award application deadline: 6/30; financial award applicants required to submit FAFSA. *Faculty research:* Discrete mathematics, mathematical social sciences. *Unit head:* Dr. Michelle Foster, Interim Chair, 334-229-4484, Fax: 334-229-4902, E-mail: mforster@alasu.edu. *Application contact:* Dr. Ed Brown, Dean of Graduate Studies, 334-229-4274, Fax: 334-229-4928, E-mail: ebrown@alasu.edu.
Website: http://www.alasu.edu/academics/colleges—departments/science-mathematics-technology/mathematics-computer-science/index.aspx

American University, College of Arts and Sciences, Department of Mathematics and Statistics, Washington, DC 22016-8050. Offers applied statistics (Certificate); biostatistics (MS); data science (Certificate); mathematics (MA); professional science: quantitative analysis (MS); statistics (MS). *Program availability:* Part-time, evening/weekend. *Faculty:* 36 full-time (13 women), 8 part-time/adjunct (1 woman). *Students:* 19 full-time (4 women), 21 part-time (9 women); includes 14 minority (7 Black or African American, non-Hispanic/Latino; 2 Asian, non-Hispanic/Latino; 4 Hispanic/Latino; 1 Two or more races, non-Hispanic/Latino), 10 international. Average age 29. 64 applicants, 92% accepted, 19 enrolled. In 2018, 10 master's, 9 other advanced degrees awarded. *Degree requirements:* For master's, comprehensive exam, thesis or alternative. *Entrance requirements:* For master's, GRE; please see website: https://www.american.edu/cas/mathstat/, statement of purpose, transcripts, 2 letters of recommendation, resume; for Certificate, bachelor's degree, statement of purpose, transcripts, resume. Additional exam requirements/recommendations for international students: Required—TOEFL (minimum score 600 paper-based; 100 iBT). Application fee: $55. *Expenses:* Contact institution. *Financial support:* Scholarships/grants and unspecified assistantships available. Financial award applicants required to submit FAFSA. *Unit head:* Dr. Stephen Casey, Department Chair, 202-885-3120, E-mail: mathstat@american.edu. *Application contact:* Jonathan Harper, Assistant Director, Graduate Recruitment, 202-855-3620, E-mail: casgrad@american.edu.
Website: http://www.american.edu/cas/mathstat/

American University of Beirut, Graduate Programs, Faculty of Arts and Sciences, Beirut 1107 2020, Lebanon. Offers anthropology (MA); Arab and Middle Eastern history (PhD); Arabic language and literature (MA, PhD); archaeology (MA); art history and curating (MA); biology (MS); cell and molecular biology (PhD); chemistry (MS); clinical psychology (MA); computational sciences (MS); computer science (MS); economics (MA); education (MA), including administration and policy studies, elementary education, mathematics education, psychology school guidance, psychology test and measurements, science education, teaching English as a foreign language; English language (MA); English literature (MA); environmental policy planning (MS); financial economics (MAFE); general psychology (MA); geology (MS); history (MA); Islamic studies (MA); mathematics (MS); media studies (MA); Middle East studies (MA); philosophy (MA); physics (MS); political studies (MA); public administration (MA); public policy and international affairs (MA); sociology (MA); theoretical physics (PhD). *Program availability:* Part-time. *Faculty:* 187 full-time (64 women), 27 part-time/adjunct (15 women). *Students:* 292 full-time (215 women), 216 part-time (148 women). Average age 27. 422 applicants, 64% accepted, 124 enrolled. In 2018, 90 master's, 3 doctorates awarded. *Degree requirements:* For master's, comprehensive exam, thesis (for some programs), project; for doctorate, comprehensive exam, thesis/dissertation (for some programs). *Entrance requirements:* For master's, GRE General Test (for archaeology, clinical psychology, general psychology, economics, financial economics and biology); for doctorate, GRE General Test for all PhD programs, GRE Subject Test for theoretical physics. Additional exam requirements/recommendations for international students: Required—TOEFL (minimum score 583 paper-based; 97 iBT), IELTS (minimum score 7). *Application deadline:* For fall admission, 3/18 for domestic students; for spring admission, 11/5 for domestic students. Application fee: $50. Electronic applications accepted. *Expenses:* MA/MS: Humanities and social sciences=$912/credit. Sciences=$943/credit. Financial economics=$986/credit. Thesis: Humanities/social sciences=$6565 and sciences=$6865. *Financial support:* In 2018–19, 227 fellowships with full tuition reimbursements, 17 research assistantships with full tuition reimbursements, 83 teaching assistantships with full tuition reimbursements were awarded; scholarships/grants, tuition waivers (full and partial), and unspecified assistantships also available. Financial award application deadline: 3/18. *Faculty research:* Sciences: Physics: High energy, Particle, Polymer and Soft Matter, Thermal, Plasma; String Theory, Mathematical physics, Astrophysics (stellar evolution, planet and galaxy formation and evolution, astrophysical dynamics), Solid State physics/thin films, Spintronics, Magnetic properties of materials, Mineralogy, Petrology, and Geochemistry of Hard Rocks, Geophysics and Petrophysics, Hydrogeology, Micropaleontology, Sedimentology, and Stratigraphy, Structural Geology and Geotectonics. Renewable en. *Total annual research expenditures:* $4.3 million. *Unit head:* Dr. Nadia Maria El Cheikh, Dean, Faculty of Arts and Sciences, 961-1-350000 Ext. 3800, Fax: 961-1-744461, E-mail: nmcheikh@aub.edu.lb. *Application contact:* Adriana Michelle Zanaty, Curriculum and Graduate Studies Officer, 961-1-350000 Ext. 3833, Fax: 961-1-744461, E-mail: az48@aub.edu.lb.
Website: https://www.aub.edu.lb/fas/Pages/default.aspx

American University of Sharjah, Graduate Programs, Sharjah, United Arab Emirates. Offers accounting (MS); biomedical engineering (MSBME); business administration (MBA); chemical engineering (MS Ch E); civil engineering (MSCE); computer engineering (MS); electrical engineering (MSEE); engineering systems management (MS, PhD); mathematics (MS); mechanical engineering (MSME); mechatronics engineering (MS); teaching English to speakers of other languages (MA); translation and interpreting (MA); urban planning (MUP). *Program availability:* Part-time, evening/weekend. *Degree requirements:* For master's, thesis (for some programs). *Entrance requirements:* For master's, GMAT (for MBA). Additional exam requirements/recommendations for international students: Required—TOEFL (minimum score 550 paper-based; 80 iBT), TWE (minimum score 5); Recommended—IELTS (minimum score 6.5). Electronic applications accepted. *Faculty research:* Water pollution, management and waste water treatment, energy and sustainability, air pollution, Islamic finance, family business and small and medium enterprises.

Appalachian State University, Cratis D. Williams School of Graduate Studies, Department of Mathematical Sciences, Boone, NC 28608. Offers mathematics (MA). *Program availability:* Part-time, online learning. *Degree requirements:* For master's, comprehensive exam, thesis optional. *Entrance requirements:* For master's, GRE General Test, 3 letters of recommendation. Additional exam requirements/recommendations for international students: Required—TOEFL (minimum score 570 paper-based; 79 iBT), IELTS (minimum score 6.5). Electronic applications accepted. *Expenses: Tuition, area resident:* Full-time $4839; part-time $237 per credit hour. Tuition, state resident: full-time $4839; part-time $237 per credit hour. Tuition, nonresident: full-time $18,271; part-time $895.50 per credit hour. *Faculty research:* Graph theory, differential equations, logic, geometry, complex analysis, topology, algebra, mathematics education.

Arizona State University at the Tempe campus, College of Liberal Arts and Sciences, School of Mathematical and Statistical Sciences, Tempe, AZ 85287-1804. Offers applied mathematics (PhD); mathematics (MA, PhD); mathematics education (PhD); statistics (MS, PhD, Graduate Certificate). *Program availability:* Part-time. Terminal master's awarded for partial completion of doctoral program. *Degree requirements:* For master's, thesis or alternative, interactive Program of Study (iPOS) submitted before completing 50 percent of required credit hours; for doctorate, comprehensive exam, thesis/dissertation, interactive Program of Study (iPOS) submitted before completing 50 percent of required credit hours. *Entrance requirements:* For master's and doctorate, GRE General Test, minimum GPA of 3.0 or equivalent in last 2 years of work leading to bachelor's degree. Additional exam requirements/recommendations for international students: Required—TOEFL, IELTS, or PTE. Electronic applications accepted. *Expenses:* Contact institution.

Arkansas State University, Graduate School, College of Sciences and Mathematics, Department of Mathematics and Statistics, State University, AR 72467. Offers mathematics (MS); mathematics education (MSE). *Program availability:* Part-time. *Degree requirements:* For master's, comprehensive exam, thesis or alternative. *Entrance requirements:* For master's, GRE General Test or MAT, appropriate bachelor's degree, official transcripts, immunization records, valid teaching certificate (for MSE). Additional exam requirements/recommendations for international students: Required—TOEFL (minimum score 550 paper-based; 79 iBT), IELTS (minimum score 6), PTE (minimum score 56). Electronic applications accepted.

Auburn University, Graduate School, College of Sciences and Mathematics, Department of Mathematics and Statistics, Auburn University, AL 36849. Offers applied mathematics (MAM, MS); mathematics (MS, PhD); probability and statistics (M Prob S); statistics (MS). *Degree requirements:* For doctorate, thesis/dissertation. *Entrance requirements:* For master's, GRE General Test, undergraduate mathematics background; for doctorate, GRE General Test, GRE Subject Test. Electronic applications accepted. *Expenses:* Tuition, state resident: full-time $11,282; part-time $535 per credit hour. Tuition, nonresident: full-time $30,542; part-time $1605 per credit hour. *Required fees:* $826 per semester. Tuition and fees vary according to degree level and program. *Faculty research:* Pure and applied mathematics.

Augustana University, MA in Education Program, Sioux Falls, SD 57197. Offers instructional strategies (MA); reading (MA); special populations (MA); STEM (MA); technology (MA). *Accreditation:* NCATE. *Program availability:* Part-time-only, evening/weekend, online only, 100% online. *Degree requirements:* For master's, thesis. *Entrance requirements:* For master's, appropriate bachelor's degree, minimum GPA of 3.0, teaching certificate. Additional exam requirements/recommendations for international students: Required—TOEFL (minimum score 550 paper-based). Electronic applications accepted. *Expenses:* Contact institution. *Faculty research:* Multicultural education, education of students with autism, well-being in school settings, factors that predict academic hopefulness.

Aurora University, School of Arts and Sciences, Aurora, IL 60506-4892. Offers homeland security (MS); mathematics (MS); mathematics and science education for elementary teachers (MA); mathematics education (MA); science education (MA). *Program availability:* Part-time, evening/weekend, 100% online. *Faculty:* 3 full-time (1 woman), 10 part-time/adjunct (4 women). *Students:* 9 full-time (4 women), 76 part-time (52 women); includes 13 minority (6 Black or African American, non-Hispanic/Latino; 1 Asian, non-Hispanic/Latino; 5 Hispanic/Latino; 1 Two or more races, non-Hispanic/Latino). Average age 36. 54 applicants, 98% accepted, 24 enrolled. In 2018, 6 master's awarded. *Degree requirements:* For master's, research seminars, capstone project. *Entrance requirements:* For master's, bachelor's degree in mathematics or in some other field with extensive course work in mathematics (for MS in mathematics). Additional exam requirements/recommendations for international students: Required—TOEFL (minimum score 550 paper-based; 79 iBT). *Application deadline:* For fall admission, 6/1 for international students; for spring admission, 10/1 for international students. Applications are processed on a rolling basis. Application fee: $0. Electronic applications accepted. *Expenses:* Contact institution. *Financial support:* In 2018–19, 2 students received support. Federal Work-Study, scholarships/grants, and unspecified assistantships available. Financial award applicants required to submit FAFSA. *Unit head:* Dr. Frank Buscher, Vice President for Academic Affairs, 630-844-5252, E-mail: fbuscher@aurora.edu. *Application contact:* Center for Graduate Studies, 630-947-0955, E-mail: AUadmission@aurora.edu.

Ball State University, Graduate School, College of Sciences and Humanities, Department of Mathematical Sciences, Program in Mathematics, Muncie, IN 47306. Offers MA, MS. *Program availability:* Part-time. *Degree requirements:* For master's, thesis (for some programs). *Entrance requirements:* For master's, minimum baccalaureate GPA of 2.75 or 3.0 in latter half of baccalaureate. Additional exam requirements/recommendations for international students: Required—TOEFL (minimum score 550 paper-based; 79 iBT), IELTS (minimum score 6.5). Electronic applications accepted.

Peterson's Graduate Programs in the Physical Sciences, Mathematics, Agricultural Sciences, the Environment & Natural Resources 2020

www.petersons.com **207**

Mathematics

Baylor University, Graduate School, College of Arts and Sciences, Department of Mathematics, Waco, TX 76798. Offers MS, PhD. *Faculty:* 23 full-time (0 women). *Students:* 23 full-time (9 women), 4 part-time (1 woman); includes 6 minority (1 American Indian or Alaska Native, non-Hispanic/Latino; 1 Hispanic/Latino; 1 Native Hawaiian or other Pacific Islander, non-Hispanic/Latino; 3 Two or more races, non-Hispanic/Latino), 3 international. Average age 26. 42 applicants, 19% accepted, 8 enrolled. In 2018, 5 doctorates awarded. Terminal master's awarded for partial completion of doctoral program. *Degree requirements:* For master's, comprehensive exam, final oral exam; for doctorate, comprehensive exam, thesis/dissertation. *Entrance requirements:* For master's and doctorate, GRE General Test. Additional exam requirements/recommendations for international students: Required—TOEFL (minimum score 85 iBT). *Application deadline:* For fall admission, 1/1 for domestic and international students. Applications are processed on a rolling basis. Application fee: $50. Electronic applications accepted. *Financial support:* In 2018–19, 28 students received support, including 2 research assistantships with full tuition reimbursements available (averaging $25,000 per year), 26 teaching assistantships with full tuition reimbursements available (averaging $25,000 per year). Financial award application deadline: 1/1. *Faculty research:* Algebra, analysis, PDE's, mathematical physics, topology, representation theory, applied mathematics, numerical analysis. *Unit head:* Dr. Mark Spenski, Graduate Program Director, 254-710-6577, Fax: 254-710-3569, E-mail: mark_sepanski@baylor.edu. *Application contact:* Judy Dees, Graduate Program Coordinator, 254-710-3146, Fax: 254-710-3569, E-mail: Judy_Dees@baylor.edu.
Website: http://www.baylor.edu/math/

Bemidji State University, School of Graduate Studies, Bemidji, MN 56601. Offers biology (MS); education (MS); English (MA, MS); environmental studies (MS); mathematics (MS); mathematics (elementary and middle level education) (MS); special education (M Sp Ed). *Program availability:* Part-time, online learning. *Degree requirements:* For master's, comprehensive exam, thesis (for some programs). *Entrance requirements:* For master's, GRE; GMAT, letters of recommendation, letters of interest. Additional exam requirements/recommendations for international students: Required—TOEFL (minimum score 550 paper-based; 80 iBT). Electronic applications accepted. *Expenses:* Contact institution. *Faculty research:* Human performance, sport, and health: physical education teacher education, continuum models, spiritual health, intellectual health, resiliency, health priorities; psychology: health psychology, college student drinking behavior, micro-aggressions, infant cognition, false memories, leadership assessment; biology: structure and dynamics of forest communities, aquatic and riverine ecology, interaction between animal populations and aquatic environments, cellular motility.

Binghamton University, State University of New York, Graduate School, Harpur College of Arts and Sciences, Department of Mathematical Sciences, Binghamton, NY 13902-6000. Offers mathematical sciences (MA, PhD); statistics (MA). *Program availability:* Part-time. Terminal master's awarded for partial completion of doctoral program. *Degree requirements:* For master's, comprehensive exam (for some programs), thesis or alternative; for doctorate, 2 foreign languages, thesis/dissertation. *Entrance requirements:* For master's and doctorate, GRE General Test. Additional exam requirements/recommendations for international students: Required—TOEFL (minimum score 550 paper-based; 80 iBT). Electronic applications accepted.

Boise State University, College of Arts and Sciences, Department of Mathematics, Boise, ID 83725-0399. Offers mathematics (MS); mathematics education (MS). *Program availability:* Part-time. *Degree requirements:* For master's, thesis optional. *Entrance requirements:* For master's, GRE General Test. Additional exam requirements/recommendations for international students: Required—TOEFL (minimum score 550 paper-based; 80 iBT), IELTS (minimum score 6). Electronic applications accepted.

Boston College, Morrissey Graduate School of Arts and Sciences, Department of Mathematics, Chestnut Hill, MA 02467-3800. Offers PhD, MBA/MA. Terminal master's awarded for partial completion of doctoral program. *Degree requirements:* For doctorate, comprehensive exam, thesis/dissertation. *Entrance requirements:* Additional exam requirements/recommendations for international students: Required—TOEFL (minimum score 600 paper-based; 100 iBT), IELTS (minimum score 8). Electronic applications accepted. *Faculty research:* Number theory, algebraic geometry, representation theory, topology, geometry.

Boston University, Graduate School of Arts and Sciences, Department of Mathematics and Statistics, Boston, MA 02215. Offers MA, MS, PhD. *Students:* 142 full-time (70 women), 38 part-time (24 women); includes 13 minority (11 Asian, non-Hispanic/Latino; 1 Hispanic/Latino; 1 Two or more races, non-Hispanic/Latino), 132 international. Average age 24. 1,081 applicants, 34% accepted, 92 enrolled. In 2018, 45 master's, 5 doctorates awarded. Terminal master's awarded for partial completion of doctoral program. *Degree requirements:* For master's, comprehensive exam (for some programs); for doctorate, comprehensive exam, thesis/dissertation. *Entrance requirements:* For master's and doctorate, GRE General Test, GRE Subject Test (mathematics), 3 letters of recommendation, transcripts, personal statement. Additional exam requirements/recommendations for international students: Required—TOEFL (minimum score 550 paper-based; 84 iBT). *Application deadline:* For fall admission, 1/6 for domestic and international students. Application fee: $95. Electronic applications accepted. *Financial support:* In 2018–19, 72 students received support, including 6 fellowships with full tuition reimbursements available (averaging $22,660 per year), 10 research assistantships with full tuition reimbursements available (averaging $22,660 per year), 48 teaching assistantships with full tuition reimbursements available (averaging $22,660 per year); Federal Work-Study, scholarships/grants, and health care benefits also available. Support available to part-time students. Financial award application deadline: 1/6. *Unit head:* David Rohrlich, Interim Chair, 617-353-9545, Fax: 617-353-8100, E-mail: rohrlich@bu.edu. *Application contact:* Sean Grogg, Graduate Program Administrator, 617-353-2560, Fax: 617-353-8100, E-mail: skgrogg@bu.edu.
Website: http://math.bu.edu/

Bowling Green State University, Graduate College, College of Arts and Sciences, Department of Mathematics and Statistics, Bowling Green, OH 43403. Offers mathematics (MA, MAT, PhD); statistics (PhD). *Program availability:* Part-time. *Degree requirements:* For master's, thesis or alternative; for doctorate, comprehensive exam, thesis/dissertation. *Entrance requirements:* For master's and doctorate, GRE General Test. Additional exam requirements/recommendations for international students: Required—TOEFL. Electronic applications accepted. *Faculty research:* Statistics and probability, algebra, analysis.

Brandeis University, Graduate School of Arts and Sciences, Department of Mathematics, Waltham, MA 02454-9110. Offers MA, PhD. *Program availability:* Part-time. *Faculty:* 16 full-time (1 woman), 3 part-time/adjunct (2 women). *Students:* 30 full-time (3 women), 3 part-time (2 women); includes 4 minority (3 Asian, non-Hispanic/Latino; 1 Hispanic/Latino), 16 international. Average age 27. 170 applicants, 18% accepted, 7 enrolled. In 2018, 10 master's, 6 doctorates awarded. Terminal master's awarded for partial completion of doctoral program. *Degree requirements:* For master's, one foreign language; for doctorate, one foreign language, comprehensive exam, thesis/dissertation, qualifying exam. *Entrance requirements:* For master's and doctorate, GRE General Test; GRE Subject Test (recommended), resume, letters of recommendation, statement of purpose, transcripts. Additional exam requirements/recommendations for international students: Required—TOEFL, IELTS, PTE. *Application deadline:* For fall admission, 1/15 priority date for domestic students; for spring admission, 11/1 for domestic students. Applications are processed on a rolling basis. Application fee: $75. Electronic applications accepted. *Financial support:* In 2018–19, 24 fellowships with full tuition reimbursements (averaging $24,480 per year), 25 teaching assistantships with full tuition reimbursements (averaging $6,400 per year) were awarded; scholarships/grants, health care benefits, and tuition waivers (full and partial) also available. Support available to part-time students. *Faculty research:* Algebra, analysis, topology, combinatorics. *Unit head:* Dr. Olivier Bernardi, Director of Graduate Studies, 781-736-3061, E-mail: bernardi@brandeis.edu. *Application contact:* Maryanna Aldrich, Administrator, 781-736-2352, E-mail: scigradoffice@brandeis.edu.
Website: http://www.brandeis.edu/gsas/programs/math.html

Brigham Young University, Graduate Studies, College of Physical and Mathematical Sciences, Department of Mathematics, Provo, UT 84602. Offers MS, PhD. *Program availability:* Part-time. *Faculty:* 34 full-time (2 women). *Students:* 21 full-time (5 women), 15 part-time (3 women); includes 7 minority (1 Black or African American, non-Hispanic/Latino; 6 Asian, non-Hispanic/Latino). Average age 24. 18 applicants, 78% accepted, 12 enrolled. In 2018, 14 master's, 2 doctorates awarded. Terminal master's awarded for partial completion of doctoral program. *Degree requirements:* For master's, comprehensive exam, thesis, project; qualifying exams in algebra and analysis; for doctorate, comprehensive exam, thesis/dissertation, qualifying exams. *Entrance requirements:* For master's, GRE General Test, GRE Subject Test (math; minimum score of 600), minimum GPA of 3.0 in last 60 hours, bachelor's degree in mathematics; for doctorate, GRE General Test, GRE Subject Test (math; minimum score of 600), master's degree in mathematics or related field. Additional exam requirements/recommendations for international students: Required—TOEFL (minimum score 600 paper-based; 85 iBT), We accept IELTS and English3 exams. *Application deadline:* For fall admission, 1/15 priority date for domestic and international students; for winter admission, 9/15 priority date for domestic and international students; for spring admission, 1/15 priority date for domestic and international students; for summer admission, 1/15 priority date for domestic and international students. Applications are processed on a rolling basis. Application fee: $50. Electronic applications accepted. *Expenses:* 10620-21240 (average 15930) per year. *Financial support:* In 2018–19, 37 students received support, including 4 research assistantships with full tuition reimbursements available (averaging $18,000 per year), 34 teaching assistantships with full tuition reimbursements available (averaging $18,000 per year); institutionally sponsored loans also available. Support available to part-time students. Financial award application deadline: 1/15. *Faculty research:* Algebraic geometry/number theory, applied math/nonlinear PDEs, combinatorics/matrix theory, geometric group theory/topology. *Total annual research expenditures:* $107,000. *Unit head:* Dr. Paul M Jenkins, Chairperson, 801-422-5868, Fax: 801-422-0504, E-mail: jenkins@mathematics.byu.edu. *Application contact:* Lonette Stoddard, Graduate Secretary, 801-422-2062, Fax: 801-422-0504, E-mail: lonettes@byu.edu.
Website: https://math.byu.edu

Brock University, Faculty of Graduate Studies, Faculty of Mathematics and Science, Program in Mathematics and Statistics, St. Catharines, ON L2S 3A1, Canada. Offers M Sc. *Program availability:* Part-time. *Degree requirements:* For master's, thesis or project. *Entrance requirements:* For master's, honors degree. Additional exam requirements/recommendations for international students: Required—TOEFL (minimum score 550 paper-based; 80 iBT), IELTS (minimum score 6.5), TWE (minimum score 4). Electronic applications accepted.

Brooklyn College of the City University of New York, School of Natural and Behavioral Sciences, Department of Mathematics, Brooklyn, NY 11210-2889. Offers MA. *Program availability:* Part-time, evening/weekend. *Degree requirements:* For master's, comprehensive exam (for mathematics). *Entrance requirements:* For master's, minimum GPA of 3.0, 2 letters of recommendation. Additional exam requirements/recommendations for international students: Required—TOEFL (minimum score 500 paper-based; 61 iBT). Electronic applications accepted. *Faculty research:* Differential geometry, gauge theory, complex analysis, orthogonal functions.

Brown University, Graduate School, Department of Mathematics, Providence, RI 02912. Offers PhD. *Degree requirements:* For doctorate, one foreign language, thesis/dissertation. *Entrance requirements:* For doctorate, GRE. Additional exam requirements/recommendations for international students: Required—TOEFL (minimum score 600 paper-based; 100 iBT) or IELTS (minimum score 7). Electronic applications accepted. *Expenses:* Contact institution. *Faculty research:* Algebraic geometry, number theory, functional analysis, geometry, topology.

Bryn Mawr College, Graduate School of Arts and Sciences, Department of Mathematics, Bryn Mawr, PA 19010-2899. Offers MA, PhD. *Program availability:* Part-time. Terminal master's awarded for partial completion of doctoral program. *Degree requirements:* For master's, one foreign language, thesis; for doctorate, one foreign language, comprehensive exam, thesis/dissertation. *Entrance requirements:* For master's and doctorate, GRE General Test, transcripts, three letters of recommendation, statement of interest, resume or curriculum vitae. Additional exam requirements/recommendations for international students: Required—TOEFL (minimum score 600 paper-based; 100 iBT), IELTS (minimum score 7). Electronic applications accepted.

Bucknell University, Graduate Studies, College of Arts and Sciences, Department of Mathematics, Lewisburg, PA 17837. Offers MA, MS. *Degree requirements:* For master's, comprehensive exam, thesis or alternative. *Entrance requirements:* For master's, GRE General Test, GRE Subject Test, minimum GPA of 3.0. Additional exam requirements/recommendations for international students: Required—TOEFL (minimum score 600 paper-based).

Cabrini University, Academic Affairs, Radnor, PA 19087. Offers accounting (M Acc); autism spectrum disorder (M Ed); biological sciences (MS), including civic leadership; criminology and criminal justice (MA); curriculum, instruction, and assessment (M Ed); educational leadership (M Ed, Ed D), including curriculum and instructional leadership (Ed D), preK-12 leadership (Ed D); English as a second language (M Ed); organizational leadership (DBA, PhD); preK to 4 (M Ed); reading specialist (M Ed); secondary education (M Ed), including biology, chemistry, English, English/communication, mathematics, social studies; special education grades 7-12 (M Ed); special education preK-8 (M Ed); teaching and learning (M Ed). *Program availability:* Part-time, evening/weekend. *Degree requirements:* For master's, comprehensive exam (for some programs), thesis (for some programs); for doctorate, comprehensive exam (for some programs), thesis/dissertation. *Entrance requirements:* For master's, professional resume, personal statement, two recommendations, official transcripts; for doctorate, official transcripts, minimum master's GPA of 3.0, two recommendations, interview with admissions committee. Additional exam requirements/recommendations for international students: Required—TOEFL (minimum score 80 iBT). Electronic applications accepted. Application fee is waived when completed online. *Expenses:* Contact institution.

California Institute of Technology, Division of Physics, Mathematics and Astronomy, Department of Mathematics, Pasadena, CA 91125-0001. Offers PhD. *Degree requirements:* For doctorate, one foreign language, thesis/dissertation, candidacy and final exams. *Entrance requirements:* For doctorate, GRE General Test, GRE Subject Test. Additional exam requirements/recommendations for international students: Required—TOEFL. *Faculty research:* Number theory, combinatorics, differential geometry, dynamical systems, finite groups.

California Polytechnic State University, San Luis Obispo, College of Science and Mathematics, Department of Mathematics, San Luis Obispo, CA 93407. Offers MS. *Program availability:* Part-time. *Faculty:* 12 full-time (1 woman), 1 (woman) part-time/ adjunct. *Students:* 5 full-time (2 women), 5 part-time (3 women); includes 3 minority (2 Asian, non-Hispanic/Latino; 1 Hispanic/Latino), 2 international. Average age 26. 15 applicants, 40% accepted, 2 enrolled. In 2018, 5 master's awarded. *Degree requirements:* For master's, comprehensive exam. *Entrance requirements:* For master's, GRE. Additional exam requirements/recommendations for international students: Required—TOEFL (minimum score 80 iBT). *Application deadline:* For fall admission, 4/1 for domestic and international students. Applications are processed on a rolling basis. Application fee: $55. *Expenses: Tuition, area resident:* Full-time $7176; part-time $4164 per year. Tuition, state resident: full-time $10,965. Tuition, nonresident: full-time $10,965. *Required fees:* $6336; $3711. *Financial support:* Fellowships, teaching assistantships, career-related internships or fieldwork, Federal Work-Study, and scholarships/grants available. Support available to part-time students. Financial award application deadline: 3/2; financial award applicants required to submit FAFSA. *Faculty research:* Combinatorics, dynamical systems, ordinary and partial differential equations, operator theory, topology. *Unit head:* Dr. Morgan Sherman, Graduate Coordinator, 805-756-1676, E-mail: sherman1@calpoly.edu. *Application contact:* Dr. Morgan Sherman, Graduate Coordinator, 805-756-1676, E-mail: sherman1@calpoly.edu.
Website: http://math.calpoly.edu/

California State Polytechnic University, Pomona, Program in Mathematics, Pomona, CA 91768-2557. Offers mathematics (MS). *Program availability:* Part-time, evening/ weekend. *Students:* 14 full-time (5 women), 42 part-time (14 women); includes 33 minority (2 Black or African American, non-Hispanic/Latino; 9 Asian, non-Hispanic/ Latino; 19 Hispanic/Latino; 3 Two or more races, non-Hispanic/Latino), 7 international. Average age 27. 67 applicants, 58% accepted, 25 enrolled. In 2018, 14 master's awarded. *Entrance requirements:* Additional exam requirements/recommendations for international students: Required—TOEFL (minimum score 550 paper-based). *Application deadline:* Applications are processed on a rolling basis. Application fee: $55. Electronic applications accepted. *Expenses:* Contact institution. *Financial support:* Application deadline: 3/2; applicants required to submit FAFSA. *Unit head:* Dr. Adam King, Assistant Professor/Graduate Coordinator, 909-979-5595, Fax: 909-869-4904, E-mail: king@cpp.edu. *Application contact:* Dr. Adam King, Assistant Professor/ Graduate Coordinator, 909-979-5595, Fax: 909-869-4904, E-mail: king@cpp.edu.
Website: http://www.cpp.edu/~sci/mathematics-statistics/graduate-students/

California State University Channel Islands, Extended University and International Programs, MS Mathematics, Camarillo, CA 93012. Offers MS. *Program availability:* Part-time, evening/weekend. *Students:* 20 full-time (5 women); includes 9 minority (1 Black or African American, non-Hispanic/Latino; 4 Asian, non-Hispanic/Latino; 3 Hispanic/Latino; 1 Two or more races, non-Hispanic/Latino). *Degree requirements:* For master's, thesis. *Entrance requirements:* Additional exam requirements/ recommendations for international students: Required—TOEFL (minimum score 550 paper-based; 80 iBT), IELTS (minimum score 6.5). *Application deadline:* For fall admission, 5/1 for domestic and international students; for spring admission, 11/1 for domestic and international students. Application fee: $55. Electronic applications accepted. *Financial support:* Applicants required to submit FAFSA. *Unit head:* Dr. Jorge Garcia, Program Director, 805-437-2769, E-mail: jorge.garcia@csuci.edu. *Application contact:* Andrew Conley, Graduate Programs Recruiter, 805-437-2652, E-mail: andrew.conley@csuci.edu.
Website: https://ext.csuci.edu/

California State University, East Bay, Office of Graduate Studies, College of Science, Department of Mathematics, Hayward, CA 94542-3000. Offers mathematics teaching (MS); pure mathematics (MS). *Program availability:* Part-time, evening/weekend. *Degree requirements:* For master's, comprehensive exam or thesis. *Entrance requirements:* For master's, minimum GPA of 3.0 in field. Additional exam requirements/ recommendations for international students: Required—TOEFL (minimum score 550 paper-based). Electronic applications accepted.

California State University, Fresno, Division of Research and Graduate Studies, College of Science and Mathematics, Department of Mathematics, Fresno, CA 93740-8027. Offers mathematics (MA); mathematics teaching (MA). *Program availability:* Part-time. *Degree requirements:* For master's, thesis or alternative. *Entrance requirements:* For master's, GRE General Test. Additional exam requirements/recommendations for international students: Required—TOEFL. Electronic applications accepted. *Faculty research:* Diagnostic testing project.

California State University, Fullerton, Graduate Studies, College of Natural Science and Mathematics, Department of Mathematics, Fullerton, CA 92831-3599. Offers applied mathematics (MA); mathematics education (MA). *Program availability:* Part-time. *Entrance requirements:* For master's, minimum GPA of 2.5 in last 60 units of course work, major in mathematics or related field.

California State University, Long Beach, Graduate Studies, College of Natural Sciences and Mathematics, Department of Mathematics and Statistics, Long Beach, CA 90840. Offers mathematics (MS), including applied mathematics, applied statistics, mathematics education for secondary school teachers. *Program availability:* Part-time. *Degree requirements:* For master's, comprehensive exam or thesis. *Application deadline:* For fall admission, 6/1 for domestic students; for spring admission, 11/1 for domestic students. Applications are processed on a rolling basis. Application fee: $55. Electronic applications accepted. *Expenses: Required fees:* $2628 per term. Tuition and fees vary according to class time, course level, course load, degree level, campus/ location and program. *Financial support:* Teaching assistantships, Federal Work-Study, institutionally sponsored loans, scholarships/grants, and traineeships available. Financial award application deadline: 3/2; financial award applicants required to submit FAFSA. *Faculty research:* Algebra, functional analysis, partial differential equations, operator theory, numerical analysis. *Unit head:* Dr. Tangan Gao, Chair, 562-985-4721, Fax: 562-985-8227, E-mail: tangan.gao@csulb.edu. *Application contact:* Dr. Tangan Gao, Chair, 562-985-4721, Fax: 562-985-8227, E-mail: tangan.gao@csulb.edu.

California State University, Los Angeles, Graduate Studies, College of Natural and Social Sciences, Department of Mathematics, Los Angeles, CA 90032-8530. Offers mathematics (MS), including applied mathematics. *Program availability:* Part-time, evening/weekend. *Degree requirements:* For master's, comprehensive exam or thesis. *Entrance requirements:* For master's, previous course work in mathematics. Additional exam requirements/recommendations for international students: Required—TOEFL

(minimum score 500 paper-based). Electronic applications accepted. *Faculty research:* Group theory, functional analysis, convexity theory, ordered geometry.

California State University, Northridge, Graduate Studies, College of Science and Mathematics, Department of Mathematics, Northridge, CA 91330. Offers applied mathematics (MS); mathematics (MS). *Program availability:* Part-time, evening/ weekend. *Degree requirements:* For master's, thesis (for some programs). *Entrance requirements:* For master's, GRE (if cumulative undergraduate GPA less than 3.0). Additional exam requirements/recommendations for international students: Required— TOEFL.

California State University, Sacramento, College of Natural Sciences and Mathematics, Department of Mathematics and Statistics, Sacramento, CA 95819. Offers mathematics (MA). *Program availability:* Part-time. *Degree requirements:* For master's, comprehensive exam, writing proficiency exam. *Entrance requirements:* For master's, minimum GPA of 3.0 in mathematics, 2.5 overall during previous 2 years; BA in mathematics or equivalent. Additional exam requirements/recommendations for international students: Required—TOEFL (minimum score 550 paper-based; 80 iBT); Recommended—IELTS, TSE. Electronic applications accepted. *Expenses:* Contact institution. *Faculty research:* Algebra, applied mathematics, methods in mathematical finance, subelliptic analysis, topology.

California State University, San Bernardino, Graduate Studies, College of Natural Sciences, Program in Mathematics, San Bernardino, CA 92407. Offers mathematics (MA); teaching mathematics (MAT). *Program availability:* Part-time. *Faculty:* 7 full-time (3 women). *Students:* 4 full-time (2 women), 33 part-time (17 women); includes 24 minority (1 Black or African American, non-Hispanic/Latino; 1 Asian, non-Hispanic/ Latino; 21 Hispanic/Latino; 1 Two or more races, non-Hispanic/Latino), 2 international. Average age 29. 23 applicants, 52% accepted, 10 enrolled. In 2018, 15 master's awarded. *Degree requirements:* For master's, advancement to candidacy. *Entrance requirements:* Additional exam requirements/recommendations for international students: Required—TOEFL. *Application deadline:* For fall admission, 7/16 for domestic students; for winter admission, 10/16 for domestic students; for spring admission, 1/22 for domestic students. Application fee: $55. *Faculty research:* Mathematics education, technology in education, algebra, combinatorics, real analysis. *Unit head:* Corey Dunn, Coordinator, 909-537-5368, E-mail: cmdunn@csusb.edu. *Application contact:* Dr. Dorota Huizinga, Assistant Dean of Graduate Studies, 909-537-3064, E-mail: dorota.huizinga@csusb.edu.

California State University, San Marcos, College of Science and Mathematics, Program in Mathematics, San Marcos, CA 92096-0001. Offers MS. *Program availability:* Part-time, evening/weekend. *Degree requirements:* For master's, comprehensive exam, thesis optional. *Entrance requirements:* Additional exam requirements/ recommendations for international students: Required—TOEFL, TWE. *Application deadline:* For fall admission, 4/15 priority date for domestic students; for spring admission, 8/31 for domestic students. Applications are processed on a rolling basis. Application fee: $55. *Financial support:* Applicants required to submit FAFSA. *Faculty research:* Combinatorics, graph theory, partial differential equations, numerical analysis, computational linear algebra. *Unit head:* Dr. Amber Puha, Graduate Program Coordinator, Mathematics, 760-750-4201, E-mail: apuha@csusm.edu. *Application contact:* Dr. Wesley Schultz, Dean of Office of Graduate Studies and Research, 760-750-8045, Fax: 760-750-8045, E-mail: apply@csusm.edu.
Website: http://www.csusm.edu/math/msdegree/

Carleton University, Faculty of Graduate Studies, Faculty of Science, School of Mathematics and Statistics, Ottawa, ON K1S 5B6, Canada. Offers mathematics (M Sc, PhD). Programs offered jointly with University of Ottawa. *Degree requirements:* For master's, thesis optional; for doctorate, one foreign language, comprehensive exam, thesis/dissertation. *Entrance requirements:* For master's, honors degree; for doctorate, master's degree. Additional exam requirements/recommendations for international students: Required—TOEFL. *Faculty research:* Pure mathematics, applied mathematics, probability and statistics.

Carlow University, College of Learning and Innovation, Program in Curriculum and Instruction, Pittsburgh, PA 15213-3165. Offers autism (M Ed); early childhood leadership (M Ed); online learning instructional design (M Ed); STEM (M Ed). *Program availability:* Part-time, evening/weekend. *Entrance requirements:* For master's, personal essay; resume or curriculum vitae; two recommendations; official transcripts; interview; minimum undergraduate GPA of 3.0. Additional exam requirements/recommendations for international students: Required—TOEFL (minimum score 550 paper-based). *Application deadline:* Applications are processed on a rolling basis. Electronic applications accepted. *Expenses: Tuition:* Full-time $13,090; part-time $5100 per semester. *Required fees:* $215; $84. Tuition and fees vary according to course load, degree level and program. *Financial support:* Application deadline: 4/1; applicants required to submit FAFSA. *Unit head:* Dr. Keeley Baronak, Chair, 412-578-6135, Fax: 412-578-6326, E-mail: kobaronak@carlow.edu. *Application contact:* Dr. Keeley Baronak, Chair, 412-578-6135, Fax: 412-578-6326, E-mail: kobaronak@carlow.edu.
Website: http://www.carlow.edu/Curriculum_and_Instruction_MEd.aspx

Carnegie Mellon University, Mellon College of Science, Department of Mathematical Sciences, Pittsburgh, PA 15213-3891. Offers algorithms, combinatorics, and optimization (PhD); computational finance (MS); mathematical finance (PhD); mathematical sciences (DA, PhD); pure and applied logic (PhD). *Program availability:* Part-time. Terminal master's awarded for partial completion of doctoral program. *Degree requirements:* For doctorate, thesis/dissertation. *Entrance requirements:* For master's and doctorate, GRE General Test, GRE Subject Test. Additional exam requirements/ recommendations for international students: Required—TOEFL. Electronic applications accepted. *Faculty research:* Continuum mechanics, discrete mathematics, applied and computational mathematics.

Case Western Reserve University, School of Graduate Studies, Department of Mathematics, Applied Mathematics and Statistics, Cleveland, OH 44106. Offers applied mathematics (MS, PhD); mathematics (MS, PhD). *Program availability:* Part-time. *Faculty:* 33 full-time (15 women), 2 part-time/adjunct (both women). *Students:* 35 full-time (15 women); includes 6 minority (1 Black or African American, non-Hispanic/Latino; 4 Asian, non-Hispanic/Latino; 1 Hispanic/Latino), 16 international. Average age 26. 185 applicants, 17% accepted, 15 enrolled. In 2018, 13 master's, 3 doctorates awarded. Terminal master's awarded for partial completion of doctoral program. *Degree requirements:* For master's, thesis or alternative; for doctorate, comprehensive exam, thesis/dissertation. *Entrance requirements:* For master's and doctorate, GRE General Test, 3 letters of recommendation. Additional exam requirements/recommendations for international students: Required—TOEFL (minimum score 577 paper-based; 90 iBT); Recommended—IELTS (minimum score 7). *Application deadline:* For fall admission, 4/1 priority date for domestic students; for spring admission, 11/1 priority date for domestic students. Applications are processed on a rolling basis. Application fee: $50. Electronic applications accepted. *Expenses: Tuition:* Full-time $45,168; part-time $1939 per credit hour. *Required fees:* $36; $18 per semester. $18 per semester. *Financial support:* Research assistantships, teaching assistantships, institutionally sponsored loans, health

Peterson's Graduate Programs in the Physical Sciences, Mathematics, Agricultural Sciences, the Environment & Natural Resources 2020

www.petersons.com   **209**

care benefits, and unspecified assistantships available. Financial award application deadline: 12/1; financial award applicants required to submit CSS PROFILE or FAFSA. *Faculty research:* Probability theory, convexity and high-dimensional phenomena, imaging, geometric evaluation of curves, dynamical systems, large scale scientific computing, life sciences. *Unit head:* Mary Ann Horn, Professor and Chair, 216-216.368.0470, Fax: 216-368-5163, E-mail: maryann.horn@case.edu. *Application contact:* Sakeenah Bari-Harold, Department Administrator, 216-368-0463, Fax: 216-368-5163, E-mail: sakeenah.bari-harold@case.edu.
Website: http://math.case.edu/

Central Connecticut State University, School of Graduate Studies, School of Engineering, Science and Technology, Department of Mathematical Sciences, New Britain, CT 06050-4010. Offers data mining (MS, Certificate); mathematics (MA, MS), including actuarial science (MA), computer science (MA), statistics (MA); mathematics education leadership (Sixth Year Certificate); mathematics for secondary education (Certificate). *Program availability:* Part-time, evening/weekend, 100% online. *Faculty:* 13 full-time (4 women). *Students:* 14 full-time (9 women), 70 part-time (39 women); includes 21 minority (8 Black or African American, non-Hispanic/Latino; 9 Asian, non-Hispanic/Latino; 3 Hispanic/Latino; 1 Two or more races, non-Hispanic/Latino), 2 international. Average age 33. 57 applicants, 70% accepted, 20 enrolled. In 2018, 20 master's, 3 other advanced degrees awarded. *Degree requirements:* For master's, comprehensive exam, thesis or alternative, special project; for other advanced degree, qualifying exam. *Entrance requirements:* For master's, minimum undergraduate GPA of 2.7; for other advanced degree, minimum undergraduate GPA of 3.0, essay, letters of recommendation. Additional exam requirements/recommendations for international students: Required—TOEFL (minimum score 550 paper-based; 79 iBT); Recommended—IELTS (minimum score 6.5). *Application deadline:* For fall admission, 6/1 for domestic students, 5/1 for international students; for spring admission, 11/1 for domestic and international students. Applications are processed on a rolling basis. Application fee: $50. Electronic applications accepted. *Expenses: Tuition, area resident:* Full-time $7027; part-time $388 per credit. Tuition, state resident: full-time $9750; part-time $388 per credit. Tuition, nonresident: full-time $18,102; part-time $388 per credit. *International tuition:* $18,102 full-time. *Required fees:* $266 per semester. *Financial support:* In 2018–19, 22 students received support. Career-related internships or fieldwork, Federal Work-Study, scholarships/grants, and unspecified assistantships available. Support available to part-time students. Financial award application deadline: 3/1; financial award applicants required to submit FAFSA. *Faculty research:* Statistics, actuarial mathematics, computer systems and engineering, computer programming techniques, operations research. *Unit head:* Dr. Robin Kalder, Chair, 860-832-2835, E-mail: kalderr@ccsu.edu. *Application contact:* Patricia Gardner, Associate Director of Graduate Studies, 860-832-2350, Fax: 860-832-2362.
Website: http://www.ccsu.edu/mathematics/

Central European University, Department of Mathematics and its Applications, 1051, Hungary. Offers mathematics and its applications (MS, PhD). *Degree requirements:* For master's, one foreign language, thesis (for some programs); for doctorate, comprehensive exam, thesis/dissertation. *Entrance requirements:* For master's and doctorate, entrance exam or GRE, statement of purpose. Additional exam requirements/recommendations for international students: Required—TOEFL (minimum score 570 paper-based); Recommended—IELTS (minimum score 6.5). Electronic applications accepted. *Faculty research:* Algebra, algebraic geometry, bioinformatics, calculus of variations, computational biology, cryptography, discrete mathematics, evolutions equations, fluid mechanics, geometry, number theory, numerical analysis, optimization, ordinary and partial differential equations, probability theory, quantum mechanics, statistics, stochastic processes.

Central Michigan University, College of Graduate Studies, College of Science and Engineering, Department of Mathematics, Mount Pleasant, MI 48859. Offers mathematics (MA, PhD), including teaching of college mathematics (PhD). *Program availability:* Part-time. *Degree requirements:* For master's, thesis or alternative; for doctorate, thesis/dissertation. *Entrance requirements:* For master's, minimum GPA of 2.7, 20 hours of course work in mathematics; for doctorate, GRE, minimum GPA of 3.0, 20 hours of course work in mathematics. Electronic applications accepted. *Faculty research:* Combinatorics, approximation theory, applied mathematics, statistics, functional analysis and operator theory.

Chicago State University, School of Graduate and Professional Studies, College of Arts and Sciences, Department of Mathematics and Computer Science, Chicago, IL 60628. Offers computer science (MS); mathematics (MS). *Degree requirements:* For master's, thesis optional, oral exam. *Entrance requirements:* For master's, minimum GPA of 2.75.

City College of the City University of New York, Graduate School, Division of Science, Department of Mathematics, New York, NY 10031-9198. Offers MS. *Program availability:* Part-time. *Degree requirements:* For master's, one foreign language. *Entrance requirements:* Additional exam requirements/recommendations for international students: Required—TOEFL (minimum score 500 paper-based; 61 iBT). Electronic applications accepted. *Faculty research:* Group theory, number theory, logic, statistics, computational geometry.

Claremont Graduate University, Graduate Programs, Institute of Mathematical Sciences, Claremont, CA 91711-6160. Offers computational and systems biology (PhD); computational mathematics and numerical analysis (MA, MS); computational science (PhD); engineering and industrial applied mathematics (PhD); mathematics (PhD); operations research and statistics (MA, MS); physical applied mathematics (MA, MS); pure mathematics (MA, MS); scientific computing (MA, MS); systems and control theory (MA, MS). PhD programs offered jointly with San Diego State University and California State University, Long Beach. *Program availability:* Part-time. Terminal master's awarded for partial completion of doctoral program. *Entrance requirements:* For master's and doctorate, GRE General Test. Additional exam requirements/recommendations for international students: Required—TOEFL (minimum score 75 iBT). Electronic applications accepted.

Clark Atlanta University, School of Arts and Sciences, Department of Mathematical Sciences, Atlanta, GA 30314. Offers MS. *Program availability:* Part-time. *Degree requirements:* For master's, one foreign language, thesis optional. *Entrance requirements:* For master's, GRE General Test, minimum GPA of 2.5. Additional exam requirements/recommendations for international students: Required—TOEFL (minimum score 500 paper-based; 61 iBT). *Faculty research:* Numerical methods for operator equations, ADA language development.

Clarkson University, School of Arts and Sciences, Department of Mathematics, Potsdam, NY 13699. Offers MS, PhD. *Faculty:* 15 full-time (6 women), 5 part-time/adjunct (2 women). *Students:* 24 full-time (9 women), 1 part-time (0 women); includes 2 minority (1 Hispanic/Latino; 1 Two or more races, non-Hispanic/Latino), 15 international. 32 applicants, 78% accepted, 7 enrolled. In 2018, 9 master's, 5 doctorates awarded. *Degree requirements:* For master's, thesis; for doctorate, comprehensive exam, thesis/dissertation. *Entrance requirements:* For master's and doctorate, GRE. Additional exam requirements/recommendations for international students: Required—TOEFL (minimum score 550 paper-based, 80 iBT) or IELTS (6.5). *Application deadline:* Applications are processed on a rolling basis. Application fee: $50. Electronic applications accepted. *Expenses: Tuition:* Full-time $24,984; part-time $1388 per credit hour. *Required fees:* $225. Tuition and fees vary according to campus/location and program. *Financial support:* Scholarships/grants and unspecified assistantships available. *Unit head:* Dr. Joseph Skufca, Chair of Mathematics, 315-268-2399, E-mail: jskufca@clarkson.edu. *Application contact:* Dan Capogna, Director of Graduate Admissions & Recruitment, 518-631-9910, E-mail: graduate@clarkson.edu.
Website: https://www.clarkson.edu/academics/graduate

Clemson University, Graduate School, College of Science, School of Mathematical & Statistical Sciences, Clemson, SC 29634. Offers MS, PhD. *Program availability:* Part-time. *Faculty:* 47 full-time (9 women). *Students:* 123 full-time (48 women), 3 part-time (2 women); includes 8 minority (2 Black or African American, non-Hispanic/Latino; 3 Hispanic/Latino; 3 Two or more races, non-Hispanic/Latino), 43 international. Average age 26. 100 applicants, 92% accepted, 26 enrolled. In 2018, 12 master's, 12 doctorates awarded. *Degree requirements:* For master's, thesis or alternative; for doctorate, comprehensive exam, thesis/dissertation, 3 preliminary exams during first two years. *Entrance requirements:* For master's and doctorate, GRE General Test, GRE Subject Test (mathematics), unofficial transcripts, letters of recommendation, statement of purpose. Additional exam requirements/recommendations for international students: Required—TOEFL (minimum score 90 iBT); Recommended—IELTS (minimum score 6.5), TSE (minimum score 54). *Application deadline:* For fall admission, 1/15 priority date for domestic and international students; for spring admission, 10/1 priority date for domestic and international students. Applications are processed on a rolling basis. Application fee: $80 ($90 for international students). Electronic applications accepted. *Expenses: Tuition, area resident:* Full-time $11,270; part-time $8688 per credit hour. Tuition, state resident: full-time $11,796. Tuition, nonresident: full-time $23,802; part-time $17,412 per credit hour. *International tuition:* $23,246 full-time. *Required fees:* $1196; $497 per semester. Tuition and fees vary according to course load, degree level, campus/location and program. *Financial support:* In 2018–19, 113 students received support, including 2 fellowships with full and partial tuition reimbursements available (averaging $5,000 per year), 6 research assistantships with full and partial tuition reimbursements available (averaging $21,467 per year), 98 teaching assistantships with full and partial tuition reimbursements available (averaging $20,805 per year); career-related internships or fieldwork and unspecified assistantships also available. Financial award application deadline: 1/15. *Faculty research:* Pure and applied analysis, algebra and discrete mathematics, computational mathematics, operations research, statistics. *Total annual research expenditures:* $1.5 million. *Unit head:* Dr. Kevin James, Interim Director, 864-656-1517, E-mail: kevja@clemson.edu. *Application contact:* Dr. Taufiquar Khan, Associate Director for Graduate Studies, 864-656-1516, E-mail: mthgrad@clemson.edu.
Website: https://www.clemson.edu/science/departments/mathematical-sciences/

Cleveland State University, College of Graduate Studies, College of Sciences and Health Professions, Department of Mathematics, Cleveland, OH 44115. Offers applied statistics (MS); mathematics (MS). *Program availability:* Part-time, evening/weekend. *Faculty:* 17 full-time (7 women), 1 part-time/adjunct (0 women). *Students:* 22 full-time (9 women), 18 part-time (9 women); includes 3 minority (2 Black or African American, non-Hispanic/Latino; 1 Asian, non-Hispanic/Latino), 13 international. Average age 29. 66 applicants, 86% accepted, 18 enrolled. In 2018, 23 master's awarded. *Entrance requirements:* Additional exam requirements/recommendations for international students: Required—TOEFL (minimum score 550 paper-based; 78 iBT). *Application deadline:* Applications are processed on a rolling basis. Application fee: $40. Electronic applications accepted. *Expenses:* Tuition, state resident: full-time $7232.55; part-time $6676 per credit hour. Tuition, nonresident: full-time $12,375. *International tuition:* $18,914 full-time. *Required fees:* $80; $80 $40. Tuition and fees vary according to program. *Financial support:* In 2018–19, 14 students received support, including 12 teaching assistantships with full tuition reimbursements available (averaging $6,960 per year); unspecified assistantships also available. Financial award application deadline: 3/15. *Faculty research:* Algebraic topology, algebraic geometry, statistics, mathematical biology, applied mathematics. *Total annual research expenditures:* $132,202. *Unit head:* Dr. Ivan Soprunov, Chairperson/Professor, 216-687-4681, Fax: 216-523-7340, E-mail: i.soprunov@csuohio.edu. *Application contact:* Elaine Chuha, Administrative Coordinator, 216-523-7162, Fax: 216-523-7340, E-mail: e.hoff@csuohio.edu.
Website: http://www.csuohio.edu/sciences/dept/mathematics/

The College at Brockport, State University of New York, School of Arts and Sciences, Department of Mathematics, Brockport, NY 14420-2997. Offers MA. *Program availability:* Part-time. *Faculty:* 9 full-time (4 women). *Students:* 8 full-time (4 women), 9 part-time (2 women). 12 applicants, 100% accepted, 6 enrolled. In 2018, 5 master's awarded. *Degree requirements:* For master's, comprehensive exam. *Entrance requirements:* For master's, minimum GPA of 3.0, letters of recommendation, statement of objectives. Additional exam requirements/recommendations for international students: Required—TOEFL (minimum score 550 paper-based; 79 iBT), IELTS (minimum score 6.5). *Application deadline:* For fall admission, 4/15 priority date for domestic and international students; for spring admission, 11/15 priority date for domestic and international students; for summer admission, 4/15 for domestic and international students. Application fee: $50. Electronic applications accepted. *Expenses:* Tuition, state resident: part-time $471 per credit. Tuition, nonresident: part-time $963 per credit. *Financial support:* In 2018–19, 4 teaching assistantships with full tuition reimbursements (averaging $6,000 per year) were awarded; Federal Work-Study, scholarships/grants, and unspecified assistantships also available. Support available to part-time students. Financial award application deadline: 3/15; financial award applicants required to submit FAFSA. *Faculty research:* Mathematical modeling, dynamical systems, complex/functional analysis, graph theory and combinations, algebra and number theory. *Unit head:* Dr. Rebecca Smith, Chairperson, 585-395-5183, Fax: 585-395-2304, E-mail: rnsmith@brockport.edu. *Application contact:* Dr. Nathan Reff, Graduate Director, 585-395-5298, Fax: 585-395-2304, E-mail: nreff@brockport.edu.
Website: https://www.brockport.edu/academics/mathematics/graduate/masters.html

College of Charleston, Graduate School, School of Sciences and Mathematics, Program in Mathematics, Charleston, SC 29424-0001. Offers mathematics (MS). *Program availability:* Part-time, evening/weekend. *Degree requirements:* For master's, thesis optional. *Entrance requirements:* For master's, GRE, BS in mathematics or equivalent, 2 letters of recommendation. Additional exam requirements/recommendations for international students: Required—TOEFL (minimum score 81 iBT). Electronic applications accepted. *Faculty research:* Algebra, dynamical systems, probability, analysis and topology, combinatorics.

Colorado State University, College of Natural Sciences, Department of Mathematics, Fort Collins, CO 80523-1874. Offers MS, PhD. *Program availability:* Part-time. Terminal master's awarded for partial completion of doctoral program. *Degree requirements:* For master's, comprehensive exam (for some programs), thesis (for some programs); for doctorate, comprehensive exam, thesis/dissertation. *Entrance requirements:* For master's, GRE, minimum GPA of 3.0; transcripts; letters of recommendation; for doctorate, GRE, minimum GPA of 3.0; letters of recommendation. Additional exam requirements/recommendations for international students: Required—TOEFL (minimum score 550 paper-based; 80 iBT), IELTS (minimum score 6.5). Electronic applications accepted. *Expenses:* Tuition, state resident: full-time $10,520; part-time $4675 per credit hour. Tuition, nonresident: full-time $25,791; part-time $11,462 per credit hour. *International tuition:* *Required fees:* $2392; $576 $288. Tuition and fees vary according to course level, course load, degree level, program and student level. *Faculty research:* Algebra, analysis, geometry, topology, math education.

Columbia University, Graduate School of Arts and Sciences, New York, NY 10027. Offers African-American studies (MA); American studies (MA); anthropology (MA, PhD); art history and archaeology (MA, PhD); astronomy (PhD); biological sciences (PhD); biotechnology (MA); chemical physics (PhD); chemistry (PhD); classical studies (MA, PhD); classics (MA, PhD); climate and society (MA); conservation biology (MA); earth and environmental sciences (PhD); East Asia: regional studies (MA); East Asian languages and cultures (MA, PhD); ecology, evolution and environmental biology (MA), including conservation biology; ecology, evolution, and environmental biology (PhD), including ecology and evolutionary biology, evolutionary primatology; economics (MA, PhD); English and comparative literature (MA, PhD); French and Romance philology (MA, PhD); Germanic languages (MA, PhD); global French studies (MA); global thought (MA); Hispanic cultural studies (MA); history (PhD); history and literature (MA); human rights studies (MA); Islamic studies (MA); Italian (MA, PhD); Japanese pedagogy (MA); Jewish studies (MA); Latin America and the Caribbean: regional studies (MA); Latin American and Iberian cultures (PhD); mathematics (MA, PhD), including finance (MA); medieval and Renaissance studies (MA); Middle Eastern, South Asian, and African studies (MA, PhD); modern art: critical and curatorial studies (MA); modern European studies (MA); museum anthropology (MA); music (DMA, PhD); oral history (MA); philosophical foundations of physics (MA); philosophy (MA, PhD); physics (PhD); political science (MA, PhD); psychology (PhD); quantitative methods in the social sciences (MA); religion (MA, PhD); Russia, Eurasia and East Europe: regional studies (MA); Russian translation (MA); Slavic cultures (MA); Slavic languages (MA, PhD); sociology (MA, PhD); South Asian studies (MA); statistics (MA, PhD); theatre (PhD). Dual-degree programs require admission to both Graduate School of Arts and Sciences and another Columbia school. *Program availability:* Part-time. Terminal master's awarded for partial completion of doctoral program. *Degree requirements:* For master's, variable foreign language requirement, comprehensive exam (for some programs), thesis (for some programs); for doctorate, variable foreign language requirement, comprehensive exam (for some programs), thesis/dissertation. *Entrance requirements:* For master's and doctorate, GRE General Test, GRE Subject Test (for some programs). Additional exam requirements/recommendations for international students: Required—TOEFL, IELTS. Electronic applications accepted.

Columbus State University, Graduate Studies, College of Education and Health Professions, Department of Teacher Education, Columbus, GA 31907-5645. Offers curriculum and instruction in accomplished teaching (M Ed); early childhood education (M Ed, MAT, Ed S); middle grades education (M Ed, MAT, Ed S); secondary education (M Ed, MAT, Ed S), including biology (MAT), chemistry (MAT), earth and space science (MAT), English/language arts, general science (M Ed), history (MAT), mathematics, science (Ed S), social science (M Ed, Ed S); special education (M Ed, MAT, Ed S), including general curriculum (M Ed, MAT); teacher leadership (M Ed). *Accreditation:* NCATE. *Program availability:* Part-time, evening/weekend, 100% online, blended/hybrid learning. *Faculty:* 20 full-time (12 women), 20 part-time/adjunct (15 women). *Students:* 110 full-time (84 women), 143 part-time (115 women); includes 105 minority (96 Black or African American, non-Hispanic/Latino; 4 Hispanic/Latino; 5 Two or more races, non-Hispanic/Latino). Average age 33. 147 applicants, 56% accepted, 62 enrolled. In 2018, 112 master's, 11 other advanced degrees awarded. *Degree requirements:* For Ed S, thesis or alternative. *Entrance requirements:* For master's, GRE General Test, minimum undergraduate GPA of 2.75; for Ed S, GRE General Test, minimum undergraduate GPA of 2.75, graduate 3.0. Additional exam requirements/recommendations for international students: Required—TOEFL (minimum score 550 paper-based; 79 iBT). *Application deadline:* For fall admission, 6/30 for domestic students, 5/1 for international students; for spring admission, 11/1 for domestic and international students; for summer admission, 3/1 for domestic and international students. Applications are processed on a rolling basis. Application fee: $50. Electronic applications accepted. *Expenses: Tuition, area resident:* Full-time $4924; part-time $618 per credit hour. Tuition, state resident: full-time $4924; part-time $618 per credit hour. Tuition, nonresident: full-time $19,218; part-time $2403 per credit hour. *International tuition:* $19,218 full-time. *Required fees:* $1870; $802. Tuition and fees vary according to course level, degree level and program. *Financial support:* In 2018–19, 29 students received support, including 7 research assistantships with partial tuition reimbursements available (averaging $3,000 per year); career-related internships or fieldwork, Federal Work-Study, institutionally sponsored loans, scholarships/grants, tuition waivers (partial), and unspecified assistantships also available. Support available to part-time students. Financial award application deadline: 5/1; financial award applicants required to submit FAFSA. *Unit head:* Dr. Jan Burcham, Department Chair, 706-507-8519, Fax: 706-568-3134, E-mail: burcham_jan@columbusstate.edu. *Application contact:* Catrina Smith-Edmond, Assistant Director for Graduate and Global Admission, 706-507-8824, Fax: 706-568-5091, E-mail: smithedmond_catrina@columbusstate.edu.
Website: http://te.columbusstate.edu/

Concordia University, School of Graduate Studies, Faculty of Arts and Science, Department of Mathematics and Statistics, Montréal, QC H3G 1M8, Canada. Offers mathematics (PhD); mathematics and statistics (M Sc, MA); teaching of mathematics (MTM). *Degree requirements:* For master's, thesis optional; for doctorate, comprehensive exam, thesis/dissertation. *Entrance requirements:* For master's, honors degree in mathematics or equivalent. *Faculty research:* Number theory, computational algebra, mathematical physics, differential geometry, dynamical systems and statistics.

Cornell University, Graduate School, Graduate Fields of Arts and Sciences, Field of Mathematics, Ithaca, NY 14853. Offers PhD. *Degree requirements:* For doctorate, one foreign language, comprehensive exam, thesis/dissertation, teaching experience. *Entrance requirements:* For doctorate, GRE General Test, GRE Subject Test (mathematics), 3 letters of recommendation. Additional exam requirements/recommendations for international students: Required—TOEFL (minimum score 600 paper-based; 95 iBT). Electronic applications accepted. *Faculty research:* Analysis, dynamical systems, Lie theory, logic, topology and geometry.

Dalhousie University, Faculty of Science, Department of Mathematics and Statistics, Program in Mathematics, Halifax, NS B3H 4R2, Canada. Offers M Sc, PhD. *Degree requirements:* For master's, thesis; for doctorate, thesis/dissertation. *Entrance requirements:* Additional exam requirements/recommendations for international students: Required—TOEFL, IELTS, CANTEST, CAEL, or Michigan English Language Assessment Battery. Electronic applications accepted. *Faculty research:* Applied mathematics, category theory, algebra, analysis, graph theory.

Dartmouth College, Guarini School of Graduate and Advanced Studies, Department of Mathematics, Hanover, NH 03755. Offers AM, PhD. *Faculty:* 19 full-time (6 women), 9 part-time/adjunct (1 woman). *Students:* 26 full-time (10 women); includes 2 minority (1 American Indian or Alaska Native, non-Hispanic/Latino; 1 Two or more races, non-Hispanic/Latino), 6 international. Average age 25. 93 applicants, 24% accepted, 5 enrolled. In 2018, 6 master's, 3 doctorates awarded. Terminal master's awarded for partial completion of doctoral program. *Entrance requirements:* For doctorate, GRE General Test, GRE Subject Test. Additional exam requirements/recommendations for international students: Required—TOEFL. For fall admission, 2/8 priority date for domestic students. Application fee: $25. Electronic applications accepted. *Financial support:* Fellowships, research assistantships, teaching assistantships, institutionally sponsored loans, scholarships/grants, tuition waivers (full), and unspecified assistantships available. *Faculty research:* Mathematical logic, set theory, combinations, number theory. *Unit head:* Dr. Scott Pauls, Chair, 603-646-1047, Fax: 603-646-1312. *Application contact:* Traci Flynn-Moloney, Department Administrator, 603-646-3723, Fax: 603-646-1312.
Website: http://math.dartmouth.edu/

Delaware State University, Graduate Programs, Department of Mathematics, Program in Mathematics, Dover, DE 19901-2277. Offers MS. *Entrance requirements:* Additional exam requirements/recommendations for international students: Required—TOEFL (minimum score 550 paper-based). Electronic applications accepted.

DePaul University, College of Science and Health, Chicago, IL 60604-2287. Offers applied mathematics (MS); applied statistics (MS); biological sciences (MA, MS); chemistry (MS); environmental science (MS); mathematics education (MA); mathematics for teaching (MS); nursing (MS); nursing practice (DNP); physics (MS); polymer and coatings science (MS); psychology (MS); pure mathematics (MS); science education (MS); MA/PhD. *Accreditation:* AACN. Electronic applications accepted.

Drew University, Caspersen School of Graduate Studies, Madison, NJ 07940-1493. Offers conflict resolution and leadership (Certificate), including community leadership, moderation, peace building; education (M Ed); finance (MA); history and culture (MA, PhD), including American history, book history, British history, European history, intellectual history, Irish history, print culture, public history; K-12 education (MAT), including art, biology, chemistry, elementary education, English, French, Italian, math, secondary education, special education, teacher of students with disabilities; liberal studies (M Litt, D Litt), including history, Irish/Irish-American studies, literature (M Litt, MMH, D Litt, DMH, CMH), religion, spirituality, teaching in the two-year college, writing; medical humanities (MMH, DMH, CMH), including arts, health, healthcare, literature (M Litt, MMH, D Litt, DMH, CMH), scientific research; poetry (MFA). *Program availability:* Part-time, evening/weekend. *Faculty:* 3 full-time (2 women), 27 part-time/adjunct (13 women). *Students:* 66 full-time (38 women), 179 part-time (117 women); includes 37 minority (15 Black or African American, non-Hispanic/Latino; 2 Asian, non-Hispanic/Latino; 15 Hispanic/Latino; 5 Two or more races, non-Hispanic/Latino), 14 international. Average age 42. 157 applicants, 82% accepted, 57 enrolled. In 2018, 34 master's, 24 doctorates, 17 other advanced degrees awarded. Terminal master's awarded for partial completion of doctoral program. *Degree requirements:* For master's and other advanced degree, thesis (for some programs); for doctorate, one foreign language, comprehensive exam (for some programs), thesis/dissertation. *Entrance requirements:* For master's, PRAXIS Core and Subject Area tests (for MAT), GRE/GMAT (for MFin MS in Data Analytics), resume, transcripts, writing sample, personal statement, letters of recommendation; for doctorate, GRE (PhD in history and culture), resume, transcripts, writing sample, personal statement, letters of recommendation; for other advanced degree, resume, transcripts, personal statement. Additional exam requirements/recommendations for international students: Required—TOEFL (minimum score 587 paper-based; 80 iBT), IELTS (minimum score 6), TWE (minimum score 4). *Application deadline:* For fall admission, 8/1 for domestic students, 6/1 for international students; for spring admission, 12/1 for domestic students, 10/1 for international students. Applications are processed on a rolling basis. Application fee: $35. Electronic applications accepted. *Financial support:* Fellowships, research assistantships, teaching assistantships, career-related internships or fieldwork, Federal Work-Study, scholarships/grants, and unspecified assistantships available. Support available to part-time students. Financial award applicants required to submit FAFSA. *Unit head:* Dr. Debra Liebowitz, Provost and Dean of the College of Liberal Arts & Caspersen School of Graduate Studies, 973-4080100, E-mail: dliebowi@drew.edu. *Application contact:* Amo-Augustus Kubeyinje, Associate Vice President for Graduate Enrollment, 973-408-3111, E-mail: akubeyinje@drew.edu.
Website: http://www.drew.edu/caspersen

Drexel University, College of Arts and Sciences, Department of Mathematics, Philadelphia, PA 19104-2875. Offers MS, PhD. *Program availability:* Part-time. *Degree requirements:* For doctorate, one foreign language, thesis/dissertation. *Entrance requirements:* For master's and doctorate, GRE. Additional exam requirements/recommendations for international students: Required—TOEFL. Electronic applications accepted. *Faculty research:* Probability and statistics, combinatorics, special functions, functional analysis, parallel processing, computer algebra.

Duke University, Graduate School, Department of Mathematics, Durham, NC 27708. Offers PhD. *Degree requirements:* For doctorate, 2 foreign languages, thesis/dissertation. *Entrance requirements:* For doctorate, GRE General Test, GRE Subject Test. Additional exam requirements/recommendations for international students: Required—TOEFL (minimum score 577 paper-based; 90 iBT) or IELTS (minimum score 7). Electronic applications accepted.

Duquesne University, Graduate School of Liberal Arts, Program in Computational Mathematics, Pittsburgh, PA 15282-0001. Offers MS. *Faculty:* 26 full-time (8 women), 11 part-time/adjunct (5 women). *Students:* 8 full-time (4 women), 3 part-time (0 women); includes 1 minority (Black or African American, non-Hispanic/Latino), 1 international. Average age 26. 6 applicants, 83% accepted, 4 enrolled. In 2018, 5 master's awarded. *Degree requirements:* For master's, thesis optional. *Entrance requirements:* For master's, GRE General Test. Additional exam requirements/recommendations for international students: Required—TOEFL. *Application deadline:* For fall admission, 8/1 for domestic students, 5/1 for international students. Applications are processed on a rolling basis. Application fee: $0. Electronic applications accepted. *Expenses: Tuition:* Full-time $23,112; part-time $1284 per credit. Tuition and fees vary according to program. *Financial support:* In 2018–19, 6 students received support, including 6 teaching assistantships with full tuition reimbursements available (averaging $12,500 per year); Federal Work-Study, institutionally sponsored loans, scholarships/grants, and unspecified assistantships also available. Financial award application deadline: 5/1. *Unit head:* Dr. Stacey Levine, Chair, 412-396-6468, E-mail: levines@duq.edu. *Application contact:* Linda Rendulic, Assistant to the Dean, 412-396-6400, Fax: 412-396-5265, E-mail: rendulic@duq.edu.
Website: http://www.duq.edu/academics/schools/liberal-arts/graduate-school/programs/computational-math

Mathematics

East Carolina University, Graduate School, Thomas Harriot College of Arts and Sciences, Department of Mathematics, Greenville, NC 27858-4353. Offers mathematics (MA), including mathematics in the community college, statistics. *Program availability:* Part-time, evening/weekend. *Application deadline:* For fall admission, 6/1 priority date for domestic students, 2/1 priority date for international students; for spring admission, 10/15 priority date for domestic students, 10/1 priority date for international students. *Expenses: Tuition, area resident:* Full-time $4749. Tuition, state resident: full-time $4749. Tuition, nonresident: full-time $17,898. *International tuition:* $17,898 full-time. *Required fees:* $2787. Part-time tuition and fees vary according to course load and program. *Financial support:* Application deadline: 3/1. *Unit head:* Dr. Johannes H. Hattingh, Chair, 252-328-6461, E-mail: hattinghj@ecu.edu. *Application contact:* Graduate School Admissions, 252-328-6012, Fax: 252-328-6071, E-mail: gradschool@ecu.edu.
Website: http://www.ecu.edu/cs-cas/math/

Eastern Illinois University, Graduate School, College of Liberal Arts and Sciences, Department of Mathematics and Computer Science, Charleston, IL 61920. Offers elementary/middle school mathematics education (MA); mathematics (MA); secondary mathematics education (MA). *Program availability:* Part-time, evening/weekend. *Degree requirements:* For master's, comprehensive exam (for some programs), thesis (for some programs). *Entrance requirements:* For master's, GMAT or GRE. Additional exam requirements/recommendations for international students: Required—TOEFL (minimum score 500 paper-based; 61 iBT), IELTS (minimum score 6). Electronic applications accepted. *Expenses:* Tuition, state resident: part-time $299 per credit hour. Tuition, nonresident: part-time $718 per credit hour. *Required fees:* $214.50 per credit hour.

Eastern Kentucky University, The Graduate School, College of Arts and Sciences, Department of Mathematics and Statistics, Richmond, KY 40475-3102. Offers mathematical sciences (MS). *Program availability:* Part-time. *Degree requirements:* For master's, comprehensive exam. *Entrance requirements:* For master's, GRE General Test, minimum GPA of 2.5. *Faculty research:* Graph theory, number theory, ring theory, topology, statistics, Abstract Algebra.

Eastern Michigan University, Graduate School, College of Arts and Sciences, Department of Mathematics and Statistics, Ypsilanti, MI 48197. Offers MA. *Program availability:* Part-time, evening/weekend, online learning. *Faculty:* 25 full-time (9 women). *Students:* 9 full-time (3 women), 23 part-time (11 women); includes 7 minority (1 Black or African American, non-Hispanic/Latino; 2 Asian, non-Hispanic/Latino; 2 Hispanic/Latino; 2 Two or more races, non-Hispanic/Latino), 2 international. Average age 32. 29 applicants, 72% accepted, 9 enrolled. In 2018, 10 master's awarded. *Entrance requirements:* Additional exam requirements/recommendations for international students: Required—TOEFL. *Application deadline:* Applications are processed on a rolling basis. Application fee: $45. *Financial support:* Fellowships, research assistantships with full tuition reimbursements, teaching assistantships with full tuition reimbursements, career-related internships or fieldwork, Federal Work-Study, institutionally sponsored loans, scholarships/grants, tuition waivers (partial), and unspecified assistantships available. Support available to part-time students. Financial award applicants required to submit FAFSA. *Unit head:* Dr. Debra Ingram, Department Head, 734-487-1444, Fax: 734-487-2489, E-mail: dingra12@emich.edu. *Application contact:* Dr. Bingwu Wang, Graduate Advisor, 734-487-5044, Fax: 734-487-2489, E-mail: bwang@emich.edu.
Website: http://www.math.emich.edu

East Tennessee State University, School of Graduate Studies, College of Arts and Sciences, Department of Mathematics and Statistics, Johnson City, TN 37614. Offers mathematical modeling in bioscience (Postbaccalaureate Certificate); mathematical sciences (MS). *Program availability:* Part-time, evening/weekend. *Degree requirements:* For master's, comprehensive exam, thesis. *Entrance requirements:* For master's, GRE General Test, bachelor's degree in math or related area, three letters of recommendation. Additional exam requirements/recommendations for international students: Required—TOEFL (minimum score 550 paper-based; 79 iBT). Electronic applications accepted. *Faculty research:* Applied mathematics, applied statistics, discrete mathematics, graph theory, mathematics education, mathematical epidemiology, probability.

Elizabeth City State University, Department of Mathematics and Computer Science, Master of Science in Mathematics Program, Elizabeth City, NC 27909-7806. Offers applied mathematics (MS); community college teaching (MS); mathematics education (MS); remote sensing (MS). *Program availability:* Part-time, evening/weekend. *Degree requirements:* For master's, thesis. *Entrance requirements:* For master's, MAT and/or GRE, minimum GPA of 3.0, 3 letters of recommendation, two official transcripts from all undergraduate/graduate schools attended, typewritten one-page request for entry into program that includes description of student's educational preparation. Additional exam requirements/recommendations for international students: Required—TOEFL (minimum score 550 paper-based, 80 iBT) or IELTS (minimum score 6.5). Electronic applications accepted. *Faculty research:* Oceanic temperature effects, mathematics strategies in elementary schools, multimedia, Antarctic temperature mapping, computer networks, water quality, remote sensing, polar ice, satellite imagery.

Emory University, Laney Graduate School, Department of Mathematics and Computer Science, Atlanta, GA 30322-1100. Offers computer science (MS); computer science and informatics (PhD); mathematics (MS, PhD). Terminal master's awarded for partial completion of doctoral program. *Degree requirements:* For master's, thesis; for doctorate, one foreign language, comprehensive exam, thesis/dissertation. *Entrance requirements:* For master's and doctorate, GRE General Test. Additional exam requirements/recommendations for international students: Recommended—TOEFL. Electronic applications accepted.

Emporia State University, Department of Mathematics and Economics, Emporia, KS 66801-5415. Offers mathematics (MS). *Program availability:* Part-time, evening/weekend, online only, 100% online. *Degree requirements:* For master's, comprehensive exam or thesis. *Entrance requirements:* For master's, appropriate undergraduate degree. Additional exam requirements/recommendations for international students: Required—TOEFL (minimum score 520 paper-based; 68 iBT). Electronic applications accepted.

Fairfield University, College of Arts and Sciences, Fairfield, CT 06824. Offers American studies (MA); communication (MA); creative writing (MFA); mathematics (MS); public administration (MPA). *Program availability:* Part-time, evening/weekend, online learning. *Degree requirements:* For master's, capstone research course. *Entrance requirements:* For master's, minimum GPA of 3.0, 2 letters of recommendation, resume, personal statement. Additional exam requirements/recommendations for international students: Required—TOEFL (minimum score 550 paper-based; 80 iBT) or IELTS (minimum score 6.5). Electronic applications accepted. *Expenses:* Contact institution. *Faculty research:* Nutrition and physiology, media industries, community-based teaching and learning, non commutative algebra and partial differential equations, cancer research in biology and physics.

Fairleigh Dickinson University, Metropolitan Campus, University College: Arts, Sciences, and Professional Studies, School of Computer Sciences and Engineering, Program in Mathematical Foundation, Teaneck, NJ 07666-1914. Offers MS.

Florida Atlantic University, Charles E. Schmidt College of Science, Department of Mathematical Sciences, Boca Raton, FL 33431-0991. Offers applied mathematics and statistics (MS); mathematics (MST, PhD). *Program availability:* Part-time. *Faculty:* 36 full-time (7 women), 1 part-time/adjunct (0 women). *Students:* 20 full-time (7 women), 38 part-time (10 women); includes 23 minority (7 Black or African American, non-Hispanic/Latino; 3 Asian, non-Hispanic/Latino; 9 Hispanic/Latino; 4 Two or more races, non-Hispanic/Latino), 16 international. Average age 31. 47 applicants, 21% accepted, 10 enrolled. In 2018, 15 master's, 6 doctorates awarded. Terminal master's awarded for partial completion of doctoral program. *Entrance requirements:* For master's and doctorate, GRE General Test, minimum GPA of 3.0. Additional exam requirements/recommendations for international students: Required—TOEFL (minimum score 500 paper-based; 61 iBT), IELTS (minimum score 6). *Application deadline:* For fall admission, 7/1 priority date for domestic students, 2/15 priority date for international students; for spring admission, 11/1 priority date for domestic students, 7/15 priority date for international students. Applications are processed on a rolling basis. Application fee: $30. Electronic applications accepted. *Expenses: Tuition, area resident:* Full-time $7400; part-time $369.82 per credit. Tuition, state resident: full-time $7400; part-time $369.82 per credit. Tuition, nonresident: full-time $20,496; part-time $1024.81 per credit. *Financial support:* Fellowships, teaching assistantships, and Federal Work-Study available. Financial award application deadline: 4/1. *Faculty research:* Cryptography, statistics, algebra, analysis, combinatorics. *Application contact:* Sonia Clayton, 561-297-4629, E-mail: mathgraduate@fau.edu.
Website: http://www.math.fau.edu/

Florida Gulf Coast University, College of Arts and Sciences, Program in Mathematics, Fort Myers, FL 33965-6565. Offers MS. *Degree requirements:* For master's, comprehensive exam, research seminar. *Entrance requirements:* For master's, GRE. Additional exam requirements/recommendations for international students: Required—TOEFL (minimum score 550 paper-based). Electronic applications accepted.

Florida International University, College of Arts, Sciences, and Education, Department of Mathematics and Statistics, Miami, FL 33199. Offers mathematical sciences (MS); statistics (MS). *Program availability:* Part-time, evening/weekend. *Faculty:* 58 full-time (18 women), 37 part-time/adjunct (12 women). *Students:* 10 full-time (2 women), 7 part-time (2 women); includes 11 minority (all Hispanic/Latino), 6 international. Average age 30. 25 applicants, 48% accepted, 11 enrolled. In 2018, 10 master's awarded. *Degree requirements:* For master's, thesis or alternative, project. *Entrance requirements:* For master's, GRE General Test, minimum GPA of 3.0, letter of intent, letters of recommendation. Additional exam requirements/recommendations for international students: Required—TOEFL (minimum score 550 paper-based; 80 iBT). *Application deadline:* For fall admission, 6/1 for domestic students, 4/1 for international students; for spring admission, 10/1 for domestic students, 9/1 for international students. Applications are processed on a rolling basis. Application fee: $30. Electronic applications accepted. *Financial support:* Institutionally sponsored loans and scholarships/grants available. Financial award application deadline: 3/1; financial award applicants required to submit FAFSA. *Unit head:* Dr. Laura De Carli, Chair, 305-348-0278, Fax: 305-348-6158, E-mail: laura.decarli@fiu.edu. *Application contact:* Nanett Rojas, Manager, Admissions Operations, 305-348-7464, Fax: 305-348-7441, E-mail: gradadm@fiu.edu.
Website: http://mathstat.fiu.edu

George Mason University, College of Science, Department of Mathematical Sciences, Fairfax, VA 22030. Offers MS, PhD. *Faculty:* 37 full-time (12 women), 12 part-time/adjunct (4 women). *Students:* 29 full-time (9 women), 20 part-time (6 women); includes 10 minority (3 Black or African American, non-Hispanic/Latino; 5 Asian, non-Hispanic/Latino; 1 Hispanic/Latino; 1 Two or more races, non-Hispanic/Latino), 8 international. Average age 34. 61 applicants, 82% accepted, 14 enrolled. In 2018, 10 master's, 3 doctorates awarded. *Degree requirements:* For master's, comprehensive exam, thesis optional; for doctorate, comprehensive exam, thesis/dissertation. *Entrance requirements:* For master's, GRE, 3 letters of recommendation; official college transcripts; expanded goals statement; resume; for doctorate, GRE (recommended), master's degree in math or undergraduate coursework with math preparation with minimum GPA of 3.0 in last 60 credits; 2 copies of official transcripts; 3 letters of recommendation; expanded goals statement. Additional exam requirements/recommendations for international students: Required—TOEFL (minimum score 575 paper-based; 88 iBT), IELTS (minimum score 6.5), PTE (minimum score 59). Application fee: $75 ($80 for international students). Electronic applications accepted. *Financial support:* In 2018–19, 27 students received support, including 9 research assistantships with tuition reimbursements available (averaging $22,444 per year), 18 teaching assistantships with tuition reimbursements available (averaging $18,633 per year); career-related internships or fieldwork, Federal Work-Study, scholarships/grants, unspecified assistantships, and health care benefits (for full-time research or teaching assistantship recipients) also available. Support available to part-time students. Financial award application deadline: 3/1; financial award applicants required to submit FAFSA. *Faculty research:* Nonlinear dynamics and topology, with an emphasis on global bifurcations and chaos; numerical and theoretical methods of dynamical systems. *Total annual research expenditures:* $940,059. *Unit head:* David Walnut, Chair, 703-993-1478, Fax: 703-993-1491, E-mail: dwalnut@gmu.edu. *Application contact:* Flavia Colonna, Professor and Graduate Coordinator, 703-993-1465, E-mail: fcolonna@gmu.edu.
Website: http://math.gmu.edu/

Georgetown University, Graduate School of Arts and Sciences, Department of Mathematics and Statistics, Washington, DC 20057. Offers mathematics (MS); statistics (MS). *Program availability:* Part-time, evening/weekend. *Entrance requirements:* Additional exam requirements/recommendations for international students: Required—TOEFL or IELTS. Electronic applications accepted. *Faculty research:* Partial differential equations, mathematical biology, inverse problems, statistics.

The George Washington University, Columbian College of Arts and Sciences, Department of Mathematics, Washington, DC 20052. Offers applied mathematics (MS); financial mathematics (Graduate Certificate); mathematics (MA, PhD, Graduate Certificate). *Program availability:* Part-time, evening/weekend. *Students:* 29 full-time (10 women), 15 part-time (5 women); includes 9 minority (1 Black or African American, non-Hispanic/Latino; 4 Asian, non-Hispanic/Latino; 4 Hispanic/Latino), 21 international. Average age 27. 86 applicants, 73% accepted, 20 enrolled. In 2018, 7 master's, 6 doctorates awarded. Terminal master's awarded for partial completion of doctoral program. *Degree requirements:* For master's, comprehensive exam; for doctorate, one foreign language, thesis/dissertation, general exam. *Entrance requirements:* For master's and doctorate, GRE General Test, minimum GPA of 3.0, interview. Additional exam requirements/recommendations for international students: Required—TOEFL (minimum score 550 paper-based; 80 iBT). *Application deadline:* For fall admission, 1/15 priority date for domestic and international students; for spring admission, 10/1 priority

date for domestic students, 9/1 priority date for international students. Applications are processed on a rolling basis. Application fee: $75. Electronic applications accepted. *Financial support:* In 2018–19, 17 students received support. Fellowships with full tuition reimbursements available, teaching assistantships, Federal Work-Study, and tuition waivers available. Financial award application deadline: 1/15. *Unit head:* Frank Baginski, Chair, 202-994-6269, E-mail: baginski@gwu.edu. *Application contact:* Frank Baginski, Chair, 202-994-6269, E-mail: baginski@gwu.edu.
Website: http://math.columbian.gwu.edu/

Georgia Institute of Technology, Graduate Studies, College of Sciences, School of Mathematics, Atlanta, GA 30332-0001. Offers MS, PhD. *Program availability:* Part-time. Terminal master's awarded for partial completion of doctoral program. *Degree requirements:* For master's, thesis optional; for doctorate, one foreign language, comprehensive exam, thesis/dissertation. *Entrance requirements:* For master's, GRE General Test; for doctorate, GRE General Test, GRE Subject Test. Additional exam requirements/recommendations for international students: Required—TOEFL (minimum score 590 paper-based; 96 iBT). Electronic applications accepted. *Faculty research:* Dynamical systems, discrete mathematics, probability and statistics, mathematical physics.

Georgia Institute of Technology, Graduate Studies, Multidisciplinary Program in Algorithms, Combinatorics, and Optimization, Atlanta, GA 30332-0001. Offers PhD. Program offered jointly with College of Computing, School of Mathematics, and School of Industrial and Systems Engineering. *Program availability:* Part-time. *Degree requirements:* For doctorate, comprehensive exam, thesis/dissertation. *Entrance requirements:* For doctorate, GRE General Test, GRE Subject Test (computer science, mathematics or physics). Additional exam requirements/recommendations for international students: Required—TOEFL (minimum score 600 paper-based; 100 iBT). Electronic applications accepted. *Faculty research:* Complexity, graph minors, combinatorial optimization, mathematical programming, probabilistic methods.

Georgia Southern University, Jack N. Averitt College of Graduate Studies, College of Science and Mathematics, Program in Mathematics, Statesboro, GA 30458. Offers applied mathematics (MS). *Program availability:* Part-time. *Faculty:* 41 full-time (12 women). *Students:* 34 full-time (10 women), 3 part-time (1 woman); includes 6 minority (4 Black or African American, non-Hispanic/Latino; 2 Asian, non-Hispanic/Latino), 17 international. Average age 28. 22 applicants, 86% accepted, 12 enrolled. In 2018, 14 *Degree requirements:* For master's, comprehensive exam, thesis, terminal exam, project. *Entrance requirements:* For master's, GRE, BS in engineering, science, or mathematics; course work in calculus, probability, and linear algebra; proficiency in a computer programming language. Additional exam requirements/recommendations for international students: Required—TOEFL (minimum score 550 paper-based; 80 iBT), IELTS (minimum score 6). *Application deadline:* For fall admission, 3/1 priority date for domestic and international students; for spring admission, 10/1 priority date for domestic students, 10/1 for international students. Applications are processed on a rolling basis. Application fee: $50. Electronic applications accepted. *Expenses: Tuition, area resident:* Part-time $3324 per semester. Tuition, state resident: full-time $5814; part-time $3324 per semester. Tuition, nonresident: full-time $23,204; part-time $13,260 per semester. *Required fees:* $2092; $2092. Tuition and fees vary according to course load, degree level, campus/location and program. *Financial support:* In 2018–19, 28 students received support, including 23 teaching assistantships with full tuition reimbursements available (averaging $7,750 per year); career-related internships or fieldwork, Federal Work-Study, scholarships/grants, tuition waivers (full), and unspecified assistantships also available. Support available to part-time students. Financial award application deadline: 4/15; financial award applicants required to submit FAFSA. *Faculty research:* Algebra, number theory, and combinatorics; analysis and differential equations, approximation, optimization and computational mathematics; geometry and topology; mathematics education; statistics. *Total annual research expenditures:* $21,950. *Unit head:* Dr. Sabrina Hessinger, Interim Chair, 912-478-5132, Fax: 912-478-0654, E-mail: shessinger@georgiasouthern.edu.
Website: http://cosm.georgiasouthern.edu/math/student-resources/graduate-degree/

Georgia State University, College of Arts and Sciences, Department of Mathematics and Statistics, Atlanta, GA 30302-3083. Offers bioinformatics (MS, PhD); biostatistics (MS, PhD); discrete mathematics (MS); mathematics (MS, PhD); scientific computing (MS); statistics (MS). *Program availability:* Part-time. *Faculty:* 28 full-time (8 women), 1 part-time/adjunct (0 women). *Students:* 88 full-time (46 women), 15 part-time (8 women); includes 27 minority (7 Black or African American, non-Hispanic/Latino; 14 Asian, non-Hispanic/Latino; 4 Hispanic/Latino; 2 Two or more races, non-Hispanic/Latino), 57 international. Average age 32. 109 applicants, 65% accepted, 37 enrolled. In 2018, 29 master's, 11 doctorates awarded. Terminal master's awarded for partial completion of doctoral program. *Entrance requirements:* exam requirements/recommendations for international students: Required—TOEFL (minimum score 550 paper-based; 80 iBT). *Application deadline:* For fall admission, 7/1 priority date for domestic and international students; for spring admission, 11/15 priority date for domestic and international students. Application fee: $50. Electronic applications accepted. *Expenses: Tuition, area resident:* Full-time $9360; part-time $390 per credit hour. Tuition, state resident: full-time $9360; part-time $390 per credit hour. Tuition, nonresident: full-time $30,024; part-time $1251 per credit hour. *International tuition:* $30,024 full-time. $2128. *Financial support:* In 2018–19, fellowships with full tuition reimbursements (averaging $22,000 per year), research assistantships with full tuition reimbursements (averaging $9,000 per year), teaching assistantships with full tuition reimbursements (averaging $9,000 per year) were awarded; institutionally sponsored loans, scholarships/grants, health care benefits, and unspecified assistantships also available. Financial award application deadline: 2/1. *Faculty research:* Algebra, matrix theory, graph theory and combinatorics; applied mathematics and analysis; collegiate mathematics education; statistics, biostatistics and applications; bioinformatics, dynamical systems. *Unit head:* Dr. Guantao Chen, Chair, 404-413-6436, Fax: 404-413-6403, E-mail: gchen@gsu.edu. *Application contact:* Dr. Guantao Chen, Chair, 404-413-6436, Fax: 404-413-6403, E-mail: gchen@gsu.edu.
Website: https://www.mathstat.gsu.edu/

Governors State University, College of Arts and Sciences, Program in Mathematics, University Park, IL 60484. Offers actuarial science (MS). *Program availability:* Part-time. *Faculty:* 39 full-time (14 women), 29 part-time/adjunct (12 women). *Students:* 3 full-time (2 women), 20 part-time (13 women); includes 7 minority (5 Black or African American, non-Hispanic/Latino; 2 Hispanic/Latino). Average age 35. 13 applicants, 77% accepted, 7 enrolled. In 2018, 9 master's awarded. *Application deadline:* For fall admission, 4/1 for domestic students. Applications are processed on a rolling basis. Application fee: $50. Electronic applications accepted. *Financial support:* Application deadline: 5/1; applicants required to submit FAFSA. *Unit head:* Mary Carrington, Interim Chair, Division of Science, Mathematics, and Technology, 708-534-5000 Ext. 4532, E-mail: mcarrington@govst.edu. *Application contact:* Mary Carrington, Interim Chair, Division of Science, Mathematics, and Technology, 708-534-5000 Ext. 4532, E-mail:

The Graduate Center, City University of New York, Graduate Studies, Program in Mathematics, New York, NY 10016-4039. Offers PhD. *Degree requirements:* For doctorate, 2 foreign languages, thesis/dissertation. *Entrance requirements:* doctorate, GRE General Test. Additional exam requirements/recommendations for international students: Required—TOEFL. Electronic applications accepted.

Harvard University, Graduate School of Arts and Sciences, Department of Mathematics, Cambridge, MA 02138. Offers PhD. *Degree requirements:* For doctorate, 2 foreign languages, thesis/dissertation, qualifying exam. *Entrance requirements:* For doctorate, GRE General Test, GRE Subject Test. Additional exam requirements/recommendations for international students: Required—TOEFL.

Hofstra University, School of Education, Programs in Teacher Education, Hempstead, NY 11549. Offers bilingual education (MA); bilingual extension (Advanced Certificate); business education (MS Ed); curriculum studies (MS Ed); early childhood and childhood education (MS Ed); early childhood education (MA, MS Ed); educational technology (Advanced Certificate); elementary education (MA, MS Ed); English education (MS Ed); family and consumer science (MS Ed); fine arts and music education (Advanced Certificate); fine arts education (MS Ed); foreign language and TESOL (MS Ed); foreign language education (MA, MS Ed); languages other than English and teaching English as a second language (MA); learning and teaching (Ed D); mathematics education (MA, MS Ed); middle childhood extension (Advanced Certificate); music education (MA, MS Ed); science education (MA); secondary education (Advanced Certificate); social studies education (MA, MS Ed); teaching languages other than English and TESOL (MS Ed); technology for learning (MA); TESOL (MS Ed, Advanced Certificate); TESOL with specialization in STEM (MA); work based learning extension (Advanced Certificate). *Program availability:* Part-time, evening/weekend, blended/hybrid learning. *Students:* 138 full-time (94 women), 109 part-time (78 women); includes 66 minority (16 Black or African American, non-Hispanic/Latino; 17 Asian, non-Hispanic/Latino; 31 Hispanic/Latino; 2 Native Hawaiian or other Pacific Islander, non-Hispanic/Latino), 6 international. Average age 29. 217 applicants, 86% accepted, 113 enrolled. In 2018, 105 master's, 11 doctorates, 25 other advanced degrees awarded. *Degree requirements:* For master's, comprehensive exam, thesis (for some programs), exit project, student teaching, fieldwork, electronic portfolio, curriculum project, minimum GPA of 3.0; for doctorate, dissertation; for Advanced Certificate, 3 foreign languages, comprehensive exam (for some programs), thesis project. *Entrance requirements:* For master's, GRE, 2 letters of recommendation, portfolio, teacher certification (MA), interview, essay; for doctorate, GMAT, GRE, LSAT, or MAT; for Advanced Certificate, 2 letters of recommendation, essay, interview and/or portfolio, teaching certificate. Additional exam requirements/recommendations for international students: Required—TOEFL (minimum score 550 paper-based; 80 iBT). *Application deadline:* Applications are processed on a rolling basis. Application fee: $75. Electronic applications accepted. *Financial support:* In 2018–19, 86 students received support, including 51 fellowships with full and partial tuition reimbursements available (averaging $5,080 per year), 2 research assistantships with full and partial tuition reimbursements available (averaging $3,470 per year); career-related internships or fieldwork, Federal Work-Study, institutionally sponsored loans, scholarships/grants, traineeships, tuition waivers (full and partial), unspecified assistantships, and scholarships and endowed scholarships also available. Support available to part-time students. Financial award applicants required to submit FAFSA. *Faculty research:* Impact of memory on learning; brain function, cognitive-development, learning, and achievement; student activism and civic education; using children's literature to promote diversity; 2nd language acquisition. *Unit head:* Dr. Alan Singer, Chairperson, 516-463-5853, Fax: 516-463-6275, E-mail: alan.j.singer@hofstra.edu. *Application contact:* Sunil Samuel, Assistant Vice President of Admissions, 516-463-4723, Fax: 516-463-4664, E-mail: graduateadmission@hofstra.edu.
Website: http://www.hofstra.edu/education/

Houston Baptist University, College of Education and Behavioral Sciences, Programs in Education, Houston, TX 77074-3298. Offers bilingual education (M Ed); counselor education (M Ed); curriculum and instruction (M Ed); curriculum and instruction (EC-6 bilingual) (M Ed); curriculum and instruction in all-level art, Spanish, music, or physical education (M Ed); curriculum and instruction in EC-6 and special education (EC-12) (M Ed); curriculum and instruction in instructional technology (M Ed); curriculum and instruction in mathematics, science, or social studies (4-8) (M Ed); curriculum and instruction with EC-6 generalist (M Ed); curriculum and instruction with English language arts and reading (4-8) (M Ed); educational administration (M Ed); educational diagnostician (M Ed); executive educational leadership (Ed D); higher education in business management (M Ed); higher education in Christian studies (M Ed); higher education in counseling (M Ed); higher education in educational technology (M Ed); reading (M Ed); special educational leadership (Ed D). *Program availability:* Part-time, evening/weekend, 100% online, blended/hybrid learning. *Degree requirements:* For master's, comprehensive exam; for doctorate, thesis/dissertation. *Entrance requirements:* For master's, minimum GPA of 2.75, two recommendations, resume, bachelor's degree conferred transcript; interview (for non-certified teachers); for doctorate, GRE, 5 letters of recommendation. Additional exam requirements/recommendations for international students: Required—TOEFL (minimum score 80 iBT), IELTS (minimum score 6.5). Electronic applications accepted. Application fee is waived when completed online. *Expenses:* Contact institution. *Faculty research:* Autism and inclusion, integrating technology into instruction, school change and leadership trust.

Houston Baptist University, School of Humanities, Program in Liberal Arts, Houston, TX 77074-3298. Offers education (EC-12 art, music, physical education, or Spanish) (MLA); education (EC-6 generalist) (MLA); general liberal arts (MLA); specialization in education (4-8 or 7-12) (MLA). *Program availability:* Part-time, evening/weekend. *Entrance requirements:* For master's, minimum GPA of 2.5, essay/personal statement, resume, bachelor's degree transcript. Additional exam requirements/recommendations for international students: Required—TOEFL (minimum score 80 iBT), IELTS (minimum score 6.5). Electronic applications accepted. Application fee is waived when completed online. *Expenses:* Contact institution.

Howard University, Graduate School, Department of Mathematics, Washington, DC 20059-0002. Offers applied mathematics (MS, PhD); mathematics (MS, PhD). *Program availability:* Part-time. Terminal master's awarded for partial completion of doctoral program. *Degree requirements:* For master's, comprehensive exam, thesis or alternative, qualifying exam; for doctorate, 2 foreign languages, comprehensive exam, thesis/dissertation, qualifying exams. *Entrance requirements:* For master's, GRE General Test, minimum GPA of 3.0; for doctorate, GRE General Test. Additional exam requirements/recommendations for international students: Required—TOEFL. Electronic applications accepted.

Hunter College of the City University of New York, Graduate School, School of Arts and Sciences, Department of Mathematics and Statistics, New York, NY 10065-5085. Offers adolescent mathematics education (MA); applied mathematics (MA); bioinformatics (MA); pure mathematics (MA); statistics (MA). *Program availability:* Part-time, evening/weekend. *Degree requirements:* For master's, one foreign language, comprehensive exam, thesis (for some programs). *Entrance requirements:* For master's,

GRE General Test, 24 credits in mathematics. Additional exam requirements/recommendations for international students: Required—TOEFL. *Faculty research:* Data analysis, dynamical systems, computer graphics, topology, statistical decision theory.

Idaho State University, Graduate School, College of Science and Engineering, Department of Mathematics and Statistics, Pocatello, ID 83209-8085. Offers mathematics (MS, DA); mathematics for secondary teachers (MA). *Program availability:* Part-time. *Degree requirements:* For master's, comprehensive exam, thesis (for some programs), oral and written exams; for doctorate, comprehensive exam, thesis/dissertation, teaching internships. *Entrance requirements:* For master's, GRE General Test, GRE Subject Test, course work in modern algebra, differential equations, advanced calculus, introductory analysis; for doctorate, GRE General Test, GRE Subject Test, minimum graduate GPA of 3.5, MS in mathematics, teaching experience, 3 letters of recommendation. Additional exam requirements/recommendations for international students: Required—TOEFL (minimum score 550 paper-based; 80 iBT). Electronic applications accepted. *Faculty research:* Algebra, analysis geometry, statistics, applied mathematics.

Illinois State University, Graduate School, College of Arts and Sciences, Department of Mathematics, Program in Mathematics, Normal, IL 61790. Offers MA, MS. *Faculty:* 47 full-time (26 women), 14 part-time/adjunct (5 women). *Students:* 32 full-time (15 women), 3 part-time (all women); includes 6 minority (1 Black or African American, non-Hispanic/Latino; 1 Asian, non-Hispanic/Latino; 2 Hispanic/Latino; 2 Two or more races, non-Hispanic/Latino), 19 international. Average age 30. 109 applicants, 94% accepted, 35 enrolled. In 2018, 20 master's awarded. *Degree requirements:* For master's, thesis or alternative. *Entrance requirements:* For master's, GRE General Test, minimum GPA of 2.8 in last 60 hours of course work. *Application deadline:* Applications are processed on a rolling basis. Application fee: $40. *Expenses: Tuition, area resident:* Full-time $7264.62. Tuition, state resident: full-time $9466. Tuition, nonresident: full-time $17,290. *International tuition:* $15,089.40 full-time. *Required fees:* $1481.04. *Financial support:* In 2018–19, 30 teaching assistantships were awarded; tuition waivers (full) and unspecified assistantships also available. Financial award application deadline: 4/1. *Unit head:* Dr. George Seelinger, Department Chair, 309-438-8781, E-mail: gfseeli@IllinoisState.edu. *Application contact:* Dr. Amin Bahmanian, Graduate Coordinator, 309-438-7707, E-mail: mbahman@IllinoisState.edu.

Indiana State University, College of Graduate and Professional Studies, College of Arts and Sciences, Department of Mathematics and Computer Science, Terre Haute, IN 47809. Offers computer science (MS); mathematics (MA, MS). *Program availability:* Part-time. *Degree requirements:* For master's, thesis or alternative. *Entrance requirements:* For master's, 24 semester hours of course work in undergraduate mathematics. Electronic applications accepted.

Indiana University Bloomington, University Graduate School, College of Arts and Sciences, Department of Mathematics, Bloomington, IN 47405. Offers applied mathematics (MA); mathematical physics (PhD); mathematics education (MAT); pure mathematics (MA, PhD). Terminal master's awarded for partial completion of doctoral program. *Degree requirements:* For doctorate, one foreign language, thesis/dissertation. *Entrance requirements:* For master's and doctorate, GRE General Test, GRE Subject Test. Additional exam requirements/recommendations for international students: Required—TOEFL. Electronic applications accepted. *Expenses:* Contact institution. *Faculty research:* Topology, geometry, algebra, applied mathematics, analysis.

Indiana University of Pennsylvania, School of Graduate Studies and Research, College of Natural Sciences and Mathematics, Department of Mathematics, Indiana, PA 15705. Offers applied mathematics (MS); elementary and middle school mathematics education (M Ed); secondary mathematics education (M Ed). *Program availability:* Part-time. *Faculty:* 11 full-time (4 women). *Students:* 8 full-time (3 women), 27 part-time (16 women); includes 3 minority (1 Black or African American, non-Hispanic/Latino; 1 Asian, non-Hispanic/Latino; 1 Two or more races, non-Hispanic/Latino), 2 international. Average age 29. 23 applicants, 87% accepted, 8 enrolled. In 2018, 17 master's awarded. *Degree requirements:* For master's, thesis optional. *Entrance requirements:* For master's, 2 letters of recommendation. Additional exam requirements/recommendations for international students: Required—TOEFL (minimum score 540 paper-based). *Application deadline:* Applications are processed on a rolling basis. Application fee: $50. Electronic applications accepted. *Expenses:* Tuition, state resident: full-time $12,384; part-time $516 per credit hour. Tuition, nonresident: full-time $18,576; part-time $774 per credit hour. *Required fees:* $4454; $186 per credit hour. $65 per semester. Tuition and fees vary according to program and reciprocity agreements. *Financial support:* In 2018–19, 5 research assistantships with tuition reimbursements (averaging $4,500 per year) were awarded; fellowships with partial tuition reimbursements, career-related internships or fieldwork, Federal Work-Study, scholarships/grants, and unspecified assistantships also available. Support available to part-time students. Financial award application deadline: 4/15; financial award applicants required to submit FAFSA. *Unit head:* Dr. Francisco E Alarcon, Chairperson, 724-357-2608, E-mail: falarcon@iup.edu. *Application contact:* Dr. Yu-Ju Kuo, Graduate Coordinator, 724-357-3797, E-mail: yjkuo@iup.edu.
Website: http://www.iup.edu/math

Indiana University–Purdue University Indianapolis, School of Science, Department of Mathematical Sciences, Indianapolis, IN 46202-3216. Offers mathematics (MS, PhD), including applied mathematics, applied statistics (MS), mathematical statistics (PhD), mathematics, mathematics education (MS). *Program availability:* Part-time, evening/weekend. *Degree requirements:* For master's, thesis optional; for doctorate, one foreign language, comprehensive exam, thesis/dissertation. *Entrance requirements:* For doctorate, GRE General Test (recommended). Additional exam requirements/recommendations for international students: Required—TOEFL (minimum score 79 iBT), IELTS (minimum score 6.5), GRE General Test. Electronic applications accepted. *Faculty research:* Mathematical physics, integral systems, partial differential equations, noncommutative geometry, biomathematics, computational neuroscience.

Instituto Tecnologico de Santo Domingo, Graduate School, Area of Basic And Environmental Sciences, Santo Domingo, Dominican Republic. Offers environmental science (M En S), including environmental education, environmental management, marine resources, natural resources management; mathematics (MS, PhD); renewable energy technology (MS, Certificate).

Iowa State University of Science and Technology, Department of Mathematics, Ames, IA 50011. Offers applied mathematics (MS, PhD); mathematics (MS, PhD); school mathematics (MSM). *Degree requirements:* For master's, thesis or alternative; for doctorate, thesis/dissertation. *Entrance requirements:* For master's and doctorate, GRE General Test. Additional exam requirements/recommendations for international students: Required—TOEFL (minimum score 550 paper-based; 79 iBT), IELTS (minimum score 6.5). Electronic applications accepted.

Jackson State University, Graduate School, College of Science, Engineering and Technology, Department of Mathematics and Statistical Sciences, Jackson, MS 39217. Offers applied mathematics (MS); mathematics education (MST); pure mathematics (MS). *Program availability:* Part-time, evening/weekend. *Degree requirements:* For master's, comprehensive exam, thesis (for some programs). *Entrance requirements:* For master's, GRE General Test. Additional exam requirements/recommendations for international students: Required—TOEFL (minimum score 520 paper-based; 67 iBT).

Jacksonville State University, Graduate Studies, School of Science, Program in Mathematics, Jacksonville, AL 36265-1602. Offers MS. *Program availability:* Part-time, evening/weekend. *Degree requirements:* For master's, comprehensive exam, thesis (for some programs). *Entrance requirements:* For master's, GRE General Test or MAT. Additional exam requirements/recommendations for international students: Required—TOEFL (minimum score 500 paper-based; 61 iBT). Electronic applications accepted.

Jacksonville University, College of Arts and Sciences, MA in Mathematics Program, Jacksonville, FL 32211. Offers MA. *Program availability:* Part-time. *Degree requirements:* For master's, comprehensive exam, minimum 30 credit hours (thesis); 36 credit hours including 6 credit hours outside department (non-thesis). *Entrance requirements:* For master's, official transcripts of academic work, statement of intent, resume, three letters of recommendation, interview with program advisor, demonstration of adequate understanding of basic differential and integral calculus, successful completion of calculus I and II. Additional exam requirements/recommendations for international students: Required—TOEFL (minimum score 540 paper-based; 76 iBT). Electronic applications accepted. *Expenses:* Contact institution. *Faculty research:* Teaching of college mathematics, particularly college calculus.

John Carroll University, Graduate Studies, Department of Mathematics, University Heights, OH 44118. Offers MA. *Program availability:* Part-time, evening/weekend. *Degree requirements:* For master's, research essay. *Entrance requirements:* Additional exam requirements/recommendations for international students: Required—TOEFL. *Application deadline:* Applications are processed on a rolling basis. Application fee: $0. Electronic applications accepted. *Expenses: Tuition:* Full-time $13,140; part-time $730 per credit hour. Tuition and fees vary according to program. *Financial support:* Scholarships/grants and unspecified assistantships available. Financial award applicants required to submit FAFSA. *Faculty research:* Algebraic topology, algebra, differential geometry, combinatorics, Lie groups. *Unit head:* Dr. Barbara K D'Ambrosia, Chair, 216-397-4682, Fax: 216-397-3033, E-mail: bdambrosia@jcu.edu. *Application contact:* Colleen K. Sommerfeld, Assistant Dean for Graduate Admission & Retention, 216-397-4902, Fax: 216-297-1835, E-mail: csommerfeld@jcu.edu.
Website: http://sites.jcu.edu/graduatestudies/pages/graduate-programs/masters-programs/mathematics/

Johns Hopkins University, Zanvyl Krieger School of Arts and Sciences, Department of Mathematics, Baltimore, MD 21218. Offers PhD. *Faculty:* 29 full-time (5 women). *Students:* 34 full-time (8 women). 97 applicants, 32% accepted, 17 enrolled. In 2018, 3 doctorates awarded. *Degree requirements:* For doctorate, thesis/dissertation, 3 qualifying exams. *Entrance requirements:* For doctorate, GRE General Test, GRE Subject Test. Additional exam requirements/recommendations for international students: Required—TOEFL (minimum score 600 paper-based; 100 iBT), IELTS. *Application deadline:* For fall admission, 12/15 for domestic and international students. Application fee: $75. Electronic applications accepted. *Financial support:* In 2018–19, 32 students received support, including 32 teaching assistantships with full tuition reimbursements available; fellowships with full tuition reimbursements available, research assistantships, Federal Work-Study, and institutionally sponsored loans also available. Financial award application deadline: 4/15; financial award applicants required to submit FAFSA. *Faculty research:* Algebraic geometry, number theory, algebraic topology, differential geometry, partial differential equations. *Unit head:* Dr. David Savitt, Chair, 410-516-7688, E-mail: savitt@math.jhu.edu. *Application contact:* Richard Helman, Director of Graduate Admissions, 410-516-7125, E-mail: rhelman@jhu.edu.
Website: http://www.mathematics.jhu.edu/

Kansas State University, Graduate School, College of Arts and Sciences, Department of Mathematics, Manhattan, KS 66506. Offers MS, PhD, Graduate Certificate. *Program availability:* Part-time. Terminal master's awarded for partial completion of doctoral program. *Degree requirements:* For master's, thesis or alternative; for doctorate, one foreign language, thesis/dissertation. *Entrance requirements:* For master's and doctorate, bachelor's degree in mathematics; 21 semester hours of work beyond the calculus level; minimum B average in courses taken in mathematics and in all work taken during one's last two years of university study. Additional exam requirements/recommendations for international students: Required—TOEFL (minimum score 550 paper-based; 79 iBT); Recommended—IELTS (minimum score 6.5), TSE (minimum score 58). Electronic applications accepted. *Faculty research:* Low-dimensional topology, geometry, complex and harmonic analysis, group and representation theory, noncommunicative spaces.

Kent State University, College of Arts and Sciences, Department of Mathematical Sciences, Kent, OH 44242-0001. Offers applied mathematics (MA, MS, PhD); mathematics for secondary teachers (MA); pure mathematics (MA, MS, PhD). *Program availability:* Part-time. *Faculty:* 23 full-time (7 women). *Students:* 84 full-time (33 women), 39 part-time (17 women); includes 7 minority (2 Black or African American, non-Hispanic/Latino; 4 Asian, non-Hispanic/Latino; 1 Hispanic/Latino), 43 international. Average age 31. 66 applicants, 79% accepted, 12 enrolled. In 2018, 16 master's, 10 doctorates awarded. *Degree requirements:* For master's, comprehensive exam (for some programs), thesis (for some programs); for doctorate, comprehensive exam, thesis/dissertation. *Entrance requirements:* For master's, bachelor's degree with proficiency in numerical analysis and statistics, goal statement, resume or vita, 3 letters of recommendation; for doctorate, official transcript(s), goal statement, three letters of recommendation, resume or vita, passage of the departmental qualifying examination at the master's level. Additional exam requirements/recommendations for international students: Required—TOEFL (minimum score 525 paper-based, 71 iBT), Michigan English Language Assessment Battery (minimum score 74), IELTS (minimum score 6.0) or PTE (minimum score 50). *Application deadline:* For fall admission, 5/1 for domestic and international students; for spring admission, 10/1 for domestic and international students; for summer admission, 2/1 for domestic and international students. Applications are processed on a rolling basis. Application fee: $45 ($70 for international students). Electronic applications accepted. *Expenses:* Tuition, state resident: full-time $11,766; part-time $536 per credit. Tuition, nonresident: full-time $21,952; part-time $999 per credit. *International tuition:* $21,952 full-time. Tuition and fees vary according to course load. *Financial support:* Fellowships with full tuition reimbursements, research assistantships with full tuition reimbursements, teaching assistantships with full tuition reimbursements, scholarships/grants, and unspecified assistantships available. Financial award application deadline: 1/31. *Unit head:* Dr. Andrew Tonge, Professor and Chair, 330-672-9046, E-mail: atonge@kent.edu. *Application contact:* Artem Zvavitch, Professor and Graduate Coordinator, 330-672-3316, E-mail: zvavitch@math.kent.edu.
Website: http://www.kent.edu/math/

Kent State University, College of Education, Health and Human Services, School of Teaching, Learning and Curriculum Studies, Kent, OH 44242-0001. Offers career technical teacher education (M Ed); curriculum and instruction (M Ed, PhD, Ed S); early

childhood education (M Ed, MA, MAT); junior high/middle school (M Ed, MA); math specialization (M Ed, MA); reading specialization (M Ed, MA); secondary education (MAT). *Program availability:* Part-time, evening/weekend. *Faculty:* 43 full-time (25 women), 7 part-time/adjunct (6 women). *Students:* 116 full-time (88 women), 110 part-time (83 women); includes 23 minority (6 Black or African American, non-Hispanic/Latino; 1 American Indian or Alaska Native, non-Hispanic/Latino; 13 Asian, non-Hispanic/Latino; 1 Hispanic/Latino; 2 Native Hawaiian or other Pacific Islander, non-Hispanic/Latino), 17 international. 202 applicants, 35% accepted. In 2018, 71 master's, 13 doctorates, 2 other advanced degrees awarded. *Degree requirements:* For master's, thesis (for some programs); for doctorate, comprehensive exam, thesis/dissertation. *Entrance requirements:* For doctorate and Ed S, GRE General Test. Additional exam requirements/recommendations for international students. Required—TOEFL (minimum score 550 paper-based; 80 iBT). *Application deadline:* Applications are processed on a rolling basis. Application fee: $45 ($60 for international students). Electronic applications accepted. *Expenses:* Tuition, state resident: full-time $11,766; part-time $536 per credit. Tuition, nonresident: full-time $21,952; part-time $999 per credit. *International tuition:* $21,952 full-time. Tuition and fees vary according to course load. *Financial support:* In 2018–19, 21 research assistantships with full tuition reimbursements (averaging $12,642 per year), 3 teaching assistantships with full tuition reimbursements (averaging $13,500 per year) were awarded; Federal Work-Study, scholarships/grants, unspecified assistantships, and 3 administrative assistantships (averaging $10,500 per year) also available. Financial award application deadline: 4/1. *Unit head:* Dr. Alexa Sandmann, Director, 330-672-0652, E-mail: asandmann@kent.edu. *Application contact:* Cheryl Slusarczyk, Academic Program Director, Office of Graduate Student Services, 330-672-2576, Fax: 330-672-9162, E-mail: ogs@kent.edu.
Website: http://www.kent.edu/ehhs/tlcs/

Kutztown University of Pennsylvania, College of Education, Program in Secondary Education, Kutztown, PA 19530-0730. Offers biology (M Ed); curriculum and instruction (M Ed); English (M Ed); mathematics (M Ed); middle level (M Ed); social studies (M Ed); teaching (M Ed); transformational teaching and learning (Ed D). *Accreditation:* NCATE. *Program availability:* Part-time, evening/weekend, 100% online, blended/hybrid learning. *Faculty:* 5 full-time (3 women), 3 part-time/adjunct (0 women). *Students:* 25 full-time (16 women), 80 part-time (51 women); includes 8 minority (1 Black or African American, non-Hispanic/Latino; 5 Hispanic/Latino; 2 Two or more races, non-Hispanic/Latino), 1 international. Average age 32. 86 applicants, 93% accepted, 45 enrolled. In 2018, 3,531 master's awarded. *Degree requirements:* For master's, comprehensive exam, thesis optional; for doctorate, thesis/dissertation. *Entrance requirements:* For master's, GRE General Test, minimum undergraduate major GPA of 3.0, 3 letters of recommendation, copy of PRAXIS II or valid instructional I or II teaching certificate; for doctorate, master's or specialist degree in education or related field from regionally-accredited institution of higher learning with minimum graduate GPA of 3.25, significant educational experience, employment in an education setting (preferred). Additional exam requirements/recommendations for international students: Required—TOEFL (minimum score 550 paper-based, 79 iBT), IELTS (minimum score 6.5), or PTE (minimum score 53). *Application deadline:* For fall admission, 8/1 for domestic and international students; for spring admission, 12/1 for domestic and international students. Application fee: $35. Electronic applications accepted. *Expenses:* Tuition, state resident: part-time $516 per credit. Tuition, nonresident: part-time $774 per credit. *Required fees:* $119 per credit. One-time fee: $50 part-time. Tuition and fees vary according to degree level. *Financial support:* Career-related internships or fieldwork, Federal Work-Study, scholarships/grants, and unspecified assistantships available. Financial award application deadline: 3/1; financial award applicants required to submit FAFSA. *Unit head:* Dr. Georgeos Sirrakos, Department Chair, 610-683-4279, Fax: 610-683-1338, E-mail: sirrakos@kutztown.edu. *Application contact:* Dr. Patricia Walsh Coates, Graduate Coordinator, 610-638-4289, Fax: 610-683-1338, E-mail: coates@kutztown.edu.
Website: https://www.kutztown.edu/academcs/graduate-programs/secondary-education.htm

Lakehead University, Graduate Studies, School of Mathematical Sciences, Thunder Bay, ON P7B 5E1, Canada. Offers computer science (M Sc); mathematical science (MA). *Program availability:* Part-time, evening/weekend. *Degree requirements:* For master's, thesis optional. *Entrance requirements:* For master's, minimum B average, honours degree in mathematics or computer science. Additional exam requirements/recommendations for international students: Required—TOEFL. *Faculty research:* Numerical analysis, classical analysis, theoretical computer science, abstract harmonic analysis, functional analysis.

Lamar University, College of Graduate Studies, College of Arts and Sciences, Department of Mathematics, Beaumont, TX 77710. Offers MS. *Faculty:* 25 full-time (8 women), 15 part-time/adjunct (8 women). *Students:* 14 full-time (3 women), 1 part-time (0 women); includes 2 minority (1 Asian, non-Hispanic/Latino; 1 Hispanic/Latino), 5 international. Average age 28. 13 applicants, 100% accepted, 8 enrolled. In 2018, 6 master's awarded. *Degree requirements:* For master's, comprehensive exam (for some programs), thesis optional. *Entrance requirements:* For master's, GRE General Test, minimum GPA of 2.5 in last 60 hours of undergraduate course work. Additional exam requirements/recommendations for international students: Required—TOEFL (minimum score 550 paper-based; 79 iBT), IELTS (minimum score 6.5). *Application deadline:* Applications are processed on a rolling basis. Application fee: $25 ($50 for international students). Electronic applications accepted. *Expenses:* Tuition, state resident: full-time $6234; part-time $346 per credit hour. Tuition, nonresident: full-time $6852; part-time $761 per credit hour. *International tuition:* $6852 full-time. *Required fees:* $1940; $327 per credit hour. Tuition and fees vary according to course load, campus/location, program and reciprocity agreements. *Financial support:* In 2018–19, 4 students received support, including 4 teaching assistantships (averaging $12,000 per year); fellowships and research assistantships also available. Financial award application deadline: 4/1. *Faculty research:* Complex analysis, differential equations, algebra, topology statistics. *Total annual research expenditures:* $7,203. *Unit head:* Dr. Jeremy Alm, Department Chair, 409-880-8792, Fax: 409-880-8794, E-mail: chair@math.lamar.edu. *Application contact:* Celeste Contreas, Director, Admissions and Academic Services, 409-880-8888, Fax: 409-880-7419, E-mail: gradmissions@lamar.edu.
Website: http://artssciences.lamar.edu/mathematics

Lee University, Program in Education, Cleveland, TN 37320-3450. Offers art (MAT); curriculum and instruction (M Ed, Ed S); early childhood (MAT); educational leadership (M Ed, Ed S); elementary education (MAT); English and math (MAT); English and science (MAT); English and social studies (MAT); higher education administration (MS); history (MAT); history and economics (MAT); math and science (MAT); math and social studies (MAT); middle grades (MAT); science and social studies (MASW); secondary education (MAT); Spanish (MAT); special education (M Ed, MAT); TESOL (MAT). *Accreditation:* NCATE. *Program availability:* Part-time. *Faculty:* 13 full-time (5 women), 13 part-time/adjunct (7 women). *Students:* 32 full-time (26 women), 73 part-time (49 women); includes 13 minority (10 Black or African American, non-Hispanic/Latino; 3 Two or more races, non-Hispanic/Latino), 3 international. Average age 30. 56 applicants, 73% accepted, 34 enrolled. In 2018, 60 master's, 3 other advanced degrees awarded.

Degree requirements: For master's, variable foreign language requirement, thesis optional, internship. *Entrance requirements:* For master's, MAT or GRE General Test, minimum undergraduate GPA of 2.75, 3 letters of recommendation, interview, writing sample, official transcripts, background check; for Ed S, minimum undergraduate and master's GPA of 2.75, official transcripts for undergraduate and master's degrees. Additional exam requirements/recommendations for international students: Required—TOEFL (minimum score 61 iBT). *Application deadline:* For fall admission, 6/1 priority date for domestic and international students; for spring admission, 11/1 priority date for domestic and international students; for summer admission, 4/1 priority date for domestic and international students. Applications are processed on a rolling basis. Application fee: $25. Electronic applications accepted. *Financial support:* In 2018–19, 43 students received support. Career-related internships or fieldwork, Federal Work-Study, institutionally sponsored loans, scholarships/grants, and unspecified assistantships available. Financial award application deadline: 3/1; financial award applicants required to submit FAFSA. *Unit head:* Dr. William Kamm, Director, 423-614-8544, E-mail: wkamm@leeuniversity.edu. *Application contact:* Jeffery McGirt, Director of Graduate Enrollment, 423-614-8691, Fax: 423-614-8317, E-mail: jmcgirt@leeuniversity.edu.
Website: http://www.leeuniversity.edu/academics/graduate/education

Lehigh University, College of Arts and Sciences, Department of Mathematics, Bethlehem, PA 18015. Offers applied mathematics (MS, PhD); mathematics (MS, PhD); statistics (MS). *Program availability:* Part-time. *Faculty:* 23 full-time (5 women). *Students:* 37 full-time (10 women), 4 part-time (1 woman); includes 4 minority (1 Black or African American, non-Hispanic/Latino; 1 Asian, non-Hispanic/Latino; 1 Hispanic/Latino; 1 Two or more races, non-Hispanic/Latino), 22 international. Average age 24. 127 applicants, 53% accepted, 13 enrolled. In 2018, 14 master's, 3 doctorates awarded. Terminal master's awarded for partial completion of doctoral program. *Degree requirements:* For master's, comprehensive exam, thesis optional; for doctorate, comprehensive exam, thesis/dissertation, qualifying examination, general examination, advanced topic examination. *Entrance requirements:* For master's and doctorate, GRE General Test (strongly recommended), minimum undergraduate GPA of 2.75, 3.0 for last two semesters; adequate background in math. Additional exam requirements/recommendations for international students: Required—TOEFL. *Application deadline:* For fall admission, 1/1 for domestic and international students; for spring admission, 12/1 for domestic and international students. Application fee: $75. Electronic applications accepted. *Expenses:* $1500 per credit. *Financial support:* In 2018–19, 35 students received support, including fellowships with full tuition reimbursements available (averaging $25,000 per year), 2 research assistantships with full tuition reimbursements available (averaging $21,800 per year), 26 teaching assistantships with full tuition reimbursements available (averaging $21,500 per year); scholarships/grants and tuition waivers (full and partial) also available. Support available to part-time students. Financial award application deadline: 1/1. *Faculty research:* Probability and statistics, geometry and topology, algebra, discrete mathematics, differential equations. *Total annual research expenditures:* $173,233. *Unit head:* Dr. Garth Isaak, Chairman, 610-758-3732, Fax: 610-758-3767, E-mail: gisaak@lehigh.edu. *Application contact:* Dr. Robert Neel, Graduate Director, 610-758-5531, E-mail: robert.neel@lehigh.edu.
Website: http://www.math.cas2.lehigh.edu/graduate-programs-mathematics

Lehman College of the City University of New York, School of Natural and Social Sciences, Department of Mathematics and Computer Science, Program in Mathematics, Bronx, NY 10468-1589. Offers MA. *Program availability:* Part-time, evening/weekend. *Degree requirements:* For master's, one foreign language, thesis or alternative.

Louisiana State University and Agricultural & Mechanical College, Graduate School, College of Science, Department of Mathematics, Baton Rouge, LA 70803. Offers MS, PhD.

Louisiana Tech University, Graduate School, College of Education, Ruston, LA 71272. Offers counseling and guidance (MA), including clinical mental health counseling, human services, orientation and mobility; counseling psychology (PhD); curriculum and instruction (M Ed); cyber education (Graduate Certificate); dynamics of domestic and family violence (Graduate Certificate); early childhood education - PreK-3 (MAT); educational leadership (M Ed, Ed D); elementary education and special education mild/moderate grades 1-5 (MAT); higher education administration (Graduate Certificate); industrial/organizational psychology (MA, PhD); kinesiology (MS); middle school education (MAT), including mathematics; orientation and mobility (Graduate Certificate); rehabilitation teaching for the blind (Graduate Certificate); secondary education (MAT), including agriculture, biology, business, chemistry, English; special education: visually impaired (MAT); teacher leader education (Graduate Certificate); visual impairments - blind education (Graduate Certificate). *Accreditation:* NCATE. *Program availability:* Part-time. *Degree requirements:* For master's, thesis; for doctorate, thesis/dissertation. *Entrance requirements:* For master's and doctorate, GRE General Test. Additional exam requirements/recommendations for international students: Required—TOEFL (minimum score 550 paper-based; 80 iBT), IELTS (minimum score 6.5). Electronic applications accepted. *Faculty research:* Blindness and the best methods for increasing independence for individuals who are blind or visually impaired; educating and investigating factors contributing to improvements in human performance across the lifespan and a reduction in injury rates during training.

Louisiana Tech University, Graduate School, College of Engineering and Science, Ruston, LA 71272. Offers applied physics (MS); biomedical engineering (PhD); computer science (MS); engineering (MS, PhD), including cyberspace engineering (PhD), engineering education (PhD), engineering physics (PhD), materials and infrastructure systems (PhD), micro/nanoscale systems (PhD); engineering and technology management (MS); mathematics (MS); molecular science and nanotechnology (MS, PhD). *Program availability:* Part-time-only. Terminal master's awarded for partial completion of doctoral program. *Degree requirements:* For master's, thesis (for some programs); for doctorate, thesis/dissertation. *Entrance requirements:* For master's and Graduate Certificate, GRE General Test, minimum GPA of 3.0 in last 60 hours. Additional exam requirements/recommendations for international students: Required—TOEFL (minimum score 550 paper-based; 80 iBT), IELTS (minimum score 6.5). Electronic applications accepted. *Faculty research:* Trenchless technology, micromanufacturing, radionuclide transport, microbial liquefaction, hazardous waste treatment.

Loyola University Chicago, Graduate School, Department of Mathematics and Statistics, Chicago, IL 60660. Offers applied statistics (MS); mathematics (MS). *Program availability:* Part-time. *Faculty:* 19 full-time (3 women). *Students:* 41 full-time (21 women), 7 part-time (1 woman); includes 10 minority (1 Black or African American, non-Hispanic/Latino; 7 Asian, non-Hispanic/Latino; 1 Hispanic/Latino; 1 Two or more races, non-Hispanic/Latino), 9 international. Average age 26. 69 applicants, 62% accepted, 22 enrolled. In 2018, 28 master's awarded. *Entrance requirements:* For master's, GRE General Test. Additional exam requirements/recommendations for international students: Required—TOEFL (minimum score 550 paper-based; 79 iBT), IELTS (minimum score 6.5). *Application deadline:* For fall admission, 8/1 for domestic students; for spring admission, 12/1 for domestic students. Applications are processed on a rolling

Peterson's Graduate Programs in the Physical Sciences, Mathematics, Agricultural Sciences, the Environment & Natural Resources 2020

www.petersons.com 215

basis. Application fee: $0. Electronic applications accepted. *Expenses:* Contact institution. *Financial support:* In 2018–19, 12 students received support, including 4 fellowships with full and partial tuition reimbursements available (averaging $12,000 per year), 6 teaching assistantships with tuition reimbursements available (averaging $10,000 per year); career-related internships or fieldwork, Federal Work-Study, institutionally sponsored loans, and tuition waivers (partial) also available. Financial award application deadline: 3/15; financial award applicants required to submit FAFSA. *Faculty research:* Nonlinear analysis and partial differential equations, algebra and combinatorics, knot theory, control theory and engineering, probability and applied statistics. *Total annual research expenditures:* $70,000. *Unit head:* Dr. Timothy O'Brien, Graduate Program Director for Applied Statistics, 773-508-2129, Fax: 773-508-2123, E-mail: tobrie1@luc.edu. *Application contact:* Dr. Rafal Goebel, Graduate Program Director for Mathematics, 773-508-3558, E-mail: rgoebel1@luc.edu.
Website: http://www.luc.edu/math/

Manhattan College, Graduate Programs, School of Education and Health, Program in Special Education, Riverdale, NY 10471. Offers adolescence education students with disabilities generalist extension in English or math or social studies - grades 7-12 (MS Ed); bilingual education (Advanced Certificate); dual childhood/students with disabilities - grades 1-6 (MS Ed); students with disabilities - grades 1-6 (MS Ed). *Program availability:* Part-time, evening/weekend. *Degree requirements:* For master's, thesis, internship (if not certified). *Entrance requirements:* For master's, GRE, minimum GPA of 3.0. Additional exam requirements/recommendations for international students: Required—TOEFL (minimum score 550 paper-based; 80 iBT), IELTS (minimum score 6). Electronic applications accepted. Application fee is waived when completed online. *Expenses:* Contact institution.

Manhattan College, Graduate Programs, School of Science, Program in Mathematics, Riverdale, NY 10471. Offers MS. *Program availability:* Part-time. *Faculty:* 14 full-time (7 women). *Students:* 1 (woman) full-time, all international. Average age 24. 5 applicants, 80% accepted, 1 enrolled. *Degree requirements:* For master's, comprehensive exam, research seminar. *Entrance requirements:* Additional exam requirements/recommendations for international students: Required—TOEFL (minimum score 550 paper-based; 80 iBT), IELTS (minimum score 6.5), TOEFL or IELTS. *Application deadline:* Applications are processed on a rolling basis. Application fee: $75. Electronic applications accepted. *Expenses:* *Financial support:* Unspecified assistantships available. *Faculty research:* Algebra, topology, hyperbolic geometry, operations research, statistics and modeling. *Unit head:* Dr. Constantine Theodosiou, Dean, 718-862-7368, E-mail: constantine.theodosiou@manhattan.edu. *Application contact:* Doina Lawler, Assistant Director of Graduate Admissions, 718-862-8649, E-mail: dlawler01@manhattan.edu.

Manhattanville College, School of Education, Jump Start Program, Purchase, NY 10577-2132. Offers childhood education and special education (grades 1-6) (MPS); early childhood education (birth-grade 2) (MAT); education (Advanced Certificate); English and special education (grades 5-12) (MPS); mathematics and special education (grades 5-12) (MPS); science and special education (grades 5-12) (MPS); social studies and special education (grades 5-12) (MPS); Spanish (grades 7-12) (MAT); tesol - teaching English as a second language (all grades) (MPS). *Program availability:* Part-time, evening/weekend. *Faculty:* 11 full-time (7 women), 78 part-time/adjunct (50 women). *Students:* 3 full-time (2 women), 16 part-time (11 women); includes 5 minority (1 Black or African American, non-Hispanic/Latino; 3 Hispanic/Latino; 1 Native Hawaiian or other Pacific Islander, non-Hispanic/Latino). Average age 31. 48 applicants, 54% accepted, 22 enrolled. In 2018, 23 master's, 1 other advanced degree awarded. *Degree requirements:* For master's, comprehensive exam (for some programs), thesis (for some programs), student teaching, research seminars, portfolios, internships, writing assessment; for Advanced Certificate, comprehensive exam (for some programs). *Entrance requirements:* For master's, for programs leading to certification, candidates must submit scores from GRE or MAT(miller analogies test), minimum undergraduate GPA of 3.0, all transcripts from all colleges and universities attended, 2 letters of recommendation, interview, essay (2-3 page personal statement that describes reasons for choosing education as profession and personal philosophy of education), proof of immunization (for those born after 1957). Additional exam requirements/recommendations for international students: Required—TOEFL (minimum score 600 paper-based; 110 iBT); Recommended—IELTS (minimum score 8). *Application deadline:* Applications are processed on a rolling basis. Application fee: $75. Electronic applications accepted. *Expenses:* 935 per credit. *Financial support:* Teaching assistantships, career-related internships or fieldwork, Federal Work-Study, institutionally sponsored loans, scholarships/grants, and unspecified assistantships available. Financial award application deadline: 3/15; financial award applicants required to submit FAFSA. *Faculty research:* Early childhood and technology, professional development schools and community schools, students with emotional difficulties, literacy and adolescents, mindfulness, changing suburbs institute, and community schools, studying the effects of the environment on special populations, the most difficult cases, students who are presented with multiple challenges: learning, behavioral and ACE experiences who see criminal behavior as a way to cope; working on giving them the tools they need to succeed. *Unit head:* Dr. Shelley Wepner, Dean, 914-323-3153, E-mail: Shelly.Wepner@mville.edu. *Application contact:* Alissa Wilson, Director, SOE Graduate Enrollment Management, 914-323-3150, Fax: 914-694-1732, E-mail: edschool@mville.edu.
Website: http://www.mville.edu/programs/jump-start

Manhattanville College, School of Education, Program in Middle Childhood/Adolescence Education (Grades 5-12), Purchase, NY 10577-2132. Offers biology and special education (MPS); chemistry and special education (MPS); education for sustainability (Advanced Certificate); English and special education (MPS); literacy and special education (MPS); literacy specialist (MPS); math and special education (MPS); mathematics (Advanced Certificate); middle childhood/adolescence ed science (biology or chemistry grades 5-12) or (physics grades 7-12) (MAT), middle childhood/adolescence education (grades 5-12) English (MAT, Advanced Certificate); middle childhood/adolescence education (grades 5-12) mathematics (MAT, Advanced Certificate); middle childhood/adolescence education (grades 5-12) science (biology chemistry, physics, earth science) (Advanced Certificate); middle childhood/adolescence education (grades 5-12) social studies (MAT, Advanced Certificate); physics (MAT, Advanced Certificate); social studies (MAT); social studies and special education (MPS); special education generalist (MPS). *Program availability:* Part-time, evening/weekend. *Faculty:* 3 full-time (2 women), 9 part-time/adjunct (4 women). *Students:* 11 full-time (6 women), 17 part-time (12 women); includes 3 minority (1 Black or African American, non-Hispanic/Latino; 2 Hispanic/Latino). Average age 31. 17 applicants, 71% accepted, 7 enrolled. In 2018, 8 master's, 3 other advanced degrees awarded. *Degree requirements:* For master's, comprehensive exam (for some programs), thesis (for some programs), student teaching, research seminars, portfolios, internships, writing assessment; for Advanced Certificate, comprehensive exam (for some programs). *Entrance requirements:* For master's, for programs leading to certification, candidates must submit scores from GRE or MAT(Miller Analogies Test), minimum undergraduate GPA of 3.0, all transcripts from all colleges and universities attended, 2 letters of recommendation, interview, essay (2-3 page personal statement that describes reasons for choosing education as profession and personal philosophy of education), proof of immunization (for those born after 1957). Additional exam requirements/recommendations for international students: Required—TOEFL (minimum score 600 paper-based; 110 iBT); Recommended—IELTS (minimum score 8). *Application deadline:* Applications are processed on a rolling basis. Application fee: $75. Electronic applications accepted. *Expenses:* 935 per credit. *Financial support:* Teaching assistantships, career-related internships or fieldwork, Federal Work-Study, institutionally sponsored loans, scholarships/grants, and unspecified assistantships available. Financial award application deadline: 3/15; financial award applicants required to submit FAFSA. *Faculty research:* Education for sustainability. *Unit head:* Dr. Shelley Wepner, Dean, 914-323-3153, Fax: 914-323-5493, E-mail: Shelley.Wepner@mville.edu. *Application contact:* Alissa Wilson, Director, Graduate Admissions, 914-323-3150, Fax: 914-694-1732, E-mail: edschool@mville.edu.
Website: http://www.mville.edu/programs#/search/19

Marquette University, Graduate School, College of Arts and Sciences, Department of Mathematics, Statistics, and Computer Science, Milwaukee, WI 53201-1881. Offers bioinformatics (MS); computational sciences (MS, PhD); computing (MS); mathematics education (MS). *Program availability:* Part-time, evening/weekend, online learning. Terminal master's awarded for partial completion of doctoral program. *Degree requirements:* For master's, thesis (for some programs), essay with oral presentation; for doctorate, comprehensive exam, thesis/dissertation, qualifying examination. *Entrance requirements:* For master's, official transcripts from all current and previous colleges/universities except Marquette, three letters of recommendation; for doctorate, GRE General Test, official transcripts from all current and previous colleges/universities except Marquette, three letters of recommendation. Additional exam requirements/recommendations for international students: Required—TOEFL (minimum score 530 paper-based). Electronic applications accepted. *Faculty research:* Models of physiological systems, mathematical immunology, computational group theory, mathematical logic, computational science.

Marshall University, Academic Affairs Division, College of Science, Department of Mathematics, Huntington, WV 25755. Offers MA. *Degree requirements:* For master's, thesis (for some programs). *Entrance requirements:* For master's, GRE General Test.

Marygrove College, Graduate Studies, Detroit, MI 48221-2599. Offers autism spectrum disorders (M Ed, Certificate); curriculum instruction and assessment (MAT); educational leadership (MA); educational technology (M Ed); effective teaching in the 21st century-classroom focus (MAT); effective teaching in the 21st century-technology focus (MAT); human resource management (MA, Certificate); mathematics 6-8 (MAT); mathematics K-5 (MAT); reading and literacy K-6 (MAT); reading specialist (M Ed); school administrator (Certificate); social justice (MA); special education (MAT); special education - learning disabilities (M Ed); teaching - pre-elementary education (M Ed); teaching - pre-secondary education (M Ed). *Program availability:* Part-time, evening/weekend, 100% online, blended/hybrid learning. *Entrance requirements:* For master's, all official bachelor's transcripts. Additional exam requirements/recommendations for international students: Required—TOEFL (minimum score 550 paper-based; 80 iBT). Electronic applications accepted.

Massachusetts Institute of Technology, School of Science, Department of Mathematics, Cambridge, MA 02139. Offers PhD. *Degree requirements:* For doctorate, one foreign language, comprehensive exam, thesis/dissertation. *Entrance requirements:* For doctorate, GRE General Test, GRE Subject Test. Additional exam requirements/recommendations for international students: Required—IELTS. Electronic applications accepted. *Expenses: Tuition:* Full-time $51,520; part-time $800 per credit hour. *Required fees:* $312. *Faculty research:* Analysis, geometry and topology; algebra and number theory; representation theory; combinatorics, theoretical computer science and computational biology; physical applied mathematics and computational science.

McGill University, Faculty of Graduate and Postdoctoral Studies, Faculty of Science, Department of Mathematics and Statistics, Montréal, QC H3A 2T5, Canada. Offers computational science and engineering (M Sc); mathematics and statistics (M Sc, MA, PhD), including applied mathematics (M Sc, MA), pure mathematics (M Sc, MA), statistics (M Sc, MA).

McMaster University, School of Graduate Studies, Faculty of Science, Department of Mathematics and Statistics, Hamilton, ON L8S 4M2, Canada. Offers mathematics (M Sc, PhD); statistics (M Sc), including applied statistics, medical statistics, statistical theory. *Program availability:* Part-time. *Degree requirements:* For master's, thesis or alternative, oral exam; for doctorate, comprehensive exam, thesis/dissertation. *Entrance requirements:* For master's, minimum B+ average in last year of honors degree; for doctorate, minimum B+ average, M Sc in mathematics or statistics. Additional exam requirements/recommendations for international students: Required—TOEFL (minimum score 550 paper-based). *Faculty research:* Algebra, analysis, applied mathematics, geometry and topology, probability and statistics.

McNeese State University, Doré School of Graduate Studies, College of Science and Agriculture, Department of Mathematical Sciences, Lake Charles, LA 70609. Offers computer science (MS); mathematics (MS); statistics (MS). *Program availability:* Evening/weekend. *Degree requirements:* For master's, comprehensive exam, thesis or alternative, written exam. *Entrance requirements:* For master's, GRE.

Memorial University of Newfoundland, School of Graduate Studies, Department of Mathematics and Statistics, St. John's, NL A1C 5S7, Canada. Offers mathematics (M Sc, PhD); statistics (M Sc, MAS, PhD). *Program availability:* Part-time. *Degree requirements:* For master's, thesis, practicum and report (MAS); for doctorate, comprehensive exam, thesis/dissertation, oral defense of thesis. *Entrance requirements:* For master's, 2nd class honors degree (MAS, M Sc); for doctorate, MAS or M Sc in mathematics and statistics. Electronic applications accepted. *Faculty research:* Algebra, topology, applied mathematics, mathematical statistics, applied statistics and probability.

Mercer University, Graduate Studies, Macon Campus, Tift College of Education (Macon), Macon, GA 31207. Offers curriculum and instruction (PhD); early childhood education (M Ed, Ed S); educational leadership (M Ed, PhD, Ed S), including higher education (PhD), P-12; higher education leadership (M Ed); independent and charter school leadership (M Ed); secondary education (MAT), including STEM; teacher leadership (Ed S). *Accreditation:* NCATE. *Program availability:* Part-time, evening/weekend, 100% online, blended/hybrid learning. *Degree requirements:* For master's, research project report; for doctorate, comprehensive exam, thesis/dissertation. *Entrance requirements:* For master's, GRE or MAT, minimum GPA of 2.75; for doctorate, GRE, minimum GPA of 3.5; interview; writing sample; 3 recommendations; for Ed S, GRE or MAT, minimum GPA of 3.5 (for teacher leadership), 3.0 (for educational leadership). Additional exam requirements/recommendations for international students: Required—TOEFL (minimum score 80 iBT). Electronic applications accepted. *Expenses:* Contact institution. *Faculty research:* Teacher effectiveness, specific learning disabilities, inclusion.

Miami University, College of Arts and Science, Department of Mathematics, Oxford, OH 45056. Offers MA, MAT, MS. *Faculty:* 30 full-time (8 women). *Students:* 19 full-time (8 women), 8 part-time (7 women); includes 1 minority (Hispanic/Latino), 8 international. Average age 26. In 2018, 12 master's awarded. *Unit head:* Dr. Patrick Dowling, Department Chair, 513-529-5831, E-mail: dowlinpn@miamioh.edu. *Application contact:* Dr. Paul Larson, Director of Graduate Studies, 513-529-9248, E-mail: larsonpb@miamioh.edu.
Website: http://www.MiamiOH.edu/mathematics

Michigan State University, The Graduate School, College of Natural Science, Department of Mathematics, East Lansing, MI 48824. Offers applied mathematics (MS, PhD); industrial mathematics (MS); mathematics (MAT, MS, PhD). *Entrance requirements:* Additional exam requirements/recommendations for international students: Required—TOEFL. Electronic applications accepted.

Michigan Technological University, Graduate School, College of Sciences and Arts, Department of Mathematical Sciences, Houghton, MI 49931. Offers MS, PhD. *Program availability:* Part-time, 100% online, blended/hybrid learning. *Faculty:* 36 full-time (12 women), 4 part-time/adjunct. *Students:* 41 full-time (19 women), 2 part-time; includes 1 minority (Two or more races, non-Hispanic/Latino), 31 international. Average age 28. 108 applicants, 51% accepted, 16 enrolled. In 2018, 10 master's, 8 doctorates awarded. Terminal master's awarded for partial completion of doctoral program. *Degree requirements:* For master's, comprehensive exam (for some programs), thesis (for some programs); for doctorate, comprehensive exam, thesis/dissertation, qualifying exam. *Entrance requirements:* For master's and doctorate, GRE (Michigan Tech students exempt), statement of purpose, personal statement, official transcripts, 3 letters of recommendation, resume/curriculum vitae. Additional exam requirements/recommendations for international students: Required—TOEFL (recommended minimum score 79 iBT) or IELTS (recommended minimum score of 6.5) required. *Application deadline:* For fall admission, 2/15 priority date for domestic and international students. Applications are processed on a rolling basis. Electronic applications accepted. *Expenses: Tuition, area resident:* Full-time $18,126; part-time $1007 per credit. Tuition, state resident: full-time $18,126; part-time $1007 per credit. Tuition, nonresident: full-time $18,126; part-time $1007 per credit. *International tuition:* $18,126 full-time. *Required fees:* $248; $124 per semester. Tuition and fees vary according to course load and program. *Financial support:* In 2018–19, 41 students received support, including 4 fellowships with tuition reimbursements available (averaging $16,590 per year), 7 research assistantships with tuition reimbursements available (averaging $16,590 per year), 27 teaching assistantships with tuition reimbursements available (averaging $16,590 per year); career-related internships or fieldwork, Federal Work-Study, scholarships/grants, health care benefits, unspecified assistantships, and cooperative program also available. Financial award application deadline: 2/15; financial award applicants required to submit FAFSA. *Faculty research:* Fluid dynamics, mathematical modeling, design theory, coding theory, statistical genetics, computational mathematics, numerical analysis, econometrics, algebra, combinatorics. *Total annual research expenditures:* $274,499. *Unit head:* Dr. Mark S. Gockenbach, Chair, 906-487-2068, Fax: 906-487-3133, E-mail: msgocken@mtu.edu. *Application contact:* Dr. Qiuying Sha, Professor, 906-487-2146, Fax: 906-487-3133, E-mail: qsha@mtu.edu.
Website: http://www.mtu.edu/math/

Middle Tennessee State University, College of Graduate Studies, College of Basic and Applied Sciences, Department of Mathematical Sciences, Murfreesboro, TN 37132. Offers mathematics (MS, MST). *Program availability:* Part-time, evening/weekend, online learning. *Degree requirements:* For master's, comprehensive exam, thesis optional. *Entrance requirements:* For master's, GRE General Test or MAT. Additional exam requirements/recommendations for international students: Required—TOEFL (minimum score 525 paper-based; 71 iBT) or IELTS (minimum score 6). Electronic applications accepted.

Minnesota State University Mankato, College of Graduate Studies and Research, College of Science, Engineering and Technology, Department of Mathematics and Statistics, Program in Mathematics, Mankato, MN 56001. Offers mathematics (MA); mathematics education (MS). *Degree requirements:* For master's, one foreign language, comprehensive exam (for some programs), thesis or alternative. *Entrance requirements:* For master's, GRE General Test, minimum GPA of 3.0 during previous 2 years. Additional exam requirements/recommendations for international students: Required—TOEFL. Electronic applications accepted.

Mississippi College, Graduate School, College of Arts and Sciences, School of Science and Mathematics, Department of Mathematics, Clinton, MS 39058. Offers M Ed, MCS, MS. *Program availability:* Part-time. *Degree requirements:* For master's, comprehensive exam, thesis optional. *Entrance requirements:* For master's, GRE or NTE, minimum GPA of 2.5. Additional exam requirements/recommendations for international students: Recommended—TOEFL, IELTS. Electronic applications accepted.

Mississippi State University, College of Arts and Sciences, Department of Mathematics and Statistics, Mississippi State, MS 39762. Offers mathematical sciences (PhD); mathematics (MS); statistics (MS). *Program availability:* Part-time. *Faculty:* 19 full-time (4 women). *Students:* 40 full-time (16 women), 3 part-time (1 woman); includes 4 minority (2 Black or African American, non-Hispanic/Latino; 2 Asian, non-Hispanic/Latino), 25 international. Average age 29. 54 applicants, 57% accepted, 10 enrolled. In 2018, 10 master's, 1 doctorate awarded. Terminal master's awarded for partial completion of doctoral program. *Degree requirements:* For master's, thesis optional, comprehensive oral or written exam; for doctorate, one foreign language, thesis/dissertation, comprehensive oral and written exam. *Entrance requirements:* For master's, minimum GPA of 2.75 on last two years of undergraduate courses; for doctorate, GRE. Additional exam requirements/recommendations for international students: Required—TOEFL (minimum score 477 paper-based; 53 iBT); Recommended—IELTS (minimum score 4.5). *Application deadline:* For fall admission, 3/15 priority date for domestic students, 5/1 for international students; for spring admission, 11/1 for domestic students, 9/1 for international students. Applications are processed on a rolling basis. Application fee: $60 ($80 for international students). Electronic applications accepted. *Expenses:* Tuition, state resident: full-time $8450; part-time $360.59 per credit hour. Tuition, nonresident: full-time $23,140; part-time $969.09 per credit hour. *Required fees:* $110. One-time fee: $55 full-time. Part-time tuition and fees vary according to course load, degree level, campus/location and reciprocity agreements. *Financial support:* In 2018–19, 29 teaching assistantships with full tuition reimbursements (averaging $14,738 per year) were awarded; Federal Work-Study, institutionally sponsored loans, tuition waivers (partial), and unspecified assistantships also available. Financial award application deadline: 4/1; financial award applicants required to submit FAFSA. *Faculty research:* Differential equations, algebra, numerical analysis, functional analysis, applied statistics. *Total annual research expenditures:* $1.3 million. *Unit head:* Dr. Mohsen Razzaghi, Professor and Head, 662-325-3414, Fax: 662-325-0005, E-mail: razzaghi@math.msstate.edu. *Application contact:* Nathan Drake, Admissions and Enrollment Assistant, 662-325-3804, E-mail: ndrake@grad.msstate.edu.
Website: http://www.math.msstate.edu

Missouri State University, Graduate College, College of Natural and Applied Sciences, Department of Mathematics, Springfield, MO 65897. Offers mathematics (MS); natural and applied science (MNAS), including mathematics (MNAS, MS Ed); secondary education (MS Ed), including mathematics (MNAS, MS Ed). *Program availability:* Part-time. *Faculty:* 21 full-time (4 women). *Students:* 13 full-time (4 women), 15 part-time (10 women); includes 2 minority (1 American Indian or Alaska Native, non-Hispanic/Latino; 1 Hispanic/Latino), 6 international. Average age 24. 18 applicants, 56% accepted. In 2018, 11 master's awarded. *Degree requirements:* For master's, comprehensive exam, thesis or alternative. *Entrance requirements:* For master's, GRE (MS, MNAS), minimum undergraduate GPA of 3.0 (MS, MNAS), 9-12 teacher certification (MS Ed). Additional exam requirements/recommendations for international students: Required—TOEFL (minimum score 550 paper-based; 79 iBT), IELTS (minimum score 6). *Application deadline:* For fall admission, 7/20 priority date for domestic students, 5/1 for international students; for spring admission, 12/20 priority date for domestic students, 9/1 for international students. Applications are processed on a rolling basis. Application fee: $55 ($60 for international students). Electronic applications accepted. Tuition and fees vary according to class time, course level, course load, degree level, campus/location, program and student level. *Financial support:* In 2018–19, 11 teaching assistantships with full tuition reimbursements (averaging $10,672 per year) were awarded; Federal Work-Study, institutionally sponsored loans, scholarships/grants, and unspecified assistantships also available. Financial award application deadline: 1/31; financial award applicants required to submit FAFSA. *Faculty research:* Harmonic analysis, commutative algebra, number theory, K-theory, probability. *Unit head:* Dr. William Bray, Department Head, 417-836-5112, Fax: 417-836-6966, E-mail: mathematics@missouristate.edu. *Application contact:* Lakan Drinker, Director, Graduate Enrollment Management, 417-836-5330, Fax: 417-836-6200, E-mail: lakandrinker@missouristate.edu.
Website: http://math.missouristate.edu/

Missouri University of Science and Technology, Department of Mathematics and Statistics, Rolla, MO 65401. Offers applied mathematics (MS); mathematics (MST, PhD), including mathematics (PhD), mathematics education (MST), statistics (PhD). Terminal master's awarded for partial completion of doctoral program. *Degree requirements:* For master's, thesis or alternative; for doctorate, one foreign language, thesis/dissertation. *Entrance requirements:* For master's and doctorate, GRE General Test, GRE Subject Test. Additional exam requirements/recommendations for international students: Required—TOEFL (minimum score 550 paper-based). Electronic applications accepted. *Expenses:* Tuition, state resident: full-time $7545.60; part-time $419.20 per credit hour. Tuition, nonresident: full-time $22,169; part-time $1231.60 per credit hour. *International tuition:* $23,518.80 full-time. *Required fees:* $4523.05. Full-time tuition and fees vary according to course load, campus/location, program and reciprocity agreements. *Faculty research:* Analysis, differential equations, topology, statistics.

Montana State University, The Graduate School, College of Letters and Science, Department of Mathematical Sciences, Bozeman, MT 59717. Offers mathematics (MS, PhD), including mathematics education option (MS); statistics (MS, PhD). *Program availability:* Part-time, online learning. *Degree requirements:* For master's, comprehensive exam, thesis (for some programs); for doctorate, comprehensive exam, thesis/dissertation. *Entrance requirements:* For master's and doctorate, GRE General Test. Additional exam requirements/recommendations for international students: Required—TOEFL (minimum score 550 paper-based). Electronic applications accepted. *Faculty research:* Applied mathematics, dynamical systems, statistics, mathematics education, mathematical and computational biology.

Montclair State University, The Graduate School, College of Science and Mathematics, Program in Mathematics, Montclair, NJ 07043-1624. Offers mathematics education (MS); pure and applied mathematics (MS). *Program availability:* Part-time, evening/weekend. *Degree requirements:* For master's, comprehensive exam. *Entrance requirements:* For master's, GRE General Test, 2 letters of recommendation, essay. Additional exam requirements/recommendations for international students: Required—TOEFL (minimum score 83 iBT), IELTS (minimum score 6.5). Electronic applications accepted. *Faculty research:* Computation, applied analysis.

Morgan State University, School of Graduate Studies, School of Computer, Mathematical, and Natural Sciences, Department of Mathematics, Baltimore, MD 21251. Offers industrial and computational mathematics (PhD); mathematics (MA). *Program availability:* Part-time, evening/weekend. *Degree requirements:* For master's, comprehensive exam, thesis. *Entrance requirements:* For master's, GRE. Additional exam requirements/recommendations for international students: Required—TOEFL (minimum score 550 paper-based). *Faculty research:* Number theory, semigroups, analysis, operations research.

Murray State University, Jesse D. Jones College of Science, Engineering and Technology, Department of Mathematics and Statistics, Murray, KY 42071. Offers mathematics (MA, MS); mathematics teacher leader (MAT). *Program availability:* Part-time. *Entrance requirements:* For master's, GRE or GMAT, minimum university GPA of 2.75. Additional exam requirements/recommendations for international students: Required—TOEFL (minimum score 527 paper-based; 71 iBT). Electronic applications accepted.

New Jersey Institute of Technology, College of Science and Liberal Arts, Newark, NJ 07102. Offers applied mathematics (MS); applied physics (MS, PhD); applied statistics (MS, Certificate); biology (MS, PhD); biostatistics (MS); chemistry (MS, PhD); environmental and sustainability policy (MS); environmental science (MS, PhD); history (MA, MAT); materials science and engineering (MS, PhD); mathematical and computational finance (MS); mathematical sciences (PhD); pharmaceutical chemistry (MS); professional and technical communications (MS); technical communication essentials (Certificate). *Program availability:* Part-time, evening/weekend. *Faculty:* 150 full-time (43 women), 115 part-time/adjunct (47 women). *Students:* 200 full-time (79 women), 63 part-time (29 women); includes 61 minority (17 Black or African American, non-Hispanic/Latino; 29 Asian, non-Hispanic/Latino; 11 Hispanic/Latino; 4 Two or more races, non-Hispanic/Latino), 136 international. Average age 28. 429 applicants, 49% accepted, 89 enrolled. In 2018, 43 master's, 16 doctorates, 2 other advanced degrees awarded. Terminal master's awarded for partial completion of doctoral program. *Degree requirements:* For master's, thesis (for some programs); for doctorate, thesis/dissertation. *Entrance requirements:* For master's and doctorate, GRE General Test, Minimum GPA of 3.0, personal statement, three (3) letters of recommendation, and transcripts. Additional exam requirements/recommendations for international students: Required—TOEFL (minimum score 550 paper-based; 79 iBT), IELTS (minimum score 6.5). *Application deadline:* For fall admission, 6/1 priority date for domestic students, 5/1 priority date for international students; for spring admission, 11/15 priority date for domestic and international students. Applications are processed on a rolling basis. Application fee: $75. Electronic applications accepted. *Expenses:* $22,690 per year (in-state), $32,136 per year (out-of-state). *Financial support:* In 2018–19, 134 students received support, including 17 fellowships with full tuition reimbursements available (averaging $22,000 per year), 74 research assistantships with full tuition reimbursements available (averaging $22,000 per year), 71 teaching assistantships with

full tuition reimbursements available (averaging $22,000 per year); scholarships/grants, traineeships, health care benefits, and unspecified assistantships also available. Financial award application deadline: 1/15. *Faculty research:* Biophotonics and bioimaging, morphogenetic patterning, embryogenesis, biological fluid dynamics, applied research in the mathematical sciences. *Total annual research expenditures:* $29.2 million. *Unit head:* Dr. Kevin Belfield, Dean, 973-596-3676, Fax: 973-565-0586, E-mail: kevin.d.belfield@njit.edu. *Application contact:* Stephen Eck, Director of Admissions, 973-596-3300, Fax: 973-596-3461, E-mail: admissions@njit.edu.
Website: http://csla.njit.edu/

New Mexico Institute of Mining and Technology, Center for Graduate Studies, Department of Mathematics, Socorro, NM 87801. Offers applied and industrial mathematics (PhD); industrial mathematics (MS); mathematics (MS); operations research and statistics (MS). *Degree requirements:* For master's, thesis optional; for doctorate, thesis/dissertation. *Entrance requirements:* For master's, GRE General Test. Additional exam requirements/recommendations for international students: Required—TOEFL (minimum score 540 paper-based). *Faculty research:* Applied mathematics, differential equations, industrial mathematics, numerical analysis, stochastic processes.

New York University, Graduate School of Arts and Science, Courant Institute of Mathematical Sciences, Department of Mathematics, New York, NY 10012-1019. Offers mathematics (MS); mathematics and statistics/operations research (MS); mathematics in finance (MS); scientific computing (MS). *Program availability:* Part-time, evening/weekend. *Students:* 195 full-time (78 women), 55 part-time (9 women); includes 32 minority (1 Black or African American, non-Hispanic/Latino; 21 Asian, non-Hispanic/Latino; 7 Hispanic/Latino; 3 Two or more races, non-Hispanic/Latino), 208 international. Average age 25. 1,477 applicants, 27% accepted, 122 enrolled. In 2018, 86 master's, 12 doctorates awarded. *Degree requirements:* For master's, thesis optional; for doctorate, one foreign language, thesis/dissertation, oral and written exams. *Entrance requirements:* For master's, GRE General Test, GRE Subject Test; for doctorate, GRE General Test, GRE Subject Test (recommended). Additional exam requirements/recommendations for international students: Required—TOEFL, IELTS. *Application deadline:* For fall admission, 1/4 for domestic and international students; for spring admission, 12/1 for domestic and international students. Application fee: $110. *Financial support:* Fellowships, research assistantships, teaching assistantships, Federal Work-Study, institutionally sponsored loans, scholarships/grants, health care benefits, and unspecified assistantships available. Financial award application deadline: 1/4; financial award applicants required to submit FAFSA. *Faculty research:* Partial differential equations, computational science, applied mathematics, geometry and topology, probability and stochastic processes. *Unit head:* Fedor Bogomolov, Director of Graduate Studies, 212-998-3238, Fax: 212-995-4121, E-mail: admissions@math.nyu.edu. *Application contact:* Tamar Arnon, Graduate Program Administrator, 212-998-3238, Fax: 212-995-4121, E-mail: admissions@math.nyu.edu.
Website: http://www.math.nyu.edu/

See Close-Up on page 253.

North Carolina Agricultural and Technical State University, The Graduate College, College of Science and Technology, Department of Mathematics, Greensboro, NC 27411. Offers applied mathematics (MS), including secondary education; mathematics (MAT). *Accreditation:* NCATE (one or more programs are accredited). *Program availability:* Part-time, evening/weekend. *Degree requirements:* For master's, comprehensive exam, thesis or alternative, qualifying exam. *Entrance requirements:* For master's, GRE General Test, minimum GPA of 3.0.

North Carolina Central University, College of Arts and Sciences, Department of Mathematics and Physics, Durham, NC 27707-3129. Offers mathematics (MS); physics (MS). *Program availability:* Part-time, evening/weekend. *Degree requirements:* For master's, one foreign language, comprehensive exam, thesis. *Entrance requirements:* For master's, minimum GPA of 3.0 in major, 2.5 overall. Additional exam requirements/recommendations for international students: Required—TOEFL.

North Carolina State University, Graduate School, College of Agriculture and Life Sciences and College of Engineering and College of Sciences, Program in Financial Mathematics, Raleigh, NC 27695. Offers MFM. *Program availability:* Part-time. *Degree requirements:* For master's, thesis optional, project/internship. *Entrance requirements:* For master's, GRE General Test. Additional exam requirements/recommendations for international students: Required—TOEFL (minimum score 550 paper-based). Electronic applications accepted. *Faculty research:* Financial mathematics modeling and computation, futures, options and commodities markets, real options, credit risk, portfolio optimization.

North Carolina State University, Graduate School, College of Sciences, Department of Mathematics, Raleigh, NC 27695. Offers MS, PhD. *Program availability:* Part-time. Terminal master's awarded for partial completion of doctoral program. *Degree requirements:* For master's, thesis (for some programs); for doctorate, one foreign language, thesis/dissertation. *Entrance requirements:* For master's and doctorate, GRE General Test, GRE Subject Test. Electronic applications accepted. *Faculty research:* Numerical and applied mathematics, industrial mathematics, algebra including symbolic and Lie, dynamical systems, analysis.

North Dakota State University, College of Graduate and Interdisciplinary Studies, College of Science and Mathematics, Department of Mathematics, Fargo, ND 58102. Offers applied mathematics (MS, PhD); mathematics (MS, PhD). *Entrance requirements:* For master's and doctorate, GRE General Test. Additional exam requirements/recommendations for international students: Required—TOEFL (minimum score 525 paper-based; 71 iBT), IELTS. Electronic applications accepted.

Northeastern Illinois University, College of Graduate Studies and Research, College of Arts and Sciences, Program in Mathematics, Chicago, IL 60625. Offers mathematics (MS), including applied mathematics. *Program availability:* Part-time, evening/weekend. *Degree requirements:* For master's, comprehensive exam, thesis optional, project. *Entrance requirements:* For master's, minimum GPA of 2.75, 6 undergraduate courses in mathematics. Additional exam requirements/recommendations for international students: Required—TOEFL (minimum score 550 paper-based; 79 iBT). Electronic applications accepted. *Faculty research:* Numerical analysis, mathematical biology, operations research, statistics, geometry and mathematics of finance.

Northeastern University, College of Science, Boston, MA 02115-5096. Offers applied mathematics (MS); bioinformatics (MS); biology (PhD); biotechnology (MS); chemistry and chemical biology (MS, PhD); environmental science and policy (MS); marine and environmental sciences (PhD); marine biology (MS); mathematics (MS, PhD); operations research (MSOR); physics (MS, PhD); psychology (PhD). *Program availability:* Part-time. Terminal master's awarded for partial completion of doctoral program. *Degree requirements:* For master's, comprehensive exam (for some programs), thesis; for doctorate, comprehensive exam (for some programs), thesis/dissertation. *Entrance requirements:* For master's, GRE General Test. Electronic applications accepted. *Expenses:* Contact institution.

Northern Arizona University, College of Environment, Forestry, and Natural Sciences, Department of Mathematics and Statistics, Flagstaff, AZ 86011. Offers applied statistics (Graduate Certificate); mathematics (MS); mathematics education (MS); statistics (MS); teaching introductory community college mathematics (Graduate Certificate). *Program availability:* Part-time. *Degree requirements:* For master's, variable foreign language requirement, comprehensive exam (for some programs), thesis (for some programs); for Graduate Certificate, comprehensive exam (for some programs). *Entrance requirements:* Additional exam requirements/recommendations for international students: Required—TOEFL (minimum score 80 iBT), IELTS (minimum score 6.5), TOEFL minimum iBT score of 89 (for MS and Graduate Certificate). Electronic applications accepted.

Northern Illinois University, Graduate School, College of Liberal Arts and Sciences, Department of Mathematical Sciences, De Kalb, IL 60115-2854. Offers mathematical sciences (PhD); mathematics (MS); statistics (MS). *Program availability:* Part-time. *Faculty:* 43 full-time (10 women), 4 part-time/adjunct (0 women). *Students:* 49 full-time (19 women), 27 part-time (6 women); includes 9 minority (2 Black or African American, non-Hispanic/Latino; 5 Asian, non-Hispanic/Latino; 2 Hispanic/Latino), 23 international. Average age 32. 44 applicants, 61% accepted, 13 enrolled. In 2018, 31 master's, 3 doctorates awarded. Terminal master's awarded for partial completion of doctoral program. *Degree requirements:* For master's, comprehensive exam, thesis optional; for doctorate, one foreign language, thesis/dissertation, candidacy exam, dissertation defense, internship. *Entrance requirements:* For master's, GRE General Test, minimum GPA of 2.75; for doctorate, GRE General Test, minimum GPA of 2.75 (undergraduate), 3.2 (graduate). Additional exam requirements/recommendations for international students: Required—TOEFL (minimum score 550 paper-based). *Application deadline:* For fall admission, 6/1 for domestic students, 5/1 for international students; for spring admission, 11/1 for domestic students, 10/1 for international students. Applications are processed on a rolling basis. Application fee: $40. Electronic applications accepted. *Financial support:* In 2018–19, 37 teaching assistantships with full tuition reimbursements were awarded; fellowships with full tuition reimbursements, research assistantships with full tuition reimbursements, career-related internships or fieldwork, Federal Work-Study, scholarships/grants, tuition waivers (full), and unspecified assistantships also available. Support available to part-time students. Financial award applicants required to submit FAFSA. *Faculty research:* Numerical linear algebra, noncommutative rings, nonlinear partial differential equations, finite group theory, abstract harmonic analysis. *Unit head:* Dr. Jeff Thunder, Chair, 815-753-6763, Fax: 815-753-1112, E-mail: jthunder@niu.edu. *Application contact:* Dr. John Ye, Director, Graduate Studies, 815-753-0568, E-mail: ye@math.niu.edu.
Website: http://www.math.niu.edu/

Northwestern University, The Graduate School, Judd A. and Marjorie Weinberg College of Arts and Sciences, Department of Mathematics, Evanston, IL 60208. Offers PhD. Admissions and degrees offered through The Graduate School. *Program availability:* Part-time. *Degree requirements:* For doctorate, thesis/dissertation, preliminary exam. *Entrance requirements:* For doctorate, GRE General Test, GRE Subject Test. Additional exam requirements/recommendations for international students: Required—TOEFL. *Faculty research:* Algebra, algebraic topology, analysis dynamical systems, partial differential equations.

Northwest Missouri State University, Graduate School, College of Arts and Sciences, Maryville, MO 64468-6001. Offers biology (MS); elementary mathematics specialist (MS Ed); English (MA); English education (MS Ed); English pedagogy (MA); geographic information science (MS, Certificate); history (MS Ed); mathematics (MS); mathematics education (MS Ed); teaching: science (MS Ed). *Program availability:* Part-time. *Faculty:* 20 full-time (9 women). *Students:* 15 full-time (9 women), 66 part-time (30 women); includes 6 minority (2 Black or African American, non-Hispanic/Latino; 1 American Indian or Alaska Native, non-Hispanic/Latino; 1 Hispanic/Latino; 2 Two or more races, non-Hispanic/Latino), 2 international. Average age 34. 32 applicants, 66% accepted, 19 enrolled. In 2018, 17 master's awarded. *Degree requirements:* For master's, comprehensive exam. *Entrance requirements:* For master's, GRE General Test, writing sample. Additional exam requirements/recommendations for international students: Required—TOEFL (minimum score 550 paper-based). *Application deadline:* For fall admission, 7/1 for domestic and international students; for spring admission, 11/15 for domestic and international students. Applications are processed on a rolling basis. Application fee: $0 ($75 for international students). Electronic applications accepted. *Expenses: Tuition, area resident:* Full-time $4551; part-time $252.86 per credit hour. Tuition, state resident: full-time $4551; part-time $252.86 per credit hour. Tuition, nonresident: full-time $9103; part-time $505.72 per credit hour. *International tuition:* $9103 full-time. *Required fees:* $2668; $148.20 per credit hour. Tuition and fees vary according to program. *Financial support:* Research assistantships with full tuition reimbursements, teaching assistantships with full tuition reimbursements, and administrative assistantships, tutorial assistantships available. Financial award application deadline: 4/1; financial award applicants required to submit FAFSA. *Unit head:* Dr. Michael Steiner, Dean, 660-562-1197. *Application contact:* Dr. Michael Steiner, Dean, 660-562-1197.
Website: https://www.nwmissouri.edu/academics/undergraduate/majors/liberal-arts-sciences.htm

Oakland University, Graduate Study and Lifelong Learning, College of Arts and Sciences, Department of Mathematics and Statistics, Program in Mathematics, Rochester, MI 48309-4401. Offers MA. *Entrance requirements:* Additional exam requirements/recommendations for international students: Required—TOEFL (minimum score 550 paper-based). Electronic applications accepted. *Expenses:* Contact institution.

The Ohio State University, Graduate School, College of Arts and Sciences, Division of Natural and Mathematical Sciences, Department of Mathematics, Columbus, OH 43210. Offers actuarial and quantitative risk management (MAQRM); computational sciences (MMS); mathematical biosciences (MMS); mathematics (PhD); mathematics for educators (MMS). *Faculty:* 61. *Students:* 150 full-time (32 women); includes 16 minority (9 Asian, non-Hispanic/Latino; 5 Hispanic/Latino; 2 Two or more races, non-Hispanic/Latino), 84 international. Average age 26. In 2018, 24 master's, 21 doctorates awarded. *Degree requirements:* For master's, thesis optional; for doctorate, one foreign language, thesis/dissertation. *Entrance requirements:* For master's, GRE General Test; for doctorate, GRE General Test (recommended), GRE Subject Test (mathematics). Additional exam requirements/recommendations for international students: Required—TOEFL (minimum score 550 paper-based; 79 iBT), Michigan English Language Assessment Battery (minimum score 82); Recommended—IELTS (minimum score 7). *Application deadline:* For fall admission, 12/15 priority date for domestic and international students. Applications are processed on a rolling basis. Application fee: $60 ($70 for international students). Electronic applications accepted. *Financial support:* Fellowships, research assistantships, teaching assistantships, Federal Work-Study, institutionally sponsored loans, and unspecified assistantships available. Support available to part-time students. *Unit head:* Dr. Jean-Francois Lafont, Chair, 614-292-7173, E-mail: lafont.1@osu.edu. *Application contact:* Erin Anthony, Graduate Studies Coordinator, 614-292-6274, Fax: 614-292-1479, E-mail: grad-info@math.osu.edu.
Website: http://www.math.osu.edu/

Ohio University, Graduate College, College of Arts and Sciences, Department of Mathematics, Athens, OH 45701-2979. Offers MS, PhD. *Program availability:* Part-time, evening/weekend. Terminal master's awarded for partial completion of doctoral program. *Degree requirements:* For master's, thesis optional; for doctorate, comprehensive exam, thesis/dissertation. *Entrance requirements:* For master's and doctorate, minimum GPA of 3.0. Additional exam requirements/recommendations for international students: Required—TOEFL (minimum score 550 paper-based; 80 iBT) or IELTS (minimum score 6.5). Electronic applications accepted. *Faculty research:* Algebra (group and ring theory), functional analysis, topology, differential equations, computational math.

Oklahoma State University, College of Arts and Sciences, Department of Mathematics, Stillwater, OK 74078. Offers applied mathematics (MS, PhD). *Faculty:* 44 full-time (10 women), 9 part-time/adjunct (6 women). *Students:* 15 full-time (3 women), 32 part-time (13 women); includes 10 minority (4 Black or African American, non-Hispanic/Latino; 2 American Indian or Alaska Native, non-Hispanic/Latino; 2 Hispanic/Latino; 2 Two or more races, non-Hispanic/Latino), 17 international. Average age 29. 50 applicants, 32% accepted, 14 enrolled. In 2018, 5 master's awarded. *Entrance requirements:* For master's and doctorate, GRE (recommended). Additional exam requirements/recommendations for international students: Required—TOEFL (minimum score 550 paper-based; 79 iBT). *Application deadline:* For fall admission, 3/1 for domestic and international students; for spring admission, 10/15 for domestic students, 10/15 priority date for international students. Applications are processed on a rolling basis. Application fee: $40 ($75 for international students). Electronic applications accepted. *Expenses: Tuition, area resident:* Full-time $4148. Tuition, state resident: full-time $4148. Tuition, nonresident: full-time $10,517. *International tuition:* $10,517 full-time. *Required fees:* $4394; $2929 per credit hour. Tuition and fees vary according to course load and program. *Financial support:* Research assistantships, teaching assistantships, health care benefits, and tuition waivers (partial) available. Financial award application deadline: 3/1; financial award applicants required to submit FAFSA. *Unit head:* Dr. Willam Jaco, Department Head, 405-744-5688, Fax: 405-744-8225, E-mail: william.jaco@okstate.edu. *Application contact:* Dr. Sheryl Tucker, Dean, 405-744-6368, Fax: 405-744-0355, E-mail: gradi@okstate.edu. Website: http://math.okstate.edu/

Old Dominion University, College of Sciences, Programs in Computational and Applied Mathematics, Norfolk, VA 23529. Offers applied mathematics (MS, PhD); biostatistics (MS); statistics (MS); statistics/biostatistics (PhD). *Program availability:* Part-time. Terminal master's awarded for partial completion of doctoral program. *Degree requirements:* For master's, project; for doctorate, comprehensive exam, thesis/dissertation, candidacy exam. *Entrance requirements:* For master's, minimum GPA of 3.0 in major, 2.8 overall; for doctorate, GRE General Test, 3 recommendation letters, transcripts, essay. Additional exam requirements/recommendations for international students: Required—TOEFL (minimum score 550 paper-based; 79 iBT); Recommended—IELTS (minimum score 6.5). Electronic applications accepted. *Faculty research:* Numerical analysis, integral equations, continuum mechanics, statistics, direct and inverse scattering.

Oregon State University, College of Education, Program in Teaching, Corvallis, OR 97331. Offers clinically based elementary education (MAT); elementary education (MAT); language arts (MAT); mathematics (MAT); music education (MAT); science (MAT); social studies (MAT). *Program availability:* Part-time, blended/hybrid learning. *Entrance requirements:* For master's, CBEST. Additional exam requirements/recommendations for international students: Required—TOEFL (minimum score 575 paper-based). *Expenses:* Contact institution.

Oregon State University, College of Science, Program in Mathematics, Corvallis, OR 97331. Offers differential geometry (MA, MS, PhD); financial and actuarial mathematics (MA, MS, PhD); mathematical biology (MA, MS, PhD); mathematics education (MS, PhD); number theory (MA, MS, PhD); numerical analysis (MA, MS, PhD); probability (MA). Terminal master's awarded for partial completion of doctoral program. *Degree requirements:* For master's, thesis or alternative; for doctorate, thesis/dissertation, qualifying exams. *Entrance requirements:* For master's and doctorate, GRE. Additional exam requirements/recommendations for international students: Required—TOEFL (minimum score 100 iBT). Electronic applications accepted.

Pace University, School of Education, New York, NY 10038. Offers adolescent education (MST), including biology, chemistry, earth science, English, foreign languages, mathematics, physics, social studies; childhood education (MST); early childhood development, learning and intervention (MST); educational technology studies (MS); inclusive adolescent education (MST), including biology, chemistry, earth science, English, foreign languages, mathematics, physics, social studies; integrated instruction for educational technology (Certificate); integrated instruction for literacy and technology (Certificate); literacy (MS Ed); special education (MS Ed). *Accreditation:* NCATE. *Program availability:* Part-time, evening/weekend, 100% online, blended/hybrid learning. *Faculty:* 19 full-time (13 women), 86 part-time/adjunct (49 women). *Students:* 98 full-time (82 women), 542 part-time (391 women); includes 256 minority (116 Black or African American, non-Hispanic/Latino; 2 American Indian or Alaska Native, non-Hispanic/Latino; 45 Asian, non-Hispanic/Latino; 83 Hispanic/Latino; 10 Two or more races, non-Hispanic/Latino), 4 international. Average age 30. 223 applicants, 89% accepted, 130 enrolled. In 2018, 269 master's, 12 other advanced degrees awarded. *Degree requirements:* For master's and Certificate, certification exams. *Entrance requirements:* For master's, GRE (for initial certification programs only), teaching certificate (for MS Ed in literacy and special education programs only). Additional exam requirements/recommendations for international students: Required—TOEFL (minimum score 88 iBT), IELTS or PTE. *Application deadline:* For fall admission, 8/1 priority date for domestic students, 6/1 for international students; for spring admission, 12/1 priority date for domestic students, 10/1 for international students. Applications are processed on a rolling basis. Application fee: $70. Electronic applications accepted. *Expenses:* Contact institution. *Financial support:* In 2018–19, 17 students received support, including 17 research assistantships with partial tuition reimbursements available (averaging $6,020 per year); career-related internships or fieldwork, Federal Work-Study, scholarships/grants, and unspecified assistantships also available. Financial award application deadline: 9/1; financial award applicants required to submit FAFSA. *Faculty research:* STEM education, TESOL, teacher education, special education, language and literary development. *Total annual research expenditures:* $1.4 million. *Unit head:* Dr. Harriet Feldman, Dean, School of Education, 914-773-3829, E-mail: hfeldman@pace.edu. *Application contact:* Susan Ford-Goldschein, Director of Graduate Admissions, 212-346-1531, Fax: 212-346-1585, E-mail: graduateadmission@pace.edu. Website: http://www.pace.edu/school-of-education

Penn State University Park, Graduate School, Eberly College of Science, Department of Mathematics, University Park, PA 16802. Offers M Ed, MA, D Ed, PhD.

Pittsburg State University, Graduate School, College of Arts and Sciences, Department of Mathematics, Pittsburg, KS 66762. Offers MS. *Program availability:* Part-time. *Degree requirements:* For master's, thesis or alternative. *Entrance requirements:*

Additional exam requirements/recommendations for international students: Required—TOEFL (minimum score 520 paper-based; 68 iBT), IELTS (minimum score 6), PTE (minimum score 47). Electronic applications accepted. *Expenses:* Contact institution. *Faculty research:* Operations research, numerical analysis, applied analysis, applied algebra.

Portland State University, Graduate Studies, College of Liberal Arts and Sciences, Fariborz Maseeh Department of Mathematics and Statistics, Portland, OR 97207-0751. Offers applied statistics (Certificate); mathematical sciences (PhD); mathematics education (PhD); mathematics for middle school (Certificate); mathematics for teachers (MS); statistics (MS); MA/MS. *Degree requirements:* For master's, comprehensive exam, thesis or alternative, 2 written examinations; for doctorate, thesis/dissertation, preliminary and comprehensive examinations. *Entrance requirements:* For master's, GRE General Test, GRE Subject Test, minimum GPA of 3.0 in upper-division course work or 2.75 cumulative undergraduate; for doctorate, GRE General Test. Additional exam requirements/recommendations for international students: Required—TOEFL (minimum score 550 paper-based; 80 iBT). *Faculty research:* Algebra, topology, statistical distribution theory, control theory, statistical robustness.

Portland State University, Graduate Studies, College of Liberal Arts and Sciences, Systems Science Program, Portland, OR 97207-0751. Offers computational intelligence (Certificate); computer modeling and simulation (Certificate); systems science (MS); systems science/anthropology (PhD); systems science/business administration (PhD); systems science/civil engineering (PhD); systems science/economics (PhD); systems science/engineering management (PhD); systems science/general (PhD); systems science/mathematical sciences (PhD); systems science/mechanical engineering (PhD); systems science/psychology (PhD); systems science/sociology (PhD). *Degree requirements:* For master's, comprehensive exam (for some programs), thesis optional; for doctorate, variable foreign language requirement, comprehensive exam (for some programs), thesis/dissertation. *Entrance requirements:* For master's, GRE/GMAT (recommended), minimum GPA of 3.0 on undergraduate or graduate work, 2 letters of recommendation, statement of interest; for doctorate, GMAT, GRE General Test, minimum GPA of 3.0 undergraduate, 3.25 graduate; 3 letters of recommendation, statement of interest. Additional exam requirements/recommendations for international students: Required—TOEFL (minimum score 550 paper-based; 80 iBT). Electronic applications accepted. *Faculty research:* Systems theory and methodology, artificial intelligence neural networks, information theory, nonlinear dynamics/chaos, modeling and simulation.

Princeton University, Graduate School, Department of Mathematics, Princeton, NJ 08544-1019. Offers PhD. *Degree requirements:* For doctorate, 2 foreign languages, thesis/dissertation. *Entrance requirements:* For doctorate, GRE General Test, GRE Subject Test, 3 letters of recommendation. Additional exam requirements/recommendations for international students: Required—TOEFL (minimum score 600 paper-based). Electronic applications accepted.

Purdue University, Graduate School, College of Science, Department of Mathematics, West Lafayette, IN 47907. Offers MS, PhD. *Faculty:* 83 full-time (14 women), 2 part-time/adjunct (0 women). *Students:* 155 full-time (39 women), 6 part-time (3 women); includes 24 minority (1 Black or African American, non-Hispanic/Latino; 9 Asian, non-Hispanic/Latino; 12 Hispanic/Latino; 1 Native Hawaiian or other Pacific Islander, non-Hispanic/Latino; 1 Two or more races, non-Hispanic/Latino), 60 international. Average age 26. 274 applicants, 26% accepted, 26 enrolled. In 2018, 10 master's, 17 doctorates awarded. Terminal master's awarded for partial completion of doctoral program. *Degree requirements:* For doctorate, one foreign language, thesis/dissertation, oral and written exams. *Entrance requirements:* For master's and doctorate, GRE General Test, GRE Subject Test in advanced mathematics (strongly recommended), minimum undergraduate GPA of 3.0 or equivalent. Additional exam requirements/recommendations for international students: Required—TOEFL (minimum score 570 paper-based; 77 iBT). *Application deadline:* For fall admission, 1/15 for domestic and international students; for spring admission, 12/1 for domestic students, 10/15 for international students. Application fee: $60 ($75 for international students). Electronic applications accepted. *Financial support:* In 2018–19, fellowships with full and partial tuition reimbursements (averaging $16,000 per year), teaching assistantships with partial tuition reimbursements (averaging $16,020 per year) were awarded. Support available to part-time students. Financial award application deadline: 3/1; financial award applicants required to submit FAFSA. *Faculty research:* Algebra, analysis, topology, differential equations, applied mathematics. *Unit head:* Plamen Stefanov, Head, 765-494-1954, E-mail: Plamen-Stefanov@purdue.edu. *Application contact:* Shannon Cassady, Graduate Contact, 765-494-1961, E-mail: scassady@purdue.edu. Website: http://www.math.purdue.edu/

Purdue University Fort Wayne, College of Arts and Sciences, Department of Mathematical Sciences, Fort Wayne, IN 46805-1499. Offers applied mathematics (MS); applied statistics (Certificate); mathematics (MS); operations research (MS); teaching (MAT). *Program availability:* Part-time, evening/weekend. *Entrance requirements:* For master's, minimum GPA of 3.0, major or minor in mathematics, three letters of recommendation. Additional exam requirements/recommendations for international students: Required—TOEFL (minimum score 550 paper-based; 79 iBT); Recommended—TWE. Electronic applications accepted. *Faculty research:* Eves' Theorem, paired-placements for student teaching, holomorphic maps.

Purdue University Northwest, Graduate Studies Office, School of Engineering, Mathematics, and Science, Department of Mathematics, Computer Science, and Statistics, Hammond, IN 46323-2094. Offers computer science (MS); mathematics (MAT, MS). *Program availability:* Part-time. *Entrance requirements:* Additional exam requirements/recommendations for international students: Required—TOEFL. *Faculty research:* Topology, analysis, algebra, mathematics education.

Queens College of the City University of New York, Mathematics and Natural Sciences Division, Department of Mathematics, Queens, NY 11367-1597. Offers applied mathematics (MA); pure mathematics (MA). *Program availability:* Part-time, evening/weekend. *Faculty:* 34 full-time (8 women), 65 part-time/adjunct (26 women). *Students:* 3 full-time (0 women), 34 part-time (12 women); includes 19 minority (5 Black or African American, non-Hispanic/Latino; 11 Asian, non-Hispanic/Latino; 3 Hispanic/Latino), 2 international. Average age 33. 39 applicants, 62% accepted, 13 enrolled. In 2018, 11 master's awarded. *Degree requirements:* For master's, comprehensive exam, oral exam (for pure mathematics), written exam (for applied mathematics). *Entrance requirements:* For master's, minimum GPA of 3.0. Additional exam requirements/recommendations for international students: Required—TOEFL (minimum score 61 iBT), IELTS (minimum score 5). *Application deadline:* For fall admission, 4/1 for domestic and international students; for spring admission, 11/1 for domestic and international students. Applications are processed on a rolling basis. Application fee: $125. Electronic applications accepted. *Financial support:* Career-related internships or fieldwork and Federal Work-Study available. Financial award application deadline: 4/1; financial award applicants required to submit FAFSA. *Faculty research:* Number theory, probability, complex analysis, algebra, topology. *Unit head:* Dr. Alan Sultan, Chair, 718-997-5811,

Peterson's Graduate Programs in the Physical Sciences, Mathematics, Agricultural Sciences, the Environment & Natural Resources 2020

www.petersons.com **219**

Fax: 718-997-5882, E-mail: alan.sultan@qc.cuny.edu. *Application contact:* Elizabeth D'Amico-Ramirez, Assistant Director of Graduate Admissions, 718-997-5203, E-mail: elizabeth.damicoramirez@qc.cuny.edu.

Queen's University at Kingston, School of Graduate Studies, Faculty of Arts and Science, Department of Mathematics and Statistics, Kingston, ON K7L 3N6, Canada. Offers mathematics (M Sc, PhD); statistics (M Sc, PhD). *Program availability:* Part-time. *Degree requirements:* For master's, thesis; for doctorate, comprehensive exam, thesis/dissertation. *Entrance requirements:* Additional exam requirements/recommendations for international students: Required—TOEFL. *Faculty research:* Algebra, analysis, applied mathematics, statistics.

Regent University, Graduate School, School of Education, Virginia Beach, VA 23464-9800. Offers education (M Ed, Ed D, PhD), including adult education (Ed D, PhD, Ed S), advanced educational leadership (Ed D, PhD, Ed S), character education (Ed D, PhD, Ed S), Christian education leadership (Ed D, PhD, Ed S), Christian school administration (M Ed), curriculum and instruction (Ed D, PhD, Ed S), curriculum and instruction - adult education (M Ed), curriculum and instruction - Christian school (M Ed), curriculum and instruction - gifted and talented (M Ed), curriculum and instruction - STEM education (M Ed), curriculum and instruction - teacher leader (M Ed), discipleship for ministry (M Ed), educational leadership (M Ed), educational psychology (Ed D, PhD, Ed S), educational technology and online learning (Ed D, PhD, Ed S), elementary education (M Ed), exceptional education executive leadership (Ed D, PhD, Ed S), higher education (Ed D, PhD, Ed S), higher education leadership and management (Ed D, PhD, Ed S), instructional design and technology (M Ed), K-12 school leadership (Ed D, PhD, Ed S), K-12 special education (M Ed), leadership in mathematics education (M Ed), reading specialist (M Ed), special education (Ed D, PhD, Ed S), student affairs (M Ed), TESOL - adult education (M Ed), TESOL - K-12 (M Ed); educational specialist (Ed S), including adult education (Ed D, PhD, Ed S), advanced educational leadership (Ed D, PhD, Ed S), character education (Ed D, PhD, Ed S), Christian education leadership (Ed D, PhD, Ed S), curriculum and instruction (Ed D, PhD, Ed S), educational psychology (Ed D, PhD, Ed S), educational technology and online learning (Ed D, PhD, Ed S), exceptional education executive leadership (Ed D, PhD, Ed S), higher education (Ed D, PhD, Ed S), higher education leadership and management (Ed D, PhD, Ed S), K-12 school leadership (Ed D, PhD, Ed S), special education (Ed D, PhD, Ed S). *Accreditation:* TEAC. *Program availability:* Part-time, evening/weekend, 100% online, blended/hybrid learning. *Degree requirements:* For master's, thesis or alternative; for doctorate, comprehensive exam, thesis/dissertation. *Entrance requirements:* For master's, Virginia Communication and Literacy Assessment (VCLA), PRAXIS, college transcripts, writing sample, interview; for doctorate, GRE, writing sample, resume, transcripts, interview. Additional exam requirements/recommendations for international students: Required—TOEFL (minimum score 577 paper-based). Electronic applications accepted. *Expenses:* Contact institution. *Faculty research:* Christian school administration, curriculum and instruction, educational technology and online learning, higher education, special education.

Rensselaer Polytechnic Institute, Graduate School, School of Science, Program in Mathematics, Troy, NY 12180-3590. Offers MS, PhD. *Faculty:* 24 full-time (5 women). *Students:* 49 full-time (15 women), 1 part-time (0 women); includes 5 minority (3 Hispanic/Latino; 2 Two or more races, non-Hispanic/Latino), 13 international. Average age 25. 102 applicants, 60% accepted, 17 enrolled. In 2018, 7 master's, 5 doctorates awarded. Terminal master's awarded for partial completion of doctoral program. *Degree requirements:* For doctorate, comprehensive exam, thesis/dissertation. *Entrance requirements:* For master's and doctorate, GRE. Additional exam requirements/recommendations for international students: Required—TOEFL (minimum score 600 paper-based; 100 iBT), IELTS (minimum score 7), PTE (minimum score 68). *Application deadline:* For fall admission, 1/1 priority date for domestic and international students; for spring admission, 8/15 priority date for domestic and international students. Applications are processed on a rolling basis. Application fee: $75. Electronic applications accepted. *Financial support:* In 2018–19, research assistantships (averaging $23,000 per year), teaching assistantships (averaging $23,000 per year) were awarded; fellowships also available. Financial award application deadline: 1/1. *Faculty research:* Acoustics, applied geometry, approximation theory, bioinformatics, biomathematics, chemically-reacting flows, data-driven modeling, dynamical systems, environmental problems, fluid dynamics, inverse problem, machine learning, math education, mathematical physics, multiphase flows, nonlinear analysis, nonlinear materials, nonlinear waves, operations research and mathematical programming, optimization, perturbation methods, scientific computing. *Total annual research expenditures:* $1.9 million. *Unit head:* Dr. John Mitchell, Graduate Program Director, 518-276-6519, E-mail: mitchj@rpi.edu. *Application contact:* Jarron Decker, Director of Graduate Admissions, 518-276-6216, Fax: 518-276-4072, E-mail: gradadmissions@rpi.edu.
Website: https://science.rpi.edu/mathematical-sciences

Rhode Island College, School of Graduate Studies, Faculty of Arts and Sciences, Department of Mathematics and Computer Science, Providence, RI 02908-1991. Offers mathematics (MA); mathematics content specialist (CGS). *Program availability:* Part-time, evening/weekend. *Faculty:* 3 full-time (1 woman). *Students:* 6 part-time (3 women); includes 4 minority (2 Black or African American, non-Hispanic/Latino; 2 Hispanic/Latino). Average age 28. In 2018, 4 master's, 1 other advanced degree awarded. *Degree requirements:* For master's, comprehensive exam. *Entrance requirements:* For master's, GRE General Test or MAT, minimum of 30 hours beyond pre-calculus math, 3 letters of recommendation, interview. Additional exam requirements/recommendations for international students: Required—TOEFL (minimum score 550 paper-based; 80 iBT). *Application deadline:* For fall admission, 3/1 for domestic students; for spring admission, 11/1 for domestic students. Applications are processed on a rolling basis. Application fee: $50. Electronic applications accepted. *Expenses: Tuition, area resident:* Part-time $407 per credit. Tuition, nonresident: part-time $792 per credit. *Required fees:* $29 per credit. $100 per semester. *Financial support:* Teaching assistantships, Federal Work-Study, scholarships/grants, health care benefits, and unspecified assistantships available. Support available to part-time students. Financial award application deadline: 5/15; financial award applicants required to submit FAFSA. *Unit head:* Dr. Stephanie Costa, Chair, 401-456-8038. *Application contact:* Dr. Stephanie Costa, Chair, 401-456-8038.
Website: http://www.ric.edu/mathcomputerscience/Pages/Mathematics-Program.aspx

Rice University, Graduate Programs, Wiess School of Natural Sciences, Department of Mathematics, Houston, TX 77251-1892. Offers PhD. Terminal master's awarded for partial completion of doctoral program. *Degree requirements:* For doctorate, one foreign language, comprehensive exam, thesis/dissertation. *Entrance requirements:* For doctorate, GRE Subject Test, GRE General Test. Additional exam requirements/recommendations for international students: Required—TOEFL (minimum score 600 paper-based; 90 iBT). Electronic applications accepted. *Faculty research:* Algebraic geometry/algebra, complex analysis and Teichmuller theory, dynamical systems and Ergodic theory, topology, differential geometry and geometric analysis.

Rivier University, School of Graduate Studies, Department of Computer Science and Mathematics, Nashua, NH 03060. Offers computer science (MS); mathematics (MAT). *Program availability:* Part-time, evening/weekend. *Entrance requirements:* For master's, GRE Subject Test. Electronic applications accepted.

Rochester Institute of Technology, Graduate Enrollment Services, College of Science, School of Mathematical Sciences, Rochester, NY 14623-5603. Offers applied and computational mathematics (MS); applied statistics (MS, Advanced Certificate); mathematical modeling (PhD). *Program availability:* Part-time, evening/weekend. *Students:* 48 full-time (27 women), 57 part-time (23 women); includes 17 minority (1 Black or African American, non-Hispanic/Latino; 9 Asian, non-Hispanic/Latino; 4 Hispanic/Latino; 3 Two or more races, non-Hispanic/Latino), 31 international. Average age 28. 181 applicants, 48% accepted, 30 enrolled. In 2018, 23 master's awarded. *Entrance requirements:* For master's, minimum GPA of 3.0 (recommended). *Application deadline:* For fall admission, 2/15 priority date for domestic and international students; for spring admission, 12/15 priority date for domestic and international students. Applications are processed on a rolling basis. Application fee: $65. Electronic applications accepted. *Expenses:* Contact institution. *Financial support:* In 2018–19, 64 students received support. Research assistantships with partial tuition reimbursements available, teaching assistantships with partial tuition reimbursements available, career-related internships or fieldwork, scholarships/grants, and unspecified assistantships available. Support available to part-time students. Financial award applicants required to submit FAFSA. *Faculty research:* Mathematical biology; dynamical systems and fluid dynamics; discrete mathematics; applied inverse problems; geometry, relativity and gravitation; earth systems modeling; graph theory. *Unit head:* Matthew Coppenbarger, Interim School Head, 585-475-5887, E-mail: mecsma@rit.edu. *Application contact:* Diane Ellison, Senior Associate Vice President, Graduate Enrollment Services, 585-475-2229, Fax: 585-475-7164, E-mail: gradinfo@rit.edu.
Website: http://www.rit.edu/cos/sms/

Roosevelt University, Graduate Division, College of Arts and Sciences, Department of Math, Actuarial Science, and Economics, Chicago, IL 60605. Offers actuarial science (MS); mathematics (MS), including mathematical sciences. Electronic applications accepted.

Rowan University, Graduate School, College of Science and Mathematics, Department of Mathematics, Program in Mathematics, Glassboro, NJ 08028-1701. Offers MA. Electronic applications accepted.

Royal Military College of Canada, Division of Graduate Studies, Faculty of Science, Department of Mathematics and Computer Science, Kingston, ON K7K 7B4, Canada. Offers computer science (M Sc); mathematics (M Sc). *Degree requirements:* For master's, thesis. *Entrance requirements:* For master's, honours degree with second-class standing. Electronic applications accepted.

Rutgers University–Camden, Graduate School of Arts and Sciences, Program in Mathematical Sciences, Camden, NJ 08102. Offers industrial mathematics (MBS); industrial/applied mathematics (MS); mathematical computer science (MS); pure mathematics (MS); teaching in mathematical sciences (MS). *Program availability:* Part-time, evening/weekend. *Degree requirements:* For master's, comprehensive exam, thesis optional, survey paper, 30 credits. *Entrance requirements:* For master's, GRE, BS/BA in math or related subject, 2 letters of recommendation. Additional exam requirements/recommendations for international students: Required—TOEFL (minimum score 550 paper-based), IELTS. Electronic applications accepted. *Faculty research:* Differential geometry, dynamical systems, vertex operator algebra, automorphic forms, CR-structures.

Rutgers University–Newark, Graduate School, Program in Mathematical Sciences, Newark, NJ 07102. Offers PhD. *Degree requirements:* For doctorate, thesis/dissertation, written qualifying exam. *Entrance requirements:* For doctorate, GRE General Test, minimum B average. Additional exam requirements/recommendations for international students: Required—TOEFL. Electronic applications accepted. *Faculty research:* Number theory, automorphic form, low-dimensional topology, Kleinian groups, representation theory.

Rutgers University–New Brunswick, Graduate School-New Brunswick, Department of Mathematics, Piscataway, NJ 08854-8097. Offers applied mathematics (MS, PhD); mathematics (MS, PhD). *Program availability:* Part-time. *Degree requirements:* For doctorate, one foreign language, comprehensive exam, thesis/dissertation. *Entrance requirements:* For master's and doctorate, GRE General Test, GRE Subject Test. Additional exam requirements/recommendations for international students: Required—TOEFL. *Faculty research:* Logic and set theory, number theory, mathematical physics, control theory, partial differential equations.

St. John's University, St. John's College of Liberal Arts and Sciences, Department of Mathematics and Computer Science, Queens, NY 11439. Offers applied and computational mathematics (MA). *Program availability:* Part-time, evening/weekend. *Degree requirements:* For master's, comprehensive exam. *Entrance requirements:* For master's, letters of recommendation, transcripts, resume, personal statement. Additional exam requirements/recommendations for international students: Required—TOEFL (minimum score 80 iBT), IELTS (minimum score 6.5). Electronic applications accepted.

Saint Joseph's University, College of Arts and Sciences, Department of Computer Science, Philadelphia, PA 19131-1395. Offers computer science (MS); mathematics and computer science (Post-Master's Certificate). *Program availability:* Part-time, evening/weekend. *Entrance requirements:* For master's, 2 letters of recommendation, resume, personal statement, official transcripts. Additional exam requirements/recommendations for international students: Required—TOEFL (minimum score 550 paper-based; 80 iBT), IELTS (minimum score 6.5). Electronic applications accepted. *Expenses:* Contact institution. *Faculty research:* Computer vision, artificial intelligence, computer graphics, database modelling, computer security.

Saint Louis University, Graduate Programs, College of Arts and Sciences, Department of Mathematics and Statistics, St. Louis, MO 63103. Offers mathematics (MA, PhD). *Program availability:* Part-time. *Degree requirements:* For master's, comprehensive exam, thesis (for some programs); for doctorate, one foreign language, thesis/dissertation, preliminary exams. *Entrance requirements:* For master's, GRE General Test, letters of recommendation, resume, interview; for doctorate, GRE General Test, letters of recommendation, resumé, interview, transcripts, goal statement. Additional exam requirements/recommendations for international students: Required—TOEFL (minimum score 525 paper-based). Electronic applications accepted. *Faculty research:* Algebra, groups and rings, analysis, differential geometry, topology.

Salem State University, School of Graduate Studies, Program in Mathematics, Salem, MA 01970-5353. Offers MAT, MS. *Program availability:* Part-time, evening/weekend. *Entrance requirements:* For master's, GRE or MAT. Additional exam requirements/recommendations for international students: Required—TOEFL (minimum score 550 paper-based; 80 iBT) or IELTS (minimum score 5.5).

Sam Houston State University, College of Sciences, Department of Mathematics and Statistics, Huntsville, TX 77341. Offers mathematics (MA, MS); statistics (MS). *Program* *availability:* Part-time. *Degree requirements:* For master's, comprehensive exam, thesis optional. *Entrance requirements:* For master's, GRE General Test, letters of recommendation. Additional exam requirements/recommendations for international students: Required—TOEFL (minimum score 550 paper-based; 79 iBT), IELTS (minimum score 6.5). Electronic applications accepted.

San Diego State University, Graduate and Research Affairs, College of Sciences, Department of Mathematics and Statistics, San Diego, CA 92182. Offers applied mathematics (MS); mathematics (MA); mathematics and science education (PhD); statistics (MS). PhD offered jointly wtih University of California, San Diego. *Program availability:* Part-time. *Degree requirements:* For doctorate, thesis/dissertation. *Entrance requirements:* For master's, GRE General Test; for doctorate, GRE, minimum GPA of 3.25 in last 30 undergraduate semester units, minimum graduate GPA of 3.5, MSE recommendation form, 3 letters of recommendation. Additional exam requirements/recommendations for international students: Required—TOEFL. Electronic applications accepted. *Faculty research:* Teacher education in mathematics.

San Francisco State University, Division of Graduate Studies, College of Science and Engineering, Department of Mathematics, San Francisco, CA 94132-1722. Offers MA. *Application deadline:* Applications are processed on a rolling basis. *Unit head:* Dr. Serkan Hosten, Chair, 415-338-2251, Fax: 415-338-1461, E-mail: serkan@sfsu.edu. *Application contact:* Dr. Joseph Gubeladze, Graduate Coordinator, 415-338-7722, Fax: 415-338-1461, E-mail: soso@sfsu.edu.
Website: http://math.sfsu.edu

Simon Fraser University, Office of Graduate Studies and Postdoctoral Fellows, Faculty of Science, Department of Mathematics, Burnaby, BC V5A 1S6, Canada. Offers applied and computational mathematics (M Sc, PhD); mathematics (M Sc, PhD); operations research (M Sc, PhD). *Degree requirements:* For master's, thesis or alternative; for doctorate, comprehensive exam, thesis/dissertation. *Entrance requirements:* For master's, GRE General Test, GRE Subject Test (mathematics), minimum GPA of 3.0 (on scale of 4.33) or 3.33 based on last 60 credits of undergraduate courses; for doctorate, GRE General Test, GRE Subject Test (mathematics), minimum GPA of 3.5 (on scale of 4.33). Additional exam requirements/recommendations for international students: Recommended—TOEFL (minimum score 580 paper-based; 93 iBT), IELTS (minimum score 7), TWE (minimum score 5). Electronic applications accepted. *Faculty research:* Computer algebra, discrete mathematics, fluid dynamics, nonlinear partial differential equations and variation methods, numerical analysis and scientific computing.

Smith College, Graduate and Special Programs, Center for Women in Mathematics Post-Baccalaureate Program, Northampton, MA 01063. Offers Postbaccalaureate Certificate. *Students:* 8 full-time (all women); includes 5 minority (2 Black or African American, non-Hispanic/Latino; 2 Asian, non-Hispanic/Latino; 1 Hispanic/Latino). Average age 24. 28 applicants, 43% accepted, 8 enrolled. In 2018, 8 Postbaccalaureate Certificates awarded. *Entrance requirements:* Additional exam requirements/ recommendations for international students: Required—TOEFL (minimum score 595 paper-based; 97 iBT), IELTS (minimum score 7.5). *Application deadline:* For fall admission, 3/15 for domestic students; for spring admission, 10/15 for domestic students. Application fee: $60. *Expenses: Tuition:* Full-time $39,120; part-time $1630 per credit. Tuition and fees vary according to course load and program. *Financial support:* In 2018–19, 8 students received support. Scholarships/grants and tuition waivers (full) available. Financial award application deadline: 3/15. *Unit head:* Julianna Tymoczko, Director, 413-585-3775, E-mail: jtymoczko@smith.edu. *Application contact:* Ruth Morgan, Program Coordinator, 413-585-3050, Fax: 413-585-3054, E-mail: rmorgan@smith.edu.

South Carolina State University, College of Graduate and Professional Studies, Department of Education, Orangeburg, SC 29117-0001. Offers early childhood education (MAT); education (M Ed); elementary education (M Ed, MAT); English (MAT); general science/biology (MAT); mathematics (MAT); secondary education (M Ed), including biology education, business education, counselor education, English education, home economics education, industrial education, mathematics education, science education, social studies education; special education (M Ed), including emotionally handicapped, learning disabilities, mentally handicapped. *Accreditation:* NCATE. *Program availability:* Part-time, evening/weekend. *Faculty:* 17 full-time (6 women), 12 part-time/adjunct (5 women). *Students:* 42 full-time (32 women), 93 part-time (64 women); includes 121 minority (119 Black or African American, non-Hispanic/ Latino; 2 Asian, non-Hispanic/Latino), 2 international. Average age 40. 50 applicants, 98% accepted, 39 enrolled. In 2018, 9 master's awarded. *Degree requirements:* For master's, thesis optional, departmental qualifying exam. *Entrance requirements:* For master's, GRE General Test, NTE, interview, teaching certificate. *Application deadline:* For fall admission, 6/15 priority date for domestic students, 6/15 for international students; for spring admission, 11/1 for domestic and international students. Application fee: $25. Electronic applications accepted. *Expenses: Tuition, area resident:* Full-time $9928; part-time $552 per credit hour. Tuition, state resident: full-time $9928. Tuition, nonresident: full-time $21,038; part-time $1169 per credit hour. *Required fees:* $1532; $85 per credit hour. *Financial support:* Fellowships, career-related internships or fieldwork, Federal Work-Study, and scholarships/grants available. Financial award application deadline: 6/1. *Unit head:* Dr. Charlie Spell, Chair, Department of Education, 803-536-8963, Fax: 803-516-4568, E-mail: cspell@scsu.edu. *Application contact:* Curtis Foskey, Coordinator of Graduate Studies, 803-536-8419, Fax: 803-536-8812, E-mail: cfoskey@scsu.edu.

South Dakota State University, Graduate School, Jerome J. Lohr College of Engineering, Department of Mathematics and Statistics, Brookings, SD 57007. Offers computational science and statistics (PhD); mathematics (MS); statistics (MS). *Program availability:* Part-time. Terminal master's awarded for partial completion of doctoral program. *Degree requirements:* For master's, thesis (for some programs), oral exam; for doctorate, comprehensive exam, thesis/dissertation, oral and written exams. *Entrance requirements:* Additional exam requirements/recommendations for international students: Required—TOEFL (minimum score 550 paper-based; 80 iBT); Recommended—IELTS. *Faculty research:* Financial mathematics, predictive analytics, operations research, bioinformatics, biostatistics, computational science, statistics, number theory, abstract algebra.

Southeast Missouri State University, School of Graduate Studies, Department of Mathematics, Cape Girardeau, MO 63701-4799. Offers MNS. *Program availability:* Part-time, evening/weekend, online learning. *Faculty:* 12 full-time (2 women). *Students:* 2 full-time (0 women), 5 part-time (4 women); includes 1 minority (Black or African American, non-Hispanic/Latino). Average age 33. 2 applicants, 100% accepted, 1 enrolled. In 2018, 4 master's awarded. *Degree requirements:* For master's, paper and comprehensive exam, or thesis. *Entrance requirements:* For master's, minimum undergraduate GPA of 2.75. Additional exam requirements/recommendations for international students: Required—TOEFL (minimum score 550 paper-based; 79 iBT), IELTS (minimum score 6), PTE (minimum score 53). *Application deadline:* For fall admission, 8/1 for domestic students, 6/1 for international students; for spring

admission, 11/21 for domestic students, 10/1 for international students; for summer admission, 5/15 for domestic students. Applications are processed on a rolling basis. Application fee: $30 ($40 for international students). Electronic applications accepted. *Expenses:* Contact institution. *Financial support:* In 2018–19, 7 teaching assistantships with full tuition reimbursements were awarded; career-related internships or fieldwork, Federal Work-Study, scholarships/grants, traineeships, tuition waivers (full), and unspecified assistantships also available. Support available to part-time students. Financial award application deadline: 6/30; financial award applicants required to submit FAFSA. *Faculty research:* Algebraic geometry, combinatorics, differential equations, mathematics education, statistics. *Unit head:* Dr. Daniel Daly, Interim Chairperson, 573-651-2164, Fax: 573-986-6811, E-mail: ddaly@semo.edu. *Application contact:* Dr. Emmanuel Thompson, Graduate Program Associate Professor, 573-651-2721, E-mail: ethompson@semo.edu.
Website: http://www.semo.edu/math/

Southern Connecticut State University, School of Graduate Studies, School of Arts and Sciences, Department of Mathematics, New Haven, CT 06515-1355. Offers MS. *Program availability:* Part-time, evening/weekend. *Degree requirements:* For master's, thesis or alternative. *Entrance requirements:* For master's, interview. Electronic applications accepted.

Southern Illinois University Carbondale, Graduate School, College of Science, Department of Mathematics, Carbondale, IL 62901-4701. Offers MA, MS, PhD. PhD offered jointly with Southeast Missouri State University. *Program availability:* Part-time. *Degree requirements:* For master's, thesis; for doctorate, 2 foreign languages, thesis/dissertation. *Entrance requirements:* For master's, GRE General Test, minimum GPA of 2.7; for doctorate, GRE General Test, minimum GPA of 3.25. Additional exam requirements/recommendations for international students: Required—TOEFL. *Faculty research:* Differential equations, combinatorics, probability, algebra, numerical analysis.

Southern Illinois University Edwardsville, Graduate School, College of Arts and Sciences, Department of Mathematics and Statistics, Program in Pure Mathematics, Edwardsville, IL 62026. Offers MS. *Program availability:* Part-time. *Degree requirements:* For master's, thesis (for some programs), special project. *Entrance requirements:* Additional exam requirements/recommendations for international students: Required—TOEFL (minimum score 550 paper-based, 79 iBT), IELTS (minimum score 6.5), Michigan Test of English Language Proficiency or PTE. Electronic applications accepted.

Southern Methodist University, Dedman College of Humanities and Sciences, Department of Mathematics, Dallas, TX 75275. Offers computational and applied mathematics (MS, PhD). *Degree requirements:* For master's, oral exams; for doctorate, thesis/dissertation, oral and written exams. *Entrance requirements:* For master's and doctorate, GRE General Test, minimum GPA of 3.0, 18 undergraduate hours in mathematics beyond first- and second-year calculus. Additional exam requirements/ recommendations for international students: Required—TOEFL. Electronic applications accepted. *Faculty research:* Numerical analysis and scientific computation, fluid dynamics, optics, wave propagation, mathematical biology.

Southern University and Agricultural and Mechanical College, Graduate School, College of Sciences and Engineering, Program in Mathematics, Baton Rouge, LA 70813. Offers MS. *Degree requirements:* For master's, comprehensive exam, thesis optional. *Entrance requirements:* For master's, GMAT, GRE General Test. Additional exam requirements/recommendations for international students: Required—TOEFL. *Faculty research:* Algebraic number theory, abstract algebra, computer analysis, probability, mathematics education.

Stanford University, School of Engineering, Institute for Computational and Mathematical Engineering, Stanford, CA 94305-2004. Offers MS, PhD. *Expenses: Tuition:* Full-time $50,703; part-time $32,970 per year. *Required fees:* $651.
Website: http://icme.stanford.edu/

Stanford University, School of Humanities and Sciences, Department of Mathematics, Stanford, CA 94305-2004. Offers PhD. *Expenses: Tuition:* Full-time $50,703; part-time $32,970 per year. *Required fees:* $651.
Website: http://math.stanford.edu/

State University of New York College at Cortland, Graduate Studies, School of Arts and Sciences, Programs in Adolescence Education, Cortland, NY 13045. Offers biology (MAT); chemistry (MAT); English (MAT, MS Ed); mathematics (MAT); mathematics and physics (MS Ed); physics (MAT, MS Ed). *Accreditation:* NCATE. *Program availability:* Part-time, evening/weekend. *Degree requirements:* For master's, one foreign language, comprehensive exam (for some programs), thesis (for some programs). *Entrance requirements:* For master's, GRE General Test.

State University of New York College at Potsdam, School of Arts and Sciences, Department of Mathematics, Potsdam, NY 13676. Offers MA. *Program availability:* Part-time, evening/weekend. *Entrance requirements:* For master's, minimum GPA of 3.0 in all undergraduate math courses, 2.75 in last 60 hours of undergraduate coursework. Additional exam requirements/recommendations for international students: Required— TOEFL (minimum score 550 paper-based; 80 iBT), IELTS (minimum score 6). Electronic applications accepted.

Stephen F. Austin State University, Graduate School, College of Sciences and Mathematics, Department of Mathematics and Statistics, Nacogdoches, TX 75962. Offers mathematics (MS); mathematics education (MS); statistics (MS). *Degree requirements:* For master's, comprehensive exam, thesis optional. *Entrance requirements:* For master's, GRE General Test, minimum GPA of 2.8 in last 60 hours, 2.5 overall. Additional exam requirements/recommendations for international students: Required—TOEFL. *Faculty research:* Kernel type estimators, fractal mappings, spline curve fitting, robust regression continua theory.

Stevens Institute of Technology, Graduate School, Charles V. Schaefer Jr. School of Engineering and Science, Department of Mathematical Sciences, Program in Mathematics, Hoboken, NJ 07030. Offers MS, PhD. *Program availability:* Part-time, evening/weekend. *Faculty:* 21 full-time (2 women), 1 part-time/adjunct (0 women). *Students:* 19 full-time (5 women), 2 part-time (1 woman); includes 3 minority (2 Asian, non-Hispanic/Latino; 1 Hispanic/Latino), 8 international. Average age 33. In 2018, 5 master's awarded. Terminal master's awarded for partial completion of doctoral program. *Degree requirements:* For master's, thesis optional, minimum B average in major field and overall; for doctorate, comprehensive exam (for some programs), thesis/ dissertation. *Entrance requirements:* For master's, GRE/GMAT scores: GRE scores are required for all applicants applying to a full-time graduate program in the Schaefer School of Engineering and Science (SES). International applicants must submit TOEFL/ IELTS scores and fulfill the English Language Proficiency Requirements in order to be considered. Additional exam requirements/recommendations for international students: Required—TOEFL (minimum score 74 iBT), IELTS (minimum score 6). *Application deadline:* For fall admission, 4/15 for domestic and international students; for spring admission, 11/1 for domestic and international students; for summer admission, 5/1 for

Peterson's Graduate Programs in the Physical Sciences, Mathematics, Agricultural Sciences, the Environment & Natural Resources 2020

www.petersons.com **221**

domestic students. Applications are processed on a rolling basis. Application fee: $60. Electronic applications accepted. *Expenses: Tuition:* Full-time $35,960; part-time $1620 per credit. *Required fees:* $1290; $600 per semester. Tuition and fees vary according to course load. *Financial support:* Fellowships, research assistantships, teaching assistantships, career-related internships or fieldwork, Federal Work-Study, scholarships/grants, and unspecified assistantships available. Financial award application deadline: 2/15; financial award applicants required to submit FAFSA. *Unit head:* Dr. Jean Zu, Dean of SES, 201-216.8233, Fax: 201-216.8372, E-mail: Jean.Zu@stevens.edu. *Application contact:* Graduate Admission, 888-783-8367, Fax: 888-511-1306, E-mail: graduate@stevens.edu.

Stony Brook University, State University of New York, Graduate School, College of Arts and Sciences, Department of Mathematics, Stony Brook, NY 11794. Offers MA, MAT, PhD. *Faculty:* 40 full-time (10 women), 11 part-time/adjunct (4 women). *Students:* 74 full-time (12 women), 8 part-time (6 women); includes 8 minority (6 Asian, non-Hispanic/Latino; 1 Hispanic/Latino; 1 Two or more races, non-Hispanic/Latino), 51 international. Average age 25. 316 applicants, 14% accepted, 21 enrolled. In 2018, 6 master's, 8 doctorates awarded. *Degree requirements:* For doctorate, 2 foreign languages, thesis/dissertation. *Entrance requirements:* For master's and doctorate, GRE General Test. Additional exam requirements/recommendations for international students: Required—TOEFL (minimum score 90 iBT). *Application deadline:* For fall admission, 1/15 for domestic students; for spring admission, 10/1 for domestic students. Application fee: $100. Electronic applications accepted. *Expenses:* Contact institution. *Financial support:* In 2018–19, 10 fellowships, 11 research assistantships, 42 teaching assistantships were awarded. *Faculty research:* Mathematics, algebra, topology, polynomials, geometry. *Total annual research expenditures:* $2.2 million. *Unit head:* Dr. Alexander Kirillov, Chair, 631-632-8260, E-mail: chair@math.stonybrook.edu. *Application contact:* Donna McWilliams, Coordinator, 631-632-8282, Fax: 631-632-7631, E-mail: donna.mcwilliams@stonybrook.edu.
Website: http://www.math.stonybrook.edu/

Syracuse University, College of Arts and Sciences, Department of Mathematics, Syracuse, NY 13244. Offers math education (PhD); mathematics (MS, PhD); mathematics education (MS). *Program availability:* Part-time. In 2018, 11 master's, 3 doctorates awarded. Terminal master's awarded for partial completion of doctoral program. *Degree requirements:* For doctorate, 2 foreign languages, comprehensive exam, thesis/dissertation. *Entrance requirements:* For master's and doctorate, GRE General Test, GRE Subject Test (recommended), brief (about 500 words) statement indicating why applicant wishes to pursue graduate study and why Syracuse is a good fit, curriculum vitae or resume, transcripts from each post-secondary institution, three letters of recommendation. Additional exam requirements/recommendations for international students: Required—TOEFL (minimum score 100 iBT). *Application deadline:* For fall admission, 1/20 priority date for domestic and international students. Application fee: $75. Electronic applications accepted. *Financial support:* Teaching assistantships, scholarships/grants, and tuition waivers available. Financial award applicants required to submit FAFSA. *Faculty research:* Pure mathematics, numerical mathematics, computing statistics. *Unit head:* Dr. Uday Banerjee, Chair, 315-443-1471, E-mail: banerjee@syr.edu. *Application contact:* Graham Leuschke, Professor and Associate Chair for Graduate Affairs, 315-443-1500, E-mail: gjleusch@syr.edu.
Website: http://math.syr.edu

Tarleton State University, College of Graduate Studies, College of Science and Technology, Department of Mathematics, Stephenville, TX 76402. Offers MS. *Program availability:* Part-time, evening/weekend. *Faculty:* 4 full-time (2 women). *Students:* 3 full-time (0 women), 10 part-time (3 women). Average age 27. 6 applicants, 100% accepted, 5 enrolled. In 2018, 10 master's awarded. *Degree requirements:* For master's, comprehensive exam, thesis (for some programs). *Entrance requirements:* For master's, GRE General Test, minimum GPA of 3.0. Additional exam requirements/recommendations for international students: Required—TOEFL (minimum score 520 paper-based; 69 iBT); Recommended—IELTS (minimum score 6), TSE (minimum score 50). *Application deadline:* For fall admission, 8/15 priority date for domestic students; for spring admission, 1/7 for domestic students. Applications are processed on a rolling basis. Application fee: $50 ($130 for international students). Electronic applications accepted. *Expenses:* Contact institution. *Financial support:* Research assistantships, teaching assistantships, career-related internships or fieldwork, and Federal Work-Study available. Support available to part-time students. Financial award application deadline: 5/1; financial award applicants required to submit FAFSA. *Unit head:* Dr. Bowen Brawner, Department Head, 254-968-9167, Fax: 254-968-9534, E-mail: brawner@tarleton.edu. *Application contact:* Information Contact, 254-968-9104, Fax: 254-968-9670, E-mail: gradoffice@tarleton.edu.
Website: http://www.tarleton.edu/degrees/masters/ms-mathematics/

Temple University, College of Science and Technology, Department of Mathematics, Philadelphia, PA 19122. Offers applied and computational mathematics (MS); mathematics (MS, PhD). *Program availability:* Part-time. *Faculty:* 30 full-time (3 women). *Students:* 32 full-time (12 women), 2 part-time (1 woman); includes 6 minority (5 Asian, non-Hispanic/Latino; 1 Hispanic/Latino), 17 international. 74 applicants, 35% accepted, 10 enrolled. In 2018, 6 master's, 6 doctorates awarded. *Degree requirements:* For master's, thesis optional; for doctorate, comprehensive exam, thesis/dissertation. *Entrance requirements:* For master's, GRE General Test, 3 letters of recommendation, statement of goals, resume; for doctorate, GRE General Test, GRE Subject Test, 3 letters of recommendation, statement of goals, resume. Additional exam requirements/recommendations for international students: Required—TOEFL (minimum score 79 iBT), IELTS (minimum score 6.5), PTE (minimum score 53), one of three is required. *Application deadline:* Applications are processed on a rolling basis. Application fee: $60. Electronic applications accepted. *Expenses:* Contact institution. *Financial support:* Research assistantships, teaching assistantships, Federal Work-Study, health care benefits, and unspecified assistantships available. Financial award applicants required to submit FAFSA. *Faculty research:* Complex analysis, partial differential equations, low dimensional topology, geometric group theory, applied mathematics. *Unit head:* Brian Rider, Department Chair, 215-204-7589, E-mail: brian.rider@temple.edu. *Application contact:* David Futer, Graduate Chairperson, 215-204-7854, E-mail: grad.math@temple.edu.
Website: http://math.temple.edu/

Tennessee State University, The School of Graduate Studies and Research, College of Engineering, Nashville, TN 37209-1561. Offers biomedical engineering (ME); civil engineering (ME); computer and information systems engineering (MS, PhD); electrical engineering (ME); environmental engineering (ME); manufacturing engineering (ME); mathematical sciences (MS); mechanical engineering (ME). *Program availability:* Part-time, evening/weekend. *Degree requirements:* For master's, project; for doctorate, comprehensive exam, thesis/dissertation. *Entrance requirements:* For doctorate, minimum GPA of 3.3. *Faculty research:* Robotics, intelligent systems, human-computer interaction software systems, biomedical engineering, signal/image processing, probabilistic design, intelligent manufacturing, cooperative mobile robots, condition based maintenance, sensor fusion.

Tennessee Technological University, College of Graduate Studies, College of Arts and Sciences, Department of Mathematics, Cookeville, TN 38505. Offers MS. *Program availability:* Part-time. *Faculty:* 17 full-time (4 women). *Students:* 8 full-time (2 women), 1 (woman) part-time, 1 international. 11 applicants, 82% accepted, 4 enrolled. In 2018, 4 master's awarded. *Degree requirements:* For master's, thesis or alternative. *Entrance requirements:* For master's, GRE General Test. Additional exam requirements/recommendations for international students: Required—TOEFL (minimum score 527 paper-based; 71 iBT), IELTS (minimum score 5.5), PTE (minimum score 48), or TOEIC (Test of English as an International Communication). *Application deadline:* For fall admission, 8/1 for domestic students, 5/1 for international students; for spring admission, 12/1 for domestic students, 10/1 for international students; for summer admission, 5/1 for domestic students, 2/1 for international students. Applications are processed on a rolling basis. Application fee: $35 ($40 for international students). Electronic applications accepted. *Financial support:* In 2018–19, 8 teaching assistantships (averaging $9,600 per year) were awarded; research assistantships also available. Financial award application deadline: 4/1. *Unit head:* Dr. Allan Mills, Chairperson, 931-372-3441, Fax: 931-372-6353, E-mail: amills@tntech.edu. *Application contact:* Shelia K. Kendrick, Coordinator of Graduate Studies, 931-372-3808, Fax: 931-372-3497, E-mail: skendrick@tntech.edu.

Texas A&M International University, Office of Graduate Studies and Research, College of Arts and Sciences, Department of Mathematics and Physics, Laredo, TX 78041. Offers mathematics (MS). *Degree requirements:* For master's, comprehensive exam, thesis (for some programs). *Entrance requirements:* For master's, GRE General Test. Additional exam requirements/recommendations for international students: Required—TOEFL (minimum score 550 paper-based; 79 iBT).

Texas A&M University, College of Science, Department of Mathematics, College Station, TX 77843. Offers mathematics (MS, PhD); quantitative finance (MS). *Program availability:* Part-time, online learning. *Faculty:* 70. *Students:* 135 full-time (35 women), 36 part-time (21 women); includes 21 minority (8 Asian, non-Hispanic/Latino; 9 Hispanic/Latino; 4 Two or more races, non-Hispanic/Latino), 74 international. Average age 29. 164 applicants, 42% accepted, 30 enrolled. In 2018, 38 master's, 15 doctorates awarded. Terminal master's awarded for partial completion of doctoral program. *Degree requirements:* For master's, comprehensive exam, thesis optional; for doctorate, one foreign language, comprehensive exam, thesis/dissertation. *Entrance requirements:* For master's and doctorate, GRE General Test. Additional exam requirements/recommendations for international students: Required—TOEFL (minimum score 550 paper-based). *Application deadline:* For fall admission, 12/15 for domestic and international students; for spring admission, 8/1 for domestic and international students; for summer admission, 11/1 for domestic and international students. Applications are processed on a rolling basis. Application fee: $50 ($90 for international students). Electronic applications accepted. *Expenses:* Contact institution. *Financial support:* In 2018–19, 134 students received support, including 11 fellowships with tuition reimbursements available (averaging $6,841 per year), 12 research assistantships with tuition reimbursements available (averaging $13,216 per year), 103 teaching assistantships with tuition reimbursements available (averaging $17,836 per year); career-related internships or fieldwork, institutionally sponsored loans, scholarships/grants, traineeships, health care benefits, tuition waivers (full and partial), and unspecified assistantships also available. Support available to part-time students. Financial award application deadline: 3/1; financial award applicants required to submit FAFSA. *Faculty research:* Algebra and combinatorics, applied mathematics and interdisciplinary research, approximation theory, functional analysis, geometry and topology. *Unit head:* Dr. Emil Straube, Head, 979-845-9424, Fax: 979-845-6028, E-mail: straube@math.tamu.edu. *Application contact:* Monique Stewart, Academic Advisor, 979-862-4137, Fax: 979-862-4190, E-mail: stewart@math.tamu.edu.
Website: http://www.math.tamu.edu/

Texas A&M University–Central Texas, Graduate Studies and Research, Killeen, TX 76549. Offers accounting (MS); business administration (MBA); clinical mental health counseling (MS); criminal justice (MCJ); curriculum and instruction (M Ed); educational administration (M Ed); educational psychology - experimental psychology (MS); history (MA); human resource management (MS); information systems (MS); liberal studies (MS); management and leadership (MS); marriage and family therapy (MS); mathematics (MS); political science (MA); school counseling (M Ed); school psychology (Ed S).

Texas A&M University–Commerce, College of Science and Engineering, Commerce, TX 75429. Offers biological sciences (MS); broadfield science biology (MS); broadfield science chemistry (MS); broadfield science physics (MS); chemistry (MS); computational linguistics (Graduate Certificate); computational science (MS); computer science (MS); environmental science (Graduate Certificate); mathematics (MS); physics (MS); technology management (MS). *Program availability:* Part-time. *Faculty:* 44 full-time (7 women), 7 part-time/adjunct (0 women). *Students:* 178 full-time (67 women), 234 part-time (104 women); includes 82 minority (19 Black or African American, non-Hispanic/Latino; 1 American Indian or Alaska Native, non-Hispanic/Latino; 14 Asian, non-Hispanic/Latino; 37 Hispanic/Latino; 11 Two or more races, non-Hispanic/Latino), 158 international. Average age 30. 481 applicants, 52% accepted, 105 enrolled. In 2018, 218 master's awarded. *Degree requirements:* For master's, comprehensive exam, thesis optional. *Entrance requirements:* For master's, GRE, official transcripts, letters of recommendation, resume, statement of goals. Additional exam requirements/recommendations for international students: Required—TOEFL (minimum score 550 paper-based; 79 iBT), IELTS (minimum score 6), PTE (minimum score 53). *Application deadline:* For fall admission, 6/1 priority date for international students; for spring admission, 10/15 priority date for international students; for summer admission, 3/15 priority date for international students. Applications are processed on a rolling basis. Application fee: $50 ($75 for international students). Electronic applications accepted. *Expenses:* Contact institution. *Financial support:* In 2018–19, 46 students received support, including 43 research assistantships with partial tuition reimbursements available (averaging $2,418 per year), 135 teaching assistantships with partial tuition reimbursements available (averaging $3,376 per year); scholarships/grants, health care benefits, and unspecified assistantships also available. Financial award application deadline: 5/1; financial award applicants required to submit FAFSA. *Faculty research:* Biomedical, Catalytic Material & Processes, Nuclear Theory/Astrophysics, Cybersecurity, STEM Education. *Total annual research expenditures:* $1.8 million. *Unit head:* Dr. Brent L. Donham, Dean, 903-886-5321, Fax: 903-886-5199, E-mail: brent.donham@tamuc.edu. *Application contact:* Dayla Burgin, Graduate Student Services Coordinator, 903-886-5134, E-mail: dayla.burgin@tamuc.edu.
Website: https://new.tamuc.edu/science-engineering/

Texas A&M University–Corpus Christi, College of Graduate Studies, College of Science and Engineering, Program in Mathematics, Corpus Christi, TX 78412. Offers MS. *Program availability:* Part-time. *Degree requirements:* For master's, thesis (for some programs), capstone. *Entrance requirements:* For master's, essay (300-500 words). Additional exam requirements/recommendations for international students: Required—TOEFL (minimum score 550 paper-based; 79 iBT), IELTS (minimum score 6.5). Electronic applications accepted.

Texas A&M University–Kingsville, College of Graduate Studies, College of Arts and Sciences, Department of Mathematics, Kingsville, TX 78363. Offers mathematics (MS); statistical analytics, computing and modeling (MS). *Entrance requirements:* Additional exam requirements/recommendations for international students: Required—TOEFL (minimum score 550 paper-based; 79 iBT); Recommended—IELTS. Electronic applications accepted.

Texas Christian University, College of Science and Engineering, Department of Mathematics, Fort Worth, TX 76129-0002. Offers applied mathematics (MS); mathematics (MAT, PhD); pure mathematics (MS). *Program availability:* Part-time, evening/weekend. *Faculty:* 13 full-time (2 women). *Students:* 12 full-time (5 women), 1 part-time (0 women); includes 4 minority (1 Asian, non-Hispanic/Latino; 2 Hispanic/Latino; 1 Two or more races, non-Hispanic/Latino), 2 international. Average age 28. 11 applicants, 45% accepted, 4 enrolled. In 2018, 2 master's awarded. Terminal master's awarded for partial completion of doctoral program. *Degree requirements:* For master's, thesis optional; for doctorate, comprehensive exam, thesis/dissertation. *Entrance requirements:* For master's and doctorate, GRE General Test, 24 hours of math, including courses in elementary calculus of one and several variables, linear algebra, abstract algebra and real analysis. Additional exam requirements/recommendations for international students: Recommended—TOEFL (minimum score 550 paper-based; 80 iBT), IELTS (minimum score 6.5). *Application deadline:* For fall admission, 1/1 priority date for domestic and international students; for spring admission, 9/1 priority date for domestic and international students. Application fee: $60. Electronic applications accepted. *Financial support:* In 2018–19, 9 students received support, including 9 teaching assistantships with full tuition reimbursements available (averaging $15,000 per year); tuition waivers (full) also available. Support available to part-time students. Financial award application deadline: 1/1. *Faculty research:* Algebraic geometry, differential geometry and global analysis, algebraic topology, K-theory and operator algebras, number theory. *Total annual research expenditures:* $60,000. *Unit head:* Dr. Greg Friedman, Professor/Chair, 817-257-6343, Fax: 817-257-7766, E-mail: g.friedman@tcu.edu. *Application contact:* Dr. Ken Richardson, Professor/Director, Graduate Program, 817-257-6128, E-mail: k.richardson@tcu.edu.
Website: http://mathematics.tcu.edu/

Texas Southern University, School of Science and Technology, Department of Mathematics, Houston, TX 77004-4584. Offers MS. *Program availability:* Part-time, evening/weekend. *Degree requirements:* For master's, comprehensive exam, thesis. *Entrance requirements:* For master's, GRE General Test, minimum GPA of 2.5. Additional exam requirements/recommendations for international students: Required—TOEFL. Electronic applications accepted. *Faculty research:* Statistics, number theory, topology, differential equations, numerical analysis.

Texas State University, The Graduate College, College of Science and Engineering, Program in Mathematics, San Marcos, TX 78666. Offers M Ed, MS. *Program availability:* Part-time. *Faculty:* 22 full-time (7 women). *Students:* 17 full-time (7 women), 7 part-time (4 women); includes 9 minority (1 Asian, non-Hispanic/Latino; 8 Hispanic/Latino), 3 international. Average age 32. 47 applicants, 64% accepted, 14 enrolled. In 2018, 6 master's awarded. *Degree requirements:* For master's, comprehensive exam, thesis (for some programs). *Entrance requirements:* For master's, official GRE (general test only) required with competitive scores in the verbal reasoning and quantitative reasoning sections, baccalaureate degree in mathematics or related field from regionally-accredited university with minimum GPA of 2.75 on last 60 undergraduate semester hours, resume, statement of purpose, 3 letters of recommendation addressing the substance and quality of preparation for graduate study. Additional exam requirements/recommendations for international students: Required—TOEFL (minimum score 550 paper-based; 78 iBT), IELTS (minimum score 6.5). *Application deadline:* For fall admission, 2/1 priority date for domestic and international students; for spring admission, 8/15 priority date for domestic and international students; for summer admission, 4/15 for domestic students, 3/15 for international students. Applications are processed on a rolling basis. Application fee: $55 ($90 for international students). Electronic applications accepted. *Expenses:* Tuition, state resident: full-time $8102; part-time $4051 per semester. Tuition, nonresident: full-time $18,229; part-time $9115 per semester. *International tuition:* $18,229 full-time. *Required fees:* $2116; $120 per credit hour. Tuition and fees vary according to course load. *Financial support:* In 2018–19, 14 students received support, including 1 research assistantship (averaging $18,000 per year), 10 teaching assistantships (averaging $14,514 per year); Federal Work-Study, institutionally sponsored loans, scholarships/grants, health care benefits, and unspecified assistantships also available. Support available to part-time students. Financial award application deadline: 1/15; financial award applicants required to submit FAFSA. *Faculty research:* Orbits in finite group actions, modeling and simulations of complex fluids and atomistic strain, innovative weak galerkin finite element methods with application in fluorescence. *Total annual research expenditures:* $15,100. *Unit head:* Dr. Stewart Welsh, Graduate Advisor, 512-245-3426, Fax: 512-245-3425, E-mail: mathgrad@txstate.edu. *Application contact:* Dr. Andrea Golato, Dean of the Graduate College, 512-245-3446, Fax: 512-245-3425, E-mail: gp02@txstate.edu.
Website: http://www.math.txstate.edu/degrees-programs/masters.html

Texas Tech University, Graduate School, College of Arts and Sciences, Department of Mathematics and Statistics, Lubbock, TX 79409-1042. Offers mathematics (MA, MS, PhD); statistics (MS). *Program availability:* Part-time. *Faculty:* 62 full-time (17 women). *Students:* 95 full-time (45 women), 7 part-time (2 women); includes 15 minority (7 Asian, non-Hispanic/Latino; 5 Hispanic/Latino; 3 Two or more races, non-Hispanic/Latino), 69 international. Average age 29. 81 applicants, 54% accepted, 24 enrolled. In 2018, 31 master's, 23 doctorates awarded. Terminal master's awarded for partial completion of doctoral program. *Degree requirements:* For master's, comprehensive exam (for some programs), thesis (for some programs); for doctorate, comprehensive exam, thesis/dissertation. *Entrance requirements:* For master's, GRE (for MS and assistantship applications only), official transcripts, 3 letters of recommendation, resume/CV, cover letter; for doctorate, GRE General Test, official transcripts, 3 letters of recommendation, resume/CV, cover letter. Additional exam requirements/recommendations for international students: Required—TOEFL (minimum score 550 paper-based; 79 iBT), IELTS (minimum score 6.5). *Application deadline:* For fall admission, 6/1 priority date for domestic students, 1/15 priority date for international students; for spring admission, 9/1 priority date for domestic students, 6/15 priority date for international students. Applications are processed on a rolling basis. Application fee: $65. Electronic applications accepted. *Expenses:* Contact institution. *Financial support:* In 2018–19, 105 students received support, including 92 fellowships (averaging $2,171 per year), 6 research assistantships (averaging $17,386 per year), 95 teaching assistantships (averaging $17,841 per year). Financial award application deadline: 12/15; financial award applicants required to submit FAFSA. *Faculty research:* Applied math, biomathematics, complex analysis, computational mathematics, statistics. *Total annual research expenditures:* $525,707. *Unit head:* Dr. Magdalena Toda, Professor & Department Chair, 806-834-7944, Fax: 806-742-1112, E-mail: magda.toda@ttu.edu. *Application contact:* David Cannon, Program Manager, Graduate Studies, 806-834-7393, Fax: 806-742-1112, E-mail: david.cannon@ttu.edu.
Website: www.math.ttu.edu/

Texas Woman's University, Graduate School, College of Arts and Sciences, Department of Mathematics and Computer Science, Denton, TX 76204. Offers emphasis in mathematics or computer science (MAT); informatics (MS); mathematics (MS); mathematics teaching (MS). *Program availability:* Part-time, evening/weekend, blended/hybrid learning. *Faculty:* 11 full-time (7 women), 1 part-time/adjunct (0 women). *Students:* 17 full-time (13 women), 71 part-time (49 women); includes 53 minority (22 Black or African American, non-Hispanic/Latino; 16 Asian, non-Hispanic/Latino; 13 Hispanic/Latino; 2 Two or more races, non-Hispanic/Latino), 2 international. Average age 36. 37 applicants, 78% accepted, 24 enrolled. In 2018, 23 master's awarded. *Degree requirements:* For master's, comprehensive exam, thesis (for some programs), professional paper, capstone or thesis (depending on degree). *Entrance requirements:* For master's, minimum GPA of 3.0 in last 60 undergraduate credit hours, 2 semesters of calculus, 2 additional advanced math courses, 2 letters of reference (for MS in mathematics, mathematics teaching); minimum GPA of 3.0, statement of intent, resume, 2 letters of recommendation (for MS in informatics). Additional exam requirements/recommendations for international students: Required—TOEFL (minimum score 79 iBT); Recommended—IELTS (minimum score 6.5), TSE (minimum score 53). *Application deadline:* Applications are processed on a rolling basis. Application fee: $50 ($75 for international students). Electronic applications accepted. *Expenses:* Tuition, area resident: Full-time $4852; part-time $270 per semester hour. Tuition, state resident: full-time $4852; part-time $270 per semester hour. Tuition, nonresident: full-time $12,322; part-time $685 per semester hour. *International tuition:* $12,322 full-time. *Required fees:* $2714; $113 per semester hour. $296 per semester. Tuition and fees vary according to course level, course load, degree level, campus/location and program. *Financial support:* In 2018–19, 16 students received support, including 12 teaching assistantships (averaging $10,987 per year); career-related internships or fieldwork, Federal Work-Study, institutionally sponsored loans, scholarships/grants, traineeships, health care benefits, and unspecified assistantships also available. Support available to part-time students. Financial award application deadline: 3/1; financial award applicants required to submit FAFSA. *Faculty research:* Optimal control theory and differential games, information security, statistics and modern approaches, knot theory, math and computer science education. *Unit head:* Dr. Don E. Edwards, Chair, 940-898-2166, Fax: 940-898-2179, E-mail: mathcs@twu.edu. *Application contact:* Korie Hawkins, Associate Director of Admissions, Graduate Recruitment, 940-898-3188, Fax: 940-898-3081, E-mail: admissions@twu.edu.
Website: http://www.twu.edu/math-computer-science/

Tufts University, Graduate School of Arts and Sciences, Department of Mathematics, Medford, MA 02155. Offers mathematics (MS, PhD). Terminal master's awarded for partial completion of doctoral program. *Degree requirements:* For master's, thesis; for doctorate, comprehensive exam, thesis/dissertation. *Entrance requirements:* For master's, GRE General Test; for doctorate, GRE General Test, GRE Subject Test. Additional exam requirements/recommendations for international students: Required—TOEFL (minimum score 550 paper-based; 80 iBT), IELTS (minimum score 6.5). Electronic applications accepted. *Expenses:* Contact institution.

Tulane University, School of Science and Engineering, Department of Mathematics, New Orleans, LA 70118-5669. Offers MS, PhD. *Degree requirements:* For master's, thesis (for some programs); for doctorate, thesis/dissertation. *Entrance requirements:* For master's, GRE General Test, minimum B average in undergraduate course work; for doctorate, GRE General Test. Additional exam requirements/recommendations for international students: Required—TOEFL. Electronic applications accepted. *Expenses: Tuition:* Full-time $52,856; part-time $2937 per credit hour. *Required fees:* $2040; $44.50 per credit hour. $580 per term. Tuition and fees vary according to course load, degree level and program.

Université de Moncton, Faculty of Sciences, Department of Mathematics and Statistics, Moncton, NB E1A 3E9, Canada. Offers mathematics (M Sc). *Degree requirements:* For master's, one foreign language, thesis. *Entrance requirements:* For master's, minimum GPA of 3.0. Electronic applications accepted. *Faculty research:* Statistics, numerical analysis, fixed point theory, mathematical physics.

Université de Montréal, Faculty of Arts and Sciences, Department of Mathematics and Statistics, Montréal, QC H3C 3J7, Canada. Offers mathematical and computational finance (M Sc, DESS); mathematics (M Sc, PhD); statistics (M Sc, PhD). *Degree requirements:* For master's, thesis; for doctorate, thesis/dissertation, general exam. *Entrance requirements:* For master's and doctorate, proficiency in French. Electronic applications accepted. *Faculty research:* Pure and applied mathematics, actuarial mathematics.

Université de Sherbrooke, Faculty of Sciences, Department of Mathematics, Sherbrooke, QC J1K 2R1, Canada. Offers M Sc, PhD. *Degree requirements:* For master's, thesis; for doctorate, comprehensive exam, thesis/dissertation. *Entrance requirements:* For doctorate, master's degree. Electronic applications accepted. *Faculty research:* Measure theory, differential equations, probability, statistics, error control codes.

Université du Québec à Montréal, Graduate Programs, Program in Mathematics, Montréal, QC H3C 3P8, Canada. Offers M Sc, PhD. *Program availability:* Part-time. *Degree requirements:* For master's, thesis; for doctorate, thesis/dissertation. *Entrance requirements:* For master's, appropriate bachelor's degree or equivalent, proficiency in French; for doctorate, appropriate master's degree or equivalent, proficiency in French.

Université du Québec à Trois-Rivières, Graduate Programs, Program in Mathematics and Computer Science, Trois-Rivières, QC G9A 5H7, Canada. Offers M Sc. *Faculty research:* Probability, statistics.

Université Laval, Faculty of Sciences and Engineering, Department of Mathematics and Statistics, Programs in Mathematics, Québec, QC G1K 7P4, Canada. Offers M Sc, PhD. Terminal master's awarded for partial completion of doctoral program. *Degree requirements:* For master's, thesis (for some programs); for doctorate, comprehensive exam, thesis/dissertation. *Entrance requirements:* For master's and doctorate, knowledge of French and English. Electronic applications accepted.

University at Albany, State University of New York, College of Arts and Sciences, Department of Mathematics and Statistics, Albany, NY 12222-0001. Offers mathematics (MA, PhD). *Faculty:* 24 full-time (2 women). *Students:* 18 full-time (1 woman); includes 15 minority (2 Black or African American, non-Hispanic/Latino; 1 American Indian or Alaska Native, non-Hispanic/Latino; 5 Asian, non-Hispanic/Latino; 5 Hispanic/Latino; 2 Two or more races, non-Hispanic/Latino), 31 international. 61 applicants, 39% accepted, 12 enrolled. In 2018, 8 master's awarded. *Degree requirements:* For doctorate, one foreign language, thesis/dissertation. *Entrance requirements:* For doctorate, GRE General Test. Additional exam requirements/recommendations for international students: Required—TOEFL (minimum score 550 paper-based). *Application deadline:* For fall admission, 3/15 for domestic students, 5/1 for international students; for spring admission, 11/1 for international students. Applications are processed on a rolling basis. Application fee: $75. Electronic applications accepted. *Financial support:* Fellowships, research assistantships, teaching assistantships, and minority assistantships available.

Peterson's Graduate Programs in the Physical Sciences, Mathematics, Agricultural Sciences, the Environment & Natural Resources 2020

www.petersons.com **223**

Financial award application deadline: 3/15. *Unit head:* Michael Stessin, Chair, 518-442-4600, Fax: 518-442-4731, E-mail: mstessin@albany.edu. *Application contact:* Michael DeRensis, Director, Graduate Admissions, 518-442-3980, Fax: 518-442-3922, E-mail: graduate@albany.edu.
Website: http://mathalbany.edu/default.html

University at Buffalo, the State University of New York, Graduate School, College of Arts and Sciences, Department of Mathematics, Buffalo, NY 14260. Offers MA, PhD. Terminal master's awarded for partial completion of doctoral program. *Degree requirements:* For master's, comprehensive exam (for some programs), thesis (for some programs), project (for some programs); for doctorate, comprehensive exam, thesis/dissertation. *Entrance requirements:* Additional exam requirements/recommendations for international students: Required—TOEFL (minimum score 550 paper-based, 79 iBT), IELTS (minimum score 6.5), or PTE (minimum score 55 with all areas not less than 50). Electronic applications accepted. *Expenses:* Contact institution. *Faculty research:* Algebra, analysis, applied mathematics, logic, number theory, topology.

The University of Akron, Graduate School, Buchtel College of Arts and Sciences, Department of Mathematics, Program in Mathematics, Akron, OH 44325. Offers MS. *Program availability:* Part-time, evening/weekend. *Degree requirements:* For master's, seminar and comprehensive exam or thesis. *Entrance requirements:* For master's, minimum GPA of 2.75, three letters of recommendation, statement of purpose. Additional exam requirements/recommendations for international students: Required—TOEFL (minimum score 79 iBT), IELTS (minimum score 6.5). Electronic applications accepted.

The University of Alabama, Graduate School, College of Arts and Sciences, Department of Mathematics, Tuscaloosa, AL 35487. Offers applied mathematics (PhD); mathematics (MA, PhD); pure mathematics (PhD). Terminal master's awarded for partial completion of doctoral program. *Degree requirements:* For master's, thesis or alternative, 24 semester hours of course work, plus thesis in mathematics, or 27 semester hours of courses plus 3 hours of work on project supervised by member of graduate faculty in mathematics; for doctorate, comprehensive exam, thesis/dissertation, 48 hours of coursework with minimum of 39 hours in mathematics; qualifying exams in two areas of mathematics; candidacy; completion of at least 24 semester hours of dissertation research; written dissertation and oral defense. *Entrance requirements:* For master's and doctorate, GRE (minimum of 300 total combined Verbal/Quantitative subscores), statement of purpose; three letters of recommendation; official transcripts; BA, BS or B Sc in mathematics or closely-related subject with minimum GPA of 3.0. Additional exam requirements/recommendations for international students: Recommended—TOEFL (minimum score 550 paper-based; 79 iBT), IELTS (minimum score 6.5). Electronic applications accepted. *Faculty research:* Algebra, analysis, topology, mathematics education, applied and computational mathematics, statistics.

The University of Alabama at Birmingham, College of Arts and Sciences, Program in Mathematics, Birmingham, AL 35294. Offers MS. Terminal master's awarded for partial completion of doctoral program. *Degree requirements:* For master's, thesis or alternative. *Entrance requirements:* For master's, GRE General Test, minimum GPA of 3.0, letters of recommendation. Additional exam requirements/recommendations for international students: Required—TOEFL, TWE. Electronic applications accepted. *Expenses: Tuition, area resident:* Full-time $8100; part-time $8100 per year. Tuition, state resident: full-time $8100. Tuition, nonresident: full-time $19,188; part-time $19,188 per year. Tuition and fees vary according to program. *Faculty research:* Differential equations, topology, mathematical physics, dynamic systems.

The University of Alabama in Huntsville, School of Graduate Studies, College of Science, Department of Mathematical Sciences, Huntsville, AL 35899. Offers applied mathematics (PhD); education (MA); mathematics (MA, MS). PhD offered jointly with The University of Alabama (Tuscaloosa) and The University of Alabama at Birmingham. *Program availability:* Part-time. *Faculty:* 7 full-time. *Students:* 18 full-time (4 women), 12 part-time (4 women); includes 5 minority (3 Black or African American, non-Hispanic/Latino; 2 Asian, non-Hispanic/Latino), 2 international. Average age 31. 25 applicants, 80% accepted, 10 enrolled. In 2018, 6 master's, 3 doctorates awarded. *Degree requirements:* For master's, comprehensive exam, thesis or alternative, oral and written exams; for doctorate, comprehensive exam, thesis/dissertation, oral and written exams. *Entrance requirements:* For master's and doctorate, GRE General Test, minimum GPA of 3.0. Additional exam requirements/recommendations for international students: Required—TOEFL (minimum score 550 paper-based; 80 iBT), IELTS (minimum score 6.5). *Application deadline:* For fall admission, 7/15 priority date for domestic students, 4/1 priority date for international students; for spring admission, 11/30 priority date for domestic students, 9/1 priority date for international students. Applications are processed on a rolling basis. Application fee: $50. Electronic applications accepted. *Expenses: Tuition, area resident:* Full-time $10,632; part-time $412 per credit hour. Tuition, state resident: full-time $10,632. Tuition, nonresident: full-time $23,604; part-time $412 per credit hour. *Required fees:* $582; $582. Tuition and fees vary according to course load and program. *Financial support:* In 2018–19, 7 students received support, including 6 teaching assistantships with full tuition reimbursements available (averaging $6,000 per year); career-related internships or fieldwork, Federal Work-Study, institutionally sponsored loans, scholarships/grants, health care benefits, and unspecified assistantships also available. Support available to part-time students. Financial award application deadline: 4/1; financial award applicants required to submit FAFSA. *Faculty research:* Combinatorics and graph theory, computational mathematics, differential equations and applications, mathematical biology, probability and stochastic processes. *Unit head:* Dr. Toka Diagana, Professor and Chair, 256-824-6470, Fax: 256-824-6173, E-mail: mathchair@uah.edu. *Application contact:* Kim Gray, Graduate Studies Admissions Coordinator, 256-824-6002, Fax: 256-824-6405, E-mail: deangrad@uah.edu.
Website: http://www.math.uah.edu/

University of Alaska Fairbanks, College of Natural Science and Mathematics, Department of Mathematics and Statistics, Fairbanks, AK 99775-6660. Offers mathematics (PhD); statistics (MS, Graduate Certificate). *Program availability:* Part-time. *Faculty:* 17 full-time (6 women). *Students:* 15 full-time (4 women), 1 (woman) part-time; includes 4 minority (3 Asian, non-Hispanic/Latino; 1 Hispanic/Latino), 5 international. Average age 31. 16 applicants, 44% accepted, 4 enrolled. In 2018, 7 master's, 1 other advanced degree awarded. *Degree requirements:* For master's, comprehensive exam, thesis (for some programs), oral defense of project or thesis; for doctorate, comprehensive exam, thesis/dissertation, oral defense of dissertation. *Entrance requirements:* For master's, GRE General Test, bachelor's degree from accredited institution with minimum cumulative undergraduate and major GPA of 3.0; for doctorate, GRE Subject Test (mathematics), bachelor's degree from accredited institution with minimum cumulative undergraduate and major GPA of 3.0. Additional exam requirements/recommendations for international students: Required—TOEFL (minimum score 550 paper-based; 79 iBT), IELTS (minimum score 6.5). *Application deadline:* For fall admission, 6/1 for domestic students, 3/1 for international students; for spring admission, 10/15 for domestic students, 9/1 for international students. Applications are processed on a rolling basis. Application fee: $60. Electronic applications accepted. *Expenses: Tuition, area resident:* Full-time $8802; part-time $5868 per credit hour. Tuition, state resident: full-time $8802; part-time $5868 per credit hour. Tuition, nonresident: full-time $18,504; part-time $12,336 per credit hour. *International tuition:* $18,504 full-time. *Required fees:* $1416; $944 per credit hour. $472 per semester. Tuition and fees vary according to course load and program. *Financial support:* In 2018–19, 1 research assistantship with full tuition reimbursement (averaging $9,404 per year), 10 teaching assistantships with full tuition reimbursements (averaging $18,550 per year) were awarded; fellowships with full tuition reimbursements, career-related internships or fieldwork, Federal Work-Study, scholarships/grants, health care benefits, and unspecified assistantships also available. Support available to part-time students. Financial award application deadline: 2/15; financial award applicants required to submit FAFSA. *Faculty research:* Kriging, arrangements of hyperplanes, bifurcation analysis of time-periodic differential-delay equations, inverse problems, phylogenic tree construction. *Unit head:* Dr. Anthony Rickard, Department Chair, 907-474-5374, E-mail: uaf-mathandstat-dept@alaska.edu. *Application contact:* Samara Taber, Director of Admissions, 907-474-7500, E-mail: uaf-admissions@alaska.edu.
Website: http://www.uaf.edu/dms/

University of Alberta, Faculty of Graduate Studies and Research, Department of Mathematical and Statistical Sciences, Edmonton, AB T6G 2E1, Canada. Offers applied mathematics (M Sc, PhD); biostatistics (M Sc); mathematical finance (M Sc, PhD); mathematical physics (M Sc, PhD); mathematics (M Sc, PhD); statistics (M Sc, PhD, Postgraduate Diploma). *Program availability:* Part-time. Terminal master's awarded for partial completion of doctoral program. *Degree requirements:* For master's, thesis (for some programs); for doctorate, comprehensive exam, thesis/dissertation. *Entrance requirements:* Additional exam requirements/recommendations for international students: Required—TOEFL (minimum score 580 paper-based). Electronic applications accepted. *Faculty research:* Classical and functional analysis, algebra, differential equations, geometry.

The University of Arizona, College of Science, Department of Mathematics, Tucson, AZ 85721. Offers mathematics (MA, MS, PhD); secondary mathematics education (MA). *Program availability:* Part-time. *Degree requirements:* For master's, thesis; for doctorate, 2 foreign languages, thesis/dissertation. *Entrance requirements:* For master's, GRE; for doctorate, GRE, statement of purpose. Additional exam requirements/recommendations for international students: Required—TOEFL (minimum score 550 paper-based; 79 iBT). Electronic applications accepted. *Faculty research:* Algebra/number theory, computational science, dynamical systems, geometry, analysis.

The University of Arizona, Graduate Interdisciplinary Programs, Graduate Interdisciplinary Program in Applied Mathematics, Tucson, AZ 85721. Offers applied mathematics (MS, PhD); mathematical sciences (PMS). Terminal master's awarded for partial completion of doctoral program. *Degree requirements:* For master's, thesis (for some programs); for doctorate, comprehensive exam, thesis/dissertation. *Entrance requirements:* For master's, GRE, 3 letters of recommendation; for doctorate, GRE, 3 letters of recommendation, statement of purpose. Additional exam requirements/recommendations for international students: Required—TOEFL (minimum score 575 paper-based; 80 iBT). Electronic applications accepted. *Faculty research:* Dynamical systems and chaos, partial differential equations, pattern formation, fluid dynamics and turbulence, scientific computation, mathematical physics, mathematical biology, medical imaging, applied probability and stochastic processes.

University of Arkansas, Graduate School, J. William Fulbright College of Arts and Sciences, Department of Mathematical Sciences, Program in Mathematics, Fayetteville, AR 72701. Offers MS, PhD. In 2018, 7 master's, 2 doctorates awarded. *Degree requirements:* For master's, thesis or alternative; for doctorate, 2 foreign languages, thesis/dissertation. *Application deadline:* For fall admission, 8/1 for domestic students, 4/1 for international students; for spring admission, 12/1 for domestic students, 10/1 for international students; for summer admission, 4/15 for domestic students, 3/1 for international students. Applications are processed on a rolling basis. Application fee: $60. Electronic applications accepted. *Financial support:* In 2018–19, 2 research assistantships, 44 teaching assistantships were awarded; fellowships with tuition reimbursements, career-related internships or fieldwork, and Federal Work-Study also available. Support available to part-time students. Financial award application deadline: 4/1; financial award applicants required to submit FAFSA. *Unit head:* Dr. Mark Johnson, Department Chair, 479-575-3351, Fax: 479-575-8630, E-mail: markj@uark.edu. *Application contact:* Dr. Maria Tjani, Graduate Coordinator, 479-575-7309, Fax: 479-575-8630, E-mail: mtjani@uark.edu.
Website: https://fulbright.uark.edu/departments/math/

University of Arkansas at Little Rock, Graduate School, College of Arts, Letters, and Sciences, Department of Mathematics and Statistics, Little Rock, AR 72204-1099. Offers applied statistics (Graduate Certificate); mathematical sciences (MS). *Program availability:* Part-time, evening/weekend. *Degree requirements:* For master's, comprehensive exam. *Entrance requirements:* For master's, GRE General Test, GRE Subject Test, minimum GPA of 2.7, previous course work in advanced mathematics.

The University of British Columbia, Faculty of Science, Department of Mathematics, Vancouver, BC V6T 1Z2, Canada. Offers M Sc, PhD. *Program availability:* Part-time. *Degree requirements:* For master's, thesis or alternative, essay, qualifying exam; for doctorate, comprehensive exam, thesis/dissertation, qualifying exam, thesis proposal. *Entrance requirements:* Additional exam requirements/recommendations for international students: Required—TOEFL. Electronic applications accepted. *Expenses:* Contact institution. *Faculty research:* Applied mathematics, financial mathematics, pure mathematics.

University of Calgary, Faculty of Graduate Studies, Faculty of Science, Program in Math and Statistics, Calgary, AB T2N 1N4, Canada. Offers M Sc, PhD. *Degree requirements:* For master's, comprehensive exam, thesis; for doctorate, thesis/dissertation, candidacy exam, preliminary exams. *Entrance requirements:* For master's, honors degree in applied math, pure math, or statistics; for doctorate, MA or M Sc. Additional exam requirements/recommendations for international students: Required—TOEFL (minimum score 600 paper-based) or IELTS (minimum score 7). *Faculty research:* Combinatorics, applied mathematics, statistics, probability, analysis.

University of California, Berkeley, Graduate Division, College of Letters and Science, Department of Mathematics, Berkeley, CA 94720. Offers applied mathematics (PhD); mathematics (MA, PhD). Terminal master's awarded for partial completion of doctoral program. *Degree requirements:* For master's, exam or thesis; for doctorate, 2 foreign languages, thesis/dissertation, qualifying exam. *Entrance requirements:* For master's and doctorate, GRE General Test, GRE Subject Test, minimum GPA of 3.0, 3 letters of recommendation. Electronic applications accepted. *Faculty research:* Algebra, analysis, logic, geometry/topology.

University of California, Davis, Graduate Studies, Program in Mathematics, Davis, CA 95616. Offers MA, MAT, PhD. Terminal master's awarded for partial completion of doctoral program. *Degree requirements:* For master's, comprehensive exam; for doctorate, one foreign language, thesis/dissertation. *Entrance requirements:* For master's and doctorate, GRE General Test, GRE Subject Test, minimum GPA of 3.0. Additional exam requirements/recommendations for international students: Required—TOEFL (minimum score 550 paper-based). Electronic applications accepted. *Faculty research:* Mathematical physics, geometric topology, probability, partial differential equations, applied mathematics.

University of California, Irvine, School of Physical Sciences, Department of Mathematics, Irvine, CA 92697. Offers MS, PhD. *Students:* 105 full-time (18 women), 1 part-time (0 women); includes 27 minority (1 American Indian or Alaska Native, non-Hispanic/Latino; 13 Asian, non-Hispanic/Latino; 11 Hispanic/Latino; 2 Two or more races, non-Hispanic/Latino), 37 international. Average age 27. 249 applicants, 26% accepted, 22 enrolled. In 2018, 11 master's, 8 doctorates awarded. *Entrance requirements:* For master's and doctorate, GRE General Test, GRE Subject Test, minimum GPA of 3.0. Additional exam requirements/recommendations for international students: Required—TOEFL (minimum score 550 paper-based). *Application deadline:* For fall admission, 1/15 priority date for domestic and international students. Applications are processed on a rolling basis. Application fee: $105 ($125 for international students). Electronic applications accepted. *Financial support:* Fellowships, research assistantships with full tuition reimbursements, teaching assistantships, institutionally sponsored loans, traineeships, health care benefits, and unspecified assistantships available. Financial award application deadline: 3/1; financial award applicants required to submit FAFSA. *Faculty research:* Algebra and logic, geometry and topology, probability, mathematical physics. *Unit head:* Karl Rubin, Chair, 949-824-1645, Fax: 949-824-7993, E-mail: krubin@math.uci.edu. *Application contact:* Donna M. McConnell, Graduate Affairs Officer, 949-824-5544, Fax: 949-824-7993, E-mail: dmcconne@uci.edu.
Website: http://www.math.uci.edu/

University of California, Los Angeles, Graduate Division, College of Letters and Science, Department of Mathematics, Los Angeles, CA 90095. Offers MA, MAT, PhD. Terminal master's awarded for partial completion of doctoral program. *Degree requirements:* For master's, comprehensive exam or thesis; for doctorate, one foreign language, thesis/dissertation, oral and written qualifying exams. *Entrance requirements:* For master's, GRE General Test; GRE Subject Test (mathematics), bachelor's degree; minimum undergraduate GPA of 3.0, 3.2 in upper-division mathematics courses (or its equivalent if letter grade system not used); for doctorate, GRE General Test; GRE Subject Test (mathematics), bachelor's degree; minimum undergraduate GPA of 3.0, 3.5 in upper-division mathematics courses (or its equivalent if letter grade system not used). Additional exam requirements/recommendations for international students: Required—TOEFL. Electronic applications accepted.

University of California, Riverside, Graduate Division, Department of Mathematics, Riverside, CA 92521-0102. Offers MS, PhD. *Program availability:* Part-time. Terminal master's awarded for partial completion of doctoral program. *Degree requirements:* For master's, comprehensive exam; for doctorate, thesis/dissertation, qualifying exams. *Entrance requirements:* For master's and doctorate, GRE General Test, minimum GPA of 3.2. Additional exam requirements/recommendations for international students: Required—TOEFL (minimum score 550 paper-based; 80 iBT). Electronic applications accepted. *Faculty research:* Algebraic geometry, commutative algebra, Lie algebra, differential equations, differential geometry.

University of California, San Diego, Graduate Division, Department of Mathematics, La Jolla, CA 92093. Offers applied mathematics (MA); computational science (PhD); mathematics (MA, PhD); statistics (MS, PhD). *Students:* 171 full-time (36 women), 3 part-time (1 woman). 713 applicants, 25% accepted, 55 enrolled. In 2018, 12 master's, 13 doctorates awarded. Terminal master's awarded for partial completion of doctoral program. *Degree requirements:* For master's, comprehensive exam; for doctorate, comprehensive exam, thesis/dissertation. *Entrance requirements:* For master's, GRE General Test; GRE Subject Test (for MA), minimum GPA of 3.0; for doctorate, GRE General Test, GRE Subject Test, minimum GPA of 3.0. Additional exam requirements/recommendations for international students: Required—TOEFL (minimum score 550 paper-based; 80 iBT), IELTS (minimum score 7); Recommended—TSE. *Application deadline:* For fall admission, 1/16 for domestic students. Application fee: $105 ($125 for international students). Electronic applications accepted. *Financial support:* Fellowships, research assistantships, teaching assistantships, and scholarships/grants available. Financial award applicants required to submit FAFSA. *Faculty research:* Combinatorics, bioinformatics, differential equations, logic and computational complexity, probability theory and statistics, Algebra, Algebraic Geometry, Analysis, Applied Math, Combinatorics, Computational Science, Geometry, Math Physics, Number Theory, Other, Partial Differential Equations, Probability, Representation Theory, Statistics, Topology. *Unit head:* Lei Ni, Chair, 858-534-2734, E-mail: lni@math.ucsd.edu. *Application contact:* Mark Whelan, Admissions Specialist, 858-534-2642, E-mail: mathgradadmissions@math.ucsd.edu.
Website: http://math.ucsd.edu/

University of California, Santa Barbara, Graduate Division, College of Letters and Sciences, Division of Mathematics, Life, and Physical Sciences, Department of Mathematics, Santa Barbara, CA 93106-3080. Offers applied mathematics (MA), including computational science and engineering; mathematics (MA, PhD), including computational science and engineering (PhD), mathematics (MA); MA/PhD. Terminal master's awarded for partial completion of doctoral program. *Degree requirements:* For master's, comprehensive exam (for some programs), thesis (for some programs); for doctorate, comprehensive exam, thesis/dissertation. *Entrance requirements:* For master's and doctorate, GRE General Test, GRE Subject Test (math). Additional exam requirements/recommendations for international students: Required—TOEFL (minimum score 575 paper-based; 80 iBT), IELTS (minimum score 7). Electronic applications accepted. *Faculty research:* Topology, differential geometry, algebra, applied mathematics, partial differential equations.

University of California, Santa Cruz, Division of Graduate Studies, Division of Physical and Biological Sciences, Department of Mathematics, Santa Cruz, CA 95064. Offers MA, PhD. Terminal master's awarded for partial completion of doctoral program. *Degree requirements:* For master's, thesis; for doctorate, one foreign language, thesis/dissertation, qualifying exam. *Entrance requirements:* For doctorate, GRE General Test, GRE Subject Test. Additional exam requirements/recommendations for international students: Required—TOEFL (minimum score 550 paper-based; 83 iBT); Recommended—IELTS (minimum score 8). Electronic applications accepted. *Faculty research:* Vertex operator algebras, algebraic topology, elliptic cohomology, quantum field theory, automorphic forms, dynamical systems, celestial mechanics, geometric mechanics, bifurcation theory, control theory, representations of Lie and p-adic groups, applications to number theory, Bessel functions, Rankin-Selberg integrals, Gelfand-Graev models, differential geometry, nonlinear analysis, harmonic maps, Ginzburg-Landau problem.

University of Central Arkansas, Graduate School, College of Natural Sciences and Math, Department of Mathematics, Conway, AR 72035-0001. Offers applied mathematics (MS); math education (MA). *Program availability:* Part-time. *Degree requirements:* For master's, comprehensive exam, thesis optional. *Entrance requirements:* For master's, GRE General Test, minimum GPA of 2.7. Additional exam requirements/recommendations for international students: Required—TOEFL (minimum score 550 paper-based; 80 iBT). Electronic applications accepted.

University of Central Florida, College of Sciences, Department of Mathematics, Orlando, FL 32816. Offers MS, PhD, Certificate. *Program availability:* Part-time, evening/weekend. *Students:* 63 full-time (21 women), 19 part-time (9 women); includes 17 minority (5 Black or African American, non-Hispanic/Latino; 8 Asian, non-Hispanic/Latino; 4 Hispanic/Latino), 31 international. Average age 31. 95 applicants, 49% accepted, 20 enrolled. In 2018, 13 master's, 2 doctorates, 4 other advanced degrees awarded. *Degree requirements:* For master's, thesis or alternative; for doctorate, thesis/dissertation, candidacy exam. *Entrance requirements:* For master's, GRE General Test, minimum GPA of 3.0 in last 60 hours; for doctorate, GRE Subject Test, letters of recommendation, goal statement, resume. Additional exam requirements/recommendations for international students: Required—TOEFL. *Application deadline:* For fall admission, 7/15 for domestic students; for spring admission, 12/1 for domestic students. Application fee: $30. Electronic applications accepted. *Financial support:* In 2018–19, 56 students received support, including 10 fellowships with partial tuition reimbursements available (averaging $11,400 per year), 10 research assistantships with partial tuition reimbursements available (averaging $4,640 per year), 61 teaching assistantships with partial tuition reimbursements available (averaging $13,555 per year); career-related internships or fieldwork, Federal Work-Study, institutionally sponsored loans, health care benefits, tuition waivers (partial), and unspecified assistantships also available. Financial award application deadline: 3/1; financial award applicants required to submit FAFSA. *Faculty research:* Applied mathematics, dynamical systems, mathematical biology, partial differential equations, mathematical statistics. *Unit head:* Dr. Xin Li, Chair, 407-823-2135, Fax: 407-823-6253, E-mail: xin.li@ucf.edu. *Application contact:* Associate Director, Graduate Admissions, 407-823-2766, Fax: 407-823-6442, E-mail: gradadmissions@ucf.edu.
Website: http://www.math.ucf.edu/

University of Central Missouri, The Graduate School, Warrensburg, MO 64093. Offers accountancy (MA); accounting (MBA); applied mathematics (MS); aviation safety (MA); biology (MS); business administration (MBA); career and technical education leadership (MS); college student personnel administration (MS); communication (MA); computer science (MS); counseling (MS); criminal justice (MS); educational leadership (Ed D); educational technology (MS); elementary and early childhood education (MSE); English (MA); environmental studies (MA); finance (MBA); history (MA); human services/educational technology (Ed S); human services/learning resources (Ed S); human services/professional counseling (Ed S); industrial hygiene (MS); industrial management (MS); information systems (MBA); information technology (MS); kinesiology (MS); library science and information services (MS); literacy education (MSE); marketing (MBA); mathematics (MS); music (MA); occupational safety management (MS); psychology (MS); rural family nursing (MS); school administration (MSE); social gerontology (MS); sociology (MA); special education (MSE); speech language pathology (MS); superintendency (Ed S); teaching (MAT); teaching English as a second language (MA); technology (MS); technology management (PhD); theatre (MA). *Accreditation:* ASHA. *Program availability:* Part-time, 100% online, blended/hybrid learning. *Degree requirements:* For master's and Ed S, comprehensive exam (for some programs), thesis (for some programs). *Entrance requirements:* Additional exam requirements/recommendations for international students: Required—TOEFL (minimum score 550 paper-based; 79 iBT). Electronic applications accepted.

University of Central Oklahoma, The Jackson College of Graduate Studies, College of Mathematics and Science, Department of Mathematics and Statistics, Edmond, OK 73034-5209. Offers applied mathematical science (MS), including mathematics, statistics, teaching; applied mathematics and computer science (MS). *Program availability:* Part-time. *Degree requirements:* For master's, comprehensive exam (for some programs), thesis (for some programs). *Entrance requirements:* Additional exam requirements/recommendations for international students: Required—TOEFL (minimum score 550 paper-based; 79 iBT), IELTS (minimum score 6.5). Electronic applications accepted.

University of Chicago, Division of the Physical Sciences, Department of Mathematics, Chicago, IL 60637. Offers mathematics (PhD). *Degree requirements:* For doctorate, comprehensive exam, thesis/dissertation. *Entrance requirements:* For doctorate, GRE General Test, GRE Subject Test, research statement, 3 letters of recommendation, transcripts for all previous degrees and institutions attended. Additional exam requirements/recommendations for international students: Required—TOEFL (minimum score 600 paper-based; 90 iBT), IELTS (minimum score 7). Electronic applications accepted. *Faculty research:* Analysis, differential geometry, algebra number theory, topology, algebraic geometry.

University of Cincinnati, Graduate School, McMicken College of Arts and Sciences, Department of Mathematical Sciences, Cincinnati, OH 45221. Offers applied mathematics (MS, PhD); mathematics education (MAT); pure mathematics (MS, PhD); statistics (MS, PhD). *Program availability:* Part-time. *Faculty:* 39 full-time (4 women), 12 part-time/adjunct (4 women). *Students:* 44 full-time (24 women), 19 part-time (9 women); includes 28 minority (2 Black or African American, non-Hispanic/Latino; 25 Asian, non-Hispanic/Latino; 1 Hispanic/Latino), 42 international. 91 applicants, 35% accepted, 27 enrolled. In 2018, 5 master's, 4 doctorates awarded. Terminal master's awarded for partial completion of doctoral program. *Degree requirements:* For master's, comprehensive exam, thesis or alternative; for doctorate, comprehensive exam, thesis/dissertation. *Entrance requirements:* For master's and doctorate, GRE. Additional exam requirements/recommendations for international students: Required—TOEFL, IELTS. *Application deadline:* For fall admission, 2/1 priority date for domestic and international students. Applications are processed on a rolling basis. Application fee: $65. Electronic applications accepted. *Financial support:* In 2018–19, 51 students received support, including 2 fellowships with full tuition reimbursements available (averaging $13,500 per year), 2 research assistantships with full tuition reimbursements available (averaging $13,000 per year), 26 teaching assistantships with full tuition reimbursements available (averaging $18,500 per year); career-related internships or fieldwork, scholarships/grants, and unspecified assistantships also available. Support available to part-time students. Financial award application deadline: 2/1. *Faculty research:* Algebra, analysis, differential equations, numerical analysis, statistics. *Unit head:* Dr. Shuang Zhang, Professor and Department Head, 513-556-4052, Fax: 513-556-3417, E-mail: zhangs@ucmail.uc.edu. *Application contact:* Kamellia Smith, Program Coordinator, 513-5564053, Fax: 513-556-3417, E-mail: kamellia.smith@uc.edu.
Website: https://www.artsci.uc.edu/departments/math.html

University of Colorado Boulder, Graduate School, College of Arts and Sciences, Department of Mathematics, Boulder, CO 80309. Offers MA, MS, PhD. Terminal master's awarded for partial completion of doctoral program. *Degree requirements:* For master's, comprehensive exam, thesis or alternative; for doctorate, one foreign language, comprehensive exam, thesis/dissertation, 2 preliminary exams. *Entrance requirements:* For master's and doctorate, minimum undergraduate GPA of 3.0.

Electronic applications accepted. Application fee is waived when completed online. *Faculty research:* Mathematics; analysis and functional analysis; geometry; algebra; number theory.

University of Colorado Colorado Springs, College of Letters, Arts and Sciences, Program in Interdisciplinary Applied Sciences, Colorado Springs, CO 80918. Offers applied sciences (PhD), including math, physics. *Program availability:* Part-time, evening/weekend. *Faculty:* 10 full-time (2 women), 10 part-time/adjunct (0 women). *Students:* 2 full-time (1 woman), 43 part-time (14 women); includes 6 minority (1 American Indian or Alaska Native, non-Hispanic/Latino; 2 Asian, non-Hispanic/Latino; 1 Hispanic/Latino; 2 Two or more races, non-Hispanic/Latino), 6 international. Average age 31. 13 applicants, 92% accepted, 12 enrolled. In 2018, 3 doctorates awarded. *Degree requirements:* For doctorate, comprehensive exam, thesis/dissertation. *Entrance requirements:* For doctorate, GRE or minimum GPA of 3.0 with baccalaureate degree in biological sciences, mathematics, physics or equivalent from accredited college or university and appropriate background of undergraduate physics courses. Additional exam requirements/recommendations for international students: Required—TOEFL (minimum score 80 iBT), IELTS (minimum score 6.5). *Application deadline:* Applications are processed on a rolling basis. Application fee: $60 ($100 for international students). Electronic applications accepted. *Expenses:* Tuition and fees vary by program, course load, and residency type. Please visit the University of Colorado Colorado Springs Student Financial Services website to estimate current program costs: https://www.uccs.edu/bursar/index.php/estimate-your-bill. *Financial support:* In 2018–19, 15 students received support, including 11 teaching assistantships (averaging $3,500 per year); Federal Work-Study, scholarships/grants, and unspecified assistantships also available. Support available to part-time students. Financial award application deadline: 3/1; financial award applicants required to submit FAFSA. *Faculty research:* Solid-state/condensed-matter physics, surface science, electron spectroscopies, nonlinear physics. *Total annual research expenditures:* $695,442. *Unit head:* Dr. Robert Camley, Professor, 719-255-3512, E-mail: rcamley@uccs.edu. *Application contact:* Dr. Karen Livesey, Assistant Professor, 719-255-5116, E-mail: klivesey@uccs.edu.

University of Colorado Denver, College of Liberal Arts and Sciences, Department of Mathematical and Statistical Sciences, Denver, CO 80217. Offers applied mathematics (MS, PhD), including applied mathematics, applied probability (MS), applied statistics (MS), computational biology (PhD), computational mathematics (PhD), discrete mathematics, finite geometry (PhD), mathematics education (PhD), mathematics of engineering and science (MS), numerical analysis, operations research (MS), optimization and operations research (PhD), probability (PhD), statistics (PhD). *Program availability:* Part-time. *Degree requirements:* For master's, comprehensive exam, thesis optional, 30 hours of course work with minimum GPA of 3.0; for doctorate, comprehensive exam, thesis/dissertation, 42 hours of course work with minimum GPA of 3.25. *Entrance requirements:* For master's, GRE General Test; GRE Subject Test in math (recommended), 30 hours of course work in mathematics (24 of which must be upper-division mathematics), bachelor's degree with minimum GPA of 3.0; for doctorate, GRE General Test; GRE Subject Test in math (recommended), 30 hours of course work in mathematics (24 of which must be upper-division mathematics), master's degree with minimum GPA of 3.25. Additional exam requirements/recommendations for international students: Required—TOEFL (minimum score 537 paper-based; 75 iBT); Recommended—IELTS (minimum score 6.5). Electronic applications accepted. *Expenses:* Tuition, state resident: full-time $6786; part-time $337 per credit hour. Tuition, nonresident: full-time $22,590; part-time $1255 per credit hour. *Required fees:* $1231; $137 per credit hour. Tuition and fees vary according to program and reciprocity agreements. *Faculty research:* Computational mathematics, computational biology, discrete mathematics and geometry, probability and statistics, optimization.

University of Colorado Denver, College of Liberal Arts and Sciences, Program in Integrated Sciences, Denver, CO 80217. Offers applied science (MIS); computer science (MIS); mathematics (MIS). *Program availability:* Part-time, evening/weekend. *Entrance requirements:* For master's, GRE if undergraduate GPA is 3.0 or less, minimum of 40 semester hours in mathematics, computer science, physics, biology, chemistry and/or geology; essay; three letters of recommendation. *Expenses:* Tuition, state resident: full-time $6786; part-time $337 per credit hour. Tuition, nonresident: full-time $22,590; part-time $1255 per credit hour. *Required fees:* $1231; $137 per credit hour. Tuition and fees vary according to program and reciprocity agreements. *Faculty research:* Computer science, applied science, mathematics.

University of Delaware, College of Arts and Sciences, Department of Mathematical Sciences, Newark, DE 19716. Offers applied mathematics (MS, PhD); mathematics (MS, PhD). *Program availability:* Part-time. Terminal master's awarded for partial completion of doctoral program. *Degree requirements:* For master's, thesis (for some programs); for doctorate, one foreign language, thesis/dissertation, qualifying exam. *Entrance requirements:* For master's and doctorate, GRE General Test. Additional exam requirements/recommendations for international students: Required—TOEFL. Electronic applications accepted. *Faculty research:* Scattering theory, inverse problems, fluid dynamics, numerical analysis, combinatorics.

University of Denver, Division of Natural Sciences and Mathematics, Department of Mathematics, Denver, CO 80208. Offers MA, MS, PhD. *Program availability:* Part-time. *Faculty:* 18 full-time (6 women). *Students:* 24 part-time (8 women); includes 4 minority (1 Asian, non-Hispanic/Latino; 3 Two or more races, non-Hispanic/Latino), 7 international. Average age 26. 46 applicants, 93% accepted, 8 enrolled. In 2018, 5 master's awarded. Terminal master's awarded for partial completion of doctoral program. *Degree requirements:* For doctorate, 2 foreign languages, comprehensive exam, thesis/dissertation. *Entrance requirements:* For master's and doctorate, GRE General Test, bachelor's degree in mathematics or related field, transcripts, personal statement, three letters of recommendation. Additional exam requirements/recommendations for international students: Required—TOEFL (minimum score 550 paper-based; 80 iBT). *Application deadline:* For fall admission, 2/15 priority date for domestic and international students; for winter admission, 11/1 for domestic students, 10/1 for international students. Applications are processed on a rolling basis. Application fee: $65. Electronic applications accepted. *Expenses:* $33,183 per year full-time. *Financial support:* In 2018–19, 18 students received support, including 15 teaching assistantships with tuition reimbursements available (averaging $18,648 per year); career-related internships or fieldwork, Federal Work-Study, institutionally sponsored loans, scholarships/grants, and unspecified assistantships also available. Support available to part-time students. Financial award application deadline: 2/15; financial award applicants required to submit FAFSA. *Faculty research:* Foundations of mathematics, dynamical systems, functional analysis, nonassociative algebra, probabilistic combinatorics. *Unit head:* Dr. Petr Vojtechovsky, Professor and Chair, 303-871-3314, E-mail: petr.vojtechovsky@du.edu. *Application contact:* Susan Bolton, Assistant to the Chair, 303-871-3344, E-mail: susan.bolton@du.edu.
Website: http://www.du.edu/nsm/departments/mathematics

The University of Findlay, Office of Graduate Admissions, Findlay, OH 45840-3653. Offers applied security and analytics (MSAS); athletic training (MAT); business (MBA), including certified management accountant, certified public accountant, health care management, hospitality management; education (MA Ed, Ed D), including children's literature (MA Ed), curriculum and teaching (MA Ed), education (MA Ed), educational administration (MA Ed), human resource development (MA Ed), mathematics (MA Ed), reading (MA Ed), science education (MA Ed), superintendent (Ed D), teaching (Ed D), technology (MA Ed); environmental, safety, and health management (MSEM); health informatics (MS); occupational therapy (MOT); pharmacy (Pharm D); physical therapy (DPT); physician assistant (MPA); rhetoric and writing (MA); teaching English to speakers of other languages (TESOL) and applied linguistics (MA). *Program availability:* Part-time, evening/weekend, 100% online, blended/hybrid learning. *Degree requirements:* For master's, comprehensive exam (for some programs), thesis (for some programs), cumulative project, capstone project; for doctorate, thesis/dissertation (for some programs). *Entrance requirements:* For master's, GRE/GMAT, bachelor's degree from accredited institution, minimum undergraduate GPA of 2.5 in last 64 hours of course work; for doctorate, GRE, MAT, minimum cumulative GPA of 3.0. Additional exam requirements/recommendations for international students: Required—TOEFL (minimum score 79 iBT), IELTS (minimum score 7), PTE (minimum score 61). Electronic applications accepted.

University of Florida, Graduate School, College of Liberal Arts and Sciences, Department of Mathematics, Gainesville, FL 32611. Offers mathematics (MAT, MS, MST, PhD), including imaging science and technology (PhD), mathematics (PhD), quantitative finance (PhD). *Program availability:* Part-time. Terminal master's awarded for partial completion of doctoral program. *Degree requirements:* For master's, comprehensive exam, thesis optional, first-year exam; for doctorate, one foreign language, comprehensive exam, thesis/dissertation. *Entrance requirements:* For master's and doctorate, GRE General Test, GRE Subject Test (math), minimum GPA of 3.0. Additional exam requirements/recommendations for international students: Required—TOEFL (minimum score 550 paper-based; 80 iBT), IELTS (minimum score 6). Electronic applications accepted. *Faculty research:* Applied mathematics, including imaging, optimization and biomathematics; analysis and probability; combinatorics and number theory; topology and foundations; group theory.

University of Georgia, Franklin College of Arts and Sciences, Department of Mathematics, Athens, GA 30602. Offers applied mathematical science (MAMS); mathematics (MA, PhD). *Degree requirements:* For master's, one foreign language, thesis (for some programs); for doctorate, 2 foreign languages, thesis/dissertation. *Entrance requirements:* For master's and doctorate, GRE General Test. Electronic applications accepted.

University of Guelph, Office of Graduate and Postdoctoral Studies, College of Physical and Engineering Science, Department of Mathematics and Statistics, Guelph, ON N1G 2W1, Canada. Offers applied mathematics (PhD); applied statistics (PhD); mathematics and statistics (M Sc). *Program availability:* Part-time. *Degree requirements:* For master's, thesis (for some programs); for doctorate, thesis/dissertation. *Entrance requirements:* For master's, minimum B- average during previous 2 years of course work; for doctorate, minimum B average. Additional exam requirements/recommendations for international students: Required—TOEFL (minimum score 550 paper-based; 89 iBT), IELTS (minimum score 6.5). *Faculty research:* Dynamical systems, mathematical biology, numerical analysis, linear and nonlinear models, reliability and bioassay.

University of Hawaii at Manoa, Office of Graduate Education, College of Natural Sciences, Department of Mathematics, Honolulu, HI 96822. Offers MA, PhD. *Program availability:* Part-time. *Degree requirements:* For doctorate, one foreign language, comprehensive exam, thesis/dissertation. *Entrance requirements:* For master's and doctorate, GRE General Test, minimum GPA of 3.0. Additional exam requirements/recommendations for international students: Required—TOEFL (minimum score 500 paper-based; 61 iBT), IELTS (minimum score 5). *Faculty research:* Analysis, algebra, lattice theory, logic topology, differential geometry.

University of Houston, College of Natural Sciences and Mathematics, Department of Mathematics, Houston, TX 77204. Offers applied mathematics (MS); mathematics (MA, PhD). *Program availability:* Part-time. *Degree requirements:* For master's, thesis optional. *Entrance requirements:* For master's and doctorate, GRE (Verbal and Quantitative). Additional exam requirements/recommendations for international students: Required—TOEFL (minimum score 550 paper-based; 79 iBT), IELTS (minimum score 6.5). Electronic applications accepted. *Faculty research:* Applied mathematics, modern analysis, computational science, geometry, dynamical systems.

University of Houston–Clear Lake, School of Science and Computer Engineering, Program in Mathematical Sciences, Houston, TX 77058-1002. Offers MS. *Program availability:* Part-time, evening/weekend. *Entrance requirements:* For master's, GRE General Test. Additional exam requirements/recommendations for international students: Required—TOEFL (minimum score 550 paper-based).

University of Idaho, College of Graduate Studies, College of Science, Department of Mathematics, Moscow, ID 83844-1103. Offers MAT, MS, PhD. *Faculty:* 7 full-time. *Students:* 18. Average age 29. In 2018, 3 master's awarded. *Degree requirements:* For doctorate, thesis/dissertation. *Entrance requirements:* For master's, minimum GPA of 3.0; for doctorate, GRE, minimum GPA of 3.0. Additional exam requirements/recommendations for international students: Required—TOEFL (minimum score 79 iBT). *Application deadline:* For fall admission, 8/1 for domestic students; for spring admission, 12/15 for domestic students. Applications are processed on a rolling basis. Application fee: $60. Electronic applications accepted. *Expenses:* Tuition, state resident: full-time $7266.44; part-time $474.50 per credit hour. Tuition, nonresident: full-time $24,902; part-time $1453.50 per credit hour. *Required fees:* $2085.56; $45.50 per credit hour. *Financial support:* Research assistantships and teaching assistantships available. Financial award applicants required to submit FAFSA. *Faculty research:* Bioinformatics and mathematical biology, analysis and differential equations, statistical genetics, probability and stochastic processes, discrete geometry. *Unit head:* Dr. Christopher J. Williams, Chair, 208-885-6742, E-mail: math@uidaho.edu. *Application contact:* Dr. Christopher J. Williams, Chair, 208-885-6742, E-mail: math@uidaho.edu.
Website: https://www.uidaho.edu/sci/math

University of Illinois at Chicago, College of Liberal Arts and Sciences, Department of Mathematics, Statistics, and Computer Science, Chicago, IL 60607-7128. Offers mathematics (DA); probability and statistics (PhD); secondary school mathematics (MST); statistics (MS). *Program availability:* Part-time. *Degree requirements:* For master's, comprehensive exam; for doctorate, one foreign language, thesis/dissertation. *Entrance requirements:* For master's and doctorate, GRE General Test, minimum GPA of 3.0. Additional exam requirements/recommendations for international students: Required—TOEFL (minimum score 100 iBT). Electronic applications accepted.

University of Illinois at Urbana–Champaign, Graduate College, College of Liberal Arts and Sciences, Department of Mathematics, Champaign, IL 61820. Offers applied mathematics (MS); applied mathematics: actuarial science (MS); mathematics (MS, PhD); teaching of mathematics (MS).

The University of Iowa, Graduate College, College of Liberal Arts and Sciences, Department of Mathematics, Iowa City, IA 52242-1316. Offers MS, PhD. *Degree requirements:* For master's, thesis optional, exam; for doctorate, comprehensive exam, thesis/dissertation. *Entrance requirements:* For master's and doctorate, GRE General Test, minimum GPA of 3.0. Additional exam requirements/recommendations for international students: Required—TOEFL (minimum score 620 paper-based; 105 iBT). Electronic applications accepted.

The University of Kansas, Graduate Studies, College of Liberal Arts and Sciences, Department of Mathematics, Lawrence, KS 66045. Offers applied mathematics (Graduate Certificate); mathematics (MA, PhD); PhD/MA. *Program availability:* Part-time. *Students:* 73 full-time (17 women); includes 5 minority (4 Asian, non-Hispanic/Latino; 1 Two or more races, non-Hispanic/Latino), 32 international. Average age 28. 83 applicants, 49% accepted, 15 enrolled. In 2018, 9 master's, 7 doctorates, 1 other advanced degree awarded. Terminal master's awarded for partial completion of doctoral program. *Entrance requirements:* For master's and doctorate, GRE, official transcripts, three letters of recommendation, resume/curriculum vitae, statement of purpose. Additional exam requirements/recommendations for international students: Required—TOEFL, IELTS. *Application deadline:* For fall admission, 12/31 priority date for domestic and international students; for spring admission, 10/15 for domestic and international students. Application fee: $65 ($85 for international students). Electronic applications accepted. *Financial support:* Fellowships, research assistantships, teaching assistantships, institutionally sponsored loans, scholarships/grants, health care benefits, and unspecified assistantships available. Support available to part-time students. Financial award application deadline: 12/31. *Faculty research:* Algebra and algebraic geometry; analysis, partial differential equations and dynamical systems; probability, stochastic analysis and stochastic control; numerical analysis; geometry. *Unit head:* Weizhang Huang, Chair, 785-864-3651, E-mail: whuang@ku.edu. *Application contact:* Lori Springs, Graduate Admissions Contact, 785-864-7300, E-mail: lsprings@ku.edu. Website: http://www.math.ku.edu/

University of Kentucky, Graduate School, College of Arts and Sciences, Program in Mathematics, Lexington, KY 40506-0032. Offers applied mathematics (MS); mathematics (MA, MS, PhD). *Degree requirements:* For master's, comprehensive exam, thesis optional; for doctorate, one foreign language, comprehensive exam, thesis/dissertation. *Entrance requirements:* For master's, GRE General Test, minimum undergraduate GPA of 2.75; for doctorate, GRE General Test, minimum graduate GPA of 3.0. Additional exam requirements/recommendations for international students: Required—TOEFL (minimum score 550 paper-based). Electronic applications accepted. *Faculty research:* Numerical analysis, combinatorics, partial differential equations, algebra and number theory, real and complex analysis.

University of Lethbridge, School of Graduate Studies, Lethbridge, AB T1K 3M4, Canada. Offers addictions counseling (M Sc); agricultural biotechnology (M Sc); agricultural studies (M Sc, MA); anthropology (MA); archaeology (M Sc, MA); art (MA, MFA); biochemistry (M Sc); biological sciences (M Sc); biomolecular science (PhD); biosystems and biodiversity (PhD); Canadian studies (MA); chemistry (M Sc); computer science (M Sc); computer science and geographical information science (M Sc); counseling (MC); counseling psychology (M Ed); dramatic arts (MA); earth, space, and physical science (PhD); economics (MA); education (MA, PhD); educational leadership (M Ed); English (MA); environmental science (M Sc); evolution and behavior (PhD); exercise science (M Sc); French (MA); French/German (MA); French/Spanish (MA); general education (M Ed); geography (M Sc, MA); German (MA); health sciences (M Sc); individualized multidisciplinary (M Sc, MA); kinesiology (M Sc, MA); management (M Sc), including accounting, finance, human resource management and labor relations, information systems, international management, marketing, policy and strategy; mathematics (M Sc); music (M Mus, MA); Native American studies (MA); neuroscience (M Sc, PhD); new media (MA, MFA); nursing (M Sc, MN); philosophy (MA); physics (M Sc); political science (MA); psychology (M Sc, MA); religious studies (MA); sociology (MA); theatre and dramatic arts (MFA); theoretical and computational science (PhD); urban and regional studies (MA); women and gender studies (MA). *Program availability:* Part-time, evening/weekend. *Degree requirements:* For master's, thesis (for some programs); for doctorate, comprehensive exam, thesis/dissertation. *Entrance requirements:* For master's, GMAT (for M Sc in management), bachelor's degree in related field, minimum GPA of 3.0 during previous 20 graded semester courses, 2 years' teaching or related experience (M Ed); for doctorate, master's degree, minimum graduate GPA of 3.5. Additional exam requirements/recommendations for international students: Required—TOEFL (minimum score 580 paper-based; 93 iBT). Electronic applications accepted. *Faculty research:* Movement and brain plasticity, gibberellin physiology, photosynthesis, carbon cycling, molecular properties of main-group ring components.

University of Louisiana at Lafayette, College of Sciences, Department of Mathematics, Lafayette, LA 70504. Offers MS, PhD. Terminal master's awarded for partial completion of doctoral program. *Degree requirements:* For master's, thesis or alternative; for doctorate, 2 foreign languages, comprehensive exam, thesis/dissertation. *Entrance requirements:* For master's, GRE General Test, minimum GPA of 2.75; for doctorate, GRE General Test, minimum GPA of 3.0. Additional exam requirements/recommendations for international students: Required—TOEFL (minimum score 550 paper-based). Electronic applications accepted. *Faculty research:* Topology, algebra, applied mathematics, analysis.

University of Louisville, Graduate School, College of Arts and Sciences, Department of Mathematics, Louisville, KY 40292. Offers applied and industrial mathematics (PhD); mathematics (MA). *Program availability:* Part-time. *Faculty:* 32 full-time (6 women). *Students:* 28 full-time (9 women), 7 part-time (1 woman); includes 4 minority (2 Asian, non-Hispanic/Latino; 1 Hispanic/Latino; 1 Two or more races, non-Hispanic/Latino), 6 international. Average age 30. 21 applicants, 86% accepted, 13 enrolled. In 2018, 5 master's awarded. Terminal master's awarded for partial completion of doctoral program. *Degree requirements:* For master's, variable foreign language requirement, thesis or alternative; for doctorate, comprehensive exam, thesis/dissertation. *Entrance requirements:* For master's and doctorate, GRE. Additional exam requirements/recommendations for international students: Required—TOEFL (minimum score 550 paper-based; 79 iBT), IELTS (minimum score 6.5). *Application deadline:* For fall admission, 3/1 priority date for domestic and international students; for winter admission, 11/1 priority date for domestic and international students; for spring admission, 11/1 priority date for domestic and international students; for summer admission, 3/1 priority date for domestic and international students. Applications are processed on a rolling basis. Application fee: $65. Electronic applications accepted. *Expenses: Tuition, area resident:* Full-time $6500; part-time $723 per credit hour. Tuition, state resident: full-time $6500. Tuition, nonresident: full-time $13,557; part-time $1507 per credit hour. Tuition and fees vary according to course load and program. *Financial support:* In 2018–19, 32 students received support, including 3 fellowships with full tuition reimbursements available (averaging $22,000 per year), 1 research assistantship with partial tuition reimbursement available (averaging $20,000 per year), 24 teaching assistantships with full tuition reimbursements available (averaging $20,000 per year); health care benefits and unspecified assistantships also available. Financial award application deadline: 2/3. *Faculty research:* Mathematical biology, partial differential equations, statistics, combinatorics, analysis. *Total annual research expenditures:* $135,462. *Unit head:* Dr. David Swanson, Chair, 502-852-6234, E-mail: david.swanson@louisville.edu. *Application contact:* Dr. Hamid Kulosman, Graduate Director/Professor, 502-852-3403, E-mail: hamid.kulosman@louisville.edu. Website: http://www.math.louisville.edu

University of Lynchburg, Graduate Studies, M Ed Program in Science Education, Lynchburg, VA 24501-3199. Offers science education (M Ed), including earth science, math. *Program availability:* Part-time, evening/weekend. *Degree requirements:* For master's, comprehensive exam. *Entrance requirements:* For master's, GRE, minimum GPA of 3.0 (preferred), official transcripts (bachelor's, others as relevant), three letters of recommendation, career goals statement. Additional exam requirements/recommendations for international students: Required—TOEFL (minimum score 550 paper-based; 80 iBT), IELTS (minimum score 6). Electronic applications accepted. Application fee is waived when completed online. *Expenses:* Contact institution.

University of Maine, Graduate School, College of Liberal Arts and Sciences, Department of Mathematics and Statistics, Orono, ME 04469. Offers mathematics (MA). *Faculty:* 19 full-time (3 women). *Students:* 8 full-time (3 women), 3 part-time (1 woman); includes 3 minority (1 Asian, non-Hispanic/Latino; 2 Two or more races, non-Hispanic/Latino), 1 international. Average age 27. 4 applicants, 100% accepted, 3 enrolled. In 2018, 1 master's awarded. *Entrance requirements:* For master's, GRE General Test. Additional exam requirements/recommendations for international students: Required—TOEFL (minimum score 80 iBT), IELTS (minimum score 6.5). *Application deadline:* For fall admission, 1/20 for domestic and international students. Applications are processed on a rolling basis. Application fee: $65. Electronic applications accepted. *Financial support:* In 2018–19, 13 students received support, including 1 research assistantship with full tuition reimbursement available (averaging $15,000 per year), 11 teaching assistantships with full tuition reimbursements available (averaging $15,600 per year); tuition waivers (full and partial) also available. Financial award application deadline: 3/1. *Faculty research:* Analysis, number theory, dynamical systems, mathematical biology, statistics. *Total annual research expenditures:* $121,125. *Unit head:* Dr. Nigel Pitt, Co-Chair, 207-581-3916, Fax: 207-581-4977, E-mail: pitt@math.umaine.edu. *Application contact:* Scott G. Delcourt, Assistant Vice President for Graduate Studies and Senior Associate Dean, 207-581-3291, Fax: 207-581-3232, E-mail: graduate@maine.edu. Website: http://umaine.edu/mathematics/

The University of Manchester, School of Mathematics, Manchester, United Kingdom. Offers actuarial science (PhD); applied mathematics (M Phil, PhD); applied numerical computing (M Phil, PhD); financial mathematics (M Phil, PhD); mathematical logic (M Phil); probability (M Phil, PhD); pure mathematics (M Phil, PhD); statistics (M Phil, PhD).

University of Manitoba, Faculty of Graduate Studies, Faculty of Science, Department of Mathematics, Winnipeg, MB R3T 2N2, Canada. Offers M Sc, PhD. *Degree requirements:* For master's, one foreign language, thesis or alternative; for doctorate, one foreign language, thesis/dissertation.

University of Manitoba, Faculty of Graduate Studies, Faculty of Science, Program in Mathematical, Computational and Statistical Sciences, Winnipeg, MB R3T 2N2, Canada. Offers MMCSS.

University of Maryland, College Park, Academic Affairs, College of Computer, Mathematical and Natural Sciences, Department of Mathematics, Program in Mathematics, College Park, MD 20742. Offers MA, PhD. *Program availability:* Part-time, evening/weekend. Terminal master's awarded for partial completion of doctoral program. *Degree requirements:* For master's, thesis or alternative; for doctorate, one foreign language, thesis/dissertation, written exam, oral exam. *Entrance requirements:* For master's, GRE General Test, GRE Subject Test, minimum GPA of 3.0, 3 letters of recommendation; for doctorate, GRE General Test, GRE Subject Test, 3 letters of recommendation. Electronic applications accepted.

University of Massachusetts Amherst, Graduate School, College of Natural Sciences, Department of Mathematics and Statistics, Amherst, MA 01003. Offers applied mathematics (MS); mathematics (MS, PhD); statistics (MS, PhD). Terminal master's awarded for partial completion of doctoral program. *Degree requirements:* For master's, thesis or alternative; for doctorate, comprehensive exam, thesis/dissertation. *Entrance requirements:* For master's and doctorate, GRE General Test, GRE Subject Test (mathematics). Additional exam requirements/recommendations for international students: Required—TOEFL (minimum score 550 paper-based; 80 iBT), IELTS (minimum score 6.5). Electronic applications accepted.

University of Massachusetts Lowell, College of Sciences, Department of Mathematical Sciences, Lowell, MA 01854. Offers Ed D. *Program availability:* Part-time.

University of Memphis, Graduate School, College of Arts and Sciences, Department of Mathematical Sciences, Memphis, TN 38152. Offers applied mathematics (MS); applied statistics (PhD); mathematics (MS, PhD); statistics (MS); teaching of mathematics (MS). *Program availability:* Part-time. *Students:* 35 full-time (11 women), 41 part-time (13 women); includes 33 minority (14 Black or African American, non-Hispanic/Latino; 12 Asian, non-Hispanic/Latino; 5 Hispanic/Latino; 2 Two or more races, non-Hispanic/Latino), 22 international. Average age 34. 35 applicants, 83% accepted, 17 enrolled. In 2018, 10 master's, 5 doctorates awarded. Terminal master's awarded for partial completion of doctoral program. *Degree requirements:* For master's, comprehensive exam, thesis or alternative; for doctorate, one foreign language, comprehensive exam, thesis/dissertation, qualifying exam, final exam. *Entrance requirements:* For master's, GRE General Test, minimum GPA of 2.5, undergraduate degree in math or statistics, two letters of recommendation; for doctorate, GRE General Test, minimum GPA of 2.5, three letters of recommendation. Additional exam requirements/recommendations for international students: Required—TOEFL (minimum score 550 paper-based; 79 iBT). *Application deadline:* For fall admission, 8/1 for domestic students, 5/1 priority date for international students; for spring admission, 12/1 for domestic students, 9/1 priority date for international students. Applications are processed on a rolling basis. Application fee: $35 ($60 for international students). Electronic applications accepted. *Expenses: Tuition, area resident:* Full-time $10,240; part-time $503 per credit hour. Tuition, state resident: full-time $10,464. Tuition, nonresident: full-time $20,224; part-time $991 per credit hour. *Required fees:* $850; $106 per credit hour. *Financial support:* Fellowships with full tuition reimbursements, research assistantships with full tuition reimbursements, teaching assistantships with full tuition reimbursements, career-related internships or fieldwork, Federal Work-Study, scholarships/grants, and unspecified assistantships available. Financial award application deadline: 2/1; financial award applicants required to submit FAFSA. *Faculty research:* Combinatorics, ergodic theory, graph theory, Ramsey theory, applied statistics. *Unit head:* Dr. Irena Lasiecka, Chair, 901-678-2482, Fax: 901-678-2480, E-mail: lasiecka@memphis.edu. *Application contact:* Dr. Fernanda Botelho, Graduate Advising Coordinator, 901-678-3131, Fax: 901-678-2480, E-mail: mbotelho@memphis.edu.
Website: https://www.memphis.edu/msci

University of Memphis, Graduate School, College of Education, Department of Instruction and Curriculum Leadership, Memphis, TN 38152. Offers advanced studies in teaching and learning (M Ed); applied behavior analysis (Graduate Certificate); autism studies (Graduate Certificate); early childhood education (MAT, MS, Ed D); elementary education (MAT); instruction and curriculum (MS, Ed D); instruction design and technology (MS, Ed D); instructional design and technology (Graduate Certificate); literacy, leadership, and coaching (Graduate Certificate); reading (MS, Ed D); school library information specialist (Graduate Certificate); secondary education (MAT); special education (MAT, MS, Ed D); STEM teacher leadership (Graduate Certificate); urban education (Graduate Certificate). *Accreditation:* NCATE (one or more programs are accredited). *Program availability:* Part-time. *Students:* 62 full-time (45 women), 412 part-time (326 women); includes 209 minority (179 Black or African American, non-Hispanic/Latino; 1 American Indian or Alaska Native, non-Hispanic/Latino; 5 Asian, non-Hispanic/Latino; 17 Hispanic/Latino; 7 Two or more races, non-Hispanic/Latino), 4 international. Average age 35. 195 applicants, 91% accepted, 143 enrolled. In 2018, 122 master's, 13 doctorates, 29 other advanced degrees awarded. Terminal master's awarded for partial completion of doctoral program. *Degree requirements:* For master's, comprehensive exam, thesis or alternative; for doctorate, comprehensive exam, thesis/dissertation. *Entrance requirements:* For master's, GRE General Test, PRAXIS, minimum GPA of 2.5, letters of reference; for doctorate, GRE General Test, GRE Subject Test, 2 years of teaching experience, letters of reference, statement of purpose, interview. Additional exam requirements/recommendations for international students: Required—TOEFL (minimum score 550 paper-based; 79 iBT). *Application deadline:* For fall admission, 4/1 priority date for domestic students; for spring admission, 10/1 priority date for domestic students; for summer admission, 2/1 priority date for domestic students. Applications are processed on a rolling basis. Application fee: $35 ($60 for international students). Electronic applications accepted. *Expenses: Tuition, area resident:* Full-time $10,240; part-time $503 per credit hour. Tuition, state resident: full-time $10,464. Tuition, nonresident: full-time $20,224; part-time $991 per credit hour. *Required fees:* $850; $106 per credit hour. *Financial support:* Research assistantships with full tuition reimbursements, teaching assistantships with full tuition reimbursements, career-related internships or fieldwork, Federal Work-Study, institutionally sponsored loans, scholarships/grants, traineeships, and unspecified assistantships available. Support available to part-time students. Financial award application deadline: 2/1; financial award applicants required to submit FAFSA. *Faculty research:* Effective urban teachers, preparation and retention of urban teachers, technology utilization in schools, field-based teacher preparation programs, effective use of online instruction. *Unit head:* Dr. Christian Mueller, Chair, 901-678-2365, E-mail: cemuellr@memphis.edu. *Application contact:* Dr. Lee Allen, Director of Graduate Programs, 901-678-4073, E-mail: allenlee@memphis.edu.
Website: http://www.memphis.edu/icl/

University of Miami, Graduate School, College of Arts and Sciences, Department of Mathematics, Coral Gables, FL 33124. Offers mathematical finance (MS); mathematics (MA, MS, PhD). *Program availability:* Part-time, evening/weekend. Terminal master's awarded for partial completion of doctoral program. *Degree requirements:* For master's, comprehensive exam, qualifying exams; for doctorate, one foreign language, thesis/dissertation, qualifying exams. *Entrance requirements:* For master's and doctorate, GRE General Test, minimum GPA of 3.0. Additional exam requirements/recommendations for international students: Required—TOEFL (minimum score 550 paper-based; 59 iBT). Electronic applications accepted. *Faculty research:* Applied mathematics, probability, geometric analysis, differential equations, algebraic combinatorics.

University of Michigan, Rackham Graduate School, College of Literature, Science, and the Arts, Department of Mathematics, Ann Arbor, MI 48109. Offers applied and interdisciplinary mathematics (AM, MS, PhD); mathematics (AM, MS, PhD); quantitative finance and risk management (MS). *Program availability:* Part-time. *Degree requirements:* For doctorate, one foreign language, comprehensive exam, thesis/dissertation, oral defense of dissertation, preliminary exam. *Entrance requirements:* For master's and doctorate, GRE General Test, GRE Subject Test. Additional exam requirements/recommendations for international students: Required—TOEFL (minimum score 560 paper-based; 84 iBT). Electronic applications accepted. *Expenses:* Contact institution. *Faculty research:* Algebra, analysis, topology, applied mathematics, geometry.

University of Michigan–Flint, College of Arts and Sciences, Program in Mathematics, Flint, MI 48502-1950. Offers MA. MA in Mathematics program currently on program moratorium. *Program availability:* Part-time. *Faculty:* 11 full-time (3 women), 10 part-time/adjunct (4 women). *Students:* 4 part-time (3 women); includes 1 minority (Hispanic/Latino). Average age 31. 2 applicants, 50% accepted. In 2018, 1 master's awarded. *Entrance requirements:* Additional exam requirements/recommendations for international students: Required—TOEFL (minimum score 84 iBT), IELTS (minimum score 6.5). *Application deadline:* Applications are processed on a rolling basis. Application fee: $55. Electronic applications accepted. *Unit head:* Dr. Cam McLeman, Director, 810-767-6689, E-mail: mclemanc@umflint.edu. *Application contact:* Matt Bohlem, Director of Graduate Admissions, 810-762-3171, Fax: 810-766-6789, E-mail: mbohlen@umflint.edu.
Website: https://www.umflint.edu/graduateprograms/mathematics-ma

University of Minnesota, Twin Cities Campus, College of Science and Engineering, School of Mathematics, Minneapolis, MN 55455-0213. Offers mathematics (MS, PhD); quantitative finance (Certificate). *Program availability:* Part-time. Terminal master's awarded for partial completion of doctoral program. *Degree requirements:* For master's, thesis (for some programs); for doctorate, 2 foreign languages, thesis/dissertation. *Entrance requirements:* For master's, GRE Subject Test (recommended); for doctorate, GRE Subject Test. Additional exam requirements/recommendations for international students: Required—TOEFL. Electronic applications accepted. *Faculty research:* Partial and ordinary differential equations, algebra and number theory, geometry, combinatorics, numerical analysis, probability, financial mathematics.

University of Minnesota, Twin Cities Campus, Graduate School, College of Education and Human Development, Department of Curriculum and Instruction, Program in Teaching, Minneapolis, MN 55455-0213. Offers teaching (M Ed), including arts in education, elementary education, English education, mathematics, science, second language education, social studies. *Students:* 249 full-time (182 women), 101 part-time (59 women); includes 57 minority (5 Black or African American, non-Hispanic/Latino; 16 Asian, non-Hispanic/Latino; 25 Hispanic/Latino; 11 Two or more races, non-Hispanic/Latino), 12 international. Average age 28. 383 applicants, 79% accepted, 261 enrolled. In 2018, 292 master's awarded. Application fee: $75 ($95 for international students). *Unit head:* Dr. Mark Vagle, Chair, 612-625-4006, Fax: 612-624-8277, E-mail: mvagle@umn.edu. *Application contact:* Dr. Mark Vagle, Chair, 612-625-4006, Fax: 612-624-8277, E-mail: mvagle@umn.edu.
Website: http://www.cehd.umn.edu/ci/

University of Mississippi, Graduate School, College of Liberal Arts, University, MS 38677-1848. Offers anthropology (MA); biology (MS, PhD); chemistry (MS, DA, PhD); creative writing (MFA); documentary expression (MFA); economics (MA, PhD); English (MA, PhD); experimental psychology (PhD); history (MA, PhD); mathematics (MS, PhD); modern languages (MA); music (MM); philosophy (MA); physics (MA, MS, PhD); political science (MA, PhD); Southern studies (MA); studio art (MFA). *Program availability:* Part-time. *Faculty:* 474 full-time (209 women), 71 part-time/adjunct (38 women). *Students:* 471 full-time (241 women), 80 part-time (39 women); includes 90 minority (43 Black or African American, non-Hispanic/Latino; 14 Asian, non-Hispanic/Latino; 23 Hispanic/Latino; 10 Two or more races, non-Hispanic/Latino), 136 international. *Degree requirements:* For doctorate, thesis/dissertation. *Entrance requirements:* For master's, GRE General Test, minimum GPA of 3.0; for doctorate, GRE General Test. Additional exam requirements/recommendations for international students: Required—TOEFL. *Application deadline:* Applications are processed on a rolling basis. Application fee: $50. Electronic applications accepted. *Financial support:* Fellowships, research assistantships, teaching assistantships, career-related internships or fieldwork, Federal Work-Study, institutionally sponsored loans, scholarships/grants, and unspecified assistantships available. Financial award application deadline: 3/1; financial award applicants required to submit FAFSA. *Unit head:* Dr. Lee Michael Cohen, Dean, 662-915-7177, Fax: 662-915-5792, E-mail: libarts@olemiss.edu. *Application contact:* Tameka Smith, Graduate Activities Specialist for Admissions, 662-915-7474, Fax: 662-915-7577, E-mail: gschool@olemiss.edu.
Website: ventress@olemiss.edu

University of Missouri, Office of Research and Graduate Studies, College of Arts and Science, Department of Mathematics, Columbia, MO 65211. Offers applied mathematics (MS); mathematics (MA, PhD). *Entrance requirements:* For master's and doctorate, GRE General Test, minimum GPA of 3.0; bachelor's degree from accredited institution. *Faculty research:* Algebraic geometry, analysis (real, complex, functional and harmonic), analytic functions, applied mathematics, financial mathematics and mathematics of insurance, commutative rings, scattering theory, differential equations (ordinary and partial), differential geometry, dynamical systems, general relativity, mathematical physics, number theory, probabilistic analysis and topology.

University of Missouri–Kansas City, College of Arts and Sciences, Department of Mathematics and Statistics, Kansas City, MO 64110-2499. Offers MA, MS, PhD. PhD (interdisciplinary) offered through the School of Graduate Studies. *Program availability:* Part-time. Terminal master's awarded for partial completion of doctoral program. *Degree requirements:* For master's, written exam; for doctorate, 2 foreign languages, thesis/dissertation, oral and written exams. *Entrance requirements:* For master's, bachelor's degree in mathematics, minimum GPA of 3.0; for doctorate, GMAT or GRE General Test. Additional exam requirements/recommendations for international students: Required—TOEFL (minimum score 550 paper-based; 80 iBT). Electronic applications accepted. *Faculty research:* Numerical analysis, statistics, biostatistics, commutative algebra, differential equations.

University of Missouri–St. Louis, College of Arts and Sciences, Department of Mathematics and Computer Science, St. Louis, MO 63121. Offers computer science (MS); mathematical and computational sciences (PhD); mathematics (MA). *Program availability:* Part-time, evening/weekend. *Degree requirements:* For master's, thesis optional; for doctorate, thesis/dissertation. *Entrance requirements:* For master's, GRE (for teaching assistantships), 2 letters of recommendation; C programming, C++ or Java (for computer science); for doctorate, GRE General Test, 3 letters of recommendation. Additional exam requirements/recommendations for international students: Required—TOEFL (minimum score 550 paper-based; 79 iBT), IELTS (minimum score 6.5). Electronic applications accepted. *Faculty research:* Probability and statistics; algebra, geometry, and topology; evolutionary computation; computer graphics and image manipulations; networking and communications; computational mathematics; biological data.

University of Montana, Graduate School, College of Humanities and Sciences, Department of Mathematical Sciences, Missoula, MT 59812. Offers mathematics (MA, PhD), including college mathematics teaching (PhD), mathematical sciences research (PhD); mathematics education (MA). *Program availability:* Part-time. Terminal master's awarded for partial completion of doctoral program. *Degree requirements:* For doctorate, thesis/dissertation. *Entrance requirements:* For master's and doctorate, GRE General Test. Additional exam requirements/recommendations for international students: Required—TOEFL (minimum score 525 paper-based).

University of Nebraska at Omaha, Graduate Studies, College of Arts and Sciences, Department of Mathematics, Omaha, NE 68182. Offers MA, MAT, MS. *Program availability:* Part-time. *Degree requirements:* For master's, comprehensive exam, thesis (for some programs). *Entrance requirements:* For master's, minimum GPA of 3.0, 15 undergraduate math hours beyond calculus, official transcripts. Additional exam requirements/recommendations for international students: Required—TOEFL, IELTS, PTE. Electronic applications accepted.

University of Nebraska–Lincoln, Graduate College, College of Arts and Sciences, Department of Mathematics, Lincoln, NE 68588. Offers mathematics (MA, MAT, MS, PhD); mathematics and computer science (PhD). *Degree requirements:* For master's, thesis optional; for doctorate, variable foreign language requirement, comprehensive exam, thesis/dissertation. *Entrance requirements:* Additional exam requirements/recommendations for international students: Required—TOEFL (minimum score 550 paper-based). Electronic applications accepted. *Faculty research:* Applied mathematics, commutative algebra, algebraic geometry, Bayesian statistics, biostatistics.

University of Nevada, Las Vegas, Graduate College, College of Sciences, Department of Mathematical Sciences, Las Vegas, NV 89154-4020. Offers MS, PhD. *Program availability:* Part-time. *Faculty:* 19 full-time (3 women). *Students:* 39 full-time (9 women), 16 part-time (6 women); includes 11 minority (5 Asian, non-Hispanic/Latino; 5 Hispanic/Latino; 1 Two or more races, non-Hispanic/Latino), 17 international. Average age 30. 27 applicants, 59% accepted, 9 enrolled. In 2018, 7 master's, 3 doctorates awarded. *Degree requirements:* For master's, comprehensive exam (for some programs), thesis (for some programs); for doctorate, comprehensive exam, thesis/dissertation. *Entrance requirements:* For master's, bachelor's degree; 2 letters of recommendation; statement of purpose; for doctorate, GRE General Test (minimum score in the top 35% of the quantitative), bachelor's degree/master's degree; 3 letters of recommendation; statement of purpose. Additional exam requirements/recommendations for international students: Required—TOEFL (minimum score 550 paper-based; 79 iBT), IELTS (minimum score 7). *Application deadline:* For fall admission, 2/1 for domestic and international students; for spring admission, 10/1 for domestic and international students. Application fee: $60 ($95 for international students). Electronic applications accepted. *Expenses:* Contact institution. *Financial support:* In 2018–19, 40 students received support, including 1 fellowship with full tuition reimbursement available (averaging $25,000 per year), 1 research assistantship with full tuition reimbursement available (averaging $11,250 per year), 39 teaching assistantships with full tuition reimbursements available (averaging $18,231 per year); institutionally sponsored loans, scholarships/grants, health care benefits, and unspecified assistantships also available. Financial award application deadline: 3/15; financial award applicants required to submit FAFSA. *Faculty research:* Scientific computing, computer simulation, numerical analysis

for differential equations; partial differential equations; mathematical logic, foundations of mathematics, set theory, large cardinals; statistics, biostatistics, statistical computing; number theory, arithmetic geometry, algebraic geometry. *Total annual research expenditures:* $89,905. *Unit head:* Dr. Zhijian Wu, Chair/Professor, 702-895-1618, Fax: 702-895-4343, E-mail: math.chair@unlv.edu. *Application contact:* Dr. Jichun Li, Graduate Coordinator, 702-895-0365, Fax: 702-895-4343, E-mail: math.gradcoord@unlv.edu.
Website: http://math.unlv.edu/

University of Nevada, Reno, Graduate School, College of Science, Department of Mathematics and Statistics, Reno, NV 89557. Offers mathematics (MS); teaching mathematics (MATM). *Degree requirements:* For master's, thesis optional. *Entrance requirements:* For master's, GRE General Test, minimum GPA of 2.75. Additional exam requirements/recommendations for international students: Required—TOEFL (minimum score 500 paper-based; 61 iBT), IELTS (minimum score 6). Electronic applications accepted. *Faculty research:* Operator algebra, nonlinear systems, differential equations.

University of New Brunswick Fredericton, School of Graduate Studies, Faculty of Science, Department of Mathematics and Statistics, Fredericton, NB E3B 5A3, Canada. Offers M Sc, PhD. *Degree requirements:* For master's, thesis; for doctorate, comprehensive exam, thesis/dissertation. *Entrance requirements:* For master's and doctorate, minimum GPA of 3.0. Additional exam requirements/recommendations for international students: Required—TOEFL (minimum score 550 paper-based), TWE (minimum score 4); Recommended—IELTS (minimum score 7). Electronic applications accepted. *Faculty research:* Commutative and non-commutative algebra, combinatorics, mathematical modeling and computation, mathematical biology, classical and quantum gravity, multivariate statistics and spatial statistics.

University of New Hampshire, Graduate School, College of Engineering and Physical Sciences, Department of Mathematics and Statistics, Durham, NH 03824. Offers applied mathematics (PhD); industrial statistics (Certificate); mathematics (MS, MST, PhD); mathematics education (PhD); mathematics: applied mathematics (MS); mathematics: statistics (MS, PhD). Terminal master's awarded for partial completion of doctoral program. *Entrance requirements:* Additional exam requirements/recommendations for international students: Required—TOEFL (minimum score 550 paper-based; 80 iBT). Electronic applications accepted.

University of New Mexico, Graduate Studies, College of Arts and Sciences, Department of Mathematics and Statistics, Albuquerque, NM 87131-2039. Offers mathematics (MS, PhD); statistics (MS, PhD). *Program availability:* Part-time. *Students:* Average age 31. 92 applicants, 47% accepted, 22 enrolled. In 2018, 19 master's, 13 doctorates awarded. Terminal master's awarded for partial completion of doctoral program. *Degree requirements:* For master's, comprehensive exam (for some programs), thesis or alternative; for doctorate, one foreign language, comprehensive exam, thesis/dissertation, 4 department seminars. *Entrance requirements:* For master's and doctorate, minimum GPA of 3.0, 3 letters of recommendation, letter of intent. Additional exam requirements/recommendations for international students: Required—TOEFL (minimum score 550 paper-based). *Application deadline:* For fall admission, 2/15 priority date for domestic and international students; for spring admission, 11/1 priority date for domestic and international students. Application fee: $50. Electronic applications accepted. *Financial support:* Research assistantships, teaching assistantships, health care benefits, and unspecified assistantships available. Financial award application deadline: 2/15; financial award applicants required to submit FAFSA. *Faculty research:* Pure and applied mathematics, applied statistics, numerical analysis, biostatistics, differential geometry, fluid dynamics, nonparametric curve estimation. *Total annual research expenditures:* $1.2 million. *Unit head:* Dr. Terry Loring, Chair, 505-277-4613, Fax: 505-277-5505, E-mail: loring@math.unm.edu. *Application contact:* Ana Parra Lombard, Coordinator, Program Advisement, 505-277-5250, Fax: 505-277-5505, E-mail: aparra@math.unm.edu.
Website: http://math.unm.edu/

University of New Orleans, Graduate School, College of Sciences, Department of Mathematics, New Orleans, LA 70148. Offers MS. *Program availability:* Part-time. *Entrance requirements:* For master's, BA or BS in mathematics. Additional exam requirements/recommendations for international students: Required—TOEFL (minimum score 550 paper-based; 79 iBT), IELTS (minimum score 6.5). Electronic applications accepted. *Faculty research:* Differential equations, combinatorics, statistics, complex analysis, algebra.

The University of North Carolina at Chapel Hill, Graduate School, College of Arts and Sciences, Department of Mathematics, Chapel Hill, NC 27599. Offers MA, MS, PhD. *Degree requirements:* For master's, comprehensive exam, thesis or alternative, computer language proficiency; for doctorate, one foreign language, thesis/dissertation, 3 comprehensive exams, computer language proficiency, instructional service. *Entrance requirements:* For master's and doctorate, GRE General Test, minimum GPA of 3.0. Additional exam requirements/recommendations for international students: Required—TOEFL. Electronic applications accepted. *Faculty research:* Algebraic geometry, topology, analysis, lie theory, applied math.

The University of North Carolina at Charlotte, Cato College of Education, Department of Reading and Elementary Education, Charlotte, NC 28223-0001. Offers elementary education (M Ed, Graduate Certificate); elementary mathematics education (Graduate Certificate); reading education (M Ed). *Program availability:* Part-time, evening/weekend, 100% online, blended/hybrid learning. *Students:* 58 part-time (all women); includes 15 minority (12 Black or African American, non-Hispanic/Latino; 1 American Indian or Alaska Native, non-Hispanic/Latino; 2 Two or more races, non-Hispanic/Latino). Average age 31. 39 applicants, 95% accepted, 35 enrolled. In 2018, 29 master's, 23 other advanced degrees awarded. *Entrance requirements:* For master's, GRE or MAT, three letters of recommendation, official transcripts, academic and professional goals statement, valid teacher's license, bachelor's degree in elementary education; NC A-level license or its equivalent in another state (for reading education). Additional exam requirements/recommendations for international students: Required—TOEFL (minimum score 523 paper-based; 70 iBT), IELTS (minimum score 6), TOEFL (minimum score 523 paper-based, 70 iBT) or IELTS (6). *Application deadline:* Applications are processed on a rolling basis. Application fee: $75. Electronic applications accepted. Tuition and fees vary according to course load and program. *Financial support:* Research assistantships, career-related internships or fieldwork, institutionally sponsored loans, scholarships/grants, and unspecified assistantships available. Support available to part-time students. Financial award application deadline: 3/1; financial award applicants required to submit FAFSA. *Total annual research expenditures:* $146,699. *Unit head:* Dr. Mike Putman, Chair, 704-687-8019, E-mail: michael.putman@uncc.edu. *Application contact:* Kathy B. Giddings, Director of Graduate Admissions, 704-687-5503, Fax: 704-687-1668, E-mail: gradadm@uncc.edu.
Website: http://reel.uncc.edu/

The University of North Carolina at Charlotte, College of Liberal Arts and Sciences, Department of Mathematics and Statistics, Charlotte, NC 28223-0001. Offers applied mathematics (PhD); mathematics (MS). *Program availability:* Part-time, evening/weekend. *Students:* 48 full-time (20 women), 20 part-time (13 women); includes 8 minority (2 Black or African American, non-Hispanic/Latino; 5 Asian, non-Hispanic/Latino; 1 Hispanic/Latino), 38 international. Average age 29. 48 applicants, 92% accepted, 20 enrolled. In 2018, 14 master's, 6 doctorates awarded. Terminal master's awarded for partial completion of doctoral program. *Entrance requirements:* For master's, GRE General Test, bachelor's degree, or its U.S. equivalent, from regionally-accredited college or university; minimum overall GPA of 3.0 on all previous work beyond high school; for doctorate, GRE General Test, at least 27 hours of courses in the mathematical sciences, as approved by the department Graduate Committee, with minimum C grades and minimum overall GPA in mathematics or statistics courses of 3.0. Additional exam requirements/recommendations for international students: Required—TOEFL (minimum score 523 paper-based; 70 iBT), IELTS (minimum score 6), TOEFL (minimum score 523 paper-based, 70 iBT) or IELTS (6). *Application deadline:* Applications are processed on a rolling basis. Application fee: $75. Electronic applications accepted. Tuition and fees vary according to course load and program. *Financial support:* Fellowships, research assistantships, teaching assistantships, career-related internships or fieldwork, Federal Work-Study, institutionally sponsored loans, scholarships/grants, and unspecified assistantships available. Support available to part-time students. Financial award application deadline: 3/1; financial award applicants required to submit FAFSA. *Total annual research expenditures:* $844,249. *Unit head:* Dr. Yuanan Diao, Chair, 704-687-0620, E-mail: ydiao@uncc.edu. *Application contact:* Kathy B. Giddings, Director of Graduate Admissions, 704-687-5503, Fax: 704-687-1668, E-mail: gradadm@uncc.edu.
Website: http://math.uncc.edu/

The University of North Carolina at Greensboro, Graduate School, College of Arts and Sciences, Department of Mathematics and Statistics, Greensboro, NC 27412-5001. Offers mathematics (MA, PhD). *Program availability:* Part-time. *Degree requirements:* For master's, comprehensive exam, thesis (for some programs). *Entrance requirements:* For master's, GRE General Test. Additional exam requirements/recommendations for international students: Required—TOEFL. Electronic applications accepted. *Faculty research:* General and geometric topology, statistics, computer networks, symbolic logic, mathematics education.

The University of North Carolina Wilmington, College of Arts and Sciences, Department of Mathematics and Statistics, Wilmington, NC 28403-3297. Offers applied statistics (Professional Certificate); mathematics (MS). *Program availability:* Part-time. *Degree requirements:* For master's, comprehensive exam, thesis (for some programs). *Entrance requirements:* For master's, GRE General Test, 3 letters of recommendation. Additional exam requirements/recommendations for international students: Required—TOEFL (minimum score 550 paper-based; 79 iBT), IELTS (minimum score 6.5). Electronic applications accepted.

University of North Dakota, Graduate School, College of Arts and Sciences, Department of Mathematics, Grand Forks, ND 58202. Offers M Ed, MS. *Program availability:* Part-time. *Degree requirements:* For master's, thesis or alternative, final exam. *Entrance requirements:* For master's, minimum GPA of 3.0. Additional exam requirements/recommendations for international students: Required—TOEFL (minimum score 550 paper-based; 79 iBT), IELTS (minimum score 6.5). Electronic applications accepted. *Faculty research:* Statistics, measure theory, topological vector spaces, algebra, applied math.

University of Northern British Columbia, Office of Graduate Studies, Prince George, BC V2N 4Z9, Canada. Offers business administration (Diploma); community health science (M Sc); disability management (MA); education (M Ed); first nations studies (MA); gender studies (MA); history (MA); interdisciplinary studies (MA); international studies (MA); mathematical, computer and physical sciences (M Sc); natural resources and environmental studies (M Sc, MA, MNRES, PhD); political science (MA); psychology (M Sc, PhD); social work (MSW). *Program availability:* Part-time, evening/weekend, online learning. *Degree requirements:* For master's, thesis; for doctorate, thesis/dissertation. *Entrance requirements:* For master's, GRE, minimum B average in undergraduate course work; for doctorate, candidacy exam, minimum A average in graduate course work.

University of Northern Colorado, Graduate School, College of Natural and Health Sciences, School of Mathematical Sciences, Greeley, CO 80639. Offers educational mathematics (PhD); mathematical teaching (MA); mathematics (MA). *Program availability:* Part-time. *Degree requirements:* For master's, comprehensive exam, thesis or alternative; for doctorate, comprehensive exam, thesis/dissertation. *Entrance requirements:* For master's, GRE General Test (for liberal arts), 3 letters of recommendation; for doctorate, GRE General Test, 3 letters of recommendation. Electronic applications accepted.

University of Northern Iowa, Graduate College, College of Humanities, Arts and Sciences, Department of Mathematics, MA Program in Mathematics, Cedar Falls, IA 50614. Offers community college teaching (MA); mathematics (MA); secondary teaching (MA).

University of North Florida, College of Arts and Sciences, Department of Mathematics and Statistics, Jacksonville, FL 32224. Offers mathematical sciences (MS); statistics (MS). *Program availability:* Part-time, evening/weekend. *Faculty:* 13 full-time (5 women). *Students:* 17 full-time (7 women), 4 part-time (2 women); includes 3 minority (1 Asian, non-Hispanic/Latino; 1 Hispanic/Latino; 1 Two or more races, non-Hispanic/Latino), 6 international. Average age 27. 25 applicants, 44% accepted, 9 enrolled. In 2018, 8 master's awarded. *Degree requirements:* For master's, comprehensive exam, thesis optional. *Entrance requirements:* For master's, GRE General Test, minimum GPA of 3.0 in last 60 hours of course work. Additional exam requirements/recommendations for international students: Required—TOEFL (minimum score 500 paper-based; 61 iBT). *Application deadline:* For fall admission, 8/1 priority date for domestic students, 6/1 for international students; for spring admission, 12/1 priority date for domestic students, 10/1 for international students; for summer admission, 3/15 priority date for domestic students, 2/1 for international students. Application fee: $30. Electronic applications accepted. *Expenses: Tuition, area resident:* Part-time $408.10 per credit hour. Tuition, state resident: part-time $408.10 per credit hour. Tuition, nonresident: part-time $932.61 per credit hour. *Required fees:* $111.81 per credit hour. Tuition and fees vary according to course load, campus/location and program. *Financial support:* In 2018–19, 21 students received support, including 3 teaching assistantships (averaging $5,922 per year); Federal Work-Study, scholarships/grants, tuition waivers (partial), and unspecified assistantships also available. Support available to part-time students. Financial award application deadline: 4/1; financial award applicants required to submit FAFSA. *Faculty research:* Real analysis, number theory, Euclidean geometry. *Total annual research expenditures:* $300. *Unit head:* Dr. Scott H. Hochwald, Chair, 904-620-2653, Fax: 904-620-2818, E-mail: shochwal@unf.edu. *Application contact:* Dr. Amanda Pascale, Director, The Graduate School, 904-620-1360, Fax: 904-620-1362, E-mail: graduateschool@unf.edu.
Website: http://www.unf.edu/coas/math-stat/

University of North Texas, Toulouse Graduate School, Denton, TX 76203-5459. Offers accounting (MS); applied anthropology (MA, MS); applied behavior analysis (Certificate); applied geography (MA); applied technology and performance improvement (M Ed, MS); art education (MA); art history (MA); arts leadership (Certificate); audiology (Au D); behavior analysis (MS); behavioral science (PhD); biochemistry and molecular biology (MS); biology (MA, MS); biomedical engineering (MS); business analysis (MS); chemistry (MS); clinical health psychology (PhD); communication studies (MA, MS); computer engineering (MS); computer science (MS); counseling (M Ed, MS), including clinical mental health counseling (MS), college and university counseling, elementary school counseling, secondary school counseling; creative writing (MA); criminal justice (MS); curriculum and instruction (M Ed); decision sciences (MBA); design (MA, MFA), including fashion design (MFA), innovation studies, interior design (MFA); early childhood studies (MS); economics (MS); educational leadership (M Ed, Ed D); educational psychology (MS, PhD), including family studies (MS), gifted and talented (MS), human development (MS), learning and cognition (MS), research, measurement and evaluation (MS); electrical engineering (MS); emergency management (MPA); engineering technology (MS); English (MA); English as a second language (MA); environmental science (MS); finance (MBA, MS); financial management (MPA); French (MA); health services management (MBA); higher education (M Ed, Ed D); history (MA, MS); hospitality management (MS); human resources management (MPA); information science (MS); information systems (PhD); information technologies (MBA); interdisciplinary studies (MA, MS); international studies (MA); international sustainable tourism (MS); jazz studies (MM); journalism (MA, MJ, Graduate Certificate), including interactive and virtual digital communication (Graduate Certificate), narrative journalism (Graduate Certificate), public relations (Graduate Certificate); kinesiology (MS); linguistics (MA); local government management (MPA); logistics (PhD); logistics and supply chain management (MBA); long-term care, senior housing, and aging services (MA); management (PhD); marketing (MBA); mathematics (MA, MS); mechanical and energy engineering (MS, PhD); music (MA), including ethnomusicology, music theory, musicology, performance; music composition (PhD); music education (MM Ed, PhD); nonprofit management (MPA); operations and supply chain management (MBA); performance (MM, DMA); philosophy (MA); political science (MA); professional and technical communication (MA); radio, television and film (MA, MFA); rehabilitation counseling (Certificate); sociology (MA); Spanish (MA); special education (M Ed); speech-language pathology (MA); strategic management (MBA); studio art (MFA); teaching (M Ed); MBA/MS. *Program availability:* Part-time, evening/weekend, online learning. Terminal master's awarded for partial completion of doctoral program. *Degree requirements:* For master's, variable foreign language requirement, comprehensive exam (for some programs), thesis (for some programs); for doctorate, variable foreign language requirement, comprehensive exam (for some programs), thesis/dissertation; for other advanced degree, variable foreign language requirement, comprehensive exam (for some programs). *Entrance requirements:* For master's and doctorate, GRE, GMAT. Additional exam requirements/recommendations for international students: Required—TOEFL (minimum score 550 paper-based; 79 iBT). Electronic applications accepted.

University of Notre Dame, The Graduate School, College of Science, Department of Mathematics, Notre Dame, IN 46556. Offers algebra (PhD); algebraic geometry (PhD); applied mathematics (MSAM); complex analysis (PhD); differential geometry (PhD); logic (PhD); partial differential equations (PhD); topology (PhD). Terminal master's awarded for partial completion of doctoral program. *Degree requirements:* For doctorate, one foreign language, thesis/dissertation, qualifying exam. *Entrance requirements:* For master's and doctorate, GRE General Test, GRE Subject Test. Additional exam requirements/recommendations for international students: Required—TOEFL (minimum

score 600 paper-based; 80 iBT). Electronic applications accepted. *Faculty research:* Algebra, analysis, geometry/topology, logic, applied math.

University of Oklahoma, College of Arts and Sciences, Department of Mathematics, Norman, OK 73019. Offers MA, MS, PhD, MBA/MS. *Program availability:* Part-time. *Faculty:* 35 full-time (6 women). *Students:* 38 full-time (11 women), 20 part-time (7 women); includes 12 minority (3 Asian, non-Hispanic/Latino; 7 Hispanic/Latino; 2 Two or more races, non-Hispanic/Latino), 16 international. Average age 28. 16 applicants, 81% accepted, 12 enrolled. In 2018, 6 master's, 11 doctorates awarded. Terminal master's awarded for partial completion of doctoral program. *Degree requirements:* For master's, comprehensive exam; for doctorate, one foreign language, comprehensive exam, thesis/dissertation. *Entrance requirements:* For master's and doctorate, undergraduate degree. Additional exam requirements/recommendations for international students: Required—TOEFL (minimum score 79 iBT) or IELTS (minimum score 6.5). *Application deadline:* For fall admission, 1/31 for domestic and international students. Applications are processed on a rolling basis. Application fee: $50 ($100 for international students). Electronic applications accepted. *Expenses:* Tuition, state resident: full-time $5683.20; part-time $236.80 per credit hour. Tuition, nonresident: full-time $20,342; part-time $847.60 per credit hour. *International tuition:* $20,342.40 full-time. *Required fees:* $2894.20; $110.05 per credit hour. $126.50 per semester. Tuition and fees vary according to course load and program. *Financial support:* Fellowships, research assistantships, teaching assistantships, scholarships/grants, and health care benefits available. Financial award application deadline: 6/1; financial award applicants required to submit FAFSA. *Faculty research:* Algebra and number theory; analysis and applied mathematics; geometry; topology; research in undergraduate mathematics education. *Unit head:* Dr. Noel Brady, Chair, 405-325-6711, Fax: 405-325-7484, E-mail: nbrady@ou.edu. *Application contact:* Michael Jablonski, Graduate Director, 405-325-6711, Fax: 405-325-7484, E-mail: jablo@math.ou.edu. Website: http://math.ou.edu

See Display below and Close-Up on page 255.

University of Oregon, Graduate School, College of Arts and Sciences, Department of Mathematics, Eugene, OR 97403. Offers MA, MS, PhD. *Program availability:* Part-time. Terminal master's awarded for partial completion of doctoral program. *Degree requirements:* For doctorate, 2 foreign languages, thesis/dissertation. *Entrance requirements:* For master's and doctorate, GRE General Test, GRE Subject Test. Additional exam requirements/recommendations for international students: Required—TOEFL. *Faculty research:* Algebra, topology, analytic geometry, numerical analysis, statistics.

University of Ottawa, Faculty of Graduate and Postdoctoral Studies, Faculty of Science, Ottawa-Carleton Institute of Mathematics and Statistics, Ottawa, ON K1N 6N5, Canada. Offers M Sc, PhD. M Sc, PhD offered jointly with Carleton University. *Program availability:* Part-time. *Degree requirements:* For master's, thesis optional; for doctorate, one foreign language, comprehensive exam, thesis/dissertation. *Entrance requirements:* For master's, honors B Sc degree or equivalent, minimum B average; for doctorate, M Sc, minimum B+ average. Electronic applications accepted. *Faculty research:* Pure mathematics, applied mathematics, probability and statistics.

University of Pennsylvania, School of Arts and Sciences, Graduate Group in Mathematics, Philadelphia, PA 19104. Offers AM, PhD. *Faculty:* 28 full-time (4 women), 6 part-time/adjunct (0 women). *Students:* 62 full-time (13 women); includes 11 minority (2 Black or African American, non-Hispanic/Latino; 4 Asian, non-Hispanic/Latino; 5 Hispanic/Latino), 35 international. Average age 26. 299 applicants, 11% accepted, 15 enrolled. In 2018, 10 master's, 5 doctorates awarded. Terminal master's awarded for partial completion of doctoral program. *Degree requirements:* For master's, thesis or

---

Department of Mathematics
The University of Oklahoma

Thank you for your interest in our department and in the University of Oklahoma! The **Mathematics Department** at the University of Oklahoma has a long and rich academic tradition dating back to the mid-1890s. We awarded our first master's degree in 1927 and our first doctorate in 1947. We offer a wide range of options leading to the Master of Arts, Master of Science, and Ph.D. degrees. You will be able to select from a broad **range of options** in pure and applied mathematics and in research in mathematics education for your graduate degree:

1. **Algebra and Number Theory.** Algebraic Geometry, Algebraic Groups, Combinatorics, Modular Forms, Representation Theory (real, p-adic, Lie, automorphic).
2. **Analysis.** Global Analysis, Harmonic Analysis, Integrable Systems, PDEs, Signal Processing, Spectral Theory, Wavelets and Frames.
3. **Applied Mathematics and Mathematical Physics.** Control Theory, Dynamical Systems, Modeling.
4. **Geometry.** Convexity, Harmonic Maps, Riemannian Geometry, Group Actions and Non-negative Curvature.
5. **RUME.** Research in Undergraduate Mathematics Education, Diversity and Equity, International Comparative Education.
6. **Topology.** Algebraic and Geometric Topology, Dimension Theory, Geometric Group Theory, Hyperbolic Geometry, Low Dimensional Topology, Teichmuller Theory.

For more information, contact:
Cristin Yates, Assistant to the Graduate Director
Department of Mathematics
The University of Oklahoma
Norman, OK 73019
cyates@ou.edu
www.math.ou.edu/grad/

230 www.petersons.com

Peterson's Graduate Programs in the Physical Sciences, Mathematics, Agricultural Sciences, the Environment & Natural Resources 2020

alternative; for doctorate, thesis/dissertation. Application fee: $80. *Financial support:* Application deadline: 12/15.
Website: http://www.sas.upenn.edu/graduate-division

University of Pittsburgh, Kenneth P. Dietrich School of Arts and Sciences, Department of Mathematics, Pittsburgh, PA 15260. Offers applied mathematics (MA, MS); mathematics (MA, MS, PhD). *Program availability:* Part-time. Terminal master's awarded for partial completion of doctoral program. *Degree requirements:* For master's, thesis; for doctorate, comprehensive exam, thesis/dissertation. *Entrance requirements:* For master's and doctorate, GRE General Test; GRE Subject Test (recommended), minimum GPA of 3.0. Additional exam requirements/recommendations for international students: Required—TOEFL (minimum score 90 iBT) or IELTS (minimum score 7.0). Electronic applications accepted. *Faculty research:* Algebra, combinatorics, and geometry; analysis and partial differential equations; applied analysis; complex biological systems; mathematical finance.

University of Puerto Rico–Mayagüez, Graduate Studies, College of Arts and Sciences, Department of Mathematical Sciences, Mayagüez, PR 00681-9000. Offers applied mathematics (MS); pre-college math education (MS); pure mathematics (MS); scientific computing (MS); statistics (MS). *Program availability:* Part-time. *Degree requirements:* For master's, one foreign language, comprehensive exam, thesis. *Entrance requirements:* For master's, undergraduate degree in mathematics or its equivalent. Electronic applications accepted. *Faculty research:* Automata theory, linear algebra, logic.

University of Puerto Rico–Río Piedras, College of Natural Sciences, Department of Mathematics, San Juan, PR 00931-3300. Offers MS, PhD. *Program availability:* Part-time. *Degree requirements:* For master's, comprehensive exam, thesis; for doctorate, comprehensive exam, thesis/dissertation. *Entrance requirements:* For master's and doctorate, GRE General Test and GRE Subject Test, interview, minimum GPA of 3.0, 3 letters of recommendation. *Faculty research:* Investigation of database logistics, cryptograph systems, distribution and spectral theory, Boolean function, differential equations.

University of Regina, Faculty of Graduate Studies and Research, Faculty of Science, Department of Mathematics and Statistics, Regina, SK S4S 0A2, Canada. Offers mathematics (M Sc, PhD); statistics (M Sc, PhD). *Program availability:* Part-time. *Faculty:* 24 full-time (4 women), 7 part-time/adjunct (4 women). *Students:* 31 full-time (16 women), 5 part-time (1 woman). Average age 30. 45 applicants, 67% accepted, 6 enrolled. In 2018, 8 master's, 1 doctorate awarded. *Degree requirements:* For master's, thesis (for some programs), course work; for doctorate, comprehensive exam, thesis/dissertation, course work, seminar, original research. *Entrance requirements:* For master's, graduating average of 75% from 4 years bachelor degree (or equivalent); for doctorate, applicants must have obtained a thesis-based Master's degree in the discipline to qualify as a doctoral student. Applicants must have academic credentials consistent with being fully-qualified to undertake graduate work at the doctoral level. Additional exam requirements/recommendations for international students: Required—TOEFL (minimum score 580 paper-based; 80 iBT), IELTS (minimum score 6.5), PTE (minimum score 59), other options are CAEL, MELAB, Cantest and U of R ESL. *Application deadline:* For fall admission, 1/31 for domestic and international students; for winter admission, 6/30 for domestic and international students. Application fee: $100. Electronic applications accepted. *Expenses:* Estimated tuition and fees for one academic year is 6,702.90 for master's. The fee will vary base on your choice program. For doctoral program one academic year is estimated 14,129.40. International students will pay additional 1,191.75 for international surcharge per semester. *Financial support:* Fellowships, research assistantships, teaching assistantships, career-related internships or fieldwork, Federal Work-Study, scholarships/grants, unspecified assistantships, and travel award and Graduate Scholarship Base funds available. Support available to part-time students. Financial award application deadline: 9/30. *Faculty research:* Actuarial mathematics, algebra, discrete mathematics, number theory, analysis, geometry and topology, statistics and probability theory. *Unit head:* Dr. Shaun Fallat, Department Head, 306-585-4148, Fax: 306-585-4020, E-mail: mathstat.head@uregina.ca. *Application contact:* Dr. Donald Stanley, Graduate Coordinator, 306-585-4343, Fax: 306-585-4020, E-mail: Donald.Stanley@uregina.ca.
Website: http://www.uregina.ca/science/mathstat/

University of Rhode Island, Graduate School, College of Arts and Sciences, Department of Mathematics, Kingston, RI 02881. Offers applied analysis (MS); applied mathematical sciences (PhD); combinatorics and graph theory (MS); complex dynamical systems (MS); difference equations (MS); numerical analysis (MS); pure mathematics (PhD). *Program availability:* Part-time. *Faculty:* 24 full-time (8 women). *Students:* 17 full-time (7 women), 6 part-time (1 woman); includes 3 minority (2 Black or African American, non-Hispanic/Latino; 1 Hispanic/Latino), 1 international. 27 applicants, 81% accepted, 8 enrolled. In 2018, 3 master's, 3 doctorates awarded. *Entrance requirements:* For master's and doctorate, 2 letters of reference, one of which must address the candidate's abilities to teach in English (3 for international candidates). Additional exam requirements/recommendations for international students: Required—TOEFL. *Application deadline:* For fall admission, 7/15 for domestic students, 2/1 for international students; for spring admission, 11/15 for domestic students, 7/15 for international students. Application fee: $65. Electronic applications accepted. *Expenses: Tuition, area resident:* Full-time $13,226; part-time $735 per credit. Tuition, state resident: full-time $13,226; part-time $735 per credit. Tuition, nonresident: full-time $25,854; part-time $1436 per credit. *International tuition:* $25,854 full-time. *Required fees:* $1698; $50 per credit. $35 per semester. One-time fee: $165. *Financial support:* In 2018–19, 14 teaching assistantships with tuition reimbursements (averaging $17,996 per year) were awarded. Financial award application deadline: 2/1; financial award applicants required to submit FAFSA. *Unit head:* Dr. James Baglama, Chair, 401-874-2709, Fax: 401-874-4454, E-mail: jbaglama@math.uri.edu. *Application contact:* Dr. Tom Sharland, Director of Graduate Studies, 401-874-2314, E-mail: tsharland@uri.edu.
Website: http://www.math.uri.edu/

University of Rochester, School of Arts and Sciences, Department of Mathematics, Rochester, NY 14627. Offers PhD. *Faculty:* 20 full-time (2 women). *Students:* 45 full-time (8 women), 2 part-time (1 woman); includes 2 minority (both Hispanic/Latino), 27 international. Average age 28. 79 applicants, 20% accepted, 10 enrolled. In 2018, 3 doctorates awarded. Terminal master's awarded for partial completion of doctoral program. *Degree requirements:* For doctorate, comprehensive exam, thesis/dissertation, oral qualifying exam. *Entrance requirements:* For doctorate, GRE General Test, GRE Subject Test. Additional exam requirements/recommendations for international students: Required—TOEFL (minimum score 100 iBT), IELTS (minimum score 9.5). *Application deadline:* For fall admission, 1/15 for domestic and international students. Application fee: $60. Electronic applications accepted. *Expenses: Tuition:* Full-time $52,974; part-time $1654 per credit hour. *Required fees:* $612. One-time fee: $30 part-time. Tuition and fees vary according to campus/location and program. *Financial support:* In 2018–19, 48 students received support, including 6 fellowships (averaging $21,000 per year), 42 teaching assistantships (averaging $18,000 per year); institutionally sponsored loans, scholarships/grants, traineeships, tuition waivers (full and partial), and unspecified assistantships also available. Financial award application deadline: 1/15. *Faculty research:* Algebra and number theory, analysis, geometry, mathematical physics and probability, topology. *Total annual research expenditures:* $362,460. *Unit head:* Thomas Tucker, Professor and Chair, 585-275-9421, E-mail: thomas.tucker@rochester.edu. *Application contact:* Cynthia Spencer, Administrative Assistant, 585-275-9422, E-mail: cynthia.spencer@rochester.edu.
Website: http://www.sas.rochester.edu/mth/graduate/index.html

University of San Diego, School of Leadership and Education Sciences, Department of Learning and Teaching, San Diego, CA 92110-2492. Offers curriculum and instruction (M Ed), including inclusive learning, literacy and digital learning, school leadership, steam (science, technology, engineering, arts, and mathematics); inclusive learning (M Ed); literacy and digital learning (M Ed); school leadership (M Ed); special education (M Ed); STEAM (science, technology, engineering, arts, and mathematics) (M Ed); TESOL, literacy and culture (M Ed). *Program availability:* Part-time, evening/weekend. *Faculty:* 9 full-time (7 women), 34 part-time/adjunct (26 women). *Students:* 136 full-time (102 women), 223 part-time (177 women); includes 130 minority (17 Black or African American, non-Hispanic/Latino; 21 Asian, non-Hispanic/Latino; 74 Hispanic/Latino; 3 Native Hawaiian or other Pacific Islander, non-Hispanic/Latino; 15 Two or more races, non-Hispanic/Latino), 10 international. Average age 33. 391 applicants, 85% accepted, 190 enrolled. In 2018, 201 master's awarded. *Degree requirements:* For master's, thesis (for some programs), international experience. *Entrance requirements:* For master's, California Basic Educational Skills Test, California Subject Examination for Teachers. Additional exam requirements/recommendations for international students: Required—TOEFL (minimum score 580 paper-based; 83 iBT), TWE. *Application deadline:* Applications are processed on a rolling basis. Application fee: $45. Electronic applications accepted. *Financial support:* In 2018–19, 127 students received support. Career-related internships or fieldwork, Federal Work-Study, institutionally sponsored loans, scholarships/grants, and stipends available. Financial award application deadline: 4/1; financial award applicants required to submit FAFSA. *Faculty research:* Action research methodology, cultural studies, instructional theories and practices, second language acquisition, school reform. *Unit head:* Dr. Reyes Quezada, Chair, 619-260-7655, E-mail: rquezada@sandiego.edu. *Application contact:* Erika Garwood, Associate Director of Graduate Admissions, 619-260-4524, Fax: 619-260-4158, E-mail: grads@sandiego.edu.
Website: http://www.sandiego.edu/soles/learning-and-teaching/

University of Saskatchewan, College of Graduate and Postdoctoral Studies, College of Arts and Science, Department of Mathematics and Statistics, Saskatoon, SK S7N 5A2, Canada. Offers M Math, M Sc, PhD. *Degree requirements:* For master's, thesis (for some programs); for doctorate, comprehensive exam (for some programs), thesis/dissertation. *Entrance requirements:* Additional exam requirements/recommendations for international students: Required—TOEFL (minimum score 80 iBT); Recommended—IELTS (minimum score 6.5). Electronic applications accepted.

University of South Alabama, College of Arts and Sciences, Department of Mathematics and Statistics, Mobile, AL 36688. Offers mathematics (MS). *Program availability:* Part-time, evening/weekend. *Degree requirements:* For master's, comprehensive exam, thesis optional. *Entrance requirements:* For master's, GRE, BS in mathematics or a mathematics-related field. Additional exam requirements/recommendations for international students: Required—TOEFL (minimum score 525 paper-based; 71 iBT), IELTS (minimum score 6). Electronic applications accepted. *Faculty research:* Finite groups, numerical analysis, potential theory, approximation theory, operator theory.

University of South Carolina, The Graduate School, College of Arts and Sciences, Department of Mathematics, Columbia, SC 29208. Offers mathematics (MA, MS, PhD); mathematics education (M Math, MAT). MAT offered in cooperation with the College of Education. *Program availability:* Part-time. Terminal master's awarded for partial completion of doctoral program. *Degree requirements:* For master's, comprehensive exam, thesis (for some programs); for doctorate, one foreign language, comprehensive exam, thesis/dissertation, admission to candidacy exam, residency. *Entrance requirements:* For master's and doctorate, GRE General Test. Additional exam requirements/recommendations for international students: Required—TOEFL (minimum score 600 paper-based; 100 iBT). Electronic applications accepted. *Faculty research:* Computational mathematics, analysis (classical/modern), discrete mathematics, algebra, number theory.

University of South Dakota, Graduate School, College of Arts and Sciences, Department of Mathematics, Vermillion, SD 57069. Offers MA, MS. *Program availability:* Part-time. *Degree requirements:* For master's, thesis (for some programs). *Entrance requirements:* For master's, GRE, minimum GPA of 2.7. Additional exam requirements/recommendations for international students: Required—TOEFL (minimum score 550 paper-based; 79 iBT). Electronic applications accepted.

University of Southern California, Graduate School, Dana and David Dornsife College of Letters, Arts and Sciences, Department of Mathematics, Los Angeles, CA 90089. Offers applied mathematics (MA, MS, PhD); mathematical finance (MS); mathematics (MA, PhD); statistics (MS). *Program availability:* Part-time. Terminal master's awarded for partial completion of doctoral program. *Degree requirements:* For master's, comprehensive exam (for some programs), thesis (for some programs); for doctorate, one foreign language, comprehensive exam, thesis/dissertation. *Entrance requirements:* For master's, GRE General Test, GMAT; for doctorate, GRE General Test, GRE Subject Test (mathematics). Additional exam requirements/recommendations for international students: Required—TOEFL (minimum score 100 iBT). Electronic applications accepted. *Faculty research:* Algebra, algebraic geometry and number theory, analysis/partial differential equations, applied mathematics, financial mathematics, probability, combinatorics and statistics.

University of Southern Mississippi, College of Arts and Sciences, Department of Mathematics, Hattiesburg, MS 39406-0001. Offers computational science (PhD), including mathematics; mathematics (MS). *Program availability:* Part-time. *Degree requirements:* For master's, comprehensive exam, thesis or alternative; for doctorate, comprehensive exam, thesis/dissertation. *Entrance requirements:* For master's, GRE General Test, minimum GPA of 2.75 in last 60 hours; for doctorate, GRE General Test, minimum GPA of 3.5. Additional exam requirements/recommendations for international students: Required—TOEFL, IELTS. Electronic applications accepted. *Faculty research:* Dynamical systems, numerical analysis and multigrid methods, random number generation, matrix theory, group theory.

University of South Florida, College of Arts and Sciences, Department of Mathematics and Statistics, Tampa, FL 33620-9951. Offers mathematics (MA, PhD), including pure and applied mathematics, statistics (PhD); statistics (MA). *Program availability:* Part-time, evening/weekend. *Faculty:* 24 full-time (2 women). *Students:* 65 full-time (24 women), 16 part-time (3 women); includes 8 minority (2 Black or African American, non-Hispanic/Latino; 2 Asian, non-Hispanic/Latino; 1 Hispanic/Latino; 3 Two or more races, non-Hispanic/Latino), 43 international. Average age 29. 77 applicants, 57% accepted, 22 enrolled. In 2018, 14 master's, 11 doctorates awarded. Terminal master's awarded

for partial completion of doctoral program. *Degree requirements:* For master's, comprehensive exam, thesis (for some programs); for doctorate, comprehensive exam, thesis/dissertation. *Entrance requirements:* For master's, GRE (minimum 55th percentile Quantitative score; Verbal and Analytical Writing scores also considered), BA in mathematical sciences, statistics, or related area. 3.00 GPA in undergraduate math courses, and in Elementary Abstract Algebra, Bridge to Abstract Mathematics, and Intermediate Analysis (for Math) 3.50 GPA (for Statistics). 3 letters of recommendation; Dept Application with goals statement; TA application; for doctorate, GRE (minimum 55th percentile Quantitative; Verbal and Analytical Writing scores also considered), minimum GPA of 3.5 in graduate mathematics courses, three letters of recommendation, statement of goals, master's or bachelor's degree in mathematical sciences or related field. Department Application, TA Application. Additional exam requirements/recommendations for international students: Required—TOEFL, TOEFL (minimum score 550 paper-based; 79 iBT) or IELTS (minimum score 6.5). *Application deadline:* For fall admission, 2/1 priority date for domestic and international students; for spring admission, 10/1 priority date for domestic students, 9/15 for international students. Application fee: $30. Electronic applications accepted. *Expenses:* Tuition, state resident: full-time $6350. Tuition, nonresident: full-time $19,048. *International tuition:* $19,048 full-time. *Required fees:* $2079. *Financial support:* In 2018–19, 9 students received support, including 6 research assistantships (averaging $16,990 per year), 55 teaching assistantships with partial tuition reimbursements available (averaging $13,742 per year); unspecified assistantships also available. Financial award application deadline: 2/1. *Faculty research:* Mathematics: algebra and number theory, harmonic and complex analysis, approximation theory, theory of orthogonal polynomials, Banach space theory and operator theory, differential equations and nonlinear analysis, discrete mathematics, geometry and topology; statistics: linear and nonlinear statistical models for health sciences, operations research problems, economic systems; stochastic control problems; dynamic reliability analysis and control. *Total annual research expenditures:* $654,045. *Unit head:* Dr. Leslaw Skrzypek, Associate Professor and Chairperson, 813-974-1268, Fax: 813-974-2700, E-mail: skrzypek@usf.edu. *Application contact:* Dr. Brian Curtin, Professor/Director of Graduate Mathematics Program, 813-974-4929, E-mail: bcurtin@usf.edu.
Website: http://math.usf.edu/

University of South Florida, Innovative Education, Tampa, FL 33620-9951. Offers adult, career and higher education (Graduate Certificate), including college teaching, leadership in developing human resources, leadership in higher education; Africana studies (Graduate Certificate), including diasporas and health disparities, genocide and human rights; aging studies (Graduate Certificate), including gerontology; art research (Graduate Certificate), including museum studies; business foundations (Graduate Certificate); chemical and biomedical engineering (Graduate Certificate), including materials science and engineering, water, health and sustainability; child and family studies (Graduate Certificate), including positive behavior support; civil and industrial engineering (Graduate Certificate), including transportation systems analysis; community and family health (Graduate Certificate), including maternal and child health, social marketing and public health, violence and injury: prevention and intervention, women's health; criminology (Graduate Certificate), including criminal justice administration; data science for public administration (Graduate Certificate); digital humanities (Graduate Certificate); educational measurement and research (Graduate Certificate), including evaluation; English (Graduate Certificate), including comparative literary studies, creative writing, professional and technical communication; entrepreneurship (Graduate Certificate); environmental health (Graduate Certificate), including safety management; epidemiology and biostatistics (Graduate Certificate), including applied biostatistics, biostatistics, concepts and tools of epidemiology, epidemiology, epidemiology of infectious diseases; geography, environment and planning (Graduate Certificate), including community development, environmental policy and management, geographical information systems; geology (Graduate Certificate), including hydrogeology; global health (Graduate Certificate), including disaster management, global health and Latin American and Caribbean studies, global health practice, humanitarian assistance, infection control; government and international affairs (Graduate Certificate), including Cuban studies, globalization studies; health policy and management (Graduate Certificate), including health management and leadership, public health policy and programs; hearing specialist: early intervention (Graduate Certificate); industrial and management systems engineering (Graduate Certificate), including systems engineering, technology management; information studies (Graduate Certificate), including school library media specialist; information systems/decision sciences (Graduate Certificate), including analytics and business intelligence; instructional technology (Graduate Certificate), including distance education, Florida digital/virtual educator, instructional design, multimedia design, Web design; internal medicine, bioethics and medical humanities (Graduate Certificate), including biomedical ethics; Latin American and Caribbean studies (Graduate Certificate); leadership for coastal resiliency planning (Graduate Certificate); mass communications (Graduate Certificate), including multimedia journalism; mathematics and statistics (Graduate Certificate), including mathematics; medicine (Graduate Certificate), including aging and neuroscience, bioinformatics, biotechnology, brain fitness and memory management, clinical investigation, hand and upper limb rehabilitation, health informatics, health sciences, integrative weight management, intellectual property, medicine and gender, metabolic and nutritional medicine, metabolic cardiology, pharmacy sciences; national and competitive intelligence (Graduate Certificate); nursing (Graduate Certificate), including simulation based academic fellowship in advanced pain management; psychological and social foundations (Graduate Certificate), including career counseling, college teaching, diversity in education, mental health counseling, school counseling; public affairs (Graduate Certificate), including nonprofit management, public management, research administration; public health (Graduate Certificate), including assessing chemical toxicity and public health risks, health equity, pharmacoepidemiology, public health generalist, toxicology, translational research in adolescent behavioral health; public health practices (Graduate Certificate), including planning for healthy communities; rehabilitation and mental health counseling (Graduate Certificate), including integrative mental health care, marriage and family therapy, rehabilitation technology; secondary education (Graduate Certificate), including ESOL, foreign language education: culture and content, foreign language education: professional; social work (Graduate Certificate), including geriatric social work/clinical gerontology; special education (Graduate Certificate), including autism spectrum disorder, disabilities education: severe/profound; world languages (Graduate Certificate), including teaching English as a second language (TESL) or foreign language. *Expenses:* Tuition, state resident: full-time $6350. Tuition, nonresident: full-time $19,048. *International tuition:* $19,048 full-time. *Required fees:* $2079. *Unit head:* Dr. Cynthia DeLuca, Associate Vice President and Assistant Vice Provost, 813-974-3077, Fax: 813-974-7061, E-mail: deluca@usf.edu. *Application contact:* Owen Hooper, Director, Summer and Alternative Calendar Programs, 813-974-6917, E-mail: hooper@usf.edu.
Website: http://www.usf.edu/innovative-education/

The University of Tennessee, Graduate School, College of Arts and Sciences, Department of Mathematics, Knoxville, TN 37996. Offers applied mathematics (MS); mathematical ecology (PhD); mathematics (M Math, MS, PhD). *Program availability:* Part-time. *Degree requirements:* For master's, thesis or alternative; for doctorate, one foreign language, thesis/dissertation. *Entrance requirements:* For master's and doctorate, minimum GPA of 2.7. Additional exam requirements/recommendations for international students: Required—TOEFL. Electronic applications accepted.

The University of Tennessee at Chattanooga, Program in Mathematics, Chattanooga, TN 37403. Offers applied mathematics (MS); applied statistics (MS); mathematics education (MS); pre-professional mathematics (MS). *Program availability:* Part-time. *Degree requirements:* For master's, internship or thesis. *Entrance requirements:* For master's, GRE (if applying for an assistantship), two letters of recommendation. Additional exam requirements/recommendations for international students: Required—TOEFL (minimum score 550 paper-based; 61 iBT), IELTS (minimum score 6). Electronic applications accepted. *Expenses:* Contact institution.

The University of Texas at Arlington, Graduate School, College of Science, Department of Mathematics, Arlington, TX 76019. Offers applied math (MS); mathematics (PhD); mathematics education (MA). *Program availability:* Part-time, evening/weekend. *Degree requirements:* For master's, comprehensive exam, thesis or alternative; for doctorate, comprehensive exam, thesis/dissertation, preliminary examinations. *Entrance requirements:* For master's, GRE General Test (minimum score 350 verbal, 650 quantitative); for doctorate, GRE General Test (minimum score 350 verbal, 700 quantitative), 30 hours of graduate course work in mathematics, minimum GPA of 3.0 in last 60 hours of course work. Additional exam requirements/recommendations for international students: Required—TOEFL (minimum score 550 paper-based; 79 iBT). Electronic applications accepted. *Faculty research:* Algebra, combinatorics and geometry, applied mathematics and mathematical biology, computational mathematics, mathematics education, probability and statistics.

The University of Texas at Austin, Graduate School, College of Natural Sciences, Department of Mathematics, Austin, TX 78712-1111. Offers MA, PhD. *Entrance requirements:* For master's and doctorate, GRE General Test. Electronic applications accepted.

The University of Texas at Dallas, School of Natural Sciences and Mathematics, Department of Mathematical Sciences, Richardson, TX 75080. Offers actuarial science (MS); mathematics (MS, PhD), including applied mathematics, data science (MS), engineering mathematics (MS), mathematics (MS); statistics (MS, PhD). *Program availability:* Part-time, evening/weekend. *Faculty:* 29 full-time (6 women), 3 part-time/adjunct (0 women). *Students:* 155 full-time (58 women), 35 part-time (9 women); includes 34 minority (4 Black or African American, non-Hispanic/Latino; 19 Asian, non-Hispanic/Latino; 7 Hispanic/Latino; 4 Two or more races, non-Hispanic/Latino), 116 international. Average age 32. 264 applicants, 37% accepted, 48 enrolled. In 2018, 48 master's, 11 doctorates awarded. *Degree requirements:* For master's, thesis optional; for doctorate, thesis/dissertation. *Entrance requirements:* For master's, GRE General Test, minimum GPA of 3.0 in upper-level course work in field; for doctorate, GRE General Test, minimum GPA of 3.5 in upper-level course work in field. Additional exam requirements/recommendations for international students: Required—TOEFL (minimum score 550 paper-based). *Application deadline:* For fall admission, 7/15 for domestic students, 5/1 priority date for international students; for spring admission, 11/15 for domestic students, 9/1 priority date for international students. Applications are processed on a rolling basis. Application fee: $50 ($100 for international students). Electronic applications accepted. *Expenses: Tuition, area resident:* Full-time $13,458. Tuition, state resident: full-time $13,458. Tuition, nonresident: full-time $26,852. *International tuition:* $26,852 full-time. Tuition and fees vary according to course load. *Financial support:* In 2018–19, 92 students received support, including 10 research assistantships (averaging $24,110 per year), 89 teaching assistantships with partial tuition reimbursements available (averaging $17,110 per year); fellowships, career-related internships or fieldwork, Federal Work-Study, institutionally sponsored loans, scholarships/grants, and unspecified assistantships also available. Support available to part-time students. Financial award application deadline: 4/30; financial award applicants required to submit FAFSA. *Faculty research:* Sequential analysis, applications in semiconductor manufacturing, medical image analysis, computational anatomy, information theory, probability theory. *Unit head:* Dr. Vladimir Dragovic, Department Head, 972-883-2161, Fax: 972-883-6622, E-mail: utdmath@utdallas.edu. *Application contact:* Evangelina Bustamante, Graduate Student Coordinator, 972-883-2163, Fax: 972-883-6622, E-mail: utdmath@utdallas.edu.
Website: http://www.utdallas.edu/math

The University of Texas at El Paso, Graduate School, College of Science, Department of Mathematical Sciences, El Paso, TX 79968-0001. Offers mathematics (MAT, MS); statistics (MS). *Program availability:* Part-time, evening/weekend. *Degree requirements:* For master's, thesis optional. *Entrance requirements:* For master's, minimum GPA of 3.0, letters of recommendation. Additional exam requirements/recommendations for international students: Required—TOEFL; Recommended—IELTS. Electronic applications accepted.

The University of Texas at San Antonio, College of Sciences, Department of Mathematics, San Antonio, TX 78249-0617. Offers applied mathematics (MS), including industrial mathematics; mathematics (MS); mathematics education (MS). *Program availability:* Part-time, evening/weekend. *Degree requirements:* For master's, comprehensive exam (for some programs), thesis or alternative. *Entrance requirements:* For master's, GRE General Test, minimum GPA of 3.0 in last 60 hours. Additional exam requirements/recommendations for international students: Required—TOEFL (minimum score 550 paper-based; 79 iBT), IELTS (minimum score 6.5). Electronic applications accepted. *Faculty research:* Differential equations, functional analysis, numerical analysis, number theory, logic.

The University of Texas at Tyler, College of Arts and Sciences, Department of Mathematics, Tyler, TX 75799-0001. Offers MS, MSIS. *Faculty:* 10 full-time (0 women). *Students:* 6 full-time (1 woman), 1 (woman) part-time; includes 1 minority (Hispanic/Latino), 3 international. Average age 26. 4 applicants, 100% accepted, 4 enrolled. In 2018, 2 master's awarded. *Degree requirements:* For master's, comprehensive exam, thesis optional. *Entrance requirements:* For master's, GRE General Test. Additional exam requirements/recommendations for international students: Required—TOEFL. *Application deadline:* For fall admission, 8/17 priority date for domestic students, 7/1 priority date for international students; for spring admission, 12/21 priority date for domestic students, 11/1 priority date for international students. Applications are processed on a rolling basis. Application fee: $25 ($50 for international students). *Financial support:* In 2018–19, 7 students received support, including 7 teaching assistantships (averaging $10,000 per year); fellowships, research assistantships, and unspecified assistantships also available. Financial award application deadline: 7/1; financial award applicants required to submit FAFSA. *Faculty research:* Discrete geometry, knot theory, commutative algebra, noncommutative rings, group theory, mathematical biology, mathematical physics. *Unit head:* Dr. Sheldon Davis, Chair, 903-566-7210, E-mail: sdavis@uttyler.edu. *Application contact:* Dr. Sheldon Davis, Chair, 903-566-7210, E-mail: sdavis@uttyler.edu.
Website: https://www.uttyler.edu/math/

The University of Texas Rio Grande Valley, College of Sciences, School of Mathematical and Statistical Sciences, Edinburg, TX 78539. Offers mathematics (MS). *Program availability:* Part-time, evening/weekend. *Entrance requirements:* For master's, GRE General Test, bachelor's degree in mathematics or related field with minimum of 12 hours of upper-division mathematics or statistics course work and minimum GPA of 3.0; official transcripts from each institution attended. Additional exam requirements/recommendations for international students: Required—TOEFL (minimum score 550 paper-based, 61 iBT) or IELTS (6.5). Electronic applications accepted. *Expenses: Tuition, area resident:* Full-time $6888. Tuition, state resident: full-time $6888. Tuition, nonresident: full-time $14,484. *International tuition:* $14,484 full-time. *Required fees:* $1468. *Faculty research:* Differential equations, group theory, functional analysis, analytic number theory, combinatorics and discrete geometry.

University of the Incarnate Word, School of Mathematics, Science, and Engineering, San Antonio, TX 78209-6397. Offers applied statistics (MS); biology (MA, MS); mathematics (MA), including teaching; multidisciplinary sciences (MA); nutrition (MS). *Program availability:* Part-time, evening/weekend. *Faculty:* 6 full-time (4 women), 1 (woman) part-time/adjunct. *Students:* 30 full-time (24 women), 9 part-time (7 women); includes 20 minority (1 Black or African American, non-Hispanic/Latino; 1 American Indian or Alaska Native, non-Hispanic/Latino; 1 Asian, non-Hispanic/Latino; 17 Hispanic/Latino), 5 international. 34 applicants, 88% accepted, 13 enrolled. In 2018, 10 master's awarded. *Degree requirements:* For master's, comprehensive exam (for some programs), thesis optional, capstone. *Entrance requirements:* For master's, GRE, recommendation letter. Additional exam requirements/recommendations for international students: Required—TOEFL (minimum score 560 paper-based; 83 iBT). *Application deadline:* Applications are processed on a rolling basis. Application fee: $20. Electronic applications accepted. *Expenses: Tuition:* Full-time $22,560; part-time $940 per credit hour. *Required fees:* $2484; $94 per credit hour. Tuition and fees vary according to degree level, program and student level. *Financial support:* Research assistantships, Federal Work-Study, scholarships/grants, tuition waivers (partial), and unspecified assistantships available. Financial award applicants required to submit FAFSA. *Faculty research:* Neural morphallaxis in lumbriculus variegatus, igneous and metamorphic petrology, applied cloud and precipitation physics, DNA-protein interactions, evolution of adenoviruses and picornaviruses. *Unit head:* Dr. Carlos A. Garcia, Dean, 210-829-2717, Fax: 210-829-3153, E-mail: cagarci9@uiwtx.edu. *Application contact:* Jessica Delarosa, Associate Director of Admissions, 210-8296005, Fax: 210-829-3921, E-mail: admis@uiwtx.edu.
Website: https://www.uiw.edu/smse/index.html

University of the Virgin Islands, College of Science and Mathematics, St. Thomas, VI 00802. Offers marine and environmental science (MS); mathematics for secondary teachers (MA). *Faculty:* 5 full-time (4 women), 7 part-time/adjunct (2 women). *Students:* 16 full-time (13 women), 19 part-time (13 women); includes 10 minority (4 Black or African American, non-Hispanic/Latino; 1 American Indian or Alaska Native, non-Hispanic/Latino; 2 Hispanic/Latino; 1 Native Hawaiian or other Pacific Islander, non-Hispanic/Latino; 2 Two or more races, non-Hispanic/Latino), 1 international. Average age 27. In 2018, 8 master's awarded. *Degree requirements:* For master's, comprehensive exam, thesis. *Entrance requirements:* For master's, GRE, minimum GPA of 2.5. Additional exam requirements/recommendations for international students: Required—TOEFL (minimum score 550 paper-based). *Application deadline:* For fall admission, 4/30 for domestic and international students; for spring admission, 10/30 for domestic and international students. Application fee: $30. Electronic applications accepted. *Expenses:* Tuition, state resident: full-time $6948; part-time $386 per credit. Tuition, nonresident: full-time $13,230; part-time $735 per credit. *International tuition:* $13,230 full-time. *Required fees:* $508. *Financial support:* Fellowships, research assistantships, teaching assistantships, career-related internships or fieldwork, and scholarships/grants available. Financial award application deadline: 4/15; financial award applicants required to submit FAFSA. *Unit head:* Dr. Sandra Romano, Dean, 340-693-1230, Fax: 340-693-1245, E-mail: sromano@uvi.edu. *Application contact:* Charmaine Smith, Director of Admissions, 340-690-4070, E-mail: csmith@uvi.edu.

The University of Toledo, College of Graduate Studies, College of Natural Sciences and Mathematics, Department of Mathematics, Toledo, OH 43606-3390. Offers applied mathematics (MS, PhD); statistics (MS, PhD). *Program availability:* Part-time. *Degree requirements:* For master's, comprehensive exam (for some programs), thesis (for some programs); for doctorate, 2 foreign languages, thesis/dissertation. *Entrance requirements:* For master's and doctorate, GRE General Test, GRE Subject Test, minimum cumulative point-hour ratio of 2.7 for all previous academic work, three letters of recommendation, statement of purpose, transcripts from all prior institutions attended. Additional exam requirements/recommendations for international students: Required—TOEFL (minimum score 550 paper-based; 80 iBT). Electronic applications accepted.

University of Toronto, School of Graduate Studies, Faculty of Arts and Science, Department of Mathematics, Toronto, ON M5S 1A1, Canada. Offers mathematical finance (MMF); mathematics (M Sc, PhD). *Program availability:* Part-time. *Degree requirements:* For master's, thesis optional, research project; for doctorate, thesis/dissertation. *Entrance requirements:* For master's, minimum B average in final year, bachelor's degree in mathematics or a related area, 3 letters of reference; for doctorate, master's degree in mathematics or a related area, minimum A- average, 3 letters of reference. Additional exam requirements/recommendations for international students: Required—TOEFL (minimum score 580 paper-based; 93 iBT), TWE (minimum score 4). Electronic applications accepted.

The University of Tulsa, Graduate School, College of Engineering and Natural Sciences, Department of Mathematics, Tulsa, OK 74104-3189. Offers MS, MTA, PhD, MSF/MSAM. *Program availability:* Part-time. *Faculty:* 18 full-time (6 women), 3 part-time/adjunct (2 women). *Students:* 6 full-time (2 women), 3 part-time (0 women); includes 2 minority (1 Hispanic/Latino; 1 Two or more races, non-Hispanic/Latino). Average age 31. 12 applicants, 33% accepted, 1 enrolled. In 2018, 1 master's, 1 doctorate awarded. Terminal master's awarded for partial completion of doctoral program. *Degree requirements:* For master's, thesis (for some programs); for doctorate, comprehensive exam, thesis/dissertation. *Entrance requirements:* For master's, GRE General Test. Additional exam requirements/recommendations for international students: Required—TOEFL (minimum score 550 paper-based; 80 iBT), IELTS (minimum score 6). *Application deadline:* Applications are processed on a rolling basis. Application fee: $55. Electronic applications accepted. *Expenses: Tuition:* Full-time $22,230; part-time $1235 per credit hour. *Required fees:* $2100; $6 per credit hour. One-time fee: $400 full-time. Tuition and fees vary according to course level, course load and program. *Financial support:* In 2018–19, 7 students received support, including 3 fellowships with full tuition reimbursements available (averaging $2,075 per year), 2 research assistantships with full tuition reimbursements available (averaging $6,717 per year), 6 teaching assistantships with full tuition reimbursements available (averaging $11,689 per year); career-related internships or fieldwork, Federal Work-Study, scholarships/grants, health care benefits, tuition waivers (full and partial), and unspecified assistantships also available. Support available to part-time students. Financial award application deadline: 2/1; financial award applicants required to submit FAFSA. *Faculty research:* Optimization theory, numerical analysis, mathematical physics, modeling, Bayesian statistical inference. *Unit head:* Dr. Bill Coberly, Department Chair, 918-631-3119, Fax: 918-631-3077, E-mail: coberly@utulsa.edu. *Application contact:* Dr. Dale Doty, Advisor, 918-631-2983, Fax: 918-631-3077, E-mail: dale-doty@utulsa.edu.
Website: http://engineering.utulsa.edu/academics/mathematics/

University of Utah, Graduate School, College of Science, Department of Mathematics, Salt Lake City, UT 84112-0090. Offers mathematics (MA, MS, PhD); mathematics teaching (MS); statistics (M Stat). *Program availability:* Part-time. *Faculty:* 45 full-time (4 women), 17 part-time/adjunct (6 women). *Students:* 112 full-time (40 women), 26 part-time (12 women); includes 7 minority (1 Black or African American, non-Hispanic/Latino; 6 Asian, non-Hispanic/Latino), 40 international. Average age 28. 288 applicants, 20% accepted, 25 enrolled. In 2018, 9 master's, 16 doctorates awarded. Terminal master's awarded for partial completion of doctoral program. *Degree requirements:* For master's, comprehensive exam, thesis or alternative, written or oral exam; for doctorate, comprehensive exam, thesis/dissertation, written and oral exam. *Entrance requirements:* For master's and doctorate, GRE Subject Test in math (recommended), Minimum undergraduate GPA of 3.0. Additional exam requirements/recommendations for international students: Required—TOEFL (minimum score 550 paper-based; 80 iBT), GRE (recommended). *Application deadline:* For fall admission, 1/1 for domestic and international students; for spring admission, 11/1 for domestic and international students; for summer admission, 3/15 for domestic and international students. Application fee: $55 ($65 for international students). Electronic applications accepted. *Expenses: Tuition, area resident:* Full-time $7190.66; part-time $2112.48 per year. Tuition, state resident: full-time $7190.66. Tuition, nonresident: full-time $25,195. *Required fees:* $558; $555.04 per unit. Tuition and fees vary according to course level, course load, degree level, program and student level. *Financial support:* In 2018–19, 106 students received support, including 1 fellowship (averaging $20,000 per year), 22 research assistantships with full tuition reimbursements available (averaging $20,000 per year), 73 teaching assistantships with full tuition reimbursements available (averaging $20,000 per year); health care benefits and unspecified assistantships also available. Financial award application deadline: 1/1; financial award applicants required to submit FAFSA. *Faculty research:* Algebraic geometry, applied mathematics, commutative algebra, data science, geometry and topology, materials and microstructure, mathematical biology, number theory, probability, statistics. *Total annual research expenditures:* $4.7 million. *Unit head:* Dr. Davar Khoshnevisan, Chair, 801-581-7870, E-mail: chair@math.utah.edu. *Application contact:* Dr. Elena Cherkaev, Director of Graduate Studies, 801-581-7315, Fax: 801-581-6841, E-mail: elena@math.utah.edu.
Website: http://www.math.utah.edu/

University of Vermont, Graduate College, College of Engineering and Mathematical Sciences, Department of Mathematics and Statistics, Program in Mathematics, Burlington, VT 05401. Offers MS, MST, PhD. *Degree requirements:* For doctorate, thesis/dissertation. *Entrance requirements:* Additional exam requirements/recommendations for international students: Required—TOEFL (minimum score 550 paper-based, 90 iBT) or IELTS (6.5). Electronic applications accepted. *Expenses:* Contact institution.

University of Victoria, Faculty of Graduate Studies, Faculty of Science, Department of Mathematics and Statistics, Victoria, BC V8W 2Y2, Canada. Offers M Sc, MA, PhD. *Program availability:* Part-time. *Degree requirements:* For master's, thesis; for doctorate, one foreign language, thesis/dissertation, 3 qualifying exams, candidacy exam. *Entrance requirements:* Additional exam requirements/recommendations for international students: Required—TOEFL (minimum score 575 paper-based), IELTS (minimum score 7). Electronic applications accepted. *Faculty research:* Functional analysis and operator theory, applied ordinary and partial differential equations, discrete mathematics and graph theory.

University of Virginia, College and Graduate School of Arts and Sciences, Department of Mathematics, Charlottesville, VA 22903. Offers math education (MA); mathematics (MA, MS, PhD). *Degree requirements:* For master's, one foreign language, comprehensive exam, thesis optional; for doctorate, one foreign language, comprehensive exam, thesis/dissertation. *Entrance requirements:* For master's and doctorate, GRE General Test, GRE Subject Test, 2-3 letters of recommendation. Additional exam requirements/recommendations for international students: Required—TOEFL (minimum score 600 paper-based; 90 iBT), IELTS. Electronic applications accepted.

University of Washington, Graduate School, College of Arts and Sciences, Department of Mathematics, Seattle, WA 98195. Offers mathematics (MA, MS, PhD); numerical analysis (MS); optimization (MS). *Program availability:* Part-time. Terminal master's awarded for partial completion of doctoral program. *Degree requirements:* For master's, thesis optional; for doctorate, 2 foreign languages, thesis/dissertation. *Entrance requirements:* For master's, GRE, minimum GPA of 3.0; for doctorate, GRE General Test, GRE Subject Test (mathematics), minimum GPA of 3.0. Additional exam requirements/recommendations for international students: Required—TOEFL. Electronic applications accepted. *Faculty research:* Algebra, analysis, probability, combinatorics and geometry.

University of Washington, Graduate School, Interdisciplinary Graduate Program in Quantitative Ecology and Resource Management, Seattle, WA 98195. Offers MS, PhD. *Degree requirements:* For master's, thesis; for doctorate, thesis/dissertation. *Entrance requirements:* For master's and doctorate, GRE General Test, minimum GPA of 3.0. Additional exam requirements/recommendations for international students: Required—TOEFL. Electronic applications accepted. *Faculty research:* Population dynamics, statistical analysis, ecological modeling and systems analysis of aquatic and terrestrial ecosystems.

University of Waterloo, Graduate Studies and Postdoctoral Affairs, Faculty of Mathematics, Department of Combinatorics and Optimization, Waterloo, ON N2L 3G1, Canada. Offers M Math, PhD. *Degree requirements:* For master's, research paper or thesis; for doctorate, comprehensive exam, thesis/dissertation. *Entrance requirements:* For master's, GRE General Test, honors degree in field, minimum B+ average; for doctorate, GRE General Test, master's degree, minimum A average. Additional exam requirements/recommendations for international students: Required—TOEFL, IELTS, PTE. *Application deadline:* Applications are processed on a rolling basis. Application fee: $125 Canadian dollars. Electronic applications accepted. *Financial support:* Research assistantships, teaching assistantships, career-related internships or fieldwork, and scholarships/grants available. *Faculty research:* Algebraic and enumerative combinatorics, continuous optimization, cryptography, discrete optimization and graph theory.
Website: https://uwaterloo.ca/combinatorics-and-optimization/

University of Waterloo, Graduate Studies and Postdoctoral Affairs, Faculty of Mathematics, Department of Pure Mathematics, Waterloo, ON N2L 3G1, Canada. Offers M Math, PhD. *Program availability:* Part-time. Terminal master's awarded for partial completion of doctoral program. *Degree requirements:* For master's, thesis

optional; for doctorate, comprehensive exam, thesis/dissertation. *Entrance requirements:* For master's, honors degree in field, minimum B+ average; for doctorate, master's degree, minimum B+ average. Additional exam requirements/ recommendations for international students: Required—TOEFL, IELTS, PTE. *Application deadline:* Applications are processed on a rolling basis. Application fee: $125 Canadian dollars. Electronic applications accepted. *Financial support:* Research assistantships, teaching assistantships, scholarships/grants, and unspecified assistantships available. *Faculty research:* Algebra, algebraic and differential geometry, functional and harmonic analysis, logic and universal algebra, number theory.
Website: https://uwaterloo.ca/pure-mathematics/

The University of Western Ontario, School of Graduate and Postdoctoral Studies, Faculty of Science, Department of Mathematics, London, ON N6A 3K7, Canada. Offers M Sc, PhD. Terminal master's awarded for partial completion of doctoral program. *Degree requirements:* For master's, thesis or alternative; for doctorate, one foreign language, comprehensive exam, thesis/dissertation, qualifying exam. *Entrance requirements:* For master's, minimum B average, honors degree; for doctorate, master's degree. Additional exam requirements/recommendations for international students: Required—TOEFL (minimum score 550 paper-based). *Faculty research:* Algebra and number theory, analysis, geometry and topology.

University of West Florida, Hal Marcus College of Science and Engineering, Department of Mathematics and Statistics, Pensacola, FL 32514-5750. Offers mathematical sciences (MS). *Program availability:* Part-time, evening/weekend. *Degree requirements:* For master's, thesis optional. *Entrance requirements:* For master's, GRE (minimum score: verbal 420; quantitative 580), minimum GPA of 3.0; official transcripts. Additional exam requirements/recommendations for international students: Required—TOEFL (minimum score 550 paper-based).

University of West Georgia, College of Science and Mathematics, Carrollton, GA 30118. Offers biology (MS); computer science (MS); geographic information systems (Postbaccalaureate Certificate); mathematics (MS). *Program availability:* Part-time, evening/weekend, 100% online, blended/hybrid learning. *Faculty:* 47 full-time (16 women). *Students:* 14 full-time (12 women), 93 part-time (26 women); includes 35 minority (21 Black or African American, non-Hispanic/Latino; 1 American Indian or Alaska Native, non-Hispanic/Latino; 7 Asian, non-Hispanic/Latino; 3 Hispanic/Latino; 3 Two or more races, non-Hispanic/Latino), 11 international. Average age 34. 97 applicants, 91% accepted, 71 enrolled. In 2018, 27 master's, 4 other advanced degrees awarded. *Entrance requirements:* Additional exam requirements/recommendations for international students: Required—TOEFL (minimum score 523 paper-based; 69 iBT); Recommended—IELTS (minimum score 6.5). *Application deadline:* For fall admission, 6/1 for domestic and international students; for spring admission, 11/15 for domestic students, 10/15 for international students; for summer admission, 4/1 for domestic students, 3/30 for international students. Applications are processed on a rolling basis. Application fee: $40. Electronic applications accepted. Tuition and fees vary according to course load, degree level, campus/location and program. *Financial support:* Fellowships, research assistantships, teaching assistantships, career-related internships or fieldwork, Federal Work-Study, institutionally sponsored loans, scholarships/grants, and unspecified assistantships available. Support available to part-time students. Financial award application deadline: 4/1; financial award applicants required to submit FAFSA. *Unit head:* Dr. Pauline Gagnon, Interim Dean of Science and Mathematics, Dean of COAH, 678-839-5190, Fax: 678-839-5191, E-mail: pgagnon@westga.edu. *Application contact:* Dr. Toby Ziglar, Assistant Dean of the Graduate School, 678-839-1394, Fax: 678-839-1395, E-mail: graduate@westga.edu.
Website: http://www.westga.edu/cosm

University of Windsor, Faculty of Graduate Studies, Faculty of Science, Department of Mathematics and Statistics, Windsor, ON N9B 3P4, Canada. Offers mathematics (M Sc); statistics (M Sc, PhD). *Degree requirements:* For master's, thesis or alternative; for doctorate, comprehensive exam, thesis/dissertation. *Entrance requirements:* For master's, minimum B average; for doctorate, minimum A average. Additional exam requirements/recommendations for international students: Required—TOEFL (minimum score 560 paper-based). Electronic applications accepted. *Faculty research:* Applied mathematics, operational research, fluid dynamics.

University of Wisconsin–Madison, Graduate School, College of Letters and Science, Department of Mathematics, Madison, WI 53706. Offers PhD. *Degree requirements:* For doctorate, comprehensive exam, thesis/dissertation, classes in a minor field; minimum GPA of 3.3. *Entrance requirements:* For doctorate, GRE General Test, GRE Subject Test (math). Additional exam requirements/recommendations for international students: Required—TOEFL (minimum score 580 paper-based; 92 iBT), IELTS. Electronic applications accepted. *Faculty research:* Analysis, applied/computational mathematics, geometry/topology, logic, algebra/number theory, probability.

University of Wisconsin–Milwaukee, Graduate School, College of Letters and Science, Department of Mathematical Sciences, Milwaukee, WI 53201-0413. Offers mathematics (MS, PhD), including actuarial science, algebra (PhD), applied and computational mathematics (PhD), atmospheric science, foundations of advanced studies (MS), industrial mathematics, probability and statistics (PhD), standard mathematics (MS), statistics (MS), topology (PhD). *Students:* 56 full-time (11 women), 10 part-time (2 women); includes 4 minority (2 Black or African American, non-Hispanic/ Latino; 1 Asian, non-Hispanic/Latino; 1 Two or more races, non-Hispanic/Latino), 28 international. Average age 30. 136 applicants, 22% accepted, 20 enrolled. In 2018, 16 master's, 8 doctorates awarded. *Degree requirements:* For master's, comprehensive exam, thesis optional; for doctorate, 2 foreign languages, thesis/dissertation. *Entrance requirements:* Additional exam requirements/recommendations for international students: Required—TOEFL (minimum score 550 paper-based; 79 iBT), IELTS (minimum score 6.5). *Application deadline:* For fall admission, 1/1 priority date for domestic students; for spring admission, 9/1 for domestic students. Application fee: $56 ($96 for international students). Electronic applications accepted. *Financial support:* Fellowships, research assistantships, teaching assistantships, career-related internships or fieldwork, health care benefits, and unspecified assistantships available. Support available to part-time students. Financial award application deadline: 4/15; financial award applicants required to submit FAFSA. *Faculty research:* Algebra, applied mathematics, atmospheric science, probability and statistics, topology. *Unit head:* Richard Stockbridge, Department Chair, 414-229-4568, E-mail: stockbri@uwm.edu. *Application contact:* General Information Contact, 414-229-4982, Fax: 414-229-6967, E-mail: gradschool@uwm.edu.
Website: http://www.uwm.edu/dept/math/

University of Wyoming, College of Arts and Sciences, Department of Mathematics and Statistics, Laramie, WY 82071. Offers applied statistics (MS); mathematics (MA, MAT, MS, MST, PhD). *Program availability:* Part-time. Terminal master's awarded for partial completion of doctoral program. *Degree requirements:* For master's, comprehensive exam, thesis, qualifying exam; for doctorate, comprehensive exam, thesis/dissertation, preliminary exam. *Entrance requirements:* For master's and doctorate, GRE General Test, minimum GPA of 3.0. Additional exam requirements/recommendations for international students: Required—TOEFL (minimum score 540 paper-based; 76 iBT). *Expenses: Tuition, area resident:* Full-time $6504; part-time $271 per credit hour. Tuition, state resident: full-time $6504; part-time $271 per credit hour. Tuition, nonresident: full-time $19,464; part-time $811 per credit hour. *International tuition:* $19,464 full-time. *Required fees:* $1410.94; $343.82 per semester. $343.82 per semester. Tuition and fees vary according to course load, program and reciprocity agreements. *Faculty research:* Numerical analysis, classical analysis, mathematical modeling, algebraic combinations.

Utah State University, School of Graduate Studies, College of Science, Department of Mathematics and Statistics, Logan, UT 84322. Offers industrial mathematics (MS); mathematical sciences (PhD); mathematics (M Math, MS); statistics (MS). *Program availability:* Part-time. Terminal master's awarded for partial completion of doctoral program. *Degree requirements:* For master's, thesis optional, qualifying exam; for doctorate, one foreign language, comprehensive exam, thesis/dissertation. *Entrance requirements:* For master's and doctorate, GRE General Test, minimum GPA of 3.0. Additional exam requirements/recommendations for international students: Required—TOEFL. *Faculty research:* Differential equations, computational mathematics, dynamical systems, probability and statistics, pure mathematics.

Vanderbilt University, Department of Mathematics, Nashville, TN 37240-1001. Offers MA, MAT, MS, PhD. *Faculty:* 30 full-time (2 women). *Students:* 40 full-time (5 women); includes 2 minority (1 Black or African American, non-Hispanic/Latino; 1 Two or more races, non-Hispanic/Latino), 22 international. Average age 26. 85 applicants, 21% accepted, 10 enrolled. In 2018, 2 master's, 8 doctorates awarded. *Degree requirements:* For master's, one foreign language, thesis or alternative; for doctorate, one foreign language, comprehensive exam, thesis/dissertation. *Entrance requirements:* For master's and doctorate, GRE General Test, GRE Subject Test. Additional exam requirements/recommendations for international students: Required—TOEFL (minimum score 570 paper-based; 88 iBT). *Application deadline:* For fall admission, 1/1 for domestic and international students. Application fee: $0. Electronic applications accepted. *Expenses: Tuition:* Full-time $47,208; part-time $2026 per credit hour. *Required fees:* $478. *Financial support:* Fellowships, research assistantships with full tuition reimbursements, teaching assistantships with full tuition reimbursements, Federal Work-Study, institutionally sponsored loans, scholarships/grants, and health care benefits available. Financial award application deadline: 1/15; financial award applicants required to submit CSS PROFILE or FAFSA. *Faculty research:* Algebra, topology, applied mathematics, graph theory, analytical mathematics. *Unit head:* Dr. Mike Neamtu, Chair, 615-322-6672, Fax: 615-343-0215, E-mail: mike.neamtu@vanderbilt.edu. *Application contact:* Alexander Powell, Director of Graduate Studies, 615-322-6650, Fax: 315-343-0215, E-mail: alexander.m.powell@vanderbilt.edu.
Website: http://www.vanderbilt.edu/math/

Villanova University, Graduate School of Liberal Arts and Sciences, Department of Mathematics and Statistics, Villanova, PA 19085-1699. Offers applied statistics (MS); mathematics (MA). *Program availability:* Part-time, evening/weekend. *Degree requirements:* For master's, comprehensive exam. *Entrance requirements:* For master's, GRE, minimum GPA of 3.0. Additional exam requirements/recommendations for international students: Required—TOEFL. Electronic applications accepted.

Virginia Commonwealth University, Graduate School, College of Humanities and Sciences, Department of Mathematics and Applied Mathematics, Richmond, VA 23284-9005. Offers applied mathematics (MS). *Degree requirements:* For master's, thesis optional. *Entrance requirements:* For master's, GRE General Test, GRE Subject Test, 30 undergraduate semester credits in the mathematical sciences or closely-related fields. Additional exam requirements/recommendations for international students: Required—TOEFL (minimum score 600 paper-based; 100 iBT); Recommended—IELTS (minimum score 6.5). Electronic applications accepted. *Faculty research:* Mathematics, applied mathematics.

Virginia Polytechnic Institute and State University, Graduate School, College of Science, Blacksburg, VA 24061. Offers biological sciences (MS, PhD); biomedical technology development and management (MS); chemistry (MS, PhD); data analysis and applied statistics (MA); economics (PhD); geosciences (MS, PhD); mathematics (MS, PhD); physics (MS, PhD); psychology (MS, PhD); statistics (MS, PhD). *Faculty:* 349 full-time (109 women), 3 part-time/adjunct (2 women). *Students:* 542 full-time (202 women), 39 part-time (19 women); includes 71 minority (11 Black or African American, non-Hispanic/Latino; 1 American Indian or Alaska Native, non-Hispanic/Latino; 18 Asian, non-Hispanic/Latino; 32 Hispanic/Latino; 9 Two or more races, non-Hispanic/ Latino), 220 international. Average age 27. 977 applicants, 25% accepted, 110 enrolled. In 2018, 75 master's, 69 doctorates awarded. *Degree requirements:* For master's, comprehensive exam (for some programs), thesis (for some programs); for doctorate, comprehensive exam (for some programs), thesis/dissertation (for some programs). *Entrance requirements:* For master's and doctorate, GRE/GMAT. Additional exam requirements/recommendations for international students: Required—TOEFL (minimum score 90 iBT). *Application deadline:* For fall admission, 8/1 for domestic students, 4/1 for international students; for spring admission, 1/1 for domestic students, 9/1 for international students. Applications are processed on a rolling basis. Application fee: $75. Electronic applications accepted. *Expenses:* Tuition, state resident: full-time $15,510; part-time $739.50 per credit hour. Tuition, nonresident: full-time $29,629; part-time $1490.25 per credit hour. *Required fees:* $2804; $550 per semester. Tuition and fees vary according to course load, campus/location and program. *Financial support:* In 2018–19, 7 fellowships with full tuition reimbursements (averaging $29,657 per year), 260 research assistantships with full tuition reimbursements (averaging $15,888 per year), 383 teaching assistantships with full tuition reimbursements (averaging $18,063 per year) were awarded; unspecified assistantships also available. Financial award application deadline: 3/1; financial award applicants required to submit FAFSA. *Total annual research expenditures:* $27.3 million. *Unit head:* Dr. Sally C. Morton, Dean, 540-231-5422, Fax: 540-231-3380, E-mail: scmorton@vt.edu. *Application contact:* Allison Craft, Executive Assistant, 540-231-6394, Fax: 540-231-3380, E-mail: crafta@vt.edu.
Website: http://www.science.vt.edu/

Virginia State University, College of Graduate Studies, College of Engineering and Technology, Department of Mathematics and Economics, Petersburg, VA 23806-0001. Offers economics (MA); mathematics (MS). *Degree requirements:* For master's, thesis (for some programs).

Wake Forest University, Graduate School of Arts and Sciences, Department of Mathematics and Statistics, Winston-Salem, NC 27109. Offers mathematics (MA). *Program availability:* Part-time. *Degree requirements:* For master's, one foreign language, thesis optional. *Entrance requirements:* For master's, GRE General Test. Additional exam requirements/recommendations for international students: Required—TOEFL (minimum score 79 iBT). Electronic applications accepted. *Faculty research:* Algebra, ring theory, topology, differential equations.

Washington State University, College of Arts and Sciences, Department of Mathematics, Pullman, WA 99164. Offers applied mathematics (MS, PhD); mathematics

(MS, PhD); mathematics teaching (MS, PhD). Programs offered at the Pullman campus. *Program availability:* Part-time. Terminal master's awarded for partial completion of doctoral program. *Degree requirements:* For master's, comprehensive exam (for some programs), thesis or alternative, oral exam, project; for doctorate, 2 foreign languages, comprehensive exam, thesis/dissertation, oral exam, written exam. *Entrance requirements:* For master's and doctorate, minimum GPA of 3.0, 3 letters of recommendation. Additional exam requirements/recommendations for international students: Required—TOEFL (minimum score 600 paper-based; 100 iBT) or IELTS (minimum score 7). Electronic applications accepted. *Faculty research:* Computational mathematics, operations research, modeling in the natural sciences, applied statistics.

Washington University in St. Louis, The Graduate School, Department of Mathematics, St. Louis, MO 63130-4899. Offers mathematics (MA, PhD); statistics (MA, PhD). Terminal master's awarded for partial completion of doctoral program. *Degree requirements:* For master's, thesis or alternative; for doctorate, thesis/dissertation. *Entrance requirements:* For master's and doctorate, GRE General Test. Additional exam requirements/recommendations for international students: Required—TOEFL. Electronic applications accepted. *Faculty research:* Algebra, algebraic geometry, real and complex analysis, differential geometry, topology, statistics, mathematical statistics, survival analysis, modeling, statistical computing for massive data, Bayesian regularization, bioinformatics, longitudinal and functional data analysis, statistical computation, application of statistics to medicine.

Wayne State University, College of Education, Division of Teacher Education, Detroit, MI 48202. Offers art education (M Ed); bilingual/bicultural education (Certificate); curriculum and instruction (Ed D, PhD, Ed S), including English as a second language (MAT, Ed D, Ed S), K-12 curriculum (PhD); elementary education (MAT), including bilingual/bicultural education (M Ed, MAT), early childhood education (M Ed, MAT), English as a second language (MAT, Ed D, Ed S), foreign language education, science education (M Ed, MAT), special education (M Ed, MAT); elementary mathematics specialist (Certificate); English as a second language (Certificate); reading (M Ed, Ed S); reading, language and literature (Ed D); secondary education (MAT), including bilingual/bicultural education (M Ed, MAT), early childhood education (M Ed, MAT), English as a second language (MAT, Ed D, Ed S), English education, foreign language education, mathematics education (M Ed, MAT), science education (M Ed, MAT), social studies education (M Ed, MAT); special education (MAT), including career and technical education; teaching and learning (M Ed), including bilingual/bicultural education (M Ed, MAT), early childhood education (M Ed, MAT), elementary education, foreign language, mathematics education (M Ed, MAT), science education (M Ed, MAT), social studies education (M Ed, MAT), special education (M Ed, MAT). *Program availability:* Part-time, evening/weekend. *Faculty:* 20. *Students:* 121 full-time (94 women), 251 part-time (209 women); includes 116 minority (83 Black or African American, non-Hispanic/Latino; 3 American Indian or Alaska Native, non-Hispanic/Latino; 3 Asian, non-Hispanic/Latino; 14 Hispanic/Latino; 13 Two or more races, non-Hispanic/Latino), 11 international. Average age 37. 171 applicants, 23% accepted, 32 enrolled. In 2018, 112 master's, 8 doctorates, 11 other advanced degrees awarded. *Degree requirements:* For master's, thesis (for some programs), essay or project (for some M Ed programs), professional field experience (for MAT programs); for doctorate, comprehensive exam, thesis/dissertation. *Entrance requirements:* For master's, undergraduate degree, verification of participation in group work with children, Michigan State Police criminal background check, negative tb test, personal statement (for MAT programs); for all other master's programs: undergraduate degree, personal statement; for doctorate, minimum undergraduate GPA of 3.0, graduate 3.5; interview; curriculum vitae; references; writing sample; letter of application; master's degree (for most programs); for other advanced degree, education specialist certificate: undergraduate with GPA of 2.5 or better and master's degree with GPA of 2.75 or better; personal statement. Additional exam requirements/recommendations for international students: Required—TOEFL (minimum score 550 paper-based; 79 iBT); Recommended—IELTS (minimum score 6.5), TWE (minimum score 5.5), TSE (minimum score 58). *Application deadline:* Applications are processed on a rolling basis. Application fee: $50. Electronic applications accepted. *Financial support:* In 2018–19, 85 students received support, including 3 fellowships (averaging $14,275 per year); research assistantships with tuition reimbursements available, Federal Work-Study, scholarships/grants, and unspecified assistantships also available. Support available to part-time students. Financial award applicants required to submit FAFSA. *Faculty research:* Improving students' skill achievement in mathematics, improving elementary children's understanding of informational text, teachers' use of their pedagogical and mathematical knowledge in the interactive work of teaching, the intersection of identity construction in teaching and learning, identifying effective methods of literacy instruction and assessments for bilingual students in elementary language arts classrooms. *Unit head:* Dr. Roland Coloma, Assistant Dean for Teacher Education, 313-577-0902, E-mail: rscoloma@wayne.edu. *Application contact:* Dr. Mary L. Waker, Graduate Admissions Officer, 313-577-1601, Fax: 313-577-7904, E-mail: m.waker@wayne.edu.
Website: http://coe.wayne.edu/ted/index.php

Wesleyan University, Graduate Studies, Department of Mathematics and Computer Science, Middletown, CT 06459. Offers computer science (MA); mathematics (MA, PhD). *Faculty:* 22 full-time (7 women). *Students:* 19 full-time (8 women); includes 3 minority (1 Black or African American, non-Hispanic/Latino; 1 Asian, non-Hispanic/Latino; 1 Hispanic/Latino), 4 international. Average age 25. 66 applicants, 11% accepted, 6 enrolled. In 2018, 4 master's, 2 doctorates awarded. Terminal master's awarded for partial completion of doctoral program. *Degree requirements:* For master's, one foreign language, thesis; for doctorate, 2 foreign languages, comprehensive exam (for some programs), thesis/dissertation. *Entrance requirements:* For master's, GRE General Test, GRE Subject Test; for doctorate, GRE Subject Test. Additional exam requirements/recommendations for international students: Recommended—TOEFL. *Application deadline:* For fall admission, 2/15 for domestic and international students. Applications are processed on a rolling basis. Application fee: $0. Electronic applications accepted. *Financial support:* In 2018–19, 17 teaching assistantships with full tuition reimbursements (averaging $23,000 per year) were awarded; tuition waivers (full) also available. Financial award application deadline: 4/15. *Faculty research:* Topology, analysis, algebra, geometry, number theory. *Unit head:* Dr. Karen Collins, Chair, 860-685-2196, E-mail: kcollins@wesleyan.edu. *Application contact:* Caryn Canalia, Administrative Assistant, 860-685-2182, Fax: 860-685-2571, E-mail: ccanalia@wesleyan.edu.
Website: http://www.wesleyan.edu/mathcs/index.html

West Chester University of Pennsylvania, College of the Sciences and Mathematics, Department of Mathematics, West Chester, PA 19383. Offers applied and computational mathematics (MS); applied statistics (MS, Certificate); mathematics (MA, Teaching Certificate); mathematics education (MA). *Program availability:* Part-time, evening/weekend. *Degree requirements:* For master's, comprehensive exam or thesis (for MA). *Entrance requirements:* For master's, GMAT or GRE General Test (for MA in mathematics, may be waived under certain circumstances), interview (for MA in mathematics); for other advanced degree, GMAT or GRE General Test (for Certificate in applied statistics). Additional exam requirements/recommendations for international

students: Required—TOEFL or IELTS. Electronic applications accepted. *Faculty research:* Teachers teaching with technology in service training program, biostatistics, hierarchical linear models, clustered binary outcome data, mathematics biology, stochastic analysis.

Western Connecticut State University, Division of Graduate Studies, Maricostas School of Arts and Sciences, Department of Mathematics, Danbury, CT 06810-6885. Offers MA. *Program availability:* Part-time. *Students:* 7 part-time (4 women). Average age 35. *Degree requirements:* For master's, comprehensive exam, thesis, completion of program in 6 years. *Entrance requirements:* For master's, minimum GPA of 2.5. Additional exam requirements/recommendations for international students: Recommended—TOEFL (minimum score 550 paper-based; 79 iBT), IELTS (minimum score 6). *Application deadline:* For fall admission, 8/5 priority date for domestic students; for spring admission, 1/5 priority date for domestic students. Applications are processed on a rolling basis. Application fee: $50. *Financial support:* Application deadline: 5/1; applicants required to submit FAFSA. *Faculty research:* Eulerian mathematical principles. *Unit head:* Dr. Charles Rocca, Graduate Coordinator, 203-837-9360, Fax: 203-837-8527, E-mail: roccac@wcsu.edu. *Application contact:* Dr. Chris Shankle, Associate Director of Graduate Studies, 203-837-9005, Fax: 203-837-8326, E-mail: shanklec@wcsu.edu.
Website: http://www.wcsu.edu/math/

Western Illinois University, School of Graduate Studies, College of Arts and Sciences, Department of Mathematics, Macomb, IL 61455-1390. Offers mathematics (MS). *Program availability:* Part-time. *Students:* 11 full-time (2 women), 4 part-time (1 woman); includes 2 minority (both Asian, non-Hispanic/Latino), 9 international. Average age 30. 12 applicants, 50% accepted, 4 enrolled. In 2018, 8 master's awarded. *Entrance requirements:* Additional exam requirements/recommendations for international students: Required—TOEFL (minimum score 500 paper-based; 61 iBT). *Application deadline:* Applications are processed on a rolling basis. Application fee: $30. Electronic applications accepted. *Financial support:* In 2018–19, 4 students received support, including 2 teaching assistantships with full tuition reimbursements available (averaging $8,688 per year). Financial award applicants required to submit FAFSA. *Unit head:* Dr. Victoria Baramidze, Chairperson, 309-298-1054. *Application contact:* Dr. Mark Mossman, Associate Provost and Director of Graduate Studies, 309-298-1806, Fax: 309-298-2345, E-mail: grad-office@wiu.edu.
Website: http://wiu.edu/mathematics

Western Kentucky University, Graduate School, Ogden College of Science and Engineering, Department of Mathematics, Bowling Green, KY 42101. Offers MA, MS. *Degree requirements:* For master's, comprehensive exam, thesis optional, written exam. *Entrance requirements:* For master's, GRE General Test, minimum GPA of 2.75. Additional exam requirements/recommendations for international students: Required—TOEFL (minimum score 555 paper-based; 79 iBT). *Faculty research:* Differential equations numerical analysis, probability statistics, algebra, typology, knot theory.

Western Michigan University, Graduate College, College of Arts and Sciences, Department of Mathematics, Kalamazoo, MI 49008. Offers applied and computational mathematics (MS); mathematics education (MA, PhD), including collegiate mathematics education (PhD). *Degree requirements:* For doctorate, one foreign language, thesis/dissertation.

Western Washington University, Graduate School, College of Sciences and Technology, Department of Mathematics, Bellingham, WA 98225-5996. Offers MS. *Program availability:* Part-time. *Degree requirements:* For master's, thesis (for some programs), project, qualifying examination. *Entrance requirements:* For master's, GRE General Test, minimum GPA of 3.0 in last 60 semester hours or last 90 quarter hours. Additional exam requirements/recommendations for international students: Required—TOEFL (minimum score 567 paper-based). Electronic applications accepted. *Faculty research:* Numerical analysis, combinatorics, harmonic analysis, inverse problems, reliability testing.

West Texas A&M University, School of Engineering, Computer Science and Mathematics, Program in Mathematics, Canyon, TX 79015. Offers MS. *Program availability:* Part-time. *Degree requirements:* For master's, comprehensive exam, thesis optional. *Entrance requirements:* For master's, GRE General Test. Additional exam requirements/recommendations for international students: Required—TOEFL (minimum score 550 paper-based). Electronic applications accepted.

West Virginia University, Eberly College of Arts and Sciences, Morgantown, WV 26506. Offers biology (MS, PhD); chemistry (MS, PhD); communication studies (MA, PhD); computational statistics (PhD); creative writing (MFA); English (MA, PhD); forensic and investigative science (MS); forensic science (PhD); geography (MA); geology (MA, PhD); history (MA, PhD); legal studies (MLS); mathematics (MS); physics (MS, PhD); political science (MA, PhD); professional writing and editing (MA); psychology (MA); public administration (MPA); social work (MSW); sociology (MA, PhD); statistics (MS). *Program availability:* Part-time, evening/weekend, online learning. *Students:* 803 full-time (434 women), 237 part-time (138 women); includes 99 minority (31 Black or African American, non-Hispanic/Latino; 1 American Indian or Alaska Native, non-Hispanic/Latino; 16 Asian, non-Hispanic/Latino; 25 Hispanic/Latino; 26 Two or more races, non-Hispanic/Latino), 208 international. In 2018, 285 master's, 63 doctorates awarded. Terminal master's awarded for partial completion of doctoral program. *Degree requirements:* For master's, thesis (for some programs); for doctorate, comprehensive exam, thesis/dissertation. *Entrance requirements:* For master's and doctorate, GRE. Additional exam requirements/recommendations for international students: Required—TOEFL (minimum score 600 paper-based); Recommended—TWE. *Application deadline:* For spring admission, 2/15 priority date for domestic and international students. Applications are processed on a rolling basis. Application fee: $45. Electronic applications accepted. *Financial support:* Fellowships with full tuition reimbursements, research assistantships with full tuition reimbursements, teaching assistantships with full tuition reimbursements, career-related internships or fieldwork, Federal Work-Study, institutionally sponsored loans, scholarships/grants, health care benefits, tuition waivers (full and partial), unspecified assistantships, and administrative assistantships available. Financial award application deadline: 2/1; financial award applicants required to submit FAFSA. *Faculty research:* Humanities, social sciences, life science, physical sciences, mathematics. *Unit head:* Dr. Gregory Dunaway, Dean, 304-293-4611, Fax: 304-293-6858, E-mail: gregory.dunaway@mail.wvu.edu. *Application contact:* Dr. Jessica Queener, Director of Graduate Studies, 304-293-7476 Ext. 5205, Fax: 304-293-6858, E-mail: Jessica.queener@mail.wvu.edu.
Website: http://www.as.wvu.edu/

Wichita State University, Graduate School, Fairmount College of Liberal Arts and Sciences, Department of Mathematics, Statistics and Physics, Wichita, KS 67260. Offers applied mathematics (PhD); mathematics (MS); physics (MS). *Program availability:* Part-time. *Unit head:* Dr. Ziqi Sun, Interim Chair, 316-978-3160, Fax: 316-978-3748, E-mail: ziqi.sun@wichita.edu. *Application contact:* Jordan Oleson, Admissions Coordinator, 316-978-3095, Fax: 316-978-3253, E-mail: jordan.oleson@wichita.edu.
Website: http://www.wichita.edu/math

Peterson's Graduate Programs in the Physical Sciences, Mathematics, Agricultural Sciences, the Environment & Natural Resources 2020

www.petersons.com **235**

Wilfrid Laurier University, Faculty of Graduate and Postdoctoral Studies, Faculty of Science, Department of Mathematics, Waterloo, ON N2L 3C5, Canada. Offers mathematics for science and finance (M Sc). *Program availability:* Part-time. *Degree requirements:* For master's, thesis optional. *Entrance requirements:* For master's, 4-year honors degree in mathematics, minimum B+ average. Additional exam requirements/recommendations for international students: Required—TOEFL (minimum score 89 iBT). Electronic applications accepted. *Faculty research:* Modeling, analysis, resolution, and generalization of financial and scientific problems.

Wilkes University, College of Graduate and Professional Studies, College of Science and Engineering, Department of Mathematics and Computer Science, Wilkes-Barre, PA 18766-0002. Offers mathematics (MS). *Program availability:* Part-time. *Students:* 2 full-time (0 women), 1 part-time (0 women); includes 1 minority (Asian, non-Hispanic/Latino). Average age 33. In 2018, 1 master's awarded. *Entrance requirements:* For master's, GRE General Test. Additional exam requirements/recommendations for international students: Required—TOEFL (minimum score 550 paper-based; 79 iBT). *Application deadline:* Applications are processed on a rolling basis. Application fee: $45 ($65 for international students). Electronic applications accepted. Tuition and fees vary according to course load, degree level and program. *Financial support:* Unspecified assistantships available. Financial award application deadline: 3/1; financial award applicants required to submit FAFSA. *Unit head:* Dr. Prahlad Murthy, Interim Dean, 570-408-4600, Fax: 570-408-7883, E-mail: prahlad.murthy@wilkes.edu. *Application contact:* Kristin Donati, Associate Director of Graduate Admissions, 570-408-3338, Fax: 570-408-7846, E-mail: kristin.donati@wilkes.edu.
Website: http://www.wilkes.edu/academics/colleges/science-and-engineering/mathematics-computer-science/index.aspx

Worcester Polytechnic Institute, Graduate Admissions, Department of Mathematical Sciences, Worcester, MA 01609-2280. Offers applied mathematics (MS); applied statistics (MS); financial mathematics (MS); industrial mathematics (MS); mathematical sciences (PhD, Graduate Certificate); mathematics for educators (MME). *Program availability:* Part-time, evening/weekend. *Students:* 56 full-time (26 women), 34 part-time (13 women); includes 3 minority (1 Black or African American, non-Hispanic/Latino; 1 Asian, non-Hispanic/Latino; 1 Hispanic/Latino), 51 international. Average age 27. 284 applicants, 63% accepted, 33 enrolled. In 2018, 35 master's, 6 doctorates awarded. Terminal master's awarded for partial completion of doctoral program. *Degree requirements:* For master's, thesis (for some programs); for doctorate, comprehensive exam, thesis/dissertation. *Entrance requirements:* For master's, GRE Subject Test in math (for teaching assistantship; strongly recommended for all others), 3 letters of recommendation; for doctorate, GRE General Test, GRE Subject Test (math), 3 letters of recommendation. Additional exam requirements/recommendations for international students: Required—TOEFL (minimum score 563 paper-based; 84 iBT), IELTS (minimum score 7). *Application deadline:* For fall admission, 1/1 priority date for domestic students, 1/1 for international students; for spring admission, 10/1 priority date for domestic students, 10/1 for international students. Applications are processed on a rolling basis. Application fee: $70. Electronic applications accepted. *Financial support:* Fellowships, research assistantships, teaching assistantships, career-related internships or fieldwork, institutionally sponsored loans, scholarships/grants, and unspecified assistantships available. Financial award application deadline: 1/1. *Unit head:* Dr. Luca Capogna, Department Head, 508-831-5241, Fax: 508-831-5824, E-mail: lcapogna@wpi.edu. *Application contact:* Dr. Sarah Olsen, Graduate Coordinator, 508-831-5241, Fax: 508-831-5824, E-mail: sdolsen@wpi.edu.
Website: https://www.wpi.edu/academics/departments/mathematical-sciences

Wright State University, Graduate School, College of Science and Mathematics, Department of Mathematics and Statistics, Program in Mathematics, Dayton, OH 45435. Offers MS. *Degree requirements:* For master's, comprehensive exam. *Entrance requirements:* For master's, previous course work in mathematics beyond calculus. Additional exam requirements/recommendations for international students: Required—TOEFL. *Faculty research:* Analysis, algebraic combinatorics, graph theory, operator theory.

Yale University, Graduate School of Arts and Sciences, Department of Mathematics, New Haven, CT 06520. Offers M Phil, MS, PhD. *Degree requirements:* For doctorate, 2 foreign languages, thesis/dissertation. *Entrance requirements:* For doctorate, GRE General Test, GRE Subject Test.

Yeshiva University, The Katz School, Program in Mathematics, New York, NY 10033-3201. Offers MA.

York University, Faculty of Graduate Studies, Faculty of Science, Program in Mathematics and Statistics, Toronto, ON M3J 1P3, Canada. Offers industrial and applied mathematics (M Sc); mathematics and statistics (MA, PhD). *Program availability:* Part-time. *Degree requirements:* For master's, thesis optional; for doctorate, one foreign language, comprehensive exam, thesis/dissertation. Electronic applications accepted.

Youngstown State University, College of Graduate Studies, College of Science, Technology, Engineering and Mathematics, Department of Mathematics and Statistics, Youngstown, OH 44555-0001. Offers actuarial science (MS); applied mathematics (MS); computer science (MS); mathematics (MS); secondary/community college mathematics (MS); statistics (MS). *Program availability:* Part-time. *Degree requirements:* For master's, comprehensive exam, thesis optional. *Entrance requirements:* For master's, minimum GPA of 2.7 in computer science and mathematics. Additional exam requirements/recommendations for international students: Required—TOEFL. *Faculty research:* Regression analysis, numerical analysis, statistics, Markov chain, topology and fuzzy sets.

Statistics

Acadia University, Faculty of Pure and Applied Science, Department of Mathematics and Statistics, Wolfville, NS B4P 2R6, Canada. Offers applied mathematics and statistics (M Sc). *Entrance requirements:* For master's, honors degree in mathematics, statistics or equivalent. Additional exam requirements/recommendations for international students: Required—TOEFL (minimum score 580 paper-based; 93 iBT), IELTS (minimum score 6.5). *Faculty research:* Geophysical fluid dynamics, machine scheduling problems, control theory, stochastic optimization, survival analysis.

American University, College of Arts and Sciences, Department of Mathematics and Statistics, Washington, DC 22016-8050. Offers applied statistics (Certificate); biostatistics (MS); data science (Certificate); mathematics (MA); professional science: quantitative analysis (MS); statistics (MS). *Program availability:* Part-time, evening/weekend. *Faculty:* 36 full-time (13 women), 8 part-time/adjunct (1 woman). *Students:* 19 full-time (4 women), 21 part-time (9 women); includes 14 minority (7 Black or African American, non-Hispanic/Latino; 2 Asian, non-Hispanic/Latino; 4 Hispanic/Latino; 1 Two or more races, non-Hispanic/Latino), 10 international. Average age 29. 64 applicants, 92% accepted, 19 enrolled. In 2018, 10 master's, 9 other advanced degrees awarded. *Degree requirements:* For master's, comprehensive exam, thesis or alternative. *Entrance requirements:* For master's, GRE; please see website: https://www.american.edu/cas/mathstat/, statement of purpose, transcripts, 2 letters of recommendation, resume; for Certificate, bachelor's degree, statement of purpose, transcripts, resume. Additional exam requirements/recommendations for international students: Required—TOEFL (minimum score 600 paper-based; 100 iBT). Application fee: $55. *Expenses:* Contact institution. *Financial support:* Scholarships/grants and unspecified assistantships available. Financial award applicants required to submit FAFSA. *Unit head:* Dr. Stephen Casey, Department Chair, 202-885-3120, E-mail: mathstat@american.edu. *Application contact:* Jonathan Harper, Assistant Director, Graduate Recruitment, 202-855-3620, E-mail: casgrad@american.edu.
Website: http://www.american.edu/cas/mathstat/

Arizona State University at the Tempe campus, College of Liberal Arts and Sciences, School of Mathematical and Statistical Sciences, Tempe, AZ 85287-1804. Offers applied mathematics (PhD); mathematics (MA, PhD); mathematics education (PhD); statistics (MS, PhD, Graduate Certificate). *Program availability:* Part-time. Terminal master's awarded for partial completion of doctoral program. *Degree requirements:* For master's, thesis or alternative, interactive Program of Study (iPOS) submitted before completing 50 percent of required credit hours; for doctorate, comprehensive exam, thesis/dissertation, interactive Program of Study (iPOS) submitted before completing 50 percent of required credit hours. *Entrance requirements:* For master's and doctorate, GRE General Test, minimum GPA of 3.0 or equivalent in last 2 years of work leading to bachelor's degree. Additional exam requirements/recommendations for international students: Required—TOEFL, IELTS, or PTE. Electronic applications accepted. *Expenses:* Contact institution.

Auburn University, Graduate School, College of Sciences and Mathematics, Department of Mathematics and Statistics, Auburn University, AL 36849. Offers applied mathematics (MAM, MS); mathematics (MS, PhD); probability and statistics (M Prob S); statistics (MS). *Degree requirements:* For doctorate, thesis/dissertation. *Entrance requirements:* For master's, GRE General Test, undergraduate mathematics background; for doctorate, GRE General Test, GRE Subject Test. Electronic applications accepted. *Expenses:* Tuition, state resident: full-time $11,282; part-time $535 per credit hour. Tuition, nonresident: full-time $30,542; part-time $1605 per credit hour. *Required fees:* $826 per semester. Tuition and fees vary according to degree level and program. *Faculty research:* Pure and applied mathematics.

Ball State University, Graduate School, College of Sciences and Humanities, Department of Mathematical Sciences, Program in Statistics, Muncie, IN 47306. Offers statistics (MA, MS). *Program availability:* Part-time. *Degree requirements:* For master's, thesis (for some programs). *Entrance requirements:* For master's, minimum baccalaureate GPA of 2.75 or 3.0 in latter half of baccalaureate. Additional exam requirements/recommendations for international students: Required—TOEFL (minimum score 550 paper-based; 79 iBT), IELTS (minimum score 6.5). Electronic applications accepted. *Faculty research:* Robust methods.

Baruch College of the City University of New York, Zicklin School of Business, Department of Statistics and Computer Information Systems, Program in Statistics, New York, NY 10010-5585. Offers MBA, MS. *Program availability:* Part-time, evening/weekend. *Entrance requirements:* For master's, GMAT, 2 letters of recommendation, resume, 2 years of work experience. Additional exam requirements/recommendations for international students: Required—TOEFL (minimum score 590 paper-based), TWE.

Baylor University, Graduate School, College of Arts and Sciences, Department of Statistical Science, Waco, TX 76798. Offers MA, PhD. *Faculty:* 9 full-time (2 women). *Students:* 27 full-time (8 women), 3 part-time (all women); includes 7 minority (1 Black or African American, non-Hispanic/Latino; 3 Asian, non-Hispanic/Latino; 1 Hispanic/Latino; 2 Two or more races, non-Hispanic/Latino), 5 international. Average age 24. 74 applicants, 14% accepted, 8 enrolled. In 2018, 4 master's, 2 doctorates awarded. *Degree requirements:* For master's, comprehensive exam; for doctorate, comprehensive exam, thesis/dissertation. *Entrance requirements:* For master's and doctorate, GRE General Test, foundation in calculus and statistics, including multivariable calculus, linear algebra, and at least one statistics course. Additional exam requirements/recommendations for international students: Required—TOEFL. *Application deadline:* For fall admission, 1/15 for domestic and international students; for summer admission, 1/15 for domestic and international students. Applications are processed on a rolling basis. Application fee: $50. Electronic applications accepted. *Financial support:* In 2018–19, 22 students received support, including 11 fellowships with full tuition reimbursements available (averaging $21,000 per year), 5 research assistantships with full tuition reimbursements available (averaging $24,000 per year), 6 teaching assistantships with full tuition reimbursements available (averaging $24,000 per year). Financial award application deadline: 1/15. *Faculty research:* Bayesian methods, biostatistics, time series, spatial statistics, biopharmaceutical statistics. *Unit head:* Dr. James Stamey, Chair, 254-710-7405, Fax: 254-710-4477, E-mail: james_stamey@baylor.edu. *Application contact:* Dr. Jane Harvill, Graduate Program Director, 254-710-1517, E-mail: jane_harvill@baylor.edu.
Website: http://www.baylor.edu/statistics/

Binghamton University, State University of New York, Graduate School, Harpur College of Arts and Sciences, Department of Mathematical Sciences, Binghamton, NY 13902-6000. Offers mathematical sciences (MA, PhD); statistics (MA). *Program availability:* Part-time. Terminal master's awarded for partial completion of doctoral program. *Degree requirements:* For master's, comprehensive exam (for some programs), thesis or alternative; for doctorate, 2 foreign languages, thesis/dissertation. *Entrance requirements:* For master's and doctorate, GRE General Test. Additional exam requirements/recommendations for international students: Required—TOEFL (minimum score 550 paper-based; 80 iBT). Electronic applications accepted.

Bowling Green State University, Graduate College, College of Arts and Sciences, Department of Mathematics and Statistics, Bowling Green, OH 43403. Offers mathematics (MA, MAT, PhD); statistics (PhD). *Program availability:* Part-time. *Degree requirements:* For master's, thesis or alternative; for doctorate, comprehensive exam, thesis/dissertation. *Entrance requirements:* For master's and doctorate, GRE General Test. Additional exam requirements/recommendations for international students: Required—TOEFL. Electronic applications accepted. *Faculty research:* Statistics and probability, algebra, analysis.

Brigham Young University, Graduate Studies, College of Physical and Mathematical Sciences, Department of Statistics, Provo, UT 84602-1001. Offers applied statistics (MS). *Faculty:* 17 full-time (3 women). *Students:* 24 full-time (9 women); includes 2 minority (both Asian, non-Hispanic/Latino). Average age 25. 17 applicants, 18% accepted, 3 enrolled. In 2018, 17 master's awarded. *Degree requirements:* For master's, comprehensive exam, thesis (for some programs). *Entrance requirements:* For master's, GRE General Test, bachelor's degree from an accredited US university or equivalent, minimum 3.3 undergraduate GPA, 2 methods courses beyond introductory statistics, 2 courses in calculus-based statistical theory, differential calculus, integral calculus, multivariate calculus, a course in linear algebra. Additional exam requirements/recommendations for international students: Required—TOEFL (minimum score 580 paper-based; 85 iBT). *Application deadline:* For fall admission, 2/1 for domestic and international students. Application fee: $50. Electronic applications accepted. *Expenses:* Contact institution. *Financial support:* In 2018–19, 15 students received support, including 11 research assistantships (averaging $11,500 per year), 10 teaching assistantships (averaging $11,500 per year); scholarships/grants and tuition waivers also available. Financial award application deadline: 3/1. *Faculty research:* Statistical genetics, reliability and pollution monitoring, Bayesian methods. *Total annual research expenditures:* $750,637. *Unit head:* Dr. Scott D Grimshaw, Chair, 801-422-6251, Fax: 801-422-0635, E-mail: sdg@stat.byu.edu. *Application contact:* Dr. David B Dahl, Graduate Coordinator, 801-422-9222, Fax: 801-422-0635, E-mail: dahl@stat.byu.edu.
Website: http://statistics.byu.edu/

Brock University, Faculty of Graduate Studies, Faculty of Mathematics and Science, Program in Mathematics and Statistics, St. Catharines, ON L2S 3A1, Canada. Offers M Sc. *Program availability:* Part-time. *Degree requirements:* For master's, thesis or project. *Entrance requirements:* For master's, honors degree. Additional exam requirements/recommendations for international students: Required—TOEFL (minimum score 550 paper-based; 80 iBT), IELTS (minimum score 6.5), TWE (minimum score 4). Electronic applications accepted.

California State University, East Bay, Office of Graduate Studies, College of Science, Department of Statistics and Biostatistics, Statistics Program, Hayward, CA 94542-3000. Offers actuarial science (MS); applied statistics (MS); computational statistics (MS); mathematical statistics (MS). *Program availability:* Part-time, evening/weekend. *Degree requirements:* For master's, comprehensive exam. *Entrance requirements:* For master's, letters of recommendation, minimum GPA of 3.0, math through lower-division calculus. Additional exam requirements/recommendations for international students: Required—TOEFL (minimum score 550 paper-based). Electronic applications accepted.

Carnegie Mellon University, Dietrich College of Humanities and Social Sciences, Department of Statistics, Pittsburgh, PA 15213-3891. Offers machine learning and statistics (PhD); mathematical finance (PhD); statistics (MS, PhD), including applied statistics (PhD), computational statistics (PhD), theoretical statistics (PhD); statistics and public policy (PhD). Terminal master's awarded for partial completion of doctoral program. *Degree requirements:* For doctorate, comprehensive exam, thesis/dissertation. *Entrance requirements:* For master's and doctorate, GRE General Test. Additional exam requirements/recommendations for international students: Required—TOEFL. *Faculty research:* Stochastic processes, Bayesian statistics, statistical computing, decision theory, psychiatric statistics.

Central Connecticut State University, School of Graduate Studies, School of Engineering, Science and Technology, Department of Mathematical Sciences, New Britain, CT 06050-4010. Offers data mining (MS, Certificate); mathematics (MA, MS), including actuarial science (MA), computer science (MA), statistics (MA); mathematics education leadership (Sixth Year Certificate); mathematics for secondary education (Certificate). *Program availability:* Part-time, evening/weekend, 100% online. *Faculty:* 13 full-time (4 women). *Students:* 14 full-time (9 women), 70 part-time (39 women); includes 21 minority (8 Black or African American, non-Hispanic/Latino; 9 Asian, non-Hispanic/Latino; 3 Hispanic/Latino; 1 Two or more races, non-Hispanic/Latino), 2 international. Average age 33. 57 applicants, 70% accepted, 20 enrolled. In 2018, 20 master's, 3 other advanced degrees awarded. *Degree requirements:* For master's, comprehensive exam, thesis or alternative, special project; for other advanced degree, qualifying exam. *Entrance requirements:* For master's, minimum undergraduate GPA of 2.7; for other advanced degree, minimum undergraduate GPA of 3.0, essay, letters of recommendation. Additional exam requirements/recommendations for international students: Required—TOEFL (minimum score 550 paper-based; 79 iBT); Recommended—IELTS (minimum score 6.5). *Application deadline:* For fall admission, 6/1 for domestic students, 5/1 for international students; for spring admission, 11/1 for domestic and international students. Applications are processed on a rolling basis. Application fee: $50. Electronic applications accepted. *Expenses: Tuition, area resident:* Full-time $7027; part-time $388 per credit. Tuition, state resident: full-time $9750; part-time $388 per credit. Tuition, nonresident: full-time $18,102; part-time $388 per credit. *International tuition:* $18,102 full-time. *Required fees:* $266 per semester. *Financial support:* In 2018–19, 22 students received support. Career-related internships or fieldwork, Federal Work-Study, scholarships/grants, and unspecified assistantships available. Support available to part-time students. Financial award application deadline: 3/1; financial award applicants required to submit FAFSA. *Faculty research:* Statistics, actuarial mathematics, computer systems and engineering, computer programming techniques, operations research. *Unit head:* Dr. Robin Kalder, Chair, 860-832-2835, E-mail: kalderr@ccsu.edu. *Application contact:* Patricia Gardner, Associate Director of Graduate Studies, 860-832-2350, Fax: 860-832-2362.
Website: http://www.ccsu.edu/mathematics/

Claremont Graduate University, Graduate Programs, Institute of Mathematical Sciences, Claremont, CA 91711-6160. Offers computational and systems biology (PhD); computational mathematics and numerical analysis (MA, MS); computational science (PhD); engineering and industrial applied mathematics (PhD); mathematics (PhD); operations research and statistics (MA, MS); physical applied mathematics (MA, MS); pure mathematics (MA, MS); scientific computing (MA, MS); systems and control theory (MA, MS). PhD programs offered jointly with San Diego State University and California State University, Long Beach. *Program availability:* Part-time. Terminal master's awarded for partial completion of doctoral program. *Entrance requirements:* For master's and doctorate, GRE General Test. Additional exam requirements/recommendations for international students: Required—TOEFL (minimum score 75 iBT). Electronic applications accepted.

Clemson University, Graduate School, College of Agriculture, Forestry and Life Sciences, Department of Agricultural Sciences, Clemson, SC 29634. Offers agricultural education (M Ag Ed); applied economics (PhD); applied economics and statistics (MS). *Program availability:* Part-time. *Faculty:* 18 full-time (3 women). *Students:* 20 full-time (14 women), 12 part-time (6 women); includes 2 minority (both Black or African American, non-Hispanic/Latino). Average age 29. 39 applicants, 64% accepted, 15 enrolled. In 2018, 30 master's awarded. *Degree requirements:* For master's, thesis optional; for doctorate, comprehensive exam, thesis/dissertation. *Entrance requirements:* For master's and doctorate, GRE General Test, unofficial transcripts, letters of recommendation. Additional exam requirements/recommendations for international students: Required—TOEFL (minimum score 80 paper-based; 80 iBT), IELTS (minimum score 6.5), PTE (minimum score 5). *Application deadline:* For fall admission, 6/1 for domestic students, 7/1 for international students; for spring admission, 10/1 for domestic students, 11/1 for international students. Applications are processed on a rolling basis. Application fee: $80 ($90 for international students). Electronic applications accepted. *Expenses:* $5898 per semester full-time resident, $11623 per semester full-time non-resident, $724 per credit hour part-time resident, $1451 per credit hour part-time non-resident, online $955 per credit hour, $4938 doctoral programs resident, $10405 doctoral programs non-resident, $1144 full-time graduate assistant, other fees may apply per session. *Financial support:* In 2018–19, 17 students received support, including 2 fellowships with full and partial tuition reimbursements available (averaging $8,750 per year), 2 research assistantships with full and partial tuition reimbursements available (averaging $12,000 per year), 5 teaching assistantships with full and partial tuition reimbursements available (averaging $13,188 per year); career-related internships or fieldwork and unspecified assistantships also available. Financial award application deadline: 6/1. *Faculty research:* Agricultural education, agricultural economics, agricultural statistics, agribusiness. *Total annual research expenditures:* $427,800. *Unit head:* Dr. Charles Privette, Department Chair, 864-656-6247, E-mail: privett@clemson.edu. *Application contact:* Dr. Charles Privette, Department Chair, 864-656-6247, E-mail: privett@clemson.edu.
Website: http://www.clemson.edu/cafls/departments/agricultural-sciences/index.html

Colorado State University, College of Natural Sciences, Department of Statistics, Fort Collins, CO 80523-1877. Offers MAS, MS, PhD. *Program availability:* Part-time, evening/weekend, 100% online. Terminal master's awarded for partial completion of doctoral program. *Degree requirements:* For master's, capstone; for doctorate, comprehensive exam, thesis/dissertation. *Entrance requirements:* For master's, GRE General Test; entrance exam preferred (for MAS), at least three semesters of calculus, course in linear algebra, at least one undergraduate statistics course; for doctorate, GRE General Test, transcripts; letters of recommendation; resume; statement of purpose. Additional exam requirements/recommendations for international students: Required—TOEFL (minimum score 550 paper-based; 80 iBT). Electronic applications accepted. *Expenses:* Contact institution. *Faculty research:* Analytic inference for complex surveys; statistical consulting; model selection and model uncertainty; nonparametric function and density estimation; developing statistical methods for environmental health research.

Columbia University, Graduate School of Arts and Sciences, New York, NY 10027. Offers African-American studies (MA); American studies (MA); anthropology (MA, PhD); art history and archaeology (MA, PhD); astronomy (PhD); biological sciences (PhD); biotechnology (MA); chemical physics (PhD); chemistry (PhD); classical studies (MA, PhD); classics (MA, PhD); climate and society (MA); conservation biology (MA); earth and environmental sciences (PhD); East Asia: regional studies (MA); East Asian languages and cultures (MA, PhD); ecology, evolution and environmental biology (MA), including conservation biology; ecology, evolution, and environmental biology (PhD), including ecology and evolutionary biology, evolutionary primatology; economics (MA, PhD); English and comparative literature (MA, PhD); French and Romance philology (MA, PhD); Germanic languages (MA, PhD); global French studies (MA); global thought (MA); Hispanic cultural studies (MA); history (PhD); history and literature (MA); human rights studies (MA); Islamic studies (MA); Italian (MA, PhD); Japanese pedagogy (MA); Jewish studies (MA); Latin America and the Caribbean: regional studies (MA); Latin American and Iberian cultures (PhD); mathematics (MA, PhD), including finance (MA); medieval and Renaissance studies (MA); Middle Eastern, South Asian, and African studies (MA, PhD); modern art: critical and curatorial studies (MA); modern European studies (MA); museum anthropology (MA); music (DMA, PhD); oral history (MA); philosophical foundations of physics (MA); philosophy (MA, PhD); physics (PhD); political science (MA, PhD); psychology (PhD); quantitative methods in the social sciences (MA); religion (MA, PhD); Russia, Eurasia and East Europe: regional studies (MA); Russian translation (MA); Slavic cultures (MA); Slavic languages (MA, PhD); sociology (MA, PhD); South Asian studies (MA); statistics (MA, PhD); theatre (PhD). Dual-degree programs require admission to both Graduate School of Arts and Sciences and another Columbia school. *Program availability:* Part-time. Terminal master's awarded for partial completion of doctoral program. *Degree requirements:* For master's, variable foreign language requirement, comprehensive exam (for some programs), thesis (for some programs); for doctorate, variable foreign language requirement, comprehensive exam (for some programs), thesis/dissertation. *Entrance requirements:* For master's and doctorate, GRE General Test, GRE Subject Test (for some programs). Additional exam requirements/recommendations for international students: Required—TOEFL, IELTS. Electronic applications accepted.

Concordia University, School of Graduate Studies, Faculty of Arts and Science, Department of Mathematics and Statistics, Montréal, QC H3G 1M8, Canada. Offers mathematics (PhD); mathematics and statistics (M Sc, MA); teaching of mathematics (MTM). *Degree requirements:* For master's, thesis optional; for doctorate, comprehensive exam, thesis/dissertation. *Entrance requirements:* For master's, honors degree in mathematics or equivalent. *Faculty research:* Number theory, computational algebra, mathematical physics, differential geometry, dynamical systems and statistics.

Cornell University, Graduate School, Graduate Fields of Engineering, Field of Operations Research and Information Engineering, Ithaca, NY 14853. Offers applied probability and statistics (PhD); manufacturing systems engineering (PhD); mathematical programming (PhD); operations research and industrial engineering (M Eng). *Degree requirements:* For doctorate, comprehensive exam, thesis/dissertation. *Entrance requirements:* For master's and doctorate, GRE General Test, 3 letters of recommendation. Additional exam requirements/recommendations for international students: Required—TOEFL (minimum score 600 paper-based; 100 iBT). Electronic applications accepted. *Faculty research:* Mathematical programming and combinatorial optimization, statistics, stochastic processes, mathematical finance, simulation, manufacturing, e-commerce.

Cornell University, Graduate School, Graduate Fields of Engineering, Field of Statistics, Ithaca, NY 14853. Offers applied statistics (MPS); biometry (MS, PhD); decision theory (MS, PhD); economic and social statistics (MS, PhD); engineering statistics (MS, PhD); experimental design (MS, PhD); mathematical statistics (MS, PhD); probability (MS, PhD); sampling (MS, PhD); statistical computing (MS, PhD); stochastic processes (MS, PhD). Terminal master's awarded for partial completion of doctoral program. *Degree requirements:* For master's, project (MPS), thesis (MS); for doctorate, one foreign language, thesis/dissertation. *Entrance requirements:* For master's, GRE General Test (for MS), 2 letters of recommendation (MS, MPS); for doctorate, GRE General Test, 2 letters of recommendation. Additional exam requirements/recommendations for international students: Required—TOEFL (minimum score 550 paper-based; 77 iBT). Electronic applications accepted. *Faculty research:* Bayesian analysis, survival analysis, nonparametric statistics, stochastic processes, mathematical statistics.

Dalhousie University, Faculty of Science, Department of Mathematics and Statistics, Program in Statistics, Halifax, NS B3H 4R2, Canada. Offers M Sc, PhD. *Degree requirements:* For master's, thesis, 50 hours of consulting; for doctorate, thesis/dissertation, 50 hours of consulting. *Entrance requirements:* Additional exam requirements/recommendations for international students: Required—TOEFL, IELTS, CANTEST, CAEL, or Michigan English Language Assessment Battery. Electronic applications accepted. *Faculty research:* Data analysis, multivariate analysis, robustness, time series, statistical genetics.

Duke University, Graduate School, Department of Statistical Science, Durham, NC 27708. Offers MSS, PhD. *Program availability:* Part-time. *Degree requirements:* For doctorate, thesis/dissertation. *Entrance requirements:* For doctorate, GRE General Test. Additional exam requirements/recommendations for international students: Required—TOEFL (minimum score 577 paper-based; 90 iBT) or IELTS (minimum score 7). Electronic applications accepted.

Duke University, Graduate School, Program in Statistical and Economic Modeling, Durham, NC 27708. Offers econometrics (MS); financial economics (MS). Program offered jointly by the Departments of Statistical Science and Economics. *Entrance requirements:* For master's, GRE General Test. Additional exam requirements/recommendations for international students: Required—TOEFL (minimum score 577 paper-based; 90 iBT) or IELTS (minimum score 7). Electronic applications accepted.

East Carolina University, Graduate School, Thomas Harriot College of Arts and Sciences, Department of Mathematics, Greenville, NC 27858-4353. Offers mathematics (MA), including mathematics in the community college, statistics. *Program availability:* Part-time, evening/weekend. *Application deadline:* For fall admission, 6/1 priority date for domestic students, 2/1 priority date for international students; for spring admission, 10/15 priority date for domestic students, 10/1 priority date for international students. *Expenses: Tuition, area resident:* Full-time $4749. Tuition, state resident: full-time $4749. Tuition, nonresident: full-time $17,898. *International tuition:* $17,898 full-time. *Required fees:* $2787. Part-time tuition and fees vary according to course load and program. *Financial support:* Application deadline: 3/1. *Unit head:* Dr. Johannes H. Hattingh, Chair, 252-328-6461, E-mail: hattinghj@ecu.edu. *Application contact:* Graduate School Admissions, 252-328-6012, Fax: 252-328-6071, E-mail: gradschool@ecu.edu.
Website: http://www.ecu.edu/cs-cas/math/

Florida Atlantic University, Charles E. Schmidt College of Science, Department of Mathematical Sciences, Boca Raton, FL 33431-0991. Offers applied mathematics and statistics (MS); mathematics (MST, PhD). *Program availability:* Part-time. *Faculty:* 36 full-time (7 women), 1 part-time/adjunct (0 women). *Students:* 20 full-time (7 women), 38 part-time (10 women); includes 23 minority (7 Black or African American, non-Hispanic/Latino; 3 Asian, non-Hispanic/Latino; 9 Hispanic/Latino; 4 Two or more races, non-Hispanic/Latino), 16 international. Average age 31. 47 applicants, 21% accepted, 10 enrolled. In 2018, 15 master's, 6 doctorates awarded. Terminal master's awarded for partial completion of doctoral program. *Entrance requirements:* For master's and doctorate, GRE General Test, minimum GPA of 3.0. Additional exam requirements/recommendations for international students: Required—TOEFL (minimum score 500 paper-based; 61 iBT), IELTS (minimum score 6). *Application deadline:* For fall admission, 7/1 priority date for domestic students, 2/15 priority date for international students; for spring admission, 11/1 priority date for domestic students, 7/15 priority date for international students. Applications are processed on a rolling basis. Application fee: $30. Electronic applications accepted. *Expenses: Tuition, area resident:* Full-time $7400; part-time $369.82 per credit. Tuition, state resident: full-time $7400; part-time $369.82 per credit. Tuition, nonresident: full-time $20,496; part-time $1024.81 per credit. *Financial support:* Fellowships, teaching assistantships, and Federal Work-Study available. Financial award application deadline: 4/1. *Faculty research:* Cryptography, statistics, algebra, analysis, combinatorics. *Application contact:* Sonia Clayton, 561-297-4629, E-mail: mathgraduate@fau.edu.
Website: http://www.math.fau.edu/

Florida International University, College of Arts, Sciences, and Education, Department of Mathematics and Statistics, Miami, FL 33199. Offers mathematical sciences (MS); statistics (MS). *Program availability:* Part-time, evening/weekend. *Faculty:* 58 full-time (18 women), 37 part-time/adjunct (12 women). *Students:* 10 full-time (2 women), 7 part-time (2 women); includes 11 minority (all Hispanic/Latino), 6 international. Average age 30. 25 applicants, 48% accepted, 11 enrolled. In 2018, 10 master's awarded. *Degree requirements:* For master's, thesis or alternative, project. *Entrance requirements:* For master's, GRE General Test, minimum GPA of 3.0, letter of intent, letters of recommendation. Additional exam requirements/recommendations for international students: Required—TOEFL (minimum score 550 paper-based; 80 iBT). *Application deadline:* For fall admission, 6/1 for domestic students, 4/1 for international students; for spring admission, 10/1 for domestic students, 9/1 for international students. Applications are processed on a rolling basis. Application fee: $30. Electronic applications accepted. *Financial support:* Institutionally sponsored loans and scholarships/grants available. Financial award application deadline: 3/1; financial award applicants required to submit FAFSA. *Unit head:* Dr. Laura De Carli, Chair, 305-348-0278, Fax: 305-348-6158, E-mail: laura.decarli@fiu.edu. *Application contact:* Nanett Rojas, Manager, Admissions Operations, 305-348-7464, Fax: 305-348-7441, E-mail: gradadm@fiu.edu.
Website: http://mathstat.fiu.edu

George Mason University, Volgenau School of Engineering, Department of Statistics, Fairfax, VA 22030. Offers biostatistics (MS); statistical science (MS, PhD); statistics (Certificate). *Faculty:* 17 full-time (4 women), 5 part-time/adjunct (0 women). *Students:* 35 full-time (16 women), 30 part-time (14 women); includes 13 minority (3 Black or African American, non-Hispanic/Latino; 8 Asian, non-Hispanic/Latino; 1 Hispanic/Latino; 1 Two or more races, non-Hispanic/Latino), 28 international. Average age 29. 71 applicants, 77% accepted, 23 enrolled. In 2018, 24 master's, 3 doctorates, 5 other advanced degrees awarded. *Degree requirements:* For master's, thesis optional; for doctorate, comprehensive exam, thesis/dissertation, qualifying exams. *Entrance requirements:* For master's, GRE/GMAT, bachelor's degree from accredited institution with minimum GPA of 3.0 in major that includes calculus, matrix algebra, calculus-based probability and statistics; personal goal statement; 2 official copies of transcripts; 3 letters of recommendation; resume; official bank statement; proof of financial support; photocopy of passport; for doctorate, GRE, MS in math-intensive discipline with minimum GPA of 3.5, personal goals statement, 2 official copies of transcripts, 3 letters of recommendation, resume, official bank statement, proof of financial support, photocopy of passport; for Certificate, bachelor's degree with 2 courses in calculus and probability or statistics, personal goals statement, 2 official copies of transcripts, 1-3 letters of recommendation (depending on program), resume, official bank statement, proof of financial support, photocopy of passport. Additional exam requirements/recommendations for international students: Required—TOEFL (minimum score 575 paper-based; 80 iBT), IELTS (minimum score 6.5), PTE. *Application deadline:* For fall admission, 12/15 priority date for domestic and international students; for spring admission, 8/15 priority date for domestic and international students. Application fee: $65 ($80 for international students). Electronic applications accepted. *Expenses:* $589 per credit in-state, $1,346.75 per credit out-of-state. *Financial support:* In 2018–19, 25 students received support, including 9 research assistantships with tuition reimbursements available (averaging $17,522 per year), 16 teaching assistantships with tuition reimbursements available (averaging $17,851 per year); career-related internships or fieldwork, Federal Work-Study, scholarships/grants, unspecified assistantships, and health care benefits (for full-time research or teaching assistantship recipients) also available. Support available to part-time students. Financial award application deadline: 3/1; financial award applicants required to submit FAFSA. *Faculty research:* Data analytics; visualization; biostatistics; time series; statistical modeling. *Total annual research expenditures:* $368,545. *Unit head:* William F. Rosenberger, Chair, 703-993-3645, Fax: 703-993-1700, E-mail: wrosenbe@gmu.edu. *Application contact:* Elizabeth Quigley, Administrative Assistant, 703-993-9107, Fax: 703-993-1700, E-mail: equigley@gmu.edu.
Website: http://statistics.gmu.edu/

Georgetown University, Graduate School of Arts and Sciences, Department of Mathematics and Statistics, Washington, DC 20057. Offers mathematics (MS); statistics (MS). *Program availability:* Part-time, evening/weekend. *Entrance requirements:* Additional exam requirements/recommendations for international students: Required—TOEFL or IELTS. Electronic applications accepted. *Faculty research:* Partial differential equations, mathematical biology, inverse problems, statistics.

The George Washington University, Columbian College of Arts and Sciences, Department of Statistics, Washington, DC 20052. Offers statistics (MS, PhD); survey design and data analysis (Graduate Certificate). *Program availability:* Part-time, evening/weekend. *Faculty:* 19 full-time (4 women), 17 part-time/adjunct (5 women). *Students:* 302 full-time (162 women), 118 part-time (46 women); includes 62 minority (12 Black or African American, non-Hispanic/Latino; 1 American Indian or Alaska Native, non-Hispanic/Latino; 32 Asian, non-Hispanic/Latino; 14 Hispanic/Latino; 1 Native Hawaiian or other Pacific Islander, non-Hispanic/Latino; 2 Two or more races, non-Hispanic/Latino), 294 international. Average age 27. 1,258 applicants, 51% accepted, 159 enrolled. In 2018, 200 master's, 9 doctorates, 10 other advanced degrees awarded. Terminal master's awarded for partial completion of doctoral program. *Degree requirements:* For master's, comprehensive exam; for doctorate, thesis/dissertation, general exam. *Entrance requirements:* For master's and doctorate, GRE General Test, interview, minimum GPA of 3.0. Additional exam requirements/recommendations for international students: Required—TOEFL (minimum score 550 paper-based; 80 iBT). *Application deadline:* For fall admission, 1/15 priority date for domestic and international students; for spring admission, 10/1 priority date for domestic students, 9/1 priority date for international students. Applications are processed on a rolling basis. Application fee: $75. Electronic applications accepted. *Financial support:* In 2018–19, 13 students received support. Fellowships with tuition reimbursements available, teaching assistantships with tuition reimbursements available, Federal Work-Study, and tuition waivers available. Financial award application deadline: 1/15. *Unit head:* Dr. Tapan K. Nayak, Chair, 202-994-6549, E-mail: tapan@gwu.edu. *Application contact:* Information Contact, 202-994-6356, Fax: 202-994-6917.
Website: http://www.gwu.edu/~stat/

Georgia Institute of Technology, Graduate Studies, Multidisciplinary Program in Analytics, Atlanta, GA 30332-0001. Offers MS. Program offered jointly with Scheller College of Business, College of Computing, and College of Engineering. *Program availability:* Part-time. *Degree requirements:* For master's, applied analytics practicum or approved internship. *Entrance requirements:* For master's, GRE or GMAT. Additional exam requirements/recommendations for international students: Required—TOEFL (minimum score 600 paper-based; 100 iBT). Electronic applications accepted. *Expenses:* Contact institution.

Georgia Institute of Technology, Graduate Studies, Multidisciplinary Program in Statistics, Atlanta, GA 30332-0001. Offers MS. Program offered jointly with School of Mathematics and School of Industrial and Systems Engineering. *Program availability:* Part-time. *Degree requirements:* For master's, thesis optional. *Entrance requirements:* For master's, GRE General Test. Additional exam requirements/recommendations for international students: Required—TOEFL (minimum score 590 paper-based; 96 iBT). Electronic applications accepted. *Faculty research:* Statistical control procedures, statistical modeling of transportation systems.

Georgia State University, College of Arts and Sciences, Department of Mathematics and Statistics, Atlanta, GA 30302-3083. Offers bioinformatics (MS, PhD); biostatistics (MS, PhD); discrete mathematics (MS); mathematics (MS, PhD); scientific computing (MS); statistics (MS). *Program availability:* Part-time. *Faculty:* 28 full-time (8 women), 1 part-time/adjunct (0 women). *Students:* 88 full-time (46 women), 15 part-time (8 women); includes 27 minority (7 Black or African American, non-Hispanic/Latino; 14 Asian, non-Hispanic/Latino; 4 Hispanic/Latino; 2 Two or more races, non-Hispanic/Latino), 57 international. Average age 32. 109 applicants, 65% accepted, 37 enrolled. In 2018, 29 master's, 11 doctorates awarded. Terminal master's awarded for partial completion of doctoral program. *Entrance requirements:* For master's and doctorate, GRE. Additional exam requirements/recommendations for international students: Required—TOEFL (minimum score 550 paper-based; 80 iBT). *Application deadline:* For fall admission, 7/1 priority date for domestic and international students; for spring admission, 11/15 priority date for domestic and international students. Application fee: $50. Electronic applications accepted. *Expenses: Tuition, area resident:* Full-time $9360; part-time $390 per credit hour. Tuition, state resident: full-time $9360; part-time $390 per credit hour. Tuition, nonresident: full-time $30,024; part-time $1251 per credit hour. *International tuition:* $30,024 full-time. *Required fees:* $2128. *Financial support:* In 2018–19, fellowships with full tuition reimbursements (averaging $22,000 per year), research assistantships with full tuition reimbursements (averaging $9,000 per year), teaching assistantships with full tuition reimbursements (averaging $9,000 per year) were awarded; institutionally sponsored loans, scholarships/grants, health care benefits, and unspecified assistantships also available. Financial award application deadline: 2/1. *Faculty research:* Algebra, matrix theory, graph theory and combinatorics; applied mathematics and analysis; collegiate mathematics education; statistics, biostatistics and applications; bioinformatics, dynamical systems. *Unit head:* Dr. Guantao Chen, Chair, 404-413-6436, Fax: 404-413-6403, E-mail: gchen@gsu.edu. *Application contact:* Dr. Guantao Chen, Chair, 404-413-6436, Fax: 404-413-6403, E-mail: gchen@gsu.edu.
Website: https://www.mathstat.gsu.edu/

Hampton University, School of Science, Program in Applied Mathematics, Hampton, VA 23668. Offers computational mathematics (MS); nonlinear science (MS); statistics and probability (MS). *Program availability:* Part-time. *Faculty:* 1. *Students:* 2 full-time (1 woman), 1 (woman) part-time; all minorities (all Black or African American, non-Hispanic/Latino). Average age 37. 4 applicants, 50% accepted, 2 enrolled. In 2018, 1 master's awarded. *Degree requirements:* For master's, thesis optional. *Entrance requirements:* For master's, GRE General Test. Additional exam requirements/recommendations for international students: Required—TOEFL (minimum score 525 paper-based) or IELTS (6.5). *Application deadline:* For fall admission, 6/1 priority date for domestic students, 4/1 priority date for international students; for spring admission, 11/1 priority date for domestic students, 9/1 priority date for international students; for summer admission, 4/1 priority date for domestic students, 2/1 priority date for international students. Applications are processed on a rolling basis. Application fee: $35. Electronic applications accepted. *Financial support:* Application deadline: 6/30; applicants required to submit FAFSA. *Faculty research:* Stochastic processes, nonlinear dynamics, approximation theory, hydrodynamical stability, Clifford Analysis, Functional Analysis, Operator Theory, Hilbert Space, Polyconvex Integrand, Ordinary Differential Equations, and Calculus of Variations, Longitudinal Data Analysis and Logistic Regression Modeling. *Unit head:* Dr. Arun K. Verma, Professor/Chair, 757-727-5352, Fax: 757-637-2378, E-mail: arun.verma@hamptonu.edu. *Application contact:* Dr. Arun K. Verma, Professor/Chair, 757-727-5352, Fax: 757-637-2378, E-mail: arun.verma@hamptonu.edu.

Harvard University, Graduate School of Arts and Sciences, Department of Statistics, Cambridge, MA 02138. Offers AM, PhD. Terminal master's awarded for partial completion of doctoral program. *Degree requirements:* For master's, one foreign language; for doctorate, one foreign language, thesis/dissertation, exam, qualifying paper. *Entrance requirements:* For master's and doctorate, GRE General Test, GRE Subject Test (recommended). Additional exam requirements/recommendations for international students: Required—TOEFL. *Faculty research:* Interactive graphic analysis of multidimensional data, data analysis, modeling and inference, statistical modeling of U.S. economic time series.

Hunter College of the City University of New York, Graduate School, School of Arts and Sciences, Department of Mathematics and Statistics, New York, NY 10065-5085. Offers adolescent mathematics education (MA); applied mathematics (MA); bioinformatics (MA); pure mathematics (MA); statistics (MA). *Program availability:* Part-time, evening/weekend. *Degree requirements:* For master's, one foreign language, comprehensive exam, thesis (for some programs). *Entrance requirements:* For master's, GRE General Test, 24 credits in mathematics. Additional exam requirements/recommendations for international students: Required—TOEFL. *Faculty research:* Data analysis, dynamical systems, computer graphics, topology, statistical decision theory.

Indiana University Bloomington, University Graduate School, College of Arts and Sciences, Department of Statistics, Bloomington, IN 47405. Offers applied statistics (MS); statistical science (MS, PhD). *Program availability:* Part-time. Terminal master's awarded for partial completion of doctoral program. *Degree requirements:* For master's, thesis or alternative; for doctorate, comprehensive exam, thesis/dissertation. *Entrance requirements:* For master's and doctorate, GRE. Additional exam requirements/recommendations for international students: Required—TOEFL (minimum score 100 iBT). *Faculty research:* Spatial statistics, Bayesian statistics, statistical learning, network science, applied statistics.

Indiana University–Purdue University Indianapolis, School of Science, Department of Mathematical Sciences, Indianapolis, IN 46202-3216. Offers mathematics (MS, PhD), including applied mathematics, applied statistics (MS), mathematical statistics (PhD), mathematics, mathematics education (MS). *Program availability:* Part-time, evening/weekend. *Degree requirements:* For master's, thesis optional; for doctorate, one foreign language, comprehensive exam, thesis/dissertation. *Entrance requirements:* For doctorate, GRE General Test (recommended). Additional exam requirements/recommendations for international students: Required—TOEFL (minimum score 79 iBT), IELTS (minimum score 6.5), GRE General Test. Electronic applications accepted. *Faculty research:* Mathematical physics, integral systems, partial differential equations, noncommutative geometry, biomathematics, computational neurosciences.

Iowa State University of Science and Technology, Department of Statistics, Ames, IA 50011. Offers MS, PhD, MBA/MS. *Entrance requirements:* For master's and doctorate, GRE General Test. Additional exam requirements/recommendations for international students: Required—TOEFL (minimum score 570 paper-based; 79 iBT), IELTS (minimum score 6.5). Electronic applications accepted.

Jackson State University, Graduate School, College of Science, Engineering and Technology, Department of Mathematics and Statistical Sciences, Jackson, MS 39217. Offers applied mathematics (MS); mathematics education (MST); pure mathematics (MS). *Program availability:* Part-time, evening/weekend. *Degree requirements:* For master's, comprehensive exam, thesis (for some programs). *Entrance requirements:* For master's, GRE General Test. Additional exam requirements/recommendations for international students: Required—TOEFL (minimum score 520 paper-based; 67 iBT).

Johns Hopkins University, G. W. C. Whiting School of Engineering, Department of Applied Mathematics and Statistics, Baltimore, MD 21218. Offers computational medicine (PhD); discrete mathematics (MA, MSE, PhD); financial mathematics (MSE); operations research/optimization (MA, MSE, PhD); statistics/probability (MA, MSE, PhD). *Faculty:* 25 full-time (4 women). *Students:* 173 full-time (67 women), 13 part-time (10 women). 1,406 applicants, 25% accepted, 89 enrolled. In 2018, 60 master's, 5 doctorates awarded. Terminal master's awarded for partial completion of doctoral program. *Degree requirements:* For master's, thesis (for some programs); for doctorate, thesis/dissertation, oral exam, introductory exam. *Entrance requirements:* For master's and doctorate, GRE General Test, 3 letters of recommendation, statement of purpose, transcripts. Additional exam requirements/recommendations for international students: Required—TOEFL (minimum score 600 paper-based; 100 iBT), IELTS (minimum score 7). *Application deadline:* For fall admission, 1/15 for domestic and international students; for spring admission, 9/15 for domestic and international students. Application fee: $75. Electronic applications accepted. *Financial support:* In 2018–19, 57 students received support, including 14 fellowships with full tuition reimbursements available (averaging $24,750 per year), 13 research assistantships with full tuition reimbursements available (averaging $23,000 per year), 30 teaching assistantships with full tuition reimbursements available (averaging $2,300 per year); Federal Work-Study, health care benefits, and tuition waivers (full and partial) also available. Financial award application deadline: 1/15; financial award applicants required to submit FAFSA. *Faculty research:* Matrix and numerical analysis, differential equation modeling, optimization and operations research, probability and statistics, discrete mathematics, financial mathematics. *Unit head:* Dr. Laurent Younes, Chair, 410-516-5103, Fax: 410-516-7459, E-mail: laurent.younes@jhu.edu. *Application contact:* Kristin Bechtel, Academic Program Coordinator, 410-516-7198, Fax: 410-516-7459, E-mail: kbechtel@jhu.edu. Website: http://engineering.jhu.edu/ams

Johns Hopkins University, G. W. C. Whiting School of Engineering, Master of Science in Engineering Management Program, Baltimore, MD 21218. Offers biomaterials (MSEM); civil engineering (MSEM); communications science (MSEM); computer science (MSEM); environmental systems analysis, economics and public policy (MSEM); fluid mechanics (MSEM); materials science and engineering (MSEM); mechanical engineering (MSEM); mechanics and materials (MSEM); nano-biotechnology (MSEM); nanomaterials and nanotechnology (MSEM); operations research (MSEM); probability and statistics (MSEM); smart product and device design (MSEM). *Students:* 34 full-time (12 women), 18 part-time (7 women). 233 applicants, 39% accepted, 33 enrolled. In 2018, 27 master's awarded. *Entrance requirements:* For master's, GRE, 3 letters of recommendation, statement of purpose, transcripts. Additional exam requirements/recommendations for international students: Required—TOEFL (minimum score 600 paper-based, 100 iBT) or IELTS (7). *Application deadline:* For fall admission, 2/15 for domestic and international students. Application fee: $75. Electronic applications accepted. *Financial support:* In 2018–19, 43 research assistantships (averaging $43,344 per year) were awarded; health care benefits also available. *Unit head:* Dr. Pamela Sheff, Director, 410-516-7056, Fax: 410-516-4880, E-mail: pamsheff@gmail.com. *Application contact:* Lindsey Conklin, Sr. Academic Program Coordinator, 410-516-1108, Fax: 410-516-0780, E-mail: lconkli4@jhu.edu. Website: http://engineering.jhu.edu/msem/

Kansas State University, Graduate School, College of Arts and Sciences, Department of Statistics, Manhattan, KS 66506. Offers MS, PhD, Graduate Certificate. Terminal master's awarded for partial completion of doctoral program. *Degree requirements:* For master's, thesis or alternative, exam or research paper; for doctorate, comprehensive exam, thesis/dissertation, qualifying and preliminary exams. *Entrance requirements:* For master's and doctorate, previous course work in statistics and mathematics; for Graduate Certificate, statement of objectives, transcripts, 2 letters of reference. Additional exam requirements/recommendations for international students: Required—TOEFL (minimum score 550 paper-based; 79 iBT), IELTS (minimum score 6.5), PTE (minimum score 58). Electronic applications accepted. *Faculty research:* Linear and nonlinear statistical models, design analysis of experiments, nonparametric methods, high-dimensional data, Bayesian methods, categorical data analysis.

Lehigh University, College of Arts and Sciences, Department of Mathematics, Bethlehem, PA 18015. Offers applied mathematics (MS, PhD); mathematics (MS, PhD); statistics (MS). *Program availability:* Part-time. *Faculty:* 23 full-time (5 women). *Students:* 37 full-time (10 women), 4 part-time (1 woman); includes 4 minority (1 Black or African American, non-Hispanic/Latino; 1 Asian, non-Hispanic/Latino; 1 Hispanic/Latino; 1 Two or more races, non-Hispanic/Latino), 22 international. Average age 24. 127 applicants, 53% accepted, 13 enrolled. In 2018, 14 master's, 3 doctorates awarded. Terminal master's awarded for partial completion of doctoral program. *Degree requirements:* For master's, comprehensive exam, thesis optional; for doctorate, comprehensive exam, thesis/dissertation, qualifying examination, general examination, advanced topic examination. *Entrance requirements:* For master's and doctorate, GRE General Test (strongly recommended), minimum undergraduate GPA of 2.75, 3.0 for last two semesters; adequate background in math. Additional exam requirements/recommendations for international students: Required—TOEFL. *Application deadline:* For fall admission, 1/1 for domestic and international students; for spring admission, 12/1 for domestic and international students. Application fee: $75. Electronic applications accepted. *Expenses:* $1500 per credit. *Financial support:* In 2018–19, 35 students received support, including fellowships with full tuition reimbursements available (averaging $25,000 per year), 2 research assistantships with full tuition reimbursements available (averaging $21,800 per year), 26 teaching assistantships with full tuition reimbursements available (averaging $21,500 per year); scholarships/grants and tuition waivers (full and partial) also available. Support available to part-time students. Financial award application deadline: 1/1. *Faculty research:* Probability and statistics, geometry and topology, algebra, discrete mathematics, differential equations. *Total annual research expenditures:* $173,233. *Unit head:* Dr. Garth Isaak, Chairman, 610-758-3732, Fax: 610-758-3767, E-mail: gisaak@lehigh.edu. *Application contact:* Dr. Robert Neel, Graduate Director, 610-758-5531, E-mail: robert.neel@lehigh.edu. Website: http://www.math.cas2.lehigh.edu/graduate-programs-mathematics

Louisiana State University and Agricultural & Mechanical College, Graduate School, College of Agriculture, Department of Experimental Statistics, Baton Rouge, LA 70803. Offers applied statistics (M App St).

Loyola University Chicago, Graduate School, Department of Mathematics and Statistics, Chicago, IL 60660. Offers applied statistics (MS); mathematics (MS). *Program availability:* Part-time. *Faculty:* 19 full-time (3 women). *Students:* 41 full-time (21 women), 7 part-time (1 woman); includes 10 minority (1 Black or African American, non-Hispanic/Latino; 7 Asian, non-Hispanic/Latino; 1 Hispanic/Latino; 1 Two or more races, non-Hispanic/Latino), 9 international. Average age 26. 69 applicants, 62% accepted, 22 enrolled. In 2018, 28 master's awarded. *Entrance requirements:* For master's, GRE General Test. Additional exam requirements/recommendations for international students: Required—TOEFL (minimum score 550 paper-based; 79 iBT), IELTS (minimum score 6.5). *Application deadline:* For fall admission, 8/1 for domestic students; for spring admission, 12/1 for domestic students. Applications are processed on a rolling basis. Application fee: $0. Electronic applications accepted. *Expenses:* Contact institution. *Financial support:* In 2018–19, 12 students received support, including 4 fellowships with full and partial tuition reimbursements available (averaging $12,000 per year), 6 teaching assistantships with tuition reimbursements available (averaging $10,000 per year); career-related internships or fieldwork, Federal Work-Study, institutionally sponsored loans, and tuition waivers (partial) also available. Financial award application deadline: 3/15; financial award applicants required to submit FAFSA. *Faculty research:* Nonlinear analysis and partial differential equations, algebra and combinatorics, knot theory, control theory and engineering, probability and applied statistics. *Total annual research expenditures:* $70,000. *Unit head:* Dr. Timothy O'Brien, Graduate Program Director for Applied Statistics, 773-508-2129, Fax: 773-508-2123, E-mail: tobrie1@luc.edu. *Application contact:* Dr. Rafal Goebel, Graduate Program Director for Mathematics, 773-508-3558, E-mail: rgoebel1@luc.edu. Website: http://www.luc.edu/math/

McGill University, Faculty of Graduate and Postdoctoral Studies, Faculty of Arts, Department of Economics, Montréal, QC H3A 2T5, Canada. Offers economics (MA, PhD); social statistics (MA).

McGill University, Faculty of Graduate and Postdoctoral Studies, Faculty of Arts, Department of Sociology, Montréal, QC H3A 2T5, Canada. Offers medical sociology (MA); neo-tropical environment (MA); social statistics (MA); sociology (MA, PhD, Diploma).

McGill University, Faculty of Graduate and Postdoctoral Studies, Faculty of Science, Department of Mathematics and Statistics, Montréal, QC H3A 2T5, Canada. Offers computational science and engineering (M Sc); mathematics and statistics (M Sc, MA, PhD), including applied mathematics (M Sc, MA), pure mathematics (M Sc, MA), statistics (M Sc, MA).

McMaster University, School of Graduate Studies, Faculty of Science, Department of Mathematics and Statistics, Program in Statistics, Hamilton, ON L8S 4M2, Canada. Offers applied statistics (M Sc); medical statistics (M Sc); statistical theory (M Sc).

Degree requirements: For master's, thesis or alternative. *Entrance requirements:* For master's, honors degree background in mathematics and statistics. Additional exam requirements/recommendations for international students: Required—TOEFL (minimum score 550 paper-based). *Faculty research:* Development of polymer production technology, quality of life in patients who use pharmaceutical agents, mathematical modeling, order statistics from progressively censored samples, nonlinear stochastic model in genetics.

McNeese State University, Doré School of Graduate Studies, College of Science and Agriculture, Department of Mathematical Sciences, Lake Charles, LA 70609. Offers computer science (MS); mathematics (MS); statistics (MS). *Program availability:* Evening/weekend. *Degree requirements:* For master's, comprehensive exam, thesis or alternative, written exam. *Entrance requirements:* For master's, GRE.

Memorial University of Newfoundland, School of Graduate Studies, Department of Mathematics and Statistics, St. John's, NL A1C 5S7, Canada. Offers mathematics (M Sc, PhD); statistics (M Sc, MAS, PhD). *Program availability:* Part-time. *Degree requirements:* For master's, thesis, practicum and report (MAS); for doctorate, comprehensive exam, thesis/dissertation, oral defense of thesis. *Entrance requirements:* For master's, 2nd class honors degree (MAS, M Sc); for doctorate, MAS or M Sc in mathematics and statistics. Electronic applications accepted. *Faculty research:* Algebra, topology, applied mathematics, mathematical statistics, applied statistics and probability.

Miami University, College of Arts and Science, Department of Statistics, Oxford, OH 45056. Offers MS Stat. *Faculty:* 12 full-time (6 women). *Students:* 26 full-time (10 women), 2 part-time (0 women); includes 1 minority (Two or more races, non-Hispanic/Latino), 16 international. Average age 25. In 2018, 14 master's awarded. *Unit head:* Dr. A. John Bailer, Professor/Chair, 513-529-7828, E-mail: baileraj@miamioh.edu. *Application contact:* Dr. A. John Bailer, Professor/Chair, 513-529-7828, E-mail: baileraj@miamioh.edu.
Website: http://miamioh.edu/cas/academics/departments/statistics/index.html

Michigan State University, The Graduate School, College of Natural Science, Department of Statistics and Probability, East Lansing, MI 48824. Offers applied statistics (MS); statistics (MS, PhD). *Entrance requirements:* Additional exam requirements/recommendations for international students: Required—TOEFL. Electronic applications accepted.

Minnesota State University Mankato, College of Graduate Studies and Research, College of Science, Engineering and Technology, Department of Mathematics and Statistics, Program in Statistics, Mankato, MN 56001. Offers applied statistics (MS). *Degree requirements:* For master's, one foreign language, comprehensive exam, thesis or alternative. *Entrance requirements:* For master's, GRE General Test, minimum GPA of 3.0 during previous 2 years. Additional exam requirements/recommendations for international students: Required—TOEFL. Electronic applications accepted.

Mississippi State University, College of Arts and Sciences, Department of Mathematics and Statistics, Mississippi State, MS 39762. Offers mathematical sciences (PhD); mathematics (MS); statistics (MS). *Program availability:* Part-time. *Faculty:* 19 full-time (4 women). *Students:* 40 full-time (16 women), 3 part-time (1 woman); includes 4 minority (2 Black or African American, non-Hispanic/Latino; 2 Asian, non-Hispanic/Latino), 25 international. Average age 29. 54 applicants, 57% accepted, 10 enrolled. In 2018, 10 master's, 1 doctorate awarded. Terminal master's awarded for partial completion of doctoral program. *Degree requirements:* For master's, thesis optional, comprehensive oral or written exam; for doctorate, one foreign language, thesis/dissertation, comprehensive oral and written exam. *Entrance requirements:* For master's, minimum GPA of 2.75 on last two years of undergraduate courses; for doctorate, GRE. Additional exam requirements/recommendations for international students: Required—TOEFL (minimum score 477 paper-based; 53 iBT); Recommended—IELTS (minimum score 4.5). *Application deadline:* For fall admission, 3/15 priority date for domestic students, 5/1 for international students; for spring admission, 11/1 for domestic students, 9/1 for international students. Applications are processed on a rolling basis. Application fee: $60 ($80 for international students). Electronic applications accepted. *Expenses:* Tuition, state resident: full-time $8450; part-time $360.59 per credit hour. Tuition, nonresident: full-time $23,140; part-time $969.09 per credit hour. *Required fees:* $110. One-time fee: $55 full-time. Part-time tuition and fees vary according to course load, degree level, campus/location and reciprocity agreements. *Financial support:* In 2018–19, 29 teaching assistantships with full tuition reimbursements (averaging $14,738 per year) were awarded; Federal Work-Study, institutionally sponsored loans, tuition waivers (partial), and unspecified assistantships also available. Financial award application deadline: 4/1; financial award applicants required to submit FAFSA. *Faculty research:* Differential equations, algebra, numerical analysis, functional analysis, applied statistics. *Total annual research expenditures:* $1.3 million. *Unit head:* Dr. Mohsen Razzaghi, Professor and Head, 662-325-3414, Fax: 662-325-0005, E-mail: razzaghi@math.msstate.edu. *Application contact:* Nathan Drake, Admissions and Enrollment Assistant, 662-325-3804, E-mail: ndrake@grad.msstate.edu.
Website: http://www.math.msstate.edu

Missouri University of Science and Technology, Department of Mathematics and Statistics, Rolla, MO 65401. Offers applied mathematics (MS); mathematics (MST, PhD), including mathematics (PhD), mathematics education (MST), statistics (PhD). Terminal master's awarded for partial completion of doctoral program. *Degree requirements:* For master's, thesis or alternative; for doctorate, one foreign language, thesis/dissertation. *Entrance requirements:* For master's and doctorate, GRE General Test, GRE Subject Test. Additional exam requirements/recommendations for international students: Required—TOEFL (minimum score 550 paper-based). Electronic applications accepted. *Expenses:* Tuition, state resident: full-time $7545.60; part-time $419.20 per credit hour. Tuition, nonresident: full-time $22,169; part-time $1231.60 per credit hour. *International tuition:* $23,518.80 full-time. *Required fees:* $4523.05. Full-time tuition and fees vary according to course load, campus/location, program and reciprocity agreements. *Faculty research:* Analysis, differential equations, topology, statistics.

Montana State University, The Graduate School, College of Letters and Science, Department of Ecology, Bozeman, MT 59717. Offers ecological and environmental statistics (MS); ecology and environmental sciences (PhD); fish and wildlife biology (PhD); fish and wildlife management (MS). *Program availability:* Part-time. *Degree requirements:* For master's, comprehensive exam, thesis (for some programs); for doctorate, comprehensive exam, thesis/dissertation. *Entrance requirements:* For master's and doctorate, GRE, minimum GPA of 3.0, letters of recommendation, essay. Additional exam requirements/recommendations for international students: Required—TOEFL (minimum score 550 paper-based). Electronic applications accepted. *Faculty research:* Community ecology, population ecology, land-use effects, management and conservation, environmental modeling.

Montana State University, The Graduate School, College of Letters and Science, Department of Mathematical Sciences, Bozeman, MT 59717. Offers mathematics (MS, PhD), including mathematics education option (MS); statistics (MS, PhD). *Program availability:* Part-time, online learning. *Degree requirements:* For master's, comprehensive exam, thesis (for some programs); for doctorate, comprehensive exam, thesis/dissertation. *Entrance requirements:* For master's and doctorate, GRE General Test. Additional exam requirements/recommendations for international students: Required—TOEFL (minimum score 550 paper-based). Electronic applications accepted. *Faculty research:* Applied mathematics, dynamical systems, statistics, mathematics education, mathematical and computational biology.

Montclair State University, The Graduate School, College of Science and Mathematics, Program in Statistics, Montclair, NJ 07043-1624. Offers MS. *Program availability:* Part-time, evening/weekend. *Degree requirements:* For master's, comprehensive exam, thesis or alternative. *Entrance requirements:* For master's, GRE General Test, 2 letters of recommendation, essay. Additional exam requirements/recommendations for international students: Required—TOEFL (minimum score 83 iBT), IELTS (minimum score 6.5). Electronic applications accepted. *Faculty research:* Biostatistics, time series.

Murray State University, Jesse D. Jones College of Science, Engineering and Technology, Department of Mathematics and Statistics, Murray, KY 42071. Offers mathematics (MA, MS); mathematics teacher leader (MAT). *Program availability:* Part-time. *Entrance requirements:* For master's, GRE or GMAT, minimum university GPA of 2.75. Additional exam requirements/recommendations for international students: Required—TOEFL (minimum score 527 paper-based; 71 iBT). Electronic applications accepted.

New Jersey Institute of Technology, Ying Wu College of Computing, Newark, NJ 07102. Offers big data management and mining (Certificate); business and information systems (Certificate); computer science (PhD); computing and business (MS); data mining (Certificate); data science (MS); information security (Certificate); information systems (PhD); information technology administration and security (MS); IT administration (Certificate); network security and information assurance (Certificate); software engineering (MS), including information systems; software engineering analysis/design (Certificate); Web systems development (Certificate). *Program availability:* Part-time, evening/weekend. *Faculty:* 69 full-time (13 women), 38 part-time/adjunct (4 women). *Students:* 699 full-time (229 women), 269 part-time (67 women); includes 260 minority (44 Black or African American, non-Hispanic/Latino; 145 Asian, non-Hispanic/Latino; 59 Hispanic/Latino; 12 Two or more races, non-Hispanic/Latino), 614 international. Average age 26. 2,216 applicants, 55% accepted, 366 enrolled. In 2018, 418 master's, 5 doctorates, 13 other advanced degrees awarded. Terminal master's awarded for partial completion of doctoral program. *Degree requirements:* For master's, thesis optional; for doctorate, thesis/dissertation. *Entrance requirements:* For master's, GRE General Test; for doctorate, GRE General Test, minimum graduate GPA of 3.5. Additional exam requirements/recommendations for international students: Required—TOEFL (minimum score 550 paper-based; 79 iBT), IELTS (minimum score 6.5). *Application deadline:* For fall admission, 6/1 priority date for domestic students, 5/1 priority date for international students; for spring admission, 11/15 priority date for domestic and international students. Applications are processed on a rolling basis. Application fee: $75. Electronic applications accepted. *Expenses:* $22,690 per year (in-state), $32,136 per year (out-of-state). *Financial support:* In 2018–19, 366 students received support, including 10 fellowships with full tuition reimbursements available (averaging $22,000 per year), 47 research assistantships with full tuition reimbursements available (averaging $22,000 per year), 28 teaching assistantships with full tuition reimbursements available (averaging $22,000 per year); career-related internships or fieldwork, Federal Work-Study, scholarships/grants, and unspecified assistantships also available. Financial award application deadline: 1/15. *Faculty research:* Computer systems, communications and networking, artificial intelligence, database engineering, systems analysis, analytics and optimization in crowdsourcing. *Total annual research expenditures:* $4.9 million. *Unit head:* Dr. Craig Gotsman, Dean, 973-596-3366, Fax: 973-596-5777, E-mail: craig.gotsman@njit.edu. *Application contact:* Stephen Eck, Director of Admissions, 973-596-3300, Fax: 973-596-3461, E-mail: admissions@njit.edu.
Website: http://computing.njit.edu/

New Mexico Institute of Mining and Technology, Center for Graduate Studies, Department of Mathematics, Socorro, NM 87801. Offers applied and industrial mathematics (PhD); industrial mathematics (MS); mathematics (MS); operations research and statistics (MS). *Degree requirements:* For master's, thesis optional; for doctorate, thesis/dissertation. *Entrance requirements:* For master's, GRE General Test. Additional exam requirements/recommendations for international students: Required—TOEFL (minimum score 540 paper-based). *Faculty research:* Applied mathematics, differential equations, industrial mathematics, numerical analysis, stochastic processes.

New York University, Leonard N. Stern School of Business, Department of Information, Operations and Management Sciences, New York, NY 10012-1019. Offers information systems (MBA, PhD); operations management (MBA, PhD); statistics (MBA, PhD). *Faculty research:* Knowledge management, economics of information, computer-supported groups and communities financial information systems, data mining and business intelligence.

North Carolina State University, Graduate School, College of Sciences, Department of Statistics, Raleigh, NC 27695. Offers M Stat, MS, PhD. *Program availability:* Part-time. *Degree requirements:* For master's, comprehensive exam, thesis (for some programs), final oral exam; for doctorate, thesis/dissertation, final oral and written exams, written and oral preliminary exams. *Entrance requirements:* For master's and doctorate, GRE General Test. Additional exam requirements/recommendations for international students: Required—TOEFL. Electronic applications accepted. *Faculty research:* Biostatistics; nonlinear models.

North Dakota State University, College of Graduate and Interdisciplinary Studies, College of Science and Mathematics, Department of Statistics, Fargo, ND 58102. Offers sports statistics (PhD); statistics (MS). *Entrance requirements:* Additional exam requirements/recommendations for international students: Required—TOEFL. Electronic applications accepted.

Northern Arizona University, College of Environment, Forestry, and Natural Sciences, Department of Mathematics and Statistics, Flagstaff, AZ 86011. Offers applied statistics (Graduate Certificate); mathematics (MS); mathematics education (MS); statistics (MS); teaching introductory community college mathematics (Graduate Certificate). *Program availability:* Part-time. *Degree requirements:* For master's, variable foreign language requirement, comprehensive exam (for some programs), thesis (for some programs); for Graduate Certificate, comprehensive exam (for some programs). *Entrance requirements:* Additional exam requirements/recommendations for international students: Required—TOEFL (minimum score 80 iBT), IELTS (minimum score 6.5), TOEFL minimum iBT score of 89 (for MS and Graduate Certificate). Electronic applications accepted.

Northern Illinois University, Graduate School, College of Liberal Arts and Sciences, Department of Mathematical Sciences, Division of Statistics, De Kalb, IL 60115-2854. Offers MS. *Program availability:* Part-time. *Faculty:* 8 full-time (1 woman), 1 part-time/adjunct (0 women). *Students:* 16 full-time (8 women), 5 part-time (1 woman); includes 1 minority (Asian, non-Hispanic/Latino), 8 international. Average age 28. 15 applicants, 87% accepted, 9 enrolled. In 2018, 20 master's awarded. *Degree requirements:* For master's, comprehensive exam, thesis optional. *Entrance requirements:* For master's, GRE General Test, minimum GPA of 2.75; course work in statistics, calculus, and linear algebra. Additional exam requirements/recommendations for international students: Required—TOEFL (minimum score 550 paper-based). *Application deadline:* For fall admission, 6/1 for domestic students, 5/1 for international students; for spring admission, 11/1 for domestic students, 10/1 for international students. Applications are processed on a rolling basis. Application fee: $40. Electronic applications accepted. *Financial support:* In 2018–19, 1 research assistantship with full tuition reimbursement, 18 teaching assistantships with full tuition reimbursements were awarded; fellowships with full tuition reimbursements, career-related internships or fieldwork, Federal Work-Study, scholarships/grants, tuition waivers (full), and unspecified assistantships also available. Support available to part-time students. Financial award applicants required to submit FAFSA. *Faculty research:* Reality and life testing, quality control, statistical inference from stochastic process, nonparametric statistics. *Unit head:* Dr. Barbara Gonzalez, Chair, 815-753-6714, E-mail: bgonzalez4@niu.edu. *Application contact:* Dr. Barbara Gonzalez, Chair, 815-753-6714, E-mail: bgonzalez4@niu.edu.
Website: http://www.niu.edu/stat/

Northwestern University, The Graduate School, Judd A. and Marjorie Weinberg College of Arts and Sciences, Department of Statistics, Evanston, IL 60208. Offers MS, PhD. Admissions and degrees offered through The Graduate School. *Program availability:* Part-time. Terminal master's awarded for partial completion of doctoral program. *Degree requirements:* For master's, final exam; for doctorate, thesis/dissertation, preliminary exam, final exam. *Entrance requirements:* For master's and doctorate, GRE General Test. Additional exam requirements/recommendations for international students: Required—TOEFL. *Faculty research:* Theoretical statistics, applied statistics, computational methods, statistical designs, complex models.

Northwestern University, McCormick School of Engineering and Applied Science, Department of Industrial Engineering and Management Sciences, MS in Analytics Program, Evanston, IL 60208. Offers MS. *Entrance requirements:* For master's, GRE or GMAT. Additional exam requirements/recommendations for international students: Required—TOEFL (minimum score 80 iBT), IELTS (minimum score 7). Electronic applications accepted.

Northwestern University, School of Professional Studies, Program in Data Science, Evanston, IL 60208. Offers computer-based data mining (MS); marketing analytics (MS); predictive modeling (MS); risk analytics (MS); Web analytics (MS). *Program availability:* Online learning. *Entrance requirements:* For master's, official transcripts, two letters of recommendation, statement of purpose, current resume or curriculum vitae. Additional exam requirements/recommendations for international students: Required—TOEFL (minimum score 600 paper-based; 100 iBT) or IELTS (minimum score 7).

Oakland University, Graduate Study and Lifelong Learning, College of Arts and Sciences, Department of Mathematics and Statistics, Program in Statistical Methods, Rochester, MI 48309-4401. Offers Certificate. *Entrance requirements:* Additional exam requirements/recommendations for international students: Required—TOEFL (minimum score 550 paper-based). *Expenses:* Contact institution.

The Ohio State University, Graduate School, College of Arts and Sciences, Division of Natural and Mathematical Sciences, Department of Statistics, Columbus, OH 43210. Offers biostatistics (PhD); statistics (M Appl Stat, MS, PhD). *Program availability:* Part-time. *Faculty:* 25. *Students:* 72 (30 women). Average age 26. In 2018, 19 master's, 12 doctorates awarded. Terminal master's awarded for partial completion of doctoral program. *Entrance requirements:* For master's and doctorate, GRE General Test. Additional exam requirements/recommendations for international students: Required—TOEFL (minimum score 600 paper-based; 100 iBT); Recommended—IELTS (minimum score 8). *Application deadline:* For fall admission, 1/1 priority date for domestic students, 12/1 priority date for international students; for spring admission, 12/1 for domestic students, 11/1 for international students. Applications are processed on a rolling basis. Application fee: $60 ($70 for international students). Electronic applications accepted. *Financial support:* Fellowships, research assistantships, teaching assistantships, Federal Work-Study, and institutionally sponsored loans available. Support available to part-time students. *Unit head:* Dr. Steve MacEachern, Chair, 614-292-5843, Fax: 614-292-2096, E-mail: maceachern.1@osu.edu. *Application contact:* Graduate and Professional Admissions, 614-292-9444, Fax: 614-292-3895, E-mail: gpadmissions@osu.edu.
Website: http://www.stat.osu.edu/

Oklahoma State University, College of Arts and Sciences, Department of Statistics, Stillwater, OK 74078. Offers MS, PhD. *Faculty:* 11 full-time (3 women), 1 (woman) part-time/adjunct. *Students:* 12 full-time (5 women), 11 part-time (6 women); includes 3 minority (1 American Indian or Alaska Native, non-Hispanic/Latino; 2 Hispanic/Latino), 13 international. Average age 28. 40 applicants, 25% accepted, 7 enrolled. In 2018, 3 master's, 1 doctorate awarded. *Entrance requirements:* For master's and doctorate, GRE. Additional exam requirements/recommendations for international students: Required—TOEFL (minimum score 550 paper-based), IELTS (minimum score 7). *Application deadline:* For fall admission, 3/1 priority date for international students; for spring admission, 8/1 priority date for international students. Applications are processed on a rolling basis. Application fee: $40 ($75 for international students). Electronic applications accepted. *Expenses: Tuition, area resident:* Full-time $4148. Tuition, state resident: full-time $4148. Tuition, nonresident: full-time $10,517. *International tuition:* $10,517 full-time. *Required fees:* $4394; $2929 per credit hour. Tuition and fees vary according to course load and program. *Financial support:* Research assistantships, teaching assistantships, career-related internships or fieldwork, Federal Work-Study, scholarships/grants, health care benefits, tuition waivers (partial), and unspecified assistantships available. Support available to part-time students. Financial award application deadline: 3/1; financial award applicants required to submit FAFSA. *Faculty research:* Linear models, sampling methods, ranking and selections procedures, categorical data, multiple comparisons. *Unit head:* Dr. Melinda H Mccann, Interim Department Head, 405-744-5684, Fax: 405-744-3533. *Application contact:* Dr. Sheryl Tucker, Dean, 405-744-6368, Fax: 405-744-0355, E-mail: gradi@okstate.edu.
Website: http://statistics.okstate.edu

Old Dominion University, College of Sciences, Programs in Computational and Applied Mathematics, Norfolk, VA 23529. Offers applied mathematics (MS, PhD); biostatistics (MS); statistics (MS); statistics/biostatistics (PhD). *Program availability:* Part-time. Terminal master's awarded for partial completion of doctoral program. *Degree requirements:* For master's, project; for doctorate, comprehensive exam, thesis/dissertation, candidacy exam. *Entrance requirements:* For master's, minimum GPA of 3.0 in major, 2.8 overall; for doctorate, GRE General Test, 3 recommendation letters, transcripts, essay. Additional exam requirements/recommendations for international students: Required—TOEFL (minimum score 550 paper-based; 79 iBT); Recommended—IELTS (minimum score 6.5). Electronic applications accepted. *Faculty research:* Numerical analysis, integral equations, continuum mechanics, statistics, direct and inverse scattering.

Oregon State University, College of Science, Program in Statistics, Corvallis, OR 97331. Offers MA, MS, PhD. *Program availability:* Part-time. *Degree requirements:* For master's, consulting experience; for doctorate, thesis/dissertation, consulting experience. *Entrance requirements:* For master's and doctorate, GRE. Additional exam requirements/recommendations for international students: Required—TOEFL (minimum score 80 iBT), IELTS (minimum score 6.5). *Faculty research:* Analysis of enumerative data, nonparametric statistics, asymptotics, experimental design, generalized regression models, linear model theory, reliability theory, survival analysis, wildlife and general survey methodology.

Penn State University Park, Graduate School, Eberly College of Science, Department of Statistics, University Park, PA 16802. Offers applied statistics (MAS); statistics (MA, MS, PhD).

Portland State University, Graduate Studies, College of Liberal Arts and Sciences, Fariborz Maseeh Department of Mathematics and Statistics, Portland, OR 97207-0751. Offers applied statistics (Certificate); mathematical sciences (PhD); mathematics education (PhD); mathematics for middle school (Certificate), mathematics for teachers (MS); statistics (MS); MA/MS. *Degree requirements:* For master's, comprehensive exam, thesis or alternative, 2 written examinations; for doctorate, thesis/dissertation, preliminary and comprehensive examinations. *Entrance requirements:* For master's, GRE General Test, GRE Subject Test, minimum GPA of 3.0 in upper-division course work or 2.75 cumulative undergraduate; for doctorate, GRE General Test. Additional exam requirements/recommendations for international students: Required—TOEFL (minimum score 550 paper-based; 80 iBT). *Faculty research:* Algebra, topology, statistical distribution theory, control theory, statistical robustness.

Purdue University, Graduate School, College of Science, Department of Statistics, West Lafayette, IN 47909. Offers applied statistics, mathematical statistics and probability, joint statistics and computer science, computational finance (MS). *Faculty:* 34 full-time (6 women). *Students:* 144 full-time (54 women); includes 125 minority (4 Black or African American, non-Hispanic/Latino; 116 Asian, non-Hispanic/Latino; 3 Hispanic/Latino; 2 Native Hawaiian or other Pacific Islander, non-Hispanic/Latino). Average age 25. 523 applicants, 6% accepted, 29 enrolled. In 2018, 29 master's, 14 doctorates awarded. Terminal master's awarded for partial completion of doctoral program. *Degree requirements:* For master's, comprehensive exam; for doctorate, comprehensive exam, thesis/dissertation, qualifying exams, preliminary oral exam. *Entrance requirements:* For master's and doctorate, GRE General Test. Additional exam requirements/recommendations for international students: Required—TOEFL (minimum score 80 iBT), IELTS (minimum score 7). *Application deadline:* For fall admission, 12/31 for domestic and international students; for spring admission, 10/15 for domestic and international students. Application fee: $60 ($75 for international students). Electronic applications accepted. *Expenses:* This degree take 4-8 years depending on each individual student. Tuition and Fees are approximately $36,000 per year for all international students and $12,500 for Indiana residents. *Financial support:* In 2018–19, 5 students received support, including 5 fellowships with full tuition reimbursements available (averaging $25,000 per year), 19 research assistantships with full tuition reimbursements available (averaging $20,000 per year), 70 teaching assistantships with full tuition reimbursements available (averaging $20,000 per year); career-related internships or fieldwork, health care benefits, and unspecified assistantships also available. Financial award application deadline: 1/15. *Faculty research:* Statistical computing, bioinformatics, statistical theory, computational finance, spatial statistics. *Total annual research expenditures:* $2 million. *Unit head:* Dr. Hao Zhang, Head, 765-494-3141, Fax: 765-494-0558, E-mail: zhanghao@purdue.edu. *Application contact:* Patti Foster, Graduate Coordinator, 765-494-5794, Fax: 765-494-0558, E-mail: foster43@purdue.edu.
Website: http://www.stat.purdue.edu/

Queen's University at Kingston, School of Graduate Studies, Faculty of Arts and Science, Department of Mathematics and Statistics, Kingston, ON K7L 3N6, Canada. Offers mathematics (M Sc, PhD); statistics (M Sc, PhD). *Program availability:* Part-time. *Degree requirements:* For master's, thesis; for doctorate, comprehensive exam, thesis/dissertation. *Entrance requirements:* Additional exam requirements/recommendations for international students: Required—TOEFL. *Faculty research:* Algebra, analysis, applied mathematics, statistics.

Rice University, Graduate Programs, George R. Brown School of Engineering, Department of Statistics, Houston, TX 77251-1892. Offers bioinformatics (PhD); biostatistics (PhD); computational finance (PhD); general statistics (PhD); statistics (M Stat, MA); MBA/M Stat. *Program availability:* Part-time. *Degree requirements:* For master's, comprehensive exam; for doctorate, comprehensive exam, thesis/dissertation. *Entrance requirements:* For master's and doctorate, GRE General Test, minimum GPA of 3.0. Additional exam requirements/recommendations for international students: Required—TOEFL (minimum score 630 paper-based; 90 iBT). Electronic applications accepted. *Faculty research:* Statistical genetics, non parametric function estimation, computational statistics and visualization, stochastic processes.

Rochester Institute of Technology, Graduate Enrollment Services, Kate Gleason College of Engineering, Center for Quality and Applied Statistics, Advanced Certificate Program in Lean Six Sigma, Rochester, NY 14623-5603. Offers Advanced Certificate. *Program availability:* Part-time, evening/weekend, 100% online. In 2018, 4 Advanced Certificates awarded. *Entrance requirements:* For degree, GRE, baccalaureate degree from accredited institution with minimum GPA of 3.0, satisfactory background in statistics, official transcripts, one letter of recommendation, current resume. Additional exam requirements/recommendations for international students: Required—TOEFL (minimum score 550 paper-based; 79 iBT), IELTS (minimum score 6.5), PTE (minimum score 58). *Application deadline:* Applications are processed on a rolling basis. Application fee: $65. Electronic applications accepted. *Expenses:* Contact institution. *Financial support:* Available to part-time students. Applicants required to submit FAFSA. *Faculty research:* Design of experiments, statistical process control, lean six sigma, process optimization, value stream mapping. *Unit head:* Rebecca Ziebarth, Project Manager, 585-475-2033, E-mail: razeqa@rit.edu. *Application contact:* Diane Ellison, Senior Associate Vice President, Graduate Enrollment Services, 585-475-2229, Fax: 585-475-7164, E-mail: gradinfo@rit.edu.
Website: https://www.rit.edu/study/lean-six-sigma-adv-cert

Rutgers University–New Brunswick, Graduate School-New Brunswick, Program in Statistics, Piscataway, NJ 08854-8097. Offers applied statistics (MS); biostatistics (MS); data mining (MS); quality and productivity management (MS); statistics (MS, PhD). *Program availability:* Part-time. Terminal master's awarded for partial completion of doctoral program. *Degree requirements:* For master's, comprehensive exam, essay, exam, non-thesis essay paper; for doctorate, one foreign language, thesis/dissertation, qualifying oral and written exams. *Entrance requirements:* For master's, GRE General Test; for doctorate, GRE General Test, GRE Subject Test (recommended). Additional exam requirements/recommendations for international students: Required—TOEFL (minimum score 550 paper-based). Electronic applications accepted. *Faculty research:* Probability, decision theory, linear models, multivariate statistics, statistical computing.

St. John's University, College of Professional Studies, Department of Computer Science, Mathematics and Science, Queens, NY 11439. Offers data mining and predictive analytics (MS). *Entrance requirements:* For master's, letters of recommendation, transcripts, resume, personal statement, prerequisites: calculus, probability and statistics. Additional exam requirements/recommendations for international students: Required—TOEFL (minimum score 80 iBT), IELTS (minimum score 6.5). Electronic applications accepted.

Sam Houston State University, College of Sciences, Department of Mathematics and Statistics, Huntsville, TX 77341. Offers mathematics (MA, MS); statistics (MS). *Program availability:* Part-time. *Degree requirements:* For master's, comprehensive exam, thesis optional. *Entrance requirements:* For master's, GRE General Test, letters of recommendation. Additional exam requirements/recommendations for international students: Required—TOEFL (minimum score 550 paper-based; 79 iBT), IELTS (minimum score 6.5). Electronic applications accepted.

San Diego State University, Graduate and Research Affairs, College of Sciences, Department of Mathematics and Statistics, Program in Statistics, San Diego, CA 92182. Offers MS. *Program availability:* Part-time. *Degree requirements:* For master's, comprehensive exam. *Entrance requirements:* For master's, GRE General Test. Additional exam requirements/recommendations for international students: Required—TOEFL. Electronic applications accepted.

Simon Fraser University, Office of Graduate Studies and Postdoctoral Fellows, Faculty of Science, Department of Statistics and Actuarial Science, Burnaby, BC V5A 1S6, Canada. Offers actuarial science (M Sc); statistics (M Sc, PhD). *Degree requirements:* For master's, participation in consulting, project; for doctorate, comprehensive exam, thesis/dissertation. *Entrance requirements:* For master's, minimum GPA of 3.0 (on scale of 4.33) or 3.33 based on last 60 credits of undergraduate courses; for doctorate, minimum GPA of 3.5 (on scale of 4.33). Additional exam requirements/recommendations for international students: Recommended—TOEFL (minimum score 580 paper-based; 93 iBT), IELTS (minimum score 7), TWE (minimum score 5). Electronic applications accepted. *Faculty research:* Biostatistics, experimental design, envirometrics, statistical computing, statistical theory.

South Dakota State University, Graduate School, Jerome J. Lohr College of Engineering, Department of Mathematics and Statistics, Brookings, SD 57007. Offers computational science and statistics (PhD); mathematics (MS); statistics (MS). *Program availability:* Part-time. Terminal master's awarded for partial completion of doctoral program. *Degree requirements:* For master's, thesis (for some programs), oral exam; for doctorate, comprehensive exam, thesis/dissertation, oral and written exams. *Entrance requirements:* Additional exam requirements/recommendations for international students: Required—TOEFL (minimum score 550 paper-based; 80 iBT); Recommended—IELTS. *Faculty research:* Financial mathematics, predictive analytics, operations research, bioinformatics, biostatistics, computational science, statistics, number theory, abstract algebra.

Southern Illinois University Edwardsville, Graduate School, College of Arts and Sciences, Department of Mathematics and Statistics, Program in Statistics and Operations Research, Edwardsville, IL 62026. Offers MS. *Program availability:* Part-time. *Degree requirements:* For master's, thesis (for some programs), special project. *Entrance requirements:* Additional exam requirements/recommendations for international students: Required—TOEFL (minimum score 550 paper-based, 79 iBT), IELTS (minimum score 6.5), Michigan Test of English Language Proficiency or PTE. Electronic applications accepted.

Southern Methodist University, Dedman College of Humanities and Sciences, Department of Statistical Science, Dallas, TX 75275-0332. Offers applied statistics and data analytics (MS); biostatistics (PhD); statistical science (PhD). *Program availability:* Part-time. *Degree requirements:* For master's, thesis, oral and written exams; for doctorate, thesis/dissertation, oral and written exams. *Entrance requirements:* For master's, GRE General Test, 12 hours of advanced math courses; for doctorate, GRE General Test, minimum GPA of 3.0. Additional exam requirements/recommendations for international students: Required—TOEFL. Electronic applications accepted. *Faculty research:* Regression, time series, linear models sampling, nonparametrics, biostatistics.

Stanford University, School of Humanities and Sciences, Department of Statistics, Stanford, CA 94305-2004. Offers data science (MS); financial mathematics (MS); statistics (PhD). *Expenses: Tuition:* Full-time $50,703; part-time $32,970 per year. *Required fees:* $651.
Website: https://statistics.stanford.edu/

Stephen F. Austin State University, Graduate School, College of Sciences and Mathematics, Department of Mathematics and Statistics, Nacogdoches, TX 75962. Offers mathematics (MS); mathematics education (MS); statistics (MS). *Degree requirements:* For master's, comprehensive exam, thesis optional. *Entrance requirements:* For master's, GRE General Test, minimum GPA of 2.8 in last 60 hours, 2.5 overall. Additional exam requirements/recommendations for international students: Required—TOEFL. *Faculty research:* Kernel type estimators, fractal mappings, spline curve fitting, robust regression continua theory.

Stevens Institute of Technology, Graduate School, Charles V. Schaefer Jr. School of Engineering and Science, Department of Mathematical Sciences, Program in Stochastic Systems, Hoboken, NJ 07030. Offers MS, Certificate. *Program availability:* Part-time, evening/weekend. *Faculty:* 21 full-time (2 women), 1 part-time/adjunct (0 women). *Students:* 3 full-time (1 woman), 2 international. Average age 23. In 2018, 3 master's awarded. *Degree requirements:* For master's, thesis optional, minimum B average in major field and overall; for Certificate, minimum B average. *Entrance requirements:* For master's, GRE/GMAT scores: GRE scores are required for all applicants applying to a full-time graduate program in the Schaefer School of Engineering and Science (SES). International applicants must submit TOEFL/IELTS scores and fulfill the English Language Proficiency Requirements in order to be considered. Additional exam requirements/recommendations for international students: Required—TOEFL (minimum score 74 iBT), IELTS (minimum score 6). *Application deadline:* For fall admission, 4/15 for domestic and international students; for spring admission, 11/1 for domestic and international students; for summer admission, 5/1 for domestic students. Applications are processed on a rolling basis. Application fee: $60. Electronic applications accepted. *Expenses: Tuition:* Full-time $35,960; part-time $1620 per credit. *Required fees:* $1290; $600 per semester. Tuition and fees vary according to course load. *Financial support:* Fellowships, research assistantships, teaching assistantships, career-related internships or fieldwork, Federal Work-Study, scholarships/grants, and unspecified assistantships available. Financial award application deadline: 2/15; financial award applicants required to submit FAFSA. *Unit head:* Dr. Jean Zu, Dean of SES, 201-216.8233, Fax: 201-216.8372, E-mail: Jean.Zu@stevens.edu. *Application contact:* Graduate Admission, 888-783-8367, Fax: 888-511-1306, E-mail: graduate@stevens.edu.

Stony Brook University, State University of New York, Graduate School, College of Engineering and Applied Sciences, Department of Applied Mathematics and Statistics, Stony Brook, NY 11794. Offers MS, PhD, Advanced Certificate. *Faculty:* 28 full-time (6 women), 5 part-time/adjunct (0 women). *Students:* 242 full-time (79 women), 30 part-time (15 women); includes 29 minority (23 Asian, non-Hispanic/Latino; 5 Hispanic/Latino; 1 Two or more races, non-Hispanic/Latino), 195 international. Average age 26. 388 applicants, 70% accepted, 58 enrolled. In 2018, 47 master's, 28 doctorates awarded. *Degree requirements:* For master's, thesis or alternative; for doctorate, one foreign language, comprehensive exam, thesis/dissertation. *Entrance requirements:* For master's and doctorate, GRE General Test. Additional exam requirements/recommendations for international students: Required—TOEFL (minimum score 90 iBT). *Application deadline:* For fall admission, 1/15 for domestic students; for spring admission, 10/1 for domestic students. Application fee: $100. *Expenses:* Contact institution. *Financial support:* In 2018–19, 3 fellowships, 36 research assistantships, 47 teaching assistantships were awarded. *Faculty research:* Computational mathematics, computational modeling, applied mathematics, computational physics, computational chemistry. *Total annual research expenditures:* $2.8 million. *Unit head:* Dr. Joseph Mitchell, Chair, 631-632-8366, Fax: 631-632-8490, E-mail: joseph.mitchell@stonybrook.edu. *Application contact:* Christine Rota, Coordinator, 631-632-8360, Fax: 631-632-8490, E-mail: christine.rota@stonybrook.edu.
Website: https://www.stonybrook.edu/commcms/ams/

Temple University, Fox School of Business, Doctoral Programs in Business, Philadelphia, PA 19122-6096. Offers accounting (PhD); entrepreneurship (PhD); finance (PhD); international business (PhD); management information systems (PhD); marketing (PhD); risk management and insurance (PhD); statistics (PhD); strategic management (PhD); tourism and sport (PhD). *Accreditation:* AACSB. *Degree requirements:* For doctorate, thesis/dissertation. *Entrance requirements:* For doctorate, GRE General Test, GMAT, minimum GPA of 3.0, master's degree. Additional exam requirements/recommendations for international students: Required—TOEFL (minimum score 600 paper-based; 100 iBT), IELTS (minimum score 7.5). Electronic applications accepted.

Temple University, Fox School of Business, Specialized Master's Programs, Philadelphia, PA 19122-6096. Offers accountancy (MS); actuarial science (MS); finance (MS); financial engineering (MS); human resource management (MS); innovation management and entrepreneurship (MS); marketing (MS); statistics (MS). MS in innovation management and entrepreneurship delivered jointly with College of Engineering. *Accreditation:* AACSB. *Program availability:* Part-time. *Entrance requirements:* For master's, GRE General Test or GMAT, minimum undergraduate GPA of 3.0. Additional exam requirements/recommendations for international students: Required—TOEFL (minimum score 600 paper-based; 100 iBT), IELTS (minimum score 7.5).

Texas A&M University, College of Science, Department of Statistics, College Station, TX 77843. Offers analytics (MS); statistics (MS, PhD). MS in analytics offered in partnership with Mays Business School. *Program availability:* Part-time. *Faculty:* 35. *Students:* 83 full-time (28 women), 364 part-time (120 women); includes 141 minority (17 Black or African American, non-Hispanic/Latino; 73 Asian, non-Hispanic/Latino; 41 Hispanic/Latino; 10 Two or more races, non-Hispanic/Latino), 70 international. Average age 34. 148 applicants, 97% accepted, 124 enrolled. In 2018, 104 master's, 10 doctorates awarded. Terminal master's awarded for partial completion of doctoral program. *Entrance requirements:* For master's and doctorate, GRE General Test. Additional exam requirements/recommendations for international students: Required—TOEFL. *Application deadline:* For fall admission, 3/1 priority date for domestic students; for spring admission, 8/1 for domestic students. Applications are processed on a rolling basis. Application fee: $50 ($90 for international students). *Expenses:* Contact institution. *Financial support:* In 2018–19, 122 students received support, including 24 fellowships with tuition reimbursements available (averaging $2,738 per year), 36 research assistantships with tuition reimbursements available (averaging $12,000 per year), 51 teaching assistantships with tuition reimbursements available (averaging $18,418 per year); career-related internships or fieldwork, institutionally sponsored loans, scholarships/grants, traineeships, health care benefits, tuition waivers (full and partial), and unspecified assistantships also available. Support available to part-time students. Financial award application deadline: 3/1; financial award applicants required to submit FAFSA. *Faculty research:* Time series, applied probability and stochastic processes, factor models, statistics education, microarrays. *Unit head:* Dr. Valen E. Johnson, Department Head, 979-845-3141, Fax: 979-845-3144, E-mail: vjohnson@stat.tamu.edu. *Application contact:* Dr. Jianhua Huang, Graduate Director, 979-845-3141, Fax: 979-845-3144, E-mail: grecruiting@stat.tamu.edu.
Website: http://www.stat.tamu.edu/

Texas A&M University–Kingsville, College of Graduate Studies, College of Arts and Sciences, Department of Mathematics, Kingsville, TX 78363. Offers mathematics (MS); statistical analytics, computing and modeling (MS). *Entrance requirements:* Additional exam requirements/recommendations for international students: Required—TOEFL (minimum score 550 paper-based; 79 iBT); Recommended—IELTS. Electronic applications accepted.

Texas Tech University, Graduate School, College of Arts and Sciences, Department of Mathematics and Statistics, Lubbock, TX 79409-1042. Offers mathematics (MA, MS, PhD); statistics (MS). *Program availability:* Part-time. *Faculty:* 62 full-time (17 women). *Students:* 95 full-time (45 women), 7 part-time (2 women); includes 15 minority (7 Asian, non-Hispanic/Latino; 5 Hispanic/Latino; 3 Two or more races, non-Hispanic/Latino), 60 international. Average age 29. 81 applicants, 54% accepted, 24 enrolled. In 2018, 31 master's, 23 doctorates awarded. Terminal master's awarded for partial completion of doctoral program. *Degree requirements:* For master's, comprehensive exam (for some programs), thesis (for some programs); for doctorate, comprehensive exam, thesis/dissertation. *Entrance requirements:* For master's, GRE (for MS and assistantship applications only), official transcripts, 3 letters of recommendation, resume/CV, cover letter; for doctorate, GRE General Test, official transcripts, 3 letters of recommendation, resume/CV, cover letter. Additional exam requirements/recommendations for international students: Required—TOEFL (minimum score 550 paper-based; 79 iBT), IELTS (minimum score 6.5). *Application deadline:* For fall admission, 6/1 priority date for domestic students, 1/15 priority date for international students; for spring admission, 9/1 priority date for domestic students, 6/15 priority date for international students. Applications are processed on a rolling basis. Application fee: $65. Electronic applications accepted. *Expenses:* Contact institution. *Financial support:* In 2018–19, 105 students received support, including 92 fellowships (averaging $2,171 per year), 6 research assistantships (averaging $17,386 per year), 95 teaching assistantships (averaging $17,841 per year). Financial award application deadline: 12/15; financial award applicants required to submit FAFSA. *Faculty research:* Applied math, biomathematics, complex analysis, computational mathematics, statistics. *Total annual research expenditures:* $525,707. *Unit head:* Dr. Magdalena Toda, Professor & Department Chair, 806-834-7944, Fax: 806-742-1112, E-mail: magda.toda@ttu.edu. *Application contact:* David Cannon, Program Manager, Graduate Studies, 806-834-7393, Fax: 806-742-1112, E-mail: david.cannon@ttu.edu. Website: www.math.ttu.edu/

Université de Montréal, Faculty of Arts and Sciences, Department of Mathematics and Statistics, Montréal, QC H3C 3J7, Canada. Offers mathematical and computational finance (M Sc, DESS); mathematics (M Sc, PhD); statistics (M Sc, PhD). *Degree requirements:* For master's, thesis; for doctorate, thesis/dissertation, general exam. *Entrance requirements:* For master's and doctorate, proficiency in French. Electronic applications accepted. *Faculty research:* Pure and applied mathematics, actuarial mathematics.

Université Laval, Faculty of Sciences and Engineering, Department of Mathematics and Statistics, Program in Statistics, Québec, QC G1K 7P4, Canada. Offers M Sc. *Degree requirements:* For master's, thesis (for some programs). *Entrance requirements:* For master's, knowledge of French and English. Electronic applications accepted.

The University of Akron, Graduate School, Buchtel College of Arts and Sciences, Department of Statistics, Akron, OH 44325. Offers MS. *Program availability:* Part-time, evening/weekend. *Degree requirements:* For master's, thesis optional. *Entrance requirements:* For master's, minimum GPA of 2.75; baccalaureate degree in statistics, mathematics, or related area; three letters of recommendation; one semester of applied statistics; three semesters of calculus, linear algebra, or equivalent. Additional exam requirements/recommendations for international students: Required—TOEFL (minimum score 79 iBT), IELTS (minimum score 6.5). Electronic applications accepted. *Faculty research:* Experimental design, sampling, actuarial science, biostatistics.

University of Alaska Fairbanks, College of Natural Science and Mathematics, Department of Mathematics and Statistics, Fairbanks, AK 99775-6660. Offers mathematics (PhD); statistics (MS, Graduate Certificate). *Program availability:* Part-time. *Faculty:* 17 full-time (6 women). *Students:* 15 full-time (4 women), 1 (woman) part-time; includes 4 minority (3 Asian, non-Hispanic/Latino; 1 Hispanic/Latino), 5 international. Average age 31. 16 applicants, 44% accepted, 4 enrolled. In 2018, 7 master's, 1 other advanced degree awarded. *Degree requirements:* For master's, comprehensive exam, thesis (for some programs), oral defense of project or thesis; for doctorate, comprehensive exam, thesis/dissertation, oral defense of dissertation. *Entrance requirements:* For master's, GRE General Test, bachelor's degree from accredited institution with minimum cumulative undergraduate and major GPA of 3.0; for doctorate, GRE Subject Test (mathematics), bachelor's degree from accredited institution with minimum cumulative undergraduate and major GPA of 3.0. Additional exam requirements/recommendations for international students: Required—TOEFL (minimum score 550 paper-based; 79 iBT), IELTS (minimum score 6.5). *Application deadline:* For fall admission, 6/1 for domestic students, 3/1 for international students; for spring admission, 10/15 for domestic students, 9/1 for international students. Applications are processed on a rolling basis. Application fee: $60. Electronic applications accepted. *Expenses: Tuition, area resident:* Full-time $8802; part-time $5868 per credit hour. Tuition, state resident: full-time $8802; part-time $5868 per credit hour. Tuition, nonresident: full-time $18,504; part-time $12,336 per credit hour. *International tuition:* $18,504 full-time. *Required fees:* $1416; $944 per credit hour. $472 per semester. Tuition and fees vary according to course load and program. *Financial support:* In 2018–19, 1 research assistantship with full tuition reimbursement (averaging $9,404 per year), 10 teaching assistantships with full tuition reimbursements (averaging $18,550 per year) were awarded; fellowships with full tuition reimbursements, career-related internships or fieldwork, Federal Work-Study, scholarships/grants, health care benefits, and unspecified assistantships also available. Support available to part-time students. Financial award application deadline: 2/15; financial award applicants required to submit FAFSA. *Faculty research:* Kriging, arrangements of hyperplanes, bifurcation analysis of time-periodic differential-delay equations, inverse problems, phylogenic tree construction. *Unit head:* Dr. Anthony Rickard, Department Chair, 907-474-5374, E-mail: uaf-mathandstat-dept@alaska.edu. *Application contact:* Samara Taber, Director of Admissions, 907-474-7500, E-mail: uaf-admissions@alaska.edu. Website: http://www.uaf.edu/dms/

University of Alberta, Faculty of Graduate Studies and Research, Department of Mathematical and Statistical Sciences, Edmonton, AB T6G 2E1, Canada. Offers applied mathematics (M Sc, PhD); biostatistics (M Sc); mathematical finance (M Sc, PhD); mathematical physics (M Sc, PhD); mathematics (M Sc, PhD); statistics (M Sc, PhD, Postgraduate Diploma). *Program availability:* Part-time. Terminal master's awarded for partial completion of doctoral program. *Degree requirements:* For master's, thesis (for some programs); for doctorate, comprehensive exam, thesis/dissertation. *Entrance requirements:* Additional exam requirements/recommendations for international students: Required—TOEFL (minimum score 580 paper-based). Electronic applications accepted. *Faculty research:* Classical and functional analysis, algebra, differential equations, geometry.

The University of Arizona, Graduate Interdisciplinary Programs, Graduate Interdisciplinary Program in Statistics, Tucson, AZ 85721. Offers MS, PhD. *Entrance requirements:* Additional exam requirements/recommendations for international students: Required—TOEFL, IELTS.

University of Arkansas, Graduate School, J. William Fulbright College of Arts and Sciences, Department of Mathematical Sciences, Program in Statistics, Fayetteville, AR 72701. Offers MS. *Application deadline:* For fall admission, 8/1 for domestic students, 4/1 for international students; for spring admission, 12/1 for domestic students, 10/1 for international students; for summer admission, 4/15 for domestic students, 3/1 for international students. Applications are processed on a rolling basis. Application fee: $60. Electronic applications accepted. *Financial support:* In 2018–19, 4 research assistantships, 65 teaching assistantships were awarded; fellowships, career-related internships or fieldwork, and Federal Work-Study also available. Support available to part-time students. Financial award application deadline: 4/1; financial award applicants required to submit FAFSA. *Unit head:* Dr. Mark Johnson, Department Chair, 479-575-3351, E-mail: markj@uark.edu. *Application contact:* Dr. Maria Tjani, Graduate Coordinator, E-mail: mtjani@uark.edu. Website: https://fulbright.uark.edu/departments/math/

The University of British Columbia, Faculty of Science, Department of Computer Science, Vancouver, BC V6T 1Z4, Canada. Offers computer science (M Sc, PhD); data science (MDS). *Program availability:* Part-time. *Degree requirements:* For doctorate, comprehensive exam, thesis/dissertation. *Entrance requirements:* Additional exam requirements/recommendations for international students: Required—TOEFL. Electronic applications accepted. *Expenses:* Contact institution. *Faculty research:* Computational intelligence, data management and mining, theory, graphics, network security and systems.

The University of British Columbia, Faculty of Science, Department of Statistics, Vancouver, BC V6T 1Z2, Canada. Offers M Sc, PhD. *Degree requirements:* For master's, thesis or alternative, seminar; for doctorate, comprehensive exam, thesis/dissertation. *Entrance requirements:* Additional exam requirements/recommendations for international students: Required—TOEFL, IELTS. Electronic applications accepted. *Expenses:* Contact institution. *Faculty research:* Theoretical statistics, applied statistics, biostatistics, computational statistics, data science.

University of Calgary, Faculty of Graduate Studies, Faculty of Science, Program in Math and Statistics, Calgary, AB T2N 1N4, Canada. Offers M Sc, PhD. *Degree requirements:* For master's, comprehensive exam, thesis; for doctorate, thesis/dissertation, candidacy exam, preliminary exams. *Entrance requirements:* For master's, honors degree in applied math, pure math, or statistics; for doctorate, MA or M Sc. Additional exam requirements/recommendations for international students: Required—TOEFL (minimum score 600 paper-based) or IELTS (minimum score 7). *Faculty research:* Combinatorics, applied mathematics, statistics, probability, analysis.

University of California, Berkeley, Graduate Division, College of Letters and Science, Department of Statistics, Berkeley, CA 94720. Offers MA, PhD. *Degree requirements:* For doctorate, thesis/dissertation, qualifying exam, written preliminary exam. *Entrance requirements:* For master's and doctorate, GRE General Test, minimum GPA of 3.0, 3 letters of recommendation. Electronic applications accepted.

University of California, Davis, Graduate Studies, Program in Statistics, Davis, CA 95616. Offers MS, PhD. Terminal master's awarded for partial completion of doctoral program. *Degree requirements:* For master's, comprehensive exam; for doctorate, thesis/dissertation. *Entrance requirements:* For master's and doctorate, GRE General Test, minimum GPA of 3.0. Additional exam requirements/recommendations for international students: Required—TOEFL (minimum score 550 paper-based). Electronic applications accepted. *Faculty research:* Nonparametric analysis, time series analysis, biostatistics, curve estimation, reliability.

University of California, Irvine, Donald Bren School of Information and Computer Sciences, Department of Statistics, Irvine, CA 92697. Offers MS, PhD. *Students:* 60 full-time (29 women), 1 part-time (0 women); includes 11 minority (1 Black or African American, non-Hispanic/Latino; 1 American Indian or Alaska Native, non-Hispanic/Latino; 6 Asian, non-Hispanic/Latino; 2 Hispanic/Latino; 1 Two or more races, non-Hispanic/Latino), 35 international. Average age 26. 284 applicants, 25% accepted, 20 enrolled. In 2018, 22 master's, 5 doctorates awarded. Application fee: $105 ($125 for international students). *Unit head:* Daniel Gillen, Chair, 949-824-9862, E-mail: dgillen@uci.edu. *Application contact:* Yaming Yu, Vice Chair for Graduate Studies, 949-824-7361, E-mail: yamingy@uci.edu. Website: http://www.stat.uci.edu/

University of California, Los Angeles, Graduate Division, College of Letters and Science, Department of Statistics, Los Angeles, CA 90095. Offers MS, PhD. Terminal master's awarded for partial completion of doctoral program. *Degree requirements:* For master's, comprehensive exam, thesis; for doctorate, thesis/dissertation, oral and written qualifying exams; 1 quarter of teaching experience. *Entrance requirements:* For master's, GRE General Test, bachelor's degree; minimum undergraduate GPA of 3.0, 3.2 in upper-division courses (or its equivalent if letter grade system not used); for doctorate, GRE General Test, bachelor's degree; minimum GPA of 3.5 (or its equivalent if letter grade system not used). Additional exam requirements/recommendations for international students: Required—TOEFL. Electronic applications accepted.

University of California, Riverside, Graduate Division, Department of Statistics, Riverside, CA 92521. Offers MS. Terminal master's awarded for partial completion of doctoral program. *Degree requirements:* For master's, comprehensive exam. *Entrance requirements:* For master's, GRE (minimum score 300), strong background in statistics and sufficient training in mathematics or upper-division statistical courses to meet deficiencies; minimum GPA of 3.0. Additional exam requirements/recommendations for international students: Required—TOEFL (minimum score 550 paper-based; 80 iBT); Recommended—IELTS. Electronic applications accepted. *Faculty research:* Design and analysis of gene expression experiments using DNA microarrays, statistical design and analysis of experiments, linear models, probability models and statistical inference, genetic mapping.

University of California, San Diego, Graduate Division, Department of Mathematics, La Jolla, CA 92093. Offers applied mathematics (MA); computational science (PhD); mathematics (MA, PhD); statistics (MS, PhD). *Students:* 171 full-time (36 women), 3 part-time (1 woman). 713 applicants, 25% accepted, 55 enrolled. In 2018, 12 master's, 13 doctorates awarded. Terminal master's awarded for partial completion of doctoral program. *Degree requirements:* For master's, comprehensive exam; for doctorate, comprehensive exam, thesis/dissertation. *Entrance requirements:* For master's, GRE General Test; GRE Subject Test (for MA), minimum GPA of 3.0; for doctorate, GRE General Test, GRE Subject Test, minimum GPA of 3.0. Additional exam requirements/recommendations for international students: Required—TOEFL (minimum score 550 paper-based; 80 iBT), IELTS (minimum score 7); Recommended—TSE. *Application deadline:* For fall admission, 1/16 for domestic students. Application fee: $105 ($125 for international students). Electronic applications accepted. *Financial support:* Fellowships, research assistantships, teaching assistantships, and scholarships/grants available. Financial award applicants required to submit FAFSA. *Faculty research:* Combinatorics, bioinformatics, differential equations, logic and computational complexity, probability theory and statistics, Algebra, Algebraic Geometry, Analysis, Applied Math, Combinatorics, Computational Science, Geometry, Math Physics, Number Theory, Other, Partial Differential Equations, Probability, Representation Theory, Statistics, Topology. *Unit head:* Lei Ni, Chair, 858-534-2734, E-mail: lni@math.ucsd.edu. *Application contact:* Mark Whelan, Admissions Specialist, 858-534-2642, E-mail: mathgradadmissions@math.ucsd.edu. Website: http://math.ucsd.edu/

University of California, Santa Barbara, Graduate Division, College of Letters and Sciences, Division of Mathematics, Life, and Physical Sciences, Department of Statistics and Applied Probability, Santa Barbara, CA 93106-3110. Offers bioengineering (PhD); financial mathematics and statistics (PhD); quantitative methods in the social sciences (PhD); statistics (MA), including applied statistics, mathematical statistics; statistics and applied probability (PhD); MA/PhD. Terminal master's awarded for partial completion of doctoral program. *Degree requirements:* For master's, comprehensive exam, thesis optional; for doctorate, comprehensive exam, thesis/dissertation. *Entrance requirements:* For master's and doctorate, GRE General Test. Additional exam requirements/recommendations for international students: Required—TOEFL (minimum score 550 paper-based; 80 iBT), IELTS (minimum score 7). Electronic applications accepted. *Faculty research:* Bayesian inference, financial mathematics, stochastic processes, environmental statistics, biostatistical modeling.

University of California, Santa Cruz, Jack Baskin School of Engineering, Department of Applied Mathematics, Santa Cruz, CA 95064. Offers scientific computing and applied mathematics (MS); statistics and applied mathematics (MS, PhD), including applied

Peterson's Graduate Programs in the Physical Sciences, Mathematics, Agricultural Sciences, the Environment & Natural Resources 2020

www.petersons.com **243**

mathematics, statistics. *Program availability:* Part-time. Terminal master's awarded for partial completion of doctoral program. *Degree requirements:* For master's, thesis, seminar, capstone project; for doctorate, thesis/dissertation, seminar, first-year exam, qualifying exam. *Entrance requirements:* For master's and doctorate, GRE General Test; GRE Subject Test in math (recommended). Additional exam requirements/recommendations for international students: Required—TOEFL (minimum score 570 paper-based; 89 iBT); Recommended—IELTS (minimum score 8). Electronic applications accepted. *Expenses:* Contact institution. *Faculty research:* Bayesian nonparametric methods; computationally intensive Bayesian inference, prediction, and decision-making; envirometrics; fluid mechanics; mathematical biology.

University of Central Oklahoma, The Jackson College of Graduate Studies, College of Mathematics and Science, Department of Mathematics and Statistics, Edmond, OK 73034-5209. Offers applied mathematical science (MS), including mathematics, statistics, teaching; applied mathematics and computer science (MS). *Program availability:* Part-time. *Degree requirements:* For master's, comprehensive exam (for some programs), thesis (for some programs). *Entrance requirements:* Additional exam requirements/recommendations for international students: Required—TOEFL (minimum score 550 paper-based; 79 iBT), IELTS (minimum score 6.5). Electronic applications accepted.

University of Chicago, Booth School of Business, Full-Time MBA Program, Chicago, IL 60637. Offers accounting (MBA); analytic finance (MBA); analytic management (MBA); econometrics and statistics (MBA); economics (MBA); entrepreneurship (MBA); finance (MBA); general management (MBA); health administration and policy (Certificate); international business (MBA); managerial and organizational behavior (MBA); marketing analytics (MBA); marketing management (MBA); operations management (MBA); strategic management (MBA); MBA/AM; MBA/JD; MBA/MA; MBA/MD; MBA/MPP. *Accreditation:* AACSB. *Entrance requirements:* For master's, GMAT or GRE, transcripts, resume, 2 letters of recommendation, essays, interview. Additional exam requirements/recommendations for international students: Required—TOEFL, IELTS, or PTE. Electronic applications accepted. *Expenses:* Contact institution.

University of Chicago, Division of the Physical Sciences, Department of Statistics, Chicago, IL 60637. Offers MS, PhD. *Program availability:* Part-time. Terminal master's awarded for partial completion of doctoral program. *Degree requirements:* For master's, thesis; for doctorate, thesis/dissertation, preliminary examinations. *Entrance requirements:* For master's, GRE General Test, research statement, 3 letters of recommendation, transcripts for all previous degrees and institutions attended; for doctorate, GRE General Test; GRE Subject Test in mathematics (strongly encouraged), research statement, 3 letters of recommendation, transcripts for all previous degrees and institutions attended. Additional exam requirements/recommendations for international students: Required—TOEFL (minimum score 90 iBT), IELTS (minimum score 7). Electronic applications accepted. *Faculty research:* Probability; theory, methodology, and application of statistics; computational mathematics and machine learning.

University of Cincinnati, Graduate School, McMicken College of Arts and Sciences, Department of Mathematical Sciences, Cincinnati, OH 45221. Offers applied mathematics (MS, PhD); mathematics education (MAT); pure mathematics (MS, PhD); statistics (MS, PhD). *Program availability:* Part-time. *Faculty:* 39 full-time (4 women), 12 part-time/adjunct (4 women). *Students:* 44 full-time (24 women), 19 part-time (9 women); includes 28 minority (2 Black or African American, non-Hispanic/Latino; 25 Asian, non-Hispanic/Latino; 1 Hispanic/Latino), 42 international. 91 applicants, 35% accepted, 27 enrolled. In 2018, 5 master's, 4 doctorates awarded. Terminal master's awarded for partial completion of doctoral program. *Degree requirements:* For master's, comprehensive exam, thesis or alternative; for doctorate, comprehensive exam, thesis/dissertation. *Entrance requirements:* For master's and doctorate, GRE. Additional exam requirements/recommendations for international students: Required—TOEFL, IELTS. *Application deadline:* For fall admission, 2/1 priority date for domestic and international students. Applications are processed on a rolling basis. Application fee: $65. Electronic applications accepted. *Financial support:* In 2018–19, 51 students received support, including 2 fellowships with full tuition reimbursements available (averaging $13,500 per year), 2 research assistantships with full tuition reimbursements available (averaging $13,000 per year), 26 teaching assistantships with full tuition reimbursements available (averaging $18,500 per year); career-related internships or fieldwork, scholarships/grants, and unspecified assistantships also available. Support available to part-time students. Financial award application deadline: 2/1. *Faculty research:* Algebra, analysis, differential equations, numerical analysis, statistics. *Unit head:* Dr. Shuang Zhang, Professor and Department Head, 513-556-4052, Fax: 513-556-3417, E-mail: zhangs@ucmail.uc.edu. *Application contact:* Kamellia Smith, Program Coordinator, 513-5564053, Fax: 513-556-3417, E-mail: kamellia.smith@uc.edu.
Website: https://www.artsci.uc.edu/departments/math.html

University of Colorado Denver, College of Liberal Arts and Sciences, Department of Mathematical and Statistical Sciences, Denver, CO 80217. Offers applied mathematics (MS, PhD), including applied mathematics, applied probability (MS), applied statistics (MS), computational biology (PhD), computational mathematics (PhD), discrete mathematics, finite geometry (PhD), mathematics education (PhD), mathematics of engineering and science (MS), numerical analysis, operations research (MS), optimization and operations research (PhD), probability (PhD), statistics (PhD). *Program availability:* Part-time. *Degree requirements:* For master's, comprehensive exam, thesis optional, 30 hours of course work with minimum GPA of 3.0; for doctorate, comprehensive exam, thesis/dissertation, 42 hours of course work with minimum GPA of 3.25. *Entrance requirements:* For master's, GRE General Test; GRE Subject Test in math (recommended), 30 hours of course work in mathematics (24 of which must be upper-division mathematics), bachelor's degree with minimum GPA of 3.0; for doctorate, GRE General Test; GRE Subject Test in math (recommended), 30 hours of course work in mathematics (24 of which must be upper-division mathematics), master's degree with minimum GPA of 3.25. Additional exam requirements/recommendations for international students: Required—TOEFL (minimum score 537 paper-based; 75 iBT); Recommended—IELTS (minimum score 6.5). Electronic applications accepted. *Expenses:* Tuition, state resident: full-time $6786; part-time $337 per credit hour. Tuition, nonresident: full-time $22,590; part-time $1255 per credit hour. *Required fees:* $1231; $137 per credit hour. Tuition and fees vary according to program and reciprocity agreements. *Faculty research:* Computational mathematics, computational biology, discrete mathematics and geometry, probability and statistics, optimization.

University of Connecticut, Graduate School, College of Liberal Arts and Sciences, Department of Statistics, Storrs, CT 06269. Offers MS, PhD. Terminal master's awarded for partial completion of doctoral program. *Degree requirements:* For master's, comprehensive exam; for doctorate, thesis/dissertation. *Entrance requirements:* For master's and doctorate, GRE General Test. Additional exam requirements/recommendations for international students: Required—TOEFL (minimum score 550 paper-based). Electronic applications accepted.

University of Delaware, College of Agriculture and Natural Resources, Department of Food and Resource Economics, Program in Statistics, Newark, DE 19716. Offers MS. *Program availability:* Part-time. *Entrance requirements:* For master's, GRE General Test, 3 letters of recommendation. Additional exam requirements/recommendations for international students: Required—TOEFL (minimum score 550 paper-based). Electronic applications accepted.

University of Florida, Graduate School, College of Liberal Arts and Sciences, Department of Statistics, Gainesville, FL 32611. Offers quantitative finance (PhD); statistics (M Stat, MS Stat, PhD). *Program availability:* Part-time. Terminal master's awarded for partial completion of doctoral program. *Degree requirements:* For master's, variable foreign language requirement, comprehensive exam, final oral exam; thesis (for MS Stat); for doctorate, comprehensive exam, thesis/dissertation. *Entrance requirements:* For master's and doctorate, GRE General Test, minimum GPA of 3.0. Additional exam requirements/recommendations for international students: Required—TOEFL (minimum score 550 paper-based; 80 iBT), IELTS (minimum score 6). Electronic applications accepted. *Faculty research:* Bayesian statistics, biostatistics, Markov Chain Monte Carlo (MCMC), nonparametric statistics, statistical genetics/genomics.

University of Georgia, Franklin College of Arts and Sciences, Department of Statistics, Athens, GA 30602. Offers MS, PhD. *Degree requirements:* For master's, thesis (for some programs); for doctorate, one foreign language, thesis/dissertation. *Entrance requirements:* For master's and doctorate, GRE General Test. Electronic applications accepted.

University of Guelph, Office of Graduate and Postdoctoral Studies, College of Physical and Engineering Science, Department of Mathematics and Statistics, Guelph, ON N1G 2W1, Canada. Offers applied mathematics (PhD); applied statistics (PhD); mathematics and statistics (M Sc). *Program availability:* Part-time. *Degree requirements:* For master's, thesis (for some programs); for doctorate, thesis/dissertation. *Entrance requirements:* For master's, minimum B- average during previous 2 years of course work; for doctorate, minimum B average. Additional exam requirements/recommendations for international students: Required—TOEFL (minimum score 550 paper-based; 89 iBT), IELTS (minimum score 6.5). *Faculty research:* Dynamical systems, mathematical biology, numerical analysis, linear and nonlinear models, reliability and bioassay.

University of Houston–Clear Lake, School of Science and Computer Engineering, Program in Statistics, Houston, TX 77058-1002. Offers MS. *Entrance requirements:* For master's, GRE General Test. Additional exam requirements/recommendations for international students: Required—TOEFL (minimum score 550 paper-based).

University of Idaho, College of Graduate Studies, College of Science, Department of Statistical Science, Moscow, ID 83844-1104. Offers MS. *Faculty:* 6. *Students:* 10 full-time, 9 part-time. Average age 32. In 2018, 4 master's awarded. *Degree requirements:* For master's, thesis or alternative. *Entrance requirements:* For master's, minimum GPA of 3.0. Additional exam requirements/recommendations for international students: Required—TOEFL (minimum score 79 iBT). *Application deadline:* For fall admission, 8/1 for domestic students; for spring admission, 12/15 for domestic students. Applications are processed on a rolling basis. Application fee: $60. Electronic applications accepted. *Expenses:* Tuition, state resident: full-time $7266.44; part-time $474.50 per credit hour. Tuition, nonresident: full-time $24,902; part-time $1453.50 per credit hour. *Required fees:* $2085.56; $45.50 per credit hour. *Financial support:* Research assistantships and teaching assistantships available. Financial award applicants required to submit FAFSA. *Faculty research:* Statistical ecology, psychometrics, multivariate analysis, epidemiology, study design. *Unit head:* Dr. Christopher J. Williams, Chair, 208-885-2929, E-mail: stat@uidaho.edu. *Application contact:* Dr. Christopher J. Williams, Chair, 208-885-2929, E-mail: stat@uidaho.edu.
Website: http://www.uidaho.edu/sci/stat/

University of Illinois at Chicago, College of Liberal Arts and Sciences, Department of Mathematics, Statistics, and Computer Science, Chicago, IL 60607-7128. Offers mathematics (DA); probability and statistics (PhD); secondary school mathematics (MST); statistics (MS). *Program availability:* Part-time. *Degree requirements:* For master's, comprehensive exam; for doctorate, one foreign language, thesis/dissertation. *Entrance requirements:* For master's and doctorate, GRE General Test, minimum GPA of 3.0. Additional exam requirements/recommendations for international students: Required—TOEFL (minimum score 100 iBT). Electronic applications accepted.

University of Illinois at Urbana–Champaign, Graduate College, College of Liberal Arts and Sciences, Department of Statistics, Champaign, IL 61820. Offers analytics (MS); applied statistics (MS); statistics (MS, PhD).

The University of Iowa, Graduate College, College of Education, Department of Psychological and Quantitative Foundations, Iowa City, IA 52242-1316. Offers counseling psychology (PhD); educational measurement and statistics (MA, PhD); educational psychology (MA, PhD); school psychology (PhD, Ed S). *Accreditation:* APA. *Degree requirements:* For master's, thesis optional, exam; for doctorate, comprehensive exam, thesis/dissertation; for Ed S, exam. *Entrance requirements:* For master's, doctorate, and Ed S, GRE General Test, minimum GPA of 3.0. Additional exam requirements/recommendations for international students: Required—TOEFL (minimum score 550 paper-based; 81 iBT). Electronic applications accepted.

The University of Iowa, Graduate College, College of Liberal Arts and Sciences, Department of Statistics and Actuarial Science, Iowa City, IA 52242-1316. Offers actuarial science (MS); statistics (MS, PhD). *Degree requirements:* For master's, thesis optional, exam; for doctorate, comprehensive exam, thesis/dissertation. *Entrance requirements:* For master's and doctorate, GRE General Test, minimum GPA of 3.0. Additional exam requirements/recommendations for international students: Required—TOEFL (minimum score 550 paper-based; 81 iBT). Electronic applications accepted.

The University of Kansas, University of Kansas Medical Center, School of Medicine, Department of Biostatistics & Data Science, Kansas City, KS 66160. Offers applied statistics and analytics (MS); biostatistics (MS, PhD, Graduate Certificate); statistical applications (Graduate Certificate). *Faculty:* 21. *Students:* 36 full-time (16 women), 86 part-time (32 women); includes 32 minority (10 Black or African American, non-Hispanic/Latino; 12 Asian, non-Hispanic/Latino; 6 Hispanic/Latino; 4 Two or more races, non-Hispanic/Latino), 23 international. Average age 31. 52 applicants, 88% accepted, 42 enrolled. In 2018, 10 master's, 2 doctorates, 1 other advanced degree awarded. *Degree requirements:* For master's, comprehensive exam; for doctorate, comprehensive exam, thesis/dissertation. *Entrance requirements:* For master's, GRE, coursework in calculus, computer programming, linear algebra, differential equations, and numerical analysis; for doctorate, master's degree. Additional exam requirements/recommendations for international students: Required—TOEFL. Application fee: $60. Electronic applications accepted. *Financial support:* In 2018–19, 1 fellowship with full tuition reimbursement (averaging $25,000 per year), 25 research assistantships with full and partial tuition reimbursements (averaging $19,200 per year) were awarded; scholarships/grants, traineeships, and unspecified assistantships also available. Financial award application deadline: 3/1; financial award applicants required to submit FAFSA. *Faculty research:*

Biostatistics, clinical trials. *Total annual research expenditures:* $451,667. *Unit head:* Dr. Matthew Mayo, Professor and Chair, 913-588-4735 Ext. 913, Fax: 913-588-0252, E-mail: mmayo@kumc.edu. *Application contact:* Dr. Jo A. Wick, Assistant Director of Graduate Education, 913-588-4790, Fax: 913-588-0252, E-mail: jwick@kumc.edu. Website: http://www.kumc.edu/school-of-medicine/department-of-biostatistics.html

University of Kentucky, Graduate School, College of Arts and Sciences, Program in Statistics, Lexington, KY 40506-0032. Offers MS, PhD. *Degree requirements:* For master's, comprehensive exam, thesis optional; for doctorate, comprehensive exam, thesis/dissertation. *Entrance requirements:* For master's, GRE General Test, minimum undergraduate GPA of 2.75; for doctorate, GRE General Test, minimum graduate GPA of 3.0. Additional exam requirements/recommendations for international students: Required—TOEFL (minimum score 550 paper-based). Electronic applications accepted. *Faculty research:* Computer intensive statistical inference, biostatistics, mathematical and applied statistics, applied probability.

The University of Manchester, School of Mathematics, Manchester, United Kingdom. Offers actuarial science (PhD); applied mathematics (M Phil, PhD); applied numerical computing (M Phil, PhD); financial mathematics (M Phil, PhD); mathematical logic (M Phil); probability (M Phil, PhD); pure mathematics (M Phil, PhD); statistics (M Phil, PhD).

The University of Manchester, School of Social Sciences, Manchester, United Kingdom. Offers ethnographic documentary (M Phil); interdisciplinary study of culture (PhD); philosophy (PhD); politics (PhD); social anthropology (PhD); social anthropology with visual media (PhD); social change (PhD); social statistics (PhD); sociology (PhD); visual anthropology (M Phil).

University of Manitoba, Faculty of Graduate Studies, Faculty of Science, Department of Statistics, Winnipeg, MB R3T 2N2, Canada. Offers M Sc, PhD. *Degree requirements:* For master's, thesis or alternative; for doctorate, one foreign language, thesis/dissertation.

University of Manitoba, Faculty of Graduate Studies, Faculty of Science, Program in Mathematical, Computational and Statistical Sciences, Winnipeg, MB R3T 2N2, Canada. Offers MMCSS.

University of Maryland, Baltimore County, The Graduate School, College of Natural and Mathematical Sciences, Department of Mathematics and Statistics, Program in Statistics, Baltimore, MD 21250. Offers biostatistics (PhD); environmental statistics (MS); statistics (MS, PhD). *Program availability:* Part-time, evening/weekend. Terminal master's awarded for partial completion of doctoral program. *Degree requirements:* For master's, comprehensive exam (for some programs), thesis (for some programs); for doctorate, comprehensive exam, thesis/dissertation. *Entrance requirements:* For master's and doctorate, GRE General Test, minimum GPA of 3.0. Additional exam requirements/recommendations for international students: Required—TOEFL (minimum score 600 paper-based; 100 iBT). Electronic applications accepted. *Faculty research:* Design of experiments, statistical decision theory and inference, time series analysis, biostatistics and environmental statistics, bioinformatics.

University of Maryland, College Park, Academic Affairs, College of Computer, Mathematical and Natural Sciences, Department of Mathematics, Program in Mathematical Statistics, College Park, MD 20742. Offers MA, PhD. *Program availability:* Part-time, evening/weekend. Terminal master's awarded for partial completion of doctoral program. *Degree requirements:* For master's, thesis or comprehensive exams, scholarly paper; for doctorate, one foreign language, thesis/dissertation, written and oral exams. *Entrance requirements:* For master's and doctorate, GRE General Test, GRE Subject Test (mathematics), minimum GPA of 3.0, 3 letters of recommendation. Electronic applications accepted. *Faculty research:* Statistics and probability, stochastic processes, nonparametric statistics, space-time statistics.

University of Massachusetts Amherst, Graduate School, College of Natural Sciences, Department of Mathematics and Statistics, Amherst, MA 01003. Offers applied mathematics (MS); mathematics (MS, PhD); statistics (MS, PhD). Terminal master's awarded for partial completion of doctoral program. *Degree requirements:* For master's, thesis or alternative; for doctorate, comprehensive exam, thesis/dissertation. *Entrance requirements:* For master's and doctorate, GRE General Test, GRE Subject Test (mathematics). Additional exam requirements/recommendations for international students: Required—TOEFL (minimum score 550 paper-based; 80 iBT), IELTS (minimum score 6.5). Electronic applications accepted.

University of Memphis, Graduate School, College of Arts and Sciences, Department of Mathematical Sciences, Memphis, TN 38152. Offers applied mathematics (MS); applied statistics (PhD); mathematics (MS, PhD); statistics (MS); teaching of mathematics (MS). *Program availability:* Part-time. *Students:* 35 full-time (11 women), 41 part-time (13 women); includes 33 minority (14 Black or African American, non-Hispanic/Latino; 12 Asian, non-Hispanic/Latino; 5 Hispanic/Latino; 2 Two or more races, non-Hispanic/Latino), 22 international. Average age 34. 35 applicants, 83% accepted, 17 enrolled. In 2018, 10 master's, 5 doctorates awarded. Terminal master's awarded for partial completion of doctoral program. *Degree requirements:* For master's, comprehensive exam, thesis or alternative; for doctorate, one foreign language, comprehensive exam, thesis/dissertation, qualifying exam, final exam. *Entrance requirements:* For master's, GRE General Test, minimum GPA of 2.5, undergraduate degree in math or statistics, two letters of recommendation; for doctorate, GRE General Test, minimum GPA of 2.5, three letters of recommendation. Additional exam requirements/recommendations for international students: Required—TOEFL (minimum score 550 paper-based; 79 iBT). *Application deadline:* For fall admission, 8/1 for domestic students, 5/1 priority date for international students; for spring admission, 12/1 for domestic students, 9/1 priority date for international students. Applications are processed on a rolling basis. Application fee: $35 ($60 for international students). Electronic applications accepted. *Expenses: Tuition, area resident:* Full-time $10,240; part-time $503 per credit hour. *Tuition, state resident:* full-time $10,464. *Tuition,* nonresident: full-time $20,224; part-time $991 per credit hour. *Required fees:* $850; $106 per credit hour. *Financial support:* Fellowships with full tuition reimbursements, research assistantships with full tuition reimbursements, teaching assistantships with full tuition reimbursements, career-related internships or fieldwork, Federal Work-Study, scholarships/grants, and unspecified assistantships available. Financial award application deadline: 2/1; financial award applicants required to submit FAFSA. *Faculty research:* Combinatorics, ergodic theory, graph theory, Ramsey theory, applied statistics. *Unit head:* Dr. Irena Lasiecka, Chair, 901-678-2482, Fax: 901-678-2480, E-mail: lasiecka@memphis.edu. *Application contact:* Dr. Fernanda Botelho, Graduate Advising Coordinator, 901-678-3131, Fax: 901-678-2480, E-mail: mbotelho@memphis.edu. Website: https://www.memphis.edu/msci

University of Michigan, Rackham Graduate School, College of Literature, Science, and the Arts, Department of Statistics, Ann Arbor, MI 48109. Offers applied statistics (MS); data science (MS); statistics (AM, PhD). *Faculty:* 23 full-time (5 women). *Students:* 216 full-time (88 women), 1 part-time (0 women); includes 25 minority (1 Black or African American, non-Hispanic/Latino; 20 Asian, non-Hispanic/Latino; 2 Hispanic/Latino; 2 Two

or more races, non-Hispanic/Latino), 157 international. 1,267 applicants, 27% accepted, 102 enrolled. In 2018, 70 master's, 14 doctorates awarded. Terminal master's awarded for partial completion of doctoral program. *Degree requirements:* For doctorate, comprehensive exam, thesis/dissertation, oral defense of dissertation, preliminary exams. *Entrance requirements:* For master's and doctorate, GRE General Test. Additional exam requirements/recommendations for international students: Required—TOEFL (minimum score 560 paper-based; 84 iBT), IELTS (minimum score 6.5). *Application deadline:* For fall admission, 12/31 for domestic and international students. Application fee: $75 ($90 for international students). Electronic applications accepted. *Financial support:* Fellowships, research assistantships, teaching assistantships, career-related internships or fieldwork, Federal Work-Study, institutionally sponsored loans, scholarships/grants, health care benefits, and unspecified assistantships available. *Faculty research:* Reliability and degradation modeling, biological and legal applications, bioinformatics, statistical computing, covariance estimation. *Unit head:* Prof. Xuming He, Chair, 734-7645981, E-mail: statchair@umich.edu. *Application contact:* Andrea Nashar, PhD Program Coordinator, 734-763-3520, E-mail: statsphdprogram@umich.edu. Website: http://www.lsa.umich.edu/stats/

University of Michigan, Rackham Graduate School, Program in Survey Methodology, Ann Arbor, MI 48109. Offers data science (MS, PhD); social and psychological (MS, PhD); statistical (MS, PhD); survey methodology (Certificate). *Program availability:* Part-time. *Faculty:* 12 full-time (2 women), 8 part-time/adjunct (3 women). *Students:* 26 full-time (16 women), 4 part-time (3 women); includes 24 minority (1 Black or African American, non-Hispanic/Latino; 14 Asian, non-Hispanic/Latino; 1 Hispanic/Latino; 8 Two or more races, non-Hispanic/Latino). Average age 26. 42 applicants, 48% accepted, 13 enrolled. In 2018, 6 master's, 3 doctorates, 2 other advanced degrees awarded. Terminal master's awarded for partial completion of doctoral program. *Degree requirements:* For master's, internships; for doctorate, comprehensive exam, thesis/dissertation. *Entrance requirements:* For master's and doctorate, GRE, 3 letters of recommendation, academic statement of purpose, personal statement, resume or curriculum vitae, academic transcripts; for Certificate, 3 letters of recommendation, academic statement of purpose, personal statement, resume or curriculum vitae, academic transcripts. Additional exam requirements/recommendations for international students: Required—TOEFL (minimum score 560 paper-based; 84 iBT). *Application deadline:* For fall admission, 1/1 for domestic and international students. Application fee: $75 ($90 for international students). Electronic applications accepted. *Expenses:* Contact institution. *Financial support:* In 2018–19, 11 students received support, including 11 research assistantships with full tuition reimbursements available; teaching assistantships, career-related internships or fieldwork, institutionally sponsored loans, scholarships/grants, traineeships, health care benefits, and unspecified assistantships also available. Support available to part-time students. Financial award application deadline: 1/1. *Faculty research:* Survey methodology, web surveys, survey non-response, sample design methods, adaptive survey design. *Total annual research expenditures:* $2.5 million. *Unit head:* Dr. Frederick Conrad, Director, 734-936-1019, Fax: 734-764-8263, E-mail: fconrad@umich.edu. *Application contact:* Jill Esau, Educational Programs Administrator, 734-647-4620, Fax: 734-764-8263, E-mail: jesau@umich.edu. Website: http://psm.isr.umich.edu/

University of Minnesota, Twin Cities Campus, Graduate School, College of Liberal Arts, School of Statistics, Minneapolis, MN 55455-0213. Offers MS, PhD. *Program availability:* Part-time. Terminal master's awarded for partial completion of doctoral program. *Degree requirements:* For doctorate, comprehensive exam, thesis/dissertation. *Entrance requirements:* For master's and doctorate, GRE General Test. Additional exam requirements/recommendations for international students: Required—TOEFL (minimum score 100 iBT). Electronic applications accepted. *Faculty research:* Data analysis, statistical computing, experimental design, probability theory, Bayesian inference, risk analysis.

University of Missouri, Office of Research and Graduate Studies, College of Arts and Science, Department of Statistics, Columbia, MO 65211. Offers MA, PhD. *Entrance requirements:* For master's, GRE General Test, minimum GPA of 3.0 in math and statistics courses; bachelor's degree from accredited college/university in related area; for doctorate, GRE General Test, minimum GPA of 3.0, 3.5 in math/statistics. Additional exam requirements/recommendations for international students: Required—TOEFL.

University of Missouri–Kansas City, College of Arts and Sciences, Department of Mathematics and Statistics, Kansas City, MO 64110-2499. Offers MA, MS, PhD. PhD (interdisciplinary) offered through the School of Graduate Studies. *Program availability:* Part-time. Terminal master's awarded for partial completion of doctoral program. *Degree requirements:* For master's, written exam; for doctorate, 2 foreign languages, thesis/dissertation, oral and written exams. *Entrance requirements:* For master's, bachelor's degree in mathematics, minimum GPA of 3.0; for doctorate, GMAT or GRE General Test. Additional exam requirements/recommendations for international students: Required—TOEFL (minimum score 550 paper-based; 80 iBT). Electronic applications accepted. *Faculty research:* Numerical analysis, statistics, biostatistics, commutative algebra, differential equations.

University of Nebraska–Lincoln, Graduate College, College of Agricultural Sciences and Natural Resources, Department of Statistics, Lincoln, NE 68588. Offers MS, PhD. *Degree requirements:* For master's, thesis optional. *Entrance requirements:* For master's, GRE General Test. Additional exam requirements/recommendations for international students: Required—TOEFL (minimum score 550 paper-based). Electronic applications accepted. *Faculty research:* Design of experiments, linear models, spatial variability, statistical modeling and inference, sampling.

University of New Brunswick Fredericton, School of Graduate Studies, Faculty of Science, Department of Mathematics and Statistics, Fredericton, NB E3B 5A3, Canada. Offers M Sc, PhD. *Degree requirements:* For master's, thesis; for doctorate, comprehensive exam, thesis/dissertation. *Entrance requirements:* For master's and doctorate, minimum GPA of 3.0. Additional exam requirements/recommendations for international students: Required—TOEFL (minimum score 550 paper-based), TWE (minimum score 4); Recommended—IELTS (minimum score 7). Electronic applications accepted. *Faculty research:* Commutative and non-commutative algebra, combinatorics, mathematical modeling and computation, mathematical biology, classical and quantum gravity, multivariate statistics and spatial statistics.

University of New Mexico, Graduate Studies, College of Arts and Sciences, Department of Mathematics and Statistics, Albuquerque, NM 87131-2039. Offers mathematics (MS, PhD); statistics (MS, PhD). *Program availability:* Part-time. *Students:* Average age 31. 92 applicants, 47% accepted, 22 enrolled. In 2018, 19 master's, 13 doctorates awarded. Terminal master's awarded for partial completion of doctoral program. *Degree requirements:* For master's, comprehensive exam (for some programs), thesis or alternative; for doctorate, one foreign language, comprehensive exam, thesis/dissertation, 4 department seminars. *Entrance requirements:* For master's and doctorate, minimum GPA of 3.0, 3 letters of recommendation, letter of intent.

Peterson's Graduate Programs in the Physical Sciences, Mathematics, Agricultural Sciences, the Environment & Natural Resources 2020

www.petersons.com **245**

Additional exam requirements/recommendations for international students: Required—TOEFL (minimum score 550 paper-based). *Application deadline:* For fall admission, 2/15 priority date for domestic and international students; for spring admission, 11/1 priority date for domestic and international students. Application fee: $50. Electronic applications accepted. *Financial support:* Research assistantships, teaching assistantships, health care benefits, and unspecified assistantships available. Financial award application deadline: 2/15; financial award applicants required to submit FAFSA. *Faculty research:* Pure and applied mathematics, applied statistics, numerical analysis, biostatistics, differential geometry, fluid dynamics, nonparametric curve estimation. *Total annual research expenditures:* $1.2 million. *Unit head:* Dr. Terry Loring, Chair, 505-277-4613, Fax: 505-277-5505, E-mail: loring@math.unm.edu. *Application contact:* Ana Parra Lombard, Coordinator, Program Advisement, 505-277-5250, Fax: 505-277-5505, E-mail: aparra@math.unm.edu.
Website: http://math.unm.edu/

The University of North Carolina at Chapel Hill, Graduate School, College of Arts and Sciences, Department of Statistics and Operations Research, Chapel Hill, NC 27599. Offers operations research (MS, PhD); statistics (MS, PhD). *Degree requirements:* For master's, comprehensive exam, essay or thesis; for doctorate, comprehensive exam, thesis/dissertation. *Entrance requirements:* For master's and doctorate, GRE General Test, GRE Subject Test, minimum GPA of 3.0. Additional exam requirements/recommendations for international students: Required—TOEFL.

The University of North Carolina Wilmington, College of Arts and Sciences, Department of Mathematics and Statistics, Wilmington, NC 28403-3297. Offers applied statistics (Professional Certificate); mathematics (MS). *Program availability:* Part-time. *Degree requirements:* For master's, comprehensive exam, thesis (for some programs). *Entrance requirements:* For master's, GRE General Test, 3 letters of recommendation. Additional exam requirements/recommendations for international students: Required—TOEFL (minimum score 550 paper-based; 79 iBT), IELTS (minimum score 6.5). Electronic applications accepted.

University of North Florida, College of Arts and Sciences, Department of Mathematics and Statistics, Jacksonville, FL 32224. Offers mathematical sciences (MS); statistics (MS). *Program availability:* Part-time, evening/weekend. *Faculty:* 13 full-time (5 women). *Students:* 17 full-time (7 women), 4 part-time (2 women); includes 3 minority (1 Asian, non-Hispanic/Latino; 1 Hispanic/Latino; 1 Two or more races, non-Hispanic/Latino), 6 international. Average age 27. 25 applicants, 44% accepted, 9 enrolled. In 2018, 8 master's awarded. *Degree requirements:* For master's, comprehensive exam, thesis optional. *Entrance requirements:* For master's, GRE General Test, minimum GPA of 3.0 in last 60 hours of course work. Additional exam requirements/recommendations for international students: Required—TOEFL (minimum score 500 paper-based; 61 iBT). *Application deadline:* For fall admission, 8/1 priority date for domestic students, 6/1 for international students; for spring admission, 12/1 priority date for domestic students, 10/1 for international students; for summer admission, 3/15 priority date for domestic students, 2/1 for international students. Application fee: $30. Electronic applications accepted. *Expenses: Tuition, area resident:* Part-time $408.10 per credit hour. Tuition, state resident: part-time $408.10 per credit hour. Tuition, nonresident: part-time $932.61 per credit hour. *Required fees:* $111.81 per credit hour. Tuition and fees vary according to course load, campus/location and program. *Financial support:* In 2018–19, 21 students received support, including 3 teaching assistantships (averaging $5,922 per year); Federal Work-Study, scholarships/grants, tuition waivers (partial), and unspecified assistantships also available. Support available to part-time students. Financial award application deadline: 4/1; financial award applicants required to submit FAFSA. *Faculty research:* Real analysis, number theory, Euclidean geometry. *Total annual research expenditures:* $300. *Unit head:* Dr. Scott H. Hochwald, Chair, 904-620-2653, Fax: 904-620-2818, E-mail: shochwal@unf.edu. *Application contact:* Dr. Amanda Pascale, Director, The Graduate School, 904-620-1360, Fax: 904-620-1362, E-mail: graduateschool@unf.edu.
Website: http://www.unf.edu/coas/math-stat/

University of Notre Dame, The Graduate School, College of Science, Department of Applied and Computational Mathematics and Statistics, Notre Dame, IN 46556. Offers applied and computational mathematics and statistics (PhD); applied statistics (MS); computational finance (MS).

University of Ottawa, Faculty of Graduate and Postdoctoral Studies, Faculty of Science, Ottawa-Carleton Institute of Mathematics and Statistics, Ottawa, ON K1N 6N5, Canada. Offers M Sc, PhD. M Sc, PhD offered jointly with Carleton University. *Program availability:* Part-time. *Degree requirements:* For master's, thesis optional; for doctorate, one foreign language, comprehensive exam, thesis/dissertation. *Entrance requirements:* For master's, honors B Sc degree or equivalent, minimum B average; for doctorate, M Sc, minimum B+ average. Electronic applications accepted. *Faculty research:* Pure mathematics, applied mathematics, probability and statistics.

University of Pennsylvania, Wharton School, Department of Statistics, Philadelphia, PA 19104. Offers MBA, PhD. *Degree requirements:* For doctorate, comprehensive exam, thesis/dissertation. *Entrance requirements:* For master's and doctorate, GRE. Additional exam requirements/recommendations for international students: Required—TOEFL, TWE. *Faculty research:* Nonparametric function estimation, analysis of algorithms, time series analysis, observational studies, inference.

University of Pittsburgh, Kenneth P. Dietrich School of Arts and Sciences, Department of Statistics, Pittsburgh, PA 15260. Offers applied statistics (MA, MS); statistics (MA, MS, PhD). *Program availability:* Part-time. Terminal master's awarded for partial completion of doctoral program. *Degree requirements:* For master's, thesis (for some programs); for doctorate, comprehensive exam, thesis/dissertation. *Entrance requirements:* For master's and doctorate, 3 semesters of calculus, 1 semester of linear algebra, 1 year of mathematical statistics. Additional exam requirements/recommendations for international students: Required—TOEFL (minimum score 90 iBT). Electronic applications accepted. *Faculty research:* Multivariate analysis, time series, quantile research analysis, stochastic models, high dimensional statistical inference.

University of Regina, Faculty of Graduate Studies and Research, Faculty of Science, Department of Mathematics and Statistics, Regina, SK S4S 0A2, Canada. Offers mathematics (M Sc, PhD); statistics (M Sc, PhD). *Program availability:* Part-time. *Faculty:* 24 full-time (4 women), 7 part-time/adjunct (4 women). *Students:* 31 full-time (16 women), 5 part-time (1 woman). Average age 30. 45 applicants, 67% accepted, 6 enrolled. In 2018, 8 master's, 1 doctorate awarded. *Degree requirements:* For master's, thesis (for some programs), course work; for doctorate, comprehensive exam, thesis/dissertation, course work, seminar, original research. *Entrance requirements:* For master's, graduating average of 75% from 4 years bachelor degree (or equivalent); for doctorate, applicants must have obtained a thesis-based Master's degree in the discipline to qualify as a doctoral student. Applicants must have academic credentials consistent with being fully-qualified to undertake graduate work at the doctoral level. Additional exam requirements/recommendations for international students: Required—TOEFL (minimum score 580 paper-based; 80 iBT), IELTS (minimum score 6.5), PTE (minimum score 59), other options are CAEL, MELAB, Cantest and U of R ESL. *Application deadline:* For fall admission, 1/31 for domestic and international students; for winter admission, 6/30 for domestic and international students. Application fee: $100. Electronic applications accepted. *Expenses:* Estimated tuition and fees for one academic year is 6,702.90 for master's. The fee will vary base on your choice program. For doctoral program one academic year is estimated 14,129.40. International students will pay additional 1,191.75 for international surcharge per semester. *Financial support:* Fellowships, research assistantships, teaching assistantships, career-related internships or fieldwork, Federal Work-Study, scholarships/grants, unspecified assistantships, and travel award and Graduate Scholarship Base funds available. Support available to part-time students. Financial award application deadline: 9/30. *Faculty research:* Actuarial mathematics, algebra, discrete mathematics, number theory, analysis, geometry and topology, statistics and probability theory. *Unit head:* Dr. Shaun Fallat, Department Head, 306-585-4148, Fax: 306-585-4020, E-mail: mathstat.head@uregina.ca. *Application contact:* Dr. Donald Stanley, Graduate Coordinator, 306-585-4343, Fax: 306-585-4020, E-mail: Donald.Stanley@uregina.ca.
Website: http://www.uregina.ca/science/mathstat/

University of Rhode Island, Graduate School, College of Arts and Sciences, Department of Computer Science and Statistics, Kingston, RI 02881. Offers computer science (MS, PhD); cyber security (PSM, Graduate Certificate); digital forensics (Graduate Certificate). *Program availability:* Part-time, evening/weekend, 100% online, blended/hybrid learning. *Faculty:* 18 full-time (5 women). *Students:* 27 full-time (15 women), 98 part-time (22 women); includes 16 minority (3 Black or African American, non-Hispanic/Latino; 5 Asian, non-Hispanic/Latino; 8 Hispanic/Latino), 14 international. 78 applicants, 88% accepted, 50 enrolled. In 2018, 34 master's, 2 doctorates, 23 other advanced degrees awarded. Terminal master's awarded for partial completion of doctoral program. *Entrance requirements:* Additional exam requirements/recommendations for international students: Required—TOEFL. *Application deadline:* For fall admission, 7/15 for domestic students, 2/1 for international students; for spring admission, 11/15 for domestic students, 7/15 for international students. Application fee: $65. Electronic applications accepted. *Expenses: Tuition, area resident:* Full-time $13,226; part-time $735 per credit. Tuition, state resident: full-time $13,226; part-time $735 per credit. Tuition, nonresident: full-time $25,854; part-time $1436 per credit. *International tuition:* $25,854 full-time. *Required fees:* $1698; $50 per credit. $35 per semester. One-time fee: $165. *Financial support:* In 2018–19, 1 research assistantship with tuition reimbursement (averaging $8,862 per year), 12 teaching assistantships with tuition reimbursements (averaging $16,443 per year) were awarded; unspecified assistantships also available. Financial award application deadline: 2/1; financial award applicants required to submit FAFSA. *Unit head:* Dr. Lisa DiPippo, Chair, 401-874-2701, Fax: 401-874-4617, E-mail: dipippo@cs.uri.edu. *Application contact:* Lutz Hamel, Graduate Program Director, 401-874-2701, E-mail: lutzhamel@uri.edu.
Website: http://www.cs.uri.edu/

University of Rochester, School of Medicine and Dentistry, Graduate Programs in Medicine and Dentistry, Department of Biostatistics and Computational Biology, Programs in Statistics, Rochester, NY 14642. Offers bioinformatics and computational biology (PhD). *Expenses: Tuition:* Full-time $52,974; part-time $1654 per credit hour. *Required fees:* $612. One-time fee: $30 part-time. Tuition and fees vary according to campus/location and program.

University of Saskatchewan, College of Graduate and Postdoctoral Studies, College of Arts and Science, Department of Mathematics and Statistics, Saskatoon, SK S7N 5A2, Canada. Offers M Math, M Sc, PhD. *Degree requirements:* For master's, thesis (for some programs); for doctorate, comprehensive exam (for some programs), thesis/dissertation. *Entrance requirements:* Additional exam requirements/recommendations for international students: Required—TOEFL (minimum score 80 iBT); Recommended—IELTS (minimum score 6.5). Electronic applications accepted.

University of South Africa, College of Economic and Management Sciences, Pretoria, South Africa. Offers accounting (D Admin, D Com); accounting science (DA); auditing (D Admin, D Com); business administration (M Tech); business economics (D Admin); business leadership (DBL); business management (D Admin, D Com); economic management analysis (M Tech); economics (D Admin, D Com, PhD); human resource development (M Tech); industrial psychology (D Admin, D Com, PhD); logistics (D Com); marketing (M Tech); public administration (D Admin, D Com, DPA, PhD); public management (M Tech); quantitative management (D Admin, D Com); real estate (M Tech); statistics (D Admin, PhD); tourism management (D Admin, D Com); transport economics (D Admin, D Com).

University of South Carolina, The Graduate School, College of Arts and Sciences, Department of Statistics, Columbia, SC 29208. Offers applied statistics (CAS); industrial statistics (MIS); statistics (MS, PhD). *Program availability:* Part-time, evening/weekend, online learning. Terminal master's awarded for partial completion of doctoral program. *Degree requirements:* For master's, thesis; for doctorate, comprehensive exam, thesis/dissertation. *Entrance requirements:* For master's, GRE General Test or GMAT, 2 years of work experience (MIS); for doctorate, GRE General Test; for CAS, GRE General Test or GMAT. Additional exam requirements/recommendations for international students: Required—TOEFL (minimum score 600 paper-based; 100 iBT). Electronic applications accepted. *Expenses:* Contact institution. *Faculty research:* Reliability, environmentrics, statistics computing, psychometrics, bioinformatics.

University of Southern California, Graduate School, Dana and David Dornsife College of Letters, Arts and Sciences, Department of Mathematics, Los Angeles, CA 90089. Offers applied mathematics (MA, MS, PhD); mathematical finance (MS); mathematics (MA, PhD); statistics (MS). *Program availability:* Part-time. Terminal master's awarded for partial completion of doctoral program. *Degree requirements:* For master's, comprehensive exam (for some programs), thesis (for some programs); for doctorate, one foreign language, comprehensive exam, thesis/dissertation. *Entrance requirements:* For master's, GRE General Test, GMAT; for doctorate, GRE General Test, GRE Subject Test (mathematics). Additional exam requirements/recommendations for international students: Required—TOEFL (minimum score 100 iBT). Electronic applications accepted. *Faculty research:* Algebra, algebraic geometry and number theory, analysis/partial differential equations, applied mathematics, financial mathematics, probability, combinatorics and statistics.

University of Southern Maine, College of Science, Technology, and Health, Program in Statistics, Portland, ME 04103. Offers MS, CGS. *Faculty research:* Environmental statistics, statistical quality control, survival and reliability analysis, design of experiments, statistical data mining, queueing system, operations research, generalized linear models.

University of South Florida, College of Arts and Sciences, Department of Mathematics and Statistics, Tampa, FL 33620-9951. Offers mathematics (MA, PhD), including pure and applied mathematics, statistics (PhD); statistics (MA). *Program availability:* Part-time, evening/weekend. *Faculty:* 24 full-time (2 women). *Students:* 65 full-time (24 women), 16 part-time (3 women); includes 8 minority (2 Black or African American, non-Hispanic/Latino; 2 Asian, non-Hispanic/Latino; 1 Hispanic/Latino; 3 Two or more races,

non-Hispanic/Latino), 43 international. Average age 29. 77 applicants, 57% accepted, 22 enrolled. In 2018, 14 master's, 11 doctorates awarded. Terminal master's awarded for partial completion of doctoral program. *Degree requirements:* For master's, comprehensive exam, thesis (for some programs); for doctorate, comprehensive exam, thesis/dissertation. *Entrance requirements:* For master's, GRE (minimum 55th percentile Quantitative score; Verbal and Analytical Writing scores also considered), BA in mathematical sciences, statistics, or related area. 3.00 GPA in undergraduate math courses, and in Elementary Abstract Algebra, Bridge to Abstract Mathematics, and Intermediate Analysis (for Math) 3.50 GPA (for Statistics). 3 letters of recommendation; Dept Application with goals statement; TA application; for doctorate, GRE (minimum 55th percentile Quantitative; Verbal and Analytical Writing scores also considered), minimum GPA of 3.5 in graduate mathematics courses, three letters of recommendation, statement of goals, master's or bachelor's degree in mathematical sciences or related field. Department Application, TA Application. Additional exam requirements/recommendations for international students: Required—TOEFL, TOEFL (minimum score 550 paper-based; 79 iBT) or IELTS (minimum score 6.5). *Application deadline:* For fall admission, 2/1 priority date for domestic and international students; for spring admission, 10/1 priority date for domestic students, 9/15 for international students. Application fee: $30. Electronic applications accepted. *Expenses:* Tuition, state resident: full-time $6350. Tuition, nonresident: full-time $19,048. *International tuition:* $19,048 full-time. *Required fees:* $2079. *Financial support:* In 2018–19, 9 students received support, including 6 research assistantships (averaging $16,990 per year), 55 teaching assistantships with partial tuition reimbursements available (averaging $13,742 per year); unspecified assistantships also available. Financial award application deadline: 2/1. *Faculty research:* Mathematics: algebra and number theory, harmonic and complex analysis, approximation theory, theory of orthogonal polynomials, Banach space theory and operator theory, differential equations and nonlinear analysis, discrete mathematics, geometry and topology; statistics: linear and nonlinear statistical models for health sciences, operations research problems, economic systems; stochastic control problems; dynamic reliability analysis and control. *Total annual research expenditures:* $654,045. *Unit head:* Dr. Leslaw Skrzypek, Associate Professor and Chairperson, 813-974-1268, Fax: 813-974-2700, E-mail: skrzypek@usf.edu. *Application contact:* Dr. Brian Curtin, Professor/Director of Graduate Mathematics Program, 813-974-4929, E-mail: bcurtin@usf.edu.
Website: http://math.usf.edu/

The University of Tennessee, Graduate School, College of Business Administration, Department of Statistics, Knoxville, TN 37996. Offers industrial statistics (MS); statistics (MS). *Program availability:* Part-time. *Degree requirements:* For master's, thesis or alternative. *Entrance requirements:* For master's, GMAT or GRE General Test, minimum GPA of 2.7. Additional exam requirements/recommendations for international students: Required—TOEFL. Electronic applications accepted.

The University of Tennessee, Graduate School, College of Business Administration, Program in Business Administration, Knoxville, TN 37996. Offers accounting (PhD); finance (MBA, PhD); logistics and transportation (MBA, PhD); management (PhD); marketing (MBA, PhD); operations management (MBA); professional business administration (MBA); statistics (PhD); JD/MBA; MS/MBA; Pharm D/MBA. Pharm D/MBA offered jointly with The University of Tennessee Health Science Center. *Accreditation:* AACSB. *Program availability:* Online learning. *Degree requirements:* For master's, thesis or alternative; for doctorate, thesis/dissertation. *Entrance requirements:* For master's and doctorate, GMAT, minimum GPA of 2.7. Additional exam requirements/recommendations for international students: Required—TOEFL. Electronic applications accepted.

The University of Texas at Austin, Graduate School, College of Natural Sciences, Division of Statistics and Scientific Computation, Austin, TX 78712-1111. Offers statistics (MS, PhD). *Entrance requirements:* For master's, GRE General Test; for doctorate, GRE General Test, letters of recommendation, bachelor's degree from accredited college or university, minimum GPA of 3.0, statement of purpose, curriculum vitae or resume. Additional exam requirements/recommendations for international students: Required—TOEFL or IELTS.

The University of Texas at Dallas, School of Natural Sciences and Mathematics, Department of Mathematical Sciences, Richardson, TX 75080. Offers actuarial science (MS); mathematics (MS, PhD), including applied mathematics, data science (MS), engineering mathematics (MS), mathematics (MS); statistics (MS, PhD). *Program availability:* Part-time, evening/weekend. *Faculty:* 29 full-time (6 women), 3 part-time/adjunct (0 women). *Students:* 155 full-time (58 women), 35 part-time (9 women); includes 34 minority (4 Black or African American, non-Hispanic/Latino; 19 Asian, non-Hispanic/Latino; 7 Hispanic/Latino; 4 Two or more races, non-Hispanic/Latino), 116 international. Average age 32. 264 applicants, 37% accepted, 48 enrolled. In 2018, 48 master's, 11 doctorates awarded. *Degree requirements:* For master's, thesis optional; for doctorate, thesis/dissertation. *Entrance requirements:* For master's, GRE General Test, minimum GPA of 3.0 in upper-level course work in field; for doctorate, GRE General Test, minimum GPA of 3.5 in upper-level course work in field. Additional exam requirements/recommendations for international students: Required—TOEFL (minimum score 550 paper-based). *Application deadline:* For fall admission, 7/15 for domestic students, 5/1 priority date for international students; for spring admission, 11/15 for domestic students, 9/1 priority date for international students. Applications are processed on a rolling basis. Application fee: $50 ($100 for international students). Electronic applications accepted. *Expenses: Tuition, area resident:* Full-time $13,458. Tuition, state resident: full-time $13,458. Tuition, nonresident: full-time $26,852. *International tuition:* $26,852 full-time. Tuition and fees vary according to course load. *Financial support:* In 2018–19, 92 students received support, including 10 research assistantships (averaging $24,110 per year), 89 teaching assistantships with partial tuition reimbursements available (averaging $17,110 per year); fellowships, career-related internships or fieldwork, Federal Work-Study, institutionally sponsored loans, scholarships/grants, and unspecified assistantships also available. Support available to part-time students. Financial award application deadline: 4/30; financial award applicants required to submit FAFSA. *Faculty research:* Sequential analysis, applications in semiconductor manufacturing, medical image analysis, computational anatomy, information theory, probability theory. *Unit head:* Dr. Vladimir Dragovic, Department Head, 972-883-2161, Fax: 972-883-6622, E-mail: utdmath@utdallas.edu. *Application contact:* Evangelina Bustamante, Graduate Student Coordinator, 972-883-2163, Fax: 972-883-6622, E-mail: utdmath@utdallas.edu.
Website: http://www.utdallas.edu/math

The University of Texas at El Paso, Graduate School, College of Science, Department of Mathematical Sciences, El Paso, TX 79968-0001. Offers mathematics (MAT, MS); statistics (MS). *Program availability:* Part-time, evening/weekend. *Degree requirements:* For master's, thesis optional. *Entrance requirements:* For master's, minimum GPA of 3.0, letters of recommendation. Additional exam requirements/recommendations for international students: Required—TOEFL; Recommended—IELTS. Electronic applications accepted.

The University of Texas at San Antonio, College of Business, Department of Management Science and Statistics, San Antonio, TX 78249-0617. Offers applied statistics (MS, PhD); management science (MBA). *Accreditation:* AACSB. *Program availability:* Part-time, evening/weekend. *Degree requirements:* For master's, comprehensive exam (for some programs), thesis or alternative; for doctorate, comprehensive exam, thesis/dissertation. *Entrance requirements:* For master's, GMAT, minimum of 36 semester credit hours of coursework beyond any hours acquired in the MBA-leveling courses; statement of purpose; for doctorate, GRE, minimum cumulative GPA of 3.3 in the last 60 hours of coursework; transcripts from all colleges and universities attended; curriculum vitae; statement of academic work experiences, interests, and goals; three letters of recommendation, BA, BS, or MS in mathematics, statistics, or closely-related field. Additional exam requirements/recommendations for international students: Required—TOEFL (minimum score 550 paper-based; 79 iBT), IELTS (minimum score 6.5). Electronic applications accepted. *Faculty research:* Statistical signal processing, reliability and life-testing experiments, modeling decompression sickness using survival analysis.

The University of Toledo, College of Graduate Studies, College of Natural Sciences and Mathematics, Department of Mathematics, Toledo, OH 43606-3390. Offers applied mathematics (MS, PhD); statistics (MS, PhD). *Program availability:* Part-time. *Degree requirements:* For master's, comprehensive exam (for some programs), thesis (for some programs); for doctorate, 2 foreign languages, thesis/dissertation. *Entrance requirements:* For master's and doctorate, GRE General Test, GRE Subject Test, minimum cumulative point-hour ratio of 2.7 for all previous academic work, three letters of recommendation, statement of purpose, transcripts from all prior institutions attended. Additional exam requirements/recommendations for international students: Required—TOEFL (minimum score 550 paper-based; 80 iBT). Electronic applications accepted.

University of Toronto, School of Graduate Studies, Faculty of Arts and Science, Department of Statistical Sciences, Toronto, ON M5S 1A1, Canada. Offers M Sc, PhD. *Program availability:* Part-time. *Degree requirements:* For doctorate, comprehensive exam, thesis/dissertation. *Entrance requirements:* For master's, GRE (recommended for students educated outside of Canada), 3 letters of reference; for doctorate, GRE (recommended for students educated outside of Canada), 3 letters of reference, M Stat or equivalent, minimum B+ average. Additional exam requirements/recommendations for international students: Required—TOEFL (minimum score 580 paper-based; 93 iBT), TWE (minimum score 4). Electronic applications accepted.

University of Utah, Graduate School, College of Education, Department of Educational Psychology, Salt Lake City, UT 84112. Offers clinical mental health counseling (M Ed); counseling psychology (PhD); elementary education (M Ed); instructional design and educational technology (M Ed); instructional design and technology (MS); learning and cognition (MS, PhD); reading and literacy (M Ed, PhD); school counseling (M Ed); school psychology (M Ed, PhD, Ed S); statistics (M Stat). *Accreditation:* APA (one or more programs are accredited). *Faculty:* 20 full-time (12 women), 50 part-time/adjunct (34 women). *Students:* 127 full-time (93 women), 92 part-time (63 women); includes 33 minority (1 Black or African American, non-Hispanic/Latino; 7 Asian, non-Hispanic/Latino; 18 Hispanic/Latino; 1 Native Hawaiian or other Pacific Islander, non-Hispanic/Latino; 6 Two or more races, non-Hispanic/Latino), 5 international. Average age 32. 296 applicants, 27% accepted, 73 enrolled. In 2018, 68 master's, 10 doctorates, 3 other advanced degrees awarded. Terminal master's awarded for partial completion of doctoral program. *Degree requirements:* For master's, thesis (for some programs); for doctorate, thesis/dissertation. *Entrance requirements:* For master's and doctorate, GRE General Test, minimum GPA of 3.0. Additional exam requirements/recommendations for international students: Required—TOEFL (minimum score 80 iBT). *Application deadline:* For fall admission, 12/15 for domestic and international students; for winter admission, 11/1 for domestic and international students; for spring admission, 3/15 for domestic and international students. Application fee: $55 ($65 for international students). Electronic applications accepted. *Expenses:* Contact institution. *Financial support:* In 2018–19, 72 students received support, including 6 fellowships with full and partial tuition reimbursements available (averaging $17,000 per year), 14 research assistantships with full and partial tuition reimbursements available (averaging $15,750 per year), 27 teaching assistantships with full and partial tuition reimbursements available (averaging $15,500 per year); career-related internships or fieldwork, scholarships/grants, traineeships, health care benefits, and unspecified assistantships also available. Financial award application deadline: 4/1; financial award applicants required to submit FAFSA. *Faculty research:* Autism, computer technology and instruction, cognitive behavior, aging, group counseling. *Total annual research expenditures:* $620,935. *Unit head:* Dr. Anne E. Cook, Chair, 801-581-7148, Fax: 801-581-5566, E-mail: anne.cook@utah.edu. *Application contact:* JoLynn N. Yates, Academic Coordinator, 801-581-7148, Fax: 801-581-5566, E-mail: jo.yates@utah.edu.
Website: http://www.ed.utah.edu/edps/

University of Utah, Graduate School, College of Science, Department of Mathematics, Salt Lake City, UT 84112-0090. Offers mathematics (MA, MS, PhD); mathematics teaching (MS); statistics (M Stat). *Program availability:* Part-time. *Faculty:* 45 full-time (4 women), 17 part-time/adjunct (6 women). *Students:* 112 full-time (40 women), 26 part-time (12 women); includes 7 minority (1 Black or African American, non-Hispanic/Latino; 6 Asian, non-Hispanic/Latino), 40 international. Average age 28. 288 applicants, 20% accepted, 25 enrolled. In 2018, 9 master's, 16 doctorates awarded. Terminal master's awarded for partial completion of doctoral program. *Degree requirements:* For master's, comprehensive exam, thesis or alternative, written or oral exam; for doctorate, comprehensive exam, thesis/dissertation, written and oral exam. *Entrance requirements:* For master's and doctorate, GRE Subject Test in math (recommended), Minimum undergraduate GPA of 3.0. Additional exam requirements/recommendations for international students: Required—TOEFL (minimum score 550 paper-based; 80 iBT), GRE (recommended). *Application deadline:* For fall admission, 1/1 for domestic and international students; for spring admission, 11/1 for domestic and international students; for summer admission, 3/15 for domestic and international students. Application fee: $55 ($65 for international students). Electronic applications accepted. *Expenses: Tuition, area resident:* Full-time $7190.66; part-time $2112.48 per year. Tuition, state resident: full-time $7190.66. Tuition, nonresident: full-time $25,195. *Required fees:* $558; $555.04 per unit. Tuition and fees vary according to course level, course load, degree level, program and student level. *Financial support:* In 2018–19, 106 students received support, including 1 fellowship (averaging $20,000 per year), 22 research assistantships with full tuition reimbursements available (averaging $20,000 per year), 73 teaching assistantships with full tuition reimbursements available (averaging $20,000 per year); health care benefits and unspecified assistantships also available. Financial award application deadline: 1/1; financial award applicants required to submit FAFSA. *Faculty research:* Algebraic geometry, applied mathematics, commutative algebra, data science, geometry and topology, materials and microstructure, mathematical biology, number theory, probability, statistics. *Total annual research expenditures:* $4.7 million. *Unit head:* Dr. Davar Khoshnvesian, Chair, 801-581-7870, E-mail: chair@math.utah.edu. *Application contact:* Dr. Elena Cherkaev, Director of Graduate Studies, 801-581-7315, Fax: 801-581-6841, E-mail: elena@math.utah.edu.
Website: http://www.math.utah.edu/

Statistics

University of Utah, Graduate School, Professional Master of Science and Technology Program, Salt Lake City, UT 84112-9016. Offers biotechnology (PSM); computational science (PSM); environmental science (PSM); science instrumentation (PSM). *Program availability:* Part-time. *Degree requirements:* For master's, professional experience project (internship). *Entrance requirements:* For master's, GRE (recommended), minimum undergraduate GPA of 3.0, bachelor's degree from accredited university or college. Additional exam requirements/recommendations for international students: Required—TOEFL (minimum score 550 paper-based; 80 iBT), IELTS (minimum score 6.5). Electronic applications accepted. *Expenses:* Contact institution.

University of Vermont, Graduate College, College of Engineering and Mathematical Sciences, Department of Mathematics and Statistics, Program in Statistics, Burlington, VT 05401. Offers MS. *Entrance requirements:* For master's, GRE General Test. Additional exam requirements/recommendations for international students: Required—TOEFL (minimum score 550 paper-based, 90 iBT) or IELTS (6.5). Electronic applications accepted. *Faculty research:* Applied statistics.

University of Victoria, Faculty of Graduate Studies, Faculty of Science, Department of Mathematics and Statistics, Victoria, BC V8W 2Y2, Canada. Offers M Sc, MA, PhD. *Program availability:* Part-time. *Degree requirements:* For master's, thesis; for doctorate, one foreign language, thesis/dissertation, 3 qualifying exams, candidacy exam. *Entrance requirements:* Additional exam requirements/recommendations for international students: Required—TOEFL (minimum score 575 paper-based), IELTS (minimum score 7). Electronic applications accepted. *Faculty research:* Functional analysis and operator theory, applied ordinary and partial differential equations, discrete mathematics and graph theory.

University of Virginia, College and Graduate School of Arts and Sciences, Department of Statistics, Charlottesville, VA 22903. Offers MS, PhD. *Degree requirements:* For master's, exam; for doctorate, comprehensive exam, thesis/dissertation. *Entrance requirements:* For master's and doctorate, GRE General Test, 3 letters of recommendation. Additional exam requirements/recommendations for international students: Required—TOEFL (minimum score 600 paper-based; 90 iBT), IELTS (minimum score 7). Electronic applications accepted.

University of Washington, Graduate School, College of Arts and Sciences, Department of Statistics, Seattle, WA 98195. Offers MS, PhD. Terminal master's awarded for partial completion of doctoral program. *Degree requirements:* For master's, thesis optional; for doctorate, one foreign language, thesis/dissertation. *Entrance requirements:* For master's and doctorate, GRE General Test, minimum GPA of 3.0. Additional exam requirements/recommendations for international students: Required—TOEFL. *Faculty research:* Mathematical statistics, stochastic modeling, spatial statistics, statistical computing.

University of Washington, Graduate School, School of Public Health, Department of Biostatistics, Seattle, WA 98195. Offers biostatistics (MPH, MS, PhD); statistical genetics (PhD). *Faculty:* 40 full-time (18 women), 6 part-time/adjunct (4 women). *Students:* 80 full-time (44 women), 4 part-time (2 women); includes 13 minority (2 Black or African American, non-Hispanic/Latino; 10 Asian, non-Hispanic/Latino; 1 Hispanic/Latino), 48 international. Average age 27. 357 applicants, 15% accepted, 18 enrolled. In 2018, 7 master's, 8 doctorates awarded. Terminal master's awarded for partial completion of doctoral program. *Degree requirements:* For master's, thesis (for some programs); for doctorate, thesis/dissertation. *Entrance requirements:* Additional exam requirements/recommendations for international students: Required—TOEFL (minimum score 500 paper-based; 80 iBT). *Application deadline:* For fall admission, 12/1 for domestic and international students. Application fee: $85. Electronic applications accepted. *Financial support:* In 2018–19, 14 research assistantships with full tuition reimbursements (averaging $26,592 per year), 28 teaching assistantships with full tuition reimbursements (averaging $62,048 per year) were awarded; traineeships, health care benefits, and tuition for employed students also available. Financial award application deadline: 12/1. *Faculty research:* Cystic Fibrosis, survival analysis, decision theory, biomarkers, longitudinal and multilevel data. *Unit head:* Dr. Patrick Heagerty, Chair/Professor, 206-543-1044, E-mail: bchair@uw.edu. *Application contact:* Biostatistics Admissions, E-mail: bioadmit@uw.edu. Website: http://www.biostat.washington.edu/

University of Waterloo, Graduate Studies and Postdoctoral Affairs, Faculty of Mathematics, Department of Statistics and Actuarial Science, Waterloo, ON N2L 3G1, Canada. Offers actuarial science (M Math, MAS, PhD); biostatistics (PhD); statistics (M Math, PhD); statistics-biostatistics (M Math); statistics-computing (M Math); statistics-finance (M Math). *Degree requirements:* For master's, research paper or thesis; for doctorate, comprehensive exam, thesis/dissertation. *Entrance requirements:* For master's, honors degree in field, minimum B+ average; for doctorate, master's degree, minimum B+ average. Additional exam requirements/recommendations for international students: Required—TOEFL, IELTS, PTE. *Application deadline:* Applications are processed on a rolling basis. Application fee: $125 Canadian dollars. Electronic applications accepted. *Financial support:* Fellowships, research assistantships, teaching assistantships, career-related internships or fieldwork, and scholarships/grants available. *Faculty research:* Data analysis, risk theory, inference, stochastic processes, quantitative finance. Website: https://uwaterloo.ca/statistics-and-actuarial-science/

The University of Western Ontario, School of Graduate and Postdoctoral Studies, Faculty of Science, Department of Statistical and Actuarial Sciences, London, ON N6A 3K7, Canada. Offers M Sc, PhD. *Degree requirements:* For master's, thesis (for some programs); for doctorate, comprehensive exam, thesis/dissertation. *Entrance requirements:* For master's, honours BA with B+ average. Additional exam requirements/recommendations for international students: Required—TOEFL. *Faculty research:* Statistical theory, statistical applications, probability, actuarial science.

University of Windsor, Faculty of Graduate Studies, Faculty of Science, Department of Mathematics and Statistics, Windsor, ON N9B 3P4, Canada. Offers mathematics (M Sc); statistics (M Sc, PhD). *Degree requirements:* For master's, thesis or alternative; for doctorate, comprehensive exam, thesis/dissertation. *Entrance requirements:* For master's, minimum B average; for doctorate, minimum A average. Additional exam requirements/recommendations for international students: Required—TOEFL (minimum score 560 paper-based). Electronic applications accepted. *Faculty research:* Applied mathematics, operational research, fluid dynamics.

University of Wisconsin–Madison, Graduate School, College of Letters and Science, Department of Statistics, Madison, WI 53706-1380. Offers biometry (MS); statistics (MS, PhD). *Program availability:* Part-time. *Degree requirements:* For master's, exam; for doctorate, thesis/dissertation. *Entrance requirements:* For master's and doctorate, GRE. Additional exam requirements/recommendations for international students: Required—TOEFL. Electronic applications accepted. *Faculty research:* Biostatistics, bootstrap and other resampling theory and methods, linear and nonlinear models, nonparametrics, time series and stochastic processes.

University of Wisconsin–Milwaukee, Graduate School, College of Letters and Science, Department of Mathematical Sciences, Milwaukee, WI 53201-0413. Offers mathematics (MS, PhD), including actuarial science, algebra (PhD), applied and computational mathematics (PhD), atmospheric science, foundations of advanced studies (MS), industrial mathematics, probability and statistics (PhD), standard mathematics (MS), statistics (MS), topology (PhD). *Students:* 56 full-time (11 women), 10 part-time (2 women); includes 4 minority (2 Black or African American, non-Hispanic/Latino; 1 Asian, non-Hispanic/Latino; 1 Two or more races, non-Hispanic/Latino), 28 international. Average age 30. 136 applicants, 22% accepted, 20 enrolled. In 2018, 16 master's, 8 doctorates awarded. *Degree requirements:* For master's, comprehensive exam, thesis optional; for doctorate, 2 foreign languages, thesis/dissertation. *Entrance requirements:* Additional exam requirements/recommendations for international students: Required—TOEFL (minimum score 550 paper-based; 79 iBT), IELTS (minimum score 6.5). *Application deadline:* For fall admission, 1/1 priority date for domestic students; for spring admission, 9/1 for domestic students. Application fee: $56 ($96 for international students). Electronic applications accepted. *Financial support:* Fellowships, research assistantships, teaching assistantships, career-related internships or fieldwork, health care benefits, and unspecified assistantships available. Support available to part-time students. Financial award application deadline: 4/15; financial award applicants required to submit FAFSA. *Faculty research:* Algebra, applied mathematics, atmospheric science, probability and statistics, topology. *Unit head:* Richard Stockbridge, Department Chair, 414-229-4568, E-mail: stockbri@uwm.edu. *Application contact:* General Information Contact, 414-229-4982, Fax: 414-229-6967, E-mail: gradschool@uwm.edu. Website: http://www.uwm.edu/dept/math/

Utah State University, School of Graduate Studies, College of Science, Department of Mathematics and Statistics, Logan, UT 84322. Offers industrial mathematics (MS); mathematical sciences (PhD); mathematics (M Math, MS); statistics (MS). *Program availability:* Part-time. Terminal master's awarded for partial completion of doctoral program. *Degree requirements:* For master's, thesis optional, qualifying exam; for doctorate, one foreign language, comprehensive exam, thesis/dissertation. *Entrance requirements:* For master's and doctorate, GRE General Test, minimum GPA of 3.0. Additional exam requirements/recommendations for international students: Required—TOEFL. *Faculty research:* Differential equations, computational mathematics, dynamical systems, probability and statistics, pure mathematics.

Virginia Polytechnic Institute and State University, Graduate School, College of Science, Blacksburg, VA 24061. Offers biological sciences (MS, PhD); biomedical technology development and management (MS); chemistry (MS, PhD); data analysis and applied statistics (MA); economics (PhD); geosciences (MS, PhD); mathematics (MS, PhD); physics (MS, PhD); psychology (MS, PhD); statistics (MS, PhD). *Faculty:* 349 full-time (109 women), 3 part-time/adjunct (2 women). *Students:* 542 full-time (202 women), 39 part-time (19 women); includes 71 minority (11 Black or African American, non-Hispanic/Latino; 1 American Indian or Alaska Native, non-Hispanic/Latino; 18 Asian, non-Hispanic/Latino; 32 Hispanic/Latino; 9 Two or more races, non-Hispanic/Latino), 220 international. Average age 27. 977 applicants, 25% accepted, 110 enrolled. In 2018, 75 master's, 69 doctorates awarded. *Degree requirements:* For master's, comprehensive exam (for some programs), thesis (for some programs); for doctorate, comprehensive exam (for some programs), thesis/dissertation (for some programs). *Entrance requirements:* For master's and doctorate, GRE/GMAT. Additional exam requirements/recommendations for international students: Required—TOEFL (minimum score 90 iBT). *Application deadline:* For fall admission, 8/1 for domestic students, 4/1 for international students; for spring admission, 1/1 for domestic students, 9/1 for international students. Applications are processed on a rolling basis. Application fee: $75. Electronic applications accepted. *Expenses:* Tuition, state resident: full-time $15,510; part-time $739.50 per credit hour. Tuition, nonresident: full-time $29,629; part-time $1490.25 per credit hour. *Required fees:* $2804; $550 per semester. Tuition and fees vary according to course load, campus/location and program. *Financial support:* In 2018–19, 7 fellowships with full tuition reimbursements (averaging $29,657 per year), 260 research assistantships with full tuition reimbursements (averaging $15,888 per year), 383 teaching assistantships with full tuition reimbursements (averaging $18,063 per year) were awarded; unspecified assistantships also available. Financial award application deadline: 3/1; financial award applicants required to submit FAFSA. *Total annual research expenditures:* $27.3 million. *Unit head:* Dr. Sally C. Morton, Dean, 540-231-5422, Fax: 540-231-3380, E-mail: scmorton@vt.edu. *Application contact:* Allison Craft, Executive Assistant, 540-231-6394, Fax: 540-231-3380, E-mail: crafta@vt.edu. Website: http://www.science.vt.edu/

Washington University in St. Louis, The Graduate School, Department of Mathematics, St. Louis, MO 63130-4899. Offers mathematics (MA, PhD); statistics (MA, PhD). Terminal master's awarded for partial completion of doctoral program. *Degree requirements:* For master's, thesis or alternative; for doctorate, thesis/dissertation. *Entrance requirements:* For master's and doctorate, GRE General Test. Additional exam requirements/recommendations for international students: Required—TOEFL. Electronic applications accepted. *Faculty research:* Algebra, algebraic geometry, real and complex analysis, differential geometry, topology, statistics, mathematical statistics, survival analysis, modeling, statistical computing for massive data, Bayesian regularization, bioinformatics, longitudinal and functional data analysis, statistical computation, application of statistics to medicine.

Wayne State University, College of Liberal Arts and Sciences, Department of Mathematics, Detroit, MI 48202. Offers applied mathematics (MA); mathematical statistics (MA); mathematics (MA, MS, PhD). *Faculty:* 18. *Students:* 33 full-time (12 women), 17 part-time (5 women); includes 7 minority (1 Black or African American, non-Hispanic/Latino; 2 Asian, non-Hispanic/Latino; 1 Hispanic/Latino; 3 Two or more races, non-Hispanic/Latino), 28 international. Average age 30. 70 applicants, 40% accepted, 8 enrolled. In 2018, 16 master's, 4 doctorates awarded. *Degree requirements:* For master's, comprehensive exam, thesis (for some programs), essays, oral exams; for doctorate, comprehensive exam, thesis/dissertation. *Entrance requirements:* For master's, twelve semester credits in mathematics beyond sophomore calculus, including advanced calculus and linear or modern algebra; for doctorate, master's degree in mathematics or equivalent level of advancement. Additional exam requirements/recommendations for international students: Required—TOEFL (minimum score 550 paper-based; 79 iBT), TWE (minimum score 5.5), Michigan English Language Assessment Battery (minimum score 85); Recommended—IELTS (minimum score 6.5). Application fee: $50. Electronic applications accepted. *Financial support:* In 2018–19, 33 students received support, including 2 fellowships with tuition reimbursements available (averaging $20,000 per year), 3 research assistantships with tuition reimbursements available (averaging $21,107 per year), 25 teaching assistantships with tuition reimbursements available (averaging $20,216 per year); scholarships/grants, health care benefits, and unspecified assistantships also available. Financial award applicants required to submit FAFSA. *Faculty research:* Algebra, analysis, applied mathematics, geometry and topology, probability and statistics. *Unit head:* Dr. Hengguang Li, Associate Professor and Chair, 313-577-2479, E-mail: li@wayne.edu. *Application contact:* Dr. Hengguang Li, Associate Professor and Chair, 313-577-2479, E-mail: li@wayne.edu. Website: http://clas.wayne.edu/math/

Western Michigan University, Graduate College, College of Arts and Sciences, Department of Statistics, Kalamazoo, MI 49008. Offers MS, PhD, Graduate Certificate.

West Virginia University, Eberly College of Arts and Sciences, Morgantown, WV 26506. Offers biology (MS, PhD); chemistry (MS, PhD); communication studies (MA, PhD); computational statistics (PhD); creative writing (MFA); English (MA, PhD); forensic and investigative science (MS); forensic science (PhD); geography (MA); geology (MA, PhD); history (MA, PhD); legal studies (MLS); mathematics (MS); physics (MS, PhD); political science (MA, PhD); professional writing and editing (MA); psychology (MA); public administration (MPA); social work (MSW); sociology (MA, PhD); statistics (MS). *Program availability:* Part-time, evening/weekend, online learning. *Students:* 803 full-time (434 women), 237 part-time (138 women); includes 99 minority (31 Black or African American, non-Hispanic/Latino; 1 American Indian or Alaska Native, non-Hispanic/Latino; 16 Asian, non-Hispanic/Latino; 25 Hispanic/Latino; 26 Two or more races, non-Hispanic/Latino), 208 international. In 2018, 285 master's, 63 doctorates awarded. Terminal master's awarded for partial completion of doctoral program. *Degree requirements:* For master's, thesis (for some programs); for doctorate, comprehensive exam, thesis/dissertation. *Entrance requirements:* For master's and doctorate, GRE. Additional exam requirements/recommendations for international students: Required—TOEFL (minimum score 600 paper-based); Recommended—TWE. *Application deadline:* For spring admission, 2/15 priority date for domestic and international students. Applications are processed on a rolling basis. Application fee: $45. Electronic applications accepted. *Financial support:* Fellowships with full tuition reimbursements, research assistantships with full tuition reimbursements, teaching assistantships with full tuition reimbursements, career-related internships or fieldwork, Federal Work-Study, institutionally sponsored loans, scholarships/grants, health care benefits, tuition waivers (full and partial), unspecified assistantships, and administrative assistantships available. Financial award application deadline: 2/1; financial award applicants required to submit FAFSA. *Faculty research:* Humanities, social sciences, life science, physical sciences, mathematics. *Unit head:* Dr. Gregory Dunaway, Dean, 304-293-4611, Fax: 304-293-6858, E-mail: gregory.dunaway@mail.wvu.edu. *Application contact:* Dr. Jessica Queener, Director of Graduate Studies, 304-293-7476 Ext. 5205, Fax: 304-293-6858, E-mail: Jessica.queener@mail.wvu.edu.
Website: http://www.as.wvu.edu/

Yale University, Graduate School of Arts and Sciences, Department of Statistics, New Haven, CT 06520. Offers MA, PhD. Terminal master's awarded for partial completion of doctoral program. *Degree requirements:* For doctorate, thesis/dissertation. *Entrance requirements:* For doctorate, GRE General Test, GRE Subject Test.

York University, Faculty of Graduate Studies, Faculty of Science, Program in Mathematics and Statistics, Toronto, ON M3J 1P3, Canada. Offers industrial and applied mathematics (M Sc); mathematics and statistics (MA, PhD). *Program availability:* Part-time. *Degree requirements:* For master's, thesis; for doctorate, one foreign language, comprehensive exam, thesis/dissertation. Electronic applications accepted.

Youngstown State University, College of Graduate Studies, College of Science, Technology, Engineering and Mathematics, Department of Mathematics and Statistics, Youngstown, OH 44555-0001. Offers actuarial science (MS); applied mathematics (MS); computer science (MS); mathematics (MS); secondary/community college mathematics (MS); statistics (MS). *Program availability:* Part-time. *Degree requirements:* For master's, comprehensive exam, thesis optional. *Entrance requirements:* For master's, minimum GPA of 2.7 in computer science and mathematics. Additional exam requirements/recommendations for international students: Required—TOEFL. *Faculty research:* Regression analysis, numerical analysis, statistics, Markov chain, topology and fuzzy sets.

Peterson's Graduate Programs in the Physical Sciences, Mathematics, Agricultural Sciences, the Environment & Natural Resources 2020

www.petersons.com **249**

CHAPMAN UNIVERSITY

Schmid College of Science and Technology
Computational and Data Sciences Program

CHAPMAN
UNIVERSITY
SCHMID COLLEGE OF SCIENCE
AND TECHNOLOGY

Programs of Study

Chapman University's M.S. and Ph.D. in Computational and Data Sciences programs follow a uniquely interdisciplinary approach to solving critically important problems using mathematics, physics, chemistry, biology, statistics, and computing. Whereas computer science involves the pursuit of new frontiers chiefly within the realm of computer software and hardware, computational science practitioners apply the knowledge and power of computing to other science disciplines, whether it be running a costly physics experiment through a computer simulation to save millions, or creating new software that can sift through raw data with a far more strategic and sophisticated eye.

Through modeling, simulation, and study of specific phenomena via computer analysis, data mining and software engineering, students learn to apply extraordinary technology and processes to answer the world's most complex questions in fields including:

- Earth Systems Science
- Bioinformatics and Biotechnology
- Genomics and Drug Design
- Population Genetics
- Economic Science

According to academic forecasters and business analysts, computational and data science is one of the most rapidly emerging areas of study in the nation. Chapman University's graduate programs in computational and data sciences help students find their place in this ever-growing field. Upon graduation, students are greeted with a diverse range of career options: graduates go on to work in aerospace engineering, data science, environmental modeling, medical development, gene sequencing, geology, and meteorology.

More information about this cutting-edge program is available online at chapman.edu/CADS.

Research Facilities

Chapman University is in a period of significant expansion. To further distinguish itself, Chapman University has invested in the new, 140,000 square-foot Keck Center for Science and Technology which opened in fall 2018. The Center features research and teaching labs, a specialized computational sciences laboratory with super-computing room, collaboration areas for student/faculty exchange, graduate student lounges, and much more. More details can be found at chapman.edu/forward.

Chapman University's Schmid College of Science and Technology, home to the computational and date sciences program, is also home to various centers for research, including the Center of Excellence in Computation, Algebra, and Topology (CECAT); the Center of Excellence in Complex and Hyper-complex Analysis (CECHA); and the Center of Excellence in Earth Systems Modeling and Observations (CEESMO). Schmid College faculty are also affiliated with the Institute for Quantum Studies, which hosts a distinguished list of world-renowned physicists, including 2013 Nobel Prize recipient Francois Englert and 2010 Presidential Medal of Honor winner Yakir Aharonov.

Financial Aid

Financial assistance is available in the form of federal loans, department scholarships, teaching assistantships, and research assistantships. Most students receive some form of financial support from the University, and some receive additional aid through the School's industry partnerships.

All students who submit a complete application are automatically considered for a department scholarship. Admitted students are notified of scholarships soon after receiving confirmation of admission.

More information is available at chapman.edu/financial-aid.

Cost of Study

Tuition for the 2019-2020 academic year for both the M.S. and Ph.D. in Computational and Data Sciences programs is $1630 per credit. Tuition amounts are subject to change. Additional details can be found at chapman.edu/GraduatePrograms.

Living and Housing Costs

Information on graduate student housing is available at chapman.edu/students/services/housing-and-residence/on-campus/applying-housing or by calling 714-997-6603.

Location

Chapman University is located in the heart of Orange County, California. Orange County's natural landscape provides endless opportunities for intellectual and recreational exploration. Whether it's a bonfire at the beach or the study of desert habitat, Southern California offers access to both marine and mountain experiences. Whether prospective students are interested in business, the arts, science, or social entrepreneurship, they will find opportunities to learn, acquire skills, and build a resume in Southern California.

Chapman University occupies 76 park-like acres lined with palm and shade trees. A mix of historical and modern buildings makes Chapman one of the most beautiful university campuses in the nation.

Peterson's Graduate Programs in the Physical Sciences, Mathematics, Agricultural Sciences, the Environment & Natural Resources 2020

www.petersons.com **251**

The University and The College

The mission of Chapman University's Schmid College of Science and Technology is to mentor and grow leaders through a curriculum that develops outstanding problem-solving skills in the context of the grand, interdisciplinary challenges facing the world today. As Chapman University moves toward the future, the Schmid College of Science and Technology will be leading the pack with innovative research and hands-on learning experiences.

Faculty

Faculty conduct high-quality research and run several research labs that not only produce excellent research, but also actively involve students in the research process. Students receive first-hand experience in funded research projects of societal importance, have the chance to co-author papers in national recognized journals, and are able to present at national conferences.

In their research, faculty members combine interdisciplinary breadth and collaboration with rigorous disciplinary depth and scholarship. This approach provides students with a modern view of problem solving in today's technologically focused world. Students are encouraged to collaborate with faculty in research, and to experience the exhilaration of making new discoveries or developing advanced software and hardware tools. Additional information is available at chapman.edu/CADS.

Admission Requirements

Applicants to the M.S. and Ph.D. programs in Computational and Data Sciences must complete the following prerequisite courses:

- Differential Equations
- Computer Programming (Data Structures preferred)
- Probability and Statistics

Minimum GRE scores are verbal: 500/153, quantitative: 680/146, and analytical writing: 4.0. For international students, minimum scores on the Test of English as a Foreign Language (TOEFL) are 550 (paper-based) or 80 (Internet-based); International English Language Testing System (IELTS): 6.5; Pearson Test of English (PTE) 53; or Cambridge English Advanced Exam (CAE) 180 minimum.

Further information regarding these and other requirements can be found at chapman.edu/CADS.

Applying

Prospective students should contact the Office of Graduate Admission at 714-997-6711 or gradadmit@chapman.edu with questions or for more information.

Applicants must submit the following:

- Online application for admission ($60 nonrefundable application fee).
- Official transcripts from degree-granting institution, as well as any other institutions where any program prerequisites were taken.
- Graduate Record Exam (GRE) scores are required. GMAT scores may be accepted in lieu of GRE.
- Two letters of recommendation, including one from an academic source which describes the applicant's professional and academic abilities.
- Statement of Intent
- Resume or CV
- Language test scores (international students only)
- Financial Certification Form (international students only)

The application deadline for fall semester enrollment is May 1 for the M.S. and March 15 for the Ph.D. Prospective students should contact the Office of Graduate Admission at 714-997-6711 or gradadmit@chapman.edu for more information.

Correspondence and Information:

Chapman University
One University Drive
Orange, California 92866
United States
Phone: 714-997-6730
E-mail: CADS@chapman.edu
Website: chapman.edu/CADS

252 www.petersons.com

Peterson's Graduate Programs in the Physical Sciences, Mathematics, Agricultural Sciences, the Environment & Natural Resources 2020

NEW YORK UNIVERSITY
Courant Institute of Mathematical Sciences
Department of Mathematics

Programs of Study

New York University's (NYU) Courant Institute of Mathematical Sciences (CIMS) is a highly respected center for research and advanced training in mathematics and computer science. NYU's world-class interdisciplinary graduate programs are known for their cutting-edge training in analysis and applied mathematics, including partial differential equations, differential geometry, dynamical systems, probability and stochastic processes, scientific computation, mathematical physics, and fluid dynamics.

The interdisciplinary focus is one of the greatest strengths of the Courant Institute's graduate programs. Courses, seminars, and research collaborations go far beyond traditional areas of pure and applied mathematics, covering diverse areas such as visual neural science, materials science, atmosphere/ocean science, cardiac fluid dynamics, plasma physics, mathematical genomics, and mathematical finance. Analysis plays a central role that provides a natural bridge between these subjects.

The Mathematics Department at the Courant Institute offers programs leading to Ph.D. degrees in mathematics and atmosphere/ocean science. It also offers Master of Science degrees in mathematics, scientific computing, and mathematical finance.

The Ph.D. degrees in mathematics and in atmosphere/ocean science and mathematics are open to students who wish to pursue a career in academic research and teaching, as well as in the private and public sectors. Consistent with its scientific breadth, the Institute welcomes applicants whose primary background is in quantitative fields such as economics, engineering, physics, or biology, as well as mathematics. Doctoral students take advanced courses in their areas of specialization, followed by a period of research and the preparation and defense of the doctoral thesis. Detailed information about the Ph.D. program in mathematics is available at http://math.nyu.edu/degree/phd/phd.html.

The M.S. degree in mathematics encompasses the basic graduate curriculum in mathematics, and also offers the opportunity of some more specialized training in an area of interest. A typical master's program involves basic courses in real analysis, complex analysis, and linear algebra, followed by other fundamental courses such as probability, scientific computing, and differential equations. Depending on their mathematical interests, students will then be able to take more advanced graduate courses in pure and applied mathematics.

The M.S. degree in scientific computing program provides broad yet rigorous training in areas of mathematics and computer science related to scientific computing. It aims to prepare students with the right talents and background for a technical career doing practical computing. The program accommodates both full-time and part-time students, with most courses meeting in the evening. The program is self-contained and terminal, providing a complete set of skills in a field where the need is greater than the supply. The master's program focuses on computational science, which includes modeling and numerical simulation as used in engineering design, development, and optimization.

The master's degree in mathematics in finance has a strong pragmatic component, including practically oriented courses and student mentoring by finance professionals. Graduates of the program know more finance than most science graduates and have stronger quantitative skills than most business graduates. They start with undergraduate degrees in quantitative subjects such as mathematics, physics, or engineering and are admitted to the program through a highly selective process. Courant's tightly integrated curriculum provides an efficient introduction to the theoretical and computational skills that are genuinely used and valued in the financial industry. The programs special strengths include its ensemble of courses, most created specifically for this program; great depth in relevant areas of applied mathematics; its extensive involvement of Fellows and other finance professionals; and strong participation by permanent faculty in teaching and mentoring students. Response from the finance industry has been very encouraging, with graduates finding excellent jobs in a wide range of quantitative areas.

Areas of Research

The Courant Institute has a tradition of research, which combines pure and applied mathematics, with a high level of interaction between different areas. Below are some of the current areas of research. The choice of categories is somewhat arbitrary, as many faculty have interests that cut across boundaries, and the fields continue to evolve.

- **Algebraic Geometry:** The research focus of the algebraic geometry group at Courant lies at the interface of geometry, topology, and number theory. Of particular interest are problems concerning the existence and distribution of rational points and rational curves on higher-dimensional varieties, group actions and hidden symmetries, as well as rationality, unirationality, and hyperbolicity properties of algebraic varieties.

- **Analysis and PDE:** Most, if not all, physical systems can be modeled by partial differential equations (PDE)—from continuum mechanics (including fluid mechanics and material science) to quantum mechanics or general relativity. The study of PDE has been a central research theme at the Courant Institute since its foundation. Themes are extremely varied, ranging from abstract questions (existence, uniqueness of solutions) to more concrete ones (qualitative or quantitative information on the behavior of solutions, often in relation with simulations).

- **Computational and Mathematical Biology:** Biological applications of mathematics and computing at Courant include genome analysis, biomolecular structure and dynamics, systems biology, embryology, immunology, neuroscience, heart physiology, biofluid dynamics, and medical imaging. The students, researchers, and faculty who work on these questions are pure and applied mathematicians and computer scientists working in close collaboration with biological and medical colleagues at NYU and elsewhere.

- **Dynamical Systems and Ergodic Theory:** The subject of dynamical systems is concerned with systems that evolve over time according to a well-defined rule, which could be either deterministic or probabilistic; examples of such systems arise in almost any field of science. Ergodic theory is a branch of dynamical systems concerned with measure preserving transformation of measure spaces, such as the dynamical systems associated with Hamiltonian mechanics. The theory of dynamical systems has applications in many areas of mathematics, including number theory, PDE, geometry, topology, and mathematical physics.

- **Geometry:** Geometry research at Courant blends differential and metric geometry with analysis and topology. The geometry group has strong ties with analysis and partial differential equations, as there are many PDEs and techniques of interest to both groups, such as Einstein's equations, the minimal surface equation, calculus of variations, and geometric measure theory.

- **Physical Applied Mathematics:** A central theme at the Courant Institute is the study of physical systems using advanced methods of applied mathematics. Currently, areas of focus include fluid dynamics, plasma physics, statistical mechanics, molecular dynamics and dynamical systems. The tradition at the Institute is to investigate fundamental questions as well as to solve problems with direct, real-world applications. In doing so, the people looking into these questions build on the strong synergies and fresh ideas that emerge in the frequent collaboration with analysis and PDE specialists as well as experts in scientific computing at the institute.

- **Probability Theory:** Domains of interest range from stochastic processes to random discrete structures to statistical physics (percolation, random matrices, etc.), which has become more and more central in recent years. Probability theory has natural connections with a number of fields (computational methods, financial mathematics, mathematical physics, dynamical systems, graph theory) since a great number of phenomena can be best modeled or understood by probabilistic means.

- **Scientific Computing:** Courant faculty have interests in stochastic modeling in statistical and quantum mechanics, nonlinear optimization, matrix analysis, high-dimensional data analysis, and numerical solutions of the partial differential equations that lie at the heart of fluid and solid mechanics, plasma physics, acoustics, and electromagnetism. Central to much of this work is the development of robust and efficient algorithms. As these algorithms are applied to increasingly complex problems, significant attention is being devoted to the design of effective and supportable software.

Research Facilities

The Courant Institute Library has one of the nation's most complete and retrospectively rich mathematics collections, including many hard-to-obtain items in languages other than English. Its collection comprises more than 64,000 volumes, including a burgeoning spectrum of electronic books and journals. The library is a campus wireless access point and has a campus network-compatible printing facility.

Peterson's Graduate Programs in the Physical Sciences, Mathematics, Agricultural Sciences, the Environment & Natural Resources 2020

www.petersons.com 253

New York University

Financial Support

Financial support is awarded to students engaging in full-time Ph.D. study, covering tuition, fees, and NYU's individual comprehensive student insurance. In the 2017–18 academic year, it offered a 9-month stipend of $29,408. Summer positions involving teaching, research, or computational projects are available to a number of the Ph.D. students.

Cost of Study

In 2018–19, tuition was calculated at $1,787 per point. Associated fees were $499 for the first point in fall 2017 and spring 2018, and $70 per point thereafter. A full-time program of study normally consists of 24 points per year (four 3-credit courses per term).

Living and Housing Costs

University housing for graduate students is limited. It consists mainly of shared studio apartments in buildings on campus and shared suites in residence halls within walking distance of the University. Information about University housing, including location options and current costs, can be found online at http://www.nyu.edu/life/living-at-nyu.html.

Student Group

In 2019–20, tuition was calculated at $1,856 per point. Associated fees were $509 for the first point in fall 2019 and spring 2020, and $70 per point thereafter. A full-time program of study normally consists of 24 points per year (four 3-credit courses per term).

Faculty

A detailed list of the faculty members and their research can be found at http://www.math.nyu.edu/people/.

Location

The graduate programs at the Courant Institute are offered in the very heart of the world's leading artistic and financial center in downtown Manhattan. The NYU campus is located in historic Greenwich Village, the long-time creative magnet for artists, writers, actors, musicians, and free thinkers.

Applying

The online application can be accessed at http://gsas.nyu.edu/object/grad.admissions.onlineapp. Specific information about admission requirements and applying to the Ph.D. programs in mathematics can be found at http://www.math.nyu.edu/degree/phd/application.html. Application details and admission requirements for the master's degree programs are available at http://www.math.nyu.edu/degree/ms/application.html.

Correspondence and Information

For questions regarding the graduate admissions process:

Graduate School of Arts and Science
Graduate Enrollment Services
New York University
Post Office Box 907, Cooper Station
New York, New York 10276-0907
Phone: 212-998-8050

For further information and questions regarding the programs:

Department of Mathematics
Courant Institute of Mathematical Sciences
New York University
251 Mercer Street
New York, New York 10012-1110
Phone: 212 998-3005
E-mail: admissions@math.nyu.edu
Website: http://www.math.nyu.edu/

254 www.petersons.com

Peterson's Graduate Programs in the Physical Sciences, Mathematics, Agricultural Sciences, the Environment & Natural Resources 2020

UNIVERSITY OF OKLAHOMA
Department of Mathematics

Programs of Study

While the Mathematics Department at the University of Oklahoma (OU) offers three different graduate degrees—M.S., M.A., and Ph.D.—students are considered to be on either of two tracks, the M.S. track or the M.A./Ph.D. track.

The M.A./Ph.D track is the standard program for most students seeking a Ph.D. in mathematics. All students in the program (regardless of their future specialization) need to pass the three Ph.D. qualifying examinations in algebra, analysis, and topology. Each of these exams is associated with a two-semester graduate course sequence that forms the core of the M.A. degree and also count toward the Ph.D. degree. Students who pass all three qualifying examinations can go into the Ph.D. program in one of the following two options.

Ph.D. program (traditional option): This is essentially the same as the M.A./Ph.D. program above. The main difference is that students who already have a master's degree in mathematics may apply directly to this program. Students with a baccalaureate degree apply to the M.A./Ph.D. program and move into the Ph.D. program on successful completion of the Ph.D. qualifying examinations. The student's ultimate goal in this program is to write and defend a dissertation representing an original contribution to research in mathematics.

Ph.D. program (RUME—research in undergraduate mathematics—option): As is the case with the traditional option, students who already have a master's degree in mathematics may apply to this program, while students with a baccalaureate degree apply to the M.A./Ph.D. program. The student's ultimate goal in this program is to write and defend a dissertation representing an original contribution to research in undergraduate mathematics education.

Students with strong mathematical backgrounds are encouraged to take "free shot" attempts at the Ph.D. qualifying examinations, usually held in August, the week before classes start. These attempts are only offered to students when they first enter the program, and results do not go on the student's record unless they pass.

The M.S. track (Master of Science program) is offered by the Mathematics Department for students who want to pursue studies in mathematics beyond the undergraduate level, but who do not plan to obtain a doctorate in mathematics. Recent graduates of the M.S. program have gone on to careers as actuaries, statistical analysts, and software engineers. Some become mathematics teachers in settings ranging from middle school to two- and four-year colleges. Still others have gone on to obtain doctorates and academic positions in fields other than mathematics, such as economics, mathematics education, and computer science.

Students will be able to select from a broad range of options in pure and applied mathematics and in research in undergraduate mathematics education as they pursue their graduate degree, including: (1) Algebra and Number Theory: algebraic geometry, algebraic groups, combinatorics, modular forms, representation theory (real, p-adic, Lie, automorphic); (2) Analysis: global analysis, harmonic analysis, integrable systems, PDEs, signal processing, spectral theory, wavelets and frames; (3) Applied Mathematics and Mathematical Physics: control theory, dynamical systems, modeling; (4) Geometry: convexity, harmonic maps, Riemannian geometry, group actions, non-negative curvature; (5) RUME: research in undergraduate mathematics education, diversity and equity, international comparative education; (6) Topology: algebraic and geometric topology, dimension theory, geometric group theory, hyperbolic geometry, low-dimensional topology, Teichmuller theory.

Additional information about the University's graduate programs in mathematics can be found at http://math.ou.edu/grad.

Research Facilities

Students in the Department have a wide range of facilities and resources to support their study and research efforts. The department maintains Linux file and web servers. There is a workstation cluster for graduate students in the main Department office suite, and smaller computer labs on various floors of the physical sciences building.

At the University level, the OU Information Technology office provides a variety of services to support research and teaching: https://itscnorman.ou.edu.

The OU Supercomputing Center for Education and Research (OSCER) provides top-of-the-line resources to faculty and students. http://www.ou.edu/oscer.

The University Library's LORA system gives students access to MathSciNet, the definitive database of mathematics literature reviews and bibliographical information (available in BibTeX format); JSTOR, and numerous other online databases and resources from off-campus locations.

Graduate students can use the facilities of the Zarrow Family Faculty and Graduate Student Center, located in the lower level of the Bizzell library. Additional resources in the Bizzell library include the Digital Scholarship Lab, Innovation @ the Edge, and the Data Analytics, Visualization and Informatics Syndicate. These facilities are a conveniently located two-minute walk from the Mathematics Department. See https://libraries.ou.edu/services for more details.

Financial Aid

Most students are employed as graduate teaching assistants while earning their degrees. The students' transition into their new roles as educators is facilitated by a robust summer orientation and participation in a highly coordinated course during their first year. Other graduate teaching assistant duties include grading, working in the Mathematics Help Center, and assisting in multi-section courses.

Stipends for graduate teaching assistants start at $19,500 and students are automatically nominated by the graduate committee for addition fellowships of up to $5,000.

Summer support is available in the form of teaching assistantships (with stipends of $3,500-4,500 per course) and research awards (either provided by the Department or by individual faculty research grants).

Further details regarding financial support for graduate students can be found at http://math.ou.edu/grad/financial.php.

Peterson's Graduate Programs in the Physical Sciences, Mathematics, Agricultural Sciences, the Environment & Natural Resources 2020

www.petersons.com   255

University of Oklahoma

Cost of Study

A/Y 2019-20 tuition and fees for graduate students can be found at http://www.ou.edu/admissions/affordability/cost.

Living and Housing Costs

The University offers several on-campus apartment choices. In addition, there are a large number of privately-owned apartments, duplexes, and houses available in Norman. Many off-campus housing locations are served by CART, the Cleveland Area Rapid Transit system, which is free for OU students.

Student Group

The OU mathematics graduate program is composed of about 60 students, representing over a dozen different countries from around the globe. There is an active Mathematics Graduate Student Association which provides guidance and mentoring and organizes various events for graduate students. Additional details about the association can be found online at http://math.ou.edu/~mgsa.

Location

As part of the Southern Great Plains, Oklahoma benefits from both its rich historic heritage and the vital and modern growth of its metropolitan areas. Although by location a suburb of Oklahoma City, Norman is an independent community with a permanent population of more than 110,000. Norman residents enjoy extensive parks and recreation programs and a 10,000-acre lake and park area. Money magazine named Norman as the nation's sixth best place to live in the 2008 edition of its annual rankings.

The University and The Department

The Mathematics Department at the University of Oklahoma has a long and rich academic tradition dating back to the formation of the University in the mid-1890s. We awarded our first master's degree in 1927 and our first doctorate in 1947.

Students who pursue a graduate degree in mathematics at OU become part of a team that is responsible for the instruction of more than 13,000 OU undergraduate students annually. The Department's faculty members maintain a vibrant and collegial research atmosphere and also serve as sources of inspiration, mentoring, and advice. The strong sense of community is enhanced by having faculty, postdoctoral, and student offices, as well as a common room, seminar and conference rooms and instructional classrooms, all housed in the same building.

Prospective graduate students can experience the Mathematics Department in person during OU MathFest, an annual two-day open house held in the spring semester.

Applying

Prospective students should submit their online application and required documents at http://math.ou.edu/grad/admissions.php. If you have any questions, please contact Cristin Sloan, Assistant to the Graduate Director, either by e-mail csloan@ou.edu or by telephone 405-325-2719.

Correspondence and Information

Director of Graduate Studies
University of Oklahoma
Department of Mathematics
601 Elm Street, PHSC 423
Norman, Oklahoma 73019
Phone: 800-522-0772 (toll-free)
E-mail: mathgraddir@ou.edu
Website: http://www.math.ou.edu

THE FACULTY

The Mathematics Department at the University of Oklahoma has 34 permanent faculty members, 8 visiting faculty members, and a support staff of 5 (including a full-time undergraduate adviser). Virtually all of the department's faculty have active research programs (many externally funded) and regularly publish articles in mathematical journals and participate in conferences around the world.

Additional details regarding the Mathematics Department faculty can be found at http://www.math.ou.edu/people/faculty_research.html.

Students walk to class on the Norman campus.

256   www.petersons.com

Peterson's Graduate Programs in the Physical Sciences, Mathematics, Agricultural Sciences, the Environment & Natural Resources 2020

ACADEMIC AND PROFESSIONAL PROGRAMS IN THE AGRICULTURAL SCIENCES

Section 8
Agricultural and Food Sciences

This section contains a directory of institutions offering graduate work in agricultural and food sciences. Additional information about programs listed in the directory may be obtained by writing directly to the dean of a graduate school or chair of a department at the address given in the directory.

For programs offering related work, see also in this book *Natural Resources*. In the other guides in this series:

Graduate Programs in the Humanities, Arts & Social Sciences

See *Architecture (Landscape Architecture)* and *Economics (Agricultural Economics and Agribusiness)*

Graduate Programs in the Biological/Biomedical Sciences & Health-Related Medical Professions

See *Biological and Biomedical Sciences; Botany and Plant Biology; Ecology, Environmental Biology, and Evolutionary Biology; Entomology; Genetics, Developmental Biology, and Reproductive Biology; Nutrition; Pathology and Pathobiology; Physiology; Veterinary Medicine and Sciences; and Zoology*

Graduate Programs in Engineering & Applied Sciences

See *Agricultural Engineering and Bioengineering* and *Biomedical Engineering and Biotechnology*

Graduate Programs in Business, Education, Information Studies, Law & Social Work

See *Education (Agricultural Education)*

CONTENTS

Program Directories

Featured School: Display and Close-Up

Agricultural Sciences—General

Alabama Agricultural and Mechanical University, School of Graduate Studies, College of Agricultural, Life and Natural Sciences, Huntsville, AL 35811. Offers MS, MURP, PhD. *Program availability:* Part-time, evening/weekend. Terminal master's awarded for partial completion of doctoral program. *Degree requirements:* For doctorate, one foreign language, thesis/dissertation. *Entrance requirements:* For master's, GRE General Test; for doctorate, GRE General Test, MS. Additional exam requirements/recommendations for international students: Required—TOEFL (minimum score 500 paper-based; 61 iBT). Electronic applications accepted. *Faculty research:* Remote sensing, environmental pollutants, food biotechnology, plant growth.

Alcorn State University, School of Graduate Studies, School of Agriculture and Applied Sciences, Lorman, MS 39096-7500. Offers agricultural economics (MS Ag); agronomy (MS Ag); animal science (MS Ag). *Degree requirements:* For master's, thesis optional. *Faculty research:* Aquatic systems, dairy herd improvement, fruit production, alternative farming practices.

Angelo State University, College of Graduate Studies and Research, College of Science and Engineering, Department of Agriculture, San Angelo, TX 76909. Offers agriculture (M Ag). *Program availability:* Part-time, evening/weekend. *Students:* 15 full-time (9 women), 5 part-time (2 women); includes 3 minority (all Hispanic/Latino). Average age 25. *Degree requirements:* For master's, comprehensive exam, thesis (for MS). *Entrance requirements:* For master's, GRE General Test, essay. *Application deadline:* For fall admission, 7/15 priority date for domestic students, 6/10 for international students; for spring admission, 12/1 priority date for domestic students, 11/1 for international students. Applications are processed on a rolling basis. Application fee: $40 ($50 for international students). Electronic applications accepted. *Expenses: Tuition, area resident:* Full-time $3964; part-time $220 per credit hour. Tuition, state resident: full-time $3964; part-time $220 per credit hour. Tuition, nonresident: full-time $11,434; part-time $635 per credit hour. *International tuition:* $11,434 full-time. *Financial support:* Research assistantships, Federal Work-Study, scholarships/grants, and unspecified assistantships available. Support available to part-time students. Financial award application deadline: 3/1. *Faculty research:* Effect of protein and energy on feedlot performance, bitterweed toxicosis in sheep, meat laboratory, North Concho Watershed Project, baseline vegetation. *Unit head:* Dr. Micheal Salisbury, Chair, 325-942-2027, E-mail: mike.salisbury@angelo.edu. *Application contact:* Dr. Loree Branham, Graduate Advisor, 325-486-6749, E-mail: loree.branham@angelo.edu.
Website: http://www.angelo.edu/dept/agriculture/

Arkansas State University, Graduate School, College of Agriculture and Technology, State University, AR 72467. Offers agricultural education (SCCT); agriculture (MSA); vocational-technical administration (SCCT). *Program availability:* Part-time. *Degree requirements:* For master's, comprehensive exam, thesis or alternative; for SCCT, comprehensive exam. *Entrance requirements:* For master's, GRE General Test or MAT, appropriate bachelor's degree, official transcripts, immunization records; for SCCT, GRE General Test or MAT, interview, master's degree, official transcript, immunization records. Additional exam requirements/recommendations for international students: Required—TOEFL (minimum score 550 paper-based; 79 iBT), IELTS (minimum score 6), PTE (minimum score 56). Electronic applications accepted.

Auburn University, Graduate School, College of Agriculture, Auburn University, AL 36849. Offers M Ag, M Aq, MS, PhD. *Program availability:* Part-time. *Degree requirements:* For doctorate, thesis/dissertation. *Entrance requirements:* For master's and doctorate, GRE General Test. Electronic applications accepted. *Expenses:* Tuition, state resident: full-time $11,282; part-time $535 per credit hour. Tuition, nonresident: full-time $30,542; part-time $1605 per credit hour. *Required fees:* $826 per semester. Tuition and fees vary according to degree level and program.

Brigham Young University, Graduate Studies, College of Life Sciences, Provo, UT 84602. Offers MPH, MS, PhD. *Degree requirements:* For master's, comprehensive exam, thesis, prospectus. defense of research, defense of thesis; for doctorate, comprehensive exam, thesis/dissertation, prospectus, defense of research, defense of dissertation. *Entrance requirements:* For master's, GRE General Test, minimum GPA of 3.2 for last 60 hours of course work; for doctorate, GRE General Test, GRE Subject Test (biology), minimum GPA of 3.2 for last 60 hours of course work. Additional exam requirements/recommendations for international students: Required—TOEFL (minimum score 580 paper-based; 85 iBT), IELTS (minimum score 7). Electronic applications accepted. *Expenses:* Contact institution. *Faculty research:* Biology, microbiology, molecular biology, physiology, environmental science.

California Polytechnic State University, San Luis Obispo, College of Agriculture, Food and Environmental Sciences, Department of Agriculture, San Luis Obispo, CA 93407. Offers MS. *Program availability:* Part-time. *Faculty:* 16 full-time (5 women). *Students:* 27 full-time (19 women), 15 part-time (8 women); includes 14 minority (7 Asian, non-Hispanic/Latino; 6 Hispanic/Latino; 1 Two or more races, non-Hispanic/Latino), 1 international. Average age 26. 35 applicants, 40% accepted, 14 enrolled. In 2018, 29 master's awarded. *Degree requirements:* For master's, thesis. *Entrance requirements:* For master's, GRE. Additional exam requirements/recommendations for international students: Required—TOEFL (minimum score 80 iBT). *Application deadline:* For fall admission, 4/1 for domestic and international students; for winter admission, 10/1 for domestic students, 6/30 for international students; for spring admission, 10/1 for domestic students. Applications are processed on a rolling basis. Application fee: $55. Electronic applications accepted. *Expenses: Tuition, area resident:* Full-time $7176; part-time $4164 per year. Tuition, state resident: full-time $10,965. Tuition, nonresident: full-time $10,965. *Required fees:* $6336; $3711. *Financial support:* Fellowships, research assistantships, teaching assistantships, career-related internships or fieldwork, institutionally sponsored loans, scholarships/grants, health care benefits, and unspecified assistantships available. Financial award application deadline: 3/2; financial award applicants required to submit FAFSA. *Faculty research:* Sustainability; specialty crops; dairy products technology; irrigation training and water engineering; animal science. *Unit head:* Dr. Jim Prince, Associate Dean, 805-756-2161, E-mail: jpprince@calpoly.edu. *Application contact:* Dr. Jim Prince, Associate Dean, 805-756-2161, E-mail: jpprince@calpoly.edu.

California State Polytechnic University, Pomona, Program in Agriculture, Pomona, CA 91768-2557. Offers agriculture (MS). *Program availability:* Part-time, evening/weekend. *Students:* 28 full-time (16 women), 28 part-time (14 women); includes 36 minority (3 Black or African American, non-Hispanic/Latino; 8 Asian, non-Hispanic/Latino; 21 Hispanic/Latino; 4 Two or more races, non-Hispanic/Latino), 3 international. Average age 31. 48 applicants, 71% accepted, 26 enrolled. In 2018, 11 master's awarded. *Degree requirements:* For master's, thesis or alternative. *Entrance requirements:* Additional exam requirements/recommendations for international students: Required—TOEFL (minimum score 550 paper-based). *Application deadline:* Applications are processed on a rolling basis. Application fee: $55. Electronic applications accepted. *Expenses:* Contact institution. *Financial support:* Application deadline: 3/2; applicants required to submit FAFSA. *Faculty research:* Equine nutrition, physiology, and reproduction; leadership development; bioartificial pancreas; plant science; ruminant and human nutrition. *Unit head:* Dr. Harmit Singh, Associate Professor/Director of Research and Graduate Studies, 909-869-3023, Fax: 909-869-5078, E-mail: harmitsingh@cpp.edu. *Application contact:* Dr. Harmit Singh, Associate Professor/Director of Research and Graduate Studies, 909-869-3023, Fax: 909-869-5078, E-mail: harmitsingh@cpp.edu.
Website: http://www.cpp.edu/~agri/agmasters/index.shtml

California State University, Chico, Office of Graduate Studies, College of Agriculture, Chico, CA 95929-0722. Offers agricultural education (MS). *Students:* 1 full-time (0 women). 3 applicants, 67% accepted. In 2018, 10 master's awarded. *Degree requirements:* For master's, thesis or alternative, the culminating activity can be in the form of thesis, project or oral exam. *Entrance requirements:* For master's, GRE or MAT, 3 letters of recommendation, three departmental recommendation forms, statement of purpose. Additional exam requirements/recommendations for international students: Required—TOEFL (minimum score 550 paper-based; 80 iBT), IELTS (minimum score 6.5), PTE (minimum score 59). *Application deadline:* For fall admission, 6/1 priority date for domestic students, 7/1 priority date for international students. Application fee: $55. Electronic applications accepted. *Expenses: Tuition, area resident:* Full-time $4622; part-time $3116 per unit. Tuition, state resident: full-time $4622; part-time $3116 per unit. Tuition, nonresident: full-time $10,634. *Required fees:* $2160; $1620 per year. Tuition and fees vary according to class time and program. *Financial support:* Fellowships, research assistantships, teaching assistantships, career-related internships or fieldwork, Federal Work-Study, scholarships/grants, traineeships, health care benefits, unspecified assistantships, and stipends available. Support available to part-time students. Financial award application deadline: 3/2; financial award applicants required to submit FAFSA. *Unit head:* Mollie Aschenbrener, MS Education Coordinator, 530-898-4568, Fax: 530-898-5844, E-mail: maschenbrener@csuchico.edu. *Application contact:* Micah Lehner, Graduate Admissions Coordinator, 530-898-5416, Fax: 530-898-3342, E-mail: mlehner@csuchico.edu.
Website: http://www.csuchico.edu/ag/

Clemson University, Graduate School, College of Agriculture, Forestry and Life Sciences, Department of Agricultural Sciences, Clemson, SC 29634. Offers agricultural education (M Ag Ed); applied economics (PhD); applied economics and statistics (MS). *Program availability:* Part-time. *Faculty:* 18 full-time (3 women). *Students:* 20 full-time (14 women), 12 part-time (6 women); includes 2 minority (both Black or African American, non-Hispanic/Latino). Average age 29. 39 applicants, 64% accepted, 15 enrolled. In 2018, 30 master's awarded. *Degree requirements:* For master's, thesis optional; for doctorate, comprehensive exam, thesis/dissertation. *Entrance requirements:* For master's and doctorate, GRE General Test, unofficial transcripts, letters of recommendation. Additional exam requirements/recommendations for international students: Required—TOEFL (minimum score 80 paper-based; 80 iBT), IELTS (minimum score 6.5), PTE (minimum score 5). *Application deadline:* For fall admission, 6/1 for domestic students, 7/1 for international students; for spring admission, 10/1 for domestic students, 11/1 for international students. Applications are processed on a rolling basis. Application fee: $80 ($90 for international students). Electronic applications accepted. *Expenses:* $5898 per semester full-time resident, $11623 per semester full-time non-resident, $724 per credit hour part-time resident, $1451 per credit hour part-time non-resident, online $955 per credit hour, $4938 doctoral programs resident, $10405 doctoral programs non-resident, $1144 full-time graduate assistant, other fees may apply per session. *Financial support:* In 2018–19, 17 students received support, including 2 fellowships with full and partial tuition reimbursements available (averaging $8,750 per year), 2 research assistantships with full and partial tuition reimbursements available (averaging $12,000 per year), 5 teaching assistantships with full and partial tuition reimbursements available (averaging $13,188 per year); career-related internships or fieldwork and unspecified assistantships also available. Financial award application deadline: 6/1. *Faculty research:* Agricultural education, agricultural economics, agricultural statistics, agribusiness. *Total annual research expenditures:* $427,800. *Unit head:* Dr. Charles Privette, Department Chair, 864-656-6247, E-mail: privett@clemson.edu. *Application contact:* Dr. Charles Privette, Department Chair, 864-656-6247, E-mail: privett@clemson.edu.
Website: http://www.clemson.edu/cafls/departments/agricultural-sciences/index.html

Colorado State University, College of Agricultural Sciences, Fort Collins, CO 80523-1101. Offers M Agr, M Ext Ed, MAEE, MLA, MS, PhD. *Program availability:* Part-time, evening/weekend, 100% online, blended/hybrid learning. Terminal master's awarded for partial completion of doctoral program. *Degree requirements:* For master's, comprehensive exam (for some programs), thesis (for some programs); for doctorate, comprehensive exam (for some programs), thesis/dissertation. *Entrance requirements:* Additional exam requirements/recommendations for international students: Required—TOEFL (minimum score 550 paper-based; 80 iBT); Recommended—IELTS (minimum score 6.5). Electronic applications accepted. *Expenses:* Contact institution. *Faculty research:* Water and environmental economics; plant breeding and genetics; livestock management systems; crop rotations and management; agri-food system analysis.

Dalhousie University, Faculty of Agriculture, Halifax, NS B3H 4R2, Canada. Offers agriculture (M Sc), including air quality, animal behavior, animal molecular genetics, animal nutrition, animal technology, aquaculture, botany, crop management, crop physiology, ecology, environmental microbiology, food science, horticulture, nutrient management, pest management, physiology, plant biotechnology, plant pathology, soil chemistry, soil fertility, waste management and composting, water quality. *Program availability:* Part-time. *Degree requirements:* For master's, thesis, ATC Exam Teaching Assistantship. *Entrance requirements:* For master's, honors B Sc, minimum GPA of 3.0. Additional exam requirements/recommendations for international students: Required—TOEFL (minimum score 580 paper-based; 92 iBT), IELTS, Michigan English Language Assessment Battery, CanTEST, CAEL. *Faculty research:* Bio-product development, organic agriculture, nutrient management, air and water quality, agricultural biotechnology.

Illinois State University, Graduate School, College of Applied Science and Technology, Department of Agriculture, Normal, IL 61790. Offers agribusiness (MS). *Faculty:* 18 full-time (6 women), 7 part-time/adjunct (2 women). *Students:* 8 full-time (2 women), 4 part-time (3 women); includes 1 minority (Two or more races, non-Hispanic/Latino), 4 international. Average age 24. 11 applicants, 36% accepted, 2 enrolled. In 2018, 3 master's awarded. *Degree requirements:* For master's, comprehensive exam

(for some programs), thesis optional. *Entrance requirements:* For master's, GRE General Test, minimum GPA of 3.0 in last 60 hours. *Application deadline:* Applications are processed on a rolling basis. Application fee: $40. *Expenses: Tuition, area resident:* Full-time $7264.62. Tuition, state resident: full-time $9466. Tuition, nonresident: full-time $17,290. *International tuition:* $15,089.40 full-time. *Required fees:* $1481.04. *Financial support:* Research assistantships, teaching assistantships, tuition waivers (full), and unspecified assistantships available. Financial award application deadline: 4/1. *Faculty research:* Engineering-economic system models for rural ethanol production facilities, development and evaluation of a propane-fueled, production scale, on-site thermal destruction system C-FAR 2007; field scale evaluation and technology transfer of economically, ecologically systems; sound liquid swine manure treatment and application. *Unit head:* Dr. Robert Rhykerd, Department Chair, 309-438-8550, E-mail: rrhyker@ilstu.edu. *Application contact:* Dr. Robert Rhykerd, Department Chair, 309-438-8550, E-mail: rrhyker@ilstu.edu.
Website: http://agriculture.illinoisstate.edu/

Instituto Tecnológico y de Estudios Superiores de Monterrey, Campus Monterrey, Graduate and Research Division, Program in Agriculture, Monterrey, Mexico. Offers agricultural parasitology (PhD); agricultural sciences (MS); farming productivity (MS); food processing engineering (MS); phytopathology (MS). *Program availability:* Part-time. *Degree requirements:* For master's, one foreign language, thesis; for doctorate, one foreign language, thesis/dissertation. *Entrance requirements:* For master's, EXADEP; for doctorate, GMAT or GRE, master's degree in related field. Additional exam requirements/recommendations for international students: Required—TOEFL. *Faculty research:* Animal embryos and reproduction, crop entomology, tropical agriculture, agricultural productivity, induced mutation in oleaginous plants.

Iowa State University of Science and Technology, Program in Sustainable Agriculture, Ames, IA 50011. Offers MS, PhD. *Entrance requirements:* For master's and doctorate, GRE General Test. Additional exam requirements/recommendations for international students: Required—TOEFL (minimum score 570 paper-based; 80 iBT), IELTS (minimum score 6.5). Electronic applications accepted.

Kansas State University, Graduate School, College of Agriculture, Manhattan, KS 66506. Offers MAB, MS, PhD, Certificate. *Program availability:* Part-time, online learning. Terminal master's awarded for partial completion of doctoral program. *Degree requirements:* For doctorate, thesis/dissertation. *Entrance requirements:* For master's, GRE, minimum undergraduate GPA of 3.0; for doctorate, GRE, minimum undergraduate GPA of 3.5. Additional exam requirements/recommendations for international students: Required—TOEFL (minimum score 550 paper-based). Electronic applications accepted. *Faculty research:* Plant production, animal production, food, grain processing, agricultural economics.

Louisiana State University and Agricultural & Mechanical College, Graduate School, College of Agriculture, Baton Rouge, LA 70803. Offers M App St, MS, PhD.

Louisiana Tech University, Graduate School, College of Education, Ruston, LA 71272. Offers counseling and guidance (MA), including clinical mental health counseling, human services, orientation and mobility; counseling psychology (PhD); curriculum and instruction (M Ed); cyber education (Graduate Certificate); dynamics of domestic and family violence (Graduate Certificate); early childhood education - PreK-3 (MAT); educational leadership (M Ed, Ed D); elementary education and special education mild/moderate grades 1-5 (MAT); higher education administration (Graduate Certificate); industrial/organizational psychology (MA, PhD); kinesiology (MS); middle school education (MAT), including mathematics; orientation and mobility (Graduate Certificate); rehabilitation teaching for the blind (Graduate Certificate); secondary education (MAT), including agriculture, biology, business, chemistry, English; special education: visually impaired (MAT); teacher leader education (Graduate Certificate); visual impairments - blind education (Graduate Certificate). *Accreditation:* NCATE. *Program availability:* Part-time. *Degree requirements:* For master's, thesis; for doctorate, thesis/dissertation. *Entrance requirements:* For master's and doctorate, GRE General Test. Additional exam requirements/recommendations for international students: Required—TOEFL (minimum score 550 paper-based; 80 iBT), IELTS (minimum score 6.5). Electronic applications accepted. *Faculty research:* Blindness and the best methods for increasing independence for individuals who are blind or visually impaired; educating and investigating factors contributing to improvements in human performance across the lifespan and a reduction in injury rates during training.

McGill University, Faculty of Graduate and Postdoctoral Studies, Faculty of Agricultural and Environmental Sciences, Montréal, QC H3A 2T5, Canada. Offers M Sc, M Sc A, PhD, Certificate, Graduate Diploma.

McNeese State University, Doré School of Graduate Studies, College of Science and Agriculture, Harold and Pearl Dripps School of Agricultural Sciences, Program in Environmental and Chemical Sciences, Lake Charles, LA 70609. Offers agricultural sciences (MS); environmental science (MS). *Program availability:* Evening/weekend. *Degree requirements:* For master's, comprehensive exam, thesis or alternative. *Entrance requirements:* For master's, GRE.

Michigan State University, The Graduate School, College of Agriculture and Natural Resources, East Lansing, MI 48824. Offers MA, MIPS, MS, MURP, PhD. *Faculty research:* Plant science, animal sciences, forestry, fisheries and wildlife, recreation and tourism.

Mississippi State University, College of Agriculture and Life Sciences, Department of Animal and Dairy Sciences, Mississippi State, MS 39762. Offers agricultural life sciences (MS), including animal physiology (MS, PhD), genetics (MS, PhD); agricultural science (PhD), including animal dairy sciences, animal nutrition (MS, PhD); agriculture (MS), including animal nutrition (MS, PhD), animal science; life sciences (PhD), including animal physiology (MS, PhD), genetics (MS, PhD). *Faculty:* 19 full-time (6 women). *Students:* 18 full-time (13 women), 11 part-time (6 women); includes 3 minority (1 Black or African American, non-Hispanic/Latino; 1 American Indian or Alaska Native, non-Hispanic/Latino; 1 Hispanic/Latino), 6 international. Average age 26. 28 applicants, 39% accepted, 10 enrolled. In 2018, 8 master's, 2 doctorates awarded. *Degree requirements:* For master's, comprehensive exam (for some programs), thesis, written proposal of intended research area; for doctorate, comprehensive exam, thesis/dissertation, written proposal of intended research area. *Entrance requirements:* For master's, GRE General Test, minimum GPA of 3.0; for doctorate, GRE General Test. Additional exam requirements/recommendations for international students: Required—TOEFL (minimum score 575 paper-based; 84 iBT), IELTS (minimum score 7). *Application deadline:* For fall admission, 7/1 for domestic students, 5/1 for international students; for spring admission, 11/1 for domestic students, 9/1 for international students. Applications are processed on a rolling basis. Application fee: $60 ($80 for international students). Electronic applications accepted. *Expenses:* Tuition, state resident: full-time $8450; part-time $360.59 per credit hour. Tuition, nonresident: full-time $23,140; part-time $969.09 per credit hour. *Required fees:* $110. One-time fee: $55 full-time. Part-time tuition and fees vary according to course load, degree level, campus/location and reciprocity agreements. *Financial support:* In 2018–19, 13 research assistantships (averaging $13,167 per year) were awarded; Federal Work-Study, institutionally sponsored loans, and unspecified assistantships also available. Financial award application deadline: 4/1; financial award applicants required to submit FAFSA. *Faculty research:* Ecology and population dynamics, physiology, biochemistry and behavior, systematics. *Unit head:* Dr. John Blanton, Professor and Head, 662-325-2802, Fax: 662-325-8873, E-mail: john.blanton@msstate.edu. *Application contact:* Ryan King, Admissions and Enrollment Assistant, 662-325-8951, E-mail: rjk101@grad.msstate.edu.
Website: http://www.ads.msstate.edu/

Mississippi State University, College of Agriculture and Life Sciences, Department of Poultry Science, Mississippi State, MS 39762. Offers agricultural sciences (MS, PhD), including poultry science. *Faculty:* 8 full-time (3 women). *Students:* 12 full-time (5 women), 3 part-time (2 women); includes 1 minority (Black or African American, non-Hispanic/Latino), 8 international. Average age 30. 3 applicants, 67% accepted, 2 enrolled. In 2018, 1 master's, 3 doctorates awarded. *Degree requirements:* For master's, comprehensive exam, thesis optional; for doctorate, comprehensive exam, thesis/dissertation. *Entrance requirements:* Additional exam requirements/recommendations for international students: Required—TOEFL (minimum score 477 paper-based; 53 iBT); Recommended—IELTS (minimum score 4.5). *Application deadline:* For fall admission, 7/1 for domestic students, 5/1 for international students; for spring admission, 10/1 for domestic students, 11/1 for international students. Applications are processed on a rolling basis. Application fee: $60 ($80 for international students). Electronic applications accepted. *Expenses:* Tuition, state resident: full-time $8450; part-time $360.59 per credit hour. Tuition, nonresident: full-time $23,140; part-time $969.09 per credit hour. *Required fees:* $110. One-time fee: $55 full-time. Part-time tuition and fees vary according to course load, degree level, campus/location and reciprocity agreements. *Financial support:* In 2018–19, 11 research assistantships with partial tuition reimbursements (averaging $14,798 per year) were awarded; Federal Work-Study, institutionally sponsored loans, scholarships/grants, and unspecified assistantships also available. Financial award application deadline: 4/1; financial award applicants required to submit FAFSA. *Unit head:* Dr. Mary Beck, Professor and Head, 662-325-3416, Fax: 662-325-8292, E-mail: mmb485@msstate.edu. *Application contact:* Ryan King, Admissions and Enrollment Assistant, 662-325-8951, E-mail: rjk101@grad.msstate.edu.
Website: http://www.poultry.msstate.edu/

Mississippi State University, College of Agriculture and Life Sciences, School of Human Sciences, Mississippi State, MS 39762. Offers agriculture and extension education (MS), including communication, leadership; agriculture science (PhD), including agriculture and extension education; fashion design and merchandising (MS), including design and product development, merchandising; human development and family studies (MS, PhD). *Accreditation:* NCATE (one or more programs are accredited). *Program availability:* Part-time. *Faculty:* 21 full-time (12 women). *Students:* 30 full-time (28 women), 51 part-time (35 women); includes 17 minority (13 Black or African American, non-Hispanic/Latino; 1 Hispanic/Latino; 3 Two or more races, non-Hispanic/Latino), 4 international. Average age 34. 26 applicants, 62% accepted, 16 enrolled. In 2018, 8 master's, 12 doctorates awarded. *Degree requirements:* For master's, thesis optional, comprehensive oral or written exam. *Entrance requirements:* For master's, GRE, minimum GPA of 2.75 in last 4 semesters of course work; for doctorate, minimum GPA of 3.0 on prior graduate work. Additional exam requirements/recommendations for international students: Required—TOEFL (minimum score 477 paper-based; 53 iBT); Recommended—IELTS (minimum score 4.5). *Application deadline:* For fall admission, 7/1 for domestic students, 5/1 for international students; for spring admission, 11/1 for domestic students, 9/1 for international students. Applications are processed on a rolling basis. Application fee: $60 ($80 for international students). Electronic applications accepted. *Expenses:* Tuition, state resident: full-time $8450; part-time $360.59 per credit hour. Tuition, nonresident: full-time $23,140; part-time $969.09 per credit hour. *Required fees:* $110. One-time fee: $55 full-time. Part-time tuition and fees vary according to course load, degree level, campus/location and reciprocity agreements. *Financial support:* In 2018–19, 14 research assistantships (averaging $12,575 per year) were awarded; Federal Work-Study, institutionally sponsored loans, and unspecified assistantships also available. Financial award application deadline: 4/1; financial award applicants required to submit FAFSA. *Faculty research:* Animal welfare, agroscience, information technology, learning styles, problem solving. *Unit head:* Dr. Michael Newman, Professor and Director, 662-325-2950, E-mail: mnewman@humansci.msstate.edu. *Application contact:* Ryan King, Admissions and Enrollment Assistant, 662-325-8951, E-mail: rjk101@grad.msstate.edu.
Website: http://www.humansci.msstate.edu

Missouri State University, Graduate College, Darr College of Agriculture, Springfield, MO 65897. Offers plant science (MS); secondary education (MS Ed), including agriculture. *Program availability:* Part-time. *Faculty:* 16 full-time (5 women), 1 part-time/adjunct (0 women). *Students:* 22 full-time (9 women), 32 part-time (17 women); includes 3 minority (1 American Indian or Alaska Native, non-Hispanic/Latino; 2 Two or more races, non-Hispanic/Latino). Average age 23. 24 applicants, 42% accepted. In 2018, 21 master's awarded. *Degree requirements:* For master's, comprehensive exam, thesis or alternative. *Entrance requirements:* For master's, GRE (MS in plant science, MNAS), 9-12 teacher certification (MS Ed), minimum GPA of 3.0 (MS plant science, MNAS). Additional exam requirements/recommendations for international students: Required—TOEFL (minimum score 550 paper-based; 79 iBT), IELTS (minimum score 6). *Application deadline:* For fall admission, 7/20 priority date for domestic students, 5/1 for international students; for spring admission, 12/20 priority date for domestic students, 9/1 for international students; for summer admission, 5/20 priority date for domestic students. Applications are processed on a rolling basis. Application fee: $55 ($60 for international students). Electronic applications accepted. Tuition and fees vary according to class time, course level, course load, degree level, campus/location, program and student level. *Financial support:* In 2018–19, 7 research assistantships with full tuition reimbursements (averaging $9,365 per year), 6 teaching assistantships with full tuition reimbursements (averaging $8,450 per year) were awarded; Federal Work-Study, institutionally sponsored loans, scholarships/grants, and unspecified assistantships also available. Financial award application deadline: 1/31; financial award applicants required to submit FAFSA. *Faculty research:* Grapevine biotechnology, agricultural marketing, Asian elephant reproduction, poultry science, integrated pest management. *Unit head:* Dr. Ronald Del Vecchio, Dean, 417-836-5050, E-mail: darr@missouristate.edu. *Application contact:* Lakan Drinker, Director, Graduate Enrollment Management, 417-836-5330, Fax: 417-836-6200, E-mail: lakandrinker@missouristate.edu.
Website: http://ag.missouristate.edu/

Montana State University, The Graduate School, College of Agriculture, Bozeman, MT 59717. Offers MS, PhD. *Program availability:* Part-time, online learning. *Degree requirements:* For master's, comprehensive exam; for doctorate, comprehensive exam, thesis/dissertation. *Entrance requirements:* For master's and doctorate, GRE General Test. Additional exam requirements/recommendations for international students: Required—TOEFL (minimum score 550 paper-based). Electronic applications accepted.

Morehead State University, Graduate School, College of Science, Department of Agricultural Sciences, Morehead, KY 40351. Offers career and technical agricultural education (MS). *Program availability:* Part-time, evening/weekend. *Degree requirements:* For master's, comprehensive exam, thesis or alternative, exit exam. *Entrance requirements:* For master's, GRE, minimum GPA of 3.0 for undergraduate major. Additional exam requirements/recommendations for international students: Required—TOEFL (minimum score 500 paper-based). Electronic applications accepted.

Murray State University, Hutson School of Agriculture, Murray, KY 42071. Offers agriculture (MS), including agribusiness economics, agriculture education, sustainable agriculture, veterinary hospital management; veterinary hospital management (Certificate). *Program availability:* Part-time, 100% online, blended/hybrid learning. *Entrance requirements:* For master's, GRE or GMAT, minimum university GPA of 2.75. Additional exam requirements/recommendations for international students: Required—TOEFL (minimum score 527 paper-based; 71 iBT). Electronic applications accepted.

New Mexico State University, College of Agricultural, Consumer and Environmental Sciences, Department of Animal and Range Sciences, Las Cruces, NM 88003-8001. Offers agriculture (M Ag), including domestic animal biology; animal science (MS, PhD); range science (MS, PhD). *Program availability:* Part-time. *Faculty:* 18 full-time (7 women). *Students:* 31 full-time (19 women), 8 part-time (4 women); includes 10 minority (1 American Indian or Alaska Native, non-Hispanic/Latino; 9 Hispanic/Latino), 8 international. Average age 30. 19 applicants, 58% accepted, 9 enrolled. In 2018, 11 master's, 3 doctorates awarded. *Degree requirements:* For master's, thesis, seminar, experimental statistics; for doctorate, thesis/dissertation, research tool. *Entrance requirements:* For master's, minimum GPA of 3.0 in last 60 hours of undergraduate course work (MS), 3 reference letters, personal statement, resume, BS in animal science; for doctorate, minimum graduate GPA of 3.2, MS with thesis, 3 reference letters, personal statement, resume, BS in animal science. Additional exam requirements/recommendations for international students: Required—TOEFL (minimum score 550 paper-based; 79 iBT), IELTS (minimum score 6.5). *Application deadline:* For fall admission, 2/15 priority date for domestic and international students; for spring admission, 10/1 priority date for domestic and international students. Applications are processed on a rolling basis. Application fee: $40 ($50 for international students). Electronic applications accepted. *Expenses: Tuition, area resident:* Full-time $4216.70; part-time $252.70 per credit hour. Tuition, state resident: full-time $4216.70; part-time $252.70 per credit hour. Tuition, nonresident: full-time $12,769; part-time $881.10 per credit hour. *International tuition:* $12,769.30 full-time. *Required fees:* $878.40; $48.80 per credit hour. Full-time tuition and fees vary according to course load and reciprocity agreements. *Financial support:* In 2018–19, 33 students received support, including 3 fellowships (averaging $4,548 per year), 13 research assistantships (averaging $13,038 per year), 16 teaching assistantships (averaging $9,486 per year); career-related internships or fieldwork, Federal Work-Study, scholarships/grants, traineeships, health care benefits, and unspecified assistantships also available. Support available to part-time students. Financial award application deadline: 3/1. *Faculty research:* Reproductive physiology, ruminant nutrition, nutrition toxicology, range ecology, land use hydrology. *Total annual research expenditures:* $3.3 million. *Unit head:* Dr. Shanna Ivey, Department Head, 575-646-2514, Fax: 575-646-5441, E-mail: sivey@nmsu.edu. *Application contact:* Jenny Castillo, Graduate Advising, 575-646-2515, Fax: 575-646-5441, E-mail: cjenny@nmsu.edu.
Website: http://aces.nmsu.edu/academics/anrs

North Carolina Agricultural and Technical State University, The Graduate College, College of Agriculture and Environmental Sciences, Greensboro, NC 27411. Offers MAT, MS. *Program availability:* Part-time, evening/weekend. *Degree requirements:* For master's, comprehensive exam, qualifying exam. *Entrance requirements:* For master's, GRE General Test. *Faculty research:* Aid for small farmers, agricultural technology, housing, food science, nutrition.

North Carolina State University, Graduate School, College of Agriculture and Life Sciences, Raleigh, NC 27695. Offers MBAE, MFG, MFM, MFS, MMB, MN, MP, MS, PhD, Certificate. *Program availability:* Part-time. Electronic applications accepted.

North Dakota State University, College of Graduate and Interdisciplinary Studies, College of Agriculture, Food Systems, and Natural Resources, Fargo, ND 58102. Offers MS, PhD. *Program availability:* Part-time. *Entrance requirements:* Additional exam requirements/recommendations for international students: Required—TOEFL. Electronic applications accepted. *Faculty research:* Horticulture and forestry, plant and wheat breeding, diseases of insects, animal and range sciences, soil science, veterinary medicine.

Northwest Missouri State University, Graduate School, School of Agricultural Sciences, Maryville, MO 64468-6001. Offers agricultural economics (MBA); agricultural education (MS Ed); agriculture (MS); teaching: agriculture (MS Ed). *Program availability:* Part-time. *Faculty:* 6 full-time (1 woman). *Students:* 9 full-time (7 women), 4 international. Average age 23. 8 applicants, 63% accepted, 4 enrolled. In 2018, 1 master's awarded. *Degree requirements:* For master's, comprehensive exam, thesis (for some programs). *Entrance requirements:* For master's, GRE General Test, minimum undergraduate GPA of 2.5, writing sample. Additional exam requirements/recommendations for international students: Required—TOEFL (minimum score 550 paper-based). *Application deadline:* For fall admission, 7/1 for domestic and international students; for spring admission, 11/15 for domestic and international students. Applications are processed on a rolling basis. Application fee: $0 ($75 for international students). Electronic applications accepted. *Expenses: Tuition, area resident:* Full-time $4551; part-time $252.86 per credit hour. Tuition, state resident: full-time $4551; part-time $252.86 per credit hour. Tuition, nonresident: full-time $9103; part-time $505.72 per credit hour. *International tuition:* $9103 full-time. *Required fees:* $2668; $148.20 per credit hour. Tuition and fees vary according to program. *Financial support:* Research assistantships with full tuition reimbursements, teaching assistantships with full tuition reimbursements, and unspecified assistantships available. Financial award application deadline: 4/1; financial award applicants required to submit FAFSA. *Unit head:* Rodney Barr, Director, 660-562-1620. *Application contact:* Rodney Barr, Director, 660-562-1620.
Website: http://www.nwmissouri.edu/ag/

The Ohio State University, Graduate School, College of Food, Agricultural, and Environmental Sciences, Columbus, OH 43210. Offers M Ed, MAS, MENR, MPHM, MS, PhD. *Program availability:* Part-time. *Faculty:* 327. *Students:* 478 full-time (273 women), 58 part-time (32 women); includes 73 minority (18 Black or African American, non-Hispanic/Latino; 17 Asian, non-Hispanic/Latino; 26 Hispanic/Latino; 12 Two or more races, non-Hispanic/Latino), 166 international. Average age 28. In 2018, 112 master's, 59 doctorates awarded. *Entrance requirements:* Additional exam requirements/recommendations for international students: Required—TOEFL (minimum score 550 paper-based; 79 iBT), Michigan English Language Assessment Battery (minimum score 82); Recommended—IELTS (minimum score 7). *Application deadline:* Applications are processed on a rolling basis. Application fee: $60 ($70 for international students). Electronic applications accepted. *Financial support:* Fellowships with tuition reimbursements, research assistantships with tuition reimbursements, teaching assistantships with tuition reimbursements, career-related internships or fieldwork, Federal Work-Study, institutionally sponsored loans, and unspecified assistantships available. Support available to part-time students. *Unit head:* Dr. Cathann A. Kress, Vice President and Dean, 614-292-6164, E-mail: kress.98@osu.edu. *Application contact:* Graduate and Professional Admissions, 614-292-9444, Fax: 614-292-3895, E-mail: gpadmissions@osu.edu.
Website: http://cfaes.osu.edu/

Oklahoma State University, College of Agricultural Science and Natural Resources, Stillwater, OK 74078. Offers M Ag, MS, PhD. *Program availability:* Online learning. *Faculty:* 213 full-time (55 women), 5 part-time/adjunct (2 women). *Students:* 117 full-time (68 women), 271 part-time (138 women); includes 51 minority (15 Black or African American, non-Hispanic/Latino; 7 American Indian or Alaska Native, non-Hispanic/Latino; 4 Asian, non-Hispanic/Latino; 13 Hispanic/Latino; 12 Two or more races, non-Hispanic/Latino), 103 international. Average age 28. 209 applicants, 55% accepted, 100 enrolled. In 2018, 128 master's, 35 doctorates awarded. *Degree requirements:* For master's, thesis (for some programs); for doctorate, comprehensive exam, thesis/dissertation. *Entrance requirements:* For master's and doctorate, GRE or GMAT. Additional exam requirements/recommendations for international students: Required—TOEFL (minimum score 550 paper-based; 79 iBT). *Application deadline:* For fall admission, 3/1 priority date for domestic and international students; for spring admission, 8/1 priority date for domestic and international students. Applications are processed on a rolling basis. Application fee: $40 ($75 for international students). Electronic applications accepted. *Expenses: Tuition, area resident:* Full-time $4148. Tuition, state resident: full-time $4148. Tuition, nonresident: full-time $10,517. *International tuition:* $10,517 full-time. *Required fees:* $4394; $2929 per credit hour. Tuition and fees vary according to course load and program. *Financial support:* In 2018–19, 220 research assistantships (averaging $3,640 per year), 53 teaching assistantships (averaging $3,144 per year) were awarded; fellowships, career-related internships or fieldwork, Federal Work-Study, scholarships/grants, health care benefits, tuition waivers (partial), and unspecified assistantships also available. Support available to part-time students. Financial award application deadline: 3/1; financial award applicants required to submit FAFSA. *Unit head:* Dr. Thomas Coon, Vice President/Dean, 405-744-2474, E-mail: thomas.coon@okstate.edu. *Application contact:* Dr. Sheryl Tucker, Vice Prov/Dean/Prof, 405-744-6368, Fax: 405-744-0355, E-mail: gradi@okstate.edu.
Website: http://casnr.okstate.edu

Penn State University Park, Graduate School, College of Agricultural Sciences, University Park, PA 16802. Offers M Ed, MPS, MS, PhD, Certificate. *Program availability:* Part-time. *Entrance requirements:* Additional exam requirements/recommendations for international students: Required—TOEFL (minimum score 550 paper-based; 80 iBT), IELTS. Electronic applications accepted. *Expenses:* Contact institution.

Prairie View A&M University, College of Agriculture and Human Sciences, Prairie View, TX 77446. Offers MS. *Program availability:* Part-time, evening/weekend. *Students:* Average age 31. 57 applicants, 88% accepted, 36 enrolled. In 2018, 24 master's awarded. *Degree requirements:* For master's, comprehensive exam, thesis (for some programs), field placement. *Entrance requirements:* For master's, GRE General Test, minimum GPA of 2.45. Additional exam requirements/recommendations for international students: Required—TOEFL (minimum score 550 paper-based; 79 iBT). *Application deadline:* For fall admission, 5/1 priority date for domestic and international students; for spring admission, 10/11 priority date for domestic students, 9/1 priority date for international students; for summer admission, 3/1 priority date for domestic students, 2/1 priority date for international students. Applications are processed on a rolling basis. Application fee: $50. Electronic applications accepted. *Expenses:* Contact institution. *Financial support:* Research assistantships, career-related internships or fieldwork, Federal Work-Study, institutionally sponsored loans, scholarships/grants, tuition waivers (full and partial), and unspecified assistantships available. Support available to part-time students. Financial award application deadline: 4/1; financial award applicants required to submit FAFSA. *Faculty research:* Domestic violence prevention, water quality, food growth regulators, wetland dynamics, biochemistry, obesity and nutrition, family therapy. *Unit head:* Dr. Ali Fares, Interim Dean and Director of Land-Grant Programs, 936-261-5019, E-mail: alfares@pvamu.edu. *Application contact:* Pauline Walker, Administrative Assistant II, 936-261-3521, Fax: 936-261-3529, E-mail: gradadmissions@pvamu.edu.

Purdue University, Graduate School, College of Agriculture, West Lafayette, IN 47907. Offers EMBA, M Agr, MA, MS, MSF, PhD. *Program availability:* Part-time. *Faculty:* 285 full-time (75 women), 12 part-time/adjunct (4 women). *Students:* 550 full-time (255 women), 119 part-time (51 women); includes 77 minority (14 Black or African American, non-Hispanic/Latino; 5 American Indian or Alaska Native, non-Hispanic/Latino; 18 Asian, non-Hispanic/Latino; 25 Hispanic/Latino; 1 Native Hawaiian or other Pacific Islander, non-Hispanic/Latino; 14 Two or more races, non-Hispanic/Latino), 284 international. Average age 28. 620 applicants, 32% accepted, 141 enrolled. In 2018, 127 master's, 88 doctorates awarded. *Degree requirements:* For doctorate, thesis/dissertation. *Entrance requirements:* Additional exam requirements/recommendations for international students: Required—TOEFL. *Application deadline:* Applications are processed on a rolling basis. Application fee: $60 ($75 for international students). Electronic applications accepted. *Financial support:* Fellowships with tuition reimbursements, research assistantships with tuition reimbursements, teaching assistantships with tuition reimbursements, career-related internships or fieldwork, and tuition waivers (partial) available. Support available to part-time students. Financial award applicants required to submit FAFSA. *Unit head:* Karen Plaut, Dean, 765-494-7420, E-mail: kplaut@purdue.edu. *Application contact:* Graduate School Admissions, 765-494-2600, Fax: 765-494-0136, E-mail: gradinfo@purdue.edu.
Website: http://www.ag.purdue.edu/Pages/default.aspx

Sam Houston State University, College of Sciences, Department of Agricultural Sciences and Engineering Technology, Huntsville, TX 77341. Offers agriculture (MS). *Program availability:* Part-time. *Degree requirements:* For master's, comprehensive exam, thesis optional. *Entrance requirements:* For master's, GRE General Test, letters of recommendation. Additional exam requirements/recommendations for international students: Required—TOEFL (minimum score 550 paper-based; 79 iBT), IELTS (minimum score 6.5). Electronic applications accepted.

South Dakota State University, Graduate School, College of Agriculture, Food and Environmental Sciences, Brookings, SD 57007. Offers MS, PhD. *Program availability:* Part-time. *Degree requirements:* For master's, thesis, oral exam; for doctorate, thesis/dissertation, preliminary oral and written exams. *Entrance requirements:* Additional exam requirements/recommendations for international students: Required—TOEFL.

Southern Arkansas University–Magnolia, School of Graduate Studies, Magnolia, AR 71753. Offers agriculture (MS); business administration (MBA), including agribusiness, social entrepreneurship, supply chain management; clinical and mental health counseling (MS); computer and information sciences (MS), including cyber security and privacy, data science, information technology; gifted and talented (M Ed), including curriculum and instruction, educational administration and supervision, gifted and

talented P-8/7-12, instructional specialist P-4; higher, adult and lifelong education (M Ed); kinesiology (M Ed), including coaching; library media and information specialist (M Ed); public administration (MPA); school counseling K-12 (M Ed); student affairs and college counseling (M Ed); teaching (MAT). *Accreditation:* NCATE. *Program availability:* Part-time, 100% online, blended/hybrid learning. *Faculty:* 36 full-time (21 women), 32 part-time/adjunct (15 women). *Students:* 164 full-time (77 women), 762 part-time (510 women); includes 192 minority (163 Black or African American, non-Hispanic/Latino; 7 American Indian or Alaska Native, non-Hispanic/Latino; 13 Asian, non-Hispanic/Latino; 1 Hispanic/Latino; 8 Two or more races, non-Hispanic/Latino), 213 international. Average age 28. 363 applicants, 100% accepted, 237 enrolled. In 2018, 716 master's awarded. *Degree requirements:* For master's, comprehensive exam (for some programs), thesis optional. *Entrance requirements:* For master's, GRE, MAT or GMAT, minimum GPA of 2.5. Additional exam requirements/recommendations for international students: Required—TOEFL (minimum score 550 paper-based), IELTS (minimum score 6). *Application deadline:* For fall admission, 8/1 for domestic and international students; for spring admission, 12/1 for domestic students, 11/15 for international students; for summer admission, 4/1 for domestic students, 5/10 for international students. Applications are processed on a rolling basis. Application fee: $25 ($90 for international students). Electronic applications accepted. *Expenses: Tuition, area resident:* Full-time $5130; part-time $3420 per year. Tuition, state resident: full-time $5130; part-time $3420 per year. Tuition, nonresident: full-time $7866; part-time $5244 per year. *International tuition:* $7866 full-time. *Required fees:* $1052; $710 per unit. Tuition and fees vary according to course load. *Financial support:* Career-related internships or fieldwork, Federal Work-Study, scholarships/grants, tuition waivers (full), and unspecified assistantships available. Financial award applicants required to submit FAFSA. *Faculty research:* Alternative certification for teachers, supervision of instruction, instructional leadership, counseling. *Unit head:* Dr. Kim Bloss, Dean, School of Graduate Studies, 870-235-4150, Fax: 870-235-5227, E-mail: kkbloss@saumag.edu. *Application contact:* Talia Jett, Admissions Coordinator, 870-2355450, Fax: 870-235-5227, E-mail: taliajett@saumag.edu.
Website: http://www.saumag.edu/graduate

Southern Illinois University Carbondale, Graduate School, College of Agriculture, Carbondale, IL 62901-4701. Offers MS, MBA/MS. *Program availability:* Part-time. *Entrance requirements:* For master's, minimum GPA of 2.7. Additional exam requirements/recommendations for international students: Required—TOEFL. *Faculty research:* Production and studies in crops, animal nutrition, agribusiness economics and management, forest biology and ecology, microcomputers in agriculture.

Southern University and Agricultural and Mechanical College, Graduate School, College of Agricultural, Family and Consumer Sciences, Baton Rouge, LA 70813. Offers urban forestry (MS). *Degree requirements:* For master's, thesis. *Entrance requirements:* For master's, GRE, minimum GPA of 3.0. Additional exam requirements/recommendations for international students: Required—TOEFL (minimum score 525 paper-based). *Faculty research:* Urban forest interactions with environment, social and economic impacts of urban forests, tree biology/pathology, development of urban forest management tools.

Stephen F. Austin State University, Graduate School, Arthur Temple College of Forestry and Agriculture, Department of Agriculture, Nacogdoches, TX 75962. Offers MS. *Accreditation:* NCATE. *Degree requirements:* For master's, comprehensive exam, thesis (for some programs). *Entrance requirements:* For master's, GRE General Test, minimum GPA of 2.8 in last half of major, 2.5 overall. Additional exam requirements/recommendations for international students: Required—TOEFL (minimum score 550 paper-based). *Faculty research:* Asian vegetables, soil fertility, animal breeding, animal nutrition.

Tarleton State University, College of Graduate Studies, College of Agricultural and Environmental Sciences, Department of Agricultural and Consumer Sciences, Stephenville, TX 76402. Offers agricultural and consumer resources (MS). *Program availability:* Part-time, evening/weekend, 100% online, blended/hybrid learning. *Faculty:* 9 full-time (1 woman), 3 part-time/adjunct (1 woman). *Students:* 49 full-time (33 women), 22 part-time (14 women). Average age 25. 36 applicants, 97% accepted, 28 enrolled. In 2018, 25 master's awarded. *Degree requirements:* For master's, comprehensive exam, thesis (for some programs). *Entrance requirements:* For master's, GRE General Test, minimum GPA of 3.0. Additional exam requirements/recommendations for international students: Required—TOEFL (minimum score 520 paper-based; 69 iBT); Recommended—IELTS (minimum score 6), TSE (minimum score 50). *Application deadline:* For fall admission, 8/5 priority date for domestic students; for spring admission, 12/1 for domestic students. Applications are processed on a rolling basis. Application fee: $50 ($130 for international students). Electronic applications accepted. *Expenses:* Contact institution. *Financial support:* Research assistantships, Federal Work-Study, institutionally sponsored loans, scholarships/grants, and unspecified assistantships available. Financial award application deadline: 5/1; financial award applicants required to submit FAFSA. *Unit head:* Dr. Wayne Atchley, Department Head, 254-968-9601, Fax: 254-968-9199, E-mail: watchley@tarleton.edu. *Application contact:* Information Contact, 254-968-9104, Fax: 254-968-9670, E-mail: gradoffice@tarleton.edu.
Website: http://www.tarleton.edu/agservices/

Tarleton State University, College of Graduate Studies, College of Agricultural and Environmental Sciences, Department of Wildlife, Sustainability, and Ecosystem Sciences, Stephenville, TX 76402. Offers agricultural and natural resource sciences (MS). *Program availability:* Part-time, evening/weekend. *Faculty:* 4 full-time (2 women), 2 part-time/adjunct (0 women). *Students:* 10 full-time (5 women), 7 part-time (4 women). Average age 28. 7 applicants, 86% accepted, 4 enrolled. In 2018, 5 master's awarded. *Degree requirements:* For master's, comprehensive exam, thesis (for some programs). *Entrance requirements:* For master's, GRE General Test, minimum GPA of 3.0. Additional exam requirements/recommendations for international students: Required—TOEFL (minimum score 520 paper-based; 69 iBT); Recommended—IELTS (minimum score 6), TSE (minimum score 50). *Application deadline:* For fall admission, 8/1 priority date for domestic students; for spring admission, 12/1 for domestic students. Applications are processed on a rolling basis. Application fee: $50 ($130 for international students). Electronic applications accepted. *Expenses:* Contact institution. *Financial support:* Research assistantships, teaching assistantships, career-related internships or fieldwork, Federal Work-Study, and institutionally sponsored loans available. Support available to part-time students. Financial award application deadline: 5/1; financial award applicants required to submit FAFSA. *Unit head:* Dr. T. Wayne Schwertner, Department Head, 254-968-9219, E-mail: schwertner@tarleton.edu. *Application contact:* Information Contact, 254-968-9104, Fax: 254-968-9670, E-mail: gradoffice@tarleton.edu.

Tennessee State University, The School of Graduate Studies and Research, College of Agriculture, Human and Natural Sciences, Nashville, TN 37209-1561. Offers agricultural sciences (MS), including agribusiness, agricultural and extension education, animal science, plant and soil science; biological sciences (MS, PhD); biotechnology (PhD); chemistry (MS). *Program availability:* Part-time, evening/weekend. *Degree requirements:* For master's, thesis. *Entrance requirements:* For master's, GRE General Test, GRE Subject Test, MAT. *Faculty research:* Small farm economics, ornamental horticulture, beef cattle production, rural elderly.

Tennessee Technological University, College of Graduate Studies, College of Interdisciplinary Studies, School of Environmental Studies, Department of Environmental Sciences, Cookeville, TN 38505. Offers agriculture (PhD); biology (PhD); chemistry (PhD); geosciences (PhD); integrated research (PhD). *Program availability:* Part-time. *Students:* 3 full-time (all women), 17 part-time (6 women); includes 2 minority (1 Asian, non-Hispanic/Latino; 1 Two or more races, non-Hispanic/Latino), 5 international. 14 applicants, 29% accepted, 2 enrolled. In 2018, 3 doctorates awarded. *Degree requirements:* For doctorate, comprehensive exam, thesis/dissertation. *Entrance requirements:* For doctorate, GRE. Additional exam requirements/recommendations for international students: Required—TOEFL (minimum score 527 paper-based; 71 iBT), IELTS (minimum score 5.5), PTE (minimum score 48), or TOEIC (Test of English as an International Communication). *Application deadline:* For fall admission, 7/1 for domestic students, 5/1 for international students; for spring admission, 12/1 for domestic students, 10/2 for international students; for summer admission, 5/1 for domestic students, 2/1 for international students. Applications are processed on a rolling basis. Application fee: $35 ($40 for international students). Electronic applications accepted. *Financial support:* Fellowships, research assistantships, and teaching assistantships available. Financial award application deadline: 4/1. *Unit head:* Dr. Hayden Mattingly, Interim Director, 931-372-6246, E-mail: hmattingly@tntech.edu. *Application contact:* Shelia K. Kendrick, Coordinator of Graduate Studies, 931-372-3808, Fax: 931-372-3497, E-mail: skendrick@tntech.edu.

Texas A&M University, College of Agriculture and Life Sciences, College Station, TX 77843. Offers M Agr, M Ed, M Engr, MEIM, MNRD, MRRD, MS, MWSc, Ed D, PhD. *Program availability:* Part-time, blended/hybrid learning. *Faculty:* 349. *Students:* 978 full-time (512 women), 279 part-time (141 women); includes 204 minority (36 Black or African American, non-Hispanic/Latino; 3 American Indian or Alaska Native, non-Hispanic/Latino; 27 Asian, non-Hispanic/Latino; 121 Hispanic/Latino; 1 Native Hawaiian or other Pacific Islander, non-Hispanic/Latino; 16 Two or more races, non-Hispanic/Latino), 416 international. Average age 30. 515 applicants, 61% accepted, 238 enrolled. In 2018, 224 master's, 102 doctorates awarded. *Entrance requirements:* Additional exam requirements/recommendations for international students: Required—TOEFL (minimum score 550 paper-based; 80 iBT), IELTS (minimum score 6), PTE (minimum score 53). *Application deadline:* For fall admission, 7/21 priority date for domestic students, 6/1 priority date for international students; for spring admission, 12/1 priority date for domestic students, 10/1 priority date for international students. Applications are processed on a rolling basis. Application fee: $50 ($90 for international students). Electronic applications accepted. *Expenses:* Contact institution. *Financial support:* In 2018–19, 1,013 students received support, including 159 fellowships with tuition reimbursements available (averaging $13,554 per year), 575 research assistantships with tuition reimbursements available (averaging $14,017 per year), 337 teaching assistantships with tuition reimbursements available (averaging $13,020 per year); career-related internships or fieldwork, institutionally sponsored loans, scholarships/grants, traineeships, health care benefits, tuition waivers (full and partial), and unspecified assistantships also available. Support available to part-time students. Financial award application deadline: 3/15; financial award applicants required to submit FAFSA. *Faculty research:* Plant sciences, animal sciences, environmental natural resources, biological and agricultural engineering, agricultural economics. *Unit head:* Dr. Mark A. Hussey, Vice Chancellor and Dean for Agriculture and Life Sciences, 979-845-4747, Fax: 979-845-9938, E-mail: mhussey@tamu.edu. *Application contact:* Graduate Admissions, 979-845-1044, E-mail: graduate-admissions@tamu.edu.
Website: http://aglifesciences.tamu.edu/

Texas A&M University–Commerce, College of Agricultural Sciences and Natural Resources, Commerce, TX 75429. Offers agricultural sciences (MS). *Program availability:* Part-time, evening/weekend, 100% online, blended/hybrid learning. *Faculty:* 9 full-time (1 woman), 1 (woman) part-time/adjunct. *Students:* 21 full-time (14 women), 31 part-time (24 women); includes 15 minority (1 Black or African American, non-Hispanic/Latino; 1 American Indian or Alaska Native, non-Hispanic/Latino; 1 Asian, non-Hispanic/Latino; 7 Hispanic/Latino; 5 Two or more races, non-Hispanic/Latino), 3 international. Average age 27. 27 applicants, 59% accepted, 13 enrolled. In 2018, 21 master's awarded. *Degree requirements:* For master's, comprehensive exam, thesis (for some programs). *Entrance requirements:* For master's, GRE or GMAT. Additional exam requirements/recommendations for international students: Required—TOEFL (minimum score 550 paper-based; 79 iBT), IELTS (minimum score 6), PTE (minimum score 53). *Application deadline:* For fall admission, 6/1 priority date for international students; for spring admission, 10/15 priority date for international students; for summer admission, 10/15 priority date for international students. Applications are processed on a rolling basis. Application fee: $50 ($75 for international students). Electronic applications accepted. *Expenses: Tuition, area resident:* Full-time $3630. Tuition, state resident: full-time $3630. Tuition, nonresident: full-time $11,100. *International tuition:* $11,100 full-time. *Required fees:* $2794. Tuition and fees vary according to course load, degree level and program. *Financial support:* In 2018–19, 17 students received support, including 45 research assistantships with partial tuition reimbursements available (averaging $2,736 per year), 1 teaching assistantship with partial tuition reimbursement available (averaging $4,725 per year); career-related internships or fieldwork, Federal Work-Study, institutionally sponsored loans, scholarships/grants, health care benefits, and unspecified assistantships also available. Financial award application deadline: 5/1; financial award applicants required to submit FAFSA. *Faculty research:* Fruits and vegetable trade and demand and price analysis, feeder cattle pricing at auctions, coupons and market shares of food product brands, food product demand and price analysis, Texas wheat uniform variety trials, landscape fabric performance and effect on soil organic matter, performance of ornamental plants and crops, effect of fertilizers on ornamental plants and crops, agricultural teachers and agricultural mechanical competencies, cross-cultural immersion in agricultural education. *Total annual research expenditures:* $98,890. *Unit head:* Dr. Randy Harp, Dean, 903-886-5351, Fax: 903-886-5990, E-mail: randy.harp@tamuc.edu. *Application contact:* Vicky Turner, Doctoral Degree and Special Programs Coordinator, 903-886-5167, E-mail: vicky.turner@tamuc.edu.
Website: https://new.tamuc.edu/agriculture/

Texas A&M University–Kingsville, College of Graduate Studies, Dick and Mary Lewis Kleberg College of Agriculture, Natural Resources and Human Sciences, Kingsville, TX 78363. Offers MS, PhD. *Degree requirements:* For master's, variable foreign language requirement, comprehensive exam, thesis (for some programs); for doctorate, variable foreign language requirement, comprehensive exam, thesis/dissertation. *Entrance requirements:* For master's and doctorate, GRE, GMAT, MAT. Additional exam requirements/recommendations for international students: Required—TOEFL. Electronic applications accepted. *Faculty research:* Mesquite cloning; genesis of soil salinity; dove management; bone development; egg, meat, and milk consumption versus price.

Agricultural Sciences—General

Texas A&M University–Kingsville, College of Graduate Studies, Dick and Mary Lewis Kleberg College of Agriculture, Natural Resources and Human Sciences, Department of Agriculture, Agribusiness, and Environmental Sciences, Program in Agricultural Science, Kingsville, TX 78363. Offers MS. *Degree requirements:* For master's, variable foreign language requirement, comprehensive exam, thesis (for some programs). *Entrance requirements:* For master's, GRE (minimum combined Math & Verbal score of 290), MAT, GMAT, minimum GPA of 2.5. Additional exam requirements/recommendations for international students: Required—TOEFL (minimum score 550 paper-based; 79 iBT). Electronic applications accepted.

Texas Tech University, Graduate School, College of Agricultural Sciences and Natural Resources, Lubbock, TX 79409-2123. Offers MAB, MLA, MS, Ed D, PhD, JD/MS. *Program availability:* Part-time, 100% online, blended/hybrid learning. *Faculty:* 125 full-time (44 women), 19 part-time/adjunct (4 women). *Students:* 304 full-time (162 women), 118 part-time (57 women); includes 51 minority (2 Black or African American, non-Hispanic/Latino; 4 Asian, non-Hispanic/Latino; 34 Hispanic/Latino; 11 Two or more races, non-Hispanic/Latino), 121 international. Average age 29. 176 applicants, 65% accepted, 93 enrolled. In 2018, 88 master's, 31 doctorates awarded. *Degree requirements:* For master's, comprehensive exam (for some programs), thesis or alternative; for doctorate, comprehensive exam, thesis/dissertation. *Entrance requirements:* For master's and doctorate, GRE General Test, formal approval from departmental committee. Additional exam requirements/recommendations for international students: Required—TOEFL (minimum score 550 paper-based; 79 iBT). *Application deadline:* For fall admission, 6/1 priority date for domestic students, 1/15 priority date for international students; for spring admission, 9/1 priority date for domestic students, 6/15 priority date for international students. Applications are processed on a rolling basis. Application fee: $65. Electronic applications accepted. *Expenses:* Contact institution. *Financial support:* In 2018–19, 372 students received support, including 310 fellowships (averaging $3,561 per year), 254 research assistantships (averaging $15,078 per year), 36 teaching assistantships (averaging $15,284 per year); scholarships/grants, health care benefits, and unspecified assistantships also available. Support available to part-time students. Financial award application deadline: 4/15; financial award applicants required to submit FAFSA. *Faculty research:* Biopolymers, sustainable land and water use, food safety, agricultural policy, ecology and land management. *Total annual research expenditures:* $12.8 million. *Unit head:* Dr. William Brown, Dean, 806-742-2808, Fax: 806-742-2836, E-mail: william.f.brown@ttu.edu. *Application contact:* Dr. Christy Bratcher, Associate Dean for Research, 806-834-1364, Fax: 806-742-2836, E-mail: christy.bratcher@ttu.edu.
Website: www.depts.ttu.edu/agriculturalsciences/

Tropical Agriculture Research and Higher Education Center, Graduate School, Turrialba, Costa Rica. Offers agribusiness management (MS); agroforestry systems (PhD); development practices (MS); ecological agriculture (MS); environmental socioeconomics (MS); forestry in tropical and subtropical zones (PhD); integrated watershed management (MS); international sustainable tourism (MS); management and conservation of tropical rainforests and biodiversity (MS); tropical agriculture (PhD); tropical agroforestry (MS). *Entrance requirements:* For master's, GRE, 2 years of related professional experience, letters of recommendation; for doctorate, GRE, 4 letters of recommendation, letter of support from employing organization, master's degree in agronomy, biological sciences, forestry, natural resources or related field. Additional exam requirements/recommendations for international students: Required—TOEFL (minimum score 550 paper-based). Electronic applications accepted. *Faculty research:* Biodiversity in fragmented landscapes, ecosystem management, integrated pest management, environmental livestock production, biotechnology carbon balances in diverse land uses.

Universidad Nacional Pedro Henriquez Urena, Graduate School, Santo Domingo, Dominican Republic. Offers agricultural diversity (MS), including horticultural/fruit production, tropical animal production; conservation of monuments and cultural assets (M Arch); ecology and environment (MS); environmental engineering (MEE); international relations (MA); natural resource management (MS); political science (MA); project optimization (MPM); project feasibility (MPM); project management (MPM); sanitation engineering (ME); science for teachers (MS); tropical Caribbean architecture (M Arch).

Université Laval, Faculty of Agricultural and Food Sciences, Québec, QC G1K 7P4, Canada. Offers M Sc, PhD, Diploma. *Program availability:* Part-time. *Degree requirements:* For doctorate, comprehensive exam, thesis/dissertation. Electronic applications accepted.

University of Alberta, Faculty of Graduate Studies and Research, Department of Agricultural, Food and Nutritional Science, Edmonton, AB T6G 2E1, Canada. Offers M Ag, M Eng, M Sc, PhD, MBA/M Ag. *Degree requirements:* For master's, thesis; for doctorate, comprehensive exam, thesis/dissertation. *Entrance requirements:* For master's, minimum GPA of 3.3; for doctorate, minimum GPA of 3.5. Additional exam requirements/recommendations for international students: Required—IELTS (minimum score 6.5), TOEFL (minimum score of 550 paper-based or a total iBT score of 88 with a score of at least 20 on each of the individual skill areas), Michigan English Language Assessment Battery (minimum score 85); CAEL (overall minimum score 60). *Faculty research:* Animal science, food science, nutrition and metabolism, bioresource engineering, plant science and range management.

The University of Arizona, College of Agriculture and Life Sciences, Tucson, AZ 85721. Offers MAE, MHE Ed, MS, PhD, Graduate Certificate. *Program availability:* Part-time. *Degree requirements:* For doctorate, thesis/dissertation. *Entrance requirements:* For master's, GRE, GMAT, or MAT, bachelor's degree or equivalent, minimum GPA of 3.0. Additional exam requirements/recommendations for international students: Required—TOEFL (minimum score 550 paper-based; 79 iBT). Electronic applications accepted. *Faculty research:* Regulation of skeletal muscle mass during growth, bone health and osteoporosis prevention, regulation of gene expression, development of new crops for arid and semi-arid lands, molecular genetics and pathogenesis of the opportunistic pathogen.

University of Arkansas, Graduate School, Dale Bumpers College of Agricultural, Food and Life Sciences, Fayetteville, AR 72701. Offers MS, PhD. *Students:* 164 applicants, 59% accepted. In 2018, 80 master's, 16 doctorates awarded. *Application deadline:* For fall admission, 8/1 for domestic students, 4/1 for international students; for spring admission, 12/1 for domestic students, 10/1 for international students; for summer admission, 4/15 for domestic students, 3/1 for international students. Applications are processed on a rolling basis. Application fee: $60. Electronic applications accepted. *Financial support:* In 2018–19, 167 research assistantships, 7 teaching assistantships were awarded; fellowships with tuition reimbursements, career-related internships or fieldwork, Federal Work-Study, scholarships/grants, and unspecified assistantships also available. Support available to part-time students. Financial award application deadline: 4/1; financial award applicants required to submit FAFSA. *Unit head:* Dr. Deacue Fields, Dean, 479-575-2034, E-mail: dcfields@uark.edu. *Application contact:* Dausen Garet Duncan, Coordinator of Recruitment, 479-575-2253, E-mail: dgduncan@uark.edu.
Website: http://bumperscollege.uark.edu/

The University of British Columbia, Faculty of Land and Food Systems, Vancouver, BC V6T 1Z4, Canada. Offers M Sc, MFRE, MFS, MLWS, PhD. *Program availability:* Part-time. *Degree requirements:* For master's, thesis; for doctorate, comprehensive exam, thesis/dissertation. *Entrance requirements:* Additional exam requirements/recommendations for international students: Required—TOEFL (minimum score 577 paper-based; 90 iBT), IELTS (minimum score 6.5). Electronic applications accepted.

University of California, Davis, Graduate Studies, Graduate Group in International Agricultural Development, Davis, CA 95616. Offers MS. *Degree requirements:* For master's, comprehensive exam (for some programs), thesis (for some programs). *Entrance requirements:* For master's, GRE General Test, minimum GPA of 3.0. Additional exam requirements/recommendations for international students: Required—TOEFL (minimum score 550 paper-based). Electronic applications accepted. *Faculty research:* Aspects of agricultural, environmental and social sciences on agriculture and related issues in developing countries.

University of Connecticut, Graduate School, College of Agriculture, Health and Natural Resources, Storrs, CT 06269. Offers MS, PhD. Terminal master's awarded for partial completion of doctoral program. *Degree requirements:* For master's, comprehensive exam; for doctorate, comprehensive exam, thesis/dissertation. *Entrance requirements:* For master's and doctorate, GRE General Test. Additional exam requirements/recommendations for international students: Required—TOEFL (minimum score 550 paper-based). Electronic applications accepted.

University of Delaware, College of Agriculture and Natural Resources, Newark, DE 19716. Offers MA, MS, PhD. *Program availability:* Part-time. *Degree requirements:* For master's, thesis; for doctorate, thesis/dissertation. *Entrance requirements:* For master's and doctorate, GRE General Test. Electronic applications accepted.

University of Florida, Graduate School, College of Agricultural and Life Sciences, Gainesville, FL 32611. Offers MAB, MFAS, MFRC, MS, DPM, PhD, Certificate, JD/MFRC, JD/MS, JD/PhD. *Program availability:* Part-time. *Degree requirements:* For master's, comprehensive exam (for some programs), thesis (for some programs); for doctorate, comprehensive exam, thesis/dissertation. *Entrance requirements:* For master's and doctorate, GRE General Test, minimum GPA of 3.0; for Certificate, GRE. Additional exam requirements/recommendations for international students: Required—TOEFL (minimum score 550 paper-based; 80 iBT), IELTS (minimum score 6). Electronic applications accepted. *Faculty research:* Agriculture, human and natural resources, the life sciences.

University of Georgia, College of Agricultural and Environmental Sciences, Athens, GA 30602. Offers MAE, MS, PhD. *Degree requirements:* For doctorate, thesis/dissertation. *Entrance requirements:* For master's and doctorate, GRE General Test. Electronic applications accepted.

University of Guelph, Office of Graduate and Postdoctoral Studies, Ontario Agricultural College, Guelph, ON N1G 2W1, Canada. Offers M Sc, MLA, PhD, Diploma, MA/M Sc. *Program availability:* Part-time, online learning. *Degree requirements:* For doctorate, thesis/dissertation.

University of Hawaii at Manoa, Office of Graduate Education, College of Tropical Agriculture and Human Resources, Honolulu, HI 96822. Offers MS, PhD. *Program availability:* Part-time. *Entrance requirements:* Additional exam requirements/recommendations for international students: Required—TOEFL or IELTS.

University of Illinois at Urbana–Champaign, Graduate College, College of Agricultural, Consumer and Environmental Sciences, Program in Agricultural Production, Champaign, IL 61820. Offers MS. Applications accepted for Fall semester only.

The University of Iowa, Graduate College, College of Public Health, Department of Occupational and Environmental Health, Iowa City, IA 52242-1316. Offers agricultural safety and health (MS, PhD); ergonomics (MPH); industrial hygiene (MS, PhD); occupational and environmental health (MPH, MS, PhD, Certificate); MS/MA; MS/MS. *Accreditation:* ABET (one or more programs are accredited). *Degree requirements:* For master's, thesis optional, exam; for doctorate, comprehensive exam, thesis/dissertation. *Entrance requirements:* For master's and doctorate, GRE General Test, minimum GPA of 3.0. Additional exam requirements/recommendations for international students: Required—TOEFL (minimum score 600 paper-based; 100 iBT). Electronic applications accepted.

University of Kentucky, Graduate School, College of Agriculture, Food and Environment, Lexington, KY 40506-0032. Offers MS, MSFOR, PhD. *Program availability:* Part-time. Terminal master's awarded for partial completion of doctoral program. *Degree requirements:* For master's, comprehensive exam, thesis (for some programs); for doctorate, comprehensive exam, thesis/dissertation. *Entrance requirements:* For master's, GRE General Test, minimum undergraduate GPA of 2.75; for doctorate, GRE General Test, minimum undergraduate GPA of 2.75, graduate 3.0. Additional exam requirements/recommendations for international students: Required—TOEFL (minimum score 550 paper-based). Electronic applications accepted.

University of Lethbridge, School of Graduate Studies, Lethbridge, AB T1K 3M4, Canada. Offers addictions counseling (M Sc); agricultural biotechnology (M Sc); agricultural studies (M Sc, MA); anthropology (MA); archaeology (M Sc, MA); art (MA, MFA); biochemistry (M Sc); biological sciences (M Sc); biomolecular science (PhD); biosystems and biodiversity (PhD); Canadian studies (MA); chemistry (M Sc); computer science (M Sc); computer science and geographical information science (M Sc); counseling (MC); counseling psychology (M Ed); dramatic arts (MA); earth, space, and physical science (PhD); economics (MA); education (MA, PhD); educational leadership (M Ed); English (MA); environmental science (M Sc); evolution and behavior (PhD); exercise science (M Sc); French (MA); French/German (MA); French/Spanish (MA); general education (M Ed); geography (M Sc, MA); German (MA); health sciences (M Sc); individualized multidisciplinary (M Sc, MA); kinesiology (M Sc, MA); management (M Sc), including accounting, finance, human resource management and labor relations, information systems, international management, marketing, policy and strategy; mathematics (M Sc); music (M Mus, MA); Native American studies (MA); neuroscience (M Sc, PhD); new media (MA, MFA); nursing (M Sc, MN); philosophy (MA); physics (M Sc); political science (MA); psychology (M Sc, MA); religious studies (MA); sociology (MA); theatre and dramatic arts (MFA); theoretical and computational science (PhD); urban and regional studies (MA); women and gender studies (MA). *Program availability:* Part-time, evening/weekend. *Degree requirements:* For master's, thesis (for some programs); for doctorate, comprehensive exam, thesis/dissertation. *Entrance requirements:* For master's, GMAT (for M Sc in management), bachelor's degree in related field, minimum GPA of 3.0 during previous 20 graded semester courses, 2 years' teaching or related experience (M Ed); for doctorate, master's degree, minimum graduate GPA of 3.5. Additional exam requirements/recommendations for international students: Required—TOEFL (minimum score 580 paper-based; 93 iBT). Electronic applications accepted. *Faculty research:* Movement and brain plasticity, gibberellin physiology, photosynthesis, carbon cycling, molecular properties of main-group ring components.

University of Maine, Graduate School, College of Natural Sciences, Forestry, and Agriculture, Orono, ME 04469. Offers MA, MF, MPS, MS, MSW, MWC, PSM, PhD, CAS, CGS. *Accreditation:* SAF (one or more programs are accredited). *Program availability:* Part-time, evening/weekend. *Faculty:* 193 full-time (86 women), 122 part-time/adjunct (45 women). *Students:* 500 full-time (339 women), 59 part-time (45 women); includes 46 minority (4 Black or African American, non-Hispanic/Latino; 10 American Indian or Alaska Native, non-Hispanic/Latino; 11 Asian, non-Hispanic/Latino; 13 Hispanic/Latino; 8 Two or more races, non-Hispanic/Latino), 72 international. Average age 30. 562 applicants, 56% accepted, 188 enrolled. In 2018, 129 master's, 21 doctorates, 9 other advanced degrees awarded. Terminal master's awarded for partial completion of doctoral program. *Degree requirements:* For master's, thesis (for some programs); for doctorate, comprehensive exam, thesis/dissertation. *Entrance requirements:* For master's and doctorate, GRE General Test. Additional exam requirements/recommendations for international students: Required—TOEFL. *Application deadline:* For fall admission, 2/1 priority date for domestic students. Applications are processed on a rolling basis. Application fee: $65. Electronic applications accepted. *Financial support:* In 2018–19, 347 students received support, including 7 fellowships (averaging $23,900 per year), 190 research assistantships (averaging $19,700 per year), 93 teaching assistantships (averaging $16,000 per year); career-related internships or fieldwork, Federal Work-Study, institutionally sponsored loans, scholarships/grants, health care benefits, tuition waivers (full and partial), and unspecified assistantships also available. Support available to part-time students. Financial award application deadline: 3/1. *Total annual research expenditures:* $25.8 million. *Unit head:* Dr. Fred Servello, Interim Dean, 207-581-3206, Fax: 207-581-3207. *Application contact:* Scott G. Delcourt, Assistant Vice President for Graduate Studies and Senior Associate Dean, 207-581-3291, Fax: 207-581-3232, E-mail: graduate@maine.edu.
Website: http://nsfa.umaine.edu

University of Manitoba, Faculty of Graduate Studies, Faculty of Agricultural and Food Sciences, Winnipeg, MB R3T 2N2, Canada. Offers M Sc, PhD. *Degree requirements:* For master's, thesis or alternative; for doctorate, variable foreign language requirement, thesis/dissertation.

University of Maryland, College Park, Academic Affairs, College of Agriculture and Natural Resources, College Park, MD 20742. Offers MS, DVM, PhD. *Program availability:* Part-time, evening/weekend. *Degree requirements:* For doctorate, thesis/dissertation. *Entrance requirements:* For master's, minimum GPA of 3.0. Additional exam requirements/recommendations for international students: Required—TOEFL. Electronic applications accepted.

University of Maryland Eastern Shore, Graduate Programs, Department of Agriculture, Food and Resource Sciences, Program in Food and Agricultural Sciences, Princess Anne, MD 21853. Offers MS. *Degree requirements:* For master's, comprehensive exam, thesis or alternative, oral exams. *Entrance requirements:* For master's, GRE General Test, minimum GPA of 3.0. Additional exam requirements/recommendations for international students: Required—TOEFL (minimum score 80 iBT). Electronic applications accepted. *Faculty research:* Poultry and swine nutrition and management, soybean specialty products, farm management practices, agriculture technology.

University of Minnesota, Twin Cities Campus, Graduate School, College of Food, Agricultural and Natural Resource Sciences, Saint Paul, MN 55108. Offers MS, PhD. *Program availability:* Part-time. Terminal master's awarded for partial completion of doctoral program. *Degree requirements:* For master's, comprehensive exam, thesis; for doctorate, comprehensive exam, thesis/dissertation. *Entrance requirements:* For master's and doctorate, GRE General Test. Additional exam requirements/recommendations for international students: Required—TOEFL (minimum score 550 paper-based; 79 iBT), IELTS (minimum score 6.5). Electronic applications accepted. *Expenses:* Contact institution. *Faculty research:* All aspects of agriculture: forestry, soils, ento, plant path, agron/hort, nutrition, food science, animal science, applied econ, bioproducts/systems engineering/management, water resources, cons bio.

University of Missouri, Office of Research and Graduate Studies, College of Agriculture, Food and Natural Resources, Columbia, MO 65211. Offers MS, PhD, PhD/MD. *Program availability:* Part-time. Terminal master's awarded for partial completion of doctoral program. *Entrance requirements:* For master's and doctorate, GRE General Test, minimum GPA of 3.0.

University of Nebraska–Lincoln, Graduate College, College of Agricultural Sciences and Natural Resources, Lincoln, NE 68588. Offers M Ag, MA, MBA, MS, PhD. *Degree requirements:* For doctorate, comprehensive exam, thesis/dissertation. *Entrance requirements:* Additional exam requirements/recommendations for international students: Required—TOEFL. Electronic applications accepted. *Faculty research:* Environmental sciences, animal sciences, human resources and family sciences, plant breeding and genetics, food and nutrition.

University of Nevada, Reno, Graduate School, College of Agriculture, Biotechnology and Natural Resources, Reno, NV 89557. Offers MS, PhD. Terminal master's awarded for partial completion of doctoral program. *Degree requirements:* For master's, thesis optional; for doctorate, thesis/dissertation. *Entrance requirements:* For master's, GRE General Test, minimum GPA of 2.75; for doctorate, GRE General Test, minimum GPA of 3.0. Additional exam requirements/recommendations for international students: Required—TOEFL (minimum score 500 paper-based; 61 iBT), IELTS (minimum score 6). Electronic applications accepted.

University of New Hampshire, Graduate School, College of Life Sciences and Agriculture, Department of Molecular, Cellular and Biomedical Sciences, Program in Animal and Nutritional Sciences, Durham, NH 03824. Offers agricultural sciences (MS, PhD); nutritional sciences (MS, PhD). *Program availability:* Part-time. *Entrance requirements:* For master's and doctorate, GRE. Additional exam requirements/recommendations for international students: Required—TOEFL (minimum score 550 paper-based; 80 iBT). Electronic applications accepted.

University of Puerto Rico–Mayagüez, Graduate Studies, College of Agricultural Sciences, Mayagüez, PR 00681-9000. Offers MS. *Program availability:* Part-time. *Degree requirements:* For master's, comprehensive exam, thesis.

University of Saskatchewan, College of Graduate and Postdoctoral Studies, College of Agriculture and Bioresources, Saskatoon, SK S7N 5A2, Canada. Offers M Ag, M Sc, MA, PhD, Diploma, PGD. *Program availability:* Part-time. *Degree requirements:* For master's, thesis (for some programs); for doctorate, comprehensive exam (for some programs), thesis/dissertation. *Entrance requirements:* Additional exam requirements/

recommendations for international students: Required—TOEFL (minimum score 80 iBT); Recommended—IELTS (minimum score 6.5).

University of South Africa, College of Agriculture and Environmental Sciences, Pretoria, South Africa. Offers agriculture (MS); consumer science (MCS); environmental management (MA, MS, PhD); environmental science (MA, MS, PhD); geography (MA, MS, PhD); horticulture (M Tech); human ecology (MHE); life sciences (MS); nature conservation (M Tech).

The University of Tennessee, Graduate School, College of Agricultural Sciences and Natural Resources, Knoxville, TN 37996. Offers MS, PhD. *Program availability:* Part-time, online learning. *Degree requirements:* For master's, thesis (for some programs), for doctorate, thesis/dissertation. *Entrance requirements:* For master's and doctorate, minimum GPA of 2.7. Additional exam requirements/recommendations for international students: Required—TOEFL. Electronic applications accepted.

The University of Tennessee at Martin, Graduate Programs, College of Agriculture and Applied Sciences, Program in Agricultural and Natural Resources Management, Martin, TN 38238. Offers MSANR. *Program availability:* Part-time, online only, 100% online. *Faculty:* 15. *Students:* 3 full-time (all women), 19 part-time (9 women). Average age 29. 22 applicants, 41% accepted, 6 enrolled. In 2018, 9 master's awarded. *Degree requirements:* For master's, comprehensive exam, thesis optional. *Entrance requirements:* For master's, GRE General Test, minimum GPA of 2.5. Additional exam requirements/recommendations for international students: Required—TOEFL (minimum score 525 paper-based; 71 iBT). *Application deadline:* For fall admission, 7/27 priority date for domestic and international students; for spring admission, 12/17 priority date for domestic and international students; for summer admission, 5/10 priority date for domestic and international students. Applications are processed on a rolling basis. Application fee: $30 ($130 for international students). Electronic applications accepted. *Expenses: Tuition, area resident:* Full-time $8918; part-time $495 per credit hour. Tuition, state resident: full-time $8918; part-time $485 per credit hour. Tuition, nonresident: full-time $14,958; part-time $831 per credit hour. *International tuition:* $22,862 full-time. *Required fees:* $1446; $81 per credit hour. Part-time tuition and fees vary according to course load. *Financial support:* In 2018–19, 9 students received support, including 1 teaching assistantship with full tuition reimbursement available (averaging $3,431 per year); research assistantships, scholarships/grants, and tuition waivers (full and partial) also available. Financial award application deadline: 2/1; financial award applicants required to submit FAFSA. *Unit head:* Dr. Joey Mehlhorn, Interim Coordinator, 731-881-7275, Fax: 731-881-7968, E-mail: mehlhorn@utm.edu. *Application contact:* Jolene L. Cunningham, Student Services Specialist, 731-881-7012, Fax: 731-881-7499, E-mail: jcunningham@utm.edu.
Website: http://www.utm.edu/departments/caas/msanr

The University of Texas Rio Grande Valley, College of Sciences, School of Earth, Environmental, and Marine Sciences, Edinburg, TX 78539. Offers agricultural, environmental, and sustainability sciences (MS); ocean, coastal, and earth sciences (MS). *Expenses: Tuition, area resident:* Full-time $6888. Tuition, state resident: full-time $6888. Tuition, nonresident: full-time $14,484. *International tuition:* $14,484 full-time. *Required fees:* $1468.

University of Vermont, Graduate College, College of Agriculture and Life Sciences, Burlington, VT 05405. Offers MPA, MS, PhD, Graduate Certificate. *Program availability:* Part-time. *Degree requirements:* For doctorate, one foreign language, thesis/dissertation. *Entrance requirements:* For master's and doctorate, GRE General Test. Additional exam requirements/recommendations for international students: Required—TOEFL (minimum score 550 paper-based; 90 iBT), IELTS (minimum score 6.5). Electronic applications accepted.

University of Wisconsin–Madison, Graduate School, College of Agricultural and Life Sciences, Madison, WI 53706-1380. Offers MA, MPS, MS, PhD. *Program availability:* Part-time. *Entrance requirements:* For master's and doctorate, GRE. Additional exam requirements/recommendations for international students: Required—TOEFL. Electronic applications accepted.

University of Wisconsin–River Falls, Outreach and Graduate Studies, College of Agriculture, Food, and Environmental Sciences, River Falls, WI 54022. Offers MS. *Program availability:* Part-time. *Degree requirements:* For master's, comprehensive exam, thesis (for some programs). *Entrance requirements:* For master's, minimum GPA of 2.75. Additional exam requirements/recommendations for international students: Required—TOEFL (minimum score 500 paper-based; 65 iBT), IELTS (minimum score 5.4). Electronic applications accepted.

University of Wyoming, College of Agriculture and Natural Resources, Laramie, WY 82071. Offers MA, MS, PhD. *Program availability:* Part-time. Terminal master's awarded for partial completion of doctoral program. *Degree requirements:* For doctorate, thesis/dissertation. *Entrance requirements:* For master's and doctorate, GRE General Test, minimum GPA of 3.0. Electronic applications accepted. *Expenses: Tuition, area resident:* Full-time $6504; part-time $271 per credit hour. Tuition, state resident: full-time $6504; part-time $271 per credit hour. Tuition, nonresident: full-time $19,464; part-time $811 per credit hour. *International tuition:* $19,464 full-time. *Required fees:* $1410.94; $343.82 per semester. $343.82 per semester. Tuition and fees vary according to course load, program and reciprocity agreements. *Faculty research:* Nutrition, molecular biology, animal science, plant science, entomology.

Utah State University, School of Graduate Studies, College of Agriculture and Applied Sciences, Logan, UT 84322. Offers MAE, MDA, MLA, MPS, MS, PhD. *Program availability:* Part-time, online learning. Terminal master's awarded for partial completion of doctoral program. *Degree requirements:* For doctorate, thesis/dissertation. *Entrance requirements:* For master's and doctorate, GRE General Test, minimum GPA of 3.0. Additional exam requirements/recommendations for international students: Required—TOEFL. *Faculty research:* Low-input agriculture, anti-viral chemotherapy, lactic culture, environmental biophysics and climate.

Virginia Polytechnic Institute and State University, Graduate School, College of Agriculture and Life Sciences, Blacksburg, VA 24061. Offers agricultural and applied economics (MS, PhD); agricultural and life sciences (MS); agriculture, leadership, and community education (MS, PhD); animal and poultry science (MS, PhD); biochemistry (MS, PhD); crop and soil environmental sciences (MS, PhD); dairy science (MS, PhD); entomology (MS, PhD); food science and technology (MS, PhD); horticulture (PhD); human nutrition, foods and exercise (MS, PhD); plant pathology, physiology, and weed science (MS, PhD). *Faculty:* 244 full-time (79 women), 1 (woman) part-time/adjunct. *Students:* 360 full-time (195 women), 110 part-time (73 women); includes 70 minority (24 Black or African American, non-Hispanic/Latino; 1 American Indian or Alaska Native, non-Hispanic/Latino; 15 Asian, non-Hispanic/Latino; 12 Hispanic/Latino; 18 Two or more races, non-Hispanic/Latino), 110 international. Average age 28. 296 applicants, 54% accepted, 105 enrolled. In 2018, 92 master's, 59 doctorates awarded. *Degree requirements:* For master's, comprehensive exam (for some programs), thesis (for some programs); for doctorate, comprehensive exam (for some programs), thesis/dissertation (for some programs). *Entrance requirements:* For master's and doctorate, GRE/GMAT.

Peterson's Graduate Programs in the Physical Sciences, Mathematics, Agricultural Sciences, the Environment & Natural Resources 2020

www.petersons.com **265**

Additional exam requirements/recommendations for international students: Required—TOEFL (minimum score 90 iBT). *Application deadline:* For fall admission, 8/1 for domestic students, 4/1 for international students; for spring admission, 1/1 for domestic students, 9/1 for international students. Applications are processed on a rolling basis. Application fee: $75. Electronic applications accepted. *Expenses:* Tuition, state resident: full-time $15,510; part-time $739.50 per credit hour. Tuition, nonresident: full-time $29,629; part-time $1490.25 per credit hour. *Required fees:* $2804; $550 per semester. Tuition and fees vary according to course load, campus/location and program. *Financial support:* In 2018–19, 3 fellowships with full tuition reimbursements (averaging $25,731 per year), 249 research assistantships with full tuition reimbursements (averaging $19,826 per year), 105 teaching assistantships with full tuition reimbursements (averaging $19,277 per year) were awarded; scholarships/grants and unspecified assistantships also available. Financial award application deadline: 3/1; financial award applicants required to submit FAFSA. *Total annual research expenditures:* $42.4 million. *Unit head:* Dr. Alan L. Grant, Dean, 540-231-4152, Fax: 540-231-4163, E-mail: algrant@vt.edu. *Application contact:* Crystal Tawney, Administrative Assistant, 540-231-4152, Fax: 540-231-4163, E-mail: cdtawney@vt.edu.
Website: http://www.cals.vt.edu/

Virginia Polytechnic Institute and State University, VT Online, Blacksburg, VA 24061. Offers advanced transportation systems (Certificate); aerospace engineering (MS); agricultural and life sciences (MSLFS); business information systems (Graduate Certificate); career and technical education (MS); civil engineering (MS); computer engineering (M Eng, MS); decision support systems (Graduate Certificate); eLearning leadership (MA); electrical engineering (M Eng, MS); engineering administration (MEA); environmental engineering (Certificate); environmental politics and policy (Graduate Certificate); environmental sciences and engineering (MS); foundations of political analysis (Graduate Certificate); health product risk management (Graduate Certificate); industrial and systems engineering (MS); information policy and society (Graduate Certificate); information security (Graduate Certificate); information technology (MIT); instructional technology (MA); integrative STEM education (MA Ed); liberal arts (Graduate Certificate); life sciences: health product risk management (MS); natural resources (MNR, Graduate Certificate); networking (Graduate Certificate); nonprofit and nongovernmental organization management (Graduate Certificate); ocean engineering (MS); political science (MA); security studies (Graduate Certificate); software development (Graduate Certificate). *Expenses:* Tuition, state resident: full-time $15,510; part-time $739.50 per credit hour. Tuition, nonresident: full-time $29,629; part-time $1490.25 per credit hour. *Required fees:* $2804; $550 per semester. Tuition and fees vary according to course load, campus/location and program. *Application contact:* Graduate Admissions and Academic Progress, 540-231-8636, E-mail: grads@vt.edu.
Website: http://www.vto.vt.edu/

Western Kentucky University, Graduate School, Ogden College of Science and Engineering, Department of Agriculture, Bowling Green, KY 42101. Offers MA Ed, MS. *Program availability:* Part-time, evening/weekend. *Degree requirements:* For master's, comprehensive exam, thesis optional. *Entrance requirements:* For master's, GRE General Test, minimum GPA of 2.75. Additional exam requirements/recommendations for international students: Required—TOEFL (minimum score 555 paper-based; 79 iBT). *Faculty research:* Establishment of warm season grasses, heat composting, enrichment activities in agricultural education.

West Texas A&M University, College of Agriculture and Natural Sciences, Department of Agricultural Sciences, Canyon, TX 79015. Offers agricultural business and economics (MS); agriculture (MS, PhD); animal science (MS); plant, soil and environmental science (MS). *Program availability:* Part-time. *Degree requirements:* For master's, comprehensive exam, thesis optional. *Entrance requirements:* For master's, GRE General Test. Additional exam requirements/recommendations for international students: Required—TOEFL (minimum score 550 paper-based). Electronic applications accepted.

West Virginia University, Davis College of Agriculture, Forestry and Consumer Sciences, Morgantown, WV 26506. Offers agricultural and extension education (MS, PhD); agriculture and resource management (MS); agriculture, natural resources and design (M Agr); agronomy (MS); animal and food science (PhD); animal physiology (MS); applied and environmental microbiology (MS); design and merchandising (MS); entomology (MS); forest resource science (PhD); forestry (MSF); genetics and developmental biology (MS, PhD); horticulture (MS); human and community development (PhD); landscape architecture (MLA); natural resource economics (PhD); nutritional and food science (MS); plant and soil science (PhD); plant pathology (MS); recreation, parks and tourism resources (MS); reproductive physiology (MS, PhD); wildlife and fisheries resources (PhD). *Accreditation:* ASLA. *Program availability:* Part-time. *Students:* 188 full-time (86 women), 47 part-time (30 women); includes 22 minority (5 Black or African American, non-Hispanic/Latino; 5 Asian, non-Hispanic/Latino; 8 Hispanic/Latino; 4 Two or more races, non-Hispanic/Latino), 60 international. In 2018, 56 master's, 14 doctorates awarded. *Degree requirements:* For master's, thesis; for doctorate, thesis/dissertation. *Entrance requirements:* Additional exam requirements/recommendations for international students: Required—TOEFL (minimum score 550 paper-based). *Application deadline:* For fall admission, 6/1 priority date for domestic students, 6/1 for international students; for spring admission, 1/5 for domestic and international students. Applications are processed on a rolling basis. Application fee: $60. Electronic applications accepted. *Financial support:* Fellowships, research assistantships, teaching assistantships, career-related internships or fieldwork, Federal Work-Study, institutionally sponsored loans, tuition waivers (full and partial), and unspecified assistantships available. Financial award application deadline: 2/1; financial award applicants required to submit FAFSA. *Faculty research:* Reproductive physiology, soil and water quality, human nutrition, aquaculture, wildlife management. *Unit head:* Dr. Ken Blemings, Interim Dean, 304-293-2395, Fax: 304-293-3740, E-mail: ken.blemings@mail.wvu.edu. *Application contact:* Dr. J. Todd Petty, Associate Dean, 304-293-2278, Fax: 304-293-3740, E-mail: jtpetty@mail.wvu.edu.
Website: https://www.davis.wvu.edu

Agronomy and Soil Sciences

Alabama Agricultural and Mechanical University, School of Graduate Studies, College of Agricultural, Life and Natural Sciences, Department of Biological and Environmental Sciences, Huntsville, AL 35811. Offers biology (MS); plant and soil science (MS, PhD). *Program availability:* Evening/weekend. Terminal master's awarded for partial completion of doctoral program. *Degree requirements:* For master's, thesis optional; for doctorate, one foreign language, thesis/dissertation optional. *Entrance requirements:* For master's, GRE General Test, BS in agriculture; for doctorate, GRE General Test, master's degree. Additional exam requirements/recommendations for international students: Required—TOEFL (minimum score 500 paper-based; 61 iBT). Electronic applications accepted. *Faculty research:* Plant breeding, cytogenetics, crop production, soil chemistry and fertility, remote sensing.

Alcorn State University, School of Graduate Studies, School of Agriculture and Applied Sciences, Lorman, MS 39096-7500. Offers agricultural economics (MS Ag); agronomy (MS Ag); animal science (MS Ag). *Degree requirements:* For master's, thesis optional. *Faculty research:* Aquatic systems, dairy herd improvement, fruit production, alternative farming practices.

Auburn University, Graduate School, College of Agriculture, Department of Agronomy and Soils, Auburn University, AL 36849. Offers M Ag, MS, PhD. *Program availability:* Part-time. *Degree requirements:* For master's, thesis (for some programs); for doctorate, thesis/dissertation. *Entrance requirements:* For master's and doctorate, GRE General Test. Electronic applications accepted. *Expenses:* Tuition, state resident: full-time $11,282; part-time $535 per credit hour. Tuition, nonresident: full-time $30,542; part-time $1605 per credit hour. *Required fees:* $826 per semester. Tuition and fees vary according to degree level and program. *Faculty research:* Plant breeding and genetics; weed science; crop production; soil fertility and plant nutrition; soil genesis, morphology, and classification.

Colorado State University, College of Agricultural Sciences, Department of Bioagricultural Sciences and Pest Management, Fort Collins, CO 80523-1177. Offers entomology (MS, PhD); pest management (MS); plant pathology (MS, PhD); weed science (MS, PhD). Terminal master's awarded for partial completion of doctoral program. *Degree requirements:* For master's, thesis; for doctorate, thesis/dissertation. *Entrance requirements:* For master's and doctorate, minimum GPA of 3.0, three letters of recommendation, essay, transcripts, short essay outlining experience and career goals. Additional exam requirements/recommendations for international students: Required—TOEFL (minimum score 550 paper-based). Electronic applications accepted. *Expenses:* Tuition, state resident: full-time $10,520; part-time $4675 per credit hour. Tuition, nonresident: full-time $25,791; part-time $11,462 per credit hour. *International tuition:* $25,791 full-time. *Required fees:* $2392; $576 $288. Tuition and fees vary according to course level, course load, degree level, program and student level. *Faculty research:* Genomics and molecular biology, ecology and genetics, ecology and evolution of pest organisms, herbicide resistant weeds.

Colorado State University, College of Agricultural Sciences, Department of Soil and Crop Sciences, Fort Collins, CO 80523-1170. Offers MS, PhD. *Program availability:* Part-time. Terminal master's awarded for partial completion of doctoral program. *Degree requirements:* For master's, thesis; for doctorate, comprehensive exam, teaching/dissertation. *Entrance requirements:* For master's and doctorate, GRE. Additional exam requirements/recommendations for international students: Required—TOEFL (minimum score 550 paper-based), IELTS (minimum score 6.5). Electronic applications accepted. *Expenses:* Tuition, state resident: full-time $10,520; part-time $4675 per credit hour. Tuition, nonresident: full-time $25,791; part-time $11,462 per credit hour. *International tuition:* $25,791 full-time. *Required fees:* $2392; $576 $288. Tuition and fees vary according to course level, course load, degree level, program and student level. *Faculty research:* Agroecosystem management, plant breeding and genetics, soil science.

Cornell University, Graduate School, Graduate Fields of Agriculture and Life Sciences, Field of Soil and Crop Sciences, Ithaca, NY 14853. Offers agronomy (MS, PhD); environmental information science (MS, PhD); environmental management (MPS); field crop science (MS, PhD); soil science (MS, PhD). *Degree requirements:* For master's, thesis (MS); for doctorate, comprehensive exam, thesis/dissertation. *Entrance requirements:* For master's and doctorate, GRE General Test, 2 letters of recommendation. Additional exam requirements/recommendations for international students: Required—TOEFL (minimum score 550 paper-based; 77 iBT). Electronic applications accepted. *Faculty research:* Soil chemistry, physics and biology; crop physiology and management; environmental information science and modeling; international agriculture; weed science.

Dalhousie University, Faculty of Agriculture, Halifax, NS B3H 4R2, Canada. Offers agriculture (M Sc), including air quality, animal behavior, animal molecular genetics, animal nutrition, animal technology, aquaculture, botany, crop management, crop physiology, ecology, environmental microbiology, food science, horticulture, nutrient management, pest management, physiology, plant biotechnology, plant pathology, soil chemistry, soil fertility, waste management and composting, water quality. *Program availability:* Part-time. *Degree requirements:* For master's, thesis, ATC Exam Teaching Assistantship. *Entrance requirements:* For master's, honors B Sc, minimum GPA of 3.0. Additional exam requirements/recommendations for international students: Required—TOEFL (minimum score 580 paper-based; 92 iBT), IELTS, Michigan English Language Assessment Battery, CanTEST, CAEL. *Faculty research:* Bio-product development, organic agriculture, nutrient management, air and water quality, agricultural biotechnology.

Iowa State University of Science and Technology, Department of Agronomy, Ames, IA 50011. Offers agricultural meteorology (MS, PhD); agronomy (MS); crop production and physiology (MS, PhD); plant breeding (MS, PhD); soil science (MS, PhD). *Degree requirements:* For master's, thesis or alternative. *Entrance requirements:* Additional exam requirements/recommendations for international students: Recommended—TOEFL (minimum score 550 paper-based; 79 iBT), IELTS (minimum score 6.5). Electronic applications accepted.

Iowa State University of Science and Technology, Program in Crop Production and Physiology, Ames, IA 50011. Offers MS, PhD. *Entrance requirements:* Additional exam requirements/recommendations for international students: Required—TOEFL (minimum score 550 paper-based; 79 iBT), IELTS (minimum score 6.5). Electronic applications accepted.

Iowa State University of Science and Technology, Program in Soil Science, Ames, IA 50011. Offers MS, PhD. *Entrance requirements:* Additional exam requirements/recommendations for international students: Required—TOEFL (minimum score 550 paper-based; 79 iBT), IELTS (minimum score 6.5). Electronic applications accepted.

Kansas State University, Graduate School, College of Agriculture, Department of Agronomy, Manhattan, KS 66506. Offers crop science (MS, PhD); grassland management (Certificate); plant breeding and genetics (MS, PhD); range and forage science (MS, PhD); soil and environmental science (MS, PhD); weed science (MS, PhD). *Program availability:* Part-time. *Degree requirements:* For master's, thesis or alternative, oral exam; for doctorate, thesis/dissertation, preliminary exams. *Entrance requirements:* For master's, minimum GPA of 3.0 in BS; for doctorate, minimum GPA of 3.0 in master's program. Additional exam requirements/recommendations for international students: Required—TOEFL (minimum score 79 iBT). Electronic applications accepted. *Expenses:* Contact institution. *Faculty research:* Range and forage science; soil and environmental science; weed science; plant breeding and genetics; crop physiology, ecology and production.

Louisiana State University and Agricultural & Mechanical College, Graduate School, College of Agriculture, School of Plant, Environmental and Soil Sciences, Baton Rouge, LA 70803. Offers agronomy (MS, PhD); horticulture (MS, PhD); soil science (MS, PhD).

McGill University, Faculty of Graduate and Postdoctoral Studies, Faculty of Agricultural and Environmental Sciences, Department of Bioresource Engineering, Montréal, QC H3A 2T5, Canada. Offers computer applications (M Sc, M Sc A, PhD); food engineering (M Sc, M Sc A, PhD); grain drying (M Sc, M Sc A, PhD); irrigation and drainage (M Sc, M Sc A, PhD); machinery (M Sc, M Sc A, PhD); pollution control (M Sc, M Sc A, PhD); post-harvest technology (M Sc, M Sc A, PhD); soil dynamics (M Sc, M Sc A, PhD); structure and environment (M Sc, M Sc A, PhD); vegetable and fruit storage (M Sc, M Sc A, PhD).

McGill University, Faculty of Graduate and Postdoctoral Studies, Faculty of Agricultural and Environmental Sciences, Department of Natural Resource Sciences, Montréal, QC H3A 2T5, Canada. Offers entomology (M Sc, PhD); environmental assessment (M Sc); forest science (M Sc, PhD); microbiology (M Sc, PhD); micrometeorology (M Sc, PhD); neotropical environment (M Sc, PhD); soil science (M Sc, PhD); wildlife biology (M Sc, PhD).

Michigan State University, The Graduate School, College of Agriculture and Natural Resources, Department of Plant, Soil and Microbial Sciences, East Lansing, MI 48824. Offers crop and soil sciences (MS, PhD); crop and soil sciences-environmental toxicology (PhD); plant breeding and genetics-crop and soil sciences (MS); plant breeding, genetics and biotechnology-crop and soil sciences (PhD); plant pathology (MS, PhD). *Entrance requirements:* Additional exam requirements/recommendations for international students: Required—TOEFL (minimum score 550 paper-based), Michigan State University ELT (minimum score 85), Michigan Michigan English Language Assessment Battery (minimum score 83). Electronic applications accepted.

Michigan State University, The Graduate School, College of Natural Science, MSU-DOE Plant Research Laboratory, East Lansing, MI 48824. Offers biochemistry and molecular biology (PhD); cellular and molecular biology (PhD); crop and soil sciences (PhD); genetics (PhD); microbiology and molecular genetics (PhD); plant biology (PhD); plant physiology (PhD). Offered jointly with the Department of Energy. *Degree requirements:* For doctorate, comprehensive exam, thesis/dissertation, laboratory rotation, defense of dissertation. *Entrance requirements:* For doctorate, GRE General Test, acceptance into one of the affiliated department programs; 3 letters of recommendation; bachelor's degree or equivalent in life sciences, chemistry, biochemistry, or biophysics; research experience. Electronic applications accepted. *Faculty research:* Role of hormones in the regulation of plant development and physiology, molecular mechanisms associated with signal recognition, development and application of genetic methods and materials, protein routing and function.

Mississippi State University, College of Agriculture and Life Sciences, Department of Plant and Soil Sciences, Mississippi State, MS 39762. Offers weed science (MS, PhD), including agronomy, horticulture, weed science. *Faculty:* 43 full-time (6 women). *Students:* 47 full-time (16 women), 32 part-time (9 women); includes 3 minority (all Black or African American, non-Hispanic/Latino), 21 international. Average age 29. 21 applicants, 43% accepted, 9 enrolled. In 2018, 18 master's, 11 doctorates awarded. *Degree requirements:* For master's, comprehensive exam, thesis, oral and/or written exams; for doctorate, comprehensive exam, thesis/dissertation, minimum of 20 semester hours of research for dissertation. *Entrance requirements:* For master's, GRE (for weed science), minimum GPA of 2.75 (agronomy/horticulture), 3.0 (weed science); for doctorate, GRE (for weed science), minimum GPA of 3.0 (agronomy/horticulture), 3.25 (weed science). Additional exam requirements/recommendations for international students: Required—TOEFL (minimum score 500 paper-based; 61 iBT), TOEFL minimum score 550 paper-based, 79 iBT or IELTS minimum score 6.5 (for weed science); Recommended—IELTS (minimum score 5.5). *Application deadline:* For fall admission, 7/1 for domestic students, 5/1 for international students; for spring admission, 10/1 for domestic students, 9/1 for international students. Applications are processed on a rolling basis. Application fee: $60 ($80 for international students). Electronic applications accepted. *Expenses:* Tuition, state resident: full-time $8450; part-time $360.59 per credit hour. Tuition, nonresident: full-time $23,140; part-time $969.09 per credit hour. *Required fees:* $110. One-time fee: $55 full-time. Part-time tuition and fees vary according to course load, degree level, campus/location and reciprocity agreements. *Financial support:* In 2018–19, 40 research assistantships with full tuition reimbursements (averaging $15,736 per year), 4 teaching assistantships with partial tuition reimbursements (averaging $14,888 per year) were awarded; Federal Work-Study, institutionally sponsored loans, scholarships/grants, and unspecified assistantships also available. Financial award application deadline: 4/1; financial award applicants required to submit FAFSA. *Faculty research:* Bioenergy crops, cotton breeding, environmental plant pathology, row crop weed control, genomics. *Unit head:* Dr. J. Michael Phillips, Professor and Head, 662-325-2311, Fax: 662-325-8742, E-mail: jmp657@msstate.edu. *Application contact:* Ryan King, Admissions and Enrollment Assistant, 662-325-8951, E-mail: rjk101@grad.msstate.edu.
Website: http://www.pss.msstate.edu/

North Carolina Agricultural and Technical State University, The Graduate College, College of Agriculture and Environmental Sciences, Department of Natural Resources and Environmental Design, Greensboro, NC 27411. Offers plant, soil and environmental science (MS). *Program availability:* Part-time, evening/weekend. *Degree requirements:* For master's, comprehensive exam, thesis optional, qualifying exam. *Entrance requirements:* For master's, GRE General Test, minimum GPA of 3.0. *Faculty research:* Soil parameters and compaction of forest site, controlled traffic effects on soil, improving soybean and vegetable crops.

North Carolina State University, Graduate School, College of Agriculture and Life Sciences, Department of Crop and Soil Sciences, Raleigh, NC 27695. Offers soil science (MS, PhD). *Program availability:* Part-time. Terminal master's awarded for partial completion of doctoral program. *Degree requirements:* For master's, thesis; for doctorate, thesis/dissertation. *Entrance requirements:* For master's and doctorate, GRE. Electronic applications accepted. *Faculty research:* Crop breeding and genetics, application of biotechnology to crop improvement, plant physiology, crop physiology and management, agroecology.

North Dakota State University, College of Graduate and Interdisciplinary Studies, College of Agriculture, Food Systems, and Natural Resources, Department of Soil Science, Fargo, ND 58102. Offers soil sciences (MS, PhD). *Program availability:* Part-time. *Degree requirements:* For master's, comprehensive exam, thesis, classroom teaching; for doctorate, comprehensive exam, thesis/dissertation, classroom teaching. *Entrance requirements:* Additional exam requirements/recommendations for international students: Required—TOEFL (minimum score 525 paper-based; 71 iBT). Electronic applications accepted. *Faculty research:* Microclimate, nitrogen management, landscape studies, water quality, soil management.

The Ohio State University, Graduate School, College of Food, Agricultural, and Environmental Sciences, School of Environment and Natural Resources, Columbus, OH 43210. Offers ecological restoration (MS, PhD); ecosystem science (MS, PhD); environment and natural resources (MENR); environmental social sciences (MS, PhD); fisheries and wildlife science (MS, PhD); forest science (MS, PhD); rural sociology (MS, PhD); soil science (MS, PhD). *Faculty:* 38. *Students:* 106 (64 women). Average age 29. In 2018, 21 master's, 5 doctorates awarded. *Entrance requirements:* For master's and doctorate, GRE. Additional exam requirements/recommendations for international students: Required—TOEFL (minimum score 550 paper-based; 79 iBT), Michigan English Language Assessment Battery (minimum score 82); Recommended—IELTS (minimum score 7). *Application deadline:* For fall admission, 1/1 priority date for domestic students, 12/15 priority date for international students; for spring admission, 11/1 for domestic students, 9/15 for international students. Applications are processed on a rolling basis. Application fee: $60 ($70 for international students). Electronic applications accepted. *Financial support:* Fellowships, research assistantships, teaching assistantships, health care benefits, and unspecified assistantships available. *Unit head:* Dr. Jeff S. Sharp, Director, 614-292-9410, E-mail: sharp.123@osu.edu. *Application contact:* Graduate and Professional Admissions, 614-292-9444, Fax: 614-292-3895, E-mail: gpadmissions@osu.edu.
Website: http://senr.osu.edu/

Oklahoma State University, College of Agricultural Science and Natural Resources, Department of Horticulture and Landscape Architecture, Stillwater, OK 74078. Offers crop science (PhD); horticulture (M Ag, MS). *Faculty:* 17 full-time (5 women), 1 (woman) part-time/adjunct. *Students:* 1 full-time (0 women), 8 part-time (5 women); includes 3 minority (1 American Indian or Alaska Native, non-Hispanic/Latino; 2 Two or more races, non-Hispanic/Latino), 3 international. Average age 28. 5 applicants, 60% accepted, 3 enrolled. In 2018, 7 master's awarded. *Entrance requirements:* For master's and doctorate, GRE or GMAT. Additional exam requirements/recommendations for international students: Required—TOEFL (minimum score 550 paper-based; 79 iBT). *Application deadline:* For fall admission, 3/1 priority date for international students; for spring admission, 8/1 priority date for international students. Applications are processed on a rolling basis. Application fee: $40 ($75 for international students). Electronic applications accepted. *Expenses: Tuition, area resident:* Full-time $4148. Tuition, state resident: full-time $4148. Tuition, nonresident: full-time $10,517. *International tuition:* $10,517 full-time. *Required fees:* $4394; $2929 per credit hour. Tuition and fees vary according to course load and program. *Financial support:* Research assistantships, teaching assistantships, career-related internships or fieldwork, Federal Work-Study, scholarships/grants, health care benefits, tuition waivers (partial), and unspecified assistantships available. Support available to part-time students. Financial award application deadline: 3/1; financial award applicants required to submit FAFSA. *Faculty research:* Stress and postharvest physiology; water utilization and runoff; integrated pest management (IPM) systems and nursery, turf, floriculture, vegetable, net and fruit produces and natural resources, food extraction, and processing; public garden management. *Unit head:* Dr. Janet Cole, Department Head, 405-744-5415, Fax: 405-744-9709. *Application contact:* Dr. Sheryl Tucker, Dean, 405-744-7099, Fax: 405-744-0355, E-mail: gradi@okstate.edu.
Website: http://www.hortla.okstate.edu/

Oklahoma State University, College of Agricultural Science and Natural Resources, Department of Plant and Soil Sciences, Stillwater, OK 74078. Offers crop science (PhD); plant and soil sciences (MS); soil science (M Ag). *Faculty:* 27 full-time (4 women). *Students:* 14 full-time (5 women), 42 part-time (16 women); includes 5 minority (3 Black or African American, non-Hispanic/Latino; 1 Hispanic/Latino; 1 Two or more races, non-Hispanic/Latino), 29 international. Average age 28. 15 applicants, 33% accepted, 5 enrolled. In 2018, 11 master's, 7 doctorates awarded. *Entrance requirements:* For master's and doctorate, GRE or GMAT. Additional exam requirements/recommendations for international students: Required—TOEFL (minimum score 550 paper-based; 79 iBT). *Application deadline:* For fall admission, 3/1 priority date for international students; for spring admission, 8/1 priority date for international students. Applications are processed on a rolling basis. Application fee: $40 ($75 for international students). Electronic applications accepted. *Expenses: Tuition, area resident:* Full-time $4148. Tuition, state resident: full-time $4148. Tuition, nonresident: full-time $10,517. *International tuition:* $10,517 full-time. *Required fees:* $4394; $2929 per credit hour. Tuition and fees vary according to course load and program. *Financial support:* Research assistantships, teaching assistantships, career-related internships or fieldwork, Federal Work-Study, scholarships/grants, health care benefits, tuition waivers (partial), and unspecified assistantships available. Support available to part-time students. Financial award application deadline: 3/1; financial award applicants required to submit FAFSA. *Faculty research:* Crop science, weed science, rangeland ecology and management, biotechnology, breeding and genetics. *Unit head:* Dr. Jeff Edwards, Department Head, 405-744-6130, Fax: 405-744-0354, E-mail: jeff.edwards@okstate.edu. *Application contact:* Dr. Sheryl Tucker, Dean, 405-744-6368, Fax: 405-744-0355, E-mail: gradi@okstate.edu.
Website: http://pss.okstate.edu

Oregon State University, College of Agricultural Sciences, Program in Crop Science, Corvallis, OR 97331. Offers MS, PhD. *Program availability:* Part-time. *Degree requirements:* For master's, thesis (for some programs); for doctorate, variable foreign language requirement, thesis/dissertation. *Entrance requirements:* For master's and doctorate, GRE, minimum GPA of 3.0 in last 90 hours of course work. Additional exam requirements/recommendations for international students: Required—TOEFL (minimum score 80 iBT), IELTS (minimum score 6.5). *Faculty research:* Cereal and new crops breeding and genetics; weed science; seed technology and production; potato, new crops, and general crop production; plant physiology.

Oregon State University, College of Agricultural Sciences, Program in Soil Science, Corvallis, OR 97331. Offers environmental soil science (MS, PhD). *Program availability:* Part-time. *Entrance requirements:* Additional exam requirements/recommendations for international students: Required—TOEFL (minimum score 80 iBT), IELTS (minimum score 6.5).

Penn State University Park, Graduate School, College of Agricultural Sciences, Department of Ecosystem Science and Management, University Park, PA 16802. Offers forest resources (MS, PhD); soil science (MS, PhD); wildlife and fisheries science (MS, PhD).

Agronomy and Soil Sciences

Purdue University, Graduate School, College of Agriculture, Department of Agronomy, West Lafayette, IN 47907. Offers MS, PhD. *Program availability:* Part-time. *Faculty:* 33 full-time (7 women). *Students:* 44 full-time (16 women), 17 part-time (9 women); includes 7 minority (2 American Indian or Alaska Native, non-Hispanic/Latino; 2 Asian, non-Hispanic/Latino; 2 Hispanic/Latino; 1 Two or more races, non-Hispanic/Latino), 21 international. Average age 29. 31 applicants, 32% accepted, 9 enrolled. In 2018, 11 master's, 5 doctorates awarded. *Degree requirements:* For doctorate, thesis/dissertation. *Entrance requirements:* For master's and doctorate, GRE General Test, minimum undergraduate GPA of 3.0 or equivalent. Additional exam requirements/recommendations for international students: Required—TOEFL (minimum score 550 paper-based, 77 iBT), IELTS (minimum score 6.5) or PTE (minimum score 58). *Application deadline:* For fall admission, 4/15 for domestic and international students; for spring admission, 10/15 for domestic students, 9/15 for international students; for summer admission, 4/15 for domestic students, 2/15 for international students. Applications are processed on a rolling basis. Application fee: $60 ($75 for international students). Electronic applications accepted. *Financial support:* Fellowships with tuition reimbursements, research assistantships with tuition reimbursements, and teaching assistantships with tuition reimbursements available. Support available to part-time students. Financial award applicants required to submit FAFSA. *Faculty research:* Plant genetics and breeding, crop physiology and ecology, agricultural meteorology, soil microbiology. *Unit head:* Ronald F. Turco, Head of the Graduate Program, 765-494-8077, E-mail: rturco@purdue.edu. *Application contact:* Patti Oliver, Graduate Contact, 765-494-4774, E-mail: poliver@purdue.edu.
Website: https://ag.purdue.edu/agry

Southern Illinois University Carbondale, Graduate School, College of Agriculture, Department of Plant, Soil, and General Agriculture, Carbondale, IL 62901-4701. Offers MS. *Degree requirements:* For master's, thesis. *Entrance requirements:* For master's, minimum GPA of 2.7. Additional exam requirements/recommendations for international students: Required—TOEFL. *Faculty research:* Herbicides, fertilizers, agriculture education, landscape design, plant breeding.

Tennessee State University, The School of Graduate Studies and Research, College of Agriculture, Human and Natural Sciences, Nashville, TN 37209-1561. Offers agricultural sciences (MS), including agribusiness, agricultural and extension education, animal science, plant and soil science; biological sciences (MS, PhD); biotechnology (PhD); chemistry (MS). *Program availability:* Part-time, evening/weekend. *Degree requirements:* For master's, thesis. *Entrance requirements:* For master's, GRE General Test, GRE Subject Test, MAT. *Faculty research:* Small farm economics, ornamental horticulture, beef cattle production, rural elderly.

Texas A&M University, College of Agriculture and Life Sciences, Department of Soil and Crop Sciences, College Station, TX 77843. Offers soil science (MS, PhD). *Faculty:* 33. *Students:* 107 full-time (44 women), 38 part-time (12 women); includes 17 minority (1 Black or African American, non-Hispanic/Latino; 1 Asian, non-Hispanic/Latino; 12 Hispanic/Latino; 3 Two or more races, non-Hispanic/Latino), 59 international. Average age 30. 29 applicants, 100% accepted, 28 enrolled. In 2018, 24 master's, 16 doctorates awarded. *Degree requirements:* For master's, thesis; for doctorate, thesis/dissertation. *Entrance requirements:* For master's and doctorate, GRE General Test. Additional exam requirements/recommendations for international students: Required—TOEFL (minimum score 550 paper-based; 80 iBT), IELTS (minimum score 6), PTE (minimum score 53). *Application deadline:* For fall admission, 3/1 priority date for domestic students; for spring admission, 8/1 for domestic students. Applications are processed on a rolling basis. Application fee: $50 ($90 for international students). Electronic applications accepted. *Expenses:* Contact institution. *Financial support:* In 2018–19, 112 students received support, including 14 fellowships with tuition reimbursements available (averaging $8,934 per year), 87 research assistantships with tuition reimbursements available (averaging $14,775 per year), 87 teaching assistantships with tuition reimbursements available (averaging $15,636 per year); career-related internships or fieldwork, institutionally sponsored loans, scholarships/grants, traineeships, health care benefits, tuition waivers (full and partial), and unspecified assistantships also available. Support available to part-time students. Financial award application deadline: 3/15; financial award applicants required to submit FAFSA. *Faculty research:* Soil and crop management, turf grass science, weed science, cereal chemistry, food protein chemistry. *Unit head:* Dr. David D. Baltensperger, Department Head, 979-845-3041, E-mail: dbaltensperger@ag.tamu.edu. *Application contact:* Megan Teel, Academic Advisor III, 979-862-4165, Fax: 979-458-0533, E-mail: megan_teel@tamu.edu.
Website: http://soilcrop.tamu.edu

Texas A&M University–Kingsville, College of Graduate Studies, Dick and Mary Lewis Kleberg College of Agriculture, Natural Resources and Human Sciences, Department of Agriculture, Agribusiness, and Environmental Sciences, Program in Plant and Soil Science, Kingsville, TX 78363. Offers MS. *Degree requirements:* For master's, variable foreign language requirement, comprehensive exam, thesis (for some programs). *Entrance requirements:* For master's, GRE (minimum combined Math & Verbal score of 290), MAT, GMAT, minimum GPA of 2.5. Additional exam requirements/recommendations for international students: Required—TOEFL (minimum score 550 paper-based; 79 iBT). Electronic applications accepted.

Texas Tech University, Graduate School, College of Agricultural Sciences and Natural Resources, Department of Plant and Soil Science, Lubbock, TX 79409-2122. Offers horticulture science (MS); plant and soil science (MS, PhD). *Program availability:* Part-time, evening/weekend, 100% online, blended/hybrid learning. *Faculty:* 28 full-time (9 women), 10 part-time/adjunct (3 women). *Students:* 71 full-time (33 women), 41 part-time (12 women); includes 14 minority (3 Asian, non-Hispanic/Latino; 7 Hispanic/Latino; 4 Two or more races, non-Hispanic/Latino), 47 international. Average age 30. 47 applicants, 53% accepted, 20 enrolled. In 2018, 19 master's, 8 doctorates awarded. Terminal master's awarded for partial completion of doctoral program. *Degree requirements:* For master's, comprehensive exam (for some programs), thesis (for some programs); for doctorate, comprehensive exam, thesis/dissertation. *Entrance requirements:* For master's and doctorate, GRE. Additional exam requirements/recommendations for international students: Required—TOEFL (minimum score 550 paper-based; 79 iBT). *Application deadline:* For fall admission, 6/1 priority date for domestic students, 1/15 priority date for international students; for spring admission, 9/1 priority date for domestic students, 6/15 priority date for international students. Applications are processed on a rolling basis. Application fee: $65. Electronic applications accepted. *Expenses:* Contact institution. *Financial support:* In 2018–19, 101 students received support, including 92 fellowships (averaging $2,907 per year), 58 research assistantships (averaging $16,900 per year), 12 teaching assistantships (averaging $14,673 per year); scholarships/grants, health care benefits, and unspecified assistantships also available. Financial award application deadline: 4/15; financial award applicants required to submit FAFSA. *Faculty research:* Crop protection, crop science, fibers and biopolymers, soil science, horticulture, turf grass science, genetics. *Total annual research expenditures:* $5 million. *Unit head:* Dr. Glen Ritchie, Department Chair and Associate Professor, 806-742-2838, Fax: 806-742-0775, E-mail: glen.ritchie@ttu.edu. *Application contact:* Diann Merriman, Lead Academic Advisor, 806-834-7044, Fax: 806-742-0775, E-mail: diann.merriman@ttu.edu.
Website: www.pssc.ttu.edu

Tuskegee University, Graduate Programs, College of Agriculture, Environment and Nutrition Sciences, Department of Agricultural and Environmental Sciences, Program in Plant and Soil Sciences, Tuskegee, AL 36088. Offers MS. *Degree requirements:* For master's, thesis. *Entrance requirements:* For master's, GRE General Test. Additional exam requirements/recommendations for international students: Required—TOEFL (minimum score 500 paper-based).

Université Laval, Faculty of Agricultural and Food Sciences, Department of Soils and Agricultural Engineering, Programs in Soils and Environment Science, Québec, QC G1K 7P4, Canada. Offers environmental technology (M Sc); soils and environment science (M Sc, PhD). Terminal master's awarded for partial completion of doctoral program. *Degree requirements:* For master's, thesis (for some programs); for doctorate, comprehensive exam, thesis/dissertation. *Entrance requirements:* For master's and doctorate, knowledge of French and English. Electronic applications accepted.

Université Laval, Faculty of Forestry, Geography and Geomatics, Program in Agroforestry, Québec, QC G1K 7P4, Canada. Offers M Sc. *Degree requirements:* For master's, thesis (for some programs). *Entrance requirements:* For master's, English exam (comprehension of English), knowledge of French, knowledge of a third language. Electronic applications accepted.

University of Alberta, Faculty of Graduate Studies and Research, Department of Renewable Resources, Edmonton, AB T6G 2E1, Canada. Offers agroforestry (M Ag, M Sc, MF); conservation biology (M Sc, PhD); forest biology and management (M Sc, PhD); land reclamation and remediation (M Sc, PhD); protected areas and wildlands management (M Sc, PhD); soil science (M Ag, M Sc, PhD); water and land resources (M Ag, M Sc, PhD); wildlife ecology and management (M Sc, PhD); MBA/M Ag; MBA/MF. *Program availability:* Part-time. *Degree requirements:* For master's, thesis (for some programs); for doctorate, comprehensive exam, thesis/dissertation. *Entrance requirements:* For master's, minimum 2 years of relevant professional experiences, minimum GPA of 3.0; for doctorate, minimum GPA of 3.0. Additional exam requirements/recommendations for international students: Required—TOEFL (minimum score 550 paper-based). Electronic applications accepted. *Faculty research:* Natural and managed landscapes.

The University of Arizona, College of Agriculture and Life Sciences, Department of Soil, Water and Environmental Science, Tucson, AZ 85721. Offers MS, PhD, Graduate Certificate. *Degree requirements:* For master's, thesis; for doctorate, comprehensive exam, thesis/dissertation. *Entrance requirements:* For master's, GRE (recommended), minimum GPA of 3.0, letter of interest, 3 letters of recommendation; for doctorate, GRE (recommended), MS, minimum GPA of 3.0, letter of interest, 3 letters of recommendation. Additional exam requirements/recommendations for international students: Required—TOEFL (minimum score 550 paper-based; 80 iBT). Electronic applications accepted. *Faculty research:* Plant production, environmental microbiology, contaminant flow and transport, aquaculture.

University of Arkansas, Graduate School, Dale Bumpers College of Agricultural, Food and Life Sciences, Department of Crop, Soil and Environmental Sciences, Fayetteville, AR 72701. Offers agronomy (MS, PhD). In 2018, 13 master's, 7 doctorates awarded. *Degree requirements:* For master's, thesis optional; for doctorate, variable foreign language requirement, thesis/dissertation. *Application deadline:* For fall admission, 8/1 for domestic students, 4/1 for international students; for spring admission, 12/1 for domestic students, 10/1 for international students; for summer admission, 4/15 for domestic students, 3/1 for international students. Applications are processed on a rolling basis. Application fee: $60. Electronic applications accepted. *Financial support:* In 2018–19, 36 research assistantships were awarded; fellowships with tuition reimbursements, teaching assistantships, career-related internships or fieldwork, and Federal Work-Study also available. Support available to part-time students. Financial award application deadline: 4/1; financial award applicants required to submit FAFSA. *Unit head:* Dr. Robert Bacon, Department Head, 479-575-2354, Fax: 479-575-7465, E-mail: rbacon@uark.edu. *Application contact:* Daniela Kidd, Graduate Coordinator, 479-575-2347, Fax: 479-575-7465, E-mail: drkidd@uark.edu.
Website: https://crop-soil-environmental-sciences.uark.edu/

The University of British Columbia, Faculty of Land and Food Systems, Program in Soil Science, Vancouver, BC V6T 1Z4, Canada. Offers M Sc, PhD. *Degree requirements:* For master's, thesis; for doctorate, comprehensive exam, thesis/dissertation. *Entrance requirements:* Additional exam requirements/recommendations for international students: Required—TOEFL, IELTS. Electronic applications accepted. *Expenses:* Contact institution. *Faculty research:* Soil and water conservation, land use, land use and land classification, soil physics, soil chemistry and mineralogy.

University of California, Davis, Graduate Studies, Graduate Group in Horticulture and Agronomy, Davis, CA 95616. Offers MS. *Degree requirements:* For master's, comprehensive exam (for some programs), thesis (for some programs). *Entrance requirements:* For master's, GRE General Test. Additional exam requirements/recommendations for international students: Required—TOEFL (minimum score 550 paper-based). Electronic applications accepted. *Faculty research:* Postharvest physiology, mineral nutrition, crop improvement, plant growth and development.

University of California, Davis, Graduate Studies, Graduate Group in Soils and Biogeochemistry, Davis, CA 95616. Offers MS, PhD. Terminal master's awarded for partial completion of doctoral program. *Degree requirements:* For master's, comprehensive exam (for some programs), thesis (for some programs); for doctorate, thesis/dissertation. *Entrance requirements:* For master's, minimum GPA of 3.3; for doctorate, GRE, minimum GPA of 3.3. Additional exam requirements/recommendations for international students: Required—TOEFL (minimum score 550 paper-based). Electronic applications accepted. *Faculty research:* Rhizosphere ecology, soil transport processes, biogeochemical cycling, sustainable agriculture.

University of California, Riverside, Graduate Division, Environmental Sciences Department, Riverside, CA 92521-0102. Offers MS, PhD. *Degree requirements:* For doctorate, thesis/dissertation. *Entrance requirements:* For master's and doctorate, minimum GPA of 3.2. Additional exam requirements/recommendations for international students: Required—TOEFL (minimum score 550 paper-based; 80 iBT). Electronic applications accepted. *Faculty research:* Environmental chemistry and ecotoxicology, environmental microbiology, environmental and natural resource economics and policy, soil and water science, environmental sciences and management.

University of Connecticut, Graduate School, College of Agriculture, Health and Natural Resources, Department of Plant Science and Landscape Architecture, Storrs, CT 06269. Offers MS, PhD. Terminal master's awarded for partial completion of doctoral program. *Degree requirements:* For master's, comprehensive exam; for doctorate, thesis/dissertation. *Entrance requirements:* For master's and doctorate, GRE General Test, GRE Subject Test. Additional exam requirements/recommendations for international students: Required—TOEFL (minimum score 550 paper-based). Electronic applications accepted.

University of Delaware, College of Agriculture and Natural Resources, Department of Plant and Soil Sciences, Newark, DE 19716. Offers MS, PhD. *Program availability:* Part-time. Terminal master's awarded for partial completion of doctoral program. *Degree requirements:* For master's, thesis; for doctorate, thesis/dissertation. *Entrance requirements:* For master's and doctorate, GRE General Test. Additional exam requirements/recommendations for international students: Required—TOEFL (minimum score 550 paper-based). Electronic applications accepted. *Faculty research:* Soil chemistry, plant and cell tissue culture, plant breeding and genetics, soil physics, soil biochemistry, plant molecular biology, soil microbiology.

University of Florida, Graduate School, College of Agricultural and Life Sciences, Department of Agronomy, Gainesville, FL 32611. Offers agroecology (MS); agronomy (MS, PhD); geographic information systems (MS); toxicology (PhD); tropical conservation and development (MS, PhD). *Program availability:* Part-time, online learning. Terminal master's awarded for partial completion of doctoral program. *Degree requirements:* For master's, thesis (for some programs); for doctorate, comprehensive exam, thesis/dissertation (for some programs). *Entrance requirements:* For master's and doctorate, GRE General Test, minimum GPA of 3.0, statement of purpose, 3 letters of recommendation. Additional exam requirements/recommendations for international students: Required—TOEFL (minimum score 550 paper-based; 80 iBT), IELTS (minimum score 6). Electronic applications accepted. *Faculty research:* Invasive and aquatic weed ecology, grassland ecology and management, genomics and molecular genetics, plant drought stress tolerance, sustainable food production systems.

University of Florida, Graduate School, College of Agricultural and Life Sciences, Department of Soil and Water Science, Gainesville, FL 32611. Offers soil and water science (MS, PhD), including agroecology (MS), geographic information systems, hydrologic sciences, tropical conservation and development, wetland sciences. *Program availability:* Part-time, evening/weekend, online learning. Terminal master's awarded for partial completion of doctoral program. *Degree requirements:* For master's, thesis optional; for doctorate, comprehensive exam, thesis/dissertation. *Entrance requirements:* For master's and doctorate, GRE General Test, minimum GPA of 3.0. Additional exam requirements/recommendations for international students: Required—TOEFL (minimum score 550 paper-based; 80 iBT), IELTS (minimum score 6). Electronic applications accepted. *Faculty research:* Carbon dynamics and ecosystem services; landscape analysis and modeling; nutrient pesticide and waste management; soil, water, and aquifer remediation; wetlands and aquatic ecosystems.

University of Georgia, College of Agricultural and Environmental Sciences, Department of Crop and Soil Sciences, Athens, GA 30602. Offers crop and soil sciences (MS, PhD). *Program availability:* Part-time. *Degree requirements:* For master's, thesis (MS); for doctorate, comprehensive exam, thesis/dissertation. *Entrance requirements:* For master's and doctorate, GRE General Test. Additional exam requirements/recommendations for international students: Required—TOEFL (minimum score 550 paper-based). Electronic applications accepted. *Faculty research:* Plant breeding, genomics, nutrient management, water quality, soil chemistry.

University of Guelph, Office of Graduate and Postdoctoral Studies, Ontario Agricultural College, Department of Land Resource Science, Guelph, ON N1G 2W1, Canada. Offers atmospheric science (M Sc, PhD); environmental and agricultural earth sciences (M Sc, PhD); land resources management (M Sc, PhD); soil science (M Sc, PhD). *Program availability:* Part-time. *Degree requirements:* For master's, thesis (for some programs), research project (non-thesis track); for doctorate, comprehensive exam, thesis/dissertation. *Entrance requirements:* For master's, minimum B- average during previous 2 years of course work; for doctorate, minimum B average during previous 2 years of course work. Additional exam requirements/recommendations for international students: Required—TOEFL (minimum score 550 paper-based). Electronic applications accepted. *Faculty research:* Soil science, environmental earth science, land resource management.

University of Idaho, College of Graduate Studies, College of Agricultural and Life Sciences, Department of Soil and Water Systems, Moscow, ID 83844-2340. Offers soil and land resources (MS, PhD). *Faculty:* 8. *Students:* 9. Average age 30. In 2018, 1 master's awarded. *Degree requirements:* For doctorate, thesis/dissertation. *Entrance requirements:* For master's and doctorate, GRE General Test, minimum GPA of 3.0. Additional exam requirements/recommendations for international students: Required—TOEFL (minimum score 79 iBT). *Application deadline:* For fall admission, 8/1 for domestic students; for spring admission, 12/15 for domestic students. Applications are processed on a rolling basis. Application fee: $60. Electronic applications accepted. *Expenses:* Tuition, state resident: full-time $7266.44; part-time $474.50 per credit hour. Tuition, nonresident: full-time $24,902; part-time $1453.50 per credit hour. *Required fees:* $2085.56; $45.50 per credit hour. *Financial support:* Applicants required to submit FAFSA. *Faculty research:* Impacts of water conservation, soil health, soil fertility and plant nutrition, soil physics. *Unit head:* Jodi Johnson-Maynard, Head, 208-885-0111, E-mail: cals-sws@uidaho.edu. *Application contact:* Jodi Johnson-Maynard, Head, 208-885-0111, E-mail: cals-sws@uidaho.edu.
Website: https://www.uidaho.edu/cals/soil-and-water-systems

University of Illinois at Urbana–Champaign, Graduate College, College of Agricultural, Consumer and Environmental Sciences, Department of Crop Sciences, Champaign, IL 61820. Offers bioinformatics: crop sciences (MS); crop sciences (MS, PhD). *Program availability:* Online learning.

University of Kentucky, Graduate School, College of Agriculture, Food and Environment, Program in Plant and Soil Science, Lexington, KY 40506-0032. Offers integrated plant and soil sciences (MS, PhD). *Degree requirements:* For master's, comprehensive exam, thesis optional. *Entrance requirements:* For master's, GRE General Test, minimum undergraduate GPA of 2.75, graduate 3.0. Additional exam requirements/recommendations for international students: Required—TOEFL (minimum score 550 paper-based). Electronic applications accepted.

University of Manitoba, Faculty of Graduate Studies, Faculty of Agricultural and Food Sciences, Department of Plant Science, Winnipeg, MB R3T 2N2, Canada. Offers agronomy and plant protection (M Sc, PhD); horticulture (M Sc, PhD); plant breeding and genetics (M Sc, PhD); plant physiology-biochemistry (M Sc, PhD). *Degree requirements:* For master's, thesis; for doctorate, one foreign language, thesis/dissertation.

University of Manitoba, Faculty of Graduate Studies, Faculty of Agricultural and Food Sciences, Department of Soil Science, Winnipeg, MB R3T 2N2, Canada. Offers M Sc, PhD. *Degree requirements:* For master's, thesis; for doctorate, one foreign language, thesis/dissertation.

University of Minnesota, Twin Cities Campus, Graduate School, College of Food, Agricultural and Natural Resource Sciences, Land and Atmospheric Science Graduate Program, Saint Paul, MN 55108. Offers MS, PhD. Terminal master's awarded for partial completion of doctoral program. *Degree requirements:* For master's, comprehensive exam, thesis; for doctorate, comprehensive exam, thesis/dissertation. *Entrance requirements:* For master's and doctorate, GRE General Test, minimum GPA of 3.0.

Additional exam requirements/recommendations for international students: Required—TOEFL (minimum score 550 paper-based; 79 iBT), IELTS (minimum score 6.5). Electronic applications accepted. *Faculty research:* Soil water and atmospheric resources, soil physical management, agricultural chemicals and their management, plant nutrient management, biological nitrogen fixation.

University of Missouri, Office of Research and Graduate Studies, College of Agriculture, Food and Natural Resources, Division of Plant Sciences, Columbia, MO 65211. Offers crop, soil and pest management (MS, PhD); entomology (MS, PhD); horticulture (MS, PhD); plant breeding, genetics and genomics (MS, PhD); plant stress biology (MS, PhD). Terminal master's awarded for partial completion of doctoral program. *Degree requirements:* For master's, thesis; for doctorate, comprehensive exam, thesis/dissertation. *Entrance requirements:* For master's and doctorate, GRE General Test, minimum GPA of 3.0; bachelor's degree from accredited college. Additional exam requirements/recommendations for international students: Required—TOEFL (minimum score 500 paper-based; 61 iBT), IELTS (minimum score 5.5). Electronic applications accepted. *Faculty research:* Crop, soil and pest management; entomology; horticulture; plant biology and genetics; plant microbiology and pathology.

University of Missouri, Office of Research and Graduate Studies, College of Agriculture, Food and Natural Resources, School of Natural Resources, Columbia, MO 65211. Offers agroforestry (MS, Certificate); conservation biology (Certificate); fisheries and wildlife sciences (MS, PhD); forestry (MS, PhD); geographical information science (Certificate); human dimensions of natural resources (MS, PhD); parks, recreation and tourism (MS); society and ecosystems (Certificate); soil, environmental and atmospheric sciences (MS, PhD); water resources (MS, PhD). *Program availability:* Part-time. *Degree requirements:* For doctorate, thesis/dissertation. *Entrance requirements:* For master's and doctorate, GRE General Test (minimum score 1200 Verbal and Quantitative), minimum GPA of 3.2. Additional exam requirements/recommendations for international students: Required—TOEFL (minimum score 550 paper-based; 80 iBT), IELTS (minimum score 6.5). Electronic applications accepted.

University of Nebraska–Lincoln, Graduate College, College of Agricultural Sciences and Natural Resources, Department of Agronomy and Horticulture, Program in Agronomy, Lincoln, NE 68588. Offers MS, PhD. *Degree requirements:* For master's, thesis; for doctorate, comprehensive exam, thesis/dissertation. *Entrance requirements:* Additional exam requirements/recommendations for international students: Required—TOEFL (minimum score 500 paper-based). Electronic applications accepted. *Faculty research:* Crop physiology and production, plant breeding and genetics, range and forage management, soil and water science, weed science.

University of Puerto Rico–Mayagüez, Graduate Studies, College of Agricultural Sciences, Department of Crops and Agroenvironmental Sciences, Mayagüez, PR 00681-9000. Offers agronomy (MS); crop protection (MS); horticulture (MS); soils (MS). *Program availability:* Part-time. *Degree requirements:* For master's, comprehensive exam, thesis. Electronic applications accepted. *Faculty research:* Ecology of tropical forests, population dynamics, processing and sensing analysis of food, physiology of plants, phytopathology.

University of Saskatchewan, College of Graduate and Postdoctoral Studies, College of Agriculture and Bioresources, Department of Soil Science, Saskatoon, SK S7N 5A2, Canada. Offers M Sc, PhD. *Degree requirements:* For master's, thesis (for some programs); for doctorate, comprehensive exam (for some programs), thesis/dissertation. *Entrance requirements:* Additional exam requirements/recommendations for international students: Required—TOEFL (minimum score 80 iBT); Recommended—IELTS (minimum score 6.5).

University of Vermont, Graduate College, College of Agriculture and Life Sciences, Department of Plant and Soil Science, Burlington, VT 05405. Offers agroecology (Graduate Certificate); plant and soil science (MS, PhD), including agroecology, agronomy (MS), ecological landscape design, entomology, horticulture (MS), plant pathology (MS), soil science. *Degree requirements:* For master's, thesis; for doctorate, one foreign language, thesis/dissertation. *Entrance requirements:* For master's and doctorate, GRE General Test. Additional exam requirements/recommendations for international students: Required—TOEFL (minimum score 550 paper-based; 90 iBT), IELTS (minimum score 6.5). Electronic applications accepted. *Faculty research:* Soil chemistry, plant nutrition.

University of Wisconsin–Madison, Graduate School, College of Agricultural and Life Sciences, Department of Agronomy, Madison, WI 53706-1380. Offers agronomy (MS, PhD); plant breeding and plant genetics (MS, PhD). *Degree requirements:* For master's, thesis or alternative; for doctorate, thesis/dissertation. *Entrance requirements:* For master's and doctorate, GRE, minimum GPA of 3.0. Additional exam requirements/recommendations for international students: Required—TOEFL (minimum score 580 paper-based). Electronic applications accepted. *Faculty research:* Plant breeding and genetics, plant molecular biology and physiology, cropping systems and management, weed science.

University of Wisconsin–Madison, Graduate School, College of Agricultural and Life Sciences, Department of Soil Science, Madison, WI 53706. Offers MS, PhD. *Degree requirements:* For master's, comprehensive exam, thesis; for doctorate, comprehensive exam, thesis/dissertation. *Entrance requirements:* For master's and doctorate, GRE General Test. Additional exam requirements/recommendations for international students: Required—TOEFL. Electronic applications accepted. *Faculty research:* Soil characterization and mapping, fate of toxicants in the environment, soil microbiology, permafrost, water quality and quantity.

University of Wyoming, College of Agriculture and Natural Resources, Department of Ecosystem Science and Management, Laramie, WY 82071. Offers ecology (MS); entomology (MS, PhD); rangeland ecology and watershed management (MS, PhD), including soil sciences (PhD), soil sciences and water resources (MS); soil science (MS, PhD); water resources (MS, PhD). *Program availability:* Part-time. *Degree requirements:* For master's, comprehensive exam, thesis, oral examination; for doctorate, comprehensive exam, thesis/dissertation, preliminary oral and written exam, oral final exam. *Entrance requirements:* For master's and doctorate, GRE General Test, minimum GPA of 3.0. Additional exam requirements/recommendations for international students: Required—TOEFL. Electronic applications accepted. *Expenses: Tuition, area resident:* Full-time $6504; part-time $271 per credit hour. *Tuition, state resident:* full-time $6504; part-time $271 per credit hour. *Tuition, nonresident:* full-time $19,464; part-time $811 per credit hour. *International tuition:* $19,464 full-time. *Required fees:* $1410.94; $343.82 per semester. $343.82 per semester. Tuition and fees vary according to course load, program and reciprocity agreements. *Faculty research:* Plant control, grazing management, riparian restoration, riparian management, reclamation.

University of Wyoming, College of Agriculture and Natural Resources, Department of Plant Sciences, Laramie, WY 82071. Offers agronomy (MS, PhD). *Degree requirements:* For master's, thesis; for doctorate, thesis/dissertation. *Entrance requirements:* For master's and doctorate, GRE General Test, minimum GPA of 3.0. Additional exam requirements/recommendations for international students: Required—

Peterson's Graduate Programs in the Physical Sciences, Mathematics, Agricultural Sciences, the Environment & Natural Resources 2020

www.petersons.com **269**

TOEFL (minimum score 525 paper-based). Electronic applications accepted. *Expenses: Tuition, area resident:* Full-time $6504; part-time $271 per credit hour. Tuition, state resident: full-time $6504; part-time $271 per credit hour. Tuition, nonresident: full-time $19,464; part-time $811 per credit hour. *International tuition:* $19,464 full-time. *Required fees:* $1410.94; $343.82 per semester. $343.82 per semester. Tuition and fees vary according to course load, program and reciprocity agreements. *Faculty research:* Crops, weeds, plant diseases.

Utah State University, School of Graduate Studies, College of Agriculture and Applied Sciences, Department of Plants, Soils and Climate, Logan, UT 84322. Offers climate sciences (MS, PhD); ecology (MS, PhD); horticulture (MPS); plant science (MS, PhD); soil science (MS, PhD). *Program availability:* Part-time. Terminal master's awarded for partial completion of doctoral program. *Degree requirements:* For master's, thesis; for doctorate, thesis/dissertation. *Entrance requirements:* For master's, GRE General Test, BS in plant, soil, atmospheric science, or related field; minimum GPA of 3.0; for doctorate, GRE General Test, minimum GPA of 3.0. Additional exam requirements/recommendations for international students: Required—TOEFL. Electronic applications accepted. *Faculty research:* Biotechnology and genomics, plant physiology and biology, nutrient and water efficient landscapes, physical-chemical-biological processes in soil, environmental biophysics and climate.

Virginia Polytechnic Institute and State University, Graduate School, College of Agriculture and Life Sciences, Blacksburg, VA 24061. Offers agricultural and applied economics (MS, PhD); agricultural and life sciences (MS); agriculture, leadership, and community education (MS, PhD); animal and poultry science (MS, PhD); biochemistry (MS, PhD); crop and soil environmental sciences (MS, PhD); dairy science (MS, PhD); entomology (MS, PhD); food science and technology (MS, PhD); horticulture (PhD); human nutrition, foods and exercise (MS, PhD); plant pathology, physiology, and weed science (MS, PhD). *Faculty:* 244 full-time (79 women), 1 (woman) part-time/adjunct. *Students:* 360 full-time (195 women), 110 part-time (73 women); includes 70 minority (24 Black or African American, non-Hispanic/Latino; 1 American Indian or Alaska Native, non-Hispanic/Latino; 15 Asian, non-Hispanic/Latino; 12 Hispanic/Latino; 18 Two or more races, non-Hispanic/Latino), 110 international. Average age 28. 296 applicants, 54% accepted, 105 enrolled. In 2018, 92 master's, 59 doctorates awarded. *Degree requirements:* For master's, comprehensive exam (for some programs), thesis (for some programs); for doctorate, comprehensive exam (for some programs), thesis/dissertation (for some programs). *Entrance requirements:* For master's and doctorate, GRE/GMAT. Additional exam requirements/recommendations for international students: Required—TOEFL (minimum score 90 iBT). *Application deadline:* For fall admission, 8/1 for domestic students, 4/1 for international students; for spring admission, 1/1 for domestic students, 9/1 for international students. Applications are processed on a rolling basis. Application fee: $75. Electronic applications accepted. *Expenses:* Tuition, state resident: full-time $15,510; part-time $739.50 per credit hour. Tuition, nonresident: full-time $29,629; part-time $1490.25 per credit hour. *Required fees:* $2804; $550 per semester. Tuition and fees vary according to course load, campus/location and program. *Financial support:* In 2018–19, 3 fellowships with full tuition reimbursements (averaging $25,731 per year), 249 research assistantships with full tuition reimbursements (averaging $19,826 per year), 105 teaching assistantships with full tuition reimbursements (averaging $19,277 per year) were awarded; scholarships/grants and unspecified assistantships also available. Financial award application deadline: 3/1; financial award applicants required to submit FAFSA. *Total annual research expenditures:* $42.4 million. *Unit head:* Dr. Alan L. Grant, Dean, 540-231-4152, Fax: 540-231-4163, E-mail: algrant@vt.edu. *Application contact:* Crystal Tawney, Administrative Assistant, 540-231-4152, Fax: 540-231-4163, E-mail: cdtawney@vt.edu. Website: http://www.cals.vt.edu/

Washington State University, College of Agricultural, Human, and Natural Resource Sciences, Department of Crop and Soil Sciences, Pullman, WA 99164. Offers crop sciences (MS, PhD); soil sciences (MS, PhD). Programs offered at the Pullman campus. Terminal master's awarded for partial completion of doctoral program. *Degree requirements:* For master's, comprehensive exam (for some programs), thesis (for some programs), oral exam; for doctorate, comprehensive exam, thesis/dissertation, oral exam, written exam. *Entrance requirements:* For master's, GRE, personal statement of educational goals and professional expectations, minimum GPA of 3.0, 3 letters of recommendation; for doctorate, GRE, personal statement of educational goals and professional expectations, minimum GPA of 3.0. Additional exam requirements/recommendations for international students: Required—TOEFL (minimum score 550 paper-based), IELTS. Electronic applications accepted. *Faculty research:* Environmental soils, soil/water quality, plant breeding genetics, plant nutrition/nutrient cycling, plant/seed metabolism.

West Virginia University, Davis College of Agriculture, Forestry and Consumer Sciences, Morgantown, WV 26506. Offers agricultural and extension education (MS, PhD); agriculture and resource management (MS); agriculture, natural resources and design (M Agr); agronomy (MS); animal and food science (PhD); animal physiology (MS); applied and environmental microbiology (MS); design and merchandising (MS); entomology (MS); forest resource science (PhD); forestry (MSF); genetics and developmental biology (MS, PhD); horticulture (MS); human and community development (PhD); landscape architecture (MLA); natural resource economics (PhD); nutritional and food science (MS); plant and soil science (PhD); plant pathology (MS); recreation, parks and tourism resources (MS); reproductive physiology (MS, PhD); wildlife and fisheries resources (PhD). *Accreditation:* ASLA. *Program availability:* Part-time. *Students:* 188 full-time (86 women), 47 part-time (30 women); includes 22 minority (5 Black or African American, non-Hispanic/Latino; 5 Asian, non-Hispanic/Latino; 8 Hispanic/Latino; 4 Two or more races, non-Hispanic/Latino), 60 international. In 2018, 56 master's, 14 doctorates awarded. *Degree requirements:* For master's, thesis; for doctorate, thesis/dissertation. *Entrance requirements:* Additional exam requirements/recommendations for international students: Required—TOEFL (minimum score 550 paper-based). *Application deadline:* For fall admission, 6/1 priority date for domestic students, 6/1 for international students; for spring admission, 1/5 for domestic and international students. Applications are processed on a rolling basis. Application fee: $60. Electronic applications accepted. *Financial support:* Fellowships, research assistantships, teaching assistantships, career-related internships or fieldwork, Federal Work-Study, institutionally sponsored loans, tuition waivers (full and partial), and unspecified assistantships available. Financial award application deadline: 2/1; financial award applicants required to submit FAFSA. *Faculty research:* Reproductive physiology, soil and water quality, human nutrition, aquaculture, wildlife management. *Unit head:* Dr. Ken Blemings, Interim Dean, 304-293-2395, Fax: 304-293-3740, E-mail: ken.blemings@mail.wvu.edu. *Application contact:* Dr. J. Todd Petty, Associate Dean, 304-293-2278, Fax: 304-293-3740, E-mail: jtpetty@mail.wvu.edu. Website: https://www.davis.wvu.edu

Animal Sciences

Alcorn State University, School of Graduate Studies, School of Agriculture and Applied Sciences, Lorman, MS 39096-7500. Offers agricultural economics (MS Ag); agronomy (MS Ag); animal science (MS Ag). *Degree requirements:* For master's, thesis optional. *Faculty research:* Aquatic systems, dairy herd improvement, fruit production, alternative farming practices.

American University of Beirut, Graduate Programs, Faculty of Agricultural and Food Sciences, Beirut, Lebanon. Offers agricultural economics (MS); animal science (MS); ecosystem management (MSES); food safety (MS); food security (MS); food technology (MS); irrigation (MS); nutrition (MS); plant protection (MS); plant science (MS); poultry science (MS); public health nutrition (MS); rural community development (MS). *Program availability:* Part-time. *Faculty:* 24 full-time (4 women). *Students:* 30 full-time (22 women), 90 part-time (69 women); includes 9 minority (all Black or African American, non-Hispanic/Latino). Average age 25. 238 applicants, 77% accepted, 37 enrolled. In 2018, 19 master's awarded. *Degree requirements:* For master's, one foreign language, comprehensive exam, thesis (for some programs). *Entrance requirements:* Additional exam requirements/recommendations for international students: Required—TOEFL (minimum score 600 paper-based; 100 iBT), IELTS (minimum score 7.5). *Application deadline:* For fall admission, 2/10 for domestic and international students; for spring admission, 11/2 for domestic and international students. Application fee: $50. Electronic applications accepted. *Expenses: Tuition:* Full-time $17,748; part-time $986 per credit. *Required fees:* $762. Tuition and fees vary according to course load and program. *Financial support:* In 2018–19, 2 fellowships with full and partial tuition reimbursements (averaging $11,637 per year), 12 research assistantships with full and partial tuition reimbursements (averaging $3,840 per year), 73 teaching assistantships with full and partial tuition reimbursements were awarded; scholarships/grants, health care benefits, and unspecified assistantships also available. Financial award application deadline: 2/2. *Faculty research:* Plant science; animal science; landscape for culture and socio-ecological health; diet, obesity and non communicable diseases; water, agriculture, ecosystem & remote sensing; water-energy-food-health nexus. *Total annual research expenditures:* $1.2 million. *Unit head:* Prof. Rabi Hassan Mohtar, Dean of Faculty of Agricultural and Food Sciences, 961-1-350000 Ext. 4400, Fax: 961-1-744460, E-mail: mohtar@aub.edu.lb. *Application contact:* Prof. Zaher Dawy, Associate Provost, 961-1-374374 Ext. 4386, Fax: 961-1-374374, E-mail: graduate.council@aub.edu.lb. Website: http://www.aub.edu.lb/fafs/pages/default.aspx

Auburn University, Graduate School, College of Agriculture, Department of Animal Sciences, Auburn University, AL 36849. Offers M Ag, MS, PhD. *Program availability:* Part-time. *Degree requirements:* For master's, thesis (for some programs); for doctorate, thesis/dissertation. *Entrance requirements:* For master's and doctorate, GRE General Test. Electronic applications accepted. *Expenses:* Tuition, state resident: full-time $11,282; part-time $535 per credit hour. Tuition, nonresident: full-time $30,542; part-time $1605 per credit hour. *Required fees:* $826 per semester. Tuition and fees vary according to degree level and program. *Faculty research:* Animal breeding and genetics, animal biochemistry and nutrition, physiology of reproduction, animal production.

Auburn University, Graduate School, College of Agriculture, Department of Poultry Science, Auburn University, AL 36849. Offers M Ag, MS, PhD. *Program availability:* Part-time. *Degree requirements:* For master's, thesis (for some programs); for doctorate, thesis/dissertation. *Entrance requirements:* For master's, GRE General Test; for doctorate, GRE General Test, MS. Electronic applications accepted. *Expenses:* Tuition, state resident: full-time $11,282; part-time $535 per credit hour. Tuition, nonresident: full-time $30,542; part-time $1605 per credit hour. *Required fees:* $826 per semester. Tuition and fees vary according to degree level and program. *Faculty research:* Poultry nutrition, poultry breeding, poultry physiology, poultry diseases and parasites, processing/food science.

Bergin University of Canine Studies, Program in Canine Life Sciences, Rohnert Park, CA 94928. Offers MS. *Program availability:* Online learning. *Degree requirements:* For master's, thesis or culminating project. *Entrance requirements:* For master's, official transcript, personal essay, two letters of reference.

Boise State University, College of Arts and Sciences, Department of Biological Sciences, Boise, ID 83725. Offers biology (MA, MS); biomolecular sciences (PhD); raptor biology (MS). *Program availability:* Part-time. *Degree requirements:* For master's, thesis. *Entrance requirements:* For master's, GRE General Test, minimum GPA of 3.0. Additional exam requirements/recommendations for international students: Required—TOEFL (minimum score 550 paper-based; 80 iBT), IELTS (minimum score 6). Electronic applications accepted. *Faculty research:* Soil and stream microbial ecology, avian ecology.

Brigham Young University, Graduate Studies, College of Life Sciences, Department of Plant and Wildlife Sciences, Provo, UT 84602-1001. Offers environmental science (MS); genetics and biotechnology (MS); wildlife and wildlands conservation (MS, PhD). *Faculty:* 24 full-time (1 woman). *Students:* 12 full-time (7 women), 42 part-time (12 women); includes 2 minority (both Hispanic/Latino). Average age 30. 29 applicants, 59% accepted, 17 enrolled. In 2018, 18 master's, 1 doctorate awarded. *Degree requirements:* For master's, thesis, no C grades or below, 30 hours (24 coursework, 6 thesis); for doctorate, comprehensive exam, thesis/dissertation, no C grades or below, 54 hours (18 dissertation, 36 coursework). *Entrance requirements:* For master's, GRE General Test, minimum GPA of 3.2; for doctorate, GRE, minimum GPA of 3.2. Additional exam requirements/recommendations for international students: Required—TOEFL (minimum score 580 paper-based; 85 iBT). *Application deadline:* 2/1 for domestic and international students; for summer admission, 2/1 for domestic and international students. Application fee: $50. Electronic applications accepted. *Financial support:* In 2018–19, 54 students received support, including 71 research assistantships with partial tuition reimbursements available (averaging $18,081 per year), 42 teaching assistantships with partial tuition reimbursements available (averaging $16,478 per year); scholarships/grants and tuition waivers (partial) also available. Financial award application deadline: 3/1. *Faculty research:* Environmental science, plant genetics, plant ecology, plant nutrition and pathology, wildlife and wildlands conservation. *Total annual research*

expenditures: $2.1 million. *Unit head:* Neil Hansen, Chair, 801-422-2491, E-mail: neil_hansen@byu.edu. *Application contact:* Bradley D. Geary, Graduate Coordinator, 801-422-1228, Fax: 801-422-0008, E-mail: bradley_geary@byu.edu.
Website: http://pws.byu.edu

California State University, Fresno, Division of Research and Graduate Studies, Jordan College of Agricultural Sciences and Technology, Department of Animal Sciences and Agricultural Education, Fresno, CA 93740-8027. Offers animal science (MS). *Program availability:* Part-time, evening/weekend. *Degree requirements:* For master's, thesis. *Entrance requirements:* For master's, GRE General Test, minimum GPA of 3.0 in last 60 hours. Additional exam requirements/recommendations for international students: Required—TOEFL. Electronic applications accepted. *Faculty research:* Horse nutrition, animal health and welfare, electronic monitoring.

Clemson University, Graduate School, College of Agriculture, Forestry and Life Sciences, Department of Animal and Veterinary Sciences, Clemson, SC 29634. Offers MS, PhD. *Program availability:* Part-time. *Faculty:* 19 full-time (11 women). *Students:* 23 full-time (16 women), 3 part-time (1 woman); includes 2 minority (1 Black or African American, non-Hispanic/Latino; 1 Hispanic/Latino), 4 international. Average age 28. 17 applicants, 94% accepted, 12 enrolled. In 2018, 8 master's, 3 doctorates awarded. *Degree requirements:* For master's, thesis optional; for doctorate, comprehensive exam, thesis/dissertation. *Entrance requirements:* For master's and doctorate, GRE General Test, unofficial transcripts, letters of recommendation. Additional exam requirements/recommendations for international students: Required—TOEFL (minimum score 80 paper-based; 80 iBT); Recommended—IELTS (minimum score 6.5), TSE (minimum score 54). *Application deadline:* For fall admission, 4/15 for international students; for spring admission, 10/15 for international students. Applications are processed on a rolling basis. Application fee: $80 ($90 for international students). Electronic applications accepted. *Expenses:* $5898 per semester full-time resident, $11623 per semester full-time non-resident, $724 per credit hour part-time resident, $1451 per credit hour part-time non-resident, online $955 per credit hour, $4938 doctoral programs resident, $10405 doctoral programs non-resident, $1144 full-time graduate assistant, other fees may apply per session. *Financial support:* In 2018–19, 21 students received support, including 2 fellowships with full and partial tuition reimbursements available (averaging $7,000 per year), 10 research assistantships with full and partial tuition reimbursements available (averaging $12,938 per year), 9 teaching assistantships with full and partial tuition reimbursements available (averaging $12,931 per year); career-related internships or fieldwork also available. *Faculty research:* Reproduction, ruminant nutrition, muscle biology/biochemistry, fetal growth and development, immunology. *Total annual research expenditures:* $254,309. *Unit head:* Dr. James Strickland, Department Chair, 864-656-3138, E-mail: jrstric@clemson.edu. *Application contact:* Dr. Jeryl Jones, Graduate Program Coordinator, 864-656-2142, E-mail: jerylj@clemson.edu.
Website: http://www.clemson.edu/cafls/departments/animal_vet_science/

Colorado State University, College of Agricultural Sciences, Department of Animal Sciences, Fort Collins, CO 80523-1171. Offers MS, PhD. *Degree requirements:* For master's, comprehensive exam (for some programs), thesis (for some programs); for doctorate, comprehensive exam (for some programs), thesis/dissertation. *Entrance requirements:* Additional exam requirements/recommendations for international students: Required—TOEFL (minimum score 550 paper-based; 80 iBT); Recommended—IELTS (minimum score 6.5). Electronic applications accepted. *Expenses:* Tuition, state resident: full-time $10,520; part-time $4675 per credit hour. Tuition, nonresident: full-time $25,791; part-time $11,462 per credit hour. *International tuition:* $25,791 full-time. *Required fees:* $2392; $576 $288. Tuition and fees vary according to course level, course load, degree level, program and student level. *Faculty research:* Breeding and genetics, equine reproduction, meat safety and quality, livestock behavior and welfare, beef and dairy management systems.

Cornell University, Graduate School, Graduate Fields of Agriculture and Life Sciences, Field of Animal Science, Ithaca, NY 14853. Offers animal genetics (MPS, MS, PhD); animal genomics (MPS, MS, PhD); animal nutrition (MPS, MS, PhD); animal science (MPS, MS); physiology of reproduction (MPS, MS, PhD). *Degree requirements:* For master's, thesis, teaching experience; for doctorate, comprehensive exam, thesis/dissertation, teaching experience. *Entrance requirements:* For master's and doctorate, 2 letters of recommendation. Additional exam requirements/recommendations for international students: Required—TOEFL (minimum score 550 paper-based; 77 iBT). Electronic applications accepted. *Faculty research:* Quantitative genetics, genetic improvement of animal populations, statistical genetics.

Dalhousie University, Faculty of Agriculture, Halifax, NS B3H 4R2, Canada. Offers agriculture (M Sc), including air quality, animal behavior, animal molecular genetics, animal nutrition, animal technology, aquaculture, botany, crop management, crop physiology, ecology, environmental microbiology, food science, horticulture, nutrient management, pest management, physiology, plant biotechnology, plant pathology, soil chemistry, soil fertility, waste management and composting, water quality. *Program availability:* Part-time. *Degree requirements:* For master's, thesis, ATC Exam Teaching Assistantship. *Entrance requirements:* For master's, honors B Sc, minimum GPA of 3.0. Additional exam requirements/recommendations for international students: Required—TOEFL (minimum score 580 paper-based; 92 iBT), IELTS, Michigan English Language Assessment Battery, CanTEST, CAEL. *Faculty research:* Bio-product development, organic agriculture, nutrient management, air and water quality, agricultural biotechnology.

Fort Valley State University, College of Graduate Studies and Extended Education, Program in Animal Science, Fort Valley, GA 31030. Offers MS. *Degree requirements:* For master's, thesis. *Entrance requirements:* For master's, GRE General Test. Additional exam requirements/recommendations for international students: Recommended—TOEFL.

Iowa State University of Science and Technology, Department of Animal Science, Ames, IA 50011. Offers animal breeding and genetics (MS, PhD); animal physiology (MS); animal psychology (PhD); animal science (MS, PhD); meat science (MS, PhD). *Degree requirements:* For master's, thesis or alternative; for doctorate, thesis/dissertation. *Entrance requirements:* For master's and doctorate, GRE General Test. Additional exam requirements/recommendations for international students: Required—TOEFL (minimum score 550 paper-based; 80 iBT), IELTS (minimum score 6.5). Electronic applications accepted. *Faculty research:* Animal breeding, animal nutrition, meat science, muscle biology, nutritional physiology.

Iowa State University of Science and Technology, Program in Animal Breeding and Genetics, Ames, IA 50011. Offers animal breeding and genetics (MS); immunogenetics (PhD); molecular genetics (PhD); quantitative genetics (PhD). *Entrance requirements:* For master's and doctorate, GRE. Additional exam requirements/recommendations for international students: Required—TOEFL (minimum score 550 paper-based; 80 iBT), IELTS (minimum score 6.5). Electronic applications accepted.

Iowa State University of Science and Technology, Program in Animal Physiology, Ames, IA 50011. Offers MS, PhD. *Entrance requirements:* For master's and doctorate, GRE. Additional exam requirements/recommendations for international students: Required—TOEFL (minimum score 550 paper-based; 80 iBT), IELTS (minimum score 6.5). Electronic applications accepted.

Iowa State University of Science and Technology, Program in Meat Science, Ames, IA 50011. Offers MS, PhD. *Entrance requirements:* For master's and doctorate, GRE. Additional exam requirements/recommendations for international students: Required—TOEFL (minimum score 550 paper-based; 80 iBT), IELTS (minimum score 6.5). Electronic applications accepted.

Kansas State University, Graduate School, College of Agriculture, Department of Animal Sciences and Industry, Manhattan, KS 66506. Offers genetics (MS, PhD); meat science (MS, PhD); monogastric nutrition (MS, PhD); physiology (MS, PhD); ruminant nutrition (MS, PhD). *Degree requirements:* For master's, comprehensive exam, thesis, oral exam; for doctorate, comprehensive exam, thesis/dissertation, preliminary exams. *Entrance requirements:* Additional exam requirements/recommendations for international students: Required—TOEFL (minimum score 550 paper-based; 79 iBT). Electronic applications accepted. *Faculty research:* Animal nutrition, animal physiology, meat science, animal genetics.

Louisiana State University and Agricultural & Mechanical College, Graduate School, College of Agriculture, School of Animal Sciences, Baton Rouge, LA 70803. Offers MS, PhD.

McGill University, Faculty of Graduate and Postdoctoral Studies, Faculty of Agricultural and Environmental Sciences, Department of Animal Science, Montréal, QC H3A 2T5, Canada. Offers M Sc, M Sc A, PhD.

Michigan State University, College of Veterinary Medicine and The Graduate School, Graduate Programs in Veterinary Medicine, Department of Large Animal Clinical Sciences, East Lansing, MI 48824. Offers MS, PhD. *Entrance requirements:* Additional exam requirements/recommendations for international students: Required—TOEFL (minimum score 550 paper-based), Michigan State University ELT (minimum score 85), Michigan English Language Assessment Battery (minimum score 83). Electronic applications accepted.

Michigan State University, College of Veterinary Medicine and The Graduate School, Graduate Programs in Veterinary Medicine, Department of Small Animal Clinical Sciences, East Lansing, MI 48824. Offers MS. *Degree requirements:* For master's, thesis. *Entrance requirements:* Additional exam requirements/recommendations for international students: Required—TOEFL, Michigan State University ELT (minimum score 85), Michigan English Language Assessment Battery (minimum score 83).

Michigan State University, The Graduate School, College of Agriculture and Natural Resources, Department of Animal Science, East Lansing, MI 48824. Offers animal science (MS, PhD); animal science-environmental toxicology (PhD). *Entrance requirements:* Additional exam requirements/recommendations for international students: Required—TOEFL (minimum score 550 paper-based), Michigan State University ELT (minimum score 85), Michigan English Language Assessment Battery (minimum score 83). Electronic applications accepted.

Mississippi State University, College of Agriculture and Life Sciences, Department of Animal and Dairy Sciences, Mississippi State, MS 39762. Offers agricultural life sciences (MS), including animal physiology (MS, PhD), genetics (MS, PhD); agricultural science (PhD), including animal dairy sciences, animal nutrition (MS, PhD); agriculture (MS), including animal nutrition (MS, PhD), animal science; life sciences (PhD), including animal physiology (MS, PhD), genetics (MS, PhD). *Faculty:* 19 full-time (6 women). *Students:* 18 full-time (13 women), 11 part-time (6 women); includes 3 minority (1 Black or African American, non-Hispanic/Latino; 1 American Indian or Alaska Native, non-Hispanic/Latino; 1 Hispanic/Latino), 6 international. Average age 26. 28 applicants, 39% accepted, 10 enrolled. In 2018, 8 master's, 2 doctorates awarded. *Degree requirements:* For master's, comprehensive exam (for some programs), thesis, written proposal of intended research area; for doctorate, comprehensive exam, thesis/dissertation, written proposal of intended research area. *Entrance requirements:* For master's, GRE General Test, minimum GPA of 3.0; for doctorate, GRE General Test. Additional exam requirements/recommendations for international students: Required—TOEFL (minimum score 575 paper-based; 84 iBT), IELTS (minimum score 7). *Application deadline:* For fall admission, 7/1 for domestic students, 5/1 for international students; for spring admission, 11/1 for domestic students, 9/1 for international students. Applications are processed on a rolling basis. Application fee: $60 ($80 for international students). Electronic applications accepted. *Expenses:* Tuition, state resident: full-time $8450; part-time $360.59 per credit hour. Tuition, nonresident: full-time $23,140; part-time $969.09 per credit hour. *Required fees:* $110. One-time fee: $55 full-time. Part-time tuition and fees vary according to course level, degree level, campus/location and reciprocity agreements. *Financial support:* In 2018–19, 13 research assistantships (averaging $13,167 per year) were awarded; Federal Work-Study, institutionally sponsored loans, and unspecified assistantships also available. Financial award application deadline: 4/1; financial award applicants required to submit FAFSA. *Faculty research:* Ecology and population dynamics, physiology, biochemistry and behavior, systematics. *Unit head:* Dr. John Blanton, Professor and Head, 662-325-2802, Fax: 662-325-8873, E-mail: john.blanton@msstate.edu. *Application contact:* Ryan King, Admissions and Enrollment Assistant, 662-325-8951, E-mail: rjk101@grad.msstate.edu.
Website: http://www.ads.msstate.edu/

Mississippi State University, College of Agriculture and Life Sciences, Department of Poultry Science, Mississippi State, MS 39762. Offers agricultural sciences (MS, PhD), including poultry science. *Faculty:* 8 full-time (3 women). *Students:* 12 full-time (5 women), 3 part-time (2 women); includes 1 minority (Black or African American, non-Hispanic/Latino), 8 international. Average age 30. 3 applicants, 67% accepted, 2 enrolled. In 2018, 1 master's, 3 doctorates awarded. *Degree requirements:* For master's, comprehensive exam, thesis optional; for doctorate, comprehensive exam, thesis/dissertation. *Entrance requirements:* Additional exam requirements/recommendations for international students: Required—TOEFL (minimum score 477 paper-based; 53 iBT); Recommended—IELTS (minimum score 4.5). *Application deadline:* For fall admission, 7/1 for domestic students, 5/1 for international students; for spring admission, 10/1 for domestic students, 11/1 for international students. Applications are processed on a rolling basis. Application fee: $60 ($80 for international students). Electronic applications accepted. *Expenses:* Tuition, state resident: full-time $8450; part-time $360.59 per credit hour. Tuition, nonresident: full-time $23,140; part-time $969.09 per credit hour. *Required fees:* $110. One-time fee: $55 full-time. Part-time tuition and fees vary according to course load, degree level, campus/location and reciprocity agreements. *Financial support:* In 2018–19, 11 research assistantships with partial tuition reimbursements (averaging $14,798 per year) were awarded; Federal Work-Study, institutionally sponsored loans, scholarships/grants, and unspecified assistantships also available. Financial award application deadline: 4/1; financial award applicants required to submit FAFSA. *Unit head:* Dr. Mary Beck, Professor and Head, 662-325-3416, Fax: 662-325-8292, E-mail: mmb485@msstate.edu. *Application contact:* Ryan King, Admissions and Enrollment Assistant, 662-325-8951, E-mail: rjk101@grad.msstate.edu.
Website: http://www.poultry.msstate.edu/

Animal Sciences

Missouri Western State University, Program in Business Administration, St. Joseph, MO 64507-2294. Offers animal and life sciences (MBA); enterprise resource planning (MBA); forensic accounting (MBA); general business (MBA). *Program availability:* Part-time, 100% online. *Students:* 25 full-time (12 women), 41 part-time (17 women); includes 8 minority (3 Black or African American, non-Hispanic/Latino; 2 American Indian or Alaska Native, non-Hispanic/Latino; 2 Asian, non-Hispanic/Latino; 1 Two or more races, non-Hispanic/Latino), 1 international. Average age 32. 45 applicants, 93% accepted, 25 enrolled. In 2018, 19 master's awarded. *Entrance requirements:* Additional exam requirements/recommendations for international students: Recommended—TOEFL (minimum score 79 iBT), IELTS (minimum score 6). *Application deadline:* For fall admission, 7/15 for domestic and international students; for spring admission, 11/1 for domestic and international students; for summer admission, 4/29 for domestic and international students. Applications are processed on a rolling basis. Application fee: $45 ($50 for international students). Electronic applications accepted. *Expenses: Tuition, area resident:* Part-time $359.39 per credit hour. Tuition, state resident: part-time $359.39 per credit hour. Tuition, nonresident: part-time $643.39 per credit hour. Tuition and fees vary according to program. *Financial support:* Scholarships/grants and unspecified assistantships available. Support available to part-time students. *Unit head:* Dr. Logan Jones, Dean of Craig School of Business, 816-271-4338, E-mail: jones@missouriwestern.edu. *Application contact:* Dr. Susan Bashinski, Dean of the Graduate School, 816-271-4394, Fax: 816-271-4525, E-mail: graduate@missouriwestern.edu.
Website: https://www.missouriwestern.edu/business/mba/

Montana State University, The Graduate School, College of Agriculture, Department of Animal and Range Sciences, Bozeman, MT 59717. Offers MS, PhD. *Program availability:* Part-time. *Degree requirements:* For master's, comprehensive exam; for doctorate, comprehensive exam, thesis/dissertation. *Entrance requirements:* For master's, GRE, minimum GPA of 3.0; undergraduate coursework in animal science, range science or closely-related field; faculty adviser; for doctorate, GRE. Additional exam requirements/recommendations for international students: Required—TOEFL (minimum score 550 paper-based; 80 iBT). Electronic applications accepted. *Faculty research:* Rangeland ecology, wildlife habitat management, residual feed intake, post-partum effect of bulls, increasing efficiency of sheep production systems.

North Carolina Agricultural and Technical State University, The Graduate College, College of Agriculture and Environmental Sciences, Department of Animal Sciences, Greensboro, NC 27411. Offers integrated animal health systems (MS).

North Carolina State University, Graduate School, College of Agriculture and Life Sciences, Department of Animal Science, Raleigh, NC 27695. Offers animal and poultry science (PhD); animal science (MS). *Degree requirements:* For master's, thesis optional. *Entrance requirements:* For master's, GRE, minimum GPA of 3.0. Electronic applications accepted. *Faculty research:* Nutrient utilization, mineral nutrition, genomics, endocrinology, reproductive physiology.

North Carolina State University, Graduate School, College of Agriculture and Life Sciences, Department of Poultry Science, Raleigh, NC 27695. Offers MS. *Program availability:* Part-time. *Degree requirements:* For master's, thesis. Electronic applications accepted. *Faculty research:* Reproductive physiology, nutrition, toxicology, immunology, molecular biology.

North Dakota State University, College of Graduate and Interdisciplinary Studies, College of Agriculture, Food Systems, and Natural Resources, Department of Animal Sciences, Fargo, ND 58102. Offers MS, PhD. *Degree requirements:* For master's, thesis; for doctorate, comprehensive exam, thesis/dissertation. *Entrance requirements:* For master's and doctorate, GRE General Test. Additional exam requirements/recommendations for international students: Required—TOEFL (minimum score 71 iBT). *Faculty research:* Reproduction, nutrition, meat and muscle biology, breeding/genetics.

The Ohio State University, Graduate School, College of Food, Agricultural, and Environmental Sciences, Department of Animal Sciences, Columbus, OH 43210. Offers MAS, MS, PhD. *Faculty:* 21. *Students:* 30 (23 women). Average age 27. In 2018, 10 master's, 6 doctorates awarded. *Entrance requirements:* For master's and doctorate, GRE General Test. Additional exam requirements/recommendations for international students: Required—TOEFL (minimum score 550 paper-based; 79 iBT), Michigan English Language Assessment Battery (minimum score 82); Recommended—IELTS (minimum score 7). *Application deadline:* For fall admission, 12/1 priority date for domestic and international students; for spring admission, 12/12 for domestic students, 11/10 for international students. Applications are processed on a rolling basis. Application fee: $60 ($70 for international students). Electronic applications accepted. *Financial support:* Fellowships with tuition reimbursements, research assistantships with tuition reimbursements, teaching assistantships with tuition reimbursements, Federal Work-Study, and institutionally sponsored loans available. Support available to part-time students. *Unit head:* Dr. John C. Foltz, Chair, 614-292-1242, E-mail: foltz.75@osu.edu. *Application contact:* Graduate and Professional Admissions, 614-292-9444, Fax: 614-292-3895, E-mail: gpadmissions@osu.edu.
Website: http://ansci.osu.edu/

Oklahoma State University, College of Agricultural Science and Natural Resources, Department of Animal Science, Stillwater, OK 74078. Offers animal sciences (M Ag, MS); food science (PhD). *Faculty:* 26 full-time (5 women), 2 part-time/adjunct (1 woman). *Students:* 18 full-time (12 women), 56 part-time (35 women); includes 8 minority (1 Black or African American, non-Hispanic/Latino; 2 Asian, non-Hispanic/Latino; 3 Hispanic/Latino; 2 Two or more races, non-Hispanic/Latino), 16 international. Average age 26. 51 applicants, 27% accepted, 14 enrolled. In 2018, 14 master's, 4 doctorates awarded. *Entrance requirements:* For master's and doctorate, GRE or GMAT. Additional exam requirements/recommendations for international students: Required—TOEFL (minimum score 550 paper-based; 79 iBT). *Application deadline:* For fall admission, 3/1 priority date for international students; for spring admission, 8/1 priority date for international students. Applications are processed on a rolling basis. Application fee: $40 ($75 for international students). Electronic applications accepted. *Expenses: Tuition, area resident:* Full-time $4148. Tuition, state resident: full-time $4148. Tuition, nonresident: full-time $10,517. *International tuition:* $10,517 full-time. *Required fees:* $4394; $2929 per credit hour. Tuition and fees vary according to course load and program. *Financial support:* Research assistantships, teaching assistantships, career-related internships or fieldwork, Federal Work-Study, scholarships/grants, health care benefits, tuition waivers (partial), and unspecified assistantships available. Support available to part-time students. Financial award application deadline: 3/1; financial award applicants required to submit FAFSA. *Faculty research:* Quantitative trait loci identification for economical traits in swing/beef; waste management strategies in livestock; endocrine control of reproductive processes in farm animals; cholesterol synthesis, inhibition, and reduction; food safety research. *Unit head:* Dr. Clint Rusk, Department Head, 405-744-6062, Fax: 405-744-7390, E-mail: clint.rusk@okstate.edu. *Application contact:* Dr. Sheryl Tucker, Dean, 405-744-6368, Fax: 405-744-0355, E-mail: gradi@okstate.edu.
Website: http://www.ansi.okstate.edu

Oregon State University, College of Agricultural Sciences, Programs in Animal and Rangeland Sciences, Corvallis, OR 97331. Offers animal science (MS); poultry science (MS). *Program availability:* Part-time. *Entrance requirements:* For master's, GRE. Additional exam requirements/recommendations for international students: Required—TOEFL (minimum score 80 iBT), IELTS (minimum score 6.5).

Penn State University Park, Graduate School, College of Agricultural Sciences, Department of Animal Science, University Park, PA 16802. Offers MPS, MS, PhD.

Purdue University, Graduate School, College of Agriculture, Department of Animal Sciences, West Lafayette, IN 47907. Offers MS, PhD. *Program availability:* Part-time. *Faculty:* 25 full-time (7 women), 3 part-time/adjunct (2 women). *Students:* 54 full-time (32 women), 2 part-time (1 woman); includes 3 minority (1 Black or African American, non-Hispanic/Latino; 1 Hispanic/Latino; 1 Two or more races, non-Hispanic/Latino), 22 international. Average age 27. 40 applicants, 53% accepted, 16 enrolled. In 2018, 10 master's, 9 doctorates awarded. Terminal master's awarded for partial completion of doctoral program. *Degree requirements:* For master's, thesis optional; for doctorate, thesis/dissertation. *Entrance requirements:* For master's, GRE General Test, minimum undergraduate GPA of 3.0 or equivalent; for doctorate, GRE General Test, minimum undergraduate GPA of 3.0 or equivalent; master's degree with minimum GPA of 3.0 or equivalent. Additional exam requirements/recommendations for international students: Required—TOEFL (minimum score 550 paper-based; 77 iBT), TWE. *Application deadline:* For fall admission, 5/1 priority date for domestic students, 4/1 for international students; for spring admission, 10/1 priority date for domestic students, 8/1 for international students; for summer admission, 3/1 priority date for domestic students, 1/1 for international students. Applications are processed on a rolling basis. Application fee: $60 ($75 for international students). Electronic applications accepted. *Financial support:* In 2018–19, 35 students received support, including fellowships with full tuition reimbursements available (averaging $17,475 per year), 29 research assistantships with full tuition reimbursements available (averaging $18,577 per year). Support available to part-time students. Financial award applicants required to submit FAFSA. *Faculty research:* Genetics, meat science, nutrition, management, ethology. *Unit head:* Alan G. Mathew, Head, 765-494-4806, E-mail: agmathew@purdue.edu. *Application contact:* Kimberly See, Graduate Contact, 765-494-4863, E-mail: see2@purdue.edu.
Website: http://www.ansc.purdue.edu/

Purdue University, Graduate School, College of Health and Human Sciences, Department of Nutrition Science, West Lafayette, IN 47907. Offers animal health (MS, PhD); biochemical and molecular nutrition (MS, PhD); growth and development (MS, PhD); human and clinical nutrition (MS, PhD); public health and education (MS, PhD). *Faculty:* 18 full-time (12 women), 1 part-time/adjunct (0 women). *Students:* 44 full-time (36 women), 2 part-time (1 woman); includes 4 minority (2 Black or African American, non-Hispanic/Latino; 1 Asian, non-Hispanic/Latino; 1 Two or more races, non-Hispanic/Latino), 17 international. Average age 26. 51 applicants, 29% accepted, 11 enrolled. In 2018, 3 master's, 13 doctorates awarded. *Degree requirements:* For master's, thesis; for doctorate, thesis/dissertation. *Entrance requirements:* For master's and doctorate, GRE General Test (minimum scores in verbal and quantitative areas of 1000 or 300 on new scoring), minimum undergraduate GPA of 3.0 or equivalent. Additional exam requirements/recommendations for international students: Required—TOEFL (minimum score 600 paper-based; 77 iBT). *Application deadline:* For fall admission, 1/10 for domestic and international students. Applications are processed on a rolling basis. Application fee: $60 ($75 for international students). Electronic applications accepted. *Financial support:* Fellowships, research assistantships, and teaching assistantships available. Support available to part-time students. Financial award applicants required to submit FAFSA. *Faculty research:* Nutrient requirements, nutrient metabolism, nutrition and disease prevention. *Unit head:* Michele R. Forman, Head, 765-494-9921, E-mail: mforman@purdue.edu. *Application contact:* Kim Buhman, Graduate Contact for Admissions, 765-496-6872, E-mail: kbuhman@purdue.edu.
Website: http://www.cfs.purdue.edu/fn/

Rutgers University–New Brunswick, Graduate School-New Brunswick, Program in Endocrinology and Animal Biosciences, Piscataway, NJ 08854-8097. Offers MS, PhD. Terminal master's awarded for partial completion of doctoral program. *Degree requirements:* For master's, thesis; for doctorate, comprehensive exam, thesis/dissertation. *Entrance requirements:* For master's and doctorate, GRE General Test. Additional exam requirements/recommendations for international students: Required—TOEFL. Electronic applications accepted. *Faculty research:* Comparative and behavioral endocrinology, epigenetic regulation of the endocrine system, exercise physiology and immunology, fetal and neonatal developmental programming, mammary gland biology and breast cancer, neuroendocrinology and alcohol studies, reproductive and developmental toxicology.

South Dakota State University, Graduate School, College of Agriculture, Food and Environmental Sciences, Department of Animal Science, Brookings, SD 57007. Offers animal science (MS, PhD); biological sciences (PhD). *Program availability:* Part-time. *Degree requirements:* For master's, thesis, oral exam; for doctorate, comprehensive exam, thesis/dissertation, preliminary oral and written exams. *Entrance requirements:* Additional exam requirements/recommendations for international students: Required—TOEFL (minimum score 550 paper-based; 79 iBT). *Faculty research:* Ruminant and nonruminant nutrition, meat science, reproductive physiology, range utilization, ecology genetics, muscle biology, animal production.

South Dakota State University, Graduate School, College of Agriculture, Food and Environmental Sciences, Department of Dairy and Food Science, Brookings, SD 57007. Offers dairy science (MS, PhD); food science (MS, PhD). *Program availability:* Part-time. *Degree requirements:* For master's, thesis, oral exam; for doctorate, comprehensive exam, thesis/dissertation, preliminary oral and written exams. *Entrance requirements:* Additional exam requirements/recommendations for international students: Required—TOEFL (minimum score 550 paper-based). *Faculty research:* Dairy cattle nutrition, energy metabolism, food safety, dairy processing technology.

Southern Illinois University Carbondale, Graduate School, College of Agriculture, Department of Animal Science, Food and Nutrition, Program in Animal Science, Carbondale, IL 62901-4701. Offers MS. *Degree requirements:* For master's, thesis. *Entrance requirements:* For master's, GRE, minimum GPA of 2.7. Additional exam requirements/recommendations for international students: Required—TOEFL. *Faculty research:* Nutrition, reproductive physiology, animal biotechnology, phytoestrogens and animal reproduction.

Sul Ross State University, Division of Agricultural and Natural Resource Science, Program in Animal Science, Alpine, TX 79832. Offers M Ag, MS. *Program availability:* Part-time. *Degree requirements:* For master's, thesis (for some programs). *Entrance requirements:* For master's, GRE General Test, minimum GPA of 2.5 in last 60 hours of undergraduate work. *Faculty research:* Reproductive physiology, meat processing, animal nutrition, equine foot and motion studies, Spanish goat and Barbado sheep studies.

Texas A&M University, College of Agriculture and Life Sciences, Department of Animal Science, College Station, TX 77843. Offers animal breeding, animal science (MS); animal science (M Agr); equine industry management (MEIM); physiology of reproduction (PhD). *Faculty:* 37 full-time (11 women). *Students:* 100 full-time (68 women), 25 part-time (14 women); includes 12 minority (1 Black or African American, non-Hispanic/Latino; 2 American Indian or Alaska Native, non-Hispanic/Latino; 9 Hispanic/Latino), 26 international. Average age 27. 21 applicants, 95% accepted, 18 enrolled. In 2018, 39 master's, 8 doctorates awarded. *Degree requirements:* For master's, thesis; for doctorate, thesis/dissertation. *Entrance requirements:* For master's and doctorate, GRE General Test. Additional exam requirements/recommendations for international students: Required—TOEFL (minimum score 550 paper-based; 80 iBT), IELTS (minimum score 6), PTE (minimum score 53). *Application deadline:* For fall admission, 2/1 priority date for domestic students; for spring admission, 10/1 priority date for domestic students. Applications are processed on a rolling basis. Application fee: $50 ($90 for international students). Electronic applications accepted. *Expenses:* Contact institution. *Financial support:* In 2018–19, 112 students received support, including 33 fellowships with tuition reimbursements available (averaging $4,101 per year), 56 research assistantships with tuition reimbursements available (averaging $11,921 per year), 41 teaching assistantships with tuition reimbursements available (averaging $10,290 per year); career-related internships or fieldwork, institutionally sponsored loans, scholarships/grants, traineeships, health care benefits, tuition waivers (full and partial), and unspecified assistantships also available. Support available to part-time students. Financial award application deadline: 3/15; financial award applicants required to submit FAFSA. *Faculty research:* Genetic engineering/gene markers, dietary effects on colon cancer, biotechnology. *Unit head:* Dr. H. Russell Cross, Professor and Head, 979-845-1543, Fax: 979-845-6433, E-mail: hrcross@tamu.edu. *Application contact:* Dr. David Forrest, Professor and Associate Head for Academic Programs, 979-845-1542, E-mail: d-forrest@tamu.edu.
Website: http://animalscience.tamu.edu/

Texas A&M University, College of Agriculture and Life Sciences, Department of Poultry Science, College Station, TX 77843. Offers poultry science (PhD). *Program availability:* Part-time, evening/weekend, blended/hybrid learning. *Faculty:* 15. *Students:* 41 full-time (21 women), 15 part-time (5 women); includes 10 minority (2 Black or African American, non-Hispanic/Latino; 2 Asian, non-Hispanic/Latino; 6 Hispanic/Latino), 9 international. Average age 30. 8 applicants, 100% accepted, 8 enrolled. In 2018, 4 master's, 5 doctorates awarded. Terminal master's awarded for partial completion of doctoral program. *Degree requirements:* For master's, thesis (for some programs); for doctorate, thesis/dissertation. *Entrance requirements:* For master's and doctorate, GRE General Test. Additional exam requirements/recommendations for international students: Required—TOEFL (minimum score 550 paper-based; 80 iBT), IELTS (minimum score 6), PTE (minimum score 53). *Application deadline:* Applications are processed on a rolling basis. Application fee: $50 ($90 for international students). Electronic applications accepted. *Expenses:* Contact institution. *Financial support:* In 2018–19, 37 students received support, including 9 fellowships with tuition reimbursements available (averaging $9,838 per year), 32 research assistantships with tuition reimbursements available (averaging $11,270 per year), 1 teaching assistantship with tuition reimbursement available (averaging $10,000 per year); career-related internships or fieldwork, institutionally sponsored loans, scholarships/grants, traineeships, health care benefits, tuition waivers (full and partial), and unspecified assistantships also available. Support available to part-time students. Financial award application deadline: 3/15; financial award applicants required to submit FAFSA. *Faculty research:* Poultry diseases and immunology, avian genetics and physiology, nutrition and metabolism, poultry processing and food safety, waste management. *Unit head:* Dr. David Caldwell, Department Head/Professor, 979-845-1931, E-mail: caldwell@tamu.edu. *Application contact:* Graduate Admissions, 979-845-1060, E-mail: admissions@tamu.edu.
Website: http://posc.tamu.edu/

Texas A&M University–Kingsville, College of Graduate Studies, Dick and Mary Lewis Kleberg College of Agriculture, Natural Resources and Human Sciences, Department of Animal, Rangeland, and Wildlife Sciences, Program in Animal Science, Kingsville, TX 78363. Offers MS. *Degree requirements:* For master's, variable foreign language requirement, comprehensive exam, thesis or alternative. *Entrance requirements:* For master's, GRE (minimum score of 150 for each of the math and verbal sections), MAT, GMAT, minimum GPA of 3.0 for coursework from a previous degree. Additional exam requirements/recommendations for international students: Required—TOEFL (minimum score 550 paper-based; 79 iBT). Electronic applications accepted.

Texas Tech University, Graduate School, College of Agricultural Sciences and Natural Resources, Department of Animal and Food Sciences, Lubbock, TX 79409-2141. Offers animal science (MS, PhD); food science (MS). *Faculty:* 35 full-time (18 women), 2 part-time/adjunct (1 woman). *Students:* 81 full-time (46 women), 6 part-time (4 women); includes 10 minority (9 Hispanic/Latino; 1 Two or more races, non-Hispanic/Latino), 23 international. Average age 26. 45 applicants, 62% accepted, 22 enrolled. In 2018, 21 master's, 9 doctorates awarded. *Degree requirements:* For master's, thesis or alternative; for doctorate, thesis/dissertation. *Entrance requirements:* For master's and doctorate, GRE. Additional exam requirements/recommendations for international students: Required—TOEFL (minimum score 550 paper-based; 79 iBT). *Application deadline:* For fall admission, 6/1 priority date for domestic students, 1/15 priority date for international students; for spring admission, 9/1 priority date for domestic students, 6/15 priority date for international students. Applications are processed on a rolling basis. Application fee: $65. Electronic applications accepted. *Expenses:* Contact institution. *Financial support:* In 2018–19, 94 students received support, including 65 fellowships (averaging $3,316 per year), 79 research assistantships (averaging $13,833 per year), 6 teaching assistantships (averaging $21,756 per year); scholarships/grants and unspecified assistantships also available. Financial award applicants required to submit FAFSA. *Faculty research:* Nutrition, welfare and behavior, physiology and reproduction, muscle and meat biology, food safety, food security, companion animal, health and well-being. *Total annual research expenditures:* $4.2 million. *Unit head:* Dr. Michael Orth, Department Chair and Professor, 806-834-5653, Fax: 806-742-0898, E-mail: michael.orth@ttu.edu. *Application contact:* Charles Cooke, Administrative Business Assistant, 806-834-8977, E-mail: charles.cooke@ttu.edu.
Website: www.depts.ttu.edu/afs

Tufts University, Cummings School of Veterinary Medicine, Program in Conservation Medicine, Medford, MA 02155. Offers MS. *Degree requirements:* For master's, case study, preceptorship. *Entrance requirements:* For master's, GRE, official transcripts, curriculum vitae. Additional exam requirements/recommendations for international students: Required—TOEFL or IELTS. Electronic applications accepted. *Expenses: Tuition:* Full-time $51,288; part-time $1710 per credit hour. *Required fees:* $904. Full-time tuition and fees vary according to degree level, program and student level. Part-time tuition and fees vary according to course load. *Faculty research:* Non-invasive saliva collection techniques for free-ranging mountain gorillas and captive eastern gorillas, animal sentinels for infectious diseases.

Tuskegee University, Graduate Programs, College of Agriculture, Environment and Nutrition Sciences, Department of Agricultural and Environmental Sciences, Program in Animal and Poultry Sciences, Tuskegee, AL 36088. Offers animal and poultry breeding (MS); animal and poultry nutrition (MS); animal and poultry physiology (MS). *Degree requirements:* For master's, thesis. *Entrance requirements:* For master's, GRE General Test. Additional exam requirements/recommendations for international students: Required—TOEFL (minimum score 500 paper-based).

Universidad Nacional Pedro Henriquez Urena, Graduate School, Santo Domingo, Dominican Republic. Offers agricultural diversity (MS), including horticultural/fruit production, tropical animal production; conservation of monuments and cultural assets (M Arch); ecology and environment (MS); environmental engineering (MEE); international relations (MA); natural resource management (MS); political science (MA); project optimization (MPM); project feasibility (MPM); project management (MPM); sanitation engineering (ME); science for teachers (MS); tropical Caribbean architecture (M Arch).

Université Laval, Faculty of Agricultural and Food Sciences, Department of Animal Sciences, Programs in Animal Sciences, Québec, QC G1K 7P4, Canada. Offers M Sc, PhD. *Program availability:* Part-time. Terminal master's awarded for partial completion of doctoral program. *Degree requirements:* For master's, thesis; for doctorate, comprehensive exam, thesis/dissertation. *Entrance requirements:* For master's and doctorate, knowledge of French and English. Electronic applications accepted.

The University of Arizona, College of Agriculture and Life Sciences, Department of Animal Sciences, Tucson, AZ 85721. Offers MS, PhD. *Program availability:* Part-time. *Degree requirements:* For master's, thesis; for doctorate, thesis/dissertation. *Entrance requirements:* For master's, GRE Subject Test, 3 letters of recommendation, minimum GPA of 3.0; for doctorate, GRE Subject Test (biology or chemistry recommended), 3 letters of recommendation, statement of purpose, minimum GPA of 3.0. Additional exam requirements/recommendations for international students: Required—TOEFL (minimum score 550 paper-based; 79 iBT). Electronic applications accepted. *Faculty research:* Nutrition of beef and dairy cattle, reproduction and breeding, muscle growth and function, animal stress, meat science.

The University of Arizona, College of Agriculture and Life Sciences, School of Animal and Comparative Biomedical Sciences, Tucson, AZ 85721. Offers MS, PhD. *Degree requirements:* For master's, thesis; for doctorate, comprehensive exam, thesis/dissertation. *Entrance requirements:* For master's and doctorate, GRE, minimum GPA of 3.0, 3 letters of recommendation, letter of intent. Additional exam requirements/recommendations for international students: Required—TOEFL (minimum score 550 paper-based; 79 iBT). Electronic applications accepted.

University of Arkansas, Graduate School, Dale Bumpers College of Agricultural, Food and Life Sciences, Department of Animal Science, Fayetteville, AR 72701. Offers MS, PhD. In 2018, 7 master's, 3 doctorates awarded. *Degree requirements:* For master's, thesis; for doctorate, variable foreign language requirement, thesis/dissertation. *Entrance requirements:* For master's, GRE General Test or minimum GPA of 2.7. *Application deadline:* For fall admission, 8/1 for domestic students, 4/1 for international students; for spring admission, 12/1 for domestic students, 10/1 for international students; for summer admission, 4/15 for domestic students, 3/1 for international students. Applications are processed on a rolling basis. Application fee: $60. Electronic applications accepted. *Financial support:* In 2018–19, 11 research assistantships, 2 teaching assistantships were awarded; fellowships with tuition reimbursements, career-related internships or fieldwork, and Federal Work-Study also available. Support available to part-time students. Financial award application deadline: 4/1; financial award applicants required to submit FAFSA. *Unit head:* Dr. Michael L. Looper, Department Head, 479-575-3745, E-mail: looper@uark.edu. *Application contact:* Dr. Charles Rosenkrans, Graduate Coordinator, 479-575-4376, E-mail: crosenkr@uark.edu.
Website: https://animal-science.uark.edu/

University of Arkansas, Graduate School, Dale Bumpers College of Agricultural, Food and Life Sciences, Department of Poultry Science, Fayetteville, AR 72701. Offers MS, PhD. In 2018, 3 master's, 3 doctorates awarded. *Degree requirements:* For master's, thesis; for doctorate, variable foreign language requirement, thesis/dissertation. *Application deadline:* For fall admission, 8/1 for domestic students, 4/1 for international students; for spring admission, 12/1 for domestic students, 10/1 for international students; for summer admission, 4/15 for domestic students, 3/1 for international students. Applications are processed on a rolling basis. Application fee: $60. Electronic applications accepted. *Financial support:* In 2018–19, 25 research assistantships were awarded; fellowships with tuition reimbursements, teaching assistantships, career-related internships or fieldwork, and Federal Work-Study also available. Support available to part-time students. Financial award application deadline: 4/1; financial award applicants required to submit FAFSA. *Unit head:* Dr. Michael T. Kidd, Department Head, 479-575-3699, Fax: 479-575-3026, E-mail: mkidd@uark.edu. *Application contact:* Dr. John Marcy, Graduate Coordinator, 479-575-2211, Fax: 479-8775, E-mail: jmarcy@uark.edu.
Website: https://poultry-science.uark.edu/

The University of British Columbia, Faculty of Land and Food Systems, Applied Animal Biology Program, Vancouver, BC V6T 1Z4, Canada. Offers M Sc, PhD. *Degree requirements:* For master's, thesis; for doctorate, comprehensive exam, thesis/dissertation. *Entrance requirements:* Additional exam requirements/recommendations for international students: Required—TOEFL, IELTS. Electronic applications accepted. *Expenses:* Contact institution. *Faculty research:* Animal production, animal behavior and welfare, reproductive physiology, animal genetics, aquaculture and fish physiology.

University of California, Davis, Graduate Studies, Graduate Group in Animal Biology, Davis, CA 95616. Offers MAM, MS, PhD. Terminal master's awarded for partial completion of doctoral program. *Degree requirements:* For master's, comprehensive exam (for some programs), thesis (for some programs); for doctorate, thesis/dissertation. *Entrance requirements:* For master's, GRE General Test, minimum GPA of 3.0. Additional exam requirements/recommendations for international students: Required—TOEFL (minimum score 550 paper-based). Electronic applications accepted. *Faculty research:* Genetics, nutrition, physiology and behavior in domestic and aquatic animals.

University of Connecticut, Graduate School, College of Agriculture, Health and Natural Resources, Department of Animal Science, Storrs, CT 06269. Offers MS, PhD. Terminal master's awarded for partial completion of doctoral program. *Degree requirements:* For master's, comprehensive exam, thesis; for doctorate, comprehensive exam, thesis/dissertation. *Entrance requirements:* For master's and doctorate, GRE General Test, GRE Subject Test. Additional exam requirements/recommendations for international students: Required—TOEFL (minimum score 550 paper-based). Electronic applications accepted.

University of Delaware, College of Agriculture and Natural Resources, Department of Animal and Food Sciences, Newark, DE 19716. Offers animal sciences (MS, PhD); food sciences (MS). *Program availability:* Part-time. Terminal master's awarded for partial completion of doctoral program. *Degree requirements:* For master's, thesis; for doctorate, comprehensive exam, thesis/dissertation. *Entrance requirements:* For master's and doctorate, GRE General Test. Additional exam requirements/recommendations for international students: Required—TOEFL. Electronic applications accepted. *Faculty research:* Food chemistry, food microbiology, process engineering technology, packaging, food analysis, microbial genetics, molecular endocrinology, growth physiology, avian immunology and virology, monogastric nutrition, avian genomics.

University of Florida, Graduate School, College of Agricultural and Life Sciences, Department of Animal Sciences, Gainesville, FL 32611. Offers animal molecular and cellular biology (MS, PhD); animal sciences (MS, PhD). *Program availability:* Part-time. *Degree requirements:* For master's, variable foreign language requirement, comprehensive exam (for some programs), thesis optional, one departmental and one exit seminar; for doctorate, comprehensive exam, thesis/dissertation, two departmental seminars, one exit seminar. *Entrance requirements:* For master's and doctorate, GRE General Test, minimum GPA of 3.0, 3 letters of recommendation. Additional exam requirements/recommendations for international students: Required—TOEFL (minimum score 550 paper-based; 80 iBT), IELTS (minimum score 6). Electronic applications accepted. *Faculty research:* Improving the quality, preservation and utilization of livestock feeds; reducing effects of stress on embryonic function, growth and lactation; optimizing muscle growth and composition and meat palatability and quality; improving lactation performance, health and fertility of beef and dairy cows; genetic and genomic analysis of production, reproduction, and health traits in livestock.

University of Georgia, College of Agricultural and Environmental Sciences, Department of Animal and Dairy Sciences, Athens, GA 30602. Offers animal and dairy science (PhD); animal science (MS). *Degree requirements:* For master's, thesis; for doctorate, one foreign language, thesis/dissertation. *Entrance requirements:* For master's and doctorate, GRE General Test. Electronic applications accepted.

University of Georgia, College of Agricultural and Environmental Sciences, Department of Poultry Science, Athens, GA 30602. Offers animal nutrition (PhD); poultry science (MS, PhD). *Degree requirements:* For master's, thesis; for doctorate, one foreign language, thesis/dissertation. *Entrance requirements:* For master's and doctorate, GRE General Test. Electronic applications accepted.

University of Guelph, Office of Graduate and Postdoctoral Studies, Ontario Agricultural College, Department of Animal and Poultry Science, Guelph, ON N1G 2W1, Canada. Offers M Sc, PhD. *Program availability:* Part-time. *Degree requirements:* For master's, thesis (for some programs); for doctorate, comprehensive exam, thesis/dissertation. *Entrance requirements:* For master's, minimum B- average during previous 2 years of course work; for doctorate, minimum B- average. Additional exam requirements/recommendations for international students: Required—TOEFL (minimum score 550 paper-based; 89 iBT), IELTS (minimum score 6.5). *Faculty research:* Animal breeding and genetics (quantitative or molecular), animal nutrition (monogastric or ruminant), animal physiology (environmental, reproductive or behavioral), behavior and welfare.

University of Hawaii at Manoa, Office of Graduate Education, College of Tropical Agriculture and Human Resources, Department of Human Nutrition, Food and Animal Sciences, Program in Animal Sciences, Honolulu, HI 96822. Offers MS. *Program availability:* Part-time. *Entrance requirements:* For master's, GRE General Test. Additional exam requirements/recommendations for international students: Required—TOEFL (minimum score 580 paper-based; 100 iBT), IELTS (minimum score 5). *Faculty research:* Nutritional biochemistry, food composition, nutrition education, nutritional epidemiology, international nutrition, food toxicology.

University of Idaho, College of Graduate Studies, College of Agricultural and Life Sciences, Department of Animal and Veterinary Science, Moscow, ID 83844-2330. Offers MS, PhD. *Faculty:* 6 full-time. *Students:* 20 full-time (15 women), 13 part-time (7 women). Average age 27. In 2018, 8 master's, 2 doctorates awarded. *Degree requirements:* For doctorate, thesis/dissertation. *Entrance requirements:* For master's and doctorate, minimum GPA of 3.0. Additional exam requirements/recommendations for international students: Required—TOEFL (minimum score 79 iBT). *Application deadline:* For fall admission, 8/1 for domestic students; for spring admission, 12/15 for domestic students. Applications are processed on a rolling basis. Application fee: $60. Electronic applications accepted. *Expenses:* Tuition, state resident: full-time $7266.44; part-time $474.50 per credit hour. Tuition, nonresident: full-time $24,902; part-time $1453.50 per credit hour. *Required fees:* $2085.56; $45.50 per credit hour. *Financial support:* Research assistantships and teaching assistantships available. Financial award applicants required to submit FAFSA. *Faculty research:* Reproductive biology, muscle and growth physiology, meat science, milk quality, ruminant nutrition. *Unit head:* Dr. Amin Ahmadzadeh, Department Head, 208-885-6345, E-mail: avs@uidaho.edu. *Application contact:* Dr. Amin Ahmadzadeh, Department Head, 208-885-6345, E-mail: avs@uidaho.edu.
Website: https://www.uidaho.edu/cals/animal-and-veterinary-science

University of Illinois at Urbana–Champaign, Graduate College, College of Agricultural, Consumer and Environmental Sciences, Department of Animal Sciences, Champaign, IL 61820. Offers animal sciences (MS, PhD); bioinformatics: animal sciences (MS).

University of Kentucky, Graduate School, College of Agriculture, Food and Environment, Program in Animal and Food Sciences, Lexington, KY 40506-0032. Offers MS, PhD. Terminal master's awarded for partial completion of doctoral program. *Degree requirements:* For master's, comprehensive exam, thesis optional; for doctorate, comprehensive exam, thesis/dissertation. *Entrance requirements:* For master's, GRE General Test, minimum undergraduate GPA of 2.75; for doctorate, GRE General Test, minimum graduate GPA of 3.0. Additional exam requirements/recommendations for international students: Required—TOEFL (minimum score 550 paper-based). Electronic applications accepted. *Faculty research:* Nutrition of horses, cattle, swine, poultry, and sheep; physiology of reproduction and lactation; food science; microbiology.

University of Manitoba, Faculty of Graduate Studies, Faculty of Agricultural and Food Sciences, Department of Animal Science, Winnipeg, MB R3T 2N2, Canada. Offers M Sc, PhD. *Degree requirements:* For master's, thesis; for doctorate, one foreign language, thesis/dissertation.

University of Maryland, College Park, Academic Affairs, College of Agriculture and Natural Resources, Department of Animal and Avian Sciences, Program in Animal Sciences, College Park, MD 20742. Offers MS, PhD. *Degree requirements:* For master's, thesis, oral exam or written comprehensive exam; for doctorate, thesis/dissertation, journal publication, scientific paper. *Entrance requirements:* For master's, GRE General Test, minimum GPA of 3.0; for doctorate, GRE General Test. Additional exam requirements/recommendations for international students: Required—TOEFL. Electronic applications accepted. *Faculty research:* Animal physiology, cell biology and biochemistry, reproduction, biometrics, animal behavior.

University of Massachusetts Amherst, Graduate School, College of Natural Sciences, Department of Animal Biotechnology and Biomedical Sciences, Amherst, MA 01003. Offers MS, PhD. *Program availability:* Part-time. Terminal master's awarded for partial completion of doctoral program. *Degree requirements:* For master's, thesis or alternative; for doctorate, comprehensive exam, thesis/dissertation. *Entrance requirements:* For doctorate, GRE General Test. Additional exam requirements/recommendations for international students: Required—TOEFL (minimum score 550 paper-based; 80 iBT), IELTS (minimum score 6.5). Electronic applications accepted.

University of Minnesota, Twin Cities Campus, Graduate School, College of Food, Agricultural and Natural Resource Sciences, Animal Sciences Graduate Program, St. Paul, MN 55108. Offers MS, PhD. *Program availability:* Part-time. Terminal master's awarded for partial completion of doctoral program. *Degree requirements:* For master's, comprehensive exam, thesis; for doctorate, comprehensive exam, thesis/dissertation. *Entrance requirements:* For master's and doctorate, GRE. Additional exam requirements/recommendations for international students: Required—TOEFL (minimum score 550 paper-based; 79 iBT), IELTS (minimum score 6.5). Electronic applications accepted. *Faculty research:* Physiology, growth biology, nutrition, genetics, production systems.

University of Missouri, Office of Research and Graduate Studies, College of Agriculture, Food and Natural Resources, Department of Animal Sciences, Columbia, MO 65211. Offers MS, PhD. Terminal master's awarded for partial completion of doctoral program. *Entrance requirements:* For master's, GRE General Test (minimum scores: 146 verbal and 146 quantitative), minimum GPA of 3.0; for doctorate, GRE General Test (minimum score: Verbal 146, Quantitative 146), minimum GPA of 3.0; MS with thesis; 3 letters of recommendation. *Faculty research:* Reproductive and environmental physiology; ruminant and monogastric nutrition; genetics/genomics; meat science and livestock production across swine, dairy cattle, beef cattle, poultry, companion animals and horses.

University of Nebraska–Lincoln, Graduate College, College of Agricultural Sciences and Natural Resources, Department of Animal Science, Lincoln, NE 68588. Offers MS, PhD. *Degree requirements:* For master's, thesis; for doctorate, comprehensive exam, thesis/dissertation. *Entrance requirements:* For master's and doctorate, GRE General Test. Additional exam requirements/recommendations for international students: Required—TOEFL (minimum score 525 paper-based). Electronic applications accepted. *Faculty research:* Animal breeding and genetics, meat and poultry products, nonruminant and ruminant nutrition, physiology.

University of Nevada, Reno, Graduate School, College of Agriculture, Biotechnology and Natural Resources, Program in Animal and Rangeland Science, Reno, NV 89557. Offers MS. *Degree requirements:* For master's, thesis optional. *Entrance requirements:* For master's, GRE, minimum GPA of 2.75. Additional exam requirements/recommendations for international students: Required—TOEFL (minimum score 500 paper-based; 61 iBT), IELTS (minimum score 6). Electronic applications accepted. *Faculty research:* Sperm fertility, embryo development, ruminant utilization of forages.

University of New Hampshire, Graduate School, College of Life Sciences and Agriculture, Department of Molecular, Cellular and Biomedical Sciences, Program in Animal and Nutritional Sciences, Durham, NH 03824. Offers agricultural sciences (MS, PhD); nutritional sciences (MS, PhD). *Program availability:* Part-time. *Entrance requirements:* For master's and doctorate, GRE. Additional exam requirements/recommendations for international students: Required—TOEFL (minimum score 550 paper-based; 80 iBT). Electronic applications accepted.

University of Puerto Rico–Mayagüez, Graduate Studies, College of Agricultural Sciences, Department of Animal Science, Mayagüez, PR 00681-9000. Offers MS. *Program availability:* Part-time. *Degree requirements:* For master's, comprehensive exam, thesis. Electronic applications accepted. *Faculty research:* Swine production and nutrition, poultry production, dairy science and technology, microbiology.

University of Rhode Island, Graduate School, College of the Environment and Life Sciences, Department of Fisheries, Animal and Veterinary Sciences, Kingston, RI 02881. Offers animal health and disease (MS); animal science (MS); aquaculture (MS); aquatic pathology (MS); environmental sciences (PhD), including animal science, aquaculture science, aquatic pathology, fisheries science; fisheries (MS). *Faculty:* 12 full-time (7 women). *Entrance requirements:* Additional exam requirements/recommendations for international students: Required—TOEFL. *Application deadline:* For fall admission, 7/15 for domestic students, 2/1 for international students; for spring admission, 11/15 for domestic students, 7/15 for international students. Application fee: $65. Electronic applications accepted. *Expenses: Tuition, area resident:* Full-time $13,226; part-time $735 per credit. Tuition, state resident: full-time $13,226; part-time $735 per credit. Tuition, nonresident: full-time $25,854; part-time $1436 per credit. *International tuition:* $25,854 full-time. *Required fees:* $1698; $50 per credit. $35 per semester. One-time fee: $165. *Financial support:* Application deadline: 2/1; applicants required to submit FAFSA. *Unit head:* Dr. Marta Gomez-Chiarri, Chair, 401-874-2917, Fax: 401-874-7575, E-mail: gomezchi@uri.edu. *Application contact:* Dr. Marta Gomez-Chiarri, Chair, 401-874-2917, Fax: 401-874-7575, E-mail: gomezchi@uri.edu.
Website: http://web.uri.edu/favs/

University of Saskatchewan, College of Graduate and Postdoctoral Studies, College of Agriculture and Bioresources, Department of Animal and Poultry Science, Saskatoon, SK S7N 5A2, Canada. Offers M Sc, PhD. *Degree requirements:* For master's, thesis; for doctorate, thesis/dissertation. *Entrance requirements:* Additional exam requirements/recommendations for international students: Required—TOEFL.

University of Saskatchewan, Western College of Veterinary Medicine and College of Graduate and Postdoctoral Studies, Graduate Programs in Veterinary Medicine, Department of Large Animal Clinical Sciences, Saskatoon, SK S7N 5A2, Canada. Offers M Sc, M Vet Sc, PhD. *Degree requirements:* For master's, thesis (for some programs); for doctorate, comprehensive exam (for some programs), thesis/dissertation. *Entrance requirements:* Additional exam requirements/recommendations for international students: Required—TOEFL (minimum score 80 iBT); Recommended—IELTS (minimum score 6.5). Electronic applications accepted. *Faculty research:* Reproduction, infectious diseases, epidemiology, food safety.

University of Saskatchewan, Western College of Veterinary Medicine and College of Graduate and Postdoctoral Studies, Graduate Programs in Veterinary Medicine, Department of Small Animal Clinical Sciences, Saskatoon, SK S7N 5A2, Canada. Offers small animal clinical sciences (M Sc, PhD); veterinary anesthesiology, radiology and surgery (M Vet Sc); veterinary internal medicine (M Vet Sc). *Degree requirements:* For master's, thesis (for some programs); for doctorate, comprehensive exam (for some programs), thesis/dissertation. *Entrance requirements:* Additional exam requirements/recommendations for international students: Required—TOEFL (minimum score 80 iBT); Recommended—IELTS (minimum score 6.5). Electronic applications accepted. *Faculty research:* Orthopedics, wildlife, cardiovascular exercise/myelopathy, ophthalmology.

The University of Tennessee, Graduate School, College of Agricultural Sciences and Natural Resources, Department of Animal Science, Knoxville, TN 37996. Offers animal anatomy (PhD); breeding (MS, PhD); management (MS, PhD); nutrition (MS, PhD); physiology (MS, PhD). *Program availability:* Part-time. *Degree requirements:* For master's, thesis; for doctorate, thesis/dissertation. *Entrance requirements:* For master's and doctorate, GRE General Test, minimum GPA of 2.7. Additional exam requirements/recommendations for international students: Required—TOEFL. Electronic applications accepted.

University of Vermont, Graduate College, College of Agriculture and Life Sciences, Department of Animal and Veterinary Sciences, Burlington, VT 05405-0148. Offers animal science (MS); animal, nutrition and food sciences (PhD). *Degree requirements:* For master's, thesis; for doctorate, one foreign language, thesis/dissertation. *Entrance requirements:* For master's and doctorate, GRE General Test. Additional exam requirements/recommendations for international students: Required—TOEFL (minimum score 550 paper-based, 90 iBT) or IELTS (6.5). Electronic applications accepted. *Faculty research:* Animal nutrition, dairy production.

University of Wisconsin–Madison, Graduate School, College of Agricultural and Life Sciences, Department of Animal Sciences, Madison, WI 53706-1380. Offers MS, PhD. *Program availability:* Part-time. Terminal master's awarded for partial completion of doctoral program. *Degree requirements:* For master's, thesis; for doctorate, thesis/dissertation. *Entrance requirements:* For master's and doctorate, GRE General Test. Additional exam requirements/recommendations for international students: Required—TOEFL (minimum score 550 paper-based; 80 iBT). Electronic applications accepted. *Faculty research:* Animal biology, immunity and toxicology, endocrinology and reproductive physiology, genetics-animal breeding, meat science, muscle biology.

University of Wisconsin–Madison, Graduate School, College of Agricultural and Life Sciences, Department of Dairy Science, Madison, WI 53706-1380. Offers MS, PhD. *Program availability:* Part-time. Terminal master's awarded for partial completion of doctoral program. *Degree requirements:* For master's, thesis; for doctorate, thesis/dissertation. *Entrance requirements:* For master's and doctorate, GRE General Test. Additional exam requirements/recommendations for international students: Required—TOEFL (minimum score 550 paper-based; 80 iBT). Electronic applications accepted. *Faculty research:* Genetics, nutrition, lactation, reproduction, management of dairy cattle.

University of Wyoming, College of Agriculture and Natural Resources, Department of Animal Science, Program in Animal Sciences, Laramie, WY 82071. Offers MS, PhD. *Degree requirements:* For master's, comprehensive exam, thesis; for doctorate, comprehensive exam, thesis/dissertation. *Entrance requirements:* For master's, GRE General Test, minimum GPA of 3.0; for doctorate, GRE General Test or MS degree, minimum GPA of 3.0. Additional exam requirements/recommendations for international students: Required—TOEFL (minimum score 525 paper-based). *Expenses: Tuition, area resident:* Full-time $6504; part-time $271 per credit hour. Tuition, state resident: full-time $6504; part-time $271 per credit hour. Tuition, nonresident: full-time $19,464; part-time $811 per credit hour. *International tuition:* $19,464 full-time. *Required fees:* $1410.94; $343.82 per semester. $343.82 per semester. Tuition and fees vary according to course load, program and reciprocity agreements. *Faculty research:* Reproductive biology, ruminant nutrition meat science, muscle biology, food microbiology, lipid metabolism.

Utah State University, School of Graduate Studies, College of Agriculture and Applied Sciences, Department of Animal, Dairy and Veterinary Sciences, Logan, UT 84322. Offers animal science (MS, PhD); bioveterinary science (MS, PhD); dairy science (MS). *Program availability:* Part-time. *Degree requirements:* For master's, thesis (for some programs); for doctorate, comprehensive exam, thesis/dissertation. *Entrance requirements:* For master's and doctorate, GRE General Test, minimum GPA of 3.0. Additional exam requirements/recommendations for international students: Required—TOEFL. Electronic applications accepted. *Faculty research:* Monoclonal antibodies, antiviral chemotherapy, management systems, biotechnology, rumen fermentation manipulation.

Virginia Polytechnic Institute and State University, Graduate School, College of Agriculture and Life Sciences, Blacksburg, VA 24061. Offers agricultural and applied economics (MS, PhD); agricultural and life sciences (MS); agriculture, leadership, and community education (MS, PhD); animal and poultry science (MS, PhD); biochemistry (MS, PhD); crop and soil environmental sciences (MS, PhD); dairy science (MS, PhD); entomology (MS, PhD); food science and technology (MS, PhD); horticulture (PhD); human nutrition, foods and exercise (MS, PhD); plant pathology, physiology, and weed science (MS, PhD). *Faculty:* 244 full-time (79 women), 1 (woman) part-time/adjunct. *Students:* 360 full-time (195 women), 110 part-time (73 women); includes 70 minority (24 Black or African American, non-Hispanic/Latino; 1 American Indian or Alaska Native, non-Hispanic/Latino; 15 Asian, non-Hispanic/Latino; 12 Hispanic/Latino; 18 Two or more races, non-Hispanic/Latino), 110 international. Average age 28. 296 applicants, 54% accepted, 105 enrolled. In 2018, 92 master's, 59 doctorates awarded. *Degree requirements:* For master's, comprehensive exam (for some programs), thesis (for some programs); for doctorate, comprehensive exam (for some programs), thesis/dissertation (for some programs). *Entrance requirements:* For master's and doctorate, GRE/GMAT. Additional exam requirements/recommendations for international students: Required—TOEFL (minimum score 90 iBT). *Application deadline:* For fall admission, 8/1 for domestic students, 4/1 for international students; for spring admission, 1/1 for domestic students, 9/1 for international students. Applications are processed on a rolling basis. Application fee: $75. Electronic applications accepted. *Expenses:* Tuition, state resident: full-time $15,510; part-time $739.50 per credit hour. Tuition, nonresident: full-time $20,620; part-time $1400.25 per credit hour. *Required fees:* $2804; $550 per semester. Tuition and fees vary according to course load, campus/location and program. *Financial support:* In 2018–19, 3 fellowships with full tuition reimbursements (averaging $25,731 per year), 249 research assistantships with full tuition reimbursements (averaging $19,826 per year), 105 teaching assistantships with full tuition reimbursements (averaging $19,277 per year) were awarded; scholarships/grants and unspecified assistantships also available. Financial award application deadline: 3/1; financial award applicants required to submit FAFSA. *Total annual research expenditures:* $42.4 million. *Unit head:* Dr. Alan L. Grant, Dean, 540-231-4152, Fax: 540-231-4163, E-mail: algrant@vt.edu. *Application contact:* Crystal Tawney, Administrative Assistant, 540-231-4152, Fax: 540-231-4163, E-mail: cdtawney@vt.edu. Website: http://www.cals.vt.edu/

Washington State University, College of Agricultural, Human, and Natural Resource Sciences, Department of Animal Sciences, Pullman, WA 99164. Offers MS, PhD. Programs offered at the Pullman campus. *Program availability:* Part-time. *Degree requirements:* For master's, comprehensive exam, thesis, oral exam; for doctorate, comprehensive exam, thesis/dissertation, oral and written exam. *Entrance requirements:* For master's, GRE, minimum GPA of 3.0, 3 letters of recommendation, department questionnaire; for doctorate, GRE General Test, minimum GPA of 3.0. Additional exam requirements/recommendations for international students: Required—TOEFL, IELTS. Electronic applications accepted. *Faculty research:* Animal genomics, nutrition, reproduction, muscle biology and growth.

West Texas A&M University, College of Agriculture and Natural Sciences, Department of Agricultural Sciences, Emphasis in Animal Science, Canyon, TX 79015. Offers MS. *Program availability:* Part-time. *Degree requirements:* For master's, comprehensive exam, thesis optional. *Entrance requirements:* For master's, GRE General Test. Additional exam requirements/recommendations for international students: Required—TOEFL (minimum score 550 paper-based). Electronic applications accepted. *Faculty research:* Nutrition, animal breeding, meat science, reproduction physiology, feedlots.

West Virginia University, Davis College of Agriculture, Forestry and Consumer Sciences, Morgantown, WV 26506. Offers agricultural and extension education (MS, PhD); agriculture and resource management (MS); agriculture, natural resources and design (M Agr); agronomy (MS); animal and food science (PhD); animal physiology (MS); applied and environmental microbiology (MS); design and merchandising (MS); entomology (MS); forest resource science (PhD); forestry (MSF); genetics and developmental biology (MS, PhD); horticulture (MS); human and community development (PhD); landscape architecture (MLA); natural resource economics (PhD); nutritional and food science (MS); plant and soil science (PhD); plant pathology (MS); recreation, parks and tourism resources (MS); reproductive physiology (MS, PhD); wildlife and fisheries resources (PhD). *Accreditation:* ASLA. *Program availability:* Part-time. *Students:* 188 full-time (86 women), 47 part-time (30 women); includes 22 minority (5 Black or African American, non-Hispanic/Latino; 5 Asian, non-Hispanic/Latino; 8 Hispanic/Latino; 4 Two or more races, non-Hispanic/Latino), 60 international. In 2018, 56 master's, 14 doctorates awarded. *Degree requirements:* For master's, thesis; for doctorate, thesis/dissertation. *Entrance requirements:* Additional exam requirements/recommendations for international students: Required—TOEFL (minimum score 550 paper-based). *Application deadline:* For fall admission, 6/1 priority date for domestic students, 6/1 for international students; for spring admission, 1/5 for domestic and international students. Applications are processed on a rolling basis. Application fee: $60. Electronic applications accepted. *Financial support:* Fellowships, research assistantships, teaching assistantships, career-related internships or fieldwork, Federal Work-Study, institutionally sponsored loans, tuition waivers (full and partial), and unspecified assistantships available. Financial award application deadline: 2/1; financial award applicants required to submit FAFSA. *Faculty research:* Reproductive physiology, soil and water quality, human nutrition, aquaculture, wildlife management. *Unit head:* Dr. Ken Blemings, Interim Dean, 304-293-2395, Fax: 304-293-3740, E-mail: ken.blemings@mail.wvu.edu. *Application contact:* Dr. J. Todd Petty, Associate Dean, 304-293-2278, Fax: 304-293-3740, E-mail: jtpetty@mail.wvu.edu. Website: https://www.davis.wvu.edu

Aquaculture

American University of Beirut, Graduate Programs, Faculty of Agricultural and Food Sciences, Beirut, Lebanon. Offers agricultural economics (MS); animal science (MS); ecosystem management (MSES); food safety (MS); food security (MS); food technology (MS); irrigation (MS); nutrition (MS); plant protection (MS); plant science (MS); poultry science (MS); public health nutrition (MS); rural community development (MS). *Program availability:* Part-time. *Faculty:* 24 full-time (4 women). *Students:* 30 full-time (22 women), 90 part-time (69 women); includes 9 minority (all Black or African American, non-Hispanic/Latino). Average age 25. 238 applicants, 77% accepted, 37 enrolled. In 2018, 19 master's awarded. *Degree requirements:* For master's, one foreign language, comprehensive exam, thesis (for some programs). *Entrance requirements:* Additional exam requirements/recommendations for international students: Required—TOEFL (minimum score 600 paper-based; 100 iBT), IELTS (minimum score 7.5). *Application deadline:* For fall admission, 2/10 for domestic and international students; for spring admission, 11/2 for domestic and international students. Application fee: $50. Electronic applications accepted. *Expenses: Tuition:* Full-time $17,748; part-time $986 per credit. *Required fees:* $762. Tuition and fees vary according to course load and program. *Financial support:* In 2018–19, 2 fellowships with full and partial tuition reimbursements (averaging $11,637 per year), 12 research assistantships with full and partial tuition reimbursements (averaging $3,840 per year), 73 teaching assistantships with full and partial tuition reimbursements were awarded; scholarships/grants, health care benefits, and unspecified assistantships also available. Financial award application deadline: 2/2. *Faculty research:* Plant science; animal science; landscape for culture and socio-ecological health; diet, obesity and non communicable diseases; water, agriculture, ecosystem & remote sensing; water-energy-food-health nexus. *Total annual research expenditures:* $1.2 million. *Unit head:* Prof. Rabi Hassan Mohtar, Dean of Faculty of Agricultural and Food Sciences, 961-1-350000 Ext. 4400, Fax: 961-1-744460, E-mail: mohtar@aub.edu.lb. *Application contact:* Prof. Zaher Dawy, Associate Provost, 961-1-374374 Ext. 4386, Fax: 961-1-374374, E-mail: graduate.council@aub.edu.lb. Website: http://www.aub.edu.lb/fafs/pages/default.aspx

Auburn University, Graduate School, College of Agriculture, Department of Fisheries and Allied Aquacultures, Auburn University, AL 36849. Offers M Aq, MS, PhD. *Program availability:* Part-time. *Degree requirements:* For master's, thesis (for some programs); for doctorate, 2 foreign languages, thesis/dissertation. *Entrance requirements:* For master's and doctorate, GRE General Test. Electronic applications accepted. *Expenses:* Tuition, state resident: full-time $11,282; part-time $535 per credit hour. Tuition, nonresident: full-time $30,542; part-time $1605 per credit hour. *Required fees:* $826 per semester. Tuition and fees vary according to degree level and program. *Faculty research:* Channel catfish production; aquatic animal health; community and population ecology; pond management; production hatching, breeding and genetics.

Dalhousie University, Faculty of Agriculture, Halifax, NS B3H 4R2, Canada. Offers agriculture (M Sc), including air quality, animal behavior, animal molecular genetics, animal nutrition, animal technology, aquaculture, botany, crop management, crop physiology, ecology, environmental microbiology, food science, horticulture, nutrient management, pest management, physiology, plant biotechnology, plant pathology, soil chemistry, soil fertility, waste management and composting, water quality. *Program* *availability:* Part-time. *Degree requirements:* For master's, thesis, ATC Exam Teaching Assistantship. *Entrance requirements:* For master's, honors B Sc, minimum GPA of 3.0. Additional exam requirements/recommendations for international students: Required—TOEFL (minimum score 580 paper-based; 92 iBT), IELTS, Michigan English Language Assessment Battery, CanTEST, CAEL. *Faculty research:* Bio-product development, organic agriculture, nutrient management, air and water quality, agricultural biotechnology.

Memorial University of Newfoundland, School of Graduate Studies, Interdisciplinary Program in Aquaculture, St. John's, NL A1C 5S7, Canada. Offers M Sc. *Program availability:* Part-time. *Degree requirements:* For master's, thesis, seminar or thesis topic. *Entrance requirements:* For master's, honors B Sc or diploma in aquaculture from the Marine Institute of Memorial University of Newfoundland. Electronic applications accepted. *Faculty research:* Marine fish larval biology, fin fish nutrition, shellfish culture, fin fish virology, fin fish reproductive biology.

Oregon State University, College of Agricultural Sciences, Program in Fisheries Science, Corvallis, OR 97331. Offers aquaculture (MS); conservation biology (MS, PhD); fish genetics (MS, PhD); ichthyology (MS, PhD); limnology (MS, PhD); parasites and diseases (MS, PhD); physiology and ecology of marine and freshwater fishes (MS, PhD); stream ecology (MS, PhD); toxicology (MS, PhD); water pollution biology (MS, PhD). *Program availability:* Part-time. *Entrance requirements:* For master's and doctorate, GRE, minimum GPA of 3.0 in last 90 hours. Additional exam requirements/recommendations for international students: Required—TOEFL (minimum score 80 iBT), IELTS (minimum score 6.5). *Faculty research:* Fisheries ecology, fish toxicology, stream ecology, quantitative analyses of marine and freshwater fish populations.

Purdue University, Graduate School, College of Agriculture, Department of Forestry and Natural Resources, West Lafayette, IN 47907. Offers fisheries and aquatic sciences (MS, MSF, PhD); forest biology (MS, MSF, PhD); natural resource social science (MS, PhD); natural resources social science (MSF); quantitative ecology (MS, MSF, PhD); wildlife science (MS, MSF, PhD); wood products and wood products manufacturing (MS, MSF, PhD). *Faculty:* 25 full-time (5 women), 1 part-time/adjunct (0 women). *Students:* 58 full-time (32 women), 5 part-time (1 woman); includes 12 minority (2 American Indian or Alaska Native, non-Hispanic/Latino; 1 Asian, non-Hispanic/Latino; 4 Hispanic/Latino; 1 Native Hawaiian or other Pacific Islander, non-Hispanic/Latino; 4 Two or more races, non-Hispanic/Latino), 12 international. Average age 27. 51 applicants, 27% accepted, 14 enrolled. In 2018, 13 master's, 11 doctorates awarded. *Degree requirements:* For master's, thesis; for doctorate, thesis/dissertation. *Entrance requirements:* For master's and doctorate, GRE General Test (minimum score: verbal 50th percentile; quantitative 50th percentile; analytical writing 4.0), minimum undergraduate GPA of 3.2 or equivalent. Additional exam requirements/recommendations for international students: Required—TOEFL (minimum score 550 paper-based; 77 iBT). *Application deadline:* For fall admission, 1/5 for domestic students, 1/15 for international students; for spring admission, 9/15 for domestic and international students. Applications are processed on a rolling basis. Application fee: $60 ($75 for international students). Electronic applications accepted. *Financial support:* In 2018–19, 10 research assistantships (averaging $15,259 per year) were awarded; fellowships, teaching assistantships, career-related internships or fieldwork, and scholarships/grants also available. Support available to part-time students. Financial award application deadline: 1/5; financial award applicants required to submit FAFSA. *Faculty research:* Wildlife management, forest management, forest ecology, forest soils, limnology. *Unit head:* Robert G. Wagner, Head of the Graduate Program, 765-494-3590, E-mail: rgwagner@purdue.edu. *Application contact:* Christine Hofmeyer, Graduate Contact, 765-494-3572, E-mail: chofmeye@purdue.edu.
Website: https://ag.purdue.edu/fnr

Texas A&M University–Corpus Christi, College of Graduate Studies, College of Science and Engineering, Program in Fisheries and Mariculture, Corpus Christi, TX 78412. Offers MS. *Degree requirements:* For master's, comprehensive exam, thesis (for some programs), thesis or project. *Entrance requirements:* For master's, GRE (taken within 5 years), essay (minimum of 300 words); 3 letters of recommendation. Additional exam requirements/recommendations for international students: Required—TOEFL (minimum score 550 paper-based; 79 iBT), IELTS (minimum score 6.5). Electronic applications accepted.

University of Arkansas at Pine Bluff, School of Agriculture, Fisheries and Human Sciences, Pine Bluff, AR 71601-2799. Offers agricultural regulations (MS); aquaculture and fisheries (MS, PhD).

University of Florida, Graduate School, College of Agricultural and Life Sciences, School of Forest Resources and Conservation, Department of Fisheries and Aquatic Sciences, Gainesville, FL 32611. Offers MFAS, MS, PhD. *Program availability:* Part-time, online learning. *Degree requirements:* For master's, thesis (for MS); technical paper (for MFAS); for doctorate, comprehensive exam, thesis/dissertation. *Entrance requirements:* For master's and doctorate, GRE General Test, minimum GPA of 3.0. Additional exam requirements/recommendations for international students: Required—TOEFL (minimum score 550 paper-based; 80 iBT), IELTS (minimum score 6). Electronic applications accepted.

University of Guelph, Office of Graduate and Postdoctoral Studies, Ontario Agricultural College, Program in Aquaculture, Guelph, ON N1G 2W1, Canada. Offers M Sc. *Degree requirements:* For master's, practicum, research project. *Entrance requirements:* For master's, minimum B- average during previous 2 years of course work. *Faculty research:* Protein and amino acid metabolism, genetics, gamete cryogenics, pathology, epidemiology.

University of Rhode Island, Graduate School, College of the Environment and Life Sciences, Department of Fisheries, Animal and Veterinary Sciences, Kingston, RI 02881. Offers animal health and disease (MS); animal science (MS); aquaculture (MS); aquatic pathology (MS); environmental sciences (PhD), including animal science, aquaculture science, aquatic pathology, fisheries science; fisheries (MS). *Faculty:* 12 full-time (7 women). *Entrance requirements:* Additional exam requirements/recommendations for international students: Required—TOEFL. *Application deadline:* For fall admission, 7/15 for domestic students, 2/1 for international students; for spring admission, 11/15 for domestic students, 7/15 for international students. Application fee: $65. Electronic applications accepted. *Expenses: Tuition, area resident:* Full-time $13,226; part-time $735 per credit. Tuition, state resident: full-time $13,226; part-time $735 per credit. Tuition, nonresident: full-time $25,854; part-time $1436 per credit. *International tuition:* $25,854 full-time. *Required fees:* $1698; $50 per credit. $35 per semester. One-time fee: $165. *Financial support:* Application deadline: 2/1; applicants required to submit FAFSA. *Unit head:* Dr. Marta Gomez-Chiarri, Chair, 401-874-2917, Fax: 401-874-7575, E-mail: gomezchi@uri.edu. *Application contact:* Dr. Marta Gomez-Chiarri, Chair, 401-874-2917, Fax: 401-874-7575, E-mail: gomezchi@uri.edu.
Website: http://web.uri.edu/favs/

Food Science and Technology

Alabama Agricultural and Mechanical University, School of Graduate Studies, College of Agricultural, Life and Natural Sciences, Department of Food and Animal Sciences, Huntsville, AL 35811. Offers food science (MS, PhD). *Entrance requirements:* Additional exam requirements/recommendations for international students: Required—TOEFL (minimum score 500 paper-based; 61 iBT).

American University of Beirut, Graduate Programs, Faculty of Agricultural and Food Sciences, Beirut, Lebanon. Offers agricultural economics (MS); animal science (MS); ecosystem management (MSES); food safety (MS); food security (MS); food technology (MS); irrigation (MS); nutrition (MS); plant protection (MS); plant science (MS); poultry science (MS); public health nutrition (MS); rural community development (MS). *Program availability:* Part-time. *Faculty:* 24 full-time (4 women). *Students:* 30 full-time (22 women), 90 part-time (69 women); includes 9 minority (all Black or African American, non-Hispanic/Latino). Average age 25. 238 applicants, 77% accepted, 37 enrolled. In 2018, 19 master's awarded. *Degree requirements:* For master's, one foreign language, comprehensive exam, thesis (for some programs). *Entrance requirements:* Additional exam requirements/recommendations for international students: Required—TOEFL (minimum score 600 paper-based; 100 iBT), IELTS (minimum score 7.5). *Application deadline:* For fall admission, 2/10 for domestic and international students; for spring admission, 11/2 for domestic and international students. Application fee: $50. Electronic applications accepted. *Expenses: Tuition:* Full-time $17,748; part-time $986 per credit. *Required fees:* $762. Tuition and fees vary according to course load and program. *Financial support:* In 2018–19, 2 fellowships with full and partial tuition reimbursements (averaging $11,637 per year), 12 research assistantships with full and partial tuition reimbursements (averaging $3,840 per year), 73 teaching assistantships with full and partial tuition reimbursements were awarded; scholarships/grants, health care benefits, and unspecified assistantships also available. Financial award application deadline: 2/2. *Faculty research:* Plant science; animal science; landscape for culture and socio-ecological health; diet, obesity and non communicable diseases; water, agriculture, ecosystem & remote sensing; water-energy-food-health nexus. *Total annual research expenditures:* $1.2 million. *Unit head:* Prof. Rabi Hassan Mohtar, Dean of Faculty of Agricultural and Food Sciences, 961-1-350000 Ext. 4400, Fax: 961-1-744460, E-mail: mohtar@aub.edu.lb. *Application contact:* Prof. Zaher Dawy, Associate Provost, 961-1-374374 Ext. 4386, Fax: 961-1-374374, E-mail: graduate.council@aub.edu.lb.
Website: http://www.aub.edu.lb/fafs/pages/default.aspx

The American University of Rome, Graduate School, Rome, Italy. Offers arts management (MA); food studies (MA); peace studies (MA); sustainable cultural heritage (MA). *Degree requirements:* For master's, thesis, internship. *Entrance requirements:* For master's, bachelor's degree in the liberal arts, humanities or social sciences; minimum GPA of 2.75. Additional exam requirements/recommendations for international students: Required—TOEFL (minimum score 550 paper-based; 80 iBT), IELTS (minimum score 6.5). Electronic applications accepted. *Faculty research:* Sustainable cultural heritage, archaeology in Europe and Italy.

Auburn University, Graduate School, College of Human Sciences, Department of Nutrition and Food Science, Auburn University, AL 36849. Offers MS, PhD, Graduate Certificate. *Program availability:* Part-time. *Degree requirements:* For master's, thesis (for some programs); for doctorate, thesis/dissertation. *Entrance requirements:* For master's and doctorate, GRE General Test. Electronic applications accepted. *Expenses:* Tuition, state resident: full-time $11,282; part-time $535 per credit hour. Tuition, nonresident: full-time $30,542; part-time $1605 per credit hour. *Required fees:* $826 per semester. Tuition and fees vary according to degree level and program. *Faculty research:* Food quality and safety, diet, food supply, physical activity in maintenance of health, prevention of selected chronic disease states.

Boston University, Metropolitan College, Program in Gastronomy, Boston, MA 02215. Offers communications (MLA); history and culture (MLA). *Program availability:* Part-time, evening/weekend. *Faculty:* 3 full-time (2 women), 6 part-time/adjunct (3 women). *Students:* 4 full-time (2 women), 47 part-time (43 women); includes 10 minority (1 Black or African American, non-Hispanic/Latino; 4 Asian, non-Hispanic/Latino; 5 Hispanic/Latino), 4 international. Average age 33. 44 applicants, 93% accepted, 17 enrolled. In 2018, 30 master's awarded. *Entrance requirements:* Additional exam requirements/recommendations for international students: Required—TOEFL. *Application deadline:* Applications are processed on a rolling basis. Application fee: $85. Electronic applications accepted. *Expenses:* Contact institution. *Financial support:* In 2018–19, 5 research assistantships (averaging $4,200 per year) were awarded; career-related internships or fieldwork, scholarships/grants, and unspecified assistantships also available. Support available to part-time students. Financial award applicants required to submit FAFSA. *Faculty research:* Food entrepreneurship, food writing, sustainable food systems, cross-cultural perspectives on human right to food, biocultural determinants of food and nutrition intake, economic, urban and cultural sociology, wine studies. *Unit head:* Dr. Megan Elias, Associate Professor of the Practice and Director, 617-353-6916, Fax: 617-353-4130, E-mail: gastrmla@bu.edu. *Application contact:* Barbara Rotger, Program Manager, 617-353-6916, Fax: 617-353-4130, E-mail: brotger@bu.edu.
Website: http://www.bu.edu/met/gastronomy

Brigham Young University, Graduate Studies, College of Life Sciences, Department of Nutrition, Dietetics and Food Science, Provo, UT 84602-1001. Offers food science (MS); nutrition (MS), including dietetics, nutritional science. *Faculty:* 16 full-time (6 women). *Students:* 27 full-time (20 women); includes 4 minority (3 Hispanic/Latino; 1 Two or more races, non-Hispanic/Latino), 2 international. Average age 27. 12 applicants, 50% accepted, 4 enrolled. In 2018, 10 master's awarded. *Degree requirements:* For master's, thesis, MS/DI program requires a project and internship instead of a thesis. *Entrance requirements:* For master's, GRE, MCAT, DAT, GMAT, LSAT. Additional exam requirements/recommendations for international students: Required—TOEFL (minimum score 580 paper-based; 85 iBT); Recommended—IELTS (minimum score 7). *Application deadline:* For fall admission, 3/1 priority date for domestic and international students; for winter admission, 6/30 priority date for domestic and international students; for spring admission,

3/1 priority date for domestic and international students; for summer admission, 3/1 priority date for domestic and international students. Application fee: $50. Electronic applications accepted. *Financial support:* In 2018–19, 30 students received support, including 30 research assistantships with partial tuition reimbursements available (averaging $9,887 per year); teaching assistantships, institutionally sponsored loans, and scholarships/grants also available. Financial award application deadline: 4/1; financial award applicants required to submit FAFSA. *Faculty research:* Nutrition assessment, diabetes research, product development, cancer, food microbiology. *Total annual research expenditures:* $521,258. *Unit head:* Dr. Merrill J. Christensen, Chair, 801-422-5255, Fax: 801-422-0258, E-mail: merrill_christensen@byu.edu. *Application contact:* Judy Stoudt, Graduate Program Manager, 801-422-4296, Fax: 801-422-0258, E-mail: judy.stoudt@byu.edu. Website: http://ndfs.byu.edu/

California Polytechnic State University, San Luis Obispo, College of Agriculture, Food and Environmental Sciences, Department of Food Science and Nutrition, San Luis Obispo, CA 93407. Offers food science (MS); nutrition (MS). *Students:* 5 full-time (all women), 2 part-time (1 woman); includes 2 minority (1 Asian, non-Hispanic/Latino; 1 Hispanic/Latino). Average age 30. 13 applicants, 46% accepted, 1 enrolled. In 2018, 3 master's awarded. *Degree requirements:* For master's, thesis. *Entrance requirements:* For master's, GRE. Additional exam requirements/recommendations for international students: Required—TOEFL (minimum score 80 iBT). *Application deadline:* For fall admission, 4/1 for domestic students. Application fee: $55. *Expenses: Tuition, area resident:* Full-time $7176; part-time $4164 per year. Tuition, state resident: full-time $10,965. Tuition, nonresident: full-time $10,965. *Required fees:* $6336; $3711. *Financial support:* Fellowships, research assistantships, teaching assistantships, scholarships/grants, health care benefits, tuition waivers, and unspecified assistantships available. Financial award application deadline: 3/2; financial award applicants required to submit FAFSA. *Unit head:* Dr. Johan Ubbink, Head, 805-756-2660, E-mail: jubbink@calpoly.edu. *Application contact:* Dr. Jim Prince, Associate Dean, Research and Graduate Programs, 805-756-5104, E-mail: jpprince@calpoly.edu. Website: http://www.fsn.calpoly.edu

Chapman University, Schmid College of Science and Technology, Food Science Program, Orange, CA 92866. Offers MS, MS/MBA. *Program availability:* Part-time, evening/weekend. *Degree requirements:* For master's, thesis or alternative. *Entrance requirements:* For master's, GRE or GMAT. Electronic applications accepted. *Expenses:* Contact institution.

See Display on this page and Close-Up on page 291.

Clemson University, Graduate School, College of Agriculture, Forestry and Life Sciences, Department of Food, Nutrition and Packaging Sciences, Clemson, SC 29634. Offers food technology (PhD); food, nutrition and culinary sciences (MS); packaging science (MS). *Program availability:* Part-time. *Faculty:* 24 full-time (12 women), 1 (woman) part-time/adjunct. *Students:* 38 full-time (21 women), 8 part-time (6 women); includes 3 minority (1 Black or African American, non-Hispanic/Latino, 1 Hispanic/Latino; 1 Two or more races, non-Hispanic/Latino), 20 international. Average age 30. 79 applicants, 39% accepted, 24 enrolled. In 2018, 12 master's, 4 doctorates awarded. *Degree requirements:* For master's, thesis or alternative; for doctorate, comprehensive exam, thesis/dissertation. *Entrance requirements:* For master's and doctorate, GRE General Test, unofficial transcripts, letters of recommendation. Additional exam requirements/recommendations for international students: Required—TOEFL (minimum score 80 paper-based; 80 iBT); Recommended—IELTS (minimum score 6.5), TSE (minimum score 54). *Application deadline:* For fall admission, 4/15 for international students; for spring admission, 10/15 for international students. Applications are processed on a rolling basis. Application fee: $80 ($90 for international students). Electronic applications accepted. *Expenses:* $5198 per semester full-time resident, $10123 per semester full-time non-resident, $556 per credit hour part-time resident, $1109 per credit hour part-time non-resident, online $770 per credit hour, $4938 doctoral programs resident, $10405 doctoral programs non-resident, $1144 full-time graduate assistant, other fees may apply per session; Packaging Science MS: $6823 per semester full-time resident, $14023 per semester full-time non-resident, $833 per credit hour part-time resident, $1731 per credit hour part-time non-resident, online $1264 per credit hour, $1144 full-time graduate assistant, other fees may apply per session. *Financial support:* In 2018–19, 37 students received support, including 1 fellowship with full and partial tuition reimbursement available (averaging $5,000 per year), 15 research assistantships with full and partial tuition reimbursements available (averaging $13,366 per year), 15 teaching assistantships with full and partial tuition reimbursements available (averaging $11,008 per year); career-related internships or fieldwork and unspecified assistantships also available. *Faculty research:* Food chemistry, food processing, microbiology, muscle foods, packaging. *Total annual research expenditures:* $659,372. *Unit head:* Dr. E. Jeffery Rhodehamel, Department Chair, 864-656-1211, E-mail: jrhode@clemson.edu. *Application contact:* Dr. Paul Dawson, Graduate Coordinator, 864-656-1138, E-mail: pdawson@clemson.edu. Website: http://www.clemson.edu/cafls/departments/fnps/

Colorado State University, College of Health and Human Sciences, Department of Food Science and Human Nutrition, Fort Collins, CO 80523-1571. Offers dietetics (MS); food science and human nutrition (PhD); food science and nutrition (MS); nutrition and exercise science (MS). *Accreditation:* AND. *Program availability:* Part-time, 100% online, blended/hybrid learning. Terminal master's awarded for partial completion of doctoral program. *Degree requirements:* For master's, thesis; for doctorate, thesis/dissertation. *Entrance requirements:* For master's and doctorate, GRE (minimum 50th percentile), minimum GPA of 3.0; statement of purpose; resume; letters of recommendation; transcript. Additional exam requirements/recommendations for international students: Required—TOEFL (minimum score 550 paper-based; 80 iBT), IELTS (minimum score 6.5). Electronic applications accepted. *Expenses:* Contact institution. *Faculty research:* Community-based interventions on public health outcomes; consumer food handling behavior; adult learning and assessment; food and culture issues; role of microbes in ecosystem functioning.

Cornell University, Graduate School, Graduate Fields of Agriculture and Life Sciences, Field of Food Science and Technology, Ithaca, NY 14853. Offers dairy science (MPS, MS, PhD); enology (MS, PhD); food chemistry (MPS, MS, PhD); food engineering (MPS, MS, PhD); food microbiology (MPS, MS, PhD); food processing waste technology (MPS, MS, PhD); food science (MFS, MPS, MS, PhD); international food science (MPS, MS, PhD); sensory evaluation (MPS, MS, PhD). Terminal master's awarded for partial completion of doctoral program. *Degree requirements:* For master's, thesis (MS), teaching experience; for doctorate, comprehensive exam, thesis/dissertation, teaching experience. *Entrance requirements:* For master's and doctorate, GRE General Test, 3 letters of recommendation. Additional exam requirements/recommendations for international students: Required—TOEFL (minimum score 550 paper-based; 77 iBT). Electronic applications accepted. *Faculty research:* Food microbiology/biotechnology, food engineering/processing, food safety/toxicology, sensory science/flavor chemistry, food packaging.

Dalhousie University, Faculty of Agriculture, Halifax, NS B3H 4R2, Canada. Offers agriculture (M Sc), including air quality, animal behavior, animal molecular genetics,

Peterson's Graduate Programs in the Physical Sciences, Mathematics, Agricultural Sciences, the Environment & Natural Resources 2020

www.petersons.com 277

animal nutrition, animal technology, aquaculture, botany, crop management, crop physiology, ecology, environmental microbiology, food science, horticulture, nutrient management, pest management, physiology, plant biotechnology, plant pathology, soil chemistry, soil fertility, waste management and composting, water quality. *Program availability:* Part-time. *Degree requirements:* For master's, thesis, ATC Exam Teaching Assistantship. *Entrance requirements:* For master's, honors B Sc, minimum GPA of 3.0. Additional exam requirements/recommendations for international students: Required—TOEFL (minimum score 580 paper-based; 92 iBT), IELTS, Michigan English Language Assessment Battery, CanTEST, CAEL. *Faculty research:* Bio-product development, organic agriculture, nutrient management, air and water quality, agricultural biotechnology.

Dalhousie University, Faculty of Engineering, Department of Process Engineering and Applied Science, Halifax, NS B3J 1Z1, Canada. Offers biological engineering (M Eng, MA Sc, PhD); chemical engineering (M Eng, MA Sc, PhD); food science (M Sc, PhD). *Degree requirements:* For master's, thesis; for doctorate, thesis/dissertation. *Entrance requirements:* Additional exam requirements/recommendations for international students: Required—TOEFL, IELTS, CANTEST, CAEL, or Michigan English Language Assessment Battery. Electronic applications accepted. *Faculty research:* Explosions, process optimization, combustion synthesis of materials, waste minimization, treatment of industrial wastewater.

Drexel University, Goodwin College of Professional Studies, School of Technology and Professional Studies, Philadelphia, PA 19104-2875. Offers construction management (MS); creativity and innovation (MS); engineering technology (MS); food science (MS); hospitality management (MS); professional studies: creativity studies (MS); professional studies: e-learning leadership (MS); professional studies: homeland security management (MS); project management (MS); property management (MS); sport management (MS). *Program availability:* Part-time, evening/weekend. *Entrance requirements:* Additional exam requirements/recommendations for international students: Required—TOEFL, IELTS. Electronic applications accepted. Application fee is waived when completed online.

Florida State University, The Graduate School, College of Human Sciences, Department of Nutrition, Food and Exercise Sciences, Tallahassee, FL 32306-1493. Offers exercise physiology (MS, PhD); nutrition and food science (MS, PhD), including nutrition education and health promotion (MS); sports nutrition (MS); sports sciences (MS). *Program availability:* Part-time. *Faculty:* 26 full-time (12 women). *Students:* 71 full-time (49 women), 15 part-time (7 women); includes 15 minority (1 Black or African American, non-Hispanic/Latino; 2 Asian, non-Hispanic/Latino; 1 Hispanic/Latino; 11 Two or more races, non-Hispanic/Latino), 12 international. 177 applicants, 37% accepted, 31 enrolled. In 2018, 24 master's, 6 doctorates awarded. *Degree requirements:* For master's, thesis optional; for doctorate, thesis/dissertation, preliminary examination, minimum of 24 credit hours dissertation, dissertation defense. *Entrance requirements:* For master's, GRE General Test, minimum upper-division GPA of 3.0; for doctorate, GRE General Test, minimum upper-division GPA of 3.0 or awarded master's degree. Additional exam requirements/recommendations for international students: Required—TOEFL (minimum score 550 paper-based; 80 iBT). *Application deadline:* For fall admission, 4/1 for domestic and international students; for spring admission, 10/1 for domestic and international students. Applications are processed on a rolling basis. Application fee: $30. Electronic applications accepted. *Expenses: Tuition, area resident:* Part-time $479.32 per credit hour. Tuition and fees vary according to campus/location and program. *Financial support:* In 2018–19, 45 students received support, including 12 research assistantships with full tuition reimbursements available (averaging $25,000 per year), 30 teaching assistantships with full tuition reimbursements available (averaging $25,000 per year); career-related internships or fieldwork, Federal Work-Study, institutionally sponsored loans, scholarships/grants, and unspecified assistantships also available. Financial award application deadline: 2/1; financial award applicants required to submit FAFSA. *Faculty research:* Nutrition and health, sports nutrition, energy and human performance, strength training, functional performance, cardiovascular physiology, sarcopenia, chronic disease and aging, functional food, food safety, food allergy, and food safety/quality detection methods. *Total annual research expenditures:* $1.1 million. *Unit head:* Dr. Chester Ray, Department Chair, 850-644-1850, Fax: 850-645-5000, E-mail: caray@fsu.edu. *Application contact:* Mary-Sue McLemore, Academic Support Assistant, 850-644-1117, E-mail: mmclemore@fsu.edu.
Website: https://humansciences.fsu.edu/nutrition-food-exercise-sciences/students/graduate-programs/

Illinois Institute of Technology, Graduate College, School of Applied Technology, Institute for Food Safety and Health, Bedford Park, IL 60501-1957. Offers food process engineering (MFPE, MS); food safety and technology (MFST, MS). *Program availability:* Part-time. *Degree requirements:* For master's, comprehensive exam (for some programs), thesis (for some programs). *Entrance requirements:* For master's, GRE (minimum score 304), minimum undergraduate GPA of 3.0. Additional exam requirements/recommendations for international students: Required—TOEFL (minimum score 550 paper-based; 80 iBT). Electronic applications accepted. *Faculty research:* Microbial food safety and security, food virology, interfacial colloidal phenomena, development of DNA-based methods for detection, differentiation and tracking of food borne pathogens in food systems and environment, appetite and obesity management and vascular disease.

Iowa State University of Science and Technology, Department of Food Science and Human Nutrition, Ames, IA 50011. Offers food science and technology (MS, PhD); nutrition (MS, PhD). *Accreditation:* AND. *Degree requirements:* For master's, thesis; for doctorate, thesis/dissertation. *Entrance requirements:* For master's and doctorate, GRE General Test. Additional exam requirements/recommendations for international students: Required—TOEFL (minimum score 550 paper-based; 79 iBT), IELTS (minimum score 6.5). Electronic applications accepted.

Kansas State University, Graduate School, College of Agriculture, Food Science Institute, Manhattan, KS 66506. Offers MS, PhD. *Program availability:* Part-time, online learning. *Degree requirements:* For master's, thesis, residency; for doctorate, thesis/dissertation, preliminary exams, residency. *Entrance requirements:* For master's, GRE General Test, minimum undergraduate GPA of 3.0; course each in calculus, statistics, biology, organic chemistry, microbiology, biochemistry and physics; for doctorate, GRE General Test, minimum GPA of 3.5 in master's course work. Additional exam requirements/recommendations for international students: Required—TOEFL (minimum score 550 paper-based; 90 iBT), IELTS (minimum score 7). Electronic applications accepted. *Faculty research:* Food safety and defense, food chemistry, ingredient technology, food nutrients and bioactive compounds, food analysis, quality assurance, new product development, meat and dairy technology, sensory evaluation, food microbiology.

London Metropolitan University, Graduate Programs, London, United Kingdom. Offers applied psychology (M Sc); architecture (MA); biomedical science (M Sc); blood science (M Sc); cancer pharmacology (M Sc); computer networking and cyber security (M Sc); computing and information systems (M Sc); conference interpreting (MA); counter-terrorism studies (M Sc); creative, digital and professional writing (MA); crime, violence and prevention (M Sc); criminology (M Sc); curating contemporary art (MA); data analytics (M Sc); digital media (MA); early childhood studies (MA); education (MA, Ed D); financial services law, regulation and compliance (LL M); food science (M Sc); forensic psychology (M Sc); health and social care management and policy (M Sc); human nutrition (M Sc); human resource management (MA); human rights and international conflict (MA); information technology (M Sc); intelligence and security studies (M Sc); international oil, gas and energy law (LL M); international relations (MA); interpreting (MA); learning and teaching in higher education (MA); legal practice (LL M); media and entertainment law (LL M); organizational and consumer psychology (M Sc); psychological therapy (M Sc); psychology of mental health (M Sc); public health (M Sc); public policy and management (MPA); security studies (M Sc); social work (M Sc); spatial planning and urban design (MA); sports therapy (M Sc); supporting older children and young people with dyslexia (MA); teaching languages (MA), including Arabic, English; translation (MA); woman and child abuse (MA).

Louisiana State University and Agricultural & Mechanical College, Graduate School, College of Agriculture, School of Nutrition and Food Sciences, Baton Rouge, LA 70803. Offers MS, PhD.

McGill University, Faculty of Graduate and Postdoctoral Studies, Faculty of Agricultural and Environmental Sciences, Department of Food Science and Agricultural Chemistry, Montréal, QC H3A 2T5, Canada. Offers M Sc, PhD.

Memorial University of Newfoundland, School of Graduate Studies, Department of Biochemistry, St. John's, NL A1C 5S7, Canada. Offers biochemistry (M Sc, PhD); food science (M Sc, PhD). *Program availability:* Part-time. *Degree requirements:* For master's, thesis; for doctorate, comprehensive exam, thesis/dissertation, oral defense of thesis. *Entrance requirements:* For master's, 2nd class degree in related field; for doctorate, M Sc. Electronic applications accepted. *Faculty research:* Toxicology, cell and molecular biology, food engineering, marine biotechnology, lipid biology.

Michigan State University, College of Veterinary Medicine and The Graduate School, Graduate Programs in Veterinary Medicine, National Food Safety and Toxicology Center, East Lansing, MI 48824. Offers food safety (MS). *Entrance requirements:* Additional exam requirements/recommendations for international students: Required—TOEFL, Michigan State University ELT (minimum score 85), Michigan English Language Assessment Battery (minimum score 83). Electronic applications accepted.

Michigan State University, The Graduate School, College of Agriculture and Natural Resources, Department of Food Science and Human Nutrition, East Lansing, MI 48824. Offers food science (MS, PhD); food science - environmental toxicology (PhD); human nutrition (MS, PhD); human nutrition-environmental toxicology (PhD). *Entrance requirements:* Additional exam requirements/recommendations for international students: Required—TOEFL (minimum score 550 paper-based), Michigan State University ELT (minimum score 85), Michigan English Language Assessment Battery (minimum score 83). Electronic applications accepted.

Mississippi State University, College of Agriculture and Life Sciences, Department of Food Science, Nutrition and Health Promotion, Mississippi State, MS 39762. Offers food science and technology (MS, PhD); health promotion (MS); nutrition (MS, PhD). *Program availability:* Blended/hybrid learning. *Faculty:* 16 full-time (6 women). *Students:* 53 full-time (41 women), 32 part-time (23 women); includes 9 minority (5 Black or African American, non-Hispanic/Latino; 2 Asian, non-Hispanic/Latino; 2 Hispanic/Latino), 17 international. Average age 28. 57 applicants, 51% accepted, 20 enrolled. In 2018, 24 master's, 5 doctorates awarded. *Degree requirements:* For master's, comprehensive exam, thesis; for doctorate, comprehensive exam, thesis/dissertation. *Entrance requirements:* For master's, GRE General Test, minimum GPA of 2.75; for doctorate, GRE General Test, minimum GPA of 2.75 undergraduate, 3.0 graduate. Additional exam requirements/recommendations for international students: Required—TOEFL (minimum score 550 paper-based; 79 iBT); Recommended—IELTS (minimum score 6.5). *Application deadline:* For fall admission, 7/1 for domestic students, 5/1 for international students; for spring admission, 11/1 for domestic students, 9/1 for international students. Applications are processed on a rolling basis. Application fee: $60 ($80 for international students). Electronic applications accepted. *Expenses:* Tuition, state resident: full-time $8450; part-time $360.59 per credit hour. Tuition, nonresident: full-time $23,140; part-time $969.09 per credit hour. *Required fees:* $110. One-time fee: $55 full-time. Part-time tuition and fees vary according to course load, degree level, campus/location and reciprocity agreements. *Financial support:* In 2018–19, 15 research assistantships (averaging $14,495 per year) were awarded; Federal Work-Study, institutionally sponsored loans, scholarships/grants, and unspecified assistantships also available. Financial award application deadline: 4/1; financial award applicants required to submit FAFSA. *Faculty research:* Food preservation, food chemistry, food safety, food processing, product development. *Unit head:* Dr. Marion Will Evans, Professor and Head, 662-325-5508, Fax: 662-325-8728, E-mail: mwe59@msstate.edu. *Application contact:* Ryan King, Admissions and Enrollment Assistant, 662-325-8951, E-mail: rjk101@grad.msstate.edu.
Website: http://www.fsnhp.msstate.edu

New Mexico State University, College of Agricultural, Consumer and Environmental Sciences, Department of Family and Consumer Sciences, Las Cruces, NM 88003-8001. Offers clothing, textiles, and merchandising (MS); family and child science (MS); family and consumer science education (MS); family and consumer sciences (MS); food science and technology (MS); hotel, restaurant, and tourism management (MS); human nutrition and dietetic sciences (MS). *Program availability:* Part-time. *Faculty:* 11 full-time (8 women), 1 (woman) part-time/adjunct. *Students:* 35 full-time (27 women), 7 part-time (6 women); includes 28 minority (2 Black or African American, non-Hispanic/Latino; 25 Hispanic/Latino; 1 Two or more races, non-Hispanic/Latino), 1 international. Average age 30. 21 applicants, 76% accepted, 14 enrolled. In 2018, 19 master's awarded. *Degree requirements:* For master's, comprehensive exam (for some programs), thesis (for some programs), oral exam. *Entrance requirements:* For master's, GRE, 3 letters of reference from faculty members or employers, resume, letter of interest. Additional exam requirements/recommendations for international students: Required—TOEFL (minimum score 550 paper-based; 79 iBT), IELTS (minimum score 6.5). *Application deadline:* For fall admission, 2/1 priority date for domestic and international students; for spring admission, 10/1 for domestic and international students. Applications are processed on a rolling basis. Application fee: $40 ($50 for international students). Electronic applications accepted. *Expenses: Tuition, area resident:* Full-time $4216.70; part-time $252.70 per credit hour. Tuition, state resident: full-time $4216.70; part-time $252.70 per credit hour. Tuition, nonresident: full-time $12,769; part-time $881.10 per credit hour. *International tuition:* $12,769.30 full-time. *Required fees:* $878.40; $48.80 per credit hour. Full-time tuition and fees vary according to course load and reciprocity agreements. *Financial support:* In 2018–19, 27 students received support, including 6 research assistantships (averaging $11,417 per year), 8 teaching assistantships (averaging $11,913 per year); career-related internships or fieldwork, Federal Work-Study, scholarships/grants, traineeships, health care benefits, and unspecified assistantships also available. Support available to part-time students. Financial award application deadline: 3/1. *Faculty research:* Food product analysis, childhood obesity, dietary decision-making, military families, equine assisted psychotherapy. *Total annual research expenditures:* $432,486. *Application contact:* Dr.

Kourtney Vaillancourt, Graduate Program Contact, 575-646-3383, Fax: 575-646-1889, E-mail: kvaillan@nmsu.edu.
Website: http://aces.nmsu.edu/academics/fcs

New York University, Steinhardt School of Culture, Education, and Human Development, Department of Nutrition, Food Studies, and Public Health, Program in Food Studies, New York, NY 10012. Offers food studies (MA, PhD), including food culture (MA), food systems (MA). *Program availability:* Part-time. *Degree requirements:* For master's, thesis (for some programs); for doctorate, thesis/dissertation. *Entrance requirements:* For doctorate, GRE General Test, interview. Additional exam requirements/recommendations for international students: Required—TOEFL (minimum score 100 iBT). Electronic applications accepted. *Faculty research:* Cultural and social history of food, food systems and agriculture, food and aesthetics, political economy of food.

North Carolina Agricultural and Technical State University, The Graduate College, College of Agriculture and Environmental Sciences, Department of Family and Consumer Sciences, Greensboro, NC 27411. Offers child development, early education and family studies (MAT); family and consumer sciences education (MAT); food and nutritional sciences (MS). *Program availability:* Part-time, evening/weekend. *Degree requirements:* For master's, comprehensive exam, thesis or alternative, qualifying exam. *Entrance requirements:* For master's, GRE General Test, minimum GPA of 2.6.

North Carolina State University, Graduate School, College of Agriculture and Life Sciences, Department of Food, Bioprocessing and Nutrition Sciences, Raleigh, NC 27695. Offers MFS, MS, PhD. *Degree requirements:* For master's, thesis (for some programs); for doctorate, thesis/dissertation. *Entrance requirements:* For master's and doctorate, GRE. Electronic applications accepted. *Faculty research:* Food safety, value-added food products, environmental quality, nutrition and health, biotechnology.

North Dakota State University, College of Graduate and Interdisciplinary Studies, College of Agriculture, Food Systems, and Natural Resources, Program in Cereal Science, Fargo, ND 58102. Offers MS, PhD. *Program availability:* Part-time. Terminal master's awarded for partial completion of doctoral program. *Degree requirements:* For master's, comprehensive exam, thesis; for doctorate, comprehensive exam, thesis/dissertation. *Entrance requirements:* Additional exam requirements/recommendations for international students: Required—TOEFL (minimum score 550 paper-based; 79 iBT), IELTS (minimum score 6). *Faculty research:* Legume food products, cereal proteins and product quality, oilseeds functional components.

North Dakota State University, College of Graduate and Interdisciplinary Studies, Interdisciplinary Program in Food Safety, Fargo, ND 58102. Offers food safety (MS, PhD). *Program availability:* Part-time, online learning. Terminal master's awarded for partial completion of doctoral program. *Degree requirements:* For master's, thesis; for doctorate, comprehensive exam, thesis/dissertation. *Entrance requirements:* Additional exam requirements/recommendations for international students: Required—TOEFL, IELTS, TWE. Electronic applications accepted. *Faculty research:* Mycotoxins in grain, pathogens in meat systems, sensor development for food pathogens.

The Ohio State University, Graduate School, College of Food, Agricultural, and Environmental Sciences, Department of Food Science and Technology, Columbus, OH 43210. Offers MS, PhD. *Accreditation:* AND. *Faculty:* 20. *Students:* 84 (58 women). Average age 25. In 2018, 8 master's, 8 doctorates awarded. *Entrance requirements:* For master's and doctorate, GRE General Test. Additional exam requirements/recommendations for international students: Required—TOEFL (minimum score 550 paper-based; 79 iBT), Michigan English Language Assessment Battery (minimum score 82); Recommended—IELTS (minimum score 7). *Application deadline:* For fall admission, 12/15 priority date for domestic students, 12/1 priority date for international students; for spring admission, 11/15 for domestic students, 11/1 for international students; for summer admission, 4/5 for domestic students, 3/1 for international students. Applications are processed on a rolling basis. Application fee: $60 ($70 for international students). Electronic applications accepted. *Financial support:* Fellowships with tuition reimbursements, research assistantships with tuition reimbursements, Federal Work-Study, and institutionally sponsored loans available. Support available to part-time students. *Unit head:* Dr. Sheryl Barringer, Chair, 614-688-3642, E-mail: barringer.11@osu.edu. *Application contact:* Graduate and Professional Admissions, 614-292-9444, Fax: 614-292-3895, E-mail: gpadmissions@osu.edu.
Website: http://fst.osu.edu/

Oklahoma State University, College of Agricultural Science and Natural Resources, Department of Animal Science, Stillwater, OK 74078. Offers animal sciences (M Ag, MS); food science (PhD). *Faculty:* 26 full-time (5 women), 2 part-time/adjunct (1 woman). *Students:* 18 full-time (12 women), 56 part-time (35 women); includes 8 minority (1 Black or African American, non-Hispanic/Latino; 2 Asian, non-Hispanic/Latino; 3 Hispanic/Latino; 2 Two or more races, non-Hispanic/Latino), 16 international. Average age 26. 51 applicants, 27% accepted, 14 enrolled. In 2018, 14 master's, 4 doctorates awarded. *Entrance requirements:* For master's and doctorate, GRE or GMAT. Additional exam requirements/recommendations for international students: Required—TOEFL (minimum score 550 paper-based; 79 iBT). *Application deadline:* For fall admission, 3/1 priority date for international students; for spring admission, 8/1 priority date for international students. Applications are processed on a rolling basis. Application fee: $40 ($75 for international students). Electronic applications accepted. *Expenses: Tuition, area resident:* Full-time $4148. Tuition, state resident: full-time $4148. Tuition, nonresident: full-time $10,517. *International tuition:* $10,517 full-time. *Required fees:* $4394; $2929 per credit hour. Tuition and fees vary according to course load and program. *Financial support:* Research assistantships, teaching assistantships, career-related internships or fieldwork, Federal Work-Study, scholarships/grants, health care benefits, tuition waivers (partial), and unspecified assistantships available. Support available to part-time students. Financial award application deadline: 3/1; financial award applicants required to submit FAFSA. *Faculty research:* Quantitative trait loci identification for economical traits in swing/beef; waste management strategies in livestock; endocrine control of reproductive processes in farm animals; cholesterol synthesis, inhibition, and reduction; food safety research. *Unit head:* Dr. Clint Rusk, Department Head, 405-744-6062, Fax: 405-744-7390, E-mail: clint.rusk@okstate.edu. *Application contact:* Dr. Sheryl Tucker, Dean, 405-744-6368, Fax: 405-744-0355, E-mail: gradi@okstate.edu.
Website: http://www.ansi.okstate.edu

Oregon State University, College of Agricultural Sciences, Program in Food Science and Technology, Corvallis, OR 97331. Offers brewing (MS, PhD); enology (MS, PhD); flavor chemistry (MS, PhD); food and seafood processing (MS, PhD); food chemistry/biochemistry (MS, PhD); food engineering (MS, PhD); food microbiology/biotechnology (MS, PhD); sensory evaluation (MS, PhD). *Entrance requirements:* For master's and doctorate, GRE (minimum Verbal and Quantitative scores of 300), minimum GPA of 3.0 in last 90 hours. Additional exam requirements/recommendations for international students: Required—TOEFL (minimum score 80 iBT), IELTS (minimum score 6.5).

Penn State University Park, Graduate School, College of Agricultural Sciences, Department of Food Science, University Park, PA 16802. Offers MS, PhD.

Portland State University, Graduate Studies, College of Urban and Public Affairs, Hatfield School of Government, Department of Public Administration, Portland, OR 97207-0751. Offers collaborative governance (Certificate); energy policy and management (Certificate); global management and leadership (MPA); health administration (MPA); human resource management (MPA); local government (MPA); natural resource policy and administration (MPA); nonprofit and public management (Certificate); nonprofit management (MPA); public administration (EMPA); public affairs and policy (PhD); sustainable food systems (Certificate). *Accreditation:* CAHME; NASPAA (one or more programs are accredited). *Program availability:* Part-time, evening/weekend. *Degree requirements:* For master's, integrative field experience (MPA), practicum (MPH); for doctorate, comprehensive exam, thesis/dissertation. *Entrance requirements:* For master's, GRE (minimum scores: verbal 150, quantitative 149, and analytic writing 4.5), minimum GPA of 3.0, 3 recommendation letters, resume, 500-word statement of intent; for doctorate, GRE, 3 recommendation letters, resume, 500-word personal essay. Additional exam requirements/recommendations for international students: Required—TOEFL (minimum score 550 paper-based; 80 iBT), IELTS (minimum score 7). *Faculty research:* Public budgeting, program evaluation, nonprofit management, natural resources policy and administration.

Portland State University, Graduate Studies, College of Urban and Public Affairs, Nohad A. Toulan School of Urban Studies and Planning, Portland, OR 97207-0751. Offers applied social demography (Certificate); energy policy and management (Certificate); real estate development (Certificate); sustainable food systems (Certificate); transportation (Certificate); urban design (Certificate); urban studies (PhD); urban studies and planning (MRED, MURP, MUS); urban studies: regional science (PhD). *Program availability:* Part-time, evening/weekend. *Degree requirements:* For doctorate, comprehensive exam, thesis/dissertation, residency. *Entrance requirements:* For doctorate, GRE General Test, minimum GPA of 2.75, statement of purpose, 3 letters of recommendation, resume/curriculum vitae. Additional exam requirements/recommendations for international students: Required—TOEFL (minimum score 550 paper-based; 80 iBT). Electronic applications accepted.

Purdue University, Graduate School, College of Agriculture, Department of Food Science, West Lafayette, IN 47907. Offers MS, PhD. *Faculty:* 21 full-time (8 women), 1 (woman) part-time/adjunct. *Students:* 58 full-time (31 women), 10 part-time (5 women); includes 7 minority (2 Black or African American, non-Hispanic/Latino; 2 Asian, non-Hispanic/Latino; 2 Hispanic/Latino; 1 Two or more races, non-Hispanic/Latino), 45 international. Average age 28. 101 applicants, 9% accepted, 8 enrolled. In 2018, 10 master's, 10 doctorates awarded. *Degree requirements:* For master's, thesis (for some programs); for doctorate, thesis/dissertation, teaching assistantship. *Entrance requirements:* For master's, GRE General Test (minimum score Verbal 400, Quantitative 500, Analytical 4.0 old scoring; 146/144/4.0 new scoring), minimum undergraduate GPA of 3.0 or equivalent; for doctorate, GRE General Test (minimum score Verbal 400, Quantitative 500, Analytical 4.0 old scoring; 146/144/4.0 new scoring), minimum undergraduate GPA of 3.0 or equivalent; master's degree with minimum GPA of 3.0 or equivalent. Additional exam requirements/recommendations for international students: Required—TOEFL (minimum score 575 paper-based; 77 iBT). *Application deadline:* For fall admission, 7/15 priority date for domestic students, 7/15 for international students; for spring admission, 11/15 for domestic and international students. Applications are processed on a rolling basis. Application fee: $60 ($75 for international students). Electronic applications accepted. *Financial support:* In 2018–19, 4 fellowships (averaging $24,500 per year), 38 research assistantships (averaging $13,500 per year), 1 teaching assistantship (averaging $13,500 per year) were awarded; career-related internships or fieldwork also available. Support available to part-time students. Financial award application deadline: 4/1; financial award applicants required to submit FAFSA. *Faculty research:* Processing, technology, microbiology, chemistry of foods, carbohydrate chemistry. *Unit head:* Brian E. Farkas, Head, 765-494-8256, E-mail: bfarkas@purdue.edu. *Application contact:* Mitzi L. Barnett, Graduate Contact for Enrolled Students, 765-494-8258, E-mail: mbarnett@purdue.edu.
Website: https://ag.purdue.edu/foodsci

Rutgers University–New Brunswick, Graduate School-New Brunswick, Program in Food Science, Piscataway, NJ 08854-8097. Offers M Phil, MS, PhD. *Program availability:* Part-time, evening/weekend, online learning. *Degree requirements:* For master's, thesis or alternative; for doctorate, thesis/dissertation. *Entrance requirements:* For master's and doctorate, GRE General Test. *Faculty research:* Nutraceuticals and functional foods, food and flavor analysis, food chemistry and biochemistry, food nanotechnology, food engineering and processing.

South Dakota State University, Graduate School, College of Agriculture, Food and Environmental Sciences, Department of Dairy and Food Science, Brookings, SD 57007. Offers dairy science (MS, PhD); food science (MS, PhD). *Program availability:* Part-time. *Degree requirements:* For master's, thesis, oral exam; for doctorate, comprehensive exam, thesis/dissertation, preliminary oral and written exams. *Entrance requirements:* Additional exam requirements/recommendations for international students: Required—TOEFL (minimum score 550 paper-based). *Faculty research:* Dairy cattle nutrition, energy metabolism, food safety, dairy processing technology.

Texas A&M University, College of Agriculture and Life Sciences, Department of Nutrition and Food Science, College Station, TX 77843. Offers food science and technology (M Agr, MS); nutrition (MS, PhD). *Faculty:* 15. *Students:* 52 full-time (34 women), 4 part-time (0 women); includes 13 minority (5 Black or African American, non-Hispanic/Latino; 8 Hispanic/Latino), 32 international. Average age 30. 77 applicants, 17% accepted, 10 enrolled. In 2018, 5 master's, 6 doctorates awarded. *Degree requirements:* For master's, thesis; for doctorate, thesis/dissertation. *Entrance requirements:* For master's and doctorate, GRE General Test. Additional exam requirements/recommendations for international students: Required—TOEFL (minimum score 550 paper-based; 80 iBT), IELTS (minimum score 6), PTE (minimum score 53). *Application deadline:* For fall admission, 12/1 priority date for domestic students, 12/1 for international students; for spring admission, 6/1 for domestic and international students; for summer admission, 12/1 priority date for domestic students, 12/1 for international students. Applications are processed on a rolling basis. Application fee: $50 ($90 for international students). Electronic applications accepted. *Expenses:* Contact institution. *Financial support:* In 2018–19, 47 students received support, including 2 fellowships with tuition reimbursements available (averaging $9,582 per year), 22 research assistantships with tuition reimbursements available (averaging $12,876 per year), 19 teaching assistantships with tuition reimbursements available (averaging $12,857 per year); career-related internships or fieldwork, institutionally sponsored loans, scholarships/grants, traineeships, health care benefits, tuition waivers (full and partial), and unspecified assistantships also available. Support available to part-time students. Financial award application deadline: 3/15; financial award applicants required to submit FAFSA. *Faculty research:* Food safety, microbiology, product development. *Unit head:* Dr. Boon Chew, Department Head, 979-862-6655, E-mail: boon.chew@tamu.edu. *Application contact:* Graduate Admissions, 979-845-1044, E-mail: admissions@tamu.edu.
Website: http://nfs.tamu.edu

Food Science and Technology

Texas Tech University, Graduate School, College of Agricultural Sciences and Natural Resources, Department of Animal and Food Sciences, Lubbock, TX 79409-2141. Offers animal science (MS, PhD); food science (MS). *Faculty:* 35 full-time (18 women), 2 part-time/adjunct (1 woman). *Students:* 81 full-time (46 women), 6 part-time (4 women); includes 10 minority (9 Hispanic/Latino; 1 Two or more races, non-Hispanic/Latino), 23 international. Average age 26. 45 applicants, 62% accepted, 22 enrolled. In 2018, 21 master's, 9 doctorates awarded. *Degree requirements:* For master's, thesis or alternative; for doctorate, thesis/dissertation. *Entrance requirements:* For master's and doctorate, GRE. Additional exam requirements/recommendations for international students: Required—TOEFL (minimum score 550 paper-based; 79 iBT). *Application deadline:* For fall admission, 6/1 priority date for domestic students, 1/15 priority date for international students; for spring admission, 9/1 priority date for domestic students, 6/15 priority date for international students. Applications are processed on a rolling basis. Application fee: $65. Electronic applications accepted. *Expenses:* Contact institution. *Financial support:* In 2018–19, 94 students received support, including 65 fellowships (averaging $3,316 per year), 79 research assistantships (averaging $13,833 per year), 6 teaching assistantships (averaging $21,756 per year); scholarships/grants and unspecified assistantships also available. Financial award applicants required to submit FAFSA. *Faculty research:* Nutrition, welfare and behavior, physiology and reproduction, muscle and meat biology, food safety, food security, companion animal, health and well-being. *Total annual research expenditures:* $4.2 million. *Unit head:* Dr. Michael Orth, Department Chair and Professor, 806-834-5653, Fax: 806-742-0898, E-mail: michael.orth@ttu.edu. *Application contact:* Charles Cooke, Administrative Business Assistant, 806-834-8977, E-mail: charles.cooke@ttu.edu.
Website: www.depts.ttu.edu/afs

Texas Woman's University, Graduate School, College of Health Sciences, Department of Nutrition and Food Sciences, Denton, TX 76204. Offers exercise and sports nutrition (MS); food science and flavor chemistry (MS); food systems administration (MS); nutrition (MS, PhD). *Program availability:* Part-time, evening/weekend, 100% online. *Faculty:* 14 full-time (9 women), 3 part-time/adjunct (all women). *Students:* 84 full-time (72 women), 80 part-time (75 women); includes 52 minority (7 Black or African American, non-Hispanic/Latino; 13 Asian, non-Hispanic/Latino; 25 Hispanic/Latino; 7 Two or more races, non-Hispanic/Latino), 10 international. Average age 28. 76 applicants, 82% accepted, 44 enrolled. In 2018, 77 master's, 3 doctorates awarded. *Degree requirements:* For master's, thesis or alternative, thesis (for food and flavor chemistry); thesis or coursework (for exercise and sports nutrition, nutrition), capstone; for doctorate, comprehensive exam, thesis/dissertation, qualifying exam, 50% of all required hours must be earned at TWU. *Entrance requirements:* For master's, GRE General Test (preferred minimum score 143 [350 old version] Verbal, 141 [450 old version] Quantitative), minimum GPA of 3.25 for last 60 undergraduate hours, resume, personal statement of interest (food science and flavor chemistry only); for doctorate, GRE General Test (preferred minimum score 153 [450 old version] Verbal, 146 [550 old version] Quantitative), minimum GPA of 3.5 on last 60 undergraduate hours and graduate course work, 2 letters of reference, resume, statement of purpose. Additional exam requirements/recommendations for international students: Required—TOEFL (minimum score 79 iBT); Recommended—IELTS (minimum score 6.5), TSE (minimum score 53). *Application deadline:* For fall admission, 6/15 for domestic students, 3/1 priority date for international students; for spring admission, 10/1 for domestic students, 7/1 priority date for international students; for summer admission, 4/1 for domestic students, 2/1 priority date for international students. Application fee: $50 ($75 for international students). Electronic applications accepted. *Expenses:* Contact institution. *Financial support:* In 2018–19, 60 students received support, including 1 research assistantship, 18 teaching assistantships (averaging $6,858 per year); career-related internships or fieldwork, Federal Work-Study, institutionally sponsored loans, scholarships/grants, traineeships, health care benefits, and unspecified assistantships also available. Support available to part-time students. Financial award application deadline: 3/1; financial award applicants required to submit FAFSA. *Faculty research:* Bio-active food components and cancer, functional foods in diabetes, obesity and bone health, flavor chemistry, obesity prevention in children. *Unit head:* Dr. K. Shane Broughton, Chair, 940-898-2636, Fax: 940-898-2634, E-mail: nutrfdsci@twu.edu. *Application contact:* Korie Hawkins, Associate Director of Admissions, Graduate Recruitment, 940-898-3188, Fax: 940-898-3081, E-mail: admissions@twu.edu.
Website: http://www.twu.edu/nutrition-food-sciences/

Tuskegee University, Graduate Programs, College of Agriculture, Environment and Nutrition Sciences, Department of Food and Nutritional Sciences, Tuskegee, AL 36088. Offers MS. *Degree requirements:* For master's, thesis. *Entrance requirements:* For master's, GRE General Test. Additional exam requirements/recommendations for international students: Required—TOEFL (minimum score 500 paper-based).

Universidad de las Américas Puebla, Division of Graduate Studies, School of Engineering, Program in Chemical Engineering, Puebla, Mexico. Offers chemical engineering (MS); food technology (MS). *Program availability:* Part-time, evening/weekend. *Degree requirements:* For master's, one foreign language, thesis. *Faculty research:* Food science, reactors, oil industry, biotechnology.

Universidad de las Américas Puebla, Division of Graduate Studies, School of Engineering, Program in Food Sciences, Puebla, Mexico. Offers MS.

Université de Moncton, School of Food Science, Nutrition and Family Studies, Moncton, NB E1A 3E9, Canada. Offers foods/nutrition (M Sc). *Program availability:* Part-time. *Degree requirements:* For master's, one foreign language, thesis. *Entrance requirements:* For master's, previous course work in statistics. Electronic applications accepted. *Faculty research:* Clinic nutrition (anemia, elderly, osteoporosis), applied nutrition, metabolic activities of lactic bacteria, solubility of low density lipoproteins, bile acids.

Université Laval, Faculty of Agricultural and Food Sciences, Department of Food Sciences and Nutrition, Programs in Food Sciences and Technology, Québec, QC G1K 7P4, Canada. Offers M Sc, PhD. Terminal master's awarded for partial completion of doctoral program. *Degree requirements:* For master's, thesis (for some programs); for doctorate, comprehensive exam, thesis/dissertation. *Entrance requirements:* For master's and doctorate, knowledge of French and English. Electronic applications accepted.

University at Buffalo, the State University of New York, Graduate School, School of Architecture and Planning, Department of Urban and Regional Planning, Buffalo, NY 14214. Offers economic development (MUP); environment/land use (MUP); health and food systems (MUP); historic preservation (MUP, Certificate); neighborhood/community development (MUP); real estate development (MSRED); urban and regional planning (PhD); urban design (MUP); JD/MUP; M Arch/MUP. *Accreditation:* ACSP. *Program availability:* Part-time. *Faculty:* 13 full-time (5 women), 14 part-time/adjunct (6 women). *Students:* 75 full-time (33 women), 27 part-time (14 women); includes 21 minority (10 Black or African American, non-Hispanic/Latino; 1 Asian, non-Hispanic/Latino; 4 Hispanic/Latino; 6 Two or more races, non-Hispanic/Latino), 19 international. Average age 27. 189 applicants, 21% accepted, 30 enrolled. In 2018, 39 master's, 2 doctorates, 4 other advanced degrees awarded. *Degree requirements:* For master's, thesis or alternative, project; for doctorate, comprehensive exam, thesis/dissertation. *Entrance requirements:* For master's, resume, two letters of recommendation, personal statement, transcripts; for doctorate, GRE, transcripts, three letters of recommendation, resume, research statement, writing sample. Additional exam requirements/recommendations for international students: Required—TOEFL (minimum score 79 iBT), IELTS (minimum score 6.5). *Application deadline:* For fall admission, 3/1 priority date for domestic and international students; for spring admission, 10/31 priority date for domestic students, 10/1 priority date for international students. Applications are processed on a rolling basis. Application fee: $75. Electronic applications accepted. *Financial support:* In 2018–19, 44 students received support, including 3 fellowships with full tuition reimbursements available (averaging $15,600 per year), 2 research assistantships with partial tuition reimbursements available (averaging $10,920 per year), 16 teaching assistantships with partial tuition reimbursements available (averaging $6,563 per year); career-related internships or fieldwork, Federal Work-Study, institutionally sponsored loans, scholarships/grants, health care benefits, tuition waivers (full and partial), and unspecified assistantships also available. Financial award application deadline: 3/1; financial award applicants required to submit FAFSA. *Faculty research:* Economic and international development, environmental and land use planning, GIS and spatial analysis, urban design and physical planning, neighborhood planning and community development, historic preservation. *Total annual research expenditures:* $616,211. *Unit head:* Dr. Daniel B. Hess, Professor and Chair, 716-829-5326, Fax: 716-829-3256, E-mail: dbhess@buffalo.edu. *Application contact:* Norma Everett, Assistant to the Chair, 716-829-3283, Fax: 716-829-3256, E-mail: norma.everett@buffalo.edu.
Website: http://www.ap.buffalo.edu/planning/

University of Arkansas, Graduate School, Dale Bumpers College of Agricultural, Food and Life Sciences, Department of Food Science, Fayetteville, AR 72704. Offers MS, PhD. In 2018, 9 master's, 3 doctorates awarded. *Application deadline:* For fall admission, 8/1 for domestic students, 4/1 for international students; for spring admission, 12/1 for domestic students, 10/1 for international students; for summer admission, 4/15 for domestic students, 3/1 for international students. Applications are processed on a rolling basis. Application fee: $60. Electronic applications accepted. *Financial support:* In 2018–19, 25 research assistantships were awarded; fellowships with tuition reimbursements, teaching assistantships, career-related internships or fieldwork, Federal Work-Study, scholarships/grants, and unspecified assistantships also available. Support available to part-time students. Financial award application deadline: 4/1; financial award applicants required to submit FAFSA. *Unit head:* Dr. Jeyam Subbiah, Department Head, 479-575-4605, Fax: 479-575-6936, E-mail: jsubbiah@uark.edu. *Application contact:* Dr. Ya-Jane Wang, Professor, Carbohydrate Chemistry, 479-575-3871, Fax: 479-575-6936, E-mail: yjwan@uark.edu.
Website: https://food-science.uark.edu/

University of Arkansas, Graduate School, Dale Bumpers College of Agricultural, Food and Life Sciences, Food Safety Program, Fayetteville, AR 72701. Offers MS. *Program availability:* Part-time, evening/weekend, online learning. In 2018, 5 master's awarded. *Application deadline:* For fall admission, 8/1 for domestic students, 4/1 for international students; for spring admission, 12/1 for domestic students, 10/1 for international students; for summer admission, 4/15 for domestic students, 3/1 for international students. Applications are processed on a rolling basis. Application fee: $60. Electronic applications accepted. *Financial support:* Fellowships, research assistantships, teaching assistantships, career-related internships or fieldwork, and Federal Work-Study available. Support available to part-time students. Financial award application deadline: 4/1; financial award applicants required to submit FAFSA. *Unit head:* Dr. Deacue Fields, Dean, 479-575-2034, E-mail: dcfields@uark.edu. *Application contact:* Kristin Seals, Program Coordinator, 479-575-3163, E-mail: kdseals@uark.edu.
Website: https://bumperscollege.uark.edu/future-students/food-safety.php

The University of British Columbia, Faculty of Land and Food Systems, Integrated Studies in Land and Food Systems Program, Vancouver, BC V6T 1Z1, Canada. Offers M Sc, PhD. *Degree requirements:* For doctorate, thesis/dissertation.

The University of British Columbia, Faculty of Land and Food Systems, Program in Food Science, Vancouver, BC V6T 1Z4, Canada. Offers M Sc, MFS, PhD. *Degree requirements:* For master's, thesis; for doctorate, comprehensive exam, thesis/dissertation. *Entrance requirements:* Additional exam requirements/recommendations for international students: Required—TOEFL, IELTS. Electronic applications accepted. *Expenses:* Contact institution. *Faculty research:* Food chemistry and biochemistry, food process science, food toxicology and safety, food microbiology, food biotechnology.

University of California, Davis, Graduate Studies, Graduate Group in Food Science, Davis, CA 95616. Offers MS, PhD. Terminal master's awarded for partial completion of doctoral program. *Degree requirements:* For master's, comprehensive exam (for some programs), thesis (for some programs); for doctorate, thesis/dissertation. *Entrance requirements:* For master's and doctorate, GRE General Test, minimum GPA of 3.0. Additional exam requirements/recommendations for international students: Required—TOEFL (minimum score 550 paper-based). Electronic applications accepted.

University of Delaware, College of Agriculture and Natural Resources, Department of Animal and Food Sciences, Newark, DE 19716. Offers animal sciences (MS, PhD); food sciences (MS). *Program availability:* Part-time. Terminal master's awarded for partial completion of doctoral program. *Degree requirements:* For master's, thesis; for doctorate, comprehensive exam, thesis/dissertation. *Entrance requirements:* For master's and doctorate, GRE General Test. Additional exam requirements/recommendations for international students: Required—TOEFL. Electronic applications accepted. *Faculty research:* Food chemistry, food microbiology, process engineering technology, packaging, food analysis, microbial genetics, molecular endocrinology, growth physiology, avian immunology and virology, monogastric nutrition, avian genomics.

University of Florida, Graduate School, College of Agricultural and Life Sciences, Department of Food Science and Human Nutrition, Gainesville, FL 32611. Offers food science (PhD), including toxicology; food science and human nutrition (MS), including nutritional sciences; nutritional sciences (MS, PhD), including clinical and translational science (PhD). *Degree requirements:* For master's, thesis optional; for doctorate, thesis/dissertation. *Entrance requirements:* For master's and doctorate, GRE General Test, minimum GPA of 3.0. Additional exam requirements/recommendations for international students: Required—TOEFL. Electronic applications accepted. *Faculty research:* Pesticide research, nutritional biochemistry and microbiology, food safety and toxicology assessment and dietetics, food chemistry.

University of Georgia, College of Agricultural and Environmental Sciences, Department of Food Science and Technology, Athens, GA 30602. Offers food science (MS, PhD). *Program availability:* Part-time. *Degree requirements:* For master's, thesis; for doctorate, thesis/dissertation. *Entrance requirements:* For master's and doctorate, GRE General Test. Additional exam requirements/recommendations for international students: Required—TOEFL (minimum score 550 paper-based). Electronic applications accepted.

University of Guelph, Office of Graduate and Postdoctoral Studies, Ontario Agricultural College, Department of Food Science, Guelph, ON N1G 2W1, Canada. Offers food safety and quality assurance (M Sc); food science (M Sc, PhD). *Degree requirements:* For master's, thesis; for doctorate, comprehensive exam, thesis/dissertation. *Entrance requirements:* For master's, minimum B- average during previous 2 years of honors B Sc degree; for doctorate, minimum B average. Additional exam requirements/recommendations for international students: Required—TOEFL (minimum score 550 paper-based), IELTS (minimum score 6.5). Electronic applications accepted. *Faculty research:* Food chemistry, food microbiology, food processing, preservation and utilization.

University of Hawaii at Manoa, Office of Graduate Education, College of Tropical Agriculture and Human Resources, Department of Human Nutrition, Food and Animal Sciences, Program in Food Science, Honolulu, HI 96822. Offers MS. *Program availability:* Part-time. *Degree requirements:* For master's, thesis optional. *Entrance requirements:* For master's, GRE General Test. Additional exam requirements/recommendations for international students: Required—TOEFL (minimum score 580 paper-based; 92 iBT), IELTS (minimum score 5). *Faculty research:* Biochemistry of natural products, sensory evaluation, food processing, food chemistry, food safety.

University of Idaho, College of Graduate Studies, College of Agricultural and Life Sciences, Bistate School of Food Science, Moscow, ID 83844-2312. Offers MS, PhD. *Faculty:* 7 full-time. *Students:* 14. Average age 28. In 2018, 3 master's, 1 doctorate awarded. *Entrance requirements:* For master's, minimum GPA of 3.0. Additional exam requirements/recommendations for international students: Required—TOEFL (minimum score 79 iBT). *Application deadline:* For fall admission, 8/1 for domestic students; for spring admission, 12/15 for domestic students. Applications are processed on a rolling basis. Application fee: $60. Electronic applications accepted. *Expenses:* Tuition, state resident: full-time $7266.44; part-time $474.50 per credit hour. Tuition, nonresident: full-time $24,902; part-time $1453.50 per credit hour. *Required fees:* $2085.56; $45.50 per credit hour. *Financial support:* Research assistantships and teaching assistantships available. Financial award applicants required to submit FAFSA. *Faculty research:* Analytical methods to predict the safety and quality of food products, wheat health, food processing. *Unit head:* Dr. Barbara Rasco, Director, 208-885-0707, E-mail: foodscience@uidaho.edu. *Application contact:* Dr. Barbara Rasco, Director, 208-885-0707, E-mail: foodscience@uidaho.edu.
Website: http://sfs.wsu.edu/

University of Illinois at Urbana–Champaign, Graduate College, College of Agricultural, Consumer and Environmental Sciences, Department of Food Science and Human Nutrition, Champaign, IL 61820. Offers food science (MS); food science and human nutrition (MS, PhD), including professional science (MS); human nutrition (MS). *Program availability:* Part-time, online learning.

University of Kentucky, Graduate School, College of Agriculture, Food and Environment, Program in Animal and Food Sciences, Lexington, KY 40506-0032. Offers MS, PhD. Terminal master's awarded for partial completion of doctoral program. *Degree requirements:* For master's, comprehensive exam, thesis optional; for doctorate, comprehensive exam, thesis/dissertation. *Entrance requirements:* For master's, GRE General Test, minimum undergraduate GPA of 2.75; for doctorate, GRE General Test, minimum graduate GPA of 3.0. Additional exam requirements/recommendations for international students: Required—TOEFL (minimum score 550 paper-based). Electronic applications accepted. *Faculty research:* Nutrition of horses, cattle, swine, poultry, and sheep; physiology of reproduction and lactation; food science; microbiology.

University of Manitoba, Faculty of Graduate Studies, Faculty of Agricultural and Food Sciences, Department of Food and Human Nutritional Sciences, Winnipeg, MB R3T 2N2, Canada. Offers food science (M Sc, PhD); human nutritional sciences (M Sc, PhD). *Degree requirements:* For master's, thesis.

University of Maryland, College Park, Academic Affairs, College of Agriculture and Natural Resources, Department of Nutrition and Food Science, Program in Food Science, College Park, MD 20742. Offers MS, PhD. *Degree requirements:* For master's, comprehensive exam, research-based thesis or equivalent paper; for doctorate, comprehensive exam, thesis/dissertation. *Entrance requirements:* For master's, GRE General Test, minimum GPA of 3.0, professional experience, 3 letters of recommendation; for doctorate, GRE General Test, minimum GPA of 3.0. Additional exam requirements/recommendations for international students: Required—TOEFL. Electronic applications accepted. *Faculty research:* Food chemistry, engineering, microbiology, and processing technology; quality assurance; membrane separations, rheology and texture measurement.

University of Maryland Eastern Shore, Graduate Programs, Department of Agriculture, Food and Resource Sciences, Program in Food and Agricultural Sciences, Princess Anne, MD 21853. Offers MS. *Degree requirements:* For master's, comprehensive exam, thesis or alternative, oral exams. *Entrance requirements:* For master's, GRE General Test, minimum GPA of 3.0. Additional exam requirements/recommendations for international students: Required—TOEFL (minimum score 80 iBT). Electronic applications accepted. *Faculty research:* Poultry and swine nutrition and management, soybean specialty products, farm management practices, agriculture technology.

University of Maryland Eastern Shore, Graduate Programs, Department of Agriculture, Food and Resource Sciences, Program in Food Science and Technology, Princess Anne, MD 21853. Offers PhD. *Degree requirements:* For doctorate, comprehensive exam, thesis/dissertation. *Entrance requirements:* For doctorate, minimum GPA of 3.0, strong background in food science and related fields, intended dissertation research. Additional exam requirements/recommendations for international students: Required—TOEFL (minimum score 80 iBT). Electronic applications accepted. *Faculty research:* Prevalence, growth, survival and control of listeria; microbial models of the effect of storage temperature.

University of Massachusetts Amherst, Graduate School, College of Natural Sciences, Department of Food Science, Amherst, MA 01003. Offers MS, PhD. *Program availability:* Part-time. Terminal master's awarded for partial completion of doctoral program. *Degree requirements:* For master's, thesis or alternative; for doctorate, comprehensive exam, thesis/dissertation. *Entrance requirements:* For master's and doctorate, GRE General Test. Additional exam requirements/recommendations for international students: Required—TOEFL (minimum score 550 paper-based; 80 iBT), IELTS (minimum score 6.5). Electronic applications accepted.

University of Minnesota, Twin Cities Campus, Graduate School, College of Food, Agricultural and Natural Resource Sciences, Program in Food Science, St. Paul, MN 55455-0213. Offers MS, PhD. *Program availability:* Part-time. *Faculty:* 20 full-time (6 women), 10 part-time/adjunct (4 women). *Students:* 40 full-time (34 women), 15 part-time (10 women); includes 6 minority (1 American Indian or Alaska Native, non-Hispanic/Latino; 4 Asian, non-Hispanic/Latino; 1 Hispanic/Latino), 26 international. Average age 25. 80 applicants, 25% accepted, 16 enrolled. In 2018, 15 master's, 3 doctorates awarded. Terminal master's awarded for partial completion of doctoral program. *Degree requirements:* For master's, comprehensive exam, thesis; for doctorate, comprehensive exam, thesis/dissertation. *Entrance requirements:* For master's, GRE General Test, previous course work in general chemistry, organic chemistry, calculus, physics, and biology; for doctorate, GRE General Test, previous course work in general chemistry, organic chemistry, calculus, physics, and biology; MS or demonstrated research capabilities. Additional exam requirements/recommendations for international students: Required—TOEFL (minimum score 550 paper-based; 79 iBT), IELTS (minimum score 6.5). *Application deadline:* Applications are processed on a rolling basis. Application fee: $75 ($95 for international students). Electronic applications accepted. *Expenses:* Contact institution. *Financial support:* In 2018–19, fellowships with full tuition reimbursements (averaging $40,000 per year), research assistantships with tuition reimbursements (averaging $40,000 per year), teaching assistantships with tuition reimbursements (averaging $40,000 per year) were awarded; career-related internships or fieldwork, scholarships/grants, traineeships, health care benefits, and unspecified assistantships also available. Support available to part-time students. *Faculty research:* Food chemistry, food microbiology, food technology, grain science, dairy science, food safety. *Total annual research expenditures:* $2 million. *Unit head:* Dr. Joellen Feirtag, Director of Graduate Studies, 612-624-3629, Fax: 612-625-5272, E-mail: jfeirtag@umn.edu. *Application contact:* Toed, Program Coordinator, 612-624-6753, Fax: 612-625-5272, E-mail: fscngrad@umn.edu.
Website: http://fscn.cfans.umn.edu/graduate-programs/food-science

University of Mississippi, Graduate School, School of Applied Sciences, University, MS 38677. Offers communicative disorders (MS); criminal justice (MCJ); exercise science (MS); food and nutrition services (MS); health and kinesiology (PhD); health promotion (MS); nutrition and hospitality management (PhD); park and recreation management (MA); social welfare (PhD); social work (MSW). *Faculty:* 66 full-time (36 women), 27 part-time/adjunct (13 women). *Students:* 192 full-time (148 women), 40 part-time (25 women); includes 50 minority (41 Black or African American, non-Hispanic/Latino; 1 American Indian or Alaska Native, non-Hispanic/Latino; 1 Asian, non-Hispanic/Latino; 5 Hispanic/Latino; 2 Two or more races, non-Hispanic/Latino), 16 international. Average age 26. In 2018, 72 master's, 5 doctorates awarded. *Entrance requirements:* For master's, GRE General Test, minimum GPA of 3.0. Additional exam requirements/recommendations for international students: Required—TOEFL. *Application deadline:* Applications are processed on a rolling basis. Application fee: $50. Electronic applications accepted. *Financial support:* Scholarships/grants available. Financial award application deadline: 3/1; financial award applicants required to submit FAFSA. *Unit head:* Dr. Peter Grandjean, Dean of Applied Sciences, 662-915-7900, Fax: 662-915-7901, E-mail: applsci@olemiss.edu. *Application contact:* Temeka Smith, Graduate Activities Specialist for Admissions, 662-915-7474, Fax: 662-915-7577, E-mail: gschool@olemiss.edu.

University of Missouri, Office of Research and Graduate Studies, College of Agriculture, Food and Natural Resources, Department of Food Science, Columbia, MO 65211. Offers MS, PhD. Terminal master's awarded for partial completion of doctoral program. *Entrance requirements:* For master's, GRE General Test (minimum score: Verbal and Quantitative 1000 with neither section below 400, 297 combined under new scoring; Analytical 3.5), minimum GPA of 3.0; BS in food science from accredited university; for doctorate, GRE General Test (minimum score: Verbal and Quantitative 1000 with neither section below 400, Analytical 3.5), minimum GPA of 3.0; BS and MS in food science from accredited university. *Faculty research:* Food chemistry, food analysis, food microbiology, food engineering and process control, functional foods, meat science and processing technology.

University of Nebraska–Lincoln, Graduate College, College of Agricultural Sciences and Natural Resources, Department of Food Science and Technology, Lincoln, NE 68588. Offers MS, PhD. *Degree requirements:* For master's, thesis optional; for doctorate, comprehensive exam, thesis/dissertation. *Entrance requirements:* For master's and doctorate, GRE General Test. Additional exam requirements/recommendations for international students: Required—TOEFL (minimum score 505 paper-based). Electronic applications accepted. *Faculty research:* Food chemistry, microbiology, processing, engineering, and biotechnology.

University of Puerto Rico–Mayagüez, Graduate Studies, College of Agricultural Sciences, Department of Food Science and Technology, Mayagüez, PR 00681-9000. Offers MS. *Program availability:* Part-time. *Degree requirements:* For master's, comprehensive exam, thesis. Electronic applications accepted. *Faculty research:* Food microbiology, food science, seafood technology, food engineering and packaging, fermentation.

University of Rhode Island, Graduate School, College of Health Sciences, Department of Nutrition and Food Sciences, Kingston, RI 02881. Offers dietetic internship (MS); nutrition (MS); online dietetics (MS). *Program availability:* Part-time, 100% online. *Faculty:* 10 full-time (9 women), 1 (woman) part-time/adjunct. *Students:* 47 full-time (44 women), 42 part-time (38 women); includes 12 minority (2 Black or African American, non-Hispanic/Latino; 10 Asian, non-Hispanic/Latino), 2 international. 65 applicants, 77% accepted, 47 enrolled. In 2018, 43 master's awarded. *Entrance requirements:* Additional exam requirements/recommendations for international students: Required—TOEFL. *Application deadline:* For fall admission, 2/15 for domestic students, 2/1 for international students. Application fee: $65. Electronic applications accepted. *Expenses: Tuition, area resident:* Full-time $13,226; part-time $735 per credit. Tuition, state resident: full-time $13,226; part-time $735 per credit. Tuition, nonresident: full-time $25,854; part-time $1436 per credit. *International tuition:* $25,854 full-time. *Required fees:* $1698; $50 per credit. $35 per semester. One-time fee: $165. *Financial support:* In 2018–19, 1 research assistantship with tuition reimbursement (averaging $18,080 per year), 6 teaching assistantships (averaging $15,449 per year) were awarded. Financial award application deadline: 2/1; financial award applicants required to submit FAFSA. *Unit head:* Dr. Cathy English, Chair, 401-874-5689, Fax: 401-874-5974, E-mail: cathy@uri.edu. *Application contact:* Dr. Ingrid Lofgren, Graduate Coordinator, 401-874-5706, E-mail: ingridlofgren@uri.edu.
Website: http://web.uri.edu/nfs/

University of Rhode Island, Graduate School, College of the Environment and Life Sciences, Department of Biological Sciences, Kingston, RI 02881. Offers cell and molecular biology (MS, PhD); earth and environmental sciences (MS, PhD); ecology and ecosystem sciences (MS, PhD); evolutionary and marine biology (MS, PhD); sustainable agriculture and food systems (MS, PhD). *Program availability:* Part-time. *Faculty:* 20 full-time (10 women). *Students:* 105 full-time (65 women), 7 part-time (3 women); includes 10 minority (4 Black or African American, non-Hispanic/Latino; 3 Asian, non-Hispanic/Latino; 2 Hispanic/Latino; 1 Two or more races, non-Hispanic/Latino), 23 international. 121 applicants, 31% accepted, 28 enrolled. In 2018, 17 master's, 11 doctorates awarded. *Entrance requirements:* Additional exam requirements/recommendations for international students: Required—TOEFL. *Application deadline:* For fall admission, 1/15 for domestic and international students. Application fee: $65. Electronic applications accepted. *Expenses: Tuition, area resident:* Full-time $13,226; part-time $735 per credit. Tuition, state resident: full-time $13,226; part-time $735 per credit. Tuition, nonresident: full-time $25,854; part-time $1436 per

credit. *International tuition:* $25,854 full-time. *Required fees:* $1698; $50 per credit. $35 per semester. One-time fee: $165. *Financial support:* In 2018–19, 11 research assistantships with tuition reimbursements (averaging $10,985 per year) were awarded. Financial award application deadline: 1/15; financial award applicants required to submit FAFSA. *Faculty research:* Physiological constraints on predators in the Antarctic, effects of CO2 absorption in salt water particularly as it impacts pteropods. *Unit head:* Dr. Evan Preisser, Chair, 401-874-2120, E-mail: preisser@uri.edu. *Application contact:* Dr. Evan Preisser, Chair, 401-874-2120, E-mail: preisser@uri.edu.
Website: http://web.uri.edu/bio/

University of Saskatchewan, College of Graduate and Postdoctoral Studies, College of Agriculture and Bioresources, Department of Food and Bioproduct Sciences, Saskatoon, SK S7N 5A2, Canada. Offers applied microbiology (M Sc, PhD); food science (M Sc, PhD). *Degree requirements:* For master's, thesis; for doctorate, comprehensive exam (for some programs), thesis/dissertation. *Entrance requirements:* Additional exam requirements/recommendations for international students: Required—TOEFL (minimum score 80 iBT); Recommended—IELTS (minimum score 6.5).

University of Southern California, Graduate School, School of Pharmacy, Regulatory Science Programs, Los Angeles, CA 90089. Offers clinical research design and management (Graduate Certificate); food safety (Graduate Certificate); patient and product safety (Graduate Certificate); preclinical drug development (Graduate Certificate); regulatory and clinical affairs (Graduate Certificate); regulatory science (MS, DRSc). *Program availability:* Part-time, evening/weekend, online learning. Terminal master's awarded for partial completion of doctoral program. *Degree requirements:* For master's, thesis optional; for doctorate, comprehensive exam, thesis/dissertation. *Entrance requirements:* For master's, GRE. Additional exam requirements/recommendations for international students: Required—TOEFL (minimum score 603 paper-based; 100 iBT). Electronic applications accepted.

University of Southern Mississippi, College of Education and Human Sciences, Department of Nutrition and Food Systems, Hattiesburg, MS 39406-0001. Offers MS. *Program availability:* Part-time, online learning. *Degree requirements:* For master's, comprehensive exam, thesis (for some programs). *Entrance requirements:* For master's, GRE General Test, minimum GPA of 2.75 on last 60 hours. Additional exam requirements/recommendations for international students: Required—TOEFL, IELTS. Electronic applications accepted.

The University of Tennessee, Graduate School, College of Agricultural Sciences and Natural Resources, Department of Food Science and Technology, Knoxville, TN 37996. Offers food science and technology (MS, PhD), including food chemistry (PhD), food microbiology (PhD), food processing (PhD), sensory evaluation of foods (PhD). *Program availability:* Part-time. *Degree requirements:* For master's, thesis or alternative; for doctorate, thesis/dissertation. *Entrance requirements:* For master's and doctorate, GRE General Test, minimum GPA of 2.7. Additional exam requirements/recommendations for international students: Required—TOEFL. Electronic applications accepted.

The University of Tennessee at Martin, Graduate Programs, College of Agriculture and Applied Sciences, Department of Family and Consumer Sciences, Martin, TN 38238. Offers dietetics (MSFCS); general family and consumer sciences (MSFCS). *Program availability:* Part-time, 100% online. *Faculty:* 7. *Students:* 5 full-time (1 woman), 29 part-time (27 women); includes 2 minority (both Black or African American, non-Hispanic/Latino). Average age 29. 54 applicants, 70% accepted, 17 enrolled. In 2018, 9 master's awarded. *Degree requirements:* For master's, comprehensive exam, thesis optional. *Entrance requirements:* For master's, GRE General Test, minimum GPA of 2.5. Additional exam requirements/recommendations for international students: Required—TOEFL (minimum score 525 paper-based; 71 iBT). *Application deadline:* For fall admission, 7/27 priority date for domestic and international students; for spring admission, 12/17 priority date for domestic and international students; for summer admission, 5/10 priority date for domestic and international students. Applications are processed on a rolling basis. Application fee: $30 ($130 for international students). Electronic applications accepted. *Expenses: Tuition, area resident:* Full-time $8918; part-time $495 per credit hour. Tuition, state resident: full-time $8918; part-time $485 per credit hour. Tuition, nonresident: full-time $14,958; part-time $831 per credit hour. *International tuition:* $22,862 full-time. *Required fees:* $1446; $81 per credit hour. Part-time tuition and fees vary according to course load. *Financial support:* In 2018–19, 11 students received support, including 4 teaching assistantships with full tuition reimbursements available (averaging $7,087 per year); research assistantships with full tuition reimbursements available, scholarships/grants, and tuition waivers (full and partial) also available. Financial award application deadline: 2/1; financial award applicants required to submit FAFSA. *Faculty research:* Children with developmental disabilities, regional food product development and marketing, parent education. *Unit head:* Dr. Lisa LeBleu, Coordinator, 731-881-7116, Fax: 731-881-7106, E-mail: llcblou@utm.edu. *Application contact:* Jolene L. Cunningham, Student Services Specialist, 731-881-7012, Fax: 731-881-7499, E-mail: jcunningham@utm.edu.
Website: http://www.utm.edu/departments/caas/fcs/index.php

University of Vermont, Graduate College, College of Agriculture and Life Sciences, Department of Animal and Veterinary Sciences, Burlington, VT 05405-0148. Offers animal science (MS); animal, nutrition and food sciences (PhD). *Degree requirements:* For master's, thesis; for doctorate, one foreign language, thesis/dissertation. *Entrance requirements:* For master's and doctorate, GRE General Test. Additional exam requirements/recommendations for international students: Required—TOEFL (minimum score 550 paper-based, 90 iBT) or IELTS (6.5). Electronic applications accepted. *Faculty research:* Animal nutrition, dairy production.

University of Vermont, Graduate College, Cross-College Interdisciplinary Program, Program in Food Systems, Burlington, VT 05405. Offers MS, PhD. *Entrance requirements:* For master's and doctorate, GRE General Test. Additional exam requirements/recommendations for international students: Required—TOEFL (minimum score 550 paper-based, 90 iBT) or IELTS (6.5). Electronic applications accepted.

University of Wisconsin–Madison, Graduate School, College of Agricultural and Life Sciences, Department of Food Science, Madison, WI 53706-1380. Offers MS, PhD. *Program availability:* Part-time. *Degree requirements:* For master's, thesis; for doctorate, thesis/dissertation. *Entrance requirements:* For master's and doctorate, GRE General Test. Additional exam requirements/recommendations for international students: Required—TOEFL. Electronic applications accepted. *Faculty research:* Food chemistry, food engineering, food microbiology, food processing.

University of Wisconsin–Stout, Graduate School, College of Education, Health and Human Sciences, Program in Food and Nutritional Sciences, Menomonie, WI 54751. Offers MS. *Program availability:* Part-time. *Degree requirements:* For master's, thesis. *Entrance requirements:* For master's, minimum GPA of 3.0. Additional exam requirements/recommendations for international students: Required—TOEFL (minimum score 500 paper-based; 61 iBT). Electronic applications accepted. *Faculty research:* Disease states and nutrition, childhood obesity, nutraceuticals, food safety, nanotechnology.

University of Wyoming, College of Agriculture and Natural Resources, Department of Animal Science, Program in Food Science and Human Nutrition, Laramie, WY 82071. Offers MS. *Degree requirements:* For master's, thesis. *Entrance requirements:* For master's, GRE General Test, minimum GPA of 3.0. Additional exam requirements/recommendations for international students: Required—TOEFL (minimum score 525 paper-based). Electronic applications accepted. *Expenses: Tuition, area resident:* Full-time $6504; part-time $271 per credit hour. Tuition, state resident: full-time $6504; part-time $271 per credit hour. Tuition, nonresident: full-time $19,464; part-time $811 per credit hour. *International tuition:* $19,464 full-time. *Required fees:* $1410.94; $343.82 per semester. $343.82 per semester. Tuition and fees vary according to course load, program and reciprocity agreements. *Faculty research:* Protein and lipid metabolism, food microbiology, food safety, meat science.

Utah State University, School of Graduate Studies, College of Agriculture and Applied Sciences, Department of Nutrition, Dietetics, and Food Sciences, Logan, UT 84322. Offers dietetic administration (MDA); nutrition and food sciences (MS, PhD). *Program availability:* Online learning. *Degree requirements:* For master's, thesis; for doctorate, comprehensive exam, thesis/dissertation, teaching experience. *Entrance requirements:* For master's, GRE General Test, minimum GPA of 3.0, course work in chemistry, biochemistry, physics, math, bacteriology, physiology; for doctorate, GRE General Test, minimum GPA of 3.2, course work in chemistry, MS or manuscript in referred journal. Additional exam requirements/recommendations for international students: Required—TOEFL (minimum score 550 paper-based). Electronic applications accepted. *Faculty research:* Mineral balance, meat microbiology and nitrate interactions, milk ultrafiltration, lactic culture, milk coagulation.

Washington State University, College of Agricultural, Human, and Natural Resource Sciences, School of Food Science, Pullman, WA 99164-6376. Offers MS, PhD. Programs offered at the Pullman campus. *Program availability:* Part-time. *Degree requirements:* For master's, comprehensive exam, thesis, oral exam, written exam; for doctorate, comprehensive exam, thesis/dissertation, oral exam, written exam. *Entrance requirements:* For master's, GRE General Test, BS; official transcripts; letter of interest; minimum GPA of 3.0; resume; 3 letters of recommendation, 1 from major advisor; for doctorate, GRE General Test, MS demonstrating ability to conduct and report research; minimum GPA of 3.0; resume; 3 letters of recommendation, 1 from major advisor. Additional exam requirements/recommendations for international students: Required—TOEFL (minimum score 550 paper-based; 80 iBT). Electronic applications accepted. *Faculty research:* Food microbiology and chemistry of food; starch and protein chemistry; food processing and engineering; food safety; microbiological, chemical, and quality aspects of food; dairy, wine processes.

Wayne State University, College of Liberal Arts and Sciences, Department of Nutrition and Food Science, Detroit, MI 48202. Offers dietetics (Postbaccalaureate Certificate); food science (PhD); nutrition (PhD); nutrition and food science (MA, MS); MA/MPH. Postbaccalaureate certificate program admits only in fall with April 1 application deadline. *Faculty:* 5. *Students:* 30 full-time (25 women), 7 part-time (4 women); includes 5 minority (2 Asian, non-Hispanic/Latino; 1 Hispanic/Latino; 2 Two or more races, non-Hispanic/Latino), 14 international. Average age 30. 55 applicants, 38% accepted, 16 enrolled. In 2018, 10 master's, 4 doctorates awarded. *Degree requirements:* For master's, thesis (for some programs), essay (for MA); for doctorate, thesis/dissertation. *Entrance requirements:* For master's, GRE General Test (recommended), two letters of recommendation; minimum GPA of 3.0; undergraduate degree in science; for doctorate, GRE (recommended), MS in nutrition and/or food science or in a cognate science with minimum GPA of 3.5; three letters of recommendation; personal statement; interview (live or Web-based). Additional exam requirements/recommendations for international students: Required—TOEFL (minimum score 550 paper-based; 79 iBT), TWE (minimum score 5.5), Michigan English Language Assessment Battery (minimum score 85); Recommended—IELTS (minimum score 6.5). *Application deadline:* For fall admission, 3/1 priority date for domestic and international students. Applications are processed on a rolling basis. Application fee: $50. Electronic applications accepted. *Financial support:* In 2018–19, 15 students received support, including 1 fellowship with tuition reimbursement available (averaging $20,000 per year), 1 research assistantship with tuition reimbursement available (averaging $24,200 per year), 8 teaching assistantships with tuition reimbursements available (averaging $20,516 per year); scholarships/grants, health care benefits, and unspecified assistantships also available. Financial award applicants required to submit FAFSA. *Faculty research:* Metabolomics and the study of nutrition and disease; understanding the effect of nutrition intervention (i.e., caloric restriction, folate deficiency) on the molecular mechanisms of aging and cancer; obesity and diabetes; study of how different dietary constituents (e.g. fatty acids) interact with each other to modulate key parameters related to plasma lipoprotein metabolism. *Unit head:* Dr. Ahmad R. Heydari, Professor and Chair, 313-577-2500, E-mail: ahmad.heydari@wayne.edu. *Application contact:* Dr. Diane Cress, Associate Professor and Graduate Officer, 313-577-5978, E-mail: gradprogramnfs@wayne.edu.
Website: http://clas.wayne.edu/nfs/

West Virginia University, Davis College of Agriculture, Forestry and Consumer Sciences, Morgantown, WV 26506. Offers agricultural and extension education (MS, PhD); agriculture and resource management (MS); agriculture, natural resources and design (M Agr); agronomy (MS); animal and food science (PhD); animal physiology (MS); applied and environmental microbiology (MS); design and merchandising (MS); entomology (MS); forest resource science (PhD); forestry (MSF); genetics and developmental biology (MS, PhD); horticulture (MS); human and community development (PhD); landscape architecture (MLA); natural resource economics (PhD); nutritional and food science (MS); plant and soil science (PhD); plant pathology (MS); recreation, parks and tourism resources (MS); reproductive physiology (MS, PhD); wildlife and fisheries resources (PhD). *Accreditation:* ASLA. *Program availability:* Part-time. *Students:* 188 full-time (86 women), 47 part-time (30 women); includes 22 minority (5 Black or African American, non-Hispanic/Latino; 5 Asian, non-Hispanic/Latino; 8 Hispanic/Latino; 4 Two or more races, non-Hispanic/Latino), 60 international. In 2018, 56 master's, 14 doctorates awarded. *Degree requirements:* For master's, thesis; for doctorate, thesis/dissertation. *Entrance requirements:* Additional exam requirements/recommendations for international students: Required—TOEFL (minimum score 550 paper-based). *Application deadline:* For fall admission, 6/1 priority date for domestic students, 6/1 for international students; for spring admission, 1/5 for domestic and international students. Applications are processed on a rolling basis. Application fee: $60. Electronic applications accepted. *Financial support:* Fellowships, research assistantships, teaching assistantships, career-related internships or fieldwork, Federal Work-Study, institutionally sponsored loans, tuition waivers (full and partial), and unspecified assistantships available. Financial award application deadline: 2/1; financial award applicants required to submit FAFSA. *Faculty research:* Reproductive physiology, soil and water quality, human nutrition, aquaculture, wildlife management. *Unit head:* Dr. Ken Blemings, Interim Dean, 304-293-2395, Fax: 304-293-3740, E-mail: ken.blemings@mail.wvu.edu. *Application contact:* Dr. J. Todd Petty, Associate Dean, 304-293-2278, Fax: 304-293-3740, E-mail: jtpetty@mail.wvu.edu.
Website: https://www.davis.wvu.edu

Horticulture

Auburn University, Graduate School, College of Agriculture, Department of Horticulture, Auburn University, AL 36849. Offers M Ag, MS, PhD. *Program availability:* Part-time. *Degree requirements:* For master's, thesis (for some programs); for doctorate, thesis/dissertation. *Entrance requirements:* For master's and doctorate, GRE General Test. Electronic applications accepted. *Expenses:* Tuition, state resident: full-time $11,282; part-time $535 per credit hour. Tuition, nonresident: full-time $30,542; part-time $1605 per credit hour. *Required fees:* $826 per semester. Tuition and fees vary according to degree level and program. *Faculty research:* Environmental regulators, water quality, weed control, growth regulators, plasticulture.

Colorado State University, College of Agricultural Sciences, Department of Horticulture and Landscape Architecture, Fort Collins, CO 80523-1173. Offers MLA, MS, PhD. Terminal master's awarded for partial completion of doctoral program. *Degree requirements:* For master's, thesis (for some programs), research paper; for doctorate, thesis/dissertation. *Entrance requirements:* For master's, GRE General Test (minimum score of 300 combined Verbal and Quantitative sections), minimum GPA of 3.0, letters of reference, transcripts, resume/curriculum vitae, statement of purpose; for doctorate, GRE General Test (minimum score of 300 combined Verbal and Quantitative sections), minimum GPA of 3.0, letters of reference, statement of purpose, resume/curriculum vitae, transcripts. Additional exam requirements/recommendations for international students: Required—TOEFL (minimum score 550 paper-based), IELTS. Electronic applications accepted. *Expenses:* Tuition, state resident: full-time $10,520; part-time $4675 per credit hour. Tuition, nonresident: full-time $25,791; part-time $11,462 per credit hour. *International tuition:* $25,791 full-time. *Required fees:* $2392; $576 $288. Tuition and fees vary according to course level, course load, degree level, program and student level. *Faculty research:* Specialty crops, environmental physiology, water requirements for plant life, biochemical diversity, land reclamation within post-mined landscapes.

Cornell University, Graduate School, Graduate Fields of Agriculture and Life Sciences, Field of Horticulture, Ithaca, NY 14853. Offers breeding of horticultural crops (MPS); horticultural crop management systems (MPS); human-plant interactions (MPS, PhD); physiology and ecology of horticultural crops (MPS, MS, PhD). *Degree requirements:* For master's, thesis (MS); for doctorate, comprehensive exam, thesis/dissertation. *Entrance requirements:* For master's and doctorate, GRE General Test, 3 letters of recommendation. Additional exam requirements/recommendations for international students: Required—TOEFL (minimum score 550 paper-based; 77 iBT). Electronic applications accepted. *Faculty research:* Plant selection/plant materials, greenhouse management, greenhouse crop production, urban landscape management, turfgrass management.

Dalhousie University, Faculty of Agriculture, Halifax, NS B3H 4R2, Canada. Offers agriculture (M Sc), including air quality, animal behavior, animal molecular genetics, animal nutrition, animal technology, aquaculture, botany, crop management, crop physiology, ecology, environmental microbiology, food science, horticulture, nutrient management, pest management, physiology, plant biotechnology, plant pathology, soil chemistry, soil fertility, waste management and composting, water quality. *Program availability:* Part-time. *Degree requirements:* For master's, thesis, ATC Exam Teaching Assistantship. *Entrance requirements:* For master's, honors B Sc, minimum GPA of 3.0. Additional exam requirements/recommendations for international students: Required—TOEFL (minimum score 580 paper-based; 92 iBT), IELTS, Michigan English Language Assessment Battery, CanTEST, CAEL. *Faculty research:* Bio-product development, organic agriculture, nutrient management, air and water quality, agricultural biotechnology.

Iowa State University of Science and Technology, Department of Horticulture, Ames, IA 50011. Offers MS, PhD. *Degree requirements:* For master's, thesis; for doctorate, thesis/dissertation. *Entrance requirements:* For master's and doctorate, GRE General Test. Additional exam requirements/recommendations for international students: Required—TOEFL (minimum score 550 paper-based; 79 iBT), IELTS (minimum score 6.5). Electronic applications accepted.

Kansas State University, Graduate School, College of Agriculture, Department of Horticulture and Natural Resources, Manhattan, KS 66506. Offers horticulture and natural resources (MS, PhD), including horticulture and natural resources, urban food systems (MS). *Program availability:* Part-time, online learning. *Degree requirements:* For master's, thesis, oral exam; for doctorate, thesis/dissertation, preliminary exams. *Entrance requirements:* For master's and doctorate, GRE General Test. Additional exam requirements/recommendations for international students: Required—TOEFL (minimum score 550 paper-based; 79 iBT); Recommended—IELTS (minimum score 6.5). Electronic applications accepted. *Faculty research:* Environmental stress, phytochemicals and health, postharvest technology, sustainable production, turf grass science.

Louisiana State University and Agricultural & Mechanical College, Graduate School, College of Agriculture, School of Plant, Environmental and Soil Sciences, Baton Rouge, LA 70803. Offers agronomy (MS, PhD); horticulture (MS, PhD); soil science (MS, PhD).

Michigan State University, The Graduate School, College of Agriculture and Natural Resources, Department of Horticulture, East Lansing, MI 48824. Offers horticulture (MS, PhD); plant breeding, genetics and biotechnology-horticulture (MS, PhD). *Entrance requirements:* Additional exam requirements/recommendations for international students: Required—TOEFL. Electronic applications accepted.

Mississippi State University, College of Agriculture and Life Sciences, Department of Plant and Soil Sciences, Mississippi State, MS 39762. Offers weed science (MS, PhD), including agronomy, horticulture, weed science. *Faculty:* 43 full-time (6 women). *Students:* 47 full-time (16 women), 32 part-time (9 women); includes 3 minority (all Black or African American, non-Hispanic/Latino), 21 international. Average age 29. 21 applicants, 43% accepted, 9 enrolled. In 2018, 18 master's, 11 doctorates awarded. *Degree requirements:* For master's, comprehensive exam, thesis, oral and/or written exams; for doctorate, comprehensive exam, thesis/dissertation, minimum of 20 semester hours of research for dissertation. *Entrance requirements:* For master's, GRE (for weed science), minimum GPA of 2.75 (agronomy/horticulture), 3.0 (weed science); for doctorate, GRE (for weed science), minimum GPA of 3.0 (agronomy/horticulture), 3.25 (weed science). Additional exam requirements/recommendations for international students: Required—TOEFL (minimum score 500 paper-based; 61 iBT), TOEFL minimum score 550 paper-based, 79 iBT or IELTS minimum score 6.5 (for weed science); Recommended—IELTS (minimum score 5.5). *Application deadline:* For fall admission, 7/1 for domestic students, 5/1 for international students; for spring

admission, 10/1 for domestic students, 9/1 for international students. Applications are processed on a rolling basis. Application fee: $60 ($80 for international students). Electronic applications accepted. *Expenses:* Tuition, state resident: full-time $8450; part-time $360.59 per credit hour. Tuition, nonresident: full-time $23,140; part-time $969.09 per credit hour. *Required fees:* $110. One-time fee: $55 full-time. Part-time tuition and fees vary according to course load, degree level, campus/location and reciprocity agreements. *Financial support:* In 2018–19, 40 research assistantships with full tuition reimbursements (averaging $15,736 per year), 4 teaching assistantships with partial tuition reimbursements (averaging $14,888 per year) were awarded; Federal Work-Study, institutionally sponsored loans, scholarships/grants, and unspecified assistantships also available. Financial award application deadline: 4/1; financial award applicants required to submit FAFSA. *Faculty research:* Bioenergy crops, cotton breeding, environmental plant pathology, row crop weed control, genomics. *Unit head:* Dr. J. Michael Phillips, Professor and Head, 662-325-2311, Fax: 662-325-8742, E-mail: jmp657@msstate.edu. *Application contact:* Ryan King, Admissions and Enrollment Assistant, 662-325-8951, E-mail: rjk101@grad.msstate.edu.
Website: http://www.pss.msstate.edu/

North Carolina State University, Graduate School, College of Agriculture and Life Sciences, Department of Horticultural Science, Raleigh, NC 27695. Offers MS, PhD, Certificate. *Program availability:* Online learning. Terminal master's awarded for partial completion of doctoral program. *Degree requirements:* For master's, thesis (for some programs); for doctorate, thesis/dissertation. *Entrance requirements:* For master's and doctorate, GRE General Test, bachelor's degree in agriculture or biology, minimum GPA of 3.0. Electronic applications accepted. *Faculty research:* Plant physiology, breeding and genetics, tissue culture, herbicide physiology, propagation.

North Dakota State University, College of Graduate and Interdisciplinary Studies, College of Agriculture, Food Systems, and Natural Resources, Department of Plant Sciences, Fargo, ND 58102. Offers horticulture (MS); plant sciences (MS, PhD). *Program availability:* Part-time. *Entrance requirements:* Additional exam requirements/recommendations for international students: Required—TOEFL (minimum score 525 paper-based; 71 iBT). Electronic applications accepted. *Faculty research:* Biotechnology, weed control science, plant breeding, plant genetics, crop physiology.

The Ohio State University, Graduate School, College of Food, Agricultural, and Environmental Sciences, Department of Horticulture and Crop Science, Columbus, OH 43210. Offers MS, PhD. *Faculty:* 22. *Students:* 43 (18 women). Average age 27. In 2018, 12 master's, 4 doctorates awarded. *Entrance requirements:* For master's and doctorate, GRE General Test. Additional exam requirements/recommendations for international students: Required—TOEFL (minimum score 550 paper-based; 79 iBT), Michigan English Language Assessment Battery (minimum score 82); Recommended—IELTS (minimum score 7). *Application deadline:* For fall admission, 12/13 priority date for domestic students, 11/30 priority date for international students; for spring admission, 12/1 for domestic students, 10/31 for international students; for summer admission, 4/1 for domestic students, 2/28 for international students. Applications are processed on a rolling basis. Application fee: $60 ($70 for international students). Electronic applications accepted. *Financial support:* Fellowships, research assistantships, teaching assistantships, Federal Work-Study, and institutionally sponsored loans available. Support available to part-time students. *Unit head:* Dr. Jim Metzger, Chair, 614-292-3854, E-mail: metzger.72@osu.edu. *Application contact:* Graduate and Professional Admissions, 614-292-9444, Fax: 614-292-3895, E-mail: gpadmissions@osu.edu.
Website: http://hcs.osu.edu/

Oklahoma State University, College of Agricultural Science and Natural Resources, Department of Horticulture and Landscape Architecture, Stillwater, OK 74078. Offers crop science (PhD); horticulture (M Ag, MS). *Faculty:* 17 full-time (5 women), 1 (woman) part-time/adjunct. *Students:* 1 full-time (0 women), 8 part-time (5 women); includes 3 minority (1 American Indian or Alaska Native, non-Hispanic/Latino; 2 Two or more races, non-Hispanic/Latino), 3 international. Average age 28. 5 applicants, 60% accepted, 3 enrolled. In 2018, 7 master's awarded. *Entrance requirements:* For master's and doctorate, GRE or GMAT. Additional exam requirements/recommendations for international students: Required—TOEFL (minimum score 550 paper-based; 79 iBT). *Application deadline:* For fall admission, 3/1 priority date for international students; for spring admission, 8/1 priority date for international students. Applications are processed on a rolling basis. Application fee: $40 ($75 for international students). Electronic applications accepted. *Expenses:* Tuition, area resident: Full-time $4148. Tuition, state resident: full-time $4148. Tuition, nonresident: full-time $10,517. *International tuition:* $10,517 full-time. *Required fees:* $4394; $2929 per credit hour. Tuition and fees vary according to course load and program. *Financial support:* Research assistantships, teaching assistantships, career-related internships or fieldwork, Federal Work-Study, scholarships/grants, health care benefits, tuition waivers (partial), and unspecified assistantships available. Support available to part-time students. Financial award application deadline: 3/1; financial award applicants required to submit FAFSA. *Faculty research:* Stress and postharvest physiology; water utilization and runoff; integrated pest management (IPM) systems and nursery, turf, floriculture, vegetable, net and fruit produces and natural resources, food extraction, and processing; public garden management. *Unit head:* Dr. Janet Cole, Department Head, 405-744-5415, Fax: 405-744-9709. *Application contact:* Dr. Sheryl Tucker, Dean, 405-744-7099, Fax: 405-744-0355, E-mail: gradi@okstate.edu.
Website: http://www.hortla.okstate.edu/

Oregon State University, College of Agricultural Sciences, Program in Horticulture, Corvallis, OR 97331. Offers breeding, genetics, and biotechnology (MS, PhD); community and landscape horticultural systems (MS, PhD); sustainable crop production (MS, PhD). *Degree requirements:* For master's, thesis (for some programs); for doctorate, thesis/dissertation. *Entrance requirements:* For master's and doctorate, GRE General Test, minimum GPA of 3.0 in last 90 hours. Additional exam requirements/recommendations for international students: Required—TOEFL (minimum score 80 iBT), IELTS (minimum score 6.5).

Penn State University Park, Graduate School, College of Agricultural Sciences, Department of Plant Science, University Park, PA 16802. Offers agronomy (MS, PhD); horticulture (MS, PhD).

Purdue University, Graduate School, College of Agriculture, Department of Horticulture, West Lafayette, IN 47907. Offers M Agr, MS, PhD. *Program availability:* Part-time. *Faculty:* 27 full-time (8 women). *Students:* 24 full-time (10 women), 3 part-time (1 woman); includes 3 minority (1 Black or African American, non-Hispanic/Latino; 1 American Indian or Alaska Native, non-Hispanic/Latino; 1 Hispanic/Latino), 19 international. Average age 28. 20 applicants, 30% accepted, 4 enrolled. In 2018, 5

Peterson's Graduate Programs in the Physical Sciences, Mathematics, Agricultural Sciences, the Environment & Natural Resources 2020

www.petersons.com **283**

master's, 5 doctorates awarded. Terminal master's awarded for partial completion of doctoral program. *Degree requirements:* For master's, thesis optional; for doctorate, thesis/dissertation. *Entrance requirements:* For master's and doctorate, GRE General Test, minimum undergraduate GPA of 3.0 or equivalent. Additional exam requirements/recommendations for international students: Required—TOEFL (minimum score 550 paper-based; 77 iBT); Recommended—TWE. *Application deadline:* For fall admission, 5/1 for domestic and international students; for spring admission, 10/1 for domestic and international students; for summer admission, 3/1 for domestic and international students. Applications are processed on a rolling basis. Application fee: $60 ($75 for international students). Electronic applications accepted. *Financial support:* Fellowships, research assistantships with tuition reimbursements, and teaching assistantships with tuition reimbursements available. Support available to part-time students. Financial award applicants required to submit FAFSA. *Faculty research:* Floral scent and plant volatile biosynthesis, mineral nutrient utilization from cellular to global scales, hormone signaling and transport, regulation of plant architecture and reproduction, plant cell cycle regulation, water utilization and stress responses, sustainable biofuel production, enhancement of salt tolerance in crop plants, natural genetic variation, plant epigenetics, mechanisms of heterosis, hybridization and species breeding barriers. *Unit head:* Aaron J. Patton, Interim Head of the Graduate Program, 765-494-1306, E-mail: ajpatton@purdue.edu. *Application contact:* Jamie Moffatt, Graduate Contact, 765-494-1301, E-mail: jmoffat@purdue.edu.
Website: https://ag.purdue.edu/hla/Hort

Rutgers University–New Brunswick, Graduate School-New Brunswick, Program in Plant Biology, Piscataway, NJ 08854-8097. Offers horticulture and plant technology (MS, PhD); molecular and cellular biology (MS, PhD); organismal and population biology (MS, PhD); plant pathology (MS, PhD). *Program availability:* Part-time. Terminal master's awarded for partial completion of doctoral program. *Degree requirements:* For master's, comprehensive exam, thesis or alternative; for doctorate, comprehensive exam, thesis/dissertation. *Entrance requirements:* For master's and doctorate, GRE General Test, GRE Subject Test (recommended). Additional exam requirements/recommendations for international students: Required—TOEFL (minimum score 600 paper-based). Electronic applications accepted. *Faculty research:* Molecular biology and biochemistry of plants, plant development and genomics, plant protection, plant improvement, plant management of horticultural and field crops.

Texas A&M University, College of Agriculture and Life Sciences, Department of Horticultural Sciences, College Station, TX 77843. Offers horticulture (M Agr). *Faculty:* 18. *Students:* 48 full-time (27 women), 14 part-time (8 women); includes 10 minority (1 Black or African American, non-Hispanic/Latino; 3 Asian, non-Hispanic/Latino; 6 Hispanic/Latino), 26 international. Average age 31. 16 applicants, 100% accepted, 16 enrolled. In 2018, 7 master's, 1 doctorate awarded. Terminal master's awarded for partial completion of doctoral program. *Degree requirements:* For master's, thesis (for some programs), professional internship; for doctorate, thesis/dissertation. *Entrance requirements:* For master's and doctorate, GRE General Test. Additional exam requirements/recommendations for international students: Required—TOEFL (minimum score 550 paper-based; 80 iBT), IELTS (minimum score 6), PTE (minimum score 53). *Application deadline:* For fall admission, 12/15 priority date for domestic and international students; for spring admission, 9/1 priority date for domestic and international students; for summer admission, 9/1 priority date for domestic students, 9/1 for international students. Applications are processed on a rolling basis. Application fee: $50 ($90 for international students). Electronic applications accepted. *Expenses:* Contact institution. *Financial support:* In 2018–19, 50 students received support, including 10 fellowships with tuition reimbursements available (averaging $8,913 per year), 38 research assistantships with tuition reimbursements available (averaging $11,808 per year), 10 teaching assistantships with tuition reimbursements available (averaging $14,663 per year); career-related internships or fieldwork, institutionally sponsored loans, scholarships/grants, traineeships, health care benefits, tuition waivers (full and partial), and unspecified assistantships also available. Support available to part-time students. Financial award application deadline: 3/15; financial award applicants required to submit FAFSA. *Faculty research:* Plant breeding, molecular biology, plant nutrition, post-harvest physiology, plant physiology. *Unit head:* Dr. Dan Lineberger, Professor and Head, 979-845-5278, Fax: 979-845-0627, E-mail: dan-lineberger@tamu.edu. *Application contact:* Dr. Patricia Klein, Associate Professor/Associate Head for Graduate Studies, 979-862-6308, Fax: 979-845-0627, E-mail: pklein@tamu.edu.
Website: http://hortsciences.tamu.edu/

Texas A&M University–Kingsville, College of Graduate Studies, Dick and Mary Lewis Kleberg College of Agriculture, Natural Resources and Human Sciences, Department of Agriculture, Agribusiness, and Environmental Sciences, Kingsville, TX 78363. Offers agribusiness (MS); agricultural science (MS); horticulture (PhD); plant and soil science (MS); ranch management (MS). Electronic applications accepted.

Texas Tech University, Graduate School, College of Agricultural Sciences and Natural Resources, Department of Plant and Soil Science, Lubbock, TX 79409-2122. Offers horticulture science (MS); plant and soil science (MS, PhD). *Program availability:* Part-time, evening/weekend, 100% online, blended/hybrid learning. *Faculty:* 28 full-time (9 women), 10 part-time/adjunct (3 women). *Students:* 71 full-time (33 women), 41 part-time (12 women); includes 14 minority (3 Asian, non-Hispanic/Latino; 7 Hispanic/Latino; 4 Two or more races, non-Hispanic/Latino), 47 international. Average age 30. 47 applicants, 53% accepted, 20 enrolled. In 2018, 19 master's, 8 doctorates awarded. Terminal master's awarded for partial completion of doctoral program. *Degree requirements:* For master's, comprehensive exam (for some programs), thesis (for some programs); for doctorate, comprehensive exam, thesis/dissertation. *Entrance requirements:* For master's and doctorate, GRE. Additional exam requirements/recommendations for international students: Required—TOEFL (minimum score 550 paper-based; 79 iBT). *Application deadline:* For fall admission, 6/1 priority date for domestic students, 1/15 priority date for international students; for spring admission, 9/1 priority date for domestic students, 6/15 priority date for international students. Applications are processed on a rolling basis. Application fee: $65. Electronic applications accepted. *Expenses:* Contact institution. *Financial support:* In 2018–19, 101 students received support, including 92 fellowships (averaging $2,907 per year), 58 research assistantships (averaging $16,900 per year), 12 teaching assistantships (averaging $14,673 per year); scholarships/grants, health care benefits, and unspecified assistantships also available. Financial award application deadline: 4/15; financial award applicants required to submit FAFSA. *Faculty research:* Crop protection, crop science, fibers and biopolymers, soil science, horticulture, turf grass science, genetics. *Total annual research expenditures:* $5 million. *Unit head:* Dr. Glen Ritchie, Department Chair and Associate Professor, 806-742-2838, Fax: 806-742-0775, E-mail: glen.ritchie@ttu.edu. *Application contact:* Diann Merriman, Lead Academic Advisor, 806-834-7044, Fax: 806-742-0775, E-mail: diann.merriman@ttu.edu.
Website: www.pssc.ttu.edu

Universidad Nacional Pedro Henriquez Urena, Graduate School, Santo Domingo, Dominican Republic. Offers agricultural diversity (MS), including horticultural/fruit production, tropical animal production; conservation of monuments and cultural assets (M Arch); ecology and environment (MS); environmental engineering (MEE); international relations (MA); natural resource management (MS); political science (MA); project optimization (MPM); project feasibility (MPM); project management (MPM); sanitation engineering (ME); science for teachers (MS); tropical Caribbean architecture (M Arch).

University of Arkansas, Graduate School, Dale Bumpers College of Agricultural, Food and Life Sciences, Department of Horticulture, Fayetteville, AR 72701. Offers MS. In 2018, 6 master's awarded. *Application deadline:* For fall admission, 8/1 for domestic students, 4/1 for international students; for spring admission, 12/1 for domestic students, 10/1 for international students; for summer admission, 4/15 for domestic students, 3/1 for international students. Applications are processed on a rolling basis. Application fee: $60. Electronic applications accepted. *Financial support:* In 2018–19, 7 research assistantships were awarded; fellowships, teaching assistantships, career-related internships or fieldwork, and Federal Work-Study also available. Support available to part-time students. Financial award application deadline: 4/1; financial award applicants required to submit FAFSA. *Unit head:* Dr. Wayne A. Mackay, Department Head, 479-575-7319, E-mail: mackay@uark.edu. *Application contact:* Dr. Wayne Mackay, Graduate Coordinator, 479-575-7319, E-mail: mackay@uark.edu.
Website: https://horticulture.uark.edu/

University of California, Davis, Graduate Studies, Graduate Group in Horticulture and Agronomy, Davis, CA 95616. Offers MS. *Degree requirements:* For master's, comprehensive exam (for some programs), thesis (for some programs). *Entrance requirements:* For master's, GRE General Test. Additional exam requirements/recommendations for international students: Required—TOEFL (minimum score 550 paper-based). Electronic applications accepted. *Faculty research:* Postharvest physiology, mineral nutrition, crop improvement, plant growth and development.

University of Delaware, College of Agriculture and Natural Resources, Longwood Graduate Program in Public Horticulture, Newark, DE 19716. Offers MS. *Degree requirements:* For master's, thesis, internship. *Entrance requirements:* For master's, GRE General Test, introductory taxonomy course. Additional exam requirements/recommendations for international students: Required—TOEFL. Electronic applications accepted. *Faculty research:* Management and development of publicly oriented horticultural institutions.

University of Florida, Graduate School, College of Agricultural and Life Sciences, Department of Environmental Horticulture, Gainesville, FL 32611. Offers MS, PhD. *Program availability:* Part-time, online learning. Terminal master's awarded for partial completion of doctoral program. *Degree requirements:* For master's, comprehensive exam, thesis optional, teaching experience; for doctorate, comprehensive exam, thesis/dissertation, teaching experience. *Entrance requirements:* For master's and doctorate, GRE General Test, minimum GPA of 3.0. Additional exam requirements/recommendations for international students: Required—TOEFL (minimum score 550 paper-based; 80 iBT), IELTS (minimum score 6). Electronic applications accepted. *Faculty research:* Breeding and genetics, conservation and restoration horticulture, landscape design and ecology, floriculture, nursery and foliage crop production, turf grasses and urban horticulture, arboriculture.

University of Florida, Graduate School, College of Agricultural and Life Sciences, Department of Horticultural Sciences, Gainesville, FL 32611. Offers horticultural sciences (MS, PhD), including environmental horticulture, horticultural sciences, toxicology (PhD). *Degree requirements:* For master's, thesis optional; for doctorate, comprehensive exam, thesis/dissertation. *Entrance requirements:* For master's and doctorate, GRE General Test, minimum GPA of 3.0. Additional exam requirements/recommendations for international students: Required—TOEFL (minimum score 550 paper-based; 80 iBT), IELTS (minimum score 6). Electronic applications accepted. *Faculty research:* Breeding and genetics, crop production and nutrition, organic/sustainable agriculture, physiology and biochemistry.

University of Georgia, College of Agricultural and Environmental Sciences, Department of Horticulture, Athens, GA 30602. Offers horticulture (MS, PhD). *Program availability:* Part-time. *Degree requirements:* For master's, thesis (MS); for doctorate, one foreign language, thesis/dissertation. *Entrance requirements:* For master's and doctorate, GRE General Test. Electronic applications accepted.

University of Guelph, Office of Graduate and Postdoctoral Studies, Ontario Agricultural College, Department of Plant Agriculture, Guelph, ON N1G 2W1, Canada. Offers M Sc, PhD. *Program availability:* Part-time. *Degree requirements:* For master's, thesis; for doctorate, comprehensive exam, thesis/dissertation. *Entrance requirements:* For master's, minimum B average during previous 2 years of course work; for doctorate, minimum B average. Additional exam requirements/recommendations for international students: Required—TOEFL (minimum score 550 paper-based; 89 iBT), IELTS (minimum score 6.5), Michigan English Language Assessment Battery (minimum score: 85). Electronic applications accepted. *Faculty research:* Plant physiology, biochemistry, taxonomy, morphology, genetics, production, ecology, breeding and biotechnology.

University of Hawaii at Manoa, Office of Graduate Education, College of Tropical Agriculture and Human Resources, Department of Tropical Plant and Soil Sciences, Honolulu, HI 96822. Offers MS, PhD. *Program availability:* Part-time. *Degree requirements:* For master's, thesis optional; for doctorate, comprehensive exam, thesis/dissertation. *Entrance requirements:* For master's and doctorate, GRE General Test. Additional exam requirements/recommendations for international students: Required—TOEFL (minimum score 520 paper-based; 79 iBT), IELTS (minimum score 5). *Faculty research:* Genetics and breeding; physiology, culture, and management; weed science; turf grass and landscape; sensory evaluation.

University of Maine, Graduate School, College of Natural Sciences, Forestry, and Agriculture, School of Food and Agriculture, Orono, ME 04469. Offers horticulture (MS). *Program availability:* Part-time. *Faculty:* 27 full-time (13 women). *Students:* 46 full-time (38 women), 11 part-time (9 women); includes 6 minority (1 American Indian or Alaska Native, non-Hispanic/Latino; 2 Asian, non-Hispanic/Latino; 3 Hispanic/Latino), 15 international. Average age 27. 47 applicants, 55% accepted, 17 enrolled. In 2018, 13 master's, 2 doctorates awarded. *Degree requirements:* For master's, thesis (for some programs); for doctorate, comprehensive exam, thesis/dissertation. *Entrance requirements:* For master's and doctorate, GRE General Test. Additional exam requirements/recommendations for international students: Required—TOEFL (minimum score 88 iBT). *Application deadline:* For fall admission, 2/1 priority date for domestic students. Applications are processed on a rolling basis. Application fee: $65. Electronic applications accepted. *Financial support:* In 2018–19, 8 students received support, including 5 teaching assistantships with full tuition reimbursements available (averaging $15,600 per year); Federal Work-Study, institutionally sponsored loans, tuition waivers (full and partial), and unspecified assistantships also available. Financial award application deadline: 3/1. *Faculty research:* Nutrition education for adults and children, food processing, food safety, sustainable crop and soil management, animal health and nutrition. *Total annual research expenditures:* $2.1 million. *Unit head:* Dr. Sue Erich, Chair, 207-581-2947, Fax: 207-581-2770. *Application contact:* Scott G. Delcourt,

Assistant Vice President for Graduate Studies and Senior Associate Dean, 207-581-3291, Fax: 207-581-3232, E-mail: graduate@maine.edu.
Website: https://umaine.edu/foodandagriculture/graduate-programs/

University of Manitoba, Faculty of Graduate Studies, Faculty of Agricultural and Food Sciences, Department of Plant Science, Winnipeg, MB R3T 2N2, Canada. Offers agronomy and plant protection (M Sc, PhD); horticulture (M Sc, PhD); plant breeding and genetics (M Sc, PhD); plant physiology-biochemistry (M Sc, PhD). *Degree requirements:* For master's, thesis; for doctorate, one foreign language, thesis/dissertation.

University of Maryland, College Park, Academic Affairs, College of Agriculture and Natural Resources, Department of Plant Science and Landscape Architecture, Plant Science Program, College Park, MD 20742. Offers MS, PhD. *Entrance requirements:* For doctorate, GRE General Test. Additional exam requirements/recommendations for international students: Required—TOEFL. Electronic applications accepted. *Faculty research:* Mineral nutrition, genetics and breeding, chemical growth, histochemistry, postharvest physiology.

University of Missouri, Office of Research and Graduate Studies, College of Agriculture, Food and Natural Resources, Division of Plant Sciences, Columbia, MO 65211. Offers crop, soil and pest management (MS, PhD); entomology (MS, PhD); horticulture (MS, PhD); plant breeding, genetics and genomics (MS, PhD); plant stress biology (MS, PhD). Terminal master's awarded for partial completion of doctoral program. *Degree requirements:* For master's, thesis; for doctorate, comprehensive exam, thesis/dissertation. *Entrance requirements:* For master's and doctorate, GRE General Test, minimum GPA of 3.0; bachelor's degree from accredited college. Additional exam requirements/recommendations for international students: Required—TOEFL (minimum score 500 paper-based; 61 iBT), IELTS (minimum score 5.5). Electronic applications accepted. *Faculty research:* Crop, soil and pest management; entomology; horticulture; plant biology and genetics; plant microbiology and pathology.

University of Nebraska–Lincoln, Graduate College, College of Agricultural Sciences and Natural Resources, Department of Agronomy and Horticulture, Program in Horticulture, Lincoln, NE 68588. Offers MS, PhD. *Degree requirements:* For master's, thesis optional. *Entrance requirements:* For master's, GRE General Test. Additional exam requirements/recommendations for international students: Required—TOEFL (minimum score 600 paper-based). Electronic applications accepted. *Faculty research:* Horticultural crops: production, management, cultural, and ecological aspects; tissue and cell culture; plant nutrition and anatomy; postharvest physiology and ecology.

University of Puerto Rico–Mayagüez, Graduate Studies, College of Agricultural Sciences, Department of Crops and Agroenvironmental Sciences, Mayagüez, PR 00681-9000. Offers agronomy (MS); crop protection (MS); horticulture (MS); soils (MS). *Program availability:* Part-time. *Degree requirements:* For master's, comprehensive exam, thesis. Electronic applications accepted. *Faculty research:* Ecology of tropical forests, population dynamics, processing and sensing analysis of food, physiology of plants, phytopathology.

University of South Africa, College of Agriculture and Environmental Sciences, Pretoria, South Africa. Offers agriculture (MS); consumer science (MCS); environmental management (MA, MS, PhD); environmental science (MA, MS, PhD); geography (MA, MS, PhD); horticulture (M Tech); human ecology (MHE); life sciences (MS); nature conservation (M Tech).

University of Vermont, Graduate College, College of Agriculture and Life Sciences, Department of Plant and Soil Science, Burlington, VT 05405. Offers agroecology (Graduate Certificate); plant and soil science (MS, PhD), including agroecology, agronomy (MS), ecological landscape design, entomology, horticulture (MS), plant pathology (MS), soil science. *Degree requirements:* For master's, thesis; for doctorate, one foreign language, thesis/dissertation. *Entrance requirements:* For master's and doctorate, GRE General Test. Additional exam requirements/recommendations for international students: Required—TOEFL (minimum score 550 paper-based; 90 iBT), IELTS (minimum score 6.5). Electronic applications accepted. *Faculty research:* Soil chemistry, plant nutrition.

University of Washington, Graduate School, College of the Environment, School of Environmental and Forest Sciences, Seattle, WA 98195. Offers bioresource science and engineering (MS, PhD); environmental horticulture (MEH); forest ecology (MS, PhD); forest management (MFR); forest soils (MS, PhD); restoration ecology (MS, PhD); restoration ecology and environmental horticulture (MS, PhD); social sciences (MS, PhD); sustainable resource management (MS, PhD); wildlife science (MS, PhD); MFR/MAIS; MPA/MS. *Accreditation:* SAF. *Program availability:* Part-time. *Degree requirements:* For master's, thesis; for doctorate, comprehensive exam, thesis/dissertation. *Entrance requirements:* For master's and doctorate, GRE, minimum GPA of 3.0. Additional exam requirements/recommendations for international students: Required—TOEFL. Electronic applications accepted. *Faculty research:* Ecosystem analysis, silviculture and forest protection, paper science and engineering, environmental horticulture and urban forestry, natural resource policy and economics, restoration ecology and environment horticulture, conservation, human dimensions, wildlife, bioresource science and engineering.

University of Wisconsin–Madison, Graduate School, College of Agricultural and Life Sciences, Department of Horticulture, Madison, WI 53706-1380. Offers MS, PhD. *Program availability:* Part-time. Terminal master's awarded for partial completion of doctoral program. *Degree requirements:* For master's, comprehensive exam, thesis (for some programs); for doctorate, comprehensive exam, thesis/dissertation. *Entrance requirements:* For master's and doctorate, minimum GPA of 3.0. Additional exam requirements/recommendations for international students: Required—TOEFL (minimum score 580 paper-based). Electronic applications accepted. *Faculty research:* Biotechnology, crop breeding/genetics, environmental physiology, crop management, cytogenetics.

Utah State University, School of Graduate Studies, College of Agriculture and Applied Sciences, Department of Plants, Soils and Climate, Logan, UT 84322. Offers climate sciences (MS, PhD); ecology (MS, PhD); horticulture (MPS); plant science (MS, PhD); soil science (MS, PhD). *Program availability:* Part-time. Terminal master's awarded for partial completion of doctoral program. *Degree requirements:* For master's, thesis; for doctorate, thesis/dissertation. *Entrance requirements:* For master's, GRE General Test, BS in plant, soil, atmospheric science, or related field; minimum GPA of 3.0; for doctorate, GRE General Test, minimum GPA of 3.0. Additional exam requirements/recommendations for international students: Required—TOEFL. Electronic applications accepted. *Faculty research:* Biotechnology and genomics, plant physiology and biology, nutrient and water efficient landscapes, physical-chemical-biological processes in soil, environmental biophysics and climate.

Virginia Polytechnic Institute and State University, Graduate School, College of Agriculture and Life Sciences, Blacksburg, VA 24061. Offers agricultural and applied economics (MS, PhD); agricultural and life sciences (MS); agriculture, leadership, and community education (MS, PhD); animal and poultry science (MS, PhD); biochemistry (MS, PhD); crop and soil environmental sciences (MS, PhD); dairy science (MS, PhD); entomology (MS, PhD); food science and technology (MS, PhD); horticulture (PhD); human nutrition, foods and exercise (MS, PhD); plant pathology, physiology, and weed science (MS, PhD). *Faculty:* 244 full-time (79 women), 1 (woman) part-time/adjunct. *Students:* 360 full-time (195 women), 110 part-time (73 women); includes 70 minority (24 Black or African American, non-Hispanic/Latino; 1 American Indian or Alaska Native, non-Hispanic/Latino; 15 Asian, non-Hispanic/Latino; 12 Hispanic/Latino; 18 Two or more races, non-Hispanic/Latino), 110 international. Average age 28. 296 applicants, 54% accepted, 105 enrolled. In 2018, 92 master's, 59 doctorates awarded. *Degree requirements:* For master's, comprehensive exam (for some programs), thesis (for some programs); for doctorate, comprehensive exam (for some programs), thesis/dissertation (for some programs). *Entrance requirements:* For master's and doctorate, GRE/GMAT. Additional exam requirements/recommendations for international students: Required—TOEFL (minimum score 90 iBT). *Application deadline:* For fall admission, 8/1 for domestic students, 4/1 for international students; for spring admission, 1/1 for domestic students, 9/1 for international students. Applications are processed on a rolling basis. Application fee: $75. Electronic applications accepted. *Expenses:* Tuition, state resident: full-time $15,510; part-time $739.50 per credit hour. Tuition, nonresident: full-time $29,629; part-time $1490.25 per credit hour. *Required fees:* $2804; $550 per semester. Tuition and fees vary according to course load, campus/location and program. *Financial support:* In 2018–19, 3 fellowships with full tuition reimbursements (averaging $25,731 per year), 249 research assistantships with full tuition reimbursements (averaging $19,826 per year), 105 teaching assistantships with full tuition reimbursements (averaging $19,277 per year) were awarded; scholarships/grants and unspecified assistantships also available. Financial award application deadline: 3/1; financial award applicants required to submit FAFSA. *Total annual research expenditures:* $42.4 million. *Unit head:* Dr. Alan L. Grant, Dean, 540-231-4152, Fax: 540-231-4163, E-mail: algrant@vt.edu. *Application contact:* Crystal Tawney, Administrative Assistant, 540-231-4152, Fax: 540-231-4163, E-mail: cdtawney@vt.edu.
Website: http://www.cals.vt.edu/

Washington State University, College of Agricultural, Human, and Natural Resource Sciences, Department of Horticulture, Pullman, WA 99164. Offers MS, PhD. Programs offered at the Pullman campus. *Program availability:* Part-time. *Degree requirements:* For master's, comprehensive exam (for some programs), thesis (for some programs), oral exam; for doctorate, comprehensive exam, thesis/dissertation, oral exam, written exam. *Entrance requirements:* For master's and doctorate, GRE General Test, GRE Subject Test, minimum GPA of 3.0, 3 letters of recommendation, statement of purpose/intent. Additional exam requirements/recommendations for international students: Required—TOEFL (minimum score 550 paper-based). Electronic applications accepted. *Faculty research:* Post-harvest physiology, genetics/plant breeding, molecular biology.

West Virginia University, Davis College of Agriculture, Forestry and Consumer Sciences, Morgantown, WV 26506. Offers agricultural and extension education (MS, PhD); agriculture and resource management (MS); agriculture, natural resources and design (M Agr); agronomy (MS); animal and food science (PhD); animal physiology (MS); applied and environmental microbiology (MS); design and merchandising (MS); entomology (MS); forest resource science (PhD); forestry (MSF); genetics and developmental biology (MS, PhD); horticulture (MS); human and community development (PhD), landscape architecture (MLA); natural resource economics (PhD); nutritional and food science (MS); plant and soil science (PhD); plant pathology (MS); recreation, parks and tourism resources (MS); reproductive physiology (MS, PhD); wildlife and fisheries resources (PhD). *Accreditation:* ASLA. *Program availability:* Part-time. *Students:* 188 full-time (86 women), 47 part-time (30 women); includes 22 minority (5 Black or African American, non-Hispanic/Latino; 5 Asian, non-Hispanic/Latino; 8 Hispanic/Latino; 4 Two or more races, non-Hispanic/Latino), 60 international. In 2018, 56 master's, 14 doctorates awarded. *Degree requirements:* For master's, thesis; for doctorate, thesis/dissertation. *Entrance requirements:* Additional exam requirements/recommendations for international students: Required—TOEFL (minimum score 550 paper-based). *Application deadline:* For fall admission, 6/1 priority date for domestic students, 6/1 for international students; for spring admission, 1/5 for domestic and international students. Applications are processed on a rolling basis. Application fee: $60. Electronic applications accepted. *Financial support:* Fellowships, research assistantships, teaching assistantships, career-related internships or fieldwork, Federal Work-Study, institutionally sponsored loans, tuition waivers (full and partial), and unspecified assistantships available. Financial award application deadline: 2/1; financial award applicants required to submit FAFSA. *Faculty research:* Reproductive physiology, soil and water quality, human nutrition, aquaculture, wildlife management. *Unit head:* Dr. Ken Blemings, Interim Dean, 304-293-2395, Fax: 304-293-3740, E-mail: ken.blemings@mail.wvu.edu. *Application contact:* Dr. J. Todd Petty, Associate Dean, 304-293-2278, Fax: 304-293-3740, E-mail: jtpetty@mail.wvu.edu.
Website: https://www.davis.wvu.edu

Plant Sciences

Alabama Agricultural and Mechanical University, School of Graduate Studies, College of Agricultural, Life and Natural Sciences, Department of Biological and Environmental Sciences, Huntsville, AL 35811. Offers biology (MS); plant and soil science (MS, PhD). *Program availability:* Evening/weekend. Terminal master's awarded for partial completion of doctoral program. *Degree requirements:* For master's, thesis optional; for doctorate, one foreign language, thesis/dissertation optional. *Entrance requirements:* For master's, GRE General Test, BS in agriculture; for doctorate, GRE General Test, master's degree. Additional exam requirements/recommendations for international students: Required—TOEFL (minimum score 500 paper-based; 61 iBT). Electronic applications accepted. *Faculty research:* Plant breeding, cytogenetics, crop production, soil chemistry and fertility, remote sensing.

Plant Sciences

American University of Beirut, Graduate Programs, Faculty of Agricultural and Food Sciences, Beirut, Lebanon. Offers agricultural economics (MS); animal science (MS); ecosystem management (MSES); food safety (MS); food security (MS); food technology (MS); irrigation (MS); nutrition (MS); plant protection (MS); plant science (MS); poultry science (MS); public health nutrition (MS); rural community development (MS). *Program availability:* Part-time. *Faculty:* 24 full-time (4 women). *Students:* 30 full-time (22 women), 90 part-time (69 women); includes 9 minority (all Black or African American, non-Hispanic/Latino). Average age 25. 238 applicants, 77% accepted, 37 enrolled. In 2018, 19 master's awarded. *Degree requirements:* For master's, one foreign language, comprehensive exam, thesis (for some programs). *Entrance requirements:* Additional exam requirements/recommendations for international students: Required—TOEFL (minimum score 600 paper-based; 100 iBT), IELTS (minimum score 7.5). *Application deadline:* For fall admission, 2/10 for domestic and international students; for spring admission, 11/2 for domestic and international students. Application fee: $50. Electronic applications accepted. *Expenses: Tuition:* Full-time $17,748; part-time $986 per credit. *Required fees:* $762. Tuition and fees vary according to course load and program. *Financial support:* In 2018–19, 2 fellowships with full and partial tuition reimbursements (averaging $11,637 per year), 12 research assistantships with full and partial tuition reimbursements (averaging $3,840 per year), 73 teaching assistantships with full and partial tuition reimbursements were awarded; scholarships/grants, health care benefits, and unspecified assistantships also available. Financial award application deadline: 2/2. *Faculty research:* Plant science; animal science; landscape for culture and socio-ecological health; diet, obesity and non communicable diseases; water, agriculture, ecosystem & remote sensing; water-energy-food-health nexus. *Total annual research expenditures:* $1.2 million. *Unit head:* Prof. Rabi Hassan Mohtar, Dean of Faculty of Agricultural and Food Sciences, 961-1-350000 Ext. 4400, Fax: 961-1-744460, E-mail: mohtar@aub.edu.lb. *Application contact:* Prof. Zaher Dawy, Associate Provost, 961-1-374374 Ext. 4386, Fax: 961-1-374374, E-mail: graduate.council@aub.edu.lb.
Website: http://www.aub.edu.lb/fafs/pages/default.aspx

Brigham Young University, Graduate Studies, College of Life Sciences, Department of Plant and Wildlife Sciences, Provo, UT 84602-1001. Offers environmental science (MS); genetics and biotechnology (MS); wildlife and wildlands conservation (MS, PhD). *Faculty:* 24 full-time (1 woman). *Students:* 12 full-time (7 women), 42 part-time (12 women); includes 2 minority (both Hispanic/Latino). Average age 30. 29 applicants, 59% accepted, 17 enrolled. In 2018, 18 master's, 1 doctorate awarded. *Degree requirements:* For master's, thesis, no C grades or below, 30 hours (24 coursework, 6 thesis); for doctorate, comprehensive exam, thesis/dissertation, no C grades or below, 54 hours (18 dissertation, 36 coursework). *Entrance requirements:* For master's, GRE General Test, minimum GPA of 3.2; for doctorate, GRE, minimum GPA of 3.2. Additional exam requirements/recommendations for international students: Required—TOEFL (minimum score 580 paper-based; 85 iBT). *Application deadline:* 2/1 for domestic and international students; for summer admission, 2/1 for domestic and international students. Application fee: $50. Electronic applications accepted. *Financial support:* In 2018–19, 54 students received support, including 71 research assistantships with partial tuition reimbursements available (averaging $18,081 per year), 42 teaching assistantships with partial tuition reimbursements available (averaging $16,478 per year); scholarships/grants and tuition waivers (partial) also available. Financial award application deadline: 3/1. *Faculty research:* Environmental science, plant genetics, plant ecology, plant nutrition and pathology, wildlife and wildlands conservation. *Total annual research expenditures:* $2.1 million. *Unit head:* Neil Hansen, Chair, 801-422-2491, E-mail: neil_hansen@byu.edu. *Application contact:* Bradley D. Geary, Graduate Coordinator, 801-422-1228, Fax: 801-422-0008, E-mail: bradley_geary@byu.edu.
Website: http://pws.byu.edu

California State University, Fresno, Division of Research and Graduate Studies, Jordan College of Agricultural Sciences and Technology, Department of Plant Science, Fresno, CA 93740-8027. Offers MS. *Program availability:* Part-time. *Degree requirements:* For master's, thesis. *Entrance requirements:* For master's, GRE General Test, minimum GPA of 2.5. Additional exam requirements/recommendations for international students: Required—TOEFL. Electronic applications accepted. *Faculty research:* Crop patterns, small watershed management, electronic monitoring of feedlot cattle, disease control, dairy operations.

Colorado State University, College of Agricultural Sciences, Department of Soil and Crop Sciences, Fort Collins, CO 80523-1170. Offers MS, PhD. *Program availability:* Part-time. Terminal master's awarded for partial completion of doctoral program. *Degree requirements:* For master's, thesis; for doctorate, comprehensive exam, teaching/dissertation. *Entrance requirements:* For master's and doctorate, GRE. Additional exam requirements/recommendations for international students: Required—TOEFL (minimum score 550 paper-based), IELTS (minimum score 6.5). Electronic applications accepted. *Expenses:* Tuition, state resident: full-time $10,520; part-time $4675 per credit hour. Tuition, nonresident: full-time $25,791; part-time $11,462 per credit hour. *International tuition:* $25,791 full-time. *Required fees:* $2392; $576 $288. Tuition and fees vary according to course level, course load, degree level, program and student level. *Faculty research:* Agroecosystem management, plant breeding and genetics, soil science.

Cornell University, Graduate School, Graduate Fields of Agriculture and Life Sciences, Field of Plant Breeding, Ithaca, NY 14853. Offers plant breeding (MPS, MS, PhD); plant genetics (MPS, MS, PhD). Terminal master's awarded for partial completion of doctoral program. *Degree requirements:* For master's, thesis (MS), project paper (MPS); for doctorate, comprehensive exam, thesis/dissertation. *Entrance requirements:* For master's and doctorate, GRE General Test, GRE Subject Test (recommended), 3 letters of recommendation. Additional exam requirements/recommendations for international students: Required—TOEFL (minimum score 550 paper-based; 77 iBT). Electronic applications accepted. *Faculty research:* Crop breeding for improved yield, stress resistance and quality; genetics and genomics of crop plants; applications of molecular biology and bioinformatics to crop improvement; genetic diversity and utilization of wild germplasm; international agriculture.

Cornell University, Graduate School, Graduate Fields of Agriculture and Life Sciences, Field of Plant Protection, Ithaca, NY 14853. Offers MPS. *Degree requirements:* For master's, internship, final exam. *Entrance requirements:* For master's, GRE General Test, 3 letters of recommendation. Additional exam requirements/recommendations for international students: Required—TOEFL (minimum score 550 paper-based; 77 iBT). Electronic applications accepted. *Faculty research:* Fruit and vegetable crop insects and diseases, systems modeling, biological control, plant protection economics, integrated pest management.

Delaware State University, Graduate Programs, Department of Agriculture and Natural Resources, Program in Plant Science, Dover, DE 19901-2277. Offers MS. *Entrance requirements:* For master's, GRE. Additional exam requirements/recommendations for international students: Required—TOEFL (minimum score 550 paper-based).

Illinois State University, Graduate School, College of Arts and Sciences, School of Biological Sciences, Normal, IL 61790. Offers animal behavior (MS); bacteriology (MS); biochemistry (MS); biological sciences (MS); biology (PhD); biophysics (MS); biotechnology (MS); botany (MS, PhD); cell biology (MS); conservation biology (MS); developmental biology (MS); ecology (MS, PhD); entomology (MS); evolutionary biology (MS); genetics (MS, PhD); immunology (MS); microbiology (MS, PhD); molecular biology (MS); molecular genetics (MS); neurobiology (MS); neuroscience (MS); parasitology (MS); physiology (MS, PhD); plant biology (MS); plant molecular biology (MS); plant sciences (MS); structural biology (MS); zoology (MS, PhD). *Program availability:* Part-time. *Faculty:* 27 full-time (8 women), 7 part-time/adjunct (4 women). *Students:* 48 full-time (29 women), 15 part-time (12 women); includes 11 minority (2 Black or African American, non-Hispanic/Latino; 1 Asian, non-Hispanic/Latino; 4 Hispanic/Latino; 4 Two or more races, non-Hispanic/Latino), 6 international. Average age 26. 58 applicants, 40% accepted, 13 enrolled. In 2018, 15 master's, 6 doctorates awarded. *Degree requirements:* For master's, thesis or alternative; for doctorate, variable foreign language requirement, thesis/dissertation, 2 terms of residency. *Entrance requirements:* For master's, GRE General Test, minimum GPA of 2.6 in last 60 hours of course work; for doctorate, GRE General Test. *Application deadline:* Applications are processed on a rolling basis. Application fee: $40. *Expenses: Tuition, area resident:* Full-time $7264.62. Tuition, state resident: full-time $9466. Tuition, nonresident: full-time $17,290. *International tuition:* $15,089.40 full-time. *Required fees:* $1481.04. *Financial support:* In 2018–19, 5 research assistantships, 49 teaching assistantships were awarded; Federal Work-Study, tuition waivers (full), and unspecified assistantships also available. Financial award application deadline: 4/1. *Faculty research:* Redoc balance and drug development in schistosoma mansoni, control of the growth of listeria monocytogenes at low temperature, regulation of cell expansion and microtubule function by SPRI, CRUI: physiology and fitness consequences of different life history phenotypes. *Unit head:* Dr. Craig Gatto, School Director, 309-438-3087, E-mail: cgatto@IllinoisState.edu. *Application contact:* Dr. Ben Sadd, Assistant Chair for Graduate Studies, 309-438-2651, E-mail: bmsadd@IllinoisState.edu.
Website: http://www.bio.ilstu.edu/

Iowa State University of Science and Technology, Program in Plant Breeding, Ames, IA 50011. Offers MS, PhD. *Degree requirements:* For master's, thesis optional. *Entrance requirements:* For master's and doctorate, GRE. Additional exam requirements/recommendations for international students: Required—TOEFL (minimum score 550 paper-based; 79 iBT), IELTS (minimum score 6.5). Electronic applications accepted.

Kansas State University, Graduate School, College of Agriculture, Department of Agronomy, Manhattan, KS 66506. Offers crop science (MS, PhD); grassland management (Certificate); plant breeding and genetics (MS, PhD); range and forage science (MS, PhD); soil and environmental science (MS, PhD); weed science (MS, PhD). *Program availability:* Part-time. *Degree requirements:* For master's, thesis or alternative, oral exam; for doctorate, thesis/dissertation, preliminary exams. *Entrance requirements:* For master's, minimum GPA of 3.0 in BS; for doctorate, minimum GPA of 3.0 in master's program. Additional exam requirements/recommendations for international students: Required—TOEFL (minimum score 79 iBT). Electronic applications accepted. *Expenses:* Contact institution. *Faculty research:* Range and forage science; soil and environmental science; weed science; plant breeding and genetics; crop physiology, ecology and production.

McGill University, Faculty of Graduate and Postdoctoral Studies, Faculty of Agricultural and Environmental Sciences, Department of Plant Science, Montréal, QC H3A 2T5, Canada. Offers M Sc, M Sc A, PhD, Certificate.

Michigan State University, The Graduate School, College of Agriculture and Natural Resources, Program in Plant Breeding and Genetics, East Lansing, MI 48824. Offers MS, PhD. *Entrance requirements:* Additional exam requirements/recommendations for international students: Required—TOEFL. Electronic applications accepted. *Faculty research:* Applied plant breeding and genetics; disease, insect and herbicide resistances; gene isolation and genomics; abiotic stress factors; molecular mapping.

Michigan State University, The Graduate School, College of Natural Science, MSU-DOE Plant Research Laboratory, East Lansing, MI 48824. Offers biochemistry and molecular biology (PhD); cellular and molecular biology (PhD); crop and soil sciences (PhD); genetics (PhD); microbiology and molecular genetics (PhD); plant biology (PhD); plant physiology (PhD). Offered jointly with the Department of Energy. *Degree requirements:* For doctorate, comprehensive exam, thesis/dissertation, laboratory rotation, defense of dissertation. *Entrance requirements:* For doctorate, GRE General Test, acceptance into one of the affiliated department programs; 3 letters of recommendation; bachelor's degree or equivalent in life sciences, chemistry, biochemistry, or biophysics; research experience. Electronic applications accepted. *Faculty research:* Role of hormones in the regulation of plant development and physiology, molecular mechanisms associated with signal recognition, development and application of genetic methods and materials, protein routing and function.

Mississippi State University, College of Agriculture and Life Sciences, Department of Plant and Soil Sciences, Mississippi State, MS 39762. Offers weed science (MS, PhD), including agronomy, horticulture, weed science. *Faculty:* 43 full-time (6 women). *Students:* 47 full-time (16 women), 32 part-time (9 women); includes 3 minority (all Black or African American, non-Hispanic/Latino), 21 international. Average age 29. 21 applicants, 43% accepted, 9 enrolled. In 2018, 18 master's, 11 doctorates awarded. *Degree requirements:* For master's, comprehensive exam, thesis, oral and/or written exams; for doctorate, comprehensive exam, thesis/dissertation, minimum of 20 semester hours of research for dissertation. *Entrance requirements:* For master's, GRE (for weed science), minimum GPA of 2.75 (agronomy/horticulture), 3.0 (weed science); for doctorate, GRE (for weed science), minimum GPA of 3.0 (agronomy/horticulture), 3.25 (weed science). Additional exam requirements/recommendations for international students: Required—TOEFL (minimum score 500 paper-based; 61 iBT), TOEFL minimum score 550 paper-based, 79 iBT or IELTS minimum score 6.5 (for weed science); Recommended—IELTS (minimum score 5.5). *Application deadline:* For fall admission, 7/1 for domestic students, 5/1 for international students; for spring admission, 10/1 for domestic students, 9/1 for international students. Applications are processed on a rolling basis. Application fee: $60 ($80 for international students). Electronic applications accepted. *Expenses:* Tuition, state resident: full-time $8450; part-time $360.59 per credit hour. Tuition, nonresident: full-time $23,140; part-time $969.09 per credit hour. *Required fees:* $110. One-time fee: $55 full-time. Part-time tuition and fees vary according to course load, degree level, campus/location and reciprocity agreements. *Financial support:* In 2018–19, 40 research assistantships with full tuition reimbursements (averaging $15,736 per year), 4 teaching assistantships with partial tuition reimbursements (averaging $14,888 per year) were awarded; Federal Work-Study, institutionally sponsored loans, scholarships/grants, and unspecified assistantships also available. Financial award application deadline: 4/1; financial award applicants required to submit FAFSA. *Faculty research:* Bioenergy crops, cotton breeding, environmental plant pathology, row crop weed control, genomics. *Unit head:* Dr. J. Michael Phillips, Professor and Head, 662-325-2311, Fax: 662-325-8742, E-mail: jmp657@msstate.edu. *Application contact:* Ryan King, Admissions and Enrollment Assistant, 662-325-8951, E-mail: rjk101@grad.msstate.edu.
Website: http://www.pss.msstate.edu/

Missouri State University, Graduate College, Darr College of Agriculture, Springfield, MO 65897. Offers plant science (MS); secondary education (MS Ed), including agriculture. *Program availability:* Part-time. *Faculty:* 16 full-time (5 women), 1 part-time/adjunct (0 women). *Students:* 22 full-time (9 women), 32 part-time (17 women); includes 3 minority (1 American Indian or Alaska Native, non-Hispanic/Latino; 2 Two or more races, non-Hispanic/Latino). Average age 23. 24 applicants, 42% accepted. In 2018, 21 master's awarded. *Degree requirements:* For master's, comprehensive exam, thesis or alternative. *Entrance requirements:* For master's, GRE (MS in plant science, MNAS), 9-12 teacher certification (MS Ed), minimum GPA of 3.0 (MS plant science, MNAS). Additional exam requirements/recommendations for international students: Required—TOEFL (minimum score 550 paper-based; 79 iBT), IELTS (minimum score 6). *Application deadline:* For fall admission, 7/20 priority date for domestic students, 5/1 for international students; for spring admission, 12/20 priority date for domestic students, 9/1 for international students; for summer admission, 5/20 priority date for domestic students. Applications are processed on a rolling basis. Application fee: $55 ($60 for international students). Electronic applications accepted. Tuition and fees vary according to class time, course level, course load, degree level, campus/location, program and student level. *Financial support:* In 2018–19, 7 research assistantships with full tuition reimbursements (averaging $9,365 per year), 6 teaching assistantships with full tuition reimbursements (averaging $8,450 per year) were awarded; Federal Work-Study, institutionally sponsored loans, scholarships/grants, and unspecified assistantships also available. Financial award application deadline: 1/31; financial award applicants required to submit FAFSA. *Faculty research:* Grapevine biotechnology, agricultural marketing, Asian elephant reproduction, poultry science, integrated pest management. *Unit head:* Dr. Ronald Del Vecchio, Dean, 417-836-5050, E-mail: darr@missouristate.edu. *Application contact:* Lakan Drinker, Director, Graduate Enrollment Management, 417-836-5330, Fax: 417-836-6200, E-mail: lakandrinker@missouristate.edu.
Website: http://ag.missouristate.edu/

Montana State University, The Graduate School, College of Agriculture, Department of Plant Sciences and Plant Pathology, Bozeman, MT 59717. Offers plant pathology (MS); plant sciences (MS, PhD), including plant genetics (PhD), plant pathology (PhD). *Program availability:* Part-time. *Degree requirements:* For master's, comprehensive exam; for doctorate, comprehensive exam, thesis/dissertation. *Entrance requirements:* For master's, GRE General Test, minimum GPA of 3.0; for doctorate, GRE General Test. Additional exam requirements/recommendations for international students: Required—TOEFL (minimum score 550 paper-based). Electronic applications accepted. *Faculty research:* Plant genetics, plant metabolism, plant microbe interactions, plant pathology, entomology research.

North Carolina Agricultural and Technical State University, The Graduate College, College of Agriculture and Environmental Sciences, Department of Natural Resources and Environmental Design, Greensboro, NC 27411. Offers plant, soil and environmental science (MS). *Program availability:* Part-time, evening/weekend. *Degree requirements:* For master's, comprehensive exam, thesis optional, qualifying exam. *Entrance requirements:* For master's, GRE General Test, minimum GPA of 3.0. *Faculty research:* Soil parameters and compaction of forest site, controlled traffic effects on soil, improving soybean and vegetable crops.

North Dakota State University, College of Graduate and Interdisciplinary Studies, College of Agriculture, Food Systems, and Natural Resources, Department of Plant Sciences, Fargo, ND 58102. Offers horticulture (MS); plant sciences (MS, PhD). *Program availability:* Part-time. *Entrance requirements:* Additional exam requirements/recommendations for international students: Required—TOEFL (minimum score 525 paper-based; 71 iBT). Electronic applications accepted. *Faculty research:* Biotechnology, weed control science, plant breeding, plant genetics, crop physiology.

The Ohio State University, Graduate School, Center for Applied Plant Sciences, Columbus, OH 43210. Offers PhD. *Students:* 9 full-time (5 women). Average age 27. In 2018, 3 doctorates awarded. *Degree requirements:* For doctorate, thesis/dissertation. *Entrance requirements:* Additional exam requirements/recommendations for international students: Required—TOEFL (minimum score 550 paper-based; 79 iBT), IELTS (minimum score 7), Michigan English Language Assessment Battery (minimum score 82). *Application deadline:* For fall admission, 11/15 priority date for domestic and international students. Applications are processed on a rolling basis. Application fee: $60 ($70 for international students). Electronic applications accepted. *Financial support:* Fellowships with tuition reimbursements and research assistantships with tuition reimbursements available. *Unit head:* Dr. Thomas Mitchell, Graduate Studies Committee Chair, 614-292-1728, E-mail: mitchell.815@osu.edu. *Application contact:* Graduate and Professional Admissions, 614-292-9444, Fax: 614-292-3895, E-mail: gpadmissions@osu.edu.
Website: http://tpsgp.osu.edu/

Oklahoma State University, College of Agricultural Science and Natural Resources, Department of Plant and Soil Sciences, Stillwater, OK 74078. Offers crop science (PhD); plant and soil sciences (MS); soil science (M Ag). *Faculty:* 27 full-time (4 women). *Students:* 14 full-time (5 women), 42 part-time (16 women); includes 5 minority (3 Black or African American, non-Hispanic/Latino; 1 Hispanic/Latino; 1 Two or more races, non-Hispanic/Latino), 29 international. Average age 28. 15 applicants, 33% accepted, 5 enrolled. In 2018, 11 master's, 7 doctorates awarded. *Entrance requirements:* For master's and doctorate, GRE or GMAT. Additional exam requirements/recommendations for international students: Required—TOEFL (minimum score 550 paper-based; 79 iBT). *Application deadline:* For fall admission, 3/1 priority date for international students; for spring admission, 8/1 priority date for international students. Applications are processed on a rolling basis. Application fee: $40 ($75 for international students). Electronic applications accepted. *Expenses: Tuition, area resident:* Full-time $4148. Tuition, state resident: full-time $4148. Tuition, nonresident: full-time $10,517. *International tuition:* $10,517 full-time. *Required fees:* $4394; $2929 per credit hour. Tuition and fees vary according to course load and program. *Financial support:* Research assistantships, teaching assistantships, career-related internships or fieldwork, Federal Work-Study, scholarships/grants, health care benefits, tuition waivers (partial), and unspecified assistantships available. Support available to part-time students. Financial award application deadline: 3/1; financial award applicants required to submit FAFSA. *Faculty research:* Crop science, weed science, rangeland ecology and management, biotechnology, breeding and genetics. *Unit head:* Dr. Jeff Edwards, Department Head, 405-744-6130, Fax: 405-744-0354, E-mail: jeff.edwards@okstate.edu. *Application contact:* Dr. Sheryl Tucker, Dean, 405-744-6368, Fax: 405-744-0355, E-mail: gradi@okstate.edu.
Website: http://pss.okstate.edu

Penn State University Park, Graduate School, College of Agricultural Sciences, Department of Plant Science, University Park, PA 16802. Offers agronomy (MS, PhD); horticulture (MS, PhD).

Purdue University, Graduate School, PULSe - Purdue University Life Sciences Program, West Lafayette, IN 47907. Offers biomolecular structure and biophysics (PhD); biotechnology (PhD); chemical biology (PhD); chromatin and regulation of gene expression (PhD); integrative neuroscience (PhD); integrative plant sciences (PhD); membrane biology (PhD); microbiology (PhD); molecular evolutionary and cancer biology (PhD); molecular evolutionary genetics (PhD); molecular virology (PhD). *Students:* 43 full-time (24 women); includes 8 minority (1 Black or African American, non-Hispanic/Latino; 2 Asian, non-Hispanic/Latino; 2 Hispanic/Latino; 3 Two or more races, non-Hispanic/Latino), 25 international. Average age 25. 181 applicants, 25% accepted, 17 enrolled. *Entrance requirements:* For doctorate, GRE, minimum undergraduate GPA of 3.0. Additional exam requirements/recommendations for international students: Required—TOEFL (minimum score 550 paper-based; 77 iBT). *Application deadline:* For fall admission, 1/15 priority date for domestic and international students. Applications are processed on a rolling basis. Application fee: $60 ($75 for international students). Electronic applications accepted. *Financial support:* In 2018–19, research assistantships with tuition reimbursements (averaging $22,500 per year), teaching assistantships with tuition reimbursements (averaging $22,500 per year) were awarded. *Unit head:* Dr. Jason R. Cannon, Head of the Graduate Program, 765-494-0794, E-mail: cannonjr@purdue.edu. *Application contact:* Lindsey Springer, Graduate Contact for Admissions, 765-496-9667, E-mail: lbcampbe@purdue.edu.
Website: http://www.gradschool.purdue.edu/pulse

South Dakota State University, Graduate School, College of Agriculture, Food and Environmental Sciences, Department of Agronomy, Horticulture and Plant Science, Brookings, SD 57007. Offers biological sciences (PhD); plant science (MS, PhD). *Degree requirements:* For master's, thesis (for some programs), oral exam; for doctorate, comprehensive exam, thesis/dissertation, preliminary oral and written exams. *Entrance requirements:* Additional exam requirements/recommendations for international students: Required—TOEFL (minimum score 560 paper-based; 83 iBT).

Southern Illinois University Carbondale, Graduate School, College of Agriculture, Department of Plant, Soil, and General Agriculture, Carbondale, IL 62901-4701. Offers MS. *Degree requirements:* For master's, thesis. *Entrance requirements:* For master's, minimum GPA of 2.7. Additional exam requirements/recommendations for international students: Required—TOEFL. *Faculty research:* Herbicides, fertilizers, agriculture education, landscape design, plant breeding.

State University of New York College of Environmental Science and Forestry, Department of Environmental and Forest Biology, Syracuse, NY 13210-2779. Offers applied ecology (MPS); chemical ecology (MPS, MS, PhD); conservation biology (MPS, MS, PhD); ecology (MPS, MS, PhD); entomology (MPS, MS, PhD); environmental interpretation (MPS, MS, PhD); environmental physiology (MPS, MS, PhD); fish and wildlife biology and management (MPS, MS, PhD); forest pathology and mycology (MPS, MS, PhD); plant biotechnology (MPS); plant science and biotechnology (MPS, MS, PhD). *Program availability:* Part-time. *Faculty:* 35 full-time (10 women), 4 part-time/adjunct (3 women). *Students:* 107 full-time (57 women), 21 part-time (8 women); includes 9 minority (6 American Indian or Alaska Native, non-Hispanic/Latino; 2 Asian, non-Hispanic/Latino; 1 Hispanic/Latino), 18 international. Average age 30. 79 applicants, 49% accepted, 24 enrolled. In 2018, 30 master's, 3 doctorates awarded. Terminal master's awarded for partial completion of doctoral program. *Degree requirements:* For master's, thesis (for some programs), capstone seminar; for doctorate, comprehensive exam, thesis/dissertation, capstone seminar. *Entrance requirements:* For master's and doctorate, GRE General Test, minimum GPA of 3.0. Additional exam requirements/recommendations for international students: Required—TOEFL (minimum score 550 paper-based; 80 iBT), IELTS (minimum score 6). *Application deadline:* For fall admission, 2/1 priority date for domestic and international students; for spring admission, 11/1 priority date for domestic and international students. Applications are processed on a rolling basis. Application fee: $60. Electronic applications accepted. *Expenses: Tuition, area resident:* Full-time $11,090; part-time $462 per credit hour. Tuition, state resident: full-time $11,090; part-time $462 per credit hour. Tuition, nonresident: full-time $22,650; part-time $944 per credit hour. *International tuition:* $22,650 full-time. *Required fees:* $1733; $178.58 per credit hour. *Financial support:* In 2018–19, 46 students received support. Unspecified assistantships available. Financial award application deadline: 6/30; financial award applicants required to submit FAFSA. *Faculty research:* Ecology, conservation biology, fish and wildlife biology and management, plant science, entomology. *Total annual research expenditures:* $5.9 million. *Unit head:* Dr. Melissa K. Fierke, Chair, 315-470-6809, Fax: 315-470-6743, E-mail: mkfierke@esf.edu. *Application contact:* Scott Shannon, Associate Provost for Instruction/Dean of the Graduate School, 315-470-6599, E-mail: esfgrad@esf.edu.
Website: http://www.esf.edu/efb/grad/default.asp

Tennessee State University, The School of Graduate Studies and Research, College of Agriculture, Human and Natural Sciences, Nashville, TN 37209-1561. Offers agricultural sciences (MS), including agribusiness, agricultural and extension education, animal science, plant and soil science; biological sciences (MS, PhD); biotechnology (PhD); chemistry (MS). *Program availability:* Part-time, evening/weekend. *Degree requirements:* For master's, thesis. *Entrance requirements:* For master's, GRE General Test, GRE Subject Test, MAT. *Faculty research:* Small farm economics, ornamental horticulture, beef cattle production, rural elderly.

Texas A&M University–Kingsville, College of Graduate Studies, Dick and Mary Lewis Kleberg College of Agriculture, Natural Resources and Human Sciences, Department of Agriculture, Agribusiness, and Environmental Sciences, Program in Plant and Soil Science, Kingsville, TX 78363. Offers MS. *Degree requirements:* For master's, variable foreign language requirement, comprehensive exam, thesis (for some programs). *Entrance requirements:* For master's, GRE (minimum combined Math & Verbal score of 290), MAT, GMAT, minimum GPA of 2.5. Additional exam requirements/recommendations for international students: Required—TOEFL (minimum score 550 paper-based; 79 iBT). Electronic applications accepted.

Texas Tech University, Graduate School, College of Agricultural Sciences and Natural Resources, Department of Plant and Soil Science, Lubbock, TX 79409-2122. Offers horticulture science (MS); plant and soil science (MS, PhD). *Program availability:* Part-time, evening/weekend, 100% online, blended/hybrid learning. *Faculty:* 28 full-time (9 women), 10 part-time/adjunct (3 women). *Students:* 71 full-time (33 women), 41 part-time (12 women); includes 14 minority (3 Asian, non-Hispanic/Latino; 7 Hispanic/Latino; 4 Two or more races, non-Hispanic/Latino), 47 international. Average age 30. 47 applicants, 53% accepted, 20 enrolled. In 2018, 19 master's, 8 doctorates awarded. Terminal master's awarded for partial completion of doctoral program. *Degree requirements:* For master's, comprehensive exam (for some programs), thesis (for some programs); for doctorate, comprehensive exam, thesis/dissertation. *Entrance requirements:* For master's and doctorate, GRE. Additional exam requirements/recommendations for international students: Required—TOEFL (minimum score 550 paper-based; 79 iBT). *Application deadline:* For fall admission, 6/1 priority date for domestic students, 1/15 priority date for international students; for spring admission, 9/1 priority date for domestic students, 6/15 priority date for international students. Applications are processed on a rolling basis. Application fee: $65. Electronic applications accepted. *Expenses:* Contact institution. *Financial support:* In 2018–19,

Peterson's Graduate Programs in the Physical Sciences, Mathematics, Agricultural Sciences, the Environment & Natural Resources 2020

www.petersons.com **287**

101 students received support, including 92 fellowships (averaging $2,907 per year), 58 research assistantships (averaging $16,900 per year), 12 teaching assistantships (averaging $14,673 per year); scholarships/grants, health care benefits, and unspecified assistantships also available. Financial award application deadline: 4/15; financial award applicants required to submit FAFSA. *Faculty research:* Crop protection, crop science, fibers and biopolymers, soil science, horticulture, turf grass science, genetics. *Total annual research expenditures:* $5 million. *Unit head:* Dr. Glen Ritchie, Department Chair and Associate Professor, 806-742-2838, Fax: 806-742-0775, E-mail: glen.ritchie@ttu.edu. *Application contact:* Diann Merriman, Lead Academic Advisor, 806-834-7044, Fax: 806-742-0775, E-mail: diann.merriman@ttu.edu.
Website: www.pssc.ttu.edu

Tuskegee University, Graduate Programs, College of Agriculture, Environment and Nutrition Sciences, Department of Agricultural and Environmental Sciences, Program in Plant and Soil Sciences, Tuskegee, AL 36088. Offers MS. *Degree requirements:* For master's, thesis. *Entrance requirements:* For master's, GRE General Test. Additional exam requirements/recommendations for international students: Required—TOEFL (minimum score 500 paper-based).

The University of Arizona, College of Agriculture and Life Sciences, School of Plant Sciences, Program in Plant Sciences, Tucson, AZ 85721. Offers MS, PhD. *Entrance requirements:* Additional exam requirements/recommendations for international students: Required—TOEFL (minimum score 550 paper-based; 79 iBT). Electronic applications accepted. *Faculty research:* Biochemistry and physiology, biodiversity and evolutionarily biology, cell and developmental biology, controlled environmental agriculture, crop and horticultural management and production, environmental and stress biology.

University of Arkansas, Graduate School, Dale Bumpers College of Agricultural, Food and Life Sciences, Interdepartmental Program in Plant Science, Fayetteville, AR 72701. Offers PhD. *Application deadline:* For fall admission, 8/1 for domestic students, 4/1 for international students; for spring admission, 12/1 for domestic students, 10/1 for international students; for summer admission, 4/15 for domestic students, 3/1 for international students. Applications are processed on a rolling basis. Application fee: $60. Electronic applications accepted. *Financial support:* In 2018–19, 9 research assistantships were awarded; fellowships with tuition reimbursements, teaching assistantships, career-related internships or fieldwork, and Federal Work-Study also available. Support available to part-time students. Financial award application deadline: 4/1; financial award applicants required to submit FAFSA. *Unit head:* Dr. Ken Korth, Interim Department Head, 479-575-2445, E-mail: kkorth@uark.edu. *Application contact:* Dr. Ken Korth, Interim Department Head, 479-575-2445, E-mail: kkorth@uark.edu.
Website: https://plant-pathology.uark.edu/academics/degrees/phd-in-plant-science.php

The University of British Columbia, Faculty of Land and Food Systems, Plant Science Program, Vancouver, BC V6T 1Z4, Canada. Offers M Sc, PhD. *Program availability:* Part-time. *Degree requirements:* For master's, thesis; for doctorate, comprehensive exam, thesis/dissertation. *Entrance requirements:* Additional exam requirements/recommendations for international students: Required—TOEFL, IELTS. Electronic applications accepted. *Expenses:* Contact institution. *Faculty research:* Plant physiology and biochemistry, biotechnology, plant protection (insect, weeds, and diseases), plant breeding, plant-environment interaction.

University of California, Riverside, Graduate Division, Department of Botany and Plant Sciences, Riverside, CA 92521-0102. Offers plant biology (MS, PhD), including plant cell, molecular, and developmental biology (PhD), plant ecology (PhD), plant genetics (PhD). *Program availability:* Part-time. Terminal master's awarded for partial completion of doctoral program. *Degree requirements:* For master's, comprehensive exams or thesis; for doctorate, thesis/dissertation, qualifying exams. *Entrance requirements:* For master's and doctorate, GRE General Test, minimum GPA of 3.2. Additional exam requirements/recommendations for international students: Required—TOEFL (minimum score 550 paper-based, 80 iBT) or IELTS. Electronic applications accepted. *Faculty research:* Agricultural plant biology; biochemistry and physiology; cellular, molecular and developmental biology; ecology, evolution, systematics and ethnobotany; genetics, genomics and bioinformatics.

University of Connecticut, Graduate School, College of Agriculture, Health and Natural Resources, Department of Plant Science and Landscape Architecture, Storrs, CT 06269. Offers MS, PhD. Terminal master's awarded for partial completion of doctoral program. *Degree requirements:* For master's, comprehensive exam; for doctorate, thesis/dissertation. *Entrance requirements:* For master's and doctorate, GRE General Test, GRE Subject Test. Additional exam requirements/recommendations for international students: Required—TOEFL (minimum score 550 paper-based). Electronic applications accepted.

University of Delaware, College of Agriculture and Natural Resources, Department of Plant and Soil Sciences, Newark, DE 19716. Offers MS, PhD. *Program availability:* Part-time. Terminal master's awarded for partial completion of doctoral program. *Degree requirements:* For master's, thesis; for doctorate, thesis/dissertation. *Entrance requirements:* For master's and doctorate, GRE General Test. Additional exam requirements/recommendations for international students: Required—TOEFL (minimum score 550 paper-based). Electronic applications accepted. *Faculty research:* Soil chemistry, plant and cell tissue culture, plant breeding and genetics, soil physics, soil biochemistry, plant molecular biology, soil microbiology.

University of Florida, Graduate School, College of Agricultural and Life Sciences, Program in Plant Medicine, Gainesville, FL 32611. Offers plant medicine (DPM); tropical conservation and development (DPM). *Program availability:* Part-time. *Degree requirements:* For doctorate, comprehensive exam. *Entrance requirements:* For doctorate, GRE General Test (minimum combined score 300), minimum GPA of 3.0, BS or BA. Additional exam requirements/recommendations for international students: Required—TOEFL (minimum score 550 paper-based; 80 iBT), IELTS (minimum score 6).

University of Georgia, College of Agricultural and Environmental Sciences, Institute of Plant Breeding, Genetics and Genomics, Athens, GA 30602. Offers MS, PhD.

University of Hawaii at Manoa, Office of Graduate Education, College of Tropical Agriculture and Human Resources, Department of Plant and Environmental Protection Sciences, Honolulu, HI 96822. Offers entomology (MS, PhD); tropical plant pathology (MS, PhD). *Program availability:* Part-time. Terminal master's awarded for partial completion of doctoral program. *Degree requirements:* For master's, thesis optional; for doctorate, comprehensive exam, thesis/dissertation. *Entrance requirements:* For master's and doctorate, GRE General Test. Additional exam requirements/recommendations for international students: Required—TOEFL (minimum score 500 paper-based; 61 iBT), IELTS (minimum score 5). *Faculty research:* Nematology, virology, mycology, bacteriology, epidemiology.

University of Idaho, College of Graduate Studies, College of Agricultural and Life Sciences, Department of Entomology, Plant Pathology and Nematology, Moscow, ID 83844-2329. Offers plant science (MS). *Faculty:* 14 full-time (5 women). *Students:* 17. Average age 32. In 2018, 1 master's, 2 doctorates awarded. *Entrance requirements:* For master's and doctorate, minimum GPA of 3.0. Additional exam requirements/recommendations for international students: Required—TOEFL (minimum score 550 paper-based; 79 iBT). *Application deadline:* For fall admission, 8/15 for domestic students; for spring admission, 12/15 for domestic students. Applications are processed on a rolling basis. Application fee: $60. Electronic applications accepted. *Expenses:* Tuition, state resident: full-time $7266.44; part-time $474.50 per credit hour. Tuition, nonresident: full-time $24,902; part-time $1453.50 per credit hour. *Required fees:* $2085.56; $45.50 per credit hour. *Financial support:* Research assistantships and teaching assistantships available. Financial award applicants required to submit FAFSA. *Faculty research:* Seed potato production, wheat production, insect pests, plant pathogens, chemical ecology. *Unit head:* Dr. Edwin Lewis, Department Head, 208-885-3776, E-mail: mclaughlin@uidaho.edu. *Application contact:* Dr. Edwin Lewis, Department Head, 208-885-3776, E-mail: mclaughlin@uidaho.edu.
Website: https://www.uidaho.edu/cals/entomology-plant-pathology-and-nematology

University of Idaho, College of Graduate Studies, College of Agricultural and Life Sciences, Department of Plant Sciences, Moscow, ID 83844-2333. Offers MS, PhD. *Faculty:* 15 full-time, 8 part-time/adjunct. *Students:* 29 full-time, 9 part-time. Average age 30. In 2018, 7 master's, 3 doctorates awarded. *Degree requirements:* For master's, thesis (for some programs). *Entrance requirements:* For master's and doctorate, GRE General Test, minimum GPA of 3.0. Additional exam requirements/recommendations for international students: Required—TOEFL (minimum score 79 iBT). *Application deadline:* For fall admission, 8/1 for domestic students; for spring admission, 12/15 for domestic students. Application fee: $60. *Expenses:* Tuition, state resident: full-time $7266.44; part-time $474.50 per credit hour. Tuition, nonresident: full-time $24,902; part-time $1453.50 per credit hour. *Required fees:* $2085.56; $45.50 per credit hour. *Financial support:* Applicants required to submit FAFSA. *Faculty research:* Controlling root diseases in wheat and barley, domestication of plants, reduced herbicide rates control weeds in grain, wheat breeding program. *Unit head:* Robert Tripepi, Head, 208-885-2122, E-mail: plantsciences@uidaho.edu. *Application contact:* Robert Tripepi, Head, 208-885-2122, E-mail: plantsciences@uidaho.edu.
Website: https://www.uidaho.edu/cals/plant-sciences

University of Kentucky, Graduate School, College of Agriculture, Food and Environment, Program in Plant and Soil Science, Lexington, KY 40506-0032. Offers integrated plant and soil sciences (MS, PhD). *Degree requirements:* For master's, comprehensive exam, thesis optional. *Entrance requirements:* For master's, GRE General Test, minimum undergraduate GPA of 2.75, graduate 3.0. Additional exam requirements/recommendations for international students: Required—TOEFL (minimum score 550 paper-based). Electronic applications accepted.

The University of Manchester, School of Biological Sciences, Manchester, United Kingdom. Offers adaptive organismal biology (M Phil, PhD); animal biology (M Phil, PhD); biochemistry (M Phil, PhD); bioinformatics (M Phil, PhD); biomolecular sciences (M Phil, PhD); biotechnology (M Phil, PhD); cell biology (M Phil, PhD); cell matrix research (M Phil, PhD); channels and transporters (M Phil, PhD); developmental biology (M Phil, PhD); environmental biology (M Phil, PhD); evolutionary biology (M Phil, PhD); gene expression (M Phil, PhD); genetics (M Phil, PhD); history of science, technology and medicine (M Phil, PhD); immunology (M Phil, PhD); integrative neurobiology and behavior (M Phil, PhD); membrane trafficking (M Phil, PhD); microbiology (M Phil, PhD); molecular and cellular neuroscience (M Phil, PhD); molecular biology (M Phil, PhD); molecular cancer studies (M Phil, PhD); neuroscience (M Phil, PhD); ophthalmology (M Phil, PhD); optometry (M Phil, PhD); organelle function (M Phil, PhD); pharmacology (M Phil, PhD); physiology (M Phil, PhD); plant sciences (M Phil, PhD); stem cell research (M Phil, PhD); structural biology (M Phil, PhD); systems neuroscience (M Phil, PhD); toxicology (M Phil, PhD).

University of Manitoba, Faculty of Graduate Studies, Faculty of Agricultural and Food Sciences, Department of Plant Science, Winnipeg, MB R3T 2N2, Canada. Offers agronomy and plant protection (M Sc, PhD); horticulture (M Sc, PhD); plant breeding and genetics (M Sc, PhD); plant physiology-biochemistry (M Sc, PhD). *Degree requirements:* For master's, thesis; for doctorate, one foreign language, thesis/dissertation.

University of Massachusetts Amherst, Graduate School, Interdisciplinary Programs, Program in Plant Biology, Amherst, MA 01003. Offers biochemistry and metabolism (MS, PhD); cell biology and physiology (MS, PhD); environmental, ecological and integrative biology (MS, PhD); genetics and evolution (MS, PhD). *Degree requirements:* For master's, thesis; for doctorate, 2 foreign languages, comprehensive exam, thesis/dissertation. *Entrance requirements:* For master's and doctorate, GRE General Test. Additional exam requirements/recommendations for international students: Required—TOEFL (minimum score 550 paper-based; 80 iBT), IELTS (minimum score 6.5). Electronic applications accepted.

University of Minnesota, Twin Cities Campus, Graduate School, College of Food, Agricultural and Natural Resource Sciences, Program in Applied Plant Sciences, St. Paul, MN 55108. Offers MS, PhD. *Program availability:* Part-time. Terminal master's awarded for partial completion of doctoral program. *Degree requirements:* For master's, comprehensive exam, thesis; for doctorate, comprehensive exam, thesis/dissertation. *Entrance requirements:* For master's and doctorate, GRE General Test. Additional exam requirements/recommendations for international students: Required—TOEFL (minimum score 550 paper-based; 79 iBT), IELTS (minimum score 6.5). Electronic applications accepted. *Faculty research:* Weed science, horticulture, crop management, sustainable agriculture, biotechnology, plant breeding.

University of Missouri, Office of Research and Graduate Studies, College of Agriculture, Food and Natural Resources, Division of Plant Sciences, Columbia, MO 65211. Offers crop, soil and pest management (MS, PhD); entomology (MS, PhD); horticulture (MS, PhD); plant breeding, genetics and genomics (MS, PhD); plant stress biology (MS, PhD). Terminal master's awarded for partial completion of doctoral program. *Degree requirements:* For master's, thesis; for doctorate, comprehensive exam, thesis/dissertation. *Entrance requirements:* For master's and doctorate, GRE General Test, minimum GPA of 3.0; bachelor's degree from accredited college. Additional exam requirements/recommendations for international students: Required—TOEFL (minimum score 500 paper-based; 61 iBT), IELTS (minimum score 5.5). Electronic applications accepted. *Faculty research:* Crop, soil and pest management; entomology; horticulture; plant biology and genetics; plant microbiology and pathology.

University of Saskatchewan, College of Graduate and Postdoctoral Studies, College of Agriculture and Bioresources, Department of Plant Sciences, Saskatoon, SK S7N 5A2, Canada. Offers M Sc, PhD. *Degree requirements:* For master's, thesis; for doctorate, comprehensive exam (for some programs), thesis/dissertation. *Entrance requirements:* Additional exam requirements/recommendations for international students: Required—TOEFL (minimum score 80 iBT); Recommended—IELTS (minimum score 6.5).

The University of Tennessee, Graduate School, College of Agricultural Sciences and Natural Resources, Department of Plant Sciences, Knoxville, TN 37996. Offers floriculture (MS); landscape design (MS); public horticulture (MS); turfgrass (MS); woody ornamentals (MS). *Program availability:* Part-time. *Degree requirements:* For master's, thesis or alternative. *Entrance requirements:* For master's, minimum GPA of 2.7. Additional exam requirements/recommendations for international students: Required—TOEFL. Electronic applications accepted.

University of Vermont, Graduate College, College of Agriculture and Life Sciences, Department of Plant and Soil Science, Burlington, VT 05405. Offers agroecology (Graduate Certificate); plant and soil science (MS, PhD), including agroecology, agronomy (MS), ecological landscape design, entomology, horticulture (MS), plant pathology (MS), soil science. *Degree requirements:* For master's, thesis; for doctorate, one foreign language, thesis/dissertation. *Entrance requirements:* For master's and doctorate, GRE General Test. Additional exam requirements/recommendations for international students: Required—TOEFL (minimum score 550 paper-based; 90 iBT), IELTS (minimum score 6.5). Electronic applications accepted. *Faculty research:* Soil chemistry, plant nutrition.

University of Wisconsin–Madison, Graduate School, College of Agricultural and Life Sciences, Department of Agronomy, Madison, WI 53706-1380. Offers agronomy (MS, PhD); plant breeding and plant genetics (MS, PhD). *Degree requirements:* For master's, thesis or alternative; for doctorate, thesis/dissertation. *Entrance requirements:* For master's and doctorate, GRE, minimum GPA of 3.0. Additional exam requirements/recommendations for international students: Required—TOEFL (minimum score 580 paper-based). Electronic applications accepted. *Faculty research:* Plant breeding and genetics, plant molecular biology and physiology, cropping systems and management, weed science.

University of Wisconsin–Madison, Graduate School, College of Agricultural and Life Sciences, Plant Breeding and Plant Genetics Program, Madison, WI 53706-1380. Offers MS, PhD. *Program availability:* Part-time. Terminal master's awarded for partial completion of doctoral program. *Degree requirements:* For master's, comprehensive exam, thesis; for doctorate, comprehensive exam, thesis/dissertation, formal exit seminar. *Entrance requirements:* For master's and doctorate, GRE, minimum GPA of 3.0. Additional exam requirements/recommendations for international students: Required—TOEFL (minimum: 550 paper, 80 iBT), IELTS (minimum: 6) or Michigan English Language Assessment Battery (minimum: 77). Electronic applications accepted. *Faculty research:* Plant improvement, classical and molecular genetics, quantitative and statistical genetics, cytogenetics, stress and pest resistances.

Utah State University, School of Graduate Studies, College of Agriculture and Applied Sciences, Department of Plants, Soils and Climate, Logan, UT 84322. Offers climate sciences (MS, PhD); ecology (MS, PhD); horticulture (MPS); plant science (MS, PhD); soil science (MS, PhD). *Program availability:* Part-time. Terminal master's awarded for partial completion of doctoral program. *Degree requirements:* For master's, thesis; for doctorate, thesis/dissertation. *Entrance requirements:* For master's, GRE General Test,

BS in plant, soil, atmospheric science, or related field; minimum GPA of 3.0; for doctorate, GRE General Test, minimum GPA of 3.0. Additional exam requirements/recommendations for international students: Required—TOEFL. Electronic applications accepted. *Faculty research:* Biotechnology and genomics, plant physiology and biology, nutrient and water efficient landscapes, physical-chemical-biological processes in soil, environmental biophysics and climate.

West Texas A&M University, College of Agriculture and Natural Sciences, Department of Agricultural Sciences, Emphasis in Plant, Soil and Environmental Science, Canyon, TX 79015. Offers MS. *Program availability:* Part-time. *Degree requirements:* For master's, comprehensive exam, thesis optional. *Entrance requirements:* For master's, GRE General Test. Additional exam requirements/recommendations for international students: Required—TOEFL (minimum score 550 paper-based). Electronic applications accepted. *Faculty research:* Crop and soil disciplines.

West Virginia University, Davis College of Agriculture, Forestry and Consumer Sciences, Morgantown, WV 26506. Offers agricultural and extension education (MS, PhD); agriculture and resource management (MS); agriculture, natural resources and design (M Agr); agronomy (MS); animal and food science (PhD); animal physiology (MS); applied and environmental microbiology (MS); design and merchandising (MS); entomology (MS); forest resource science (PhD); forestry (MSF); genetics and developmental biology (MS, PhD); horticulture (MS); human and community development (PhD); landscape architecture (MLA); natural resource economics (PhD); nutritional and food science (MS); plant and soil science (PhD); plant pathology (MS); recreation, parks and tourism resources (MS); reproductive physiology (MS, PhD); wildlife and fisheries resources (PhD). *Accreditation:* ASLA. *Program availability:* Part-time. *Students:* 188 full-time (86 women), 47 part-time (30 women); includes 22 minority (5 Black or African American, non-Hispanic/Latino; 5 Asian, non-Hispanic/Latino; 8 Hispanic/Latino; 4 Two or more races, non-Hispanic/Latino), 60 international. In 2018, 56 master's, 14 doctorates awarded. *Degree requirements:* For master's, thesis; for doctorate, thesis/dissertation. *Entrance requirements:* Additional exam requirements/recommendations for international students: Required—TOEFL (minimum score 550 paper-based). *Application deadline:* For fall admission, 6/1 priority date for domestic students, 6/1 for international students; for spring admission, 1/5 for domestic and international students. Applications are processed on a rolling basis. Application fee: $60. Electronic applications accepted. *Financial support:* Fellowships, research assistantships, teaching assistantships, career-related internships or fieldwork, Federal Work-Study, institutionally sponsored loans, tuition waivers (full and partial), and unspecified assistantships available. Financial award application deadline: 2/1; financial award applicants required to submit FAFSA. *Faculty research:* Reproductive physiology, soil and water quality, human nutrition, aquaculture, wildlife management. *Unit head:* Dr. Ken Blemings, Interim Dean, 304-293-2395, Fax: 304-293-3740, E-mail: ken.blemings@mail.wvu.edu. *Application contact:* Dr. J. Todd Petty, Associate Dean, 304-293-2278, Fax: 304-293-3740, E-mail: jtpetty@mail.wvu.edu. Website: https://www.davis.wvu.edu

Viticulture and Enology

California State University, Fresno, Division of Research and Graduate Studies, Jordan College of Agricultural Sciences and Technology, Department of Viticulture and Enology, Fresno, CA 93740-8027. Offers MS. *Program availability:* Part-time, evening/weekend. *Degree requirements:* For master's, comprehensive exam (for some programs), thesis (for some programs). *Entrance requirements:* For master's, GRE General Test, minimum GPA of 2.5. Additional exam requirements/recommendations for international students: Required—TOEFL. Electronic applications accepted. *Faculty research:* Ethel carbonate formation, clinical an physiological characterization, grape and wine quality.

Cornell University, Graduate School, Graduate Fields of Agriculture and Life Sciences, Field of Food Science and Technology, Ithaca, NY 14050. Offers dairy science (MPS, MS, PhD); enology (MS, PhD); food chemistry (MPS, MS, PhD); food engineering (MPS, MS, PhD); food microbiology (MPS, MS, PhD); food processing waste technology (MPS, MS, PhD); food science (MFS, MPS, MS, PhD); international food science (MPS, MS, PhD); sensory evaluation (MPS, MS, PhD). Terminal master's awarded for partial completion of doctoral program. *Degree requirements:* For master's, thesis (MS), teaching experience; for doctorate, comprehensive exam, thesis/dissertation, teaching experience. *Entrance requirements:* For master's and doctorate, GRE General Test, 3 letters of recommendation. Additional exam requirements/recommendations for

international students: Required—TOEFL (minimum score 550 paper-based; 77 iBT). Electronic applications accepted. *Faculty research:* Food microbiology/biotechnology, food engineering/processing, food safety/toxicology, sensory science/flavor chemistry, food packaging.

Oregon State University, College of Agricultural Sciences, Program in Food Science and Technology, Corvallis, OR 97331. Offers brewing (MS, PhD); enology (MS, PhD); flavor chemistry (MS, PhD); food and seafood processing (MS, PhD); food chemistry/biochemistry (MS, PhD); food engineering (MS, PhD); food microbiology/biotechnology (MS, PhD); sensory evaluation (MS, PhD). *Entrance requirements:* For master's and doctorate, GRE (minimum Verbal and Quantitative scores of 300), minimum GPA of 3.0 in last 90 hours. Additional exam requirements/recommendations for international students: Required—TOEFL (minimum score 80 iBT), IELTS (minimum score 6.5).

University of California, Davis, Graduate Studies, Graduate Group in Viticulture and Enology, Davis, CA 95616. Offers MS, PhD. *Degree requirements:* For master's, comprehensive exam (for some programs), thesis (for some programs). *Entrance requirements:* Additional exam requirements/recommendations for international students: Required—TOEFL (minimum score 550 paper-based).

Peterson's Graduate Programs in the Physical Sciences, Mathematics, Agricultural Sciences, the Environment & Natural Resources 2020

www.petersons.com **289**

CHAPMAN UNIVERSITY
Schmid College of Science and Technology
Food Sciences Program

CHAPMAN
UNIVERSITY
**SCHMID COLLEGE OF SCIENCE
AND TECHNOLOGY**

Programs of Study

Chapman University's Master of Science (M.S.) in Food Science is the perfect graduate degree program to turn passion for science and food into a rewarding career. Students in the program learn how to apply scientific principles to study the properties of food and to develop innovative ways to process and package foods.

The Food Science program uses biology, chemistry, physical sciences, psychology and engineering to study the properties of foods. Food scientists develop innovative ways to process, preserve, or package food, thereby making the world's food supply safer, sustainable, and more nutritious. The food science industry represents one of the healthiest industries in the world, with segments from food processing to food sales contributing close to $42.2 billion to the U.S. economy. According to the Bureau of Labor Statistics, the demand for food scientists is projected to increase 10 percent until 2020, and job prospects in Southern California especially continue to grow steadily.

More than 1,500 food-processing companies are located within a 90-mile radius of Chapman University's campus in Orange County, California. Most students in the program obtain work experience via internships, and the program's job placement rate is close to 100 percent. Graduates have found employment with firms such as Baskin-Robbins; Carl Karcher Enterprises, Inc.; Cheesecake Factory; Con-Agra; Contessa Foods; Disney Consumer Products; Dole; Dr. Pepper/Seven-Up; Fresh Express; Hain Celestial; Kellogg's; Masterfoods USA; Nestle, USA; Nutrilite; PepsiCo; Ready Pac Foods, Inc.; Starbucks; Sunkist Growers, Inc.; Taco Bell; Unilever; Ventura Foods; and many others.

Chapman University also offers two dual degree programs: an MBA/M.S. in Food Science and a J.D./M.S. in Food Science. More information is available at chapman.edu/food-science.

Research Facilities

Chapman University has invested in the new, 140,000 square-foot Keck Center for Science and Technology which opened in fall 2018. The Center features research and teaching labs; equipment to support molecular biology, microbiology, biogeochemistry research, organic and physical chemistry; graduate student lounges; collaboration areas; and more. Additional information can be found at chapman.edu/forward.

Financial Aid

Financial assistance is available in the form of federal loans, department scholarships, teaching assistantships and research assistantships. Most students receive some form of financial support from the University, and some receive additional aid through the School's industry partnerships.

All students who submit a complete application are automatically considered for a department scholarship. Admitted students are notified of scholarships soon after receiving confirmation of admission.

Additional information regarding financial aid is available at chapman.edu/financial-aid.

Cost of Study

Tuition for the 2019-2020 academic year is $1,055 per credit for the M.S. in Food Science program and $1485 per credit for the MBA/M.S. in Food Science dual-degree program. Tuition is subject to change; the most current details can be found online at chapman.edu/GraduatePrograms.

Living and Housing Costs

Information on graduate student housing is available at chapman.edu/students/services/housing-and-residence/on-campus/applying-housing, or by calling 714-997-6603.

Location

Chapman University is located in the heart of Orange County, California. Orange County's natural landscape provides extensive opportunities for intellectual and recreational exploration. Whether it's a bonfire at the beach or the study of desert habitat, Southern California offers access to both marine and mountain experiences. Whether students are studying business, the arts, science, or social entrepreneurship, they will find opportunities to learn, acquire skills, and build a resume in Southern California.

Chapman University occupies 76 park-like acres lined with palm and shade trees. A mix of historical and modern buildings makes Chapman one of the most beautiful university campuses in the nation.

The University and the College

The mission of Chapman University's Schmid College of Science and Technology, home of the Food Science program, is to mentor and grow leaders through a curriculum that develops outstanding problem-solving skills in the context of the grand, interdisciplinary challenges facing the world today. As Chapman University moves toward the future, the Schmid College of Science and Technology will be leading the pack with innovative research and hands-on learning experiences.

Peterson's Graduate Programs in the Physical Sciences, Mathematics, Agricultural Sciences, the Environment & Natural Resources 2020

www.petersons.com **291**

Faculty

Faculty conduct high-quality research and run several research labs that not only produce important research, but also actively involve students in the research process. Students receive first-hand experience in funded research projects of societal importance, have the chance to co-author papers in nationally recognized journals, and are able to present at national conferences.

In their research, faculty members combine interdisciplinary breadth and collaboration with rigorous disciplinary depth and scholarship. This approach provides students with a modern view of problem solving in today's technologically focused world. Students are encouraged to collaborate with faculty in research, and to experience the exhilaration of making new discoveries or developing advanced software and hardware tools.

Admission Requirements

Admitted students hold degrees in chemistry, biology, pharmacy, business, chemical, mechanical engineering, and food science and nutrition. Applicants must have earned a minimum GPA of 3.00 and provide evidence of satisfactory coursework in the following areas: general chemistry with laboratory (two semesters); organic chemistry with laboratory (two semesters or one semester organic and one semester biochemistry); microbiology with laboratory (one semester); statistics (one semester); and human nutrition (one semester). Additional details can be found at chapman.edu/food-science.

Minimum GRE scores are verbal: 500/153, quantitative: 680/153, and analytical writing: 3.5. For international students, minimum scores on the Test of English as a Foreign Language (TOEFL) are 550 (paper-based) or 80 (Internet-based); International English Language Testing System (IELTS): 6.5; Pearson Test of English (PTE) 53; or Cambridge English Advanced Exam (CAE) 180 minimum.

Applying

Applicants must submit the following:

- Online application for admission (including $60 nonrefundable application fee)

- Official transcripts (see chapman.edu/food-science for details)

- Graduate Record Exam (GRE) scores are required (GMAT scores may be accepted in lieu of GRE)

- Two letters of recommendation which describe the applicant's professional and academic abilities

- Statement of intent

- Resume or CV

- Language test (international students only)

- Financial Certification Form (international students only)

The application deadline is May 1 for fall semester enrollment. Prospective students should contact the Office of Graduate Admission at 714-997-6711 or gradadmit@chapman.edu for more information.

Correspondence and Information:

Chapman University

One University Drive

Orange, California 92866

United States

Phone: 714-997-6730

E-mail: SchmidCollege@chapman.edu

Website: chapman.edu/food-science

292   www.petersons.com

Peterson's Graduate Programs in the Physical Sciences, Mathematics, Agricultural Sciences, the Environment & Natural Resources 2020

ACADEMIC AND PROFESSIONAL PROGRAMS IN THE ENVIRONMENT AND NATURAL SCIENCES

Section 9
Environmental Sciences and Management

This section contains a directory of institutions offering graduate work in environmental sciences and management, followed by an in-depth entry submitted by an institution that chose to prepare a detailed program description. Additional information about programs listed in the directory but not augmented by an in-depth entry may be obtained by writing directly to the dean of a graduate school or chair of a department at the address given in the directory.

For programs offering related work, see also in this book *Natural Resources*. In the other guides in this series:

Graduate Programs in the Humanities, Arts & Social Sciences
See *Political Science and International Affairs* and *Public, Regional, and Industrial Affairs*

Graduate Programs in the Biological/Biomedical Sciences & Health-Related Medical Professions
See *Ecology, Environmental Biology, and Evolutionary Biology*
Graduate Programs in Engineering & Applied Sciences
See *Management of Engineering and Technology*

CONTENTS

Program Directories

Environmental Management and Policy

Adelphi University, College of Arts and Sciences, Program in Environmental Studies, Garden City, NY 11530-0701. Offers MS. *Students:* 2 full-time (0 women), 5 part-time (3 women); includes 3 minority (2 Black or African American, non-Hispanic/Latino; 1 Asian, non-Hispanic/Latino), 3 international. Average age 33. 34 applicants, 29% accepted, 4 enrolled. In 2018, 9 master's awarded. *Entrance requirements:* For master's, GRE General Test, 2 letters of recommendation; course work in microeconomics, political science, statistics/calculus, and either chemistry or physics; computer literacy. Additional exam requirements/recommendations for international students: Required—TOEFL (minimum score 550 paper-based; 80 iBT), IELTS (minimum score 6.5). *Application deadline:* For fall admission, 3/1 for international students; for spring admission, 11/1 for international students. Applications are processed on a rolling basis. Application fee: $50. Electronic applications accepted. *Expenses:* Contact institution. *Financial support:* Research assistantships with full and partial tuition reimbursements, teaching assistantships, career-related internships or fieldwork, institutionally sponsored loans, scholarships/grants, traineeships, and unspecified assistantships available. Support available to part-time students. Financial award application deadline: 1/1; financial award applicants required to submit FAFSA. *Faculty research:* Contaminates sites, workplace exposure level of contaminants, climate change and human health. *Unit head:* Aaren Freeman, Graduate Coordinator of Environmental Studies Program, 516-237-8546, E-mail: afreeman@adelphi.edu. *Application contact:* Aaren Freeman, Graduate Coordinator of Environmental Studies Program, 516-237-8546, E-mail: afreeman@adelphi.edu.
Website: http://environmental-studies.adelphi.edu/ms-in-environmental-studies/

Air Force Institute of Technology, Graduate School of Engineering and Management, Department of Systems and Engineering Management, Dayton, OH 45433-7765. Offers cost analysis (MS); environmental and engineering management (MS); environmental engineering science (MS); information resource/systems management (MS). *Accreditation:* ABET. *Program availability:* Part-time. *Degree requirements:* For master's, thesis. *Entrance requirements:* For master's, GRE, GMAT, minimum GPA of 3.0.

American Public University System, AMU/APU Graduate Programs, Charles Town, WV 25414. Offers accounting (MS); applied business analytics (MS); business administration (MBA); criminal justice (MA); cybersecurity studies (MS); educational leadership (M Ed); environmental policy and management (MS); global security (DGS); health information management (MS); history (MA), including American military history, American Revolution, civil war, war since 1945, World War II; information technology (MS); international relations and conflict resolution (MA), including American politics and government, comparative government and development, general, international relations, public policy; national security studies (MA); nursing (MSN); political science (MA); public policy (MPP); reverse logistics management (MA), including comparative and security issues, conflict resolution, international and transnational security issues, peacekeeping; space studies (MS); sports management (MS); strategic intelligence (DSI); teaching (M Ed), including secondary social studies; transportation and logistics management (MA). *Program availability:* Part-time, evening/weekend, online only, 100% online. *Students:* 406 full-time (180 women), 7,826 part-time (3,329 women); includes 2,781 minority (1,438 Black or African American, non-Hispanic/Latino; 44 American Indian or Alaska Native, non-Hispanic/Latino; 193 Asian, non-Hispanic/Latino; 747 Hispanic/Latino; 53 Native Hawaiian or other Pacific Islander, non-Hispanic/Latino; 306 Two or more races, non-Hispanic/Latino), 121 international. Average age 38. In 2018, 2,717 master's awarded. *Degree requirements:* For master's, comprehensive exam or practicum; for doctorate, practicum. *Entrance requirements:* For master's, official transcript showing earned bachelor's degree from institution accredited by recognized accrediting body. Additional exam requirements/recommendations for international students: Required—TOEFL (minimum score 550 paper-based), IELTS (minimum score 6.5). *Application deadline:* Applications are processed on a rolling basis. Application fee: $0. Electronic applications accepted. *Financial support:* Scholarships/grants available. Financial award applicants required to submit FAFSA. *Unit head:* Dr. Wallace Boston, President, 877-468-6268, Fax: 304-728-2348, E-mail: president@apus.edu. *Application contact:* Yoci Deal, Associate Vice President, Graduate and International Admissions, 877-468-6268, Fax: 304-724-3764, E-mail: info@apus.edu.
Website: http://www.apus.edu

American University, College of Arts and Sciences, Department of Environmental Science, Washington, DC 20016. Offers environmental assessment (Graduate Certificate); environmental science (MS); professional science: environmental assessment (MS). *Faculty:* 7 full-time (5 women), 5 part-time/adjunct (1 woman). *Students:* 12 full-time (10 women), 5 part-time (2 women); includes 3 minority (all Hispanic/Latino), 1 international. Average age 25. 17 applicants, 94% accepted, 7 enrolled. In 2018, 7 master's, 1 other advanced degree awarded. *Degree requirements:* For master's, comprehensive exam, thesis (for some programs). *Entrance requirements:* For master's, GRE General Test, GRE Subject Test, one year of calculus, lab science, statement of purpose, transcripts, 2 letters of recommendation, resume. Additional exam requirements/recommendations for international students: Required—TOEFL. Application fee: $55. Electronic applications accepted. *Expenses:* Contact institution. *Financial support:* Research assistantships, teaching assistantships, and unspecified assistantships available. Financial award applicants required to submit FAFSA. *Unit head:* Dr. Stephen MacAvoy, Department Chair, 202-885-1751, E-mail: environ@american.edu. *Application contact:* Jonathan Harper, Assistant Director, Graduate Recruitment, 202-855-3620, E-mail: casgrad@american.edu.
Website: http://www.american.edu/cas/environmental/

American University, School of International Service, Washington, DC 20016-8071. Offers comparative and regional studies (Certificate); cross-cultural communication (Certificate); development management (MS); ethics, peace, and global affairs (MA); European studies (Certificate); global environmental policy (MA, Certificate); global information technology (Certificate); global media (MA); international affairs (MA), including comparative and regional studies, global governance, politics, and security, international economic relations, natural resources and sustainable development, U.S. foreign policy and national security; international arts management (Certificate); international communication (MA, Certificate); international development (MA); international economic policy (Certificate); international economic relations (Certificate); international economics (MA); international peace and conflict resolution (MA, Certificate); international politics (Certificate); international relations (MA, PhD); international service (MIS); peacebuilding (Certificate); social enterprise (MA); the Americas (Certificate); United States foreign policy (Certificate); JD/MA. *Program availability:* Part-time, evening/weekend, 100% online, blended/hybrid learning. *Faculty:* 115 full-time (48 women), 50 part-time/adjunct (22 women). *Students:* 496 full-time (320 women), 477 part-time (242 women); includes 410 minority (83 Black or African American, non-Hispanic/Latino; 2 American Indian or Alaska Native, non-Hispanic/Latino; 51 Asian, non-Hispanic/Latino; 242 Hispanic/Latino; 32 Two or more races, non-Hispanic/Latino), 93 international. Average age 30. 1,280 applicants, 82% accepted, 356 enrolled. In 2018, 400 master's, 3 doctorates, 8 other advanced degrees awarded. Terminal master's awarded for partial completion of doctoral program. *Degree requirements:* For master's, one foreign language, comprehensive exam, thesis or alternative; for doctorate, one foreign language, comprehensive exam, thesis/dissertation. *Entrance requirements:* For master's, Please visit the website for details: https://www.american.edu/sis/admissions/, transcripts, resume, 2 letters of recommendation, statement of purpose; for doctorate, GRE, transcripts, resume, 3 letters of recommendation, statement of purpose. Additional exam requirements/recommendations for international students: Required—TOEFL. Application fee: $55. Electronic applications accepted. *Expenses:* Contact institution. *Financial support:* Research assistantships, teaching assistantships, institutionally sponsored loans, scholarships/grants, and unspecified assistantships available. Financial award applicants required to submit FAFSA. *Unit head:* Christine BN Chin, 202-885-1600, E-mail: sisgrad@american.edu. *Application contact:* Jia Jiang, Director, Graduate Enrollment Management, 202-885-1689, E-mail: jiang@american.edu.
Website: http://www.american.edu/sis/

American University of Beirut, Graduate Programs, Faculty of Arts and Sciences, Beirut 1107 2020, Lebanon. Offers anthropology (MA); Arab and Middle Eastern history (PhD); Arabic language and literature (MA, PhD); archaeology (MA); art history and curating (MA); biology (MS); cell and molecular biology (PhD); chemistry (MS); clinical psychology (MA); computational sciences (MS); computer science (MS); economics (MA); education (MA), including administration and policy studies, elementary education, mathematics education, psychology school guidance, psychology test and measurements, science education, teaching English as a foreign language; English language (MA); English literature (MA); environmental policy planning (MS); financial economics (MAFE); general psychology (MA); geology (MS); history (MA); Islamic studies (MA); mathematics (MS); media studies (MA); Middle East studies (MA); philosophy (MA); physics (MS); political studies (MA); public administration (MA); public policy and international affairs (MA); sociology (MA); theoretical physics (PhD). *Program availability:* Part-time. *Faculty:* 187 full-time (64 women), 27 part-time/adjunct (15 women). *Students:* 292 full-time (215 women), 216 part-time (148 women). Average age 27. 422 applicants, 64% accepted, 124 enrolled. In 2018, 90 master's, 3 doctorates awarded. *Degree requirements:* For master's, comprehensive exam, thesis (for some programs), project; for doctorate, comprehensive exam, thesis/dissertation (for some programs). *Entrance requirements:* For master's, GRE General Test (for archaeology, clinical psychology, general psychology, economics, financial economics and biology); for doctorate, GRE General Test for all PhD programs, GRE Subject Test for theoretical physics. Additional exam requirements/recommendations for international students: Required—TOEFL (minimum score 583 paper-based; 97 iBT), IELTS (minimum score 7). *Application deadline:* For fall admission, 3/18 for domestic students; for spring admission, 11/5 for domestic students. Application fee: $50. Electronic applications accepted. *Expenses:* MA/MS: Humanities and social sciences=$912/credit. Sciences=$943/credit. Financial economics=$986/credit. Thesis: Humanities/social sciences=$6565 and sciences=$6865. *Financial support:* In 2018–19, 227 fellowships with full tuition reimbursements, 17 research assistantships with full tuition reimbursements, 83 teaching assistantships with full tuition reimbursements were awarded; scholarships/grants, tuition waivers (full and partial), and unspecified assistantships also available. Financial award application deadline: 3/18. *Faculty research:* Sciences: Physics: High energy, Particle, Polymer and Soft Matter, Thermal, Plasma; String Theory, Mathematical physics, Astrophysics (stellar evolution, planet and galaxy formation and evolution, astrophysical dynamics), Solid State physics/thin films, Spintronics, Magnetic properties of materials, Mineralogy, Petrology, and Geochemistry of Hard Rocks, Geophysics and Petrophysics, Hydrogeology, Micropaleontology, Sedimentology, and Stratigraphy, Structural Geology and Geotectonics, Renewable en. *Total annual research expenditures:* $4.3 million. *Unit head:* Dr. Nadia Maria El Cheikh, Dean, Faculty of Arts and Sciences, 961-1-350000 Ext. 3800, Fax: 961-1-744461, E-mail: nmcheikh@aub.edu.lb. *Application contact:* Adriana Michelle Zanaty, Curriculum and Graduate Studies Officer, 961-1-350000 Ext. 3833, Fax: 961-1-744461, E-mail: az48@aub.edu.lb.
Website: https://www.aub.edu.lb/fas/Pages/default.aspx

Antioch University New England, Graduate School, Department of Environmental Studies, Doctoral Program in Environmental Studies, Keene, NH 03431-3552. Offers PhD. *Degree requirements:* For doctorate, thesis/dissertation, practicum. *Entrance requirements:* For doctorate, master's degree and previous experience in the environmental field. Additional exam requirements/recommendations for international students: Required—TOEFL (minimum score 550 paper-based). Electronic applications accepted. *Expenses:* Contact institution. *Faculty research:* Environmental history, green politics, ecopsychology.

Antioch University New England, Graduate School, Department of Environmental Studies, Program in Resource Management and Conservation, Keene, NH 03431-3552. Offers MS. *Degree requirements:* For master's, thesis optional, practicum. *Entrance requirements:* For master's, previous undergraduate course work in science and math. Additional exam requirements/recommendations for international students: Required—TOEFL (minimum score 550 paper-based). Electronic applications accepted. *Expenses:* Contact institution.

Antioch University New England, Graduate School, Department of Environmental Studies, Self-Designed Studies Program, Keene, NH 03431-3552. Offers MS. *Degree requirements:* For master's, practicum, seminar, thesis or project. *Entrance requirements:* For master's, detailed proposal. Additional exam requirements/recommendations for international students: Required—TOEFL (minimum score 550 paper-based).

Antioch University New England, Graduate School, Department of Management, Program in Sustainability (Green MBA), Keene, NH 03431-3552. Offers MBA. *Program availability:* Part-time. *Entrance requirements:* For master's, GRE, resume, 3 letters of recommendation. Additional exam requirements/recommendations for international students: Required—TOEFL (minimum score 600 paper-based).

Arizona State University at the Tempe campus, Ira A. Fulton Schools of Engineering, The Polytechnic School, Programs in Technology Management, Mesa, AZ 85212. Offers aviation management and human factors (MS); environmental technology management (MS); global technology and development (MS); graphic information technology (MS); management of technology (MS). *Program availability:* Part-time, evening/weekend, online learning. *Degree requirements:* For master's, thesis or applied project and oral defense; interactive Program of Study (iPOS) submitted before completing 50 percent of required credit hours. *Entrance requirements:* For master's, GRE, minimum GPA of 3.0 or equivalent in last 2 years of work leading to bachelor's degree. Additional exam requirements/recommendations for international students: Required—TOEFL, IELTS, or PTE. Electronic applications accepted. *Faculty research:* Digital imaging, digital publishing, Internet development/e-commerce, information aviation human factors, pilot selection, databases, multimedia, commercial digital photography, digital workflow, computer graphics modeling and animation, information design, sociotechnology, visual and technical literacy, environmental management, quality management, project management, industrial ethics, hazardous materials, environmental chemistry.

Ball State University, Graduate School, College of Sciences and Humanities, Department of Natural Resources and Environmental Management, Muncie, IN 47306. Offers emergency management and homeland security (Certificate); natural resources and environmental management (MA, MS). *Program availability:* Part-time. *Degree requirements:* For master's, thesis (for some programs). *Entrance requirements:* For master's, GRE General Test, minimum baccalaureate GPA of 2.75 or 3.0 in latter half of baccalaureate, two letters of reference. Additional exam requirements/recommendations for international students: Required—TOEFL (minimum score 550 paper-based; 79 iBT), IELTS (minimum score 6.5). Electronic applications accepted. *Faculty research:* Acid rain, indoor air pollution, land reclamation.

Bard College, Bard Center for Environmental Policy, Annandale-on-Hudson, NY 12504. Offers climate science and policy (MS, Professional Certificate), including agriculture (MS), ecosystems (MS); environmental policy (MS, Professional Certificate); sustainability (MBA); MS/JD; MS/MAT. *Program availability:* Part-time. *Degree requirements:* For master's, thesis, 4-month, full-time internship. *Entrance requirements:* For master's, GRE, coursework in statistics, chemistry and one other semester of college science; personal statement; curriculum vitae; 3 letters of recommendation; sample of written work. Additional exam requirements/recommendations for international students: Required—TOEFL (minimum score 600 paper-based; 100 iBT). Electronic applications accepted. *Expenses:* Contact institution. *Faculty research:* Climate and agriculture, alternative energy, environmental economics, environmental toxicology, EPA law, sustainable development, international relations, literature and composition, human rights, agronomy, advocacy, leadership.

Baylor University, Graduate School, College of Arts and Sciences, Department of Environmental Science, Waco, TX 76798. Offers MES, MS, PhD. *Students:* 24 full-time (14 women), 1 (woman) part-time; includes 8 minority (2 Black or African American, non-Hispanic/Latino; 2 Asian, non-Hispanic/Latino; 3 Hispanic/Latino; 1 Two or more races, non-Hispanic/Latino), 5 international. In 2018, 1 master's, 1 doctorate awarded. *Degree requirements:* For master's, thesis; for doctorate, comprehensive exam, thesis/dissertation. *Entrance requirements:* For master's, GRE General Test. Additional exam requirements/recommendations for international students: Required—TOEFL. *Application deadline:* For fall admission, 1/2 priority date for domestic students; for spring admission, 5/2 for domestic students. Applications are processed on a rolling basis. Application fee: $25. *Financial support:* Research assistantships, teaching assistantships, career-related internships or fieldwork, Federal Work-Study, and institutionally sponsored loans available. Financial award application deadline: 1/2. *Faculty research:* Environmental toxicology, environmental chemistry. *Unit head:* Dr. Erica Bruce, Graduate Program Director, 254-710-4877, Fax: 254-710-3409, E-mail: erica_bruce@baylor.edu. *Application contact:* Kristie Curttright, Administrative Assistant, 254-710-3405, Fax: 254-710-3870, E-mail: kristie_curttright@baylor.edu. Website: https://www.baylor.edu/environmentalscience/

Bemidji State University, School of Graduate Studies, Bemidji, MN 56601. Offers biology (MS); education (MS), English (MA, MS); environmental studies (MS); mathematics (MS); mathematics (elementary and middle level education) (MS); special education (M Sp Ed). *Program availability:* Part-time, online learning. *Degree requirements:* For master's, comprehensive exam, thesis (for some programs). *Entrance requirements:* For master's, GRE; GMAT, letters of recommendation, letters of interest. Additional exam requirements/recommendations for international students: Required—TOEFL (minimum score 550 paper-based; 80 iBT). Electronic applications accepted. *Expenses:* Contact institution. *Faculty research:* Human performance, sport, and health: physical education teacher education, continuum models, spiritual health, intellectual health, resiliency, health priorities; psychology: health psychology, college student drinking behavior, micro-aggressions, infant cognition, false memories, leadership assessment; biology: structure and dynamics of forest communities, aquatic and riverine ecology, interaction between animal populations and aquatic environments, cellular motility.

Binghamton University, State University of New York, Graduate School, Harpur College of Arts and Sciences, Department of Geological Sciences and Environmental Studies, Binghamton, NY 13902-6000. Offers environmental studies (MS); geological sciences (MS, PhD). *Program availability:* Part-time. Terminal master's awarded for partial completion of doctoral program. *Degree requirements:* For master's, thesis; for doctorate, one foreign language, comprehensive exam, thesis/dissertation. *Entrance requirements:* For master's and doctorate, GRE General Test. Additional exam requirements/recommendations for international students: Required—TOEFL (minimum score 550 paper-based; 80 iBT). Electronic applications accepted.

California State University, Fullerton, Graduate Studies, College of Humanities and Social Sciences, Program in Environmental Studies, Fullerton, CA 92831-3599. Offers MS. *Program availability:* Part-time. *Entrance requirements:* For master's, minimum GPA of 2.5 in last 60 units of course work.

Central European University, Department of Environmental Sciences and Policy, 1051, Hungary. Offers MS, PhD. *Program availability:* Part-time. Terminal master's awarded for partial completion of doctoral program. *Degree requirements:* For master's, one foreign language, thesis; for doctorate, one foreign language, comprehensive exam, thesis/dissertation. *Entrance requirements:* For master's and doctorate, essay, interview, statement of purpose. Additional exam requirements/recommendations for international students: Required—TOEFL (minimum score 570 paper-based); Recommended—IELTS (minimum score 6.5). Electronic applications accepted. *Faculty research:* Management of ecological systems, environmental impact assessment, energy conservation, climate change policy, forest policy in countries in transition.

Central Washington University, School of Graduate Studies and Research, College of the Sciences, Program in Cultural and Environmental Resource Management, Ellensburg, WA 98926. Offers anthropology (MS); geography (MS). *Entrance requirements:* For master's, GRE, minimum GPA of 3.0. Additional exam requirements/recommendations for international students: Required—TOEFL (minimum score 550 paper-based; 79 iBT). Electronic applications accepted.

The Citadel, The Military College of South Carolina, Citadel Graduate College, School of Science and Mathematics, Department of Biology, Charleston, SC 29409. Offers biology (MA); environmental studies (Graduate Certificate). *Accreditation:* NCATE (one or more programs are accredited). *Program availability:* Part-time, evening/weekend. *Entrance requirements:* For master's, GRE (minimum combined score of 290 verbal and quantitative) or MAT (minimum raw score of 396), official transcript reflecting highest degree earned from regionally-accredited college or university; for Graduate Certificate, official transcript reflecting highest degree earned from regionally-accredited college or university. Additional exam requirements/recommendations for international students: Required—TOEFL (minimum score 550 paper-based; 79 iBT). Electronic applications accepted. *Expenses:* Tuition, state resident: part-time $595 per credit hour. Tuition, nonresident: part-time $1020 per credit hour. *Required fees:* $90 per term.

Clarkson University, Institute for a Sustainable Environment, Program in Environmental Politics and Governance, Potsdam, NY 13699. Offers MS. *Program availability:* Part-time. *Students:* 2 full-time (both women), 1 international. 5 applicants. *Degree requirements:* For master's, thesis. *Entrance requirements:* For master's, GRE. Additional exam requirements/recommendations for international students: Required—TOEFL (minimum score 550 paper-based, 80 iBT) or IELTS (6.5). *Application deadline:* Applications are processed on a rolling basis. Application fee: $50. Electronic applications accepted. *Expenses: Tuition:* Full-time $24,984; part-time $1388 per credit hour. *Required fees:* $225. Tuition and fees vary according to campus/location and program. *Financial support:* Scholarships/grants and unspecified assistantships available. *Unit head:* Dr. Susan Powers, Director of the Institute for a Sustainable Environment/Associate Director of Sustainability, 315-268-6542, E-mail: spowers@clarkson.edu. *Application contact:* Dan Capogna, Director of Graduate Admissions & Recruitment, 518-631-9910, E-mail: graduate@clarkson.edu. Website: https://www.clarkson.edu/academics/graduate

Clark University, Graduate School, Department of International Development, Community, and Environment, Program in Environmental Science and Policy, Worcester, MA 01610-1477. Offers MS, MBA/MS. *Degree requirements:* For master's, thesis. *Entrance requirements:* For master's, 2 references, resume or curriculum vitae, personal statement. Additional exam requirements/recommendations for international students: Required—TOEFL (minimum score 575 paper-based; 90 iBT), IELTS (minimum score 6.5). Electronic applications accepted. *Expenses:* Contact institution. *Faculty research:* Environmental justice, children's health and risk assessment, smart grids and energy technology transitions, uncertainty-risk analysis, climate variability modeling.

Clark University, Graduate School, Department of International Development, Community, and Environment, Program in Geographic Information Science for Development and Environment, Worcester, MA 01610-1477. Offers MS. *Degree requirements:* For master's, thesis. *Entrance requirements:* For master's, 2 references, resume or curriculum vitae, personal statement. Additional exam requirements/recommendations for international students: Required—TOEFL (minimum score 575 paper-based; 90 iBT), IELTS (minimum score 6.5). Electronic applications accepted. *Expenses:* Contact institution. *Faculty research:* Land-use change, the effects of environmental influences on child health and development, quantitative methods, watershed management, brownfields redevelopment, human/environment interactions, biodiversity conservation, climate change.

Clemson University, Graduate School, College of Agriculture, Forestry and Life Sciences, Department of Plant and Environmental Sciences, Clemson, SC 29634. Offers entomology (MS, PhD); plant and environmental sciences (MS, PhD). *Program availability:* Part-time. *Faculty:* 35 full-time (10 women). *Students:* 76 full-time (31 women), 19 part-time (3 women); includes 4 minority (1 Asian, non-Hispanic/Latino; 3 Two or more races, non-Hispanic/Latino), 29 international. Average age 29. 66 applicants, 65% accepted, 28 enrolled. In 2018, 12 master's, 8 doctorates awarded. *Degree requirements:* For master's, thesis (for some programs); for doctorate, comprehensive exam, thesis/dissertation. *Entrance requirements:* For master's and doctorate, GRE General Test, unofficial transcripts, letters of recommendation. Additional exam requirements/recommendations for international students: Required—TOEFL (minimum score 80 paper-based; 80 iBT); Recommended—IELTS (minimum score 6.5), TSE (minimum score 54). *Application deadline:* For fall admission, 4/15 for international students; for spring admission, 10/15 for international students. Applications are processed on a rolling basis. Application fee: $80 ($90 for international students). Electronic applications accepted. *Expenses: Tuition, area resident:* Full-time $11,270; part-time $8688 per credit hour. Tuition, state resident: full-time $11,796. Tuition, nonresident: full-time $20,002, part-time $17,412 per credit hour. *International tuition:* $23,246 full-time. *Required fees:* $1196; $497 per semester. Tuition and fees vary according to course load, degree level, campus/location and program. *Financial support:* In 2018–19, 45 students received support, including 6 fellowships with full and partial tuition reimbursements available (averaging $4,167 per year), 29 research assistantships with full and partial tuition reimbursements available (averaging $16,620 per year), 10 teaching assistantships with full and partial tuition reimbursements available (averaging $15,148 per year). *Faculty research:* Agronomy, horticulture, plant pathology, plant physiology, entomology. *Total annual research expenditures:* $3.6 million. *Unit head:* Dr. Carlyle Brewster, Department Chair, 864-656-3352, E-mail: carlylb@clemson.edu. *Application contact:* Dr. Guido Schnabel, Graduate Program Coordinator, 864-656-6705, E-mail: schnabel@clemson.edu. Website: http://www.clemson.edu/cafls/departments/plant-environmental-sciences/index.html

Cleveland State University, College of Graduate Studies, Maxine Goodman Levin College of Urban Affairs, Program in Environmental Studies, Cleveland, OH 44115. Offers environmental nonprofit management (MAES); environmental planning (MAES); policy and administration (MAES); sustainable economic development (MAES); urban economic development (Certificate); JD/MAES. *Program availability:* Part-time, evening/weekend. *Faculty:* 16 full-time (8 women), 13 part-time/adjunct (5 women). *Students:* 8 full-time (4 women), 6 part-time (2 women); includes 3 minority (2 Black or African American, non-Hispanic/Latino; 1 Asian, non-Hispanic/Latino). Average age 29. 10 applicants, 100% accepted, 5 enrolled. In 2018, 5 master's awarded. *Degree requirements:* For master's, thesis or alternative, exit project. *Entrance requirements:* For master's, GRE General Test (minimum score: verbal and quantitative combined 40th percentile, analytical writing 4.0), minimum GPA of 3.0. Additional exam requirements/recommendations for international students: Required—TOEFL (minimum score 550 paper-based; 78 iBT), IELTS (6.0), or International Test of English Proficiency (iTEP). *Application deadline:* For fall admission, 7/1 priority date for domestic students, 5/15 for international students; for spring admission, 11/15 for domestic students, 11/1 for international students; for summer admission, 4/1 for domestic students, 3/15 for international students. Applications are processed on a rolling basis. Application fee: $40. Electronic applications accepted. *Expenses:* Contact institution. *Financial support:* In 2018–19, 4 students received support. Research assistantships, teaching assistantships with partial tuition reimbursements available, scholarships/grants, tuition waivers (full and partial), and unspecified assistantships available. Support available to part-time students. Financial award application deadline: 3/1; financial award applicants required to submit FAFSA. *Faculty research:* Environmental policy and administration, environmental planning, geographic information systems (GIS), urban sustainability planning and management, energy policy, land re-use. *Unit head:* Dr. Sanda Kaufman, Professor/Program Director, 216-687-2367, Fax: 216-687-9239, E-mail: s.kaufman@csuohio.edu. *Application contact:* David Arrighi, Graduate Academic Advisor, 216-523-7522, Fax: 216-687-5398, E-mail: d.arrighi@csuohio.edu. Website: http://urban.csuohio.edu/academics/graduate/maes/

Cleveland State University, College of Graduate Studies, Maxine Goodman Levin College of Urban Affairs, Program in Urban Planning and Development, Cleveland, OH 44115. Offers economic development (MUPD); environmental sustainability (MUPD); historic preservation (MUPD); housing and neighborhood development (MUPD); real estate development and finance (MUPD); urban economic development (Certificate); urban geographic information systems (MUPD); JD/MUPDD. *Accreditation:* ACSP. *Program availability:* Part-time, evening/weekend. *Faculty:* 16 full-time (8 women), 13 part-time/adjunct (5 women). *Students:* 27 full-time (11 women), 21 part-time (11 women); includes 7 minority (5 Black or African American, non-Hispanic/Latino; 1 Hispanic/Latino; 1 Two or more races, non-Hispanic/Latino), 2 international. Average age 28. 48 applicants, 56% accepted, 14 enrolled. In 2018, 7 master's awarded. *Degree requirements:* For master's, thesis or alternative, exit project. *Entrance requirements:* For master's, GRE General Test (minimum score: 50th percentile combined verbal and quantitative, 4.0 analytical writing), minimum GPA of 3.0. Additional exam requirements/recommendations for international students: Required—TOEFL (minimum score 550 paper-based; 78 iBT), IELTS (6.0), or International Test of English Proficiency (iTEP). *Application deadline:* For fall admission, 7/1 priority date for domestic students, 5/15 for international students; for spring admission, 11/15 for domestic students, 11/1 for international students; for summer admission, 4/1 for domestic students, 3/15 for international students. Applications are processed on a rolling basis. Application fee: $40. Electronic applications accepted. *Expenses:* Contact institution. *Financial support:* In 2018–19, 10 students received support, including 5 research assistantships with full tuition reimbursements available (averaging $7,200 per year), 3 teaching assistantships with partial tuition reimbursements available (averaging $2,400 per year); scholarships/grants, tuition waivers (full and partial), and unspecified assistantships also available. Support available to part-time students. Financial award application deadline: 3/1; financial award applicants required to submit FAFSA. *Faculty research:* Housing and neighborhood development, urban housing policy, environmental sustainability, economic development, GIS and planning decision support. *Unit head:* Dr. Stephanie Ryberg-Webster, Assistant Professor/Program Director, 216-802-3386, Fax: 216-687-2013, E-mail: s.ryberg@csuohio.edu. *Application contact:* David Arrighi, Graduate Academic Advisor, 216-523-7522, Fax: 216-687-5398, E-mail: d.arrighi@csuohio.edu. Website: http://www.csuohio.edu/urban/mupd/mupd

College of the Atlantic, Program in Human Ecology, Bar Harbor, ME 04609-1198. Offers M Phil. *Degree requirements:* For master's, thesis. *Faculty research:* Conservation of endangered species, public policy/community planning, environmental education, history, philosophy.

Colorado State University, College of Liberal Arts, Department of Political Science, Fort Collins, CO 80523-1782. Offers environmental politics and policy (PhD); political science (MA). *Program availability:* Part-time. Terminal master's awarded for partial completion of doctoral program. *Degree requirements:* For master's, thesis (for some programs), methods; for doctorate, comprehensive exam, thesis/dissertation, methods. *Entrance requirements:* For master's, GRE General Test (minimum verbal and quantitative scores of 301 [1080 on old scoring system] and analytical score of 5.0), bachelor's degree; for doctorate, GRE General Test (minimum verbal and quantitative scores of 308 [1200 on old scoring system] and analytical score of 5.0), minimum graduate-level GPA of 3.5; 15-page writing sample. Additional exam requirements/recommendations for international students: Required—TOEFL (minimum score 600 paper-based). Electronic applications accepted. *Expenses:* Tuition, state resident: full-time $10,520; part-time $4675 per credit hour. Tuition, nonresident: full-time $25,791; part-time $11,462 per credit hour. *International tuition:* $25,791 full-time. *Required fees:* $2392; $576 $288. Tuition and fees vary according to course level, course load, degree level, program and student level. *Faculty research:* Environmental politics and policy; political institutions; political behavior; democracy; political power.

Colorado State University, Warner College of Natural Resources, Department of Forest and Rangeland Stewardship, Fort Collins, CO 80523-1472. Offers ecological restoration (MNRS); forest sciences (MS); rangeland ecosystem science (PhD). *Program availability:* Part-time, 100% online. *Degree requirements:* For master's, thesis (for some programs); for doctorate, comprehensive exam, thesis/dissertation. *Entrance requirements:* For master's and doctorate, GRE General Test, minimum GPA of 3.0; statement of purpose; resume/curriculum vitae; 3 references. Additional exam requirements/recommendations for international students: Required—TOEFL (minimum score 550 paper-based; 80 iBT), IELTS (minimum score 6.5), PTE (minimum score 58). Electronic applications accepted. *Expenses:* Contact institution. *Faculty research:* Wildland restoration/management; natural resource policy; biometrics; wildland fire; climate change.

Columbia University, School of International and Public Affairs, Program in Environmental Science and Policy, New York, NY 10027. Offers MPA. Program admits applicants for late May/early June start only. *Degree requirements:* For master's, workshops. *Entrance requirements:* For master's, GRE, previous course work in biology and chemistry, earth sciences (recommended), economics (strongly recommended). Additional exam requirements/recommendations for international students: Required—TOEFL. Electronic applications accepted. *Faculty research:* Ecological management of enclosed ecosystems vegetation dynamics, environmental policy and management, energy policy, nuclear waste policy, environmental and natural resource economics and policy, carbon sequestration, urban planning, environmental risk assessment/toxicology, environmental justice.

Columbus State University, Graduate Studies, College of Letters and Sciences, Department of Political Science and Public Administration, Columbus, GA 31907-5645. Offers public administration (MPA), including criminal justice, environmental policy, government administration, health services administration, political campaigning, urban policy. *Program availability:* Part-time, evening/weekend, 100% online, blended/hybrid learning. *Faculty:* 4 full-time (2 women), 6 part-time/adjunct (1 woman). *Students:* 18 full-time (12 women), 35 part-time (18 women); includes 20 minority (15 Black or African American, non-Hispanic/Latino; 1 Asian, non-Hispanic/Latino; 3 Hispanic/Latino; 1 Two or more races, non-Hispanic/Latino), 2 international. Average age 31. 35 applicants, 40% accepted, 10 enrolled. In 2018, 37 master's awarded. *Degree requirements:* For master's, comprehensive exam. *Entrance requirements:* For master's, GRE General Test, minimum GPA of 2.75, three letters of recommendation. Additional exam requirements/recommendations for international students: Required—TOEFL (minimum score 550 paper-based; 79 iBT). *Application deadline:* For fall admission, 6/30 for domestic students, 5/1 for international students; for spring admission, 11/1 for domestic and international students; for summer admission, 3/1 for domestic and international students. Applications are processed on a rolling basis. Application fee: $50. Electronic applications accepted. *Expenses: Tuition, area resident:* Full-time $4924; part-time $618 per credit hour. Tuition, state resident: full-time $4924; part-time $618 per credit hour. Tuition, nonresident: full-time $19,218; part-time $2403 per credit hour. *International tuition:* $19,218 full-time. *Required fees:* $1870; $802. Tuition and fees vary according to course load, degree level and program. *Financial support:* In 2018–19, 3 students received support, including 7 research assistantships with partial tuition reimbursements available (averaging $3,000 per year); career-related internships or fieldwork, Federal Work-Study, institutionally sponsored loans, scholarships/grants, tuition waivers (partial), and unspecified assistantships also available. Support available to part-time students. Financial award application deadline: 5/1; financial award applicants required to submit FAFSA. *Unit head:* Dr. Frederick Gordon, Director, 706-565-7875, E-mail: gordon_frederick@colstate.edu. *Application contact:* Catrina Smith-Edmond, Assistant Director for Graduate and Global Admission, 706-507-8824, Fax: 706-568-5091, E-mail: smithedmond_catrina@columbusstate.edu.
Website: http://politicalscience.columbusstate.edu/

Concordia University, School of Graduate Studies, Faculty of Arts and Science, Department of Geography, Planning and Environment, Montréal, QC H3G 1M8, Canada. Offers environmental assessment (M Env, Diploma); geography, urban and environmental studies (M Sc, PhD).

Cornell University, Graduate School, Graduate Fields of Agriculture and Life Sciences, Field of Natural Resources, Ithaca, NY 14853. Offers community-based natural resources management (MS, PhD); conservation biology (MS, PhD); ecosystem biology and biogeochemistry (MPS, MS, PhD); environmental management (MPS); fishery and aquatic science (MPS, MS, PhD); forest science (MPS, MS, PhD); human dimensions of natural resources management (MPS, MS, PhD); policy and institutional analysis (MS, PhD); program development and evaluation (MPS, MS, PhD); quantitative ecology (MS, PhD); wildlife science (MPS, MS, PhD). *Degree requirements:* For master's, thesis (MS), project paper (MPS); for doctorate, comprehensive exam, thesis/dissertation. *Entrance requirements:* For master's and doctorate, GRE General Test, 2 letters of recommendation. Additional exam requirements/recommendations for international students: Required—TOEFL (minimum score 550 paper-based; 77 iBT). Electronic applications accepted. *Faculty research:* Ecosystem-level dynamics, systems modeling, conservation biology/management, resource management's human dimensions, biogeochemistry.

Cornell University, Graduate School, Graduate Fields of Agriculture and Life Sciences, Field of Soil and Crop Sciences, Ithaca, NY 14853. Offers agronomy (MS, PhD); environmental information science (MS, PhD); environmental management (MPS); field crop science (MS, PhD); soil science (MS, PhD). *Degree requirements:* For master's, thesis (MS); for doctorate, comprehensive exam, thesis/dissertation. *Entrance requirements:* For master's and doctorate, GRE General Test, 2 letters of recommendation. Additional exam requirements/recommendations for international students: Required—TOEFL (minimum score 550 paper-based; 77 iBT). Electronic applications accepted. *Faculty research:* Soil chemistry, physics and biology; crop physiology and management; environmental information science and modeling; international agriculture; weed science.

Cornell University, Graduate School, Graduate Fields of Architecture, Art and Planning, Field of Regional Science, Ithaca, NY 14853. Offers environmental studies (MA, MS, PhD); international spatial problems (MA, MS, PhD); location theory (MA, MS, PhD); multiregional economic analysis (MA, MS, PhD); peace science (MA, MS, PhD); planning methods (MA, MS, PhD); urban and regional economics (MA, MS, PhD). Terminal master's awarded for partial completion of doctoral program. *Degree requirements:* For master's, thesis; for doctorate, comprehensive exam, thesis/dissertation. *Entrance requirements:* For master's and doctorate, GRE General Test, 2 letters of recommendation. Additional exam requirements/recommendations for international students: Required—TOEFL (minimum score 600 paper-based; 77 iBT). Electronic applications accepted. *Faculty research:* Urban and regional growth, spatial economics, formation of spatial patterns by socioeconomic systems, non-linear dynamics and complex systems, environmental-economic systems.

Cornell University, Graduate School, Graduate Fields of Arts and Sciences, Field of Archaeology, Ithaca, NY 14853. Offers environmental archaeology (MA); historical archaeology (MA); Latin American archaeology (MA); medieval archaeology (MA); Mediterranean and Near Eastern archaeology (MA); Stone Age archaeology (MA). *Degree requirements:* For master's, one foreign language, thesis. *Entrance requirements:* For master's, GRE General Test, 3 letters of recommendation, sample of written work. Additional exam requirements/recommendations for international students: Required—TOEFL (minimum score 550 paper-based; 77 iBT). Electronic applications accepted. *Faculty research:* Anatolia, Lydia, Sardis, classical and Hellenistic Greece, science in archaeology, North American Indians, Stone Age Africa, Mayan trade.

Dalhousie University, Faculty of Agriculture, Halifax, NS B3H 4R2, Canada. Offers agriculture (M Sc), including air quality, animal behavior, animal molecular genetics, animal nutrition, animal technology, aquaculture, botany, crop management, crop physiology, ecology, environmental microbiology, food science, horticulture, nutrient management, pest management, physiology, plant biotechnology, plant pathology, soil chemistry, soil fertility, waste management and composting, water quality. *Program availability:* Part-time. *Degree requirements:* For master's, thesis, ATC Exam Teaching Assistantship. *Entrance requirements:* For master's, honors B Sc, minimum GPA of 3.0. Additional exam requirements/recommendations for international students: Required—TOEFL (minimum score 580 paper-based; 92 iBT), IELTS, Michigan English Language Assessment Battery, CanTEST, CAEL. *Faculty research:* Bio-product development, organic agriculture, nutrient management, air and water quality, agricultural biotechnology.

Dalhousie University, Faculty of Management, School for Resource and Environmental Studies, Halifax, NS B3H 3J5, Canada. Offers MES, MREM, MLIS/MREM. *Program availability:* Part-time. *Degree requirements:* For master's, thesis. *Entrance requirements:* For master's, honors degree. Additional exam requirements/recommendations for international students: Required—TOEFL, IELTS, CANTEST, CAEL, or Michigan English Language Assessment Battery. Electronic applications accepted. *Faculty research:* Resource management and ecology, aboriginal resource rights, management of toxic substances, environmental impact assessment, forest management, policy, coastal zone management.

Drexel University, College of Arts and Sciences, Program in Environmental Policy, Philadelphia, PA 19104-2875. Offers MS. *Program availability:* Part-time, evening/weekend. *Degree requirements:* For master's, thesis optional. Electronic applications accepted.

Duke University, Graduate School, University Program in Environmental Policy, Durham, NC 27708. Offers PhD. *Degree requirements:* For doctorate, comprehensive exam, thesis/dissertation. *Entrance requirements:* For doctorate, GRE General Test. Additional exam requirements/recommendations for international students: Required—TOEFL (minimum score 577 paper-based; 90 iBT) or IELTS (minimum score 7). Electronic applications accepted.

Duquesne University, Bayer School of Natural and Environmental Sciences, Environmental Science and Management Program, Pittsburgh, PA 15282-0001. Offers MS, Certificate, JD/MS, MBA/MS. *Program availability:* Part-time, evening/weekend. *Faculty:* 7 full-time (2 women), 10 part-time/adjunct (3 women). *Students:* 16 full-time (10 women), 10 part-time (9 women); includes 5 minority (2 Asian, non-Hispanic/Latino; 1 Hispanic/Latino; 2 Two or more races, non-Hispanic/Latino). Average age 27. 18 applicants, 94% accepted, 9 enrolled. In 2018, 25 master's awarded. *Degree requirements:* For master's, thesis (for some programs), minimum of 37 credit hours (for conservation biology); for Certificate, minimum of 18 credit hours. *Entrance requirements:* For master's, GRE General Test, course work in biology, chemistry, and calculus or statistics; 2 letters of reference; official transcripts; statement of purpose; for Certificate, undergraduate degree, 2 letters of reference, official transcripts, statement of purpose. Additional exam requirements/recommendations for international students: Required—TOEFL (minimum score 90 iBT), TOEFL (minimum score 90 iBT) or IELTS. *Application deadline:* For fall admission, 7/1 priority date for domestic students, 4/1 for international students; for spring admission, 10/1 priority date for domestic students, 10/1 for international students. Applications are processed on a rolling basis. Application fee: $0. Electronic applications accepted. *Expenses:* $1376/credit hour. *Financial support:* In 2018–19, 23 students received support, including 1 fellowship with full tuition reimbursement available (averaging $18,000 per year), 7 research assistantships with full and partial tuition reimbursements available (averaging $14,500 per year), 1 teaching assistantship with full tuition reimbursement available (averaging $14,000 per year); career-related internships or fieldwork, scholarships/grants, tuition waivers (partial), and unspecified assistantships also available. Financial award application deadline: 5/31. *Faculty research:* Watershed management systems, environmental analytical chemistry, environmental endocrinology, environmental microbiology, aquatic biology. *Unit head:* Dr. John Stolz, Director, 412-396-6333, Fax: 412-396-5907, E-mail: stolz@duq.edu. *Application contact:* Heather Costello, Senior Graduate Academic Advisor, 412-396-6339, E-mail: costelloh@duq.edu.
Website: http://www.duq.edu/academics/schools/natural-and-environmental-sciences/academic-programs/environmental-science-and-management

The Evergreen State College, Graduate Programs, Program in Environmental Studies, Olympia, WA 98505. Offers MES. *Program availability:* Part-time, evening/weekend. *Faculty:* 5 full-time (3 women), 5 part-time/adjunct (2 women). *Students:* 61 full-time (38 women), 38 part-time (27 women); includes 22 minority (3 Black or African American, non-Hispanic/Latino; 1 American Indian or Alaska Native, non-Hispanic/Latino; 2 Asian, non-Hispanic/Latino; 11 Hispanic/Latino; 5 Two or more races, non-Hispanic/Latino). Average age 31. 77 applicants, 91% accepted, 46 enrolled. In 2018, 29 master's awarded. *Degree requirements:* For master's, thesis. *Entrance requirements:* For master's, BA or BS; Minimum GPA of 3.0 on 4.0 scale for last 90 graded quarter hours or 60 graded semester hours; 4 quarter or 3 semester hour credits: social science, natural science and statistics; 3 letters of recommendation; evidence of writing, analytical and general communication skills of high quality and at level appropriate for graduate study. Additional exam requirements/recommendations for international students: Required—TOEFL (minimum score 600 paper-based; 100 iBT), TOEFL (minimum score 600 paper-based; 100 iBT) or IELTS (minimum score 7.5). *Application deadline:* For fall admission, 1/15 priority date for domestic and international students. Applications are processed on a rolling basis. Application fee: $50. Electronic applications accepted. *Expenses:* Contact institution. *Financial support:* In 2018–19, 46 students received support, including 13 fellowships with partial tuition reimbursements available (averaging $3,495 per year); career-related internships or fieldwork, Federal Work-Study, institutionally sponsored loans, scholarships/grants, and tuition waivers (partial) also available. Support available to part-time students. Financial award application deadline: 2/1; financial award applicants required to submit FAFSA. *Faculty research:* History of science and technology, environmental sociology, energy and climate change, social science research methods, environmental chemistry, molecular biology and ecology, oceanography, energy and environmental policy, political ecology, social impacts of energy choices, landscape ecology, conservation biology, avian ecology, native wildlife response to land use and climate change, empirical field studies, ecological modeling, physics, math, astrophysics, Geographic Information Systems (GIS). *Unit head:* Dr. Kevin Francis, Director, 360-867-5831, Fax: 360-867-5430, E-mail: francisk@evergreen.edu. *Application contact:* Andrea Martin, Assistant Director, 360-867-6225, Fax: 360-867-5430, E-mail: martina@evergreen.edu.
Website: http://www.evergreen.edu/mes/

Florida Gulf Coast University, College of Arts and Sciences, Program in Environmental Studies, Fort Myers, FL 33965-6565. Offers MA. *Program availability:* Part-time. *Degree requirements:* For master's, internship. *Entrance requirements:* Additional exam requirements/recommendations for international students: Required—TOEFL (minimum score 550 paper-based).

Florida Gulf Coast University, College of Arts and Sciences, Program in Public Administration, Fort Myers, FL 33965-6565. Offers environmental policy (MPA); management (MPA). *Accreditation:* NASPAA. *Program availability:* Part-time. *Degree requirements:* For master's, thesis. *Entrance requirements:* For master's, GRE General Test, MAT, minimum GPA of 3.0. Additional exam requirements/recommendations for international students: Required—TOEFL (minimum score 550 paper-based). Electronic applications accepted. *Faculty research:* Personnel, public policy, public finance, housing policy.

Florida Institute of Technology, College of Engineering and Science, Program in Environmental Resource Management, Melbourne, FL 32901-6975. Offers MS. *Program availability:* Part-time. *Students:* 1 full-time (0 women), 2 part-time (1 woman), all international. Average age 26. In 2018, 2 master's awarded. *Degree requirements:* For master's, internship. *Entrance requirements:* For master's, GRE General Test, 3 letters of recommendation, resume, statement of objectives, conference with faculty and the program chair (highly recommended). Additional exam requirements/recommendations for international students: Required—TOEFL (minimum score 550 paper-based; 79 iBT). *Application deadline:* Applications are processed on a rolling basis. Application fee: $50. Electronic applications accepted. *Expenses: Tuition:* Full-time $22,338; part-time $1241 per credit hour. Tuition and fees vary according to degree level, campus/location and program. *Financial support:* Research assistantships, teaching assistantships, career-related internships or fieldwork, and tuition remissions available. Financial award application deadline: 3/1; financial award applicants required to submit FAFSA. *Faculty research:* Coastal management issues, environmental policy, land use, impacts of growth, managing aquatic resources. *Unit head:* Dr. Richard Aronson, Department Head, 321-674-9034, E-mail: raronson@fit.edu. *Application contact:* Mike Perry, Executive Director of Admissions, 321-674-7127, E-mail: perrymj@fit.edu.
Website: https://www.fit.edu/programs/environmental-resource-management-ms/

Florida International University, College of Arts, Sciences, and Education, Department of Earth and Environment, Miami, FL 33199. Offers earth science (PhD); environmental studies (MS); geosciences (MS, PhD); natural resources management and policy (PSM). *Program availability:* Part-time, evening/weekend. *Faculty:* 33 full-time (11 women), 15 part-time/adjunct (5 women). *Students:* 92 full-time (45 women), 6 part-time (4 women); includes 42 minority (5 Black or African American, non-Hispanic/Latino; 1 Asian, non-Hispanic/Latino; 32 Hispanic/Latino; 4 Two or more races, non-Hispanic/Latino), 22 international. Average age 30. 80 applicants, 55% accepted, 27 enrolled. In 2018, 22 master's, 4 doctorates awarded. *Degree requirements:* For master's, thesis; for doctorate, comprehensive exam, thesis/dissertation. *Entrance requirements:* For master's and doctorate, GRE General Test, 3 letters of recommendation, minimum GPA of 3.0, resume. Additional exam requirements/recommendations for international students: Required—TOEFL (minimum score 550 paper-based; 80 iBT). *Application deadline:* For fall admission, 2/15 for domestic and international students; for spring admission, 9/1 for domestic and international students. Applications are processed on a rolling basis. Application fee: $30. Electronic applications accepted. *Financial support:* Institutionally sponsored loans and scholarships/grants available. Financial award application deadline: 3/1; financial award applicants required to submit FAFSA. *Faculty research:* Determination of dispersivity and hydraulic conductivity in the Biscayne Aquifer. *Unit head:* Dr. Rene Price, Chair, 305-348-3119, E-mail: rene.price@fiu.edu. *Application contact:* Nanett Rojas, Manager, Admissions Operations, 305-348-7464, Fax: 305-348-7441, E-mail: gradadm@fiu.edu.

George Mason University, College of Science, Department of Environmental Science and Policy, Fairfax, VA 22030. Offers MS, PhD. *Faculty:* 17 full-time (9 women), 10 part-time/adjunct (2 women). *Students:* 51 full-time (37 women), 62 part-time (39 women); includes 17 minority (3 Black or African American, non-Hispanic/Latino; 9 Asian, non-Hispanic/Latino; 2 Hispanic/Latino; 3 Two or more races, non-Hispanic/Latino), 6 international. Average age 31. 50 applicants, 82% accepted, 22 enrolled. In 2018, 12 master's, 15 doctorates awarded. *Degree requirements:* For master's, variable foreign language requirement, comprehensive exam (for some programs), thesis (for some programs); for doctorate, variable foreign language requirement, comprehensive exam, thesis/dissertation. *Entrance requirements:* For master's, GRE, BA or BS; for doctorate, GRE, advanced degree or equivalent research experience. Additional exam requirements/recommendations for international students: Required—TOEFL (minimum score 575 paper-based; 88 iBT), IELTS (minimum score 6.5), PTE (minimum score 59). Application fee: $75 ($80 for international students). Electronic applications accepted. *Financial support:* In 2018–19, 40 students received support, including 9 research assistantships with tuition reimbursements available (averaging $15,944 per year), 31 teaching assistantships with tuition reimbursements available (averaging $17,032 per year); career-related internships or fieldwork, Federal Work-Study, scholarships/grants, unspecified assistantships, and health care benefits (for full-time research or teaching assistantship recipients) also available. Support available to part-time students. Financial award application deadline: 3/1; financial award applicants required to submit FAFSA. *Faculty research:* Conservation of species and ecosystems; water and watersheds; one health and sustainability; climate change; interdisciplinary (including natural and social science). *Total annual research expenditures:* $300,156. *Unit head:* Dr. Alonso Aguirre, Chair, 703-993-7590, E-mail: aaguirr3@gmu.edu. *Application contact:* Sharon Bloomquist, Graduate Program Coordinator, 703-993-3187, Fax: 703-993-1066, E-mail: sbloomqu@gmu.edu.
Website: http://esp.gmu.edu/

The George Washington University, Columbian College of Arts and Sciences, Program in Environmental and Resource Policy, Washington, DC 20052. Offers MA. *Students:* 19 full-time (10 women), 9 part-time (6 women); includes 7 minority (1 Black or African American, non-Hispanic/Latino; 4 Asian, non-Hispanic/Latino; 2 Hispanic/Latino), 1 international. Average age 26. 67 applicants, 84% accepted, 18 enrolled. In 2018, 13 master's awarded. *Entrance requirements:* For master's, GRE General Test, minimum GPA of 3.0, two letters of recommendation. Additional exam requirements/recommendations for international students: Required—TOEFL (minimum score 600 paper-based; 100 iBT). *Application deadline:* For fall admission, 4/1 priority date for domestic and international students; for spring admission, 10/1 priority date for domestic students, 9/1 priority date for international students. Applications are processed on a rolling basis. Application fee: $60. Electronic applications accepted. *Financial support:* In 2018–19, 2 students received support. Fellowships, institutionally sponsored loans, and tuition waivers available. Financial award application deadline: 1/15. *Unit head:* Prof. Peter Linquiti, Director, 202-994-5837, E-mail: linquiti@gwu.edu. *Application contact:* Prof. Peter Linquiti, Director, 202-994-5837, E-mail: linquiti@gwu.edu.
Website: http://www.gwu.edu/~tspppa/academics/affiliated_environment_policy.cfm

Georgia Institute of Technology, Graduate Studies, College of Design, School of City and Regional Planning, Atlanta, GA 30332-0001. Offers city and regional planning (PhD); economic development (MCRP); environmental planning and management (MCRP); geographic information systems (MCRP); land and community development (MCRP); land use planning (MCRP); transportation (MCRP); urban design (MCRP); MCP/MSCE. *Accreditation:* ACSP. *Degree requirements:* For master's, thesis, internship. *Entrance requirements:* For master's, GRE General Test, minimum GPA of 2.7. Additional exam requirements/recommendations for international students: Required—TOEFL. Electronic applications accepted.

Georgia State University, Andrew Young School of Policy Studies, Department of Economics, Atlanta, GA 30302-3083. Offers economics (MA); environmental economics (PhD); experimental economics (PhD); labor economics (PhD); policy (MA); public finance (PhD); urban and regional economics (PhD). MA offered through the College of Arts and Sciences. *Program availability:* Part-time. *Faculty:* 19 full-time (4 women). *Students:* 116 full-time (47 women), 10 part-time (5 women); includes 33 minority (14 Black or African American, non-Hispanic/Latino; 9 Asian, non-Hispanic/Latino; 7 Hispanic/Latino; 3 Two or more races, non-Hispanic/Latino), 57 international. Average age 28. 263 applicants, 43% accepted, 38 enrolled. In 2018, 21 master's, 11 doctorates awarded. Terminal master's awarded for partial completion of doctoral program. *Degree requirements:* For master's, thesis optional; for doctorate, comprehensive exam, thesis/dissertation. *Entrance requirements:* For master's and doctorate, GRE. Additional exam requirements/recommendations for international students: Required—TOEFL (minimum score 603 paper-based; 100 iBT) or IELTS (minimum score 7). *Application deadline:* For fall admission, 1/15 for domestic and international students. Application fee: $50. Electronic applications accepted. *Expenses: Tuition, area resident:* Full-time $9360; part-time $390 per credit hour. *Tuition, state resident:* full-time $9360; part-time $390 per credit hour. *Tuition, nonresident:* full-time $30,024; part-time $1251 per credit hour. *International tuition:* $30,024 full-time. *Required fees:* $2128. *Financial support:* In 2018–19, fellowships with full tuition reimbursements (averaging $11,333 per year), research assistantships with full tuition reimbursements (averaging $9,788 per year), teaching assistantships with full tuition reimbursements (averaging $3,000 per year) were awarded; career-related internships or fieldwork also available. Financial award application deadline: 2/15; financial award applicants required to submit FAFSA. *Faculty research:* Public, experimental, urban/environmental, labor, and health economics. *Unit head:* Dr. Rusty Tchernis, Director of the Doctoral Program, 404-413-0154, Fax: 404-413-0145, E-mail: rtchernis@gsu.edu. *Application contact:* Dr. Rusty Tchernis, Director of the Doctoral Program, 404-413-0154, Fax: 404-413-0145, E-mail: rtchernis@gsu.edu.
Website: http://economics.gsu.edu/

Georgia State University, Andrew Young School of Policy Studies, Department of Public Management and Policy, Atlanta, GA 30303. Offers criminal justice (MPA); disaster

Peterson's Graduate Programs in the Physical Sciences, Mathematics, Agricultural Sciences, the Environment & Natural Resources 2020

www.petersons.com **299**

management (Certificate); disaster policy (MPA); environmental policy (PhD); health policy (PhD); management and finance (MPA); nonprofit management (MPA, Certificate); nonprofit policy (MPA); planning and economic development (MPP, Certificate); policy analysis and evaluation (MPA), including planning and economic development; public and nonprofit management (PhD); public finance and budgeting (PhD), including science and technology policy, urban and regional economic development; public finance policy (MPA), including social policy; public health (MPA). *Accreditation:* NASPAA (one or more programs are accredited). *Program availability:* Part-time. *Faculty:* 13 full-time (6 women), 2 part-time/adjunct (0 women). *Students:* 126 full-time (77 women), 96 part-time (65 women); includes 104 minority (80 Black or African American, non-Hispanic/Latino; 4 Asian, non-Hispanic/Latino; 10 Hispanic/Latino; 10 Two or more races, non-Hispanic/Latino), 32 international. Average age 32. 304 applicants, 59% accepted, 99 enrolled. In 2018, 57 master's, 7 doctorates, 8 other advanced degrees awarded. Terminal master's awarded for partial completion of doctoral program. *Degree requirements:* For master's, thesis optional; for doctorate, comprehensive exam, thesis/dissertation. *Entrance requirements:* For master's and doctorate, GRE. Additional exam requirements/recommendations for international students: Required—TOEFL (minimum score 603 paper-based; 100 iBT) or IELTS (minimum score 7). *Application deadline:* For fall admission, 1/15 for domestic and international students. Application fee: $50. Electronic applications accepted. *Expenses: Tuition, area resident:* Full-time $9360; part-time $390 per credit hour. Tuition, state resident: full-time $9360; part-time $390 per credit hour. Tuition, nonresident: full-time $30,024; part-time $1251 per credit hour. *International tuition:* $30,024 full-time. *Required fees:* $2128. *Financial support:* In 2018–19, fellowships (averaging $8,194 per year), research assistantships (averaging $8,068 per year), teaching assistantships (averaging $3,600 per year) were awarded; institutionally sponsored loans, scholarships/grants, health care benefits, and unspecified assistantships also available. Financial award application deadline: 2/1. *Faculty research:* Public budgeting and finance, public management, nonprofit management, performance measurement and management, urban development. *Unit head:* Dr. Greg Lewis, Chair and Professor, 404-413-0014, Fax: 404-413-0104, E-mail: glewis@gsu.edu. *Application contact:* Dr. Greg Lewis, Chair and Professor, 404-413-0014, Fax: 404-413-0104, E-mail: glewis@gsu.edu.
Website: https://aysps.gsu.edu/public-management-policy/

Harvard University, Extension School, Cambridge, MA 02138-3722. Offers applied sciences (CAS); biotechnology (ALM); educational technologies (ALM); educational technology (CET); English for graduate and professional studies (DGP); environmental management (ALM, CEM); information technology (ALM); journalism (ALM); liberal arts (ALM); management (ALM, CM); mathematics for teaching (ALM); museum studies (ALM); premedical studies (Diploma); publication and communication (CPC). *Program availability:* Part-time, evening/weekend. *Degree requirements:* For master's, thesis. *Entrance requirements:* For master's, 3 completed graduate courses with grade of B or higher. Additional exam requirements/recommendations for international students: Required—TOEFL (minimum score 600 paper-based), TWE (minimum score 5). *Expenses:* Contact institution.

Humboldt State University, Academic Programs, College of Natural Resources and Sciences, Programs in Environmental Systems, Arcata, CA 95521-8299. Offers environmental systems (MS), including energy, environment and society, environmental resources engineering, geology, math modeling. *Faculty:* 34 full-time (14 women), 37 part-time/adjunct (17 women). *Students:* 18 full-time (8 women), 6 part-time (2 women); includes 7 minority (3 Asian, non-Hispanic/Latino; 3 Hispanic/Latino; 1 Two or more races, non-Hispanic/Latino), 4 international. Average age 28. 48 applicants, 52% accepted, 11 enrolled. In 2018, 12 master's awarded. *Degree requirements:* For master's, thesis. *Entrance requirements:* For master's, GRE, appropriate bachelor's degree, minimum GPA of 2.5, 3 letters of recommendation. Additional exam requirements/recommendations for international students: Required—TOEFL. *Application deadline:* For fall admission, 2/15 for domestic students; for spring admission, 10/15 for domestic students. Applications are processed on a rolling basis. Application fee: $55. *Expenses: Tuition:* Part-time $4649 per semester. *Required fees:* $2121; $1673. Tuition and fees vary according to program. *Financial support:* Application deadline: 3/1; applicants required to submit FAFSA. *Faculty research:* Mathematical modeling, international development technology, geology, environmental resources engineering. *Unit head:* Dr. Margaret Lang, Graduate Program Coordinator, 707-826-3256, E-mail: CNRSmast@humboldt.edu. *Application contact:* Dr. Margaret Lang, Graduate Program Coordinator, 707-826-3256, E-mail: CNRSmast@humboldt.edu.

Idaho State University, Graduate School, College of Science and Engineering, Department of Civil and Environmental Engineering, Pocatello, ID 83209-8060. Offers civil engineering (MS); environmental engineering (MS); environmental science and management (MS). *Program availability:* Part-time. *Degree requirements:* For master's, comprehensive exam (for some programs), thesis optional, thesis project, 2 semesters of seminar. *Entrance requirements:* For master's, GRE. Additional exam requirements/recommendations for international students: Required—TOEFL (minimum score 550 paper-based; 80 iBT). Electronic applications accepted. *Faculty research:* Floor vibration investigations, earthquake engineering, base isolation systems and seismic risk assessment, infrastructure revitalization (building foundations and damage, bridge structures, highways, and dams), slope stability and soil erosion, pavement rehabilitation, computational fluid dynamics and flood control structures, microbial fuel cells, water treatment and water quality modeling, environmental risk assessment, biotechnology, nanotechnology.

Illinois Institute of Technology, Stuart School of Business, Program in Environmental Management and Sustainability, Chicago, IL 60661. Offers MS, JD/MS, MBA/MS. *Program availability:* Part-time, evening/weekend. *Entrance requirements:* For master's, GRE (minimum score 298) or GMAT (500), one semester of general chemistry and mathematics through calculus. Additional exam requirements/recommendations for international students: Required—TOEFL (minimum score 600 paper-based; 85 iBT); Recommended—IELTS (minimum score 7). Electronic applications accepted. *Expenses:* Contact institution. *Faculty research:* Wind energy, carbon footprint reduction, critical asset management, solar energy, water quality management.

Indiana University Bloomington, School of Public and Environmental Affairs, Public Affairs Programs, Bloomington, IN 47405. Offers economic development (MPA); energy (MPA); environmental policy (PhD); environmental policy and natural resource management (MPA); information systems (MPA); international development (MPA); local government management (MPA); nonprofit management (MPA, Certificate); policy analysis (MPA); public budgeting and financial management (Certificate); public finance (PhD); public financial administration (MPA); public management (MPA, PhD, Certificate); public policy analysis (PhD); social entrepreneurship (Certificate); specialized public affairs (MPA); sustainability and sustainable development (MPA); JD/MPA; MPA/MA; MPA/MIS; MPA/MLS; MSES/MPA. *Accreditation:* NASPAA (one or more programs are accredited). *Program availability:* Part-time. *Degree requirements:* For master's, capstone, internship; for doctorate, comprehensive exam, thesis/dissertation. *Entrance requirements:* For master's, GRE General Test or GMAT, official transcripts, 3 letters of recommendation, resume, personal statement; for doctorate, GRE General Test, official transcripts, 3 letters of recommendation, statement of purpose. Additional exam requirements/recommendations for international students: Required—TOEFL (minimum score 600 paper-based; 96 iBT); Recommended—IELTS (minimum score 7). Electronic applications accepted. *Faculty research:* International development, environmental policy and resource management, policy analysis, public finance, public management, urban management, nonprofit management, energy policy, social policy, public finance.

Indiana University Northwest, School of Public and Environmental Affairs, Gary, IN 46408. Offers criminal justice (MPA); environmental affairs (Graduate Certificate); health services (MPA); nonprofit management (Certificate); public management (MPA, Graduate Certificate). *Accreditation:* NASPAA (one or more programs are accredited). *Program availability:* Part-time. *Entrance requirements:* For master's, GRE General Test (minimum combined verbal and quantitative score of 280), GMAT, or LSAT, letters of recommendation. Electronic applications accepted. *Faculty research:* Employment in income security policies, evidence in criminal justice, equal employment law, social welfare policy and welfare reform, public finance in developing countries.

Indiana University of Pennsylvania, School of Graduate Studies and Research, College of Humanities and Social Sciences, Department of Geography and Regional Planning, Environmental Planning Track, Indiana, PA 15705. Offers MS. *Program availability:* Part-time. *Faculty:* 8 full-time (2 women), 1 part-time/adjunct (0 women). *Students:* 4 full-time (3 women). Average age 29. 9 applicants, 78% accepted, 3 enrolled. In 2018, 2 master's awarded. *Degree requirements:* For master's, thesis optional. *Entrance requirements:* Additional exam requirements/recommendations for international students: Required—TOEFL (minimum score 550 paper-based). *Application deadline:* Applications are processed on a rolling basis. Application fee: $50. Electronic applications accepted. *Expenses:* Tuition, state resident: full-time $12,384; part-time $516 per credit hour. Tuition, nonresident: full-time $18,576; part-time $774 per credit hour. *Required fees:* $4454; $186 per credit hour. $65 per semester. Tuition and fees vary according to program and reciprocity agreements. *Financial support:* In 2018–19, 4 research assistantships with tuition reimbursements (averaging $4,370 per year) were awarded; career-related internships or fieldwork, Federal Work-Study, scholarships/grants, and unspecified assistantships also available. Financial award application deadline: 4/15; financial award applicants required to submit FAFSA. *Unit head:* Dr. Jennifer Smith, Graduate Coordinator, 724-357-2250, E-mail: jsmith@iup.edu. *Application contact:* Dr. Jennifer Smith, Graduate Coordinator, 724-357-2250, E-mail: jsmith@iup.edu.

Instituto Tecnologico de Santo Domingo, Graduate School, Area of Basic And Environmental Sciences, Santo Domingo, Dominican Republic. Offers environmental science (M En S), including environmental education, environmental management, marine resources, natural resources management; mathematics (MS, PhD); renewable energy technology (MS, Certificate).

Instituto Tecnológico y de Estudios Superiores de Monterrey, Campus Estado de México, Professional and Graduate Division, Estado de Mexico, Mexico. Offers administration of information technologies (MITA); architecture (M Arch); business administration (GMBA, MBA); computer sciences (MCS, PhD); education (M Ed); educational institution administration (MAD); educational technology and innovation (PhD); electronic commerce (MEC); environmental systems (MS); finance (MAF); humanistic studies (MHS); information sciences and knowledge management (MISKM); information systems (MS); manufacturing systems (MS); marketing (MEM); quality systems and productivity (MS); science and materials engineering (PhD); telecommunications management (MTM). *Program availability:* Part-time, online learning. *Degree requirements:* For master's, one foreign language, thesis (for some programs); for doctorate, one foreign language, thesis/dissertation. *Entrance requirements:* For master's, E-PAEP 500, interview; for doctorate, E-PAEP 500, research proposal. Additional exam requirements/recommendations for international students: Required—TOEFL (minimum score 550 paper-based). *Faculty research:* Surface treatments by plasmas, mechanical properties, robotics, graphical computing, mechatronics security protocols.

Instituto Tecnológico y de Estudios Superiores de Monterrey, Campus Irapuato, Graduate Programs, Irapuato, Mexico. Offers administration (MBA); administration of information technology (MAIT); administration of telecommunications (MAT); architecture (M Arch); computer science (MCS); education (M Ed); educational administration (MEA); educational innovation and technology (DEIT); educational technology (MET); electronic commerce (MBA); environmental administration and planning (MEAP); environmental systems (MES); finances (MBA); humanistic studies (MHS); international management for Latin American executives (MIMLAE); library and information science (MLIS); manufacturing quality management (MMQM); marketing research (MBA).

Inter American University of Puerto Rico, Metropolitan Campus, Graduate Programs, Program in Environmental Evaluation and Protection, San Juan, PR 00919-1293. Offers MS.

James Madison University, The Graduate School, College of Integrated Science and Engineering, Program in Environmental Management and Sustainability, Harrisonburg, VA 22807. Offers MS. *Students:* 3 part-time (1 woman), 1 international. Average age 30. In 2018, 15 master's awarded. Electronic applications accepted. *Expenses:* Tuition, state resident: full-time $10,848. Tuition, nonresident: full-time $27,888. *Required fees:* $1128. *Financial support:* Fellowships, Federal Work-Study, and unspecified assistantships available. Financial award application deadline: 3/1; financial award applicants required to submit FAFSA. *Unit head:* Dr. Eric H. Maslen, Department Head, 540-568-2740, E-mail: masleneh@jmu.edu. *Application contact:* Lynette D. Michael, Director of Graduate Admissions, 540-568-6131 Ext. 6395, Fax: 540-568-7860, E-mail: michaeld@jmu.edu.
Website: http://www.jmu.edu/mems-malta/index.shtml

Johns Hopkins University, Advanced Academic Programs, Program in Environmental Sciences and Policy, Washington, DC 21218. Offers energy policy and climate (MS); environmental sciences (MS); geographic information systems (MS, Certificate). *Program availability:* Part-time, evening/weekend, online learning. *Students:* 13 full-time (11 women), 192 part-time (148 women). 81 applicants, 78% accepted, 36 enrolled. In 2018, 66 master's awarded. *Entrance requirements:* For master's, minimum GPA of 3.0, coursework in chemistry and calculus. Additional exam requirements/recommendations for international students: Required—TOEFL (minimum score 100 iBT). *Application deadline:* For fall admission, 5/31 priority date for domestic students, 4/30 priority date for international students; for spring admission, 10/31 priority date for domestic and international students. Applications are processed on a rolling basis. Application fee: $75. Electronic applications accepted. *Financial support:* Applicants required to submit FAFSA. *Unit head:* Dr. Jerry Burgess, Program Director, 202-452-1915, E-mail: jerry.burgess@jhu.edu. *Application contact:* Melissa Edwards, Admissions Manager, 202-452-1941, Fax: 202-452-1970, E-mail: aapadmissions@jhu.edu.
Website: http://advanced.jhu.edu/academics/graduate-degree-programs/environmental-sciences-and-policy/

Johns Hopkins University, Engineering Program for Professionals, Part-time Program in Environmental Planning and Management, Baltimore, MD 21218. Offers MS, Graduate Certificate, Post-Master's Certificate. *Program availability:* Part-time, evening/weekend, online only, 100% online. *Faculty:* 7 part-time/adjunct (2 women). *Students:* 33 part-time (21 women). 14 applicants, 21% accepted, 2 enrolled. In 2018, 13 master's awarded. *Entrance requirements:* Additional exam requirements/recommendations for international students: Required—TOEFL (minimum score 600 paper-based; 100 iBT). Application fee: $0. *Unit head:* Dr. Hedy Alavi, Program Chair, 410-516-7091, Fax: 410-516-8996, E-mail: hedy.alavi@jhu.edu. *Application contact:* Doug Schiller, Admissions Manager, 410-516-2300, Fax: 410-579-8049, E-mail: schiller@jhu.edu. Website: http://www.ep.jhu.edu

Johns Hopkins University, G. W. C. Whiting School of Engineering, Master of Science in Engineering Management Program, Baltimore, MD 21218. Offers biomaterials (MSEM); civil engineering (MSEM); communications science (MSEM); computer science (MSEM); environmental systems analysis, economics and public policy (MSEM); fluid mechanics (MSEM); materials science and engineering (MSEM); mechanical engineering (MSEM); mechanics and materials (MSEM); nano-biotechnology (MSEM); nanomaterials and nanotechnology (MSEM); operations research (MSEM); probability and statistics (MSEM); smart product and device design (MSEM). *Students:* 34 full-time (12 women), 18 part-time (7 women). 233 applicants, 39% accepted, 33 enrolled. In 2018, 27 master's awarded. *Entrance requirements:* For master's, GRE, 3 letters of recommendation, statement of purpose, transcripts. Additional exam requirements/recommendations for international students: Required—TOEFL (minimum score 600 paper-based, 100 iBT) or IELTS (7). *Application deadline:* For fall admission, 2/15 for domestic and international students. Application fee: $75. Electronic applications accepted. *Financial support:* In 2018–19, 43 research assistantships (averaging $43,344 per year) were awarded; health care benefits also available. *Unit head:* Dr. Pamela Sheff, Director, 410-516-7056, Fax: 410-516-4880, E-mail: pamsheff@gmail.com. *Application contact:* Lindsey Conklin, Sr. Academic Program Coordinator, 410-516-1108, Fax: 410-516-0780, E-mail: lconkli4@jhu.edu. Website: http://engineering.jhu.edu/msem/

Lake Forest College, Graduate Program in Liberal Studies, Lake Forest, IL 60045. Offers American studies (MLS); cinema in East Asia (MLS); environmental studies (MLS); history (MLS); Medieval and Renaissance art (MLS); philosophy (MLS); Spanish (MLS); writing (MLS). *Program availability:* Part-time, evening/weekend. *Degree requirements:* For master's, thesis optional, 8 courses, including at least 3 interdisciplinary seminars. *Entrance requirements:* For master's, transcript, essay, interview. Additional exam requirements/recommendations for international students: Required—TOEFL (minimum score 550 paper-based; 83 iBT); Recommended—IELTS (minimum score 6.5). Electronic applications accepted. *Expenses:* Contact institution. *Faculty research:* Religion in America, Asian philosophy, cinema studies, theater studies, sociology of religion.

Lehigh University, College of Arts and Sciences, Environmental Policy Program, Bethlehem, PA 18015. Offers environmental health (Graduate Certificate); environmental justice (Graduate Certificate); environmental policy and law (Graduate Certificate); environmental policy design (MA); sustainable development (Graduate Certificate); urban environmental policy (Graduate Certificate). *Faculty:* 7 full-time (3 women). *Students:* 10 full-time (7 women), 3 part-time (2 women); includes 2 minority (1 Asian, non-Hispanic/Latino; 1 Hispanic/Latino), 1 international. Average age 24. 12 applicants, 100% accepted, 9 enrolled. In 2018, 3 master's awarded. *Degree requirements:* For master's, thesis or additional course work. *Entrance requirements:* For master's, GRE, minimum GPA of 2.75, 3.0 for last two undergraduate semesters; essay; 2 letters of recommendation. Additional exam requirements/recommendations for international students: Required—TOEFL (minimum score 85 iBT), IELTS (minimum score 6.5). *Application deadline:* For fall admission, 1/1 for domestic and international students; for spring admission, 12/1 for domestic and international students. Application fee: $75. Tuition and fees vary according to program. *Financial support:* Application deadline: 1/1. *Faculty research:* Environmental policy, environmental law, urban policy, urban politics, urban environmental policy, sustainability, sustainable development, international environmental law, international environmental policy, environmental justice, social justice. *Unit head:* Dr. Karen B. Pooley, Director, 610-758-1238, E-mail: kbp312@lehigh.edu. *Application contact:* Mandy Fraley, Academic Coordinator, 610-758-5837, Fax: 610-758-6232, E-mail: amf518@lehigh.edu. Website: http://ei.cas2.lehigh.edu/

Long Island University–LIU Post, College of Liberal Arts and Sciences, Brookville, NY 11548-1300. Offers applied mathematics (MS); behavior analysis (MA); biology (MS); criminal justice (MS); earth science (MS); English (MA); environmental sustainability (MS); genetic counseling (MS); history (MA); interdisciplinary studies (MA, MS); political science (MA); psychology (MA). *Program availability:* Part-time, evening/weekend, blended/hybrid learning. Terminal master's awarded for partial completion of doctoral program. *Degree requirements:* For master's, comprehensive exam (for some programs), thesis (for some programs). *Entrance requirements:* Additional exam requirements/recommendations for international students: Required—TOEFL, IELTS, or PTE. Electronic applications accepted. *Faculty research:* Biology, environmental sustainability, mathematics, psychology, genetic counseling.

Louisiana State University and Agricultural & Mechanical College, Graduate School, School of the Coast and Environment, Department of Environmental Sciences, Baton Rouge, LA 70803. Offers environmental planning and management (MS); environmental science (PhD); environmental toxicology (MS).

McGill University, Faculty of Graduate and Postdoctoral Studies, Faculty of Agricultural and Environmental Sciences, Department of Natural Resource Sciences, Montréal, QC H3A 2T5, Canada. Offers entomology (M Sc, PhD); environmental assessment (M Sc); forest science (M Sc, PhD); microbiology (M Sc, PhD); micrometeorology (M Sc, PhD); neotropical environment (M Sc, PhD); soil science (M Sc, PhD); wildlife biology (M Sc, PhD).

Middlebury Institute of International Studies at Monterey, Graduate School of International Policy and Management, Program in International Environmental Policy, Monterey, CA 93940-2691. Offers MA. *Degree requirements:* For master's, one foreign language. *Entrance requirements:* For master's, minimum GPA of 3.0, proficiency in a foreign language. Additional exam requirements/recommendations for international students: Required—TOEFL (minimum score 550 paper-based; 80 iBT). Electronic applications accepted.

Millersville University of Pennsylvania, College of Graduate Studies and Adult Learning, College of Science and Technology, Department of Earth Sciences, Millersville, PA 17551-0302. Offers integrated scientific applications (MS). *Program availability:* Part-time. *Faculty:* 3 full-time (0 women), 5 part-time/adjunct (1 woman). *Students:* 7 full-time (3 women), 7 part-time (3 women); includes 3 minority (1 Black or African American, non-Hispanic/Latino; 1 Asian, non-Hispanic/Latino; 1 Hispanic/Latino). Average age 26. 10 applicants, 100% accepted, 8 enrolled. In 2018, 3 master's awarded. *Degree requirements:* For master's, thesis optional, capstone experience such

as internship or applied research. *Entrance requirements:* For master's, GRE or MAT or GMAT, required only if cumulative GPA is lower than 3.0, Resume. Additional exam requirements/recommendations for international students: Required—TOEFL, IELTS (minimum score 6), PTE (minimum score 60). *Application deadline:* Applications are processed on a rolling basis. Application fee: $40. Electronic applications accepted. *Expenses: Tuition, area resident:* Full-time $9288; part-time $516 per credit. Tuition, state resident: full-time $9288; part-time $516 per credit. Tuition, nonresident: full-time $13,932; part-time $774 per credit. *International tuition:* $13,932 full-time. *Required fees:* $2623.50; $145.75 per credit. Tuition and fees vary according to course load, degree level and program. *Financial support:* In 2018–19, 4 students received support. Unspecified assistantships available. Financial award application deadline: 3/15; financial award applicants required to submit FAFSA. *Faculty research:* Meteorology, ocean sciences and coastal studies, physical oceanography, geology, earth sciences, environmental geology, earth sciences education, heliophysics and space weather. *Total annual research expenditures:* $50,000. *Unit head:* Dr. Richard D. Clark, Chairperson and Graduate Program Coordinator, 717-871-7434, Fax: 717-871-7918, E-mail: richard.clark@millersville.edu. *Application contact:* Dr. James A. Delle, Acting Dean of College of Graduate Studies and Adult Learning/Associate Provost, Academic Administration, 717-871-7462, E-mail: James.Delle@millersville.edu. Website: https://www.millersville.edu/esci/index.php

Missouri State University, Graduate College, Interdisciplinary Program in Professional Studies, Springfield, MO 65897. Offers administrative studies (Certificate); applied communication (MS); criminal justice (MS); environmental management (MS); homeland security (MS); individualized (MS); professional studies (MS); screenwriting and producing (MS); sports management (MS). *Program availability:* Part-time, evening/weekend, 100% online, blended/hybrid learning. *Students:* 94 full-time (61 women), 81 part-time (44 women); includes 17 minority (7 Black or African American, non-Hispanic/Latino; 1 American Indian or Alaska Native, non-Hispanic/Latino; 1 Asian, non-Hispanic/Latino; 5 Hispanic/Latino; 3 Two or more races, non-Hispanic/Latino), 62 international. Average age 24. 71 applicants, 63% accepted. In 2018, 62 master's awarded. *Degree requirements:* For master's, comprehensive exam, thesis or alternative. *Entrance requirements:* For master's, GRE, GMAT (if GPA less than 3.0). Additional exam requirements/recommendations for international students: Required—TOEFL (minimum score 550 paper-based; 79 iBT), IELTS (minimum score 6). *Application deadline:* For fall admission, 7/15 priority date for domestic students; for spring admission, 12/1 priority date for domestic students; for summer admission, 5/1 for domestic students. Applications are processed on a rolling basis. Application fee: $55 ($60 for international students). Electronic applications accepted. Tuition and fees vary according to class time, course level, course load, degree level, campus/location, program and student level. *Financial support:* Career-related internships or fieldwork, Federal Work-Study, institutionally sponsored loans, scholarships/grants, and unspecified assistantships available. Support available to part-time students. Financial award application deadline: 1/31; financial award applicants required to submit FAFSA. *Unit head:* Dr. Gerald Masterson, Program Director, 417-836-5251, Fax: 417-836-6888, E-mail: mps@missouristate.edu. *Application contact:* Lakan Drinker, Director, Graduate Enrollment Management, 417-836-5330, Fax: 417-836-6200, E-mail: lakandrinker@missouristate.edu. Website: https://gip.missouristate.edu/mps/

Montclair State University, The Graduate School, College of Science and Mathematics, PhD Program in Environmental Management, Montclair, NJ 07043-1624. Offers PhD. *Degree requirements:* For doctorate, thesis/dissertation. *Entrance requirements:* For doctorate, GRE General Test, 3 letters of recommendation, essay. Additional exam requirements/recommendations for international students: Required—TOEFL (minimum score 83 iBT) or IELTS (minimum score 6.5). Electronic applications accepted. *Faculty research:* Environmental geochemistry/remediation/forensics, environmental law and policy, regional climate modeling, remote sensing, Cenozoic marine sediment records from polar regions, sustainability science.

Montclair State University, The Graduate School, College of Science and Mathematics, Program in Environmental Studies, Montclair, NJ 07043-1624. Offers environmental education (MA); environmental management (MA); environmental science (MA). *Program availability:* Part-time, evening/weekend. *Degree requirements:* For master's, thesis. *Entrance requirements:* For master's, GRE General Test, 2 letters of recommendation, essay. Additional exam requirements/recommendations for international students: Required—TOEFL (minimum score 83 iBT), IELTS (minimum score 6.5). Electronic applications accepted. *Faculty research:* Environmental geochemistry/remediation/forensics, environmental law and policy, regional climate modeling, remote sensing, Cenozoic marine sediment records from polar regions, sustainability science.

Morehead State University, Graduate School, College of Science, Department of Biology and Chemistry, Morehead, KY 40351. Offers biology (MS); biology regional analysis (MS). *Program availability:* Part-time. *Degree requirements:* For master's, comprehensive exam, thesis optional, oral and written final exams. *Entrance requirements:* For master's, GRE General Test, minimum GPA of 3.0 in biology, 2.5 overall; undergraduate major/minor in biology, environmental science, or equivalent. Additional exam requirements/recommendations for international students: Required—TOEFL (minimum score 525 paper-based). Electronic applications accepted. *Faculty research:* Atherosclerosis, RNA evolution, cancer biology, water quality/ecology, immunoparasitology.

New Jersey Institute of Technology, College of Science and Liberal Arts, Newark, NJ 07102. Offers applied mathematics (MS); applied physics (MS, PhD); applied statistics (MS, Certificate); biology (MS, PhD); biostatistics (MS); chemistry (MS, PhD); environmental and sustainability policy (MS); environmental science (MS, PhD); history (MA, MAT); materials science and engineering (MS, PhD); mathematical and computational finance (MS); mathematical sciences (PhD); pharmaceutical chemistry (MS); professional and technical communications (MS); technical communication essentials (Certificate). *Program availability:* Part-time, evening/weekend. *Faculty:* 150 full-time (43 women), 115 part-time/adjunct (47 women). *Students:* 200 full-time (79 women), 63 part-time (29 women); includes 61 minority (17 Black or African American, non-Hispanic/Latino; 29 Asian, non-Hispanic/Latino; 11 Hispanic/Latino; 4 Two or more races, non-Hispanic/Latino), 136 international. Average age 28. 429 applicants, 49% accepted, 89 enrolled. In 2018, 43 master's, 16 doctorates, 2 other advanced degrees awarded. Terminal master's awarded for partial completion of doctoral program. *Degree requirements:* For master's, thesis (for some programs); for doctorate, thesis/dissertation. *Entrance requirements:* For master's and doctorate, GRE General Test, Minimum GPA of 3.0, personal statement, three (3) letters of recommendation, and transcripts. Additional exam requirements/recommendations for international students: Required—TOEFL (minimum score 550 paper-based; 79 iBT), IELTS (minimum score 6.5). *Application deadline:* For fall admission, 6/1 priority date for domestic students, 5/1 priority date for international students; for spring admission, 11/15 priority date for domestic and international students. Applications are processed on a rolling basis. Application fee: $75. Electronic applications accepted. *Expenses:* $22,690 per year (in-state), $32,136 per year (out-of-state). *Financial support:* In 2018–19, 134 students

Peterson's Graduate Programs in the Physical Sciences, Mathematics, Agricultural Sciences, the Environment & Natural Resources 2020

www.petersons.com **301**

received support, including 17 fellowships with full tuition reimbursements available (averaging $22,000 per year), 74 research assistantships with full tuition reimbursements available (averaging $22,000 per year), 71 teaching assistantships with full tuition reimbursements available (averaging $22,000 per year); scholarships/grants, traineeships, health care benefits, and unspecified assistantships also available. Financial award application deadline: 1/15. *Faculty research:* Biophotonics and bioimaging, morphogenetic patterning, embryogenesis, biological fluid dynamics, applied research in the mathematical sciences. *Total annual research expenditures:* $29.2 million. *Unit head:* Dr. Kevin Belfield, Dean, 973-596-3676, Fax: 973-565-0586, E-mail: kevin.d.belfield@njit.edu. *Application contact:* Stephen Eck, Director of Admissions, 973-596-3300, Fax: 973-596-3461, E-mail: admissions@njit.edu.
Website: http://csla.njit.edu/

The New School, Schools of Public Engagement, Program in Environmental Policy and Sustainability Management, New York, NY 10011. Offers environmental policy and sustainability management (MS). *Program availability:* Part-time, evening/weekend. *Degree requirements:* For master's, thesis. *Entrance requirements:* For master's, two letters of recommendation, statement of purpose, resume, transcripts. Additional exam requirements/recommendations for international students: Required—TOEFL (minimum score 92 iBT), IELTS (minimum score 7), PTE (minimum score 68). Electronic applications accepted. *Expenses:* Contact institution.

New York Institute of Technology, College of Engineering and Computing Sciences, Department of Energy Management, Old Westbury, NY 11568-8000. Offers energy technology (Advanced Certificate); environmental management (Advanced Certificate); facilities management (Advanced Certificate); infrastructure security management (Advanced Certificate). *Program availability:* Part-time, evening/weekend, 100% online, blended/hybrid learning. *Faculty:* 2 full-time (0 women), 6 part-time/adjunct (1 woman). *Students:* 30 full-time (4 women), 46 part-time (11 women); includes 27 minority (7 Black or African American, non-Hispanic/Latino; 10 Asian, non-Hispanic/Latino; 9 Hispanic/Latino; 1 Two or more races, non-Hispanic/Latino), 22 international. Average age 32. 96 applicants, 75% accepted, 24 enrolled. In 2018, 3 Advanced Certificates awarded. *Entrance requirements:* For degree, BS or equivalent; minimum undergraduate GPA of 2.85. Additional exam requirements/recommendations for international students: Required—TOEFL (minimum score 79 iBT), IELTS (minimum score 6), PTE (minimum score 53). *Application deadline:* For fall admission, 7/1 for domestic students, 6/1 for international students; for spring admission, 12/1 for domestic and international students. Applications are processed on a rolling basis. Application fee: $50. Electronic applications accepted. *Expenses: Tuition:* Full-time $1285; part-time $1285 per credit. *Required fees:* $215; $175 per unit. Tuition and fees vary according to course load, degree level and campus/location. *Financial support:* Fellowships with partial tuition reimbursements, teaching assistantships with partial tuition reimbursements, career-related internships or fieldwork, Federal Work-Study, scholarships/grants, tuition waivers (full and partial), and unspecified assistantships available. Support available to part-time students. Financial award application deadline: 2/15; financial award applicants required to submit FAFSA. *Faculty research:* Alternative energy systems; energy policy, master planning, and auditing; facilities management; lighting technology; cogeneration; utility rate structures; smart homes; monitoring systems; building information modeling; sustainability. *Unit head:* Dr. Robert Amundsen, Department Chair, 516-686-7578, E-mail: ramundse@nyit.edu. *Application contact:* Alice Dolitsky, Director, Graduate Admissions, 516-686-7520, Fax: 516-686-1116, E-mail: admissions@nyit.edu.
Website: http://www.nyit.edu/engineering/department_of_energy_management

New York University, School of Professional Studies, Center for Global Affairs, New York, NY 10012-1019. Offers global affairs (MS), including environment/energy policy, global gender studies, human rights and international law, international development and humanitarian assistance, international relations/global futures, peace building, private sector, transnational security. *Program availability:* Part-time, evening/weekend. *Degree requirements:* For master's, thesis. *Entrance requirements:* For master's, GRE or GMAT (only upon request), bachelor's degree, resume with relevant professional work, internship or volunteer experience, two letters of recommendation, statement of purpose. Additional exam requirements/recommendations for international students: Required—TOEFL (minimum score 600 paper-based; 100 iBT), IELTS (minimum score 7). Electronic applications accepted. *Expenses:* Contact institution.

Northeastern Illinois University, College of Graduate Studies and Research, College of Arts and Sciences, Program in Geography and Environmental Studies, Chicago, IL 60625. Offers geographic information science (Graduate Certificate); geography and environmental studies (MA). *Program availability:* Part-time, evening/weekend. *Degree requirements:* For master's, comprehensive exam, thesis optional. *Entrance requirements:* For master's, undergraduate minor in geography or environmental studies, minimum GPA of 2.75. Additional exam requirements/recommendations for international students: Required—TOEFL (minimum score 550 paper-based; 79 iBT). Electronic applications accepted. *Faculty research:* Segregation and urbanization of minority groups in the Chicago area, scale dependence and parameterization in nonpoint source pollution modeling, ecological land classification and mapping, ecosystem restoration, soil-vegetation relationships.

Northeastern University, College of Science, Boston, MA 02115-5096. Offers applied mathematics (MS); bioinformatics (MS); biology (PhD); biotechnology (MS); chemistry and chemical biology (MS, PhD); environmental science and policy (MS); marine and environmental sciences (PhD); marine biology (MS); mathematics (MS, PhD); operations research (MSOR); physics (MS, PhD); psychology (PhD). *Program availability:* Part-time. Terminal master's awarded for partial completion of doctoral program. *Degree requirements:* For master's, comprehensive exam (for some programs), thesis; for doctorate, comprehensive exam (for some programs), thesis/dissertation. *Entrance requirements:* For master's, GRE General Test. Electronic applications accepted. *Expenses:* Contact institution.

Northern Arizona University, College of Environment, Forestry, and Natural Sciences, School of Earth Sciences and Environmental Sustainability, Flagstaff, AZ 86011. Offers climate science and solutions (MS); conservation ecology (Graduate Certificate); earth sciences and environmental sustainability (PhD); environmental sciences and policy (MS); geology (MS). *Program availability:* Part-time. *Degree requirements:* For master's, variable foreign language requirement, comprehensive exam (for some programs), thesis (for some programs); for doctorate, variable foreign language requirement, comprehensive exam (for some programs), thesis/dissertation (for some programs); for Graduate Certificate, comprehensive exam (for some programs). *Entrance requirements:* For master's and doctorate, GRE General Test. Additional exam requirements/recommendations for international students: Required—TOEFL (minimum score 80 iBT), IELTS (minimum score 6.5). Electronic applications accepted.

The Ohio State University, Graduate School, College of Food, Agricultural, and Environmental Sciences, School of Environment and Natural Resources, Columbus, OH 43210. Offers ecological restoration (MS, PhD); ecosystem science (MS, PhD); environment and natural resources (MENR); environmental social sciences (MS, PhD); fisheries and wildlife science (MS, PhD); forest science (MS, PhD); rural sociology (MS, PhD); soil science (MS, PhD). *Faculty:* 38. *Students:* 106 (64 women). Average age 29. In 2018, 21 master's, 5 doctorates awarded. *Entrance requirements:* For master's and doctorate, GRE. Additional exam requirements/recommendations for international students: Required—TOEFL (minimum score 550 paper-based; 79 iBT), Michigan English Language Assessment Battery (minimum score 82); Recommended—IELTS (minimum score 7). *Application deadline:* For fall admission, 1/1 priority date for domestic students, 12/15 priority date for international students; for spring admission, 11/1 for domestic students, 9/15 for international students. Applications are processed on a rolling basis. Application fee: $60 ($70 for international students). Electronic applications accepted. *Financial support:* Fellowships, research assistantships, teaching assistantships, health care benefits, and unspecified assistantships available. *Unit head:* Dr. Jeff S. Sharp, Director, 614-292-9410, E-mail: sharp.123@osu.edu. *Application contact:* Graduate and Professional Admissions, 614-292-9444, Fax: 614-292-3895, E-mail: gpadmissions@osu.edu.
Website: http://senr.osu.edu/

Ohio University, Graduate College, College of Arts and Sciences, Department of Geological Sciences, Athens, OH 45701-2979. Offers environmental geochemistry (MS). *Program availability:* Part-time. *Degree requirements:* For master's, thesis. *Entrance requirements:* Additional exam requirements/recommendations for international students: Required—TOEFL (minimum score 550 paper-based; 80 iBT) or IELTS (minimum score 6.5). Electronic applications accepted. *Faculty research:* Geoscience education, tectonics, fluvial geomorphology, invertebrate paleontology, mine/hydrology.

Ohio University, Graduate College, Voinovich School of Leadership and Public Affairs, Program in Environmental Studies, Athens, OH 45701-2979. Offers MS, Certificate. *Program availability:* Part-time. *Degree requirements:* For master's, comprehensive exam (for some programs), written exams or thesis, research project. *Entrance requirements:* For master's, minimum GPA of 3.0. Additional exam requirements/recommendations for international students: Required—TOEFL (minimum score 600 paper-based; 100 iBT) or IELTS (minimum score 7). Electronic applications accepted. *Faculty research:* Air quality modeling, conservation biology, environmental policy, geographical information systems, land management and watershed restoration.

Oregon State University, College of Liberal Arts, Program in Environmental Arts and Humanities, Corvallis, OR 97331. Offers environmental action (MA).

Oregon State University, College of Liberal Arts, Program in Public Policy, Corvallis, OR 97331. Offers energy policy (MPP, PhD); environmental policy (MPP, PhD); international policy (MPP, PhD); law, crime and policy (MPP, PhD); rural policy (MPP, PhD); science and technology policy (MPP, PhD); social policy (MPP, PhD). *Accreditation:* NASPAA. *Program availability:* Part-time, 100% online. *Entrance requirements:* For master's and doctorate, GRE. Additional exam requirements/recommendations for international students: Required—TOEFL, IELTS (minimum score 6.5).

Pace University, Dyson College of Arts and Sciences, Department of Environmental Studies and Science, New York, NY 10038. Offers environmental science (MS). Offered at Pleasantville, NY location only. *Program availability:* Part-time, evening/weekend. *Students:* 12 full-time (5 women), 15 part-time (10 women); includes 7 minority (1 Asian, non-Hispanic/Latino; 4 Hispanic/Latino; 2 Two or more races, non-Hispanic/Latino), 1 international. Average age 28. 20 applicants, 75% accepted, 7 enrolled. In 2018, 4 master's awarded. *Degree requirements:* For master's, thesis, research project. *Entrance requirements:* For master's, GRE, two letters of recommendation, resume, personal statement, all official transcripts. Additional exam requirements/recommendations for international students: Required—TOEFL (minimum score 88 iBT), IELTS (minimum score 7) or PTE (minimum score 60). *Application deadline:* For fall admission, 8/1 priority date for domestic students, 6/1 for international students; for spring admission, 12/1 priority date for domestic students, 10/1 for international students. Applications are processed on a rolling basis. Application fee: $70. Electronic applications accepted. *Financial support:* Fellowships, research assistantships, career-related internships or fieldwork, scholarships/grants, and unspecified assistantships available. Support available to part-time students. Financial award application deadline: 2/15; financial award applicants required to submit FAFSA. *Unit head:* Dr. E. Melanie DuPuis, Chair, Environmental Studies and Science Program, 914-773-3522, E-mail: edupuis@pace.edu. *Application contact:* Susan Ford-Goldschein, Director of Graduate Admissions, 914-422-4283, Fax: 212-346-1585, E-mail: graduateadmission@pace.edu.
Website: http://www.pace.edu/dyson/departments/environmental-studies-science

Penn State University Park, Graduate School, Intercollege Graduate Programs, Intercollege Program in Environmental Pollution Control, University Park, PA 16802. Offers MEPC, MS.

Point Park University, School of Arts and Sciences, Department of Natural Sciences, Engineering and Technology, Pittsburgh, PA 15222-1984. Offers engineering management (MS); environmental studies (MS). *Program availability:* Part-time, evening/weekend. *Degree requirements:* For master's, comprehensive exam (for some programs), thesis or alternative. *Entrance requirements:* For master's, minimum QPA of 2.75, 2 letters of recommendation, minimum B average in engineering technology or a related field, official undergraduate transcript, statement of intent, resume. Additional exam requirements/recommendations for international students: Required—TOEFL. Electronic applications accepted.

Polytechnic University of Puerto Rico, Graduate School, Hato Rey, PR 00918. Offers business administration (MBA), including computer information systems, general management, management of information systems, management of international enterprises; civil engineering (ME, MS); computer engineering (ME, MS); computer science (MCS, MS); electrical engineering (ME, MS); engineering management (MEM); environmental management (MEM); landscape architecture (M Land Arch); manufacturing competitiveness (MMC, MS); manufacturing engineering (ME, MS); mechanical engineering (M Mech E). *Accreditation:* ASLA. *Program availability:* Part-time, evening/weekend. *Entrance requirements:* For master's, 3 letters of recommendation.

Polytechnic University of Puerto Rico, Miami Campus, Graduate School, Miami, FL 33166. Offers accounting (MBA); business administration (MBA); construction management (MEM); environmental management (MEM); finance (MBA); human resources management (MBA); logistics and supply chain management (MBA); management of international enterprises (MBA); manufacturing management (MEM); marketing management (MBA); project management (MBA). *Program availability:* Part-time, evening/weekend, online learning. *Entrance requirements:* For master's, minimum GPA of 3.0. Electronic applications accepted.

Polytechnic University of Puerto Rico, Orlando Campus, Graduate School, Orlando, FL 32825. Offers accounting (MBA); business administration (MBA); construction management (MEM); engineering management (MEM); environmental management (MEM); finance (MBA); human resources management (MBA); management of international enterprises (MBA); management of technology (MBA); manufacturing management (MEM). *Program availability:* Part-time, evening/weekend, online learning. *Entrance requirements:* For master's, minimum GPA of 3.0. Additional exam requirements/recommendations for international students: Recommended—TOEFL. Electronic applications accepted.

Portland State University, Graduate Studies, College of Liberal Arts and Sciences, Department of Environmental Sciences and Management, Portland, OR 97207-0751. Offers environmental management (MEM); environmental science and management (PSM); environmental sciences/biology (PhD); environmental sciences/chemistry (PhD); environmental sciences/civil engineering (PhD); environmental sciences/geography (PhD); environmental sciences/geology (PhD); environmental sciences/physics (PhD); environmental studies (MS); hydrology (Certificate). *Program availability:* Part-time. *Degree requirements:* For master's, thesis or alternative; for doctorate, variable foreign language requirement, comprehensive exam, thesis/dissertation, oral and qualifying exams. *Entrance requirements:* For master's, GRE General Test, science-based BA/BS or equivalent training, 3 letters of recommendation, identification of potential advisor; for doctorate, minimum GPA of 3.0 in upper-division course work or 2.75 overall. Additional exam requirements/recommendations for international students: Required—TOEFL (minimum score 550 paper-based; 80 iBT), IELTS (minimum score 6.5). *Faculty research:* Environmental aspects of biology, chemistry, civil engineering, geology, physics.

Prescott College, Graduate Programs, Program in Environmental Studies, Prescott, AZ 86301. Offers environmental studies (MA); student-directed independent study (MA). *Program availability:* Part-time, online learning. *Degree requirements:* For master's, thesis, fieldwork or internship, practicum. *Entrance requirements:* For master's, 2 letters of recommendation, resume. Additional exam requirements/recommendations for international students: Required—TOEFL (minimum score 500 paper-based). Electronic applications accepted.

Purdue University, Graduate School, College of Agriculture, Department of Forestry and Natural Resources, West Lafayette, IN 47907. Offers fisheries and aquatic sciences (MS, MSF, PhD); forest biology (MS, MSF, PhD); natural resource social science (MS, PhD); natural resources social science (MSF); quantitative ecology (MS, MSF, PhD); wildlife science (MS, MSF, PhD); wood products and wood products manufacturing (MS, MSF, PhD). *Faculty:* 25 full-time (5 women), 1 part-time/adjunct (0 women). *Students:* 58 full-time (32 women), 5 part-time (1 woman); includes 12 minority (2 American Indian or Alaska Native, non-Hispanic/Latino; 1 Asian, non-Hispanic/Latino; 4 Hispanic/Latino; 1 Native Hawaiian or other Pacific Islander, non-Hispanic/Latino; 4 Two or more races, non-Hispanic/Latino), 12 international. Average age 27. 51 applicants, 27% accepted, 14 enrolled. In 2018, 13 master's, 11 doctorates awarded. *Degree requirements:* For master's, thesis; for doctorate, thesis/dissertation. *Entrance requirements:* For master's and doctorate, GRE General Test (minimum score: verbal 50th percentile; quantitative 50th percentile; analytical writing 4.0), minimum undergraduate GPA of 3.2 or equivalent. Additional exam requirements/recommendations for international students: Required—TOEFL (minimum score 550 paper-based; 77 iBT). *Application deadline:* For fall admission, 1/5 for domestic students, 1/15 for international students; for spring admission, 9/15 for domestic and international students. Applications are processed on a rolling basis. Application fee: $60 ($75 for international students). Electronic applications accepted. *Financial support:* In 2018–19, 10 research assistantships (averaging $15,259 per year) were awarded; fellowships, teaching assistantships, career-related internships or fieldwork, and scholarships/grants also available. Support available to part-time students. Financial award application deadline: 1/5; financial award applicants required to submit FAFSA. *Faculty research:* Wildlife management, forest management, forest ecology, forest soils, limnology. *Unit head:* Robert G. Wagner, Head of the Graduate Program, 765-494-3590, E-mail: rgwagner@purdue.edu. *Application contact:* Christine Hofmeyer, Graduate Contact, 765-494-3572, E-mail: chofmeye@purdue.edu.
Website: https://ag.purdue.edu/fnr

Rice University, Graduate Programs, Wiess School–Professional Science Master's Programs, Professional Master's Program in Environmental Analysis and Decision Making, Houston, TX 77251-1892. Offers MS. *Program availability:* Part-time. *Degree requirements:* For master's, internship. *Entrance requirements:* For master's, GRE General Test, letters of recommendation (4). Additional exam requirements/recommendations for international students: Required—TOEFL (minimum score 600 paper-based; 90 iBT). Electronic applications accepted. *Faculty research:* Environmental biotechnology, environmental nanochemistry, environmental statistics, remote sensing.

Royal Roads University, Graduate Studies, Environment and Sustainability Program, Victoria, BC V9B 5Y2, Canada. Offers environment and management (M Sc, MA); environment and sustainability (MAIS); environmental education and communication (MA, G Dip, Graduate Certificate); MA/MS. *Program availability:* Blended/hybrid learning. *Degree requirements:* For master's, thesis. *Entrance requirements:* For master's, 5-7 years of related work experience. Electronic applications accepted. *Expenses:* Tuition, area resident: Full-time $27,000 Canadian dollars. Tuition, state resident: full-time $27,000 Canadian dollars. Tuition, nonresident: full-time $33,000 Canadian dollars. *Required fees:* $662 Canadian dollars. *Faculty research:* Sustainable development, atmospheric processes, sustainable communities, chemical fate and transport of persistent organic pollutants, educational technology.

St. Edward's University, School of Behavioral and Social Sciences, Austin, TX 78704. Offers environmental management and sustainability (PSM). *Entrance requirements:* Additional exam requirements/recommendations for international students: Required—TOEFL, IELTS. Electronic applications accepted.

Samford University, Howard College of Arts and Sciences, Birmingham, AL 35229. Offers energy (MSEM); environmental management (MSEM); public health (MSEM); JD/MSEM. *Program availability:* Part-time, online only, 100% online. *Faculty:* 8 full-time (2 women), 1 part-time/adjunct (0 women). *Students:* 7 full-time (3 women); includes 4 minority (3 Black or African American, non-Hispanic/Latino; 1 Asian, non-Hispanic/Latino). Average age 28. 18 applicants, 28% accepted, 4 enrolled. In 2018, 4 master's awarded. *Entrance requirements:* For master's, 2 letters of recommendation; minimum overall GPA of 3.0 (3 years or less since undergraduate degree); minimum overall GPA of 2.5 (after 3 years' relevant work experience). Additional exam requirements/recommendations for international students: Required—TOEFL (minimum score 520 paper-based). Application fee: $40. *Expenses: Tuition:* Full-time $17,255; part-time $837 per credit. *Required fees:* $610; $305 per term. Tuition and fees vary according to course load, degree level, program and student level. *Financial support:* Application deadline: 2/15; applicants required to submit FAFSA. *Faculty research:* Genetics, environmental science, animal biology, ecology, biodiversity. *Unit head:* Dr. Anthony Scott Overton, Professor and Chair, 205-726-4537, E-mail: aoverton@samford.edu. *Application contact:* David Frings, Assistant Graduate Director, 205-726-4537, E-mail: dmfrings@samford.edu.
Website: http://howard.samford.edu/

San Francisco State University, Division of Graduate Studies, College of Health and Social Sciences, Public Administration Program, San Francisco, CA 94132-1722. Offers criminal justice administration (MPA); environmental administration and policy (MPA); gerontology (MPA); nonprofit administration (MPA); public management (MPA); public policy (MPA); urban administration (MPA). *Accreditation:* NASPAA.

San Francisco State University, Division of Graduate Studies, College of Science and Engineering, Department of Geography and Environment, San Francisco, CA 94132-1722. Offers geographic information science (MS); geography (MA); resource management and environmental planning (MA). *Unit head:* Dr. Andrew Oliphant, Chair, 415-405-2143, Fax: 415-338-6243, E-mail: andrewo@sfsu.edu. *Application contact:* Dr. Nancy Wilkinson, Graduate Coordinator, 415-338-1439, Fax: 415-338-6243, E-mail: nancyw@sfsu.edu.
Website: http://geog.sfsu.edu/

San Jose State University, Program in Environmental Studies, San Jose, CA 95192-0001. Offers MS. *Program availability:* Part-time. *Degree requirements:* For master's, comprehensive exam, thesis or alternative. *Entrance requirements:* Additional exam requirements/recommendations for international students: Required—TOEFL (minimum score 580 paper-based). Electronic applications accepted. *Faculty research:* Remote sensing, land use/land cover mapping.

Shippensburg University of Pennsylvania, School of Graduate Studies, College of Arts and Sciences, Department of Geography and Earth Science, Shippensburg, PA 17257-2299. Offers geoenvironmental studies (MS). *Program availability:* Part-time, evening/weekend. *Faculty:* 7 full-time (1 woman), 1 part-time/adjunct (0 women). *Students:* 9 full-time (1 woman), 6 part-time (3 women); includes 1 minority (Hispanic/Latino), 1 international. Average age 29. 26 applicants, 77% accepted, 7 enrolled. In 2018, 8 master's awarded. *Degree requirements:* For master's, comprehensive exam, thesis (6 credits) or 1 semester research project (3 credits) and internship (6 credits); practicum exam. *Entrance requirements:* For master's, GRE (if GPA less than 2.75), 12 credit hours in geography or earth sciences, or a combined total of 18 credit hours in the two fields, or 15 credit hours in social sciences including 6 credit hours in geography plus 15 credit hours in the natural sciences including 6 credit hours in the earth sciences. Additional exam requirements/recommendations for international students: Required—TOEFL (minimum score 550 paper-based; 68 iBT), IELTS (minimum score 6), TOEFL (minimum score 550 paper-based, 68 iBT) or IELTS (minimum score 6). *Application deadline:* For fall admission, 3/30 for international students; for spring admission, 9/30 for international students. Applications are processed on a rolling basis. Application fee: $45. Electronic applications accepted. *Expenses:* Tuition, state resident: part-time $516 per credit. Tuition, nonresident: part-time $750 per credit. *Required fees:* $149 per credit. *Financial support:* In 2018–19, 8 students received support. Career-related internships or fieldwork, scholarships/grants, unspecified assistantships, and resident hall director and student payroll positions available. Support available to part-time students. Financial award application deadline: 3/1; financial award applicants required to submit FAFSA. *Unit head:* Dr. Thomas P. Feeney, Professor and Program Coordinator, 717-477-1685, Fax: 717-477-4029, E-mail: tpfeen@ship.edu. *Application contact:* Maya T. Mapp, Director of Admissions, 717-477-1231, Fax: 717-477-4016, E-mail: mtmapp@ship.edu.
Website: http://www.ship.edu/geo-ess/

Simon Fraser University, Office of Graduate Studies and Postdoctoral Fellows, Faculty of Environment, School of Resource and Environmental Management, Burnaby, BC V5A 1S6, Canada. Offers quantitative methods in fisheries management (Graduate Diploma); resource and environmental management (MRM, PhD); resource and environmental planning (MRM). *Degree requirements:* For master's, thesis (for some programs); for doctorate, comprehensive exam, thesis/dissertation. *Entrance requirements:* For master's and Graduate Diploma, minimum GPA of 3.0 (on scale of 4.33) or 3.33 based on last 60 credits of undergraduate courses; for doctorate, minimum GPA of 3.5 (on scale of 4.33). Additional exam requirements/recommendations for international students: Recommended—TOEFL (minimum score 580 paper-based; 93 iBT), IELTS (minimum score 7), TWE (minimum score 5). Electronic applications accepted. *Faculty research:* Climate, coastal marine ecology and conservation, environmental toxicology, fisheries science and management, forest ecology.

SIT Graduate Institute, Graduate Programs, Master's Program in Global Leadership and Social Innovation, Brattleboro, VT 05302-0676. Offers MA. *Program availability:* Online learning.

Slippery Rock University of Pennsylvania, Graduate Studies (Recruitment), College of Health, Environment, and Science, Department of Parks, Conservation and Recreation Therapy, Slippery Rock, PA 16057-1383. Offers environmental education (M Ed); park and resource management (MS). *Program availability:* Part-time, evening/weekend, online only, 100% online. *Faculty:* 2 full-time (1 woman), 2 part-time/adjunct (1 woman). *Students:* 4 full-time (3 women), 69 part-time (44 women); includes 5 minority (1 Black or African American, non-Hispanic/Latino; 3 Hispanic/Latino; 1 Two or more races, non-Hispanic/Latino). Average age 33. 44 applicants, 73% accepted, 20 enrolled. In 2018, 34 master's awarded. *Degree requirements:* For master's, comprehensive exam (for some programs), thesis (for some programs), internship. *Entrance requirements:* For master's, official transcripts, minimum GPA of 2.75, personal statement. Additional exam requirements/recommendations for international students: Required—TOEFL (minimum score 550 paper-based; 80 iBT). *Application deadline:* For fall admission, 3/1 priority date for domestic students, 5/1 priority date for international students; for spring admission, 10/1 priority date for domestic students, 9/1 priority date for international students. Applications are processed on a rolling basis. Application fee: $25 ($30 for international students). Electronic applications accepted. *Expenses:* Contact institution. *Financial support:* In 2018–19, 4 students received support. Career-related internships or fieldwork, Federal Work-Study, institutionally sponsored loans, scholarships/grants, tuition waivers (partial), and unspecified assistantships available. Support available to part-time students. Financial award application deadline: 5/1; financial award applicants required to submit FAFSA. *Unit head:* Dr. John Lisco, Graduate Coordinator, 724-738-2596, Fax: 724-738-2938, E-mail: john.lisco@sru.edu. *Application contact:* Brandi Weber-Mortimer, Director of Graduate Admissions, 724-738-2051, Fax: 724-738-2146, E-mail: graduate.admissions@sru.edu.
Website: http://www.sru.edu/academics/colleges-and-departments/ches/departments/parks-and-recreation

Southeast Missouri State University, School of Graduate Studies, Department of Human Environmental Studies, Cape Girardeau, MO 63701-4799. Offers MA. *Program availability:* Part-time, evening/weekend. *Faculty:* 11 full-time (6 women). *Students:* 8 full-time (1 woman), 5 part-time (1 woman), 5 international. Average age 33. 3 applicants, 100% accepted, 3 enrolled. In 2018, 3 master's awarded. *Degree requirements:* For master's, comprehensive exam (for some programs), thesis (for some programs). *Entrance requirements:* For master's, minimum undergraduate GPA of 2.75; 15 hours of course work in specialization. Additional exam requirements/recommendations for international students: Required—TOEFL (minimum score 550 paper-based; 79 iBT), IELTS (minimum score 6), PTE (minimum score 53). *Application*

Peterson's Graduate Programs in the Physical Sciences, Mathematics, Agricultural Sciences, the Environment & Natural Resources 2020

www.petersons.com 303

deadline: For fall admission, 8/1 for domestic students, 6/1 for international students; for spring admission, 11/21 for domestic students, 10/1 for international students; for summer admission, 5/15 for domestic students. Applications are processed on a rolling basis. Application fee: $30 ($40 for international students). Electronic applications accepted. *Expenses:* Contact institution. *Financial support:* In 2018–19, 5 students received support, including 3 teaching assistantships with full tuition reimbursements available; career-related internships or fieldwork, Federal Work-Study, scholarships/grants, traineeships, tuition waivers (full), and unspecified assistantships also available. Financial award application deadline: 6/30; financial award applicants required to submit FAFSA. *Faculty research:* Veteran families and relationships, suicide and domestic violence, child abuse and neglect, school system environmental design, obesity and college students. *Unit head:* Dr. Victor R. Wilburn, Professor/Chair, Human Environmental Studies, 573-986-4907, Fax: 573-651-2949, E-mail: vwilburn@semo.edu. *Application contact:* Dr. Victor R. Wilburn, Professor/Chair, Human Environmental Studies, 573-986-4907, Fax: 573-651-2949, E-mail: vwilburn@semo.edu.
Website: http://www.semo.edu/hes/

Southern Illinois University Carbondale, Graduate School, College of Liberal Arts, Department of Geography, Carbondale, IL 62901-4701. Offers MS, PhD. *Degree requirements:* For master's, thesis; for doctorate, thesis/dissertation. *Entrance requirements:* For master's, GRE (recommended), minimum GPA of 2.7; for doctorate, minimum GPA of 3.25. Additional exam requirements/recommendations for international students: Required—TOEFL. *Faculty research:* Natural resources management emphasizing water resources and environmental quality of air, water, and land systems.

Southern Illinois University Edwardsville, Graduate School, College of Arts and Sciences, Program in Environmental Science Management, Edwardsville, IL 62026. Offers PSM. *Program availability:* Part-time, evening/weekend. *Degree requirements:* For master's, thesis, internship. *Entrance requirements:* For master's, GRE. Additional exam requirements/recommendations for international students: Required—TOEFL (minimum score 550 paper-based; 79 iBT), IELTS (minimum score 6.5). Electronic applications accepted.

Southern New Hampshire University, School of Business, Manchester, NH 03106-1045. Offers accounting (MBA, Graduate Certificate); accounting finance (MS); accounting/auditing (MS); accounting/forensic accounting (MS); accounting/management accounting (MS); accounting/taxation (MS); applied economics (MS); athletic administration (MBA, Graduate Certificate); business administration (IMBA, Certificate), including business information systems (Certificate), human resource management (Certificate); business analytics (MBA); business intelligence (MBA); communication (MA), including new media and marketing, public relations; community economic development (MBA); criminal justice (MBA); data analytics (MS); economics (MBA); engineering management (MBA); entrepreneurship (MBA); finance (MBA, MS, Graduate Certificate); finance/corporate finance (MS); finance/investments (MS); forensic accounting (MBA); forensic accounting and fraud examination (Graduate Certificate); healthcare informatics (MBA); healthcare management (MBA); human resource management (MS); human resources (MBA); information technology (MS); information technology management (MBA); international business (PhD); Internet marketing (MBA); leadership (MBA); leadership of nonprofit organizations (Graduate Certificate); management (MS); marketing (MBA, MS, Graduate Certificate); music business (MBA); operations and project management (MS); operations and supply chain management (MBA, Graduate Certificate); organizational leadership (MS); project management (MBA, Graduate Certificate); public administration (MBA, Graduate Certificate); quantitative analysis (MBA); Six Sigma (Graduate Certificate); Six Sigma quality (MBA); social media marketing (MBA, Graduate Certificate); sport management (MBA, MS, Graduate Certificate); sustainability and environmental compliance (MBA); MBA/Certificate. *Accreditation:* ACBSP. *Program availability:* Part-time, evening/weekend, online learning. Terminal master's awarded for partial completion of doctoral program. *Degree requirements:* For master's, one foreign language, comprehensive exam (for some programs), thesis or alternative; for doctorate, one foreign language, comprehensive exam, thesis/dissertation. *Entrance requirements:* For master's, minimum GPA of 2.5; for doctorate, GMAT. Additional exam requirements/recommendations for international students: Required—TOEFL (minimum score 500 paper-based). Electronic applications accepted.

State University of New York College of Environmental Science and Forestry, Department of Environmental Resources Engineering, Syracuse, NY 13210-2779. Offers ecological engineering (MPS, MS, PhD); environmental management (MPS); environmental resources engineering (MPS, MS, PhD); geospatial information science and engineering (MPS, MS, PhD); water resources engineering (MPS, MS, PhD). *Program availability:* Part-time. *Faculty:* 9 full-time (1 woman), 3 part-time/adjunct (0 women). *Students:* 32 full-time (12 women), 8 part-time (0 women); includes 2 minority (1 Black or African American, non-Hispanic/Latino; 1 Asian, non-Hispanic/Latino), 19 international. Average age 41. 31 applicants, 58% accepted, 7 enrolled. In 2018, 11 master's, 1 doctorate awarded. Terminal master's awarded for partial completion of doctoral program. *Degree requirements:* For master's, thesis (for some programs); for doctorate, comprehensive exam, thesis/dissertation. *Entrance requirements:* For master's and doctorate, GRE General Test, minimum GPA of 3.0. Additional exam requirements/recommendations for international students: Required—TOEFL (minimum score 550 paper-based; 80 iBT), IELTS (minimum score 6). *Application deadline:* For fall admission, 1/15 priority date for domestic and international students; for spring admission, 11/1 priority date for domestic and international students. Applications are processed on a rolling basis. Application fee: $60. Electronic applications accepted. *Expenses: Tuition, area resident:* Full-time $11,090; part-time $462 per credit hour. Tuition, state resident: full-time $11,090; part-time $462 per credit hour. Tuition, nonresident: full-time $22,650; part-time $944 per credit hour. *International tuition:* $22,650 full-time. *Required fees:* $1733; $178.58 per credit hour. *Financial support:* In 2018–19, 9 students received support. Unspecified assistantships available. Financial award application deadline: 6/30; financial award applicants required to submit FAFSA. *Faculty research:* Ecological engineering, environmental resources engineering, geospatial information science and engineering, water resources engineering, environmental science. *Total annual research expenditures:* $508,995. *Unit head:* Dr. Lindi Quackenbush, Chair, 315-470-4727, Fax: 315-470-4710, E-mail: ljquackc@esf.edu. *Application contact:* Scott Shannon, Associate Provost for Instruction/Dean of the Graduate School, 315-470-6599, Fax: 315-470-6978, E-mail: esfgrad@esf.edu.
Website: http://www.esf.edu/ere

State University of New York College of Environmental Science and Forestry, Department of Environmental Studies, Syracuse, NY 13210-2779. Offers environmental communication (MPS, MS); environmental policy (MPS, MS). *Program availability:* Part-time. *Faculty:* 10 full-time (7 women), 3 part-time/adjunct (2 women). *Students:* 8 full-time (6 women), 2 part-time (both women), 1 international. Average age 26. 9 applicants, 78% accepted, 5 enrolled. In 2018, 3 master's awarded. *Degree requirements:* For master's, thesis (for some programs). *Entrance requirements:* For master's, GRE General Test. Additional exam requirements/recommendations for international students: Required—TOEFL (minimum score 550 paper-based), IELTS (minimum score 6). *Application deadline:* Applications are processed on a rolling basis. Application fee: $60. Electronic applications accepted. *Expenses: Tuition, area resident:* Full-time $11,090; part-time $462 per credit hour. Tuition, state resident: full-time $11,090; part-time $462 per credit hour. Tuition, nonresident: full-time $22,650; part-time $944 per credit hour. *International tuition:* $22,650 full-time. *Required fees:* $1733; $178.58 per credit hour. *Financial support:* In 2018–19, 2 students received support. Unspecified assistantships available. Financial award application deadline: 6/30; financial award applicants required to submit FAFSA. *Total annual research expenditures:* $257,781. *Unit head:* Dr. Bennette Whitmore, Chair, 315-470-6636, E-mail: bwhitmor@esf.edu. *Application contact:* Scott Shannon, Associate Provost for Instruction/Dean of the Graduate School, 315-470-6599, Fax: 315-470-6978, E-mail: esfgrad@esf.edu.
Website: http://www.esf.edu/es/

State University of New York College of Environmental Science and Forestry, Program in Environmental Science, Syracuse, NY 13210-2779. Offers biophysical and ecological economics (MPS); coupled natural and human systems (MPS); ecosystem restoration (MPS); environmental and community land planning (MPS, MS); environmental and natural resources policy (PhD); environmental communication and participatory processes (PhD); environmental monitoring and modeling (MPS); water and wetland resource studies (MPS, MS). *Program availability:* Part-time. *Faculty:* 1 full-time (0 women), 1 (woman) part-time/adjunct. *Students:* 52 full-time (30 women), 13 part-time (9 women); includes 3 minority (1 Asian, non-Hispanic/Latino; 2 Hispanic/Latino), 26 international. Average age 32. 51 applicants, 73% accepted, 17 enrolled. In 2018, 14 master's, 8 doctorates awarded. Terminal master's awarded for partial completion of doctoral program. *Degree requirements:* For master's, thesis (for some programs); for doctorate, comprehensive exam, thesis/dissertation. *Entrance requirements:* For master's and doctorate, GRE General Test, minimum GPA of 3.0. Additional exam requirements/recommendations for international students: Required—TOEFL (minimum score 550 paper-based; 80 iBT), IELTS (minimum score 6). *Application deadline:* For fall admission, 2/1 priority date for domestic and international students; for spring admission, 11/1 priority date for domestic and international students. Applications are processed on a rolling basis. Application fee: $60. Electronic applications accepted. *Expenses: Tuition, area resident:* Full-time $11,090; part-time $462 per credit hour. Tuition, state resident: full-time $11,090; part-time $462 per credit hour. Tuition, nonresident: full-time $22,650; part-time $944 per credit hour. *International tuition:* $22,650 full-time. *Required fees:* $1733; $178.58 per credit hour. *Financial support:* In 2018–19, 24 students received support. Unspecified assistantships available. Financial award application deadline: 6/30; financial award applicants required to submit FAFSA. *Faculty research:* Environmental education/communications, water resources, land resources, waste management. *Unit head:* Dr. Russell Briggs, Director of the Division of Environmental Science, 315-470-6989, Fax: 315-470-6700, E-mail: rdbriggs@esf.edu. *Application contact:* Scott Shannon, Associate Provost for Instruction/Dean of the Graduate School, 315-470-6599, Fax: 315-470-6978, E-mail: esfgrad@esf.edu.
Website: http://www.esf.edu/environmentalscience/graduate/

Stony Brook University, State University of New York, School of Professional Development, Stony Brook, NY 11794. Offers coaching (Graduate Certificate); environmental management (MPS); German (MAT); higher education administration (MA, Certificate); human resource management (MS, Graduate Certificate); Italian (MAT); liberal studies (MA); mathematics (MAT); school district business leadership (Advanced Certificate); social studies (MAT); Spanish (MAT). *Program availability:* Part-time, evening/weekend, online learning. *Faculty:* 3 full-time (2 women), 94 part-time/adjunct (40 women). *Students:* 214 full-time (138 women), 1,100 part-time (813 women); includes 313 minority (117 Black or African American, non-Hispanic/Latino; 2 American Indian or Alaska Native, non-Hispanic/Latino; 32 Asian, non-Hispanic/Latino; 140 Hispanic/Latino; 3 Native Hawaiian or other Pacific Islander, non-Hispanic/Latino; 19 Two or more races, non-Hispanic/Latino), 7 international. Average age 33. 483 applicants, 89% accepted, 337 enrolled. In 2018, 315 master's, 178 other advanced degrees awarded. *Entrance requirements:* Additional exam requirements/recommendations for international students: Required—TOEFL (minimum score 85 iBT). *Application deadline:* For fall admission, 1/15 for domestic students, 6/1 for international students; for spring admission, 10/1 for domestic and international students. Applications are processed on a rolling basis. Application fee: $100. *Expenses:* Contact institution. *Financial support:* Fellowships, research assistantships, teaching assistantships, and career-related internships or fieldwork available. Support available to part-time students. *Unit head:* Patricia Malone, Associate Vice President for Professional Education and Assistant Provost for Engaged Learning, 631-632-7512, Fax: 631-632-9046, E-mail: patricia.malone@stonybrook.edu. *Application contact:* Melissa Jordan, Assistant Dean, 631-632-7751, E-mail: melissa.jordan@stonybrook.edu.
Website: http://www.stonybrook.edu/spd/

Tennessee Technological University, College of Graduate Studies, College of Interdisciplinary Studies, School of Environmental Studies, Professional Science Master's Program, Cookeville, TN 38505. Offers environmental informatics (PSM); manufacturing sustainability (PSM). *Program availability:* Part-time. *Students:* 8 full-time (4 women), 7 part-time (1 woman); includes 1 minority (Black or African American, non-Hispanic/Latino). 6 applicants, 67% accepted, 6 enrolled. In 2018, 2 master's awarded. *Degree requirements:* For master's, comprehensive exam, thesis or alternative, internship. *Entrance requirements:* For master's, GRE General Test. Additional exam requirements/recommendations for international students: Required—TOEFL (minimum score 527 paper-based; 71 iBT), IELTS (minimum score 5.5), PTE (minimum score 48), or TOEIC (Test of English as an International Communication). *Application deadline:* For fall admission, 7/1 for domestic students, 5/1 for international students; for spring admission, 2/1 for domestic students, 10/1 for international students; for summer admission, 5/1 for domestic students, 2/1 for international students. Applications are processed on a rolling basis. Application fee: $35 ($40 for international students). Electronic applications accepted. *Financial support:* Research assistantships available. Financial award application deadline: 4/1. *Unit head:* Dr. Hayden Mattingly, Interim Director, 931-372-6246, E-mail: hmattingly@tntech.edu. *Application contact:* Shelia K. Kendrick, Coordinator of Graduate Studies, 931-372-3808, Fax: 931-372-3497, E-mail: skendrick@tntech.edu.
Website: https://www.tntech.edu/is/ses/psm/psmei

Texas Southern University, Barbara Jordan-Mickey Leland School of Public Affairs, Program in Urban Planning and Environmental Policy, Houston, TX 77004-4584. Offers MS, PhD. *Accreditation:* ACSP. *Program availability:* Part-time, evening/weekend. *Degree requirements:* For master's, comprehensive exam, thesis optional. *Entrance requirements:* For master's, GRE General Test, minimum GPA of 2.5. Additional exam requirements/recommendations for international students: Required—TOEFL. Electronic applications accepted.

Texas Tech University, Graduate School, College of Architecture, Lubbock, TX 79409-2091. Offers architecture (M Arch, MS); land-use planning, management, and design

(PhD); MBA/M Arch. *Program availability:* Part-time. *Faculty:* 34 full-time (13 women), 11 part-time/adjunct (3 women). *Students:* 70 full-time (29 women), 13 part-time (1 woman); includes 31 minority (4 Black or African American, non-Hispanic/Latino; 1 Asian, non-Hispanic/Latino; 26 Hispanic/Latino), 16 international. Average age 26. 49 applicants, 57% accepted, 16 enrolled. In 2018, 41 master's, 1 doctorate awarded. *Degree requirements:* For master's, comprehensive exam (for some programs), thesis (for some programs); for doctorate, comprehensive exam, thesis/dissertation. *Entrance requirements:* For master's, GRE General Test, portfolio; for doctorate, GRE General Test. Additional exam requirements/recommendations for international students: Required—TOEFL (minimum score 550 paper-based; 79 iBT). *Application deadline:* For fall admission, 6/1 priority date for domestic students, 1/15 priority date for international students; for spring admission, 9/1 priority date for domestic students, 6/15 priority date for international students. Applications are processed on a rolling basis. Application fee: $65. Electronic applications accepted. *Expenses:* Contact institution. *Financial support:* In 2018–19, 70 students received support, including 70 fellowships (averaging $4,305 per year); research assistantships, teaching assistantships, career-related internships or fieldwork, Federal Work-Study, institutionally sponsored loans, scholarships/grants, traineeships, health care benefits, and unspecified assistantships also available. Support available to part-time students. Financial award application deadline: 2/1; financial award applicants required to submit FAFSA. *Faculty research:* Architectural Design, Digital Design and Fabrication, Community Development and Urban Design, Health and Wellness Design, Historic Preservation. *Total annual research expenditures:* $58,777. *Unit head:* Prof. James P. Williamson, Dean, 806-742-3136, Fax: 806-742-1400, E-mail: james.p.williamson@ttu.edu. *Application contact:* Sarah Hatley, Unit Manager, College Advising, 806-834-5704, Fax: 806-742-1400, E-mail: sarah.hatley@ttu.edu. Website: arch.ttu.edu/

Texas Tech University, Graduate School, College of Arts and Sciences, Department of Biological Sciences, Lubbock, TX 79409-3131. Offers biology (MS, PhD); environmental sustainability and natural resource management (PSM); microbiology (MS); zoology (MS, PhD). *Program availability:* Part-time, blended/hybrid learning. *Faculty:* 45 full-time (16 women). *Students:* 118 full-time (65 women), 16 part-time (6 women); includes 20 minority (3 Black or African American, non-Hispanic/Latino; 3 Asian, non-Hispanic/Latino; 11 Hispanic/Latino; 3 Two or more races, non-Hispanic/Latino), 56 international. Average age 29. 69 applicants, 62% accepted, 23 enrolled. In 2018, 13 master's, 6 doctorates awarded. *Degree requirements:* For master's, comprehensive exam, thesis or alternative; for doctorate, comprehensive exam, thesis/dissertation. *Entrance requirements:* For master's and doctorate, GRE General Test. Additional exam requirements/recommendations for international students: Required—TOEFL (minimum score 550 paper-based; 79 iBT). *Application deadline:* For fall admission, 6/1 priority date for domestic students, 1/15 priority date for international students; for spring admission, 9/1 priority date for domestic students, 6/15 priority date for international students. Applications are processed on a rolling basis. Application fee: $65. Electronic applications accepted. *Expenses:* Contact institution. *Financial support:* In 2018–19, 123 students received support, including 102 fellowships (averaging $1,678 per year), 31 research assistantships (averaging $18,374 per year), 89 teaching assistantships (averaging $16,281 per year); Federal Work-Study and health care benefits also available. Financial award application deadline: 2/15; financial award applicants required to submit FAFSA. *Faculty research:* Biodiversity, genomics and evolution; climate change in arid ecosystems, plant biology and biotechnology; animal communication and behavior; microbiomes, zoonosis and emerging diseases. *Total annual research expenditures:* $1.6 million. *Unit head:* Dr. John Zak, Professor, Chair & Associate Dean, 806-834-2682, Fax: 806-742-2963, E-mail: john.zak@ttu.edu. *Application contact:* Dr. Lou Densmore, Graduate Adviser, 806-834-6479, Fax: 806-742-2963, E-mail: lou.densmore@ttu.edu. Website: www.depts.ttu.edu/biology/

Thomas Edison State University, John S. Watson School of Public Service and Continuing Studies, Trenton, NJ 08608. Offers community and economic development (MSM); environmental policy/environmental justice (MSM); homeland security (MSHS, MSM); information and technology for public service (MSM); nonprofit management (MSM); public and municipal finance (MSM); public health (MSM); public service administration and leadership (MSM); public service leadership (MPSL). *Program availability:* Part-time, online learning. *Entrance requirements:* Additional exam requirements/recommendations for international students: Required—TOEFL (minimum score 550 paper-based; 79 iBT). Electronic applications accepted.

Towson University, College of Liberal Arts, Program in Geography and Environmental Planning, Towson, MD 21252-0001. Offers MA. *Program availability:* Part-time, evening/weekend. *Degree requirements:* For master's, thesis optional. *Entrance requirements:* For master's, bachelor's degree with minimum of 9 credits of course work in geography, minimum GPA of 3.0 overall and in all geography courses, 2 letters of recommendation, essay. Electronic applications accepted. *Expenses: Tuition, area resident:* Full-time $9196; part-time $418 per unit. Tuition, state resident: full-time $9196; part-time $418 per unit. Tuition, nonresident: full-time $19,030; part-time $865 per unit. *International tuition:* $19,030 full-time. *Required fees:* $3102; $141 per year. $423 per term. Tuition and fees vary according to campus/location and program.

Trent University, Graduate Studies, Program in Environmental and Life Sciences, Environmental and Resource Studies Program, Peterborough, ON K9J 7B8, Canada. Offers M Sc, PhD. *Degree requirements:* For master's, thesis; for doctorate, thesis/dissertation. *Entrance requirements:* For master's, honours degree; for doctorate, master's degree. *Faculty research:* Environmental biogeochemistry, aquatic organic contaminants, fisheries, wetland ecology, renewable resource management.

Tropical Agriculture Research and Higher Education Center, Graduate School, Turrialba, Costa Rica. Offers agribusiness management (MS); agroforestry systems (PhD); development practices (MS); ecological agriculture (MS); environmental socioeconomics (MS); forestry in tropical and subtropical zones (PhD); integrated watershed management (MS); international sustainable tourism (MS); management and conservation of tropical rainforests and biodiversity (MS); tropical agriculture (PhD); tropical agroforestry (MS). *Entrance requirements:* For master's, GRE, 2 years of related professional experience, letters of recommendation; for doctorate, GRE, 4 letters of recommendation, letter of support from employing organization, master's degree in agronomy, biological sciences, forestry, natural resources or related field. Additional exam requirements/recommendations for international students: Required—TOEFL (minimum score 550 paper-based). Electronic applications accepted. *Faculty research:* Biodiversity in fragmented landscapes, ecosystem management, integrated pest management, environmental livestock production, biotechnology carbon balances in diverse land uses.

Troy University, Graduate School, College of Arts and Sciences, Program in Environmental and Biological Sciences, Troy, AL 36082. Offers MS. *Program availability:* Part-time, evening/weekend, 100% online, blended/hybrid learning. *Faculty:* 1 full-time (0 women), 1 (woman) part-time/adjunct. *Students:* 3 full-time (2 women), 21 part-time (10 women); includes 1 minority (Two or more races, non-Hispanic/Latino), 6 international. Average age 29. 31 applicants, 74% accepted, 4 enrolled. In 2018, 9 master's awarded. *Degree requirements:* For master's, comprehensive exam (for some programs), thesis (for some programs), comprehensive exam or thesis, minimum GPA of 3.0, admission to candidacy. *Entrance requirements:* For master's, GRE (minimum score of 850 on old exam or 290 on new exam), MAT (minimum score of 385) or GMAT (minimum score of 380), bachelor's degree; minimum undergraduate GPA of 2.5 or 3.0 on last 30 semester hours. Additional exam requirements/recommendations for international students: Required—TOEFL (minimum score 523 paper-based; 70 iBT), IELTS (minimum score 6). *Application deadline:* Applications are processed on a rolling basis. Application fee: $50. Electronic applications accepted. *Expenses: Tuition, area resident:* Full-time $425; part-time $425 per credit hour. Tuition, state resident: full-time $425; part-time $425 per credit hour. Tuition, nonresident: full-time $850; part-time $850 per credit hour. *International tuition:* $850 full-time. *Required fees:* $50 per semester. Tuition and fees vary according to campus/location and program. *Financial support:* Fellowships, career-related internships or fieldwork, and scholarships/grants available. Support available to part-time students. Financial award applicants required to submit FAFSA. *Unit head:* Dr. Sig Harden, Chairman, Department of Biology, 334-670-3660, Fax: 334-670-3626, E-mail: sbharden@troy.edu. *Application contact:* Jessica A. Kimbro, Assistant Director of Graduate Programs, 334-670-3189, E-mail: jacord@troy.edu. Website: https://www.troy.edu/academics/academic-programs/environmental-science.html

Tufts University, Graduate School of Arts and Sciences, Department of Urban and Environmental Policy and Planning, Medford, MA 02155. Offers community development (MA); environmental policy (MA); health and human welfare (MA); housing policy (MA); international environment/development policy (MA); public policy (MPP); MA/JD; MA/MBA; MA/MPH; MA/MS; MALD/MA. MALD/MA offered in connection with The Fletcher School of Law and Diplomacy; MA/MPH with School of Medicine; MA/MS with School of Nutrition Science and Policy or School of Engineering; MA/MBA with Boston College, Carroll School of Management; MA/JD with Boston College Law School. *Accreditation:* ACSP (one or more programs are accredited). *Program availability:* Part-time. *Degree requirements:* For master's, thesis or alternative, internship. *Entrance requirements:* For master's, GRE General Test. Additional exam requirements/recommendations for international students: Required—TOEFL (minimum score 550 paper-based; 80 iBT), IELTS (minimum score 6.5). Electronic applications accepted. *Expenses:* Contact institution.

Tufts University, Graduate School of Arts and Sciences, Graduate Certificate Programs, Community Environmental Studies Program, Medford, MA 02155. Offers Certificate. *Program availability:* Part-time, evening/weekend. Electronic applications accepted. *Expenses:* Contact institution.

Tufts University, Graduate School of Arts and Sciences, Graduate Certificate Programs, Environmental Management Program, Medford, MA 02155. Offers Certificate. *Program availability:* Part-time, evening/weekend. Electronic applications accepted. *Expenses: Tuition:* Full-time $51,288; part-time $1710 per credit hour. *Required fees:* $904. Full-time tuition and fees vary according to degree level, program and student level. Part-time tuition and fees vary according to course load.

Tufts University, School of Engineering, Department of Civil and Environmental Engineering, Medford, MA 02155. Offers bioengineering (MS), including environmental biotechnology; civil and environmental engineering (MS, PhD), including applied data science, environmental and water resources engineering, environmental health, geosystems engineering, structural engineering and mechanics; PhD/PhD. *Program availability:* Part-time. Terminal master's awarded for partial completion of doctoral program. *Degree requirements:* For master's, thesis (for some programs); for doctorate, thesis/dissertation. *Entrance requirements:* For master's and doctorate, GRE General Test. Additional exam requirements/recommendations for international students: Required—TOEFL (minimum score 550 paper-based; 80 iBT), IELTS (minimum score 6.5). Electronic applications accepted. *Expenses: Tuition:* Full-time $51,288; part-time $1710 per credit hour. *Required fees:* $904. Full-time tuition and fees vary according to degree level, program and student level. Part-time tuition and fees vary according to course load. *Faculty research:* Environmental and water resources engineering, environmental health, geotechnical and geoenvironmental engineering, structural engineering and mechanics, water diplomacy.

Universidad Autonoma de Guadalajara, Graduate Programs, Guadalajara, Mexico. Offers administrative law and justice (LL M); advertising and corporate communications (MA); architecture (M Arch); business (MBA); computational science (MCC); education (Ed M, Ed D); English-Spanish translation (MA); entrepreneurship and management (MBA); integrated management of digital animation (MA); international business (MIB); international corporate law (LL M); Internet technologies (MS); manufacturing systems (MMS); occupational health (MS); philosophy (MA, PhD); power electronics (MS); quality systems (MQS); renewable energy (MS); social evaluation of projects (MBA); strategic market research (MBA); tax law (MA); teaching mathematics (MA).

Universidad del Turabo, Graduate Programs, Programs in Science and Technology, Gurabo, PR 00778-3030. Offers environmental analysis (MSE), including environmental chemistry; environmental management (MSE), including pollution management; environmental science (D Sc), including environmental biology. *Entrance requirements:* For master's, GRE, EXADEP, GMAT, interview, official transcript, essay, recommendation letters; for doctorate, GRE, EXADEP, GMAT, official transcript, recommendation letters, essay, curriculum vitae, interview. Electronic applications accepted.

Universidad Metropolitana, School of Environmental Affairs, Program in Environmental Planning, San Juan, PR 00928-1150. Offers MP. *Program availability:* Part-time. *Degree requirements:* For master's, thesis. *Entrance requirements:* For master's, EXADEP, interview. Electronic applications accepted.

Universidad Metropolitana, School of Environmental Affairs, Program in Environmental Studies, San Juan, PR 00928-1150. Offers MAES. *Program availability:* Part-time. *Degree requirements:* For master's, thesis or alternative. *Entrance requirements:* For master's, EXADEP, interview. Electronic applications accepted.

Université de Montréal, Faculty of Medicine, Programs in Environment and Prevention, Montréal, QC H3C 3J7, Canada. Offers environment, health and disaster management (DESS). Electronic applications accepted. *Faculty research:* Health, environment, pollutants, protection, waste.

Université du Québec à Chicoutimi, Graduate Programs, Program in Renewable Resources, Chicoutimi, QC G7H 2B1, Canada. Offers M Sc. *Program availability:* Part-time. *Degree requirements:* For master's, thesis. *Entrance requirements:* For master's, appropriate bachelor's degree, proficiency in French.

Université du Québec, Institut National de la Recherche Scientifique, Graduate Programs, Research Center–Water Earth Environment, Québec, QC G1K 9A9, Canada. Offers earth sciences (M Sc, PhD); earth sciences - environmental technologies (M Sc); water sciences (M Sc, PhD). *Program availability:* Part-time. *Faculty:* 34 full-time.

Peterson's Graduate Programs in the Physical Sciences, Mathematics, Agricultural Sciences, the Environment & Natural Resources 2020

www.petersons.com **305**

Students: 169 full-time (87 women), 19 part-time (11 women), 132 international. Average age 33. 58 applicants, 66% accepted, 32 enrolled. In 2018, 34 master's, 24 doctorates awarded. *Degree requirements:* For master's, thesis (for some programs); for doctorate, thesis/dissertation. *Entrance requirements:* For master's, appropriate bachelor's degree, proficiency in French; for doctorate, appropriate master's degree, proficiency in French. *Application deadline:* For fall admission, 3/30 for domestic and international students; for winter admission, 11/1 for domestic and international students; for spring admission, 3/1 for domestic and international students. Application fee: $45. Electronic applications accepted. *Financial support:* In 2018–19, fellowships (averaging $16,500 per year) were awarded; research assistantships also available. *Faculty research:* Land use, impacts of climate change, adaptation to climate change, integrated management of resources (mineral and water). *Unit head:* Jean-François Blais, Director, 418-654-2575, Fax: 418-654-2600, E-mail: jean-francois.blais@ete.inrs.ca. *Application contact:* Sean Otto, Registrar, 418-654-2518, Fax: 418-654-3858, E-mail: sean.otto@inrs.ca.
Website: http://www.ete.inrs.ca/

Université Laval, Faculty of Administrative Sciences, Programs in Business Administration, Québec, QC G1K 7P4, Canada. Offers accounting (MBA); agri-food management (MBA); electronic business (MBA, Diploma); factory management and logistics (MBA); finance (MBA); firm management (MBA); geomatic management (MBA); information technology management (MBA); international management (MBA); management (MBA); management accounting (MBA, Diploma); marketing (MBA); modeling and organizational decision (MBA); occupational health and safety management (MBA); pharmacy management (MBA); social and environmental responsibility (MBA); technological entrepreneurship (Diploma). *Accreditation:* AACSB. *Program availability:* Part-time, evening/weekend, online learning. *Entrance requirements:* For master's and Diploma, knowledge of French and English. Electronic applications accepted.

Université Laval, Faculty of Agricultural and Food Sciences, Department of Soils and Agricultural Engineering, Programs in Agri-Food Engineering, Québec, QC G1K 7P4, Canada. Offers agri-food engineering (M Sc); environmental technology (M Sc). *Degree requirements:* For master's, thesis (for some programs). *Entrance requirements:* For master's, knowledge of French. Electronic applications accepted.

Université Laval, Faculty of Agricultural and Food Sciences, Department of Soils and Agricultural Engineering, Programs in Soils and Environment Science, Québec, QC G1K 7P4, Canada. Offers environmental technology (M Sc); soils and environment science (M Sc, PhD). Terminal master's awarded for partial completion of doctoral program. *Degree requirements:* For master's, thesis (for some programs); for doctorate, comprehensive exam, thesis/dissertation. *Entrance requirements:* For master's and doctorate, knowledge of French and English. Electronic applications accepted.

University of Alaska Fairbanks, College of Liberal Arts, Department of Arctic and Northern Studies, Fairbanks, AK 99775-6460. Offers Arctic policy (MA); environmental politics and policy (MA); Northern history (MA). *Program availability:* Part-time, blended/hybrid learning. *Students:* 8 full-time (6 women), 13 part-time (7 women); includes 3 minority (1 American Indian or Alaska Native, non-Hispanic/Latino; 1 Hispanic/Latino; 1 Two or more races, non-Hispanic/Latino), 3 international. Average age 37. 12 applicants, 33% accepted, 3 enrolled. In 2018, 6 master's awarded. *Degree requirements:* For master's, comprehensive exam, oral defense of project or thesis. *Entrance requirements:* For master's, bachelor's degree from accredited institution, preference given to applicants with 3.0 GPA or higher. Additional exam requirements/recommendations for international students: Required—TOEFL (minimum score 550 paper-based; 79 iBT), IELTS (minimum score 6.5). *Application deadline:* For fall admission, 6/1 for domestic students, 3/1 for international students; for spring admission, 10/15 for domestic students, 9/1 for international students. Applications are processed on a rolling basis. Application fee: $60. Electronic applications accepted. *Expenses: Tuition, area resident:* Full-time $8802; part-time $5868 per credit hour. Tuition, state resident: full-time $8802; part-time $5868 per credit hour. Tuition, nonresident: full-time $18,504; part-time $12,336 per credit hour. *International tuition:* $18,504 full-time. *Required fees:* $1416; $944 per credit hour. $472 per semester. Tuition and fees vary according to course load and program. *Financial support:* In 2018–19, 6 teaching assistantships with full tuition reimbursements (averaging $4,463 per year) were awarded; fellowships with full tuition reimbursements, research assistantships with full tuition reimbursements, career-related internships or fieldwork, Federal Work-Study, scholarships/grants, health care benefits, and unspecified assistantships also available. Support available to part-time students. Financial award application deadline: 1/1; financial award applicants required to submit FAFSA. *Faculty research:* Wide-ranging topics in the social sciences and humanities in the circumpolar north, especially addressing current challenges we face, within historical and cultural perspectives. *Total annual research expenditures:* $18,000. *Unit head:* Dr. Mary Ehrlander, Director, 907-474-7126, E-mail: uaf-northern@alaska.edu. *Application contact:* Samara Taber, Director of Admissions, 907-474-7500, E-mail: uaf-admissions@alaska.edu.
Website: http://www.uaf.edu/northern/

University of Alberta, Faculty of Graduate Studies and Research, Department of Economics, Edmonton, AB T6G 2E1, Canada. Offers economics (MA, PhD); economics and finance (MA); environmental and natural resource economics (PhD). *Program availability:* Part-time. *Degree requirements:* For doctorate, thesis/dissertation. *Entrance requirements:* For master's and doctorate, GRE. Additional exam requirements/recommendations for international students: Required—TOEFL. *Faculty research:* Public finance, international trade, industrial organization, Pacific Rim economics, monetary economics.

The University of Arizona, College of Agriculture and Life Sciences, School of Natural Resources and the Environment, Watershed Resources Program, Tucson, AZ 85721. Offers water, society, and policy (MS); watershed management (MS, PhD). *Degree requirements:* For master's, thesis; for doctorate, comprehensive exam, thesis/dissertation. *Entrance requirements:* For master's, GRE General Test, minimum GPA of 3.0, 3 letters of recommendation; for doctorate, GRE General Test, minimum GPA of 3.0, 3 letters of recommendation, MA or MS. Additional exam requirements/recommendations for international students: Required—TOEFL (minimum score 550 paper-based; 79 iBT). Electronic applications accepted. *Faculty research:* Forest fuel characteristics, prescribed fire, tree ring-fire scar analysis, erosion, sedimentation.

The University of British Columbia, Faculty of Forestry, Program in Geomatics for Environmental Management, Vancouver, BC V6T 1Z1, Canada. Offers MGEM.

The University of British Columbia, Faculty of Science, Institute for Resources, Environment and Sustainability, Vancouver, BC V6T 1Z4, Canada. Offers M Sc, MA, PhD. *Degree requirements:* For master's, thesis; for doctorate, comprehensive exam, thesis/dissertation. *Entrance requirements:* Additional exam requirements/recommendations for international students: Required—TOEFL. Electronic applications accepted. *Expenses:* Contact institution. *Faculty research:* Land management, water resources, energy, environmental assessment, risk evaluation.

University of Calgary, Faculty of Graduate Studies, Faculty of Law, Certificate Program in Natural Resources, Energy and Environmental Law, Calgary, AB T2N 1N4, Canada. Offers LL M, Postbaccalaureate Certificate. *Program availability:* Part-time, evening/weekend. *Degree requirements:* For master's, thesis optional. *Entrance requirements:* For master's, JD or LL B. Additional exam requirements/recommendations for international students: Required—TOEFL (minimum score 100 iBT), IELTS (minimum score 7). Electronic applications accepted. *Faculty research:* Natural resources law and regulations; environmental law, ethics and policies; oil and gas and energy law; water and municipal law; Aboriginal law.

University of Calgary, Faculty of Graduate Studies, Interdisciplinary Graduate Programs, Calgary, AB T2N 1N4, Canada. Offers interdisciplinary research (M Sc, MA, PhD); resources and the environment (M Sc, MA, PhD). *Program availability:* Part-time. *Degree requirements:* For master's, thesis; for doctorate, thesis/dissertation, written and oral candidacy exam. *Entrance requirements:* Additional exam requirements/recommendations for international students: Required—TOEFL (minimum score 600 paper-based).

University of Calgary, Faculty of Graduate Studies, Schulich School of Engineering, Program in Chemical and Petroleum Engineering, Calgary, AB T2N 1N4, Canada. Offers chemical engineering (M Eng, M Sc, PhD); energy and environment engineering (M Eng, M Sc, PhD); energy and environmental systems (M Eng, M Sc, PhD); environmental engineering (M Eng, M Sc, PhD); petroleum engineering (M Eng, M Sc, PhD); reservoir characterization (M Eng, M Sc). *Program availability:* Part-time. *Degree requirements:* For master's, thesis (for some programs); for doctorate, comprehensive exam, thesis/dissertation, candidacy exam. *Entrance requirements:* For master's, minimum GPA of 3.0 or equivalent; for doctorate, minimum GPA of 3.5 or equivalent. Additional exam requirements/recommendations for international students: Required—TOEFL (minimum score 550 paper-based; 80 iBT), IELTS (minimum score 7). Electronic applications accepted. *Faculty research:* Environmental engineering, biomedical engineering modeling, simulation and control, petroleum recovery and reservoir engineering, phase equilibria and transport properties.

University of California, Berkeley, Graduate Division, College of Natural Resources, Department of Environmental Science, Policy, and Management, Berkeley, CA 94720. Offers environmental science, policy, and management (MS, PhD); forestry (MF). Terminal master's awarded for partial completion of doctoral program. *Degree requirements:* For master's, thesis optional; for doctorate, thesis/dissertation, qualifying exam. *Entrance requirements:* For master's and doctorate, GRE General Test, minimum GPA of 3.0, 3 letters of recommendation. Additional exam requirements/recommendations for international students: Required—TOEFL. Electronic applications accepted. *Faculty research:* Biology and ecology of insects; ecosystem function and environmental issues of soils; plant health/interactions from molecular to ecosystem levels; range management and ecology; forest and resource policy, sustainability, and management.

University of California, Berkeley, UC Berkeley Extension, Certificate Programs in Sustainability Studies, Berkeley, CA 94720. Offers leadership in sustainability and environmental management (Professional Certificate); solar energy and green building (Professional Certificate); sustainable design (Professional Certificate).

University of California, San Diego, Graduate Division, School of Global Policy and Strategy, Master of Public Policy Program, La Jolla, CA 92093. Offers American policy in global context (MPP); business, government and regulation (MPP); energy and environmental policy (MPP); health policy (MPP); program design and evaluation (MPP); security policy (MPP). *Entrance requirements:* For master's, GMAT or GRE General Test. Additional exam requirements/recommendations for international students: Required—TOEFL (minimum score 90 iBT), IELTS (minimum score 7). Electronic applications accepted. *Expenses:* Contact institution.

University of California, Santa Barbara, Graduate Division, College of Letters and Sciences, Division of Social Sciences, Department of Global Studies, Santa Barbara, CA 93106-7065. Offers global culture, ideology, and religion (MA, PhD); global government, human rights, and civil society (MA, PhD); political economy, sustainable development, and the environment (MA, PhD). *Degree requirements:* For master's, one foreign language, thesis, 2 years of a second language; for doctorate, one foreign language, thesis/dissertation, reading proficiency in at least one language other than English. *Entrance requirements:* For master's, GRE, 2 years of a second language with minimum B grade in the final term, statement of purpose, resume or curriculum vitae, 3 letters of recommendation, transcripts (from all post-secondary institutions attended), writing sample (15-20 pages); for doctorate, GRE, statement of purpose, personal achievements/contributions statement, resume or curriculum vitae, 3 letters of recommendation, transcripts from all post-secondary institutions attended, writing sample (15-20 pages). Additional exam requirements/recommendations for international students: Required—TOEFL (minimum score 600 paper-based; 94 iBT), IELTS (minimum score 7). Electronic applications accepted.

University of California, Santa Barbara, Graduate Division, College of Letters and Sciences, Division of Social Sciences, Department of Sociology, Santa Barbara, CA 93106-9430. Offers interdisciplinary emphasis: Black studies (PhD); interdisciplinary emphasis: environment and society (PhD); interdisciplinary emphasis: feminist studies (PhD); interdisciplinary emphasis: global studies (PhD); interdisciplinary emphasis: language, interaction and social organization (PhD); interdisciplinary emphasis: quantitative methods in the social sciences (PhD); interdisciplinary emphasis: technology and society (PhD); sociology (PhD); MA/PhD. Terminal master's awarded for partial completion of doctoral program. *Degree requirements:* For doctorate, comprehensive exam, thesis/dissertation. *Entrance requirements:* For doctorate, GRE General Test. Additional exam requirements/recommendations for international students: Required—TOEFL (minimum score 550 paper-based; 80 iBT), IELTS (minimum score 7). Electronic applications accepted. *Faculty research:* Gender and sexualities, race/ethnicity, social movements, conversation analysis, global sociology.

University of California, Santa Barbara, Graduate Division, Donald Bren School of Environmental Science and Management, Santa Barbara, CA 93106-5131. Offers economics and environmental science (PhD); environmental science and management (MESM, PhD); technology and society (PhD). *Degree requirements:* For master's, thesis; for doctorate, thesis/dissertation. *Entrance requirements:* For master's and doctorate, GRE. Additional exam requirements/recommendations for international students: Required—TOEFL (minimum score 550 paper-based; 80 iBT), IELTS (minimum score 7). Electronic applications accepted. *Faculty research:* Coastal marine resources management, conservation planning, corporate environmental management, economics and politics of the environment, energy and climate, pollution prevention and remediation, water resources management.

University of California, Santa Cruz, Division of Graduate Studies, Division of Social Sciences, Program in Environmental Studies, Santa Cruz, CA 95064. Offers PhD. *Degree requirements:* For doctorate, thesis/dissertation, qualifying exam. *Entrance requirements:* For doctorate, GRE General Test. Additional exam requirements/

recommendations for international students: Required—TOEFL (minimum score 550 paper-based; 83 iBT); Recommended—IELTS (minimum score 8). Electronic applications accepted. *Faculty research:* Political economy and sustainability, conservation biology, agroecology, environmental policy analysis.

University of Central Missouri, The Graduate School, Warrensburg, MO 64093. Offers accountancy (MA); accounting (MBA); applied mathematics (MS); aviation safety (MA); biology (MS); business administration (MBA); career and technical education leadership (MS); college student personnel administration (MS); communication (MA); computer science (MS); counseling (MS); criminal justice (MS); educational leadership (Ed D); educational technology (MS); elementary and early childhood education (MSE); English (MA); environmental studies (MA); finance (MBA); history (MA); human services/educational technology (Ed S); human services/learning resources (Ed S); human services/professional counseling (Ed S); industrial hygiene (MS); industrial management (MS); information systems (MBA); information technology (MS); kinesiology (MS); library science and information services (MS); literacy education (MSE); marketing (MBA); mathematics (MS); music (MA); occupational safety management (MS); psychology (MS); rural family nursing (MS); school administration (MSE); social gerontology (MS); sociology (MA); special education (MSE); speech language pathology (MS); superintendency (Ed S); teaching (MAT); teaching English as a second language (MA); technology (MS); technology management (PhD); theatre (MA). *Accreditation:* ASHA. *Program availability:* Part-time, 100% online, blended/hybrid learning. *Degree requirements:* For master's and Ed S, comprehensive exam (for some programs), thesis (for some programs). *Entrance requirements:* Additional exam requirements/recommendations for international students: Required—TOEFL (minimum score 550 paper-based; 79 iBT). Electronic applications accepted.

University of Chicago, Harris School of Public Policy, Master of Science Program in Environmental Science and Policy, Chicago, IL 60637. Offers MS. Offered in partnership with the Argonne National Laboratory. *Entrance requirements:* For master's, GRE General Test, transcripts, resume, 3 letters of recommendation. Additional exam requirements/recommendations for international students: Required—TOEFL (minimum score 104 iBT), IELTS (minimum score 7). Electronic applications accepted.

University of Colorado Boulder, Graduate School, College of Arts and Sciences, Program in Environmental Studies, Boulder, CO 80309. Offers MS, PhD. *Entrance requirements:* For master's, minimum undergraduate GPA of 3.0. Electronic applications accepted. Application fee is waived when completed online. *Faculty research:* Environmental planning/policy; environmental conservation; environmental studies; behavioral/social sciences; conservation biology.

University of Colorado Denver, College of Architecture and Planning, Program in Urban and Regional Planning, Denver, CO 80217. Offers economic and community development planning (MURP); land use and environmental planning (MURP); urban place making (MURP). *Accreditation:* ACSP. *Program availability:* Part-time. *Degree requirements:* For master's, thesis, minimum of 51 semester hours. *Entrance requirements:* For master's, GRE (for students with an undergraduate GPA below 3.0), sample of writing or work project; statement of interest; resume; three letters of recommendation. Additional exam requirements/recommendations for international students: Required—TOEFL (minimum score 75 iBT). Electronic applications accepted. *Expenses:* Contact institution. *Faculty research:* Physical planning, environmental planning, economic development planning.

University of Colorado Denver, College of Liberal Arts and Sciences, Program in Humanities, Denver, CO 80217. Offers community health (MSS); ethnic studies (MH, MSS); humanities (MH, Graduate Certificate); international studies (MSS); philosophy and theory (MH); social justice (MH, MSS); society and the environment (MSS); visual studies (MH); women's and gender studies (MH, MSS). *Program availability:* Part-time, evening/weekend. *Degree requirements:* For master's, 36 credit hours, project or thesis. *Entrance requirements:* For master's, writing sample, statement of purpose/letter of intent, three letters of recommendation. Additional exam requirements/recommendations for international students: Required—TOEFL (minimum score 537 paper-based; 75 iBT); Recommended—IELTS (minimum score 6.5). Electronic applications accepted. *Expenses:* Tuition, state resident: full-time $6786; part-time $337 per credit hour. Tuition, nonresident: full-time $22,590; part-time $1255 per credit hour. *Required fees:* $1231; $137 per credit hour. Tuition and fees vary according to program and reciprocity agreements. *Faculty research:* Women and gender in the classical Mediterranean, communication theory and democracy, relationship between psychology and philosophy.

University of Colorado Denver, School of Public Affairs, Program in Public Affairs and Administration, Denver, CO 80127. Offers public administration (MPA), including domestic violence, emergency management and homeland security, environmental policy, management and law, homeland security and defense, local government, nonprofit management, public administration; public affairs (PhD). *Accreditation:* NASPAA. *Program availability:* Part-time, evening/weekend, online learning. *Expenses:* Tuition, state resident: full-time $6786; part-time $337 per credit hour. Tuition, nonresident: full-time $22,590; part-time $1255 per credit hour. *Required fees:* $1231; $137 per credit hour. Tuition and fees vary according to program and reciprocity agreements.

University of Dayton, Department of Mechanical and Aerospace Engineering, Dayton, OH 45469. Offers aerospace engineering (MSAE, PhD); mechanical engineering (MSME, PhD); renewable and clean energy (MS). *Program availability:* Part-time, 100% online, blended/hybrid learning. *Degree requirements:* For master's, variable foreign language requirement, comprehensive exam (for some programs), thesis; for doctorate, variable foreign language requirement, comprehensive exam, thesis/dissertation, departmental qualifying exam. *Entrance requirements:* For master's, BS in engineering, math, or physics; minimum GPA of 3.0; for doctorate, GRE. Additional exam requirements/recommendations for international students: Required—TOEFL (minimum score 550 paper-based; 80 iBT), IELTS (minimum score 6.5). Electronic applications accepted. *Faculty research:* Biomechanics, combustion, renewable energy, mechatronics, aerodynamics.

University of Delaware, Center for Energy and Environmental Policy, Newark, DE 19716. Offers energy and environmental policy (MA, MEEP, PhD); urban affairs and public policy (PhD), including technology, environment, and society. *Degree requirements:* For master's, analytical paper or thesis; for doctorate, comprehensive exam, thesis/dissertation. *Entrance requirements:* For master's, GRE General Test, minimum GPA of 3.0; for doctorate, GRE General Test, minimum GPA of 3.5. Additional exam requirements/recommendations for international students: Required—TOEFL. Electronic applications accepted. *Faculty research:* Sustainable development, renewable energy, climate change, environmental policy, environmental justice, disaster policy.

University of Denver, Sturm College of Law, Programs in Environmental and Natural Resources Law and Policy, Denver, CO 80208. Offers environmental and natural resources law and policy (LL M, MLS); natural resources law and policy (Certificate). *Students:* 3 full-time (1 woman), 7 part-time (3 women); includes 1 minority (Black or African American, non-Hispanic/Latino), 2 international. Average age 33. In 2018, 15 master's awarded. *Degree requirements:* For master's, capstone. *Entrance requirements:* For master's, bachelor's degree (for MRLS), JD (for LLM), transcripts, two letters of recommendation, resume, personal statement. Additional exam requirements/recommendations for international students: Required—TOEFL (minimum score 550 paper-based; 80 iBT). *Application deadline:* For fall admission, 8/5 for domestic and international students; for spring admission, 12/23 for domestic and international students; for summer admission, 5/18 for domestic and international students. Applications are processed on a rolling basis. Application fee: $65. Electronic applications accepted. *Expenses:* $40,700 per year full-time. *Financial support:* In 2018–19, 10 students received support. Federal Work-Study, institutionally sponsored loans, scholarships/grants, and unspecified assistantships available. Support available to part-time students. Financial award application deadline: 2/15; financial award applicants required to submit FAFSA.
Website: http://www.law.du.edu/index.php/graduate-legal-studies/masters-programs/mls-enrlp

The University of Findlay, Office of Graduate Admissions, Findlay, OH 45840-3653. Offers applied security and analytics (MSAS); athletic training (MAT); business (MBA), including certified management accountant, certified public accountant, health care management, hospitality management; education (MA Ed, Ed D), including children's literature (MA Ed), curriculum and teaching (MA Ed), education (MA Ed), educational administration (MA Ed), human resource development (MA Ed), mathematics (MA Ed), reading (MA Ed), science education (MA Ed), superintendent (Ed D), teaching (Ed D), technology (MA Ed); environmental, safety, and health management (MSEM); health informatics (MS); occupational therapy (MOT); pharmacy (Pharm D); physical therapy (DPT); physician assistant (MPA); rhetoric and writing (MA); teaching English to speakers of other languages (TESOL) and applied linguistics (MA). *Program availability:* Part-time, evening/weekend, 100% online, blended/hybrid learning. *Degree requirements:* For master's, comprehensive exam (for some programs), thesis (for some programs), cumulative project, capstone project; for doctorate, thesis/dissertation (for some programs). *Entrance requirements:* For master's, GRE/GMAT, bachelor's degree from accredited institution, minimum undergraduate GPA of 2.5 in last 64 hours of course work; for doctorate, GRE, MAT, minimum cumulative GPA of 3.0. Additional exam requirements/recommendations for international students: Required—TOEFL (minimum score 79 iBT), IELTS (minimum score 7), PTE (minimum score 61). Electronic applications accepted.

University of Guelph, Office of Graduate and Postdoctoral Studies, Ontario Agricultural College, Department of Land Resource Science, Guelph, ON N1G 2W1, Canada. Offers atmospheric science (M Sc, PhD); environmental and agricultural earth sciences (M Sc, PhD); land resources management (M Sc, PhD); soil science (M Sc, PhD). *Program availability:* Part-time. *Degree requirements:* For master's, thesis (for some programs), research project (non-thesis track); for doctorate, comprehensive exam, thesis/dissertation. *Entrance requirements:* For master's, minimum B- average during previous 2 years of course work; for doctorate, minimum B average during previous 2 years of course work. Additional exam requirements/recommendations for international students: Required—TOEFL (minimum score 550 paper-based). Electronic applications accepted. *Faculty research:* Soil science, environmental earth science, land resource management.

University of Hawaii at Manoa, Office of Graduate Education, College of Social Sciences, Department of Urban and Regional Planning, Honolulu, HI 96822. Offers community planning (MURP); disaster management and humanitarian assistance (Graduate Certificate); environmental planning and sustainability (MURP); international development planning (MURP); land use, transportation and infrastructure planning (MURP); planning studies (Graduate Certificate); urban and regional planning (PhD, Graduate Certificate). *Accreditation:* ACSP. *Program availability:* Part-time. *Entrance requirements:* For master's, GRE General Test, minimum GPA of 3.0; for doctorate, GRE General Test. Additional exam requirements/recommendations for international students: Required—TOEFL (minimum score 500 paper-based; 61 iBT), IELTS (minimum score 5).

University of Hawaii at Manoa, Office of Graduate Education, College of Tropical Agriculture and Human Resources, Department of Natural Resources and Environmental Management, Honolulu, HI 96822. Offers MS, PhD. *Program availability:* Part-time. Terminal master's awarded for partial completion of doctoral program. *Degree requirements:* For master's, thesis optional; for doctorate, comprehensive exam, thesis/dissertation. *Entrance requirements:* For master's and doctorate, GRE General Test, minimum GPA of 3.0 in last 4 semesters of course work. Additional exam requirements/recommendations for international students: Required—TOEFL (minimum score 600 paper-based; 100 iBT), IELTS (minimum score 7). *Faculty research:* Bioeconomics, natural resource management.

University of Houston–Clear Lake, School of Business, Program in Administrative Science, Houston, TX 77058-1002. Offers environmental management (MS); human resource management (MA). *Program availability:* Part-time, evening/weekend. *Degree requirements:* For master's, thesis optional. *Entrance requirements:* For master's, GMAT. Additional exam requirements/recommendations for international students: Required—TOEFL (minimum score 550 paper-based). Electronic applications accepted.

University of Illinois at Springfield, Graduate Programs, College of Public Affairs and Administration, Program in Environmental Studies, Springfield, IL 62703-5407. Offers environmental science (MS); environmental studies (MA). *Program availability:* Part-time, evening/weekend, 100% online. *Faculty:* 6 full-time (3 women), 2 part-time/adjunct (1 woman). *Students:* 12 full-time (7 women), 43 part-time (23 women); includes 12 minority (3 Black or African American, non-Hispanic/Latino; 2 Asian, non-Hispanic/Latino; 4 Hispanic/Latino; 3 Two or more races, non-Hispanic/Latino), 2 international. Average age 30. 44 applicants, 41% accepted, 15 enrolled. In 2018, 33 master's awarded. *Degree requirements:* For master's, thesis, project, or capstone closure course. *Entrance requirements:* For master's, minimum undergraduate GPA of 3.0, 2 letters of recommendation, goals essay, completion of ecology course with lab with minimum B grade, undergraduate or work background sufficient for advanced course work in environmental studies. Additional exam requirements/recommendations for international students: Required—TOEFL (minimum score 500 paper-based; 61 iBT). *Application deadline:* Applications are processed on a rolling basis. Application fee: $60 ($75 for international students). Electronic applications accepted. *Financial support:* In 2018–19, research assistantships with full tuition reimbursements (averaging $10,384 per year), teaching assistantships with full tuition reimbursements (averaging $10,303 per year) were awarded; fellowships, career-related internships or fieldwork, Federal Work-Study, scholarships/grants, health care benefits, and unspecified assistantships also available. Support available to part-time students. Financial award application deadline: 11/15; financial award applicants required to submit FAFSA. *Unit head:* Dr. Dennis Ruez, Jr., Program Administrator, 217-206-8424, E-mail: druez2@uis.edu. *Application contact:* Dr. Dennis Ruez, Jr., Program Administrator, 217-206-8424, E-mail: druez2@uis.edu.
Website: http://www.uis.edu/environmentalstudies/

Environmental Management and Policy

University of Maine, Graduate School, College of Liberal Arts and Sciences, Department of Anthropology, Orono, ME 04469. Offers anthropology and environmental policy (PhD). *Faculty:* 10 full-time (5 women). *Students:* 11 full-time (7 women); includes 1 minority (American Indian or Alaska Native, non-Hispanic/Latino), 1 international. Average age 30. 18 applicants, 67% accepted, 2 enrolled. *Degree requirements:* For doctorate, comprehensive exam, thesis/dissertation. *Entrance requirements:* For doctorate, GRE General Test. Additional exam requirements/recommendations for international students: Required—TOEFL (minimum score 80 iBT), IELTS (minimum score 6.5). *Application deadline:* For fall admission, 1/15 for domestic and international students. Application fee: $65. Electronic applications accepted. *Financial support:* In 2018–19, 16 students received support, including 4 research assistantships with full tuition reimbursements available (averaging $15,600 per year), 6 teaching assistantships with full tuition reimbursements available (averaging $15,600 per year); scholarships/grants and unspecified assistantships also available. Financial award application deadline: 3/1. *Faculty research:* Historical ecology, human dimensions of climate change, conservation, indigenous studies. *Total annual research expenditures:* $219,811. *Unit head:* Gregory Zaro, Chair, 207-581-1857, Fax: 207-581-1823, E-mail: gregory.zaro@umit.maine.edu. *Application contact:* Scott G. Delcourt, Assistant Vice President for Graduate Studies and Senior Associate Dean, 207-581-3291, Fax: 207-581-3232, E-mail: graduate@maine.edu.
Website: http://www.umaine.edu/anthropology/graduate-programs/

The University of Manchester, School of Environment, Education and Development, Manchester, United Kingdom. Offers architecture (M Phil, PhD); development policy and management (M Phil, PhD); human geography (M Phil, PhD); physical geography (M Phil, PhD); planning and landscape (M Phil, PhD).

University of Maryland, Baltimore County, The Graduate School, College of Arts, Humanities and Social Sciences, Department of Geography and Environmental Systems, Program in Geography and Environmental Systems, Baltimore, MD 21250. Offers MS, PhD. *Program availability:* Part-time. Terminal master's awarded for partial completion of doctoral program. *Degree requirements:* For master's, thesis optional, annual faculty evaluation, research paper; for doctorate, comprehensive exam, thesis/dissertation, annual faculty evaluation, qualifying exams, proposal and dissertation defense. *Entrance requirements:* For master's and doctorate, GRE, minimum GPA of 3.0 overall, 3.3 in major. Additional exam requirements/recommendations for international students: Required—TOEFL (minimum score 550 paper-based; 80 iBT); Recommended—IELTS. Electronic applications accepted. *Expenses:* Contact institution. *Faculty research:* Watershed processes; political ecology; land change and land use; conservation and development; urbanization; economic geography; climate and weather systems; ecology and biogeography; landscape ecology; urban sustainability; environmental health; environmental policy; geographic information science and remote sensing.

University of Maryland, Baltimore County, The Graduate School, College of Arts, Humanities and Social Sciences, School of Public Policy, Baltimore, MD 21250. Offers public policy (MPP, PhD), including economics (PhD), educational policy, emergency services (PhD), environmental policy (MPP), evaluation and analytical methods, health policy, policy history (PhD), public management, urban policy. *Program availability:* Part-time, evening/weekend. Terminal master's awarded for partial completion of doctoral program. *Degree requirements:* For master's, thesis, policy analysis paper, internship for pre-service; for doctorate, comprehensive exam, thesis/dissertation, comprehensive and field qualifying exams. *Entrance requirements:* For master's, GRE General Test, 3 academic letters of reference, resume, official transcripts; for doctorate, GRE General Test, 3 academic letters of reference, resume, research paper, official transcripts. Additional exam requirements/recommendations for international students: Required—TOEFL (minimum score 550 paper-based; 80 iBT), IELTS (minimum score 6.5). Electronic applications accepted. *Expenses:* Contact institution. *Faculty research:* Education policy, health policy, urban and environmental policy, public management, evaluation and analytical method.

University of Maryland Eastern Shore, Graduate Programs, Department of Natural Sciences, Princess Anne, MD 21853. Offers chemistry (MS); quantitative fisheries and resource economics (PMS); toxicology (MS, PhD). *Degree requirements:* For master's, thesis; for doctorate, comprehensive exam, thesis/dissertation. *Entrance requirements:* For master's and doctorate, GRE General Test, minimum GPA of 3.0. Additional exam requirements/recommendations for international students: Required—TOEFL (minimum score 80 iBT). Electronic applications accepted. *Faculty research:* Environmental chemistry (air/water pollution), fin fish ecology.

University of Maryland University College, The Graduate School, Program in Environmental Management, Adelphi, MD 20783. Offers MS. *Program availability:* Part-time, online learning. *Students:* 1 full-time (0 women), 214 part-time (125 women); includes 81 minority (42 Black or African American, non-Hispanic/Latino; 1 American Indian or Alaska Native, non-Hispanic/Latino; 8 Asian, non-Hispanic/Latino; 22 Hispanic/Latino; 1 Native Hawaiian or other Pacific Islander, non-Hispanic/Latino; 7 Two or more races, non-Hispanic/Latino), 3 international. Average age 35. 47 applicants, 100% accepted, 37 enrolled. In 2018, 43 master's awarded. *Degree requirements:* For master's, thesis or alternative, capstone course. *Application deadline:* Applications are processed on a rolling basis. Application fee: $50. Electronic applications accepted. *Financial support:* Scholarships/grants available. Support available to part-time students. Financial award application deadline: 6/1; financial award applicants required to submit FAFSA. *Unit head:* Robert Ouellette, Program Chair, 240-684-2400. *Application contact:* Admissions, 800-888-8682, E-mail: studentfirst@umuc.edu.
Website: https://www.umuc.edu/academic-programs/masters-degrees/environmental-management.cfm

University of Massachusetts Amherst, Graduate School, College of Natural Sciences, Department of Environmental Conservation, Amherst, MA 01003. Offers building systems (MS, PhD); environmental policy and human dimensions (MS, PhD); forest resources (MS, PhD); sustainability science (MS); water, wetlands and watersheds (MS, PhD); wildlife and fisheries conservation (MS, PhD). *Program availability:* Part-time. Terminal master's awarded for partial completion of doctoral program. *Degree requirements:* For master's, thesis or alternative; for doctorate, comprehensive exam, thesis/dissertation. *Entrance requirements:* For master's and doctorate, GRE General Test. Additional exam requirements/recommendations for international students: Required—TOEFL (minimum score 550 paper-based; 80 iBT), IELTS (minimum score 6.5). Electronic applications accepted.

University of Massachusetts Dartmouth, Graduate School, College of Arts and Sciences, Department of Public Policy, North Dartmouth, MA 02747-2300. Offers educational policy (Graduate Certificate); environmental policy (Graduate Certificate); public management (Graduate Certificate); public policy (MPP). *Program availability:* Part-time, 100% online, blended/hybrid learning. *Faculty:* 4 full-time (0 women), 1 part-time/adjunct (0 women). *Students:* 11 full-time (10 women), 60 part-time (37 women); includes 16 minority (6 Black or African American, non-Hispanic/Latino; 2 Asian, non-Hispanic/Latino; 7 Hispanic/Latino; 1 Two or more races, non-Hispanic/Latino). Average age 35. 55 applicants, 95% accepted, 33 enrolled. In 2018, 16 master's, 24 other advanced degrees awarded. *Degree requirements:* For master's, e-portfolio. *Entrance requirements:* For master's, GRE or GMAT (waived if applicant has already earned a graduate degree from accredited school or if applicant has successfully completed the educational, environmental or public management certificate program), statement of purpose (minimum of 300 words), resume, 2 letters of recommendation, official transcripts; for Graduate Certificate, statement of purpose (minimum of 300 words), resume, official transcripts. Additional exam requirements/recommendations for international students: Required—TOEFL (minimum score 600 paper-based; 100 iBT). *Application deadline:* Applications are processed on a rolling basis. Application fee: $60. Electronic applications accepted. *Financial support:* Health care benefits available. Financial award application deadline: 3/1; financial award applicants required to submit FAFSA. *Faculty research:* Environmental justice, sustainability, international trade and finance, corporate social responsibility, global governance. *Total annual research expenditures:* $9,000. *Unit head:* Chad McGuire, Graduate Program Director, Public Policy, 508-999-8520, E-mail: cmcguire@umassd.edu. *Application contact:* Scott Webster, Director of Graduate Studies & Admissions, 508-999-8604, Fax: 508-999-8183, E-mail: graduate@umassd.edu.
Website: http://www.umassd.edu/cas/departmentsanddegreeprograms/publicpolicy/

University of Michigan, School for Environment and Sustainability, Program in Environment and Sustainability, Ann Arbor, MI 48109. Offers behavior, education and communication (MS); conservation ecology (MS); environment and sustainability (PhD); environmental informatics (MS); environmental justice (MS); environmental policy and planning (MS); sustainable systems (MS); MS/JD; MS/MBA; MS/MPH; MS/MPP; MS/MSE; MS/MURP. *Faculty:* 39 full-time (15 women), 19 part-time/adjunct (3 women). *Students:* 332 full-time (184 women); includes 52 minority (6 Black or African American, non-Hispanic/Latino; 1 American Indian or Alaska Native, non-Hispanic/Latino; 14 Asian, non-Hispanic/Latino; 17 Hispanic/Latino; 1 Native Hawaiian or other Pacific Islander, non-Hispanic/Latino; 13 Two or more races, non-Hispanic/Latino), 57 international. Average age 26. 485 applicants. In 2018, 113 master's, 4 doctorates awarded. Terminal master's awarded for partial completion of doctoral program. *Degree requirements:* For master's, thesis, practicum, or group project; for doctorate, comprehensive exam, thesis/dissertation, oral defense of dissertation, preliminary exam. *Entrance requirements:* For master's, GRE General Test (must be taken within 5 years of application submission); for doctorate, GRE General Test (must be taken within 5 years of application submission), Master's Degree. Additional exam requirements/recommendations for international students: Required—TOEFL (minimum score 560 paper-based; 84 iBT). *Application deadline:* For fall admission, 4/30 for domestic and international students. Applications are processed on a rolling basis. Application fee: $75 ($90 for international students). Electronic applications accepted. *Financial support:* Fellowships, research assistantships, teaching assistantships, career-related internships or fieldwork, Federal Work-Study, scholarships/grants, health care benefits, and unspecified assistantships available. Financial award application deadline: 1/7; financial award applicants required to submit FAFSA. *Faculty research:* 1) Climate Change, Energy, and Sustainable Systems 2) Environmental Justice 3) Environmental Behavior, Communications, and Policy 4) Conservation Ecology, Ecosystems Management, and Geographic Information Systems (GIS) 5) Cities, Mobility, and Built Environment. *Unit head:* Dr. Jonathan Overpeck, Samuel A. Graham Dean, 734-764-2550, Fax: 734-763-8965, E-mail: overpeck@umich.edu. *Application contact:* Jung Koral, Associate Director of Enrollment Services, 734-764-6453, Fax: 734-936-2195, E-mail: seas-admissions@umich.edu.
Website: https://seas.umich.edu/academics/ms

University of Minnesota, Twin Cities Campus, Graduate School, College of Food, Agricultural and Natural Resource Sciences, Program in Natural Resources Science and Management, St. Paul, MN 55108. Offers assessment, monitoring, and geospatial analysis (MS, PhD); economics, policy, management, and society (MS, PhD); forest hydrology and watershed management (MS, PhD); forest products (MS, PhD); forests: biology, ecology, conservation, and management (MS, PhD); natural resources science and management (MS, PhD); paper science and engineering (MS, PhD); recreation resources, tourism, and environmental education (MS, PhD). *Program availability:* Part-time. Terminal master's awarded for partial completion of doctoral program. *Degree requirements:* For master's, comprehensive exam, thesis (for some programs); for doctorate, comprehensive exam, thesis/dissertation. *Entrance requirements:* For master's and doctorate, GRE General Test. Additional exam requirements/recommendations for international students: Required—TOEFL (minimum score 550 paper-based; 79 iBT); Recommended—IELTS (minimum score 6.5). Electronic applications accepted. *Faculty research:* Forest hydrology, biology, ecology, conservation, and management; recreation resources and environmental education; wildlife ecology; economics, policy, and society; geographic information systems (GIS); forest products and paper science.

University of Minnesota, Twin Cities Campus, Graduate School, Humphrey School of Public Affairs, PhD Program in Public Affairs, Minneapolis, MN 55455. Offers management and governance (PhD); public policy (PhD); science, technology, and environmental policy (PhD); urban planning (PhD). *Program availability:* Part-time. *Degree requirements:* For doctorate, comprehensive exam, thesis/dissertation. *Entrance requirements:* For doctorate, GRE General Test. Additional exam requirements/recommendations for international students: Required—TOEFL (minimum score 650 paper-based; 100 iBT), IELTS (minimum score 7). Electronic applications accepted. *Expenses:* Contact institution. *Faculty research:* Public policy, urban/regional planning, public/nonprofit management and governance, science/technology/environmental policy.

University of Minnesota, Twin Cities Campus, Graduate School, Humphrey School of Public Affairs, Program in Science, Technology, and Environmental Policy, Minneapolis, MN 55455. Offers MS, JD/MS. *Program availability:* Part-time. *Degree requirements:* For master's, thesis. *Entrance requirements:* For master's, GRE General Test, undergraduate training in the biological or physical sciences or engineering, minimum undergraduate GPA of 3.0. Additional exam requirements/recommendations for international students: Required—TOEFL (minimum score 600 paper-based; 100 iBT), IELTS (minimum score 7). Electronic applications accepted. *Expenses:* Contact institution. *Faculty research:* Economics, history, philosophy, and politics of science and technology; organization and management of science and technology.

University of Montana, Graduate School, College of Humanities and Sciences, Program in Environmental Studies (EVST), Missoula, MT 59812. Offers MS, JD/MS. *Program availability:* Part-time. *Degree requirements:* For master's, thesis, portfolio or professional paper. *Entrance requirements:* Additional exam requirements/recommendations for international students: Required—TOEFL (minimum score 580 paper-based; 92 iBT). Electronic applications accepted. *Faculty research:* Pollution ecology, sustainable agriculture, environmental writing, environmental policy, environmental justice, environmental history, habitat-land management, traditional ecological knowledge of Native Peoples.

University of Nevada, Reno, Graduate School, College of Science, Mackay School of Earth Sciences and Engineering, Department of Geography, Program in Land Use Planning, Reno, NV 89557. Offers MS. *Degree requirements:* For master's, thesis. *Entrance requirements:* For master's, GRE General Test, minimum GPA of 3.0. Additional exam requirements/recommendations for international students: Required—TOEFL (minimum score 500 paper-based; 61 iBT), IELTS (minimum score 6). Electronic applications accepted. *Faculty research:* Contemporary planning, environmental planning.

University of New Brunswick Fredericton, School of Graduate Studies, Faculty of Engineering, Department of Chemical Engineering, Fredericton, NB E3B 5A3, Canada. Offers chemical engineering (M Eng, M Sc E, PhD); environmental studies (M Eng). *Program availability:* Part-time. *Degree requirements:* For master's, thesis; for doctorate, comprehensive exam, thesis/dissertation, qualifying exam. *Entrance requirements:* For master's and doctorate, minimum GPA of 3.0. Additional exam requirements/recommendations for international students: Required—TOEFL (minimum score 580 paper-based), TWE (minimum score 5), Michigan English Language Assessment Battery (minimum score 85) or CanTest (minimum score 4.5). Electronic applications accepted. *Faculty research:* Processing and characterizing nanoengineered composite materials based on carbon nanotubes, enhanced oil recovery processes and oil sweep strategies for conventional and heavy oils, pulp and paper, waste-water treatment, chemistry and corrosion of high and lower temperature water systems, adsorption, aquaculture systems, bioprocessing and biomass refining, nanotechnologies, nuclear, oil and gas, polymer and recirculation.

University of New Brunswick Fredericton, School of Graduate Studies, Faculty of Engineering, Department of Civil Engineering, Fredericton, NB E3B 5A3, Canada. Offers construction engineering and management (M Eng, M Sc E, PhD); environmental engineering (M Eng, M Sc E, PhD); environmental studies (M Eng); geotechnical engineering (M Eng, M Sc E, PhD); groundwater/hydrology (M Eng, M Sc E, PhD); materials (M Eng, M Sc E, PhD); pavements (M Eng, M Sc E, PhD); structures (M Eng, M Sc E, PhD); transportation (M Eng, M Sc E, PhD). *Program availability:* Part-time. *Degree requirements:* For master's, thesis; for doctorate, comprehensive exam, thesis/dissertation, qualifying exam; 27 credit hours of courses. *Entrance requirements:* For master's, minimum GPA of 3.0; B Sc E in civil engineering or related engineering degree; for doctorate, minimum GPA of 3.0; graduate degree in engineering or applied science. Additional exam requirements/recommendations for international students: Required—IELTS (minimum score 7.5), TWE (minimum score 4), Michigan English Language Assessment Battery (minimum score 85) or CanTest (minimum score 4.5); Recommended—TOEFL (minimum score 580 paper-based). Electronic applications accepted. *Faculty research:* Construction engineering and management; engineering materials and infrastructure renewal; highway and pavement research; structures and solid mechanics; geotechnical and geoenvironmental engineering; structure interaction; transportation and planning; environment, solid waste management; structural engineering; water and environmental engineering.

University of New Brunswick Fredericton, School of Graduate Studies, Faculty of Forestry and Environmental Management, Fredericton, NB E3B 5A3, Canada. Offers ecological foundations of forest management (PhD); environmental management (MEM); forest engineering (M Sc FE, MFE); forest products marketing (MBA); forest resources (M Sc F, MF, PhD). *Program availability:* Part-time. *Degree requirements:* For master's, thesis; for doctorate, thesis/dissertation. *Entrance requirements:* For master's and doctorate, minimum GPA of 3.0. Additional exam requirements/recommendations for international students: Required—TOEFL (minimum score 550 paper-based; 80 iBT), IELTS (minimum score 7), TWE (minimum score 4). Electronic applications accepted. *Faculty research:* Forest machines, soils, and ecosystems; integrated forest management; forest meteorology; wood engineering; stream ecosystems dynamics; forest and natural resources policy; forest operations planning; wood technology and mechanics; forest road construction and engineering; forest, wildlife, insect, bird, and fire ecology; remote sensing; insect impacts; silviculture; LiDAR analytics; integrated pest management; forest tree genetics; genetic resource conservation and sustainable management.

University of New Hampshire, Graduate School, College of Life Sciences and Agriculture, Department of Natural Resources and the Environment, Durham, NH 03824. Offers environmental conservation (MS); environmental economics (MS); forestry (MS); natural resources (MS); resource administration and management (MS); soil and water resource management (MS); wildlife and conservation biology (MS). *Program availability:* Part-time. *Entrance requirements:* For master's, GRE General Test. Additional exam requirements/recommendations for international students: Required—TOEFL (minimum score 550 paper-based; 80 iBT). Electronic applications accepted.

University of New Haven, Graduate School, College of Arts and Sciences, Program in Environmental Science, West Haven, CT 06516. Offers environmental ecology (MS); environmental geoscience (MS); environmental health and management (MS); environmental science (MS); geographical information systems (MS). *Program availability:* Part-time, evening/weekend. *Students:* 14 full-time (8 women), 13 part-time (6 women); includes 7 minority (3 Black or African American, non-Hispanic/Latino; 3 Hispanic/Latino; 1 Native Hawaiian or other Pacific Islander, non-Hispanic/Latino), 4 international. Average age 29. 59 applicants, 86% accepted, 10 enrolled. In 2018, 17 master's awarded. *Entrance requirements:* Additional exam requirements/recommendations for international students: Required—TOEFL (minimum score 80 iBT), IELTS, PTE. *Application deadline:* Applications are processed on a rolling basis. Application fee: $50. Electronic applications accepted. Application fee is waived when completed online. *Expenses: Tuition:* Full-time $16,470; part-time $915 per credit hour. *Required fees:* $230; $95 per term. *Financial support:* Research assistantships with partial tuition reimbursements, teaching assistantships with partial tuition reimbursements, Federal Work-Study, scholarships/grants, and unspecified assistantships available. Support available to part-time students. Financial award applicants required to submit FAFSA. *Unit head:* Dr. Roman Zajac, Professor, 203-932-7114, E-mail: rzajac@newhaven.edu. *Application contact:* Selina O'Toole, Senior Associate Director of Graduate Admissions, 203-932-7337, E-mail: SOToole@newhaven.edu.
Website: https://www.newhaven.edu/arts-sciences/graduate-programs/environmental-science/

University of New Mexico, Graduate Studies, College of Arts and Sciences, Program in Geography and Environmental Studies, Albuquerque, NM 87131-2039. Offers MS. *Program availability:* Part-time. *Students:* Average age 32. 20 applicants, 75% accepted, 11 enrolled. In 2018, 6 master's awarded. *Degree requirements:* For master's, comprehensive exam (for some programs), thesis (for some programs). *Entrance requirements:* For master's, GRE. Additional exam requirements/recommendations for international students: Required—TOEFL. *Application deadline:* For fall admission, 2/1 priority date for domestic students, 1/1 priority date for international students; for spring admission, 11/15 for domestic and international students. Application fee: $50. Electronic applications accepted. *Financial support:* Research assistantships with full tuition reimbursements, teaching assistantships with full tuition reimbursements, health care benefits, and tuition waivers (full and partial) available. Financial award applicants required to submit FAFSA. *Faculty research:* Geographic information science, environmental management. *Unit head:* Dr. Scott M. Freundschuh, Chair, 505-277-0058, Fax: 505-277-3614, E-mail: sfreunds@unm.edu. *Application contact:* Dr. Maria D. Lane, Director of Graduate Studies, 505-277-4075, Fax: 505-277-3614, E-mail: mdlane@unm.edu.
Website: http://geography.unm.edu

University of New Mexico, Graduate Studies, Water Resources Program, Albuquerque, NM 87131-2039. Offers hydroscience (MWR); policy management (MWR). *Program availability:* Part-time. *Students:* Average age 34. 16 applicants, 69% accepted, 11 enrolled. In 2018, 5 master's awarded. *Entrance requirements:* For master's, minimum GPA of 3.0 during last 2 years of undergraduate work, 3 letters of reference. Additional exam requirements/recommendations for international students: Required—TOEFL (minimum score 550 paper-based). *Application deadline:* For fall admission, 7/15 for domestic students; for spring admission, 11/15 for domestic students. Applications are processed on a rolling basis. Application fee: $50. Electronic applications accepted. *Financial support:* Research assistantships, career-related internships or fieldwork, institutionally sponsored loans, scholarships/grants, and unspecified assistantships available. Financial award application deadline: 3/1; financial award applicants required to submit FAFSA. *Faculty research:* Sustainable water resources, transboundary water resources, economics, water law, hydrology, developing countries, hydrogeology. *Unit head:* Dr. Robert Berrens, Director, 505-277-7759, Fax: 505-277-5226, E-mail: rberrens@unm.edu. *Application contact:* Annamarie Cordova, Administrative Assistant II, 505-277-7759, Fax: 505-277-5226, E-mail: acordova@unm.edu.
Website: http://www.unm.edu/~wrp/

The University of North Carolina Wilmington, College of Arts and Sciences, Department of Environmental Sciences, Wilmington, NC 28403-3297. Offers environmental studies (MS). *Program availability:* Part-time. *Degree requirements:* For master's, final project or practicum. *Entrance requirements:* For master's, GRE General Test, 3 letters of recommendation, essay. Additional exam requirements/recommendations for international students: Required—TOEFL (minimum score 550 paper-based; 79 iBT), IELTS (minimum score 6.5). Electronic applications accepted. *Faculty research:* Coastal management, environmental management, environmental education, environmental law, natural resource management.

University of Northern British Columbia, Office of Graduate Studies, Prince George, BC V2N 4Z9, Canada. Offers business administration (Diploma); community health science (M Sc); disability management (MA); education (M Ed); first nations studies (MA); gender studies (MA); history (MA); interdisciplinary studies (MA); international studies (MA); mathematical, computer and physical sciences (M Sc); natural resources and environmental studies (M Sc, MA, MNRES, PhD); political science (MA); psychology (M Sc, PhD); social work (MSW). *Program availability:* Part-time, evening/weekend, online learning. *Degree requirements:* For master's, thesis; for doctorate, thesis/dissertation. *Entrance requirements:* For master's, GRE, minimum B average in undergraduate course work; for doctorate, candidacy exam, minimum A average in graduate course work.

University of Oregon, Graduate School, College of Arts and Sciences, Environmental Studies Program, Eugene, OR 97403. Offers environmental science, studies, and policy (PhD); environmental studies (MA, MS). *Degree requirements:* For master's, one foreign language, thesis; for doctorate, comprehensive exam, thesis/dissertation. *Entrance requirements:* For master's, GRE General Test, minimum GPA of 3.0; for doctorate, GRE General Test. Additional exam requirements/recommendations for international students: Required—TOEFL (minimum score 550 paper-based). Electronic applications accepted.

University of Pennsylvania, School of Arts and Sciences, College of Liberal and Professional Studies, Philadelphia, PA 19104. Offers applied geosciences (MSAG); applied positive psychology (MAP); chemical sciences (MCS); environmental studies (MES); individualized study (MLA); liberal arts (M Phil); medical physics (MMP); organization dynamics (M Phil). *Students:* 219 full-time (144 women), 295 part-time (178 women); includes 101 minority (31 Black or African American, non-Hispanic/Latino; 1 American Indian or Alaska Native, non-Hispanic/Latino; 35 Asian, non-Hispanic/Latino; 16 Hispanic/Latino; 1 Native Hawaiian or other Pacific Islander, non-Hispanic/Latino; 17 Two or more races, non-Hispanic/Latino), 103 international. Average age 34. 633 applicants, 52% accepted, 249 enrolled. In 2018, 180 master's awarded. *Unit head:* Nora Lewis, Vice Dean, Professional and Liberal Education, 215-898-7326, E-mail: nlewis@sas.upenn.edu. *Application contact:* Nora Lewis, Vice Dean, Professional and Liberal Education, 215-898-7326, E-mail: nlewis@sas.upenn.edu.
Website: http://www.sas.upenn.edu/lps/graduate

University of Puerto Rico–Río Piedras, Graduate School of Planning, San Juan, PR 00931-3300. Offers economic planning systems (MP); environmental planning (MP); social policy and planning (MP); urban and territorial planning (MP). *Accreditation:* ACSP. *Program availability:* Part-time. *Degree requirements:* For master's, comprehensive exam, thesis, planning project defense. *Entrance requirements:* For master's, PAEG, GRE, minimum GPA of 3.0, 2 letters of recommendation. *Faculty research:* Municipalities, historic Atlas, Puerto Rico, economic future.

University of Rhode Island, Graduate School, College of the Environment and Life Sciences, Department of Environmental and Natural Resource Economics, Kingston, RI 02881. Offers MS, PhD. *Program availability:* Part-time. *Faculty:* 7 full-time (2 women). *Students:* 16 full-time (7 women), 3 part-time (all women); includes 2 minority (1 Black or African American, non-Hispanic/Latino; 1 Asian, non-Hispanic/Latino), 8 international. 33 applicants, 85% accepted, 6 enrolled. In 2018, 2 master's, 6 doctorates awarded. *Entrance requirements:* Additional exam requirements/recommendations for international students: Required—TOEFL. *Application deadline:* For fall admission, 2/1 for domestic and international students. Application fee: $65. Electronic applications accepted. *Expenses: Tuition, area resident:* Full-time $13,226; part-time $735 per credit. Tuition, state resident: full-time $13,226; part-time $735 per credit. Tuition, nonresident: full-time $25,854; part-time $1436 per credit. *International tuition:* $25,854 full-time. *Required fees:* $1698; $50 per credit. $35 per semester. One-time fee: $165. *Financial support:* In 2018–19, 16 research assistantships with tuition reimbursements (averaging $11,641 per year) were awarded. Financial award application deadline: 2/1; financial award applicants required to submit FAFSA. *Unit head:* Dr. Hirotsugu Uchida, Chair, 401-874-4586, Fax: 401-874-4766, E-mail: enre_chair@etal.uri.edu. *Application contact:* Corey Lang, Graduate Program Director, 401-874-4569, E-mail: clang@uri.edu.
Website: http://web.uri.edu/enre/

University of South Africa, College of Agriculture and Environmental Sciences, Pretoria, South Africa. Offers agriculture (MS); consumer science (MCS); environmental management (MA, MS, PhD); environmental science (MA, MS, PhD); geography (MA, MS, PhD); horticulture (M Tech); human ecology (MHE); life sciences (MS); nature conservation (M Tech).

Environmental Management and Policy

University of South Alabama, College of Arts and Sciences, Department of Marine Sciences, Mobile, AL 36688. Offers marine conservation and resource management (MS); marine sciences (MS, PhD). *Degree requirements:* For master's, comprehensive exam, thesis optional; for doctorate, comprehensive exam, thesis/dissertation, research project. *Entrance requirements:* For master's, GRE, minimum GPA of 3.0, BS in marine sciences or related discipline; for doctorate, GRE, BS or MS in marine sciences or related discipline; minimum undergraduate GPA of 3.0, graduate 3.25. Additional exam requirements/recommendations for international students: Required—TOEFL (minimum score 525 paper-based; 71 iBT). Electronic applications accepted. *Faculty research:* Marine ecosystem response, coastal ecosystems, marine fisheries ecology, overfishing, climate change.

University of South Carolina, The Graduate School, School of the Environment, Program in Earth and Environmental Resources Management, Columbia, SC 29208. Offers MEERM, JD/MEERM. *Program availability:* Part-time, online learning. *Degree requirements:* For master's, thesis optional. *Entrance requirements:* For master's, GRE General Test. Additional exam requirements/recommendations for international students: Required—TOEFL. Electronic applications accepted. *Faculty research:* Hydrology, sustainable development, environmental geology and engineering, energy/environmental resources management.

University of South Florida, College of Arts and Sciences, School of Geosciences, Tampa, FL 33620-9951. Offers environmental science and policy (MS); geography (MA), including environmental geography, geographic information science and spatial analysis, human geography; geography and environmental science and policy (PhD); geology (MS, PhD). *Program availability:* Part-time, evening/weekend. *Faculty:* 33 full-time (6 women). *Students:* 93 full-time (43 women), 48 part-time (23 women); includes 24 minority (8 Black or African American, non-Hispanic/Latino; 6 Asian, non-Hispanic/Latino; 5 Hispanic/Latino; 5 Two or more races, non-Hispanic/Latino), 42 international. Average age 31. 107 applicants, 50% accepted, 23 enrolled. In 2018, 14 master's, 11 doctorates awarded. *Degree requirements:* For master's, comprehensive exam, thesis (for some programs); for doctorate, comprehensive exam, thesis/dissertation. *Entrance requirements:* For master's, GRE General Test, minimum GPA of 3.0, letter of intent, 3 letters of recommendation; for doctorate, GRE General Test, master's in geography, environmental science and policy or related field; GPA of at least 3.2 in graduate credits; letter of intent; 3 letters of recommendation. Additional exam requirements/recommendations for international students: Required—TOEFL, TOEFL minimum score 550 paper-based; 79 iBT or IELTS minimum score 6.5 (for MA and MURP); TOEFL minimum score 600 paper-based (for MS and PhD). *Application deadline:* For fall admission, 2/15 priority date for domestic students, 2/15 for international students; for spring admission, 10/15 priority date for domestic students, 9/15 for international students; for summer admission, 2/15 priority date for domestic students, 1/15 for international students. Application fee: $30. Electronic applications accepted. *Expenses:* Tuition, state resident: full-time $6350. Tuition, nonresident: full-time $19,048. International tuition: $19,048 full-time. Required fees: $2079. *Financial support:* In 2018–19, 45 students received support, including 3 research assistantships (averaging $12,345 per year), 25 teaching assistantships with tuition reimbursements available (averaging $12,807 per year); unspecified assistantships also available. Financial award application deadline: 3/1. *Faculty research:* Geography: human geography, environmental geography, geographic information science and spatial analysis, urban geography, social theory; environmental science, policy, and planning: water resources, wildlife ecology, Karst and wetland environments, natural hazards, soil contamination, meteorology and climatology, environmental sustainability and policy, urban and regional planning. *Total annual research expenditures:* $3 million. *Unit head:* Dr. Mark Rains, Professor and Chair, 813-974-3310, Fax: 813-974-5911, E-mail: mrains@usf.edu. *Application contact:* Dr. Ruiliang Pu, Associate Professor and Graduate Program Coordinator, 813-974-1508, Fax: 813-974-5911, E-mail: rpu@usf.edu.
Website: http://hennarot.forest.usf.edu/main/depts/geosci/

University of South Florida, Innovative Education, Tampa, FL 33620-9951. Offers adult, career and higher education (Graduate Certificate), including college teaching, leadership in developing human resources, leadership in higher education; Africana studies (Graduate Certificate), including diasporas and health disparities, genocide and human rights; aging studies (Graduate Certificate), including gerontology; art research (Graduate Certificate), including museum studies; business foundations (Graduate Certificate); chemical and biomedical engineering (Graduate Certificate), including materials science and engineering, water, health and sustainability; child and family studies (Graduate Certificate), including positive behavior support; civil and industrial engineering (Graduate Certificate), including transportation systems analysis; community and family health (Graduate Certificate), including maternal and child health, social marketing and public health, violence and injury: prevention and intervention, women's health; criminology (Graduate Certificate), including criminal justice administration; data science for public administration (Graduate Certificate); digital humanities (Graduate Certificate); educational measurement and research (Graduate Certificate), including evaluation; English (Graduate Certificate), including comparative literary studies, creative writing, professional and technical communication; entrepreneurship (Graduate Certificate); environmental health (Graduate Certificate), including safety management; epidemiology and biostatistics (Graduate Certificate), including applied biostatistics, biostatistics, concepts and tools of epidemiology, epidemiology, epidemiology of infectious diseases; geography, environment and planning (Graduate Certificate), including community development, environmental policy and management, geographical information systems; geology (Graduate Certificate), including hydrogeology; global health (Graduate Certificate), including disaster management, global health and Latin American and Caribbean studies, global health practice, humanitarian assistance, infection control; government and international affairs (Graduate Certificate), including Cuban studies, globalization studies; health policy and management (Graduate Certificate), including health management and leadership, public health policy and programs; hearing specialist: early intervention (Graduate Certificate); industrial and management systems engineering (Graduate Certificate), including systems engineering, technology management; information studies (Graduate Certificate), including school library media specialist; information systems/decision sciences (Graduate Certificate), including analytics and business intelligence; instructional technology (Graduate Certificate), including distance education, Florida digital/virtual educator, instructional design, multimedia design, Web design; internal medicine, bioethics and medical humanities (Graduate Certificate), including biomedical ethics; Latin American and Caribbean studies (Graduate Certificate); leadership for coastal resiliency planning (Graduate Certificate); mass communications (Graduate Certificate), including multimedia journalism; mathematics and statistics (Graduate Certificate), including mathematics; medicine (Graduate Certificate), including aging and neuroscience, bioinformatics, biotechnology, brain fitness and memory management, clinical investigation, hand and upper limb rehabilitation, health informatics, health sciences, integrative weight management, intellectual property, medicine and gender, metabolic and nutritional medicine, metabolic cardiology, pharmacy sciences; national and competitive intelligence (Graduate Certificate); nursing (Graduate Certificate), including simulation based academic fellowship in advanced pain management;

psychological and social foundations (Graduate Certificate), including career counseling, college teaching, diversity in education, mental health counseling, school counseling; public affairs (Graduate Certificate), including nonprofit management, public management, research administration; public health (Graduate Certificate), including assessing chemical toxicity and public health risks, health equity, pharmacoepidemiology, public health generalist, toxicology, translational research in adolescent behavioral health; public health practices (Graduate Certificate), including planning for healthy communities; rehabilitation and mental health counseling (Graduate Certificate), including integrative mental health care, marriage and family therapy, rehabilitation technology; secondary education (Graduate Certificate), including ESOL, foreign language education: culture and content, foreign language education: professional; social work (Graduate Certificate), including geriatric social work/clinical gerontology; special education (Graduate Certificate), including autism spectrum disorder, disabilities education: severe/profound; world languages (Graduate Certificate), including teaching English as a second language (TESL) or foreign language. *Expenses:* Tuition, state resident: full-time $6350. Tuition, nonresident: full-time $19,048. International tuition: $19,048 full-time. Required fees: $2079. *Unit head:* Dr. Cynthia DeLuca, Associate Vice President and Assistant Vice Provost, 813-974-3077, Fax: 813-974-7061, E-mail: deluca@usf.edu. *Application contact:* Owen Hooper, Director, Summer and Alternative Calendar Programs, 813-974-6917, E-mail: hooper@usf.edu.
Website: http://www.usf.edu/innovative-education/

University of South Florida, St. Petersburg, College of Arts and Sciences, St. Petersburg, FL 33701. Offers digital journalism and design (MA); environmental science and policy (MA, MS); Florida studies (MLA); journalism and media studies (MA); liberal studies (MLA); psychology (MA). *Program availability:* Part-time, online learning. *Degree requirements:* For master's, comprehensive exam, thesis or project. *Entrance requirements:* For master's, GRE, LSAT, MCAT (varies by program), letter of intent, 3 letters of recommendation, writing samples, bachelor's degree from regionally-accredited institution with minimum GPA of 3.0 overall or in upper two years. Additional exam requirements/recommendations for international students: Required—TOEFL (minimum score 550 paper-based; 79 iBT); Recommended—IELTS. Electronic applications accepted.

The University of Tennessee, Graduate School, College of Arts and Sciences, Department of Sociology, Knoxville, TN 37996. Offers criminology (MA, PhD); energy, environment, and resource policy (MA, PhD); political economy (MA, PhD). *Program availability:* Part-time. *Degree requirements:* For master's, thesis or alternative; for doctorate, thesis/dissertation. *Entrance requirements:* For master's, GRE General Test, minimum GPA of 3.0; for doctorate, GRE General Test, minimum GPA of 3.5. Additional exam requirements/recommendations for international students: Required—TOEFL. Electronic applications accepted.

The University of Texas at Austin, Graduate School, College of Liberal Arts, Teresa Lozano Long Institute of Latin American Studies, Austin, TX 78712-1111. Offers cultural politics of Afro-Latin and indigenous peoples (MA); development studies (MA); environmental studies (MA); human rights (MA); Latin American and international law (LL M); JD/MA; MA/MA; MBA/MA; MP Aff/MA; MSCRP/MA. LL M offered jointly with The University of Texas School of Law. *Entrance requirements:* For master's, GRE General Test.

University of Washington, Graduate School, Interdisciplinary Graduate Program in Quantitative Ecology and Resource Management, Seattle, WA 98195. Offers MS, PhD. *Degree requirements:* For master's, thesis; for doctorate, thesis/dissertation. *Entrance requirements:* For master's and doctorate, GRE General Test, minimum GPA of 3.0. Additional exam requirements/recommendations for international students: Required—TOEFL. Electronic applications accepted. *Faculty research:* Population dynamics, statistical analysis, ecological modeling and systems analysis of aquatic and terrestrial ecosystems.

University of Waterloo, Graduate Studies and Postdoctoral Affairs, Faculty of Environment, Department of Geography and Environmental Management, Waterloo, ON N2L 3G1, Canada. Offers MA, PhD. MA, PhD offered jointly with Wilfrid Laurier University. *Degree requirements:* For master's, thesis optional; for doctorate, one foreign language, comprehensive exam, thesis/dissertation. *Entrance requirements:* For master's, honors degree, minimum B average; for doctorate, master's degree, minimum A- average. Additional exam requirements/recommendations for international students: Required—TOEFL, IELTS, PTE. *Application deadline:* Applications are processed on a rolling basis. Application fee: $125 Canadian dollars. Electronic applications accepted. *Financial support:* Research assistantships, teaching assistantships, career-related internships or fieldwork, and scholarships/grants available. *Faculty research:* Urban economic geography; physical geography; resource management; cultural, regional, historical geography; spatial data.
Website: https://uwaterloo.ca/geography-environmental-management/

University of Waterloo, Graduate Studies and Postdoctoral Affairs, Faculty of Environment, School of Environment, Resources and Sustainability, Waterloo, ON N2L 3G1, Canada. Offers MES, PhD. *Program availability:* Part-time. *Degree requirements:* For master's, thesis. *Entrance requirements:* For master's, honors degree, minimum B average, resume. Additional exam requirements/recommendations for international students: Required—TOEFL, IELTS, PTE. Application fee: $125 Canadian dollars. Electronic applications accepted. *Financial support:* Research assistantships, teaching assistantships, and scholarships/grants available. *Faculty research:* Applied sustainability; sustainable water policy; food, agriculture, and the environment; biology studies; environment and business; ecological monitoring; soil ecosystem dynamics; urban water demand management; demand response.
Website: https://uwaterloo.ca/environment-resources-and-sustainability/

University of Wisconsin–Green Bay, Graduate Studies, Program in Environmental Science and Policy, Green Bay, WI 54311-7001. Offers MS. *Program availability:* Part-time. *Degree requirements:* For master's, thesis or alternative. *Entrance requirements:* For master's, GRE General Test, minimum GPA of 3.0. Electronic applications accepted. *Faculty research:* Bald eagle, parasitic population of domestic and wild animals, resource recovery, anaerobic digestion of organic waste.

Utah State University, School of Graduate Studies, S.J. and Jessie E. Quinney College of Natural Resources, Department of Environment and Society, Logan, UT 84322. Offers bioregional planning (MS); geography (MA, MS); human dimensions of ecosystem science and management (MS, PhD); recreation resource management (MS, PhD). *Degree requirements:* For master's, comprehensive exam, thesis (for some programs). *Entrance requirements:* For master's and doctorate, GRE General Test, minimum GPA of 3.0. Additional exam requirements/recommendations for international students: Required—TOEFL. Electronic applications accepted. *Faculty research:* Geographic information systems/geographic and environmental education, bioregional planning, natural resource and environmental policy, outdoor recreation and tourism, natural resource and environmental management.

Vanderbilt University, School of Engineering, Department of Civil and Environmental Engineering, Program in Environmental Engineering, Nashville, TN 37240-1001. Offers environmental engineering (M Eng); environmental management (MS, PhD). MS and PhD offered through the Graduate School. *Program availability:* Part-time. Terminal master's awarded for partial completion of doctoral program. *Degree requirements:* For master's, thesis or alternative; for doctorate, thesis/dissertation. *Entrance requirements:* For master's and doctorate, GRE General Test. Additional exam requirements/recommendations for international students: Required—TOEFL. Electronic applications accepted. *Expenses: Tuition:* Full-time $47,208; part-time $2026 per credit hour. *Required fees:* $478. *Faculty research:* Waste treatment, hazardous waste management, chemical waste treatment, water quality.

Vermont Law School, Graduate and Professional Programs, Master's Programs, South Royalton, VT 05068-0096. Offers American legal studies (LL M); energy law (LL M); energy regulation and law (MERL); environmental law (LL M); environmental law and policy (MELP); food and agriculture law (LL M); food and agriculture law and policy (MFALP); JD/MELP; JD/MERL; JD/MFALP. *Program availability:* Part-time, 100% online, blended/hybrid learning. *Entrance requirements:* Additional exam requirements/recommendations for international students: Required—TOEFL. *Faculty research:* Environment and new economy; takings; international environmental law; interaction among science, law, and environmental policy; climate change and the law.

Virginia Commonwealth University, Graduate School, School of Life Sciences, Center for Environmental Studies, Richmond, VA 23284-9005. Offers M Env Sc, MS. *Degree requirements:* For master's, thesis. *Entrance requirements:* For master's, GRE General Test. Additional exam requirements/recommendations for international students: Required—TOEFL (minimum score 600 paper-based; 100 iBT). Electronic applications accepted.

Virginia Polytechnic Institute and State University, Graduate School, College of Architecture and Urban Studies, Blacksburg, VA 24061. Offers architecture (M Arch, MS); architecture and design research (PhD); building construction science management (MS); creative technologies (MFA); environmental design and planning (PhD); government and international affairs (MPIA); landscape architecture (MLA, PhD); planning, governance, and globalization (PhD); public administration and public affairs (MPA, PhD); urban and regional planning (MURPL). *Accreditation:* ASLA (one or more programs are accredited). *Faculty:* 145 full-time (56 women), 2 part-time/adjunct (1 woman). *Students:* 334 full-time (167 women), 188 part-time (99 women); includes 112 minority (43 Black or African American, non-Hispanic/Latino; 1 American Indian or Alaska Native, non-Hispanic/Latino; 26 Asian, non-Hispanic/Latino; 30 Hispanic/Latino; 12 Two or more races, non-Hispanic/Latino; 134 international. Average age 33. 521 applicants, 65% accepted, 111 enrolled. In 2018, 130 master's, 23 doctorates awarded. *Degree requirements:* For master's, comprehensive exam (for some programs), thesis (for some programs); for doctorate, comprehensive exam (for some programs), thesis/dissertation (for some programs). *Entrance requirements:* For master's and doctorate, GRE/GMAT. Additional exam requirements/recommendations for international students: Required—TOEFL (minimum score 90 iBT). *Application deadline:* For fall admission, 8/1 for domestic students, 4/1 for international students; for spring admission, 1/1 for domestic students, 9/1 for international students. Applications are processed on a rolling basis. Application fee: $75. Electronic applications accepted. *Expenses:* Tuition, state resident: full-time $15,510; part-time $739.50 per credit hour. Tuition, nonresident: full-time $29,629; part-time $1490.25 per credit hour. *Required fees:* $2804; $550 per semester. Tuition and fees vary according to course load, campus/location and program. *Financial support:* In 2018–19, 1 fellowship with full tuition reimbursement (averaging $28,977 per year), 34 research assistantships with full tuition reimbursements (averaging $15,814 per year), 140 teaching assistantships with full tuition reimbursements (averaging $10,971 per year) were awarded; scholarships/grants and unspecified assistantships also available. Financial award application deadline: 3/1; financial award applicants required to submit FAFSA. *Total annual research expenditures:* $3 million. *Unit head:* Dr. Richard Blythe, Dean, 540-231-6416, Fax: 540-231-6332, E-mail: richbl1@vt.edu. *Application contact:* Christine Mattsson-Coon, Executive Assistant, 540-231-6416, Fax: 540-231-6332, E-mail: cmattsso@vt.edu. Website: http://www.caus.vt.edu/

Virginia Polytechnic Institute and State University, VT Online, Blacksburg, VA 24061. Offers advanced transportation systems (Certificate); aerospace engineering (MS); agricultural and life sciences (MSLFS); business information systems (Graduate Certificate); career and technical education (MS); civil engineering (MS); computer engineering (M Eng, MS); decision support systems (Graduate Certificate); eLearning leadership (MA); electrical engineering (M Eng, MS); engineering administration (MEA); environmental engineering (Certificate); environmental politics and policy (Graduate Certificate); environmental sciences and engineering (MS); foundations of political analysis (Graduate Certificate); health product risk management (Graduate Certificate); industrial and systems engineering (MS); information policy and society (Graduate Certificate); information security (Graduate Certificate); information technology (MIT); instructional technology (MA); integrative STEM education (MA Ed); liberal arts (Graduate Certificate); life sciences: health product risk management (MS); natural resources (MNR, Graduate Certificate); networking (Graduate Certificate); nonprofit and nongovernmental organization management (Graduate Certificate); ocean engineering (MS); political science (MA); security studies (Graduate Certificate); software development (Graduate Certificate). *Expenses:* Tuition, state resident: full-time $15,510; part-time $739.50 per credit hour. Tuition, nonresident: full-time $29,629; part-time $1490.25 per credit hour. *Required fees:* $2804; $550 per semester. Tuition and fees vary according to course load, campus/location and program. *Application contact:* Graduate Admissions and Academic Progress, 540-231-8636, E-mail: grads@vt.edu. Website: http://www.vto.vt.edu/

Webster University, College of Arts and Sciences, Department of Biological Sciences, St. Louis, MO 63119-3194. Offers biological sciences (MS); environmental management (MS). *Program availability:* Part-time, online learning. *Degree requirements:* For master's, comprehensive exam (for some programs), thesis (for some programs). *Entrance requirements:* Additional exam requirements/recommendations for international students: Required—TOEFL. *Expenses: Tuition:* Full-time $22,500; part-time $750 per credit hour. Tuition and fees vary according to degree level, campus/location and program.

Webster University, George Herbert Walker School of Business and Technology, Department of Business, St. Louis, MO 63119-3194. Offers business and organizational security management (MBA); decision support systems (MBA); environmental management (MBA); finance (MBA, MS); forensic accounting (MS); gerontology (MBA); human resources development (MBA); human resources management (MBA); information technology management (MBA); international business (MA, MBA); international relations (MBA); management and leadership (MBA); marketing (MBA); media communications (MBA); procurement and acquisitions management (MBA); Web services (MBA). *Accreditation:* ACBSP. *Program availability:* Part-time, evening/weekend, online learning. *Degree requirements:* For master's, comprehensive exam (for some programs), thesis (for some programs). *Entrance requirements:* Additional exam requirements/recommendations for international students: Required—TOEFL. *Expenses: Tuition:* Full-time $22,500; part-time $750 per credit hour. Tuition and fees vary according to degree level, campus/location and program.

Wesley College, Business Program, Dover, DE 19901-3875. Offers environmental management (MBA); executive leadership (MBA); management (MBA). Executive leadership concentration also offered at New Castle, DE location. *Program availability:* Part-time, evening/weekend. *Entrance requirements:* For master's, GMAT or GRE, minimum undergraduate GPA of 2.75.

Wesley College, Environmental Studies Program, Dover, DE 19901-3875. Offers MS. *Program availability:* Part-time, evening/weekend. *Entrance requirements:* For master's, BA/BSM in science or engineering field, portfolio.

Western State Colorado University, Program in Environmental Management, Gunnison, CO 81231. Offers integrative land management (MEM); sustainable and resilient communities (MEM). *Program availability:* Online learning. *Degree requirements:* For master's, project, portfolio. *Entrance requirements:* Additional exam requirements/recommendations for international students: Required—TOEFL.

Wilfrid Laurier University, Faculty of Graduate and Postdoctoral Studies, Faculty of Arts, Department of Geography and Environmental Studies, Waterloo, ON N2L 3C5, Canada. Offers environmental and resource management (MA, MES, PhD); environmental science (M Sc, MES, PhD); geomatics (M Sc, MES, PhD); human geography (MES, PhD). *Program availability:* Part-time. *Degree requirements:* For master's, thesis optional; for doctorate, thesis/dissertation. *Entrance requirements:* For master's, honors BA in geography, minimum B average in undergraduate course work; honors BSc with minimum B+ or honors BES or BA in physical geography, environmental or earth sciences or the equivalent; for doctorate, MA in geography, minimum A- average. Additional exam requirements/recommendations for international students: Required—TOEFL (minimum score 89 iBT). Electronic applications accepted. *Faculty research:* Resources management, urban, economic, physical, cultural, earth surfaces, geomatics, historical, regional, spatial data handling.

Wilfrid Laurier University, Faculty of Graduate and Postdoctoral Studies, School of International Policy and Governance, International Public Policy Program, Waterloo, ON N2L 3C5, Canada. Offers global governance (MIPP); human security (MIPP); international economic relations (MIPP); international environmental policy (MIPP). Offered jointly with University of Waterloo. *Entrance requirements:* For master's, honours BA with minimum B average. Additional exam requirements/recommendations for international students: Required—TOEFL (minimum score 89 iBT). Electronic applications accepted. *Faculty research:* International environmental policy, international economic relations, human security, global governance.

Wilmington University, College of Business, New Castle, DE 19720-6491. Offers accounting (MBA, MS); business administration (MBA, DBA); environmental stewardship (MBA); finance (MBA); health care administration (MBA, MSM); homeland security (MBA, MSM); human resource management (MSM); management information systems (MBA, MSN); marketing (MSM); marketing management (MBA); military leadership (MSM); organizational leadership (MBA, MSM); public administration (MSM). *Program availability:* Part-time, evening/weekend. *Entrance requirements:* Additional exam requirements/recommendations for international students: Required—TOEFL (minimum score 500 paper-based). Electronic applications accepted.

Yale University, Graduate School of Arts and Sciences, Department of Forestry and Environmental Studies, New Haven, CT 06520. Offers environmental sciences (PhD); forestry (PhD). *Degree requirements:* For doctorate, thesis/dissertation. *Entrance requirements:* For doctorate, GRE General Test.

Yale University, School of Forestry and Environmental Studies, New Haven, CT 06511. Offers environmental management (MEM), including business and the environment, ecosystem and conservation management, energy and the environment, environmental policy analysis; environmental science (MES); forest science (MFS); forestry (MF); forestry and environmental studies (PhD); JD/MEM; MBA/MEM; MBA/MF; MEM/M Arch; MEM/M Div; MEM/MA; MEM/MAR; MEM/MPH. *Accreditation:* SAF (one or more programs are accredited). *Program availability:* Part-time. Terminal master's awarded for partial completion of doctoral program. *Degree requirements:* For master's, internship and capstone project (for MEM and MF); research project and thesis (for MES and MFS); for doctorate, comprehensive exam, thesis/dissertation. *Entrance requirements:* For master's, GRE General Test, GMAT or LSAT; for doctorate, GRE General Test. Additional exam requirements/recommendations for international students: Required—TOEFL (minimum score 600 paper-based; 100 iBT) or IELTS (minimum score 7). Electronic applications accepted. *Expenses:* Contact institution. *Faculty research:* Environmental policy, social ecology, industrial environmental management, forestry, environmental health, urban ecology, water science policy.

York University, Faculty of Graduate Studies, Program in Environmental Studies, Toronto, ON M3J 1P3, Canada. Offers MES, PhD, MES/LL B, MES/MA. *Program availability:* Part-time. *Degree requirements:* For master's, thesis optional; for doctorate, comprehensive exam, thesis/dissertation, research seminar. Electronic applications accepted.

Youngstown State University, College of Graduate Studies, College of Science, Technology, Engineering and Mathematics, Program in Environmental Studies, Youngstown, OH 44555-0001. Offers environmental studies (MS); industrial/institutional management (Certificate); risk management (Certificate). *Degree requirements:* For master's, comprehensive exam, thesis, oral defense of dissertation. *Entrance requirements:* For master's, GRE General Test or minimum GPA of 2.7. Additional exam requirements/recommendations for international students: Required—TOEFL.

Peterson's Graduate Programs in the Physical Sciences, Mathematics, Agricultural Sciences, the Environment & Natural Resources 2020

www.petersons.com 311

Environmental Sciences

Adelphi University, College of Arts and Sciences, Program in Environmental Studies, Garden City, NY 11530-0701. Offers MS. *Students:* 2 full-time (0 women), 5 part-time (3 women); includes 3 minority (2 Black or African American, non-Hispanic/Latino; 1 Asian, non-Hispanic/Latino), 3 international. Average age 33. 34 applicants, 29% accepted, 4 enrolled. In 2018, 9 master's awarded. *Entrance requirements:* For master's, GRE General Test, 2 letters of recommendation; course work in microeconomics, political science, statistics/calculus, and either chemistry or physics; computer literacy. Additional exam requirements/recommendations for international students: Required—TOEFL (minimum score 550 paper-based; 80 iBT), IELTS (minimum score 6.5). *Application deadline:* For fall admission, 3/1 for international students; for spring admission, 11/1 for international students. Applications are processed on a rolling basis. Application fee: $50. Electronic applications accepted. *Expenses:* Contact institution. *Financial support:* Research assistantships with full and partial tuition reimbursements, teaching assistantships, career-related internships or fieldwork, institutionally sponsored loans, scholarships/grants, traineeships, and unspecified assistantships available. Support available to part-time students. Financial award application deadline: 1/1; financial award applicants required to submit FAFSA. *Faculty research:* Contaminates sites, workplace exposure level of contaminants, climate change and human health. *Unit head:* Aaren Freeman, Graduate Coordinator of Environmental Studies Program, 516-237-8546, E-mail: afreeman@adelphi.edu. *Application contact:* Aaren Freeman, Graduate Coordinator of Environmental Studies Program, 516-237-8546, E-mail: afreeman@adelphi.edu.
Website: http://environmental-studies.adelphi.edu/ms-in-environmental-studies/

Alaska Pacific University, Graduate Programs, Environmental Science Department, Program in Environmental Science, Anchorage, AK 99508-4672. Offers MSES. *Program availability:* Part-time. *Degree requirements:* For master's, thesis. *Entrance requirements:* For master's, GRE General Test, minimum GPA of 3.0. Additional exam requirements/recommendations for international students: Required—TOEFL (minimum score 550 paper-based).

American University, College of Arts and Sciences, Department of Environmental Science, Washington, DC 20016. Offers environmental assessment (Graduate Certificate); environmental science (MS); professional science: environmental assessment (MS). *Faculty:* 7 full-time (5 women), 5 part-time/adjunct (1 woman). *Students:* 12 full-time (10 women), 5 part-time (2 women); includes 3 minority (all Hispanic/Latino), 1 international. Average age 25. 17 applicants, 94% accepted, 7 enrolled. In 2018, 7 master's, 1 other advanced degree awarded. *Degree requirements:* For master's, comprehensive exam, thesis (for some programs). *Entrance requirements:* For master's, GRE General Test, GRE Subject Test, one year of calculus, lab science, statement of purpose, transcripts, 2 letters of recommendation, resume. Additional exam requirements/recommendations for international students: Required—TOEFL. Application fee: $55. Electronic applications accepted. *Expenses:* Contact institution. *Financial support:* Research assistantships, teaching assistantships, and unspecified assistantships available. Financial award applicants required to submit FAFSA. *Unit head:* Dr. Stephen MacAvoy, Department Chair, 202-885-1751, E-mail: environ@american.edu. *Application contact:* Jonathan Harper, Assistant Director, Graduate Recruitment, 202-855-3620, E-mail: casgrad@american.edu.
Website: http://www.american.edu/cas/environmental/

American University of Beirut, Graduate Programs, Faculty of Agricultural and Food Sciences, Beirut, Lebanon. Offers agricultural economics (MS); animal science (MS); ecosystem management (MSES); food safety (MS); food security (MS); food technology (MS); irrigation (MS); nutrition (MS); plant protection (MS); plant science (MS); poultry science (MS); public health nutrition (MS); rural community development (MS). *Program availability:* Part-time. *Faculty:* 24 full-time (4 women). *Students:* 30 full-time (22 women), 90 part-time (69 women); includes 9 minority (all Black or African American, non-Hispanic/Latino). Average age 25. 238 applicants, 77% accepted, 37 enrolled. In 2018, 19 master's awarded. *Degree requirements:* For master's, one foreign language, comprehensive exam, thesis (for some programs). *Entrance requirements:* Additional exam requirements/recommendations for international students: Required—TOEFL (minimum score 600 paper-based; 100 iBT), IELTS (minimum score 7.5). *Application deadline:* For fall admission, 2/10 for domestic and international students; for spring admission, 11/2 for domestic and international students. Application fee: $50. Electronic applications accepted. *Expenses: Tuition:* Full-time $17,748; part-time $986 per credit. *Required fees:* $762. Tuition and fees vary according to course load and program. *Financial support:* In 2018–19, 2 fellowships with full and partial tuition reimbursements (averaging $11,637 per year), 12 research assistantships with full and partial tuition reimbursements (averaging $3,840 per year), 73 teaching assistantships with full and partial tuition reimbursements were awarded; scholarships/grants, health care benefits, and unspecified assistantships also available. Financial award application deadline: 2/2. *Faculty research:* Plant science; animal science; landscape for culture and socio-ecological health; diet, obesity and non communicable diseases; water, agriculture, ecosystem & remote sensing; water-energy-food-health nexus. *Total annual research expenditures:* $1.2 million. *Unit head:* Prof. Rabi Hassan Mohtar, Dean of Faculty of Agricultural and Food Sciences, 961-1-350000 Ext. 4400, Fax: 961-1-744460, E-mail: mohtar@aub.edu.lb. *Application contact:* Prof. Zaher Dawy, Associate Provost, 961-1-374374 Ext. 4386, Fax: 961-1-374374, E-mail: graduate.council@aub.edu.lb.
Website: http://www.aub.edu.lb/fafs/pages/default.aspx

American University of Beirut, Graduate Programs, Faculty of Health Sciences, Beirut 1107 2020, Lebanon. Offers environmental sciences (MS), including environmental health; epidemiology (MS, PhD); epidemiology and biostatistics (MPH); health care leadership (EMHCL); health management and policy (MPH), including health service administration; health promotion and community health (MPH); health research (MS); public health nutrition (MS). *Program availability:* Part-time, evening/weekend. *Faculty:* 33 full-time (20 women), 10 part-time/adjunct (5 women). *Students:* 65 full-time (56 women), 84 part-time (77 women). Average age 26. 391 applicants, 42% accepted, 64 enrolled. In 2018, 136 master's awarded. *Degree requirements:* For master's, one foreign language, comprehensive exam, thesis, no thesis is required for the MPH program; for doctorate, one foreign language, comprehensive exam, thesis/dissertation. *Entrance requirements:* For master's, 2 letters of recommendations, personal statement for each program, transcript of grades, letter explaining the grading system and passing grade; for doctorate, GRE, Official transcripts(all levels) and certified copies of degrees, 3 letters of recommendations, personal statement, CV, interview. Additional exam requirements/recommendations for international students: Required—TOEFL (minimum score 97 iBT), IELTS (minimum score 7). *Application deadline:* For fall admission, 4/4 for domestic and international students; for spring admission, 11/5 for domestic and international students. Application fee: $50. Electronic applications accepted. *Expenses: Tuition:* Full-time $17,748; part-time $986 per credit. *Required fees:* $762. Tuition and fees vary according to course load and program. *Financial support:* In 2018–19, 50 students received support, including 3 fellowships with full and partial tuition reimbursements available (averaging $14,400 per year), 9 research assistantships with full and partial tuition reimbursements available (averaging $6,816 per year), 6 teaching assistantships with full and partial tuition reimbursements available (averaging $3,808 per year); scholarships/grants and unspecified assistantships also available. Financial award application deadline: 4/4. *Faculty research:* Conflict and health; refugees health; sexual and reproductive health; tobacco control; health care quality and access and environmental management. *Total annual research expenditures:* $2.3 million. *Unit head:* Prof. Iman Adel Nuwayhid, Dean/Professor, 961-1-759683 Ext. 4600, Fax: 961-1-744470, E-mail: nuwayhid@aub.edu.lb. *Application contact:* Lama El Kadi, Administrative Coordinator, 961-1-350000 Ext. 4687, E-mail: le19@aub.edu.lb.
Website: http://www.aub.edu.lb/fhs/Pages/default.aspx

American University of Beirut, Graduate Programs, Maroun Semaan Faculty of Engineering and Architecture, Beirut, Lebanon. Offers applied energy (ME); civil engineering (PhD); electrical and computer engineering (PhD); energy studies (MS); engineering management (MEM); environmental and water resources (ME); environmental technology (MSES); mechanical engineering (ME, PhD); urban design (MUD); urban planning and policy (MUPP). For progreen diploma: LAU/AUC. *Program availability:* Part-time, 100% online. *Faculty:* 105 full-time (25 women), 102 part-time/adjunct (33 women). *Students:* 380 full-time (186 women), 100 part-time (38 women). Average age 27. 489 applicants, 64% accepted, 127 enrolled. In 2018, 109 master's, 14 doctorates awarded. Terminal master's awarded for partial completion of doctoral program. *Degree requirements:* For master's, one foreign language, comprehensive exam, thesis optional; for doctorate, one foreign language, comprehensive exam, thesis/dissertation. *Entrance requirements:* For doctorate, GRE. Additional exam requirements/recommendations for international students: Required—TOEFL (minimum score 575 paper-based; 88 iBT), AUB-EN; Recommended—IELTS (minimum score 7). *Application deadline:* For fall admission, 4/4 for domestic and international students; for spring admission, 11/3 for domestic and international students; for summer admission, 4/4 for domestic and international students. Application fee: $50. *Expenses: Tuition:* Full-time $17,748; part-time $986 per credit. *Required fees:* $762. Tuition and fees vary according to course load and program. *Financial support:* In 2018–19, 15 students received support, including 92 fellowships with full tuition reimbursements available (averaging $14,400 per year), 80 research assistantships with full and partial tuition reimbursements available (averaging $5,300 per year), 162 teaching assistantships with full and partial tuition reimbursements available (averaging $1,400 per year); scholarships/grants, tuition waivers (full and partial), and unspecified assistantships also available. Financial award application deadline: 4/4. *Faculty research:* All areas in engineering, architecture and design. *Total annual research expenditures:* $1.5 million. *Unit head:* Prof. Alan Shihade, Dean, 961-1-374374 Ext. 3400, Fax: 961-1-744462, E-mail: as20@aub.edu.lb. *Application contact:* Dr. Salim Kanaan, Director, Admissions Office, 961-1-374374 Ext. 2590, Fax: 961-1-750775, E-mail: sk00@aub.edu.lb.
Website: https://www.aub.edu.lb/msfea/pages/default.aspx

Antioch University New England, Graduate School, Department of Environmental Studies, Doctoral Program in Environmental Studies, Keene, NH 03431-3552. Offers PhD. *Degree requirements:* For doctorate, thesis/dissertation, practicum. *Entrance requirements:* For doctorate, master's degree and previous experience in the environmental field. Additional exam requirements/recommendations for international students: Required—TOEFL (minimum score 550 paper-based). Electronic applications accepted. *Expenses:* Contact institution. *Faculty research:* Environmental history, green politics, ecopsychology.

Antioch University New England, Graduate School, Department of Environmental Studies, Program in Environmental Education, Keene, NH 03431-3552. Offers MS. *Degree requirements:* For master's, practicum. *Entrance requirements:* For master's, previous undergraduate course work in biology, chemistry, and mathematics; resume; 3 letters of recommendation. Additional exam requirements/recommendations for international students: Required—TOEFL (minimum score 550 paper-based). Electronic applications accepted. *Expenses:* Contact institution. *Faculty research:* Sustainability, natural resources inventory.

Arizona State University at the Tempe campus, College of Liberal Arts and Sciences, School of Human Evolution and Social Change, Tempe, AZ 85287-2402. Offers anthropology (MA, PhD), including anthropology (PhD), archaeology (PhD), bioarchaeology (PhD), evolutionary (PhD), museum studies (MA), sociocultural (PhD); applied mathematics for the life and social sciences (PhD); environmental social science (PhD), including environmental social science, urbanism; global health (MA, PhD), including complex adaptive systems science (PhD), evolutionary global health sciences (PhD), health and culture (PhD), urbanism (PhD); immigration studies (Graduate Certificate). Terminal master's awarded for partial completion of doctoral program. *Degree requirements:* For master's, thesis or alternative, interactive Program of Study (iPOS) submitted before completing 50 percent of required credit hours; for doctorate, comprehensive exam, thesis/dissertation, interactive Program of Study (iPOS) submitted before completing 50 percent of required credit hours. *Entrance requirements:* For master's and doctorate, GRE, minimum GPA of 3.0 or equivalent in last 2 years of work leading to bachelor's degree. Additional exam requirements/recommendations for international students: Required—TOEFL, IELTS, or PTE. Electronic applications accepted.

Arkansas State University, Graduate School, College of Sciences and Mathematics, Program in Environmental Sciences, State University, AR 72467. Offers environmental sciences (MS, PhD). *Program availability:* Part-time. *Degree requirements:* For master's, comprehensive exam, thesis (for some programs); for doctorate, comprehensive exam, thesis/dissertation. *Entrance requirements:* For master's, GRE General Test, appropriate bachelor's degree, letters of recommendation, interview, official transcript, immunization records, letter of intent, resume, statement of purpose; for doctorate, GRE, appropriate bachelor's or master's degree, interview, letters of recommendation, personal statement, official transcript, immunization records, resume, statement of purpose. Additional exam requirements/recommendations for international students: Required—TOEFL (minimum score 550 paper-based; 79 iBT), IELTS (minimum score 6), PTE (minimum score 56). Electronic applications accepted.

Ball State University, Graduate School, College of Sciences and Humanities, Interdepartmental Program in Environmental Sciences, Muncie, IN 47306. Offers environmental science (PhD), including biology, chemistry, geological sciences. *Program availability:* Part-time. *Degree requirements:* For doctorate, thesis/dissertation. *Entrance requirements:* For doctorate, GRE General Test, minimum cumulative GPA of

3.0 (chemistry), 3.2 (biology and geological sciences); acknowledged arrangement for doctoral environmental sciences research with faculty mentor; three letters of recommendation. Additional exam requirements/recommendations for international students: Required—TOEFL (minimum score 550 paper-based; 79 iBT), IELTS (minimum score 6.5). Electronic applications accepted.

Baylor University, Graduate School, College of Arts and Sciences, The Institute of Ecological, Earth and Environmental Sciences, Waco, TX 76798. Offers PhD. *Faculty:* 24 full-time (4 women). *Students:* 5 full-time (1 woman); includes 2 minority (1 Asian, non-Hispanic/Latino; 1 Hispanic/Latino), 2 international. Average age 25. 8 applicants, 25% accepted, 1 enrolled. In 2018, 1 doctorate awarded. *Degree requirements:* For doctorate, comprehensive exam, thesis/dissertation. *Entrance requirements:* For doctorate, GRE. Additional exam requirements/recommendations for international students: Required—TOEFL (minimum score 550 paper-based; 80 iBT); Recommended—IELTS (minimum score 6.5). *Application deadline:* For fall admission, 2/15 priority date for domestic and international students. Application fee: $40. Electronic applications accepted. *Expenses:* Contact institution. *Financial support:* In 2018–19, 5 students received support, including 5 research assistantships with full and partial tuition reimbursements available (averaging $22,000 per year), 5 teaching assistantships with full and partial tuition reimbursements available (averaging $22,000 per year); scholarships/grants, health care benefits, tuition waivers (partial), and unspecified assistantships also available. Financial award application deadline: 2/15. *Faculty research:* Ecosystem processes, environmental toxicology and risk assessment, biogeochemical cycling, chemical fate and transport, conservation management. *Unit head:* Dr. Joe C. Yelderman, Jr., Director, 254-710-2185, E-mail: joe_yelderman@baylor.edu. *Application contact:* Shannon Koehler, Office Manager, 254-710-2224, Fax: 254-710-2298, E-mail: shannon_koehler@baylor.edu.
Website: http://www.baylor.edu/TIEEES/

Boston University, Graduate School of Arts and Sciences, Department of Earth and Environment, Boston, MA 02215. Offers earth and environment (MA, PhD); energy and environment (MA); remote sensing and geospatial sciences (MA). *Students:* 73 full-time (41 women), 5 part-time (3 women); includes 7 minority (3 Asian, non-Hispanic/Latino; 4 Hispanic/Latino), 38 international. Average age 25. 195 applicants, 53% accepted, 31 enrolled. In 2018, 30 master's, 4 doctorates awarded. Terminal master's awarded for partial completion of doctoral program. *Degree requirements:* For master's, comprehensive exam (for some programs), thesis (for some programs); for doctorate, comprehensive exam, thesis/dissertation. *Entrance requirements:* For master's and doctorate, GRE General Test, 3 letters of recommendation, official transcripts, personal statement. Additional exam requirements/recommendations for international students: Required—TOEFL (minimum score 550 paper-based; 84 iBT). *Application deadline:* For fall admission, 12/19 for domestic and international students; for winter admission, 11/1 for domestic and international students. Application fee: $95. Electronic applications accepted. *Financial support:* In 2018–19, 50 students received support, including 4 fellowships with full tuition reimbursements available (averaging $22,660 per year), 24 research assistantships with full tuition reimbursements available (averaging $22,660 per year), 12 teaching assistantships with full tuition reimbursements available (averaging $22,660 per year); Federal Work-Study, scholarships/grants, traineeships, and health care benefits also available. Financial award application deadline: 12/19. *Faculty research:* Biogeosciences, climate and surface processes; energy, environment and society; geographical sciences; geology, geochemistry and geophysics. *Unit head:* Guido Salvucci, Interim Chair, 617-353-8344, E-mail: gdsalvuc@bu.edu. *Application contact:* Matt DiCintio, Graduate Program Coordinator, 617-353-2529, Fax: 617-353-8399, E-mail: dicintio@bu.edu.
Website: http://www.bu.edu/earth/

Brigham Young University, Graduate Studies, College of Life Sciences, Department of Plant and Wildlife Sciences, Provo, UT 84602-1001. Offers environmental science (MS); genetics and biotechnology (MS), wildlife and wildlands conservation (MS, PhD). *Faculty:* 24 full-time (1 woman). *Students:* 12 full-time (7 women), 42 part-time (12 women); includes 2 minority (both Hispanic/Latino). Average age 30. 29 applicants, 59% accepted, 17 enrolled. In 2018, 18 master's, 1 doctorate awarded. *Degree requirements:* For master's, thesis, no C grades or below, 30 hours (24 coursework, 6 thesis); for doctorate, comprehensive exam, thesis/dissertation, no C grades or below, 54 hours (18 dissertation, 36 coursework). *Entrance requirements:* For master's, GRE General Test, minimum GPA of 3.2; for doctorate, GRE, minimum GPA of 3.2. Additional exam requirements/recommendations for international students: Required—TOEFL (minimum score 580 paper-based; 85 iBT). *Application deadline:* 2/1 for domestic and international students; for summer admission, 2/1 for domestic and international students. Application fee: $50. Electronic applications accepted. *Financial support:* In 2018–19, 54 students received support, including 71 research assistantships with partial tuition reimbursements available (averaging $18,081 per year), 42 teaching assistantships with partial tuition reimbursements available (averaging $16,478 per year); scholarships/grants and tuition waivers (partial) also available. Financial award application deadline: 3/1. *Faculty research:* Environmental science, plant genetics, plant ecology, plant nutrition and pathology, wildlife and wildlands conservation. *Total annual research expenditures:* $2.1 million. *Unit head:* Neil Hansen, Chair, 801-422-2491, E-mail: neil_hansen@byu.edu. *Application contact:* Bradley D. Geary, Graduate Coordinator, 801-422-1228, Fax: 801-422-0008, E-mail: bradley_geary@byu.edu.
Website: http://pws.byu.edu

California Institute of Technology, Division of Geological and Planetary Sciences, Pasadena, CA 91125-0001. Offers environmental science and engineering (MS, PhD); geobiology (MS, PhD); geochemistry (MS, PhD); geology (MS, PhD); geophysics (MS, PhD); planetary science (MS, PhD). *Degree requirements:* For doctorate, thesis/dissertation. *Entrance requirements:* For doctorate, GRE General Test. Additional exam requirements/recommendations for international students: Required—TOEFL; Recommended—IELTS, TWE. Electronic applications accepted. *Faculty research:* Planetary surfaces, evolution of anaerobic respiratory processes, structural geology and tectonics, theoretical and numerical seismology, global biogeochemical cycles.

California State Polytechnic University, Pomona, John T. Lyle Center for Regenerative Studies, Pomona, CA 91768-2557. Offers MS. *Program availability:* Part-time. *Students:* 11 full-time (5 women), 9 part-time (5 women); includes 10 minority (2 Black or African American, non-Hispanic/Latino; 2 Asian, non-Hispanic/Latino; 5 Hispanic/Latino; 1 Two or more races, non-Hispanic/Latino), 1 international. Average age 32. 18 applicants, 100% accepted, 13 enrolled. In 2018, 6 master's awarded. *Entrance requirements:* Additional exam requirements/recommendations for international students: Required—TOEFL (minimum score 550 paper-based). *Application deadline:* Applications are processed on a rolling basis. Application fee: $55. Electronic applications accepted. *Expenses:* Contact institution. *Financial support:* Application deadline: 3/2; applicants required to submit FAFSA. *Unit head:* Dr. Pablo La Roche, Interim Director/Graduate Coordinator, 909-869-2700, Fax: 909-869-4331, E-mail: pmlaroche@cpp.edu. *Application contact:* Dr. Pablo La Roche, Interim Director/Graduate Coordinator, 909-869-2700, Fax: 909-869-4331, E-mail: pmlaroche@cpp.edu.
Website: https://env.cpp.edu/rs/rs

California State University, Chico, Office of Graduate Studies, College of Natural Sciences, Department of Geological and Environmental Sciences, Program in Environmental Science, Chico, CA 95929-0722. Offers MS, PSM. *Program availability:* Part-time. *Students:* 4 full-time (1 woman). 6 applicants, 33% accepted, 2 enrolled. *Degree requirements:* For master's, comprehensive exam, thesis or project plan. *Entrance requirements:* For master's, GRE, identification of faculty mentor, 2 letters of recommendation, statement of purpose, curriculum vitae, department letter of recommendation access waiver form. Additional exam requirements/recommendations for international students: Required—TOEFL (minimum score 550 paper-based; 80 iBT), IELTS (minimum score 6.5), PTE (minimum score 59). *Application deadline:* For fall admission, 3/1 priority date for domestic students, 3/1 for international students; for spring admission, 9/15 priority date for domestic students, 9/15 for international students. Application fee: $55. Electronic applications accepted. *Expenses: Tuition, area resident:* Full-time $4622; part-time $3116 per unit. Tuition, state resident: full-time $4622; part-time $3116 per unit. Tuition, nonresident: full-time $10,634. *Required fees:* $2160; $1620 per year. Tuition and fees vary according to class time and program. *Financial support:* Fellowships, research assistantships, teaching assistantships, career-related internships or fieldwork, Federal Work-Study, scholarships/grants, traineeships, health care benefits, unspecified assistantships, and stipends available. Support available to part-time students. Financial award application deadline: 3/2; financial award applicants required to submit FAFSA. *Unit head:* Dr. Todd J. Greene, Chair, 530-898-5262, E-mail: geos@csuchico.edu. *Application contact:* Micah Lehner, Graduate Admissions Coordinator, 530-898-5416, Fax: 530-898-3342, E-mail: mlehner@csuchico.edu.
Website: http://catalog.csuchico.edu/viewer/19/GEOS/ENSCNONEMS.html

California State University, East Bay, Office of Graduate Studies, College of Science, Department of Earth and Environmental Sciences, Hayward, CA 94542-3000. Offers geology (MS), including environmental geology, geology. *Program availability:* Part-time, evening/weekend. *Degree requirements:* For master's, thesis or project. *Entrance requirements:* For master's, GRE, minimum GPA of 2.75 in field, 2.5 overall; 2 letters of recommendation. Additional exam requirements/recommendations for international students: Required—TOEFL (minimum score 550 paper-based). Electronic applications accepted. *Faculty research:* Hydrology, seismic activity; origins of life.

California State University, Northridge, Graduate Studies, College of Science and Mathematics, Department of Chemistry and Biochemistry, Northridge, CA 91330. Offers biochemistry (MS); chemistry (MS), including chemistry, environmental chemistry. *Degree requirements:* For master's, thesis. *Entrance requirements:* For master's, GRE General Test or minimum GPA of 3.0. Additional exam requirements/recommendations for international students: Required—TOEFL. Electronic applications accepted.

California State University, San Bernardino, Graduate Studies, College of Natural Sciences, Program in Earth and Environmental Sciences, San Bernardino, CA 92407. Offers MS. *Faculty:* 1 (woman) full-time. *Students:* 8 full-time (3 women), 1 (woman) part-time; includes 6 minority (all Hispanic/Latino). Average age 27. 9 applicants, 44% accepted, 2 enrolled. *Entrance requirements:* Additional exam requirements/recommendations for international students: Required—TOEFL. *Application deadline:* For fall admission, 7/16 for domestic students; for winter admission, 10/16 for domestic students; for spring admission, 1/22 for domestic students. Application fee: $55. *Unit head:* Dr. Joan E. Fryxell, Graduate Coordinator, 909-537-5311, E-mail: jfryxell@csusb.edu. *Application contact:* Dr. Dorota Huizinga, Dean of Graduate Studies, 909-537-3064, E-mail: dorota.huizinga@csusb.edu.

Carnegie Mellon University, Mellon College of Science, Department of Chemistry, Pittsburgh, PA 15213-3891. Offers atmospheric chemistry (PhD); bioinorganic chemistry (PhD); bioorganic chemistry and chemical biology (PhD); biophysical chemistry (PhD); catalysis (PhD); green and environmental chemistry (PhD); materials and nanoscience (PhD); renewable energy (PhD); sensors, probes, and imaging (PhD); spectroscopy and single molecule analysis (PhD); theoretical and computational chemistry (PhD). *Program availability:* Part-time. Terminal master's awarded for partial completion of doctoral program. *Degree requirements:* For doctorate, thesis/dissertation, departmental qualifying and oral exams, teaching experience. *Entrance requirements:* For doctorate, GRE General Test, GRE Subject Test. Additional exam requirements/recommendations for international students: Required—TOEFL. Electronic applications accepted. *Faculty research:* Physical and theoretical chemistry, chemical synthesis, biophysical/bioinorganic chemistry.

Christopher Newport University, Graduate Studies, Environmental Science Program, Newport News, VA 23606-3072. Offers MS. *Program availability:* Part-time. *Degree requirements:* For master's, comprehensive exam, thesis (for some programs). *Entrance requirements:* For master's, GRE General Test, minimum GPA of 3.0. Additional exam requirements/recommendations for international students: Required—TOEFL (minimum score 580 paper-based; 92 iBT), IELTS (minimum score 7). Electronic applications accepted. *Faculty research:* Wetlands ecology and restoration, aquatic ecology, wetlands mitigation, greenhouse gases.

Clarkson University, Institute for a Sustainable Environment, Program in Environmental Science and Engineering, Potsdam, NY 13699. Offers MS, PhD. *Program availability:* Part-time. *Students:* 17 full-time (8 women), 9 international. 18 applicants, 72% accepted, 4 enrolled. In 2018, 1 master's, 3 doctorates awarded. *Degree requirements:* For master's, thesis; for doctorate, comprehensive exam, thesis/dissertation. *Entrance requirements:* For master's and doctorate, GRE. Additional exam requirements/recommendations for international students: Required—TOEFL (minimum score 550 paper-based, 80 iBT) or IELTS (6.5). *Application deadline:* Applications are processed on a rolling basis. Application fee: $50. Electronic applications accepted. *Expenses: Tuition:* Full-time $24,984; part-time $1388 per credit hour. *Required fees:* $225. Tuition and fees vary according to campus/location and program. *Financial support:* Scholarships/grants and unspecified assistantships available. *Unit head:* Dr. Susan Powers, Director of the Institute for a Sustainable Environment/Associate Director of Sustainability, 315-268-6542, E-mail: spowers@clarkson.edu. *Application contact:* Dan Capogna, Director of Graduate Admissions & Recruitment, 518-631-9910, E-mail: graduate@clarkson.edu.
Website: https://www.clarkson.edu/academics/graduate

Clark University, Graduate School, Department of International Development, Community, and Environment, Worcester, MA 01610-1477. Offers community and global health (MHS); community development and planning (MA); environmental science and policy (MS); geographic information science for development and environment (MS); international development and social change (MA); MA/MBA; MBA/MS. *Entrance requirements:* For master's, 3 references, resume or curriculum vitae. Additional exam requirements/recommendations for international students: Required—TOEFL (minimum score 575 paper-based; 90 iBT) or IELTS (minimum score 6.5). *Expenses: Tuition:* Full-time $34,110. *Required fees:* $40. Tuition and fees vary according to course load and program. *Faculty research:* Community action research, gender analysis, environmental risk assessment, land-use planning, geographic information systems, HIV and AIDS, global health and social justice, environmental health, climate change and sustainability.

Environmental Sciences

Clemson University, Graduate School, College of Agriculture, Forestry and Life Sciences, Department of Plant and Environmental Sciences, Clemson, SC 29634. Offers entomology (MS, PhD); plant and environmental sciences (MS, PhD). *Program availability:* Part-time. *Faculty:* 35 full-time (10 women). *Students:* 76 full-time (31 women), 19 part-time (3 women); includes 4 minority (1 Asian, non-Hispanic/Latino; 3 Two or more races, non-Hispanic/Latino), 29 international. Average age 29. 66 applicants, 65% accepted, 28 enrolled. In 2018, 12 master's, 8 doctorates awarded. *Degree requirements:* For master's, thesis (for some programs); for doctorate, comprehensive exam, thesis/dissertation. *Entrance requirements:* For master's and doctorate, GRE General Test, unofficial transcripts, letters of recommendation. Additional exam requirements/recommendations for international students: Required—TOEFL (minimum score 80 paper-based; 80 iBT); Recommended—IELTS (minimum score 6.5), TSE (minimum score 54). *Application deadline:* For fall admission, 4/15 for international students; for spring admission, 10/15 for international students. Applications are processed on a rolling basis. Application fee: $80 ($90 for international students). Electronic applications accepted. *Expenses: Tuition, area resident:* Full-time $11,270; part-time $8688 per credit hour. Tuition, state resident: full-time $11,796. Tuition, nonresident: full-time $23,802; part-time $17,412 per credit hour. *International tuition:* $23,246 full-time. *Required fees:* $1196; $497 per semester. Tuition and fees vary according to course load, degree level, campus/location and program. *Financial support:* In 2018–19, 45 students received support, including 6 fellowships with full and partial tuition reimbursements available (averaging $4,167 per year), 29 research assistantships with full and partial tuition reimbursements available (averaging $16,620 per year), 10 teaching assistantships with full and partial tuition reimbursements available (averaging $15,148 per year). *Faculty research:* Agronomy, horticulture, plant pathology, plant physiology, entomology. *Total annual research expenditures:* $3.6 million. *Unit head:* Dr. Carlyle Brewster, Department Chair, 864-656-3352, E-mail: carlylb@clemson.edu. *Application contact:* Dr. Guido Schnabel, Graduate Program Coordinator, 864-656-6705, E-mail: schnabel@clemson.edu.
Website: http://www.clemson.edu/cafls/departments/plant-environmental-sciences/index.html

Cleveland State University, College of Graduate Studies, College of Sciences and Health Professions, Department of Biological, Geological, and Environmental Sciences, Cleveland, OH 44115. Offers MS, PhD. *Program availability:* Part-time. *Faculty:* 18 full-time (5 women), 54 part-time/adjunct (22 women). *Students:* 57 full-time (32 women), 16 part-time (9 women); includes 6 minority (5 Black or African American, non-Hispanic/Latino; 1 Hispanic/Latino), 26 international. Average age 28. 56 applicants, 54% accepted, 16 enrolled. In 2018, 10 master's, 3 doctorates awarded. Terminal master's awarded for partial completion of doctoral program. *Entrance requirements:* For master's, GRE General Test, 3 letters of recommendation; for doctorate, GRE General Test, 3 letters of recommendation; 1-2 page essay; statement of career goals and research interests. Additional exam requirements/recommendations for international students: Required—TOEFL (minimum score 550 paper-based; 78 iBT), IELTS. *Application deadline:* Applications are processed on a rolling basis. Application fee: $40. Electronic applications accepted. *Expenses:* Tuition, state resident: full-time $7232.55; part-time $6676 per credit hour. Tuition, nonresident: full-time $12,375. *International tuition:* $18,914 full-time. *Required fees:* $80; $80 $40. Tuition and fees vary according to program. *Financial support:* In 2018–19, 33 students received support, including 1 fellowship with full tuition reimbursement available (averaging $21,000 per year), 14 research assistantships with full tuition reimbursements available (averaging $11,800 per year), 29 teaching assistantships with full tuition reimbursements available (averaging $9,500 per year); tuition waivers (full and partial) and unspecified assistantships also available. Financial award applicants required to submit FAFSA. *Faculty research:* Cardiopulmonary pathology, signaling pathways and RNA interference, toxoplasmosis, plant ecology, biology and biochemistry of nitric oxide. *Unit head:* Dr. Crystal M. Weyman, Chairperson/Professor, 216-687-6971, Fax: 216-687-6972, E-mail: c.weyman@csuohio.edu. *Application contact:* Dr. Girish C. Shukla, Associate Professor and Graduate Program Director, 216-687-2395, Fax: 216-687-6972, E-mail: g.shukla@csuohio.edu.
Website: http://www.csuohio.edu/sciences/bges

The College at Brockport, State University of New York, School of Arts and Sciences, Department of Environmental Science and Biology, Brockport, NY 14420-2997. Offers MS. *Program availability:* Part-time. *Faculty:* 5 full-time (2 women), 2 part-time/adjunct (1 woman). *Students:* 6 full-time (all women), 24 part-time (10 women). 12 applicants, 75% accepted, 8 enrolled. In 2018, 13 master's awarded. *Degree requirements:* For master's, comprehensive exam, thesis. *Entrance requirements:* For master's, minimum GPA of 3.0, letters of recommendation, sample of scientific writing, statement of objectives. Additional exam requirements/recommendations for international students: Required—TOEFL (minimum score 550 paper-based; 79 iBT), IELTS (minimum score 6.5). *Application deadline:* For fall admission, 4/15 priority date for domestic and international students; for spring admission, 11/15 priority date for domestic and international students; for summer admission, 4/15 priority date for domestic and international students. Application fee: $50. Electronic applications accepted. *Expenses:* Tuition, state resident: part-time $471 per credit. Tuition, nonresident: part-time $963 per credit. *Financial support:* In 2018–19, 2 research assistantships with full tuition reimbursements (averaging $6,000 per year) were awarded; Federal Work-Study, scholarships/grants, and unspecified assistantships also available. Support available to part-time students. Financial award application deadline: 3/15; financial award applicants required to submit FAFSA. *Faculty research:* Aquatic and terrestrial ecology/organismal biology, watersheds and wetlands, persistent toxic chemicals, soil-plant interactions, aquaculture. *Unit head:* Dr. Kathryn Amatangelo, Graduate Program Director, 585-395-5743, Fax: 585-395-5969, E-mail: kamatang@brockport.edu. *Application contact:* Danielle A. Welch, Graduate Counselor, 585-395-2525, E-mail: dwelch@brockport.edu.
Website: http://www.brockport.edu/envsci/grad/

College of Charleston, Graduate School, School of Sciences and Mathematics, Program in Environmental Studies, Charleston, SC 29424-0001. Offers MS. *Program availability:* Part-time, evening/weekend. *Degree requirements:* For master's, thesis or research internship. *Entrance requirements:* For master's, GRE, minimum GPA of 3.0, 3 letters of recommendation. Additional exam requirements/recommendations for international students: Required—TOEFL (minimum score 81 iBT). Electronic applications accepted. *Expenses:* Contact institution.

College of Staten Island of the City University of New York, Graduate Programs, Division of Science and Technology, Program in Environmental Science, Staten Island, NY 10314-6600. Offers MS. *Program availability:* Part-time, evening/weekend. *Students:* 16. 17 applicants, 59% accepted, 4 enrolled. In 2018, 4 master's awarded. *Degree requirements:* For master's, thesis, 30 credits in approved courses with minimum GPA of 3.0 including thesis project for a minimum of 3-6 credits. *Entrance requirements:* For master's, GRE General Test, bachelor's degree; 1 year of course work in chemistry, physics, differential and integral calculus, and ecology; minimum overall grade of B-, or the equivalent, in undergraduate work; minimum B average, or the equivalent, in undergraduate science and engineering courses; interview with faculty of program. Additional exam requirements/recommendations for international students: Required—TOEFL (minimum score 550 paper-based; 79 iBT), IELTS (minimum score 6.5). *Application deadline:* For fall admission, 4/25 priority date for domestic and international students; for spring admission, 11/25 priority date for domestic and international students. Applications are processed on a rolling basis. Application fee: $75. Electronic applications accepted. *Expenses: Tuition, area resident:* Full-time $10,770; part-time $455 per credit. Tuition, state resident: full-time $10,770; part-time $455 per credit. Tuition, nonresident: full-time $19,920; part-time $830 per credit. *International tuition:* $19,920 full-time. *Required fees:* $559.20; $181.10 per semester. Tuition and fees vary according to program. *Unit head:* Dr. Alfred Levine, Graduate Program Coordinator, 718-982-2822, E-mail: alfred.levine@csi.cuny.edu. *Application contact:* Sasha Spence, Associate Director for Graduate Admissions, 718-982-2019, Fax: 718-982-2500, E-mail: sasha.spence@csi.cuny.edu.
Website: https://www.csi.cuny.edu/sites/default/files/pdf/admissions/grad/pdf/Environmental%20Science%20Fact%20Sheet.pdf

Colorado School of Mines, Office of Graduate Studies, Department of Geology and Geological Engineering, Golden, CO 80401. Offers environmental geochemistry (PMS); geochemistry (MS, PhD); geological engineering (ME, MS, PhD); geology (MS, PhD); hydrology (MS, PhD); mineral exploration (PMS); petroleum reservoir systems (PMS); underground construction and tunneling (MS). *Program availability:* Part-time. *Faculty:* 30 full-time (12 women), 6 part-time/adjunct (5 women). *Students:* 129 full-time (44 women), 32 part-time (12 women); includes 20 minority (1 Black or African American, non-Hispanic/Latino; 2 American Indian or Alaska Native, non-Hispanic/Latino; 3 Asian, non-Hispanic/Latino; 10 Hispanic/Latino; 4 Two or more races, non-Hispanic/Latino), 30 international. Average age 29. 244 applicants, 41% accepted, 54 enrolled. In 2018, 39 master's, 11 doctorates awarded. *Degree requirements:* For master's, thesis (for some programs); for doctorate, comprehensive exam, thesis/dissertation. *Entrance requirements:* For master's and doctorate, GRE General Test. Additional exam requirements/recommendations for international students: Required—TOEFL (minimum score 550 paper-based; 79 iBT). *Application deadline:* For fall admission, 12/15 priority date for domestic and international students; for spring admission, 9/1 priority date for domestic and international students. Application fee: $60 ($80 for international students). Electronic applications accepted. *Expenses:* Tuition, state resident: full-time $16,650; part-time $925 per contact hour. Tuition, nonresident: full-time $36,270; part-time $2015 per contact hour. *International tuition:* $36,270 full-time. *Required fees:* $2314; $2314 per semester. *Financial support:* In 2018–19, 48 research assistantships with full tuition reimbursements, 20 teaching assistantships with full tuition reimbursements were awarded; fellowships, scholarships/grants, health care benefits, and unspecified assistantships also available. Financial award application deadline: 12/15; financial award applicants required to submit FAFSA. *Faculty research:* Predictive sediment modeling, petrophysics, aquifer-contaminant flow modeling, water-rock interactions, geotechnical engineering. *Unit head:* Dr. Wendy Bohrson, Head, 303-273-3066, E-mail: bohrson@mines.edu. *Application contact:* Dr. Christian Shorey, Lecturer/Program Manager, 303-273-3556, E-mail: cshorey@mines.edu.
Website: http://geology.mines.edu

Columbia University, Graduate School of Arts and Sciences, New York, NY 10027. Offers African-American studies (MA); American studies (MA); anthropology (MA, PhD); art history and archaeology (MA, PhD); astronomy (PhD); biological sciences (PhD); biotechnology (MA); chemical physics (PhD); chemistry (PhD); classical studies (MA, PhD); classics (MA, PhD); climate and society (MA); conservation biology (MA); earth and environmental sciences (PhD); East Asia: regional studies (MA); East Asian languages and cultures (MA, PhD); ecology, evolution and environmental biology (MA), including conservation biology; ecology, evolution, and environmental biology (PhD), including ecology and evolutionary biology, evolutionary primatology; economics (MA, PhD); English and comparative literature (MA, PhD); French and Romance philology (MA, PhD); Germanic languages (MA, PhD); global French studies (MA); global thought (MA); Hispanic cultural studies (MA); history (PhD); history and literature (MA); human rights studies (MA); Islamic studies (MA); Italian (MA, PhD); Japanese pedagogy (MA); Jewish studies (MA); Latin America and the Caribbean: regional studies (MA); Latin American and Iberian cultures (PhD); mathematics (MA, PhD), including finance (MA); medieval and Renaissance studies (MA); Middle Eastern, South Asian, and African studies (MA, PhD); modern art: critical and curatorial studies (MA); modern European studies (MA); museum anthropology (MA); music (DMA, PhD); oral history (MA); philosophical foundations of physics (MA); philosophy (MA, PhD); physics (PhD); political science (MA, PhD); psychology (PhD); quantitative methods in the social sciences (MA); religion (MA, PhD); Russia, Eurasia and East Europe: regional studies (MA); Russian translation (MA); Slavic cultures (MA); Slavic languages (MA, PhD); sociology (MA, PhD); South Asian studies (MA); statistics (MA, PhD); theatre (PhD). Dual-degree programs require admission to both Graduate School of Arts and Sciences and another Columbia school. *Program availability:* Part-time. Terminal master's awarded for partial completion of doctoral program. *Degree requirements:* For master's, variable foreign language requirement, comprehensive exam (for some programs), thesis (for some programs); for doctorate, variable foreign language requirement, comprehensive exam (for some programs), thesis/dissertation. *Entrance requirements:* For master's and doctorate, GRE General Test, GRE Subject Test (for some programs). Additional exam requirements/recommendations for international students: Required—TOEFL, IELTS. Electronic applications accepted.

Columbia University, School of International and Public Affairs, Program in Environmental Science and Policy, New York, NY 10027. Offers MPA. Program admits applicants for late May/early June start only. *Degree requirements:* For master's, workshops. *Entrance requirements:* For master's, GRE, previous course work in biology and chemistry, earth sciences (recommended), economics (strongly recommended). Additional exam requirements/recommendations for international students: Required—TOEFL. Electronic applications accepted. *Faculty research:* Ecological management of enclosed ecosystems vegetation dynamics, environmental policy and management, energy policy, nuclear waste policy, environmental and natural resource economics and policy, carbon sequestration, urban planning, environmental risk assessment/toxicology, environmental justice.

Columbus State University, Graduate Studies, College of Education and Health Professions, Department of Teacher Education, Columbus, GA 31907-5645. Offers curriculum and instruction in accomplished teaching (M Ed); early childhood education (M Ed, MAT, Ed S); middle grades education (M Ed, MAT, Ed S); secondary education (M Ed, MAT, Ed S), including biology (MAT), chemistry (MAT), earth and space science (MAT), English/language arts, general science (M Ed), history (MAT), mathematics, science (Ed S), social science (M Ed, Ed S); special education (M Ed, MAT, Ed S), including general curriculum (M Ed, MAT); teacher leadership (M Ed). *Accreditation:* NCATE. *Program availability:* Part-time, evening/weekend, 100% online, blended/hybrid learning. *Faculty:* 20 full-time (12 women), 20 part-time/adjunct (15 women). *Students:* 110 full-time (84 women), 143 part-time (115 women); includes 105 minority (96 Black or African American, non-Hispanic/Latino; 4 Hispanic/Latino; 5 Two or more races, non-Hispanic/Latino). Average age 33. 147 applicants, 56% accepted, 62 enrolled. In 2018, 112 master's, 11 other advanced degrees awarded. *Degree requirements:* For Ed S,

thesis or alternative. *Entrance requirements:* For master's, GRE General Test, minimum undergraduate GPA of 2.75; for Ed S, GRE General Test, minimum undergraduate GPA of 2.75, graduate 3.0. Additional exam requirements/recommendations for international students: Required—TOEFL (minimum score 550 paper-based; 79 iBT). *Application deadline:* For fall admission, 6/30 for domestic students, 5/1 for international students; for spring admission, 11/1 for domestic and international students; for summer admission, 3/1 for domestic and international students. Applications are processed on a rolling basis. Application fee: $50. Electronic applications accepted. *Expenses: Tuition, area resident:* Full-time $4924; part-time $618 per credit hour. Tuition, state resident: full-time $4924; part-time $618 per credit hour. Tuition, nonresident: full-time $19,218; part-time $2403 per credit hour. *International tuition:* $19,218 full-time. *Required fees:* $1870; $802. Tuition and fees vary according to course load, degree level and program. *Financial support:* In 2018–19, 29 students received support, including 7 research assistantships with partial tuition reimbursements available (averaging $3,000 per year); career-related internships or fieldwork, Federal Work-Study, institutionally sponsored loans, scholarships/grants, tuition waivers (partial), and unspecified assistantships also available. Support available to part-time students. Financial award application deadline: 5/1; financial award applicants required to submit FAFSA. *Unit head:* Dr. Jan Burcham, Department Chair, 706-507-8519, Fax: 706-568-3134, E-mail: burcham_jan@columbusstate.edu. *Application contact:* Catrina Smith-Edmond, Assistant Director for Graduate and Global Admission, 706-507-8824, Fax: 706-568-5091, E-mail: smithedmond_catrina@columbusstate.edu.
Website: http://te.columbusstate.edu/

Columbus State University, Graduate Studies, College of Letters and Sciences, Department of Earth and Space Sciences, Columbus, GA 31907-5645. Offers natural sciences (MS), including biology, chemistry, environmental science, geosciences. *Program availability:* Part-time, evening/weekend. *Faculty:* 5 full-time (2 women), 8 part-time/adjunct (0 women). *Students:* 19 full-time (7 women), 10 part-time (5 women); includes 7 minority (4 Black or African American, non-Hispanic/Latino; 2 Hispanic/Latino; 1 Two or more races, non-Hispanic/Latino), 4 international. Average age 27. 21 applicants, 48% accepted, 7 enrolled. In 2018, 6 master's awarded. *Degree requirements:* For master's, thesis. *Entrance requirements:* For master's, GRE General Test, minimum GPA of 3.0. Additional exam requirements/recommendations for international students: Required—TOEFL (minimum score 550 paper-based; 79 iBT). *Application deadline:* For fall admission, 6/30 priority date for domestic students, 5/1 for international students; for spring admission, 11/1 for domestic and international students; for summer admission, 3/1 for domestic and international students. Applications are processed on a rolling basis. Application fee: $50. Electronic applications accepted. *Expenses: Tuition, area resident:* Full-time $4924; part-time $618 per credit hour. Tuition, state resident: full-time $4924; part-time $618 per credit hour. Tuition, nonresident: full-time $19,218; part-time $2403 per credit hour. *International tuition:* $19,218 full-time. *Required fees:* $1870; $802. Tuition and fees vary according to course load, degree level and program. *Financial support:* In 2018–19, 1 student received support, including 15 research assistantships with partial tuition reimbursements available (averaging $3,000 per year); career-related internships or fieldwork, Federal Work-Study, institutionally sponsored loans, scholarships/grants, and unspecified assistantships also available. Support available to part-time students. Financial award application deadline: 5/1; financial award applicants required to submit FAFSA. *Unit head:* Dr. Clint Barineau, Department Chair, 706-569-3026, E-mail: barineau_clinton@columbusstate.edu. *Application contact:* Catrina Smith-Edmond, Assistant Director for Graduate and Global Admission, 706-507-8824, Fax: 706-568-5091, E-mail: smithedmond_catrina@columbusstate.edu.
Website: http://ess.columbusstate.edu/

Cornell University, Graduate School, Graduate Fields of Agriculture and Life Sciences, Field of Soil and Crop Sciences, Ithaca, NY 14853. Offers agronomy (MS, PhD); environmental information science (MS, PhD); environmental management (MPS); field crop science (MS, PhD); soil science (MS, PhD). *Degree requirements:* For master's, thesis (MS); for doctorate, comprehensive exam, thesis/dissertation. *Entrance requirements:* For master's and doctorate, GRE General Test, 2 letters of recommendation. Additional exam requirements/recommendations for international students: Required—TOEFL (minimum score 550 paper-based; 77 iBT). Electronic applications accepted. *Faculty research:* Soil chemistry, physics and biology; crop physiology and management; environmental information science and modeling; international agriculture; weed science.

Dalhousie University, Faculty of Agriculture, Halifax, NS B3H 4R2, Canada. Offers agriculture (M Sc), including air quality, animal behavior, animal molecular genetics, animal nutrition, animal technology, aquaculture, botany, crop management, crop physiology, ecology, environmental microbiology, food science, horticulture, nutrient management, pest management, physiology, plant biotechnology, plant pathology, soil chemistry, soil fertility, waste management and composting, water quality. *Program availability:* Part-time. *Degree requirements:* For master's, thesis, ATC Exam Teaching Assistantship. *Entrance requirements:* For master's, honors B Sc, minimum GPA of 3.0. Additional exam requirements/recommendations for international students: Required—TOEFL (minimum score 580 paper-based; 92 iBT), IELTS, Michigan English Language Assessment Battery, CanTEST, CAEL. *Faculty research:* Bio-product development, organic agriculture, nutrient management, air and water quality, agricultural biotechnology.

DePaul University, College of Science and Health, Chicago, IL 60604-2287. Offers applied mathematics (MS); applied statistics (MS); biological sciences (MA, MS); chemistry (MS); environmental science (MS); mathematics education (MA); mathematics for teaching (MS); nursing (MS); nursing practice (DNP); physics (MS); polymer and coatings science (MS); psychology (MS); pure mathematics (MS); science education (MS); MA/PhD. *Accreditation:* AACN. Electronic applications accepted.

Drexel University, College of Arts and Sciences, Program in Environmental Science, Philadelphia, PA 19104-2875. Offers MS, PhD. *Program availability:* Part-time, evening/weekend. Terminal master's awarded for partial completion of doctoral program. *Degree requirements:* For master's, thesis optional; for doctorate, thesis/dissertation. Electronic applications accepted.

Duke University, Graduate School, Doctoral Program in Environment, Durham, NC 27708-0328. Offers PhD. *Degree requirements:* For doctorate, variable foreign language requirement, thesis/dissertation. *Entrance requirements:* For doctorate, GRE General Test. Additional exam requirements/recommendations for international students: Required—TOEFL (minimum score 577 paper-based; 90 iBT) or IELTS (minimum score 7). Electronic applications accepted.

Duke University, Nicholas School of the Environment, Durham, NC 27708. Offers earth and ocean sciences (PhD); environment (MEM, MF, PhD); marine science and conservation (PhD). *Faculty:* 50. *Students:* 365 full-time (243 women); includes 67 minority (7 Black or African American, non-Hispanic/Latino; 4 American Indian or Alaska Native, non-Hispanic/Latino; 36 Asian, non-Hispanic/Latino; 20 Hispanic/Latino), 93 international. Average age 27. 428 applicants, 83% accepted, 151 enrolled. In 2018, 181 master's awarded. *Degree requirements:* For master's, project; for doctorate, variable foreign language requirement, thesis/dissertation. *Entrance requirements:* For master's, GRE General Test, previous course work in natural or social sciences relevant to environmental interests; college calculus, college statistics, and concentration-specific prerequisites. Additional exam requirements/recommendations for international students: Required—TOEFL, IELTS. *Application deadline:* For fall admission, 12/15 priority date for domestic and international students. Application fee: $400. Electronic applications accepted. *Financial support:* Research assistantships, career-related internships or fieldwork, Federal Work-Study, institutionally sponsored loans, scholarships/grants, and unspecified assistantships available. Financial award application deadline: 12/15; financial award applicants required to submit CSS PROFILE or FAFSA. *Faculty research:* Global environmental change, energy and the environment, water resource management, ecosystem science and conservation, ecotoxicology and environmental health, business and environment, environmental economics and policy, coastal environmental management, forest resource management. *Unit head:* Sherri Nevius, Associate Dean, Student Services, 919-613-8063, E-mail: sherri.nevius@duke.edu. *Application contact:* Benjamin Spain, Associate Director of Enrollment Services, 919-684-1155, E-mail: admissions@nicholas.duke.edu.
Website: http://nicholas.duke.edu/

Duquesne University, Bayer School of Natural and Environmental Sciences, Environmental Science and Management Program, Pittsburgh, PA 15282-0001. Offers MS, Certificate, JD/MS, MBA/MS. *Program availability:* Part-time, evening/weekend. *Faculty:* 7 full-time (2 women), 10 part-time/adjunct (3 women). *Students:* 16 full-time (10 women), 10 part-time (9 women), includes 5 minority (2 Asian, non-Hispanic/Latino; 1 Hispanic/Latino; 2 Two or more races, non-Hispanic/Latino). Average age 27. 18 applicants, 94% accepted, 9 enrolled. In 2018, 25 master's awarded. *Degree requirements:* For master's, thesis (for some programs), minimum of 37 credit hours (for conservation biology); for Certificate, minimum of 18 credit hours. *Entrance requirements:* For master's, GRE General Test, course work in biology, chemistry, and calculus or statistics; 2 letters of reference; official transcripts; statement of purpose; for Certificate, undergraduate degree, 2 letters of reference, official transcripts, statement of purpose. Additional exam requirements/recommendations for international students: Required—TOEFL (minimum score 90 iBT), TOEFL (minimum score 90 iBT) or IELTS. *Application deadline:* For fall admission, 7/1 priority date for domestic students, 4/1 for international students; for spring admission, 10/1 priority date for domestic students, 10/1 for international students. Applications are processed on a rolling basis. Application fee: $0. Electronic applications accepted. *Expenses:* $1376/credit hour. *Financial support:* In 2018–19, 23 students received support, including 1 fellowship with full tuition reimbursement available (averaging $18,000 per year), 7 research assistantships with full and partial tuition reimbursements available (averaging $14,500 per year), 1 teaching assistantship with full tuition reimbursement available (averaging $14,000 per year); career-related internships or fieldwork, scholarships/grants, tuition waivers (partial), and unspecified assistantships also available. Financial award application deadline: 5/31. *Faculty research:* Watershed management systems, environmental analytical chemistry, environmental endocrinology, environmental microbiology, aquatic biology. *Unit head:* Dr. John Stolz, Director, 412-396-6333, Fax: 412-396-5907, E-mail: stolz@duq.edu. *Application contact:* Heather Costello, Senior Graduate Academic Advisor, 412-396-6339, E-mail: costelloh@duq.edu.
Website: http://www.duq.edu/academics/schools/natural-and-environmental-sciences/academic-programs/environmental-science-and-management

Florida Agricultural and Mechanical University, School of the Environment, Tallahassee, FL 32307. Offers MS, PhD. *Degree requirements:* For master's, thesis; for doctorate, comprehensive exam, thesis/dissertation, oral exam. *Entrance requirements:* For master's and doctorate, GRE General Test, minimum GPA of 3.0. Additional exam requirements/recommendations for international students: Required—TOEFL. Electronic applications accepted. *Faculty research:* Environmental chemistry, environmental policy and risk management, aquatic and terrestrial ecology, biomolecular sciences, environmental restoration and waste management.

Florida Gulf Coast University, College of Arts and Sciences, Program in Environmental Science, Fort Myers, FL 33965-6565. Offers MS. *Program availability:* Part-time. *Entrance requirements:* For master's, GRE General Test, minimum GPA of 3.0. Additional exam requirements/recommendations for international students: Required—TOEFL (minimum score 550 paper-based). Electronic applications accepted. *Faculty research:* Political issues in environmental science, recycling, environmentally-friendly buildings, pathophysiology, immunotoxicology of marine organisms.

Florida Institute of Technology, College of Engineering and Science, Program in Environmental Science, Melbourne, FL 32901-6975. Offers MS, PhD. *Program availability:* Part-time. *Students:* 7 full-time (1 woman), 4 international. Average age 29. 5 applicants, 80% accepted, 2 enrolled. In 2018, 1 master's, 1 doctorate awarded. *Degree requirements:* For master's, comprehensive exam (for some programs), thesis optional, 30 credit hours, seminar, oral presentation of research results; for doctorate, comprehensive exam, thesis/dissertation, research proposal, seminar presentation on said research, publication of dissertation in refereed national or international journals, 24 credit hours coursework, 24 credit hours beyond master's degree. *Entrance requirements:* For master's, GRE General Test, 3 letters of recommendation, resume, statement of objectives; for doctorate, GRE General Test, 3 letters of recommendation (one from master's degree thesis adviser), resume, statement of objectives, bachelor's or master's degree in science curriculum, on-campus interview (highly recommended). Additional exam requirements/recommendations for international students: Required—TOEFL (minimum score 550 paper-based; 79 iBT). *Application deadline:* Applications are processed on a rolling basis. Application fee: $50. Electronic applications accepted. *Expenses: Tuition:* Full-time $22,338; part-time $1241 per credit hour. Tuition and fees vary according to degree level, campus/location and program. *Financial support:* Career-related internships or fieldwork and tuition remissions available. Financial award application deadline: 3/1; financial award applicants required to submit FAFSA. *Faculty research:* Offshore oil spills and drilling impacts, drinking water resources, rising sea levels, natural resource management, water and wastewater treatment, air quality, ecological surveys, nuclear waste, effects of local weather on ecosystems. *Unit head:* Dr. Richard Aronson, Department Head, 321-674-8034, E-mail: raronson@fit.edu. *Application contact:* Mike Perry, Executive Director of Admissions, 321-674-7127, E-mail: perrymj@fit.edu.
Website: https://www.fit.edu/programs/environmental-science-ms/

Florida State University, The Graduate School, Department of Anthropology, Department of Earth, Ocean and Atmospheric Science, Program in Oceanography, Tallahassee, FL 32306-4320. Offers aquatic environmental science (MS, PSM); oceanography (MS, PhD). *Faculty:* 15 full-time (4 women). *Students:* 49 full-time (29 women), 4 part-time (2 women); includes 5 minority (1 Black or African American, non-Hispanic/Latino; 2 Asian, non-Hispanic/Latino; 2 Hispanic/Latino), 9 international. Average age 26. 77 applicants, 34% accepted, 22 enrolled. In 2018, 13 master's, 2 doctorates awarded. *Degree requirements:* For master's, thesis; for doctorate, comprehensive exam, thesis/dissertation. *Entrance requirements:* For master's and doctorate, GRE General Test, minimum upper-division GPA of 3.0. Additional exam

Peterson's Graduate Programs in the Physical Sciences, Mathematics, Agricultural Sciences, the Environment & Natural Resources 2020

www.petersons.com **315**

requirements/recommendations for international students: Required—TOEFL (minimum score 550 paper-based; 80 iBT). *Application deadline:* For fall admission, 2/15 priority date for domestic and international students; for spring admission, 9/15 priority date for domestic and international students. Applications are processed on a rolling basis. Application fee: $35. Electronic applications accepted. *Expenses: Tuition, area resident:* Part-time $479.32 per credit hour. Tuition and fees vary according to campus/location and program. *Financial support:* In 2018–19, 38 students received support, including 2 fellowships with full tuition reimbursements available, 24 research assistantships with full tuition reimbursements available, 12 teaching assistantships with full tuition reimbursements available. Financial award application deadline: 2/15; financial award applicants required to submit FAFSA. *Faculty research:* Trace metals in seawater, currents and waves, modeling, benthic ecology, marine biogeochemistry. *Unit head:* Dr. Jeffrey Chanton, Area Coordinator, 850-644-6205, Fax: 850-644-2581, E-mail: jchanton@fsu.edu. *Application contact:* Michaela Lupiani, Academic Coordinator, 850-644-6205, Fax: 850-644-2581, E-mail: mlupiani@fsu.edu.
Website: http://www.eoas.fsu.edu

Gannon University, School of Graduate Studies, College of Engineering and Business, School of Engineering and Computer Science, Program in Environmental Science and Engineering, Erie, PA 16541-0001. Offers environmental health (MSEH); environmental health and engineering (MS). *Program availability:* Part-time, evening/weekend. *Degree requirements:* For master's, thesis (for some programs), research paper or project (for some programs). *Entrance requirements:* For master's, GRE, bachelor's degree in science or engineering from an accredited college or university. Additional exam requirements/recommendations for international students: Required—TOEFL (minimum score 79 iBT), GRE. Electronic applications accepted. Application fee is waived when completed online.

George Mason University, College of Science, Department of Environmental Science and Policy, Fairfax, VA 22030. Offers MS, PhD. *Faculty:* 17 full-time (9 women), 10 part-time/adjunct (2 women). *Students:* 51 full-time (37 women), 62 part-time (39 women); includes 17 minority (3 Black or African American, non-Hispanic/Latino; 9 Asian, non-Hispanic/Latino; 2 Hispanic/Latino; 3 Two or more races, non-Hispanic/Latino), 6 international. Average age 31. 50 applicants, 82% accepted, 22 enrolled. In 2018, 12 master's, 15 doctorates awarded. *Degree requirements:* For master's, variable foreign language requirement, comprehensive exam (for some programs), thesis (for some programs); for doctorate, variable foreign language requirement, comprehensive exam, thesis/dissertation. *Entrance requirements:* For master's, GRE, BA or BS; for doctorate, GRE, advanced degree or equivalent research experience. Additional exam requirements/recommendations for international students: Required—TOEFL (minimum score 575 paper-based; 88 iBT), IELTS (minimum score 6.5), PTE (minimum score 59). Application fee: $75 ($80 for international students). Electronic applications accepted. *Financial support:* In 2018–19, 40 students received support, including 9 research assistantships with tuition reimbursements available (averaging $15,944 per year), 31 teaching assistantships with tuition reimbursements available (averaging $17,032 per year); career-related internships or fieldwork, Federal Work-Study, scholarships/grants, unspecified assistantships, and health care benefits (for full-time research or teaching assistantship recipients) also available. Support available to part-time students. Financial award application deadline: 3/1; financial award applicants required to submit FAFSA. *Faculty research:* Conservation of species and ecosystems; water and watersheds; one health and sustainability; climate change; interdisciplinary (including natural and social science). *Total annual research expenditures:* $300,156. *Unit head:* Dr. Alonso Aguirre, Chair, 703-993-7590, E-mail: aaguirr3@gmu.edu. *Application contact:* Sharon Bloomquist, Graduate Program Coordinator, 703-993-3187, Fax: 703-993-1066, E-mail: sbloomqu@gmu.edu.
Website: http://esp.gmu.edu/

The Graduate Center, City University of New York, Graduate Studies, Program in Earth and Environmental Sciences, New York, NY 10016-4039. Offers PhD. *Degree requirements:* For doctorate, one foreign language, comprehensive exam, thesis/dissertation. *Entrance requirements:* For doctorate, GRE General Test. Additional exam requirements/recommendations for international students: Required—TOEFL. Electronic applications accepted.

Harvard University, Cyprus International Institute for the Environment and Public Health in Association with Harvard School of Public Health, Cambridge, MA 02138. Offers environmental health (MS); environmental/public health (PhD); epidemiology and biostatistics (MS). *Entrance requirements:* For master's and doctorate, GRE, resume/curriculum vitae, 3 letters of recommendation, BA or BS (including diploma and official transcripts). Additional exam requirements/recommendations for international students: Required—TOEFL, IELTS (minimum score 7). Electronic applications accepted. *Faculty research:* Air pollution, climate change, biostatistics, sustainable development, environmental management.

Harvard University, Graduate School of Arts and Sciences, Harvard John A. Paulson School of Engineering and Applied Sciences, Cambridge, MA 02138. Offers applied mathematics (PhD); applied physics (PhD); computational science and engineering (ME, SM); computer science (PhD); data science (SM); design engineering (MDE); engineering science (ME), including electrical engineering (ME, SM, PhD); engineering sciences (SM, PhD), including bioengineering (PhD), electrical engineering (ME, SM, PhD), environmental science and engineering (PhD), materials science and mechanical engineering (PhD). MDE offered in collaboration with Graduate School of Design. *Program availability:* Part-time. Terminal master's awarded for partial completion of doctoral program. *Degree requirements:* For master's, thesis (for ME); for doctorate, comprehensive exam, thesis/dissertation. *Entrance requirements:* For master's and doctorate, GRE General Test, GRE Subject Test (recommended), 3 letters of recommendation. Additional exam requirements/recommendations for international students: Required—TOEFL (minimum score 80 iBT). Electronic applications accepted. *Expenses:* Contact institution. *Faculty research:* Applied mathematics, applied physics, computer science and electrical engineering, environmental engineering, mechanical and biomedical engineering.

Howard University, Graduate School, Department of Chemistry, Washington, DC 20059-0002. Offers analytical chemistry (MS, PhD); atmospheric (MS, PhD); biochemistry (MS, PhD); environmental (MS, PhD); inorganic chemistry (MS, PhD); organic chemistry (MS, PhD); physical chemistry (MS, PhD). Terminal master's awarded for partial completion of doctoral program. *Degree requirements:* For master's, comprehensive exam, thesis, teaching experience; for doctorate, comprehensive exam, thesis/dissertation, teaching experience. *Entrance requirements:* For master's, GRE General Test, minimum GPA of 2.7; for doctorate, GRE General Test, minimum GPA of 3.0. Additional exam requirements/recommendations for international students: Required—TOEFL. Electronic applications accepted. *Faculty research:* Synthetic organics, materials, natural products, mass spectrometry.

Humboldt State University, Academic Programs, College of Natural Resources and Sciences, Programs in Environmental Systems, Arcata, CA 95521-8299. Offers environmental systems (MS), including energy, environment and society, environmental resources engineering, geology, math modeling. *Faculty:* 34 full-time (14 women), 37 part-time/adjunct (17 women). *Students:* 18 full-time (8 women), 6 part-time (2 women); includes 7 minority (3 Asian, non-Hispanic/Latino; 3 Hispanic/Latino; 1 Two or more races, non-Hispanic/Latino), 4 international. Average age 28. 48 applicants, 52% accepted, 11 enrolled. In 2018, 12 master's awarded. *Degree requirements:* For master's, thesis. *Entrance requirements:* For master's, GRE, appropriate bachelor's degree, minimum GPA of 2.5, 3 letters of recommendation. Additional exam requirements/recommendations for international students: Required—TOEFL. *Application deadline:* For fall admission, 2/15 for domestic students; for spring admission, 10/15 for domestic students. Applications are processed on a rolling basis. Application fee: $55. *Expenses: Tuition:* Part-time $4649 per semester. *Required fees:* $2121; $1673. Tuition and fees vary according to program. *Financial support:* Application deadline: 3/1; applicants required to submit FAFSA. *Faculty research:* Mathematical modeling, international development technology, geology, environmental resources engineering. *Unit head:* Dr. Margaret Lang, Graduate Program Coordinator, 707-826-3256, E-mail: CNRSmast@humboldt.edu. *Application contact:* Dr. Margaret Lang, Graduate Program Coordinator, 707-826-3256, E-mail: CNRSmast@humboldt.edu.

Idaho State University, Graduate School, College of Science and Engineering, Department of Civil and Environmental Engineering, Pocatello, ID 83209-8060. Offers civil engineering (MS); environmental engineering (MS); environmental science and management (MS). *Program availability:* Part-time. *Degree requirements:* For master's, comprehensive exam (for some programs), thesis optional, thesis project, 2 semesters of seminar. *Entrance requirements:* For master's, GRE. Additional exam requirements/recommendations for international students: Required—TOEFL (minimum score 550 paper-based; 80 iBT). Electronic applications accepted. *Faculty research:* Floor vibration investigations, earthquake engineering, base isolation systems and seismic risk assessment, infrastructure revitalization (building foundations and damage, bridge structures, highways, and dams), slope stability and soil erosion, pavement rehabilitation, computational fluid dynamics and flood control structures, microbial fuel cells, water treatment and water quality modeling, environmental risk assessment, biotechnology, nanotechnology.

Idaho State University, Graduate School, College of Science and Engineering, Department of Geosciences, Pocatello, ID 83209-8072. Offers geographic information science (MS); geology (MNS, MS); geology with emphasis in environmental geoscience (MS); geophysics/hydrology/geology (MS); geotechnology (Postbaccalaureate Certificate). *Program availability:* Part-time. *Degree requirements:* For master's, comprehensive exam, thesis, oral colloquium; for Postbaccalaureate Certificate, thesis optional, minimum 19 credits. *Entrance requirements:* For master's, GRE General Test (minimum 50th percentile in 2 sections), 3 letters of recommendation; for Postbaccalaureate Certificate, GRE General Test, 3 letters of recommendation, bachelor's degree, statement of goals. Additional exam requirements/recommendations for international students: Required—TOEFL (minimum score 550 paper-based; 80 iBT). Electronic applications accepted. *Faculty research:* Quantitative field mapping and sampling: microscopic, geochemical, and isotopic analysis of rocks, minerals and water; remote sensing, geographic information systems, and global positioning systems: environmental and watershed management; surficial and fluvial processes: landscape change; regional tectonics, structural geology; planetary geology.

Indiana University Bloomington, School of Public and Environmental Affairs, Environmental Science Programs, Bloomington, IN 47405. Offers applied ecology (MSES); energy (MSES); environmental chemistry, toxicology, and risk assessment (MSES); environmental science (PhD); hazardous materials management (Certificate); specialized environmental science (MSES); water resources (MSES); JD/MSES; MSES/MA; MSES/MPA; MSES/MS. *Program availability:* Part-time. Terminal master's awarded for partial completion of doctoral program. *Degree requirements:* For master's, capstone or thesis; internship; for doctorate, comprehensive exam, thesis/dissertation. *Entrance requirements:* For master's, GRE General Test or GMAT, official transcripts, 3 letters of recommendation, resume, personal statement; for doctorate, GRE General Test or LSAT, official transcripts, 3 letters of recommendation, resume or curriculum vitae, statement of purpose. Additional exam requirements/recommendations for international students: Required—TOEFL (minimum score 600 paper-based; 96 iBT); Recommended—IELTS (minimum score 7). Electronic applications accepted. *Faculty research:* Applied ecology, bio-geochemistry, toxicology, wetlands ecology, environmental microbiology, forest ecology, environmental chemistry.

Instituto Tecnologico de Santo Domingo, Graduate School, Area of Basic And Environmental Sciences, Santo Domingo, Dominican Republic. Offers environmental science (M En S), including environmental education, environmental management, marine resources, natural resources management; mathematics (MS, PhD); renewable energy technology (MS, Certificate).

Instituto Tecnológico y de Estudios Superiores de Monterrey, Campus Ciudad de México, Virtual University Division, Ciudad de Mexico, Mexico. Offers administration of information technologies (MA); computer sciences (MA); education (MA, PhD); educational technology (MA); environmental engineering (MA); environmental systems (MA); humanistic studies (MA); industrial engineering (MA); international business for Latin America (MA); quality systems (MA); quality systems and productivity (MA). *Program availability:* Part-time, evening/weekend, online learning. *Entrance requirements:* For master's and doctorate, Instituto entrance exam. Additional exam requirements/recommendations for international students: Required—TOEFL.

Inter American University of Puerto Rico, San Germán Campus, Graduate Studies Center, Program in Environmental Sciences, San Germán, PR 00683-5008. Offers MS. *Program availability:* Part-time, evening/weekend. *Degree requirements:* For master's, comprehensive exam, thesis. *Entrance requirements:* For master's, GRE General Test or EXADEP, minimum GPA of 3.0. *Expenses: Tuition:* Full-time $212; part-time $212 per credit. *Required fees:* $366 per semester. One-time fee: $31. Tuition and fees vary according to degree level and program. *Faculty research:* Environmental biology, environmental chemistry, water resources and unit operations.

Iowa State University of Science and Technology, Department of Geological and Atmospheric Sciences, Ames, IA 50011. Offers earth science (MS, PhD); environmental science (MS, PhD); geology (MS, PhD); meteorology (MS, PhD). *Degree requirements:* For master's, thesis (for some programs); for doctorate, thesis/dissertation. *Entrance requirements:* For master's and doctorate, GRE General Test. Additional exam requirements/recommendations for international students: Required—TOEFL (minimum score 550 paper-based; 79 iBT), IELTS (minimum score 6.5). Electronic applications accepted.

Iowa State University of Science and Technology, Program in Environmental Sciences, Ames, IA 50011. Offers MS, PhD. *Degree requirements:* For master's, thesis; for doctorate, thesis/dissertation. *Entrance requirements:* For master's and doctorate, GRE General Test. Additional exam requirements/recommendations for international students: Required—TOEFL (minimum score 550 paper-based; 79 iBT), IELTS (minimum score 6.5). Electronic applications accepted.

Jackson State University, Graduate School, College of Science, Engineering and Technology, Department of Biology, Jackson, MS 39217. Offers biology (MS); environmental science (MS). *Program availability:* Part-time, evening/weekend. *Degree requirements:* For master's, comprehensive exam, thesis. *Entrance requirements:* For master's, GRE General Test. Additional exam requirements/recommendations for international students: Required—TOEFL (minimum score 520 paper-based; 67 iBT). *Faculty research:* Comparative studies on the carbohydrate composition of marine macroalgae, host-parasite relationship between the spruce budworm and entomepathogen fungus.

Johns Hopkins University, Advanced Academic Programs, Program in Environmental Sciences and Policy, Washington, DC 21218. Offers energy policy and climate (MS); environmental sciences (MS); geographic information systems (MS, Certificate). *Program availability:* Part-time, evening/weekend, online learning. *Students:* 10 full-time (11 women), 192 part-time (148 women). 81 applicants, 78% accepted, 36 enrolled. In 2018, 66 master's awarded. *Entrance requirements:* For master's, minimum GPA of 3.0, coursework in chemistry and calculus. Additional exam requirements/recommendations for international students: Required—TOEFL (minimum score 100 iBT). *Application deadline:* For fall admission, 5/31 priority date for domestic students, 4/30 priority date for international students; for spring admission, 10/31 priority date for domestic and international students. Applications are processed on a rolling basis. Application fee: $75. Electronic applications accepted. *Financial support:* Applicants required to submit FAFSA. *Unit head:* Dr. Jerry Burgess, Program Director, 202-452-1915, E-mail: jerry.burgess@jhu.edu. *Application contact:* Melissa Edwards, Admissions Manager, 202-452-1941, Fax: 202-452-1970, E-mail: aapadmissions@jhu.edu.
Website: http://advanced.jhu.edu/academics/graduate-degree-programs/environmental-sciences-and-policy/

Kansas State University, Graduate School, College of Agriculture, Department of Agronomy, Manhattan, KS 66506. Offers crop science (MS, PhD); grassland management (Certificate); plant breeding and genetics (MS, PhD); range and forage science (MS, PhD); soil and environmental science (MS, PhD); weed science (MS, PhD). *Program availability:* Part-time. *Degree requirements:* For master's, thesis or alternative, oral exam; for doctorate, thesis/dissertation, preliminary exams. *Entrance requirements:* For master's, minimum GPA of 3.0 in BS; for doctorate, minimum GPA of 3.0 in master's program. Additional exam requirements/recommendations for international students: Required—TOEFL (minimum score 79 iBT). Electronic applications accepted. *Expenses:* Contact institution. *Faculty research:* Range and forage science; soil and environmental science; weed science; plant breeding and genetics; crop physiology, ecology and production.

Laurentian University, School of Graduate Studies and Research, Programme in Chemistry and Biochemistry, Sudbury, ON P3E 2C6, Canada. Offers analytical chemistry (M Sc); biochemistry (M Sc); environmental chemistry (M Sc); organic chemistry (M Sc); physical/theoretical chemistry (M Sc). *Program availability:* Part-time. *Degree requirements:* For master's, thesis or alternative. *Entrance requirements:* For master's, honors degree with minimum second class. *Faculty research:* Cell cycle checkpoints, kinetic modeling, toxicology to metal stress, quantum chemistry, biogeochemistry metal speciation.

Lehigh University, College of Arts and Sciences, Department of Earth and Environmental Sciences, Bethlehem, PA 18015. Offers MS, PhD. *Faculty:* 15 full-time (3 women). *Students:* 21 full-time (9 women); includes 1 minority (Hispanic/Latino), 5 international. Average age 31. 24 applicants, 33% accepted, 4 enrolled. In 2018, 2 master's, 1 doctorate awarded. Terminal master's awarded for partial completion of doctoral program. *Degree requirements:* For master's, thesis; for doctorate, thesis/dissertation. *Entrance requirements:* For master's and doctorate, GRE General Test, transcripts, recommendation letters, research statement, faculty advocates. Additional exam requirements/recommendations for international students: Required—TOEFL (minimum score 85 iBT). *Application deadline:* For fall admission, 1/1 for domestic and international students. Application fee: $75. Tuition and fees vary according to program. *Financial support:* In 2018–19, 14 students received support, including 6 fellowships with full tuition reimbursements available (averaging $21,310 per year), 10 research assistantships with partial tuition reimbursements available (averaging $21,310 per year), 18 teaching assistantships with full tuition reimbursements available (averaging $21,310 per year); scholarships/grants also available. Financial award application deadline: 1/1. *Faculty research:* Geochemistry, petrology, climate modeling, seismology, geomorphology, tectonics, surficial processes, ecology, environmental change, remote sensing. *Total annual research expenditures:* $851,337. *Unit head:* Dr. Gray E. Bebout, Chairman, 610-758-5831, Fax: 610-758-3677, E-mail: geb0@lehigh.edu. *Application contact:* Dr. Robert K. Booth, Graduate Coordinator, 610-758-6580, Fax: 610-758-3677, E-mail: rkb205@lehigh.edu.
Website: http://www.ees.lehigh.edu/

Lincoln University, Graduate Studies, Jefferson City, MO 65101. Offers business administration (MBA); counseling (M Ed); environmental science (MS); higher education (MA); history (MA); natural sciences (MS); school teaching middle school with certification (M Ed); school teaching-elementary (M Ed); school teaching-secondary (M Ed); sociology (MA); sociology/criminal justice (MA); sustainable agriculture (MS). *Program availability:* Part-time, evening/weekend, 100% online, blended/hybrid learning. *Students:* 37 full-time (23 women), 52 part-time (25 women); includes 26 minority (24 Black or African American, non-Hispanic/Latino; 1 Asian, non-Hispanic/Latino; 1 Two or more races, non-Hispanic/Latino), 11 international. Average age 34. 67 applicants, 52% accepted, 29 enrolled. In 2018, 48 master's awarded. *Degree requirements:* For master's, comprehensive exam, thesis optional. *Entrance requirements:* For master's, GRE, MAT, or GMAT, minimum GPA of 2.75 overall, 3.0 in courses related to specialization; 3 letters of recommendation; minimum C average in English composition; personal statement of purpose. Additional exam requirements/recommendations for international students: Required—TOEFL (minimum score 500 paper-based; 61 iBT), IELTS (minimum score 5.5), Michigan English Language Assessment Battery (minimum score 80). *Application deadline:* For fall admission, 7/1 priority date for domestic students, 5/1 priority date for international students; for spring admission, 11/1 priority date for domestic students, 10/1 priority date for international students; for summer admission, 6/1 priority date for domestic students. Applications are processed on a rolling basis. Application fee: $30. Electronic applications accepted. *Expenses: Tuition, area resident:* Full-time $6984; part-time $291 per credit. Tuition, state resident: full-time $6984; part-time $291 per credit. Tuition, nonresident: full-time $12,996; part-time $541.50 per credit. *International tuition:* $12,996 full-time. *Required fees:* $1242.20. *Financial support:* In 2018–19, 9 research assistantships with tuition reimbursements (averaging $4,050 per year) were awarded; fellowships with tuition reimbursements, Federal Work-Study, scholarships/grants, and unspecified assistantships also available. Support available to part-time students. Financial award application deadline: 3/1; financial award applicants required to submit FAFSA. *Unit head:* Dr. Benjamin Arnold, Assistant Vice President of Academic Affairs, 573-681-5247, Fax: 573-681-5106, E-mail: gradschool@lincolnu.edu. *Application contact:* Sarah Robinett, Administrative Assistant, 573-681-5247, Fax: 573-681-5106, E-mail: gradschool@lincolnu.edu.
Website: http://www.lincolnu.edu/web/graduate-studies/graduate-studies

Louisiana State University and Agricultural & Mechanical College, Graduate School, College of Agriculture, School of Renewable Natural Resources, Baton Rouge, LA 70803. Offers fisheries (MS); forestry (MS, PhD); wildlife (MS); wildlife and fisheries science (PhD).

Louisiana State University and Agricultural & Mechanical College, Graduate School, School of the Coast and Environment, Department of Environmental Sciences, Baton Rouge, LA 70803. Offers environmental planning and management (MS); environmental science (PhD); environmental toxicology (MS).

Loyola Marymount University, Frank R. Seaver College of Science and Engineering, Program in Environmental Science, Los Angeles, CA 90045. Offers MS. *Unit head:* Dr. Jeremy Pal, Graduate Program Director, Civil Engineering and Environmental Science, 310-568-6241, E-mail: jpal@lmu.edu. *Application contact:* Ammar Dalal, Assistant Vice Provost for Graduate Enrollment, 310-338-2721, Fax: 310-338-6086, E-mail: graduateinfo@lmu.edu.
Website: http://cse.lmu.edu/graduateprograms/msinenvironmentalscience

Marshall University, Academic Affairs Division, College of Information Technology and Engineering, Division of Applied Science and Technology, Program in Environmental Science, Huntington, WV 25755. Offers MS. *Program availability:* Part-time, evening/weekend. *Degree requirements:* For master's, final project, oral exam. *Entrance requirements:* For master's, GRE General Test or MAT, minimum GPA of 2.5, course work in calculus.

Massachusetts Institute of Technology, School of Engineering, Department of Civil and Environmental Engineering, Cambridge, MA 02139. Offers biological oceanography (PhD, Sc D); chemical oceanography (PhD, Sc D); civil and environmental engineering (M Eng, SM, PhD, Sc D); civil and environmental systems (PhD, Sc D); civil engineering (PhD, Sc D, CE); civil engineering and computation (PhD); coastal engineering (PhD, Sc D); construction engineering and management (PhD, Sc D); environmental biology (PhD, Sc D); environmental chemistry (PhD, Sc D); environmental engineering (PhD, Sc D); environmental engineering and computation (PhD); environmental fluid mechanics (PhD, Sc D); geotechnical and geoenvironmental engineering (PhD, Sc D); hydrology (PhD, Sc D); information technology (PhD, Sc D); oceanographic engineering (PhD, Sc D); structures and materials (PhD, Sc D); transportation (PhD, Sc D); SM/MBA. *Degree requirements:* For master's, thesis; for doctorate, comprehensive exam, thesis/dissertation; for CE, comprehensive exam, thesis. *Entrance requirements:* For master's, doctorate, and CE, GRE General Test. Additional exam requirements/recommendations for international students: Required—TOEFL, IELTS. Electronic applications accepted. *Expenses: Tuition:* Full-time $51,520; part-time $800 per credit hour. *Required fees:* $312. *Faculty research:* Environmental chemistry, environmental fluid mechanics and coastal engineering, environmental microbiology, geotechnical engineering and geomechanics, hydrology and hydro climatology, infrastructure systems, mechanics of materials and structures, transportation systems.

McNeese State University, Doré School of Graduate Studies, College of Science and Agriculture, Harold and Pearl Dripps School of Agricultural Sciences, Program in Environmental and Chemical Sciences, Lake Charles, LA 70609. Offers agricultural sciences (MS); environmental science (MS). *Program availability:* Evening/weekend. *Degree requirements:* For master's, comprehensive exam, thesis or alternative. *Entrance requirements:* For master's, GRE.

Memorial University of Newfoundland, School of Graduate Studies, Interdisciplinary Program in Environmental Science, St. John's, NL A1C 5S7, Canada. Offers M Env Sc, M Sc, PhD. *Program availability:* Part-time. *Degree requirements:* For master's, thesis (MSc), project (M Env Sci). *Entrance requirements:* For master's, 2nd class honours bachelor's degree; for doctorate, master's degree. Electronic applications accepted. *Faculty research:* Earth and ocean systems, environmental chemistry and toxicology, environmental engineering.

Mercer University, Graduate Studies, Macon Campus, School of Engineering, Macon, GA 31207. Offers biomedical engineering (MSE); computer engineering (MSE); electrical engineering (MSE); engineering management (MSE); environmental engineering (MSE); environmental systems (MS); mechanical engineering (MSE); software engineering (MSE); software systems (MS); technical communications management (MS); technical management (MS). *Program availability:* Part-time-only, evening/weekend, online learning. *Degree requirements:* For master's, thesis or alternative. *Entrance requirements:* For master's, GRE (minimum score 300), minimum undergraduate GPA of 3.0. Additional exam requirements/recommendations for international students: Required—TOEFL (minimum score 550 paper-based; 80 iBT). *Expenses:* Contact institution. *Faculty research:* Designing prostheses and orthotics, oxygen transfer and limitations in biological systems, low-cost groundwater development, lung airway and transport, autonomous mobile robots.

Miami University, Institute for the Environment and Sustainability, Oxford, OH 45056. Offers M Env. *Faculty:* 1 (woman) full-time. *Students:* 22 full-time (14 women), 19 part-time (8 women); includes 4 minority (1 Black or African American, non-Hispanic/Latino; 1 American Indian or Alaska Native, non-Hispanic/Latino; 1 Hispanic/Latino; 1 Two or more races, non-Hispanic/Latino), 7 international. Average age 26. In 2018, 17 master's awarded. Electronic applications accepted. *Unit head:* Dr. Jonathan Levy, Director/Associate Professor of Geology and Environmental Earth Science, 513-529-1947, E-mail: levyj@miamioh.edu. *Application contact:* Dr. Jonathan Levy, Director/Associate Professor of Geology and Environmental Earth Science, 513-529-1947, E-mail: levyj@miamioh.edu.
Website: http://www.MiamiOH.edu/ies/

Michigan State University, The Graduate School, College of Natural Science, Department of Earth and Environmental Sciences, East Lansing, MI 48824. Offers environmental geosciences (MS, PhD); environmental geosciences-environmental toxicology (PhD); geological sciences (MS, PhD). *Degree requirements:* For master's, thesis (for those without prior thesis work); for doctorate, thesis/dissertation. *Entrance requirements:* For master's, GRE General Test, minimum GPA of 3.0, course work in geoscience, 3 letters of recommendation; for doctorate, GRE General Test, 3 letters of recommendation. Additional exam requirements/recommendations for international students: Required—TOEFL (minimum score 550 paper-based), Michigan State University ELT (minimum score 85), Michigan English Language Assessment Battery (minimum score 83). Electronic applications accepted. *Faculty research:* Water in the environment, global and biological change, crystal dynamics.

Minnesota State University Mankato, College of Graduate Studies and Research, College of Science, Engineering and Technology, Department of Biological Sciences, Program in Environmental Sciences, Mankato, MN 56001. Offers MS. *Degree requirements:* For master's, one foreign language, comprehensive exam, thesis or alternative. *Entrance requirements:* For master's, minimum GPA of 3.0. Additional exam requirements/recommendations for international students: Required—TOEFL. Electronic applications accepted.

Environmental Sciences

Montana State University, The Graduate School, College of Agriculture, Department of Land Resources and Environmental Sciences, Bozeman, MT 59717. Offers land rehabilitation (interdisciplinary) (MS); land resources and environmental sciences (MS), including land rehabilitation (interdisciplinary), land resources and environmental sciences. *Program availability:* Part-time. *Degree requirements:* For master's, comprehensive exam. *Entrance requirements:* For master's, GRE General Test. Additional exam requirements/recommendations for international students: Required—TOEFL (minimum score 550 paper-based). Electronic applications accepted. *Faculty research:* Soil nutrient management and plant nutrition, isotope biogeochemistry of soils, biodegradation of hydrocarbons in soils and natural waters, remote sensing, GIS systems, managed and natural ecosystems, microbial and metabolic diversity in geothermally heated soils, integrated management of weeds, diversified cropping systems, insect behavior and ecology, river ecology, microbial biogeochemistry, weed ecology.

Montana State University, The Graduate School, College of Letters and Science, Department of Ecology, Bozeman, MT 59717. Offers ecological and environmental statistics (MS); ecology and environmental sciences (PhD); fish and wildlife biology (PhD); fish and wildlife management (MS). *Program availability:* Part-time. *Degree requirements:* For master's, comprehensive exam, thesis (for some programs); for doctorate, comprehensive exam, thesis/dissertation. *Entrance requirements:* For master's and doctorate, GRE, minimum GPA of 3.0, letters of recommendation, essay. Additional exam requirements/recommendations for international students: Required—TOEFL (minimum score 550 paper-based). Electronic applications accepted. *Faculty research:* Community ecology, population ecology, land-use effects, management and conservation, environmental modeling.

Montclair State University, The Graduate School, College of Science and Mathematics, Program in Environmental Studies, Montclair, NJ 07043-1624. Offers environmental education (MA); environmental management (MA); environmental science (MA). *Program availability:* Part-time, evening/weekend. *Degree requirements:* For master's, thesis. *Entrance requirements:* For master's, GRE General Test, 2 letters of recommendation, essay. Additional exam requirements/recommendations for international students: Required—TOEFL (minimum score 83 iBT), IELTS (minimum score 6.5). Electronic applications accepted. *Faculty research:* Environmental geochemistry/remediation/forensics, environmental law and policy, regional climate modeling, remote sensing, Cenozoic marine sediment records from polar regions, sustainability science.

Murray State University, Jesse D. Jones College of Science, Engineering and Technology, Department of Earth and Environmental Sciences, Murray, KY 42071. Offers geosciences (MS); geospatial data science (Certificate). *Program availability:* Part-time. *Entrance requirements:* For master's and Certificate, GRE or GMAT, minimum university GPA of 2.75. Additional exam requirements/recommendations for international students: Required—TOEFL (minimum score 527 paper-based; 71 iBT). Electronic applications accepted.

Murray State University, Jesse D. Jones College of Science, Engineering and Technology, Department of Occupational Safety and Health, Murray, KY 42071. Offers environmental science (MS). *Program availability:* Part-time, evening/weekend, 100% online, blended/hybrid learning. *Entrance requirements:* For master's, GRE or GMAT, minimum university GPA of 2.75. Additional exam requirements/recommendations for international students: Required—TOEFL (minimum score 527 paper-based; 71 iBT). Electronic applications accepted.

New Jersey Institute of Technology, College of Science and Liberal Arts, Newark, NJ 07102. Offers applied mathematics (MS); applied physics (MS, PhD); applied statistics (MS, Certificate); biology (MS, PhD); biostatistics (MS); chemistry (MS, PhD); environmental and sustainability policy (MS); environmental science (MS, PhD); history (MA, MAT); materials science and engineering (MS, PhD); mathematical and computational finance (MS); mathematical sciences (PhD); pharmaceutical chemistry (MS); professional and technical communications (MS); technical communication essentials (Certificate). *Program availability:* Part-time, evening/weekend. *Faculty:* 150 full-time (43 women), 115 part-time/adjunct (47 women). *Students:* 200 full-time (79 women), 63 part-time (29 women); includes 61 minority (17 Black or African American, non-Hispanic/Latino; 29 Asian, non-Hispanic/Latino; 11 Hispanic/Latino; 4 Two or more races, non-Hispanic/Latino), 136 international. Average age 28. 429 applicants, 49% accepted, 89 enrolled. In 2018, 43 master's, 16 doctorates, 2 other advanced degrees awarded. Terminal master's awarded for partial completion of doctoral program. *Degree requirements:* For master's, thesis (for some programs); for doctorate, thesis/dissertation. *Entrance requirements:* For master's and doctorate, GRE General Test, Minimum GPA of 3.0, personal statement, three (3) letters of recommendation, and transcripts. Additional exam requirements/recommendations for international students: Required—TOEFL (minimum score 550 paper-based; 79 iBT), IELTS (minimum score 6.5). *Application deadline:* For fall admission, 6/1 priority date for domestic students, 5/1 priority date for international students; for spring admission, 11/15 priority date for domestic and international students. Applications are processed on a rolling basis. Application fee: $75. Electronic applications accepted. *Expenses:* $22,690 per year (in-state), $32,136 per year (out-of-state). *Financial support:* In 2018–19, 134 students received support, including 17 fellowships with full tuition reimbursements available (averaging $22,000 per year), 74 research assistantships with full tuition reimbursements available (averaging $22,000 per year), 71 teaching assistantships with full tuition reimbursements available (averaging $22,000 per year); scholarships/grants, traineeships, health care benefits, and unspecified assistantships also available. Financial award application deadline: 1/15. *Faculty research:* Biophotonics and bioimaging, morphogenetic patterning, embryogenesis, biological fluid dynamics, applied research in the mathematical sciences. *Total annual research expenditures:* $29.2 million. *Unit head:* Dr. Kevin Belfield, Dean, 973-596-3676, Fax: 973-565-0586, E-mail: kevin.d.belfield@njit.edu. *Application contact:* Stephen Eck, Director of Admissions, 973-596-3300, Fax: 973-596-3461, E-mail: admissions@njit.edu. Website: http://csla.njit.edu/

North Carolina Agricultural and Technical State University, The Graduate College, College of Agriculture and Environmental Sciences, Greensboro, NC 27411. Offers MAT, MS. *Program availability:* Part-time, evening/weekend. *Degree requirements:* For master's, comprehensive exam, qualifying exam. *Entrance requirements:* For master's, GRE General Test. *Faculty research:* Aid for small farmers, agricultural technology, housing, food science, nutrition.

North Carolina Central University, College of Arts and Sciences, Department of Environmental, Earth and Geospatial Sciences, Durham, NC 27707-3129. Offers earth sciences (MS); environmental and geographic sciences (MS). *Degree requirements:* For master's, one foreign language, comprehensive exam. *Entrance requirements:* For master's, GRE, minimum GPA of 3.0 in major, 2.5 overall. Additional exam requirements/recommendations for international students: Required—TOEFL.

North Dakota State University, College of Graduate and Interdisciplinary Studies, College of Engineering, Doctoral Program in Engineering, Fargo, ND 58102. Offers environmental and conservation science (PhD); materials and nanotechnology (PhD); natural resource management (PhD); STEM education (PhD); transportation and logistics (PhD). *Degree requirements:* For doctorate, comprehensive exam, thesis/ dissertation. *Entrance requirements:* For doctorate, bachelor's degree in engineering, minimum GPA of 3.0. Additional exam requirements/recommendations for international students: Required—TOEFL. Electronic applications accepted. *Expenses:* Contact institution.

North Dakota State University, College of Graduate and Interdisciplinary Studies, Interdisciplinary Program in Environmental and Conservation Sciences, Fargo, ND 58102. Offers MS, PhD. *Entrance requirements:* Additional exam requirements/ recommendations for international students: Required—TOEFL.

Northeastern University, College of Science, Boston, MA 02115-5096. Offers applied mathematics (MS); bioinformatics (MS); biology (PhD); biotechnology (MS); chemistry and chemical biology (MS, PhD); environmental science and policy (MS); marine and environmental sciences (PhD); marine biology (MS); mathematics (MS, PhD); operations research (MSOR); physics (MS, PhD); psychology (PhD). *Program availability:* Part-time. Terminal master's awarded for partial completion of doctoral program. *Degree requirements:* For master's, comprehensive exam (for some programs), thesis; for doctorate, comprehensive exam (for some programs), thesis/ dissertation. *Entrance requirements:* For master's, GRE General Test. Electronic applications accepted. *Expenses:* Contact institution.

Northern Arizona University, College of Environment, Forestry, and Natural Sciences, School of Earth Sciences and Environmental Sustainability, Flagstaff, AZ 86011. Offers climate science and solutions (MS); conservation ecology (Graduate Certificate); earth sciences and environmental sustainability (PhD); environmental sciences and policy (MS); geology (MS). *Program availability:* Part-time. *Degree requirements:* For master's, variable foreign language requirement, comprehensive exam (for some programs), thesis (for some programs); for doctorate, variable foreign language requirement, comprehensive exam (for some programs), thesis/dissertation (for some programs); for Graduate Certificate, comprehensive exam (for some programs). *Entrance requirements:* For master's and doctorate, GRE General Test. Additional exam requirements/recommendations for international students: Required—TOEFL (minimum score 80 iBT), IELTS (minimum score 6.5). Electronic applications accepted.

Oakland University, Graduate Study and Lifelong Learning, College of Arts and Sciences, Department of Chemistry, Rochester, MI 48309-4479. Offers biomedical sciences (PhD), including health and environmental chemistry; chemistry (MS). *Degree requirements:* For master's, thesis; for doctorate, thesis/dissertation. *Entrance requirements:* For master's, minimum GPA of 3.0; for doctorate, GRE Subject Test, minimum GPA of 3.0. Additional exam requirements/recommendations for international students: Required—TOEFL (minimum score 550 paper-based). Electronic applications accepted.

The Ohio State University, Graduate School, College of Food, Agricultural, and Environmental Sciences, Program in Environmental Science, Columbus, OH 43210. Offers MS, PhD. *Students:* 41 (26 women). Average age 26. In 2018, 8 master's, 7 doctorates awarded. *Degree requirements:* For master's, one foreign language, thesis optional; for doctorate, one foreign language, thesis/dissertation. *Entrance requirements:* For master's and doctorate, GRE General Test. Additional exam requirements/recommendations for international students: Required—TOEFL (minimum score 550 paper-based; 79 iBT), IELTS (minimum score 7), Michigan English Language Assessment Battery (minimum score 82). *Application deadline:* For fall admission, 12/15 priority date for domestic students, 11/30 priority date for international students. Applications are processed on a rolling basis. Application fee: $60 ($70 for international students). Electronic applications accepted. *Financial support:* Fellowships, research assistantships, teaching assistantships, Federal Work-Study, and institutionally sponsored loans available. Support available to part-time students. *Unit head:* Dr. Nicholas Basta, Co-Director, 614-292-6282, E-mail: basta.4@osu.edu. *Application contact:* Graduate and Professional Admissions, 614-292-9444, Fax: 614-292-3895, E-mail: gpadmissions@osu.edu. Website: http://www.esgp.osu.edu

The Ohio State University, Graduate School, College of Food, Agricultural, and Environmental Sciences, School of Environment and Natural Resources, Columbus, OH 43210. Offers ecological restoration (MS, PhD); ecosystem science (MS, PhD); environment and natural resources (MENR); environmental social sciences (MS, PhD); fisheries and wildlife science (MS, PhD); forest science (MS, PhD); rural sociology (MS, PhD); soil science (MS, PhD). *Faculty:* 38. *Students:* 106 (64 women). Average age 29. In 2018, 21 master's, 5 doctorates awarded. *Entrance requirements:* For master's and doctorate, GRE. Additional exam requirements/recommendations for international students: Required—TOEFL (minimum score 550 paper-based; 79 iBT), Michigan English Language Assessment Battery (minimum score 82); Recommended—IELTS (minimum score 7). *Application deadline:* For fall admission, 1/1 priority date for domestic students, 12/15 priority date for international students; for spring admission, 11/1 for domestic students, 9/15 for international students. Applications are processed on a rolling basis. Application fee: $60 ($70 for international students). Electronic applications accepted. *Financial support:* Fellowships, research assistantships, teaching assistantships, health care benefits, and unspecified assistantships available. *Unit head:* Dr. Jeff S. Sharp, Director, 614-292-9410, E-mail: sharp.123@osu.edu. *Application contact:* Graduate and Professional Admissions, 614-292-9444, Fax: 614-292-3895, E-mail: gpadmissions@osu.edu. Website: http://senr.osu.edu/

Oklahoma State University, College of Arts and Sciences, Department of Plant Biology, Ecology, and Evolution, Stillwater, OK 74078. Offers botany (MS); environmental science (PhD). *Faculty:* 15 full-time (5 women). *Students:* 1 full-time (0 women), 11 part-time (7 women), 4 international. Average age 30. 3 applicants, 67% accepted, 2 enrolled. In 2018, 1 master's, 3 doctorates awarded. *Entrance requirements:* For master's and doctorate, GRE or GMAT. Additional exam requirements/recommendations for international students: Required—TOEFL (minimum score 550 paper-based; 79 iBT). *Application deadline:* For fall admission, 3/1 priority date for international students; for spring admission, 8/1 priority date for international students. Applications are processed on a rolling basis. Application fee: $40 ($75 for international students). Electronic applications accepted. *Expenses: Tuition, area resident:* Full-time $4148. Tuition, state resident: full-time $4148. Tuition, nonresident: full-time $10,517. *International tuition:* $10,517 full-time. *Required fees:* $4394; $2929 per credit hour. Tuition and fees vary according to course load and program. *Financial support:* Research assistantships, teaching assistantships, career-related internships or fieldwork, Federal Work-Study, scholarships/grants, health care benefits, tuition waivers (partial), and unspecified assistantships available. Support available to part-time students. Financial award application deadline: 3/1; financial award applicants required to submit FAFSA. *Faculty research:* Ethnobotany, developmental genetics of Arabidopsis, biological roles of plasmodesmata, community ecology and biodiversity, nutrient cycling in grassland ecosystems. *Unit head:* Dr. Andrew Doust, Department

Head, 405-744-2544, Fax: 405-744-7074, E-mail: andrew.doust@okstate.edu. *Application contact:* Dr. Sheryl Tucker, Dean, 405-744-6368, Fax: 405-744-0355, E-mail: gradi@okstate.edu.
Website: http://plantbio.okstate.edu

Oklahoma State University, Graduate College, Stillwater, OK 74078. Offers aerospace security (Graduate Certificate); bioenergy and sustainable technology (Graduate Certificate); business data mining (Graduate Certificate); business sustainability (Graduate Certificate); environmental science (MS); international studies (MS); non-profit management (Graduate Certificate); teaching English to speakers of other languages (Graduate Certificate); telecommunications management (MS). Programs are interdisciplinary. *Degree requirements:* For master's, thesis (for some programs); for doctorate, comprehensive exam, thesis/dissertation. *Entrance requirements:* For master's and doctorate, GRE or GMAT. Additional exam requirements/recommendations for international students: Required—TOEFL (minimum score 550 paper-based; 79 iBT). Electronic applications accepted. *Expenses: Tuition, area resident:* Full-time $4148. Tuition, state resident: full-time $4148. Tuition, nonresident: full-time $10,517. *International tuition:* $10,517 full-time. *Required fees:* $4394; $2929 per credit hour. Tuition and fees vary according to course load and program.

Old Dominion University, College of Sciences, Program in Chemistry, Norfolk, VA 23529. Offers analytical chemistry (MS, PhD); biochemistry (MS, PhD); environmental chemistry (MS, PhD); inorganic chemistry (MS, PhD); organic chemistry (MS, PhD); physical chemistry (MS, PhD). *Program availability:* Part-time. Terminal master's awarded for partial completion of doctoral program. *Degree requirements:* For master's, comprehensive exam, thesis (for some programs); for doctorate, comprehensive exam, thesis/dissertation. *Entrance requirements:* For master's and doctorate, GRE General Test, minimum GPA of 3.0 in major, 2.5 overall, transcripts, essay, three letters of recommendation, resume. Additional exam requirements/recommendations for international students: Required—TOEFL (minimum score 84 iBT). Electronic applications accepted. *Expenses:* Contact institution. *Faculty research:* Biogeochemistry, materials chemistry, computational chemistry, organic chemistry, biofuels.

Oregon Health & Science University, School of Medicine, Graduate Programs in Medicine, Department of Environmental and Biomolecular Systems, Portland, OR 97239-3098. Offers biochemistry and molecular biology (MS, PhD); environmental science and engineering (MS, PhD). This program is no longer admitting new students. *Program availability:* Part-time. *Faculty:* 13 full-time (4 women). *Students:* 5 full-time (4 women), 2 part-time (0 women). Average age 31. In 2018, 13 master's, 3 doctorates awarded. Terminal master's awarded for partial completion of doctoral program. *Degree requirements:* For master's, thesis (for some programs); for doctorate, comprehensive exam, thesis/dissertation, qualifying exam. *Entrance requirements:* For master's and doctorate, GRE General Test (minimum scores: 153 Verbal/148 Quantitative/4.5 Analytical) or MCAT (for some programs). *Application deadline:* For fall admission, 7/15 for domestic students, 5/15 for international students; for winter admission, 10/15 for domestic students, 9/15 for international students; for spring admission, 1/15 for domestic students, 12/15 for international students. Applications are processed on a rolling basis. Application fee: $70. Electronic applications accepted. *Financial support:* Health care benefits and full-tuition and stipends (for PhD students) available. Financial award application deadline: 3/1; financial award applicants required to submit FAFSA. *Faculty research:* Metalloprotein biochemistry, molecular microbiology, environmental microbiology, environmental chemistry, biogeochemistry. *Unit head:* Dr. Michiko Nakano, Program Director. *Application contact:* Dr. Michiko Nakano, Program Director.

Oregon State University, College of Agricultural Sciences, Program in Toxicology, Corvallis, OR 97331. Offers environmental chemistry and ecotoxicology (MS, PhD); mechanistic toxicology (MS, PhD); molecular and cellular toxicology (MS, PhD); neurotoxicology (MS, PhD). *Degree requirements:* For master's, thesis; for doctorate, thesis/dissertation. *Entrance requirements:* For master's and doctorate, GRE, bachelor's degree in chemistry or biological sciences, minimum GPA of 3.0 in last 90 hours of course work. Additional exam requirements/recommendations for international students: Required—TOEFL (minimum score 80 iBT), IELTS (minimum score 6.5).

Oregon State University, Interdisciplinary/Institutional Programs, Program in Environmental Sciences, Corvallis, OR 97331. Offers biogeochemistry (MA, MS, PSM, PhD); ecology (MA, MS, PSM, PhD); environmental education (MA, MS, PhD); quantitative analysis (PSM); social science (MA, MS, PSM, PhD); water resources (MA, MS, PhD). *Program availability:* Part-time. *Degree requirements:* For master's, variable foreign language requirement, thesis; for doctorate, thesis/dissertation. *Entrance requirements:* For master's and doctorate, GRE. Additional exam requirements/recommendations for international students: Required—TOEFL (minimum score 80 iBT), IELTS (minimum score 6.5).

Pace University, Dyson College of Arts and Sciences, Department of Environmental Studies and Science, New York, NY 10038. Offers environmental science (MS). Offered at Pleasantville, NY location only. *Program availability:* Part-time, evening/weekend. *Students:* 12 full-time (5 women), 15 part-time (10 women); includes 7 minority (1 Asian, non-Hispanic/Latino; 4 Hispanic/Latino; 2 Two or more races, non-Hispanic/Latino), 1 international. Average age 28. 20 applicants, 75% accepted, 7 enrolled. In 2018, 4 master's awarded. *Degree requirements:* For master's, thesis, research project. *Entrance requirements:* For master's, GRE, two letters of recommendation, resume, personal statement, all official transcripts. Additional exam requirements/recommendations for international students: Required—TOEFL (minimum score 88 iBT), IELTS (minimum score 7) or PTE (minimum score 60). *Application deadline:* For fall admission, 8/1 priority date for domestic students, 6/1 for international students; for spring admission, 12/1 priority date for domestic students, 10/1 for international students. Applications are processed on a rolling basis. Application fee: $70. Electronic applications accepted. *Financial support:* Fellowships, research assistantships, career-related internships or fieldwork, scholarships/grants, and unspecified assistantships available. Support available to part-time students. Financial award application deadline: 2/15; financial award applicants required to submit FAFSA. *Unit head:* Dr. E. Melanie DuPuis, Chair, Environmental Studies and Science Program, 914-773-3522, E-mail: edupuis@pace.edu. *Application contact:* Susan Ford-Goldschein, Director of Graduate Admissions, 914-422-4283, Fax: 212-346-1585, E-mail: graduateadmission@pace.edu.
Website: http://www.pace.edu/dyson/departments/environmental-studies-science

Penn State Harrisburg, Graduate School, School of Science, Engineering and Technology, Middletown, PA 17057. Offers civil engineering (MS); computer science (MS); electrical engineering (M Eng, MS); engineering management (MPS); engineering science (M Eng); environmental engineering (M Eng); environmental pollution control (MEPC, MS); mechanical engineering (MS); structural engineering (Certificate). *Program availability:* Part-time, evening/weekend.

Penn State University Park, Graduate School, Intercollege Graduate Programs, Intercollege Program in Environmental Pollution Control, University Park, PA 16802. Offers MEPC, MS.

Pontifical Catholic University of Puerto Rico, College of Sciences, Department of Biology, Ponce, PR 00717-0777. Offers environmental sciences (MS). *Degree requirements:* For master's, thesis. *Entrance requirements:* For master's, GRE, 2 letters of recommendation, interview, minimum GPA of 2.75.

Portland State University, Graduate Studies, College of Liberal Arts and Sciences, Department of Environmental Sciences and Management, Portland, OR 97207-0751. Offers environmental management (MEM); environmental science and management (PSM); environmental sciences/biology (PhD); environmental sciences/chemistry (PhD); environmental sciences/civil engineering (PhD); environmental sciences/geography (PhD); environmental sciences/geology (PhD); environmental sciences/physics (PhD); environmental studies (MS); hydrology (Certificate). *Program availability:* Part-time. *Degree requirements:* For master's, thesis or alternative; for doctorate, variable foreign language requirement, comprehensive exam, thesis/dissertation, oral and qualifying exams. *Entrance requirements:* For master's, GRE General Test, science-based BA/BS or equivalent training, 3 letters of recommendation, identification of potential advisor; for doctorate, minimum GPA of 3.0 in upper-division course work or 2.75 overall. Additional exam requirements/recommendations for international students: Required—TOEFL (minimum score 550 paper-based; 80 iBT), IELTS (minimum score 6.5). *Faculty research:* Environmental aspects of biology, chemistry, civil engineering, geology, physics.

Portland State University, Graduate Studies, College of Liberal Arts and Sciences, Department of Geology, Portland, OR 97207-0751. Offers environmental sciences and resources (PhD); geology (MA, MS, Certificate); science/geology (MAT, MST). *Program availability:* Part-time. *Degree requirements:* For master's, comprehensive exam, thesis or alternative, field comprehensive; for doctorate, thesis/dissertation. *Entrance requirements:* For master's, GRE General Test, GRE Subject Test, BA/BS in geology, minimum GPA of 3.0 in geology-related and allied sciences, resume, statement of intent, 2 letters of recommendation. Additional exam requirements/recommendations for international students: Required—TOEFL (minimum score 550 paper-based; 80 iBT). Electronic applications accepted. *Faculty research:* Sediment transport, volcanic environmental geology, coastal and fluvial processes.

Queens College of the City University of New York, Mathematics and Natural Sciences Division, School of Earth and Environmental Sciences, Queens, NY 11367-1597. Offers applied environmental geosciences (MS); geological and environmental sciences (MA). *Program availability:* Part-time, evening/weekend. *Faculty:* 17 full-time (5 women), 16 part-time/adjunct (8 women). *Students:* 1 (woman) full-time, 14 part-time (5 women); includes 3 minority (2 Black or African American, non-Hispanic/Latino; 1 Asian, non-Hispanic/Latino), 1 international. Average age 28. 11 applicants, 73% accepted, 6 enrolled. In 2018, 11 master's awarded. *Degree requirements:* For master's, thesis (for some programs), internship (MS) or thesis (MA) required. *Entrance requirements:* For master's, previous course work in calculus, physics, geology, and chemistry; minimum GPA of 3.0. Additional exam requirements/recommendations for international students: Required—TOEFL, IELTS. *Application deadline:* For fall admission, 4/1 for domestic students; for spring admission, 11/1 for domestic students. Applications are processed on a rolling basis. Application fee: $125. Electronic applications accepted. *Financial support:* In 2018–19, 10 teaching assistantships (averaging $11,968 per year) were awarded; career-related internships or fieldwork and unspecified assistantships also available. Financial award application deadline: 4/1; financial award applicants required to submit FAFSA. *Unit head:* Jeffrey Bird, Chair, 718-997-3300, E-mail: jeffrey.bird@qc.cuny.edu. *Application contact:* Gregory O'Mullan, Graduate Advisor, 718-997-997-3452, E-mail: gomullan@qc.cuny.edu.
Website: http://www.qc.cuny.edu/Academics/Degrees/DMNS/sees/Pages/default.aspx

Rice University, Graduate Programs, George R. Brown School of Engineering, Department of Civil and Environmental Engineering, Houston, TX 77251-1892. Offers civil engineering (MCE, MS, PhD); environmental engineering (MEE, MES, MS, PhD); environmental science (MEE, MES, MS, PhD). *Program availability:* Part-time. *Degree requirements:* For master's, thesis (for some programs); for doctorate, thesis/dissertation. *Entrance requirements:* For master's and doctorate, GRE General Test, GRE Subject Test, minimum GPA of 3.25. Additional exam requirements/recommendations for international students: Required—TOEFL (minimum score 600 paper-based; 90 iBT). Electronic applications accepted. *Faculty research:* Biology and chemistry of groundwater, pollutant fate in groundwater systems, water quality monitoring, urban storm water runoff, urban air quality.

Rice University, Graduate Programs, Wiess School–Professional Science Master's Programs, Houston, TX 77251-1892. Offers MS.

Rochester Institute of Technology, Graduate Enrollment Services, College of Science, School of Life Sciences, MS Program in Environmental Science, Rochester, NY 14623-5603. Offers MS. *Program availability:* Part-time. *Students:* 7 full-time (4 women), 4 part-time (3 women); includes 1 minority (Two or more races, non-Hispanic/Latino), 2 international. Average age 24. 15 applicants, 47% accepted, 2 enrolled. In 2018, 3 master's awarded. *Degree requirements:* For master's, thesis or alternative, Thesis or Project. *Entrance requirements:* For master's, GRE required for applicants with degrees from international universities., minimum GPA of 3.0 (recommended) overall and in math/science, personal statement, three letters of recommendation. Additional exam requirements/recommendations for international students: Required—TOEFL (minimum score 550 paper-based; 79 iBT), IELTS (minimum score 6.5), PTE (minimum score 58). *Application deadline:* For fall admission, 2/15 priority date for domestic and international students; for spring admission, 12/15 priority date for domestic and international students. Applications are processed on a rolling basis. Application fee: $65. Electronic applications accepted. *Financial support:* In 2018–19, 8 students received support. Research assistantships with partial tuition reimbursements available, teaching assistantships with partial tuition reimbursements available, career-related internships or fieldwork, scholarships/grants, and unspecified assistantships available. Support available to part-time students. Financial award applicants required to submit FAFSA. *Faculty research:* Aquatic ecology, global warming, microbial degradation of pharmaceuticals, GIS applications, nutrition of migratory birds. *Unit head:* Jeffery Lodge, Graduate Program Director, 585-475-2489, Fax: 585-475-5000, E-mail: jslsbi@rit.edu. *Application contact:* Diane Ellison, Senior Associate Vice President, Graduate Enrollment Services, 585-475-2229, Fax: 585-475-7164, E-mail: gradinfo@rit.edu.
Website: https://www.rit.edu/study/environmental-science-ms

Rutgers University–Newark, Graduate School, Program in Environmental Science, Newark, NJ 07102. Offers MS, PhD. MS, PhD offered jointly with New Jersey Institute of Technology. *Entrance requirements:* For master's and doctorate, GRE, minimum B average.

Rutgers University–New Brunswick, Graduate School-New Brunswick, Department of Environmental Sciences, Piscataway, NJ 08854-8097. Offers air pollution and resources (MS, PhD); aquatic biology (MS, PhD); aquatic chemistry (MS, PhD); atmospheric science (MS, PhD); chemistry and physics of aerosol and hydrosol systems (MS, PhD); environmental chemistry (MS, PhD); environmental microbiology (MS, PhD);

environmental toxicology (PhD); exposure assessment (PhD); fate and effects of pollutants (MS, PhD); pollution prevention and control (MS, PhD); water and wastewater treatment (MS, PhD); water resources (MS, PhD). Terminal master's awarded for partial completion of doctoral program. *Degree requirements:* For master's, comprehensive exam, thesis or alternative, oral final exam; for doctorate, comprehensive exam, thesis/dissertation, thesis defense, qualifying exam. *Entrance requirements:* For master's and doctorate, GRE General Test. Additional exam requirements/recommendations for international students: Required—TOEFL. Electronic applications accepted. *Faculty research:* Biological waste treatment; contaminant fate and transport; air, soil and water quality.

Rutgers University–New Brunswick, Graduate School of Biomedical Sciences, Program in Exposure Science and Assessment, Piscataway, NJ 08854-5635. Offers PhD, MD/PhD. PhD offered jointly with Rutgers, The State University of New Jersey, New Brunswick. *Entrance requirements:* Additional exam requirements/recommendations for international students: Required—TOEFL. Electronic applications accepted.

Sitting Bull College, Graduate Programs, Fort Yates, ND 58538-9701. Offers curriculum and instruction (M Ed); environmental science (MS). *Entrance requirements:* For master's, GRE, official transcripts from all previous colleges and universities, three letters of recommendation, curriculum vitae, letter of intent.

South Dakota School of Mines and Technology, Graduate Division, PhD Program in Atmospheric and Environmental Sciences, Rapid City, SD 57701-3995. Offers PhD. Program offered jointly with South Dakota State University. *Program availability:* Part-time. *Degree requirements:* For doctorate, comprehensive exam, thesis/dissertation. *Entrance requirements:* For doctorate, GRE General Test, GRE Subject Test. Additional exam requirements/recommendations for international students: Required—TOEFL (minimum score 520 paper-based; 68 iBT), TWE. Electronic applications accepted.

Southeast Missouri State University, School of Graduate Studies, Program in Environmental Science, Cape Girardeau, MO 63701-4799. Offers MS. *Program availability:* Part-time. *Faculty:* 16 full-time (5 women). *Students:* 8 full-time (1 woman), 5 part-time (1 woman), 5 international. Average age 33. 5 applicants, 100% accepted, 3 enrolled. In 2018, 3 master's awarded. *Degree requirements:* For master's, comprehensive exam (for some programs), thesis (for some programs). *Entrance requirements:* For master's, GRE General Test, 30 hours of natural science, minimum GPA of 3.0. Additional exam requirements/recommendations for international students: Required—TOEFL (minimum score 550 paper-based; 79 iBT), IELTS (minimum score 6), PTE (minimum score 53). *Application deadline:* For fall admission, 8/1 for domestic students, 6/1 for international students; for spring admission, 11/21 for domestic students, 10/1 for international students; for summer admission, 5/15 for domestic students. Applications are processed on a rolling basis. Application fee: $30 ($40 for international students). Electronic applications accepted. *Expenses:* Contact institution. *Financial support:* In 2018–19, 5 students received support, including 3 teaching assistantships with full tuition reimbursements available; career-related internships or fieldwork, Federal Work-Study, scholarships/grants, traineeships, tuition waivers (full), and unspecified assistantships also available. Financial award application deadline: 6/30; financial award applicants required to submit FAFSA. *Faculty research:* Asthma and indoor air, mussels and water quality, metals in wildlife, paths in environmental samples, genesis of arctic soils. *Unit head:* Dr. John Kraemer, Director, 573-651-2355, E-mail: jkraemer@semo.edu. *Application contact:* Dr. John Kraemer, Director, 573-651-2355, E-mail: jkraemer@semo.edu.

Southern Connecticut State University, School of Graduate Studies, School of Arts and Sciences, Department of Environment, Geography and Marine Sciences, New Haven, CT 06515-1355. Offers environmental education (MS); science education (MS, Diploma). *Accreditation:* NCATE. *Program availability:* Part-time, evening/weekend. *Degree requirements:* For master's, thesis or alternative. *Entrance requirements:* For master's, interview; for Diploma, master's degree. Electronic applications accepted.

Southern Illinois University Carbondale, Graduate School, College of Science, Department of Geology and Department of Geography, Program in Environmental Resources and Policy, Carbondale, IL 62901-4701. Offers PhD. *Degree requirements:* For doctorate, thesis/dissertation. *Entrance requirements:* For doctorate, GRE, minimum GPA of 3.25.

Southern Illinois University Edwardsville, Graduate School, College of Arts and Sciences, Program in Environmental Sciences, Edwardsville, IL 62026. Offers MS. *Program availability:* Part-time, evening/weekend. *Degree requirements:* For master's, thesis (for some programs), final exam, oral exam. *Entrance requirements:* For master's, GRE. Additional exam requirements/recommendations for international students: Required—TOEFL (minimum score 550 paper-based; 79 iBT), IELTS (minimum score 6.5). Electronic applications accepted.

Southern University and Agricultural and Mechanical College, Graduate School, College of Sciences and Engineering, Program in Chemistry, Baton Rouge, LA 70813. Offers analytical chemistry (MS); biochemistry (MS); environmental sciences (MS); inorganic chemistry (MS); organic chemistry (MS); physical chemistry (MS). *Degree requirements:* For master's, thesis. *Entrance requirements:* For master's, GMAT or GRE General Test. Additional exam requirements/recommendations for international students: Required—TOEFL (minimum score 525 paper-based). *Faculty research:* Synthesis of macrocyclic ligands, latex accelerators, anticancer drugs, biosensors, absorption isotheums, isolation of specific enzymes from plants.

Stanford University, School of Earth, Energy and Environmental Sciences, Stanford, CA 94305-2004. Offers MS, PhD, Eng. *Expenses: Tuition:* Full-time $50,703; part-time $32,970 per year. *Required fees:* $651.

Stanford University, School of Humanities and Sciences, Department of Anthropology, Stanford, CA 94305-2004. Offers anthropology (MA); archaeology (PhD); culture and society (PhD); ecology and environment (PhD). *Expenses: Tuition:* Full-time $50,703; part-time $32,970 per year. *Required fees:* $651.
Website: http://www.stanford.edu/dept/anthsci/

State University of New York College of Environmental Science and Forestry, Department of Chemistry, Syracuse, NY 13210-2779. Offers biochemistry (MPS, MS, PhD); environmental chemistry (MPS, MS, PhD); organic chemistry of natural products (MPS, MS, PhD); polymer chemistry (MPS, MS, PhD). *Program availability:* Part-time. *Faculty:* 14 full-time (1 woman), 1 part-time/adjunct (0 women). *Students:* 37 full-time (14 women), 3 part-time (2 women); includes 1 minority (Asian, non-Hispanic/Latino), 13 international. Average age 28. 51 applicants, 53% accepted, 13 enrolled. In 2018, 4 master's, 5 doctorates awarded. Terminal master's awarded for partial completion of doctoral program. *Degree requirements:* For master's, thesis; for doctorate, comprehensive exam, thesis/dissertation. *Entrance requirements:* For master's and doctorate, GRE General Test, GRE Subject Test, minimum GPA of 3.0. Additional exam requirements/recommendations for international students: Required—TOEFL (minimum score 550 paper-based; 80 iBT), IELTS (minimum score 6). *Application deadline:* For fall admission, 2/1 priority date for domestic and international students; for spring admission, 11/1 priority date for domestic and international students. Applications are processed on a rolling basis. Application fee: $60. Electronic applications accepted. *Expenses: Tuition, area resident:* Full-time $11,090; part-time $462 per credit hour. Tuition, state resident: full-time $11,090; part-time $462 per credit hour. Tuition, nonresident: full-time $22,650; part-time $944 per credit hour. *International tuition:* $22,650 full-time. *Required fees:* $1733; $178.58 per credit hour. *Financial support:* In 2018–19, 13 students received support. Unspecified assistantships available. Financial award application deadline: 6/30; financial award applicants required to submit FAFSA. *Faculty research:* Polymer chemistry, biochemistry, environmental chemistry, natural products chemistry. *Total annual research expenditures:* $1.3 million. *Unit head:* Dr. Avik Chatterjee, Chair, 315-470-4747, Fax: 315-470-6855, E-mail: achatter@esf.edu. *Application contact:* Scott Shannon, Associate Provost for Instruction/Dean of the Graduate School, 315-470-6599, Fax: 315-470-6978, E-mail: sshannon@esf.edu.
Website: http://www.esf.edu/chemistry

State University of New York College of Environmental Science and Forestry, Department of Environmental and Forest Biology, Syracuse, NY 13210-2779. Offers applied ecology (MPS); chemical ecology (MPS, MS, PhD); conservation biology (MPS, MS, PhD); ecology (MPS, MS, PhD); entomology (MPS, MS, PhD); environmental interpretation (MPS, MS, PhD); environmental physiology (MPS, MS, PhD); fish and wildlife biology and management (MPS, MS, PhD); forest pathology and mycology (MPS, MS, PhD); plant biotechnology (MPS); plant science and biotechnology (MPS, MS, PhD). *Program availability:* Part-time. *Faculty:* 35 full-time (10 women), 4 part-time/adjunct (3 women). *Students:* 107 full-time (57 women), 21 part-time (8 women); includes 9 minority (6 American Indian or Alaska Native, non-Hispanic/Latino; 2 Asian, non-Hispanic/Latino; 1 Hispanic/Latino), 18 international. Average age 30. 79 applicants, 49% accepted, 24 enrolled. In 2018, 30 master's, 3 doctorates awarded. Terminal master's awarded for partial completion of doctoral program. *Degree requirements:* For master's, thesis (for some programs), capstone seminar; for doctorate, comprehensive exam, thesis/dissertation, capstone seminar. *Entrance requirements:* For master's and doctorate, GRE General Test, minimum GPA of 3.0. Additional exam requirements/recommendations for international students: Required—TOEFL (minimum score 550 paper-based; 80 iBT), IELTS (minimum score 6). *Application deadline:* For fall admission, 2/1 priority date for domestic and international students; for spring admission, 11/1 priority date for domestic and international students. Applications are processed on a rolling basis. Application fee: $60. Electronic applications accepted. *Expenses: Tuition, area resident:* Full-time $11,090; part-time $462 per credit hour. Tuition, state resident: full-time $11,090; part-time $462 per credit hour. Tuition, nonresident: full-time $22,650; part-time $944 per credit hour. *International tuition:* $22,650 full-time. *Required fees:* $1733; $178.58 per credit hour. *Financial support:* In 2018–19, 46 students received support. Unspecified assistantships available. Financial award application deadline: 6/30; financial award applicants required to submit FAFSA. *Faculty research:* Ecology, conservation biology, fish and wildlife biology and management, plant science, entomology. *Total annual research expenditures:* $5.9 million. *Unit head:* Dr. Melissa K. Fierke, Chair, 315-470-6809, Fax: 315-470-6743, E-mail: mkfierke@esf.edu. *Application contact:* Scott Shannon, Associate Provost for Instruction/Dean of the Graduate School, 315-470-6599, E-mail: esfgrad@esf.edu.
Website: http://www.esf.edu/efb/grad/default.asp

State University of New York College of Environmental Science and Forestry, Program in Environmental Science, Syracuse, NY 13210-2779. Offers biophysical and ecological economics (MPS); coupled natural and human systems (MPS); ecosystem restoration (MPS); environmental and community land planning (MPS, MS); environmental and natural resources policy (PhD); environmental communication and participatory processes (PhD); environmental monitoring and modeling (MPS); water and wetland resource studies (MPS, MS). *Program availability:* Part-time. *Faculty:* 1 full-time (0 women), 1 (woman) part-time/adjunct. *Students:* 52 full-time (30 women), 13 part-time (9 women); includes 3 minority (1 Asian, non-Hispanic/Latino; 2 Hispanic/Latino), 26 international. Average age 32. 51 applicants, 73% accepted, 17 enrolled. In 2018, 14 master's, 8 doctorates awarded. Terminal master's awarded for partial completion of doctoral program. *Degree requirements:* For master's, thesis (for some programs); for doctorate, comprehensive exam, thesis/dissertation. *Entrance requirements:* For master's and doctorate, GRE General Test, minimum GPA of 3.0. Additional exam requirements/recommendations for international students: Required—TOEFL (minimum score 550 paper-based; 80 iBT), IELTS (minimum score 6). *Application deadline:* For fall admission, 2/1 priority date for domestic and international students; for spring admission, 11/1 priority date for domestic and international students. Applications are processed on a rolling basis. Application fee: $60. Electronic applications accepted. *Expenses: Tuition, area resident:* Full-time $11,090; part-time $462 per credit hour. Tuition, state resident: full-time $11,090; part-time $462 per credit hour. Tuition, nonresident: full-time $22,650; part-time $944 per credit hour. *International tuition:* $22,650 full-time. *Required fees:* $1733; $178.58 per credit hour. *Financial support:* In 2018–19, 24 students received support. Unspecified assistantships available. Financial award application deadline: 6/30; financial award applicants required to submit FAFSA. *Faculty research:* Environmental education/communications, water resources, land resources, waste management. *Unit head:* Dr. Russell Briggs, Director of the Division of Environmental Science, 315-470-6989, Fax: 315-470-6700, E-mail: rdbriggs@esf.edu. *Application contact:* Scott Shannon, Associate Provost for Instruction/Dean of the Graduate School, 315-470-6599, Fax: 315-470-6978, E-mail: esfgrad@esf.edu.
Website: http://www.esf.edu/environmentalscience/graduate/

Stephen F. Austin State University, Graduate School, College of Sciences and Mathematics, Division of Environmental Science, Nacogdoches, TX 75962. Offers MS. *Degree requirements:* For master's, comprehensive exam. *Entrance requirements:* For master's, GRE General Test, minimum GPA of 2.8 in last 60 hours, 2.5 overall. Additional exam requirements/recommendations for international students: Required—TOEFL.

Stockton University, Office of Graduate Studies, Program in Environmental Science, Galloway, NJ 08205-9441. Offers PSM. *Program availability:* Part-time, evening/weekend. *Faculty:* 12 full-time (4 women), 1 part-time/adjunct (0 women). *Students:* 7 full-time (4 women), 6 part-time (2 women); includes 1 minority (Asian, non-Hispanic/Latino). Average age 27. 6 applicants, 83% accepted, 3 enrolled. In 2018, 11 master's awarded. *Entrance requirements:* For master's, GRE. Additional exam requirements/recommendations for international students: Required—TOEFL. *Application deadline:* For fall admission, 7/1 for domestic and international students; for spring admission, 12/1 for domestic students, 11/1 for international students. Applications are processed on a rolling basis. Application fee: $50. Electronic applications accepted. *Expenses:* Contact institution. *Financial support:* Fellowships, research assistantships, career-related internships or fieldwork, Federal Work-Study, scholarships/grants, and unspecified assistantships available. Financial award application deadline: 3/1; financial award applicants required to submit FAFSA. *Unit head:* Dr. Kathy Sedia, Program Director, 609-626-3640, E-mail: gradschool@stockton.edu. *Application contact:* Tara Williams,

Assistant Director of Graduate Enrollment Management, 609-626-3640, Fax: 609-626-6050, E-mail: gradschool@stockton.edu. Website: http://www.stockton.edu/grad

Tarleton State University, College of Graduate Studies, College of Science and Technology, Department of Chemistry, Geosciences and Physics, Stephenville, TX 76402. Offers environmental science (MS). *Program availability:* Part-time, evening/weekend. *Faculty:* 3 full-time (2 women), 1 part-time/adjunct (0 women). *Students:* 8 full-time (3 women), 3 part-time (0 women). Average age 31. 4 applicants, 50% accepted, 1 enrolled. In 2018, 4 master's awarded. *Degree requirements:* For master's, comprehensive exam, thesis optional. *Entrance requirements:* For master's, GRE General Test, minimum GPA of 3.0. Additional exam requirements/recommendations for international students: Required—TOEFL (minimum score 520 paper-based; 69 iBT); Recommended—IELTS (minimum score 6), TSE (minimum score 50). *Application deadline:* For fall admission, 8/15 priority date for domestic students; for spring admission, 1/7 for domestic students. Applications are processed on a rolling basis. Application fee: $50 ($130 for international students). Electronic applications accepted. *Expenses:* Contact institution. *Financial support:* Research assistantships, teaching assistantships, career-related internships or fieldwork, and Federal Work-Study available. Support available to part-time students. Financial award application deadline: 5/1; financial award applicants required to submit FAFSA. *Unit head:* Dr. Ryan Morgan, Department Head, 254-968-9143, Fax: 254-968-9953, E-mail: rmorgan@tarleton.edu. *Application contact:* Information Contact, 254-968-9104, Fax: 254-968-9670, E-mail: gradoffice@tarleton.edu.

Tennessee Technological University, College of Graduate Studies, College of Interdisciplinary Studies, School of Environmental Studies, Department of Environmental Sciences, Cookeville, TN 38505. Offers agriculture (PhD); biology (PhD); chemistry (PhD); geosciences (PhD); integrated research (PhD). *Program availability:* Part-time. *Students:* 3 full-time (all women), 17 part-time (6 women); includes 2 minority (1 Asian, non-Hispanic/Latino; 1 Two or more races, non-Hispanic/Latino), 5 international. 14 applicants, 29% accepted, 2 enrolled. In 2018, 3 doctorates awarded. *Degree requirements:* For doctorate, comprehensive exam, thesis/dissertation. *Entrance requirements:* For doctorate, GRE. Additional exam requirements/recommendations for international students: Required—TOEFL (minimum score 527 paper-based; 71 iBT), IELTS (minimum score 5.5), PTE (minimum score 48), or TOEIC (Test of English as an International Communication). *Application deadline:* For fall admission, 7/1 for domestic students, 5/1 for international students; for spring admission, 12/1 for domestic students, 10/2 for international students; for summer admission, 5/1 for domestic students, 2/1 for international students. Applications are processed on a rolling basis. Application fee: $35 ($40 for international students). Electronic applications accepted. *Financial support:* Fellowships, research assistantships, and teaching assistantships available. Financial award application deadline: 4/1. *Unit head:* Dr. Hayden Mattingly, Interim Director, 931-372-6246, E-mail: hmattingly@tntech.edu. *Application contact:* Shelia K. Kendrick, Coordinator of Graduate Studies, 931-372-3808, Fax: 931-372-3497, E-mail: skendrick@tntech.edu.

Tennessee Technological University, College of Graduate Studies, College of Interdisciplinary Studies, School of Environmental Studies, Professional Science Master's Program, Cookeville, TN 38505. Offers environmental informatics (PSM); manufacturing sustainability (PSM). *Program availability:* Part-time. *Students:* 8 full-time (4 women), 7 part-time (1 woman); includes 1 minority (Black or African American, non-Hispanic/Latino). 6 applicants, 67% accepted, 6 enrolled. In 2018, 2 master's awarded. *Degree requirements:* For master's, comprehensive exam, thesis or alternative, internship. *Entrance requirements:* For master's, GRE General Test. Additional exam requirements/recommendations for international students: Required—TOEFL (minimum score 527 paper-based; 71 iBT), IELTS (minimum score 5.5), PTE (minimum score 48), or TOEIC (Test of English as an International Communication). *Application deadline:* For fall admission, 7/1 for domestic students, 5/1 for international students; for spring admission, 2/1 for domestic students, 10/1 for international students; for summer admission, 5/1 for domestic students, 2/1 for international students. Applications are processed on a rolling basis. Application fee: $35 ($40 for international students). Electronic applications accepted. *Financial support:* Research assistantships available. Financial award application deadline: 4/1. *Unit head:* Dr. Hayden Mattingly, Interim Director, 931-372-6246, E-mail: hmattingly@tntech.edu. *Application contact:* Shelia K. Kendrick, Coordinator of Graduate Studies, 931-372-3808, Fax: 931-372-3497, E-mail: skendrick@tntech.edu. Website: https://www.tntech.edu/is/ses/psm/psmei

Texas A&M University-Commerce, College of Science and Engineering, Commerce, TX 75429. Offers biological sciences (MS); broadfield science biology (MS); broadfield science chemistry (MS); broadfield science physics (MS); chemistry (MS); computational linguistics (Graduate Certificate); computational science (MS); computer science (MS); environmental science (Graduate Certificate); mathematics (MS); physics (MS); technology management (MS). *Program availability:* Part-time. *Faculty:* 44 full-time (7 women), 7 part-time/adjunct (0 women). *Students:* 178 full-time (67 women), 234 part-time (104 women); includes 82 minority (19 Black or African American, non-Hispanic/Latino; 1 American Indian or Alaska Native, non-Hispanic/Latino; 14 Asian, non-Hispanic/Latino; 37 Hispanic/Latino; 11 Two or more races, non-Hispanic/Latino), 158 international. Average age 30. 481 applicants, 52% accepted, 105 enrolled. In 2018, 218 master's awarded. *Degree requirements:* For master's, comprehensive exam, thesis optional. *Entrance requirements:* For master's, GRE, official transcripts, letters of recommendation, resume, statement of goals. Additional exam requirements/recommendations for international students: Required—TOEFL (minimum score 550 paper-based; 79 iBT), IELTS (minimum score 6), PTE (minimum score 53). *Application deadline:* For fall admission, 6/1 priority date for international students; for spring admission, 10/15 priority date for international students; for summer admission, 3/15 priority date for international students. Applications are processed on a rolling basis. Application fee: $50 ($75 for international students). Electronic applications accepted. *Expenses:* Contact institution. *Financial support:* In 2018–19, 46 students received support, including 43 research assistantships with partial tuition reimbursements available (averaging $2,418 per year), 135 teaching assistantships with partial tuition reimbursements available (averaging $3,376 per year); scholarships/grants, health care benefits, and unspecified assistantships also available. Financial award application deadline: 5/1; financial award applicants required to submit FAFSA. *Faculty research:* Biomedical, Catalytic Material & Processes, Nuclear Theory/Astrophysics, Cybersecurity, STEM Education. *Total annual research expenditures:* $1.8 million. *Unit head:* Dr. Brent L. Donham, Dean, 903-886-5321, Fax: 903-886-5199, E-mail: brent.donham@tamuc.edu. *Application contact:* Dayla Burgin, Graduate Student Services Coordinator, 903-886-5134, E-mail: dayla.burgin@tamuc.edu. Website: https://new.tamuc.edu/science-engineering/

Texas A&M University–Corpus Christi, College of Graduate Studies, College of Science and Engineering, Program in Environmental Science, Corpus Christi, TX 78412. Offers MS. *Program availability:* Part-time, evening/weekend. *Degree requirements:* For master's, comprehensive exam, thesis (for some programs) thesis or project. *Entrance requirements:* For master's, GRE (taken within 5 years; waived for

students who have earned previous graduate degree), essay (minimum of 300 words); 3 letters of recommendation. Additional exam requirements/recommendations for international students: Required—TOEFL (minimum score 550 paper-based; 79 iBT), IELTS (minimum score 6.5). Electronic applications accepted.

Texas Christian University, College of Science and Engineering, Department of Environmental Science, Fort Worth, TX 76129-0002. Offers MA, MEM, MS, MBA/MEM. *Program availability:* Part-time. *Degree requirements:* For master's, comprehensive exam, thesis (MS). *Entrance requirements:* For master's, GRE General Test, 1 year each of course work in biology and chemistry, 1 semester each in calculus and statistics. Additional exam requirements/recommendations for international students: Required—TOEFL (minimum score 550 paper-based; 80 iBT).

Texas Tech University, Graduate School, College of Arts and Sciences, Department of Environmental Toxicology, Lubbock, TX 79409-1163. Offers MS, PhD, JD/MS, MBA/MS. *Program availability:* Part-time. *Faculty:* 16 full-time (5 women). *Students:* 47 full-time (33 women), 6 part-time (4 women); includes 11 minority (4 Black or African American, non-Hispanic/Latino; 1 Asian, non-Hispanic/Latino; 4 Hispanic/Latino; 2 Two or more races, non-Hispanic/Latino), 14 international. Average age 29. 32 applicants, 69% accepted, 17 enrolled. In 2018, 18 master's, 7 doctorates awarded. Terminal master's awarded for partial completion of doctoral program. *Degree requirements:* For master's, thesis; for doctorate, comprehensive exam, thesis/dissertation. *Entrance requirements:* For master's and doctorate, GRE. Additional exam requirements/recommendations for international students: Required—TOEFL (minimum score 550 paper-based; 79 iBT); Recommended—IELTS (minimum score 6.5), TSE (minimum score 60). *Application deadline:* For fall admission, 6/1 priority date for domestic students, 1/15 priority date for international students; for spring admission, 9/1 priority date for domestic students, 6/15 priority date for international students. Applications are processed on a rolling basis. Application fee: $65. Electronic applications accepted. *Expenses:* Contact institution. *Financial support:* In 2018–19, 58 students received support, including 51 fellowships (averaging $2,050 per year), 42 research assistantships (averaging $12,440 per year); teaching assistantships, Federal Work-Study, institutionally sponsored loans, scholarships/grants, health care benefits, and unspecified assistantships also available. Financial award application deadline: 5/15; financial award applicants required to submit FAFSA. *Faculty research:* Wildlife toxicology; human health epidemiology and toxicology; endangered species toxicology; reproductive, molecular, and developmental toxicology; environmental and forensic chemistry. *Total annual research expenditures:* $1.1 million. *Unit head:* Dr. Steven M. Presley, Chair and Professor, 806-885-4567 Ext. 236, Fax: 806-885-2132, E-mail: steve.presley@ttu.edu. *Application contact:* Dr. Kamaleshwar Singh, Graduate Officer, 806-834-8407, Fax: 806-885-2132, E-mail: kamaleshwar.singh@ttu.edu. Website: www.tiehh.ttu.edu/

Thompson Rivers University, Program in Environmental Science, Kamloops, BC V2C 0C8, Canada. Offers MS. *Entrance requirements:* For master's, personal resume, 2 letters of recommendation. Additional exam requirements/recommendations for international students: Required—TOEFL.

Towson University, Jess and Mildred Fisher College of Science and Mathematics, Program in Environmental Science, Towson, MD 21252-0001. Offers MS, Postbaccalaureate Certificate. *Program availability:* Part-time, evening/weekend. *Entrance requirements:* For master's, 3 letters of recommendation, bachelor's degree in related field, minimum GPA of 3.0, personal statement; for Postbaccalaureate Certificate, 3 letters of recommendation, bachelor's degree in related field, minimum GPA of 3.0. Electronic applications accepted. *Expenses:* Tuition, area resident: Full-time $9196; part-time $418 per unit. Tuition, state resident: full-time $9196; part-time $418 per unit. Tuition, nonresident: full-time $19,030; part-time $865 per unit. International tuition: $19,030 full-time. *Required fees:* $3102; $141 per year; $420 per term. Tuition and fees vary according to campus/location and program.

Tuskegee University, Graduate Programs, College of Agriculture, Environment and Nutrition Sciences, Department of Agricultural and Environmental Sciences, Program in Environmental Sciences, Tuskegee, AL 36088. Offers MS. *Degree requirements:* For master's, thesis. *Entrance requirements:* For master's, GRE General Test. Additional exam requirements/recommendations for international students: Required—TOEFL (minimum score 500 paper-based).

Universidad del Turabo, Graduate Programs, Programs in Science and Technology, Gurabo, PR 00778-3030. Offers environmental analysis (MSE), including environmental chemistry; environmental management (MSE), including pollution management; environmental science (D Sc), including environmental biology. *Entrance requirements:* For master's, GRE, EXADEP, GMAT, interview, official transcript, essay, recommendation letters; for doctorate, GRE, EXADEP, GMAT, official transcript, recommendation letters, essay, curriculum vitae, interview. Electronic applications accepted.

Universidad Nacional Pedro Henriquez Urena, Graduate School, Santo Domingo, Dominican Republic. Offers agricultural diversity (MS), including horticultural/fruit production, tropical animal production; conservation of monuments and cultural assets (M Arch); ecology and environment (MS); environmental engineering (MEE); international relations (MA); natural resource management (MS); political science (MA); project optimization (MPM); project feasibility (MPM); project management (MPM); sanitation engineering (ME); science for teachers (MS); tropical Caribbean architecture (M Arch).

Université de Sherbrooke, Faculty of Sciences, Centre Universitaire de Formation en Environnement, Sherbrooke, QC J1K 2R1, Canada. Offers M Sc, Diploma. *Program availability:* Online learning. Electronic applications accepted. *Faculty research:* Environmental studies.

Université du Québec à Montréal, Graduate Programs, Program in Environmental Sciences, Montréal, QC H3C 3P8, Canada. Offers M Sc, PhD, Certificate. *Program availability:* Part-time. *Degree requirements:* For master's, research report; for doctorate, thesis/dissertation. *Entrance requirements:* For master's, appropriate bachelor's degree or equivalent, proficiency in French; for doctorate, appropriate master's degree or equivalent, proficiency in French.

Université du Québec à Trois-Rivières, Graduate Programs, Program in Environmental Sciences, Trois-Rivières, QC G9A 5H7, Canada. Offers M Sc, PhD. *Program availability:* Part-time. *Degree requirements:* For master's, thesis. *Entrance requirements:* For master's, appropriate bachelor's degree, proficiency in French.

Université du Québec en Abitibi-Témiscamingue, Graduate Programs, Program in Environmental Sciences, Rouyn-Noranda, QC J9X 5E4, Canada. Offers biology (MS); environmental sciences (PhD); sustainable forest ecosystem management (MS).

Université Laval, Faculty of Sciences and Engineering, Department of Geology and Geological Engineering, Programs in Earth Sciences, Québec, QC G1K 7P4, Canada. Offers earth sciences (M Sc, PhD); environmental technologies (M Sc). Offered jointly

Peterson's Graduate Programs in the Physical Sciences, Mathematics, Agricultural Sciences, the Environment & Natural Resources 2020

www.petersons.com **321**

with INRS-Géressources. Terminal master's awarded for partial completion of doctoral program. *Degree requirements:* For master's, thesis (for some programs); for doctorate, comprehensive exam, thesis/dissertation. *Entrance requirements:* For master's and doctorate, knowledge of French. Electronic applications accepted.

University at Buffalo, the State University of New York, Graduate School, College of Arts and Sciences, Department of Geography, Buffalo, NY 14260. Offers earth systems science (MA, MS); economic geography and business geographics (MS); environmental modeling and analysis (MA); geographic information science (MA, MS); geography (MA, PhD); health geography (MS); international trade (MA); urban and regional analysis (MA). *Program availability:* Part-time. Terminal master's awarded for partial completion of doctoral program. *Degree requirements:* For master's, thesis (for some programs), project or portfolio; for doctorate, thesis/dissertation. *Entrance requirements:* For master's, GRE General Test, minimum GPA of 2.9; for doctorate, GRE General Test, minimum GPA of 3.0. Additional exam requirements/recommendations for international students: Required—TOEFL (minimum score 550 paper-based; 79 iBT). Electronic applications accepted. *Expenses:* Contact institution. *Faculty research:* International business and world trade, geographic information systems and cartography, transportation, urban and regional analysis, physical and environmental geography.

University of Alberta, Faculty of Graduate Studies and Research, Department of Civil and Environmental Engineering, Edmonton, AB T6G 2E1, Canada. Offers construction engineering and management (M Eng, M Sc, PhD); environmental engineering (M Eng, M Sc, PhD); environmental science (M Sc, PhD); geoenvironmental engineering (M Eng, M Sc, PhD); geotechnical engineering (M Eng, M Sc, PhD); mining engineering (M Eng, M Sc, PhD); petroleum engineering (M Eng, M Sc, PhD); structural engineering (M Eng, M Sc, PhD); water resources (M Eng, M Sc, PhD). *Program availability:* Part-time, online learning. *Degree requirements:* For master's, thesis (for some programs); for doctorate, thesis/dissertation. *Entrance requirements:* For master's, minimum GPA of 3.0 in last 2 years of undergraduate studies; for doctorate, minimum GPA of 3.0. Additional exam requirements/recommendations for international students: Required—TOEFL (minimum score 550 paper-based). Electronic applications accepted. *Faculty research:* Mining.

The University of Arizona, College of Agriculture and Life Sciences, Department of Soil, Water and Environmental Science, Tucson, AZ 85721. Offers MS, PhD, Graduate Certificate. *Degree requirements:* For master's, thesis; for doctorate, comprehensive exam, thesis/dissertation. *Entrance requirements:* For master's, GRE (recommended), minimum GPA of 3.0, letter of interest, 3 letters of recommendation; for doctorate, GRE (recommended), MS, minimum GPA of 3.0, letter of interest, 3 letters of recommendation. Additional exam requirements/recommendations for international students: Required—TOEFL (minimum score 550 paper-based; 80 iBT). Electronic applications accepted. *Faculty research:* Plant production, environmental microbiology, contaminant flow and transport, aquaculture.

The University of Arizona, College of Agriculture and Life Sciences, Graduate Interdisciplinary Program in Arid Lands Resource Sciences, Tucson, AZ 85721. Offers PhD. *Degree requirements:* For doctorate, one foreign language, comprehensive exam, thesis/dissertation. *Entrance requirements:* For doctorate, GRE. Additional exam requirements/recommendations for international students: Required—TOEFL (minimum score 550 paper-based; 79 iBT). Electronic applications accepted. *Faculty research:* International development; famine, famine early warning systems, and food security; land use, history, change, degradation, desertification, management, and policy; sustainable agriculture and farming systems; remote sensing and spatial analysis; carbon sequestration; political-ecology of natural resources; ethnoecology and other ethno-sciences; economic and agricultural policy and development; economic botany; borderlands issues; globalization; civil conflict; urban development.

University of California, Berkeley, Graduate Division, College of Natural Resources, Department of Environmental Science, Policy, and Management, Berkeley, CA 94720. Offers environmental science, policy, and management (MS, PhD); forestry (MF). Terminal master's awarded for partial completion of doctoral program. *Degree requirements:* For master's, thesis optional; for doctorate, thesis/dissertation, qualifying exam. *Entrance requirements:* For master's and doctorate, GRE General Test, minimum GPA of 3.0, 3 letters of recommendation. Additional exam requirements/recommendations for international students: Required—TOEFL. Electronic applications accepted. *Faculty research:* Biology and ecology of insects; ecosystem function and environmental issues of soils; plant health/interactions from molecular to ecosystem levels; range management and ecology; forest and resource policy, sustainability, and management.

University of California, Davis, Graduate Studies, Graduate Group in Soils and Biogeochemistry, Davis, CA 95616. Offers MS, PhD. Terminal master's awarded for partial completion of doctoral program. *Degree requirements:* For master's, comprehensive exam (for some programs), thesis (for some programs); for doctorate, thesis/dissertation. *Entrance requirements:* For master's, minimum GPA of 3.3; for doctorate, GRE, minimum GPA of 3.3. Additional exam requirements/recommendations for international students: Required—TOEFL (minimum score 550 paper-based). Electronic applications accepted. *Faculty research:* Rhizosphere ecology, soil transport processes, biogeochemical cycling, sustainable agriculture.

University of California, Los Angeles, Graduate Division, Fielding School of Public Health, Department of Environmental Health Sciences, Los Angeles, CA 90095. Offers environmental health sciences (MS, PhD); environmental science and engineering (D Env); molecular toxicology (PhD); JD/MPH. *Accreditation:* ABET (one or more programs are accredited); CEPH. *Degree requirements:* For master's, comprehensive exam or thesis; for doctorate, thesis/dissertation, oral and written qualifying exams. *Entrance requirements:* For master's, GRE General Test, minimum GPA of 3.0; for doctorate, GRE General Test, minimum undergraduate GPA of 3.0. Electronic applications accepted.

University of California, Los Angeles, Graduate Division, Institute of the Environment and Sustainability, Los Angeles, CA 90095-1496. Offers environmental science and engineering (D Env). *Degree requirements:* For doctorate, thesis/dissertation, oral and written qualifying exams. *Entrance requirements:* For doctorate, GRE General Test, minimum undergraduate GPA of 3.0, master's degree or equivalent in a natural science, engineering, or public health. *Faculty research:* Toxic and hazardous substances, air and water pollution, risk assessment/management, water resources, marine science.

University of California, Riverside, Graduate Division, Materials Science and Engineering Program, Riverside, CA 92521. Offers MS. *Entrance requirements:* For master's, GRE. Additional exam requirements/recommendations for international students: Required—TOEFL (minimum score 550 paper-based; 80 iBT). Electronic applications accepted.

University of California, Santa Barbara, Graduate Division, Donald Bren School of Environmental Science and Management, Santa Barbara, CA 93106-5131. Offers economics and environmental science (PhD); environmental science and management (MESM, PhD); technology and society (PhD). *Degree requirements:* For master's, thesis; for doctorate, thesis/dissertation. *Entrance requirements:* For master's and doctorate, GRE. Additional exam requirements/recommendations for international students: Required—TOEFL (minimum score 550 paper-based; 80 iBT), IELTS (minimum score 7). Electronic applications accepted. *Faculty research:* Coastal marine resources management, conservation planning, corporate environmental management, economics and politics of the environment, energy and climate, pollution prevention and remediation, water resources management.

University of Chicago, Harris School of Public Policy, Master of Science Program in Environmental Science and Policy, Chicago, IL 60637. Offers MS. Offered in partnership with the Argonne National Laboratory. *Entrance requirements:* For master's, GRE General Test, transcripts, resume, 3 letters of recommendation. Additional exam requirements/recommendations for international students: Required—TOEFL (minimum score 104 iBT), IELTS (minimum score 7). Electronic applications accepted.

University of Cincinnati, Graduate School, College of Engineering and Applied Science, Department of Biomedical, Chemical and Environmental Engineering, Program in Environmental Sciences, Cincinnati, OH 45221. Offers MS, PhD. *Program availability:* Part-time. *Degree requirements:* For master's, thesis or alternative; for doctorate, one foreign language, thesis/dissertation. *Entrance requirements:* For master's and doctorate, GRE General Test. Additional exam requirements/recommendations for international students: Required—TOEFL (minimum score 580 paper-based; 92 iBT). Electronic applications accepted. *Faculty research:* Environmental microbiology, solid-waste management, air pollution control, water pollution control, aerosols.

University of Colorado Colorado Springs, College of Letters, Arts and Sciences, Department of Geography and Environmental Studies, Colorado Springs, CO 80918. Offers MA. *Program availability:* Part-time. *Faculty:* 14 full-time (7 women), 9 part-time/adjunct (6 women). *Students:* 7 full-time (2 women), 11 part-time (5 women); includes 4 minority (3 Hispanic/Latino; 1 Two or more races, non-Hispanic/Latino). Average age 36. 16 applicants, 75% accepted, 10 enrolled. In 2018, 3 master's awarded. *Degree requirements:* For master's, comprehensive exam (for some programs), thesis (for some programs). *Entrance requirements:* For master's, beyond the Feb. 1, 2019 GES MA application deadline, the GRE is no longer a required component of the MA application, minimum undergraduate GPA of 3.0, statement of intent (essay). Additional exam requirements/recommendations for international students: Required—Applicants who have completed a post-secondary degree at U.S. institution also meet the English proficiency requirements. Applicants with combined sco; Recommended—TOEFL (minimum score 89 iBT), IELTS (minimum score 6.5). *Application deadline:* For fall admission, 2/1 priority date for domestic and international students. Applications are processed on a rolling basis. Application fee: $60 ($100 for international students). Electronic applications accepted. *Expenses:* Program tuition and fees vary by course load and residency classification. Please visit the University of Colorado Colorado Springs Student Financial Services website to see current program costs: https://www.uccs.edu/bursar/index.php/estimate-your-bill. *Financial support:* In 2018–19, 9 students received support. Federal Work-Study, scholarships/grants, and unspecified assistantships available. Support available to part-time students. Financial award application deadline: 3/1; financial award applicants required to submit FAFSA. *Faculty research:* Socio-ecological implications of conservation strategies, cultural geography, militarized spaces, geovisualization, geographic information systems, hydrology, biogeography, human-environment interactions, geomorphology, population. *Total annual research expenditures:* $142,630. *Unit head:* Dr. Brandon Vogt, Director of Graduate Studies in GES, 719-255-5146, E-mail: bvogt@uccs.edu. *Application contact:* Monica Killebrew, Department of Geography and Environmental Studies, Administrative Assistant, 719-255-3016, Fax: 719-255-4066, E-mail: mkillebr@uccs.edu.
Website: http://www.uccs.edu/geography/

University of Colorado Denver, College of Liberal Arts and Sciences, Department of Geography and Environmental Sciences, Denver, CO 80217. Offers environmental sciences (MS), including air quality, ecosystems, environmental health, geospatial analysis, hazardous waste, water quality. *Program availability:* Part-time, evening/weekend. *Degree requirements:* For master's, thesis or alternative, 30 credits including 21 of core requirements and 9 of environmental science electives. *Entrance requirements:* For master's, GRE General Test, BA in one of the natural/physical sciences or engineering (or equivalent background); prerequisite coursework in calculus and physics (one semester each); general chemistry with lab and general biology with lab (two semesters each); three letters of recommendation. Additional exam requirements/recommendations for international students: Required—TOEFL (minimum score 537 paper-based; 75 iBT); Recommended—IELTS (minimum score 6.5). Electronic applications accepted. *Expenses:* Tuition, state resident: full-time $6786; part-time $337 per credit hour. Tuition, nonresident: full-time $22,590; part-time $1255 per credit hour. *Required fees:* $1231; $137 per credit hour. Tuition and fees vary according to program and reciprocity agreements. *Faculty research:* Air quality, environmental health, ecosystems, hazardous waste, water quality, geospatial analysis and environmental science education.

University of Guam, Office of Graduate Studies, College of Natural and Applied Sciences, Program in Environmental Science, Mangilao, GU 96923. Offers MS. *Program availability:* Part-time. *Degree requirements:* For master's, thesis. *Entrance requirements:* For master's, GRE General Test. Additional exam requirements/recommendations for international students: Required—TOEFL. *Faculty research:* Water resources, ecology, karst formations, hydrogeology, meteorology.

University of Guelph, Office of Graduate and Postdoctoral Studies, Ontario Agricultural College, Department of Land Resource Science, Guelph, ON N1G 2W1, Canada. Offers atmospheric science (M Sc, PhD); environmental and agricultural earth sciences (M Sc, PhD); land resources management (M Sc, PhD); soil science (M Sc, PhD). *Program availability:* Part-time. *Degree requirements:* For master's, thesis (for some programs), research project (non-thesis track); for doctorate, comprehensive exam, thesis/dissertation. *Entrance requirements:* For master's, minimum B- average during previous 2 years of course work; for doctorate, minimum B average during previous 2 years of course work. Additional exam requirements/recommendations for international students: Required—TOEFL (minimum score 550 paper-based). Electronic applications accepted. *Faculty research:* Soil science, environmental earth science, land resource management.

University of Hawaii at Hilo, Program in Tropical Conservation Biology and Environmental Science, Hilo, HI 96720-4091. Offers MS. *Entrance requirements:* Additional exam requirements/recommendations for international students: Required—TOEFL, IELTS. Electronic applications accepted.

University of Houston–Clear Lake, School of Science and Computer Engineering, Program in Environmental Science, Houston, TX 77058-1002. Offers MS. *Program availability:* Part-time, evening/weekend. *Entrance requirements:* For master's, GRE General Test. Additional exam requirements/recommendations for international students: Required—TOEFL (minimum score 550 paper-based).

University of Idaho, College of Graduate Studies, College of Natural Resources, Environmental Science Program, Moscow, ID 83844-1139. Offers MS, PhD. *Faculty:* 27. *Students:* 26 full-time (19 women), 60 part-time (33 women). Average age 33. In 2018, 21 master's, 1 doctorate awarded. *Entrance requirements:* For master's, minimum GPA of 3.0. Additional exam requirements/recommendations for international students: Required—TOEFL (minimum score 79 iBT). *Application deadline:* For fall admission, 8/1 for domestic students; for spring admission, 12/15 for domestic students. Applications are processed on a rolling basis. Application fee: $60. Electronic applications accepted. *Expenses:* Tuition, state resident: full-time $7266.44; part-time $474.50 per credit hour. Tuition, nonresident: full-time $24,902; part-time $1453.50 per credit hour. *Required fees:* $2085.56; $45.50 per credit hour. *Financial support:* Research assistantships and teaching assistantships available. Financial award applicants required to submit FAFSA. *Unit head:* Dr. J.D. Wulfhorst, Director, 208-885-6113, E-mail: envs@uidaho.edu. *Application contact:* Dr. J.D. Wulfhorst, Director, 208-885-6113, E-mail: envs@uidaho.edu.
Website: https://www.uidaho.edu/cnr/departments/environmental-science-program

University of Illinois at Springfield, Graduate Programs, College of Public Affairs and Administration, Program in Environmental Studies, Springfield, IL 62703-5407. Offers environmental science (MS); environmental studies (MA). *Program availability:* Part-time, evening/weekend, 100% online. *Faculty:* 6 full-time (3 women), 2 part-time/adjunct (1 woman). *Students:* 12 full-time (7 women), 43 part-time (23 women); includes 12 minority (3 Black or African American, non-Hispanic/Latino; 2 Asian, non-Hispanic/Latino; 4 Hispanic/Latino; 3 Two or more races, non-Hispanic/Latino), 2 international. Average age 30. 44 applicants, 41% accepted, 15 enrolled. In 2018, 33 master's awarded. *Degree requirements:* For master's, thesis, project, or capstone closure course. *Entrance requirements:* For master's, minimum undergraduate GPA of 3.0, 2 letters of recommendation, goals essay, completion of ecology course with lab with minimum B grade, undergraduate or work background sufficient for advanced course work in environmental studies. Additional exam requirements/recommendations for international students: Required—TOEFL (minimum score 500 paper-based; 61 iBT). *Application deadline:* Applications are processed on a rolling basis. Application fee: $60 ($75 for international students). Electronic applications accepted. *Financial support:* In 2018–19, research assistantships with full tuition reimbursements (averaging $10,384 per year), teaching assistantships with full tuition reimbursements (averaging $10,303 per year) were awarded; fellowships, career-related internships or fieldwork, Federal Work-Study, scholarships/grants, health care benefits, and unspecified assistantships also available. Support available to part-time students. Financial award application deadline: 11/15; financial award applicants required to submit FAFSA. *Unit head:* Dr. Dennis Ruez, Jr., Program Administrator, 217-206-8424, E-mail: druez2@uis.edu. *Application contact:* Dr. Dennis Ruez, Jr., Program Administrator, 217-206-8424, E-mail: druez2@uis.edu.
Website: http://www.uis.edu/environmentalstudies/

University of Illinois at Urbana–Champaign, Graduate College, College of Agricultural, Consumer and Environmental Sciences, Department of Natural Resources and Environmental Science, Champaign, IL 61820. Offers MS, PhD, MS/JD. *Program availability:* Part-time, online learning.

The University of Kansas, Graduate Studies, School of Engineering, Program in Environmental Science, Lawrence, KS 66045. Offers MS, PhD. *Program availability:* Part-time. *Students:* 2 full-time (both women), 2 part-time (0 women), 1 international. Average age 33. 4 applicants, 25% accepted, 1 enrolled. In 2018, 2 master's awarded. Terminal master's awarded for partial completion of doctoral program. *Entrance requirements:* For master's, GRE, minimum GPA of 3.0, recommendations, resume, statement of purpose; for doctorate, GRE, minimum GPA of 3.5, recommendations, resume, statement of purpose. Additional exam requirements/recommendations for international students: Required—TOEFL, IELTS. *Application deadline:* For fall admission, 12/15 priority date for domestic and international students; for spring admission, 9/15 priority date for domestic and international students. Application fee: $65 ($85 for international students). Electronic applications accepted. *Financial support:* Fellowships, research assistantships, teaching assistantships, career-related internships or fieldwork, and scholarships/grants available. Financial award application deadline: 12/15. *Faculty research:* Water quality, water treatment, wastewater treatment, air quality, air pollution control, solid waste, hazardous waste, water resources engineering, water resources science. *Unit head:* David Darwin, Chair, 785-864-3827, Fax: 785-864-5631, E-mail: daved@ku.edu. *Application contact:* Susan Scott, Administrative Assistant, 785-864-3826, E-mail: sbscott@ku.edu.
Website: http://ceae.ku.edu/overview-8

University of Lethbridge, School of Graduate Studies, Lethbridge, AB T1K 3M4, Canada. Offers addictions counseling (M Sc); agricultural biotechnology (M Sc); agricultural studies (M Sc, MA); anthropology (MA); archaeology (M Sc, MA); art (MA, MFA); biochemistry (M Sc); biological sciences (M Sc); biomolecular science (PhD); biosystems and biodiversity (PhD); Canadian studies (MA); chemistry (M Sc); computer science (M Sc); computer science and geographical information science (M Sc); counseling (MC); counseling psychology (M Ed); dramatic arts (MA); earth, space, and physical science (PhD); economics (MA); education (MA, PhD); educational leadership (M Ed); English (MA); environmental science (M Sc); evolution and behavior (PhD); exercise science (M Sc); French (MA); French/German (MA); French/Spanish (MA); general education (M Ed); geography (M Sc, MA); German (MA); health sciences (M Sc); individualized multidisciplinary (M Sc, MA); kinesiology (M Sc, MA); management (M Sc), including accounting, finance, human resource management and labor relations, information systems, international management, marketing, policy and strategy; mathematics (M Sc); music (M Mus, MA); Native American studies (MA); neuroscience (M Sc, PhD); new media (MA, MFA); nursing (M Sc, MN); philosophy (MA); physics (M Sc); political science (MA); psychology (M Sc, MA); religious studies (MA); sociology (MA); theatre and dramatic arts (MFA); theoretical and computational science (PhD); urban and regional studies (MA); women and gender studies (MA). *Program availability:* Part-time, evening/weekend. *Degree requirements:* For master's, thesis (for some programs); for doctorate, comprehensive exam, thesis/dissertation. *Entrance requirements:* For master's, GMAT (for M Sc in management), bachelor's degree in related field, minimum GPA of 3.0 during previous 20 graded semester courses, 2 years' teaching or related experience (M Ed); for doctorate, master's degree, minimum graduate GPA of 3.5. Additional exam requirements/recommendations for international students: Required—TOEFL (minimum score 580 paper-based; 93 iBT). Electronic applications accepted. *Faculty research:* Movement and brain plasticity, gibberellin physiology, photosynthesis, carbon cycling, molecular properties of main-group ring components.

University of Louisiana at Lafayette, College of Sciences, School of Geosciences, Lafayette, LA 70504. Offers environmental resource science (MS); geosciences (MS). *Program availability:* Part-time. *Degree requirements:* For master's, comprehensive exam, thesis. *Entrance requirements:* For master's, GRE General Test, minimum GPA of 2.75. Additional exam requirements/recommendations for international students: Required—TOEFL (minimum score 550 paper-based). Electronic applications accepted. *Faculty research:* Aquifer contamination, coastal erosion, geochemistry of peat, petroleum geology and geophysics, remote sensing and geographic information systems applications.

The University of Manchester, School of Earth and Environmental Sciences, Manchester, United Kingdom. Offers atmospheric sciences (M Phil, M Sc, PhD); basin studies and petroleum geosciences (M Phil, M Sc, PhD); earth, atmospheric and environmental sciences (M Phil, M Sc, PhD); environmental geochemistry and cosmochemistry (M Phil, M Sc, PhD); isotope geochemistry and cosmochemistry (M Phil, M Sc, PhD); paleontology (M Phil, M Sc, PhD); physics and chemistry of minerals and fluids (M Phil, M Sc, PhD); structural and petrological geosciences (M Phil, M Sc, PhD).

University of Manitoba, Faculty of Graduate Studies, Clayton H. Riddell Faculty of Environment, Earth, and Resources, Department of Environment and Geography, Winnipeg, MB R3T 2N2, Canada. Offers environment (M Env); environment and geography (M Sc); geography (MA, PhD). *Degree requirements:* For master's, thesis; for doctorate, one foreign language, thesis/dissertation.

University of Maryland, Baltimore, Graduate School, Program in Marine-Estuarine-Environmental Sciences, College Park, MD 20740. Offers MS, PhD. *Program availability:* Part-time. Terminal master's awarded for partial completion of doctoral program. *Degree requirements:* For doctorate, comprehensive exam, thesis/dissertation, proposal defense, oral defense. *Entrance requirements:* For doctorate, GRE General Test, minimum GPA of 3.0, curriculum vitae, essay, 3 letters of recommendation. Additional exam requirements/recommendations for international students: Required—TOEFL (minimum score 80 iBT); Recommended—IELTS (minimum score 7). Electronic applications accepted.

University of Maryland, Baltimore County, The Graduate School, Marine-Estuarine-Environmental Sciences Graduate Program, College Park, MD 20742. Offers MS, PhD. *Program availability:* Part-time. *Degree requirements:* For master's, thesis, oral defense; for doctorate, comprehensive exam, thesis/dissertation, proposal defense, oral defense. *Entrance requirements:* For master's and doctorate, GRE General Test, minimum GPA of 3.0. Additional exam requirements/recommendations for international students: Required—TOEFL. Electronic applications accepted.

University of Maryland, College Park, Academic Affairs, College of Agriculture and Natural Resources, Department of Environmental Science and Technology, College Park, MD 20742. Offers MS, PhD. Electronic applications accepted.

University of Maryland, College Park, Academic Affairs, College of Computer, Mathematical and Natural Sciences, Program in Marine-Estuarine-Environmental Sciences, College Park, MD 20742. Offers MS, PhD. *Program availability:* Part-time. Terminal master's awarded for partial completion of doctoral program. *Degree requirements:* For master's, thesis, oral defense; for doctorate, comprehensive exam, thesis/dissertation, proposal defense, oral defense. *Entrance requirements:* For master's and doctorate, GRE General Test, minimum GPA of 3.0. Additional exam requirements/recommendations for international students: Required—TOEFL. Electronic applications accepted. *Faculty research:* Ecology, environmental chemistry, environmental molecular biology/biotechnology, environmental sciences, fisheries science, oceanography.

University of Maryland Eastern Shore, Graduate Programs, Program in Marine-Estuarine-Environmental Sciences, College Park, MD 20740. Offers MS, PhD. *Program availability:* Part-time. *Degree requirements:* For master's, thesis; for doctorate, comprehensive exam, thesis/dissertation, proposal defense. *Entrance requirements:* For master's and doctorate, GRE General Test, minimum GPA of 3.0. Additional exam requirements/recommendations for international students: Required—TOEFL. Electronic applications accepted.

University of Massachusetts Boston, School for the Environment, Program in Environmental Sciences, Boston, MA 02125-3393. Offers MS, PhD. *Program availability:* Part-time, evening/weekend. *Students:* 25 full-time (15 women), 17 part-time (11 women); includes 6 minority (1 Asian, non-Hispanic/Latino; 3 Hispanic/Latino; 2 Two or more races, non-Hispanic/Latino), 5 international. Average age 31. 21 applicants, 62% accepted, 10 enrolled. In 2018, 9 master's, 4 doctorates awarded. *Entrance requirements:* For doctorate, GRE General Test, minimum GPA of 2.75. *Application deadline:* For fall admission, 6/15 for domestic students; for spring admission, 10/15 for domestic students. *Expenses: Tuition, area resident:* Full-time $17,896. Tuition, state resident: full-time $17,896. Tuition, nonresident: full-time $34,932. *International tuition:* $34,932 full-time. *Required fees:* $355. *Financial support:* Research assistantships, teaching assistantships, career-related internships or fieldwork, Federal Work-Study, and unspecified assistantships available. Support available to part-time students. Financial award application deadline: 3/1; financial award applicants required to submit FAFSA. *Faculty research:* Polychoets biology, predator and prey relationships, population and evolutionary biology, neurobiology, biodiversity. *Unit head:* Dr. Juanita Urban-Rich, Associate Professor, 617-287.7485, Fax: 617-287.7485, E-mail: Juanita.Urban-Rich@umb.edu. *Application contact:* Graduate Admissions Coordinator, 617-287-6400, Fax: 617-287-6236, E-mail: graduate.admissions@umb.edu.

University of Massachusetts Lowell, College of Health Sciences, Department of Work Environment, Lowell, MA 01854. Offers cleaner production and pollution prevention (Sc D). *Program availability:* Part-time. Terminal master's awarded for partial completion of doctoral program. *Degree requirements:* For doctorate, thesis/dissertation. *Entrance requirements:* For doctorate, GRE General Test. Additional exam requirements/recommendations for international students: Required—TOEFL.

University of Massachusetts Lowell, College of Sciences, Department of Chemistry, Lowell, MA 01854. Offers analytical chemistry (PhD); biochemistry (PhD); chemistry (MS, PhD); environmental studies (PhD); green chemistry (PhD); inorganic chemistry (PhD); organic chemistry (PhD); polymer science (MS). Terminal master's awarded for partial completion of doctoral program. *Degree requirements:* For master's, thesis; for doctorate, 2 foreign languages, thesis/dissertation. *Entrance requirements:* For master's and doctorate, GRE General Test. Electronic applications accepted.

University of Massachusetts Lowell, Francis College of Engineering, Department of Civil and Environmental Engineering and College of Sciences, Program in Environmental Studies, Lowell, MA 01854. Offers MS, PhD. *Program availability:* Part-time. *Degree requirements:* For master's, thesis optional. *Entrance requirements:* For master's, GRE General Test. *Faculty research:* Remote sensing of air pollutants, atmospheric deposition of toxic metals, contaminant transport in groundwater, soil remediation.

University of Michigan, Rackham Graduate School, College of Literature, Science, and the Arts, Department of Earth and Environmental Sciences, Ann Arbor, MI 48109-1005. Offers MS, PhD. Terminal master's awarded for partial completion of doctoral program. *Degree requirements:* For master's, thesis; for doctorate, comprehensive exam, thesis/dissertation, oral defense of dissertation. *Entrance requirements:* For master's and doctorate, GRE General Test. Additional exam requirements/recommendations for international students: Required—TOEFL (minimum score 100 iBT). Electronic applications accepted. *Faculty research:* Isotope geochemistry, paleoclimatology, mineral physics, tectonics, paleontology.

Environmental Sciences

University of Michigan, School for Environment and Sustainability, Program in Environment and Sustainability, Ann Arbor, MI 48109. Offers behavior, education and communication (MS); conservation ecology (MS); environment and sustainability (PhD); environmental informatics (MS); environmental justice (MS); environmental policy and planning (MS); sustainable systems (MS); MS/JD; MS/MBA; MS/MPH; MS/MPP; MS/MSE; MS/MURP. *Faculty:* 39 full-time (15 women), 19 part-time/adjunct (3 women). *Students:* 332 full-time (184 women); includes 52 minority (6 Black or African American, non-Hispanic/Latino; 1 American Indian or Alaska Native, non-Hispanic/Latino; 14 Asian, non-Hispanic/Latino; 17 Hispanic/Latino; 1 Native Hawaiian or other Pacific Islander, non-Hispanic/Latino; 13 Two or more races, non-Hispanic/Latino), 57 international. Average age 26. 485 applicants. In 2018, 113 master's, 4 doctorates awarded. Terminal master's awarded for partial completion of doctoral program. *Degree requirements:* For master's, thesis, practicum, or group project; for doctorate, comprehensive exam, thesis/dissertation, oral defense of dissertation, preliminary exam. *Entrance requirements:* For master's, GRE General Test (must be taken within 5 years of application submission); for doctorate, GRE General Test (must be taken within 5 years of application submission), Master's Degree. Additional exam requirements/recommendations for international students: Required—TOEFL (minimum score 560 paper-based; 84 iBT). *Application deadline:* For fall admission, 4/30 for domestic and international students. Applications are processed on a rolling basis. Application fee: $75 ($90 for international students). Electronic applications accepted. *Financial support:* Fellowships, research assistantships, teaching assistantships, career-related internships or fieldwork, Federal Work-Study, scholarships/grants, health care benefits, and unspecified assistantships available. Financial award application deadline: 1/7; financial award applicants required to submit FAFSA. *Faculty research:* 1) Climate Change, Energy, and Sustainable Systems 2) Environmental Justice 3) Environmental Behavior, Communications, and Policy 4) Conservation Ecology, Ecosystems Management, and Geographic Information Systems (GIS) 5) Cities, Mobility, and Built Environment. *Unit head:* Dr. Jonathan Overpeck, Samuel A. Graham Dean, 734-764-2550, Fax: 734-763-8965, E-mail: overpeck@umich.edu. *Application contact:* Jung Koral, Associate Director of Enrollment Services, 734-764-6453, Fax: 734-936-2195, E-mail: seas-admissions@umich.edu.
Website: https://seas.umich.edu/academics/ms

University of Michigan–Dearborn, College of Arts, Sciences, and Letters, Master of Science in Environmental Science Program, Dearborn, MI 48128. Offers MS. *Program availability:* Part-time, evening/weekend. *Faculty:* 12 full-time (5 women), 3 part-time/adjunct (1 woman). *Students:* 1 (woman) full-time, 8 part-time (5 women); includes 4 minority (1 Black or African American, non-Hispanic/Latino; 3 Asian, non-Hispanic/Latino), 1 international. Average age 28. 16 applicants, 56% accepted, 6 enrolled. In 2018, 9 master's awarded. *Degree requirements:* For master's, thesis optional. *Entrance requirements:* For master's, 3 letters of reference, minimum GPA of 3.0. Additional exam requirements/recommendations for international students: Required—TOEFL (minimum score 560 paper-based; 84 iBT), IELTS (minimum score 6.5). *Application deadline:* For fall admission, 8/1 priority date for domestic students, 5/1 priority date for international students; for winter admission, 12/1 priority date for domestic students, 9/1 priority date for international students; for spring admission, 4/1 priority date for domestic students, 1/1 priority date for international students. Applications are processed on a rolling basis. Application fee: $60. Electronic applications accepted. *Expenses:* $12,140 (typical full-time in-state); $20,708 (typical full-time out-of-state). *Financial support:* In 2018–19, 2 students received support. Scholarships/grants and non-resident tuition scholarships available. Financial award application deadline: 3/1; financial award applicants required to submit FAFSA. *Faculty research:* Fate and transport of heavy metals, land use and impact on surface and ground water, ecosystem and management, natural resources, plant, animal and microbial diversity. *Unit head:* Dr. Jacop Napieralski, Director, 313-593-5157, E-mail: jnapiera@umich.edu. *Application contact:* Office of Graduate Studies, 313-583-6321, E-mail: umd-graduatestudies@umich.edu.
Website: http://umdearborn.edu/casl/envsci_ms/

University of Missouri, Office of Research and Graduate Studies, College of Agriculture, Food and Natural Resources, School of Natural Resources, Columbia, MO 65211. Offers agroforestry (MS, Certificate); conservation biology (Certificate); fisheries and wildlife sciences (MS, PhD); forestry (MS, PhD); geographical information science (Certificate); human dimensions of natural resources (MS, PhD); parks, recreation and tourism (MS); society and ecosystems (Certificate); soil, environmental and atmospheric sciences (MS, PhD); water resources (MS, PhD). *Program availability:* Part-time. *Degree requirements:* For doctorate, thesis/dissertation. *Entrance requirements:* For master's and doctorate, GRE General Test (minimum score 1200 Verbal and Quantitative), minimum GPA of 3.2. Additional exam requirements/recommendations for international students: Required—TOEFL (minimum score 550 paper-based; 80 iBT), IELTS (minimum score 6.5). Electronic applications accepted.

University of Montana, Graduate School, College of Humanities and Sciences, Program in Environmental Studies (EVST), Missoula, MT 59812. Offers MS, JD/MS. *Program availability:* Part-time. *Degree requirements:* For master's, thesis, portfolio or professional paper. *Entrance requirements:* Additional exam requirements/recommendations for international students: Required—TOEFL (minimum score 580 paper-based; 92 iBT). Electronic applications accepted. *Faculty research:* Pollution ecology, sustainable agriculture, environmental writing, environmental policy, environmental justice, environmental history, habitat-land management, traditional ecological knowledge of Native Peoples.

University of Nevada, Las Vegas, Graduate College, Greenspun College of Urban Affairs, School of Public Policy and Leadership, Las Vegas, NV 89154-4030. Offers crisis and emergency management (MS); emergency crisis management cybersecurity (Certificate); environmental science (MS, PhD); non-profit management (Certificate); public administration (MPA); public affairs (PhD); public management (Certificate); urban leadership (MA). *Program availability:* Part-time. *Faculty:* 14 full-time (6 women), 11 part-time/adjunct (4 women). *Students:* 61 full-time (33 women), 113 part-time (74 women); includes 95 minority (29 Black or African American, non-Hispanic/Latino; 1 American Indian or Alaska Native, non-Hispanic/Latino; 9 Asian, non-Hispanic/Latino; 41 Hispanic/Latino; 3 Native Hawaiian or other Pacific Islander, non-Hispanic/Latino; 12 Two or more races, non-Hispanic/Latino), 2 international. Average age 37. 96 applicants, 68% accepted, 55 enrolled. In 2018, 59 master's, 6 doctorates, 19 other advanced degrees awarded. *Degree requirements:* For master's, comprehensive exam (for some programs), thesis (for some programs), oral exam; for doctorate, comprehensive exam, thesis/dissertation; for Certificate, portfolio. *Entrance requirements:* For master's, GRE General Test or GMAT, bachelor's degree with minimum GPA 2.75; statement of purpose; 3 letters of recommendation; for doctorate, GRE General Test, master's degree with minimum GPA of 3.5; 3 letters of recommendation; statement of purpose; writing sample; personal interview; for Certificate, bachelor's degree; 2 letters of recommendation; writing sample. Additional exam requirements/recommendations for international students: Required—TOEFL (minimum score 550 paper-based; 80 iBT), IELTS (minimum score 7). *Application deadline:* For fall admission, 6/1 for domestic and international students; for spring admission, 11/1 for domestic and international students; for summer admission, 3/1 for domestic students. Application fee: $60 ($95 for international students). Electronic applications accepted. *Expenses:* Contact institution. *Financial support:* In 2018–19, 23 students received support, including 8 research assistantships with full tuition reimbursements available (averaging $16,719 per year), 15 teaching assistantships with full tuition reimbursements available (averaging $13,500 per year); institutionally sponsored loans, scholarships/grants, health care benefits, and unspecified assistantships also available. Financial award application deadline: 3/15; financial award applicants required to submit FAFSA. *Total annual research expenditures:* $109,177. *Unit head:* Dr. Christopher Stream, Director, 702-895-5120, Fax: 702-895-4436, E-mail: sppl.chair@unlv.edu. *Application contact:* Dr. Jayce Farmer, Graduate Coordinator, 702-895-4828, E-mail: sppl.gradcoord@unlv.edu.
Website: https://www.unlv.edu/publicpolicy

University of Nevada, Reno, Graduate School, College of Agriculture, Biotechnology and Natural Resources, Department of Natural Resources and Environmental Science, Reno, NV 89557. Offers MS. *Degree requirements:* For master's, thesis optional. *Entrance requirements:* For master's, GRE, minimum GPA of 2.75. Additional exam requirements/recommendations for international students: Required—TOEFL (minimum score 500 paper-based; 61 iBT), IELTS (minimum score 6). Electronic applications accepted. *Faculty research:* Range management, plant physiology, remote sensing, soils, wildlife.

University of Nevada, Reno, Graduate School, Interdisciplinary Program in Environmental Sciences and Health, Reno, NV 89557. Offers MS, PhD. Terminal master's awarded for partial completion of doctoral program. *Degree requirements:* For master's, thesis; for doctorate, thesis/dissertation. *Entrance requirements:* For master's, GRE General Test, minimum GPA of 2.75; for doctorate, GRE General Test, minimum GPA of 3.0. Additional exam requirements/recommendations for international students: Required—TOEFL (minimum score 500 paper-based; 61 iBT), IELTS (minimum score 6). Electronic applications accepted. *Faculty research:* Environmental chemistry, environmental toxicology, ecological toxicology.

University of New Haven, Graduate School, College of Arts and Sciences, Program in Environmental Science, West Haven, CT 06516. Offers environmental ecology (MS); environmental geoscience (MS); environmental health and management (MS); environmental science (MS); geographical information systems (MS). *Program availability:* Part-time, evening/weekend. *Students:* 14 full-time (8 women), 13 part-time (6 women); includes 7 minority (3 Black or African American, non-Hispanic/Latino; 3 Hispanic/Latino; 1 Native Hawaiian or other Pacific Islander, non-Hispanic/Latino), 4 international. Average age 29. 59 applicants, 86% accepted, 10 enrolled. In 2018, 17 master's awarded. *Entrance requirements:* Additional exam requirements/recommendations for international students: Required—TOEFL (minimum score 80 iBT), IELTS, PTE. *Application deadline:* Applications are processed on a rolling basis. Application fee: $50. Electronic applications accepted. Application fee is waived when completed online. *Expenses: Tuition:* Full-time $16,470; part-time $915 per credit hour. *Required fees:* $230; $95 per term. *Financial support:* Research assistantships with partial tuition reimbursements, teaching assistantships with partial tuition reimbursements, Federal Work-Study, scholarships/grants, and unspecified assistantships available. Support available to part-time students. Financial award applicants required to submit FAFSA. *Unit head:* Dr. Roman Zajac, Professor, 203-932-7114, E-mail: rzajac@newhaven.edu. *Application contact:* Selina O'Toole, Senior Associate Director of Graduate Admissions, 203-932-7337, E-mail: SOToole@newhaven.edu.
Website: https://www.newhaven.edu/arts-sciences/graduate-programs/environmental-science/

University of New Orleans, Graduate School, College of Sciences, Department of Earth and Environmental Sciences, New Orleans, LA 70148. Offers MS, PhD. *Program availability:* Evening/weekend. *Degree requirements:* For master's, thesis. *Entrance requirements:* For master's, GRE General Test. Additional exam requirements/recommendations for international students: Required—TOEFL (minimum score 550 paper-based; 79 iBT), IELTS. Electronic applications accepted. *Faculty research:* Continental margin structure and seismology, tectonics at convergent plate margins, continental shelf sediment stability, early diagenesis of carbonates.

The University of North Carolina at Chapel Hill, Graduate School, Gillings School of Global Public Health, Department of Environmental Sciences and Engineering, Chapel Hill, NC 27599-7431. Offers environmental engineering (MPH, MS, MSEE, MSPH); environmental health sciences (MPH, MS, MSPH, PhD); MPH/MCRP; MS/MCRP; MSPH/MCRP. *Faculty:* 26 full-time (10 women), 36 part-time/adjunct (10 women). *Students:* 72 full-time (46 women), 25 part-time (14 women); includes 13 minority (3 Black or African American, non-Hispanic/Latino; 3 Asian, non-Hispanic/Latino; 3 Hispanic/Latino; 4 Two or more races, non-Hispanic/Latino), 16 international. Average age 29. 150 applicants, 43% accepted, 33 enrolled. In 2018, 25 master's, 6 doctorates awarded. Terminal master's awarded for partial completion of doctoral program. *Degree requirements:* For master's, comprehensive exam, thesis (for some programs), research paper; for doctorate, comprehensive exam, thesis/dissertation. *Entrance requirements:* For master's and doctorate, GRE General Test, 3 letters of recommendation (academic and/or professional; at least one academic). Additional exam requirements/recommendations for international students: Required—TOEFL (minimum score 90 iBT), IELTS (minimum score 7). *Application deadline:* For fall admission, 4/9 for domestic and international students. Application fee: $90. Electronic applications accepted. *Financial support:* Fellowships with tuition reimbursements, research assistantships with tuition reimbursements, teaching assistantships with tuition reimbursements, career-related internships or fieldwork, Federal Work-Study, scholarships/grants, traineeships, health care benefits, and unspecified assistantships available. Support available to part-time students. Financial award application deadline: 12/10; financial award applicants required to submit FAFSA. *Faculty research:* Air, radiation and industrial hygiene, aquatic and atmospheric sciences, environmental health sciences, environmental management and policy, water resources engineering. *Unit head:* Dr. Barbara J. Turpin, Professor and Chair, 919-966-1024, Fax: 919-966-7911, E-mail: esechair@unc.edu. *Application contact:* Adia Ware, Academic Coordinator, 919-966-3844, Fax: 919-966-7911, E-mail: aware@unc.edu.
Website: https://sph.unc.edu/envr/environmental-sciences-and-engineering-home/

The University of North Carolina Wilmington, College of Arts and Sciences, Department of Environmental Sciences, Wilmington, NC 28403-3297. Offers environmental studies (MS). *Program availability:* Part-time. *Degree requirements:* For master's, final project or practicum. *Entrance requirements:* For master's, GRE General Test, 3 letters of recommendation, essay. Additional exam requirements/recommendations for international students: Required—TOEFL (minimum score 550 paper-based; 79 iBT), IELTS (minimum score 6.5). Electronic applications accepted. *Faculty research:* Coastal management, environmental management, environmental education, environmental law, natural resource management.

University of North Texas, Toulouse Graduate School, Denton, TX 76203-5459. Offers accounting (MS); applied anthropology (MA, MS); applied behavior analysis

(Certificate); applied geography (MA); applied technology and performance improvement (M Ed, MS); art education (MA); art history (MA); arts leadership (Certificate); audiology (Au D); behavior analysis (MS); behavioral science (PhD); biochemistry and molecular biology (MS); biology (MA, MS); biomedical engineering (MS); business analysis (MS); chemistry (MS); clinical health psychology (PhD); communication studies (MA, MS); computer engineering (MS); computer science (MS); counseling (M Ed, MS), including clinical mental health counseling (MS), college and university counseling, elementary school counseling, secondary school counseling; creative writing (MA); criminal justice (MS); curriculum and instruction (M Ed); decision sciences (MBA); design (MA, MFA), including fashion design (MFA), innovation studies, interior design (MFA); early childhood studies (MS); economics (MS); educational leadership (M Ed, Ed D); educational psychology (MS, PhD), including family studies (MS), gifted and talented (MS), human development (MS), learning and cognition (MS), research, measurement and evaluation (MS); electrical engineering (MS); emergency management (MPA); engineering technology (MS); English (MA); English as a second language (MA); environmental science (MS); finance (MBA, MS); financial management (MPA); French (MA); health services management (MBA); higher education (M Ed, Ed D); history (MA, MS); hospitality management (MS); human resources management (MPA); information science (MS); information systems (PhD); information technologies (MBA); interdisciplinary studies (MA, MS); international studies (MA); international sustainable tourism (MS); jazz studies (MM); journalism (MA, MJ, Graduate Certificate), including interactive and virtual digital communication (Graduate Certificate), narrative journalism (Graduate Certificate), public relations (Graduate Certificate); kinesiology (MS); linguistics (MA); local government management (MPA); logistics (PhD); logistics and supply chain management (MBA); long-term care, senior housing, and aging services (MA); management (PhD); marketing (MBA); mathematics (MA, MS); mechanical and energy engineering (MS, PhD); music (MA), including ethnomusicology, music theory, musicology, performance; music composition (PhD); music education (MM Ed, PhD); nonprofit management (MPA); operations and supply chain management (MBA); performance (MM, DMA); philosophy (MA); political science (MA); professional and technical communication (MA); radio, television and film (MA, MFA); rehabilitation counseling (Certificate); sociology (MA); Spanish (MA); special education (M Ed); speech-language pathology (MA); strategic management (MBA); studio art (MFA); teaching (M Ed); MBA/MS. *Program availability:* Part-time, evening/weekend, online learning. Terminal master's awarded for partial completion of doctoral program. *Degree requirements:* For master's, variable foreign language requirement, comprehensive exam (for some programs), thesis (for some programs); for doctorate, variable foreign language requirement, comprehensive exam (for some programs), thesis/dissertation; for other advanced degree, variable foreign language requirement, comprehensive exam (for some programs). *Entrance requirements:* For master's and doctorate, GRE, GMAT. Additional exam requirements/recommendations for international students: Required—TOEFL (minimum score 550 paper-based; 79 iBT). Electronic applications accepted.

University of Oklahoma, Gallogly College of Engineering, School of Civil Engineering and Environmental Science, Norman, OK 73019-0390. Offers civil engineering (MS, PhD), including civil engineering; environmental engineering (MS, PhD); environmental science (M Env Sc, PhD), including environmental science. *Program availability:* Part-time. *Faculty:* 24 full-time (4 women), 3 part-time/adjunct (2 women). *Students:* 33 full-time (11 women), 61 part-time (22 women); includes 21 minority (6 Black or African American, non-Hispanic/Latino; 2 American Indian or Alaska Native, non-Hispanic/Latino; 2 Asian, non-Hispanic/Latino; 7 Hispanic/Latino; 4 Two or more races, non-Hispanic/Latino), 27 international. Average age 30. 154 applicants, 68% accepted, 52 enrolled. In 2018, 9 master's, 4 doctorates awarded. Terminal master's awarded for partial completion of doctoral program. *Degree requirements:* For master's, thesis; for doctorate, comprehensive exam, thesis/dissertation, general exam. *Entrance requirements:* For master's and doctorate, GRE. Additional exam requirements/recommendations for international students: Required—TOEFL (minimum score 79 iBT) or IELTS (minimum score 6.5). *Application deadline:* For fall admission, 1/15 for domestic and international students; for spring admission, 5/15 for domestic and international students. Application fee: $50 ($100 for international students). Electronic applications accepted. *Expenses:* Tuition, state resident: full-time $5683.20; part-time $236.80 per credit hour. Tuition, nonresident: full-time $20,342; part-time $847.60 per credit hour. *International tuition:* $20,342.40 full-time. *Required fees:* $2894.20; $110.05 per credit hour. $126.50 per semester. Tuition and fees vary according to course load and program. *Financial support:* Fellowships, research assistantships, teaching assistantships, and scholarships/grants available. Financial award application deadline: 6/1; financial award applicants required to submit FAFSA. *Faculty research:* Intelligent structures, composites, earthquake engineering, intelligent compaction, bridge engineering. *Unit head:* Dr. Randall Kolar, Director, 405-325-4267, Fax: 405-325-4217, E-mail: kolar@ou.edu. *Application contact:* Graduate Studies Coordinator, 405-325-2344, Fax: 405-325-4217, E-mail: ceesgradstudies@ou.edu.
Website: http://www.ou.edu/coe/cees.html

University of Pennsylvania, School of Arts and Sciences, Graduate Group in Earth and Environmental Science, Philadelphia, PA 19104. Offers MS, PhD. *Program availability:* Part-time. *Faculty:* 10 full-time (3 women), 2 part-time/adjunct (0 women). *Students:* 13 full-time (4 women); includes 6 minority (2 Black or African American, non-Hispanic/Latino; 4 Two or more races, non-Hispanic/Latino), 2 international. Average age 27. 57 applicants, 18% accepted, 2 enrolled. In 2018, 1 doctorate awarded. Application fee: $80.
Website: http://www.sas.upenn.edu/graduate-division

University of Pittsburgh, Kenneth P. Dietrich School of Arts and Sciences, Department of Geology and Environmental Science, Pittsburgh, PA 15260. Offers geographical information systems and remote sensing (Pro-MS); geology and environmental science (MS, PhD). *Program availability:* Part-time. *Degree requirements:* For master's, comprehensive exam, thesis; for doctorate, comprehensive exam, thesis/dissertation. *Entrance requirements:* For master's and doctorate, GRE. Additional exam requirements/recommendations for international students: Required—TOEFL (minimum score 100 iBT); Recommended—IELTS (minimum score 7). Electronic applications accepted. *Expenses:* Contact institution. *Faculty research:* Volcanology; sedimentary geology; geochemistry; hydrology; geophysics; geomorphology; remote sensing.

University of Prince Edward Island, Faculty of Science, Charlottetown, PE C1A 4P3, Canada. Offers environmental sciences (M Sc, PhD); human biology (M Sc); molecular and macromolecular sciences (M Sc, PhD); sustainable design engineering (M Sc). *Degree requirements:* For master's, thesis. *Entrance requirements:* Additional exam requirements/recommendations for international students: Required—TOEFL (minimum score 550 paper-based, 80 iBT), Canadian Academic English Language Assessment, Michigan English Language Assessment Battery, Canadian Test of English for Scholars and Trainees. *Faculty research:* Ecology and wildlife biology, molecular, genetics and biotechnology, organometallic, bio-organic, supramolecular and synthetic organic chemistry, neurobiology and stoke materials science.

University of Puerto Rico–Mayagüez, Graduate Studies, College of Arts and Sciences, Department of Chemistry, Mayagüez, PR 00681-9000. Offers applied chemistry (MS, PhD), including biophysical chemistry (PhD), chemistry of materials (PhD), environmental chemistry (PhD). *Program availability:* Part-time. Terminal master's awarded for partial completion of doctoral program. *Degree requirements:* For master's, one foreign language, comprehensive exam, thesis; for doctorate, one foreign language, comprehensive exam, thesis/dissertation. *Entrance requirements:* For master's, GRE General Test or minimum GPA of 2.0, BS in chemistry or the equivalent; minimum GPA of 2.8; for doctorate, GRE General Test or minimum GPA of 2.0. Electronic applications accepted. *Faculty research:* Synthesis of heterocyclic moieties, protein structure and function, chemistry of explosives, bio-nanocomposites, process analytical technology.

University of Puerto Rico–Río Piedras, College of Natural Sciences, Department of Environmental Sciences, San Juan, PR 00931-3300. Offers MS, PhD.

University of Rhode Island, Graduate School, College of the Environment and Life Sciences, Department of Biological Sciences, Kingston, RI 02881. Offers cell and molecular biology (MS, PhD); earth and environmental sciences (MS, PhD); ecology and ecosystem sciences (MS, PhD); evolutionary and marine biology (MS, PhD); sustainable agriculture and food systems (MS, PhD). *Program availability:* Part-time. *Faculty:* 20 full-time (10 women). *Students:* 105 full-time (65 women), 7 part-time (3 women); includes 10 minority (4 Black or African American, non-Hispanic/Latino; 3 Asian, non-Hispanic/Latino; 2 Hispanic/Latino; 1 Two or more races, non-Hispanic/Latino), 23 international. 121 applicants, 31% accepted, 28 enrolled. In 2018, 17 master's, 11 doctorates awarded. *Entrance requirements:* Additional exam requirements/recommendations for international students: Required—TOEFL. *Application deadline:* For fall admission, 1/15 for domestic and international students. Application fee: $65. Electronic applications accepted. *Expenses: Tuition, area resident:* Full-time $13,226; part-time $735 per credit. Tuition, state resident: full-time $13,226; part-time $735 per credit. Tuition, nonresident: full-time $25,854; part-time $1436 per credit. *International tuition:* $25,854 full-time. *Required fees:* $1698; $50 per credit. $35 per semester. One-time fee: $165. *Financial support:* In 2018–19, 11 research assistantships with tuition reimbursements (averaging $10,985 per year) were awarded. Financial award application deadline: 1/15; financial award applicants required to submit FAFSA. *Faculty research:* Physiological constraints on predators in the Antarctic, effects of CO2 absorption in salt water particularly as it impacts pteropods. *Unit head:* Dr. Evan Preisser, Chair, 401-874-2120, E-mail: preisser@uri.edu. *Application contact:* Dr. Evan Preisser, Chair, 401-874-2120, E-mail: preisser@uri.edu.
Website: http://web.uri.edu/bio/

University of Rhode Island, Graduate School, College of the Environment and Life Sciences, Department of Fisheries, Animal and Veterinary Sciences, Kingston, RI 02881. Offers animal health and disease (MS); animal science (MS); aquaculture (MS); aquatic pathology (MS); environmental sciences (PhD), including animal science, aquaculture science, aquatic pathology, fisheries science; fisheries (MS). *Faculty:* 12 full-time (7 women). *Entrance requirements:* Additional exam requirements/recommendations for international students: Required—TOEFL. *Application deadline:* For fall admission, 7/15 for domestic students, 2/1 for international students; for spring admission, 11/15 for domestic students, 7/15 for international students. Application fee: $65. Electronic applications accepted. *Expenses: Tuition, area resident:* Full-time $13,226; part-time $735 per credit. Tuition, state resident: full-time $13,226; part-time $735 per credit. Tuition, nonresident: full-time $25,854; part-time $1436 per credit. *International tuition:* $25,854 full-time. *Required fees:* $1698; $50 per credit. $35 per semester. One-time fee: $165. *Financial support:* Application deadline: 2/1; applicants required to submit FAFSA. *Unit head:* Dr. Marta Gomez-Chiarri, Chair, 401-874-2917, Fax: 401-874-7575, E-mail: gomezchi@uri.edu. *Application contact:* Dr. Marta Gomez-Chiarri, Chair, 401-874-2917, Fax: 401-874-7575, E-mail: gomezchi@uri.edu.
Website: http://web.uri.edu/favs/

University of San Diego, College of Arts and Sciences, Environmental and Ocean Sciences Program, San Diego, CA 92110-2492. Offers MS. *Program availability:* Part-time. *Faculty:* 6 full-time (3 women), 1 part-time/adjunct (0 women). *Students:* 5 full-time (all women), 13 part-time (10 women); includes 4 minority (2 Asian, non-Hispanic/Latino; 2 Two or more races, non-Hispanic/Latino), 1 international. Average age 27. 17 applicants, 41% accepted, 4 enrolled. In 2018, 6 master's awarded. *Degree requirements:* For master's, thesis. *Entrance requirements:* For master's, GRE General Test, minimum GPA of 3.0; 1 semester each of biology with lab, physics with lab, and calculus; 1 year of chemistry with lab. Additional exam requirements/recommendations for international students: Required—TOEFL (minimum score 580 paper-based; 83 iBT), TWE. *Application deadline:* For fall admission, 4/1 for domestic and international students. Applications are processed on a rolling basis. Application fee: $45. Electronic applications accepted. *Financial support:* In 2018–19, 12 students received support. Teaching assistantships, career-related internships or fieldwork, Federal Work-Study, institutionally sponsored loans, scholarships/grants, and unspecified assistantships available. Support available to part-time students. Financial award application deadline: 4/1; financial award applicants required to submit FAFSA. *Faculty research:* Marine biology and ecology, environmental geology and geochemistry, climatology and geomorphology, physiological ecology, fisheries and aquaculture. *Unit head:* Dr. Ronald S. Kaufmann, Director, 619-260-4795, Fax: 619-260-6874, E-mail: soroya@sandiego.edu. *Application contact:* Erika Garwood, Associate Director of Graduate Admissions, 619-260-4524, Fax: 619-260-4158, E-mail: grads@sandiego.edu.
Website: http://www.sandiego.edu/cas/ms-environmental-ocean-sciences/

University of Saskatchewan, College of Graduate and Postdoctoral Studies, School of Environment and Sustainability, Saskatoon, SK S7N 5A2, Canada. Offers MES, PhD.

University of South Africa, College of Agriculture and Environmental Sciences, Pretoria, South Africa. Offers agriculture (MS); consumer science (MCS); environmental management (MA, MS, PhD); environmental science (MA, MS, PhD); geography (MA, MS, PhD); horticulture (M Tech); human ecology (MHE); life sciences (MS); nature conservation (M Tech).

University of South Florida, College of Arts and Sciences, School of Geosciences, Tampa, FL 33620-9951. Offers environmental science and policy (MS); geography (MA), including environmental geography, geographic information science and spatial analysis, human geography; geography and environmental science and policy (PhD); geology (MS, PhD). *Program availability:* Part-time, evening/weekend. *Faculty:* 33 full-time (6 women). *Students:* 93 full-time (43 women), 48 part-time (23 women); includes 24 minority (8 Black or African American, non-Hispanic/Latino; 6 Asian, non-Hispanic/Latino; 5 Hispanic/Latino; 5 Two or more races, non-Hispanic/Latino), 42 international. Average age 31. 107 applicants, 50% accepted, 23 enrolled. In 2018, 14 master's, 11 doctorates awarded. *Degree requirements:* For master's, comprehensive exam, thesis (for some programs); for doctorate, comprehensive exam, thesis/dissertation. *Entrance requirements:* For master's, GRE General Test, minimum GPA of 3.0, letter of intent, 3 letters of recommendation; for doctorate, GRE General Test, master's in geography, environmental science and policy or related field; GPA of at least 3.2 in graduate credits; letter of intent; 3 letters of recommendation. Additional exam requirements/

recommendations for international students: Required—TOEFL, TOEFL minimum score 550 paper-based; 79 iBT or IELTS minimum score 6.5 (for MA and MURP); TOEFL minimum score 600 paper-based (for MS and PhD). *Application deadline:* For fall admission, 2/15 priority date for domestic students, 2/15 for international students; for spring admission, 10/15 priority date for domestic students, 9/15 for international students; for summer admission, 2/15 priority date for domestic students, 1/15 for international students. Application fee: $30. Electronic applications accepted. *Expenses:* Tuition, state resident: full-time $6350. Tuition, nonresident: full-time $19,048. *International tuition:* $19,048 full-time. *Required fees:* $2079. *Financial support:* In 2018–19, 45 students received support, including 3 research assistantships (averaging $12,345 per year), 25 teaching assistantships with tuition reimbursements available (averaging $12,807 per year); unspecified assistantships also available. Financial award application deadline: 3/1. *Faculty research:* Geography: human geography, environmental geography, geographic information science and spatial analysis, urban geography, social theory; environmental science, policy, and planning: water resources, wildlife ecology, Karst and wetland environments, natural hazards, soil contamination, meteorology and climatology, environmental sustainability and policy, urban and regional planning. *Total annual research expenditures:* $3 million. *Unit head:* Dr. Mark Rains, Professor and Chair, 813-974-3310, Fax: 813-974-5911, E-mail: mrains@usf.edu. *Application contact:* Dr. Ruiliang Pu, Associate Professor and Graduate Program Coordinator, 813-974-1508, Fax: 813-974-5911, E-mail: rpu@usf.edu.
Website: http://hennarot.forest.usf.edu/main/depts/geosci/

University of South Florida, St. Petersburg, College of Arts and Sciences, St. Petersburg, FL 33701. Offers digital journalism and design (MA); environmental science and policy (MA, MS); Florida studies (MLA); journalism and media studies (MA); liberal studies (MLA); psychology (MA). *Program availability:* Part-time, online learning. *Degree requirements:* For master's, comprehensive exam, thesis or project. *Entrance requirements:* For master's, GRE, LSAT, MCAT (varies by program), letter of intent, 3 letters of recommendation, writing samples, bachelor's degree from regionally-accredited institution with minimum GPA of 3.0 overall or in upper two years. Additional exam requirements/recommendations for international students: Required—TOEFL (minimum score 550 paper-based; 79 iBT); Recommended—IELTS. Electronic applications accepted.

The University of Tennessee at Chattanooga, Program in Environmental Science, Chattanooga, TN 37403. Offers MS. *Program availability:* Part-time. *Degree requirements:* For master's, internship or thesis. *Entrance requirements:* For master's, GRE General Test, minimum undergraduate GPA of 2.75 or 3.0 for last 60 credit hours. Additional exam requirements/recommendations for international students: Required—TOEFL (minimum score 550 paper-based; 79 iBT), IELTS (minimum score 6). Electronic applications accepted. *Expenses:* Contact institution. *Faculty research:* Bioremediation, stream fish ecology and conservation, environmental law and policy, avian conservation and management.

The University of Texas at Arlington, Graduate School, College of Science, Department of Earth and Environmental Sciences, Arlington, TX 76019. Offers MS, PhD. *Program availability:* Part-time, evening/weekend. Terminal master's awarded for partial completion of doctoral program. *Degree requirements:* For master's, thesis optional; for doctorate, comprehensive exam, thesis/dissertation. *Entrance requirements:* For master's, GRE General Test. Additional exam requirements/recommendations for international students: Required—TOEFL (minimum score 550 paper-based). Electronic applications accepted. *Faculty research:* Hydrology, aqueous geochemistry, biostratigraphy, structural geology, petroleum geology.

The University of Texas at El Paso, Graduate School, College of Engineering, Department of Mechanical Engineering, El Paso, TX 79968-0001. Offers environmental science and engineering (PhD); mechanical engineering (MS). *Program availability:* Part-time. *Degree requirements:* For master's, thesis optional; for doctorate, thesis/dissertation. *Entrance requirements:* For master's, GRE, minimum GPA of 3.0, letter of reference; for doctorate, GRE, minimum GPA of 3.5, letters of reference, BS or equivalent. Additional exam requirements/recommendations for international students: Required—TOEFL; Recommended—IELTS. Electronic applications accepted. *Faculty research:* Aerospace, energy, combustion and propulsion, design engineering, high temperature materials.

The University of Texas at San Antonio, College of Engineering, Department of Civil and Environmental Engineering, San Antonio, TX 78249-0617. Offers civil engineering (MCE, MSCE); environmental science and engineering (PhD). *Program availability:* Part-time. *Degree requirements:* For master's, comprehensive exam, thesis (for some programs); for doctorate, comprehensive exam, thesis/dissertation, written qualifying exam, dissertation proposal. *Entrance requirements:* For master's, GRE General Test, BS in civil engineering or related field from accredited institution, statement of research/specialization interest, recommendation by the Civil Engineering Master's Program Admissions Committee; for doctorate, GRE, BS and MS from accredited institution, minimum GPA of 3.0 in upper-division and graduate courses, three letters of recommendation, letter of research interest, resume/curriculum vitae. Additional exam requirements/recommendations for international students: Required—TOEFL (minimum score 550 paper-based; 79 iBT), IELTS (minimum score 6.5). Electronic applications accepted. *Expenses:* Contact institution. *Faculty research:* Structures, application of geographic information systems in water resources, geotechnical engineering, pavement traffic loading, hydrogeology.

The University of Texas at San Antonio, College of Sciences, Department of Environmental Science and Ecology, San Antonio, TX 78249-0617. Offers MS. *Entrance requirements:* For master's, GRE, bachelor's degree in biology, ecology, environmental science, chemistry, geology, engineering, or some other related scientific discipline; one semester each of general statistics, organic chemistry, and environmental science or ecology; undergraduate transcripts; resume; two recommendation letters; statement of purpose. Additional exam requirements/recommendations for international students: Required—TOEFL (minimum score 550 paper-based; 79 iBT), IELTS (minimum score 6.5). Electronic applications accepted. *Faculty research:* Conservation biology, environmental chemistry and toxicology, freshwater ecology, natural resource policy and administration, river restoration.

The University of Texas at San Antonio, College of Sciences, Department of Geological Sciences, San Antonio, TX 78249-0617. Offers MS. *Program availability:* Part-time. *Degree requirements:* For master's, comprehensive exam, thesis (for some programs). *Entrance requirements:* For master's, GRE General Test, three letters of recommendation, statement of research interest, undergraduate transcripts. Additional exam requirements/recommendations for international students: Required—TOEFL (minimum score 550 paper-based; 79 iBT), IELTS (minimum score 6.5). Electronic applications accepted. *Faculty research:* Hydrogeology, sedimentary and stratigraphy, structure, paleontology, geographic information science.

The University of Texas Rio Grande Valley, College of Sciences, School of Earth, Environmental, and Marine Sciences, Edinburg, TX 78539. Offers agricultural, environmental, and sustainability sciences (MS); ocean, coastal, and earth sciences (MS). *Expenses: Tuition, area resident:* Full-time $6888. Tuition, state resident: full-time $6888. Tuition, nonresident: full-time $14,484. *International tuition:* $14,484 full-time. *Required fees:* $1468.

University of the Virgin Islands, College of Science and Mathematics, St. Thomas, VI 00802. Offers marine and environmental science (MS); mathematics for secondary teachers (MA). *Faculty:* 5 full-time (4 women), 7 part-time/adjunct (2 women). *Students:* 16 full-time (13 women), 19 part-time (13 women); includes 10 minority (4 Black or African American, non-Hispanic/Latino; 1 American Indian or Alaska Native, non-Hispanic/Latino; 2 Hispanic/Latino; 1 Native Hawaiian or other Pacific Islander, non-Hispanic/Latino; 2 Two or more races, non-Hispanic/Latino), 1 international. Average age 27. In 2018, 8 master's awarded. *Degree requirements:* For master's, comprehensive exam, thesis. *Entrance requirements:* For master's, GRE, minimum GPA of 2.5. Additional exam requirements/recommendations for international students: Required—TOEFL (minimum score 550 paper-based). *Application deadline:* For fall admission, 4/30 for domestic and international students; for spring admission, 10/30 for domestic and international students. Application fee: $30. Electronic applications accepted. *Expenses:* Tuition, state resident: full-time $6948; part-time $386 per credit. Tuition, nonresident: full-time $13,230; part-time $735 per credit. *International tuition:* $13,230 full-time. *Required fees:* $508. *Financial support:* Fellowships, research assistantships, teaching assistantships, career-related internships or fieldwork, and scholarships/grants available. Financial award application deadline: 4/15; financial award applicants required to submit FAFSA. *Unit head:* Dr. Sandra Romano, Dean, 340-693-1230, Fax: 340-693-1245, E-mail: sromano@uvi.edu. *Application contact:* Charmaine Smith, Director of Admissions, 340-690-4070, E-mail: csmith@uvi.edu.

The University of Toledo, College of Graduate Studies, College of Natural Sciences and Mathematics, Department of Environmental Sciences, Toledo, OH 43606-3390. Offers biology (MS, PhD), including ecology; geology (MS), including earth surface processes. *Program availability:* Part-time. *Degree requirements:* For master's, thesis or alternative. *Entrance requirements:* For master's, GRE General Test, minimum cumulative point-hour ratio of 2.7 for all previous academic work, three letters of recommendation, statement of purpose, transcripts from all prior institutions attended. Additional exam requirements/recommendations for international students: Required—TOEFL (minimum score 550 paper-based; 80 iBT). Electronic applications accepted. *Faculty research:* Environmental geochemistry, geophysics, petrology and mineralogy, paleontology, geohydrology.

University of Toronto, School of Graduate Studies, Department of Physical and Environmental Sciences, Toronto, ON M5S 1A1, Canada. Offers environmental science (M Env Sc, PhD). *Entrance requirements:* For master's, bachelor's degree (B Sc or B Eng), minimum B average in last two years of undergraduate program, two half-courses or one full-course each in chemistry, physics, calculus and biology. Additional exam requirements/recommendations for international students: Required—TOEFL (minimum score 580 paper-based; 93 iBT), TWE (minimum score 4). Electronic applications accepted.

University of Utah, Graduate School, Professional Master of Science and Technology Program, Salt Lake City, UT 84112-9016. Offers biotechnology (PSM); computational science (PSM); environmental science (PSM); science instrumentation (PSM). *Program availability:* Part-time. *Degree requirements:* For master's, professional experience project (internship). *Entrance requirements:* For master's, GRE (recommended), minimum undergraduate GPA of 3.0, bachelor's degree from accredited university or college. Additional exam requirements/recommendations for international students: Required—TOEFL (minimum score 550 paper-based; 80 iBT), IELTS (minimum score 6.5). Electronic applications accepted. *Expenses:* Contact institution.

University of Vermont, Graduate College, College of Agriculture and Life Sciences, Field Naturalist Program, Burlington, VT 05405. Offers plant biology (MS), including field naturalist. *Degree requirements:* For master's, thesis, final exam, project. *Entrance requirements:* For master's, GRE General Test, interview. Additional exam requirements/recommendations for international students: Required—TOEFL (minimum score 550 paper-based, 90 iBT) or IELTS (6.5). Electronic applications accepted. *Faculty research:* Integrative field science, environmental problem-solving.

University of Virginia, College and Graduate School of Arts and Sciences, Department of Environmental Sciences, Charlottesville, VA 22903. Offers MA, MS, PhD. *Degree requirements:* For master's, thesis; for doctorate, comprehensive exam, thesis/dissertation. *Entrance requirements:* For master's and doctorate, GRE General Test, 2 letters of recommendation. Additional exam requirements/recommendations for international students: Required—TOEFL (minimum score 600 paper-based; 90 iBT), IELTS (minimum score 7). Electronic applications accepted.

University of Waterloo, Graduate Studies and Postdoctoral Affairs, Faculty of Science, Department of Earth and Environmental Sciences, Waterloo, ON N2L 3G1, Canada. Offers M Sc, PhD. *Program availability:* Part-time. *Degree requirements:* For master's, research paper or thesis; for doctorate, comprehensive exam, thesis/dissertation. *Entrance requirements:* For master's, GRE, honors degree, minimum B average; for doctorate, GRE, master's degree, minimum B average. Additional exam requirements/recommendations for international students: Required—TOEFL, IELTS, PTE. *Application deadline:* Applications are processed on a rolling basis. Application fee: $125 Canadian dollars. Electronic applications accepted. *Financial support:* Research assistantships, teaching assistantships, career-related internships or fieldwork, and institutionally sponsored loans available. *Faculty research:* Environmental geology, soil physics.
Website: https://uwaterloo.ca/earth-environmental-sciences/

The University of Western Ontario, School of Graduate and Postdoctoral Studies, Faculty of Science, Department of Earth Sciences, London, ON N6A 3K7, Canada. Offers environment and sustainability (MES); geology (M Sc, PhD); geology and environmental science (M Sc, PhD); geophysics (M Sc, PhD); geophysics and environmental science (M Sc, PhD). *Degree requirements:* For master's, thesis; for doctorate, thesis/dissertation, qualifying exam. *Entrance requirements:* For master's, honors in B Sc; for doctorate, M Sc. Additional exam requirements/recommendations for international students: Required—TOEFL. *Faculty research:* Geophysics, geochemistry, paleontology, sedimentology/stratigraphy, glaciology/quaternary.

University of West Florida, Hal Marcus College of Science and Engineering, Department of Earth and Environmental Sciences, Pensacola, FL 32514-5750. Offers environmental science (MS); geographic information science administration (MS). *Program availability:* Part-time. *Entrance requirements:* For master's, GRE (minimum score: 50th percentile for verbal; 40th percentile for quantitative), official transcripts; formal letter of interest, background, and professional goals; three letters of recommendation by individuals in professionally-relevant fields (waived for graduates of UWF Department of Environmental Sciences); current curriculum vitae/resume. Additional exam requirements/recommendations for international students: Required—TOEFL (minimum score 550 paper-based).

University of Windsor, Faculty of Graduate Studies, GLIER-Great Lakes Institute for Environmental Research, Windsor, ON N9B 3P4, Canada. Offers environmental science (M Sc, PhD). *Degree requirements:* For master's, thesis; for doctorate, thesis/dissertation. *Entrance requirements:* For master's, minimum B+ average; for doctorate, M Sc degree, minimum B+ average. Additional exam requirements/recommendations for international students: Required—TOEFL (minimum score 560 paper-based). Electronic applications accepted. *Faculty research:* Environmental chemistry and toxicology, conservation and resource management, iron formation geochemistry.

University of Wisconsin–Green Bay, Graduate Studies, Program in Environmental Science and Policy, Green Bay, WI 54311-7001. Offers MS. *Program availability:* Part-time. *Degree requirements:* For master's, thesis or alternative. *Entrance requirements:* For master's, GRE General Test, minimum GPA of 3.0. Electronic applications accepted. *Faculty research:* Bald eagle, parasitic population of domestic and wild animals, resource recovery, anaerobic digestion of organic waste.

University of Wisconsin–Madison, Graduate School, College of Engineering, Department of Civil and Environmental Engineering, Madison, WI 53706-1380. Offers construction engineering and management (MS); environmental science and engineering (MS); geological/geotechnical engineering (MS); structural engineering (MS); transportation engineering (MS); water resources engineering (MS). *Program availability:* Part-time. *Faculty:* 31 full-time (8 women). *Students:* 97 full-time (28 women), 39 part-time (15 women); includes 12 minority (2 Black or African American, non-Hispanic/Latino; 3 Asian, non-Hispanic/Latino; 6 Hispanic/Latino; 1 Two or more races, non-Hispanic/Latino), 62 international. Average age 28. 261 applicants, 45% accepted, 29 enrolled. In 2018, 33 master's awarded. Terminal master's awarded for partial completion of doctoral program. *Degree requirements:* For master's, thesis (for some programs), minimum of 30 credits; minimum overall GPA of 3.0. *Entrance requirements:* For master's, GRE General Test, bachelor's degree; minimum GPA of 3.0 for last 60 credits of course work. Additional exam requirements/recommendations for international students: Required—TOEFL (minimum score 580 paper-based; 92 iBT). *Application deadline:* For fall admission, 12/15 priority date for domestic and international students; for spring admission, 10/1 for domestic and international students. Application fee: $75 ($81 for international students). Electronic applications accepted. *Expenses:* In-state tuition (Full-time): $10,728; Out-of-state tuition (full-time): $24,054; Fees: $1282; In-state tuition (per credit): $670; Out-of-state tuition (per credit): $1503; Fees (per credit): $126. *Financial support:* In 2018–19, 90 students received support, including 8 fellowships with full tuition reimbursements available (averaging $28,704 per year), 54 research assistantships with full tuition reimbursements available (averaging $23,784 per year), 21 teaching assistantships with full tuition reimbursements available (averaging $16,584 per year); Federal Work-Study, scholarships/grants, health care benefits, unspecified assistantships, and project assistantships also available. Support available to part-time students. Financial award application deadline: 12/1; financial award applicants required to submit FAFSA. *Faculty research:* Construction engineering and management; environmental engineering; structural engineering; transportation and city planning; water resources engineering; water chemistry. *Total annual research expenditures:* $12.5 million. *Unit head:* Dr. William Likos, Chair, 608-263-9490, Fax: 608-262-5199, E-mail: frontdesk@cee.wisc.edu. *Application contact:* Cheryl Loschko, Student Services Coordinator, 608-890-2420, E-mail: loschko@wisc.edu.
Website: https://www.engr.wisc.edu/department/civil-environmental-engineering/academics/ms-phd-civil-and-environmental-engineering/

University of Wisconsin–Milwaukee, Graduate School, College of Letters and Science, Department of Geography, Milwaukee, WI 53201-0413. Offers international interests (MA, MS, PhD); physical geography and environmental studies (MA, MS, PhD); urban development (MA, MS, PhD). *Students:* 10 full-time (6 women), 8 part-time (5 women); includes 2 minority (1 Black or African American, non-Hispanic/Latino; 1 Asian, non-Hispanic/Latino), 8 international. Average age 32. 19 applicants, 42% accepted, 2 enrolled. In 2018, 8 master's, 2 doctorates awarded. *Degree requirements:* For master's, comprehensive exam, thesis; for doctorate, thesis/dissertation. *Entrance requirements:* For master's and doctorate, GRE. Additional exam requirements/recommendations for international students: Required—TOEFL (minimum score 550 paper-based; 79 iBT), IELTS (minimum score 6.5). *Application deadline:* For fall admission, 1/1 priority date for domestic students; for spring admission, 9/1 for domestic students. Application fee: $56 ($96 for international students). Electronic applications accepted. *Financial support:* Fellowships, research assistantships, teaching assistantships, career-related internships or fieldwork, unspecified assistantships, and project assistantships available. Support available to part-time students. Financial award application deadline: 4/15; financial award applicants required to submit FAFSA. *Unit head:* Mark Schwartz, Department Chair, 414-229-3740, E-mail: mds@uwm.edu. *Application contact:* General Information Contact, 414-229-4982, Fax: 414-229-6967, E-mail: gradschool@uwm.edu.
Website: http://www4.uwm.edu/letsci/geography/

Vanderbilt University, Department of Earth and Environmental Sciences, Nashville, TN 37240-1001. Offers MAT, MS. *Faculty:* 9 full-time (2 women), 1 part-time/adjunct. *Students:* 13 full-time (8 women), 4 part-time (1 woman); includes 2 minority (both Hispanic/Latino). Average age 26. 39 applicants, 13% accepted, 4 enrolled. In 2018, 5 master's awarded. *Degree requirements:* For master's, thesis. *Entrance requirements:* For master's, GRE General Test, GRE Subject Test (recommended). Additional exam requirements/recommendations for international students: Required—TOEFL (minimum score 570 paper-based; 88 iBT). *Application deadline:* For fall admission, 1/15 for domestic and international students. Application fee: $0. Electronic applications accepted. *Expenses: Tuition:* Full-time $47,208; part-time $2026 per credit hour. *Required fees:* $478. *Financial support:* Fellowships with tuition reimbursements, research assistantships with tuition reimbursements, teaching assistantships with full tuition reimbursements, career-related internships or fieldwork, Federal Work-Study, institutionally sponsored loans, and health care benefits available. Financial award application deadline: 1/15; financial award applicants required to submit CSS PROFILE or FAFSA. *Faculty research:* Geochemical processes, magmatic processes and crustal evolution, paleoecology and paleo environments, sedimentary systems, transport phenomena, environmental policy. *Unit head:* Dr. Steven Goodbred, Chair, 615-322-2976, E-mail: g.gualda@vanderbilt.edu. *Application contact:* David Furbish, Director of Graduate Studies, 615-322-2137, E-mail: david.j.furbish@vanderbilt.edu.
Website: http://www.vanderbilt.edu/ees/

Virginia Polytechnic Institute and State University, VT Online, Blacksburg, VA 24061. Offers advanced transportation systems (Certificate); aerospace engineering (MS); agricultural and life sciences (MSLFS); business information systems (Graduate Certificate); career and technical education (MS); civil engineering (MS); computer engineering (M Eng, MS); decision support systems (Graduate Certificate); eLearning leadership (MA); electrical engineering (M Eng, MS); engineering administration (MEA); environmental engineering (Certificate); environmental politics and policy (Graduate Certificate); environmental sciences and engineering (MS); foundations of political analysis (Graduate Certificate); health product risk management (Graduate Certificate); industrial and systems engineering (MS); information policy and society (Graduate

Certificate); information security (Graduate Certificate); information technology (MIT); instructional technology (MA); integrative STEM education (MA Ed); liberal arts (Graduate Certificate); life sciences: health product risk management (MS); natural resources (MNR, Graduate Certificate); networking (Graduate Certificate); nonprofit and nongovernmental organization management (Graduate Certificate); ocean engineering (MS); political science (MA); security studies (Graduate Certificate); software development (Graduate Certificate). *Expenses:* Tuition, state resident: full-time $15,510; part-time $739.50 per credit hour. Tuition, nonresident: full-time $29,629; part-time $1490.25 per credit hour. *Required fees:* $2804; $550 per semester. Tuition and fees vary according to course load, campus/location and program. *Application contact:* Graduate Admissions and Academic Progress, 540-231-8636, E-mail: grads@vt.edu.
Website: http://www.vto.vt.edu/

Washington State University, College of Agricultural, Human, and Natural Resource Sciences, School of the Environment, Pullman, WA 99164. Offers environmental and natural resource sciences (PhD); natural resource sciences (MS). Program applications must be made through the Pullman campus. *Degree requirements:* For master's, comprehensive exam (for some programs), thesis (for some programs), oral exam; for doctorate, comprehensive exam, thesis/dissertation, oral exam. *Entrance requirements:* For master's, GRE General Test, official copies of all college transcripts, three letters of recommendation. Additional exam requirements/recommendations for international students: Required—TOEFL, IELTS. *Faculty research:* Environmental and natural resources conservation and sustainability; earth sciences: earth systems and geology; wildlife ecology and conservation sciences.

Washington State University, College of Arts and Sciences, School of the Environment, Pullman, WA 99164. Offers environmental and natural resource sciences (PhD); environmental science (MS); geology (MS, PhD); natural resource science (MS). *Degree requirements:* For master's, comprehensive exam (for some programs), thesis (for some programs), oral exam; for doctorate, comprehensive exam, thesis/dissertation, oral exam, written exam. *Entrance requirements:* For master's, 3 undergraduate semester hours each in sociology or cultural anthropology, environmental science, biological sciences, and calculus or statistics; 4 in general ecology; and 6 in general chemistry or general physics; for doctorate, minimum GPA of 3.0. Additional exam requirements/recommendations for international students: Required—TOEFL, IELTS.

Wesleyan University, Graduate Studies, Department of Earth and Environmental Sciences, Middletown, CT 06459. Offers MA. *Degree requirements:* For master's, thesis. *Entrance requirements:* For master's, GRE General Test, official transcripts, three recommendation letters, essay. Additional exam requirements/recommendations for international students: Required—TOEFL. Electronic applications accepted. *Faculty research:* Tectonics, volcanology, stratigraphy, coastal processes, geochemistry.

Western Illinois University, School of Graduate Studies, College of Arts and Sciences, Program in Environmental Science: Large River Ecosystems, Macomb, IL 61455-1390. Offers PhD. *Students:* 4 full-time (3 women), 2 part-time (both women), 2 international. Average age 37. 1 applicant, 100% accepted, 1 enrolled. *Entrance requirements:* For doctorate, GRE, three letters of recommendation, official transcripts, statement of research intent, curriculum vitae. Additional exam requirements/recommendations for international students: Required—TOEFL. *Application deadline:* Applications are processed on a rolling basis. Application fee: $30. *Financial support:* In 2018–19, 4 students received support, including 1 research assistantship with full tuition reimbursement available (averaging $7,544 per year), 3 teaching assistantships with full tuition reimbursements available (averaging $8,688 per year). *Unit head:* Dr. Roger Viadero, Director, Institute for Environmental Sciences, 309-298-2040. *Application contact:* Dr. Mark Mossman, Associate Provost and Director of Graduate Studies, 309-298-1806, Fax: 309-298-2345, E-mail: grad-office@wiu.edu.
Website: http://wiu.edu/graduate_studies/programs_of_study/environsci_profile.php

Western Washington University, Graduate School, Huxley College of the Environment, Department of Environmental Sciences, Bellingham, WA 98225-5996. Offers environmental science (MS); marine and estuarine science (MS). *Program availability:* Part-time. *Degree requirements:* For master's, thesis. *Entrance requirements:* For master's, GRE General Test, minimum GPA of 3.0 in last 60 semester hours or last 90 quarter hours. Additional exam requirements/recommendations for international students: Required—TOEFL (minimum score 567 paper-based). Electronic applications accepted. *Faculty research:* Landscape ecology, climate change, watershed studies, environmental toxicology and risk assessment, aquatic toxicology, toxic algae, invasive species.

Western Washington University, Graduate School, Huxley College of the Environment, Department of Environmental Studies, Bellingham, WA 98225-5996. Offers environmental education (M Ed); geography (MS). *Program availability:* Part-time. *Degree requirements:* For master's, thesis. *Entrance requirements:* For master's, GRE General Test, minimum GPA of 3.0 in last 60 semester hours or last 90 quarter hours. Additional exam requirements/recommendations for international students: Required—TOEFL (minimum score 567 paper-based). Electronic applications accepted. *Faculty research:* Geomorphology; pedogenesis; quaternary studies and climate change in the western U.S. landscape ecology, biogeography, pyrogeography, and spatial analysis.

West Texas A&M University, College of Agriculture and Natural Sciences, Department of Agricultural Sciences, Emphasis in Plant, Soil and Environmental Science, Canyon, TX 79015. Offers MS. *Program availability:* Part-time. *Degree requirements:* For master's, comprehensive exam, thesis optional. *Entrance requirements:* For master's, GRE General Test. Additional exam requirements/recommendations for international students: Required—TOEFL (minimum score 550 paper-based). Electronic applications accepted. *Faculty research:* Crop and soil disciplines.

West Texas A&M University, College of Agriculture and Natural Sciences, Department of Life, Earth and Environmental Sciences, Program in Environmental Science, Canyon, TX 79015. Offers MS. *Program availability:* Part-time. *Degree requirements:* For master's, comprehensive exam, thesis optional. *Entrance requirements:* For master's, GRE General Test. Additional exam requirements/recommendations for international students: Required—TOEFL (minimum score 550 paper-based). Electronic applications accepted.

Wichita State University, Graduate School, Fairmount College of Liberal Arts and Sciences, Department of Geology, Wichita, KS 67260. Offers earth, environmental, and physical sciences (MS). *Program availability:* Part-time. *Unit head:* Dr. William Parcell, Chair, 316-978-3140, E-mail: william.parcell@wichita.edu. *Application contact:* Jordan Oleson, Admissions Coordinator, 316-978-3095, Fax: 316-978-3253, E-mail: jordan.oleson@wichita.edu.
Website: http://www.wichita.edu/geology

Wilfrid Laurier University, Faculty of Graduate and Postdoctoral Studies, Faculty of Arts, Department of Geography and Environmental Studies, Waterloo, ON N2L 3C5, Canada. Offers environmental and resource management (MA, MES, PhD); environmental science (M Sc, MES, PhD); geomatics (M Sc, MES, PhD); human

Peterson's Graduate Programs in the Physical Sciences, Mathematics, Agricultural Sciences, the Environment & Natural Resources 2020

www.petersons.com **327**

geography (MES, PhD). *Program availability:* Part-time. *Degree requirements:* For master's, thesis optional; for doctorate, thesis/dissertation. *Entrance requirements:* For master's, honors BA in geography, minimum B average in undergraduate course work; honors BSc with minimum B+ or honors BES or BA in physical geography, environmental or earth sciences or the equivalent; for doctorate, MA in geography, minimum A- average. Additional exam requirements/recommendations for international students: Required—TOEFL (minimum score 89 iBT). Electronic applications accepted. *Faculty research:* Resources management, urban, economic, physical, cultural, earth surfaces, geomatics, historical, regional, spatial data handling.

Wright State University, Graduate School, College of Science and Mathematics, Program in Environmental Sciences, Dayton, OH 45435. Offers PhD.

Yale University, Graduate School of Arts and Sciences, Department of Forestry and Environmental Studies, New Haven, CT 06520. Offers environmental sciences (PhD); forestry (PhD). *Degree requirements:* For doctorate, thesis/dissertation. *Entrance requirements:* For doctorate, GRE General Test.

Yale University, School of Forestry and Environmental Studies, New Haven, CT 06511. Offers environmental management (MEM), including business and the environment, ecosystem and conservation management, energy and the environment, environmental policy analysis; environmental science (MES); forest science (MFS); forestry (MF); forestry and environmental studies (PhD); JD/MEM; MBA/MEM; MBA/MF; MEM/M Arch; MEM/M Div; MEM/MA; MEM/MAR; MEM/MPH. *Accreditation:* SAF (one or more programs are accredited). *Program availability:* Part-time. Terminal master's awarded for partial completion of doctoral program. *Degree requirements:* For master's, internship and capstone project (for MEM and MF); research project and thesis (for MES and MFS); for doctorate, comprehensive exam, thesis/dissertation. *Entrance requirements:* For master's, GRE General Test, GMAT or LSAT; for doctorate, GRE General Test. Additional exam requirements/recommendations for international students: Required—TOEFL (minimum score 600 paper-based; 100 iBT) or IELTS (minimum score 7). Electronic applications accepted. *Expenses:* Contact institution. *Faculty research:* Environmental policy, social ecology, industrial environmental management, forestry, environmental health, urban ecology, water science policy.

Marine Affairs

Dalhousie University, Faculty of Management, Marine Affairs Program, Halifax, NS B3H 3J5, Canada. Offers MMM. *Degree requirements:* For master's, project. *Entrance requirements:* For master's, minimum GPA of 3.0. Additional exam requirements/recommendations for international students: Required—TOEFL, IELTS, CANTEST, CAEL, or Michigan English Language Assessment Battery. Electronic applications accepted. *Faculty research:* Coastal zone management, sea use planning, development of non-living resources, protection and preservation of the coastal and marine environment, marine law and policy, fisheries management, maritime transport, conflict management.

Louisiana State University and Agricultural & Mechanical College, Graduate School, School of the Coast and Environment, Department of Oceanography and Coastal Sciences, Baton Rouge, LA 70803. Offers MS, PhD.

Memorial University of Newfoundland, School of Graduate Studies, Department of Sociology, St. John's, NL A1C 5S7, Canada. Offers gender (PhD); maritime sociology (PhD); sociology (M Phil, MA); work and development (PhD). *Program availability:* Part-time. *Degree requirements:* For master's, comprehensive exam, thesis optional, program journal (M Phil); for doctorate, one foreign language, comprehensive exam, thesis/dissertation, oral defense of thesis. *Entrance requirements:* For master's, 2nd class degree from university of recognized standing in area of study; for doctorate, MA, M Phil, or equivalent. Electronic applications accepted. *Faculty research:* Work and development, gender, maritime sociology.

Memorial University of Newfoundland, School of Graduate Studies, Interdisciplinary Program in Marine Studies, St. John's, NL A1C 5S7, Canada. Offers fisheries resource management (MMS, Graduate Diploma); marine spatial planning and management (MMS). *Program availability:* Part-time. *Degree requirements:* For master's, report. *Entrance requirements:* For master's, high 2nd class degree from a recognized university; demonstrated commitment to the fishery through employment or experience in a sector of the fishery, in a regulatory agency or government department connected to the fisheries, in a non-governmental agency, or through self-employment or relevant professional consulting activities; for Graduate Diploma, high 2nd class degree from a recognized university. Electronic applications accepted. *Faculty research:* Biological, ecological and oceanographic aspects of world fisheries; economics; political science; sociology.

Oregon State University, College of Earth, Ocean, and Atmospheric Sciences, Program in Marine Resource Management, Corvallis, OR 97331. Offers MS. *Program availability:* Part-time. *Entrance requirements:* For master's, GRE, minimum GPA of 3.0 in last 90 hours of course work. Additional exam requirements/recommendations for international students: Required—TOEFL (minimum score 575 paper-based). *Faculty research:* Ocean and coastal resources, fisheries resources, marine pollution, marine recreation and tourism.

Stony Brook University, State University of New York, Graduate School, School of Marine and Atmospheric Sciences, Program in Marine Conservation and Policy, Stony Brook, NY 11794. Offers MA. *Students:* 15 full-time (9 women), 2 part-time (1 woman); includes 4 minority (1 Asian, non-Hispanic/Latino; 2 Hispanic/Latino; 1 Two or more races, non-Hispanic/Latino). Average age 28. 18 applicants, 89% accepted, 13 enrolled. In 2018, 12 master's awarded. *Entrance requirements:* For master's, GRE General Test, minimum GPA of 3.0; one semester of college-level biology and three additional semester courses in college-level math or science; personal statement; 3 letters of reference; official transcripts. Additional exam requirements/recommendations for international students: Required—TOEFL. *Application deadline:* For fall admission, 1/15 for domestic students; for spring admission, 10/1 for domestic students. Application fee: $100. Electronic applications accepted. *Expenses:* Contact institution. *Financial support:* In 2018–19, 1 teaching assistantship was awarded. *Unit head:* Dr. Larry Swanson, Interim Dean, 631-632-8700, E-mail: larry.swanson@stonybrook.edu. *Application contact:* Ginny Clancy, Educational Programs Coordinator, 631-632-8681, Fax: 631-632-8915, E-mail: ginny.clancy@stonybrook.edu.
Website: http://www.somas.stonybrook.edu/mcp/

Université du Québec à Rimouski, Graduate Programs, Program in Management of Marine Resources, Rimouski, QC G5L 3A1, Canada. Offers M Sc, Diploma. *Program availability:* Part-time. *Entrance requirements:* For master's, appropriate bachelor's degree, proficiency in French.

University of Delaware, College of Earth, Ocean, and Environment, School of Marine Science and Policy, Newark, DE 19716. Offers marine policy (MMP); marine studies (MS, PhD), including marine biosciences, oceanography, physical ocean science and engineering; oceanography (PhD).

University of Massachusetts Dartmouth, Graduate School, School for Marine Science and Technology, New Bedford, MA 02747-2300. Offers coastal and ocean administration science and technology (MS); marine science and technology (MS, PhD). *Program availability:* Part-time. *Faculty:* 14 full-time (1 woman). *Students:* 21 full-time (13 women), 31 part-time (15 women); includes 3 minority (1 Asian, non-Hispanic/Latino; 2 Two or more races, non-Hispanic/Latino), 8 international. Average age 31. 30 applicants, 73% accepted, 10 enrolled. In 2018, 7 master's, 4 doctorates awarded. Terminal master's awarded for partial completion of doctoral program. *Degree requirements:* For master's, thesis; for doctorate, comprehensive exam, thesis/dissertation. *Entrance requirements:* For master's, GRE, statement of interest (minimum of 300 words), resume, 3 letters of recommendation, official transcripts; for doctorate, GRE, statement of intent (minimum of 300 words), statement of interest (minimum of 300 words), resume, 3 letters of recommendation, official transcripts. Additional exam requirements/recommendations for international students: Required—TOEFL (minimum score 577 paper-based; 90 iBT). *Application deadline:* For fall admission, 2/15 priority date for domestic students, 1/15 priority date for international students; for spring admission, 11/15 priority date for domestic students, 10/15 priority date for international students. Application fee: $60. Electronic applications accepted. *Financial support:* In 2018–19, 3 fellowships (averaging $14,000 per year), 30 research assistantships (averaging $17,994 per year), 1 teaching assistantship (averaging $9,250 per year) were awarded; tuition waivers (full and partial) and doctoral support, dissertation writing support also available. Financial award application deadline: 3/1; financial award applicants required to submit FAFSA. *Faculty research:* Major marine biogeochemical cycles, atmospheric co2 concentration, resource assessment and bycatch avoidance, air sea interaction, dynamics/kinematics of coastal fonts, estuarian circulation, storm-force and internal wave dynamics stock assessment, oceanic frontal processes, arctic ocean and climate change. *Total annual research expenditures:* $11.1 million. *Unit head:* Steven Lohrenz, Dean, School for Marine Science and Technology, 508-910-6550, E-mail: slohrenz@umassd.edu. *Application contact:* Scott Webster, Director of Graduate Studies and Admissions, 508-999-8604, Fax: 508-999-8183, E-mail: graduate@umassd.edu.
Website: http://www.umassd.edu/smast

University of Miami, Graduate School, Rosenstiel School of Marine and Atmospheric Science, Division of Marine Affairs and Policy, Coral Gables, FL 33124. Offers MA, MS, JD/MA. *Program availability:* Part-time. *Degree requirements:* For master's, comprehensive exam, thesis (for some programs), internship, paper. *Entrance requirements:* For master's, GRE General Test. Additional exam requirements/recommendations for international students: Required—TOEFL (minimum score 550 paper-based). Electronic applications accepted.

University of Rhode Island, Graduate School, College of the Environment and Life Sciences, Department of Marine Affairs, Kingston, RI 02881. Offers MA, MMA, PhD. *Program availability:* Part-time. *Faculty:* 9 full-time (4 women). *Students:* 36 full-time (25 women), 7 part-time (3 women); includes 3 minority (1 American Indian or Alaska Native, non-Hispanic/Latino; 1 Asian, non-Hispanic/Latino; 1 Native Hawaiian or other Pacific Islander, non-Hispanic/Latino), 4 international. 34 applicants, 79% accepted, 20 enrolled. In 2018, 17 master's, 2 doctorates awarded. *Entrance requirements:* Additional exam requirements/recommendations for international students: Required—TOEFL. *Application deadline:* For fall admission, 4/15 for domestic students, 2/1 for international students. Application fee: $65. Electronic applications accepted. *Expenses: Tuition, area resident:* Full-time $13,226; part-time $735 per credit. Tuition, state resident: full-time $13,226; part-time $735 per credit. Tuition, nonresident: full-time $25,854; part-time $1436 per credit. *International tuition:* $25,854 full-time. *Required fees:* $1698; $50 per credit. $35 per semester. One-time fee: $165. *Financial support:* In 2018–19, 16 research assistantships (averaging $11,641 per year) were awarded. Financial award application deadline: 1/15; financial award applicants required to submit FAFSA. *Unit head:* Dr. Tracy Dalton, Chair, 401-874-2434, E-mail: dalton@uri.edu. *Application contact:* Dr. Austin Becker, Graduate Program Coordinator, 401-874-4192, E-mail: abecker@uri.edu.
Website: https://web.uri.edu/maf/

University of Washington, Graduate School, College of the Environment, School of Marine and Environmental Affairs, Seattle, WA 98195. Offers MMA, Graduate Certificate. *Degree requirements:* For master's, thesis. *Entrance requirements:* For master's, GRE General Test, minimum GPA of 3.0. Additional exam requirements/recommendations for international students: Required—TOEFL. Electronic applications accepted. *Faculty research:* Marine pollution, port authorities, fisheries management, global climate change, marine environmental protection.

Section 10
Natural Resources

This section contains a directory of institutions offering graduate work in natural resources. Additional information about programs listed in the directory may be obtained by writing directly to the dean of a graduate school or chair of a department at the address given in the directory.

For programs offering related work, see also in this book *Environmental Sciences and Management* and *Meteorology and Atmospheric Sciences*. In the other guides in this series:

Graduate Programs in the Humanities, Arts & Social Sciences

See *Architecture (Landscape Architecture)* and *Public, Regional, and Industrial Affairs*

Graduate Programs in the Biological/Biomedical Sciences & Health-Related Medical Professions

See *Biological and Biomedical Sciences; Botany and Plant Biology; Ecology, Environmental Biology, and Evolutionary Biology; Entomology; Genetics, Developmental Biology, and Reproductive Biology; Nutrition; Pathology and Pathobiology; Pharmacology and Toxicology; Physiology; Veterinary Medicine and Sciences;* and *Zoology*

Graduate Programs in Engineering & Applied Sciences

See *Agricultural Engineering and Bioengineering; Civil and Environmental Engineering; Geological, Mineral/Mining, and Petroleum Engineering; Management of Engineering and Technology;* and *Ocean Engineering*

CONTENTS

Program Directories

Fish, Game, and Wildlife Management

Arkansas Tech University, College of Natural and Health Sciences, Russellville, AR 72801. Offers fisheries and wildlife biology (MS); health informatics (MS); nursing (MSN). *Program availability:* Part-time, evening/weekend, 100% online, blended/hybrid learning. *Students:* 11 full-time (7 women), 46 part-time (30 women); includes 10 minority (9 Black or African American, non-Hispanic/Latino; 1 Asian, non-Hispanic/Latino), 1 international. Average age 35. In 2018, 22 master's awarded. *Degree requirements:* For master's, thesis (for some programs), project. *Entrance requirements:* Additional exam requirements/recommendations for international students: Required—TOEFL (minimum score 550 paper-based; 79 iBT), IELTS (minimum score 6.5), PTE (minimum score 58). *Application deadline:* For fall admission, 3/1 priority date for domestic students, 5/1 priority date for international students; for spring admission, 10/1 priority date for domestic and international students. Applications are processed on a rolling basis. Application fee: $40 ($90 for international students). Electronic applications accepted. *Expenses: Tuition, area resident:* Full-time $6816; part-time $284 per credit hour. Tuition, state resident: full-time $6816; part-time $284 per credit hour. Tuition, nonresident: full-time $13,632; part-time $568 per credit hour. *International tuition:* $13,632 full-time. *Required fees:* $457.50 per semester. Tuition and fees vary according to course load and degree level. *Financial support:* In 2018–19, research assistantships with full and partial tuition reimbursements (averaging $4,800 per year), teaching assistantships with full and partial tuition reimbursements (averaging $4,800 per year) were awarded; career-related internships or fieldwork, Federal Work-Study, scholarships/grants, health care benefits, and unspecified assistantships also available. Support available to part-time students. Financial award application deadline: 4/15; financial award applicants required to submit FAFSA. *Unit head:* Dr. Jeff Robertson, Dean, 479-968-0498, E-mail: jrobertson@atu.edu. *Application contact:* Dr. Jeff Robertson, Interim Dean of Graduate College, 479-968-0398, Fax: 479-964-0542, E-mail: gradcollege@atu.edu.
Website: http://www.atu.edu/nhs/

Auburn University, Graduate School, College of Agriculture, Department of Fisheries and Allied Aquacultures, Auburn University, AL 36849. Offers M Aq, MS, PhD. *Program availability:* Part-time. *Degree requirements:* For master's, thesis (for some programs); for doctorate, 2 foreign languages, thesis/dissertation. *Entrance requirements:* For master's and doctorate, GRE General Test. Electronic applications accepted. *Expenses:* Tuition, state resident: full-time $11,282; part-time $535 per credit hour. Tuition, nonresident: full-time $30,542; part-time $1605 per credit hour. *Required fees:* $826 per semester. Tuition and fees vary according to degree level and program. *Faculty research:* Channel catfish production; aquatic animal health; community and population ecology; pond management; production hatching, breeding and genetics.

Auburn University, Graduate School, School of Forestry and Wildlife Sciences, Auburn University, AL 36849. Offers forestry (MS); natural resource conservation (MNR); wildlife sciences (MS, PhD). *Accreditation:* SAF. *Program availability:* Part-time. *Degree requirements:* For master's, thesis (MS); for doctorate, thesis/dissertation. *Entrance requirements:* For master's and doctorate, GRE General Test. Electronic applications accepted. *Expenses:* Tuition, state resident: full-time $11,282; part-time $535 per credit hour. Tuition, nonresident: full-time $30,542; part-time $1605 per credit hour. *Required fees:* $826 per semester. Tuition and fees vary according to degree level and program. *Faculty research:* Forest nursery management, silviculture and vegetation management, biological processes and ecological relationships, growth and yield of plantations and natural stands, urban forestry, forest taxation, law and policy.

Brigham Young University, Graduate Studies, College of Life Sciences, Department of Plant and Wildlife Sciences, Provo, UT 84602-1001. Offers environmental science (MS); genetics and biotechnology (MS); wildlife and wildlands conservation (MS, PhD). *Faculty:* 24 full-time (1 woman). *Students:* 12 full-time (7 women), 42 part-time (12 women); includes 2 minority (both Hispanic/Latino). Average age 30. 29 applicants, 59% accepted, 17 enrolled. In 2018, 18 master's, 1 doctorate awarded. *Degree requirements:* For master's, thesis, no C grades or below, 30 hours (24 coursework, 6 thesis); for doctorate, comprehensive exam, thesis/dissertation, no C grades or below, 54 hours (18 dissertation, 36 coursework). *Entrance requirements:* For master's, GRE General Test, minimum GPA of 3.2; for doctorate, GRE, minimum GPA of 3.2. Additional exam requirements/recommendations for international students: Required—TOEFL (minimum score 580 paper-based; 85 iBT). *Application deadline:* 2/1 for domestic and international students; for summer admission, 2/1 for domestic and international students. Application fee: $50. Electronic applications accepted. *Financial support:* In 2018–19, 54 students received support, including 71 research assistantships with partial tuition reimbursements available (averaging $18,081 per year), 42 teaching assistantships with partial tuition reimbursements available (averaging $16,478 per year); scholarships/grants and tuition waivers (partial) also available. Financial award application deadline: 3/1. *Faculty research:* Environmental science, plant genetics, plant ecology, plant nutrition and pathology, wildlife and wildlands conservation. *Total annual research expenditures:* $2.1 million. *Unit head:* Neil Hansen, Chair, 801-422-2491, E-mail: neil_hansen@byu.edu. *Application contact:* Bradley D. Geary, Graduate Coordinator, 801-422-1228, Fax: 801-422-0008, E-mail: bradley_geary@byu.edu.
Website: http://pws.byu.edu

Central Washington University, School of Graduate Studies and Research, College of the Sciences, Department of Biological Sciences, Ellensburg, WA 98926. Offers botany (MS); microbiology and parasitology (MS); stream ecology and fisheries (MS); terrestrial ecology (MS). *Program availability:* Part-time. *Entrance requirements:* For master's, GRE General Test, minimum GPA of 3.0. Additional exam requirements/recommendations for international students: Required—TOEFL (minimum score 550 paper-based; 79 iBT). Electronic applications accepted.

Clemson University, Graduate School, College of Agriculture, Forestry and Life Sciences, Department of Forestry and Environmental Conservation, Clemson, SC 29634. Offers forest resources (MFR, MS, PhD); wildlife and fisheries biology (MS, PhD). *Program availability:* Part-time, 100% online. *Faculty:* 29 full-time (7 women). *Students:* 71 full-time (26 women), 54 part-time (25 women); includes 12 minority (2 Black or African American, non-Hispanic/Latino; 3 Hispanic/Latino; 7 Two or more races, non-Hispanic/Latino), 8 international. Average age 28. 100 applicants, 83% accepted, 74 enrolled. In 2018, 14 master's, 5 doctorates awarded. *Degree requirements:* For master's, thesis optional; for doctorate, comprehensive exam, thesis/dissertation. *Entrance requirements:* For master's and doctorate, GRE General Test, unofficial transcripts, letters of recommendation. Additional exam requirements/recommendations for international students: Required—TOEFL (minimum score 80 paper-based; 80 iBT); Recommended—IELTS (minimum score 6.5), TSE (minimum score 54). *Application deadline:* For fall admission, 4/15 for international students; for spring admission, 10/15 for international students. Applications are processed on a rolling basis. Application fee: $80 ($90 for international students). Electronic applications accepted. *Expenses: Tuition, area resident:* Full-time $11,270; part-time $8688 per credit hour. Tuition, state resident: full-time $11,796. Tuition, nonresident: full-time $23,802; part-time $17,412 per credit hour. *International tuition:* $23,246 full-time. *Required fees:* $1196; $497 per semester. Tuition and fees vary according to course load, degree level, campus/location and program. *Financial support:* In 2018–19, 41 students received support, including 5 fellowships with full and partial tuition reimbursements available (averaging $2,000 per year), 31 research assistantships with full and partial tuition reimbursements available (averaging $16,095 per year), 5 teaching assistantships with full and partial tuition reimbursements available (averaging $13,560 per year); career-related internships or fieldwork and unspecified assistantships also available. *Faculty research:* Wildlife ecology and management, forest ecology and management, environmental and natural resources, wetlands conservation, ecotoxicology and risk mitigation. *Total annual research expenditures:* $2.1 million. *Unit head:* Dr. Gregg Yarrow, Department Chair, 864-656-3302, E-mail: gyarrow@clemson.edu. *Application contact:* Dr. Kyle Barrett, Graduate Program Coordinator, 864-642-1847, E-mail: rbarre2@clemson.edu.
Website: http://www.clemson.edu/cafls/departments/fec/index.html

Colorado State University, Warner College of Natural Resources, Department of Fish, Wildlife, and Conservation Biology, Fort Collins, CO 80523-1474. Offers MFWCB, MS, PhD. *Program availability:* 100% online. *Degree requirements:* For master's, comprehensive exam, thesis (for some programs); for doctorate, comprehensive exam, thesis/dissertation. *Entrance requirements:* For master's, GRE, minimum cumulative undergraduate GPA of 3.0; faculty advisor; statement of purpose; related degree; 2 years of relevant employment (for online program); for doctorate, GRE, minimum cumulative undergraduate GPA of 3.0; faculty advisor; statement of purpose; related degree. Additional exam requirements/recommendations for international students: Required—TOEFL (minimum score 550 paper-based; 79 iBT), IELTS (minimum score 6.5). Electronic applications accepted. *Expenses:* Contact institution. *Faculty research:* Impacts and management of exotics; endangered species management; capture-mark-recapture methods; conservation and management of aquatic ecosystems; wildlife disease ecology.

Cornell University, Graduate School, Graduate Fields of Agriculture and Life Sciences, Field of Natural Resources, Ithaca, NY 14853. Offers community-based natural resources management (MS, PhD); conservation biology (MS, PhD); ecosystem biology and biogeochemistry (MPS, MS, PhD); environmental management (MPS); fishery and aquatic science (MPS, MS, PhD); forest science (MPS, MS, PhD); human dimensions of natural resources management (MPS, MS, PhD); policy and institutional analysis (MS, PhD); program development and evaluation (MPS, MS, PhD); quantitative ecology (MS, PhD); wildlife science (MPS, MS, PhD). *Degree requirements:* For master's, thesis (MS), project paper (MPS); for doctorate, comprehensive exam, thesis/dissertation. *Entrance requirements:* For master's and doctorate, GRE General Test, 2 letters of recommendation. Additional exam requirements/recommendations for international students: Required—TOEFL (minimum score 550 paper-based; 77 iBT). Electronic applications accepted. *Faculty research:* Ecosystem-level dynamics, systems modeling, conservation biology/management, resource management's human dimensions, biogeochemistry.

Frostburg State University, College of Liberal Arts and Sciences, Department of Biology, Program in Fisheries and Wildlife Management, Frostburg, MD 21532-1099. Offers MS. *Program availability:* Part-time, evening/weekend. *Degree requirements:* For master's, thesis. *Entrance requirements:* For master's, GRE General Test, resume. Additional exam requirements/recommendations for international students: Required—TOEFL. Electronic applications accepted. *Faculty research:* Evolution and systematics of freshwater fishes, biochemical mechanisms of temperature adaptation in freshwater fishes, wildlife and fish parasitology, biology of freshwater invertebrates, remote sensing.

Humboldt State University, Academic Programs, College of Natural Resources and Sciences, Programs in Natural Resources, Arcata, CA 95521-8299. Offers natural resources (MS), including fisheries, forestry, natural resources planning and interpretation, rangeland resources and wildland soils, wastewater utilization, watershed management, wildlife. *Faculty:* 22 full-time (5 women), 20 part-time/adjunct (7 women). *Students:* 43 full-time (22 women), 45 part-time (21 women); includes 24 minority (1 Black or African American, non-Hispanic/Latino; 2 American Indian or Alaska Native, non-Hispanic/Latino; 1 Asian, non-Hispanic/Latino; 16 Hispanic/Latino; 4 Two or more races, non-Hispanic/Latino), 1 international. Average age 28. 38 applicants, 37% accepted, 14 enrolled. In 2018, 21 master's awarded. *Degree requirements:* For master's, thesis or alternative. *Entrance requirements:* For master's, GRE, appropriate bachelor's degree, minimum GPA of 2.5, 3 letters of recommendation, resume. Additional exam requirements/recommendations for international students: Required—TOEFL (minimum score 500 paper-based). *Application deadline:* For fall admission, 2/1 for domestic and international students; for spring admission, 9/30 for domestic and international students. Applications are processed on a rolling basis. Application fee: $55. *Expenses: Tuition:* Part-time $4649 per semester. *Required fees:* $2121; $1673. Tuition and fees vary according to program. *Financial support:* Fellowships, career-related internships or fieldwork, and Federal Work-Study available. Support available to part-time students. Financial award application deadline: 3/1; financial award applicants required to submit FAFSA. *Faculty research:* Spotted owl habitat, pre-settlement vegetation, hardwood utilization, tree physiology, fisheries. *Unit head:* Dr. Andrew Stubblefield, Graduate Program Coordinator, 707-826-3258, E-mail: andrew.stubblefield@humboldt.edu. *Application contact:* Dr. Andrew Stubblefield, Graduate Program Coordinator, 707-826-3258, E-mail: andrew.stubblefield@humboldt.edu.
Website: http://www.humboldt.edu/cnrs/graduate_programs

Iowa State University of Science and Technology, Department of Natural Resource Ecology and Management, Ames, IA 50011. Offers forestry (MS, PhD); wildlife ecology (MS, PhD). *Entrance requirements:* For master's and doctorate, GRE General Test. Additional exam requirements/recommendations for international students: Required—TOEFL (minimum score 550 paper-based; 79 iBT), IELTS (minimum score 6.5). Electronic applications accepted.

Iowa State University of Science and Technology, Program in Fisheries Biology, Ames, IA 50011. Offers MS, PhD. *Entrance requirements:* For master's and doctorate, GRE. Additional exam requirements/recommendations for international students: Required—TOEFL (minimum score 550 paper-based; 79 iBT), IELTS (minimum score 6.5). Electronic applications accepted.

Louisiana State University and Agricultural & Mechanical College, Graduate School, College of Agriculture, School of Renewable Natural Resources, Baton Rouge, LA 70803. Offers fisheries (MS); forestry (MS, PhD); wildlife (MS); wildlife and fisheries science (PhD).

McGill University, Faculty of Graduate and Postdoctoral Studies, Faculty of Agricultural and Environmental Sciences, Department of Natural Resource Sciences, Montréal, QC H3A 2T5, Canada. Offers entomology (M Sc, PhD); environmental assessment (M Sc); forest science (M Sc, PhD); microbiology (M Sc, PhD); micrometeorology (M Sc, PhD); neotropical environment (M Sc, PhD); soil science (M Sc, PhD); wildlife biology (M Sc, PhD).

Memorial University of Newfoundland, School of Graduate Studies, Interdisciplinary Program in Marine Studies, St. John's, NL A1C 5S7, Canada. Offers fisheries resource management (MMS, Graduate Diploma); marine spatial planning and management (MMS). *Program availability:* Part-time. *Degree requirements:* For master's, report. *Entrance requirements:* For master's, high 2nd class degree from a recognized university; demonstrated commitment to the fishery through employment or experience in a sector of the fishery, in a regulatory agency or government department connected to the fisheries, in a non-governmental agency, or through self-employment or relevant professional consulting activities; for Graduate Diploma, high 2nd class degree from a recognized university. Electronic applications accepted. *Faculty research:* Biological, ecological and oceanographic aspects of world fisheries; economics; political science; sociology.

Michigan State University, The Graduate School, College of Agriculture and Natural Resources, Department of Fisheries and Wildlife, East Lansing, MI 48824. Offers fisheries and wildlife (MS, PhD); fisheries and wildlife - environmental toxicology (PhD). *Entrance requirements:* Additional exam requirements/recommendations for international students: Required—TOEFL (minimum score 550 paper-based), Michigan State University ELT (minimum score 85), Michigan English Language Assessment Battery (minimum score 83). Electronic applications accepted.

Mississippi State University, College of Forest Resources, Department of Wildlife, Fisheries and Aquaculture, Mississippi State, MS 39762. Offers MS, PhD. *Program availability:* Part-time. *Faculty:* 27 full-time (4 women). *Students:* 38 full-time (12 women), 15 part-time (2 women); includes 2 minority (both Hispanic/Latino), 4 international. Average age 29. 14 applicants, 57% accepted, 8 enrolled. In 2018, 23 master's, 7 doctorates awarded. *Degree requirements:* For master's, thesis, comprehensive oral or written exam; for doctorate, comprehensive exam, thesis/dissertation. *Entrance requirements:* For master's, GRE, bachelor's degree, minimum GPA of 3.0 on last 60 hours of undergraduate courses; for doctorate, GRE, master's degree, minimum GPA of 3.2 on prior graduate studies. Additional exam requirements/recommendations for international students: Required—TOEFL (minimum score 550 paper-based; 79 iBT); Recommended—IELTS (minimum score 6.5). *Application deadline:* For fall admission, 7/1 for domestic students, 5/1 for international students; for spring admission, 11/1 for domestic students, 9/1 for international students. Applications are processed on a rolling basis. Application fee: $60 ($80 for international students). Electronic applications accepted. *Expenses:* Tuition, state resident: full-time $8450; part-time $360.59 per credit hour. Tuition, nonresident: full-time $23,140; part-time $969.09 per credit hour. *Required fees:* $110. One-time fee: $55 full-time. Part-time tuition and fees vary according to course load, degree level, campus/location and reciprocity agreements. *Financial support:* In 2018–19, 31 research assistantships with partial tuition reimbursements (averaging $15,700 per year) were awarded; Federal Work-Study, institutionally sponsored loans, and unspecified assistantships also available. Financial award application deadline: 4/1; financial award applicants required to submit FAFSA. *Faculty research:* Spatial technology, habitat restoration, aquaculture, fisheries, wildlife management. *Unit head:* Dr. Andrew Kouba, Professor and Head, 662-325-2378, Fax: 662-325-0720, E-mail: ak260@msstate.edu. *Application contact:* Nathan Drake, Admissions and Enrollment Assistant, 662-325-3804, E-mail: ndrake@grad.msstate.edu.
Website: http://www.cfr.msstate.edu/wildlife/index.asp

Montana State University, The Graduate School, College of Letters and Science, Department of Ecology, Bozeman, MT 59717. Offers ecological and environmental statistics (MS); ecology and environmental sciences (PhD); fish and wildlife biology (PhD); fish and wildlife management (MS). *Program availability:* Part-time. *Degree requirements:* For master's, comprehensive exam, thesis (for some programs); for doctorate, comprehensive exam, thesis/dissertation. *Entrance requirements:* For master's and doctorate, GRE, minimum GPA of 3.0, letters of recommendation, essay. Additional exam requirements/recommendations for international students: Required—TOEFL (minimum score 550 paper-based). Electronic applications accepted. *Faculty research:* Community ecology, population ecology, land-use effects, management and conservation, environmental modeling.

The Ohio State University, Graduate School, College of Food, Agricultural, and Environmental Sciences, School of Environment and Natural Resources, Columbus, OH 43210. Offers ecological restoration (MS, PhD); ecosystem science (MS, PhD); environment and natural resources (MENR); environmental social sciences (MS, PhD); fisheries and wildlife science (MS, PhD); forest science (MS, PhD); rural sociology (MS, PhD); soil science (MS, PhD). *Faculty:* 38. *Students:* 106 (64 women). Average age 29. In 2018, 21 master's, 5 doctorates awarded. *Entrance requirements:* For master's and doctorate, GRE. Additional exam requirements/recommendations for international students: Required—TOEFL (minimum score 550 paper-based; 79 iBT), Michigan English Language Assessment Battery (minimum score 82); Recommended—IELTS (minimum score 7). *Application deadline:* For fall admission, 1/1 priority date for domestic students, 12/15 priority date for international students; for spring admission, 11/1 for domestic students, 9/15 for international students. Applications are processed on a rolling basis. Application fee: $60 ($70 for international students). Electronic applications accepted. *Financial support:* Fellowships, research assistantships, teaching assistantships, health care benefits, and unspecified assistantships available. *Unit head:* Dr. Jeff S. Sharp, Director, 614-292-9410, E-mail: sharp.123@osu.edu. *Application contact:* Graduate and Professional Admissions, 614-292-9444, Fax: 614-292-3895, E-mail: gpadmissions@osu.edu.
Website: http://senr.osu.edu/

Oregon State University, College of Agricultural Sciences, Program in Fisheries and Wildlife Administration, Corvallis, OR 97331. Offers PSM. *Program availability:* Part-time, 100% online. *Entrance requirements:* For master's, GRE. Additional exam requirements/recommendations for international students: Required—TOEFL (minimum score 80 iBT), IELTS (minimum score 6.5).

Oregon State University, College of Agricultural Sciences, Program in Fisheries Science, Corvallis, OR 97331. Offers aquaculture (MS); conservation biology (MS, PhD); fish genetics (MS, PhD); ichthyology (MS, PhD); limnology (MS, PhD); parasites and diseases (MS, PhD); physiology and ecology of marine and freshwater fishes (MS, PhD); stream ecology (MS, PhD); toxicology (MS, PhD); water pollution biology (MS, PhD). *Program availability:* Part-time. *Entrance requirements:* For master's and doctorate, GRE, minimum GPA of 3.0 in last 90 hours. Additional exam requirements/recommendations for international students: Required—TOEFL (minimum score 80 iBT), IELTS (minimum score 6.5). *Faculty research:* Fisheries ecology, fish toxicology, stream ecology, quantitative analyses of marine and freshwater fish populations.

Oregon State University, College of Agricultural Sciences, Program in Wildlife Science, Corvallis, OR 97331. Offers animal-habitat relationships (MS, PhD). *Program availability:* Part-time. *Entrance requirements:* For master's and doctorate, GRE, minimum GPA of 3.0 in last 90 hours. Additional exam requirements/recommendations for international students: Required—TOEFL (minimum score 80 iBT), IELTS (minimum score 6.5).

Penn State University Park, Graduate School, College of Agricultural Sciences, Department of Ecosystem Science and Management, University Park, PA 16802. Offers forest resources (MS, PhD); soil science (MS, PhD); wildlife and fisheries science (MS, PhD).

Purdue University, Graduate School, College of Agriculture, Department of Forestry and Natural Resources, West Lafayette, IN 47907. Offers fisheries and aquatic sciences (MS, MSF, PhD); forest biology (MS, MSF, PhD); natural resource social science (MS, PhD); natural resources social science (MSF); quantitative ecology (MS, MSF, PhD); wildlife science (MS, MSF, PhD); wood products and wood products manufacturing (MS, MSF, PhD). *Faculty:* 25 full-time (5 women), 1 part-time/adjunct (0 women). *Students:* 58 full-time (32 women), 5 part-time (1 woman); includes 12 minority (2 American Indian or Alaska Native, non-Hispanic/Latino; 1 Asian, non-Hispanic/Latino; 4 Hispanic/Latino; 1 Native Hawaiian or other Pacific Islander, non-Hispanic/Latino; 4 Two or more races, non-Hispanic/Latino), 12 international. Average age 27. 51 applicants, 27% accepted, 14 enrolled. In 2018, 13 master's, 11 doctorates awarded. *Degree requirements:* For master's, thesis; for doctorate, thesis/dissertation. *Entrance requirements:* For master's and doctorate, GRE General Test (minimum score: verbal 50th percentile; quantitative 50th percentile; analytical writing 4.0), minimum undergraduate GPA of 3.2 or equivalent. Additional exam requirements/recommendations for international students: Required—TOEFL (minimum score 550 paper-based; 77 iBT). *Application deadline:* For fall admission, 1/5 for domestic students, 1/15 for international students; for spring admission, 9/15 for domestic and international students. Applications are processed on a rolling basis. Application fee: $60 ($75 for international students). Electronic applications accepted. *Financial support:* In 2018–19, 10 research assistantships (averaging $15,259 per year) were awarded; fellowships, teaching assistantships, career-related internships or fieldwork, and scholarships/grants also available. Support available to part-time students. Financial award application deadline: 1/5; financial award applicants required to submit FAFSA. *Faculty research:* Wildlife management, forest management, forest ecology, forest soils, limnology. *Unit head:* Robert G. Wagner, Head of the Graduate Program, 765-494-3590, E-mail: rgwagner@purdue.edu. *Application contact:* Christine Hofmeyer, Graduate Contact, 765-494-3572, E-mail: chofmeye@purdue.edu.
Website: https://ag.purdue.edu/fnr

Simon Fraser University, Office of Graduate Studies and Postdoctoral Fellows, Faculty of Environment, School of Resource and Environmental Management, Burnaby, BC V5A 1S6, Canada. Offers quantitative methods in fisheries management (Graduate Diploma); resource and environmental management (MRM, PhD); resource and environmental planning (MRM). *Degree requirements:* For master's, thesis (for some programs); for doctorate, comprehensive exam, thesis/dissertation. *Entrance requirements:* For master's and Graduate Diploma, minimum GPA of 3.0 (on scale of 4.33) or 3.33 based on last 60 credits of undergraduate courses; for doctorate, minimum GPA of 3.5 (on scale of 4.33). Additional exam requirements/recommendations for international students: Recommended—TOEFL (minimum score 500 paper-based; 93 iBT), IELTS (minimum score 7), TWE (minimum score 5). Electronic applications accepted. *Faculty research:* Climate, coastal marine ecology and conservation, environmental toxicology, fisheries science and management, forest ecology.

South Dakota State University, Graduate School, College of Agriculture, Food and Environmental Sciences, Department of Natural Resource Management, Brookings, SD 57007. Offers biological sciences (MS, PhD); wildlife and fisheries sciences (MS, PhD). *Program availability:* Part-time. *Degree requirements:* For master's, thesis, oral exam; for doctorate, comprehensive exam, thesis/dissertation, interim exam, oral and written comprehensive exams. *Entrance requirements:* For master's and doctorate, GRE. Additional exam requirements/recommendations for international students: Required—TOEFL (minimum score 525 paper-based; 71 iBT). *Faculty research:* Agriculture interactions, wetland conservation, biostress, wildlife and fisheries ecology and techniques.

State University of New York College of Environmental Science and Forestry, Department of Environmental and Forest Biology, Syracuse, NY 13210-2779. Offers applied ecology (MPS); chemical ecology (MPS, MS, PhD); conservation biology (MPS, MS, PhD); ecology (MPS, MS, PhD); entomology (MPS, MS, PhD); environmental interpretation (MPS, MS, PhD); environmental physiology (MPS, MS, PhD); fish and wildlife biology and management (MPS, MS, PhD); forest pathology and mycology (MPS, MS, PhD); plant biotechnology (MPS); plant science and biotechnology (MPS, MS, PhD). *Program availability:* Part-time. *Faculty:* 35 full-time (10 women), 4 part-time/adjunct (3 women). *Students:* 107 full-time (57 women), 21 part-time (8 women); includes 9 minority (6 American Indian or Alaska Native, non-Hispanic/Latino; 2 Asian, non-Hispanic/Latino; 1 Hispanic/Latino), 18 international. Average age 30. 79 applicants, 49% accepted, 24 enrolled. In 2018, 30 master's, 3 doctorates awarded. Terminal master's awarded for partial completion of doctoral program. *Degree requirements:* For master's, thesis (for some programs), capstone seminar; for doctorate, comprehensive exam, thesis/dissertation, capstone seminar. *Entrance requirements:* For master's and doctorate, GRE General Test, minimum GPA of 3.0. Additional exam requirements/recommendations for international students: Required—TOEFL (minimum score 550 paper-based; 80 iBT), IELTS (minimum score 6). *Application deadline:* For fall admission, 2/1 priority date for domestic and international students; for spring admission, 11/1 priority date for domestic and international students. Applications are processed on a rolling basis. Application fee: $60. Electronic applications accepted. *Expenses: Tuition, area resident:* Full-time $11,090; part-time $462 per credit hour. Tuition, state resident: full-time $11,090; part-time $462 per credit hour. Tuition, nonresident: full-time $22,650; part-time $944 per credit hour. *International tuition:* $22,650 full-time. *Required fees:* $1733; $178.58 per credit hour. *Financial support:* In 2018–19, 46 students received support. Unspecified assistantships available. Financial award application deadline: 6/30; financial award applicants required to submit FAFSA. *Faculty research:* Ecology, conservation biology, fish and wildlife biology and management, plant science, entomology. *Total annual research expenditures:* $5.9 million. *Unit head:* Dr. Melissa K. Fierke, Chair, 315-470-6809, Fax: 315-470-6743, E-mail: mkfierke@esf.edu. *Application contact:* Scott Shannon, Associate Provost for Instruction/Dean of the Graduate School, 315-470-6599, E-mail: esfgrad@esf.edu.
Website: http://www.esf.edu/efb/grad/default.asp

Peterson's Graduate Programs in the Physical Sciences, Mathematics, Agricultural Sciences, the Environment & Natural Resources 2020

www.petersons.com **331**

Fish, Game, and Wildlife Management

Sul Ross State University, Division of Agricultural and Natural Resource Science, Programs in Natural Resource Management, Alpine, TX 79832. Offers range and wildlife management (M Ag, MS). *Program availability:* Part-time. *Degree requirements:* For master's, thesis (for some programs). *Entrance requirements:* For master's, GRE General Test, minimum undergraduate GPA of 2.5 in last 60 hours.

Tarleton State University, College of Graduate Studies, College of Agricultural and Environmental Sciences, Department of Wildlife, Sustainability, and Ecosystem Sciences, Stephenville, TX 76402. Offers agricultural and natural resource sciences (MS). *Program availability:* Part-time, evening/weekend. *Faculty:* 4 full-time (2 women), 2 part-time/adjunct (0 women). *Students:* 10 full-time (5 women), 7 part-time (4 women). Average age 28. 7 applicants, 86% accepted, 4 enrolled. In 2018, 5 master's awarded. *Degree requirements:* For master's, comprehensive exam, thesis (for some programs). *Entrance requirements:* For master's, GRE General Test, minimum GPA of 3.0. Additional exam requirements/recommendations for international students: Required—TOEFL (minimum score 520 paper-based; 69 iBT); Recommended—IELTS (minimum score 6), TSE (minimum score 50). *Application deadline:* For fall admission, 8/1 priority date for domestic students; for spring admission, 12/1 for domestic students. Applications are processed on a rolling basis. Application fee: $50 ($130 for international students). Electronic applications accepted. *Expenses:* Contact institution. *Financial support:* Research assistantships, teaching assistantships, career-related internships or fieldwork, Federal Work-Study, and institutionally sponsored loans available. Support available to part-time students. Financial award application deadline: 5/1; financial award applicants required to submit FAFSA. *Unit head:* Dr. T. Wayne Schwertner, Department Head, 254-968-9219, E-mail: schwertner@tarleton.edu. *Application contact:* Information Contact, 254-968-9104, Fax: 254-968-9670, E-mail: gradoffice@tarleton.edu.

Tennessee Technological University, College of Graduate Studies, College of Arts and Sciences, Department of Biology, Cookeville, TN 38505. Offers fish, game, and wildlife management (MS). *Program availability:* Part-time. *Faculty:* 22 full-time (2 women). *Students:* 4 full-time (3 women), 15 part-time (5 women). 12 applicants, 25% accepted, 3 enrolled. In 2018, 7 master's awarded. *Degree requirements:* For master's, thesis. *Entrance requirements:* For master's, GRE. Additional exam requirements/recommendations for international students: Required—TOEFL (minimum score 527 paper-based; 71 iBT), IELTS (minimum score 5.5), PTE (minimum score 48), or TOEIC (Test of English as an International Communication). *Application deadline:* For fall admission, 8/1 for domestic students, 5/1 for international students; for spring admission, 12/1 for domestic students, 10/1 for international students; for summer admission, 5/1 for domestic students, 2/1 for international students. Applications are processed on a rolling basis. Application fee: $35 ($40 for international students). Electronic applications accepted. *Financial support:* In 2018–19, 7 research assistantships, 14 teaching assistantships (averaging $7,500 per year) were awarded. Financial award application deadline: 4/1. *Faculty research:* Aquatics, environmental studies. *Unit head:* Dr. Chris Brown, Interim Chairperson, 931-372-3134, Fax: 931-372-6257, E-mail: cabrown@tntech.edu. *Application contact:* Shelia K. Kendrick, Coordinator of Graduate Studies, 931-372-3808, Fax: 931-372-3497, E-mail: skendrick@tntech.edu.

Texas A&M University, College of Agriculture and Life Sciences, Department of Wildlife and Fisheries Sciences, College Station, TX 77843. Offers wildlife and fisheries sciences (MS); wildlife science (MWSc). *Program availability:* Part-time, blended/hybrid learning. *Faculty:* 26. *Students:* 57 full-time (35 women), 34 part-time (25 women); includes 20 minority (1 Black or African American, non-Hispanic/Latino; 1 Asian, non-Hispanic/Latino; 17 Hispanic/Latino; 1 Two or more races, non-Hispanic/Latino), 16 international. Average age 32. 26 applicants, 54% accepted, 14 enrolled. In 2018, 19 master's, 10 doctorates awarded. Terminal master's awarded for partial completion of doctoral program. *Degree requirements:* For master's, thesis, final oral defense; for doctorate, thesis/dissertation, final oral defense. *Entrance requirements:* For master's and doctorate, GRE General Test, minimum GPA of 3.0. Additional exam requirements/recommendations for international students: Required—TOEFL (minimum score 550 paper-based; 80 iBT), IELTS (minimum score 6), PTE (minimum score 53). *Application deadline:* For fall admission, 5/1 for domestic students, 2/1 for international students; for spring admission, 9/1 for domestic and international students. Applications are processed on a rolling basis. Application fee: $50 ($90 for international students). Electronic applications accepted. *Expenses:* Contact institution. *Financial support:* In 2018–19, 66 students received support, including 21 fellowships with tuition reimbursements available (averaging $8,249 per year), 575 research assistantships with tuition reimbursements available (averaging $14,017 per year), 337 teaching assistantships with tuition reimbursements available (averaging $13,020 per year); career-related internships or fieldwork, institutionally sponsored loans, scholarships/grants, traineeships, health care benefits, tuition waivers (full and partial), and unspecified assistantships also available. Support available to part-time students. Financial award application deadline: 3/15; financial award applicants required to submit FAFSA. *Faculty research:* Wildlife ecology and management, fisheries ecology and management, aquaculture, biological inventories and museum collections, biosystematics and genome analysis. *Unit head:* Dr. Michael Masser, Professor and Department Head, 979-845-6295, Fax: 979-845-3786, E-mail: mmasser@tamu.edu. *Application contact:* Dr. Delbert Gatlin, Professor/Associate Department Head for Research and Graduate Programs, 979-847-9333, Fax: 979-845-3786, E-mail: d-gatlin@tamu.edu.
Website: http://wfsc.tamu.edu/

Texas A&M University–Kingsville, College of Graduate Studies, Dick and Mary Lewis Kleberg College of Agriculture, Natural Resources and Human Sciences, Department of Animal, Rangeland, and Wildlife Sciences, Program in Range and Wildlife Management, Kingsville, TX 78363. Offers MS. *Degree requirements:* For master's, variable foreign language requirement, comprehensive exam, thesis (for some programs). *Entrance requirements:* For master's, GRE (minimum of 150 for each of the math and verbal sections), MAT, GMAT, minimum GPA of 3.0 for coursework from previous degree. Additional exam requirements/recommendations for international students: Required—TOEFL (minimum score 550 paper-based; 79 iBT). Electronic applications accepted.

Texas A&M University–Kingsville, College of Graduate Studies, Dick and Mary Lewis Kleberg College of Agriculture, Natural Resources and Human Sciences, Department of Animal, Rangeland, and Wildlife Sciences, Program in Wildlife Science, Kingsville, TX 78363. Offers PhD. *Degree requirements:* For doctorate, variable foreign language requirement, comprehensive exam, thesis/dissertation. *Entrance requirements:* For doctorate, GRE, MAT, GMAT, 3 letters of recommendation. Additional exam requirements/recommendations for international students: Required—TOEFL (minimum score 550 paper-based; 79 iBT). Electronic applications accepted.

Texas State University, The Graduate College, College of Science and Engineering, Program in Wildlife Ecology, San Marcos, TX 78666. Offers MS. *Program availability:* Part-time. *Faculty:* 10 full-time (4 women), 1 part-time/adjunct (0 women). *Students:* 17 full-time (6 women), 8 part-time (5 women); includes 5 minority (all Hispanic/Latino). Average age 27. 14 applicants, 57% accepted, 8 enrolled. In 2018, 9 master's awarded. *Degree requirements:* For master's, comprehensive exam, thesis. *Entrance requirements:* For master's, official GRE (general test only) required with competitive scores in the verbal reasoning and quantitative reasoning sections, baccalaureate degree in biology or related discipline from regionally-accredited university with minimum GPA of 3.0 on last 60 undergraduate semester hours, current resume, statement of purpose, 3 letters of recommendation, letter of intent to mentor from biology department faculty member. Additional exam requirements/recommendations for international students: Required—TOEFL (minimum score 550 paper-based; 78 iBT), IELTS (minimum score 6.5). *Application deadline:* For fall admission, 2/1 priority date for domestic and international students; for spring admission, 10/15 for domestic students, 10/1 for international students; for summer admission, 4/15 for domestic students, 3/15 for international students. Applications are processed on a rolling basis. Application fee: $55 ($90 for international students). Electronic applications accepted. *Expenses:* Tuition, state resident: full-time $8102; part-time $4051 per semester. Tuition, nonresident: full-time $18,229; part-time $9115 per semester. *International tuition:* $18,229 full-time. *Required fees:* $2116; $120 per credit hour. Tuition and fees vary according to course load. *Financial support:* In 2018–19, 17 students received support, including 1 research assistantship (averaging $12,152 per year), 15 teaching assistantships (averaging $13,702 per year); Federal Work-Study, institutionally sponsored loans, health care benefits, and unspecified assistantships also available. Support available to part-time students. Financial award application deadline: 1/15; financial award applicants required to submit FAFSA. *Faculty research:* Disease Ecology (Zoonotic diseases, Hantavirus ecology), Community Ecology (Temporal Niche Overlap, Metacommunity Theory), Mammal Ecology, Invasive Species; using modern statistical methods to monitor spatial and temporal alterations in wildlife population demographics; Behavioral Ecology, Sexual Selection in the context of speciation and predator-prey dynamics; understand how ecological processes and how they affect the structure and health of populations and communities in rivers. *Total annual research expenditures:* $514,418. *Unit head:* Dr. Floyd Weckerly, Graduate Advisor, 512-245-3353, Fax: 512-245-8713, E-mail: fw11@txstate.edu. *Application contact:* Dr. Andrea Golato, Dean of the Graduate School, 512-245-2581, Fax: 512-245-8365, E-mail: jw02@swt.edu.
Website: http://www.bio.txstate.edu/Graduate-Programs/M-S—Wildlife-Ecology-Program-.html

Texas Tech University, Graduate School, College of Agricultural Sciences and Natural Resources, Department of Natural Resources Management, Lubbock, TX 79409-2125. Offers wildlife, aquatic, and wildlands science and management (MS, PhD). *Program availability:* Part-time. *Faculty:* 18 full-time (3 women), 1 part-time/adjunct (0 women). *Students:* 43 full-time (18 women), 12 part-time (3 women); includes 7 minority (4 Hispanic/Latino; 3 Two or more races, non-Hispanic/Latino), 3 international. Average age 30. 12 applicants, 83% accepted, 8 enrolled. In 2018, 11 master's, 3 doctorates awarded. *Degree requirements:* For master's, comprehensive exam, thesis (for some programs); for doctorate, comprehensive exam, thesis/dissertation. *Entrance requirements:* For master's and doctorate, GRE General Test, formal approval from departmental committee. Additional exam requirements/recommendations for international students: Required—TOEFL (minimum score 550 paper-based; 79 iBT). *Application deadline:* For fall admission, 6/1 priority date for domestic students, 1/15 priority date for international students; for spring admission, 9/1 priority date for domestic students, 6/15 priority date for international students. Applications are processed on a rolling basis. Application fee: $65. Electronic applications accepted. *Expenses:* Contact institution. *Financial support:* In 2018–19, 50 students received support, including 41 fellowships (averaging $4,687 per year), 38 research assistantships (averaging $14,456 per year), 5 teaching assistantships (averaging $13,036 per year); Federal Work-Study, scholarships/grants, and unspecified assistantships also available. Financial award application deadline: 4/15; financial award applicants required to submit FAFSA. *Faculty research:* Applying ecological knowledge in decision-making about sustainable resource use, community (plant or animal) response to disturbances, population dynamics, climate change, habitat restoration, wildlife management, range management, fisheries ecology, fire ecology, aquatic systems. *Total annual research expenditures:* $2.1 million. *Unit head:* Dr. Mark Wallace, Professor and Chair, 806-834-6979, Fax: 806-742-2280, E-mail: mark.wallace@ttu.edu. *Application contact:* Melissa S Moore, Administrative Assistant, 806-834-2628, Fax: 806-742-2280, E-mail: melissa.s.moore@ttu.edu.
Website: www.nrm.ttu.edu/

Université du Québec à Rimouski, Graduate Programs, Program in Wildlife Resources Management, Rimouski, QC G5L 3A1, Canada. Offers biology (PhD); wildlife resources management (M Sc, Diploma). PhD offered jointly with Université du Québec à Montréal, Université du Québec à Trois-Rivières, and Université du Québec en Abitibi-Témiscamingue. *Entrance requirements:* For degree, appropriate bachelor's degree, proficiency in French.

University of Alaska Fairbanks, College of Fisheries and Ocean Sciences, Program in Fisheries, Fairbanks, AK 99775-7220. Offers MS, PhD. *Program availability:* Part-time, Zoom. *Faculty:* 8 full-time (4 women). *Students:* 28 full-time (20 women), 35 part-time (19 women); includes 5 minority (1 Black or African American, non-Hispanic/Latino; 1 American Indian or Alaska Native, non-Hispanic/Latino; 3 Hispanic/Latino), 3 international. Average age 32. 16 applicants, 56% accepted, 9 enrolled. In 2018, 9 master's, 5 doctorates awarded. *Degree requirements:* For master's, comprehensive exam, thesis, oral defense of thesis; for doctorate, comprehensive exam, thesis/dissertation, oral defense of dissertation. *Entrance requirements:* For master's, GRE General Test, bachelor's degree from accredited institution with minimum cumulative undergraduate and major GPA of 3.0; for doctorate, GRE General Test, degree in a fisheries-related field with minimum cumulative GPA of 3.0. Additional exam requirements/recommendations for international students: Required—TOEFL (minimum score 550 paper-based; 79 iBT), IELTS (minimum score 6.5). *Application deadline:* For fall admission, 6/1 for domestic students, 3/1 for international students; for spring admission, 10/15 for domestic students, 8/15 for international students. Applications are processed on a rolling basis. Application fee: $60. Electronic applications accepted. *Expenses: Tuition, area resident:* Full-time $8802; part-time $5868 per credit hour. Tuition, state resident: full-time $8802; part-time $5868 per credit hour. Tuition, nonresident: full-time $18,504; part-time $12,336 per credit hour. *International tuition:* $18,504 full-time. *Required fees:* $1416; $944 per credit hour. $472 per semester. Tuition and fees vary according to course load and program. *Financial support:* In 2018–19, 15 research assistantships with full tuition reimbursements (averaging $13,654 per year), 4 teaching assistantships with full tuition reimbursements (averaging $7,763 per year) were awarded; fellowships with full tuition reimbursements, career-related internships or fieldwork, Federal Work-Study, scholarships/grants, health care benefits, and unspecified assistantships also available. Support available to part-time students. Financial award application deadline: 7/1; financial award applicants required to submit FAFSA. *Total annual research expenditures:* $3.1 million. *Unit head:* Dr. Milo Adkison, Chair, 907-796-5452, E-mail: info@sfos.uaf.edu. *Application contact:* Samara Taber, Director of Admissions, 907-474-7500, E-mail: uaf-admissions@alaska.edu.
Website: http://www.uaf.edu/cfos/academics/graduate/fisheries/

University of Alaska Fairbanks, College of Natural Science and Mathematics, Department of Biology and Wildlife, Fairbanks, AK 99775-6100. Offers biological sciences (MS, PhD); wildlife biology and conservation (MS). *Program availability:* Part-time. *Faculty:* 20 full-time (8 women). *Students:* 41 full-time (24 women), 20 part-time (13 women); includes 7 minority (1 American Indian or Alaska Native, non-Hispanic/Latino; 2 Hispanic/Latino; 1 Native Hawaiian or other Pacific Islander, non-Hispanic/Latino; 3 Two or more races, non-Hispanic/Latino), 2 international. Average age 31. 36 applicants, 33% accepted, 10 enrolled. In 2018, 12 master's, 5 doctorates awarded. *Degree requirements:* For master's, comprehensive exam, thesis, oral defense of thesis; for doctorate, comprehensive exam, thesis/dissertation, oral defense of dissertation. *Entrance requirements:* For master's and doctorate, GRE General Test, GRE Subject Test (biology), bachelor's degree from accredited institution with minimum cumulative undergraduate and major GPA of 3.0. Additional exam requirements/recommendations for international students: Required—TOEFL (minimum score 550 paper-based; 79 iBT), TWE. *Application deadline:* For fall admission, 1/15 for domestic and international students; for spring admission, 9/15 for domestic students, 9/1 for international students. Application fee: $60. Electronic applications accepted. *Expenses: Tuition, area resident:* Full-time $8802; part-time $5868 per credit hour. Tuition, state resident: full-time $8802; part-time $5868 per credit hour. Tuition, nonresident: full-time $18,504; part-time $12,336 per credit hour. *International tuition:* $18,504 full-time. *Required fees:* $1416; $944 per credit hour. $472 per semester. Tuition and fees vary according to course load and program. *Financial support:* In 2018–19, 18 research assistantships with full tuition reimbursements (averaging $15,377 per year), 11 teaching assistantships with full tuition reimbursements (averaging $9,005 per year) were awarded; fellowships with full tuition reimbursements, career-related internships or fieldwork, Federal Work-Study, scholarships/grants, health care benefits, and unspecified assistantships also available. Support available to part-time students. Financial award application deadline: 7/1; financial award applicants required to submit FAFSA. *Faculty research:* Plant-herbivore interactions, plant metabolic defenses, insect manufacture of glycerol, ice nucleators, structure and functions of arctic and subarctic freshwater ecosystems. *Total annual research expenditures:* $820,000. *Unit head:* Diane Wagner, Department Chair, 907-474-7671, E-mail: uaf-bw-dept@alaska.edu. *Application contact:* Samara Taber, Director of Admissions, 907-474-7500, E-mail: uaf-admissions@alaska.edu.
Website: http://www.bw.uaf.edu

University of Arkansas at Pine Bluff, School of Agriculture, Fisheries and Human Sciences, Pine Bluff, AR 71601-2799. Offers agricultural regulations (MS); aquaculture and fisheries (MS, PhD).

University of Delaware, College of Agriculture and Natural Resources, Department of Entomology and Wildlife Ecology, Newark, DE 19716. Offers entomology and applied ecology (MS, PhD), including avian ecology, evolution and taxonomy, insect biological control, insect ecology and behavior (MS), insect genetics, pest management, plant-insect interactions, wildlife ecology and management. *Program availability:* Part-time. *Degree requirements:* For master's, comprehensive exam, thesis, oral exam, seminar; for doctorate, comprehensive exam, thesis/dissertation, qualifying exam, seminar. *Entrance requirements:* For master's, GRE General Test, minimum GPA of 3.0 in field, 2.8 overall; for doctorate, GRE General Test, GRE Subject Test (biology), minimum GPA of 3.0 in field, 2.8 overall. Additional exam requirements/recommendations for international students: Required—TOEFL. Electronic applications accepted. *Faculty research:* Ecology and evolution of plant-insect interactions, ecology of wildlife conservation management, habitat restoration, biological control, applied ecosystem management.

University of Florida, Graduate School, College of Agricultural and Life Sciences, Department of Wildlife Ecology and Conservation, Gainesville, FL 32611. Offers environmental education and communications (Certificate); wildlife ecology and conservation (MS, PhD), including geographic information systems, tropical conservation and development, wetland sciences. *Degree requirements:* For master's, comprehensive exam, thesis optional; for doctorate, comprehensive exam, thesis/dissertation. *Entrance requirements:* For master's and doctorate, GRE General Test (minimum 34th percentile for Quantitative), minimum GPA of 3.3. Additional exam requirements/recommendations for international students: Required—TOEFL (minimum score 550 paper-based; 80 iBT), IELTS (minimum score 6). Electronic applications accepted. *Faculty research:* Conservation biology, spatial ecology, wildlife conservation and management, wetlands ecology and conservation, human dimensions in wildlife conservation.

University of Maine, Graduate School, College of Natural Sciences, Forestry, and Agriculture, Department of Wildlife, Fisheries, and Conservation Biology, Orono, ME 04469. Offers wildlife ecology (PhD). *Program availability:* Part-time. *Faculty:* 11 full-time (5 women). *Students:* 18 full-time (10 women), 1 part-time (0 women), 1 international. Average age 29. 14 applicants, 50% accepted, 3 enrolled. In 2018, 4 master's, 3 doctorates awarded. Terminal master's awarded for partial completion of doctoral program. *Degree requirements:* For master's, thesis (for some programs); for doctorate, one foreign language, comprehensive exam, thesis/dissertation. *Entrance requirements:* For master's and doctorate, GRE General Test. Additional exam requirements/recommendations for international students: Required—TOEFL. *Application deadline:* For fall admission, 2/1 priority date for domestic students. Applications are processed on a rolling basis. Application fee: $65. Electronic applications accepted. *Financial support:* In 2018–19, 36 students received support, including 25 research assistantships with full tuition reimbursements available (averaging $16,800 per year), 8 teaching assistantships with full tuition reimbursements available (averaging $15,600 per year); career-related internships or fieldwork, Federal Work-Study, institutionally sponsored loans, and tuition waivers (full and partial) also available. Financial award application deadline: 3/1. *Faculty research:* GIS applications, human dimensions of natural resources, wildlife-habitat relationships associated with forest management practices, migratory fish ecology, vernal pool ecology and conservation, population dynamics. *Total annual research expenditures:* $1.3 million. *Unit head:* Dr. Daniel Harrison, Chair, 207-581-2867, Fax: 207-581-2858. *Application contact:* Scott G. Delcourt, Assistant Vice President for Graduate Studies and Senior Associate Dean, 207-581-3291, Fax: 207-581-3232, E-mail: graduate@maine.edu.
Website: http://umaine.edu/wle/

University of Maryland Eastern Shore, Graduate Programs, Department of Natural Sciences, Princess Anne, MD 21853. Offers chemistry (MS); quantitative fisheries and resource economics (PMS); toxicology (MS, PhD). *Degree requirements:* For master's, thesis; for doctorate, comprehensive exam, thesis/dissertation. *Entrance requirements:* For master's and doctorate, GRE General Test, minimum GPA of 3.0. Additional exam requirements/recommendations for international students: Required—TOEFL (minimum score 80 iBT). Electronic applications accepted. *Faculty research:* Environmental chemistry (air/water pollution), fin fish ecology.

University of Massachusetts Amherst, Graduate School, College of Natural Sciences, Department of Environmental Conservation, Amherst, MA 01003. Offers building systems (MS, PhD); environmental policy and human dimensions (MS, PhD); forest resources (MS, PhD); sustainability science (MS); water, wetlands and watersheds (MS, PhD); wildlife and fisheries conservation (MS, PhD). *Program availability:* Part-time. Terminal master's awarded for partial completion of doctoral program. *Degree requirements:* For master's, thesis or alternative; for doctorate, comprehensive exam, thesis/dissertation. *Entrance requirements:* For master's and doctorate, GRE General Test. Additional exam requirements/recommendations for international students: Required—TOEFL (minimum score 550 paper-based; 80 iBT), IELTS (minimum score 6.5). Electronic applications accepted.

University of Miami, Graduate School, Rosenstiel School of Marine and Atmospheric Science, Division of Marine Biology and Fisheries, Coral Gables, FL 33124. Offers MA, MS, PhD. Terminal master's awarded for partial completion of doctoral program. *Degree requirements:* For master's, comprehensive exam, thesis; for doctorate, comprehensive exam, thesis/dissertation. *Entrance requirements:* For master's and doctorate, GRE General Test. Additional exam requirements/recommendations for international students: Required—TOEFL (minimum score 550 paper-based). Electronic applications accepted. *Faculty research:* Biochemistry, physiology, plankton, coral, biology.

University of Missouri, Office of Research and Graduate Studies, College of Agriculture, Food and Natural Resources, School of Natural Resources, Columbia, MO 65211. Offers agroforestry (MS, Certificate); conservation biology (Certificate); fisheries and wildlife sciences (MS, PhD); forestry (MS, PhD); geographical information science (Certificate); human dimensions of natural resources (MS, PhD); parks, recreation and tourism (MS); society and ecosystems (Certificate); soil, environmental and atmospheric sciences (MS, PhD); water resources (MS, PhD). *Program availability:* Part-time. *Degree requirements:* For doctorate, thesis/dissertation. *Entrance requirements:* For master's and doctorate, GRE General Test (minimum score 1200 Verbal and Quantitative), minimum GPA of 3.2. Additional exam requirements/recommendations for international students: Required—TOEFL (minimum score 550 paper-based; 80 iBT), IELTS (minimum score 6.5). Electronic applications accepted.

University of Montana, Graduate School, College of Forestry and Conservation, Missoula, MT 59812. Offers fish and wildlife biology (PhD); forest and conservation sciences (PhD); forestry (MS); recreation management (MS); resource conservation (MS); systems ecology (MS, PhD); wildlife biology (MS). *Degree requirements:* For doctorate, thesis/dissertation. *Entrance requirements:* For master's and doctorate, GRE General Test. Additional exam requirements/recommendations for international students: Required—TOEFL (minimum score 575 paper-based).

University of New Hampshire, Graduate School, College of Life Sciences and Agriculture, Department of Natural Resources and the Environment, Durham, NH 03824. Offers environmental conservation (MS); environmental economics (MS); forestry (MS); natural resources (MS); resource administration and management (MS); soil and water resource management (MS); wildlife and conservation biology (MS). *Program availability:* Part-time. *Entrance requirements:* For master's, GRE General Test. Additional exam requirements/recommendations for international students: Required—TOEFL (minimum score 550 paper-based; 80 iBT). Electronic applications accepted.

University of North Dakota, Graduate School, College of Arts and Sciences, Department of Biology, Grand Forks, ND 58202. Offers biology (MS); fisheries/wildlife (PhD); genetics (PhD); zoology (PhD). Terminal master's awarded for partial completion of doctoral program. *Degree requirements:* For master's, thesis, final exam; for doctorate, comprehensive exam, thesis/dissertation, final exam. *Entrance requirements:* For master's, GRE General Test, GRE Subject Test, minimum GPA of 3.0; for doctorate, GRE General Test, GRE Subject Test, minimum GPA of 3.5. Additional exam requirements/recommendations for international students: Required—TOEFL (minimum score 550 paper-based; 79 iBT), IELTS (minimum score 6.5). Electronic applications accepted. *Faculty research:* Population biology, wildlife ecology, RNA processing, hormonal control of behavior.

University of Rhode Island, Graduate School, College of the Environment and Life Sciences, Department of Fisheries, Animal and Veterinary Sciences, Kingston, RI 02881. Offers animal health and disease (MS); animal science (MS); aquaculture (MS); aquatic pathology (MS); environmental sciences (PhD), including animal science, aquaculture science, aquatic pathology, fisheries science; fisheries (MS). *Faculty:* 12 full-time (7 women). *Entrance requirements:* Additional exam requirements/recommendations for international students: Required—TOEFL. *Application deadline:* For fall admission, 7/15 for domestic students, 2/1 for international students; for spring admission, 11/15 for domestic students, 7/15 for international students. Application fee: $65. Electronic applications accepted. *Expenses: Tuition, area resident:* Full-time $13,226; part-time $735 per credit. Tuition, state resident: full-time $13,226; part-time $735 per credit. Tuition, nonresident: full-time $25,854; part-time $1436 per credit. *International tuition:* $25,854 full-time. *Required fees:* $1698; $50 per credit. $35 per semester. One-time fee: $165. *Financial support:* Application deadline: 2/1; applicants required to submit FAFSA. *Unit head:* Dr. Marta Gomez-Chiarri, Chair, 401-874-2917, Fax: 401-874-7575, E-mail: gomezchi@uri.edu. *Application contact:* Dr. Marta Gomez-Chiarri, Chair, 401-874-2917, Fax: 401-874-7575, E-mail: gomezchi@uri.edu.
Website: http://web.uri.edu/favs/

The University of Tennessee, Graduate School, College of Agricultural Sciences and Natural Resources, Department of Forestry, Wildlife, and Fisheries, Program in Wildlife and Fisheries Science, Knoxville, TN 37996. Offers MS. *Degree requirements:* For master's, thesis. *Entrance requirements:* For master's, GRE General Test, minimum GPA of 2.7. Additional exam requirements/recommendations for international students: Required—TOEFL. Electronic applications accepted.

University of Washington, Graduate School, College of the Environment, School of Aquatic and Fishery Sciences, Seattle, WA 98195. Offers MS, PhD. *Degree requirements:* For master's, thesis; for doctorate, thesis/dissertation. *Entrance requirements:* For master's and doctorate, GRE General Test, minimum GPA of 3.0. Additional exam requirements/recommendations for international students: Required—TOEFL. Electronic applications accepted. *Faculty research:* Fish and shellfish ecology, fisheries management, aquatic ecology, conservation biology, genetics.

University of Washington, Graduate School, College of the Environment, School of Environmental and Forest Sciences, Seattle, WA 98195. Offers bioresource science and engineering (MS, PhD); environmental horticulture (MEH); forest ecology (MS, PhD); forest management (MFR); forest soils (MS, PhD); restoration ecology (MS, PhD); restoration ecology and environmental horticulture (MS, PhD); social sciences (MS, PhD); sustainable resource management (MS, PhD); wildlife science (MS, PhD); MFR/MAIS; MPA/MS. *Accreditation:* SAF. *Program availability:* Part-time. *Degree requirements:* For master's, thesis; for doctorate, comprehensive exam, thesis/dissertation. *Entrance requirements:* For master's and doctorate, GRE, minimum GPA of 3.0. Additional exam requirements/recommendations for international students: Required—TOEFL. Electronic applications accepted. *Faculty research:* Ecosystem analysis, silviculture and forest protection, paper science and engineering, environmental horticulture and urban forestry, natural resource policy and economics, restoration ecology and environment horticulture, conservation, human dimensions, wildlife, bioresource science and engineering.

University of Wisconsin–Madison, Graduate School, College of Agricultural and Life Sciences, Department of Forest and Wildlife Ecology, Program in Wildlife Ecology, Madison, WI 53706-1380. Offers MS, PhD.

Utah State University, School of Graduate Studies, S.J. and Jessie E. Quinney College of Natural Resources, Department of Watershed Sciences, Logan, UT 84322. Offers ecology (MS, PhD); fisheries biology (MS, PhD); watershed science (MS, PhD). *Degree requirements:* For master's, thesis (for some programs); for doctorate, thesis/dissertation. *Entrance requirements:* For master's and doctorate, GRE General Test, minimum GPA of 3.2. Additional exam requirements/recommendations for international students: Required—TOEFL. Electronic applications accepted. *Faculty research:* Behavior, population ecology, habitat, conservation biology, restoration, aquatic ecology, fisheries management, fluvial geomorphology, remote sensing, conservation biology.

Utah State University, School of Graduate Studies, S.J. and Jessie E. Quinney College of Natural Resources, Department of Wildland Resources, Logan, UT 84322. Offers ecology (MS, PhD); forestry (MS, PhD); range science (MS, PhD); wildlife biology (MS, PhD). *Program availability:* Part-time. *Degree requirements:* For master's, thesis; for doctorate, comprehensive exam, thesis/dissertation. *Entrance requirements:* For master's and doctorate, GRE General Test, minimum GPA of 3.0. Additional exam requirements/recommendations for international students: Required—TOEFL. *Faculty research:* Range plant ecophysiology, plant community ecology, ruminant nutrition, population ecology.

Virginia Polytechnic Institute and State University, Graduate School, College of Natural Resources and Environment, Blacksburg, VA 24061. Offers fisheries and wildlife (MS, PhD); forest products (MS/MF); forestry (PhD); geography (MS); geospatial and environmental analysis (PhD); natural resources (MNR); MS/MF. *Faculty:* 80 full-time (18 women). *Students:* 179 full-time (80 women), 75 part-time (40 women); includes 34 minority (3 Black or African American, non-Hispanic/Latino; 7 Asian, non-Hispanic/Latino; 17 Hispanic/Latino; 1 Native Hawaiian or other Pacific Islander, non-Hispanic/Latino; 6 Two or more races, non-Hispanic/Latino), 33 international. Average age 32. 110 applicants, 58% accepted, 50 enrolled. In 2018, 93 master's, 13 doctorates awarded. *Degree requirements:* For master's, comprehensive exam (for some programs), thesis (for some programs); for doctorate, comprehensive exam (for some programs), thesis/dissertation (for some programs). *Entrance requirements:* For master's and doctorate, GRE/GMAT. Additional exam requirements/recommendations for international students: Required—TOEFL (minimum score 90 iBT). *Application deadline:* For fall admission, 8/1 for domestic students, 4/1 for international students; for spring admission, 1/1 for domestic students, 9/1 for international students. Applications are processed on a rolling basis. Application fee: $75. Electronic applications accepted. *Expenses:* Tuition, state resident: full-time $15,510; part-time $739.50 per credit hour. Tuition, nonresident: full-time $29,629; part-time $1490.25 per credit hour. *Required fees:* $2804; $550 per semester. Tuition and fees vary according to course load, campus/location and program. *Financial support:* In 2018–19, 4 fellowships with full tuition reimbursements (averaging $29,791 per year), 97 research assistantships with full tuition reimbursements (averaging $18,686 per year), 47 teaching assistantships with full tuition reimbursements (averaging $17,302 per year) were awarded; scholarships/grants also available. Financial award application deadline: 3/1; financial award applicants required to submit FAFSA. *Total annual research expenditures:* $16.1 million. *Unit head:* Dr. Paul M. Winistorfer, Dean, 540-231-5481, Fax: 540-231-7664, E-mail: pstorfer@vt.edu. *Application contact:* Arlice Banks, Executive Assistant, 540-231-7051, Fax: 540-231-7664, E-mail: arbanks@vt.edu.
Website: http://cnre.vt.edu/

West Virginia University, Davis College of Agriculture, Forestry and Consumer Sciences, Morgantown, WV 26506. Offers agricultural and extension education (MS, PhD); agriculture and resource management (MS); agriculture, natural resources and design (M Agr); agronomy (MS); animal and food science (PhD); animal physiology (MS); applied and environmental microbiology (MS); design and merchandising (MS); entomology (MS); forest resource science (PhD); forestry (MSF); genetics and developmental biology (MS, PhD); horticulture (MS); human and community development (PhD); landscape architecture (MLA); natural resource economics (PhD); nutritional and food science (MS); plant and soil science (PhD); plant pathology (MS); recreation, parks and tourism resources (MS); reproductive physiology (MS, PhD); wildlife and fisheries resources (PhD). *Accreditation:* ASLA. *Program availability:* Part-time. *Students:* 188 full-time (86 women), 47 part-time (30 women); includes 22 minority (5 Black or African American, non-Hispanic/Latino; 5 Asian, non-Hispanic/Latino; 8 Hispanic/Latino; 4 Two or more races, non-Hispanic/Latino), 60 international. In 2018, 56 master's, 14 doctorates awarded. *Degree requirements:* For master's, thesis; for doctorate, thesis/dissertation. *Entrance requirements:* Additional exam requirements/recommendations for international students: Required—TOEFL (minimum score 550 paper-based). *Application deadline:* For fall admission, 6/1 priority date for domestic students, 6/1 for international students; for spring admission, 1/5 for domestic and international students. Applications are processed on a rolling basis. Application fee: $60. Electronic applications accepted. *Financial support:* Fellowships, research assistantships, teaching assistantships, career-related internships or fieldwork, Federal Work-Study, institutionally sponsored loans, tuition waivers (full and partial), and unspecified assistantships available. Financial award application deadline: 2/1; financial award applicants required to submit FAFSA. *Faculty research:* Reproductive physiology, soil and water quality, human nutrition, aquaculture, wildlife management. *Unit head:* Dr. Ken Blemings, Interim Dean, 304-293-2395, Fax: 304-293-3740, E-mail: ken.blemings@mail.wvu.edu. *Application contact:* Dr. J. Todd Petty, Associate Dean, 304-293-2278, Fax: 304-293-3740, E-mail: jtpetty@mail.wvu.edu.
Website: https://www.davis.wvu.edu

Forestry

Auburn University, Graduate School, School of Forestry and Wildlife Sciences, Auburn University, AL 36849. Offers forestry (MS); natural resource conservation (MNR); wildlife sciences (MS, PhD). *Accreditation:* SAF. *Program availability:* Part-time. *Degree requirements:* For master's, thesis (MS); for doctorate, thesis/dissertation. *Entrance requirements:* For master's and doctorate, GRE General Test. Electronic applications accepted. *Expenses:* Tuition, state resident: full-time $11,282; part-time $535 per credit hour. Tuition, nonresident: full-time $30,542; part-time $1605 per credit hour. *Required fees:* $826 per semester. Tuition and fees vary according to degree level and program. *Faculty research:* Forest nursery management, silviculture and vegetation management, biological processes and ecological relationships, growth and yield of plantations and natural stands, urban forestry, forest taxation, law and policy.

California Polytechnic State University, San Luis Obispo, College of Agriculture, Food and Environmental Sciences, Department of Natural Resources Management and Environmental Sciences, San Luis Obispo, CA 93407. Offers forestry sciences (MS). *Program availability:* Part-time. *Faculty:* 5 full-time (2 women). *Students:* 1 full-time (0 women), 4 part-time (2 women); includes 2 minority (both Hispanic/Latino). Average age 33. 8 applicants, 50% accepted, 4 enrolled. In 2018, 4 master's awarded. *Degree requirements:* For master's, thesis. *Entrance requirements:* For master's, GRE. Additional exam requirements/recommendations for international students: Required—TOEFL (minimum score 80 iBT). *Application deadline:* For fall admission, 4/1 for domestic and international students; for winter admission, 10/1 for domestic students, 6/30 for international students; for spring admission, 10/1 for domestic students. Applications are processed on a rolling basis. Application fee: $55. Electronic applications accepted. *Expenses: Tuition, area resident:* Full-time $7176; part-time $4164 per year. Tuition, state resident: full-time $10,965. Tuition, nonresident: full-time $10,965. *Required fees:* $6336; $3711. *Financial support:* Fellowships, research assistantships, teaching assistantships, career-related internships or fieldwork, institutionally sponsored loans, scholarships/grants, health care benefits, and unspecified assistantships available. Financial award application deadline: 3/2; financial award applicants required to submit FAFSA. *Faculty research:* Hydrology, biometrics, forest health and management, fire science, urban and community forestry. *Unit head:* Dr. Richard Thompson, Department Head, 805-756-2898, E-mail: rpthomps@calpoly.edu. *Application contact:* Dr. Richard Thompson, Department Head, 805-756-2898, E-mail: rpthomps@calpoly.edu.
Website: http://nres.calpoly.edu/

Clemson University, Graduate School, College of Agriculture, Forestry and Life Sciences, Department of Forestry and Environmental Conservation, Clemson, SC 29634. Offers forest resources (MFR, MS, PhD); wildlife and fisheries biology (MS, PhD). *Program availability:* Part-time, 100% online. *Faculty:* 29 full-time (7 women). *Students:* 71 full-time (26 women), 54 part-time (25 women); includes 12 minority (2 Black or African American, non-Hispanic/Latino; 3 Hispanic/Latino; 7 Two or more races, non-Hispanic/Latino), 8 international. Average age 28. 100 applicants, 83% accepted, 74 enrolled. In 2018, 14 master's, 5 doctorates awarded. *Degree requirements:* For master's, thesis optional; for doctorate, comprehensive exam, thesis/dissertation. *Entrance requirements:* For master's and doctorate, GRE General Test, unofficial transcripts, letters of recommendation. Additional exam requirements/recommendations for international students: Required—TOEFL (minimum score 80 paper-based; 80 iBT); Recommended—IELTS (minimum score 6.5), TSE (minimum score 54). *Application deadline:* For fall admission, 4/15 for international students; for spring admission, 10/15 for international students. Applications are processed on a rolling basis. Application fee: $80 ($90 for international students). Electronic applications accepted. *Expenses: Tuition, area resident:* Full-time $11,270; part-time $8688 per credit hour. Tuition, state resident: full-time $11,796. Tuition, nonresident: full-time $23,802; part-time $17,412 per credit hour. *International tuition:* $23,246 full-time. *Required fees:* $1196; $497 per semester. Tuition and fees vary according to course load, degree level, campus/location and program. *Financial support:* In 2018–19, 41 students received support, including 5 fellowships with full and partial tuition reimbursements available (averaging $2,000 per year), 31 research assistantships with full and partial tuition reimbursements available (averaging $16,095 per year), 5 teaching assistantships with full and partial tuition reimbursements available (averaging $13,560 per year); career-related internships or fieldwork and unspecified assistantships also available. *Faculty research:* Wildlife ecology and management, forest ecology and management, environmental and natural resources, wetlands conservation, ecotoxicology and risk mitigation. *Total annual research expenditures:* $2.1 million. *Unit head:* Dr. Gregg Yarrow, Department Chair, 864-656-3302, E-mail: gyarrow@clemson.edu. *Application contact:* Dr. Kyle Barrett, Graduate Program Coordinator, 864-642-1847, E-mail: rbarre2@clemson.edu.
Website: http://www.clemson.edu/cafls/departments/fec/index.html

Cornell University, Graduate School, Graduate Fields of Agriculture and Life Sciences, Field of Natural Resources, Ithaca, NY 14853. Offers community-based natural resources management (MPS, PhD); conservation biology (MS, PhD); ecosystem biology and biogeochemistry (MPS, MS, PhD); environmental management (MPS); fishery and aquatic science (MPS, MS, PhD); forest science (MPS, MS, PhD); human dimensions of natural resources management (MPS, MS, PhD); policy and institutional analysis (MS, PhD); program development and evaluation (MPS, MS, PhD); quantitative ecology (MS, PhD); wildlife science (MPS, MS, PhD). *Degree requirements:* For master's, thesis (MS), project paper (MPS); for doctorate, comprehensive exam, thesis/dissertation. *Entrance requirements:* For master's and doctorate, GRE General Test, 2 letters of recommendation. Additional exam requirements/recommendations for international students: Required—TOEFL (minimum score 550 paper-based; 77 iBT). Electronic applications accepted. *Faculty research:* Ecosystem-level dynamics, systems modeling, conservation biology/management, resource management's human dimensions, biogeochemistry.

Harvard University, Graduate School of Arts and Sciences, Department of Forestry, Cambridge, MA 02138. Offers forest science (MFS). *Degree requirements:* For master's, thesis. *Entrance requirements:* For master's, GRE General Test, bachelor's degree in biology or forestry. Additional exam requirements/recommendations for international students: Required—TOEFL. *Faculty research:* Forest ecology, planning, and physiology; forest microbiology.

Humboldt State University, Academic Programs, College of Natural Resources and Sciences, Programs in Natural Resources, Arcata, CA 95521-8299. Offers natural resources (MS), including fisheries, forestry, natural resources planning and interpretation, rangeland resources and wildland soils, wastewater utilization, watershed management, wildlife. *Faculty:* 22 full-time (5 women), 20 part-time/adjunct (7 women). *Students:* 43 full-time (22 women), 45 part-time (21 women); includes 24 minority (1 Black or African American, non-Hispanic/Latino; 2 American Indian or Alaska Native, non-Hispanic/Latino; 1 Asian, non-Hispanic/Latino; 16 Hispanic/Latino; 4 Two or more races, non-Hispanic/Latino), 1 international. Average age 28. 38 applicants, 37% accepted, 14 enrolled. In 2018, 21 master's awarded. *Degree requirements:* For master's, thesis or alternative. *Entrance requirements:* For master's, GRE, appropriate bachelor's degree, minimum GPA of 2.5, 3 letters of recommendation, resume.

Additional exam requirements/recommendations for international students: Required—TOEFL (minimum score 500 paper-based). *Application deadline:* For fall admission, 2/1 for domestic and international students; for spring admission, 9/30 for domestic and international students. Applications are processed on a rolling basis. Application fee: $55. *Expenses: Tuition:* Part-time $4649 per semester. *Required fees:* $2121; $1673. Tuition and fees vary according to program. *Financial support:* Fellowships, career-related internships or fieldwork, and Federal Work-Study available. Support available to part-time students. Financial award application deadline: 3/1; financial award applicants required to submit FAFSA. *Faculty research:* Spotted owl habitat, pre-settlement vegetation, hardwood utilization, tree physiology, fisheries. *Unit head:* Dr. Andrew Stubblefield, Graduate Program Coordinator, 707-826-3258, E-mail: andrew.stubblefield@humboldt.edu. *Application contact:* Dr. Andrew Stubblefield, Graduate Program Coordinator, 707-826-3258, E-mail: andrew.stubblefield@humboldt.edu.
Website: http://www.humboldt.edu/cnrs/graduate_programs

Iowa State University of Science and Technology, Department of Natural Resource Ecology and Management, Ames, IA 50011. Offers forestry (MS, PhD); wildlife ecology (MS, PhD). *Entrance requirements:* For master's and doctorate, GRE General Test. Additional exam requirements/recommendations for international students: Required—TOEFL (minimum score 550 paper-based; 79 iBT), IELTS (minimum score 6.5). Electronic applications accepted.

Iowa State University of Science and Technology, Program in Forestry, Ames, IA 50011. Offers MS, PhD. *Entrance requirements:* For master's and doctorate, GRE. Additional exam requirements/recommendations for international students: Required—TOEFL (minimum score 550 paper-based; 79 iBT), IELTS (minimum score 6.5). Electronic applications accepted.

Lakehead University, Graduate Studies, Faculty of Natural Resources Management, Thunder Bay, ON P7B 5E1, Canada. Offers forest sciences (PhD); forestry (M Sc F). *Program availability:* Part-time. *Degree requirements:* For master's, thesis. *Entrance requirements:* For master's, minimum B average. Additional exam requirements/recommendations for international students: Required—TOEFL. *Faculty research:* Soils, silviculture, wildlife, ecology, genetics.

Louisiana State University and Agricultural & Mechanical College, Graduate School, College of Agriculture, School of Renewable Natural Resources, Baton Rouge, LA 70803. Offers fisheries (MS); forestry (MS, PhD); wildlife (MS); wildlife and fisheries science (PhD).

McGill University, Faculty of Graduate and Postdoctoral Studies, Faculty of Agricultural and Environmental Sciences, Department of Natural Resource Sciences, Montréal, QC H3A 2T5, Canada. Offers entomology (M Sc, PhD); environmental assessment (M Sc); forest science (M Sc, PhD); microbiology (M Sc, PhD); micrometeorology (M Sc, PhD); neotropical environment (M Sc, PhD); soil science (M Sc, PhD); wildlife biology (M Sc, PhD).

Michigan State University, The Graduate School, College of Agriculture and Natural Resources, Department of Forestry, East Lansing, MI 48824. Offers forestry (MS, PhD); forestry-environmental toxicology (PhD); plant breeding, genetics and biotechnology-forestry (MS, PhD). *Entrance requirements:* Additional exam requirements/recommendations for international students: Required—TOEFL (minimum score 550 paper-based), Michigan State University ELT (minimum score 85), Michigan English Language Assessment Battery (minimum score 83). Electronic applications accepted.

Michigan Technological University, Graduate School, School of Forest Resources and Environmental Science, Houghton, MI 49931. Offers forest resources and environmental science (MGIS). *Accreditation:* SAF. *Program availability:* Part-time. *Faculty:* 38 full-time (11 women), 24 part-time/adjunct (7 women). *Students:* 60 full-time (21 women), 16 part-time (7 women); includes 4 minority (1 Black or African American, non-Hispanic/Latino; 3 Two or more races, non-Hispanic/Latino), 13 international. Average age 30. 110 applicants, 30% accepted, 22 enrolled. In 2018, 20 master's, 6 doctorates awarded. Terminal master's awarded for partial completion of doctoral program. *Degree requirements:* For master's, thesis (for some programs), comprehensive exam (for non-research degrees); for doctorate, comprehensive exam, thesis/dissertation. *Entrance requirements:* For master's and doctorate, GRE, statement of purpose, personal statement, official transcripts, 3 letters of recommendation, resume/curriculum vitae. Additional exam requirements/recommendations for international students: Required—TOEFL, IELTS, TOEFL (recommended minimum score 79 iBT) or IELTS (recommended minimum score of 6.5). *Application deadline:* Applications are processed on a rolling basis. Electronic applications accepted. *Expenses: Tuition, area resident:* Full-time $18,126; part-time $1007 per credit. Tuition, state resident: full-time $18,126; part-time $1007 per credit. Tuition, nonresident: full-time $18,126; part-time $1007 per credit. *International tuition:* $18,126 full-time. *Required fees:* $248; $124 per semester. Tuition and fees vary according to course load and program. *Financial support:* In 2018–19, 41 students received support, including 2 fellowships with tuition reimbursements available (averaging $16,590 per year), 18 research assistantships with tuition reimbursements available (averaging $16,590 per year), 8 teaching assistantships with tuition reimbursements available (averaging $16,590 per year); career-related internships or fieldwork, Federal Work-Study, scholarships/grants, health care benefits, unspecified assistantships, and cooperative program also available. Financial award applicants required to submit FAFSA. *Faculty research:* Forestry, wildlife ecology and management; natural resources, applied ecology and environmental science; biotechnology and molecular genetics; forest biomaterials; geospatial science and technology. *Total annual research expenditures:* $3.4 million. *Unit head:* Dr. Andrew J. Storer, Dean, 906-487-3470, Fax: 906-487-2915, E-mail: storer@mtu.edu. *Application contact:* Dr. Audrey L. Mayer, Graduate Director/Professor, 906-487-3448, Fax: 906-487-2915, E-mail: almayer@mtu.edu.
Website: http://www.mtu.edu/forest/

Mississippi State University, College of Forest Resources, Department of Forestry, Mississippi State, MS 39762. Offers forestry (MS). *Program availability:* Part-time. *Faculty:* 22 full-time (4 women). *Students:* 22 full-time (10 women), 13 part-time (4 women); includes 2 minority (1 Black or African American, non-Hispanic/Latino; 1 American Indian or Alaska Native, non-Hispanic/Latino), 10 international. Average age 31. 23 applicants, 48% accepted, 10 enrolled. In 2018, 7 master's, 2 doctorates awarded. *Degree requirements:* For master's, thesis optional, comprehensive oral or written exam; for doctorate, comprehensive exam, thesis/dissertation. *Entrance requirements:* For master's, GRE, BS with minimum GPA of 3.0 on last 60 hours of undergraduate study; for doctorate, minimum GPA of 3.1 on prior graduate courses or 3.25 on last 60 hours of undergraduate study. Additional exam requirements/recommendations for international students: Required—TOEFL (minimum score 550 paper-based; 79 iBT); Recommended—IELTS (minimum score 6.5). *Application deadline:* For fall admission, 7/1 for domestic students, 5/1 for international students; for spring admission, 11/1 for domestic students, 9/1 for international students. Applications are processed on a rolling basis. Application fee: $60 ($80 for international students). Electronic applications accepted. *Expenses:* Tuition, state resident: full-time $8450; part-time $360.59 per credit hour. Tuition, nonresident: full-time $23,140; part-time $969.09 per credit hour. *Required fees:* $110. One-time fee: $55 full-time. Part-time tuition and fees vary according to course load, degree level, campus/location and reciprocity agreements. *Financial support:* In 2018–19, 22 research assistantships with full tuition reimbursements (averaging $13,348 per year) were awarded; Federal Work-Study, institutionally sponsored loans, and unspecified assistantships also available. Financial award application deadline: 4/1; financial award applicants required to submit FAFSA. *Faculty research:* Forest hydrology, forest biometry, forest management/economics, forest biology, industrial forest operations. *Unit head:* Dr. Donal Grebner, Professor and Head, 662-325-0928, Fax: 662-325-8762, E-mail: dlg26@msstate.edu. *Application contact:* Nathan Drake, Admissions and Enrollment Assistant, 662-325-3804, E-mail: ndrake@grad.msstate.edu.
Website: http://www.cfr.msstate.edu/forestry/

Mississippi State University, College of Forest Resources, Department of Sustainable Bioproducts, Mississippi State, MS 39762. Offers forest resources (PhD), including sustainable biproducts; sustainable bioproducts (MS). *Faculty:* 12 full-time (1 woman), 1 part-time/adjunct (0 women). *Students:* 32 full-time (16 women), 2 part-time (0 women); includes 4 minority (2 Black or African American, non-Hispanic/Latino; 1 Asian, non-Hispanic/Latino; 1 Two or more races, non-Hispanic/Latino), 21 international. Average age 29. 19 applicants, 58% accepted, 8 enrolled. In 2018, 5 master's, 5 doctorates awarded. *Degree requirements:* For master's, thesis optional; for doctorate, comprehensive exam, thesis/dissertation. *Entrance requirements:* For master's, GRE (if undergraduate GPA of last two years less than 3.0); for doctorate, GRE if undergraduate GPA of last two years is below 3.0. Additional exam requirements/recommendations for international students: Required—TOEFL (minimum score 550 paper-based; 79 iBT); Recommended—IELTS (minimum score 6.5). *Application deadline:* For fall admission, 7/1 for domestic students, 5/1 for international students; for spring admission, 11/1 for domestic students, 9/1 for international students. Applications are processed on a rolling basis. Application fee: $60 ($80 for international students). Electronic applications accepted. *Expenses:* Tuition, state resident: full-time $8450; part-time $360.59 per credit hour. Tuition, nonresident: full-time $23,140; part-time $969.09 per credit hour. *Required fees:* $110. One-time fee: $55 full-time. Part-time tuition and fees vary according to course load, degree level, campus/location and reciprocity agreements. *Financial support:* In 2018–19, 100 students received support, including 32 research assistantships with full tuition reimbursements available (averaging $16,968 per year); Federal Work-Study, institutionally sponsored loans, and unspecified assistantships also available. Financial award application deadline: 4/1; financial award applicants required to submit FAFSA. *Faculty research:* Wood property enhancement and durability, environmental science and chemistry, wood-based composites, primary wood production, furniture manufacturing and management. *Unit head:* Dr. Rubin Shmulsky, Department Head and Graduate Coordinator, 662-325-2116, Fax: 662-325-8126, E-mail: rshmulsky@cfr.msstate.edu. *Application contact:* Nathan Drake, Admissions and Enrollment Assistant, 662-325-3804, E-mail: ndrake@grad.msstate.edu.
Website: http://www.cfr.msstate.edu/forestp//index.asp

North Carolina State University, Graduate School, College of Natural Resources, Department of Forestry and Environmental Resources, Raleigh, NC 27695. Offers MF, MS, PhD. *Program availability:* Part-time. *Degree requirements:* For master's, thesis (for some programs), teaching experience; for doctorate, thesis/dissertation, teaching experience. *Entrance requirements:* For master's and doctorate, GRE General Test. Additional exam requirements/recommendations for international students: Required—TOEFL. Electronic applications accepted. *Faculty research:* Forest genetics, forest ecology and silviculture, forest economics/management/policy, international forestry, remote sensing/geographic information systems.

Northern Arizona University, College of Environment, Forestry, and Natural Sciences, School of Forestry, Flagstaff, AZ 86011. Offers forest science (PhD); forestry (MF, MSF). *Program availability:* Part-time. *Degree requirements:* For master's, variable foreign language requirement, comprehensive exam (for some programs), thesis (for some programs); for doctorate, variable foreign language requirement, comprehensive exam (for some programs), thesis/dissertation (for some programs). *Entrance requirements:* For master's and doctorate, GRE General Test. Additional exam requirements/recommendations for international students: Required—TOEFL (minimum score 80 iBT), IELTS (minimum score 6.5). Electronic applications accepted.

The Ohio State University, Graduate School, College of Food, Agricultural, and Environmental Sciences, School of Environment and Natural Resources, Columbus, OH 43210. Offers ecological restoration (MS, PhD); ecosystem science (MS, PhD); environment and natural resources (MENR); environmental social sciences (MS, PhD); fisheries and wildlife science (MS, PhD); forest science (MS, PhD); rural sociology (MS, PhD); soil science (MS, PhD). *Faculty:* 38. *Students:* 106 (64 women). Average age 29. In 2018, 21 master's, 5 doctorates awarded. *Entrance requirements:* For master's and doctorate, GRE. Additional exam requirements/recommendations for international students: Required—TOEFL (minimum score 550 paper-based; 79 iBT), Michigan English Language Assessment Battery (minimum score 82); Recommended—IELTS (minimum score 7). *Application deadline:* For fall admission, 1/1 priority date for domestic students, 12/15 priority date for international students; for spring admission, 11/1 for domestic students, 9/15 for international students. Applications are processed on a rolling basis. Application fee: $60 ($70 for international students). Electronic applications accepted. *Financial support:* Fellowships, research assistantships, teaching assistantships, health care benefits, and unspecified assistantships available. *Unit head:* Dr. Jeff S. Sharp, Director, 614-292-9410, E-mail: sharp.123@osu.edu. *Application contact:* Graduate and Professional Admissions, 614-292-9444, Fax: 614-292-3895, E-mail: gpadmissions@osu.edu.
Website: http://senr.osu.edu/

Oklahoma State University, College of Agricultural Science and Natural Resources, Department of Natural Resource Ecology and Management, Stillwater, OK 74078. Offers M Ag, MS, PhD. *Faculty:* 26 full-time (4 women), 1 (woman) part-time/adjunct. *Students:* 1 full-time (0 women), 41 part-time (16 women); includes 6 minority (1 American Indian or Alaska Native, non-Hispanic/Latino; 1 Asian, non-Hispanic/Latino; 2 Hispanic/Latino; 2 Two or more races, non-Hispanic/Latino), 5 international. Average age 27. 10 applicants, 90% accepted, 9 enrolled. In 2018, 14 master's, 4 doctorates awarded. *Entrance requirements:* For master's and doctorate, GRE or GMAT. Additional exam requirements/recommendations for international students: Required—TOEFL (minimum score 550 paper-based; 79 iBT). *Application deadline:* For fall admission, 3/1 priority date for international students; for spring admission, 8/1 priority date for international students. Applications are processed on a rolling basis. Application fee: $40 ($75 for international students). Electronic applications accepted. *Expenses: Tuition, area resident:* Full-time $4148. Tuition, state resident: full-time $4148. Tuition, nonresident: full-time $10,517. *International tuition:* $10,517 full-time. *Required fees:* $4394; $2929 per credit hour. Tuition and fees vary according to course load and program. *Financial support:* Research assistantships, teaching assistantships, career-related internships or fieldwork, Federal Work-Study, scholarships/grants, health care benefits, tuition waivers (partial), and unspecified assistantships available. Support available to part-time students. Financial award application deadline: 3/1; financial

award applicants required to submit FAFSA. *Faculty research:* Forest ecology, upland bird ecology, forest ecophysiology, urban forestry, molecular forest genetics/biotechnology/tree breeding. *Unit head:* Dr. Jim Ansley, Department Head, 405-744-3014, Fax: 405-744-3530, E-mail: jim.ansley@okstate.edu. *Application contact:* Dr. Sheryl Tucker, Dean, 405-744-6368, Fax: 405-744-0355, E-mail: gradi@okstate.edu.
Website: http://nrem.okstate.edu/

Oregon State University, College of Forestry, Program in Forest Ecosystems and Society, Corvallis, OR 97331. Offers forest biology (MF); forest, wildlife and landscape ecology (MS, PhD); genetics and physiology (MS, PhD); integrated social and ecological systems (MS, PhD); science of conservation, restoration and sustainable management (MS, PhD); silviculture (MF); social science, policy, and natural resources (MS, PhD); soil-plant-atmosphere continuum (MS, PhD); sustainable recreation and tourism (MS). *Program availability:* Part-time. *Entrance requirements:* For master's and doctorate, GRE. Additional exam requirements/recommendations for international students: Required—TOEFL (minimum score 80 iBT), IELTS (minimum score 6.5). *Faculty research:* Ecosystem structure and function, nutrient cycling, biotechnology, vegetation management, integrated forest protection.

Oregon State University, College of Forestry, Program in Natural Resources, Corvallis, OR 97331. Offers fisheries management (MNR); forests and climate change (MNR); geographic information science (MNR); sustainable natural resources (MNR); urban forestry (MNR); water conflict management and transformation (MNR); wildlife management (MNR). *Program availability:* Part-time, online only, 100% online. *Entrance requirements:* For master's, GRE. Additional exam requirements/recommendations for international students: Required—TOEFL (minimum score 80 iBT), IELTS (minimum score 6.5). *Expenses:* Contact institution.

Oregon State University, College of Forestry, Program in Sustainable Forest Management, Corvallis, OR 97331. Offers engineering for sustainable forestry (MF, MS, PhD). *Program availability:* Part-time. *Entrance requirements:* For master's and doctorate, GRE. Additional exam requirements/recommendations for international students: Required—TOEFL (minimum score 80 iBT), IELTS (minimum score 6.5).

Oregon State University, College of Forestry, Program in Wood Science, Corvallis, OR 97331. Offers biodeterioration and materials protection (MS, PhD). *Program availability:* Part-time. *Entrance requirements:* For master's and doctorate, GRE General Test, minimum GPA of 3.0 in last 90 hours. Additional exam requirements/recommendations for international students: Required—TOEFL (minimum score 575 paper-based; 93 iBT), IELTS (minimum score 7).

Penn State University Park, Graduate School, College of Agricultural Sciences, Department of Ecosystem Science and Management, University Park, PA 16802. Offers forest resources (MS, PhD); soil science (MS, PhD); wildlife and fisheries science (MS, PhD).

Purdue University, Graduate School, College of Agriculture, Department of Forestry and Natural Resources, West Lafayette, IN 47907. Offers fisheries and aquatic sciences (MS, MSF, PhD); forest biology (MS, MSF, PhD); natural resource social science (MS, PhD); natural resources social science (MSF); quantitative ecology (MS, MSF, PhD); wildlife science (MS, MSF, PhD); wood products and wood products manufacturing (MS, MSF, PhD). *Faculty:* 25 full-time (5 women), 1 part-time/adjunct (0 women). *Students:* 58 full-time (32 women), 5 part-time (1 woman); includes 12 minority (2 American Indian or Alaska Native, non-Hispanic/Latino; 1 Asian, non-Hispanic/Latino; 4 Hispanic/Latino; 1 Native Hawaiian or other Pacific Islander, non-Hispanic/Latino; 4 Two or more races, non-Hispanic/Latino), 12 international. Average age 27. 51 applicants, 27% accepted, 14 enrolled. In 2018, 13 master's, 11 doctorates awarded. *Degree requirements:* For master's, thesis; for doctorate, thesis/dissertation. *Entrance requirements:* For master's and doctorate, GRE General Test (minimum score: verbal 50th percentile; quantitative 50th percentile; analytical writing 4.0), minimum undergraduate GPA of 3.2 or equivalent. Additional exam requirements/recommendations for international students: Required—TOEFL (minimum score 550 paper-based; 77 iBT). *Application deadline:* For fall admission, 1/5 for domestic students, 1/15 for international students; for spring admission, 9/15 for domestic and international students. Applications are processed on a rolling basis. Application fee: $60 ($75 for international students). Electronic applications accepted. *Financial support:* In 2018–19, 10 research assistantships (averaging $15,259 per year) were awarded; fellowships, teaching assistantships, career-related internships or fieldwork, and scholarships/grants also available. Support available to part-time students. Financial award application deadline: 1/5; financial award applicants required to submit FAFSA. *Faculty research:* Wildlife management, forest management, forest ecology, forest soils, limnology. *Unit head:* Robert G. Wagner, Head of the Graduate Program, 765-494-3590, E-mail: rgwagner@purdue.edu. *Application contact:* Christine Hofmeyer, Graduate Contact, 765-494-3572, E-mail: chofmeye@purdue.edu.
Website: https://ag.purdue.edu/fnr

Southern Illinois University Carbondale, Graduate School, College of Agriculture, Department of Forestry, Carbondale, IL 62901-4701. Offers MS. *Program availability:* Part-time. *Degree requirements:* For master's, thesis. *Entrance requirements:* For master's, GRE, minimum GPA of 2.7. Additional exam requirements/recommendations for international students: Required—TOEFL. *Faculty research:* Forest recreation, forest ecology, remote sensing, forest management and economics.

Southern University and Agricultural and Mechanical College, Graduate School, College of Agricultural, Family and Consumer Sciences, Department of Urban Forestry and Natural Resources, Baton Rouge, LA 70813. Offers MS. *Degree requirements:* For master's, thesis. *Entrance requirements:* For master's, GRE, minimum GPA of 3.0. Additional exam requirements/recommendations for international students: Required—TOEFL (minimum score 525 paper-based). *Faculty research:* Biology of plant pathogen, water resources, plant pathology.

State University of New York College of Environmental Science and Forestry, Department of Environmental and Forest Biology, Syracuse, NY 13210-2779. Offers applied ecology (MPS); chemical ecology (MPS, MS, PhD); conservation biology (MPS, MS, PhD); ecology (MPS, MS, PhD); entomology (MPS, MS, PhD); environmental interpretation (MPS, MS, PhD); environmental physiology (MPS, MS, PhD); fish and wildlife biology and management (MPS, MS, PhD); forest pathology and mycology (MPS, MS, PhD); plant biotechnology (MPS); plant science and biotechnology (MPS, MS, PhD). *Program availability:* Part-time. *Faculty:* 35 full-time (10 women), 4 part-time/adjunct (3 women). *Students:* 107 full-time (57 women), 21 part-time (8 women); includes 9 minority (6 American Indian or Alaska Native, non-Hispanic/Latino; 2 Asian, non-Hispanic/Latino; 1 Hispanic/Latino), 18 international. Average age 30. 79 applicants, 49% accepted, 24 enrolled. In 2018, 30 master's, 3 doctorates awarded. Terminal master's awarded for partial completion of doctoral program. *Degree requirements:* For master's, thesis (for some programs), capstone seminar; for doctorate, comprehensive exam, thesis/dissertation, capstone seminar. *Entrance requirements:* For master's and doctorate, GRE General Test, minimum GPA of 3.0. Additional exam requirements/recommendations for international students: Required—TOEFL (minimum score 550 paper-based; 80 iBT), IELTS (minimum score 6). *Application deadline:* For fall admission, 2/1 priority date for domestic and international students; for spring admission, 11/1 priority date for domestic and international students. Applications are processed on a rolling basis. Application fee: $60. Electronic applications accepted. *Expenses: Tuition, area resident:* Full-time $11,090; part-time $462 per credit hour. Tuition, state resident: full-time $11,090; part-time $462 per credit hour. Tuition, nonresident: full-time $22,650; part-time $944 per credit hour. *International tuition:* $22,650 full-time. *Required fees:* $1733; $178.58 per credit hour. *Financial support:* In 2018–19, 46 students received support. Unspecified assistantships available. Financial award application deadline: 6/30; financial award applicants required to submit FAFSA. *Faculty research:* Ecology, conservation biology, fish and wildlife biology and management, plant science, entomology. *Total annual research expenditures:* $5.9 million. *Unit head:* Dr. Melissa K. Fierke, Chair, 315-470-6809, Fax: 315-470-6743, E-mail: mkfierke@esf.edu. *Application contact:* Scott Shannon, Associate Provost for Instruction/Dean of the Graduate School, 315-470-6599, E-mail: esfgrad@esf.edu.
Website: http://www.esf.edu/efb/grad/default.asp

State University of New York College of Environmental Science and Forestry, Department of Forest and Natural Resources Management, Syracuse, NY 13210-2779. Offers ecology and ecosystems (MPS, MS, PhD); economics, governance and human dimensions (MPS, MS, PhD); forest and natural resources management (MPS, MS, PhD); forest resources management (MF); monitoring, analysis and modeling (MPS, MS, PhD). *Accreditation:* SAF. *Program availability:* Part-time. *Faculty:* 33 full-time (8 women), 7 part-time/adjunct (0 women). *Students:* 42 full-time (19 women), 5 part-time (2 women); includes 5 minority (1 Black or African American, non-Hispanic/Latino; 1 American Indian or Alaska Native, non-Hispanic/Latino; 2 Asian, non-Hispanic/Latino; 1 Hispanic/Latino), 13 international. Average age 30. 26 applicants, 81% accepted, 4 enrolled. In 2018, 14 master's awarded. Terminal master's awarded for partial completion of doctoral program. *Degree requirements:* For master's, thesis (for some programs); for doctorate, comprehensive exam, thesis/dissertation. *Entrance requirements:* For master's and doctorate, GRE General Test, minimum GPA of 3.0. Additional exam requirements/recommendations for international students: Required—TOEFL (minimum score 550 paper-based; 80 iBT), IELTS (minimum score 6). *Application deadline:* For fall admission, 2/1 priority date for domestic and international students; for spring admission, 11/1 priority date for domestic and international students. Applications are processed on a rolling basis. Application fee: $60. *Expenses: Tuition, area resident:* Full-time $11,090; part-time $462 per credit hour. Tuition, state resident: full-time $11,090; part-time $462 per credit hour. Tuition, nonresident: full-time $22,650; part-time $944 per credit hour. *International tuition:* $22,650 full-time. *Required fees:* $1733; $178.58 per credit hour. *Financial support:* In 2018–19, 13 students received support. Unspecified assistantships available. Financial award application deadline: 6/30; financial award applicants required to submit FAFSA. *Faculty research:* Silviculture recreation management, tree improvement, operations management, economics. *Total annual research expenditures:* $3.2 million. *Unit head:* Dr. Christopher Nowak, Chair, 315-470-6575, Fax: 315-470-6536, E-mail: canowak@esf.edu. *Application contact:* Scott Shannon, Associate Provost for Instruction/Dean of the Graduate School, 315-470-6599, Fax: 315-470-6978, E-mail: esfgrad@esf.edu.
Website: http://www.esf.edu/fnrm/

Stephen F. Austin State University, Graduate School, Arthur Temple College of Forestry and Agriculture, Department of Forestry, Nacogdoches, TX 75962. Offers MF, MS, PhD. *Program availability:* Part-time. *Degree requirements:* For master's, thesis; for doctorate, thesis/dissertation. *Entrance requirements:* For master's and doctorate, GRE General Test. Additional exam requirements/recommendations for international students: Required—TOEFL. *Faculty research:* Wildlife management, basic plant science, forest recreation, multipurpose land management.

Texas A&M University, College of Agriculture and Life Sciences, Department of Ecosystem Science and Management, College Station, TX 77843. Offers ecosystem science and management (M Agr, MNRD, MS, PhD). *Program availability:* Part-time. *Faculty:* 26. *Students:* 45 full-time (24 women), 19 part-time (11 women); includes 15 minority (2 Black or African American, non-Hispanic/Latino; 2 Asian, non-Hispanic/Latino; 9 Hispanic/Latino; 2 Two or more races, non-Hispanic/Latino), 13 international. Average age 29. 20 applicants, 90% accepted, 18 enrolled. In 2018, 8 master's, 7 doctorates awarded. Terminal master's awarded for partial completion of doctoral program. *Degree requirements:* For master's, thesis (for some programs); for doctorate, thesis/dissertation. *Entrance requirements:* For master's and doctorate, GRE General Test. Additional exam requirements/recommendations for international students: Required—TOEFL (minimum score 550 paper-based; 80 iBT), IELTS (minimum score 6), PTE (minimum score 53). *Application deadline:* For fall admission, 3/15 priority date for domestic students; for spring admission, 10/15 priority date for domestic students. Applications are processed on a rolling basis. Application fee: $50 ($90 for international students). Electronic applications accepted. *Expenses:* Contact institution. *Financial support:* In 2018–19, 51 students received support, including 13 fellowships with tuition reimbursements available (averaging $7,762 per year), 22 research assistantships with tuition reimbursements available (averaging $8,294 per year), 29 teaching assistantships with tuition reimbursements available (averaging $12,140 per year); career-related internships or fieldwork, institutionally sponsored loans, scholarships/grants, traineeships, health care benefits, tuition waivers (full and partial), and unspecified assistantships also available. Support available to part-time students. Financial award application deadline: 3/15; financial award applicants required to submit FAFSA. *Faculty research:* Expert systems, geographic information systems, economics, biology, genetics. *Unit head:* Dr. Kathleen Kavanagh, Professor and Department Head, 979-845-5000, Fax: 979-845-6049, E-mail: katyk@tamu.edu. *Application contact:* Heather Haliburton Janke, Senior Academic Advisor II, 979-862-8993, Fax: 979-845-6049, E-mail: hjanke@tamu.edu.
Website: http://essm.tamu.edu

Tropical Agriculture Research and Higher Education Center, Graduate School, Turrialba, Costa Rica. Offers agribusiness management (MS); agroforestry systems (PhD); development practices (MS); ecological agriculture (MS); environmental socioeconomics (MS); forestry in tropical and subtropical zones (PhD); integrated watershed management (MS); international sustainable tourism (MS); management and conservation of tropical rainforests and biodiversity (MS); tropical agriculture (PhD); tropical agroforestry (MS). *Entrance requirements:* For master's, GRE, 2 years of related professional experience, letters of recommendation; for doctorate, GRE, 4 letters of recommendation, letter of support from employing organization, master's degree in agronomy, biological sciences, forestry, natural resources or related field. Additional exam requirements/recommendations for international students: Required—TOEFL (minimum score 550 paper-based). Electronic applications accepted. *Faculty research:* Biodiversity in fragmented landscapes, ecosystem management, integrated pest management, environmental livestock production, biotechnology carbon balances in diverse land uses.

Université du Québec en Abitibi-Témiscamingue, Graduate Programs, Program in Environmental Sciences, Rouyn-Noranda, QC J9X 5E4, Canada. Offers biology (MS); environmental sciences (PhD); sustainable forest ecosystem management (MS).

Université Laval, Faculty of Forestry, Geography and Geomatics, Department of Wood and Forest Sciences, Programs in Forestry Sciences, Québec, QC G1K 7P4, Canada. Offers M Sc, PhD. Terminal master's awarded for partial completion of doctoral program. *Degree requirements:* For master's, thesis (for some programs); for doctorate, comprehensive exam, thesis/dissertation. *Entrance requirements:* For master's and doctorate, knowledge of French. Additional exam requirements/recommendations for international students: Required—TOEIC or TOEFL. Electronic applications accepted.

Université Laval, Faculty of Forestry, Geography and Geomatics, Department of Wood and Forest Sciences, Programs in Wood Sciences, Québec, QC G1K 7P4, Canada. Offers M Sc, PhD. Terminal master's awarded for partial completion of doctoral program. *Degree requirements:* For master's, thesis; for doctorate, comprehensive exam, thesis/dissertation. *Entrance requirements:* For master's and doctorate, knowledge of French. Electronic applications accepted.

Université Laval, Faculty of Forestry, Geography and Geomatics, Program in Agroforestry, Québec, QC G1K 7P4, Canada. Offers M Sc. *Degree requirements:* For master's, thesis (for some programs). *Entrance requirements:* For master's, English exam (comprehension of English), knowledge of French, knowledge of a third language. Electronic applications accepted.

University of Alberta, Faculty of Graduate Studies and Research, Department of Rural Economy, Edmonton, AB T6G 2E1, Canada. Offers agricultural economics (M Ag, M Sc, PhD); forest economics (M Ag, M Sc, PhD); rural sociology (M Ag, M Sc); MBA/M Ag. *Program availability:* Part-time. *Degree requirements:* For doctorate, thesis/dissertation. *Entrance requirements:* Additional exam requirements/recommendations for international students: Required—TOEFL. *Faculty research:* Agroforestry, development, extension education, marketing and trade, natural resources and environment, policy, production economics.

The University of Arizona, College of Agriculture and Life Sciences, School of Natural Resources and the Environment, Watershed Resources Program, Tucson, AZ 85721. Offers water, society, and policy (MS); watershed management (MS, PhD). *Degree requirements:* For master's, thesis; for doctorate, comprehensive exam, thesis/dissertation. *Entrance requirements:* For master's, GRE General Test, minimum GPA of 3.0, 3 letters of recommendation; for doctorate, GRE General Test, minimum GPA of 3.0, 3 letters of recommendation, MA or MS. Additional exam requirements/recommendations for international students: Required—TOEFL (minimum score 550 paper-based; 79 iBT). Electronic applications accepted. *Faculty research:* Forest fuel characteristics, prescribed fire, tree ring-fire scar analysis, erosion, sedimentation.

University of Arkansas at Monticello, School of Forest Resources, Monticello, AR 71656. Offers MS. *Program availability:* Part-time. *Degree requirements:* For master's, comprehensive exam, thesis. *Entrance requirements:* For master's, GRE General Test, minimum GPA of 2.7. Additional exam requirements/recommendations for international students: Required—TOEFL (minimum score 550 paper-based). Electronic applications accepted. *Faculty research:* Geographic information systems/remote sensing, forest ecology, wildlife ecology and management.

The University of British Columbia, Faculty of Forestry, Program in Forestry, Vancouver, BC V6T 1Z1, Canada. Offers M Sc, MA Sc, MF, PhD.

The University of British Columbia, Faculty of Forestry, Program in International Forestry, Vancouver, BC V6T 1Z1, Canada. Offers MIF.

The University of British Columbia, Faculty of Forestry, Program in Sustainable Forest Management, Vancouver, BC V6T 1Z1, Canada. Offers MSFM.

University of California, Berkeley, Graduate Division, College of Natural Resources, Department of Environmental Science, Policy, and Management, Berkeley, CA 94720. Offers environmental science, policy, and management (MS, PhD); forestry (MF). Terminal master's awarded for partial completion of doctoral program. *Degree requirements:* For master's, thesis optional; for doctorate, thesis/dissertation, qualifying exam. *Entrance requirements:* For master's and doctorate, GRE General Test, minimum GPA of 3.0, 3 letters of recommendation. Additional exam requirements/recommendations for international students: Required—TOEFL. Electronic applications accepted. *Faculty research:* Biology and ecology of insects; ecosystem function and environmental issues of soils; plant health/interactions from molecular to ecosystem levels; range management and ecology; forest and resource policy, sustainability, and management.

University of Florida, Graduate School, College of Agricultural and Life Sciences, School of Forest Resources and Conservation, Gainesville, FL 32611. Offers fisheries and aquatic sciences (MFAS, MS, PhD), including ecological restoration (MFAS, MFRC, MS, PhD), geographic information systems (MFAS, MFRC, MS, PhD), natural resource policy and administration (MFAS, MFRC, MS, PhD), wetland sciences (MFAS, MFRC, MS, PhD); forest resources and conservation (MFRC, MS, PhD), including agroforestry, ecological restoration (MFAS, MFRC, MS, PhD), geographic information systems (MFAS, MFRC, MS, PhD), geomatics, hydrologic sciences (MS, PhD), natural resource policy and administration (MFAS, MFRC, MS, PhD), toxicology (PhD), tropical conservation and development, wetland sciences (MFAS, MFRC, MS, PhD); JD/MFRC; JD/MS; JD/PhD. *Program availability:* Part-time, evening/weekend, online learning. Terminal master's awarded for partial completion of doctoral program. *Degree requirements:* For master's, comprehensive exam, thesis optional, project (for MFRC); for doctorate, comprehensive exam, thesis/dissertation. *Entrance requirements:* For master's, GRE General Test, minimum GPA of 3.0, curriculum vitae, 3 letters of recommendation; for doctorate, GRE General Test, minimum GPA of 3.25, curriculum vitae, 3 letters of recommendation. Additional exam requirements/recommendations for international students: Required—TOEFL (minimum score 550 paper-based; 80 iBT), IELTS (minimum score 6). Electronic applications accepted. *Faculty research:* Quantitative and integrative fisheries science, ecology and management of aquatic systems, finfish, invertebrate and ornamental aquaculture, aquatic animal health, geomatics and GIS, natural resource conservation, tropical forestry, economics and policy, environmental education, forest biology and ecology, forest management, hydrology, silviculture.

University of Georgia, Warnell School of Forestry and Natural Resources, Athens, GA 30602. Offers MFR, MS, PhD. *Accreditation:* SAF. *Degree requirements:* For master's, thesis (MS), for doctorate, one foreign language, thesis/dissertation. *Entrance requirements:* For master's and doctorate, GRE General Test. Electronic applications accepted.

University of Kentucky, Graduate School, College of Agriculture, Food and Environment, Program in Forestry, Lexington, KY 40506-0032. Offers MSFOR. *Degree requirements:* For master's, comprehensive exam, thesis optional. *Entrance requirements:* For master's, GRE General Test, minimum undergraduate GPA of 2.75. Additional exam requirements/recommendations for international students: Required—TOEFL (minimum score 550 paper-based). Electronic applications accepted. *Faculty research:* Forest ecology, silviculture, watershed management, forest products utilization, wildlife habitat management.

University of Maine, Graduate School, College of Natural Sciences, Forestry, and Agriculture, School of Forest Resources, Orono, ME 04469. Offers MF, MS, PhD. *Accreditation:* SAF (one or more programs are accredited). *Program availability:* Part-time. *Faculty:* 23 full-time (8 women), 59 part-time/adjunct (16 women). *Students:* 47 full-time (19 women), 2 part-time (1 woman); includes 6 minority (1 Black or African American, non-Hispanic/Latino; 2 American Indian or Alaska Native, non-Hispanic/Latino; 2 Asian, non-Hispanic/Latino; 1 Hispanic/Latino), 15 international. Average age 29. 45 applicants, 84% accepted, 21 enrolled. In 2018, 10 master's, 4 doctorates awarded. *Degree requirements:* For master's, thesis; for doctorate, one foreign language, comprehensive exam, thesis/dissertation. *Entrance requirements:* For master's and doctorate, GRE General Test. Additional exam requirements/recommendations for international students: Required—TOEFL (minimum score 80 iBT), IELTS (minimum score 6.5), PTE (minimum score 60). *Application deadline:* For fall admission, 1/15 priority date for domestic students, 1/15 for international students. Applications are processed on a rolling basis. Application fee: $65. Electronic applications accepted. *Financial support:* In 2018–19, 56 students received support, including 42 research assistantships with full tuition reimbursements available (averaging $16,000 per year), 9 teaching assistantships with full tuition reimbursements available (averaging $15,600 per year); career-related internships or fieldwork, Federal Work-Study, institutionally sponsored loans, scholarships/grants, and unspecified assistantships also available. Financial award application deadline: 3/1. *Faculty research:* Forest Ecosystem Science, Human Dimensions of Natural Resources, Forest Economics & Policy, Parks, Recreation & Tourism, Bioproducts Engineering. *Total annual research expenditures:* $3.7 million. *Unit head:* Dr. Stephen Shaler, Director, 207-581-4737. *Application contact:* Scott G. Delcourt, Assistant Vice President for Graduate Studies and Senior Associate Dean, 207-581-3291, Fax: 207-581-3232, E-mail: graduate@maine.edu.
Website: http://forest.umaine.edu/

University of Massachusetts Amherst, Graduate School, College of Natural Sciences, Department of Environmental Conservation, Amherst, MA 01003. Offers building systems (MS, PhD); environmental policy and human dimensions (MS, PhD); forest resources (MS, PhD); sustainability science (MS); water, wetlands and watersheds (MS, PhD); wildlife and fisheries conservation (MS, PhD). *Program availability:* Part-time. Terminal master's awarded for partial completion of doctoral program. *Degree requirements:* For master's, thesis or alternative; for doctorate, comprehensive exam, thesis/dissertation. *Entrance requirements:* For master's and doctorate, GRE General Test. Additional exam requirements/recommendations for international students: Required—TOEFL (minimum score 550 paper-based; 80 iBT), IELTS (minimum score 6.5). Electronic applications accepted.

University of Minnesota, Twin Cities Campus, Graduate School, College of Food, Agricultural and Natural Resource Sciences, Program in Natural Resources Science and Management, St. Paul, MN 55108. Offers assessment, monitoring, and geospatial analysis (MS, PhD); economics, policy, management, and society (MS, PhD); forest hydrology and watershed management (MS, PhD); forest products (MS, PhD); forests: biology, ecology, conservation, and management (MS, PhD); natural resources science and management (MS, PhD); paper science and engineering (MS, PhD); recreation resources, tourism, and environmental education (MS, PhD). *Program availability:* Part-time. Terminal master's awarded for partial completion of doctoral program. *Degree requirements:* For master's, comprehensive exam, thesis (for some programs); for doctorate, comprehensive exam, thesis/dissertation. *Entrance requirements:* For master's and doctorate, GRE General Test. Additional exam requirements/recommendations for international students: Required—TOEFL (minimum score 550 paper-based; 79 iBT); Recommended—IELTS (minimum score 6.5). Electronic applications accepted. *Faculty research:* Forest hydrology, biology, ecology, conservation, and management; recreation resources and environmental education; wildlife ecology; economics, policy, and society; geographic information systems (GIS); forest products and paper science.

University of Missouri, Office of Research and Graduate Studies, College of Agriculture, Food and Natural Resources, School of Natural Resources, Columbia, MO 65211. Offers agroforestry (MS, Certificate); conservation biology (Certificate), fisheries and wildlife sciences (MS, PhD); forestry (MS, PhD); geographical information science (Certificate); human dimensions of natural resources (MS, PhD); parks, recreation and tourism (MS); society and ecosystems (Certificate); soil, environmental and atmospheric sciences (MS, PhD); water resources (MS, PhD). *Program availability:* Part-time. *Degree requirements:* For doctorate, thesis/dissertation. *Entrance requirements:* For master's and doctorate, GRE General Test (minimum score 1200 Verbal and Quantitative), minimum GPA of 3.2. Additional exam requirements/recommendations for international students: Required—TOEFL (minimum score 550 paper-based; 80 iBT), IELTS (minimum score 6.5). Electronic applications accepted.

University of Montana, Graduate School, College of Forestry and Conservation, Missoula, MT 59812. Offers fish and wildlife biology (PhD); forest and conservation sciences (PhD); forestry (MS); recreation management (MS); resource conservation (MS); systems ecology (MS, PhD); wildlife biology (MS). *Degree requirements:* For doctorate, thesis/dissertation. *Entrance requirements:* For master's and doctorate, GRE General Test. Additional exam requirements/recommendations for international students: Required—TOEFL (minimum score 575 paper-based).

University of New Brunswick Fredericton, School of Graduate Studies, Faculty of Forestry and Environmental Management, Fredericton, NB E3B 5A3, Canada. Offers ecological foundations of forest management (PhD); environmental management (MEM); forest engineering (M Sc FE, MFE); forest products marketing (MBA); forest resources (M Sc F, MF, PhD). *Program availability:* Part-time. *Degree requirements:* For master's, thesis; for doctorate, thesis/dissertation. *Entrance requirements:* For master's and doctorate, minimum GPA of 3.0. Additional exam requirements/recommendations for international students: Required—TOEFL (minimum score 550 paper-based; 80 iBT), IELTS (minimum score 7), TWE (minimum score 4). Electronic applications accepted. *Faculty research:* Forest machines, soils, and ecosystems; integrated forest management; forest meteorology; wood engineering; stream ecosystems dynamics; forest and natural resources policy; forest operations planning; wood technology and mechanics; forest road construction and engineering; forest, wildlife, insect, bird, and fire ecology; remote sensing; insect impacts; silviculture; LiDAR analytics; integrated pest management; forest tree genetics; genetic resource conservation and sustainable management.

University of New Hampshire, Graduate School, College of Life Sciences and Agriculture, Department of Natural Resources and the Environment, Durham, NH 03824. Offers environmental conservation (MS); environmental economics (MS); forestry (MS); natural resources (MS); resource administration and management (MS);

soil and water resource management (MS); wildlife and conservation biology (MS). *Program availability:* Part-time. *Entrance requirements:* For master's, GRE General Test. Additional exam requirements/recommendations for international students: Required—TOEFL (minimum score 550 paper-based; 80 iBT). Electronic applications accepted.

The University of Tennessee, Graduate School, College of Agricultural Sciences and Natural Resources, Department of Forestry, Wildlife, and Fisheries, Program in Forestry, Knoxville, TN 37996. Offers MS. *Degree requirements:* For master's, thesis or alternative. *Entrance requirements:* For master's, GRE General Test, minimum GPA of 2.7. Additional exam requirements/recommendations for international students: Required—TOEFL. Electronic applications accepted.

University of Toronto, School of Graduate Studies, Faculty of Forestry, Toronto, ON M5S 1A1, Canada. Offers M Sc F, MFC, PhD. *Degree requirements:* For master's, comprehensive exam, thesis, oral thesis/research paper defense; for doctorate, thesis/dissertation, oral defense of thesis. *Entrance requirements:* For master's, bachelor's degree in a related area, minimum B average in final year (M Sc F), final 2 years (MFC); resume, 3 letters of reference; for doctorate, writing sample, minimum A- average, master's in a related area, 3 letters of reference, resume. Additional exam requirements/recommendations for international students: Required—TOEFL (minimum score 580 paper-based; 93 iBT), TWE (minimum score 5). Electronic applications accepted.

University of Vermont, Graduate College, The Rubenstein School of Environment and Natural Resources, Program in Natural Resources, Burlington, VT 05405. Offers ecological economics (Certificate); natural resources (MS), including aquatic ecology and watershed science, environment thought and culture, environment, science and public affairs, forestry; natural resources (PhD); MELP/MS. MELP/MS offered in collaboration with Vermont Law School. *Degree requirements:* For master's, thesis or alternative; for doctorate, thesis/dissertation. *Entrance requirements:* For master's and doctorate, GRE General Test. Additional exam requirements/recommendations for international students: Required—TOEFL (minimum score 550 paper-based; 90 iBT), IELTS (minimum score 6.5). Electronic applications accepted.

University of Washington, Graduate School, College of the Environment, School of Environmental and Forest Sciences, Seattle, WA 98195. Offers bioresource science and engineering (MS, PhD); environmental horticulture (MEH); forest ecology (MS, PhD); forest management (MFR); forest soils (MS, PhD); restoration ecology (MS, PhD); restoration ecology and environmental horticulture (MS, PhD); social sciences (MS, PhD); sustainable resource management (MS, PhD); wildlife science (MS, PhD); MFR/MAIS; MPA/MS. *Accreditation:* SAF. *Program availability:* Part-time. *Degree requirements:* For master's, thesis; for doctorate, comprehensive exam, thesis/dissertation. *Entrance requirements:* For master's and doctorate, GRE, minimum GPA of 3.0. Additional exam requirements/recommendations for international students: Required—TOEFL. Electronic applications accepted. *Faculty research:* Ecosystem analysis, silviculture and forest protection, paper science and engineering, environmental horticulture and urban forestry, natural resource policy and economics, restoration ecology and environment horticulture, conservation, human dimensions, wildlife, bioresource science and engineering.

University of Wisconsin–Madison, Graduate School, College of Agricultural and Life Sciences, Department of Forest and Wildlife Ecology, Program in Forestry, Madison, WI 53706-1380. Offers MS, PhD.

Utah State University, School of Graduate Studies, S.J. and Jessie E. Quinney College of Natural Resources, Department of Wildland Resources, Logan, UT 84322. Offers ecology (MS, PhD); forestry (MS, PhD); range science (MS, PhD); wildlife biology (MS, PhD). *Program availability:* Part-time. *Degree requirements:* For master's, thesis; for doctorate, comprehensive exam, thesis/dissertation. *Entrance requirements:* For master's and doctorate, GRE General Test, minimum GPA of 3.0. Additional exam requirements/recommendations for international students: Required—TOEFL. *Faculty research:* Range plant ecophysiology, plant community ecology, ruminant nutrition, population ecology.

Virginia Polytechnic Institute and State University, Graduate School, College of Natural Resources and Environment, Blacksburg, VA 24061. Offers fisheries and wildlife (MS, PhD); forest products (MS/MF); forestry (PhD); geography (MS); geospatial and environmental analysis (PhD); natural resources (MNR); MS/MF. *Faculty:* 80 full-time (18 women). *Students:* 179 full-time (80 women), 75 part-time (40 women); includes 34 minority (3 Black or African American, non-Hispanic/Latino; 7 Asian, non-Hispanic/Latino; 17 Hispanic/Latino; 1 Native Hawaiian or other Pacific Islander, non-Hispanic/Latino; 6 Two or more races, non-Hispanic/Latino), 33 international. Average age 32. 110 applicants, 58% accepted, 50 enrolled. In 2018, 93 master's, 13 doctorates awarded. *Degree requirements:* For master's, comprehensive exam (for some programs), thesis (for some programs); for doctorate, comprehensive exam (for some programs), thesis/dissertation (for some programs). *Entrance requirements:* For master's and doctorate, GRE/GMAT. Additional exam requirements/recommendations for international students: Required—TOEFL (minimum score 90 iBT). *Application deadline:* For fall admission, 8/1 for domestic students, 4/1 for international students; for spring admission, 1/1 for domestic students, 9/1 for international students. Applications are processed on a rolling basis. Application fee: $75. Electronic applications accepted. *Expenses:* Tuition, state resident: full-time $15,510; part-time $739.50 per credit hour. Tuition, nonresident: full-time $29,629; part-time $1490.25 per credit hour. *Required fees:* $2804; $550 per semester. Tuition and fees vary according to course load, campus/location and program. *Financial support:* In 2018–19, 4 fellowships with full tuition reimbursements (averaging $29,791 per year), 97 research assistantships with full tuition reimbursements (averaging $18,686 per year), 47 teaching assistantships with full tuition reimbursements (averaging $17,302 per year) were awarded; scholarships/grants also available. Financial award application deadline: 3/1; financial award applicants required to submit FAFSA. *Total annual research expenditures:* $16.1 million. *Unit head:* Dr. Paul M. Winistorfer, Dean, 540-231-5481, Fax: 540-231-7664, E-mail: pstorfer@vt.edu. *Application contact:* Arlice Banks, Executive Assistant, 540-231-7051, Fax: 540-231-7664, E-mail: arbanks@vt.edu.
Website: http://cnre.vt.edu/

West Virginia University, Davis College of Agriculture, Forestry and Consumer Sciences, Morgantown, WV 26506. Offers agricultural and extension education (MS, PhD); agriculture and resource management (MS); agriculture, natural resources and design (M Agr); agronomy (MS); animal and food science (PhD); animal physiology (MS); applied and environmental microbiology (MS); design and merchandising (MS); entomology (MS); forest resource science (PhD); forestry (MSF); genetics and developmental biology (MS, PhD); horticulture (MS); human and community development (PhD); landscape architecture (MLA); natural resource economics (PhD); nutritional and food science (MS); plant and soil science (PhD); plant pathology (MS); recreation, parks and tourism resources (MS); reproductive physiology (MS, PhD); wildlife and fisheries resources (PhD). *Accreditation:* ASLA. *Program availability:* Part-time. *Students:* 188 full-time (86 women), 47 part-time (30 women); includes 22 minority (5 Black or African American, non-Hispanic/Latino; 5 Asian, non-Hispanic/Latino; 8 Hispanic/Latino; 4 Two or more races, non-Hispanic/Latino), 60 international. In 2018, 56 master's, 14 doctorates awarded. *Degree requirements:* For master's, thesis; for doctorate, thesis/dissertation. *Entrance requirements:* Additional exam requirements/recommendations for international students: Required—TOEFL (minimum score 550 paper-based). *Application deadline:* For fall admission, 6/1 priority date for domestic students, 6/1 for international students; for spring admission, 1/5 for domestic and international students. Applications are processed on a rolling basis. Application fee: $60. Electronic applications accepted. *Financial support:* Fellowships, research assistantships, teaching assistantships, career-related internships or fieldwork, Federal Work-Study, institutionally sponsored loans, tuition waivers (full and partial), and unspecified assistantships available. Financial award application deadline: 2/1; financial award applicants required to submit FAFSA. *Faculty research:* Reproductive physiology, soil and water quality, human nutrition, aquaculture, wildlife management. *Unit head:* Dr. Ken Blemings, Interim Dean, 304-293-2395, Fax: 304-293-3740, E-mail: ken.blemings@mail.wvu.edu. *Application contact:* Dr. J. Todd Petty, Associate Dean, 304-293-2278, Fax: 304-293-3740, E-mail: jtpetty@mail.wvu.edu.
Website: https://www.davis.wvu.edu

Yale University, Graduate School of Arts and Sciences, Department of Forestry and Environmental Studies, New Haven, CT 06520. Offers environmental sciences (PhD); forestry (PhD). *Degree requirements:* For doctorate, thesis/dissertation. *Entrance requirements:* For doctorate, GRE General Test.

Yale University, School of Forestry and Environmental Studies, New Haven, CT 06511. Offers environmental management (MEM), including business and the environment, ecosystem and conservation management, energy and the environment, environmental policy analysis; environmental science (MES); forest science (MFS); forestry (MF); forestry and environmental studies (PhD); JD/MEM; MBA/MEM; MBA/MF; MEM/M Arch; MEM/M Div; MEM/MA; MEM/MAR; MEM/MPH. *Accreditation:* SAF (one or more programs are accredited). *Program availability:* Part-time. Terminal master's awarded for partial completion of doctoral program. *Degree requirements:* For master's, internship and capstone project (for MEM and MF); research project and thesis (for MES and MFS); for doctorate, comprehensive exam, thesis/dissertation. *Entrance requirements:* For master's, GRE General Test, GMAT or LSAT; for doctorate, GRE General Test. Additional exam requirements/recommendations for international students: Required—TOEFL (minimum score 600 paper-based; 100 iBT) or IELTS (minimum score 7). Electronic applications accepted. *Expenses:* Contact institution. *Faculty research:* Environmental policy, social ecology, industrial environmental management, forestry, environmental health, urban ecology, water science policy.

Natural Resources

American University, School of International Service, Washington, DC 20016-8071. Offers comparative and regional studies (Certificate); cross-cultural communication (Certificate); development management (MS); ethics, peace, and global affairs (MA); European studies (Certificate); global environmental policy (MA, Certificate); global information technology (Certificate); global media (MA); international affairs (MA), including comparative and regional studies, global governance, politics, and security, international economic relations, natural resources and sustainable development, U.S. foreign policy and national security; international arts management (Certificate); international communication (MA, Certificate); international development (MA); international economic policy (Certificate); international economic relations (Certificate); international economics (MA); international peace and conflict resolution (MA, Certificate); international politics (Certificate); international relations (MA, PhD); international service (MIS); peacebuilding (Certificate); social enterprise (MA); the Americas (Certificate); United States foreign policy (Certificate); JD/MA. *Program availability:* Part-time, evening/weekend, 100% online, blended/hybrid learning. *Faculty:* 115 full-time (48 women), 50 part-time/adjunct (22 women). *Students:* 496 full-time (320 women), 477 part-time (242 women); includes 410 minority (83 Black or African American, non-Hispanic/Latino; 2 American Indian or Alaska Native, non-Hispanic/Latino; 51 Asian, non-Hispanic/Latino; 242 Hispanic/Latino; 32 Two or more races, non-Hispanic/Latino), 93 international. Average age 30. 1,280 applicants, 82% accepted, 356 enrolled. In 2018, 400 master's, 3 doctorates, 8 other advanced degrees awarded. Terminal master's awarded for partial completion of doctoral program. *Degree requirements:* For master's, one foreign language, comprehensive exam, thesis or alternative; for doctorate, one foreign language, comprehensive exam, thesis/dissertation. *Entrance requirements:* For master's, Please visit the website for details: https://www.american.edu/sis/admissions/, transcripts, resume, 2 letters of recommendation, statement of purpose; for doctorate, GRE, transcripts, resume, 3 letters of recommendation, statement of purpose. Additional exam requirements/recommendations for international students: Required—TOEFL. Application fee: $55. Electronic applications accepted. *Expenses:* Contact institution. *Financial support:* Research assistantships, teaching assistantships, institutionally sponsored loans, scholarships/grants, and unspecified assistantships available. Financial award applicants required to submit FAFSA. *Unit head:* Christine BN Chin, 202-885-1600, E-mail: sisgrad@american.edu. *Application contact:* Jia Jiang, Director, Graduate Enrollment Management, 202-885-1689, E-mail: jiang@american.edu.
Website: http://www.american.edu/sis/

Auburn University, Graduate School, School of Forestry and Wildlife Sciences, Auburn University, AL 36849. Offers forestry (MS); natural resource conservation (MNR); wildlife sciences (MS, PhD). *Accreditation:* SAF. *Program availability:* Part-time. *Degree requirements:* For master's, thesis (MS); for doctorate, thesis/dissertation. *Entrance requirements:* For master's and doctorate, GRE General Test. Electronic applications accepted. *Expenses:* Tuition, state resident: full-time $11,282; part-time $535 per credit hour. Tuition, nonresident: full-time $30,542; part-time $1605 per credit hour. *Required fees:* $826 per semester. Tuition and fees vary according to degree level and program.

Faculty research: Forest nursery management, silviculture and vegetation management, biological processes and ecological relationships, growth and yield of plantations and natural stands, urban forestry, forest taxation, law and policy.

Ball State University, Graduate School, College of Sciences and Humanities, Department of Natural Resources and Environmental Management, Muncie, IN 47306. Offers emergency management and homeland security (Certificate); natural resources and environmental management (MA, MS). *Program availability:* Part-time. *Degree requirements:* For master's, thesis (for some programs). *Entrance requirements:* For master's, GRE General Test, minimum baccalaureate GPA of 2.75 or 3.0 in latter half of baccalaureate, two letters of reference. Additional exam requirements/recommendations for international students: Required—TOEFL (minimum score 550 paper-based; 79 iBT), IELTS (minimum score 6.5). Electronic applications accepted. *Faculty research:* Acid rain, indoor air pollution, land reclamation.

Boise State University, School of Public Service, Department of Public Policy and Administration, Boise, ID 83725-0399. Offers public policy and administration (MPA, PhD, Graduate Certificate), including environmental, natural resource and energy policy and administration (MPA), general public administration (MPA), state and local government policy and administration (MPA). *Accreditation:* NASPAA. *Program availability:* Part-time. Terminal master's awarded for partial completion of doctoral program. *Degree requirements:* For master's, comprehensive exam, thesis optional, directed research project, internship; for doctorate, thesis/dissertation. *Entrance requirements:* For master's, GRE General Test, minimum GPA of 3.0. Additional exam requirements/recommendations for international students: Required—TOEFL (minimum score 550 paper-based; 80 iBT), IELTS (minimum score 6). Electronic applications accepted.

California Polytechnic State University, San Luis Obispo, College of Agriculture, Food and Environmental Sciences, Department of Natural Resources Management and Environmental Sciences, San Luis Obispo, CA 93407. Offers forestry sciences (MS). *Program availability:* Part-time. *Faculty:* 5 full-time (2 women). *Students:* 1 full-time (0 women), 4 part-time (2 women); includes 2 minority (both Hispanic/Latino). Average age 33. 8 applicants, 50% accepted, 4 enrolled. In 2018, 4 master's awarded. *Degree requirements:* For master's, thesis. *Entrance requirements:* For master's, GRE. Additional exam requirements/recommendations for international students: Required—TOEFL (minimum score 80 iBT). *Application deadline:* For fall admission, 4/1 for domestic and international students; for winter admission, 10/1 for domestic students, 6/30 for international students; for spring admission, 10/1 for domestic students. Applications are processed on a rolling basis. Application fee: $55. Electronic applications accepted. *Expenses: Tuition, area resident:* Full-time $7176; part-time $4164 per year. Tuition, state resident: full-time $10,965. Tuition, nonresident: full-time $10,965. *Required fees:* $6336; $3711. *Financial support:* Fellowships, research assistantships, teaching assistantships, career-related internships or fieldwork, institutionally sponsored loans, scholarships/grants, health care benefits, and unspecified assistantships available. Financial award application deadline: 3/2; financial award applicants required to submit FAFSA. *Faculty research:* Hydrology, biometrics, forest health and management, fire science, urban and community forestry. *Unit head:* Dr. Richard Thompson, Department Head, 805-756-2898, E-mail: rpthomps@calpoly.edu. *Application contact:* Dr. Richard Thompson, Department Head, 805-756-2898, E-mail: rpthomps@calpoly.edu.
Website: http://nres.calpoly.edu/

Central Washington University, School of Graduate Studies and Research, College of the Sciences, Program in Cultural and Environmental Resource Management, Ellensburg, WA 98926. Offers anthropology (MS); geography (MS). *Entrance requirements:* For master's, GRE, minimum GPA of 3.0. Additional exam requirements/recommendations for international students: Required—TOEFL (minimum score 550 paper-based; 79 iBT). Electronic applications accepted.

Colorado State University, College of Natural Sciences, Programs in Natural Sciences Education, Fort Collins, CO 80523. Offers material science and engineering (PhD); natural science education (MNSE); zoo, aquarium, and animal shelter management (MS). *Program availability:* 100% online. *Degree requirements:* For master's, comprehensive exam (for some programs), thesis (for some programs); for doctorate, comprehensive exam (for some programs), thesis/dissertation. *Entrance requirements:* Additional exam requirements/recommendations for international students: Required—TOEFL (minimum score 550 paper-based). Electronic applications accepted. *Expenses:* Contact institution.

Colorado State University, Warner College of Natural Resources, Department of Human Dimensions of Natural Resources, Fort Collins, CO 80523-1480. Offers human dimensions of natural resources (MS, PhD); tourism management (MTM). *Program availability:* Part-time, evening/weekend, 100% online. Terminal master's awarded for partial completion of doctoral program. *Degree requirements:* For master's, thesis (for some programs); for doctorate, comprehensive exam, thesis/dissertation. *Entrance requirements:* For master's, GRE General Test, minimum GPA of 3.0, 3 letters of recommendation, statement of interest, official transcripts; for doctorate, GRE General Test, minimum GPA of 3.0, 3 letters of recommendation, copy of master's thesis or professional paper, statement of interest, official transcripts. Electronic applications accepted. *Expenses:* Contact institution. *Faculty research:* Biocultural approaches to conservation; conservation governance; dimensions of wildlife management; marine conservation; park recreation and management.

Cornell University, Graduate School, Graduate Fields of Agriculture and Life Sciences, Field of Natural Resources, Ithaca, NY 14853. Offers community-based natural resources management (MS, PhD); conservation biology (MS, PhD); ecosystem biology and biogeochemistry (MPS, MS, PhD); environmental management (MPS); fishery and aquatic science (MPS, MS, PhD); forest science (MPS, MS, PhD); human dimensions of natural resources management (MPS, MS, PhD); policy and institutional analysis (MS, PhD); program development and evaluation (MPS, MS, PhD); quantitative ecology (MS, PhD); wildlife science (MPS, MS, PhD). *Degree requirements:* For master's, thesis (MS), project paper (MPS); for doctorate, comprehensive exam, thesis/dissertation. *Entrance requirements:* For master's and doctorate, GRE General Test, 2 letters of recommendation. Additional exam requirements/recommendations for international students: Required—TOEFL (minimum score 550 paper-based; 77 iBT). Electronic applications accepted. *Faculty research:* Ecosystem-level dynamics, systems modeling, conservation biology/management, resource management's human dimensions, biogeochemistry.

Dalhousie University, Faculty of Management, Centre for Advanced Management Education, Halifax, NS B3H 3J5, Canada. Offers financial services (MBA); information management (MIM); management (MPA); natural resources (MBA). *Program availability:* Part-time, online learning. *Entrance requirements:* For master's, GMAT, minimum GPA of 3.0, resume. Additional exam requirements/recommendations for international students: Required—TOEFL, IELTS, CANTEST, CAEL, or Michigan English Language Assessment Battery. Electronic applications accepted.

Delaware State University, Graduate Programs, Department of Agriculture and Natural Resources, Program in Natural Resources, Dover, DE 19901-2277. Offers MS. *Entrance requirements:* For master's, GRE. Additional exam requirements/recommendations for international students: Required—TOEFL (minimum score 550 paper-based).

Duke University, Nicholas School of the Environment, Durham, NC 27708. Offers earth and ocean sciences (PhD); environment (MEM, MF, PhD); marine science and conservation (PhD). *Faculty:* 50. *Students:* 365 full-time (243 women); includes 67 minority (7 Black or African American, non-Hispanic/Latino; 4 American Indian or Alaska Native, non-Hispanic/Latino; 36 Asian, non-Hispanic/Latino; 20 Hispanic/Latino), 93 international. Average age 27. 428 applicants, 83% accepted, 151 enrolled. In 2018, 181 master's awarded. *Degree requirements:* For master's, project; for doctorate, variable foreign language requirement, thesis/dissertation. *Entrance requirements:* For master's, GRE General Test, previous course work in natural or social sciences relevant to environmental interests; college calculus, college statistics, and concentration-specific prerequisites. Additional exam requirements/recommendations for international students: Required—TOEFL, IELTS. *Application deadline:* For fall admission, 12/15 priority date for domestic and international students. Application fee: $400. Electronic applications accepted. *Financial support:* Research assistantships, career-related internships or fieldwork, Federal Work-Study, institutionally sponsored loans, scholarships/grants, and unspecified assistantships available. Financial award application deadline: 12/15; financial award applicants required to submit CSS PROFILE or FAFSA. *Faculty research:* Global environmental change, energy and the environment, water resource management, ecosystem science and conservation, ecotoxicology and environmental health, business and environment, environmental economics and policy, coastal environmental management, forest resource management. *Unit head:* Sherri Nevius, Associate Dean, Student Services, 919-613-8063, E-mail: sherri.nevius@duke.edu. *Application contact:* Benjamin Spain, Associate Director of Enrollment Services, 919-684-1155, E-mail: admissions@nicholas.duke.edu. Website: http://nicholas.duke.edu/

Florida International University, College of Arts, Sciences, and Education, Department of Earth and Environment, Miami, FL 33199. Offers earth science (PhD); environmental studies (MS); geosciences (MS, PhD); natural resources management and policy (PSM). *Program availability:* Part-time, evening/weekend. *Faculty:* 33 full-time (11 women), 15 part-time/adjunct (5 women). *Students:* 92 full-time (45 women), 6 part-time (4 women); includes 42 minority (5 Black or African American, non-Hispanic/Latino; 1 Asian, non-Hispanic/Latino; 32 Hispanic/Latino; 4 Two or more races, non-Hispanic/Latino), 22 international. Average age 30. 80 applicants, 55% accepted, 27 enrolled. In 2018, 22 master's, 4 doctorates awarded. *Degree requirements:* For master's, thesis; for doctorate, comprehensive exam, thesis/dissertation. *Entrance requirements:* For master's and doctorate, GRE General Test, 3 letters of recommendation, minimum GPA of 3.0, resume. Additional exam requirements/recommendations for international students: Required—TOEFL (minimum score 550 paper-based; 80 iBT). *Application deadline:* For fall admission, 2/15 for domestic and international students; for spring admission, 9/1 for domestic and international students. Applications are processed on a rolling basis. Application fee: $30. Electronic applications accepted. *Financial support:* Institutionally sponsored loans and scholarships/grants available. Financial award application deadline: 3/1; financial award applicants required to submit FAFSA. *Faculty research:* Determination of dispersivity and hydraulic conductivity in the Biscayne Aquifer. *Unit head:* Dr. Rene Price, Chair, 305-348-3119, E-mail: rene.price@fiu.edu. *Application contact:* Nanett Rojas, Manager, Admissions Operations, 305-348-7464, Fax: 305-348-7441, E-mail: gradadm@fiu.edu.

Humboldt State University, Academic Programs, College of Natural Resources and Sciences, Programs in Natural Resources, Arcata, CA 95521-8299. Offers natural resources (MS), including fisheries, forestry, natural resources planning and interpretation, rangeland resources and wildland soils, wastewater utilization, watershed management, wildlife. *Faculty:* 22 full-time (5 women), 20 part-time/adjunct (7 women). *Students:* 43 full-time (22 women), 45 part-time (21 women); includes 24 minority (1 Black or African American, non-Hispanic/Latino; 2 American Indian or Alaska Native, non-Hispanic/Latino; 1 Asian, non-Hispanic/Latino; 16 Hispanic/Latino; 4 Two or more races, non-Hispanic/Latino), 1 international. Average age 28. 38 applicants, 37% accepted, 14 enrolled. In 2018, 21 master's awarded. *Degree requirements:* For master's, thesis or alternative. *Entrance requirements:* For master's, GRE, appropriate bachelor's degree, minimum GPA of 2.5, 3 letters of recommendation, resume. Additional exam requirements/recommendations for international students: Required—TOEFL (minimum score 500 paper-based). *Application deadline:* For fall admission, 2/1 for domestic and international students; for spring admission, 9/30 for domestic and international students. Applications are processed on a rolling basis. Application fee: $55. *Expenses: Tuition:* Part-time $4649 per semester. *Required fees:* $2121; $1673. Tuition and fees vary according to program. *Financial support:* Fellowships, career-related internships or fieldwork, and Federal Work-Study available. Support available to part-time students. Financial award application deadline: 3/1; financial award applicants required to submit FAFSA. *Faculty research:* Spotted owl habitat, pre-settlement vegetation, hardwood utilization, tree physiology, fisheries. *Unit head:* Dr. Andrew Stubblefield, Graduate Program Coordinator, 707-826-3258, E-mail: andrew.stubblefield@humboldt.edu. *Application contact:* Dr. Andrew Stubblefield, Graduate Program Coordinator, 707-826-3258, E-mail: andrew.stubblefield@humboldt.edu.
Website: http://www.humboldt.edu/cnrs/graduate_programs

Indiana University–Purdue University Indianapolis, Robert H. McKinney School of Law, Indianapolis, IN 46202. Offers advocacy skills (Certificate); American law for foreign lawyers (LL M); civil and human rights (Certificate); corporate and commercial law (LL M, Certificate); criminal law (Certificate); environmental and natural resources (Certificate); health law (Certificate); health law, policy and bioethics (LL M); intellectual property law (LL M, Certificate); international and comparative law (LL M, Certificate); international human rights law (LL M); law (MJ, JD, SJD); JD/M Phil; JD/MBA; JD/MD; JD/MHA; JD/MLS; JD/MPA; JD/MPH; JD/MSW. *Accreditation:* ABA. *Program availability:* Part-time. *Entrance requirements:* For doctorate, LSAT. Additional exam requirements/recommendations for international students: Required—TOEFL (minimum score 79 iBT), IELTS (minimum score 6.5). Electronic applications accepted. *Expenses:* Contact institution.

Instituto Tecnologico de Santo Domingo, Graduate School, Area of Basic And Environmental Sciences, Santo Domingo, Dominican Republic. Offers environmental science (M En S), including environmental education, environmental management, marine resources, natural resources management; mathematics (MS, PhD); renewable energy technology (MS, Certificate).

Iowa State University of Science and Technology, Program In Biorenewable Resources and Technology, Ames, IA 50011. Offers MS, PhD. *Degree requirements:* For master's, thesis or alternative; for doctorate, thesis/dissertation. *Entrance requirements:* For master's and doctorate, GRE General Test. Additional exam requirements/recommendations for international students: Required—TOEFL (minimum score 550 paper-based; 79 iBT), IELTS (minimum score 6.5). Electronic applications accepted.

Peterson's Graduate Programs in the Physical Sciences, Mathematics, Agricultural Sciences, the Environment & Natural Resources 2020

www.petersons.com **339**

Natural Resources

Kansas State University, Graduate School, College of Agriculture, Department of Horticulture and Natural Resources, Manhattan, KS 66506. Offers horticulture and natural resources (MS, PhD), including horticulture and natural resources, urban food systems (MS). *Program availability:* Part-time, online learning. *Degree requirements:* For master's, thesis, oral exam; for doctorate, thesis/dissertation, preliminary exams. *Entrance requirements:* For master's and doctorate, GRE General Test. Additional exam requirements/recommendations for international students: Required—TOEFL (minimum score 550 paper-based; 79 iBT); Recommended—IELTS (minimum score 6.5). Electronic applications accepted. *Faculty research:* Environmental stress, phytochemicals and health, postharvest technology, sustainable production, turf grass science.

Laurentian University, School of Graduate Studies and Research, School of Engineering, Sudbury, ON P3E 2C6, Canada. Offers mineral resources engineering (M Eng, MA Sc); natural resources engineering (PhD). *Program availability:* Part-time. *Faculty research:* Mining engineering, rock mechanics (tunneling, rockbursts, rock support), metallurgy (mineral processing, hydro and pyrometallurgy), simulations and remote mining, simulations and scheduling.

Louisiana State University and Agricultural & Mechanical College, Graduate School, College of Agriculture, School of Renewable Natural Resources, Baton Rouge, LA 70803. Offers fisheries (MS); forestry (MS, PhD); wildlife (MS); wildlife and fisheries science (PhD).

McGill University, Faculty of Graduate and Postdoctoral Studies, Faculty of Agricultural and Environmental Sciences, Department of Natural Resource Sciences, Montréal, QC H3A 2T5, Canada. Offers entomology (M Sc, PhD); environmental assessment (M Sc); forest science (M Sc, PhD); microbiology (M Sc, PhD); micrometeorology (M Sc, PhD); neotropical environment (M Sc, PhD); soil science (M Sc, PhD); wildlife biology (M Sc, PhD).

Michigan State University, The Graduate School, College of Agriculture and Natural Resources, Department of Community Sustainability, East Lansing, MI 48824. Offers MS, PhD. *Entrance requirements:* Additional exam requirements/recommendations for international students: Required—TOEFL. Electronic applications accepted.

Montana State University, The Graduate School, College of Agriculture, Department of Land Resources and Environmental Sciences, Bozeman, MT 59717. Offers land rehabilitation (interdisciplinary) (MS); land resources and environmental sciences (MS), including land rehabilitation (interdisciplinary), land resources and environmental sciences. *Program availability:* Part-time. *Degree requirements:* For master's, comprehensive exam. *Entrance requirements:* For master's, GRE General Test. Additional exam requirements/recommendations for international students: Required—TOEFL (minimum score 550 paper-based). Electronic applications accepted. *Faculty research:* Soil nutrient management and plant nutrition, isotope biogeochemistry of soils, biodegradation of hydrocarbons in soils and natural waters, remote sensing, GIS systems, managed and natural ecosystems, microbial and metabolic diversity in geothermally heated soils, integrated management of weeds, diversified cropping systems, insect behavior and ecology, river ecology, microbial biogeochemistry, weed ecology.

New Mexico Highlands University, Graduate Studies, College of Arts and Sciences, Department of Natural Resources Management, Las Vegas, NM 87701. Offers natural science (MS), including chemistry.

North Carolina Agricultural and Technical State University, The Graduate College, College of Agriculture and Environmental Sciences, Department of Natural Resources and Environmental Design, Greensboro, NC 27411. Offers plant, soil and environmental science (MS). *Program availability:* Part-time, evening/weekend. *Degree requirements:* For master's, comprehensive exam, thesis optional, qualifying exam. *Entrance requirements:* For master's, GRE General Test, minimum GPA of 3.0. *Faculty research:* Soil parameters and compaction of forest site, controlled traffic effects on soil, improving soybean and vegetable crops.

North Carolina State University, Graduate School, College of Natural Resources, Department of Parks, Recreation and Tourism Management, Raleigh, NC 27695. Offers natural resource management (MPRTM, MS); park and recreation management (MPRTM, MS); parks, recreation and tourism management (PhD); recreational sport management (MPRTM, MS); spatial information science (MPRTM, MS); tourism policy and development (MPRTM, MS). *Degree requirements:* For master's, thesis (for some programs); for doctorate, thesis/dissertation. *Entrance requirements:* For master's and doctorate, GRE General Test. Additional exam requirements/recommendations for international students: Required—TOEFL. Electronic applications accepted. *Faculty research:* Tourism policy and development, spatial information systems, natural resource management, recreational sports management, park and recreation management.

North Dakota State University, College of Graduate and Interdisciplinary Studies, College of Agriculture, Food Systems, and Natural Resources, Program in Natural Resources Management, Fargo, ND 58102. Offers MS, PhD. *Program availability:* Part-time. *Degree requirements:* For master's, thesis; for doctorate, comprehensive exam, thesis/dissertation. *Entrance requirements:* Additional exam requirements/recommendations for international students: Required—TOEFL. Electronic applications accepted. *Faculty research:* Natural resources economics, wetlands issues, wildlife, prairie ecology, range management.

North Dakota State University, College of Graduate and Interdisciplinary Studies, College of Engineering, Doctoral Program in Engineering, Fargo, ND 58102. Offers environmental and conservation science (PhD); materials and nanotechnology (PhD); natural resource management (PhD); STEM education (PhD); transportation and logistics (PhD). *Degree requirements:* For doctorate, comprehensive exam, thesis/dissertation. *Entrance requirements:* For doctorate, bachelor's degree in engineering, minimum GPA of 3.0. Additional exam requirements/recommendations for international students: Required—TOEFL. Electronic applications accepted. *Expenses:* Contact institution.

Northeastern State University, College of Science and Health Professions, Department of Natural Sciences, Program in Natural Sciences, Tahlequah, OK 74464-2399. Offers MS. *Faculty:* 14 full-time (8 women), 1 (woman) part-time/adjunct. *Students:* 7 full-time (2 women), 6 part-time (5 women); includes 6 minority (1 American Indian or Alaska Native, non-Hispanic/Latino; 1 Asian, non-Hispanic/Latino; 2 Hispanic/Latino; 2 Two or more races, non-Hispanic/Latino); 1 international. Average age 29. In 2018, 2 master's awarded. *Degree requirements:* For master's, thesis, project. *Application deadline:* For fall admission, 3/1 for domestic students; for spring admission, 10/1 for domestic students. Applications are processed on a rolling basis. Electronic applications accepted. *Expenses: Tuition, area resident:* Full-time $4500; part-time $250 per credit hour. Tuition, state resident: full-time $4500; part-time $250 per credit hour. Tuition, nonresident: full-time $9999; part-time $555.50 per credit hour. *International tuition:* $9999 full-time. *Required fees:* $601.20; $33.40 per credit hour. *Unit head:* Dr.

Christopher Burba, Program Chair, 918-444-3835, E-mail: burba@nsuok.edu. *Application contact:* Josh McCollum, Graduate Coordinator, 918-444-2093, E-mail: mccolluj@nsuok.edu. Website: http://academics.nsuok.edu/naturalsciences/Degrees/Graduate/MSNaturalScience.aspx

The Ohio State University, Graduate School, College of Food, Agricultural, and Environmental Sciences, School of Environment and Natural Resources, Columbus, OH 43210. Offers ecological restoration (MS, PhD); ecosystem science (MS, PhD); environment and natural resources (MENR); environmental social sciences (MS, PhD); fisheries and wildlife science (MS, PhD); forest science (MS, PhD); rural sociology (MS, PhD); soil science (MS, PhD). *Faculty:* 38. *Students:* 106 (64 women). Average age 29. In 2018, 21 master's, 5 doctorates awarded. *Entrance requirements:* For master's and doctorate, GRE. Additional exam requirements/recommendations for international students: Required—TOEFL (minimum score 550 paper-based; 79 iBT), Michigan English Language Assessment Battery (minimum score 82); Recommended—IELTS (minimum score 7). *Application deadline:* For fall admission, 1/1 priority date for domestic students, 12/15 priority date for international students; for spring admission, 11/1 for domestic students, 9/15 for international students. Applications are processed on a rolling basis. Application fee: $60 ($70 for international students). Electronic applications accepted. *Financial support:* Fellowships, research assistantships, teaching assistantships, health care benefits, and unspecified assistantships available. *Unit head:* Dr. Jeff S. Sharp, Director, 614-292-9410, E-mail: sharp.123@osu.edu. *Application contact:* Graduate and Professional Admissions, 614-292-9444, Fax: 614-292-3895, E-mail: gpadmissions@osu.edu. Website: http://senr.osu.edu/

Oklahoma State University, College of Agricultural Science and Natural Resources, Stillwater, OK 74078. Offers M Ag, MS, PhD. *Program availability:* Online learning. *Faculty:* 213 full-time (55 women), 5 part-time/adjunct (2 women). *Students:* 117 full-time (68 women), 271 part-time (138 women); includes 51 minority (15 Black or African American, non-Hispanic/Latino; 7 American Indian or Alaska Native, non-Hispanic/Latino; 4 Asian, non-Hispanic/Latino; 13 Hispanic/Latino; 12 Two or more races, non-Hispanic/Latino), 103 international. Average age 28. 209 applicants, 55% accepted, 100 enrolled. In 2018, 128 master's, 35 doctorates awarded. *Degree requirements:* For master's, thesis (for some programs); for doctorate, comprehensive exam, thesis/dissertation. *Entrance requirements:* For master's and doctorate, GRE or GMAT. Additional exam requirements/recommendations for international students: Required—TOEFL (minimum score 550 paper-based; 79 iBT). *Application deadline:* For fall admission, 3/1 priority date for domestic and international students; for spring admission, 8/1 priority date for domestic and international students. Applications are processed on a rolling basis. Application fee: $40 ($75 for international students). Electronic applications accepted. *Expenses: Tuition, area resident:* Full-time $4148. Tuition, state resident: full-time $4148. Tuition, nonresident: full-time $10,517. *International tuition:* $10,517 full-time. *Required fees:* $4394; $2929 per credit hour. Tuition and fees vary according to course load and program. *Financial support:* In 2018–19, 220 research assistantships (averaging $3,640 per year), 53 teaching assistantships (averaging $3,144 per year) were awarded; fellowships, career-related internships or fieldwork, Federal Work-Study, scholarships/grants, health care benefits, tuition waivers (partial), and unspecified assistantships also available. Support available to part-time students. Financial award application deadline: 3/1; financial award applicants required to submit FAFSA. *Unit head:* Dr. Thomas Coon, Vice President/Dean, 405-744-2474, E-mail: thomas.coon@okstate.edu. *Application contact:* Dr. Sheryl Tucker, Vice Prov/Dean/Prof, 405-744-6368, Fax: 405-744-0355, E-mail: gradi@okstate.edu. Website: http://casnr.okstate.edu

Oregon State University, College of Forestry, Program in Natural Resources, Corvallis, OR 97331. Offers fisheries management (MNR); forests and climate change (MNR); geographic information science (MNR); sustainable natural resources (MNR); urban forestry (MNR); water conflict management and transformation (MNR); wildlife management (MNR). *Program availability:* Part-time, online only, 100% online. *Entrance requirements:* For master's, GRE. Additional exam requirements/recommendations for international students: Required—TOEFL (minimum score 80 iBT), IELTS (minimum score 6.5). *Expenses:* Contact institution.

Purdue University, Graduate School, College of Agriculture, Department of Forestry and Natural Resources, West Lafayette, IN 47907. Offers fisheries and aquatic sciences (MS, MSF, PhD); forest biology (MS, MSF, PhD); natural resource social science (MS, PhD); natural resources social science (MSF); quantitative ecology (MS, MSF, PhD); wildlife science (MS, MSF, PhD); wood products and wood products manufacturing (MS, MSF, PhD). *Faculty:* 25 full-time (5 women), 1 part-time/adjunct (0 women). *Students:* 58 full-time (32 women), 5 part-time (1 woman); includes 12 minority (2 American Indian or Alaska Native, non-Hispanic/Latino; 1 Asian, non-Hispanic/Latino; 4 Hispanic/Latino; 1 Native Hawaiian or other Pacific Islander, non-Hispanic/Latino; 4 Two or more races, non-Hispanic/Latino), 12 international. Average age 27. 51 applicants, 27% accepted, 14 enrolled. In 2018, 13 master's, 11 doctorates awarded. *Degree requirements:* For master's, thesis; for doctorate, thesis/dissertation. *Entrance requirements:* For master's and doctorate, GRE General Test (minimum score: verbal 50th percentile; quantitative 50th percentile; analytical writing 4.0), minimum undergraduate GPA of 3.2 or equivalent. Additional exam requirements/recommendations for international students: Required—TOEFL (minimum score 550 paper-based; 77 iBT). *Application deadline:* For fall admission, 1/5 for domestic students, 1/15 for international students; for spring admission, 9/15 for domestic and international students. Applications are processed on a rolling basis. Application fee: $60 ($75 for international students). Electronic applications accepted. *Financial support:* In 2018–19, 10 research assistantships (averaging $15,259 per year) were awarded; fellowships, teaching assistantships, career-related internships or fieldwork, and scholarships/grants also available. Support available to part-time students. Financial award application deadline: 1/5; financial award applicants required to submit FAFSA. *Faculty research:* Wildlife management, forest management, forest ecology, forest soils, limnology. *Unit head:* Robert G. Wagner, Head of the Graduate Program, 765-494-3590, E-mail: rgwagner@purdue.edu. *Application contact:* Christine Hofmeyer, Graduate Contact, 765-494-3572, E-mail: chofmeye@purdue.edu. Website: https://ag.purdue.edu/fnr

State University of New York College of Environmental Science and Forestry, Department of Environmental Resources Engineering, Syracuse, NY 13210-2779. Offers ecological engineering (MPS, MS, PhD); environmental management (MPS); environmental resources engineering (MPS, MS, PhD); geospatial information science and engineering (MPS, MS, PhD); water resources engineering (MPS, MS, PhD). *Program availability:* Part-time. *Faculty:* 9 full-time (1 woman), 3 part-time/adjunct (0 women). *Students:* 32 full-time (12 women), 8 part-time (0 women); includes 2 minority (1 Black or African American, non-Hispanic/Latino; 1 Asian, non-Hispanic/Latino), 19 international. Average age 41. 31 applicants, 58% accepted, 7 enrolled. In 2018, 11 master's, 1 doctorate awarded. Terminal master's awarded for partial completion of doctoral program. *Degree requirements:* For master's, thesis (for some programs); for

doctorate, comprehensive exam, thesis/dissertation. *Entrance requirements:* For master's and doctorate, GRE General Test, minimum GPA of 3.0. Additional exam requirements/recommendations for international students: Required—TOEFL (minimum score 550 paper-based; 80 iBT), IELTS (minimum score 6). *Application deadline:* For fall admission, 1/15 priority date for domestic and international students; for spring admission, 11/1 priority date for domestic and international students. Applications are processed on a rolling basis. Application fee: $60. Electronic applications accepted. *Expenses: Tuition, area resident:* Full-time $11,090; part-time $462 per credit hour. Tuition, state resident: full-time $11,090; part-time $462 per credit hour. Tuition, nonresident: full-time $22,650; part-time $944 per credit hour. *International tuition:* $22,650 full-time. *Required fees:* $1733; $178.58 per credit hour. *Financial support:* In 2018–19, 9 students received support. Unspecified assistantships available. Financial award application deadline: 6/30; financial award applicants required to submit FAFSA. *Faculty research:* Ecological engineering, environmental resources engineering, geospatial information science and engineering, water resources engineering, environmental science. *Total annual research expenditures:* $508,995. *Unit head:* Dr. Lindi Quackenbush, Chair, 315-470-4727, Fax: 315-470-4710, E-mail: ljquackc@esf.edu. *Application contact:* Scott Shannon, Associate Provost for Instruction/Dean of the Graduate School, 315-470-6599, Fax: 315-470-6978, E-mail: esfgrad@esf.edu.
Website: http://www.esf.edu/ere

State University of New York College of Environmental Science and Forestry, Department of Forest and Natural Resources Management, Syracuse, NY 13210-2779. Offers ecology and ecosystems (MPS, MS, PhD); economics, governance and human dimensions (MPS, MS, PhD); forest and natural resources management (MPS, MS, PhD); forest resources management (MF); monitoring, analysis and modeling (MPS, MS, PhD). *Accreditation:* SAF. *Program availability:* Part-time. *Faculty:* 33 full-time (8 women), 7 part-time/adjunct (0 women). *Students:* 42 full-time (19 women), 5 part-time (2 women); includes 5 minority (1 Black or African American, non-Hispanic/Latino; 1 American Indian or Alaska Native, non-Hispanic/Latino; 2 Asian, non-Hispanic/Latino; 1 Hispanic/Latino), 13 international. Average age 30. 26 applicants, 81% accepted, 4 enrolled. In 2018, 14 master's awarded. Terminal master's awarded for partial completion of doctoral program. *Degree requirements:* For master's, thesis (for some programs); for doctorate, comprehensive exam, thesis/dissertation. *Entrance requirements:* For master's and doctorate, GRE General Test, minimum GPA of 3.0. Additional exam requirements/recommendations for international students: Required— TOEFL (minimum score 550 paper-based; 80 iBT), IELTS (minimum score 6). *Application deadline:* For fall admission, 2/1 priority date for domestic and international students; for spring admission, 11/1 priority date for domestic and international students. Applications are processed on a rolling basis. Application fee: $60. *Expenses: Tuition, area resident:* Full-time $11,090; part-time $462 per credit hour. Tuition, state resident: full-time $11,090; part-time $462 per credit hour. Tuition, nonresident: full-time $22,650; part-time $944 per credit hour. *International tuition:* $22,650 full-time. *Required fees:* $1733; $178.58 per credit hour. *Financial support:* In 2018–19, 13 students received support. Unspecified assistantships available. Financial award application deadline: 6/30; financial award applicants required to submit FAFSA. *Faculty research:* Silviculture recreation management, tree improvement, operations management, economics. *Total annual research expenditures:* $3.2 million. *Unit head:* Dr. Christopher Nowak, Chair, 315-470-6575, Fax: 315-470-6536, E-mail: canowak@esf.edu. *Application contact:* Scott Shannon, Associate Provost for Instruction/Dean of the Graduate School, 315-470-6599, Fax: 315-470-6978, E-mail: esfgrad@esf.edu.
Website: http://www.esf.edu/fnrm/

Sul Ross State University, Division of Agricultural and Natural Resource Science, Programs in Natural Resource Management, Alpine, TX 79832. Offers range and wildlife management (M Ag, MS). *Program availability:* Part-time. *Degree requirements:* For master's, thesis (for some programs). *Entrance requirements:* For master's, GRE General Test, minimum undergraduate GPA of 2.5 in last 60 hours.

Tarleton State University, College of Graduate Studies, College of Agricultural and Environmental Sciences, Department of Wildlife, Sustainability, and Ecosystem Sciences, Stephenville, TX 76402. Offers agricultural and natural resource sciences (MS). *Program availability:* Part-time, evening/weekend. *Faculty:* 4 full-time (2 women), 2 part-time/adjunct (0 women). *Students:* 10 full-time (5 women), 7 part-time (4 women). Average age 28. 7 applicants, 86% accepted, 4 enrolled. In 2018, 5 master's awarded. *Degree requirements:* For master's, comprehensive exam, thesis (for some programs). *Entrance requirements:* For master's, GRE General Test, minimum GPA of 3.0. Additional exam requirements/recommendations for international students: Required—TOEFL (minimum score 520 paper based, 69 iBT); Recommended—IELTS (minimum score 6), TSE (minimum score 50). *Application deadline:* For fall admission, 8/1 priority date for domestic students; for spring admission, 12/1 for domestic students. Applications are processed on a rolling basis. Application fee: $50 ($130 for international students). Electronic applications accepted. *Expenses:* Contact institution. *Financial support:* Research assistantships, teaching assistantships, career-related internships or fieldwork, Federal Work-Study, and institutionally sponsored loans available. Support available to part-time students. Financial award application deadline: 5/1; financial award applicants required to submit FAFSA. *Unit head:* Dr. T. Wayne Schwertner, Department Head, 254-968-9219, E-mail: schwertner@tarleton.edu. *Application contact:* Information Contact, 254-968-9104, Fax: 254-968-9670, E-mail: gradoffice@tarleton.edu.

Texas A&M University, College of Agriculture and Life Sciences, Department of Ecosystem Science and Management, College Station, TX 77843. Offers ecosystem science and management (M Agr, MNRD, MS, PhD). *Program availability:* Part-time. *Faculty:* 26. *Students:* 45 full-time (24 women), 19 part-time (11 women); includes 15 minority (2 Black or African American, non-Hispanic/Latino; 2 Asian, non-Hispanic/Latino; 9 Hispanic/Latino; 2 Two or more races, non-Hispanic/Latino), 13 international. Average age 29. 20 applicants, 90% accepted, 18 enrolled. In 2018, 8 master's, 7 doctorates awarded. Terminal master's awarded for partial completion of doctoral program. *Degree requirements:* For master's, thesis (for some programs); for doctorate, thesis/dissertation. *Entrance requirements:* For master's and doctorate, GRE General Test. Additional exam requirements/recommendations for international students: Required—TOEFL (minimum score 550 paper-based; 80 iBT), IELTS (minimum score 6), PTE (minimum score 53). *Application deadline:* For fall admission, 3/15 priority date for domestic students; for spring admission, 10/15 priority date for domestic students. Applications are processed on a rolling basis. Application fee: $50 ($90 for international students). Electronic applications accepted. *Expenses:* Contact institution. *Financial support:* In 2018–19, 51 students received support, including 13 fellowships with tuition reimbursements available (averaging $7,762 per year), 22 research assistantships with tuition reimbursements available (averaging $8,294 per year), 29 teaching assistantships with tuition reimbursements available (averaging $12,140 per year); career-related internships or fieldwork, institutionally sponsored loans, scholarships/ grants, traineeships, health care benefits, tuition waivers (full and partial), and unspecified assistantships also available. Support available to part-time students. Financial award application deadline: 3/15; financial award applicants required to submit

FAFSA. *Faculty research:* Expert systems, geographic information systems, economics, biology, genetics. *Unit head:* Dr. Kathleen Kavanagh, Professor and Department Head, 979-845-5000, Fax: 979-845-6049, E-mail: katyk@tamu.edu. *Application contact:* Heather Haliburton Janke, Senior Academic Advisor II, 979-862-8993, Fax: 979-845-6049, E-mail: hjanke@tamu.edu.
Website: http://essm.tamu.edu

Texas Tech University, Graduate School, College of Agricultural Sciences and Natural Resources, Department of Natural Resources Management, Lubbock, TX 79409-2125. Offers wildlife, aquatic, and wildlands science and management (MS, PhD). *Program availability:* Part-time. *Faculty:* 18 full-time (3 women), 1 part-time/adjunct (0 women). *Students:* 43 full-time (18 women), 12 part-time (3 women); includes 7 minority (4 Hispanic/Latino; 3 Two or more races, non-Hispanic/Latino), 3 international. Average age 30. 12 applicants, 83% accepted, 8 enrolled. In 2018, 11 master's, 3 doctorates awarded. *Degree requirements:* For master's, comprehensive exam, thesis (for some programs); for doctorate, comprehensive exam, thesis/dissertation. *Entrance requirements:* For master's and doctorate, GRE General Test, formal approval from departmental committee. Additional exam requirements/recommendations for international students: Required—TOEFL (minimum score 550 paper-based; 79 iBT). *Application deadline:* For fall admission, 6/1 priority date for domestic students, 1/15 priority date for international students; for spring admission, 9/1 priority date for domestic students, 6/15 priority date for international students. Applications are processed on a rolling basis. Application fee: $65. Electronic applications accepted. *Expenses:* Contact institution. *Financial support:* In 2018–19, 50 students received support, including 41 fellowships (averaging $4,687 per year), 38 research assistantships (averaging $14,456 per year), 5 teaching assistantships (averaging $13,036 per year); Federal Work-Study, scholarships/grants, and unspecified assistantships also available. Financial award application deadline: 4/15; financial award applicants required to submit FAFSA. *Faculty research:* Applying ecological knowledge in decision-making about sustainable resource use, community (plant or animal) response to disturbances, population dynamics, climate change, habitat restoration, wildlife management, range management, fisheries ecology, fire ecology, aquatic systems. *Total annual research expenditures:* $2.1 million. *Unit head:* Dr. Mark Wallace, Professor and Chair, 806-834-6979, Fax: 806-742-2280, E-mail: mark.wallace@ttu.edu. *Application contact:* Melissa S Moore, Administrative Assistant, 806-834-2628, Fax: 806-742-2280, E-mail: melissa.s.moore@ttu.edu.
Website: www.nrm.ttu.edu/

Texas Tech University, Graduate School, Interdisciplinary Programs, Lubbock, TX 79409-1030. Offers arid land studies (MS); biotechnology (MS); heritage and museum sciences (MA); interdisciplinary studies (MA, MS); wind science and engineering (PhD); JD/MS. *Program availability:* Part-time, 100% online, blended/hybrid learning. *Faculty:* 10 full-time (5 women). *Students:* 98 full-time (50 women), 82 part-time (52 women); includes 75 minority (33 Black or African American, non-Hispanic/Latino; 1 American Indian or Alaska Native, non-Hispanic/Latino; 7 Asian, non-Hispanic/Latino; 31 Hispanic/ Latino; 3 Two or more races, non-Hispanic/Latino), 19 international. Average age 30. 96 applicants, 76% accepted, 55 enrolled. In 2018, 64 master's, 1 doctorate awarded. Terminal master's awarded for partial completion of doctoral program. *Degree requirements:* For master's, comprehensive exam (for some programs), thesis (for some programs); for doctorate, comprehensive exam, thesis/dissertation (for some programs). *Entrance requirements:* Additional exam requirements/recommendations for international students: Required—TOEFL (minimum score 550 paper-based; 79 iBT), IELTS (minimum score 6.5), PTE (minimum score 60), Cambridge Advanced (B), Cambridge Proficiency (C), ELS English for Academic Purposes (Level 112). *Application deadline:* For fall admission, 6/1 priority date for domestic students, 1/15 priority date for international students; for spring admission, 9/1 priority date for domestic students, 6/15 priority date for international students. Applications are processed on a rolling basis. Application fee: $65. Electronic applications accepted. *Expenses:* Tuition, state resident: full-time $7776; part-time $324 per credit hour. Tuition, nonresident: full-time $17,736; part-time $739 per credit hour. *Required fees:* $2504; $53.50 per credit hour. $610 per semester. Tuition and fees vary according to program. *Financial support:* In 2018–19, 124 students received support, including 111 fellowships (averaging $4,942 per year), 27 research assistantships (averaging $17,595 per year), 8 teaching assistantships (averaging $13,758 per year); scholarships/grants and unspecified assistantships also available. Financial award application deadline: 4/15; financial award applicants required to submit FAFSA. *Total annual research expenditures:* $2.3 million. *Unit head:* Dr. Mark A. Sheridan, Vice Provost for Graduate and Postdoctoral Affairs/ Dean of the Graduate School, 806-742-2787, Fax: 806-742-1746, E-mail: mark.sheridan@ttu.edu. *Application contact:* David Doerfert, Associate Dean, 806-834-4477, Fax: 806-742-4038, E-mail: david.doerfert@ttu.edu.
Website: www.depts.ttu.edu/gradschool/

Unity College, Program in Professional Science, Unity, ME 04988. Offers sustainability science (MS); sustainable natural resource management (MS). *Program availability:* Online learning.

Universidad Metropolitana, School of Environmental Affairs, Program in Environmental Management, San Juan, PR 00928-1150. Offers MSEM. *Program availability:* Part-time. *Degree requirements:* For master's, thesis. Electronic applications accepted.

Universidad Nacional Pedro Henriquez Urena, Graduate School, Santo Domingo, Dominican Republic. Offers agricultural diversity (MS), including horticultural/fruit production, tropical animal production; conservation of monuments and cultural assets (M Arch); ecology and environment (MS); environmental engineering (MEE); international relations (MA); natural resource management (MS); political science (MA); project optimization (MPM); project feasibility (MPM); project management (MPM); sanitation engineering (ME); science for teachers (MS); tropical Caribbean architecture (M Arch).

Université du Québec à Montréal, Graduate Programs, Program in Earth Sciences, Montreal, QC H3C 3P8, Canada. Offers earth sciences (M Sc); mineral resources (PhD); non-renewable resources (DESS). *Program availability:* Part-time. Terminal master's awarded for partial completion of doctoral program. *Degree requirements:* For master's, thesis (for some programs); for doctorate, thesis/dissertation. *Entrance requirements:* For master's, appropriate bachelor's degree or equivalent, proficiency in French. *Faculty research:* Economic geology, structural geology, geochemistry, Quaternary geology, isotopic geochemistry.

Université du Québec en Abitibi-Témiscamingue, Graduate Programs, Program in Environmental Sciences, Rouyn-Noranda, QC J9X 5E4, Canada. Offers biology (MS); environmental sciences (PhD); sustainable forest ecosystem management (MS).

University of Alaska Fairbanks, School of Natural Resources and Extension, Fairbanks, AK 99775-7140. Offers natural resources and sustainability (PhD); natural resources management (MS). *Program availability:* Part-time. *Faculty:* 34 full-time (18 women), 1 (woman) part-time/adjunct. *Students:* 11 full-time (8 women), 15 part-time (7 women); includes 5 minority (1 Black or African American, non-Hispanic/Latino; 1 Hispanic/Latino; 3 Two or more races, non-Hispanic/Latino), 1 international. Average

Peterson's Graduate Programs in the Physical Sciences, Mathematics, Agricultural Sciences, the Environment & Natural Resources 2020

www.petersons.com **341**

age 39. 11 applicants, 36% accepted, 3 enrolled. In 2018, 7 master's, 2 doctorates awarded. *Degree requirements:* For master's, comprehensive exam, thesis (for some programs), oral defense of project or thesis; for doctorate, comprehensive exam, thesis/dissertation, defense of the dissertation. *Entrance requirements:* For master's, GRE General Test, bachelor's degree from accredited institution with minimum cumulative undergraduate and major GPA of 3.0; for doctorate, minimum cumulative GPA of 3.0. Additional exam requirements/recommendations for international students: Required—TOEFL (minimum score 550 paper-based; 89 iBT), IELTS (minimum score 6.5). *Application deadline:* For fall admission, 6/1 for domestic students, 3/1 for international students; for spring admission, 10/15 for domestic students, 9/1 for international students. Applications are processed on a rolling basis. Application fee: $60. Electronic applications accepted. *Expenses: Tuition, area resident:* Full-time $8802; part-time $5868 per credit hour. Tuition, state resident: full-time $8802; part-time $5868 per credit hour. Tuition, nonresident: full-time $18,504; part-time $12,336 per credit hour. *International tuition:* $18,504 full-time. *Required fees:* $1416; $944 per credit hour. $472 per semester. Tuition and fees vary according to course load and program. *Financial support:* In 2018–19, 4 research assistantships with full tuition reimbursements (averaging $11,999 per year), 1 teaching assistantship with full tuition reimbursement (averaging $5,034 per year) were awarded; fellowships with full tuition reimbursements, career-related internships or fieldwork, Federal Work-Study, scholarships/grants, health care benefits, and unspecified assistantships also available. Support available to part-time students. Financial award application deadline: 2/15; financial award applicants required to submit FAFSA. *Faculty research:* Conservation biology, soil/water conservation, land use policy and planning in the arctic and subarctic, forest ecosystem management, subarctic agricultural production. *Total annual research expenditures:* $3.8 million. *Unit head:* Milan Shipka, Director, 907-474-7429, E-mail: uaf-snre@alaska.edu. *Application contact:* Samara Taber, Director of Admissions, 907-474-7500, E-mail: uaf-admissions@alaska.edu.
Website: http://www.uaf.edu/snre/

University of Alberta, Faculty of Graduate Studies and Research, Department of Renewable Resources, Edmonton, AB T6G 2E1, Canada. Offers agroforestry (M Ag, M Sc, MF); conservation biology (M Sc, PhD); forest biology and management (M Sc, PhD); land reclamation and remediation (M Sc, PhD); protected areas and wildlands management (M Sc, PhD); soil science (M Ag, M Sc, PhD); water and land resources (M Ag, M Sc, PhD); wildlife ecology and management (M Sc, PhD); MBA/M Ag; MBA/MF. *Program availability:* Part-time. *Degree requirements:* For master's, thesis (for some programs); for doctorate, comprehensive exam, thesis/dissertation. *Entrance requirements:* For master's, minimum 2 years of relevant professional experiences, minimum GPA of 3.0; for doctorate, minimum GPA of 3.0. Additional exam requirements/recommendations for international students: Required—TOEFL (minimum score 550 paper-based). Electronic applications accepted. *Faculty research:* Natural and managed landscapes.

University of Alberta, Faculty of Graduate Studies and Research, Program in Business Administration, Edmonton, AB T6G 2E1, Canada. Offers international business (MBA); leisure and sport management (MBA); natural resources and energy (MBA); technology commercialization (MBA); MBA/LL B; MBA/M Ag; MBA/M Eng; MBA/MF; MBA/PhD. *Accreditation:* AACSB. *Program availability:* Part-time, evening/weekend. *Degree requirements:* For master's, thesis or alternative. *Entrance requirements:* For master's, GMAT. Additional exam requirements/recommendations for international students: Required—TOEFL (minimum score 600 paper-based). Electronic applications accepted. *Faculty research:* Natural resources and energy/management and policy/family enterprise/international business/healthcare research management.

The University of Arizona, College of Agriculture and Life Sciences, School of Natural Resources and the Environment, Program in Natural Resources, Tucson, AZ 85721. Offers MS, PhD. *Degree requirements:* For master's, thesis; for doctorate, comprehensive exam, thesis/dissertation. *Entrance requirements:* For master's and doctorate, GRE General Test, minimum GPA of 3.0. Additional exam requirements/recommendations for international students: Required—TOEFL (minimum score 550 paper-based; 79 iBT). Electronic applications accepted. *Faculty research:* Criteria for defining, mapping, and evaluating range sites; methods of establishing forage plants on southwestern range lands; plants for pollution and erosion control, beautification, and browse.

University of Arkansas at Monticello, School of Forest Resources, Monticello, AR 71656. Offers MS. *Program availability:* Part-time. *Degree requirements:* For master's, comprehensive exam, thesis. *Entrance requirements:* For master's, GRE General Test, minimum GPA of 2.7. Additional exam requirements/recommendations for international students: Required—TOEFL (minimum score 550 paper-based). Electronic applications accepted. *Faculty research:* Geographic information systems/remote sensing, forest ecology, wildlife ecology and management.

The University of British Columbia, Faculty of Land and Food Systems, Program in Land and Water Systems, Vancouver, BC V6T 1Z1, Canada. Offers MLWS.

The University of British Columbia, Faculty of Science, Institute for Resources, Environment and Sustainability, Vancouver, BC V6T 1Z4, Canada. Offers M Sc, MA, PhD. *Degree requirements:* For master's, thesis; for doctorate, comprehensive exam, thesis/dissertation. *Entrance requirements:* Additional exam requirements/recommendations for international students: Required—TOEFL. Electronic applications accepted. *Expenses:* Contact institution. *Faculty research:* Land management, water resources, energy, environmental assessment, risk evaluation.

University of California, Berkeley, Graduate Division, College of Natural Resources, Group in Energy and Resources, Berkeley, CA 94720. Offers MA, MS, PhD. *Degree requirements:* For master's, project or thesis; for doctorate, one foreign language, thesis/dissertation, qualifying exam. *Entrance requirements:* For master's and doctorate, GRE General Test, minimum GPA of 3.0, 3 letters of recommendation. Electronic applications accepted. *Faculty research:* Technical, economic, environmental, and institutional aspects of energy conservation in residential and commercial buildings; international patterns of energy use; renewable energy sources; assessment of valuation of energy and environmental resources pricing.

University of Connecticut, Graduate School, College of Agriculture, Health and Natural Resources, Department of Natural Resources and the Environment, Storrs, CT 06269. Offers MS, PhD. Terminal master's awarded for partial completion of doctoral program. *Degree requirements:* For master's, comprehensive exam. *Entrance requirements:* For master's, GRE General Test, GRE Subject Test. Additional exam requirements/recommendations for international students: Required—TOEFL (minimum score 550 paper-based). Electronic applications accepted.

University of Delaware, College of Agriculture and Natural Resources, Department of Bioresources Engineering, Newark, DE 19716. Offers MS.

University of Florida, Graduate School, College of Agricultural and Life Sciences, School of Forest Resources and Conservation, Gainesville, FL 32611. Offers fisheries and aquatic sciences (MFAS, MS, PhD), including ecological restoration (MFAS, MFRC, MS, PhD), geographic information systems (MFAS, MFRC, MS, PhD), natural resource policy and administration (MFAS, MFRC, MS, PhD), wetland sciences (MFAS, MFRC, MS, PhD); forest resources and conservation (MFRC, MS, PhD), including agroforestry, ecological restoration (MFAS, MFRC, MS, PhD), geographic information systems (MFAS, MFRC, MS, PhD), geomatics, hydrologic sciences (MS, PhD), natural resource policy and administration (MFAS, MFRC, MS, PhD), toxicology (PhD), tropical conservation and development, wetland sciences (MFAS, MFRC, MS, PhD); JD/MFRC; JD/MS; JD/PhD. *Program availability:* Part-time, evening/weekend, online learning. Terminal master's awarded for partial completion of doctoral program. *Degree requirements:* For master's, comprehensive exam, thesis optional, project (for MFRC); for doctorate, comprehensive exam, thesis/dissertation. *Entrance requirements:* For master's, GRE General Test, minimum GPA of 3.0, curriculum vitae, 3 letters of recommendation; for doctorate, GRE General Test, minimum GPA of 3.25, curriculum vitae, 3 letters of recommendation. Additional exam requirements/recommendations for international students: Required—TOEFL (minimum score 550 paper-based; 80 iBT), IELTS (minimum score 6). Electronic applications accepted. *Faculty research:* Quantitative and integrative fisheries science, ecology and management of aquatic systems, finfish, invertebrate and ornamental aquaculture, aquatic animal health, geomatics and GIS, natural resource conservation, tropical forestry, economics and policy, environmental education, forest biology and ecology, forest management, hydrology, silviculture.

University of Florida, Graduate School, School of Natural Resources and Environment, Gainesville, FL 32611. Offers interdisciplinary ecology (MS, PhD). *Degree requirements:* For master's, comprehensive exam, thesis; for doctorate, comprehensive exam, thesis/dissertation. *Entrance requirements:* For master's and doctorate, GRE General Test, minimum GPA of 3.0. Additional exam requirements/recommendations for international students: Required—TOEFL (minimum score 550 paper-based; 80 iBT), IELTS (minimum score 6). Electronic applications accepted. *Faculty research:* Natural sciences, social sciences, sustainability studies, research design and methods.

University of Georgia, Warnell School of Forestry and Natural Resources, Athens, GA 30602. Offers MFR, MS, PhD. *Accreditation:* SAF. *Degree requirements:* For master's, thesis (MS); for doctorate, one foreign language, thesis/dissertation. *Entrance requirements:* For master's and doctorate, GRE General Test. Electronic applications accepted.

University of Guelph, Office of Graduate and Postdoctoral Studies, Ontario Agricultural College, Department of Land Resource Science, Guelph, ON N1G 2W1, Canada. Offers atmospheric science (M Sc, PhD); environmental and agricultural earth sciences (M Sc, PhD); land resources management (M Sc, PhD); soil science (M Sc, PhD). *Program availability:* Part-time. *Degree requirements:* For master's, thesis (for some programs), research project (non-thesis track); for doctorate, comprehensive exam, thesis/dissertation. *Entrance requirements:* For master's, minimum B- average during previous 2 years of course work; for doctorate, minimum B average during previous 2 years of course work. Additional exam requirements/recommendations for international students: Required—TOEFL (minimum score 550 paper-based). Electronic applications accepted. *Faculty research:* Soil science, environmental earth science, land resource management.

University of Hawaii at Manoa, Office of Graduate Education, College of Tropical Agriculture and Human Resources, Department of Natural Resources and Environmental Management, Honolulu, HI 96822. Offers MS, PhD. *Program availability:* Part-time. Terminal master's awarded for partial completion of doctoral program. *Degree requirements:* For master's, thesis optional; for doctorate, comprehensive exam, thesis/dissertation. *Entrance requirements:* For master's and doctorate, GRE General Test, minimum GPA of 3.0 in last 4 semesters of course work. Additional exam requirements/recommendations for international students: Required—TOEFL (minimum score 600 paper-based; 100 iBT), IELTS (minimum score 7). *Faculty research:* Bioeconomics, natural resource management.

University of Idaho, College of Graduate Studies, College of Natural Resources, Moscow, ID 83844-2282. Offers MNR, MS, PSM, PhD. *Faculty:* 60. *Students:* 130 full-time (77 women), 146 part-time (67 women). Average age 33. 146 applicants, 67% accepted, 74 enrolled. In 2018, 79 master's, 6 doctorates awarded. *Entrance requirements:* For master's and doctorate, minimum GPA of 3.0. Additional exam requirements/recommendations for international students: Required—TOEFL. *Application deadline:* For fall admission, 8/1 for domestic students; for spring admission, 12/15 for domestic students. Applications are processed on a rolling basis. Application fee: $60. Electronic applications accepted. *Expenses:* Tuition, state resident: full-time $7266.44; part-time $474.50 per credit hour. Tuition, nonresident: full-time $24,902; part-time $1453.50 per credit hour. *Required fees:* $2085.56; $45.50 per credit hour. *Financial support:* Fellowships, research assistantships, teaching assistantships, and Federal Work-Study available. Support available to part-time students. Financial award applicants required to submit FAFSA. *Faculty research:* Fisheries and wildlife, forest nursery and seedling research, remote sensing and GIS research, wilderness research, combustion physics. *Unit head:* Dr. Dennis Becker, Dean, 208-885-8981, Fax: 208-885-5534, E-mail: cnr@uidaho.edu. *Application contact:* Dr. Dennis Becker, Dean, 208-885-8981, Fax: 208-885-5534, E-mail: cnr@uidaho.edu.
Website: https://www.uidaho.edu/cnr

University of Illinois at Urbana–Champaign, Graduate College, College of Agricultural, Consumer and Environmental Sciences, Department of Natural Resources and Environmental Science, Champaign, IL 61820. Offers MS, PhD, MS/JD. *Program availability:* Part-time, online learning.

University of Louisiana at Lafayette, College of Sciences, School of Geosciences, Lafayette, LA 70504. Offers environmental resource science (MS); geosciences (MS). *Program availability:* Part-time. *Degree requirements:* For master's, comprehensive exam, thesis. *Entrance requirements:* For master's, GRE General Test, minimum GPA of 2.75. Additional exam requirements/recommendations for international students: Required—TOEFL (minimum score 550 paper-based). Electronic applications accepted. *Faculty research:* Aquifer contamination, coastal erosion, geochemistry of peat, petroleum geology and geophysics, remote sensing and geographic information systems applications.

The University of Manchester, School of Materials, Manchester, United Kingdom. Offers advanced aerospace materials engineering (M Sc); advanced metallic systems (PhD); biomedical materials (M Phil, M Sc, PhD); ceramics and glass (M Phil, M Sc, PhD); composite materials (M Sc, PhD); corrosion and protection (M Phil, M Sc, PhD); materials (M Phil, PhD); metallic materials (M Phil, M Sc, PhD); nanostructural materials (M Phil, M Sc, PhD); paper science (M Phil, M Sc, PhD); polymer science and engineering (M Phil, M Sc, PhD); technical textiles (M Sc); textile design, fashion and management (M Phil, M Sc, PhD); textile science and technology (M Phil, M Sc, PhD); textiles (M Phil, PhD); textiles and fashion (M Ent).

University of Manitoba, Faculty of Graduate Studies, Clayton H. Riddell Faculty of Environment, Earth, and Resources, Natural Resources Institute, Winnipeg, MB R3T 2N2, Canada. Offers natural resources and environmental management (PhD); natural resources management (MNRM).

University of Maryland, College Park, Academic Affairs, College of Agriculture and Natural Resources, Department of Plant Science and Landscape Architecture, Natural Resource Sciences Program, College Park, MD 20742. Offers MS, PhD. *Faculty research:* Wetland soils, acid mine drainage, acid sulfate soil.

University of Michigan, School for Environment and Sustainability, Program in Environment and Sustainability, Ann Arbor, MI 48109. Offers behavior, education and communication (MS); conservation ecology (MS); environment and sustainability (PhD); environmental informatics (MS); environmental justice (MS); environmental policy and planning (MS); sustainable systems (MS); MS/JD; MS/MBA; MS/MPH; MS/MPP; MS/MSE; MS/MURP. *Faculty:* 39 full-time (15 women), 19 part-time/adjunct (3 women). *Students:* 332 full-time (184 women); includes 52 minority (6 Black or African American, non-Hispanic/Latino; 1 American Indian or Alaska Native, non-Hispanic/Latino; 14 Asian, non-Hispanic/Latino; 17 Hispanic/Latino; 1 Native Hawaiian or other Pacific Islander, non-Hispanic/Latino; 13 Two or more races, non-Hispanic/Latino), 57 international. Average age 26. 485 applicants. In 2018, 113 master's, 4 doctorates awarded. Terminal master's awarded for partial completion of doctoral program. *Degree requirements:* For master's, thesis, practicum, or group project; for doctorate, comprehensive exam, thesis/dissertation, oral defense of dissertation, preliminary exam. *Entrance requirements:* For master's, GRE General Test (must be taken within 5 years of application submission); for doctorate, GRE General Test (must be taken within 5 years of application submission), Master's Degree. Additional exam requirements/recommendations for international students: Required—TOEFL (minimum score 560 paper-based; 84 iBT). *Application deadline:* For fall admission, 4/30 for domestic and international students. Applications are processed on a rolling basis. Application fee: $75 ($90 for international students). Electronic applications accepted. *Financial support:* Fellowships, research assistantships, teaching assistantships, career-related internships or fieldwork, Federal Work-Study, scholarships/grants, health care benefits, and unspecified assistantships available. Financial award application deadline: 1/7; financial award applicants required to submit FAFSA. *Faculty research:* 1) Climate Change, Energy, and Sustainable Systems 2) Environmental Justice 3) Environmental Behavior, Communications, and Policy 4) Conservation Ecology, Ecosystems Management, and Geographic Information Systems (GIS) 5) Cities, Mobility, and Built Environment. *Unit head:* Dr. Jonathan Overpeck, Samuel A. Graham Dean, 734-764-2550, Fax: 734-763-8965, E-mail: overpeck@umich.edu. *Application contact:* Jung Koral, Associate Director of Enrollment Services, 734-764-6453, Fax: 734-936-2195, E-mail: seas-admissions@umich.edu.
Website: https://seas.umich.edu/academics/ms

University of Minnesota, Twin Cities Campus, Graduate School, College of Food, Agricultural and Natural Resource Sciences, Program in Natural Resources Science and Management, St. Paul, MN 55108. Offers assessment, monitoring, and geospatial analysis (MS, PhD); economics, policy, management, and society (MS, PhD); forest hydrology and watershed management (MS, PhD); forest products (MS, PhD); forests: biology, ecology, conservation, and management (MS, PhD); natural resources science and management (MS, PhD); paper science and engineering (MS, PhD); recreation resources, tourism, and environmental education (MS, PhD). *Program availability:* Part-time. Terminal master's awarded for partial completion of doctoral program. *Degree requirements:* For master's, comprehensive exam, thesis (for some programs); for doctorate, comprehensive exam, thesis/dissertation. *Entrance requirements:* For master's and doctorate, GRE General Test. Additional exam requirements/recommendations for international students: Required—TOEFL (minimum score 550 paper-based; 79 iBT); Recommended—IELTS (minimum score 6.5). Electronic applications accepted. *Faculty research:* Forest hydrology, biology, ecology, conservation, and management; recreation resources and environmental education; wildlife ecology; economics, policy, and society; geographic information systems (GIS); forest products and paper science.

University of Montana, Graduate School, College of Forestry and Conservation, Missoula, MT 59812. Offers fish and wildlife biology (PhD); forest and conservation sciences (PhD); forestry (MS); recreation management (MS); resource conservation (MS); systems ecology (MS, PhD); wildlife biology (MS). *Degree requirements:* For doctorate, thesis/dissertation. *Entrance requirements:* For master's and doctorate, GRE General Test. Additional exam requirements/recommendations for international students: Required—TOEFL (minimum score 575 paper-based).

University of Nebraska–Lincoln, Graduate College, College of Agricultural Sciences and Natural Resources, Department of Agricultural Economics, Lincoln, NE 68588. Offers agribusiness (MBA); agricultural economics (MS, PhD); community development (M Ag). *Degree requirements:* For master's, thesis optional; for doctorate, comprehensive exam, thesis/dissertation. *Entrance requirements:* For master's and doctorate, GRE General Test. Additional exam requirements/recommendations for international students: Required—TOEFL (minimum score 550 paper-based). Electronic applications accepted. *Faculty research:* Marketing and agribusiness, production economics, resource law, international trade and development, rural policy and revitalization.

University of Nebraska–Lincoln, Graduate College, College of Agricultural Sciences and Natural Resources, School of Natural Resources, Lincoln, NE 68588. Offers geography (PhD); natural resources (MS, PhD). *Degree requirements:* For master's, thesis optional. *Entrance requirements:* For master's, GRE General Test. Additional exam requirements/recommendations for international students: Required—TOEFL. Electronic applications accepted. *Faculty research:* Wildlife biology, aquatic sciences, landscape ecology, agroforestry.

University of New Brunswick Saint John, Faculty of Business, Saint John, NB E2L 4L5, Canada. Offers administration (MBA); electronic commerce (MBA); international business (MBA); natural resource management (MBA). *Program availability:* Part-time. *Entrance requirements:* For master's, GMAT (minimum score of 550) or GRE (minimum 54th percentile), minimum GPA of 3.0. Additional exam requirements/recommendations for international students: Required—TOEFL (minimum score 580 paper-based; 93 iBT), TWE (minimum score 4.5). Electronic applications accepted. *Expenses:* Contact institution. *Faculty research:* International business, project management, innovation and technology management; business use of Weblogs and podcasts to communicate; corporate governance; high-involvement work systems; international competitiveness; supply chain management and logistics.

University of New Hampshire, Graduate School, College of Life Sciences and Agriculture, Department of Natural Resources and the Environment, Program in Resource Administration and Management, Durham, NH 03824. Offers MS. *Program availability:* Part-time. *Entrance requirements:* For master's, GRE General Test. Additional exam requirements/recommendations for international students: Required—TOEFL (minimum score 550 paper-based; 80 iBT). Electronic applications accepted.

University of New Hampshire, Graduate School, Interdisciplinary Programs, Doctoral Program in Natural Resources and Earth Systems Science, Durham, NH 03824. Offers earth and environmental sciences (PhD), including geology; natural resources and environmental studies (PhD). *Entrance requirements:* For doctorate, GRE. Additional exam requirements/recommendations for international students: Required—TOEFL (minimum score 550 paper-based; 80 iBT). Electronic applications accepted.

University of New Mexico, Graduate Studies, College of Arts and Sciences, Program in Economics, Albuquerque, NM 87131-2039. Offers econometrics (MA); economic theory (MA); environmental/natural resource economics (MA, PhD); international/development and sustainability economics (MA, PhD); public economics (MA, PhD). *Program availability:* Part-time. *Students:* Average age 33. 49 applicants, 20% accepted, 10 enrolled. In 2018, 7 master's, 4 doctorates awarded. Terminal master's awarded for partial completion of doctoral program. *Degree requirements:* For master's, comprehensive exam, thesis (for some programs); for doctorate, comprehensive exam, thesis/dissertation. *Entrance requirements:* For master's and doctorate, GRE General Test, 3 letters of recommendation, letter of intent, curriculum vitae. Additional exam requirements/recommendations for international students: Required—TOEFL (minimum score 520 paper-based; 68 iBT). *Application deadline:* For fall admission, 3/1 priority date for domestic students, 3/1 for international students. Applications are processed on a rolling basis. Application fee: $50. Electronic applications accepted. *Financial support:* Fellowships, research assistantships, teaching assistantships, career-related internships or fieldwork, Federal Work-Study, scholarships/grants, health care benefits, and unspecified assistantships available. Support available to part-time students. Financial award application deadline: 3/1; financial award applicants required to submit FAFSA. *Faculty research:* Core theory, econometrics, public finance, international/development economics, labor/human resource economics, environmental/natural resource economics. *Total annual research expenditures:* $167,690. *Unit head:* Dr. Janie Chermak, Chair, 505-277-2037, Fax: 505-277-9445, E-mail: jchermak@unm.edu. *Application contact:* Jeff Newcomer Miller, Academic Advisor, 505-277-3056, Fax: 505-277-9445, E-mail: econgrad@unm.edu.
Website: http://econ.unm.edu

University of Northern British Columbia, Office of Graduate Studies, Prince George, BC V2N 4Z9, Canada. Offers business administration (Diploma); community health science (M Sc); disability management (MA); education (M Ed); first nations studies (MA); gender studies (MA); history (MA); interdisciplinary studies (MA); international studies (MA); mathematical, computer and physical sciences (M Sc); natural resources and environmental studies (M Sc, MA, MNRES, PhD); political science (MA); psychology (M Sc, PhD); social work (MSW). *Program availability:* Part-time, evening/weekend, online learning. *Degree requirements:* For master's, thesis; for doctorate, thesis/dissertation. *Entrance requirements:* For master's, GRE, minimum B average in undergraduate course work; for doctorate, candidacy exam, minimum A average in graduate course work.

University of Rhode Island, Graduate School, College of the Environment and Life Sciences, Department of Environmental and Natural Resource Economics, Kingston, RI 02881. Offers MS, PhD. *Program availability:* Part-time. *Faculty:* 7 full-time (2 women). *Students:* 16 full-time (7 women), 3 part-time (all women); includes 2 minority (1 Black or African American, non-Hispanic/Latino; 1 Asian, non-Hispanic/Latino), 8 international. 33 applicants, 85% accepted, 6 enrolled. In 2018, 2 master's, 6 doctorates awarded. *Entrance requirements:* Additional exam requirements/recommendations for international students: Required—TOEFL. *Application deadline:* For fall admission, 2/1 for domestic and international students. Application fee: $65. Electronic applications accepted. *Expenses: Tuition, area resident:* Full-time $13,226; part-time $735 per credit. Tuition, state resident: full-time $13,226; part-time $735 per credit. Tuition, nonresident: full-time $25,854; part-time $1436 per credit. *International tuition:* $25,854 full-time. *Required fees:* $1698; $50 per credit. $35 per semester. One-time fee: $165. *Financial support:* In 2018–19, 16 research assistantships with tuition reimbursements (averaging $11,641 per year) were awarded. Financial award application deadline: 2/1; financial award applicants required to submit FAFSA. *Unit head:* Dr. Hirotsugu Uchida, Chair, 401-874-4586, Fax: 401-874-4766, E-mail: enre_chair@etal.uri.edu. *Application contact:* Corey Lang, Graduate Program Director, 401-874-4569, E-mail: clang@uri.edu.
Website: http://web.uri.edu/enre/

University of Rhode Island, Graduate School, College of the Environment and Life Sciences, Department of Natural Resources Science, Kingston, RI 02881. Offers MS, PhD. *Program availability:* Part-time. *Faculty:* 14 full-time (3 women). *Students:* 41 full-time (20 women), 6 part-time (3 women); includes 4 minority (1 Asian, non-Hispanic/Latino; 1 Hispanic/Latino; 2 Two or more races, non-Hispanic/Latino), 5 international. 46 applicants, 91% accepted, 22 enrolled. In 2018, 22 master's awarded. *Entrance requirements:* For master's and doctorate, GRE, 3 letters of recommendation. Additional exam requirements/recommendations for international students: Required—TOEFL. *Application deadline:* For fall admission, 7/15 for domestic students, 2/1 for international students; for spring admission, 11/15 for domestic students, 7/15 for international students; for summer admission, 4/15 for domestic students. Application fee: $65. Electronic applications accepted. *Expenses: Tuition, area resident:* Full-time $13,226; part-time $735 per credit. Tuition, state resident: full-time $13,226; part-time $735 per credit. Tuition, nonresident: full-time $25,854; part-time $1436 per credit. *International tuition:* $25,854 full-time. *Required fees:* $1698; $50 per credit. $35 per semester. One-time fee: $165. *Financial support:* In 2018–19, 16 research assistantships with tuition reimbursements (averaging $11,641 per year) were awarded. Financial award application deadline: 2/1; financial award applicants required to submit FAFSA. *Unit head:* Dr. Arthur Gold, Chair, 401-874-2903, Fax: 401-874-4561, E-mail: agold@uri.edu. *Application contact:* Dr. Peter August, Co-Director of the CELS Master of Environmental Science and Management Graduate Program, 401-874-4794, Fax: 401-874-4561, E-mail: pete@edc.uri.edu.
Website: http://web.uri.edu/nrs/

University of San Francisco, College of Arts and Sciences, Program in Environmental Management, San Francisco, CA 94117. Offers MS. *Program availability:* Evening/weekend. *Students:* 76 full-time (50 women), 16 part-time (14 women); includes 37 minority (4 Black or African American, non-Hispanic/Latino; 11 Asian, non-Hispanic/Latino; 14 Hispanic/Latino; 1 Native Hawaiian or other Pacific Islander, non-Hispanic/Latino; 7 Two or more races, non-Hispanic/Latino), 6 international. Average age 29. 132 applicants, 62% accepted, 39 enrolled. In 2018, 44 master's awarded. *Degree requirements:* For master's, thesis, project. *Entrance requirements:* For master's, 3 semesters of course work in chemistry, minimum GPA of 2.7, work experience in environmental field. Additional exam requirements/recommendations for international students: Required—TOEFL (minimum score 90 iBT), IELTS (minimum score 6.5), PTE (minimum score 61). *Application deadline:* For fall admission, 2/15 for domestic and international students. Applications are processed on a rolling basis. Application fee: $55. Electronic applications accepted. *Financial support:* Teaching assistantships with partial tuition reimbursements, career-related internships or fieldwork, and scholarships/grants available. Financial award applicants required to submit FAFSA. *Faculty research:* Ecology, environmental health and hazards, water management, energy and climate, environmental law, applied ecology, california ecosystems, restoration ecology, wetland ecology, wetland delineation, marine resources, environmental health, environmental toxicology, environmental risk management, hydrology, sustainable design, GIS, renewable energy. *Unit head:* Sindy Vela, Graduate Director, 415-422-4119, E-mail: msem@usfca.edu. *Application contact:* Information Contact, 415-422-5101, E-mail: asgraduate@usfca.edu.
Website: https://www.usfca.edu/arts-sciences/graduate-programs/environmental-management

Natural Resources

University of South Africa, College of Agriculture and Environmental Sciences, Pretoria, South Africa. Offers agriculture (MS); consumer science (MCS); environmental management (MA, MS, PhD); environmental science (MA, MS, PhD); geography (MA, MS, PhD); horticulture (M Tech); human ecology (MHE); life sciences (MS); nature conservation (M Tech).

The University of Texas at Austin, Graduate School, Cockrell School of Engineering, Department of Petroleum and Geosystems Engineering, Program in Energy and Earth Resources, Austin, TX 78712-1111. Offers MA. *Degree requirements:* For master's, thesis, seminar. *Entrance requirements:* For master's, GRE General Test. Additional exam requirements/recommendations for international students: Required—TOEFL. Electronic applications accepted.

University of Vermont, Graduate College, The Rubenstein School of Environment and Natural Resources, Program in Natural Resources, Burlington, VT 05405. Offers ecological economics (Certificate); natural resources (MS), including aquatic ecology and watershed science, environment thought and culture, environment, science and public affairs, forestry; natural resources (PhD); MELP/MS. MELP/MS offered in collaboration with Vermont Law School. *Degree requirements:* For master's, thesis or alternative; for doctorate, thesis/dissertation. *Entrance requirements:* For master's and doctorate, GRE General Test. Additional exam requirements/recommendations for international students: Required—TOEFL (minimum score 550 paper-based; 90 iBT), IELTS (minimum score 6.5). Electronic applications accepted.

University of Washington, Graduate School, College of the Environment, School of Environmental and Forest Sciences, Seattle, WA 98195. Offers bioresource science and engineering (MS, PhD); environmental horticulture (MEH); forest ecology (MS, PhD); forest management (MFR); forest soils (MS, PhD); restoration ecology (MS, PhD); restoration ecology and environmental horticulture (MS, PhD); social sciences (MS, PhD); sustainable resource management (MS, PhD); wildlife science (MS, PhD); MFR/MAIS; MPA/MS. *Accreditation:* SAF. *Program availability:* Part-time. *Degree requirements:* For master's, thesis; for doctorate, comprehensive exam, thesis/dissertation. *Entrance requirements:* For master's and doctorate, GRE, minimum GPA of 3.0. Additional exam requirements/recommendations for international students: Required—TOEFL. Electronic applications accepted. *Faculty research:* Ecosystem analysis, silviculture and forest protection, paper science and engineering, environmental horticulture and urban forestry, natural resource policy and economics, restoration ecology and environment horticulture, conservation, human dimensions, wildlife, bioresource science and engineering.

University of Wisconsin–Madison, Graduate School, Gaylord Nelson Institute for Environmental Studies, Environment and Resources Program, Madison, WI 53706-1380. Offers MS, PhD. *Program availability:* Part-time. *Degree requirements:* For master's, thesis; for doctorate, comprehensive exam, thesis/dissertation. *Entrance requirements:* For master's and doctorate, GRE General Test. Additional exam requirements/recommendations for international students: Required—TOEFL (minimum score 550 paper-based, 80 iBT) or IELTS (6.5). Electronic applications accepted. *Expenses:* Contact institution. *Faculty research:* Land use/tenure, watershed management, geographic information systems, remote sensing, environmental law/justice, restoration ecology, agroecology, political ecology, energy resources, climate science, public health, sustainability, human-wildlife conflict, conservation biology, environmental history.

University of Wisconsin–Stevens Point, College of Natural Resources, Stevens Point, WI 54481-3897. Offers MNR, MS. *Program availability:* Part-time. *Degree requirements:* For master's, thesis or alternative. *Entrance requirements:* For master's, GRE. *Faculty research:* Wildlife management, environmental education, fisheries, forestry, resource policy and planning.

University of Wyoming, College of Agriculture and Natural Resources, Department of Ecosystem Science and Management, Laramie, WY 82071. Offers ecology (MS); entomology (MS, PhD); rangeland ecology and watershed management (MS, PhD), including soil sciences (PhD), soil sciences and water resources (MS); soil science (MS, PhD); water resources (MS, PhD). *Program availability:* Part-time. *Degree requirements:* For master's, comprehensive exam, thesis, oral examination; for doctorate, comprehensive exam, thesis/dissertation, preliminary oral and written exam, oral final exam. *Entrance requirements:* For master's and doctorate, GRE General Test, minimum GPA of 3.0. Additional exam requirements/recommendations for international students: Required—TOEFL. Electronic applications accepted. *Expenses: Tuition, area resident:* Full-time $6504; part-time $271 per credit hour. Tuition, state resident: full-time $6504; part-time $271 per credit hour. Tuition, nonresident: full-time $19,464; part-time $811 per credit hour. *International tuition:* $19,464 full-time. *Required fees:* $1410.94; $343.82 per semester. $343.82 per semester. Tuition and fees vary according to course load, program and reciprocity agreements. *Faculty research:* Plant control, grazing management, riparian restoration, riparian management, reclamation.

University of Wyoming, College of Arts and Sciences, Department of Geography, Program in Rural Planning and Natural Resources, Laramie, WY 82071. Offers community and regional planning and natural resources (MP). *Degree requirements:* For master's, thesis or alternative. *Entrance requirements:* For master's, GRE General Test, minimum GPA of 3.0. Additional exam requirements/recommendations for international students: Required—TOEFL. *Expenses: Tuition, area resident:* Full-time $6504; part-time $271 per credit hour. Tuition, state resident: full-time $6504; part-time $271 per credit hour. Tuition, nonresident: full-time $19,464; part-time $811 per credit hour. *International tuition:* $19,464 full-time. *Required fees:* $1410.94; $343.82 per semester. $343.82 per semester. Tuition and fees vary according to course load, program and reciprocity agreements. *Faculty research:* Rural and small town planning, public land management.

Utah State University, School of Graduate Studies, S.J. and Jessie E. Quinney College of Natural Resources, Interdisciplinary Program in Natural Resources, Logan, UT 84322. Offers MNR. *Entrance requirements:* For master's, GRE General Test, minimum GPA of 3.0. Additional exam requirements/recommendations for international students: Required—TOEFL. *Faculty research:* Ecosystem management, human dimensions, quantitative methods, informative management.

Virginia Polytechnic Institute and State University, Graduate School, College of Natural Resources and Environment, Blacksburg, VA 24061. Offers fisheries and wildlife (MS, PhD); forest products (MS/MF); forestry (PhD); geography (MS); geospatial and environmental analysis (PhD); natural resources (MNR); MS/MF. *Faculty:* 80 full-time (18 women). *Students:* 179 full-time (80 women), 75 part-time (40 women); includes 34 minority (3 Black or African American, non-Hispanic/Latino; 7 Asian, non-Hispanic/Latino; 17 Hispanic/Latino; 1 Native Hawaiian or other Pacific Islander, non-Hispanic/Latino; 6 Two or more races, non-Hispanic/Latino), 33 international. Average age 32. 110 applicants, 58% accepted, 50 enrolled. In 2018, 93 master's, 13 doctorates awarded. *Degree requirements:* For master's, comprehensive exam (for some programs), thesis (for some programs); for doctorate, comprehensive exam (for some programs), thesis/dissertation (for some programs). *Entrance requirements:* For master's and doctorate, GRE/GMAT. Additional exam requirements/recommendations for international students: Required—TOEFL (minimum score 90 iBT). *Application deadline:* For fall admission, 8/1 for domestic students, 4/1 for international students; for spring admission, 1/1 for domestic students, 9/1 for international students. Applications are processed on a rolling basis. Application fee: $75. Electronic applications accepted. *Expenses:* Tuition, state resident: full-time $15,510; part-time $739.50 per credit hour. Tuition, nonresident: full-time $29,629; part-time $1490.25 per credit hour. *Required fees:* $2804; $550 per semester. Tuition and fees vary according to course load, campus/location and program. *Financial support:* In 2018–19, 4 fellowships with full tuition reimbursements (averaging $29,791 per year), 97 research assistantships with full tuition reimbursements (averaging $18,686 per year), 47 teaching assistantships with full tuition reimbursements (averaging $17,302 per year) were awarded; scholarships/grants also available. Financial award application deadline: 3/1; financial award applicants required to submit FAFSA. *Total annual research expenditures:* $16.1 million. *Unit head:* Dr. Paul M. Winistorfer, Dean, 540-231-5481, Fax: 540-231-7664, E-mail: pstorfer@vt.edu. *Application contact:* Arlice Banks, Executive Assistant, 540-231-7051, Fax: 540-231-7664, E-mail: arbanks@vt.edu.
Website: http://cnre.vt.edu/

Virginia Polytechnic Institute and State University, VT Online, Blacksburg, VA 24061. Offers advanced transportation systems (Certificate); aerospace engineering (MS); agricultural and life sciences (MSLFS); business information systems (Graduate Certificate); career and technical education (MS); civil engineering (MS); computer engineering (M Eng, MS); decision support systems (Graduate Certificate); eLearning leadership (MA); electrical engineering (M Eng, MS); engineering administration (MEA); environmental engineering (Certificate); environmental politics and policy (Graduate Certificate); environmental sciences and engineering (MS); foundations of political analysis (Graduate Certificate); health product risk management (Graduate Certificate); industrial and systems engineering (MS); information policy and society (Graduate Certificate); information security (Graduate Certificate); information technology (MIT); instructional technology (MA); integrative STEM education (MA Ed); liberal arts (Graduate Certificate); life sciences: health product risk management (MS); natural resources (MNR, Graduate Certificate); networking (Graduate Certificate); nonprofit and nongovernmental organization management (Graduate Certificate); ocean engineering (MS); political science (MA); security studies (Graduate Certificate); software development (Graduate Certificate). *Expenses:* Tuition, state resident: full-time $15,510; part-time $739.50 per credit hour. Tuition, nonresident: full-time $29,629; part-time $1490.25 per credit hour. *Required fees:* $2804; $550 per semester. Tuition and fees vary according to course load, campus/location and program. *Application contact:* Graduate Admissions and Academic Progress, 540-231-8636, E-mail: grads@vt.edu.
Website: http://www.vto.vt.edu/

Washington State University, College of Agricultural, Human, and Natural Resource Sciences, School of the Environment, Pullman, WA 99164. Offers environmental and natural resource sciences (PhD); natural resource sciences (MS). Program applications must be made through the Pullman campus. *Degree requirements:* For master's, comprehensive exam (for some programs), thesis (for some programs), oral exam; for doctorate, comprehensive exam, thesis/dissertation, oral exam. *Entrance requirements:* For master's, GRE General Test, official copies of all college transcripts, three letters of recommendation. Additional exam requirements/recommendations for international students: Required—TOEFL, IELTS. *Faculty research:* Environmental and natural resources conservation and sustainability; earth sciences: earth systems and geology; wildlife ecology and conservation sciences.

Washington State University, College of Arts and Sciences, School of the Environment, Pullman, WA 99164. Offers environmental and natural resource sciences (PhD); environmental science (MS); geology (MS, PhD); natural resource science (MS). *Degree requirements:* For master's, comprehensive exam (for some programs), thesis (for some programs), oral exam; for doctorate, comprehensive exam, thesis/dissertation, oral exam, written exam. *Entrance requirements:* For master's, 3 undergraduate semester hours each in sociology or cultural anthropology, environmental science, biological sciences, and calculus or statistics; 4 in general ecology; and 6 in general chemistry or general physics; for doctorate, minimum GPA of 3.0. Additional exam requirements/recommendations for international students: Required—TOEFL, IELTS.

West Virginia University, Davis College of Agriculture, Forestry and Consumer Sciences, Morgantown, WV 26506. Offers agricultural and extension education (MS, PhD); agriculture and resource management (MS); agriculture, natural resources and design (M Agr); agronomy (MS); animal and food science (PhD); animal physiology (MS); applied and environmental microbiology (MS); design and merchandising (MS); entomology (MS); forest resource science (PhD); forestry (MSF); genetics and developmental biology (MS, PhD); horticulture (MS); human and community development (PhD); landscape architecture (MLA); natural resource economics (PhD); nutritional and food science (MS); plant and soil science (PhD); plant pathology (MS); recreation, parks and tourism resources (MS); reproductive physiology (MS, PhD); wildlife and fisheries resources (PhD). *Accreditation:* ASLA. *Program availability:* Part-time. *Students:* 188 full-time (86 women), 47 part-time (30 women); includes 22 minority (5 Black or African American, non-Hispanic/Latino; 5 Asian, non-Hispanic/Latino; 8 Hispanic/Latino; 4 Two or more races, non-Hispanic/Latino), 60 international. In 2018, 56 master's, 14 doctorates awarded. *Degree requirements:* For master's, thesis; for doctorate, thesis/dissertation. *Entrance requirements:* Additional exam requirements/recommendations for international students: Required—TOEFL (minimum score 550 paper-based). *Application deadline:* For fall admission, 6/1 priority date for domestic students, 6/1 for international students; for spring admission, 1/5 for domestic and international students. Applications are processed on a rolling basis. Application fee: $60. Electronic applications accepted. *Financial support:* Fellowships, research assistantships, teaching assistantships, career-related internships or fieldwork, Federal Work-Study, institutionally sponsored loans, tuition waivers (full and partial), and unspecified assistantships available. Financial award application deadline: 2/1; financial award applicants required to submit FAFSA. *Faculty research:* Reproductive physiology, soil and water quality, human nutrition, aquaculture, wildlife management. *Unit head:* Dr. Ken Blemings, Interim Dean, 304-293-2395, Fax: 304-293-3740, E-mail: ken.blemings@mail.wvu.edu. *Application contact:* Dr. J. Todd Petty, Associate Dean, 304-293-2278, Fax: 304-293-3740, E-mail: jtpetty@mail.wvu.edu.
Website: https://www.davis.wvu.edu

Range Science

Kansas State University, Graduate School, College of Agriculture, Department of Agronomy, Manhattan, KS 66506. Offers crop science (MS, PhD); grassland management (Certificate); plant breeding and genetics (MS, PhD); range and forage science (MS, PhD); soil and environmental science (MS, PhD); weed science (MS, PhD). *Program availability:* Part-time. *Degree requirements:* For master's, thesis or alternative, oral exam; for doctorate, thesis/dissertation, preliminary exams. *Entrance requirements:* For master's, minimum GPA of 3.0 in BS; for doctorate, minimum GPA of 3.0 in master's program. Additional exam requirements/recommendations for international students: Required—TOEFL (minimum score 79 iBT). Electronic applications accepted. *Expenses:* Contact institution. *Faculty research:* Range and forage science; soil and environmental science; weed science; plant breeding and genetics; crop physiology, ecology and production.

Montana State University, The Graduate School, College of Agriculture, Department of Animal and Range Sciences, Bozeman, MT 59717. Offers MS, PhD. *Program availability:* Part-time. *Degree requirements:* For master's, comprehensive exam; for doctorate, comprehensive exam, thesis/dissertation. *Entrance requirements:* For master's, GRE, minimum GPA of 3.0; undergraduate coursework in animal science, range science or closely-related field; faculty adviser; for doctorate, GRE. Additional exam requirements/recommendations for international students: Required—TOEFL (minimum score 550 paper-based; 80 iBT). Electronic applications accepted. *Faculty research:* Rangeland ecology, wildlife habitat management, residual feed intake, post-partum effect of bulls, increasing efficiency of sheep production systems.

Oregon State University, College of Agricultural Sciences, Program in Rangeland Ecology and Management, Corvallis, OR 97331. Offers agroforestry (MS, PhD). *Program availability:* Part-time. Terminal master's awarded for partial completion of doctoral program. *Entrance requirements:* Additional exam requirements/recommendations for international students: Required—TOEFL (minimum score 80 iBT), IELTS (minimum score 6.5). *Faculty research:* Range ecology, watershed science, animal grazing, agroforestry.

Sul Ross State University, Division of Agricultural and Natural Resource Science, Programs in Natural Resource Management, Alpine, TX 79832. Offers range and wildlife management (M Ag, MS). *Program availability:* Part-time. *Degree requirements:* For master's, thesis (for some programs). *Entrance requirements:* For master's, GRE General Test, minimum undergraduate GPA of 2.5 in last 60 hours.

Texas A&M University–Kingsville, College of Graduate Studies, Dick and Mary Lewis Kleberg College of Agriculture, Natural Resources and Human Sciences, Department of Agriculture, Agribusiness, and Environmental Sciences, King Ranch Institute for Ranch Management, Kingsville, TX 78363. Offers MS. *Entrance requirements:* Additional exam requirements/recommendations for international students: Required—TOEFL (minimum score 550 paper-based; 79 iBT); Recommended—IELTS. Electronic applications accepted.

Texas A&M University–Kingsville, College of Graduate Studies, Dick and Mary Lewis Kleberg College of Agriculture, Natural Resources and Human Sciences, Department of Animal, Rangeland, and Wildlife Sciences, Program in Range and Wildlife Management, Kingsville, TX 78363. Offers MS. *Degree requirements:* For master's, variable foreign language requirement, comprehensive exam, thesis (for some programs). *Entrance requirements:* For master's, GRE (minimum of 150 for each of the math and verbal sections), MAT, GMAT, minimum GPA of 3.0 for coursework from previous degree. Additional exam requirements/recommendations for international students: Required—TOEFL (minimum score 550 paper-based; 79 iBT). Electronic applications accepted.

The University of Arizona, College of Agriculture and Life Sciences, School of Natural Resources and the Environment, Program in Natural Resources, Tucson, AZ 85721. Offers MS, PhD. *Degree requirements:* For master's, thesis; for doctorate, comprehensive exam, thesis/dissertation. *Entrance requirements:* For master's and doctorate, GRE General Test, minimum GPA of 3.0. Additional exam requirements/recommendations for international students: Required—TOEFL (minimum score 550 paper-based; 79 iBT). Electronic applications accepted. *Faculty research:* Criteria for defining, mapping, and evaluating range sites; methods of establishing forage plants on southwestern range lands; plants for pollution and erosion control, beautification, and browse.

University of California, Berkeley, Graduate Division, College of Natural Resources, Group in Range Management, Berkeley, CA 94720. Offers MS. *Degree requirements:* For master's, thesis. *Entrance requirements:* For master's, GRE General Test, minimum GPA of 3.0, 3 letters of recommendation. Additional exam requirements/recommendations for international students: Required—TOEFL. Electronic applications accepted. *Faculty research:* Grassland and Savannah ecology, wetland ecology, oak woodland classification, wildlife habitat management.

University of Nevada, Reno, Graduate School, College of Agriculture, Biotechnology and Natural Resources, Program in Animal and Rangeland Science, Reno, NV 89557. Offers MS. *Degree requirements:* For master's, thesis optional. *Entrance requirements:* For master's, GRE, minimum GPA of 2.75. Additional exam requirements/recommendations for international students: Required—TOEFL (minimum score 500 paper-based; 61 iBT), IELTS (minimum score 6). Electronic applications accepted. *Faculty research:* Sperm fertility, embryo development, ruminant utilization of forages.

University of Wyoming, College of Agriculture and Natural Resources, Department of Ecosystem Science and Management, Laramie, WY 82071. Offers ecology (MS); entomology (MS, PhD); rangeland ecology and watershed management (MS, PhD), including soil sciences (PhD), soil sciences and water resources (MS); soil science (MS, PhD); water resources (MS, PhD). *Program availability:* Part-time. *Degree requirements:* For master's, comprehensive exam, thesis, oral examination; for doctorate, comprehensive exam, thesis/dissertation, preliminary oral and written exam, oral final exam. *Entrance requirements:* For master's and doctorate, GRE General Test, minimum GPA of 3.0. Additional exam requirements/recommendations for international students: Required—TOEFL. Electronic applications accepted. *Expenses: Tuition, area resident:* Full-time $6504; part-time $271 per credit hour. Tuition, state resident: full-time $6504; part-time $271 per credit hour. Tuition, nonresident: full-time $19,464; part-time $811 per credit hour. *International tuition:* $19,464 full-time. *Required fees:* $1410.94; $343.82 per semester. $343.82 per semester. Tuition and fees vary according to course load, program and reciprocity agreements. *Faculty research:* Plant control, grazing management, riparian restoration, riparian management, reclamation.

Utah State University, School of Graduate Studies, S.J. and Jessie E. Quinney College of Natural Resources, Department of Wildland Resources, Logan, UT 84322. Offers ecology (MS, PhD); forestry (MS, PhD); range science (MS, PhD); wildlife biology (MS, PhD). *Program availability:* Part-time. *Degree requirements:* For master's, thesis; for doctorate, comprehensive exam, thesis/dissertation. *Entrance requirements:* For master's and doctorate, GRE General Test, minimum GPA of 3.0. Additional exam requirements/recommendations for international students: Required—TOEFL. *Faculty research:* Range plant ecophysiology, plant community ecology, ruminant nutrition, population ecology.

Water Resources

Albany State University, College of Arts and Humanities, Albany, GA 31705-2717. Offers criminal justice (MS); English education (M Ed); public administration (MPA), including community and economic development, criminal justice administration, health administration and policy, human resources management, public management, public policy, water resources management and policy; social work (MSW). *Accreditation:* NASPAA. *Program availability:* Part-time. *Degree requirements:* For master's, comprehensive exam, professional portfolio (for MPA), internship, capstone report. *Entrance requirements:* For master's, GRE, MAT, minimum GPA of 3.0, official transcript, pre-medical record/certificate of immunization, letters of reference. Electronic applications accepted. *Faculty research:* HIV prevention for minority students.

California State University, Monterey Bay, College of Science, Program in Applied Marine and Watershed Science, Seaside, CA 93955-8001. Offers MS. *Program availability:* Part-time. *Degree requirements:* For master's, thesis, thesis defense. *Entrance requirements:* For master's, GRE, recommendations, interview. Additional exam requirements/recommendations for international students: Required—TOEFL (minimum score 525 paper-based; 71 iBT). Electronic applications accepted. *Faculty research:* Remote sensing and geospatial technology, efficacy and management, marine science and ecology, watershed process, hydrology, restoration, sedimentology, ecosystem modeling.

Colorado State University, Warner College of Natural Resources, Department of Ecosystem Science and Sustainability, Fort Collins, CO 80523-1476. Offers greenhouse gas management and accounting (MGMA); watershed science (MS). *Degree requirements:* For master's, thesis (for some programs). *Entrance requirements:* For master's, GRE (70th percentile or higher), minimum GPA of 3.0; resume; transcript; letters of recommendation; statement of purpose; undergraduate degree in a related field. Additional exam requirements/recommendations for international students: Required—TOEFL (minimum score 550 paper-based; 80 iBT), IELTS (minimum score 6.5). Electronic applications accepted. *Expenses:* Contact institution. *Faculty research:* Animal-habitat relationships; pastoral ecology and simulation; solving applied problems in ecosystem science and sustainable ecosystem management; intersections and boundaries of human activities, physical processes, and ecosystems; theoretical and applied ecology.

Colorado State University, Warner College of Natural Resources, Department of Geosciences, Fort Collins, CO 80523-1482. Offers earth sciences (PhD), including geosciences, watershed science. Terminal master's awarded for partial completion of doctoral program. *Degree requirements:* For master's, thesis; for doctorate, comprehensive exam, thesis/dissertation. *Entrance requirements:* For master's, GRE General Test, minimum GPA of 3.3, letters of recommendation; for doctorate, GRE General Test, minimum GPA of 3.3, letters of recommendation; MS (preferred). Additional exam requirements/recommendations for international students: Required—TOEFL (minimum score 550 paper-based; 80 iBT), IELTS (minimum score 6.5). Electronic applications accepted. *Expenses:* Tuition, state resident: full-time $10,520; part-time $4675 per credit hour. Tuition, nonresident: full-time $25,791; part-time $11,462 per credit hour. *International tuition:* $25,791 full-time. *Required fees:* $2392; $576 $288. Tuition and fees vary according to course level, course load, degree level, program and student level. *Faculty research:* Geophysics, cryosphere, hydrogeology, geomorphology, geology.

Cornell University, Graduate School, Graduate Fields of Agriculture and Life Sciences and Graduate Fields of Engineering, Field of Biological and Environmental Engineering, Ithaca, NY 14853. Offers bioenergy and integrated energy systems (M Eng, MPS, MS, PhD); biological engineering (M Eng, MPS, MS, PhD); bioprocess engineering (M Eng, MPS, MS, PhD); ecohydrology (M Eng, MPS, MS, PhD); environmental engineering (M Eng, MPS, MS, PhD); environmental management (MPS); food engineering (M Eng, MPS, MS, PhD); industrial biotechnology (M Eng, MPS, MS, PhD); nanobiotechnology (M Eng, MPS, MS, PhD); sustainable systems (M Eng, MPS, MS, PhD); synthetic biology (MS); syntheticbiology (M Eng, MPS, PhD). Terminal master's awarded for partial completion of doctoral program. *Degree requirements:* For master's, thesis (MS); for doctorate, comprehensive exam, thesis/dissertation. *Entrance requirements:* For master's, letters of recommendation (3 for MS, 2 for M Eng and MPS); for doctorate, GRE General Test, 3 letters of recommendation. Additional exam requirements/recommendations for international students: Required—TOEFL (minimum score 550 paper-based; 77 iBT). Electronic applications accepted. *Faculty research:* Biological and food engineering, environmental, soil and water engineering, international agricultural engineering, structures and controlled environments, machine systems and energy.

Dalhousie University, Faculty of Agriculture, Halifax, NS B3H 4R2, Canada. Offers agriculture (M Sc), including air quality, animal behavior, animal molecular genetics,

Peterson's Graduate Programs in the Physical Sciences, Mathematics, Agricultural Sciences, the Environment & Natural Resources 2020

www.petersons.com **345**

animal nutrition, animal technology, aquaculture, botany, crop management, crop physiology, ecology, environmental microbiology, food science, horticulture, nutrient management, pest management, physiology, plant biotechnology, plant pathology, soil chemistry, soil fertility, waste management and composting, water quality. *Program availability:* Part-time. *Degree requirements:* For master's, thesis, ATC Exam Teaching Assistantship. *Entrance requirements:* For master's, honors B Sc, minimum GPA of 3.0. Additional exam requirements/recommendations for international students: Required—TOEFL (minimum score 580 paper-based; 92 iBT), IELTS, Michigan English Language Assessment Battery, CanTEST, CAEL. *Faculty research:* Bio-product development, organic agriculture, nutrient management, air and water quality, agricultural biotechnology.

Humboldt State University, Academic Programs, College of Natural Resources and Sciences, Programs in Natural Resources, Arcata, CA 95521-8299. Offers natural resources (MS), including fisheries, forestry, natural resources planning and interpretation, rangeland resources and wildland soils, wastewater utilization, watershed management, wildlife. *Faculty:* 22 full-time (5 women), 20 part-time/adjunct (7 women). *Students:* 43 full-time (22 women), 45 part-time (21 women); includes 24 minority (1 Black or African American, non-Hispanic/Latino; 2 American Indian or Alaska Native, non-Hispanic/Latino; 1 Asian, non-Hispanic/Latino; 16 Hispanic/Latino; 4 Two or more races, non-Hispanic/Latino), 1 international. Average age 28. 38 applicants, 37% accepted, 14 enrolled. In 2018, 21 master's awarded. *Degree requirements:* For master's, thesis or alternative. *Entrance requirements:* For master's, GRE, appropriate bachelor's degree, minimum GPA of 2.5, 3 letters of recommendation, resume. Additional exam requirements/recommendations for international students: Required—TOEFL (minimum score 500 paper-based). *Application deadline:* For fall admission, 2/1 for domestic and international students; for spring admission, 9/30 for domestic and international students. Applications are processed on a rolling basis. Application fee: $55. *Expenses: Tuition:* Part-time $4649 per semester. *Required fees:* $2121; $1673. Tuition and fees vary according to program. *Financial support:* Fellowships, career-related internships or fieldwork, and Federal Work-Study available. Support available to part-time students. Financial award application deadline: 3/1; financial award applicants required to submit FAFSA. *Faculty research:* Spotted owl habitat, pre-settlement vegetation, hardwood utilization, tree physiology, fisheries. *Unit head:* Dr. Andrew Stubblefield, Graduate Program Coordinator, 707-826-3258, E-mail: andrew.stubblefield@humboldt.edu. *Application contact:* Dr. Andrew Stubblefield, Graduate Program Coordinator, 707-826-3258, E-mail: andrew.stubblefield@humboldt.edu.
Website: http://www.humboldt.edu/cnrs/graduate_programs

Marquette University, Graduate School, College of Engineering, Department of Civil and Environmental Engineering, Milwaukee, WI 53201-1881. Offers construction engineering and management (MS, PhD, Certificate); environmental engineering (MS, PhD); structural design (Certificate); structural engineering and structural mechanics (MS, PhD); transportation (Certificate); transportation engineering and materials (MS, PhD); waste and wastewater treatment processes (Certificate); water resources engineering (Certificate). *Program availability:* Part-time, evening/weekend. Terminal master's awarded for partial completion of doctoral program. *Degree requirements:* For master's, comprehensive exam (for some programs), thesis or alternative; for doctorate, thesis/dissertation. *Entrance requirements:* For master's, GRE General Test (recommended), minimum GPA of 3.0, official transcripts from all current and previous colleges/universities except Marquette, three letters of recommendation; for doctorate, GRE General Test, minimum GPA of 3.0, official transcripts from all current and previous colleges/universities except Marquette, three letters of recommendation, brief statement of purpose, submission of any English language publications authored by applicant (strongly recommended). Additional exam requirements/recommendations for international students: Required—TOEFL (minimum score 530 paper-based). Electronic applications accepted. *Faculty research:* Highway safety, highway performance, and intelligent transportation systems; surface mount technology; watershed management.

Missouri University of Science and Technology, Department of Geosciences and Geological and Petroleum Engineering, Rolla, MO 65401. Offers geological engineering (MS, DE, PhD); geology and geophysics (MS, PhD), including geochemistry, geology, geophysics, groundwater and environmental geology; petroleum engineering (MS, DE, PhD). *Program availability:* Part-time. *Degree requirements:* For master's, thesis optional; for doctorate, comprehensive exam, thesis/dissertation. *Entrance requirements:* For master's, GRE General Test (minimum score 600 quantitative, writing 3.5), minimum GPA of 3.0 in last 4 semesters; for doctorate, GRE General Test (minimum scores: Quantitative 600, Writing 3.5). Additional exam requirements/recommendations for international students: Required—TOEFL (minimum score 550 paper-based). Electronic applications accepted. *Expenses:* Tuition, state resident: full-time $7545.60; part-time $419.20 per credit hour. Tuition, nonresident: full-time $22,169; part-time $1231.60 per credit hour. *International tuition:* $23,518.80 full-time. *Required fees:* $4523.05. Full-time tuition and fees vary according to course load, campus/location, program and reciprocity agreements. *Faculty research:* Digital image processing and geographic information systems, mineralogy, igneous and sedimentary petrology-geochemistry, sedimentology groundwater hydrology and contaminant transport.

Montclair State University, The Graduate School, College of Science and Mathematics, Water Resource Management Certificate Program, Montclair, NJ 07043-1624. Offers Certificate. *Program availability:* Part-time, evening/weekend. *Entrance requirements:* Additional exam requirements/recommendations for international students: Required—TOEFL (minimum score 550 paper-based).

New Mexico State University, Graduate School, Program in Water Science Management, Las Cruces, NM 88003-8001. Offers MS, PhD. *Program availability:* Part-time. *Faculty:* 4 full-time (0 women). *Students:* 22 full-time (8 women), 14 part-time (4 women); includes 9 minority (1 American Indian or Alaska Native, non-Hispanic/Latino; 8 Hispanic/Latino), 12 international. Average age 34. 28 applicants, 57% accepted, 7 enrolled. In 2018, 2 doctorates awarded. *Degree requirements:* For master's, comprehensive exam, thesis; for doctorate, comprehensive exam, thesis/dissertation, written and oral comprehensive exams. *Entrance requirements:* For master's, letter of intent or personal statement; resume or curriculum vitae; 3 letters of recommendation; minimum GPA of 3.0; for doctorate, letter of intent or personal statement; resume or curriculum vitae; 3 letters of recommendation; minimum GPA of 3.5. Additional exam requirements/recommendations for international students: Required—TOEFL (minimum score 550 paper-based; 79 iBT), IELTS (minimum score 6.5). *Application deadline:* For fall admission, 2/15 for domestic and international students; for spring admission, 10/1 for domestic and international students. Application fee: $40 ($50 for international students). Electronic applications accepted. *Expenses: Tuition, area resident:* Full-time $4216.70; part-time $252.70 per credit hour. Tuition, state resident: full-time $4216.70; part-time $252.70 per credit hour. Tuition, nonresident: full-time $12,769; part-time $881.10 per credit hour. *International tuition:* $12,769.30 full-time. *Required fees:* $878.40; $48.80 per credit hour. Full-time tuition and fees vary according to course load and reciprocity agreements. *Financial support:* In 2018–19, 28 students received support, including 6 research assistantships (averaging $20,063 per year); career-related internships or fieldwork, Federal Work-Study, scholarships/grants, traineeships, health care benefits, and unspecified assistantships also available. Support available to part-time students. Financial award application deadline: 3/1. *Faculty research:* Agricultural and water resources, watersheds riparian and aquatic systems, water quality and treatment, water economics and policy, water informatics. *Unit head:* Dr. Alexander Fernald, Program Chair, 575-646-4198, Fax: 575-646-2842, E-mail: wsm@nmsu.edu. *Application contact:* Dr. Marcus Gay, Student Program Coordinator, 575-646-4198, Fax: 575-646-2842, E-mail: wsm@nmsu.edu.
Website: http://wsm.research.nmsu.edu

Old Dominion University, Frank Batten College of Engineering and Technology, Program in Civil Engineering, Norfolk, VA 23529. Offers civil engineering (ME, MS), including coastal engineering, geotechnical engineering, hydraulics and water resources, structural engineering, transportation engineering. *Program availability:* Part-time, evening/weekend, blended/hybrid learning. *Degree requirements:* For master's, comprehensive exam, thesis optional. *Entrance requirements:* For master's, GRE, minimum GPA of 3.0. Additional exam requirements/recommendations for international students: Required—TOEFL (minimum score 550 paper-based, 80 iBT) or IELTS (6.5). Electronic applications accepted. *Expenses:* Contact institution. *Faculty research:* Structural engineering, coastal engineering, geotechnical engineering, water resources, transportation engineering.

Oregon State University, Interdisciplinary/Institutional Programs, Program in Water Resources Policy and Management, Corvallis, OR 97331. Offers MS. *Entrance requirements:* For master's, GRE. Additional exam requirements/recommendations for international students: Required—TOEFL (minimum score 80 iBT), IELTS (minimum score 6.5).

Oregon State University, Interdisciplinary/Institutional Programs, Program in Water Resources Science, Corvallis, OR 97331. Offers MS, PhD. *Entrance requirements:* For master's and doctorate, GRE. Additional exam requirements/recommendations for international students: Required—TOEFL (minimum score 80 iBT), IELTS (minimum score 6.5).

Rutgers University–New Brunswick, Graduate School-New Brunswick, Department of Environmental Sciences, Piscataway, NJ 08854-8097. Offers air pollution and resources (MS, PhD); aquatic biology (MS, PhD); aquatic chemistry (MS, PhD); atmospheric science (MS, PhD); chemistry and physics of aerosol and hydrosol systems (MS, PhD); environmental chemistry (MS, PhD); environmental microbiology (MS, PhD); environmental toxicology (PhD); exposure assessment (PhD); fate and effects of pollutants (MS, PhD); pollution prevention and control (MS, PhD); water and wastewater treatment (MS, PhD); water resources (MS, PhD). Terminal master's awarded for partial completion of doctoral program. *Degree requirements:* For master's, comprehensive exam, thesis or alternative, oral final exam; for doctorate, comprehensive exam, thesis/dissertation, thesis defense, qualifying exam. *Entrance requirements:* For master's and doctorate, GRE General Test. Additional exam requirements/recommendations for international students: Required—TOEFL. Electronic applications accepted. *Faculty research:* Biological waste treatment; contaminant fate and transport; air, soil and water quality.

State University of New York College of Environmental Science and Forestry, Program in Environmental Science, Syracuse, NY 13210-2779. Offers biophysical and ecological economics (MPS); coupled natural and human systems (MPS); ecosystem restoration (MPS); environmental and community land planning (MPS, MS); environmental and natural resources policy (PhD); environmental communication and participatory processes (PhD); environmental monitoring and modeling (MPS); water and wetland resource studies (MPS, MS). *Program availability:* Part-time. *Faculty:* 1 full-time (0 women), 1 (woman) part-time/adjunct. *Students:* 52 full-time (30 women), 13 part-time (9 women); includes 3 minority (1 Asian, non-Hispanic/Latino; 2 Hispanic/Latino), 26 international. Average age 32. 51 applicants, 73% accepted, 17 enrolled. In 2018, 14 master's, 8 doctorates awarded. Terminal master's awarded for partial completion of doctoral program. *Degree requirements:* For master's, thesis (for some programs); for doctorate, comprehensive exam, thesis/dissertation. *Entrance requirements:* For master's and doctorate, GRE General Test, minimum GPA of 3.0. Additional exam requirements/recommendations for international students: Required—TOEFL (minimum score 550 paper-based; 80 iBT), IELTS (minimum score 6). *Application deadline:* For fall admission, 2/1 priority date for domestic and international students; for spring admission, 11/1 priority date for domestic and international students. Applications are processed on a rolling basis. Application fee: $60. Electronic applications accepted. *Expenses: Tuition, area resident:* Full-time $11,090; part-time $462 per credit hour. Tuition, state resident: full-time $11,090; part-time $462 per credit hour. Tuition, nonresident: full-time $22,650; part-time $944 per credit hour. *International tuition:* $22,650 full-time. *Required fees:* $1733; $178.58 per credit hour. *Financial support:* In 2018–19, 24 students received support. Unspecified assistantships available. Financial award application deadline: 6/30; financial award applicants required to submit FAFSA. *Faculty research:* Environmental education/communications, water resources, land resources, waste management. *Unit head:* Dr. Russell Briggs, Director of the Division of Environmental Science, 315-470-6989, Fax: 315-470-6700, E-mail: rdbriggs@esf.edu. *Application contact:* Scott Shannon, Associate Provost for Instruction/Dean of the Graduate School, 315-470-6599, Fax: 315-470-6978, E-mail: esfgrad@esf.edu.
Website: http://www.esf.edu/environmentalscience/graduate/

Tropical Agriculture Research and Higher Education Center, Graduate School, Turrialba, Costa Rica. Offers agribusiness management (MS); agroforestry systems (PhD); development practices (MS); ecological agriculture (MS); environmental socioeconomics (MS); forestry in tropical and subtropical zones (PhD); integrated watershed management (MS); international sustainable tourism (MS); management and conservation of tropical rainforests and biodiversity (MS); tropical agriculture (PhD); tropical agroforestry (MS). *Entrance requirements:* For master's, GRE, 2 years of related professional experience, letters of recommendation; for doctorate, GRE, 4 letters of recommendation, letter of support from employing organization, master's degree in agronomy, biological sciences, forestry, natural resources or related field. Additional exam requirements/recommendations for international students: Required—TOEFL (minimum score 550 paper-based). Electronic applications accepted. *Faculty research:* Biodiversity in fragmented landscapes, ecosystem management, integrated pest management, environmental livestock production, biotechnology carbon balances in diverse land uses.

Tufts University, The Gerald J. and Dorothy R. Friedman School of Nutrition Science and Policy, Boston, MA 02111. Offers agriculture, food and environment (MS, PhD); biochemical and molecular nutrition (MS, PhD); dietetic internship (MS); food and nutrition policy (MS, PhD); humanitarian assistance (MAHA); nutrition (MS, PhD); nutrition data science (MS, PhD); nutrition interventions, communication, and behavior change (MS, PhD); sustainable water management (MS). *Program availability:* Part-time. *Degree requirements:* For doctorate, comprehensive exam, thesis/dissertation. *Entrance requirements:* For master's and doctorate, GRE General Test. Additional exam requirements/recommendations for international students: Required—TOEFL.

Electronic applications accepted. *Expenses:* Contact institution. *Faculty research:* Nutritional biochemistry and metabolism, cell and molecular biochemistry, epidemiology, policy/planning, applied nutrition.

The University of Arizona, College of Agriculture and Life Sciences, Department of Soil, Water and Environmental Science, Tucson, AZ 85721. Offers MS, PhD, Graduate Certificate. *Degree requirements:* For master's, thesis; for doctorate, comprehensive exam, thesis/dissertation. *Entrance requirements:* For master's, GRE (recommended), minimum GPA of 3.0, letter of interest, 3 letters of recommendation; for doctorate, GRE (recommended), MS, minimum GPA of 3.0, letter of interest, 3 letters of recommendation. Additional exam requirements/recommendations for international students: Required—TOEFL (minimum score 550 paper-based; 80 iBT). Electronic applications accepted. *Faculty research:* Plant production, environmental microbiology, contaminant flow and transport, aquaculture.

The University of Arizona, College of Agriculture and Life Sciences, School of Natural Resources and the Environment, Watershed Resources Program, Tucson, AZ 85721. Offers water, society, and policy (MS); watershed management (MS, PhD). *Degree requirements:* For master's, thesis; for doctorate, comprehensive exam, thesis/dissertation. *Entrance requirements:* For master's, GRE General Test, minimum GPA of 3.0, 3 letters of recommendation; for doctorate, GRE General Test, minimum GPA of 3.0, 3 letters of recommendation, MA or MS. Additional exam requirements/recommendations for international students: Required—TOEFL (minimum score 550 paper-based; 79 iBT). Electronic applications accepted. *Faculty research:* Forest fuel characteristics, prescribed fire, tree ring-fire scar analysis, erosion, sedimentation.

The University of Arizona, College of Science, Department of Hydrology and Water Resources, Tucson, AZ 85721. Offers hydrology (PhD). *Program availability:* Part-time. *Degree requirements:* For doctorate, thesis/dissertation. *Entrance requirements:* For doctorate, GRE General Test, minimum undergraduate GPA of 3.2, graduate 3.4; 3 letters of recommendation; master's degree in related field; master's thesis abstract. Additional exam requirements/recommendations for international students: Required—TOEFL (minimum score 550 paper-based; 79 iBT). Electronic applications accepted. *Faculty research:* Subsurface and surface hydrology, hydrometeorology/climatology, applied remote sensing, water resource systems, environmental hydrology and water quality.

The University of British Columbia, Faculty of Land and Food Systems, Program in Land and Water Systems, Vancouver, BC V6T 1Z1, Canada. Offers MLWS.

University of Calgary, Faculty of Graduate Studies, Schulich School of Engineering, Program in Civil Engineering, Calgary, AB T2N 1N4, Canada. Offers avalanche mechanics (M Sc, PhD); civil engineering (M Eng, M Sc, PhD); energy and environment engineering (M Eng, M Sc, PhD); environmental engineering (M Eng, M Sc, PhD); geotechnical engineering (M Eng, M Sc, PhD); materials science (M Eng, M Sc, PhD); project management (M Eng, M Sc, PhD); structures and solid mechanics (M Eng, M Sc, PhD); transportation engineering (M Eng, M Sc, PhD); water resources (M Eng, M Sc, PhD). *Program availability:* Part-time. *Degree requirements:* For master's, thesis; for doctorate, thesis/dissertation, written and oral candidacy exam. *Entrance requirements:* For master's, minimum GPA of 3.0; for doctorate, minimum GPA of 3.5. Additional exam requirements/recommendations for international students: Required—TOEFL (minimum score 580 paper-based; 93 iBT), IELTS (minimum score 7). Electronic applications accepted. *Faculty research:* Geotechnical engineering, energy and environment, transportation, project management, structures and solid mechanics.

University of California, Riverside, Graduate Division, Environmental Sciences Department, Riverside, CA 92521-0102. Offers MS, PhD. *Degree requirements:* For doctorate, thesis/dissertation. *Entrance requirements:* For master's and doctorate, minimum GPA of 3.2. Additional exam requirements/recommendations for international students: Required—TOEFL (minimum score 550 paper-based; 80 iBT). Electronic applications accepted. *Faculty research:* Environmental chemistry and ecotoxicology, environmental microbiology, environmental and natural resource economics and policy, soil and water science, environmental sciences and management.

University of Colorado Denver, College of Liberal Arts and Sciences, Department of Geography and Environmental Sciences, Denver, CO 80217. Offers environmental sciences (MS), including air quality, ecosystems, environmental health, geospatial analysis, hazardous waste, water quality. *Program availability:* Part-time, evening/weekend. *Degree requirements:* For master's, thesis or alternative, 30 credits including 21 of core requirements and 9 of environmental science electives. *Entrance requirements:* For master's, GRE General Test, BA in one of the natural/physical sciences or engineering (or equivalent background); prerequisite coursework in calculus and physics (one semester each); general chemistry with lab and general biology with lab (two semesters each); three letters of recommendation. Additional exam requirements/recommendations for international students: Required—TOEFL (minimum score 537 paper-based; 75 iBT); Recommended—IELTS (minimum score 6.5). Electronic applications accepted. *Expenses:* Tuition, state resident: full-time $6786; part-time $337 per credit hour. Tuition, nonresident: full-time $22,590; part-time $1255 per credit hour. *Required fees:* $1231; $137 per credit hour. Tuition and fees vary according to program and reciprocity agreements. *Faculty research:* Air quality, environmental health, ecosystems, hazardous waste, water quality, geospatial analysis and environmental science education.

University of Florida, Graduate School, College of Agricultural and Life Sciences, Department of Soil and Water Science, Gainesville, FL 32611. Offers soil and water science (MS, PhD), including agroecology (MS), geographic information systems, hydrologic sciences, tropical conservation and development, wetland sciences. *Program availability:* Part-time, evening/weekend, online learning. Terminal master's awarded for partial completion of doctoral program. *Degree requirements:* For master's, thesis optional; for doctorate, comprehensive exam, thesis/dissertation. *Entrance requirements:* For master's and doctorate, GRE General Test, minimum GPA of 3.0. Additional exam requirements/recommendations for international students: Required—TOEFL (minimum score 550 paper-based; 80 iBT), IELTS (minimum score 6). Electronic applications accepted. *Faculty research:* Carbon dynamics and ecosystem services; landscape analysis and modeling; nutrient pesticide and waste management; soil, water, and aquifer remediation; wetlands and aquatic ecosystems.

University of Idaho, College of Graduate Studies, College of Agricultural and Life Sciences, Water Resources Program, Moscow, ID 83844-300. Offers engineering and science (MS, PhD); law, management and policy (MS, PhD); science and management (MS, PhD). *Faculty:* 20 full-time (5 women). *Students:* 23 full-time, 7 part-time. Average age 32. In 2018, 7 master's, 2 doctorates awarded. *Entrance requirements:* For master's, minimum GPA of 3.0. Additional exam requirements/recommendations for international students: Required—TOEFL (minimum score 550 paper-based; 79 iBT), IELTS (minimum score 6.5), Michigan English Language Assessment Battery (minimum score of 77). *Application deadline:* For fall admission, 8/1 for domestic students; for spring admission, 12/15 for domestic students. Applications are processed on a rolling basis. Application fee: $60. Electronic applications accepted. *Expenses:* Tuition, state resident: full-time $7266.44; part-time $474.50 per credit hour. Tuition, nonresident: full-

time $24,902; part-time $1453.50 per credit hour. *Required fees:* $2085.56; $45.50 per credit hour. *Financial support:* Applicants required to submit FAFSA. *Faculty research:* Water management, biological wastewater treatment and water reclamation, invasive species, aquatics ecosystem restoration, Fish ecology. Website: https://www.uidaho.edu/cals/water-resources

The University of Iowa, Graduate College, College of Engineering, Department of Civil and Environmental Engineering, Iowa City, IA 52242-1316. Offers environmental engineering and science (MS, PhD); hydraulics and water resources (MS, PhD); structures, mechanics and materials (MS, PhD); sustainable water development (MS, PhD); transportation engineering (MS, PhD). *Program availability:* Part-time. Terminal master's awarded for partial completion of doctoral program. *Degree requirements:* For master's, thesis optional, exam; for doctorate, comprehensive exam, thesis/dissertation, exam. *Entrance requirements:* For master's, GRE (minimum combined score of 301 on verbal and quantitative), minimum undergraduate GPA of 3.0; for doctorate, GRE (minimum combined score of 301 on verbal and quantitative), minimum graduate GPA of 3.0. Additional exam requirements/recommendations for international students: Required—TOEFL (minimum score 550 paper-based; 81 iBT), IELTS (minimum score 7). Electronic applications accepted. *Faculty research:* Water resources; environmental engineering and science; hydraulics and hydrology; structures, mechanics, and materials; transportation engineering.

University of Maine, Graduate School, College of Natural Sciences, Forestry, and Agriculture, School of Earth and Climate Sciences, Orono, ME 04469. Offers MS, PhD. *Program availability:* Part-time. *Faculty:* 23 full-time (6 women), 28 part time/adjunct (8 women). *Students:* 37 full-time (18 women), 5 part-time (2 women); includes 3 minority (1 Asian, non-Hispanic/Latino; 2 Hispanic/Latino), 5 international. Average age 31. 55 applicants, 33% accepted, 13 enrolled. In 2018, 6 master's, 2 doctorates awarded. *Degree requirements:* For master's, thesis; for doctorate, one foreign language, comprehensive exam, thesis/dissertation. *Entrance requirements:* For master's and doctorate, GRE General Test. Additional exam requirements/recommendations for international students: Required—TOEFL (minimum score 80 iBT). *Application deadline:* For fall admission, 1/15 for domestic and international students. Applications are processed on a rolling basis. Application fee: $65. Electronic applications accepted. *Financial support:* In 2018–19, 54 students received support, including 1 fellowship with full tuition reimbursement available (averaging $16,000 per year), 37 research assistantships with full tuition reimbursements available (averaging $18,500 per year), 10 teaching assistantships with full tuition reimbursements available (averaging $15,600 per year); Federal Work-Study, institutionally sponsored loans, tuition waivers (full and partial), and unspecified assistantships also available. Financial award application deadline: 3/1. *Faculty research:* Geodynamics, climate change, environmental geology, marine geology. *Total annual research expenditures:* $2.2 million. *Unit head:* Dr. Scott Johnson, Chair, 207-581-2142, Fax: 207-581-2202. *Application contact:* Scott G. Delcourt, Assistant Vice President for Graduate Studies and Senior Associate Dean, 207-581-3291, Fax: 207-581-3232, E-mail: graduate@maine.edu. Website: http://umaine.edu/earthclimate/

University of Massachusetts Amherst, Graduate School, College of Natural Sciences, Department of Environmental Conservation, Amherst, MA 01003. Offers building systems (MS, PhD); environmental policy and human dimensions (MS, PhD); forest resources (MS, PhD); sustainability science (MS); water, wetlands and watersheds (MS, PhD); wildlife and fisheries conservation (MS, PhD). *Program availability:* Part-time. Terminal master's awarded for partial completion of doctoral program. *Degree requirements:* For master's, thesis or alternative; for doctorate, comprehensive exam, thesis/dissertation. *Entrance requirements:* For master's and doctorate, GRE General Test. Additional exam requirements/recommendations for international students: Required—TOEFL (minimum score 550 paper-based; 80 iBT), IELTS (minimum score 6.5). Electronic applications accepted

University of Minnesota, Twin Cities Campus, Graduate School, College of Food, Agricultural and Natural Resource Sciences, Program in Natural Resources Science and Management, St. Paul, MN 55108. Offers assessment, monitoring, and geospatial analysis (MS, PhD); economics, policy, management, and society (MS, PhD); forest hydrology and watershed management (MS, PhD); forest products (MS, PhD); forests: biology, ecology, conservation, and management (MS, PhD); natural resources science and management (MS, PhD); paper science and engineering (MS, PhD); recreation resources, tourism, and environmental education (MS, PhD). *Program availability:* Part-time. Terminal master's awarded for partial completion of doctoral program. *Degree requirements:* For master's, comprehensive exam, thesis (for some programs); for doctorate, comprehensive exam, thesis/dissertation. *Entrance requirements:* For master's and doctorate, GRE General Test. Additional exam requirements/recommendations for international students: Required—TOEFL (minimum score 550 paper-based; 79 iBT); Recommended—IELTS (minimum score 6.5). Electronic applications accepted. *Faculty research:* Forest hydrology, biology, ecology, conservation, and management; recreation resources and environmental education; wildlife ecology; economics, policy, and society; geographic information systems (GIS); forest products and paper science.

University of Minnesota, Twin Cities Campus, Graduate School, College of Food, Agricultural and Natural Resource Sciences, Program in Water Resources Science, St. Paul, MN 55108. Offers MS, PhD. *Program availability:* Part-time. *Degree requirements:* For master's, comprehensive exam, thesis or project; for doctorate, comprehensive exam, thesis/dissertation. *Entrance requirements:* For master's, GRE, minimum GPA of 3.0 and bachelor's degree in physical, chemical, biological, or environmental science or engineering (preferred); at least two courses each in calculus, chemistry, and physics, and one course in the biological sciences (recommended); for doctorate, GRE, minimum GPA of 3.0 and master's degree in water resources, or physical, chemical, biological, or environmental science or engineering (preferred); at least two courses each in calculus, chemistry, and physics, and one course in the biological sciences (recommended). Additional exam requirements/recommendations for international students: Required—TOEFL (minimum score 550 paper-based; 79 iBT), IELTS (minimum score 6.5), Michigan English Language Assessment Battery (minimum score 80). Electronic applications accepted. *Expenses:* Contact institution. *Faculty research:* Hydrologic science, limnology, water quality, environmental chemistry, aquatic biology.

University of Missouri, Office of Research and Graduate Studies, College of Agriculture, Food and Natural Resources, School of Natural Resources, Columbia, MO 65211. Offers agroforestry (MS, Certificate); conservation biology (Certificate); fisheries and wildlife sciences (MS, PhD); forestry (MS, PhD); geographical information science (Certificate); human dimensions of natural resources (MS, PhD); parks, recreation and tourism (MS); society and ecosystems (Certificate); soil, environmental and atmospheric sciences (MS, PhD); water resources (MS, PhD). *Program availability:* Part-time. *Degree requirements:* For doctorate, thesis/dissertation. *Entrance requirements:* For master's and doctorate, GRE General Test (minimum score 1200 Verbal and Quantitative), minimum GPA of 3.2. Additional exam requirements/recommendations for international students: Required—TOEFL (minimum score 550 paper-based; 80 iBT), IELTS (minimum score 6.5). Electronic applications accepted.

Peterson's Graduate Programs in the Physical Sciences, Mathematics, Agricultural Sciences, the Environment & Natural Resources 2020

www.petersons.com **347**

Water Resources

University of Nevada, Las Vegas, Graduate College, College of Sciences, Program in Water Resources Management, Las Vegas, NV 89154-4029. Offers MS. *Program availability:* Part-time. *Students:* 1 full-time (0 women), 2 part-time (1 woman); includes 2 minority (1 Black or African American, non-Hispanic/Latino; 1 Two or more races, non-Hispanic/Latino). Average age 34. 3 applicants, 100% accepted, 2 enrolled. In 2018, 2 master's awarded. *Degree requirements:* For master's, comprehensive exam, thesis, oral exam. *Entrance requirements:* For master's, GRE General Test, bachelor's degree; 3 letters of recommendation; statement of purpose. Additional exam requirements/recommendations for international students: Required—TOEFL (minimum score 550 paper-based; 80 iBT), IELTS (minimum score 7). *Application deadline:* For fall admission, 4/1 for domestic and international students; for spring admission, 11/1 for domestic students, 10/1 for international students. Application fee: $60 ($95 for international students). Electronic applications accepted. *Expenses:* Contact institution. *Financial support:* In 2018–19, 1 student received support, including 1 research assistantship with full tuition reimbursement available (averaging $12,375 per year); institutionally sponsored loans, scholarships/grants, health care benefits, and unspecified assistantships also available. Financial award application deadline: 3/15; financial award applicants required to submit FAFSA. *Faculty research:* Hydrogeology, water conservation, environmental chemistry, invasive species control, ecosystem management and restoration. *Unit head:* Dr. Michael Nicholl, Chair/Associate Professor, 702-895-4616, Fax: 702-895-4064, E-mail: wrm.chair@unlv.edu. *Application contact:* Dr. Michael Nicholl, Chair/Associate Professor, 702-895-4616, Fax: 702-895-4064, E-mail: wrm.chair@unlv.edu.
Website: http://www.unlv.edu/sciences/wrm/

University of New Brunswick Fredericton, School of Graduate Studies, Faculty of Engineering, Department of Civil Engineering, Fredericton, NB E3B 5A3, Canada. Offers construction engineering and management (M Eng, M Sc E, PhD); environmental engineering (M Eng, M Sc E, PhD); environmental studies (M Eng); geotechnical engineering (M Eng, M Sc E, PhD); groundwater/hydrology (M Eng, M Sc E, PhD); materials (M Eng, M Sc E, PhD); pavements (M Eng, M Sc E, PhD); structures (M Eng, M Sc E, PhD); transportation (M Eng, M Sc E, PhD). *Program availability:* Part-time. *Degree requirements:* For master's, thesis; for doctorate, comprehensive exam, thesis/dissertation, qualifying exam; 27 credit hours of courses. *Entrance requirements:* For master's, minimum GPA of 3.0; B Sc E in civil engineering or related engineering degree; for doctorate, minimum GPA of 3.0; graduate degree in engineering or applied science. Additional exam requirements/recommendations for international students: Required—IELTS (minimum score 7.5), TWE (minimum score 4), Michigan English Language Assessment Battery (minimum score 85) or CanTest (minimum score 4.5); Recommended—TOEFL (minimum score 580 paper-based). Electronic applications accepted. *Faculty research:* Construction engineering and management; engineering materials and infrastructure renewal; highway and pavement research; structures and solid mechanics; geotechnical and geoenvironmental engineering; structure interaction; transportation and planning; environment, solid waste management; structural engineering; water and environmental engineering.

University of New Hampshire, Graduate School, College of Life Sciences and Agriculture, Department of Natural Resources and the Environment, Durham, NH 03824. Offers environmental conservation (MS); environmental economics (MS); forestry (MS); natural resources (MS); resource administration and management (MS); soil and water resource management (MS); wildlife and conservation biology (MS). *Program availability:* Part-time. *Entrance requirements:* For master's, GRE General Test. Additional exam requirements/recommendations for international students: Required—TOEFL (minimum score 550 paper-based; 80 iBT). Electronic applications accepted.

University of New Mexico, Graduate Studies, Water Resources Program, Albuquerque, NM 87131-2039. Offers hydroscience (MWR); policy management (MWR). *Program availability:* Part-time. *Students:* Average age 34. 16 applicants, 69% accepted, 11 enrolled. In 2018, 5 master's awarded. *Entrance requirements:* For master's, minimum GPA of 3.0 during last 2 years of undergraduate work, 3 letters of reference. Additional exam requirements/recommendations for international students: Required—TOEFL (minimum score 550 paper-based). *Application deadline:* For fall admission, 7/15 for domestic students; for spring admission, 11/15 for domestic students. Applications are processed on a rolling basis. Application fee: $50. Electronic applications accepted. *Financial support:* Research assistantships, career-related internships or fieldwork, institutionally sponsored loans, scholarships/grants, and unspecified assistantships available. Financial award application deadline: 3/1; financial award applicants required to submit FAFSA. *Faculty research:* Sustainable water resources, transboundary water resources, economics, water law, hydrology, developing countries, hydrogeology. *Unit head:* Dr. Robert Berrens, Director, 505-277-7759, Fax: 505-277-5226, E-mail: rberrens@unm.edu. *Application contact:* Annamarie Cordova, Administrative Assistant II, 505-277-7759, Fax: 505-277-5226, E-mail: acordova@unm.edu.
Website: http://www.unm.edu/~wrp/

University of Southern California, Graduate School, Viterbi School of Engineering, Sonny Astani Department of Civil and Environmental Engineering, Los Angeles, CA 90089. Offers applied mechanics (MS); civil engineering (MS, PhD); computer-aided engineering (ME, Graduate Certificate); construction management (MCM); engineering technology commercialization (Graduate Certificate); environmental engineering (MS, PhD); environmental quality management (ME); structural design (ME); sustainable cities (Graduate Certificate); transportation systems (MS, Graduate Certificate); water and waste management (MS). *Program availability:* Part-time, evening/weekend. Terminal master's awarded for partial completion of doctoral program. *Degree requirements:* For master's, thesis optional; for doctorate, thesis/dissertation. *Entrance requirements:* For master's and doctorate, GRE General Test. Additional exam requirements/recommendations for international students: Required—TOEFL. Electronic applications accepted. *Faculty research:* Geotechnical engineering, transportation engineering, structural engineering, construction management, environmental engineering, water resources.

University of the District of Columbia, College of Agriculture, Urban Sustainability and Environmental Sciences, Program in Water Resources Management, Washington, DC 20008-1175. Offers PSM.

University of the Pacific, McGeorge School of Law, Sacramento, CA 95817. Offers advocacy (JD); international water resources law (JSD); public policy and law (LL M); JD/MBA; JD/MPPA. *Accreditation:* ABA. *Program availability:* Part-time, evening/weekend. *Degree requirements:* For master's, thesis (for some programs); for doctorate, thesis/dissertation (for some programs). *Entrance requirements:* For master's, JD; for doctorate, LSAT (for JD), LL M (for JSD). Additional exam requirements/recommendations for international students: Required—TOEFL (minimum score 600 paper-based; 100 iBT). Electronic applications accepted. *Expenses:* Contact institution. *Faculty research:* International legal studies, public policy and law, advocacy, intellectual property law, taxation, criminal law.

University of Wisconsin–Madison, Graduate School, Gaylord Nelson Institute for Environmental Studies, Water Resources Management Program, Madison, WI 53706-1380. Offers MS. *Program availability:* Part-time. *Degree requirements:* For master's, summer group practicum workshop. *Entrance requirements:* For master's, GRE General Test. Additional exam requirements/recommendations for international students: Required—TOEFL (minimum score 550 paper-based, 80 iBT) or IELTS (6.5). Electronic applications accepted. *Expenses:* Contact institution. *Faculty research:* Geology, hydrogeology, hydrology, fluvial geography, water chemistry, limnology, aquatic ecology, rural sociology, water law and policy.

University of Wisconsin–Milwaukee, Graduate School, School of Freshwater Sciences, Milwaukee, WI 53201-0413. Offers MS, PhD. *Students:* 36 full-time (23 women), 19 part-time (8 women); includes 3 minority (1 Hispanic/Latino; 2 Two or more races, non-Hispanic/Latino), 2 international. Average age 31. 54 applicants, 56% accepted, 25 enrolled. In 2018, 21 master's awarded. Application fee: $56 ($96 for international students). Electronic applications accepted. *Financial support:* Fellowships, research assistantships, teaching assistantships, and unspecified assistantships available. Financial award applicants required to submit FAFSA. *Unit head:* J. Val Klump, Dean, 414-382-1715, E-mail: vklump@uwm.edu. *Application contact:* Dr. Harvey Bootsma, Graduate Program Representative, 414-382-1717, E-mail: hbootsma@uwm.edu.
Website: http://uwm.edu/freshwater/

University of Wyoming, College of Agriculture and Natural Resources, Department of Ecosystem Science and Management, Laramie, WY 82071. Offers ecology (MS); entomology (MS, PhD); rangeland ecology and watershed management (MS, PhD), including soil sciences (PhD), soil sciences and water resources (MS); soil science (MS, PhD); water resources (MS, PhD). *Program availability:* Part-time. *Degree requirements:* For master's, comprehensive exam, thesis, oral examination; for doctorate, comprehensive exam, thesis/dissertation, preliminary oral and written exam, oral final exam. *Entrance requirements:* For master's and doctorate, GRE General Test, minimum GPA of 3.0. Additional exam requirements/recommendations for international students: Required—TOEFL. Electronic applications accepted. *Expenses: Tuition, area resident:* Full-time $6504; part-time $271 per credit hour. Tuition, state resident: full-time $6504; part-time $271 per credit hour. Tuition, nonresident: full-time $19,464; part-time $811 per credit hour. *International tuition:* $19,464 full-time. *Required fees:* $1410.94; $343.82 per semester. $343.82 per semester. Tuition and fees vary according to course load, program and reciprocity agreements. *Faculty research:* Plant control, grazing management, riparian restoration, riparian management, reclamation.

Utah State University, School of Graduate Studies, S.J. and Jessie E. Quinney College of Natural Resources, Department of Watershed Sciences, Logan, UT 84322. Offers ecology (MS, PhD); fisheries biology (MS, PhD); watershed science (MS, PhD). *Degree requirements:* For master's, thesis (for some programs); for doctorate, thesis/dissertation. *Entrance requirements:* For master's and doctorate, GRE General Test, minimum GPA of 3.2. Additional exam requirements/recommendations for international students: Required—TOEFL. Electronic applications accepted. *Faculty research:* Behavior, population ecology, habitat, conservation biology, restoration, aquatic ecology, fisheries management, fluvial geomorphology, remote sensing, conservation biology.

348 www.petersons.com

Peterson's Graduate Programs in the Physical Sciences, Mathematics, Agricultural Sciences, the Environment & Natural Resources 2020

APPENDIXES

Institutional Changes Since the 2019 Edition

Following is an alphabetical listing of institutions that have recently closed, merged with other institutions, or changed their names or status. In the case of a name change, the former name appears first, followed by the new name.

Argosy University, Dallas (Farmers Branch, TX): *closed.*

Argosy University, Denver (Denver, CO): *closed.*

Argosy University, Inland Empire (Ontario, CA): *closed.*

Argosy University, Nashville (Nashville, TN): *closed.*

Argosy University, Salt Lake City (Draper, UT): *closed.*

Argosy University, San Diego (San Diego, CA): *closed.*

Argosy University, San Francisco Bay Area (Alameda, CA): *closed.*

Argosy University, Sarasota (Sarasota, FL): *closed.*

Argosy University, Schaumburg (Schaumburg, IL): *closed.*

Arlington Baptist College (Arlington, TX): *name changed to Arlington Baptist University.*

Armstrong State University (Savannah, GA): *name changed to Georgia Southern University–Armstrong Campus.*

Art Center College of Design (Pasadena, CA): *name changed to ArtCenter College of Design.*

The Art Institute of California–San Francisco, a campus of Argosy University (San Francisco, CA): *closed.*

Augsburg College (Minneapolis, MN): *name changed to Augsburg University.*

Bristol University (Anaheim, CA): *closed.*

Claremont McKenna College (Claremont, CA): *merged into The Claremont Colleges (Claremont, CA).*

Coleman University (San Diego, CA): *closed.*

Digital Media Arts College (Boca Raton, FL): *closed.*

Everest University (Tampa, FL): *no longer offers graduate degrees.*

Fairleigh Dickinson University, College at Florham (Madison, NJ): *name changed to Fairleigh Dickinson University, Florham Campus.*

Faith Evangelical College & Seminary (Tacoma, WA): *name changed to Faith International University.*

Frank Lloyd Wright School of Architecture (Scottsdale, AZ): *name changed to School of Architecture at Taliesin.*

Future Generations Graduate School (Franklin, WV): *name changed to Future Generations University.*

Grace University (Omaha, NE): *closed.*

Greenville College (Greenville, IL): *name changed to Greenville University.*

Hazelden Graduate School of Addiction Studies (Center City, MN): *name changed to Hazelden Betty Ford Graduate School of Addiction.*

Henley-Putnam University (San Jose, CA): *name changed to Henley-Putnam School of Strategic Security.*

Huntington College of Health Sciences (Knoxville, TN): *name changed to Huntington University of Health Sciences.*

The Institute for the Psychological Sciences (Arlington, VA): *name changed to Divine Mercy University.*

International College of the Cayman Islands (Newlands, Cayman Islands): *not accredited by an agency recognized by USDE or CHEA at the time of publication.*

Johnson State College (Johnson, VT): *name changed to Northern Vermont University–Johnson.*

John Wesley University (High Point, NC): *closed.*

Kaplan University, Davenport Campus (Davenport, IA): *name changed to Purdue University Global.*

Knowledge Systems Institute (Skokie, IL): no longer degree granting.

Long Island University–Hudson at Westchester (Purchase, NY): *name changed to Long Island University–Hudson.*

Lutheran Theological Seminary at Gettysburg (Gettysburg, PA): *name changed to United Lutheran Seminary.*

Lynchburg College (Lynchburg, VA): *name changed to University of Lynchburg.*

Lyndon State College (Lyndonville, VT): *name changed to Northern Vermont University–Lyndon.*

Marylhurst University (Marylhurst, OR): *closed.*

McNally Smith College of Music (Saint Paul, MN): *closed.*

Memphis College of Art (Memphis, TN): *closed.*

Mirrer Yeshiva (Brooklyn, NY): *name changed to Mirror Yeshiva Central Institute.*

Moody Theological Seminary–Michigan (Plymouth, MI): *name changed to Moody Theological Seminary Michigan.*

Mount Ida College (Newton, MA): *closed.*

National American University (Rapid City, SD): no longer offers graduate degrees.

The Ohio State University–Mansfield Campus (Mansfield, OH): *name changed to The Ohio State University at Mansfield.*

The Ohio State University–Newark Campus (Newark, OH): *name changed to The Ohio State University at Newark.*

Our Lady of the Lake College (Baton Rouge, LA): *name changed to Franciscan Missionaries of Our Lady University.*

Philadelphia University (Philadelphia, PA): *closed.*

Rudolf Steiner College (Fair Oaks, CA): *not accredited by an agency recognized by USDE or CHEA at the time of publication.*

Sacred Heart School of Theology (Hales Corners, WI): *name changed to Sacred Heart Seminary and School of Theology.*

Sewanee: The University of the South (Sewanee, TN): *name changed to The University of the South.*

Shepherd University (Los Angeles, CA): *closed.*

Silicon Valley University (San Jose, CA): *closed.*

South University (Novi, MI): *closed.*

South University (High Point, NC): *closed.*

South University (Cleveland, OH): *closed.*

University of Great Falls (Great Falls, MT): *name changed to University of Providence.*

University of Phoenix–Atlanta Campus (Sandy Springs, GA): *closed.*

University of Phoenix–Augusta Campus (Augusta, GA): *closed.*

University of Phoenix–Central Florida Campus (Orlando, FL): *closed.*

University of Phoenix–Charlotte Campus (Charlotte, NC): *closed.*

University of Phoenix–Colorado Campus (Lone Tree, CO): *closed.*

University of Phoenix–Colorado Springs Downtown Campus (Colorado Springs, CO): *closed.*

University of Phoenix–Columbus Georgia Campus (Columbus, GA): *closed.*

University of Phoenix–Jersey City Campus (Jersey City, NJ): *closed.*

University of Phoenix–New Mexico Campus (Albuquerque, NM): *closed.*

University of Phoenix–North Florida Campus (Jacksonville, FL): *closed.*

University of Phoenix–Southern Arizona Campus (Tucson, AZ): *closed.*

University of Phoenix–Southern California Campus (Costa Mesa, CA): *closed.*

University of Phoenix–South Florida Campus (Miramar, FL): *closed.*

University of Phoenix–Utah Campus (Salt Lake City, UT): *closed.*

University of Phoenix–Washington D.C. Campus (Washington, DC): *closed.*

University of Phoenix–Western Washington Campus (Tukwila, WA): *closed.*

University of Puerto Rico, Mayagüez Campus (Mayagüez, PR): *name changed to University of Puerto Rico–Mayagüez.*

University of Puerto Rico, Medical Sciences Campus (San Juan, PR): *name changed to University of Puerto Rico–Medical Sciences Campus.*

University of Puerto Rico, Río Piedras Campus (San Juan, PR): *name changed to University of Puerto Rico–Río Piedras.*

The University of South Dakota (Vermillion, SD): *name changed to University of South Dakota.*

Urbana University (Urbana, OH): *name changed to Urbana University–A Branch Campus of Franklin University.*

Virginia College in Birmingham (Birmingham, AL): *closed.*

Warner Pacific College (Portland, OR): *name changed to Warner Pacific University.*

Wheelock College (Boston, MA): *merged into Boston University (Boston, MA).*

Wright Institute (Berkeley, CA): *name changed to The Wright Institute.*

Yeshiva Karlin Stolin Rabbinical Institute (Brooklyn, NY): *name changed to Yeshiva Karlin Stolin.*

Abbreviations Used in the Guides

The following list includes abbreviations of degree names used in the profiles in the 2020 edition of the guides. Because some degrees (e.g., Doctor of Education) can be abbreviated in more than one way (e.g., D.Ed. or Ed.D.), and because the abbreviations used in the guides reflect the preferences of the individual colleges and universities, the list may include two or more abbreviations for a single degree.

DEGREES

A Mus D	Doctor of Musical Arts
AC	Advanced Certificate
AD	Artist's Diploma
	Doctor of Arts
ADP	Artist's Diploma
Adv C	Advanced Certificate
AGC	Advanced Graduate Certificate
AGSC	Advanced Graduate Specialist Certificate
ALM	Master of Liberal Arts
AM	Master of Arts
AMBA	Accelerated Master of Business Administration
APC	Advanced Professional Certificate
APMPH	Advanced Professional Master of Public Health
App Sc	Applied Scientist
App Sc D	Doctor of Applied Science
AstE	Astronautical Engineer
ATC	Advanced Training Certificate
Au D	Doctor of Audiology
B Th	Bachelor of Theology
CAES	Certificate of Advanced Educational Specialization
CAGS	Certificate of Advanced Graduate Studies
CAL	Certificate in Applied Linguistics
CAPS	Certificate of Advanced Professional Studies
CAS	Certificate of Advanced Studies
CATS	Certificate of Achievement in Theological Studies
CE	Civil Engineer
CEM	Certificate of Environmental Management
CET	Certificate in Educational Technologies
CGS	Certificate of Graduate Studies
Ch E	Chemical Engineer
Clin Sc D	Doctor of Clinical Science
CM	Certificate in Management
CMH	Certificate in Medical Humanities
CMM	Master of Church Ministries
CMS	Certificate in Ministerial Studies
CNM	Certificate in Nonprofit Management
CPC	Certificate in Publication and Communication
CPH	Certificate in Public Health
CPS	Certificate of Professional Studies
CScD	Doctor of Clinical Science

CSD	Certificate in Spiritual Direction
CSS	Certificate of Special Studies
CTS	Certificate of Theological Studies
D Ac	Doctor of Acupuncture
D Admin	Doctor of Administration
D Arch	Doctor of Architecture
D Be	Doctor in Bioethics
D Com	Doctor of Commerce
D Couns	Doctor of Counseling
D Des	Doctorate of Design
D Div	Doctor of Divinity
D Ed	Doctor of Education
D Ed Min	Doctor of Educational Ministry
D Eng	Doctor of Engineering
D Engr	Doctor of Engineering
D Ent	Doctor of Enterprise
D Env	Doctor of Environment
D Law	Doctor of Law
D Litt	Doctor of Letters
D Med Sc	Doctor of Medical Science
D Mgt	Doctor of Management
D Min	Doctor of Ministry
D Miss	Doctor of Missiology
D Mus	Doctor of Music
D Mus A	Doctor of Musical Arts
D Phil	Doctor of Philosophy
D Prof	Doctor of Professional Studies
D Ps	Doctor of Psychology
D Sc	Doctor of Science
D Sc D	Doctor of Science in Dentistry
D Sc IS	Doctor of Science in Information Systems
D Sc PA	Doctor of Science in Physician Assistant Studies
D Th	Doctor of Theology
D Th P	Doctor of Practical Theology
DA	Doctor of Accounting
	Doctor of Arts
DACM	Doctor of Acupuncture and Chinese Medicine
DAIS	Doctor of Applied Intercultural Studies
DAOM	Doctorate in Acupuncture and Oriental Medicine
DAT	Doctorate of Athletic Training
	Professional Doctor of Art Therapy
DBA	Doctor of Business Administration
DBH	Doctor of Behavioral Health
DBL	Doctor of Business Leadership
DC	Doctor of Chiropractic
DCC	Doctor of Computer Science
DCD	Doctor of Communications Design

DCE	Doctor of Computer Engineering
DCJ	Doctor of Criminal Justice
DCL	Doctor of Civil Law
	Doctor of Comparative Law
DCM	Doctor of Church Music
DCN	Doctor of Clinical Nutrition
DCS	Doctor of Computer Science
DDN	Diplôme du Droit Notarial
DDS	Doctor of Dental Surgery
DE	Doctor of Education
	Doctor of Engineering
DED	Doctor of Economic Development
DEIT	Doctor of Educational Innovation and Technology
DEL	Doctor of Executive Leadership
DEM	Doctor of Educational Ministry
DEPD	Diplôme Études Spécialisées
DES	Doctor of Engineering Science
DESS	Diplôme Études Supérieures Spécialisées
DET	Doctor of Educational Technology
DFA	Doctor of Fine Arts
DGP	Diploma in Graduate and Professional Studies
DGS	Doctor of Global Security
DH Sc	Doctor of Health Sciences
DHA	Doctor of Health Administration
DHCE	Doctor of Health Care Ethics
DHL	Doctor of Hebrew Letters
DHPE	Doctorate of Health Professionals Education
DHS	Doctor of Health Science
DHSc	Doctor of Health Science
DIT	Doctor of Industrial Technology
	Doctor of Information Technology
DJS	Doctor of Jewish Studies
DLS	Doctor of Liberal Studies
DM	Doctor of Management
	Doctor of Music
DMA	Doctor of Musical Arts
DMD	Doctor of Dental Medicine
DME	Doctor of Manufacturing Management
	Doctor of Music Education
DMFT	Doctor of Marital and Family Therapy
DMH	Doctor of Medical Humanities
DML	Doctor of Modern Languages
DMP	Doctorate in Medical Physics
DMPNA	Doctor of Management Practice in Nurse Anesthesia
DN Sc	Doctor of Nursing Science
DNAP	Doctor of Nurse Anesthesia Practice
DNP	Doctor of Nursing Practice
DNP-A	Doctor of Nursing Practice - Anesthesia
DNS	Doctor of Nursing Science
DO	Doctor of Osteopathy

DOL	Doctorate of Organizational Leadership
DOM	Doctor of Oriental Medicine
DOT	Doctor of Occupational Therapy
DPA	Diploma in Public Administration
	Doctor of Public Administration
DPDS	Doctor of Planning and Development Studies
DPH	Doctor of Public Health
DPM	Doctor of Plant Medicine
	Doctor of Podiatric Medicine
DPPD	Doctor of Policy, Planning, and Development
DPS	Doctor of Professional Studies
DPT	Doctor of Physical Therapy
DPTSc	Doctor of Physical Therapy Science
Dr DES	Doctor of Design
Dr NP	Doctor of Nursing Practice
Dr OT	Doctor of Occupational Therapy
Dr PH	Doctor of Public Health
Dr Sc PT	Doctor of Science in Physical Therapy
DRSc	Doctor of Regulatory Science
DS	Doctor of Science
DS Sc	Doctor of Social Science
DScPT	Doctor of Science in Physical Therapy
DSI	Doctor of Strategic Intelligence
DSJS	Doctor of Science in Jewish Studies
DSL	Doctor of Strategic Leadership
DSNS	Doctorate of Statecraft and National Security
DSS	Doctor of Strategic Security
DSW	Doctor of Social Work
DTL	Doctor of Talmudic Law
	Doctor of Transformational Leadership
DV Sc	Doctor of Veterinary Science
DVM	Doctor of Veterinary Medicine
DWS	Doctor of Worship Studies
EAA	Engineer in Aeronautics and Astronautics
EASPh D	Engineering and Applied Science Doctor of Philosophy
ECS	Engineer in Computer Science
Ed D	Doctor of Education
Ed DCT	Doctor of Education in College Teaching
Ed L D	Doctor of Education Leadership
Ed M	Master of Education
Ed S	Specialist in Education
Ed Sp	Specialist in Education
EDB	Executive Doctorate in Business
EDM	Executive Doctorate in Management
EE	Electrical Engineer
EJD	Executive Juris Doctor
EMBA	Executive Master of Business Administration
EMFA	Executive Master of Forensic Accounting
EMHA	Executive Master of Health Administration
EMHCL	Executive Master in Healthcare Leadership

354 www.petersons.com

Peterson's Graduate Programs in the Physical Sciences, Mathematics, Agricultural Sciences, the Environment & Natural Resources 2020

EMIB	Executive Master of International Business	M Ac	Master of Accountancy
EMIR	Executive Master in International Relations		Master of Accounting
EML	Executive Master of Leadership		Master of Acupuncture
EMPA	Executive Master of Public Administration	M Ac OM	Master of Acupuncture and Oriental Medicine
EMPL	Executive Master in Policy Leadership	M Acc	Master of Accountancy
	Executive Master in Public Leadership		Master of Accounting
EMS	Executive Master of Science	M Acct	Master of Accountancy
EMTM	Executive Master of Technology Management		Master of Accounting
Eng	Engineer	M Accy	Master of Accountancy
Eng Sc D	Doctor of Engineering Science	M Actg	Master of Accounting
Engr	Engineer	M Acy	Master of Accountancy
Exec MHA	Executive Master of Health Administration	M Ad	Master of Administration
Exec Ed D	Executive Doctor of Education	M Ad Ed	Master of Adult Education
Exec MBA	Executive Master of Business Administration	M Adm	Master of Administration
Exec MPA	Executive Master of Public Administration	M Adm Mgt	Master of Administrative Management
Exec MPH	Executive Master of Public Health	M Admin	Master of Administration
Exec MS	Executive Master of Science	M ADU	Master of Architectural Design and Urbanism
Executive MA	Executive Master of Arts	M Adv	Master of Advertising
G Dip	Graduate Diploma	M Ag	Master of Agriculture
GBC	Graduate Business Certificate	M Ag Ed	Master of Agricultural Education
GDM	Graduate Diploma in Management	M Agr	Master of Agriculture
GDPA	Graduate Diploma in Public Administration	M App Comp Sc	Master of Applied Computer Science
GEMBA	Global Executive Master of Business Administration	M App St	Master of Applied Statistics
GM Acc	Graduate Master of Accountancy	M Appl Stat	Master of Applied Statistics
GMBA	Global Master of Business Administration	M Aq	Master of Aquaculture
GP LL M	Global Professional Master of Laws	M Ar	Master of Architecture
GPD	Graduate Performance Diploma	M Arch	Master of Architecture
GSS	Graduate Special Certificate for Students in Special Situations	M Arch I	Master of Architecture I
		M Arch II	Master of Architecture II
IEMBA	International Executive Master of Business Administration	M Arch E	Master of Architectural Engineering
IMA	Interdisciplinary Master of Arts	M Arch H	Master of Architectural History
IMBA	International Master of Business Administration	M Bioethics	Master in Bioethics
		M Cat	Master of Catechesis
IMES	International Master's in Environmental Studies	M Ch E	Master of Chemical Engineering
		M Cl D	Master of Clinical Dentistry
Ingeniero	Engineer	M Cl Sc	Master of Clinical Science
JCD	Doctor of Canon Law	M Comm	Master of Communication
JCL	Licentiate in Canon Law	M Comp	Master of Computing
JD	Juris Doctor	M Comp Sc	Master of Computer Science
JM	Juris Master	M Coun	Master of Counseling
JSD	Doctor of Juridical Science	M Dent	Master of Dentistry
	Doctor of Jurisprudence	M Dent Sc	Master of Dental Sciences
	Doctor of the Science of Law	M Des	Master of Design
JSM	Master of the Science of Law	M Des S	Master of Design Studies
L Th	Licentiate in Theology	M Div	Master of Divinity
LL B	Bachelor of Laws	M E Sci	Master of Earth Science
LL CM	Master of Comparative Law	M Ec	Master of Economics
LL D	Doctor of Laws	M Econ	Master of Economics
LL M	Master of Laws	M Ed	Master of Education
LL M in Tax	Master of Laws in Taxation	M Ed T	Master of Education in Teaching
LL M CL	Master of Laws in Common Law	M En	Master of Engineering

Peterson's Graduate Programs in the Physical Sciences, Mathematics, Agricultural Sciences, the Environment & Natural Resources 2020

www.petersons.com **355**

M En S	Master of Environmental Sciences	M Sc E	Master of Science in Engineering
M Eng	Master of Engineering	M Sc Eng	Master of Science in Engineering
M Eng Mgt	Master of Engineering Management	M Sc Engr	Master of Science in Engineering
M Engr	Master of Engineering	M Sc F	Master of Science in Forestry
M Ent	Master of Enterprise	M Sc FE	Master of Science in Forest Engineering
M Env	Master of Environment	M Sc Geogr	Master of Science in Geography
M Env Des	Master of Environmental Design	M Sc N	Master of Science in Nursing
M Env E	Master of Environmental Engineering	M Sc OT	Master of Science in Occupational Therapy
M Env Sc	Master of Environmental Science	M Sc P	Master of Science in Planning
M Ext Ed	Master of Extension Education	M Sc Pl	Master of Science in Planning
M Fin	Master of Finance	M Sc PT	Master of Science in Physical Therapy
M Geo E	Master of Geological Engineering	M Sc T	Master of Science in Teaching
M Geoenv E	Master of Geoenvironmental Engineering	M SEM	Master of Sustainable Environmental Management
M Geog	Master of Geography		
M Hum	Master of Humanities	M Serv Soc	Master of Social Service
M IDST	Master's in Interdisciplinary Studies	M Soc	Master of Sociology
M Jur	Master of Jurisprudence	M Sp Ed	Master of Special Education
M Kin	Master of Kinesiology	M Stat	Master of Statistics
M Land Arch	Master of Landscape Architecture	M Sys E	Master of Systems Engineering
M Litt	Master of Letters	M Sys Sc	Master of Systems Science
M Mark	Master of Marketing	M Tax	Master of Taxation
M Mat SE	Master of Material Science and Engineering	M Tech	Master of Technology
M Math	Master of Mathematics	M Th	Master of Theology
M Mech E	Master of Mechanical Engineering	M Trans E	Master of Transportation Engineering
M Med Sc	Master of Medical Science	M U Ed	Master of Urban Education
M Mgmt	Master of Management	M Urb	Master of Urban Planning
M Mgt	Master of Management	M Vet Sc	Master of Veterinary Science
M Min	Master of Ministries	MA	Master of Accounting
M Mtl E	Master of Materials Engineering		Master of Administration
M Mu	Master of Music		Master of Arts
M Mus	Master of Music	MA Comm	Master of Arts in Communication
M Mus Ed	Master of Music Education	MA Ed	Master of Arts in Education
M Music	Master of Music	MA Ed/HD	Master of Arts in Education and Human Development
M Pet E	Master of Petroleum Engineering		
M Pharm	Master of Pharmacy	MA Islamic	Master of Arts in Islamic Studies
M Phil	Master of Philosophy	MA Min	Master of Arts in Ministry
M Phil F	Master of Philosophical Foundations	MA Miss	Master of Arts in Missiology
M Pl	Master of Planning	MA Past St	Master of Arts in Pastoral Studies
M Plan	Master of Planning	MA Ph	Master of Arts in Philosophy
M Pol	Master of Political Science	MA Psych	Master of Arts in Psychology
M Pr Met	Master of Professional Meteorology	MA Sc	Master of Applied Science
M Prob S	Master of Probability and Statistics	MA Sp	Master of Arts (Spirituality)
M Psych	Master of Psychology	MA Th	Master of Arts in Theology
M Pub	Master of Publishing	MA-R	Master of Arts (Research)
M Rel	Master of Religion	MAA	Master of Applied Anthropology
M Sc	Master of Science		Master of Applied Arts
M Sc A	Master of Science (Applied)		Master of Arts in Administration
M Sc AC	Master of Science in Applied Computing	MAAA	Master of Arts in Arts Administration
M Sc AHN	Master of Science in Applied Human Nutrition	MAAD	Master of Advanced Architectural Design
		MAAE	Master of Arts in Art Education
M Sc BMC	Master of Science in Biomedical Communications	MAAPPS	Master of Arts in Asia Pacific Policy Studies
		MAAS	Master of Arts in Aging and Spirituality
M Sc CS	Master of Science in Computer Science	MAASJ	Master of Arts in Applied Social Justice

MAAT	Master of Arts in Applied Theology		Master of Architectural Engineering
MAB	Master of Agribusiness		Master of Art Education
	Master of Applied Bioengineering		Master of Arts in Education
	Master of Arts in Business		Master of Arts in English
MABA	Master's in Applied Behavior Analysis	MAEd	Master of Arts Education
MABC	Master of Arts in Biblical Counseling	MAEE	Master of Agricultural and Extension Education
MABE	Master of Arts in Bible Exposition		
MABL	Master of Arts in Biblical Languages	MAEL	Master of Arts in Educational Leadership
MABM	Master of Agribusiness Management	MAEM	Master of Arts in Educational Ministries
MABS	Master of Arts in Biblical Studies	MAEP	Master of Arts in Economic Policy
MABT	Master of Arts in Bible Teaching		Master of Arts in Educational Psychology
MAC	Master of Accountancy	MAES	Master of Arts in Environmental Sciences
	Master of Accounting	MAET	Master of Arts in English Teaching
	Master of Arts in Communication	MAF	Master of Arts in Finance
	Master of Arts in Counseling	MAFE	Master of Arts in Financial Economics
MACC	Master of Arts in Christian Counseling	MAFM	Master of Accounting and Financial Management
MACCT	Master of Accounting		
MACD	Master of Arts in Christian Doctrine	MAFS	Master of Arts in Family Studies
MACE	Master of Arts in Christian Education	MAG	Master of Applied Geography
MACH	Master of Arts in Church History	MAGU	Master of Urban Analysis and Management
MACI	Master of Arts in Curriculum and Instruction	MAH	Master of Arts in Humanities
MACIS	Master of Accounting and Information Systems	MAHA	Master of Arts in Humanitarian Assistance
		MAHCM	Master of Arts in Health Care Mission
MACJ	Master of Arts in Criminal Justice	MAHG	Master of American History and Government
MACL	Master of Arts in Christian Leadership		
	Master of Arts in Community Leadership	MAHL	Master of Arts in Hebrew Letters
MACM	Master of Arts in Christian Ministries	MAHN	Master of Applied Human Nutrition
	Master of Arts in Christian Ministry	MAHR	Master of Applied Historical Research
	Master of Arts in Church Music	MAHS	Master of Arts in Human Services
	Master of Arts in Counseling Ministries	MAHSR	Master in Applied Health Services Research
MACML	Master of Arts in Christian Ministry and Leadership	MAIA	Master of Arts in International Administration
MACN	Master of Arts in Counseling		Master of Arts in International Affairs
MACO	Master of Arts in Counseling	MAICS	Master of Arts in Intercultural Studies
MAcOM	Master of Acupuncture and Oriental Medicine	MAIDM	Master of Arts in Interior Design and Merchandising
MACP	Master of Arts in Christian Practice	MAIH	Master of Arts in Interdisciplinary Humanities
	Master of Arts in Church Planting		
	Master of Arts in Counseling Psychology	MAIOP	Master of Applied Industrial/Organizational Psychology
MACS	Master of Applied Computer Science	MAIS	Master of Arts in Intercultural Studies
	Master of Arts in Catholic Studies		Master of Arts in Interdisciplinary Studies
	Master of Arts in Christian Studies		Master of Arts in International Studies
MACSE	Master of Arts in Christian School Education	MAIT	Master of Administration in Information Technology
MACT	Master of Arts in Communications and Technology	MAJ	Master of Arts in Journalism
MAD	Master in Educational Institution Administration	MAJCS	Master of Arts in Jewish Communal Service
		MAJPS	Master of Arts in Jewish Professional Studies
	Master of Art and Design	MAJS	Master of Arts in Jewish Studies
MADR	Master of Arts in Dispute Resolution	MAL	Master of Athletic Leadership
MADS	Master of Applied Disability Studies	MALA	Master of Arts in Liberal Arts
MAE	Master of Aerospace Engineering	MALCM	Master in Arts Leadership and Cultural Management
	Master of Agricultural Economics		
	Master of Agricultural Education	MALD	Master of Arts in Law and Diplomacy
	Master of Applied Economics	MALER	Master of Arts in Labor and Employment Relations

Peterson's Graduate Programs in the Physical Sciences, Mathematics, Agricultural Sciences, the Environment & Natural Resources 2020

www.petersons.com   **357**

MALL	Master of Arts in Language Learning		Mar Eng	Marine Engineer
MALLT	Master of Arts in Language, Literature, and Translation		MARC	Master of Arts in Rehabilitation Counseling
MALP	Master of Arts in Language Pedagogy		MARE	Master of Arts in Religious Education
MALS	Master of Arts in Liberal Studies		MARL	Master of Arts in Religious Leadership
MAM	Master of Acquisition Management		MARS	Master of Arts in Religious Studies
	Master of Agriculture and Management		MAS	Master of Accounting Science
	Master of Applied Mathematics			Master of Actuarial Science
	Master of Arts in Management			Master of Administrative Science
	Master of Arts in Ministry			Master of Advanced Study
	Master of Arts Management			Master of American Studies
	Master of Aviation Management			Master of Animal Science
MAMC	Master of Arts in Mass Communication			Master of Applied Science
	Master of Arts in Ministry and Culture			Master of Applied Statistics
	Master of Arts in Ministry for a Multicultural Church			Master of Archival Studies
MAME	Master of Arts in Missions/Evangelism		MASA	Master of Advanced Studies in Architecture
MAMFC	Master of Arts in Marriage and Family Counseling		MASC	Master of Arts in School Counseling
MAMFT	Master of Arts in Marriage and Family Therapy		MASD	Master of Arts in Spiritual Direction
			MASE	Master of Arts in Special Education
MAMHC	Master of Arts in Mental Health Counseling		MASF	Master of Arts in Spiritual Formation
MAMS	Master of Applied Mathematical Sciences		MASJ	Master of Arts in Systems of Justice
	Master of Arts in Ministerial Studies		MASLA	Master of Advanced Studies in Landscape Architecture
	Master of Arts in Ministry and Spirituality		MASM	Master of Aging Services Management
MAMT	Master of Arts in Mathematics Teaching			Master of Arts in Specialized Ministries
MAN	Master of Applied Nutrition		MASS	Master of Applied Social Science
MANT	Master of Arts in New Testament		MASW	Master of Aboriginal Social Work
MAOL	Master of Arts in Organizational Leadership		MAT	Master of Arts in Teaching
MAOM	Master of Acupuncture and Oriental Medicine			Master of Arts in Theology
				Master of Athletic Training
	Master of Arts in Organizational Management			Master's in Administration of Telecommunications
MAOT	Master of Arts in Old Testament		Mat E	Materials Engineer
MAP	Master of Applied Politics		MATCM	Master of Acupuncture and Traditional Chinese Medicine
	Master of Applied Psychology		MATDE	Master of Arts in Theology, Development, and Evangelism
	Master of Arts in Planning			
	Master of Psychology		MATDR	Master of Territorial Management and Regional Development
	Master of Public Administration		MATE	Master of Arts for the Teaching of English
MAP Min	Master of Arts in Pastoral Ministry		MATESL	Master of Arts in Teaching English as a Second Language
MAPA	Master of Arts in Public Administration			
MAPC	Master of Arts in Pastoral Counseling		MATESOL	Master of Arts in Teaching English to Speakers of Other Languages
MAPE	Master of Arts in Physics Education			
MAPM	Master of Arts in Pastoral Ministry		MATF	Master of Arts in Teaching English as a Foreign Language/Intercultural Studies
	Master of Arts in Pastoral Music			
	Master of Arts in Practical Ministry		MATFL	Master of Arts in Teaching Foreign Language
MAPP	Master of Arts in Public Policy		MATH	Master of Arts in Therapy
MAPS	Master of Applied Psychological Sciences		MATI	Master of Administration of Information Technology
	Master of Arts in Pastoral Studies			
	Master of Arts in Public Service		MATL	Master of Arts in Teaching of Languages
MAPW	Master of Arts in Professional Writing			Master of Arts in Transformational Leadership
MAQRM	Master's of Actuarial and Quantitative Risk Management		MATM	Master of Arts in Teaching of Mathematics
			MATRN	Master of Athletic Training
MAR	Master of Arts in Reading		MATS	Master of Arts in Theological Studies
	Master of Arts in Religion			

	Master of Arts in Transforming Spirituality		Master of Business Taxation
MAUA	Master of Arts in Urban Affairs	MBV	Master of Business for Veterans
MAUD	Master of Arts in Urban Design	MC	Master of Classics
MAURP	Master of Arts in Urban and Regional Planning		Master of Communication
			Master of Counseling
MAW	Master of Arts in Worship	MC Ed	Master of Continuing Education
MAWSHP	Master of Arts in Worship	MC Sc	Master of Computer Science
MAYM	Master of Arts in Youth Ministry	MCA	Master of Commercial Aviation
MB	Master of Bioinformatics		Master of Communication Arts
MBA	Master of Business Administration		Master of Criminology (Applied)
MBA-AM	Master of Business Administration in Aviation Management	MCAM	Master of Computational and Applied Mathematics
MBA-EP	Master of Business Administration–Experienced Professionals	MCC	Master of Computer Science
MBAA	Master of Business Administration in Aviation	MCD	Master of Communications Disorders
			Master of Community Development
MBAE	Master of Biological and Agricultural Engineering	MCE	Master in Electronic Commerce
			Master of Chemistry Education
	Master of Biosystems and Agricultural Engineering		Master of Christian Education
			Master of Civil Engineering
MBAH	Master of Business Administration in Health		Master of Control Engineering
MBAi	Master of Business Administration–International	MCEM	Master of Construction Engineering Management
MBAICT	Master of Business Administration in Information and Communication Technology	MCEPA	Master of Chinese Economic and Political Affairs
MBC	Master of Building Construction	MCHE	Master of Chemical Engineering
MBE	Master of Bilingual Education	MCIS	Master of Communication and Information Studies
	Master of Bioengineering		Master of Computer and Information Science
	Master of Bioethics		
	Master of Biomedical Engineering		Master of Computer Information Systems
	Master of Business Economics	MCIT	Master of Computer and Information Technology
	Master of Business Education		
MBEE	Master in Biotechnology Enterprise and Entrepreneurship	MCJ	Master of Criminal Justice
MBET	Master of Business, Entrepreneurship and Technology	MCL	Master in Communication Leadership
			Master of Canon Law
MBI	Master in Business Informatics		Master of Christian Leadership
MBIOT	Master of Biotechnology		Master of Comparative Law
MBiotech	Master of Biotechnology	MCM	Master of Christian Ministry
MBL	Master of Business Leadership		Master of Church Music
MBLE	Master in Business Logistics Engineering		Master of Communication Management
MBME	Master's in Biomedical Engineering		Master of Community Medicine
MBMSE	Master of Business Management and Software Engineering		Master of Construction Management
			Master of Contract Management
MBOE	Master of Business Operational Excellence	MCMin	Master of Christian Ministry
MBS	Master of Biblical Studies	MCMM	Master in Communications and Media Management
	Master of Biological Science		
	Master of Biomedical Sciences	MCMP	Master of City and Metropolitan Planning
	Master of Bioscience	MCMS	Master of Clinical Medical Science
	Master of Building Science	MCN	Master of Clinical Nutrition
	Master of Business and Science	MCOL	Master of Arts in Community and Organizational Leadership
	Master of Business Statistics		
MBST	Master of Biostatistics	MCP	Master of City Planning
MBT	Master of Biomedical Technology		Master of Community Planning
			Master of Counseling Psychology
	Master of Biotechnology		Master of Cytopathology Practice

Peterson's Graduate Programs in the Physical Sciences, Mathematics, Agricultural Sciences, the Environment & Natural Resources 2020

www.petersons.com **359**

	Master of Science in Quality Systems and Productivity
MCPD	Master of Community Planning and Development
MCR	Master in Clinical Research
MCRP	Master of City and Regional Planning
	Master of Community and Regional Planning
MCRS	Master of City and Regional Studies
MCS	Master of Chemical Sciences
	Master of Christian Studies
	Master of Clinical Science
	Master of Combined Sciences
	Master of Communication Studies
	Master of Computer Science
	Master of Consumer Science
MCSE	Master of Computer Science and Engineering
MCSL	Master of Catholic School Leadership
MCSM	Master of Construction Science and Management
MCT	Master of Commerce and Technology
MCTM	Master of Clinical Translation Management
MCTP	Master of Communication Technology and Policy
MCTS	Master of Clinical and Translational Science
MCVS	Master of Cardiovascular Science
MD	Doctor of Medicine
MDA	Master of Dietetic Administration
MDB	Master of Design-Build
MDE	Master in Design Engineering
	Master of Developmental Economics
	Master of Distance Education
	Master of the Education of the Deaf
MDH	Master of Dental Hygiene
MDI	Master of Disruptive Innovation
MDM	Master of Design Methods
	Master of Digital Media
MDP	Master in Sustainable Development Practice
	Master of Development Practice
MDR	Master of Dispute Resolution
MDS	Master in Data Science
	Master of Dental Surgery
	Master of Design Studies
	Master of Digital Sciences
MDSPP	Master in Data Science for Public Policy
ME	Master of Education
	Master of Engineering
	Master of Entrepreneurship
ME Sc	Master of Engineering Science
ME-PD	Master of Education–Professional Development
MEA	Master of Educational Administration
	Master of Engineering Administration

MEAE	Master of Entertainment Arts and Engineering
MEAP	Master of Environmental Administration and Planning
MEB	Master of Energy Business
MEBD	Master in Environmental Building Design
MEBT	Master in Electronic Business Technologies
MEC	Master of Electronic Commerce
Mech E	Mechanical Engineer
MEDS	Master of Environmental Design Studies
MEE	Master in Education
	Master of Electrical Engineering
	Master of Energy Engineering
	Master of Environmental Engineering
MEECON	Master of Energy Economics
MEEM	Master of Environmental Engineering and Management
MEENE	Master of Engineering in Environmental Engineering
MEEP	Master of Environmental and Energy Policy
MEERM	Master of Earth and Environmental Resource Management
MEH	Master in Humanistic Studies
	Master of Environmental Health
	Master of Environmental Horticulture
MEHS	Master of Environmental Health and Safety
MEIM	Master of Entertainment Industry Management
	Master of Equine Industry Management
MEL	Master of Educational Leadership
	Master of Engineering Leadership
	Master of English Literature
MELP	Master of Environmental Law and Policy
MEM	Master of Engineering Management
	Master of Environmental Management
	Master of Marketing
MEME	Master of Engineering in Manufacturing Engineering
	Master of Engineering in Mechanical Engineering
MENR	Master of Environment and Natural Resources
MENVEGR	Master of Environmental Engineering
MEP	Master of Engineering Physics
MEPC	Master of Environmental Pollution Control
MEPD	Master of Environmental Planning and Design
MER	Master of Employment Relations
MERE	Master of Entrepreneurial Real Estate
MERL	Master of Energy Regulation and Law
MES	Master of Education and Science
	Master of Engineering Science
	Master of Environment and Sustainability
	Master of Environmental Science
	Master of Environmental Studies
	Master of Environmental Systems

MESM	Master of Environmental Science and Management
MET	Master of Educational Technology
	Master of Engineering Technology
	Master of Entertainment Technology
	Master of Environmental Toxicology
METM	Master of Engineering and Technology Management
MEVE	Master of Environmental Engineering
MF	Master of Finance
	Master of Forestry
MFA	Master of Financial Administration
	Master of Fine Arts
MFALP	Master of Food and Agriculture Law and Policy
MFAS	Master of Fisheries and Aquatic Science
MFC	Master of Forest Conservation
MFCS	Master of Family and Consumer Sciences
MFE	Master of Financial Economics
	Master of Financial Engineering
	Master of Forest Engineering
MFES	Master of Fire and Emergency Services
MFG	Master of Functional Genomics
MFHD	Master of Family and Human Development
MFM	Master of Financial Management
	Master of Financial Mathematics
MFPE	Master of Food Process Engineering
MFR	Master of Forest Resources
MFRC	Master of Forest Resources and Conservation
MFRE	Master of Food and Resource Economics
MFS	Master of Food Science
	Master of Forensic Sciences
	Master of Forest Science
	Master of Forest Studies
	Master of French Studies
MFST	Master of Food Safety and Technology
MFT	Master of Family Therapy
MFWCB	Master of Fish, Wildlife and Conservation Biology
MFYCS	Master of Family, Youth and Community Sciences
MGA	Master of Global Affairs
	Master of Government Administration
	Master of Governmental Administration
MGBA	Master of Global Business Administration
MGC	Master of Genetic Counseling
MGCS	Master of Genetic Counselor Studies
MGD	Master of Graphic Design
MGE	Master of Geotechnical Engineering
MGEM	Master of Geomatics for Environmental Management
	Master of Global Entrepreneurship and Management
MGIS	Master of Geographic Information Science
	Master of Geographic Information Systems

MGM	Master of Global Management
MGMA	Master of Greenhouse Gas Management and Accounting
MGP	Master of Gestion de Projet
MGPS	Master of Global Policy Studies
MGREM	Master of Global Real Estate Management
MGS	Master of Gender Studies
	Master of Gerontological Studies
	Master of Global Studies
MH	Master of Humanities
MH Sc	Master of Health Sciences
MHA	Master of Health Administration
	Master of Healthcare Administration
	Master of Hospital Administration
	Master of Hospitality Administration
MHB	Master of Human Behavior
MHC	Master of Mental Health Counseling
MHCA	Master of Health Care Administration
MHCD	Master of Health Care Design
MHCI	Master of Human-Computer Interaction
MHCL	Master of Health Care Leadership
MHCM	Master of Health Care Management
MHE	Master of Health Education
	Master of Higher Education
	Master of Human Ecology
MHE Ed	Master of Home Economics Education
MHEA	Master of Higher Education Administration
MHHS	Master of Health and Human Services
MHI	Master of Health Informatics
	Master of Healthcare Innovation
MHID	Master of Healthcare Interior Design
MHIHIM	Master of Health Informatics and Health Information Management
MHIIM	Master of Health Informatics and Information Management
MHK	Master of Human Kinetics
MHM	Master of Healthcare Management
MHMS	Master of Health Management Systems
MHP	Master of Health Physics
	Master of Heritage Preservation
	Master of Historic Preservation
MHPA	Master of Heath Policy and Administration
MHPCTL	Master of High Performance Coaching and Technical Leadership
MHPE	Master of Health Professions Education
MHR	Master of Human Resources
MHRD	Master in Human Resource Development
MHRIR	Master of Human Resources and Industrial Relations
MHRLR	Master of Human Resources and Labor Relations
MHRM	Master of Human Resources Management
MHS	Master of Health Science
	Master of Health Sciences

Peterson's Graduate Programs in the Physical Sciences, Mathematics, Agricultural Sciences, the Environment & Natural Resources 2020

www.petersons.com   **361**

	Master of Health Studies
	Master of Hispanic Studies
	Master of Human Services
	Master of Humanistic Studies
MHSA	Master of Health Services Administration
MHSM	Master of Health Systems Management
MI	Master of Information
	Master of Instruction
MI Arch	Master of Interior Architecture
MIA	Master of Interior Architecture
	Master of International Affairs
MIAA	Master of International Affairs and Administration
MIAM	Master of International Agribusiness Management
MIAPD	Master of Interior Architecture and Product Design
MIB	Master of International Business
MIBS	Master of International Business Studies
MICLJ	Master of International Criminal Law and Justice
MICM	Master of International Construction Management
MID	Master of Industrial Design
	Master of Industrial Distribution
	Master of Innovation Design
	Master of Interior Design
	Master of International Development
MIDA	Master of International Development Administration
MIDP	Master of International Development Policy
MIDS	Master of Information and Data Science
MIE	Master of Industrial Engineering
MIF	Master of International Forestry
MIHTM	Master of International Hospitality and Tourism Management
MIJ	Master of International Journalism
MILR	Master of Industrial and Labor Relations
MIM	Master in Ministry
	Master of Information Management
	Master of International Management
	Master of International Marketing
MIMFA	Master of Investment Management and Financial Analysis
MIMLAE	Master of International Management for Latin American Executives
MIMS	Master of Information Management and Systems
	Master of Integrated Manufacturing Systems
MIP	Master of Infrastructure Planning
	Master of Intellectual Property
	Master of International Policy
MIPA	Master of International Public Affairs
MIPD	Master of Integrated Product Design
MIPER	Master of International Political Economy of Resources

MIPM	Master of International Policy Management
MIPP	Master of International Policy and Practice
	Master of International Public Policy
MIPS	Master of International Planning Studies
MIR	Master of Industrial Relations
	Master of International Relations
MIRD	Master of International Relations and Diplomacy
MIRHR	Master of Industrial Relations and Human Resources
MIS	Master of Imaging Science
	Master of Industrial Statistics
	Master of Information Science
	Master of Information Systems
	Master of Integrated Science
	Master of Interdisciplinary Studies
	Master of International Service
	Master of International Studies
MISE	Master of Industrial and Systems Engineering
MISKM	Master of Information Sciences and Knowledge Management
MISM	Master of Information Systems Management
MISW	Master of Indigenous Social Work
MIT	Master in Teaching
	Master of Industrial Technology
	Master of Information Technology
	Master of Initial Teaching
	Master of International Trade
MITA	Master of Information Technology Administration
MITM	Master of Information Technology and Management
MJ	Master of Journalism
	Master of Jurisprudence
MJ Ed	Master of Jewish Education
MJA	Master of Justice Administration
MJM	Master of Justice Management
MJS	Master of Judaic Studies
	Master of Judicial Studies
	Master of Juridical Studies
MK	Master of Kinesiology
MKM	Master of Knowledge Management
ML	Master of Latin
	Master of Law
ML Arch	Master of Landscape Architecture
MLA	Master of Landscape Architecture
	Master of Liberal Arts
MLAS	Master of Laboratory Animal Science
	Master of Liberal Arts and Sciences
MLAUD	Master of Landscape Architecture in Urban Development
MLD	Master of Leadership Development
	Master of Leadership Studies
MLE	Master of Applied Linguistics and Exegesis

MLER	Master of Labor and Employment Relations
MLI Sc	Master of Library and Information Science
MLIS	Master of Library and Information Science
	Master of Library and Information Studies
MLM	Master of Leadership in Ministry
MLPD	Master of Land and Property Development
MLRHR	Master of Labor Relations and Human Resources
MLS	Master of Leadership Studies
	Master of Legal Studies
	Master of Liberal Studies
	Master of Library Science
	Master of Life Sciences
	Master of Medical Laboratory Sciences
MLSCM	Master of Logistics and Supply Chain Management
MLT	Master of Language Technologies
MLTCA	Master of Long Term Care Administration
MLW	Master of Studies in Law
MLWS	Master of Land and Water Systems
MM	Master of Management
	Master of Mediation
	Master of Ministry
	Master of Music
MM Ed	Master of Music Education
MM Sc	Master of Medical Science
MM St	Master of Museum Studies
MMA	Master of Marine Affairs
	Master of Media Arts
	Master of Musical Arts
MMAL	Master of Maritime Administration and Logistics
MMAS	Master of Military Art and Science
MMB	Master of Microbial Biotechnology
MMC	Master of Manufacturing Competitiveness
	Master of Mass Communications
MMCM	Master of Music in Church Music
MMCSS	Master of Mathematical Computational and Statistical Sciences
MME	Master of Management in Energy
	Master of Manufacturing Engineering
	Master of Mathematics Education
	Master of Mathematics for Educators
	Master of Mechanical Engineering
	Master of Mining Engineering
	Master of Music Education
MMEL	Master's in Medical Education Leadership
MMF	Master of Mathematical Finance
MMFC/T	Master of Marriage and Family Counseling/ Therapy
MMFT	Master of Marriage and Family Therapy
MMG	Master of Management
MMH	Master of Management in Hospitality
	Master of Medical Humanities

MMI	Master of Management of Innovation
MMIS	Master of Management Information Systems
MML	Master of Managerial Logistics
MMM	Master of Manufacturing Management
	Master of Marine Management
	Master of Medical Management
MMP	Master of Marine Policy
	Master of Medical Physics
	Master of Music Performance
MMPA	Master of Management and Professional Accounting
MMQM	Master of Manufacturing Quality Management
MMR	Master of Marketing Research
MMRM	Master of Marine Resources Management
MMS	Master in Migration Studies
	Master of Management Science
	Master of Management Studies
	Master of Manufacturing Systems
	Master of Marine Studies
	Master of Materials Science
	Master of Mathematical Sciences
	Master of Medical Science
	Master of Medieval Studies
MMSE	Master of Manufacturing Systems Engineering
MMSM	Master of Music in Sacred Music
MMT	Master in Marketing
	Master of Math for Teaching
	Master of Music Therapy
	Master's in Marketing Technology
MMus	Master of Music
MN	Master of Nursing
	Master of Nutrition
MN NP	Master of Nursing in Nurse Practitioner
MNA	Master of Nonprofit Administration
	Master of Nurse Anesthesia
MNAE	Master of Nanoengineering
MNAL	Master of Nonprofit Administration and Leadership
MNAS	Master of Natural and Applied Science
MNCL	Master of Nonprofit and Civic Leadership
MNCM	Master of Network and Communications Management
MNE	Master of Nuclear Engineering
MNL	Master in International Business for Latin America
MNM	Master of Nonprofit Management
MNO	Master of Nonprofit Organization
MNPL	Master of Not-for-Profit Leadership
MNpS	Master of Nonprofit Studies
MNR	Master of Natural Resources
MNRD	Master of Natural Resources Development
MNRES	Master of Natural Resources and Environmental Studies

Peterson's Graduate Programs in the Physical Sciences, Mathematics, Agricultural Sciences, the Environment & Natural Resources 2020

www.petersons.com   **363**

MNRM	Master of Natural Resource Management
MNRMG	Master of Natural Resource Management and Geography
MNRS	Master of Natural Resource Stewardship
MNS	Master of Natural Science
MNSE	Master of Natural Sciences Education
MO	Master of Oceanography
MOD	Master of Organizational Development
MOGS	Master of Oil and Gas Studies
MOL	Master of Organizational Leadership
MOM	Master of Organizational Management
	Master of Oriental Medicine
MOR	Master of Operations Research
MOT	Master of Occupational Therapy
MP	Master of Physiology
	Master of Planning
MP Ac	Master of Professional Accountancy
MP Acc	Master of Professional Accountancy
	Master of Professional Accounting
	Master of Public Accounting
MP Aff	Master of Public Affairs
MP Th	Master of Pastoral Theology
MPA	Master of Performing Arts
	Master of Physician Assistant
	Master of Professional Accountancy
	Master of Professional Accounting
	Master of Public Administration
	Master of Public Affairs
MPAC	Master of Professional Accounting
MPAID	Master of Public Administration and International Development
MPAP	Master of Physician Assistant Practice
	Master of Public Administration and Policy
	Master of Public Affairs and Politics
MPAS	Master of Physician Assistant Science
	Master of Physician Assistant Studies
MPC	Master of Professional Communication
MPD	Master of Product Development
	Master of Public Diplomacy
MPDS	Master of Planning and Development Studies
MPE	Master of Physical Education
MPEM	Master of Project Engineering and Management
MPFM	Master of Public Financial Management
MPH	Master of Public Health
MPHE	Master of Public Health Education
MPHM	Master in Plant Health Management
MPHS	Master of Population Health Sciences
MPHTM	Master of Public Health and Tropical Medicine
MPI	Master of Public Informatics
MPIA	Master of Public and International Affairs
MPL	Master of Pastoral Leadership
MPM	Master of Pastoral Ministry
	Master of Pest Management
	Master of Policy Management
	Master of Practical Ministries
	Master of Professional Management
	Master of Project Management
	Master of Public Management
MPNA	Master of Public and Nonprofit Administration
MPNL	Master of Philanthropy and Nonprofit Leadership
MPO	Master of Prosthetics and Orthotics
MPOD	Master of Positive Organizational Development
MPP	Master of Public Policy
MPPA	Master of Public Policy Administration
	Master of Public Policy and Administration
MPPAL	Master of Public Policy, Administration and Law
MPPGA	Master of Public Policy and Global Affairs
MPPM	Master of Public Policy and Management
MPR	Master of Public Relations
MPRTM	Master of Parks, Recreation, and Tourism Management
MPS	Master of Pastoral Studies
	Master of Perfusion Science
	Master of Planning Studies
	Master of Political Science
	Master of Preservation Studies
	Master of Prevention Science
	Master of Professional Studies
	Master of Public Service
MPSA	Master of Public Service Administration
MPSG	Master of Population and Social Gerontology
MPSIA	Master of Political Science and International Affairs
MPSL	Master of Public Safety Leadership
MPT	Master of Pastoral Theology
	Master of Physical Therapy
	Master of Practical Theology
MPVM	Master of Preventive Veterinary Medicine
MPW	Master of Professional Writing
	Master of Public Works
MQF	Master of Quantitative Finance
MQM	Master of Quality Management
	Master of Quantitative Management
MQS	Master of Quality Systems
MR	Master of Recreation
	Master of Retailing
MRA	Master in Research Administration
	Master of Regulatory Affairs
MRC	Master of Rehabilitation Counseling
MRCP	Master of Regional and City Planning

364 www.petersons.com

Peterson's Graduate Programs in the Physical Sciences, Mathematics, Agricultural Sciences, the Environment & Natural Resources 2020

	Master of Regional and Community Planning
MRD	Master of Rural Development
MRE	Master of Real Estate
	Master of Religious Education
MRED	Master of Real Estate Development
MREM	Master of Resource and Environmental Management
MRLS	Master of Resources Law Studies
MRM	Master of Resources Management
MRP	Master of Regional Planning
MRRD	Master in Recreation Resource Development
MRS	Master of Religious Studies
MRSc	Master of Rehabilitation Science
MRUD	Master of Resilient Design
MS	Master of Science
MS Cmp E	Master of Science in Computer Engineering
MS Kin	Master of Science in Kinesiology
MS Acct	Master of Science in Accounting
MS Accy	Master of Science in Accountancy
MS Aero E	Master of Science in Aerospace Engineering
MS Ag	Master of Science in Agriculture
MS Arch	Master of Science in Architecture
MS Arch St	Master of Science in Architectural Studies
MS Bio E	Master of Science in Bioengineering
MS Bm E	Master of Science in Biomedical Engineering
MS Ch E	Master of Science in Chemical Engineering
MS Cp E	Master of Science in Computer Engineering
MS Eco	Master of Science in Economics
MS Econ	Master of Science in Economics
MS Ed	Master of Science in Education
MS Ed Admin	Master of Science in Educational Administration
MS El	Master of Science in Educational Leadership and Administration
MS En E	Master of Science in Environmental Engineering
MS Eng	Master of Science in Engineering
MS Engr	Master of Science in Engineering
MS Env E	Master of Science in Environmental Engineering
MS Exp Surg	Master of Science in Experimental Surgery
MS Mat SE	Master of Science in Material Science and Engineering
MS Met E	Master of Science in Metallurgical Engineering
MS Mgt	Master of Science in Management
MS Min	Master of Science in Mining
MS Min E	Master of Science in Mining Engineering
MS Mt E	Master of Science in Materials Engineering
MS Otol	Master of Science in Otolaryngology
MS Pet E	Master of Science in Petroleum Engineering
MS Sc	Master of Social Science
MS Sp Ed	Master of Science in Special Education
MS Stat	Master of Science in Statistics
MS Surg	Master of Science in Surgery
MS Tax	Master of Science in Taxation
MS Tc E	Master of Science in Telecommunications Engineering
MS-R	Master of Science (Research)
MSA	Master of School Administration
	Master of Science in Accountancy
	Master of Science in Accounting
	Master of Science in Administration
	Master of Science in Aeronautics
	Master of Science in Agriculture
	Master of Science in Analytics
	Master of Science in Anesthesia
	Master of Science in Architecture
	Master of Science in Aviation
	Master of Sports Administration
	Master of Surgical Assisting
MSAA	Master of Science in Astronautics and Aeronautics
MSABE	Master of Science in Agricultural and Biological Engineering
MSAC	Master of Science in Acupuncture
MSACC	Master of Science in Accounting
MSACS	Master of Science in Applied Computer Science
MSAE	Master of Science in Aeronautical Engineering
	Master of Science in Aerospace Engineering
	Master of Science in Applied Economics
	Master of Science in Applied Engineering
	Master of Science in Architectural Engineering
MSAEM	Master of Science in Aerospace Engineering and Mechanics
MSAF	Master of Science in Aviation Finance
MSAG	Master of Science in Applied Geosciences
MSAH	Master of Science in Allied Health
MSAL	Master of Sport Administration and Leadership
MSAM	Master of Science in Applied Mathematics
MSANR	Master of Science in Agriculture and Natural Resources
MSAS	Master of Science in Administrative Studies
	Master of Science in Applied Statistics
	Master of Science in Architectural Studies
MSAT	Master of Science in Accounting and Taxation
	Master of Science in Advanced Technology
	Master of Science in Athletic Training
MSB	Master of Science in Biotechnology
MSBA	Master of Science in Business Administration
	Master of Science in Business Analysis
MSBAE	Master of Science in Biological and Agricultural Engineering

Peterson's Graduate Programs in the Physical Sciences, Mathematics, Agricultural Sciences, the Environment & Natural Resources 2020

www.petersons.com 365

	Master of Science in Biosystems and Agricultural Engineering
MSBCB	Master's in Bioinformatics and Computational Biology
MSBE	Master of Science in Biological Engineering
	Master of Science in Biomedical Engineering
MSBENG	Master of Science in Bioengineering
MSBH	Master of Science in Behavioral Health
MSBM	Master of Sport Business Management
MSBME	Master of Science in Biomedical Engineering
MSBMS	Master of Science in Basic Medical Science
MSBS	Master of Science in Biomedical Sciences
MSBTM	Master of Science in Biotechnology and Management
MSC	Master of Science in Commerce
	Master of Science in Communication
	Master of Science in Counseling
	Master of Science in Criminology
	Master of Strategic Communication
MSCC	Master of Science in Community Counseling
MSCD	Master of Science in Communication Disorders
	Master of Science in Community Development
MSCE	Master of Science in Chemistry Education
	Master of Science in Civil Engineering
	Master of Science in Clinical Epidemiology
	Master of Science in Computer Engineering
	Master of Science in Continuing Education
MSCEE	Master of Science in Civil and Environmental Engineering
MSCF	Master of Science in Computational Finance
MSCH	Master of Science in Chemical Engineering
MSChE	Master of Science in Chemical Engineering
MSCI	Master of Science in Clinical Investigation
MSCID	Master of Science in Community and International Development
MSCIS	Master of Science in Computer and Information Science
	Master of Science in Computer and Information Systems
	Master of Science in Computer Information Science
	Master of Science in Computer Information Systems
MSCIT	Master of Science in Computer Information Technology
MSCJ	Master of Science in Criminal Justice
MSCJA	Master of Science in Criminal Justice Administration
MSCJS	Master of Science in Crime and Justice Studies
MSCLS	Master of Science in Clinical Laboratory Studies
MSCM	Master of Science in Church Management
	Master of Science in Conflict Management

	Master of Science in Construction Management
	Master of Supply Chain Management
MSCMP	Master of Science in Cybersecurity Management and Policy
MSCNU	Master of Science in Clinical Nutrition
MSCP	Master of Science in Clinical Psychology
	Master of Science in Community Psychology
	Master of Science in Computer Engineering
	Master of Science in Counseling Psychology
MSCPE	Master of Science in Computer Engineering
MSCPharm	Master of Science in Pharmacy
MSCR	Master of Science in Clinical Research
MSCRP	Master of Science in City and Regional Planning
	Master of Science in Community and Regional Planning
MSCS	Master of Science in Clinical Science
	Master of Science in Computer Science
	Master of Science in Cyber Security
MSCSD	Master of Science in Communication Sciences and Disorders
MSCSE	Master of Science in Computer Science and Engineering
MSCTE	Master of Science in Career and Technical Education
MSD	Master of Science in Dentistry
	Master of Science in Design
	Master of Science in Dietetics
MSDM	Master of Security and Disaster Management
MSE	Master of Science Education
	Master of Science in Economics
	Master of Science in Education
	Master of Science in Engineering
	Master of Science in Engineering Management
	Master of Software Engineering
	Master of Special Education
	Master of Structural Engineering
MSECE	Master of Science in Electrical and Computer Engineering
MSED	Master of Sustainable Economic Development
MSEE	Master of Science in Electrical Engineering
	Master of Science in Environmental Engineering
MSEH	Master of Science in Environmental Health
MSEL	Master of Science in Educational Leadership
MSEM	Master of Science in Engineering and Management
	Master of Science in Engineering Management
	Master of Science in Engineering Mechanics
	Master of Science in Environmental Management
MSENE	Master of Science in Environmental Engineering

Peterson's Graduate Programs in the Physical Sciences, Mathematics, Agricultural Sciences, the Environment & Natural Resources 2020

MSEO	Master of Science in Electro-Optics
MSES	Master of Science in Embedded Software Engineering
	Master of Science in Engineering Science
	Master of Science in Environmental Science
	Master of Science in Environmental Studies
	Master of Science in Exercise Science
MSESE	Master of Science in Energy Systems Engineering
MSET	Master of Science in Educational Technology
	Master of Science in Engineering Technology
MSEV	Master of Science in Environmental Engineering
MSF	Master of Science in Finance
	Master of Science in Forestry
MSFA	Master of Science in Financial Analysis
MSFCS	Master of Science in Family and Consumer Science
MSFE	Master of Science in Financial Engineering
MSFM	Master of Sustainable Forest Management
MSFOR	Master of Science in Forestry
MSFP	Master of Science in Financial Planning
MSFS	Master of Science in Financial Sciences
	Master of Science in Forensic Science
MSFSB	Master of Science in Financial Services and Banking
MSFT	Master of Science in Family Therapy
MSGC	Master of Science in Genetic Counseling
MSH	Master of Science in Health
	Master of Science in Hospice
MSHA	Master of Science in Health Administration
MSHCA	Master of Science in Health Care Administration
MSHCPM	Master of Science in Health Care Policy and Management
MSHE	Master of Science in Health Education
MSHES	Master of Science in Human Environmental Sciences
MSHFID	Master of Science in Human Factors in Information Design
MSHFS	Master of Science in Human Factors and Systems
MSHI	Master of Science in Health Informatics
MSHP	Master of Science in Health Professions
MSHR	Master of Science in Human Resources
MSHRL	Master of Science in Human Resource Leadership
MSHRM	Master of Science in Human Resource Management
MSHROD	Master of Science in Human Resources and Organizational Development
MSHS	Master of Science in Health Science
	Master of Science in Health Services
	Master of Science in Homeland Security
MSHSR	Master of Science in Human Security and Resilience

MSI	Master of Science in Information
	Master of Science in Instruction
	Master of System Integration
MSIA	Master of Science in Industrial Administration
	Master of Science in Information Assurance
MSIDM	Master of Science in Interior Design and Merchandising
MSIE	Master of Science in Industrial Engineering
MSIEM	Master of Science in Information Engineering and Management
MSIM	Master of Science in Industrial Management
	Master of Science in Information Management
	Master of Science in International Management
MSIMC	Master of Science in Integrated Marketing Communications
MSIMS	Master of Science in Identity Management and Security
MSIS	Master of Science in Information Science
	Master of Science in Information Studies
	Master of Science in Information Systems
	Master of Science in Interdisciplinary Studies
MSISE	Master of Science in Infrastructure Systems Engineering
MSISM	Master of Science in Information Systems Management
MSISPM	Master of Science in Information Security Policy and Management
MSIST	Master of Science in Information Systems Technology
MSIT	Master of Science in Industrial Technology
	Master of Science in Information Technology
	Master of Science in Instructional Technology
MSITM	Master of Science in Information Technology Management
MSJ	Master of Science in Journalism
	Master of Science in Jurisprudence
MSJC	Master of Social Justice and Criminology
MSJFP	Master of Science in Juvenile Forensic Psychology
MSJJ	Master of Science in Juvenile Justice
MSJPS	Master of Science in Justice and Public Safety
MSK	Master of Science in Kinesiology
MSL	Master in the Study of Law
	Master of School Leadership
	Master of Science in Leadership
	Master of Science in Limnology
	Master of Sports Leadership
	Master of Strategic Leadership
	Master of Studies in Law
MSLA	Master of Science in Legal Administration
MSLB	Master of Sports Law and Business

Peterson's Graduate Programs in the Physical Sciences, Mathematics, Agricultural Sciences, the Environment & Natural Resources 2020

www.petersons.com **367**

MSLFS	Master of Science in Life Sciences
MSLP	Master of Speech-Language Pathology
MSLS	Master of Science in Library Science
MSLSCM	Master of Science in Logistics and Supply Chain Management
MSLT	Master of Second Language Teaching
MSM	Master of Sacred Ministry
	Master of Sacred Music
	Master of School Mathematics
	Master of Science in Management
	Master of Science in Medicine
	Master of Science in Organization Management
	Master of Security Management
	Master of Strategic Ministry
	Master of Supply Management
MSMA	Master of Science in Marketing Analysis
MSMAE	Master of Science in Materials Engineering
MSMC	Master of Science in Management and Communications
	Master of Science in Mass Communications
MSME	Master of Science in Mathematics Education
	Master of Science in Mechanical Engineering
	Master of Science in Medical Ethics
MSMHC	Master of Science in Mental Health Counseling
MSMIT	Master of Science in Management and Information Technology
MSMLS	Master of Science in Medical Laboratory Science
MSMOT	Master of Science in Management of Technology
MSMP	Master of Science in Medical Physics
	Master of Science in Molecular Pathology
MSMS	Master of Science in Management Science
	Master of Science in Marine Science
	Master of Science in Medical Sciences
MSMSE	Master of Science in Manufacturing Systems Engineering
	Master of Science in Material Science and Engineering
	Master of Science in Material Science Engineering
	Master of Science in Mathematics and Science Education
MSMus	Master of Sacred Music
MSN	Master of Science in Nursing
MSNA	Master of Science in Nurse Anesthesia
MSNE	Master of Science in Nuclear Engineering
MSNS	Master of Science in Natural Science
	Master of Science in Nutritional Science
MSOD	Master of Science in Organization Development
	Master of Science in Organizational Development

MSOEE	Master of Science in Outdoor and Environmental Education
MSOES	Master of Science in Occupational Ergonomics and Safety
MSOH	Master of Science in Occupational Health
MSOL	Master of Science in Organizational Leadership
MSOM	Master of Science in Oriental Medicine
MSOR	Master of Science in Operations Research
MSOT	Master of Science in Occupational Technology
	Master of Science in Occupational Therapy
MSP	Master of Science in Pharmacy
	Master of Science in Planning
	Master of Speech Pathology
	Master of Sustainable Peacebuilding
MSPA	Master of Science in Physician Assistant
MSPAS	Master of Science in Physician Assistant Studies
MSPC	Master of Science in Professional Communications
MSPE	Master of Science in Petroleum Engineering
MSPH	Master of Science in Public Health
MSPHR	Master of Science in Pharmacy
MSPM	Master of Science in Professional Management
	Master of Science in Project Management
MSPNGE	Master of Science in Petroleum and Natural Gas Engineering
MSPPM	Master of Science in Public Policy and Management
MSPS	Master of Science in Pharmaceutical Science
	Master of Science in Political Science
	Master of Science in Psychological Services
MSPT	Master of Science in Physical Therapy
MSRA	Master of Science in Recreation Administration
MSRE	Master of Science in Real Estate
	Master of Science in Religious Education
MSRED	Master of Science in Real Estate Development
	Master of Sustainable Real Estate Development
MSRLS	Master of Science in Recreation and Leisure Studies
MSRM	Master of Science in Risk Management
MSRMP	Master of Science in Radiological Medical Physics
MSRS	Master of Science in Radiological Sciences
	Master of Science in Rehabilitation Science
MSS	Master of Security Studies
	Master of Social Science
	Master of Social Services
	Master of Sports Science
	Master of Strategic Studies
	Master's in Statistical Science
MSSA	Master of Science in Social Administration

MSSCM	Master of Science in Supply Chain Management		MTA	Master of Tax Accounting
				Master of Teaching Arts
MSSD	Master of Arts in Software Driven Systems Design			Master of Tourism Administration
	Master of Science in Sustainable Design		MTC	Master of Technical Communications
MSSE	Master of Science in Software Engineering		MTCM	Master of Traditional Chinese Medicine
	Master of Science in Special Education		MTD	Master of Training and Development
MSSEM	Master of Science in Systems and Engineering Management		MTE	Master in Educational Technology
				Master of Technological Entrepreneurship
MSSI	Master of Science in Security Informatics		MTESOL	Master in Teaching English to Speakers of Other Languages
	Master of Science in Strategic Intelligence			
MSSIS	Master of Science in Security and Intelligence Studies		MTHM	Master of Tourism and Hospitality Management
MSSL	Master of Science in School Leadership		MTI	Master of Information Technology
MSSLP	Master of Science in Speech Language Pathology		MTID	Master of Tangible Interaction Design
			MTL	Master of Talmudic Law
MSSM	Master of Science in Sports Medicine		MTM	Master of Technology Management
	Master of Science in Systems Management			Master of Telecommunications Management
MSSP	Master of Science in Social Policy			Master of the Teaching of Mathematics
MSSS	Master of Science in Safety Science			Master of Transformative Ministry
	Master of Science in Systems Science			Master of Translational Medicine
MSST	Master of Science in Security Technologies		MTMH	Master of Tropical Medicine and Hygiene
MSSW	Master of Science in Social Work		MTMS	Master in Teaching Mathematics and Science
MSSWE	Master of Science in Software Engineering			
MST	Master of Science and Technology		MTOM	Master of Traditional Oriental Medicine
	Master of Science in Taxation		MTPC	Master of Technical and Professional Communication
	Master of Science in Teaching			
	Master of Science in Technology		MTR	Master of Translational Research
	Master of Science in Telecommunications		MTS	Master of Theatre Studies
	Master of Science Teaching			Master of Theological Studies
MSTC	Master of Science in Technical Communication		MTW	Master of Teaching Writing
			MTWM	Master of Trust and Wealth Management
	Master of Science in Telecommunications		MUA	Master of Urban Affairs
MSTCM	Master of Science in Traditional Chinese Medicine		MUAP	Master's of Urban Affairs and Policy
			MUCD	Master of Urban and Community Design
MSTE	Master of Science in Telecommunications Engineering		MUD	Master of Urban Design
			MUDS	Master of Urban Design Studies
	Master of Science in Transportation Engineering		MUEP	Master of Urban and Environmental Planning
MSTL	Master of Science in Teacher Leadership		MUP	Master of Urban Planning
MSTM	Master of Science in Technology Management		MUPD	Master of Urban Planning and Development
			MUPP	Master of Urban Planning and Policy
	Master of Science in Transfusion Medicine		MUPRED	Master of Urban Planning and Real Estate Development
MSTOM	Master of Science in Traditional Oriental Medicine			
MSUASE	Master of Science in Unmanned and Autonomous Systems Engineering		MURP	Master of Urban and Regional Planning
				Master of Urban and Rural Planning
MSUD	Master of Science in Urban Design		MURPL	Master of Urban and Regional Planning
MSUS	Master of Science in Urban Studies		MUS	Master of Urban Studies
MSW	Master of Social Work		Mus M	Master of Music
MSWE	Master of Software Engineering		MUSA	Master of Urban Spatial Analytics
MSWREE	Master of Science in Water Resources and Environmental Engineering		MVP	Master of Voice Pedagogy
			MVS	Master of Visual Studies
MT	Master of Taxation		MWBS	Master of Won Buddhist Studies
	Master of Teaching		MWC	Master of Wildlife Conservation
	Master of Technology		MWR	Master of Water Resources
	Master of Textiles			

Peterson's Graduate Programs in the Physical Sciences, Mathematics, Agricultural Sciences, the Environment & Natural Resources 2020

www.petersons.com   369

MWS	Master of Women's Studies	Psy D	Doctor of Psychology
	Master of Worship Studies	Psy M	Master of Psychology
MWSc	Master of Wildlife Science	Psy S	Specialist in Psychology
Nav Arch	Naval Architecture	Psya D	Doctor of Psychoanalysis
Naval E	Naval Engineer	S Psy S	Specialist in Psychological Services
ND	Doctor of Naturopathic Medicine	Sc D	Doctor of Science
	Doctor of Nursing	Sc M	Master of Science
NE	Nuclear Engineer	SCCT	Specialist in Community College Teaching
Nuc E	Nuclear Engineer	ScDPT	Doctor of Physical Therapy Science
OD	Doctor of Optometry	SD	Specialist Degree
OTD	Doctor of Occupational Therapy	SJD	Doctor of Juridical Sciences
PBME	Professional Master of Biomedical Engineering	SLPD	Doctor of Speech-Language Pathology
		SM	Master of Science
PC	Performer's Certificate	SM Arch S	Master of Science in Architectural Studies
PD	Professional Diploma	SMACT	Master of Science in Art, Culture and Technology
PGC	Post-Graduate Certificate		
PGD	Postgraduate Diploma	SMBT	Master of Science in Building Technology
Ph L	Licentiate of Philosophy	SP	Specialist Degree
Pharm D	Doctor of Pharmacy	Sp Ed	Specialist in Education
PhD	Doctor of Philosophy	Sp LIS	Specialist in Library and Information Science
PhD Otol	Doctor of Philosophy in Otolaryngology		
PhD Surg	Doctor of Philosophy in Surgery	SPA	Specialist in Arts
PhDEE	Doctor of Philosophy in Electrical Engineering	Spec	Specialist's Certificate
		Spec M	Specialist in Music
PMBA	Professional Master of Business Administration	Spt	Specialist Degree
		SSP	Specialist in School Psychology
PMC	Post Master Certificate	STB	Bachelor of Sacred Theology
PMD	Post-Master's Diploma	STD	Doctor of Sacred Theology
PMS	Professional Master of Science	STL	Licentiate of Sacred Theology
	Professional Master's	STM	Master of Sacred Theology
Post-Doctoral MS	Post-Doctoral Master of Science	tDACM	Transitional Doctor of Acupuncture and Chinese Medicine
Post-MSN Certificate	Post-Master of Science in Nursing Certificate		
		TDPT	Transitional Doctor of Physical Therapy
PPDPT	Postprofessional Doctor of Physical Therapy	Th D	Doctor of Theology
Pro-MS	Professional Science Master's	Th M	Master of Theology
Professional MA	Professional Master of Arts	TOTD	Transitional Doctor of Occupational Therapy
Professional MBA	Professional Master of Business Administration		
		VMD	Doctor of Veterinary Medicine
Professional MS	Professional Master of Science	WEMBA	Weekend Executive Master of Business Administration
PSM	Professional Master of Science		
	Professional Science Master's	XMA	Executive Master of Arts

370 www.petersons.com

Peterson's Graduate Programs in the Physical Sciences, Mathematics, Agricultural Sciences, the Environment & Natural Resources 2020

INDEXES

Displays and Close-Ups

Directories and Subject Areas

Following is an alphabetical listing of directories and subject areas. Also listed are cross-references for subject area names not used in the directory structure of the guides, for example, "City and Regional Planning (*see* Urban and Regional Planning)."

Graduate Programs in the Humanities, Arts & Social Sciences

Addictions/Substance Abuse Counseling
Administration (*see* Arts Administration; Public Administration)
African-American Studies
African Languages and Literatures (*see* African Studies)
African Studies
Agribusiness (*see* Agricultural Economics and Agribusiness)
Agricultural Economics and Agribusiness
Alcohol Abuse Counseling (*see* Addictions/Substance Abuse Counseling)
American Indian/Native American Studies
American Studies
Anthropology
Applied Arts and Design—General
Applied Behavior Analysis
Applied Economics
Applied History (*see* Public History)
Applied Psychology
Applied Social Research
Arabic (*see* Near and Middle Eastern Languages)
Arab Studies (*see* Near and Middle Eastern Studies)
Archaeology
Architectural History
Architecture
Archives Administration (*see* Public History)
Area and Cultural Studies (*see* African-American Studies; African Studies; American Indian/Native American Studies; American Studies; Asian-American Studies; Asian Studies; Canadian Studies; Cultural Studies; East European and Russian Studies; Ethnic Studies; Folklore; Gender Studies; Hispanic Studies; Holocaust Studies; Jewish Studies; Latin American Studies; Near and Middle Eastern Studies; Northern Studies; Pacific Area/Pacific Rim Studies; Western European Studies; Women's Studies)
Art/Fine Arts
Art History
Arts Administration
Arts Journalism
Art Therapy
Asian-American Studies
Asian Languages
Asian Studies
Behavioral Sciences (*see* Psychology)
Bible Studies (*see* Religion; Theology)
Biological Anthropology
Black Studies (*see* African-American Studies)
Broadcasting (*see* Communication; Film, Television, and Video Production)
Broadcast Journalism
Building Science
Canadian Studies

Celtic Languages
Ceramics (*see* Art/Fine Arts)
Child and Family Studies
Child Development
Chinese
Chinese Studies (*see* Asian Languages; Asian Studies)
Christian Studies (*see* Missions and Missiology; Religion; Theology)
Cinema (*see* Film, Television, and Video Production)
City and Regional Planning (*see* Urban and Regional Planning)
Classical Languages and Literatures (*see* Classics)
Classics
Clinical Psychology
Clothing and Textiles
Cognitive Psychology (*see* Psychology—General; Cognitive Sciences)
Cognitive Sciences
Communication—General
Community Affairs (*see* Urban and Regional Planning; Urban Studies)
Community Planning (*see* Architecture; Environmental Design; Urban and Regional Planning; Urban Design; Urban Studies)
Community Psychology (*see* Social Psychology)
Comparative and Interdisciplinary Arts
Comparative Literature
Composition (*see* Music)
Computer Art and Design
Conflict Resolution and Mediation/Peace Studies
Consumer Economics
Corporate and Organizational Communication
Corrections (*see* Criminal Justice and Criminology)
Counseling (*see* Counseling Psychology; Pastoral Ministry and Counseling)
Counseling Psychology
Crafts (*see* Art/Fine Arts)
Creative Arts Therapies (*see* Art Therapy; Therapies—Dance, Drama, and Music)
Criminal Justice and Criminology
Cultural Anthropology
Cultural Studies
Dance
Decorative Arts
Demography and Population Studies
Design (*see* Applied Arts and Design; Architecture; Art/Fine Arts; Environmental Design; Graphic Design; Industrial Design; Interior Design; Textile Design; Urban Design)
Developmental Psychology
Diplomacy (*see* International Affairs)
Disability Studies
Drama Therapy (*see* Therapies—Dance, Drama, and Music)
Dramatic Arts (*see* Theater)
Drawing (*see* Art/Fine Arts)
Drug Abuse Counseling (*see* Addictions/Substance Abuse Counseling)
Drug and Alcohol Abuse Counseling (*see* Addictions/Substance Abuse Counseling)
East Asian Studies (*see* Asian Studies)
East European and Russian Studies
Economic Development
Economics

Educational Theater (*see* Theater; Therapies—Dance, Drama, and Music)

Emergency Management

English

Environmental Design

Ethics

Ethnic Studies

Ethnomusicology (*see* Music)

Experimental Psychology

Family and Consumer Sciences—General

Family Studies (*see* Child and Family Studies)

Family Therapy (*see* Child and Family Studies; Clinical Psychology; Counseling Psychology; Marriage and Family Therapy)

Filmmaking (*see* Film, Television, and Video Production)

Film Studies (*see* Film, Television, and Video Production)

Film, Television, and Video Production

Film, Television, and Video Theory and Criticism

Fine Arts (*see* Art/Fine Arts)

Folklore

Foreign Languages (*see* specific language)

Foreign Service (*see* International Affairs; International Development)

Forensic Psychology

Forensic Sciences

Forensics (*see* Speech and Interpersonal Communication)

French

Gender Studies

General Studies (*see* Liberal Studies)

Genetic Counseling

Geographic Information Systems

Geography

German

Gerontology

Graphic Design

Greek (*see* Classics)

Health Communication

Health Psychology

Hebrew (*see* Near and Middle Eastern Languages)

Hebrew Studies (*see* Jewish Studies)

Hispanic and Latin American Languages

Hispanic Studies

Historic Preservation

History

History of Art (*see* Art History)

History of Medicine

History of Science and Technology

Holocaust and Genocide Studies

Home Economics (*see* Family and Consumer Sciences—General)

Homeland Security

Household Economics, Sciences, and Management (*see* Family and Consumer Sciences—General)

Human Development

Humanities

Illustration

Industrial and Labor Relations

Industrial and Organizational Psychology

Industrial Design

Interdisciplinary Studies

Interior Design

International Affairs

International Development

International Economics

International Service (*see* International Affairs; International Development)

International Trade Policy

Internet and Interactive Multimedia

Interpersonal Communication (*see* Speech and Interpersonal Communication)

Interpretation (*see* Translation and Interpretation)

Islamic Studies (*see* Near and Middle Eastern Studies; Religion)

Italian

Japanese

Japanese Studies (*see* Asian Languages; Asian Studies; Japanese)

Jewelry (*see* Art/Fine Arts)

Jewish Studies

Journalism

Judaic Studies (*see* Jewish Studies; Religion)

Labor Relations (*see* Industrial and Labor Relations)

Landscape Architecture

Latin American Studies

Latin (*see* Classics)

Law Enforcement (*see* Criminal Justice and Criminology)

Liberal Studies

Lighting Design

Linguistics

Literature (*see* Classics; Comparative Literature; specific language)

Marriage and Family Therapy

Mass Communication

Media Studies

Medical Illustration

Medieval and Renaissance Studies

Metalsmithing (*see* Art/Fine Arts)

Middle Eastern Studies (*see* Near and Middle Eastern Studies)

Military and Defense Studies

Mineral Economics

Ministry (*see* Pastoral Ministry and Counseling; Theology)

Missions and Missiology

Motion Pictures (*see* Film, Television, and Video Production)

Museum Studies

Music

Musicology (*see* Music)

Music Therapy (*see* Therapies—Dance, Drama, and Music)

National Security

Native American Studies (*see* American Indian/Native American Studies)

Near and Middle Eastern Languages

Near and Middle Eastern Studies

Northern Studies

Organizational Psychology (*see* Industrial and Organizational Psychology)

Oriental Languages (*see* Asian Languages)

Oriental Studies (*see* Asian Studies)

Pacific Area/Pacific Rim Studies

Painting (*see* Art/Fine Arts)

Pastoral Ministry and Counseling

Philanthropic Studies

Philosophy

Photography

Playwriting (*see* Theater; Writing)

Policy Studies (*see* Public Policy)

Political Science

Population Studies (*see* Demography and Population Studies)

Portuguese

Printmaking (*see* Art/Fine Arts)

Product Design (*see* Industrial Design)

Psychoanalysis and Psychotherapy

Psychology—General

Public Administration

Public Affairs

Public History

Public Policy

Public Speaking (*see* Mass Communication; Rhetoric; Speech and Interpersonal Communication)

Publishing

Regional Planning (*see* Architecture; Urban and Regional Planning; Urban Design; Urban Studies)

Rehabilitation Counseling

Religion

Renaissance Studies (*see* Medieval and Renaissance Studies)

Rhetoric

Romance Languages

Romance Literatures (*see* Romance Languages)

Rural Planning and Studies

Rural Sociology

Russian

Scandinavian Languages

School Psychology

Sculpture (*see* Art/Fine Arts)

Security Administration (*see* Criminal Justice and Criminology)

Slavic Languages

Slavic Studies (*see* East European and Russian Studies; Slavic Languages)

Social Psychology

Social Sciences

Sociology

Southeast Asian Studies (*see* Asian Studies)

Soviet Studies (*see* East European and Russian Studies; Russian)

Spanish

Speech and Interpersonal Communication

Sport Psychology

Studio Art (*see* Art/Fine Arts)

Substance Abuse Counseling (*see* Addictions/Substance Abuse Counseling)

Survey Methodology

Sustainable Development

Technical Communication

Technical Writing

Telecommunications (*see* Film, Television, and Video Production)

Television (*see* Film, Television, and Video Production)

Textile Design

Textiles (*see* Clothing and Textiles; Textile Design)

Thanatology

Theater

Theater Arts (*see* Theater)

Theology

Therapies—Dance, Drama, and Music

Translation and Interpretation

Transpersonal and Humanistic Psychology

Urban and Regional Planning

Urban Design

Urban Planning (*see* Architecture; Urban and Regional Planning; Urban Design; Urban Studies)

Urban Studies

Video (*see* Film, Television, and Video Production)

Visual Arts (*see* Applied Arts and Design; Art/Fine Arts; Film, Television, and Video Production; Graphic Design; Illustration; Photography)

Western European Studies

Women's Studies

World Wide Web (*see* Internet and Interactive Multimedia)

Writing

Graduate Programs in the Biological/Biomedical Sciences & Health-Related Medical Professions

Acupuncture and Oriental Medicine

Acute Care/Critical Care Nursing Administration (*see* Health Services Management and Hospital Administration; Nursing and Healthcare Administration; Pharmaceutical Administration)

Adult Nursing

Advanced Practice Nursing (*see* Family Nurse Practitioner Studies)

Allied Health—General

Allied Health Professions (*see* Clinical Laboratory Sciences/Medical Technology; Clinical Research; Communication Disorders; Dental Hygiene; Emergency Medical Services; Occupational Therapy; Physical Therapy; Physician Assistant Studies; Rehabilitation Sciences)

Allopathic Medicine

Anatomy

Anesthesiologist Assistant Studies

Animal Behavior

Bacteriology

Behavioral Sciences (*see* Biopsychology; Neuroscience; Zoology)

Biochemistry

Bioethics

Biological and Biomedical Sciences—General Biological Chemistry (*see* Biochemistry)

Biological Oceanography (*see* Marine Biology)

Biophysics

Biopsychology

Botany

Breeding (*see* Botany; Plant Biology; Genetics)

Cancer Biology/Oncology

Cardiovascular Sciences

Cell Biology

Cellular Physiology (*see* Cell Biology; Physiology)

Child-Care Nursing (*see* Maternal and Child/Neonatal Nursing)

Chiropractic

Clinical Laboratory Sciences/Medical Technology

Clinical Research

Community Health

Community Health Nursing

Computational Biology

Conservation (*see* Conservation Biology; Environmental Biology)

Conservation Biology

Crop Sciences (*see* Botany; Plant Biology)

Cytology (*see* Cell Biology)

Dental and Oral Surgery (*see* Oral and Dental Sciences)

Dental Assistant Studies (*see* Dental Hygiene)

Dental Hygiene

Dental Services (*see* Dental Hygiene)

Dentistry

Developmental Biology Dietetics (*see* Nutrition)

Peterson's Graduate Programs in the Physical Sciences, Mathematics, Agricultural Sciences, the Environment & Natural Resources 2020

www.petersons.com **377**

Ecology
Embryology (*see* Developmental Biology)
Emergency Medical Services
Endocrinology (*see* Physiology)
Entomology
Environmental Biology
Environmental and Occupational Health
Epidemiology
Evolutionary Biology
Family Nurse Practitioner Studies
Foods (*see* Nutrition)
Forensic Nursing
Genetics
Genomic Sciences
Gerontological Nursing
Health Physics/Radiological Health
Health Promotion
Health-Related Professions (*see* individual allied health professions)
Health Services Management and Hospital Administration
Health Services Research
Histology (*see* Anatomy; Cell Biology)
HIV/AIDS Nursing
Hospice Nursing
Hospital Administration (*see* Health Services Management and Hospital Administration)
Human Genetics
Immunology
Industrial Hygiene
Infectious Diseases
International Health
Laboratory Medicine (*see* Clinical Laboratory Sciences/Medical Technology; Immunology; Microbiology; Pathology)
Life Sciences (*see* Biological and Biomedical Sciences)
Marine Biology
Maternal and Child Health
Maternal and Child/Neonatal Nursing
Medical Imaging
Medical Microbiology
Medical Nursing (*see* Medical/Surgical Nursing)
Medical Physics
Medical/Surgical Nursing
Medical Technology (*see* Clinical Laboratory Sciences/Medical Technology)
Medical Sciences (*see* Biological and Biomedical Sciences)
Medical Science Training Programs (*see* Biological and Biomedical Sciences)
Medicinal and Pharmaceutical Chemistry
Medicinal Chemistry (*see* Medicinal and Pharmaceutical Chemistry)
Medicine (*see* Allopathic Medicine; Naturopathic Medicine; Osteopathic Medicine; Podiatric Medicine)
Microbiology
Midwifery (*see* Nurse Midwifery)
Molecular Biology
Molecular Biophysics
Molecular Genetics
Molecular Medicine
Molecular Pathogenesis
Molecular Pathology
Molecular Pharmacology
Molecular Physiology
Molecular Toxicology
Naturopathic Medicine

Neural Sciences (*see* Biopsychology; Neurobiology; Neuroscience)
Neurobiology
Neuroendocrinology (*see* Biopsychology; Neurobiology; Neuroscience; Physiology)
Neuropharmacology (*see* Biopsychology; Neurobiology; Neuroscience; Pharmacology)
Neurophysiology (*see* Biopsychology; Neurobiology; Neuroscience; Physiology)
Neuroscience
Nuclear Medical Technology (*see* Clinical Laboratory Sciences/ Medical Technology)
Nurse Anesthesia
Nurse Midwifery
Nurse Practitioner Studies (*see* Family Nurse Practitioner Studies)
Nursing Administration (*see* Nursing and Healthcare Administration)
Nursing and Healthcare Administration
Nursing Education
Nursing—General
Nursing Informatics
Nutrition
Occupational Health (*see* Environmental and Occupational Health; Occupational Health Nursing)
Occupational Health Nursing
Occupational Therapy
Oncology (*see* Cancer Biology/Oncology)
Oncology Nursing
Optometry
Oral and Dental Sciences
Oral Biology (*see* Oral and Dental Sciences)
Oral Pathology (*see* Oral and Dental Sciences)
Organismal Biology (*see* Biological and Biomedical Sciences; Zoology)
Oriental Medicine and Acupuncture (*see* Acupuncture and Oriental Medicine)
Orthodontics (*see* Oral and Dental Sciences)
Osteopathic Medicine
Parasitology
Pathobiology
Pathology
Pediatric Nursing
Pedontics (*see* Oral and Dental Sciences)
Perfusion
Pharmaceutical Administration
Pharmaceutical Chemistry (*see* Medicinal and Pharmaceutical Chemistry)
Pharmaceutical Sciences
Pharmacology
Pharmacy
Photobiology of Cells and Organelles (*see* Botany; Cell Biology; Plant Biology)
Physical Therapy
Physician Assistant Studies
Physiological Optics (*see* Vision Sciences)
Podiatric Medicine
Preventive Medicine (*see* Community Health and Public Health)
Physiological Optics (*see* Physiology)
Physiology
Plant Biology
Plant Molecular Biology
Plant Pathology
Plant Physiology
Pomology (*see* Botany; Plant Biology)
Psychiatric Nursing
Public Health—General
Public Health Nursing (*see* Community Health Nursing)
Psychiatric Nursing
Psychobiology (*see* Biopsychology)
Psychopharmacology (*see* Biopsychology; Neuroscience; Pharmacology)
Radiation Biology
Radiological Health (*see* Health Physics/Radiological Health)

Rehabilitation Nursing
Rehabilitation Sciences
Rehabilitation Therapy (*see* Physical Therapy)
Reproductive Biology
School Nursing
Sociobiology (*see* Evolutionary Biology)
Structural Biology
Surgical Nursing (*see* Medical/Surgical Nursing)
Systems Biology
Teratology
Therapeutics
Theoretical Biology (*see* Biological and Biomedical Sciences)
Therapeutics (*see* Pharmaceutical Sciences; Pharmacology; Pharmacy)
Toxicology
Transcultural Nursing
Translational Biology
Tropical Medicine (*see* Parasitology)
Veterinary Medicine
Veterinary Sciences
Virology
Vision Sciences
Wildlife Biology (*see* Zoology)
Women's Health Nursing
Zoology

Graduate Programs in the Physical Sciences, Mathematics, Agricultural Sciences, the Environment & Natural Resources

Acoustics
Agricultural Sciences
Agronomy and Soil Sciences
Analytical Chemistry
Animal Sciences
Applied Mathematics
Applied Physics
Applied Statistics
Aquaculture
Astronomy
Astrophysical Sciences (*see* Astrophysics; Atmospheric Sciences; Meteorology; Planetary and Space Sciences)
Astrophysics
Atmospheric Sciences
Biological Oceanography (*see* Marine Affairs; Marine Sciences; Oceanography)
Biomathematics
Biometry
Biostatistics
Chemical Physics
Chemistry
Computational Sciences
Condensed Matter Physics
Dairy Science (*see* Animal Sciences)
Earth Sciences (*see* Geosciences)
Environmental Management and Policy
Environmental Sciences
Environmental Studies (*see* Environmental Management and Policy)
Experimental Statistics (*see* Statistics)
Fish, Game, and Wildlife Management
Food Science and Technology

Forestry
General Science (*see* specific topics)
Geochemistry
Geodetic Sciences
Geological Engineering (*see* Geology)
Geological Sciences (*see* Geology)
Geology
Geophysical Fluid Dynamics (*see* Geophysics)
Geophysics
Geosciences
Horticulture
Hydrogeology
Hydrology
Inorganic Chemistry
Limnology
Marine Affairs
Marine Geology
Marine Sciences
Marine Studies (*see* Marine Affairs; Marine Geology; Marine Sciences; Oceanography)
Mathematical and Computational Finance
Mathematical Physics
Mathematical Statistics (*see* Applied Statistics; Statistics)
Mathematics
Meteorology
Mineralogy
Natural Resource Management (*see* Environmental Management and Policy; Natural Resources)
Natural Resources
Nuclear Physics (*see* Physics)
Ocean Engineering (*see* Marine Affairs; Marine Geology; Marine Sciences; Oceanography)
Oceanography
Optical Sciences
Optical Technologies (*see* Optical Sciences)
Optics (*see* Applied Physics; Optical Sciences; Physics)
Organic Chemistry
Paleontology
Paper Chemistry (*see* Chemistry)
Photonics
Physical Chemistry
Physics
Planetary and Space Sciences
Plant Sciences
Plasma Physics
Poultry Science (*see* Animal Sciences)
Radiological Physics (*see* Physics)
Range Management (*see* Range Science)
Range Science
Resource Management (*see* Environmental Management and Policy; Natural Resources)
Solid-Earth Sciences (*see* Geosciences)
Space Sciences (*see* Planetary and Space Sciences)
Statistics
Theoretical Chemistry
Theoretical Physics
Viticulture and Enology
Water Resources

Peterson's Graduate Programs in the Physical Sciences, Mathematics, Agricultural Sciences, the Environment & Natural Resources 2020

www.petersons.com **379**

Graduate Programs in Engineering & Applied Sciences

Aeronautical Engineering (*see* Aerospace/Aeronautical Engineering)

Aerospace/Aeronautical Engineering

Aerospace Studies (*see* Aerospace/Aeronautical Engineering)

Agricultural Engineering

Applied Mechanics (*see* Mechanics)

Applied Science and Technology

Architectural Engineering

Artificial Intelligence/Robotics

Astronautical Engineering (*see* Aerospace/Aeronautical Engineering)

Automotive Engineering

Aviation

Biochemical Engineering

Bioengineering

Bioinformatics

Biological Engineering (*see* Bioengineering)

Biomedical Engineering

Biosystems Engineering

Biotechnology

Ceramic Engineering (*see* Ceramic Sciences and Engineering)

Ceramic Sciences and Engineering

Ceramics (*see* Ceramic Sciences and Engineering)

Chemical Engineering

Civil Engineering

Computer and Information Systems Security

Computer Engineering

Computer Science

Computing Technology (*see* Computer Science)

Construction Engineering

Construction Management

Database Systems

Electrical Engineering

Electronic Materials

Electronics Engineering (*see* Electrical Engineering)

Energy and Power Engineering

Energy Management and Policy

Engineering and Applied Sciences

Engineering and Public Affairs (*see* Technology and Public Policy)

Engineering and Public Policy (*see* Energy Management and Policy; Technology and Public Policy)

Engineering Design

Engineering Management

Engineering Mechanics (*see* Mechanics)

Engineering Metallurgy (*see* Metallurgical Engineering and Metallurgy)

Engineering Physics

Environmental Design (*see* Environmental Engineering)

Environmental Engineering

Ergonomics and Human Factors

Financial Engineering

Fire Protection Engineering

Food Engineering (*see* Agricultural Engineering)

Game Design and Development

Gas Engineering (*see* Petroleum Engineering)

Geological Engineering

Geophysics Engineering (*see* Geological Engineering)

Geotechnical Engineering

Hazardous Materials Management

Health Informatics

Health Systems (*see* Safety Engineering; Systems Engineering)

Highway Engineering (*see* Transportation and Highway Engineering)

Human-Computer Interaction

Human Factors (*see* Ergonomics and Human Factors)

Hydraulics

Hydrology (*see* Water Resources Engineering)

Industrial Engineering (*see* Industrial/Management Engineering)

Industrial/Management Engineering

Information Science

Internet Engineering

Macromolecular Science (*see* Polymer Science and Engineering)

Management Engineering (*see* Engineering Management; Industrial/Management Engineering)

Management of Technology

Manufacturing Engineering

Marine Engineering (*see* Civil Engineering)

Materials Engineering

Materials Sciences

Mechanical Engineering

Mechanics

Medical Informatics

Metallurgical Engineering and Metallurgy

Metallurgy (*see* Metallurgical Engineering and Metallurgy)

Mineral/Mining Engineering

Modeling and Simulation

Nanotechnology

Nuclear Engineering

Ocean Engineering

Operations Research

Paper and Pulp Engineering

Petroleum Engineering

Pharmaceutical Engineering

Plastics Engineering (*see* Polymer Science and Engineering)

Polymer Science and Engineering

Public Policy (*see* Energy Management and Policy; Technology and Public Policy)

Reliability Engineering

Robotics (*see* Artificial Intelligence/Robotics)

Safety Engineering

Software Engineering

Solid-State Sciences (*see* Materials Sciences)

Structural Engineering

Surveying Science and Engineering

Systems Analysis (*see* Systems Engineering)

Systems Engineering

Systems Science

Technology and Public Policy

Telecommunications

Telecommunications Management

Textile Sciences and Engineering

Textiles (*see* Textile Sciences and Engineering)

Transportation and Highway Engineering

Urban Systems Engineering (*see* Systems Engineering)

Waste Management (*see* Hazardous Materials Management)

Water Resources Engineering

Peterson's Graduate Programs in the Physical Sciences, Mathematics, Agricultural Sciences, the Environment & Natural Resources 2020

Graduate Programs in Business, Education, Information Studies, Law & Social Work

Accounting
Actuarial Science
Adult Education
Advertising and Public Relations
Agricultural Education
Alcohol Abuse Counseling (*see* Counselor Education)
Archival Management and Studies
Art Education
Athletics Administration (*see* Kinesiology and Movement Studies)
Athletic Training and Sports Medicine
Audiology (*see* Communication Disorders)
Aviation Management
Banking (*see* Finance and Banking)
Business Administration and Management—General
Business Education
Communication Disorders
Community College Education
Computer Education
Continuing Education (*see* Adult Education)
Counseling (*see* Counselor Education)
Counselor Education
Curriculum and Instruction
Developmental Education
Distance Education Development
Drug Abuse Counseling (*see* Counselor Education)
Early Childhood Education
Educational Leadership and Administration
Educational Measurement and Evaluation
Educational Media/Instructional Technology
Educational Policy
Educational Psychology
Education—General
Education of the Blind (*see* Special Education)
Education of the Deaf (*see* Special Education)
Education of the Gifted
Education of the Hearing Impaired (*see* Special Education)
Education of the Learning Disabled (*see* Special Education)
Education of the Mentally Retarded (*see* Special Education)
Education of the Physically Handicapped (*see* Special Education)
Education of Students with Severe/Multiple Disabilities
Education of the Visually Handicapped (*see* Special Education)
Electronic Commerce
Elementary Education
English as a Second Language
English Education
Entertainment Management
Entrepreneurship
Environmental Education
Environmental Law
Exercise and Sports Science
Exercise Physiology (*see* Kinesiology and Movement Studies)
Facilities and Entertainment Management
Finance and Banking
Food Services Management (*see* Hospitality Management)
Foreign Languages Education
Foundations and Philosophy of Education
Guidance and Counseling (*see* Counselor Education)

Health Education
Health Law
Hearing Sciences (*see* Communication Disorders)
Higher Education
Home Economics Education
Hospitality Management
Hotel Management (*see* Travel and Tourism)
Human Resources Development
Human Resources Management
Human Services
Industrial Administration (*see* Industrial and Manufacturing Management)
Industrial and Manufacturing Management
Industrial Education (*see* Vocational and Technical Education)
Information Studies
Instructional Technology (*see* Educational Media/Instructional Technology)
Insurance
Intellectual Property Law
International and Comparative Education
International Business
International Commerce (*see* International Business)
International Economics (*see* International Business)
International Trade (*see* International Business)
Investment and Securities (*see* Business Administration and Management; Finance and Banking; Investment Management)
Investment Management
Junior College Education (*see* Community College Education)
Kinesiology and Movement Studies
Law
Legal and Justice Studies
Leisure Services (*see* Recreation and Park Management)
Leisure Studies
Library Science
Logistics
Management (*see* Business Administration and Management)
Management Information Systems
Management Strategy and Policy
Marketing
Marketing Research
Mathematics Education
Middle School Education
Movement Studies (*see* Kinesiology and Movement Studies)
Multilingual and Multicultural Education
Museum Education
Music Education
Nonprofit Management
Nursery School Education (*see* Early Childhood Education)
Occupational Education (*see* Vocational and Technical Education)
Organizational Behavior
Organizational Management
Parks Administration (*see* Recreation and Park Management)
Personnel (*see* Human Resources Development; Human Resources Management; Organizational Behavior; Organizational Management; Student Affairs)
Philosophy of Education (*see* Foundations and Philosophy of Education)
Physical Education
Project Management
Public Relations (*see* Advertising and Public Relations)
Quality Management
Quantitative Analysis

Peterson's Graduate Programs in the Physical Sciences, Mathematics, Agricultural Sciences, the Environment & Natural Resources 2020

www.petersons.com **381**

Reading Education

Real Estate

Recreation and Park Management

Recreation Therapy (*see* Recreation and Park Management)

Religious Education

Remedial Education (*see* Special Education)

Restaurant Administration (*see* Hospitality Management)

Science Education

Secondary Education

Social Sciences Education

Social Studies Education (*see* Social Sciences Education)

Social Work

Special Education

Speech-Language Pathology and Audiology (*see* Communication Disorders)

Sports Management

Sports Medicine (*see* Athletic Training and Sports Medicine)

Sports Psychology and Sociology (*see* Kinesiology and Movement Studies)

Student Affairs

Substance Abuse Counseling (*see* Counselor Education)

Supply Chain Management

Sustainability Management

Systems Management (*see* Management Information Systems)

Taxation

Teacher Education (*see* specific subject areas)

Teaching English as a Second Language (*see* English as a Second Language)

Technical Education (*see* Vocational and Technical Education)

Transportation Management

Travel and Tourism

Urban Education

Vocational and Technical Education

Vocational Counseling (*see* Counselor Education)

382 www.petersons.com

Peterson's Graduate Programs in the Physical Sciences, Mathematics, Agricultural Sciences, the Environment & Natural Resources 2020

Directories and Subject Areas in This Book

NOTES

NOTES

NOTES

NOTES

NOTES

NOTES

NOTES

NOTES

NOTES

NOTES

NOTES